O'CONNOR'S TEXAS FAMILY CODE PLUS

AUTHORS
JOAN FOOTE JENKINS
RANDALL B. WILHITE

O'CONNOR'S
HOUSTON, TEXAS

O'CONNOR'S ANNOTATED CODES SERIES

Suggested cite form: ***O'Connor's Texas Family Code Plus*** (2017-18)

O'CONNOR'S®

Mailing address:
P.O. Box 3348
Houston, TX 77253-3348

Shipping address:
9364 Wallisville Rd., Ste. 150
Houston, TX 77013

Phone: (713) 335-8200
(800) OCONNOR (626-6667)
Fax: (713) 335-8201

www.oconnors.com

Print date: July 7, 2017
Printed in the United States of America

ISBN 978-1-59839-275-3

This book is intended to provide attorneys with current and accurate information about selected Texas codes, rules, and statutes. The information in this book, however, may not be sufficient in dealing with a client's particular legal problem, and O'Connor's, Michol O'Connor, Joan Jenkins, and Randall Wilhite do not warrant or represent its suitability for this purpose. Attorneys using this book do so with the understanding that the information published in it should not be relied on as a substitute for independent research using original sources of authority.

Subscription Notice: By ordering this book, you are enrolled in our subscription program, which entitles you to a lower annual price. Before we send you an updated book, we send you a letter and reply card confirming that you want the new edition. You have the option at that time to change or cancel your order. If you do not change or cancel your order, the book will be shipped to you. If you decide to return the book, the return postage is your responsibility. You can change your subscription status at any time in writing. If you want to order a product but do not wish to enroll in the subscription program, please call 1-800-OCONNOR for pricing details.

ABOUT THIS BOOK

This book contains the Texas Family Code, Texas Rules of Civil Procedure, and Texas Rules of Evidence—all with up-to-date case annotations—as well as "plus" selections from other codes and statutes that are often used in daily family-law practice.

Family lawyers will find this book particularly useful because its contents and design have been chosen with the practitioner in mind. The book allows you to carry only one volume to the courthouse and still have all the necessary codes, statutes, and rules at your fingertips. Cross-references and caution notes have been included in the Rules of Civil Procedure and Evidence to guide you to sections of the Family Code that override or affect the rules. In addition, we provide annotations in the Rules of Civil Procedure and Evidence that relate specifically to family-law practice. Finally, we developed a comprehensive yet easy-to-use index, so you can find the information you need quickly.

You will also find cross-references frm the Family Code to ***O'Connor's Texas Family Law Handbook***. The ***Family Law Handbook*** is a practice manual that provides in-depth explanation and analysis of how the codes, rules, and case law work together. Written in ***O'Connor's*** easy-to-read commentary format, this comprehensive guide walks you step by step through the substantive and procedural issues essential to practicing family law in Texas.

CURRENCY

The statutes in this book are current through the 85th Legislature, Regular Session (2017). The case law is current through April 2017, and the court rules are current through May 2017. The Public Laws are current through P.L. 115-41.

At the time of printing, the 85th Legislature had convened a special session to address certain sunset provisions and potentially 19 other items identified by the governor. If any Family Code sections are affected by laws passed during this session, you can receive an update to the code if you register to be notified at www.oconnors.com. Customers who subscribe to O'Connor's Online will be able to access the revised code sections before they take effect at www.oconnors.com/online.

CONVENTIONS & LEGISLATIVE CONFLICTS

In this book, 2017 legislative changes are marked with Ⓐ, Ⓔ, or Ⓒ, depending on whether the section was amended, enacted, or codified (or recodified) from another statute. Statutory language added by the Legislature is underlined, and language removed by the Legislature is shown in ~~strikethrough~~ text. Italicized editor's notes explain the effect of legislative changes (e.g., effective dates, savings clauses).

Occasionally, the Legislature enacts multiple code sections with the same number. The identically numbered sections are marked with ☠ and accompanied by an editor's note describing the duplicate numbering. Each section is also labeled with a bracketed letter or number (e.g., [A*]) to help distinguish it. Likewise, when the Legislature passes a bill that amends a section or subsection without reference to another bill's conflicting amendment to the same section or subsection, both versions of the section or subsection are presented. Each version is marked with ☠ and accompanied by an editor's note describing the conflict.

When multiple amendments to the same section or subsection are enacted during the same legislative session, the amendments should be harmonized unless they are irreconcilable. Tex. Gov't Code §311.025(b); ***Burke v. Union Pac. Res.***, 138 S.W.3d 46, 75 (Tex.App.—Texarkana 2004, pet. denied). Conflicting amendments are irreconcilable only if both provisions cannot be complied with at the same time. ***State v. Jackson***, 370 S.W.2d 797, 800 (Tex.App.—Houston [1st Dist.] 1963), *aff'd*, 376 S.W.2d 341 (Tex.1964). In that circumstance, the amendment enacted last will prevail. Tex. Gov't Code §311.025(b). For this reason, the editor's note accompanying each conflict includes the date each bill was enacted, which in most cases is the date of the last vote on the bill (not the bill's effective date). *See* Tex. Gov't Code §311.025(d), (e).

To determine whether conflicting statutory provisions can be harmonized, you should review the text carefully and consult the Code Construction Act (Government Code ch. 311), the canons of statutory construction, and the legis-

lative history for those provisions. Legislative history for recent bills can be found on the Texas Legislature Online (TLO) website at www.capitol.state.tx.us. To find a bill analysis on TLO, select the correct legislative session in the drop-down box under "Search Legislation," enter the bill number (e.g., HB 387) in the box below that, select "Go," click on the "Text" tab, and then select the latest document under the "Bill Analysis" column. Other legislative history, such as passed and rejected amendments, floor journals, fiscal notes, and audio or video recordings of hearings, can also be found on the TLO website.

Because some conflicting versions of sections and subsections persist beyond the following legislative session, editor's notes may contain references to session laws (e.g., Acts 2003, 78th Leg., ch. 213 …) rather than bill numbers. To find a bill number from past session laws, use the "Bill-chapter cross reference" function on the Legislative Reference Library website at www.lrl.state.tx.us.

ABOUT THE AUTHORS

Joan Foote Jenkins is a founding partner in the firm of Jenkins & Kamin, LLP, and is board-certified in family law by the Texas Board of Legal Specialization. She has received numerous honors in recognition of her achievements over the course of her long career, including being selected as a "Super Lawyer" by *Texas Monthly* magazine each year since the inception of the award and being recognized by the publisher as one of the "Top 50 Women Lawyers in Texas" and "Top 100 in the Houston Region." In addition, Ms. Jenkins has been listed in "Best Lawyers in America" for over 20 years and was named by that publication as Houston's "Best Family Lawyer for 2010." She has also received the annual David A. Gibson Award for Professionalism and Excellence in the Practice of Family Law, presented by the Gulf Coast Family Law Specialists. Ms. Jenkins has served as Chair of the Family Law Council of the State Bar of Texas, President of the Gulf Coast Family Law Specialists, Chair of the Family Law Section of the Houston Bar Association, and longtime Chair of the Pattern Jury Charge Committee – Family, Probate. Ms. Jenkins is also past Chair of the Texas Family Law Foundation, an organization devoted to promotion of laws that benefit and protect Texas families and children in the area of family law.

Ms. Jenkins is one of the most frequent lecturers at continuing legal education seminars in the area of family law, having authored over 100 comprehensive articles on the subject. Ms. Jenkins was the Co-Course Director for the Advanced Family Law Course and the Course Director for the New Frontiers in Marital Property both sponsored by the State Bar of Texas. Ms. Jenkins is also past Chair of the Texas Family Practice Manual Drafting Committee and has worked on numerous other projects for the State Bar of Texas. Licensed since 1982, Ms. Jenkins is a graduate of the University of Texas at Austin and South Texas College of Law.

Randall B. Wilhite is a shareholder with the law firm of Fullenweider Wilhite, P.C., and is board-certified in family law by the Texas Board of Legal Specialization. Mr. Wilhite is also an Adjunct Professor of Law at the University of Texas School of Law in Austin, where he has taught for over ten years. For five consecutive years, *Texas Monthly* magazine has named Mr. Wilhite as one of the "Top 100 Lawyers in Texas," and he is a recipient of the prestigious David A. Gibson Award for Professionalism and Excellence in the Practice of Family Law, presented by the Gulf Coast Family Law Specialists. He was also named the Frank G. Evans Mediator of the Year, an award presented by the State Bar of Texas. Mr. Wilhite earned that honor by handling over 2,600 complex family-law mediations. He is a Fellow in the American Academy of Matrimonial Lawyers and the International Academy of Matrimonial Lawyers. And for many years, Mr. Wilhite has sat on the Texas Board of Legal Specialization, which writes and grades the examination for board certification in Texas family law.

Mr. Wilhite is a Certified Public Accountant and one of the very few practicing attorneys in the United States who is "Accredited in Business Valuation" by the American Institute of Certified Public Accountants.

Mr. Wilhite has spoken at more than 120 continuing legal education seminars and institutes in Texas and other states on the topics of division of property, reimbursement, characterization, economic contribution, retirement assets, mediation, arbitration, collaborative law, ethics, taxation, valuation, accounting, evidence, and discovery. He has been presented with the Texas Academy of Family Law Specialists Award for the "Best Continuing Legal Education Presentation in Texas Family Law" for his article *Valuation of Closely Held Businesses & Professional Practices*.

ACKNOWLEDGMENT

We would like to thank the National Conference of Commissioners on Uniform State Laws for use of the official comments to uniform acts adopted by the Texas Legislature.

YOUR SUGGESTIONS

We welcome your comments. If you think we should have included (or excluded) something, or if you see anything that needs to be corrected, please let us know. Send your comments to the mailing address or fax number shown on the copyright page, or by e-mail to Lauren Sacra Harvey, Managing Legal Editor, at lharvey@oconnors.com.

CAVEAT

This book provides citations to important opinions that interpret the Texas Family Code, portions of other codes, the Texas Rules of Civil Procedure, and the Texas Rules of Evidence, as well as charts that summarize information from codes, statutes, and cases. Because you may disagree with the choice of cases for the codes and rules in this book, you should use the book only as a research guide. Read the codes, the rules, and the cases in full and make your own evaluation of them.

EDITORIAL & PRODUCTION STAFF

As always, the staff of O'Connor's worked hard to prepare this publication, both in its substance and in its layout. The people who worked on this edition of ***O'Connor's Texas Family Code Plus*** are listed below.

MANAGING LEGAL EDITOR
Lauren Sacra Harvey, J.D.

CONTENT EDITORS
Kelly L. Beam, J.D.
Gregory S. Otterson, J.D.

LEGAL EDITORS
Sharon McCord Cozort, J.D.
Kristen N. Ellis, J.D.
Jessica Younger Field, J.D.
Jordyn Johnson, J.D.
Jamie Milne, J.D.
John R. Passmore, J.D.
Courtney Drake Shaarawi, J.D.

LEGAL EDITORIAL ASSISTANTS
Erin Gage, J.D.
Victoria R. Guzman, J.D.
Erwin K. Kristel, J.D.
Patrick M. Miller, J.D.
Colin K. Morrison, J.D.
Alejandro Mota, J.D.
Amanda D. Pesonen, J.D.
Christian Eric Engelbrecht Ryholt

PRODUCTION MANAGER
Donna E. Vass

PRODUCTION EDITOR
Annabelle M. Wilde

PRODUCTION STAFF
Sara Rhodes Bean
Evan Gabriel Bernard
Nicole E. Hammond
Clare Jensen
Rachel L. Jobe
Sara C. Rolater
Sarah M. Rutledge
Daniel Spence
Emily J. Viehman

PROOFREADERS
Sara Rhodes Bean
Evan Gabriel Bernard
Clare Jensen
Kathryn A. Ritcheske, J.D.
Sarah M. Rutledge
Annabelle M. Wilde

JOAN FOOTE JENKINS
RANDALL B. WILHITE

Master Table of Contents

Abortion – definition. Family Code §§33.001 and 161.006 were both amended to remove the current definition of "abortion" and to replace it with the definition under Health & Safety Code §245.002, which was also amended this session.

Adoption – access to information. Family Code §162.0062 was amended to authorize a prospective adoptive parent to examine any record or other information relating to a child's health history if the child has been placed with the prospective adoptive parent before adoption. The amended law also outlines who is responsible for informing the prospective adoptive parents of this right and redacting the necessary information from the relevant documents to protect the identity of the biological parents.

Adoption – custody transfer of adopted child. Family Code §162.026 was enacted to specify the limited circumstances in which a parent, managing conservator, or guardian of an adopted child can transfer permanent physical custody of the child.

Adoption – health history of child. Family Code §162.007 was amended to add new information that must be provided in the child's health history. Under the amended law, the child's health history must include, if known, whether the child's birth mother consumed alcohol during pregnancy and whether the child has been diagnosed with fetal alcohol spectrum disorder.

Adoption – health & social report. Family Code §162.005 was amended to require that the TDFPS ensure that each licensed child-placing agency, single-source continuum contractor, or other person placing a child for adoption receives a copy of any portion of the health, social, educational, and genetic history report that has been prepared by the department.

Adoption – notice of sibling access. Family Code §162.0086 was enacted to require disclosure by the TDFPS to any person seeking to adopt a child who is placed for adoption by the department about the right of a child's sibling to file a suit for access under Family Code §§102.0045 and 153.551.

Adoption – postadoption support information. Family Code §162.603 was enacted to require a licensed child-placing agency to provide prospective adoptive parents with information about the community services and other resources available to support a parent who adopts a child and the options available to the adoptive parent if the parent is unable to care for the adopted child.

Appellate review – accelerated appeals. Family Code §109.002 was amended to clarify that an appeal from a final order rendered under Family Code ch. 152 (UCCJEA) must comply with Family Code §152.314, which governs accelerated appeals.

Associate judge – powers. Family Code §201.007 was amended to establish that certain final orders rendered and signed by an associate judge become final after the deadline to request a de novo hearing with the referring court expires. Further, the amended law authorizes an associate judge to render a final order in a SAPCR if the parties waive, in writing and before the start of a hearing conducted by the associate judge, their right to a de novo hearing with the referring court. Section 201.007 also retroactively allows an associate judge to render certain final orders.

Associate judge – powers in Title IV-D cases. Family Code §201.104 was amended to clarify that an associate judge can hear and render an order on any matter necessary to be decided in connection with a Title IV-D service, including a SAPCR and a modification suit under Family Code ch. 156. Family Code §201.204 was similarly amended to clarify that an associate judge can hear and render an order in an adoption suit for a child whose managing conservator is the TDFPS.

Attorney ad litem – continuation of appointment in government suit. Family Code §107.016 was amended to limit the amount of a time a court can extend an attorney ad litem appointment. Under the amended law, an order that appoints the TDFPS as a child's managing conservator can also order the continuation of the attorney ad litem appointment, but the appointment can no longer continue beyond when the child leaves the conservatorship of the TDFPS.

Attorney ad litem – powers & duties. Family Code §107.003 was amended to require an attorney ad litem to determine whether a child who is at least 16 has received the following: a certified copy of the child's birth certificate, a Social Security card, a driver's license or personal identification certificate, and any other personal document the TDFPS determines to be appropriate.

Child abuse – abbreviated investigation & administrative closure of certain cases. Family Code §261.3017[A*] was enacted to allow a caseworker to refer a reported case of child abuse or neglect within 60 days after receiving the report to a department supervisor for an abbreviated investigation or administrative closure. The code section outlines the necessary requirements and protocols.

Child abuse – abuse redefined. Family Code §261.001 was amended to expand the definition of "abuse" to include forcing or coercing a child to enter into a marriage.

Child abuse – anonymous report. Family Code §261.304 was amended to create an exception to the authorization to visit a child's home as part of an investigation of an anonymous report. Under the amended law, a home visit should not be done if the alleged abuse or neglect can be confirmed or clearly ruled out without a home visit.

Child abuse – investigating agencies. Family Code §261.401 was amended to remove the definitions of "abuse," "exploitation," and "neglect" from the statute.

Child abuse – investigating juvenile justice programs & facilities. Family Code §261.405 was amended to include definitions of "abuse," "exploitation," and "neglect."

Child abuse – central registry. Family Code §261.002 was amended to specify when and under what circumstances a person's name must be removed from the central registry

Child abuse – exploitation defined. Family Code §261.001 was amended to include a definition of "exploitation."

Child abuse – investigation of report. Family Code §261.301 was amended to require the TDFPS to determine whether an alleged abuser who is responsible for a child's care, custody, or welfare is an active-duty member of the U.S. armed forces or the spouse of an active-duty member, and if so, to notify the U.S. Department of Defense Family Advocacy Program at the closest active-duty military installation of the investigation. The code section was further amended to require the department to designate employees to serve as investigators and responders for after-hours reports of child abuse or neglect in geographic areas that have demonstrated a need for such services.

Child abuse – neglect. Family Code §261.001 was amended to expand the definition of "neglect" to include a negligent act or omission by an employee, volunteer, or other individual working under the auspices of a facility or program that causes or may cause substantial emotional harm or physical injury to, or the death of, a child served by the facility or program.

Child abuse – person responsible for child's care, custody, or welfare. Family Code §261.001 was amended to expand the definition of "person responsible for child's care, custody, or welfare" to include an employee, volunteer, or other person working under the supervision of a licensed or unlicensed child-care facility.

Child abuse – TDFPS protective order. Family Code ch. 261, subchapter F (§§261.501-261.505), was enacted as "Protective Order in Certain Cases of Abuse or Neglect." The new law allows the TDFPS to file an application for a protective order to protect a child if the department (1) has temporary managing conservatorship of the child, (2) determines that the child is a victim of abuse or neglect, has a history of being abused or neglected, or lives in certain threatening circumstances, and (3) is not otherwise authorized to apply for a protective order under Family Code ch. 82.

Child-custody evaluation – elements of evaluation. Family Code §107.109 was amended to prohibit a child-custody evaluator from offering an opinion about the conservatorship of a child until the evaluator first completes any additional elements ordered by the court, as well as the statutorily required basic elements. Section 107.109 was further amended to narrow the interview requirement to only those parties seeking conservatorship, possession of, or access to the child, and the statute no longer requires the evaluator to interview a child who is under the age of four.

Also, the language in the subsections that required the evaluator to assess a party's "home environment" was changed to make this an optional evaluation of a party's "residence" that can be ordered by the court.

Child-custody evaluation – evaluator immunity. Family Code §107.009 was amended to give a child-custody evaluator who is appointed under Family Code ch. 107 immunity from civil liability unless gross negligence, conscious indifference, or bad faith can be proved.

Child-custody evaluation – powers & duties. Family Code §107.1111 was enacted to allow a child-custody evaluator to obtain records that relate to any person living in a residence subject to a child-custody evaluation. The new code section further outlines the parameters of disclosing this information and the consequences for recklessly disclosing confidential information.

Child-custody evaluation – providing completed report. Family Code §107.113 was amended to remove the language that required the child-custody evaluator to file the evaluation report with the court at a time set by the court and also to remove the language that required the report to be included as part of the case record. Under the amended law, the statute requires the evaluator to file notice with the court when the report is complete. Further, the statute specifies who must be provided with copies of the report and the necessary timeline. Family Code §107.114 was also amended to reflect that disclosure of the child-custody evaluation report to the court is subject to the rules of evidence.

Child-custody evaluation – requirements for order. Family Code §107.103 was amended to exclude the order requirements of subsection (c) for child-custody evaluators who are qualified under Family Code §107.104(b)(3). Further, §107.103 was amended to require that an order for a child-custody evaluation include a list of the statutorily required elements of the evaluation, as well as a list of any additional elements the court requires.

Child support – property subject to child-support liens. Family Code §157.317 was amended to clarify that proceeds from the sale of oil or gas production from a well located in Texas are subject to a child-support lien.

Dissolution of marriage – findings of fact. Family Code §6.711 was amended to clarify that the written findings of fact and conclusions of law required under this section, in a dissolution suit in which the court has rendered a judgment dividing the parties' estate, must include the characterization and value of all assets, liabilities, claims, and offsets on which disputed evidence has been presented. Further, the amended statute states that findings under this code section should be completed in addition to any other findings and conclusions required by law.

Dissolution of marriage – petition requirements. Family Code §6.405 was amended to expand the kinds of protective orders that must be referenced in a petition to dissolve a marriage. Under the amended section, a petitioner must now state whether a protective order under Code of Criminal Procedure (CCP) ch. 7A or an order for emergency protection under CCP art. 17.292 is in effect or pending and attach a copy of each order to the petition.

Domestic violence & sexual abuse. Family Code §153.004 was amended to replace "physical or sexual abuse" with "abuse" and to add "family violence" throughout. Further, the law was amended to expand the rebuttable presumption that it is not in the child's best interest for a parent to have unsupervised visitation with the child if there is evidence of neglect, abuse, or family violence by the parent to also include the same evidence of neglect, abuse, or family violence by any person who resides in that parent's household or who is permitted by that parent to have unsupervised access to the child during the parent's periods of possession.

Embryo donation. Family Code ch. 162, subchapter H (§§162.701 and 162.702), was enacted as "Embryo Donation Information." The new subchapter requires the TDFPS to post information about embryo donation on the department's website that includes contact information for nonprofit organizations that facilitate embryo donation.

Enforcement – indigency hearing for court-appointed attorney. Family Code §157.163 was amended to allow the court to conduct an indigency hearing through the use of teleconferencing, videoconferencing, or other remote electronic means if the court determines that doing so will facilitate the hearing.

Enforcement – release hearing. Family Code §157.105 was amended to allow the court to conduct a release hearing through the use of teleconferencing, videoconferencing, or other remote electronic means if the court determines that doing so will facilitate the hearing.

Family violence & abuse – defined. Family Code §261.001 was amended to expand the definition of "abuse" to include forcing or coercing a child to enter into a marriage. The definition of "family violence" under Family Code §71.004 was also amended to include this form of abuse.

Family violence – confidential communications. Family Code ch. 93 (§§93.001-93.004), was enacted as "Confidential & Privileged Communications." The new chapter establishes the confidential and privileged nature of any written or oral communications between an advocate and a victim of family violence.

Foster care – defined. Family Code §101.0133 was amended to remove "agency foster group home," "foster group home," and "foster home" from the list of possible foster-care placement destinations and added "residential child-care facility," which includes an agency foster home, specialized child-care home, cottage home operation, general residential operation, or another facility licensed or certified under Human Resources Code ch. 42. Commensurate changes were made to Family Code §101.017, which defines "licensed child placing agency."

Foster parent – standing to intervene in suit requesting possessory conservatorship. Family Code §102.004 was amended to limit the ability of a foster parent to intervene in a pending suit requesting possessory conservatorship. Under the amended law, a foster parent can be granted leave to intervene in such a suit only if the foster parent would have standing to file an original suit as provided by Family Code §102.003(a)(12).

Guardian ad litem – continuation of appointment in TDFPS case. Family Code §107.016 was amended to limit the amount of a time a court can extend a guardian ad litem appointment for child. Under the amended law, an order appointing the TDFPS as a child's managing conservator can also order continuation of the guardian ad litem appointment as set by the court, but the appointment can now continue only while the child remains in TDFPS conservatorship.

Guardian ad litem – powers & duties. Family Code §107.002 was amended to require a guardian ad litem to determine whether a child who is at least 16 has received the following: a certified copy of the child's birth certificate, a Social Security card, a driver's license or personal identification certificate, and any other personal document the TDFPS determines to be appropriate. Further, under the amended law, the guardian ad litem is entitled to have access to the child's placement, be consulted about placement decisions, evaluate whether child-welfare service providers are protecting the child's best interest, receive notice and be invited to attend meetings related to the child's service plan, and attend court-ordered mediation in the child's case.

Mandatory transfer of SAPCR involving government suit. Family Code §155.201 was amended to require that a court with continuing, exclusive jurisdiction transfer the proceedings upon receiving notice that a court exercising jurisdiction under Family Code ch. 262 (i.e., government suit filed to protect a child) has ordered the transfer under Family Code §262.203(a)(2). Section 262.203 was similarly amended to allow a court exercising jurisdiction under ch. 262 to order this transfer. And Family Code §155.204 was amended to require, as opposed to authorize, the TDFPS to file a ch. 262 transfer order with the clerk of the court of continuing, exclusive jurisdiction and to further clarify that the clerk must transfer the order within the time frame required under Family Code §155.207(a), with no hearing or order from the court of continuing, exclusive jurisdiction.

Marriage – minor. Family Code §6.205 was amended, along with other Family Code sections, to ensure that a person under the age of 16 cannot be married in Texas. Under the new law, a marriage is void if either party to the marriage is under 18, unless the underage party has been granted a court order removing the disabilities of minority for general purposes.

Marriage – underage applicants. Family Code §§2.102 and 2.103 were repealed and §2.101 was amended to prohibit a person under the age of 16 from getting married and to ensure that a minor who petitions the court to marry has access to an attorney and has the same legal protections as the person she is marrying. Under the new law, a

county clerk cannot issue a marriage license if either applicant is under 18, unless each underage applicant can show that the applicant has been granted a court order removing the disabilities of minority for general purposes.

Marriage license – age of absent applicant. Family Code §2.006 was amended to increase the age requirement of an absent applicant to 18. A person under 18 can no longer have another person apply for a marriage license on her behalf.

Marriage license – application by minor. Family Code §2.003 was amended, along with other Family Code sections, to prohibit a person under the age of 16 from getting married and to ensure that a minor who petitions the court to marry has access to an attorney and has the same legal protections as the person she is marrying. Under the new law, a person under 18 can marry only if she (1) has been granted a court order removing the disabilities of minority for general purposes and (2) provides the order to the county clerk with the marriage application. An out-of-state order must be certified and filed with the State of Texas under Family Code §31.007.

Marriage license – information on license. Family Code §2.009 was amended to require that a license issued under this section identify the county in which it was issued. The license can now also include the name of the county clerk.

Marriage license – who can apply. Family Code §2.009 was amended, along with other Family Code sections, to prohibit a person under the age of 16 from getting married and to ensure that a minor who petitions to marry has access to an attorney and has the same legal protections as the person she is marrying. Under the new law, an applicant for a marriage license must be at least 18 or, if under 18, have been granted a court order removing the disabilities of minority for general purposes. A county clerk may no longer issue a marriage license to a person who is 16 or 17 based on parental consent or the dissolution of a former marriage.

Mediated settlement agreement – court review. Family Code §153.0071 was amended to provide a new rationale for a court to decline to enter judgment on a mediated settlement agreement. Under the amended law, a court can decline to enter judgment on a mediated settlement agreement if the court finds that the agreement (1) would permit a person to reside in the same household as the child or otherwise have unsupervised access to the child if that person is subject to registration under Code of Criminal Procedure ch. 62, based on an offense committed when she was at least 17 years old, or if the person otherwise has a history or pattern of past or present physical or sexual abuse directed against any person, and (2) is not in the child's best interest.

Modification suit – frivolous finding. Family Code §156.005 was amended to require that a court state in its order its finding that a modification suit has been filed frivolously or is designed to harass a party.

Modification suit – temporary orders. Family Code §156.006 was amended to clarify that generally a temporary order issued while a modification suit is pending cannot have the effect of (1) creating a designation of the person who has the exclusive right to designate the child's primary residence or (2) creating a geographic area, or changing or eliminating the geographic area, within which a conservator must maintain the child's primary residence under the final order.

Nonparent authorization agreement – applicability. Former Family Code ch. 34, "Authorization Agreement for Nonparent Relative," was amended to read "Authorization Agreement for Nonparent Adult Caregiver." Family Code §34.001, which listed the family members who could enter into an authorization agreement, was repealed, and §34.0015 was enacted to define both "adult caregiver" and "parent."

Nonparent authorization agreement – contents. Family Code §34.003 was amended to require that an authorization agreement include a statement indicating that the agreement is for a term of six months with automatic six-month renewals or for a specific term less than six months, as well as a statement identifying the circumstances under which the agreement may be terminated or continued beyond its stated term.

Nonparent authorization agreement – not foster care. Family Code §34.0022 was enacted to provide that an adult caregiver who is a party to an authorization agreement is not subject to any law or rule governing the licensing or regulation of a residential child-care facility under Human Resources Code ch. 42. Further, the new code section

provides that a child who is the subject of an authorization agreement is not considered to be placed in foster care and that the parties to the agreement are not subject to any law or rule governing foster-care providers.

Nonparent authorization agreement – notice for nonparty parent. Family Code §34.005 was amended to require that two copies of the executed authorization agreement be mailed simultaneously by two separate means to a parent who was not a party to the agreement.

Nonparent authorization agreement – powers. Family Code §34.002 was amended to expand the authority of an adult caregiver who is a party to an authorization agreement to include obtaining state-issued personal identification documents for the child, including the child's birth certificate, and federally issued personal identification documents for the child, including the child's Social Security card.

Nonparent authorization agreement – term. Family Code §34.0075 was enacted to establish automatically renewing six-month terms that apply unless a shorter term is specified, the agreement is terminated, or a court permits the agreement to continue under Family Code §34.008(b).

Parentage – petition requirements for suit to adjudicate. Family Code §160.6035 was enacted to require that any party, except the TDFPS, who files a petition in a proceeding to adjudicate parentage must state in the petition whether certain protective orders, in regard to a party or a child of a party, are currently in effect or whether an application for those orders is pending. Specifically, the petition must provide information about protective orders under Family Code title 4 and Code of Criminal Procedure (CCP) ch. 7A, as well as orders for emergency protection under CCP art. 17.292. If (1) an order is in effect, (2) a party to the suit or a child of a party to the suit was the applicant or the victim of the alleged conduct, and (3) the other party was the respondent or defendant in an action regarding the alleged conduct, the petitioner must attach a copy of each relevant order to the petition.

Property division – limits on power to enforce or clarify. Family Code §9.007 was amended to remove the statutory provision requiring the temporary abatement of a court's power to render further orders to assist in the implementation or clarification of a property division ordered in a divorce or annulment decree while appellate proceedings were pending. Instead, the section now prohibits a court from rendering such an order until 30 days after the final judgment is signed. The court is further prohibited from rendering such an order if a timely motion for a new trial or to vacate, modify, correct, or reform the decree is filed. In that case, the court cannot render an order to assist in the implementation or clarification of the property division until the 30th day after an order overruling the motion is signed or the motion is overruled by operation of law.

Protective orders – access to confidential information. Family Code §85.007 was amended to allow a law-enforcement agency to access the confidential record of information for a person protected by a protective order for the purpose of entering the information into a statewide law-enforcement information system.

Protective orders – confidentiality of applicant's mailing address. Family Code §82.011 was enacted to allow an applicant for a protective order who is not represented by an attorney to designate another person to receive court-related correspondence and to prohibit the court clerk from releasing the applicant's mailing address to the respondent. Family Code §82.041, which specifies the requirements for notice of an application for a protective order, was also amended to allow for this new protection.

Protective orders – motion to terminate. Family Code §85.025 was amended to limit the number of times a person who is the subject of a protective order can file a motion asking the court to determine whether there is a continuing need for the protective order. Under the amended law, a person who is the subject of a protective order that is effective for more than two years can now file only one motion of this kind. Further, §85.025 was amended to prohibit a person who is the subject of a protective order issued under Code of Criminal Procedure ch. 7A from asking the court for a continuing need determination at all.

Receiver – appointment. Family Code §6.502 was amended to require a court to issue written findings of fact and conclusions of law in support of appointing a receiver under this section within seven days of the appointment. If the court chooses to dispense with the issuance of the bond under Family Code §6.503, the amended section further requires the court to include its rationale for this decision.

SAPCR – petition requirements. Family Code §102.008 was amended to require that any party, except the TDFPS, who files a SACPR must state in the petition whether certain protective orders, in regard to a party or a child of a party, are currently in effect or whether an application for those orders is pending. Specifically, the petition must provide information about protective orders under Family Code title 4 and Code of Criminal Procedure (CCP) ch. 7A, as well as orders for emergency protection under CCP art. 17.292. If (1) an order is in effect, (2) a party to the suit or a child of a party to the suit was the applicant or the victim of the alleged conduct, and (3) the other party was the respondent or defendant in an action regarding the alleged conduct, the petitioner must attach a copy of each relevant order to the petition.

SAPCR – request for findings related to child-support order. Family Code §154.130 was amended to change the time period during which a party can file a written request for findings of fact. Under the amended law, a party must file a request for findings of fact before the final order is signed and no later than 20 days after the court has rendered its order. As amended, the code section no longer provides a deadline for the court to comply with a request for findings, and the court does not have to state the obligee's monthly net resources unless evidence of the net resources have been offered.

SAPCR – request for findings related to possession order. Family Code §§153.254 and 153.258 were amended to create one standard for requesting findings when a parent contests possession of a child and the possession order varies from the standard possession order. Section 153.258 no longer has a deadline for filing a request for findings, and this code section now addresses a possession order for a child under the age of three. Further, a request for findings of fact under this code section must now conform to the Texas Rules of Civil Procedure.

Temporary authorization for care of minor child – no parental consent. Family Code ch. 35 (§§35.001-35.007), was enacted to allow a person to seek a court order for temporary authorization for the care of a child if (1) the person's relationship to the child would make the person eligible to consent to the child's medical, dental, psychological, or surgical treatment under Family Code §32.001 or eligible to enter an authorization agreement under Family Code ch. 34, (2) the child has resided with the person for at least 30 days before filing the petition, and (3) the person does not have authorization under ch. 34 or other written permission from a parent, conservator, or guardian that enables the person to provide necessary care for the child.

Temporary orders during appeal. Family Code §6.709, for dissolution suits, and §109.001, for SAPCRs, were amended to remove the 30-day deadline for a court to render a temporary order pending appeal and to instead give the court jurisdiction to conduct a hearing and sign an original temporary order up to 60 days after an eligible party has filed notice of appeal from a final judgment under the Texas Rules of Appellate Procedure. Under both statutes, the standard for an award of attorney fees was also changed to require that the fees be necessary as well as reasonable. Section 6.709 amendments clarify that a temporary order under this section can be directed toward one or both parties and add a new requirement that a temporary order must be considered equitable as well as necessary. Section 6.709 was also amended to allow a temporary order to (1) enjoin a party from dissipating or transferring property that was awarded to the other party as part of the court's property division and (2) suspend the operation of all or part of the property division that is being appealed. Both §§6.709 and 109.001 provide the necessary parameters of these orders and establish the requirements for modifying a temporary order under each section.

Termination of parent-child relationship – child support. Family Code §154.001 was amended to expand the conditions under which a court can order a parent who is financially able and whose parental rights have been terminated to support the child. Under the amended law, if the TDFPS has been appointed managing conservator of the child because the parent has been convicted of sexual assault or aggravated sexual assault of the other parent or has been placed on community supervision for being criminally responsible for the sexual assault or aggravated sexual assault of the other parent, the offending parent can be required to pay child support.

Termination of parent-child relationship – ground related to family service plans. Family Code §161.001 was amended to prohibit a court from terminating the parent-child relationship under §161.001(b)(1)(O) based on a parent's failure to comply with a specific court-ordered provision if the parent proves by a preponderance of evidence that (1) the parent was unable to comply with specific provisions of the court order and (2) the parent made a good-faith effort to comply with the order and failure to comply is not attributable to any fault of the parent.

Termination of parent-child relationship – limitations on certain evidence. Family Code §161.001 was amended to prohibit the court from making a finding and ordering termination of the parent-child relationship based on evidence that the parent homeschooled a child, is economically disadvantaged, has been charged with a certain nonviolent misdemeanor offense, administered prescribed low-THC cannabis to a child, or declined immunization for a child for reasons of conscience, including a religious belief.

Termination of parent-child relationship – new grounds. Family Code §161.001 was amended to add two new grounds for terminating the parent-child relationship. Under the amended law, a court can order the termination of the parent-child relationship if there is a finding by clear and convincing evidence that the parent has been convicted of, or has been placed on community supervision for being criminally responsible for, the sexual assault or aggravated sexual assault of the child's other parent.

Termination of parent-child relationship – parental rights. Family Code §161.206 was amended to clarify that in a termination suit filed by the TDFPS that seeks to terminate the parent-child relationship for more than one parent, the court must find grounds for termination for each parent by clear and convincing evidence.

Title IV-D suit – affidavit required with suit to take possession of child. Family Code §262.113 was amended to require more specific assertions in the necessary affidavit when filing a suit to take possession of a child based on the potential harm the child could experience. Specifically, the affidavit must assert the following: (1) there is a continuing danger to the physical health or safety of the child caused by an act or failure to act of the person entitled to possession of the child, (2) allowing the child to remain in the home would be contrary to the child's welfare, and (3) reasonable efforts, consistent with the circumstances and providing for the safety of the child, have been made to prevent or eliminate the need to remove the child from the home.

Title IV-D suit – appointment of surrogate parent for child with disabilities. Family Code §263.0025 was amended to do the following: eliminate the requirement that a court give preferential consideration to a foster parent of a child with a disability when assigning a surrogate parent for the child, expand the qualifications necessary to become a surrogate parent, and provide a clarified list of people who cannot serve as a surrogate parent under the statute.

Title IV-D suit – assessment of child's needs. Family Code §264.1075 was amended to require the TDFPS to refer a child who has been assessed as potentially having an intellectual disability for a formal determination of intellectual disability as soon as possible and to ensure that the determination is conducted by an authorized provider before the child's 16th birthday. If the child who is placed in the managing conservatorship of the department is already 16, the determination must be conducted as soon as possible after the initial assessment.

Title IV-D suit – assessment of proposed placement. Family Code §264.754 was amended to define "low-risk criminal offense" and to give a person who was convicted of a low-risk criminal offense the right to appeal being disqualified from serving as a relative caregiver or other designated caregiver for a child if the disqualification was based on the low-risk criminal offense.

Title IV-D suit – caregiver assistance agreement. Family Code §264.755 was amended to change the way the amount of money provided to a person under a caregiver assistance agreement is calculated. Family Code §264.7551 was enacted to make it a criminal offense to knowingly, and with intent to defraud or deceive the TDFPS, make or cause to be made a false statement or misrepresentation of a material fact that allows a person to enter into a caregiver assistance agreement.

Title IV-D suit – child fatality & near-fatality data. Family Code §§264.5031 and 264.5032 were enacted to define "near fatality" and to require the TDFPS to collect data on near-fatality child abuse or neglect cases and to further produce a detailed report relating to child fatality and near-fatality cases.

Title IV-D suit – child fatality report. Family Code §261.204 was amended to specify a date, March 1, as the annual deadline for the TDFPS to publish the aggregated child fatality report.

Title IV-D suit – child-fatality review-team committee members. Family Code §264.502 was amended to require that the child-fatality review-team committee have three new members. Under the amended law, the committee must include a person appointed by and representing the speaker of the house of representatives, the lieutenant governor, and the governor.

Title IV-D suit – community-based care. Family Code ch. 264, subchapter B-1 (§§264.151-264.170), was enacted as "Community-Based Care" to provide the mandate and parameters to the TDFPS for contracting with community-based nonprofit and local governmental entities that have the ability to provide child-welfare services.

Title IV-D suit – confirmation of agreed child-support review order. Family Code §233.024 was amended to state that an agreed child-support review order will be considered confirmed by the court, by operation of law, on the fourth day after the order was filed, even if the court has not signed the order by the third day after the order has been filed as otherwise required by the statute.

Title IV-D suit – court review of placement. Family Code §262.0022 was enacted to require a court at each hearing under Family Code ch. 262 to review the placement of each child in the temporary or permanent managing conservatorship of the TDFPS who is not placed with a relative caregiver or designated caregiver as defined by Family Code §264.751. Further the court must include in its findings a statement on whether the department has the option of placing the child with a relative or other designated caregiver.

Title IV-D suit – definitions related to placement of child. Family Code §263.001 was amended to add a definition of "least restrictive setting" and to provide more guidance for determining the least restrictive setting depending on a child's age. The same definition of "least restrictive setting" was also added to Family Code §264.001 in the chapter addressing child welfare services.

Title IV-D suit – disclosure of certain evidence. Family Code §262.014 was enacted to require disclosure by the TDFPS of witness names, copies of relevant offense reports, and a copy of any photograph, video, or recording that will be presented as evidence, if the attorney for a parent who is a party to the SAPCR or an attorney ad litem for the parent's child requests this information.

Title IV-D suit – filing requirement. Family Code §262.013[A*] was enacted to require that any suit filed under Family Code ch. 262 based on allegations of abuse or neglect arising from the same incident or occurrence and involving children that live in the same home must be filed in the same court.

Title IV-D suit – findings on health-care consultation. Family Code §266.005 was enacted to require a court to make findings in the record supporting the court's order if the court declines to follow the recommendation of a health-care professional that the court has found to have been consulted about a health-care service, procedure, or treatment for a child in the TDFPS's conservatorship.

Title IV-D suit – full adversary hearing. Family Code §262.201 was amended to allow the court to postpone the full adversary hearing if a parent appears in opposition to the suit. The code section was further amended to require that the full adversary hearing be held no later than 30 days after the suit is filed.

Title IV-D suit – independent-living-skills assessment. Family Code §264.121 was amended to require the TDFPS to conduct an independent-living-skills assessment for all youth in the department's (1) permanent conservatorship who are between 14 and 16 and (2) conservatorship who are 16 or older. The amended statute also outlines how to update these assessments.

Title IV-D suit – insurer reporting. Family Code §231.015 was amended to create additional exemptions for insurer disclosures that otherwise help the AG's Child Support Division intercept awards or claims to satisfy child-support payments that are owed. Under the amended law, an insurer can no longer be required to report or identify claims for benefits that are (1) assigned to be paid to a funeral-service provider or facility for funeral expenses owed by the insured, (2) assigned to be paid to a health-care provider or facility for medical expenses owed by the insured, or (3) to be paid under a limited-benefit insurance policy that provides coverage for diseases, dental or vision benefits, or hospital indemnity or other fixed indemnity coverage.

Title IV-D suit – jurisdiction after one year. Family Code §263.401 was amended to allow for the automatic termination of a court's jurisdiction over a SAPCR that seeks to terminate the parent-child relationship or appoint the TDFPS as the child's managing conservator. Under the amended law, the court's jurisdiction over such a suit will automatically terminate and the suit will be dismissed on the first Monday after the first anniversary of the date the court rendered a temporary order appointing the department as temporary managing conservator, unless the court has commenced the trial on the merits or granted an extension. Under the amended law, the court must provide notice of the automatic dismissal date to all parties at least 60 days before that date. The code section was further amended to terminate the court's jurisdiction in the event of a court-ordered extension if the court does not commence the trial on the merits before the extended dismissal date.

Title IV-D suit – medical examination for child. Family Code §264.1076 was enacted to require the TDFPS to ensure that certain children who are removed from their homes receive a medical examination from a physician or other health-care provider no later than the end of the third business day after the child was removed.

Title IV-D suit – monitored return of child. Family Code §263.403 was amended to add a new rationale for keeping jurisdiction, despite the automatic dismissal required by Family Code §263.401. Under the amended law, a court can keep jurisdiction, without dismissing the suit, if the court renders a temporary order that transitions the child from substitute care to the parent while the parent completes the necessary service plan requirements. The code section was further amended to allow the TDFPS or the parent to ask the court to retain jurisdiction for an additional six months to allow the parent time to complete the service plan.

Title IV-D suit – no ex parte hearings. Family Code §262.206 was enacted to prohibit ex parte hearings in a suit under Family Code ch. 262.

Title IV-D suit – no investigation based on request for information. Family Code §264.2043 was enacted to prohibit the initiation of an investigation of child abuse or neglect based solely on a request submitted to the TDFPS by a child's parent for information related to services provided for families in crisis.

Title IV-D suit – notice of hearing & presenting evidence for placing child. Family Code §263.0021 was amended to require that notice of a hearing for individuals listed under §263.0021(b)(2) state that the individual may, but is not required to, attend the hearing and can ask to be heard at the hearing. The code section was further amended to require the court to determine whether the child's caregiver is present at the hearing and, if so, to let the caregiver testify about the child if the caregiver wishes to do so.

Title IV-D suit – permanency hearing. Family Code §263.306 was amended to specify additional determinations that must be made by a court at a permanency hearing for a child whose permanency goal is another planned permanent living arrangement. Family Code §263.4041 was enacted to verify the child's information related to this same transition. These standards were also added to Family Code §263.5031.

Title IV-D suit – petition after taking possession of child in emergency. Family Code §262.105 was amended to include a requirement that in an original SAPCR filed after taking possession of a child in an emergency to protect the child, the TDFPS must include an affidavit stating facts sufficient to satisfy a person of ordinary prudence and caution that when the child was taken (1) the child faced an immediate danger, (2) continuation of the child in the home would have been contrary to the child's welfare, (3) there was no time for a full adversary hearing, and (4) reasonable efforts were made to avoid removing the child.

Title IV-D suit – placement of child. Family Code §264.107 was amended to include a new factor to consider when selecting a placement for a child—whether the placement is in the child's best interest. Under the amended statute, factors that reflect best interest include whether the placement is the least restrictive setting for the child, is the closest in geographic proximity to the child's home, is the most able to meet the identified needs of the child, and satisfies any expressed interests of the child relating to placement when developmentally appropriate.

Title IV-D suit – removal limits. Family Code §262.116 was enacted to prohibit the TDFPS from taking possession of a child based on evidence that a parent homeschooled a child, is economically disadvantaged, has been charged

with certain nonviolent misdemeanor offenses, administered prescribed low-THC cannabis to a child, or declined immunization for a child for reasons of conscience, including a religious belief.

Title IV-D suit – service of citation. Family Code §231.118 was amended to prohibit the inclusion of the address served in a return of process if (1) a pleading filed in the suit requests a finding under Family Code §105.006(c) or (2) the court has already made a finding and ordered nondisclosure under §105.006(c) relating to the parties and the order has not been superseded.

Title IV-D suit – standard for returning child who was taken in emergency. Family Code §262.107 was amended to include two new distinct rationales for not returning a child who was taken into TDFPS possession in an emergency to include (1) the parent or person who has possession of the child is currently using a controlled substance and constitutes an immediate danger to the child and (2) the parent or person who has possession of the child has permitted the child to remain on premises used for the manufacture of methamphetamine.

Title IV-D suit – temporary restraining order before full adversary hearing. Family Code §262.1131 was enacted to allow a court to render a temporary restraining order in a suit filed under Family Code §262.113.

Title IV-D suit – Title IV-D case redefined. Family Code §101.034 was amended to define "Title IV-D case" to include modification suits filed by the Title IV-D agency under Family Code §231.101 and any other action relating to services provided under that section.

Title IV-D suit – voluntary temporary managing conservatorship. Family Code §262.013[B*] was enacted to assert that a parent's voluntary agreement to temporarily place the parent's child in the managing conservatorship of the department is not an admission by the parent that the parent engaged in conduct that endangered the child.

Volunteer advocates – surrogate parent requirements. Family Code §107.031 was amended to add an additional requirement for a volunteer advocate to become a surrogate parent for a child. Under the amended law, a volunteer advocate can only become a surrogate parent if she completes a training program for surrogate parents that complies with the minimum standards established by the Texas Education Agency.

FAMILY CODE SECTIONS AFFECTED BY 2017 LEGISLATION

Legend: Ⓐ Amended Ⓔ Enacted Ⓡ Repealed

§	HEADING	ACTION
Marriage		
2.003	Application for license by minor	A
2.006	Absent applicant	A
2.009	Issuance of license	A
2.014	Family trust fund	A
2.101	General age requirement	A
2.102	Parental consent for underage applicant	R
2.103	Court order for underage applicant	R
Marital Property		
3.406	Equitable lien	A
Homesteads		
5.002	Sale of separate homestead after spouse judicially declared incapacitated	A
5.003	Sale of community homestead after spouse judicially declared incapacitated	A
Dissolution of Marriage		
6.111	Death of party to voidable marriage	A
6.205	Marriage to minor	A
6.405	Protective order & related orders	A
6.502	Temporary injunction & other temporary orders	A
6.709	Temporary orders during appeal	A
6.711	Findings of fact & conclusions of law	A
Post-decree Proceedings		
9.007	Limitation on power of court to enforce	A
Consent to Abortion		
33.001	Definitions	A
Authorization Agreements		
34.001	Applicability	R
34.0015	Definitions	A
34.002	Authorization agreement	A
34.0021	Authorization agreement by parent in child protective services case	A

§	HEADING	ACTION
Authorization Agreements (continued)		
34.0022	Inapplicability of certain laws	E
34.003	Contents of authorization agreement	A
34.004	Execution of authorization agreement	A
34.005	Duties of parties to authorization agreement	A
34.007	Effect of authorization agreement	A
34.0075	Term of authorization agreement	E
34.008	Termination of authorization agreement	A
Temporary Authorization for Care of Child		
35.001	Applicability	E
35.002	Temporary authorization	E
35.003	Petition for temporary authorization for care of child	E
35.004	Notice; hearing	E
35.005	Order for temporary authorization	E
35.006	Renewal or termination of temporary authorization	E
35.007	Effect of temporary authorization	E
Title 2 – General		
47.003	Use of digitized signature	A
Juvenile Justice Code – General		
51.03	Delinquent conduct; conduct indicating a need for supervision	A
51.13	Effect of adjudication or disposition	A
Juvenile Justice Proceedings		
52.011	Duty of law enforcement officer to notify probate court	E
52.031	First offender program	A
53.01	Preliminary investigation & determinations; notice to parents	A
53.011	Services provided to certain children & families	E
54.04	Disposition hearing	A
54.04012	Trafficked persons program	A

Summary of 2017 Legislation

Family Code Sections Affected by 2017 Legislation

§	HEADING	ACTION
Juvenile Justice Proceedings (continued)		
54.0404	Electronic transmission of certain visual material depicting minor: educational programs	A
54.10	Hearings before referee	A
Juvenile Justice Records		
58.001	Law enforcement collection & transmittal of records of children	A
58.002	Photographs & fingerprints of children	A
58.0021	Fingerprints or photographs for comparison in investigation	A
58.003	Sealing of records	A
58.004	Redaction of victim's personally identifiable information	A
58.005	Confidentiality of facility records	A
58.0051	Interagency sharing of educational records	A
58.0052	Interagency sharing of certain noneducational records	A
58.006	Destruction of certain records	R
58.007	Confidentiality of probation department, prosecutor, & court records	A
58.0071	Destruction of certain physical records & files	R
58.00711	Records relating to children charged with, convicted of, or receiving deferred disposition for fine-only misdemeanors	R
58.0072	[Renumbered as §58.009]	A
58.008	Confidentiality of law enforcement records	E
58.009	Dissemination of juvenile justice information by the Texas Juvenile Justice Department	A
58.102	Juvenile justice information system	A
58.104	Types of information collected	A
58.106	Dissemination of confidential information in juvenile justice information system	A
58.112	[Transferred to HumRes §203.019]	A
58.201	Definition	R
58.202	Exempted records	R

§	HEADING	ACTION
Juvenile Justice Records (continued)		
58.203	Certification	R
58.204	Restricted access on certification	R
58.205	Request to the Federal Bureau of Investigation on certification	R
58.206	Effect of certification in relation to the protected person	R
58.207	Juvenile court orders on certification	R
58.208	Information to child on discharge	R
58.209	Information to child by probation officer or Texas Juvenile Justice Department	R
58.210	Sealing or destruction of records not affected	R
58.211	Rescinding restricted access	R
58.251	Definitions	E
58.252	Exempted records	E
58.253	Sealing records without application: delinquent conduct	E
58.254	Certification of eligibility for sealing records without application for delinquent conduct	E
58.255	Sealing records without application: conduct indicating need for supervision	E
58.256	Application for sealing records	E
58.257	Hearing regarding sealing of records	E
58.258	Order sealing records	E
58.259	Actions taken on receipt of order to seal records	E
58.260	Inspection & release of sealed records	E
58.261	Effect of sealing records	E
58.262	Information given to child regarding sealing of records	E
58.263	Destruction of records: no probable cause	E
58.264	Permissible destruction of records	E
58.265	Juvenile records not subject to expunction	E
58.301	Definitions	A

FAMILY CODE SECTIONS AFFECTED BY 2017 LEGISLATION

§	HEADING	ACTION
Juvenile Justice Records (continued)		
58.303	Local juvenile justice information system	A
58.304	Types of information contained in a local juvenile information system	A
58.305	Partner agencies	A
58.306	Access to information; levels	A
58.307	Confidentiality of information	A
Protective Orders		
71.004	Family violence	A
82.011	Confidentiality of certain information	E
82.041	Contents of notice of application	A
85.007	Confidentiality of certain information	A
85.025	Duration of protective order	A
Confidential & Privileged Communications		
93.001	Definitions	E
93.002	Confidential communications	E
93.003	Privileged communications	E
93.004	Exceptions	E
Title 5 – Definitions		
101.0133	Foster care	A
101.017	Licensed child placing agency	A
101.034	Title IV-D case	A
Filing Suit		
102.004	Standing for grandparent or other person	A
102.008	Contents of petition	A
Settings, Hearings & Orders		
105.002	Jury	A
Court Appointments		
107.002	Powers & duties of guardian ad litem for child	A
107.003	Powers & duties of attorney ad litem for child & amicus attorney	A
107.004	Additional duties of attorney ad litem for child	A

§	HEADING	ACTION
Court Appointments (continued)		
107.009	Immunity	A
107.016	Continued representation; duration of appointment	A
107.031	Volunteer advocates	A
107.061-107.072 (Subch. E)	[Renumbered as §§107.251-107.262 and redesignated as Subch. G]	A
107.101-107.108 (Subch. F)	[Renumbered as §§107.301-107.308 and redesignated as Subch. H]	A
107.103	Order for child custody evaluation	A
107.109	Elements of child custody evaluation	A
107.110	Psychometric testing	A
107.1101	Effect of potentially undiagnosed serious mental illness	A
107.1111	Child custody evaluator access to other records	E
107.113	Child custody evaluation report required	A
107.114	Introduction & provision of child custody evaluation report	A
107.152	Applicability	A
107.154	Adoption evaluator: minimum qualifications	A
107.159	Requirements for pre-placement portion of adoption evaluation & report	A
107.160	Requirements for post-placement portion of adoption evaluation & report	A
107.251-107.262 (Subch. G)	Office of Child Representation & Office of Parent Representation	A
107.301-107.308 (Subch. H)	Managed Assigned Counsel Program for the Representation of Certain Children & Parents	A
Appeals		
109.001	Temporary orders during pendency of appeal	A
109.002	Appellate review	A
109.003	Payment for court reporter's record	A

Summary of 2017 Legislation

Family Code Sections Affected by 2017 Legislation

§	HEADING	ACTION
UCCJEA		
152.314	Accelerated appeals	A
Conservatorship, Possession & Access		
153.004	History of domestic violence or sexual abuse	A
153.0071	Alternate dispute resolution procedures	A
153.254	Child less than three years of age	A
153.258	Request for findings when order varies from standard order	A
Child Support		
154.001	Support of child	A
154.013	Continuation of duty to pay support after death of obligee	A
154.015	Acceleration of unpaid child support obligation	A
154.130	Findings in child support order	A
Jurisdiction; Transfer		
155.201	Mandatory transfer	A
155.204	Procedure for transfer	A
Modification Suits		
156.005	Frivolous filing of suit for modification	A
156.006	Temporary orders	A
Enforcement Suits		
157.105	Release hearing	A
157.163	Appointment of attorney	A
157.317	Property to which lien attaches	A
UPA		
160.6035	Contents of petition; statement relating to certain protective orders required	E
Termination Suits		
161.001	Involuntary termination of parent-child relationship	A
161.006	Termination after abortion	A
161.206	Order terminating parental rights	A

§	HEADING	ACTION
Adoption Suits		
162.005	Preparation of health, social, educational, & genetic history report	A
162.0062	Access to information	A
162.007	Contents of health, social, educational, & genetic history report	A
162.0086	Information regarding sibling access	E
162.026	Regulated custody transfer of adopted child	E
162.304	Financial & medical assistance	A
162.3041	Continuation of assistance after child's 18th birthday	A
162.603	Post-adoption support information provided by licensed child-placing agencies	E
162.701	Definitions	E
162.702	Information regarding embryo donation	E
Associate Judges		
201.007	Powers of associate judge	A
201.013	Order of court	A
201.014	Judicial action on associate judge's proposed order or judgment	A
201.016	Appellate review	A
201.104	Powers of associate judge	A
201.204	General powers of associate judge	A
Title IV-D Services		
231.013	Information resources steering committee	R
231.015	Insurance reporting program	A
231.118	Service of citation	A
Child Support Review Process		
233.024	Confirmation of agreed order	A
Competitive Bidding for Child Support Services		
236.001	Definition	R
236.002	Powers & duties of council	R
236.003	Child support collection agreement	R

Family Code Sections Affected by 2017 Legislation

§	HEADING	ACTION
Reports of Child Abuse or Neglect		
261.001	Definitions	A
261.002	Central registry	A
261.004[A*]	Tracking of recurrence of child abuse or neglect reports	E
261.004[B*]	Reference to executive commissioner or commission	E
261.101	Persons required to report; time to report	A
261.204	Annual child fatality report	A
261.301	Investigation of report	A
261.3017[A*]	Abbreviated investigation & administrative closure of certain cases	E
261.3017[B*]	Consultation with physician networks & systems regarding certain medical conditions	E
261.3023	Law enforcement response to child safety check alert	A
261.3024	Removal from child safety check alert list	A
261.3025	Child safety check alert list progress report	A
261.304	Investigation of anonymous report	A
261.401	Agency investigation	A
261.405	Investigations in juvenile justice programs & facilities	A
261.501	Filing application for protective order in certain cases of abuse or neglect	E
261.502	Certification of findings	E
261.503	Temporary ex parte order	E
261.504	Required findings; issuance of protective order	E
261.505	Application of other law	E
Suits by Governmental Entity		
262.0022	Review of placement; findings	E
262.011	Placement in secure agency foster home	A
262.012	Sealing of court records filed electronically	A
262.013[A*]	Filing requirement for petition regarding more than one child	E

§	HEADING	ACTION
Suits by Governmental Entity (continued)		
262.013[B*]	Voluntary temporary managing conservatorship	E
262.014	Disclosure of certain evidence	E
262.101	Filing petition before taking possession of child	A
262.1015	Removal of alleged perpetrator; offense	A
262.102	Emergency order authorizing possession of child	A
262.103	Duration of temporary order, temporary restraining order, & attachment	A
262.105	Filing petition after taking possession of child in emergency	A
262.106	Initial hearing after taking possession of child in emergency without court order	A
262.107	Standard for decision at initial hearing after taking possession of child without a court order in emergency	A
262.109	Notice to parent, conservator, or guardian	A
262.113	Filing suit without taking possession of child	A
262.1131	Temporary restraining order before full adversary hearing	E
262.116	Limits on removal	E
262.201	Full adversary hearing; findings of the court	A
262.203	Transfer of suit	A
262.205	Hearing when child not in possession of governmental entity	R
262.206	Ex parte hearings prohibited	E
262.353	Study to develop alternatives to relinquishment of custody to obtain mental health services	R
Child Under Care of DFPS		
263.001	Definitions	A
263.002	Review of placements by court; findings	A
263.0021	Notice of hearing; presentation of evidence	A

FAMILY CODE SECTIONS AFFECTED BY 2017 LEGISLATION

§	HEADING	ACTION
Child Under Care of DFPS (continued)		
263.0025	Special education decision-making for children in foster care	A
263.008	Foster children's bill of rights	A
263.009	Permanency planning meetings	A
263.306	Permanency hearings before final order	A
263.401	Dismissal after one year; new trials; extension	A
263.402	Limit on extension	A
263.403	Monitored return of child to parent	A
263.4041	Verification of transition plan	E
263.4055	Supreme court rules	E
263.5031	Permanency hearings following final order	A
263.603	Extended jurisdiction to determine guardianship	A
Child Welfare Services		
264.001	Definitions	A
264.0011	Reference to executive commissioner or commission	E
264.0111	Money earned by child	A
264.017	Required reporting	A
264.018	Required notifications	A
264.107	Placement of children	A
264.1075	Assessing needs of child	A
264.1076	Medical examination required	E
264.121	Transitional Living Services Program	A
264.1211[A*]	Career development & education program	E
264.1211[B*]	Records & documents for children aging out of foster care	E
264.1211[C*]	Facilitation of transition to institution of higher education	E
264.1251	Summer internship pilot program	E
264.1252	Foster parent recruitment study	E
264.126	[Renumbered as §264.153]	A
264.1261	Foster care capacity needs plan	E
264.128	Single child plan of service initiative	E

§	HEADING	ACTION
Child Welfare Services (continued)		
264.151	Legislative intent	E
264.152	Definitions	E
264.153	Community-based care implementation plan	A
264.154	Qualifications of single source continuum contractor; selection	E
264.155	Required contract provisions	E
264.156	Readiness review process for community-based care contractor	E
264.157	Expansion of community-based care	E
264.158	Transfer of case management services to single source continuum contractor	E
264.159	Data access & standards governance council	E
264.160	Liability insurance requirements	E
264.161	Statutory duties assumed by contractor	E
264.162	Review of contractor performance	E
264.163	Continuing duties of department	E
264.164	Confidentiality	E
264.165	Notice required for early termination of contract	E
264.166	Contingency plan in event of early contract termination	E
264.167	Attorney-client privilege	E
264.168	Review of contractor recommendations by department	E
264.169	Pilot program for family-based safety services	E
264.170	Limited liability for single source continuum contractor & related personnel	E
264.201	Services by department	A
264.2042[A*]	Grants for faith-based community collaborative programs	E
264.2042[B*]	Nonprofit organizations providing child & family services	E
264.2043	Prohibition on abuse or neglect investigation based solely on request for information	E

§	HEADING	ACTION
Child Welfare Services (continued)		
264.304	Hearing; determination of at-risk child	R
264.4061	Multidisciplinary team response required	E
264.502	Committee	A
264.503	Purpose & duties of committee & specified state agencies	A
264.5031	Collection of near fatality data	E
264.5032	Report of child fatality & near fatality data	E
264.505	Establishment of review team	A
264.506	Purpose & duties of review team	A
264.509	Access to information	A
264.514	Procedure in the event of reportable death	A
264.751	Definitions	A
264.754	Assessment of proposed placement	A
264.755	Caregiver assistance agreement	A
264.7551	Fraudulent agreement; criminal offense; civil penalty	E
264.760	Eligibility for foster care payments & permanency care assistance	A
264.762	Annual report	E
264.8521	Notice to applicants	A
264.857	Deadline for new agreements	R
264.903	Caregiver evaluation	A

§	HEADING	ACTION
Prevention & Early Intervention Services		
265.004	Use of evidence-based programs for at-risk families	A
265.0041	Collaboration with institutions of higher education	E
265.005	Strategic plan	A
265.007	Improving provision of prevention & early intervention services	E
265.008	Evaluation of prevention & early intervention services	E
265.101-265.105 (Subch. C)	[Renumbered as §§265.151-265.155 and redesignated as Subch. D]	A
265.106	Partnership program standards	A
265.109	Program monitoring & evaluation; annual committee reports	A
265.151-265.155 (Subch. D)	Parenting Education	A
Medical Care & Educational Services for Foster Children		
266.001	Definitions	A
266.003	Medical services for child abuse & neglect victims	A
266.005	Finding on health care consultation	E
266.006	Health passport	A
266.008	Education passport	A
266.012	Comprehensive assessments	A
266.013	Continuity of services provided by commission	E

FAMILY CODE—TITLE 1

THE MARRIAGE RELATIONSHIP

TABLE OF CONTENTS

FAMILY CODE—TITLE 1
THE MARRIAGE RELATIONSHIP
TABLE OF CONTENTS

FAMILY CODE—TITLE 1

THE MARRIAGE RELATIONSHIP

TABLE OF CONTENTS

TITLE 1. THE MARRIAGE RELATIONSHIP

SUBTITLE A. MARRIAGE

CHAPTER 1. GENERAL PROVISIONS

SUBCHAPTER A. DEFINITIONS

FAM §1.001. APPLICABILITY OF DEFINITIONS

(a) The definitions in this subchapter apply to this title.

(b) Except as provided by this subchapter, the definitions in Chapter 101 apply to terms used in this title.

(c) If, in another part of this title, a term defined by this subchapter has a meaning different from the meaning provided by this subchapter, the meaning of that other provision prevails.

History of Fam. Code §1.001: Acts 1997, 75th Leg., ch. 7, §1, eff. Apr. 17, 1997.

FAM §1.002. COURT

"Court" means the district court, juvenile court having the jurisdiction of a district court, or other court expressly given jurisdiction of a suit under this title.

History of Fam. Code §1.002: Acts 1997, 75th Leg., ch. 7, §1, eff. Apr. 17, 1997.

FAM §1.003. SUIT FOR DISSOLUTION OF MARRIAGE

"Suit for dissolution of a marriage" includes a suit for divorce or annulment or to declare a marriage void.

History of Fam. Code §1.003: Acts 1997, 75th Leg., ch. 7, §1, eff. Apr. 17, 1997.

Sections 1.004-1.100 reserved for expansion

SUBCHAPTER B. PUBLIC POLICY

FAM §1.101. EVERY MARRIAGE PRESUMED VALID

In order to promote the public health and welfare and to provide the necessary records, this code specifies detailed rules to be followed in establishing the marriage relationship. However, in order to provide stability for those entering into the marriage relationship in good faith and to provide for an orderly determination of parentage and security for the children of the relationship, it is the policy of this state to preserve and uphold each marriage against claims of invalidity unless a strong reason exists for holding the marriage void or voidable. Therefore, every marriage entered into in this state is presumed to be valid unless expressly made void by Chapter 6 or unless expressly made voidable by Chapter 6 and annulled as provided by that chapter.

History of Fam. Code §1.101: Acts 1997, 75th Leg., ch. 7, §1, eff. Apr. 17, 1997. Source: Former Fam. Code §2.01.

See also ***O'Connor's Texas Family Law Handbook*** (2017), "Applying presumption of validity," ch. 3-A, §3.1.2, p. 215.

ANNOTATIONS

Texas Employers' Ins. v. Elder, 282 S.W.2d 371, 373 (Tex.1955). "The presumption in favor of the validity of a marriage which, as in this case, has been duly shown to have been contracted is one of the strongest, if, indeed, not the strongest, known to law. The presumption is, in itself, evidence, and may even outweigh positive evidence to the contrary. The strength of the presumption increases with the lapse of time, acknowledgments by the parties to the marriage, and the birth of children; and the fact that the legitimacy of a child may be involved is a factor in sustaining the validity of the marriage. It is well that the presumption should be so regarded, for it is grounded upon a sound public policy which favors morality, innocence, marriage, and legitimacy rather than immorality, guilt, concubinage, and bastardy." (Internal quotes omitted.)

FAM §1.102. MOST RECENT MARRIAGE PRESUMED VALID

When two or more marriages of a person to different spouses are alleged, the most recent marriage is presumed to be valid as against each marriage that precedes the most recent marriage until one who asserts the validity of a prior marriage proves the validity of the prior marriage.

History of Fam. Code §1.102: Acts 1997, 75th Leg., ch. 7, §1, eff. Apr. 17, 1997. Source: Former Fam. Code §2.01.

See also ***O'Connor's Texas Family Law Handbook*** (2017), "Most recent marriage presumed valid," ch. 3-C, §3.2.1, p. 288.

ANNOTATIONS

Estate of Claveria v. Claveria, 615 S.W.2d 164, 165 (Tex.1981). "The presumption that the most recent marriage is a valid one continues until one proves the

impediment of a prior marriage and its continuing validity. *At 166:* After some evidence of a prior and continuing marriage has been introduced, the weight of such evidence must be determined by the finder of fact." *See also* ***Bailey-Mason v. Mason***, 122 S.W.3d 894, 898 (Tex.App.—Dallas 2003, pet. denied).

Davis v. Davis, 521 S.W.2d 603, 605 (Tex.1975). "It is not necessary in order to rebut the presumption that [respondent] prove the nonexistence of divorce in every jurisdiction where proceedings could have been possible; it is only necessary to rule out those proceedings where [decedent-H] might reasonably have been expected to have pursued them." *See also* ***Jordan v. Jordan***, 938 S.W.2d 177, 179 (Tex.App.—Houston [1st Dist.] 1997, no writ).

Chandler v. Chandler, 842 S.W.2d 829, 834 (Tex. App.—El Paso 1992, writ denied). "While it is unclear from a cursory reading of the statute whether the above presumption only applies when the most recent marriage was performed in Texas, the portion of [Fam. Code] §2.01 [now §1.102] providing for the presumption does not limit it solely to Texas marriages. Moreover, cases prior and subsequent to enactment of §2.01 have applied the presumption to 'foreign' marriages."

Loera v. Loera, 815 S.W.2d 910, 911 (Tex.App.—Corpus Christi 1991, no writ). "Because the presumption is, in itself, considered evidence, the party attacking the validity of the marriage has a burden to 'introduce sufficient evidence, standing alone, to negate the dissolution of the prior marriage.' *At 912:* To prevail, [H] was required to adduce evidence establishing the continued validity of the prior marriage at the time of the parties' marriage. Death terminates marriage as a matter of law, and death is presumed after seven years of absence; therefore, [H's] failure to present any evidence establishing that [former H] was alive within seven years before the parties' marriage, or thereafter, requires us to sustain [respondent's] point of error."

FAM §1.103. PERSONS MARRIED ELSEWHERE

The law of this state applies to persons married elsewhere who are domiciled in this state.

History of Fam. Code §1.103: Acts 1997, 75th Leg., ch. 7, §1, eff. Apr. 17, 1997. Source: Former Fam. Code §4.01.

ANNOTATIONS

Seth v. Seth, 694 S.W.2d 459, 462 (Tex.App.—Fort Worth 1985, no writ). "Traditionally, courts have chosen and used the law of the place a divorce or marriage purportedly occurs to determine the validity of the ceremony. Two recent decisions by the Supreme Court of Texas, however, indicate that choice-of-law decisions should not be made on the basis of the mechanical test of where the act occurred (lex loci) but should instead be made on the basis of the most significant relationship approach, using the factors set forth in the Restatement (2d) of Conflict of Laws §6 (1971). Thus, based on [these decisions], we hold that §6 criteria, and not the place of celebration test, should be applied to determine choice of law in a marriage or divorce context. *At 463:* We now list the §6 choice of law principles: ... (1) A court, subject to constitutional restrictions, will follow a statutory directive of its own state on choice of law. (2) When there is no such directive, the factors relevant to the choice of the applicable rule of law include (a) the needs of the interstate and international systems, (b) the relevant policies of the forum, (c) the relevant policies of other interested states and the relative interests of those states in the determination of the particular issue, (d) the protection of justified expectations, (e) the basic policies underlying the particular field of law, (f) certainty, predictability and uniformity of result, and (g) ease in the determination and application of the law to be applied."

FAM §1.104. CAPACITY OF SPOUSE

Except as expressly provided by statute or by the constitution, a person, regardless of age, who has been married in accordance with the law of this state has the capacity and power of an adult, including the capacity to contract.

History of Fam. Code §1.104: Acts 1997, 75th Leg., ch. 7, §1, eff. Apr. 17, 1997. Source: Former Fam. Code §4.03.

See also *O'Connor's Texas Family Law Handbook* (2017), "Getting married," ch. 1-B, §5.2.2, p. 33.

FAM §1.105. JOINDER IN CIVIL SUITS

(a) A spouse may sue and be sued without the joinder of the other spouse.

(b) When claims or liabilities are joint and several, the spouses may be joined under the rules relating to joinder of parties generally.

History of Fam. Code §1.105: Acts 1997, 75th Leg., ch. 7, §1, eff. Apr. 17, 1997. Source: Former Fam. Code §4.04.

ANNOTATIONS

Cooper v. Texas Gulf Indus., 513 S.W.2d 200, 202 (Tex.1974). While Fam. Code §4.04, now §1.105, provides that "a spouse may sue and be sued without the

joinder of the other, *neither* spouse may virtually represent the other. The rights of the wife, like the rights of the husband and the rights of any other joint owner, may be affected only by a suit in which the wife is called to answer. If one of the spouses wishes the other to represent him or her, [Fam. Code] §5.22(c) [now §3.102(c)] permits that arrangement provided the consenting spouse authorizes that representation by a power of attorney or other agreement in writing."

FAM §1.106. CRIMINAL CONVERSATION NOT AUTHORIZED

A right of action by one spouse against a third party for criminal conversation is not authorized in this state.

History of Fam. Code §1.106: Acts 1997, 75th Leg., ch. 7, §1, eff. Apr. 17, 1997. Source: Former Fam. Code §4.05.

FAM §1.107. ALIENATION OF AFFECTION NOT AUTHORIZED

A right of action by one spouse against a third party for alienation of affection is not authorized in this state.

History of Fam. Code §1.107: Acts 1997, 75th Leg., ch. 7, §1, eff. Apr. 17, 1997. Source: Former Fam. Code §4.06.

ANNOTATIONS

Helena Lab. v. Snyder, 886 S.W.2d 767, 768-69 (Tex.1994). The Texas Supreme Court "has never recognized an independent cause of action for negligent interference with the familial relationship. In some circumstances, damages may be recovered for such injuries; but, such recovery is allowed only in connection with some recognized tort. [¶] An independent cause of action for negligent interference with the familial relationship would allow an employer to be held responsible for an employee's conduct, even though the employee is shielded from responsibility for that conduct by [Fam. Code] §4.06 [now §1.107]. Exposing employers to this form of liability would be inconsistent with §4.06." *See also* ***Stites v. Gillum***, 872 S.W.2d 786, 791-92 (Tex.App.—Fort Worth 1994, writ denied).

FAM §1.108. PROMISE OR AGREEMENT MUST BE IN WRITING

A promise or agreement made on consideration of marriage or nonmarital conjugal cohabitation is not enforceable unless the promise or agreement or a memorandum of the promise or agreement is in writing and signed by the person obligated by the promise or agreement.

History of Fam. Code §1.108: Acts 1997, 75th Leg., ch. 7, §1, eff. Apr. 17, 1997. Source: B&CC §26.01.

See also ***O'Connor's Texas Family Law Handbook*** (2017), "Other Agreements," ch. 2-D, §5, p. 178.

ANNOTATIONS

Curtis v. Anderson, 106 S.W.3d 251, 254-55 (Tex. App.—Austin 2003, pet. denied). "Although §1.108 was obviously intended to apply to prenuptial agreements, its plain language is broad enough to include [woman's] alleged promise to return [man's] ring. [E]ngagement rings are traditionally given in contemplation of marriage or 'on consideration of marriage.' We hold that [man's] allegation that he and [woman] had expressed their 'mutual understanding' that the ring would be returned if the marriage did not occur comes within the scope of this statute as written. Therefore, to be enforceable any such agreement must be in writing. [T]he [conditional-gift] rule operates to require that the ring be returned to the donor if the donee is at fault in terminating the engagement.... 'A gift to a person to whom the donor is engaged to be married, made in contemplation of marriage, although absolute in form, is conditional; and on breach of the marriage engagement by the donee the property may be recovered by the donor.' *At 256:* We believe that the same rule should apply when the donor defaults. We hold that absent a written agreement a donor is not entitled to the return of an engagement ring if he terminates the engagement."

Tatum v. Tatum, 606 S.W.2d 31, 33 (Tex.App.—Corpus Christi 1980, no writ). "It is settled in Texas that an oral promise based upon a consideration of marriage is unenforceable under the statute of frauds. Furthermore, the rendition of services by the plaintiff spouse is not sufficient part performance to render the promise enforceable."

FAM §1.109. USE OF DIGITIZED SIGNATURE

(a) A digitized signature on an original petition under this title or any other pleading or order in a proceeding under this title satisfies the requirements for and imposes the duties of signatories to pleadings, motions, and other papers identified under Rule 13, Texas Rules of Civil Procedure.

(b) A digitized signature under this section may be applied only by, and must remain under the sole control of, the person whose signature is represented.

History of Fam. Code §1.109: Acts 2015, 84th Leg., ch. 1165, §1, eff. Sept. 1, 2015.

CHAPTER 2. THE MARRIAGE RELATIONSHIP

SUBCHAPTER A. APPLICATION FOR MARRIAGE LICENSE

FAM §2.001. MARRIAGE LICENSE

*In **Obergefell v. Hodges**, ___ U.S. ___, 135 S.Ct. 2584 (2015), the U.S. Supreme Court held that same-sex couples may exercise the fundamental right to marry in all states, and that there is no lawful basis for a state to refuse to recognize a lawful same-sex marriage performed in another state on the ground of its same-sex character. See annotation under Family Code §6.204, p. 65.*

(a) A man and a woman desiring to enter into a ceremonial marriage must obtain a marriage license from the county clerk of any county of this state.

(b) A license may not be issued for the marriage of persons of the same sex.

History of Fam. Code §2.001: Acts 1997, 75th Leg., ch. 7, §1, eff. Apr. 17, 1997. Source: Former Fam. Code §1.01.

FAM §2.002. APPLICATION FOR LICENSE

Except as provided by Section 2.006, each person applying for a license must:

(1) appear before the county clerk;

(2) submit the person's proof of identity and age as provided by Section 2.005(b);

(3) provide the information applicable to that person for which spaces are provided in the application for a marriage license;

(4) mark the appropriate boxes provided in the application; and

(5) take the oath printed on the application and sign the application before the county clerk.

History of Fam. Code §2.002: Acts 1997, 75th Leg., ch. 7, §1, eff. Apr. 17, 1997. Amended by Acts 2009, 81st Leg., ch. 978, §1, eff. Sept. 1, 2009. Source: Former Fam. Code §1.02.

See also ***O'Connor's Texas Family Law Handbook*** (2017), "How to apply for license," ch. 1-A, §2.2.1(4), p. 8.

FAM §2.003. APPLICATION FOR LICENSE BY MINOR

The amended text in §2.003 is effective for applications for a marriage license filed on or after Sept. 1, 2017. Applications filed before Sept. 1, 2017, are governed by the former law in effect at that time.

(a) A person under 18 years of age may not marry unless the person has been granted by this state or another state a court order removing the disabilities of minority of the person for general purposes.

(b) In addition to the other requirements provided by this chapter, a person under 18 years of age applying for a license must provide to the county clerk:

(1) [~~documents establishing, as provided by Section 2.102, parental consent for the person to the marriage;~~]

[~~(2)~~] [~~documents establishing that a prior marriage of the person has been dissolved; or~~]

[~~(3)~~] a court order granted by this state under Chapter 31 removing the disabilities of minority of the person for general purposes; or

(2) if the person is a nonresident minor, a certified copy of an order removing the disabilities of minority of the person for general purposes filed with this state under Section 31.007 [~~Section 2.103 authorizing the marriage of the person~~].

History of Fam. Code §2.003: Acts 1997, 75th Leg., ch. 7, §1, eff. Apr. 17, 1997. Amended by S.B. 1705, §1, 85th Leg., eff. Sept. 1, 2017. Source: Former Fam. Code §1.02(2)(B).

FAM §2.004. APPLICATION FORM

(a) The county clerk shall furnish the application form as prescribed by the bureau of vital statistics.

(b) The application form must contain:

(1) a heading entitled "Application for Marriage License, ______________ County, Texas";

(2) spaces for each applicant's full name, including the woman's maiden surname, address, social security number, if any, date of birth, and place of birth, including city, county, and state;

(3) a space for indicating the document tendered by each applicant as proof of identity and age;

(4) spaces for indicating whether each applicant has been divorced within the last 30 days;

(5) printed boxes for each applicant to check "true" or "false" in response to the following statement: "I am not presently married and the other applicant is not presently married.";

(6) printed boxes for each applicant to check "true" or "false" in response to the following statement: "The other applicant is not related to me as:

(A) an ancestor or descendant, by blood or adoption;

(B) a brother or sister, of the whole or half blood or by adoption;

(C) a parent's brother or sister, of the whole or half blood or by adoption;

(D) a son or daughter of a brother or sister, of the whole or half blood or by adoption;

(E) a current or former stepchild or stepparent; or

(F) a son or daughter of a parent's brother or sister, of the whole or half blood or by adoption.";

(7) printed boxes for each applicant to check "true" or "false" in response to the following statement: "I am not presently delinquent in the payment of court-ordered child support.";

(8) a printed oath reading: "I SOLEMNLY SWEAR (OR AFFIRM) THAT THE INFORMATION I HAVE GIVEN IN THIS APPLICATION IS CORRECT.";

(9) spaces immediately below the printed oath for the applicants' signatures;

(10) a certificate of the county clerk that:

(A) each applicant made the oath and the date and place that it was made; or

(B) an applicant did not appear personally but the prerequisites for the license have been fulfilled as provided by this chapter;

(11) spaces for indicating the date of the marriage and the county in which the marriage is performed;

(12) a space for the address to which the applicants desire the completed license to be mailed; and

(13) a printed box for each applicant to check indicating that the applicant wishes to make a voluntary contribution of $5 to promote healthy early childhood by supporting the Texas Home Visiting Program administered by the Office of Early Childhood Coordination of the Health and Human Services Commission.

(c) An applicant commits an offense if the applicant knowingly provides false information under Subsection (b)(1), (2), (3), or (4). An offense under this subsection is a Class C misdemeanor.

(d) An applicant commits an offense if the applicant knowingly provides false information under Subsection (b)(5) or (6). An offense under this subsection is a Class A misdemeanor.

History of Fam. Code §2.004: Acts 1997, 75th Leg., ch. 7, §1, eff. Apr. 17, 1997. Amended by Acts 1997, 75th Leg., ch. 776, §1, eff. Sept. 1, 1997; Acts 2005, 79th Leg., ch. 268, §4.05, eff. Sept. 1, 2005; Acts 2013, 83rd Leg., ch. 820, §1, eff. June 14, 2013. Source: Former Fam. Code §1.03.

FAM §2.005. PROOF OF IDENTITY & AGE

(a) The county clerk shall require proof of the identity and age of each applicant.

(b) The proof must be established by:

(1) a driver's license or identification card issued by this state, another state, or a Canadian province that is current or has expired not more than two years preceding the date the identification is submitted to the county clerk in connection with an application for a license;

(2) a United States passport;

(3) a current passport issued by a foreign country or a consular document issued by a state or national government;

(4) an unexpired Certificate of United States Citizenship, Certificate of Naturalization, United States Citizen Identification Card, Permanent Resident Card, Temporary Resident Card, Employment Authorization Card, or other document issued by the federal Department of Homeland Security or the United States Department of State including an identification photograph;

(5) an unexpired military identification card for active duty, reserve, or retired personnel with an identification photograph;

(6) an original or certified copy of a birth certificate issued by a bureau of vital statistics for a state or a foreign government;

(7) an original or certified copy of a Consular Report of Birth Abroad or Certificate of Birth Abroad issued by the United States Department of State;

(8) an original or certified copy of a court order relating to the applicant's name change or sex change;

(9) school records from a secondary school or institution of higher education;

(10) an insurance policy continuously valid for the two years preceding the date of the application for a license;

(11) a motor vehicle certificate of title;

(12) military records, including documentation of release or discharge from active duty or a draft record;

(13) an unexpired military dependent identification card;

(14) an original or certified copy of the applicant's marriage license or divorce decree;

(15) a voter registration certificate;

(16) a pilot's license issued by the Federal Aviation Administration or another authorized agency of the United States;

(17) a license to carry a handgun under Subchapter H, Chapter 411, Government Code;

(18) a temporary driving permit or a temporary identification card issued by the Department of Public Safety; or

(19) an offender identification card issued by the Texas Department of Criminal Justice.

(c) A person commits an offense if the person knowingly provides false, fraudulent, or otherwise inaccurate proof of an applicant's identity or age under this section. An offense under this subsection is a Class A misdemeanor.

History of Fam. Code §2.005: Acts 1997, 75th Leg., ch. 7, §1, eff. Apr. 17, 1997. Amended by Acts 2005, 79th Leg., ch. 268, §4.06, eff. Sept. 1, 2005; Acts 2009, 81st Leg., ch. 978, §2, eff. Sept. 1, 2009; Acts 2015, 84th Leg., ch. 437, §10, eff. Jan. 1, 2016. Source: Former Fam. Code §1.04.

ANNOTATIONS

In re McReynolds, 502 S.W.3d 884, 886 (Tex. App.—Dallas 2016, no pet.). Family Code "§2.005(b)(8) does not authorize Texas courts to render sex change orders. *At 888:* [T]here is no statutory scheme expressly authorizing sex change orders or establishing procedures for obtaining such an order. We presume that, when the legislature adopted §2.005(b)(8), it knew there was already a statutory procedure for judicial name change orders and no statutory procedure for judicial sex change orders. The legislature's decision not to establish a scheme for sex change orders comparable to [Fam. Code] Ch. 45 suggests a lack of legislative intent to grant Texas courts the authority to make such orders. [¶] [H]olding that §2.005(b)(8) does not authorize Texas courts to render sex change orders does not mean that such orders cannot exist elsewhere. Other states (or countries) may have procedures for sex change orders. [Section] 2.005(b) means that sex change orders from jurisdictions that provide for such orders are proper means for establishing a marriage license applicant's age or identity."

A FAM §2.006. ABSENT APPLICANT

The amended text in §2.006 is effective for applications for a marriage license filed on or after Sept. 1, 2017. Applications filed before Sept. 1, 2017, are governed by the former law in effect at that time.

(a) If an applicant who is 18 years of age or older is unable to appear personally before the county clerk to apply for a marriage license, any adult person or the other applicant may apply on behalf of the absent applicant.

(b) The person applying on behalf of an absent applicant shall provide to the clerk:

(1) notwithstanding Section 132.001, Civil Practice and Remedies Code, the notarized affidavit of the absent applicant as provided by this subchapter; and

(2) proof of the identity and age of the absent applicant under Section 2.005(b) [~~; and~~]

[~~(3)~~] [~~if required because the absent applicant is a person under 18 years of age, documents establishing that a prior marriage has been dissolved, a court order authorizing the marriage of the absent, underage appli-~~]

~~cant, or documents establishing consent by a parent or a person who has legal authority to consent to the marriage, including:~~]

[~~(A)~~] [~~proof of identity of the parent or person with legal authority to consent to the marriage under Section 2.005(b); and~~]

[~~(B)~~] [~~proof that the parent or person has the legal authority to consent to the marriage for the applicant under rules adopted under Section 2.102(j)~~].

(c) Notwithstanding Subsection (a), the clerk may not issue a marriage license for which both applicants are absent unless the person applying on behalf of each absent applicant provides to the clerk an affidavit of the applicant declaring that the applicant is a member of the armed forces of the United States stationed in another country in support of combat or another military operation.

History of Fam. Code §2.006: Acts 1997, 75th Leg., ch. 7, §1, eff. Apr. 17, 1997. Amended by Acts 2005, 79th Leg., ch. 947, §1, eff. Sept. 1, 2005; Acts 2009, 81st Leg., ch. 978, §3, eff. Sept. 1, 2009; Acts 2013, 83rd Leg., ch. 650, §1, eff. Sept. 1, 2013; S.B. 1705, §2, 85th Leg., eff. Sept. 1, 2017. Source: Former Fam. Code §1.05(a), (b).

FAM §2.007. AFFIDAVIT OF ABSENT APPLICANT

The affidavit of an absent applicant must include:

(1) the absent applicant's full name, including the maiden surname of a female applicant, address, date of birth, place of birth, including city, county, and state, citizenship, and social security number, if any;

(2) a declaration that the absent applicant has not been divorced within the last 30 days;

(3) a declaration that the absent applicant is:

(A) not presently married; or

(B) married to the other applicant and they wish to marry again;

(4) a declaration that the other applicant is not presently married and is not related to the absent applicant as:

(A) an ancestor or descendant, by blood or adoption;

(B) a brother or sister, of the whole or half blood or by adoption;

(C) a parent's brother or sister, of the whole or half blood or by adoption;

(D) a son or daughter of a brother or sister, of the whole or half blood or by adoption;

(E) a current or former stepchild or stepparent; or

(F) a son or daughter of a parent's brother or sister, of the whole or half blood or by adoption;

(5) a declaration that the absent applicant desires to marry and the name, age, and address of the person to whom the absent applicant desires to be married;

(6) the approximate date on which the marriage is to occur;

(7) the reason the absent applicant is unable to appear personally before the county clerk for the issuance of the license; and

(8) the appointment of any adult, other than the other applicant, to act as proxy for the purpose of participating in the ceremony, if the absent applicant is:

(A) a member of the armed forces of the United States stationed in another country in support of combat or another military operation; and

(B) unable to attend the ceremony.

History of Fam. Code §2.007: Acts 1997, 75th Leg., ch. 7, §1, eff. Apr. 17, 1997. Amended by Acts 2005, 79th Leg., ch. 268, §4.07, eff. Sept. 1, 2005; Acts 2013, 83rd Leg., ch. 650, §2, eff. Sept. 1, 2013. Source: Former Fam. Code §1.05(c).

FAM §2.0071. MAINTENANCE OF RECORDS BY CLERK RELATING TO LICENSE FOR ABSENT APPLICANT

A county clerk who issues a marriage license for an absent applicant shall maintain the affidavit of the absent applicant and the application for the marriage license in the same manner that the clerk maintains an application for a marriage license submitted by two applicants in person.

History of Fam. Code §2.0071: Acts 2013, 83rd Leg., ch. 650, §3, eff. Sept. 1, 2013.

FAM §2.008. EXECUTION OF APPLICATION BY CLERK

(a) The county clerk shall:

(1) determine that all necessary information, other than the date of the marriage ceremony, the county in which the ceremony is conducted, and the name of the person who performs the ceremony, is recorded on the application and that all necessary documents are submitted;

(2) administer the oath to each applicant appearing before the clerk;

(3) have each applicant appearing before the clerk sign the application in the clerk's presence; and

(4) execute the clerk's certificate on the application.

(b) A person appearing before the clerk on behalf of an absent applicant is not required to take the oath on behalf of the absent applicant.

History of Fam. Code §2.008: Acts 1997, 75th Leg., ch. 7, §1, eff. Apr. 17, 1997. Source: Former Fam. Code §1.06.

A FAM §2.009. ISSUANCE OF LICENSE

The amended text in subsection (a) is effective for applications for a marriage license filed on or after Sept. 1, 2017. Applications filed before Sept. 1, 2017, are governed by the former law in effect at that time.

(a) Except as provided by Subsections (b) and (d), the county clerk may not issue a license if either applicant:

(1) fails to provide the information required by this subchapter;

(2) fails to submit proof of age and identity;

(3) [~~is under 16 years of age and has not been granted a court order as provided by Section 2.103;~~]

[~~(4)~~] is [~~16 years of age or older but~~] under 18 years of age and has not presented [~~at least one of the following~~]:

(A) [~~parental consent as provided by Section 2.102;~~]

[~~(B)~~] [~~documents establishing that a prior marriage of the applicant has been dissolved; or~~]

[~~(C)~~] a court order granted by this state under Chapter 31 removing the disabilities of minority of the applicant for general purposes; or

(B) if the applicant is a nonresident minor, a certified copy of an order removing the disabilities of minority of the applicant for general purposes filed with this state under Section 31.007 [~~as provided by Section 2.103~~];

(4) [~~(5)~~] checks "false" in response to a statement in the application, except as provided by Subsection (b) or (d), or fails to make a required declaration in an affidavit required of an absent applicant; or

(5) [~~(6)~~] indicates that the applicant has been divorced within the last 30 days, unless:

(A) the applicants were divorced from each other; or

(B) the prohibition against remarriage is waived as provided by Section 6.802.

(b) If an applicant checks "false" in response to the statement "I am not presently married and the other applicant is not presently married," the county clerk shall inquire as to whether the applicant is presently married to the other applicant. If the applicant states that the applicant is currently married to the other applicant, the county clerk shall record that statement on the license before the administration of the oath. The county clerk may not refuse to issue a license on the ground that the applicants are already married to each other.

(c) On the proper execution of the application, the clerk shall:

(1) prepare the license;

(2) enter on the license the names of the licensees, the date that the license is issued, and, if applicable, the name of the person appointed to act as proxy for an absent applicant, if any;

(3) record the time at which the license was issued;

(4) distribute to each applicant written notice of the online location of the information prepared under Section 2.010 regarding acquired immune deficiency syndrome (AIDS) and human immunodeficiency virus (HIV) and note on the license that the distribution was made; and

(5) inform each applicant:

(A) that a premarital education handbook developed by the child support division of the office of the attorney general under Section 2.014 is available on the child support division's Internet website; or

(B) if the applicant does not have Internet access, how the applicant may obtain a paper copy of the handbook described by Paragraph (A).

(d) The county clerk may not refuse to issue a license to an applicant on the ground that the applicant checked "false" in response to the statement "I am not presently delinquent in the payment of court-ordered child support."

Subsection (e) is effective for marriage licenses issued on or after Jan. 1, 2019. Marriage licenses issued before Jan. 1, 2019, are governed by the former law in effect immediately before June 12, 2017.

(e) A license issued by a county clerk under this section:

(1) must identify the county in which the license is issued; and

(2) may include the name of the county clerk.

History of Fam. Code §2.009: Acts 1997, 75th Leg., ch. 7, §1, eff. Apr. 17, 1997. Amended by Acts 1997, 75th Leg., ch. 776, §2, eff. Sept. 1, 1997; Acts 1999, 76th Leg., ch. 62, §6.01(a) (eff. Sept. 1, 1999), ch. 185, §1 (eff. Sept. 1, 1999); Acts 2005, 79th Leg., ch. 268, §4.08, eff. Sept. 1, 2005; Acts 2009, 81st Leg., ch. 978, §4, eff. Sept. 1, 2009; Acts 2013, 83rd Leg., ch. 742, §1 (eff. Sept. 1, 2013), ch. 890, §1 (eff. Sept. 1, 2013); H.B. 555, §1, 85th Leg., eff. June 12, 2017; S.B. 1705, §3, 85th Leg., eff. Sept. 1, 2017. Source: Former Fam. Code §1.07.

FAM §2.010. AIDS INFORMATION; POSTING ON INTERNET

The Department of State Health Services shall prepare and make available to the public on its Internet website information about acquired immune deficiency syndrome (AIDS) and human immunodeficiency virus (HIV). The information must be designed to inform an applicant for a marriage license about:

(1) the incidence and mode of transmission of AIDS and HIV;

(2) the local availability of medical procedures, including voluntary testing, designed to show or help show whether a person has AIDS or HIV infection, antibodies to HIV, or infection with any other probable causative agent of AIDS; and

(3) available and appropriate counseling services regarding AIDS and HIV infection.

History of Fam. Code §2.010: Acts 1997, 75th Leg., ch. 7, §1, eff. Apr. 17, 1997. Amended by Acts 2013, 83rd Leg., ch. 890, §2, eff. Sept. 1, 2013. Source: Former Fam. Code §1.07(e).

FAM §2.011. REPEALED

Repealed by Acts 2009, 81st Leg., ch. 978, §10, eff. Sept. 1, 2009.

FAM §2.012. VIOLATION BY COUNTY CLERK; PENALTY

A county clerk or deputy county clerk who violates or fails to comply with this subchapter commits an offense. An offense under this section is a misdemeanor punishable by a fine of not less than $200 and not more than $500.

History of Fam. Code §2.012: Acts 1997, 75th Leg., ch. 7, §1, eff. Apr. 17, 1997. Source: Former Fam. Code §1.09.

FAM §2.013. PREMARITAL EDUCATION COURSES

(a) Each person applying for a marriage license is encouraged to attend a premarital education course of at least eight hours during the year preceding the date of the application for the license.

(b) A premarital education course must include instruction in:

(1) conflict management;

(2) communication skills; and

(3) the key components of a successful marriage.

(c) A course under this section should be offered by instructors trained in a skills-based and research-based marriage preparation curricula. The following individuals and organizations may provide courses:

(1) marriage educators;

(2) clergy or their designees;

(3) licensed mental health professionals;

(4) faith-based organizations; and

(5) community-based organizations.

(d) The curricula of a premarital education course must meet the requirements of this section and provide the skills-based and research-based curricula of:

(1) the United States Department of Health and Human Services healthy marriage initiative;

(2) the National Healthy Marriage Resource Center;

(3) criteria developed by the Health and Human Services Commission; or

(4) other similar resources.

(e) The Health and Human Services Commission shall maintain an Internet website on which individuals and organizations described by Subsection (c) may electronically register with the commission to indicate the skills-based and research-based curriculum in which the registrant is trained.

(f) A person who provides a premarital education course shall provide a signed and dated completion certificate to each individual who completes the course. The certificate must include the name of the course, the name of the course provider, and the completion date.

History of Fam. Code §2.013: Acts 1999, 76th Leg., ch. 185, §2, eff. Sept. 1, 1999. Amended by Acts 2007, 80th Leg., ch. 327, §1, eff. Sept. 1, 2008.

Ⓐ FAM §2.014. FAMILY TRUST FUND

(a) The family trust fund is created as a trust fund with the state comptroller and shall be administered by the attorney general for the beneficiaries of the fund.

(b) Money in the trust fund is derived from depositing $3 of each marriage license fee as authorized under Section 118.018(c), Local Government Code, and may be used only for:

(1) the development of a premarital education handbook;

(2) grants to institutions of higher education having academic departments that are capable of research on marriage and divorce that will assist in determining programs, courses, and policies to help strengthen families and assist children whose parents are divorcing;

(3) support for counties to create or administer free or low-cost premarital education courses;

(4) programs intended to reduce the amount of delinquent child support; and

(5) other programs the attorney general determines will assist families in this state.

(c) The premarital education handbook under Subsection (b)(1) must:

(1) as provided by Section 2.009(c)(5), be made available to each applicant for a marriage license in an electronic form on the Internet website of the child support division of the office of the attorney general or, for an applicant who does not have Internet access, in paper copy form; and

(2) contain information on:

(A) conflict management;

(B) communication skills;

(C) children and parenting responsibilities; and

(D) financial responsibilities.

(d) Repealed by S.B. 526, §6(b), 85th Leg., eff. Sept. 1, 2017; S.B. 1731, §15(b), 85th Leg., eff. Sept. 1, 2017.

[~~(d)~~] [~~The attorney general shall appoint an advisory committee to assist in the development of the premarital education handbook. The advisory committee shall consist of nine members, including at least three members who are eligible under Section 2.013(d) to provide a premarital education course. A member of the advisory committee is not entitled to reimbursement of the member's expenses.~~]

History of Fam. Code §2.014: Acts 1999, 76th Leg., ch. 185, §2, eff. Sept. 1, 1999. Amended by Acts 2013, 83rd Leg., ch. 742, §2 (eff. Sept. 1, 2013), ch. 890, §3 (eff. Sept. 1, 2013); S.B. 526, §6(b), 85th Leg., eff. Sept. 1, 2017; S.B. 1731, §15(b), 85th Leg., eff. Sept. 1, 2017.

Sections 2.015-2.100 reserved for expansion

SUBCHAPTER B. UNDERAGE APPLICANTS

A FAM §2.101. GENERAL AGE REQUIREMENT

The amended text in §2.101 is effective for applications for a marriage license filed on or after Sept. 1, 2017. Applications filed before Sept. 1, 2017, are governed by the former law in effect at that time.

A [~~Except as otherwise provided by this subchapter or on a showing that a prior marriage has been dissolved, a~~] county clerk may not issue a marriage license if either applicant is under 18 years of age, unless each underage applicant shows that the applicant has been granted by this state or another state a court order removing the disabilities of minority of the applicant for general purposes.

History of Fam. Code §2.101: Acts 1997, 75th Leg., ch. 7, §1, eff. Apr. 17, 1997. Amended by S.B. 1705, §4, 85th Leg., eff. Sept. 1, 2017. Source: Former Fam. Code §1.51.

FAM §2.102. REPEALED [~~PARENTAL CONSENT FOR UNDERAGE APPLICANT~~]

[~~(a)~~] [~~If an applicant is 16 years of age or older but under 18 years of age, the county clerk shall issue the license if parental consent is given as provided by this section.~~]

[~~(b)~~] [~~Parental consent must be evidenced by a written declaration on a form supplied by the county clerk in which the person consents to the marriage and swears that the person is a parent (if there is no person who has the court-ordered right to consent to marriage for the applicant) or a person who has the court-ordered right to consent to marriage for the applicant (whether an individual, authorized agency, or court).~~]

[~~(c)~~] [~~Except as otherwise provided by this section, consent must be acknowledged before a county clerk.~~]

[~~(d)~~] [~~If the person giving parental consent resides in another state, the consent may be acknowledged before an officer authorized to issue marriage licenses in that state.~~]

[~~(e)~~] [~~If the person giving parental consent is unable because of illness or incapacity to comply with the provisions of Subsection (c) or (d), the consent may be acknowledged before any officer authorized to take acknowledgments. A consent under this subsection must be accompanied by a physician's affidavit stating that the person giving parental consent is unable to comply because of illness or incapacity.~~]

[~~(f)~~] [~~Parental consent must be given at the time the application for the marriage license is made or not earlier than the 30th day preceding the date the application is made.~~]

[~~(g)~~] [~~A person commits an offense if the person knowingly provides parental consent for an underage applicant under this section and the person is not a parent or a person who has the court-ordered right to consent to marriage for the applicant. An offense under this subsection is a Class A misdemeanor.~~]

[~~(h)~~] [~~A parent or a person who has the court-ordered right to consent to marriage for the applicant commits an offense if the parent or other person knowingly provides parental consent under this section for an applicant who is younger than 16 years of age or who~~

is presently married to a person other than the person the applicant desires to marry. An offense under this subsection is a felony of the third degree.]

[(i)] [A parent or person who has the legal authority to consent to marriage for an underage applicant who gives consent under this section shall provide:]

[(1)] [proof of the parent's or person's identity under Section 2.005(b); and]

[(2)] [proof that the parent or person has the legal authority to consent to marriage for the applicant under rules adopted under Subsection (j).]

[(j)] [The executive commissioner of the Health and Human Services Commission shall adopt rules detailing acceptable proof of the legal authority to consent to the marriage of an underage applicant. In adopting rules, the executive commissioner shall ensure that the rules:]

[(1)] [adequately protect against fraud; and]

[(2)] [do not create an undue burden on any class of person legally entitled to consent to the marriage of an underage applicant.]

Repealed by S.B. 1705, §6, 85th Leg., eff. Sept. 1, 2017.

FAM §2.103. REPEALED [COURT ORDER FOR UNDERAGE APPLICANT]

[(a)] [A minor may petition the court in the minor's own name for an order granting permission to marry. In a suit under this section, the trial judge may advance the suit if the best interest of the applicant would be served by an early hearing.]

[(b)] [The petition must be filed in the county where a parent resides if a court has not awarded another person the right to consent to marriage for the minor. If a court has awarded another person the right to consent to marriage for the minor, the petition must be filed in the county where that person resides. If no parent or person who has the court-ordered right to consent to marriage for the minor resides in this state, the petition must be filed in the county where the minor lives.]

[(c)] [The petition must include:]

[(1)] [a statement of the reasons the minor desires to marry;]

[(2)] [a statement of whether each parent is living or is dead;]

[(3)] [the name and residence address of each living parent; and]

[(4)] [a statement of whether a court has awarded to a person other than a parent of the minor the right to consent to marriage for the minor.]

[(d)] [Process shall be served as in other civil cases on each living parent of the minor or on a person who has the court-ordered right to consent to marriage for the minor, as applicable. Citation may be given by publication as in other civil cases, except that notice shall be published one time only.]

[(e)] [The court shall appoint an amicus attorney or an attorney ad litem to represent the minor in the proceeding. The court shall specify a fee to be paid by the minor for the services of the amicus attorney or attorney ad litem. The fee shall be collected in the same manner as other costs of the proceeding.]

[(f)] [If after a hearing the court, sitting without a jury, believes marriage to be in the best interest of the minor, the court, by order, shall grant the minor permission to marry.]

Repealed by S.B. 1705, §6, 85th Leg., eff. Sept. 1, 2017.

Sections 2.104-2.200 reserved for expansion

SUBCHAPTER C. CEREMONY & RETURN OF LICENSE

FAM §2.201. EXPIRATION OF LICENSE

If a marriage ceremony has not been conducted before the 90th day after the date the license is issued, the marriage license expires.

History of Fam. Code §2.201: Acts 1997, 75th Leg., ch. 7, §1, eff. Apr. 17, 1997. Amended by Acts 2013, 83rd Leg., ch. 1350, §1, eff. Sept. 1, 2013. Source: Former Fam. Code §1.81(a).

FAM §2.202. PERSONS AUTHORIZED TO CONDUCT CEREMONY

(a) The following persons are authorized to conduct a marriage ceremony:

(1) a licensed or ordained Christian minister or priest;

(2) a Jewish rabbi;

(3) a person who is an officer of a religious organization and who is authorized by the organization to conduct a marriage ceremony;

(4) a justice of the supreme court, judge of the court of criminal appeals, justice of the courts of appeals, judge of the district, county, and probate courts, judge of the county courts at law, judge of the courts of domestic relations, judge of the juvenile courts, retired justice or judge of those courts, justice of the peace, retired justice

of the peace, judge of a municipal court, retired judge of a municipal court, associate judge of a statutory probate court, retired associate judge of a statutory probate court, associate judge of a county court at law, retired associate judge of a county court at law, or judge or magistrate of a federal court of this state; and

(5) a retired judge or magistrate of a federal court of this state.

(b) For the purposes of Subsection (a)(4), a retired judge or justice is a former judge or justice who is vested in the Judicial Retirement System of Texas Plan One or the Judicial Retirement System of Texas Plan Two or who has an aggregate of at least 12 years of service as judge or justice of any type listed in Subsection (a)(4).

(b-1) For the purposes of Subsection (a)(5), a retired judge or magistrate is a former judge or magistrate of a federal court of this state who is fully vested in the Federal Employees Retirement System under 28 U.S.C. Section 371 or 377.

(c) Except as provided by Subsection (d), a person commits an offense if the person knowingly conducts a marriage ceremony without authorization under this section. An offense under this subsection is a Class A misdemeanor.

(d) A person commits an offense if the person knowingly conducts a marriage ceremony of a minor whose marriage is prohibited by law or of a person who by marrying commits an offense under Section 25.01, Penal Code. An offense under this subsection is a felony of the third degree.

History of Fam. Code §2.202: Acts 1997, 75th Leg., ch. 7, §1, eff. Apr. 17, 1997. Amended by Acts 2005, 79th Leg., ch. 268, §4.10, eff. Sept. 1, 2005; Acts 2009, 81st Leg., ch. 134, §1, eff. Sept. 1, 2009; Acts 2013, 83rd Leg., ch. 1350, §2, eff. Sept. 1, 2013; Acts 2015, 84th Leg., ch. 1069, §1, eff. Sept. 1, 2015. Source: Former Fam. Code §1.83(a), (b).

ANNOTATIONS

Husband v. Pierce, 800 S.W.2d 661, 664 (Tex. App.—Tyler 1990, orig. proceeding). "[E]ven in the absence of a valid marriage license authorizing a marriage ceremony, whether conducted by a person authorized by [Fam. Code] §1.83 [now §2.202] or not, is nevertheless valid 'if there was a reasonable appearance of authority by that person, and at least one party to the marriage participated in the ceremony in good faith and that party treats the marriage as valid.'"

FAM §2.203. CEREMONY

(a) On receiving an unexpired marriage license, an authorized person may conduct the marriage ceremony as provided by this subchapter.

(b) A person may assent to marriage by the appearance of a proxy appointed in the affidavit authorized by Subchapter A if the person is:

(1) a member of the armed forces of the United States stationed in another country in support of combat or another military operation; and

(2) unable to attend the ceremony.

History of Fam. Code §2.203: Acts 1997, 75th Leg., ch. 7, §1, eff. Apr. 17, 1997. Amended by Acts 2013, 83rd Leg., ch. 650, §4, eff. Sept. 1, 2013. Source: Former Fam. Code §1.82(a), (b).

See also ***O'Connor's Texas Family Law Handbook*** (2017), "Marriage ceremony," ch. 1-A, §2.2.2, p. 11.

ANNOTATIONS

Coulter v. Melady, 489 S.W.2d 156, 158 (Tex. App.—Texarkana 1972, writ ref'd n.r.e.). "The [Family] Code prescribes no set form for a marriage ceremony or the procedure therein. The official conducting the ceremony is not required to elicit particular or specific information or answers from a party to the marriage, nor are participants required to speak or respond in a given way. [Purported W's] failure to audibly respond to questions during the ceremony does not raise a fact issue as to her consent to the marriage, as her prior action shows consent as a matter of law."

FAM §2.204. 72-HOUR WAITING PERIOD; EXCEPTIONS

(a) Except as provided by this section, a marriage ceremony may not take place during the 72-hour period immediately following the issuance of the marriage license.

(b) The 72-hour waiting period after issuance of a marriage license does not apply to an applicant who:

(1) is a member of the armed forces of the United States and on active duty;

(2) is not a member of the armed forces of the United States but performs work for the United States Department of Defense as a department employee or under a contract with the department;

(3) obtains a written waiver under Subsection (c); or

(4) completes a premarital education course described by Section 2.013, and who provides to the county clerk a premarital education course completion certificate indicating completion of the premarital

education course not more than one year before the date the marriage license application is filed with the clerk.

(c) An applicant may request a judge of a court with jurisdiction in family law cases, a justice of the supreme court, a judge of the court of criminal appeals, a county judge, or a judge of a court of appeals for a written waiver permitting the marriage ceremony to take place during the 72-hour period immediately following the issuance of the marriage license. If the judge finds that there is good cause for the marriage to take place during the period, the judge shall sign the waiver. Notwithstanding any other provision of law, a judge under this section has the authority to sign a waiver under this section.

History of Fam. Code §2.204: Acts 1997, 75th Leg., ch. 7, §1, eff. Apr. 17, 1997. Amended by Acts 1999, 76th Leg., ch. 1052, §1, eff. Sept. 1, 1999; Acts 2005, 79th Leg., ch. 1196, §1, eff. June 18, 2005; Acts 2007, 80th Leg., ch. 327, §2, eff. Sept. 1, 2008. Source: Former Fam. Code §1.82(c), (d).

FAM §2.205. DISCRIMINATION IN CONDUCTING MARRIAGE PROHIBITED

(a) A person authorized to conduct a marriage ceremony by this subchapter is prohibited from discriminating on the basis of race, religion, or national origin against an applicant who is otherwise competent to be married.

(b) On a finding by the State Commission on Judicial Conduct that a person has intentionally violated Subsection (a), the commission may recommend to the supreme court that the person be removed from office.

History of Fam. Code §2.205: Acts 1997, 75th Leg., ch. 7, §1, eff. Apr. 17, 1997. Source: Former Fam. Code §1.83(c), (d).

FAM §2.206. RETURN OF LICENSE; PENALTY

(a) The person who conducts a marriage ceremony shall record on the license the date on which and the county in which the ceremony is performed and the person's name, subscribe the license, and return the license to the county clerk who issued it not later than the 30th day after the date the ceremony is conducted.

(b) A person who fails to comply with this section commits an offense. An offense under this section is a misdemeanor punishable by a fine of not less than $200 and not more than $500.

History of Fam. Code §2.206: Acts 1997, 75th Leg., ch. 7, §1, eff. Apr. 17, 1997. Source: Former Fam. Code §1.84.

FAM §2.207. MARRIAGE CONDUCTED AFTER LICENSE EXPIRED; PENALTY

(a) A person who is to conduct a marriage ceremony shall determine whether the license has expired from the county clerk's endorsement on the license.

(b) A person who conducts a marriage ceremony after the marriage license has expired commits an offense. An offense under this section is a misdemeanor punishable by a fine of not less than $200 and not more than $500.

History of Fam. Code §2.207: Acts 1997, 75th Leg., ch. 7, §1, eff. Apr. 17, 1997. Source: Former Fam. Code §1.81.

FAM §2.208. RECORDING & DELIVERY OF LICENSE

(a) The county clerk shall record a returned marriage license and mail the license to the address indicated on the application.

(b) On the application form the county clerk shall record:

(1) the date of the marriage ceremony;

(2) the county in which the ceremony was conducted; and

(3) the name of the person who conducted the ceremony.

History of Fam. Code §2.208: Acts 1997, 75th Leg., ch. 7, §1, eff. Apr. 17, 1997. Source: Former Fam. Code §1.85.

FAM §2.209. DUPLICATE LICENSE

(a) On request, the county clerk shall issue a certified copy of a recorded marriage license.

(b) If a marriage license issued by a county clerk is lost, destroyed, or rendered useless, the clerk shall issue a duplicate license.

(c) If one or both parties to a marriage license discover an error on the recorded marriage license, both parties to the marriage shall execute a notarized affidavit stating the error. The county clerk shall file and record the affidavit as an amendment to the marriage license, and the affidavit is considered part of the marriage license. The clerk shall include a copy of the affidavit with any future certified copy of the marriage license issued by the clerk.

(d) The executive commissioner of the Health and Human Services Commission by rule shall prescribe the form of the affidavit under Subsection (c).

History of Fam. Code §2.209: Acts 1997, 75th Leg., ch. 7, §1, eff. Apr. 17, 1997. Amended by Acts 2009, 81st Leg., ch. 978, §6, eff. Sept. 1, 2009. Source: Former Fam. Code §1.86.

Sections 2.210-2.300 reserved for expansion

SUBCHAPTER D. VALIDITY OF MARRIAGE

FAM §2.301. FRAUD, MISTAKE, OR ILLEGALITY IN OBTAINING LICENSE

Except as otherwise provided by this chapter, the validity of a marriage is not affected by any fraud, mistake, or illegality that occurred in obtaining the marriage license.

History of Fam. Code §2.301: Acts 1997, 75th Leg., ch. 7, §1, eff. Apr. 17, 1997. Source: Former Fam. Code §2.02.

ANNOTATIONS

Foster v. State, 20 S.W. 823, 824 (Tex.Crim.App. 1892). "That the officer signed the license as district clerk instead as county clerk could not and did not operate to render the marriage void. The evidence clearly manifests a sufficient marriage, duly solemnized by a Catholic priest according to the ritual of that church. This was sufficient. This court cannot agree to the proposition that a mistake of the clerk in issuing a marriage license can invalidate a marriage solemnly consummated between the parties."

Williams v. White, 263 S.W.2d 666, 668 (Tex. App.—Austin 1953, writ ref'd n.r.e.). "[O]ur courts have held that statutes regulating the mode of entering into the marriage relations including the consent of the parents and provisions requiring that a license be obtained before performance of the marriage ceremony, are merely directory, and that, although marriage is entered into otherwise than in accordance with the provisions of such statutes, it is nevertheless a valid marriage unless, of course, the statute declares that its violation shall render the marriage void."

FAM §2.302. CEREMONY CONDUCTED BY UNAUTHORIZED PERSON

The validity of a marriage is not affected by the lack of authority of the person conducting the marriage ceremony if:

(1) there was a reasonable appearance of authority by that person;

(2) at least one party to the marriage participated in the ceremony in good faith and that party treats the marriage as valid; and

(3) neither party to the marriage:

(A) is a minor whose marriage is prohibited by law; or

(B) by marrying commits an offense under Section 25.01, Penal Code.

History of Fam. Code §2.302: Acts 1997, 75th Leg., ch. 7, §1, eff. Apr. 17, 1997. Amended by Acts 2005, 79th Leg., ch. 268, §4.11, eff. Sept. 1, 2005. Source: Former Fam. Code §2.03.

ANNOTATIONS

Husband v. Pierce, 800 S.W.2d 661, 664 (Tex. App.—Tyler 1990, orig. proceeding). See annotation under Family Code §2.202, p. 16.

Sections 2.303-2.400 reserved for expansion

SUBCHAPTER E. MARRIAGE WITHOUT FORMALITIES

FAM §2.401. PROOF OF INFORMAL MARRIAGE

☠ *In **Obergefell v. Hodges**, ___ U.S. ___, 135 S.Ct. 2584 (2015), the U.S. Supreme Court held that same-sex couples may exercise the fundamental right to marry in all states, and that there is no lawful basis for a state to refuse to recognize a lawful same-sex marriage performed in another state on the ground of its same-sex character. See annotation under Family Code §6.204, p. 65.*

(a) In a judicial, administrative, or other proceeding, the marriage of a man and woman may be proved by evidence that:

(1) a declaration of their marriage has been signed as provided by this subchapter; or

(2) the man and woman agreed to be married and after the agreement they lived together in this state as husband and wife and there represented to others that they were married.

(b) If a proceeding in which a marriage is to be proved as provided by Subsection (a)(2) is not commenced before the second anniversary of the date on which the parties separated and ceased living together, it is rebuttably presumed that the parties did not enter into an agreement to be married.

(c) A person under 18 years of age may not:

(1) be a party to an informal marriage; or

(2) execute a declaration of informal marriage under Section 2.402.

(d) A person may not be a party to an informal marriage or execute a declaration of an informal marriage if the person is presently married to a person who is not the other party to the informal marriage or declaration of an informal marriage, as applicable.

History of Fam. Code §2.401: Acts 1997, 75th Leg., ch. 7, §1, eff. Apr. 17, 1997. Amended by Acts 1997, 75th Leg., ch. 1362, §1, eff. Sept. 1, 1997; Acts 2005, 79th Leg., ch. 268, §4.12, eff. Sept. 1, 2005. Source: Former Fam. Code §1.91.

See also *O'Connor's Texas Family Law Handbook* (2017), "Informal Marriage," ch. 1-A, §3, p. 13.

ANNOTATIONS

Generally

Villegas v. Griffin Indus., 975 S.W.2d 745, 750 (Tex.App.—Corpus Christi 1998, pet. denied). "Informal marriages, like ceremonial marriages, can only be dissolved by legal proceedings decreeing annulment or divorce, or by the death of one spouse." *See also* ***Tatum v. Tatum***, 478 S.W.2d 629, 631 (Tex.App.—Fort Worth 1972, writ dism'd).

Texas Employers' Ins. v. Borum, 834 S.W.2d 395, 399 (Tex.App.—San Antonio 1992, writ denied). "Proof of a common-law marriage pursuant to the [Family] Code requires: (1) an agreement presently to be married; (2) living together *in this state* as husband and wife; and (3) holding each other out to the public *in this state* as husband and wife. The language in subsections (2) and (3) preclude[s] proof of a common-law marriage when the acts occurred in a state other than Texas."

Agreement

Russell v. Russell, 865 S.W.2d 929, 933 (Tex.1993). "Proof of cohabitation and representations to others that the couple are married may constitute circumstantial evidence of an agreement to be married. However, the circumstances of each case must be determined based upon its own facts. We conclude that [Fam. Code] §1.91 [now §2.401] does not require direct evidence of an agreement to be married in order to establish a common law marriage, but that the agreement may be proved by circumstantial evidence."

Collora v. Navarro, 574 S.W.2d 65, 68 (Tex.1978). "The only direct evidence relating to the first element ... was [alleged W's] testimony that she and [alleged H] had 'agreed to a marriage.' Her testimony was direct, positive, and uncontradicted. [H's attorney] chose not to cross-examine her, nor did he call her as an adverse witness. There was no other direct evidence produced at trial that proved or disproved her testimony. Under these circumstances, the court of civil appeals held that [alleged W's] testimony, standing alone, could do no more than raise a fact issue of credibility and could not support a directed verdict. With this conclusion we cannot agree. *At 70:* When all of the evidence points only to the truthfulness of the witness, a directed verdict cannot automatically be rejected solely because the witness' testimony cannot be contradicted."

Assoun v. Gustafson, 493 S.W.3d 156, 163 (Tex.App.—Dallas 2016, pet. filed 7-29-16). Woman and man "submitted their sworn statements that each does not have, and has never had, an agreement to be married to the other in conjunction with their representations to government agencies made under oath that they were single. Based on this they moved for summary judgment that they were not informally married as a matter of law because they negated the first element of an informal marriage that they had no agreement to be married. The circumstantial evidence of a marriage presented by [petitioner] fails to create a fact issue on the first element of an informal marriage—an agreement to be married—in light of [woman's and man's] direct evidence that the parties never agreed to be married and informed government agencies that each was single. [¶] [Woman's and man's] counsel conceded in oral argument that there could be a genuine issue of material fact in some cases even where two people sign affidavits averring they are not married but that the evidence raised by [petitioner] failed to do so in this case. We agree and decide [woman and man] are correct when they argued in the motion for summary judgment...."

In re C.M.V., 479 S.W.3d 352, 360 (Tex.App.—El Paso 2015, no pet.). "To establish that the parties agreed to be husband and wife, it must be shown that [both parties] intended to create an immediate and permanent marriage relationship, not merely a temporary cohabitation that may be ended by either party. An agreement to be married cannot be inferred from the mere evidence of cohabitation and representations of marriage to others, but such evidence may be circumstantial evidence of an agreement to be married. The circumstances of each case must be determined from the facts of that case."

Flores v. Flores, 847 S.W.2d 648, 650 (Tex.App.—Waco 1993, writ denied). "The evidence must show that the parties intended to have a present, immediate, and permanent marital relationship and that they did in fact agree to be husband and wife. *At 652:* Occasional references to 'my wife' or 'my husband' do not prove a tacit agreement to be married without corroboration. If the statement is made in a self-serving context ... it may

not have great weight. On the other hand, a forthright assertion of marriage with the consequences of liability ... may be far more probative of such an agreement."

Cohabitation

Ex parte Threet, 333 S.W.2d 361, 363 (Tex.1960). "All of the acts of intercourse ... occurred at [P's] parents' house or at the home of [D's] parents. After such meetings, the one away from home would 'go home.' [¶] [P] candidly admitted that she and [D] never established a home together. She never moved in with [D] at his house, nor he into hers. She continued to give her parents' residence as her residence. Neither moved any of his or her clothes or personal effects into any common room or apartment. *At 364:* It is our opinion that the facts above set out do not constitute evidence that the couple lived together *as man and wife....*"

Farrell v. Farrell, 459 S.W.3d 114, 117 (Tex.App.—El Paso 2015, no pet.). "[T]here was no Texas common law marriage because [when man and woman, who were previously legally married, began living together], all of the parties were residing in New Mexico, not Texas. And while [woman] claimed that at various points right after the first divorce, [man] was spending entire weekends with her in El Paso, it is clear from her testimony that the parties did not *agree* to be married until [a later date]. The Family Code requires cohabitation in the state of Texas *after the parties agree to be married.*"

Omodele v. Adams, No. 14-01-00999-CV (Tex. App.—Houston [14th Dist.] 2003, no pet.) (memo op.; 1-16-03). "[N]either the Family Code nor the common law provide a bright-line test to determine the length of time a couple must cohabitate to satisfy this requirement. Rather, the cohabitation element is determined on a case-by-case basis. In the case at hand, uncontroverted testimony established that the parties lived together from August 1998 to April 2000. Further, the parties purchased a home and insurance together as husband and wife in September 1999. [H] submitted no evidence to contradict these facts. After considering all the evidence, we find it is legally and factually sufficient to support the element of living together as husband and wife." *See also* ***Allen v. Allen***, 966 S.W.2d 658, 661 (Tex.App.—San Antonio 1998, pet. denied) (situations involving frequent overnight guest do not, alone, establish cohabitation).

Holding Out

Estate of Claveria v. Claveria, 615 S.W.2d 164, 166 (Tex.1981). "[P]roof of common-law marriage may be shown by the conduct of the parties, or by such circumstances as their addressing each other as husband and wife, acknowledging their children as legitimate, joining in conveyances as spouses, and occupying the same dwelling place. [¶] When two persons not living together occasionally refer to each other as a spouse, those isolated references have been held, in some instances as a matter of law, not to have established a common-law marriage. Further, the act of one of the parties to an alleged common-law marriage in celebrating a ceremonial marriage with another person without having first obtained a divorce tends to discredit the first relationship and to show that it was not valid. Still, the circumstances of each case must be determined based upon its own facts."

Ex parte Threet, 333 S.W.2d 361, 364-65 (Tex. 1960). "[T]he introduction of [D] as her husband to two close friends, and telling two or three others that she was married to [D], constituted no evidence that [P] and [D] were living together as husband and wife and holding themselves out to the public as man and wife. Under the Texas decisions, there can be no secret common law marriage as such. The secrecy is inconsistent and irreconcilable with the requirement of a public holding out that the couple are living together as husband and wife." *See also* ***Eris v. Phares***, 39 S.W.3d 708, 714-15 (Tex.App.—Houston [1st Dist.] 2001, pet. denied).

Small v. McMaster, 352 S.W.3d 280, 284-85 (Tex. App.—Houston [14th Dist.] 2011, pet. denied). "The statutory requirement of 'presenting to others' [under §2.401(a)(2)] is synonymous with the judicial requirement of 'holding out to the public.' 'Holding out' may be established by the conduct and actions of the parties. Occasional introductions as husband and wife are not sufficient to establish the element of holding out. [¶] Whether the evidence is sufficient to establish that a couple held themselves out as husband and wife turns on whether the couple had a reputation in the community for being married. Proving a reputation for being married requires evidence that the couple 'consistently conducted themselves as husband and wife in the public eye or that the community viewed them as married.' [¶] Further, the element of presenting to others requires both parties to have represented themselves as

married." *See also* ***Mills v. Mest***, 94 S.W.3d 72, 75 (Tex. App.—Houston [14th Dist.] 2002, pet. denied) (to prove concept of "holding out," evidence must show couple's behavior was intended as communication to third parties, not just intimate behavior in general); ***Lee v. Lee***, 981 S.W.2d 903, 906 (Tex.App.—Houston [1st Dist.] 1998, no pet.) (spoken words are not necessary to establish representation as H and W).

Capacity

Kingery v. Hintz, 124 S.W.3d 875, 877 (Tex.App.—Houston [14th Dist.] 2003, no pet.). "The Family Code plainly provides that a person under the age of 18 may not be a party to an informal marriage. *At 878:* [T]he Family Code emancipates a minor only after she has been married in accordance with the laws of Texas. Hence, [respondent] could only have been emancipated after she entered into a legal marriage[, which did not occur in this case]."

FAM §2.402. DECLARATION & REGISTRATION OF INFORMAL MARRIAGE

(a) A declaration of informal marriage must be signed on a form prescribed by the bureau of vital statistics and provided by the county clerk. Each party to the declaration shall provide the information required in the form.

(b) The declaration form must contain:

(1) a heading entitled "Declaration and Registration of Informal Marriage, ___________ County, Texas";

(2) spaces for each party's full name, including the woman's maiden surname, address, date of birth, place of birth, including city, county, and state, and social security number, if any;

(3) a space for indicating the type of document tendered by each party as proof of age and identity;

(4) printed boxes for each party to check "true" or "false" in response to the following statement: "The other party is not related to me as:

(A) an ancestor or descendant, by blood or adoption;

(B) a brother or sister, of the whole or half blood or by adoption;

(C) a parent's brother or sister, of the whole or half blood or by adoption;

(D) a son or daughter of a brother or sister, of the whole or half blood or by adoption;

(E) a current or former stepchild or stepparent; or

(F) a son or daughter of a parent's brother or sister, of the whole or half blood or by adoption.";

(5) a printed declaration and oath reading: "I SOLEMNLY SWEAR (OR AFFIRM) THAT WE, THE UNDERSIGNED, ARE MARRIED TO EACH OTHER BY VIRTUE OF THE FOLLOWING FACTS: ON OR ABOUT (DATE) WE AGREED TO BE MARRIED, AND AFTER THAT DATE WE LIVED TOGETHER AS HUSBAND AND WIFE AND IN THIS STATE WE REPRESENTED TO OTHERS THAT WE WERE MARRIED. SINCE THE DATE OF MARRIAGE TO THE OTHER PARTY I HAVE NOT BEEN MARRIED TO ANY OTHER PERSON. THIS DECLARATION IS TRUE AND THE INFORMATION IN IT WHICH I HAVE GIVEN IS CORRECT.";

(6) spaces immediately below the printed declaration and oath for the parties' signatures; and

(7) a certificate of the county clerk that the parties made the declaration and oath and the place and date it was made.

(c) Repealed by Acts 1997, 75th Leg., ch. 1362, §4, eff. Sept. 1, 1997.

History of Fam. Code §2.402: Acts 1997, 75th Leg., ch. 7, §1, eff. Apr. 17, 1997. Amended by Acts 1997, 75th Leg., ch. 1362, §4, eff. Sept. 1, 1997; Acts 2005, 79th Leg., ch. 268, §4.13, eff. Sept. 1, 2005. Source: Former Fam. Code §1.92.

ANNOTATIONS

Amaye v. Oravetz, 57 S.W.3d 581, 584 n.3 (Tex. App.—Houston [14th Dist.] 2001, pet. denied). "A declaration and registration is simply a method of establishing a common law marriage; it is not an independent basis, as [petitioner] suggests, upon which a marriage may be founded. Accordingly, [petitioner's] failure to present evidence to rebut the presumption of no common law marriage negates this 'basis' as well."

FAM §2.403. PROOF OF IDENTITY & AGE; OFFENSE

(a) The county clerk shall require proof of the identity and age of each party to the declaration of informal marriage to be established by a document listed in Section 2.005(b).

(b) A person commits an offense if the person knowingly provides false, fraudulent, or otherwise inaccurate proof of the person's identity or age under this section. An offense under this subsection is a Class A misdemeanor.

History of Fam. Code §2.403: Acts 1997, 75th Leg., ch. 7, §1, eff. Apr. 17, 1997. Amended by Acts 2005, 79th Leg., ch. 268, §4.14, eff. Sept. 1, 2005; Acts 2009, 81st Leg., ch. 978, §7, eff. Sept. 1, 2009. Source: Former Fam. Code §1.93.

FAM §2.404. RECORDING OF CERTIFICATE OR DECLARATION OF INFORMAL MARRIAGE

(a) The county clerk shall:

(1) determine that all necessary information is recorded on the declaration of informal marriage form and that all necessary documents are submitted to the clerk;

(2) administer the oath to each party to the declaration;

(3) have each party sign the declaration in the clerk's presence; and

(4) execute the clerk's certificate to the declaration.

(a-1) On the proper execution of the declaration, the clerk may:

(1) prepare a certificate of informal marriage;

(2) enter on the certificate the names of the persons declaring their informal marriage and the date the certificate or declaration is issued; and

(3) record the time at which the certificate or declaration is issued.

(b) The county clerk may not certify the declaration or issue or record the certificate of informal marriage or declaration if:

(1) either party fails to supply any information or provide any document required by this subchapter;

(2) either party is under 18 years of age; or

(3) either party checks "false" in response to the statement of relationship to the other party.

(c) On execution of the declaration, the county clerk shall record the declaration or certificate of informal marriage, deliver the original of the declaration to the parties, deliver the original of the certificate of informal marriage to the parties, if a certificate was prepared, and send a copy of the declaration of informal marriage to the bureau of vital statistics.

(d) An executed declaration or a certificate of informal marriage recorded as provided in this section is prima facie evidence of the marriage of the parties.

(e) At the time the parties sign the declaration, the clerk shall distribute to each party printed materials about acquired immune deficiency syndrome (AIDS) and human immunodeficiency virus (HIV). The clerk shall note on the declaration that the distribution was made. The materials shall be prepared and provided to the clerk by the Texas Department of Health and shall be designed to inform the parties about:

(1) the incidence and mode of transmission of AIDS and HIV;

(2) the local availability of medical procedures, including voluntary testing, designed to show or help show whether a person has AIDS or HIV infection, antibodies to HIV, or infection with any other probable causative agent of AIDS; and

(3) available and appropriate counseling services regarding AIDS and HIV infection.

History of Fam. Code §2.404: Acts 1997, 75th Leg., ch. 7, §1, eff. Apr. 17, 1997. Amended by Acts 1997, 75th Leg., ch. 1362, §2, eff. Sept. 1, 1997; Acts 2009, 81st Leg., ch. 978, §§8, 9, eff. Sept. 1, 2009. Source: Former Fam. Code §1.94.

ANNOTATIONS

Colburn v. State, 966 S.W.2d 511, 514 (Tex.Crim. App.1998). "A properly recorded declaration of informal marriage constitutes *prima facie* proof of the informal marriage. Thus, the trial court may find the common law marriage proven based upon the declaration alone, but evidence may be offered rebutting the existence of the marriage as sworn to or stated in the declaration. In other words, the trial court is not bound to find a marriage as stated in the declaration when there is evidence to the contrary."

FAM §2.405. VIOLATION BY COUNTY CLERK; PENALTY

A county clerk or deputy county clerk who violates this subchapter commits an offense. An offense under this section is a misdemeanor punishable by a fine of not less than $200 and not more than $500.

History of Fam. Code §2.405: Acts 1997, 75th Leg., ch. 7, §1, eff. Apr. 17, 1997. Source: Former Fam. Code §1.95.

Sections 2.406-2.500 reserved for expansion

SUBCHAPTER F. RIGHTS & DUTIES OF SPOUSES

FAM §2.501. DUTY TO SUPPORT

(a) Each spouse has the duty to support the other spouse.

(b) A spouse who fails to discharge the duty of support is liable to any person who provides necessaries to the spouse to whom support is owed.

History of Fam. Code §2.501: Acts 1997, 75th Leg., ch. 7, §1, eff. Apr. 17, 1997. Source: Former Fam. Code §4.02.

See also ***O'Connor's Texas Family Law Handbook*** (2017), "Duty of support – provide necessaries," ch. 1-C, §2.2.1, p. 36.

ANNOTATIONS

Tedder v. Gardner Aldrich, LLP, 421 S.W.3d 651, 655 (Tex.2013). "'[M]arriage itself does not create

joint and several liability.' [O]ne spouse's liability for debts incurred by or for the other is determined by statute. [¶] [Under Fam. Code §§2.501 and 3.201,] one spouse is not liable for the other's debt unless the other incurred it as the one's agent or the one failed to support the other and the debt is for necessaries. *At 656:* [A] spouse's necessaries are things like food, clothing, and habitation—that is, sustenance—and we have squarely rejected the view that a spouse's legal fees in a divorce proceeding fall into this category. ... '[I]t is not a correct approach ... to classify the wife's attorney's fees as a necessity, and then apply the rule that necessities are primarily the obligations of the community and secondarily of the husband's separate estate.... [T]he trial court [has discretion] in determining the proper division of the community estate of the parties.... The attorney's fee is but a factor to be considered by the court in making an equitable division of the estate, considering the conditions and needs of the parties and all of the surrounding circumstances.'"

Ex parte Hall, 854 S.W.2d 656, 658 (Tex.1993). "The obligation which the law imposes on spouses to support one another ... is not considered a 'debt' within [Tex. Const.] art. 1, §18, but a legal duty arising out of the status of the parties. ... However, a person may also contract to support his spouse ..., and that obligation, to the extent it exceeds his legal duty, is a debt."

Sections 2.502-2.600 blank

SUBCHAPTER G. FREEDOM OF RELIGION WITH RESPECT TO RECOGNIZING OR PERFORMING CERTAIN MARRIAGES

FAM §2.601. RIGHTS OF CERTAIN RELIGIOUS ORGANIZATIONS

A religious organization, an organization supervised or controlled by or in connection with a religious organization, an individual employed by a religious organization while acting in the scope of that employment, or a clergy or minister may not be required to solemnize any marriage or provide services, accommodations, facilities, goods, or privileges for a purpose related to the solemnization, formation, or celebration of any marriage if the action would cause the organization or individual to violate a sincerely held religious belief.

History of Fam. Code §2.601: Acts 2015, 84th Leg., ch. 434, §1, eff. June 11, 2015.

ANNOTATIONS

Obergefell v. Hodges, ___ U.S. ___, 135 S.Ct. 2584, 2607 (2015). "[R]eligions, and those who adhere to religious doctrines, may continue to advocate with utmost, sincere conviction that, by divine precepts, same-sex marriage should not be condoned. The First Amendment ensures that religious organizations and persons are given proper protection as they seek to teach the principles that are so fulfilling and so central to their lives and faiths, and to their own deep aspirations to continue the family structure they have long revered. The same is true of those who oppose same-sex marriage for other reasons. In turn, those who believe allowing same-sex marriage is proper or indeed essential, whether as a matter of religious conviction or secular belief, may engage those who disagree with their view in an open and searching debate. The Constitution, however, does not permit the State to bar same-sex couples from marriage on the same terms as accorded to couples of the opposite sex."

FAM §2.602. DISCRIMINATION AGAINST RELIGIOUS ORGANIZATION PROHIBITED

A refusal to provide services, accommodations, facilities, goods, or privileges under Section 2.601 is not the basis for a civil or criminal cause of action or any other action by this state or a political subdivision of this state to penalize or withhold benefits or privileges, including tax exemptions or governmental contracts, grants, or licenses, from any protected organization or individual.

History of Fam. Code §2.602: Acts 2015, 84th Leg., ch. 434, §1, eff. June 11, 2015.

SUBTITLE B. PROPERTY RIGHTS & LIABILITIES

CHAPTER 3. MARITAL PROPERTY RIGHTS & LIABILITIES

SUBCHAPTER A. GENERAL RULES FOR SEPARATE & COMMUNITY PROPERTY

FAM §3.001. SEPARATE PROPERTY

A spouse's separate property consists of:

(1) the property owned or claimed by the spouse before marriage;

(2) the property acquired by the spouse during marriage by gift, devise, or descent; and

(3) the recovery for personal injuries sustained by the spouse during marriage, except any recovery for loss of earning capacity during marriage.

History of Fam. Code §3.001: Acts 1997, 75th Leg., ch. 7, §1, eff. Apr. 17, 1997. Source: Former Fam. Code §5.01(a).

See also ***O'Connor's Texas Family Law Handbook*** (2017), "Separate property," ch. 2-A, §2.1, p. 94.

ANNOTATIONS

Generally

Welder v. Lambert, 44 S.W. 281, 286 (Tex.1898). "In this cause the title [to disputed land] originated in the contract of [father] with the state of ... Texas. That contract ... was the 'cause' of the title. [Father] was single when it was entered into, and the right to earn the lands acquired by it was his separate property. The title relates to its origin, and must take the impress of its character from it."

Rusk v. Rusk, 5 S.W.3d 299, 303 (Tex.App.—Houston [14th Dist.] 1999, pet. denied). "The characterization of property as either 'community' or 'separate' is determined by the inception of title to the property. The major consideration in determining the characterization of property as community or separate is the intention of spouses shown by the circumstances surrounding the inception of title. Inception of title occurs when a party first has right of claim to the property by virtue of which title is finally vested."

Lipsey v. Lipsey, 983 S.W.2d 345, 350 (Tex.App.—Fort Worth 1998, no pet.). "[W]hen separate property produces income and that income is acquired by a spouse, it is community property. However, an increase in the value of an item of separate property is an inherent part of the item and cannot be separated from it."

Ridgell v. Ridgell, 960 S.W.2d 144, 148 (Tex.App.—Corpus Christi 1997, no pet.). "Property acquired in exchange for separate property becomes the separate property of the spouse who exchanged the property."

Harris v. Harris, 765 S.W.2d 798, 803 (Tex.App.—Houston [14th Dist.] 1989, writ denied). "As in the case of stock splits and increases, analogous to this situation involving 'units' of a partnership, mutations and increases in separate property remain separate property."

Cook v. Cook, 679 S.W.2d 581, 583 (Tex.App.—San Antonio 1984, no writ). "Where property is purchased partly with community funds and partly with separate funds, the property is community property to the extent and in the proportion that the purchase price is paid by the community, while the spouse providing the separate funds will have a separate interest in the property to the amount of investment of separate funds."

Property Owned Before Marriage

Jensen v. Jensen, 665 S.W.2d 107, 109 (Tex.1984). "[A]ll property held by either a husband or a wife before marriage remains the separate property of such spouse and the status of the property is to be determined by the origin of the title to the property, and not by the acquisition of the final title."

Langston v. Langston, 82 S.W.3d 686, 688 (Tex. App.—Eastland 2002, no pet.). "Property owned by a spouse before marriage remains the separate property of that spouse during marriage. Once property is characterized as separate property, that character does not change although the property is improved with community funds."

Gift, Devise, or Descent

Stearns v. Martens, 476 S.W.3d 541, 548 (Tex. App.—Houston [14th Dist.] 2015, no pet.). "[I]f the instrument [in which one spouse transfers property (whether separate or community) to the other spouse] contains no separate-property recitals, then parol evidence is admissible regarding the marital-property issue. Because the [Stock Transfer] Agreement contains no separate-property recitals, parol evidence is admissible regarding the marital-property issue, and there is no irrebuttable presumption that the transferred shares are [W's] separate property."

In re Marriage of Moncey, 404 S.W.3d 701, 710 (Tex.App.—Texarkana 2013, no pet.). "'An attempted gift by a third party to the community estate vests each partner with a one-half undivided interest in the property as his or her separate property.' [¶] A gift is a voluntary transfer of property to another made gratuitously and without consideration. Three elements are required to establish the existence of a gift: (1) intent to make a gift, (2) delivery of the property, and (3) acceptance of the property. Generally, the burden of proof rests on the person claiming the existence of a gift. '[T]he intent must exist at the time of the transfer.'" *See also* ***Roosth v. Roosth***, 889 S.W.2d 445, 457 (Tex. App.—Houston [14th Dist.] 1994, writ denied) (each spouse gets one-half undivided separate interest in wedding gifts).

In re Marriage of Skarda, 345 S.W.3d 665, 671 (Tex.App.—Amarillo 2011, no pet.). "A deed for property from one spouse as grantor to the other spouse as grantee creates a rebuttable presumption that the grantee spouse received the property as separate property by gift. ... The intent of the donor is the principal issue in determining whether a gift was made." *See also* ***Magness v. Magness***, 241 S.W.3d 910, 912-13 (Tex.App.—Dallas 2007, pet. denied) (presumption of gift may be rebutted by proof that deed was procured by fraud, accident, or mistake).

In re Marriage of Case, 28 S.W.3d 154, 158-59 (Tex.App.—Texarkana 2000, no pet.). "The general rule in divorce cases is that, when a spouse uses separate property to acquire property during marriage and takes title to that property in the names of both spouses, a presumption arises that the purchasing spouse intended to make a gift of one half of the separate funds to the other spouse. [¶] However, in 1979 the Nontestamentary Transfers Chapter of the ... Probate Code [now Estates Code ch. 113] was adopted. This chapter ... contains specific provisions governing the ownership of joint bank accounts. The provisions govern the basic ownership and withdrawal rights both during and after the life of a depositor. [¶] The [Estates] Code ... provides, '[During the lifetime of all parties to a joint account, the account belongs] to the parties in proportion to the net contributions by each [party] to the sums on deposit[] unless there is clear and convincing evidence of a different intent.' This statutory provision of the [Estates] Code has the effect of overriding any common-law gift presumptions on bank accounts. The [Estates] Code specifically spells out how the ownership of the property is to be determined."

Pemelton v. Pemelton, 809 S.W.2d 642, 646 (Tex. App.—Corpus Christi 1991), *rev'd on other grounds sub nom.* ***Heggen v. Pemelton***, 836 S.W.2d 145 (Tex.1992). "Proof that the property was acquired by gift during the marriage may rebut the community presumption. A presumption of separate property arises when (1) one spouse is grantor and the other spouse is grantee, or (2) one spouse furnishes separate property consideration and title is taken in the name of the other spouse, or (3) the instrument of conveyance contains a significant recital that states that the consideration is paid from the separate funds of a spouse or that the property is conveyed to a spouse as his or her separate property. Furthermore, a grantor may make a gift of encumbered property and a conveyance may be a gift even if the grantee assumes an obligation to extinguish the encumbrance. *At 647:* A gift is a transfer of property made voluntarily and gratuitously, without consideration. The burden of proving a gift is on the person claiming the gift was made. Although a conveyance of title from parent to child is presumed a gift, such presumption is rebuttable by evidence showing the facts and circumstances surrounding the deed's execution in addition to the deed's recitations. [¶] Lack of consideration is

an essential characteristic of a gift. An exchange of consideration precludes a gift. Gift and onerous consideration are exact antitheses. A recital of onerous consideration in a deed negatives the idea of a gift." (Internal quotes omitted.)

Personal Injury

Douglas v. Delp, 987 S.W.2d 879, 883 (Tex.1999). "Any mental anguish damages recovered are part of the injured spouse's separate property."

Lewis v. Lewis, 944 S.W.2d 630, 630 (Tex.1997). "The character of [workers'] compensation benefits paid during marriage is determined not by when the injury occurred, but by when the loss of earning capacity occurred."

Graham v. Franco, 488 S.W.2d 390, 397 (Tex. 1972). "[T]he reason for the rule that the negligence of the husband should be imputed to the wife (that he would profit from his own wrong) falls where the recovery for her injuries is her separate property. We have held that such recovery is her separate property, and the recovery will not be to him or the community. Therefore, the contributory negligence of the husband does not bar the recovery by the wife."

Harrell v. Hochderffer, 345 S.W.3d 652, 659-60 (Tex.App.—Austin 2011, no pet.). Respondents argue "that a recovery for exemplary damages [in a personal-injury case] is characterized as community property. ... A recovery for personal injuries ... is expressly characterized as separate property under the family code, with a statutory exception for any recovery for loss of earning capacity during the marriage. The only additional exceptions acknowledged by Texas courts are funds recovered for 'medical expenses incurred during marriage, and ... other expenses associated with injury to the community estate.' Unlike lost earning capacity and medical expenses, however, exemplary damages do not represent income to which the community is entitled or an expense for which the community is liable. An exemplary damages recovery is merely 'a private windfall,' levied for the public purpose of punishment and deterrence, and is not associated with an injury to the community estate. Because an exemplary-damages award does not fall under any exception to the general rule that the recovery for personal injuries is separate property, such damages must be characterized as separate property under ... §3.001(3)."

In re Marriage of Franklin, No. 07-04-0515-CV (Tex.App.—Amarillo 2006, pet. denied) (memo op.; 6-19-06). "Unlike the potential recovery in ***Osborn*** [below], we deal here with an asset acquired during marriage from the settlement of a lawsuit in which both [H's] separate property claims and community property claims were asserted and settled. The trial court here properly placed on [H] the burden to show that the annuity he claimed as separate property was obtained as a result of his personal injuries and was not compensation for lost earning capacity during marriage or medical expenses." *See also* ***Munoz v. Munoz***, No. 08-01-00443-CV (Tex.App.—El Paso 2003, no pet.) (memo op.; 12-19-03) (because there was no evidence establishing which portion of personal-injury settlement was separate property, entire settlement proceeds were presumed to be community property).

Slaton v. Slaton, 987 S.W.2d 180, 184 (Tex.App.—Houston [14th Dist.] 1999, pet. denied). "[M]oney received as the result of a settlement agreement for personal injuries sustained by a spouse during the marriage has been found to be separate property, minus loss of earnings and other consequential damages to the community estate. Thus, we reject [H's] contention that the settlement agreement was merely a contract that proceeds should be viewed as community property."

Osborn v. Osborn, 961 S.W.2d 408, 414 (Tex. App.—Houston [1st Dist.] 1997, pet. denied). "There is no presumption that a potential recovery for ... personal injuries to the body of a spouse is community property. ... The damages that are the separate property of the injured spouse include those for disfigurement and for physical pain and suffering in the past and in the future. [¶] To the extent the marital partnership was injured, the community estate is entitled to recover damages. The damages that belong to the community estate include lost wages of the injured spouse, damages for medical expenses, and other expenses associated with the injury to the community estate. To the extent the other spouse was injured by loss of consortium, those damages are the separate property of the other spouse." *See also* ***Cottone v. Cottone***, 122 S.W.3d 211, 213 (Tex. App.—Houston [1st Dist.] 2003, no pet.).

FAM §3.002. COMMUNITY PROPERTY

Community property consists of the property, other than separate property, acquired by either spouse during marriage.

History of Fam. Code §3.002: Acts 1997, 75th Leg., ch. 7, §1, eff. Apr. 17, 1997. Source: Former Fam. Code §5.01(b).

See also ***O'Connor's Texas Family Law Handbook*** (2017), "Community property," ch. 2-A, §2.2, p. 96.

ANNOTATIONS

Generally

Lee v. Lee, 247 S.W. 828, 832-33 (Tex.1923). "The word 'acquired' is not to be construed in any restricted sense, but must necessarily have that broad signification as will include all effects or gains or property of every kind coming to the husband or wife during coverture in any manner other than by 'gift, devise or descent.'"

McClary v. Thompson, 65 S.W.3d 829, 836 (Tex. App.—Fort Worth 2002, pet. denied). Although this court agrees with ***Dewey v. Dewey***, 745 S.W.2d 514 (Tex.App.—Corpus Christi 1988, writ denied), "that the inception-of-title rule has no application in the context of retirement benefits, the fact is that whether we characterize the Texas rule as one of apportionment or inception-of-title, the result is the same, i.e., apportionment. Therefore, we reject [petitioner's] argument that the character of the entire retirement account must be determined based on the inception-of-title rule. We conclude that, under either theory, the contributions and interest earned during the marriage constituted community property."

Wilson v. Wilson, 44 S.W.3d 597, 601 (Tex.App.—Fort Worth 2001, no pet.). "Because [the parties] were still married even after their separation in 1990, the property they continued to acquire between the date of separation and divorce was still considered community property, unless either spouse could establish that the property was separate property under [Fam. Code] §3.001."

Camp v. Camp, 972 S.W.2d 906, 908 n.1 (Tex. App.—Corpus Christi 1998, pet. denied). "The characterization of property as either 'community' or 'separate' is determined by the inception of title to the property. Inception of title occurs when a party first has right of claim to the property by virtue of which title is finally vested."

Business Interest—Corporation

Young v. Young, 168 S.W.3d 276, 281-82 (Tex. App.—Dallas 2005, no pet.). "Under certain circumstances, a spouse may be able to reach the assets of the other spouse's separately owned corporation. A finding of alter ego allows piercing of the corporate veil. Piercing the corporate veil, in turn, allows the trial court to characterize as community property assets that would otherwise be the separate property of a spouse. In the divorce context, piercing the corporate veil allows the trial court to achieve an equitable result. [¶] In a divorce case, a finding of alter ego sufficient to justify piercing the corporate veil requires: (1) unity between the separate property corporation and the spouse such that the separateness has ceased to exist; and (2) the spouse's improper use of the corporation damaged the community estate beyond that which might be remedied by a claim for reimbursement." *See also* ***Lifshutz v. Lifshutz***, 61 S.W.3d 511, 517-18 (Tex.App.—San Antonio 2001, pet. denied) (corporate veil not pierced because H's misuse and dominance of corporation did not result in harm to community estate); ***Zisblatt v. Zisblatt***, 693 S.W.2d 944, 955 (Tex.App.—Fort Worth 1985, writ dism'd) (court found that upholding corporation as separate property would materially prejudice community estate).

Hunt v. Hunt, 952 S.W.2d 564, 567 (Tex.App.—Eastland 1997, no writ). "When a corporation is funded with separate property, the corporation is separate property."

Siefkas v. Siefkas, 902 S.W.2d 72, 79 (Tex.App.—El Paso 1995, no writ). "[U]nless the corporation is a spouse's alter ego, a court may only award a spouse's interest in the corporation, not specific corporate property."

Thomas v. Thomas, 738 S.W.2d 342, 343 (Tex. App.—Houston [1st Dist.] 1987, writ denied). Petitioner "admits that in an ordinary corporation, retained earnings are a corporate asset. They are not marital property, separate or community. [Petitioner] contends, however, that retained earnings of a Subchapter S corporation should be treated as community property because the community has paid federal income tax on them. This, she argues, justifies the recognition of a community interest in the retained earnings. We disagree. [¶] Subchapter S status does not determine who owns the corporation's earnings. It merely provides an alternate method to tax the corporation's income. A Subchapter S corporation may distribute its income, but, like any other corporation, it is not required to do so. Corporate distributions, regardless of form, are controlled by state law. The shareholder in a Sub-

chapter S corporation has no greater rights over corporate property than a shareholder in any other corporation."

Business Interest—Goodwill

Salinas v. Rafati, 948 S.W.2d 286, 290 (Tex.1997). "To the extent that the valuation of the dissolved partnership was based on the goodwill attributable to the personal skills and talents of the former partners, it improperly took into account intangibles that were not partnership assets. *At 291:* [T]here may be goodwill in a professional partnership that is separate from the skills or attributes of an individual member. [¶] [But in this case,] a valuation based on the earnings of the [former partners] improperly takes into account goodwill that is attributable only to the professionals personally."

Nail v. Nail, 486 S.W.2d 761, 764 (Tex.1972). It cannot be said that "the accrued good will in [a professional practice] was an earned or vested property right at the time of the divorce or that it qualifies as property subject to division by decree of the court. It did not possess value or constitute an asset separate and apart from his person, or from his individual ability to practice his profession. It would be extinguished in event of his death, or retirement, or disablement, as well as in event of the sale of his practice or the loss of his patients, whatever the cause. ... Accordingly, we hold that the [personal] good will of petitioner's medical practice that may have accrued at the time of the divorce was not property in the estate of the parties...."

Finn v. Finn, 658 S.W.2d 735, 740-41 (Tex.App.—Dallas 1983, writ ref'd n.r.e.). A two-pronged test is used "to determine whether the goodwill attached to a professional practice is subject to division upon divorce. First, goodwill must be determined to exist independently of the personal ability of the professional spouse. Second, if such goodwill is found to exist, then it must be determined whether that goodwill has a commercial value in which the community estate is entitled to share. [¶] Evidence in the present case indicates that [H's] law firm has goodwill independent of his professional ability. [¶] The inquiry does not stop here ..., but must continue to determine whether his goodwill has commercial value to which the community estate is entitled. [¶] The community estate is not entitled to a greater interest than that to which [H] is entitled in the firm's goodwill. The extent of [H's] interest is governed by the partnership agreement. *At 742:* The [partnership] agreement does not provide any compensation for accrued goodwill to a partner who ceases to practice law with the firm, nor does it provide any mechanism to realize the value of the firm's goodwill. [¶] The lack of any legal right of [H] to realize the value of the firm's goodwill is a decisive factor. ... Such realization in the future is no more than an expectancy entirely dependent on [H's] continued participation in the firm, and, therefore, is not property in the community estate." *See also* ***Hill v. Hill***, No. 02-12-00332-CV (Tex.App.—Fort Worth 2014, no pet.) (memo op.; 1-9-14).

Austin v. Austin, 619 S.W.2d 290, 292 (Tex.App.—Austin 1981, no writ). "Once a professional practice is sold, the good will is no longer attached to the person of the professional man or woman. The seller's actions will no longer have significant effect on the good will. The value of the good will is fixed and it is now property that may be divided as community property."

Business Interest—Partnership

Harris v. Harris, 765 S.W.2d 798, 802 (Tex.App.—Houston [14th Dist.] 1989, writ denied). "Under the entity theory of partnership, adopted by Texas in the Uniform Partnership Act [now Texas Revised Partnership Act], partnership property is owned by the partnership entity, not the individual partners. A partner's rights in specific partnership property are wholly subordinated to the rights of the partnership entity as owner of the property. He may possess the property only for partnership purposes. Partnership property is therefore neither separate nor community in character. The only partnership property right the partner has which is subject to a community or separate property characterization is his interest in the partnership, that is his right to receive his share of the partnership profits and surplus. Distributions of the partner's share of profits and surplus (income) received during marriage are community property even if the partner's interest in the partnership is separate property."

Business Interest—Sole Proprietorship

In re Marriage of York, 613 S.W.2d 764, 770 (Tex.App.—Amarillo 1981, no writ). "In Texas, the profits derived from a business enterprise carried on by either the husband or wife are community property, even though the capital of the business is the separate property of one of the spouses."

Debts & Loans

Tedder v. Gardner Aldrich, LLP, 421 S.W.3d 651, 654 (Tex.2013). The "concept [of 'community debt' is] often misused to impose liability on a spouse who did not incur the debt. Confusion over the significance of 'community debt' has been ascribed to our opinion in ***Cockerham v. Cockerham***[, 527 S.W.2d 162 (Tex. 1975)], where we said that 'debts contracted during marriage are presumed to be on the credit of the community and thus are joint community obligations, unless it is shown the creditor agreed to look solely to the separate estate of the contracting spouse for satisfaction.' We immediately added: '[T]he fact that the debts are community liabilities would not, without more, necessarily lead to the conclusion they were joint liabilities. Characterization of the debts as community liabilities is only one aspect of the circumstances to be considered in determining whether the debts are joint.' But the first statement, and the entire analysis, has proved misleading. *At 655:* '[M]arriage itself does not create joint and several liability.' [O]ne spouse's liability for debts incurred by or for the other is determined by statute."

Nesmith v. Berger, 64 S.W.3d 110, 117 (Tex.App.—Austin 2001, pet. denied). "[W] contends that the mortgage signed by [H] lacks the 'magic words' stating that the creditor agreed to look solely to [H's] separate property for satisfaction. [¶] A question of fact is raised as to the character of the property when the documentary evidence fails to reflect an express agreement by the lender to look only to the purchasing spouse's separate estate for payment. We must look to the totality of the circumstances in which the debt arose to determine the character of the debt. Evidence showing, for example, that the down payment was paid with separate funds, and the parties agreed that the property would remain separate property and the balance of the debt was to be paid from separate funds is sufficient to overcome the presumption of community debt. 'The effect of such proof would not be altered by the fact that [nonpurchasing spouse] joined in the promise to pay the balance of the purchase money.'"

Jones v. Jones, 890 S.W.2d 471, 475-76 (Tex. App.—Corpus Christi 1994, writ denied). "When establishing whether the debt incurred and the property purchased during marriage was the separate property of one of the spouses, the lender's knowledge of the spouses' intentions is of significant importance. The intention of one spouse alone to repay a loan out of separate funds and then hold the property purchased with the proceeds of that loan as separate property has never been controlling. Therefore, the intention of the lender to look solely to the property of one spouse is an evidentiary factor of prime importance in showing by clear and convincing evidence that the spouses intended to hold the property as one spouse's separate property, especially where there is no evidence of such an agreement."

Goodridge v. Goodridge, 591 S.W.2d 571, 574 (Tex. App.—Dallas 1979, writ dism'd). "Property acquired on the credit of the community is community property." *See also* ***Uranga v. Uranga***, 527 S.W.2d 761, 765 (Tex. App.—San Antonio 1975, writ dism'd) (money borrowed during marriage is presumed to be community property).

Brooks v. Brooks, 515 S.W.2d 730, 733 (Tex.App.—Eastland 1974, writ ref'd n.r.e.). "Texas statutes do not define the term 'community debt.' We hold that the term does not include a potential income tax obligation."

Income—Child's

Insurance Co. of Tex. v. Stratton, 287 S.W.2d 320, 323 (Tex.App.—Waco 1956, writ ref'd n.r.e.). "[E]arnings of an unemancipated minor, as well as any property that might be purchased with proceeds derived from such earnings, belong to and become a part of the community property of the father and mother of such minor."

Income—Intellectual Property

Alsenz v. Alsenz, 101 S.W.3d 648, 653 (Tex.App.—Houston [1st Dist.] 2003, pet. denied). "In general, income produced from separate property is considered community property. This is usually true regardless of the nature of the separate property, whether the separate property generating income is stock or shares in a corporation, a trust, real estate, livestock, or other assets. [W] argues that the royalties here are in the nature of such income. [¶] An exception to the general rule that income from separate property is community property concerns oil-and-gas royalties. Because such royalties are payment for the extraction of the separate property, the royalties are also considered separate property. [H] argues that the royalties paid on a patent are equivalent to oil-and-gas royalties because the value of a patent diminishes over time. We must decide whether the income stream generated from intellectual

property should be treated under the general rule or in the same manner as oil-and-gas royalties. *At 654:* We hold that the income stream generated during the marriage from [H's] inventions patented before the marriage was a 'revenue' and a 'fruit' of his separate property; therefore, we hold that it was community property."

Income—Property

McElwee v. McElwee, 911 S.W.2d 182, 188-89 (Tex.App.—Houston [1st Dist.] 1995, writ denied). "Rents and revenues from separate property are community property." *See also* ***Smith v. Lanier***, 998 S.W.2d 324, 332 (Tex.App.—Austin 1999, pet. denied) (cash dividends on separately held stock); ***Ridgell v. Ridgell***, 960 S.W.2d 144, 148 (Tex.App.—Corpus Christi 1997, no pet.) (income from trust); ***Gutierrez v. Gutierrez***, 791 S.W.2d 659, 664-65 (Tex.App.—San Antonio 1990, no writ) (offspring born to cattle during marriage); ***Harris v. Harris***, 765 S.W.2d 798, 802 (Tex.App.—Houston [14th Dist.] 1989, writ denied) (profit-sharing distributions).

Income—Spouse's

Keller v. Keller, 141 S.W.2d 308, 311 (Tex.1940). "It is urged on [H's] behalf that under the trial court's findings the community owned no claim for salary at the time of the divorce. It is undisputed that the item was not paid by the corporation until a few days after the divorce was granted. [¶] Whether the salaries were drawn during the current year is immaterial. When paid they were paid for that year and were paid as salaries. [¶] The parties at interest, including [H], treated the amounts received as salary, according to the undisputed testimony. [¶] Regardless of whether the corporation could have elected to treat the item in question as dividends on the stock, it did not do so; nor could [H] lawfully waive his claim to salary already set up and by his mere ipse dixit convert it into dividends, or some form of profit incident to stock ownership, and thereby convert his salary, which was community property, into his separate property."

Loya v. Loya, 473 S.W.3d 362, 368-69 (Tex.App.—Houston [14th Dist.] 2015), *rev'd on other grounds*, ___ S.W.3d ___ (Tex.2017) (No. 15-0763; 5-12-17). "[T]here is no bright line rule for bonuses: a bonus paid during marriage may be based in part on work performed prior to the marriage, which would make that portion of the bonus a spouse's separate property. [A] bonus paid post-divorce, but alleged to be based in part on work performed during the marriage, could be subject to proof that some portion of this bonus is community property." *See also* ***Moore v. Moore***, 192 S.W.2d 929, 930 (Tex.App.—Fort Worth 1946, no writ) (money received by spouse after marriage for services rendered prior to marriage becomes spouse's separate property).

Chubb Lloyds Ins. v. Kizer, 943 S.W.2d 946, 952 n.3 (Tex.App.—Fort Worth 1997, writ denied). "The personal earnings of either spouse during marriage are characterized as community property."

Life Insurance

Brown v. Lee, 371 S.W.2d 694, 696 (Tex.1963). "[T]he right to receive insurance proceeds payable at a future but uncertain date is 'property.' Such property is said to be in the nature of a chose in action which matures at the death of the insured. [¶] When purchased with community funds, the ownership of the unmatured chose logically belongs to the community, unless it has been irrevocably given away under the terms of the policy, i.e., where the purchaser has, without fraud, foreclosed any right to change the named beneficiary.... The proceeds at maturity are likewise community in character, except where the named beneficiary is in fact surviving, in which case a gift of the policy rights to such beneficiary is presumed to have been intended and completed by the death of the insured. [¶] Under circumstances where the uninsured spouse predeceases the insured spouse, settlement of the decedent's community interest in the unmatured chose has ordinarily been resolved by allocating one-half of the cash surrender value to the deceased's estate and the other one-half, plus ownership of the unmatured chose, to the surviving spouse. But ... where settlement of the deceased [W's] community interest in the policies was not made prior to the death of the insured and her heirs were not guilty of laches in failing to seek such compensation, [W's] community interest was never extinguished and the policies retained their community status up to the time of maturity. Consequently, the proceeds are community."

Camp v. Camp, 972 S.W.2d 906, 908-09 (Tex.App.—Corpus Christi 1998, pet. denied). Decedent's mother "contended that the inception of title rule governs the disposition of this case, *i.e.*, because [decedent] acquired title to the insurance policy before his marriage to [W], it is his separate property and his designation of his mother as beneficiary stands. It is undisputed that [decedent] acquired title to the insur-

ance policy through his employment compensation prior to his marriage to [W] and that [his mother] is the named beneficiary. Texas case law supports the conclusions that the policy was his separate property with [W] entitled to reimbursement for her share of the premiums paid with community funds ([decedent's] earnings during the marriage). [¶] [W] would argue that, as applied to the instant case, inception of title analysis is inapposite because term life insurance is too ephemeral to constitute property. ... As per the government code, property contemplated by family code provisions relating to the characterization of marital property must be understood to include not only life insurance policies, but also 'the effects of life insurance policies.' The undisputed effect of the term life policy [decedent] acquired was that it would pay $35,000 to a named beneficiary upon his ... death. Thus, even if it does not build up cash value, the term life insurance policy produces a tangible effect, and [decedent's] title to it relates back to a time prior to his marriage to [W]."

Seaman v. Seaman, 756 S.W.2d 56, 58 (Tex.App.—Texarkana 1988, no writ). "A life insurance policy that is an incident of employment during marriage is community property. This is true even if premiums are not deducted from the employee's salary because the policy is a benefit earned by employment. Even though the policy provides only for term insurance and has no cash value, it is still a property right that can be awarded to one of the spouses on divorce."

Dent v. Dent, 689 S.W.2d 521, 522 (Tex.App.—Fort Worth 1985, no writ). "The proceeds of life insurance policies purchased during the marriage on the life of a third person with one of the spouses named as the beneficiary are community property."

Givens v. Girard Life Ins., 480 S.W.2d 421, 423 (Tex.App.—Dallas 1972, writ ref'd n.r.e.). "Life insurance is defined as property ..., and earnings during marriage are community property.... Since the premiums paid by [H's] employer were part of the compensation for his services, this insurance is deemed to be purchased out of his earnings and therefore community property."

Mineral Interest

Norris v. Vaughan, 260 S.W.2d 676, 679 (Tex.1953). "When royalty is paid for oil or gas produced from the separate property of the lessor, the courts of this state have held that such royalty is payment for the extraction or waste of the separate estate and therefore remains separate property."

Cone v. Cone, 266 S.W.2d 480, 483-84 (Tex.App.—Amarillo 1953), *writ dism'd*, 266 S.W.2d 860 (Tex.1954). "No citation of authority should be required as to the proposition that oil in place is a part of the realty and that if such oil is separate property when a part of the realty it remains separate property when produced and separated therefrom."

McGarraugh v. McGarraugh, 177 S.W.2d 296, 301 (Tex.App.—Amarillo 1943, writ dism'd). "Inasmuch as the items here involved were delay rentals and accrued merely by lapse of time like other rentals, did not depend upon the finding or production of oil or gas, and did not exhaust the substance of the land, we think they constituted personal property and belonged to the community estate."

Real Property

In re Marriage of Morris, 12 S.W.3d 877, 881-82 (Tex.App.—Texarkana 2000, no pet.). "Once separate property character attaches, that character does not change because community funds are spent to improve the property. Any improvements made on separate property, including a residence, are considered the separate property of the land owner." (Internal quotes omitted.)

Wilkerson v. Wilkerson, 992 S.W.2d 719, 722 (Tex.App.—Austin 1999, no pet.). "Real property acquired before marriage is separate property. ... When real property is acquired under a contract for deed or installment contract, the inception of title relates back to the time the contract was executed, not the time when legal title is conveyed. Thus, if one spouse entered into a contract for deed before marriage, the property is separate property even if the conveyance of legal title occurs during the marriage and the deed names both spouses as grantees."

Carter v. Carter, 736 S.W.2d 775, 779 (Tex.App.—Houston [14th Dist.] 1987, no writ). "Ownership of real property is governed by the rule that 'the character of title to property as separate or community depends upon the existence or nonexistence of the marriage at the time of the incipiency of the right in virtue of which the title is finally extended, and that the title, when extended, relates back to that time.' [H] acquired a right to title to the property when he entered into the earnest money contract. As the date of execution of the earnest money contract was prior to the marriage, [H's] right

to title preceded the marriage and the separate character of the property was thereby established."

Stocks

Legrand-Brock v. Brock, 246 S.W.3d 318, 321 (Tex.App.—Beaumont 2008, pet. denied). "Generally, when a spouse owns separate-property stock in a dissolving corporation and receives distributions of liquidated assets, the distributions remain the stockholder's separate property. ... Distributions received in exchange for the cancellation of stock upon the corporation's dissolution retain the character of the stock. [¶] [W] argues that because [company] distributed the cash from its retained earnings, the distributions were dividends and therefore community property. *At 322 n.3:* A 'liquidation dividend' is defined as '[a] dividend paid to a dissolving corporation's shareholders, [usually] from the capital of the corporation, upon the decision to suspend all or part of its business operations.' *At 322:* Cash dividends from stock are treated like income, and when distributed during marriage are community property. A distribution by a corporation to its shareholders may constitute a dividend in law even though not formally designated as a dividend by the board of directors. The corporation's earnings or surplus funds normally do not constitute a dividend while they are retained by the corporation, however. *At 324:* The trial court properly characterized the liquidating distributions as [H's] separate property."

Bakken v. Bakken, 503 S.W.2d 315, 317-18 (Tex. App.—Dallas 1973, no writ). "Mutual funds assets usually consist of the stocks, bonds and other securities of a number of other corporations. Their income is generally of two kinds: (1) cash dividends received from the corporations whose stock they own, and (2) the profit or gain realized from the sale of such stocks. When these cash dividends are passed on to married owners of mutual fund shares who hold them as separate property, there is no question that these dividends become community property of the spouses. The question before us is whether the distributed capital gains retain their nature as separate property or become community property when passed on to married owners of the mutual fund shares. [¶] We hold that since [W's] original shares in the two mutual funds were admittedly her separate property the profit or gain realized from the sale of capital assets of the mutual funds is also her separate property."

Wohlenberg v. Wohlenberg, 485 S.W.2d 342, 347 (Tex.App.—El Paso 1972, no writ). "A stock dividend normally is separate if the stock ownership out of which it springs is separate."

Trusts

Benavides v. Mathis, 433 S.W.3d 59, 63 (Tex. App.—San Antonio 2014, pet. denied). "'[I]n the context of a distribution of trust income under an irrevocable trust during marriage, income distributions are community property only if the recipient has a present possessory right to part of the corpus, even if the recipient has chosen not to exercise that right, because the recipient's possessory right to access the corpus means that the recipient is effectively an owner of the trust corpus.'" *See also* **Sharma v. Routh**, 302 S.W.3d 355, 364 (Tex.App.—Houston [14th Dist.] 2009, no pet.); ***In re Marriage of Burns***, this page.

Lipsey v. Lipsey, 983 S.W.2d 345, 351 (Tex.App.—Fort Worth 1998, no pet.). "Absent fraud, a spouse may create a trust from separate property, and so long as the income remains undistributed during marriage and there is no right to compel distribution, the income is not acquired during marriage and remains separate trust property."

In re Marriage of Burns, 573 S.W.2d 555, 557-58 (Tex.App.—Texarkana 1978, writ dism'd). The issue presented "is whether *the property was acquired by either spouse* during the marriage. By definition, the undistributed trust and estate income had not been distributed to [H] nor did he have a present or past right to require its distribution so as to compel a finding that there was a constructive acquisition. The income was actually acquired by the trusts and estates and not by either [party]. As stated, there was no constructive acquisition. Since neither spouse actually or constructively acquired the undistributed trust and estate income during the marriage, such income, though earned during the marriage, remained a part of the respective trust or estate and was not subject to division by the court. Such income was not community property." *See also* **Ridgell v. Ridgell**, 960 S.W.2d 144, 148 (Tex.App.—Corpus Christi 1997, no pet.) (if spouse does not receive income from trust and has no more than expectancy interest in corpus, income remains separate property); ***Benavides v. Mathis***, this page.

FAM §3.003. PRESUMPTION OF COMMUNITY PROPERTY

(a) Property possessed by either spouse during or on dissolution of marriage is presumed to be community property.

(b) The degree of proof necessary to establish that property is separate property is clear and convincing evidence.

History of Fam. Code §3.003: Acts 1997, 75th Leg., ch. 7, §1, eff. Apr. 17, 1997. Source: Former Fam. Code §5.02.

See also ***O'Connor's Texas Family Law Handbook*** (2017), "Community-property presumption," ch. 2-A, §3.2, p. 97; "Rebutting community-property presumption," ch. 2-A, §3.3, p. 97; "Clear & Convincing Evidence," ch. 2-A, §6, p. 106.

ANNOTATIONS

Generally

Tarver v. Tarver, 394 S.W.2d 780, 783 (Tex.1965). "The plain wording of the statute creates a rebuttable presumption that all property possessed by a husband and wife when their marriage is dissolved is their community property and imposes the burden upon one asserting otherwise to prove the contrary by satisfactory evidence. [¶] The general rule is that to discharge the burden imposed by the statute, a spouse, or one claiming through a spouse, must trace and clearly identify property claimed as separate property, and that when the evidence shows that separate and community property have been so commingled as to defy resegregation and identification, the burden is not discharged and the statutory presumption that the entire mass is community controls its disposition."

Sink v. Sink, 364 S.W.3d 340, 344-45 (Tex.App.—Dallas 2012, no pet.). "Separate property will retain its character through a series of exchanges so long as the party asserting separate ownership can overcome the presumption of community property by tracing the assets on hand during the marriage back to property that, because of its time and manner of acquisition, is separate in character. ... Any doubt as to the character of property should be resolved in favor of the community estate."

Rebutting the Presumption

Pearson v. Fillingim, 332 S.W.3d 361, 363 (Tex. 2011). "The issue ... is whether the mineral rights were characterized as community property at the time of the [original] divorce decree. [H] claims the mineral rights were a gift from his parents. ... Parties claiming certain property as their separate property have the burden of rebutting the presumption of community property. To do so, they must trace and clearly identify the property in question as separate by clear and convincing evidence. [H] did not attend the final hearing, much less offer proof that the deeds were his separate property. Thus, the deeds must be characterized as community property, even if the characterization was mistaken.... *At 364:* This is not a divestiture of separate property, but a necessary classification of property as set by the community presumption." *See also* ***Cockerham v. Cockerham***, 527 S.W.2d 162, 167 (Tex.1975).

In re Marriage of Everse, 440 S.W.3d 749, 751 (Tex.App.—Amarillo 2013, no pet.). "Tracing involves establishing the separate origin of property through evidence showing the time and means by which the spouse originally obtained possession of the property. To overcome the community property presumption, the party asserting separate ownership must clearly trace the original separate property into the particular assets on hand during the marriage. The burden of tracing is a difficult, but not impossible, burden to sustain. As a general rule, mere testimony that funds came from a separate source, without any tracing of the funds, will not constitute the clear and convincing evidence necessary to rebut the community presumption." *See also* ***Sink v. Sink***, 364 S.W.3d 340, 344-45 (Tex.App.—Dallas 2012, no pet.); ***Graves v. Tomlinson***, 329 S.W.3d 128, 139 (Tex.App.—Houston [14th Dist.] 2010, pet. denied).

In re Marriage of Moore, 890 S.W.2d 821, 834 (Tex.App.—Amarillo 1994, no writ). "The burden of proof of rebutting this presumption rests on the party who claims separate ownership of such property. ... A necessary corollary of this burden is that [the party rebutting the presumption has] the obligation of requesting the necessary and proper jury questions as to the separate or community status of the [property]."

Latham v. Allison, 560 S.W.2d 481, 485 (Tex. App.—Fort Worth 1977, writ ref'd n.r.e.). "When tracing separate property, it is not enough to show that separate funds *could have been* the source of a subsequent deposit of funds. Such conjecture does not constitute sufficient evidence to sustain [petitioner's] burden of tracing to overcome the community property presumption of [Fam. Code] §5.02 [now §3.003]."

Method of Tracing—Clearinghouse

Estate of Hanau v. Hanau, 730 S.W.2d 663, 667 (Tex.1987). "The account here has not been commingled, as it was stipulated that the decedent had always kept the property in his own name and that his [W] had no power over the account. It certainly does not appear that the property has so radically changed as to 'defy resegregation and identification'.... Further, the petitioner has shown the chain of events leading from the [sale of one stock to the purchase of another] and shown that no other transactions occurred on the days in question, which would have planted the seeds of doubt upon the possible source of the funds used to buy the stocks." *See also* ***McKinley v. McKinley***, 496 S.W.2d 540, 542-43 (Tex.1973).

Peterson v. Peterson, 595 S.W.2d 889, 892 (Tex. App.—Austin 1980, writ dism'd). "[H] testified that he sold inherited property and deposited funds in excess of $35,000 into his personal bank account. He subsequently paid the balance of the purchase price from that same account. [W] argues that no evidence was introduced to establish the beginning balance of that account on the date of marriage or to establish what deposits or withdrawals were made between the date of the marriage and the date of closing. [¶] [W]e find probative evidence to support the trial court's finding that the community property presumption was overcome by tracing the entire purchase price to [H's] separate funds."

Method of Tracing—Community-Out-First

Smith v. Smith, 22 S.W.3d 140, 146 (Tex.App.—Houston [14th Dist.] 2000, no pet.). "Generally, when separate property and community property are commingled in a single bank account, we presume that the community funds are drawn out first, before separate funds are withdrawn, and where there are sufficient funds at all times to cover the separate property balance in the account at the time of divorce, we presume that the balance remains separate property. *At 147:* We assume, without deciding, that the community-out-first presumption is a rebuttable one. *At 147 n.5:* We also note that a blind application of the community-out-first presumption does not uphold the policy reason for the presumption's original application. [M]echanical application of the community-out-first presumption leads to [H's] preserving his separate estate at the expense of the community. Were we to view [H] as a trustee acting in the best interest of the beneficiary, we would apply not the community-out-first presumption, but a separate-out-first presumption. We would presume [H] spent his own funds before spending the community funds thus leaving community funds in the account for possible disbursement to the beneficiary—[W]—upon dissolution of the marriage. [H] would have the burden of rebutting the separate-out-first presumption. We apply the community-out-first presumption because it seems to be established law." *See also* ***Zagorski v. Zagorski***, 116 S.W.3d 309, 316-17 (Tex.App.—Houston [14th Dist.] 2003, pet. denied).

Welder v. Welder, 794 S.W.2d 420, 434 (Tex.App.—Corpus Christi 1990, no writ). Respondent "argues that the community-out-first presumption should be limited to situations where one party is acting in a special position of trust with regard to the other's funds, over and above the trust relationship inherent in the very nature of a joint account. ***Sibley*** [***v. Sibley***, 286 S.W.2d 657 (Tex.App.—Dallas 1955, writ dism'd)], however, does not limit itself in this way. As in the present case, ***Sibley*** determined rights to a joint account held by the parties during marriage and used to pay community expenditures, in which one of the parties had deposited separate funds. The only requirement for tracing and the application of the community-out-first presumption is that the party attempting to overcome the community presumption produce clear evidence of the transactions affecting the commingled account."

Method of Tracing—Item Tracing

Cockerham v. Cockerham, 527 S.W.2d 162, 167 (Tex.1975). "In order to overcome [the community-property] presumption, the party asserting separate ownership must clearly trace the original separate property into the particular assets on hand during the marriage." *See also* ***Nelson v. Nelson***, 193 S.W.3d 624, 630-31 (Tex.App.—Eastland 2006, no pet.).

Mortenson v. Trammell, 604 S.W.2d 269, 274 (Tex. App.—Corpus Christi 1980, writ ref'd n.r.e.). "To prove by clear and convincing evidence that a certain asset is the separate property of one spouse, it is generally necessary to trace the origin of the asset. Value tracing is commonly accepted as the means by which cash assets are traced, while item tracing is required of other assets. This requirement for tracing to the origin not only necessitates a showing of how one spouse obtained the property but also requires evidence which clearly establishes the origin of the asset."

Method of Tracing—Minimum-Sum Balance

Padon v. Padon, 670 S.W.2d 354, 357 (Tex. App.—San Antonio 1984, no writ). "The evidence elicited at trial shows the following: During the marriage of the parties, [H's] father died leaving [H] an amount in excess of $160,000.00. On February 25, 1977, $160,490.00 was deposited ... to open an account styled [in both H's and W's names]. Both parties agree [H] inherited and deposited $160,000.00 into this account. Both parties also agree that in early 1977 a house was purchased for $89,900.00, which was paid for by check. The March bank statement of [couple's] account shows no additional deposits from the time of the initial $160,490.00 deposit until March 4, 1977. On March 1, 1977, the statement shows a check cleared the account in the amount of $89,900.00. [¶] Both parties testified that all monies received from all sources during the marriage were subsequently deposited into this account. The March 1977 statement is the only statement in evidence. [¶] We hold [H] established as a matter of law that the house ... is his separate property...."

Snider v. Snider, 613 S.W.2d 8, 11 (Tex.App.—Dallas 1981, no writ). "On the date of the marriage, the balance in the account was $27,642.45. Upon dissolution of the community by [H's] death, the balance was $35,809.80. The account grew by *interest* from time to time, as well as by new deposits, and was reduced by withdrawals from time to time. The witness ... testified that an additional deposit of $10,000.00 of separate funds of [H] was made after the marriage and that the remaining deposits, as well as withdrawals, were made by the community. The passbook for this account was introduced into evidence and supports the separate character and balance of the account on the date of marriage. ... We hold that this record traces and identifies [H's] separate interest in the ... account to the extent of $29,642.45 with the remainder of the account being deemed community for want of tracing or identity."

Method of Tracing—Pro Rata

Marineau v. General Am. Life Ins., 898 S.W.2d 397, 403 (Tex.App.—Fort Worth 1995, writ denied). Once insurance company "proved that embezzled funds were commingled into [H's account that was] used to pay the insurance policy premiums, the burden shifted to [W] to prove that part or all of the insurance premiums were paid with funds belonging to [H]. [Insurance company] contends that [W] failed to meet this burden by only offering evidence of the proportion of embezzled money to personal money deposited into the Account used to pay the insurance premiums. In [insurance company's] view, [W] would have had to prove the ownership proportion of each payment to calculate the ownership of the policy, and absent such proof, the presumption is that all of the commingled funds are held in trust. We disagree. Neither party has cited any Texas case addressing the proof necessary to rebut the presumption that the commingled funds belong to the trust, or the extent of recovery allowed the owner of the embezzled funds when those funds only paid for part of the premiums. After reviewing the case law of other jurisdictions on this point, we feel the reasoning of the court in ***G&M Motor Co. v. Thompson***, 567 P.2d 80 (Okla.1977), is appropriate in this case. The court there held that the employer of the embezzling employee was entitled to a pro rata share of the life insurance policy proceeds where the wrongfully acquired funds were partially used to pay the premiums. Recovery was limited to the total amount of embezzled monies, interest, and costs."

Method of Tracing—Value Tracing

Trawick v. Trawick, 671 S.W.2d 105, 110 (Tex. App.—El Paso 1984, no writ). "The party with the burden of tracing is aided by the rule that one dollar has the same value as another. Under the law, there can be no commingling by the mixing of dollars where the number owned by each claimant is known." *See also* ***In re Marriage of Tandy***, 532 S.W.2d 714, 717 (Tex. App.—Amarillo 1976, no writ).

Mortenson v. Trammell, 604 S.W.2d 269, 274 (Tex. App.—Corpus Christi 1980, writ ref'd n.r.e.). "To prove by clear and convincing evidence that a certain asset is the separate property of one spouse, it is generally necessary to trace the origin of the asset. Value tracing is commonly accepted as the means by which cash assets are traced, while item tracing is required of other assets. This requirement for tracing to the origin not only necessitates a showing of how one spouse obtained the property but also requires evidence which clearly establishes the origin of the asset."

FAM §3.004. RECORDATION OF SEPARATE PROPERTY

(a) A subscribed and acknowledged schedule of a spouse's separate property may be recorded in the deed records of the county in which the parties, or one of them, reside and in the county or counties in which the real property is located.

(b) A schedule of a spouse's separate real property is not constructive notice to a good faith purchaser for value or a creditor without actual notice unless the instrument is acknowledged and recorded in the deed records of the county in which the real property is located.

History of Fam. Code §3.004: Acts 1997, 75th Leg., ch. 7, §1, eff. Apr. 17, 1997. Source: Former Fam. Code §5.03.

FAM §3.005. GIFTS BETWEEN SPOUSES

If one spouse makes a gift of property to the other spouse, the gift is presumed to include all the income and property that may arise from that property.

History of Fam. Code §3.005: Acts 1997, 75th Leg., ch. 7, §1, eff. Apr. 17, 1997. Source: Former Fam. Code §5.04.

See also *O'Connor's Texas Family Law Handbook* (2017), "Income from separate-property gift," ch. 2-A, §7.2.2(1), p. 108.

ANNOTATIONS

Roberts v. Roberts, 999 S.W.2d 424, 432 (Tex. App.—El Paso 1999, no pet.). "Generally speaking, one who is claiming the existence of a gift has the burden of proof. However, where the conveyance is from one spouse to the other spouse, there is a presumption of gift. [¶] A gift by one spouse to another may be set aside if it is induced by duress or undue influence. In such a case, the burden rests with the donee to show that the gift was fair and equitable."

FAM §3.006. PROPORTIONAL OWNERSHIP OF PROPERTY BY MARITAL ESTATES

If the community estate of the spouses and the separate estate of a spouse have an ownership interest in property, the respective ownership interests of the marital estates are determined by the rule of inception of title.

History of Fam. Code §3.006: Acts 1999, 76th Leg., ch. 692, §1, eff. Sept. 1, 1999. Amended by Acts 2001, 77th Leg., ch. 838, §3, eff. Sept. 1, 2001.

FAM §3.007. PROPERTY INTEREST IN CERTAIN EMPLOYEE BENEFITS

(a), (b) Repealed by Acts 2009, 81st Leg., ch. 768, §11(1), eff. Sept. 1, 2009.

(c) The separate property interest of a spouse in a defined contribution retirement plan may be traced using the tracing and characterization principles that apply to a nonretirement asset.

(d) A spouse who is a participant in an employer-provided stock option plan or an employer-provided restricted stock plan has a separate property interest in the options or restricted stock granted to the spouse under the plan as follows:

(1) if the option or stock was granted to the spouse before marriage but required continued employment during marriage before the grant could be exercised or the restriction removed, the spouse's separate property interest is equal to the fraction of the option or restricted stock in which:

(A) the numerator is the sum of:

(i) the period from the date the option or stock was granted until the date of marriage; and

(ii) if the option or stock also required continued employment following the date of dissolution of the marriage before the grant could be exercised or the restriction removed, the period from the date of dissolution of the marriage until the date the grant could be exercised or the restriction removed; and

(B) the denominator is the period from the date the option or stock was granted until the date the grant could be exercised or the restriction removed; and

(2) if the option or stock was granted to the spouse during the marriage but required continued employment following the date of dissolution of the marriage before the grant could be exercised or the restriction removed, the spouse's separate property interest is equal to the fraction of the option or restricted stock in which:

(A) the numerator is the period from the date of dissolution of the marriage until the date the grant could be exercised or the restriction removed; and

(B) the denominator is the period from the date the option or stock was granted until the date the grant could be exercised or the restriction removed.

(e) The computation described by Subsection (d) applies to each component of the benefit requiring varying periods of employment before the grant could be exercised or the restriction removed.

(f) Repealed by Acts 2009, 81st Leg., ch. 768, §11(1), eff. Sept. 1, 2009.

History of Fam. Code §3.007: Acts 2005, 79th Leg., ch. 490, §1, eff. Sept. 1, 2005. Amended by Acts 2009, 81st Leg., ch. 768, §§1, 11(1), eff. Sept. 1, 2009.

Author's comment: The 2009 repeal of Family Code §3.007(a) and (b) effectively reinstates the common-law formula for calculating the community's interest in defined-benefit plans as described in ***Berry v. Berry***, 647 S.W.2d 945 (Tex.1983), and ***Taggart v. Taggart***, 552 S.W.2d 422 (Tex.1977).

See also *O'Connor's Texas Family Law Handbook* (2017), "Dividing & Confirming Qualified Private Retirement Benefits," ch. 7-E, p. 871.

ANNOTATIONS

Generally

In re Marriage of Reinauer, 946 S.W.2d 853, 857 (Tex.App.—Amarillo 1997, writ denied). "[R]etirement pay ... connotes an earned property right that accrued by reason of years of service or deferred compensation earned during each month of service. In other words, the payment must, at the very least, be a form of compensation accruing to the individual due to his years of service with the employer. Discretionary payments made for purposes other than as compensation earned during an employee's tenure do not satisfy these criteria and, thus, are not retirement pay or benefits. Nor do mere gratuities or gifts from one's employer satisfy the requisite criteria."

Dividing Defined-Benefits Plans

Berry v. Berry, 647 S.W.2d 945, 946 (Tex.1983). "***Taggart*** only held that the divorced wife 'owned as her part of the community estate a share in the contingent right to military benefits even though that right had not matured at the time of the divorce.' ... We did not, however, determine whether the community's interest in retirement benefits should be valued as of the date of divorce, as opposed to the time the benefits were actually received. *At 947:* Retirement and pension benefits are a mode of employee compensation. It is clear from the record in this case that 12 additional years of work following divorce, which included some 12 to 14 pay raises, plus union contract negotiations for an improved benefits plan, brought about the increase in retirement benefits paid to [H]. These post-divorce increases cannot be awarded to [W], for to do so would invade [H's] separate property, which cannot be done. [¶] We are not to be understood as overruling ***Taggart*** ... or disapproving of its progeny insofar as those opinions approve an apportionment formula for determining the *extent* of the community interest in retirement benefits. When the value of such benefits is in issue, however, the benefits are to be apportioned to the spouses based upon the value of the community's interest at the time of divorce."

Taggart v. Taggart, 552 S.W.2d 422, 423 (Tex. 1977). "[R]etirement benefits are subject to division as vested contingent community property rights even though the present right has not fully matured. [¶] [W]e hold that [W] owned as her part of the community estate a share in the contingent right to military benefits even though that right had not matured at the time of the divorce. *At 424:* The trial court computed [W's] one-half interest in [H's] retirement benefits upon the basis of his 20 years of service as a member of the regular Navy. At the end of the 20 years, he was not entitled to receive any retirement benefits based upon his term of service, because he had to serve in the Fleet Reserve for an additional ten years. It was, therefore, his 360 months of service that entitled him to the retirement benefits. According to the undisputed evidence, [couple's] marriage coincided with his service in the Navy for a period of 246 months. The correct computation of [W's] vested interest is that she was entitled only to one-half of 246/360th's of the retirement pay."

Limbaugh v. Limbaugh, 71 S.W.3d 1, 16 n.12 (Tex. App.—Waco 2002, no pet.). "Under ***Taggart***, the community interest in a fully matured retirement plan is calculated by dividing the number of months the parties were married during the employee spouse's employment by the total number of months of service of the employee spouse. The resulting percentage represents the community estate's interest in the retirement benefits. ***Berry*** applies in those cases where the employee spouse's service will continue after the divorce. In this situation, the community interest is determined as of the time of divorce. The ***Berry*** formula prevents a divorce court from awarding the non-employee spouse any portion of a post-divorce increase in retirement attributable to raises, promotions, services rendered or contributions as such an increase would be the employee spouse's separate property. Conversely, a divorce court may award the non-employee spouse her respective share of any post-divorce cost-of-living increase in the retirement benefit."

Albrecht v. Albrecht, 974 S.W.2d 262, 263-64 (Tex. App.—San Antonio 1998, no pet.). "The formulas for apportioning retirement benefits differ depending on whether the value of the pension plan is at issue. The formula used when the value of the pension plan *is not in issue* was set out in ***Taggart*** as follows: ½ × ((# years of service while married) ÷ (# years of service at retirement)) × value of accrued benefit at date of retirement = non-employee spouse's share. This formula is called the ***Taggart*** formula. The formula was used by the Supreme Court of Texas to determine the non-employee spouse's community interest in military retirement benefits. [¶] When the value of the plan *is in issue*, the

following formula is used: ½ × ((# years married under pension plan) ÷ (# years employed under plan as of date of divorce)) × value of plan on date of divorce = non-employee spouse's share. This formula is called the *Berry* formula."

Military Retirement Benefits

Mansell v. Mansell, 490 U.S. 581, 588-89 (1989). Uniformed Services Former Spouses' Protection Act §1408(c)(1) "affirmatively grants state courts the power to divide military retirement pay, yet its language is both precise and limited. It provides that 'a court may treat disposable retired or retainer pay ... either as property solely of the member or as property of the member and his spouse in accordance with the law of the jurisdiction of such court.' The Act's definitional section specifically defines the term 'disposable retired or retainer pay' to exclude, *inter alia*, military retirement pay waived in order to receive veterans' disability payments. Thus, under the Act's plain and precise language, state courts have been granted the authority to treat disposable retired pay as community property; they have not been granted the authority to treat total retired pay as community property."

Havlen v. McDougall, 22 S.W.3d 343, 345 (Tex. 2000). "[I]n 1981, the U.S. Supreme Court [in ***McCarty v. McCarty***, 453 U.S. 210 (1981),] held that federal military pension law prohibited state courts from dividing military retirement benefits.... [¶] Congress reacted to ***McCarty*** by enacting legislation[, the Uniformed Services Former Spouses' Protection Act,] that reversed ***McCarty***'s effect and once again allowed state courts to treat military retirement pay as marital property subject to division under state law. Congress set June 25, 1981, the day before the ***McCarty*** decision, to begin the period in which military retirement benefits could be divided under the new legislation. *At 346:* Subsequently, in 1990, Congress amended the Act to limit the power of state courts that were abusing the original act by reopening finalized divorces from the pre-*McCarty* period. [¶] The sole question we consider today is whether a court may divide military benefits as community property in a former spouse's partition suit when a final divorce decree issued before June 25, 1981, did not divide or reserve jurisdiction to divide those benefits. We hold that it may not. [¶] [W] argues that the operation of Texas law, which converts an undivided asset such as military retirement pay into a tenancy in common, is sufficient to 'treat' [i.e., divide] the asset for the Act's purposes. We disagree. *At 347:* The 1990 Amendment provides that the 'final decree' must treat or reserve jurisdiction to treat the military retirement benefits. ... The court of appeals did not consider that the Amendment expressly requires that *the decree* itself treat the asset. The Amendment does not provide any other way to treat an asset. Therefore, because the decree itself does not treat or reserve jurisdiction to treat the military benefits, they are not subject to subsequent partition."

FAM §3.008. PROPERTY INTEREST IN CERTAIN INSURANCE PROCEEDS

(a) Insurance proceeds paid or payable that arise from a casualty loss to property during marriage are characterized in the same manner as the property to which the claim is attributable.

(b) If a person becomes disabled or is injured, any disability insurance payment or workers' compensation payment is community property to the extent it is intended to replace earnings lost while the disabled or injured person is married. To the extent that any insurance payment or workers' compensation payment is intended to replace earnings while the disabled or injured person is not married, the recovery is the separate property of the disabled or injured spouse.

History of Fam. Code §3.008: Acts 2005, 79th Leg., ch. 490, §1, eff. Sept. 1, 2005.

See also ***O'Connor's Texas Family Law Handbook*** (2017), "Compensation for lost earning capacity," ch. 2-A, §11.1, p. 122; "Casualty insurance," ch. 2-A, §12.2, p. 125.

ANNOTATIONS

In re Marriage of Bradshaw, 487 S.W.3d 306, 310 (Tex.App.—Texarkana 2016, pet. filed 5-6-16). "'If [an insurance] policy insures both community and separate property, the proceeds of the policy will be apportioned between the community and separate estates.' Here, [W] failed to introduce any evidence establishing the value of [previous] house or the amount of the insurance proceeds specifically attributable to the loss of the home. *At 311:* In the absence of additional evidence, we find no error in the trial court's determination that [W] (1) failed to establish, by clear and convincing evidence, that [current] property was entirely purchased with separate property funds, and (2) assuming that a portion of the property was purchased with separate property funds, failed to establish, by clear and convincing evidence, what percentage of the property was purchased with separate property funds."

Sections 3.009-3.100 reserved for expansion

SUBCHAPTER B. MANAGEMENT, CONTROL, & DISPOSITION OF MARITAL PROPERTY

FAM §3.101. MANAGING SEPARATE PROPERTY

Each spouse has the sole management, control, and disposition of that spouse's separate property.

History of Fam. Code §3.101: Acts 1997, 75th Leg., ch. 7, §1, eff. Apr. 17, 1997. Source: Former Fam. Code §5.21.

See also ***O'Connor's Texas Family Law Handbook*** (2017), "Management Rights over Separate Property," ch. 2-B, §3, p. 143.

ANNOTATIONS

Vallone v. Vallone, 644 S.W.2d 455, 458 (Tex.1982). "It is fundamental that any property or rights acquired by one of the spouses after marriage by toil, talent, industry or other productive faculty belongs to the community estate. Nevertheless, the law contemplates that a spouse may expend a reasonable amount of talent or labor in the management and preservation of his or her separate estate without impressing a community character upon that estate."

Whittlesey v. Miller, 572 S.W.2d 665, 669 (Tex. 1978). "In the absence of evidence showing authority, the mere relationship of husband and wife does not give the husband authority to contract with regard to the wife's separate property."

FAM §3.102. MANAGING COMMUNITY PROPERTY

(a) During marriage, each spouse has the sole management, control, and disposition of the community property that the spouse would have owned if single, including:

(1) personal earnings;

(2) revenue from separate property;

(3) recoveries for personal injuries; and

(4) the increase and mutations of, and the revenue from, all property subject to the spouse's sole management, control, and disposition.

(b) If community property subject to the sole management, control, and disposition of one spouse is mixed or combined with community property subject to the sole management, control, and disposition of the other spouse, then the mixed or combined community property is subject to the joint management, control, and disposition of the spouses, unless the spouses provide otherwise by power of attorney in writing or other agreement.

(c) Except as provided by Subsection (a), community property is subject to the joint management, control, and disposition of the spouses unless the spouses provide otherwise by power of attorney in writing or other agreement.

History of Fam. Code §3.102: Acts 1997, 75th Leg., ch. 7, §1, eff. Apr. 17, 1997. Source: Former Fam. Code §5.22.

See also ***O'Connor's Texas Family Law Handbook*** (2017), "Management Rights over Community Property," ch. 2-B, §2, p. 140.

ANNOTATIONS

Sole Management

Douglas v. Delp, 987 S.W.2d 879, 883 (Tex.1999). "[H's] loss of earning capacity during the marriage constitutes his sole-management community property. [H's] credit reputation is also his sole-management community property, as it was acquired, at least in part, during the marriage and would have belonged solely to him were he not married."

Medenco, Inc. v. Myklebust, 615 S.W.2d 187, 189 (Tex.1981). "During marriage, community property employment benefits acquired through employment are subject to the sole management, control and disposition of the employee spouse."

Valdez v. Ramirez, 574 S.W.2d 748, 750 (Tex.1978). "While [W] was employed by the federal government and earning future rights to a retirement annuity, those contingent rights were community property, but such inchoate rights are characterized by the Family Code as 'special community' under [W's] sole management and control. *At 751:* Thus, while being earned, the right to a future Civil Service retirement annuity was the special community of [W], subject to her sole management, control and disposition. As manager of this 'special community' asset, she had the contract right to select a mode of payment."

Jean v. Tyson-Jean, 118 S.W.3d 1, 5 (Tex.App.—Houston [14th Dist.] 2003, pet. denied). "In general, community property is subject to the 'joint management, control and disposition of the spouses unless the spouses provide otherwise by power of attorney in writing or other agreement.' To effectuate a valid conveyance, both spouses must necessarily be joined in a transaction. [¶] However, where community property is held in one spouse's name only, there is a presumption that the property is *sole-management* community property. [Family Code] §3.104 therefore trumps [Fam. Code] §3.102. Absent a showing of fraud or notice on the part of persons dealing with the named spouse, this

sole-management presumption protects third parties who rely on the spouse's authority to deal with the property."

Madrigal v. Madrigal, 115 S.W.3d 32, 34-35 (Tex. App.—San Antonio 2003, no pet.). "Proceeds from a life insurance policy acquired as a benefit of employment during marriage are community property. The policy is the sole management community property of the employee spouse, and that spouse may designate the beneficiary of the policy. [¶] A surviving spouse establishes a prima facie case of constructive fraud on the community by proof that the life insurance policy was purchased with community funds for the benefit of a person outside the community. The donor spouse or the designated beneficiary, seeking to overcome a prima facie case of fraud and sustain the gift, has the burden of proof to show that the disposition of the surviving spouse's one-half community interest is fair."

Bell v. Moores, 832 S.W.2d 749, 752 (Tex.App.—Houston [14th Dist.] 1992, writ denied). "Personal earnings are subject to the sole management, control, and disposition of the employee spouse. [¶] Courts have held that an employee spouse, because of his exclusive managerial power over personal earnings, has the sole authority to bring an action for recovery of the community property under his sole management. *At 753:* At the time [W] intervened in the suit against the appellees, she was still married to [H]. At that time, the royalties in question were community property under his sole management. ... Thus, when the suit was commenced by [W], she was without standing to assert such a claim. The property involved was subject to the sole management of [H], and as such, only he had the power to sue for recovery of the royalties because of his management power."

Joint Management

Cockerham v. Cockerham, 527 S.W.2d 162, 170 (Tex.1975). "With regard to the 320-acre tract, the record reveals [H] and [W] in effect borrowed the cash necessary to purchase the community interest by giving a note secured by a deed of trust on the property in return. Title to the property was taken in the name of both [H] and [W]; both [H] and [W] were obligated on the note. Under virtually identical circumstances these facts were considered sufficient to establish that the community interest was subject to the joint management of [H] and [W]."

Cooper v. Texas Gulf Indus., 513 S.W.2d 200, 202 (Tex.1974). Family Code §5.22, now §3.102, "takes away the husband's sole right to manage all of the couple's community property. When joint management community property is involved, the husband and wife are now *joint* managers. The wife is her husband's equal with respect to management; she stands in the same position as any other joint owner of property. While another section provides that a spouse may sue and be sued without the joinder of the other, *neither* spouse may virtually represent the other. The rights of the wife, like the rights of the husband and the rights of any other joint owner, may be affected only by a suit in which the wife is called to answer. If one of the spouses wishes the other to represent him or her, §5.22(c) ... permits that arrangement provided the consenting spouse authorizes that representation by a power of attorney or other agreement in writing. No such writing is in evidence here. [¶] [W] was not a party to the first suit; the doctrine of virtual representation was abolished by the new Family Code; there was no writing authorizing [H] to represent her. Accordingly, her interest in [their] joint management community property is untouched by the judgment of dismissal with prejudice of the first suit."

Caulley v. Caulley, 777 S.W.2d 147, 150 (Tex. App.—Houston [14th Dist.] 1989), *rev'd in part on other grounds*, 806 S.W.2d 795 (Tex.1991). "Absent evidence that the community property farm is subject to [W's] sole management, control, and disposition, the farm is presumed to be jointly managed."

Vallone v. Miller, 663 S.W.2d 97, 99 (Tex.App.—Houston [14th Dist.] 1983, writ ref'd n.r.e.). "One spouse cannot alone convey or encumber joint management community property unless the spouses have otherwise agreed. ... Without a 'power of attorney in writing or other agreement' to the contrary, [H] had no authority to contract to dispose of the entire joint management community property without [W] joining in the contract."

LeBlanc v. Waller, 603 S.W.2d 265, 267 (Tex. App.—Houston [14th Dist.] 1980, no writ). "This 'agreement' referred to in [Fam. Code §5.22(c), now §3.102(c),] is not a partition agreement of the community, but rather an agreement to transfer the power of management, control, and disposition over certain community property assets from one spouse to the other. Appellant contends that the oral agreement for

division of their property falls within the 'other agreement' provision of subsection (c) above. We agree. ... Applying the standard rules of statutory construction, it is apparent that the Texas Legislature chose to remove the requirement that such an agreement be in writing."

FAM §3.103. MANAGING EARNINGS OF MINOR

Except as provided by Section 264.0111, during the marriage of the parents of an unemancipated minor for whom a managing conservator has not been appointed, the earnings of the minor are subject to the joint management, control, and disposition of the parents of the minor, unless otherwise provided by agreement of the parents or by judicial order.

History of Fam. Code §3.103: Acts 1997, 75th Leg., ch. 7, §1, eff. Apr. 17, 1997. Amended by Acts 2001, 77th Leg., ch. 964, §1, eff. Sept. 1, 2001. Source: Former Fam. Code §5.23.

FAM §3.104. PROTECTION OF THIRD PERSONS

(a) During marriage, property is presumed to be subject to the sole management, control, and disposition of a spouse if it is held in that spouse's name, as shown by muniment, contract, deposit of funds, or other evidence of ownership, or if it is in that spouse's possession and is not subject to such evidence of ownership.

(b) A third person dealing with a spouse is entitled to rely, as against the other spouse or anyone claiming from that spouse, on that spouse's authority to deal with the property if:

(1) the property is presumed to be subject to the sole management, control, and disposition of the spouse; and

(2) the person dealing with the spouse:

(A) is not a party to a fraud on the other spouse or another person; and

(B) does not have actual or constructive notice of the spouse's lack of authority.

History of Fam. Code §3.104: Acts 1997, 75th Leg., ch. 7, §1, eff. Apr. 17, 1997. Source: Former Fam. Code §5.24.

ANNOTATIONS

Ifiesimama v. Haile, ___ S.W.3d ___ (Tex.App.—Houston [1st Dist.] 2017, n.p.h.) (No. 01-15-00829-CV; 3-30-17). Respondents, H and W, "argue that because the property was their community property, [H] lacked the authority to sell or encumber [W's] interest in the property. [¶] [Petitioners] presented evidence ... that [H] is the sole owner of the property. And [respondents] failed to produce the general warranty deed from the time they purchased the property showing whether [H] individually or [respondents] jointly purchased the property. However, the deed of trust corresponding to the mortgage on the property ... shows that [H] mortgaged the property individually, and [W] signed a waiver of any interest she might have in the property. [Respondents] did not introduce any evidence at trial indicating that [W] had an interest in the property or that the property was subject to their joint management, control, or disposition. Furthermore, [petitioner] testified that [H] represented to [agent] that he had authority to sell the property. There is no indication in the record that [petitioners] knew before the title company refused to close on the sale that [W] had any interest in the property or that she did not agree that the property should be sold. [¶] [Petitioners] presented evidence that the property was subject to [H's] sole management, control, and disposition and that they did not have notice that [H] lacked authority to sell the property on [W's] behalf. ... We hold that the trial court did not err in concluding that [petitioners] entered into a valid and enforceable contract with [H]." *See also* ***Williams v. Portland State Bank***, 514 S.W.2d 124, 126 (Tex.App.—Beaumont 1974, writ dism'd) ("Whatever puts a person on inquiry ordinarily amounts in law to notice, provided inquiry has become a duty and would lead to knowledge of the facts by the exercise of ordinary diligence and understanding.").

Jean v. Tyson-Jean, 118 S.W.3d 1, 5 (Tex.App.—Houston [14th Dist.] 2003, pet. denied). "[W]here community property is held in one spouse's name only, there is a presumption that the property is *sole-management* community property. [Family Code] §3.104 therefore trumps [Fam. Code] §3.102. Absent a showing of fraud or notice on the part of persons dealing with the named spouse, this sole-management presumption protects third parties who rely on the spouse's authority to deal with the property. *At 7:* [Intervenor] cites no authority for the proposition that merely having knowledge a person is married is, as a matter of law, the same as knowing the person lacks authority to convey property. [¶] Texas case law indicates that simply knowing someone is married—or that he or she has been married—without more, is not enough to prove notice under §3.104(b)(2)(B)."

Fajkus v. First Nat'l Bank, 735 S.W.2d 882, 886 (Tex.App.—Austin 1987, writ denied). Real property was "held in the name of [H] only, therefore, it is pre-

sumed that the property was subject to his sole management, control and disposition. [W] asserts that the presumption was rebutted by evidence that both spouses signed in all other transactions involving the property. This evidence, however, is insufficient to show joint management. [J]oint execution of documents relating to liens on property does not render that property subject to the joint management of both spouses." *See also* ***Thomas v. Rhodes***, 701 S.W.2d 943, 945 (Tex.App.—Fort Worth 1986, writ ref'd n.r.e.).

Williams v. Portland State Bank, 514 S.W.2d 124, 126 (Tex.App.—Beaumont 1974, writ dism'd). "[I]t is presumed that property held in the name of one spouse alone, is subject to the sole management, control and disposition of such spouse, and a third person dealing with that spouse is entitled to rely upon that spouse's authority to deal with the property in the absence of fraud or notice of the spouse's lack of authority. [¶] There is … no evidence in this record that the Bank had actual specific knowledge that [H] had no authority from [W] to encumber her interest in this tract of land. However, [Fam. Code §5.24, now §3.104,] does not require knowledge of lack of authority, but uses the term notice. … Whatever puts a person on inquiry ordinarily amounts in law to notice, provided inquiry has become a duty and would lead to knowledge of the facts by the exercise of ordinary diligence and understanding. In other words, one who has knowledge of such facts as would cause a prudent man to make further inquiry, is chargeable with notice of the facts which, by use of ordinary intelligence, he would have ascertained. [¶] [W]e hold the actual knowledge by the Bank that [W] had refused to sign the first note and deed of trust was sufficient as a matter of law to put the Bank on notice to make further inquiry as to the extent to [H's] authority to encumber [W's] interest in this tract of land." (Internal quotes omitted.) *See also* ***Flack v. First Nat'l Bank***, 226 S.W.2d 628, 632 (Tex.1950).

Sections 3.105-3.200 reserved for expansion

SUBCHAPTER C. MARITAL PROPERTY LIABILITIES

FAM §3.201. SPOUSAL LIABILITY

(a) A person is personally liable for the acts of the person's spouse only if:

(1) the spouse acts as an agent for the person; or

(2) the spouse incurs a debt for necessaries as provided by Subchapter F, Chapter 2.

(b) Except as provided by this subchapter, community property is not subject to a liability that arises from an act of a spouse.

(c) A spouse does not act as an agent for the other spouse solely because of the marriage relationship.

History of Fam. Code §3.201: Acts 1997, 75th Leg., ch. 7, §1, eff. Apr. 17, 1997. Source: Former Fam. Code §4.031.

See also *O'Connor's Texas Family Law Handbook* (2017), "Liability of Spouses," ch. 1-D, §2, p. 51.

ANNOTATIONS

Tedder v. Gardner Aldrich, LLP, 421 S.W.3d 651, 655 (Tex.2013). See annotation under Family Code §2.501, p. 22.

Mock v. Mock, 216 S.W.3d 370, 374 (Tex.App.—Eastland 2006, pet. denied). "Unless it is shown that [a] creditor agreed to look solely to the separate estate of the contracting spouse for satisfaction, §3.201 has no effect on the long-standing presumption that debts contracted during the marriage are presumed to be on the credit of the community and, thus, are joint community obligations."

Patel v. Kuciemba, 82 S.W.3d 589, 598 (Tex.App.—Corpus Christi 2002, pet. denied). "The trial court erred … in rendering judgment against [W], individually, … because there was no evidence that [H] acted as [W's] agent in executing the promissory notes under apparent authority or that [W] ratified the promissory notes."

Nationwide of Brian, Inc. v. Dyer, 969 S.W.2d 518, 520 (Tex.App.—Austin 1998, no pet.). "[H] signed both the sales contract and arbitration addendum; [W] signed neither. We find the absence of her signature has no legal significance due to her status as a third-party beneficiary.… As a third-party beneficiary, [W] is bound by the terms of the sales contract, including the arbitration agreement."

Kimsey v. Kimsey, 965 S.W.2d 690, 695 (Tex. App.—El Paso 1998, pet. denied). "Generally, both spouses are jointly and severally liable for the tax due on a joint return. Thus, a spouse may be liable for the entire tax liability although the income was totally earned by the other spouse. If a husband and wife file as married filing separately, each is liable only for the tax due on his or her own return. [¶] Generally if husband and wife are separated, they are considered married for the entire year if no final decree of divorce has been entered by the last day of the tax year. If they are considered married, they may file jointly or as married

filing separately and they may file a joint return even if one had no income or deductions. The difficulty here is that for the years prior to the year of divorce, the trial court made no order as to whether the parties are to file jointly or as married filing separately. As for the year of divorce, if the final decree is obtained on or before the last day of the tax year, the parties are considered unmarried and cannot file a joint return. As a result, each spouse is still liable for taxes on half of the community income for the part of the year before dissolution."

FAM §3.202. RULES OF MARITAL PROPERTY LIABILITY

(a) A spouse's separate property is not subject to liabilities of the other spouse unless both spouses are liable by other rules of law.

(b) Unless both spouses are personally liable as provided by this subchapter, the community property subject to a spouse's sole management, control, and disposition is not subject to:

(1) any liabilities that the other spouse incurred before marriage; or

(2) any nontortious liabilities that the other spouse incurs during marriage.

(c) The community property subject to a spouse's sole or joint management, control, and disposition is subject to the liabilities incurred by the spouse before or during marriage.

(d) All community property is subject to tortious liability of either spouse incurred during marriage.

(e) For purposes of this section, all retirement allowances, annuities, accumulated contributions, optional benefits, and money in the various public retirement system accounts of this state that are community property subject to the participating spouse's sole management, control, and disposition are not subject to any claim for payment of a criminal restitution judgment entered against the nonparticipant spouse except to the extent of the nonparticipant spouse's interest as determined in a qualified domestic relations order under Chapter 804, Government Code.

History of Fam. Code §3.202: Acts 1997, 75th Leg., ch. 7, §1, eff. Apr. 17, 1997. Amended by Acts 2009, 81st Leg., ch. 1244, §1, eff. Sept. 1, 2009. Source: Former Fam. Code §5.61.

See also ***O'Connor's Texas Family Law Handbook*** (2017), "Liability of Marital Property," ch. 2-C, p. 150.

ANNOTATIONS

Tedder v. Gardner Aldrich, LLP, 421 S.W.3d 651, 654 (Tex.2013). See annotation under Family Code §3.002, *Debts & Loans*, p. 29.

Carlton v. Estate of Estes, 664 S.W.2d 322, 323 (Tex.1983). "[A] spouse's interest in community property subject to joint management, control, and disposition may be reached to satisfy the liabilities of the other spouse without joinder of both spouses in the suit."

Knoderer v. State Farm Lloyds, 515 S.W.3d 21, ___ (Tex.App.—Texarkana 2017, pet. filed 5-22-17). Petitioners "argue that the monetary sanctions [against H] effectively sanction [W] since she has been married to [H] for 35 years and the sanctions necessarily reach their community property. … Since [W] was not the offender, they reason, the trial court could not assess monetary sanctions against [H] since it would subject [W's] community assets to satisfy the monetary sanctions. [¶] The [TRCPs] impose duties upon parties to a lawsuit during the process of discovery and allow a trial court to impose sanctions on a party who breaches those duties, i.e., abuses the discovery process. While not a tort in the traditional sense, discovery abuse may be viewed as a tort. [¶] [H] not only breached the duties imposed on him by the [TRCPs], he blatantly disobeyed the orders of the trial court by altering … hard drives. At a minimum, his behavior for which he incurred liability was tortious. Therefore, even though [W] is not personally liable for [H's] tortious and sanctionable conduct, her community property may be subject to the liability resulting from it."

Drake Interiors, L.L.C. v. Thomas, 433 S.W.3d 841, 849 (Tex.App.—Houston [14th Dist.] 2014, pet. denied). Under §3.202(c), "[i]f a husband incurs a debt before he marries, the creditor may reach his marital property in satisfaction of the debt, even if that property is jointly managed by his non-debtor wife. [Here,] the [p]roperty was [H] and [W's] joint management community property. Accordingly, if the [judgment creditor's] lien attached during marriage, then [creditor] can reach any nonexempt community interest in the [p]roperty. [W] cannot invalidate the lien simply because the debt was not hers. [¶] [W] did not need to be named in the earlier lawsuit or judgment for [creditor] to reach community assets jointly managed by her and [H]. … Thus, to the extent it is not impressed with homestead rights, the [p]roperty may be reached in satisfaction of [H's] premarital debt. *At 850-51:* [In comparison, under §3.202(d),] if a husband is adjudged negligent during marriage, the entire marital estate is placed at risk—the husband's sole manage-

ment community property, the wife's sole management community property, and both spouses' joint management community property. This contrasts with §3.202(c), which restricts the types of marital property subject to nontortious liabilities. Under §3.202(c), if a husband incurs a debt before or during marriage, the creditor may reach the husband's sole management community property and both spouses' joint management community property—but not the wife's sole management community property."

Rancho Mi Hacienda v. Bryant, 365 S.W.3d 127, 130 (Tex.App.—Texarkana 2012, no pet.). Petitioner's "contention that all community property is subject to claims of tortious liability incurred by the community during marriage is ... accurate. Where [petitioner's] reasoning is erroneous regards whether a judgment taken after dissolution of the community solely against one former spouse is enforceable against [former community] property awarded to the other (nonjudgment) former spouse. *At 131:* It [is] not. [¶] [T]he property awarded to [W] in her divorce ... is not liable to satisfy the post-divorce judgment taken solely against her former husband...."

Blake v. Amoco Fed. Credit Un., 900 S.W.2d 108, 111 (Tex.App.—Houston [14th Dist.] 1995, no writ). "It is well-settled law in Texas that divorce courts cannot disturb the rights of a creditor to collect from either of the divorcing parties on a joint obligation. *At 112:* [T]he divorce court could not prejudice the creditor's right to take a judgment against both spouses when dividing responsibility for payment of debts."

Nelson v. Citizens Bank & Trust Co., 881 S.W.2d 128, 131 (Tex.App.—Houston [14th Dist.] 1994, no writ). "[E]ither spouse can incur contractual liability that will bind the share of the noncontracting spouse's community property subject to the sole or joint control of the contracting spouse, but the noncontracting spouse is not 'personally liable' for the obligation."

FAM §3.203. ORDER IN WHICH PROPERTY IS SUBJECT TO EXECUTION

(a) A judge may determine, as deemed just and equitable, the order in which particular separate or community property is subject to execution and sale to satisfy a judgment, if the property subject to liability for a judgment includes any combination of:

(1) a spouse's separate property;

(2) community property subject to a spouse's sole management, control, and disposition;

(3) community property subject to the other spouse's sole management, control, and disposition; and

(4) community property subject to the spouses' joint management, control, and disposition.

(b) In determining the order in which particular property is subject to execution and sale, the judge shall consider the facts surrounding the transaction or occurrence on which the suit is based.

History of Fam. Code §3.203: Acts 1997, 75th Leg., ch. 7, §1, eff. Apr. 17, 1997. Source: Former Fam. Code §5.62.

Sections 3.204-3.300 reserved for expansion

SUBCHAPTER D. MANAGEMENT, CONTROL, & DISPOSITION OF MARITAL PROPERTY UNDER UNUSUAL CIRCUMSTANCES

FAM §3.301. MISSING, ABANDONED, OR SEPARATED SPOUSE

(a) A spouse may file a sworn petition stating the facts that make it desirable for the petitioning spouse to manage, control, and dispose of community property described or defined in the petition that would otherwise be subject to the sole or joint management, control, and disposition of the other spouse if:

(1) the other spouse has disappeared and that spouse's location remains unknown to the petitioning spouse, unless the spouse is reported to be a prisoner of war or missing on public service;

(2) the other spouse has permanently abandoned the petitioning spouse; or

(3) the spouses are permanently separated.

(b) The petition may be filed in a court in the county in which the petitioner resided at the time the separation began, or the abandonment or disappearance occurred, not earlier than the 60th day after the date of the occurrence of the event. If both spouses are nonresidents of this state at the time the petition is filed, the petition may be filed in a court in a county in which any part of the described or defined community property is located.

History of Fam. Code §3.301: Acts 1997, 75th Leg., ch. 7, §1, eff. Apr. 17, 1997. Amended by Acts 2001, 77th Leg., ch. 217, §23, eff. Sept. 1, 2001. Source: Former Fam. Code §5.25(a), (b).

FAM §3.302. SPOUSE MISSING ON PUBLIC SERVICE

(a) If a spouse is reported by an executive department of the United States to be a prisoner of war or

missing on the public service of the United States, the spouse of the prisoner of war or missing person may file a sworn petition stating the facts that make it desirable for the petitioner to manage, control, and dispose of the community property described or defined in the petition that would otherwise be subject to the sole or joint management, control, and disposition of the imprisoned or missing spouse.

(b) The petition may be filed in a court in the county in which the petitioner resided at the time the report was made not earlier than six months after the date of the notice that a spouse is reported to be a prisoner of war or missing on public service. If both spouses were nonresidents of this state at the time the report was made, the petition shall be filed in a court in a county in which any part of the described or defined property is located.

History of Fam. Code §3.302: Acts 1997, 75th Leg., ch. 7, §1, eff. Apr. 17, 1997. Source: Former Fam. Code §5.26(a), (b).

FAM §3.303. APPOINTMENT OF ATTORNEY

(a) Except as provided by Subsection (b), the court may appoint an attorney in a suit filed under this subchapter for the respondent.

(b) The court shall appoint an attorney in a suit filed under this subchapter for a respondent reported to be a prisoner of war or missing on public service.

(c) The court shall allow a reasonable fee for an appointed attorney's services as a part of the costs of the suit.

History of Fam. Code §3.303: Acts 1997, 75th Leg., ch. 7, §1, eff. Apr. 17, 1997. Source: Former Fam. Code §§5.25(c), 5.26(c).

FAM §3.304. NOTICE OF HEARING; CITATION

(a) Notice of the hearing, accompanied by a copy of the petition, shall be issued and served on the attorney representing the respondent, if an attorney has been appointed.

(b) If an attorney has not been appointed for the respondent, citation shall be issued and served on the respondent as in other civil cases.

History of Fam. Code §3.304: Acts 1997, 75th Leg., ch. 7, §1, eff. Apr. 17, 1997. Source: Former Fam. Code §§5.25(d), 5.26(d).

FAM §3.305. CITATION BY PUBLICATION

(a) If the residence of the respondent, other than a respondent reported to be a prisoner of war or missing on public service, is unknown, citation shall be published in a newspaper of general circulation published in the county in which the petition was filed. If that county has no newspaper of general circulation, citation shall be published in a newspaper of general circulation in an adjacent county or in the nearest county in which a newspaper of general circulation is published.

(b) The notice shall be published once a week for two consecutive weeks before the hearing, but the first notice may not be published after the 20th day before the date set for the hearing.

History of Fam. Code §3.305: Acts 1997, 75th Leg., ch. 7, §1, eff. Apr. 17, 1997. Source: Former Fam. Code §5.25(e).

FAM §3.306. COURT ORDER FOR MANAGEMENT, CONTROL, & DISPOSITION OF COMMUNITY PROPERTY

(a) After hearing the evidence in a suit under this subchapter, the court, on terms the court considers just and equitable, shall render an order describing or defining the community property at issue that will be subject to the management, control, and disposition of each spouse during marriage.

(b) The court may:

(1) impose any condition and restriction the court deems necessary to protect the rights of the respondent;

(2) require a bond conditioned on the faithful administration of the property; and

(3) require payment to the registry of the court of all or a portion of the proceeds of the sale of the property, to be disbursed in accordance with the court's further directions.

History of Fam. Code §3.306: Acts 1997, 75th Leg., ch. 7, §1, eff. Apr. 17, 1997. Source: Former Fam. Code §§5.25(f), 5.26(e).

FAM §3.307. CONTINUING JURISDICTION OF COURT; VACATING ORIGINAL ORDER

(a) The court has continuing jurisdiction over the court's order rendered under this subchapter.

(b) On the motion of either spouse, the court shall amend or vacate the original order after notice and hearing if:

(1) the spouse who disappeared reappears;

(2) the abandonment or permanent separation ends; or

(3) the spouse who was reported to be a prisoner of war or missing on public service returns.

History of Fam. Code §3.307: Acts 1997, 75th Leg., ch. 7, §1, eff. Apr. 17, 1997. Amended by Acts 2001, 77th Leg., ch. 217, §24, eff. Sept. 1, 2001. Source: Former Fam. Code §§5.25(g), 5.26(f).

FAM §3.308. RECORDING ORDER TO AFFECT REAL PROPERTY

An order authorized by this subchapter affecting real property is not constructive notice to a good faith purchaser for value or to a creditor without actual notice unless the order is recorded in the deed records of the county in which the real property is located.

History of Fam. Code §3.308: Acts 1997, 75th Leg., ch. 7, §1, eff. Apr. 17, 1997. Source: Former Fam. Code §§5.25(h), 5.26(g).

FAM §3.309. REMEDIES CUMULATIVE

The remedies provided in this subchapter are cumulative of other rights, powers, and remedies afforded spouses by law.

History of Fam. Code §3.309: Acts 1997, 75th Leg., ch. 7, §1, eff. Apr. 17, 1997. Source: Former Fam. Code §5.27.

Sections 3.310-3.400 blank

SUBCHAPTER E. CLAIMS FOR REIMBURSEMENT

FAM §3.401. DEFINITIONS

*In **Obergefell v. Hodges**, ___ U.S. ___, 135 S.Ct. 2584 (2015), the U.S. Supreme Court held that same-sex couples may exercise the fundamental right to marry in all states, and that there is no lawful basis for a state to refuse to recognize a lawful same-sex marriage performed in another state on the ground of its same-sex character. See annotation under Family Code §6.204, p. 65.*

In this subchapter:

(1) to **(3)** Repealed by Acts 2009, 81st Leg., ch. 768, §11(2), eff. Sept. 1, 2009.

(4) "Marital estate" means one of three estates:

(A) the community property owned by the spouses together and referred to as the community marital estate;

(B) the separate property owned individually by the husband and referred to as a separate marital estate; or

(C) the separate property owned individually by the wife, also referred to as a separate marital estate.

(5) "Spouse" means a husband, who is a man, or a wife, who is a woman. A member of a civil union or similar relationship entered into in another state between persons of the same sex is not a spouse.

History of Fam. Code §3.401: Acts 2001, 77th Leg., ch. 838, §2, eff. Sept. 1, 2001. Amended by Acts 2009, 81st Leg., ch. 768, §11(2), eff. Sept. 1, 2009. Subchapter E amended by Acts 2001, 77th Leg., ch. 838, §2, eff. Sept. 1, 2001; Acts 2009, 81st Leg., ch. 768, §2, eff. Sept. 1, 2009.

History of Former Fam. Code §3.401: Acts 1999, 76th Leg., ch. 692, §2, eff. Sept. 1, 1999. Deleted by Acts 2001, 77th Leg., ch. 838, §2, eff. Sept. 1, 2001.

FAM §3.402. CLAIM FOR REIMBURSEMENT; OFFSETS

(a) For purposes of this subchapter, a claim for reimbursement includes:

(1) payment by one marital estate of the unsecured liabilities of another marital estate;

(2) inadequate compensation for the time, toil, talent, and effort of a spouse by a business entity under the control and direction of that spouse;

(3) the reduction of the principal amount of a debt secured by a lien on property owned before marriage, to the extent the debt existed at the time of marriage;

(4) the reduction of the principal amount of a debt secured by a lien on property received by a spouse by gift, devise, or descent during a marriage, to the extent the debt existed at the time the property was received;

(5) the reduction of the principal amount of that part of a debt, including a home equity loan:

(A) incurred during a marriage;

(B) secured by a lien on property; and

(C) incurred for the acquisition of, or for capital improvements to, property;

(6) the reduction of the principal amount of that part of a debt:

(A) incurred during a marriage;

(B) secured by a lien on property owned by a spouse;

(C) for which the creditor agreed to look for repayment solely to the separate marital estate of the spouse on whose property the lien attached; and

(D) incurred for the acquisition of, or for capital improvements to, property;

(7) the refinancing of the principal amount described by Subdivisions (3)-(6), to the extent the refinancing reduces that principal amount in a manner described by the applicable subdivision;

(8) capital improvements to property other than by incurring debt; and

(9) the reduction by the community property estate of an unsecured debt incurred by the separate estate of one of the spouses.

(b) The court shall resolve a claim for reimbursement by using equitable principles, including the prin-

ciple that claims for reimbursement may be offset against each other if the court determines it to be appropriate.

(c) Benefits for the use and enjoyment of property may be offset against a claim for reimbursement for expenditures to benefit a marital estate, except that the separate estate of a spouse may not claim an offset for use and enjoyment of a primary or secondary residence owned wholly or partly by the separate estate against contributions made by the community estate to the separate estate.

(d) Reimbursement for funds expended by a marital estate for improvements to another marital estate shall be measured by the enhancement in value to the benefited marital estate.

(e) The party seeking an offset to a claim for reimbursement has the burden of proof with respect to the offset.

History of Fam. Code §3.402: Acts 2001, 77th Leg., ch. 838, §2, eff. Sept. 1, 2001. Amended by Acts 2009, 81st Leg., ch. 768, §3, eff. Sept. 1, 2009.

History of Former Fam. Code §3.402: Acts 1999, 76th Leg., ch. 692, §2, eff. Sept. 1, 1999. Deleted by Acts 2001, 77th Leg., ch. 838, §2, eff. Sept. 1, 2001.

See also *O'Connor's Texas Family Law Handbook* (2017), "Reimbursement Claims," ch. 7-F, p. 910.

ANNOTATIONS

Burden

Vallone v. Vallone, 644 S.W.2d 455, 459 (Tex.1982). "The party claiming the right of reimbursement has the burden of pleading and proving that the expenditures and improvements were made and that they are reimbursable."

Liens

Heggen v. Pemelton, 836 S.W.2d 145, 146 (Tex. 1992). "When dividing marital property on divorce, trial courts may impose equitable liens on one spouse's *separate real property* to secure the other spouse's right of reimbursement for community improvements to that property. Although courts may impress equitable liens on separate real property to secure reimbursement rights, they may not impress such liens, absent any compensable reimbursement interest, simply to ensure a just and right division. *At 148:* The lien imposed on [W's] separate property homestead was invalid for two reasons. First, it burdened her separate real property for reasons other than to secure [H's] reimbursement interest; that is, the trial court impermissibly imposed it to secure a just and right division. And second, it imposed a lien on [W's] homestead that, based on the record, did not fit into any of the categories allowed by the Texas Constitution…."

Winkle v. Winkle, 951 S.W.2d 80, 87 (Tex.App.—Corpus Christi 1997, pet. denied). "[T]rial courts generally may impose equitable liens on one spouse's separate property as a means for securing the discharge of payments owed by one spouse to the other. Such liens, however, are permissible only against the separate property to which improvement was made at community expense." *See also* ***Hinton v. Burns***, 433 S.W.3d 189, 200 (Tex.App.—Dallas 2014, no pet.) (equitable lien imposed on W's unimproved homestead was invalid).

Offsets

Penick v. Penick, 783 S.W.2d 194, 197 (Tex.1988). "The outright rejection of offsetting benefits is inconsistent with the equitable nature of a claim for reimbursement."

Grossnickle v. Grossnickle, 935 S.W.2d 830, 841 (Tex.App.—Texarkana 1996, writ denied). "Reimbursement for expenditures made on property may be offset by benefits such as usage by the party making these expenditures."

Principal Amount of Debt

Nelson v. Nelson, 193 S.W.3d 624, 628-29 (Tex. App.—Eastland 2006, no pet.). "[A] 'lien' requires more than an obligation to repay a debt. Rather, it requires some instrument, agreement, or act giving one creditor superior rights to collateral over all other unsecured creditors or creditors with a subsequently obtained judicial lien. There is no evidence that [H's] parents had any greater right to the five-acre tract [they had sold to H] than any other creditor. Consequently, §3.402(a)(1) [now §3.402(a)(3)] is inapplicable."

Time, Toil, Talent & Effort

Jensen v. Jensen, 665 S.W.2d 107, 109 (Tex.1984). The reimbursement theory "requires adoption of the rule that the community will be reimbursed for the value of time and effort expended by either or both spouses to enhance the separate estate of either, other than that reasonably necessary to manage and preserve the separate estate, less the remuneration received for that time and effort in the form of salary, bonus, dividends and other fringe benefits, those items being community property when received."

Pearce v. Pearce, 824 S.W.2d 195, 200 (Tex. App.—El Paso 1991, writ denied). "[W]hen time, toil, talent and effort have been expended for the betterment of a marital estate, it is clear that a spouse has the option of pursuing a claim for reimbursement. If the spouse has entered, as in this case, a post-nuptial agreement, one must determine whether such a claim has been waived. [¶] The Trust Indenture involved in this case does not mention 'reimbursement,' nor does it contain a release or waiver of such a claim. In fact, there is no provision in the agreement that specifically addresses the issue of future wages and/or time, toil, talent and effort of either spouse. Instead, the agreement only refers to community property and/or other rights to the separate property of [H]. Reimbursement, however, is not a property right, it is an equitable claim that arises upon dissolution of the marriage through death, divorce or annulment. [¶] We find that the language of the Trust Indenture cannot be construed as a bar to [W's] claim for reimbursement. There is no manifestation of intent to exclude such a claim."

FAM §3.403. REPEALED

Repealed by Acts 2009, 81st Leg., ch. 768, §11(3), eff. Sept. 1, 2009.

FAM §3.404. APPLICATION OF INCEPTION OF TITLE RULE; OWNERSHIP INTEREST NOT CREATED

(a) This subchapter does not affect the rule of inception of title under which the character of property is determined at the time the right to own or claim the property arises.

(b) A claim for reimbursement under this subchapter does not create an ownership interest in property, but does create a claim against the property of the benefited estate by the contributing estate. The claim matures on dissolution of the marriage or the death of either spouse.

History of Fam. Code §3.404: Acts 1999, 76th Leg., ch. 692, §2, eff. Sept. 1, 1999. Renumbered from §3.403 and amended by Acts 2001, 77th Leg., ch. 838, §2, eff. Sept. 1, 2001. Amended by Acts 2009, 81st Leg., ch. 768, §4, eff. Sept. 1, 2009.

FAM §3.405. MANAGEMENT RIGHTS

This subchapter does not affect the right to manage, control, or dispose of marital property as provided by this chapter.

History of Fam. Code §3.405: Acts 1999, 76th Leg., ch. 692, §2, eff. Sept. 1, 1999. Renumbered from §3.404 and amended by Acts 2001, 77th Leg., ch. 838, §2, eff. Sept. 1, 2001.

History of Former Fam. Code §3.405: Acts 1999, 76th Leg., ch. 692, §2, eff. Sept. 1, 1999. Deleted by Acts 2001, 77th Leg., ch. 838, §2, eff. Sept. 1, 2001.

Ⓐ FAM §3.406. EQUITABLE LIEN

(a) On dissolution of a marriage, the court may impose an equitable lien on the property of a benefited marital estate to secure a claim for reimbursement against that property by a contributing marital estate.

(b) On the death of a spouse, a court may, on application for a claim for reimbursement brought by the surviving spouse, the personal representative of the estate of the deceased spouse, or any other person interested in the estate, as defined by Chapter 22, Estates ~~[Section 3, Texas Probate]~~ Code, impose an equitable lien on the property of a benefited marital estate to secure a claim for reimbursement against that property by a contributing marital estate.

(c) Repealed by Acts 2009, 81st Leg., ch. 768, §11(4), eff. Sept. 1, 2009.

History of Fam. Code §3.406: Acts 1999, 76th Leg., ch. 692, §2, eff. Sept. 1, 1999. Amended by Acts 2001, 77th Leg., ch. 838, §2, eff. Sept. 1, 2001; Acts 2009, 81st Leg., ch. 768, §§5, 11(4), eff. Sept. 1, 2009; S.B. 1488, §22.013, 85th Leg., eff. Sept. 1, 2017.

See also ***O'Connor's Texas Family Law Handbook*** (2017), "Equitable lien," ch. 7-F, §7.3.2(2)(c), p. 923.

FAM §§3.407, 3.408. REPEALED

Repealed by Acts 2009, 81st Leg., ch. 768, §11(5), eff. Sept. 1, 2009.

FAM §3.409. NONREIMBURSABLE CLAIMS

The court may not recognize a marital estate's claim for reimbursement for:

(1) the payment of child support, alimony, or spousal maintenance;

(2) the living expenses of a spouse or child of a spouse;

(3) contributions of property of a nominal value;

(4) the payment of a liability of a nominal amount; or

(5) a student loan owed by a spouse.

History of Fam. Code §3.409: Acts 2001, 77th Leg., ch. 838, §2, eff. Sept. 1, 2001.

See also ***O'Connor's Texas Family Law Handbook*** (2017), "Nonreimbursable claims," ch. 7-F, §3.2.2, p. 917.

ANNOTATIONS

Norris v. Vaughan, 260 S.W.2d 676, 683 (Tex.1953). "It is fundamental that the husband is obligated to furnish support for the community living and if no community funds are available he should utilize his separate funds. It is his duty to provide for the community and in this instance he chose to expend a portion of his separate estate so that the community standard of living could be as it was. Separate funds spent for commu-

nity living in such a manner should be deemed a gift to the community for its well-being and use. Allowing a right of reimbursement at a later date would be inconsistent with the fundamental concept that a man should provide for his home and community."

Pelzig v. Berkebile, 931 S.W.2d 398, 400 (Tex. App.—Corpus Christi 1996, no writ). "The cases which exempt 'living expenses' from reimbursement all deal with claims for separate property expended by one spouse for the living expenses of the married couple and their family. The child support, college expenses, and alimony payments were legal obligations [of H] brought with him into the marriage. There is no evidence that [W] was deceived about these obligations. There is no evidence that [W] ever sought to require [H] to meet these obligations out of his separate estate, either during their marriage or in the form of a prenuptial agreement. There is no evidence that these expenses benefited [H's] separate estate. The trial court, therefore, did not abuse its discretion in equitably determining that no right of reimbursement attaches to these payments."

Graham v. Graham, 836 S.W.2d 308, 310-11 (Tex. App.—Texarkana 1992, no writ). "Spouses are obligated to furnish support for community living expenses using separate property, if necessary. Separate property expended for community living is deemed to be a gift for the benefit of the well-being and use of the community estate. However, no cases have applied this rule to a situation where separate funds have been used to retire a community obligation in a lump sum payment. [¶] [H] proved that the proceeds from the sale of his separate property were used to retire the corpus of a community debt. There was no evidence that any of the funds were used to pay normal living expenses. The use of separate property to retire a community debt gives rise to reimbursement regardless of the purpose of the debt." *See also* ***In re Marriage of Case***, 28 S.W.3d 154, 161 (Tex.App.—Texarkana 2000, no pet.).

FAM §3.410. EFFECT OF MARITAL PROPERTY AGREEMENTS

A premarital or marital property agreement, whether executed before, on, or after September 1, 2009, that satisfies the requirements of Chapter 4 is effective to waive, release, assign, or partition a claim for economic contribution, reimbursement, or both, under this subchapter to the same extent the agreement would have been effective to waive, release, assign, or partition a claim for economic contribution, reimbursement, or both under the law as it existed immediately before September 1, 2009, unless the agreement provides otherwise.

History of Fam. Code §3.410: Acts 2001, 77th Leg., ch. 838, §2, eff. Sept. 1, 2001. Amended by Acts 2009, 81st Leg., ch. 768, §6, eff. Sept. 1, 2009.

CHAPTER 4. PREMARITAL & MARITAL PROPERTY AGREEMENTS

SUBCHAPTER A. UNIFORM PREMARITAL AGREEMENT ACT

NCCUSL Prefatory Comment*

The number of marriages between persons previously married and the number of marriages between persons each of whom is intending to continue to pursue a career is steadily increasing. For these and other reasons, it is becoming more and more common for persons contemplating marriage to seek to resolve by agreement certain issues presented by the forthcoming marriage. However, despite a lengthy legal history for these premarital agreements, there is a substantial uncertainty as to the enforceability of all, or a portion, of the provisions of these agreements and a significant lack of uniformity of treatment of these agreements among the states. The problems caused by this un-

* **Editor's note:**

The NCCUSL comments have been edited to reflect the Texas Legislature's omission of sections and changing of section numbers from the original uniform act. The Texas Legislature did not adopt the NCCUSL comments when it adopted the Uniform Premarital Agreement Act. The full uniform act and comments can be found at www.uniformlaws.org.

certainty and nonuniformity are greatly exacerbated by the mobility of our population. Nevertheless, this uncertainty and nonuniformity seem reflective not so much of basic policy differences between the states but rather a result of spasmodic, reflexive response to varying factual circumstances at different times. Accordingly, uniform legislation conforming to modern social policy which provides both certainty and sufficient flexibility to accommodate different circumstances would appear to be both a significant improvement and a goal realistically capable of achievement.

This Act, the Uniform Premarital Agreement Act (Act), is intended to be relatively limited in scope. Section 4.001 defines a "premarital agreement" as "an agreement between prospective spouses made in contemplation of marriage and to be effective upon marriage." Section 4.002 requires that a premarital agreement be in writing and signed by both parties. Section 4.004 provides that a premarital agreement becomes effective upon the marriage of the parties. These sections establish significant parameters. That is, the Act does not deal with agreements between persons who live together but who do not contemplate marriage or who do not marry. Nor does the Act provide for postnuptial or separation agreements or with oral agreements.

On the other hand, agreements which are embraced by the Act are permitted to deal with a wide variety of matters and Section 4.003 provides an **illustrative** list of those matters, including spousal support, which may properly be dealt with in a premarital agreement.

Section 4.006 is the key operative section of the Act and sets forth the conditions under which a premarital agreement is not enforceable. An agreement is not enforceable if the party against whom enforcement is sought proves that (a) he or she did not execute the agreement voluntarily or that (b) the agreement was unconscionable when it was executed and, before execution of the agreement, he or she (1) was not provided a fair and reasonable disclosure of the property or financial obligations of the other party, (2) did not voluntarily and expressly waive, in writing, any right to disclosure of the property or financial obligations of the other party beyond the disclosure provided, **and** (3) did not have, or reasonably could not have had, an adequate knowledge of the property and financial obligations of the other party.

...

These sections form the heart of the Act; the remaining sections deal with more tangential issues. Section 4.005 prescribes the manner in which a premarital agreement may be amended or revoked; Section 4.007 provides for very limited enforcement where a marriage is subsequently determined to be void; and Section 4.008 tolls any statute of limitations applicable to an action asserting a claim for relief under a premarital agreement during the parties' marriage.

FAM §4.001. DEFINITIONS

In this subchapter:

(1) "Premarital agreement" means an agreement between prospective spouses made in contemplation of marriage and to be effective on marriage.

(2) "Property" means an interest, present or future, legal or equitable, vested or contingent, in real or personal property, including income and earnings.

History of Fam. Code §4.001: Acts 1997, 75th Leg., ch. 7, §1, eff. Apr. 17, 1997. Source: Former Fam. Code §5.41.

ANNOTATIONS

Beck v. Beck, 814 S.W.2d 745, 749 (Tex.1991). "We hold that the 1980 amendment to [Tex. Const.] art. 16, §15 ... demonstrates an intention on the part of the legislature and the people of Texas to not only authorize future premarital agreements, but to impliedly validate [Fam. Code] §5.41 [now §4.001] and all premarital agreements entered into before 1980 pursuant to that statute. The legislature and the people of Texas have made the public policy determination that premarital agreements should be enforced."

Williams v. Williams, 569 S.W.2d 867, 870 (Tex. 1978). Family Code §5.41, now §4.001, "should be construed as broadly as possible in order to allow the parties as much flexibility to contract with respect to property or other rights incident to the marriage, provided the constitutional and statutory definitions of separate and community property or the requirements of public policy are not violated."

Ahmed v. Ahmed, 261 S.W.3d 190, 194 (Tex.App.—Houston [14th Dist.] 2008, no pet.). "If the legal requirements for a ceremonial marriage are satisfied, Texas does not distinguish between civil and religious marriage ceremonies. It is the parties' marital status, rather than a specific type of ceremony, that is significant. Because the parties participated in a valid civil wedding ceremony six months before signing the ... agreement, they were already spouses, not 'prospective spouses,' and their agreement could not have been [a premarital agreement] made 'in contemplation of marriage.'"

NCCUSL Comment*

The definition of "premarital agreement" set forth in subsection (1) is limited to an agreement between prospective spouses made in contemplation of and to be effective upon marriage. Agreements between persons living together but not contemplating marriage (see *Marvin v. Marvin*, 18 Cal. 3d 660 (1976), judgment after trial modified, 122 Cal. App. 3d 871 (1981)) and postnuptial or separation agreements are outside the scope of this Act. Formal requirements are prescribed by Section 4.002. An illustrative list of matters which may be included in an agreement is set forth in Section 4.003.

Subsection (2) is designed to embrace all forms of property and interests therein. These may include rights in a professional license or practice, employee benefit plans, pension and retirement accounts, and so on. The reference to income or earnings includes both income from property and earnings from personal services.

FAM §4.002. FORMALITIES

A premarital agreement must be in writing and signed by both parties. The agreement is enforceable without consideration.

History of Fam. Code §4.002: Acts 1997, 75th Leg., ch. 7, §1, eff. Apr. 17, 1997. Source: Former Fam. Code §5.42.

NCCUSL Comment*

Section 4.002 restates the common requirement that a premarital agreement be reduced to writing and signed by both parties (see Ariz. Rev. Stats. §25-201; Ark. Stats. §55-310; Cal. Civ. C. §5134; 13 Dela. Code 1974 §301; Idaho Code §32-917; Ann. Laws Mass. ch. 209, §25; Minn. Stats. Ann. §519.11; Montana Rev. C. §36-123; New Mex Stats. Ann. 1978 40-2-4; Ore. Rev. Stats. §108.140; Vernon's Texas Codes Ann. §5.44; Vermont Stats. Ann. Title 12, §181). Many states also require other formalities, including notarization or an acknowledgment (see, e.g., Arizona, Arkansas, California, Idaho, Montana, New Mexico) but may then permit the formal statutory requirement to be avoided or satisfied subsequent to execution (see *In re Marriage of Cleveland*,

* See footnote on p. 49.

76 Cal. App. 3d 357 (1977) (premarital agreement never acknowledged but "proved" by sworn testimony of parties in dissolution proceeding)). This act dispenses with all formal requirements except a writing signed by both parties. Although the section is framed in the singular, the agreement may consist of one or more documents intended to be part of the agreement and executed as required by this section.

Section 4.002 also restates what appears to be the almost universal rule regarding the marriage as consideration for a premarital agreement (see, e.g., Ga. Code §20-303; *Barnhill v. Barnhill*, 386 So. 2d 749 (Ala. Civ. App. 1980); *Estate of Gillilan v. Estate of Gillilan*, 406 N.E.2d 981 (Ind. App. 1980); *Friedlander v. Friedlander*, 494 P.2d 208 (Wash. 1972); but cf. *Wilson v. Wilson*, 170 A.2d 679, 685 (Me. 1961)). The primary importance of this rule has been to provide a degree of mutuality of benefits to support the enforceability of a premarital agreement. A marriage is a prerequisite for the effectiveness of a premarital agreement under this act (see Section 4.004). This requires that there be a ceremonial marriage. Even if this marriage is subsequently determined to have been void, Section 4.007 may provide limits of enforceability of an agreement entered into in contemplation of that marriage. Consideration as such is not required and the standards for enforceability are established by Sections 4.006 and 4.007. Nevertheless, this provision is retained here as a desirable, if not essential, restatement of the law. On the other hand, the fact that marriage is deemed to be consideration for the purpose of this act does not change the rules applicable in other areas of law (see, e.g., 26 U.S.C.A. §2043 (release of certain marital rights not treated as consideration for federal estate tax), 2512; *Merrill v. Fahs*, 324 U.S. 308, rehearing denied 324 U.S. 888 (release of marital rights in premarital agreement not adequate and full consideration for purposes of federal gift tax)).

Finally, a premarital agreement is a contract. As required for any other contract, the parties must have the capacity to contract in order to enter into a binding agreement. Those persons who lack the capacity to contract but who under other provisions of law are permitted to enter into a binding agreement may enter into a premarital agreement under those other provisions of law.

FAM §4.003. CONTENT

(a) The parties to a premarital agreement may contract with respect to:

(1) the rights and obligations of each of the parties in any of the property of either or both of them whenever and wherever acquired or located;

(2) the right to buy, sell, use, transfer, exchange, abandon, lease, consume, expend, assign, create a security interest in, mortgage, encumber, dispose of, or otherwise manage and control property;

(3) the disposition of property on separation, marital dissolution, death, or the occurrence or nonoccurrence of any other event;

(4) the modification or elimination of spousal support;

(5) the making of a will, trust, or other arrangement to carry out the provisions of the agreement;

(6) the ownership rights in and disposition of the death benefit from a life insurance policy;

(7) the choice of law governing the construction of the agreement; and

(8) any other matter, including their personal rights and obligations, not in violation of public policy or a statute imposing a criminal penalty.

(b) The right of a child to support may not be adversely affected by a premarital agreement.

History of Fam. Code §4.003: Acts 1997, 75th Leg., ch. 7, §1, eff. Apr. 17, 1997. Source: Former Fam. Code §5.43.

See also *O'Connor's Texas Family Law Handbook* (2017), "Scope of premarital agreement," ch. 2-D, §3.2.3, p. 163.

ANNOTATIONS

Williams v. Williams, 569 S.W.2d 867, 870 (Tex. 1978). Spouse may waive rights to the homestead and exempt property in a premarital agreement.

In re Knott, 118 S.W.3d 899, 903-04 (Tex.App.—Texarkana 2003, no pet.). Section 4.003(b) "reflects the Legislature's intent to discourage an obligor from fraudulently characterizing his or her assets so as to diminish or extinguish the amount of the child support obligation. Such a reading of §4.003(b) is consistent with the constitutional mandate that premarital agreements not be made for the purpose of committing fraud. Moreover, §4.003(b) … does not override the Texas Constitution's general express approval of premarital agreements that are not made for fraudulent purposes."

Dokmanovic v. Schwarz, 880 S.W.2d 272, 275-76 (Tex.App.—Houston [14th Dist.] 1994, no writ). "The agreement in this case … indicated the parties' intent to exchange their community interests in income from separate property and in earnings. [¶] [W]e hold that the antenuptial agreement in this case was valid as an exchange of income to be acquired by the parties during their future marriage. Because the agreement was valid, there were no commingled funds with which property was acquired during marriage. Furthermore, no partition was required where a valid exchange occurred." *See also* ***Winger v. Pianka***, 831 S.W.2d 853, 858 (Tex.App.—Austin 1992, writ denied) (couples who intend to marry can partition or exchange between themselves salaries and earnings to be acquired during marriage).

NCCUSL Comment*

Section 4.003 permits the parties to contract in a premarital agreement with respect to any matter listed and any other matter not in violation of public policy or any statute imposing a criminal penalty. The matters are intended to be illustrative, not exclusive. Paragraph (4) of subsection (a) specifically authorizes the parties to deal with spousal support obligations. There is a split in authority among the states as to whether an premarital agreement may control the issue of spousal support. Some few states do not permit a premarital agreement to control this issue (see, e.g., *In re Marriage of Winegard*, 278 N.W.2d 505 (Iowa 1979); *Fricke v. Fricke*, 42 N.W. 2d 500 (Wis. 1950)). However, the better view and growing trend is to permit a premarital agreement to govern this matter if the agreement and the circumstances of its execution satisfy certain stan-

* See footnote on p. 49.

dards (see, e.g., *Newman v. Newman*, 653 P.2d 728 (Colo. Sup. Ct. 1982); *Parniawski v. Parniawski*, 359 A.2d 719 (Conn. 1976); *Volid v. Volid*, 286 N.E.2d 42 (Ill. 1972); *Osborne v. Osborne*, 428 N.E.2d 810 (Mass. 1981); *Hudson v. Hudson*, 350 P.2d 596 (Okla. 1960); *Unander v. Unander*, 506 P.2d 719 (Ore. 1973)) (see Sections 4.007 and 4.008).

Paragraph (8) of subsection (a) makes clear that the parties may also contract with respect to other matters, including personal rights and obligations, not in violation of public policy or a criminal statute. Hence, subject to this limitation, an agreement may provide for such matters as the choice of abode, the freedom to pursue career opportunities, the upbringing of children, and so on. However, subsection (b) of this section makes clear that an agreement may not adversely affect what would otherwise be the obligation of a party to a child.

FAM §4.004. EFFECT OF MARRIAGE

A premarital agreement becomes effective on marriage.

History of Fam. Code §4.004: Acts 1997, 75th Leg., ch. 7, §1, eff. Apr. 17, 1997. Source: Former Fam. Code §5.44.

NCCUSL Comment*

This section establishes a marriage as a prerequisite for the effectiveness of a premarital agreement. As a consequence, the act does not provide for a situation where persons live together without marrying. In that situation, the parties must look to the other law of the jurisdiction (see *Marvin v. Marvin*, 18 Cal. 3d 660 (1976); judgment after trial modified, 122 Cal. App. 3d 871 (1981)).

FAM §4.005. AMENDMENT OR REVOCATION

After marriage, a premarital agreement may be amended or revoked only by a written agreement signed by the parties. The amended agreement or the revocation is enforceable without consideration.

History of Fam. Code §4.005: Acts 1997, 75th Leg., ch. 7, §1, eff. Apr. 17, 1997. Source: Former Fam. Code §5.45.

NCCUSL Comment*

This section requires the same formalities of execution for an amendment or revocation of a premarital agreement as are required for its original execution (cf. *Estate of Gillilan v. Estate of Gillilan*, 406 N.E.2d 981 (Ind. App. 1980) (agreement may be altered by subsequent agreement but not simply by inconsistent acts)).

FAM §4.006. ENFORCEMENT

(a) A premarital agreement is not enforceable if the party against whom enforcement is requested proves that:

(1) the party did not sign the agreement voluntarily; or

(2) the agreement was unconscionable when it was signed and, before signing the agreement, that party:

(A) was not provided a fair and reasonable disclosure of the property or financial obligations of the other party;

(B) did not voluntarily and expressly waive, in writing, any right to disclosure of the property or financial obligations of the other party beyond the disclosure provided; and

* See footnote on p. 49.

(C) did not have, or reasonably could not have had, adequate knowledge of the property or financial obligations of the other party.

(b) An issue of unconscionability of a premarital agreement shall be decided by the court as a matter of law.

(c) The remedies and defenses in this section are the exclusive remedies or defenses, including common law remedies or defenses.

History of Fam. Code §4.006: Acts 1997, 75th Leg., ch. 7, §1, eff. Apr. 17, 1997. Source: Former Fam. Code §5.46.

See also ***O'Connor's Texas Family Law Handbook*** (2017), "Contesting enforcement of premarital agreement," ch. 2-D, §3.5, p. 166.

ANNOTATIONS

Moore v. Moore, 383 S.W.3d 190, 195 (Tex.App.—Dallas 2012, pet. denied). "The Uniform Premarital Agreement Act does not define voluntariness and there are relatively few Texas cases discussing the meaning of the term as used in the Act. Texas courts have construed 'voluntarily' to mean an action that is taken intentionally or by the free exercise of one's will. The parameters of involuntary execution of a premarital agreement may not be clear in every case and will tend to depend on the circumstances. In determining whether any evidence of involuntariness existed, this Court has considered (1) whether a party has had the advice of counsel, (2) misrepresentations made in procuring the agreement, (3) the amount of information provided and (4) whether information has been withheld. Evidence of fraud and duress may also provide proof of involuntariness. However, fraud and duress are not themselves defenses to a premarital agreement."

Fazakerly v. Fazakerly, 996 S.W.2d 260, 265 (Tex. App.—Eastland 1999, pet. denied). "The issue of unconscionability must be decided by the trial court as a matter of law before the disclosure questions are addressed."

Marsh v. Marsh, 949 S.W.2d 734, 739 (Tex.App.—Houston [14th Dist.] 1997, no writ). "[N]either the legislature nor Texas courts have defined 'unconscionable' in the context of marital or premarital property agreements. *At 741-42:* In reviewing the validity of a marital property agreement, this court has considered such factors as the maturity of the individuals, their business backgrounds, their educational levels, their experiences in prior marriages, their respective ages and their motivations to protect their respective children. [¶] The fact that the premarital agreement was signed shortly before the wedding does not make the

agreement unconscionable. Likewise, the fact that [H] was not represented by independent counsel is not dispositive. [¶] [Additionally,] even though a premarital agreement may be disproportionate, unfairness is not material to the enforceability of the agreement. A factual finding that a premarital agreement is unfair does not satisfy the burden of proof required to establish unconscionability. [¶] [Further,] [t]he fact that [H] denied reading the premarital agreement is not grounds for avoiding the contract. [¶] [Finally,] [f]or an agreement to be unconscionable, it must be 'so far one-sided that no reasonable person could consider it to be an arm's length transaction.'"

NCCUSL Comment*

This section sets forth the conditions which must be proven to avoid the enforcement of a premarital agreement. If prospective spouses enter into a premarital agreement and their subsequent marriage is determined to be void, the enforceability of the agreement is governed by Section 4.007.

The conditions stated under subsection (a) are comparable to concepts which are expressed in the statutory and decisional law of many jurisdictions. Enforcement based on disclosure and voluntary execution is perhaps most common (see, e.g., Ark. Stats. §55-309; Minn. Stats. Ann. §519.11; *In re Kaufmann's Estate*, 171 A.2d 48 (Pa. 1961) (alternate holding)). However, knowledge or reason to know, together with voluntary execution, may also be sufficient (see, e.g., Tenn. Code Ann. §36-606; *Barnhill v. Barnhill*, 386 So. 2d 749 (Ala. Civ. App. 1980); *Del Vecchio v. Del Vecchio*, 143 So. 2d 17 (Fla. 1962); *Coward and Coward*, 582 P.2d 834 (Or. App. 1978); but see *Matter of Estate of Lebsock*, 618 P.2d 683 (Colo. App. 1980)) and so may a voluntary, knowing waiver (see *Hafner v. Hafner*, 295 N.W.2d 567 (Minn. 1980)). In each of these situations, it should be underscored that execution must have been voluntary (see *Lutgert v. Lutgert*, 338 So. 2d 1111 (Fla. 1976); see also 13 Dela. Code 1974 §301 (10 day waiting period)). Finally, a premarital agreement is enforceable if enforcement would not have been unconscionable at the time the agreement was executed (cf. *Hartz v. Hartz*, 234 A.2d 865 (Md. 1967) (premarital agreement upheld if no disclosure but agreement was fair and equitable under the circumstances)).

The test of "unconscionability" is drawn from Section 306 of the Uniform Marriage and Divorce Act (UMDA) (see *Ferry v. Ferry*, 586 S.W.2d 782 (Mo. 1979); see also *Newman v. Newman*, 653 P.2d 728 (Colo. Sup. Ct. 1982) (maintenance provisions of premarital agreement tested for unconscionability at time of marriage termination)). The following discussion set forth in the Commissioner's Note to Section 306 of the UMDA is equally appropriate here:

The standard of unconscionability is used in commercial law, where its meaning includes protection against onesidedness, oppression, or unfair surprise (see section 2-302, Uniform Commercial Code), and in contract law, *Scott v. U.S.*, 12 Wall (U.S.) 443 (1870) ('contract ... unreasonable and unconscionable but not void for fraud'); *Stiefler v. McCullough*, 174 N.E. 823, 97 Ind.App. 123 (1931); *Terre Haute Cooperage v. Branscome*, 35 So.2d 537, 203 Miss. 493 (1948); *Carter v. Boone County Trust Co.*, 92 S.W.2d 647, 338 Mo. 629 (1936). It has been used in cases respecting divorce settlements or awards. *Bell v. Bell*, 371 P.2d 773, 150 Colo. 174 (1962) ('this division of property is manifestly unfair, inequitable and unconscionable'). Hence the act does not introduce a novel standard unknown to the law. In the context of negotiations between spouses as to the financial incidents of their marriage, the standard includes protection against overreaching, concealment of assets, and sharp dealing not consistent with the obligations of marital partners to deal fairly with each other.

"In order to determine whether the agreement is unconscionable, the court may look to the economic circumstances of the parties resulting from the agreement, and any other relevant evidence such as the conditions under which the agreement was made, including the knowledge of the other party. If the court finds the agreement not unconscionable, its terms respecting property division and maintenance may not be altered by the court at the hearing." (Commissioner's Note, Sec. 306, Uniform Marriage and Divorce Act.)

Nothing in Section 4.006 makes the absence of assistance of independent legal counsel a condition for the unenforceability of a premarital agreement. However, lack of that assistance may well be a factor in determining whether the conditions stated in Section 4.006 may have existed (see, e.g., *Del Vecchio v. Del Vecchio*, 143 So.2d 17 (Fla. 1962)).

No special provision is made for enforcement of provisions of a premarital agreement relating to personal rights and obligations. However, a premarital agreement is a contract and these provisions may be enforced to the extent that they are enforceable are under otherwise applicable law (see *Avitzur v. Avitzur*, 459 N.Y.S.2d 572 (Ct. App.)).

Section 4.006 is framed in a manner to require the party who alleges that a premarital agreement is not enforceable to bear the burden of proof as to that allegation. The statutory law conflicts on the issue of where the burden of proof lies (contrast Ark. Stats. §55-313; 31 Minn. Stats. Ann. §519.11 with Vernon's Texas Codes Ann. §5.45). Similarly, some courts have placed the burden on the attacking spouse to prove the invalidity of the agreement. *Linker v. Linker*, 470 P.2d 921 (Colo. 1970); *Matter of Estate of Benker*, 296 N.W.2d 167 (Mich. App. 1980); *In re Kauffmann's Estate*, 171 A.2d 48 (Pa. 1961). Some have placed the burden upon those relying upon the agreement to prove its validity. *Hartz v. Hartz*, 234 A.2d 865 (Md. 1967). Finally, several have adopted a middle ground by stating that a premarital agreement is presumptively valid but if a disproportionate disposition is made for the wife, the husband bears the burden of proof of showing adequate disclosure. (*Del Vecchio v. Del Vecchio*, 143 So.2d 17 (Fla. 1962); *Christians v. Christians*, 44 N.W.2d 431 (Iowa 1950); *In re Neis' Estate*, 225 P.2d 110 (Kan. 1950); *Truitt v. Truitt's Adm'r*, 162 S.W.2d 31 (Ky. 1942); *In re Estate of Strickland*, 149 N.W.2d 344 (Neb. 1967); *Kosik v. George*, 452 P.2d 560 (Or. 1969); *Friedlander v. Friedlander*, 494 P.2d 208 (Wash. 1972).)

FAM §4.007. ENFORCEMENT: VOID MARRIAGE

If a marriage is determined to be void, an agreement that would otherwise have been a premarital agreement is enforceable only to the extent necessary to avoid an inequitable result.

History of Fam. Code §4.007: Acts 1997, 75th Leg., ch. 7, §1, eff. Apr. 17, 1997. Source: Former Fam. Code §5.47.

NCCUSL Comment*

Under section 4.007, a void marriage does not completely invalidate a premarital agreement but does substantially limit its enforceability. Where parties have married and lived together for a substantial period of time and one or both have relied on the existence of a premarital agreement, the failure to enforce the agreement may well be inequitable. This section, accordingly, provides the court discretion to enforce the agreement to the extent necessary to avoid the inequitable result (see Annot., 46 A.L.R. 3d 1403).

FAM §4.008. LIMITATION OF ACTIONS

A statute of limitations applicable to an action asserting a claim for relief under a premarital agreement is tolled during the marriage of the parties to the agreement. However, equitable defenses limiting the time for enforcement, including laches and estoppel, are available to either party.

History of Fam. Code §4.008: Acts 1997, 75th Leg., ch. 7, §1, eff. Apr. 17, 1997. Source: Former Fam. Code §5.48.

ANNOTATIONS

Fazakerly v. Fazakerly, 996 S.W.2d 260, 264 (Tex. App.—Eastland 1999, pet. denied). "It is clear that [W] argued limitations ... despite her erroneous assertion

* See footnote on p. 49.

that the antenuptial agreement was 'barred by limitations pursuant to [Fam. Code] §4.008....' The applicable statutes of limitations ... provide for a four-year period. Section 4.008 and its predecessor ... deal with the tolling of limitations; these sections are not statutes of limitations. *At 264 n.3:* Claims of fraud in connection with a contract are governed by the four-year limitation in [CPRC] §16.051."

NCCUSL Comment*

In order to avoid the potentially disruptive effect of compelling litigation between the spouses in order to escape the running of an applicable statute of limitations, Section 4.008 tolls any applicable statute during the marriage of the parties (contrast *Dykema v. Dykema*, 412 N.E.2d 13 (Ill. App. 1980) (statute of limitations not tolled where fraud not adequately pleaded, hence premarital agreement enforced at death)). However, a party is not completely free to sit on his or her rights because the section does preserve certain equitable defenses.

FAM §4.009. APPLICATION & CONSTRUCTION

This subchapter shall be applied and construed to effect its general purpose to make uniform the law with respect to the subject of this subchapter among states enacting these provisions.

History of Fam. Code §4.009: Acts 1997, 75th Leg., ch. 7, §1, eff. Apr. 17, 1997. Source: Former Fam. Code §5.49.

FAM §4.010. SHORT TITLE

This subchapter may be cited as the Uniform Premarital Agreement Act.

History of Fam. Code §4.010: Acts 1997, 75th Leg., ch. 7, §1, eff. Apr. 17, 1997. Source: Former Fam. Code §5.50.

Sections 4.011-4.100 reserved for expansion

SUBCHAPTER B. MARITAL PROPERTY AGREEMENT

FAM §4.101. DEFINITION

In this subchapter, "property" has the meaning assigned by Section 4.001.

History of Fam. Code §4.101: Acts 1997, 75th Leg., ch. 7, §1, eff. Apr. 17, 1997. Source: Former Fam. Code §5.51.

FAM §4.102. PARTITION OR EXCHANGE OF COMMUNITY PROPERTY

At any time, the spouses may partition or exchange between themselves all or part of their community property, then existing or to be acquired, as the spouses may desire. Property or a property interest transferred to a spouse by a partition or exchange agreement becomes that spouse's separate property. The partition or exchange of property may also provide that future earnings and income arising from the transferred property shall be the separate property of the owning spouse.

* See footnote on p. 49.

History of Fam. Code §4.102: Acts 1997, 75th Leg., ch. 7, §1, eff. Apr. 17, 1997. Amended by Acts 2003, 78th Leg., ch. 230, §2, eff. Sept. 1, 2003; Acts 2005, 79th Leg., ch. 477, §1, eff. Sept. 1, 2005. Source: Former Fam. Code §5.52.

See also ***O'Connor's Texas Family Law Handbook*** (2017), "Partition/exchange agreements – community to separate," ch. 2-D, §4.1, p. 171.

ANNOTATIONS

Byrnes v. Byrnes, 19 S.W.3d 556, 559 (Tex.App.—Fort Worth 2000, no pet.). "The term 'partition' as used in [§4.102] contemplates a division of property among the parties, not a complete forfeiture or assignment. Absent a specific reference to a partition or language indicating that such a division was intended, Texas courts have refused to uphold transactions between spouses as partitions. [¶] Because the parties' agreement makes no specific reference to a partition, contains no language indicating that the parties intended a partition, and provides for a forfeiture of [H's] interest, the document is not a valid partition under §4.102.... *At 559 n.2:* The parties' agreement also specifically provides that it is subject to judicial approval. A partition agreement does not require judicial approval, while an agreement incident to divorce does."

In re Marriage of Morrison, 913 S.W.2d 689, 693 (Tex.App.—Texarkana 1995, writ denied). "Although a partition and exchange agreement is one mechanism by which spouses may convert community property into their separate property, it is not the only method by which such a transformation can be effected."

FAM §4.103. AGREEMENT BETWEEN SPOUSES CONCERNING INCOME OR PROPERTY FROM SEPARATE PROPERTY

At any time, the spouses may agree that the income or property arising from the separate property that is then owned by one of them, or that may thereafter be acquired, shall be the separate property of the owner.

History of Fam. Code §4.103: Acts 1997, 75th Leg., ch. 7, §1, eff. Apr. 17, 1997. Source: Former Fam. Code §5.53.

FAM §4.104. FORMALITIES

A partition or exchange agreement under Section 4.102 or an agreement under Section 4.103 must be in writing and signed by both parties. Either agreement is enforceable without consideration.

History of Fam. Code §4.104: Acts 1997, 75th Leg., ch. 7, §1, eff. Apr. 17, 1997. Amended by Acts 2005, 79th Leg., ch. 477, §2, eff. Sept. 1, 2005. Source: Former Fam. Code §5.54.

ANNOTATIONS

Collins v. Collins, 752 S.W.2d 636, 637 (Tex.App.—Fort Worth 1988, writ ref'd). "[W]e find that a joint income tax return signed by both spouses, in which the

income of various assets is listed as separate and community, absent specific language indicating that the document is intended by the parties to constitute an agreement to partition, as a matter of law does not constitute a partition agreement in writing and signed by the parties as required by [Fam. Code] §5.54 [now §4.104]. [¶] We do not find the requirements of the Statute of Frauds to be applicable to the requirements for the writing required by [§5.54], because §5.54 requires an agreement in writing signed by both parties, whereas the Statute of Frauds requires only a memorandum of an agreement and not an agreement itself. *At 638:* To allow the establishment of the existence of the agreement by parol evidence would be to destroy the requirement set forth by [§5.54] that the agreement be in writing."

Dalton v. Don J. Jackson, Inc., 691 S.W.2d 765, 768 (Tex.App.—Austin 1985, no pet.). "[O]ne spouse may not convey his or her interest in joint community property to a third party [without the other spouse's consent], so as to effectuate a partition by creating a tenancy-in-common between the remaining spouse and the third party."

FAM §4.105. ENFORCEMENT

(a) A partition or exchange agreement is not enforceable if the party against whom enforcement is requested proves that:

(1) the party did not sign the agreement voluntarily; or

(2) the agreement was unconscionable when it was signed and, before execution of the agreement, that party:

(A) was not provided a fair and reasonable disclosure of the property or financial obligations of the other party;

(B) did not voluntarily and expressly waive, in writing, any right to disclosure of the property or financial obligations of the other party beyond the disclosure provided; and

(C) did not have, or reasonably could not have had, adequate knowledge of the property or financial obligations of the other party.

(b) An issue of unconscionability of a partition or exchange agreement shall be decided by the court as a matter of law.

(c) The remedies and defenses in this section are the exclusive remedies or defenses, including common law remedies or defenses.

History of Fam. Code §4.105: Acts 1997, 75th Leg., ch. 7, §1, eff. Apr. 17, 1997. Source: Former Fam. Code §5.55.

See also *O'Connor's Texas Family Law Handbook* (2017), "Contesting enforcement of partition/exchange agreement," ch. 2-D, §4.1.3, p. 174.

ANNOTATIONS

Sheshunoff v. Sheshunoff, 172 S.W.3d 686, 697 (Tex.App.—Austin 2005, pet. denied). "[A]lthough the presence of such factors as fraud, duress, and undue influence may bear upon the inquiry, [respondent] does not have to prove each element of these common-law defenses to establish the ultimate issue of involuntary execution. *At 698:* Subsection (c) was intended to clarify merely that ... parties cannot assert common-law defenses *in addition* to the defenses enumerated in §4.105. It does not prohibit us from considering as potential evidence of involuntary execution proof of conduct that [respondent] asserts constitutes fraud or duress. [¶] In sum, we conclude that §4.105 sets out the exclusive remedies available to prevent enforcement of a postmarital agreement, and that, although common-law defenses may inform our analysis of 'voluntariness,' they will not necessarily control." *See also* ***Sanders v. Sanders***, No. 02-08-00201-CV (Tex.App.—Fort Worth 2010, no pet.) (memo op.; 10-14-10) (common-law defense of mental incapacity informed court's analysis of whether W voluntarily signed postnuptial agreements).

In re Marriage of Smith, 115 S.W.3d 126, 135-36 (Tex.App.—Texarkana 2003, pet. denied). "While the value of the property that each party received under the contract now seems quite disproportionate, we do not evaluate whether the contract is unconscionable years later. Rather, we look to the circumstances at the time the parties entered into the contract. No evidence was presented as to the value of the retirement benefits as of 1982. Likely, such value was uncertain at that time. Likewise, the parties could not predict any appreciation or depreciation in value of any of the property received under the agreement. So, while we note the marked difference in the current value of the property received by [parties], we cannot say the contract under which each received the property was an unconscionable one."

Pletcher v. Goetz, 9 S.W.3d 442, 445 (Tex.App.—Fort Worth 1999, pet. denied). "The party challenging the enforceability of a partition and exchange agreement bears the burden of proving the agreement was involuntary or unconscionable. However, neither the legislature nor the supreme court has defined the term 'unconscionable' in the context of marital property

agreements. As a result, appellate courts have turned to the commercial context for guidance in evaluating 'unconscionability.' [¶] The issue of whether a partition and exchange agreement is unconscionable is a question of law for the court. In assessing the conscionability of an agreement, the court should consider all of the circumstances in which the agreement was made."

FAM §4.106. RIGHTS OF CREDITORS & RECORDATION UNDER PARTITION OR EXCHANGE AGREEMENT

(a) A provision of a partition or exchange agreement made under this subchapter is void with respect to the rights of a preexisting creditor whose rights are intended to be defrauded by it.

(b) A partition or exchange agreement made under this subchapter may be recorded in the deed records of the county in which a party resides and in the county in which the real property affected is located. An agreement made under this subchapter is constructive notice to a good faith purchaser for value or a creditor without actual notice only if the instrument is acknowledged and recorded in the county in which the real property is located.

History of Fam. Code §4.106: Acts 1997, 75th Leg., ch. 7, §1, eff. Apr. 17, 1997. Source: Former Fam. Code §5.56.

Sections 4.107-4.200 blank

SUBCHAPTER C. AGREEMENT TO CONVERT SEPARATE PROPERTY TO COMMUNITY PROPERTY

FAM §4.201. DEFINITION

In this subchapter, "property" has the meaning assigned by Section 4.001.

History of Fam. Code §4.201: Acts 1999, 76th Leg., ch. 692, §3, eff. Jan. 1, 2000.

FAM §4.202. AGREEMENT TO CONVERT TO COMMUNITY PROPERTY

At any time, spouses may agree that all or part of the separate property owned by either or both spouses is converted to community property.

History of Fam. Code §4.202: Acts 1999, 76th Leg., ch. 692, §3, eff. Jan. 1, 2000.

See also *O'Connor's Texas Family Law Handbook* (2017), "Conversion agreements – separate to community," ch. 2-D, §4.2, p. 175.

FAM §4.203. FORMALITIES OF AGREEMENT

(a) An agreement to convert separate property to community property:

(1) must be in writing and:

(A) be signed by the spouses;

(B) identify the property being converted; and

(C) specify that the property is being converted to the spouses' community property; and

(2) is enforceable without consideration.

(b) The mere transfer of a spouse's separate property to the name of the other spouse or to the name of both spouses is not sufficient to convert the property to community property under this subchapter.

History of Fam. Code §4.203: Acts 1999, 76th Leg., ch. 692, §3, eff. Jan. 1, 2000.

See also *O'Connor's Texas Family Law Handbook* (2017), "Drafting conversion agreement," ch. 2-D, §4.2.2, p. 176.

ANNOTATIONS

In re Estate of Cunningham, 390 S.W.3d 685, 687 (Tex.App.—Dallas 2012, no pet.). Deceased husband's son "challenges the trial court's conclusions that the … agreement [between H and W] (1) complied with the requirements of [Fam. Code] §4.203 … and (2) converted [H's] separate property into the community property of [H] and [W]. *At 688-89:* The document in this case is a fill-in-the-blank form, entitled 'Agreement to Establish Right of Survivorship to Community Property between Spouses.' It recites that the Texas Constitution was amended in 1987 to allow spouses to agree in writing that all or part of their community property be passed on the death of one spouse to the surviving spouse and states '[t]his form is intended for that purpose.' [T]he form states: '*Community Property*—The parties agree that the following is held as their community property: … Home and other real property locate[d] at: [address] *including all inheritance property*[.]' [¶] [W]e conclude this agreement fails to comply with [Fam. Code] §§4.203 and 4.205…. Specifically, the agreement does not state the spouses agree to convert all or a part of one spouse's separate property into community property. [And] there is nothing in the record to show [H] or [W] received a 'fair and reasonable disclosure of the legal effect of converting separate property to community property.' [T]he agreement … did not convert [H's] separate property into community property."

FAM §4.204. MANAGEMENT OF CONVERTED PROPERTY

Except as specified in the agreement to convert the property and as provided by Subchapter B, Chapter 3, and other law, property converted to community property under this subchapter is subject to:

(1) the sole management, control, and disposition of the spouse in whose name the property is held;

(2) the sole management, control, and disposition of the spouse who transferred the property if the property is not subject to evidence of ownership;

(3) the joint management, control, and disposition of the spouses if the property is held in the name of both spouses; or

(4) the joint management, control, and disposition of the spouses if the property is not subject to evidence of ownership and was owned by both spouses before the property was converted to community property.

History of Fam. Code §4.204: Acts 1999, 76th Leg., ch. 692, §3, eff. Jan. 1, 2000.

FAM §4.205. ENFORCEMENT

(a) An agreement to convert property to community property under this subchapter is not enforceable if the spouse against whom enforcement is sought proves that the spouse did not:

(1) execute the agreement voluntarily; or

(2) receive a fair and reasonable disclosure of the legal effect of converting the property to community property.

(b) An agreement that contains the following statement, or substantially similar words, prominently displayed in bold-faced type, capital letters, or underlined, is rebuttably presumed to provide a fair and reasonable disclosure of the legal effect of converting property to community property:

"THIS INSTRUMENT CHANGES SEPARATE PROPERTY TO COMMUNITY PROPERTY. THIS MAY HAVE ADVERSE CONSEQUENCES DURING MARRIAGE AND ON TERMINATION OF THE MARRIAGE BY DEATH OR DIVORCE. FOR EXAMPLE:

"EXPOSURE TO CREDITORS. IF YOU SIGN THIS AGREEMENT, ALL OR PART OF THE SEPARATE PROPERTY BEING CONVERTED TO COMMUNITY PROPERTY MAY BECOME SUBJECT TO THE LIABILITIES OF YOUR SPOUSE. IF YOU DO NOT SIGN THIS AGREEMENT, YOUR SEPARATE PROPERTY IS GENERALLY NOT SUBJECT TO THE LIABILITIES OF YOUR SPOUSE UNLESS YOU ARE PERSONALLY LIABLE UNDER ANOTHER RULE OF LAW.

"LOSS OF MANAGEMENT RIGHTS. IF YOU SIGN THIS AGREEMENT, ALL OR PART OF THE SEPARATE PROPERTY BEING CONVERTED TO COMMUNITY PROPERTY MAY BECOME SUBJECT TO EITHER THE JOINT MANAGEMENT, CONTROL, AND DISPOSITION OF YOU AND YOUR SPOUSE OR THE SOLE MANAGEMENT, CONTROL, AND DISPOSITION OF YOUR SPOUSE ALONE. IN THAT EVENT, YOU WILL LOSE YOUR MANAGEMENT RIGHTS OVER THE PROPERTY. IF YOU DO NOT SIGN THIS AGREEMENT, YOU WILL GENERALLY RETAIN THOSE RIGHTS."

"LOSS OF PROPERTY OWNERSHIP. IF YOU SIGN THIS AGREEMENT AND YOUR MARRIAGE IS SUBSEQUENTLY TERMINATED BY THE DEATH OF EITHER SPOUSE OR BY DIVORCE, ALL OR PART OF THE SEPARATE PROPERTY BEING CONVERTED TO COMMUNITY PROPERTY MAY BECOME THE SOLE PROPERTY OF YOUR SPOUSE OR YOUR SPOUSE'S HEIRS. IF YOU DO NOT SIGN THIS AGREEMENT, YOU GENERALLY CANNOT BE DEPRIVED OF OWNERSHIP OF YOUR SEPARATE PROPERTY ON TERMINATION OF YOUR MARRIAGE, WHETHER BY DEATH OR DIVORCE."

(c) If a proceeding regarding enforcement of an agreement under this subchapter occurs after the death of the spouse against whom enforcement is sought, the proof required by Subsection (a) may be made by an heir of the spouse or the personal representative of the estate of that spouse.

History of Fam. Code §4.205: Acts 1999, 76th Leg., ch. 692, §3, eff. Jan. 1, 2000. Amended by Acts 2003, 78th Leg., ch. 230, §3, eff. Sept. 1, 2003.

See also *O'Connor's Texas Family Law Handbook* (2017), "Contesting enforcement of conversion agreement," ch. 2-D, §4.2.3, p. 178.

ANNOTATIONS

In re Estate of Cunningham, 390 S.W.3d 685, 687 (Tex.App.—Dallas 2012, no pet.). See annotation under Family Code §4.203, p. 56.

FAM §4.206. RIGHTS OF CREDITORS; RECORDING

(a) A conversion of separate property to community property does not affect the rights of a preexisting creditor of the spouse whose separate property is being converted.

(b) A conversion of separate property to community property may be recorded in the deed records of the county in which a spouse resides and of the county in which any real property is located.

(c) A conversion of real property from separate property to community property is constructive notice to a good faith purchaser for value or a creditor without actual notice only if the agreement to convert the prop-

erty is acknowledged and recorded in the deed records of the county in which the real property is located.

History of Fam. Code §4.206: Acts 1999, 76th Leg., ch. 692, §3, eff. Jan. 1, 2000.

CHAPTER 5. HOMESTEAD RIGHTS

SUBCHAPTER A. SALE OF HOMESTEAD; GENERAL RULE

FAM §5.001. SALE, CONVEYANCE, OR ENCUMBRANCE OF HOMESTEAD

Whether the homestead is the separate property of either spouse or community property, neither spouse may sell, convey, or encumber the homestead without the joinder of the other spouse except as provided in this chapter or by other rules of law.

History of Fam. Code §5.001: Acts 1997, 75th Leg., ch. 7, §1, eff. Apr. 17, 1997. Source: Former Fam. Code §5.81.

See also ***O'Connor's Texas Family Law Handbook*** (2017), "Homestead Protections," ch. 2-E, §3, p. 184.

ANNOTATIONS

Benchmark Bank v. Crowder, 919 S.W.2d 657, 662 (Tex.1996). "When a homestead is subject to foreclosure of a federal tax lien on an indebtedness owed by a taxpayer, the taxpayer's spouse, who does not owe any of that indebtedness, has a separate homestead interest and must be compensated for the loss of the homestead estate. [T]he [foreclosing] Bank must compensate [non-debtor spouse] for the loss of her separate, vested interest in the homestead upon foreclosure."

Grissom v. Anderson, 79 S.W.2d 619, 621 (Tex. 1935). "A conveyance by a husband, not joined by his wife, of the homestead property, is merely inoperative while the property continues to be a homestead, or until such time as the homestead may be abandoned, or the deed ratified in accordance with law."

FAM §5.002. SALE OF SEPARATE HOMESTEAD AFTER SPOUSE JUDICIALLY DECLARED INCAPACITATED

If the homestead is the separate property of a spouse and the other spouse has been judicially declared incapacitated by a court exercising original jurisdiction over guardianship and other matters under Title 3, Estates ~~[Chapter XIII, Texas Probate]~~ Code, the owner may sell, convey, or encumber the homestead without the joinder of the other spouse.

History of Fam. Code §5.002: Acts 1997, 75th Leg., ch. 7, §1, eff. Apr. 17, 1997. Amended by Acts 2001, 77th Leg., ch. 217, §25, eff. Sept. 1, 2001; S.B. 1488, §22.014, 85th Leg., eff. Sept. 1, 2017. Source: Former Fam. Code §5.82.

FAM §5.003. SALE OF COMMUNITY HOMESTEAD AFTER SPOUSE JUDICIALLY DECLARED INCAPACITATED

If the homestead is the community property of the spouses and one spouse has been judicially declared incapacitated by a court exercising original jurisdiction over guardianship and other matters under Title 3, Estates ~~[Chapter XIII, Texas Probate]~~ Code, the competent spouse may sell, convey, or encumber the homestead without the joinder of the other spouse.

History of Fam. Code §5.003: Acts 1997, 75th Leg., ch. 7, §1, eff. Apr. 17, 1997. Renumbered from §5.107 and amended by Acts 2001, 77th Leg., ch. 217, §29, eff. Sept. 1, 2001. Amended by S.B. 1488, §22.015, 85th Leg., eff. Sept. 1, 2017. Source: Former Fam. Code §5.84.

Sections 5.004-5.100 reserved for expansion

SUBCHAPTER B. SALE OF HOMESTEAD UNDER UNUSUAL CIRCUMSTANCES

FAM §5.101. SALE OF SEPARATE HOMESTEAD UNDER UNUSUAL CIRCUMSTANCES

If the homestead is the separate property of a spouse, that spouse may file a sworn petition that gives a description of the property, states the facts that make it desirable for the spouse to sell, convey, or encumber the homestead without the joinder of the other spouse, and alleges that the other spouse:

(1) has disappeared and that the location of the spouse remains unknown to the petitioning spouse;

(2) has permanently abandoned the homestead and the petitioning spouse;

(3) has permanently abandoned the homestead and the spouses are permanently separated; or

(4) has been reported by an executive department of the United States to be a prisoner of war or missing on public service of the United States.

History of Fam. Code §5.101: Acts 1997, 75th Leg., ch. 7, §1, eff. Apr. 17, 1997. Amended by Acts 2001, 77th Leg., ch. 217, §26, eff. Sept. 1, 2001. Source: Former Fam. Code §§5.83(a), 5.831(a).

ANNOTATIONS

Caulley v. Caulley, 806 S.W.2d 795, 797 (Tex.1991). "Once homestead rights are shown to exist in property, they are presumed to continue, and anyone asserting abandonment has the burden of proving it by competent evidence."

FAM §5.102. SALE OF COMMUNITY HOMESTEAD UNDER UNUSUAL CIRCUMSTANCES

If the homestead is the community property of the spouses, one spouse may file a sworn petition that gives a description of the property, states the facts that make it desirable for the petitioning spouse to sell, convey, or encumber the homestead without the joinder of the other spouse, and alleges that the other spouse:

(1) has disappeared and that the location of the spouse remains unknown to the petitioning spouse;

(2) has permanently abandoned the homestead and the petitioning spouse;

(3) has permanently abandoned the homestead and the spouses are permanently separated; or

(4) has been reported by an executive department of the United States to be a prisoner of war or missing on public service of the United States.

History of Fam. Code §5.102: Acts 1997, 75th Leg., ch. 7, §1, eff. Apr. 17, 1997. Amended by Acts 2001, 77th Leg., ch. 217, §27, eff. Sept. 1, 2001. Source: Former Fam. Code §§5.85(a), 5.87(a).

FAM §5.103. TIME FOR FILING PETITION

The petitioning spouse may file the petition in a court of the county in which any portion of the property is located not earlier than the 60th day after the date of the occurrence of an event described by Sections 5.101(1)-(3) and 5.102(1)-(3) or not less than six months after the date the other spouse has been reported to be a prisoner of war or missing on public service.

History of Fam. Code §5.103: Acts 1997, 75th Leg., ch. 7, §1, eff. Apr. 17, 1997. Amended by Acts 2001, 77th Leg., ch. 217, §28, eff. Sept. 1, 2001. Source: Former Fam. Code §§5.83(b), 5.831(b), 5.85, 5.87(b).

FAM §5.104. APPOINTMENT OF ATTORNEY

(a) Except as provided by Subsection (b), the court may appoint an attorney in a suit filed under this subchapter for the respondent.

(b) The court shall appoint an attorney in a suit filed under this subchapter for a respondent reported to be a prisoner of war or missing on public service.

(c) The court shall allow a reasonable fee for the appointed attorney's services as a part of the costs of the suit.

History of Fam. Code §5.104: Acts 1997, 75th Leg., ch. 7, §1, eff. Apr. 17, 1997. Source: Former Fam. Code §§5.83(b), 5.831(b), 5.85(b), 5.87(b).

FAM §5.105. CITATION; NOTICE OF HEARING

Citation and notice of hearing for a suit filed as provided by this subchapter shall be issued and served in the manner provided in Subchapter D, Chapter 3.

History of Fam. Code §5.105: Acts 1997, 75th Leg., ch. 7, §1, eff. Apr. 17, 1997. Source: Former Fam. Code §§5.83(b), 5.831(b), 5.85(b), 5.87(b).

FAM §5.106. COURT ORDER

(a) After notice and hearing, the court shall render an order the court deems just and equitable with respect to the sale, conveyance, or encumbrance of a separate property homestead.

(b) After hearing the evidence, the court, on terms the court deems just and equitable, shall render an order describing or defining the community property at issue that will be subject to the management, control, and disposition of each spouse during marriage.

(c) The court may:

(1) impose any conditions and restrictions the court deems necessary to protect the rights of the respondent;

(2) require a bond conditioned on the faithful administration of the property; and

(3) require payment to the registry of the court of all or a portion of the proceeds of the sale of the property to be disbursed in accordance with the court's further directions.

History of Fam. Code §5.106: Acts 1997, 75th Leg., ch. 7, §1, eff. Apr. 17, 1997. Source: Former Fam. Code §§5.83(c), 5.831(c), 5.85(c), 5.87(c).

FAM §5.107. RENUMBERED

Renumbered as §5.003 by Acts 2001, 77th Leg., ch. 217, §29, eff. Sept. 1, 2001.

FAM §5.108. REMEDIES & POWERS CUMULATIVE

The remedies and the powers of a spouse provided by this subchapter are cumulative of the other rights, powers, and remedies afforded the spouses by law.

History of Fam. Code §5.108: Acts 1997, 75th Leg., ch. 7, §1, eff. Apr. 17, 1997. Source: Former Fam. Code §5.86.

SUBTITLE C. DISSOLUTION OF MARRIAGE

CHAPTER 6. SUIT FOR DISSOLUTION OF MARRIAGE

SUBCHAPTER A. GROUNDS FOR DIVORCE & DEFENSES

FAM §6.001. INSUPPORTABILITY

On the petition of either party to a marriage, the court may grant a divorce without regard to fault if the marriage has become insupportable because of discord or conflict of personalities that destroys the legitimate ends of the marital relationship and prevents any reasonable expectation of reconciliation.

History of Fam. Code §6.001: Acts 1997, 75th Leg., ch. 7, §1, eff. Apr. 17, 1997. Source: Former Fam. Code §3.01.

See also *O'Connor's Texas Family Law Handbook* (2017), "Insupportability," ch. 3-A, §4.1.1, p. 222.

ANNOTATIONS

In re Marriage of Wellington, No. 10-07-00181-CV (Tex.App.—Waco 2008, no pet.) (memo op.; 8-27-08). "[H] asserts that [W's] one-word responses ('yes' or 'no') to her attorney's questions [in the face of H's controverting testimony] do not create a record that re-

veals sufficient facts upon which the trial court could have rationally exercised its discretion [under §6.001]. [¶] [T]he decision to protect society's interests by allowing one spouse to seek and be granted a divorce without a showing of fault was made by the Legislature when it enacted the statute establishing insupportability as a grounds. [W]hen the statutory grounds asserted were proven by satisfactory evidence, the trial court had no discretion to deny the divorce."

In re Marriage of Beach, 97 S.W.3d 706, 709 (Tex. App.—Dallas 2003, no pet.). "[W]e hold that a spouse does not have a legal duty to reconcile."

In re Marriage of Richards, 991 S.W.2d 32, 37-38 (Tex.App.—Amarillo 1999, pet. dism'd). The insupportability "ground, also known as no-fault divorce ... has three elements. They are (1) that the marriage has become insupportable because of discord or conflict, (2) that discord or conflict destroys the legitimate ends of the marriage, and (3) there is no reasonable expectation of reconciliation. There is nothing in the language of the statute to support the conclusion that these are not questions of fact. [¶] Even assuming, arguendo, that the trial court's statement that there is 'no defense' to a petition for divorce on the ground of insupportability were a correct statement of the law, that would not relieve the petitioner of his duty to establish the statutory elements with adequate evidence. Any attempt to determine those factual issues without giving [appellant] an opportunity to respond would violate due process. ... While the adoption of 'no-fault' divorce dispenses with any burden to establish the source of the conflict rendering the marriage insupportable, it does not relieve the petitioner of the burden to establish the existence of the statutory elements."

FAM §6.002. CRUELTY

The court may grant a divorce in favor of one spouse if the other spouse is guilty of cruel treatment toward the complaining spouse of a nature that renders further living together insupportable.

History of Fam. Code §6.002: Acts 1997, 75th Leg., ch. 7, §1, eff. Apr. 17, 1997. Source: Former Fam. Code §3.02.

See also *O'Connor's Texas Family Law Handbook* (2017), "Cruelty," ch. 3-A, §4.2.1, p. 223.

ANNOTATIONS

Villalpando v. Villalpando, 480 S.W.3d 801, 805 (Tex.App.—Houston [14th Dist.] 2015, no pet.). "Section 6.002 does not require a trial court to grant a divorce on the basis of cruel treatment even if the record reveals evidence of cruelty. Instead, the trial court has the discretion to choose among reasons supported by the evidence for granting a divorce."

Newberry v. Newberry, 351 S.W.3d 552, 557 (Tex. App.—El Paso 2011, no pet.). "A spouse's conduct rises to the level of cruel treatment when his or her conduct renders the couple's living together insupportable. 'Insupportable' means 'incapable of being borne, unendurable, insufferable, intolerable.' Mere disagreements or trifling matters will not justify granting a divorce for cruelty. If, for instance, the complaining spouse suffers only nervousness or embarrassment, a trial court may not grant the divorce on the ground of cruelty. Abuse need not be limited to bodily injury; nonetheless, physical abuse will support granting a divorce on cruelty grounds. Acts occurring after separation may be used to support a finding of cruelty. [¶] Adultery may be considered to be cruelty sufficient to support the grant of a divorce on that ground. The accumulation of several different acts of cruelty may constitute sufficient grounds on which to grant a divorce." *See also* ***Henry v. Henry***, 48 S.W.3d 468, 473-74 (Tex.App.—Houston [14th Dist.] 2001, no pet.).

FAM §6.003. ADULTERY

The court may grant a divorce in favor of one spouse if the other spouse has committed adultery.

History of Fam. Code §6.003: Acts 1997, 75th Leg., ch. 7, §1, eff. Apr. 17, 1997. Source: Former Fam. Code §3.03.

See also *O'Connor's Texas Family Law Handbook* (2017), "Adultery," ch. 3-A, §4.2.2, p. 224.

ANNOTATIONS

In re Marriage of C.A.S., 405 S.W.3d 373, 383 (Tex.App.—Dallas 2013, no pet.). "Adultery means the 'voluntary sexual intercourse of a married person with one not the spouse.' Adultery is not limited to actions committed before the parties separated."

FAM §6.004. CONVICTION OF FELONY

(a) The court may grant a divorce in favor of one spouse if during the marriage the other spouse:

(1) has been convicted of a felony;

(2) has been imprisoned for at least one year in the Texas Department of Criminal Justice, a federal penitentiary, or the penitentiary of another state; and

(3) has not been pardoned.

(b) The court may not grant a divorce under this section against a spouse who was convicted on the testimony of the other spouse.

History of Fam. Code §6.004: Acts 1997, 75th Leg., ch. 7, §1, eff. Apr. 17, 1997. Amended by Acts 2009, 81st Leg., ch. 87, §25.056, eff. Sept. 1, 2009. Source: Former Fam. Code §3.04.

See also ***O'Connor's Texas Family Law Handbook*** (2017), "Felony conviction," ch. 3-A, §4.2.3, p. 224.

FAM §6.005. ABANDONMENT

The court may grant a divorce in favor of one spouse if the other spouse:

(1) left the complaining spouse with the intention of abandonment; and

(2) remained away for at least one year.

History of Fam. Code §6.005: Acts 1997, 75th Leg., ch. 7, §1, eff. Apr. 17, 1997. Source: Former Fam. Code §3.05.

See also ***O'Connor's Texas Family Law Handbook*** (2017), "Abandonment," ch. 3-A, §4.2.4, p. 224.

FAM §6.006. LIVING APART

The court may grant a divorce in favor of either spouse if the spouses have lived apart without cohabitation for at least three years.

History of Fam. Code §6.006: Acts 1997, 75th Leg., ch. 7, §1, eff. Apr. 17, 1997. Source: Former Fam. Code §3.06.

See also ***O'Connor's Texas Family Law Handbook*** (2017), "Living apart," ch. 3-A, §4.1.2, p. 223.

FAM §6.007. CONFINEMENT IN MENTAL HOSPITAL

The court may grant a divorce in favor of one spouse if at the time the suit is filed:

(1) the other spouse has been confined in a state mental hospital or private mental hospital, as defined in Section 571.003, Health and Safety Code, in this state or another state for at least three years; and

(2) it appears that the hospitalized spouse's mental disorder is of such a degree and nature that adjustment is unlikely or that, if adjustment occurs, a relapse is probable.

History of Fam. Code §6.007: Acts 1997, 75th Leg., ch. 7, §1, eff. Apr. 17, 1997. Source: Former Fam. Code §3.07.

See also ***O'Connor's Texas Family Law Handbook*** (2017), "Confinement in mental hospital," ch. 3-A, §4.1.3, p. 223.

FAM §6.008. DEFENSES

(a) The defenses to a suit for divorce of recrimination and adultery are abolished.

(b) Condonation is a defense to a suit for divorce only if the court finds that there is a reasonable expectation of reconciliation.

History of Fam. Code §6.008: Acts 1997, 75th Leg., ch. 7, §1, eff. Apr. 17, 1997. Source: Former Fam. Code §3.08.

Sections 6.009-6.100 reserved for expansion

SUBCHAPTER B. GROUNDS FOR ANNULMENT

FAM §6.101. REPEALED

Repealed by Acts 2007, 80th Leg., ch. 52, §8, eff. Sept. 1, 2007.

FAM §6.102. ANNULMENT OF MARRIAGE OF PERSON UNDER AGE 18

(a) The court may grant an annulment of a marriage of a person 16 years of age or older but under 18 years of age that occurred without parental consent or without a court order as provided by Subchapters B and E, Chapter 2.

(b) A petition for annulment under this section may be filed by:

(1) a next friend for the benefit of the underage party;

(2) a parent; or

(3) the judicially designated managing conservator or guardian of the person of the underage party, whether an individual, authorized agency, or court.

(c) A suit filed under this subsection by a next friend is barred unless it is filed within 90 days after the date of the marriage.

History of Fam. Code §6.102: Acts 1997, 75th Leg., ch. 7, §1, eff. Apr. 17, 1997. Amended by Acts 2005, 79th Leg., ch. 268, §4.16, eff. Sept. 1, 2005; Acts 2007, 80th Leg., ch. 52, §3, eff. Sept. 1, 2007. Source: Former Fam. Code §2.41(b).

See also ***O'Connor's Texas Family Law Handbook*** (2017), "Suit for Annulment," ch. 3-B, p. 277.

FAM §6.103. UNDERAGE ANNULMENT BARRED BY ADULTHOOD

A suit to annul a marriage may not be filed under Section 6.102 by a parent, managing conservator, or guardian of a person after the 18th birthday of the person.

History of Fam. Code §6.103: Acts 1997, 75th Leg., ch. 7, §1, eff. Apr. 17, 1997. Amended by Acts 2007, 80th Leg., ch. 52, §4, eff. Sept. 1, 2007. Source: Former Fam. Code §2.41(a), (b).

FAM §6.104. DISCRETIONARY ANNULMENT OF UNDERAGE MARRIAGE

(a) An annulment under Section 6.102 of a marriage may be granted at the discretion of the court sitting without a jury.

(b) In exercising its discretion, the court shall consider the pertinent facts concerning the welfare of the parties to the marriage, including whether the female is pregnant.

History of Fam. Code §6.104: Acts 1997, 75th Leg., ch. 7, §1, eff. Apr. 17, 1997. Amended by Acts 2007, 80th Leg., ch. 52, §5, eff. Sept. 1, 2007. Source: Former Fam. Code §2.41(c).

FAM §6.105. UNDER INFLUENCE OF ALCOHOL OR NARCOTICS

The court may grant an annulment of a marriage to a party to the marriage if:

(1) at the time of the marriage the petitioner was under the influence of alcoholic beverages or narcotics and as a result did not have the capacity to consent to the marriage; and

(2) the petitioner has not voluntarily cohabited with the other party to the marriage since the effects of the alcoholic beverages or narcotics ended.

History of Fam. Code §6.105: Acts 1997, 75th Leg., ch. 7, §1, eff. Apr. 17, 1997. Source: Former Fam. Code §2.42.

FAM §6.106. IMPOTENCY

The court may grant an annulment of a marriage to a party to the marriage if:

(1) either party, for physical or mental reasons, was permanently impotent at the time of the marriage;

(2) the petitioner did not know of the impotency at the time of the marriage; and

(3) the petitioner has not voluntarily cohabited with the other party since learning of the impotency.

History of Fam. Code §6.106: Acts 1997, 75th Leg., ch. 7, §1, eff. Apr. 17, 1997. Source: Former Fam. Code §2.43.

FAM §6.107. FRAUD, DURESS, OR FORCE

The court may grant an annulment of a marriage to a party to the marriage if:

(1) the other party used fraud, duress, or force to induce the petitioner to enter into the marriage; and

(2) the petitioner has not voluntarily cohabited with the other party since learning of the fraud or since being released from the duress or force.

History of Fam. Code §6.107: Acts 1997, 75th Leg., ch. 7, §1, eff. Apr. 17, 1997. Source: Former Fam. Code §2.44.

ANNOTATIONS

Desta v. Anyaoha, 371 S.W.3d 596, 599 (Tex. App.—Dallas 2012, no pet.). "Wife [argues] that fraud to secure a marriage for immigration purposes and misrepresentations concerning love, affection, and a desire for children do not affect the 'essentials of a marital relationship.' In so doing, Wife not only seeks to have us impose an additional standard beyond what the statute requires, but also delineate the boundaries of what such an amorphous standard might entail. [¶] We decline this invitation to expand the scope of §6.107 to impose more than what the statute requires." *See also* ***Manjlai v. Manjlai***, 447 S.W.3d 376, 380-81 (Tex.App.—Houston [14th Dist.] 2014, pet. denied) (annulment was properly granted based on H's use of fraud to induce W to enter marriage so H could obtain green card).

Leax v. Leax, 305 S.W.3d 22, 30 (Tex.App.—Houston [1st Dist.] 2009, pet. denied). "Several courts [outside of Texas] have held that the nondisclosure of a prior marriage and divorce does not qualify as an extreme enough fraud to annul a marriage. *At 31:* [But] the extreme number of [W's five] concealed previous marriages was sufficient to justify annulment based on [W's] use of fraud 'to induce [H] to enter into the marriage' under §6.107…."

Coulter v. Melady, 489 S.W.2d 156, 158 (Tex. App.—Texarkana 1972, writ ref'd n.r.e.). "Want of consent to marriage, standing alone, is not listed in the Family Code as a cause that renders a marriage either void or voidable. Nevertheless this court is persuaded that free consent and agreement of the parties is essential to a valid ceremonial marriage. … A party's knowing compliance with the Code's requirements … evidences voluntary consent to marriage and by force of law is conclusive that such party voluntarily consented. And such marriage may be annulled only when it is judicially ascertained to be void or voidable for a reason listed in the statutes."

FAM §6.108. MENTAL INCAPACITY

(a) The court may grant an annulment of a marriage to a party to the marriage on the suit of the party or the party's guardian or next friend, if the court finds it to be in the party's best interest to be represented by a guardian or next friend, if:

(1) at the time of the marriage the petitioner did not have the mental capacity to consent to marriage or to understand the nature of the marriage ceremony because of a mental disease or defect; and

(2) since the marriage ceremony, the petitioner has not voluntarily cohabited with the other party during a period when the petitioner possessed the mental capacity to recognize the marriage relationship.

(b) The court may grant an annulment of a marriage to a party to the marriage if:

(1) at the time of the marriage the other party did not have the mental capacity to consent to marriage or to understand the nature of the marriage ceremony because of a mental disease or defect;

(2) at the time of the marriage the petitioner neither knew nor reasonably should have known of the mental disease or defect; and

(3) since the date the petitioner discovered or reasonably should have discovered the mental disease or defect, the petitioner has not voluntarily cohabited with the other party.

History of Fam. Code §6.108: Acts 1997, 75th Leg., ch. 7, §1, eff. Apr. 17, 1997. Source: Former Fam. Code §2.45.

FAM §6.109. CONCEALED DIVORCE

(a) The court may grant an annulment of a marriage to a party to the marriage if:

(1) the other party was divorced from a third party within the 30-day period preceding the date of the marriage ceremony;

(2) at the time of the marriage ceremony the petitioner did not know, and a reasonably prudent person would not have known, of the divorce; and

(3) since the petitioner discovered or a reasonably prudent person would have discovered the fact of the divorce, the petitioner has not voluntarily cohabited with the other party.

(b) A suit may not be brought under this section after the first anniversary of the date of the marriage.

History of Fam. Code §6.109: Acts 1997, 75th Leg., ch. 7, §1, eff. Apr. 17, 1997. Source: Former Fam. Code §2.46.

FAM §6.110. MARRIAGE LESS THAN 72 HOURS AFTER ISSUANCE OF LICENSE

(a) The court may grant an annulment of a marriage to a party to the marriage if the marriage ceremony took place in violation of Section 2.204 during the 72-hour period immediately following the issuance of the marriage license.

(b) A suit may not be brought under this section after the 30th day after the date of the marriage.

History of Fam. Code §6.110: Acts 1997, 75th Leg., ch. 7, §1, eff. Apr. 17, 1997. Source: Former Fam. Code §2.48.

Ⓐ FAM §6.111. DEATH OF PARTY TO VOIDABLE MARRIAGE

Except as provided by Subchapter C, Chapter 123, Estates [~~Section 47A, Texas Probate~~] Code, a marriage subject to annulment may not be challenged in a proceeding instituted after the death of either party to the marriage.

History of Fam. Code §6.111: Acts 1997, 75th Leg., ch. 7, §1, eff. Apr. 17, 1997. Amended by Acts 2007, 80th Leg., ch. 1170, §4.03, eff. Sept. 1, 2007; S.B. 1488, §22.016, 85th Leg., eff. Sept. 1, 2017. Source: Former Fam. Code §2.47.

Sections 6.112-6.200 reserved for expansion

SUBCHAPTER C. DECLARING A MARRIAGE VOID

FAM §6.201. CONSANGUINITY

A marriage is void if one party to the marriage is related to the other as:

(1) an ancestor or descendant, by blood or adoption;

(2) a brother or sister, of the whole or half blood or by adoption;

(3) a parent's brother or sister, of the whole or half blood or by adoption; or

(4) a son or daughter of a brother or sister, of the whole or half blood or by adoption.

History of Fam. Code §6.201: Acts 1997, 75th Leg., ch. 7, §1, eff. Apr. 17, 1997. Source: Former Fam. Code §2.21.

See also *O'Connor's Texas Family Law Handbook* (2017), "Incest," ch. 3-C, §3.1, p. 287.

FAM §6.202. MARRIAGE DURING EXISTENCE OF PRIOR MARRIAGE

(a) A marriage is void if entered into when either party has an existing marriage to another person that has not been dissolved by legal action or terminated by the death of the other spouse.

(b) The later marriage that is void under this section becomes valid when the prior marriage is dissolved if, after the date of the dissolution, the parties have lived together as husband and wife and represented themselves to others as being married.

History of Fam. Code §6.202: Acts 1997, 75th Leg., ch. 7, §1, eff. Apr. 17, 1997. Source: Former Fam. Code §2.22.

See also *O'Connor's Texas Family Law Handbook* (2017), "Bigamy," ch. 3-C, §3.2, p. 288.

ANNOTATIONS

Loera v. Loera, 815 S.W.2d 910, 911 (Tex.App.—Corpus Christi 1991, no writ). The most recent marriage "places the burden of proof on appellee to establish (1) the prior marriage and (2) its continuing validity at the time of the subsequent marriage. Because the presumption is, in itself, considered evidence, the party attacking the validity of the marriage has a burden to 'introduce sufficient evidence, standing alone, to negate the dissolution of the prior marriage.'"

FAM §6.203. CERTAIN VOID MARRIAGES VALIDATED

Except for a marriage that would have been void under Section 6.201, a marriage that was entered into before January 1, 1970, in violation of the prohibitions of Article 496, Penal Code of Texas, 1925, is validated from

the date the marriage commenced if the parties continued until January 1, 1970, to live together as husband and wife and to represent themselves to others as being married.

History of Fam. Code §6.203: Acts 1997, 75th Leg., ch. 7, §1, eff. Apr. 17, 1997. Source: Former Fam. Code §2.23.

FAM §6.204. RECOGNITION OF SAME-SEX MARRIAGE OR CIVIL UNION

In ***Obergefell v. Hodges***, *___ U.S. ___, 135 S.Ct. 2584 (2015), the U.S. Supreme Court held that same-sex couples may exercise the fundamental right to marry in all states, and that there is no lawful basis for a state to refuse to recognize a lawful same-sex marriage performed in another state on the ground of its same-sex character. See annotation below.*

(a) In this section, "civil union" means any relationship status other than marriage that:

(1) is intended as an alternative to marriage or applies primarily to cohabitating persons; and

(2) grants to the parties of the relationship legal protections, benefits, or responsibilities granted to the spouses of a marriage.

(b) A marriage between persons of the same sex or a civil union is contrary to the public policy of this state and is void in this state.

(c) The state or an agency or political subdivision of the state may not give effect to a:

(1) public act, record, or judicial proceeding that creates, recognizes, or validates a marriage between persons of the same sex or a civil union in this state or in any other jurisdiction; or

(2) right or claim to any legal protection, benefit, or responsibility asserted as a result of a marriage between persons of the same sex or a civil union in this state or in any other jurisdiction.

History of Fam. Code §6.204: Acts 2003, 78th Leg., ch. 124, §1, eff. Sept. 1, 2003.

ANNOTATIONS

Obergefell v. Hodges, ___ U.S. ___, 135 S.Ct. 2584, 2604-05 (2015). "[T]he right to marry is a fundamental right inherent in the liberty of the person, and under the Due Process and Equal Protection Clauses of the 14th Amendment couples of the same-sex may not be deprived of that right and that liberty. The Court now holds that same-sex couples may exercise the fundamental right to marry. [T]he State laws challenged by Petitioners … are now held invalid to the extent they exclude same-sex couples from civil marriage on the same terms and conditions as opposite-sex couples. *At 2607-08:* The Court, in this decision, holds same-sex couples may exercise the fundamental right to marry in all States. It follows that the Court also must hold—and it now does hold—that there is no lawful basis for a State to refuse to recognize a lawful same-sex marriage performed in another State on the ground of its same-sex character."

De Leon v. Abbott, 791 F.3d 619, 625 (5th Cir.2015). "In response to ***Obergefell*** [***v. Hodges***, ___ U.S. ___, 135 S.Ct. 2584 (2015)], … the district court *a quo* issued a one-paragraph order … stating that it 'hereby … enjoins [the State] from enforcing [Tex. Const.] Art. 1, §32 …, any related provisions in the Texas Family Code, and any other laws or regulations prohibiting a person from marrying another person of the same sex or recognizing same-sex marriage.' [T]he preliminary injunction is AFFIRMED." *See also* ***Parker v. Pidgeon***, 477 S.W.3d 353, 354-55 (Tex.App.—Houston [14th Dist.] 2015, pet. argued 3-1-17) (interpreting ***De Leon*** as finding Tex. Const. art. 1, §32 and Fam. Code §6.204 unconstitutional and enjoining State from enforcing them).

A FAM §6.205. MARRIAGE TO MINOR

The amended text in §6.205 is effective for marriages entered into on or after Sept. 1, 2017. Marriages entered into before Sept. 1, 2017, are governed by the former law in effect at that time.

A marriage is void if either party to the marriage is younger than 18 [~~16~~] years of age, unless a court order removing the disabilities of minority of the party for general purposes has been obtained in this state or in another state [~~under Section 2.103~~].

History of Fam. Code §6.205: Acts 2005, 79th Leg., ch. 268, §4.17, eff. Sept. 1, 2005. Amended by Acts 2007, 80th Leg., ch. 52, §6, eff. Sept. 1, 2007; S.B. 1705, §5, 85th Leg., eff. Sept. 1, 2017.

See also ***O'Connor's Texas Family Law Handbook*** (2017), "Marriage to minor," ch. 3-C, §3.4, p. 290.

FAM §6.206. MARRIAGE TO STEPCHILD OR STEPPARENT

A marriage is void if a party is a current or former stepchild or stepparent of the other party.

History of Fam. Code §6.206: Acts 2005, 79th Leg., ch. 268, §4.17, eff. Sept. 1, 2005.

See also ***O'Connor's Texas Family Law Handbook*** (2017), "Marriage to stepchild or stepparent," ch. 3-C, §3.5, p. 290.

Sections 6.207-6.300 reserved for expansion

SUBCHAPTER D. JURISDICTION, VENUE, & RESIDENCE QUALIFICATIONS

FAM §6.301. GENERAL RESIDENCY RULE FOR DIVORCE SUIT

A suit for divorce may not be maintained in this state unless at the time the suit is filed either the petitioner or the respondent has been:

(1) a domiciliary of this state for the preceding six-month period; and

(2) a resident of the county in which the suit is filed for the preceding 90-day period.

History of Fam. Code §6.301: Acts 1997, 75th Leg., ch. 7, §1, eff. Apr. 17, 1997. Source: Former Fam. Code §3.21.

See also ***O'Connor's Texas Family Law Handbook*** (2017), "Filing Suit in Proper Court," ch. 3-A, §2, p. 207.

ANNOTATIONS

In re Milton, 420 S.W.3d 245, 252 (Tex.App.—Houston [1st Dist.] 2013, orig. proceeding). Section 6.301 "is not jurisdictional, but it controls a petitioner's right to sue for a divorce; it is a mandatory requirement that cannot be waived. [¶] Typically, when the residency requirements have not been met, the trial court abates the suit so that either the petitioner or the respondent can meet the residency requirements. Once a party files a plea in abatement, the trial court should abate the proceedings until at least one of the parties has completed the mandatory residency requirements. When, however, the record indicates that neither party intends to reside in the county of suit, abating the suit will not cure a failure to meet the residency requirements."

In re Green, 385 S.W.3d 665, 669 (Tex.App.—San Antonio 2012, orig. proceeding). "The test for residence or domicile typically involves an inquiry into a person's intent. When determining where a person resides, volition, intention and action are all elements to be equally considered. In order to be a resident, there must be an intention to establish a permanent domicile or home, and the intention must be accompanied by some act done in the execution of the intent. With regards to a soldier in the military, the soldier does not acquire a new domicile merely by being stationed at a particular place in the line of duty. Rather, a soldier's domicile remains the same as when he or she entered the service, unless proof of clear and unequivocal intention to change domicile is shown. *At 670:* Even if the trial court had found the disputed testimony as to [H's] intent in favor of [W], such intent is not enough to establish Texas as [H's] residence when not accompanied by an act showing such intent." (Internal quotes omitted.)

Griffith v. Griffith, 341 S.W.3d 43, 53 (Tex.App.—San Antonio 2011, no pet.). "[T]he trial court found [W] to be a domiciliary of Texas for the preceding six-month period and a resident of [a Texas] County for the preceding 90-day period. [H argues] that the trial court abused its discretion in finding such because [W] traveled between Texas and Florida [in that same time period]. However, '[t]here are no limits on the number of residences that a party may maintain at any one time.' Thus, there is no abuse of discretion by the trial court in finding that [W] met §6.301's residency requirements." *See also* ***Stallworth v. Stallworth***, 201 S.W.3d 338, 345 (Tex.App.—Dallas 2006, no pet.).

Palau v. Sanchez, No. 03-08-00136-CV (Tex. App.—Austin 2010, pet. denied) (memo op.; 11-10-10). "[S]ection 6.301 [does not require] that a petitioner be a ... citizen of the U.S. or carry a certain type of visa. [In this case, W had a tourist visa, but she] testified that she had lived in a house in Austin [for several years] and that at the time of moving there, she intended to live there. Thus, she satisfies the definition of 'domiciliary.' [Further,] 'a resident is not necessarily either a citizen or a domiciliary.' [W] also satisfies the definition of a 'resident.'"

In re Rowe, 182 S.W.3d 424, 426 (Tex.App.—Eastland 2005, orig. proceeding). "Because §6.301 requires a petitioner to establish residency before filing suit, as opposed to before receiving a divorce, the mere fact that time will pass during the pendency of this proceeding does not deprive relator of the opportunity to appeal the trial court's decision to deny his plea in abatement. Per the plain language of the statute, residency must be established as of the date the suit is filed. Relator can effectively raise this issue on appeal. Therefore, the application of §6.301 alone does not deprive him of an adequate remedy at law. [¶] [T]he Texas Supreme Court has consistently held that ... venue decisions in two-party suits, except for [SAPCRs], are incidental trial rulings correctable by appeal. *At 427:* We conclude ... that mandamus is not available to review the trial court's venue determination...." *But see* ***Cook v. Mayfield***, 886 S.W.2d 840, 841 (Tex.App.—Waco 1994, orig. proceeding) (passage of time will defeat venue argument, making mandamus appropriate).

Gonzales v. Gonzales, No. 12-03-00225-CV (Tex. App.—Tyler 2003, no pet.) (memo op.; 12-23-03). Section 6.301's "residency requirement has been defined as a physical presence in a county, accompanied by a good faith intention to remain and permanently and definitely make that county his home. There is no reason an inmate may not maintain a divorce action in the county where he is imprisoned."

Lutes v. Lutes, 538 S.W.2d 256, 258 (Tex.App.—Houston [14th Dist.] 1976, no writ). Under Fam. Code §3.21, now §6.301, "the petitioner may ... bring suit in either the county of his residence or in that of the respondent's. But the choice of in which of those counties the suit is to be filed is still given to the petitioner."

FAM §6.302. SUIT FOR DIVORCE BY NONRESIDENT SPOUSE

If one spouse has been a domiciliary of this state for at least the last six months, a spouse domiciled in another state or nation may file a suit for divorce in the county in which the domiciliary spouse resides at the time the petition is filed.

History of Fam. Code §6.302: Acts 1997, 75th Leg., ch. 7, §1, eff. Apr. 17, 1997. Source: Former Fam. Code §3.24.

FAM §6.303. ABSENCE ON PUBLIC SERVICE

Time spent by a Texas domiciliary outside this state or outside the county of residence of the domiciliary while in the service of the armed forces or other service of the United States or of this state, or while accompanying the domiciliary's spouse in the spouse's service of the armed forces or other service of the United States or of this state, is considered residence in this state and in that county.

History of Fam. Code §6.303: Acts 1997, 75th Leg., ch. 7, §1, eff. Apr. 17, 1997. Amended by Acts 2011, 82nd Leg., ch. 436, §1, eff. June 17, 2011. Source: Former Fam. Code §3.22.

FAM §6.304. ARMED FORCES PERSONNEL NOT PREVIOUSLY RESIDENTS

A person not previously a resident of this state who is serving in the armed forces of the United States and has been stationed at one or more military installations in this state for at least the last six months and at a military installation in a county of this state for at least the last 90 days, or who is accompanying the person's spouse during the spouse's military service in those locations and for those periods, is considered to be a Texas domiciliary and a resident of that county for those periods for the purpose of filing suit for dissolution of a marriage.

History of Fam. Code §6.304: Acts 1997, 75th Leg., ch. 7, §1, eff. Apr. 17, 1997. Amended by Acts 2011, 82nd Leg., ch. 436, §1, eff. June 17, 2011. Source: Former Fam. Code §3.23.

ANNOTATIONS

Fox v. Fox, 559 S.W.2d 407, 410 (Tex.App.—Austin 1977, no writ). "Divorce jurisdiction is extended to Texas courts regarding military personnel stationed in the state meeting certain requirements, pursuant to [Fam. Code] §3.23 [now §6.304]. Even though the spouses are domiciled in different states, a Texas court may grant an *ex parte* divorce under [§3.23] if one of the parties falls within the statute."

FAM §6.305. ACQUIRING JURISDICTION OVER NONRESIDENT RESPONDENT

(a) If the petitioner in a suit for dissolution of a marriage is a resident or a domiciliary of this state at the time the suit for dissolution is filed, the court may exercise personal jurisdiction over the respondent or over the respondent's personal representative although the respondent is not a resident of this state if:

(1) this state is the last marital residence of the petitioner and the respondent and the suit is filed before the second anniversary of the date on which marital residence ended; or

(2) there is any basis consistent with the constitutions of this state and the United States for the exercise of the personal jurisdiction.

(b) A court acquiring jurisdiction under this section also acquires jurisdiction over the respondent in a suit affecting the parent-child relationship.

History of Fam. Code §6.305: Acts 1997, 75th Leg., ch. 7, §1, eff. Apr. 17, 1997. Source: Former Fam. Code §3.26.

See also ***O'Connor's Texas Family Law Handbook*** (2017), "Filing Suit in Proper Court," ch. 3-A, §2, p. 207.

ANNOTATIONS

Dawson-Austin v. Austin, 968 S.W.2d 319, 326 (Tex.1998). "The U.S. Constitution permits 'a state court [to] take personal jurisdiction over a defendant only if it has some minimum, purposeful contacts with the state, and the exercise of jurisdiction will not offend traditional notions of fair play and substantial justice.' *At 327:* In the present case, the location in Texas of property that either is or is claimed to be part of the marital estate does not supply the minimum contacts required for the court to exercise jurisdiction over [W]. ... We do not believe that one spouse may leave the other, move to another state in which neither has ever lived, buy a home or open a bank account or store a

stock certificate there, and by those unilateral actions, and nothing more, compel the other spouse to litigate their divorce in the new domicile consistent with due process. One spouse cannot, solely by actions in which the other spouse is not involved, create the contacts between a state and the other spouse necessary for jurisdiction over a divorce action."

Aduli v. Aduli, 368 S.W.3d 805, 816 (Tex.App.—Houston [14th Dist.] 2012, no pet.). "A single act can support jurisdiction as long as there is a substantial connection with the forum state. However, a single act or occasional acts may be insufficient to establish jurisdiction if the nature, quality, and circumstances surrounding their commission only create an attenuated connection with the state, diminishing reasonable foreseeability of litigation in the forum state." *See also* ***Reynolds v. Reynolds***, 2 S.W.3d 429, 431 (Tex.App.—Houston [1st Dist.] 1999, no pet.).

Goodenbour v. Goodenbour, 64 S.W.3d 69, 76-77 (Tex.App.—Austin 2001, pet. denied). "In applying the term 'last marital residence,' we should acknowledge that more and more frequently one spouse may, by choice or necessity, work in a state or country apart from the family unit for a period of time. A work separation, where spouses live apart to pursue professional opportunities, must be distinguished from a marital separation when spouses have decided to dissolve their marriage. Much as a military member may be on temporary assignment elsewhere, one spouse may, for a time, pursue a work assignment away from the other family members. The family decision to endure a work separation may include consideration of what schooling or other opportunities are best for the children. Because the family has made the decision to remain an intact unit, the fact that the spouses live apart does not mean that a marital residence no longer exists. As long as the parties choose to maintain a marriage, there will be a marital residence somewhere."

Bloom v. Bloom, 935 S.W.2d 942, 948 (Tex. App.—San Antonio 1996, no writ). "[W] does not contest the trial court's subject matter jurisdiction over the divorce proceeding. She does, however, contend that the trial court lacked subject matter jurisdiction to determine child visitation and custody, child support, and the division of marital property. What [W] fails to recognize is that the two are inextricably interrelated. The trial court acquires subject matter jurisdiction over a divorce proceeding if the suit is filed by a qualified resident, 'this state is the last marital residence of the petitioner and the respondent,' and 'the suit is commenced within two years after the date on which the marital residence ended.' And, once the trial court acquires subject matter jurisdiction in this manner, it 'shall' divide the community estate. Additionally, a trial court that obtains subject matter jurisdiction under [Fam. Code] §3.26(a) [now §6.305] 'also acquires jurisdiction over the respondent in a [SAPCR],' including jurisdiction 'to make a child custody determination by initial decree … if … this state … is the home state of the child on the date of the commencement of the proceeding….'"

Hoffman v. Hoffman, 821 S.W.2d 3, 5 (Tex.App.—Fort Worth 1992, no writ). "Where the trial court in a divorce proceeding has no personal jurisdiction over the respondent, the trial court has the jurisdiction to grant the divorce, but not to determine the managing conservatorship of children or divide property outside the State of Texas. It may also lack jurisdiction to divide property within the state."

FAM §6.306. JURISDICTION TO ANNUL MARRIAGE

(a) A suit for annulment of a marriage may be maintained in this state only if the parties were married in this state or if either party is domiciled in this state.

(b) A suit for annulment is a suit in rem, affecting the status of the parties to the marriage.

History of Fam. Code §6.306: Acts 1997, 75th Leg., ch. 7, §1, eff. Apr. 17, 1997. Source: Former Fam. Code §3.25.

FAM §6.307. JURISDICTION TO DECLARE MARRIAGE VOID

(a) Either party to a marriage made void by this chapter may sue to have the marriage declared void, or the court may declare the marriage void in a collateral proceeding.

(b) The court may declare a marriage void only if:

(1) the purported marriage was contracted in this state; or

(2) either party is domiciled in this state.

(c) A suit to have a marriage declared void is a suit in rem, affecting the status of the parties to the purported marriage.

History of Fam. Code §6.307: Acts 1997, 75th Leg., ch. 7, §1, eff. Apr. 17, 1997. Source: Former Fam. Code §§2.24, 3.25.

FAM §6.308. EXERCISING PARTIAL JURISDICTION

(a) A court in which a suit for dissolution of a marriage is filed may exercise its jurisdiction over those portions of the suit for which it has authority.

(b) The court's authority to resolve the issues in controversy between the parties may be restricted because the court lacks:

(1) the required personal jurisdiction over a nonresident party in a suit for dissolution of the marriage;

(2) the required jurisdiction under Chapter 152; or

(3) the required jurisdiction under Chapter 159.

History of Fam. Code §6.308: Acts 1997, 75th Leg., ch. 7, §1, eff. Apr. 17, 1997.

ANNOTATIONS

Dawson-Austin v. Austin, 968 S.W.2d 319, 324 (Tex.1998). "The cases that hold adjudication of divorce and division of the marital estate to be non-severable claims all do so in the context of [TRCP] 41 ('Misjoinder and Non-Joinder of Parties'), 174 ('Consolidation; Separate Trials'), and 320 ('Motion [for New Trial] and Action of Court Thereon'). [¶] No case holds that claims of divorce and division of property do not involve severable *jurisdictional* issues. The U.S. Supreme Court recognized long ago that a court could have jurisdiction to grant a divorce—an adjudication of parties' status—without having jurisdiction to divide their property—an adjudication of parties' rights."

Sections 6.309-6.400 reserved for expansion

SUBCHAPTER E. FILING SUIT

FAM §6.401. CAPTION

(a) Pleadings in a suit for divorce or annulment shall be styled "In the Matter of the Marriage of __________ and __________."

(b) Pleadings in a suit to declare a marriage void shall be styled "A Suit To Declare Void the Marriage of __________ and __________."

History of Fam. Code §6.401: Acts 1997, 75th Leg., ch. 7, §1, eff. Apr. 17, 1997. Source: Former Fam. Code §3.51.

See also *O'Connor's Texas Family Law Handbook* (2017), "Contents of petition," ch. 3-A, §5.4, p. 225; "Contents of petition," ch. 3-C, §4.4, p. 290.

FAM §6.402. PLEADINGS

(a) A petition in a suit for dissolution of a marriage is sufficient without the necessity of specifying the underlying evidentiary facts if the petition alleges the grounds relied on substantially in the language of the statute.

(b) Allegations of grounds for relief, matters of defense, or facts relied on for a temporary order that are stated in short and plain terms are not subject to special exceptions because of form or sufficiency.

(c) The court shall strike an allegation of evidentiary fact from the pleadings on the motion of a party or on the court's own motion.

History of Fam. Code §6.402: Acts 1997, 75th Leg., ch. 7, §1, eff. Apr. 17, 1997. Source: Former Fam. Code §3.52.

ANNOTATIONS

In re Marriage of Richards, 991 S.W.2d 32, 36 (Tex.App.—Amarillo 1999, pet. dism'd). "The thrust of [W's] argument is that [§6.402(b)] denies her a legal and factual test of [H's] pleadings before trial[;] therefore [W] is denied honest and fair adjudication of her defense that [H's] facts do not support his allegations. [¶] [W] presents no argument showing that she could not obtain the facts necessary for her defense through discovery, or that summary judgment did not provide an adequate method to avoid the burdens of trial if the facts did not support the action asserted. Because these procedures were available to her, §6.402 … neither denies her access to the courts of this state or deprives her of equal protection of the laws." (Internal quotes omitted.)

FAM §6.403. ANSWER

The respondent in a suit for dissolution of a marriage is not required to answer on oath or affirmation.

History of Fam. Code §6.403: Acts 1997, 75th Leg., ch. 7, §1, eff. Apr. 17, 1997. Source: Former Fam. Code §3.53.

ANNOTATIONS

Considine v. Considine, 726 S.W.2d 253, 254 (Tex. App.—Austin 1987, no writ). "In the usual case, the defendant who fails to file an answer is said to confess to the facts properly pleaded in the petition. In such a case, the non-answering defendant cannot mount an evidentiary attack against the judgment on motion for new trial or on appeal. [¶] In a divorce case, however, the petition is not taken as confessed for want of an answer. Even if the respondent fails to file an answer, the petitioner must adduce proof to support the material allegations in the petition. Accordingly, the judgment of divorce is subject to an evidentiary attack on motion for new trial and appeal."

FAM §6.4035. WAIVER OF SERVICE

(a) A party to a suit for the dissolution of a marriage may waive the issuance or service of process after

the suit is filed by filing with the clerk of the court in which the suit is filed the waiver of the party acknowledging receipt of a copy of the filed petition.

(b) The waiver must contain the mailing address of the party who executed the waiver.

(c) Notwithstanding Section 132.001, Civil Practice and Remedies Code, the waiver must be sworn before a notary public who is not an attorney in the suit. This subsection does not apply if the party executing the waiver is incarcerated.

(d) The Texas Rules of Civil Procedure do not apply to a waiver executed under this section.

(e) The party executing the waiver may not sign the waiver using a digitized signature.

(f) For purposes of this section, "digitized signature" has the meaning assigned by Section 101.0096.

History of Fam. Code §6.4035: Acts 1997, 75th Leg., ch. 614, §1, eff. Sept. 1, 1997. Amended by Acts 2013, 83rd Leg., ch. 916, §2, eff. Sept. 1, 2013; Acts 2015, 84th Leg., ch. 198, §1, eff. Sept. 1, 2015.

FAM §6.404. INFORMATION REGARDING PROTECTIVE ORDERS

At any time while a suit for dissolution of a marriage is pending, if the court believes, on the basis of any information received by the court, that a party to the suit or a member of the party's family or household may be a victim of family violence, the court shall inform that party of the party's right to apply for a protective order under Title 4.

History of Fam. Code §6.404: Acts 2005, 79th Leg., ch. 361, §2, eff. June 17, 2005.

History of Former Fam. Code §6.404: Repealed by Acts 2003, 78th Leg., ch. 1313, §1, eff. Sept. 1, 2003.

A FAM §6.405. PROTECTIVE ORDER & RELATED ORDERS

The amended text in §6.405 is effective for petitions filed on or after Sept. 1, 2017. Petitions filed before Sept. 1, 2017, are governed by the former law in effect at that time.

(a) The petition in a suit for dissolution of a marriage must state whether, in regard to a party to the suit or a child of a party to the suit:

(1) there is in effect:

(A) a protective order under Title 4;

(B) a protective order under Chapter 7A, Code of Criminal Procedure; or

(C) an order for emergency protection under Article 17.292, Code of Criminal Procedure; [~~is in effect~~] or

(2) [~~if~~] an application for an [~~a protective~~] order described by Subdivision (1) is pending [~~with regard to the parties to the suit~~].

(b) The petitioner shall attach to the petition a copy of each [~~protective~~] order described by Subsection (a)(1) [~~issued under Title 4~~] in which a party [~~one of the parties~~] to the suit or the child of a party to the suit was the applicant or victim of the conduct alleged in the application or order and the other party was the respondent or defendant of an action regarding the conduct alleged in the application or order without regard to the date of the order. If a copy of the [~~protective~~] order is not available at the time of filing, the petition must state that a copy of the order will be filed with the court before any hearing.

History of Fam. Code §6.405: Acts 1997, 75th Leg., ch. 7, §1, eff. Apr. 17, 1997. Amended by Acts 1999, 76th Leg., ch. 62, §6.04, eff. Sept. 1, 1999; H.B. 3052, §1, 85th Leg., eff. Sept. 1, 2017. Source: Former Fam. Code §3.522.

FAM §6.406. MANDATORY JOINDER OF SUIT AFFECTING PARENT-CHILD RELATIONSHIP

(a) The petition in a suit for dissolution of a marriage shall state whether there are children born or adopted of the marriage who are under 18 years of age or who are otherwise entitled to support as provided by Chapter 154.

(b) If the parties are parents of a child, as defined by Section 101.003, and the child is not under the continuing jurisdiction of another court as provided by Chapter 155, the suit for dissolution of a marriage must include a suit affecting the parent-child relationship under Title 5.

History of Fam. Code §6.406: Acts 1997, 75th Leg., ch. 7, §1, eff. Apr. 17, 1997. Source: Former Fam. Code §3.55(a), (b).

See also *O'Connor's Texas Family Law Handbook* (2017), "Filing SAPCR with dissolution suit," ch. 4-A, §3.3, p. 347.

ANNOTATIONS

In re B.T.G., 494 S.W.3d 839, 842 (Tex.App.—Dallas 2016, no pet.). Section 6.406's "specific mandate, without limitation, that the divorce and SAPCR must be joined controls and means the two suits cannot be severed. '[T]he Family Code operates as a statutory trump to the procedural rules,' and a trial court is unable to sever a divorce from a SAPCR. A severance splits a single suit into two or more independent actions, each action resulting in an appealable final judgment. Thus, a severance is the opposite of what the family code requires when it mandates that a divorce suit must include a SAPCR."

Osteen v. Osteen, 999 S.W.2d 28, 29 (Tex.App.—Houston [14th Dist.] 1999, no pet.). "If there are children of the marriage, and the children are not under the continuing jurisdiction of any other court, the code requires the suit for divorce to include a [SAPCR]. However, if a [SAPCR] is filed separately from a suit for divorce, the district court that handles the divorce action will acquire dominant jurisdiction over the parent-child suit."

In re Marriage of Morales, 968 S.W.2d 508, 511 (Tex.App.—Corpus Christi 1998, no pet.). "A divorce case involving children of the marriage actually constitutes two separate and distinct lawsuits. Thus, when the parties to a divorce action are *parents* of a child, the suit for dissolution of the marriage must include a [SAPCR] under [Fam. Code] Title 5."

FAM §6.407. TRANSFER OF SUIT AFFECTING PARENT-CHILD RELATIONSHIP TO DIVORCE COURT

(a) If a suit affecting the parent-child relationship is pending at the time the suit for dissolution of a marriage is filed, the suit affecting the parent-child relationship shall be transferred as provided by Section 103.002 to the court in which the suit for dissolution is filed.

(b) If the parties are parents of a child, as defined by Section 101.003, and the child is under the continuing jurisdiction of another court under Chapter 155, either party to the suit for dissolution of a marriage may move that court for transfer of the suit affecting the parent-child relationship to the court having jurisdiction of the suit for dissolution. The court with continuing jurisdiction shall transfer the proceeding as provided by Chapter 155. On the transfer of the proceedings, the court with jurisdiction of the suit for dissolution of a marriage shall consolidate the two causes of action.

(c) After transfer of a suit affecting the parent-child relationship as provided in Chapter 155, the court with jurisdiction of the suit for dissolution of a marriage has jurisdiction to render an order in the suit affecting the parent-child relationship as provided by Title 5.

History of Fam. Code §6.407: Acts 1997, 75th Leg., ch. 7, §1, eff. Apr. 17, 1997. Source: Former Fam. Code §3.55(b)-(d).

See also ***O'Connor's Texas Family Law Handbook*** (2017), "Challenging Venue," ch. 4-B, §3, p. 350.

ANNOTATIONS

Neal v. Avey, 853 S.W.2d 707, 709 (Tex.App.—Houston [14th Dist.] 1993, writ denied). "If the children are under the continuing jurisdiction of a court under a parent-child suit, [Fam. Code] §3.55(c) [now §6.407] allows either of the parties to the divorce to move the court where the parent-child suit is pending for transfer of that suit to the court having jurisdiction of the divorce. Upon proper motion and showing that venue is proper in another county, this transfer is mandatory."

Garza v. Texas DHS, 757 S.W.2d 44, 46-47 (Tex.App.—San Antonio 1988, writ denied). Held: Trial court has discretion to deny motion to transfer when mandatory transfer provisions are abused.

Ortiz v. Aranda, 716 S.W.2d 692, 693 (Tex.App.—Corpus Christi 1986, no writ). "The suit for divorce was filed in the 225th District Court and the motion to modify child custody was filed in the 150th District Court. The 150th District Court was the court of continuing jurisdiction over the child.... The motion to modify stated that a divorce action had been filed, and requested the 150th District Court to consolidate the two actions. Neither an order of transfer nor an order of consolidation is in the record. [¶] [T]he decree of divorce ... was entered by the 225th District Court.... [¶] We have determined ... that the divorce decree is void insofar as it purports to modify the conservatorship of the child. The decree recites on its face that it was entered by the 225th District Court, and the record contains no transfer of the modification action from the 150th District Court as required by [Fam. Code] §3.55(c) [now §6.407]."

FAM §6.408. SERVICE OF CITATION

Citation on the filing of an original petition in a suit for dissolution of a marriage shall be issued and served as in other civil cases. Citation may also be served on any other person who has or who may assert an interest in the suit for dissolution of the marriage.

History of Fam. Code §6.408: Acts 1997, 75th Leg., ch. 7, §1, eff. Apr. 17, 1997.

See also ***O'Connor's Texas Family Law Handbook*** (2017), "Service of Process," ch. 3-A, §8, p. 233.

ANNOTATIONS

Ackerly v. Ackerly, 13 S.W.3d 454, 457-58 (Tex.App.—Corpus Christi 2000, no pet.). "In the present case [involving a motion for reduction to money judgment under Fam. Code §9.010], the record contains no indication of service by citation. The docket sheet reflects no citation was ever issued, served, or returned for filing with the court. The only indication of any notice to [respondent] is a 'Certificate of Service' in the

motion, which was signed by counsel, and states, 'this will certify that a copy of the above and foregoing has been mailed to Respondent at his last known address on this 26 day of June, 1998.' This notice does not comply with the citation requirements set forth in the [TRCPs]. Therefore, the default judgment is not supported by proper service of process."

Avila v. Avila, 843 S.W.2d 280, 281 (Tex.App.—El Paso 1992, no writ). "There are no presumptions in favor of valid issuance, service and return of citation in this situation. Moreover, failure to affirmatively show strict compliance with the [TRCPs] renders the attempted service of process invalid and of no effect."

FAM §6.409. CITATION BY PUBLICATION

(a) Citation in a suit for dissolution of a marriage may be by publication as in other civil cases, except that notice shall be published one time only.

(b) The notice shall be sufficient if given in substantially the following form:

"STATE OF TEXAS

To (name of person to be served with citation), and to all whom it may concern (if the name of any person to be served with citation is unknown), Respondent(s),

"You have been sued. You may employ an attorney. If you or your attorney do not file a written answer with the clerk who issued this citation by 10 a.m. on the Monday next following the expiration of 20 days after you were served this citation and petition, a default judgment may be taken against you. The petition of __________, Petitioner, was filed in the Court of __________ County, Texas, on the ______ day of __________, against __________, Respondent(s), numbered ______, and entitled 'In the Matter of Marriage of __________ and __________. The suit requests __________ (statement of relief sought).'

"The Court has authority in this suit to enter any judgment or decree dissolving the marriage and providing for the division of property that will be binding on you.

"Issued and given under my hand and seal of said Court at __________, Texas, this the ______ day of __________, ______.

"
____

Clerk of the __________ Court of

__________ County, Texas

By ______, Deputy."

(c) The form authorized in this section and the form authorized by Section 102.010 may be combined in appropriate situations.

(d) If the citation is for a suit in which a parent-child relationship does not exist, service by publication may be completed by posting the citation at the courthouse door for seven days in the county in which the suit is filed.

(e) If the petitioner or the petitioner's attorney of record makes an oath that no child presently under 18 years of age was born or adopted by the spouses and that no appreciable amount of property was accumulated by the spouses during the marriage, the court may dispense with the appointment of an attorney ad litem. In a case in which citation was by publication, a statement of the evidence, approved and signed by the judge, shall be filed with the papers of the suit as a part of the record.

History of Fam. Code §6.409: Acts 1997, 75th Leg., ch. 7, §1, eff. Apr. 17, 1997. Source: Former Fam. Code §3.521.

ANNOTATIONS

In re A.Y., 16 S.W.3d 387, 389 (Tex.App.—El Paso 2000, no pet.). "The Family Code allows for citation by publication as in other civil cases. Therefore, the [TRCPs] apply and [TRCP] 116 makes citation by publication proper if published in the county where suit is pending." *See also* ***Jones v. Jones***, No. 09-06-238-CV (Tex.App.—Beaumont 2007, no pet.) (memo op.; 8-16-07) (analyzing facts under TRCP 244 in addition to Fam. Code §6.409(e)).

FAM §6.410. REPORT TO ACCOMPANY PETITION

At the time a petition for divorce or annulment of a marriage is filed, the petitioner shall also file a completed report that may be used by the district clerk, at the time the petition is granted, to comply with Section 194.002, Health and Safety Code.

History of Fam. Code §6.410: Acts 2003, 78th Leg., ch. 1128, §4, eff. Sept. 1, 2003.

FAM §6.411. CONFIDENTIALITY OF PLEADINGS

(a) This section applies only in a county with a population of 3.4 million or more.

(b) Except as otherwise provided by law, all pleadings and other documents filed with the court in a suit for dissolution of a marriage are confidential, are excepted from required public disclosure under Chapter 552, Government Code, and may not be released to a

person who is not a party to the suit until after the date of service of citation or the 31st day after the date of filing the suit, whichever date is sooner.

History of Fam. Code §6.411: Acts 2003, 78th Leg., ch. 1314, §1, eff. Sept. 1, 2003. Renumbered from §6.410 by Acts 2005, 79th Leg., ch. 728, §23.001(24), eff. Sept. 1, 2005.

Sections 6.412-6.500 reserved for expansion

SUBCHAPTER F. TEMPORARY ORDERS

FAM §6.501. TEMPORARY RESTRAINING ORDER

(a) After the filing of a suit for dissolution of a marriage, on the motion of a party or on the court's own motion, the court may grant a temporary restraining order without notice to the adverse party for the preservation of the property and for the protection of the parties as necessary, including an order prohibiting one or both parties from:

(1) intentionally communicating in person or in any other manner, including by telephone or another electronic voice transmission, video chat, in writing, or electronic messaging, with the other party by use of vulgar, profane, obscene, or indecent language or in a coarse or offensive manner, with intent to annoy or alarm the other party;

(2) threatening the other party in person or in any other manner, including by telephone or another electronic voice transmission, video chat, in writing, or electronic messaging, to take unlawful action against any person, intending by this action to annoy or alarm the other party;

(3) placing a telephone call, anonymously, at an unreasonable hour, in an offensive and repetitious manner, or without a legitimate purpose of communication with the intent to annoy or alarm the other party;

(4) intentionally, knowingly, or recklessly causing bodily injury to the other party or to a child of either party;

(5) threatening the other party or a child of either party with imminent bodily injury;

(6) intentionally, knowingly, or recklessly destroying, removing, concealing, encumbering, transferring, or otherwise harming or reducing the value of the property of the parties or either party with intent to obstruct the authority of the court to order a division of the estate of the parties in a manner that the court deems just and right, having due regard for the rights of each party and any children of the marriage;

(7) intentionally falsifying a writing or record, including an electronic record, relating to the property of either party;

(8) intentionally misrepresenting or refusing to disclose to the other party or to the court, on proper request, the existence, amount, or location of any tangible or intellectual property of the parties or either party, including electronically stored or recorded information;

(9) intentionally or knowingly damaging or destroying the tangible or intellectual property of the parties or either party, including electronically stored or recorded information;

(10) intentionally or knowingly tampering with the tangible or intellectual property of the parties or either party, including electronically stored or recorded information, and causing pecuniary loss or substantial inconvenience to the other party;

(11) except as specifically authorized by the court:

(A) selling, transferring, assigning, mortgaging, encumbering, or in any other manner alienating any of the property of the parties or either party, regardless of whether the property is:

(i) personal property, real property, or intellectual property; or

(ii) separate or community property;

(B) incurring any debt, other than legal expenses in connection with the suit for dissolution of marriage;

(C) withdrawing money from any checking or savings account in a financial institution for any purpose;

(D) spending any money in either party's possession or subject to either party's control for any purpose;

(E) withdrawing or borrowing money in any manner for any purpose from a retirement, profit sharing, pension, death, or other employee benefit plan, employee savings plan, individual retirement account, or Keogh account of either party; or

(F) withdrawing or borrowing in any manner all or any part of the cash surrender value of a life insurance policy on the life of either party or a child of the parties;

(12) entering any safe deposit box in the name of or subject to the control of the parties or either party, whether individually or jointly with others;

(13) changing or in any manner altering the beneficiary designation on any life insurance policy on the life of either party or a child of the parties;

(14) canceling, altering, failing to renew or pay premiums on, or in any manner affecting the level of coverage that existed at the time the suit was filed of, any life, casualty, automobile, or health insurance policy insuring the parties' property or persons, including a child of the parties;

(15) opening or diverting mail or e-mail or any other electronic communication addressed to the other party;

(16) signing or endorsing the other party's name on any negotiable instrument, check, or draft, including a tax refund, insurance payment, and dividend, or attempting to negotiate any negotiable instrument payable to the other party without the personal signature of the other party;

(17) taking any action to terminate or limit credit or charge credit cards in the name of the other party;

(18) discontinuing or reducing the withholding for federal income taxes from either party's wages or salary;

(19) destroying, disposing of, or altering any financial records of the parties, including a canceled check, deposit slip, and other records from a financial institution, a record of credit purchases or cash advances, a tax return, and a financial statement;

(20) destroying, disposing of, or altering any e-mail, text message, video message, or chat message or other electronic data or electronically stored information relevant to the subject matter of the suit for dissolution of marriage, regardless of whether the information is stored on a hard drive, in a removable storage device, in cloud storage, or in another electronic storage medium;

(21) modifying, changing, or altering the native format or metadata of any electronic data or electronically stored information relevant to the subject matter of the suit for dissolution of marriage, regardless of whether the information is stored on a hard drive, in a removable storage device, in cloud storage, or in another electronic storage medium;

(22) deleting any data or content from any social network profile used or created by either party or a child of the parties;

(23) using any password or personal identification number to gain access to the other party's e-mail account, bank account, social media account, or any other electronic account;

(24) terminating or in any manner affecting the service of water, electricity, gas, telephone, cable television, or any other contractual service, including security, pest control, landscaping, or yard maintenance at the residence of either party, or in any manner attempting to withdraw any deposit paid in connection with any of those services;

(25) excluding the other party from the use and enjoyment of a specifically identified residence of the other party; or

(26) entering, operating, or exercising control over a motor vehicle in the possession of the other party.

(b) A temporary restraining order under this subchapter may not include a provision:

(1) the subject of which is a requirement, appointment, award, or other order listed in Section 64.104, Civil Practice and Remedies Code; or

(2) that:

(A) excludes a spouse from occupancy of the residence where that spouse is living except as provided in a protective order made in accordance with Title 4;

(B) prohibits a party from spending funds for reasonable and necessary living expenses; or

(C) prohibits a party from engaging in acts reasonable and necessary to conduct that party's usual business and occupation.

History of Fam. Code §6.501: Acts 1997, 75th Leg., ch. 7, §1, eff. Apr. 17, 1997. Amended by Acts 1999, 76th Leg., ch. 1081, §6, eff. Sept. 1, 1999; Acts 2015, 84th Leg., ch. 43, §1, eff. Sept. 1, 2015. Source: Former Fam. Code §3.58(a), (b).

See also ***O'Connor's Texas Family Law Handbook*** (2017), "Temporary Restraining Orders," ch. 5-B, p. 677.

Ⓐ FAM §6.502. TEMPORARY INJUNCTION & OTHER TEMPORARY ORDERS

(a) While a suit for dissolution of a marriage is pending and on the motion of a party or on the court's own motion after notice and hearing, the court may render an appropriate order, including the granting of a temporary injunction for the preservation of the property and protection of the parties as deemed necessary and equitable and including an order directed to one or both parties:

(1) requiring a sworn inventory and appraisement of the real and personal property owned or claimed by the parties and specifying the form, manner, and substance of the inventory and appraisal and list of debts and liabilities;

(2) requiring payments to be made for the support of either spouse;

(3) requiring the production of books, papers, documents, and tangible things by a party;

(4) ordering payment of reasonable attorney's fees and expenses;

(5) appointing a receiver for the preservation and protection of the property of the parties;

(6) awarding one spouse exclusive occupancy of the residence during the pendency of the case;

(7) prohibiting the parties, or either party, from spending funds beyond an amount the court determines to be for reasonable and necessary living expenses;

(8) awarding one spouse exclusive control of a party's usual business or occupation; or

(9) prohibiting an act described by Section 6.501(a).

(b) Not later than the 30th day after the date a receiver is appointed under Subsection (a)(5), the receiver shall give notice of the appointment to each lienholder of any property under the receiver's control.

(c) Not later than the seventh day after the date a receiver is appointed under Subsection (a)(5), the court shall issue written findings of fact and conclusions of law in support of the receiver's appointment. If the court dispenses with the issuance of a bond between the spouses as provided by Section 6.503(b) in connection with the receiver's appointment, the court shall include in the court's findings an explanation of the reasons the court dispensed with the issuance of a bond.

History of Fam. Code §6.502: Acts 1997, 75th Leg., ch. 7, §1, eff. Apr. 17, 1997. Amended by Acts 2001, 77th Leg., ch. 695, §1, eff. Sept. 1, 2001; H.B. 2703, §1, 85th Leg., eff. Sept. 1, 2017. Source: Former Fam. Code §§3.58(c), 3.59.

See also *O'Connor's Texas Family Law Handbook* (2017), "General Concepts," ch. 5-A, p. 671; "Temporary Injunctions," ch. 5-C, p. 688; "Temporary Orders," ch. 5-D, p. 695.

ANNOTATIONS

Generally

In re Vitol, Inc., No. 14-10-00049-CV (Tex.App.—Houston [14th Dist.] 2010, orig. proceeding) (memo op.; 1-28-10). The "'requirement of a hearing [under §6.502] implies that the opposing spouse will be afforded the normal right to participate in an adversarial hearing, rather than merely the right to be present as a spectator at an *ex parte* hearing.' [¶] '[T]he trial court may impose reasonable limitations upon the parties' presentation of evidence in a temporary injunction hearing; however, a party may not be deprived of the right to offer any evidence.' If the trial court's limitation is arbitrary in its nature, it will be considered an abuse of discretion on the part of the trial judge." *See also* ***Post v. Garza***, 867 S.W.2d 88, 90 (Tex.App.—Corpus Christi 1993, orig. proceeding).

Attorney Fees

In re Bielefeld, 143 S.W.3d 924, 930 (Tex.App.—Fort Worth 2004, orig. proceeding). "Unlike the order sought to be enforced in ***Kimsey***, the order for payment of attorney's fees and expenses to [W's] attorney in the instant case does not characterize the fees ordered to be paid as 'temporary' or for 'spousal support.' *At 931:* We hold that the trial court did not have authority to enforce its written order for payment of advance interim attorney's fees ... to [W's] divorce lawyer by contempt because it did not characterize those fees and expenses as spousal support, thus making them attorney's fees which may not be enforced by contempt. Therefore, the contempt order is void." *See also* ***Ex parte Kimsey***, 915 S.W.2d 523, 527 (Tex.App.—El Paso 1995, orig. proceeding) (fees ordered to be paid were spousal support, not debt, so H's confinement was valid).

Herschberg v. Herschberg, 994 S.W.2d 273, 279 (Tex.App.—Corpus Christi 1999, pet. denied). "With regard to attorney's fees, there is no specific guidance in §6.502 to suggest how the amount of expected attorney's fees is to be calculated. We conclude that, as with temporary support, the award of temporary attorney's fees must be based on the needs of the applicant as weighed against the ability of the opposing party to pay such fees. [¶] Because of the uncertainties of future litigation and of the legal and factual issues that may arise, temporary orders are only an estimate of the actual attorney's fees and costs. As long as there is a credible showing of the need for attorney's fees in the amount requested and the ability of the opposing spouse to meet that need, the trial court has authority by temporary orders to require the payment of such fees. However, the trial court may not make the opposing party destitute in order to pay the applicant's support and fees."

Inventory

Ismail v. Ismail, 702 S.W.2d 216, 224 (Tex.App.—Houston [1st Dist.] 1985, writ ref'd n.r.e.). "The Family Code provides that the trial court may issue temporary orders requiring either party to file a sworn inventory.

If a party fails to comply with a temporary order, the party may be punished under the court's contempt power. We hold that the request for an inventory in a divorce case is a specie of discovery, and that the sanctions provided for in [TRCP] 215, as well as those granted in [Fam. Code] §3.58(c)(1) [now §6.502(1)], are available to the trial court to punish or secure compliance with its order to furnish an inventory."

Receiver

Norem v. Norem, 105 S.W.3d 213, 216 (Tex.App.—Dallas 2003, no pet.). "Under the family code, the trial court appoints a receiver when it deems it necessary and equitable for the preservation and protection of the marital property. Thus, for the court to appoint a receiver pursuant to the family code there must be evidence that the receivership is for the protection and preservation of the marital estate. *At 217:* Here, [W] presented evidence that the value of the community estate had diminished in value during the pendency of the divorce suit. [W's] testimony established that [H] had not followed orders to deliver property and pay attorney's fees from community property. The evidence demonstrated that many of the community assets had been sold and the funds dispersed. [W] testified that [H] had moved, sold, transferred, and encumbered property in violation of court orders and injunctions. The evidence supports the appointment of a receivership…." *See also* ***Stoker v. Stoker***, No. 12-07-00334-CV (Tex.App.—Tyler 2008, no pet.) (memo op.; 5-14-08) (order appointing receiver under §6.502(a)(5) must be supported by evidence).

Mallou v. Payne & Vendig, 750 S.W.2d 251, 254-55 (Tex.App.—Dallas 1988, writ denied). "'Parties' in the context of [Fam. Code] §3.58 [now §6.502(5)] *means the spouses*. 'Parties' does not include third-party creditors…. The family courts do not have unbridled discretion in appointing a receiver. As this court has stated previously: 'In recognition of the fact that appointment of a receiver without notice is one of the most drastic actions known to law or equity and should be exercised with extreme caution and only where great emergency or imperative necessity requires it, our courts have uniformly been reluctant to grant such harsh relief.' The appointment of a receiver is disfavored in the law and is only permitted if it is conclusively shown that: (1) the property is in danger of being lost, removed, or materially injured; (2) the trial court considered other available options; and (3) from the evidence before it, the trial court concluded that a less harsh remedy was unavailable."

Readhimer v. Readhimer, 728 S.W.2d 872, 873-74 (Tex.App.—Houston [1st Dist.] 1987, no writ). "Unlike receiverships authorized by the [CPRC], the Family Code does not set out the predicate necessary to support a receivership order. This Court is aware of cases reciting that, in a divorce case, the court may appoint a receiver without any showing that the property is in danger of being lost, removed, or materially injured. The better rule, however, would require a showing that the parties' property was in danger and that a less harsh remedy was unavailable before a receiver is appointed. It certainly would require some evidence and a record demonstrating the options that the court could or did consider."

Spousal Support

Ex parte Hall, 854 S.W.2d 656, 658 (Tex.1993). "The temporary support order in this case was issued solely on the basis of the parties' prenuptial agreement and not on the authority of the Family Code. … For this reason the trial court did not consider it necessary to complete the hearing required by statute before granting temporary support. It did not determine whether the spousal support ordered was 'necessary and equitable,' as required by [Fam. Code] §3.58(c) [now §6.502], nor whether the temporary child support was 'for the safety and welfare of the child,' as required by [Fam. Code] §11.11(a) [now §105.001]. It did not take into account the guidelines and factors required for setting child support. … It calculated the arrearage due without any evidentiary basis. Under these circumstances, the temporary support order was not enforceable by contempt."

In re Eaton, No. 02-14-00239-CV (Tex.App.—Fort Worth 2014, orig. proceeding) (memo op.; 9-25-14). "The purpose of temporary spousal maintenance is to protect the welfare of a 'financially dependent' spouse or to maintain the status quo of the family until the final divorce decree. Here, the parties' status quo under the terms of the presumptively enforceable [partition or exchange agreement (PEA)] was that there was no community estate and that [W] received no monetary support from [H]. [B]y ordering temporary spousal support and interim attorney's fees even though there was a presumptively valid PEA, which provided for no community

estate and no monetary support ..., the trial court incorrectly applied the law, thereby abusing its discretion. [¶] [T]he presumptively enforceable agreement should have controlled and superseded the court's jurisdiction to order temporary spousal support and interim attorney's fees. Although [the] agreement did not specifically mention temporary spousal support or interim attorney's fees, the agreement did specify that the agreement fully satisfied *any* and *all* claims one would have to the other's separate property and that there was no community estate after the date of the agreement. This language necessarily precluded any award of temporary spousal support or interim attorney's fees."

Herschberg v. Herschberg, 994 S.W.2d 273, 278 (Tex.App.—Corpus Christi 1999, pet. denied). "[T]emporary support pending divorce has for its purpose the maintenance of the family until the final decree. It is not a property right, but is to be determined by the consideration of the needs of the applicant. Therefore, temporary support should be awarded based on considerations of both the degree to which the applicant is destitute of means to pay for his or her necessities during the pendency of the suit, and the ability of the requested spouse to pay. [¶] [T]emporary support is only meant to pay for necessary expenses. Therefore, it is not proper to use a temporary support order to make an interim division of the property or to equalize the standard of living for each party pending a final division."

Grossnickle v. Grossnickle, 935 S.W.2d 830, 848 (Tex.App.—Texarkana 1996, writ denied). "Temporary spousal support ends when the divorce is final. A trial court may properly award temporary spousal support pending an appeal of a divorce. [H]owever, [W] did not appeal the divorce itself, so she was not entitled to spousal support during the appeal on other issues."

FAM §6.503. AFFIDAVIT, VERIFIED PLEADING, & BOND NOT REQUIRED

(a) A temporary restraining order or temporary injunction under this subchapter:

(1) may be granted without an affidavit or a verified pleading stating specific facts showing that immediate and irreparable injury, loss, or damage will result before notice can be served and a hearing can be held; and

(2) need not:

(A) define the injury or state why it is irreparable;

(B) state why the order was granted without notice; or

(C) include an order setting the suit for trial on the merits with respect to the ultimate relief sought.

(b) In a suit for dissolution of a marriage, the court may dispense with the issuance of a bond between the spouses in connection with temporary orders for the protection of the parties and their property.

History of Fam. Code §6.503: Acts 1997, 75th Leg., ch. 7, §1, eff. Apr. 17, 1997. Source: Former Fam. Code §3.58(d), (e).

FAM §6.504. PROTECTIVE ORDERS

On the motion of a party to a suit for dissolution of a marriage, the court may render a protective order as provided by Subtitle B, Title 4.

History of Fam. Code §6.504: Acts 1997, 75th Leg., ch. 7, §1, eff. Apr. 17, 1997. Amended by Acts 1997, 75th Leg., ch. 1193, §1, eff. Sept. 1, 1997. Source: Former Fam. Code §3.581.

FAM §6.505. COUNSELING

(a) While a divorce suit is pending, the court may direct the parties to counsel with a person named by the court.

(b) The person named by the court to counsel the parties shall submit a written report to the court and to the parties before the final hearing. In the report, the counselor shall give only an opinion as to whether there exists a reasonable expectation of reconciliation of the parties and, if so, whether further counseling would be beneficial. The sole purpose of the report is to aid the court in determining whether the suit for divorce should be continued pending further counseling.

(c) A copy of the report shall be furnished to each party.

(d) If the court believes that there is a reasonable expectation of the parties' reconciliation, the court may by written order continue the proceedings and direct the parties to a person named by the court for further counseling for a period fixed by the court not to exceed 60 days, subject to any terms, conditions, and limitations the court considers desirable. In ordering counseling, the court shall consider the circumstances of the parties, including the needs of the parties' family and the availability of counseling services. At the expiration of the period specified by the court, the counselor to whom the parties were directed shall report to the court whether the parties have complied with the court's order. Thereafter, the court shall proceed as in a divorce suit generally.

(e) If the court orders counseling under this section and the parties to the marriage are the parents of a child under 18 years of age born or adopted during the

marriage, the counseling shall include counseling on issues that confront children who are the subject of a suit affecting the parent-child relationship.

History of Fam. Code §6.505: Acts 1997, 75th Leg., ch. 7, §1, eff. Apr. 17, 1997. Amended by Acts 1997, 75th Leg., ch. 1325, §1, eff. Sept. 1, 1997. Source: Former Fam. Code §3.54(a)-(c).

FAM §6.506. CONTEMPT

The violation of a temporary restraining order, temporary injunction, or other temporary order issued under this subchapter is punishable as contempt.

History of Fam. Code §6.506: Acts 1997, 75th Leg., ch. 7, §1, eff. Apr. 17, 1997. Source: Former Fam. Code §3.58(f).

ANNOTATIONS

Ex parte Hall, 854 S.W.2d 656, 658 (Tex.1993). "An order requiring temporary support payments is enforceable by contempt."

Ex parte Threet, 333 S.W.2d 361, 362 (Tex.1960). Relator "has been held in contempt by a district court for refusing to make support payments [in accordance with a temporary order] pending a divorce action. [Relator] denied that he had been married, and here contends that the district court was without power to require such payments because there was no evidence introduced at the hearing that there had ever been any marriage. *At 363-64:* A valid marriage is a prerequisite to a support order in an action for divorce. The existence of the marriage must be admitted or shown before such a decree or order properly can be made. Where the marriage is denied, as it was here, the marriage must be at least tentatively established. Stated differently, when the marriage is put in issue, the burden is upon the party seeking support to establish at least a prima facie case of marriage."

Ex parte Kimsey, 915 S.W.2d 523, 525 (Tex.App.—El Paso 1995, orig. proceeding). Family Code §3.58(f), now §6.506, "allows the trial court to punish by contempt the violation of any temporary order. Thus, it is clear that Relator can be punished by contempt for his violation of the trial court's temporary order requiring him to pay sums into the registry of the court for the payment of attorney's fees. The question remains, however, whether that punishment can take the form of imprisonment in light of [Tex. Const.] art. 1, §18.... [¶] While the constitution clearly prohibits imprisonment for debt, the courts have consistently recognized that obligations incurred for the support of children and spouses do not constitute a debt. *At 526:* Thus, an order of contempt arising from the failure to pay those obligations may be enforced by incarceration without running afoul of the constitutional prohibition."

FAM §6.507. INTERLOCUTORY APPEAL

An order under this subchapter, except an order appointing a receiver, is not subject to interlocutory appeal.

History of Fam. Code §6.507: Acts 1997, 75th Leg., ch. 7, §1, eff. Apr. 17, 1997. Source: Former Fam. Code §3.58(g).

ANNOTATIONS

Hudson v. Aceves, ___ S.W.3d ___ (Tex.App.—Corpus Christi 2016, n.p.h.) (No. 13-14-00400-CV; 12-1-16). "A temporary injunction is generally subject to interlocutory appeal. But an order under [Fam. Code Ch. 6,] Subch. F ..., regarding temporary orders in divorce cases, is not subject to interlocutory appeal. [¶] [F]amily code §6.507 [takes] precedence over [CPRC] §51.014(a)(4) ... and prohibit[s] an interlocutory appeal of a temporary injunction in a divorce case."

Sections 6.508-6.600 reserved for expansion

SUBCHAPTER G. ALTERNATIVE DISPUTE RESOLUTION

FAM §6.601. ARBITRATION PROCEDURES

(a) On written agreement of the parties, the court may refer a suit for dissolution of a marriage to arbitration. The agreement must state whether the arbitration is binding or nonbinding.

(b) If the parties agree to binding arbitration, the court shall render an order reflecting the arbitrator's award.

History of Fam. Code §6.601: Acts 1997, 75th Leg., ch. 7, §1, eff. Apr. 17, 1997.

See also ***O'Connor's Texas Family Law Handbook*** (2017), "Arbitration," ch. 3-A, §13.1.4, p. 257; "Arbitration," ch. 4-D, §10.1.3, p. 427.

ANNOTATIONS

Cooper v. Bushong, 10 S.W.3d 20, 24-25 (Tex. App.—Austin 1999, pet. denied). "A court can set aside an arbitration award only if: (1) the award was procured by corruption, fraud or other undue means; (2) the rights of a party were prejudiced by evident partiality, corruption, misconduct, or willful misbehavior by an arbitrator; (3) the arbitrator exceeded his powers, refused to postpone the hearing after a showing of sufficient cause for the postponement, refused to hear evidence material to the controversy, or conducted the hearing, contrary to the General Arbitration Act, in a

manner that substantially prejudiced the rights of a party; or (4) there was no agreement to arbitrate, the issue was not adversely determined in a proceeding to compel or stay arbitration, and the party did not participate in the arbitration hearing without raising the objection."

FAM §6.6015. DETERMINATION OF VALIDITY & ENFORCEABILITY OF CONTRACT CONTAINING AGREEMENT TO ARBITRATE

(a) If a party to a suit for dissolution of a marriage opposes an application to compel arbitration or makes an application to stay arbitration and asserts that the contract containing the agreement to arbitrate is not valid or enforceable, notwithstanding any provision of the contract to the contrary, the court shall try the issue promptly and may order arbitration only if the court determines that the contract containing the agreement to arbitrate is valid and enforceable against the party seeking to avoid arbitration.

(b) A determination under this section that a contract is valid and enforceable does not affect the court's authority to stay arbitration or refuse to compel arbitration on any other ground provided by law.

(c) This section does not apply to:

(1) a court order;

(2) a mediated settlement agreement described by Section 6.602;

(3) a collaborative law agreement described by Section 6.603;[1]

(4) a written settlement agreement reached at an informal settlement conference described by Section 6.604; or

(5) any other agreement between the parties that is approved by a court.

1. **Editor's note:** Family Code §6.603 was repealed by Acts 2011, 82nd Leg., ch. 1048, §2, eff. Sept. 1, 2011. Title 1-A, Collaborative Family Law, was enacted by Acts 2011, 82nd Leg., ch. 1048, §1, eff. Sept. 1, 2011.

History of Fam. Code §6.6015: Acts 2011, 82nd Leg., ch. 1088, §1, eff. June 17, 2011.

See also ***O'Connor's Texas Family Law Handbook*** (2017), "Effect of arbitration clause," ch. 2-D, §3.5.4, p. 171.

FAM §6.602. MEDIATION PROCEDURES

(a) On the written agreement of the parties or on the court's own motion, the court may refer a suit for dissolution of a marriage to mediation.

(b) A mediated settlement agreement is binding on the parties if the agreement:

(1) provides, in a prominently displayed statement that is in boldfaced type or capital letters or underlined, that the agreement is not subject to revocation;

(2) is signed by each party to the agreement; and

(3) is signed by the party's attorney, if any, who is present at the time the agreement is signed.

(c) If a mediated settlement agreement meets the requirements of this section, a party is entitled to judgment on the mediated settlement agreement notwithstanding Rule 11, Texas Rules of Civil Procedure, or another rule of law.

(d) A party may at any time prior to the final mediation order file a written objection to the referral of a suit for dissolution of a marriage to mediation on the basis of family violence having been committed against the objecting party by the other party. After an objection is filed, the suit may not be referred to mediation unless, on the request of the other party, a hearing is held and the court finds that a preponderance of the evidence does not support the objection. If the suit is referred to mediation, the court shall order appropriate measures be taken to ensure the physical and emotional safety of the party who filed the objection. The order shall provide that the parties not be required to have face-to-face contact and that the parties be placed in separate rooms during mediation.

History of Fam. Code §6.602: Acts 1997, 75th Leg., ch. 7, §1, eff. Apr. 17, 1997. Amended by Acts 1999, 76th Leg., ch. 178, §2 (eff. Aug. 30, 1999), ch. 1351, §1 (eff. Sept. 1, 1999).

See also ***O'Connor's Texas Family Law Handbook*** (2017), "Mediation," ch. 3-A, §13.1.1, p. 244; "Mediation," ch. 4-D, §10.1.1, p. 425.

ANNOTATIONS

Milner v. Milner, 361 S.W.3d 615, 618 (Tex.2012). "Unlike other settlement agreements in family law, the trial court is not required to determine if the property division is 'just and right' before approving an MSA [under §6.602]. And once signed, [the] MSA cannot be revoked like other settlement agreements. *At 618 n.2:* [MSAs] that comply with … §6.602 are an exception to [the] general rule [that a party can revoke consent to a settlement agreement anytime before the court renders judgment on the agreement]." After evaluating the MSA, the Court remanded the property-division issue so the MSA's ambiguity could be resolved and a judgment could be rendered.

Morse v. Morse, 349 S.W.3d 55, 56 (Tex.App.—El Paso 2010, no pet.). "[H] does not dispute that the MSA meets all of the requirements of §6.602. Unless he can establish a ground for revocation, it is binding. The

only ground [H] alleges is that [W] intentionally breached the [MSA] with malice by damaging certain items of property. He cites no authority that an MSA can be revoked due to a party's alleged intentional breach. Because [H] has failed to assert a viable ground for setting aside or revoking the MSA, we deny his motion."

In re Marriage of Joyner, 196 S.W.3d 883, 891 (Tex.App.—Texarkana 2006, pet. denied). "Section 6.602 has been classified as a 'procedural shortcut' for enforcement of mediated settlement agreements in divorce cases. ... Here, the parties were entitled to a judgment incorporating the provisions of the mediated settlement agreement and, since no allegation was presented that the agreement was illegal, or procured by fraud, duress, or coercion, and there is no indication the trial court sua sponte questioned the legality of the agreement, the trial court was required to enter a judgment based on the mediated agreement. ... We hold that the judgment granting the divorce was rendered [by oral pronouncement], and since the trial court had no authority (absent an issue on illegality, duress, etc. raised either by the parties or the court sua sponte) to do otherwise, the mediated settlement agreement was a part of the divorce rendition." *See also* ***Toler v. Sanders***, 371 S.W.3d 477, 479-80 (Tex.App.—Houston [1st Dist.] 2012, no pet.) (court cannot alter or modify property division in valid MSA).

Lee v. Lee, 158 S.W.3d 612, 613-14 (Tex.App.—Fort Worth 2005, no pet.). "Given that [Fam. Code] §7.006(a) ... already allows divorcing parties to enter into written agreements without requiring mediation concerning the division of the community assets and liabilities as well as spousal maintenance, we decline to carve a common-law exception into [Fam. Code] §6.602(b) that allows an unmediated settlement agreement to morph into a mediated settlement agreement based on mere form. We hold that a mediated settlement agreement necessarily requires mediation and a mediator. [¶] Because there was no third party present at the settlement conference between [parties], there was no mediated settlement agreement. Instead, the couple's agreement is simply an agreement under §7.006(a). Such agreements may be revised or repudiated before the divorce is rendered unless the agreement is binding under another rule of law. The trial court abused its discretion in preventing [H] from revoking his consent to the settlement on the basis that the agreement was a binding mediated settlement agreement."

Mailhot v. Mailhot, 124 S.W.3d 775, 777 (Tex.App.—Houston [1st Dist.] 2003, no pet.). "It is well-settled that a judgment entered on the agreement of the parties cures all non-jurisdictional defects. A party who asks the trial court to accept a settlement agreement and to enter judgment accordingly may not later attack that judgment. To preserve error for appeal, a party who signs a judgment must specify that his agreement with the judgment is *as to form*, but not as to substance and outcome."

Boyd v. Boyd, 67 S.W.3d 398, 403 (Tex.App.—Fort Worth 2002, no pet.). "Construing the phrase 'notwithstanding rule 11 or another rule of law' to mean that a mediated settlement agreement that complies with §6.602(b) must be enforced no matter what the circumstances could require enforcement of an agreement that was illegal or that was procured by fraud, duress, coercion, or other dishonest means. We do not believe that the legislature intended such an absurd result in enacting §6.602. Rather, we construe this phrase to mean that the requirements of rule 11 and the common law that ordinarily apply to the enforcement of settlement agreements do not apply to [MSAs] in divorce proceedings, if the agreements meet the three requirements listed in §6.602(b)." *See also* ***Brooks v. Brooks***, 257 S.W.3d 418, 422 (Tex.App.—Fort Worth 2008, pet. denied) (court may refuse to enforce MSA if procured by intentional failure to disclose material information).

FAM §6.603. REPEALED

Repealed by Acts 2011, 82nd Leg., ch. 1048, §2, eff. Sept. 1, 2011.

FAM §6.604. INFORMAL SETTLEMENT CONFERENCE

(a) The parties to a suit for dissolution of a marriage may agree to one or more informal settlement conferences and may agree that the settlement conferences may be conducted with or without the presence of the parties' attorneys, if any.

(b) A written settlement agreement reached at an informal settlement conference is binding on the parties if the agreement:

(1) provides, in a prominently displayed statement that is in boldfaced type or in capital letters or underlined, that the agreement is not subject to revocation;

(2) is signed by each party to the agreement; and

(3) is signed by the party's attorney, if any, who is present at the time the agreement is signed.

(c) If a written settlement agreement meets the requirements of Subsection (b), a party is entitled to judgment on the settlement agreement notwithstanding Rule 11, Texas Rules of Civil Procedure, or another rule of law.

(d) If the court finds that the terms of the written informal settlement agreement are just and right, those terms are binding on the court. If the court approves the agreement, the court may set forth the agreement in full or incorporate the agreement by reference in the final decree.

(e) If the court finds that the terms of the written informal settlement agreement are not just and right, the court may request the parties to submit a revised agreement or set the case for a contested hearing.

History of Fam. Code §6.604: Acts 2005, 79th Leg., ch. 477, §3, eff. Sept. 1, 2005.

See also ***O'Connor's Texas Family Law Handbook*** (2017), "Informal settlement conference," ch. 3-A, §13.1.3, p. 257.

Sections 6.605-6.700 reserved for expansion

SUBCHAPTER H. TRIAL & APPEAL

FAM §6.701. FAILURE TO ANSWER

In a suit for divorce, the petition may not be taken as confessed if the respondent does not file an answer.

History of Fam. Code §6.701: Acts 1997, 75th Leg., ch. 7, §1, eff. Apr. 17, 1997. Source: Former Fam. Code §3.53.

See also ***O'Connor's Texas Family Law Handbook*** (2017), "Effect of no answer," ch. 3-A, §9.3.2, p. 240.

ANNOTATIONS

Vazquez v. Vazquez, 292 S.W.3d 80, 83-84 (Tex. App.—Houston [14th Dist.] 2007, no pet.). "[I]f a respondent in a divorce case fails to answer or appear, the petitioner must still present evidence to support the material allegations in the petition. Therefore, a default judgment of divorce is subject to an evidentiary attack on appeal." *See also* ***In re E.M.V.***, 312 S.W.3d 288, 291 (Tex.App.—Dallas 2010, no pet.).

Morris v. Morris, 717 S.W.2d 189, 190 (Tex.App.—Austin 1986, no writ). "[H's] failure to appear or answer is taken as an admission of the allegations in [W's] petition regarding residence and domicile." *But see* ***Reavis v. Reavis***, No. 01-02-00809-CV (Tex.App.—Houston [1st Dist.] 2003, no pet.) (memo op.; 12-11-03) (residency and domicile are not deemed admitted when respondent defaults).

FAM §6.702. WAITING PERIOD

(a) Except as provided by Subsection (c), the court may not grant a divorce before the 60th day after the date the suit was filed. A decree rendered in violation of this subsection is not subject to collateral attack.

(b) A waiting period is not required before a court may grant an annulment or declare a marriage void other than as required in civil cases generally.

(c) A waiting period is not required under Subsection (a) before a court may grant a divorce in a suit in which the court finds that:

(1) the respondent has been finally convicted of or received deferred adjudication for an offense involving family violence as defined by Section 71.004 against the petitioner or a member of the petitioner's household; or

(2) the petitioner has an active protective order under Title 4 or an active magistrate's order for emergency protection under Article 17.292, Code of Criminal Procedure, based on a finding of family violence, against the respondent because of family violence committed during the marriage.

History of Fam. Code §6.702: Acts 1997, 75th Leg., ch. 7, §1, eff. Apr. 17, 1997. Amended by Acts 2009, 81st Leg., ch. 896, §1, eff. June 19, 2009. Source: Former Fam. Code §3.60.

ANNOTATIONS

Gutierrez v. Davila, No. 04-09-00745-CV (Tex. App.—San Antonio 2010, no pet.) (memo op.; 12-1-10). "[H] filed a supplemental petition for divorce, which stated that he met the residency requirements for filing suit ... two months after he filed his original petition for divorce. [W] claims that when [H] supplemented his petition ..., he corrected the defect in his original filing, and the 60-day waiting period began on that date. [¶] Either [H's] supplemental petition constitutes an amended pleading filed after the residency requirements were met, and the 60 day period began at that time, or he still has not met the residency requirements of [Fam. Code] §6.301. We hold that [H's] supplemental petition constitutes an amended petition and the filing of a new suit."

In re Marriage of Gillman, 507 S.W.2d 610, 612 (Tex.App.—Amarillo 1974, writ dism'd). "[R]espondent's motion to vacate is a collateral attack upon the divorce decree. [¶] We hold that this collateral attack is precluded by the provision contained in the second sentence of [Fam. Code] §3.60 [now §6.702] which in effect states that although a divorce is granted before 60 days have elapsed since the suit was filed, the decree is

not subject to collateral attack. In the light of this statutory declaration of public policy, we hold that the noncompliance with the waiting period provision of §3.60 was procedural, not jurisdictional. Thus, such matter could only be challenged or corrected by direct appeal."

FAM §6.703. JURY

In a suit for dissolution of a marriage, either party may demand a jury trial unless the action is a suit to annul an underage marriage under Section 6.102.

History of Fam. Code §6.703: Acts 1997, 75th Leg., ch. 7, §1, eff. Apr. 17, 1997. Amended by Acts 2007, 80th Leg., ch. 52, §7, eff. Sept. 1, 2007. Source: Former Fam. Code §3.61.

See also TRCP 216.

ANNOTATIONS

In re Baker, 495 S.W.3d 393, 396 (Tex.App.—Houston [14th Dist.] 2016, orig. proceeding). "[W]e hold that [W's] waiver of a jury in the first trial did not preclude her from demanding a jury after remand for the second trial." *See also* ***In re Marriage of Stein***, 190 S.W.3d 73, 76 (Tex.App.—Amarillo 2005, no pet.) (failure to request jury trial does not bar right to jury trial on remand).

Teixeira v. Teixeira, No. 04-02-00603-CV (Tex. App.—San Antonio 2004, no pet.) (memo op.; 8-18-04). "Under [Fam. Code] §6.703, in a suit for the dissolution of a marriage, either party may demand a jury trial. [TRCP 216], however, [mandates] that in order for a jury demand to be proper, the party requesting a jury must file its written request not less than 30 days before the date set for trial and must deposit a jury fee with the clerk of the court."

In re Marriage of Richards, 991 S.W.2d 32, 36 (Tex.App.—Amarillo 1999, pet. dism'd). "We initially note §6.703 ... expressly provides that in a suit of this type, 'either party may demand a jury trial.' *At 37-38:* [H argues] that under the statute, there were no questions of material fact for resolution by the jury. We disagree. [¶] While the adoption of 'no-fault' divorce dispenses with any burden to establish the source of the conflict rendering the marriage insupportable, it does not relieve the petitioner of the burden to establish the existence of the statutory elements. Therefore, at the time of [W's] jury demand, there were questions of material fact to be resolved and it was error to deny her request."

Marr v. Marr, 905 S.W.2d 331, 333-34 (Tex.App.—Waco 1995, no writ). "Parties to divorce proceedings are entitled to a jury trial upon proper request; the jury alone decides whether contested assets will be characterized as either community or separate; and, while the question of a just and right division of the marital estate rests solely within the sound discretion of the court, the jury's findings on the factual issues underlying the division of the marital estate, including the valuation of the assets, are conclusive."

FAM §6.704. TESTIMONY OF HUSBAND OR WIFE

(a) In a suit for dissolution of a marriage, the husband and wife are competent witnesses for and against each other. A spouse may not be compelled to testify as to a matter that will incriminate the spouse.

(b) If the husband or wife testifies, the court or jury trying the case shall determine the credibility of the witness and the weight to be given the witness's testimony.

History of Fam. Code §6.704: Acts 1997, 75th Leg., ch. 7, §1, eff. Apr. 17, 1997. Source: Former Fam. Code §3.62.

FAM §6.705. TESTIMONY BY MARRIAGE COUNSELOR

(a) The report by the person named by the court to counsel the parties to a suit for divorce may not be admitted as evidence in the suit.

(b) The person named by the court to counsel the parties is not competent to testify in any suit involving the parties or their children.

(c) The files, records, and other work products of the counselor are privileged and confidential for all purposes and may not be admitted as evidence in any suit involving the parties or their children.

History of Fam. Code §6.705: Acts 1997, 75th Leg., ch. 7, §1, eff. Apr. 17, 1997. Source: Former Fam. Code §3.54(b), (d).

FAM §6.706. CHANGE OF NAME

(a) In a decree of divorce or annulment, the court shall change the name of a party specifically requesting the change to a name previously used by the party unless the court states in the decree a reason for denying the change of name.

(b) The court may not deny a change of name solely to keep the last name of family members the same.

(c) A change of name does not release a person from liability incurred by the person under a previous name or defeat a right the person held under a previous name.

(d) A person whose name is changed under this section may apply for a change of name certificate from the clerk of the court as provided by Section 45.106.

History of Fam. Code §6.706: Acts 1997, 75th Leg., ch. 7, §1, eff. Apr. 17, 1997. Source: Former Fam. Code §3.64.

FAM §6.707. TRANSFERS & DEBTS PENDING DECREE

(a) A transfer of real or personal community property or a debt incurred by a spouse while a suit for divorce or annulment is pending that subjects the other spouse or the community property to liability is void with respect to the other spouse if the transfer was made or the debt incurred with the intent to injure the rights of the other spouse.

(b) A transfer or debt is not void if the person dealing with the transferor or debtor spouse did not have notice of the intent to injure the rights of the other spouse.

(c) The spouse seeking to void a transfer or debt incurred while a suit for divorce or annulment is pending has the burden of proving that the person dealing with the transferor or debtor spouse had notice of the intent to injure the rights of the spouse seeking to void the transaction.

History of Fam. Code §6.707: Acts 1997, 75th Leg., ch. 7, §1, eff. Apr. 17, 1997. Source: Former Fam. Code §3.57.

ANNOTATIONS

Estate of Korzekwa v. Prudential Ins., 669 S.W.2d 775, 777 (Tex.App.—San Antonio 1984, writ dism'd). "It is undisputed that the life insurance policy in question was community property. ... The named insured has the right to designate the beneficiary under the insurance policy. In the instant case, the questioned change of the designated beneficiary occurred during the pendency of the divorce proceedings. [P] seeks to void the change of beneficiary, but failed to discharge her burden to show that ... the prevailing last beneficiary, had notice of any intent to injure [P's] community property rights. Therefore, under the provisions of [Fam. Code] §3.57 [now §6.707], the transfer or change of beneficiary under the subject life insurance policy is not void."

FAM §6.708. COSTS; ATTORNEY'S FEES & EXPENSES

(a) In a suit for dissolution of a marriage, the court as it considers reasonable may award costs to a party. Costs may not be adjudged against a party against whom a divorce is granted for confinement in a mental hospital under Section 6.007.

(b) The expenses of counseling may be taxed as costs against either or both parties.

(c) In a suit for dissolution of a marriage, the court may award reasonable attorney's fees and expenses. The court may order the fees and expenses and any postjudgment interest to be paid directly to the attorney, who may enforce the order in the attorney's own name by any means available for the enforcement of a judgment for debt.

History of Fam. Code §6.708: Acts 1997, 75th Leg., ch. 7, §1, eff. Apr. 17, 1997. Amended by Acts 2013, 83rd Leg., ch. 916, §§3, 4, eff. Sept. 1, 2013. Source: Former Fam. Code §§3.54(e), 3.65.

ANNOTATIONS

Campbell v. Wilder, 487 S.W.3d 146, 147 (Tex. 2016). "The trial court temporarily enjoined the District Clerk ... from billing court costs to parties who had filed uncontested affidavits of indigency. *At 151-52:* The District Clerk argues that Petitioners' divorce decrees require them to pay costs. But the decrees only allocate costs between the parties to each case, requiring each party to bear his or her own costs—whatever they are. For a party who files an affidavit of inability to pay costs, there are no costs to bill; under [TRCP] 145 ..., the affidavit is '[i]n lieu of paying or giving security for costs.' The Petitioners here all had uncontested affidavits; those affidavits are 'in lieu of' paying costs. There are no costs. [¶] The District Clerk argues that because [Fam. Code §§6.708 and 106.001 provide] courts with increased latitude to award costs, it is conceivable that a family court could order costs despite an affidavit of inability to pay. This argument flies in the face of our Constitution and case law. Rule 145 is but one manifestation of the open courts guarantee that 'every person ... shall have remedy by due course of law.' It is an abuse of discretion for any judge, including a family law judge, to order costs in spite of an uncontested affidavit of indigence. [¶] In any case, the family courts here did not order costs. The language in the judgment merely lays out the division of any costs, not an amount to be charged. It is the ministerial duty of the District Clerk to tabulate the costs and apply the affidavit of indigency. *At 154:* The temporary injunction is proper."

Smith v. Deneve, 285 S.W.3d 904, 917 (Tex.App.—Dallas 2009, no pet.). Alleged H "argues that [alleged W] cannot rely on §6.708 ... to support the award of attorneys' fees because the trial court ruled that no infor-

mal marriage existed. [¶] The plain meaning of §6.708(a) is that it applies to any 'suit' in which the plaintiff prays for 'dissolution of a marriage.' Thus, we conclude that §6.708(a) applies [here] because [alleged H] sought the dissolution of a marriage, even though the trial court ultimately ruled that no marriage actually existed. *At 918:* [S]ection 6.708 … authorizes an award of costs without expressly requiring that a marriage be proved as a prerequisite for the award." *But see* ***Mattox v. Buentello***, 800 S.W.2d 320, 328 (Tex.App.—Corpus Christi 1990, no writ) (existence of marriage relationship must be proved before court can award attorney fees in divorce action).

Ⓐ FAM §6.709. TEMPORARY ORDERS DURING APPEAL

The amended text in §6.709 is effective for orders rendered on or after Sept. 1, 2017. Orders rendered before Sept. 1, 2017, are governed by the former law in effect at that time. If any eligible parties have filed a notice of appeal from a final judgment before Sept. 1, 2017, any party to the appeal may file a motion in the trial court for an original temporary order under the former law, and until Oct. 30, 2017, the trial court has jurisdiction to conduct a hearing and sign an original temporary order under the former law.

(a) In a suit for dissolution of a marriage [~~Not later than the 30th day after the date an appeal is perfected~~], on the motion of a party or on the court's own motion, after notice and hearing, the trial court may render a temporary order as considered equitable and necessary for the preservation of the property and for the protection of the parties during an [~~the~~] appeal, including an order directed toward one or both parties [~~to~~]:

(1) requiring [~~require~~] the support of either spouse;

(2) requiring [~~require~~] the payment of reasonable and necessary attorney's fees and expenses;

(3) appointing [~~appoint~~] a receiver for the preservation and protection of the property of the parties; [~~or~~]

(4) awarding [~~award~~] one spouse exclusive occupancy of the parties' residence pending the appeal;

(5) enjoining a party from dissipating or transferring the property awarded to the other party in the trial court's property division; or

(6) suspending the operation of all or part of the property division that is being appealed.

(b) A temporary order under this section enjoining a party from dissipating or transferring the property awarded to the other party in the trial court's property division:

(1) may be rendered without:

(A) the issuance of a bond between the spouses; or

(B) an affidavit or a verified pleading stating specific facts showing that immediate and irreparable injury, loss, or damage will result;

(2) is not required to:

(A) define the injury or state why the injury is irreparable; or

(B) include an order setting the suit for trial on the merits with respect to the ultimate relief sought; and

(3) may not prohibit a party's use, transfer, conveyance, or dissipation of the property awarded to the other party in the trial court's property division if the use, transfer, conveyance, or dissipation of the property is for the purpose of suspending the enforcement of the property division that is the subject of the appeal.

(c) A temporary order under this section that suspends the operation of all or part of the property division that is the subject of the appeal may not be rendered unless the trial court takes reasonable steps to ensure that the party awarded property in the trial court's property division is protected from the other party's dissipation or transfer of that property.

(d) In considering a party's request to suspend the enforcement of the property division, the trial court shall consider whether:

(1) any relief granted under Subsection (a) is adequate to protect the party's interest in the property awarded to the party; or

(2) the party who was not awarded the property should also be required to provide security for the appeal in addition to any relief granted under Subsection (a).

(e) If the trial court determines that the party awarded the property can be adequately protected from the other party's dissipation of assets during the appeal only if the other party provides security for the appeal, the trial court shall set the appropriate amount of security, taking into consideration any relief granted under Subsection (a) and the amount of security that the other party would otherwise have to provide by law if relief under Subsection (a) was not granted.

(f) In rendering a temporary order under this section that suspends enforcement of all or part of the prop-

erty division, the trial court may grant any relief under Subsection (a), in addition to requiring the party who was not awarded the property to post security for that part of the property division to be suspended. The trial court may require that the party who was not awarded the property post all or only part of the security that would otherwise be required by law.

(g) This section does not prevent a party who was not awarded the property from exercising that party's right to suspend the enforcement of the property division as provided by law.

(h) A motion seeking an original temporary order under this section:

(1) may be filed before trial; and

(2) may not be filed by a party after the date by which that party is required to file the party's notice of appeal under the Texas Rules of Appellate Procedure.

(i) The trial court retains jurisdiction to conduct a hearing and sign an original temporary order under this section until the 60th day after the date any eligible party has filed a notice of appeal from final judgment under the Texas Rules of Appellate Procedure.

(j) The trial court retains jurisdiction to modify and enforce a temporary order under this section unless the appellate court, on a proper showing, supersedes the trial court's order.

(k) On the motion of a party or on the court's own motion, after notice and hearing, the trial court may modify a previous temporary order rendered under this section if:

(1) the circumstances of a party have materially and substantially changed since the rendition of the previous order; and

(2) modification is equitable and necessary for the preservation of the property or for the protection of the parties during the appeal.

(*l*) A party may seek review of the trial court's temporary order under this section by:

(1) motion filed in the court of appeals with jurisdiction or potential jurisdiction over the appeal from the judgment in the case;

(2) proper assignment in the party's brief; or

(3) petition for writ of mandamus.

(m) A temporary order rendered under this section is not subject to interlocutory appeal.

(n) The remedies provided in this section are cumulative of all other remedies allowed by law.

History of Fam. Code §6.709: Acts 1997, 75th Leg., ch. 7, §1, eff. Apr. 17, 1997. Amended by S.B. 1237, §1, 85th Leg., eff. Sept. 1, 2017. Source: Former Fam. Code §3.58(h), (i).

See also ***O'Connor's Texas Family Law Handbook*** (2017), "Temporary Orders," ch. 5-D, p. 695.

ANNOTATIONS

Rodriguez v. Borrego, ___ S.W.3d ___ (Tex. App.—El Paso 2016, pet. denied) (No. 08-15-00340-CV; 9-23-16). "[W] filed a motion to dismiss [H's] appeal [of the divorce decree] because [H] has not paid the temporary spousal support, the retroactive spousal support, or the attorney's fees ordered by the trial court. [¶] The [TRAPs] authorize a court of appeals to dismiss an appeal when the appellant fails to comply with a court order. [¶] [H] claims that his appeal should not be dismissed because he intends to appeal the temporary orders.... [S]everal of our sister courts have read [Fam. Code] §6.709(b) [now §6.709(j)] as vesting the appellate courts with the power to review the validity of ancillary §6.709 temporary orders concurrent with the underlying appeal from a final divorce decree. Other courts have held that mandamus is the exclusive remedy. ... It is undisputed that [H] has not made any payments required by the temporary orders, and his only excuses are that he cannot obtain the funds ... and he does not agree with the temporary orders. We are unaware of any law which permits a party to ignore temporary orders simply because he disagrees with the order and intends to appeal it. [¶] Even though this appeal has been pending for ten months and the temporary orders have been in place for approximately nine months, [H] has not made a single payment ordered by the trial court. ... Accordingly, we deny [H's] motions to modify the temporary orders and to reconsider our order that the appeal would be dismissed if he failed to comply with the temporary orders. Finding that [H] has failed to comply with a court order, we dismiss the appeal."

Thornton v. Cash, No. 14-11-01092-CV (Tex. App.—Houston [14th Dist.] 2013, no pet.) (memo op.; 4-18-13). "According to [mother], by seeking to enforce provisions found in the Temporary Orders and the Final Divorce Decree, [non-parent PCs] have accepted the benefits of the order they are seeking to reverse on appeal and, as a result, their appeal must be dismissed. [¶] [T]he [acceptance of benefits] doctrine is most commonly applied in divorce cases in which one spouse accepts certain assets awarded by the judgment and then seeks to appeal the remainder of the judgment.

[¶] While the present case does involve a divorce and property settlement, this appeal does not relate to those provisions.... Instead, it arises solely out of the trial court's decisions regarding [child]. [¶] We conclude [non-parent PCs'] efforts to enforce the trial court's determination of what was in the best interest of [child] and to ensure that [mother] fulfilled her continuing statutory duties under those orders, [do] not invoke the acceptance of the benefits doctrine. Applying the doctrine here would encourage parties to disregard a trial court's orders in [SAPCRs] that have been appealed and thereby thwart the Legislature's directive that the best interest of the child is the primary consideration in those proceedings." *See also* ***McAlister v. McAlister***, 75 S.W.3d 481, 484 (Tex.App.—San Antonio 2002, pet. denied) (acceptance of benefits doctrine does not apply to orders under §6.709(a)).

In re Garza, 153 S.W.3d 97, 103 (Tex.App.—San Antonio 2004, orig. proceeding). Mandamus was conditionally granted to "vacate the part of [court's] temporary order that requires the award of contingent appellate attorney's fees to [H] to be paid out of the funds in the registry of the court. This aspect of the trial court's temporary order substantively modifies the property division after the trial court's plenary power over its judgment had expired and requires [W] to pay attorney's fees with the exempt proceeds from the transfer of her equity interest in the homestead."

McAlister v. McAlister, 75 S.W.3d 481, 483-84 (Tex.App.—San Antonio 2002, pet. denied). Although H argues that §6.709 "does not afford the court authority to make such orders retroactive to the date of the decree, we find no such limitation in the [Family] Code. Such an interpretation could hamstring both the court and the appellant during the time of post-decree hearings and the appeal thereby abrogating the legislature's intent to maintain the status quo and provide for spousal and child support, as necessary, during the appeal. We find that the trial court has the authority under §6.709 to issue post-judgment temporary orders retroactive to the decree."

Herschberg v. Herschberg, 994 S.W.2d 273, 277 (Tex.App.—Corpus Christi 1999, pet. denied). "[T]he majority of the courts of appeals to examine whether a spouse is entitled to temporary support on appeal under [Fam. Code] §3.58(h) [now §6.709] have concluded that it is irrelevant that neither spouse has challenged the underlying divorce and that the property division is the only issue on appeal." *See also* ***In re Marriage of Joiner***, 755 S.W.2d 496, 499 (Tex.App.—Amarillo 1988, no writ). *But see* ***Grossnickle v. Grossnickle***, 935 S.W.2d 830, 848 (Tex.App.—Texarkana 1996, writ denied) (temporary spousal support not permitted if neither party appeals divorce).

FAM §6.710. NOTICE OF FINAL DECREE

The clerk of the court shall mail a notice of the signing of the final decree of dissolution of a marriage to the party who waived service of process under Section 6.4035 at the mailing address contained in the waiver or the office of the party's attorney of record. The notice must state that a copy of the decree is available at the office of the clerk of the court and include the physical address of that office.

History of Fam. Code §6.710: Acts 1997, 75th Leg., ch. 614, §2, eff. Sept. 1, 1997. Amended by Acts 2011, 82nd Leg., ch. 529, §1, eff. June 17, 2011.

A FAM §6.711. FINDINGS OF FACT & CONCLUSIONS OF LAW

The amended text in §6.711 is effective for orders rendered on or after Sept. 1, 2017. Orders rendered before Sept. 1, 2017, are governed by the former law in effect at that time.

(a) In a suit for dissolution of a marriage in which the court has rendered a judgment dividing the estate of the parties, on request by a party, the court shall state in writing its findings of fact and conclusions of law, including [~~concerning:~~]

[~~(1)~~] the characterization and value of all [~~each party's~~] assets, liabilities, claims, and offsets on which disputed evidence has been presented[~~; and~~]

[~~(2)~~] [~~the value or amount of the community estate's assets, liabilities, claims, and offsets on which disputed evidence has been presented~~].

(b) A request for findings of fact and conclusions of law under this section must conform to the Texas Rules of Civil Procedure.

(c) The findings of fact and conclusions of law required by this section are in addition to any other findings or conclusions required or authorized by law.

History of Fam. Code §6.711: Acts 2001, 77th Leg., ch. 297, §1, eff. Sept. 1, 2001. Amended by S.B. 1237, §2, 85th Leg., eff. Sept. 1, 2017.

See also ***O'Connor's Texas Family Law Handbook*** (2017), "Findings of fact & conclusions of law," ch. 7-A, §13.1, p. 811.

ANNOTATIONS

Reisler v. Reisler, 439 S.W.3d 615, 620 (Tex.App.—Dallas 2014, no pet.). "The obligation of the trial court is to make findings of fact and conclusions of law on the

ultimate or controlling issues, but not on evidentiary issues. The trial court is not obligated to detail the facts that establish fault in the break-up of the marriage or one party's separate estate that forms the basis for the disproportionate division of the property."

Panchal v. Panchal, 132 S.W.3d 465, 466-67 (Tex. App.—Eastland 2003, no pet.). "The trial court did not make any findings of fact or conclusions of law regarding the characterization and value of each party's assets, liabilities, claims, and offsets. Upon proper request, §6.711 requires that these findings and conclusions be made with respect to '... assets, liabilities, claims, and offsets *on which disputed evidence has been presented*.' Disputed evidence was presented on only a few items of the parties' property. ... The failure of the trial court to file sufficient findings of fact and conclusions of law when properly requested is presumed to be harmful unless the contrary appears on the face of the record. [¶] The remedy for the erroneous failure to file findings of fact and conclusions of law is to abate the appeal for entry of proper findings and conclusions."

Sections 6.712-6.800 reserved for expansion

SUBCHAPTER I. REMARRIAGE

FAM §6.801. REMARRIAGE

(a) Except as otherwise provided by this subchapter, neither party to a divorce may marry a third party before the 31st day after the date the divorce is decreed.

(b) The former spouses may marry each other at any time.

History of Fam. Code §6.801: Acts 1997, 75th Leg., ch. 7, §1, eff. Apr. 17, 1997. Source: Former Fam. Code §3.66(a), (b).

ANNOTATIONS

Herschberg v. Herschberg, 994 S.W.2d 273, 276-77 (Tex.App.—Corpus Christi 1999, pet. denied). "We agree with [ex-H] that the parties are actually divorced as of the date that the trial judge orally pronounces them divorced from the bench, absent some challenge to that decree on appeal. Thirty days after that decree, they are each then free to remarry someone else. [¶] Therefore, although the division of the community estate may be reversed and remanded on appeal, the marital status of the parties is not extended beyond the date of the original decree of divorce, and the nature and extent of their community property is fixed as of that date. A remand merely for division of the property ... does not prolong the marriage relationship until the decree is final after the remand."

Galbraith v. Galbraith, 619 S.W.2d 238, 240 (Tex. App.—Texarkana 1981, no writ). Petitioner's first two points of error "urge that the undisputed evidence established that [respondent's] marriage to him prior to the expiration of the 30-day waiting period prescribed by [Fam. Code] §3.66 [now §6.801] constituted an impediment to their marriage which rendered it voidable and subject to annulment. These points are overruled. The evidence shows, and the trial court here found as a fact, that a non-interlocutory oral pronouncement of a judgment of divorce was made by the trial court in [respondent's] divorce on March 12, 1976, more than 30 days prior to her marriage to [petitioner]. Although the written decree was not signed until March 24, 1976, the divorce was fully effective for all purposes, except calculation of the times for appeal, at the time it was pronounced from the bench."

FAM §6.802. WAIVER OF PROHIBITION AGAINST REMARRIAGE

For good cause shown the court may waive the prohibition against remarriage provided by this subchapter as to either or both spouses if a record of the proceedings is made and preserved or if findings of fact and conclusions of law are filed by the court.

History of Fam. Code §6.802: Acts 1997, 75th Leg., ch. 7, §1, eff. Apr. 17, 1997. Source: Former Fam. Code §3.66(c).

CHAPTER 7. AWARD OF MARITAL PROPERTY

FAM §7.001. GENERAL RULE OF PROPERTY DIVISION

In a decree of divorce or annulment, the court shall order a division of the estate of the parties in a manner that the court deems just and right, having due regard for the rights of each party and any children of the marriage.

History of Fam. Code §7.001: Acts 1997, 75th Leg., ch. 7, §1, eff. Apr. 17, 1997. Source: Former Fam. Code §3.63(a).

See also *O'Connor's Texas Family Law Handbook* (2017), "Dividing & Confirming Marital Property," ch. 7, p. 775.

ANNOTATIONS

Generally

Dawson-Austin v. Austin, 968 S.W.2d 319, 324 (Tex.1998). "It is well settled in this State that the division of a marital estate is not a claim severable from the rest of a divorce proceeding. [¶] The cases that hold adjudication of divorce and division of the marital estate to be non-severable claims all do so in the context of [TRCP] 41 ('Misjoinder and Non-Joinder of Parties'), 174 ('Consolidation; Separate Trials'), and 320 ('Motion [for New Trial] and Action of Court Thereon'). [¶] No case holds that claims of divorce and division of property do not involve severable *jurisdictional* issues. The U.S. Supreme Court recognized long ago that a court could have jurisdiction to grant a divorce—an adjudication of parties' status—without having jurisdiction to divide their property—an adjudication of parties' rights."

O'Carolan v. Hopper, 414 S.W.3d 288, 311 (Tex. App.—Austin 2013, no pet.). "The [property] division must be equitable, but the trial court does not have to divide the community property equally. The trial court has wide discretion when dividing the property, but there must be some reasonable basis for an unequal division of the property." *See also* ***Fischer-Stoker v. Stoker***, 174 S.W.3d 272, 277 (Tex.App.—Houston [1st Dist.] 2005, pet. denied) (division must not be so disproportionate as to be inequitable, and circumstances must justify awarding more than one-half to one party).

Gathe v. Gathe, 376 S.W.3d 308, 314-15 (Tex. App.—Houston [14th Dist.] 2012, no pet.). "[T]he issue of divorce and the issue of property division are not severable. Because [Fam. Code] §7.001 ... makes the division of property in a divorce action mandatory, it is error for the trial court to sever the issue of divorce from the issue of property division. [TRCP] 320 applies to divorce cases, and a trial court may grant a partial new trial on property issues. However, '[i]n the event the court seeks to grant a partial new trial on certain property issues, it must grant a new trial on all issues since they may not be severed, or treat the order granting a divorce as interlocutory and proceed to consider the property issues, or what remains of them, on new trial.'" *See also* ***In re Marriage of Johnson***, 595 S.W.2d 900, 902 (Tex.App.—Amarillo 1980, writ dism'd) (divorce decree that does not dispose of parties' property is interlocutory and therefore not appealable).

In re Marriage of Edwards, 79 S.W.3d 88, 96 (Tex. App.—Texarkana 2002, no pet.). "Section 7.001 gives the trial court broad authority to divide the marital estate in a manner it deems just and right. That authority sometimes includes the power to appoint a receiver. The appointment of a receiver is left to the trial court's sound discretion. [¶] 'In recognition of the fact that appointment of a receiver without notice is one of the most drastic actions known to law or equity and should be exercised with extreme caution and only where great emergency or imperative necessity requires it, our courts have uniformly been reluctant to grant such harsh relief.' Judicial seizure and court management of any asset should be a last resort. [¶] It appears from the record before this court the trial court's practice is to appoint a receiver when the parties cannot reach an agreement on the division of property. Such a practice constitutes an abuse of discretion insofar as it does not ... determine what can be partitioned in kind between the parties and, if necessary to achieve a just and right division, appoint a receiver to dispose of the remainder."

Rodriguez v. Rodriguez, 616 S.W.2d 383, 384 (Tex. App.—Houston [14th Dist.] 1981, no writ). "[W]here a divorce suit is submitted to the jury, the verdict as to dividing the estate of the spouses is advisory only and the trial court may in its discretion disregard jury findings and divide the property in such manner as seems just and right under facts as they appear to the court." *See also* ***Archambault v. Archambault***, 763 S.W.2d 50, 51 (Tex.App.—Beaumont 1988, no writ) (jury's determination of market value of property is binding on trial court and not advisory).

Acceptance of Benefits

Kramer v. Kastleman, 508 S.W.3d 211, 213-14 (Tex. 2017). "The acceptance-of-benefits doctrine precludes a litigant from challenging a judgment after voluntarily accepting the judgment's benefits.... [¶] [It] is a fact-dependent, estoppel-based doctrine focused on preventing unfair prejudice to the opposing party. Under this doctrine, a merits-based disposition may not be denied absent acquiescence in the judgment to the opposing party's irremediable disadvantage. *At 220:* Because judgments in marital-dissolution cases typically divide assets in which a party's right to possession and control precedes the final decree, invoking estoppel based on

dominion over that property while the litigation is ongoing presents a more complex scenario than other civil disputes. *At 227:* [B]efore denying a merits-based resolution to a dispute, courts must evaluate whether, by asserting dominion over assets awarded in the judgment under review, the appealing party clearly intended to acquiesce in the judgment; whether the assets have been so dissipated as to prevent their recovery if the judgment is reversed or modified; and whether the opposing party will be unfairly prejudiced. Equity simply will not tolerate a Catch-22 that involves a choice between relinquishing possession and control of community property and relinquishing the right to appeal. *At 228:* [M]erely using, holding, controlling, or securing possession of community property awarded in a divorce decree does not constitute clear intent to acquiesce in the judgment and will not preclude an appeal absent prejudice to the nonappealing party.... Whether estoppel of the right to appeal is warranted involves a fact-dependent inquiry entrusted to the courts' discretion."

Estate of the Parties

Pearson v. Fillingim, 332 S.W.3d 361, 362 (Tex. 2011). "The divorce decree states that 'the estate of the parties be divided as follows' and divides [the] property ... into two schedules.... *At 363:* Trial courts can only divide community property, and the phrase 'estate of the parties' encompasses the community property of a marriage, but does not reach separate property. Thus, 'estate of the parties' in the ... divorce decree refers to community property only. *At 364:* Because [H] did not provide any evidence that the deeds were separate property, they were encompassed in the 'estate of the parties' and were divided by the divorce decree's residuary clauses." *See also* ***Cameron v. Cameron***, 641 S.W.2d 210, 214 (Tex.1982).

Factors—Generally

Murff v. Murff, 615 S.W.2d 696, 699 (Tex.1981). The trial court "may consider such factors as the spouses' capacities and abilities, benefits which the party not at fault would have derived from continuation of the marriage, business opportunities, education, relative physical conditions, relative financial condition and obligations, disparity of ages, size of separate estates, and the nature of the property. We believe that the consideration of such factors by the trial court is proper in making a 'just and right' division of the property. Likewise, the consideration of a disparity in earning capacities or of incomes is proper and need not be limited by 'necessitous' circumstances."

Young v. Young, 609 S.W.2d 758, 760 (Tex.1980). Family Code §3.63, now §7.001, "specifically authorizes the trial court to have 'due regard for the rights of each party and any children of the marriage' in the just and right division of the estate of the parties. [Respondent] contends that his son's support is a 'need' and not a 'right' and hence should not be considered in the property division. We hold that an unmarried disabled adult child's right to support corresponds to his parents' duty to support and is entitled to recognition under §3.63."

Zorilla v. Wahid, 83 S.W.3d 247, 252 (Tex.App.—Corpus Christi 2002, no pet.), *disapproved on other grounds*, ***Iliff v. Iliff***, 339 S.W.3d 74 (Tex.2011). "The court may consider a spouse's dissipation of the community estate, as well as the spouse's misuse of community property. A disproportionate award may also be considered when a spouse conceals community assets. A spouse's failure to make court-ordered temporary support payments or failure to obey the court's temporary order restricting the use of community assets may also justify a disproportionate award from the community estate." *See also* ***Slicker v. Slicker***, 464 S.W.3d 850, 862 (Tex.App.—Dallas 2015, no pet.).

Factors—Alimony

Garrett v. Garrett, 534 S.W.2d 381, 382 (Tex. App.—Houston [1st Dist.] 1976, no writ). "The trial court may require one party to make monetary payments to the other party after divorce, and such payments are not construed to be in the nature of permanent alimony if they are referable to any property which either spouse may have owned or claimed. ... 'So long as the division was referable to the rights and equities of the parties in and to the properties at the time of dissolution of the marriage, such division should not be regarded as an allowance of permanent alimony....'" *See also* ***Benedict v. Benedict***, 542 S.W.2d 692, 699 (Tex.App.—Fort Worth 1976, writ dism'd).

Factors—Attorney Fees

Carle v. Carle, 234 S.W.2d 1002, 1005 (Tex.1950). "The attorney's fee is but a factor to be considered by the court in making an equitable division of the estate, considering the conditions and needs of the parties and all of the surrounding circumstances."

Grossnickle v. Grossnickle, 935 S.W.2d 830, 846-47 (Tex.App.—Texarkana 1996, writ denied). "The trial court has great discretion in deciding whether to

award attorney's fees to either party and in determining the amount of attorney's fees to be so awarded. This same principle applies to whether the trial court should consider a party's payment of attorney's fees out of community funds in the division of the property. Because the award of attorney's fees in a divorce case can be part of the property division, the trial court can award them to either party, regardless who is successful in the trial court or on appeal. [¶] The allocation of attorney's fees is a factor to be considered by the court in making an equitable division of the community estate. Prior payments out of the community estate to attorneys in the divorce action are likewise to be taken into account in the division of the marital estate. Those payments must necessarily come from the community, because the trial court has no authority to direct one party to expend separate property funds on the other's behalf for such fees, because the sole authority of a trial court to require payment of attorney's fees lies in the court's authority to divide the marital estate." *See also* ***In re Marriage of C.A.S.***, 405 S.W.3d 373, 386 (Tex.App.—Dallas 2013, no pet.) (court awarded W additional community assets to compensate her for attorney fees she incurred).

Factors—Fault

Young v. Young, 609 S.W.2d 758, 762 (Tex.1980). "Both the Legislature and the courts have traditionally considered [cruelty, adultery, and desertion] to be 'fault.' In this situation, we agree with the trial court that fault may be a consideration to be weighed in the division of property. This does not mean that fault must be considered in all cases where a divorce is granted on fault grounds. Our holding is that it may be considered."

In re Marriage of Brown, 187 S.W.3d 143, 146 (Tex.App.—Waco 2006, no pet.). When a dissolution of marriage is sought solely on the grounds of insupportability, "'a trial court should have discretion to consider proven fault' in the break-up of the marriage when making a just and right division of the community estate." *But see* ***Phillips v. Phillips***, this page.

Phillips v. Phillips, 75 S.W.3d 564, 572 (Tex.App.—Beaumont 2002, no pet.). "[W]hen dissolution of marriage is sought *solely* on the ground of insupportability, evidence of 'fault' becomes irrelevant as an analytical construct and may not be considered by the trial court in its 'just and right' division of the community estate." *But see* ***In re Marriage of Brown***, this page.

Factors—Torts

Schlueter v. Schlueter, 975 S.W.2d 584, 585 (Tex. 1998). "Because a wronged spouse has an adequate remedy for fraud on the community through the 'just and right' property division upon divorce, we hold that there is no independent tort cause of action between spouses for damages to the community estate."

Twyman v. Twyman, 855 S.W.2d 619, 625 (Tex. 1993). "[A] spouse should not be allowed to recover tort damages and a disproportionate division of the community estate based on the same conduct. Therefore, when a factfinder awards tort damages to a divorcing spouse, the court may not consider the same tortious acts when dividing the marital estate. [A]n award for tortious conduct does not replace an analysis of the remaining factors to be considered when the trial court divides the marital estate. The court may still award a disproportionate division of property for reasons other than the tortious conduct. To avoid the potential problem of double recovery, the factfinder should consider the damages awarded in the tort action when dividing the parties' property. If a jury is used to render an advisory division of the parties' estate, the judge should limit, by appropriate instruction, the jury's consideration of the alleged tortious acts and later consider the award of damages in determining a just and right division of the marital estate."

Failure to Divide

Phillips v. Phillips, 951 S.W.2d 955, 957 (Tex. App.—Waco 1997, no pet.). Where "a divorce decree fails to provide for a division of community property, the husband and wife become tenants-in-common or joint owners thereof."

Marital Agreement

Bufkin v. Bufkin, 259 S.W.3d 343, 353 (Tex.App.—Dallas 2008, pet. denied). "Since [H] and [W] have contracted how the community estate was to be divided in the event of divorce, provisions of the ... Family Code allowing evidence of fault in divisions do not apply. The Agreement's terms dictated an even division of the community estate. Accordingly, evidence of fault is not relevant and the trial judge did not abuse her discretion when she excluded it."

Mischaracterization

Brown v. Wokocha, ___ S.W.3d ___ (Tex.App.—Houston [1st Dist.] 2017, n.p.h.) (No. 01-15-00759-CV; 4-11-17). "Mischaracterizing separate property as community property is an error that may require reversal.

However, reversal is not always required. A trial court does not err in characterizing separate property as community property if the party who had the burden to establish the separate nature fails to present adequate evidence to meet that burden. And even if the spouse who is arguing that property is separate property does satisfy her burden, a mischaracterization of separate property as community property will not require reversal if the mischaracterization had only a de minimus effect on the overall division of the estate."

Roberts v. Roberts, 402 S.W.3d 833, 839 (Tex. App.—San Antonio 2013, no pet.). "[T]he trial court's mischaracterization of property upon dissolution of a marriage is not an automatic ground for reversal. The trial court abuses its discretion, and reversal is warranted, only when the error materially affects the just and right division of the community estate. A *de minimis* effect does not require reversal." *See also* ***Monroe v. Monroe***, 358 S.W.3d 711, 718-19 (Tex.App.—San Antonio 2011, pet. denied) (mischaracterization of W's jewelry collection, which was valued at $150,000, was de minimis given that community estate was valued at over $9 million); ***Tate v. Tate***, 55 S.W.3d 1, 11-12 (Tex. App.—El Paso 2000, no pet.) (mischaracterization that would result in 10% shift of property distribution in W's favor did not constitute abuse of discretion).

Money Judgment

Young v. Young, 168 S.W.3d 276, 286-87 (Tex. App.—Dallas 2005, no pet.). "A trial court may impose an equitable lien against community property to secure one spouse's obligation to pay a monetary award that represents the consideration for the other spouse's relinquishment of his or her interest in the marital estate. The trial court awarded [W] an equitable lien in certain community assets that the trial court awarded to [H]. The purpose of the lien was to secure the money judgment awarded to [W]. We conclude the trial court did not err in placing a lien on assets it found to belong to the community."

Walston v. Walston, 971 S.W.2d 687, 692-93 (Tex. App.—Waco 1998, pet. denied). "In determining if property is subject to division in kind the trial court should consider the 'nature and type of particular property involved and the relative conditions, circumstances, capabilities and experience of the parties.' These factors are also considered when the trial court must decide whether to divide community property by awarding a money judgment to one party and community assets to the other party, instead of dividing the community property in kind. Moreover, [Fam. Code] §3.63 [now §7.001] authorizes the trial court to appoint a receiver for selling property as necessary to carry out the trial court's orders and judgments."

Simpson v. Simpson, 727 S.W.2d 662, 663 (Tex. App.—Dallas 1987, no writ). "The award of a money judgment is one manner and method of dividing property in a divorce proceeding."

Partition in Kind

Hailey v. Hailey, 331 S.W.2d 299, 302-03 (Tex. 1960). "[T]he statute puts the duty on the trial court to make a partition of the community property whenever the pleadings of either party show the existence of such property. The trial court shall consider all the facts and circumstances shown by the evidence and then partition the community property, both personal and real estate, in such manner as may be just and right. ... The trial court has the duty to determine if the community property is subject to partition in kind. If [the trial court] determines that it is then [the trial court] shall equitably divide the community property between the parties. If it is not subject to partition in kind the trial court can appoint a receiver and order so much of the property as is incapable of partition to be sold and the proceeds divided between the parties in such portions as, in the discretion of the court, may be a just, fair and equitable partition, having in mind the rights of the parties and the children."

Cecola v. Ruley, 12 S.W.3d 848, 853 (Tex.App.—Texarkana 2000, no pet.). "Whether a piece of land can fairly be partitioned in kind is a question of fact for the court or jury to decide. The law favors partition in kind over partition by sale. Therefore, at trial the burden of proof falls on the party opposing partitioning in kind and seeking a partition by sale. *At 855:* If the property can be divided in kind without materially impairing its value, a sale will not be ordered, but when dividing the land into parcels causes its value to be substantially less than its value when whole, the rights of the owners are substantially prejudiced. Substantial economic loss is one of the significant factors that would warrant a sale in lieu of a partition in kind. [T]he trial court expressed a concern as to whether the property could be divided into parts of equal value. This is a proper concern and another significant factor in determining whether a partition could be fair and equitable, but even if the two parts are divided into equal value, if the

value as a part of the larger tract has been greatly diminished, this also should be considered in determining whether or not a division in kind would be fair and equitable."

Standard of Review

Richardson v. Richardson, 424 S.W.3d 691, 696 (Tex.App.—El Paso 2014, no pet.). "[T]he party challenging the division [of property] bears the burden of demonstrating from the evidence in the record that the trial court's division was so unjust and unfair as to be an abuse of discretion. [¶] We employ a two-pronged test in determining whether the trial court abused its discretion and inquire: (1) did the trial court have sufficient information upon which to exercise discretion, and (2) did the trial court abuse its discretion by making a property division that was manifestly unjust or unfair?" *See also* ***Evans v. Evans***, 14 S.W.3d 343, 345-46 (Tex.App.—Houston [14th Dist.] 2000, no pet.) (trial court abuses its discretion by acting arbitrarily or unreasonably, without reference to any guiding rules and principles; i.e., ruling without supporting evidence).

Robles v. Robles, 965 S.W.2d 605, 621 (Tex.App.—Houston [1st Dist.] 1998, pet. denied). "The role of an appellate court is only to determine whether the trial court abused its discretion in its disposition of the community property and an appellate court does not have the authority to render judgment dividing the marital property. We presume the trial court exercised its discretion properly." *See also* ***Von Hohn v. Von Hohn***, 260 S.W.3d 631, 641 (Tex.App.—Tyler 2008, no pet.) (once reversible error is found, appellate court must remand entire community estate to trial court for new division).

Valuation

Mandell v. Mandell, 310 S.W.3d 531, 537 (Tex. App.—Fort Worth 2010, pet. denied). "A straight fair market value is not an appropriate valuation method ... when a community estate owns shares in a closely held corporation and, by agreement, any sale of the shares of stock is restricted to the corporation or other stockholders. When the sale of stock is restricted by a requirement that the shares be offered first to the corporation or to other shareholders, then essentially the fair market value of the stock is zero. In this situation, the parties may show the actual value of the property interest to the owner. Such evidence might include the value of being able, by virtue of ownership of the closely held stock, to drive a new automobile, to have health insurance paid for by the company, to have a company-financed life insurance policy, to belong to a country club at company expense, and other similar financial benefits. *At 539:* A spouse is not entitled to a percentage of his or her [spouse's] future earnings. A spouse is only entitled to a division of property that the community owns at the time of divorce. *At 541:* Because the ... 'comparable sales value' for [H's] shares of ... stock was ... based on prior sales by former [shareholders] and because [that price] is the only price that [the] stock may be sold at, the trial court did not abuse its discretion by valuing the stock ... under a comparable sales valuation and as mandated by the Shareholders Agreement even though [W] did not sign it." *See also* ***R.V.K. v. L.L.K.***, 103 S.W.3d 612, 619 (Tex.App.—San Antonio 2003, no pet.) (trial court erred by not considering buy/sell agreements' restriction on marketability of stock).

Von Hohn v. Von Hohn, 260 S.W.3d 631, 638 (Tex. App.—Tyler 2008, no pet.). "[H] contends that his interest in the [law firm for which he worked] was defined by [a] partnership agreement and that the community estate was not entitled to a greater interest than that to which he was entitled in the firm's commercial goodwill. *At 640:* [We find] that the [law-firm] partnership agreement does not control the value of the individual partnership interests in the event of a divorce. The [law firm] was an ongoing partnership as of the time of divorce, ... and ... none of the triggering events specified in the partnership agreement had occurred. Consequently, the formula in the partnership agreement was not determinative of the value of [H's] interest in the [law firm]. [T]he trial court did not err when it determined that the proper measure of the value of the community interest in the [law firm] could include methods other than those set forth in the partnership agreement."

Grossnickle v. Grossnickle, 935 S.W.2d 830, 842 (Tex.App.—Texarkana 1996, writ denied). "[W]hether an appraisal is near enough in time to the date of the divorce to be considered in determining the value of the property in question for purpose of the property division is generally left to the discretion of the trial court." *See also* ***O'Carolan v. Hopper***, 414 S.W.3d 288, 312 (Tex.App.—Austin 2013, no pet.) (court correctly valued community property at time of divorce, not at time of trial on remand nine years later).

Parker v. Parker, 897 S.W.2d 918, 932 (Tex.App.—Fort Worth 1995, writ denied), *overruled on other grounds*, ***Formosa Plastics Corp. v. Presidio Eng'rs & Contractors, Inc.***, 960 S.W.2d 41 (Tex.1998). "[W]e hold the determination of whether to use the time of the divorce or the time of the division as the valuation date of an asset when the divorce and division of the property occur at different dates is in fact so specific that it should be left to the discretion of the trial judge to avoid the inequities that could result by making a bright line rule."

Finn v. Finn, 658 S.W.2d 735, 746 (Tex.App.—Dallas 1983, writ ref'd n.r.e.). "We find that the denial of discovery was such a denial of the rights of [W] as was reasonably calculated to cause and probably did cause the rendition of an improper judgment. [H's] interest in the firm was a major asset of the community estate. Lack of this discovery left the trial court's valuation of this asset without proper support in the evidence. Since this interest is the largest item of the community estate, and its value was the principal contested issue at the trial with respect to the division of the property of the parties, we conclude that without a proper valuation the trial court could not properly exercise its discretion in making a 'just and right' division within [Fam. Code] §3.63 [now §7.001]."

FAM §7.002. DIVISION & DISPOSITION OF CERTAIN PROPERTY UNDER SPECIAL CIRCUMSTANCES

(a) In addition to the division of the estate of the parties required by Section 7.001, in a decree of divorce or annulment the court shall order a division of the following real and personal property, wherever situated, in a manner that the court deems just and right, having due regard for the rights of each party and any children of the marriage:

(1) property that was acquired by either spouse while domiciled in another state and that would have been community property if the spouse who acquired the property had been domiciled in this state at the time of the acquisition; or

(2) property that was acquired by either spouse in exchange for real or personal property and that would have been community property if the spouse who acquired the property so exchanged had been domiciled in this state at the time of its acquisition.

(b) In a decree of divorce or annulment, the court shall award to a spouse the following real and personal property, wherever situated, as the separate property of the spouse:

(1) property that was acquired by the spouse while domiciled in another state and that would have been the spouse's separate property if the spouse had been domiciled in this state at the time of acquisition; or

(2) property that was acquired by the spouse in exchange for real or personal property and that would have been the spouse's separate property if the spouse had been domiciled in this state at the time of acquisition.

(c) In a decree of divorce or annulment, the court shall confirm the following as the separate property of a spouse if partitioned or exchanged by written agreement of the spouses:

(1) income and earnings from the spouses' property, wages, salaries, and other forms of compensation received on or after January 1 of the year in which the suit for dissolution of marriage was filed; or

(2) income and earnings from the spouses' property, wages, salaries, and other forms of compensation received in another year during which the spouses were married for any part of the year.

History of Fam. Code §7.002: Acts 1997, 75th Leg., ch. 7, §1, eff. Apr. 17, 1997. Amended by Acts 1999, 76th Leg., ch. 692, §4, eff. Sept. 1, 1999; Acts 2001, 77th Leg., ch. 838, §4, eff. Sept. 1, 2001; Acts 2003, 78th Leg., ch. 230, §4, eff. Sept. 1, 2003. Source: Former Fam. Code §3.63(b).

See also ***O'Connor's Texas Family Law Handbook*** (2017), "Dividing & Confirming Marital Property," ch. 7, p. 775.

ANNOTATIONS

Cayan v. Cayan, 38 S.W.3d 161, 164 (Tex.App.—Houston [14th Dist.] 2000, pet. denied). "In a final decree of divorce, a trial court is generally required to order a division of the community and quasi-community property that the court deems 'just and right.'"

Dawson-Austin v. Austin, 920 S.W.2d 776, 789-90 (Tex.App.—Dallas 1996), *rev'd on other grounds*, 968 S.W.2d 319 (Tex.1998). "[H] asserts that [Fam. Code] §3.63(b) [now §7.002] operates as a comprehensive choice-of-law provision in property characterization issues. He argues that §3.63(b)(1) should be read as providing that the characterization of property is dependent solely on Texas law. Under [H's] interpretation of §3.63(b), if property is characterized as community property in the residential state of the acquiring party but would have been separate property if the parties had resided in Texas, then in a divorce proceeding in a

Texas court, the property will be classified as separate property. [¶] We disagree with [H's] sweeping interpretation of §3.63(b). The statute by its terms acts only *to expand, not restrict, the definition of community property*. Nothing in the legislative history of the statute or the development of the law in this area suggests that §3.63(b) was intended to expand the definition of separate property and thus restrict the extent of community property. Even the popular name for the statute, the 'quasi-community' statute, suggests that it is intended to expand the definition of community property. If the legislature had intended for the statute to be a comprehensive choice-of-law provision, it would not have phrased the statute as an expanded definition of community property."

Ismail v. Ismail, 702 S.W.2d 216, 219 (Tex.App.—Houston [1st Dist.] 1985, writ ref'd n.r.e.). "The quasi-community property statute does not expressly limit its reach to situations where *both* spouses have migrated from a common law jurisdiction to Texas. [¶] We conclude that [Fam. Code] §3.63(b) [now §7.002] applies in the division of migratory spouses' property regardless of the nature of the previous domicile's legal system. [¶] [H] also argues that the statute should not be applied where only one spouse migrates to Texas. *At 221:* The real property that is the subject of this appeal is located in Texas. Texas follows the general rule that marital rights of spouses in real property are determined by the law of the place where the land is situated. Additionally, [H] has had other significant continuous business and personal contacts with Texas.... Thus, from a due process perspective, [H's] contacts with Texas, when coupled with Texas' interest in protecting the migrant spouse in this case, warrant application of Texas law to the division of the Texas property. [¶] Also, we should not interpret the language of ***Cameron*** [***v. Cameron***, 641 S.W.2d 210 (Tex.1982),] to hold that in *every* case where a party receives less in the Texas community property division than he or she would have received under the system of the previous domicile, the party has been deprived of due process. Clearly, where the Texas division of property approximates what another domicile's law requires, the nonmigrant spouse may not complain of divestment of 'separate' property. But neither can the appellant in this case complain of an unconstitutional divestment of 'separate' property under our state's constitution when, through his extensive contacts with this state, and through his personal appearance in this litigation, he has implicitly consented to Texas courts' exercising their jurisdiction in equitably dividing the marital property. *At 222:* [H] argues that the trial court erred in deciding this case under Texas law.... Property acquired by a spouse when domiciled in another jurisdiction was, under pre-***Cameron*** common law, characterized according to the previous domicile's laws. [¶] The enactment of §3.63(b), however, obviates the need to apply this anachronistic conflict-of-laws principle."

FAM §7.003. DISPOSITION OF RETIREMENT & EMPLOYMENT BENEFITS & OTHER PLANS

In a decree of divorce or annulment, the court shall determine the rights of both spouses in a pension, retirement plan, annuity, individual retirement account, employee stock option plan, stock option, or other form of savings, bonus, profit-sharing, or other employer plan or financial plan of an employee or a participant, regardless of whether the person is self-employed, in the nature of compensation or savings.

History of Fam. Code §7.003: Acts 1997, 75th Leg., ch. 7, §1, eff. Apr. 17, 1997. Source: Former Fam. Code §3.633(a).

See also ***O'Connor's Texas Family Law Handbook*** (2017), "Dividing & Confirming Qualified Private Retirement Benefits," ch. 7-E, p. 871.

ANNOTATIONS

Generally

Boggs v. Boggs, 520 U.S. 833, 835-36 (1997). "We consider whether [ERISA] pre-empts a state law allowing a nonparticipant spouse to transfer by testamentary instrument an interest in undistributed pension plan benefits. Given the pervasive significance of pension plans in the national economy, the congressional mandate for their uniform and comprehensive regulation, and the fundamental importance of community property law in defining the marital partnership in a number of States, the question is of undoubted importance. We hold ERISA pre-empts the state law. *At 844:* [Community-property] law, to the extent it provides [children] with a right to a portion of [a spouse's qualified retirement benefits], is pre-empted [by ERISA, which requires transfer of certain benefits to the employee's spouse]."

Koepke v. Koepke, 732 S.W.2d 299, 299 (Tex.1987). "The divorce decree was rendered after the decision in ***McCarty*** [***v. McCarty***, 453 U.S. 210 (1981)], but before the effective date of the Uniformed Services Former Spouses Protection Act [USFSPA], 10 U.S.C.

§1408 (February 1, 1983). *At 300:* Since the enactment of USFSPA, we have approved partition as a means to remedy certain injustices caused by ***McCarty***. Partition, however, has been limited to those post-***McCarty*** divorce decrees which did not expressly award the military retirement benefits to the serviceman. The express award of retirement benefits in a divorce decree operates as a bar to any subsequent partition suit under principles of res judicata. [¶] The court of appeals in the present case attempts to [hold] that the following language constitutes an express award of the military retirement benefits: 'All relief requested in this case and not expressly granted herein be and is hereby denied.' To construe this language, the court of appeals looked behind the judgment to the pleadings of [ex-W] which purportedly sought part of the military retirement benefits. The court of appeals then deduced that the failure to award [ex-W] a share of the military retirement benefits must have been an award of such benefits to [ex-H/serviceman] because a judgment which incorporates the above language 'expressly disposes of all parties and issues in the case'.... [¶] The divorce decree does not expressly award the military retirement benefits to [ex-H/serviceman]. The court of appeals' application of the doctrine of res judicata to bar this partition suit is erroneous...."

Ex parte Johnson, 591 S.W.2d 453, 454 (Tex.1979). "We hold that [disability compensation benefits from the Veterans' Administration for service-connected disabilities authorized by U.S.C. title 38] are not to be treated as 'property' and future benefits are not subject to division upon divorce as property."

Perez v. Perez, 587 S.W.2d 671, 672 (Tex.1979). "[W] asserts that [H's] military readjustment benefits are analogous to military retirement benefits. She argues that readjustment benefits are a property right earned during active service and, like retirement benefits earned during marriage, constitute community property. We disagree. The legislative history of the federal statute indicates a Congressional intent to provide a non-earned gratuity. *At 673:* The separate property of a spouse consists of property owned or claimed by the spouse before marriage; the property acquired by the spouse during marriage by gift, devise, or descent; and the recovery for personal injuries sustained by the spouse during the marriage, except any recovery for loss of earning capacity during marriage. It is apparent that readjustment benefits were bestowed by Congress upon an involuntarily released member of the Army Reserve as an unearned gratuity; and that to classify these benefits as a gift under Texas property rules comports with stated federal objectives."

Marsh v. Wallace, 924 S.W.2d 423, 425 (Tex. App.—Austin 1996, no writ). "[H] complains that the trial court erred in concluding that the [special separation benefit (SSB)] payment he received pursuant to [10 U.S.C.] §1174a was retirement pay and therefore divisible under the parties' divorce decree. *At 426:* SSB payments are designed to 'assist separating personnel *and their families*.' They differ from payments made upon involuntary severance from the military. In consideration of receiving an SSB payment, one voluntarily elects to separate from active duty. [¶] By its nature, an SSB payment resembles a buy-out of the service member's investment in military retirement, a sort of lump sum settlement, even though the retirement is not yet vested, in order to encourage the member's voluntary early separation from service. The recipient who reenlists and later becomes eligible for retirement has in effect received a prepayment on retirement pay because the retirement benefits are reduced by the amount of the SSB payment. Thus, one can wait to receive regular retirement benefits or opt out in favor of an SSB payment, but not both. As one court explained, an 'SSB payment [is] either retirement proceeds or a payment in lieu of retirement benefits.' *At 427:* We do not agree with an analysis which would allow one former spouse to retain all the compensation by unilaterally altering a retirement plan asset in which the other former spouse has a court-decreed interest. ... Therefore, we hold that the trial court did not err in holding that [H's] SSB payment was retirement pay in which [W] was entitled to share under the divorce decree."

Wallace v. Fuller, 832 S.W.2d 714, 716 (Tex.App.—Austin 1992, no writ). H contends "that the Former Spouses' Protection Act precludes a state court's authority to divide his military disability benefits. [H] argues that the Act expressly subjects disposable retired pay to state marital property laws but excludes military disability benefits from such treatment.... We agree that the Act's definition of disposable retired pay does not include the military disability benefits at issue in this case. The question then presented is whether Texas courts may treat as community property *only* disposable retired pay, as that term is defined in the Act.

At 718: According to ***Mansell*** [*v.* ***Mansell***, 490 U.S. 581 (1989)], state courts have authority to treat only 'disposable retired pay' as marital property. Because the Act excludes both Ch. 61 disability benefits and veterans' disability benefits from its definition of 'disposable retired pay' we are unable to avoid the applicability of ***Mansell***'s preemption doctrine. By definition, the military disability pay at issue today is not disposable retired pay. ***Mansell*** ... supports [H's] position that a state court lacks the authority to treat military disability benefits as community property subject to division in a partition proceeding."

Gallegos v. Gallegos, 788 S.W.2d 158, 160 (Tex. App.—San Antonio 1990, no writ). "[H] received V.A. Disability benefits and waived a like portion of his retirement pay. Following the holding of ***Mansell***, we hold that state courts do not have the power to treat military retirement pay that has been waived in order to receive V.A. Disability benefits as property divisible upon divorce. As a result, that portion of [H's] retirement benefit, which was waived by [H] in order to receive V.A. Disability benefits, was not divisible by the court and doing so was error. [¶] [H also] contends that the trial court erred in awarding [W] an interest in that portion of [H's] military retirement pay which was subjected to a partial defeasance because of [H's] Civil Service employment. *At 161:* [H] contends, and we agree, that [5 U.S.C.] §5532 ... requires the reduction of a retired officer's retired pay in order for him to receive the full pay of his Civil Service position. As with military retirement benefits, the [Uniformed Services Former Spouses' Protection Act] specifically defines the term 'disposable retired or retainer pay' to include 'amounts waived in order to receive compensation under Title 5....' [T]herefore, we hold that the court was without authority to divide that portion of [H's] retirement pay that was reduced in order for him to receive the full pay of his Civil Service position, as the amount waived in order to receive compensation under 5 U.S.C. §5532 must first be deducted to determine the 'disposable retired or retainer pay.' Only after such deductions are made may the court determine what portion of [H's] retirement pay is community property."

Railroad Retirement

Kamel v. Kamel, 721 S.W.2d 450, 452-53 (Tex. App.—Tyler 1986, no writ). "[H] argues that the trial court erred in awarding [W] a percentage of all retirement benefits arising out of [H's] employment with Cotton Belt Railroad. [¶] Under the Railroad Retirement Solvency Act of 1983, ... Congress added a subsection to [45 U.S.C.] §231m after the ***Hisquierdo*** [*v.* ***Hisquierdo***, 439 U.S. 572 (1979),] and ***Eichelberger*** [*v.* ***Eichelberger***, 582 S.W.2d 395 (Tex.1979),] decisions were handed down. The amendment expressly permits characterization of certain components of the [retirement] benefits as community property. The basic component of [computing] benefits under [45 U.S.C.] §231b(a), however, remains free of a trial court's division under the amendment. [¶] The record reflects that no evidence was adduced as to the value of each of the components of the appellant's retirement benefits. There was therefore no evidence as to what part of the benefits were susceptible to division by the court. It seems clear that the benefits were not calculated to exclude the exempt component set forth in §231b(a). The trial court lacked the power to divide *all* of the appellant's retirement benefits and its attempt to do so was beyond its discretion."

FAM §7.004. DISPOSITION OF RIGHTS IN INSURANCE

In a decree of divorce or annulment, the court shall specifically divide or award the rights of each spouse in an insurance policy.

History of Fam. Code §7.004: Acts 1997, 75th Leg., ch. 7, §1, eff. Apr. 17, 1997. Source: Former Fam. Code §3.632(a).

See also ***O'Connor's Texas Family Law Handbook*** (2017), "Dividing & Confirming Personal Property," ch. 7-C, p. 841.

FAM §7.005. INSURANCE COVERAGE NOT SPECIFICALLY AWARDED

(a) If in a decree of divorce or annulment the court does not specifically award all of the rights of the spouses in an insurance policy other than life insurance in effect at the time the decree is rendered, the policy remains in effect until the policy expires according to the policy's own terms.

(b) The proceeds of a valid claim under the policy are payable as follows:

(1) if the interest in the property insured was awarded solely to one former spouse by the decree, to that former spouse;

(2) if an interest in the property insured was awarded to each former spouse, to those former spouses in proportion to the interests awarded; or

(3) if the insurance coverage is directly related to the person of one of the former spouses, to that former spouse.

(c) The failure of either former spouse to change the endorsement on the policy to reflect the distribution of proceeds established by this section does not relieve the insurer of liability to pay the proceeds or any other obligation on the policy.

(d) This section does not affect the right of a former spouse to assert an ownership interest in an undivided life insurance policy, as provided by Subchapter D, Chapter 9.

History of Fam. Code §7.005: Acts 1997, 75th Leg., ch. 7, §1, eff. Apr. 17, 1997. Source: Former Fam. Code §3.632(d), (e).

FAM §7.006. AGREEMENT INCIDENT TO DIVORCE OR ANNULMENT

(a) To promote amicable settlement of disputes in a suit for divorce or annulment, the spouses may enter into a written agreement concerning the division of the property and the liabilities of the spouses and maintenance of either spouse. The agreement may be revised or repudiated before rendition of the divorce or annulment unless the agreement is binding under another rule of law.

(b) If the court finds that the terms of the written agreement in a divorce or annulment are just and right, those terms are binding on the court. If the court approves the agreement, the court may set forth the agreement in full or incorporate the agreement by reference in the final decree.

(c) If the court finds that the terms of the written agreement in a divorce or annulment are not just and right, the court may request the spouses to submit a revised agreement or may set the case for a contested hearing.

History of Fam. Code §7.006: Acts 1997, 75th Leg., ch. 7, §1, eff. Apr. 17, 1997. Source: Former Fam. Code §3.631.

Author's comment: For the current law on the division of defined-benefit plans, defined-contribution plans, stock options, and restricted stock plans, see Family Code §3.007.

See also ***O'Connor's Texas Family Law Handbook*** (2017), "Agreement incident to divorce," ch. 3-A, §13.2, p. 258.

ANNOTATIONS

Buys v. Buys, 924 S.W.2d 369, 372 (Tex.1996). "The rules of contract law govern the construction of a property settlement agreement incorporated into a divorce decree. If the agreement is worded so that we can give it a certain or definite legal meaning, it is not ambiguous and we construe it as a matter of law." *See also* ***McGoodwin v. McGoodwin***, 671 S.W.2d 880, 882 (Tex. 1984) (terms of property settlement agreement were analyzed using contract law for sale of land).

Hallsted v. McGinnis, 483 S.W.3d 72, 77 (Tex. App.—Houston [1st Dist.] 2015, no pet.). "[H's] contention that the [contractual alimony] provision [in the agreement incident to divorce] is unenforceable as a matter of public policy because it requires him to pay indefinite, 'permanent' alimony is without merit. Although public policy limits a *court's* authority to award alimony, Texas policies favoring freedom of contract and promoting the settlement of disputes allow divorcing *parties* to agree to support payments to a former spouse for any length of time, whether or not the obligation terminates on a date certain."

Abrams v. Salinas, 467 S.W.3d 606, 610 (Tex. App.—San Antonio 2015, no pet.). "'Once the agreement of the parties has been approved by the court *and made a part of its judgment*, the agreement is no longer merely a contract between private individuals but is the judgment of the court.' '[T]he divorce decree becomes a consent judgment, subject to the same degree of finality and binding force as a judgment rendered in an adversary proceeding.' *At 611:* When the terms of the agreed divorce have been incorporated into the judgment, [under CPRC §34.001,] 'an action for enforcement of [the] judgment may be brought within ten years from the date of judgment.' [¶] [However, we] hold that for an action to enforce a payment ordered by the judgment but predicated on future conditions, the [ten-year] dormant judgment statute does not begin to run on the date the judgment becomes final; rather, it begins to run when the payment becomes due."

Kendrick v. Seibert, 439 S.W.3d 408, 410 (Tex. App.—Houston [1st Dist.] 2014, no pet.). "In a divorce proceeding, the parties can enter into an agreement over the matters to be resolved in the divorce. Similarly, the parties can enter into agreements concerning matters affecting the parent-child relationship. [C]oncerning the divorce and determination of the material estate, the agreement is enforceable as a contract. *At 411:* [C]oncerning the parent-child relationship, terms of the agreement concerning conservatorship, access to the child, or child support are not enforceable as a contract. Any other terms concerning the parent-child relationship can be enforced as a contract."

In re Marriage of Western, No. 10-12-00072-CV (Tex.App.—Waco 2012, no pet.) (memo op.; 8-2-12). "[H] argues that the [settlement] agreement is unenforceable because it did not contain material terms which were later clarified after the trial court ques-

tioned the parties. [¶] Other than the provisions for attorney's fees and the couple's debt accumulated after separation, we find the trial court's clarifications to be minor in nature and not material so as to render the agreement unenforceable. [¶] With regard to additional terms or clarifications, such as the attorney's fees and the division of debts incurred after separation in this case, Texas courts have held that the court may divide the community estate of the parties upon divorce by itself partitioning the estate, by setting forth a property settlement agreement in the decree, or by incorporating such an agreement by reference in the decree. And, as to the remainder of the estate, the court must follow the mandates … of the Family Code to make a 'just and right' division of the property. [¶] We find the trial court's provisions in this case for attorney's fees and the division of the debts accumulated after separation … do not directly contradict the agreement of the parties, and we do not believe that they somehow render the agreement unenforceable." (Internal quotes omitted.) *See also* ***In re Marriage of Hallman***, No. 06-09-00089-CV (Tex.App.—Texarkana 2010, pet. denied) (memo op.; 2-23-10) (even though court enforced parties' Rule 11 agreement and incorporated it into final divorce decree, trial court was still obligated to divide community property that was not disposed of in Rule 11 agreement). *But see* ***Keim v. Anderson***, this page.

Woods v. Woods, 167 S.W.3d 932, 933 (Tex.App.—Amarillo 2005, no pet.). "[O]ne may revoke consent to a settlement agreement at any time before judgment is rendered on the agreement. This is so because a trial court cannot render a valid agreed judgment absent the consent of the parties at the time it is rendered. [C]onsent at the time judgment is rendered must still exist. *At 934:* Here, the record clearly illustrates that [W] withdrew her consent to the … agreement [that had been approved by the court] before the trial court signed the final decree. *At 935:* [T]he trial court erred by incorporating into its judgment an agreement which [W] had previously revoked." *See also* ***Cook v. Cook***, 243 S.W.3d 800, 801-02 (Tex.App.—Fort Worth 2007, no pet.) (court's oral approval of settlement agreement is not rendition of judgment).

Mailhot v. Mailhot, 124 S.W.3d 775, 777 (Tex. App.—Houston [1st Dist.] 2003, no pet.). See annotation under Family Code §6.602, p. 80.

Markowitz v. Markowitz, 118 S.W.3d 82, 88 (Tex. App.—Houston [14th Dist.] 2003, pet. denied). "While a trial court retains plenary power, it has the authority to grant a new trial after rendition of an agreed divorce. *At 89:* By vacating the original judgment, the trial court clearly withdrew its approval of the terms in the agreement. Additionally, in its Findings of Fact and Conclusions of Law, the trial court concluded that the terms of the agreement were not just and right. Thus, without approval from the trial court, there was no longer a written agreement capable of being enforced. *At 90:* After a new trial is granted, the court should have an opportunity to either accept or reject the agreement. [¶] [W]e hold that any contractual obligation arising from the decree was extinguished when the trial court concluded that it was not 'just and right.'"

Cayan v. Cayan, 38 S.W.3d 161, 164-65 (Tex. App.—Houston [14th Dist.] 2000, pet. denied). "Where parties enter into an agreement concerning the division of their property, the agreement may be revised or repudiated before rendition of the divorce '*unless the agreement is binding under another rule of law.*' If the court finds that the terms of a property division agreement are just and right, those terms are binding on the court; if not, the court may request the parties to submit a revised agreement or may set the case for a contested hearing. Once a court renders judgment on a settlement agreement, consent to the agreement cannot be revoked. [¶] Because [Fam. Code] §7.006(a) expressly recognizes that a settlement agreement can be made binding before rendition of the divorce under another rule of law, and because [Fam. Code] §6.602 expressly entitles a party to a §6.602 agreement to judgment notwithstanding other law, we interpret §6.602 simply as an exception to §7.006(a) whereby parties to a divorce may elect to make their agreement binding as of the time of its execution rather than at the subsequent time the divorce is rendered."

Keim v. Anderson, 943 S.W.2d 938, 946 (Tex. App.—El Paso 1997, no writ). "A final judgment founded upon a settlement agreement must be in strict compliance with the agreement. The trial court has no power to supply terms, provisions, or conditions not previously agreed to by the parties. It can merely approve or reject the agreement. If an appellate court determines that the decree contains terms and provisions dividing the community property that were never agreed to by the parties, it must reverse the judgment and remand the

cause. On the other hand, when the record reflects a clerical variance between a judgment announced in open court and the judgment eventually signed by the trial judge, the appellate court can modify the judgment to correct the mistake. [¶] While we believe that [the] modification [in this case] was outside of the trial court's prerogative, we also believe that the court should have an opportunity to either accept the agreement as stipulated, set aside the agreement to consider the [additional issues], or reject the agreement on the grounds that it does not constitute a just and right division of the parties' estates." *See also* ***Engineer v. Engineer***, 187 S.W.3d 625, 626-27 (Tex.App.—Houston [14th Dist.] 2006, no pet.) (court has no discretion to change parties' agreement before entering judgment). *But see* ***In re Marriage of Western***, p. 97.

Clanin v. Clanin, 918 S.W.2d 673, 676-77 (Tex. App.—Fort Worth 1996, no writ). "An agreement for judgment will not be enforced unless the agreement is reduced to writing, signed and filed with the papers as part of the record, or unless it is made in open court and entered of record. Compliance with the 'open court and entered of record' portion of [TRCP] 11 satisfies the [Fam. Code] §3.631 [now §7.006] requirement of written agreements in divorce cases. This is so because the sworn testimony of the parties given to the court reporter in open court memorializes the parties' consent and can also be reduced to writing. Therefore, this procedure has the same legal effect as a written agreement signed by the parties and, in fact, results in a written agreement that meets the requirements of ... §3.631 for agreements in divorce cases to be in writing."

FAM §7.007. DISPOSITION OF CLAIM FOR REIMBURSEMENT

In a decree of divorce or annulment, the court shall determine the rights of both spouses in a claim for reimbursement as provided by Subchapter E, Chapter 3, and shall apply equitable principles to:

(1) determine whether to recognize the claim after taking into account all the relative circumstances of the spouses; and

(2) order a division of the claim for reimbursement, if appropriate, in a manner that the court considers just and right, having due regard for the rights of each party and any children of the marriage.

History of Fam. Code §7.007: Acts 2001, 77th Leg., ch. 838, §5, eff. Sept. 1, 2001. Amended by Acts 2009, 81st Leg., ch. 768, §7, eff. Sept. 1, 2009.

See also ***O'Connor's Texas Family Law Handbook*** (2017), "Reimbursement Claims," ch. 7-F, p. 910.

FAM §7.008. CONSIDERATION OF TAXES

In ordering the division of the estate of the parties to a suit for dissolution of a marriage, the court may consider:

(1) whether a specific asset will be subject to taxation; and

(2) if the asset will be subject to taxation, when the tax will be required to be paid.

History of Fam. Code §7.008: Acts 2005, 79th Leg., ch. 168, §1, eff. Sept. 1, 2005.

See also ***O'Connor's Texas Family Law Handbook*** (2017), "Tax consequences of division," ch. 7-A, §7.2.3(4), p. 798.

ANNOTATIONS

Baccus v. Baccus, 808 S.W.2d 694, 700 (Tex.App.—Beaumont 1991, no writ). "[T]ax consequences stemming from the division of property as well as any unpaid tax liabilities are proper factors to be considered by the trial court in deriving at a fair and just division of the community properties. Furthermore, it is reversible error for a court to refuse to consider tax liability, particularly when it is substantial and one of the spouses is without means to pay the obligation." *See also* ***Able v. Able***, 725 S.W.2d 778, 780 (Tex.App.—Houston [14th Dist.] 1987, writ ref'd n.r.e.) (court can take tax liability into consideration and can even require one party to assume other party's liability or require reimbursement for taxes paid).

FAM §7.009. FRAUD ON THE COMMUNITY; DIVISION & DISPOSITION OF RECONSTITUTED ESTATE

(a) In this section, "reconstituted estate" means the total value of the community estate that would exist if an actual or constructive fraud on the community had not occurred.

(b) If the trier of fact determines that a spouse has committed actual or constructive fraud on the community, the court shall:

(1) calculate the value by which the community estate was depleted as a result of the fraud on the community and calculate the amount of the reconstituted estate; and

(2) divide the value of the reconstituted estate between the parties in a manner the court deems just and right.

(c) In making a just and right division of the reconstituted estate under Section 7.001, the court may grant any legal or equitable relief necessary to accomplish a just and right division, including:

(1) awarding to the wronged spouse an appropriate share of the community estate remaining after the actual or constructive fraud on the community;

(2) awarding a money judgment in favor of the wronged spouse against the spouse who committed the actual or constructive fraud on the community; or

(3) awarding to the wronged spouse both a money judgment and an appropriate share of the community estate.

History of Fam. Code §7.009: Acts 2011, 82nd Leg., ch. 487, §1, eff. Sept. 1, 2011.

See also ***O'Connor's Texas Family Law Handbook*** (2017), "Claim for fraud on the community," ch. 7-A, §6.2, p. 792.

ANNOTATIONS

Slicker v. Slicker, 464 S.W.3d 850, 860 (Tex.App.—Dallas 2015, no pet.). "The trial court granted judgment against [H] for $275,000 'based on [his] breach of fiduciary duty and fraud committed on the community estate.' The trial court made a finding of fact that the value of the reconstituted estate is $900,000. *At 861:* Waste occurs when one spouse, dishonestly or purposefully with the intent to deceive, deprives the community estate of assets to the detriment of the other spouse. [H] contends that because [W] was fully aware of 'the parties' financial situation, including money and bank accounts, because the parties talked about finances frequently,' there was no waste, 'especially given that [W] enjoyed the benefits of these expenditures just as did [H].' However, [H] offered no evidence to support this contention except his conclusory testimony about the parties' alleged 'lavish and extravagant lifestyle.' Although the record reflects that [H] requested money from [a] Trust for a few community expenses, there was no attempt by [H] to show that the large amounts of money he withdrew from the ... Trust were used for community purposes, or that [W] was aware of the withdrawals. *At 862:* [T]here was evidence to support the trial court's findings that [H] committed 'waste and/or constructive fraud'...."

CHAPTER 8. MAINTENANCE

SUBCHAPTER A. GENERAL PROVISIONS

FAM §8.001. DEFINITIONS

In this chapter:

(1) "Maintenance" means an award in a suit for dissolution of a marriage of periodic payments from the future income of one spouse for the support of the other spouse.

(2) "Notice of application for a writ of withholding" means the document delivered to an obligor and filed with the court as required by this chapter for the nonjudicial determination of arrears and initiation of withholding for spousal maintenance.

(3) "Obligee" means a person entitled to receive payments under the terms of an order for spousal maintenance.

(4) "Obligor" means a person required to make periodic payments under the terms of an order for spousal maintenance.

(5) "Writ of withholding" means the document issued by the clerk of a court and delivered to an employer, directing that earnings be withheld for payment of spousal maintenance as provided by this chapter.

History of Fam. Code §8.001: Acts 1997, 75th Leg., ch. 7, §1, eff. Apr. 17, 1997. Amended by Acts 2001, 77th Leg., ch. 807, §1, eff. Sept. 1, 2001. Source: Former Fam. Code §3.9601.

FAM §§8.002 TO 8.011. RENUMBERED

Renumbered as §§8.051-8.061 by Acts 2001, 77th Leg., ch. 807, §1, eff. Sept. 1, 2001.

Sections 8.012-8.050 reserved for expansion

SUBCHAPTER B. SPOUSAL MAINTENANCE

FAM §8.051. ELIGIBILITY FOR MAINTENANCE

In a suit for dissolution of a marriage or in a proceeding for maintenance in a court with personal jurisdiction over both former spouses following the dissolution of their marriage by a court that lacked personal jurisdiction over an absent spouse, the court may order maintenance for either spouse only if the spouse seeking maintenance will lack sufficient property, including the spouse's separate property, on dissolution of the marriage to provide for the spouse's minimum reasonable needs and:

(1) the spouse from whom maintenance is requested was convicted of or received deferred adjudication for a criminal offense that also constitutes an act of family violence, as defined by Section 71.004, committed during the marriage against the other spouse or the other spouse's child and the offense occurred:

(A) within two years before the date on which a suit for dissolution of the marriage is filed; or

(B) while the suit is pending; or

(2) the spouse seeking maintenance:

(A) is unable to earn sufficient income to provide for the spouse's minimum reasonable needs because of an incapacitating physical or mental disability;

(B) has been married to the other spouse for 10 years or longer and lacks the ability to earn sufficient income to provide for the spouse's minimum reasonable needs; or

(C) is the custodian of a child of the marriage of any age who requires substantial care and personal supervision because of a physical or mental disability that prevents the spouse from earning sufficient income to provide for the spouse's minimum reasonable needs.

History of Fam. Code §8.051: Acts 1997, 75th Leg., ch. 7, §1, eff. Apr. 17, 1997. Amended by Acts 1999, 76th Leg., ch. 62, §6.05 (eff. Sept. 1, 1999), ch. 304, §1 (eff. Sept. 1, 1999). Renumbered from §8.002 and amended by Acts 2001, 77th Leg., ch. 807, §1, eff. Sept. 1, 2001. Amended by Acts 2005, 79th Leg., ch. 914, §1, eff. Sept. 1, 2005; Acts 2011, 82nd Leg., ch. 486, §1, eff. Sept. 1, 2011; Acts 2013, 83rd Leg., ch. 242, §§1, 2, eff. Sept. 1, 2013. Source: Former Fam. Code §3.9602.

See also *O'Connor's Texas Family Law Handbook* (2017), "Establishing Eligibility," ch. 3-D, §2, p. 298.

ANNOTATIONS

In re Marriage of Day, 497 S.W.3d 87, 90 (Tex. App.—Houston [14th Dist.] 2016, pet. denied). "[W] requested only temporary maintenance while the divorce action was pending. *At 91:* [H] did not have fair notice that he was exposed to the additional liability of post-divorce spousal maintenance because nothing in [W's] pleadings indicated she sought such relief. [¶] [W] argues that her prayer for general relief, together with her reference to the need for support and her request for temporary relief, entitle her to an award of spousal maintenance.... *At 92:* Other than [W's] request for temporary support ..., the only arguable reference to spousal maintenance in her petition is ... where she asks the trial court to consider her 'need for future support' as one of the 'reasons' she 'should be awarded a disproportionate share of the parties' [community] estate.' Such a request is inconsistent with an award of post-divorce spousal maintenance. An award of post-divorce spousal maintenance is, in effect, an award of the husband's future separate property following the division of community property. [W's] petition asked that her need for future support be taken into account in determining her share of the community estate; there is no request for an additional award of spousal maintenance. Even under the notice pleading standard used by Texas courts, we conclude the trial court had no basis in the petition for providing such relief. [¶] We conclude the trial court abused its discretion by awarding [W] spousal maintenance because [W] did not request this relief in her petition."

Slicker v. Slicker, 464 S.W.3d 850, 860 (Tex.App.—Dallas 2015, no pet.). "The term 'minimum reasonable needs' is not defined in the Family Code. A trial court determines whether a party's minimum reasonable needs are met on a fact-specific, individualized, case-by-case basis. *At 863:* [W]e consider [W's] eligibility for maintenance at the time of the divorce, not whether she will be able to provide for her minimum reasonable needs at some point in the future with additional training or education." *See also* ***Diaz v. Diaz***, 350 S.W.3d 251, 254 (Tex.App.—San Antonio 2011, pet. denied) (list of party's expenses is helpful, but it is not determinative evidence of "minimum reasonable needs"); ***In re Marriage of Hale***, 975 S.W.2d 694, 698 (Tex.App.—Texarkana 1998, no pet.) (federal minimum-wage statute does not dictate amount that will provide for minimum reasonable needs; minimum wage is usually inadequate to support a family).

Hipolito v. Hipolito, 200 S.W.3d 805, 806 (Tex. App.—Dallas 2006, pet. denied). "[H] urges us to measure [§8.051's] ten-year requirement from the date of marriage to the filing of the divorce petition or, alternatively, to the date the parties ceased living together as husband and wife. *At 807:* The parties' marriage still existed at the time the petition for divorce was filed and when they stopped living together as man and wife. ... Because there was evidence that the parties had been married at least ten years at the time of the trial, the trial court did not err in awarding [W] spousal maintenance on this basis."

In re Marriage of McFarland, 176 S.W.3d 650, 658 (Tex.App.—Texarkana 2005, no pet.). "Other courts, in considering if a spouse is eligible for spousal maintenance, have upheld the award in situations where the spouse receiving the maintenance obtained substantial property in the divorce proceeding when those capital assets provided insufficient support. *At 659:* The primary asset awarded to [W] is the retirement account, which is subject to significant taxes for early withdrawal. [T]he trial court found the property awarded to [W] was not sufficiently liquid to enable her to meet her minimum needs. To generate any immediately accessible income from this fund would impose ... significant early withdrawal tax consequences.... While retirement benefits must be considered in determining eligibility for spousal maintenance, we cannot say, based on the facts of this case, that the trial court abused its discretion in finding the retirement account involved did not bar [W] from maintenance since her available capital assets appear to be insufficient to provide adequate support. Likewise, the home is not a readily liquid asset and is incapable of producing current income. ... Therefore, the trial court did not abuse its discretion in granting spousal maintenance."

Carlin v. Carlin, 92 S.W.3d 902, 910 (Tex.App.—Beaumont 2002, no pet.). "[B]ecause [obligee] admittedly never attempted to seek employment that would provide for her 'minimum reasonable needs,' a finding that [she] proved she was unable to support herself ... would be unreasonable."

Pickens v. Pickens, 62 S.W.3d 212, 215-16 (Tex. App.—Dallas 2001, pet. denied). "We find no authority directly addressing the quantum of evidence required to prove incapacity in a spousal maintenance action. [H]

reason[s] that because spousal maintenance is designed to replace earned income, we should consider the evidence required to receive workers' compensation benefits or federal social security disability benefits. Under both of these statutes, medical evidence is required to establish an impairment or disability. However, for both workers' compensation and federal disability, the requirement of medical evidence is statutory. There is no such statutory requirement found in the spousal maintenance provisions of the family code. If the legislature had intended to restrict eligibility for spousal maintenance by requiring a spouse to present medical evidence to prove his or her disability, it could easily have done so. [¶] Absent a statutory requirement to the contrary, testimony on incapacity need not be limited to experts; a fact finder may reasonably infer incapacity from circumstantial evidence or the competent testimony of lay witnesses. The question of the extent and duration of incapacity is an issue that can be answered by lay opinion and does not require medical testimony. In fact, the testimony of the injured party will support a finding of incapacity even if directly contradicted by expert medical testimony." *See also* ***Dunaway v. Dunaway***, No. 14-06-01042-CV (Tex.App.—Houston [14th Dist.] 2007, no pet.) (memo op.; 11-13-07) (testimony on incapacitating physical or mental disability is not limited to experts); ***Smith v. Smith***, 115 S.W.3d 303, 308-09 (Tex.App.—Corpus Christi 2003, no pet.) (some evidence of disability is causal link resulting in inability to support self through appropriate employment).

FAM §8.052. FACTORS IN DETERMINING MAINTENANCE

A court that determines that a spouse is eligible to receive maintenance under this chapter shall determine the nature, amount, duration, and manner of periodic payments by considering all relevant factors, including:

(1) each spouse's ability to provide for that spouse's minimum reasonable needs independently, considering that spouse's financial resources on dissolution of the marriage;

(2) the education and employment skills of the spouses, the time necessary to acquire sufficient education or training to enable the spouse seeking maintenance to earn sufficient income, and the availability and feasibility of that education or training;

(3) the duration of the marriage;

(4) the age, employment history, earning ability, and physical and emotional condition of the spouse seeking maintenance;

(5) the effect on each spouse's ability to provide for that spouse's minimum reasonable needs while providing periodic child support payments or maintenance, if applicable;

(6) acts by either spouse resulting in excessive or abnormal expenditures or destruction, concealment, or fraudulent disposition of community property, joint tenancy, or other property held in common;

(7) the contribution by one spouse to the education, training, or increased earning power of the other spouse;

(8) the property brought to the marriage by either spouse;

(9) the contribution of a spouse as homemaker;

(10) marital misconduct, including adultery and cruel treatment, by either spouse during the marriage; and

(11) any history or pattern of family violence, as defined by Section 71.004.

History of Fam. Code §8.052: Acts 1997, 75th Leg., ch. 7, §1, eff. Apr. 17, 1997. Renumbered from §8.003 by Acts 2001, 77th Leg., ch. 807, §1, eff. Sept. 1, 2001. Amended by Acts 2011, 82nd Leg., ch. 486, §1, eff. Sept. 1, 2011. Source: Former Fam. Code §3.9603.

See also ***O'Connor's Texas Family Law Handbook*** (2017), "Determining award," ch. 3-D, §4.2, p. 302.

ANNOTATIONS

Brown v. Brown, No. 11-12-00248-CV (Tex.App.—Eastland 2014, no pet.) (memo op.; 8-21-14). "The purpose of spousal maintenance is to provide temporary and rehabilitative support for a spouse whose ability to support herself has eroded over time while engaged in homemaking activities and whose capital assets are insufficient to provide support. [¶] Just because [W's] maintenance and child support payments are insufficient to satisfy her expenses does not automatically entitle her to a larger maintenance award. While courts frequently consider a party's monthly expenses, income, and any shortfall in determining whether a spousal maintenance award is proper, there is no requirement that a spousal maintenance award eliminate the shortfall."

Trueheart v. Trueheart, No. 14-02-01256-CV (Tex. App.—Houston [14th Dist.] 2003, no pet.) (memo op.; 9-23-03). "In considering assets awarded in the divorce, the law does not require a spouse to spend down

long-term assets, liquidate all available assets, or incur new debt simply to obtain job skills and meet needs in the short term."

FAM §8.053. PRESUMPTION

(a) It is a rebuttable presumption that maintenance under Section 8.051(2)(B) is not warranted unless the spouse seeking maintenance has exercised diligence in:

(1) earning sufficient income to provide for the spouse's minimum reasonable needs; or

(2) developing the necessary skills to provide for the spouse's minimum reasonable needs during a period of separation and during the time the suit for dissolution of the marriage is pending.

(b) Repealed by Acts 2011, 82nd Leg., ch. 486, §9(1), eff. Sept. 1, 2011.

History of Fam. Code §8.053: Acts 1997, 75th Leg., ch. 7, §1, eff. Apr. 17, 1997. Renumbered from §8.004 by Acts 2001, 77th Leg., ch. 807, §1, eff. Sept. 1, 2001. Amended by Acts 2005, 79th Leg., ch. 914, §2, eff. Sept. 1, 2005; Acts 2011, 82nd Leg., ch. 486, §§2, 9(1), eff. Sept. 1, 2011. Source: Former Fam. Code §3.9604.

See also ***O'Connor's Texas Family Law Handbook*** (2017), "Petitioner has made diligent effort to earn sufficient income or develop skills," ch. 3-D, §2.3.1(3), p. 299.

ANNOTATIONS

Day v. Day, 452 S.W.3d 430, 434 (Tex.App.—Houston [1st Dist.] 2014, pet. denied). "Unlike §8.053(a)(2), §8.053(a)(1) does not limit the diligence inquiry to 'the period of separation and ... the time the suit for dissolution of the marriage is pending.' *At 435:* [H] contends that [W] must show that she has sought additional or more lucrative employment. While an earlier version of the statute required diligence in seeking 'suitable employment,' in 2011 the Legislature broadened the inquiry to 'earning sufficient income.' [W] met this requirement by limiting her expenses, selling her separate property, exhausting her inheritance, and taking loans—all while working more than full time and being the sole caregiver to the couple's daughter. [¶] To overcome the presumption [against spousal maintenance], the spouse seeking maintenance must satisfy §8.053(a)(1) 'or' §8.053(a)(2). The statute's use of the disjunctive indicates that these are two independent methods to overcome the presumption."

FAM §8.054. DURATION OF MAINTENANCE ORDER

(a) Except as provided by Subsection (b), a court:

(1) may not order maintenance that remains in effect for more than:

(A) five years after the date of the order, if:

(i) the spouses were married to each other for less than 10 years and the eligibility of the spouse for whom maintenance is ordered is established under Section 8.051(1); or

(ii) the spouses were married to each other for at least 10 years but not more than 20 years;

(B) seven years after the date of the order, if the spouses were married to each other for at least 20 years but not more than 30 years; or

(C) 10 years after the date of the order, if the spouses were married to each other for 30 years or more; and

(2) shall limit the duration of a maintenance order to the shortest reasonable period that allows the spouse seeking maintenance to earn sufficient income to provide for the spouse's minimum reasonable needs, unless the ability of the spouse to provide for the spouse's minimum reasonable needs is substantially or totally diminished because of:

(A) physical or mental disability of the spouse seeking maintenance;

(B) duties as the custodian of an infant or young child of the marriage; or

(C) another compelling impediment to earning sufficient income to provide for the spouse's minimum reasonable needs.

(b) The court may order maintenance for a spouse to whom Section 8.051(2)(A) or (C) applies for as long as the spouse continues to satisfy the eligibility criteria prescribed by the applicable provision.

(c) On the request of either party or on the court's own motion, the court may order the periodic review of its order for maintenance under Subsection (b).

(d) The continuation of maintenance ordered under Subsection (b) is subject to a motion to modify as provided by Section 8.057.

History of Fam. Code §8.054: Acts 1997, 75th Leg., ch. 7, §1, eff. Apr. 17, 1997. Renumbered from §8.005 and amended by Acts 2001, 77th Leg., ch. 807, §1, eff. Sept. 1, 2001. Amended by Acts 2005, 79th Leg., ch. 914, §3, eff. Sept. 1, 2005; Acts 2011, 82nd Leg., ch. 486, §3, eff. Sept. 1, 2011. Source: Former Fam. Code §3.9605.

See also ***O'Connor's Texas Family Law Handbook*** (2017), "Duration of award," ch. 3-D, §4.2.2, p. 305.

ANNOTATIONS

Novick v. Shervin, 412 S.W.3d 825, 831 (Tex. App.—Dallas 2013, no pet.). "An award of spousal maintenance in a divorce decree is properly the subject

of a motion for continuation only if the decree indicates that the trial judge intended to make the award pursuant to §8.054(b) rather than §8.054(a). The necessary intent can be shown by a specific finding of disability plus a provision that the beneficiary of the award has the burden of seeking continuation of maintenance beyond a court-ordered termination date. The necessary intent can also be shown by a specific reference to §8.054(b), ... or by the fact that the award exceeds the maximum duration permitted by §8.054(a).... But an award that is within the maximum duration permitted by §8.054(a), that does not refer to §8.054(b), and that is accompanied by neither a finding of disability nor a provision for future review or continuance is presumed to be made under §8.054(a) and is not subject to extension." *See also* ***O'Carolan v. Hopper***, 414 S.W.3d 288, 309-10 (Tex.App.—Austin 2013, no pet.).

FAM §8.055. AMOUNT OF MAINTENANCE

(a) A court may not order maintenance that requires an obligor to pay monthly more than the lesser of:

(1) $5,000; or

(2) 20 percent of the spouse's average monthly gross income.

(a-1) For purposes of this chapter, gross income:

(1) includes:

(A) 100 percent of all wage and salary income and other compensation for personal services (including commissions, overtime pay, tips, and bonuses);

(B) interest, dividends, and royalty income;

(C) self-employment income;

(D) net rental income (defined as rent after deducting operating expenses and mortgage payments, but not including noncash items such as depreciation); and

(E) all other income actually being received, including severance pay, retirement benefits, pensions, trust income, annuities, capital gains, unemployment benefits, interest income from notes regardless of the source, gifts and prizes, maintenance, and alimony; and

(2) does not include:

(A) return of principal or capital;

(B) accounts receivable;

(C) benefits paid in accordance with federal public assistance programs;

(D) benefits paid in accordance with the Temporary Assistance for Needy Families program;

(E) payments for foster care of a child;

(F) Department of Veterans Affairs service-connected disability compensation;

(G) supplemental security income (SSI), social security benefits, and disability benefits; or

(H) workers' compensation benefits.

(b) to **(d)** Repealed by Acts 2011, 82nd Leg., ch. 486, §9(2), eff. Sept. 1, 2011.

History of Fam. Code §8.055: Acts 1997, 75th Leg., ch. 7, §1, eff. Apr. 17, 1997. Renumbered from §8.006 and amended by Acts 2001, 77th Leg., ch. 807, §1, eff. Sept. 1, 2001. Amended by Acts 2003, 78th Leg., ch. 1138, §1, eff. Sept. 1, 2003; Acts 2011, 82nd Leg., ch. 486, §§4, 9(2), eff. Sept. 1, 2011. Source: Former Fam. Code §3.9606.

See also ***O'Connor's Texas Family Law Handbook*** (2017), "Limiting base amount," ch. 3-D, §4.2.1(3), p. 304.

FAM §8.056. TERMINATION

(a) The obligation to pay future maintenance terminates on the death of either party or on the remarriage of the obligee.

(b) After a hearing, the court shall order the termination of the maintenance obligation if the court finds that the obligee cohabits with another person with whom the obligee has a dating or romantic relationship in a permanent place of abode on a continuing basis.

(c) Termination of the maintenance obligation does not terminate the obligation to pay any maintenance that accrued before the date of termination, whether as a result of death or remarriage under Subsection (a) or a court order under Subsection (b).

History of Fam. Code §8.056: Acts 1997, 75th Leg., ch. 7, §1, eff. Apr. 17, 1997. Renumbered from §8.007 and amended by Acts 2001, 77th Leg., ch. 807, §1, eff. Sept. 1, 2001. Amended by Acts 2011, 82nd Leg., ch. 486, §5, eff. Sept. 1, 2011. Source: Former Fam. Code §3.9607.

ANNOTATIONS

In re L.T.H., 418 S.W.3d 876, 882 (Tex.App.—Dallas 2013, pet. denied). "[W] argues contractual alimony is not subject to termination for cohabitation under §8.056.... [H's] spousal support obligation arises out of the Reformed ... Divorce Decree, as modified by the MSA; his obligation is not court-ordered spousal maintenance governed by ch. 8.... In the MSA, [W] and [H] agreed that [H] would pay [W] alimony ... 'to continue until her death or remarriage.' Neither the Reformed ... Divorce Decree nor the MSA provide that [H's] spousal support obligation shall be terminated in the event of [W's] cohabitation. Because the Reformed ... Divorce Decree and the MSA were founded upon settlement agreements reached by the parties, the trial court had no power to supply terms, provisions, or conditions not previously agreed upon by the parties."

FAM §8.057. MODIFICATION OF MAINTENANCE ORDER

(a) The amount of maintenance specified in a court order or the portion of a decree that provides for the support of a former spouse may be reduced by the filing of a motion in the court that originally rendered the order. A party affected by the order or the portion of the decree to be modified may file the motion.

(b) Notice of a motion to modify maintenance and the response, if any, are governed by the Texas Rules of Civil Procedure applicable to the filing of an original lawsuit. Notice must be given by service of citation, and a response must be in the form of an answer due on or before 10 a.m. of the first Monday after 20 days after the date of service. A court shall set a hearing on the motion in the manner provided by Rule 245, Texas Rules of Civil Procedure.

(c) After a hearing, the court may modify an original or modified order or portion of a decree providing for maintenance on a proper showing of a material and substantial change in circumstances, including circumstances reflected in the factors specified in Section 8.052, relating to either party or to a child of the marriage described by Section 8.051(2)(C), if applicable. The court shall apply the modification only to payment accruing after the filing of the motion to modify.

(d) A loss of employment or circumstances that render a former spouse unable to provide for the spouse's minimum reasonable needs by reason of incapacitating physical or mental disability that occur after the divorce or annulment are not grounds for the institution of spousal maintenance for the benefit of the former spouse.

History of Fam. Code §8.057: Acts 1997, 75th Leg., ch. 7, §1, eff. Apr. 17, 1997. Renumbered from §8.008 by Acts 2001, 77th Leg., ch. 807, §1, eff. Sept. 1, 2001. Amended by Acts 2011, 82nd Leg., ch. 486, §6, eff. Sept. 1, 2011. Source: Former Fam. Code §3.9608.

FAM §8.058. MAINTENANCE ARREARAGES

A spousal maintenance payment not timely made constitutes an arrearage.

History of Fam. Code §8.058: Acts 2001, 77th Leg., ch. 807, §1, eff. Sept. 1, 2001.

FAM §8.059. ENFORCEMENT OF MAINTENANCE ORDER

(a) The court may enforce by contempt against the obligor:

(1) the court's maintenance order; or

(2) an agreement for periodic payments of spousal maintenance under the terms of this chapter voluntarily entered into between the parties and approved by the court.

(a-1) The court may not enforce by contempt any provision of an agreed order for maintenance that exceeds the amount of periodic support the court could have ordered under this chapter or for any period of maintenance beyond the period of maintenance the court could have ordered under this chapter.

(b) On the suit to enforce by an obligee, the court may render judgment against a defaulting party for the amount of arrearages after notice by service of citation, answer, if any, and a hearing finding that the defaulting party has failed or refused to comply with the terms of the order. The judgment may be enforced by any means available for the enforcement of judgment for debts.

(c) It is an affirmative defense to an allegation of contempt of court or the violation of a condition of probation requiring payment of court-ordered maintenance that the obligor:

(1) lacked the ability to provide maintenance in the amount ordered;

(2) lacked property that could be sold, mortgaged, or otherwise pledged to raise the funds needed;

(3) attempted unsuccessfully to borrow the needed funds; and

(4) did not know of a source from which the money could have been borrowed or otherwise legally obtained.

(d) The issue of the existence of an affirmative defense does not arise until pleaded. An obligor must prove the affirmative defense by a preponderance of the evidence.

(e) Repealed by Acts 2011, 82nd Leg., ch. 486, §9(3), eff. Sept. 1, 2011.

History of Fam. Code §8.059: Acts 1997, 75th Leg., ch. 7, §1, eff. Apr. 17, 1997. Renumbered from §8.009 and amended by Acts 2001, 77th Leg., ch. 807, §1, eff. Sept. 1, 2001. Amended by Acts 2011, 82nd Leg., ch. 486, §§7, 9(3), eff. Sept. 1, 2011; Acts 2013, 83rd Leg., ch. 242, §3, eff. Sept. 1, 2013. Source: Former Fam. Code §3.9609.

ANNOTATIONS

In re Sheshtawy, 154 S.W.3d 114, 118 (Tex.2004). "The Family Code provides in §8.059 that a court may enforce a spousal maintenance order by contempt, but it is silent as to what court may do so while an appeal is pending unless the spousal support has been granted

under [Fam. Code] §6.709, which allows a trial court to grant temporary spousal support during an appeal. *At 124-25:* [W]e hold that when a final judgment has not been superseded or stayed pending an appeal, either the trial court or the court of appeals may entertain a motion for contempt. If the motion is filed in a court of appeals, it remains the better practice to refer that motion to the trial court for hearing and factfinding."

FAM §8.0591. OVERPAYMENT

(a) If an obligor is not in arrears on the obligor's maintenance obligation and the obligor's maintenance obligation has terminated, the obligee must return to the obligor any maintenance payment made by the obligor that exceeds the amount of maintenance ordered or approved by the court, regardless of whether the payment was made before, on, or after the date the maintenance obligation terminated.

(b) An obligor may file a suit to recover overpaid maintenance under Subsection (a). If the court finds that the obligee failed to return overpaid maintenance under Subsection (a), the court shall order the obligee to pay the obligor's attorney's fees and all court costs in addition to the amount of the overpaid maintenance. For good cause shown, the court may waive the requirement that the obligee pay attorney's fees and court costs if the court states in its order the reasons supporting that finding.

History of Fam. Code §8.0591: Acts 2011, 82nd Leg., ch. 486, §8, eff. Sept. 1, 2011.

See also ***O'Connor's Texas Family Law Handbook*** (2017), "Duty to Repay Overpayment," ch. 3-D, §8, p. 315.

FAM §8.060. PUTATIVE SPOUSE

In a suit to declare a marriage void, a putative spouse who did not have knowledge of an existing impediment to a valid marriage may be awarded maintenance if otherwise qualified to receive maintenance under this chapter.

History of Fam. Code §8.060: Acts 1997, 75th Leg., ch. 7, §1, eff. Apr. 17, 1997. Renumbered from §8.010 by Acts 2001, 77th Leg., ch. 807, §1, eff. Sept. 1, 2001. Source: Former Fam. Code §3.9610.

FAM §8.061. UNMARRIED COHABITANTS

An order for maintenance is not authorized between unmarried cohabitants under any circumstances.

History of Fam. Code §8.061: Acts 1997, 75th Leg., ch. 7, §1, eff. Apr. 17, 1997. Renumbered from §8.011 by Acts 2001, 77th Leg., ch. 807, §1, eff. Sept. 1, 2001. Source: Former Fam. Code §3.9611.

Sections 8.062-8.100 reserved for expansion

SUBCHAPTER C. INCOME WITHHOLDING

FAM §8.101. INCOME WITHHOLDING; GENERAL RULE

(a) In a proceeding in which periodic payments of spousal maintenance are ordered, modified, or enforced, the court may order that income be withheld from the disposable earnings of the obligor as provided by this chapter.

(a-1) The court may order that income be withheld from the disposable earnings of the obligor in a proceeding in which there is an agreement for periodic payments of spousal maintenance under the terms of this chapter voluntarily entered into between the parties and approved by the court.

(a-2) The court may not order that income be withheld from the disposable earnings of the obligor to the extent that any provision of an agreed order for maintenance exceeds the amount of periodic support the court could have ordered under this chapter or for any period of maintenance beyond the period of maintenance the court could have ordered under this chapter.

(b) This subchapter does not apply to contractual alimony or spousal maintenance, regardless of whether the alimony or maintenance is taxable, unless:

(1) the contract specifically permits income withholding; or

(2) the alimony or maintenance payments are not timely made under the terms of the contract.

(c) An order or writ of withholding for spousal maintenance may be combined with an order or writ of withholding for child support only if the obligee has been appointed managing conservator of the child for whom the child support is owed and is the conservator with whom the child primarily resides.

(d) An order or writ of withholding that combines withholding for spousal maintenance and child support must:

(1) require that the withheld amounts be paid to the appropriate place of payment under Section 154.004;

(2) be in the form prescribed by the Title IV-D agency under Section 158.106;

(3) clearly indicate the amounts withheld that are to be applied to current spousal maintenance and to any maintenance arrearages; and

(4) subject to the maximum withholding allowed under Section 8.106, order that withheld income be applied in the following order of priority:

(A) current child support;

(B) current spousal maintenance;

(C) child support arrearages; and

(D) spousal maintenance arrearages.

(e) Garnishment for the purposes of spousal maintenance does not apply to unemployment insurance benefit payments.

History of Fam. Code §8.101: Acts 2001, 77th Leg., ch. 807, §1, eff. Sept. 1, 2001. Amended by Acts 2013, 83rd Leg., ch. 242, §4, eff. Sept. 1, 2013.

See also *O'Connor's Texas Family Law Handbook* (2017), "Wage Withholding – Form & Process," ch. 3-D, §6, p. 307.

ANNOTATIONS

Pappolla v. Simovich, No. 14-12-00418-CV (Tex. App.—Houston [14th Dist.] 2013, no pet.) (memo op.; 5-21-13). "The fit between §§8.101(a) and 8.101(b) is not seamless. Subsection (a), framed permissively to allow withholding, refers to 'a proceeding in which periodic payments of spousal maintenance are ordered, modified, or enforced.' In contrast, subsection (b) is framed restrictively to exclude withholding but also provides exceptions to the exclusion; it refers to 'contractual alimony or spousal maintenance.' [¶] [W] argues that we should read §§8.101(a) and 8.101(b)(2) as independent provisions. Under this approach, withholding is permissible if either subsection can be read in isolation to allow wage withholding for contractual alimony. We reject this approach.... [¶] [T]his approach impermissibly renders superfluous subsection (a)'s affirmative grant of withholding power only in situations involving 'payments of spousal maintenance.' As written, subsection (a) encompasses withholding for spousal maintenance but not contractual alimony. Subsection (b) provides that §8.101 and the rest of Subch. C does not apply unless an exception is satisfied. [W] contends that an exception applies under subsection (b)(2). But even if this exception applies, the exception merely makes §8.101(a) operative again—and §8.101(a) still encompasses only proceedings that involve spousal maintenance. The way to reconcile and harmonize these provisions is to determine, as we do now, that income withholding may be used to enforce contractual alimony under §8.101 when contractual alimony satisfies the requirements for spousal maintenance."

FAM §8.102. WITHHOLDING FOR ARREARAGES IN ADDITION TO CURRENT SPOUSAL MAINTENANCE

(a) The court may order that, in addition to income withheld for current spousal maintenance, income be withheld from the disposable earnings of the obligor to be applied toward the liquidation of any arrearages.

(b) The additional amount withheld to be applied toward arrearages must be whichever of the following amounts will discharge the arrearages in the least amount of time:

(1) an amount sufficient to discharge the arrearages in not more than two years; or

(2) 20 percent of the amount withheld for current maintenance.

History of Fam. Code §8.102: Acts 2001, 77th Leg., ch. 807, §1, eff. Sept. 1, 2001.

FAM §8.103. WITHHOLDING FOR ARREARAGES WHEN CURRENT MAINTENANCE IS NOT DUE

A court may order income withholding to be applied toward arrearages in an amount sufficient to discharge those arrearages in not more than two years if current spousal maintenance is no longer owed.

History of Fam. Code §8.103: Acts 2001, 77th Leg., ch. 807, §1, eff. Sept. 1, 2001.

FAM §8.104. WITHHOLDING TO SATISFY JUDGMENT FOR ARREARAGES

The court, in rendering a cumulative judgment for arrearages, may order that a reasonable amount of income be withheld from the disposable earnings of the obligor to be applied toward the satisfaction of the judgment.

History of Fam. Code §8.104: Acts 2001, 77th Leg., ch. 807, §1, eff. Sept. 1, 2001.

FAM §8.105. PRIORITY OF WITHHOLDING

An order or writ of withholding under this chapter has priority over any garnishment, attachment, execution, or other order affecting disposable earnings, except for an order or writ of withholding for child support under Chapter 158.

History of Fam. Code §8.105: Acts 2001, 77th Leg., ch. 807, §1, eff. Sept. 1, 2001.

FAM §8.106. MAXIMUM AMOUNT WITHHELD FROM EARNINGS

An order or writ of withholding must direct that an obligor's employer withhold from the obligor's disposable earnings the lesser of:

(1) the amount specified in the order or writ; or

(2) an amount that, when added to the amount of income being withheld by the employer for child support, is equal to 50 percent of the obligor's disposable earnings.

History of Fam. Code §8.106: Acts 2001, 77th Leg., ch. 807, §1, eff. Sept. 1, 2001.

FAM §8.107. ORDER OR WRIT BINDING ON EMPLOYER DOING BUSINESS IN THIS STATE

An order or writ of withholding issued under this chapter and delivered to an employer doing business in this state is binding on the employer without regard to whether the obligor resides or works outside this state.

History of Fam. Code §8.107: Acts 2001, 77th Leg., ch. 807, §1, eff. Sept. 1, 2001.

FAM §8.108. VOLUNTARY WRIT OF WITHHOLDING BY OBLIGOR

(a) An obligor may file with the clerk of the court a notarized or acknowledged request signed by the obligor and the obligee for the issuance and delivery to the obligor's employer of a writ of withholding. The obligor may file the request under this section regardless of whether a writ or order has been served on any party or whether the obligor owes arrearages.

(b) On receipt of a request under this section, the clerk shall issue and deliver a writ of withholding in the manner provided by this subchapter.

(c) An employer who receives a writ of withholding issued under this section may request a hearing in the same manner and according to the same terms provided by Section 8.205.

(d) An obligor whose employer receives a writ of withholding issued under this section may request a hearing in the manner provided by Section 8.258.

(e) An obligee may contest a writ of income withholding issued under this section by requesting, not later than the 180th day after the date on which the obligee discovers that the writ was issued, a hearing to be conducted in the manner provided by Section 8.258 for a hearing on a motion to stay.

(f) A writ of withholding under this section may not reduce the total amount of spousal maintenance, including arrearages, owed by the obligor.

History of Fam. Code §8.108: Acts 2001, 77th Leg., ch. 807, §1, eff. Sept. 1, 2001.

See also ***O'Connor's Texas Family Law Handbook*** (2017), "Voluntary writ of withholding," ch. 3-D, §6.3, p. 312.

Sections 8.109-8.150 reserved for expansion

SUBCHAPTER D. PROCEDURE

FAM §8.151. TIME LIMIT

The court may issue an order or writ for withholding under this chapter at any time before all spousal maintenance and arrearages are paid.

History of Fam. Code §8.151: Acts 2001, 77th Leg., ch. 807, §1, eff. Sept. 1, 2001.

ANNOTATIONS

O'Carolan v. Hopper, 414 S.W.3d 288, 299 (Tex. App.—Austin 2013, no pet.). "[T]he question presented is whether [W's spousal-maintenance] enforcement claim was timely because the judgment in the divorce decree ordering [H] to pay ... was not dormant under [CPRC] §34.001 ..., or whether her claim should have been brought within four years of the date the last installment was due under the residual four-year limitations period provided in [CPRC] §16.051.... *At 301:* In ***Huff*** [***v. Huff***, 648 S.W.2d 286 (Tex.1983)], the court determined that because the original divorce decree precludes any further adjudication of a right to child support, these enforcement motions 'are clearly not separate claims that would come under the [four-year] catchall statute of limitation.' *At 302:* [T]he court concluded that the motion ... to reduce child-support arrearage to a judgment enforceable by any means available to enforce a debt was a motion to revive and enforce a portion of a final judgment. [T]he court held that this type of motion falls 'within the direct purview of the [ten-year] statute of limitation governing the revival and enforcement of judgments' and is therefore excluded from the scope of the four-year residual statute.... *At 303-04:* We conclude that [W's] spousal-maintenance enforcement claim should be governed by ... ***Huff***.... [W]e conclude that the ten-year dormancy period applies to the judgment in the parties' divorce decree for spousal maintenance...."

FAM §8.152. CONTENTS OF ORDER OF WITHHOLDING

(a) An order of withholding must state:

(1) the style, cause number, and court having jurisdiction to enforce the order;

(2) the name, address, and, if available, the social security number of the obligor;

(3) the amount and duration of the spousal maintenance payments, including the amount and duration of withholding for arrearages, if any; and

(4) the name, address, and, if available, the social security number of the obligee.

(b) The order for withholding must require the obligor to notify the court promptly of any material change affecting the order, including a change of employer.

(c) On request by an obligee, the court may exclude from an order of withholding the obligee's address and social security number if the obligee or a member of the obligee's family or household is a victim of family violence and is the subject of a protective order to which the obligor is also subject. On granting a request under this subsection, the court shall order the clerk to:

(1) strike the address and social security number required by Subsection (a) from the order or writ of withholding; and

(2) maintain a confidential record of the obligee's address and social security number to be used only by the court.

History of Fam. Code §8.152: Acts 2001, 77th Leg., ch. 807, §1, eff. Sept. 1, 2001.

See also *O'Connor's Texas Family Law Handbook* (2017), "Court-ordered wage withholding," ch. 3-D, §6.1, p. 307.

FAM §8.153. REQUEST FOR ISSUANCE OF ORDER OR WRIT OF WITHHOLDING

An obligor or obligee may file with the clerk of the court a request for issuance of an order or writ of withholding.

History of Fam. Code §8.153: Acts 2001, 77th Leg., ch. 807, §1, eff. Sept. 1, 2001.

FAM §8.154. ISSUANCE & DELIVERY OF ORDER OR WRIT OF WITHHOLDING

(a) On receipt of a request for issuance of an order or writ of withholding, the clerk of the court shall deliver a certified copy of the order or writ to the obligor's current employer or to any subsequent employer of the obligor. The clerk shall attach a copy of Subchapter E to the order or writ.

(b) Not later than the fourth working day after the date the order is signed or the request is filed, whichever is later, the clerk shall issue and deliver the certified copy of the order or writ by:

(1) certified or registered mail, return receipt requested, to the employer; or

(2) service of citation to:

(A) the person authorized to receive service of process for the employer in civil cases generally; or

(B) a person designated by the employer by written notice to the clerk to receive orders or notices of income withholding.

History of Fam. Code §8.154: Acts 2001, 77th Leg., ch. 807, §1, eff. Sept. 1, 2001.

Sections 8.155-8.200 reserved for expansion

SUBCHAPTER E. RIGHTS & DUTIES OF EMPLOYER

FAM §8.201. ORDER OR WRIT BINDING ON EMPLOYER

(a) An employer required to withhold income from earnings under this chapter is not entitled to notice of the proceedings before the order of withholding is rendered or writ of withholding is issued.

(b) An order or writ of withholding is binding on an employer regardless of whether the employer is specifically named in the order or writ.

History of Fam. Code §8.201: Acts 2001, 77th Leg., ch. 807, §1, eff. Sept. 1, 2001.

See also *O'Connor's Texas Family Law Handbook* (2017), "Wage Withholding – Employer Rights, Duties & Liabilities," ch. 3-D, §7, p. 313.

FAM §8.202. EFFECTIVE DATE & DURATION OF INCOME WITHHOLDING

An employer shall begin to withhold income in accordance with an order or writ of withholding not later than the first pay period after the date the order or writ was delivered to the employer. The employer shall continue to withhold income as required by the order or writ as long as the obligor is employed by the employer.

History of Fam. Code §8.202: Acts 2001, 77th Leg., ch. 807, §1, eff. Sept. 1, 2001.

FAM §8.203. REMITTING WITHHELD PAYMENTS

(a) The employer shall remit to the person or office named in the order or writ of withholding the amount of income withheld from an obligor on each pay date. The remittance must include the date on which the income withholding occurred.

(b) The employer shall include with each remittance:

(1) the cause number of the suit under which income withholding is required;

(2) the payor's name; and

(3) the payee's name, unless the remittance is made by electronic funds transfer.

History of Fam. Code §8.203: Acts 2001, 77th Leg., ch. 807, §1, eff. Sept. 1, 2001.

FAM §8.204. EMPLOYER MAY DEDUCT FEE FROM EARNINGS

An employer may deduct an administrative fee of not more than $5 each month from the obligor's disposable earnings in addition to the amount withheld as spousal maintenance.

History of Fam. Code §8.204: Acts 2001, 77th Leg., ch. 807, §1, eff. Sept. 1, 2001.

FAM §8.205. HEARING REQUESTED BY EMPLOYER

(a) Not later than the 20th day after the date an order or writ of withholding is delivered to an employer, the employer may file with the court a motion for a hearing on the applicability of the order or writ to the employer.

(b) The hearing under this section must be held on or before the 15th day after the date the motion is made.

(c) An order or writ of withholding is binding and the employer shall continue to withhold income and remit the amount withheld pending further order of the court.

History of Fam. Code §8.205: Acts 2001, 77th Leg., ch. 807, §1, eff. Sept. 1, 2001.

FAM §8.206. LIABILITY & OBLIGATION OF EMPLOYER FOR PAYMENTS

(a) An employer who complies with an order or writ of withholding under this chapter is not liable to the obligor for the amount of income withheld and remitted as required by the order or writ.

(b) An employer who receives, but does not comply with, an order or writ of withholding is liable to:

(1) the obligee for any amount of spousal maintenance not paid in compliance with the order or writ;

(2) the obligor for any amount withheld from the obligor's disposable earnings, but not remitted to the obligee; and

(3) the obligee or obligor for reasonable attorney's fees and court costs incurred in recovering an amount described by Subdivision (1) or (2).

(c) An employer shall comply with an order of withholding for spousal maintenance or alimony issued in another state that appears regular on its face in the same manner as an order issued by a tribunal of this state. The employer shall notify the employee of the order and comply with the order in the manner provided by Subchapter F, Chapter 159, with respect to an order of withholding for child support issued by another state. The employer may contest the order of withholding in the manner provided by that subchapter with respect to an order of withholding for child support issued by another state.

History of Fam. Code §8.206: Acts 2001, 77th Leg., ch. 807, §1, eff. Sept. 1, 2001.

FAM §8.207. EMPLOYER RECEIVING MULTIPLE ORDERS OR WRITS

(a) An employer who receives more than one order or writ of withholding to withhold income from the same obligor shall withhold the combined amounts due under each order or writ unless the combined amounts due exceed the maximum total amount of allowed income withholding under Section 8.106.

(b) If the combined amounts to be withheld under multiple orders or writs for the same obligor exceed the maximum total amount of allowed income withholding under Section 8.106, the employer shall pay, until that maximum is reached, in the following order of priority:

(1) an equal amount toward current child support owed by the obligor in each order or writ until the employer has complied fully with each current child support obligation;

(2) an equal amount toward current maintenance owed by the obligor in each order or writ until the employer has complied fully with each current maintenance obligation;

(3) an equal amount toward child support arrearages owed by the obligor in each order or writ until the employer has complied fully with each order or writ for child support arrearages; and

(4) an equal amount toward maintenance arrearages owed by the obligor in each order or writ until the employer has complied fully with each order or writ for spousal maintenance arrearages.

History of Fam. Code §8.207: Acts 2001, 77th Leg., ch. 807, §1, eff. Sept. 1, 2001.

FAM §8.208. EMPLOYER'S LIABILITY FOR DISCRIMINATORY HIRING OR DISCHARGE

(a) An employer may not use an order or writ of withholding as grounds in whole or part for the termination of employment of, or for any other disciplinary action against, an employee.

(b) An employer may not refuse to hire an employee because of an order or writ of withholding.

(c) An employer who intentionally discharges an employee in violation of this section is liable to that

employee for current wages, other employment benefits, and reasonable attorney's fees and court costs incurred in enforcing the employee's rights.

(d) In addition to liability imposed under Subsection (c), the court shall order with respect to an employee whose employment was suspended or terminated in violation of this section appropriate injunctive relief, including reinstatement of:

(1) the employee's position with the employer; and

(2) fringe benefits or seniority lost as a result of the suspension or termination.

(e) An employee may bring an action to enforce the employee's rights under this section.

History of Fam. Code §8.208: Acts 2001, 77th Leg., ch. 807, §1, eff. Sept. 1, 2001.

FAM §8.209. PENALTY FOR NONCOMPLIANCE

(a) In addition to the civil remedies provided by this subchapter or any other remedy provided by law, an employer who knowingly violates this chapter by failing to withhold income for spousal maintenance or to remit withheld income in accordance with an order or writ of withholding issued under this chapter commits an offense.

(b) An offense under this section is punishable by a fine not to exceed $200 for each violation.

History of Fam. Code §8.209: Acts 2001, 77th Leg., ch. 807, §1, eff. Sept. 1, 2001.

FAM §8.210. NOTICE OF TERMINATION OF EMPLOYMENT & OF NEW EMPLOYMENT

(a) An obligor who terminates employment with an employer who has been withholding income and the obligor's employer shall each notify the court and the obligee of:

(1) the termination of employment not later than the seventh day after the date of termination;

(2) the obligor's last known address; and

(3) the name and address of the obligor's new employer, if known.

(b) The obligor shall inform a subsequent employer of the order or writ of withholding after obtaining employment.

History of Fam. Code §8.210: Acts 2001, 77th Leg., ch. 807, §1, eff. Sept. 1, 2001.

Sections 8.211-8.250 reserved for expansion

SUBCHAPTER F. WRIT OF WITHHOLDING ISSUED BY CLERK

FAM §8.251. NOTICE OF APPLICATION FOR WRIT OF WITHHOLDING; FILING

(a) An obligor or obligee may file a notice of application for a writ of withholding if income withholding was not ordered at the time spousal maintenance was ordered.

(b) The obligor or obligee may file the notice of application for a writ of withholding in the court that ordered the spousal maintenance under Subchapter B.

History of Fam. Code §8.251: Acts 2001, 77th Leg., ch. 807, §1, eff. Sept. 1, 2001.

See also ***O'Connor's Texas Family Law Handbook*** (2017), "Writ of withholding," ch. 3-D, §6.2, p. 309.

FAM §8.252. CONTENTS OF NOTICE OF APPLICATION FOR WRIT OF WITHHOLDING

The notice of application for a writ of withholding must be verified and:

(1) state the amount of monthly maintenance due, including the amount of arrearages or anticipated arrearages, and the amount of disposable earnings to be withheld under a writ of withholding;

(2) state that the withholding applies to each current or subsequent employer or period of employment;

(3) state that the obligor's employer will be notified to begin the withholding if the obligor does not contest the withholding on or before the 10th day after the date the obligor receives the notice;

(4) describe the procedures for contesting the issuance and delivery of a writ of withholding;

(5) state that the obligor will be provided an opportunity for a hearing not later than the 30th day after the date of receipt of the notice of contest if the obligor contests the withholding;

(6) state that the sole ground for successfully contesting the issuance of a writ of withholding is a dispute concerning the identity of the obligor or the existence or amount of the arrearages;

(7) describe the actions that may be taken if the obligor contests the notice of application for a writ of withholding, including the procedures for suspending issuance of a writ of withholding; and

(8) include with the notice a suggested form for the motion to stay issuance and delivery of the writ of

withholding that the obligor may file with the clerk of the appropriate court.

History of Fam. Code §8.252: Acts 2001, 77th Leg., ch. 807, §1, eff. Sept. 1, 2001.

FAM §8.253. INTERSTATE REQUEST FOR WITHHOLDING

(a) The registration of a foreign order that provides for spousal maintenance or alimony as provided in Chapter 159 is sufficient for filing a notice of application for a writ of withholding.

(b) The notice must be filed with the clerk of the court having venue as provided in Chapter 159.

(c) The notice of application for a writ of withholding may be delivered to the obligor at the same time that an order is filed for registration under Chapter 159.

History of Fam. Code §8.253: Acts 2001, 77th Leg., ch. 807, §1, eff. Sept. 1, 2001.

FAM §8.254. ADDITIONAL ARREARAGES

If the notice of application for a writ of withholding states that the obligor has failed to pay more than one spousal maintenance payment according to the terms of the spousal maintenance order, the writ of withholding may include withholding for arrearages that accrue between the filing of the notice and the date of the hearing or the issuance of the writ.

History of Fam. Code §8.254: Acts 2001, 77th Leg., ch. 807, §1, eff. Sept. 1, 2001.

FAM §8.255. DELIVERY OF NOTICE OF APPLICATION FOR WRIT OF WITHHOLDING; TIME OF DELIVERY

(a) The party who files a notice of application for a writ of withholding shall deliver the notice to the obligor by:

(1) first-class or certified mail, return receipt requested, addressed to the obligor's last known address or place of employment; or

(2) service of citation as in civil cases generally.

(b) If the notice is delivered by mail, the party who filed the notice shall file with the court a certificate stating the name, address, and date the party mailed the notice.

(c) The notice is considered to have been received by the obligor:

(1) on the date of receipt, if the notice was mailed by certified mail;

(2) on the 10th day after the date the notice was mailed, if the notice was mailed by first-class mail; or

(3) on the date of service, if the notice was delivered by service of citation.

History of Fam. Code §8.255: Acts 2001, 77th Leg., ch. 807, §1, eff. Sept. 1, 2001.

FAM §8.256. MOTION TO STAY ISSUANCE OF WRIT OF WITHHOLDING

(a) The obligor may stay issuance of a writ of withholding by filing a motion to stay with the clerk of the court not later than the 10th day after the date the notice of application for a writ of withholding was received.

(b) The grounds for filing a motion to stay issuance are limited to a dispute concerning the identity of the obligor or the existence or the amount of the arrearages.

(c) The obligor shall verify that the statements of fact in the motion to stay issuance of the writ are correct.

History of Fam. Code §8.256: Acts 2001, 77th Leg., ch. 807, §1, eff. Sept. 1, 2001.

FAM §8.257. EFFECT OF FILING MOTION TO STAY

If the obligor files a motion to stay as provided by Section 8.256, the clerk of the court may not deliver the writ of withholding to the obligor's employer before a hearing is held.

History of Fam. Code §8.257: Acts 2001, 77th Leg., ch. 807, §1, eff. Sept. 1, 2001.

FAM §8.258. HEARING ON MOTION TO STAY

(a) If the obligor files a motion to stay as provided by Section 8.256, the court shall set a hearing on the motion and the clerk of the court shall notify the obligor and obligee of the date, time, and place of the hearing.

(b) The court shall hold a hearing on the motion to stay not later than the 30th day after the date the motion was filed unless the obligor and obligee agree and waive the right to have the motion heard within 30 days.

(c) After the hearing, the court shall:

(1) render an order for income withholding that includes a determination of any amount of arrearages; or

(2) grant the motion to stay.

History of Fam. Code §8.258: Acts 2001, 77th Leg., ch. 807, §1, eff. Sept. 1, 2001.

FAM §8.259. SPECIAL EXCEPTIONS

(a) A defect in a notice of application for a writ of withholding is waived unless the respondent specially

excepts in writing and cites with particularity the alleged defect, obscurity, or other ambiguity in the notice.

(b) A special exception under this section must be heard by the court before hearing the motion to stay issuance.

(c) If the court sustains an exception, the court shall provide the party filing the notice an opportunity to refile and shall continue the hearing to a specified date without requiring additional service.

History of Fam. Code §8.259: Acts 2001, 77th Leg., ch. 807, §1, eff. Sept. 1, 2001.

FAM §8.260. WRIT OF WITHHOLDING AFTER ARREARAGES ARE PAID

(a) The court may not refuse to order withholding solely on the basis that the obligor paid the arrearages after the obligor received the notice of application for a writ of withholding.

(b) The court shall order that a reasonable amount of income be withheld and applied toward the liquidation of arrearages, even though a judgment confirming arrearages was rendered against the obligor.

History of Fam. Code §8.260: Acts 2001, 77th Leg., ch. 807, §1, eff. Sept. 1, 2001.

FAM §8.261. REQUEST FOR ISSUANCE & DELIVERY OF WRIT OF WITHHOLDING

(a) If a notice of application for a writ of withholding is delivered and the obligor does not file a motion to stay within the time provided by Section 8.256, the party who filed the notice shall file with the clerk of the court a request for issuance of the writ of withholding stating the amount of current spousal maintenance, the amount of arrearages, and the amount to be withheld from the obligor's income.

(b) The party who filed the notice may not file a request for issuance before the 11th day after the date the obligor received the notice of application for a writ of withholding.

History of Fam. Code §8.261: Acts 2001, 77th Leg., ch. 807, §1, eff. Sept. 1, 2001.

FAM §8.262. ISSUANCE & DELIVERY OF WRIT OF WITHHOLDING

The clerk of the court shall, on the filing of a request for issuance of a writ of withholding, issue and deliver the writ as provided by Subchapter D not later than the second working day after the date the request is filed. The clerk shall charge a fee in the amount of $15 for issuing the writ of withholding.

History of Fam. Code §8.262: Acts 2001, 77th Leg., ch. 807, §1, eff. Sept. 1, 2001.

FAM §8.263. CONTENTS OF WRIT OF WITHHOLDING

A writ of withholding must direct that an obligor's employer or a subsequent employer withhold from the obligor's disposable earnings an amount for current spousal maintenance and arrearages consistent with this chapter.

History of Fam. Code §8.263: Acts 2001, 77th Leg., ch. 807, §1, eff. Sept. 1, 2001.

FAM §8.264. EXTENSION OF REPAYMENT SCHEDULE BY PARTY; UNREASONABLE HARDSHIP

A party who files a notice of application for a writ of withholding and who determines that the schedule for repaying arrearages would cause unreasonable hardship to the obligor or the obligor's family may extend the payment period in the writ.

History of Fam. Code §8.264: Acts 2001, 77th Leg., ch. 807, §1, eff. Sept. 1, 2001.

FAM §8.265. REMITTANCE OF AMOUNT TO BE WITHHELD

The obligor's employer shall remit the amount withheld to the person or office named in the writ on each pay date and shall include with the remittance the date on which the withholding occurred.

History of Fam. Code §8.265: Acts 2001, 77th Leg., ch. 807, §1, eff. Sept. 1, 2001.

FAM §8.266. FAILURE TO RECEIVE NOTICE OF APPLICATION FOR WRIT OF WITHHOLDING

(a) Not later than the 30th day after the date of the first pay period after the date the obligor's employer receives a writ of withholding, the obligor may file an affidavit with the court stating that:

(1) the obligor did not timely file a motion to stay because the obligor did not receive the notice of application for a writ of withholding; and

(2) grounds exist for a motion to stay.

(b) The obligor may:

(1) file with the affidavit a motion to withdraw the writ of withholding; and

(2) request a hearing on the applicability of the writ.

(c) Income withholding may not be interrupted until after the hearing at which the court renders an order denying or modifying withholding.

History of Fam. Code §8.266: Acts 2001, 77th Leg., ch. 807, §1, eff. Sept. 1, 2001.

FAM §8.267. ISSUANCE & DELIVERY OF WRIT OF WITHHOLDING TO SUBSEQUENT EMPLOYER

(a) After the clerk of the court issues a writ of withholding, a party authorized to file a notice of application for a writ of withholding under this subchapter may deliver a copy of the writ to a subsequent employer of the obligor by certified mail.

(b) Except as provided by an order under Section 8.152, the writ of withholding must include the name, address, and signature of the party and clearly indicate that the writ is being issued to a subsequent employer.

(c) The party shall file:

(1) a copy of the writ of withholding with the clerk not later than the third working day after the date of delivery of the writ to the subsequent employer; and

(2) the postal return receipt from the delivery to the subsequent employer not later than the third working day after the date the party receives the receipt.

(d) The party shall pay the clerk a fee in the amount of $15 for filing the copy of the writ.

History of Fam. Code §8.267: Acts 2001, 77th Leg., ch. 807, §1, eff. Sept. 1, 2001.

Sections 8.268-8.300 reserved for expansion

Subchapter G. Modification, Reduction, or Termination of Withholding

FAM §8.301. AGREEMENT BY PARTIES REGARDING AMOUNT OR DURATION OF WITHHOLDING

(a) An obligor and obligee may agree to reduce or terminate income withholding for spousal maintenance on the occurrence of any contingency stated in the order.

(b) The obligor and obligee may file a notarized or acknowledged request with the clerk of the court under Section 8.108 for a revised writ of withholding or notice of termination of withholding.

(c) The clerk shall issue and deliver to the obligor's employer a writ of withholding that reflects the agreed revision or a notice of termination of withholding.

(d) An agreement by the parties under this section does not modify the terms of an order for spousal maintenance.

History of Fam. Code §8.301: Acts 2001, 77th Leg., ch. 807, §1, eff. Sept. 1, 2001.

FAM §8.302. MODIFICATIONS TO OR TERMINATION OF WITHHOLDING IN VOLUNTARY WITHHOLDING CASES

(a) If an obligor initiates voluntary withholding under Section 8.108, the obligee may file with the clerk of the court a notarized request signed by the obligor and the obligee for the issuance and delivery to the obligor of:

(1) a modified writ of withholding that reduces the amount of withholding; or

(2) a notice of termination of withholding.

(b) On receipt of a request under this section, the clerk shall issue and deliver a modified writ of withholding or notice of termination in the manner provided by Section 8.301.

(c) The clerk may charge a fee in the amount of $15 for issuing and delivering the modified writ of withholding or notice of termination.

(d) An obligee may contest a modified writ of withholding or notice of termination issued under this section by requesting a hearing in the manner provided by Section 8.258 not later than the 180th day after the date the obligee discovers that the writ or notice was issued.

History of Fam. Code §8.302: Acts 2001, 77th Leg., ch. 807, §1, eff. Sept. 1, 2001.

FAM §8.303. TERMINATION OF WITHHOLDING IN MANDATORY WITHHOLDING CASES

(a) An obligor for whom withholding for maintenance owed or withholding for maintenance and child support owed is mandatory may file a motion to terminate withholding. On a showing by the obligor that the obligor has complied fully with the terms of the maintenance or child support order, as applicable, the court shall render an order for the issuance and delivery to the obligor of a notice of termination of withholding.

(b) The clerk shall issue and deliver the notice of termination ordered under this section to the obligor.

(c) The clerk may charge a fee in the amount of $15 for issuing and delivering the notice.

History of Fam. Code §8.303: Acts 2001, 77th Leg., ch. 807, §1, eff. Sept. 1, 2001.

FAM §8.304. DELIVERY OF ORDER OF REDUCTION OR TERMINATION OF WITHHOLDING

Any person may deliver to the obligor's employer a certified copy of an order that reduces the amount of

spousal maintenance to be withheld or terminates the withholding.

History of Fam. Code §8.304: Acts 2001, 77th Leg., ch. 807, §1, eff. Sept. 1, 2001.

FAM §8.305. LIABILITY OF EMPLOYERS

The provisions of this chapter regarding the liability of employers for withholding apply to an order that reduces or terminates withholding.

History of Fam. Code §8.305: Acts 2001, 77th Leg., ch. 807, §1, eff. Sept. 1, 2001.

CHAPTER 9. POST-DECREE PROCEEDINGS

SUBCHAPTER A. SUIT TO ENFORCE DECREE

FAM §9.001. ENFORCEMENT OF DECREE

(a) A party affected by a decree of divorce or annulment providing for a division of property as provided by Chapter 7, including a division of property and any contractual provisions under the terms of an agreement incident to divorce or annulment under Section 7.006 that was approved by the court, may request enforcement of that decree by filing a suit to enforce as provided by this chapter in the court that rendered the decree.

(b) Except as otherwise provided in this chapter, a suit to enforce shall be governed by the Texas Rules of Civil Procedure applicable to the filing of an original lawsuit.

(c) A party whose rights, duties, powers, or liabilities may be affected by the suit to enforce is entitled to receive notice by citation and shall be commanded to appear by filing a written answer. Thereafter, the proceedings shall be as in civil cases generally.

History of Fam. Code §9.001: Acts 1997, 75th Leg., ch. 7, §1, eff. Apr. 17, 1997. Amended by Acts 2013, 83rd Leg., ch. 242, §5, eff. Sept. 1, 2013. Source: Former Fam. Code §3.70(a), (b).

ANNOTATIONS

Brown v. Fullenweider, 52 S.W.3d 169, 170-71 (Tex.2001). "The question in this case is whether a party's attorney may file a motion under [Fam. Code §9.001] to collect fees from his own client. [¶] [T]he obvious purpose of [Fam. Code §§3.70-3.77, now §§9.001-9.014,] was to provide an expeditious procedure for enforcing and clarifying property divisions in divorce decrees. … Suffice it to say that none [of the sections] contemplates that such proceedings would involve any issues other than those related to the division of a marital estate. An attorney's claim against his client for fees is not such an issue. It is wholly implausible that the Legislature intended to deny an attorney and client the right to trial by jury in a dispute over fees related to a divorce proceeding." *See also* ***Stine v. Stewart***, 80 S.W.3d 586, 591 (Tex.2002).

FAM §9.002. CONTINUING AUTHORITY TO ENFORCE DECREE

The court that rendered the decree of divorce or annulment retains the power to enforce the property division as provided by Chapter 7, including a property division and any contractual provisions under the terms of

an agreement incident to divorce or annulment under Section 7.006 that was approved by the court.

History of Fam. Code §9.002: Acts 1997, 75th Leg., ch. 7, §1, eff. Apr. 17, 1997. Amended by Acts 2013, 83rd Leg., ch. 242, §6, eff. Sept. 1, 2013. Source: Former Fam. Code §3.70(c).

ANNOTATIONS

Chavez v. McNeely, 287 S.W.3d 840, 842 (Tex. App.—Houston [1st Dist.] 2009, no pet.). The question is "whether a district court has jurisdiction to construe a contract that is incorporated into an agreed, final divorce decree even though the court is not the same court that rendered the divorce judgment…. *At 844:* [W] argues that [Fam. Code] §§9.001 and 9.002 … create exclusive jurisdiction … in … the court that rendered the divorce decree. *At 845:* [T]he court granting a divorce does not have exclusive jurisdiction to hear a suit brought to enforce a property settlement agreement entered into upon divorce. '[O]nce the parties have agreed on a property settlement that contains a provision for periodic support payments, a suit to recover missed payments does not involve matters incident to divorce, but is instead more akin to an independent action on a contract' [that invokes the general jurisdiction of the district court]."

Beach v. Beach, 912 S.W.2d 345, 348 (Tex.App.—Houston [14th Dist.] 1995, no writ). "After rendition of a divorce decree, the trial court retains the power to enforce the property division. A court order or property division may be enforced by filing a motion in the court that rendered the decree by any party affected by the order or decree."

Dechon v. Dechon, 909 S.W.2d 950, 955 (Tex. App.—El Paso 1995, no writ). "A trial court has inherent power to clarify or enforce its previously entered decree. Such jurisdiction encompasses both subject-matter jurisdiction to adjudicate the dispute and personal jurisdiction over the parties originally affected by the decree."

FAM §9.003. FILING DEADLINES

(a) A suit to enforce the division of tangible personal property in existence at the time of the decree of divorce or annulment must be filed before the second anniversary of the date the decree was signed or becomes final after appeal, whichever date is later, or the suit is barred.

(b) A suit to enforce the division of future property not in existence at the time of the original decree must be filed before the second anniversary of the date the right to the property matures or accrues or the decree becomes final, whichever date is later, or the suit is barred.

History of Fam. Code §9.003: Acts 1997, 75th Leg., ch. 7, §1, eff. Apr. 17, 1997. Source: Former Fam. Code §3.70(c).

ANNOTATIONS

Generally

Stine v. Stewart, 80 S.W.3d 586, 588 (Tex.2002). "[P] brought a third-party beneficiary breach of contract claim against [D], her former son-in-law, for refusing to pay [P] the proceeds from the sale of property as required under an Agreement Incident to Divorce. *At 592:* [Section 9.003's] two-year statute of limitations does not apply to bar [P's] third-party … claim…. [¶] [P's] suit … is not a suit to enforce the 'division of property.' Rather, [P's] claim is that [D] breached the agreement…. Therefore, the general four-year statute of limitations for breach of contract applies."

Jenkins v. Jenkins, 991 S.W.2d 440, 445 (Tex. App.—Fort Worth 1999, pet. denied). "[S]ection 9.003(b)'s two-year statute of limitations does not apply to this case because the [bankruptcy] Trustee did not seek to compel a *division* of property via his motion to enforce. A division of property was unnecessary, because the divorce decree awarded [W] a specific amount of alimony. The Trustee merely sought a money judgment for alimony awarded but not paid…. Because the Trustee sought a reduction of the specific monetary award in the [Agreement Incident to Divorce] to judgment, rather than a division of property, the Trustee's claim is not governed by §9.003(b)." *See also* ***Bowden v. Knowlton***, 734 S.W.2d 206, 208 (Tex.App.—Houston [1st Dist.] 1987, no writ) (limitation period specified in Fam. Code §3.70(c), now §9.003, did not apply to reducing monetary award to judgment under Fam. Code §3.74, now §9.010); ***Arnold v. Eaton***, p. 118. *But see* ***Morales v. Morales***, p. 118.

Dechon v. Dechon, 909 S.W.2d 950, 961-62 (Tex. App.—El Paso 1995, no writ). Family Code §3.70(c), now §9.003, "makes little sense unless it applies to all methods of enforcement under Subchapter [A]. We decline to carve exceptions depending on the method of enforcement sought. [W]e note that while clarification is a remedy, it is in fact a prerequisite to enforcement rather than a method of enforcement. A period of several years may pass before a litigant recognizes the necessity for a clarification proceeding. [W]e apply no

statute of limitations to the clarification procedure itself. It does apply, however, to the enforcement process once clarification is obtained."

Carter v. Charles, 853 S.W.2d 667, 672 (Tex.App.—Houston [14th Dist.] 1993, no writ). The Fam. Code §3.70, now §9.003, "limitations period applies to *personal* property, not real property."

§9.003(a)

Wilke v. Phillips, No. 04-12-00604-CV (Tex.App.—San Antonio 2013, no pet.) (memo op.; 11-13-13). "The [divorce] decree ... awarded [H] '[t]he sum of $40,000 to be paid by [W] when the real property ... is sold from the proceeds of the sale. ...' [¶] Although the $40,000 awarded to [H] came from a specific source—the future sale of the house ...—it was a monetary award. The divorce decree did not award [H] an interest in the house itself. Although 'goods' are considered tangible personal property ..., money is not considered a 'good' or 'tangible chattel,' but is instead 'a currency of exchange that enables the holder to acquire goods.' We conclude the $40,000 monetary award does not constitute tangible personal property under §9.003(a). [¶] Additionally, even if an award of money were considered tangible personal property, it would not be considered 'in existence' at the time the divorce decree was signed because the divorce decree specifies the $40,000 is to be paid from the 'proceeds' of the sale of the house. 'Proceeds' are not considered to be in existence until after disposition of the property occurs. ... As a result, §9.003(a) does not apply in this case." *See also* ***Gentile v. Gentile***, No. 13-04-167-CV (Tex.App.—Corpus Christi 2007, pet. denied) (memo op.; 2-1-07).

Morales v. Morales, 195 S.W.3d 188, 191 (Tex. App.—San Antonio 2006, pet. denied). "[T]he two-year limitations provision contained in ... §9.003 [is] applicable to all enforcement motions. *At 192:* Accordingly, we ... conclude that [petitioner] was required to bring his motion to [enforce] the payments he was awarded under the divorce decree to a money judgment within two years from the date his right to those payments matured." *But see* ***Jenkins v. Jenkins***, p. 117; ***Arnold v. Eaton***, this page.

Arnold v. Eaton, 910 S.W.2d 181, 183 (Tex.App.—Eastland 1995, no writ). Respondent "argues that [movant's] motion to enforce the property award [from prior divorce] was barred by the limitations period in [Fam. Code] §3.70(c) [now §9.003(a)]. The original divorce decree awarded [movant] a debt of $20,000.00 and secured that debt by a lien. [Movant's] suit for enforcement sought to reduce the unpaid debt to a money judgment. Neither the debt nor the lien is tangible personal property." *See also* ***Jenkins v. Jenkins***, p. 117. *But see* ***Morales v. Morales***, this page.

§9.003(b)

Morales v. Rice, 388 S.W.3d 376, 385 (Tex.App.—El Paso 2012, no pet.). "Under the divorce decree, [W] was ordered to pay [H] $10,000 upon the occurrence of certain events, including if she remarried or if she had a male non-family member living with her. [Boyfriend] testified that he began living with [W] in 1996. The couple's oldest son told [H] in 1996 that [boyfriend] was living with them. [H] denied having any knowledge that [boyfriend] was living at the house with [W]. [¶] [H] had two years to enforce his claim under §9.003(b).... The issue is when the cause of action accrued. The undisputed evidence established that [boyfriend] began living with [W] in 1996. Accordingly, [H's] cause of action to enforce the division of future property accrued in 1996. [H's] motion to enforce filed in 2004 is barred by §9.003(b)...."

Preston v. Preston, No. 04-03-00333-CV (Tex. App.—San Antonio 2004, no pet.) (memo op.; 8-18-04). CPRC §16.004(a)(5) "provides that a person must bring a breach of fiduciary duty action not later than four years after the day the cause of action accrues. Here, the divorce decree designates [H] as 'a constructive trustee for the benefit of [W] for the purpose of receiving the retired pay awarded herein to [W] as [W's] sole and separate property.' Accordingly, by bringing a motion to enforce the retirement pay provisions in the divorce decree, [W] was bringing a 'breach of fiduciary duty action.' [¶] [Family Code §9.003's] two-year statute of limitations does not apply to bar [W's] breach of fiduciary duty action.... [W] did not bring suit to enforce the division of future property. Rather, she brought a breach-of-fiduciary-duty claim to enforce the divorce decree. Therefore, the four-year statute of limitations for breach-of-fiduciary-duty claims applies." *See also* ***Treuil v. Treuil***, 311 S.W.3d 114, 118 (Tex.App.—Beaumont 2010, no pet.).

Chavez v. Chavez, 12 S.W.3d 563, 564-65 (Tex. App.—San Antonio 1999, no pet.). "The proceeds from the sale of the stock constituted property not in existence at the time of the divorce decree, or future property. The statute of limitations for enforcing the division

of future property is two years from the date the right to the property matures or accrues or the decree becomes final. [H] contends that his bankruptcy discharge date serves as the first date upon which he could be charged with failing to follow the court's order. [¶] The divorce decree does not specify when [H] was required to sell the stock. Instead, the decree specifies when [H] was required to deliver the proceeds of the sale of the stock; *i.e.*, 'within ten days of the receipt of said proceeds of said stock.' As a result, the first date [H] could be charged with contempt was the 11th day after the sale of the stock.... Based on this date, the statute of limitations would have run ... unless the discovery rule applies."

In re Marriage of Reinauer, 946 S.W.2d 853, 859-60 (Tex.App.—Amarillo 1997, writ denied). "At the time the [Divorce] Decree was signed, the [spouses'] interests in the military retirement benefits had yet to mature. Nonetheless, the interests were not mere expectancies but contingent interests in future property, or choses-in-action. Given this, [W] was entitled to enforce their division at any time within two years after [H's] interests matured."

FAM §9.004. APPLICABILITY TO UNDIVIDED PROPERTY

The procedures and limitations of this subchapter do not apply to existing property not divided on divorce, which are governed by Subchapter C and by the rules applicable to civil cases generally.

History of Fam. Code §9.004: Acts 1997, 75th Leg., ch. 7, §1, eff. Apr. 17, 1997. Source: Former Fam. Code §3.70(d).

FAM §9.005. NO JURY

A party may not demand a jury trial if the procedures to enforce a decree of divorce or annulment provided by this subchapter are invoked.

History of Fam. Code §9.005: Acts 1997, 75th Leg., ch. 7, §1, eff. Apr. 17, 1997. Source: Former Fam. Code §3.70(e).

FAM §9.006. ENFORCEMENT OF DIVISION OF PROPERTY

(a) Except as provided by this subchapter and by the Texas Rules of Civil Procedure, the court may render further orders to enforce the division of property made or approved in the decree of divorce or annulment to assist in the implementation of or to clarify the prior order.

(b) The court may specify more precisely the manner of effecting the property division previously made or approved if the substantive division of property is not altered or changed.

(c) An order of enforcement does not alter or affect the finality of the decree of divorce or annulment being enforced.

History of Fam. Code §9.006: Acts 1997, 75th Leg., ch. 7, §1, eff. Apr. 17, 1997. Amended by Acts 2013, 83rd Leg., ch. 242, §7, eff. Sept. 1, 2013. Source: Former Fam. Code §3.71(a).

ANNOTATIONS

Shanks v. Treadway, 110 S.W.3d 444, 447-48 (Tex.2003). See annotation under Family Code §9.007, p. 121.

Ex parte Gorena, 595 S.W.2d 841, 844 (Tex.1979). "Despite the fact that a judgment has its genesis in an agreement between the parties, the judgment itself has an independent status. Once the agreement of the parties has been approved by the court and made a part of its judgment, the agreement is no longer merely a contract between private individuals but is the judgment of the court. [¶] 'The fact that a judgment is rendered by consent gives it neither less nor greater force or effect than it would have had it been rendered after protracted litigation....' Thus, in suits to enforce agreed judgments, parties may not raise contractual defenses because such defenses constitute impermissible collateral attacks on the prior judgments."

Perry v. Perry, 512 S.W.3d 523, 529 (Tex.App.—Houston [1st Dist.] 2016, no pet.). "[A] divorce decree by which the ex-husband agrees to pay the ex-wife a sum of money in consideration for the conveyance of her interest in real property creates an equitable vendor's lien for the ex-wife. Although the ex-wife no longer has title to the property, she can use the lien as an encumbrance against the property to satisfy the debt. If the ex-husband fails to satisfy the debt after the lien matures, the ex-wife may foreclose on and force the sale of the property."

Wright v. Eckhardt, 32 S.W.3d 891, 894 (Tex. App.—Corpus Christi 2000, no pet.). "[T]he ... Family Code provides at least two circumstances in which the trial court may issue orders clarifying [a divorce] decree. [¶] Under [Fam. Code] §9.006 ..., the court may render 'further orders to enforce the division of property made in the decree of divorce ... to assist in the implementation of or to clarify the prior order.' The court may specify more precisely the manner of effecting the property division previously made if the substantive division of property is not altered or changed. The trial court may also clarify the decree [under Fam. Code §9.008] on a finding by the court that the original

form of the division of property is not specific enough to be enforceable by contempt. [¶] [W] alleges that the trial court erred by finding that the divorce decree's division of property was not specific enough to be enforceable by contempt. We disagree with [W] that the trial court made such an implied finding, and we do not agree that such a finding is required under §9.006…."

Kimsey v. Kimsey, 965 S.W.2d 690, 694-95 (Tex. App.—El Paso 1998, pet. denied). "When a divorce decree is not a consent decree or agreed judgment, the normal rules applicable to the construction of judgments apply to its interpretation. Thus, where a decree is unambiguous, the trial court has no authority to issue an order altering or modifying the original disposition of property. If the property division in the original divorce decree is ambiguous, however, or not specific enough to be enforceable by contempt, the court may enter a clarifying order to enforce compliance with the original division of property. While the Family Code authorizes the trial court to clarify its judgment, it does not prohibit our review of [W's] complaints that the judgment is vague and unenforceable, nor is there any authority which suggests that an enforcement action is a prerequisite to raising a complaint on appeal."

Sharman v. Schuble, 846 S.W.2d 574, 575 (Tex. App.—Houston [14th Dist.] 1993, orig. proceeding). "The divorce decree stated that the net proceeds from the sale would be distributed equally to the parties '*at the time of closing*.' [The] trial [court lacks] the authority to change the property division contained in a final divorce decree. By retaining possession of these funds, the trial court has clearly departed from the terms of the divorce decree. *At 576:* By retaining the proceeds in the registry, the trial court has effectively attached the relator's property. A writ of attachment is generally unavailable in claims for unliquidated debts. … The trial court abused its discretion by refusing to distribute these funds in accordance with the terms of the divorce decree."

Ⓐ FAM §9.007. LIMITATION ON POWER OF COURT TO ENFORCE

The amended text in §9.007 is effective for orders rendered on or after Sept. 1, 2017. Orders rendered before Sept. 1, 2017, are governed by the former law in effect at that time.

(a) A court may not amend, modify, alter, or change the division of property made or approved in the decree of divorce or annulment. An order to enforce the division is limited to an order to assist in the implementation of or to clarify the prior order and may not alter or change the substantive division of property.

(b) An order under this section that amends, modifies, alters, or changes the actual, substantive division of property made or approved in a final decree of divorce or annulment is beyond the power of the divorce court and is unenforceable.

(c) The trial court may not [~~power of the court to~~] render an order [~~further orders~~] to assist in the implementation of or to clarify the property division made or approved in the decree before the 30th day after the date the final judgment is signed. If a timely motion for new trial or to vacate, modify, correct, or reform the decree is filed, the trial court may not render an order to assist in the implementation of or to clarify the property division made or approved in the decree before the 30th day after the date the order overruling the motion is signed or the motion is overruled by operation of law [~~is abated while an appellate proceeding is pending~~].

History of Fam. Code §9.007: Acts 1997, 75th Leg., ch. 7, §1, eff. Apr. 17, 1997. Amended by S.B. 1237, §3, 85th Leg., eff. Sept. 1, 2017. Source: Former Fam. Code §3.71.

ANNOTATIONS

Pearson v. Fillingim, 332 S.W.3d 361, 363 (Tex. 2011). "[T]he court that renders a divorce decree retains jurisdiction to clarify and enforce the property division within that decree. If a decree is ambiguous, that court can enter a clarification order. [But an unambiguous] judgment finalizing a divorce and dividing marital property bars relitigation of the property division, even if the decree incorrectly characterizes or divides the property." *See also* ***In re M.M. III***, 357 S.W.3d 841, 843 (Tex.App.—El Paso 2012, no pet.) (court could not modify unambiguous decree even though it awarded H's separate property to W); ***Cox v. Carter***, 145 S.W.3d 361, 366-67 (Tex.App.—Dallas 2004, no pet.) (court enforced decree even though it conflicted with applicable federal guidelines).

Hagen v. Hagen, 282 S.W.3d 899, 907 (Tex.2009). "In the case before us, the [couple's] original decree did not award [W] amounts 'calculated on' [H's] gross, or even total, retirement pay before deductions…. The [couple's] decree plainly entitled [W] only to part of the Army or military retirement pay [H] received, if, as, and when he received it. [S]uch military retirement pay did not include VA disability benefits [that H elected to receive post-divorce in lieu of retirement

pay]. Thus, the trial court ... did not modify the [couple's] decree; it only clarified that the decree did not divide VA disability pay that was or might become payable to [H]. *At 908:* On the surface, it appears that [H's post-divorce] election to receive VA benefits has worked an inequity on [W]. But the language used in divorce decrees is important, and we must presume the divorce court chose it carefully...."

Shanks v. Treadway, 110 S.W.3d 444, 447-48 (Tex. 2003). "The [divorce] decree in question identifies [H's] pension plan as arising out of past employment, but then states that [W] is entitled to a pro rata interest of any and all sums received or paid to [H] from such pension plan. The decree also defines pro rata interest as 25% of the total sum or sums paid or to be paid to [H] from such pension or retirement plan. [¶] [T]he decree is unambiguous, and [W] should receive 25% of [H's] total retirement benefits. ... The fact that the plan's value may have increased since the divorce does not affect the decree's plain language, which simply cannot reasonably be construed to award [W] an interest only in the plan benefits that had accrued on the date of divorce. *At 449:* [W]e must enforce the decree as written ... even though it conflicts with ***Taggart*** [***v. Taggart***, 552 S.W.2d 422 (Tex.1977)]. *At 449 n.7:* [W]e disagree ... that the phrase 'if, as, and when received' is a term of art evidencing an intent to value a pension plan at the time of receipt rather than at the time of divorce. ... The term ... reflects the contingent nature of the community's interest in the retirement benefits and not necessarily the value of that interest." (Internal quotes omitted.) *See also* ***Reiss v. Reiss***, 118 S.W.3d 439, 442 (Tex.2003).

Perry v. Perry, 512 S.W.3d 523, 528-29 (Tex.App.—Houston [1st Dist.] 2016, no pet.). "[I]f a divorce decree orders that property be sold, but fails to specify a price, 'the law presumes that the parties ... intended a reasonable price.' Likewise, if the decree fails to specify a time for performance, 'the law implies a reasonable time....' [¶] [T]he [receivership] order does not require that the receiver sell the House at a reasonable time and for a reasonable price. Accordingly, we hold that the receivership order modifies the division of property in [H] and [W's] decree of divorce. [¶] By appointing a receiver to sell the House 'in his sole discretion ... upon terms and conditions determined by him,' the trial court improperly modified the division of property made in [H] and [W's] decree of divorce."

Everett v. Everett, 421 S.W.3d 918, 921 (Tex. App.—El Paso 2014, no pet.). "[H] contends the trial court exceeded the permissible scope of a clarifying order by converting a responsibility for a community debt into an obligation to pay spousal maintenance. [¶] The trial court believed that the intent of the decree was for [W] to receive the additional financial assistance for 36-months whether in the form of property tax payments or additional spousal maintenance and that its order clarified this intent. However, converting a debt into spousal maintenance is not merely a clarification, it is a change in the substantive division of property and cannot be enforced under [§9.007]."

In re W.L.W., 370 S.W.3d 799, 804-05 (Tex.App.—Fort Worth 2012, orig. proceeding). "[T]he divorce decree's 'residuary clause' purports to devise a remedy for property 'that was not *disclosed or under-valued in the spreadsheet* attached to each party's Inventory and Appraisement.' [A]ccording to [W's] construction, the 'residuary clause' operates on an unwritten contingency—idling along and irrelevant when [an] asset was disclosed and properly valued in [H's] inventory and appraisement, but springing into action and 'concurrently' awarding that same asset to [W] if she proves in a post-judgment action that [H] failed to disclose the asset or undervalued it in his inventory and appraisement. [¶] [But this clause] irreconcilably conflicts with [the agreement's final asset awards]. *At 806-07:* Examining the entire divorce decree, the only reasonable construction that can be given to the 'residuary clause' as written is that it permits the post-judgment division of previously decree-divided property based upon the trial court's findings regarding the thoroughness of one side's inventory and appraisement. Unquestionably, this violates the family code's express prohibition on amending, modifying, altering, or changing a divorce decree's division of property. [W's] suit is an impermissible collateral attack on the divorce decree...."

Garcia v. Alvarez, 367 S.W.3d 784, 787-88 (Tex. App.—Houston [14th Dist.] 2012, no pet.). "[A]greed divisions of marital property contained in or incorporated into final divorce decrees are treated as contracts and their legal force and meaning are governed by the law of contracts. The fact that a decree incorporated an agreement between the parties, however, does not mean that the procedures and enforcement mechanisms provided in [Fam. Code] ch. 9 ... no longer apply

or that the trial judge has no ability to fashion an appropriate remedy within its authority. To the contrary, that chapter makes no such distinction. [¶] In its order of enforcement, the trial court stated that [ex-H] had 'overpaid … in the amount of $3,000' and [ex-W] had retained those funds. … Ordering the return of the $3,000 that was rightfully [ex-H's] under the agreed property division did not amend, modify, alter, or change the division of property. The court simply was enforcing the division of property made in the decree as authorized by the Family Code."

Sheikh v. Sheikh, 248 S.W.3d 381, 388 (Tex.App.—Houston [1st Dist.] 2007, no pet.). "Prohibited orders 'assist[ing] in the implementation of' the decree's property division encompass orders to enforce the property division that go beyond the ministerial act of execution. A turnover order is a species of post-judgment enforcement order. It is the type of enforcement order that goes beyond the ministerial act of execution. *At 391-92:* Because [trial court] had jurisdiction to enforce the unsuperseded monetary judgment against [H], the trial court had subject-matter jurisdiction to enter the turnover-and-receivership order. However, to the extent that the turnover-and-receivership order allowed the receiver to take and to dispose of the property awarded to [W] and still in [H's] possession, the order violated §9.007(c)." *See also* ***In re Phillips***, 296 S.W.3d 682, 687 (Tex.App.—El Paso 2009, orig. proceeding) (order to disburse proceeds from sale of marital home during pendency of appeal was proper ministerial act of enforcement).

Gainous v. Gainous, 219 S.W.3d 97, 108 (Tex. App.—Houston [1st Dist.] 2006, pet. denied). "[W]e hold that §9.007 is jurisdictional and that orders violating its restrictions are void. *At 111:* We hold that the divorce decree unambiguously included the DROP [deferred retirement option plan] funds in its award to [W]. Because the QDRO precluded [W] from receiving any portion of [H's] DROP funds at any time, the QDRO impermissibly altered the decree's property division and was void to the extent that it did so. Because the QDRO's provision excluding the DROP funds from [W's] award was void, [W] could properly challenge it by collateral attack, and res judicata and estoppel did not bar her challenge." *See also* ***Quijano v. Quijano***, 347 S.W.3d 345, 353-54 (Tex.App.—Houston [14th Dist.] 2011, no pet.) (QDROs, like other post-divorce enforcement or clarification orders, cannot amend, modify, alter, or change decree's property division).

Zicker v. Stewart, No. 03-04-00438-CV (Tex. App.—Austin 2006, no pet.) (memo op.; 1-27-06). Family Code §9.007 "must be read in conjunction with [TRCP] 306a and 329b. [¶] Thus, although §9.007 clearly prevents the modification of a decree once it has become final, it does not prohibit a district court from exercising its plenary power to modify the decree within 30 days of signing the judgment. Because the modified judgment in this case was issued within a week of the original decree, during which the district court maintained its plenary powers, the modification did not violate §9.007. [¶] The waiver of citation that [W] signed in relation to the filing of [H's] original petition was not effective to remove her entitlement to be notified of the pending modification." *See also* ***Fontenot v. Fontenot***, No. 09-02-00019-CV (Tex.App.—Beaumont 2002, no pet.) (memo op.; 8-15-02) (ch. 9 does not apply to correction of clerical error by judgment nunc pro tunc).

FAM §9.008. CLARIFICATION ORDER

(a) On the request of a party or on the court's own motion, the court may render a clarifying order before a motion for contempt is made or heard, in conjunction with a motion for contempt or on denial of a motion for contempt.

(b) On a finding by the court that the original form of the division of property is not specific enough to be enforceable by contempt, the court may render a clarifying order setting forth specific terms to enforce compliance with the original division of property.

(c) The court may not give retroactive effect to a clarifying order.

(d) The court shall provide a reasonable time for compliance before enforcing a clarifying order by contempt or in another manner.

History of Fam. Code §9.008: Acts 1997, 75th Leg., ch. 7, §1, eff. Apr. 17, 1997. Source: Former Fam. Code §3.72.

ANNOTATIONS

Pearson v. Fillingim, 332 S.W.3d 361, 363 (Tex. 2011). See annotation under Family Code §9.007, p. 120.

In re N.T.P., 402 S.W.3d 13, 24-25 (Tex.App.—San Antonio 2012, no pet.). Wife argues "that the trial court erred because there is no evidence or any finding that the original DRO's language was not specific enough to be enforceable by contempt or that the agency in

charge of administering military domestic relations orders had any difficulty interpreting or implementing the DRO. ... However, nothing in [Fam. Code §9.104] pertaining to [QDROs] requires such a determination by a plan administrator as a prerequisite to clarification of the order. [¶] We also disagree with [W's] argument that there must be a finding that the original order was not specific enough to be enforceable by contempt. ... Nothing in [Fam. Code] §9.1045 requires a finding that the original DRO was not enforceable by contempt as a prerequisite to clarification of the order. [¶] Next, [W] asserts there was no need for a clarification because the original DRO told the administrative agency everything it needed to know in order to pay her a percentage of [H's] retirement because the DRO specified the formula. ... However, [a] trial court [does] not abuse its discretion in clarifying a DRO by determining the actual numbers to be used in the formula."

Hollingsworth v. Hollingsworth, 274 S.W.3d 811, 818 (Tex.App.—Dallas 2008, no pet.). "The [divorce] decree orders [H] to pay the taxes, penalties, and interest timely. ... The word 'timely' is imprecise and subjective; it does not readily inform the person of the duty imposed upon him. Such an order is unenforceable and cannot support a contempt judgment. The clarification order provided a precise time and place that [H] was to pay [W] the amount of [W's] obligation to the IRS for 2003. The decree was also ambiguous in that it did not describe who [H] was to pay, that is, whether he was to pay the taxes directly to the IRS, pay [W] who would then pay the IRS, reimburse [W] for her tax payments to the IRS, or all three." (Internal quotes omitted.)

In re Marriage of Jones, 154 S.W.3d 225, 228 (Tex.App.—Texarkana 2005, no pet.). Although Fam. Code §§9.101, 9.103, and 9.104 "allow a trial court to create a QDRO where none exists, or to correct language in a QDRO that renders it defective, they do not permit a court to substantively change a property division. [¶] Under [Fam. Code] §9.008, a QDRO that is not defective, but is so abstruse as to be difficult to implement or enforce, is treated as requiring clarification, and is not handled under the subchapter controlling the creation or implementation of a QDRO. [¶] The purpose of clarification is to enforce compliance with the original division of property. In this case, QDRO Four clarified the benefit division of QDRO One after [H's] retirement date occurred and the exact formula became known. Therefore, under §9.008, clarification was available, and the trial court had the authority to render QDRO Four. *At 229:* QDRO One was not completely clear, because the complete numbers were not supplied. QDROs Two and Three both did much more than just clarify QDRO One, and thus cannot be valid orders of the trial court. QDRO Four provides exact numbers for calculation. Thus, QDRO Four is indeed the final, clarified order, and the appeal is properly before this Court."

In re Marriage of Alford, 40 S.W.3d 187, 190 (Tex.App.—Texarkana 2001, no pet.). The question is "whether the trial court had to hold a trial on the merits before issuing [a clarification order under Fam. Code §9.008]. We hold it did not. [¶] A party affected by a divorce decree that provides for a division of property may request enforcement of the decree by filing suit in the court that rendered the decree. Such a suit is governed by the [TRCPs], except as otherwise provided in [Fam. Code] Ch. 9, and any affected party is entitled to be served with notice and to file an answer. Thereafter, the proceedings are conducted as in civil cases generally, except that the parties are not entitled to a jury trial. [¶] Under §9.008(a), however, the trial court may render a clarifying order on the request of a party or on its own motion. Thus, §9.008(a) comes under the 'except as otherwise provided' provision of [Fam. Code] §9.001(b)."

FAM §9.009. DELIVERY OF PROPERTY

To enforce the division of property made or approved in a decree of divorce or annulment, the court may make an order to deliver the specific existing property awarded, without regard to whether the property is of especial value, including an award of an existing sum of money or its equivalent.

History of Fam. Code §9.009: Acts 1997, 75th Leg., ch. 7, §1, eff. Apr. 17, 1997. Amended by Acts 2013, 83rd Leg., ch. 242, §8, eff. Sept. 1, 2013. Source: Former Fam. Code §3.73.

ANNOTATIONS

Burton v. Burton, 734 S.W.2d 727, 729 (Tex.App.—Waco 1987, no writ). "The provisions of [Fam. Code] §§3.71(a) and 3.73 [now §§9.006 and 9.009] clearly authorize the court to enforce a property division by ordering the delivery of existing personal property from one party affected by the divorce decree to another party. The question is whether the court can take this action on its own motion or must await the filing of a motion to enforce under [Fam. Code] §3.70(a) [now §9.001].

The language of these sections does not expressly prohibit the court from acting on its own motion, and this court will not judicially add such a limitation."

FAM §9.010. REDUCTION TO MONEY JUDGMENT

(a) If a party fails to comply with a decree of divorce or annulment and delivery of property awarded in the decree is no longer an adequate remedy, the court may render a money judgment for the damages caused by that failure to comply.

(b) If a party did not receive payments of money as awarded in the decree of divorce or annulment, the court may render judgment against a defaulting party for the amount of unpaid payments to which the party is entitled.

(c) The remedy of a reduction to money judgment is in addition to the other remedies provided by law.

(d) A money judgment rendered under this section may be enforced by any means available for the enforcement of judgment for debt.

History of Fam. Code §9.010: Acts 1997, 75th Leg., ch. 7, §1, eff. Apr. 17, 1997. Source: Former Fam. Code §3.74.

ANNOTATIONS

Koenig v. Blaylock, 497 S.W.3d 595, 600 (Tex. App.—Austin 2016, pet. denied). "The decree here ordered [H] to pay [W] $61,500; he defaulted on that payment; [W] filed a motion to enforce; and the family court rendered an enforcement order and judgment against [H] for that very amount. When [W] petitioned the family court to enforce the divorce decree and obtained a judgment for the [full amount] that she was awarded in the decree in exchange for the award of the Residence to [H], she was made whole by receiving the very award to which she was entitled[, even if she is unable to collect on her judgment]. Under these circumstances, the enforcement order served to effectuate the property division in the decree, and [W] may not now contend that she still has rights to the Residence awarded to [H]. *At 601:* [W] was not entitled to partition because she has no enforceable property interest in the Residence, and the trial court erred in denying [H's] motion to dismiss."

DeGroot v. DeGroot, 369 S.W.3d 918, 922 (Tex. App.—Dallas 2012, no pet.). "[H] argues the enforcement order was a substantive change in the division of property because it awarded [W] her share of the 401(k) plan in cash, rather than in kind. *At 923:* [H's impermissible] liquidation of the 401(k) plan made it impossible for him to comply with the terms of the decree by delivering to [W] 50% of the 401(k) plan. The trial court, therefore, had the authority to reduce the award to a money judgment pursuant to §9.010.... [¶] [T]he trial court ... did not make an impermissible substantive change to the division of property. *At 925-26:* [W] asserts the trial court erred by ordering [H] to make monthly payments to satisfy the award rather than entering a judgment for a liquidated sum. The trial court has broad discretion in determining the appropriate relief under §9.010.... Further, it is within a trial court's discretion to order one party to pay a judgment over time to effect the division of marital property."

Morales v. Morales, 195 S.W.3d 188, 191 (Tex. App.—San Antonio 2006, pet. denied). See annotation under Family Code §9.003, *§9.003(a)*, p. 118.

de la Garza v. de la Garza, 185 S.W.3d 924, 929 (Tex.App.—Dallas 2006, no pet.). "Post-judgment interest is recoverable only on a money judgment. *At 930:* [T]hrough the [Divorce] Decree, [W] obtained a judgment ordering [H] to make three [separate] payments on or before specified dates. The Decree, however, did not award [W] a money judgment for [the total] on which post-judgment interest accrued. Once [H] failed to make the payments as ordered, [W] had the right to seek to have that portion of the decree reduced to a money judgment. [W] did not obtain a money judgment. For this reason, post-judgment interest did not accrue."

Ackerly v. Ackerly, 13 S.W.3d 454, 457 (Tex.App.—Corpus Christi 2000, no pet.). "Notably, [Fam. Code] §9.010 does not specify it is not governed by the rules of civil procedure. Accordingly, pursuant to [Fam. Code] §9.001(b), the rules which govern a motion for reduction to money judgment are the [TRCPs] applicable to the filing of an original lawsuit, and not the rules which apply to the filing of a motion (*i.e.*, [TRCP] 21 and 21a). Furthermore, any party affected by the motion is entitled to notice by citation. [¶] Because the motion for reduction to money judgment is a separate action, the trial court's judgment in this case, rendered in the absence of an answer or an appearance, is a default judgment. A default judgment is improper against a defendant who has not been served in strict compliance with the law."

Jenkins v. Jenkins, 991 S.W.2d 440, 445 (Tex. App.—Fort Worth 1999, pet. denied). See annotation under Family Code §9.003, *Generally*, p. 117.

FAM §9.011. RIGHT TO FUTURE PROPERTY

(a) The court may, by any remedy provided by this chapter, enforce an award of the right to receive installment payments or a lump-sum payment due on the maturation of an existing vested or nonvested right to be paid in the future.

(b) The subsequent actual receipt by the non-owning party of property awarded to the owner in a decree of divorce or annulment creates a fiduciary obligation in favor of the owner and imposes a constructive trust on the property for the benefit of the owner.

History of Fam. Code §9.011: Acts 1997, 75th Leg., ch. 7, §1, eff. Apr. 17, 1997. Source: Former Fam. Code §3.75.

ANNOTATIONS

Schneider v. Schneider, 5 S.W.3d 925, 930 (Tex. App.—Austin 1999, no pet.). "The Texas statute [H] cites in support of imposing a constructive trust in this situation states that the subsequent actual receipt by the non-owning party of property awarded to the owner in a divorce decree creates a fiduciary obligation and imposes a constructive trust. Here [W] has not actually received any [Armed Services Survivor's Benefit] Plan benefits. In fact, in the event the Air Force eventually recognizes the court-ordered division, or should [W] not survive [H], she will never actually receive 100% of the benefits. The entire controversy surrounding the Plan is contingent on the occurrence of future events, and a constructive trust may not be necessary in the end to carry out the court's intent. Thus, we conclude that the trial court did not act in an unreasonable and arbitrary manner or without reference to any guiding principles when it declined to impose the equitable remedy of a constructive trust on possible future Plan disbursements."

FAM §9.012. CONTEMPT

(a) The court may enforce by contempt an order requiring delivery of specific property or an award of a right to future property.

(b) The court may not enforce by contempt an award in a decree of divorce or annulment of a sum of money payable in a lump sum or in future installment payments in the nature of debt, except for:

(1) a sum of money in existence at the time the decree was rendered; or

(2) a matured right to future payments as provided by Section 9.011.

(c) This subchapter does not detract from or limit the general power of a court to enforce an order of the court by appropriate means.

History of Fam. Code §9.012: Acts 1997, 75th Leg., ch. 7, §1, eff. Apr. 17, 1997. Source: Former Fam. Code §3.76.

FAM §9.013. COSTS

The court may award costs in a proceeding to enforce a property division under this subchapter as in other civil cases.

History of Fam. Code §9.013: Acts 1997, 75th Leg., ch. 7, §1, eff. Apr. 17, 1997. Source: Former Fam. Code §3.77.

ANNOTATIONS

Messier v. Messier, 458 S.W.3d 155, 168 (Tex. App.—Houston [14th Dist.] 2015, no pet.). "[E]xpert fees have been awarded under certain provisions of the Family Code, such as chs. 6 (governing suits for dissolution of marriage) and 106 (concerning [SAPCRs]). Each of the cited chapters, however, contains provisions permitting courts to award expenses in addition to costs and attorney's fees. [Family Code] ch. 9, subch. A, governing enforcement actions ... only authorizes the award of attorney's fees and costs. Indeed, §9.013 expressly states that costs may be awarded in such actions 'as in other civil cases.' Because expert fees are neither attorney's fees nor costs, and because ch. 9, subch. A does not allow an award of expenses in an enforcement action, the trial court erred in awarding [W] her expert witness fees."

FAM §9.014. ATTORNEY'S FEES

The court may award reasonable attorney's fees in a proceeding under this subchapter. The court may order the attorney's fees to be paid directly to the attorney, who may enforce the order for fees in the attorney's own name by any means available for the enforcement of a judgment for debt.

History of Fam. Code §9.014: Acts 1997, 75th Leg., ch. 7, §1, eff. Apr. 17, 1997. Amended by Acts 2009, 81st Leg., ch. 768, §8, eff. Sept. 1, 2009. Source: Former Fam. Code §3.77.

ANNOTATIONS

Shilling v. Gough, 393 S.W.3d 555, 558 (Tex. App.—Dallas 2013, no pet.). "[H] filed a Petition for Enforcement of Permanent Injunction by Contempt [contending that W] violated the injunction [contained in

the divorce decree]. [¶] [T]he trial court concluded [W] had not violated the injunction [and] granted [W's] request for attorney's fees [under §9.014]. *At 559:* [W] contends that because [H] is a 'party affected by a decree of divorce ... providing for a division of property,' this enforcement action lies within [ch. 9, subch. A], even though [the] suit involves an injunction against speech and not a division of property. But the remainder of the subchapter makes clear that the Legislature contemplated only an enforcement action dealing with property issues when enacting [§9.014]. *At 560:* We conclude [H's] action to enforce an injunction against speech is not governed by Subchapter 9(A).... Thus, the attorney's fee provision in that subchapter, §9.014, cannot serve as authority for the award of fees to [W] in this action."

Schneider v. Schneider, 5 S.W.3d 925, 930 (Tex. App.—Austin 1999, no pet.). Section 9.014 provides that "'[t]he court *may* award reasonable attorney's fees ... in a proceeding under this chapter.' This statute does not entitle either party to attorney's fees; rather, it merely permits the court to award them. The decision to grant or deny attorney's fees under this statute is reviewed for an abuse of discretion. To prevail on this issue, [H] must prove that the trial court acted without reference to any guiding principles when it refused to award him attorney's fees."

Sections 9.015-9.100 reserved for expansion

SUBCHAPTER B. POST-DECREE QUALIFIED DOMESTIC RELATIONS ORDER

FAM §9.101. JURISDICTION FOR QUALIFIED DOMESTIC RELATIONS ORDER

(a) Notwithstanding any other provision of this chapter, the court that rendered a final decree of divorce or annulment or another final order dividing property under this title retains continuing, exclusive jurisdiction to render an enforceable qualified domestic relations order or similar order permitting payment of pension, retirement plan, or other employee benefits divisible under the law of this state or of the United States to an alternate payee or other lawful payee.

(b) Unless prohibited by federal law, a suit seeking a qualified domestic relations order or similar order under this section applies to a previously divided pension, retirement plan, or other employee benefit divisible under the law of this state or of the United States, whether the plan or benefit is private, state, or federal.

History of Fam. Code §9.101: Acts 1997, 75th Leg., ch. 7, §1, eff. Apr. 17, 1997. Source: Former Fam. Code §3.711(a), (b).

ANNOTATIONS

Araujo v. Araujo, 493 S.W.3d 232, 238 (Tex. App.—San Antonio 2016, no pet.). "[T]he trial court rendered an agreed divorce decree that divided [H's] Railroad Retirement Board pension, but it did not render or sign a QDRO. Under such circumstances, [Fam. Code] §§9.101[,] 9.103, and 9.104 'provide for limited, post-judgment jurisdiction that may be invoked only in particular circumstances, rather than for plenary, original jurisdiction.' [¶] [S]igning the Railroad Retirement Order [after the decree became final] was not a ministerial act because the trial court did not 'render' a QDRO in the divorce decree. Therefore, [W] is required to comply with the provisions of [Fam. Code] ch. 9 to obtain a post-judgment QDRO. [W] did not file a 'petition' that complies with the applicable rules of civil procedure that govern 'the filing of an original lawsuit' as required by [Fam. Code] §9.102(b). Because [W] did not comply with ... ch. 9, the Railroad Retirement Order must be reversed."

Dechon v. Dechon, 909 S.W.2d 950, 961 n.9 (Tex. App.—El Paso 1995, no writ). Family Code §3.711, now §9.101, "confers upon the trial court continuing jurisdiction to enter orders necessary to amend or correct [QDROs] in order to ensure they are qualified and enforceable. We liken this provision to [Fam. Code] §3.72 [now §9.008] clarification orders, as they both constitute prerequisites to enforcement rather than methods of enforcement."

FAM §9.102. PROCEDURE

(a) A party to a decree of divorce or annulment may petition the court for a qualified domestic relations order or similar order.

(b) Except as otherwise provided by this code, a petition under this subchapter is governed by the Texas Rules of Civil Procedure that apply to the filing of an original lawsuit.

(c) Each party whose rights may be affected by the petition is entitled to receive notice by citation and shall be commanded to appear by filing a written answer.

(d) The proceedings shall be conducted in the same manner as civil cases generally.

History of Fam. Code §9.102: Acts 1997, 75th Leg., ch. 7, §1, eff. Apr. 17, 1997. Source: Former Fam. Code §3.711(d).

FAM §9.103. PRIOR FAILURE TO RENDER QUALIFIED DOMESTIC RELATIONS ORDER

A party may petition a court to render a qualified domestic relations order or similar order if the court that rendered a final decree of divorce or annulment or another final order dividing property under this chapter did not provide a qualified domestic relations order or similar order permitting payment of benefits to an alternate payee or other lawful payee.

History of Fam. Code §9.103: Acts 1997, 75th Leg., ch. 7, §1, eff. Apr. 17, 1997. Source: Former Fam. Code §3.711(a).

FAM §9.104. DEFECTIVE PRIOR DOMESTIC RELATIONS ORDER

If a plan administrator or other person acting in an equivalent capacity determines that a domestic relations order does not satisfy the requirements of a qualified domestic relations order or similar order, the court retains continuing, exclusive jurisdiction over the parties and their property to the extent necessary to render a qualified domestic relations order.

History of Fam. Code §9.104: Acts 1997, 75th Leg., ch. 7, §1, eff. Apr. 17, 1997. Source: Former Fam. Code §3.711(c).

FAM §9.1045. AMENDMENT OF QUALIFIED DOMESTIC RELATIONS ORDER

(a) A court that renders a qualified domestic relations order retains continuing, exclusive jurisdiction to amend the order to correct the order or clarify the terms of the order to effectuate the division of property ordered by the court.

(b) An amended domestic relations order under this section must be submitted to the plan administrator or other person acting in an equivalent capacity to determine whether the amended order satisfies the requirements of a qualified domestic relations order. Section 9.104 applies to a domestic relations order amended under this section.

History of Fam. Code §9.1045: Acts 2005, 79th Leg., ch. 481, §1, eff. June 17, 2005.

FAM §9.105. LIBERAL CONSTRUCTION

The court shall liberally construe this subchapter to effect payment of retirement benefits that were divided by a previous decree that failed to contain a qualified domestic relations order or similar order or that contained an order that failed to meet the requirements of a qualified domestic relations order or similar order.

History of Fam. Code §9.105: Acts 1997, 75th Leg., ch. 7, §1, eff. Apr. 17, 1997. Source: Former Fam. Code §3.711(e).

ANNOTATIONS

Arena v. Arena, 822 S.W.2d 645, 649 (Tex.App.—Fort Worth 1991, no writ). "The domestic relations order issued by the trial court in this case recognized [W's] right to receive the vested policy benefits. The Decree of Divorce specifically identifies the name of the participant, [H], and the beneficiary, [W]; in addition, it provides the name and address of [W's] attorney. The decree specifically identifies five separate benefit plans under which [W] will be the beneficiary. The domestic relations order also states the amount of each plan and that [W] will be entitled to the entire vested portion of each. Because the Decree of Divorce includes all of the information required by [ERISA] and does not involve any of the prohibitions, the decree is deemed a QDRO."

FAM §9.106. ATTORNEY'S FEES

In a proceeding under this subchapter, the court may award reasonable attorney's fees incurred by a party to a divorce or annulment against the other party to the divorce or annulment. The court may order the attorney's fees to be paid directly to the attorney, who may enforce the order for fees in the attorney's own name by any means available for the enforcement of a judgment for debt.

History of Fam. Code §9.106: Acts 2009, 81st Leg., ch. 768, §9, eff. Sept. 1, 2009.

Sections 9.107-9.200 reserved for expansion

SUBCHAPTER C. POST-DECREE DIVISION OF PROPERTY

FAM §9.201. PROCEDURE FOR DIVISION OF CERTAIN PROPERTY NOT DIVIDED ON DIVORCE OR ANNULMENT

(a) Either former spouse may file a suit as provided by this subchapter to divide property not divided or awarded to a spouse in a final decree of divorce or annulment.

(b) Except as otherwise provided by this subchapter, the suit is governed by the Texas Rules of Civil Procedure applicable to the filing of an original lawsuit.

History of Fam. Code §9.201: Acts 1997, 75th Leg., ch. 7, §1, eff. Apr. 17, 1997. Source: Former Fam. Code §3.90(a), (b).

See also ***O'Connor's Texas Family Law Handbook*** (2017), "Postdissolution Partition of Community Property," ch. 8, p. 927.

ANNOTATIONS

Brown v. Brown, 236 S.W.3d 343, 348-49 (Tex. App.—Houston [1st Dist.] 2007, no pet.). "In contrast to a traditional lawsuit in which res judicata is an affirmative defense, as the petitioner in this statutory post-divorce action, [H] has the burden to prove that the divorce court did not consider or dispose of the 401(k) plan or the accrued bonuses in the final decree."

Burgess v. Easley, 893 S.W.2d 87, 90 (Tex.App.—Dallas 1994, no writ). "In an action brought under [Fam. Code] §3.90 [now §9.201], a trial court presumes property owned by either spouse during or at dissolution of marriage is community property."

FAM §9.202. LIMITATIONS

(a) A suit under this subchapter must be filed before the second anniversary of the date a former spouse unequivocally repudiates the existence of the ownership interest of the other former spouse and communicates that repudiation to the other former spouse.

(b) The two-year limitations period is tolled for the period that a court of this state does not have jurisdiction over the former spouses or over the property.

History of Fam. Code §9.202: Acts 1997, 75th Leg., ch. 7, §1, eff. Apr. 17, 1997. Source: Former Fam. Code §3.90(c).

See also *O'Connor's Texas Family Law Handbook* (2017), "When to file," ch. 8-A, §4.2, p. 936.

ANNOTATIONS

Mayes v. Stewart, 11 S.W.3d 440, 457 (Tex.App.—Houston [14th Dist.] 2000, pet. denied). Family Code §9.202 "does not apply to suits to partition under [Prop. Code] §23.001. The '*right to partition is absolute*.' Similarly, nothing in §9.202 suggests that it applies to tort claims against third parties."

Sagester v. Waltrip, 970 S.W.2d 767, 769 (Tex. App.—Austin 1998, pet. denied). "The statutes of limitations on divorce-related partition suits are triggered by repudiation of a claim of entitlement to a share of the undivided community property. The ... Family Code requires that all suits to divide property not divided or awarded to a spouse in a final decree of divorce be brought within two years of the date one former spouse notifies the other former spouse that he or she *unequivocally* repudiates that other spouse's ownership interest. A four-year statute of limitations applies to all cases not involving real property that do not have a shorter limitations period applicable. In partition suits not subject to the Family Code provision, the trigger for the running of the four-year limitations period is unequivocal repudiation. Absent unequivocal repudiation, the partition suit can be filed long after the divorce. [¶] This appeal turns on whether [H's] general denial ... is, as a matter of law, sufficient repudiation of [W's] claim to trigger the running of the statutes of limitations periods. [¶] We find no authority for the proposition that a general denial combined with mere failure to share benefits for 20 years proves, as a matter of law, unequivocal repudiation. [¶] A general denial is, at most, an equivocal repudiation. [H's] pleading and [W's] knowledge that she was not receiving benefits do not signify, as a matter of law, an unequivocal repudiation of [W's] claim."

Phillips v. Phillips, 951 S.W.2d 955, 957 (Tex. App.—Waco 1997, no pet.). "Even if [Fam. Code] §3.90 [now §9.202] applied to bar an enforcement action under the Family Code, that section would not operate to bar an otherwise valid partition under [Prop. Code §23.001]. The *right to partition is absolute*."

Carter v. Charles, 853 S.W.2d 667, 671 (Tex.App.—Houston [14th Dist.] 1993, no writ). "For this statute to apply, [movant] must show that (1) the property sued upon was not divided or awarded in a final decree of divorce, (2) [movant] repudiated [nonmovant's] ownership interest in the property, (3) [movant's] repudiation was unequivocal, and (4) that unequivocal repudiation was communicated to [nonmovant]."

FAM §9.203. DIVISION OF UNDIVIDED ASSETS WHEN PRIOR COURT HAD JURISDICTION

(a) If a court of this state failed to dispose of property subject to division in a final decree of divorce or annulment even though the court had jurisdiction over the spouses or over the property, the court shall divide the property in a manner that the court deems just and right, having due regard for the rights of each party and any children of the marriage.

(b) If a final decree of divorce or annulment rendered by a court in another state failed to dispose of property subject to division under the law of that state even though the court had jurisdiction to do so, a court of this state shall apply the law of the other state regarding undivided property as required by Section 1, Article IV, United States Constitution (the full faith and credit clause), and enabling federal statutes.

History of Fam. Code §9.203: Acts 1997, 75th Leg., ch. 7, §1, eff. Apr. 17, 1997. Source: Former Fam. Code §3.91.

See also *O'Connor's Texas Family Law Handbook* (2017), "Court had jurisdiction to divide," ch. 8-A, §2.1.2(1), p. 932; "Just & right division," ch. 8-A, §12.2.1, p. 948.

ANNOTATIONS

In re Ford, 435 S.W.3d 347, 350 (Tex.App.—Texarkana 2014, no pet.). "There was no evidence whether any of the income [H] received during the parties' separation was still on hand at the time of their divorce or the filing of [W's] petition [for forfeiture]. [H] did offer testimony that he had continued to help [W] financially during the separation. With no evidence any of the income was still on hand at the time of the divorce, there is nothing establishing the existence of property not disposed of in the divorce decree, as contemplated by §9.203…."

Schuchmann v. Schuchmann, 193 S.W.3d 598, 602 (Tex.App.—Fort Worth 2006, pet. denied). "[T]he question is whether the probate court had jurisdiction over [H's] new, postdivorce lawsuit to divide the stock and stock options—assets unrelated to the trusts at issue in the probate court litigation. *At 604:* The plain meaning of [§9.203(a)] is to confer jurisdiction over a postdivorce action to divide assets on the court that rendered the final decree of divorce. While the probate court may have had jurisdiction over the parties and the undivided property, it did not render the final decree of divorce. Therefore, §9.203(a) does not confer jurisdiction over the postdivorce action on the probate court."

Forgason v. Forgason, 911 S.W.2d 893, 895-96 (Tex.App.—Amarillo 1995, writ denied). The authority under Fam. Code §3.91, now §9.203, "to 'divide' property is the authority to effect its partition. In partitioning the asset among the ex-spouses, it does not divest either of title. Rather, it 'dissolves the tenancy in common,' … and apportions the asset among the tenants. It does not legally divest anyone of title to the asset. [¶] It directs the trial court to divide the subject asset in a 'just and right' manner. That standard implicitly encompasses the power to divide in less than an equal way. Depending upon the facts of each case, the court may validly apportion some, all or none of the asset to any particular party." *See also* ***In re Marriage of Moore***, 890 S.W.2d 821, 840 (Tex.App.—Amarillo 1994, no writ).

FAM §9.204. DIVISION OF UNDIVIDED ASSETS WHEN PRIOR COURT LACKED JURISDICTION

(a) If a court of this state failed to dispose of property subject to division in a final decree of divorce or annulment because the court lacked jurisdiction over a spouse or the property, and if that court subsequently acquires the requisite jurisdiction, that court may divide the property in a manner that the court deems just and right, having due regard for the rights of each party and any children of the marriage.

(b) If a final decree of divorce or annulment rendered by a court in another state failed to dispose of property subject to division under the law of that state because the court lacked jurisdiction over a spouse or the property, and if a court of this state subsequently acquires the requisite jurisdiction over the former spouses or over the property, the court in this state may divide the property in a manner that the court deems just and right, having due regard for the rights of each party and any children of the marriage.

History of Fam. Code §9.204: Acts 1997, 75th Leg., ch. 7, §1, eff. Apr. 17, 1997. Source: Former Fam. Code §3.92.

See also *O'Connor's Texas Family Law Handbook* (2017), "Court did not have jurisdiction to divide," ch. 8-A, §2.1.2(2), p. 932; "Just & right division," ch. 8-A, §12.2.1, p. 948.

FAM §9.205. ATTORNEY'S FEES

In a proceeding to divide property previously undivided in a decree of divorce or annulment as provided by this subchapter, the court may award reasonable attorney's fees. The court may order the attorney's fees to be paid directly to the attorney, who may enforce the order in the attorney's own name by any means available for the enforcement of a judgment for debt.

History of Fam. Code §9.205: Acts 1997, 75th Leg., ch. 7, §1, eff. Apr. 17, 1997. Amended by Acts 2009, 81st Leg., ch. 768, §10, eff. Sept. 1, 2009. Source: Former Fam. Code §3.93.

See also *O'Connor's Texas Family Law Handbook* (2017), "Attorney fees," ch. 8-A, §4.4.9, p. 941.

Sections 9.206-9.300 reserved for expansion

SUBCHAPTER D. DISPOSITION OF UNDIVIDED BENEFICIAL INTEREST

FAM §9.301. PRE-DECREE DESIGNATION OF EX-SPOUSE AS BENEFICIARY OF LIFE INSURANCE

(a) If a decree of divorce or annulment is rendered after an insured has designated the insured's spouse as a beneficiary under a life insurance policy in force at the time of rendition, a provision in the policy in favor of the insured's former spouse is not effective unless:

(1) the decree designates the insured's former spouse as the beneficiary;

(2) the insured redesignates the former spouse as the beneficiary after rendition of the decree; or

(3) the former spouse is designated to receive the proceeds in trust for, on behalf of, or for the benefit of a child or a dependent of either former spouse.

(b) If a designation is not effective under Subsection (a), the proceeds of the policy are payable to the named alternative beneficiary or, if there is not a named alternative beneficiary, to the estate of the insured.

(c) An insurer who pays the proceeds of a life insurance policy issued by the insurer to the beneficiary under a designation that is not effective under Subsection (a) is liable for payment of the proceeds to the person or estate provided by Subsection (b) only if:

(1) before payment of the proceeds to the designated beneficiary, the insurer receives written notice at the home office of the insurer from an interested person that the designation is not effective under Subsection (a); and

(2) the insurer has not interpleaded the proceeds into the registry of a court of competent jurisdiction in accordance with the Texas Rules of Civil Procedure.

History of Fam. Code §9.301: Acts 1997, 75th Leg., ch. 7, §1, eff. Apr. 17, 1997. Source: Former Fam. Code §3.632(b), (c).

See also ***O'Connor's Texas Family Law Handbook*** (2017), "Transferring life insurance," ch. 7-C, §10.3, p. 861.

ANNOTATIONS

Hillman v. Maretta, ___ U.S. ___, 133 S.Ct. 1943, 1951 (2013). The Federal Employees' Group Life Insurance Act (FEGLIA) "creates a scheme that gives highest priority to an insured's designated beneficiary. *At 1952:* It makes no difference whether state law requires the transfer of the proceeds ... or creates a cause of action ... that enables another person to receive the proceeds upon filing an action in state court. In either case, state law displaces the beneficiary selected by the insured ... and places someone else in her stead. [¶] FEGLIA evinces Congress' decision to accord federal employees an unfettered 'freedom of choice' in selecting the beneficiary of the insurance proceeds and to ensure the proceeds would actually 'belong' to that beneficiary. *At 1953:* [W]here a beneficiary has been duly named, the insurance proceeds she is owed under FEGLIA cannot be allocated to another person by operation of state law."

Barnett v. Barnett, 67 S.W.3d 107, 121 (Tex.2001). Had decedent "survived until divorce proceedings were concluded, [respondent] could have obtained a decree that qualified as a QDRO under ERISA. That decree would have effected a fair and just property division and could have dealt directly with the ... life insurance policy. Because [decedent] did not survive, [respondent] is relegated to a claim for constructive fraud on the community. Although preemption might result in an anomaly in this case, the reasoning in U.S. Supreme Court's decision ***Egelhoff*** compels us to conclude that [respondent's] claim is based on state law that has a connection with an ERISA plan and is accordingly preempted. *At 126:* We conclude that fraud on the community, absent actual common-law fraud, is the type of claim that Congress intended to preempt under ERISA and that fraud on the community has no counterpart in federal common law. ... Accordingly, we hold that [respondent's] claim for constructive fraud on the community and her corresponding claim for a constructive trust are preempted by ERISA." *See also* ***Egelhoff v. Egelhoff***, 532 U.S. 141, 143 (2001).

Hunt v. Jefferson-Pilot Life Ins., 900 S.W.2d 453, 456 (Tex.App.—Fort Worth 1995, writ denied). Family Code §3.632(c), now §9.301(c), "is an express limitation on the liability of an insurance company that pays the proceeds of a policy to the designated beneficiary. [¶] We find that any constructive notice the insurance company might have had upon receipt of the divorce decree does not constitute written notice under the Family Code or the Insurance Code."

FAM §9.302. PRE-DECREE DESIGNATION OF EX-SPOUSE AS BENEFICIARY IN RETIREMENT BENEFITS & OTHER FINANCIAL PLANS

(a) If a decree of divorce or annulment is rendered after a spouse, acting in the capacity of a participant, annuitant, or account holder, has designated the other spouse as a beneficiary under an individual retirement account, employee stock option plan, stock option, or other form of savings, bonus, profit-sharing, or other employer plan or financial plan of an employee or a participant in force at the time of rendition, the designating provision in the plan in favor of the other former spouse is not effective unless:

(1) the decree designates the other former spouse as the beneficiary;

(2) the designating former spouse redesignates the other former spouse as the beneficiary after rendition of the decree; or

(3) the other former spouse is designated to receive the proceeds or benefits in trust for, on behalf of, or for the benefit of a child or dependent of either former spouse.

(b) If a designation is not effective under Subsection (a), the benefits or proceeds are payable to the named alternative beneficiary or, if there is not a named alternative beneficiary, to the designating former spouse.

(c) A business entity, employer, pension trust, insurer, financial institution, or other person obligated to pay retirement benefits or proceeds of a financial plan covered by this section who pays the benefits or proceeds to the beneficiary under a designation of the other former spouse that is not effective under Subsection (a) is liable for payment of the benefits or proceeds to the person provided by Subsection (b) only if:

(1) before payment of the benefits or proceeds to the designated beneficiary, the payor receives written notice at the home office or principal office of the payor from an interested person that the designation of the beneficiary or fiduciary is not effective under Subsection (a); and

(2) the payor has not interpleaded the benefits or proceeds into the registry of a court of competent jurisdiction in accordance with the Texas Rules of Civil Procedure.

(d) This section does not affect the right of a former spouse to assert an ownership interest in an undivided pension, retirement, annuity, or other financial plan described by this section as provided by this subchapter.

(e) This section does not apply to the disposition of a beneficial interest in a retirement benefit or other financial plan of a public retirement system as defined by Section 802.001, Government Code.

History of Fam. Code §9.302: Acts 1997, 75th Leg., ch. 7, §1, eff. Apr. 17, 1997. Source: Former Fam. Code §3.633(b)-(e).

Chapters 10-14 blank

TITLE 1-A. COLLABORATIVE FAMILY LAW

Chapter 15. Collaborative Family Law Act

TITLE 1-A. COLLABORATIVE FAMILY LAW

CHAPTER 15. COLLABORATIVE FAMILY LAW ACT

NCCUSL Prefatory Note*

...

Collaborative Law—An Overview**

Definition. Collaborative law is a voluntary, contractually based alternative dispute resolution process for parties who seek to negotiate a resolution of their matter rather than having a ruling imposed upon them by a court or arbitrator. The distinctive feature of collaborative law, as compared to other forms of alternative dispute resolution such as mediation, is that parties are represented by lawyers ("collaborative lawyers") during negotiations. Collaborative lawyers do not represent the party in court, but only for the purpose of negotiating agreements. The parties agree in advance that their lawyers are disqualified from further representing parties by appearing before a tribunal if the collaborative-law process ends without complete agreement ("disqualification requirement"). *See* William H. Schwab, *Collaborative Lawyering: A Closer Look at an Emerging Practice*, 4 Pepp. Disp. Resol. L.J. 351, 358 (2004). Parties thus retain collaborative lawyers for the limited purpose of acting as advocates and counselors during the negotiation process.

The Collaborative-Law Participation Agreement. The basic ground rules for collaborative law are set forth in a written agreement ("collaborative-law participation agreement") in which parties designate collaborative lawyers and agree not to seek tribunal (usually judicial) resolution of a dispute during the collaborative-law process. Pauline H. Tesler, *Collaborative Family Law*, 4 Pepp. Disp. Resol. L.J. 317, 319 (2004). The participation agreement also provides that if a party seeks judicial intervention, or otherwise terminates the collaborative-law process, the disqualification requirement takes effect. *Id.* at 319-20. Parties agree that they have a mutual right to terminate collaborative law at any time without giving a reason.

Positional and Problem Solving Negotiations and the Disqualification Requirement. The goal of collaborative law is to encourage parties to engage in "problem-solving" rather than "positional" negotiations. *See* Roger Fisher et al., *Getting to Yes: Negotiating Agreement Without Giving In* 4-14 (2d ed. 1991). Under a positional approach to negotiation, the parties see the negotiation process as a contest to be won by one side at the expense of the other. *Id.* at 6. Parties to positional negotiations often assume an extreme starting position, and make small concessions within their predetermined bargaining range usually in response to concessions made by the other side or threats. *Id.* If they do not find a meeting point of agreement between their positions, negotiations break down and litigation ensues. Julie Macfarlane, *The New Lawyer: How Settlement is Transforming the Practice of Law* 81-84 (2007) [hereinafter Macfarlane, *New Lawyer*].

In contrast, parties who follow a problem-solving, or what is sometimes referred to as interest-based, approach to negotiation promoted by collaborative law view a dispute as the parties' joint problem that needs to be solved. Carrie Menkel-Meadow, *Toward Another View of Legal Negotiation: The Structure of Problem Solving*, 31 UCLA L. Rev. 754, 759-60 (1984). Under this approach, the negotiation process focuses on the parties' underlying "needs, desires, concerns, and fears" and not only on the parties' articulated positions. Fisher et al., *supra*, at 40. A problem-solving approach assumes that "[b]ehind opposed positions lie shared and compatible interests, as well as conflicting ones," and that looking at interests rather than positions is beneficial because "for every interest there usually exist several possible positions that could satisfy it." *Id.* at 42. Accordingly, a problem-solving negotiator focuses on "finding creative solutions that maximize the outcome for both sides." Peter Robinson, *Contending with Wolves in Sheep's Clothing: A Cautiously Cooperative Approach to Mediation Advocacy*, 50 Baylor L. Rev. 963, 965 (1998).

Lawyers can and do, of course, encourage clients to engage in problem-solving negotiations without formally labeling the process collaborative law. The distinctive feature of collaborative law is, however, the disqualification requirement—the enforcement mechanism that parties create by contract to ensure that problem-solving negotiations actually occur. The disqualification requirement enables each party to penalize the other party for unacceptable negotiation behavior if the party who wants to end the collaborative law process is willing to assume the costs of engaging new counsel. "[E]ach side knows *at the start* that the other has similarly tied its own hands by making litigation expensive. By hiring two Collaborative Law practitioners, the parties send a powerful signal to each other that they truly intend to work together to resolve their differences amicably through settlement." Scott R. Peppet, *The Ethics of Collaborative Law*, 2008 J. Disp. Resol. 131, 133 (2008) (emphasis in original).

Because of these mutually agreed upon costs of failure to agree, collaborative law is a modern method of addressing the age old dilemma for parties to a negotiation of assuring that "one's negotiating counterpart is and will continue to be a true collaborator rather than a 'sharpie.'" Ted Schneyer, *The Organized Bar and the Collaborative Law Movement: A Study in Professional Change*, 50 Ariz. L. Rev. 289, 327 (2008). It solves the age old problem for negotiators of deciding whether to cooperate or compete in a situation where each side does not know the other's intentions and "when the pursuit of self-interest by each leads

* **Editor's note:**

The NCCUSL comments have been edited to reflect the Texas Legislature's omission of sections, changing of text, and changing of section numbers from the original uniform act. The Texas Legislature did not adopt the NCCUSL comments when it adopted the Uniform Collaborative Law Act. The full uniform act and comments can be found at www.uniformlaws.org.

** **Editor's note:** The full Prefatory Note could not be included due to its length but can be found in its entirety at www.uniformlaws.org.

to a poor outcome for all"—the famous "Prisoner's Dilemma" of game theory. Robert Alexrod, *The Evolution of Cooperation* 7 (1984).

Multiple Models of Collaborative Law Practice. To encourage problem-solving negotiations, collaborative lawyers emphasize that no threats of litigation should be made during a collaborative law process and the need to maintain respectful dialogue. *See* Global Collaborative Law Council, Participation Agreement 3 (2004), *available at* http://www.collaborativelaw.us/articles/GCLC_Participation_Agreement_With_Addendum.pdf. Parties in collaborative law generally agree to disclose information voluntarily, without formal discovery requests, and to supplement responses to information requests previously made with material changes. *See id.* at 4. Many models of collaborative law require parties to engage jointly retained mental health and financial professionals in advisory and neutral roles—for example, a divorce coach, appraiser, and child's representative—rather than as consultants or trial witnesses hired by one party but not the other. *See* John Lande, *Possibilities for Collaborative Law: Ethics and Practice of Lawyer Disqualification and Process Control in a New Model of Lawyering*, 64 Ohio St. L.J. 1315, 1321 n.13 (2003) [hereinafter Lande, *Possibilities for Collaborative Law*]; Forrest S. Mosten, *Collaborative Divorce Handbook: Helping Families Without Going to Court* 106-07 (2009). Sometimes, collaborative law participation agreements require that negotiations take place in meetings in which parties are the primary negotiators and their lawyers encourage focusing on underlying interests, sharing information, and brainstorming solutions to problems. Global Collaborative Law Council, *supra*, at 2-3. Typically, in order to promote problem solving negotiations, collaborative law participation agreements provide that communications during the collaborative law process are confidential and cannot be introduced as evidence in court. *See id.* at 4-5; *see also* N.Y. Association of Collaborative Professionals, Participation Agreement.

Collaborative Law Compared to Mediation. Mediation and collaborative law are both valuable alternative dispute resolution processes that share common characteristics. They do have differences that might make one process more or less attractive to parties.

Both collaborative law and mediation offer parties the benefits of a process to promote agreement through private, confidential negotiations, the promise of cost reduction, and the potential for better relationships. Both mediation and collaborative law encourage voluntary disclosure and an ethic of fair dealing between parties. Parties in both mediation and collaborative law are likely to experience greater voice in the process of settlement than in a judicial resolution (self-determination) and are more likely to be satisfied with the process as compared to litigation. *See* Chris Guthrie & James Levin, *A "Party Satisfaction" Perspective on a Comprehensive Mediation Statute*, 13 Ohio St. J. on Disp. Resol. 885, 891 (1998).

Mediation and collaborative law do, however, have differences which might make collaborative law more or less attractive to some parties as a dispute resolution option. A neutral is not present during collaborative-law process negotiation sessions unless agreed to by the parties, while mediation sessions are facilitated by a neutral third party. *Model Standards of Conduct for Mediators* pmbl. (2005). As will be discussed *infra*, parties can participate in mediation without counsel but cannot do so in collaborative law. In many states parties do not have the protection of mediators being a licensed and regulated profession and bound by its rules of professional responsibility. Collaborative lawyers, in contrast, are licensed and regulated members of the legal profession. Mediators, as neutrals, cannot give candid legal advice to a party while collaborative lawyers can. Mediators, as neutrals, are also constrained in redressing imbalances in the knowledge and sophistication of parties. *See, e.g.*, *Model Standards of Conduct for Mediators*, Standard II(B) (2005) ("A mediator shall conduct a mediation in an impartial manner and avoid conduct that gives the appearance of partiality."); Rules of the Chief Admin. Judge, 30 N.Y. Reg. 93 (July 30, 2008) (detailing the neutrality requirement for mediators in New York); *Model Standards of Practice for Family & Divorce Mediation*, Standard IV (Symposium on Standards of Practice 2000) ("A family mediator shall conduct the mediation process in an impartial manner."). Despite their limited purpose of representation in negotiating a resolution of a dispute, collaborative lawyers are not neutrals but are advocates for their clients.

These kinds of considerations might make parties opt for collaborative law over mediation for resolution of their dispute or vice versa. Collaborative law is an attractive dispute resolution option for many parties, especially those who wish to maintain post dispute relationships with each other and minimize the costs of dispute resolution. Parties may prefer it to traditional full service representation by lawyers, which includes both settlement negotiations and representation in court, because of its reduced costs and incentives for lawyers to work hard to produce acceptable compromise while still providing the party with the support of an advocate.

...

Reducing the Costs of Divorce and Family Related Conflict for Parents and Children. Problem-solving approaches to potential settlement are especially appropriate in divorce and family disputes where economic, emotional, and parental relationships often continue after the legal process ends. Dissolution and reorganization of intimate relationships can generate intense anger, stress, and anxiety, emotions which can be exacerbated by adversary litigation and positional approaches to dispute resolution. The emotional and economic futures of children and parents, who often have limited resources, are at stake in family and divorce disputes. The needs of children are particularly implicated in divorce cases, as children exposed to high levels of inter-parental conflict "are at [a higher] risk for developing a range of emotional and behavioral problems, both during childhood and later in life." John H. Grych, *Interparental Conflict as a Risk Factor for Child Maladjustment: Implications for the Development of Prevention Programs*, 43 Fam. Ct. Rev. 97, 97 (2005); *see also Interparental Conflict and Child Development: Theory, Research, and Applications* (John H. Grych & Frank D. Fincham eds., 2001); Joan B. Kelly, *Children's Adjustment in Conflicted Marriage and Divorce: A Decade Review of Research*, 39 J. Am. Acad. Child & Adolescent Psychiatry 963-64 (2000). When conflict levels are low between parents, a child is more likely to have contact with both parents and the child support is more regularly paid. *See* Andrew I. Schepard, *Children, Courts, and Custody: Interdisciplinary Models for Divorcing Families* 35 (2004) [hereinafter Schepard, *Children, Courts, and Custody*].

Parents in divorce and family disputes have negative reactions to litigation as a method of resolving family problems. *Id.* at 42-44. Divorcing parents may well thus rationally decide that their well being and the well being of their children is better promoted by dispute resolution through collaborative law rather than more traditional courtroom proceedings and adversarial oriented positional negotiations. There are risks for parents who choose collaborative law especially of incurring the economic and emotional cost of employing a new lawyer. But there are also benefits for them and their children.

> [I]t would be a mistake to focus solely on the risks that [collaborative law] poses for clients. Other things being equal, spouses who choose court-based divorce presumably run the greater risk of harming themselves and their children in bitter litigation or rancorous negotiations. [Collaborative law] clients presumably bind themselves by a mutual commitment to good faith negotiation in hopes of reducing the risk that they will cause such harm, just as Ulysses had his crew tie him to the mast so he would not succumb to the Sirens' call and have his ship founder.

Schneyer, *supra*, at 318 n.142; *see also* Schepard, *Children, Courts, and Custody*, *supra*, at 50-51 (emphasizing the alternate dispute resolution process as the best choice for litigants who will maintain a relationship after resolution); Robert E. Emery et al., *Divorce Mediation: Research and Reflections*, 43 Fam. Ct. Rev. 22, 34 (2005) (stating parents' need to avoid becoming adversaries in divorce, especially where children are involved).

...

The Special Role of the Family and Divorce Lawyer. The importance of the role of counselor and problem solver is especially pronounced for lawyers who represent clients in divorce and family disputes where collaborative law has had its greatest growth. Indeed, the divorce bar recognizes that those disputes are particularly appropriate for the problem-solving orientation to client representation that collaborative law encourages. *Bounds of Advocacy*, a supplementary code of standards of professional responsibility for divorce law specialists who are members of the American Academy of Matrimonial Lawyers (AAML), states that: "[a]s a counselor, a problem-solving lawyer encourages problem solving in the client. ... The client's best interests include the well being of children, family peace, and economic stability." American Academy of Matrimonial Lawyers, Bounds of Advocacy: Preliminary Statement, http://www.aaml.org/library/publications/19/bounds-advocacy/preliminary-statement (last visited June 18, 2015). *Bounds of Advocacy* further states that "the emphasis on zealous representation [used] in criminal cases and some civil cases is not always appropriate in family law matters" and that "[p]ublic opinion ... increasingly support[s] other models of lawyering and goals of conflict resolution in appropriate cases." *Id.* Furthermore, *Bounds of Advocacy* states that a divorce lawyer should "consider the welfare of, and seek to minimize the adverse impact of the divorce on, the minor children." American Academy of Matrimonial

Lawyers, Bounds of Advocacy: Children, http://www.aaml.org/library/publications/19/bounds-advocacy/6-children (last visited June 18, 2015).

...

The Uniform Collaborative Law Rules and Act—An Overview

The overall goal of the Uniform Collaborative Law Rules and Act is to encourage the continued development and growth of collaborative law as a voluntary dispute resolution option. Collaborative law has thus far largely been practiced under the auspices of private collaborative-law participation agreements developed by private practice groups. These agreements vary substantially in depth and detail, and their enforcement must be accomplished by actions for breach of contract.

The Uniform Collaborative Law Rules and Act aims to standardize the most important features of collaborative-law participation agreements, both to protect consumers and to facilitate party entry into a collaborative-law process. It mandates essential elements of a process of disclosure and discussion between prospective collaborative lawyers and prospective parties to better insure that parties who sign participation agreements do so with informed consent. It requires collaborative lawyers to make reasonable inquiries and take steps to protect parties against the trauma of domestic violence. The rules/act also makes collaborative law's key features—especially the disqualification provision and voluntary disclosure of information provision—mandated provisions of participation agreements that seek the benefits of the rights and obligations of the rules/act. Finally, the rules/act creates an evidentiary privilege for collaborative-law communications to facilitate candid discussions during the collaborative-law process.

Specifically, the Uniform Collaborative Law Rules and Act:

...

- establishes minimum requirements for collaborative-law participation agreements, including written agreements that state the parties' intention to resolve their matter (collaborative matter) through a collaborative-law process under the rules/act, include a description of the matter submitted to a collaborative-law process, and designation of collaborative lawyers (§15.101);
- emphasizes that party participation in collaborative law is voluntary by prohibiting tribunals from ordering a party into a collaborative-law process over that party's objection (§15.102(b));
- specifies when and how a collaborative-law process begins and is concluded (§15.102);
- creates a stay of proceedings when parties sign a participation agreement to attempt to resolve a matter related to a proceeding pending before a tribunal while allowing the tribunal to ask for periodic status reports (§15.103);
- makes an exception to the stay of proceedings for emergency orders to protect health, safety, welfare or interests of a party, a family member or a dependent (§15.104);

...

- codifies the disqualification requirement for collaborative lawyers when a collaborative-law process concludes (§15.106);
- defines the scope of the disqualification requirement to include both the collaborative matter and a matter "related to the collaborative matter" (§15.106)—those involving the "same parties, transaction or occurrence, nucleus of operative fact, dispute, claim, or issue as the collaborative family law matter" (§15.052(12));
- extends the disqualification requirement beyond the individual collaborative lawyer to lawyers in a law firm with which the collaborative lawyer is associated (imputed disqualification) (§15.106(c));
- relaxes imputed disqualification if the firm represents low-income parties for no fee, the parties agree to the exception in advance in their collaborative-law participation agreement, and the original collaborative lawyer is screened from further participation in the matter or related matters (§15.107);
- creates a similar exception for collaborative lawyers for government agencies (§15.108(c));
- requires parties to voluntarily disclose relevant information during the collaborative-law process without formal discovery requests and update information previously disclosed that has materially changed. The parties may also agree on the scope of disclosure required during a collaborative-law process if that scope is not inconsistent with other law (§15.109);
- acknowledges that standards of professional responsibility and child abuse reporting for lawyers and other professionals are not changed by their participation in a collaborative-law process (§15.110);
- requires that lawyers disclose and discuss the material risks and benefits of a collaborative-law process as compared to other dispute resolution processes such as litigation, mediation, and arbitration to help insure parties enter into collaborative-law participation agreements with informed consent (§15.111);
- creates an obligation on collaborative lawyers to screen clients for domestic violence (defined as a "coercive or violent relationship") and, if present, to participate in a collaborative-law process only if the victim consents (§15.112);
- authorizes parties to reach an agreement on the scope of confidentiality of their collaborative-law communications (§15.113);
- creates an evidentiary privilege for collaborative-law communications which are sought to be introduced into evidence before a tribunal (§15.114);
- provides for possibility of waiver of and limited exceptions to the evidentiary privilege based on important countervailing public policies (such as the protection of bodily integrity and crime prevention) similar to those recognized for mediation communications in the Uniform Mediation Act (§§15.114, 15.115);
- authorizes tribunal discretion to enforce agreements that result from a collaborative-law process, the disqualification requirement and the evidentiary privilege provisions of the act, despite the lawyers' mistakes in required disclosures before collaborative-law participation agreements are executed and in the written participation agreements themselves (§15.116).

SUBCHAPTER A. APPLICATION & CONSTRUCTION

FAM §15.001. POLICY

It is the policy of this state to encourage the peaceable resolution of disputes, with special consideration given to disputes involving the parent-child relationship, including disputes involving the conservatorship of, possession of or access to, and support of a child, and the early settlement of pending litigation through voluntary settlement procedures.

History of Fam. Code §15.001: Acts 2011, 82nd Leg., ch. 1048, §1, eff. Sept. 1, 2011.

See also *O'Connor's Texas Family Law Handbook* (2017), "Collaborative law," ch. 3-A, §13.1.2, p. 248.

FAM §15.002. CONFLICTS BETWEEN PROVISIONS

If a provision of this chapter conflicts with another provision of this code or another statute or rule of this state and the conflict cannot be reconciled, this chapter prevails.

History of Fam. Code §15.002: Acts 2011, 82nd Leg., ch. 1048, §1, eff. Sept. 1, 2011.

FAM §15.003. UNIFORMITY OF APPLICATION & CONSTRUCTION

In applying and construing this chapter, consideration must be given to the need to promote uniformity of the law with respect to its subject matter among states that enact a collaborative law process Act for family law matters.

History of Fam. Code §15.003: Acts 2011, 82nd Leg., ch. 1048, §1, eff. Sept. 1, 2011.

NCCUSL Comment*

While the Drafting Committee recognizes that some such variations of collaborative law are inevitable given its dynamic and diverse nature and early stage of development, the specific benefits of uniformity of law should also be

* See footnote on p. 133.

emphasized. Uniform adoption of this act will make the law governing collaborative law more accessible and certain in key areas and will thus encourage parties to participate in a collaborative law process. Collaborative lawyers and parties will know the standards under which collaborative law participation agreements will be enforceable and courts can reasonably anticipate how the statute will be interpreted. Moreover, uniformity of the law will provide greater protection of collaborative law communications than any one state or choice of law doctrine has the capacity to provide. No matter how much protection one state affords confidentiality of collaborative law communications, for example, the communication will not be protected against compelled disclosure in another state if that state does not have the same level of protection.

FAM §15.004. RELATION TO ELECTRONIC SIGNATURES IN GLOBAL & NATIONAL COMMERCE ACT

This chapter modifies, limits, and supersedes the federal Electronic Signatures in Global and National Commerce Act (15 U.S.C. Section 7001 et seq.) but does not modify, limit, or supersede Section 101(c) of that Act (15 U.S.C. Section 7001(c)), or authorize electronic delivery of any of the notices described in Section 103(b) of that Act (15 U.S.C. Section 7003(b)).

History of Fam. Code §15.004: Acts 2011, 82nd Leg., ch. 1048, §1, eff. Sept. 1, 2011.

Sections 15.005-15.050 reserved for expansion

SUBCHAPTER B. GENERAL PROVISIONS

FAM §15.051. SHORT TITLE

This chapter may be cited as the Collaborative Family Law Act.

History of Fam. Code §15.051: Acts 2011, 82nd Leg., ch. 1048, §1, eff. Sept. 1, 2011.

FAM §15.052. DEFINITIONS

In this chapter:

(1) "Collaborative family law communication" means a statement made by a party or nonparty participant, whether oral or in a record, or verbal or nonverbal, that:

(A) is made to conduct, participate in, continue, or reconvene a collaborative family law process; and

(B) occurs after the parties sign a collaborative family law participation agreement and before the collaborative family law process is concluded.

(2) "Collaborative family law participation agreement" means an agreement by persons to participate in a collaborative family law process.

(3) "Collaborative family law matter" means a dispute, transaction, claim, problem, or issue for resolution that arises under Title 1 or 5 and that is described in a collaborative family law participation agreement. The term includes a dispute, claim, or issue in a proceeding.

(4) "Collaborative family law process" means a procedure intended to resolve a collaborative family law matter without intervention by a tribunal in which parties:

(A) sign a collaborative family law participation agreement; and

(B) are represented by collaborative family law lawyers.

(5) "Collaborative lawyer" means a lawyer who represents a party in a collaborative family law process.

(6) "Law firm" means:

(A) lawyers who practice law together in a partnership, professional corporation, sole proprietorship, limited liability company, or association; and

(B) lawyers employed in a legal services organization or in the legal department of a corporation or other organization or of a government or governmental subdivision, agency, or instrumentality.

(7) "Nonparty participant" means a person, including a collaborative lawyer, other than a party, who participates in a collaborative family law process.

(8) "Party" means a person who signs a collaborative family law participation agreement and whose consent is necessary to resolve a collaborative family law matter.

(9) "Proceeding" means a judicial, administrative, arbitral, or other adjudicative process before a tribunal, including related prehearing and posthearing motions, conferences, and discovery.

(10) "Prospective party" means a person who discusses with a prospective collaborative lawyer the possibility of signing a collaborative family law participation agreement.

(11) "Record" means information that is inscribed on a tangible medium or that is stored in an electronic or other medium and is retrievable in perceivable form.

(12) "Related to a collaborative family law matter" means a matter involving the same parties, transaction or occurrence, nucleus of operative fact, dispute, claim, or issue as the collaborative family law matter.

(13) "Sign" means, with present intent to authenticate or adopt a record, to:

(A) execute or adopt a tangible symbol; or

(B) attach to or logically associate with the record an electronic symbol, sound, or process.

(14) "Tribunal" means a court, arbitrator, administrative agency, or other body acting in an adjudicative

capacity that, after presentation of evidence or legal argument, has jurisdiction to render a decision affecting a party's interests in a matter.

History of Fam. Code §15.052: Acts 2011, 82nd Leg., ch. 1048, §1, eff. Sept. 1, 2011.

See also ***O'Connor's Texas Family Law Handbook*** (2017), "Collaborative law," ch. 3-A, §13.1.2, p. 248.

NCCUSL Comment*

"Collaborative family law process" and "collaborative family law participation agreement." A collaborative family law process is created by written contract, a collaborative family law participation agreement. It requires parties to engage collaborative lawyers. The minimum requirements for collaborative family law participation agreements are specified in §15.101.

"Collaborative family law communication." Section 15.114 creates an evidentiary privilege for collaborative family law communications, a term defined here.

The definition of "collaborative family law communication" parallels the definition of "mediation communication" in the Uniform Mediation Act Section 2(2). Collaborative law communications are statements that are made orally, through conduct, or in writing or other recorded activity. This definition is similar to the general rule, as reflected in Federal Rule of Evidence 801(a), which defines a "statement" as "an oral or written assertion or nonverbal conduct of a person, if it is intended by the person as an assertion." Fed. R. Evid. 801(a).

Understandable confusion has sometimes resulted because the terms "oral or ... verbal" are both used in §15.052(1) and some think the terms are synonymous. They are not. "Oral" can be defined as "[u]ttered by the mouth or in words; spoken, not written." *Black's Law Dictionary* 1095 (6th ed. 1990). Although commonly used interchangeably with "oral," "verbal" is defined strictly as "of or pertaining to words; expressed in words, whether spoken or written." *Id.* at 1558. "Thus, 'verbal' is a broader term, and it is possible for something to be verbal but not oral." *Citation omitted.*

Most generic mediation privileges cover communications but do not cover conduct that is not intended as an assertion. *Citations omitted.* The same is true of the privilege created by this act.

The mere fact that a person attended a collaborative-law session—in other words, the physical presence of a person—is not a communication. By contrast, nonverbal conduct such as nodding in response to a question would be a "communication" because it is meant as an assertion; however nonverbal conduct such as smoking a cigarette during the collaborative-law session typically would not be a "communication" because it was not meant by the actor as an assertion.

Mental impressions that are based even in part on collaborative family law communications would generally be protected by privilege. More specifically, communications include both statements and conduct meant to inform, because the purpose of the privilege is to promote candid collaborative family law communications. *But see U.S. v. Robinson*, 121 F.3d 971, 975 (5th Cir. 1997) (finding that ordinarily the act of giving a document to an attorney will not be privileged). By analogy to the attorney-client privilege, silence in response to a question may be a communication, if it is meant to inform. *But see U.S. v. White*, 950 F.2d 426, 430 & n.2 (7th Cir. 1991) (noting the distinction between communication and lack of communication). Further, conduct meant to explain or communicate a fact, such as the re-enactment of an accident, is a communication. *See* Jack B. Weinstein & Margaret A. Berger, *Weinstein's Federal Evidence* §503.14[3][a] (Joseph M. McLaughlin, ed., 2nd ed. 1997). Similarly, a client's revelation of a hidden scar to an attorney in response to a question is a communication if meant to inform. In contrast, a purely physical phenomenon, such as a tattoo or the color of a suit of clothes, observable by all, is not a communication.

If evidence of mental impressions would reveal, even indirectly, collaborative family law communications, then that evidence would be blocked by the privilege. *See Gunther v. U.S.*, 230 F.2d 222, 223-24 (D.C. Cir. 1956). For example, a party's mental impressions of the capacity of another party to enter into a binding settlement agreement would be privileged if that impression was in part based on the statements that the party made during the collaborative family law process, because the testimony might reveal the content or character of the collaborative family law communications upon which the impression is based. In contrast, the mental impression would not be privileged if it was based exclusively on the party's observation of that party wearing heavy clothes and an overcoat on a hot summer day because the choice of clothing was not meant to inform. *See, e.g., Darrow v. Gunn*, 594 F.2d 767, 774 (9th Cir. 1979) (discussing California law which states that observations and impressions of clients are not privileged).

The definition of "collaborative family law communication" has a fixed time element—it only includes communications that occur between the time a collaborative family law participation agreement is signed and before a collaborative family law process is concluded. The methods and requirements for beginning and concluding a collaborative family law process are specified in §15.102. The defined time period and methods for ascertaining are designed to make it easier for tribunals to determine the applicability of the privilege to a proposed collaborative family law communication.

The definition of collaborative family law communication does include some communications that are not made during actual negotiation sessions, such as those made for purposes of convening or continuing a negotiation session after a collaborative family law process begins. It also includes "briefs" and other reports that are prepared by the parties for the collaborative family law process.

Whether a document is prepared for a collaborative family law process is a crucial issue in determining whether it is a "collaborative family law communication." For example, a tax return brought to a collaborative-law negotiation session for a divorce settlement would not be a "collaborative family law communication," even though it may have been used extensively in the process, because it was not created for purposes of conducting, participating in, continuing, or reconvening a collaborative-law process, but rather because it is a requirement of federal law. However, a note written on the tax return to clarify a point for other participants during a negotiation session would be a collaborative family law communication. Similarly, a memorandum specifically prepared for the collaborative family law process by a party or a party's counsel explaining the rationale behind certain positions taken on the tax return would be a collaborative family law communication. Documents prepared for a collaborative-law process by experts retained by the parties would also be covered by this definition.

"Collaborative lawyer." A collaborative lawyer represents a party in a collaborative family law process. A party must be represented by a lawyer to participate in a collaborative family law process; it is not an option for the self-represented. Section 15.101(a)(5) requires that a collaborative family law participation agreement identify the collaborative lawyer who represents each party and §15.101(a)(6) requires that the agreement contain a statement by the designated lawyer confirming the representation.

"Collaborative family law matter." The act uses the term "matter" rather the narrower term "dispute" to describe what the parties may attempt to resolve through a collaborative family law process. Matter can include some or all of the issues in litigation or potential litigation, or can include issues between the parties that have not or may never ripen into litigation. The broader term emphasizes that parties have great autonomy to decide what to submit to a collaborative family law process and encourages them to use the process creatively and broadly.

Section 15.052(3) limits "collaborative family law matter" to matters which arise under Titles 1 or 5 of the Texas Family Code.

...

The parties must, however, describe the matter that they seek to resolve through a collaborative family law process in their collaborative family law participation agreement. *See* Tex. Fam. Code §15.101(a)(4). That requirement is essential to determining the scope of the disqualification requirement for collaborative lawyers under §15.106, which is applicable to the collaborative family law matter and matters "related to the collaborative family law matter," and the application of the evidentiary privilege under §15.114.

"Law firm." This definition of "law firm" is adapted from the definition of the term in the American Bar Association's Model Rules of Professional Conduct Rule 1.0(c). It includes lawyers representing governmental entities whether employed by the government or by a private law firm. It is included to help define the scope of the imputed disqualification requirement of §15.106.

"Nonparty participant." This definition parallels the definition of "nonparty participant" in the Uniform Mediation Act §2(4). It covers experts, friends, support persons, potential parties, and others who participate in the

* See footnote on p. 133.

collaborative family law process. Nonparty participants are entitled to assert a privilege before a tribunal for their own collaborative family law communications under §15.114(b). This provision is designed to encourage mental health and financial professionals to participate in a collaborative family law process without fear of becoming embroiled in litigation without their consent should the process terminate.

Nonparty participant does not, however, include a collaborative lawyer for a party. The attorney-client privilege is applicable to communications between a collaborative lawyer and the party whom he or she represents. The collaborative attorney thus has the obligation placed upon all lawyers to maintain client confidences and assert evidentiary privilege for client communications. The obligations of professional responsibility for a lawyer are not altered by the lawyer's representation of a party in collaborative law. Tex. Fam. Code §15.110. Under the Model Rules of Professional Conduct the attorney-client privilege is held by the client and can only be waived by the client, even over the attorney's objection. *Citations omitted.* An attorney does not have the right to override a client's decision to waive privilege, and including collaborative lawyers in the category of nonparty participants entitled to independently assert privilege might be thought of as changing that traditional view. *Citations omitted.* A collaborative lawyer thus does not have any additional right to independently assert privilege because of the lawyer's participation in the collaborative family law process as a "nonparty."

A few states declare ADR neutrals incompetent to testify about communications in the ADR processes. The declaration of incompetence to testify normally does not apply to lawyers representing clients, but is limited to third party neutrals, such as mediators and arbitrators. Cal. Evid. Code §703.5 (West 1995). ...

"Party." The act's definition of "party" is central to determining who has rights and obligations under the act, especially the right to assert the evidentiary privilege for collaborative family law communications. Fortunately, parties to a collaborative family law process are relatively easy to identify—they are signatories to a collaborative family law participation agreement and they engage designated collaborative lawyers.

"Proceeding." The definition of "proceeding" is drawn from §2(7) of the Uniform Mediation Act. *See* Unif. Mediation Act §2(7), 7A U.L.A. 105-06 (2006). Its purpose is to define the adjudicative type proceedings to which the act applies, and should be read broadly to effectuate the intent of the act. It was added to allow the drafters to delete repetitive language throughout the act, such as "judicial, administrative, arbitral, or other adjudicative processes, including related pre-hearing and post-hearing motions, conferences, and discovery; or ... a legislative hearing or similar process." *Id.*

"Prospective party." The definition of "prospective party" is drawn from the ABA Model Rules of Professional Conduct Rule 1.18(a) which defines a lawyer's duty to a prospective client. Model Rules of Prof'l Conduct R. 1.18(a) (2009). The act uses the term "party" rather than "client" to clarify that it does not change the standards of professional responsibility applicable to lawyers. The collaborative lawyer's obligations to prospective parties are described in §§15.111 and 15.112.

"Related to a collaborative family law matter." Under §15.106, a collaborative lawyer and lawyers in a law firm with which the collaborative lawyer is associated are disqualified from representing parties in court in a matter related to the collaborative family law matter when a collaborative family law process concludes. The definition of "related to a collaborative family law matter" thus determines the scope of the disqualification provision. The rationale and application of the definition of "related to a collaborative family law matter" is discussed in detail in the complete Prefatory Note, which can be found at www.uniformlaws.org.

"Sign." The definitions of "record" and "sign" adopt standard language approved by the Uniform Law Commission intended to conform Uniform Acts with the Uniform Electronic Transactions Act ("UETA") and its federal counterpart, Electronic Signatures in Global and National Commerce Act ("E-Sign"). *Citation omitted.* Both UETA and E-Sign were written in response to broad recognition of the commercial and other uses of electronic technologies for communications and contracting and the consensus that the choice of medium should not control the enforceability of transactions. *Citations omitted.* These sections are consistent with both UETA and E-Sign. UETA has been adopted by the Commission and received the approval of the American Bar Association House of Delegates. *Citations omitted.* As of December 2001, it had been enacted in more than 35 states. *Citation omitted.*

The practical effect of these definitions is to make clear that electronic signatures and documents have the same authority as written ones for such purposes as establishing the validity of a collaborative family law participation agreement under §15.101, notice to terminate the collaborative family law process under §15.102(d)(1), party agreements concerning the confidentiality of collaborative family law communications under §15.113, and party waiver of the collaborative family law communication privilege under §15.115(a)(2).

"Tribunal." The definition of "tribunal" is adapted from Rule 1.0(m) of the ABA Model Rules of Professional Conduct. Model Rules of Prof'l Conduct R. 1.0(m) (2009). It is included to insure the provisions of this act are applicable in judicial and other forums such as arbitration and is consistent with the broad definition of "proceeding" in subsection (9).

FAM §15.053. APPLICABILITY

This chapter applies only to a matter arising under Title 1 or 5.

History of Fam. Code §15.053: Acts 2011, 82nd Leg., ch. 1048, §1, eff. Sept. 1, 2011.

See also ***O'Connor's Texas Family Law Handbook*** (2017), "Collaborative law," ch. 3-A, §13.1.2, p. 248.

Sections 15.054-15.100 reserved for expansion

SUBCHAPTER C. COLLABORATIVE FAMILY LAW PROCESS

FAM §15.101. REQUIREMENTS FOR COLLABORATIVE FAMILY LAW PARTICIPATION AGREEMENT

(a) A collaborative family law participation agreement must:

(1) be in a record;

(2) be signed by the parties;

(3) state the parties' intent to resolve a collaborative family law matter through a collaborative family law process under this chapter;

(4) describe the nature and scope of the collaborative family law matter;

(5) identify the collaborative lawyer who represents each party in the collaborative family law process; and

(6) contain a statement by each collaborative lawyer confirming the lawyer's representation of a party in the collaborative family law process.

(b) A collaborative family law participation agreement must include provisions for:

(1) suspending tribunal intervention in the collaborative family law matter while the parties are using the collaborative family law process; and

(2) unless otherwise agreed in writing, jointly engaging any professionals, experts, or advisors serving in a neutral capacity.

(c) Parties may agree to include in a collaborative family law participation agreement additional provisions not inconsistent with this chapter.

History of Fam. Code §15.101: Acts 2011, 82nd Leg., ch. 1048, §1, eff. Sept. 1, 2011.

See also *O'Connor's Texas Family Law Handbook* (2017), "Form of agreement," ch. 3-A, §13.1.2(2)(d), p. 249; "Contents," ch. 3-A, §13.1.2(2)(e), p. 250.

NCCUSL Comment*

Subsection (a) sets minimum conditions for the validity of collaborative family law participation agreements. They are designed to insure that a written record evidences the parties' agreement and intent to participate in a collaborative family law process under the act. They were formulated to require collaborative family law participation agreements to be fundamentally fair, but simple and thus to make collaborative law more accessible to potential parties with matters in a wide variety of areas.

To qualify as a collaborative family law participation agreement, the parties must explicitly state their intention to proceed "under this chapter." The participation agreement must thus specifically reference this chapter to make its provisions such as the evidentiary privilege for collaborative family law communications applicable. This requirement is designed to help insure that parties make a deliberate decision to "opt into" in a collaborative family law process rather than participate by inadvertence. It is also designed to differentiate a collaborative family law process under this chapter from other types of cooperative or collaborative behavior or dispute resolution involving parties and lawyers.

The requirements of subsection (a) are also designed to help tribunals and parties more easily administer and interpret the disqualification and evidentiary privileges provisions of the act. It is, for example, difficult to determine the scope of the disqualification requirement unless the parties describe the matter submitted to collaborative law in their participation agreement and designate collaborative lawyers.

The requirements of subsection (a) are subject to the provisions of §15.116 which give a tribunal discretion to find that, despite flaws in their written participation agreement, parties reasonably believed they were participating in a collaborative family law process and thus to apply the provisions of the act "in the interests of justice."

Section 15.101(a)(6) requires that participation agreements "contain a statement by each collaborative lawyer confirming the lawyer's representation of a party in the collaborative family law process." The confirmation of representation required by this section does not make the collaborative lawyer to be a "party" to the participation agreement, a status which would raise professional responsibility concerns. The act explicitly notes that it does not in any way change the lawyer's responsibilities to the client under the rules of professional responsibility. Tex. Fam. Code §15.110(1). The requirement of a confirmation of representation simply is designed to identify the party's collaborative lawyer so that the disqualification provision can be more easily administered.

Many collaborative family law participation agreements are far more detailed than the minimum form requirements of subsection (a) contemplate and contain numerous additional provisions. In the interest of encouraging further continuing growth and development of collaborative law, subsection (c) authorizes additional provisions to be included in participation agreements if they are not inconsistent with the act.

Subsection (c), however, does not give unlimited discretion to add provisions to a collaborative family law participation agreement. They cannot modify the defining characteristics of the collaborative family law process or agree to waive the act's protections for prospective parties. Parties thus cannot waive a party's right to terminate collaborative law with or without cause, for any reason at any time during the process set forth in §15.102, the disqualification requirements of §§15.106-15.108, the informed consent requirements of §15.111, or the prospective collaborative lawyer's duty to inquire into a history of coercive and violent relationships between parties required by §15.112. This provision of the act should thus be interpreted as analogous to those which set minimum provisions for valid arbitration agreements, which also cannot be waived. *Citation omitted.*

Parties are, however, free to supplement the required provisions under the act with additional terms that meet their particular needs and circumstances that are not inconsistent with the fundamental nature of the collaborative family law process. For example, they may define the scope of voluntary disclosure under §15.109. They may provide for broader protection for the confidentiality of collaborative family law communications than the privilege against disclosure in legal proceedings provided in §15.113. *See supra.* They may provide, as do many models of collaborative-law practice, for the engagement of jointly retained neutral experts to participate in collaborative law and prohibit parties from retaining their own experts. They may provide that experts retained for the purpose of consulting with parties during the collaborative family law process may testify at trial if the collaborative family law process concludes. They may provide that if the collaborative family law process terminates, litigation may not be instituted for a short, set period of time, a common provision in collaborative-law participation agreements. They may agree to toll applicable statutes of limitations during the collaborative family law process or include choice of law clauses in their participation agreements. *Citations omitted.*

Appropriate bar groups should be encouraged to develop form collaborative family law participation agreements for use by lawyers and parties that comply with the requirements of this act. *Citation omitted.*

* See footnote on p. 133.

FAM §15.102. BEGINNING & CONCLUDING COLLABORATIVE FAMILY LAW PROCESS

(a) A collaborative family law process begins when the parties sign a collaborative family law participation agreement.

(b) A tribunal may not order a party to participate in a collaborative family law process over that party's objection.

(c) A collaborative family law process is concluded by:

(1) resolution of a collaborative family law matter as evidenced by a signed record;

(2) resolution of a part of a collaborative family law matter, evidenced by a signed record, in which the parties agree that the remaining parts of the matter will not be resolved in the process; or

(3) termination of the process under Subsection (d).

(d) A collaborative family law process terminates:

(1) when a party gives notice to other parties in a record that the process is ended;

(2) when a party:

(A) begins a proceeding related to a collaborative family law matter without the agreement of all parties; or

(B) in a pending proceeding related to the matter:

(i) without the agreement of all parties, initiates a pleading, motion, or request for a conference with the tribunal;

(ii) initiates an order to show cause or requests that the proceeding be put on the tribunal's active calendar; or

(iii) takes similar action requiring notice to be sent to the parties; or

(3) except as otherwise provided by Subsection (g), when a party discharges a collaborative lawyer or a collaborative lawyer withdraws from further representation of a party.

(e) A party's collaborative lawyer shall give prompt notice in a record to all other parties of the collaborative lawyer's discharge or withdrawal.

(f) A party may terminate a collaborative family law process with or without cause.

(g) Notwithstanding the discharge or withdrawal of a collaborative lawyer, a collaborative family law process continues if, not later than the 30th day after the date the notice of the collaborative lawyer's discharge or withdrawal required by Subsection (e) is sent to the parties:

(1) the unrepresented party engages a successor collaborative lawyer; and

(2) in a signed record:

(A) the parties consent to continue the process by reaffirming the collaborative family law participation agreement;

(B) the agreement is amended to identify the successor collaborative lawyer; and

(C) the successor collaborative lawyer confirms the lawyer's representation of a party in the collaborative process.

(h) A collaborative family law process does not conclude if, with the consent of the parties to a signed record resolving all or part of the collaborative matter, a party requests a tribunal to approve a resolution of the collaborative family law matter or any part of that matter as evidenced by a signed record.

(i) A collaborative family law participation agreement may provide additional methods of concluding a collaborative family law process.

History of Fam. Code §15.102: Acts 2011, 82nd Leg., ch. 1048, §1, eff. Sept. 1, 2011.

See also ***O'Connor's Texas Family Law Handbook*** (2017), "Participation agreement," ch. 3-A, §13.1.2(2), p. 248; "Concluding collaborative process," ch. 3-A, §13.1.2(8), p. 255.

NCCUSL Comment*

Section 15.102 protects a party's right to terminate participation in a collaborative family law process at any time, with or without reason or cause for any or for no reason. Subsection (b) emphasizes the voluntary nature of participation in a collaborative family law process by prohibiting tribunals from ordering a person to participate in a collaborative family law process over that person's objection.

Section 15.102 is also designed to make it as administratively easy for parties and tribunals as possible to determine when a collaborative family law process begins and ends. To the extent feasible, it links those events to signed records communicated between the parties and collaborative lawyers or events that are documented in the record of a tribunal. Establishing the beginning and end of a collaborative family law process is particularly important for application of the evidentiary privilege for collaborative family law communications recognized by §15.114 which applies only to communications in that period.

The evidentiary privilege for collaborative family law communications ends when the collaborative family law process concludes. The act specifies two methods of concluding a collaborative family law process: (1) agreement for resolution of all or part of a matter in a signed record (assuming that the parties do not agree to continue the collaborative family law process to resolve the remaining issues); and (2) termination of the process. A party can terminate the process in several ways, including sending notice in a record of termination and by taking acts that are inconsistent with the continuation of collaborative law, such as commencing or recommencing an action in court. Withdrawal or discharge of a collaborative lawyer also terminates the process, and triggers an obligation to give notice on the former collaborative lawyer. *See supra* §15.102(e).

Section 15.102(g) allows for continuation of a collaborative family law process even if a party and a collaborative lawyer terminate their lawyer-client relationship, if a successor collaborative lawyer is engaged in a defined period of time and under conditions and with documentation which indicate that the parties want the collaborative family law process to continue.

Section 15.102(h) allows the parties to agree to present an agreement resulting from a collaborative family law process to a tribunal for approval without terminating the process. For example, collaborative lawyers in divorce proceedings can present uncontested settlement agreements to the court for approval and incorporation into a court order as local practice dictates. The collaborative family law process—and the evidentiary privilege for collaborative family law communications—is not terminated by presentation of the settlement agreement to the court.

FAM §15.103. PROCEEDINGS PENDING BEFORE TRIBUNAL; STATUS REPORT

(a) The parties to a proceeding pending before a tribunal may sign a collaborative family law participation agreement to seek to resolve a collaborative family law matter related to the proceeding. The parties shall file promptly with the tribunal a notice of the agreement after the agreement is signed. Subject to Subsection (c) and Sections 15.104 and 15.105, the filing operates as a stay of the proceeding.

(b) A tribunal that is notified, not later than the 30th day before the date of a proceeding, that the parties are using the collaborative family law process to attempt to settle a collaborative family law matter may not, until a party notifies the tribunal that the collaborative family law process did not result in a settlement:

(1) set a proceeding or a hearing in the collaborative family law matter;

(2) impose discovery deadlines;

(3) require compliance with scheduling orders; or

(4) dismiss the proceeding.

(c) The parties shall notify the tribunal in a pending proceeding if the collaborative family law process results in a settlement. If the collaborative family law process does not result in a settlement, the parties shall file a status report:

(1) not later than the 180th day after the date the collaborative family law participation agreement was

---

* See footnote on p. 133.

signed or, if the proceeding was filed by agreement after the collaborative family law participation agreement was signed, not later than the 180th day after the date the proceeding was filed; and

(2) on or before the first anniversary of the date the collaborative family law participation agreement was signed or, if the proceeding was filed by agreement after the collaborative family law participation agreement was signed, on or before the first anniversary of the date the proceeding was filed, accompanied by a motion for continuance.

(d) The tribunal shall grant a motion for continuance filed under Subsection (c)(2) if the status report indicates that the parties desire to continue to use the collaborative family law process.

(e) If the collaborative family law process does not result in a settlement on or before the second anniversary of the date the proceeding was filed, the tribunal may:

(1) set the proceeding for trial on the regular docket; or

(2) dismiss the proceeding without prejudice.

(f) Each party shall file promptly with the tribunal notice in a record when a collaborative family law process concludes. The stay of the proceeding under Subsection (a) is lifted when the notice is filed. The notice may not specify any reason for termination of the process.

(g) A tribunal in which a proceeding is stayed under Subsection (a) may require the parties and collaborative lawyers to provide a status report on the collaborative family law process and the proceeding. A status report:

(1) may include only information on whether the process is ongoing or concluded; and

(2) may not include a report, assessment, evaluation, recommendation, finding, or other communication regarding a collaborative family law process or collaborative family law matter.

(h) A tribunal may not consider a communication made in violation of Subsection (g).

(i) A tribunal shall provide parties notice and an opportunity to be heard before dismissing a proceeding based on delay or failure to prosecute in which a notice of collaborative family law process is filed.

History of Fam. Code §15.103: Acts 2011, 82nd Leg., ch. 1048, §1, eff. Sept. 1, 2011.

See also ***O'Connor's Texas Family Law Handbook*** (2017), "Timely notice = automatic stay," ch. 3-A, §13.1.2(3)(b), p. 252; "Status reports," ch. 3-A, §13.1.2(7), p. 255; "Court sets matter for trial or dismisses suit," ch. 3-A, §13.1.2(8)(b)[3], p. 256; "Notice of conclusion," ch. 3-A, §13.1.2(9), p. 256.

NCCUSL Comment*

Section 15.103 regulates the relationship between the collaborative family law process and the judicial process.

This section authorizes parties to enter into a collaborative family law participation agreement to attempt to resolve matters in pending proceedings. To give the collaborative family law process time and breathing space to operate, it creates an application for a stay of proceedings upon the filing of a collaborative family law participation agreement. The stay should normally be granted from the time the tribunal receives written notice that the parties have executed a collaborative family law participation agreement until it receives written notice that the collaborative family law process is concluded.

The stay of proceedings is qualified by §15.104, which authorizes a tribunal to issue emergency orders notwithstanding the stay.

Section 15.103(g) authorizes a tribunal to ask for status reports on the collaborative family law process in pending proceedings while the stay created by party entry into a collaborative family law process is in effect. It also put limitations on the scope of the information that can be requested by the status report. The provisions of these sections are based on §7 of the Uniform Mediation Act, adapted for collaborative law. *See* Unif. Mediation Act §7, 7A U.L.A. 135-36 (2006). Section 15.103(g) and (h) recognize that the tribunal asking for the status report may rule on the matter being negotiated in the collaborative family law process and should not be influenced by the behavior of the parties or counsel therein. Its provisions would not permit the tribunal to ask in a status report whether a particular party engaged in "good faith" negotiation, or to state whether a party had been "the problem" in reaching a settlement. *Citation omitted.* The status report only can ask for non-substantive information related to scheduling and whether the collaborative family law process is ongoing.

Some jurisdictions use statistical analysis of the timeliness of case dispositions to evaluate judicial performance, and sometimes those statistics are made available to the public. *Citations omitted.* Judicial administrators are encouraged to recognize that while cases in which a collaborative family law participation agreement is signed are technically "pending," they should not be considered under active judicial management for statistical or evaluation purposes until the collaborative family law process is terminated.

FAM §15.104. EMERGENCY ORDER

During a collaborative family law process, a tribunal may issue an emergency order to protect the health, safety, welfare, or interest of a party or a family, as defined by Section 71.003. If the emergency order is granted without the agreement of all parties, the granting of the order terminates the collaborative process.

History of Fam. Code §15.104: Acts 2011, 82nd Leg., ch. 1048, §1, eff. Sept. 1, 2011.

See also ***O'Connor's Texas Family Law Handbook*** (2017), "Request or defend emergency order," ch. 3-A, §13.1.2(2)(f)[1][b], p. 251; "Limitations on stay – emergency order," ch. 3-A, §13.1.2(3)(c), p. 252; "Court grants emergency order," ch. 3-A, §13.1.2(8)(b)[4], p. 256.

NCCUSL Comment*

Section 15.104 regulates the relationship between the collaborative family law process and the judicial process.

The collaborative family law process terminates if a party seeks an emergency order of the kind authorized by this section. Section 15.102(c)(2) ends the stay of proceedings created by §15.103(a). Parties may, however, fail to provide notice of the termination of a collaborative family law process to each other and the tribunal. Additionally, an emergency order might be sought in a new proceeding after a collaborative family law process terminates.

To avoid any possible confusion, this section authorizes tribunals to issue emergency orders to do so despite the execution of a collaborative family law

* See footnote on p. 133.

participation agreement or a stay of proceedings under §15.103(a). A collaborative lawyer is also authorized to seek or defend an application for an emergency order despite the termination of the collaborative family law process under the time limited terms and conditions of §15.106(d)(2).

Section 15.104 is thus one of the act's provisions addressing the safety needs of victims of coercion and violence in collaborative law. It is based on the concern that a party in a collaborative family law process may be a victim of such violence or coercion or a dependent of a party such as a child may be threatened with abuse or abduction while a collaborative family law process is ongoing. A party should not be left without access to a tribunal during such an emergency.

The reach of this section is not limited to victims of coercion and violence themselves. It extends to members of their families and households.

The reach of this section is also not limited to emergencies involving threats to physical safety. The term "interest" encompasses financial interest or reputational interest as well. This section, in effect, authorizes a tribunal otherwise authorized to do so to issue emergency provisional relief to protect a party in any critical area as it would in any civil dispute. A party who finds out that another party is secretly looting assets from a business, for example, while participating in a collaborative family law process can seek an emergency restraining order under this section and the court is authorized to grant it despite the stay of proceedings under §15.103(f).

FAM §15.105. EFFECT OF WRITTEN SETTLEMENT AGREEMENT

(a) A settlement agreement under this chapter is enforceable in the same manner as a written settlement agreement under Section 154.071, Civil Practice and Remedies Code.

(b) Notwithstanding Rule 11, Texas Rules of Civil Procedure, or another rule or law, a party is entitled to judgment on a collaborative family law settlement agreement if the agreement:

(1) provides, in a prominently displayed statement that is in boldfaced type, capitalized, or underlined, that the agreement is not subject to revocation; and

(2) is signed by each party to the agreement and the collaborative lawyer of each party.

History of Fam. Code §15.105: Acts 2011, 82nd Leg., ch. 1048, §1, eff. Sept. 1, 2011.

See also ***O'Connor's Texas Family Law Handbook*** (2017), "Note," ch. 3-A, §13.1.2(8)(a)[1], p. 255.

FAM §15.106. DISQUALIFICATION OF COLLABORATIVE LAWYER & LAWYERS IN ASSOCIATED LAW FIRM; EXCEPTION

(a) In this section, "family" has the meaning assigned by Section 71.003.

(b) Except as provided by Subsection (d), a collaborative lawyer is disqualified from appearing before a tribunal to represent a party in a proceeding related to the collaborative family law matter regardless of whether the collaborative lawyer is representing the party for a fee.

(c) Except as provided by Subsection (d) and Sections 15.107 and 15.108, a lawyer in a law firm with which the collaborative lawyer is associated is disqualified from appearing before a tribunal to represent a party in a proceeding related to the collaborative family law matter if the collaborative lawyer is disqualified from doing so under Subsection (b).

(d) A collaborative lawyer or a lawyer in a law firm with which the collaborative lawyer is associated may represent a party:

(1) to request a tribunal to approve an agreement resulting from the collaborative family law process; or

(2) to seek or defend an emergency order to protect the health, safety, welfare, or interest of a party or a family if a successor lawyer is not immediately available to represent that party.

(e) The exception prescribed by Subsection (d) does not apply after the party is represented by a successor lawyer or reasonable measures are taken to protect the health, safety, welfare, or interest of that party or family.

History of Fam. Code §15.106: Acts 2011, 82nd Leg., ch. 1048, §1, eff. Sept. 1, 2011.

See also ***O'Connor's Texas Family Law Handbook*** (2017), "Effect on future representation," ch. 3-A, §13.1.2(2)(f), p. 250.

NCCUSL Comment*

Section 15.106 regulates who can appear before a court (tribunal) to represent a party after a collaborative family law process terminates.

The disqualification requirement for collaborative lawyers after collaborative law concludes is a fundamental defining characteristic of collaborative law. This section extends the disqualification provision to "matters related to the collaborative family matter" in addition to the matter described in the collaborative family law participation agreement. It also extends the disqualification provision to lawyers in a law firm with which the collaborative lawyer is associated in addition to the collaborative lawyer him or herself, so called "imputed disqualification." Appropriate exceptions to the disqualification requirement are made for representation to seek emergency orders for a limited time (see §15.104) and to allow collaborative lawyers to present agreements to a tribunal for approval (§15.102(h)).

FAM §15.107. EXCEPTION FROM DISQUALIFICATION FOR REPRESENTATION OF LOW-INCOME PARTIES

After a collaborative family law process concludes, another lawyer in a law firm with which a collaborative lawyer disqualified under Section 15.106(b) is associated may represent a party without a fee in the collaborative family law matter or a matter related to the collaborative family law matter if:

(1) the party has an annual income that qualifies the party for free legal representation under the criteria established by the law firm for free legal representation;

* See footnote on p. 133.

(2) the collaborative family law participation agreement authorizes that representation; and

(3) the collaborative lawyer is isolated from any participation in the collaborative family law matter or a matter related to the collaborative family law matter through procedures within the law firm that are reasonably calculated to isolate the collaborative lawyer from such participation.

History of Fam. Code §15.107: Acts 2011, 82nd Leg., ch. 1048, §1, eff. Sept. 1, 2011.

See also ***O'Connor's Texas Family Law Handbook*** (2017), "Represent low-income party," ch. 3-A, §13.1.2(2)(f)[2][c], p. 251.

NCCUSL Comment*

Section 15.107 regulates who can appear before a court (tribunal) to represent a party after a collaborative family law process terminates.

From prefatory note: Section 15.107 modifies the imputed disqualification rule for lawyers in law firms with which the collaborative lawyer is associated which represents a very low-income client without fee. The goal of this section is to allow the legal aid office, law firm, law school clinic, or the private firm doing pro bono work to continue to represent the party in the matter if collaborative law concludes. Section 15.107 only applies to parties with "an annual income that qualifies the party for free legal representation under the criteria established by the law firm for free legal representation." Tex. Fam. Code §15.107. Many legal aid offices, for example, use 125% of federal poverty guidelines as a general eligibility criterion. *Citations omitted.*

The conditions for such continued representation are that all parties to the collaborative family law participation agreement consent to this departure from the imputed disqualification rule in advance. Tex. Fam. Code §15.107(2). In addition, the collaborative lawyer must be screened from further participation in the collaborative matter and matters related to the collaborative matter. Tex. Fam. Code §15.107(3).

FAM §15.108. GOVERNMENTAL ENTITY AS PARTY

(a) In this section, "governmental entity" has the meaning assigned by Section 101.014.

(b) The disqualification prescribed by Section 15.106(b) applies to a collaborative lawyer representing a party that is a governmental entity.

(c) After a collaborative family law process concludes, another lawyer in a law firm with which the collaborative lawyer is associated may represent a governmental entity in the collaborative family law matter or a matter related to the collaborative family law matter if:

(1) the collaborative family law participation agreement authorizes that representation; and

(2) the collaborative lawyer is isolated from any participation in the collaborative family law matter or a matter related to the collaborative family law matter through procedures within the law firm that are reasonably calculated to isolate the collaborative lawyer from such participation.

History of Fam. Code §15.108: Acts 2011, 82nd Leg., ch. 1048, §1, eff. Sept. 1, 2011.

See also ***O'Connor's Texas Family Law Handbook*** (2017), "Represent governmental entity," ch. 3-A, §13.1.2(2)(f)[2][d], p. 251.

NCCUSL Comment*

Section 15.108 regulates who can appear before a court (tribunal) to represent a party after a collaborative family law process terminates.

From prefatory note: Section 15.108 creates an exception to imputed disqualification similar to that in §15.107 for lawyers in a law firm with which a collaborative lawyer is associated which represents government parties. The act's definition of "law firm" includes "the legal department of a government or government subdivision, agency, or instrumentality." Tex. Fam. Code §15.052(6).

Section 15.108 is based on the policy that taxpayers should not run the risk of the government having to pay for private outside counsel if collaborative law terminates because all the lawyers in the agency are disqualified from further representation. The conditions for the continued representation are advance consent of all parties to the continued representation and the screening of the individual collaborative lawyer from further participation in it and related matters. Tex. Fam. Code §15.108(c).

The policy behind §15.108 is supported by Rule 1.11 of the ABA Model Rules of Professional Conduct which creates an exception to the general rule of imputed disqualification for government lawyers "[b]ecause of the special problems raised by imputation within a government agency," although "ordinarily it will be prudent to screen such lawyers." Model Rules of Prof'l Conduct R. 1.11 cmt. 2 (2009). Courts also are willing to recognize screening of individual attorneys for government agencies as a desirable alternative to a wholesale disqualification of an entire agency. *Citations omitted.*

FAM §15.109. DISCLOSURE OF INFORMATION

(a) Except as provided by law other than this chapter, during the collaborative family law process, on the request of another party, a party shall make timely, full, candid, and informal disclosure of information related to the collaborative matter without formal discovery. A party shall update promptly any previously disclosed information that has materially changed.

(b) The parties may define the scope of the disclosure under Subsection (a) during the collaborative family law process.

History of Fam. Code §15.109: Acts 2011, 82nd Leg., ch. 1048, §1, eff. Sept. 1, 2011.

See also ***O'Connor's Texas Family Law Handbook*** (2017), "Informal disclosure," ch. 3-A, §13.1.2(4), p. 252.

NCCUSL Comment*

From prefatory note: The obligation of voluntary disclosure imposed by §15.109 on parties to a collaborative family law process reflects a trend in civil litigation to encourage voluntary disclosure without formal discovery requests early in a matter in the hope of encouraging careful assessment and settlement. The Federal Rules of Civil Procedure, for example, require that a party to litigation disclose names of witnesses, documents, and computation of damages "without awaiting a discovery request." Fed. R. Civ. P. 26(a)(1)(A). These early automatic disclosures were based on a consensus by an advisory committee which drafted the rule that the adversarial discovery process for obtaining information had proven to be unduly time consuming and expensive. *See generally* Fed. R. Civ. P. 26(a) advisory committee's note (1993).

...

The act does not specify sanctions for a party who does not comply with the requirements of §15.109. The Drafting Committee felt that any attempt to do so would require the act to define "bad faith" failure to disclose. The result would be the opposite of what the act seeks to encourage—more resolution of disputes without resort to the courts. Courts would have to hold contested hearings on whether party conduct met its definition of bad faith failure to disclose before awarding sanctions. Such adversarial contests would also require evidence to be presented about what transpired during the collaborative family law

* See footnote on p. 133.

process which, in turn, would require courts to breach the privilege—and the policy of confidentiality of collaborative family law communications—that the Uniform Collaborative Law Rules and Act seeks to create. *Citation omitted.*

It is important to remember that a party can unilaterally terminate collaborative law at any time and for any reason, including failure of another party to produce requested information. *See* Tex. Fam. Code §15.102(b), (f). Thus, if a party wishes to abandon collaborative law in favor of litigation for failure of voluntary disclosure, the party is free to do so and to engage in any court sanctioned discovery that might be available. Most disputed matters that reach the formal litigation system settle before trial and before completion of formal discovery. Parties to a collaborative family law process are thus no different than parties who participate in litigation or other dispute resolution processes in having to make cost-benefit assessments with the aid of their counsel about whether they have enough information from the informal process of disclosure to settle at any particular time or need or want more. *Citation omitted.*

Moreover, nothing in §15.109 changes the standards under which agreements or settlements that result from a collaborative family law process are approved by a tribunal, or can be reopened or voided because of a failure of disclosure. Those standards are determined by law other than this act. Relevant doctrines such as fraud, constructive fraud, reliance, disclosure requirements imposed by fiduciary relationships, disclosure of special facts because of superior knowledge and access to information are not affected by the act. Courts can order settlement agreements voided or rescinded because of failure of disclosure in appropriate circumstances. *Citations omitted.*

Many states, for example, mandate compulsory financial disclosure in divorce cases even without a specific request from the other party. *Citations omitted.* Resolution of divorce disputes in such states without these mandated disclosures would create a risk of a malpractice action against a collaborative lawyer who advised a party to accept such a settlement. *Citations omitted.* It would also be surprising if courts approved agreements in settlement of particular kinds of matters such as divorce, infants' estates, or class actions without the kind of pre-agreement disclosure typical for such matters. *Citations omitted.*

Section 15.109 also allows the parties to reach their own agreement on the scope of disclosure during the collaborative family law process. The standards for what must be disclosed during a collaborative family law process will thus vary depending on the nature of the matter, the participation agreement, and the assessment by parties and their counsel about their need for more information to make an informed settlement. Should the parties choose to provide more detailed standards for their voluntary disclosure or to require formal or semi formal discovery demands they can do so in their collaborative family law participation agreement. *Citation omitted.*

The standards the parties agree on for disclosure in their participation agreements are, of course, subject to the provisions of other law which are not changed by the act. As noted above, many states, for example, mandate compulsory financial disclosure in divorce cases. Federal Rule of Civil Procedure 26(c) mandates disclosure in federal civil cases, and similar provisions exist in state law in different areas. *Citations omitted.* Parties in collaborative law should take these provisions into account in devising agreements concerning the scope of their disclosure.

FAM §15.110. STANDARDS OF PROFESSIONAL RESPONSIBILITY & MANDATORY REPORTING NOT AFFECTED

This chapter does not affect:

(1) the professional responsibility obligations and standards applicable to a lawyer or other licensed professional; or

(2) the obligation of a person under other law to report abuse or neglect, abandonment, or exploitation of a child or adult.

History of Fam. Code §15.110: Acts 2011, 82nd Leg., ch. 1048, §1, eff. Sept. 1, 2011.

See also ***O'Connor's Texas Family Law Handbook*** (2017), "Note," ch. 3-A, §13.1.2(4)(b)[2], p. 252; "Note," ch. 3-A, §13.1.2(6)(a)[8][d], p. 254.

NCCUSL Comment*

In the interests of clarity, this section reaffirms that the act does not alter the professional responsibility or child abuse and neglect reporting obligations of all professionals, lawyers and non lawyers alike, who participate in a collaborative family law process.

From prefatory note: Bar association ethics opinions—including one from the American Bar Association—have concluded that collaborative lawyers are bound by the same rules of ethics as other lawyers and that the practice of collaborative law is consistent with those rules. *Citation omitted.* To avoid any possible confusion, §15.110 explicitly states the act does not change the professional responsibility obligations of collaborative lawyers.

It is important to note that the favorable bar association opinions and the act do not validate every form of collaborative family law agreement or collaborative family law practice. They still leave collaborative lawyers and collaborative family law participation agreements subject to regulation by bar ethics committees and other agencies charged with regulating lawyers and to malpractice claims by clients. Particular collaborative family law participation agreements, for example, may have provisions which raise professional responsibility concerns. The act does not require that lawyers sign the collaborative family law participation agreement as parties, a practice common in the collaborative-law community; rather, it requires only that parties identify their collaborative lawyers in participation agreements and that the lawyer sign a statement confirming the lawyer's representation of a client in collaborative law. Tex. Fam. Code §15.101(a)(6). Depending on the language and structure of a participation agreement, a lawyer who signs it may assume duties to another party to the agreement—a person with conflicting interests other than his or her client—a result that could raise ethics concerns. Scott R. Peppet, *The (New) Ethics of Collaborative Law*, 14 Disp. Resol. Mag. 23, 24-26 (2008). The act leaves questions raised by particular language and form in collaborative family law participation agreements to regulation by the same sources of authority that regulate all lawyer conduct such as ethics committees. Furthermore, to the extent that a collaborative family law participation agreement is also a lawyer-client limited retainer agreement, it must meet whatever requirements are set by state law for lawyer-client retainer agreements. *Citation omitted.*

FAM §15.111. INFORMED CONSENT

Before a prospective party signs a collaborative family law participation agreement, a prospective collaborative lawyer must:

(1) assess with the prospective party factors the lawyer reasonably believes relate to whether a collaborative family law process is appropriate for the prospective party's matter;

(2) provide the prospective party with information that the lawyer reasonably believes is sufficient for the prospective party to make an informed decision about the material benefits and risks of a collaborative family law process as compared to the material benefits and risks of other reasonably available alternatives for resolving the proposed collaborative matter, including litigation, mediation, arbitration, or expert evaluation; and

(3) advise the prospective party that:

(A) after signing an agreement, if a party initiates a proceeding or seeks tribunal intervention in a pending proceeding related to the collaborative family law matter, the collaborative family law process terminates;

* See footnote on p. 133.

(B) participation in a collaborative family law process is voluntary and any party has the right to terminate unilaterally a collaborative family law process with or without cause; and

(C) the collaborative lawyer and any lawyer in a law firm with which the collaborative lawyer is associated may not appear before a tribunal to represent a party in a proceeding related to the collaborative family law matter, except as authorized by Section 15.106(d), 15.107, or 15.108(c).

History of Fam. Code §15.111: Acts 2011, 82nd Leg., ch. 1048, §1, eff. Sept. 1, 2011.

See also ***O'Connor's Texas Family Law Handbook*** (2017), "After informed consent," ch. 3-A, §13.1.2(2)(c)[2], p. 249.

NCCUSL Comment*

From prefatory note: Section 15.111 places a duty on a potential collaborative lawyer to actively facilitate client informed consent to participate in collaborative law. The Model Rules of Professional Conduct define informed consent as "the agreement by a person to a proposed course of conduct after the lawyer has communicated adequate information and explanation about the material risks of and reasonably available alternatives to the proposed course of conduct." *Citations omitted.*

The act's requirements for a lawyer to facilitate informed client consent to participate in collaborative law are consistent with this general standard, but are more detailed and tailored to collaborative family law participation agreements. The prospective collaborative lawyer is required to "*assess with* the prospective party factors the [prospective collaborative] lawyer reasonably believes relate to whether a collaborative family law process is appropriate for the prospective party's matter." Tex. Fam. Code §15.111(1) (emphasis added). The lawyer must also "provide the prospective party with information that the lawyer reasonably believes is sufficient for the prospective party to make an informed decision about the material benefits and risks of a collaborative family law process as compared to ... other reasonably available" forms of dispute resolution such as litigation, mediation, arbitration or expert evaluation. Tex. Fam. Code §15.111(2). The act adopts the previously mentioned requirement of many states that lawyers identify and discuss the costs and benefits of other reasonable dispute resolution options with a potential party to collaborative law, including litigation, cooperative law, mediation, expert evaluation, or arbitration or some combination of these processes. *Citation omitted.* The act also requires that a lawyer describe the benefits of collaborative law to a potential party, along with its essential risk—that termination of the process, which any party has the right to do at any time, will cause the disqualification provision to take effect, imposing the economic and emotional costs on all parties of engaging new counsel. Tex. Fam. Code §15.111(3).

The act thus envisions the lawyer as an educator of a prospective party about the appropriate factors to consider in deciding whether to participate in a collaborative family law process. It also contemplates a process of discussion between lawyer and prospective party that asks that the lawyer do more than lecture a prospective party or provide written information about collaborative law and other options. Collaborative lawyers should, of course, consider how to document the process of informed consent and a party's decision to enter into a collaborative family law process through a provision of appropriate written documents. Hopefully, lawyers who seek informed consent will take steps to continuously make the information they provide to prospective parties ever easier to understand and more complete. *Citation omitted.*

The act thus specifies the overall goals and standards of the process of seeking informed client consent to participate in collaborative law. It leaves to the collaborative lawyer the specific methods of achieving informed client consent. "Lawyers should provide thorough and balanced descriptions of [collaborative law] practice, including candid discussion of possible risks." *Citation omitted.* "Lawyers may understandably worry about losing possible [collaborative law] cases if they provide more thorough and balanced information... [T]his risk of losing business is outweighed by the professional and practice benefits (and obligations) of full disclosure and truly informed consent. By providing appropriate information before parties decide whether to use [collaborative law] lawyers can have greater confidence that parties will have realistic expectations, participate in the process more constructively and will be less likely to terminate a [collaborative law] case." *Citation omitted.*

* See footnote on p. 133.

FAM §15.112. FAMILY VIOLENCE

(a) In this section:

(1) "Dating relationship" has the meaning assigned by Section 71.0021(b).

(2) "Family violence" has the meaning assigned by Section 71.004.

(3) "Household" has the meaning assigned by Section 71.005.

(4) "Member of a household" has the meaning assigned by Section 71.006.

(b) Before a prospective party signs a collaborative family law participation agreement in a collaborative family law matter in which another prospective party is a member of the prospective party's family or household or with whom the prospective party has or has had a dating relationship, a prospective collaborative lawyer must make reasonable inquiry regarding whether the prospective party has a history of family violence with the other prospective party.

(c) If a collaborative lawyer reasonably believes that the party the lawyer represents, or the prospective party with whom the collaborative lawyer consults, as applicable, has a history of family violence with another party or prospective party, the lawyer may not begin or continue a collaborative family law process unless:

(1) the party or prospective party requests beginning or continuing a process; and

(2) the collaborative lawyer or prospective collaborative lawyer determines with the party or prospective party what, if any, reasonable steps could be taken to address the concerns regarding family violence.

History of Fam. Code §15.112: Acts 2011, 82nd Leg., ch. 1048, §1, eff. Sept. 1, 2011.

See also ***O'Connor's Texas Family Law Handbook*** (2017), "Inquire into history of family violence," ch. 3-A, §13.1.2(2)(c)[2][d], p. 249.

NCCUSL Comment*

The section is a major part of the act's overall approach to assuring safety for victims of coercive and violent relationships who are prospective parties or parties in collaborative law.

From prefatory note: Section 15.112 requires a collaborative lawyer to make a reasonable effort to screen a potential party to collaborative law for a history of a coercive and violent relationship. Brief screening protocols already exist which lawyers can use to satisfy the obligation imposed by the act. *Citations omitted.* These obligations placed on collaborative lawyers by the act to incorporate screening and sensitivity to domestic violence in their representation of parties parallel obligations placed on mediators. *Citations omitted.*

Section 15.112(c) requires that the lawyer not commence or continue a collaborative family law process if the lawyer reasonably believes a potential

party or party is a victim of domestic violence unless the victim consents. This condition is designed to insure that the autonomy and decision making power of the victim of domestic violence are respected in the decision to go forward or not with collaborative law. Many state statutes allow victims of domestic violence to opt out of mediation. *Citations omitted.* Section 15.112(c)(1) extends a similar option to collaborative law by requiring the victim's consent to begin or continue the process.

FAM §15.113. CONFIDENTIALITY OF COLLABORATIVE FAMILY LAW COMMUNICATION

(a) A collaborative family law communication is confidential to the extent agreed to by the parties in a signed record or as provided by law other than this chapter.

(b) If the parties agree in a signed record, the conduct and demeanor of the parties and nonparty participants, including their collaborative lawyers, are confidential.

(c) If the parties agree in a signed record, communications related to the collaborative family law matter occurring before the signing of the collaborative family law participation agreement are confidential.

History of Fam. Code §15.113: Acts 2011, 82nd Leg., ch. 1048, §1, eff. Sept. 1, 2011.

See also ***O'Connor's Texas Family Law Handbook*** (2017), "Confidentiality," ch. 3-A, §13.1.2(5), p. 252.

NCCUSL Comment*

From prefatory note: A major contribution of the Uniform Collaborative Law Act is to create a privilege for collaborative family law communications in legal proceedings, where it would otherwise either not be available or not be available in a uniform way across the states. The Uniform Collaborative Law Act's privilege for communications made in the collaborative family law process is similar to the privilege provided to communications during mediation by the Uniform Mediation Act.

Protection for confidentiality of communications is central to collaborative law. Parties may enter collaborative law with fear that what they say during collaborative family law sessions may be used against them in later proceedings. Without assurances that communications made during the collaborative family law process will not be used to their detriment later, parties, collaborative lawyers and nonparty participants such as mental health and financial professionals will be reluctant to speak frankly, test out ideas and proposals, or freely exchange information. Undermining the confidentiality of the process would impair full use of collaborative law. *Citation omitted.*

Confidentiality of communications can also refer to broader concepts than admission of the information into the formal record of a proceeding. It is possible for collaborative family law communications to be disclosed outside of legal proceedings, for example, to family members, friends, business associates, the press and the general public. Like the Uniform Mediation Act, however, the Uniform Collaborative Law Act limits statutory protections for confidentiality to legal proceedings. It does not prohibit disclosure of collaborative family law communications to third parties outside of legal proceedings. That issue is left to the agreement of the parties as expressed in their collaborative family law participation agreements, other bodies of law and to the ethical standards of the professions involved in collaborative law. *Citation omitted.*

...

Parties can expect enforcement of their agreement to keep communications more broadly confidential through contract damages and, sometimes, specific enforcement. The courts have also enforced court orders or rules regarding nondisclosure through orders to strike pleadings and fine lawyers. *Citations omitted.*

...

The settlement negotiations privilege does not provide the same level of protection for collaborative family law communications as does the privilege created by the act. Under the Federal Rules of Evidence, and similar state rules of evidence, while a settlement offer and its accompanying negotiations may not be admitted into evidence in order to prove liability or invalidity of a claim or its amount, it may be admissible for a variety of other purposes. *Citations omitted.*

By contrast, the Uniform Collaborative Law Act provides for a broader prohibition on later disclosure of communications within the collaborative family law process in the legal process, making those communications inadmissible for any purpose other than those specified in the act. For example, the evidentiary privilege in the act applies to an array of communications, not limited to those produced in a formal four-way session such as communications before the session begins and in preparation for the session. In addition, the privilege allows parties to block not only their own testimony from future disclosure, but also communications by any other participant in the collaborative family law process such as jointly retained experts. To encourage nonparties such as mental health professionals and financial experts to participate in collaborative law, the act gives them a privilege to block their own communications from being introduced into evidence.

The act also explicitly lists the exceptions to the evidentiary privilege it creates. As with the privilege for mediation communications, the privilege for collaborative family law communications has limits and exceptions codified in §15.115, primarily to give appropriate weight to other valid justice system values, such as the protections of bodily integrity and to prosecute and protect against serious crime. They often apply to situations that arise only rarely, but might produce grave injustice in that unusual case if not excepted from the privilege.

FAM §15.114. PRIVILEGE AGAINST DISCLOSURE OF COLLABORATIVE FAMILY LAW COMMUNICATION

(a) Except as provided by Section 15.115, a collaborative family law communication, whether made before or after the institution of a proceeding, is privileged and not subject to disclosure and may not be used as evidence against a party or nonparty participant in a proceeding.

(b) Any record of a collaborative family law communication is privileged, and neither the parties nor the nonparty participants may be required to testify in a proceeding related to or arising out of the collaborative family law matter or be subject to a process requiring disclosure of privileged information or data related to the collaborative matter.

(c) An oral communication or written material used in or made a part of a collaborative family law process is admissible or discoverable if it is admissible or discoverable independent of the collaborative family law process.

(d) If this section conflicts with other legal requirements for disclosure of communications, records, or materials, the issue of privilege may be presented to the tribunal having jurisdiction of the proceeding to determine, in camera, whether the facts, circumstances, and context of the communications or materials sought to be disclosed warrant a protective order of the tribu-

* See footnote on p. 133.

nal or whether the communications or materials are subject to disclosure. The presentation of the issue of privilege under this subsection does not constitute a termination of the collaborative family law process under Section 15.102(d)(2)(B).

(e) A party or nonparty participant may disclose privileged collaborative family law communications to a party's successor counsel, subject to the terms of confidentiality in the collaborative family law participation agreement. Collaborative family law communications disclosed under this subsection remain privileged.

(f) A person who makes a disclosure or representation about a collaborative family law communication that prejudices the rights of a party or nonparty participant in a proceeding may not assert a privilege under this section. The restriction provided by this subsection applies only to the extent necessary for the person prejudiced to respond to the disclosure or representation.

History of Fam. Code §15.114: Acts 2011, 82nd Leg., ch. 1048, §1, eff. Sept. 1, 2011.

See also ***O'Connor's Texas Family Law Handbook*** (2017), "Privilege," ch. 3-A, §13.1.2(6), p. 253.

NCCUSL Comment*

Overview. Section 15.114 sets forth the act's general structure for creating a privilege prohibiting disclosure of collaborative family law communications in legal proceedings. It is based on similar provisions in the Uniform Mediation Act, whose commentary should be consulted for more expansive discussion of the issues raised here.

Holders of the Privilege for Collaborative Family Law Communications Parties. Parties are holders of the collaborative family law communications privilege. The privilege of the parties draws upon the purpose, rationale, and traditions of the attorney-client privilege, in that its paramount justification is to encourage candor by the parties, just as encouraging the client's candor is the central justification for the attorney-client privilege. Using the attorney-client privilege as a core base for the collaborative family law communications privilege is also particularly appropriate since the extensive participation of attorneys is a hallmark of collaborative law.

...

Nonparty Participants Such as Experts. Of particular note is the act's addition of a privilege for the nonparty participant, though limited to the communications by that individual in the collaborative family law process. Joint party retention of experts such as mental health professionals and financial appraisers to perform various functions is a feature of many models of collaborative law, and this provision encourages and accommodates it. Extending the privilege to nonparties for their own communications seeks to facilitate the candid participation of experts and others who may have information and perspective that would facilitate resolution of the matter. This provision would also cover statements prepared by such persons for the collaborative family law process and submitted as part of it, such as experts' reports. Any party who expects to use such an expert report prepared to submit in a collaborative family law process later in a legal proceeding would have to secure permission of all parties and the expert in order to do so. This is consistent with the treatment of reports prepared for a collaborative family law process as collaborative family law communications. *See* Tex. Fam. Code §15.052(1).

As previously discussed in the comments to §15.052, collaborative lawyers are not nonparty participants under the act, as they maintain a traditional attorney-client relationship with parties, which allocates to clients the right to waive the attorney-client privilege, even over their lawyer's objection.

---

* See footnote on p. 133.

Collaborative Family Law Communications Do Not Shield Otherwise Admissible or Discoverable Evidence. Section 15.114(c) concerning evidence otherwise discoverable and admissible makes clear that relevant evidence may not be shielded from discovery or admission at trial merely because it is communicated in a collaborative family law process. *Citations omitted.* For purposes of the collaborative family law communication privilege, it is the communication that is made in the collaborative family law process that is protected by the privilege, not the underlying evidence giving rise to the communication. Evidence that is communicated in collaborative law is subject to discovery, just as it would be if the collaborative family law process had not taken place. There is no "fruit of the poisonous tree" doctrine in the collaborative family law communication privilege. For example, a party who learns about a witness during a collaborative family law proceeding is not precluded by the privilege from subpoenaing that witness should collaborative law terminate and the matter wind up in a courtroom. *Citations omitted.*

FAM §15.115. LIMITS OF PRIVILEGE

(a) The privilege prescribed by Section 15.114 does not apply to a collaborative family law communication that is:

(1) in an agreement resulting from the collaborative family law process, evidenced in a record signed by all parties to the agreement;

(2) subject to an express waiver of the privilege in a record or orally during a proceeding if the waiver is made by all parties and nonparty participants;

(3) available to the public under Chapter 552, Government Code, or made during a session of a collaborative family law process that is open, or is required by law to be open, to the public;

(4) a threat or statement of a plan to inflict bodily injury or commit a crime of violence;

(5) a disclosure of a plan to commit or attempt to commit a crime, or conceal an ongoing crime or ongoing criminal activity;

(6) a disclosure in a report of:

(A) suspected abuse or neglect of a child to an appropriate agency under Subchapter B, Chapter 261, or in a proceeding regarding the abuse or neglect of a child, except that evidence may be excluded in the case of communications between an attorney and client under Subchapter C, Chapter 261; or

(B) abuse, neglect, or exploitation of an elderly or disabled person to an appropriate agency under Subchapter B, Chapter 48, Human Resources Code; or

(7) sought or offered to prove or disprove:

(A) a claim or complaint of professional misconduct or malpractice arising from or related to a collaborative family law process;

(B) an allegation that the settlement agreement was procured by fraud, duress, coercion, or other dishonest means or that terms of the settlement agreement are illegal;

(C) the necessity and reasonableness of attorney's fees and related expenses incurred during a collaborative family law process or to challenge or defend the enforceability of the collaborative family law settlement agreement; or

(D) a claim against a third person who did not participate in the collaborative family law process.

(b) If a collaborative family law communication is subject to an exception under Subsection (a), only the part of the communication necessary for the application of the exception may be disclosed or admitted.

(c) The disclosure or admission of evidence excepted from the privilege under Subsection (a) does not make the evidence or any other collaborative family law communication discoverable or admissible for any other purpose.

History of Fam. Code §15.115: Acts 2011, 82nd Leg., ch. 1048, §1, eff. Sept. 1, 2011.

See also *O'Connor's Texas Family Law Handbook* (2017), "Limits of privilege," ch. 3-A, §13.1.2(6)(a), p. 253.

NCCUSL Comment*

Unconditional Exceptions to Privilege. The act articulates specific and exclusive exceptions to the broad grant of privilege provided to collaborative family law communications. They are based on limited but vitally important values such as protection against serious bodily injury, crime prevention and the right of someone accused of professional misconduct to respond that outweigh the importance of confidentiality in the collaborative family law process. The exceptions are similar to those contained in the Uniform Mediation Act. *See* Unif. Mediation Act §6, 7A U.L.A. 124 (2006).

As with other privileges, when it is necessary to consider evidence in order to determine if an exception applies, the act contemplates that a court will hold an in camera proceeding at which the claim for exemption from the privilege can be confidentially asserted and defended.

Exception to Privilege for Written, But Not Oral, Agreements. Of particular note is the exception that permits evidence of a collaborative family law communication "in an agreement resulting from the collaborative family law process, evidenced in a record signed by all parties to the agreement." Tex. Fam. Code §15.115(a)(1). The exception permits such evidence to be introduced in a subsequent proceeding convened to determine whether the terms of that settlement agreement have been breached.

The words "agreement ... evidenced in a record signed by all parties" in this exception refer to written and executed agreements, those recorded by tape recording and ascribed to by the parties on the tape, and other electronic means to record and sign, as defined in §15.052(11) and (13). In other words, a party's notes about an oral agreement would not be "an agreement ... signed by all parties." On the other hand, the following situations would be considered a signed agreement: a handwritten agreement that the parties have signed, an e-mail exchange between the parties in which they agree to particular provisions, and a tape recording in which they state what constitutes their agreement.

This exception is noteworthy only for what is not included: oral agreements. The disadvantage of exempting oral settlements is that nearly everything said during a collaborative-law session could bear on either whether the parties came to an agreement or the content of the agreement. In other words, an exception for oral agreements has the potential to swallow the rule of privilege. As a result, parties might be less candid, not knowing whether a controversy later would erupt over an oral agreement.

Despite the limitation on oral agreements, the act leaves parties other means to preserve the agreement quickly. For example, parties can state their oral agreement into the tape recorder and record their assent. One would also expect that counsel will incorporate knowledge of a writing requirement into their collaborative-law representation practices.

Limited Preservation of Party Autonomy Regarding Confidentiality. Section 15.115(a)(2) allows the parties to opt for a non-privileged collaborative family law process or session of the collaborative family law process by mutual agreement and thus furthers the act's policy of party self-determination. If the parties so agree, the privilege sections of the act do not apply, thus fulfilling the parties' reasonable expectations regarding the confidentiality of that session. Parties may use this option if they wish to rely on, and therefore use in evidence, statements made during the collaborative family law process. It is the parties and their collaborative lawyers who make this choice.

FAM §15.116. AUTHORITY OF TRIBUNAL IN CASE OF NONCOMPLIANCE

(a) Notwithstanding that an agreement fails to meet the requirements of Section 15.101 or that a lawyer has failed to comply with Section 15.111 or 15.112, a tribunal may find that the parties intended to enter into a collaborative family law participation agreement if the parties:

(1) signed a record indicating an intent to enter into a collaborative family law participation agreement; and

(2) reasonably believed the parties were participating in a collaborative family law process.

(b) If a tribunal makes the findings specified in Subsection (a) and determines that the interests of justice require the following action, the tribunal may:

(1) enforce an agreement evidenced by a record resulting from the process in which the parties participated;

(2) apply the disqualification provisions of Sections 15.106, 15.107, and 15.108; and

(3) apply the collaborative family law privilege under Section 15.114.

History of Fam. Code §15.116: Acts 2011, 82nd Leg., ch. 1048, §1, eff. Sept. 1, 2011.

See also *O'Connor's Texas Family Law Handbook* (2017), "Effect of noncompliance with collaborative-law requirements," ch. 3-A, §13.1.2(10), p. 257.

NCCUSL Comment*

The act protects persons from inadvertently or inappropriately entering into a collaborative family law participation agreement by establishing protections that cannot be waived by the parties. Section 15.101 sets forth minimum standards for a collaborative family law participation agreement. Section 15.111 sets forth requirements for a lawyer's facilitating informed party consent to participate in collaborative law. Section 15.112 requires a lawyer to inquire whether there is a history of family violence.

Section 15.116 anticipates, however, that, as collaborative law expands in use and popularity, claims will be made that agreements reached in collaborative law should not be enforced, collaborative lawyers should not be disqualified and evidentiary privilege should not be recognized because of the failure of collaborative lawyers to meet these requirements. This section takes the view that, while parties should not be forced to participate in collaborative law involuntarily (see §15.102(b)), the failures of collaborative lawyers in drafting agreements and making required disclosures and inquiries should not be visited on parties whose conduct indicates an intention to participate in collaborative law.

* See footnote on p. 133.

By analogy to the doctrine established allowing enforcement of arguably flawed arbitration agreements, this section places the burden of proof on the party seeking to enforce a collaborative family law participation agreement or agreements resulting from a collaborative family law process despite the failures of form, disclosure or inquiry. *Citations omitted.*

Doubts about the parties' intentions should be resolved against enforcement. To invoke its discretion under this section the tribunal must find that a signed record of some kind—usually a written agreement—indicates that the parties intended to participate in a collaborative family law process. It cannot find that the parties entered into a collaborative family law process solely on the basis of an oral agreement. The tribunal must also find that, despite the failings of the participation agreement or the required disclosures, the parties nonetheless intended to participate in a collaborative family law process and reasonably believed that they were doing so. If the tribunal makes those findings, this section gives it the discretionary authority to enforce agreements resulting from the process the parties engaged in and the other provisions of this act if the tribunal also finds that the interests of justice so require.

Chapters 16-30 blank

Family Code—Title 2

Child in Relation to the Family

Table of Contents

Title 2. Child in Relation to the Family

TITLE 2. CHILD IN RELATION TO THE FAMILY

SUBTITLE A. LIMITATIONS OF MINORITY

CHAPTER 31. REMOVAL OF DISABILITIES OF MINORITY

FAM §31.001. REQUIREMENTS

(a) A minor may petition to have the disabilities of minority removed for limited or general purposes if the minor is:

(1) a resident of this state;

(2) 17 years of age, or at least 16 years of age and living separate and apart from the minor's parents, managing conservator, or guardian; and

(3) self-supporting and managing the minor's own financial affairs.

(b) A minor may file suit under this chapter in the minor's own name. The minor need not be represented by next friend.

History of Fam. Code §31.001: Acts 1995, 74th Leg., ch. 20, §1, eff. Apr. 20, 1995. Source: Former Fam. Code §31.01(a), (c).

See also *O'Connor's Texas Family Law Handbook* (2017), "Petitioning for removal of disabilities," ch. 1-B, §5.2.3, p. 33.

FAM §31.002. REQUISITES OF PETITION; VERIFICATION

(a) The petition for removal of disabilities of minority must state:

(1) the name, age, and place of residence of the petitioner;

(2) the name and place of residence of each living parent;

(3) the name and place of residence of the guardian of the person and the guardian of the estate, if any;

(4) the name and place of residence of the managing conservator, if any;

(5) the reasons why removal would be in the best interest of the minor; and

(6) the purposes for which removal is requested.

(b) A parent of the petitioner must verify the petition, except that if a managing conservator or guardian of the person has been appointed, the petition must be verified by that person. If the person who is to verify the petition is unavailable or that person's whereabouts are unknown, the amicus attorney or attorney ad litem shall verify the petition.

History of Fam. Code §31.002: Acts 1995, 74th Leg., ch. 20, §1, eff. Apr. 20, 1995. Amended by Acts 2005, 79th Leg., ch. 172, §13, eff. Sept. 1, 2005. Source: Former Fam. Code §31.02(a), (c).

FAM §31.003. VENUE

The petitioner shall file the petition in the county in which the petitioner resides.

History of Fam. Code §31.003: Acts 1995, 74th Leg., ch. 20, §1, eff. Apr. 20, 1995. Source: Former Fam. Code §31.03(a).

FAM §31.004. REPRESENTATION OF PETITIONER

The court shall appoint an amicus attorney or attorney ad litem to represent the interest of the petitioner at the hearing.

History of Fam. Code §31.004: Acts 1995, 74th Leg., ch. 20, §1, eff. Apr. 20, 1995. Amended by Acts 2005, 79th Leg., ch. 172, §14, eff. Sept. 1, 2005. Source: Former Fam. Code §31.04.

FAM §31.005. ORDER

The court by order, or the Texas Supreme Court by rule or order, may remove the disabilities of minority of a minor, including any restriction imposed by Chapter 32, if the court or the Texas Supreme Court finds the removal to be in the best interest of the petitioner. The order or rule must state the limited or general purposes for which disabilities are removed.

History of Fam. Code §31.005: Acts 1995, 74th Leg., ch. 20, §1, eff. Apr. 20, 1995. Amended by Acts 1999, 76th Leg., ch. 1303, §1, eff. Sept. 1, 1999. Source: Former Fam. Code §31.06.

FAM §31.006. EFFECT OF GENERAL REMOVAL

Except for specific constitutional and statutory age requirements, a minor whose disabilities are removed for general purposes has the capacity of an adult, including the capacity to contract. Except as provided by federal law, all educational rights accorded to the parent of a student, including the right to make education decisions under Section 151.001(a)(10), transfer to the minor whose disabilities are removed for general purposes.

History of Fam. Code §31.006: Acts 1995, 74th Leg., ch. 20, §1, eff. Apr. 20, 1995. Amended by Acts 2001, 77th Leg., ch. 767, §9, eff. June 13, 2001; Acts 2015, 84th Leg., ch. 1236, §7.001, eff. Sept. 1, 2015. Source: Former Fam. Code §31.07.

FAM §31.007. REGISTRATION OF ORDER OF ANOTHER STATE OR NATION

(a) A nonresident minor who has had the disabilities of minority removed in the state of the minor's

residence may file a certified copy of the order removing disabilities in the deed records of any county in this state.

(b) When a certified copy of the order of a court of another state or nation is filed, the minor has the capacity of an adult, except as provided by Section 31.006 and by the terms of the order.

History of Fam. Code §31.007: Acts 1995, 74th Leg., ch. 20, §1, eff. Apr. 20, 1995. Source: Former Fam. Code §31.08.

FAM §31.008. WAIVER OF CITATION

(a) A party to a suit under this chapter may waive the issuance or service of citation after the suit is filed by filing with the clerk of the court in which the suit is filed the waiver of the party acknowledging receipt of a copy of the filed petition.

(b) The party executing the waiver may not sign the waiver using a digitized signature.

(c) The waiver must contain the mailing address of the party executing the waiver.

(d) Notwithstanding Section 132.001, Civil Practice and Remedies Code, the waiver must be sworn before a notary public who is not an attorney in the suit. This subsection does not apply if the party executing the waiver is incarcerated.

(e) The Texas Rules of Civil Procedure do not apply to a waiver executed under this section.

(f) For purposes of this section, "digitized signature" has the meaning assigned by Section 101.0096.

History of Fam. Code §31.008: Acts 2015, 84th Leg., ch. 198, §2, eff. Sept. 1, 2015.

See also *O'Connor's Texas Family Law Handbook* (2017), "Waiver of service," ch. 1-B, §5.2.3(5), p. 34.

CHAPTER 32. CONSENT TO TREATMENT OF CHILD BY NON-PARENT OR CHILD

SUBCHAPTER A. CONSENT TO MEDICAL, DENTAL, PSYCHOLOGICAL, & SURGICAL TREATMENT

FAM §32.001. CONSENT BY NON-PARENT

(a) The following persons may consent to medical, dental, psychological, and surgical treatment of a child when the person having the right to consent as otherwise provided by law cannot be contacted and that person has not given actual notice to the contrary:

(1) a grandparent of the child;

(2) an adult brother or sister of the child;

(3) an adult aunt or uncle of the child;

(4) an educational institution in which the child is enrolled that has received written authorization to consent from a person having the right to consent;

(5) an adult who has actual care, control, and possession of the child and has written authorization to consent from a person having the right to consent;

(6) a court having jurisdiction over a suit affecting the parent-child relationship of which the child is the subject;

(7) an adult responsible for the actual care, control, and possession of a child under the jurisdiction of a juvenile court or committed by a juvenile court to the care of an agency of the state or county; or

(8) a peace officer who has lawfully taken custody of a minor, if the peace officer has reasonable grounds to believe the minor is in need of immediate medical treatment.

(b) Except as otherwise provided by this subsection, the Texas Juvenile Justice Department may consent to the medical, dental, psychological, and surgical treatment of a child committed to the department under Title 3 when the person having the right to consent has been contacted and that person has not given actual notice to the contrary. Consent for medical, dental, psychological, and surgical treatment of a child for whom the Department of Family and Protective Services has been appointed managing conservator and who is committed to the Texas Juvenile Justice Department is governed by Sections 266.004, 266.009, and 266.010.

(c) This section does not apply to consent for the immunization of a child.

(d) A person who consents to the medical treatment of a minor under Subsection (a)(7) or (8) is immune from liability for damages resulting from the examination or treatment of the minor, except to the extent of the person's own acts of negligence. A physician or dentist licensed to practice in this state, or a hospital or medical facility at which a minor is treated is immune from liability for damages resulting from the examination or treatment of a minor under this section, except to the extent of the person's own acts of negligence.

History of Fam. Code §32.001: Acts 1995, 74th Leg., ch. 20, §1, eff. Apr. 20, 1995. Amended by Acts 1995, 74th Leg., ch. 751, §5, eff. Sept. 1, 1995; Acts 2009, 81st Leg., ch. 108, §1, eff. May 23, 2009; Acts 2015, 84th Leg., ch. 734, §37, eff. Sept. 1, 2015. Source: Former Fam. Code §35.01.

See also 37 T.A.C. §380.9181; ***O'Connor's Texas Family Law Handbook*** (2017), "Medical Treatment of Child," ch. 1-E, p. 65.

ANNOTATIONS

Miller v. HCA, Inc., 118 S.W.3d 758, 767-68 (Tex. 2003). "We hold that a physician, who is confronted with emergent circumstances and provides life-sustaining treatment to a minor child, is not liable for not first obtaining consent from the parents. [¶] Providing treatment to a child under emergent circumstances does not imply consent to treatment despite actual notice of refusal to consent. Rather, it is an exception to the general rule that a physician commits a battery by providing medical treatment without consent. As such, the exception is narrowly circumscribed and arises only in emergent circumstances when there is no time to consult the parents or seek court intervention if the parents withhold consent before death is likely to result to the child. Though in situations of this character, the physician should attempt to secure parental consent if possible, the physician will not be liable under a battery or negligence theory solely for proceeding with the treatment absent consent."

FAM §32.002. CONSENT FORM

(a) Consent to medical treatment under this subchapter must be in writing, signed by the person giving consent, and given to the doctor, hospital, or other medical facility that administers the treatment.

(b) The consent must include:

(1) the name of the child;

(2) the name of one or both parents, if known, and the name of any managing conservator or guardian of the child;

(3) the name of the person giving consent and the person's relationship to the child;

(4) a statement of the nature of the medical treatment to be given; and

(5) the date the treatment is to begin.

History of Fam. Code §32.002: Acts 1995, 74th Leg., ch. 20, §1, eff. Apr. 20, 1995. Amended by Acts 1995, 74th Leg., ch. 123, §4, eff. Sept. 1, 1995. Source: Former Fam. Code §35.02.

See also ***O'Connor's Texas Family Law Handbook*** (2017), "Written consent," ch. 1-E, §2.1.1(2), p. 65.

FAM §32.003. CONSENT TO TREATMENT BY CHILD

(a) A child may consent to medical, dental, psychological, and surgical treatment for the child by a licensed physician or dentist if the child:

(1) is on active duty with the armed services of the United States of America;

(2) is:

(A) 16 years of age or older and resides separate and apart from the child's parents, managing conservator, or guardian, with or without the consent of the parents, managing conservator, or guardian and regardless of the duration of the residence; and

(B) managing the child's own financial affairs, regardless of the source of the income;

(3) consents to the diagnosis and treatment of an infectious, contagious, or communicable disease that is required by law or a rule to be reported by the licensed physician or dentist to a local health officer or the Texas Department of Health, including all diseases within the scope of Section 81.041, Health and Safety Code;

(4) is unmarried and pregnant and consents to hospital, medical, or surgical treatment, other than abortion, related to the pregnancy;

(5) consents to examination and treatment for drug or chemical addiction, drug or chemical dependency, or any other condition directly related to drug or chemical use;

(6) is unmarried, is the parent of a child, and has actual custody of his or her child and consents to medical, dental, psychological, or surgical treatment for the child; or

(7) is serving a term of confinement in a facility operated by or under contract with the Texas Department of Criminal Justice, unless the treatment would constitute a prohibited practice under Section 164.052(a)(19), Occupations Code.

(b) Consent by a child to medical, dental, psychological, and surgical treatment under this section is not subject to disaffirmance because of minority.

(c) Consent of the parents, managing conservator, or guardian of a child is not necessary in order to authorize hospital, medical, surgical, or dental care under this section.

(d) A licensed physician, dentist, or psychologist may, with or without the consent of a child who is a patient, advise the parents, managing conservator, or guardian of the child of the treatment given to or needed by the child.

(e) A physician, dentist, psychologist, hospital, or medical facility is not liable for the examination and treatment of a child under this section except for the provider's or the facility's own acts of negligence.

(f) A physician, dentist, psychologist, hospital, or medical facility may rely on the written statement of the child containing the grounds on which the child has capacity to consent to the child's medical treatment.

History of Fam. Code §32.003: Acts 1995, 74th Leg., ch. 20, §1, eff. Apr. 20, 1995. Amended by Acts 1995, 74th Leg., ch. 751, §6, eff. Sept. 1, 1995; Acts 2001, 77th Leg., ch. 821, §2.01, eff. June 14, 2001; Acts 2007, 80th Leg., ch. 1227, §2, eff. June 15, 2007. Source: Former Fam. Code §35.03(a)-(f).

See also *O'Connor's Texas Family Law Handbook* (2017), "Consent by child," ch. 1-E, §2.2.3, p. 69; "Consent by child," ch. 1-E, §3.2.3, p. 72.

FAM §32.004. CONSENT TO COUNSELING

(a) A child may consent to counseling for:

(1) suicide prevention;

(2) chemical addiction or dependency; or

(3) sexual, physical, or emotional abuse.

(b) A licensed or certified physician, psychologist, counselor, or social worker having reasonable grounds to believe that a child has been sexually, physically, or emotionally abused, is contemplating suicide, or is suffering from a chemical or drug addiction or dependency may:

(1) counsel the child without the consent of the child's parents or, if applicable, managing conservator or guardian;

(2) with or without the consent of the child who is a client, advise the child's parents or, if applicable, managing conservator or guardian of the treatment given to or needed by the child; and

(3) rely on the written statement of the child containing the grounds on which the child has capacity to consent to the child's own treatment under this section.

(c) Unless consent is obtained as otherwise allowed by law, a physician, psychologist, counselor, or social worker may not counsel a child if consent is prohibited by a court order.

(d) A physician, psychologist, counselor, or social worker counseling a child under this section is not liable for damages except for damages resulting from the person's negligence or wilful misconduct.

(e) A parent, or, if applicable, managing conservator or guardian, who has not consented to counseling treatment of the child is not obligated to compensate a physician, psychologist, counselor, or social worker for counseling services rendered under this section.

History of Fam. Code §32.004: Acts 1995, 74th Leg., ch. 20, §1, eff. Apr. 20, 1995. Source: Former Fam. Code §35.03(g).

See also *O'Connor's Texas Family Law Handbook* (2017), "Psychological Treatment," ch. 1-E, §3, p. 71.

FAM §32.005. EXAMINATION WITHOUT CONSENT OF ABUSE OR NEGLECT OF CHILD

(a) Except as provided by Subsection (c), a physician, dentist, or psychologist having reasonable grounds to believe that a child's physical or mental condition has been adversely affected by abuse or neglect may examine the child without the consent of the child, the child's parents, or other person authorized to consent to treatment under this subchapter.

(b) An examination under this section may include X-rays, blood tests, photographs, and penetration of tissue necessary to accomplish those tests.

(c) Unless consent is obtained as otherwise allowed by law, a physician, dentist, or psychologist may not examine a child:

(1) 16 years of age or older who refuses to consent; or

(2) for whom consent is prohibited by a court order.

(d) A physician, dentist, or psychologist examining a child under this section is not liable for damages except for damages resulting from the physician's or dentist's negligence.

History of Fam. Code §32.005: Acts 1995, 74th Leg., ch. 20, §1, eff. Apr. 20, 1995. Amended by Acts 1997, 75th Leg., ch. 575, §1, eff. Sept. 1, 1997. Source: Former Fam. Code §35.04.

Sections 32.006-32.100 reserved for expansion

SUBCHAPTER B. IMMUNIZATION

FAM §32.101. WHO MAY CONSENT TO IMMUNIZATION OF CHILD

(a) In addition to persons authorized to consent to immunization under Chapter 151 and Chapter 153, the following persons may consent to the immunization of a child:

(1) a guardian of the child; and

(2) a person authorized under the law of another state or a court order to consent for the child.

(b) If the persons listed in Subsection (a) are not available and the authority to consent is not denied under Subsection (c), consent to the immunization of a child may be given by:

(1) a grandparent of the child;

(2) an adult brother or sister of the child;

(3) an adult aunt or uncle of the child;

(4) a stepparent of the child;

(5) an educational institution in which the child is enrolled that has written authorization to consent for the child from a parent, managing conservator, guardian, or other person who under the law of another state or a court order may consent for the child;

(6) another adult who has actual care, control, and possession of the child and has written authorization to consent for the child from a parent, managing conservator, guardian, or other person who, under the law of another state or a court order, may consent for the child;

(7) a court having jurisdiction of a suit affecting the parent-child relationship of which the minor is the subject;

(8) an adult having actual care, control, and possession of the child under an order of a juvenile court or by commitment by a juvenile court to the care of an agency of the state or county; or

(9) an adult having actual care, control, and possession of the child as the child's primary caregiver.

(c) A person otherwise authorized to consent under Subsection (a)[1] may not consent for the child if the person has actual knowledge that a parent, managing conservator, guardian of the child, or other person who under the law of another state or a court order may consent for the child:

(1) has expressly refused to give consent to the immunization;

(2) has been told not to consent for the child; or

(3) has withdrawn a prior written authorization for the person to consent.

(d) The Texas Juvenile Justice Department may consent to the immunization of a child committed to it if a parent, managing conservator, or guardian of the minor or other person who, under the law of another state or court order, may consent for the minor has been contacted and:

(1) refuses to consent; and

(2) does not expressly deny to the department the authority to consent for the child.

(e) A person who consents under this section shall provide the health care provider with sufficient and accurate health history and other information about the minor for whom the consent is given and, if necessary, sufficient and accurate health history and information about the minor's family to enable the person who may consent to the minor's immunization and the health care provider to determine adequately the risks and benefits inherent in the proposed immunization and to determine whether immunization is advisable.

(f) Consent to immunization must meet the requirements of Section 32.002(a).

1. **Editor's note:** Enacted as such. Probably should be "(b)."

History of Fam. Code §32.101: Acts 1995, 74th Leg., ch. 20, §1, eff. Apr. 20, 1995. Amended by Acts 1995, 74th Leg., ch. 123, §1, eff. Aug. 28, 1995; Acts 1997, 75th Leg., ch. 165, §7.09(a), eff. Sept. 1, 1997; Acts 1999, 76th Leg., ch. 62, §6.02, eff. Sept. 1, 1999; Acts 2015, 84th Leg., ch. 734, §38, eff. Sept. 1, 2015. Source: Former Fam. Code §35.011.

See also 25 T.A.C. §97.91; ***O'Connor's Texas Family Law Handbook*** (2017), "Immunization," ch. 1-E, §4, p. 73.

FAM §32.1011. CONSENT TO IMMUNIZATION BY CHILD

(a) Notwithstanding Section 32.003 or 32.101, a child may consent to the child's own immunization for a disease if:

(1) the child:

(A) is pregnant; or

(B) is the parent of a child and has actual custody of that child; and

(2) the Centers for Disease Control and Prevention recommend or authorize the initial dose of an immunization for that disease to be administered before seven years of age.

(b) Consent to immunization under this section must meet the requirements of Section 32.002(a).

(c) Consent by a child to immunization under this section is not subject to disaffirmance because of minority.

(d) A health care provider or facility may rely on the written statement of the child containing the grounds on which the child has capacity to consent to the child's immunization under this section.

(e) To the extent of any conflict between this section and Section 32.003, this section controls.

History of Fam. Code §32.1011: Acts 2013, 83rd Leg., ch. 1313, §1, eff. June 14, 2013.

FAM §32.102. INFORMED CONSENT TO IMMUNIZATION

(a) A person authorized to consent to the immunization of a child has the responsibility to ensure that the consent, if given, is an informed consent. The person authorized to consent is not required to be present when the immunization of the child is requested if a consent form that meets the requirements of Section 32.002 has been given to the health care provider.

(b) The responsibility of a health care provider to provide information to a person consenting to immunization is the same as the provider's responsibility to a parent.

(c) As part of the information given in the counseling for informed consent, the health care provider shall provide information to inform the person authorized to consent to immunization of the procedures available under the National Childhood Vaccine Injury Act of 1986 (42 U.S.C. Section 300aa-1 et seq.) to seek possible recovery for unreimbursed expenses for certain injuries arising out of the administration of certain vaccines.

History of Fam. Code §32.102: Acts 1995, 74th Leg., ch. 20, §1, eff. Apr. 20, 1995. Renumbered from §32.103 and amended by Acts 1997, 75th Leg., ch. 165, §7.09(b), (d), eff. Sept. 1, 1997. Source: Former Fam. Code §35.013.

FAM §32.103. LIMITED LIABILITY FOR IMMUNIZATION

(a) In the absence of wilful misconduct or gross negligence, a health care provider who accepts the health history and other information given by a person who is delegated the authority to consent to the immunization of a child during the informed consent counseling is not liable for an adverse reaction to an immunization or for other injuries to the child resulting from factual errors in the health history or information given by the person to the health care provider.

(b) A person consenting to immunization of a child, a physician, nurse, or other health care provider, or a public health clinic, hospital, or other medical facility is not liable for damages arising from an immunization administered to a child authorized under this subchapter except for injuries resulting from the person's or facility's own acts of negligence.

History of Fam. Code §32.103: Acts 1995, 74th Leg., ch. 20, §1, eff. Apr. 20, 1995. Renumbered from §32.104 by Acts 1997, 75th Leg., ch. 165, §7.09(e), eff. Sept. 1, 1997. Source: Former Fam. Code §35.014.

FAM §32.104. RENUMBERED

Renumbered as §32.103 by Acts 1997, 75th Leg., ch. 165, §7.09(e), eff. Sept. 1, 1997.

FAM §32.105. REPEALED

Repealed by Acts 1997, 75th Leg., ch. 165, §7.09(c), eff. Sept. 1, 1997.

Sections 32.106-32.200 reserved for expansion

SUBCHAPTER C. MISCELLANEOUS PROVISIONS

FAM §32.201. EMERGENCY SHELTER OR CARE FOR MINORS

(a) An emergency shelter facility may provide shelter and care to a minor and the minor's child or children, if any.

(b) An emergency shelter facility may provide shelter or care only during an emergency constituting an immediate danger to the physical health or safety of the minor or the minor's child or children.

(c) Shelter or care provided under this section may not be provided after the 15th day after the date the shelter or care is commenced unless:

(1) the facility receives consent to continue services from the minor in accordance with Section 32.202; or

(2) the minor has qualified for financial assistance under Chapter 31, Human Resources Code, and is on the waiting list for housing assistance.

History of Fam. Code §32.201: Acts 1995, 74th Leg., ch. 20, §1, eff. Apr. 20, 1995. Amended by Acts 2003, 78th Leg., ch. 192, §1, eff. June 2, 2003. Source: Former Fam. Code §35.05.

FAM §32.202. CONSENT TO EMERGENCY SHELTER OR CARE BY MINOR

(a) A minor may consent to emergency shelter or care to be provided to the minor or the minor's child or children, if any, under Section 32.201(c) if the minor is:

(1) 16 years of age or older and:

(A) resides separate and apart from the minor's parent, managing conservator, or guardian, regardless of whether the parent, managing conservator, or guardian consents to the residence and regardless of the duration of the residence; and

(B) manages the minor's own financial affairs, regardless of the source of income; or

(2) unmarried and is pregnant or is the parent of a child.

(b) Consent by a minor to emergency shelter or care under this section is not subject to disaffirmance because of minority.

(c) An emergency shelter facility may, with or without the consent of the minor's parent, managing conservator, or guardian, provide emergency shelter or care to the minor or the minor's child or children under Section 32.201(c).

(d) An emergency shelter facility is not liable for providing emergency shelter or care to the minor or the minor's child or children if the minor consents as provided by this section, except that the facility is liable for the facility's own acts of negligence.

(e) An emergency shelter facility may rely on the minor's written statement containing the grounds on which the minor has capacity to consent to emergency shelter or care.

(f) To the extent of any conflict between this section and Section 32.003, Section 32.003 prevails.

History of Fam. Code §32.202: Acts 2003, 78th Leg., ch. 192, §2, eff. June 2, 2003.

FAM §32.203. CONSENT BY MINOR TO HOUSING OR CARE PROVIDED THROUGH TRANSITIONAL LIVING PROGRAM

(a) In this section, "transitional living program" means a residential services program for children provided in a residential child-care facility licensed or certified by the Department of Family and Protective Services under Chapter 42, Human Resources Code, that:

(1) is designed to provide basic life skills training and the opportunity to practice those skills, with a goal of basic life skills development toward independent living; and

(2) is not an independent living program.

(b) A minor may consent to housing or care provided to the minor or the minor's child or children, if any, through a transitional living program if the minor is:

(1) 16 years of age or older and:

(A) resides separate and apart from the minor's parent, managing conservator, or guardian, regardless of whether the parent, managing conservator, or guardian consents to the residence and regardless of the duration of the residence; and

(B) manages the minor's own financial affairs, regardless of the source of income; or

(2) unmarried and is pregnant or is the parent of a child.

(c) Consent by a minor to housing or care under this section is not subject to disaffirmance because of minority.

(d) A transitional living program may, with or without the consent of the parent, managing conservator, or guardian, provide housing or care to the minor or the minor's child or children.

(e) A transitional living program must attempt to notify the minor's parent, managing conservator, or guardian regarding the minor's location.

(f) A transitional living program is not liable for providing housing or care to the minor or the minor's child or children if the minor consents as provided by this section, except that the program is liable for the program's own acts of negligence.

(g) A transitional living program may rely on a minor's written statement containing the grounds on which the minor has capacity to consent to housing or care provided through the program.

(h) To the extent of any conflict between this section and Section 32.003, Section 32.003 prevails.

History of Fam. Code §32.203: Acts 2013, 83rd Leg., ch. 587, §1, eff. June 14, 2013.

FAM §32.241. REPEALED

Repealed by Acts 1997, 75th Leg., ch. 165, §7.10(c), eff. Sept. 1, 1997.

CHAPTER 33. NOTICE OF & CONSENT TO ABORTION

A FAM §33.001. DEFINITIONS

In this chapter:

(1) "Abortion" has the meaning assigned by Section 245.002, Health and Safety Code ~~[means the use of any means to terminate the pregnancy of a female~~

~~known by the attending physician to be pregnant, with the intention that the termination of the pregnancy by those means will with reasonable likelihood cause the death of the fetus~~]. This definition, as applied in this chapter, [~~applies only to an unemancipated minor known by the attending physician to be pregnant and~~] may not be construed to limit a minor's access to contraceptives.

(2) "Fetus" means an individual human organism from fertilization until birth.

(3) "Guardian" means a court-appointed guardian of the person of the minor.

(3-a) "Medical emergency" has the meaning assigned by Section 171.002, Health and Safety Code.

(4) "Physician" means an individual licensed to practice medicine in this state.

(5) "Unemancipated minor" includes a minor who:

(A) is unmarried; and

(B) has not had the disabilities of minority removed under Chapter 31.

History of Fam. Code §33.001: Acts 1999, 76th Leg., ch. 395, §1, eff. Sept. 1, 1999. Amended by Acts 2015, 84th Leg., ch. 436, §§1, 2, eff. Jan. 1, 2016; S.B. 8, §1, 85th Leg., eff. Sept. 1, 2017.

FAM §33.002. PARENTAL NOTICE

(a) A physician may not perform an abortion on a pregnant unemancipated minor unless:

(1) the physician performing the abortion gives at least 48 hours actual notice, in person or by telephone, of the physician's intent to perform the abortion to:

(A) a parent of the minor, if the minor has no managing conservator or guardian; or

(B) a court-appointed managing conservator or guardian;

(2) the physician who is to perform the abortion receives an order issued by a court under Section 33.003 or 33.004 authorizing the minor to consent to the abortion as provided by Section 33.003 or 33.004; or

(3) the physician who is to perform the abortion:

(A) concludes that a medical emergency exists;

(B) certifies in writing to the Department of State Health Services and in the patient's medical record the medical indications supporting the physician's judgment that a medical emergency exists; and

(C) provides the notice required by Section 33.0022.

(b) If a person to whom notice may be given under Subsection (a)(1) cannot be notified after a reasonable effort, a physician may perform an abortion if the physician gives 48 hours constructive notice, by certified mail, restricted delivery, sent to the last known address, to the person to whom notice may be given under Subsection (a)(1). The period under this subsection begins when the notice is mailed. If the person required to be notified is not notified within the 48-hour period, the abortion may proceed even if the notice by mail is not received.

(c) The requirement that 48 hours actual notice be provided under this section may be waived by an affidavit of:

(1) a parent of the minor, if the minor has no managing conservator or guardian; or

(2) a court-appointed managing conservator or guardian.

(d) A physician may execute for inclusion in the minor's medical record an affidavit stating that, according to the best information and belief of the physician, notice or constructive notice has been provided as required by this section. Execution of an affidavit under this subsection creates a presumption that the requirements of this section have been satisfied.

(e) The Department of State Health Services shall prepare a form to be used for making the certification required by Subsection (a)(3)(B).

(f) A certification required by Subsection (a)(3)(B) is confidential and privileged and is not subject to disclosure under Chapter 552, Government Code, or to discovery, subpoena, or other legal process. Personal or identifying information about the minor, including her name, address, or social security number, may not be included in a certification under Subsection (a)(3)(B). The physician must keep the medical records on the minor in compliance with the rules adopted by the Texas Medical Board under Section 153.003, Occupations Code.

(g) A physician who intentionally performs an abortion on a pregnant unemancipated minor in violation of this section commits an offense. An offense under this subsection is punishable by a fine not to exceed $10,000. In this subsection, "intentionally" has the meaning assigned by Section 6.03(a), Penal Code.

(h) It is a defense to prosecution under this section that the minor falsely represented her age or identity to the physician to be at least 18 years of age by dis-

playing an apparently valid proof of identity and age described by Subsection (k) such that a reasonable person under similar circumstances would have relied on the representation. The defense does not apply if the physician is shown to have had independent knowledge of the minor's actual age or identity or failed to use due diligence in determining the minor's age or identity. In this subsection, "defense" has the meaning and application assigned by Section 2.03, Penal Code.

(i) In relation to the trial of an offense under this section in which the conduct charged involves a conclusion made by the physician under Subsection (a)(3)(A), the defendant may seek a hearing before the Texas Medical Board on whether the physician's conduct was necessary because of a medical emergency. The findings of the Texas Medical Board under this subsection are admissible on that issue in the trial of the defendant. Notwithstanding any other reason for a continuance provided under the Code of Criminal Procedure or other law, on motion of the defendant, the court shall delay the beginning of the trial for not more than 30 days to permit a hearing under this subsection to take place.

(j) A physician shall use due diligence to determine that any woman on which the physician performs an abortion who claims to have reached the age of majority or to have had the disabilities of minority removed has, in fact, reached the age of majority or has had the disabilities of minority removed.

(k) For the purposes of this section, "due diligence" includes requesting proof of identity and age described by Section 2.005(b) or a copy of the court order removing disabilities of minority.

(*l*) If proof of identity and age cannot be provided, the physician shall provide information on how to obtain proof of identity and age. If the woman is subsequently unable to obtain proof of identity and age and the physician chooses to perform the abortion, the physician shall document that proof of identity and age was not obtained and report to the Department of State Health Services that proof of identity and age was not obtained for the woman on whom the abortion was performed. The department shall report annually to the legislature regarding the number of abortions performed without proof of identity and age.

History of Fam. Code §33.002: Acts 1999, 76th Leg., ch. 395, §1, eff. Sept. 1, 1999. Amended by Acts 2001, 77th Leg., ch. 1420, §14.741, eff. Sept. 1, 2001; Acts 2015, 84th Leg., ch. 436, §3, eff. Jan. 1, 2016.

See also 22 T.A.C. §165.6; 25 T.A.C. §139.5.

FAM §33.0021. CONSENT REQUIRED

A physician may not perform an abortion in violation of Section 164.052(a)(19), Occupations Code.

History of Fam. Code §33.0021: Acts 2015, 84th Leg., ch. 436, §4, eff. Jan. 1, 2016.

FAM §33.0022. MEDICAL EMERGENCY NOTIFICATION; AFFIDAVIT FOR MEDICAL RECORD

(a) If the physician who is to perform the abortion concludes under Section 33.002(a)(3)(A) that a medical emergency exists and that there is insufficient time to provide the notice required by Section 33.002 or obtain the consent required by Section 33.0021, the physician shall make a reasonable effort to inform, in person or by telephone, the parent, managing conservator, or guardian of the unemancipated minor within 24 hours after the time a medical emergency abortion is performed on the minor of:

(1) the performance of the abortion; and

(2) the basis for the physician's determination that a medical emergency existed that required the performance of a medical emergency abortion without fulfilling the requirements of Section 33.002 or 33.0021.

(b) A physician who performs an abortion as described by Subsection (a), not later than 48 hours after the abortion is performed, shall send a written notice that a medical emergency occurred and the ability of the parent, managing conservator, or guardian to contact the physician for more information and medical records, to the last known address of the parent, managing conservator, or guardian by certified mail, restricted delivery, return receipt requested. The physician may rely on last known address information if a reasonable and prudent person, under similar circumstances, would rely on the information as sufficient evidence that the parent, managing conservator, or guardian resides at that address. The physician shall keep in the minor's medical record:

(1) the return receipt from the written notice; or

(2) if the notice was returned as undeliverable, the notice.

(c) A physician who performs an abortion on an unemancipated minor during a medical emergency as described by Subsection (a) shall execute for inclusion in the medical record of the minor an affidavit that explains the specific medical emergency that necessitated the immediate abortion.

History of Fam. Code §33.0022: Acts 2015, 84th Leg., ch. 436, §4, eff. Jan. 1, 2016.

FAM §33.003. JUDICIAL APPROVAL

(a) A pregnant minor may file an application for a court order authorizing the minor to consent to the performance of an abortion without notification to and consent of a parent, managing conservator, or guardian.

(b) The application must be filed in:

(1) a county court at law, court having probate jurisdiction, or district court, including a family district court, in the minor's county of residence;

(2) if the minor's parent, managing conservator, or guardian is a presiding judge of a court described by Subdivision (1):

(A) a county court at law, court having probate jurisdiction, or district court, including a family district court, in a contiguous county; or

(B) a county court at law, court having probate jurisdiction, or district court, including a family district court, in the county where the minor intends to obtain the abortion;

(3) if the minor's county of residence has a population of less than 10,000:

(A) a court described by Subdivision (1);

(B) a county court at law, court having probate jurisdiction, or district court, including a family district court, in a contiguous county; or

(C) a county court at law, court having probate jurisdiction, or district court, including a family district court, in the county in which the facility at which the minor intends to obtain the abortion is located; or

(4) a county court at law, court having probate jurisdiction, or district court, including a family district court, in the county in which the facility at which the minor intends to obtain the abortion is located, if the minor is not a resident of this state.

(c) The application must:

(1) be made under oath;

(2) include:

(A) a statement that the minor is pregnant;

(B) a statement that the minor is unmarried, is under 18 years of age, and has not had her disabilities removed under Chapter 31;

(C) a statement that the minor wishes to have an abortion without the notification to and consent of a parent, managing conservator, or guardian;

(D) a statement as to whether the minor has retained an attorney and, if she has retained an attorney, the name, address, and telephone number of her attorney; and

(E) a statement about the minor's current residence, including the minor's physical address, mailing address, and telephone number; and

(3) be accompanied by the sworn statement of the minor's attorney under Subsection (r), if the minor has retained an attorney to assist the minor with filing the application under this section.

(d) The clerk of the court shall deliver a courtesy copy of the application made under this section to the judge who is to hear the application.

(e) The court shall appoint a guardian ad litem for the minor who shall represent the best interest of the minor. If the minor has not retained an attorney, the court shall appoint an attorney to represent the minor. The guardian ad litem may not also serve as the minor's attorney ad litem.

(f) The court may appoint to serve as guardian ad litem:

(1) a person who may consent to treatment for the minor under Sections 32.001(a)(1)-(3);

(2) a psychiatrist or an individual licensed or certified as a psychologist under Chapter 501, Occupations Code;

(3) an appropriate employee of the Department of Family and Protective Services;

(4) a member of the clergy; or

(5) another appropriate person selected by the court.

(g) The court shall fix a time for a hearing on an application filed under Subsection (a) and shall keep a record of all testimony and other oral proceedings in the action.

(g-1) The pregnant minor must appear before the court in person and may not appear using videoconferencing, telephone conferencing, or other remote electronic means.

(h) The court shall rule on an application submitted under this section and shall issue written findings of fact and conclusions of law not later than 5 p.m. on the fifth business day after the date the application is filed with the court. On request by the minor, the court shall grant an extension of the period specified by this subsection. If a request for an extension is made, the

court shall rule on an application and shall issue written findings of fact and conclusions of law not later than 5 p.m. on the fifth business day after the date the minor states she is ready to proceed to hearing. Proceedings under this section shall be given precedence over other pending matters to the extent necessary to assure that the court reaches a decision promptly, regardless of whether the minor is granted an extension under this subsection.

(i) The court shall determine by clear and convincing evidence, as described by Section 101.007, whether:

(1) the minor is mature and sufficiently well informed to make the decision to have an abortion performed without notification to or consent of a parent, managing conservator, or guardian; or

(2) the notification and attempt to obtain consent would not be in the best interest of the minor.

(i-1) In determining whether the minor meets the requirements of Subsection (i)(1), the court shall consider the experience, perspective, and judgment of the minor. The court may:

(1) consider all relevant factors, including:

(A) the minor's age;

(B) the minor's life experiences, such as working, traveling independently, or managing her own financial affairs; and

(C) steps taken by the minor to explore her options and the consequences of those options;

(2) inquire as to the minor's reasons for seeking an abortion;

(3) consider the degree to which the minor is informed about the state-published informational materials described by Chapter 171, Health and Safety Code; and

(4) require the minor to be evaluated by a licensed mental health counselor, who shall return the evaluation to the court for review within three business days.

(i-2) In determining whether the notification and the attempt to obtain consent would not be in the best interest of the minor, the court may inquire as to:

(1) the minor's reasons for not wanting to notify and obtain consent from a parent, managing conservator, or guardian;

(2) whether notification or the attempt to obtain consent may lead to physical or sexual abuse;

(3) whether the pregnancy was the result of sexual abuse by a parent, managing conservator, or guardian; and

(4) any history of physical or sexual abuse from a parent, managing conservator, or guardian.

(i-3) The court shall enter an order authorizing the minor to consent to the performance of the abortion without notification to and consent of a parent, managing conservator, or guardian and shall execute the required forms if the court finds by clear and convincing evidence, as defined by Section 101.007, that:

(1) the minor is mature and sufficiently well informed to make the decision to have an abortion performed without notification to or consent of a parent, managing conservator, or guardian; or

(2) the notification and attempt to obtain consent would not be in the best interest of the minor.

(j) If the court finds that the minor does not meet the requirements of Subsection (i-3), the court may not authorize the minor to consent to an abortion without the notification authorized under Section 33.002(a)(1) and consent under Section 33.0021.

(k) The court may not notify a parent, managing conservator, or guardian that the minor is pregnant or that the minor wants to have an abortion. The court proceedings shall be conducted in a manner that protects the confidentiality of the identity of the minor. The application and all other court documents pertaining to the proceedings are confidential and privileged and are not subject to disclosure under Chapter 552, Government Code, or to discovery, subpoena, or other legal process. Confidential records pertaining to a minor under this subsection may be disclosed to the minor.

(*l*) An order of the court issued under this section is confidential and privileged and is not subject to disclosure under Chapter 552, Government Code, or discovery, subpoena, or other legal process. The order may not be released to any person but the pregnant minor, the pregnant minor's guardian ad litem, the pregnant minor's attorney, the physician who is to perform the abortion, another person designated to receive the order by the minor, or a governmental agency or attorney in a criminal or administrative action seeking to assert or protect the interest of the minor. The supreme court may adopt rules to permit confidential docketing of an application under this section.

(*l*-1) The clerk of the court, at intervals prescribed by the Office of Court Administration of the Texas Judicial System, shall submit a report to the office that includes, for each case filed under this section:

(1) the case number and style;

(2) the applicant's county of residence;

(3) the court of appeals district in which the proceeding occurred;

(4) the date of filing;

(5) the date of disposition; and

(6) the disposition of the case.

(*l*-2) The Office of Court Administration of the Texas Judicial System shall annually compile and publish a report aggregating the data received under Subsections (*l*-1)(3) and (6). A report submitted under Subsection (*l*-1) is confidential and privileged and is not subject to disclosure under Chapter 552, Government Code, or to discovery, subpoena, or other legal process. A report under this subsection must protect the confidentiality of:

(1) the identity of all minors and judges who are the subject of the report; and

(2) the information described by Subsection (*l*-1)(1).

(m) The clerk of the supreme court shall prescribe the application form to be used by the minor filing an application under this section.

(n) A filing fee is not required of and court costs may not be assessed against a minor filing an application under this section.

(o) A minor who has filed an application under this section may not withdraw or otherwise non-suit her application without the permission of the court.

(p) Except as otherwise provided by Subsection (q), a minor who has filed an application and has obtained a determination by the court as described by Subsection (i) may not initiate a new application proceeding and the prior proceeding is res judicata of the issue relating to the determination of whether the minor may or may not be authorized to consent to the performance of an abortion without notification to and consent of a parent, managing conservator, or guardian.

(q) A minor whose application is denied may subsequently submit an application to the court that denied the application if the minor shows that there has been a material change in circumstances since the time the court denied the application.

(r) An attorney retained by the minor to assist her in filing an application under this section shall fully inform himself or herself of the minor's prior application history, including the representations made by the minor in the application regarding her address, proper venue in the county in which the application is filed, and whether a prior application has been filed and initiated. If an attorney assists the minor in the application process in any way, with or without payment, the attorney representing the minor must attest to the truth of the minor's claims regarding the venue and prior applications in a sworn statement.

History of Fam. Code §33.003: Acts 1999, 76th Leg., ch. 395, §1, eff. Sept. 1, 1999. Amended by Acts 2001, 77th Leg., ch. 1420, §14.742, eff. Sept. 1, 2001; Acts 2011, 82nd Leg., ch. 110, §1, eff. May 21, 2011; Acts 2015, 84th Leg., ch. 436, §5, eff. Jan. 1, 2016.

See also 22 T.A.C. §165.6; Rules for Judicial Bypass of Parental Notice, p. 1481.

ANNOTATIONS

Generally

In re Jane Doe 1 (I), 19 S.W.3d 249, 255 (Tex. 2000). "Because the Legislature used the imperative word 'shall,' we conclude that when a minor meets the statutory threshold, the trial court must grant the application."

In re Jane Doe, 501 S.W.3d 313, 316 (Tex.App.—Houston [14th Dist.] 2016, n.p.h.). "Based on the trial court's affirmative finding on [§33.003(i-3)](1), its negative finding on [§33.003(i-3)](2), and its denial of the application, it appears that the trial court interpreted §33.003(i-3) to require the minor to prove both subsections (1) and (2) to be entitled to relief. We disagree.... The use of 'shall' and 'or' in the statute imposes a mandatory duty on the trial court to enter a judicial bypass order if it makes either of the two stated findings."

Abuse

In re Jane Doe 2, 19 S.W.3d 278, 283 (Tex.2000). "[T]he trial court must determine whether ... the evidence supports a finding that notification *may* lead to abuse. For meaningful appellate review the trial court must make specific findings concerning the potential for abuse. Similarly, if the trial court determines that the minor's testimony about potential abuse is not credible, it should also make specific findings in that regard."

Best Interest

In re Jane Doe 2, 19 S.W.3d 278, 282 (Tex.2000). "To determine whether notification would not be in the minor's best interests, the trial court should weigh the advantages and disadvantages of parental notification in the minor's specific situation. ... In ***Holley v. Adams***, [544 S.W.2d 367 (Tex.1976),] we developed a list of non-exhaustive factors for determining a minor's best interests. Four of these factors are relevant when adapted to the parental notification context, and a trial court should consider them in determining best interests: (1) the minor's emotional or physical needs; (2) the possibility of emotional or physical danger to the minor; (3) the stability of the minor's home and whether notification would cause serious and lasting harm to the family structure; and (4) the relationship between the parent and the minor and the effect of notification on that relationship. An additional factor that courts in other jurisdictions have considered is whether notification may lead the parents to withdraw emotional and financial support from the minor. This list is not exhaustive, and in making the best-interests determination the trial court should consider all relevant circumstances. We note, however, that a minor's generalized fear of telling her parents does not, by itself, establish that notification would not be in the minor's best interests. [¶] Also, as with the maturity determination, meaningful appellate review is possible only if the trial court makes specific findings about its determination that the minor has not shown that notification is not in her best interests. Similarly, if the trial court's determination depends on its assessment of the minor's credibility, it should make specific findings on that issue."

Findings of Fact

In re Jane Doe 10, 78 S.W.3d 338, 342-43 (Tex. 2002). "Fact findings are necessary to demonstrate the trial court's careful consideration of each ground asserted for bypass, and particularized findings are essential to meaningful appellate review, at least when credibility or maturity concerns are involved. ... 'The mere fact that the trial court has checked a box on a form does not demonstrate that it has given the careful consideration necessary for such a significant decision.' Because a remand for the trial court to make fact findings is inconsistent with the expedited nature of these proceedings, it is essential that trial courts make fact findings with regard to each ground asserted for bypass. Accordingly, we renew our admonishments to the trial courts to heed the Legislature's mandate and issue fact findings and conclusions of law with regard to each ground asserted for a judicial bypass and to issue particularized findings at least when credibility or maturity issues are involved."

Hearing

In re Jane Doe 4, 19 S.W.3d 322, 325 (Tex.2000). "[B]ecause trial courts can view a witness's demeanor, they are given great latitude in believing or disbelieving a witness's testimony, particularly when the witness is interested in the outcome. Acting as factfinder, a trial judge can, therefore, reject the uncontroverted testimony of an interested witness unless it is readily controvertible, it is clear, positive, direct, and there are no circumstances tending to discredit or impeach it. The readily-controvertible prong of this test is not applicable to a parental notification proceeding under Ch. 33. Because the hearing is unopposed, the minor's testimony will rarely, if ever, be readily controvertible. The other parts of this test, however, apply to a notification proceeding as they would in any other proceeding in which the trial court acts as a factfinder."

Mature & Sufficiently Well Informed

In re Jane Doe 1 (II), 19 S.W.3d 346, 359 (Tex. 2000). "When we wrote ... that a minor must have considered the 'benefits, risks, and consequences' of the various options, we did not intend to suggest that trial courts should create checklists that a minor must recite in order to establish that she has thoughtfully considered her options. That a minor does not share the court's views about what the benefits of her alternatives might be does not mean that she has not thoughtfully considered her options or acquired sufficient information about them. ... Instead, the focus of the inquiry is whether the minor has thoughtfully considered her alternatives, and 'the examining court must weigh her situation not against the ideal but against a standard of basic understanding of her situation, her choices, and her options.' [¶] The concept of 'benefits' is inherently subjective; what one person may consider a benefit, another may not. That [applicant] does not accept and pursue the alternate benefits to abortion does not mean that she has not given those alternatives thoughtful consideration. Moreover, even though there may be generally recognized benefits to an alternative, those benefits must be considered in light of the minor's particular situation. *At 360:* [Applicant] did not

seek information or counseling from anyone who would be against her having an abortion. [The] dissent [argues] that her failure to do so supports the trial court's finding that she was not sufficiently well informed. [A] minor is not required to seek information from any particular group or viewpoint so long as 'she has obtained information on the relevant considerations from reliable sources of her choosing that enable her to make a thoughtful and informed decision.'"

In re Jane Doe 1 (I), 19 S.W.3d 249, 255 (Tex. 2000). "[A] minor is 'mature and sufficiently well informed to make the decision to have an abortion without notification to either of her parents' when the evidence demonstrates that the minor is capable of reasoned decision-making and that her decision is not the product of impulse, but is based upon careful consideration of the various options available to her and the benefits, risks, and consequences of those options. *At 256-57:* Obviously, whether a minor is mature and sufficiently well informed is a highly individualized decision that must take into account the diverse background and circumstances of each applicant for waiver of parental notification. [¶] In order to establish that she is sufficiently well informed the minor must make, at a minimum[,] three showings. [¶] First, she must show that she has obtained information from a health-care professional about the health risks associated with an abortion and that she understands those risks. [¶] Second, she must show that she understands the alternatives to abortion and their implications. [¶] Third, she must show that she is also aware of the emotional and psychological aspects of undergoing an abortion, which can be significant if not severe for some women. She must also show that she has considered how this decision might affect her family relations. [¶] A determination of maturity necessarily involves more trial court discretion. [¶] A minor who can show that she is sufficiently well informed may also establish in the process that she is mature. In making a determination of maturity, there are, however, some criteria that should not be relied upon as conclusively showing immaturity. The U.S. Supreme Court has said that one of those is the fact, standing alone, that the pregnant female is a minor. That Court has also admonished that states and courts 'may not make a blanket determination that all minors ... are too immature to make this decision or that an abortion never may be in the minor's best interests without parental approval.' A child's age, educational background or grades in school, while indicative of some level of maturity, are not conclusive on the issue of maturity. Nor is participation in extra-curricular activities. It should also go without saying that a minor's socio-economic status should not bear on the decision."

In re Jane Doe, 501 S.W.3d 313, 318-19 (Tex. App.—Houston [14th Dist.] 2016, n.p.h.). Family Code "§33.003(i-1) permits the court to consider the steps taken by the minor to explore her options and the consequences of those options. These consequences potentially would include the emotional and psychological aspects of undergoing an abortion. But the ... statute does not expressly state that the minor must prove she is aware of the emotional and psychological aspects of undergoing an abortion. *At 320:* The 2015 amendments did not change the 'sufficiently well informed' language of §33.003(i), which the supreme court interpreted in ***Doe 1*** [***(I)***] to require that the minor show that she is aware of the emotional and psychological aspects of undergoing an abortion. We therefore conclude that the 'sufficiently well informed' language mandates the three required showings identified in ***Doe 1*** [***(I)***] even after the 2015 amendments to [Fam. Code] Ch. 33 ... and the 2003 addition of [H&SC] Ch. 171.... Thus, we conclude Applicant had the burden of proving by clear and convincing evidence that she is aware of the emotional and psychological aspects of undergoing an abortion. *At 321:* Applicant's general testimony that she read the booklet is not sufficient by itself to establish the third required showing of ***Doe 1*** [***(I)***]. Applicant did not specifically testify that she read and understood the 'Emotional Side of an Abortion' section of the booklet that discusses these aspects. *At 322-23:* [T]here is no direct testimony that Applicant is aware of the emotional and psychological aspects of undergoing an abortion. ... The record does contain various general statements to the effect that Applicant understands her options, had been told 'everything' and is aware of 'the reality.' But this testimony is not clear that the terms 'options,' 'everything,' and 'reality' include the emotional and psychological aspects of undergoing an abortion."

FAM §33.004. APPEAL

(a) A minor whose application under Section 33.003 is denied may appeal to the court of appeals having jurisdiction over civil matters in the county in which the application was filed. On receipt of a notice

of appeal, the clerk of the court that denied the application shall deliver a copy of the notice of appeal and record on appeal to the clerk of the court of appeals. On receipt of the notice and record, the clerk of the court of appeals shall place the appeal on the docket of the court.

(b) The court of appeals shall rule on an appeal under this section not later than 5 p.m. on the fifth business day after the date the notice of appeal is filed with the court that denied the application. On request by the minor, the court shall grant an extension of the period specified by this subsection. If a request for an extension is made, the court shall rule on the appeal not later than 5 p.m. on the fifth business day after the date the minor states she is ready to proceed. Proceedings under this section shall be given precedence over other pending matters to the extent necessary to assure that the court reaches a decision promptly, regardless of whether the minor is granted an extension under this subsection.

(c) A ruling of the court of appeals issued under this section is confidential and privileged and is not subject to disclosure under Chapter 552, Government Code, or discovery, subpoena, or other legal process. The ruling may not be released to any person but the pregnant minor, the pregnant minor's guardian ad litem, the pregnant minor's attorney, another person designated to receive the ruling by the minor, or a governmental agency or attorney in a criminal or administrative action seeking to assert or protect the interest of the minor. The supreme court may adopt rules to permit confidential docketing of an appeal under this section.

(c-1) Notwithstanding Subsection (c), the court of appeals may publish an opinion relating to a ruling under this section if the opinion is written in a way to preserve the confidentiality of the identity of the pregnant minor.

(d) The clerk of the supreme court shall prescribe the notice of appeal form to be used by the minor appealing a judgment under this section.

(e) A filing fee is not required of and court costs may not be assessed against a minor filing an appeal under this section.

(f) An expedited confidential appeal shall be available to any pregnant minor to whom a court of appeals denies an application to authorize the minor to consent to the performance of an abortion without notification to or consent of a parent, managing conservator, or guardian.

History of Fam. Code §33.004: Acts 1999, 76th Leg., ch. 395, §1, eff. Sept. 1, 1999. Amended by Acts 2015, 84th Leg., ch. 436, §6, eff. Jan. 1, 2016.

See also 22 T.A.C. §165.6; Rules for Judicial Bypass of Parental Notice, p. 1481.

ANNOTATIONS

Generally

In re Jane Doe 11, 92 S.W.3d 511, 513 (Tex.2002). "[U]nder [§33.004(a)], it is only the denial of an application that is appealable. [¶] [T]he district court did not rule on [minor's] application within the requisite time period. And because the trial court failed to do so 'the application is deemed to be granted....' Thus, the order was not appealable."

In re Jane Doe 2, 19 S.W.3d 278, 283 (Tex.2000). "That we have provided trial courts forms for making findings of fact and conclusions of law should not prevent them from making the specific findings we require for the maturity, best interests, and potential abuse determinations. These forms are analogous to our forms allowing minors to check off that they have satisfied one or more of the statutory requirements. A minor's testimony merely parroting the language on the form is not sufficient for a judicial bypass without testimony regarding her specific circumstances. Likewise, the mere fact that the trial court has checked a box on a form does not demonstrate that it has given the careful consideration necessary for such a significant decision. Moreover, the form itself contemplates more specificity, as it includes a place for comments under each of the three statutory requirements, in which the trial court can and should detail its findings."

Best Interest

In re Jane Doe 2, 19 S.W.3d 278, 281 (Tex.2000). "[A]n appellate court should review a trial court's determination regarding whether notification is in the minor's best interests under the abuse of discretion standard. Unlike the 'mature and sufficiently well informed' determination, in which the trial court is solely making factual findings, determining the minor's best interests requires the trial court to balance the possible benefits and detriments to the minor in notifying her parents. This type of balancing necessarily involves the exercise of judicial discretion and should be reviewed on that basis."

Mature & Sufficiently Well Informed

In re Jane Doe 1 (I), 19 S.W.3d 249, 253 (Tex. 2000). "[I]n determining whether a minor is 'mature and sufficiently well informed,' the trial court is not to weigh policy considerations; it simply makes a factual determination. When the trial court acts primarily as a factfinder, appellate courts normally review its determinations under the legal and factual sufficiency standards. We therefore apply that standard of review to this appeal."

FAM §33.005. AFFIDAVIT OF PHYSICIAN

(a) A physician may execute for inclusion in the minor's medical record an affidavit stating that, after reasonable inquiry, it is the belief of the physician that:

(1) the minor has made an application or filed a notice of an appeal with a court under this chapter;

(2) the deadline for court action imposed by this chapter has passed; and

(3) the physician has been notified that the court has not denied the application or appeal.

(b) A physician who in good faith has executed an affidavit under Subsection (a) may rely on the affidavit and may perform the abortion as if the court had issued an order granting the application or appeal.

History of Fam. Code §33.005: Acts 1999, 76th Leg., ch. 395, §1, eff. Sept. 1, 1999.

See also 22 T.A.C. §165.6.

FAM §33.006. GUARDIAN AD LITEM IMMUNITY

A guardian ad litem appointed under this chapter and acting in the course and scope of the appointment is not liable for damages arising from an act or omission of the guardian ad litem committed in good faith. The immunity granted by this section does not apply if the conduct of the guardian ad litem is committed in a manner described by Sections 107.003(b)(1)-(4).[1]

1. **Editor's note:** Enacted as such. Probably should be "Sections 107.009(b)(1)-(3)."

History of Fam. Code §33.006: Acts 1999, 76th Leg., ch. 395, §1, eff. Sept. 1, 1999.

FAM §33.0065. RECORDS

The clerk of the court shall retain the records for each case before the court under this chapter in accordance with rules for civil cases and grant access to the records to the minor who is the subject of the proceeding.

History of Fam. Code §33.0065: Acts 2015, 84th Leg., ch. 436, §7, eff. Jan. 1, 2016.

FAM §33.007. COSTS PAID BY STATE

(a) A court acting under Section 33.003 or 33.004 may issue an order requiring the state to pay:

(1) the cost of any attorney ad litem and any guardian ad litem appointed for the minor;

(2) notwithstanding Sections 33.003(n) and 33.004(e), the costs of court associated with the application or appeal; and

(3) any court reporter's fees incurred.

(b) An order issued under Subsection (a) must be directed to the comptroller, who shall pay the amount ordered from funds appropriated to the Texas Department of Health.

History of Fam. Code §33.007: Acts 1999, 76th Leg., ch. 395, §1, eff. Sept. 1, 1999.

FAM §33.008. PHYSICIAN'S DUTY TO REPORT ABUSE OF A MINOR; INVESTIGATION & ASSISTANCE

(a) If a minor claims to have been physically or sexually abused or a physician or physician's agent has reason to believe that a minor has been physically or sexually abused, the physician or physician's agent shall immediately report the suspected abuse and the name of the abuser to the Department of Family and Protective Services and to a local law enforcement agency and shall refer the minor to the department for services or intervention that may be in the best interest of the minor. The local law enforcement agency shall respond and shall write a report within 24 hours of being notified of the alleged abuse. A report shall be made regardless of whether the local law enforcement agency knows or suspects that a report about the abuse may have previously been made.

(b) The appropriate local law enforcement agency and the Department of Family and Protective Services shall investigate suspected abuse reported under this section and, if warranted, shall refer the case to the appropriate prosecuting authority.

(c) When the local law enforcement agency responds to the report of physical or sexual abuse as required by Subsection (a), a law enforcement officer or appropriate agent from the Department of Family and Protective Services may take emergency possession of the minor without a court order to protect the health and safety of the minor as described by Chapter 262.

History of Fam. Code §33.008: Acts 1999, 76th Leg., ch. 395, §1, eff. Sept. 1, 1999. Amended by Acts 2011, 82nd Leg., ch. 110, §2, eff. May 21, 2011; Acts 2015, 84th Leg., ch. 436, §8, eff. Jan. 1, 2016.

FAM §33.0085. DUTY OF JUDGE OR JUSTICE TO REPORT ABUSE OF MINOR

(a) Notwithstanding any other law, a judge or justice who, as a result of court proceedings conducted under Section 33.003 or 33.004, has reason to believe that a minor has been or may be physically or sexually abused shall:

(1) immediately report the suspected abuse and the name of the abuser to the Department of Family and Protective Services and to a local law enforcement agency; and

(2) refer the minor to the department for services or intervention that may be in the best interest of the minor.

(b) The appropriate local law enforcement agency and the Department of Family and Protective Services shall investigate suspected abuse reported under this section and, if warranted, shall refer the case to the appropriate prosecuting authority.

History of Fam. Code §33.0085: Acts 2015, 84th Leg., ch. 436, §9, eff. Jan. 1, 2016.

FAM §33.009. OTHER REPORTS OF SEXUAL ABUSE OF A MINOR

A court or the guardian ad litem or attorney ad litem for the minor shall report conduct reasonably believed to violate Section 21.02, 22.011, 22.021, or 25.02, Penal Code, based on information obtained during a confidential court proceeding held under this chapter to:

(1) any local or state law enforcement agency;

(2) the Department of Family and Protective Services, if the alleged conduct involves a person responsible for the care, custody, or welfare of the child;

(3) the state agency that operates, licenses, certifies, or registers the facility in which the alleged conduct occurred, if the alleged conduct occurred in a facility operated, licensed, certified, or registered by a state agency; or

(4) an appropriate agency designated by the court.

History of Fam. Code §33.009: Acts 1999, 76th Leg., ch. 395, §1, eff. Sept. 1, 1999. Amended by Acts 2007, 80th Leg., ch. 593, §3.27, eff. Sept. 1, 2007.

FAM §33.010. CONFIDENTIALITY

Notwithstanding any other law, information obtained by the Department of Family and Protective Services or another entity under Section 33.008, 33.0085, or 33.009 is confidential except to the extent necessary to prove a violation of Section 21.02, 22.011, 22.021, or 25.02, Penal Code.

History of Fam. Code §33.010: Acts 1999, 76th Leg., ch. 395, §1, eff. Sept. 1, 1999. Amended by Acts 2007, 80th Leg., ch. 593, §3.28, eff. Sept. 1, 2007; Acts 2015, 84th Leg., ch. 436, §10, eff. Jan. 1, 2016.

FAM §33.011. INFORMATION RELATING TO JUDICIAL BYPASS

The Texas Department of Health shall produce and distribute informational materials that explain the rights of a minor under this chapter. The materials must explain the procedures established by Sections 33.003 and 33.004 and must be made available in English and in Spanish. The material provided by the department shall also provide information relating to alternatives to abortion and health risks associated with abortion.

History of Fam. Code §33.011: Acts 1999, 76th Leg., ch. 395, §1, eff. Sept. 1, 1999.

FAM §33.012. CIVIL PENALTY

(a) A person who is found to have intentionally, knowingly, recklessly, or with gross negligence violated this chapter is liable to this state for a civil penalty of not less than $2,500 and not more than $10,000.

(b) Each performance or attempted performance of an abortion in violation of this chapter is a separate violation.

(c) A civil penalty may not be assessed against:

(1) a minor on whom an abortion is performed or attempted; or

(2) a judge or justice hearing a court proceeding conducted under Section 33.003 or 33.004.

(d) It is not a defense to an action brought under this section that the minor gave informed and voluntary consent.

(e) The attorney general shall bring an action to collect a penalty under this section.

History of Fam. Code §33.012: Acts 2015, 84th Leg., ch. 436, §11, eff. Jan. 1, 2016.

FAM §33.013. CAPACITY TO CONSENT

An unemancipated minor does not have the capacity to consent to any action that violates this chapter.

History of Fam. Code §33.013: Acts 2015, 84th Leg., ch. 436, §11, eff. Jan. 1, 2016.

FAM §33.014. ATTORNEY GENERAL TO ENFORCE

The attorney general shall enforce this chapter.

History of Fam. Code §33.014: Acts 2015, 84th Leg., ch. 436, §11, eff. Jan. 1, 2016.

CHAPTER 34. AUTHORIZATION AGREEMENT FOR NONPARENT ADULT CAREGIVER [~~RELATIVE~~]

FAM §34.001. REPEALED [~~APPLICABILITY~~]

[~~This chapter applies only to:~~]

[~~(1)~~] [~~an authorization agreement between a parent of a child and a person who is the child's:~~]

[~~(A)~~] [~~grandparent;~~]

[~~(B)~~] [~~adult sibling; or~~]

[~~(C)~~] [~~adult aunt or uncle; and~~]

[~~(2)~~] [~~an authorization agreement between a parent of a child and the person with whom the child is placed under a parental child safety placement agreement.~~]

Repealed by H.B. 871, §13, 85th Leg., eff. Sept. 1, 2017.

FAM §34.0015. DEFINITIONS [~~DEFINITION~~]

In this chapter:

(1) "Adult caregiver" means an adult person whom a parent has authorized to provide temporary care for a child under this chapter.

(2) "Parent"[~~, "parent"~~] has the meaning assigned by Section 101.024.

History of Fam. Code §34.0015: Acts 2011, 82nd Leg., ch. 897, §1, eff. Sept. 1, 2011. Amended by H.B. 871, §§1, 2, 85th Leg., eff. Sept. 1, 2017.

FAM §34.002. AUTHORIZATION AGREEMENT

In 2017, two bills amended subsection (a), but only one bill, H.B. 3052, §2, saved the former law in effect at that time. The amended text from H.B. 3052, §2 is effective for authorization agreements executed on or after Sept. 1, 2017. Authorization agreements executed before Sept. 1, 2017, are governed by the former law in effect at that time. The amended text from H.B. 871, §3 is effective Sept. 1, 2017.

(a) A parent or both parents of a child may enter into an authorization agreement with an adult caregiver [~~a relative of the child listed in Section 34.001~~] to authorize the adult caregiver [~~relative~~] to perform the following acts in regard to the child:

(1) to authorize medical, dental, psychological, or surgical treatment and immunization of the child, including executing any consents or authorizations for the release of information as required by law relating to the treatment or immunization;

(2) to obtain and maintain health insurance coverage for the child and automobile insurance coverage for the child, if appropriate;

(3) to enroll the child in a day-care program or preschool or in a public or private elementary or secondary school;

(4) to authorize the child to participate in age-appropriate extracurricular, civic, social, or recreational activities, including athletic activities;

(5) to authorize the child to obtain a learner's permit, driver's license, or state-issued identification card;

(6) to authorize employment of the child; [~~and~~]

(7) to apply for and receive public benefits on behalf of the child; and

(8) to obtain:

(A) copies or originals of state-issued personal identification documents for the child, including the child's birth certificate; and

(B) to the extent authorized under federal law, copies or originals of federally issued personal identification documents for the child, including the child's social security card.

(b) To the extent of any conflict or inconsistency between this chapter and any other law relating to the eligibility requirements other than parental consent to obtain a service under Subsection (a), the other law controls.

(c) An authorization agreement under this chapter does not confer on an adult caregiver [~~a relative of the child listed in Section 34.001 or a relative or other person with whom the child is placed under a child safety placement agreement~~] the right to authorize the performance of an abortion on the child or the administration of emergency contraception to the child.

(d) Only one authorization agreement may be in effect for a child at any time. An authorization agreement is void if it is executed while a prior authorization agreement remains in effect.

History of Fam. Code §34.002: Acts 2009, 81st Leg., ch. 815, §1, eff. June 19, 2009. Amended by Acts 2011, 82nd Leg., ch. 484, §2 (eff. Sept. 1, 2011), ch. 897, §2 (eff. Sept. 1, 2011); Acts 2015, 84th Leg., ch. 1167, §1, eff. Sept. 1, 2015; H.B. 871, §3, 85th Leg., eff. Sept. 1, 2017; H.B. 3052, §2, 85th Leg., eff. Sept. 1, 2017.

A FAM §34.0021. AUTHORIZATION AGREEMENT BY PARENT IN CHILD PROTECTIVE SERVICES CASE

A parent may enter into an authorization agreement with an adult caregiver [~~a relative or other person~~] with whom a child is placed under a parental child safety placement agreement approved by the Department of Family and Protective Services to allow the person to perform the acts described by Section 34.002(a) with regard to the child:

(1) during an investigation of abuse or neglect; or

(2) while the department is providing services to the parent.

History of Fam. Code §34.0021: Acts 2011, 82nd Leg., ch. 484, §3, eff. Sept. 1, 2011. Amended by H.B. 871, §4, 85th Leg., eff. Sept. 1, 2017.

E FAM §34.0022. INAPPLICABILITY OF CERTAIN LAWS

(a) An authorization agreement executed under this chapter between a child's parent and an adult caregiver does not subject the adult caregiver to any law or rule governing the licensing or regulation of a residential child-care facility under Chapter 42, Human Resources Code.

(b) A child who is the subject of an authorization agreement executed under this chapter is not considered to be placed in foster care and the parties to the authorization agreement are not subject to any law or rule governing foster care providers.

History of Fam. Code §34.0022: Enacted by H.B. 871, §5, 85th Leg., eff. Sept. 1, 2017.

A FAM §34.003. CONTENTS OF AUTHORIZATION AGREEMENT

In 2017, two bills amended §34.003, but only one bill, H.B. 3052, §3, saved the former law in effect at that time. The amended text from H.B. 3052, §3 is effective for authorization agreements executed on or after Sept. 1, 2017. Authorization agreements executed before Sept. 1, 2017, are governed by the former law in effect at that time. The amended text from H.B. 871, §6 is effective Sept. 1, 2017.

(a) The authorization agreement must contain:

(1) the following information from the adult caregiver [~~relative of the child to whom the parent is giving authorization~~]:

(A) the name and signature of the adult caregiver [~~relative~~];

(B) the adult caregiver's [~~relative's~~] relationship to the child; and

(C) the adult caregiver's [~~relative's~~] current physical address and telephone number or the best way to contact the adult caregiver [~~relative~~];

(2) the following information from the parent:

(A) the name and signature of the parent; and

(B) the parent's current address and telephone number or the best way to contact the parent;

(3) the information in Subdivision (2) with respect to the other parent, if applicable;

(4) a statement that the adult caregiver [~~relative~~] has been given authorization to perform the functions listed in Section 34.002(a) as a result of a voluntary action of the parent and that the adult caregiver [~~relative~~] has voluntarily assumed the responsibility of performing those functions;

(5) statements that neither the parent nor the adult caregiver [~~relative~~] has knowledge that a parent, guardian, custodian, licensed child-placing agency, or other authorized agency asserts any claim or authority inconsistent with the authorization agreement under this chapter with regard to actual physical possession or care, custody, or control of the child;

(6) statements that:

(A) to the best of the parent's and adult caregiver's [~~relative's~~] knowledge:

(i) there is no court order or pending suit affecting the parent-child relationship concerning the child;

(ii) there is no pending litigation in any court concerning:

(a) custody, possession, or placement of the child; or

(b) access to or visitation with the child; and

(iii) a [~~the~~] court does not have continuing jurisdiction concerning the child; or

(B) the court with continuing jurisdiction concerning the child has given written approval for the execu-

tion of the authorization agreement accompanied by the following information:

(i) the county in which the court is located;

(ii) the number of the court; and

(iii) the cause number in which the order was issued or the litigation is pending;

(7) a statement that to the best of the parent's and adult caregiver's [~~relative's~~] knowledge there is no current, valid authorization agreement regarding the child;

(8) a statement that the authorization is made in conformance with this chapter;

(9) a statement that the parent and the adult caregiver [~~relative~~] understand that each party to the authorization agreement is required by law to immediately provide to each other party information regarding any change in the party's address or contact information;

(10) a statement by the parent that:

(A) indicates the authorization agreement is for a term of:

(i) six months from the date the parties enter into the agreement, which renews automatically for six-month terms unless the agreement is terminated as provided by Section 34.008; or

(ii) the time provided in the agreement with a specific expiration date earlier than six months after the date the parties enter into the agreement; and

(B) identifies [~~establishes~~] the circumstances under which the authorization agreement may be:

(i) terminated as provided by Section 34.008 before the term of the agreement expires; or

(ii) continued beyond the term of the agreement by a court as provided by Section 34.008(b) [~~expires, including that the authorization agreement:~~]

[~~(A)~~] [~~is valid until revoked;~~]

[~~(B)~~] [~~continues in effect after the death or during any incapacity of the parent; or~~]

[~~(C)~~] [~~expires on a date stated in the authorization agreement~~]; and

(11) space for the signature and seal of a notary public.

(b) The authorization agreement must contain the following warnings and disclosures:

(1) that the authorization agreement is an important legal document;

(2) that the parent and the adult caregiver [~~relative~~] must read all of the warnings and disclosures before signing the authorization agreement;

(3) that the persons signing the authorization agreement are not required to consult an attorney but are advised to do so;

(4) that the parent's rights as a parent may be adversely affected by placing or leaving the parent's child with another person;

(5) that the authorization agreement does not confer on the adult caregiver [~~relative~~] the rights of a managing or possessory conservator or legal guardian;

(6) that a parent who is a party to the authorization agreement may terminate the authorization agreement and resume custody, possession, care, and control of the child on demand and that at any time the parent may request the return of the child;

(7) that failure by the adult caregiver [~~relative~~] to return the child to the parent immediately on request may have criminal and civil consequences;

(8) that, under other applicable law, the adult caregiver [~~relative~~] may be liable for certain expenses relating to the child in the adult caregiver's [~~relative's~~] care but that the parent still retains the parental obligation to support the child;

(9) that, in certain circumstances, the authorization agreement may not be entered into without written permission of the court;

(10) that the authorization agreement may be terminated by certain court orders affecting the child;

(11) that the authorization agreement does not supersede, invalidate, or terminate any prior authorization agreement regarding the child;

(12) that the authorization agreement is void if a prior authorization agreement regarding the child is in effect and has not expired or been terminated;

(13) that, except as provided by Section 34.005(a-2) [~~34.005(a-1)~~], the authorization agreement is void unless not later than the 10th day after the date the authorization agreement is signed, [~~:~~]

[~~(A)~~] the parties mail [~~a copy of the authorization agreement by certified mail, return receipt requested, or international registered mail, return receipt requested, as applicable,~~] to a parent who was not a party to the authorization agreement at the parent's last known address, if the parent is living and the parent's parental rights have not been terminated:

(A) one copy of the authorization agreement by certified mail, return receipt requested, or international registered mail, return receipt requested, as applicable [~~, not later than the 10th day after the date the authorization agreement is signed~~]; and

(B) one [~~if the parties do not receive a response from the parent who is not a party to the authorization agreement before the 20th day after the date the copy of the authorization agreement is mailed under Paragraph (A), the parties mail a second~~] copy of the authorization agreement by first class mail or international first class mail, as applicable [~~, to the parent not later than the 45th day after the date the authorization agreement is signed~~]; and

(14) that the authorization agreement does not confer on an adult caregiver [~~a relative of the child~~] the right to authorize the performance of an abortion on the child or the administration of emergency contraception to the child.

History of Fam. Code §34.003: Acts 2009, 81st Leg., ch. 815, §1, eff. June 19, 2009. Amended by Acts 2011, 82nd Leg., ch. 897, §3, eff. Sept. 1, 2011; H.B. 871, §6, 85th Leg., eff. Sept. 1, 2017; H.B. 3052, §3, 85th Leg., eff. Sept. 1, 2017.

FAM §34.004. EXECUTION OF AUTHORIZATION AGREEMENT

(a) The authorization agreement must be signed and sworn to before a notary public by the parent and the adult caregiver [~~relative~~].

The amended text in subsection (b) is effective for authorization agreements executed on or after Sept. 1, 2017. Authorization agreements executed before Sept. 1, 2017, are governed by the former law in effect at that time.

(b) A parent may not execute an authorization agreement without a written order by the appropriate court if:

(1) there is a court order or pending suit affecting the parent-child relationship concerning the child;

(2) there is pending litigation in any court concerning:

(A) custody, possession, or placement of the child; or

(B) access to or visitation with the child; or

(3) a [~~the~~] court has continuing, exclusive jurisdiction over the child.

(c) An authorization agreement obtained in violation of Subsection (b) is void.

History of Fam. Code §34.004: Acts 2009, 81st Leg., ch. 815, §1, eff. June 19, 2009. Amended by H.B. 871, §7, 85th Leg., eff. Sept. 1, 2017; H.B. 3052, §4, 85th Leg., eff. Sept. 1, 2017.

FAM §34.005. DUTIES OF PARTIES TO AUTHORIZATION AGREEMENT

The amended text in §34.005 is effective for authorization agreements executed on or after Sept. 1, 2017. Authorization agreements executed before Sept. 1, 2017, are governed by the former law in effect at that time.

(a) If both parents did not sign the authorization agreement, not later than the 10th day after the date the authorization agreement is executed the parties shall mail [~~a copy of the executed authorization agreement by certified mail, return receipt requested, or international registered mail, return receipt requested, as applicable,~~] to the parent who was not a party to the authorization agreement at the parent's last known address, [~~not later than the 10th day after the date the authorization agreement is executed~~] if that parent is living and that parent's parental rights have not been terminated:

(1) one copy of the executed authorization agreement by certified mail, return receipt requested, or international registered mail, return receipt requested, as applicable; and

(2) one [~~. If the parties do not receive a response from the parent who is not a party to the authorization agreement before the 20th day after the date the copy of the authorization agreement is mailed, the parties shall mail a second~~] copy of the executed authorization agreement by first class mail or international first class mail, as applicable [~~, to the parent at the same address not later than the 45th day after the date the authorization agreement is executed~~].

(a-1) Except as otherwise provided by Subsection (a-2), an [~~An~~] authorization agreement is void if the parties fail to comply with Subsection (a) [~~this subsection~~].

(a-2) [~~(a-1)~~] Subsection (a) does not apply to an authorization agreement if the parent who was not a party to the authorization agreement:

(1) does not have court-ordered possession of or access to the child who is the subject of the authorization agreement; and

(2) has previously committed an act of family violence, as defined by Section 71.004, or assault against the parent who is a party to the authorization agreement, the child who is the subject of the authorization agreement, or another child of the parent who is a party to the authorization agreement, as documented by one or more of the following:

(A) the issuance of a protective order against the parent who was not a party to the authorization agreement as provided under Chapter 85 or under a similar law of another state; or

(B) the conviction of the parent who was not a party to the authorization agreement of an offense under Title 5, Penal Code, or of another criminal offense in this state or in another state an element of which involves a violent act or prohibited sexual conduct.

(b) A party to the authorization agreement shall immediately inform each other party of any change in the party's address or contact information. If a party fails to comply with this subsection, the authorization agreement is voidable by the other party.

History of Fam. Code §34.005: Acts 2009, 81st Leg., ch. 815, §1, eff. June 19, 2009. Amended by Acts 2011, 82nd Leg., ch. 897, §4, eff. Sept. 1, 2011; H.B. 3052, §5, 85th Leg., eff. Sept. 1, 2017.

FAM §34.006. AUTHORIZATION VOIDABLE

An authorization agreement is voidable by a party if the other party knowingly:

(1) obtained the authorization agreement by fraud, duress, or misrepresentation; or

(2) made a false statement on the authorization agreement.

History of Fam. Code §34.006: Acts 2009, 81st Leg., ch. 815, §1, eff. June 19, 2009.

A FAM §34.007. EFFECT OF AUTHORIZATION AGREEMENT

(a) A person who is not a party to the authorization agreement who relies in good faith on an authorization agreement under this chapter, without actual knowledge that the authorization agreement is void, revoked, or invalid, is not subject to civil or criminal liability to any person, and is not subject to professional disciplinary action, for that reliance if the agreement is completed as required by this chapter.

(b) The authorization agreement does not affect the rights of the child's parent or legal guardian regarding the care, custody, and control of the child, and does not mean that the adult caregiver [relative] has legal custody of the child.

(c) An authorization agreement executed under this chapter does not confer or affect standing or a right of intervention in any proceeding under Title 5.

History of Fam. Code §34.007: Acts 2009, 81st Leg., ch. 815, §1, eff. June 19, 2009. Amended by H.B. 871, §8, 85th Leg., eff. Sept. 1, 2017.

E FAM §34.0075. TERM OF AUTHORIZATION AGREEMENT

An authorization agreement executed under this chapter is for a term of six months from the date the parties enter into the agreement and renews automatically for six-month terms unless:

(1) an earlier expiration date is stated in the authorization agreement;

(2) the authorization agreement is terminated as provided by Section 34.008; or

(3) a court authorizes the continuation of the agreement as provided by Section 34.008(b).

History of Fam. Code §34.0075: Enacted by H.B. 871, §9, 85th Leg., eff. Sept. 1, 2017.

A FAM §34.008. TERMINATION OF AUTHORIZATION AGREEMENT

(a) Except as provided by Subsection (b), an authorization agreement under this chapter terminates if, after the execution of the authorization agreement, a court enters an order:

(1) affecting the parent-child relationship;

(2) concerning custody, possession, or placement of the child;

(3) concerning access to or visitation with the child; or

(4) regarding the appointment of a guardian for the child under Subchapter B, Chapter 1104, Estates [Section 676, Texas Probate] Code.

(b) An authorization agreement may continue after a court order described by Subsection (a) is entered if the court entering the order gives written permission.

(c) An authorization agreement under this chapter terminates on written revocation by a party to the authorization agreement if the party:

(1) gives each party written notice of the revocation;

(2) files the written revocation with the clerk of the county in which:

(A) the child resides;

(B) the child resided at the time the authorization agreement was executed; or

(C) the adult caregiver [relative] resides; and

(3) files the written revocation with the clerk of each court:

(A) that has continuing, exclusive jurisdiction over the child;

(B) in which there is a court order or pending suit affecting the parent-child relationship concerning the child;

(C) in which there is pending litigation concerning:

(i) custody, possession, or placement of the child; or

(ii) access to or visitation with the child; or

(D) that has entered an order regarding the appointment of a guardian for the child under Subchapter B, Chapter 1104, Estates ~~[Section 676, Texas Probate]~~ Code.

(d) Repealed by H.B. 871, §13, 85th Leg., eff. Sept. 1, 2017.

~~[(d)] [If an authorization agreement executed under this chapter does not state when the authorization agreement expires, the authorization agreement is valid until revoked.]~~

(e) If both parents have signed the authorization agreement, either parent may revoke the authorization agreement without the other parent's consent.

(f) Execution of a subsequent authorization agreement does not by itself supersede, invalidate, or terminate a prior authorization agreement.

History of Fam. Code §34.008: Acts 2009, 81st Leg., ch. 815, §1, eff. June 19, 2009. Amended by Acts 2011, 82nd Leg., ch. 897, §5, eff. Sept. 1, 2011; H.B. 871, §§10, 13, 85th Leg., eff. Sept. 1, 2017; S.B. 1488, §22.017, 85th Leg., eff. Sept. 1, 2017.

FAM §34.009. PENALTY

(a) A person commits an offense if the person knowingly:

(1) presents a document that is not a valid authorization agreement as a valid authorization agreement under this chapter;

(2) makes a false statement on an authorization agreement; or

(3) obtains an authorization agreement by fraud, duress, or misrepresentation.

(b) An offense under this section is a Class B misdemeanor.

History of Fam. Code §34.009: Acts 2009, 81st Leg., ch. 815, §1, eff. June 19, 2009.

CHAPTER 35. TEMPORARY AUTHORIZATION FOR CARE OF MINOR CHILD

FAM §35.001. APPLICABILITY

This chapter applies to a person whose relationship to a child would make the person eligible to consent to treatment under Section 32.001 or eligible to enter an authorization agreement under Section 34.001.

History of Fam. Code §35.001: Enacted by H.B. 1043, §1, 85th Leg., eff. June 1, 2017.

FAM §35.002. TEMPORARY AUTHORIZATION

A person described by Section 35.001 may seek a court order for temporary authorization for care of a child by filing a petition in the district court in the county in which the person resides if:

(1) the child has resided with the person for at least the 30 days preceding the date the petition was filed; and

(2) the person does not have an authorization agreement under Chapter 34 or other signed, written documentation from a parent, conservator, or guardian that enables the person to provide necessary care for the child.

History of Fam. Code §35.002: Enacted by H.B. 1043, §1, 85th Leg., eff. June 1, 2017.

FAM §35.003. PETITION FOR TEMPORARY AUTHORIZATION FOR CARE OF CHILD

(a) A petition for temporary authorization for care of a child must:

(1) be styled "ex parte" and be in the name of the child;

(2) be verified by the petitioner;

(3) state:

(A) the name, date of birth, and current physical address of the child;

(B) the name, date of birth, and current physical address of the petitioner; and

(C) the name and, if known, the current physical and mailing addresses of the child's parents, conservators, or guardians;

(4) describe the status and location of any court proceeding in this or another state with respect to the child;

(5) describe the petitioner's relationship to the child;

(6) provide the dates during the preceding 12 months that the child has resided with the petitioner;

(7) describe any service or action that the petitioner is unable to obtain or undertake on behalf of the child without authorization from the court;

(8) state any reason that the petitioner is unable to obtain signed, written documentation from a parent, conservator, or guardian of the child;

(9) contain a statement of the period for which the petitioner is requesting temporary authorization; and

(10) contain a statement of any reason supporting the request for the temporary authorization.

(b) If the petition identifies a court proceeding with respect to the child under Subsection (a)(4), the petitioner shall submit a copy of any court order that designates a conservator or guardian of the child.

History of Fam. Code §35.003: Enacted by H.B. 1043, §1, 85th Leg., eff. June 1, 2017.

FAM §35.004. NOTICE; HEARING

(a) On receipt of the petition, the court shall set a hearing.

(b) A copy of the petition and notice of the hearing shall be delivered to the parent, conservator, or guardian of the child by personal service or by certified mail, return receipt requested, at the last known address of the parent, conservator, or guardian.

(c) Proof of service under Subsection (b) must be filed with the court at least three days before the date of the hearing.

History of Fam. Code §35.004: Enacted by H.B. 1043, §1, 85th Leg., eff. June 1, 2017.

FAM §35.005. ORDER FOR TEMPORARY AUTHORIZATION

(a) At the hearing on the petition, the court may hear evidence relating to the child's need for care by the petitioner, any other matter raised in the petition, and any objection or other testimony of the child's parent, conservator, or guardian.

(b) The court shall award temporary authorization for care of the child to the petitioner if the court finds it is necessary to the child's welfare and no objection is made by the child's parent, conservator, or guardian. If an objection is made, the court shall dismiss the petition without prejudice.

(c) The court shall grant the petition for temporary authorization only if the court finds by a preponderance of the evidence that the child does not have a parent, conservator, guardian, or other legal representative available to give the necessary consent.

(d) The order granting temporary authorization under this chapter expires on the first anniversary of the date of issuance or at an earlier date determined by the court. The order may authorize the petitioner to:

(1) consent to medical, dental, psychological, and surgical treatment and immunization of the child;

(2) execute any consent or authorization for the release of information as required by law relating to the treatment or immunization under Subdivision (1);

(3) obtain and maintain any public benefit for the child;

(4) enroll the child in a day-care program, preschool, or public or private primary or secondary school;

(5) authorize the child to participate in age-appropriate extracurricular, civic, social, or recreational activities, including athletic activities; and

(6) authorize or consent to any other care for the child essential to the child's welfare.

(e) An order granting temporary authorization under this chapter must state:

(1) the name and date of birth of the person with temporary authorization to care for the child;

(2) the specific areas of authorization granted to the person;

(3) that the order does not supersede any rights of a parent, conservator, or guardian as provided by court order; and

(4) the expiration date of the temporary authorization order.

(f) A copy of an order for temporary authorization must:

(1) be filed under the cause number in any court that has rendered a conservatorship or guardian order regarding the child; and

(2) be sent to the last known address of the child's parent, conservator, or guardian.

History of Fam. Code §35.005: Enacted by H.B. 1043, §1, 85th Leg., eff. June 1, 2017.

FAM §35.006. RENEWAL OR TERMINATION OF TEMPORARY AUTHORIZATION

(a) A temporary authorization order may be renewed by court order for a period of not more than one year on a showing by the petitioner of a continuing need for the order.

(b) At any time, the petitioner or the child's parent, conservator, or guardian may request the court to terminate the order. The court shall terminate the order on finding that there is no longer a need for the order.

History of Fam. Code §35.006: Enacted by H.B. 1043, §1, 85th Leg., eff. June 1, 2017.

FAM §35.007. EFFECT OF TEMPORARY AUTHORIZATION

(a) A person who relies in good faith on a temporary authorization order under this chapter is not subject to:

(1) civil or criminal liability to any person; or

(2) professional disciplinary action.

(b) A temporary authorization order does not affect the rights of the child's parent, conservator, or guardian regarding the care, custody, and control of the child, and does not establish legal custody of the child.

(c) A temporary authorization order does not confer or affect standing or a right of intervention in any proceeding under Title 5.

(d) An order under this chapter is not a child custody determination and does not create a court of continuing, exclusive jurisdiction under Title 5.

History of Fam. Code §35.007: Enacted by H.B. 1043, §1, 85th Leg., eff. June 1, 2017.

Chapters 36-40 reserved for expansion

SUBTITLE B. PARENTAL LIABILITY

CHAPTER 41. LIABILITY OF PARENTS FOR CONDUCT OF CHILD

FAM §41.001. LIABILITY

A parent or other person who has the duty of control and reasonable discipline of a child is liable for any property damage proximately caused by:

(1) the negligent conduct of the child if the conduct is reasonably attributable to the negligent failure of the parent or other person to exercise that duty; or

(2) the wilful and malicious conduct of a child who is at least 10 years of age but under 18 years of age.

History of Fam. Code §41.001: Acts 1995, 74th Leg., ch. 20, §1, eff. Apr. 20, 1995. Amended by Acts 2001, 77th Leg., ch. 587, §1, eff. Sept. 1, 2001. Source: Former Fam. Code §33.01.

See also ***O'Connor's Texas Family Law Handbook*** (2017), "Property damage," ch. 1-D, §3.1.2(4), p. 56.

ANNOTATIONS

Isbell v. Ryan, 983 S.W.2d 335, 339 (Tex.App.—Houston [14th Dist.] 1998, no pet.). "As a general rule, defendants have no duty to prevent the criminal acts of a third party who does not act under defendants' supervision or control. This general rule does not apply in situations where a special relationship exists between the actor and the third person. One such exception to the rule is the parent-child relationship."

Prather v. Brandt, 981 S.W.2d 801, 806-07 (Tex. App.—Houston [1st Dist.] 1998, pet. denied). "As a general rule, minors are civilly liable for their own torts. A parent may be liable if the parent negligently allows his child to act in a manner likely to harm another, if he gives his child a dangerous instrumentality, or if he does not restrain a child known to have dangerous tendencies. A parent's duty to protect third parties from his child's acts depends on whether the injury to the third party is foreseeable. Foreseeability is evaluated by looking at the parent's knowledge of, consent to, or participation in the child's activity."

Williams v. Lavender, 797 S.W.2d 410, 412 (Tex. App.—Fort Worth 1990, writ denied). "While [D] is correct that the purpose of [Fam. Code §33.01, now §41.001,] is to protect and compensate property owners from the willful and malicious destruction of their property by minors, still, the statute expressly recognizes that a child between the ages of 12 and 18 is capable of willful and malicious conduct. Therefore, it cannot be said that as a matter of law a minor who is 14 years old cannot form the necessary malicious intent to warrant recovery of exemplary damages."

Amarillo Nat'l Bank v. Terry, 658 S.W.2d 702, 704 (Tex.App.—Amarillo 1983, no writ). "By the terms of [Fam. Code §33.01, now §41.001,] liability is imposed on the parent or other person for 'property damage.' [T]he legislative intent 'is to protect and compensate property owners from the wilful and malicious *destruction* of their property by minors.' But, giving the phrase the meaning in which it is ordinarily understood, there was no property damage proximately caused by the unauthorized withdrawals of money, for there was no damage inflicted on, much less a destruction of, the money the bank lost. Instead, the bank suffered only an economic loss and, therefore, the bank was not caused property damage within the meaning of the statute."

FAM §41.002. LIMIT OF DAMAGES

Recovery for damage caused by wilful and malicious conduct is limited to actual damages, not to exceed $25,000 per occurrence, plus court costs and reasonable attorney's fees.

History of Fam. Code §41.002: Acts 1995, 74th Leg., ch. 20, §1, eff. Apr. 20, 1995. Amended by Acts 1997, 75th Leg., ch. 783, §1, eff. Sept. 1, 1997. Source: Former Fam. Code §33.02.

FAM §41.0025. LIABILITY FOR PROPERTY DAMAGE TO AN INN OR HOTEL

(a) Notwithstanding Section 41.002, recovery of damages by an inn or hotel for wilful and malicious conduct is limited to actual damages, not to exceed $25,000 per occurrence, plus court costs and reasonable attorney's fees.

(b) In this section "occurrence" means one incident on a single day in one hotel room. The term does not include incidents in separate rooms or incidents that occur on different days.

History of Fam. Code §41.0025: Acts 1997, 75th Leg., ch. 40, §1, eff. Sept. 1, 1997.

FAM §41.003. VENUE

A suit as provided by this chapter may be filed in the county in which the conduct of the child occurred or in the county in which the defendant resides.

History of Fam. Code §41.003: Acts 1995, 74th Leg., ch. 20, §1, eff. Apr. 20, 1995. Source: Former Fam. Code §33.03.

CHAPTER 42. CIVIL LIABILITY FOR INTERFERENCE WITH POSSESSORY INTEREST IN CHILD

FAM §42.001. DEFINITIONS

In this chapter:

(1) "Order" means a temporary or final order of a court of this state or another state or nation.

(2) "Possessory right" means a court-ordered right of possession of or access to a child, including conservatorship, custody, and visitation.

History of Fam. Code §42.001: Acts 1995, 74th Leg., ch. 20, §1, eff. Apr. 20, 1995. Source: Former Fam. Code §36.01.

FAM §42.002. LIABILITY FOR INTERFERENCE WITH POSSESSORY RIGHT

(a) A person who takes or retains possession of a child or who conceals the whereabouts of a child in violation of a possessory right of another person may be liable for damages to that person.

(b) A possessory right is violated by the taking, retention, or concealment of a child at a time when another person is entitled to possession of or access to the child.

History of Fam. Code §42.002: Acts 1995, 74th Leg., ch. 20, §1, eff. Apr. 20, 1995. Source: Former Fam. Code §36.02(a), (b).

See also *O'Connor's Texas Family Law Handbook* (2017), "Petition for Interference with Possessory Interest in Child," ch. 11-E, p. 1217.

ANNOTATIONS

In re T.M.P., 417 S.W.3d 557, 566 (Tex.App.—El Paso 2013, no pet.). Mother and maternal grandparents "contend that the paternal grandparents had no possessory rights and therefore lacked standing to file suit under ch. 42.... *At 567:* The role of the paternal grandparents was merely to supervise Father's visits with the children and facilitate transportation between Texas and South Carolina. [Paternal grandparents] infer that as [court-ordered] chaperones, they were granted 'access.' We conclude that while they were certainly facilitators of Father's possessory rights, they were granted no independent rights. Because they lack standing to bring a suit for tortious interference, they are not entitled to recover damages."

FAM §42.003. AIDING OR ASSISTING INTERFERENCE WITH POSSESSORY RIGHT

(a) A person who aids or assists in conduct for which a cause of action is authorized by this chapter is jointly and severally liable for damages.

(b) A person who was not a party to the suit in which an order was rendered providing for a possessory right is not liable unless the person at the time of the violation:

(1) had actual notice of the existence and contents of the order; or

(2) had reasonable cause to believe that the child was the subject of an order and that the person's actions were likely to violate the order.

History of Fam. Code §42.003: Acts 1995, 74th Leg., ch. 20, §1, eff. Apr. 20, 1995. Source: Former Fam. Code §36.02(c), (d).

See also *O'Connor's Texas Family Law Handbook* (2017), "Aiding or assisting interference with possessory right," ch. 11-E, §3.2, p. 1219.

ANNOTATIONS

Bos v. Smith, 492 S.W.3d 361, 383 (Tex.App.—Corpus Christi 2016, pet. filed 6-24-16). "[W]hen evaluating whether a person's aiding and assisting the violation of a possession order proximately caused the claimant's damages [under §42.003], 'the relevant cause is violation of the court order, not the actions of those allegedly aiding and assisting the person violating the court order.' In other words, the relevant inquiry is not whether the defendant's aid or assistance caused the plaintiff to suffer harm, but whether the primary actor's conduct—which the defendants aided and assisted—caused the plaintiff to suffer harm."

FAM §42.004. REPEALED

Repealed by Acts 1999, 76th Leg., ch. 437, §2, eff. Sept. 1, 1999.

FAM §42.005. VENUE

A suit may be filed in a county in which:

(1) the plaintiff resides;

(2) the defendant resides;

(3) a suit affecting the parent-child relationship as provided by Chapter 102 may be brought, concerning the child who is the subject of the court order; or

(4) a court has continuing, exclusive jurisdiction as provided by Chapter 155.

History of Fam. Code §42.005: Acts 1995, 74th Leg., ch. 20, §1, eff. Apr. 20, 1995. Source: Former Fam. Code §36.05.

See also ***O'Connor's Texas Family Law Handbook*** (2017), "Where to file," ch. 11-E, §4.3, p. 1221.

FAM §42.006. DAMAGES

(a) Damages may include:

(1) the actual costs and expenses incurred, including attorney's fees, in:

(A) locating a child who is the subject of the order;

(B) recovering possession of the child if the petitioner is entitled to possession; and

(C) enforcing the order and prosecuting the suit; and

(2) mental suffering and anguish incurred by the plaintiff because of a violation of the order.

(b) A person liable for damages who acted with malice or with an intent to cause harm to the plaintiff may be liable for exemplary damages.

History of Fam. Code §42.006: Acts 1995, 74th Leg., ch. 20, §1, eff. Apr. 20, 1995. Amended by Acts 1995, 74th Leg., ch. 751, §7, eff. Sept. 1, 1995. Source: Former Fam. Code §36.03.

See also ***O'Connor's Texas Family Law Handbook*** (2017), "Relief," ch. 11-E, §4.4.7, p. 1222.

ANNOTATIONS

Bos v. Smith, 492 S.W.3d 361, 386 (Tex.App.—Corpus Christi 2016, pet. filed 6-24-16). "[I]t is apparent from the record that a significant portion of the [attorney fees] paid by [father] to [attorney's] firm was not attributable to 'recovering possession' of [children] or 'enforcing the order and prosecuting the suit' relating to [grandparents'] interference with [father's] possessory rights. Instead, the only testimony relevant to the issue provided that 'most if not all' of the ... fees incurred by [father were] attributable to defending [father] from the false charges of [child] abuse, which is not recoverable under [§42.006(a)(1)]. Accordingly, the evidence was factually insufficient to support the award."

Smith v. Smith, 720 S.W.2d 586, 601 (Tex.App.—Houston [1st Dist.] 1986, no writ). "We hold that 'actual costs and expenses,' as used in [Fam. Code] §36.03 [now §42.006], includes prospective costs and expenses that are supported by the evidence."

FAM §42.007. AFFIRMATIVE DEFENSE

The defendant may plead as an affirmative defense that the defendant acted in violation of the order with the express consent of the plaintiff.

History of Fam. Code §42.007: Acts 1995, 74th Leg., ch. 20, §1, eff. Apr. 20, 1995. Amended by Acts 1999, 76th Leg., ch. 437, §1, eff. Sept. 1, 1999. Source: Former Fam. Code §36.04.

See also ***O'Connor's Texas Family Law Handbook*** (2017), "Affirmative defenses," ch. 11-E, §6.3.3(6), p. 1224.

FAM §42.008. REMEDIES NOT AFFECTED

This chapter does not affect any other civil or criminal remedy available to any person, including the child, for interference with a possessory right, nor does it affect the power of a parent to represent the interest of a child in a suit filed on behalf of the child.

History of Fam. Code §42.008: Acts 1995, 74th Leg., ch. 20, §1, eff. Apr. 20, 1995. Source: Former Fam. Code §36.06.

FAM §42.009. FRIVOLOUS SUIT

A person sued for damages as provided by this chapter is entitled to recover attorney's fees and court costs if:

(1) the claim for damages is dismissed or judgment is awarded to the defendant; and

(2) the court or jury finds that the claim for damages is frivolous, unreasonable, or without foundation.

History of Fam. Code §42.009: Acts 1995, 74th Leg., ch. 20, §1, eff. Apr. 20, 1995. Source: Former Fam. Code §36.08.

See also *O'Connor's Texas Family Law Handbook* (2017), "Attorney fees & costs," ch. 11-E, §6.3.3(8), p. 1224.

Chapters 43 & 44 reserved for expansion

SUBTITLE C. CHANGE OF NAME

CHAPTER 45. CHANGE OF NAME

SUBCHAPTER A. CHANGE OF NAME OF CHILD

FAM §45.001. WHO MAY FILE; VENUE

A parent, managing conservator, or guardian of a child may file a petition requesting a change of name of the child in the county where the child resides.

History of Fam. Code §45.001: Acts 1995, 74th Leg., ch. 20, §1, eff. Apr. 20, 1995. Source: Former Fam. Code §§32.01, 32.02(a).

FAM §45.002. REQUIREMENTS OF PETITION

(a) A petition to change the name of a child must be verified and include:

(1) the present name and place of residence of the child;

(2) the reason a change of name is requested;

(3) the full name requested for the child;

(4) whether the child is subject to the continuing exclusive jurisdiction of a court under Chapter 155; and

(5) whether the child is subject to the registration requirements of Chapter 62, Code of Criminal Procedure.

(b) If the child is 10 years of age or older, the child's written consent to the change of name must be attached to the petition.

History of Fam. Code §45.002: Acts 1995, 74th Leg., ch. 20, §1, eff. Apr. 20, 1995. Amended by Acts 1999, 76th Leg., ch. 1390, §1, eff. Sept. 1, 1999; Acts 2003, 78th Leg., ch. 1300, §5, eff. Sept. 1, 2003. Source: Former Fam. Code §32.02.

See also *O'Connor's Texas Family Law Handbook* (2017), "Child's Name Change," ch. 1-F, §2, p. 75.

ANNOTATIONS

In re R.E.G., No. 13-08-00335-CV (Tex.App.—Corpus Christi 2009, pet. denied) (memo op.; 11-12-09). "[A] court that orders a child's name changed to a name other than the name requested [under Fam. Code §45.002] does not necessarily abuse its discretion. [Family Code] §45.004(a) provides that a trial court may order a child's name changed if the change is in the child's best interest. ... Crafting a remedy that combines the last names of both parents does not constitute an abuse of discretion where the orders are derived from the facts of the case."

FAM §45.003. CITATION

(a) The following persons are entitled to citation in a suit under this subchapter:

(1) a parent of the child whose parental rights have not been terminated;

(2) any managing conservator of the child; and

(3) any guardian of the child.

(b) Citation must be issued and served in the same manner as under Chapter 102.

History of Fam. Code §45.003: Acts 1995, 74th Leg., ch. 20, §1, eff. Apr. 20, 1995. Source: Former Fam. Code §32.03.

FAM §45.0031. WAIVER OF CITATION

(a) A party to a suit under this subchapter may waive the issuance or service of citation after the suit is filed by filing with the clerk of the court in which the suit is filed the waiver of the party acknowledging receipt of a copy of the filed petition.

(b) The party executing the waiver may not sign the waiver using a digitized signature.

(c) The waiver must contain the mailing address of the party executing the waiver.

(d) Notwithstanding Section 132.001, Civil Practice and Remedies Code, the waiver must be sworn before a notary public who is not an attorney in the suit. This subsection does not apply if the party executing the waiver is incarcerated.

(e) The Texas Rules of Civil Procedure do not apply to a waiver executed under this section.

(f) For purposes of this section, "digitized signature" has the meaning assigned by Section 101.0096.

History of Fam. Code §45.0031: Acts 2015, 84th Leg., ch. 198, §3, eff. Sept. 1, 2015.

See also *O'Connor's Texas Family Law Handbook* (2017), "Waiver of service," ch. 1-F, §2.1.6(3), p. 78.

FAM §45.004. ORDER

(a) The court may order the name of a child changed if:

(1) the change is in the best interest of the child; and

(2) for a child subject to the registration requirements of Chapter 62, Code of Criminal Procedure:

(A) the change is in the interest of the public; and

(B) the person petitioning on behalf of the child provides the court with proof that the child has notified the appropriate local law enforcement authority of the proposed name change.

(b) If the child is subject to the continuing jurisdiction of a court under Chapter 155, the court shall send a copy of the order to the central record file as provided in Chapter 108.

(c) In this section, "local law enforcement authority" has the meaning assigned by Article 62.001, Code of Criminal Procedure.

History of Fam. Code §45.004: Acts 1995, 74th Leg., ch. 20, §1, eff. Apr. 20, 1995. Amended by Acts 2003, 78th Leg., ch. 1300, §6, eff. Sept. 1, 2003; Acts 2005, 79th Leg., ch. 1008, §2.05, eff. Sept. 1, 2005. Source: Former Fam. Code §32.04.

ANNOTATIONS

In re C.M.V., 479 S.W.3d 352, 358 (Tex.App.—El Paso 2015, no pet.). See annotation under Family Code §160.636, p. 740.

Anderson v. Dainard, 478 S.W.3d 147, 151 (Tex. App.—Houston [1st Dist.] 2015, no pet.). See annotation under Family Code §160.636, p. 740.

In re H.S.B., 401 S.W.3d 77, 81 (Tex.App.—Houston [14th Dist.] 2011, no pet.). "We hold that a court may consider evidence of tradition when determining if it is in a child's best interest to order a name change, but tradition alone is an insufficient ground for changing a child's name. *At 84-85:* [Additionally,] we specifically reject three factors previously enunciated by other courts of appeals. [I]n ***In re Guthrie*** [below], the court determined that the embarrassment or inconvenience of the custodial parent was a factor.... We find such considerations have no bearing on whether a name change is in the *child's* best interest, and they inappropriately shift the inquiry to the parents' interests. [¶] We also abandon both the factor regarding the delay in requesting or objecting to a name change and the factor that considers a parent's financial support. These factors ... serve to reward or punish parents for their conduct unrelated to the name change." *See also* ***In re A.E.M.***, 455 S.W.3d 684, 690-92 (Tex.App.—Houston [1st Dist.] 2014, no pet.) (analyzing case using ***H.S.B.*** factors). *But see* ***In re Guthrie***, this page.

In re R.E.G., No. 13-08-00335-CV (Tex.App.—Corpus Christi 2009, pet. denied) (memo op.; 11-12-09). See annotation under Family Code §45.002, p. 180.

In re Guthrie, 45 S.W.3d 719, 723-24 (Tex.App.—Dallas 2001, pet. denied). "A father has no constitutional right to have his children bear his last name. The only protectable interest a father has in a child's name recognized by Texas courts is when the mother attempts to change the child's surname from the father's. [¶] The standards for changing the name of a minor are controlled by the ... Family Code. ... The general rule is that courts will exercise the power to change a child's name reluctantly and only when the substantial welfare of the child requires it. A parent's interest and desire is only a secondary consideration. Texas has no statute giving the right to name a child to either parent. However, the name chosen by one of the parents will not be changed unless the dissident parent shows a good reason for such change. *At 725-26:* Therefore, we consider the factors that address the best interest of the child, not the needs of a particular parent, or customs or traditions that reflect a constitutionally prohibited inequality [such as giving preference to one parent's name over another on the basis of whether the parent is the father or mother]. Factors that have been considered proper in a best interest test are: [1] whether the changed name or the present name would best avoid embarrassment, inconvenience, or confusion for the custodial parent or the child; [2] whether it would be more convenient or easier for the child to have the same name as or a different name from the custodial parent, either the changed name or the present name; [3] whether the changed name or the present name would help identify the child as part of a family unit; [4] the length of time the surname has been used; [5] parental misconduct, such as support or nonsupport or maintaining or failing to maintain contact with the child; [6] the degree of community respect associated with the present or changed name; [7] whether the change will positively or adversely affect the bond between the child and either parent or the parents' families; [8] any delay in requesting or objecting to name change; [9] the preferences of the child; [10] the age and maturity of the child; [11] when the

child maintains the mother's surname, assurances by the mother that she would not change her name if she married or remarried; and [12] whether the parent seeking the change is motivated by an attempt to alienate the child from the other parent." *See also* ***In re A.E.M.***, 455 S.W.3d 684, 690-92 (Tex.App.—Houston [1st Dist.] 2014, no pet.) (mere existence of another child who bears father's last name and who might periodically see child does not establish that substantial welfare of child requires name change); ***Scoggins v. Treviño***, 200 S.W.3d 832, 837-42 (Tex.App.—Corpus Christi 2006, no pet.) (analyzing case using ***Guthrie*** factors); ***Brown v. Carroll***, 683 S.W.2d 61, 63 (Tex. App.—Tyler 1984, no writ) (child's preference is not controlling when determining whether it is in child's best interest to allow name change). *But see* ***In re H.S.B.***, p. 181.

FAM §45.005. LIABILITIES & RIGHTS UNAFFECTED

A change of name does not:

(1) release a child from any liability incurred in the child's previous name; or

(2) defeat any right the child had in the child's previous name.

History of Fam. Code §45.005: Acts 1995, 74th Leg., ch. 20, §1, eff. Apr. 20, 1995. Source: Former Fam. Code §32.05.

Sections 45.006-45.100 reserved for expansion

SUBCHAPTER B. CHANGE OF NAME OF ADULT

FAM §45.101. WHO MAY FILE; VENUE

An adult may file a petition requesting a change of name in the county of the adult's place of residence.

History of Fam. Code §45.101: Acts 1995, 74th Leg., ch. 20, §1, eff. Apr. 20, 1995. Source: Former Fam. Code §32.21(a).

FAM §45.102. REQUIREMENTS OF PETITION

(a) A petition to change the name of an adult must be verified and include:

(1) the present name and place of residence of the petitioner;

(2) the full name requested for the petitioner;

(3) the reason the change in name is requested;

(4) whether the petitioner has been the subject of a final felony conviction;

(5) whether the petitioner is subject to the registration requirements of Chapter 62, Code of Criminal Procedure; and

(6) a legible and complete set of the petitioner's fingerprints on a fingerprint card format acceptable to the Department of Public Safety and the Federal Bureau of Investigation.

(b) The petition must include each of the following or a reasonable explanation why the required information is not included:

(1) the petitioner's:

(A) full name;

(B) sex;

(C) race;

(D) date of birth;

(E) driver's license number for any driver's license issued in the 10 years preceding the date of the petition;

(F) social security number; and

(G) assigned FBI number, state identification number, if known, or any other reference number in a criminal history record system that identifies the petitioner;

(2) any offense above the grade of Class C misdemeanor for which the petitioner has been charged; and

(3) the case number and the court if a warrant was issued or a charging instrument was filed or presented for an offense listed in Subsection (b)(2).

History of Fam. Code §45.102: Acts 1995, 74th Leg., ch. 20, §1, eff. Apr. 20, 1995. Amended by Acts 2003, 78th Leg., ch. 1003, §1 (eff. Sept. 1, 2003), ch. 1300, §7 (eff. Sept. 1, 2003); Acts 2005, 79th Leg., ch. 728, §6.001, eff. Sept. 1, 2005. Source: Former Fam. Code §32.21(a), (b).

See also ***O'Connor's Texas Family Law Handbook*** (2017), "Adult's Name Change," ch. 1-F, §3, p. 79.

FAM §45.103. ORDER

(a) The court shall order a change of name under this subchapter for a person other than a person with a final felony conviction or a person subject to the registration requirements of Chapter 62, Code of Criminal Procedure, if the change is in the interest or to the benefit of the petitioner and in the interest of the public.

(b) A court may order a change of name under this subchapter for a person with a final felony conviction if, in addition to the requirements of Subsection (a), the person has:

(1) received a certificate of discharge by the Texas Department of Criminal Justice or completed a period of community supervision or juvenile probation ordered by a court and not less than two years have passed from the date of the receipt of discharge or completion of community supervision or juvenile probation; or

(2) been pardoned.

(c) A court may order a change of name under this subchapter for a person subject to the registration requirements of Chapter 62, Code of Criminal Procedure, if, in addition to the requirements of Subsection (a), the person provides the court with proof that the person has notified the appropriate local law enforcement authority of the proposed name change. In this subsection, "local law enforcement authority" has the meaning assigned by Article 62.001, Code of Criminal Procedure.

History of Fam. Code §45.103: Acts 1995, 74th Leg., ch. 20, §1, eff. Apr. 20, 1995. Amended by Acts 2003, 78th Leg., ch. 1300, §8, eff. Sept. 1, 2003; Acts 2005, 79th Leg., ch. 1008, §2.06, eff. Sept. 1, 2005; Acts 2009, 81st Leg., ch. 87, §25.057, eff. Sept. 1, 2009. Source: Former Fam. Code §32.22.

ANNOTATIONS

In re Dickey, 919 S.W.2d 790, 791 (Tex.App.—Texarkana 1996, no writ). Petitioner contends "on appeal that the prohibition in [§45.103] against name changes for persons convicted of a felony refers only to felonies occurring within the State of Texas. We disagree. To limit the restrictions on name changes for felons only to convictions in Texas would subvert the purpose of the statute, *viz*, to protect the legitimate governmental interest of being able to identify persons sought on warrant and detainer and to preserve the criminal history of felons."

In re Erickson, 547 S.W.2d 357, 359 (Tex.App.—Houston [14th Dist.] 1977, no writ). "Generally, the grant of an application for change of name is a matter of judicial discretion and should be granted unless there exists some wrongful, fraudulent, or capricious purpose. [¶] It is enough that for her own proper reasons, [petitioner] conscientiously feels the necessity of being known and referred to by her previous name. To deny her this right would be a violation of equal protection under the law by creating an invalid classification based on sex. [¶] We would not like to be understood as holding that a person has the absolute right to change his name by court order. Although the petitioner is ordinarily the only party before the court, the trial judge may appropriately inquire into matters, other than sex, which would authorize him to refuse to give legal sanction to a change of name." *See also* ***In re Mayol***, 137 S.W.3d 103, 105 (Tex.App.—Houston [1st Dist.] 2004, no pet.) (not abuse of discretion to deny request for change of name when applicant could not prove he was person named on birth certificate).

FAM §45.104. LIABILITIES & RIGHTS UNAFFECTED

A change of name under this subchapter does not release a person from liability incurred in that person's previous name or defeat any right the person had in the person's previous name.

History of Fam. Code §45.104: Acts 1995, 74th Leg., ch. 20, §1, eff. Apr. 20, 1995. Source: Former Fam. Code §32.23.

FAM §45.105. CHANGE OF NAME IN DIVORCE SUIT

(a) On the final disposition of a suit for divorce, for annulment, or to declare a marriage void, the court shall enter a decree changing the name of a party specially praying for the change to a prior used name unless the court states in the decree a reason for denying the change of name. The court may not deny a change of name solely to keep last names of family members the same.

(b) A person whose name is changed under this section may apply for a change of name certificate from the clerk of the court as provided by Section 45.106.

History of Fam. Code §45.105: Acts 1997, 75th Leg., ch. 165, §7.10(a), eff. Sept. 1, 1997.

FAM §45.106. CHANGE OF NAME CERTIFICATE

(a) A person whose name is changed under Section 6.706 or 45.105 may apply to the clerk of the court ordering the name change for a change of name certificate.

(b) A certificate under this section is a one-page document that includes:

(1) the name of the person before the change of name was ordered;

(2) the name to which the person's name was changed by the court;

(3) the date on which the name change was made;

(4) the person's social security number and driver's license number, if any;

(5) the name of the court in which the name change was ordered; and

(6) the signature of the clerk of the court that issued the certificate.

(c) An applicant for a certificate under this section shall pay a $10 fee to the clerk of the court for issuance of the certificate.

(d) A certificate under this section constitutes proof of the change of name of the person named in the certificate.

History of Fam. Code §45.106: Acts 1997, 75th Leg., ch. 165, §7.10(a), eff. Sept. 1, 1997. Amended by Acts 1999, 76th Leg., ch. 62, §6.06, eff. Sept. 1, 1999.

FAM §45.107. WAIVER OF CITATION

(a) A party to a suit under this subchapter may waive the issuance or service of citation after the suit is filed by filing with the clerk of the court in which the suit is filed the waiver of the party acknowledging receipt of a copy of the filed petition.

(b) The party executing the waiver may not sign the waiver using a digitized signature.

(c) The waiver must contain the mailing address of the party executing the waiver.

(d) Notwithstanding Section 132.001, Civil Practice and Remedies Code, the waiver must be sworn before a notary public who is not an attorney in the suit. This subsection does not apply if the party executing the waiver is incarcerated.

(e) The Texas Rules of Civil Procedure do not apply to a waiver executed under this section.

(f) For purposes of this section, "digitized signature" has the meaning assigned by Section 101.0096.

History of Fam. Code §45.107: Acts 2015, 84th Leg., ch. 198, §4, eff. Sept. 1, 2015.

Subtitle D blank

SUBTITLE E. GENERAL PROVISIONS

CHAPTER 47. GENERAL PROVISIONS

FAM §47.001. APPLICABILITY OF DEFINITIONS

(a) Except as provided by Subsection (b), the definitions in Chapter 101 apply to terms used in this title.

(b) If a term defined in this title has a meaning different from the meaning provided by Chapter 101, the meaning provided by this title prevails.

History of Fam. Code §47.001: Acts 2015, 84th Leg., ch. 612, §1, eff. Sept. 1, 2015. Reenacted by S.B. 1488, §7.001, 85th Leg., eff. Sept. 1, 2017.

FAM §47.002. APPLICABILITY OF LAWS RELATING TO ATTORNEYS AD LITEM, GUARDIANS AD LITEM, & AMICUS ATTORNEYS

Chapter 107 applies to the appointment of an attorney ad litem, guardian ad litem, or amicus attorney under this title.

History of Fam. Code §47.002: Acts 2015, 84th Leg., ch. 612, §1, eff. Sept. 1, 2015. Reenacted by S.B. 1488, §7.001, 85th Leg., eff. Sept. 1, 2017.

FAM §47.003 ~~[47.001]~~. USE OF DIGITIZED SIGNATURE

(a) A digitized signature on an original petition or application under this title or any other pleading or order in a proceeding under this title satisfies the requirements for and imposes the duties of signatories to pleadings, motions, and other papers identified under Rule 13, Texas Rules of Civil Procedure.

(b) A digitized signature under this section may be applied only by, and must remain under the sole control of, the person whose signature is represented.

~~[(c)] [In this section, "digitized signature" has the meaning assigned by Section 101.0096.]~~

History of Fam. Code §47.003: Acts 2015, 84th Leg., ch. 1165, §2, eff. Sept. 1, 2015. Reenacted and amended by S.B. 1488, §7.001, 85th Leg., eff. Sept. 1, 2017.

Chapters 48-50 blank

FAMILY CODE—TITLE 3

JUVENILE JUSTICE CODE
TABLE OF CONTENTS

TITLE 3. JUVENILE JUSTICE CODE

FAMILY CODE—TITLE 3
JUVENILE JUSTICE CODE
TABLE OF CONTENTS

JUVENILE JUSTICE CODE

TABLE OF CONTENTS

TITLE 3. JUVENILE JUSTICE CODE

CHAPTER 51. GENERAL PROVISIONS

FAM §51.01. PURPOSE & INTERPRETATION

This title shall be construed to effectuate the following public purposes:

(1) to provide for the protection of the public and public safety;

(2) consistent with the protection of the public and public safety:

(A) to promote the concept of punishment for criminal acts;

(B) to remove, where appropriate, the taint of criminality from children committing certain unlawful acts; and

(C) to provide treatment, training, and rehabilitation that emphasizes the accountability and responsibility of both the parent and the child for the child's conduct;

(3) to provide for the care, the protection, and the wholesome moral, mental, and physical development of children coming within its provisions;

(4) to protect the welfare of the community and to control the commission of unlawful acts by children;

(5) to achieve the foregoing purposes in a family environment whenever possible, separating the child from the child's parents only when necessary for the child's welfare or in the interest of public safety and when a child is removed from the child's family, to give the child the care that should be provided by parents; and

(6) to provide a simple judicial procedure through which the provisions of this title are executed and enforced and in which the parties are assured a fair hearing and their constitutional and other legal rights recognized and enforced.

History of Fam. Code §51.01: Acts 1973, 63rd Leg., ch. 544, §1, eff. Sept. 1, 1973. Amended by Acts 1995, 74th Leg., ch. 262, §2, eff. Jan. 1, 1996.

FAM §51.02. DEFINITIONS

In this title:

(1) "Aggravated controlled substance felony" means an offense under Subchapter D, Chapter 481, Health and Safety Code, that is punishable by:

(A) a minimum term of confinement that is longer than the minimum term of confinement for a felony of the first degree; or

(B) a maximum fine that is greater than the maximum fine for a felony of the first degree.

(2) "Child" means a person who is:

(A) ten years of age or older and under 17 years of age; or

(B) seventeen years of age or older and under 18 years of age who is alleged or found to have engaged in

delinquent conduct or conduct indicating a need for supervision as a result of acts committed before becoming 17 years of age.

(3) "Custodian" means the adult with whom the child resides.

(4) "Guardian" means the person who, under court order, is the guardian of the person of the child or the public or private agency with whom the child has been placed by a court.

(5) "Judge" or "juvenile court judge" means the judge of a juvenile court.

(6) "Juvenile court" means a court designated under Section 51.04 of this code to exercise jurisdiction over proceedings under this title.

(7) "Law-enforcement officer" means a peace officer as defined by Article 2.12, Code of Criminal Procedure.

(8) "Nonoffender" means a child who:

(A) is subject to jurisdiction of a court under abuse, dependency, or neglect statutes under Title 5 for reasons other than legally prohibited conduct of the child; or

(B) has been taken into custody and is being held solely for deportation out of the United States.

(8-a) "Nonsecure correctional facility" means a facility described by Section 51.126.

(9) "Parent" means the mother or the father of a child, but does not include a parent whose parental rights have been terminated.

(10) "Party" means the state, a child who is the subject of proceedings under this subtitle, or the child's parent, spouse, guardian, or guardian ad litem.

(11) "Prosecuting attorney" means the county attorney, district attorney, or other attorney who regularly serves in a prosecutory capacity in a juvenile court.

(12) "Referral to juvenile court" means the referral of a child or a child's case to the office or official, including an intake officer or probation officer, designated by the juvenile board to process children within the juvenile justice system.

(13) "Secure correctional facility" means any public or private residential facility, including an alcohol or other drug treatment facility, that:

(A) includes construction fixtures designed to physically restrict the movements and activities of juveniles or other individuals held in lawful custody in the facility; and

(B) is used for the placement of any juvenile who has been adjudicated as having committed an offense, any nonoffender, or any other individual convicted of a criminal offense.

(14) "Secure detention facility" means any public or private residential facility that:

(A) includes construction fixtures designed to physically restrict the movements and activities of juveniles or other individuals held in lawful custody in the facility; and

(B) is used for the temporary placement of any juvenile who is accused of having committed an offense, any nonoffender, or any other individual accused of having committed a criminal offense.

(15) "Status offender" means a child who is accused, adjudicated, or convicted for conduct that would not, under state law, be a crime if committed by an adult, including:

(A) running away from home under Section 51.03(b)(2);

(B) a fineable only offense under Section 51.03(b)(1) transferred to the juvenile court under Section 51.08(b), but only if the conduct constituting the offense would not have been criminal if engaged in by an adult;

(C) a violation of standards of student conduct as described by Section 51.03(b)(4);

(D) a violation of a juvenile curfew ordinance or order;

(E) a violation of a provision of the Alcoholic Beverage Code applicable to minors only; or

(F) a violation of any other fineable only offense under Section 8.07(a)(4) or (5), Penal Code, but only if the conduct constituting the offense would not have been criminal if engaged in by an adult.

(16) "Traffic offense" means:

(A) a violation of a penal statute cognizable under Chapter 729, Transportation Code, except for conduct for which the person convicted may be sentenced to imprisonment or confinement in jail; or

(B) a violation of a motor vehicle traffic ordinance of an incorporated city or town in this state.

(17) "Valid court order" means a court order entered under Section 54.04 concerning a child adjudicated to have engaged in conduct indicating a need for supervision as a status offender.

History of Fam. Code §51.02: Acts 1973, 63rd Leg., ch. 544, §1, eff. Sept. 1, 1973. Amended by Acts 1975, 64th Leg., ch. 693, §1, eff. Sept. 1, 1975; Acts 1995, 74th Leg., ch. 262, §3, eff. Jan. 1, 1996; Acts 1997, 75th Leg., ch. 165, §§6.06, 30.182 (eff. Sept. 1, 1997), ch. 822, §2 (eff. Sept. 1, 1997), ch. 1013, §13 (eff. Sept. 1, 1997), ch. 1086, §§41, 47 (eff. Sept. 1, 1997); Acts 2001, 77th Leg., ch. 821, §2.02 (eff. June 14, 2001), ch. 1297, §1 (eff. Sept. 1, 2001); Acts 2003, 78th Leg., ch. 283, §1, eff. Sept. 1, 2003; Acts 2005, 79th Leg., ch. 949, §1, eff. Sept. 1, 2005; Acts 2009, 81st Leg., ch. 1187, §4.004, eff. June 19, 2009; Acts 2013, 83rd Leg., ch. 1299, §5, eff. Sept. 1, 2013; Acts 2015, 84th Leg., ch. 935, §17, eff. Sept. 1, 2015.

A FAM §51.03. DELINQUENT CONDUCT; CONDUCT INDICATING A NEED FOR SUPERVISION

The amended text in §51.03 is effective for offenses committed on or after Sept. 1, 2017. Offenses in which any element of the offense was committed before Sept. 1, 2017, are governed by the former law in effect at that time.

(a) Delinquent conduct is:

(1) conduct, other than a traffic offense, that violates a penal law of this state or of the United States punishable by imprisonment or by confinement in jail;

(2) conduct that violates a lawful order of a court under circumstances that would constitute contempt of that court in:

(A) a justice or municipal court;

(B) a county court for conduct punishable only by a fine; or

(C) a truancy court;

(3) conduct that violates Section 49.04, 49.05, 49.06, 49.07, or 49.08, Penal Code; or

(4) conduct that violates Section 106.041, Alcoholic Beverage Code, relating to driving under the influence of alcohol by a minor (third or subsequent offense).

(b) Conduct indicating a need for supervision is:

(1) subject to Subsection (f), conduct, other than a traffic offense, that violates:

(A) the penal laws of this state of the grade of misdemeanor that are punishable by fine only; or

(B) the penal ordinances of any political subdivision of this state;

(2) the voluntary absence of a child from the child's home without the consent of the child's parent or guardian for a substantial length of time or without intent to return;

(3) conduct prohibited by city ordinance or by state law involving the inhalation of the fumes or vapors of paint and other protective coatings or glue and other adhesives and the volatile chemicals itemized in Section 485.001, Health and Safety Code;

(4) an act that violates a school district's previously communicated written standards of student conduct for which the child has been expelled under Section 37.007(c), Education Code;

(5) [(6)] notwithstanding Subsection (a)(1), conduct described by Section 43.02(a) or (b), Penal Code; or

(6) [(7)] notwithstanding Subsection (a)(1), conduct that violates Section 43.261, Penal Code.

(c) Nothing in this title prevents criminal proceedings against a child for perjury.

(d) Repealed by Acts 2015, 84th Leg., ch. 935, §41(3), eff. Sept. 1, 2015.

(e) For the purposes of Subsection (b)(2), "child" does not include a person who is married, divorced, or widowed.

(e-1) Repealed by Acts 2015, 84th Leg., ch. 935, §41(3), eff. Sept. 1, 2015.

(f) Conduct described under Subsection (b)(1) does not constitute conduct indicating a need for supervision unless the child has been referred to the juvenile court under Section 51.08(b).

(g) Repealed by Acts 2015, 84th Leg., ch. 935, §41(3), eff. Sept. 1, 2015.

History of Fam. Code §51.03: Acts 1973, 63rd Leg., ch. 544, §1, eff. Sept. 1, 1973. Amended by Acts 1975, 64th Leg., ch. 693, §§2-4, eff. Sept. 1, 1975; Acts 1977, 65th Leg., ch. 340, §1, eff. June 6, 1977; Acts 1987, 70th Leg., ch. 511, §1 (eff. Sept. 1, 1987), ch. 924, §1 (eff. Sept. 1, 1987), ch. 955, §1 (eff. June 19, 1987), ch. 1040, §20 (eff. Sept. 1, 1987), ch. 1099, §48 (eff. Sept. 1, 1987); Acts 1989, 71st Leg., ch. 1100, §3.02 (eff. Aug. 28, 1989), ch. 1245, §§1, 4 (eff. Sept. 1, 1989); Acts 1991, 72nd Leg., ch. 14, §284(35) (eff. Sept. 1, 1991), ch. 16, §7.02 (eff. Aug. 26, 1991), ch. 169, §1 (eff. Sept. 1, 1991); Acts 1993, 73rd Leg., ch. 46, §1, eff. Sept. 1, 1993; Acts 1995, 74th Leg., ch. 76, §14.30 (eff. Sept. 1, 1995), ch. 262, §4 (eff. Jan. 1, 1996); Acts 1997, 75th Leg., ch. 165, §6.07 (eff. Sept. 1, 1997), ch. 1013, §14 (eff. Sept. 1, 1997), ch. 1015, §15 (eff. June 19, 1997), ch. 1086, §1 (eff. Sept. 1, 1997); Acts 2001, 77th Leg., ch. 1297, §2 (eff. Sept. 1, 2001), ch. 1514, §11 (eff. Sept. 1, 2001); Acts 2003, 78th Leg., ch. 137, §11, eff. Sept. 1, 2003; Acts 2005, 79th Leg., ch. 949, §2, eff. Sept. 1, 2005; Acts 2007, 80th Leg., ch. 908, §3, eff. Sept. 1, 2007; Acts 2009, 81st Leg., ch. 311, §3, eff. Sept. 1, 2009; Acts 2011, 82nd Leg., ch. 1098, §2 (eff. Sept. 1, 2011), ch. 1150, §1 (eff. Sept. 1, 2011), ch. 1322, §4 (eff. Sept. 1, 2011); Acts 2013, 83rd Leg., ch. 161, §7.001 (eff. Sept. 1, 2013), ch. 1299, §6 (eff. Sept. 1, 2013); Acts 2015, 84th Leg., ch. 935, §§18, 41(3) (eff. Sept. 1, 2015), ch. 944, §4 (eff. Sept. 1, 2015), ch. 1273, §3 (eff. Sept. 1, 2015); H.B. 29, §21, 85th Leg., eff. Sept. 1, 2017; S.B. 1488, §7.002, 85th Leg., eff. Sept. 1, 2017.

FAM §51.031. HABITUAL FELONY CONDUCT

(a) Habitual felony conduct is conduct violating a penal law of the grade of felony, other than a state jail felony, if:

(1) the child who engaged in the conduct has at least two previous final adjudications as having engaged in delinquent conduct violating a penal law of the grade of felony;

(2) the second previous final adjudication is for conduct that occurred after the date the first previous adjudication became final; and

(3) all appeals relating to the previous adjudications considered under Subdivisions (1) and (2) have been exhausted.

(b) For purposes of this section, an adjudication is final if the child is placed on probation or committed to the Texas Juvenile Justice Department.

(c) An adjudication based on conduct that occurred before January 1, 1996, may not be considered in a disposition made under this section.

History of Fam. Code §51.031: Acts 1995, 74th Leg., ch. 262, §5, eff. Jan. 1, 1996. Amended by Acts 1997, 75th Leg., ch. 1086, §2, eff. Sept. 1, 1997; Acts 2015, 84th Leg., ch. 734, §39, eff. Sept. 1, 2015.

FAM §51.04. JURISDICTION

(a) This title covers the proceedings in all cases involving the delinquent conduct or conduct indicating a need for supervision engaged in by a person who was a child within the meaning of this title at the time the person engaged in the conduct, and, except as provided by Subsection (h), the juvenile court has exclusive original jurisdiction over proceedings under this title.

(b) In each county, the county's juvenile board shall designate one or more district, criminal district, domestic relations, juvenile, or county courts or county courts at law as the juvenile court, subject to Subsections (c), (d), and (i).

(c) If the county court is designated as a juvenile court, at least one other court shall be designated as the juvenile court. A county court does not have jurisdiction of a proceeding involving a petition approved by a grand jury under Section 53.045 of this code.

(d) If the judge of a court designated in Subsection (b) or (c) of this section is not an attorney licensed in this state, there shall also be designated an alternate court, the judge of which is an attorney licensed in this state.

(e) A designation made under Subsection (b), (c), or (i) may be changed from time to time by the authorized boards or judges for the convenience of the people and the welfare of children. However, there must be at all times a juvenile court designated for each county. It is the intent of the legislature that in selecting a court to be the juvenile court of each county, the selection shall be made as far as practicable so that the court designated as the juvenile court will be one which is presided over by a judge who has a sympathetic understanding of the problems of child welfare and that changes in the designation of juvenile courts be made only when the best interest of the public requires it.

(f) If the judge of the juvenile court or any alternate judge named under Subsection (b) or (c) is not in the county or is otherwise unavailable, any magistrate may make a determination under Section 53.02(f) or may conduct the detention hearing provided for in Section 54.01.

(g) The juvenile board may appoint a referee to make determinations under Section 53.02(f) or to conduct hearings under this title. The referee shall be an attorney licensed to practice law in this state and shall comply with Section 54.10. Payment of any referee services shall be provided from county funds.

(h) Repealed by Acts 2015, 84th Leg., ch. 935, §41(3), eff. Sept. 1, 2015.

(i) If the court designated as the juvenile court under Subsection (b) does not have jurisdiction over proceedings under Subtitle E, Title 5, the county's juvenile board may designate at least one other court that does have jurisdiction over proceedings under Subtitle E, Title 5, as a juvenile court or alternative juvenile court.

History of Fam. Code §51.04: Acts 1973, 63rd Leg., ch. 544, §1, eff. Sept. 1, 1973. Amended by Acts 1975, 64th Leg., ch. 514, §1 (eff. June 19, 1975), ch. 693, §§5-7 (eff. Sept. 1, 1975); Acts 1977, 65th Leg., ch. 411, §1, eff. June 15, 1977; Acts 1987, 70th Leg., ch. 385, §1, eff. Sept. 1, 1987; Acts 1993, 73rd Leg., ch. 168, §4, eff. Aug. 30, 1993; Acts 1999, 76th Leg., ch. 232, §2, eff. Sept. 1, 1999; Acts 2001, 77th Leg., ch. 1297, §3 (eff. Sept. 1, 2001), ch. 1514, §12 (eff. Sept. 1, 2001); Acts 2013, 83rd Leg., ch. 186, §1, eff. Sept. 1, 2013; Acts 2015, 84th Leg., ch. 935, §41(3), eff. Sept. 1, 2015.

FAM §51.041. JURISDICTION AFTER APPEAL

(a) The court retains jurisdiction over a person, without regard to the age of the person, for conduct engaged in by the person before becoming 17 years of age if, as a result of an appeal by the person or the state under Chapter 56 of an order of the court, the order is reversed or modified and the case remanded to the court by the appellate court.

(b) If the respondent is at least 18 years of age when the order of remand from the appellate court is received by the juvenile court, the juvenile court shall proceed as provided by Sections 54.02(o)-(r) for the detention of a person at least 18 years of age in discretionary transfer proceedings. Pending retrial of the adjudication or transfer proceeding, the juvenile court may:

(1) order the respondent released from custody;

FAM §51.031

(2) order the respondent detained in a juvenile detention facility; or

(3) set bond and order the respondent detained in a county adult facility if bond is not made.

History of Fam. Code §51.041: Acts 1995, 74th Leg., ch. 262, §6, eff. Jan. 1, 1996. Amended by Acts 2001, 77th Leg., ch. 1297, §4, eff. Sept. 1, 2001; Acts 2003, 78th Leg., ch. 283, §2, eff. Sept. 1, 2003; Acts 2015, 84th Leg., ch. 74, §2, eff. Sept. 1, 2015.

FAM §51.0411. JURISDICTION FOR TRANSFER OR RELEASE HEARING

The court retains jurisdiction over a person, without regard to the age of the person, who is referred to the court under Section 54.11 for transfer to the Texas Department of Criminal Justice or release under supervision.

History of Fam. Code §51.0411: Acts 1997, 75th Leg., ch. 1086, §3, eff. June 19, 1997.

FAM §51.0412. JURISDICTION OVER INCOMPLETE PROCEEDINGS

The court retains jurisdiction over a person, without regard to the age of the person, who is a respondent in an adjudication proceeding, a disposition proceeding, a proceeding to modify disposition, a proceeding for waiver of jurisdiction and transfer to criminal court under Section 54.02(a), or a motion for transfer of determinate sentence probation to an appropriate district court if:

(1) the petition or motion was filed while the respondent was younger than 18 or 19 years of age, as applicable;

(2) the proceeding is not complete before the respondent becomes 18 or 19 years of age, as applicable; and

(3) the court enters a finding in the proceeding that the prosecuting attorney exercised due diligence in an attempt to complete the proceeding before the respondent became 18 or 19 years of age, as applicable.

History of Fam. Code §51.0412: Acts 2001, 77th Leg., ch. 1297, §5, eff. Sept. 1, 2001. Amended by Acts 2007, 80th Leg., ch. 908, §4, eff. Sept. 1, 2007; Acts 2011, 82nd Leg., ch. 438, §1, eff. Sept. 1, 2011; Acts 2013, 83rd Leg., ch. 1299, §7, eff. Sept. 1, 2013.

FAM §51.0413. JURISDICTION OVER & TRANSFER OF COMBINATION OF PROCEEDINGS

(a) A juvenile court designated under Section 51.04(b) or, if that court does not have jurisdiction over proceedings under Subtitle E, Title 5, the juvenile court designated under Section 51.04(i) may simultaneously exercise jurisdiction over proceedings under this title and proceedings under Subtitle E, Title 5, if there is probable cause to believe that the child who is the subject of those proceedings engaged in delinquent conduct or conduct indicating a need for supervision and cause to believe that the child may be the victim of conduct that constitutes an offense under Section 20A.02, Penal Code.

(b) If a proceeding is instituted under this title in a juvenile court designated under Section 51.04(b) that does not have jurisdiction over proceedings under Subtitle E, Title 5, the court shall assess the case and may transfer the proceedings to a court designated as a juvenile court or alternative juvenile court under Section 51.04(i) if the receiving court agrees and if, in the course of the proceedings, evidence is presented that constitutes cause to believe that the child who is the subject of those proceedings is a child described by Subsection (a).

History of Fam. Code §51.0413: Acts 2013, 83rd Leg., ch. 186, §2, eff. Sept. 1, 2013.

FAM §51.042. OBJECTION TO JURISDICTION BECAUSE OF AGE OF THE CHILD

(a) A child who objects to the jurisdiction of the court over the child because of the age of the child must raise the objection at the adjudication hearing or discretionary transfer hearing, if any.

(b) A child who does not object as provided by Subsection (a) waives any right to object to the jurisdiction of the court because of the age of the child at a later hearing or on appeal.

History of Fam. Code §51.042: Acts 1995, 74th Leg., ch. 262, §6, eff. Jan. 1, 1996.

FAM §51.045. JURIES IN COUNTY COURTS AT LAW

If a provision of this title requires a jury of 12 persons, that provision prevails over any other law that limits the number of members of a jury in a particular county court at law. The state and the defense are entitled to the same number of peremptory challenges allowed in a district court.

History of Fam. Code §51.045: Acts 1987, 70th Leg., ch. 385, §2, eff. Sept. 1, 1987.

FAM §51.05. COURT SESSIONS & FACILITIES

(a) The juvenile court shall be deemed in session at all times. Suitable quarters shall be provided by the commissioners court of each county for the hearing of cases and for the use of the judge, the probation officer, and other employees of the court.

(b) The juvenile court and the juvenile board shall report annually to the commissioners court on the suitability of the quarters and facilities of the juvenile court and may make recommendations for their improvement.

History of Fam. Code §51.05: Acts 1973, 63rd Leg., ch. 544, §1, eff. Sept. 1, 1973. Amended by Acts 1975, 64th Leg., ch. 693, §8, eff. Sept. 1, 1975.

FAM §51.06. VENUE

(a) A proceeding under this title shall be commenced in

(1) the county in which the alleged delinquent conduct or conduct indicating a need for supervision occurred; or

(2) the county in which the child resides at the time the petition is filed, but only if:

(A) the child was under probation supervision in that county at the time of the commission of the delinquent conduct or conduct indicating a need for supervision;

(B) it cannot be determined in which county the delinquent conduct or conduct indicating a need for supervision occurred; or

(C) the county in which the child resides agrees to accept the case for prosecution, in writing, prior to the case being sent to the county of residence for prosecution.

(b) An application for a writ of habeas corpus brought by or on behalf of a person who has been committed to an institution under the jurisdiction of the Texas Juvenile Justice Department and which attacks the validity of the judgment of commitment shall be brought in the county in which the court that entered the judgment of commitment is located.

History of Fam. Code §51.06: Acts 1973, 63rd Leg., ch. 544, §1, eff. Sept. 1, 1973. Amended by Acts 1983, 68th Leg., ch. 44, art. 1, §1, eff. Apr. 26, 1983; Acts 1995, 74th Leg., ch. 262, §7, eff. Jan. 1, 1996; Acts 1999, 76th Leg., ch. 488, §1, eff. Sept. 1, 1999; Acts 2015, 84th Leg., ch. 734, §40, eff. Sept. 1, 2015.

FAM §51.07. TRANSFER TO ANOTHER COUNTY FOR DISPOSITION

(a) When a child has been found to have engaged in delinquent conduct or conduct indicating a need for supervision under Section 54.03, the juvenile court may transfer the case and transcripts of records and documents to the juvenile court of the county where the child resides for disposition of the case under Section 54.04. Consent by the court of the county where the child resides is not required.

(b) For purposes of Subsection (a), while a child is the subject of a suit under Title 5, the child is considered to reside in the county in which the court of continuing exclusive jurisdiction over the child is located.

History of Fam. Code §51.07: Acts 1973, 63rd Leg., ch. 544, §1, eff. Sept. 1, 1973. Amended by Acts 2005, 79th Leg., ch. 949, §3, eff. Sept. 1, 2005; Acts 2013, 83rd Leg., ch. 1299, §8, eff. Sept. 1, 2013.

FAM §51.071. TRANSFER OF PROBATION SUPERVISION BETWEEN COUNTIES: COURTESY SUPERVISION PROHIBITED

Except as provided by Section 51.075, a juvenile court or juvenile probation department may not engage in the practice of courtesy supervision of a child on probation.

History of Fam. Code §51.071: Acts 2005, 79th Leg., ch. 949, §4, eff. Sept. 1, 2005.

FAM §51.072. TRANSFER OF PROBATION SUPERVISION BETWEEN COUNTIES: INTERIM SUPERVISION

(a) In this section:

(1) "Receiving county" means the county to which a child on probation has moved or intends to move.

(2) "Sending county" means the county that:

(A) originally placed the child on probation; or

(B) assumed permanent supervision of the child under an inter-county transfer of probation supervision.

(b) When a child on probation moves or intends to move from one county to another and intends to remain in the receiving county for at least 60 days, the juvenile probation department of the sending county shall request that the juvenile probation department of the receiving county provide interim supervision of the child. If the receiving county and the sending county are member counties within a judicial district served by one juvenile probation department, then a transfer of probation supervision is not required.

(c) The juvenile probation department of the receiving county may refuse the request to provide interim supervision only if:

(1) the residence of the child in the receiving county is in a residential placement facility arranged by the sending county; or

(2) the residence of the child in the receiving county is in a foster care placement arranged by the Department of Family and Protective Services.

(d) The juvenile probation department of the sending county shall initiate the request for interim supervision by electronic communication to the probation officer designated as the inter-county transfer officer for the juvenile probation department of the receiving county or, in the absence of this designation, to the chief juvenile probation officer.

(e) The juvenile probation department of the sending county shall provide the juvenile probation department of the receiving county with the following information in the request for interim supervision initiated under Subsection (d):

(1) the child's name, sex, age, race, and date of birth;

(2) the name, address, date of birth, and social security or driver's license number, and telephone number, if available, of the person with whom the child proposes to reside or is residing in the receiving county;

(3) the offense for which the child is on probation;

(4) the length of the child's probation term;

(5) a brief summary of the child's history of referrals;

(6) a brief statement of any special needs of the child;

(7) the name and telephone number of the child's school in the receiving county, if available; and

(8) the reason for the child moving or intending to move to the receiving county.

(f) Not later than 10 business days after a receiving county has agreed to provide interim supervision of a child, the juvenile probation department of the sending county shall provide the juvenile probation department of the receiving county with a copy of the following documents:

(1) the petition and the adjudication and disposition orders for the child, including the child's thumbprint;

(2) the child's conditions of probation;

(3) the social history report for the child;

(4) any psychological or psychiatric reports concerning the child;

(5) the Department of Public Safety CR 43J form or tracking incident number concerning the child;

(6) any law enforcement incident reports concerning the offense for which the child is on probation;

(7) any sex offender registration information concerning the child;

(8) any juvenile probation department progress reports concerning the child and any other pertinent documentation for the child's probation officer;

(9) case plans concerning the child;

(10) the Texas Juvenile Justice Department standard assessment tool results for the child;

(11) the computerized referral and case history for the child, including case disposition;

(12) the child's birth certificate;

(13) the child's social security number or social security card, if available;

(14) the name, address, and telephone number of the contact person in the sending county's juvenile probation department;

(15) Title IV-E eligibility screening information for the child, if available;

(16) the address in the sending county for forwarding funds collected to which the sending county is entitled;

(17) any of the child's school or immunization records that the juvenile probation department of the sending county possesses;

(18) any victim information concerning the case for which the child is on probation; and

(19) if applicable, documentation that the sending county has required the child to provide a DNA sample to the Department of Public Safety under Section 54.0405 or 54.0409 or under Subchapter G, Chapter 411, Government Code.

(f-1) The inter-county transfer officers in the sending and receiving counties shall agree on the official start date for the period of interim supervision, which must begin no later than three business days after the date the documents required under Subsection (f) have been received and accepted by the receiving county.

(f-2) On initiating a transfer of probation supervision under this section, for a child ordered to submit a DNA sample as a condition of probation, the sending county shall provide to the receiving county documentation of compliance with the requirements of Section 54.0405 or 54.0409 or of Subchapter G, Chapter 411, Government Code, as applicable. If the sending county has not provided the documentation required under this section within the time provided by Subsection (f), the receiving county may refuse to accept interim supervision until the sending county has provided the documentation.

(g) The juvenile probation department of the receiving county shall supervise the child under the probation conditions imposed by the sending county and provide services similar to those provided to a child placed on probation under the same conditions in the receiving county. On request of the juvenile probation department of the receiving county, the juvenile court of the receiving county may modify the original probation conditions and impose new conditions using the procedures in Section 54.05. The juvenile court of the receiving county may not modify a financial probation condition imposed by the juvenile court of the sending county or the length of the child's probation term. The juvenile court of the receiving county shall designate a cause number for identifying the modification proceedings.

(h) The juvenile court of the sending county may revoke probation for a violation of a condition imposed by the juvenile court of the sending county only if the condition has not been specifically modified or replaced by the juvenile court of the receiving county. The juvenile court of the receiving county may revoke probation for a violation of a condition of probation that the juvenile court of the receiving county has modified or imposed.

(i) If a child is reasonably believed to have violated a condition of probation imposed by the juvenile court of the sending county, the juvenile court of the sending or receiving county may issue a directive to apprehend or detain the child in a certified detention facility, as in other cases of probation violation. In order to respond to a probation violation under this subsection, the juvenile court of the receiving county may:

(1) modify the conditions of probation or extend the probation term; or

(2) require that the juvenile probation department of the sending county resume direct supervision for the child.

(j) On receiving a directive from the juvenile court of the receiving county under Subsection (i)(2), the juvenile probation department of the sending county shall arrange for the prompt transportation of the child back to the sending county at the expense of the sending county. The juvenile probation department in the receiving county shall provide the sending county with supporting written documentation of the incidents of violation of probation on which the request to resume direct supervision is based.

(j-1) Notwithstanding Subsection (j), the sending county may request interim supervision from the receiving county that issued a directive under Subsection (i)(2). Following the conclusion of any judicial proceedings in the sending county or on the completion of any residential placement ordered by the juvenile court of the sending county, the sending and receiving counties may mutually agree to return the child to the receiving county. The sending and receiving counties may take into consideration whether:

(1) the person having legal custody of the child resides in the receiving county;

(2) the child has been ordered by the juvenile court of the sending county to reside with a parent, guardian, or other person who resides in the sending county or any other county; and

(3) the case meets the statutory requirements for collaborative supervision.

(j-2) The period of interim supervision under Subsection (j-1) may not exceed the period under Subsection (m).

(k) The juvenile probation department of the receiving county is entitled to any probation supervision fees collected from the child or the child's parent while providing interim supervision for the child. During the period of interim supervision, the receiving county shall collect and distribute to the victim monetary restitution payments in the manner specified by the sending county. At the expiration of the period of interim supervision, the receiving county shall collect and distribute directly to the victim any remaining payments.

(*l*) The sending county is financially responsible for any special treatment program or placement that the juvenile court of the sending county requires as a condition of probation if the child's family is financially unable to pay for the program or placement.

(m) Except as provided by Subsection (n), a period of interim supervision may not exceed 180 days. Permanent supervision automatically transfers to the juvenile probation department of the receiving county after the expiration of the period of interim supervision. The juvenile probation department of the receiving county may request permanent supervision from the juvenile probation department of the sending county at any time before the 180-day interim supervision period expires. After signing and entry of an order of transfer of permanent supervision by the sending county juvenile court, the juvenile probation department shall, in accordance

with Section 51.073(b), promptly send the permanent supervision order and related documents to the receiving county.

(m-1) If a child on interim supervision moves to another county of residence or is otherwise no longer in the receiving county before the expiration of 180 days, the receiving county shall direct the sending county to resume supervision of the child.

(n) Notwithstanding Subsection (m), the period of interim supervision of a child who is placed on probation under Section 54.04(q) does not expire until the child has satisfactorily completed the greater of either 180 days or one-third of the term of probation, including one-third of the term of any extension of the probation term ordered under Section 54.05. Permanent supervision automatically transfers to the probation department of the receiving county after the expiration of the period of interim supervision under this subsection. If the state elects to initiate transfer proceedings under Section 54.051, the juvenile court of the sending county may order transfer of the permanent supervision before the expiration of the period of interim supervision under this subsection.

(o) At least once every 90 days during the period of interim supervision, the juvenile probation department of the receiving county shall provide the juvenile probation department of the sending county with a progress report of supervision concerning the child.

History of Fam. Code §51.072: Acts 2005, 79th Leg., ch. 949, §4, eff. Sept. 1, 2005. Amended by Acts 2007, 80th Leg., ch. 908, §5, eff. Sept. 1, 2007; Acts 2013, 83rd Leg., ch. 1299, §9, eff. Sept. 1, 2013.

FAM §51.073. TRANSFER OF PROBATION SUPERVISION BETWEEN COUNTIES: PERMANENT SUPERVISION

(a) In this section:

(1) "Receiving county" means the county to which a child on probation has moved or intends to move.

(2) "Sending county" means the county that:

(A) originally placed the child on probation; or

(B) assumed permanent supervision of the child under an inter-county transfer of probation supervision.

(b) On transfer of permanent supervision of a child under Section 51.072(m) or (n), the juvenile court of the sending county shall order the juvenile probation department of the sending county to provide the juvenile probation department of the receiving county with the order of transfer. On receipt of the order of transfer, the juvenile probation department of the receiving county shall ensure that the order of transfer, the petition, the order of adjudication, the order of disposition, and the conditions of probation are filed with the clerk of the juvenile court of the receiving county.

(c) The juvenile court of the receiving county shall require that the child be brought before the court in order to impose new or different conditions of probation than those originally ordered by the sending county or ordered by the receiving county during the period of interim supervision. The child shall be represented by counsel as provided by Section 51.10.

(d) Once permanent supervision is transferred to the juvenile probation department of the receiving county, the receiving county is fully responsible for selecting and imposing conditions of probation, providing supervision, modifying conditions of probation, and revoking probation. The sending county has no further jurisdiction over the child's case.

(d-1) On the final transfer of a case involving a child who has been adjudicated as having committed an offense for which registration is required under Chapter 62, Code of Criminal Procedure, the receiving county shall have jurisdiction to conduct a hearing under that chapter. This subsection does not prohibit the receiving county juvenile court from considering the written recommendations of the sending county juvenile court.

(e) This section does not affect the sending county's jurisdiction over any new offense committed by the child in the sending county.

History of Fam. Code §51.073: Acts 2005, 79th Leg., ch. 949, §4, eff. Sept. 1, 2005. Amended by Acts 2007, 80th Leg., ch. 908, §6, eff. Sept. 1, 2007.

FAM §51.074. TRANSFER OF PROBATION SUPERVISION BETWEEN COUNTIES: DEFERRED PROSECUTION

(a) A juvenile court may transfer interim supervision, but not permanent supervision, to the county where a child on deferred prosecution resides.

(b) On an extension of a previous order of deferred prosecution authorized under Section 53.03(j), the child shall remain on interim supervision for an additional period not to exceed 180 days.

(c) On a violation of the conditions of the original deferred prosecution agreement, the receiving county shall forward the case to the sending county for pros-

ecution or other action in the manner provided by Sections 51.072(i) and (j), except that the original conditions of deferred prosecution may not be modified by the receiving county.

History of Fam. Code §51.074: Acts 2005, 79th Leg., ch. 949, §4, eff. Sept. 1, 2005. Amended by Acts 2007, 80th Leg., ch. 908, §7, eff. Sept. 1, 2007.

FAM §51.075. COLLABORATIVE SUPERVISION BETWEEN ADJOINING COUNTIES

(a) If a child who is on probation in one county spends substantial time in an adjoining county, including residing, attending school, or working in the adjoining county, the juvenile probation departments of the two counties may enter into a collaborative supervision arrangement regarding the child.

(b) Under a collaborative supervision arrangement, the juvenile probation department of the adjoining county may authorize a probation officer for the county to provide supervision and other services for the child as an agent of the juvenile probation department of the county in which the child was placed on probation. The probation officer providing supervision and other services for the child in the adjoining county shall provide the probation officer supervising the child in the county in which the child was placed on probation with periodic oral, electronic, or written reports concerning the child.

(c) The juvenile court of the county in which the child was placed on probation retains sole authority to modify, amend, extend, or revoke the child's probation.

History of Fam. Code §51.075: Acts 2005, 79th Leg., ch. 949, §4, eff. Sept. 1, 2005.

FAM §51.08. TRANSFER FROM CRIMINAL COURT

(a) If the defendant in a criminal proceeding is a child who is charged with an offense other than perjury, a traffic offense, a misdemeanor punishable by fine only, or a violation of a penal ordinance of a political subdivision, unless the child has been transferred to criminal court under Section 54.02, the court exercising criminal jurisdiction shall transfer the case to the juvenile court, together with a copy of the accusatory pleading and other papers, documents, and transcripts of testimony relating to the case, and shall order that the child be taken to the place of detention designated by the juvenile court, or shall release the child to the custody of the child's parent, guardian, or custodian, to be brought before the juvenile court at a time designated by that court.

(b) A court in which there is pending a complaint against a child alleging a violation of a misdemeanor offense punishable by fine only other than a traffic offense or a violation of a penal ordinance of a political subdivision other than a traffic offense:

(1) except as provided by Subsection (d), shall waive its original jurisdiction and refer the child to juvenile court if:

(A) the complaint pending against the child alleges a violation of a misdemeanor offense under Section 43.261, Penal Code, that is punishable by fine only; or

(B) the child has previously been convicted of:

(i) two or more misdemeanors punishable by fine only other than a traffic offense;

(ii) two or more violations of a penal ordinance of a political subdivision other than a traffic offense; or

(iii) one or more of each of the types of misdemeanors described in Subparagraph (i) or (ii); and

(2) may waive its original jurisdiction and refer the child to juvenile court if the child:

(A) has not previously been convicted of a misdemeanor punishable by fine only other than a traffic offense or a violation of a penal ordinance of a political subdivision other than a traffic offense; or

(B) has previously been convicted of fewer than two misdemeanors punishable by fine only other than a traffic offense or two violations of a penal ordinance of a political subdivision other than a traffic offense.

(c) A court in which there is pending a complaint against a child alleging a violation of a misdemeanor offense punishable by fine only other than a traffic offense or a violation of a penal ordinance of a political subdivision other than a traffic offense shall notify the juvenile court of the county in which the court is located of the pending complaint and shall furnish to the juvenile court a copy of the final disposition of any matter for which the court does not waive its original jurisdiction under Subsection (b).

(d) A court that has implemented a juvenile case manager program under Article 45.056, Code of Criminal Procedure, may, but is not required to, waive its original jurisdiction under Subsection (b)(1)(B).

(e) Repealed by Acts 2015, 84th Leg., ch. 935, §41(3), eff. Sept. 1, 2015.

(f) A court shall waive original jurisdiction for a complaint against a child alleging a violation of a misdemeanor offense punishable by fine only, other than a

traffic offense, and refer the child to juvenile court if the court or another court has previously dismissed a complaint against the child under Section 8.08, Penal Code.

History of Fam. Code §51.08: Acts 1973, 63rd Leg., ch. 544, §1, eff. Sept. 1, 1973. Amended by Acts 1987, 70th Leg., ch. 1040, §21, eff. Sept. 1, 1987; Acts 1989, 71st Leg., ch. 1245, §2, eff. Sept. 1, 1989; Acts 1991, 72nd Leg., ch. 169, §2, eff. Sept. 1, 1991; Acts 2001, 77th Leg., ch. 1297, §6, eff. Sept. 1, 2001; Acts 2003, 78th Leg., ch. 283, §3 (eff. Sept. 1, 2003), ch. 1275, §3(25) (eff. Sept. 1, 2003); Acts 2005, 79th Leg., ch. 650, §1, eff. Sept. 1, 2005; Acts 2009, 81st Leg., ch. 311, §4, eff. Sept. 1, 2009; Acts 2011, 82nd Leg., ch. 1322, §16, eff. Sept. 1, 2011; Acts 2013, 83rd Leg., ch. 1407, §13, eff. Sept. 1, 2013; Acts 2015, 84th Leg., ch. 935, §41(3), eff. Sept. 1, 2015.

FAM §51.09. WAIVER OF RIGHTS

Unless a contrary intent clearly appears elsewhere in this title, any right granted to a child by this title or by the constitution or laws of this state or the United States may be waived in proceedings under this title if:

(1) the waiver is made by the child and the attorney for the child;

(2) the child and the attorney waiving the right are informed of and understand the right and the possible consequences of waiving it;

(3) the waiver is voluntary; and

(4) the waiver is made in writing or in court proceedings that are recorded.

History of Fam. Code §51.09: Acts 1973, 63rd Leg., ch. 544, §1, eff. Sept. 1, 1973. Amended by Acts 1975, 64th Leg., ch. 693, §9, eff. Sept. 1, 1975; Acts 1989, 71st Leg., ch. 84, §1, eff. Sept. 1, 1989; Acts 1991, 72nd Leg., ch. 64, §1 (eff. Sept. 1, 1991), ch. 429, §1 (eff. Sept. 1, 1991), ch. 557, §1 (eff. Sept. 1, 1991), ch. 593, §1 (eff. Aug. 26, 1991); Acts 1995, 74th Leg., ch. 262, §§8, 9, eff. Jan. 1, 1996; Acts 1997, 75th Leg., ch. 1086, §4, eff. Sept. 1, 1997.

FAM §51.095. ADMISSIBILITY OF A STATEMENT OF A CHILD

(a) Notwithstanding Section 51.09, the statement of a child is admissible in evidence in any future proceeding concerning the matter about which the statement was given if:

(1) the statement is made in writing under a circumstance described by Subsection (d) and:

(A) the statement shows that the child has at some time before the making of the statement received from a magistrate a warning that:

(i) the child may remain silent and not make any statement at all and that any statement that the child makes may be used in evidence against the child;

(ii) the child has the right to have an attorney present to advise the child either prior to any questioning or during the questioning;

(iii) if the child is unable to employ an attorney, the child has the right to have an attorney appointed to counsel with the child before or during any interviews with peace officers or attorneys representing the state; and

(iv) the child has the right to terminate the interview at any time;

(B) and:

(i) the statement must be signed in the presence of a magistrate by the child with no law enforcement officer or prosecuting attorney present, except that a magistrate may require a bailiff or a law enforcement officer if a bailiff is not available to be present if the magistrate determines that the presence of the bailiff or law enforcement officer is necessary for the personal safety of the magistrate or other court personnel, provided that the bailiff or law enforcement officer may not carry a weapon in the presence of the child; and

(ii) the magistrate must be fully convinced that the child understands the nature and contents of the statement and that the child is signing the same voluntarily, and if a statement is taken, the magistrate must sign a written statement verifying the foregoing requisites have been met;

(C) the child knowingly, intelligently, and voluntarily waives these rights before and during the making of the statement and signs the statement in the presence of a magistrate; and

(D) the magistrate certifies that the magistrate has examined the child independent of any law enforcement officer or prosecuting attorney, except as required to ensure the personal safety of the magistrate or other court personnel, and has determined that the child understands the nature and contents of the statement and has knowingly, intelligently, and voluntarily waived these rights;

(2) the statement is made orally and the child makes a statement of facts or circumstances that are found to be true and tend to establish the child's guilt, such as the finding of secreted or stolen property, or the instrument with which the child states the offense was committed;

(3) the statement was res gestae of the delinquent conduct or the conduct indicating a need for supervision or of the arrest;

(4) the statement is made:

(A) in open court at the child's adjudication hearing;

(B) before a grand jury considering a petition, under Section 53.045, that the child engaged in delinquent conduct; or

(C) at a preliminary hearing concerning the child held in compliance with this code, other than at a detention hearing under Section 54.01; or

(5) subject to Subsection (f), the statement is made orally under a circumstance described by Subsection (d) and the statement is recorded by an electronic recording device, including a device that records images, and:

(A) before making the statement, the child is given the warning described by Subdivision (1)(A) by a magistrate, the warning is a part of the recording, and the child knowingly, intelligently, and voluntarily waives each right stated in the warning;

(B) the recording device is capable of making an accurate recording, the operator of the device is competent to use the device, the recording is accurate, and the recording has not been altered;

(C) each voice on the recording is identified; and

(D) not later than the 20th day before the date of the proceeding, the attorney representing the child is given a complete and accurate copy of each recording of the child made under this subdivision.

(b) This section and Section 51.09 do not preclude the admission of a statement made by the child if:

(1) the statement does not stem from interrogation of the child under a circumstance described by Subsection (d); or

(2) without regard to whether the statement stems from interrogation of the child under a circumstance described by Subsection (d), the statement is:

(A) voluntary and has a bearing on the credibility of the child as a witness; or

(B) recorded by an electronic recording device, including a device that records images, and is obtained:

(i) in another state in compliance with the laws of that state or this state; or

(ii) by a federal law enforcement officer in this state or another state in compliance with the laws of the United States.

(c) An electronic recording of a child's statement made under Subsection (a)(5) or (b)(2)(B) shall be preserved until all juvenile or criminal matters relating to any conduct referred to in the statement are final, including the exhaustion of all appeals, or barred from prosecution.

(d) Subsections (a)(1) and (a)(5) apply to the statement of a child made:

(1) while the child is in a detention facility or other place of confinement;

(2) while the child is in the custody of an officer; or

(3) during or after the interrogation of the child by an officer if the child is in the possession of the Department of Family and Protective Services and is suspected to have engaged in conduct that violates a penal law of this state.

(e) A juvenile law referee or master may perform the duties imposed on a magistrate under this section without the approval of the juvenile court if the juvenile board of the county in which the statement of the child is made has authorized a referee or master to perform the duties of a magistrate under this section.

(f) A magistrate who provides the warnings required by Subsection (a)(5) for a recorded statement may at the time the warnings are provided request by speaking on the recording that the officer return the child and the recording to the magistrate at the conclusion of the process of questioning. The magistrate may then view the recording with the child or have the child view the recording to enable the magistrate to determine whether the child's statements were given voluntarily. The magistrate's determination of voluntariness shall be reduced to writing and signed and dated by the magistrate. If a magistrate uses the procedure described by this subsection, a child's statement is not admissible unless the magistrate determines that the statement was given voluntarily.

History of Fam. Code §51.095: Acts 1997, 75th Leg., ch. 1086, §4, eff. Sept. 1, 1997. Amended by Acts 1999, 76th Leg., ch. 982, §1 (eff. Sept. 1, 1999), ch. 1477, §1 (eff. Sept. 1, 1999); Acts 2001, 77th Leg., ch. 1297, §7 (eff. Sept. 1, 2001), ch. 1420, §21.001(29) (eff. Sept. 1, 2001); Acts 2005, 79th Leg., ch. 949, §5, eff. Sept. 1, 2005; Acts 2007, 80th Leg., ch. 908, §8, eff. Sept. 1, 2007; Acts 2011, 82nd Leg., ch. 110, §3 (eff. May 21, 2011), ch. 1158, §1 (eff. Sept. 1, 2011).

FAM §51.10. RIGHT TO ASSISTANCE OF ATTORNEY; COMPENSATION

(a) A child may be represented by an attorney at every stage of proceedings under this title, including:

(1) the detention hearing required by Section 54.01 of this code;

(2) the hearing to consider transfer to criminal court required by Section 54.02 of this code;

(3) the adjudication hearing required by Section 54.03 of this code;

(4) the disposition hearing required by Section 54.04 of this code;

(5) the hearing to modify disposition required by Section 54.05 of this code;

(6) hearings required by Chapter 55 of this code;

(7) habeas corpus proceedings challenging the legality of detention resulting from action under this title; and

(8) proceedings in a court of civil appeals or the Texas Supreme Court reviewing proceedings under this title.

(b) The child's right to representation by an attorney shall not be waived in:

(1) a hearing to consider transfer to criminal court as required by Section 54.02;

(2) an adjudication hearing as required by Section 54.03;

(3) a disposition hearing as required by Section 54.04;

(4) a hearing prior to commitment to the Texas Juvenile Justice Department as a modified disposition in accordance with Section 54.05(f); or

(5) hearings required by Chapter 55.

(c) If the child was not represented by an attorney at the detention hearing required by Section 54.01 of this code and a determination was made to detain the child, the child shall immediately be entitled to representation by an attorney. The court shall order the retention of an attorney according to Subsection (d) or appoint an attorney according to Subsection (f).

(d) The court shall order a child's parent or other person responsible for support of the child to employ an attorney to represent the child, if:

(1) the child is not represented by an attorney;

(2) after giving the appropriate parties an opportunity to be heard, the court determines that the parent or other person responsible for support of the child is financially able to employ an attorney to represent the child; and

(3) the child's right to representation by an attorney:

(A) has not been waived under Section 51.09 of this code; or

(B) may not be waived under Subsection (b) of this section.

(e) The court may enforce orders under Subsection (d) by proceedings under Section 54.07 or by appointing counsel and ordering the parent or other person responsible for support of the child to pay a reasonable attorney's fee set by the court. The order may be enforced under Section 54.07.

(f) The court shall appoint an attorney to represent the interest of a child entitled to representation by an attorney, if:

(1) the child is not represented by an attorney;

(2) the court determines that the child's parent or other person responsible for support of the child is financially unable to employ an attorney to represent the child; and

(3) the child's right to representation by an attorney:

(A) has not been waived under Section 51.09 of this code; or

(B) may not be waived under Subsection (b) of this section.

(g) The juvenile court may appoint an attorney in any case in which it deems representation necessary to protect the interests of the child.

(h) Any attorney representing a child in proceedings under this title is entitled to 10 days to prepare for any adjudication or transfer hearing under this title.

(i) Except as provided in Subsection (d) of this section, an attorney appointed under this section to represent the interests of a child shall be paid from the general fund of the county in which the proceedings were instituted according to the schedule in Article 26.05 of the Texas Code of Criminal Procedure, 1965. For this purpose, a bona fide appeal to a court of civil appeals or proceedings on the merits in the Texas Supreme Court are considered the equivalent of a bona fide appeal to the Texas Court of Criminal Appeals.

(j) The juvenile board of a county may make available to the public the list of attorneys eligible for appointment to represent children in proceedings under this title as provided in the plan adopted under Section 51.102. The list of attorneys must indicate the level of case for which each attorney is eligible for appointment under Section 51.102(b)(2).

(k) Subject to Chapter 61, the juvenile court may order the parent or other person responsible for support of the child to reimburse the county for payments the county made to counsel appointed to represent the child under Subsection (f) or (g). The court may:

(1) order payment for each attorney who has represented the child at any hearing, including a detention hearing, discretionary transfer hearing, adjudication hearing, disposition hearing, or modification of disposition hearing;

(2) include amounts paid to or on behalf of the attorney by the county for preparation time and investigative and expert witness costs; and

(3) require full or partial reimbursement to the county.

(*l*) The court may not order payments under Subsection (k) that exceed the financial ability of the parent or other person responsible for support of the child to meet the payment schedule ordered by the court.

History of Fam. Code §51.10: Acts 1973, 63rd Leg., ch. 544, §1, eff. Sept. 1, 1973. Amended by Acts 1983, 68th Leg., ch. 44, art. 1, §2, eff. Apr. 26, 1983; Acts 1995, 74th Leg., ch. 262, §11, eff. Jan. 1, 1996; Acts 2001, 77th Leg., ch. 1297, §8, eff. Sept. 1, 2001; Acts 2003, 78th Leg., ch. 283, §4, eff. Sept. 1, 2003; Acts 2015, 84th Leg., ch. 734, §41, eff. Sept. 1, 2015.

FAM §51.101. APPOINTMENT OF ATTORNEY & CONTINUATION OF REPRESENTATION

(a) If an attorney is appointed under Section 54.01(b-1) or (d) to represent a child at the initial detention hearing and the child is detained, the attorney shall continue to represent the child until the case is terminated, the family retains an attorney, or a new attorney is appointed by the juvenile court. Release of the child from detention does not terminate the attorney's representation.

(b) If there is an initial detention hearing without an attorney and the child is detained, the attorney appointed under Section 51.10(c) shall continue to represent the child until the case is terminated, the family retains an attorney, or a new attorney is appointed by the juvenile court. Release of the child from detention does not terminate the attorney's representation.

(c) The juvenile court shall determine, on the filing of a petition, whether the child's family is indigent if:

(1) the child is released by intake;

(2) the child is released at the initial detention hearing; or

(3) the case was referred to the court without the child in custody.

(d) A juvenile court that makes a finding of indigence under Subsection (c) shall appoint an attorney to represent the child on or before the fifth working day after the date the petition for adjudication or discretionary transfer hearing was served on the child. An attorney appointed under this subsection shall continue to represent the child until the case is terminated, the family retains an attorney, or a new attorney is appointed by the juvenile court.

(e) The juvenile court shall determine whether the child's family is indigent if a motion or petition is filed under Section 54.05 seeking to modify disposition by committing the child to the Texas Juvenile Justice Department or placing the child in a secure correctional facility. A court that makes a finding of indigence shall appoint an attorney to represent the child on or before the fifth working day after the date the petition or motion has been filed. An attorney appointed under this subsection shall continue to represent the child until the court rules on the motion or petition, the family retains an attorney, or a new attorney is appointed.

History of Fam. Code §51.101: Acts 2001, 77th Leg., ch. 1297, §9, eff. Sept. 1, 2001. Amended by Acts 2013, 83rd Leg., ch. 912, §3, eff. Sept. 1, 2013; Acts 2015, 84th Leg., ch. 734, §42, eff. Sept. 1, 2015.

FAM §51.102. APPOINTMENT OF COUNSEL PLAN

(a) The juvenile board in each county shall adopt a plan that:

(1) specifies the qualifications necessary for an attorney to be included on an appointment list from which attorneys are appointed to represent children in proceedings under this title; and

(2) establishes the procedures for:

(A) including attorneys on the appointment list and removing attorneys from the list; and

(B) appointing attorneys from the appointment list to individual cases.

(b) A plan adopted under Subsection (a) must:

(1) to the extent practicable, comply with the requirements of Article 26.04, Code of Criminal Procedure, except that:

(A) the income and assets of the child's parent or other person responsible for the child's support must be used in determining whether the child is indigent; and

(B) any alternative plan for appointing counsel is established by the juvenile board in the county; and

(2) recognize the differences in qualifications and experience necessary for appointments to cases in which:

(A) the allegation is:

(i) conduct indicating a need for supervision or delinquent conduct, and commitment to the Texas Juvenile Justice Department is not an authorized disposition; or

(ii) delinquent conduct, and commitment to the department without a determinate sentence is an authorized disposition; or

(B) determinate sentence proceedings have been initiated or proceedings for discretionary transfer to criminal court have been initiated.

History of Fam. Code §51.102: Acts 2001, 77th Leg., ch. 906, §11, eff. Jan. 1, 2002. Renumbered from §51.101 by Acts 2003, 78th Leg., ch. 1275, §2(51), eff. Sept. 1, 2003. Renumbered from §51.101 and amended by Acts 2003, 78th Leg., ch. 283, §5, eff. Sept. 1, 2003. Amended by Acts 2015, 84th Leg., ch. 734, §43, eff. Sept. 1, 2015.

FAM §51.11. GUARDIAN AD LITEM

(a) If a child appears before the juvenile court without a parent or guardian, the court shall appoint a guardian ad litem to protect the interests of the child. The juvenile court need not appoint a guardian ad litem if a parent or guardian appears with the child.

(b) In any case in which it appears to the juvenile court that the child's parent or guardian is incapable or unwilling to make decisions in the best interest of the child with respect to proceedings under this title, the court may appoint a guardian ad litem to protect the interests of the child in the proceedings.

(c) An attorney for a child may also be his guardian ad litem. A law-enforcement officer, probation officer, or other employee of the juvenile court may not be appointed guardian ad litem.

History of Fam. Code §51.11: Acts 1973, 63rd Leg., ch. 544, §1, eff. Sept. 1, 1973.

FAM §51.115. ATTENDANCE AT HEARING: PARENT OR OTHER GUARDIAN

(a) Each parent of a child, each managing and possessory conservator of a child, each court-appointed custodian of a child, and a guardian of the person of the child shall attend each hearing affecting the child held under:

(1) Section 54.02 (waiver of jurisdiction and discretionary transfer to criminal court);

(2) Section 54.03 (adjudication hearing);

(3) Section 54.04 (disposition hearing);

(4) Section 54.05 (hearing to modify disposition); and

(5) Section 54.11 (release or transfer hearing).

(b) Subsection (a) does not apply to:

(1) a person for whom, for good cause shown, the court waives attendance;

(2) a person who is not a resident of this state; or

(3) a parent of a child for whom a managing conservator has been appointed and the parent is not a conservator of the child.

(c) A person required under this section to attend a hearing is entitled to reasonable written or oral notice that includes a statement of the place, date, and time of the hearing and that the attendance of the person is required. The notice may be included with or attached to any other notice required by this chapter to be given the person. Separate notice is not required for a disposition hearing that convenes on the adjournment of an adjudication hearing. If a person required under this section fails to attend a hearing, the juvenile court may proceed with the hearing.

(d) A person who is required by Subsection (a) to attend a hearing, who receives the notice of the hearing, and who fails to attend the hearing may be punished by the court for contempt by a fine of not less than $100 and not more than $1,000. In addition to or in lieu of contempt, the court may order the person to receive counseling or to attend an educational course on the duties and responsibilities of parents and skills and techniques in raising children.

History of Fam. Code §51.115: Acts 1995, 74th Leg., ch. 262, §10, eff. Jan. 1, 1996.

FAM §51.116. RIGHT TO REEMPLOYMENT

(a) An employer may not terminate the employment of a permanent employee because the employee is required under Section 51.115 to attend a hearing.

(b) An employee whose employment is terminated in violation of this section is entitled to return to the same employment that the employee held when notified of the hearing if the employee, as soon as practical after the hearing, gives the employer actual notice that the employee intends to return.

(c) A person who is injured because of a violation of this section is entitled to reinstatement to the person's former position and to damages, but the damages may not exceed an amount equal to six months' com pensation at the rate at which the person was compensated when required to attend the hearing.

(d) The injured person is also entitled to reasonable attorney's fees in an amount approved by the court.

(e) It is a defense to an action brought under this section that the employer's circumstances changed while the employee attended the hearing so that reemployment was impossible or unreasonable. To establish a defense under this subsection, an employer must prove that the termination of employment was because of circumstances other than the employee's attendance at the hearing.

History of Fam. Code §51.116: Acts 1995, 74th Leg., ch. 262, §10, eff. Jan. 1, 1996.

FAM §51.12. PLACE & CONDITIONS OF DETENTION

(a) Except as provided by Subsection (h), a child may be detained only in a:

(1) juvenile processing office in compliance with Section 52.025;

(2) place of nonsecure custody in compliance with Article 45.058, Code of Criminal Procedure;

(3) certified juvenile detention facility that complies with the requirements of Subsection (f);

(4) secure detention facility as provided by Subsection (j);

(5) county jail or other facility as provided by Subsection (*l*); or

(6) nonsecure correctional facility as provided by Subsection (j-1).

(b) The proper authorities in each county shall provide a suitable place of detention for children who are parties to proceedings under this title, but the juvenile board shall control the conditions and terms of detention and detention supervision and shall permit visitation with the child at all reasonable times.

(b-1) A pre-adjudication secure detention facility may be operated only by:

(1) a governmental unit in this state as defined by Section 101.001, Civil Practice and Remedies Code; or

(2) a private entity under a contract with a governmental unit in this state.

(c) In each county, each judge of the juvenile court and a majority of the members of the juvenile board shall personally inspect all public or private juvenile pre-adjudication secure detention facilities that are located in the county at least annually and shall certify in writing to the authorities responsible for operating and giving financial support to the facilities and to the Texas Juvenile Justice Department that the facilities are suitable or unsuitable for the detention of children. In determining whether a facility is suitable or unsuitable for the detention of children, the juvenile court judges and juvenile board members shall consider:

(1) current monitoring and inspection reports and any noncompliance citation reports issued by the department, including the report provided under Subsection (c-1), and the status of any required corrective actions;

(2) current governmental inspector certification regarding the facility's compliance with local fire codes;

(3) current building inspector certification regarding the facility's compliance with local building codes;

(4) for the 12-month period preceding the inspection, the total number of allegations of abuse, neglect, or exploitation reported by the facility and a summary of the findings of any investigations of abuse, neglect, or exploitation conducted by the facility, a local law enforcement agency, and the department;

(5) the availability of health and mental health services provided to facility residents;

(6) the availability of educational services provided to facility residents; and

(7) the overall physical appearance of the facility, including the facility's security, maintenance, cleanliness, and environment.

(c-1) The Texas Juvenile Justice Department shall annually inspect each public or private juvenile pre-adjudication secure detention facility. The department shall provide a report to each juvenile court judge presiding in the same county as an inspected facility indicating whether the facility is suitable or unsuitable for the detention of children in accordance with:

(1) the requirements of Subsections (a), (f), and (g); and

(2) minimum professional standards for the detention of children in pre-adjudication secure confinement promulgated by the department or, at the election of the juvenile board of the county in which the facility is located, the current standards promulgated by the American Correctional Association.

(d) Except as provided by Subsections (j) and (*l*), a child may not be placed in a facility that has not been certified under Subsection (c) as suitable for the detention of children and registered under Subsection (i). Except as provided by Subsections (j) and (*l*), a child detained in a facility that has not been certified under Subsection (c) as suitable for the detention of children

or that has not been registered under Subsection (i) shall be entitled to immediate release from custody in that facility.

(e) If there is no certified place of detention in the county in which the petition is filed, the designated place of detention may be in another county.

(f) A child detained in a building that contains a jail, lockup, or other place of secure confinement, including an alcohol or other drug treatment facility, shall be separated by sight and sound from adults detained in the same building. Children and adults are separated by sight and sound only if they are unable to see each other and conversation between them is not possible. The separation must extend to all areas of the facility, including sally ports and passageways, and those areas used for admission, counseling, sleeping, toileting, showering, dining, recreational, educational, or vocational activities, and health care. The separation may be accomplished through architectural design. A person who has been transferred for prosecution in criminal court under Section 54.02 and is under 17 years of age is considered a child for the purposes of this subsection.

(g) Except for a child detained in a juvenile processing office, a place of nonsecure custody, a secure detention facility as provided by Subsection (j), or a facility as provided by Subsection (*l*), a child detained in a building that contains a jail or lockup may not have any contact with:

(1) part-time or full-time security staff, including management, who have contact with adults detained in the same building; or

(2) direct-care staff who have contact with adults detained in the same building.

(h) This section does not apply to a person:

(1) who has been transferred to criminal court for prosecution under Section 54.02 and is at least 17 years of age; or

(2) who is at least 17 years of age and who has been taken into custody after having:

(A) escaped from a juvenile facility operated by or under contract with the Texas Juvenile Justice Department; or

(B) violated a condition of release under supervision of the department.

(i) Except for a facility as provided by Subsection (*l*), a governmental unit or private entity that operates or contracts for the operation of a juvenile pre-adjudication secure detention facility under Subsection (b-1) in this state shall:

(1) register the facility annually with the Texas Juvenile Justice Department; and

(2) adhere to all applicable minimum standards for the facility.

(j) After being taken into custody, a child may be detained in a secure detention facility until the child is released under Section 53.01, 53.012, or 53.02 or until a detention hearing is held under Section 54.01(a), regardless of whether the facility has been certified under Subsection (c), if:

(1) a certified juvenile detention facility is not available in the county in which the child is taken into custody;

(2) the detention facility complies with:

(A) the short-term detention standards adopted by the Texas Juvenile Justice Department; and

(B) the requirements of Subsection (f); and

(3) the detention facility has been designated by the county juvenile board for the county in which the facility is located.

(j-1) After being taken into custody, a child may be detained in a nonsecure correctional facility until the child is released under Section 53.01, 53.012, or 53.02 or until a detention hearing is held under Section 54.01(a), if:

(1) the nonsecure correctional facility has been appropriately registered and certified;

(2) a certified secure detention facility is not available in the county in which the child is taken into custody;

(3) the nonsecure correctional facility complies with the short-term detention standards adopted by the Texas Juvenile Justice Department; and

(4) the nonsecure correctional facility has been designated by the county juvenile board for the county in which the facility is located.

(k) If a child who is detained under Subsection (j) or (*l*) is not released from detention at the conclusion of the detention hearing for a reason stated in Section 54.01(e), the child may be detained after the hearing only in a certified juvenile detention facility.

(*l*) A child who is taken into custody and required to be detained under Section 53.02(f) may be detained in a county jail or other facility until the child is re-

leased under Section 53.02(f) or until a detention hearing is held as required by Section 54.01(p), regardless of whether the facility complies with the requirements of this section, if:

(1) a certified juvenile detention facility or a secure detention facility described by Subsection (j) is not available in the county in which the child is taken into custody or in an adjacent county;

(2) the facility has been designated by the county juvenile board for the county in which the facility is located;

(3) the child is separated by sight and sound from adults detained in the same facility through architectural design or time-phasing;

(4) the child does not have any contact with management or direct-care staff that has contact with adults detained in the same facility on the same work shift;

(5) the county in which the child is taken into custody is not located in a metropolitan statistical area as designated by the United States Bureau of the Census; and

(6) each judge of the juvenile court and a majority of the members of the juvenile board of the county in which the child is taken into custody have personally inspected the facility at least annually and have certified in writing to the Texas Juvenile Justice Department that the facility complies with the requirements of Subdivisions (3) and (4).

(m) The Texas Juvenile Justice Department may deny, suspend, or revoke the registration of any facility required to register under Subsection (i) if the facility fails to:

(1) adhere to all applicable minimum standards for the facility; or

(2) timely correct any notice of noncompliance with minimum standards.

History of Fam. Code §51.12: Acts 1973, 63rd Leg., ch. 544, §1, eff. Sept. 1, 1973. Amended by Acts 1975, 64th Leg., ch. 693, §§10, 11, eff. Sept. 1, 1975; Acts 1985, 69th Leg., ch. 293, §1, eff. Aug. 26, 1985; Acts 1987, 70th Leg., ch. 149, §31, eff. Sept. 1, 1987; Acts 1995, 74th Leg., ch. 262, §12, eff. Jan. 1, 1996; Acts 1997, 75th Leg., ch. 772, §1 (eff. Sept. 1, 1997), ch. 1374, §1 (eff. Sept. 1, 1997); Acts 1999, 76th Leg., ch. 62, §6.07 (eff. Sept. 1, 1999), ch. 232, §3 (eff. Sept. 1, 1999), ch. 1477, §2 (eff. Sept. 1, 1999); Acts 2001, 77th Leg., ch. 1297, §10 (eff. Sept. 1, 2001), ch. 1514, §13 (eff. Sept. 1, 2001); Acts 2007, 80th Leg., ch. 263, §5, eff. June 8, 2007; Acts 2011, 82nd Leg., ch. 1087, §1, eff. Sept. 1, 2011; Acts 2013, 83rd Leg., ch. 1299, §10, eff. Sept. 1, 2013; Acts 2015, 84th Leg., ch. 734, §44, eff. Sept. 1, 2015.

FAM §51.125. POST-ADJUDICATION CORRECTIONAL FACILITIES

(a) A post-adjudication secure correctional facility for juvenile offenders may be operated only by:

(1) a governmental unit in this state as defined by Section 101.001, Civil Practice and Remedies Code; or

(2) a private entity under a contract with a governmental unit in this state.

(b) In each county, each judge of the juvenile court and a majority of the members of the juvenile board shall personally inspect all public or private juvenile post-adjudication secure correctional facilities that are not operated by the Texas Juvenile Justice Department and that are located in the county at least annually and shall certify in writing to the authorities responsible for operating and giving financial support to the facilities and to the department that the facility or facilities are suitable or unsuitable for the confinement of children. In determining whether a facility is suitable or unsuitable for the confinement of children, the juvenile court judges and juvenile board members shall consider:

(1) current monitoring and inspection reports and any noncompliance citation reports issued by the department, including the report provided under Subsection (c), and the status of any required corrective actions; and

(2) the other factors described under Sections 51.12(c)(2)-(7).

(c) The Texas Juvenile Justice Department shall annually inspect each public or private juvenile post-adjudication secure correctional facility that is not operated by the department. The department shall provide a report to each juvenile court judge presiding in the same county as an inspected facility indicating whether the facility is suitable or unsuitable for the confinement of children in accordance with minimum professional standards for the confinement of children in post-adjudication secure confinement promulgated by the department or, at the election of the juvenile board of the county in which the facility is located, the current standards promulgated by the American Correctional Association.

(d) A governmental unit or private entity that operates or contracts for the operation of a juvenile post-adjudication secure correctional facility in this state under Subsection (a), except for a facility operated by or under contract with the Texas Juvenile Justice Department, shall:

(1) register the facility annually with the department; and

(2) adhere to all applicable minimum standards for the facility.

(e) The Texas Juvenile Justice Department may deny, suspend, or revoke the registration of any facility required to register under Subsection (d) if the facility fails to:

(1) adhere to all applicable minimum standards for the facility; or

(2) timely correct any notice of noncompliance with minimum standards.

History of Fam. Code §51.125: Acts 2007, 80th Leg., ch. 263, §6, eff. June 8, 2007. Amended by Acts 2015, 84th Leg., ch. 734, §45, eff. Sept. 1, 2015.

FAM §51.126. NONSECURE CORRECTIONAL FACILITIES

(a) A nonsecure correctional facility for juvenile offenders may be operated only by:

(1) a governmental unit, as defined by Section 101.001, Civil Practice and Remedies Code; or

(2) a private entity under a contract with a governmental unit in this state.

(b) In each county, each judge of the juvenile court and a majority of the members of the juvenile board shall personally inspect, at least annually, all nonsecure correctional facilities that are located in the county and shall certify in writing to the authorities responsible for operating and giving financial support to the facilities and to the Texas Juvenile Justice Department that the facility or facilities are suitable or unsuitable for the confinement of children. In determining whether a facility is suitable or unsuitable for the confinement of children, the juvenile court judges and juvenile board members shall consider:

(1) current monitoring and inspection reports and any noncompliance citation reports issued by the Texas Juvenile Justice Department, including the report provided under Subsection (c), and the status of any required corrective actions; and

(2) the other factors described under Sections 51.12(c)(2)-(7).

(c) The Texas Juvenile Justice Department shall annually inspect each nonsecure correctional facility. The Texas Juvenile Justice Department shall provide a report to each juvenile court judge presiding in the same county as an inspected facility indicating whether the facility is suitable or unsuitable for the confinement of children in accordance with minimum professional standards for the confinement of children in nonsecure confinement promulgated by the Texas Juvenile Justice Department or, at the election of the juvenile board of the county in which the facility is located, the current standards promulgated by the American Correctional Association.

(d) A governmental unit or private entity that operates or contracts for the operation of a juvenile nonsecure correctional facility in this state under Subsection (a), except for a facility operated by or under contract with the Texas Juvenile Justice Department, shall:

(1) register the facility annually with the Texas Juvenile Justice Department; and

(2) adhere to all applicable minimum standards for the facility.

(e) The Texas Juvenile Justice Department may deny, suspend, or revoke the registration of any facility required to register under Subsection (d) if the facility fails to:

(1) adhere to all applicable minimum standards for the facility; or

(2) timely correct any notice of noncompliance with minimum standards.

(f) Expired.

History of Fam. Code §51.126: Acts 2009, 81st Leg., ch. 1187, §4.005, eff. June 19, 2009. Amended by Acts 2011, 82nd Leg., ch. 85, §2.001, eff. Sept. 1, 2011.

A FAM §51.13. EFFECT OF ADJUDICATION OR DISPOSITION

The amended text in §51.13 is effective for offenses committed on or after Sept. 1, 2017. Offenses in which any element of the offense was committed before Sept. 1, 2017, are governed by the former law in effect at that time.

(a) Except as provided by Subsections (d) and (e), an order of adjudication or disposition in a proceeding under this title is not a conviction of crime. Except as provided by Chapter 841, Health and Safety Code, an order of adjudication or disposition does not impose any civil disability ordinarily resulting from a conviction or operate to disqualify the child in any civil service application or appointment.

(b) The adjudication or disposition of a child or evidence adduced in a hearing under this title may be used only in subsequent:

(1) proceedings under this title in which the child is a party;

(2) sentencing proceedings in criminal court against the child to the extent permitted by the Texas Code of Criminal Procedure, 1965; or

(3) civil commitment proceedings under Chapter 841, Health and Safety Code.

FAM §51.13

(c) A child may not be committed or transferred to a penal institution or other facility used primarily for the execution of sentences of persons convicted of crime, except:

(1) for temporary detention in a jail or lockup pending juvenile court hearing or disposition under conditions meeting the requirements of Section 51.12;

(2) after transfer for prosecution in criminal court under Section 54.02, unless the juvenile court orders the detention of the child in a certified juvenile detention facility under Section 54.02(h);

(3) after transfer from the Texas Juvenile Justice Department under Section 245.151(c), Human Resources Code; or

(4) after transfer from a post-adjudication secure correctional facility, as that term is defined by Section 54.04011.

(d) An adjudication under Section 54.03 that a child engaged in conduct that occurred on or after January 1, 1996, and that constitutes a felony offense resulting in commitment to the Texas Juvenile Justice Department under Section 54.04(d)(2), (d)(3), or (m) or 54.05(f) or commitment to a post-adjudication secure correctional facility under Section 54.04011 for conduct that occurred on or after December 1, 2013, is a final felony conviction only for the purposes of Sections 12.42(a), (b), and (c)(1) or Section 12.425, Penal Code.

(e) A finding that a child engaged in conduct indicating a need for supervision as described by Section 51.03(b)(6) [~~51.03(b)(7)~~] is a conviction only for the purposes of Sections 43.261(c) and (d), Penal Code.

History of Fam. Code §51.13: Acts 1973, 63rd Leg., ch. 544, §1, eff. Sept. 1, 1973. Amended by Acts 1987, 70th Leg., ch. 385, §3, eff. Sept. 1, 1987; Acts 1993, 73rd Leg., ch. 799, §1, eff. June 18, 1993; Acts 1995, 74th Leg., ch. 262, §13, eff. Jan. 1, 1996; Acts 1997, 75th Leg., ch. 1086, §5, eff. Sept. 1, 1997; Acts 1999, 76th Leg., ch. 1188, §4.02, eff. Sept. 1, 1999; Acts 2003, 78th Leg., ch. 283, §6, eff. Sept. 1, 2003; Acts 2011, 82nd Leg., ch. 85, §3.004 (eff. Sept. 1, 2011), ch. 1087, §2 (eff. Sept. 1, 2011), ch. 1322, §17 (eff. Sept. 1, 2011); Acts 2013, 83rd Leg., ch. 1299, §11 (eff. Sept. 1, 2013), ch. 1323, §1 (eff. Dec. 1, 2013); Acts 2015, 84th Leg., ch. 854, §1 (eff. Sept. 1, 2015), ch. 935, §19 (eff. Sept. 1, 2015); H.B. 29, §22, 85th Leg., eff. Sept. 1, 2017; S.B. 1488, §7.003, 85th Leg., eff. Sept. 1, 2017.

FAM §§51.14, 51.15. REPEALED

Repealed by Acts 1995, 74th Leg., ch. 262, §100(A), eff. Jan. 1, 1996.

FAM §51.151. POLYGRAPH EXAMINATION

If a child is taken into custody under Section 52.01 of this code, a person may not administer a polygraph examination to the child without the consent of the child's attorney or the juvenile court unless the child is transferred to criminal court for prosecution under Section 54.02 of this code.

History of Fam. Code §51.151: Acts 1987, 70th Leg., ch. 708, §1, eff. Sept. 1, 1987.

FAM §51.16. REPEALED

Repealed by Acts 1995, 74th Leg., ch. 262, §100(A), eff. Jan. 1, 1996.

FAM §51.17. PROCEDURE & EVIDENCE

(a) Except as provided by Section 56.01(b-1) and except for the burden of proof to be borne by the state in adjudicating a child to be delinquent or in need of supervision under Section 54.03(f) or otherwise when in conflict with a provision of this title, the Texas Rules of Civil Procedure govern proceedings under this title.

(b) Discovery in a proceeding under this title is governed by the Code of Criminal Procedure and by case decisions in criminal cases.

(c) Except as otherwise provided by this title, the Texas Rules of Evidence applicable to criminal cases and Articles 33.03 and 37.07 and Chapter 38, Code of Criminal Procedure, apply in a judicial proceeding under this title.

(d) When on the motion for appointment of an interpreter by a party or on the motion of the juvenile court, in any proceeding under this title, the court determines that the child, the child's parent or guardian, or a witness does not understand and speak English, an interpreter must be sworn to interpret for the person as provided by Article 38.30, Code of Criminal Procedure.

(e) In any proceeding under this title, if a party notifies the court that the child, the child's parent or guardian, or a witness is deaf, the court shall appoint a qualified interpreter to interpret the proceedings in any language, including sign language, that the deaf person can understand, as provided by Article 38.31, Code of Criminal Procedure.

(f) Any requirement under this title that a document contain a person's signature, including the signature of a judge or a clerk of the court, is satisfied if the document contains the signature of the person as captured on an electronic device or as a digital signature. Article 2.26, Code of Criminal Procedure, applies in a proceeding held under this title.

(g) Articles 21.07, 26.07, 26.08, 26.09, and 26.10, Code of Criminal Procedure, relating to the name of an adult defendant in a criminal case, apply to a child in a proceeding held under this title.

(h) Articles 57.01 and 57.02, Code of Criminal Procedure, relating to the use of a pseudonym by a victim in a criminal case, apply in a proceeding held under this title.

(i) Except as provided by Section 56.03(f), the state is not required to pay any cost or fee otherwise imposed for court proceedings in either the trial or appellate courts.

History of Fam. Code §51.17: Acts 1973, 63rd Leg., ch. 544, §1, eff. Sept. 1, 1973. Amended by Acts 1995, 74th Leg., ch. 262, §14, eff. Jan. 1, 1996; Acts 1999, 76th Leg., ch. 1477, §3, eff. Sept. 1, 1999; Acts 2003, 78th Leg., ch. 283, §7, eff. Sept. 1, 2003; Acts 2005, 79th Leg., ch. 949, §6, eff. Sept. 1, 2005; Acts 2007, 80th Leg., ch. 908, §9, eff. Sept. 1, 2007; Acts 2009, 81st Leg., ch. 642, §1, eff. Sept. 1, 2009; Acts 2013, 83rd Leg., ch. 1299, §12, eff. Sept. 1, 2013.

FAM §51.18. ELECTION BETWEEN JUVENILE COURT & ALTERNATE JUVENILE COURT

(a) This section applies only to a child who has a right to a trial before a juvenile court the judge of which is not an attorney licensed in this state.

(b) On any matter that may lead to an order appealable under Section 56.01 of this code, a child may be tried before either the juvenile court or the alternate juvenile court.

(c) The child may elect to be tried before the alternate juvenile court only if the child files a written notice with that court not later than 10 days before the date of the trial. After the notice is filed, the child may be tried only in the alternate juvenile court. If the child does not file a notice as provided by this subsection, the child may be tried only in the juvenile court.

(d) If the child is tried before the juvenile court, the child is not entitled to a trial de novo before the alternate juvenile court.

(e) The child may appeal any order of the juvenile court or alternate juvenile court only as provided by Section 56.01 of this code.

History of Fam. Code §51.18: Acts 1977, 65th Leg., ch. 411, §2, eff. June 15, 1977. Amended by Acts 1993, 73rd Leg., ch. 168, §3, eff. Aug. 30, 1993.

FAM §51.19. LIMITATION PERIODS

(a) The limitation periods and the procedures for applying the limitation periods under Chapter 12, Code of Criminal Procedure, and other statutory law apply to proceedings under this title.

(b) For purposes of computing a limitation period, a petition filed in juvenile court for a transfer or an adjudication hearing is equivalent to an indictment or information and is treated as presented when the petition is filed in the proper court.

(c) The limitation period is two years for an offense or conduct that is not given a specific limitation period under Chapter 12, Code of Criminal Procedure, or other statutory law.

History of Fam. Code §51.19: Acts 1997, 75th Leg., ch. 1086, §6, eff. Sept. 1, 1997.

FAM §51.20. PHYSICAL OR MENTAL EXAMINATION

(a) At any stage of the proceedings under this title, including when a child is initially detained in a pre-adjudication secure detention facility or a post-adjudication secure correctional facility, the juvenile court may, at its discretion or at the request of the child's parent or guardian, order a child who is referred to the juvenile court or who is alleged by a petition or found to have engaged in delinquent conduct or conduct indicating a need for supervision to be examined by a disinterested expert, including a physician, psychiatrist, or psychologist, qualified by education and clinical training in mental health or mental retardation and experienced in forensic evaluation, to determine whether the child has a mental illness as defined by Section 571.003, Health and Safety Code, is a person with mental retardation as defined by Section 591.003, Health and Safety Code, or suffers from chemical dependency as defined by Section 464.001, Health and Safety Code. If the examination is to include a determination of the child's fitness to proceed, an expert may be appointed to conduct the examination only if the expert is qualified under Subchapter B, Chapter 46B, Code of Criminal Procedure, to examine a defendant in a criminal case, and the examination and the report resulting from an examination under this subsection must comply with the requirements under Subchapter B, Chapter 46B, Code of Criminal Procedure, for the examination and resulting report of a defendant in a criminal case.

(b) If, after conducting an examination of a child ordered under Subsection (a) and reviewing any other relevant information, there is reason to believe that the child has a mental illness or mental retardation or suffers from chemical dependency, the probation department shall refer the child to the local mental health or mental retardation authority or to another appropriate and legally authorized agency or provider for evaluation and services, unless the prosecuting attorney has filed a petition under Section 53.04.

(c) If, while a child is under deferred prosecution supervision or court-ordered probation, a qualified professional determines that the child has a mental illness

or mental retardation or suffers from chemical dependency and the child is not currently receiving treatment services for the mental illness, mental retardation, or chemical dependency, the probation department shall refer the child to the local mental health or mental retardation authority or to another appropriate and legally authorized agency or provider for evaluation and services.

(d) A probation department shall report each referral of a child to a local mental health or mental retardation authority or another agency or provider made under Subsection (b) or (c) to the Texas Juvenile Justice Department in a format specified by the department.

(e) At any stage of the proceedings under this title, the juvenile court may order a child who has been referred to the juvenile court or who is alleged by the petition or found to have engaged in delinquent conduct or conduct indicating a need for supervision to be subjected to a physical examination by a licensed physician.

History of Fam. Code §51.20: Acts 1999, 76th Leg., ch. 1477, §4, eff. Sept. 1, 1999. Amended by Acts 2001, 77th Leg., ch. 828, §5(a), eff. Sept. 1, 2001; Acts 2003, 78th Leg., ch. 35, §6, eff. Jan. 1, 2004; Acts 2005, 79th Leg., ch. 949, §7, eff. Sept. 1, 2005; Acts 2013, 83rd Leg., ch. 225, §1, eff. Sept. 1, 2013.

FAM §51.21. MENTAL HEALTH SCREENING & REFERRAL

(a) A probation department that administers the mental health screening instrument or clinical assessment required by Section 221.003, Human Resources Code, shall refer the child to the local mental health authority for assessment and evaluation if:

(1) the child's scores on the screening instrument or clinical assessment indicate a need for further mental health assessment and evaluation; and

(2) the department and child do not have access to an internal, contract, or private mental health professional.

(b) A probation department shall report each referral of a child to a local mental health authority made under Subsection (a) to the Texas Juvenile Justice Department in a format specified by the Texas Juvenile Justice Department.

History of Fam. Code §51.21: Acts 2005, 79th Leg., ch. 949, §8, eff. Sept. 1, 2005. Amended by Acts 2011, 82nd Leg., ch. 85, §3.005, eff. Sept. 1, 2011; Acts 2015, 84th Leg., ch. 734, §46, eff. Sept. 1, 2015.

CHAPTER 52. PROCEEDINGS BEFORE & INCLUDING REFERRAL TO COURT

FAM §52.01. TAKING INTO CUSTODY; ISSUANCE OF WARNING NOTICE

(a) A child may be taken into custody:

(1) pursuant to an order of the juvenile court under the provisions of this subtitle;[1]

(2) pursuant to the laws of arrest;

(3) by a law-enforcement officer, including a school district peace officer commissioned under Section 37.081, Education Code, if there is probable cause to believe that the child has engaged in:

(A) conduct that violates a penal law of this state or a penal ordinance of any political subdivision of this state;

(B) delinquent conduct or conduct indicating a need for supervision; or

(C) conduct that violates a condition of probation imposed by the juvenile court;

(4) by a probation officer if there is probable cause to believe that the child has violated a condition of probation imposed by the juvenile court;

(5) pursuant to a directive to apprehend issued as provided by Section 52.015; or

(6) by a probation officer if there is probable cause to believe that the child has violated a condition of release imposed by the juvenile court or referee under Section 54.01.

(b) The taking of a child into custody is not an arrest except for the purpose of determining the validity of taking him into custody or the validity of a search under the laws and constitution of this state or of the United States.

(c) A law-enforcement officer authorized to take a child into custody under Subdivisions (2) and (3) of Subsection (a) of this section may issue a warning notice to the child in lieu of taking the child into custody if:

(1) guidelines for warning disposition have been issued by the law-enforcement agency in which the officer works;

(2) the guidelines have been approved by the juvenile board of the county in which the disposition is made;

(3) the disposition is authorized by the guidelines;

(4) the warning notice identifies the child and describes the child's alleged conduct;

(5) a copy of the warning notice is sent to the child's parent, guardian, or custodian as soon as practicable after disposition; and

(6) a copy of the warning notice is filed with the law-enforcement agency and the office or official designated by the juvenile board.

(d) A warning notice filed with the office or official designated by the juvenile board may be used as the basis of further action if necessary.

(e) A law-enforcement officer who has probable cause to believe that a child is in violation of the compulsory school attendance law under Section 25.085, Education Code, may take the child into custody for the purpose of returning the child to the school campus of the child to ensure the child's compliance with compulsory school attendance requirements.

1. **Editor's note:** Enacted as such. Probably should be "this title."

History of Fam. Code §52.01: Acts 1973, 63rd Leg., ch. 544, §1, eff. Sept. 1, 1973. Amended by Acts 1993, 73rd Leg., ch. 115, §2, eff. May 11, 1993; Acts 1995, 74th Leg., ch. 262, §15, eff. Jan. 1, 1996; Acts 1997, 75th Leg., ch. 165, §6.08, eff. Sept. 1, 1997; Acts 2001, 77th Leg., ch. 1297, §11, eff. Sept. 1, 2001; Acts 2003, 78th Leg., ch. 283, §8, eff. Sept. 1, 2003; Acts 2005, 79th Leg., ch. 949, §9, eff. Sept. 1, 2005; Acts 2007, 80th Leg., ch. 1058, §16, eff. Sept. 1, 2007; Acts 2013, 83rd Leg., ch. 1407, §14, eff. Sept. 1, 2013.

E FAM §52.011. DUTY OF LAW ENFORCEMENT OFFICER TO NOTIFY PROBATE COURT

(a) In this section, "ward" has the meaning assigned by Section 22.033, Estates Code.

(b) As soon as practicable, but not later than the first working day after the date a law enforcement officer takes a child who is a ward into custody under Section 52.01(a)(2) or (3), the law enforcement officer or other person having custody of the child shall notify the court with jurisdiction over the child's guardianship of the child's detention or arrest.

History of Fam. Code §52.011: Enacted by S.B. 1096, §7, 85th Leg., eff. Sept. 1, 2017.

FAM §52.015. DIRECTIVE TO APPREHEND

(a) On the request of a law-enforcement or probation officer, a juvenile court may issue a directive to apprehend a child if the court finds there is probable cause to take the child into custody under the provisions of this title.

(b) On the issuance of a directive to apprehend, any law-enforcement or probation officer shall take the child into custody.

(c) An order under this section is not subject to appeal.

History of Fam. Code §52.015: Acts 1995, 74th Leg., ch. 262, §16, eff. Jan. 1, 1996.

FAM §52.0151. BENCH WARRANT; ATTACHMENT OF WITNESS IN CUSTODY

(a) If a witness is in a placement in the custody of the Texas Juvenile Justice Department, a juvenile secure detention facility, or a juvenile secure correctional facility, the court may issue a bench warrant or direct that an attachment issue to require a peace officer or probation officer to secure custody of the person at the placement and produce the person in court. Once the person is no longer needed as a witness or the period prescribed by Subsection (c) has expired without extension, the court shall order the peace officer or probation officer to return the person to the placement from which the person was released.

(b) The court may order that the person who is the witness be detained in a certified juvenile detention facility if the person is younger than 17 years of age. If the person is at least 17 years of age, the court may order that the person be detained without bond in an appropriate county facility for the detention of adults accused of criminal offenses.

(c) A witness held in custody under this section may be placed in a certified juvenile detention facility for a period not to exceed 30 days. The length of placement may be extended in 30-day increments by the court that issued the original bench warrant. If the placement is not extended, the period under this section expires and the witness may be returned as provided by Subsection (a).

History of Fam. Code §52.0151: Acts 2005, 79th Leg., ch. 949, §10, eff. Sept. 1, 2005. Amended by Acts 2013, 83rd Leg., ch. 1299, §13, eff. Sept. 1, 2013.

FAM §52.02. RELEASE OR DELIVERY TO COURT

(a) Except as provided by Subsection (c), a person taking a child into custody, without unnecessary delay and without first taking the child to any place other than a juvenile processing office designated under Section 52.025, shall do one of the following:

(1) release the child to a parent, guardian, custodian of the child, or other responsible adult upon that person's promise to bring the child before the juvenile court as requested by the court;

(2) bring the child before the office or official designated by the juvenile board if there is probable cause to believe that the child engaged in delinquent conduct, conduct indicating a need for supervision, or conduct that violates a condition of probation imposed by the juvenile court;

(3) bring the child to a detention facility designated by the juvenile board;

(4) bring the child to a secure detention facility as provided by Section 51.12(j);

(5) bring the child to a medical facility if the child is believed to suffer from a serious physical condition or illness that requires prompt treatment;

(6) dispose of the case under Section 52.03; or

(7) if school is in session and the child is a student, bring the child to the school campus to which the child is assigned if the principal, the principal's designee, or a peace officer assigned to the campus agrees to assume responsibility for the child for the remainder of the school day.

(b) A person taking a child into custody shall promptly give notice of the person's action and a statement of the reason for taking the child into custody, to:

(1) the child's parent, guardian, or custodian; and

(2) the office or official designated by the juvenile board.

(c) A person who takes a child into custody and who has reasonable grounds to believe that the child has been operating a motor vehicle in a public place while having any detectable amount of alcohol in the child's system may, before complying with Subsection (a):

(1) take the child to a place to obtain a specimen of the child's breath or blood as provided by Chapter 724, Transportation Code; and

(2) perform intoxilyzer processing and videotaping of the child in an adult processing office of a law enforcement agency.

(d) Notwithstanding Section 51.09(a), a child taken into custody as provided by Subsection (c) may submit to the taking of a breath specimen or refuse to submit to the taking of a breath specimen without the concurrence of an attorney, but only if the request made of the child to give the specimen and the child's response to that request is videotaped. A videotape made under this subsection must be maintained until the disposition of any proceeding against the child relating to the arrest is final and be made available to an attorney representing the child during that period.

History of Fam. Code §52.02: Acts 1973, 63rd Leg., ch. 544, §1, eff. Sept. 1, 1973. Amended by Acts 1991, 72nd Leg., ch. 495, §1, eff. Sept. 1, 1991; Acts 1997, 75th Leg., ch. 1013, §15 (eff. Sept. 1, 1997), ch. 1374, §2 (eff. Sept. 1, 1997); Acts 1999, 76th Leg., ch. 62, §6.08 (eff. Sept. 1, 1999), ch. 1477, §5 (eff. Sept. 1, 1999); Acts 2001, 77th Leg., ch. 1297, §12, eff. Sept. 1, 2001; Acts 2003, 78th Leg., ch. 283, §9, eff. Sept. 1, 2003; Acts 2007, 80th Leg., ch. 286, §1, eff. Sept. 1, 2007.

FAM §52.025. DESIGNATION OF JUVENILE PROCESSING OFFICE

(a) The juvenile board may designate an office or a room, which may be located in a police facility or sheriff's offices, as the juvenile processing office for the temporary detention of a child taken into custody under Section 52.01. The office may not be a cell or holding facility used for detentions other than detentions under this section. The juvenile board by written order may prescribe the conditions of the designation and limit the activities that may occur in the office during the temporary detention.

(b) A child may be detained in a juvenile processing office only for:

(1) the return of the child to the custody of a person under Section 52.02(a)(1);

(2) the completion of essential forms and records required by the juvenile court or this title;

(3) the photographing and fingerprinting of the child if otherwise authorized at the time of temporary detention by this title;

(4) the issuance of warnings to the child as required or permitted by this title; or

(5) the receipt of a statement by the child under Section 51.095(a)(1), (2), (3), or (5).

(c) A child may not be left unattended in a juvenile processing office and is entitled to be accompanied by the child's parent, guardian, or other custodian or by the child's attorney.

(d) A child may not be detained in a juvenile processing office for longer than six hours.

History of Fam. Code §52.025: Acts 1991, 72nd Leg., ch. 495, §2, eff. Sept. 1, 1991. Amended by Acts 1997, 75th Leg., ch. 1086, §48, eff. Sept. 1, 1997; Acts 2001, 77th Leg., ch. 1297, §13, eff. Sept. 1, 2001.

FAM §52.026. RESPONSIBILITY FOR TRANSPORTING JUVENILE OFFENDERS

(a) It shall be the duty of the law enforcement officer who has taken a child into custody to transport the child to the appropriate detention facility or to the school campus to which the child is assigned as provided by Section 52.02(a)(7) if the child is not released to the parent, guardian, or custodian of the child.

(b) If the juvenile detention facility is located outside the county in which the child is taken into custody, it shall be the duty of the law enforcement officer who has taken the child into custody or, if authorized by the commissioners court of the county, the sheriff of that county to transport the child to the appropriate juvenile detention facility unless the child is:

(1) detained in a secure detention facility under Section 51.12(j); or

(2) released to the parent, guardian, or custodian of the child.

(c) On adoption of an order by the juvenile board and approval of the juvenile board's order by record vote of the commissioners court, it shall be the duty of the sheriff of the county in which the child is taken into custody to transport the child to and from all scheduled juvenile court proceedings and appearances and other activities ordered by the juvenile court.

History of Fam. Code §52.026: Acts 1993, 73rd Leg., ch. 411, §1, eff. Aug. 30, 1993. Amended by Acts 1997, 75th Leg., ch. 1374, §3, eff. Sept. 1, 1997; Acts 1999, 76th Leg., ch. 62, §6.09 (eff. Sept. 1, 1999), ch. 1082, §1 (eff. June 18, 1999); Acts 2007, 80th Leg., ch. 286, §2, eff. Sept. 1, 2007.

FAM §52.027. REPEALED

Repealed by Acts 2001, 77th Leg., ch. 1297, §14 (eff. Sept. 1, 2001), ch. 1514, §19(b) (eff. Sept. 1, 2001); Acts 2003, 78th Leg., ch. 283, §61(1) (eff. Sept. 1, 2003), ch. 1276, §7.001(a) (eff. Sept. 1, 2003).

FAM §52.028. REPEALED

Repealed by Acts 2001, 77th Leg., ch. 1514, §19(b), eff. Sept. 1, 2001.

FAM §52.03. DISPOSITION WITHOUT REFERRAL TO COURT

(a) A law-enforcement officer authorized by this title to take a child into custody may dispose of the case of a child taken into custody or accused of a Class C misdemeanor, other than a traffic offense, without referral to juvenile court or charging a child in a court of competent criminal jurisdiction, if:

(1) guidelines for such disposition have been adopted by the juvenile board of the county in which the disposition is made as required by Section 52.032;

(2) the disposition is authorized by the guidelines; and

(3) the officer makes a written report of the officer's disposition to the law-enforcement agency, identifying the child and specifying the grounds for believing that the taking into custody or accusation of criminal conduct was authorized.

(b) No disposition authorized by this section may involve:

(1) keeping the child in law-enforcement custody; or

(2) requiring periodic reporting of the child to a law-enforcement officer, law-enforcement agency, or other agency.

(c) A disposition authorized by this section may involve:

(1) referral of the child to an agency other than the juvenile court;

(2) a brief conference with the child and his parent, guardian, or custodian; or

(3) referral of the child and the child's parent, guardian, or custodian for services under Section 264.302.

(d) Statistics indicating the number and kind of dispositions made by a law-enforcement agency under the authority of this section shall be reported at least annually to the office or official designated by the juvenile board, as ordered by the board.

History of Fam. Code §52.03: Acts 1973, 63rd Leg., ch. 544, §1, eff. Sept. 1, 1973. Amended by Acts 1995, 74th Leg., ch. 262, §18, eff. Jan. 1, 1996; Acts 1999, 76th Leg., ch. 48, §1, eff. Sept. 1, 1999; Acts 2001, 77th Leg., ch. 1297, §15, eff. Sept. 1, 2001; Acts 2003, 78th Leg., ch. 283, §10, eff. Sept. 1, 2003; Acts 2013, 83rd Leg., ch. 1407, §15, eff. Sept. 1, 2013.

Ⓐ FAM §52.031. FIRST OFFENDER PROGRAM

The amended text in §52.031 is effective for offenses committed or conduct that occurs on or after Sept. 1, 2017. Offenses committed or conduct that occurs in which any element of the offense was committed or the conduct occurred before Sept. 1, 2017, is governed by the former law in effect at that time.

(a) A juvenile board may establish a first offender program under this section for the referral and disposition of children taken into custody, or accused prior to the filing of a criminal charge, of:

(1) conduct indicating a need for supervision;

(2) a Class C misdemeanor, other than a traffic offense; or

(3) delinquent conduct other than conduct that constitutes:

(A) a felony of the first, second, or third degree, an aggravated controlled substance felony, or a capital felony; or

(B) a state jail felony or misdemeanor involving violence to a person or the use or possession of a firearm, location-restricted [~~illegal~~] knife, or club, as those terms are defined by Section 46.01, Penal Code, or a prohibited weapon, as described by Section 46.05, Penal Code.

(a-1) A child accused of a Class C misdemeanor, other than a traffic offense, may be referred to a first offender program established under this section prior to the filing of a complaint with a criminal court.

(b) Each juvenile board in the county in which a first offender program is established shall designate one or more law enforcement officers and agencies, which may be law enforcement agencies, to process a child under the first offender program.

(c) The disposition of a child under the first offender program may not take place until guidelines for the disposition have been adopted by the juvenile board of the county in which the disposition is made as required by Section 52.032.

Subsection (d) was amended by Acts 2013, 83rd Leg., ch. 1407, §16, enacted May 23, 2013, effective Sept. 1, 2013, without reference to the conflicting amendment made by Acts 2013, 83rd Leg., ch. 1409, §8, enacted May 20, 2013, effective Sept. 1, 2013. For harmonizing conflicts, see p. V.

(d) A law enforcement officer taking a child into custody or accusing a child of an offense described in Subsection (a)(2) may refer the child to the law enforcement officer or agency designated under Subsection (b) for disposition under the first offender program and not refer the child to juvenile court or a court of competent criminal jurisdiction only if:

(1) the child has not previously been adjudicated as having engaged in delinquent conduct;

(2) the referral complies with guidelines for disposition under Subsection (c); and

(3) the officer reports in writing the referral to the agency, identifying the child and specifying the grounds for taking the child into custody or accusing a child of an offense described in Subsection (a)(2).

Subsection (d) was amended by Acts 2013, 83rd Leg., ch. 1409, §8, enacted May 20, 2013, effective Sept. 1, 2013, without reference to the conflicting amendment made by Acts 2013, 83rd Leg., ch. 1407, §16, enacted May 23, 2013, effective Sept. 1, 2013. For harmonizing conflicts, see p. V.

(d) A law enforcement officer taking a child into custody for conduct described by Subsection (a) or before issuing a citation to a child for an offense described by Subsection (a-1) may refer the child to the law enforcement officer or agency designated under Subsection (b) for disposition under the first offender program and not refer the child to juvenile court for the conduct or file a complaint with a criminal court for the offense only if:

(1) the child has not previously been adjudicated as having engaged in delinquent conduct;

(2) the referral complies with guidelines for disposition under Subsection (c); and

(3) the officer reports in writing the referral to the agency, identifying the child and specifying the grounds for taking the child into custody or for accusing the child of an offense.

(e) A child referred for disposition under the first offender program may not be detained in law enforcement custody.

Subsection (f) was amended by Acts 2013, 83rd Leg., ch. 1407, §16, enacted May 23, 2013, effective Sept. 1, 2013, without reference to the conflicting amendment made by Acts 2013, 83rd Leg., ch. 1409, §8, enacted May 20, 2013, effective Sept. 1, 2013. For harmonizing conflicts, see p. V.

(f) The parent, guardian, or other custodian of the child must receive notice that the child has been referred for disposition under the first offender program. The notice must:

(1) state the grounds for taking the child into custody or accusing a child of an offense described in Subsection (a)(2);

(2) identify the law enforcement officer or agency to which the child was referred;

(3) briefly describe the nature of the program; and

(4) state that the child's failure to complete the program will result in the child being referred to the juvenile court or a court of competent criminal jurisdiction.

Subsection (f) was amended by Acts 2013, 83rd Leg., ch. 1409, §8, enacted May 20, 2013, effective Sept. 1, 2013, without reference to the conflicting amendment made by Acts 2013, 83rd Leg., ch. 1407, §16, enacted May 23, 2013, effective Sept. 1, 2013. For harmonizing conflicts, see p. V.

(f) The parent, guardian, or other custodian of the child must receive notice that the child has been referred for disposition under the first offender program. The notice must:

(1) state the grounds for taking the child into custody for conduct described by Subsection (a), or for accusing the child of an offense described by Subsection (a-1);

(2) identify the law enforcement officer or agency to which the child was referred;

(3) briefly describe the nature of the program; and

(4) state that the child's failure to complete the program will result in the child being referred to the juvenile court for the conduct or a complaint being filed with a criminal court for the offense.

(g) The child and the parent, guardian, or other custodian of the child must consent to participation by the child in the first offender program.

(h) Disposition under a first offender program may include:

(1) voluntary restitution by the child or the parent, guardian, or other custodian of the child to the victim of the conduct of the child;

(2) voluntary community service restitution by the child;

(3) educational, vocational training, counseling, or other rehabilitative services; and

(4) periodic reporting by the child to the law enforcement officer or agency to which the child has been referred.

(i) The case of a child who successfully completes the first offender program is closed and may not be referred to juvenile court or a court of competent criminal jurisdiction or filed with a criminal court, unless the child is taken into custody under circumstances described by Subsection (j)(3).

(j) The case of a child referred for disposition under the first offender program shall be referred to juvenile court or a court of competent criminal jurisdiction or, if the child is accused of an offense described by Subsection (a-1), filed with a criminal court if:

(1) the child fails to complete the program;

(2) the child or the parent, guardian, or other custodian of the child terminates the child's participation in the program before the child completes it; or

(3) the child completes the program but is taken into custody under Section 52.01 before the 90th day after the date the child completes the program for conduct other than the conduct for which the child was referred to the first offender program.

(k) A statement made by a child to a person giving advice or supervision or participating in the first offender program may not be used against the child in any proceeding under this title or any criminal proceeding.

(*l*) The law enforcement agency must report to the juvenile board in December of each year the following:

(1) the last known address of the child, including the census tract;

(2) the gender and ethnicity of the child referred to the program; and

(3) the offense committed by the child.

History of Fam. Code §52.031: Acts 1995, 74th Leg., ch. 262, §19, eff. Jan. 1, 1996. Amended by Acts 1999, 76th Leg., ch. 48, §2, eff. Sept. 1, 1999; Acts 2013, 83rd Leg., ch. 1407, §16 (eff. Sept. 1, 2013), ch. 1409, §8 (eff. Sept. 1, 2013); H.B. 1935, §1, 85th Leg., eff. Sept. 1, 2017.

FAM §52.032. INFORMAL DISPOSITION GUIDELINES

(a) The juvenile board of each county, in cooperation with each law enforcement agency in the county, shall adopt guidelines for the disposition of a child under Section 52.03 or 52.031. The guidelines adopted under this section shall not be considered mandatory.

(b) The guidelines adopted under Subsection (a) may not allow for the case of a child to be disposed of under Section 52.03 or 52.031 if there is probable cause to believe that the child engaged in delinquent conduct or conduct indicating a need for supervision and cause to believe that the child may be the victim of conduct that constitutes an offense under Section 20A.02, Penal Code.

History of Fam. Code §52.032: Acts 1999, 76th Leg., ch. 48, §3, eff. Sept. 1, 1999. Amended by Acts 2013, 83rd Leg., ch. 186, §3, eff. Sept. 1, 2013.

FAM §52.04. REFERRAL TO JUVENILE COURT; NOTICE TO PARENTS

(a) The following shall accompany referral of a child or a child's case to the office or official designated by the juvenile board or be provided as quickly as possible after referral:

(1) all information in the possession of the person or agency making the referral pertaining to the identity of the child and the child's address, the name and address of the child's parent, guardian, or custodian, the names and addresses of any witnesses, and the child's present whereabouts;

(2) a complete statement of the circumstances of the alleged delinquent conduct or conduct indicating a need for supervision;

(3) when applicable, a complete statement of the circumstances of taking the child into custody; and

(4) when referral is by an officer of a law-enforcement agency, a complete statement of all prior contacts with the child by officers of that law-enforcement agency.

(b) The office or official designated by the juvenile board may refer the case to a law-enforcement agency for the purpose of conducting an investigation to obtain necessary information.

(c) If the office of the prosecuting attorney is designated by the juvenile court to conduct the preliminary investigation under Section 53.01, the referring entity shall first transfer the child's case to the juvenile probation department for statistical reporting purposes only. On the creation of a statistical record or file for the case, the probation department shall within three business days forward the case to the prosecuting attorney for review under Section 53.01.

(d) On referral of the case of a child who has not been taken into custody to the office or official designated by the juvenile board, the office or official designated by the juvenile board shall promptly give notice of the referral and a statement of the reason for the referral to the child's parent, guardian, or custodian.

History of Fam. Code §52.04: Acts 1973, 63rd Leg., ch. 544, §1, eff. Sept. 1, 1973. Amended by Acts 1997, 75th Leg., ch. 1091, §1, eff. June 19, 1997; Acts 2001, 77th Leg., ch. 136, §§1, 2 (eff. Sept. 1, 2001), ch. 1297, §16 (eff. Sept. 1, 2001); Acts 2003, 78th Leg., ch. 283, §11, eff. Sept. 1, 2003.

FAM §52.041. REFERRAL OF CHILD TO JUVENILE COURT AFTER EXPULSION

(a) A school district that expels a child shall refer the child to juvenile court in the county in which the child resides.

(b) The board of the school district or a person designated by the board shall deliver a copy of the order expelling the student and any other information required by Section 52.04 on or before the second working day after the date of the expulsion hearing to the authorized officer of the juvenile court.

(c) Within five working days of receipt of an expulsion notice under this section by the office or official designated by the juvenile board, a preliminary investigation and determination shall be conducted as required by Section 53.01.

(d) The office or official designated by the juvenile board shall within two working days notify the school district that expelled the child if:

(1) a determination was made under Section 53.01 that the person referred to juvenile court was not a child within the meaning of this title;

(2) a determination was made that no probable cause existed to believe the child engaged in delinquent conduct or conduct indicating a need for supervision;

(3) no deferred prosecution or formal court proceedings have been or will be initiated involving the child;

(4) the court or jury finds that the child did not engage in delinquent conduct or conduct indicating a need for supervision and the case has been dismissed with prejudice; or

(5) the child was adjudicated but no disposition was or will be ordered by the court.

(e) In any county where a juvenile justice alternative education program is operated, no student shall be expelled without written notification by the board of the school district or its designated agent to the juvenile board's designated representative. The notification shall be made not later than two business days following the board's determination that the student is to be expelled. Failure to timely notify the designated representative of the juvenile board shall result in the child's duty to continue attending the school district's educational program, which shall be provided to that child until such time as the notification to the juvenile board's designated representative is properly made.

History of Fam. Code §52.041: Acts 1995, 74th Leg., ch. 262, §20, eff. Jan. 1, 1996. Amended by Acts 1997, 75th Leg., ch. 1015, §16, eff. June 19, 1997; Acts 2001, 77th Leg., ch. 1297, §17, eff. Sept. 1, 2001.

CHAPTER 53. PROCEEDINGS PRIOR TO JUDICIAL PROCEEDINGS

FAM §53.01. PRELIMINARY INVESTIGATION & DETERMINATIONS; NOTICE TO PARENTS

(a) On referral of a person believed to be a child or on referral of the person's case to the office or official designated by the juvenile board, the intake officer, probation officer, or other person authorized by the board shall conduct a preliminary investigation to determine whether:

(1) the person referred to juvenile court is a child within the meaning of this title; and

(2) there is probable cause to believe the person:

(A) engaged in delinquent conduct or conduct indicating a need for supervision; or

(B) is a nonoffender who has been taken into custody and is being held solely for deportation out of the United States.

(b) If it is determined that the person is not a child or there is no probable cause, the person shall immediately be released.

Subsection (b-1) is effective for children who engage in conduct that occurs on or after Sept. 1, 2017.

(b-1) The person who is conducting the preliminary investigation shall, as appropriate, refer the child's case to a community resource coordination group, a local-level interagency staffing group, or other community juvenile service provider for services under Section 53.011, if the person determines that:

(1) the child is younger than 12 years of age;

(2) there is probable cause to believe the child engaged in delinquent conduct or conduct indicating a need for supervision;

(3) the child's case does not require referral to the prosecuting attorney under Subsection (d) or (f);

(4) the child is eligible for deferred prosecution under Section 53.03; and

(5) the child and the child's family are not currently receiving services under Section 53.011 and would benefit from receiving the services.

(c) When custody of a child is given to the office or official designated by the juvenile board, the intake officer, probation officer, or other person authorized by the board shall promptly give notice of the whereabouts of the child and a statement of the reason the child was taken into custody to the child's parent, guardian, or custodian unless the notice given under Section 52.02(b) provided fair notice of the child's present whereabouts.

The amended text in subsection (d) is effective for offenses committed or conduct that occurs on or after Sept. 1, 2017. Offenses committed or conduct that occurs in which any element of the offense was committed or the conduct occurred before Sept. 1, 2017, is governed by the former law in effect at that time.

(d) Unless the juvenile board approves a written procedure proposed by the office of prosecuting attorney and chief juvenile probation officer which provides otherwise, if it is determined that the person is a child and, regardless of a finding of probable cause, or a lack thereof, there is an allegation that the child engaged in delinquent conduct of the grade of felony, or conduct constituting a misdemeanor offense involving violence to a person or the use or possession of a firearm, location-restricted [illegal] knife, or club, as those terms are defined by Section 46.01, Penal Code, or prohibited weapon, as described by Section 46.05, Penal Code, the case shall be promptly forwarded to the office of the prosecuting attorney, accompanied by:

(1) all documents that accompanied the current referral; and

(2) a summary of all prior referrals of the child to the juvenile court, juvenile probation department, or a detention facility.

(e) If a juvenile board adopts an alternative referral plan under Subsection (d), the board shall register the plan with the Texas Juvenile Justice Department.

(f) A juvenile board may not adopt an alternate referral plan that does not require the forwarding of a child's case to the prosecuting attorney as provided by Subsection (d) if probable cause exists to believe that the child engaged in delinquent conduct that violates Section 19.03, Penal Code (capital murder), or Section 19.02, Penal Code (murder).

History of Fam. Code §53.01: Acts 1973, 63rd Leg., ch. 544, §1, eff. Sept. 1, 1973. Amended by Acts 1995, 74th Leg., ch. 262, §21, eff. Jan. 1, 1996; Acts 1997, 75th Leg., ch. 1374, §5, eff. Sept. 1, 1997; Acts 2001, 77th Leg., ch. 1297, §18, eff. Sept. 1, 2001; Acts 2003, 78th Leg., ch. 283, §12, eff. Sept. 1, 2003; Acts 2015, 84th Leg., ch. 734, §47, eff. Sept. 1, 2015; H.B. 1204, §1, 85th Leg., eff. Sept. 1, 2017; H.B. 1935, §2, 85th Leg., eff. Sept. 1, 2017.

E FAM §53.011. SERVICES PROVIDED TO CERTAIN CHILDREN & FAMILIES

(a) In this section:

(1) "Community resource coordination group" has the meaning assigned by Section 531.421, Government Code.

(2) "Local-level interagency staffing group" means a group established under the memorandum of understanding described by Section 531.055, Government Code.

(b) On receipt of a referral under Section 53.01(b-1), a community resource coordination group, a local-level interagency staffing group, or another community juvenile services provider shall evaluate the child's case and make recommendations to the juvenile probation department for appropriate services for the child and the child's family.

(c) The probation officer shall create and coordinate a service plan or system of care for the child or the child's family that incorporates the service recommendations for the child or the child's family provided to the juvenile probation department under Subsection (b). The child and the child's parent, guardian, or custodian must consent to the services with knowledge that consent is voluntary.

(d) For a child who receives a service plan or system of care under this section, the probation officer may hold the child's case open for not more than three months to monitor adherence to the service plan or system of care. The probation officer may adjust the service plan or system of care as necessary during the monitoring period. The probation officer may refer the child to the prosecuting attorney if the child fails to successfully participate in required services during that period.

History of Fam. Code §53.011: Enacted by H.B. 1204, §2, 85th Leg., eff. Sept. 1, 2017.

FAM §53.012. REVIEW BY PROSECUTOR

(a) The prosecuting attorney shall promptly review the circumstances and allegations of a referral made under Section 53.01 for legal sufficiency and the desirability of prosecution and may file a petition without regard to whether probable cause was found under Section 53.01.

(b) If the prosecuting attorney does not file a petition requesting the adjudication of the child referred to the prosecuting attorney, the prosecuting attorney shall:

(1) terminate all proceedings, if the reason is for lack of probable cause; or

(2) return the referral to the juvenile probation department for further proceedings.

(c) The juvenile probation department shall promptly refer a child who has been returned to the department under Subsection (b)(2) and who fails or refuses to participate in a program of the department to the prosecuting attorney for review of the child's case and determination of whether to file a petition.

History of Fam. Code §53.012: Acts 1995, 74th Leg., ch. 262, §22, eff. Jan. 1, 1996.

FAM §53.013. PROGRESSIVE SANCTIONS PROGRAM

Each juvenile board may adopt a progressive sanctions program using the model for progressive sanctions in Chapter 59.

History of Fam. Code §53.013: Acts 1995, 74th Leg., ch. 262, §22, eff. Jan. 1, 1996. Amended by Acts 1997, 75th Leg., ch. 1086, §7, eff. Sept. 1, 1997; Acts 2003, 78th Leg., ch. 479, §1, eff. Sept. 1, 2003.

FAM §53.02. RELEASE FROM DETENTION

(a) If a child is brought before the court or delivered to a detention facility as authorized by Sections 51.12(a)(3) and (4), the intake or other authorized officer of the court shall immediately make an investigation and shall release the child unless it appears that his detention is warranted under Subsection (b). The release may be conditioned upon requirements reasonably necessary to insure the child's appearance at later proceedings, but the conditions of the release must be in writing and filed with the office or official designated by the court and a copy furnished to the child.

(b) A child taken into custody may be detained prior to hearing on the petition only if:

(1) the child is likely to abscond or be removed from the jurisdiction of the court;

(2) suitable supervision, care, or protection for the child is not being provided by a parent, guardian, custodian, or other person;

(3) the child has no parent, guardian, custodian, or other person able to return the child to the court when required;

(4) the child may be dangerous to himself or herself or the child may threaten the safety of the public if released;

(5) the child has previously been found to be a delinquent child or has previously been convicted of a penal offense punishable by a term in jail or prison and is likely to commit an offense if released; or

(6) the child's detention is required under Subsection (f).

(c) If the child is not released, a request for detention hearing shall be made and promptly presented to the court, and an informal detention hearing as provided in Section 54.01 of this code shall be held promptly, but not later than the time required by Section 54.01 of this code.

(d) A release of a child to an adult under Subsection (a) must be conditioned on the agreement of the adult to be subject to the jurisdiction of the juvenile court and to an order of contempt by the court if the adult, after notification, is unable to produce the child at later proceedings.

(e) Unless otherwise agreed in the memorandum of understanding under Section 37.011, Education Code, in a county with a population greater than 125,000, if a child being released under this section is expelled under Section 37.007, Education Code, the release shall be conditioned on the child's attending a juvenile justice alternative education program pending a deferred prosecution or formal court disposition of the child's case.

(f) A child who is alleged to have engaged in delinquent conduct and to have used, possessed, or exhibited a firearm, as defined by Section 46.01, Penal Code, in the commission of the offense shall be detained until the child is released at the direction of the judge of the juvenile court, a substitute judge authorized by Section 51.04(f), or a referee appointed under Section 51.04(g), including an oral direction by telephone, or until a detention hearing is held as required by Section 54.01.

History of Fam. Code §53.02: Acts 1973, 63rd Leg., ch. 544, §1, eff. Sept. 1, 1973. Amended by Acts 1979, 66th Leg., ch. 518, §1, eff. June 11, 1979; Acts 1981, 67th Leg., ch. 115, §1, eff. Aug. 31, 1981; Acts 1995, 74th Leg., ch. 262, §23, eff. Jan. 1, 1996; Acts 1997, 75th Leg., ch. 1015, §17 (eff. June 19, 1997), ch. 1374, §6 (eff. Sept. 1, 1997); Acts 1999, 76th Leg., ch. 232, §1, eff. Sept. 1, 1999.

FAM §53.03. DEFERRED PROSECUTION

(a) Subject to Subsections (e) and (g), if the preliminary investigation required by Section 53.01 of this code results in a determination that further proceedings in the case are authorized, the probation officer or other designated officer of the court, subject to the direction of the juvenile court, may advise the parties for a reasonable period of time not to exceed six months concerning deferred prosecution and rehabilitation of a child if:

(1) deferred prosecution would be in the interest of the public and the child;

(2) the child and his parent, guardian, or custodian consent with knowledge that consent is not obligatory; and

(3) the child and his parent, guardian, or custodian are informed that they may terminate the deferred prosecution at any point and petition the court for a court hearing in the case.

(b) Except as otherwise permitted by this title, the child may not be detained during or as a result of the deferred prosecution process.

(c) An incriminating statement made by a participant to the person giving advice and in the discussions or conferences incident thereto may not be used against the declarant in any court hearing.

(d) The juvenile board may adopt a fee schedule for deferred prosecution services and rules for the waiver of a fee for financial hardship in accordance with guidelines that the Texas Juvenile Justice Department shall provide. The maximum fee is $15 a month. If the board adopts a schedule and rules for waiver, the probation officer or other designated officer of the court shall collect the fee authorized by the schedule from the parent, guardian, or custodian of a child for whom a deferred prosecution is authorized under this section or waive the fee in accordance with the rules adopted by the board. The officer shall deposit the fees received under this section in the county treasury to the credit of a special fund that may be used only for juvenile probation or community-based juvenile corrections services or facilities in which a juvenile may be required to live while under court supervision. If the board does not adopt a schedule and rules for waiver, a fee for deferred prosecution services may not be imposed.

(e) A prosecuting attorney may defer prosecution for any child. A probation officer or other designated officer of the court:

(1) may not defer prosecution for a child for a case that is required to be forwarded to the prosecuting attorney under Section 53.01(d); and

(2) may defer prosecution for a child who has previously been adjudicated for conduct that constitutes a felony only if the prosecuting attorney consents in writing.

(f) The probation officer or other officer designated by the court supervising a program of deferred prosecution for a child under this section shall report to the juvenile court any violation by the child of the program.

(g) Prosecution may not be deferred for a child alleged to have engaged in conduct that:

(1) is an offense under Section 49.04, 49.05, 49.06, 49.07, or 49.08, Penal Code; or

(2) is a third or subsequent offense under Section 106.04 or 106.041, Alcoholic Beverage Code.

(h) If the child is alleged to have engaged in delinquent conduct or conduct indicating a need for supervision that violates Section 28.08, Penal Code, deferred prosecution under this section may include:

(1) voluntary attendance in a class with instruction in self-responsibility and empathy for a victim of an offense conducted by a local juvenile probation department, if the class is available; and

(2) voluntary restoration of the property damaged by the child by removing or painting over any markings made by the child, if the owner of the property consents to the restoration.

(h-1) If the child is alleged to have engaged in delinquent conduct or conduct indicating a need for supervision that violates Section 481.115, 481.1151, 481.116, 481.1161, 481.117, 481.118, or 481.121, Health and Safety Code, deferred prosecution under this section may include a condition that the child attend a drug education program that is designed to educate persons on the dangers of drug abuse and is approved by the Department of State Health Services in accordance with Section 521.374, Transportation Code.

(h-2) If the child is alleged to have engaged in delinquent conduct or conduct indicating a need for supervision that violates Section 106.02, 106.025, 106.04, 106.041, 106.05, or 106.07, Alcoholic Beverage Code, or Section 49.02, Penal Code, deferred prosecution under this section may include a condition that the child attend an alcohol awareness program described by Section 106.115, Alcoholic Beverage Code.

(i) The court may defer prosecution for a child at any time:

(1) for an adjudication that is to be decided by a jury trial, before the jury is sworn;

(2) for an adjudication before the court, before the first witness is sworn; or

(3) for an uncontested adjudication, before the child pleads to the petition or agrees to a stipulation of evidence.

(j) The court may add the period of deferred prosecution under Subsection (i) to a previous order of deferred prosecution, except that the court may not place the child on deferred prosecution for a combined period longer than one year.

(k) In deciding whether to grant deferred prosecution under Subsection (i), the court may consider professional representations by the parties concerning the nature of the case and the background of the respondent. The representations made under this subsection by the child or counsel for the child are not admissible against the child at trial should the court reject the application for deferred prosecution.

History of Fam. Code §53.03: Acts 1973, 63rd Leg., ch. 544, §1, eff. Sept. 1, 1973. Amended by Acts 1983, 68th Leg., ch. 565, §1, eff. Sept. 1, 1983; Acts 1987, 70th Leg., ch. 1040, §22, eff. Sept. 1, 1987; Acts 1995, 74th Leg., ch. 262, §24, eff. Jan. 1, 1996; Acts 1997, 75th Leg., ch. 593, §6 (eff. Sept. 1, 1997), ch. 1013, §16 (eff. Sept. 1, 1997); Acts 1999, 76th Leg., ch. 62, §19.01(17), eff. Sept. 1, 1999; Acts 2003, 78th Leg., ch. 283, §13, eff. Sept. 1, 2003; Acts 2005, 79th Leg., ch. 949, §11, eff. Sept. 1, 2005; Acts 2015, 84th Leg., ch. 734, §48 (eff. Sept. 1, 2015), ch. 1004, §5 (eff. Sept. 1, 2015).

FAM §53.035. GRAND JURY REFERRAL

(a) The prosecuting attorney may, before filing a petition under Section 53.04, refer an offense to a grand jury in the county in which the offense is alleged to have been committed.

(b) The grand jury has the same jurisdiction and powers to investigate the facts and circumstances concerning an offense referred to the grand jury under this section as it has to investigate other criminal activity.

(c) If the grand jury votes to take no action on an offense referred to the grand jury under this section, the prosecuting attorney may not file a petition under Section 53.04 concerning the offense unless the same or a successor grand jury approves the filing of the petition.

(d) If the grand jury votes for approval of the prosecution of an offense referred to the grand jury under this section, the prosecuting attorney may file a petition under Section 53.04.

(e) The approval of the prosecution of an offense by a grand jury under this section does not constitute approval of a petition by a grand jury for purposes of Section 53.045.

History of Fam. Code §53.035: Acts 1999, 76th Leg., ch. 1477, §6, eff. Sept. 1, 1999.

FAM §53.04. COURT PETITION; ANSWER

(a) If the preliminary investigation, required by Section 53.01 of this code results in a determination that further proceedings are authorized and warranted, a petition for an adjudication or transfer hearing of a child alleged to have engaged in delinquent conduct or conduct indicating a need for supervision may be made as promptly as practicable by a prosecuting attorney who has knowledge of the facts alleged or is informed and believes that they are true.

(b) The proceedings shall be styled "In the matter of ________________."

(c) The petition may be on information and belief.

(d) The petition must state:

(1) with reasonable particularity the time, place, and manner of the acts alleged and the penal law or standard of conduct allegedly violated by the acts;

(2) the name, age, and residence address, if known, of the child who is the subject of the petition;

(3) the names and residence addresses, if known, of the parent, guardian, or custodian of the child and of the child's spouse, if any;

(4) if the child's parent, guardian, or custodian does not reside or cannot be found in the state, or if their places of residence are unknown, the name and residence address of any known adult relative residing in the county or, if there is none, the name and residence address of the known adult relative residing nearest to the location of the court; and

(5) if the child is alleged to have engaged in habitual felony conduct, the previous adjudications in which the child was found to have engaged in conduct violating penal laws of the grade of felony.

(e) An oral or written answer to the petition may be made at or before the commencement of the hearing. If there is no answer, a general denial of the alleged conduct is assumed.

History of Fam. Code §53.04: Acts 1973, 63rd Leg., ch. 544, §1, eff. Sept. 1, 1973. Amended by Acts 1995, 74th Leg., ch. 262, §25, eff. Jan. 1, 1996.

FAM §53.045. OFFENSES ELIGIBLE FOR DETERMINATE SENTENCE

(a) Except as provided by Subsection (e), the prosecuting attorney may refer the petition to the grand jury of the county in which the court in which the petition is filed presides if the petition alleges that the child engaged in delinquent conduct that constitutes habitual felony conduct as described by Section 51.031 or that included the violation of any of the following provisions:

(1) Section 19.02, Penal Code (murder);

(2) Section 19.03, Penal Code (capital murder);

(3) Section 19.04, Penal Code (manslaughter);

(4) Section 20.04, Penal Code (aggravated kidnapping);

(5) Section 22.011, Penal Code (sexual assault) or Section 22.021, Penal Code (aggravated sexual assault);

(6) Section 22.02, Penal Code (aggravated assault);

(7) Section 29.03, Penal Code (aggravated robbery);

(8) Section 22.04, Penal Code (injury to a child, elderly individual, or disabled individual), if the offense is punishable as a felony, other than a state jail felony;

(9) Section 22.05(b), Penal Code (felony deadly conduct involving discharging a firearm);

(10) Subchapter D, Chapter 481, Health and Safety Code, if the conduct constitutes a felony of the first degree or an aggravated controlled substance felony (certain offenses involving controlled substances);

(11) Section 15.03, Penal Code (criminal solicitation);

(12) Section 21.11(a)(1), Penal Code (indecency with a child);

(13) Section 15.031, Penal Code (criminal solicitation of a minor);

(14) Section 15.01, Penal Code (criminal attempt), if the offense attempted was an offense under Section 19.02, Penal Code (murder), or Section 19.03, Penal Code (capital murder), or an offense listed by Article 42A.054(a), Code of Criminal Procedure;

(15) Section 28.02, Penal Code (arson), if bodily injury or death is suffered by any person by reason of the commission of the conduct;

(16) Section 49.08, Penal Code (intoxication manslaughter); or

(17) Section 15.02, Penal Code (criminal conspiracy), if the offense made the subject of the criminal conspiracy includes a violation of any of the provisions referenced in Subdivisions (1) through (16).

(b) A grand jury may approve a petition submitted to it under this section by a vote of nine members of the grand jury in the same manner that the grand jury votes on the presentment of an indictment.

(c) The grand jury has all the powers to investigate the facts and circumstances relating to a petition submitted under this section as it has to investigate other criminal activity but may not issue an indictment unless the child is transferred to a criminal court as provided by Section 54.02 of this code.

(d) If the grand jury approves of the petition, the fact of approval shall be certified to the juvenile court, and the certification shall be entered in the record of the case. For the purpose of the transfer of a child to the Texas Department of Criminal Justice as provided by Section 152.00161(c) or 245.151(c), Human Resources Code, as applicable, a juvenile court petition approved by a grand jury under this section is an indictment presented by the grand jury.

(e) The prosecuting attorney may not refer a petition that alleges the child engaged in conduct that violated Section 22.011(a)(2), Penal Code, or Sections 22.021(a)(1)(B) and (2)(B), Penal Code, unless the child is more than three years older than the victim of the conduct.

History of Fam. Code §53.045: Acts 1987, 70th Leg., ch. 385, §7, eff. Sept. 1, 1987. Amended by Acts 1991, 72nd Leg., ch. 574, §1, eff. Sept. 1, 1991; Acts 1995, 74th Leg., ch. 262, §§26, 27, eff. Jan. 1, 1996; Acts 1997, 75th Leg., ch. 1086, §8, eff. Sept. 1, 1997; Acts 2001, 77th Leg., ch. 1297, §19, eff. Sept. 1, 2001; Acts 2007, 80th Leg., ch. 908, §10, eff. Sept. 1, 2007; Acts 2011, 82nd Leg., ch. 85, §3.006, eff. Sept. 1, 2011; Acts 2013, 83rd Leg., ch. 1299, §14, eff. Sept. 1, 2013; Acts 2015, 84th Leg., ch. 770, §2.31 (eff. Jan. 1, 2017), ch. 854, §2 (eff. Sept. 1, 2015).

FAM §53.05. TIME SET FOR HEARING

(a) After the petition has been filed, the juvenile court shall set a time for the hearing.

(b) The time set for the hearing shall not be later than 10 working days after the day the petition was filed if:

(1) the child is in detention; or

(2) the child will be taken into custody under Section 53.06(d) of this code.

History of Fam. Code §53.05: Acts 1973, 63rd Leg., ch. 544, §1, eff. Sept. 1, 1973. Amended by Acts 1995, 74th Leg., ch. 262, §28, eff. Jan. 1, 1996.

FAM §53.06. SUMMONS

(a) The juvenile court shall direct issuance of a summons to:

(1) the child named in the petition;

(2) the child's parent, guardian, or custodian;

(3) the child's guardian ad litem; and

(4) any other person who appears to the court to be a proper or necessary party to the proceeding.

(b) The summons must require the persons served to appear before the court at the time set to answer the allegations of the petition. A copy of the petition must accompany the summons.

(c) The court may endorse on the summons an order directing the person having the physical custody or control of the child to bring the child to the hearing. A person who violates an order entered under this subsection may be proceeded against under Section 53.08 or 54.07 of this code.

(d) If it appears from an affidavit filed or from sworn testimony before the court that immediate detention of the child is warranted under Section 53.02(b) of this code, the court may endorse on the summons an order that a law-enforcement officer shall serve the summons and shall immediately take the child into custody and bring him before the court.

(e) A party, other than the child, may waive service of summons by written stipulation or by voluntary appearance at the hearing.

History of Fam. Code §53.06: Acts 1973, 63rd Leg., ch. 544, §1, eff. Sept. 1, 1973. Amended by Acts 1995, 74th Leg., ch. 262, §29, eff. Jan. 1, 1996.

FAM §53.07. SERVICE OF SUMMONS

(a) If a person to be served with a summons is in this state and can be found, the summons shall be served upon him personally at least two days before the day of the adjudication hearing. If he is in this state and cannot be found, but his address is known or can with reasonable diligence be ascertained, the summons may be served on him by mailing a copy by registered or certified mail, return receipt requested, at least five days before the day of the hearing. If he is outside this state but he can be found or his address is known, or his whereabouts or address can with reasonable diligence be ascertained, service of the summons may be made either by delivering a copy to him personally or mailing a copy to him by registered or certified mail, return receipt requested, at least five days before the day of the hearing.

(b) The juvenile court has jurisdiction of the case if after reasonable effort a person other than the child cannot be found nor his post-office address ascertained, whether he is in or outside this state.

(c) Service of the summons may be made by any suitable person under the direction of the court.

(d) The court may authorize payment from the general funds of the county of the costs of service and of necessary travel expenses incurred by persons summoned or otherwise required to appear at the hearing.

(e) Witnesses may be subpoenaed in accordance with the Texas Code of Criminal Procedure, 1965.

History of Fam. Code §53.07: Acts 1973, 63rd Leg., ch. 544, §1, eff. Sept. 1, 1973.

FAM §53.08. WRIT OF ATTACHMENT

(a) The juvenile court may issue a writ of attachment for a person who violates an order entered under Section 53.06(c).

(b) A writ of attachment issued under this section is executed in the same manner as in a criminal proceeding as provided by Chapter 24, Code of Criminal Procedure.

History of Fam. Code §53.08: Acts 1995, 74th Leg., ch. 262, §30, eff. Jan. 1, 1996.

CHAPTER 54. JUDICIAL PROCEEDINGS

FAM §54.01. DETENTION HEARING

(a) Except as provided by Subsection (p), if the child is not released under Section 53.02, a detention hearing without a jury shall be held promptly, but not later than the second working day after the child is taken into custody; provided, however, that when a child is detained on a Friday or Saturday, then such detention hearing shall be held on the first working day after the child is taken into custody.

(b) Reasonable notice of the detention hearing, either oral or written, shall be given, stating the time, place, and purpose of the hearing. Notice shall be given

to the child and, if they can be found, to his parents, guardian, or custodian. Prior to the commencement of the hearing, the court shall inform the parties of the child's right to counsel and to appointed counsel if they are indigent and of the child's right to remain silent with respect to any allegations of delinquent conduct, conduct indicating a need for supervision, or conduct that violates an order of probation imposed by a juvenile court.

(b-1) Unless the court finds that the appointment of counsel is not feasible due to exigent circumstances, the court shall appoint counsel within a reasonable time before the first detention hearing is held to represent the child at that hearing.

(c) At the detention hearing, the court may consider written reports from probation officers, professional court employees, or professional consultants in addition to the testimony of witnesses. Prior to the detention hearing, the court shall provide the attorney for the child with access to all written matter to be considered by the court in making the detention decision. The court may order counsel not to reveal items to the child or his parent, guardian, or guardian ad litem if such disclosure would materially harm the treatment and rehabilitation of the child or would substantially decrease the likelihood of receiving information from the same or similar sources in the future.

(d) A detention hearing may be held without the presence of the child's parents if the court has been unable to locate them. If no parent or guardian is present, the court shall appoint counsel or a guardian ad litem for the child, subject to the requirements of Subsection (b-1).

(e) At the conclusion of the hearing, the court shall order the child released from detention unless it finds that:

(1) he is likely to abscond or be removed from the jurisdiction of the court;

(2) suitable supervision, care, or protection for him is not being provided by a parent, guardian, custodian, or other person;

(3) he has no parent, guardian, custodian, or other person able to return him to the court when required;

(4) he may be dangerous to himself or may threaten the safety of the public if released; or

(5) he has previously been found to be a delinquent child or has previously been convicted of a penal offense punishable by a term in jail or prison and is likely to commit an offense if released.

(f) Unless otherwise agreed in the memorandum of understanding under Section 37.011, Education Code, a release may be conditioned on requirements reasonably necessary to insure the child's appearance at later proceedings, but the conditions of the release must be in writing and a copy furnished to the child. In a county with a population greater than 125,000, if a child being released under this section is expelled under Section 37.007, Education Code, the release shall be conditioned on the child's attending a juvenile justice alternative education program pending a deferred prosecution or formal court disposition of the child's case.

(g) No statement made by the child at the detention hearing shall be admissible against the child at any other hearing.

(h) A detention order extends to the conclusion of the disposition hearing, if there is one, but in no event for more than 10 working days. Further detention orders may be made following subsequent detention hearings. The initial detention hearing may not be waived but subsequent detention hearings may be waived in accordance with the requirements of Section 51.09. Each subsequent detention order shall extend for no more than 10 working days, except that in a county that does not have a certified juvenile detention facility, as described by Section 51.12(a)(3), each subsequent detention order shall extend for no more than 15 working days.

(i) A child in custody may be detained for as long as 10 days without the hearing described in Subsection (a) of this section if:

(1) a written request for shelter in detention facilities pending arrangement of transportation to his place of residence in another state or country or another county of this state is voluntarily executed by the child not later than the next working day after he was taken into custody;

(2) the request for shelter contains:

(A) a statement by the child that he voluntarily agrees to submit himself to custody and detention for a period of not longer than 10 days without a detention hearing;

(B) an allegation by the person detaining the child that the child has left his place of residence in another state or country or another county of this state, that he is

in need of shelter, and that an effort is being made to arrange transportation to his place of residence; and

(C) a statement by the person detaining the child that he has advised the child of his right to demand a detention hearing under Subsection (a) of this section; and

(3) the request is signed by the juvenile court judge to evidence his knowledge of the fact that the child is being held in detention.

(j) The request for shelter may be revoked by the child at any time, and on such revocation, if further detention is necessary, a detention hearing shall be held not later than the next working day in accordance with Subsections (a) through (g) of this section.

(k) Notwithstanding anything in this title to the contrary, the child may sign a request for shelter without the concurrence of an adult specified in Section 51.09 of this code.

(*l*) The juvenile board may appoint a referee to conduct the detention hearing. The referee shall be an attorney licensed to practice law in this state. Such payment or additional payment as may be warranted for referee services shall be provided from county funds. Before commencing the detention hearing, the referee shall inform the parties who have appeared that they are entitled to have the hearing before the juvenile court judge or a substitute judge authorized by Section 51.04(f). If a party objects to the referee conducting the detention hearing, an authorized judge shall conduct the hearing within 24 hours. At the conclusion of the hearing, the referee shall transmit written findings and recommendations to the juvenile court judge or substitute judge. The juvenile court judge or substitute judge shall adopt, modify, or reject the referee's recommendations not later than the next working day after the day that the judge receives the recommendations. Failure to act within that time results in release of the child by operation of law. A recommendation that the child be released operates to secure the child's immediate release, subject to the power of the juvenile court judge or substitute judge to reject or modify that recommendation. The effect of an order detaining a child shall be computed from the time of the hearing before the referee.

(m) The detention hearing required in this section may be held in the county of the designated place of detention where the child is being held even though the designated place of detention is outside the county of residence of the child or the county in which the alleged delinquent conduct, conduct indicating a need for supervision, or probation violation occurred.

(n) An attorney appointed by the court under Section 51.10(c) because a determination was made under this section to detain a child who was not represented by an attorney may request on behalf of the child and is entitled to a de novo detention hearing under this section. The attorney must make the request not later than the 10th working day after the date the attorney is appointed. The hearing must take place not later than the second working day after the date the attorney filed a formal request with the court for a hearing.

(o) The court or referee shall find whether there is probable cause to believe that a child taken into custody without an arrest warrant or a directive to apprehend has engaged in delinquent conduct, conduct indicating a need for supervision, or conduct that violates an order of probation imposed by a juvenile court. The court or referee must make the finding within 48 hours, including weekends and holidays, of the time the child was taken into custody. The court or referee may make the finding on any reasonably reliable information without regard to admissibility of that information under the Texas Rules of Evidence. A finding of probable cause is required to detain a child after the 48th hour after the time the child was taken into custody. If a court or referee finds probable cause, additional findings of probable cause are not required in the same cause to authorize further detention.

(p) If a child is detained in a county jail or other facility as provided by Section 51.12(*l*) and the child is not released under Section 53.02(f), a detention hearing without a jury shall be held promptly, but not later than the 24th hour, excluding weekends and holidays, after the time the child is taken into custody.

(q) If a child has not been released under Section 53.02 or this section and a petition has not been filed under Section 53.04 or 54.05 concerning the child, the court shall order the child released from detention not later than:

(1) the 30th working day after the date the initial detention hearing is held, if the child is alleged to have engaged in conduct constituting a capital felony, an aggravated controlled substance felony, or a felony of the first degree; or

(2) the 15th working day after the date the initial detention hearing is held, if the child is alleged to have

engaged in conduct constituting an offense other than an offense listed in Subdivision (1) or conduct that violates an order of probation imposed by a juvenile court.

(q-1) The juvenile board may impose an earlier deadline than the specified deadlines for filing petitions under Subsection (q) and may specify the consequences of not filing a petition by the deadline the juvenile board has established. The juvenile board may authorize but not require the juvenile court to release a respondent from detention for failure of the prosecutor to file a petition by the juvenile board's deadline.

(r) On the conditional release of a child from detention by judicial order under Subsection (f), the court, referee, or detention magistrate may order that the child's parent, guardian, or custodian present in court at the detention hearing engage in acts or omissions specified by the court, referee, or detention magistrate that will assist the child in complying with the conditions of release. The order must be in writing and a copy furnished to the parent, guardian, or custodian. An order entered under this subsection may be enforced as provided by Chapter 61.

History of Fam. Code §54.01: Acts 1973, 63rd Leg., ch. 544, §1, eff. Sept. 1, 1973. Amended by Acts 1975, 64th Leg., ch. 693, §§14, 15, eff. Sept. 1, 1975; Acts 1979, 66th Leg., ch. 518, §2, eff. June 11, 1979; Acts 1995, 74th Leg., ch. 262, §31, eff. Jan. 1, 1996; Acts 1997, 75th Leg., ch. 922, §1 (eff. Sept. 1, 1997), ch. 1015, §18 (eff. June 19, 1997), ch. 1086, §9 (eff. Sept. 1, 1997); Acts 1999, 76th Leg., ch. 232, §4 (eff. Sept. 1, 1999), ch. 1477, §7 (eff. Sept. 1, 1999); Acts 2001, 77th Leg., ch. 1297, §20 (eff. Sept. 1, 2001), ch. 1420, §21.001(30) (eff. Sept. 1, 2001); Acts 2003, 78th Leg., ch. 283, §14, eff. Sept. 1, 2003; Acts 2005, 79th Leg., ch. 949, §12, eff. Sept. 1, 2005; Acts 2013, 83rd Leg., ch. 912, §4, eff. Sept. 1, 2013.

FAM §54.011. DETENTION HEARINGS FOR STATUS OFFENDERS & NONOFFENDERS; PENALTY

(a) The detention hearing for a status offender or nonoffender who has not been released administratively under Section 53.02 shall be held before the 24th hour after the time the child arrived at a detention facility, excluding hours of a weekend or a holiday. Except as otherwise provided by this section, the judge or referee conducting the detention hearing shall release the status offender or nonoffender from secure detention.

(b) The judge or referee may order a child in detention accused of the violation of a valid court order as defined by Section 51.02 detained not longer than 72 hours after the time the detention order was entered, excluding weekends and holidays, if:

(1) the judge or referee finds at the detention hearing that there is probable cause to believe the child violated the valid court order; and

(2) the detention of the child is justified under Section 54.01(e)(1), (2), or (3).

(c) Except as provided by Subsection (d), a detention order entered under Subsection (b) may be extended for one additional 72-hour period, excluding weekends and holidays, only on a finding of good cause by the juvenile court.

(d) A detention order for a child under this section may be extended on the demand of the child's attorney only to allow the time that is necessary to comply with the requirements of Section 51.10(h), entitling the attorney to 10 days to prepare for an adjudication hearing.

(e) A status offender may be detained for a necessary period, not to exceed the period allowed under the Interstate Compact for Juveniles, to enable the child's return to the child's home in another state under Chapter 60.

(f) Except as provided by Subsection (a), a nonoffender, including a person who has been taken into custody and is being held solely for deportation out of the United States, may not be detained for any period of time in a secure detention facility or secure correctional facility, regardless of whether the facility is publicly or privately operated. A nonoffender who is detained in violation of this subsection is entitled to immediate release from the facility and may bring a civil action for compensation for the illegal detention against any person responsible for the detention. A person commits an offense if the person knowingly detains or assists in detaining a nonoffender in a secure detention facility or secure correctional facility in violation of this subsection. An offense under this subsection is a Class B misdemeanor.

History of Fam. Code §54.011: Acts 1995, 74th Leg., ch. 262, §32, eff. Jan. 1, 1996. Amended by Acts 1997, 75th Leg., ch. 1374, §7, eff. Sept. 1, 1997; Acts 2003, 78th Leg., ch. 283, §§15, 16, eff. Sept. 1, 2003; Acts 2013, 83rd Leg., ch. 1299, §15, eff. Sept. 1, 2013.

FAM §54.012. INTERACTIVE VIDEO RECORDING OF DETENTION HEARING

(a) A detention hearing under Section 54.01 may be held using interactive video equipment if:

(1) the child and the child's attorney agree to the video hearing; and

(2) the parties to the proceeding have the opportunity to cross-examine witnesses.

(b) A detention hearing may not be held using video equipment unless the video equipment for the

hearing provides for a two-way communication of image and sound among the child, the court, and other parties at the hearing.

(c) A recording of the communications shall be made. The recording shall be preserved until the earlier of:

(1) the 91st day after the date on which the recording is made if the child is alleged to have engaged in conduct constituting a misdemeanor;

(2) the 120th day after the date on which the recording is made if the child is alleged to have engaged in conduct constituting a felony; or

(3) the date on which the adjudication hearing ends.

(d) An attorney for the child may obtain a copy of the recording on payment of the reasonable costs of reproducing the copy.

History of Fam. Code §54.012: Acts 1995, 74th Leg., ch. 262, §33, eff. Jan. 1, 1996. Amended by Acts 2005, 79th Leg., ch. 949, §13, eff. Sept. 1, 2005.

FAM §54.02. WAIVER OF JURISDICTION & DISCRETIONARY TRANSFER TO CRIMINAL COURT

(a) The juvenile court may waive its exclusive original jurisdiction and transfer a child to the appropriate district court or criminal district court for criminal proceedings if:

(1) the child is alleged to have violated a penal law of the grade of felony;

(2) the child was:

(A) 14 years of age or older at the time he is alleged to have committed the offense, if the offense is a capital felony, an aggravated controlled substance felony, or a felony of the first degree, and no adjudication hearing has been conducted concerning that offense; or

(B) 15 years of age or older at the time the child is alleged to have committed the offense, if the offense is a felony of the second or third degree or a state jail felony, and no adjudication hearing has been conducted concerning that offense; and

(3) after a full investigation and a hearing, the juvenile court determines that there is probable cause to believe that the child before the court committed the offense alleged and that because of the seriousness of the offense alleged or the background of the child the welfare of the community requires criminal proceedings.

(b) The petition and notice requirements of Sections 53.04, 53.05, 53.06, and 53.07 of this code must be satisfied, and the summons must state that the hearing is for the purpose of considering discretionary transfer to criminal court.

(c) The juvenile court shall conduct a hearing without a jury to consider transfer of the child for criminal proceedings.

(d) Prior to the hearing, the juvenile court shall order and obtain a complete diagnostic study, social evaluation, and full investigation of the child, his circumstances, and the circumstances of the alleged offense.

(e) At the transfer hearing the court may consider written reports from probation officers, professional court employees, or professional consultants in addition to the testimony of witnesses. At least five days prior to the transfer hearing, the court shall provide the attorney for the child and the prosecuting attorney with access to all written matter to be considered by the court in making the transfer decision. The court may order counsel not to reveal items to the child or the child's parent, guardian, or guardian ad litem if such disclosure would materially harm the treatment and rehabilitation of the child or would substantially decrease the likelihood of receiving information from the same or similar sources in the future.

(f) In making the determination required by Subsection (a) of this section, the court shall consider, among other matters:

(1) whether the alleged offense was against person or property, with greater weight in favor of transfer given to offenses against the person;

(2) the sophistication and maturity of the child;

(3) the record and previous history of the child; and

(4) the prospects of adequate protection of the public and the likelihood of the rehabilitation of the child by use of procedures, services, and facilities currently available to the juvenile court.

(g) If the petition alleges multiple offenses that constitute more than one criminal transaction, the juvenile court shall either retain or transfer all offenses relating to a single transaction. Except as provided by Subsection (g-1), a child is not subject to criminal prosecution at any time for any offense arising out of a criminal transaction for which the juvenile court retains jurisdiction.

(g-1) A child may be subject to criminal prosecution for an offense committed under Chapter 19 or Section 49.08, Penal Code, if:

(1) the offense arises out of a criminal transaction for which the juvenile court retained jurisdiction over other offenses relating to the criminal transaction; and

(2) on or before the date the juvenile court retained jurisdiction, one or more of the elements of the offense under Chapter 19 or Section 49.08, Penal Code, had not occurred.

(h) If the juvenile court waives jurisdiction, it shall state specifically in the order its reasons for waiver and certify its action, including the written order and findings of the court, and shall transfer the person to the appropriate court for criminal proceedings and cause the results of the diagnostic study of the person ordered under Subsection (d), including psychological information, to be transferred to the appropriate criminal prosecutor. On transfer of the person for criminal proceedings, the person shall be dealt with as an adult and in accordance with the Code of Criminal Procedure, except that if detention in a certified juvenile detention facility is authorized under Section 152.0015, Human Resources Code, the juvenile court may order the person to be detained in the facility pending trial or until the criminal court enters an order under Article 4.19, Code of Criminal Procedure. A transfer of custody made under this subsection is an arrest.

(h-1) If the juvenile court orders a person detained in a certified juvenile detention facility under Subsection (h), the juvenile court shall set or deny bond for the person as required by the Code of Criminal Procedure and other law applicable to the pretrial detention of adults accused of criminal offenses.

(i) A waiver under this section is a waiver of jurisdiction over the child and the criminal court may not remand the child to the jurisdiction of the juvenile court.

(j) The juvenile court may waive its exclusive original jurisdiction and transfer a person to the appropriate district court or criminal district court for criminal proceedings if:

(1) the person is 18 years of age or older;

(2) the person was:

(A) 10 years of age or older and under 17 years of age at the time the person is alleged to have committed a capital felony or an offense under Section 19.02, Penal Code;

(B) 14 years of age or older and under 17 years of age at the time the person is alleged to have committed an aggravated controlled substance felony or a felony of the first degree other than an offense under Section 19.02, Penal Code; or

(C) 15 years of age or older and under 17 years of age at the time the person is alleged to have committed a felony of the second or third degree or a state jail felony;

(3) no adjudication concerning the alleged offense has been made or no adjudication hearing concerning the offense has been conducted;

(4) the juvenile court finds from a preponderance of the evidence that:

(A) for a reason beyond the control of the state it was not practicable to proceed in juvenile court before the 18th birthday of the person; or

(B) after due diligence of the state it was not practicable to proceed in juvenile court before the 18th birthday of the person because:

(i) the state did not have probable cause to proceed in juvenile court and new evidence has been found since the 18th birthday of the person;

(ii) the person could not be found; or

(iii) a previous transfer order was reversed by an appellate court or set aside by a district court; and

(5) the juvenile court determines that there is probable cause to believe that the child before the court committed the offense alleged.

(k) The petition and notice requirements of Sections 53.04, 53.05, 53.06, and 53.07 of this code must be satisfied, and the summons must state that the hearing is for the purpose of considering waiver of jurisdiction under Subsection (j). The person's parent, custodian, guardian, or guardian ad litem is not considered a party to a proceeding under Subsection (j) and it is not necessary to provide the parent, custodian, guardian, or guardian ad litem with notice.

(*l*) The juvenile court shall conduct a hearing without a jury to consider waiver of jurisdiction under Subsection (j). Except as otherwise provided by this subsection, a waiver of jurisdiction under Subsection (j) may be made without the necessity of conducting the diagnostic study or complying with the requirements of discretionary transfer proceedings under Subsection (d). If requested by the attorney for the person at least 10 days before the transfer hearing, the court shall order that the person be examined pursuant to Section 51.20(a) and that the results of the examina-

tion be provided to the attorney for the person and the attorney for the state at least five days before the transfer hearing.

(m) Notwithstanding any other provision of this section, the juvenile court shall waive its exclusive original jurisdiction and transfer a child to the appropriate district court or criminal court for criminal proceedings if:

(1) the child has previously been transferred to a district court or criminal district court for criminal proceedings under this section, unless:

(A) the child was not indicted in the matter transferred by the grand jury;

(B) the child was found not guilty in the matter transferred;

(C) the matter transferred was dismissed with prejudice; or

(D) the child was convicted in the matter transferred, the conviction was reversed on appeal, and the appeal is final; and

(2) the child is alleged to have violated a penal law of the grade of felony.

(n) A mandatory transfer under Subsection (m) may be made without conducting the study required in discretionary transfer proceedings by Subsection (d). The requirements of Subsection (b) that the summons state that the purpose of the hearing is to consider discretionary transfer to criminal court does not apply to a transfer proceeding under Subsection (m). In a proceeding under Subsection (m), it is sufficient that the summons provide fair notice that the purpose of the hearing is to consider mandatory transfer to criminal court.

(o) If a respondent is taken into custody for possible discretionary transfer proceedings under Subsection (j), the juvenile court shall hold a detention hearing in the same manner as provided by Section 54.01, except that the court shall order the respondent released unless it finds that the respondent:

(1) is likely to abscond or be removed from the jurisdiction of the court;

(2) may be dangerous to himself or herself or may threaten the safety of the public if released; or

(3) has previously been found to be a delinquent child or has previously been convicted of a penal offense punishable by a term of jail or prison and is likely to commit an offense if released.

(p) If the juvenile court does not order a respondent released under Subsection (o), the court shall, pending the conclusion of the discretionary transfer hearing, order that the respondent be detained in:

(1) a certified juvenile detention facility as provided by Subsection (q); or

(2) an appropriate county facility for the detention of adults accused of criminal offenses.

(q) The detention of a respondent in a certified juvenile detention facility must comply with the detention requirements under this title, except that, to the extent practicable, the person shall be kept separate from children detained in the same facility.

(r) If the juvenile court orders a respondent detained in a county facility under Subsection (p), the county sheriff shall take custody of the respondent under the juvenile court's order. The juvenile court shall set or deny bond for the respondent as required by the Code of Criminal Procedure and other law applicable to the pretrial detention of adults accused of criminal offenses.

(s) If a child is transferred to criminal court under this section, only the petition for discretionary transfer, the order of transfer, and the order of commitment, if any, are a part of the district clerk's public record.

History of Fam. Code §54.02: Acts 1973, 63rd Leg., ch. 544, §1, eff. Sept. 1, 1973. Amended by Acts 1975, 64th Leg., ch. 693, §16, eff. Sept. 1, 1975; Acts 1987, 70th Leg., ch. 140, §§1-3, eff. Sept. 1, 1987; Acts 1995, 74th Leg., ch. 262, §34, eff. Jan. 1, 1996; Acts 1999, 76th Leg., ch. 1477, §8, eff. Sept. 1, 1999; Acts 2009, 81st Leg., ch. 1354, §1, eff. Sept. 1, 2009; Acts 2011, 82nd Leg., ch. 1087, §4 (eff. Sept. 1, 2011), ch. 1103, §1 (eff. Sept. 1, 2011); Acts 2013, 83rd Leg., ch. 1299, §16, eff. Sept. 1, 2013.

FAM §54.021. REPEALED

Repealed by Acts 2015, 84th Leg., ch. 935, §41(3), eff. Sept. 1, 2015.

FAM §54.022. REPEALED

Repealed by Acts 2001, 77th Leg., ch. 1297, §71(2) (eff. Sept. 1, 2001), ch. 1514, §19(b) (eff. Sept. 1, 2001).

FAM §54.023. REPEALED

Repealed by Acts 2003, 78th Leg., ch. 283, §61(1), eff. Sept. 1, 2003.

FAM §54.03. ADJUDICATION HEARING

(a) A child may be found to have engaged in delinquent conduct or conduct indicating a need for supervision only after an adjudication hearing conducted in accordance with the provisions of this section.

(b) At the beginning of the adjudication hearing, the juvenile court judge shall explain to the child and his parent, guardian, or guardian ad litem:

(1) the allegations made against the child;

(2) the nature and possible consequences of the proceedings, including the law relating to the admissibility of the record of a juvenile court adjudication in a criminal proceeding;

(3) the child's privilege against self-incrimination;

(4) the child's right to trial and to confrontation of witnesses;

(5) the child's right to representation by an attorney if he is not already represented; and

(6) the child's right to trial by jury.

(c) Trial shall be by jury unless jury is waived in accordance with Section 51.09. If the hearing is on a petition that has been approved by the grand jury under Section 53.045, the jury must consist of 12 persons and be selected in accordance with the requirements in criminal cases. If the hearing is on a petition that alleges conduct that violates a penal law of this state of the grade of misdemeanor, the jury must consist of the number of persons required by Article 33.01(b), Code of Criminal Procedure. Jury verdicts under this title must be unanimous.

(d) Except as provided by Section 54.031, only material, relevant, and competent evidence in accordance with the Texas Rules of Evidence applicable to criminal cases and Chapter 38, Code of Criminal Procedure, may be considered in the adjudication hearing. Except in a detention or discretionary transfer hearing, a social history report or social service file shall not be viewed by the court before the adjudication decision and shall not be viewed by the jury at any time.

(e) A child alleged to have engaged in delinquent conduct or conduct indicating a need for supervision need not be a witness against nor otherwise incriminate himself. An extrajudicial statement which was obtained without fulfilling the requirements of this title or of the constitution of this state or the United States, may not be used in an adjudication hearing. A statement made by the child out of court is insufficient to support a finding of delinquent conduct or conduct indicating a need for supervision unless it is corroborated in whole or in part by other evidence. An adjudication of delinquent conduct or conduct indicating a need for supervision cannot be had upon the testimony of an accomplice unless corroborated by other evidence tending to connect the child with the alleged delinquent conduct or conduct indicating a need for supervision; and the corroboration is not sufficient if it merely shows the commission of the alleged conduct. Evidence illegally seized or obtained is inadmissible in an adjudication hearing.

(f) At the conclusion of the adjudication hearing, the court or jury shall find whether or not the child has engaged in delinquent conduct or conduct indicating a need for supervision. The finding must be based on competent evidence admitted at the hearing. The child shall be presumed to be innocent of the charges against the child and no finding that a child has engaged in delinquent conduct or conduct indicating a need for supervision may be returned unless the state has proved such beyond a reasonable doubt. In all jury cases the jury will be instructed that the burden is on the state to prove that a child has engaged in delinquent conduct or is in need of supervision beyond a reasonable doubt. A child may be adjudicated as having engaged in conduct constituting a lesser included offense as provided by Articles 37.08 and 37.09, Code of Criminal Procedure.

(g) If the court or jury finds that the child did not engage in delinquent conduct or conduct indicating a need for supervision, the court shall dismiss the case with prejudice.

(h) If the finding is that the child did engage in delinquent conduct or conduct indicating a need for supervision, the court or jury shall state which of the allegations in the petition were found to be established by the evidence. The court shall also set a date and time for the disposition hearing.

(i) In order to preserve for appellate or collateral review the failure of the court to provide the child the explanation required by Subsection (b), the attorney for the child must comply with Rule 33.1, Texas Rules of Appellate Procedure, before testimony begins or, if the adjudication is uncontested, before the child pleads to the petition or agrees to a stipulation of evidence.

(j) When the state and the child agree to the disposition of the case, in whole or in part, the prosecuting attorney shall inform the court of the agreement between the state and the child. The court shall inform the child that the court is not required to accept the agreement. The court may delay a decision on whether to accept the agreement until after reviewing a report filed under Section 54.04(b). If the court decides not to accept the agreement, the court shall inform the child of the court's decision and give the child an opportunity to withdraw the plea or stipulation of evidence. If the court rejects the agreement, no document, testimony,

or other evidence placed before the court that relates to the rejected agreement may be considered by the court in a subsequent hearing in the case. A statement made by the child before the court's rejection of the agreement to a person writing a report to be filed under Section 54.04(b) may not be admitted into evidence in a subsequent hearing in the case. If the court accepts the agreement, the court shall make a disposition in accordance with the terms of the agreement between the state and the child.

History of Fam. Code §54.03: Acts 1973, 63rd Leg., ch. 544, §1, eff. Sept. 1, 1973. Amended by Acts 1975, 64th Leg., ch. 693, §17, eff. Sept. 1, 1975; Acts 1979, 66th Leg., ch. 514, §1, eff. Aug. 27, 1979; Acts 1985, 69th Leg., ch. 590, §2, eff. Sept. 1, 1985; Acts 1987, 70th Leg., ch. 385, §8 (eff. Sept. 1, 1987), ch. 386, §3 (eff. Sept. 1, 1987); Acts 1995, 74th Leg., ch. 262, §37, eff. Jan. 1, 1996; Acts 1997, 75th Leg., ch. 1086, §10, eff. Sept. 1, 1997; Acts 1999, 76th Leg., ch. 1477, §9, eff. Sept. 1, 1999; Acts 2001, 77th Leg., ch. 1297, §22, eff. Sept. 1, 2001; Acts 2003, 78th Leg., ch. 283, §17, eff. Sept. 1, 2003; Acts 2009, 81st Leg., ch. 28, §1, eff. Sept. 1, 2009.

FAM §54.031. HEARSAY STATEMENT OF CERTAIN ABUSE VICTIMS

(a) This section applies to a hearing under this title in which a child is alleged to be a delinquent child on the basis of a violation of any of the following provisions of the Penal Code, if a child 12 years of age or younger or a person with a disability is the alleged victim of the violation:

(1) Chapter 21 (Sexual Offenses) or 22 (Assaultive Offenses);

(2) Section 25.02 (Prohibited Sexual Conduct);

(3) Section 43.25 (Sexual Performance by a Child);

(4) Section 20A.02(a)(7) or (8) (Trafficking of Persons); or

(5) Section 43.05(a)(2) (Compelling Prostitution).

(b) This section applies only to statements that describe the alleged violation that:

(1) were made by the child or person with a disability who is the alleged victim of the violation; and

(2) were made to the first person, 18 years of age or older, to whom the child or person with a disability made a statement about the violation.

(c) A statement that meets the requirements of Subsection (b) is not inadmissible because of the hearsay rule if:

(1) on or before the 14th day before the date the hearing begins, the party intending to offer the statement:

(A) notifies each other party of its intention to do so;

(B) provides each other party with the name of the witness through whom it intends to offer the statement; and

(C) provides each other party with a written summary of the statement;

(2) the juvenile court finds, in a hearing conducted outside the presence of the jury, that the statement is reliable based on the time, content, and circumstances of the statement; and

(3) the child or person with a disability who is the alleged victim testifies or is available to testify at the hearing in court or in any other manner provided by law.

(d) In this section, "person with a disability" means a person 13 years of age or older who because of age or physical or mental disease, disability, or injury is substantially unable to protect the person's self from harm or to provide food, shelter, or medical care for the person's self.

History of Fam. Code §54.031: Acts 1985, 69th Leg., ch. 590, §3, eff. Sept. 1, 1985. Amended by Acts 1995, 74th Leg., ch. 76, §14.31, eff. Sept. 1, 1995; Acts 2009, 81st Leg., ch. 284, §3, eff. June 11, 2009; Acts 2011, 82nd Leg., ch. 1, §4.01, eff. Sept. 1, 2011.

FAM §54.032. DEFERRAL OF ADJUDICATION & DISMISSAL OF CERTAIN CASES ON COMPLETION OF TEEN COURT PROGRAM

(a) A juvenile court may defer adjudication proceedings under Section 54.03 for not more than 180 days if the child:

(1) is alleged to have engaged in conduct indicating a need for supervision that violated a penal law of this state of the grade of misdemeanor that is punishable by fine only or a penal ordinance of a political subdivision of this state;

(2) waives, under Section 51.09, the privilege against self-incrimination and testifies under oath that the allegations are true;

(3) presents to the court an oral or written request to attend a teen court program; and

(4) has not successfully completed a teen court program in the two years preceding the date that the alleged conduct occurred.

(b) The teen court program must be approved by the court.

(c) A child for whom adjudication proceedings are deferred under Subsection (a) shall complete the teen court program not later than the 90th day after the date the teen court hearing to determine punishment is held

or the last day of the deferral period, whichever date is earlier. The court shall dismiss the case with prejudice at the time the child presents satisfactory evidence that the child has successfully completed the teen court program.

(d) A case dismissed under this section may not be part of the child's records for any purpose.

(e) The court may require a child who requests a teen court program to pay a fee not to exceed $10 that is set by the court to cover the costs of administering this section. The court shall deposit the fee in the county treasury of the county in which the court is located. A child who requests a teen court program and does not complete the program is not entitled to a refund of the fee.

(f) A court may transfer a case in which proceedings have been deferred as provided by this section to a court in another county if the court to which the case is transferred consents. A case may not be transferred unless it is within the jurisdiction of the court to which it is transferred.

(g) In addition to the fee authorized by Subsection (e), the court may require a child who requests a teen court program to pay a $10 fee to cover the cost to the teen court for performing its duties under this section. The court shall pay the fee to the teen court program, and the teen court program must account to the court for the receipt and disbursal of the fee. A child who pays a fee under this subsection is not entitled to a refund of the fee, regardless of whether the child successfully completes the teen court program.

(h) Notwithstanding Subsection (e) or (g), a juvenile court that is located in the Texas-Louisiana border region, as defined by Section 2056.002, Government Code, may charge a fee of $20 under those subsections.

History of Fam. Code §54.032: Acts 1989, 71st Leg., ch. 1031, §2, eff. Sept. 1, 1989. Amended by Acts 1995, 74th Leg., ch. 748, §1, eff. Sept. 1, 1995; Acts 2001, 77th Leg., ch. 216, §2, eff. Sept. 1, 2001; Acts 2003, 78th Leg., ch. 283, §18, eff. Sept. 1, 2003; Acts 2007, 80th Leg., ch. 910, §2, eff. Sept. 1, 2007.

FAM §54.0325. DEFERRAL OF ADJUDICATION & DISMISSAL OF CERTAIN CASES ON COMPLETION OF TEEN DATING VIOLENCE COURT PROGRAM

(a) In this section:

(1) "Dating violence" has the meaning assigned by Section 71.0021.

(2) "Family violence" has the meaning assigned by Section 71.004.

(3) "Teen dating violence court program" means a program that includes:

(A) a 12-week program designed to educate children who engage in dating violence and encourage them to refrain from engaging in that conduct;

(B) a dedicated teen victim advocate who assists teen victims by offering referrals to additional services, providing counseling and safety planning, and explaining the juvenile justice system;

(C) a court-employed resource coordinator to monitor children's compliance with the 12-week program;

(D) one judge who presides over all of the cases in the jurisdiction that qualify for the program; and

(E) an attorney in the district attorney's office or the county attorney's office who is assigned to the program.

(b) On the recommendation of the prosecuting attorney, the juvenile court may defer adjudication proceedings under Section 54.03 for not more than 180 days if the child is a first offender who is alleged to have engaged in conduct:

(1) that violated a penal law of this state of the grade of misdemeanor; and

(2) involving dating violence.

(c) For the purposes of Subsection (b), a first offender is a child who has not previously been referred to juvenile court for allegedly engaging in conduct constituting dating violence, family violence, or an assault.

(d) Before implementation, the teen dating violence court program must be approved by:

(1) the court; and

(2) the commissioners court of the county.

(e) A child for whom adjudication proceedings are deferred under Subsection (b) shall:

(1) complete the teen dating violence court program not later than the last day of the deferral period; and

(2) appear in court once a month for monitoring purposes.

(f) The court shall dismiss the case with prejudice at the time the child presents satisfactory evidence that the child has successfully completed the teen dating violence court program.

(g) The court may require a child who participates in a teen dating violence court program to pay a fee not to exceed $10 that is set by the court to cover the costs of administering this section. The court shall deposit the fee in the county treasury of the county in which the court is located.

(h) In addition to the fee authorized by Subsection (g), the court may require a child who participates in a teen dating violence court program to pay a fee of $10 to cover the cost to the teen dating violence court program for performing its duties under this section. The court shall pay the fee to the teen dating violence court program, and the teen dating violence court program must account to the court for the receipt and disbursal of the fee.

(i) The court shall track the number of children ordered to participate in the teen dating violence court program, the percentage of victims meeting with the teen victim advocate, and the compliance rate of the children ordered to participate in the program.

History of Fam. Code §54.0325: Acts 2011, 82nd Leg., ch. 1299, §1, eff. Sept. 1, 2011.

FAM §54.0326. DEFERRAL OF ADJUDICATION & DISMISSAL OF CERTAIN CASES ON COMPLETION OF TRAFFICKED PERSONS PROGRAM

(a) This section applies to a juvenile court or to an alternative juvenile court exercising simultaneous jurisdiction over proceedings under this title and Subtitle E, Title 5, in the manner authorized by Section 51.0413.

(b) A juvenile court may defer adjudication proceedings under Section 54.03 until the child's 18th birthday and require a child to participate in a program established under Section 152.0017, Human Resources Code, if the child:

(1) is alleged to have engaged in delinquent conduct or conduct indicating a need for supervision and may be a victim of conduct that constitutes an offense under Section 20A.02, Penal Code; and

(2) presents to the court an oral or written request to participate in the program.

(c) Following a child's completion of the program, the court shall dismiss the case with prejudice at the time the child presents satisfactory evidence that the child successfully completed the program.

History of Fam. Code §54.0326: Acts 2013, 83rd Leg., ch. 186, §4, eff. Sept. 1, 2013. Amended by Acts 2015, 84th Leg., ch. 1236, §21.002(5), eff. Sept. 1, 2015.

FAM §54.033. SEXUALLY TRANSMITTED DISEASE, AIDS, & HIV TESTING

(a) A child found at the conclusion of an adjudication hearing under Section 54.03 of this code to have engaged in delinquent conduct that included a violation of Sections 21.11(a)(1), 22.011, or 22.021, Penal Code, shall undergo a medical procedure or test at the direction of the juvenile court designed to show or help show whether the child has a sexually transmitted disease, acquired immune deficiency syndrome (AIDS), human immunodeficiency virus (HIV) infection, antibodies to HIV, or infection with any other probable causative agent of AIDS. The court may direct the child to undergo the procedure or test on the court's own motion or on the request of the victim of the delinquent conduct.

(b) If the child or another person who has the power to consent to medical treatment for the child refuses to submit voluntarily or consent to the procedure or test, the court shall require the child to submit to the procedure or test.

(c) The person performing the procedure or test shall make the test results available to the local health authority. The local health authority shall be required to notify the victim of the delinquent conduct and the person found to have engaged in the delinquent conduct of the test result.

(d) The state may not use the fact that a medical procedure or test was performed on a child under this section or use the results of the procedure or test in any proceeding arising out of the delinquent conduct.

(e) Testing under this section shall be conducted in accordance with written infectious disease control protocols adopted by the Texas Board of Health that clearly establish procedural guidelines that provide criteria for testing and that respect the rights of the child and the victim of the delinquent conduct.

(f) Nothing in this section allows a court to release a test result to anyone other than a person specifically authorized under this section. Section 81.103(d), Health and Safety Code, may not be construed to allow the disclosure of test results under this section except as provided by this section.

History of Fam. Code §54.033: Acts 1993, 73rd Leg., ch. 811, §2, eff. Sept. 1, 1993.

FAM §54.034. LIMITED RIGHT TO APPEAL: WARNING

Before the court may accept a child's plea or stipulation of evidence in a proceeding held under this title, the court shall inform the child that if the court accepts the plea or stipulation and the court makes a disposition in accordance with the agreement between the state and the child regarding the disposition of the case, the child may not appeal an order of the court entered under Section 54.03, 54.04, or 54.05, unless:

(1) the court gives the child permission to appeal; or

(2) the appeal is based on a matter raised by written motion filed before the proceeding in which the child entered the plea or agreed to the stipulation of evidence.

History of Fam. Code §54.034: Acts 1999, 76th Leg., ch. 74, §1, eff. Sept. 1, 1999.

A FAM §54.04. DISPOSITION HEARING

(a) The disposition hearing shall be separate, distinct, and subsequent to the adjudication hearing. There is no right to a jury at the disposition hearing unless the child is in jeopardy of a determinate sentence under Subsection (d)(3) or (m), in which case, the child is entitled to a jury of 12 persons to determine the sentence, but only if the child so elects in writing before the commencement of the voir dire examination of the jury panel. If a finding of delinquent conduct is returned, the child may, with the consent of the attorney for the state, change the child's election of one who assesses the disposition.

(b) At the disposition hearing, the juvenile court, notwithstanding the Texas Rules of Evidence or Chapter 37, Code of Criminal Procedure, may consider written reports from probation officers, professional court employees, or professional consultants in addition to the testimony of witnesses. On or before the second day before the date of the disposition hearing, the court shall provide the attorney for the child and the prosecuting attorney with access to all written matter to be considered by the court in disposition. The court may order counsel not to reveal items to the child or the child's parent, guardian, or guardian ad litem if such disclosure would materially harm the treatment and rehabilitation of the child or would substantially decrease the likelihood of receiving information from the same or similar sources in the future.

(c) No disposition may be made under this section unless the child is in need of rehabilitation or the protection of the public or the child requires that disposition be made. If the court or jury does not so find, the court shall dismiss the child and enter a final judgment without any disposition. No disposition placing the child on probation outside the child's home may be made under this section unless the court or jury finds that the child, in the child's home, cannot be provided the quality of care and level of support and supervision that the child needs to meet the conditions of the probation.

The amended text in subsection (d) is effective for conduct that occurs on or after Sept. 1, 2017. Conduct in which any element of the conduct occurs before Sept. 1, 2017, is governed by the former law in effect at that time.

(d) If the court or jury makes the finding specified in Subsection (c) allowing the court to make a disposition in the case:

(1) the court or jury may, in addition to any order required or authorized under Section 54.041 or 54.042, place the child on probation on such reasonable and lawful terms as the court may determine:

(A) in the child's own home or in the custody of a relative or other fit person; or

(B) subject to the finding under Subsection (c) on the placement of the child outside the child's home, in:

(i) a suitable foster home;

(ii) a suitable public or private residential treatment facility licensed by a state governmental entity or exempted from licensure by state law, except a facility operated by the Texas Juvenile Justice Department; or

(iii) a suitable public or private post-adjudication secure correctional facility that meets the requirements of Section 51.125, except a facility operated by the Texas Juvenile Justice Department;

(2) if the court or jury found at the conclusion of the adjudication hearing that the child engaged in delinquent conduct that violates a penal law of this state or the United States of the grade of felony, the court or jury made a special commitment finding under Section 54.04013, and [if] the petition was not approved by the grand jury under Section 53.045, the court may commit the child to the Texas Juvenile Justice Department under Section 54.04013, or a post-adjudication secure correctional facility under Section 54.04011(c)(1), as applicable, without a determinate sentence;

(3) if the court or jury found at the conclusion of the adjudication hearing that the child engaged in delinquent conduct that included a violation of a penal law listed in Section 53.045(a) and if the petition was approved by the grand jury under Section 53.045, the court or jury may sentence the child to commitment in the Texas Juvenile Justice Department or a post-adjudication secure correctional facility under Section 54.04011(c)(2) with a possible transfer to the Texas Department of Criminal Justice for a term of:

(A) not more than 40 years if the conduct constitutes:

(i) a capital felony;

(ii) a felony of the first degree; or

(iii) an aggravated controlled substance felony;

(B) not more than 20 years if the conduct constitutes a felony of the second degree; or

(C) not more than 10 years if the conduct constitutes a felony of the third degree;

(4) the court may assign the child an appropriate sanction level and sanctions as provided by the assignment guidelines in Section 59.003;

(5) the court may place the child in a suitable nonsecure correctional facility that is registered and meets the applicable standards for the facility as provided by Section 51.126; or

(6) if applicable, the court or jury may make a disposition under Subsection (m) or Section 54.04011(c)(2)(A).

(e) The Texas Juvenile Justice Department shall accept a person properly committed to it by a juvenile court even though the person may be 17 years of age or older at the time of commitment.

(f) The court shall state specifically in the order its reasons for the disposition and shall furnish a copy of the order to the child. If the child is placed on probation, the terms of probation shall be written in the order.

(g) If the court orders a disposition under Subsection (d)(3) or (m) and there is an affirmative finding that the defendant used or exhibited a deadly weapon during the commission of the conduct or during immediate flight from commission of the conduct, the court shall enter the finding in the order. If there is an affirmative finding that the deadly weapon was a firearm, the court shall enter that finding in the order.

(h) At the conclusion of the dispositional hearing, the court shall inform the child of:

(1) the child's right to appeal, as required by Section 56.01; and

(2) the procedures for the sealing of the child's records under Subchapter C-1, Chapter 58 [~~Section 58.003~~].

(i) If the court places the child on probation outside the child's home or commits the child to the Texas Juvenile Justice Department, the court:

(1) shall include in its order its determination that:

(A) it is in the child's best interests to be placed outside the child's home;

(B) reasonable efforts were made to prevent or eliminate the need for the child's removal from the home and to make it possible for the child to return to the child's home; and

(C) the child, in the child's home, cannot be provided the quality of care and level of support and supervision that the child needs to meet the conditions of probation; and

(2) may approve an administrative body to conduct permanency hearings pursuant to 42 U.S.C. Section 675 if required during the placement or commitment of the child.

(j) If the court or jury found that the child engaged in delinquent conduct that included a violation of a penal law of the grade of felony or jailable misdemeanor, the court:

(1) shall require that the child's thumbprint be affixed or attached to the order; and

(2) may require that a photograph of the child be attached to the order.

(k) Except as provided by Subsection (m), the period to which a court or jury may sentence a person to commitment to the Texas Juvenile Justice Department with a transfer to the Texas Department of Criminal Justice under Subsection (d)(3) applies without regard to whether the person has previously been adjudicated as having engaged in delinquent conduct.

(*l*) Except as provided by Subsection (q), a court or jury may place a child on probation under Subsection (d)(1) for any period, except that probation may not continue on or after the child's 18th birthday. Except as provided by Subsection (q), the court may, before the period of probation ends, extend the probation for any period, except that the probation may not extend to or after the child's 18th birthday.

(m) The court or jury may sentence a child adjudicated for habitual felony conduct as described by Sec-

tion 51.031 to a term prescribed by Subsection (d)(3) and applicable to the conduct adjudicated in the pending case if:

(1) a petition was filed and approved by a grand jury under Section 53.045 alleging that the child engaged in habitual felony conduct; and

(2) the court or jury finds beyond a reasonable doubt that the allegation described by Subdivision (1) in the grand jury petition is true.

(n) A court may order a disposition of secure confinement of a status offender adjudicated for violating a valid court order only if:

(1) before the order is issued, the child received the full due process rights guaranteed by the Constitution of the United States or the Texas Constitution; and

(2) the juvenile probation department in a report authorized by Subsection (b):

(A) reviewed the behavior of the child and the circumstances under which the child was brought before the court;

(B) determined the reasons for the behavior that caused the child to be brought before the court; and

(C) determined that all dispositions, including treatment, other than placement in a secure detention facility or secure correctional facility, have been exhausted or are clearly inappropriate.

(o) In a disposition under this title:

(1) a status offender may not, under any circumstances, be committed to the Texas Juvenile Justice Department for engaging in conduct that would not, under state or local law, be a crime if committed by an adult;

(2) a status offender may not, under any circumstances other than as provided under Subsection (n), be placed in a post-adjudication secure correctional facility; and

(3) a child adjudicated for contempt of a county, justice, or municipal court order may not, under any circumstances, be placed in a post-adjudication secure correctional facility or committed to the Texas Juvenile Justice Department for that conduct.

(p) Except as provided by Subsection (*l*), a court that places a child on probation under Subsection (d)(1) for conduct described by Section 54.0405(b) and punishable as a felony shall specify a minimum probation period of two years.

(q) If a court or jury sentences a child to commitment in the Texas Juvenile Justice Department or a post-adjudication secure correctional facility under Subsection (d)(3) for a term of not more than 10 years, the court or jury may place the child on probation under Subsection (d)(1) as an alternative to making the disposition under Subsection (d)(3). The court shall prescribe the period of probation ordered under this subsection for a term of not more than 10 years. The court may, before the sentence of probation expires, extend the probationary period under Section 54.05, except that the sentence of probation and any extension may not exceed 10 years. The court may, before the child's 19th birthday, discharge the child from the sentence of probation. If a sentence of probation ordered under this subsection and any extension of probation ordered under Section 54.05 will continue after the child's 19th birthday, the court shall discharge the child from the sentence of probation on the child's 19th birthday unless the court transfers the child to an appropriate district court under Section 54.051.

(r) If the judge orders a disposition under this section and there is an affirmative finding that the victim or intended victim was younger than 17 years of age at the time of the conduct, the judge shall enter the finding in the order.

(s), (t) Repealed by Acts 2007, 80th Leg., ch. 263, §64(1), eff. June 8, 2007.

(u) For the purposes of disposition under Subsection (d)(2), delinquent conduct that violates a penal law of this state of the grade of felony does not include conduct that violates a lawful order of a county, municipal, justice, or juvenile court under circumstances that would constitute contempt of that court.

(v) If the judge orders a disposition under this section for delinquent conduct based on a violation of an offense, on the motion of the attorney representing the state the judge shall make an affirmative finding of fact and enter the affirmative finding in the papers in the case if the judge determines that, regardless of whether the conduct at issue is the subject of the prosecution or part of the same criminal episode as the conduct that is the subject of the prosecution, a victim in the trial:

(1) is or has been a victim of a severe form of trafficking in persons, as defined by 22 U.S.C. Section 7102(8); or

(2) has suffered substantial physical or mental abuse as a result of having been a victim of criminal activity described by 8 U.S.C. Section 1101(a)(15)(U)(iii).

(w) That part of the papers in the case containing an affirmative finding under Subsection (v):

(1) must include specific information identifying the victim, as available;

(2) may not include information identifying the victim's location; and

(3) is confidential, unless written consent for the release of the affirmative finding is obtained from the victim or, if the victim is younger than 18 years of age, the victim's parent or guardian.

(x) A child may be detained in an appropriate detention facility following disposition of the child's case under Subsection (d) or (m) pending:

(1) transportation of the child to the ordered placement; and

(2) the provision of medical or other health care services for the child that may be advisable before transportation, including health care services for children in the late term of pregnancy.

(y) A juvenile court conducting a hearing under this section involving a child for whom the Department of Family and Protective Services has been appointed managing conservator may communicate with the court having continuing jurisdiction over the child before the disposition hearing. The juvenile court may allow the parties to the suit affecting the parent-child relationship in which the Department of Family and Protective Services is a party to participate in the communication under this subsection.

(z) Nothing in this section may be construed to prohibit a juvenile court or jury in a county to which Section 54.04011 applies from committing a child to a post-adjudication secure correctional facility in accordance with that section after a disposition hearing held in accordance with this section.

History of Fam. Code §54.04: Acts 1973, 63rd Leg., ch. 544, §1, eff. Sept. 1, 1973. Amended by Acts 1975, 64th Leg., ch. 693, §23, eff. Sept. 1, 1975; Acts 1981, 67th Leg., ch. 394, §1, eff. Aug. 31, 1981; Acts 1983, 68th Leg., ch. 44, art. 1, §3 (eff. Apr. 26, 1983), ch. 565, §2 (eff. Sept. 1, 1983); Acts 1987, 70th Leg., ch. 385, §9 (eff. Sept. 1, 1987), ch. 1052, §6.11 (eff. Sept. 1, 1987); Acts 1989, 71st Leg., ch. 2, §16.01(17) (eff. Aug. 28, 1989), ch. 80, §1 (eff. Sept. 1, 1989); Acts 1991, 72nd Leg., ch. 557, §2 (eff. Sept. 1, 1991), ch. 574, §2 (eff. Sept. 1, 1991), ch. 784, §8 (eff. Sept. 1, 1991); Acts 1993, 73rd Leg., ch. 1048, §1, eff. Sept. 1, 1993; Acts 1995, 74th Leg., ch. 262, §38, eff. Jan. 1, 1996; Acts 1997, 75th Leg., ch. 669, §2 (eff. Sept. 1, 1997), ch. 1086, §11 (eff. Sept. 1, 1997); Acts 1999, 76th Leg., ch. 1193, §9 (eff. Sept. 1, 1999), ch. 1415, §19 (eff. Sept. 1, 1999), ch. 1448, §1 (eff. Sept. 1, 1999), ch. 1477, §10 (eff. Sept. 1, 1999); Acts 2001, 77th Leg., ch. 1297, §23 (eff. Sept. 1, 2001), ch. 1420, §5.001 (eff. Sept. 1, 2001); Acts 2003, 78th Leg., ch. 137, §13, eff. Sept. 1, 2003; Acts 2007, 80th Leg., ch. 263, §§7, 64(1) (eff. June 8, 2007), ch. 849, §3 (eff. June 15, 2007), ch. 908, §11 (eff. Sept. 1, 2007); Acts 2009, 81st Leg., ch. 87, §27.001(13) (eff. Sept. 1, 2009), ch. 108, §2 (eff. May 23, 2009); Acts 2011, 82nd Leg., ch. 438, §2, eff. Sept. 1, 2011; Acts 2013, 83rd Leg., ch. 1299, §17 (eff. Sept. 1, 2013), ch. 1323, §2 (eff. Dec. 1, 2013); Acts 2015, 84th Leg., ch. 734, §49 (eff. Sept. 1, 2015), ch. 962, §1 (eff. Sept. 1, 2015); S.B. 1304, §2, 85th Leg., eff. Sept. 1, 2017.

FAM §54.0401. COMMUNITY-BASED PROGRAMS

(a) This section applies only to a county that has a population of at least 335,000.

(b) A juvenile court of a county to which this section applies may require a child who is found to have engaged in delinquent conduct that violates a penal law of the grade of misdemeanor and for whom the requirements of Subsection (c) are met to participate in a community-based program administered by the county's juvenile board.

(c) A juvenile court of a county to which this section applies may make a disposition under Subsection (b) for delinquent conduct that violates a penal law of the grade of misdemeanor:

(1) if:

(A) the child has been adjudicated as having engaged in delinquent conduct violating a penal law of the grade of misdemeanor on at least two previous occasions;

(B) of the previous adjudications, the conduct that was the basis for one of the adjudications occurred after the date of another previous adjudication; and

(C) the conduct that is the basis of the current adjudication occurred after the date of at least two previous adjudications; or

(2) if:

(A) the child has been adjudicated as having engaged in delinquent conduct violating a penal law of the grade of felony on at least one previous occasion; and

(B) the conduct that is the basis of the current adjudication occurred after the date of that previous adjudication.

(d) The Texas Juvenile Justice Department shall establish guidelines for the implementation of community-based programs described by this section. The juvenile board of each county to which this section applies shall implement a community-based program that complies with those guidelines.

(e) The Texas Juvenile Justice Department shall provide grants to selected juvenile boards to assist with the implementation of a system of community-based programs under this section.

(f) Expired.

History of Fam. Code §54.0401: Acts 2007, 80th Leg., ch. 263, §8, eff. June 8, 2007. Amended by Acts 2015, 84th Leg., ch. 734, §50, eff. Sept. 1, 2015.

FAM §54.04011. COMMITMENT TO POST-ADJUDICATION SECURE CORRECTIONAL FACILITY

(a) In this section, "post-adjudication secure correctional facility" means a facility operated by or under contract with a juvenile board or local juvenile probation department under Section 152.0016, Human Resources Code.

(b) This section applies only to a county in which the juvenile board or local juvenile probation department operates or contracts for the operation of a post-adjudication secure correctional facility.

(c) After a disposition hearing held in accordance with Section 54.04, the juvenile court of a county to which this section applies may commit a child who is found to have engaged in delinquent conduct that constitutes a felony to a post-adjudication secure correctional facility:

(1) without a determinate sentence, if:

(A) the child is found to have engaged in conduct that violates a penal law of the grade of felony and the petition was not approved by the grand jury under Section 53.045;

(B) the child is found to have engaged in conduct that violates a penal law of the grade of felony and the petition was approved by the grand jury under Section 53.045 but the court or jury does not make the finding described by Section 54.04(m)(2); or

(C) the disposition is modified under Section 54.05(f); or

(2) with a determinate sentence, if:

(A) the child is found to have engaged in conduct that included a violation of a penal law listed in Section 53.045 or that is considered habitual felony conduct as described by Section 51.031, the petition was approved by the grand jury under Section 53.045, and, if applicable, the court or jury makes the finding described by Section 54.04(m)(2); or

(B) the disposition is modified under Section 54.05(f).

(d) Nothing in this section may be construed to prohibit:

(1) a juvenile court or jury from making a disposition under Section 54.04, including:

(A) placing a child on probation on such reasonable and lawful terms as the court may determine, including placement in a public or private post-adjudication secure correctional facility under Section 54.04(d)(1)(B)(iii); or

(B) placing a child adjudicated under Section 54.04(d)(3) or (m) on probation for a term of not more than 10 years, as provided in Section 54.04(q); or

(2) the attorney representing the state from filing a motion concerning a child who has been placed on probation under Section 54.04(q) or the juvenile court from holding a hearing under Section 54.051(a).

(e) The provisions of 37 T.A.C. Section 343.610 do not apply to this section.

(f) This section expires on December 31, 2018.

History of Fam. Code §54.04011: Acts 2013, 83rd Leg., ch. 1323, §3, eff. Dec. 1, 2013.

FAM §54.04012. TRAFFICKED PERSONS PROGRAM

(a) This section applies to a juvenile court or to an alternative juvenile court exercising simultaneous jurisdiction over proceedings under this title and Subtitle E, Title 5, in the manner authorized by Section 51.0413.

(b) A juvenile court may require a child adjudicated to have engaged in delinquent conduct or conduct indicating a need for supervision and who is believed to be a victim of conduct that constitutes an offense under Section 20A.02, Penal Code, to participate in a program established under Section 152.0017, Human Resources Code.

(c) The court may require a child participating in the program to periodically appear in court for monitoring and compliance purposes.

(d) Following a child's successful completion of the program, the court may order the sealing of the records of the case in the manner provided by Subchapter C-1, Chapter 58 [~~Sections 58.003(c-7) and (c-8)~~].

History of Fam. Code §54.04012: Acts 2013, 83rd Leg., ch. 186, §5, eff. Sept. 1, 2013. Renumbered from §54.04011 and amended by Acts 2015, 84th Leg., ch. 1236, §§21.001(17), 21.002(6), eff. Sept. 1, 2015. Amended by S.B. 1304, §3, 85th Leg., eff. Sept. 1, 2017.

FAM §54.04013. SPECIAL COMMITMENT TO TEXAS JUVENILE JUSTICE DEPARTMENT

Section 54.04013 is effective for conduct that occurs on or after Sept. 1, 2017.

Notwithstanding any other provision of this code, after a disposition hearing held in accordance with Section 54.04, the juvenile court may commit a child who is found to have engaged in delinquent conduct that con-

stitutes a felony offense to the Texas Juvenile Justice Department without a determinate sentence if the court makes a special commitment finding that the child has behavioral health or other special needs that cannot be met with the resources available in the community. The court should consider the findings of a validated risk and needs assessment and the findings of any other appropriate professional assessment available to the court.

History of Fam. Code §54.04013: Acts 2015, 84th Leg., ch. 962, §2, eff. Sept. 1, 2015.

FAM §54.0402. REPEALED

Repealed by Acts 2015, 84th Leg., ch. 935, §41(3), eff. Sept. 1, 2015.

A FAM §54.0404. ELECTRONIC TRANSMISSION OF CERTAIN VISUAL MATERIAL DEPICTING MINOR: EDUCATIONAL PROGRAMS

The amended text in §54.0404 is effective for offenses committed on or after Sept. 1, 2017. Offenses in which any element of the offense was committed before Sept. 1, 2017, are governed by the former law in effect at that time.

(a) If a child is found to have engaged in conduct indicating a need for supervision described by Section 51.03(b)(6) ~~[51.03(b)(7)]~~, the juvenile court may enter an order requiring the child to attend and successfully complete an educational program described by Section 37.218, Education Code, or another equivalent educational program.

(b) A juvenile court that enters an order under Subsection (a) shall require the child or the child's parent or other person responsible for the child's support to pay the cost of attending an educational program under Subsection (a) if the court determines that the child, parent, or other person is financially able to make payment.

History of Fam. Code §54.0404: Acts 2011, 82nd Leg., ch. 1322, §18, eff. Sept. 1, 2011. Amended by Acts 2013, 83rd Leg., ch. 1299, §18, eff. Sept. 1, 2013; Acts 2015, 84th Leg., ch. 935, §20, eff. Sept. 1, 2015; H.B. 29, §23, 85th Leg., eff. Sept. 1, 2017; S.B. 1488, §7.004, 85th Leg., eff. Sept. 1, 2017.

FAM §54.0405. CHILD PLACED ON PROBATION FOR CONDUCT CONSTITUTING SEXUAL OFFENSE

(a) If a court or jury makes a disposition under Section 54.04 in which a child described by Subsection (b) is placed on probation, the court:

(1) may require as a condition of probation that the child:

(A) attend psychological counseling sessions for sex offenders as provided by Subsection (e); and

(B) submit to a polygraph examination as provided by Subsection (f) for purposes of evaluating the child's treatment progress; and

(2) shall require as a condition of probation that the child:

(A) register under Chapter 62, Code of Criminal Procedure; and

(B) submit a blood sample or other specimen to the Department of Public Safety under Subchapter G, Chapter 411, Government Code, for the purpose of creating a DNA record of the child, unless the child has already submitted the required specimen under other state law.

(b) This section applies to a child placed on probation for conduct constituting an offense for which the child is required to register as a sex offender under Chapter 62, Code of Criminal Procedure.

(c) Psychological counseling required as a condition of probation under Subsection (a) must be with an individual or organization that:

(1) provides sex offender treatment or counseling;

(2) is specified by the local juvenile probation department supervising the child; and

(3) meets minimum standards of counseling established by the local juvenile probation department.

(d) A polygraph examination required as a condition of probation under Subsection (a) must be administered by an individual who is:

(1) specified by the local juvenile probation department supervising the child; and

(2) licensed as a polygraph examiner under Chapter 1703, Occupations Code.

(e) A local juvenile probation department that specifies a sex offender treatment provider under Subsection (c) to provide counseling to a child shall:

(1) establish with the cooperation of the treatment provider the date, time, and place of the first counseling session between the child and the treatment provider;

(2) notify the child and the treatment provider, not later than the 21st day after the date the order making the disposition placing the child on probation under Section 54.04 becomes final, of the date, time, and place of the first counseling session between the child and the treatment provider; and

(3) require the treatment provider to notify the department immediately if the child fails to attend any scheduled counseling session.

(f) A local juvenile probation department that specifies a polygraph examiner under Subsection (d) to administer a polygraph examination to a child shall arrange for a polygraph examination to be administered to the child:

(1) not later than the 60th day after the date the child attends the first counseling session established under Subsection (e); and

(2) after the initial polygraph examination, as required by Subdivision (1), on the request of the treatment provider specified under Subsection (c).

(g) A court that requires as a condition of probation that a child attend psychological counseling under Subsection (a) may order the parent or guardian of the child to:

(1) attend four sessions of instruction with an individual or organization specified by the court relating to:

(A) sexual offenses;

(B) family communication skills;

(C) sex offender treatment;

(D) victims' rights;

(E) parental supervision; and

(F) appropriate sexual behavior; and

(2) during the period the child attends psychological counseling, participate in monthly treatment groups conducted by the child's treatment provider relating to the child's psychological counseling.

(h) A court that orders a parent or guardian of a child to attend instructional sessions and participate in treatment groups under Subsection (g) shall require:

(1) the individual or organization specified by the court under Subsection (g) to notify the court immediately if the parent or guardian fails to attend any scheduled instructional session; and

(2) the child's treatment provider specified under Subsection (c) to notify the court immediately if the parent or guardian fails to attend a session in which the parent or guardian is required to participate in a scheduled treatment group.

(i) A court that requires as a condition of probation that a child attend psychological counseling under Subsection (a) may, before the date the probation period ends, extend the probation for any additional period necessary to complete the required counseling as determined by the treatment provider, except that the probation may not be extended to a date after the date of the child's 18th birthday, or 19th birthday if the child is placed on determinate sentence probation under Section 54.04(q).

History of Fam. Code §54.0405: Acts 1997, 75th Leg., ch. 669, §1, eff. Sept. 1, 1997. Amended by Acts 2001, 77th Leg., ch. 211, §13 (eff. Sept. 1, 2001), ch. 1420, §14.743 (eff. Sept. 1, 2001); Acts 2011, 82nd Leg., ch. 438, §3, eff. Sept. 1, 2011.

FAM §54.0406. CHILD PLACED ON PROBATION FOR CONDUCT INVOLVING A HANDGUN

(a) If a court or jury places a child on probation under Section 54.04(d) for conduct that violates a penal law that includes as an element of the offense the possession, carrying, using, or exhibiting of a handgun, as defined by Section 46.01, Penal Code, and if at the adjudication hearing the court or jury affirmatively finds that the child personally possessed, carried, used, or exhibited the handgun, the court shall require as a condition of probation that the child, not later than the 30th day after the date the court places the child on probation, notify the juvenile probation officer who is supervising the child of the manner in which the child acquired the handgun, including the date and place of and any person involved in the acquisition.

(b) On receipt of information described by Subsection (a), a juvenile probation officer shall promptly notify the appropriate local law enforcement agency of the information.

(c) Information provided by a child to a juvenile probation officer as required by Subsection (a) and any other information derived from that information may not be used as evidence against the child in any juvenile or criminal proceeding.

History of Fam. Code §54.0406: Acts 1999, 76th Leg., ch. 1446, §1, eff. Sept. 1, 1999.

FAM §54.0407. CRUELTY TO ANIMALS: COUNSELING REQUIRED

If a child is found to have engaged in delinquent conduct constituting an offense under Section 42.09 or 42.092, Penal Code, the juvenile court shall order the child to participate in psychological counseling for a period to be determined by the court.

History of Fam. Code §54.0407: Acts 2001, 77th Leg., ch. 450, §2, eff. Sept. 1, 2001. Amended by Acts 2007, 80th Leg., ch. 886, §3, eff. Sept. 1, 2007.

FAM §54.0408. REFERRAL OF CHILD EXITING PROBATION TO MENTAL HEALTH OR MENTAL RETARDATION AUTHORITY

A juvenile probation officer shall refer a child who has been determined to have a mental illness or mental retardation to an appropriate local mental health or mental retardation authority at least three months before the child is to complete the child's juvenile probation term unless the child is currently receiving treatment from the local mental health or mental retardation authority of the county in which the child resides.

History of Fam. Code §54.0408: Acts 2005, 79th Leg., ch. 949, §14, eff. Sept. 1, 2005.

FAM §54.0409. DNA SAMPLE REQUIRED ON CERTAIN FELONY ADJUDICATIONS

(a) This section applies only to conduct constituting the commission of a felony:

(1) that is listed in Article 42A.054(a), Code of Criminal Procedure; or

(2) for which it is shown that a deadly weapon, as defined by Section 1.07, Penal Code, was used or exhibited during the commission of the conduct or during immediate flight from the commission of the conduct.

(b) If a court or jury makes a disposition under Section 54.04 in which a child is adjudicated as having engaged in conduct constituting the commission of a felony to which this section applies and the child is placed on probation, the court shall require as a condition of probation that the child provide a DNA sample under Subchapter G, Chapter 411, Government Code, for the purpose of creating a DNA record of the child, unless the child has already submitted the required sample under other state law.

History of Fam. Code §54.0409: Acts 2009, 81st Leg., ch. 1209, §3, eff. Sept. 1, 2009. Amended by Acts 2015, 84th Leg., ch. 770, §2.32, eff. Jan. 1, 2017.

FAM §54.041. ORDERS AFFECTING PARENTS & OTHERS

(a) When a child has been found to have engaged in delinquent conduct or conduct indicating a need for supervision and the juvenile court has made a finding that the child is in need of rehabilitation or that the protection of the public or the child requires that disposition be made, the juvenile court, on notice by any reasonable method to all persons affected, may:

(1) order any person found by the juvenile court to have, by a wilful act or omission, contributed to, caused, or encouraged the child's delinquent conduct or conduct indicating a need for supervision to do any act that the juvenile court determines to be reasonable and necessary for the welfare of the child or to refrain from doing any act that the juvenile court determines to be injurious to the welfare of the child;

(2) enjoin all contact between the child and a person who is found to be a contributing cause of the child's delinquent conduct or conduct indicating a need for supervision;

(3) after notice and a hearing of all persons affected order any person living in the same household with the child to participate in social or psychological counseling to assist in the rehabilitation of the child and to strengthen the child's family environment; or

(4) after notice and a hearing of all persons affected order the child's parent or other person responsible for the child's support to pay all or part of the reasonable costs of treatment programs in which the child is required to participate during the period of probation if the court finds the child's parent or person responsible for the child's support is able to pay the costs.

(b) If a child is found to have engaged in delinquent conduct or conduct indicating a need for supervision arising from the commission of an offense in which property damage or loss or personal injury occurred, the juvenile court, on notice to all persons affected and on hearing, may order the child or a parent to make full or partial restitution to the victim of the offense. The program of restitution must promote the rehabilitation of the child, be appropriate to the age and physical, emotional, and mental abilities of the child, and not conflict with the child's schooling. When practicable and subject to court supervision, the court may approve a restitution program based on a settlement between the child and the victim of the offense. An order under this subsection may provide for periodic payments by the child or a parent of the child for the period specified in the order but except as provided by Subsection (h), that period may not extend past the date of the 18th birthday of the child or past the date the child is no longer enrolled in an accredited secondary school in a program leading toward a high school diploma, whichever date is later.

(c) Restitution under this section is cumulative of any other remedy allowed by law and may be used in addition to other remedies; except that a victim of an offense is not entitled to receive more than actual damages under a juvenile court order.

(d) A person subject to an order proposed under Subsection (a) of this section is entitled to a hearing on the order before the order is entered by the court.

(e) An order made under this section may be enforced as provided by Section 54.07 of this code.

(f), (g) Repealed by Acts 2015, 84th Leg., ch. 935, §41(3), eff. Sept. 1, 2015.

(h) If the juvenile court places the child on probation in a determinate sentence proceeding initiated under Section 53.045 and transfers supervision on the child's 19th birthday to a district court for placement on community supervision, the district court shall require the payment of any unpaid restitution as a condition of the community supervision. The liability of the child's parent for restitution may not be extended by transfer to a district court for supervision.

History of Fam. Code §54.041: Acts 1975, 64th Leg., ch. 693, §18, eff. Sept. 1, 1975. Amended by Acts 1979, 66th Leg., ch. 154, §2, eff. Sept. 1, 1979; Acts 1983, 68th Leg., ch. 110, §1 (eff. Aug. 29, 1983), ch. 565, §3 (eff. Sept. 1, 1983); Acts 1989, 71st Leg., ch. 1170, §3, eff. June 16, 1989; Acts 1995, 74th Leg., ch. 262, §39, eff. Jan. 1, 1996; Acts 1997, 75th Leg., ch. 165, §6.09, eff. Sept. 1, 1997; Acts 2001, 77th Leg., ch. 1297, §15 (eff. Sept. 1, 2001), ch. 1514, §24 (eff. Sept. 1, 2001); Acts 2003, 78th Leg., ch. 283, §19, eff. Sept. 1, 2003; Acts 2011, 82nd Leg., ch. 438, §4, eff. Sept. 1, 2011; Acts 2015, 84th Leg., ch. 935, §41(3), eff. Sept. 1, 2015.

FAM §54.0411. JUVENILE PROBATION DIVERSION FUND

(a) If a disposition hearing is held under Section 54.04 of this code, the juvenile court, after giving the child, parent, or other person responsible for the child's support a reasonable opportunity to be heard, shall order the child, parent, or other person, if financially able to do so, to pay a fee as costs of court of $20.

(b) Orders for the payment of fees under this section may be enforced as provided by Section 54.07 of this code.

(c) An officer collecting costs under this section shall keep separate records of the funds collected as costs under this section and shall deposit the funds in the county treasury.

(d) Each officer collecting court costs under this section shall file the reports required under Article 103.005, Code of Criminal Procedure. If no funds due as costs under this section have been collected in any quarter, the report required for each quarter shall be filed in the regular manner, and the report must state that no funds due under this section were collected.

(e) The custodian of the county treasury may deposit the funds collected under this section in interest-bearing accounts. The custodian shall keep records of the amount of funds on deposit collected under this section and not later than the last day of the month following each calendar quarter shall send to the comptroller of public accounts the funds collected under this section during the preceding quarter. A county may retain 10 percent of the funds as a service fee and may retain the interest accrued on the funds if the custodian of a county treasury keeps records of the amount of funds on deposit collected under this section and remits the funds to the comptroller within the period prescribed under this subsection.

(f) Funds collected are subject to audit by the comptroller and funds expended are subject to audit by the State Auditor.

(g) The comptroller shall deposit the funds in a special fund to be known as the juvenile probation diversion fund.

(h) The legislature shall determine and appropriate the necessary amount from the juvenile probation diversion fund to the Texas Juvenile Justice Department for the purchase of services the department considers necessary for the diversion of any juvenile who is at risk of commitment to the department. The department shall develop guidelines for the use of the fund. The department may not purchase the services if a person responsible for the child's support or a local juvenile probation department is financially able to provide the services.

History of Fam. Code §54.0411: Acts 1987, 70th Leg., ch. 1040, §23, eff. Sept. 1, 1987. Amended by Acts 1989, 71st Leg., ch. 347, §8, eff. Oct. 1, 1989; Acts 2015, 84th Leg., ch. 734, §51, eff. Sept. 1, 2015.

FAM §54.042. LICENSE SUSPENSION

(a) A juvenile court, in a disposition hearing under Section 54.04, shall:

(1) order the Department of Public Safety to suspend a child's driver's license or permit, or if the child does not have a license or permit, to deny the issuance of a license or permit to the child if the court finds that the child has engaged in conduct that:

(A) violates a law of this state enumerated in Section 521.342(a), Transportation Code; or

(B) violates a penal law of this state or the United States, an element or elements of which involve a severe form of trafficking in persons, as defined by 22 U.S.C. Section 7102; or

(2) notify the Department of Public Safety of the adjudication, if the court finds that the child has en-

gaged in conduct that violates a law of this state enumerated in Section 521.372(a), Transportation Code.

(b) A juvenile court, in a disposition hearing under Section 54.04, may order the Department of Public Safety to suspend a child's driver's license or permit or, if the child does not have a license or permit, to deny the issuance of a license or permit to the child, if the court finds that the child has engaged in conduct that violates Section 28.08, Penal Code.

(c) The order under Subsection (a)(1) shall specify a period of suspension or denial of 365 days.

(d) The order under Subsection (b) shall specify a period of suspension or denial:

(1) not to exceed 365 days; or

(2) of 365 days if the court finds the child has been previously adjudicated as having engaged in conduct violating Section 28.08, Penal Code.

(e) A child whose driver's license or permit has been suspended or denied pursuant to this section may, if the child is otherwise eligible for, and fulfills the requirements for issuance of, a provisional driver's license or permit under Chapter 521, Transportation Code, apply for and receive an occupational license in accordance with the provisions of Subchapter L of that chapter.

(f) A juvenile court, in a disposition hearing under Section 54.04, may order the Department of Public Safety to suspend a child's driver's license or permit or, if the child does not have a license or permit, to deny the issuance of a license or permit to the child for a period not to exceed 12 months if the court finds that the child has engaged in conduct in need of supervision or delinquent conduct other than the conduct described by Subsection (a).

(g) A juvenile court that places a child on probation under Section 54.04 may require as a reasonable condition of the probation that if the child violates the probation, the court may order the Department of Public Safety to suspend the child's driver's license or permit or, if the child does not have a license or permit, to deny the issuance of a license or permit to the child for a period not to exceed 12 months. The court may make this order if a child that is on probation under this condition violates the probation. A suspension under this subsection is cumulative of any other suspension under this section.

(h) If a child is adjudicated for conduct that violates Section 49.04, 49.07, or 49.08, Penal Code, and if any conduct on which that adjudication is based is a ground for a driver's license suspension under Chapter 524 or 724, Transportation Code, each of the suspensions shall be imposed. The court imposing a driver's license suspension under this section shall credit a period of suspension imposed under Chapter 524 or 724, Transportation Code, toward the period of suspension required under this section, except that if the child was previously adjudicated for conduct that violates Section 49.04, 49.07, or 49.08, Penal Code, credit may not be given.

History of Fam. Code §54.042: Acts 1983, 68th Leg., ch. 303, §25, eff. Jan. 1, 1984. Amended by Acts 1985, 69th Leg., ch. 629, §1, eff. Sept. 1, 1985; Acts 1991, 72nd Leg., ch. 14, §284(42) (eff. Sept. 1, 1991), ch. 784, §7 (eff. Sept. 1, 1991); Acts 1993, 73rd Leg., ch. 491, §3, eff. June 15, 1993; Acts 1995, 74th Leg., ch. 76, §14.32 (eff. Sept. 1, 1995), ch. 262, §40 (eff. Jan. 1, 1996); Acts 1997, 75th Leg., ch. 165, §30.183 (eff. Sept. 1, 1997), ch. 593, §3 (eff. Sept. 1, 1997), ch. 1013, §17 (eff. Sept. 1, 1997); Acts 1999, 76th Leg., ch. 62, §19.01(18), eff. Sept. 1, 1999; Acts 2003, 78th Leg., ch. 283, §20, eff. Sept. 1, 2003; Acts 2009, 81st Leg., ch. 1146, §18.02, eff. Sept. 1, 2009.

FAM §54.043. MONITORING SCHOOL ATTENDANCE

If the court places a child on probation under Section 54.04(d) and requires as a condition of probation that the child attend school, the probation officer charged with supervising the child shall monitor the child's school attendance and report to the court if the child is voluntarily absent from school.

History of Fam. Code §54.043: Acts 1993, 73rd Leg., ch. 347, §6.02, eff. Sept. 1, 1993.

FAM §54.044. COMMUNITY SERVICE

(a) If the court places a child on probation under Section 54.04(d), the court shall require as a condition of probation that the child work a specified number of hours at a community service project approved by the court and designated by the juvenile probation department as provided by Subsection (e), unless the court determines and enters a finding on the order placing the child on probation that:

(1) the child is physically or mentally incapable of participating in the project;

(2) participating in the project will be a hardship on the child or the family of the child; or

(3) the child has shown good cause that community service should not be required.

(b) The court may also order under this section that the child's parent perform community service with the child.

(c) The court shall order that the child and the child's parent perform a total of not more than 500 hours of community service under this section.

(d) A municipality or county that establishes a program to assist children and their parents in rendering community service under this section may purchase insurance policies protecting the municipality or county against claims brought by a person other than the child or the child's parent for a cause of action that arises from an act of the child or parent while rendering community service. The municipality or county is not liable under this section to the extent that damages are recoverable under a contract of insurance or under a plan of self-insurance authorized by statute. The liability of the municipality or county for a cause of action that arises from an action of the child or the child's parent while rendering community service may not exceed $100,000 to a single person and $300,000 for a single occurrence in the case of personal injury or death, and $10,000 for a single occurrence of property damage. Liability may not extend to punitive or exemplary damages. This subsection does not waive a defense, immunity, or jurisdictional bar available to the municipality or county or its officers or employees, nor shall this section be construed to waive, repeal, or modify any provision of Chapter 101, Civil Practice and Remedies Code.

(e) For the purposes of this section, a court may submit to the juvenile probation department a list of organizations or projects approved by the court for community service. The juvenile probation department may:

(1) designate an organization or project for community service only from the list submitted by the court; and

(2) reassign or transfer a child to a different organization or project on the list submitted by the court under this subsection without court approval.

(f) A person subject to an order proposed under Subsection (a) or (b) is entitled to a hearing on the order before the order is entered by the court.

(g) On a finding by the court that a child's parents or guardians have made a reasonable good faith effort to prevent the child from engaging in delinquent conduct or engaging in conduct indicating a need for supervision and that, despite the parents' or guardians' efforts, the child continues to engage in such conduct, the court shall waive any requirement for community service that may be imposed on a parent under this section.

(h) An order made under this section may be enforced as provided by Section 54.07.

(i) In a disposition hearing under Section 54.04 in which the court finds that a child engaged in conduct violating Section 521.453, Transportation Code, the court, in addition to any other order authorized under this title and if the court is located in a municipality or county that has established a community service program, may order the child to perform eight hours of community service as a condition of probation under Section 54.04(d) unless the child is shown to have previously engaged in conduct violating Section 521.453, Transportation Code, in which case the court may order the child to perform 12 hours of community service.

History of Fam. Code §54.044: Acts 1995, 74th Leg., ch. 262, §41, eff. Jan. 1, 1996. Amended by Acts 1997, 75th Leg., ch. 1358, §2, eff. Sept. 1, 1997; Acts 2001, 77th Leg., ch. 1297, §25, eff. Sept. 1, 2001.

FAM §54.045. ADMISSION OF UNADJUDICATED CONDUCT

(a) During a disposition hearing under Section 54.04, a child may:

(1) admit having engaged in delinquent conduct or conduct indicating a need for supervision for which the child has not been adjudicated; and

(2) request the court to take the admitted conduct into account in the disposition of the child.

(b) If the prosecuting attorney agrees in writing, the court may take the admitted conduct into account in the disposition of the child.

(c) A court may take into account admitted conduct over which exclusive venue lies in another county only if the court obtains the written permission of the prosecuting attorney for that county.

(d) A child may not be adjudicated by any court for having engaged in conduct taken into account under this section, except that, if the conduct taken into account included conduct over which exclusive venue lies in another county and the written permission of the prosecuting attorney of that county was not obtained, the child may be adjudicated for that conduct, but the child's admission under this section may not be used against the child in the adjudication.

History of Fam. Code §54.045: Acts 1995, 74th Leg., ch. 262, §41, eff. Jan. 1, 1996.

FAM §54.046. CONDITIONS OF PROBATION FOR DAMAGING PROPERTY WITH GRAFFITI

(a) If a juvenile court places on probation under Section 54.04(d) a child adjudicated as having engaged

in conduct in violation of Section 28.08, Penal Code, in addition to other conditions of probation, the court:

(1) shall order the child to:

(A) reimburse the owner of the property for the cost of restoring the property; or

(B) with consent of the owner of the property, restore the property by removing or painting over any markings made by the child on the property; and

(2) if the child made markings on public property, a street sign, or an official traffic-control device in violation of Section 28.08, Penal Code, shall order the child to:

(A) make to the political subdivision that owns the public property or erected the street sign or official traffic-control device restitution in an amount equal to the lesser of the cost to the political subdivision of replacing or restoring the public property, street sign, or official traffic-control device; or

(B) with the consent of the political subdivision, restore the public property, street sign, or official traffic-control device by removing or painting over any markings made by the child on the property, sign, or device.

(a-1) For purposes of Subsection (a), "official traffic-control device" has the meaning assigned by Section 541.304, Transportation Code.

(b) In addition to a condition imposed under Subsection (a), the court may require the child as a condition of probation to attend a class with instruction in self-responsibility and empathy for a victim of an offense conducted by a local juvenile probation department.

(c) If a juvenile court orders a child to make restitution under Subsection (a) and the child, child's parent, or other person responsible for the child's support is financially unable to make the restitution, the court may order the child to perform a specific number of hours of community service, in addition to the hours required under Subsection (d), to satisfy the restitution.

(d) If a juvenile court places on probation under Section 54.04(d) a child adjudicated as having engaged in conduct in violation of Section 28.08, Penal Code, in addition to other conditions of probation, the court shall order the child to perform:

(1) at least 15 hours of community service if the amount of pecuniary loss resulting from the conduct is $50 or more but less than $500; or

(2) at least 30 hours of community service if the amount of pecuniary loss resulting from the conduct is $500 or more.

(e) The juvenile court shall direct a child ordered to make restitution under this section to deliver the amount or property due as restitution to a juvenile probation department for transfer to the owner. The juvenile probation department shall notify the juvenile court when the child has delivered the full amount of restitution ordered.

History of Fam. Code §54.046: Acts 1997, 75th Leg., ch. 593, §7, eff. Sept. 1, 1997. Amended by Acts 2007, 80th Leg., ch. 1053, §4, eff. Sept. 1, 2007; Acts 2009, 81st Leg., ch. 639, §3, eff. Sept. 1, 2009.

FAM §54.0461. PAYMENT OF JUVENILE DELINQUENCY PREVENTION FEES

(a) If a child is adjudicated as having engaged in delinquent conduct that violates Section 28.08, Penal Code, the juvenile court shall order the child, parent, or other person responsible for the child's support to pay to the court a $50 juvenile delinquency prevention fee as a cost of court.

(b) The court shall deposit fees received under this section to the credit of the county juvenile delinquency prevention fund provided for under Article 102.0171, Code of Criminal Procedure.

(c) If the court finds that a child, parent, or other person responsible for the child's support is unable to pay the juvenile delinquency prevention fee required under Subsection (a), the court shall enter into the child's case records a statement of that finding. The court may waive a fee under this section only if the court makes the finding under this subsection.

History of Fam. Code §54.0461: Acts 1999, 76th Leg., ch. 174, §1, eff. Sept. 1, 1999. Amended by Acts 2003, 78th Leg., ch. 601, §3, eff. Sept. 1, 2003; Acts 2007, 80th Leg., ch. 1053, §5, eff. Sept. 1, 2007.

FAM §54.0462. PAYMENT OF FEES FOR OFFENSES REQUIRING DNA TESTING

(a) If a child is adjudicated as having engaged in delinquent conduct that constitutes the commission of a felony and the provision of a DNA sample is required under Section 54.0409 or other law, the juvenile court shall order the child, parent, or other person responsible for the child's support to pay to the court as a cost of court:

(1) a $50 fee if the disposition of the case includes a commitment to a facility operated by or under contract with the Texas Juvenile Justice Department; and

(2) a $34 fee if the disposition of the case does not include a commitment described by Subdivision (1) and the child is required to submit a DNA sample under Section 54.0409 or other law.

(b) The clerk of the court shall transfer to the comptroller any funds received under this section. The comptroller shall credit the funds to the Department of Public Safety to help defray the cost of any analyses performed on DNA samples provided by children with respect to whom a court cost is collected under this section.

(c) If the court finds that a child, parent, or other person responsible for the child's support is unable to pay the fee required under Subsection (a), the court shall enter into the child's case records a statement of that finding. The court may waive a fee under this section only if the court makes the finding under this subsection.

History of Fam. Code §54.0462: Acts 2009, 81st Leg., ch. 1209, §4, eff. Sept. 1, 2009. Amended by Acts 2015, 84th Leg., ch. 734, §52, eff. Sept. 1, 2015.

FAM §54.047. ALCOHOL OR DRUG RELATED OFFENSE

(a) If the court or jury finds at an adjudication hearing for a child that the child engaged in delinquent conduct or conduct indicating a need for supervision that constitutes a violation of Section 481.115, 481.1151, 481.116, 481.1161, 481.117, 481.118, or 481.121, Health and Safety Code, the court may order that the child attend a drug education program that is designed to educate persons on the dangers of drug abuse and is approved by the Department of State Health Services in accordance with Section 521.374, Transportation Code.

(b) If the court or jury finds at an adjudication hearing for a child that the child engaged in delinquent conduct or conduct indicating a need for supervision that violates the alcohol-related offenses in Section 106.02, 106.025, 106.04, 106.041, 106.05, or 106.07, Alcoholic Beverage Code, or Section 49.02, Penal Code, the court may order that the child attend an alcohol awareness program described by Section 106.115, Alcoholic Beverage Code.

(c) The court shall, in addition to any order described by Subsection (a) or (b), order that, in the manner provided by Section 106.071(d), Alcoholic Beverage Code:

(1) the child perform community service; and

(2) the child's driver's license or permit be suspended or that the child be denied issuance of a driver's license or permit.

(d) An order under this section:

(1) is subject to a finding under Section 54.04(c); and

(2) may be issued in addition to any other order authorized by this title.

(e) The Department of State Health Services:

(1) is responsible for the administration of the certification of drug education programs;

(2) may charge a nonrefundable application fee for:

(A) initial certification of approval; or

(B) renewal of the certification;

(3) shall adopt rules regarding drug education programs approved under this section; and

(4) shall monitor and provide training to a person who provides a drug education program.

(f) If the court orders a child under Subsection (a) or (b) to attend a drug education program or alcohol awareness program, unless the court determines that the parent or guardian of the child is indigent and unable to pay the cost, the court shall require the child's parent or a guardian of the child to pay the cost of attending the program. The court shall allow the child's parent or guardian to pay the cost of attending the program in installments.

History of Fam. Code §54.047: Acts 1997, 75th Leg., ch. 1013, §18, eff. Sept. 1, 1997. Renumbered from §54.046 by Acts 1999, 76th Leg., ch. 62, §19.01(19), eff. Sept. 1, 1999. Amended by Acts 2015, 84th Leg., ch. 1004, §6, eff. Sept. 1, 2015.

FAM §54.048. RESTITUTION

(a) A juvenile court, in a disposition hearing under Section 54.04, may order restitution to be made by the child and the child's parents.

(b) This section applies without regard to whether the petition in the case contains a plea for restitution.

History of Fam. Code §54.048: Acts 2001, 77th Leg., ch. 1297, §26, eff. Sept. 1, 2001.

FAM §54.0481. RESTITUTION FOR DAMAGING PROPERTY WITH GRAFFITI

(a) A juvenile court, in a disposition hearing under Section 54.04 regarding a child who has been adjudicated to have engaged in delinquent conduct that violates Section 28.08, Penal Code:

(1) may order the child or a parent or other person responsible for the child's support to make restitution by:

(A) reimbursing the owner of the property for the cost of restoring the property; or

(B) with the consent of the owner of the property, personally restoring the property by removing or painting over any markings the child made; and

(2) if the child made markings on public property, a street sign, or an official traffic-control device in violation of Section 28.08, Penal Code, may order the child or a parent or other person responsible for the child's support to:

(A) make to the political subdivision that owns the public property or erected the street sign or official traffic-control device restitution in an amount equal to the lesser of the cost to the political subdivision of replacing or restoring the public property, street sign, or official traffic-control device; or

(B) with the consent of the political subdivision, restore the public property, street sign, or official traffic-control device by removing or painting over any markings made by the child on the property, sign, or device.

(b) If a juvenile court orders a child to make restitution under Subsection (a) and the child, child's parent, or other person responsible for the child's support is financially unable to make the restitution, the court may order the child to perform a specific number of hours of community service to satisfy the restitution.

(c) For purposes of Subsection (a), "official traffic-control device" has the meaning assigned by Section 541.304, Transportation Code.

History of Fam. Code §54.0481: Acts 2007, 80th Leg., ch. 1053, §6, eff. Sept. 1, 2007.

FAM §54.0482. TREATMENT OF RESTITUTION PAYMENTS

(a) A juvenile probation department that receives a payment to a victim as the result of a juvenile court order for restitution shall immediately:

(1) deposit the payment in an interest bearing account in the county treasury; and

(2) notify the victim that a payment has been received.

(b) The juvenile probation department shall promptly remit the payment to a victim who has been notified under Subsection (a) and makes a claim for payment.

(b-1) If the victim does not make a claim for payment on or before the 30th day after the date of being notified under Subsection (a), the juvenile probation department shall notify the victim by certified mail, sent to the last known address of the victim, that a payment has been received.

(c) On or before the fifth anniversary of the date the juvenile probation department receives a payment for a victim that is not claimed by the victim, the department shall make and document a good faith effort to locate and notify the victim that an unclaimed payment exists, including:

(1) confirming, if possible, the victim's most recent address with the Department of Public Safety; and

(2) making at least one additional certified mailing to the victim.

(d) A juvenile probation department satisfies the good faith requirement under Subsection (c) by sending by certified mail to the victim, during the period the child is required by the juvenile court order to make payments to the victim, a notice that the victim is entitled to an unclaimed payment.

(e) If a victim claims a payment on or before the fifth anniversary of the date on which the juvenile probation department mailed a notice to the victim under Subsection (b-1), the juvenile probation department shall pay the victim the amount of the original payment, less any interest earned while holding the payment.

(f) If a victim does not claim a payment on or before the fifth anniversary of the date on which the juvenile probation department mailed a notice to the victim under Subsection (b-1), the department:

(1) has no liability to the victim or anyone else in relation to the payment; and

(2) shall transfer the payment from the interest-bearing account to a special fund of the county treasury, the unclaimed juvenile restitution fund.

(g) The county may spend money in the unclaimed juvenile restitution fund only for the same purposes for which the county may spend juvenile state aid.

History of Fam. Code §54.0482: Acts 2007, 80th Leg., ch. 908, §12, eff. Sept. 1, 2007. Renumbered from §54.0481 by Acts 2009, 81st Leg., ch. 87, §27.001(14), eff. Sept. 1, 2009. Amended by Acts 2013, 83rd Leg., ch. 1299, §19, eff. Sept. 1, 2013.

FAM §54.049. CONDITIONS OF PROBATION FOR DESECRATING A CEMETERY OR ABUSING A CORPSE

(a) If a juvenile court places on probation under Section 54.04(d) a child adjudicated to have engaged in conduct in violation of Section 28.03(f), Penal Code, involving damage or destruction inflicted on a place of human burial or under Section 42.08, Penal Code, in addition to other conditions of probation, the court shall order the child to make restitution to a cemetery organization operating a cemetery affected by the conduct in an amount equal to the cost to the cemetery of repairing any damage caused by the conduct.

(b) If a juvenile court orders a child to make restitution under Subsection (a) and the child is financially unable to make the restitution, the court may order:

(1) the child to perform a specific number of hours of community service to satisfy the restitution; or

(2) a parent or other person responsible for the child's support to make the restitution in the amount described by Subsection (a).

(c) In this section, "cemetery" and "cemetery organization" have the meanings assigned by Section 711.001, Health and Safety Code.

History of Fam. Code §54.049: Acts 2005, 79th Leg., ch. 1025, §3, eff. June 18, 2005.

FAM §54.0491. GANG-RELATED CONDUCT

(a) In this section:

(1) "Criminal street gang" has the meaning assigned by Section 71.01, Penal Code.

(2) "Gang-related conduct" means conduct that violates a penal law of the grade of Class B misdemeanor or higher and in which a child engages with the intent to:

(A) further the criminal activities of a criminal street gang of which the child is a member;

(B) gain membership in a criminal street gang; or

(C) avoid detection as a member of a criminal street gang.

(b) A juvenile court, in a disposition hearing under Section 54.04 regarding a child who has been adjudicated to have engaged in delinquent conduct that is also gang-related conduct, shall order the child to participate in a criminal street gang intervention program that is appropriate for the child based on the child's level of involvement in the criminal activities of a criminal street gang. The intervention program:

(1) must include at least 12 hours of instruction; and

(2) may include voluntary tattoo removal.

(c) If a child required to attend a criminal street gang intervention program is committed to the Texas Juvenile Justice Department as a result of the gang-related conduct, the child must complete the intervention program before being discharged from the custody of or released under supervision by the department.

History of Fam. Code §54.0491: Acts 2009, 81st Leg., ch. 1130, §19, eff. Sept. 1, 2009. Amended by Acts 2015, 84th Leg., ch. 734, §53, eff. Sept. 1, 2015.

FAM §54.05. HEARING TO MODIFY DISPOSITION

(a) Except as provided by Subsection (a-1), any disposition, except a commitment to the Texas Juvenile Justice Department, may be modified by the juvenile court as provided in this section until:

(1) the child reaches:

(A) the child's 18th birthday; or

(B) the child's 19th birthday, if the child was placed on determinate sentence probation under Section 54.04(q); or

(2) the child is earlier discharged by the court or operation of law.

(a-1) Repealed by Acts 2015, 84th Leg., ch. 935, §41(3), eff. Sept. 1, 2015.

(b) Except for a commitment to the Texas Juvenile Justice Department or to a post-adjudication secure correctional facility under Section 54.04011 or a placement on determinate sentence probation under Section 54.04(q), all dispositions automatically terminate when the child reaches the child's 18th birthday.

(c) There is no right to a jury at a hearing to modify disposition.

(d) A hearing to modify disposition shall be held on the petition of the child and his parent, guardian, guardian ad litem, or attorney, or on the petition of the state, a probation officer, or the court itself. Reasonable notice of a hearing to modify disposition shall be given to all parties.

(e) After the hearing on the merits or facts, the court may consider written reports from probation officers, professional court employees, or professional consultants in addition to the testimony of other witnesses. On or before the second day before the date of the hear-

ing to modify disposition, the court shall provide the attorney for the child and the prosecuting attorney with access to all written matter to be considered by the court in deciding whether to modify disposition. The court may order counsel not to reveal items to the child or his parent, guardian, or guardian ad litem if such disclosure would materially harm the treatment and rehabilitation of the child or would substantially decrease the likelihood of receiving information from the same or similar sources in the future.

(f) Except as provided by Subsection (j), a disposition based on a finding that the child engaged in delinquent conduct that violates a penal law of this state or the United States of the grade of felony may be modified so as to commit the child to the Texas Juvenile Justice Department or, if applicable, a post-adjudication secure correctional facility operated under Section 152.0016, Human Resources Code, if the court after a hearing to modify disposition finds by a preponderance of the evidence that the child violated a reasonable and lawful order of the court. A disposition based on a finding that the child engaged in habitual felony conduct as described by Section 51.031 or in delinquent conduct that included a violation of a penal law listed in Section 53.045(a) may be modified to commit the child to the Texas Juvenile Justice Department or, if applicable, a post-adjudication secure correctional facility operated under Section 152.0016, Human Resources Code, with a possible transfer to the Texas Department of Criminal Justice for a definite term prescribed by, as applicable, Section 54.04(d)(3) or Section 152.0016(g), Human Resources Code, if the original petition was approved by the grand jury under Section 53.045 and if after a hearing to modify the disposition the court finds that the child violated a reasonable and lawful order of the court.

(g) Except as provided by Subsection (j), a disposition based solely on a finding that the child engaged in conduct indicating a need for supervision may not be modified to commit the child to the Texas Juvenile Justice Department. A new finding in compliance with Section 54.03 must be made that the child engaged in delinquent conduct that meets the requirements for commitment under Section 54.04.

(h) A hearing shall be held prior to placement in a post-adjudication secure correctional facility for a period longer than 30 days or commitment to the Texas Juvenile Justice Department as a modified disposition. In other disposition modifications, the child and the child's parent, guardian, guardian ad litem, or attorney may waive hearing in accordance with Section 51.09.

(i) The court shall specifically state in the order its reasons for modifying the disposition and shall furnish a copy of the order to the child.

(j) If, after conducting a hearing to modify disposition without a jury, the court finds by a preponderance of the evidence that a child violated a reasonable and lawful condition of probation ordered under Section 54.04(q), the court may modify the disposition to commit the child to the Texas Juvenile Justice Department under Section 54.04(d)(3) or, if applicable, a post-adjudication secure correctional facility operated under Section 152.0016, Human Resources Code, for a term that does not exceed the original sentence assessed by the court or jury.

(k) Repealed by Acts 2007, 80th Leg., ch. 263, §64(2), eff. June 8, 2007.

(*l*) The court may extend a period of probation under this section at any time during the period of probation or, if a motion for revocation or modification of probation is filed before the period of supervision ends, before the first anniversary of the date on which the period of probation expires.

(m) If the court places the child on probation outside the child's home or commits the child to the Texas Juvenile Justice Department or to a post-adjudication secure correctional facility operated under Section 152.0016, Human Resources Code, the court:

(1) shall include in the court's order a determination that:

(A) it is in the child's best interests to be placed outside the child's home;

(B) reasonable efforts were made to prevent or eliminate the need for the child's removal from the child's home and to make it possible for the child to return home; and

(C) the child, in the child's home, cannot be provided the quality of care and level of support and supervision that the child needs to meet the conditions of probation; and

(2) may approve an administrative body to conduct a permanency hearing pursuant to 42 U.S.C. Section 675 if required during the placement or commitment of the child.

History of Fam. Code §54.05: Acts 1973, 63rd Leg., ch. 544, §1, eff. Sept. 1, 1973. Amended by Acts 1979, 66th Leg., ch. 743, §1, eff. Aug. 27, 1979; Acts 1983, 68th Leg., ch. 44, art. 1, §4, eff. Apr. 26, 1983; Acts 1985, 69th Leg., ch. 45, §3, eff. Sept. 1, 1985; Acts 1987, 70th Leg., ch. 385, §10, eff. Sept. 1, 1987; Acts 1991, 72nd Leg., ch. 557, §3, eff. Sept. 1, 1991; Acts 1995, 74th Leg., ch. 262, §42, eff. Jan. 1, 1996; Acts 1999, 76th Leg., ch. 1448, §2 (eff. Sept. 1, 1999), ch. 1477, §11 (eff. Sept. 1, 1999); Acts 2001, 77th Leg., ch. 1297, §§27, 28 (eff. Sept. 1, 2001), ch. 1420, §5.002 (eff. Sept. 1, 2001); Acts 2003, 78th Leg., ch. 283, §21, eff. Sept. 1, 2003; Acts 2005, 79th Leg., ch. 949, §15, eff. Sept. 1, 2005; Acts 2007, 80th Leg., ch. 263, §§9, 64(2), eff. June 8, 2007; Acts 2011, 82nd Leg., ch. 438, §5 (eff. Sept. 1, 2011), ch. 1098, §5 (eff. Sept. 1, 2011); Acts 2013, 83rd Leg., ch. 1299, §20 (eff. Sept. 1, 2013), ch. 1323, §4 (eff. Dec. 1, 2013); Acts 2015, 84th Leg., ch. 734, §54 (eff. Sept. 1, 2015), ch. 935, §§21, 41(3) (eff. Sept. 1, 2015).

FAM §54.051. TRANSFER OF DETERMINATE SENTENCE PROBATION TO APPROPRIATE DISTRICT COURT

(a) On motion of the state concerning a child who is placed on probation under Section 54.04(q) for a period, including any extension ordered under Section 54.05, that will continue after the child's 19th birthday, the juvenile court shall hold a hearing to determine whether to transfer the child to an appropriate district court or discharge the child from the sentence of probation.

(b) The hearing must be conducted before the person's 19th birthday, or before the person's 18th birthday if the offense for which the person was placed on probation occurred before September 1, 2011, and must be conducted in the same manner as a hearing to modify disposition under Section 54.05.

(c) If, after a hearing, the court determines to discharge the child, the court shall specify a date on or before the child's 19th birthday to discharge the child from the sentence of probation.

(d) If, after a hearing, the court determines to transfer the child, the court shall transfer the child to an appropriate district court on the child's 19th birthday.

(d-1) After a transfer to district court under Subsection (d), only the petition, the grand jury approval, the judgment concerning the conduct for which the person was placed on determinate sentence probation, and the transfer order are a part of the district clerk's public record.

(e) A district court that exercises jurisdiction over a person transferred under Subsection (d) shall place the person on community supervision under Chapter 42A, Code of Criminal Procedure, for the remainder of the person's probationary period and under conditions consistent with those ordered by the juvenile court.

(e-1) The restrictions on a judge placing a defendant on community supervision imposed by Article 42A.054, Code of Criminal Procedure, do not apply to a case transferred from the juvenile court. The minimum period of community supervision imposed by Article 42A.053(d), Code of Criminal Procedure, does not apply to a case transferred from the juvenile court.

(e-2) If a person who is placed on community supervision under this section violates a condition of that supervision or if the person violated a condition of probation ordered under Section 54.04(q) and that probation violation was not discovered by the state before the person's 19th birthday, the district court shall dispose of the violation of community supervision or probation, as appropriate, in the same manner as if the court had originally exercised jurisdiction over the case. If the judge revokes community supervision, the judge may reduce the prison sentence to any length without regard to the minimum term imposed by Article 42A.755(a), Code of Criminal Procedure.

(e-3) The time that a person serves on probation ordered under Section 54.04(q) is the same as time served on community supervision ordered under this section for purposes of determining the person's eligibility for early discharge from community supervision under Article 42A.701, Code of Criminal Procedure.

(f) The juvenile court may transfer a child to an appropriate district court as provided by this section without a showing that the child violated a condition of probation ordered under Section 54.04(q).

(g) If the juvenile court places the child on probation for an offense for which registration as a sex offender is required by Chapter 62, Code of Criminal Procedure, and defers the registration requirement until completion of treatment for the sex offense under Subchapter H, Chapter 62, Code of Criminal Procedure, the authority under that article to reexamine the need for registration on completion of treatment is transferred to the court to which probation is transferred.

(h) If the juvenile court places the child on probation for an offense for which registration as a sex offender is required by Chapter 62, Code of Criminal Procedure, and the child registers, the authority of the court to excuse further compliance with the registration requirement under Subchapter H, Chapter 62, Code of Criminal Procedure, is transferred to the court to which probation is transferred.

(i) If the juvenile court exercises jurisdiction over a person who is 18 or 19 years of age or older, as applicable, under Section 51.041 or 51.0412, the court or jury

may, if the person is otherwise eligible, place the person on probation under Section 54.04(q). The juvenile court shall set the conditions of probation and immediately transfer supervision of the person to the appropriate court exercising criminal jurisdiction under Subsection (e).

History of Fam. Code §54.051: Acts 1999, 76th Leg., ch. 1477, §12, eff. Sept. 1, 1999. Amended by Acts 2003, 78th Leg., ch. 283, §22, eff. Sept. 1, 2003; Acts 2005, 79th Leg., ch. 1008, §2.07, eff. Sept. 1, 2005; Acts 2011, 82nd Leg., ch. 438, §6, eff. Sept. 1, 2011; Acts 2013, 83rd Leg., ch. 1299, §21, eff. Sept. 1, 2013; Acts 2015, 84th Leg., ch. 770, §2.33, eff. Jan. 1, 2017.

FAM §54.052. CREDIT FOR TIME SPENT IN DETENTION FACILITY FOR CHILD WITH DETERMINATE SENTENCE

(a) This section applies only to a child who is committed to:

(1) the Texas Juvenile Justice Department under a determinate sentence under Section 54.04(d)(3) or (m) or Section 54.05(f); or

(2) a post-adjudication secure correctional facility under a determinate sentence under Section 54.04011(c)(2).

(b) The judge of the court in which a child is adjudicated shall give the child credit on the child's sentence for the time spent by the child, in connection with the conduct for which the child was adjudicated, in a secure detention facility before the child's transfer to a Texas Juvenile Justice Department facility or a post-adjudication secure correctional facility, as applicable.

(c) If a child appeals the child's adjudication and is retained in a secure detention facility pending the appeal, the judge of the court in which the child was adjudicated shall give the child credit on the child's sentence for the time spent by the child in a secure detention facility pending disposition of the child's appeal. The court shall endorse on both the commitment and the mandate from the appellate court all credit given the child under this subsection.

(d) The Texas Juvenile Justice Department or the juvenile board or local juvenile probation department operating or contracting for the operation of the post-adjudication secure correctional facility under Section 152.0016, Human Resources Code, as applicable, shall grant any credit under this section in computing the child's eligibility for parole and discharge.

History of Fam. Code §54.052: Acts 2007, 80th Leg., ch. 263, §10, eff. June 8, 2007. Amended by Acts 2013, 83rd Leg., ch. 1323, §5, eff. Dec. 1, 2013.

FAM §54.06. JUDGMENTS FOR SUPPORT[1]

(a) At any stage of the proceeding, when a child has been placed outside the child's home, the juvenile court, after giving the parent or other person responsible for the child's support a reasonable opportunity to be heard, shall order the parent or other person to pay in a manner directed by the court a reasonable sum for the support in whole or in part of the child or the court shall waive the payment by order. The court shall order that the payment for support be made to the local juvenile probation department to be used only for residential care and other support for the child unless the child has been committed to the Texas Juvenile Justice Department, in which case the court shall order that the payment be made to the Texas Juvenile Justice Department for deposit in a special account in the general revenue fund that may be appropriated only for the care of children committed to the Texas Juvenile Justice Department.

(b) At any stage of the proceeding, when a child has been placed outside the child's home and the parent of the child is obligated to pay support for the child under a court order under Title 5, the juvenile court shall order that the person entitled to receive the support assign the person's right to support for the child placed outside the child's home to the local juvenile probation department to be used for residential care and other support for the child unless the child has been committed to the Texas Juvenile Justice Department, in which event the court shall order that the assignment be made to the Texas Juvenile Justice Department.

(c) A court may enforce an order for support under this section by ordering garnishment of the wages of the person ordered to pay support or by any other means available to enforce a child support order under Title 5.

(d) Repealed by Acts 2003, 78th Leg., ch. 283, §61(1), eff. Sept. 1, 2003.

(e) The court shall apply the child support guidelines under Subchapter C, Chapter 154, in an order requiring the payment of child support under this section. The court shall also require in an order to pay child support under this section that health insurance be provided for the child. Subchapter D, Chapter 154, applies to an order requiring health insurance for a child under this section.

(f) An order under this section prevails over any previous child support order issued with regard to the child to the extent of any conflict between the orders.

1. **Editor's note:** In 2015, the Legislature amended §54.06 to require dental insurance for a child subject to a child-support order, but the amendments are not effective until Sept. 1, 2018. For the text of the prospective amendments, see Acts 2015, 84th Leg., ch. 1150, §1, eff. Sept. 1, 2018.

History of Fam. Code §54.06: Acts 1973, 63rd Leg., ch. 544, §1, eff. Sept. 1, 1973. Amended by Acts 1983, 68th Leg., ch. 44, art. 1, §5, eff. Apr. 26, 1983; Acts 1987, 70th Leg., ch. 1040, §24, eff. Sept. 1, 1987; Acts 1993, 73rd Leg., ch. 798, §23 (eff. Sept. 1, 1993), ch. 1048, §2 (eff. Sept. 1, 1993); Acts 1995, 74th Leg., ch. 262, §43, eff. Jan. 1, 1996; Acts 1997, 75th Leg., ch. 165, §7.11, eff. Sept. 1, 1997; Acts 2003, 78th Leg., ch. 283, §61(1), eff. Sept. 1, 2003; Acts 2015, 84th Leg., ch. 734, §55, eff. Sept. 1, 2015.

FAM §54.061. PAYMENT OF PROBATION FEES

(a) If a child is placed on probation under Section 54.04(d)(1) of this code, the juvenile court, after giving the child, parent, or other person responsible for the child's support a reasonable opportunity to be heard, shall order the child, parent, or other person, if financially able to do so, to pay to the court a fee of not more than $15 a month during the period that the child continues on probation.

(b) Orders for the payment of fees under this section may be enforced as provided by Section 54.07 of this code.

(c) The court shall deposit the fees received under this section in the county treasury to the credit of a special fund that may be used only for juvenile probation or community-based juvenile corrections services or facilities in which a juvenile may be required to live while under court supervision.

(d) If the court finds that a child, parent, or other person responsible for the child's support is financially unable to pay the probation fee required under Subsection (a), the court shall enter into the records of the child's case a statement of that finding. The court may waive a fee under this section only if the court makes the finding under this subsection.

History of Fam. Code §54.061: Acts 1979, 66th Leg., ch. 154, §1, eff. Sept. 1, 1979. Amended by Acts 1981, 67th Leg., ch. 617, §4, eff. Sept. 1, 1981; Acts 1987, 70th Leg., ch. 1040, §25, eff. Sept. 1, 1987; Acts 1995, 74th Leg., ch. 262, §44, eff. Jan. 1, 1996.

FAM §54.07. ENFORCEMENT OF ORDER

(a) Except as provided by Subsection (b) or a juvenile court child support order, any order of the juvenile court may be enforced as provided by Chapter 61.

(b) A violation of any of the following orders of the juvenile court may not be enforced by contempt of court proceedings against the child:

(1) an order setting conditions of probation;

(2) an order setting conditions of deferred prosecution; and

(3) an order setting conditions of release from detention.

(c) This section and Chapter 61 do not preclude a juvenile court from summarily finding a child or other person in direct contempt of the juvenile court for conduct occurring in the presence of the judge of the court. Direct contempt of the juvenile court by a child is punishable by a maximum of 10 days' confinement in a secure juvenile detention facility or by a maximum of 40 hours of community service, or both. The juvenile court may not impose a fine on a child for direct contempt.

(d) This section and Chapter 61 do not preclude a juvenile court in an appropriate case from using a civil or coercive contempt proceeding to enforce an order.

History of Fam. Code §54.07: Acts 1973, 63rd Leg., ch. 544, §1, eff. Sept. 1, 1973. Amended by Acts 1979, 66th Leg., ch. 154, §3, eff. Sept. 1, 1979; Acts 2003, 78th Leg., ch. 283, §23, eff. Sept. 1, 2003.

FAM §54.08. PUBLIC ACCESS TO COURT HEARINGS

(a) Except as provided by this section, the court shall open hearings under this title to the public unless the court, for good cause shown, determines that the public should be excluded.

(b) The court may not prohibit a person who is a victim of the conduct of a child, or the person's family, from personally attending a hearing under this title relating to the conduct by the child unless the victim or member of the victim's family is to testify in the hearing or any subsequent hearing relating to the conduct and the court determines that the victim's or family member's testimony would be materially affected if the victim or member of the victim's family hears other testimony at trial.

(c) If a child is under the age of 14 at the time of the hearing, the court shall close the hearing to the public unless the court finds that the interests of the child or the interests of the public would be better served by opening the hearing to the public.

(d) In this section, "family" has the meaning assigned by Section 71.003.

History of Fam. Code §54.08: Acts 1973, 63rd Leg., ch. 544, §1, eff. Sept. 1, 1973. Amended by Acts 1987, 70th Leg., ch. 385, §11, eff. Sept. 1, 1987; Acts 1995, 74th Leg., ch. 262, §45, eff. Jan. 1, 1996; Acts 1997, 75th Leg., ch. 1086, §12, eff. Sept. 1, 1997.

FAM §54.09. RECORDING OF PROCEEDINGS

All judicial proceedings under this chapter except detention hearings shall be recorded by stenographic notes or by electronic, mechanical, or other appropriate means. Upon request of any party, a detention hearing shall be recorded.

History of Fam. Code §54.09: Acts 1973, 63rd Leg., ch. 544, §1, eff. Sept. 1, 1973.

A

FAM §54.10. HEARINGS BEFORE REFEREE

The amended text in §54.10 is effective for conduct that occurs on or after Sept. 1, 2017. Conduct in which any element of the conduct occurred before Sept. 1, 2017, is governed by the former law in effect at that time.

(a) Except as provided by Subsection (e), a hearing under Section 54.03, 54.04, or 54.05, including a jury trial, a hearing under Chapter 55, including a jury trial, or a hearing under the Interstate Compact for Juveniles (Chapter 60) may be held by a referee appointed in accordance with Section 51.04(g) or an associate judge appointed under Chapter 54A, Government Code, provided:

(1) the parties have been informed by the referee or associate judge that they are entitled to have the hearing before the juvenile court judge; and

(2) after each party is given an opportunity to object, no party objects to holding the hearing before the referee or associate judge.

(b) The determination under Section 53.02(f) whether to release a child may be made by a referee appointed in accordance with Section 51.04(g) if:

(1) the child has been informed by the referee that the child is entitled to have the determination made by the juvenile court judge or a substitute judge authorized by Section 51.04(f); or

(2) the child and the attorney for the child have in accordance with Section 51.09 waived the right to have the determination made by the juvenile court judge or a substitute judge.

(c) If a child objects to a referee making the determination under Section 53.02(f), the juvenile court judge or a substitute judge authorized by Section 51.04(f) shall make the determination.

(d) At the conclusion of the hearing or immediately after making the determination, the referee shall transmit written findings and recommendations to the juvenile court judge. The juvenile court judge shall adopt, modify, or reject the referee's recommendations not later than the next working day after the day that the judge receives the recommendations. Failure to act within that time results in release of the child by operation of law and a recommendation that the child be released operates to secure the child's immediate release subject to the power of the juvenile court judge to modify or reject that recommendation.

(e) Except as provided by Subsection (f), the [~~The~~] hearings provided by Sections 54.03, 54.04, and 54.05 may not be held before a referee if the grand jury has approved of the petition and the child is subject to a determinate sentence.

(f) When the state and a child who is subject to a determinate sentence agree to the disposition of the case, wholly or partly, a referee or associate judge may hold a hearing for the purpose of allowing the child to enter a plea or stipulation of evidence. After the hearing under this subsection, the referee or associate judge shall transmit the referee's or associate judge's written findings and recommendations regarding the plea or stipulation of evidence to the juvenile court judge for consideration. The juvenile court judge may accept or reject the plea or stipulation of evidence in accordance with Section 54.03(j).

History of Fam. Code §54.10: Acts 1975, 64th Leg., ch. 693, §19, eff. Sept. 1, 1975. Amended by Acts 1979, 66th Leg., ch. 743, §2, eff. Aug. 27, 1979; Acts 1987, 70th Leg., ch. 385, §12, eff. Sept. 1, 1987; Acts 1991, 72nd Leg., ch. 74, §1, eff. Sept. 1, 1991; Acts 1997, 75th Leg., ch. 1086, §13, eff. Sept. 1, 1997; Acts 1999, 76th Leg., ch. 232, §5 (eff. Sept. 1, 1999), ch. 1477, §13 (eff. Sept. 1, 1999); Acts 2011, 82nd Leg., 1st C.S., ch. 3, §6.08, eff. Jan. 1, 2012; H.B. 678, §1, 85th Leg., eff. Sept. 1, 2017.

FAM §54.11. RELEASE OR TRANSFER HEARING

(a) On receipt of a referral under Section 244.014(a), Human Resources Code, for the transfer to the Texas Department of Criminal Justice of a person committed to the Texas Juvenile Justice Department under Section 54.04(d)(3), 54.04(m), or 54.05(f), on receipt of a request by the Texas Juvenile Justice Department under Section 245.051(d), Human Resources Code, for approval of the release under supervision of a person committed to the Texas Juvenile Justice Department under Section 54.04(d)(3), 54.04(m), or 54.05(f), or on receipt of a referral under Section 152.0016(g) or (j), Human Resources Code, the court shall set a time and place for a hearing on the possible transfer or release of the person, as applicable.

(b) The court shall notify the following of the time and place of the hearing:

(1) the person to be transferred or released under supervision;

(2) the parents of the person;

(3) any legal custodian of the person, including the Texas Juvenile Justice Department or a juvenile board or local juvenile probation department if the child is committed to a post-adjudication secure correctional facility;

(4) the office of the prosecuting attorney that represented the state in the juvenile delinquency proceedings;

(5) the victim of the offense that was included in the delinquent conduct that was a ground for the disposition, or a member of the victim's family; and

(6) any other person who has filed a written request with the court to be notified of a release hearing with respect to the person to be transferred or released under supervision.

(c) Except for the person to be transferred or released under supervision and the prosecuting attorney, the failure to notify a person listed in Subsection (b) of this section does not affect the validity of a hearing conducted or determination made under this section if the record in the case reflects that the whereabouts of the persons who did not receive notice were unknown to the court and a reasonable effort was made by the court to locate those persons.

(d) At a hearing under this section the court may consider written reports and supporting documents from probation officers, professional court employees, professional consultants, employees of the Texas Juvenile Justice Department, or employees of a post-adjudication secure correctional facility in addition to the testimony of witnesses. On or before the fifth day before the date of the hearing, the court shall provide the attorney for the person to be transferred or released under supervision with access to all written matter to be considered by the court. All written matter is admissible in evidence at the hearing.

(e) At the hearing, the person to be transferred or released under supervision is entitled to an attorney, to examine all witnesses against him, to present evidence and oral argument, and to previous examination of all reports on and evaluations and examinations of or relating to him that may be used in the hearing.

(f) A hearing under this section is open to the public unless the person to be transferred or released under supervision waives a public hearing with the consent of his attorney and the court.

(g) A hearing under this section must be recorded by a court reporter or by audio or video tape recording, and the record of the hearing must be retained by the court for at least two years after the date of the final determination on the transfer or release of the person by the court.

(h) The hearing on a person who is referred for transfer under Section 152.0016(j) or 244.014(a), Human Resources Code, shall be held not later than the 60th day after the date the court receives the referral.

(i) On conclusion of the hearing on a person who is referred for transfer under Section 152.0016(j) or 244.014(a), Human Resources Code, the court may, as applicable, order:

(1) the return of the person to the Texas Juvenile Justice Department or post-adjudication secure correctional facility; or

(2) the transfer of the person to the custody of the Texas Department of Criminal Justice for the completion of the person's sentence.

(j) On conclusion of the hearing on a person who is referred for release under supervision under Section 152.0016(g) or 245.051(c), Human Resources Code, the court may, as applicable, order the return of the person to the Texas Juvenile Justice Department or post-adjudication secure correctional facility:

(1) with approval for the release of the person under supervision; or

(2) without approval for the release of the person under supervision.

(k) In making a determination under this section, the court may consider the experiences and character of the person before and after commitment to the Texas Juvenile Justice Department or post-adjudication secure correctional facility, the nature of the penal offense that the person was found to have committed and the manner in which the offense was committed, the abilities of the person to contribute to society, the protection of the victim of the offense or any member of the victim's family, the recommendations of the Texas Juvenile Justice Department, county juvenile board, local juvenile probation department, and prosecuting at-

torney, the best interests of the person, and any other factor relevant to the issue to be decided.

(*l*) Pending the conclusion of a transfer hearing, the juvenile court shall order that the person who is referred for transfer be detained in a certified juvenile detention facility as provided by Subsection (m). If the person is at least 17 years of age, the juvenile court may order that the person be detained without bond in an appropriate county facility for the detention of adults accused of criminal offenses.

(m) The detention of a person in a certified juvenile detention facility must comply with the detention requirements under this title, except that, to the extent practicable, the person must be kept separate from children detained in the same facility.

(n) If the juvenile court orders that a person who is referred for transfer be detained in a county facility under Subsection (*l*), the county sheriff shall take custody of the person under the juvenile court's order.

(o) In this section, "post-adjudication secure correctional facility" has the meaning assigned by Section 54.04011.

History of Fam. Code §54.11: Acts 1987, 70th Leg., ch. 385, §13, eff. Sept. 1, 1987. Amended by Acts 1991, 72nd Leg., ch. 574, §3, eff. Sept. 1, 1991; Acts 1995, 74th Leg., ch. 262, §46, eff. Jan. 1, 1996; Acts 2001, 77th Leg., ch. 1297, §29, eff. Sept. 1, 2001; Acts 2003, 78th Leg., ch. 283, §24, eff. Sept. 1, 2003; Acts 2009, 81st Leg., ch. 87, §25.058, eff. Sept. 1, 2009; Acts 2011, 82nd Leg., ch. 85, §3.007, eff. Sept. 1, 2011; Acts 2013, 83rd Leg., ch. 1299, §22 (eff. Sept. 1, 2013), ch. 1323, §6 (eff. Dec. 1, 2013); Acts 2015, 84th Leg., ch. 854, §3, eff. Sept. 1, 2015.

CHAPTER 55. PROCEEDINGS CONCERNING CHILDREN WITH MENTAL ILLNESS OR INTELLECTUAL DISABILITY

SUBCHAPTER A. GENERAL PROVISIONS

FAM §55.01. MEANING OF "HAVING A MENTAL ILLNESS"

For purposes of this chapter, a child who is described as having a mental illness means a child with a

mental illness as defined by Section 571.003, Health and Safety Code.

History of Fam. Code §55.01: Acts 1999, 76th Leg., ch. 1477, §14, eff. Sept. 1, 1999. Amended by Acts 2015, 84th Leg., ch. 1, §§1.001, 1.002, eff. Apr. 2, 2015.

FAM §55.02. MENTAL HEALTH & INTELLECTUAL DISABILITY JURISDICTION

For the purpose of initiating proceedings to order mental health or intellectual disability services for a child or for commitment of a child as provided by this chapter, the juvenile court has jurisdiction of proceedings under Subtitle C or D, Title 7, Health and Safety Code.

History of Fam. Code §55.02: Acts 1999, 76th Leg., ch. 1477, §14, eff. Sept. 1, 1999. Amended by Acts 2015, 84th Leg., ch. 1, §1.003, eff. Apr. 2, 2015.

FAM §55.03. STANDARDS OF CARE

(a) Except as provided by this chapter, a child for whom inpatient mental health services is ordered by a court under this chapter shall be cared for as provided by Subtitle C, Title 7, Health and Safety Code.

(b) Except as provided by this chapter, a child who is committed by a court to a residential care facility due to an intellectual disability shall be cared for as provided by Subtitle D, Title 7, Health and Safety Code.

History of Fam. Code §55.03: Acts 1999, 76th Leg., ch. 1477, §14, eff. Sept. 1, 1999. Amended by Acts 2015, 84th Leg., §1.004, eff. Apr. 2, 2015.

FAM §55.01

FAM §§55.04, 55.05. RENUMBERED

Renumbered as §§55.31, 55.32, and 55.51 by Acts 1999, 76th Leg., ch. 1477, §14, eff. Sept. 1, 1999.

Sections 55.06-55.10 reserved for expansion

SUBCHAPTER B. CHILD WITH MENTAL ILLNESS

FAM §55.11. MENTAL ILLNESS DETERMINATION; EXAMINATION

(a) On a motion by a party, the juvenile court shall determine whether probable cause exists to believe that a child who is alleged by petition or found to have engaged in delinquent conduct or conduct indicating a need for supervision has a mental illness. In making its determination, the court may:

(1) consider the motion, supporting documents, professional statements of counsel, and witness testimony; and

(2) make its own observation of the child.

(b) If the court determines that probable cause exists to believe that the child has a mental illness, the court shall temporarily stay the juvenile court proceedings and immediately order the child to be examined under Section 51.20. The information obtained from the examination must include expert opinion as to whether the child has a mental illness and whether the child meets the commitment criteria under Subtitle C, Title 7, Health and Safety Code. If ordered by the court, the information must also include expert opinion as to whether the child is unfit to proceed with the juvenile court proceedings.

(c) After considering all relevant information, including information obtained from an examination under Section 51.20, the court shall:

(1) if the court determines that evidence exists to support a finding that the child has a mental illness and that the child meets the commitment criteria under Subtitle C, Title 7, Health and Safety Code, proceed under Section 55.12; or

(2) if the court determines that evidence does not exist to support a finding that the child has a mental illness or that the child meets the commitment criteria under Subtitle C, Title 7, Health and Safety Code, dissolve the stay and continue the juvenile court proceedings.

History of Fam. Code §55.11: Acts 1999, 76th Leg., ch. 1477, §14, eff. Sept. 1, 1999.

FAM §55.12. INITIATION OF COMMITMENT PROCEEDINGS

If, after considering all relevant information, the juvenile court determines that evidence exists to support a finding that a child has a mental illness and that the child meets the commitment criteria under Subtitle C, Title 7, Health and Safety Code, the court shall:

(1) initiate proceedings as provided by Section 55.13 to order temporary or extended mental health services, as provided in Subchapter C, Chapter 574, Health and Safety Code; or

(2) refer the child's case as provided by Section 55.14 to the appropriate court for the initiation of proceedings in that court for commitment of the child under Subchapter C, Chapter 574, Health and Safety Code.

History of Fam. Code §55.12: Acts 1973, 63rd Leg., ch. 544, §1, eff. Sept. 1, 1973. Amended by Acts 1995, 74th Leg., ch. 262, §47, eff. May 31, 1995. Renumbered from §55.02(a) and amended by Acts 1999, 76th Leg., ch. 1477, §14, eff. Sept. 1, 1999.

FAM §55.13. COMMITMENT PROCEEDINGS IN JUVENILE COURT

(a) If the juvenile court initiates proceedings for temporary or extended mental health services under Section 55.12(1), the prosecuting attorney or the attor-

ney for the child may file with the juvenile court an application for court-ordered mental health services under Section 574.001, Health and Safety Code. The juvenile court shall:

(1) set a date for a hearing and provide notice as required by Sections 574.005 and 574.006, Health and Safety Code; and

(2) conduct the hearing in accordance with Subchapter C, Chapter 574, Health and Safety Code.

(b) The burden of proof at the hearing is on the party who filed the application.

(c) The juvenile court shall appoint the number of physicians necessary to examine the child and to complete the certificates of medical examination for mental illness required under Section 574.009, Health and Safety Code.

(d) After conducting a hearing on an application under this section, the juvenile court shall:

(1) if the criteria under Section 574.034, Health and Safety Code, are satisfied, order temporary mental health services for the child; or

(2) if the criteria under Section 574.035, Health and Safety Code, are satisfied, order extended mental health services for the child.

History of Fam. Code §55.13: Acts 1999, 76th Leg., ch. 1477, §14, eff. Sept. 1, 1999.

FAM §55.14. REFERRAL FOR COMMITMENT PROCEEDINGS

(a) If the juvenile court refers the child's case to the appropriate court for the initiation of commitment proceedings under Section 55.12(2), the juvenile court shall:

(1) send all papers relating to the child's mental illness to the clerk of the court to which the case is referred;

(2) send to the office of the appropriate county attorney or, if a county attorney is not available, to the office of the appropriate district attorney, copies of all papers sent to the clerk of the court under Subdivision (1); and

(3) if the child is in detention:

(A) order the child released from detention to the child's home or another appropriate place;

(B) order the child detained in an appropriate place other than a juvenile detention facility; or

(C) if an appropriate place to release or detain the child as described by Paragraph (A) or (B) is not available, order the child to remain in the juvenile detention facility subject to further detention orders of the court.

(b) The papers sent to the clerk of a court under Subsection (a)(1) constitute an application for mental health services under Section 574.001, Health and Safety Code.

History of Fam. Code §55.14: Acts 1999, 76th Leg., ch. 1477, §14, eff. Sept. 1, 1999.

FAM §55.15. STANDARDS OF CARE; EXPIRATION OF COURT ORDER FOR MENTAL HEALTH SERVICES

If the juvenile court or a court to which the child's case is referred under Section 55.12(2) orders mental health services for the child, the child shall be cared for, treated, and released in conformity to Subtitle C, Title 7, Health and Safety Code, except:

(1) a court order for mental health services for a child automatically expires on the 120th day after the date the child becomes 18 years of age; and

(2) the administrator of a mental health facility shall notify, in writing, by certified mail, return receipt requested, the juvenile court that ordered mental health services or the juvenile court that referred the case to a court that ordered the mental health services of the intent to discharge the child at least 10 days prior to discharge.

History of Fam. Code §55.15: Acts 1973, 63rd Leg., ch. 544, §1, eff. Sept. 1, 1973. Amended by Acts 1975, 64th Leg., ch. 693, §§20, 21, eff. Sept. 1, 1975; Acts 1991, 72nd Leg., ch. 76, §9, eff. Sept. 1, 1991; Acts 1995, 74th Leg., ch. 262, §47, eff. May 31, 1995. Renumbered from §55.02(c) and amended by Acts 1999, 76th Leg., ch. 1477, §14, eff. Sept. 1, 1999.

FAM §55.16. ORDER FOR MENTAL HEALTH SERVICES; STAY OF PROCEEDINGS

(a) If the court to which the child's case is referred under Section 55.12(2) orders temporary or extended inpatient mental health services for the child, the court shall immediately notify in writing the referring juvenile court of the court's order for mental health services.

(b) If the juvenile court orders temporary or extended inpatient mental health services for the child or if the juvenile court receives notice under Subsection (a) from the court to which the child's case is referred, the proceedings under this title then pending in juvenile court shall be stayed.

History of Fam. Code §55.16: Acts 1973, 63rd Leg., ch. 544, §1, eff. Sept. 1, 1973. Amended by Acts 1995, 74th Leg., ch. 262, §47, eff. May 31, 1995. Renumbered from §55.02(d) and amended by Acts 1999, 76th Leg., ch. 1477, §14, eff. Sept. 1, 1999.

FAM §55.17. MENTAL HEALTH SERVICES NOT ORDERED; DISSOLUTION OF STAY

(a) If the court to which a child's case is referred under Section 55.12(2) does not order temporary or extended inpatient mental health services for the child, the court shall immediately notify in writing the referring juvenile court of the court's decision.

(b) If the juvenile court does not order temporary or extended inpatient mental health services for the child or if the juvenile court receives notice under Subsection (a) from the court to which the child's case is referred, the juvenile court shall dissolve the stay and continue the juvenile court proceedings.

History of Fam. Code §55.17: Acts 1999, 76th Leg., ch. 1477, §14, eff. Sept. 1, 1999.

FAM §55.18. DISCHARGE FROM MENTAL HEALTH FACILITY BEFORE REACHING 18 YEARS OF AGE

If the child is discharged from the mental health facility before reaching 18 years of age, the juvenile court may:

(1) dismiss the juvenile court proceedings with prejudice; or

(2) continue with proceedings under this title as though no order of mental health services had been made.

History of Fam. Code §55.18: Acts 1973, 63rd Leg., ch. 544, §1, eff. Sept. 1, 1973. Amended by Acts 1995, 74th Leg., ch. 262, §47, eff. May 31, 1995. Renumbered from §55.02(e) by Acts 1999, 76th Leg., ch. 1477, §14, eff. Sept. 1, 1999.

FAM §55.19. TRANSFER TO CRIMINAL COURT ON 18TH BIRTHDAY

(a) The juvenile court shall transfer all pending proceedings from the juvenile court to a criminal court on the 18th birthday of a child for whom the juvenile court or a court to which the child's case is referred under Section 55.12(2) has ordered inpatient mental health services if:

(1) the child is not discharged or furloughed from the inpatient mental health facility before reaching 18 years of age; and

(2) the child is alleged to have engaged in delinquent conduct that included a violation of a penal law listed in Section 53.045 and no adjudication concerning the alleged conduct has been made.

(b) The juvenile court shall send notification of the transfer of a child under Subsection (a) to the inpatient mental health facility. The criminal court shall, within 90 days of the transfer, institute proceedings under Chapter 46B, Code of Criminal Procedure. If those or any subsequent proceedings result in a determination that the defendant is competent to stand trial, the defendant may not receive a punishment for the delinquent conduct described by Subsection (a)(2) that results in confinement for a period longer than the maximum period of confinement the defendant could have received if the defendant had been adjudicated for the delinquent conduct while still a child and within the jurisdiction of the juvenile court.

History of Fam. Code §55.19: Acts 1995, 74th Leg., ch. 262, §47, eff. May 31, 1995. Renumbered from §55.02(f), (g) and amended by Acts 1999, 76th Leg., ch. 1477, §14, eff. Sept. 1, 1999. Amended by Acts 2003, 78th Leg., ch. 35, §7, eff. Jan. 1, 2004.

Sections 55.20-55.30 reserved for expansion

SUBCHAPTER C. CHILD UNFIT TO PROCEED AS A RESULT OF MENTAL ILLNESS OR INTELLECTUAL DISABILITY

FAM §55.31. UNFITNESS TO PROCEED DETERMINATION; EXAMINATION

(a) A child alleged by petition or found to have engaged in delinquent conduct or conduct indicating a need for supervision who as a result of mental illness or an intellectual disability lacks capacity to understand the proceedings in juvenile court or to assist in the child's own defense is unfit to proceed and shall not be subjected to discretionary transfer to criminal court, adjudication, disposition, or modification of disposition as long as such incapacity endures.

(b) On a motion by a party, the juvenile court shall determine whether probable cause exists to believe that a child who is alleged by petition or who is found to have engaged in delinquent conduct or conduct indicating a need for supervision is unfit to proceed as a result of mental illness or an intellectual disability. In making its determination, the court may:

(1) consider the motion, supporting documents, professional statements of counsel, and witness testimony; and

(2) make its own observation of the child.

(c) If the court determines that probable cause exists to believe that the child is unfit to proceed, the court shall temporarily stay the juvenile court proceedings and immediately order the child to be examined under Section 51.20. The information obtained from the examination must include expert opinion as to

whether the child is unfit to proceed as a result of mental illness or an intellectual disability.

(d) After considering all relevant information, including information obtained from an examination under Section 51.20, the court shall:

(1) if the court determines that evidence exists to support a finding that the child is unfit to proceed, proceed under Section 55.32; or

(2) if the court determines that evidence does not exist to support a finding that the child is unfit to proceed, dissolve the stay and continue the juvenile court proceedings.

History of Fam. Code §55.31: Acts 1973, 63rd Leg., ch. 544, §1, eff. Sept. 1, 1973. Amended by Acts 1995, 74th Leg., ch. 262, §47, eff. May 31, 1995. Renumbered from §55.04(a), (b) and amended by Acts 1999, 76th Leg., ch. 1477, §14, eff. Sept. 1, 1999. Amended by Acts 2015, 84th Leg., ch. 1, §§1.005, 1.006, eff. Apr. 2, 2015.

FAM §55.32. HEARING ON ISSUE OF FITNESS TO PROCEED

(a) If the juvenile court determines that evidence exists to support a finding that a child is unfit to proceed as a result of mental illness or an intellectual disability, the court shall set the case for a hearing on that issue.

(b) The issue of whether the child is unfit to proceed as a result of mental illness or an intellectual disability shall be determined at a hearing separate from any other hearing.

(c) The court shall determine the issue of whether the child is unfit to proceed unless the child or the attorney for the child demands a jury before the 10th day before the date of the hearing.

(d) Unfitness to proceed as a result of mental illness or an intellectual disability must be proved by a preponderance of the evidence.

(e) If the court or jury determines that the child is fit to proceed, the juvenile court shall continue with proceedings under this title as though no question of fitness to proceed had been raised.

(f) If the court or jury determines that the child is unfit to proceed as a result of mental illness or an intellectual disability, the court shall:

(1) stay the juvenile court proceedings for as long as that incapacity endures; and

(2) proceed under Section 55.33.

(g) The fact that the child is unfit to proceed as a result of mental illness or an intellectual disability does not preclude any legal objection to the juvenile court proceedings which is susceptible of fair determination prior to the adjudication hearing and without the personal participation of the child.

History of Fam. Code §55.32: Acts 1973, 63rd Leg., ch. 544, §1, eff. Sept. 1, 1973. Amended by Acts 1995, 74th Leg., ch. 262, §47, eff. May 31, 1995. Renumbered from §55.04(c)-(f), (h) and amended by Acts 1999, 76th Leg., ch. 1477, §14, eff. Sept. 1, 1999. Amended by Acts 2015, 84th Leg., ch. 1, §1.007, eff. Apr. 2, 2015.

FAM §55.33. PROCEEDINGS FOLLOWING FINDING OF UNFITNESS TO PROCEED

(a) If the juvenile court or jury determines under Section 55.32 that a child is unfit to proceed with the juvenile court proceedings for delinquent conduct, the court shall:

(1) if the unfitness to proceed is a result of mental illness or an intellectual disability:

(A) provided that the child meets the commitment criteria under Subtitle C or D, Title 7, Health and Safety Code, order the child placed with the Department of State Health Services or the Department of Aging and Disability Services, as appropriate, for a period of not more than 90 days, which order may not specify a shorter period, for placement in a facility designated by the department; or

(B) on application by the child's parent, guardian, or guardian ad litem, order the child placed in a private psychiatric inpatient facility for a period of not more than 90 days, which order may not specify a shorter period, but only if the placement is agreed to in writing by the administrator of the facility; or

(2) if the unfitness to proceed is a result of mental illness and the court determines that the child may be adequately treated in an alternative setting, order the child to receive treatment for mental illness on an outpatient basis for a period of not more than 90 days, which order may not specify a shorter period.

(b) If the court orders a child placed in a private psychiatric inpatient facility under Subsection (a)(1)(B), the state or a political subdivision of the state may be ordered to pay any costs associated with the child's placement, subject to an express appropriation of funds for the purpose.

History of Fam. Code §55.33: Acts 1999, 76th Leg., ch. 1477, §14, eff. Sept. 1, 1999. Amended by Acts 2015, 84th Leg., ch. 1, §1.008, eff. Apr. 2, 2015.

FAM §55.34. TRANSPORTATION TO & FROM FACILITY

(a) If the court issues a placement order under Section 55.33(a)(1), the court shall order the probation

department or sheriff's department to transport the child to the designated facility.

(b) On receipt of a report from a facility to which a child has been transported under Subsection (a), the court shall order the probation department or sheriff's department to transport the child from the facility to the court. If the child is not transported to the court before the 11th day after the date of the court's order, an authorized representative of the facility shall transport the child from the facility to the court.

(c) The county in which the juvenile court is located shall reimburse the facility for the costs incurred in transporting the child to the juvenile court as required by Subsection (b).

History of Fam. Code §55.34: Acts 1999, 76th Leg., ch. 1477, §14, eff. Sept. 1, 1999.

FAM §55.35. INFORMATION REQUIRED TO BE SENT TO FACILITY; REPORT TO COURT

(a) If the juvenile court issues a placement order under Section 55.33(a), the court shall order the probation department to send copies of any information in the possession of the department and relevant to the issue of the child's mental illness or intellectual disability to the public or private facility or outpatient center, as appropriate.

(b) Not later than the 75th day after the date the court issues a placement order under Section 55.33(a), the public or private facility or outpatient center, as appropriate, shall submit to the court a report that:

(1) describes the treatment of the child provided by the facility or center; and

(2) states the opinion of the director of the facility or center as to whether the child is fit or unfit to proceed.

(c) The court shall provide a copy of the report submitted under Subsection (b) to the prosecuting attorney and the attorney for the child.

History of Fam. Code §55.35: Acts 1999, 76th Leg., ch. 1477, §14, eff. Sept. 1, 1999. Amended by Acts 2015, 84th Leg., ch. 1, §1.009, eff. Apr. 2, 2015.

FAM §55.36. REPORT THAT CHILD IS FIT TO PROCEED; HEARING ON OBJECTION

(a) If a report submitted under Section 55.35(b) states that a child is fit to proceed, the juvenile court shall find that the child is fit to proceed unless the child's attorney objects in writing or in open court not later than the second day after the date the attorney receives a copy of the report under Section 55.35(c).

(b) On objection by the child's attorney under Subsection (a), the juvenile court shall promptly hold a hearing to determine whether the child is fit to proceed, except that the hearing may be held after the date that the placement order issued under Section 55.33(a) expires. At the hearing, the court shall determine the issue of the fitness of the child to proceed unless the child or the child's attorney demands in writing a jury before the 10th day before the date of the hearing.

(c) If, after a hearing, the court or jury finds that the child is fit to proceed, the court shall dissolve the stay and continue the juvenile court proceedings as though a question of fitness to proceed had not been raised.

(d) If, after a hearing, the court or jury finds that the child is unfit to proceed, the court shall proceed under Section 55.37.

History of Fam. Code §55.36: Acts 1999, 76th Leg., ch. 1477, §14, eff. Sept. 1, 1999.

FAM §55.37. REPORT THAT CHILD IS UNFIT TO PROCEED AS A RESULT OF MENTAL ILLNESS; INITIATION OF COMMITMENT PROCEEDINGS

If a report submitted under Section 55.35(b) states that a child is unfit to proceed as a result of mental illness and that the child meets the commitment criteria for civil commitment under Subtitle C, Title 7, Health and Safety Code, the director of the public or private facility or outpatient center, as appropriate, shall submit to the court two certificates of medical examination for mental illness. On receipt of the certificates, the court shall:

(1) initiate proceedings as provided by Section 55.38 in the juvenile court for commitment of the child under Subtitle C, Title 7, Health and Safety Code; or

(2) refer the child's case as provided by Section 55.39 to the appropriate court for the initiation of proceedings in that court for commitment of the child under Subtitle C, Title 7, Health and Safety Code.

History of Fam. Code §55.37: Acts 1999, 76th Leg., ch. 1477, §14, eff. Sept. 1, 1999.

FAM §55.38. COMMITMENT PROCEEDINGS IN JUVENILE COURT FOR MENTAL ILLNESS

(a) If the juvenile court initiates commitment proceedings under Section 55.37(1), the prosecuting attorney may file with the juvenile court an application for

FAM §55.34

court-ordered mental health services under Section 574.001, Health and Safety Code. The juvenile court shall:

(1) set a date for a hearing and provide notice as required by Sections 574.005 and 574.006, Health and Safety Code; and

(2) conduct the hearing in accordance with Subchapter C, Chapter 574, Health and Safety Code.

(b) After conducting a hearing under Subsection (a)(2), the juvenile court shall:

(1) if the criteria under Section 574.034, Health and Safety Code, are satisfied, order temporary mental health services; or

(2) if the criteria under Section 574.035, Health and Safety Code, are satisfied, order extended mental health services.

History of Fam. Code §55.38: Acts 1999, 76th Leg., ch. 1477, §14, eff. Sept. 1, 1999.

FAM §55.39. REFERRAL FOR COMMITMENT PROCEEDINGS FOR MENTAL ILLNESS

(a) If the juvenile court refers the child's case to an appropriate court for the initiation of commitment proceedings under Section 55.37(2), the juvenile court shall:

(1) send all papers relating to the child's unfitness to proceed, including the verdict and judgment of the juvenile court finding the child unfit to proceed, to the clerk of the court to which the case is referred;

(2) send to the office of the appropriate county attorney or, if a county attorney is not available, to the office of the appropriate district attorney, copies of all papers sent to the clerk of the court under Subdivision (1); and

(3) if the child is in detention:

(A) order the child released from detention to the child's home or another appropriate place;

(B) order the child detained in an appropriate place other than a juvenile detention facility; or

(C) if an appropriate place to release or detain the child as described by Paragraph (A) or (B) is not available, order the child to remain in the juvenile detention facility subject to further detention orders of the court.

(b) The papers sent to a court under Subsection (a)(1) constitute an application for mental health services under Section 574.001, Health and Safety Code.

History of Fam. Code §55.39: Acts 1999, 76th Leg., ch. 1477, §14, eff. Sept. 1, 1999.

FAM §55.40. REPORT THAT CHILD IS UNFIT TO PROCEED AS A RESULT OF INTELLECTUAL DISABILITY

If a report submitted under Section 55.35(b) states that a child is unfit to proceed as a result of an intellectual disability and that the child meets the commitment criteria for civil commitment under Subtitle D, Title 7, Health and Safety Code, the director of the residential care facility shall submit to the court an affidavit stating the conclusions reached as a result of the diagnosis. On receipt of the affidavit, the court shall:

(1) initiate proceedings as provided by Section 55.41 in the juvenile court for commitment of the child under Subtitle D, Title 7, Health and Safety Code; or

(2) refer the child's case as provided by Section 55.42 to the appropriate court for the initiation of proceedings in that court for commitment of the child under Subtitle D, Title 7, Health and Safety Code.

History of Fam. Code §55.40: Acts 1999, 76th Leg., ch. 1477, §14, eff. Sept. 1, 1999. Amended by Acts 2015, 84th Leg., ch. 1, §1.010, eff. Apr. 2, 2015.

FAM §55.41. COMMITMENT PROCEEDINGS IN JUVENILE COURT FOR CHILDREN WITH INTELLECTUAL DISABILITY

(a) If the juvenile court initiates commitment proceedings under Section 55.40(1), the prosecuting attorney may file with the juvenile court an application for placement under Section 593.041, Health and Safety Code. The juvenile court shall:

(1) set a date for a hearing and provide notice as required by Sections 593.047 and 593.048, Health and Safety Code; and

(2) conduct the hearing in accordance with Sections 593.049-593.056, Health and Safety Code.

(b) After conducting a hearing under Subsection (a)(2), the juvenile court may order commitment of the child to a residential care facility if the commitment criteria under Section 593.052, Health and Safety Code, are satisfied.

(c) On receipt of the court's order, the Department of Aging and Disability Services or the appropriate community center shall admit the child to a residential care facility.

History of Fam. Code §55.41: Acts 1999, 76th Leg., ch. 1477, §14, eff. Sept. 1, 1999. Amended by Acts 2001, 77th Leg., ch. 1297, §30, eff. Sept. 1, 2001; Acts 2015, 84th Leg., ch. 1, §§1.011, 1.012, eff. Apr. 2, 2015.

FAM §55.42. REFERRAL FOR COMMITMENT PROCEEDINGS FOR CHILDREN WITH INTELLECTUAL DISABILITY

(a) If the juvenile court refers the child's case to an appropriate court for the initiation of commitment proceedings under Section 55.40(2), the juvenile court shall:

(1) send all papers relating to the child's intellectual disability to the clerk of the court to which the case is referred;

(2) send to the office of the appropriate county attorney or, if a county attorney is not available, to the office of the appropriate district attorney, copies of all papers sent to the clerk of the court under Subdivision (1); and

(3) if the child is in detention:

(A) order the child released from detention to the child's home or another appropriate place;

(B) order the child detained in an appropriate place other than a juvenile detention facility; or

(C) if an appropriate place to release or detain the child as described by Paragraph (A) or (B) is not available, order the child to remain in the juvenile detention facility subject to further detention orders of the court.

(b) The papers sent to a court under Subsection (a)(1) constitute an application for placement under Section 593.041, Health and Safety Code.

History of Fam. Code §55.42: Acts 1999, 76th Leg., ch. 1477, §14, eff. Sept. 1, 1999. Amended by Acts 2015, 84th Leg., ch. 1, §§1.013, 1.014, eff. Apr. 2, 2015.

FAM §55.43. RESTORATION HEARING

(a) The prosecuting attorney may file with the juvenile court a motion for a restoration hearing concerning a child if:

(1) the child is found unfit to proceed as a result of mental illness or an intellectual disability; and

(2) the child:

(A) is not:

(i) ordered by a court to receive inpatient mental health services;

(ii) committed by a court to a residential care facility; or

(iii) ordered by a court to receive treatment on an outpatient basis; or

(B) is discharged or currently on furlough from a mental health facility or outpatient center before the child reaches 18 years of age.

(b) At the restoration hearing, the court shall determine the issue of whether the child is fit to proceed.

(c) The restoration hearing shall be conducted without a jury.

(d) The issue of fitness to proceed must be proved by a preponderance of the evidence.

(e) If, after a hearing, the court finds that the child is fit to proceed, the court shall continue the juvenile court proceedings.

(f) If, after a hearing, the court finds that the child is unfit to proceed, the court shall dismiss the motion for restoration.

History of Fam. Code §55.43: Acts 1999, 76th Leg., ch. 1477, §14, eff. Sept. 1, 1999. Amended by Acts 2007, 80th Leg., ch. 908, §13, eff. Sept. 1, 2007; Acts 2015, 84th Leg., ch. 1, §1.015, eff. Apr. 2, 2015.

FAM §55.44. TRANSFER TO CRIMINAL COURT ON 18TH BIRTHDAY OF CHILD

(a) The juvenile court shall transfer all pending proceedings from the juvenile court to a criminal court on the 18th birthday of a child for whom the juvenile court or a court to which the child's case is referred has ordered inpatient mental health services or residential care for persons with an intellectual disability if:

(1) the child is not discharged or currently on furlough from the facility before reaching 18 years of age; and

(2) the child is alleged to have engaged in delinquent conduct that included a violation of a penal law listed in Section 53.045 and no adjudication concerning the alleged conduct has been made.

(b) The juvenile court shall send notification of the transfer of a child under Subsection (a) to the facility. The criminal court shall, before the 91st day after the date of the transfer, institute proceedings under Chapter 46B, Code of Criminal Procedure. If those or any subsequent proceedings result in a determination that the defendant is competent to stand trial, the defendant may not receive a punishment for the delinquent conduct described by Subsection (a)(2) that results in confinement for a period longer than the maximum period of confinement the defendant could have received if the defendant had been adjudicated for the delinquent conduct while still a child and within the jurisdiction of the juvenile court.

History of Fam. Code §55.44: Acts 1999, 76th Leg., ch. 1477, §14, eff. Sept. 1, 1999. Amended by Acts 2003, 78th Leg., ch. 35, §8, eff. Jan. 1, 2004; Acts 2007, 80th Leg., ch. 908, §14, eff. Sept. 1, 2007; Acts 2015, 84th Leg., ch. 1, §1.016, eff. Apr. 2, 2015.

FAM §55.45. STANDARDS OF CARE; NOTICE OF RELEASE OR FURLOUGH

(a) If the juvenile court or a court to which the child's case is referred under Section 55.37(2) orders mental health services for the child, the child shall be cared for, treated, and released in accordance with Subtitle C, Title 7, Health and Safety Code, except that the administrator of a mental health facility shall notify, in writing, by certified mail, return receipt requested, the juvenile court that ordered mental health services or that referred the case to a court that ordered mental health services of the intent to discharge the child on or before the 10th day before the date of discharge.

(b) If the juvenile court or a court to which the child's case is referred under Section 55.40(2) orders the commitment of the child to a residential care facility, the child shall be cared for, treated, and released in accordance with Subtitle D, Title 7, Health and Safety Code, except that the administrator of the residential care facility shall notify, in writing, by certified mail, return receipt requested, the juvenile court that ordered commitment of the child or that referred the case to a court that ordered commitment of the child of the intent to discharge or furlough the child on or before the 20th day before the date of discharge or furlough.

(c) If the referred child, as described in Subsection (b), is alleged to have committed an offense listed in Article 42A.054, Code of Criminal Procedure, the administrator of the residential care facility shall apply, in writing, by certified mail, return receipt requested, to the juvenile court that ordered commitment of the child or that referred the case to a court that ordered commitment of the child and show good cause for any release of the child from the facility for more than 48 hours. Notice of this request must be provided to the prosecuting attorney responsible for the case. The prosecuting attorney, the juvenile, or the administrator may apply for a hearing on this application. If no one applies for a hearing, the trial court shall resolve the application on the written submission. The rules of evidence do not apply to this hearing. An appeal of the trial court's ruling on the application is not allowed. The release of a child described in this subsection without the express approval of the trial court is punishable by contempt.

History of Fam. Code §55.45: Acts 2001, 77th Leg., ch. 1297, §31, eff. Sept. 1, 2001. Amended by Acts 2007, 80th Leg., ch. 908, §15, eff. Sept. 1, 2007; Acts 2015, 84th Leg., ch. 770, §2.34, eff. Jan. 1, 2017.

Sections 55.46-55.50 reserved for expansion

SUBCHAPTER D. LACK OF RESPONSIBILITY FOR CONDUCT AS A RESULT OF MENTAL ILLNESS OR INTELLECTUAL DISABILITY

FAM §55.51. LACK OF RESPONSIBILITY FOR CONDUCT DETERMINATION; EXAMINATION

(a) A child alleged by petition to have engaged in delinquent conduct or conduct indicating a need for supervision is not responsible for the conduct if at the time of the conduct, as a result of mental illness or an intellectual disability, the child lacks substantial capacity either to appreciate the wrongfulness of the child's conduct or to conform the child's conduct to the requirements of law.

(b) On a motion by a party in which it is alleged that a child may not be responsible as a result of mental illness or an intellectual disability for the child's conduct, the court shall order the child to be examined under Section 51.20. The information obtained from the examinations must include expert opinion as to whether the child is not responsible for the child's conduct as a result of mental illness or an intellectual disability.

(c) The issue of whether the child is not responsible for the child's conduct as a result of mental illness or an intellectual disability shall be tried to the court or jury in the adjudication hearing.

(d) Lack of responsibility for conduct as a result of mental illness or an intellectual disability must be proved by a preponderance of the evidence.

(e) In its findings or verdict the court or jury must state whether the child is not responsible for the child's conduct as a result of mental illness or an intellectual disability.

(f) If the court or jury finds the child is not responsible for the child's conduct as a result of mental illness or an intellectual disability, the court shall proceed under Section 55.52.

(g) A child found to be not responsible for the child's conduct as a result of mental illness or an intellectual disability shall not be subject to proceedings under this title with respect to such conduct, other than proceedings under Section 55.52.

History of Fam. Code §55.51: Acts 1973, 63rd Leg., ch. 544, §1, eff. Sept. 1, 1973. Amended by Acts 1995, 74th Leg., ch. 262, §47, eff. May 31, 1995. Renumbered from §55.05 and amended by Acts 1999, 76th Leg., ch. 1477, §14, eff. Sept. 1, 1999. Amended by Acts 2015, 84th Leg., ch. 1, §§1.017, 1.018, eff. Apr. 2, 2015.

FAM §55.52. PROCEEDINGS FOLLOWING FINDING OF LACK OF RESPONSIBILITY FOR CONDUCT

(a) If the court or jury finds that a child is not responsible for the child's conduct under Section 55.51, the court shall:

(1) if the lack of responsibility is a result of mental illness or an intellectual disability:

(A) provided that the child meets the commitment criteria under Subtitle C or D, Title 7, Health and Safety Code, order the child placed with the Department of State Health Services or the Department of Aging and Disability Services, as appropriate, for a period of not more than 90 days, which order may not specify a shorter period, for placement in a facility designated by the department; or

(B) on application by the child's parent, guardian, or guardian ad litem, order the child placed in a private psychiatric inpatient facility for a period of not more than 90 days, which order may not specify a shorter period, but only if the placement is agreed to in writing by the administrator of the facility; or

(2) if the child's lack of responsibility is a result of mental illness and the court determines that the child may be adequately treated in an alternative setting, order the child to receive treatment on an outpatient basis for a period of not more than 90 days, which order may not specify a shorter period.

(b) If the court orders a child placed in a private psychiatric inpatient facility under Subsection (a)(1)(B), the state or a political subdivision of the state may be ordered to pay any costs associated with the child's placement, subject to an express appropriation of funds for the purpose.

History of Fam. Code §55.52: Acts 1999, 76th Leg., ch. 1477, §14, eff. Sept. 1, 1999. Amended by Acts 2015, 84th Leg., ch. 1, §1.019, eff. Apr. 2, 2015.

FAM §55.53. TRANSPORTATION TO & FROM FACILITY

(a) If the court issues a placement order under Section 55.52(a)(1), the court shall order the probation department or sheriff's department to transport the child to the designated facility.

(b) On receipt of a report from a facility to which a child has been transported under Subsection (a), the court shall order the probation department or sheriff's department to transport the child from the facility to the court. If the child is not transported to the court before the 11th day after the date of the court's order, an authorized representative of the facility shall transport the child from the facility to the court.

(c) The county in which the juvenile court is located shall reimburse the facility for the costs incurred in transporting the child to the juvenile court as required by Subsection (b).

History of Fam. Code §55.53: Acts 1999, 76th Leg., ch. 1477, §14, eff. Sept. 1, 1999.

FAM §55.54. INFORMATION REQUIRED TO BE SENT TO FACILITY; REPORT TO COURT

(a) If the juvenile court issues a placement order under Section 55.52(a), the court shall order the probation department to send copies of any information in the possession of the department and relevant to the issue of the child's mental illness or intellectual disability to the public or private facility or outpatient center, as appropriate.

(b) Not later than the 75th day after the date the court issues a placement order under Section 55.52(a), the public or private facility or outpatient center, as appropriate, shall submit to the court a report that:

(1) describes the treatment of the child provided by the facility or center; and

(2) states the opinion of the director of the facility or center as to whether the child has a mental illness or an intellectual disability.

(c) The court shall send a copy of the report submitted under Subsection (b) to the prosecuting attorney and the attorney for the child.

History of Fam. Code §55.54: Acts 1999, 76th Leg., ch. 1477, §14, eff. Sept. 1, 1999. Amended by Acts 2015, 84th Leg., ch. 1, §1.020, eff. Apr. 2, 2015.

FAM §55.55. REPORT THAT CHILD DOES NOT HAVE MENTAL ILLNESS OR INTELLECTUAL DISABILITY; HEARING ON OBJECTION

(a) If a report submitted under Section 55.54(b) states that a child does not have a mental illness or an intellectual disability, the juvenile court shall discharge the child unless:

(1) an adjudication hearing was conducted concerning conduct that included a violation of a penal law listed in Section 53.045(a) and a petition was approved by a grand jury under Section 53.045; and

(2) the prosecuting attorney objects in writing not later than the second day after the date the attorney receives a copy of the report under Section 55.54(c).

(b) On objection by the prosecuting attorney under Subsection (a), the juvenile court shall hold a hearing

without a jury to determine whether the child has a mental illness or an intellectual disability and whether the child meets the commitment criteria for civil commitment under Subtitle C or D, Title 7, Health and Safety Code.

(c) At the hearing, the burden is on the state to prove by clear and convincing evidence that the child has a mental illness or an intellectual disability and that the child meets the commitment criteria for civil commitment under Subtitle C or D, Title 7, Health and Safety Code.

(d) If, after a hearing, the court finds that the child does not have a mental illness or an intellectual disability and that the child does not meet the commitment criteria under Subtitle C or D, Title 7, Health and Safety Code, the court shall discharge the child.

(e) If, after a hearing, the court finds that the child has a mental illness or an intellectual disability and that the child meets the commitment criteria under Subtitle C or D, Title 7, Health and Safety Code, the court shall issue an appropriate commitment order.

History of Fam. Code §55.55: Acts 1999, 76th Leg., ch. 1477, §14, eff. Sept. 1, 1999. Amended by Acts 2015, 84th Leg., ch. 1, §1.021, eff. Apr. 2, 2015.

FAM §55.56. REPORT THAT CHILD HAS MENTAL ILLNESS; INITIATION OF COMMITMENT PROCEEDINGS

If a report submitted under Section 55.54(b) states that a child has a mental illness and that the child meets the commitment criteria for civil commitment under Subtitle C, Title 7, Health and Safety Code, the director of the public or private facility or outpatient center, as appropriate, shall submit to the court two certificates of medical examination for mental illness. On receipt of the certificates, the court shall:

(1) initiate proceedings as provided by Section 55.57 in the juvenile court for commitment of the child under Subtitle C, Title 7, Health and Safety Code; or

(2) refer the child's case as provided by Section 55.58 to the appropriate court for the initiation of proceedings in that court for commitment of the child under Subtitle C, Title 7, Health and Safety Code.

History of Fam. Code §55.56: Acts 1999, 76th Leg., ch. 1477, §14, eff. Sept. 1, 1999.

FAM §55.57. COMMITMENT PROCEEDINGS IN JUVENILE COURT FOR MENTAL ILLNESS

(a) If the juvenile court initiates commitment proceedings under Section 55.56(1), the prosecuting attorney may file with the juvenile court an application for court-ordered mental health services under Section 574.001, Health and Safety Code. The juvenile court shall:

(1) set a date for a hearing and provide notice as required by Sections 574.005 and 574.006, Health and Safety Code; and

(2) conduct the hearing in accordance with Subchapter C, Chapter 574, Health and Safety Code.

(b) After conducting a hearing under Subsection (a)(2), the juvenile court shall:

(1) if the criteria under Section 574.034, Health and Safety Code, are satisfied, order temporary mental health services; or

(2) if the criteria under Section 574.035, Health and Safety Code, are satisfied, order extended mental health services.

History of Fam. Code §55.57: Acts 1999, 76th Leg., ch. 1477, §14, eff. Sept. 1, 1999.

FAM §55.58. REFERRAL FOR COMMITMENT PROCEEDINGS FOR MENTAL ILLNESS

(a) If the juvenile court refers the child's case to an appropriate court for the initiation of commitment proceedings under Section 55.56(2), the juvenile court shall:

(1) send all papers relating to the child's mental illness, including the verdict and judgment of the juvenile court finding that the child was not responsible for the child's conduct, to the clerk of the court to which the case is referred;

(2) send to the office of the appropriate county attorney or, if a county attorney is not available, to the office of the district attorney, copies of all papers sent to the clerk of the court under Subdivision (1); and

(3) if the child is in detention:

(A) order the child released from detention to the child's home or another appropriate place;

(B) order the child detained in an appropriate place other than a juvenile detention facility; or

(C) if an appropriate place to release or detain the child as described by Paragraph (A) or (B) is not available, order the child to remain in the juvenile detention facility subject to further detention orders of the court.

(b) The papers sent to a court under Subsection (a)(1) constitute an application for mental health services under Section 574.001, Health and Safety Code.

History of Fam. Code §55.58: Acts 1999, 76th Leg., ch. 1477, §14, eff. Sept. 1, 1999.

FAM §55.59. REPORT THAT CHILD HAS INTELLECTUAL DISABILITY; INITIATION OF COMMITMENT PROCEEDINGS

If a report submitted under Section 55.54(b) states that a child has an intellectual disability and that the child meets the commitment criteria for civil commitment under Subtitle D, Title 7, Health and Safety Code, the director of the residential care facility shall submit to the court an affidavit stating the conclusions reached as a result of the diagnosis. On receipt of an affidavit, the juvenile court shall:

(1) initiate proceedings in the juvenile court as provided by Section 55.60 for commitment of the child under Subtitle D, Title 7, Health and Safety Code; or

(2) refer the child's case to the appropriate court as provided by Section 55.61 for the initiation of proceedings in that court for commitment of the child under Subtitle D, Title 7, Health and Safety Code.

History of Fam. Code §55.59: Acts 1999, 76th Leg., ch. 1477, §14, eff. Sept. 1, 1999. Amended by Acts 2015, 84th Leg., ch. 1, §1.022, eff. Apr. 2, 2015.

FAM §55.60. COMMITMENT PROCEEDINGS IN JUVENILE COURT FOR CHILDREN WITH INTELLECTUAL DISABILITY

(a) If the juvenile court initiates commitment proceedings under Section 55.59(1), the prosecuting attorney may file with the juvenile court an application for placement under Section 593.041, Health and Safety Code. The juvenile court shall:

(1) set a date for a hearing and provide notice as required by Sections 593.047 and 593.048, Health and Safety Code; and

(2) conduct the hearing in accordance with Sections 593.049-593.056, Health and Safety Code.

(b) After conducting a hearing under Subsection (a)(2), the juvenile court may order commitment of the child to a residential care facility only if the commitment criteria under Section 593.052, Health and Safety Code, are satisfied.

(c) On receipt of the court's order, the Department of Aging and Disability Services or the appropriate community center shall admit the child to a residential care facility.

History of Fam. Code §55.60: Acts 1999, 76th Leg., ch. 1477, §14, eff. Sept. 1, 1999. Amended by Acts 2001, 77th Leg., ch. 1297, §32, eff. Sept. 1, 2001; Acts 2015, 84th Leg., ch. 1, §§1.023, 1.024, eff. Apr. 2, 2015.

FAM §55.61. REFERRAL FOR COMMITMENT PROCEEDINGS FOR CHILDREN WITH INTELLECTUAL DISABILITY

(a) If the juvenile court refers the child's case to an appropriate court for the initiation of commitment proceedings under Section 55.59(2), the juvenile court shall:

(1) send all papers relating to the child's intellectual disability to the clerk of the court to which the case is referred;

(2) send to the office of the appropriate county attorney or, if a county attorney is not available, to the office of the appropriate district attorney, copies of all papers sent to the clerk of the court under Subdivision (1); and

(3) if the child is in detention:

(A) order the child released from detention to the child's home or another appropriate place;

(B) order the child detained in an appropriate place other than a juvenile detention facility; or

(C) if an appropriate place to release or detain the child as described by Paragraph (A) or (B) is not available, order the child to remain in the juvenile detention facility subject to further detention orders of the court.

(b) The papers sent to a court under Subsection (a)(1) constitute an application for placement under Section 593.041, Health and Safety Code.

History of Fam. Code §55.61: Acts 1999, 76th Leg., ch. 1477, §14, eff. Sept. 1, 1999. Amended by Acts 2015, 84th Leg., ch. 1, §§1.025, 1.026, eff. Apr. 2, 2015.

CHAPTER 56. APPEAL

FAM §56.01. RIGHT TO APPEAL

(a) Except as provided by Subsection (b-1), an appeal from an order of a juvenile court is to a court of appeals and the case may be carried to the Texas Supreme Court by writ of error or upon certificate, as in civil cases generally.

(b) The requirements governing an appeal are as in civil cases generally. When an appeal is sought by filing a notice of appeal, security for costs of appeal, or an affidavit of inability to pay the costs of appeal, and the filing is made in a timely fashion after the date the disposition order is signed, the appeal must include the juvenile court adjudication and all rulings contributing to

FAM §55.58

that adjudication. An appeal of the adjudication may be sought notwithstanding that the adjudication order was signed more than 30 days before the date the notice of appeal, security for costs of appeal, or affidavit of inability to pay the costs of appeal was filed.

(b-1) A motion for new trial seeking to vacate an adjudication is:

(1) timely if the motion is filed not later than the 30th day after the date on which the disposition order is signed; and

(2) governed by Rule 21, Texas Rules of Appellate Procedure.

(c) An appeal may be taken:

(1) except as provided by Subsection (n), by or on behalf of a child from an order entered under:

(A) Section 54.02 respecting transfer of the child for prosecution as an adult;

(B) Section 54.03 with regard to delinquent conduct or conduct indicating a need for supervision;

(C) Section 54.04 disposing of the case;

(D) Section 54.05 respecting modification of a previous juvenile court disposition; or

(E) Chapter 55 by a juvenile court committing a child to a facility for the mentally ill or intellectually disabled; or

(2) by a person from an order entered under Section 54.11(i)(2) transferring the person to the custody of the Texas Department of Criminal Justice.

(d) A child has the right to:

(1) appeal, as provided by this subchapter;

(2) representation by counsel on appeal; and

(3) appointment of an attorney for the appeal if an attorney cannot be obtained because of indigency.

(e) On entering an order that is appealable under this section, the court shall advise the child and the child's parent, guardian, or guardian ad litem of the child's rights listed under Subsection (d) of this section.

(f) If the child and his parent, guardian, or guardian ad litem express a desire to appeal, the attorney who represented the child before the juvenile court shall file a notice of appeal with the juvenile court and inform the court whether that attorney will handle the appeal. Counsel shall be appointed under the standards provided in Section 51.10 of this code unless the right to appeal is waived in accordance with Section 51.09 of this code.

(g) An appeal does not suspend the order of the juvenile court, nor does it release the child from the custody of that court or of the person, institution, or agency to whose care the child is committed, unless the juvenile court so orders. However, the appellate court may provide for a personal bond.

(g-1) An appeal from an order entered under Section 54.02 respecting transfer of the child for prosecution as an adult does not stay the criminal proceedings pending the disposition of that appeal.

(h) If the order appealed from takes custody of the child from the child's parent, guardian, or custodian or waives jurisdiction under Section 54.02 and transfers the child to criminal court for prosecution, the appeal has precedence over all other cases.

(h-1) The supreme court shall adopt rules accelerating the disposition by the appellate court and the supreme court of an appeal of an order waiving jurisdiction under Section 54.02 and transferring a child to criminal court for prosecution.

(i) The appellate court may affirm, reverse, or modify the judgment or order, including an order of disposition or modified disposition, from which appeal was taken. It may reverse or modify an order of disposition or modified order of disposition while affirming the juvenile court adjudication that the child engaged in delinquent conduct or conduct indicating a need for supervision. It may remand an order that it reverses or modifies for further proceedings by the juvenile court.

(j) Neither the child nor his family shall be identified in an appellate opinion rendered in an appeal or habeas corpus proceedings related to juvenile court proceedings under this title. The appellate opinion shall be styled, "In the matter of _______," identifying the child by his initials only.

(k) The appellate court shall dismiss an appeal on the state's motion, supported by affidavit showing that the appellant has escaped from custody pending the appeal and, to the affiant's knowledge, has not voluntarily returned to the state's custody on or before the 10th day after the date of the escape. The court may not dismiss an appeal, or if the appeal has been dismissed, shall reinstate the appeal, on the filing of an affidavit of an officer or other credible person showing that the appellant voluntarily returned to custody on or before the 10th day after the date of the escape.

(*l*) The court may order the child, the child's parent, or other person responsible for support of the child

to pay the child's costs of appeal, including the costs of representation by an attorney, unless the court determines the person to be ordered to pay the costs is indigent.

(m) For purposes of determining indigency of the child under this section, the court shall consider the assets and income of the child, the child's parent, and any other person responsible for the support of the child.

(n) A child who enters a plea or agrees to a stipulation of evidence in a proceeding held under this title may not appeal an order of the juvenile court entered under Section 54.03, 54.04, or 54.05 if the court makes a disposition in accordance with the agreement between the state and the child regarding the disposition of the case, unless:

(1) the court gives the child permission to appeal; or

(2) the appeal is based on a matter raised by written motion filed before the proceeding in which the child entered the plea or agreed to the stipulation of evidence.

(o) This section does not limit a child's right to obtain a writ of habeas corpus.

History of Fam. Code §56.01: Acts 1973, 63rd Leg., ch. 544, §1, eff. Sept. 1, 1973. Amended by Acts 1987, 70th Leg., ch. 385, §14, eff. Sept. 1, 1987; Acts 1991, 72nd Leg., ch. 680, §1, eff. Sept. 1, 1991; Acts 1995, 74th Leg., ch. 262, §48, eff. Jan. 1, 1996; Acts 1997, 75th Leg., ch. 1086, §15, eff. Sept. 1, 1997; Acts 1999, 76th Leg., ch. 74, §2 (eff. Sept. 1, 1999), ch. 1477, §15 (eff. Sept. 1, 1999); Acts 2001, 77th Leg., ch. 1297, §33, eff. Sept. 1, 2001; Acts 2009, 81st Leg., ch. 87, §25.059 (eff. Sept. 1, 2009), ch. 642, §2 (eff. Sept. 1, 2009); Acts 2015, 84th Leg., ch. 74, §3, eff. Sept. 1, 2015.

FAM §56.02. TRANSCRIPT ON APPEAL

(a) An attorney retained to represent a child on appeal who desires to have included in the record on appeal a transcription of notes of the reporter has the responsibility of obtaining and paying for the transcription and furnishing it to the clerk in duplicate in time for inclusion in the record.

(b) The juvenile court shall order the reporter to furnish a transcription without charge to the attorney if the court finds, after hearing or on an affidavit filed by the child's parent or other person responsible for support of the child that the parent or other responsible person is unable to pay or to give security therefor.

(c) On certificate of the court that a transcription has been provided without charge, payment therefor shall be made from the general funds of the county in which the proceedings appealed from occurred.

(d) The court reporter shall report any portion of the proceedings requested by either party or directed by the court and shall report the proceedings in question and answer form unless a narrative transcript is requested.

History of Fam. Code §56.02: Acts 1973, 63rd Leg., ch. 544, §1, eff. Sept. 1, 1973. Amended by Acts 1991, 72nd Leg., ch. 674, §1, eff. Sept. 1, 1991.

FAM §56.03. APPEAL BY STATE IN CASES OF OFFENSES ELIGIBLE FOR DETERMINATE SENTENCE

(a) In this section, "prosecuting attorney" means the county attorney, district attorney, or criminal district attorney who has the primary responsibility of presenting cases in the juvenile court. The term does not include an assistant prosecuting attorney.

(b) The state is entitled to appeal an order of a court in a juvenile case in which the grand jury has approved of the petition under Section 53.045 if the order:

(1) dismisses a petition or any portion of a petition;

(2) arrests or modifies a judgment;

(3) grants a new trial;

(4) sustains a claim of former jeopardy; or

(5) grants a motion to suppress evidence, a confession, or an admission and if:

(A) jeopardy has not attached in the case;

(B) the prosecuting attorney certifies to the trial court that the appeal is not taken for the purpose of delay; and

(C) the evidence, confession, or admission is of substantial importance in the case.

(c) The prosecuting attorney may not bring an appeal under Subsection (b) later than the 15th day after the date on which the order or ruling to be appealed is entered by the court.

(d) The state is entitled to a stay in the proceedings pending the disposition of an appeal under Subsection (b).

(e) The court of appeals shall give preference in its docket to an appeal filed under Subsection (b).

(f) The state shall pay all costs of appeal under Subsection (b), other than the cost of attorney's fees for the respondent.

(g) If the respondent is represented by appointed counsel, the counsel shall continue to represent the respondent as appointed counsel on the appeal. If the respondent is not represented by appointed counsel, the

respondent may seek the appointment of counsel to represent the respondent on appeal. The juvenile court shall determine whether the parent or other person responsible for support of the child is financially able to obtain an attorney to represent the respondent on appeal. If the court determines that the parent or other person is financially unable to obtain counsel for the appeal, the court shall appoint counsel to represent the respondent on appeal.

(h) If the state appeals under this section and the respondent is not detained, the court shall permit the respondent to remain at large subject only to the condition that the respondent appear in court for further proceedings when required by the court. If the respondent is detained, on the state's filing of notice of appeal under this section, the respondent is entitled to immediate release from detention on the allegation that is the subject of the appeal. The court shall permit the respondent to remain at large regarding that allegation subject only to the condition that the respondent appear in court for further proceedings when required by the court.

(i) The Texas Rules of Appellate Procedure apply to a petition by the state to the supreme court for review of a decision of a court of appeals in a juvenile case.

History of Fam. Code §56.03: Acts 2003, 78th Leg., ch. 283, §25, eff. Sept. 1, 2003. Amended by Acts 2013, 83rd Leg., ch. 1299, §23, eff. Sept. 1, 2013.

CHAPTER 57. RIGHTS OF VICTIMS

FAM §57.001. DEFINITIONS

In this chapter:

(1) "Close relative of a deceased victim" means a person who was the spouse of a deceased victim at the time of the victim's death or who is a parent or adult brother, sister, or child of the deceased victim.

(2) "Guardian of a victim" means a person who is the legal guardian of the victim, whether or not the legal relationship between the guardian and victim exists because of the age of the victim or the physical or mental incompetency of the victim.

(3) "Victim" means a person who as the result of the delinquent conduct of a child suffers a pecuniary loss or personal injury or harm.

History of Fam. Code §57.001: Acts 1989, 71st Leg., ch. 633, §1, eff. June 14, 1989. Amended by Acts 1995, 74th Leg., ch. 262, §49, eff. Jan. 1, 1996; Acts 1997, 75th Leg., ch. 368, §1, eff. Sept. 1, 1997.

FAM §57.002. VICTIM'S RIGHTS

(a) A victim, guardian of a victim, or close relative of a deceased victim is entitled to the following rights within the juvenile justice system:

(1) the right to receive from law enforcement agencies adequate protection from harm and threats of harm arising from cooperation with prosecution efforts;

(2) the right to have the court or person appointed by the court take the safety of the victim or the victim's family into consideration as an element in determining whether the child should be detained before the child's conduct is adjudicated;

(3) the right, if requested, to be informed of relevant court proceedings, including appellate proceedings, and to be informed in a timely manner if those court proceedings have been canceled or rescheduled;

(4) the right to be informed, when requested, by the court or a person appointed by the court concerning the procedures in the juvenile justice system, including general procedures relating to:

(A) the preliminary investigation and deferred prosecution of a case; and

(B) the appeal of the case;

(5) the right to provide pertinent information to a juvenile court conducting a disposition hearing concerning the impact of the offense on the victim and the victim's family by testimony, written statement, or any other manner before the court renders its disposition;

(6) the right to receive information regarding compensation to victims as provided by Subchapter B, Chapter 56, Code of Criminal Procedure, including information related to the costs that may be compensated under that subchapter and the amount of com pensation, eligibility for compensation, and procedures for application for compensation under that subchapter, the payment of medical expenses under Section 56.06, Code of Criminal Procedure, for a victim of a

sexual assault, and when requested, to referral to available social service agencies that may offer additional assistance;

(7) the right to be informed, upon request, of procedures for release under supervision or transfer of the person to the custody of the Texas Department of Criminal Justice for parole, to participate in the release or transfer for parole process, to be notified, if requested, of the person's release, escape, or transfer for parole proceedings concerning the person, to provide to the Texas Juvenile Justice Department for inclusion in the person's file information to be considered by the department before the release under supervision or transfer for parole of the person, and to be notified, if requested, of the person's release or transfer for parole;

(8) the right to be provided with a waiting area, separate or secure from other witnesses, including the child alleged to have committed the conduct and relatives of the child, before testifying in any proceeding concerning the child, or, if a separate waiting area is not available, other safeguards should be taken to minimize the victim's contact with the child and the child's relatives and witnesses, before and during court proceedings;

(9) the right to prompt return of any property of the victim that is held by a law enforcement agency or the attorney for the state as evidence when the property is no longer required for that purpose;

(10) the right to have the attorney for the state notify the employer of the victim, if requested, of the necessity of the victim's cooperation and testimony in a proceeding that may necessitate the absence of the victim from work for good cause;

(11) the right to be present at all public court proceedings related to the conduct of the child as provided by Section 54.08, subject to that section; and

(12) any other right appropriate to the victim that a victim of criminal conduct has under Article 56.02 or 56.021, Code of Criminal Procedure.

(b) In notifying a victim of the release or escape of a person, the Texas Juvenile Justice Department shall use the same procedure established for the notification of the release or escape of an adult offender under Article 56.11, Code of Criminal Procedure.

History of Fam. Code §57.002: Acts 1989, 71st Leg., ch. 633, §1, eff. June 14, 1989. Amended by Acts 1995, 74th Leg., ch. 76, §5.95(110) (eff. Sept. 1, 1995), ch. 262, §50 (eff. Jan. 1, 1996); Acts 2001, 77th Leg., ch. 1034, §8, eff. Sept. 1, 2001; Acts 2009, 81st Leg., ch. 87, §25.060, eff. Sept. 1, 2009; Acts 2013, 83rd Leg., ch. 1345, §8, eff. Sept. 1, 2013; Acts 2015, 84th Leg., ch. 734, §56, eff. Sept. 1, 2015.

FAM §57.003. DUTIES OF JUVENILE BOARD & VICTIM ASSISTANCE COORDINATOR

(a) The juvenile board shall ensure to the extent practicable that a victim, guardian of a victim, or close relative of a deceased victim is afforded the rights granted by Section 57.002 and, on request, an explanation of those rights.

(b) The juvenile board may designate a person to serve as victim assistance coordinator in the juvenile board's jurisdiction for victims of juvenile offenders.

(c) The victim assistance coordinator shall ensure that a victim, or close relative of a deceased victim, is afforded the rights granted victims, guardians, and relatives by Section 57.002 and, on request, an explanation of those rights. The victim assistance coordinator shall work closely with appropriate law enforcement agencies, prosecuting attorneys, and the Texas Juvenile Justice Department in carrying out that duty.

(d) The victim assistance coordinator shall ensure that at a minimum, a victim, guardian of a victim, or close relative of a deceased victim receives:

(1) a written notice of the rights outlined in Section 57.002;

(2) an application for compensation under the Crime Victims' Compensation Act (Subchapter B, Chapter 56, Code of Criminal Procedure); and

(3) a victim impact statement with information explaining the possible use and consideration of the victim impact statement at detention, adjudication, and release proceedings involving the juvenile.

(e) The victim assistance coordinator shall, on request, offer to assist a person receiving a form under Subsection (d) to complete the form.

(f) The victim assistance coordinator shall send a copy of the victim impact statement to the court conducting a disposition hearing involving the juvenile.

(g) The juvenile board, with the approval of the commissioners court of the county, may approve a program in which the victim assistance coordinator may offer not more than 10 hours of posttrial psychological counseling for a person who serves as a juror or an alternate juror in an adjudication hearing involving graphic evidence or testimony and who requests the posttrial psychological counseling not later than the 180th day after the date on which the jury in the adjudication hearing is dismissed. The victim assistance co-

ordinator may provide the counseling using a provider that assists local juvenile justice agencies in providing similar services to victims.

History of Fam. Code §57.003: Acts 1989, 71st Leg., ch. 633, §1, eff. June 14, 1989. Amended by Acts 1995, 74th Leg., ch. 262, §51, eff. Jan. 1, 1996; Acts 2009, 81st Leg., ch. 93, §§2, 3, eff. Sept. 1, 2009; Acts 2015, 84th Leg., ch. 734, §57, eff. Sept. 1, 2015.

FAM §57.0031. NOTIFICATION OF RIGHTS OF VICTIMS OF JUVENILES

At the initial contact or at the earliest possible time after the initial contact between the victim of a reported crime and the juvenile probation office having the responsibility for the disposition of the juvenile, the office shall provide the victim a written notice:

(1) containing information about the availability of emergency and medical services, if applicable;

(2) stating that the victim has the right to receive information regarding compensation to victims of crime as provided by the Crime Victims' Compensation Act (Subchapter B, Chapter 56, Code of Criminal Procedure), including information about:

(A) the costs that may be compensated and the amount of compensation, eligibility for compensation, and procedures for application for compensation;

(B) the payment for a medical examination for a victim of a sexual assault; and

(C) referral to available social service agencies that may offer additional assistance;

(3) stating the name, address, and phone number of the victim assistance coordinator for victims of juveniles;

(4) containing the following statement: "You may call the crime victim assistance coordinator for the status of the case and information about victims' rights.";

(5) stating the rights of victims of crime under Section 57.002;

(6) summarizing each procedural stage in the processing of a juvenile case, including preliminary investigation, detention, informal adjustment of a case, disposition hearings, release proceedings, restitution, and appeals;

(7) suggesting steps the victim may take if the victim is subjected to threats or intimidation;

(8) stating the case number and assigned court for the case; and

(9) stating that the victim has the right to file a victim impact statement and to have it considered in juvenile proceedings.

History of Fam. Code §57.0031: Acts 1995, 74th Leg., ch. 262, §51, eff. Jan. 1, 1996.

FAM §57.004. NOTIFICATION

A court, a person appointed by the court, or the Texas Juvenile Justice Department is responsible for notifying a victim, guardian of a victim, or close relative of a deceased victim of a proceeding under this chapter only if the victim, guardian of a victim, or close relative of a deceased victim requests the notification in writing and provides a current address to which the notification is to be sent.

History of Fam. Code §57.004: Acts 1989, 71st Leg., ch. 633, §1, eff. June 14, 1989. Amended by Acts 2015, 84th Leg., ch. 734, §58, eff. Sept. 1, 2015.

FAM §57.005. LIABILITY

The Texas Juvenile Justice Department, a juvenile board, a court, a person appointed by a court, an attorney for the state, a peace officer, or a law enforcement agency is not liable for a failure or inability to provide a right listed under Section 57.002.

History of Fam. Code §57.005: Acts 1989, 71st Leg., ch. 633, §1, eff. June 14, 1989. Amended by Acts 2015, 84th Leg., ch. 734, §59, eff. Sept. 1, 2015.

FAM §57.006. APPEAL

The failure or inability of any person to provide a right or service listed under Section 57.002 of this code may not be used by a child as a ground for appeal or for a post conviction writ of habeas corpus.

History of Fam. Code §57.006: Acts 1989, 71st Leg., ch. 633, §1, eff. June 14, 1989.

FAM §57.007. STANDING

A victim, guardian of a victim, or close relative of a victim does not have standing to participate as a party in a juvenile proceeding or to contest the disposition of any case.

History of Fam. Code §57.007: Acts 1989, 71st Leg., ch. 633, §1, eff. June 14, 1989.

FAM §57.008. COURT ORDER FOR PROTECTION FROM JUVENILES

(a) A court may issue an order for protection from juveniles directed against a child to protect a victim of the child's conduct who, because of the victim's participation in the juvenile justice system, risks further harm by the child.

(b) In the order, the court may prohibit the child from doing specified acts or require the child to do

specified acts necessary or appropriate to prevent or reduce the likelihood of further harm to the victim by the child.

History of Fam. Code §57.008: Acts 1995, 74th Leg., ch. 262, §52, eff. Jan. 1, 1996.

CHAPTER 58. RECORDS; JUVENILE JUSTICE INFORMATION SYSTEM

SUBCHAPTER A. CREATION & CONFIDENTIALITY OF JUVENILE RECORDS

FAM §58.001. LAW ENFORCEMENT COLLECTION & TRANSMITTAL OF RECORDS OF CHILDREN

(a) Law enforcement officers and other juvenile justice personnel shall collect information described by Section 58.104 as a part of the juvenile justice information system created under Subchapter B.

(b) Repealed by S.B. 1304, §21(1), 85th Leg., eff. Sept. 1, 2017.

~~[(b)] [The information is available as provided by Subchapter B.]~~

(c) A law enforcement agency shall forward information, including fingerprints, relating to a child who has been taken into custody under Section 52.01 by the agency to the Department of Public Safety for inclusion in the juvenile justice information system created under Subchapter B, but only if the child is referred to juvenile court on or before the 10th day after the date the

child is taken into custody under Section 52.01. If the child is not referred to juvenile court within that time, the law enforcement agency shall destroy all information, including photographs and fingerprints, relating to the child unless the child is placed in a first offender program under Section 52.031 or on informal disposition under Section 52.03. The law enforcement agency may not forward any information to the Department of Public Safety relating to the child while the child is in a first offender program under Section 52.031, or during the 90 days following successful completion of the program or while the child is on informal disposition under Section 52.03. Except as provided by Subsection (f), after the date the child completes an informal disposition under Section 52.03 or after the 90th day after the date the child successfully completes a first offender program under Section 52.031, the law enforcement agency shall destroy all information, including photographs and fingerprints, relating to the child.

(d) If information relating to a child is contained in a document that also contains information relating to an adult and a law enforcement agency is required to destroy all information relating to the child under this section, the agency shall alter the document so that the information relating to the child is destroyed and the information relating to the adult is preserved.

(e) The deletion of a computer entry constitutes destruction of the information contained in the entry.

(f) A law enforcement agency may maintain information relating to a child after the 90th day after the date the child successfully completes a first offender program under Section 52.031 only to determine the child's eligibility to participate in a first offender program.

History of Fam. Code §58.001: Acts 1995, 74th Leg., ch. 262, §53, eff. Jan. 1, 1996. Amended by Acts 1997, 75th Leg., ch. 1086, §16, eff. Sept. 1, 1997; Acts 1999, 76th Leg., ch. 1477, §16, eff. Sept. 1, 1999; S.B. 1304, §§4, 5, 21(1), 85th Leg., eff. Sept. 1, 2017.

A FAM §58.002. PHOTOGRAPHS & FINGERPRINTS OF CHILDREN

(a) Except as provided by Chapter 63, Code of Criminal Procedure, a child may not be photographed or fingerprinted without the consent of the juvenile court unless the child is:

(1) taken into custody; or

(2) referred to the juvenile court for conduct that constitutes a felony or a misdemeanor punishable by confinement in jail, regardless of whether the child has been taken into custody.

(b) On or before December 31 of each year, the head of each municipal or county law enforcement agency located in a county shall certify to the juvenile board for that county that the photographs and fingerprints required to be destroyed under Section 58.001 have been destroyed. The juvenile board may [~~shall~~] conduct or cause to be conducted an audit of the records of the law enforcement agency to verify the destruction of the photographs and fingerprints and the law enforcement agency shall make its records available for this purpose. If the audit shows that the certification provided by the head of the law enforcement agency is false, that person is subject to prosecution for perjury under Chapter 37, Penal Code.

(c) This section does not prohibit a law enforcement officer from photographing or fingerprinting a child who is not in custody or who has not been referred to the juvenile court for conduct that constitutes a felony or misdemeanor punishable by confinement in jail if the child's parent or guardian voluntarily consents in writing to the photographing or fingerprinting of the child. Consent of the child's parent or guardian is not required to photograph or fingerprint a child described by Subsection (a)(1) or (2).

(d) This section does not apply to fingerprints that are required or authorized to be submitted or obtained for an application for a driver's license or personal identification card.

(e) This section does not prohibit a law enforcement officer from fingerprinting or photographing a child as provided by Section 58.0021.

History of Fam. Code §58.002: Acts 1995, 74th Leg., ch. 262, §53, eff. Jan. 1, 1996. Amended by Acts 1997, 75th Leg., ch. 1086, §17, eff. Sept. 1, 1997; Acts 1999, 76th Leg., ch. 1477, §17, eff. Sept. 1, 1999; Acts 2001, 77th Leg., ch. 1297, §34, eff. Sept. 1, 2001; S.B. 1304, §6, 85th Leg., eff. Sept. 1, 2017.

A FAM §58.0021. FINGERPRINTS OR PHOTOGRAPHS FOR COMPARISON IN INVESTIGATION

(a) A law enforcement officer may take temporary custody of a child to take the child's fingerprints if:

(1) the officer has probable cause to believe that the child has engaged in delinquent conduct;

(2) the officer has investigated that conduct and has found other fingerprints during the investigation; and

(3) the officer has probable cause to believe that the child's fingerprints will match the other fingerprints.

FAM §58.0021

(b) A law enforcement officer may take temporary custody of a child to take the child's photograph, or may obtain a photograph of a child from a juvenile probation department in possession of a photograph of the child, if:

(1) the officer has probable cause to believe that the child has engaged in delinquent conduct; and

(2) the officer has probable cause to believe that the child's photograph will be of material assistance in the investigation of that conduct.

(c) Temporary custody for the purpose described by Subsection (a) or (b):

(1) is not a taking into custody under Section 52.01; and

(2) may not be reported to the juvenile justice information system under Subchapter B.

(d) If a law enforcement officer does not take the child into custody under Section 52.01, the child shall be released from temporary custody authorized under this section as soon as the fingerprints or photographs are obtained.

(e) A law enforcement officer who under this section obtains fingerprints or photographs from a child shall:

(1) immediately destroy them if they do not lead to a positive comparison or identification; and

(2) make a reasonable effort to notify the child's parent, guardian, or custodian of the action taken.

(f) A law enforcement officer may under this section obtain fingerprints or photographs from a child at:

(1) a juvenile processing office; or

(2) a location that affords reasonable privacy to the child.

History of Fam. Code §58.0021: Acts 2001, 77th Leg., ch. 1297, §35, eff. Sept. 1, 2001. Amended by S.B. 1304, §7, 85th Leg., eff. Sept. 1, 2017.

FAM §58.0022. FINGERPRINTS OR PHOTOGRAPHS TO IDENTIFY RUNAWAYS

A law enforcement officer who takes a child into custody with probable cause to believe that the child has engaged in conduct indicating a need for supervision as described by Section 51.03(b)(2) and who after reasonable effort is unable to determine the identity of the child, may fingerprint or photograph the child to establish the child's identity. On determination of the child's identity or that the child cannot be identified by the fingerprints or photographs, the law enforcement officer shall immediately destroy all copies of the fingerprint records or photographs of the child.

History of Fam. Code §58.0022: Acts 2001, 77th Leg., ch. 1297, §36, eff. Sept. 1, 2001. Amended by Acts 2015, 84th Leg., ch. 935, §22, eff. Sept. 1, 2015.

A FAM §58.003. SEALING OF RECORDS

(a) to (c-2) Repealed by S.B. 1304, §21(2), 85th Leg., eff. Sept. 1, 2017.

[~~(a)~~] [~~Except as provided by Subsections (b), (c), and (e), the juvenile court shall order the sealing of the records in the case of a person who has been found to have engaged in delinquent conduct or conduct indicating a need for supervision, or a person taken into custody to determine whether the person engaged in delinquent conduct or conduct indicating a need for supervision, if:~~]

[~~(1)~~] [~~two years have elapsed since final discharge of the person or since the last official action in the person's case if there was no adjudication; and~~]

[~~(2)~~] [~~since the time specified in Subdivision (1), the person has not been convicted of a felony or a misdemeanor involving moral turpitude or found to have engaged in delinquent conduct or conduct indicating a need for supervision and no proceeding is pending seeking conviction or adjudication.~~]

[~~(b)~~] [~~A court may not order the sealing of the records of a person who has received a determinate sentence for engaging in delinquent conduct that violated a penal law listed in Section 53.045 or engaging in habitual felony conduct as described by Section 51.031.~~]

[~~(c)~~] [~~Subject to Subsection (b), a court may order the sealing of records concerning a person adjudicated as having engaged in delinquent conduct that violated a penal law of the grade of felony only if:~~]

[~~(1)~~] [~~the person is 19 years of age or older;~~]

[~~(2)~~] [~~the person was not transferred by a juvenile court under Section 54.02 to a criminal court for prosecution;~~]

[~~(3)~~] [~~the records have not been used as evidence in the punishment phase of a criminal proceeding under Section 3(a), Article 37.07, Code of Criminal Procedure; and~~]

[~~(4)~~] [~~the person has not been convicted of a penal law of the grade of felony after becoming age 17.~~]

[~~(c-1)~~] [~~Notwithstanding Subsections (a) and (c) and subject to Subsection (b), a juvenile court may or-~~

der the sealing of records concerning a child adjudicated as having engaged in delinquent conduct or conduct indicating a need for supervision that violated a penal law of the grade of misdemeanor or felony if the child successfully completed a drug court program under Chapter 123, Government Code, or former law. The court may:]

[(1)] [order the sealing of the records immediately and without a hearing; or]

[(2)] [hold a hearing to determine whether to seal the records.]

[(c-2)] [If the court orders the sealing of a child's records under Subsection (c-1), a prosecuting attorney or juvenile probation department may maintain until the child's 17th birthday a separate record of the child's name and date of birth and the date the child successfully completed the drug court program. The prosecuting attorney or juvenile probation department, as applicable, shall send the record to the court as soon as practicable after the child's 17th birthday to be added to the child's other sealed records.]

Subsection (c-3) was amended by H.B. 29, §24, 85th Leg., enacted May 28, 2017, effective Sept. 1, 2017, and S.B. 1488, §7.005, 85th Leg., enacted May 18, 2017, effective Sept. 1, 2017, without reference to the conflicting repeal made by S.B. 1304, §21(2), 85th Leg., enacted May 26, 2017, effective Sept. 1, 2017. For harmonizing conflicts, see p. V. The amended text in subsection (c-3) is effective for offenses committed on or after Sept. 1, 2017. Offenses in which any element of the offense was committed before Sept. 1, 2017, are governed by the former law in effect at that time.

(c-3) Notwithstanding Subsections (a) and (c) and subject to Subsection (b), a juvenile court, on the court's own motion and without a hearing, shall order the sealing of records concerning a child found to have engaged in conduct indicating a need for supervision described by Section 51.03(b)(5) [51.03(b)(6)] or taken into custody to determine whether the child engaged in conduct indicating a need for supervision described by Section 51.03(b)(5) [51.03(b)(6)]. This subsection applies only to records related to conduct indicating a need for supervision described by Section 51.03(b)(5) [51.03(b)(6)].

Subsection (c-3) was repealed by S.B. 1304, §21(2), 85th Leg., enacted May 26, 2017, effective Sept. 1, 2017, without reference to the conflicting amendments made by H.B. 29, §24, 85th Leg., enacted May 28, 2017, effective Sept. 1, 2017, and S.B. 1488, §7.005, 85th Leg., enacted May 18, 2017, effective Sept. 1, 2017. For harmonizing conflicts, see p. V.

(c-3) to **(p)** Repealed by S.B. 1304, §21(2), 85th Leg., eff. Sept. 1, 2017.

[(c-3)] [Notwithstanding Subsections (a) and (c) and subject to Subsection (b), a juvenile court, on the court's own motion and without a hearing, shall order the sealing of records concerning a child found to have engaged in conduct indicating a need for supervision described by Section 51.03(b)(6) or taken into custody to determine whether the child engaged in conduct indicating a need for supervision described by Section 51.03(b)(6). This subsection applies only to records related to conduct indicating a need for supervision described by Section 51.03(b)(6).]

[(c-4)] [A prosecuting attorney or juvenile probation department may maintain until a child's 17th birthday a separate record of the child's name and date of birth and the date on which the child's records are sealed, if the child's records are sealed under Subsection (c-3). The prosecuting attorney or juvenile probation department, as applicable, shall send the record to the court as soon as practicable after the child's 17th birthday to be added to the child's other sealed records.]

[(c-5)] [Notwithstanding Subsections (a) and (c) and subject to Subsection (b), a juvenile court may order the sealing of records concerning a child found to have engaged in conduct indicating a need for supervision that violates Section 43.261, Penal Code, or taken into custody to determine whether the child engaged in conduct indicating a need for supervision that violates Section 43.261, Penal Code, if the child attends and successfully completes an educational program described by Section 37.218, Education Code, or another equivalent educational program. The court may:]

[(1)] [order the sealing of the records immediately and without a hearing; or]

[(2)] [hold a hearing to determine whether to seal the records.]

[(c-6)] [A prosecuting attorney or juvenile probation department may maintain until a child's 17th birthday a separate record of the child's name and date of birth and the date on which the child successfully completed the educational program, if the child's records are sealed under Subsection (c-5). The pros-

FAM §58.003

~~ecuting attorney or juvenile probation department, as applicable, shall send the record to the court as soon as practicable after the child's 17th birthday to be added to the child's other sealed records.~~]

[~~(c-7)~~] [~~Notwithstanding Subsections (a) and (c) and subject to Subsection (b), a juvenile court may order the sealing of records concerning a child found to have engaged in delinquent conduct or conduct indicating a need for supervision or taken into custody to determine whether the child engaged in delinquent conduct or conduct indicating a need for supervision if the child successfully completed a trafficked persons program under Section 152.0017, Human Resources Code. The court may:~~]

[~~(1)~~] [~~order the sealing of the records immediately and without a hearing; or~~]

[~~(2)~~] [~~hold a hearing to determine whether to seal the records.~~]

[~~(c-8)~~] [~~If the court orders the sealing of a child's records under Subsection (c-7), a prosecuting attorney or juvenile probation department may maintain until the child's 18th birthday a separate record of the child's name and date of birth and the date the child successfully completed the trafficked persons program. The prosecuting attorney or juvenile probation department, as applicable, shall send the record to the court as soon as practicable after the child's 18th birthday to be added to the child's other sealed records.~~]

[~~(d)~~] [~~The court may grant to a child the relief authorized in Subsection (a), (c-1), (c-3), or (c-5) at any time after final discharge of the child or after the last official action in the case if there was no adjudication, subject, if applicable, to Subsection (e). If the child is referred to the juvenile court for conduct constituting any offense and at the adjudication hearing the child is found to be not guilty of each offense alleged, the court shall immediately and without any additional hearing order the sealing of all files and records relating to the case.~~]

[~~(e)~~] [~~The court shall give the prosecuting attorney for the juvenile court reasonable notice before a person's records become eligible for sealing under Subsection (a) or (c) and may hold a hearing before sealing the person's records if the prosecuting attorney requests a hearing. Reasonable notice of the hearing shall be given to:~~]

[~~(1)~~] [~~the person who is the subject of the records at issue;~~]

[~~(2)~~] [~~the authority granting the discharge if the final discharge was from an institution or from parole;~~]

[~~(3)~~] [~~the public or private agency or institution having custody of the person's records; and~~]

[~~(4)~~] [~~the law enforcement agency having custody of the person's files or records.~~]

[~~(f)~~] [~~A copy of the sealing order shall be sent to each agency or official named in the order.~~]

[~~(g)~~] [~~On entry of the order:~~]

[~~(1)~~] [~~all law enforcement, prosecuting attorney, clerk of court, and juvenile court records ordered sealed shall be sent before the 61st day after the date the order is received to the court issuing the order;~~]

[~~(2)~~] [~~all records of a public or private agency or institution ordered sealed shall be sent before the 61st day after the date the order is received to the court issuing the order;~~]

[~~(3)~~] [~~all index references to the records ordered sealed shall be deleted before the 61st day after the date the order is received, and verification of the deletion shall be sent before the 61st day after the date of the deletion to the court issuing the order;~~]

[~~(4)~~] [~~the juvenile court, clerk of court, prosecuting attorney, public or private agency or institution, and law enforcement officers and agencies shall properly reply that no record exists with respect to the person on inquiry in any matter; and~~]

[~~(5)~~] [~~the adjudication shall be vacated and the proceeding dismissed and treated for all purposes other than a subsequent capital prosecution, including the purpose of showing a prior finding of delinquent conduct, as if it had never occurred.~~]

[~~(g-1)~~] [~~Statistical data collected or maintained by the Texas Juvenile Justice Department, including statistical data submitted under Section 221.007, Human Resources Code, is not subject to a sealing order issued under this section.~~]

[~~(h)~~] [~~Inspection of the sealed records may be permitted by an order of the juvenile court on the petition of the person who is the subject of the records and only by those persons named in the order.~~]

[~~(i)~~] [~~On the final discharge of a child or on the last official action in the case if there is no adjudication, the child shall be given a written explanation of the child's rights under this section and a copy of the provisions of this section.~~]

[~~(j)~~] [~~A person whose records have been sealed under this section is not required in any proceeding or~~

~~in any application for employment, information, or licensing to state that the person has been the subject of a proceeding under this title and any statement that the person has never been found to be a delinquent child shall never be held against the person in any criminal or civil proceeding.~~]

[~~(k)~~] [~~A prosecuting attorney may, on application to the juvenile court, reopen at any time the files and records of a person adjudicated as having engaged in delinquent conduct that violated a penal law of the grade of felony sealed by the court under this section for the purposes of Sections 12.42(a)-(c) and (e), Penal Code.~~]

[~~(*l*)~~] [~~On the motion of a person in whose name records are kept or on the court's own motion, the court may order the destruction of records that have been sealed under this section if:~~]

[~~(1)~~] [~~the records relate to conduct that did not violate a penal law of the grade of felony or a misdemeanor punishable by confinement in jail;~~]

[~~(2)~~] [~~five years have elapsed since the person's 16th birthday; and~~]

[~~(3)~~] [~~the person has not been convicted of a felony.~~]

[~~(m)~~] [~~On request of the Department of Public Safety, a juvenile court shall reopen and allow the department to inspect the files and records of the juvenile court relating to an applicant for a license to carry a handgun under Subchapter H, Chapter 411, Government Code.~~]

[~~(n)~~] [~~A record created or maintained under Chapter 62, Code of Criminal Procedure, may not be sealed under this section if the person who is the subject of the record has a continuing obligation to register under that chapter.~~]

[~~(o)~~] [~~An agency or official named in the order that cannot seal the records because the information required in the order under Subsection (p) is incorrect or insufficient shall notify the court issuing the order before the 61st day after the date the agency or official receives the order. The court shall notify the person who is the subject of the records at issue, or the attorney for that person, before the 61st day after the date the court receives the notice that the agency or official cannot seal the records because there is incorrect or insufficient information in the order.~~]

[~~(p)~~] [~~A sealing order entered under this section must include the following information or an explanation for why one or more of the following is not included:~~]

[~~(1)~~] [~~the person's:~~]

[~~(A)~~] [~~full name;~~]

[~~(B)~~] [~~sex;~~]

[~~(C)~~] [~~race or ethnicity;~~]

[~~(D)~~] [~~date of birth;~~]

[~~(E)~~] [~~driver's license or identification card number; and~~]

[~~(F)~~] [~~social security number;~~]

[~~(2)~~] [~~the offense charged against the person or for which the person was referred to the juvenile justice system;~~]

[~~(3)~~] [~~the date on which and the county where the offense was alleged to have been committed; and~~]

[~~(4)~~] [~~if a petition was filed in the juvenile court, the cause number assigned to the petition and the court and county in which the petition was filed.~~]

History of Fam. Code §58.003: Acts 1995, 74th Leg., ch. 262, §53, eff. Jan. 1, 1996. Amended by Acts 1997, 75th Leg., ch. 165, §10.05(a) (eff. Sept. 1, 1997), ch. 1086, §18 (eff. Sept. 1, 1997); Acts 1999, 76th Leg., ch. 62, §19.01(20) (eff. Sept. 1, 1999), ch. 147, §1 (eff. Sept. 1, 1999); Acts 2003, 78th Leg., ch. 283, §26, eff. Sept. 1, 2003; Acts 2005, 79th Leg., ch. 949, §16, eff. Sept. 1, 2005; Acts 2009, 81st Leg., ch. 189, §1, eff. Sept. 1, 2009; Acts 2011, 82nd Leg., ch. 85, §3.008 (eff. Sept. 1, 2011), ch. 731, §3 (eff. June 17, 2011), ch. 1150, §2 (eff. Sept. 1, 2011), ch. 1322, §19 (eff. Sept. 1, 2011); Acts 2013, 83rd Leg., ch. 161, §§7.003, 22.001(16), 22.002(8) (eff. Sept. 1, 2013), ch. 186, §6 (eff. Sept. 1, 2013), ch. 747, §2.04 (eff. Sept. 1, 2013), ch. 1299, §§24-27 (eff. Sept. 1, 2013); Acts 2015, 84th Leg., ch. 437, §11 (eff. Jan. 1, 2016), ch. 935, §23 (eff. Sept. 1, 2015), ch. 995, §1 (eff. Sept. 1, 2015), ch. 1214, §1 (eff. Sept. 1, 2015), ch. 1236, §21.002(7) (eff. Sept. 1, 2015); H.B. 29, §24, 85th Leg., eff. Sept. 1, 2017; S.B. 1304, §21(2), 85th Leg., eff. Sept. 1, 2017; S.B. 1488, §7.005, 85th Leg., eff. Sept. 1, 2017.

Ⓐ FAM §58.004. REDACTION OF VICTIM'S PERSONALLY IDENTIFIABLE INFORMATION

(a) Notwithstanding any other law, before disclosing any juvenile court record [~~or file~~] of a child as authorized by this chapter or other law, the custodian of the record [~~or file~~] must redact any personally identifiable information about a victim of the child's delinquent conduct or conduct indicating a need for supervision who was under 18 years of age on the date the conduct occurred.

(b) This section does not apply to information that is:

(1) necessary for an agency to provide services to the victim;

(2) necessary for law enforcement purposes; [~~or~~]

(3) shared within the statewide juvenile information and case management system established under Subchapter E;

(4) shared with an attorney representing the child in a proceeding under this title; or

(5) shared with an attorney representing any other person in a juvenile or criminal court proceeding arising from the same act or conduct for which the child was referred to juvenile court.

History of Fam. Code §58.004: Acts 2015, 84th Leg., ch. 588, §1, eff. Sept. 1, 2015. Amended by S.B. 1304, §8, 85th Leg., eff. Sept. 1, 2017.

History of Former Fam. Code §58.004: Repealed by Acts 1997, 75th Leg., ch. 1086, §49(a), eff. Sept. 1, 1997.

FAM §58.005. CONFIDENTIALITY OF FACILITY RECORDS

(a) This section applies only to the inspection, copying, and maintenance of a record [~~Records and files~~] concerning a child and to the storage of information from which a record could be generated, including personally identifiable information, [~~and~~] information obtained for the purpose of diagnosis, examination, evaluation, or treatment of the child or for making a referral for treatment of the [~~a~~] child, and other records or information, created by or in the possession of:

(1) the Texas Juvenile Justice Department;

(2) an entity having custody of the child under a contract with the Texas Juvenile Justice Department; or

(3) another [~~by a~~] public or private agency or institution [~~providing supervision of a child by arrangement of the juvenile court or~~] having custody of the child under order of the juvenile court, including a facility operated by or under contract with a juvenile board or juvenile probation department.

(a-1) Except as provided by Article 15.27, Code of Criminal Procedure, the records and information to which this section applies may be disclosed only to:

(1) the professional staff or consultants of the agency or institution;

(2) the judge, probation officers, and professional staff or consultants of the juvenile court;

(3) an attorney for the child;

(4) a governmental agency if the disclosure is required or authorized by law;

(5) a person or entity to whom the child is referred for treatment or services if the agency or institution disclosing the information has entered into a written confidentiality agreement with the person or entity regarding the protection of the disclosed information;

(6) the Texas Department of Criminal Justice and the Texas Juvenile Justice Department for the purpose of maintaining statistical records of recidivism and for diagnosis and classification; or

(7) with permission from [~~leave of~~] the juvenile court, any other person, agency, or institution having a legitimate interest in the proceeding or in the work of the court.

(b) This section does not affect the collection, dissemination, or maintenance of information as provided by Subchapter B or [~~apply to information collected under Section 58.104 or under Subchapter~~] D-1.

History of Fam. Code §58.005: Acts 1995, 74th Leg., ch. 262, §53, eff. Jan. 1, 1996. Amended by Acts 2003, 78th Leg., ch. 283, §27, eff. Sept. 1, 2003; Acts 2007, 80th Leg., ch. 908, §26(a), eff. Jan. 1, 2008; Acts 2015, 84th Leg., ch. 734, §60, eff. Sept. 1, 2015; S.B. 1304, §9, 85th Leg., eff. Sept. 1, 2017.

FAM §58.0051. INTERAGENCY SHARING OF EDUCATIONAL RECORDS

(a) In this section:

(1) "Educational records" means records in the possession of a primary or secondary educational institution that contain information relating to a student, including information relating to the student's:

(A) identity;

(B) special needs;

(C) educational accommodations;

(D) assessment or diagnostic test results;

(E) attendance records;

(F) disciplinary records;

(G) medical records; and

(H) psychological diagnoses.

(2) "Juvenile service provider" means a governmental entity that provides juvenile justice or prevention, medical, educational, or other support services to a juvenile. The term includes:

(A) a state or local juvenile justice agency as defined by Section 58.101;

(B) health and human services agencies, as defined by Section 531.001, Government Code, and the Health and Human Services Commission;

(C) the Department of Family and Protective Services;

(D) the Department of Public Safety;

(E) [~~(D)~~] the Texas Education Agency;

(F) [~~(E)~~] an independent school district;

(G) [~~(F)~~] a juvenile justice alternative education program;

(H) [~~(G)~~] a charter school;

(I) [~~(H)~~] a local mental health or mental retardation authority;

(J) [~~(I)~~] a court with jurisdiction over juveniles;

(K) [~~(J)~~] a district attorney's office;

(L) [~~(K)~~] a county attorney's office; and

(M) [~~(L)~~] a children's advocacy center established under Section 264.402.

(3) "Student" means a person who:

(A) is registered or in attendance at a primary or secondary educational institution; and

(B) is younger than 18 years of age.

(b) At the request of a juvenile service provider, an independent school district or a charter school shall disclose to the juvenile service provider confidential information contained in the student's educational records if the student has been:

(1) taken into custody under Section 52.01; or

(2) referred to a juvenile court for allegedly engaging in delinquent conduct or conduct indicating a need for supervision.

(c) An independent school district or charter school that discloses confidential information to a juvenile service provider under Subsection (b) may not destroy a record of the disclosed information before the seventh anniversary of the date the information is disclosed.

(d) An independent school district or charter school shall comply with a request under Subsection (b) regardless of whether other state law makes that information confidential.

(e) A juvenile service provider that receives confidential information under this section shall:

(1) certify in writing that the juvenile service provider receiving the confidential information has agreed not to disclose it to a third party, other than another juvenile service provider; and

(2) use the confidential information only to:

(A) verify the identity of a student involved in the juvenile justice system; and

(B) provide delinquency prevention or treatment services to the student.

(f) A juvenile service provider may establish an internal protocol for sharing information with other juvenile service providers as necessary to efficiently and promptly disclose and accept the information. The protocol may specify the types of information that may be shared under this section without violating federal law, including any federal funding requirements. A juvenile service provider may enter into a memorandum of understanding with another juvenile service provider to share information according to the juvenile service provider's protocols. A juvenile service provider shall comply with this section regardless of whether the juvenile service provider establishes an internal protocol or enters into a memorandum of understanding under this subsection unless compliance with this section violates federal law.

(g) This section does not affect the confidential status of the information being shared. The information may be released to a third party only as directed by a court order or as otherwise authorized by law. Personally identifiable information disclosed to a juvenile service provider under this section is not subject to disclosure to a third party under Chapter 552, Government Code.

(h) A juvenile service provider that requests information under this section shall pay a fee to the disclosing juvenile service provider in the same amounts charged for the provision of public information under Subchapter F, Chapter 552, Government Code, unless:

(1) a memorandum of understanding between the requesting provider and the disclosing provider:

(A) prohibits the payment of a fee;

(B) provides for the waiver of a fee; or

(C) provides an alternate method of assessing a fee;

(2) the disclosing provider waives the payment of the fee; or

(3) disclosure of the information is required by law other than this subchapter.

History of Fam. Code §58.0051: Acts 1999, 76th Leg., ch. 217, §1, eff. May 24, 1999. Amended by Acts 2007, 80th Leg., ch. 908, §16, eff. Sept. 1, 2007; Acts 2011, 82nd Leg., ch. 653, §2, eff. June 17, 2011; H.B. 5, §1, 85th Leg., eff. Sept. 1, 2017.

A FAM §58.0052. INTERAGENCY SHARING OF CERTAIN NONEDUCATIONAL RECORDS

(a) In this section:

(1) "Juvenile justice agency" has the meaning assigned by Section 58.101.

(2) "Juvenile service provider" has the meaning assigned by Section 58.0051.

(3) [~~(2)~~] "Multi-system youth" means a person who:

(A) is younger than 19 years of age; and

(B) has received services from two or more juvenile service providers.

(4) [(3)] "Personal health information" means personally identifiable information regarding a multi-system youth's physical or mental health or the provision of or payment for health care services, including case management services, to a multi-system youth. The term does not include clinical psychological notes or substance abuse treatment information.

(b) Subject to Subsection (c), at [At] the request of a juvenile service provider, another juvenile service provider shall disclose to that provider a multi-system youth's personal health information or a history of governmental services provided to the multi-system youth, including:

(1) identity records;

(2) medical and dental records;

(3) assessment or diagnostic test results;

(4) special needs;

(5) program placements; [and]

(6) psychological diagnoses; and

(7) other related records or information.

Subsection (b-1) was enacted by H.B. 7, §3, 85th Leg., enacted May 26, 2017, effective Sept. 1, 2017, without reference to the conflicting enactment made by H.B. 1521, §1, 85th Leg., enacted May 28, 2017, effective June 15, 2017. For harmonizing conflicts, see p. V. Subsection (b-1) is effective for service plans filed for a full adversary hearing held under Fam. Code §262.201 or a status hearing held under Fam. Code ch. 263 on or after Jan. 1, 2018. Except as provided above, subsection (b-1) is effective for SAPCRs filed on or after Sept. 1, 2017.

(b-1) In addition to the information provided under Subsection (b), the Department of Family and Protective Services and the Texas Juvenile Justice Department shall coordinate and develop protocols for sharing with each other, on request, any other information relating to a multi-system youth necessary to:

(1) identify and coordinate the provision of services to the youth and prevent duplication of services;

(2) enhance rehabilitation of the youth; and

(3) improve and maintain community safety.

Subsection (b-1) was enacted by H.B. 1521, §1, 85th Leg., enacted May 28, 2017, effective June 15, 2017, without reference to the conflicting enactment made by H.B. 7, §3, 85th Leg., enacted May 26, 2017, effective Sept. 1, 2017. For harmonizing conflicts, see p. V.

(b-1) At the request of a state or local juvenile justice agency, the Department of Family and Protective Services or a single source continuum contractor who contracts with the department to provide foster care services shall, not later than the 14th business day after the date of the request, share with the juvenile justice agency information in the possession of the department or contractor that is necessary to improve and maintain community safety or that assists the agency in the continuation of services for or providing services to a multi-system youth who:

(1) is or has been in the temporary or permanent managing conservatorship of the department;

(2) is or was the subject of a family-based safety services case with the department;

(3) has been reported as an alleged victim of abuse or neglect to the department;

(4) is the perpetrator in a case in which the department investigation concluded that there was a reason to believe that abuse or neglect occurred; or

(5) is a victim in a case in which the department investigation concluded that there was a reason to believe that abuse or neglect occurred.

(b-2) At the request of the Department of Family and Protective Services or a single source continuum contractor who contracts with the department to provide foster care services, a state or local juvenile justice agency shall share with the department or contractor information in the possession of the juvenile justice agency that is necessary to improve and maintain community safety or that assists the department or contractor in the continuation of services for or providing services to a multi-system youth who is or has been in the custody or control of the juvenile justice agency.

(c) A juvenile service provider may disclose personally identifiable information under this section only for the purposes of:

(1) identifying a multi-system youth;

(2) coordinating and monitoring care for a multi-system youth; and

(3) improving the quality of juvenile services provided to a multi-system youth.

(d) To the extent that this section conflicts with another law of this state with respect to confidential information held by a governmental agency, this section controls.

(e) A juvenile service provider may establish an internal protocol for sharing information with other juvenile service providers as necessary to efficiently and promptly disclose and accept the information. The protocol may specify the types of information that may be shared under this section without violating federal law, including any federal funding requirements. A juvenile service provider may enter into a memorandum of understanding with another juvenile service provider to share information according to the juvenile service provider's protocols. A juvenile service provider shall comply with this section regardless of whether the juvenile service provider establishes an internal protocol or enters into a memorandum of understanding under this subsection unless compliance with this section violates federal law.

(f) This section does not affect the confidential status of the information being shared. The information may be released to a third party only as directed by a court order or as otherwise authorized by law. Personally identifiable information disclosed to a juvenile service provider under this section is not subject to disclosure to a third party under Chapter 552, Government Code.

(g) This section does not affect the authority of a governmental agency to disclose to a third party for research purposes information that is not personally identifiable as provided by the governmental agency's protocol.

(h) A juvenile service provider that requests information under this section shall pay a fee to the disclosing juvenile service provider in the same amounts charged for the provision of public information under Subchapter F, Chapter 552, Government Code, unless:

(1) a memorandum of understanding between the requesting provider and the disclosing provider:

(A) prohibits the payment of a fee;

(B) provides for the waiver of a fee; or

(C) provides an alternate method of assessing a fee;

(2) the disclosing provider waives the payment of the fee; or

(3) disclosure of the information is required by law other than this subchapter.

History of Fam. Code §58.0052: Acts 2011, 82nd Leg., ch. 653, §2, eff. June 17, 2011. Amended by Acts 2015, 84th Leg., ch. 944, §5, eff. Sept. 1, 2015; H.B. 7, §3, 85th Leg., eff. Sept. 1, 2017; H.B. 1521, §1, 85th Leg., eff. June 15, 2017; S.B. 1304, §10, 85th Leg., eff. Sept. 1, 2017.

FAM §58.0053. INTERAGENCY SHARING OF JUVENILE PROBATION RECORDS

(a) On request by the Department of Family and Protective Services, a juvenile probation officer shall disclose to the department the terms of probation of a child in the department's conservatorship.

(b) To the extent of a conflict between this section and another law of this state applicable to confidential information held by a governmental agency, this section controls.

(c) This section does not affect the confidential status of the information being shared. The information may be released to a third party only as directed by a court order or as otherwise authorized by law. Personally identifiable information disclosed to the Department of Family and Protective Services under this section is not subject to disclosure to a third party under Chapter 552, Government Code.

(d) The Department of Family and Protective Services shall enter into a memorandum of understanding with the Texas Juvenile Justice Department to adopt procedures for handling information requests under this section.

History of Fam. Code §58.0053: Acts 2015, 84th Leg., ch. 944, §6, eff. Sept. 1, 2015.

FAM §58.006. REPEALED [DESTRUCTION OF CERTAIN RECORDS]

[The court shall order the destruction of the records relating to the conduct for which a child is taken into custody, including records contained in the juvenile justice information system, if:]

[(1)] [a determination that no probable cause exists to believe the child engaged in the conduct is made under Section 53.01 and the case is not referred to a prosecutor for review under Section 53.012; or]

[(2)] [a determination that no probable cause exists to believe the child engaged in the conduct is made by a prosecutor under Section 53.012.]

Repealed by S.B. 1304, §21(3), 85th Leg., eff. Sept. 1, 2017.

A FAM §58.007. CONFIDENTIALITY OF PROBATION DEPARTMENT, PROSECUTOR, & COURT [PHYSICAL] RECORDS [OR FILES]

(a) This section applies only to the inspection, copying, and maintenance of a [physical] record [or file] concerning a child and the storage of information, by electronic means or otherwise, concerning the child

FAM §58.007

from which a [physical] record [or file] could be generated and does not affect the collection, dissemination, or maintenance of information as provided by Subchapter B or D-1. This section does not apply to a record [or file] relating to a child that is:

(1) required or authorized to be maintained under the laws regulating the operation of motor vehicles in this state;

(2) maintained by a municipal or justice court; or

(3) subject to disclosure under Chapter 62, Code of Criminal Procedure.

(b) Except as provided by Section 54.051(d-1) and by Article 15.27, Code of Criminal Procedure, the records, whether physical or electronic, [and files] of a juvenile court, a clerk of court, a juvenile probation department, or a prosecuting attorney relating to a child who is a party to a proceeding under this title may be inspected or copied only by:

(1) the judge, probation officers, and professional staff or consultants of the juvenile court;

(2) a juvenile justice agency as that term is defined by Section 58.101;

(3) an attorney representing [for] a party in a [to the] proceeding under this title;

(4) a person or entity to whom the child is referred for treatment or services, if the agency or institution disclosing the information has entered into a written confidentiality agreement with the person or entity regarding the protection of the disclosed information;

(5) a public or private agency or institution providing supervision of the child by arrangement of the juvenile court, or having custody of the child under juvenile court order; or

(6) [(5)] with permission from [leave of] the juvenile court, any other person, agency, or institution having a legitimate interest in the proceeding or in the work of the court.

(b-1) A person who is the subject of the records is entitled to access the records for the purpose of preparing and presenting a motion or application to seal the records.

(c) to **(f)** Repealed by S.B. 1304, §21(4), 85th Leg., eff. Sept. 1, 2017.

[(c)] [Except as provided by Subsection (d), law enforcement records and files concerning a child and information stored, by electronic means or otherwise, concerning the child from which a record or file could be generated may not be disclosed to the public and shall be:]

[(1)] [if maintained on paper or microfilm, kept separate from adult files and records;]

[(2)] [if maintained electronically in the same computer system as records or files relating to adults, be accessible under controls that are separate and distinct from controls to access electronic data concerning adults; and]

[(3)] [maintained on a local basis only and not sent to a central state or federal depository, except as provided by Subchapters B, D, and E.]

[(d)] [The law enforcement files and records of a person who is transferred from the Texas Juvenile Justice Department to the Texas Department of Criminal Justice may be transferred to a central state or federal depository for adult records on or after the date of transfer.]

[(e)] [Law enforcement records and files concerning a child may be inspected or copied by a juvenile justice agency as that term is defined by Section 58.101, a criminal justice agency as that term is defined by Section 411.082, Government Code, the child, and the child's parent or guardian.]

[(f)] [If a child has been reported missing by a parent, guardian, or conservator of that child, information about the child may be forwarded to and disseminated by the Texas Crime Information Center and the National Crime Information Center.]

(g) For the purpose of offering a record as evidence in the punishment phase of a criminal proceeding, a prosecuting attorney may obtain the record of a defendant's adjudication that is admissible under Section 3(a), Article 37.07, Code of Criminal Procedure, by submitting a request for the record to the juvenile court that made the adjudication. If a court receives a request from a prosecuting attorney under this subsection, the court shall, if the court possesses the requested record of adjudication, certify and provide the prosecuting attorney with a copy of the record. If a record has been sealed under this chapter, the juvenile court may not provide a copy of the record to a prosecuting attorney under this subsection.

(h) The juvenile court may disseminate to the public the following information relating to a child who is

the subject of a directive to apprehend or a warrant of arrest and who cannot be located for the purpose of apprehension:

(1) the child's name, including other names by which the child is known;

(2) the child's physical description, including sex, weight, height, race, ethnicity, eye color, hair color, scars, marks, and tattoos;

(3) a photograph of the child; and

(4) a description of the conduct the child is alleged to have committed, including the level and degree of the alleged offense.

(i) In addition to the authority to release information under Subsection (b)(6) [~~(b)(5)~~], a juvenile probation department may release information contained in its records without leave of the juvenile court pursuant to guidelines adopted by the juvenile board.

(j) Before a child or a child's parent or guardian may inspect or copy a record or file concerning the child under Subsection (e), the custodian of the record or file shall redact:

(1) any personally identifiable information about a juvenile suspect, offender, victim, or witness who is not the child; and

(2) any information that is excepted from required disclosure under Chapter 552, Government Code, or other law.

History of Fam. Code §58.007: Acts 1995, 74th Leg., ch. 262, §53, eff. Jan. 1, 1996. Amended by Acts 1997, 75th Leg., ch. 1086, §§19, 20 (eff. Sept. 1, 1997); Acts 1999, 76th Leg., ch. 815, §1 (eff. June 18, 1999), ch. 1415, §20 (eff. Sept. 1, 1999), ch. 1477, §18 (eff. Sept. 1, 1999); Acts 2001, 77th Leg., ch. 1297, §37, eff. Sept. 1, 2001; Acts 2007, 80th Leg., ch. 879, §1 (eff. Sept. 1, 2007), ch. 908, §17 (eff. Sept. 1, 2007); Acts 2009, 81st Leg., ch. 87, §25.061, eff. Sept. 1, 2009; Acts 2013, 83rd Leg., ch. 124, §1 (eff. May 24, 2013), ch. 1299, §28 (eff. Sept. 1, 2013); Acts 2015, 84th Leg., ch. 734, §61, eff. Sept. 1, 2015; S.B. 1304, §§11, 12, 21(4), 85th Leg., eff. Sept. 1, 2017.

FAM §58.0071. REPEALED [~~DESTRUCTION OF CERTAIN PHYSICAL RECORDS & FILES~~]

[~~(a)~~] [~~In this section:~~]

[~~(1)~~] [~~"Juvenile case" means:~~]

[~~(A)~~] [~~a referral for conduct indicating a need for supervision or delinquent conduct; or~~]

[~~(B)~~] [~~if a petition was filed, all charges made in the petition.~~]

[~~(2)~~] [~~"Physical records and files" include entries in a computer file or information on microfilm, microfiche, or any other electronic storage media.~~]

[~~(b)~~] [~~The custodian of physical records and files in a juvenile case may destroy the records and files if the custodian duplicates the information in the records and files in a computer file or information on microfilm, microfiche, or any other electronic storage media.~~]

[~~(c)~~] [~~The following persons may authorize, subject to Subsections (d) and (e) and any other restriction the person may impose, the destruction of the physical records and files relating to a closed juvenile case:~~]

[~~(1)~~] [~~a juvenile board in relation to the records and files in the possession of the juvenile probation department;~~]

[~~(2)~~] [~~the head of a law enforcement agency in relation to the records and files in the possession of the agency; and~~]

[~~(3)~~] [~~a prosecuting attorney in relation to the records and files in the possession of the prosecuting attorney's office.~~]

[~~(d)~~] [~~The physical records and files of a juvenile case may only be destroyed if the child who is the respondent in the case:~~]

[~~(1)~~] [~~is at least 18 years of age and:~~]

[~~(A)~~] [~~the most serious allegation adjudicated was conduct indicating a need for supervision;~~]

[~~(B)~~] [~~the most serious allegation was conduct indicating a need for supervision and there was not an adjudication; or~~]

[~~(C)~~] [~~the referral or information did not relate to conduct indicating a need for supervision or delinquent conduct and the juvenile court or the court's staff did not take action on the referral or information for that reason;~~]

[~~(2)~~] [~~is at least 21 years of age and:~~]

[~~(A)~~] [~~the most serious allegation adjudicated was delinquent conduct that violated a penal law of the grade of misdemeanor; or~~]

[~~(B)~~] [~~the most serious allegation was delinquent conduct that violated a penal law of the grade of misdemeanor or felony and there was not an adjudication; or~~]

[~~(3)~~] [~~is at least 31 years of age and the most serious allegation adjudicated was delinquent conduct that violated a penal law of the grade of felony.~~]

[~~(e)~~] [~~If a record or file contains information relating to more than one juvenile case, information relating to each case may only be destroyed if:~~]

[~~(1)~~] [~~the destruction of the information is authorized under this section; and~~]

[~~(2)~~] [~~the information can be separated from information that is not authorized to be destroyed under this section.~~]

[~~(f)~~] [~~This section does not affect the destruction of physical records and files authorized by the Texas State Library Records Retention Schedule.~~]

Repealed by S.B. 1304, §21(5), 85th Leg., eff. Sept. 1, 2017.

FAM §58.00711. REPEALED [~~RECORDS RELATING TO CHILDREN CHARGED WITH, CONVICTED OF, OR RECEIVING DEFERRED DISPOSITION FOR FINE-ONLY MISDEMEANORS~~]

[~~(a)~~] [~~This section applies only to a misdemeanor offense punishable by fine only, other than a traffic offense.~~]

[~~(b)~~] [~~Except as provided by Article 45.0217(b), Code of Criminal Procedure, all records and files and information stored by electronic means or otherwise, from which a record or file could be generated, relating to a child who is charged with, is convicted of, is found not guilty of, had a charge dismissed for, or is granted deferred disposition for an offense described by Subsection (a) are confidential and may not be disclosed to the public.~~]

Repealed by S.B. 1304, §21(6), 85th Leg., eff. Sept. 1, 2017.

FAM §58.008. CONFIDENTIALITY OF LAW ENFORCEMENT RECORDS

(a) This section applies only to the inspection, copying, and maintenance of a record concerning a child and to the storage of information, by electronic means or otherwise, concerning the child from which a record could be generated and does not affect the collection, dissemination, or maintenance of information as provided by Subchapter B. This section does not apply to a record relating to a child that is:

(1) required or authorized to be maintained under the laws regulating the operation of motor vehicles in this state;

(2) maintained by a municipal or justice court; or

(3) subject to disclosure under Chapter 62, Code of Criminal Procedure.

(b) Except as provided by Subsection (d), law enforcement records concerning a child and information concerning a child that are stored by electronic means or otherwise and from which a record could be generated may not be disclosed to the public and shall be:

(1) if maintained on paper or microfilm, kept separate from adult records;

(2) if maintained electronically in the same computer system as adult records, accessible only under controls that are separate and distinct from the controls to access electronic data concerning adults; and

(3) maintained on a local basis only and not sent to a central state or federal depository, except as provided by Subsection (c) or Subchapter B, D, or E.

(c) The law enforcement records of a person with a determinate sentence who is transferred to the Texas Department of Criminal Justice may be transferred to a central state or federal depository for adult records after the date of transfer and may be shared in accordance with the laws governing the adult records in the depository.

(d) Law enforcement records concerning a child may be inspected or copied by:

(1) a juvenile justice agency, as defined by Section 58.101;

(2) a criminal justice agency, as defined by Section 411.082, Government Code;

(3) the child; or

(4) the child's parent or guardian.

(e) Before a child or a child's parent or guardian may inspect or copy a record concerning the child under Subsection (d), the custodian of the record shall redact:

(1) any personally identifiable information about a juvenile suspect, offender, victim, or witness who is not the child; and

(2) any information that is excepted from required disclosure under Chapter 552, Government Code, or any other law.

(f) If a child has been reported missing by a parent, guardian, or conservator of that child, information about the child may be forwarded to and disseminated by the Texas Crime Information Center and the National Crime Information Center.

History of Fam. Code §58.008: Enacted by S.B. 1304, §13, 85th Leg., eff. Sept. 1, 2017.

FAM §58.009 [~~58.0072~~]. DISSEMINATION OF JUVENILE JUSTICE INFORMATION BY THE TEXAS JUVENILE JUSTICE DEPARTMENT

(a) Except as provided by this section, juvenile justice information collected and maintained by the Texas Juvenile Justice Department for statistical and re-

search purposes is confidential information for the use of the department and may not be disseminated by the department.

(b) Juvenile justice information consists of information of the type described by Section 58.104, including statistical data in any form or medium collected, maintained, or submitted to the Texas Juvenile Justice Department under Section 221.007, Human Resources Code.

(c) The Texas Juvenile Justice Department may grant the following entities access to juvenile justice information for research and statistical purposes or for any other purpose approved by the department:

(1) criminal justice agencies as defined by Section 411.082, Government Code;

(2) the Texas Education Agency, as authorized under Section 37.084, Education Code;

(3) any agency under the authority of the Health and Human Services Commission; [~~or~~]

(4) the Department of Family and Protective Services; or

(5) a public or private university.

(d) The Texas Juvenile Justice Department may grant the following entities access to juvenile justice information only for a purpose beneficial to and approved by the department to:

(1) a person working on a research or statistical project that:

(A) is funded in whole or in part by state or federal funds; and

(B) meets the requirements of and is approved by the department; or

(2) a person working on a research or statistical project that:

(A) meets the requirements of and is approved by the department; and

(B) [~~governmental entity that~~] has a specific agreement with the department that [~~, if the agreement~~]:

(i) [~~(A)~~] specifically authorizes access to information;

(ii) [~~(B)~~] limits the use of information to the purposes for which the information is given;

(iii) [~~(C)~~] ensures the security and confidentiality of the information; and

(iv) [~~(D)~~] provides for sanctions if a requirement imposed under Subparagraph (i), (ii), or (iii) [~~Paragraph (A), (B), or (C)~~] is violated.

(e) The Texas Juvenile Justice Department shall grant access to juvenile justice information for legislative purposes under Section 552.008, Government Code.

(f) The Texas Juvenile Justice Department may not release juvenile justice information in identifiable form, except for information released under Subsection (c)(1), (2), or (3) or under the terms of an agreement entered into under Subsection (d)(2). For purposes of this subsection, identifiable information means information that contains a juvenile offender's name or other personal identifiers or that can, by virtue of sample size or other factors, be reasonably interpreted as referring to a particular juvenile offender.

(g) Except as provided by Subsection (e), the [~~The~~] Texas Juvenile Justice Department is permitted but not required to release or disclose juvenile justice information to any person [~~not~~] identified under this section.

History of Fam. Code §58.009: Acts 2005, 79th Leg., ch. 949, §17, eff. Sept. 1, 2005. Amended by Acts 2007, 80th Leg., ch. 908, §18, eff. Sept. 1, 2007; Acts 2011, 82nd Leg., ch. 85, §3.009, eff. Sept. 1, 2011; Acts 2015, 84th Leg., ch. 734, §62, eff. Sept. 1, 2015. Renumbered from §58.0072 and amended by S.B. 1304, §14, 85th Leg., eff. Sept. 1, 2017. Amended by H.B. 5, §2, 85th Leg., eff. Sept. 1, 2017.

Sections 58.010-58.100 reserved for expansion

SUBCHAPTER B. JUVENILE JUSTICE INFORMATION SYSTEM

FAM §58.101. DEFINITIONS

In this subchapter:

(1) "Criminal justice agency" has the meaning assigned by Section 411.082, Government Code.

(2) "Department" means the Department of Public Safety of the State of Texas.

(3) "Disposition" means an action that results in the termination, transfer of jurisdiction, or indeterminate suspension of the prosecution of a juvenile offender.

(4) "Incident number" means a unique number assigned to a child during a specific custodial or detention period or for a specific referral to the office or official designated by the juvenile board, if the juvenile offender was not taken into custody before the referral.

(5) "Juvenile justice agency" means an agency that has custody or control over juvenile offenders.

(6) "Juvenile offender" means a child who has been assigned an incident number.

(7) "State identification number" means a unique number assigned by the department to a child in the juvenile justice information system.

(8) "Uniform incident fingerprint card" means a multiple-part form containing a unique incident number with space for information relating to the conduct for which a child has been taken into custody, detained, or referred, the child's fingerprints, and other relevant information.

History of Fam. Code §58.101: Acts 1995, 74th Leg., ch. 262, §53, eff. Jan. 1, 1996. Amended by Acts 2001, 77th Leg., ch. 1297, §39, eff. Sept. 1, 2001.

FAM §58.102. JUVENILE JUSTICE INFORMATION SYSTEM

(a) The department is responsible for recording data and maintaining a database for a computerized juvenile justice information system that serves:

(1) as the record creation point for the juvenile justice information system maintained by the state; and

(2) as the control terminal for entry of records, in accordance with federal law, rule, and policy, into the federal records system maintained by the Federal Bureau of Investigation.

(b) The department shall develop and maintain the system with the cooperation and advice of the:

(1) Texas Juvenile Justice Department; and

(2) juvenile courts and clerks of juvenile courts.

(c) The department may not collect, [~~or~~] retain, or share information relating to a juvenile except as provided by [~~if~~] this chapter [~~prohibits or restricts the collection or retention of the information~~].

(d) The database must contain the information required by this subchapter.

(e) The department shall designate the offense codes and has the sole responsibility for designating the state identification number for each juvenile whose name appears in the juvenile justice system.

History of Fam. Code §58.102: Acts 1995, 74th Leg., ch. 262, §53, eff. Jan. 1, 1996. Amended by Acts 2015, 84th Leg., ch. 734, §63, eff. Sept. 1, 2015; S.B. 1304, §15, 85th Leg., eff. Sept. 1, 2017.

FAM §58.103. PURPOSE OF SYSTEM

The purpose of the juvenile justice information system is to:

(1) provide agencies and personnel within the juvenile justice system accurate information relating to children who come into contact with the juvenile justice system of this state;

(2) provide, where allowed by law, adult criminal justice agencies accurate and easily accessible information relating to children who come into contact with the juvenile justice system;

(3) provide an efficient conversion, where appropriate, of juvenile records to adult criminal records;

(4) improve the quality of data used to conduct impact analyses of proposed legislative changes in the juvenile justice system; and

(5) improve the ability of interested parties to analyze the functioning of the juvenile justice system.

History of Fam. Code §58.103: Acts 1995, 74th Leg., ch. 262, §53, eff. Jan. 1, 1996.

FAM §58.104. TYPES OF INFORMATION COLLECTED

(a) Subject to Subsection (f), the juvenile justice information system shall consist of information relating to delinquent conduct committed or alleged to have been committed by a juvenile offender that, if the conduct had been committed by an adult, would constitute a criminal offense other than an offense punishable by a fine only, including information relating to:

(1) the juvenile offender;

(2) the intake or referral of the juvenile offender into the juvenile justice system;

(3) the detention of the juvenile offender;

(4) the prosecution of the juvenile offender;

(5) the disposition of the juvenile offender's case, including the name and description of any program to which the juvenile offender is referred; [~~and~~]

(6) the probation or commitment of the juvenile offender; and

(7) the termination of probation supervision or discharge from commitment of the juvenile offender.

(b) To the extent possible and subject to Subsection (a), the department shall include in the juvenile justice information system the following information for each juvenile offender taken into custody, detained, or referred under this title for delinquent conduct:

(1) the juvenile offender's name, including other names by which the juvenile offender is known;

(2) the juvenile offender's date and place of birth;

(3) the juvenile offender's physical description, including sex, weight, height, race, ethnicity, eye color, hair color, scars, marks, and tattoos;

(4) the juvenile offender's state identification number, and other identifying information, as determined by the department;

(5) the juvenile offender's fingerprints;

(6) the juvenile offender's last known residential address, including the census tract number designation for the address;

(7) the name and identifying number of the agency that took into custody or detained the juvenile offender;

(8) the date of detention or custody;

(9) the conduct for which the juvenile offender was taken into custody, detained, or referred, including level and degree of the alleged offense;

(10) the name and identifying number of the juvenile intake agency or juvenile probation office;

(11) each disposition by the juvenile intake agency or juvenile probation office;

(12) the date of disposition by the juvenile intake agency or juvenile probation office;

(13) the name and identifying number of the prosecutor's office;

(14) each disposition by the prosecutor;

(15) the date of disposition by the prosecutor;

(16) the name and identifying number of the court;

(17) each disposition by the court, including information concerning probation or custody of a juvenile offender by a juvenile justice agency [or probation];

(18) the date of disposition by the court;

(19) the date any probation supervision, including deferred prosecution supervision, was terminated;

(20) any commitment or release under supervision by the Texas Juvenile Justice Department;

(21) [(20)] the date of any commitment or release under supervision by the Texas Juvenile Justice Department; and

(22) [(21)] a description of each appellate proceeding.

(c) The department may designate codes relating to the information described by Subsection (b).

(d) The department shall designate a state identification number for each juvenile offender.

(e) This subchapter does not apply to a disposition that represents an administrative status notice of an agency described by Section 58.102(b).

(f) Records maintained by the department in the depository are subject to being sealed under Subchapter C-1 [Section 58.003].

History of Fam. Code §58.104: Acts 1995, 74th Leg., ch. 262, §53, eff. Jan. 1, 1996. Amended by Acts 1997, 75th Leg., ch. 1086, §21, eff. Sept. 1, 1997; Acts 2005, 79th Leg., ch. 949, §18, eff. Sept. 1, 2005; Acts 2015, 84th Leg., ch. 734, §64, eff. Sept. 1, 2015; S.B. 1304, §16, 85th Leg., eff. Sept. 1, 2017.

FAM §58.105. DUTIES OF JUVENILE BOARD

Each juvenile board shall provide for:

(1) the compilation and maintenance of records and information needed for reporting information to the department under this subchapter;

(2) the transmittal to the department, in the manner provided by the department, of all records and information required by the department under this subchapter; and

(3) access by the department to inspect records and information to determine the completeness and accuracy of information reported.

History of Fam. Code §58.105: Acts 1995, 74th Leg., ch. 262, §53, eff. Jan. 1, 1996.

A FAM §58.106. DISSEMINATION OF CONFIDENTIAL INFORMATION IN JUVENILE JUSTICE INFORMATION SYSTEM

(a) Except as otherwise provided by this section, information contained in the juvenile justice information system is confidential information for the use of the department and may not be disseminated by the department except:

(1) with the permission of the juvenile offender, to military personnel of this state or the United States;

(2) to a criminal justice agency as defined by Section 411.082, Government Code;

(3) to a noncriminal justice agency authorized by federal statute or federal executive order to receive juvenile justice record information;

(4) to a juvenile justice agency;

(5) to the Texas Juvenile Justice Department;

(6) to the office of independent ombudsman of the Texas Juvenile Justice Department;

(7) to a district, county, justice, or municipal court exercising jurisdiction over a juvenile; and

(8) to the Department of Family and Protective Services as provided by Section 411.114, Government Code.

(a-1) Repealed by S.B. 1304, §21(7), 85th Leg., eff. Sept. 1, 2017.

[~~(a-1)~~] [~~The department may disseminate information contained in the juvenile justice information system to a noncriminal justice agency or entity not listed in Subsection (a) to which the department may grant access to adult criminal history record information as provided by Section 411.083, Government Code, only if the information does not relate to conduct indicating a need for supervision or to delinquent conduct constituting a misdemeanor offense:~~]

[~~(1)~~] [~~for which a child is on deferred prosecution under Section 53.03;~~]

[~~(2)~~] [~~for which deferred prosecution was successfully completed under Section 53.03;~~]

[~~(3)~~] [~~for which a charge was dropped or not pursued for reasons other than a lack of probable cause;~~]

[~~(4)~~] [~~for which a charge is pending final adjudication under Section 54.03; or~~]

[~~(5)~~] [~~found by the juvenile court to be "not true."~~]

(a-2) Information disseminated under Subsection (a) [~~or (a-1)~~] remains confidential after dissemination and may be disclosed by the recipient only as provided by this title.

(b) Subsection (a) does [~~Subsections (a) and (a-1) do~~] not apply to a document maintained by a juvenile justice or law enforcement agency that is the source of information collected by the department.

(c) The department may, if necessary to protect the welfare of the community, disseminate to the public the following information relating to a juvenile who has escaped from the custody of the Texas Juvenile Justice Department or from another secure detention or correctional facility:

(1) the juvenile's name, including other names by which the juvenile is known;

(2) the juvenile's physical description, including sex, weight, height, race, ethnicity, eye color, hair color, scars, marks, and tattoos;

(3) a photograph of the juvenile; and

(4) a description of the conduct for which the juvenile was committed to the Texas Juvenile Justice Department or detained in the secure detention or correctional facility, including the level and degree of the alleged offense.

(d) The department may, if necessary to protect the welfare of the community, disseminate to the public the information listed under Subsection (c) relating to a juvenile offender when notified by a law enforcement agency of this state that the law enforcement agency has been issued a directive to apprehend the offender or an arrest warrant for the offender or that the law enforcement agency is otherwise authorized to arrest the offender and that the offender is suspected of having:

(1) committed a felony offense under the following provisions of the Penal Code:

(A) Title 5;

(B) Section 29.02; or

(C) Section 29.03; and

(2) fled from arrest or apprehension for commission of the offense.

History of Fam. Code §58.106: Acts 1995, 74th Leg., ch. 262, §53, eff. Jan. 1, 1996. Amended by Acts 1997, 75th Leg., ch. 380, §1, eff. Sept. 1, 1997; Acts 1999, 76th Leg., ch. 407, §1 (eff. Sept. 1, 1999), ch. 1477, §19 (eff. Sept. 1, 1999); Acts 2007, 80th Leg., ch. 263, §11, eff. June 8, 2007; Acts 2011, 82nd Leg., ch. 186, §1 (eff. Sept. 1, 2011), ch. 653, §3 (eff. June 17, 2011), ch. 1098, §11 (eff. Sept. 1, 2011); Acts 2013, 83rd Leg., ch. 161, §7.004, eff. Sept. 1, 2013; Acts 2015, 84th Leg., ch. 598, §§1, 2 (eff. Sept. 1, 2015), ch. 734, §65 (eff. Sept. 1, 2015), ch. 935, §24 (eff. Sept. 1, 2015); S.B. 1304, §§17, 21(7), 85th Leg., eff. Sept. 1, 2017.

FAM §58.107. COMPATIBILITY OF DATA

Data supplied to the juvenile justice information system must be compatible with the system and must contain both incident numbers and state identification numbers.

History of Fam. Code §58.107: Acts 1995, 74th Leg., ch. 262, §53, eff. Jan. 1, 1996.

FAM §58.108. DUTIES OF AGENCIES & COURTS

(a) A juvenile justice agency and a clerk of a juvenile court shall:

(1) compile and maintain records needed for reporting data required by the department;

(2) transmit to the department in the manner provided by the department data required by the department;

(3) give the department or its accredited agents access to the agency or court for the purpose of inspection to determine the completeness and accuracy of data reported; and

(4) cooperate with the department to enable the department to perform its duties under this chapter.

(b) A juvenile justice agency and clerk of a court shall retain documents described by this section.

History of Fam. Code §58.108: Acts 1995, 74th Leg., ch. 262, §53, eff. Jan. 1, 1996.

FAM §58.109. UNIFORM INCIDENT FINGERPRINT CARD

(a) The department may provide for the use of a uniform incident fingerprint card in the maintenance of the juvenile justice information system.

(b) The department shall design, print, and distribute to each law enforcement agency and juvenile intake agency uniform incident fingerprint cards.

(c) The incident cards must:

(1) be serially numbered with an incident number in a manner that allows each incident of referral of a juvenile offender who is the subject of the incident fingerprint card to be readily ascertained; and

(2) be multiple-part forms that can be transmitted with the juvenile offender through the juvenile justice process and that allow each agency to report required data to the department.

(d) Subject to available telecommunications capacity, the department shall develop the capability to receive by electronic means from a law enforcement agency the information on the uniform incident fingerprint card. The information must be in a form that is compatible to the form required of data supplied to the juvenile justice information system.

History of Fam. Code §58.109: Acts 1995, 74th Leg., ch. 262, §53, eff. Jan. 1, 1996.

FAM §58.110. REPORTING

(a) The department by rule shall develop reporting procedures that ensure that the juvenile offender processing data is reported from the time a juvenile offender is initially taken into custody, detained, or referred until the time a juvenile offender is released from the jurisdiction of the juvenile justice system.

(b) The law enforcement agency or the juvenile intake agency that initiates the entry of the juvenile offender into the juvenile justice information system for a specific incident shall prepare a uniform incident fingerprint card and initiate the reporting process for each incident reportable under this subchapter.

(c) The clerk of the court exercising jurisdiction over a juvenile offender's case shall report the disposition of the case to the department.

(d) In each county, the reporting agencies may make alternative arrangements for reporting the required information, including combined reporting or electronic reporting, if the alternative reporting is approved by the juvenile board and the department.

(e) Except as otherwise required by applicable state laws or regulations, information required by this chapter to be reported to the department shall be reported promptly. The information shall be reported not later than the 30th day after the date the information is received by the agency responsible for reporting the information, except that a juvenile offender's custody or detention without previous custody shall be reported to the department not later than the seventh day after the date of the custody or detention.

(f) Subject to available telecommunications capacity, the department shall develop the capability to receive by electronic means the information required under this section to be reported to the department. The information must be in a form that is compatible to the form required of data to be reported under this section.

History of Fam. Code §58.110: Acts 1995, 74th Leg., ch. 262, §53, eff. Jan. 1, 1996. Amended by Acts 2007, 80th Leg., ch. 908, §19, eff. Sept. 1, 2007; Acts 2013, 83rd Leg., ch. 1276, §2, eff. Sept. 1, 2013.

FAM §58.111. LOCAL DATA ADVISORY BOARDS

The commissioners court of each county may create a local data advisory board to perform the same duties relating to the juvenile justice information system as the duties performed by a local data advisory board in relation to the criminal history record system under Article 60.09, Code of Criminal Procedure.

History of Fam. Code §58.111: Acts 1995, 74th Leg., ch. 262, §53, eff. Jan. 1, 1996.

FAM §58.112. TRANSFERRED

Transferred to Hum. Res. Code §203.019 by S.B. 1304, §19, 85th Leg., eff. Sept. 1, 2017.

FAM §58.113. WARRANTS

The department shall maintain in a computerized database that is accessible by the same entities that may access the juvenile justice information system information relating to a warrant of arrest, as that term is defined by Article 15.01, Code of Criminal Procedure, or a directive to apprehend under Section 52.015 for any child, without regard to whether the child has been taken into custody.

History of Fam. Code §58.113: Acts 1995, 74th Leg., ch. 262, §53, eff. Jan. 1, 1996.

Sections 58.114-58.200 blank

SUBCHAPTER C. REPEALED [AUTOMATIC RESTRICTION OF ACCESS TO RECORDS]

FAM §58.201. REPEALED [DEFINITION]

[In this subchapter, "department" means the Department of Public Safety of the State of Texas.]

Repealed by S.B. 1304, §21(8), 85th Leg., eff. Sept. 1, 2017.

FAM §58.202. REPEALED [EXEMPTED RECORDS]

[The following records are exempt from this subchapter:]

[(1)] [sex offender registration records maintained by the department or a local law enforcement agency under Chapter 62, Code of Criminal Procedure; and]

[(2)] [records relating to a criminal combination or criminal street gang maintained by the department or a local law enforcement agency under Chapter 61, Code of Criminal Procedure.]

Repealed by S.B. 1304, §21(8), 85th Leg., eff. Sept. 1, 2017.

FAM §58.203. REPEALED [CERTIFICATION]

[(a)] [The department shall certify to the juvenile probation department to which a referral was made that resulted in information being submitted to the juvenile justice information system that the records relating to a person's juvenile case are subject to automatic restriction of access if:]

[(1)] [the person is at least 17 years of age;]

[(2)] [the juvenile case did not include conduct resulting in determinate sentence proceedings in the juvenile court under Section 53.045; and]

[(3)] [the juvenile case was not certified for trial in criminal court under Section 54.02.]

[(b)] [If the department's records relate to a juvenile court with multicounty jurisdiction, the department shall issue the certification described by Subsection (a) to each juvenile probation department that serves the court. On receipt of the certification, each juvenile probation department shall determine whether it received the referral and, if it received the referral, take the restrictive action notification required by law.]

[(c)] [The department may issue the certification described by Subsection (a) by electronic means, including by electronic mail.]

Repealed by S.B. 1304, §21(8), 85th Leg., eff. Sept. 1, 2017.

FAM §58.204. REPEALED [RESTRICTED ACCESS ON CERTIFICATION]

[(a)] [On certification of records in a case under Section 58.203, the department, except as provided by Subsection (b):]

[(1)] [may not disclose the existence of the records or any information from the records in response to an inquiry from:]

[(A)] [a law enforcement agency;]

[(B)] [a criminal or juvenile justice agency;]

[(C)] [a governmental or other agency given access to information under Chapter 411, Government Code; or]

[(D)] [any other person, agency, organization, or entity; and]

[(2)] [shall respond to a request for information about the records by stating that the records do not exist.]

[(b)] [On certification of records in a case under Section 58.203, the department may permit access to the information in the juvenile justice information system relating to the case of an individual only:]

[(1)] [by a criminal justice agency for a criminal justice purpose, as those terms are defined by Section 411.082, Government Code;]

[(2)] [for research purposes, by the Texas Juvenile Justice Department;]

[(3)] [by the person who is the subject of the records on an order from the juvenile court granting the petition filed by or on behalf of the person who is the subject of the records;]

[(4)] [with the permission of the juvenile court at the request of the person who is the subject of the records;]

[(5)] [with the permission of the juvenile court, by a party to a civil suit if the person who is the subject of the records has put facts relating to the person's records at issue in the suit; or]

[(6)] [with the written permission of the individual, by military personnel, including a recruiter, of this state or the United States if the individual is an applicant for enlistment in the armed forces.]

Repealed by S.B. 1304, §21(8), 85th Leg., eff. Sept. 1, 2017.

FAM §58.205. REPEALED [REQUEST TO THE FEDERAL BUREAU OF INVESTIGATION ON CERTIFICATION]

[On certification of records in a case under Section 58.203, the department shall request the Federal Bureau of Investigation to:]

[(1)] [place the information in its files on restricted status, with access only by a criminal justice agency for a criminal justice purpose, as those terms are defined by Section 411.082, Government Code; or]

[(2)] [if the action described in Subdivision (1) is not feasible, delete all information in its database concerning the case.]

Repealed by S.B. 1304, §21(8), 85th Leg., eff. Sept. 1, 2017.

FAM §58.206. REPEALED [EFFECT OF CERTIFICATION IN RELATION TO THE PROTECTED PERSON]

[(a)] [On certification of records in a case under Section 58.203:]

[(1)] [the person who is the subject of the records is not required to state in any proceeding, except as otherwise authorized by law in a criminal proceeding in which the person is testifying as a defendant, or in any application for employment, licensing, or other public or private benefit that the person has been a respondent in a case under this title and may not be punished, by perjury prosecution or otherwise, for denying:]

[(A)] [the existence of the records; or]

[(B)] [the person's participation in a juvenile proceeding related to the records; and]

[(2)] [information from the records may not be admitted against the person who is the subject of the records in a civil or criminal proceeding except a proceeding in which a juvenile adjudication was admitted under:]

[(A)] [Section 12.42, Penal Code;]

[(B)] [Article 37.07, Code of Criminal Procedure; or]

[(C)] [as otherwise authorized by criminal procedural law.]

[(b)] [A person who is the subject of records certified under this subchapter may not waive the restricted status of the records or the consequences of the restricted status.]

Repealed by S.B. 1304, §21(8), 85th Leg., eff. Sept. 1, 2017.

FAM §58.207. REPEALED [JUVENILE COURT ORDERS ON CERTIFICATION]

[(a)] [On certification of records in a case under Section 58.203, the juvenile court shall order:]

[(1)] [that the following records relating to the case may be accessed only as provided by Section 58.204(b):]

[(A)] [if the respondent was committed to the Texas Juvenile Justice Department, records maintained by the department;]

[(B)] [records maintained by the juvenile probation department;]

[(C)] [records maintained by the clerk of the court;]

[(D)] [records maintained by the prosecutor's office; and]

[(E)] [records maintained by a law enforcement agency; and]

[(2)] [the juvenile probation department to make a reasonable effort to notify the person who is the subject of records for which access has been restricted of the action restricting access and the legal significance of the action for the person, but only if the person has requested the notification in writing and has provided the juvenile probation department with a current address.]

[(b)] [Except as provided by Subsection (c), on receipt of an order under Subsection (a)(1), the agency maintaining the records:]

[(1)] [may allow access only as provided by Section 58.204(b); and]

[(2)] [shall respond to a request for information about the records by stating that the records do not exist.]

[(c)] [Notwithstanding Subsection (b) of this section and Section 58.206(b), with the written permission of the subject of the records, an agency under Subsection (a)(1) may allow military personnel, including a recruiter, of this state or the United States to access juvenile records in the same manner authorized by law for records to which access has not been restricted under this section.]

[(e)] [Subsection (b) does not apply if:]

[(1)] [the subject of an order issued under Subsection (a)(1) is under the jurisdiction of the juvenile court or the Texas Juvenile Justice Department; or]

[(2)] [the agency has received notice that the records are not subject to restricted access under Section 58.211.]

[(d)] [Notwithstanding Subsection (b) and Section 58.206(b), with the permission of the subject of the records, an agency listed in Subsection (a)(1) may permit the state military forces or the United States military forces to have access to juvenile records held by that agency. On receipt of a request from the state military forces or the United States military forces, an agency may provide access to juvenile records held by that agency in the same manner authorized by law for records that have not been restricted under Subsection (a).]

Repealed by S.B. 1304, §21(8), 85th Leg., eff. Sept. 1, 2017.

FAM §58.208. REPEALED [INFORMATION TO CHILD ON DISCHARGE]

[On the final discharge of a child from the juvenile system or on the last official action in the case, if there is no adjudication, the appropriate juvenile justice official shall provide to the child:]

[(1)] [a written explanation of how automatic restricted access under this subchapter works;]

[(2)] [a copy of this subchapter; and]

[(3)] [a statement that if the child wishes to receive notification of an action restricting access to the child's records under Section 58.207(a), the child must before the child's 17th birthday provide the juvenile probation department with a current address where the child can receive notification.]

Repealed by S.B. 1304, §21(8), 85th Leg., eff. Sept. 1, 2017.

FAM §58.209. REPEALED [INFORMATION TO CHILD BY PROBATION OFFICER OR TEXAS JUVENILE JUSTICE DEPARTMENT]

[(a)] [When a child is placed on probation for an offense that may be eligible for automatic restricted access at age 17 or when a child is received by the Texas Juvenile Justice Department on an indeterminate commitment, a probation officer or an official at the Texas Juvenile Justice Department reception center, as soon as practicable, shall explain the substance of the following information to the child:]

[(1)] [if the child was adjudicated as having committed delinquent conduct for a felony or jailable misdemeanor, that the child probably has a juvenile record with the department and the Federal Bureau of Investigation;]

[(2)] [that the child's juvenile record is a permanent record that is not destroyed or erased unless the record is eligible for sealing and the child or the child's family hires a lawyer and files a petition in court to have the record sealed;]

[(3)] [that the child's juvenile record, other than treatment records made confidential by law, can be accessed by police, sheriff's officers, prosecutors, probation officers, correctional officers, and other criminal and juvenile justice officials in this state and elsewhere;]

[(4)] [that the child's juvenile record, other than treatment records made confidential by law, can be accessed by employers, educational institutions, licensing agencies, and other organizations when the child applies for employment or educational programs;]

[(5)] [if the child's juvenile record is placed on restricted access when the child becomes 17 years of age, that access will be denied to employers, educational institutions, and others except for criminal justice agencies;]

[(6)] [that restricted access does not require any action by the child or the child's family, including the filing of a petition or hiring of a lawyer, but occurs automatically at age 17; and]

[(7)] [that if the child is under the jurisdiction of the juvenile court or the Texas Juvenile Justice Department on or after the child's 17th birthday, the law regarding restricted access will not apply until the person is discharged from the jurisdiction of the court or department, as appropriate.]

[(b)] [The probation officer or Texas Juvenile Justice Department official shall:]

[(1)] [give the child a written copy of the explanation provided; and]

[(2)] [communicate the same information to at least one of the child's parents or, if none can be found, to the child's guardian or custodian.]

[(c)] [The Texas Juvenile Justice Department shall adopt rules to implement this section and to facilitate the effective explanation of the information required to be communicated by this section.]

Repealed by S.B. 1304, §21(8), 85th Leg., eff. Sept. 1, 2017.

FAM §58.210. REPEALED [SEALING OR DESTRUCTION OF RECORDS NOT AFFECTED]

[(a)] [This subchapter does not prevent or restrict the sealing or destruction of juvenile records as authorized by law.]

~~[(b)] [Restricted access provided under this subchapter is in addition to sealing or destruction of juvenile records.]~~

~~[(c)] [A person who is the subject of records certified under this subchapter is entitled to access to the records for the purpose of preparing and presenting a motion to seal or destroy the records.]~~

Repealed by S.B. 1304, §21(8), 85th Leg., eff. Sept. 1, 2017.

FAM §58.211. REPEALED ~~[RESCINDING RESTRICTED ACCESS]~~

~~[(a)] [If the department has notified a juvenile probation department that a record has been placed on restricted access and the department later receives information in the department's criminal history system that the subject of the records has been convicted of or placed on deferred adjudication for a felony or a misdemeanor punishable by confinement in jail for an offense committed after the person reached the age of 17, the person's juvenile records are no longer subject to restricted access. The department shall notify the appropriate local juvenile probation departments in the manner described by Section 58.203 that the person's records are no longer subject to restricted access.]~~

~~[(b)] [On receipt of the notification described by Subsection (a), the juvenile probation department shall notify the agencies that maintain the person's juvenile records under Section 58.207(b) that the person's records are no longer subject to restricted access.]~~

Repealed by S.B. 1304, §21(8), 85th Leg., eff. Sept. 1, 2017.

Sections 58.212-58.250 blank

SUBCHAPTER C-1. SEALING & DESTRUCTION OF JUVENILE RECORDS

FAM §58.251. DEFINITIONS

In this subchapter:

(1) "Electronic record" means an entry in a computer file or information on microfilm, microfiche, or any other electronic storage media.

(2) "Juvenile matter" means a referral to a juvenile court or juvenile probation department and all related court proceedings and outcomes, if any.

(3) "Physical record" means a paper copy of a record.

(4) "Record" means any documentation related to a juvenile matter, including information contained in that documentation.

History of Fam. Code §58.251: Enacted by S.B. 1304, §18, 85th Leg., eff. Sept. 1, 2017.

FAM §58.252. EXEMPTED RECORDS

The following records are exempt from this subchapter:

(1) records relating to a criminal combination or criminal street gang maintained by the Department of Public Safety or a local law enforcement agency under Chapter 61, Code of Criminal Procedure;

(2) sex offender registration records maintained by the Department of Public Safety or a local law enforcement agency under Chapter 62, Code of Criminal Procedure; and

(3) records collected or maintained by the Texas Juvenile Justice Department for statistical and research purposes, including data submitted under Section 221.007, Human Resources Code, and personally identifiable information.

History of Fam. Code §58.252: Enacted by S.B. 1304, §18, 85th Leg., eff. Sept. 1, 2017.

FAM §58.253. SEALING RECORDS WITHOUT APPLICATION: DELINQUENT CONDUCT

(a) This section does not apply to the records of a child referred to a juvenile court or juvenile probation department solely for conduct indicating a need for supervision.

(b) A person who was referred to a juvenile probation department for delinquent conduct is entitled to have all records related to the person's juvenile matters, including records relating to any matters involving conduct indicating a need for supervision, sealed without applying to the juvenile court if the person:

(1) is at least 19 years of age;

(2) has not been adjudicated as having engaged in delinquent conduct or, if adjudicated for delinquent conduct, was not adjudicated for delinquent conduct violating a penal law of the grade of felony;

(3) does not have any pending delinquent conduct matters;

(4) has not been transferred by a juvenile court to a criminal court for prosecution under Section 54.02;

(5) has not as an adult been convicted of a felony or a misdemeanor punishable by confinement in jail; and

(6) does not have any pending charges as an adult for a felony or a misdemeanor punishable by confinement in jail.

History of Fam. Code §58.253: Enacted by S.B. 1304, §18, 85th Leg., eff. Sept. 1, 2017.

FAM §58.254. CERTIFICATION OF ELIGIBILITY FOR SEALING RECORDS WITHOUT APPLICATION FOR DELINQUENT CONDUCT

(a) The Department of Public Safety shall certify to a juvenile probation department that has submitted records to the juvenile justice information system that the records relating to a person referred to the juvenile probation department appear to be eligible for sealing under Section 58.253.

(b) The Department of Public Safety may issue the certification described by Subsection (a) by electronic means, including by electronic mail.

(c) Except as provided by Subsection (d), not later than the 60th day after the date the juvenile probation department receives a certification under Subsection (a), the juvenile probation department shall:

(1) give notice of the receipt of the certification to the juvenile court; and

(2) provide the court with a list of all referrals received by the department relating to that person and the outcome of each referral.

(d) If a juvenile probation department has reason to believe the records of the person for whom the department received a certification under Subsection (a) are not eligible to be sealed, the juvenile probation department shall notify the Department of Public Safety not later than the 15th day after the date the juvenile probation department received the certification. If the juvenile probation department later determines that the person's records are eligible to be sealed, the juvenile probation department shall notify the juvenile court and provide the court the information described by Subsection (c) not later than the 30th day after the date of the determination.

(e) If, after receiving a certification under Subsection (a), the juvenile probation department determines that the person's records are not eligible to be sealed, the juvenile probation department and the Department of Public Safety shall update the juvenile justice information system to reflect that determination and no further action related to the records is required.

(f) Not later than the 60th day after the date a juvenile court receives notice from a juvenile probation department under Subsection (c), the juvenile court shall issue an order sealing all records relating to the person named in the certification.

History of Fam. Code §58.254: Enacted by S.B. 1304, §18, 85th Leg., eff. Sept. 1, 2017.

FAM §58.255. SEALING RECORDS WITHOUT APPLICATION: CONDUCT INDICATING NEED FOR SUPERVISION

(a) A person who was referred to a juvenile probation department for conduct indicating a need for supervision is entitled to have all records related to all conduct indicating a need for supervision matters sealed without applying to the juvenile court if the person:

(1) is at least 18 years of age;

(2) has not been referred to the juvenile probation department for delinquent conduct;

(3) has not as an adult been convicted of a felony; and

(4) does not have any pending charges as an adult for a felony or a misdemeanor punishable by confinement in jail.

(b) The juvenile probation department shall:

(1) give the juvenile court notice that a person's records are eligible for sealing under Subsection (a); and

(2) provide the juvenile court with a list of all referrals relating to that person received by the department and the outcome of each referral.

(c) Not later than the 60th day after the date the juvenile court receives notice from the juvenile probation department under Subsection (b), the juvenile court shall issue an order sealing all records relating to the person named in the notice.

History of Fam. Code §58.255: Enacted by S.B. 1304, §18, 85th Leg., eff. Sept. 1, 2017.

FAM §58.256. APPLICATION FOR SEALING RECORDS

(a) Notwithstanding Sections 58.253 and 58.255, a person may file an application for the sealing of records related to the person in the juvenile court served by the juvenile probation department to which the person was referred. The court may not charge a fee for filing the application, regardless of the form of the application.

(b) An application filed under this section must include either the following information or the reason that one or more of the following is not included in the application:

(1) the person's:

(A) full name;

(B) sex;

(C) race or ethnicity;

(D) date of birth;

(E) driver's license or identification card number; and

(F) social security number;

(2) the conduct for which the person was referred to the juvenile probation department, including the date on which the conduct was alleged or found to have been committed;

(3) the cause number assigned to each petition relating to the person filed in juvenile court, if any, and the court in which the petition was filed; and

(4) a list of all entities the person believes have possession of records related to the person, including the applicable entities listed under Section 58.258(b).

(c) Except as provided by Subsection (d), the juvenile court may order the sealing of records related to all matters for which the person was referred to the juvenile probation department if the person:

(1) is at least 18 years of age, or is younger than 18 years of age and at least two years have elapsed after the date of final discharge in each matter for which the person was referred to the juvenile probation department;

(2) does not have any delinquent conduct matters pending with any juvenile probation department or juvenile court;

(3) was not transferred by a juvenile court to a criminal court for prosecution under Section 54.02;

(4) has not as an adult been convicted of a felony; and

(5) does not have any pending charges as an adult for a felony or a misdemeanor punishable by confinement in jail.

(d) A court may not order the sealing of the records of a person who:

(1) received a determinate sentence for engaging in:

(A) delinquent conduct that violated a penal law listed under Section 53.045; or

(B) habitual felony conduct as described by Section 51.031;

(2) is currently required to register as a sex offender under Chapter 62, Code of Criminal Procedure; or

(3) was committed to the Texas Juvenile Justice Department or to a post-adjudication secure correctional facility under Section 54.04011, unless the person has been discharged from the agency to which the person was committed.

(e) On receipt of an application under this section, the court may:

(1) order the sealing of the person's records immediately, without a hearing; or

(2) hold a hearing under Section 58.257 at the court's discretion to determine whether to order the sealing of the person's records.

History of Fam. Code §58.256: Enacted by S.B. 1304, §18, 85th Leg., eff. Sept. 1, 2017.

FAM §58.257. HEARING REGARDING SEALING OF RECORDS

(a) A hearing regarding the sealing of a person's records must be held not later than the 60th day after the date the court receives the person's application under Section 58.256.

(b) The court shall give reasonable notice of a hearing under this section to:

(1) the person who is the subject of the records;

(2) the person's attorney who made the application for sealing on behalf of the person, if any;

(3) the prosecuting attorney for the juvenile court;

(4) all entities named in the application that the person believes possess eligible records related to the person; and

(5) any individual or entity whose presence at the hearing is requested by the person or prosecutor.

History of Fam. Code §58.257: Enacted by S.B. 1304, §18, 85th Leg., eff. Sept. 1, 2017.

FAM §58.258. ORDER SEALING RECORDS

(a) An order sealing the records of a person under this subchapter must include either the following information or the reason one or more of the following is not included in the order:

(1) the person's:

(A) full name;

(B) sex;

(C) race or ethnicity;

(D) date of birth;

(E) driver's license or identification card number; and

(F) social security number;

(2) each instance of conduct indicating a need for supervision or delinquent conduct alleged against the person or for which the person was referred to the juvenile justice system;

(3) the date on which and the county in which each instance of conduct was alleged to have occurred;

(4) if any petitions relating to the person were filed in juvenile court, the cause number assigned to each petition and the court and county in which each petition was filed; and

(5) a list of the entities believed to be in possession of the records that have been ordered sealed, including the entities listed under Subsection (b).

(b) Not later than the 60th day after the date of the entry of the order, the court shall provide a copy of the order to:

(1) the Department of Public Safety;

(2) the Texas Juvenile Justice Department, if the person was committed to the department;

(3) the clerk of court;

(4) the juvenile probation department serving the court;

(5) the prosecutor's office;

(6) each law enforcement agency that had contact with the person in relation to the conduct that is the subject of the sealing order;

(7) each public or private agency that had custody of or that provided supervision or services to the person in relation to the conduct that is the subject of the sealing order; and

(8) each official, agency, or other entity that the court has reason to believe has any record containing information that is related to the conduct that is the subject of the sealing order.

(c) On entry of the order, all adjudications relating to the person are vacated and the proceedings are dismissed and treated for all purposes as though the proceedings had never occurred. The clerk of court shall:

(1) seal all court records relating to the proceedings, including any records created in the clerk's case management system; and

(2) send copies of the order to all entities listed in the order.

History of Fam. Code §58.258: Enacted by S.B. 1304, §18, 85th Leg., eff. Sept. 1, 2017.

FAM §58.259. ACTIONS TAKEN ON RECEIPT OF ORDER TO SEAL RECORDS

(a) An entity receiving an order to seal the records of a person issued under this subchapter shall, not later than the 61st day after the date of receiving the order, take the following actions, as applicable:

(1) the Department of Public Safety shall:

(A) limit access to the records relating to the person in the juvenile justice information system to only the Texas Juvenile Justice Department for the purpose of conducting research and statistical studies;

(B) destroy any other records relating to the person in the department's possession, including DNA records as provided by Section 411.151, Government Code; and

(C) send written verification of the limitation and destruction of the records to the issuing court;

(2) the Texas Juvenile Justice Department shall:

(A) seal all records relating to the person, other than those exempted from sealing under Section 58.252; and

(B) send written verification of the sealing of the records to the issuing court;

(3) a public or private agency or institution that had custody of or provided supervision or services to the person who is the subject of the records, the juvenile probation department, a law enforcement entity, or a prosecuting attorney shall:

(A) seal all records relating to the person; and

(B) send written verification of the sealing of the records to the issuing court; and

(4) any other entity that receives an order to seal a person's records shall:

(A) send any records relating to the person to the issuing court;

(B) delete all index references to the person's records; and

(C) send written verification of the deletion of the index references to the issuing court.

(b) Physical or electronic records are considered sealed if the records are not destroyed but are stored in a manner that allows access to the records only by the custodian of records for the entity possessing the records.

(c) If an entity that received an order to seal records relating to a person later receives an inquiry about a person or the matter contained in the records, the entity must respond that no records relating to the person or the matter exist.

(d) If an entity receiving an order to seal records under this subchapter is unable to comply with the order because the information in the order is incorrect or insufficient to allow the entity to identify the records that are subject to the order, the entity shall notify the

issuing court not later than the 30th day after the date of receipt of the order. The court shall take any actions necessary and possible to provide the needed information to the entity, including contacting the person who is the subject of the order or the person's attorney.

(e) If an entity receiving a sealing order under this subchapter has no records related to the person who is the subject of the order, the entity shall provide written verification of that fact to the issuing court not later than the 30th day after the date of receipt of the order.

History of Fam. Code §58.259: Enacted by S.B. 1304, §18, 85th Leg., eff. Sept. 1, 2017.

FAM §58.260. INSPECTION & RELEASE OF SEALED RECORDS

(a) A juvenile court may allow, by order, the inspection of records sealed under this subchapter or under Section 58.003, as that law existed before September 1, 2017, only by:

(1) a person named in the order, on the petition of the person who is the subject of the records;

(2) a prosecutor, on the petition of the prosecutor, for the purpose of reviewing the records for possible use:

(A) in a capital prosecution; or

(B) for the enhancement of punishment under Section 12.42, Penal Code; or

(3) a court, the Texas Department of Criminal Justice, or the Texas Juvenile Justice Department for the purposes of Article 62.007(e), Code of Criminal Procedure.

(b) After a petitioner inspects records under this section, the court may order the release of any or all of the records to the petitioner on the motion of the petitioner.

History of Fam. Code §58.260: Enacted by S.B. 1304, §18, 85th Leg., eff. Sept. 1, 2017.

FAM §58.261. EFFECT OF SEALING RECORDS

(a) A person whose records have been sealed under this subchapter or under Section 58.003, as that law existed before September 1, 2017, is not required to state in any proceeding or in any application for employment, licensing, admission, housing, or other public or private benefit that the person has been the subject of a juvenile matter.

(b) If a person's records have been sealed, the information in the records, the fact that the records once existed, or the person's denial of the existence of the records or of the person's involvement in a juvenile matter may not be used against the person in any manner, including in:

(1) a perjury prosecution or other criminal proceeding;

(2) a civil proceeding, including an administrative proceeding involving a governmental entity;

(3) an application process for licensing or certification; or

(4) an admission, employment, or housing decision.

(c) A person who is the subject of the sealed records may not waive the protected status of the records or the consequences of the protected status.

History of Fam. Code §58.261: Enacted by S.B. 1304, §18, 85th Leg., eff. Sept. 1, 2017.

FAM §58.262. INFORMATION GIVEN TO CHILD REGARDING SEALING OF RECORDS

(a) When a child is referred to the juvenile probation department, an employee of the juvenile probation department shall give the child and the child's parent, guardian, or custodian a written explanation describing the process of sealing records under this subchapter and a copy of this subchapter.

(b) On the final discharge of a child, or on the last official action in the matter if there is no adjudication, a probation officer or official at the Texas Juvenile Justice Department, as appropriate, shall give the child and the child's parent, guardian, or custodian a written explanation regarding the eligibility of the child's records for sealing under this subchapter and a copy of this subchapter.

(c) The written explanation provided to a child under Subsections (a) and (b) must include the requirements for a record to be eligible for sealing, including an explanation of the records that are exempt from sealing under Section 58.252, and the following information:

(1) that, regardless of whether the child's conduct was adjudicated, the child has a juvenile record with the Department of Public Safety and the Federal Bureau of Investigation;

(2) the child's juvenile record is a permanent record unless the record is sealed under this subchapter;

(3) except as provided by Section 58.260, the child's juvenile record, other than treatment records

made confidential by law, may be accessed by a police officer, sheriff, prosecutor, probation officer, correctional officer, or other criminal or juvenile justice official unless the record is sealed as provided by this subchapter;

(4) sealing of the child's records under Section 58.253 or Section 58.255, as applicable, does not require any action by the child or the child's family, including the filing of an application or hiring of a lawyer, but occurs automatically at age 18 or 19 as applicable based on the child's referral and adjudication history;

(5) the child's juvenile record may be eligible for an earlier sealing date under Section 58.256, but an earlier sealing requires the child or an attorney for the child to file an application with the court;

(6) the impact of sealing records on the child; and

(7) the circumstances under which a sealed record may be reopened.

(d) The Texas Juvenile Justice Department shall adopt rules to implement this section and to facilitate the effective explanation of the information required to be communicated by this section.

History of Fam. Code §58.262: Enacted by S.B. 1304, §18, 85th Leg., eff. Sept. 1, 2017.

FAM §58.263. DESTRUCTION OF RECORDS: NO PROBABLE CAUSE

The court shall order the destruction of the records relating to the conduct for which a child is taken into custody, including records contained in the juvenile justice information system, if:

(1) a determination is made under Section 53.01 that no probable cause exists to believe the child engaged in the conduct and the case is not referred to a prosecutor for review under Section 53.012; or

(2) a determination that no probable cause exists to believe the child engaged in the conduct is made by a prosecutor under Section 53.012.

History of Fam. Code §58.263: Enacted by S.B. 1304, §18, 85th Leg., eff. Sept. 1, 2017.

FAM §58.264. PERMISSIBLE DESTRUCTION OF RECORDS

(a) Subject to Subsections (b) and (c) of this section, Section 202.001, Local Government Code, and any other restrictions imposed by an entity's records retention guidelines, the following persons may authorize the destruction of records in a closed juvenile matter, regardless of the date the records were created:

(1) a juvenile board, in relation to the records in the possession of the juvenile probation department;

(2) the head of a law enforcement agency, in relation to the records in the possession of the agency; and

(3) a prosecuting attorney, in relation to the records in the possession of the prosecuting attorney's office.

(b) The records related to a person referred to a juvenile probation department may be destroyed if the person:

(1) is at least 18 years of age, and:

(A) the most serious conduct for which the person was referred was conduct indicating a need for supervision, whether or not the person was adjudicated; or

(B) the referral or information did not relate to conduct indicating a need for supervision or delinquent conduct and the juvenile probation department, prosecutor, or juvenile court did not take action on the referral or information for that reason;

(2) is at least 21 years of age, and:

(A) the most serious conduct for which the person was adjudicated was delinquent conduct that violated a penal law of the grade of misdemeanor; or

(B) the most serious conduct for which the person was referred was delinquent conduct and the person was not adjudicated as having engaged in the conduct; or

(3) is at least 31 years of age and the most serious conduct for which the person was adjudicated was delinquent conduct that violated a penal law of the grade of felony.

(c) If a record contains information relating to more than one person referred to a juvenile probation department, the record may only be destroyed if:

(1) the destruction of the record is authorized under this section; and

(2) information in the record that may be destroyed under this section can be separated from information that is not authorized to be destroyed.

(d) Electronic records are considered to be destroyed if the electronic records, including the index to the records, are deleted.

(e) Converting physical records to electronic records and subsequently destroying the physical records while maintaining the electronic records is not considered destruction of a record under this subchapter.

(f) This section does not authorize the destruction of the records of the juvenile court or clerk of court.

(g) This section does not authorize the destruction of records maintained for statistical and research purposes by the Texas Juvenile Justice Department in a juvenile information and case management system authorized under Section 58.403.

(h) This section does not affect the destruction of physical records and files authorized by the Texas State Library Records Retention Schedule.

History of Fam. Code §58.264: Enacted by S.B. 1304, §18, 85th Leg., eff. Sept. 1, 2017.

FAM §58.265. JUVENILE RECORDS NOT SUBJECT TO EXPUNCTION

Records to which this chapter applies are not subject to an order of expunction issued by any court.

History of Fam. Code §58.265: Enacted by S.B. 1304, §18, 85th Leg., eff. Sept. 1, 2017.

Sections 58.266-58.300 blank

SUBCHAPTER D. LOCAL JUVENILE JUSTICE INFORMATION SYSTEM

FAM §58.301. DEFINITIONS

In this subchapter:

(1) "County juvenile board" means a juvenile board created under Chapter 152, Human Resources Code.

(2) "Juvenile facility" means a facility that:

(A) serves juveniles under a juvenile court's jurisdiction; and

(B) is operated as a holdover facility, a pre-adjudication detention facility, a nonsecure facility, or a post-adjudication secure correctional facility.

(2-a) "Governmental juvenile [~~placement~~] facility" means a juvenile [~~residential placement~~] facility operated by a unit of government.

(3) "Governmental service provider" means a juvenile justice service provider operated by a unit of government.

(4) "Local juvenile justice information system" means a county or multicounty computerized database of information concerning children, with data entry and access by the partner agencies that are members of the system.

(5) "Partner agency" means a [~~governmental~~] service provider or juvenile [~~governmental placement~~] facility that is authorized by this subchapter to be a member of a local juvenile justice information system or that has applied to be a member of a local juvenile justice information system and has been approved by the county juvenile board or regional juvenile board committee as a member of the system.

(6) "Regional juvenile board committee" means a committee that is composed of two members from each county juvenile board in a region that comprises a multicounty local juvenile information system.

History of Fam. Code §58.301: Acts 2001, 77th Leg., ch. 1297, §41, eff. Sept. 1, 2001. Amended by Acts 2005, 79th Leg., ch. 949, §23, eff. Sept. 1, 2005; H.B. 3705, §1, 85th Leg., eff. Sept. 1, 2017.

FAM §58.302. PURPOSES OF SYSTEM

The purposes of a local juvenile justice information system are to:

(1) provide accurate information at the county or regional level relating to children who come into contact with the juvenile justice system;

(2) assist in the development and delivery of services to children in the juvenile justice system;

(3) assist in the development and delivery of services to children:

(A) who school officials have reasonable cause to believe have committed an offense for which a report is required under Section 37.015, Education Code; or

(B) who have been expelled, the expulsion of which school officials are required to report under Section 52.041;

(4) provide for an efficient transmission of juvenile records from justice and municipal courts to county juvenile probation departments and the juvenile court and from county juvenile probation departments and juvenile court to the state juvenile justice information system created by Subchapter B;

(5) provide efficient computerized case management resources to juvenile courts, prosecutors, court clerks, county juvenile probation departments, and partner agencies authorized by this subchapter;

(6) provide a directory of services available to children to the partner agencies to facilitate the delivery of services to children;

(7) provide an efficient means for municipal and justice courts to report filing of charges, adjudications, and dispositions of juveniles to the juvenile court as required by Section 51.08; and

(8) provide a method for agencies to fulfill their duties under Section 58.108, including the electronic

transmission of information required to be sent to the Department of Public Safety by Section 58.110(f).

History of Fam. Code §58.302: Acts 2001, 77th Leg., ch. 1297, §41, eff. Sept. 1, 2001. Amended by Acts 2007, 80th Leg., ch. 908, §20, eff. Sept. 1, 2007.

A FAM §58.303. LOCAL JUVENILE JUSTICE INFORMATION SYSTEM

(a) Juvenile justice agencies in a county or region of this state may jointly create and maintain a local juvenile justice information system to aid in processing the cases of children under this code, to facilitate the delivery of services to children in the juvenile justice system, and to aid in the early identification of at-risk and delinquent children.

(b) A local juvenile justice information system may contain the following components:

(1) case management resources for juvenile courts, court clerks, prosecuting attorneys, and county juvenile probation departments;

(2) reporting systems to fulfill statutory requirements for reporting in the juvenile justice system;

(3) service provider directories and indexes of agencies providing services to children;

(4) victim-witness notices required under Chapter 57;

(5) electronic filing of complaints or petitions, court orders, and other documents filed with the court, including documents containing electronic signatures;

(6) electronic offense and intake processing;

(7) case docket management and calendaring;

(8) communications by email or other electronic communications between partner agencies;

(9) reporting of charges filed, adjudications and dispositions of juveniles by municipal and justice courts and the juvenile court, and transfers of cases to the juvenile court as authorized or required by Section 51.08;

(10) reporting to schools under Article 15.27, Code of Criminal Procedure, by law enforcement agencies, prosecuting attorneys, and juvenile courts;

(11) records of adjudications and dispositions, including probation conditions ordered by the juvenile court; [~~and~~]

(12) warrant management and confirmation capabilities; and

(13) case management for juveniles in juvenile facilities.

(c) Deleted by Acts 2005, 79th Leg., ch. 949, §24, eff. Sept. 1, 2005.

(d) Repealed by H.B. 3705, §7(1), 85th Leg., eff. Sept. 1, 2017.

[~~(d)~~] [~~Membership in a local juvenile justice information system is determined by this subchapter. Membership in a regional juvenile justice information system is determined by the regional juvenile board committee from among partner agencies that have applied for membership.~~]

History of Fam. Code §58.303: Acts 2001, 77th Leg., ch. 1297, §41, eff. Sept. 1, 2001. Amended by Acts 2005, 79th Leg., ch. 949, §24, eff. Sept. 1, 2005; Acts 2007, 80th Leg., ch. 908, §21, eff. Sept. 1, 2007; H.B. 3705, §§2, 7(1), 85th Leg., eff. Sept. 1, 2017.

A FAM §58.304. TYPES OF INFORMATION CONTAINED IN A LOCAL JUVENILE INFORMATION SYSTEM

(a) A [~~Subject to Subsection (d), a~~] local juvenile justice information system must consist of:

(1) information relating to all referrals to the juvenile court of any type, including referrals for conduct indicating a need for supervision and delinquent conduct; and

(2) information relating to:

(A) the juvenile;

(B) the intake or referral of the juvenile into the juvenile justice system for any offense or conduct;

(C) the detention of the juvenile;

(D) the prosecution of the juvenile;

(E) the disposition of the juvenile's case, including the name and description of any program to which the juvenile is referred; and

(F) the probation, placement, or commitment of the juvenile.

(b) To the extent possible and subject to Subsection (a) [~~Subsections (a) and (d)~~], the local juvenile justice information system may include the following information for each juvenile taken into custody, detained, or referred under this title:

(1) the juvenile's name, including other names by which the juvenile is known;

(2) the juvenile's date and place of birth;

(3) the juvenile's physical description, including sex, weight, height, race, ethnicity, eye color, hair color, scars, marks, and tattoos;

(4) the juvenile's state identification number and other identifying information;

(5) the juvenile's fingerprints and photograph;

(6) the juvenile's last known residential address, including the census tract number designation for the address;

(7) the name, address, and phone number of the juvenile's parent, guardian, or custodian;

(8) the name and identifying number of the agency that took into custody or detained the juvenile;

(9) each date of custody or detention;

(10) a detailed description of the conduct for which the juvenile was taken into custody, detained, or referred, including the level and degree of the alleged offense;

(11) the name and identifying number of the juvenile intake agency or juvenile probation office;

(12) each disposition by the juvenile intake agency or juvenile probation office;

(13) the date of disposition by the juvenile intake agency or juvenile probation office;

(14) the name and identifying number of the prosecutor's office;

(15) each disposition by the prosecutor;

(16) the date of disposition by the prosecutor;

(17) the name and identifying number of the court;

(18) each disposition by the court, including information concerning custody of a juvenile by a juvenile justice agency or county juvenile probation department;

(19) the date of disposition by the court;

(20) any commitment or release under supervision by the Texas Juvenile Justice Department, including the date of the commitment or release;

(21) information concerning each appellate proceeding; [~~and~~]

(22) electronic copies of all documents filed with the court; and

(23) information obtained for the purpose of diagnosis, examination, evaluation, treatment, or referral for treatment of a child by a public or private agency or institution providing supervision of a child by arrangement of the juvenile court or having custody of the child under order of the juvenile court.

(c) If the Department of Public Safety assigns a state identification number for the juvenile, the identification number shall be entered in the local juvenile information system.

(d) Repealed by H.B. 3705, §7(2), 85th Leg., eff. Sept. 1, 2017.

[~~(d)~~] [~~Information obtained for the purpose of diagnosis, examination, evaluation, or treatment or for making a referral for treatment of a child by a public or private agency or institution providing supervision of a child by arrangement of the juvenile court or having custody of the child under order of the juvenile court may not be collected under Subsection (a) or (b).~~]

History of Fam. Code §58.304: Acts 2001, 77th Leg., ch. 1297, §41, eff. Sept. 1, 2001. Amended by Acts 2007, 80th Leg., ch. 908, §22, eff. Sept. 1, 2007; Acts 2015, 84th Leg., ch. 734, §67, eff. Sept. 1, 2015; H.B. 3705, §§3, 7(2), 85th Leg., eff. Sept. 1, 2017.

Ⓐ FAM §58.305. PARTNER AGENCIES

(a) A local juvenile justice information system shall to the extent possible include the following partner agencies within that county:

(1) the juvenile court and court clerk;

(2) justice of the peace and municipal courts;

(3) the county juvenile probation department;

(4) the prosecuting attorneys who prosecute juvenile cases in juvenile court, municipal court, or justice court;

(5) law enforcement agencies;

(6) each public school district in the county;

(7) [~~governmental~~] service providers approved by the county juvenile board; and

(8) juvenile [~~governmental placement~~] facilities approved by the county juvenile board.

(b) A local juvenile justice information system for a multicounty region shall to the extent possible include the partner agencies listed in Subsections (a)(1)-(6) for each county in the region and the following partner agencies from within the multicounty region that have applied for membership in the system and have been approved by the regional juvenile board committee:

(1) [~~governmental~~] service providers; and

(2) juvenile [~~governmental placement~~] facilities.

History of Fam. Code §58.305: Acts 2001, 77th Leg., ch. 1297, §41, eff. Sept. 1, 2001. Amended by Acts 2005, 79th Leg., ch. 949, §25, eff. Sept. 1, 2005; Acts 2007, 80th Leg., ch. 908, §23, eff. Sept. 1, 2007; H.B. 3705, §4, 85th Leg., eff. Sept. 1, 2017.

Ⓐ FAM §58.306. ACCESS TO INFORMATION; LEVELS

(a) This section describes the level of access to information to which each partner agency in a local juvenile justice information system is entitled.

FAM §58.306

(b) Information is at Access Level 1 if the information relates to a child:

(1) who:

(A) a school official has reasonable grounds to believe has committed an offense for which a report is required under Section 37.015, Education Code; or

(B) has been expelled, the expulsion of which is required to be reported under Section 52.041; and

(2) who has not been charged with a fineable only offense, a status offense, or delinquent conduct.

(c) Information is at Access Level 2 if the information relates to a child who:

(1) is alleged in a justice or municipal court to have committed a fineable only offense, municipal ordinance violation, or status offense; and

(2) has not been charged with delinquent conduct or conduct indicating a need for supervision.

(d) Information is at Access Level 3 if the information relates to a child who is alleged to have engaged in delinquent conduct or conduct indicating a need for supervision.

(e) Except as provided by Subsection (i), Level 1 Access is by public school districts in the county or region served by the local juvenile justice information system.

(f) Except as provided by Subsection (i), Level 2 Access is by:

(1) justice of the peace courts that process juvenile cases; and

(2) municipal courts that process juvenile cases.

(g) Except as provided by Subsection (i), Level 3 Access is by:

(1) the juvenile court and court clerk;

(2) the prosecuting attorney;

(3) the county juvenile probation department;

(4) law enforcement agencies;

(5) governmental service providers that are partner agencies; [~~and~~]

(6) governmental juvenile [~~placement~~] facilities that are partner agencies; and

(7) a private juvenile facility that is a partner agency, except the access is limited to information that relates to a child detained or placed in the custody of the facility.

(h) Access for Level 1 agencies is only to information at Level 1. Access for Level 2 agencies is only to information at Levels 1 and 2. Access for Level 3 agencies is to information at Levels 1, 2, and 3.

(i) Information described by Section 58.304(b)(23) may be accessed only by:

(1) the juvenile court and court clerk;

(2) the county juvenile probation department;

(3) a governmental juvenile facility that is a partner agency; and

(4) a private juvenile facility that is a partner agency, except the access is limited to information that relates to a child detained or placed in the custody of the facility.

History of Fam. Code §58.306: Acts 2001, 77th Leg., ch. 1297, §41, eff. Sept. 1, 2001. Amended by Acts 2007, 80th Leg., ch. 908, §24, eff. Sept. 1, 2007; H.B. 3705, §5, 85th Leg., eff. Sept. 1, 2017.

A FAM §58.307. CONFIDENTIALITY OF INFORMATION

(a) Information that is part of a local juvenile justice information system is not public information and may not be released to the public, except as authorized by law.

(b) Information that is part of a local juvenile justice information system is for the professional use of the partner agencies that are members of the system and may be used only by authorized employees of those agencies to discharge duties of those agencies.

(c) Information from a local juvenile justice information system may not be disclosed to persons, agencies, or organizations that are not members of the system except to the extent disclosure is authorized or mandated by this title.

(d) Information in a local juvenile justice information system is subject to destruction, sealing, or restricted access as provided by this title.

(e) Information in a local juvenile justice information system, including electronic signature systems, shall be protected from unauthorized access by a system of access security and any access to information in a local juvenile information system performed by browser software shall be at the level of at least 2048-bit [~~128-bit~~] encryption. A juvenile board or a regional juvenile board committee shall require all partner agencies to maintain security and restrict access in accordance with the requirements of this title.

History of Fam. Code §58.307: Acts 2001, 77th Leg., ch. 1297, §41, eff. Sept. 1, 2001. Amended by Acts 2007, 80th Leg., ch. 908, §25, eff. Sept. 1, 2007; H.B. 3705, §6, 85th Leg., eff. Sept. 1, 2017.

Sections 58.308-58.350 blank

SUBCHAPTER D-1. REPORTS ON COUNTY INTERNET WEBSITES

FAM §58.351. APPLICABILITY

This subchapter applies only to a county with a population of 600,000 or more.

History of Fam. Code §58.351: Acts 2007, 80th Leg., ch. 908, §26(b), eff. Jan. 1, 2008.

FAM §58.352. INFORMATION POSTED ON COUNTY WEBSITE

(a) A juvenile court judge in a county to which this subchapter applies shall post a report on the Internet website of the county in which the court is located. The report must include:

(1) the total number of children committed by the judge to:

(A) a correctional facility operated by the Texas Juvenile Justice Department; or

(B) a post-adjudication secure correctional facility as that term is defined by Section 54.04011; and

(2) for each child committed to a facility described by Subdivision (1):

(A) a general description of the offense committed by the child or the conduct of the child that led to the child's commitment to the facility;

(B) the year the child was committed to the facility; and

(C) the age range, race, and gender of the child.

(b) Not later than the 10th day following the first day of each quarter, a juvenile court judge shall update the information posted on a county Internet website under Subsection (a).

History of Fam. Code §58.352: Acts 2007, 80th Leg., ch. 908, §26(b), eff. Jan. 1, 2008. Amended by Acts 2015, 84th Leg., ch. 734, §68 (eff. Sept. 1, 2015), ch. 854, §4 (eff. Sept. 1, 2015).

FAM §58.353. CONFIDENTIALITY

A record posted on a county Internet website under this subchapter may not include any information that personally identifies a child.

History of Fam. Code §58.353: Acts 2007, 80th Leg., ch. 908, §26(b), eff. Jan. 1, 2008.

Sections 58.354-58.400 blank

SUBCHAPTER E. STATEWIDE JUVENILE INFORMATION & CASE MANAGEMENT SYSTEM

FAM §58.401. DEFINITIONS

In this subchapter:

(1) "Department" means the Texas Juvenile Justice Department.

(2) "Criminal justice agency" has the meaning assigned by Section 411.082, Government Code.

(3) "Juvenile justice agency" means an agency that has custody or control over juvenile offenders.

(4) "Partner agencies" means those agencies described in Section 58.305 as well as private service providers to the juvenile justice system.

(5) "System" means an automated statewide juvenile information and case management system.

History of Fam. Code §58.401: Acts 2007, 80th Leg., ch. 908, §27, eff. Sept. 1, 2007. Amended by Acts 2015, 84th Leg., ch. 734, §69, eff. Sept. 1, 2015.

FAM §58.402. PURPOSES OF SYSTEM

The purposes of the system are to:

(1) provide accurate information at the statewide level relating to children who come into contact with the juvenile justice system;

(2) facilitate communication and information sharing between authorized entities in criminal and juvenile justice agencies and partner agencies regarding effective and efficient identification of and service delivery to juvenile offenders; and

(3) provide comprehensive juvenile justice information and case management abilities that will meet the common data collection, reporting, and management needs of juvenile probation departments in this state and provide the flexibility to accommodate individualized requirements.

History of Fam. Code §58.402: Acts 2007, 80th Leg., ch. 908, §27, eff. Sept. 1, 2007.

FAM §58.403. JUVENILE INFORMATION SYSTEM

(a) Through the adoption of an interlocal contract under Chapter 791, Government Code, with one or more counties, the department may participate in and assist counties in the creation, operation, and maintenance of a system that is intended for statewide use to:

(1) aid in processing the cases of children under this title;

(2) facilitate the delivery of services to children in the juvenile justice system;

(3) aid in the early identification of at-risk and delinquent children; and

(4) facilitate cross-jurisdictional sharing of information related to juvenile offenders between authorized criminal and juvenile justice agencies and partner agencies.

(b) The department may use funds appropriated for the implementation of this section to pay costs in-

curred under an interlocal contract described by Subsection (a), including license fees, maintenance and operations costs, administrative costs, and any other costs specified in the interlocal contract.

(c) The department may provide training services to counties on the use and operation of a system created, operated, or maintained by one or more counties under Subsection (a).

(d) Subchapter L, Chapter 2054, Government Code, does not apply to the statewide juvenile information and case management system created under this subchapter.

History of Fam. Code §58.403: Acts 2007, 80th Leg., ch. 908, §27, eff. Sept. 1, 2007. Amended by Acts 2009, 81st Leg., ch. 1337, §1, eff. Sept. 1, 2009; Acts 2011, 82nd Leg., ch. 85, §2.002, eff. Sept. 1, 2011; Acts 2015, 84th Leg., ch. 734, §70, eff. Sept. 1, 2015.

FAM §58.404. INFORMATION COLLECTED BY DEPARTMENT

The department may collect and maintain all information related to juvenile offenders and all offenses committed by a juvenile offender, including all information collected and maintained under Subchapters B and D.

History of Fam. Code §58.404: Acts 2007, 80th Leg., ch. 908, §27, eff. Sept. 1, 2007. Amended by Acts 2015, 84th Leg., ch. 734, §71, eff. Sept. 1, 2015.

FAM §58.405. AUTHORITY CUMULATIVE

The authority granted by this subchapter is cumulative of all other authority granted by this chapter to a county, the department, or a juvenile justice agency and nothing in this subchapter limits the authority of a county, the department, or a juvenile justice agency under this chapter to create an information system or to share information related to a juvenile.

History of Fam. Code §58.405: Acts 2007, 80th Leg., ch. 908, §27, eff. Sept. 1, 2007. Amended by Acts 2015, 84th Leg., ch. 734, §72, eff. Sept. 1, 2015.

CHAPTER 59. PROGRESSIVE SANCTIONS MODEL

FAM §59.001. PURPOSES

The purposes of the progressive sanctions model are to:

(1) ensure that juvenile offenders face uniform and consistent consequences and punishments that correspond to the seriousness of each offender's current offense, prior delinquent history, special treatment or training needs, and effectiveness of prior interventions;

(2) balance public protection and rehabilitation while holding juvenile offenders accountable;

(3) permit flexibility in the decisions made in relation to the juvenile offender to the extent allowed by law;

(4) consider the juvenile offender's circumstances;

(5) recognize that departure of a disposition from this model is not necessarily undesirable and in some cases is highly desirable; and

(6) improve juvenile justice planning and resource allocation by ensuring uniform and consistent reporting of disposition decisions at all levels.

History of Fam. Code §59.001: Acts 1995, 74th Leg., ch. 262, §53, eff. Jan. 1, 1996. Amended by Acts 2003, 78th Leg., ch. 479, §3, eff. Sept. 1, 2003.

FAM §59.002. SANCTION LEVEL ASSIGNMENT BY PROBATION DEPARTMENT

(a) The probation department may assign a sanction level of one to a child referred to the probation department under Section 53.012.

(b) The probation department may assign a sanction level of two to a child for whom deferred prosecution is authorized under Section 53.03.

History of Fam. Code §59.002: Acts 1995, 74th Leg., ch. 262, §53, eff. Jan. 1, 1996.

FAM §59.003. SANCTION LEVEL ASSIGNMENT MODEL

(a) Subject to Subsection (e), after a child's first commission of delinquent conduct or conduct indicating a need for supervision, the probation department or prosecuting attorney may, or the juvenile court may, in a disposition hearing under Section 54.04 or a modification hearing under Section 54.05, assign a child one of the following sanction levels according to the child's conduct:

(1) for conduct indicating a need for supervision, other than conduct described in Section 51.03(b)(3) or (4) or a Class A or B misdemeanor, the sanction level is one;

(2) for conduct indicating a need for supervision under Section 51.03(b)(3) or (4) or a Class A or B misdemeanor, other than a misdemeanor involving the use or possession of a firearm, or for delinquent conduct under Section 51.03(a)(2), the sanction level is two;

(3) for a misdemeanor involving the use or possession of a firearm or for a state jail felony or a felony of the third degree, the sanction level is three;

(4) for a felony of the second degree, the sanction level is four;

(5) for a felony of the first degree, other than a felony involving the use of a deadly weapon or causing serious bodily injury, the sanction level is five;

(6) for a felony of the first degree involving the use of a deadly weapon or causing serious bodily injury, for an aggravated controlled substance felony, or for a capital felony, the sanction level is six; or

(7) for a felony of the first degree involving the use of a deadly weapon or causing serious bodily injury, for an aggravated controlled substance felony, or for a capital felony, if the petition has been approved by a grand jury under Section 53.045, or if a petition to transfer the child to criminal court has been filed under Section 54.02, the sanction level is seven.

(b) Subject to Subsection (e), if the child subsequently is found to have engaged in delinquent conduct in an adjudication hearing under Section 54.03 or a hearing to modify a disposition under Section 54.05 on two separate occasions and each involves a violation of a penal law of a classification that is less than the classification of the child's previous conduct, the juvenile court may assign the child a sanction level that is one level higher than the previously assigned sanction level, unless the child's previously assigned sanction level is six.

(c) Subject to Subsection (e), if the child's subsequent commission of delinquent conduct or conduct indicating a need for supervision involves a violation of a penal law of a classification that is the same as or greater than the classification of the child's previous conduct, the juvenile court may assign the child a sanction level authorized by law that is one level higher than the previously assigned sanction level.

(d) Subject to Subsection (e), if the child's previously assigned sanction level is four or five and the child's subsequent commission of delinquent conduct is of the grade of felony, the juvenile court may assign the child a sanction level that is one level higher than the previously assigned sanction level.

(e) The probation department may, in accordance with Section 54.05, request the extension of a period of probation specified under sanction levels one through five if the circumstances of the child warrant the extension.

(f) Before the court assigns the child a sanction level that involves the revocation of the child's probation and the commitment of the child to the Texas Juvenile Justice Department, the court shall hold a hearing to modify the disposition as required by Section 54.05.

(g) Deleted by Acts 2003, 78th Leg., ch. 479, §5, eff. Sept. 1, 2003.

History of Fam. Code §59.003: Acts 1995, 74th Leg., ch. 262, §53, eff. Jan. 1, 1996. Amended by Acts 1997, 75th Leg., ch. 1015, §19 (eff. June 19, 1997), ch. 1086, §22 (eff. Sept. 1, 1997); Acts 1999, 76th Leg., ch. 1477, §20, eff. Sept. 1, 1999; Acts 2001, 77th Leg., ch. 1297, §42, eff. Sept. 1, 2001; Acts 2003, 78th Leg., ch. 479, §§4, 5, eff. Sept. 1, 2003; Acts 2007, 80th Leg., ch. 908, §28, eff. Sept. 1, 2007; Acts 2015, 84th Leg., ch. 734, §73 (eff. Sept. 1, 2015), ch. 935, §25 (eff. Sept. 1, 2015).

FAM §59.004. SANCTION LEVEL ONE

(a) For a child at sanction level one, the juvenile court or probation department may:

(1) require counseling for the child regarding the child's conduct;

(2) inform the child of the progressive sanctions that may be imposed on the child if the child continues to engage in delinquent conduct or conduct indicating a need for supervision;

(3) inform the child's parents or guardians of the parents' or guardians' responsibility to impose reasonable restrictions on the child to prevent the conduct from recurring;

(4) provide information or other assistance to the child or the child's parents or guardians in securing needed social services;

(5) require the child or the child's parents or guardians to participate in a program for services under Section 264.302, if a program under Section 264.302 is available to the child or the child's parents or guardians;

(6) refer the child to a community-based citizen intervention program approved by the juvenile court;

(7) release the child to the child's parents or guardians; and

(8) require the child to attend and successfully complete an educational program described by Section 37.218, Education Code, or another equivalent educational program.

(b) The probation department shall discharge the child from the custody of the probation department after the provisions of this section are met.

History of Fam. Code §59.004: Acts 1995, 74th Leg., ch. 262, §53, eff. Jan. 1, 1996. Amended by Acts 1997, 75th Leg., ch. 1086, §23, eff. Sept. 1, 1997; Acts 2011, 82nd Leg., ch. 1322, §20, eff. Sept. 1, 2011.

FAM §59.005. SANCTION LEVEL TWO

(a) For a child at sanction level two, the juvenile court, the prosecuting attorney, or the probation department may, as provided by Section 53.03:

(1) place the child on deferred prosecution for not less than three months or more than six months;

(2) require the child to make restitution to the victim of the child's conduct or perform community service restitution appropriate to the nature and degree of harm caused and according to the child's ability;

(3) require the child's parents or guardians to identify restrictions the parents or guardians will impose on the child's activities and requirements the parents or guardians will set for the child's behavior;

(4) provide the information required under Sections 59.004(a)(2) and (4);

(5) require the child or the child's parents or guardians to participate in a program for services under Section 264.302, if a program under Section 264.302 is available to the child or the child's parents or guardians;

(6) refer the child to a community-based citizen intervention program approved by the juvenile court; and

(7) if appropriate, impose additional conditions of probation.

(b) The juvenile court or the probation department shall discharge the child from the custody of the probation department on the date the provisions of this section are met or on the child's 18th birthday, whichever is earlier.

History of Fam. Code §59.005: Acts 1995, 74th Leg., ch. 262, §53, eff. Jan. 1, 1996. Amended by Acts 1997, 75th Leg., ch. 1086, §24, eff. Sept. 1, 1997; Acts 1999, 76th Leg., ch. 1477, §21, eff. Sept. 1, 1999.

FAM §59.006. SANCTION LEVEL THREE

(a) For a child at sanction level three, the juvenile court may:

(1) place the child on probation for not less than six months;

(2) require the child to make restitution to the victim of the child's conduct or perform community service restitution appropriate to the nature and degree of harm caused and according to the child's ability;

(3) impose specific restrictions on the child's activities and requirements for the child's behavior as conditions of probation;

(4) require a probation officer to closely monitor the child's activities and behavior;

(5) require the child or the child's parents or guardians to participate in programs or services designated by the court or probation officer; and

(6) if appropriate, impose additional conditions of probation.

(b) The juvenile court shall discharge the child from the custody of the probation department on the date the provisions of this section are met or on the child's 18th birthday, whichever is earlier.

History of Fam. Code §59.006: Acts 1995, 74th Leg., ch. 262, §53, eff. Jan. 1, 1996. Amended by Acts 1997, 75th Leg., ch. 1086, §25, eff. Sept. 1, 1997; Acts 2003, 78th Leg., ch. 479, §6, eff. Sept. 1, 2003.

FAM §59.007. SANCTION LEVEL FOUR

(a) For a child at sanction level four, the juvenile court may:

(1) require the child to participate as a condition of probation for not less than three months or more than 12 months in an intensive services probation program that emphasizes frequent contact and reporting with a probation officer, discipline, intensive supervision services, social responsibility, and productive work;

(2) after release from the program described by Subdivision (1), continue the child on probation supervision;

(3) require the child to make restitution to the victim of the child's conduct or perform community service restitution appropriate to the nature and degree of harm caused and according to the child's ability;

(4) impose highly structured restrictions on the child's activities and requirements for behavior of the child as conditions of probation;

(5) require a probation officer to closely monitor the child;

(6) require the child or the child's parents or guardians to participate in programs or services designed to address their particular needs and circumstances; and

(7) if appropriate, impose additional sanctions.

(b) The juvenile court shall discharge the child from the custody of the probation department on the date the provisions of this section are met or on the child's 18th birthday, whichever is earlier.

History of Fam. Code §59.007: Acts 1995, 74th Leg., ch. 262, §53, eff. Jan. 1, 1996. Amended by Acts 1997, 75th Leg., ch. 1086, §26, eff. Sept. 1, 1997; Acts 2001, 77th Leg., ch. 1297, §43, eff. Sept. 1, 2001; Acts 2003, 78th Leg., ch. 479, §7, eff. Sept. 1, 2003.

FAM §59.008. SANCTION LEVEL FIVE

(a) For a child at sanction level five, the juvenile court may:

(1) as a condition of probation, place the child for not less than six months or more than 12 months in a post-adjudication secure correctional facility;

(2) after release from the program described by Subdivision (1), continue the child on probation supervision;

(3) require the child to make restitution to the victim of the child's conduct or perform community service restitution appropriate to the nature and degree of harm caused and according to the child's ability;

(4) impose highly structured restrictions on the child's activities and requirements for behavior of the child as conditions of probation;

(5) require a probation officer to closely monitor the child;

(6) require the child or the child's parents or guardians to participate in programs or services designed to address their particular needs and circumstances; and

(7) if appropriate, impose additional sanctions.

(b) The juvenile court shall discharge the child from the custody of the probation department on the date the provisions of this section are met or on the child's 18th birthday, whichever is earlier.

History of Fam. Code §59.008: Acts 1995, 74th Leg., ch. 262, §53, eff. Jan. 1, 1996. Amended by Acts 1997, 75th Leg., ch. 1086, §27, eff. Sept. 1, 1997; Acts 2003, 78th Leg., ch. 479, §8, eff. Sept. 1, 2003.

FAM §59.009. SANCTION LEVEL SIX

(a) For a child at sanction level six, the juvenile court may commit the child to the custody of the Texas Juvenile Justice Department or a post-adjudication secure correctional facility under Section 54.04011(c)(1). The department, juvenile board, or local juvenile probation department, as applicable, may:

(1) require the child to participate in a highly structured residential program that emphasizes discipline, accountability, fitness, training, and productive work for not less than nine months or more than 24 months unless the department, board, or probation department extends the period and the reason for an extension is documented;

(2) require the child to make restitution to the victim of the child's conduct or perform community service restitution appropriate to the nature and degree of the harm caused and according to the child's ability, if there is a victim of the child's conduct;

(3) require the child and the child's parents or guardians to participate in programs and services for their particular needs and circumstances; and

(4) if appropriate, impose additional sanctions.

(b) On release of the child under supervision, the Texas Juvenile Justice Department parole programs or the juvenile board or local juvenile probation department operating parole programs under Section 152.0016(c)(2), Human Resources Code, may:

(1) impose highly structured restrictions on the child's activities and requirements for behavior of the child as conditions of release under supervision;

(2) require a parole officer to closely monitor the child for not less than six months; and

(3) if appropriate, impose any other conditions of supervision.

(c) The Texas Juvenile Justice Department, juvenile board, or local juvenile probation department may discharge the child from the custody of the department, board, or probation department, as applicable, on the date the provisions of this section are met or on the child's 19th birthday, whichever is earlier.

History of Fam. Code §59.009: Acts 1995, 74th Leg., ch. 262, §53, eff. Jan. 1, 1996. Amended by Acts 1997, 75th Leg., ch. 1086, §28, eff. Sept. 1, 1997; Acts 2013, 83rd Leg., ch. 1323, §7, eff. Dec. 1, 2013.

FAM §59.010. SANCTION LEVEL SEVEN

(a) For a child at sanction level seven, the juvenile court may certify and transfer the child under Section 54.02 or sentence the child to commitment to the Texas Juvenile Justice Department under Section 54.04(d)(3), 54.04(m), or 54.05(f) or to a post-adjudication secure correctional facility under Section 54.04011(c)(2). The department, juvenile board, or local juvenile probation department, as applicable, may:

(1) require the child to participate in a highly structured residential program that emphasizes discipline, accountability, fitness, training, and productive work for not less than 12 months or more than 10 years unless the department, board, or probation department extends the period and the reason for the extension is documented;

(2) require the child to make restitution to the victim of the child's conduct or perform community service restitution appropriate to the nature and degree of harm caused and according to the child's ability, if there is a victim of the child's conduct;

(3) require the child and the child's parents or guardians to participate in programs and services for their particular needs and circumstances; and

(4) impose any other appropriate sanction.

(b) On release of the child under supervision, the Texas Juvenile Justice Department parole programs or the juvenile board or local juvenile probation department parole programs under Section 152.0016(c)(2), Human Resources Code, may:

(1) impose highly structured restrictions on the child's activities and requirements for behavior of the child as conditions of release under supervision;

(2) require a parole officer to monitor the child closely for not less than 12 months; and

(3) impose any other appropriate condition of supervision.

History of Fam. Code §59.010: Acts 1995, 74th Leg., ch. 262, §53, eff. Jan. 1, 1996. Amended by Acts 1997, 75th Leg., ch. 1086, §29, eff. Sept. 1, 1997; Acts 2013, 83rd Leg., ch. 1323, §8, eff. Dec. 1, 2013.

FAM §59.011. DUTY OF JUVENILE BOARD

A juvenile board shall require the juvenile probation department to report progressive sanction data electronically to the Texas Juvenile Justice Department in the format and time frames specified by the Texas Juvenile Justice Department.

History of Fam. Code §59.011: Acts 1995, 74th Leg., ch. 262, §53, eff. Jan. 1, 1996. Amended by Acts 2001, 77th Leg., ch. 1297, §44, eff. Sept. 1, 2001; Acts 2015, 84th Leg., ch. 734, §74, eff. Sept. 1, 2015.

FAM §59.012. REPEALED

Repealed by Acts 2013, 83rd Leg., ch. 1312, §99(9), eff. Sept. 1, 2013.

FAM §59.013. LIABILITY

The Texas Juvenile Justice Department, a juvenile board, a court, a person appointed by a court, an attorney for the state, a peace officer, or a law enforcement agency is not liable for a failure or inability to provide a service listed under Sections 59.004-59.010.

History of Fam. Code §59.013: Acts 1995, 74th Leg., ch. 262, §53, eff. Jan. 1, 1996. Amended by Acts 2015, 84th Leg., ch. 734, §75, eff. Sept. 1, 2015.

FAM §59.014. APPEAL

A child may not bring an appeal or a postconviction writ of habeas corpus based on:

(1) the failure or inability of any person to provide a service listed under Sections 59.004-59.010;

(2) the failure of a court or of any person to make a sanction level assignment as provided in Section 59.002 or 59.003;

(3) a departure from the sanction level assignment model provided by this chapter; or

(4) the failure of a juvenile court or probation department to report a departure from the model.

History of Fam. Code §59.014: Acts 1995, 74th Leg., ch. 262, §53, eff. Jan. 1, 1996. Amended by Acts 1999, 76th Leg., ch. 1011, §1 (eff. Sept. 1, 1999), ch. 1477, §22 (eff. Sept. 1, 1999); Acts 2003, 78th Leg., ch. 479, §10, Sept. 1, 2003.

FAM §59.015. WAIVER OF SANCTIONS ON PARENTS OR GUARDIANS

On a finding by the juvenile court or probation department that a child's parents or guardians have made a reasonable good faith effort to prevent the child from engaging in delinquent conduct or engaging in conduct indicating a need for supervision and that, despite the parents' or guardians' efforts, the child continues to engage in such conduct, the court or probation department shall waive any sanction that may be imposed on the parents or guardians at any sanction level.

History of Fam. Code §59.015: Acts 1995, 74th Leg., ch. 262, §53, eff. Jan. 1, 1996.

CHAPTER 60. UNIFORM INTERSTATE COMPACT ON JUVENILES

FAM §60.001. DEFINITIONS

In this chapter:

(1) "Commission" means the Interstate Commission for Juveniles.

FAM §59.010

(2) "Compact" means the Interstate Compact for Juveniles.

(3) "Compact administrator" has the meaning assigned by Article II of the compact.

History of Fam. Code §60.001: Acts 1995, 74th Leg., ch. 262, §53, eff. Jan. 1, 1996. Amended by Acts 2005, 79th Leg., ch. 1007, §2.01, eff. Aug. 26, 2008.

FAM §§60.002 TO 60.004. REPEALED

Repealed by Acts 2005, 79th Leg., ch. 1007, §3.02, eff. Aug. 26, 2008.

FAM §60.005. JUVENILE COMPACT ADMINISTRATOR

Under the compact, the governor may designate an officer as the compact administrator. The administrator, acting jointly with like officers of other party states, shall adopt regulations to carry out more effectively the terms of the compact. The compact administrator serves at the pleasure of the governor. The compact administrator shall cooperate with all departments, agencies, and officers of and in the government of this state and its subdivisions in facilitating the proper administration of the compact or of a supplementary agreement entered into by this state.

History of Fam. Code §60.005: Acts 1995, 74th Leg., ch. 262, §53, eff. Jan. 1, 1996.

FAM §60.006. SUPPLEMENTARY AGREEMENTS

A compact administrator may make supplementary agreements with appropriate officials of other states pursuant to the compact. If a supplementary agreement requires or contemplates the use of an institution or facility of this state or requires or contemplates the provision of a service of this state, the supplementary agreement has no force or effect until approved by the head of the department or agency under whose jurisdiction the institution is operated, or whose department or agency is charged with performing the service.

History of Fam. Code §60.006: Acts 1995, 74th Leg., ch. 262, §53, eff. Jan. 1, 1996.

FAM §60.007. FINANCIAL ARRANGEMENTS

The compact administrator may make or arrange for the payments necessary to discharge the financial obligations imposed upon this state by the compact or by a supplementary agreement made under the compact, subject to legislative appropriations.

History of Fam. Code §60.007: Acts 1995, 74th Leg., ch. 262, §53, eff. Jan. 1, 1996.

FAM §60.008. ENFORCEMENT

The courts, departments, agencies, and officers of this state and its subdivisions shall enforce this compact and shall do all things appropriate to effectuate its purposes and intent which are within their respective jurisdictions.

History of Fam. Code §60.008: Acts 1995, 74th Leg., ch. 262, §53, eff. Jan. 1, 1996.

FAM §60.009. ADDITIONAL PROCEDURES NOT PRECLUDED

In addition to any procedures developed under the compact for the return of a runaway juvenile, the particular states, the juvenile, or his parents, the courts, or other legal custodian involved may agree upon and adopt any plan or procedure legally authorized under the laws of this state and the other respective party states for the return of the runaway juvenile.

History of Fam. Code §60.009: Acts 1995, 74th Leg., ch. 262, §53, eff. Jan. 1, 1996. Amended by Acts 2005, 79th Leg., ch. 1007, §2.01, eff. Aug. 26, 2008.

FAM §60.010. INTERSTATE COMPACT FOR JUVENILES

Article I

PURPOSE

The compacting states to this Interstate Compact recognize that each state is responsible for the proper supervision or return of juveniles, delinquents, and status offenders who are on probation or parole and who have absconded, escaped, or run away from supervision and control and in so doing have endangered their own safety and the safety of others. The compacting states also recognize that each state is responsible for the safe return of juveniles who have run away from home and in doing so have left their state of residence. The compacting states also recognize that congress, by enacting the Crime Control Act, 4 U.S.C. Section 112 (1965), has authorized and encouraged compacts for cooperative efforts and mutual assistance in the prevention of crime.

It is the purpose of this compact, through means of joint and cooperative action among the compacting states to: (A) ensure that the juveniles who are moved under this compact to another state for probation or parole supervision and services are governed in the receiving state by the same standards that apply to juveniles receiving such supervision and services in the receiving state; (B) ensure that the public safety interests of the citizens, including the victims of juvenile offenders, in both the sending and receiving states

are adequately protected and balanced with the juvenile's and the juvenile's family's best interests and welfare when an interstate movement is under consideration; (C) return juveniles who have run away, absconded, or escaped from supervision or control or have been accused of an offense to the state requesting their return through a fair and prompt judicial review process that ensures that the requisition is in order and that the transport is properly supervised; (D) make provisions for contracts between member states for the cooperative institutionalization in public facilities in member states for delinquent youth needing special services; (E) provide for the effective tracking of juveniles who move interstate under the compact's provisions; (F) equitably allocate the costs, benefits, and obligations of the compacting states; (G) establish procedures to manage the movement between states of juvenile offenders released to the community under the jurisdiction of courts, juvenile departments, or any other criminal or juvenile justice agency which has jurisdiction over juvenile offenders, ensuring that a receiving state accepts supervision of a juvenile when the juvenile's parent or other person having legal custody resides or is undertaking residence there; (H) ensure immediate notice to jurisdictions where defined offenders are authorized to travel or to relocate across state lines; (I) establish a system of uniform data collection on information pertaining to juveniles who move interstate under this compact that prevents public disclosure of identity and individual treatment information but allows access by authorized juvenile justice and criminal justice officials and regular reporting of compact activities to heads of state executive, judicial, and legislative branches and juvenile and criminal justice administrators; (J) monitor compliance with rules governing interstate movement of juveniles and initiate interventions to address and correct noncompliance; (K) coordinate training and education regarding the regulation of interstate movement of juveniles for officials involved in such activity; and (L) coordinate the implementation and operation of the compact with the Interstate Compact for the Placement of Children, the Interstate Compact for Adult Offender Supervision and other compacts affecting juveniles particularly in those cases where concurrent or overlapping supervision issues arise. It is the policy of the compacting states that the activities conducted by the Interstate Commission created herein are the formation of public policies and therefore are public business. Furthermore, the compacting states shall cooperate and observe their individual and collective duties and responsibilities for the prompt return and acceptance of juveniles subject to the provisions of this compact. The provisions of this compact shall be reasonably and liberally construed to accomplish the purposes and policies of the compact.

Article II

DEFINITIONS

As used in this compact, unless the context clearly requires a different construction:

A. "Bylaws" means those bylaws established by the Interstate Commission for its governance or for directing or controlling the Interstate Commission's actions or conduct.

B. "Compact administrator" means the individual in each compacting state appointed pursuant to the terms of this compact responsible for the administration and management of the state's supervision and transfer of juveniles subject to the terms of this compact and to the rules adopted by the Interstate Commission under this compact.

C. "Compacting state" means any state which has enacted the enabling legislation for this compact.

D. "Commissioner" means the voting representative of each compacting state appointed pursuant to Article III of this compact.

E. "Court" means any court having jurisdiction over delinquent, neglected, or dependent children.

F. "Deputy compact administrator" means the individual, if any, in each compacting state appointed to act on behalf of a compact administrator pursuant to the terms of this compact, responsible for the administration and management of the state's supervision and transfer of juveniles subject to the terms of this compact and to the rules adopted by the Interstate Commission under this compact.

G. "Interstate Commission" means the Interstate Commission for Juveniles created by Article III of this compact.

H. "Juvenile" means any person defined as a juvenile in any member state or by the rules of the Interstate Commission, including:

(1) Accused Delinquent—a person charged with an offense that, if committed by an adult, would be a criminal offense;

(2) Adjudicated Delinquent—a person found to have committed an offense that, if committed by an adult, would be a criminal offense;

(3) Accused Status Offender—a person charged with an offense that would not be a criminal offense if committed by an adult;

(4) Adjudicated Status Offender—a person found to have committed an offense that would not be a criminal offense if committed by an adult; and

(5) Nonoffender—a person in need of supervision who has not been accused or adjudicated a status offender or delinquent.

I. "Noncompacting state" means any state which has not enacted the enabling legislation for this compact.

J. "Probation or parole" means any kind of supervision or conditional release of juveniles authorized under the laws of the compacting states.

K. "Rule" means a written statement by the Interstate Commission promulgated pursuant to Article VI of this compact that is of general applicability, implements, interprets, or prescribes a policy or provision of the compact, or an organizational, procedural, or practice requirement of the Interstate Commission, and has the force and effect of statutory law in a compacting state, and includes the amendment, repeal, or suspension of an existing rule.

L. "State" means a state of the United States, the District of Columbia (or its designee), the Commonwealth of Puerto Rico, the U.S. Virgin Islands, Guam, American Samoa, and the Northern Marianas Islands.

Article III

INTERSTATE COMMISSION FOR JUVENILES

A. The compacting states hereby create the Interstate Commission for Juveniles. The Interstate Commission shall be a body corporate and joint agency of the compacting states. The commission shall have all the responsibilities, powers, and duties set forth herein, and such additional powers as may be conferred upon it by subsequent action of the respective legislatures of the compacting states in accordance with the terms of this compact.

B. The Interstate Commission shall consist of commissioners appointed by the appropriate appointing authority in each state pursuant to the rules and requirements of each compacting state. The commissioner shall be the compact administrator, deputy compact administrator, or designee from that state who shall serve on the Interstate Commission in such capacity under or pursuant to the applicable law of the compacting state.

C. In addition to the commissioners who are the voting representatives of each state, the Interstate Commission shall include individuals who are not commissioners, but who are members of interested organizations. Such noncommissioner members must include a member of the national organizations of governors, legislators, state chief justices, attorneys general, Interstate Compact for Adult Offender Supervision, Interstate Compact for the Placement of Children, juvenile justice and juvenile corrections officials, and crime victims. All noncommissioner members of the Interstate Commission shall be ex officio (nonvoting) members. The Interstate Commission may provide in its bylaws for such additional ex officio (nonvoting) members, including members of other national organizations, in such numbers as shall be determined by the commission.

D. Each compacting state represented at any meeting of the Interstate Commission is entitled to one vote. A majority of the compacting states shall constitute a quorum for the transaction of business, unless a larger quorum is required by the bylaws of the Interstate Commission.

E. The Interstate Commission shall meet at least once each calendar year. The chairperson may call additional meetings and, upon the request of a simple majority of the compacting states, shall call additional meetings. Public notice shall be given of all meetings and meetings shall be open to the public.

F. The Interstate Commission shall establish an executive committee, which shall include commission officers, members, and others as determined by the bylaws. The executive committee shall have the power to act on behalf of the Interstate Commission during periods when the Interstate Commission is not in session, with the exception of rulemaking or amendment to the compact. The executive committee shall oversee the day-to-day activities of the administration of the compact managed by an executive director and Interstate Commission staff; administers enforcement and compliance with the provisions of the compact, its bylaws and rules, and performs such other duties as directed by the Interstate Commission or set forth in the bylaws.

G. Each member of the Interstate Commission shall have the right and power to cast a vote to which that compacting state is entitled and to participate in the

business and affairs of the Interstate Commission. A member shall vote in person and shall not delegate a vote to another compacting state. However, a commissioner shall appoint another authorized representative, in the absence of the commissioner from that state, to cast a vote on behalf of the compacting state at a specified meeting. The bylaws may provide for members' participation in meetings by telephone or other means of telecommunication or electronic communication.

H. The Interstate Commission's bylaws shall establish conditions and procedures under which the Interstate Commission shall make its information and official records available to the public for inspection or copying. The Interstate Commission may exempt from disclosure any information or official records to the extent they would adversely affect personal privacy rights or proprietary interests.

I. Public notice shall be given of all meetings and all meetings shall be open to the public, except as set forth in the rules or as otherwise provided in the compact. The Interstate Commission and any of its committees may close a meeting to the public when it determines by two-thirds vote that an open meeting would be likely to:

1. Relate solely to the Interstate Commission's internal personnel practices and procedures;

2. Disclose matters specifically exempted from disclosure by statute;

3. Disclose trade secrets or commercial or financial information which is privileged or confidential;

4. Involve accusing any person of a crime or formally censuring any person;

5. Disclose information of a personal nature where disclosure would constitute a clearly unwarranted invasion of personal privacy;

6. Disclose investigative records compiled for law enforcement purposes;

7. Disclose information contained in or related to examination, operating or condition reports prepared by, or on behalf of or for the use of, the Interstate Commission with respect to a regulated person or entity for the purpose of regulation or supervision of such person or entity;

8. Disclose information, the premature disclosure of which would significantly endanger the stability of a regulated person or entity; or

9. Specifically relate to the Interstate Commission's issuance of a subpoena, or its participation in a civil action or other legal proceeding.

J. For every meeting closed pursuant to this provision, the Interstate Commission's legal counsel shall publicly certify that, in the legal counsel's opinion, the meeting may be closed to the public, and shall reference each relevant exemptive provision. The Interstate Commission shall keep minutes which shall fully and clearly describe all matters discussed in any meeting and shall provide a full and accurate summary of any actions taken, and the reasons therefore, including a description of each of the views expressed on any item and the record of any roll call vote (reflected in the vote of each member on the question). All documents considered in connection with any action shall be identified in such minutes.

K. The Interstate Commission shall collect standardized data concerning the interstate movement of juveniles as directed through its rules which shall specify the data to be collected, the means of collection and data exchange, and reporting requirements. Such methods of data collection, exchange, and reporting shall insofar as is reasonably possible conform to up-to-date technology and coordinate the Interstate Commission's information functions with the appropriate repository of records.

Article IV
POWERS & DUTIES OF THE
INTERSTATE COMMISSION

The commission shall have the following powers and duties:

1. To provide for dispute resolution among compacting states.

2. To promulgate rules to effect the purposes and obligations as enumerated in this compact, which shall have the force and effect of statutory law and shall be binding in the compacting states to the extent and in the manner provided in this compact.

3. To oversee, supervise, and coordinate the interstate movement of juveniles subject to the terms of this compact and any bylaws adopted and rules promulgated by the Interstate Commission.

4. To enforce compliance with the compact provisions, the rules promulgated by the Interstate Commission, and the bylaws, using all necessary and proper means, including but not limited to the use of judicial process.

5. To establish and maintain offices which shall be located within one or more of the compacting states.

6. To purchase and maintain insurance and bonds.

7. To borrow, accept, hire, or contract for services of personnel.

8. To establish and appoint committees and hire staff which it deems necessary for the carrying out of its functions including, but not limited to, an executive committee as required by Article III of this compact, which shall have the power to act on behalf of the Interstate Commission in carrying out its powers and duties hereunder.

9. To elect or appoint officers, attorneys, employees, agents, or consultants, and to fix their compensation, define their duties, and determine their qualifications, and to establish the Interstate Commission's personnel policies and programs relating to, inter alia, conflicts of interest, rates of compensation, and qualifications of personnel.

10. To accept any and all donations and grants of money, equipment, supplies, materials, and services, and to receive, utilize, and dispose of same.

11. To lease, purchase, accept contributions or donations of, or otherwise to own, hold, improve, or use any property, whether real, personal, or mixed.

12. To sell, convey, mortgage, pledge, lease, exchange, abandon, or otherwise dispose of any property, whether real, personal, or mixed.

13. To establish a budget and make expenditures and levy dues as provided in Article VIII of this compact.

14. To sue and be sued.

15. To adopt a seal and bylaws governing the management and operation of the Interstate Commission.

16. To perform such functions as may be necessary or appropriate to achieve the purposes of this compact.

17. To report annually to the legislatures, governors, and judiciary of the compacting states concerning the activities of the Interstate Commission during the preceding year. Such reports shall also include any recommendations that may have been adopted by the Interstate Commission.

18. To coordinate education, training, and public awareness regarding the interstate movement of juveniles for officials involved in such activity.

19. To establish uniform standards of the reporting, collecting, and exchanging of data.

20. The Interstate Commission shall maintain its corporate books and records in accordance with the bylaws.

Article V
ORGANIZATION & OPERATION OF THE INTERSTATE COMMISSION

Sec. A. Bylaws

1. The Interstate Commission shall, by a majority of the members present and voting, within 12 months of the first Interstate Commission meeting, adopt bylaws to govern its conduct as may be necessary or appropriate to carry out the purposes of the compact, including, but not limited to:

a. Establishing the fiscal year of the Interstate Commission;

b. Establishing an executive committee and such other committees as may be necessary;

c. Providing for the establishment of committees governing any general or specific delegation of any authority or function of the Interstate Commission;

d. Providing reasonable procedures for calling and conducting meetings of the Interstate Commission and ensuring reasonable notice of each such meeting;

e. Establishing the titles and responsibilities of the officers of the Interstate Commission;

f. Providing a mechanism for concluding the operations of the Interstate Commission and the return of any surplus funds that may exist upon the termination of the compact after the payment or reserving of all of its debts and obligations;

g. Providing start-up rules for initial administration of the compact; and

h. Establishing standards and procedures for compliance and technical assistance in carrying out the compact.

Sec. B. Officers and Staff

1. The Interstate Commission shall, by a majority of the members, elect annually from among its members a chairperson and a vice chairperson, each of whom shall have such authority and duties as may be specified in the bylaws. The chairperson or, in the chairperson's absence or disability, the vice chairperson shall preside at all meetings of the Interstate Commission. The officers so elected shall serve without compensation or remuneration from the Interstate Commission, provided that, subject to the availability of budgeted funds, the officers shall be reimbursed for any ordinary and neces-

sary costs and expenses incurred by them in the performance of their duties and responsibilities as officers of the Interstate Commission.

2. The Interstate Commission shall, through its executive committee, appoint or retain an executive director for such period, upon such terms and conditions, and for such compensation as the Interstate Commission may deem appropriate. The executive director shall serve as secretary to the Interstate Commission, but shall not be a member and shall hire and supervise such other staff as may be authorized by the Interstate Commission.

Sec. C. Qualified Immunity, Defense, and Indemnification

1. The Interstate Commission's executive director and employees shall be immune from suit and liability, either personally or in their official capacity, for any claim for damage to or loss of property or personal injury or other civil liability caused or arising out of or relating to any actual or alleged act, error, or omission that occurred, or that such person had a reasonable basis for believing occurred, within the scope of Interstate Commission employment, duties, or responsibilities, provided that any such person shall not be protected from suit or liability for any damage, loss, injury, or liability caused by the intentional or wilful and wanton misconduct of any such person.

2. The liability of any commissioner, or the employee or agent of a commissioner, acting within the scope of such person's employment or duties for acts, errors, or omissions occurring within such person's state may not exceed the limits of liability set forth under the constitution and laws of that state for state officials, employees, and agents. Nothing in this subsection shall be construed to protect any such person from suit or liability for any damage, loss, injury, or liability caused by the intentional or wilful and wanton misconduct of any such person.

3. The Interstate Commission shall defend the executive director or the employees or representatives of the Interstate Commission and, subject to the approval of the attorney general of the state represented by any commissioner of a compacting state, shall defend such commissioner or the commissioner's representatives or employees in any civil action seeking to impose liability arising out of any actual or alleged act, error, or omission that occurred within the scope of Interstate Commission employment, duties, or responsibilities, or that the defendant had a reasonable basis for believing occurred within the scope of Interstate Commission employment, duties, or responsibilities, provided that the actual or alleged act, error, or omission did not result from intentional or wilful and wanton misconduct on the part of such person.

4. The Interstate Commission shall indemnify and hold the commissioner of a compacting state, or the commissioner's representatives or employees, or the Interstate Commission's representatives or employees, harmless in the amount of any settlement or judgment obtained against such persons arising out of any actual or alleged act, error, or omission that occurred within the scope of Interstate Commission employment, duties, or responsibilities, or that such persons had a reasonable basis for believing occurred within the scope of Interstate Commission employment, duties, or responsibilities, provided that the actual or alleged act, error, or omission did not result from intentional or wilful and wanton misconduct on the part of such persons.

Article VI

RULEMAKING FUNCTIONS OF THE INTERSTATE COMMISSION

A. The Interstate Commission shall promulgate and publish rules in order to effectively and efficiently achieve the purposes of the compact.

B. Rulemaking shall occur pursuant to the criteria set forth in this article and the bylaws and rules adopted pursuant thereto. Such rulemaking shall substantially conform to the principles of the "Model State Administrative Procedures Act," 1981 Act, Uniform Laws Annotated, Vol. 15, p. 1 (2000), or such other administrative procedures act, as the Interstate Commission deems appropriate consistent with due process requirements under the United States Constitution as now or hereafter interpreted by the United States Supreme Court. All rules and amendments shall become binding as of the date specified, as published with the final version of the rule as approved by the Interstate Commission.

C. When promulgating a rule, the Interstate Commission shall, at a minimum:

1. Publish the proposed rule's entire text stating the reason or reasons for that proposed rule;

2. Allow and invite persons to submit written data, facts, opinions, and arguments, which information shall be added to the record and be made publicly available;

3. Provide an opportunity for an informal hearing, if petitioned by 10 or more persons; and

4. Promulgate a final rule and its effective date, if appropriate, based on input from state or local officials, or interested parties.

D. Allow, not later than 60 days after a rule is promulgated, any interested person to file a petition in the United States District Court for the District of Columbia or in the federal district court where the Interstate Commission's principal office is located for judicial review of the rule. If the court finds that the Interstate Commission's action is not supported by substantial evidence in the rulemaking record, the court shall hold the rule unlawful and set it aside. For purposes of this subsection, evidence is substantial if it would be considered substantial evidence under the Model State Administrative Procedures Act.

E. If a majority of the legislatures of the compacting states rejects a rule, those states may, by enactment of a statute or resolution in the same manner used to adopt the compact, cause that such rule shall have no further force and effect in any compacting state.

F. The existing rules governing the operation of the Interstate Compact on Juveniles superceded by this Act shall be null and void 12 months after the first meeting of the Interstate Commission created under this compact.

G. Upon determination by the Interstate Commission that an emergency exists, the Interstate Commission may promulgate an emergency rule which shall become effective immediately upon adoption, provided that the usual rulemaking procedures provided hereunder shall be retroactively applied to said rule as soon as reasonably possible, but no later than 90 days after the effective date of the emergency rule.

Article VII
OVERSIGHT, ENFORCEMENT, & DISPUTE RESOLUTION BY THE INTERSTATE COMMISSION

Sec. A. Oversight

1. The Interstate Commission shall oversee the administration and operations of the interstate movement of juveniles subject to this compact in the compacting states and shall monitor such activities being administered in noncompacting states which may significantly affect compacting states.

2. The courts and executive agencies in each compacting state shall enforce this compact and shall take all actions necessary and appropriate to effectuate the compact's purposes and intent. The provisions of this compact and the rules promulgated hereunder shall be received by all the judges, public officers, commissions, and departments of the state government as evidence of the authorized statute and administrative rules. All courts shall take judicial notice of the compact and the rules. In any judicial or administrative proceeding in a compacting state pertaining to the subject matter of this compact which may affect the powers, responsibilities, or actions of the Interstate Commission, the Interstate Commission shall be entitled to receive all service of process in any such proceeding, and shall have standing to intervene in the proceeding for all purposes.

Sec. B. Dispute Resolution

1. The compacting states shall report to the Interstate Commission on all issues and activities necessary for the administration of the compact as well as issues and activities pertaining to compliance with the provisions of the compact and its bylaws and rules.

2. The Interstate Commission shall attempt, upon the request of a compacting state, to resolve any disputes or other issues which are subject to the compact and which may arise among compacting states and between compacting and noncompacting states. The Interstate Commission shall promulgate a rule providing for both mediation and binding dispute resolution for disputes among the compacting states.

3. The Interstate Commission, in the reasonable exercise of its discretion, shall enforce the provisions and rules of this compact using any or all means set forth in Article X of this compact.

Article VIII
FINANCE

A. The Interstate Commission shall pay or provide for the payment of the reasonable expenses of its establishment, organization, and ongoing activities.

B. The Interstate Commission shall levy on and collect an annual assessment from each compacting state to cover the cost of the internal operations and activities of the Interstate Commission and its staff which must be in a total amount sufficient to cover the Interstate Commission's annual budget as approved each year. The aggregate annual assessment amount shall be allocated based upon a formula to be determined by the Interstate Commission, taking into consideration the population of each compacting state and the volume

of interstate movement of juveniles in each compacting state. The Interstate Commission shall promulgate a rule binding upon all compacting states that governs said assessment.

C. The Interstate Commission shall not incur any obligations of any kind prior to securing the funds adequate to meet the same, nor shall the Interstate Commission pledge the credit of any of the compacting states, except by and with the authority of the compacting state.

D. The Interstate Commission shall keep accurate accounts of all receipts and disbursements. The receipts and disbursements of the Interstate Commission shall be subject to the audit and accounting procedures established under its bylaws. However, all receipts and disbursements of funds handled by the Interstate Commission shall be audited yearly by a certified or licensed public accountant and the report of the audit shall be included in and become part of the annual report of the Interstate Commission.

Article IX

COMPACTING STATES, EFFECTIVE DATE, & AMENDMENT

A. Any state, as defined in Article II of this compact, is eligible to become a compacting state.

B. The compact shall become effective and binding upon legislative enactment of the compact into law by no less than 35 of the states. The initial effective date shall be the later of July 1, 2004, or upon enactment into law by the 35th jurisdiction. Thereafter, the compact shall become effective and binding, as to any other compacting state, upon enactment of the compact into law by that state. The governors of noncompacting states or their designees shall be invited to participate in Interstate Commission activities on a nonvoting basis prior to adoption of the compact by all states.

C. The Interstate Commission may propose amendments to the compact for enactment by the compacting states. No amendment shall become effective and binding upon the Interstate Commission and the compacting states unless and until it is enacted into law by unanimous consent of the compacting states.

Article X

WITHDRAWAL, DEFAULT, TERMINATION, & JUDICIAL ENFORCEMENT

Sec. A. Withdrawal

1. Once effective, the compact shall continue in force and remain binding upon each and every compacting state, provided that a compacting state may withdraw from the compact by specifically repealing the statute which enacted the compact into law.

2. The effective date of withdrawal is the effective date of the repeal.

3. The withdrawing state shall immediately notify the chairperson of the Interstate Commission in writing upon the introduction of legislation repealing this compact in the withdrawing state. The Interstate Commission shall notify the other compacting states of the withdrawing state's intent to withdraw within 60 days of its receipt thereof.

4. The withdrawing state is responsible for all assessments, obligations, and liabilities incurred through the effective date of withdrawal, including any obligations, the performance of which extend beyond the effective date of withdrawal.

5. Reinstatement following withdrawal of any compacting state shall occur upon the withdrawing state reenacting the compact or upon such later date as determined by the Interstate Commission.

Sec. B. Technical Assistance, Fines, Suspension, Termination, and Default

1. If the Interstate Commission determines that any compacting state has at any time defaulted in the performance of any of its obligations or responsibilities under this compact, or the bylaws or duly promulgated rules, the Interstate Commission may impose any or all of the following penalties:

a. Remedial training and technical assistance as directed by the Interstate Commission;

b. Alternative dispute resolution;

c. Fines, fees, and costs in such amounts as are deemed to be reasonable as fixed by the Interstate Commission; and

d. Suspension or termination of membership in the compact, which shall be imposed only after all other reasonable means of securing compliance under the bylaws and rules have been exhausted and the Interstate Commission has determined that the offending state is in default. Immediate notice of suspension shall be given by the Interstate Commission to the governor, the chief justice or the chief judicial officer of the state, and the majority and minority leaders of the defaulting state's legislature. The grounds for default include, but are not limited to, failure of a compacting state to perform such obligations or responsibilities im-

posed upon it by this compact, the bylaws or duly promulgated rules, and any other grounds designated in commission bylaws and rules. The Interstate Commission shall immediately notify the defaulting state in writing of the penalty imposed by the Interstate Commission and of the default pending a cure of the default. The Interstate Commission shall stipulate the conditions and the time period within which the defaulting state must cure its default. If the defaulting state fails to cure the default within the time period specified by the Interstate Commission, the defaulting state shall be terminated from the compact upon an affirmative vote of a majority of the compacting states and all rights, privileges, and benefits conferred by this compact shall be terminated from the effective date of termination.

2. Within 60 days of the effective date of termination of a defaulting state, the Interstate Commission shall notify the governor, the chief justice or chief judicial officer of the state, and the majority and minority leaders of the defaulting state's legislature of such termination.

3. The defaulting state is responsible for all assessments, obligations, and liabilities incurred through the effective date of termination including any obligations, the performance of which extends beyond the effective date of termination.

4. The Interstate Commission shall not bear any costs relating to the defaulting state unless otherwise mutually agreed upon in writing between the Interstate Commission and the defaulting state.

5. Reinstatement following termination of any compacting state requires both a reenactment of the compact by the defaulting state and the approval of the Interstate Commission pursuant to the rules.

Sec. C. Judicial Enforcement

The Interstate Commission may, by majority vote of the members, initiate legal action in the United States District Court for the District of Columbia or, at the discretion of the Interstate Commission, in the federal district where the Interstate Commission has its offices, to enforce compliance with the provisions of the compact, its duly promulgated rules and bylaws, against any compacting state in default. In the event judicial enforcement is necessary the prevailing party shall be awarded all costs of such litigation including reasonable attorney's fees.

Sec. D. Dissolution of Compact

1. The compact dissolves effective upon the date of the withdrawal or default of the compacting state, which reduces membership in the compact to one compacting state.

2. Upon the dissolution of this compact, the compact becomes null and void and shall be of no further force or effect, and the business and affairs of the Interstate Commission shall be concluded and any surplus funds shall be distributed in accordance with the bylaws.

Article XI

SEVERABILITY & CONSTRUCTION

A. The provisions of this compact shall be severable, and if any phrase, clause, sentence, or provision is deemed unenforceable, the remaining provisions of the compact shall be enforceable.

B. The provisions of this compact shall be liberally construed to effectuate its purposes.

Article XII

BINDING EFFECT OF COMPACT & OTHER LAWS

Sec. A. Other Laws

1. Nothing herein prevents the enforcement of any other law of a compacting state that is not inconsistent with this compact.

2. All compacting states' laws other than state constitutions and other interstate compacts conflicting with this compact are superseded to the extent of the conflict.

Sec. B. Binding Effect of the Compact

1. All lawful actions of the Interstate Commission, including all rules and bylaws promulgated by the Interstate Commission, are binding upon the compacting states.

2. All agreements between the Interstate Commission and the compacting states are binding in accordance with their terms.

3. Upon the request of a party to a conflict over meaning or interpretation of Interstate Commission actions, and upon a majority vote of the compacting states, the Interstate Commission may issue advisory opinions regarding such meaning or interpretation.

4. In the event any provision of this compact exceeds the constitutional limits imposed on the legislature of any compacting state, the obligations, duties, powers, or jurisdiction sought to be conferred by such provision upon the Interstate Commission shall be in-

effective and such obligations, duties, powers, or jurisdiction shall remain in the compacting state and shall be exercised by the agency thereof to which such obligations, duties, powers, or jurisdiction are delegated by law in effect at the time this compact becomes effective.

History of Fam. Code §60.010: Acts 2005, 79th Leg., ch. 1007, §1.01, eff. Sept. 1, 2005.

FAM §60.011. EFFECT OF TEXAS LAWS

If the laws of this state conflict with the compact, the compact controls, except that in the event of a conflict between the compact and the Texas Constitution, as determined by the courts of this state, the Texas Constitution controls.

History of Fam. Code §60.011: Acts 2005, 79th Leg., ch. 1007, §2.02, eff. Aug. 26, 2008.

FAM §60.012. LIABILITIES FOR CERTAIN COMMISSION AGENTS

The compact administrator and each member, officer, executive director, employee, or agent of the commission acting within the scope of the person's employment or duties is, for the purpose of acts or omissions occurring within this state, entitled to the same protections under Chapter 104, Civil Practice and Remedies Code, as an employee, a member of the governing board, or any other officer of a state agency, institution, or department.

History of Fam. Code §60.012: Acts 2005, 79th Leg., ch. 1007, §2.02, eff. Aug. 26, 2008.

CHAPTER 61. RIGHTS & RESPONSIBILITIES OF PARENTS & OTHER ELIGIBLE PERSONS

SUBCHAPTER A. ENTRY OF ORDERS AGAINST PARENTS & OTHER ELIGIBLE PERSONS

FAM §61.001. DEFINITIONS

In this chapter:

(1) "Juvenile court order" means an order by a juvenile court in a proceeding to which this chapter applies requiring a parent or other eligible person to act or refrain from acting.

(2) "Other eligible person" means the respondent's guardian, the respondent's custodian, or any other person described in a provision under this title authorizing the court order.

History of Fam. Code §61.001: Acts 2003, 78th Leg., ch. 283, §28, eff. Sept. 1, 2003.

FAM §61.002. APPLICABILITY

(a) Except as provided by Subsection (b), this chapter applies to a proceeding to enter a juvenile court order:

(1) for payment of probation fees under Section 54.061;

(2) for restitution under Sections 54.041(b) and 54.048;

(3) for payment of graffiti eradication fees under Section 54.0461;

(4) for community service under Section 54.044(b);

(5) for payment of costs of court under Section 54.0411 or other provisions of law;

(6) requiring the person to refrain from doing any act injurious to the welfare of the child under Section 54.041(a)(1);

(7) enjoining contact between the person and the child who is the subject of a proceeding under Section 54.041(a)(2);

(8) ordering a person living in the same household with the child to participate in counseling under Section 54.041(a)(3);

(9) requiring a parent or other eligible person to pay reasonable attorney's fees for representing the child under Section 51.10(e);

(10) requiring the parent or other eligible person to reimburse the county for payments the county has made to an attorney appointed to represent the child under Section 51.10(j);

(11) requiring payment of deferred prosecution supervision fees under Section 53.03(d);

(12) requiring a parent or other eligible person to attend a court hearing under Section 51.115;

(13) requiring a parent or other eligible person to act or refrain from acting to aid the child in complying with conditions of release from detention under Section 54.01(r);

(14) requiring a parent or other eligible person to act or refrain from acting under any law imposing an obligation of action or omission on a parent or other eligible person because of the parent's or person's relation to the child who is the subject of a proceeding under this title;

(15) for payment of fees under Section 54.0462; or

(16) for payment of the cost of attending an educational program under Section 54.0404.

(b) This subchapter does not apply to the entry and enforcement of a child support order under Section 54.06.

History of Fam. Code §61.002: Acts 2003, 78th Leg., ch. 283, §28, eff. Sept. 1, 2003. Amended by Acts 2009, 81st Leg., ch. 1209, §5, eff. Sept. 1, 2009; Acts 2011, 82nd Leg., ch. 1322, §21, eff. Sept. 1, 2011; Acts 2015, 84th Leg., ch. 935, §26, eff. Sept. 1, 2015.

FAM §61.003. ENTRY OF JUVENILE COURT ORDER AGAINST PARENT OR OTHER ELIGIBLE PERSON

(a) To comply with the requirements of due process of law, the juvenile court shall:

(1) provide sufficient notice in writing or orally in a recorded court hearing of a proposed juvenile court order; and

(2) provide a sufficient opportunity for the parent or other eligible person to be heard regarding the proposed order.

(b) A juvenile court order must be in writing and a copy promptly furnished to the parent or other eligible person.

(c) The juvenile court may require the parent or other eligible person to provide suitable identification to be included in the court's file. Suitable identification includes fingerprints, a driver's license number, a social security number, or similar indicia of identity.

History of Fam. Code §61.003: Acts 2003, 78th Leg., ch. 283, §28, eff. Sept. 1, 2003.

FAM §61.0031. TRANSFER OF ORDER AFFECTING PARENT OR OTHER ELIGIBLE PERSON TO COUNTY OF CHILD'S RESIDENCE

(a) This section applies only when:

(1) a juvenile court has placed a parent or other eligible person under a court order under this chapter;

(2) the child who was the subject of the juvenile court proceedings in which the order was entered:

(A) resides in a county other than the county in which the order was entered;

(B) has moved to a county other than the county in which the order was entered and intends to remain in that county for at least 60 days; or

(C) intends to move to a county other than the county in which the order was entered and to remain in that county for at least 60 days; and

(3) the parent or other eligible person resides or will reside in the same county as the county in which the child now resides or to which the child has moved or intends to move.

(b) A juvenile court that enters an order described by Subsection (a)(1) may transfer the order to the juvenile court of the county in which the parent now resides or to which the parent has moved or intends to move.

(c) The juvenile court shall provide the parent or other eligible person written notice of the transfer. The notification must identify the court to which the order has been transferred.

(d) The juvenile court to which the order has been transferred shall require the parent or other eligible person to appear before the court to notify the person of the existence and terms of the order, unless the permanent supervision hearing under Section 51.073(c) has been waived. Failure to do so renders the order unenforceable.

(e) If the notice required by Subsection (d) is provided, the juvenile court to which the order has been transferred may modify, extend, or enforce the order as though the court originally entered the order.

History of Fam. Code §61.0031: Acts 2005, 79th Leg., ch. 949, §26, eff. Sept. 1, 2005. Amended by Acts 2013, 83rd Leg., ch. 1299, §33, eff. Sept. 1, 2013.

FAM §61.004. APPEAL

(a) The parent or other eligible person against whom a final juvenile court order has been entered may appeal as provided by law from judgments entered in civil cases.

(b) The movant may appeal from a judgment denying requested relief regarding a juvenile court order as provided by law from judgments entered in civil cases.

(c) The pendency of an appeal initiated under this section does not abate or otherwise affect the proceedings in juvenile court involving the child.

History of Fam. Code §61.004: Acts 2003, 78th Leg., ch. 283, §28, eff. Sept. 1, 2003.

Sections 61.005-61.050 reserved for expansion

SUBCHAPTER B. ENFORCEMENT OF ORDER AGAINST PARENT OR OTHER ELIGIBLE PERSON

FAM §61.051. MOTION FOR ENFORCEMENT

(a) A party initiates enforcement of a juvenile court order by filing a written motion. In ordinary and concise language, the motion must:

(1) identify the provision of the order allegedly violated and sought to be enforced;

(2) state specifically and factually the manner of the person's alleged noncompliance;

(3) state the relief requested; and

(4) contain the signature of the party filing the motion.

(b) The movant must allege in the same motion for enforcement each violation by the person of the juvenile court orders described by Section 61.002(a) that the movant had a reasonable basis for believing the person was violating when the motion was filed.

(c) The juvenile court retains jurisdiction to enter a contempt order if the motion for enforcement is filed not later than six months after the child's 18th birthday.

History of Fam. Code §61.051: Acts 2003, 78th Leg., ch. 283, §28, eff. Sept. 1, 2003.

FAM §61.052. NOTICE & APPEARANCE

(a) On the filing of a motion for enforcement, the court shall by written notice set the date, time, and place of the hearing and order the person against whom enforcement is sought to appear and respond to the motion.

(b) The notice must be given by personal service or by certified mail, return receipt requested, on or before the 10th day before the date of the hearing on the motion. The notice must include a copy of the motion for enforcement. Personal service must comply with the Code of Criminal Procedure.

(c) If a person moves to strike or specially excepts to the motion for enforcement, the court shall rule on the exception or motion to strike before the court hears evidence on the motion for enforcement. If an exception is sustained, the court shall give the movant an opportunity to replead and continue the hearing to a designated date and time without the requirement of additional service.

(d) If a person who has been personally served with notice to appear at the hearing does not appear, the juvenile court may not hold the person in contempt, but may issue a capias for the arrest of the person. The court shall set and enforce bond as provided by Subchapter C, Chapter 157. If a person served by certified mail, return receipt requested, with notice to appear at the hearing does not appear, the juvenile court may require immediate personal service of notice.

History of Fam. Code §61.052: Acts 2003, 78th Leg., ch. 283, §28, eff. Sept. 1, 2003.

FAM §61.053. ATTORNEY FOR THE PERSON

(a) In a proceeding on a motion for enforcement where incarceration is a possible punishment against a person who is not represented by an attorney, the court shall inform the person of the right to be represented by an attorney and, if the person is indigent, of the right to the appointment of an attorney.

(b) If the person claims indigency and requests the appointment of an attorney, the juvenile court may require the person to file an affidavit of indigency. The court may hear evidence to determine the issue of indigency.

(c) The court shall appoint an attorney to represent the person if the court determines that the person is indigent.

(d) The court shall allow an appointed or retained attorney at least 10 days after the date of the attorney's appointment or retention to respond to the movant's pleadings and to prepare for the hearing. The attorney may waive the preparation time or agree to a shorter period for preparation.

History of Fam. Code §61.053: Acts 2003, 78th Leg., ch. 283, §28, eff. Sept. 1, 2003.

FAM §61.054. COMPENSATION OF APPOINTED ATTORNEY

(a) An attorney appointed to represent an indigent person is entitled to a reasonable fee for services to be paid from the general fund of the county according to the schedule for compensation adopted by the county juvenile board. The attorney must meet the qualifications required of attorneys for appointment to Class B misdemeanor cases in juvenile court.

(b) For purposes of compensation, a proceeding in the supreme court is the equivalent of a proceeding in the court of criminal appeals.

(c) The juvenile court may order the parent or other eligible person for whom it has appointed counsel to reimburse the county for the fees the county pays to appointed counsel.

History of Fam. Code §61.054: Acts 2003, 78th Leg., ch. 283, §28, eff. Sept. 1, 2003.

FAM §61.055. CONDUCT OF ENFORCEMENT HEARING

(a) The juvenile court shall require that the enforcement hearing be recorded as provided by Section 54.09.

(b) The movant must prove beyond a reasonable doubt that the person against whom enforcement is sought engaged in conduct constituting contempt of a reasonable and lawful court order as alleged in the motion for enforcement.

(c) The person against whom enforcement is sought has a privilege not to be called as a witness or otherwise to incriminate himself or herself.

(d) The juvenile court shall conduct the enforcement hearing without a jury.

(e) The juvenile court shall include in its judgment findings as to each violation alleged in the motion for enforcement and the punishment, if any, to be imposed.

(f) If the person against whom enforcement is sought was not represented by counsel during any previous court proceeding involving a motion for enforcement, the person may through counsel raise any defense or affirmative defense to the proceeding that could have been lodged in the previous court proceeding but was not because the person was not represented by counsel.

(g) It is an affirmative defense to enforcement of a juvenile court order that the juvenile court did not provide the parent or other eligible person with due process of law in the proceeding in which the court entered the order.

History of Fam. Code §61.055: Acts 2003, 78th Leg., ch. 283, §28, eff. Sept. 1, 2003.

FAM §61.056. AFFIRMATIVE DEFENSE OF INABILITY TO PAY

(a) In an enforcement hearing in which the motion for enforcement alleges that the person against whom enforcement is sought failed to pay restitution, court costs, supervision fees, or any other payment ordered by the court, it is an affirmative defense that the person was financially unable to pay.

(b) The burden of proof to establish the affirmative defense of inability to pay is on the person asserting it.

(c) In order to prevail on the affirmative defense of inability to pay, the person asserting it must show that the person could not have reasonably paid the court-ordered obligation after the person discharged the person's other important financial obligations, including payments for housing, food, utilities, necessary clothing, education, and preexisting debts.

History of Fam. Code §61.056: Acts 2003, 78th Leg., ch. 283, §28, eff. Sept. 1, 2003.

FAM §61.057. PUNISHMENT FOR CONTEMPT

(a) On a finding of contempt, the juvenile court may commit the person to the county jail for a term not to exceed six months or may impose a fine in an amount not to exceed $500, or both.

(b) The court may impose only a single jail sentence not to exceed six months or a single fine not to exceed $500, or both, during an enforcement proceeding, without regard to whether the court has entered multiple findings of contempt.

(c) On a finding of contempt in an enforcement proceeding, the juvenile court may, instead of issuing a commitment to jail, enter an order requiring the person's future conduct to comply with the court's previous orders.

(d) Violation of an order entered under Subsection (c) may be the basis of a new enforcement proceeding.

(e) The juvenile court may assign a juvenile probation officer to assist a person in complying with a court order issued under Subsection (c).

(f) A juvenile court may reduce a term of incarceration or reduce payment of all or part of a fine at any time before the sentence is fully served or the fine fully paid.

(g) A juvenile court may reduce the burden of complying with a court order issued under Subsection (c) at any time before the order is fully satisfied, but may not increase the burden except following a new finding of contempt in a new enforcement proceeding.

History of Fam. Code §61.057: Acts 2003, 78th Leg., ch. 283, §28, eff. Sept. 1, 2003.

Sections 61.058-61.100 reserved for expansion

SUBCHAPTER C. RIGHTS OF PARENTS

FAM §61.101. DEFINITION

In this subchapter, "parent" includes the guardian or custodian of a child.

History of Fam. Code §61.101: Acts 2003, 78th Leg., ch. 283, §28, eff. Sept. 1, 2003.

FAM §61.102. RIGHT TO BE INFORMED OF PROCEEDING

(a) The parent of a child referred to a juvenile court is entitled as soon as practicable after the referral to be informed by staff designated by the juvenile board, based on the information accompanying the referral to the juvenile court, of:

(1) the date and time of the offense;

(2) the date and time the child was taken into custody;

(3) the name of the offense and its penal category;

(4) the type of weapon, if any, that was used;

(5) the type of property taken or damaged and the extent of damage, if any;

(6) the physical injuries, if any, to the victim of the offense;

(7) whether there is reason to believe that the offense was gang-related;

(8) whether there is reason to believe that the offense was related to consumption of alcohol or use of an illegal controlled substance;

(9) if the child was taken into custody with adults or other juveniles, the names of those persons;

(10) the aspects of the juvenile court process that apply to the child;

(11) if the child is in detention, the visitation policy of the detention facility that applies to the child;

(12) the child's right to be represented by an attorney and the local standards and procedures for determining whether the parent qualifies for appointment of counsel to represent the child; and

(13) the methods by which the parent can assist the child with the legal process.

(b) If the child was released on field release citation, or from the law enforcement station by the police, by intake, or by the judge or associate judge at the initial detention hearing, the information required by Subsection (a) may be communicated to the parent in person, by telephone, or in writing.

(c) If the child is not released before or at the initial detention hearing, the information required by Subsection (a) shall be communicated in person to the parent unless that is not feasible, in which event it may be communicated by telephone or in writing.

(d) Information disclosed to a parent under Subsection (a) is not admissible in a judicial proceeding under this title as substantive evidence or as evidence to impeach the testimony of a witness for the state.

History of Fam. Code §61.102: Acts 2003, 78th Leg., ch. 283, §28, eff. Sept. 1, 2003.

FAM §61.103. RIGHT OF ACCESS TO CHILD

(a) The parent of a child taken into custody for delinquent conduct, conduct indicating a need for supervision, or conduct that violates a condition of probation imposed by the juvenile court has the right to communicate in person privately with the child for reasonable periods of time while the child is in:

(1) a juvenile processing office;

(2) a secure detention facility;

(3) a secure correctional facility;

(4) a court-ordered placement facility; or

(5) the custody of the Texas Juvenile Justice Department.

(b) The time, place, and conditions of the private, in-person communication may be regulated to prevent disruption of scheduled activities and to maintain the safety and security of the facility.

History of Fam. Code §61.103: Acts 2003, 78th Leg., ch. 283, §28, eff. Sept. 1, 2003. Amended by Acts 2015, 84th Leg., ch. 734, §76, eff. Sept. 1, 2015.

FAM §61.104. PARENTAL WRITTEN STATEMENT

(a) When a petition for adjudication, a motion or petition to modify disposition, or a motion or petition for discretionary transfer to criminal court is served on a parent of the child, the parent must be provided with a form prescribed by the Texas Juvenile Justice Department on which the parent can make a written statement about the needs of the child or family or any other matter relevant to disposition of the case.

(b) The parent shall return the statement to the juvenile probation department, which shall transmit the statement to the court along with the discretionary transfer report authorized by Section 54.02(e), the disposition report authorized by Section 54.04(b), or the modification of disposition report authorized by Section 54.05(e), as applicable. The statement shall be disclosed to the parties as appropriate and may be considered by the court at the disposition, modification, or discretionary transfer hearing.

History of Fam. Code §61.104: Acts 2003, 78th Leg., ch. 283, §28, eff. Sept. 1, 2003. Amended by Acts 2015, 84th Leg., ch. 734, §77, eff. Sept. 1, 2015.

FAM §61.105. PARENTAL ORAL STATEMENT

(a) After all the evidence has been received but before the arguments of counsel at a hearing for discretionary transfer to criminal court, a disposition hearing without a jury, or a modification of disposition hearing, the court shall give a parent who is present in court a reasonable opportunity to address the court about the needs or strengths of the child or family or any other matter relevant to disposition of the case.

(b) The parent may not be required to make the statement under oath and may not be subject to cross-examination, but the court may seek clarification or expansion of the statement from the person giving the statement.

(c) The court may consider and act on the statement as the court considers appropriate.

History of Fam. Code §61.105: Acts 2003, 78th Leg., ch. 283, §28, eff. Sept. 1, 2003.

FAM §61.106. APPEAL OR COLLATERAL CHALLENGE

The failure or inability of a person to perform an act or to provide a right or service listed under this subchapter may not be used by the child or any party as a ground for:

(1) appeal;

(2) an application for a post-adjudication writ of habeas corpus; or

(3) exclusion of evidence against the child in any proceeding or forum.

History of Fam. Code §61.106: Acts 2003, 78th Leg., ch. 283, §28, eff. Sept. 1, 2003.

FAM §61.107. LIABILITY

The Texas Juvenile Justice Department, a juvenile board, a court, a person appointed by the court, an employee of a juvenile probation department, an attorney for the state, a peace officer, or a law enforcement agency is not liable for a failure or inability to provide a right listed in this chapter.

History of Fam. Code §61.107: Acts 2003, 78th Leg., ch. 283, §28, eff. Sept. 1, 2003. Amended by Acts 2015, 84th Leg., ch. 734, §78, eff. Sept. 1, 2015.

Chapters 62-64 blank

TRUANCY COURT PROCEEDINGS
TABLE OF CONTENTS

TITLE 3-A. TRUANCY COURT PROCEEDINGS

TITLE 3-A. TRUANCY COURT PROCEEDINGS

CHAPTER 65. TRUANCY COURT PROCEEDINGS

SUBCHAPTER A. GENERAL PROVISIONS

FAM §65.001. SCOPE & PURPOSE

(a) This chapter details the procedures and proceedings in cases involving allegations of truant conduct.

(b) The purpose of this chapter is to encourage school attendance by creating simple civil judicial procedures through which children are held accountable for excessive school absences.

(c) The best interest of the child is the primary consideration in adjudicating truant conduct of the child.

History of Fam. Code §65.001: Acts 2015, 84th Leg., ch. 935, §27, eff. Sept. 1, 2015.

See also Educ. Code ch. 25, subch. C.

FAM §65.002. DEFINITIONS

In this chapter:

(1) "Child" means a person who is 12 years of age or older and younger than 19 years of age.

(2) "Juvenile court" means a court designated under Section 51.04 to exercise jurisdiction over proceedings under Title 3.

(3) "Qualified telephone interpreter" means a telephone service that employs licensed court interpreters, as defined by Section 157.001, Government Code.

(4) "Truancy court" means a court designated under Section 65.004 to exercise jurisdiction over cases involving allegations of truant conduct.

History of Fam. Code §65.002: Acts 2015, 84th Leg., ch. 935, §27, eff. Sept. 1, 2015.

FAM §65.003. TRUANT CONDUCT

(a) A child engages in truant conduct if the child is required to attend school under Section 25.085, Educa-

tion Code, and fails to attend school on 10 or more days or parts of days within a six-month period in the same school year.

(b) Truant conduct may be prosecuted only as a civil case in a truancy court.

(c) It is an affirmative defense to an allegation of truant conduct that one or more of the absences required to be proven have been excused by a school official or by the court or that one or more of the absences were involuntary, but only if there is an insufficient number of unexcused or voluntary absences remaining to constitute truant conduct. The burden is on the child to show by a preponderance of the evidence that the absence has been or should be excused or that the absence was involuntary. A decision by the court to excuse an absence for purposes of this subsection does not affect the ability of the school district to determine whether to excuse the absence for another purpose.

History of Fam. Code §65.003: Acts 2015, 84th Leg., ch. 935, §27, eff. Sept. 1, 2015.

FAM §65.004. TRUANCY COURTS; JURISDICTION

(a) The following are designated as truancy courts:

(1) in a county with a population of 1.75 million or more, the constitutional county court;

(2) justice courts; and

(3) municipal courts.

(b) A truancy court has exclusive original jurisdiction over cases involving allegations of truant conduct.

(c) A municipality may enter into an agreement with a contiguous municipality or a municipality with boundaries that are within one-half mile of the municipality seeking to enter into the agreement to establish concurrent jurisdiction of the municipal courts in the municipalities and provide original jurisdiction to a municipal court in which a truancy case is brought as if the municipal court were located in the municipality in which the case arose.

(d) A truancy court retains jurisdiction over a person, without regard to the age of the person, who was referred to the court under Section 65.051 for engaging in truant conduct before the person's 19th birthday, until final disposition of the case.

History of Fam. Code §65.004: Acts 2015, 84th Leg., ch. 935, §27, eff. Sept. 1, 2015.

FAM §65.005. COURT SESSIONS

A truancy court is considered to be in session at all times.

History of Fam. Code §65.005: Acts 2015, 84th Leg., ch. 935, §27, eff. Sept. 1, 2015.

FAM §65.006. VENUE

Venue for a proceeding under this chapter is the county in which the school in which the child is enrolled is located or the county in which the child resides.

History of Fam. Code §65.006: Acts 2015, 84th Leg., ch. 935, §27, eff. Sept. 1, 2015.

FAM §65.007. RIGHT TO JURY TRIAL

(a) A child alleged to have engaged in truant conduct is entitled to a jury trial.

(b) The number of jurors in a case involving an allegation of truant conduct is six. The state and the child are each entitled to three peremptory challenges.

(c) There is no jury fee for a trial under this chapter.

History of Fam. Code §65.007: Acts 2015, 84th Leg., ch. 935, §27, eff. Sept. 1, 2015.

FAM §65.008. WAIVER OF RIGHTS

A right granted to a child by this chapter or by the constitution or laws of this state or the United States is waived in proceedings under this chapter if:

(1) the right is one that may be waived;

(2) the child and the child's parent or guardian are informed of the right, understand the right, understand the possible consequences of waiving the right, and understand that waiver of the right is not required;

(3) the child signs the waiver;

(4) the child's parent or guardian signs the waiver; and

(5) the child's attorney signs the waiver, if the child is represented by counsel.

History of Fam. Code §65.008: Acts 2015, 84th Leg., ch. 935, §27, eff. Sept. 1, 2015.

FAM §65.009. EFFECT OF ADJUDICATION

(a) An adjudication of a child as having engaged in truant conduct is not a conviction of crime. An order of adjudication does not impose any civil disability ordinarily resulting from a conviction or operate to disqualify the child in any civil service application or appointment.

(b) The adjudication of a child as having engaged in truant conduct may not be used in any subsequent

court proceedings, other than for the purposes of determining an appropriate remedial action under this chapter or in an appeal under this chapter.

History of Fam. Code §65.009: Acts 2015, 84th Leg., ch. 935, §27, eff. Sept. 1, 2015.

FAM §65.010. BURDEN OF PROOF

A court or jury may not return a finding that a child has engaged in truant conduct unless the state has proved the conduct beyond a reasonable doubt.

History of Fam. Code §65.010: Acts 2015, 84th Leg., ch. 935, §27, eff. Sept. 1, 2015.

FAM §65.011. APPLICABLE STATUTES REGARDING DISCOVERY

Discovery in a proceeding under this chapter is governed by Chapter 39, Code of Criminal Procedure, other than Articles 39.14(i) and (j).

History of Fam. Code §65.011: Acts 2015, 84th Leg., ch. 935, §27, eff. Sept. 1, 2015.

FAM §65.012. PROCEDURAL RULES

The supreme court may promulgate rules of procedure applicable to proceedings under this chapter, including guidelines applicable to the informal disposition of truancy cases.

History of Fam. Code §65.012: Acts 2015, 84th Leg., ch. 935, §27, eff. Sept. 1, 2015.

FAM §65.013. INTERPRETERS

(a) When on the motion for appointment of an interpreter by a party or on the motion of the court, in any proceeding under this chapter, the court determines that the child, the child's parent or guardian, or a witness does not understand and speak English, an interpreter must be sworn to interpret for the person. Articles 38.30(a), (b), and (c), Code of Criminal Procedure, apply in a proceeding under this chapter. A qualified telephone interpreter may be sworn to provide interpretation services if an interpreter is not available to appear in person before the court.

(b) In any proceeding under this chapter, if a party notifies the court that the child, the child's parent or guardian, or a witness is deaf, the court shall appoint a qualified interpreter to interpret the proceedings in any language, including sign language, that the deaf person can understand. Articles 38.31(d), (e), (f), and (g), Code of Criminal Procedure, apply in a proceeding under this chapter.

History of Fam. Code §65.013: Acts 2015, 84th Leg., ch. 935, §27, eff. Sept. 1, 2015.

FAM §65.014. SIGNATURES

Any requirement under this chapter that a document be signed or that a document contain a person's signature, including the signature of a judge or a clerk of the court, is satisfied if the document contains the signature of the person as captured on an electronic device or as a digital signature.

History of Fam. Code §65.014: Acts 2015, 84th Leg., ch. 935, §27, eff. Sept. 1, 2015.

FAM §65.015. PUBLIC ACCESS TO COURT HEARINGS

(a) Except as provided by Subsection (b), a truancy court shall open a hearing under this chapter to the public unless the court, for good cause shown, determines that the public should be excluded.

(b) The court may prohibit a person from personally attending a hearing if the person is expected to testify at the hearing and the court determines that the person's testimony would be materially affected if the person hears other testimony at the hearing.

History of Fam. Code §65.015: Acts 2015, 84th Leg., ch. 935, §27, eff. Sept. 1, 2015.

FAM §65.016. RECORDING OF PROCEEDINGS

(a) The proceedings in a truancy court that is not a court of record may not be recorded.

(b) The proceedings in a truancy court that is a court of record must be recorded by stenographic notes or by electronic, mechanical, or other appropriate means.

History of Fam. Code §65.016: Acts 2015, 84th Leg., ch. 935, §27, eff. Sept. 1, 2015.

FAM §65.017. JUVENILE CASE MANAGERS

A truancy court may employ a juvenile case manager in accordance with Article 45.056, Code of Criminal Procedure, to provide services to children who have been referred to the truancy court or who are in jeopardy of being referred to the truancy court.

History of Fam. Code §65.017: Acts 2015, 84th Leg., ch. 935, §27, eff. Sept. 1, 2015.

Sections 65.018-65.050 blank

SUBCHAPTER B. INITIAL PROCEDURES

FAM §65.051. INITIAL REFERRAL TO TRUANCY COURT

When a truancy court receives a referral under Section 25.0915, Education Code, and the court is not required to dismiss the referral under that section, the

court shall forward the referral to a truant conduct prosecutor who serves the court.

History of Fam. Code §65.051: Acts 2015, 84th Leg., ch. 935, §27, eff. Sept. 1, 2015.

FAM §65.052. TRUANT CONDUCT PROSECUTOR

In a justice or municipal court or a constitutional county court that is designated as a truancy court, the attorney who represents the state in criminal matters in that court shall serve as the truant conduct prosecutor.

History of Fam. Code §65.052: Acts 2015, 84th Leg., ch. 935, §27, eff. Sept. 1, 2015.

FAM §65.053. REVIEW BY PROSECUTOR

(a) The truant conduct prosecutor shall promptly review the facts described in a referral received under Section 65.051.

(b) The prosecutor may, in the prosecutor's discretion, determine whether to file a petition with the truancy court requesting an adjudication of the child for truant conduct. If the prosecutor decides not to file a petition requesting an adjudication, the prosecutor shall inform the truancy court and the school district of the decision.

(c) The prosecutor may not file a petition for an adjudication of a child for truant conduct if the referral was not made in compliance with Section 25.0915, Education Code.

History of Fam. Code §65.053: Acts 2015, 84th Leg., ch. 935, §27, eff. Sept. 1, 2015.

FAM §65.054. STATE'S PETITION

(a) A petition for an adjudication of a child for truant conduct initiates an action of the state against a child who has allegedly engaged in truant conduct.

(b) The proceedings shall be styled "In the matter of ________________, Child," identifying the child by the child's initials only.

(c) The petition may be on information and belief.

(d) The petition must state:

(1) with reasonable particularity the time, place, and manner of the acts alleged to constitute truant conduct;

(2) the name, age, and residence address, if known, of the child who is the subject of the petition;

(3) the names and residence addresses, if known, of at least one parent, guardian, or custodian of the child and of the child's spouse, if any; and

(4) if the child's parent, guardian, or custodian does not reside or cannot be found in the state, or if their places of residence are unknown, the name and residence address of any known adult relative residing in the county or, if there is none, the name and residence address of the known adult relative residing nearest to the location of the court.

(e) Filing fees may not be charged for the filing of the state's petition.

History of Fam. Code §65.054: Acts 2015, 84th Leg., ch. 935, §27, eff. Sept. 1, 2015.

FAM §65.055. LIMITATIONS PERIOD

A petition may not be filed after the 45th day after the date of the last absence giving rise to the act of truant conduct.

History of Fam. Code §65.055: Acts 2015, 84th Leg., ch. 935, §27, eff. Sept. 1, 2015.

FAM §65.056. HEARING DATE

(a) After the petition has been filed, the truancy court shall set a date and time for an adjudication hearing.

(b) The hearing may not be held on or before the 10th day after the date the petition is filed.

History of Fam. Code §65.056: Acts 2015, 84th Leg., ch. 935, §27, eff. Sept. 1, 2015.

FAM §65.057. SUMMONS

(a) After setting the date and time of an adjudication hearing, the truancy court shall direct the issuance of a summons to:

(1) the child named in the petition;

(2) the child's parent, guardian, or custodian;

(3) the child's guardian ad litem, if any; and

(4) any other person who appears to the court to be a proper or necessary party to the proceeding.

(b) The summons must require the persons served to appear before the court at the place, date, and time of the adjudication hearing to answer the allegations of the petition. A copy of the petition must accompany the summons. If a person, other than the child, required to appear under this section fails to attend a hearing, the truancy court may proceed with the hearing.

(c) The truancy court may endorse on the summons an order directing the person having the physical custody or control of the child to bring the child to the hearing.

(d) A party, other than the child, may waive service of summons by written stipulation or by voluntary appearance at the hearing.

History of Fam. Code §65.057: Acts 2015, 84th Leg., ch. 935, §27, eff. Sept. 1, 2015.

FAM §65.058. SERVICE OF SUMMONS

(a) If a person to be served with a summons is in this state and can be found, the summons shall be served on the person personally or by registered or certified mail, return receipt requested, at least five days before the date of the adjudication hearing.

(b) Service of the summons may be made by any suitable person under the direction of the court.

History of Fam. Code §65.058: Acts 2015, 84th Leg., ch. 935, §27, eff. Sept. 1, 2015.

FAM §65.059. REPRESENTATION BY ATTORNEY

(a) A child may be represented by an attorney in a case under this chapter. Representation by an attorney is not required.

(b) A child is not entitled to have an attorney appointed to represent the child, but the court may appoint an attorney if the court determines it is in the best interest of the child.

(c) The court may order a child's parent or other responsible person to pay for the cost of an attorney appointed under this section if the court determines that the person has sufficient financial resources.

History of Fam. Code §65.059: Acts 2015, 84th Leg., ch. 935, §27, eff. Sept. 1, 2015.

FAM §65.060. CHILD'S ANSWER

After the petition has been filed, the child may answer, orally or in writing, the petition at or before the commencement of the hearing. If the child does not answer, a general denial of the alleged truant conduct is assumed.

History of Fam. Code §65.060: Acts 2015, 84th Leg., ch. 935, §27, eff. Sept. 1, 2015.

FAM §65.061. GUARDIAN AD LITEM

(a) If a child appears before the truancy court without a parent or guardian, or it appears to the court that the child's parent or guardian is incapable or unwilling to make decisions in the best interest of the child with respect to proceedings under this chapter, the court may appoint a guardian ad litem to protect the interests of the child in the proceedings.

(b) An attorney for a child may also be the child's guardian ad litem. A law enforcement officer, probation officer, or other employee of the truancy court may not be appointed as a guardian ad litem.

(c) The court may order a child's parent or other person responsible to support the child to reimburse the county or municipality for the cost of the guardian ad litem. The court may issue the order only after determining that the parent or other responsible person has sufficient financial resources to offset the cost of the child's guardian ad litem wholly or partly.

History of Fam. Code §65.061: Acts 2015, 84th Leg., ch. 935, §27, eff. Sept. 1, 2015.

FAM §65.062. ATTENDANCE AT HEARING

(a) The child must be personally present at the adjudication hearing. The truancy court may not proceed with the adjudication hearing in the absence of the child.

(b) A parent or guardian of a child and any court-appointed guardian ad litem of a child is required to attend the adjudication hearing.

(c) Subsection (b) does not apply to:

(1) a person for whom, for good cause shown, the court excuses attendance;

(2) a person who is not a resident of this state; or

(3) a parent of a child for whom a managing conservator has been appointed and the parent is not a conservator of the child.

History of Fam. Code §65.062: Acts 2015, 84th Leg., ch. 935, §27, eff. Sept. 1, 2015.

FAM §65.063. RIGHT TO REEMPLOYMENT

(a) An employer may not terminate the employment of a permanent employee because the employee is required under Section 65.062(b) to attend a hearing.

(b) Notwithstanding any other law, an employee whose employment is terminated in violation of this section is entitled to return to the same employment that the employee held when notified of the hearing if the employee, as soon as practical after the hearing, gives the employer actual notice that the employee intends to return.

(c) A person who is injured because of a violation of this section is entitled to:

(1) reinstatement to the person's former position;

(2) damages not to exceed an amount equal to six times the amount of monthly compensation received by the person on the date of the hearing; and

(3) reasonable attorney's fees in an amount approved by the court.

(d) It is a defense to an action brought under this section that the employer's circumstances changed while the employee attended the hearing and caused reemployment to be impossible or unreasonable. To establish a defense under this subsection, an employer must prove that the termination of employment was because of circumstances other than the employee's attendance at the hearing.

History of Fam. Code §65.063: Acts 2015, 84th Leg., ch. 935, §27, eff. Sept. 1, 2015.

FAM §65.064. SUBPOENA OF WITNESS

A witness may be subpoenaed in accordance with the procedures for the subpoena of a witness under the Code of Criminal Procedure.

History of Fam. Code §65.064: Acts 2015, 84th Leg., ch. 935, §27, eff. Sept. 1, 2015.

FAM §65.065. CHILD ALLEGED TO BE MENTALLY ILL

(a) A party may make a motion requesting that a petition alleging a child to have engaged in truant conduct be dismissed because the child has a mental illness, as defined by Section 571.003, Health and Safety Code. In response to the motion, the truancy court shall temporarily stay the proceedings to determine whether probable cause exists to believe the child has a mental illness. In making a determination, the court may:

(1) consider the motion, supporting documents, professional statements of counsel, and witness testimony; and

(2) observe the child.

(b) If the court determines that probable cause exists to believe that the child has a mental illness, the court shall dismiss the petition. If the court determines that evidence does not exist to support a finding that the child has a mental illness, the court shall dissolve the stay and continue with the truancy court proceedings.

History of Fam. Code §65.065: Acts 2015, 84th Leg., ch. 935, §27, eff. Sept. 1, 2015.

Sections 65.066-65.100 blank

SUBCHAPTER C. ADJUDICATION HEARING & REMEDIES

FAM §65.101. ADJUDICATION HEARING; JUDGMENT

(a) A child may be found to have engaged in truant conduct only after an adjudication hearing conducted in accordance with the provisions of this chapter.

(b) At the beginning of the adjudication hearing, the judge of the truancy court shall explain to the child and the child's parent, guardian, or guardian ad litem:

(1) the allegations made against the child;

(2) the nature and possible consequences of the proceedings;

(3) the child's privilege against self-incrimination;

(4) the child's right to trial and to confrontation of witnesses;

(5) the child's right to representation by an attorney if the child is not already represented; and

(6) the child's right to a jury trial.

(c) Trial is by jury unless jury is waived in accordance with Section 65.008. Jury verdicts under this chapter must be unanimous.

(d) The Texas Rules of Evidence do not apply in a truancy proceeding under this chapter except:

(1) when the judge hearing the case determines that a particular rule of evidence applicable to criminal cases must be followed to ensure that the proceedings are fair to all parties; or

(2) as otherwise provided by this chapter.

(e) A child alleged to have engaged in truant conduct need not be a witness against nor otherwise incriminate himself or herself. An extrajudicial statement of the child that was obtained in violation of the constitution of this state or the United States may not be used in an adjudication hearing. A statement made by the child out of court is insufficient to support a finding of truant conduct unless it is corroborated wholly or partly by other evidence.

(f) At the conclusion of the adjudication hearing, the court or jury shall find whether the child has engaged in truant conduct. The finding must be based on competent evidence admitted at the hearing. The child shall be presumed to have not engaged in truant conduct and no finding that a child has engaged in truant conduct may be returned unless the state has proved the conduct beyond a reasonable doubt. In all jury cases the jury will be instructed that the burden is on the state to prove that a child has engaged in truant conduct beyond a reasonable doubt.

(g) If the court or jury finds that the child did not engage in truant conduct, the court shall dismiss the case with prejudice.

(h) If the court or jury finds that the child did engage in truant conduct, the court shall proceed to issue

a judgment finding the child has engaged in truant conduct and order the remedies the court finds appropriate under Section 65.103. The jury is not involved in ordering remedies for a child who has been adjudicated as having engaged in truant conduct.

History of Fam. Code §65.101: Acts 2015, 84th Leg., ch. 935, §27, eff. Sept. 1, 2015.

FAM §65.102. REMEDIAL ACTIONS

(a) The truancy court shall determine and order appropriate remedial actions in regard to a child who has been found to have engaged in truant conduct.

(b) The truancy court shall orally pronounce the court's remedial actions in the child's presence and enter those actions in a written order.

(c) After pronouncing the court's remedial actions, the court shall advise the child and the child's parent, guardian, or guardian ad litem of:

(1) the child's right to appeal, as detailed in Subchapter D; and

(2) the procedures for the sealing of the child's records under Section 65.201.

History of Fam. Code §65.102: Acts 2015, 84th Leg., ch. 935, §27, eff. Sept. 1, 2015.

FAM §65.103. REMEDIAL ORDER

(a) A truancy court may enter a remedial order requiring a child who has been found to have engaged in truant conduct to:

(1) attend school without unexcused absences;

(2) attend a preparatory class for the high school equivalency examination administered under Section 7.111, Education Code, if the court determines that the individual is unlikely to do well in a formal classroom environment due to the individual's age;

(3) if the child is at least 16 years of age, take the high school equivalency examination administered under Section 7.111, Education Code, if that is in the best interest of the child;

(4) attend a nonprofit, community-based special program that the court determines to be in the best interest of the child, including:

(A) an alcohol and drug abuse program;

(B) a rehabilitation program;

(C) a counseling program, including a self-improvement program;

(D) a program that provides training in self-esteem and leadership;

(E) a work and job skills training program;

(F) a program that provides training in parenting, including parental responsibility;

(G) a program that provides training in manners;

(H) a program that provides training in violence avoidance;

(I) a program that provides sensitivity training; and

(J) a program that provides training in advocacy and mentoring;

(5) complete not more than 50 hours of community service on a project acceptable to the court; and

(6) participate for a specified number of hours in a tutorial program covering the academic subjects in which the child is enrolled that are provided by the school the child attends.

(b) A truancy court may not order a child who has been found to have engaged in truant conduct to:

(1) attend a juvenile justice alternative education program, a boot camp, or a for-profit truancy class; or

(2) perform more than 16 hours of community service per week under this section.

(c) In addition to any other order authorized by this section, a truancy court may order the Department of Public Safety to suspend the driver's license or permit of a child who has been found to have engaged in truant conduct. If the child does not have a driver's license or permit, the court may order the Department of Public Safety to deny the issuance of a license or permit to the child. The period of the license or permit suspension or the order that the issuance of a license or permit be denied may not extend beyond the maximum time period that a remedial order is effective as provided by Section 65.104.

History of Fam. Code §65.103: Acts 2015, 84th Leg., ch. 935, §27, eff. Sept. 1, 2015.

FAM §65.104. MAXIMUM TIME REMEDIAL ORDER IS EFFECTIVE

A truancy court's remedial order under Section 65.103 is effective until the later of:

(1) the date specified by the court in the order, which may not be later than the 180th day after the date the order is entered; or

(2) the last day of the school year in which the order was entered.

History of Fam. Code §65.104: Acts 2015, 84th Leg., ch. 935, §27, eff. Sept. 1, 2015.

FAM §65.105. ORDERS AFFECTING PARENTS & OTHERS

(a) If a child has been found to have engaged in truant conduct, the truancy court may:

(1) order the child and the child's parent to attend a class for students at risk of dropping out of school that is designed for both the child and the child's parent;

(2) order any person found by the court to have, by a wilful act or omission, contributed to, caused, or encouraged the child's truant conduct to do any act that the court determines to be reasonable and necessary for the welfare of the child or to refrain from doing any act that the court determines to be injurious to the child's welfare;

(3) enjoin all contact between the child and a person who is found to be a contributing cause of the child's truant conduct, unless that person is related to the child within the third degree by consanguinity or affinity, in which case the court may contact the Department of Family and Protective Services, if necessary;

(4) after notice to, and a hearing with, all persons affected, order any person living in the same household with the child to participate in social or psychological counseling to assist in the child's rehabilitation;

(5) order the child's parent or other person responsible for the child's support to pay all or part of the reasonable costs of treatment programs in which the child is ordered to participate if the court finds the child's parent or person responsible for the child's support is able to pay the costs;

(6) order the child's parent to attend a program for parents of students with unexcused absences that provides instruction designed to assist those parents in identifying problems that contribute to the child's unexcused absences and in developing strategies for resolving those problems; and

(7) order the child's parent to perform not more than 50 hours of community service with the child.

(b) A person subject to an order proposed under Subsection (a) is entitled to a hearing before the order is entered by the court.

(c) On a finding by the court that a child's parents have made a reasonable good faith effort to prevent the child from engaging in truant conduct and that, despite the parents' efforts, the child continues to engage in truant conduct, the court shall waive any requirement for community service that may be imposed on a parent under this section.

History of Fam. Code §65.105: Acts 2015, 84th Leg., ch. 935, §27, eff. Sept. 1, 2015.

FAM §65.106. LIABILITY FOR CLAIMS ARISING FROM COMMUNITY SERVICE

(a) A municipality or county that establishes a program to assist children and their parents in rendering community service under this subchapter may purchase an insurance policy protecting the municipality or county against a claim brought by a person other than the child or the child's parent for a cause of action that arises from an act of the child or parent while rendering the community service. The municipality or county is not liable for the claim to the extent that damages are recoverable under a contract of insurance or under a plan of self-insurance authorized by statute.

(b) The liability of the municipality or county for a claim that arises from an action of the child or the child's parent while rendering community service may not exceed $100,000 to a single person and $300,000 for a single occurrence in the case of personal injury or death, and $10,000 for a single occurrence of property damage. Liability may not extend to punitive or exemplary damages.

(c) This section does not waive a defense, immunity, or jurisdictional bar available to the municipality or county or its officers or employees, nor shall this section be construed to waive, repeal, or modify any provision of Chapter 101, Civil Practice and Remedies Code.

History of Fam. Code §65.106: Acts 2015, 84th Leg., ch. 935, §27, eff. Sept. 1, 2015.

FAM §65.107. COURT COST

(a) If a child is found to have engaged in truant conduct, the truancy court, after giving the child, parent, or other person responsible for the child's support a reasonable opportunity to be heard, shall order the child, parent, or other person, if financially able to do so, to pay a court cost of $50 to the clerk of the court.

(b) The court's order to pay the $50 court cost is not effective unless the order is reduced to writing and signed by the judge. The written order to pay the court cost may be part of the court's order detailing the remedial actions in the case.

(c) The clerk of the court shall keep a record of the court costs collected under this section and shall forward the funds to the county treasurer, municipal treasurer, or person fulfilling the role of a county treasurer or municipal treasurer, as appropriate.

(d) The court costs collected under this section shall be deposited in a special account that can be used only to offset the cost of the operations of the truancy court.

History of Fam. Code §65.107: Acts 2015, 84th Leg., ch. 935, §27, eff. Sept. 1, 2015.

FAM §65.108. HEARING TO MODIFY REMEDY

(a) A truancy court may hold a hearing to modify any remedy imposed by the court. A remedy may only be modified during the period the order is effective under Section 65.104.

(b) There is no right to a jury at a hearing under this section.

(c) A hearing to modify a remedy imposed by the court shall be held on the petition of the state, the court, or the child and the child's parent, guardian, guardian ad litem, or attorney. Reasonable notice of a hearing to modify disposition shall be given to all parties.

(d) Notwithstanding any other law, in considering a motion to modify a remedy imposed by the court, the truancy court may consider a written report from a school district official or employee, juvenile case manager, or professional consultant in addition to the testimony of witnesses. The court shall provide the attorney for the child and the prosecuting attorney with access to all written matters to be considered by the court. The court may order counsel not to reveal items to the child or to the child's parent, guardian, or guardian ad litem if the disclosure would materially harm the treatment and rehabilitation of the child or would substantially decrease the likelihood of receiving information from the same or similar sources in the future.

(e) The truancy court shall pronounce in court, in the presence of the child, the court's changes to the remedy, if any. The court shall specifically state the new remedy and the court's reasons for modifying the remedy in a written order. The court shall furnish a copy of the order to the child.

History of Fam. Code §65.108: Acts 2015, 84th Leg., ch. 935, §27, eff. Sept. 1, 2015.

FAM §65.109. MOTION FOR NEW TRIAL

The order of a truancy court may be challenged by filing a motion for new trial. Rules 505.3(c) and (e), Texas Rules of Civil Procedure, apply to a motion for new trial.

History of Fam. Code §65.109: Acts 2015, 84th Leg., ch. 935, §27, eff. Sept. 1, 2015.

Sections 65.110-65.150 blank

SUBCHAPTER D. APPEAL

FAM §65.151. RIGHT TO APPEAL

(a) The child, the child's parent or guardian, or the state may appeal any order of a truancy court. A person subject to an order entered under Section 65.105 may appeal that order.

(b) An appeal from a truancy court shall be to a juvenile court. The case must be tried de novo in the juvenile court. This chapter applies to the de novo trial in the juvenile court. On appeal, the judgment of the truancy court is vacated.

(c) A judgment of a juvenile court in a trial conducted under Subsection (b) may be appealed in the same manner as an appeal under Chapter 56.

History of Fam. Code §65.151: Acts 2015, 84th Leg., ch. 935, §27, eff. Sept. 1, 2015.

FAM §65.152. GOVERNING LAW

Rule 506, Texas Rules of Civil Procedure, applies to the appeal of an order of a truancy court to a juvenile court in the same manner as the rule applies to an appeal of a judgment of a justice court to a county court, except an appeal bond is not required.

History of Fam. Code §65.152: Acts 2015, 84th Leg., ch. 935, §27, eff. Sept. 1, 2015.

FAM §65.153. COUNSEL ON APPEAL

(a) A child may be represented by counsel on appeal.

(b) If the child and the child's parent, guardian, or guardian ad litem request an appeal, the attorney who represented the child before the truancy court, if any, shall file a notice of appeal with the court that will hear the appeal and inform that court whether that attorney will handle the appeal.

(c) An appeal serves to vacate the order of the truancy court.

History of Fam. Code §65.153: Acts 2015, 84th Leg., ch. 935, §27, eff. Sept. 1, 2015.

Sections 65.154-65.200 blank

Subchapter E. Records

FAM §65.201. SEALING OF RECORDS

(a) A child who has been found to have engaged in truant conduct may apply, on or after the child's 18th birthday, to the truancy court that made the finding to seal the records relating to the allegation and finding of truant conduct held by:

(1) the court;

(2) the truant conduct prosecutor; and

(3) the school district.

(b) The application must include the following information or an explanation of why one or more of the following is not included:

(1) the child's:

(A) full name;

(B) sex;

(C) race or ethnicity;

(D) date of birth;

(E) driver's license or identification card number; and

(F) social security number;

(2) the dates on which the truant conduct was alleged to have occurred; and

(3) if known, the cause number assigned to the petition and the court and county in which the petition was filed.

(c) The truancy court shall order that the records be sealed after determining the child complied with the remedies ordered by the court in the case.

(d) All index references to the records of the truancy court that are ordered sealed shall be deleted not later than the 30th day after the date of the sealing order.

(e) A truancy court, clerk of the court, truant conduct prosecutor, or school district shall reply to a request for information concerning a child's sealed truant conduct case that no record exists with respect to the child.

(f) Inspection of the sealed records may be permitted by an order of the truancy court on the petition of the person who is the subject of the records and only by those persons named in the order.

(g) A person whose records have been sealed under this section is not required in any proceeding or in any application for employment, information, or licensing to state that the person has been the subject of a proceeding under this chapter. Any statement that the person has never been found to have engaged in truant conduct may not be held against the person in any criminal or civil proceeding.

(h) On or after the fifth anniversary of a child's 16th birthday, on the motion of the child or on the truancy court's own motion, the truancy court may order the destruction of the child's records that have been sealed under this section if the child has not been convicted of a felony.

History of Fam. Code §65.201: Acts 2015, 84th Leg., ch. 935, §27, eff. Sept. 1, 2015.

FAM §65.202. CONFIDENTIALITY OF RECORDS

Records and files created under this chapter may be disclosed only to:

(1) the judge of the truancy court, the truant conduct prosecutor, and the staff of the judge and prosecutor;

(2) the child or an attorney for the child;

(3) a governmental agency if the disclosure is required or authorized by law;

(4) a person or entity to whom the child is referred for treatment or services if the agency or institution disclosing the information has entered into a written confidentiality agreement with the person or entity regarding the protection of the disclosed information;

(5) the Texas Department of Criminal Justice and the Texas Juvenile Justice Department for the purpose of maintaining statistical records of recidivism and for diagnosis and classification;

(6) the agency; or

(7) with leave of the truancy court, any other person, agency, or institution having a legitimate interest in the proceeding or in the work of the court.

History of Fam. Code §65.202: Acts 2015, 84th Leg., ch. 935, §27, eff. Sept. 1, 2015.

FAM §65.203. DESTRUCTION OF CERTAIN RECORDS

A truancy court shall order the destruction of records relating to allegations of truant conduct that are held by the court or by the prosecutor if a prosecutor decides not to file a petition for an adjudication of truant conduct after a review of the referral under Section 65.053.

History of Fam. Code §65.203: Acts 2015, 84th Leg., ch. 935, §27, eff. Sept. 1, 2015.

Sections 65.204-65.250 blank

Subchapter F. Enforcement of Orders

FAM §65.251. Failure to Obey Truancy Court Order; Child in Contempt of Court

(a) If a child fails to obey an order issued by a truancy court under Section 65.103(a) or a child is in direct contempt of court, the truancy court, after providing notice and an opportunity for a hearing, may hold the child in contempt of court and order either or both of the following:

(1) that the child pay a fine not to exceed $100; or

(2) that the Department of Public Safety suspend the child's driver's license or permit or, if the child does not have a license or permit, order that the Department of Public Safety deny the issuance of a license or permit to the child until the child fully complies with the court's orders.

(b) If a child fails to obey an order issued by a truancy court under Section 65.103(a) or a child is in direct contempt of court and the child has failed to obey an order or has been found in direct contempt of court on two or more previous occasions, the truancy court, after providing notice and an opportunity for a hearing, may refer the child to the juvenile probation department as a request for truancy intervention, unless the child failed to obey the truancy court order or was in direct contempt of court while 17 years of age or older.

(c) On referral of the child to the juvenile probation department, the truancy court shall provide to the juvenile probation department:

(1) documentation of all truancy prevention measures taken by the originating school district;

(2) documentation of all truancy orders for each of the child's previous truancy referrals, including:

(A) court remedies and documentation of the child's failure to comply with the truancy court's orders, if applicable, demonstrating all interventions that were exhausted by the truancy court; and

(B) documentation describing the child's direct contempt of court, if applicable;

(3) the name, birth date, and last known address of the child and the school in which the child is enrolled; and

(4) the name and last known address of the child's parent or guardian.

(d) The juvenile probation department may, on review of information provided under Subsection (c):

(1) offer further remedies related to the local plan for truancy intervention strategies adopted under Section 25.0916, Education Code; or

(2) refer the child to a juvenile court for a hearing to be conducted under Section 65.252.

(e) A truancy court may not order the confinement of a child for the child's failure to obey an order of the court issued under Section 65.103(a).

History of Fam. Code §65.251: Acts 2015, 84th Leg., ch. 935, §27, eff. Sept. 1, 2015.

FAM §65.252. Proceedings in Juvenile Court

(a) After a referral by the local juvenile probation department, the juvenile court prosecutor shall determine if probable cause exists to believe that the child engaged in direct contempt of court or failed to obey an order of the truancy court under circumstances that would constitute contempt of court. On a finding that probable cause exists, the prosecutor shall determine whether to request an adjudication. Not later than the 20th day after the date the juvenile court receives a request for adjudication from the prosecutor, the juvenile court shall conduct a hearing to determine if the child engaged in conduct that constitutes contempt of the order issued by the truancy court or engaged in direct contempt of court.

(b) If the juvenile court finds that the child engaged in conduct that constitutes contempt of the order issued by the truancy court or direct contempt of court, the juvenile court shall:

(1) enter an order requiring the child to comply with the truancy court's order;

(2) forward a copy of the order to the truancy court within five days; and

(3) admonish the child, orally and in writing, of the consequences of subsequent referrals to the juvenile court, including:

(A) a possible charge of delinquent conduct for contempt of the truancy court's order or direct contempt of court; and

(B) a possible detention hearing.

(c) If the juvenile court prosecutor finds that probable cause does not exist to believe that the child engaged in direct contempt or in conduct that constitutes

contempt of the order issued by the truancy court, or if the juvenile probation department finds that extenuating circumstances caused the original truancy referral, the juvenile court shall enter an order requiring the child's continued compliance with the truancy court's order and notify the truancy court not later than the fifth day after the date the order is entered.

(d) This section does not limit the discretion of a juvenile prosecutor or juvenile court to prosecute a child for conduct under Section 51.03.

History of Fam. Code §65.252: Acts 2015, 84th Leg., ch. 935, §27, eff. Sept. 1, 2015.

FAM §65.253. PARENT OR OTHER PERSON IN CONTEMPT OF COURT

(a) A truancy court may enforce the following orders by contempt:

(1) an order that a parent of a child, guardian of a child, or any court-appointed guardian ad litem of a child attend an adjudication hearing under Section 65.062(b);

(2) an order requiring a person other than a child to take a particular action under Section 65.105(a);

(3) an order that a child's parent, or other person responsible to support the child, reimburse the municipality or county for the cost of the guardian ad litem appointed for the child under Section 65.061(c); and

(4) an order that a parent, or person other than the child, pay the $50 court cost under Section 65.107.

(b) A truancy court may find a parent or person other than the child in direct contempt of the court.

(c) The penalty for a finding of contempt under Subsection (a) or (b) is a fine in an amount not to exceed $100.

(d) In addition to the assessment of a fine under Subsection (c), direct contempt of the truancy court by a parent or person other than the child is punishable by:

(1) confinement in jail for a maximum of three days;

(2) a maximum of 40 hours of community service; or

(3) both confinement and community service.

History of Fam. Code §65.253: Acts 2015, 84th Leg., ch. 935, §27, eff. Sept. 1, 2015.

FAM §65.254. WRIT OF ATTACHMENT

A truancy court may issue a writ of attachment for a person who violates an order entered under Section 65.057(c). The writ of attachment is executed in the same manner as in a criminal proceeding as provided by Chapter 24, Code of Criminal Procedure.

History of Fam. Code §65.254: Acts 2015, 84th Leg., ch. 935, §27, eff. Sept. 1, 2015.

FAM §65.255. ENTRY OF TRUANCY COURT ORDER AGAINST PARENT OR OTHER ELIGIBLE PERSON

(a) The truancy court shall:

(1) provide notice to a person who is the subject of a proposed truancy court order under Section 65.253; and

(2) provide a sufficient opportunity for the person to be heard regarding the proposed order.

(b) A truancy court order under Section 65.253 must be in writing and a copy promptly furnished to the parent or other eligible person.

(c) The truancy court may require the parent or other eligible person to provide suitable identification to be included in the court's file. Suitable identification includes fingerprints, a driver's license number, a social security number, or similar indicia of identity.

History of Fam. Code §65.255: Acts 2015, 84th Leg., ch. 935, §27, eff. Sept. 1, 2015.

FAM §65.256. APPEAL

(a) The parent or other eligible person against whom a final truancy court order has been entered under Section 65.253 may appeal as provided by law from judgments entered by a justice court in civil cases.

(b) Rule 506, Texas Rules of Civil Procedure, applies to an appeal under this section, except an appeal bond is not required.

(c) The pendency of an appeal initiated under this section does not abate or otherwise affect the proceedings in the truancy court involving the child.

History of Fam. Code §65.256: Acts 2015, 84th Leg., ch. 935, §27, eff. Sept. 1, 2015.

FAM §65.257. MOTION FOR ENFORCEMENT

(a) The state may initiate enforcement of a truancy court order under Section 65.253 against a parent or person other than the child by filing a written motion. In ordinary and concise language, the motion must:

(1) identify the provision of the order allegedly violated and sought to be enforced;

(2) state specifically and factually the manner of the person's alleged noncompliance;

(3) state the relief requested; and

(4) contain the signature of the party filing the motion.

(b) The state must allege the particular violation by the person of the truancy court order that the state had a reasonable basis for believing the person was violating when the motion was filed.

(c) The truancy court may also initiate enforcement of an order under this section on its own motion.

History of Fam. Code §65.257: Acts 2015, 84th Leg., ch. 935, §27, eff. Sept. 1, 2015.

FAM §65.258. NOTICE & APPEARANCE

(a) On the filing of a motion for enforcement, the truancy court shall by written notice set the date, time, and place of the hearing and order the person against whom enforcement is sought to appear and respond to the motion.

(b) The notice must be given by personal service or by certified mail, return receipt requested, on or before the 10th day before the date of the hearing on the motion. The notice must include a copy of the motion for enforcement. Personal service must comply with the Code of Criminal Procedure.

(c) If a person moves to strike or specially excepts to the motion for enforcement, the truancy court shall rule on the exception or motion to strike before the court hears evidence on the motion for enforcement. If an exception is sustained, the court shall give the movant an opportunity to replead and continue the hearing to a designated date and time without the requirement of additional service.

(d) If a person who has been personally served with notice to appear at the hearing does not appear, the truancy court may not hold the person in contempt, but may issue a warrant for the arrest of the person.

History of Fam. Code §65.258: Acts 2015, 84th Leg., ch. 935, §27, eff. Sept. 1, 2015.

FAM §65.259. CONDUCT OF ENFORCEMENT HEARING

(a) The movant must prove beyond a reasonable doubt that the person against whom enforcement is sought engaged in conduct constituting contempt of a reasonable and lawful court order as alleged in the motion for enforcement.

(b) The person against whom enforcement is sought has a privilege not to be called as a witness or otherwise to incriminate himself or herself.

(c) The truancy court shall conduct the enforcement hearing without a jury.

(d) The truancy court shall include in the court's judgment:

(1) findings for each violation alleged in the motion for enforcement; and

(2) the punishment, if any, to be imposed.

(e) If the person against whom enforcement is sought was not represented by counsel during any previous court proceeding involving a motion for enforcement, the person may, through counsel, raise any defense or affirmative defense to the proceeding that could have been asserted in the previous court proceeding that was not asserted because the person was not represented by counsel.

(f) It is an affirmative defense to enforcement of a truancy court order under Section 65.253 that the court did not provide the parent or other eligible person with due process of law in the proceeding in which the court entered the order.

History of Fam. Code §65.259: Acts 2015, 84th Leg., ch. 935, §27, eff. Sept. 1, 2015.

Chapters 66-70 blank

PROTECTIVE ORDERS & FAMILY VIOLENCE
TABLE OF CONTENTS

TITLE 4. PROTECTIVE ORDERS & FAMILY VIOLENCE

Subtitle A. General Provisions

PROTECTIVE ORDERS & FAMILY VIOLENCE
TABLE OF CONTENTS

TITLE 4. PROTECTIVE ORDERS & FAMILY VIOLENCE

SUBTITLE A. GENERAL PROVISIONS

CHAPTER 71. DEFINITIONS

FAM §71.001. APPLICABILITY OF DEFINITIONS

(a) Definitions in this chapter apply to this title.

(b) If, in another part of this title, a term defined by this chapter has a meaning different from the meaning provided by this chapter, the meaning of that other provision prevails.

(c) Except as provided by this chapter, the definitions in Chapter 101 apply to terms used in this title.

History of Fam. Code §71.001: Acts 1997, 75th Leg., ch. 34, §1, eff. May 5, 1997. Source: Former Fam. Code §71.01(a).

FAM §71.002. COURT

"Court" means the district court, court of domestic relations, juvenile court having the jurisdiction of a district court, statutory county court, constitutional county court, or other court expressly given jurisdiction under this title.

History of Fam. Code §71.002: Acts 1997, 75th Leg., ch. 34, §1, eff. May 5, 1997. Amended by Acts 1997, 75th Leg., ch. 1220, §1, eff. Sept. 1, 1997. Source: Former Fam. Code §71.01(b)(1).

FAM §71.0021. DATING VIOLENCE

(a) "Dating violence" means an act, other than a defensive measure to protect oneself, by an actor that:

(1) is committed against a victim or applicant for a protective order:

(A) with whom the actor has or has had a dating relationship; or

(B) because of the victim's or applicant's marriage to or dating relationship with an individual with whom the actor is or has been in a dating relationship or marriage; and

(2) is intended to result in physical harm, bodily injury, assault, or sexual assault or that is a threat that reasonably places the victim or applicant in fear of imminent physical harm, bodily injury, assault, or sexual assault.

(b) For purposes of this title, "dating relationship" means a relationship between individuals who have or have had a continuing relationship of a romantic or intimate nature. The existence of such a relationship shall be determined based on consideration of:

(1) the length of the relationship;

(2) the nature of the relationship; and

(3) the frequency and type of interaction between the persons involved in the relationship.

(c) A casual acquaintanceship or ordinary fraternization in a business or social context does not constitute a "dating relationship" under Subsection (b).

History of Fam. Code §71.0021: Acts 2001, 77th Leg., ch. 91, §1, eff. Sept. 1, 2001. Amended by Acts 2011, 82nd Leg., ch. 872, §2, eff. June 17, 2011; Acts 2015, 84th Leg., ch. 117, §1, eff. Sept. 1, 2015.

See also *O'Connor's Texas Family Law Handbook* (2017), "Violence against dating partner or third party," ch. 6-A, §2.1.3, p. 719.

ANNOTATIONS

Hill v. State, No. 01-10-00926-CR (Tex.App.—Houston [1st Dist.] 2012, no pet.) (memo op.; 3-22-12). "We conclude that the inclusion of the words 'have had' [in §71.0021(b) permits a] jury to find that a dating relationship existed if it [finds] that [individuals] had a continuing relationship of a romantic or intimate nature in the past, regardless of whether that relationship was ongoing at the time of the assault."

Ochoa v. State, 355 S.W.3d 48, 52-53 (Tex. App.—Houston [1st Dist.] 2010, pet. ref'd). "Whether the statutory term 'dating relationship' [under §71.0021(b)] is ambiguous concerning its applicability to same-sex relationships is a question of first impression. ... While the statute does not explicitly state that it applies equally to same- and opposite-sex relationships, nothing in the statutory text suggests that its applicability to same-sex relationship[s] is ambiguous. *At 54:* We conclude that the statutory term 'dating relationship' plainly and unambiguously applies to both same- and opposite-sex relationships."

FAM §71.003. FAMILY

"Family" includes individuals related by consanguinity or affinity, as determined under Sections 573.022 and 573.024, Government Code, individuals who are former spouses of each other, individuals who are the parents of the same child, without regard to marriage, and a foster child and foster parent, without regard to whether those individuals reside together.

History of Fam. Code §71.003: Acts 1997, 75th Leg., ch. 34, §1, eff. May 5, 1997. Amended by Acts 2001, 77th Leg., ch. 821, §2.03, eff. June 14, 2001. Source: Former Fam. Code §71.01(b)(3).

ANNOTATIONS

James v. Hubbard, 21 S.W.3d 558, 561 (Tex. App.—San Antonio 2000, no pet.). "'Family' includes relationships established by marriage such as in-laws, as determined by [Gov't Code] §573.024.... Divorce terminates family relationships established by marriage. Thus, by operation of law, had [H] and [ex-W] been divorced then [ex-W's mother] would not have been entitled to this protective order against [H]."

Ⓐ FAM §71.004. FAMILY VIOLENCE

The amended text in §71.004 is effective for reports of suspected abuse, neglect, or exploitation of a child made on or after Sept. 1, 2017. Reports made before Sept. 1, 2017, are governed by the former law in effect at that time.

"Family violence" means:

(1) an act by a member of a family or household against another member of the family or household that is intended to result in physical harm, bodily injury, assault, or sexual assault or that is a threat that reasonably places the member in fear of imminent physical harm, bodily injury, assault, or sexual assault, but does not include defensive measures to protect oneself;

(2) abuse, as that term is defined by Sections 261.001(1)(C), (E), (G), (H), (I), (J), [~~and~~] (K), and (M), by a member of a family or household toward a child of the family or household; or

(3) dating violence, as that term is defined by Section 71.0021.

History of Fam. Code §71.004: Acts 1997, 75th Leg., ch. 34, §1, eff. May 5, 1997. Amended by Acts 2001, 77th Leg., ch. 91, §2, eff. Sept. 1, 2001; Acts 2015, 84th Leg., ch. 117, §2, eff. Sept. 1, 2015; H.B. 249, §1, 85th Leg., eff. Sept. 1, 2017; S.B. 11, §1, 85th Leg., eff. Sept. 1, 2017. Source: Former Fam. Code §71.01(b)(2).

See also ***O'Connor's Texas Family Law Handbook*** (2017), "Family Violence," ch. 6-A, §2, p. 717.

ANNOTATIONS

Burt v. Francis, ___ S.W.3d ___ (Tex.App.—Eastland 2016, no pet.) (No. 11-14-00244-CV; 8-25-16). "'Given the remedial nature of [the Family Code's protective-order provisions], courts should broadly construe its provisions so as to effectuate its humanitarian and preventative purposes.' [¶] Even in circumstances where no express threats are conveyed, the factfinder may nonetheless conclude that an individual was reasonably placed in fear."

Agbogwe v. State, 414 S.W.3d 820, 839 (Tex.App.—Houston [1st Dist.] 2013, no pet.). "Code of Criminal Procedure art. 42.013 provides that if the trial court 'determines that the offense involved family violence, as defined by [Fam. Code] §71.004 ... the court shall make an affirmative finding of that fact and enter the affirmative finding in the judgment of the case.' [¶] The State contends that the family violence finding is proper, despite the undisputed evidence that [victim] was not a member of [D's] family or household, because this offense 'only occurred in an attempt to further [D's] family violence assault on [girlfriend]' and 'the offense as a whole was committed with the intent to cause physical harm or threaten physical harm to his household member....' *At 840-41:* The focus of the family-violence finding is ... on the relationship between the defendant and the specific victim of the offense. If the victim of the specific offense is a member of the defendant's family or household, then the affirmative finding is justified. The statute is silent on whether a family violence finding is justified when the victim of the specific offense at issue is not a member of the defendant's family or household, but the criminal episode as a whole does involve a member of the defendant's household. [¶] The State ... contends that the family violence finding was proper based on the doctrine of transferred intent, arguing that '[w]hile [D] was directing an assault on his household member ... he attacked [victim] when she intervened. ...' ... The transferred intent doctrine is ... inapplicable under these circumstances. [¶] [T]he record does not support the affirmative family violence finding...."

In re Wean, No. 03-10-00383-CV (Tex.App.—Austin 2010, orig. proceeding) (memo op.; 8-31-10). "[T]he fact that a child is spanked, on its own, does not evidence family violence. A parent generally has discretion to use some amount of corporal punishment. Therefore, for corporal punishment to constitute family violence, there must be some evidence—such as severity of injury, type of instrument used, or mental or emotional state of the perpetrator—that would transcend a reasonable level of parental discretion regarding discipline."

FAM §71.005. HOUSEHOLD

"Household" means a unit composed of persons living together in the same dwelling, without regard to whether they are related to each other.

History of Fam. Code §71.005: Acts 1997, 75th Leg., ch. 34, §1, eff. May 5, 1997. Source: Former Fam. Code §71.01(b)(5).

ANNOTATIONS

Shah v. State, 414 S.W.3d 808, 813 (Tex.App.—Houston [1st Dist.] 2013, pet. ref'd). "Although no other court has expressly addressed what it means for two people to be 'living' together in the same dwelling, we note that courts ... have concluded that a complainant and a defendant were members of the same 'household,' for purposes of ... §71.005, even though there was no evidence that both individuals had a legal right to be there. *At 814:* In this case, [victim] repeatedly testified that [D] was 'living' with him in the apartment at the time of the assaults. According to [victim], [D] had moved some of his personal items into the apartment and had 'basically set[] up camp' there.... [Victim] also testified that [D] was staying in the apartment with him 'every night' and 'he never left.' [¶] [T]he State presented sufficient evidence that [D] and [victim] were members of the same 'household,' as that term is defined by ... §71.005...."

Teel v. Shifflett, 309 S.W.3d 597, 600 (Tex.App.—Houston [14th Dist.] 2010, pet. denied). Boyfriend "filed an application for a protective order alleging that he and [girlfriend] lived in the same household and that [she] had engaged in ... family violence.... *At 604:* Although the parties' cohabitation was intermittent due to their disagreements, the ... evidence is that they intended to marry and [girlfriend] moved her belongings into [boyfriend's] house. [Girlfriend] gave birth to a child ..., and both parties believe the child was fathered by [boyfriend]. [T]he evidence is ... sufficient to support the ... finding that [couple] had formed a household."

FAM §71.006. MEMBER OF A HOUSEHOLD

"Member of a household" includes a person who previously lived in a household.

History of Fam. Code §71.006: Acts 1997, 75th Leg., ch. 34, §1, eff. May 5, 1997. Source: Former Fam. Code §71.01(b)(4), (6).

FAM §71.007. PROSECUTING ATTORNEY

"Prosecuting attorney" means the attorney, determined as provided in this title, who represents the state in a district or statutory county court in the county in which venue of the application for a protective order is proper.

History of Fam. Code §71.007: Acts 1997, 75th Leg., ch. 34, §1, eff. May 5, 1997.

FAM §71.008. REPEALED

Repealed by Acts 2001, 77th Leg., ch. 48, §2, eff. Sept. 1, 2001.

CHAPTER 72. REPEALED

Repealed by Acts 1995, 74th Leg., ch. 1024, §26, eff. Sept. 1, 1995.

CHAPTER 73. REPEALED

Repealed by Acts 1997, 75th Leg., ch. 34, §2, eff. May 5, 1997.

Chapters 74-80 blank

SUBTITLE B. PROTECTIVE ORDERS

CHAPTER 81. GENERAL PROVISIONS

FAM §81.001. ENTITLEMENT TO PROTECTIVE ORDER

A court shall render a protective order as provided by Section 85.001(b) if the court finds that family violence has occurred and is likely to occur in the future.

History of Fam. Code §81.001: Acts 1997, 75th Leg., ch. 34, §1, eff. May 5, 1997. Source: Former Fam. Code §71.10(a), (b).

ANNOTATIONS

Roper v. Jolliffe, 493 S.W.3d 624, 630 (Tex.App.—Dallas 2015, pet. denied). Family Code §81.001 "did not give [respondent] the right to have a jury act as the fact finder in this case. The statute makes clear that the legislature intended that courts, not juries, act as the sole fact finders and have the responsibility for making the findings necessary for the issuance of a family violence protective order. *At 636:* [Respondent] has not shown he has a right to a jury trial under the plain meaning of [Fam. Code] Title 4, [Tex. Const.] art. 1, §15 or art. 5, §10...."

FAM §81.0015. PRESUMPTION

For purposes of this subtitle, there is a presumption that family violence has occurred and is likely to occur in the future if:

(1) the respondent has been convicted of or placed on deferred adjudication community supervision for any of the following offenses against the child for whom the petition is filed:

(A) an offense under Title 5, Penal Code, for which the court has made an affirmative finding that the offense involved family violence under Article 42.013, Code of Criminal Procedure; or

(B) an offense under Title 6, Penal Code;

(2) the respondent's parental rights with respect to the child have been terminated; and

(3) the respondent is seeking or attempting to seek contact with the child.

History of Fam. Code §81.0015: Acts 2015, 84th Leg., ch. 1241, §1, eff. Sept. 1, 2015.

See also *O'Connor's Texas Family Law Handbook* (2017), "Presumption," ch. 6-C, §2.1.2, p. 736.

FAM §81.002. NO FEE FOR APPLICANT

An applicant for a protective order or an attorney representing an applicant may not be assessed a fee, cost, charge, or expense by a district or county clerk of the court or a sheriff, constable, or other public official or employee in connection with the filing, serving, or entering of a protective order or for any other service described by this subsection, including:

(1) a fee to dismiss, modify, or withdraw a protective order;

(2) a fee for certifying copies;

(3) a fee for comparing copies to originals;

(4) a court reporter fee;

(5) a judicial fund fee;

(6) a fee for any other service related to a protective order; or

(7) a fee to transfer a protective order.

History of Fam. Code §81.002: Acts 1997, 75th Leg., ch. 34, §1, eff. May 5, 1997. Amended by Acts 1997, 75th Leg., ch. 1193, §3, eff. Sept. 1, 1997. Source: Former Fam. Code §71.041(a).

FAM §81.003. FEES & COSTS PAID BY PARTY FOUND TO HAVE COMMITTED FAMILY VIOLENCE

(a) Except on a showing of good cause or of the indigence of a party found to have committed family violence, the court shall require in a protective order that the party against whom the order is rendered pay the $16 protective order fee, the standard fees charged by the clerk of the court in a general civil proceeding for the cost of serving the order, the costs of court, and all other fees, charges, or expenses incurred in connection with the protective order.

(b) The court may order a party against whom an agreed protective order is rendered under Section 85.005 to pay the fees required in Subsection (a).

History of Fam. Code §81.003: Acts 1997, 75th Leg., ch. 34, §1, eff. May 5, 1997. Amended by Acts 1997, 75th Leg., ch. 1193, §4, eff. Sept. 1, 1997. Source: Former Fam. Code §71.041(b).

FAM §81.004. CONTEMPT FOR NONPAYMENT OF FEE

(a) A party who is ordered to pay fees and costs and who does not pay before the date specified by the order may be punished for contempt of court as provided by Section 21.002, Government Code.

(b) If a date is not specified by the court under Subsection (a), payment of costs is required before the 60th day after the date the order was rendered.

History of Fam. Code §81.004: Acts 1997, 75th Leg., ch. 34, §1, eff. May 5, 1997. Amended by Acts 1997, 75th Leg., ch. 1193, §5, eff. Sept. 1, 1997. Source: Former Fam. Code §71.041(c).

FAM §81.005. ATTORNEY'S FEES

(a) The court may assess reasonable attorney's fees against the party found to have committed family violence or a party against whom an agreed protective order is rendered under Section 85.005 as compensation for the services of a private or prosecuting attorney or an attorney employed by the Department of Family and Protective Services.

(b) In setting the amount of attorney's fees, the court shall consider the income and ability to pay of the person against whom the fee is assessed.

History of Fam. Code §81.005: Acts 1997, 75th Leg., ch. 34, §1, eff. May 5, 1997. Amended by Acts 1997, 75th Leg., ch. 1193, §6, eff. Sept. 1, 1997; Acts 2011, 82nd Leg., ch. 110, §4, eff. May 21, 2011. Source: Former Fam. Code §71.041(d).

ANNOTATIONS

In re Skero, 253 S.W.3d 884, 887 (Tex.App.—Beaumont 2008, orig. proceeding). "Although [Fam. Code] §81.005 states that attorney's fees shall be assessed 'as compensation,' the term serves to distinguish the assessment of the fee from a fine. This distinction is important, because the attorney's fees may be paid to a governmental entity, to whom the applicant may owe nothing. The order of placement of the sections logically expresses a separation between the role of attorneys in obtaining protective orders, found in [Fam. Code] §§81.005-81.0075, and other matters associated with obtaining a protective order, rather than an intention to exclude attorney's fees from the fees,

charges, and expenses generally addressed in [Fam. Code] §§81.003-81.004. We conclude that the Family Code permits the trial court to assess attorney's fees as costs, and allows the trial court to enforce its order through contempt."

FAM §81.006. PAYMENT OF ATTORNEY'S FEES

The amount of fees collected under this chapter as compensation for the fees:

(1) of a private attorney shall be paid to the private attorney who may enforce the order for fees in the attorney's own name;

(2) of a prosecuting attorney shall be paid to the credit of the county fund from which the salaries of the employees of the prosecuting attorney are paid or supplemented; and

(3) of an attorney employed by the Department of Family and Protective Services shall be deposited in the general revenue fund to the credit of the Department of Family and Protective Services.

History of Fam. Code §81.006: Acts 1997, 75th Leg., ch. 34, §1, eff. May 5, 1997. Amended by Acts 2011, 82nd Leg., ch. 110, §5, eff. May 21, 2011. Source: Former Fam. Code §71.041(d).

FAM §81.007. PROSECUTING ATTORNEY

(a) The county attorney or the criminal district attorney is the prosecuting attorney responsible for filing applications under this subtitle unless the district attorney assumes the responsibility by giving notice of that assumption to the county attorney.

(b) The prosecuting attorney responsible for filing an application under this subtitle shall provide notice of that responsibility to all law enforcement agencies in the jurisdiction of the prosecuting attorney.

(c) The prosecuting attorney shall comply with Article 5.06, Code of Criminal Procedure, in filing an application under this subtitle.

History of Fam. Code §81.007: Acts 1997, 75th Leg., ch. 34, §1, eff. May 5, 1997. Source: Former Fam. Code §71.04(c).

ANNOTATIONS

In re A.W.R., No. 10-09-00237-CV (Tex.App.—Waco 2010, no pet.) (memo op.; 8-11-10). "An applicant for a protective order may be represented by either a prosecuting attorney or a private attorney. [¶] [Respondent] argues that non-movants have greater rights when a prosecutor represents the applicant. Specifically, per [CCP] art. 2.01 …, a prosecutor must disclose exculpatory evidence. A private attorney has no such duty. Thus, [respondent] maintains that non-movants are treated disparately depending on the type of attorney representing the applicant. [¶] Because protective orders are civil proceedings, they are governed by the Family Code, not the [CCP]. Thus, we cannot say that a non-movant is treated disparately when the applicant is represented by a private attorney versus a prosecuting attorney." *But see* ***Striedel v. Striedel***, this page.

Striedel v. Striedel, 15 S.W.3d 163, 167 (Tex. App.—Corpus Christi 2000, no pet.). "[W]e express our concern regarding the trial court's failure to give consideration to the appointment of counsel for [respondent]. In this case, [respondent] filed an affidavit of indigency. Attorney for [applicant] objected to further consideration because this was a civil, not criminal proceeding. *At 167 n.2:* We note that, unlike any other 'civil' proceeding in which injunctive relief is sought, [an applicant] for a protective order is statutorily guaranteed counsel. Moreover, the statute specifically states that 'The county attorney or the criminal district attorney is the prosecuting attorney responsible for filing applications under this subtitle….' Examining the nature of a protective order, the method by which it is prosecuted, the sanctioned deprivations of liberty and property which are possible pursuant to such an order, and the possibility of incarceration, we believe the proceeding is quasi-criminal in its nature." *But see* ***In re A.W.R.***, this page.

FAM §81.0075. REPRESENTATION BY PROSECUTING ATTORNEY IN CERTAIN OTHER ACTIONS

Subject to the Texas Disciplinary Rules of Professional Conduct, a prosecuting attorney is not precluded from representing a party in a proceeding under this subtitle and the Department of Family and Protective Services in another action involving the party, regardless of whether the proceeding under this subtitle occurs before, concurrently with, or after the other action involving the party.

History of Fam. Code §81.0075: Acts 1997, 75th Leg., ch. 1193, §7, eff. Sept. 1, 1997. Amended by Acts 2011, 82nd Leg., ch. 110, §6, eff. May 21, 2011; Acts 2013, 83rd Leg., ch. 393, §1, eff. June 14, 2013.

ANNOTATIONS

In re Houston Cty., ___ S.W.3d ___ (Tex.App.—Tyler 2015, orig. proceeding) (No. 12-14-00312-CV; 8-19-15). Mother "filed a motion to disqualify [assistant county attorney] from representing the Department in the termination case because [assistant

county attorney] was [also] representing [mother] in the protective order proceeding. [¶] The County Attorney argues … that a conflict of interest is legislatively precluded [by §81.0075] when a county attorney represents a party in a family violence protective order proceeding and represents the Department in another action involving that same party. [¶] [W]e hold that the unambiguous language of the statute reflects the legislature's intent to authorize the representation described in §81.0075 unless the Texas Disciplinary Rules of Professional Conduct prohibit[] it. [¶] [Tex. Disciplinary Rules Prof'l Conduct R. 1.06 states that] a lawyer 'shall not' represent a person if the representation involves a 'substantially related matter' in which that person's interests are materially and directly adverse to the interests of another client of the lawyer or the lawyer's firm. [¶] [Mother] has shown that [father's] alleged violence and threats of violence are issues in the protective order proceeding and the termination case because of their relationship to [child's] safety. Consequently, we conclude that [mother] has met her burden to show that 'a genuine threat exists that [the County Attorney's Office] may divulge in [the termination case] confidential information obtained in the [protective order proceeding]….' Thus, [mother] has shown that the protective order proceeding and the termination case are substantially related. … Therefore, the trial court was required to disqualify the County Attorney's Office from further representation of the Department in the pending termination case."

FAM §81.008. RELIEF CUMULATIVE

Except as provided by this subtitle, the relief and remedies provided by this subtitle are cumulative of other relief and remedies provided by law.

History of Fam. Code §81.008: Acts 1997, 75th Leg., ch. 34, §1, eff. May 5, 1997. Source: Former Fam. Code §71.19.

FAM §81.009. APPEAL

(a) Except as provided by Subsections (b) and (c), a protective order rendered under this subtitle may be appealed.

(b) A protective order rendered against a party in a suit for dissolution of a marriage may not be appealed until the time the final decree of dissolution of the marriage becomes a final, appealable order.

(c) A protective order rendered against a party in a suit affecting the parent-child relationship may not be appealed until the time an order providing for support of the child or possession of or access to the child becomes a final, appealable order.

History of Fam. Code §81.009: Acts 2005, 79th Leg., ch. 916, §2, eff. June 18, 2005.

See also *O'Connor's Texas Family Law Handbook* (2017), "Appellate Review," ch. 6-C, §15, p. 758.

ANNOTATIONS

In re Keck, 329 S.W.3d 658, 661 (Tex.App.—Houston [14th Dist.] 2010, no pet.). Father "filed both an appeal and a petition for writ of mandamus, and the parties dispute which is the proper vehicle for review. … If either of the exceptions [of §81.009] applies, then appeal of the protective order must await issuance of a final, appealable order in the underlying case. There was apparently never a marriage between [father] and [mother], so the first exception does not apply. An action to terminate [father's] parental rights was pending at the time the application for a protective order was filed, and such a suit is indeed a SAPCR. However, the termination action was filed in a different court … and with a different cause number than the protective order at issue here…. It therefore cannot be said that the protective order was issued 'in' the termination action. Because neither of the §81.009 exceptions [applies] in this case, the protective order is appealable under that Family Code section."

FAM §81.010. COURT ENFORCEMENT

(a) A court of this state with jurisdiction of proceedings arising under this title may enforce a protective order rendered by another court in the same manner that the court that rendered the order could enforce the order, regardless of whether the order is transferred under Subchapter D, Chapter 85.

(b) A court's authority under this section includes the authority to enforce a protective order through contempt.

(c) A motion for enforcement of a protective order rendered under this title may be filed in:

(1) any court in the county in which the order was rendered with jurisdiction of proceedings arising under this title;

(2) a county in which the movant or respondent resides; or

(3) a county in which an alleged violation of the order occurs.

History of Fam. Code §81.010: Acts 2011, 82nd Leg., ch. 632, §1, eff. Sept. 1, 2011.

See also *O'Connor's Texas Family Law Handbook* (2017), "Motion to Transfer," ch. 6-C, §12, p. 756.

FAM §81.011. USE OF DIGITIZED SIGNATURE

(a) A digitized signature on an application for a protective order under this title or any other pleading or order in a proceeding under this title satisfies the requirements for and imposes the duties of signatories to pleadings, motions, and other papers identified under Rule 13, Texas Rules of Civil Procedure.

(b) A digitized signature under this section may be applied only by, and must remain under the sole control of, the person whose signature is represented.

History of Fam. Code §81.011: Acts 2015, 84th Leg., ch. 1165, §3, eff. Sept. 1, 2015.

CHAPTER 82. APPLYING FOR PROTECTIVE ORDER

SUBCHAPTER A. APPLICATION FOR PROTECTIVE ORDER

FAM §82.001. APPLICATION

A proceeding under this subtitle is begun by filing "An Application for a Protective Order" with the clerk of the court.

History of Fam. Code §82.001: Acts 1997, 75th Leg., ch. 34, §1, eff. May 5, 1997. Source: Former Fam. Code §§71.02, 71.04(a).

See also *O'Connor's Texas Family Law Handbook* (2017), "Application," ch. 6-B, §2, p. 721.

ANNOTATIONS

Cockerham v. Cockerham, 218 S.W.3d 298, 301 (Tex.App.—Texarkana 2007, no pet.). "A single contention has been raised ... that the trial court had no authority to enter a protective order against [daughter] because [father] did not file a petition seeking such relief. *At 304:* [I]t is clear that the trial court acted sua sponte in issuing the protective order against [daughter after finding both father and daughter engaged in family violence]. *At 308:* The purpose of the pleading requirements of [TRCP] 301 [is] to provide notice of the matters to be heard. ... Even though the notice requirements [under Fam. Code §§82.004 and 82.041] are meager, they do exist for a good reason: to allow a respondent to realize that he or she must marshal a defense. In the absence of any provision for such an opportunity and because [father] did not file such an application, we conclude that the trial court had no authority to enter the protective order sua sponte in favor of [father]."

FAM §82.002. WHO MAY FILE APPLICATION

(a) With regard to family violence under Section 71.004(1) or (2), an adult member of the family or household may file an application for a protective order to protect the applicant or any other member of the applicant's family or household.

(b) With regard to family violence under Section 71.004(3), an application for a protective order to protect the applicant may be filed by:

(1) a member of the dating relationship, regardless of whether the member is an adult or a child; or

(2) an adult member of the marriage, if the victim is or was married as described by Section 71.0021(a)(1)(B).

(c) Any adult may apply for a protective order to protect a child from family violence.

(d) In addition, an application may be filed for the protection of any person alleged to be a victim of family violence by:

(1) a prosecuting attorney; or

(2) the Department of Family and Protective Services.

(e) The person alleged to be the victim of family violence in an application filed under Subsection (c) or (d) is considered to be the applicant for a protective order under this subtitle.

History of Fam. Code §82.002: Acts 1997, 75th Leg., ch. 34, §1, eff. May 5, 1997. Amended by Acts 1997, 75th Leg., ch. 1193, §8, eff. Sept. 1, 1997; Acts 2001, 77th Leg., ch. 91, §3, eff. Sept. 1, 2001; Acts 2011, 82nd Leg., ch. 110, §7 (eff. May 21, 2011), ch. 632, §2 (eff. Sept. 1, 2011), ch. 872, §3 (eff. June 17, 2011). Source: Former Fam. Code §71.04(b).

See also 40 T.A.C. §705.3102; *O'Connor's Texas Family Law Handbook* (2017), "Who can file," ch. 6-B, §2.1, p. 721.

FAM §82.003. VENUE

An application may be filed in:

(1) the county in which the applicant resides;

(2) the county in which the respondent resides; or

(3) any county in which the family violence is alleged to have occurred.

History of Fam. Code §82.003: Acts 1997, 75th Leg., ch. 34, §1, eff. May 5, 1997. Amended by Acts 2013, 83rd Leg., ch. 392, §1, eff. June 14, 2013. Source: Former Fam. Code §71.03.

ANNOTATIONS

In re Salgado, 53 S.W.3d 752, 763 (Tex.App.—El Paso 2001, no pet.). Family Code ch. 81 "does not define residency of a child applicant for purposes of establishing venue under [Fam. Code] §82.003. In determining the elements of residence, we look for guidance to cases construing residency in various contexts. The Supreme Court has articulated the elements of residency under the general civil venue statute: (1) a fixed place of abode within the possession of the party; (2) occupied or intended to be occupied consistently over a substantial period of time; (3) which is permanent rather than temporary. An element of permanency is necessary before a party can be considered a resident of a particular county."

FAM §82.004. CONTENTS OF APPLICATION

An application must state:

(1) the name and county of residence of each applicant;

(2) the name and county of residence of each individual alleged to have committed family violence;

(3) the relationships between the applicants and the individual alleged to have committed family violence;

(4) a request for one or more protective orders; and

(5) whether an applicant is receiving services from the Title IV-D agency in connection with a child support case and, if known, the agency case number for each open case.

History of Fam. Code §82.004: Acts 1997, 75th Leg., ch. 34, §1, eff. May 5, 1997. Amended by Acts 2001, 77th Leg., ch. 296, §1, eff. Sept. 1, 2001; Acts 2013, 83rd Leg., ch. 742, §3, eff. Sept. 1, 2013. Source: Former Fam. Code §71.05(a).

See also *O'Connor's Texas Family Law Handbook* (2017), "Contents," ch. 6-B, §2.4, p. 725.

FAM §82.005. APPLICATION FILED DURING SUIT FOR DISSOLUTION OF MARRIAGE OR SUIT AFFECTING PARENT-CHILD RELATIONSHIP

A person who wishes to apply for a protective order with respect to the person's spouse and who is a party to a suit for the dissolution of a marriage or a suit affecting the parent-child relationship that is pending in a court must file the application as required by Subchapter D, Chapter 85.

History of Fam. Code §82.005: Acts 1997, 75th Leg., ch. 34, §1, eff. May 5, 1997. Amended by Acts 1997, 75th Leg., ch. 1193, §9, eff. Sept. 1, 1997. Source: Former Fam. Code §71.06.

ANNOTATIONS

Ruiz v. Ruiz, 946 S.W.2d 123, 124 (Tex.App.—El Paso 1997, no writ). Family Code §71.06(a), now §82.005, "requires that protective orders be issued under [Fam. Code] §3.581 [now §6.504] if a divorce is pending. [The] method for seeking review of a protective order entered during pendency of a divorce is mandamus."

FAM §82.006. APPLICATION FILED AFTER DISSOLUTION OF MARRIAGE

If an applicant for a protective order is a former spouse of the individual alleged to have committed family violence, the application must include:

(1) a copy of the decree dissolving the marriage; or

(2) a statement that the decree is unavailable to the applicant and that a copy of the decree will be filed with the court before the hearing on the application.

History of Fam. Code §82.006: Acts 1997, 75th Leg., ch. 34, §1, eff. May 5, 1997. Source: Former Fam. Code §71.05(c).

FAM §82.007. APPLICATION FILED FOR CHILD SUBJECT TO CONTINUING JURISDICTION

An application that requests a protective order for a child who is subject to the continuing exclusive jurisdiction of a court under Title 5 or alleges that a child who is subject to the continuing exclusive jurisdiction of a court under Title 5 has committed family violence must include:

(1) a copy of each court order affecting the conservatorship, support, and possession of or access to the child; or

(2) a statement that the orders affecting the child are unavailable to the applicant and that a copy of the

orders will be filed with the court before the hearing on the application.

History of Fam. Code §82.007: Acts 1997, 75th Leg., ch. 34, §1, eff. May 5, 1997. Source: Former Fam. Code §71.05(d).

FAM §82.008. APPLICATION FILED AFTER EXPIRATION OF FORMER PROTECTIVE ORDER

(a) An application for a protective order that is filed after a previously rendered protective order has expired must include:

(1) a copy of the expired protective order attached to the application or, if a copy of the expired protective order is unavailable, a statement that the order is unavailable to the applicant and that a copy of the order will be filed with the court before the hearing on the application;

(2) a description of either:

(A) the violation of the expired protective order, if the application alleges that the respondent violated the expired protective order by committing an act prohibited by that order before the order expired; or

(B) the threatened harm that reasonably places the applicant in fear of imminent physical harm, bodily injury, assault, or sexual assault; and

(3) if a violation of the expired order is alleged, a statement that the violation of the expired order has not been grounds for any other order protecting the applicant that has been issued or requested under this subtitle.

(b) The procedural requirements for an original application for a protective order apply to a protective order requested under this section.

History of Fam. Code §82.008: Acts 1997, 75th Leg., ch. 34, §1, eff. May 5, 1997. Amended by Acts 1999, 76th Leg., ch. 1160, §1, eff. Sept. 1, 1999. Source: Former Fam. Code §71.05(f), (g).

FAM §82.0085. APPLICATION FILED BEFORE EXPIRATION OF PREVIOUSLY RENDERED PROTECTIVE ORDER

(a) If an application for a protective order alleges that an unexpired protective order applicable to the respondent is due to expire not later than the 30th day after the date the application was filed, the application for the subsequent protective order must include:

(1) a copy of the previously rendered protective order attached to the application or, if a copy of the previously rendered protective order is unavailable, a statement that the order is unavailable to the applicant and that a copy of the order will be filed with the court before the hearing on the application; and

(2) a description of the threatened harm that reasonably places the applicant in fear of imminent physical harm, bodily injury, assault, or sexual assault.

(b) The procedural requirements for an original application for a protective order apply to a protective order requested under this section.

History of Fam. Code §82.0085: Acts 1999, 76th Leg., ch. 1160, §2, eff. Sept. 1, 1999.

ANNOTATIONS

Coffman v. Melton, 448 S.W.3d 68, 71 (Tex.App.—Houston [14th Dist.] 2014, pet. denied). "Because [W] filed her application less than a month before expiration of the original protective order, [Fam.] Code §82.0085 applies to this case[.] *At 72-74:* [H argues] that [W] was barred by the doctrine of res judicata from relying upon evidence of occurrences predating the divorce decree to prove that family violence has occurred and is likely to occur in the future. [¶] [H] posits that having relied on the pre-decree evidence for one protective order, [W] cannot rely on the same evidence in obtaining a second protective order, extending the period of protection for another two years. [¶] [T]he divorce decree in this case contains an express finding that family violence had occurred. The trial court in fact used the finding in denying [H] access to the children. Thus, in pursuing her application for a second protective order, [W] was not attempting to use pre-decree facts to prove something that was not established in the decree, she was using pre-decree facts to prove something that was, in fact, already established in the decree. [¶] An application for a new protective order under ... §82.0085 seeks new and different relief not sought in the original order (i.e., an additional period of protection) and which could not have been sought in the prior proceeding; thus, the application was not barred by res judicata. [Family Code §§82.0085 and 85.001(b)] do not prohibit proof of events occurring before issuance of the prior order."

FAM §82.009. APPLICATION FOR TEMPORARY EX PARTE ORDER

(a) An application that requests the issuance of a temporary ex parte order under Chapter 83 must:

(1) contain a detailed description of the facts and circumstances concerning the alleged family violence and the need for the immediate protective order; and

(2) be signed by each applicant under an oath that the facts and circumstances contained in the application are true to the best knowledge and belief of each applicant.

(b) For purposes of this section, a statement signed under oath by a child is valid if the statement otherwise complies with this chapter.

History of Fam. Code §82.009: Acts 1997, 75th Leg., ch. 34, §1, eff. May 5, 1997. Amended by Acts 2011, 82nd Leg., ch. 632, §3, eff. Sept. 1, 2011. Source: Former Fam. Code §71.05(e).

FAM §82.010. CONFIDENTIALITY OF APPLICATION

(a) This section applies only in a county with a population of 3.4 million or more.

(b) Except as otherwise provided by law, an application for a protective order is confidential, is excepted from required public disclosure under Chapter 552, Government Code, and may not be released to a person who is not a respondent to the application until after the date of service of notice of the application or the date of the hearing on the application, whichever date is sooner.

(c) Except as otherwise provided by law, an application requesting the issuance of a temporary ex parte order under Chapter 83 is confidential, is excepted from required public disclosure under Chapter 552, Government Code, and may not be released to a person who is not a respondent to the application until after the date that the court or law enforcement informs the respondent of the court's order.

History of Fam. Code §82.010: Acts 2003, 78th Leg., ch. 1314, §2, eff. Sept. 1, 2003.

E FAM §82.011. CONFIDENTIALITY OF CERTAIN INFORMATION

On request by an applicant, the court may protect the applicant's mailing address by rendering an order:

(1) requiring the applicant to:

(A) disclose the applicant's mailing address to the court;

(B) designate a person to receive on behalf of the applicant any notice or documents filed with the court related to the application; and

(C) disclose the designated person's mailing address to the court;

(2) requiring the court clerk to:

(A) strike the applicant's mailing address from the public records of the court, if applicable; and

(B) maintain a confidential record of the applicant's mailing address for use only by the court; and

(3) prohibiting the release of the information to the respondent.

History of Fam. Code §82.011: Enacted by S.B. 1242, §1, 85th Leg., eff. Sept. 1, 2017.

Sections 82.012-82.020 reserved for expansion

SUBCHAPTER B. PLEADINGS BY RESPONDENT

FAM §82.021. ANSWER

A respondent to an application for a protective order who is served with notice of an application for a protective order may file an answer at any time before the hearing. A respondent is not required to file an answer to the application.

History of Fam. Code §82.021: Acts 1997, 75th Leg., ch. 34, §1, eff. May 5, 1997. Source: Former Fam. Code §71.08.

FAM §82.022. REQUEST BY RESPONDENT FOR PROTECTIVE ORDER

To apply for a protective order, a respondent to an application for a protective order must file a separate application.

History of Fam. Code §82.022: Acts 1997, 75th Leg., ch. 34, §1, eff. May 5, 1997. Source: Former Fam. Code §71.121(a).

ANNOTATIONS

Cockerham v. Cockerham, 218 S.W.3d 298, 301 (Tex.App.—Texarkana 2007, no pet.). See annotation under Family Code §82.001, p. 347.

Sections 82.023-82.040 reserved for expansion

SUBCHAPTER C. NOTICE OF APPLICATION FOR PROTECTIVE ORDER

A FAM §82.041. CONTENTS OF NOTICE OF APPLICATION

(a) A notice of an application for a protective order must:

(1) be styled "The State of Texas";

(2) be signed by the clerk of the court under the court's seal;

(3) contain the name and location of the court;

(4) show the date the application was filed;

(5) show the date notice of the application for a protective order was issued;

(6) show the date, time, and place of the hearing;

(7) show the file number;

(8) show the name of each applicant and each person alleged to have committed family violence;

(9) be directed to each person alleged to have committed family violence;

(10) show:

(A) the name and address of the attorney for the applicant; or

(B) ~~[the mailing address of the applicant,]~~ if the applicant is not represented by an attorney:

(i) the mailing address of the applicant; or

(ii) if applicable, the name and mailing address of the person designated under Section 82.011; and

(11) contain the address of the clerk of the court.

(b) The notice of an application for a protective order must state: "An application for a protective order has been filed in the court stated in this notice alleging that you have committed family violence. You may employ an attorney to defend you against this allegation. You or your attorney may, but are not required to, file a written answer to the application. Any answer must be filed before the hearing on the application. If you receive this notice within 48 hours before the time set for the hearing, you may request the court to reschedule the hearing not later than 14 days after the date set for the hearing. If you do not attend the hearing, a default judgment may be taken and a protective order may be issued against you."

History of Fam. Code §82.041: Acts 1997, 75th Leg., ch. 34, §1, eff. May 5, 1997. Amended by Acts 1997, 75th Leg., ch. 1193, §10, eff. Sept. 1, 1997; S.B. 1242, §2, 85th Leg., eff. Sept. 1, 2017. Source: Former Fam. Code §71.07(d), (e).

See also *O'Connor's Texas Family Law Handbook* (2017), "Notice," ch. 6-C, §5, p. 742.

FAM §82.042. ISSUANCE OF NOTICE OF APPLICATION

(a) On the filing of an application, the clerk of the court shall issue a notice of an application for a protective order and deliver the notice as directed by the applicant.

(b) On request by the applicant, the clerk of the court shall issue a separate or additional notice of an application for a protective order.

History of Fam. Code §82.042: Acts 1997, 75th Leg., ch. 34, §1, eff. May 5, 1997. Source: Former Fam. Code §71.07(b), (c).

FAM §82.043. SERVICE OF NOTICE OF APPLICATION

(a) Each respondent to an application for a protective order is entitled to service of notice of an application for a protective order.

(b) An applicant for a protective order shall furnish the clerk with a sufficient number of copies of the application for service on each respondent.

(c) Notice of an application for a protective order must be served in the same manner as citation under the Texas Rules of Civil Procedure, except that service by publication is not authorized.

(d) Service of notice of an application for a protective order is not required before the issuance of a temporary ex parte order under Chapter 83.

(e) The requirements of service of notice under this subchapter do not apply if the application is filed as a motion in a suit for dissolution of a marriage. Notice for the motion is given in the same manner as any other motion in a suit for dissolution of a marriage.

History of Fam. Code §82.043: Acts 1997, 75th Leg., ch. 34, §1, eff. May 5, 1997. Source: Former Fam. Code §§71.06(e), 71.07(a), (f)-(h).

CHAPTER 83. TEMPORARY EX PARTE ORDERS

FAM §83.001. REQUIREMENTS FOR TEMPORARY EX PARTE ORDER

(a) If the court finds from the information contained in an application for a protective order that there is a clear and present danger of family violence, the court, without further notice to the individual alleged to have committed family violence and without a hearing, may enter a temporary ex parte order for the protection of the applicant or any other member of the family or household of the applicant.

(b) In a temporary ex parte order, the court may direct a respondent to do or refrain from doing specified acts.

History of Fam. Code §83.001: Acts 1997, 75th Leg., ch. 34, §1, eff. May 5, 1997. Amended by Acts 2001, 77th Leg., ch. 91, §4, eff. Sept. 1, 2001. Source: Former Fam. Code §71.15(a).

See also *O'Connor's Texas Family Law Handbook* (2017), "Temporary Ex Parte Protective Orders," ch. 6-B, p. 721.

FAM §83.002. DURATION OF ORDER; EXTENSION

(a) A temporary ex parte order is valid for the period specified in the order, not to exceed 20 days.

(b) On the request of an applicant or on the court's own motion, a temporary ex parte order may be extended for additional 20-day periods.

History of Fam. Code §83.002: Acts 1997, 75th Leg., ch. 34, §1, eff. May 5, 1997. Source: Former Fam. Code §71.15(b), (c).

ANNOTATIONS

Amir-Sharif v. Hawkins, 246 S.W.3d 267, 269 (Tex. App.—Dallas 2007, pet. dism'd). "The trial court extended the temporary ex parte protective order numerous times pending the outcome of [respondent's] competency evaluation.... *At 271-72:* [Respondent] contends the trial court erred in granting a 60-day extension of the ex parte protective order. [He] claims his civil rights were violated by the trial court granting an extension longer than the permitted 20 days. [¶] The family code provision for 20-day extensions for temporary ex parte protective orders is procedural, not jurisdictional. Thus, the trial court did not lose jurisdiction over [petitioner's] application for protective order by ordering a 60-day extension. [¶] [T]he trial court did not err in granting the 60-day extension."

FAM §83.003. BOND NOT REQUIRED

The court, at the court's discretion, may dispense with the necessity of a bond for a temporary ex parte order.

History of Fam. Code §83.003: Acts 1997, 75th Leg., ch. 34, §1, eff. May 5, 1997. Source: Former Fam. Code §71.15(d).

FAM §83.004. MOTION TO VACATE

Any individual affected by a temporary ex parte order may file a motion at any time to vacate the order. On the filing of the motion to vacate, the court shall set a date for hearing the motion as soon as possible.

History of Fam. Code §83.004: Acts 1997, 75th Leg., ch. 34, §1, eff. May 5, 1997. Amended by Acts 2001, 77th Leg., ch. 91, §5, eff. Sept. 1, 2001. Source: Former Fam. Code §71.15(e).

FAM §83.005. CONFLICTING ORDERS

During the time the order is valid, a temporary ex parte order prevails over any other court order made under Title 5 to the extent of any conflict between the orders.

History of Fam. Code §83.005: Acts 1997, 75th Leg., ch. 34, §1, eff. May 5, 1997. Amended by Acts 1997, 75th Leg., ch. 1193, §11, eff. Sept. 1, 1997. Source: Former Fam. Code §71.15(f).

FAM §83.006. EXCLUSION OF PARTY FROM RESIDENCE

(a) Subject to the limitations of Section 85.021(2), a person may only be excluded from the occupancy of the person's residence by a temporary ex parte order under this chapter if the applicant:

(1) files a sworn affidavit that provides a detailed description of the facts and circumstances requiring the exclusion of the person from the residence; and

(2) appears in person to testify at a temporary ex parte hearing to justify the issuance of the order without notice.

(b) Before the court may render a temporary ex parte order excluding a person from the person's residence, the court must find from the required affidavit and testimony that:

(1) the applicant requesting the excluding order either resides on the premises or has resided there within 30 days before the date the application was filed;

(2) the person to be excluded has within the 30 days before the date the application was filed committed family violence against a member of the household; and

(3) there is a clear and present danger that the person to be excluded is likely to commit family violence against a member of the household.

(c) The court may recess the hearing on a temporary ex parte order to contact the respondent by telephone and provide the respondent the opportunity to be present when the court resumes the hearing. Without regard to whether the respondent is able to be present at the hearing, the court shall resume the hearing before the end of the working day.

History of Fam. Code §83.006: Acts 1997, 75th Leg., ch. 34, §1, eff. May 5, 1997. Amended by Acts 2011, 82nd Leg., ch. 632, §4, eff. Sept. 1, 2011. Source: Former Fam. Code §71.15(g), (h).

FAM §83.007. REPEALED

Repealed by Acts 2011, 82nd Leg., ch. 632, §6(1), eff. Sept. 1, 2011.

CHAPTER 84. HEARING

FAM §84.001. TIME SET FOR HEARING

(a) On the filing of an application for a protective order, the court shall set a date and time for the hearing unless a later date is requested by the applicant. Except as provided by Section 84.002, the court may not set a date later than the 14th day after the date the application is filed.

(b) The court may not delay a hearing on an application in order to consolidate it with a hearing on a subsequently filed application.

History of Fam. Code §84.001: Acts 1997, 75th Leg., ch. 34, §1, eff. May 5, 1997. Source: Former Fam. Code §§71.09(a), 71.121(c).

ANNOTATIONS

Barbee v. Barbee, No. 12-09-00151-CV (Tex.App.—Tyler 2010, no pet.) (memo op.; 10-20-10). "The Family Code does not contain specific consequences for noncompliance with the 14-day limitation [under §84.001]. The purpose of the provision, like similar statutes, appears to be to ensure prompt resolution of the applicant's request. [T]he purpose of the statute would not be served if noncompliance resulted in dismissal for want of jurisdiction. We conclude that the final protective order, even though signed six months after the application was filed, is neither void nor voidable merely because the hearing was not held within 14 days of the date the application was filed."

FAM §84.002. EXTENDED TIME FOR HEARING IN DISTRICT COURT IN CERTAIN COUNTIES

(a) On the request of the prosecuting attorney in a county with a population of more than two million or in a county in a judicial district that is composed of more than one county, the district court shall set the hearing on a date and time not later than 20 days after the date the application is filed or 20 days after the date a request is made to reschedule a hearing under Section 84.003.

(b) The district court shall grant the request of the prosecuting attorney for an extended time in which to hold a hearing on a protective order either on a case-by-case basis or for all cases filed under this subtitle.

History of Fam. Code §84.002: Acts 1997, 75th Leg., ch. 34, §1, eff. May 5, 1997. Amended by Acts 1997, 75th Leg., ch. 1193, §12, eff. Sept. 1, 1997; Acts 2011, 82nd Leg., ch. 1163, §17, eff. Sept. 1, 2011. Source: Former Fam. Code §71.09(d).

FAM §84.003. HEARING RESCHEDULED FOR FAILURE OF SERVICE

(a) If a hearing set under this chapter is not held because of the failure of a respondent to receive service of notice of an application for a protective order, the applicant may request the court to reschedule the hearing.

(b) Except as provided by Section 84.002, the date for a rescheduled hearing shall be not later than 14 days after the date the request is made.

History of Fam. Code §84.003: Acts 1997, 75th Leg., ch. 34, §1, eff. May 5, 1997. Source: Former Fam. Code §71.09(c).

FAM §84.004. HEARING RESCHEDULED FOR INSUFFICIENT NOTICE

(a) If a respondent receives service of notice of an application for a protective order within 48 hours before the time set for the hearing, on request by the respondent, the court shall reschedule the hearing for a date not later than 14 days after the date set for the hearing.

(b) The respondent is not entitled to additional service for a hearing rescheduled under this section.

History of Fam. Code §84.004: Acts 1997, 75th Leg., ch. 34, §1, eff. May 5, 1997. Source: Former Fam. Code §71.09(b).

FAM §84.005. LEGISLATIVE CONTINUANCE

If a proceeding for which a legislative continuance is sought under Section 30.003, Civil Practice and Remedies Code, includes an application for a protective order, the continuance is discretionary with the court.

History of Fam. Code §84.005: Acts 1999, 76th Leg., ch. 62, §6.10(a), eff. Sept. 1, 1999.

FAM §84.006. HEARSAY STATEMENT OF CHILD VICTIM OF FAMILY VIOLENCE

In a hearing on an application for a protective order, a statement made by a child 12 years of age or younger that describes alleged family violence against the child is admissible as evidence in the same manner that a child's statement regarding alleged abuse against the child is admissible under Section 104.006 in a suit affecting the parent-child relationship.

History of Fam. Code §84.006: Acts 2011, 82nd Leg., ch. 59, §1, eff. Sept. 1, 2011.

CHAPTER 85. ISSUANCE OF PROTECTIVE ORDER

SUBCHAPTER A. FINDINGS & ORDERS

FAM §85.001. REQUIRED FINDINGS & ORDERS

(a) At the close of a hearing on an application for a protective order, the court shall find whether:

(1) family violence has occurred; and

(2) family violence is likely to occur in the future.

(b) If the court finds that family violence has occurred and that family violence is likely to occur in the future, the court:

(1) shall render a protective order as provided by Section 85.022 applying only to a person found to have committed family violence; and

(2) may render a protective order as provided by Section 85.021 applying to both parties that is in the best interest of the person protected by the order or member of the family or household of the person protected by the order.

(c) A protective order that requires the first applicant to do or refrain from doing an act under Section 85.022 shall include a finding that the first applicant has committed family violence and is likely to commit family violence in the future.

(d) If the court renders a protective order for a period of more than two years, the court must include in the order a finding described by Section 85.025(a-1).

History of Fam. Code §85.001: Acts 1997, 75th Leg., ch. 34, §1, eff. May 5, 1997. Amended by Acts 2001, 77th Leg., ch. 91, §6, eff. Sept. 1, 2001; Acts 2011, 82nd Leg., ch. 627, §1, eff. Sept. 1, 2011. Source: Former Fam. Code §§71.10(a), (b), 71.121(d).

See also *O'Connor's Texas Family Law Handbook* (2017), "Ruling on Application," ch. 6-C, §9, p. 747.

ANNOTATIONS

Burt v. Francis, ___ S.W.3d ___ (Tex.App.—Eastland 2016, no pet.) (No. 11-14-00244-CV; 8-25-16). See annotation under Family Code §71.004, p. 342.

Roper v. Jolliffe, 493 S.W.3d 624, 638 (Tex.App.—Dallas 2015, pet. denied). Respondent's "due process challenge is that an elevated standard of proof should apply in protective order cases. [Respondent] contends Title 4 proceedings, while classified as civil proceedings, have quasi-criminal overtones and should be based on a clear and convincing standard of proof. … The interests at stake in this case do not equate to cases that require proof by clear and convincing evidence, such as the involuntary termination of parental rights or commitment for mental illness. Because Title 4 proceedings are civil in nature, the traditional standard of proof by a preponderance of the evidence applies."

Coffman v. Melton, 448 S.W.3d 68, 71 (Tex.App.—Houston [14th Dist.] 2014, pet. denied). See annotation under Family Code §82.0085, p. 349.

Boyd v. Palmore, 425 S.W.3d 425, 432 (Tex.App.—Houston [1st Dist.] 2011, no pet.). "The statutory language of [§85.001] does not require that a likelihood finding [of future family violence] be based on more than one act of family violence. [¶] [W]hile … a pattern of family violence is sufficient to support a likelihood finding, … a pattern [is not] a necessary prerequisite to such a finding. *At 432 n.3:* [A]n episode of family violence, coupled with continued harassment, permits an inference that family violence is likely to occur in the future." *See also* ***In re J.A.T.***, No. 13-04-00477-CV (Tex.App.—Corpus Christi 2005, no pet.) (memo op.; 8-18-05) (single act of H pulling child out of W's arms was not sufficient to show likelihood of future family violence).

Teel v. Shifflett, 309 S.W.3d 597, 604 (Tex.App.—Houston [14th Dist.] 2010, pet. denied). "In parental-termination and child-custody cases, 'evidence that a parent has engaged in abusive or neglectful conduct in the past permits an inference that the parent will continue this behavior in the future.' This principle also applies in cases involving protective orders against family violence. 'Oftentimes, past is prologue; therefore, past violent conduct can be competent evidence

which is legally and factually sufficient to sustain the award of a protective order.'"

FAM §85.002. EXCEPTION FOR VIOLATION OF EXPIRED PROTECTIVE ORDER

If the court finds that a respondent violated a protective order by committing an act prohibited by the order as provided by Section 85.022, that the order was in effect at the time of the violation, and that the order has expired after the date that the violation occurred, the court, without the necessity of making the findings described by Section 85.001(a), shall render a protective order as provided by Section 85.022 applying only to the respondent and may render a protective order as provided by Section 85.021.

History of Fam. Code §85.002: Acts 1997, 75th Leg., ch. 34, §1, eff. May 5, 1997. Amended by Acts 1997, 75th Leg., ch. 1193, §13, eff. Sept. 1, 1997. Source: Former Fam. Code §71.10(c).

FAM §85.003. SEPARATE PROTECTIVE ORDERS REQUIRED

(a) A court that renders separate protective orders that apply to both parties and require both parties to do or refrain from doing acts under Section 85.022 shall render two distinct and separate protective orders in two separate documents that reflect the appropriate conditions for each party.

(b) A court that renders protective orders that apply to both parties and require both parties to do or refrain from doing acts under Section 85.022 shall render the protective orders in two separate documents. The court shall provide one of the documents to the applicant and the other document to the respondent.

(c) A court may not render one protective order under Section 85.022 that applies to both parties.

History of Fam. Code §85.003: Acts 1997, 75th Leg., ch. 34, §1, eff. May 5, 1997. Source: Former Fam. Code §71.121(a), (e), (f).

FAM §85.004. PROTECTIVE ORDER IN SUIT FOR DISSOLUTION OF MARRIAGE

A protective order in a suit for dissolution of a marriage must be in a separate document entitled "PROTECTIVE ORDER."

History of Fam. Code §85.004: Acts 1997, 75th Leg., ch. 34, §1, eff. May 5, 1997. Source: Former Fam. Code §71.06(f).

FAM §85.005. AGREED ORDER

(a) To facilitate settlement, the parties to a proceeding may agree in writing to the terms of a protective order as provided by Section 85.021. An agreement under this subsection is subject to the approval of the court.

(b) To facilitate settlement, a respondent may agree in writing to the terms of a protective order as provided by Section 85.022, subject to the approval of the court. The court may not approve an agreement that requires the applicant to do or refrain from doing an act under Section 85.022. The agreed order is enforceable civilly or criminally.

(c) If the court approves an agreement between the parties, the court shall render an agreed protective order that is in the best interest of the applicant, the family or household, or a member of the family or household.

(d) An agreed protective order is not enforceable as a contract.

(e) An agreed protective order expires on the date the court order expires.

History of Fam. Code §85.005: Acts 1997, 75th Leg., ch. 34, §1, eff. May 5, 1997. Amended by Acts 2005, 79th Leg., ch. 541, §1, eff. June 17, 2005. Source: Former Fam. Code §§71.10(d), 71.12(a), (b), (d), (e).

See also *O'Connor's Texas Family Law Handbook* (2017), "Agreed order," ch. 6-C, §9.3, p. 748.

FAM §85.006. DEFAULT ORDER

(a) A court may render a protective order that is binding on a respondent who does not attend a hearing if the respondent received service of the application and notice of the hearing.

(b) If the court reschedules the hearing under Chapter 84, a protective order may be rendered if the respondent does not attend the rescheduled hearing.

History of Fam. Code §85.006: Acts 1997, 75th Leg., ch. 34, §1, eff. May 5, 1997. Source: Former Fam. Code §71.09(e).

A FAM §85.007. CONFIDENTIALITY OF CERTAIN INFORMATION

(a) On request by a person protected by an order or member of the family or household of a person protected by an order, the court may exclude from a protective order the address and telephone number of:

(1) a person protected by the order, in which case the order shall state the county in which the person resides;

(2) the place of employment or business of a person protected by the order; or

(3) the child-care facility or school a child protected by the order attends or in which the child resides.

(b) On granting a request for confidentiality under this section, the court shall order the clerk to:

(1) strike the information described by Subsection (a) from the public records of the court; and

(2) maintain a confidential record of the information for use only by:

(A) the court; or

(B) a law enforcement agency for purposes of entering the information required by Section 411.042(b)(6), Government Code, into the statewide law enforcement information system maintained by the Department of Public Safety.

History of Fam. Code §85.007: Acts 1997, 75th Leg., ch. 34, §1, eff. May 5, 1997. Amended by Acts 2001, 77th Leg., ch. 91, §7, eff. Sept. 1, 2001; S.B. 1242, §3, 85th Leg., eff. Sept. 1, 2017. Source: Former Fam. Code §71.111.

FAM §85.008. REPEALED

Repealed by Acts 1997, 75th Leg., ch. 1193, §24, eff. Sept. 1, 1997.

FAM §85.009. ORDER VALID UNTIL SUPERSEDED

A protective order rendered under this chapter is valid and enforceable pending further action by the court that rendered the order until the order is properly superseded by another court with jurisdiction over the order.

History of Fam. Code §85.009: Acts 1997, 75th Leg., ch. 34, §1, eff. May 5, 1997. Source: Former Fam. Code §71.06(c).

See also ***O'Connor's Texas Family Law Handbook*** (2017), "Effect of Conflicting Orders," ch. 6-C, §11, p. 756.

ANNOTATIONS

Bilyeu v. Bilyeu, 86 S.W.3d 278, 282 (Tex.App.—Austin 2002, no pet.). "We hold that a protective order rendered during the pendency of the parties' divorce is not a final judgment for purposes of appeal. In effect, these orders are interlocutory orders for which the law provides no appeal. We conclude that there is no final judgment due to the ongoing power and ability of the trial court to revise *any* provision in the protective order at *any* time before it expires. ... The trial court's retained power to modify the order at any time casts doubt upon the finality of the order. When it issues a protective order while a divorce between the parties remains pending, the trial court has not *finally* disposed of all the issues and parties before the court."

In re Salgado, 53 S.W.3d 752, 761-62 (Tex.App.—El Paso 2001, no pet.). Family Code §83.005 "expressly provides that a temporary ex parte order—issued without notice or hearing—prevails to the extent of any conflict with an order issued under [Fam. Code] Title 5. [Family Code] Title 4 does not currently contain a similar provision to resolve conflicts between protective orders—issued after notice and hearing—and other existing orders. If, however, a protective order affects a party's right of possession of or access to a child, the court may transfer the protective order to the court of continuing, exclusive jurisdiction if the court finds that the transfer is in the interest of justice or for the safety or convenience of a party or witness. The transfer may be made on the court's own motion or on the motion of a party. Given these provisions, the Legislature obviously anticipated that a protective order may conflict with a valid pre-existing custody order. ... The public policy surrounding all of these provisions is to allow immediate access to a tribunal for the safety and protection of a child. While it does not appear that all of the legislative glitches have been resolved satisfactorily, we decline the invitation ... to impose our own solution by legislating from the bench." *See also* ***Brownlee v. Daniel***, No. 06-11-00136-CV (Tex.App.—Texarkana 2012, no pet.) (memo op.; 7-25-12) (post-decree protective order that contradicted conservatorship requirements in final divorce decree superseded final decree even though court issuing protective order did not have continuing, exclusive jurisdiction).

Sections 85.010-85.020 reserved for expansion

SUBCHAPTER B. CONTENTS OF PROTECTIVE ORDER

FAM §85.021. REQUIREMENTS OF ORDER APPLYING TO ANY PARTY

In a protective order, the court may:

(1) prohibit a party from:

(A) removing a child who is a member of the family or household from:

(i) the possession of a person named in the order; or

(ii) the jurisdiction of the court;

(B) transferring, encumbering, or otherwise disposing of property, other than in the ordinary course of business, that is mutually owned or leased by the parties; or

(C) removing a pet, companion animal, or assistance animal, as defined by Section 121.002, Human Resources Code, from the possession or actual or constructive care of a person named in the order;

(2) grant exclusive possession of a residence to a party and, if appropriate, direct one or more parties to vacate the residence if the residence:

(A) is jointly owned or leased by the party receiving exclusive possession and a party being denied possession;

FAM §85.007

(B) is owned or leased by the party retaining possession; or

(C) is owned or leased by the party being denied possession and that party has an obligation to support the party or a child of the party granted possession of the residence;

(3) provide for the possession of and access to a child of a party if the person receiving possession of or access to the child is a parent of the child;

(4) require the payment of support for a party or for a child of a party if the person required to make the payment has an obligation to support the other party or the child; or

(5) award to a party the use and possession of specified property that is community property or jointly owned or leased property.

History of Fam. Code §85.021: Acts 1997, 75th Leg., ch. 34, §1, eff. May 5, 1997. Amended by Acts 2011, 82nd Leg., ch. 136, §1, eff. Sept. 1, 2011; Acts 2013, 83rd Leg., ch. 543, §1, eff. Sept. 1, 2013. Source: Former Fam. Code §71.11(a)(1)-(4), (6).

See also *O'Connor's Texas Family Law Handbook* (2017), "Relief under §85.021," ch. 6-C, §3.4.11(1)(a), p. 738.

FAM §85.022. REQUIREMENTS OF ORDER APPLYING TO PERSON WHO COMMITTED FAMILY VIOLENCE

(a) In a protective order, the court may order the person found to have committed family violence to perform acts specified by the court that the court determines are necessary or appropriate to prevent or reduce the likelihood of family violence and may order that person to:

(1) complete a battering intervention and prevention program accredited under Article 42.141, Code of Criminal Procedure;

(2) beginning on September 1, 2008, if the referral option under Subdivision (1) is not available, complete a program or counsel with a provider that has begun the accreditation process described by Subsection (a-1); or

(3) if the referral option under Subdivision (1) or, beginning on September 1, 2008, the referral option under Subdivision (2) is not available, counsel with a social worker, family service agency, physician, psychologist, licensed therapist, or licensed professional counselor who has completed family violence intervention training that the community justice assistance division of the Texas Department of Criminal Justice has approved, after consultation with the licensing authorities described by Chapters 152, 501, 502, 503, and 505, Occupations Code, and experts in the field of family violence.

(a-1) Beginning on September 1, 2009, a program or provider serving as a referral option for the courts under Subsection (a)(1) or (2) must be accredited under Section 4A, Article 42.141, Code of Criminal Procedure, as conforming to program guidelines under that article.

(b) In a protective order, the court may prohibit the person found to have committed family violence from:

(1) committing family violence;

(2) communicating:

(A) directly with a person protected by an order or a member of the family or household of a person protected by an order, in a threatening or harassing manner;

(B) a threat through any person to a person protected by an order or a member of the family or household of a person protected by an order; and

(C) if the court finds good cause, in any manner with a person protected by an order or a member of the family or household of a person protected by an order, except through the party's attorney or a person appointed by the court;

(3) going to or near the residence or place of employment or business of a person protected by an order or a member of the family or household of a person protected by an order;

(4) going to or near the residence, child-care facility, or school a child protected under the order normally attends or in which the child normally resides;

(5) engaging in conduct directed specifically toward a person who is a person protected by an order or a member of the family or household of a person protected by an order, including following the person, that is reasonably likely to harass, annoy, alarm, abuse, torment, or embarrass the person;

(6) possessing a firearm, unless the person is a peace officer, as defined by Section 1.07, Penal Code, actively engaged in employment as a sworn, full-time paid employee of a state agency or political subdivision; and

(7) harming, threatening, or interfering with the care, custody, or control of a pet, companion animal, or assistance animal, as defined by Section 121.002, Human Resources Code, that is possessed by or is in the actual or constructive care of a person protected by an order or by a member of the family or household of a person protected by an order.

(c) In an order under Subsection (b)(3) or (4), the court shall specifically describe each prohibited loca-

tion and the minimum distances from the location, if any, that the party must maintain. This subsection does not apply to an order in which Section 85.007 applies.

(d) In a protective order, the court shall suspend a license to carry a handgun issued under Subchapter H, Chapter 411, Government Code, that is held by a person found to have committed family violence.

(e) In this section, "firearm" has the meaning assigned by Section 46.01, Penal Code.

History of Fam. Code §85.022: Acts 1997, 75th Leg., ch. 34, §1, eff. May 5, 1997. Amended by Acts 1997, 75th Leg., ch. 1193, §14, eff. Sept. 1, 1997; Acts 1999, 76th Leg., ch. 1412, §3, eff. Sept. 1, 1999; Acts 2001, 77th Leg., ch. 23, §3 (eff. Sept. 1, 2001), ch. 91, §8 (eff. Sept. 1, 2001); Acts 2007, 80th Leg., ch. 113, §4, eff. Sept. 1, 2007; Acts 2009, 81st Leg., ch. 1146, §11.21, eff. Sept. 1, 2009; Acts 2011, 82nd Leg., ch. 136, §2, eff. Sept. 1, 2011; Acts 2013, 83rd Leg., ch. 543, §2, eff. Sept. 1, 2013; Acts 2015, 84th Leg., ch. 437, §12, eff. Jan. 1, 2016. Source: Former Fam. Code §71.11(a)(5), (7), (b), (c).

See also *O'Connor's Texas Family Law Handbook* (2017), "Relief under §85.022," ch. 6-C, §3.4.11(1)(b), p. 739.

FAM §85.023. EFFECT ON PROPERTY RIGHTS

A protective order or an agreement approved by the court under this subtitle does not affect the title to real property.

History of Fam. Code §85.023: Acts 1997, 75th Leg., ch. 34, §1, eff. May 5, 1997. Source: Former Fam. Code §71.11(d).

FAM §85.024. ENFORCEMENT OF COUNSELING REQUIREMENT

(a) A person found to have engaged in family violence who is ordered to attend a program or counseling under Section 85.022(a)(1), (2), or (3) shall file with the court an affidavit before the 60th day after the date the order was rendered stating either that the person has begun the program or counseling or that a program or counseling is not available within a reasonable distance from the person's residence. A person who files an affidavit that the person has begun the program or counseling shall file with the court before the date the protective order expires a statement that the person completed the program or counseling not later than the 30th day before the expiration date of the protective order or the 30th day before the first anniversary of the date the protective order was issued, whichever date is earlier. An affidavit under this subsection must be accompanied by a letter, notice, or certificate from the program or counselor that verifies the person's completion of the program or counseling. A person who fails to comply with this subsection may be punished for contempt of court under Section 21.002, Government Code.

(b) A protective order under Section 85.022 must specifically advise the person subject to the order of the requirement of this section and the possible punishment if the person fails to comply with the requirement.

History of Fam. Code §85.024: Acts 1997, 75th Leg., ch. 34, §1, eff. May 5, 1997. Amended by Acts 1997, 75th Leg., ch. 1193, §15, eff. Sept. 1, 1997; Acts 2007, 80th Leg., ch. 113, §5 (eff. Sept. 1, 2007), ch. 770, §1 (eff. Sept. 1, 2007). Source: Former Fam. Code §71.11(i).

A FAM §85.025. DURATION OF PROTECTIVE ORDER

(a) Except as otherwise provided by this section, an order under this subtitle is effective:

(1) for the period stated in the order, not to exceed two years; or

(2) if a period is not stated in the order, until the second anniversary of the date the order was issued.

The amended text in subsection (a-1) is effective for applications for a protective order filed on or after Sept. 1, 2017. Applications filed before Sept. 1, 2017, are governed by the former law in effect at that time.

(a-1) The court may render a protective order sufficient to protect the applicant and members of the applicant's family or household that is effective for a period that exceeds two years if the court finds that the person who is the subject of the protective order:

(1) committed an act constituting a felony offense involving family violence against the applicant or a member of the applicant's family or household, regardless of whether the person has been charged with or convicted of the offense;

(2) caused serious bodily injury to the applicant or a member of the applicant's family or household; or

(3) [~~(2)~~] was the subject of two or more previous protective orders rendered:

(A) to protect the person on whose behalf the current protective order is sought; and

(B) after a finding by the court that the subject of the protective order:

(i) has committed family violence; and

(ii) is likely to commit family violence in the future.

The amended text in subsection (b) and the enacted text in subsections (b-1) through (b-3) are effective for protective orders issued on or after Sept. 1, 2017. Protective orders issued before Sept. 1, 2017, are governed by the former law in effect at that time.

(b) A person who is the subject of a protective order may file a motion not earlier than the first anniver-

FAM §85.022

sary of the date on which the order was rendered requesting that the court review the protective order and determine whether there is a continuing need for the order.

(b-1) Following the filing of a motion under Subsection (b), a [A] person who is the subject of a protective order issued under Subsection (a-1) that is effective for a period that exceeds two years may file not more than one [a] subsequent motion requesting that the court review the protective order and determine whether there is a continuing need for the order. The subsequent motion may not be filed earlier than the first anniversary of the date on which the court rendered an order on the [a] previous motion by the person [~~under this subsection~~].

(b-2) After a hearing on a [~~the~~] motion under Subsection (b) or (b-1), if the court does not make a finding that there is no continuing need for the protective order, the protective order remains in effect until the date the order expires under this section. Evidence of the movant's compliance with the protective order does not by itself support a finding by the court that there is no continuing need for the protective order. If the court finds there is no continuing need for the protective order, the court shall order that the protective order expires on a date set by the court.

(b-3) Subsection (b) does not apply to a protective order issued under Chapter 7A, Code of Criminal Procedure.

(c) If a person who is the subject of a protective order is confined or imprisoned on the date the protective order would expire under Subsection (a) or (a-1), or if the protective order would expire not later than the first anniversary of the date the person is released from confinement or imprisonment, the period for which the order is effective is extended, and the order expires on:

(1) the first anniversary of the date the person is released from confinement or imprisonment, if the person was sentenced to confinement or imprisonment for more than five years; or

(2) the second anniversary of the date the person is released from confinement or imprisonment, if the person was sentenced to confinement or imprisonment for five years or less.

History of Fam. Code §85.025: Acts 1997, 75th Leg., ch. 34, §1, eff. May 5, 1997. Amended by Acts 1999, 76th Leg., ch. 1160, §3, eff. Sept. 1, 1999; Acts 2011, 82nd Leg., ch. 627, §2, eff. Sept. 1, 2011; Acts 2015, 84th Leg., ch. 336, §1, eff. June 9, 2015; S.B. 257, §1, 85th Leg., eff. Sept. 1, 2017; S.B. 712, §1, 85th Leg., eff. Sept. 1, 2017. Source: Former Fam. Code §71.13.

FAM §85.026. WARNING ON PROTECTIVE ORDER

(a) Each protective order issued under this subtitle, including a temporary ex parte order, must contain the following prominently displayed statements in boldfaced type, capital letters, or underlined:

"A PERSON WHO VIOLATES THIS ORDER MAY BE PUNISHED FOR CONTEMPT OF COURT BY A FINE OF AS MUCH AS $500 OR BY CONFINEMENT IN JAIL FOR AS LONG AS SIX MONTHS, OR BOTH."

"NO PERSON, INCLUDING A PERSON WHO IS PROTECTED BY THIS ORDER, MAY GIVE PERMISSION TO ANYONE TO IGNORE OR VIOLATE ANY PROVISION OF THIS ORDER. DURING THE TIME IN WHICH THIS ORDER IS VALID, EVERY PROVISION OF THIS ORDER IS IN FULL FORCE AND EFFECT UNLESS A COURT CHANGES THE ORDER."

"IT IS UNLAWFUL FOR ANY PERSON, OTHER THAN A PEACE OFFICER, AS DEFINED BY SECTION 1.07, PENAL CODE, ACTIVELY ENGAGED IN EMPLOYMENT AS A SWORN, FULL-TIME PAID EMPLOYEE OF A STATE AGENCY OR POLITICAL SUBDIVISION, WHO IS SUBJECT TO A PROTECTIVE ORDER TO POSSESS A FIREARM OR AMMUNITION."

"A VIOLATION OF THIS ORDER BY COMMISSION OF AN ACT PROHIBITED BY THE ORDER MAY BE PUNISHABLE BY A FINE OF AS MUCH AS $4,000 OR BY CONFINEMENT IN JAIL FOR AS LONG AS ONE YEAR, OR BOTH. AN ACT THAT RESULTS IN FAMILY VIOLENCE MAY BE PROSECUTED AS A SEPARATE MISDEMEANOR OR FELONY OFFENSE. IF THE ACT IS PROSECUTED AS A SEPARATE FELONY OFFENSE, IT IS PUNISHABLE BY CONFINEMENT IN PRISON FOR AT LEAST TWO YEARS."

(b) Repealed by Acts 2011, 82nd Leg., ch. 632, §6(2), eff. Sept. 1, 2011.

Subsection (c) was amended by Acts 1999, 76th Leg., ch. 178, §3, enacted May 6, 1999, effective Aug. 30, 1999, without reference to the conflicting deletion made by Acts 1999, 76th Leg., ch. 1160, §4, enacted May 30, 1999, effective Sept. 1, 1999. For harmonizing conflicts, see p. V.

(c) Each protective order issued under this subtitle, including a temporary ex parte order, must contain the following prominently displayed statement in boldfaced type, capital letters, or underlined:

"NO PERSON, INCLUDING A PERSON WHO IS PROTECTED BY THIS ORDER, MAY GIVE PERMISSION

TO ANYONE TO IGNORE OR VIOLATE ANY PROVISION OF THIS ORDER. DURING THE TIME IN WHICH THIS ORDER IS VALID, EVERY PROVISION OF THIS ORDER IS IN FULL FORCE AND EFFECT UNLESS A COURT CHANGES THE ORDER."

History of Fam. Code §85.026: Acts 1997, 75th Leg., ch. 34, §1, eff. May 5, 1997. Amended by Acts 1999, 76th Leg., ch. 178, §3 (eff. Aug. 30, 1999), ch. 1160, §4 (eff. Sept. 1, 1999); Acts 2001, 77th Leg., ch. 23, §5, eff. Sept. 1, 2001; Acts 2011, 82nd Leg., ch. 632, §§5, 6(2), eff. Sept. 1, 2011. Source: Former Fam. Code §71.16.

Sections 85.027-85.040 reserved for expansion

SUBCHAPTER C. DELIVERY OF PROTECTIVE ORDER

FAM §85.041. DELIVERY TO RESPONDENT

(a) A protective order rendered under this subtitle shall be:

(1) delivered to the respondent as provided by Rule 21a, Texas Rules of Civil Procedure;

(2) served in the same manner as a writ of injunction; or

(3) served in open court at the close of the hearing as provided by this section.

(b) The court shall serve an order in open court to a respondent who is present at the hearing by giving to the respondent a copy of the order, reduced to writing and signed by the judge or master. A certified copy of the signed order shall be given to the applicant at the time the order is given to the respondent. If the applicant is not in court at the conclusion of the hearing, the clerk of the court shall mail a certified copy of the order to the applicant not later than the third business day after the date the hearing is concluded.

(c) If the order has not been reduced to writing, the court shall give notice orally to a respondent who is present at the hearing of the part of the order that contains prohibitions under Section 85.022 or any other part of the order that contains provisions necessary to prevent further family violence. The clerk of the court shall mail a copy of the order to the respondent and a certified copy of the order to the applicant not later than the third business day after the date the hearing is concluded.

(d) If the respondent is not present at the hearing and the order has been reduced to writing at the conclusion of the hearing, the clerk of the court shall immediately provide a certified copy of the order to the applicant and mail a copy of the order to the respondent not later than the third business day after the date the hearing is concluded.

History of Fam. Code §85.041: Acts 1997, 75th Leg., ch. 34, §1, eff. May 5, 1997. Source: Former Fam. Code §71.17(a)-(d).

ANNOTATIONS

Harvey v. State, 78 S.W.3d 368, 372-73 (Tex.Crim. App.2002). "[P]roof that an act was 'in violation of an order issued under [Fam. Code] §6.504 or ch. 85 [or] under [CCP] art. 17.292 ...,' as [Pen.] Code [§]25.07(a) requires, must be proof of either an order that was issued after service of a copy of the application and notice under the Family Code, or an order that was issued by a magistrate who warned the defendant of his rights after arrest and a copy of which was given the defendant in open court. [¶] [T]he Court of Appeals went too far in requiring that the appellant 'knew its provisions.' We think the State is right, for we find no such requirement in the procedures for protective orders. The requirements are only that the respondent be given the resources to learn the provisions; that is, that he be given a copy of the order, or notice that an order has been applied for and that a hearing will be held to decide whether it will be issued. The order is nonetheless binding on the respondent who chooses not to read the order, or who chooses not to read the notice and the application and not to attend the hearing."

FAM §85.042. DELIVERY OF ORDER TO OTHER PERSONS

(a) Not later than the next business day after the date the court issues an original or modified protective order under this subtitle, the clerk of the court shall send a copy of the order, along with the information provided by the applicant or the applicant's attorney that is required under Section 411.042(b)(6), Government Code, to:

(1) the chief of police of the municipality in which the person protected by the order resides, if the person resides in a municipality;

(2) the appropriate constable and the sheriff of the county in which the person resides, if the person does not reside in a municipality; and

(3) the Title IV-D agency, if the application for the protective order indicates that the applicant is receiving services from the Title IV-D agency.

(a-1) This subsection applies only if the respondent, at the time of issuance of an original or modified protective order under this subtitle, is a member of the

state military forces or is serving in the armed forces of the United States in an active-duty status and the applicant or the applicant's attorney provides to the clerk of the court the mailing address of the staff judge advocate or provost marshal, as applicable. In addition to complying with Subsection (a), the clerk of the court shall also provide a copy of the protective order and the information described by that subsection to the staff judge advocate at Joint Force Headquarters or the provost marshal of the military installation to which the respondent is assigned with the intent that the commanding officer will be notified, as applicable.

(b) If a protective order made under this chapter prohibits a respondent from going to or near a child-care facility or school, the clerk of the court shall send a copy of the order to the child-care facility or school.

(c) The clerk of a court that vacates an original or modified protective order under this subtitle shall notify each individual or entity who received a copy of the original or modified order from the clerk under this section that the order is vacated.

(d) The applicant or the applicant's attorney shall provide to the clerk of the court:

(1) the name and address of each law enforcement agency, child-care facility, school, and other individual or entity to which the clerk is required to send a copy of the order under this section; and

(2) any other information required under Section 411.042(b)(6), Government Code.

(e) The clerk of the court issuing an original or modified protective order under Section 85.022 that suspends a license to carry a handgun shall send a copy of the order to the appropriate division of the Department of Public Safety at its Austin headquarters. On receipt of the order suspending the license, the department shall:

(1) record the suspension of the license in the records of the department;

(2) report the suspension to local law enforcement agencies, as appropriate; and

(3) demand surrender of the suspended license from the license holder.

(f) A clerk of the court may transmit the order and any related information electronically or in another manner that can be accessed by the recipient.

(g) A clerk of the court may delay sending a copy of the order under Subsection (a) only if the clerk lacks information necessary to ensure service and enforcement.

(h) In this section, "business day" means a day other than a Saturday, Sunday, or state or national holiday.

History of Fam. Code §85.042: Acts 1997, 75th Leg., ch. 34, §1, eff. May 5, 1997. Amended by Acts 1997, 75th Leg., ch. 614, §3, eff. Sept. 1, 1997; Acts 1999, 76th Leg., ch. 1412, §4, eff. Sept. 1, 1999; Acts 2001, 77th Leg., ch. 35, §1 (eff. Sept. 1, 2001), ch. 91, §9 (eff. Sept. 1, 2001); Acts 2011, 82nd Leg., ch. 327, §1, eff. Sept. 1, 2011; Acts 2013, 83rd Leg., ch. 742, §4 (eff. Sept. 1, 2013), ch. 1276, §3 (eff. Sept. 1, 2013); Acts 2015, 84th Leg., ch. 243, §3 (eff. Sept. 1, 2015), ch. 437, §13 (eff. Jan. 1, 2016). Source: Former Fam. Code §71.17(e)-(g).

See also 37 T.A.C. §§27.71-27.76; ***O'Connor's Texas Family Law Handbook*** (2017), "Who is served," ch. 6-C, §10.2, p. 755.

Sections 85.043-85.060 blank

SUBCHAPTER D. RELATIONSHIP BETWEEN PROTECTIVE ORDER & SUIT FOR DISSOLUTION OF MARRIAGE & SUIT AFFECTING PARENT-CHILD RELATIONSHIP

FAM §85.061. DISMISSAL OF APPLICATION PROHIBITED; SUBSEQUENTLY FILED SUIT FOR DISSOLUTION OF MARRIAGE OR SUIT AFFECTING PARENT-CHILD RELATIONSHIP

If an application for a protective order is pending, a court may not dismiss the application or delay a hearing on the application on the grounds that a suit for dissolution of marriage or suit affecting the parent-child relationship is filed after the date the application was filed.

History of Fam. Code §85.061: Acts 1997, 75th Leg., ch. 1193, §16, eff. Sept. 1, 1997.

FAM §85.062. APPLICATION FILED WHILE SUIT FOR DISSOLUTION OF MARRIAGE OR SUIT AFFECTING PARENT-CHILD RELATIONSHIP PENDING

(a) If a suit for dissolution of a marriage or suit affecting the parent-child relationship is pending, a party to the suit may apply for a protective order against another party to the suit by filing an application:

(1) in the court in which the suit is pending; or

(2) in a court in the county in which the applicant resides if the applicant resides outside the jurisdiction of the court in which the suit is pending.

(b) An applicant subject to this section shall inform the clerk of the court that renders a protective order

that a suit for dissolution of a marriage or a suit affecting the parent-child relationship is pending in which the applicant is party.

(c) If a final protective order is rendered by a court other than the court in which a suit for dissolution of a marriage or a suit affecting the parent-child relationship is pending, the clerk of the court that rendered the protective order shall:

(1) inform the clerk of the court in which the suit is pending that a final protective order has been rendered; and

(2) forward a copy of the final protective order to the court in which the suit is pending.

(d) A protective order rendered by a court in which an application is filed under Subsection (a)(2) is subject to transfer under Section 85.064.

History of Fam. Code §85.062: Acts 1997, 75th Leg., ch. 1193, §16, eff. Sept. 1, 1997.

FAM §85.063. APPLICATION FILED AFTER FINAL ORDER RENDERED IN SUIT FOR DISSOLUTION OF MARRIAGE OR SUIT AFFECTING PARENT-CHILD RELATIONSHIP

(a) If a final order has been rendered in a suit for dissolution of marriage or suit affecting the parent-child relationship, an application for a protective order by a party to the suit against another party to the suit filed after the date the final order was rendered, and that is:

(1) filed in the county in which the final order was rendered, shall be filed in the court that rendered the final order; and

(2) filed in another county, shall be filed in a court having jurisdiction to render a protective order under this subtitle.

(b) A protective order rendered by a court in which an application is filed under Subsection (a)(2) is subject to transfer under Section 85.064.

History of Fam. Code §85.063: Acts 1997, 75th Leg., ch. 1193, §16, eff. Sept. 1, 1997.

ANNOTATIONS

Cooke v. Cooke, 65 S.W.3d 785, 790 (Tex.App.—Dallas 2001, no pet.). Section 85.063 "requires that all applications for protective orders involving parties to a prior divorce action must be filed in the court that rendered the final divorce decree. The plain language of the statute requires the application to be *filed* in the same court as the prior proceeding. However, the statute does not prohibit the transfer or reassignment of the case. The statute also does not require the protective order to actually be heard and ruled upon by the original divorce court."

FAM §85.064. TRANSFER OF PROTECTIVE ORDER

(a) If a protective order was rendered before the filing of a suit for dissolution of marriage or suit affecting the parent-child relationship or while the suit is pending as provided by Section 85.062, the court that rendered the order may, on the motion of a party or on the court's own motion, transfer the protective order to the court having jurisdiction of the suit if the court makes the finding prescribed by Subsection (c).

(b) If a protective order that affects a party's right to possession of or access to a child is rendered after the date a final order was rendered in a suit affecting the parent-child relationship, on the motion of a party or on the court's own motion, the court may transfer the protective order to the court of continuing, exclusive jurisdiction if the court makes the finding prescribed by Subsection (c).

(c) A court may transfer a protective order under this section if the court finds that the transfer is:

(1) in the interest of justice; or

(2) for the safety or convenience of a party or a witness.

(d) The transfer of a protective order under this section shall be conducted according to the procedures provided by Section 155.207.

(e) Except as provided by Section 81.002, the fees or costs associated with the transfer of a protective order shall be paid by the movant.

History of Fam. Code §85.064: Acts 1997, 75th Leg., ch. 1193, §16, eff. Sept. 1, 1997.

See also ***O'Connor's Texas Family Law Handbook*** (2017), "Motion to Transfer," ch. 6-C, §12, p. 756.

FAM §85.065. EFFECT OF TRANSFER

(a), (b) Repealed by Acts 2011, 82nd Leg., ch. 632, §6(3), eff. Sept. 1, 2011.

(c) A protective order that is transferred is subject to modification by the court that receives the order to the same extent modification is permitted under Chapter 87 by a court that rendered the order.

History of Fam. Code §85.065: Acts 1997, 75th Leg., ch. 1193, §16, eff. Sept. 1, 1997. Amended by Acts 2011, 82nd Leg., ch. 632, §6(3), eff. Sept. 1, 2011.

CHAPTER 86. LAW ENFORCEMENT DUTIES RELATING TO PROTECTIVE ORDERS

FAM §86.001. ADOPTION OF PROCEDURES BY LAW ENFORCEMENT AGENCY

(a) To ensure that law enforcement officers responding to calls are aware of the existence and terms of protective orders issued under this subtitle, each law enforcement agency shall establish procedures in the agency to provide adequate information or access to information for law enforcement officers of the names of each person protected by an order issued under this subtitle and of each person against whom protective orders are directed.

(b) A law enforcement agency may enter a protective order in the agency's computer records of outstanding warrants as notice that the order has been issued and is currently in effect. On receipt of notification by a clerk of court that the court has vacated or dismissed an order, the law enforcement agency shall remove the order from the agency's computer record of outstanding warrants.

History of Fam. Code §86.001: Acts 1997, 75th Leg., ch. 34, §1, eff. May 5, 1997. Source: Former Fam. Code §71.18(a), (b).

FAM §86.0011. DUTY TO ENTER INFORMATION INTO STATEWIDE LAW ENFORCEMENT INFORMATION SYSTEM

(a) On receipt of an original or modified protective order from the clerk of the issuing court, a law enforcement agency shall immediately, but not later than the third business day after the date the order is received, enter the information required by Section 411.042(b)(6), Government Code, into the statewide law enforcement information system maintained by the Department of Public Safety.

(b) In this section, "business day" means a day other than a Saturday, Sunday, or state or national holiday.

History of Fam. Code §86.0011: Acts 2001, 77th Leg., ch. 35, §2, eff. Sept. 1, 2001. Amended by Acts 2015, 84th Leg., ch. 243, §4, eff. Sept. 1, 2015.

See also *O'Connor's Texas Family Law Handbook* (2017), "Entering orders into statewide system," ch. 6-E, §4.1, p. 773.

FAM §86.002. DUTY TO PROVIDE INFORMATION TO FIREARMS DEALERS

(a) On receipt of a request for a law enforcement information system record check of a prospective transferee by a licensed firearms dealer under the Brady Handgun Violence Prevention Act, 18 U.S.C. Section 922, the chief law enforcement officer shall determine whether the Department of Public Safety has in the department's law enforcement information system a record indicating the existence of an active protective order directed to the prospective transferee.

(b) If the department's law enforcement information system indicates the existence of an active protective order directed to the prospective transferee, the chief law enforcement officer shall immediately advise the dealer that the transfer is prohibited.

History of Fam. Code §86.002: Acts 1997, 75th Leg., ch. 34, §1, eff. May 5, 1997. Source: Former Fam. Code §71.18(c).

See also *O'Connor's Texas Family Law Handbook* (2017), "Providing information to firearm dealers," ch. 6-E, §4.2, p. 773.

FAM §86.003. COURT ORDER FOR LAW ENFORCEMENT ASSISTANCE UNDER TEMPORARY ORDER

On request by an applicant obtaining a temporary ex parte protective order that excludes the respondent from the respondent's residence, the court granting the temporary order shall render a written order to the sheriff, constable, or chief of police to provide a law enforcement officer from the department of the chief of police, constable, or sheriff to:

(1) accompany the applicant to the residence covered by the order;

(2) inform the respondent that the court has ordered that the respondent be excluded from the residence;

(3) protect the applicant while the applicant takes possession of the residence; and

(4) protect the applicant if the respondent refuses to vacate the residence while the applicant takes possession of the applicant's necessary personal property.

History of Fam. Code §86.003: Acts 1997, 75th Leg., ch. 34, §1, eff. May 5, 1997. Amended by Acts 1997, 75th Leg., ch. 852, §1, eff. June 18, 1997. Source: Former Fam. Code §71.18(c).

See also *O'Connor's Texas Family Law Handbook* (2017), "Removing respondent from residence," ch. 6-E, §4.3, p. 773.

FAM §86.004. COURT ORDER FOR LAW ENFORCEMENT ASSISTANCE UNDER FINAL ORDER

On request by an applicant obtaining a final protective order that excludes the respondent from the respondent's residence, the court granting the final order shall render a written order to the sheriff, constable, or chief of police to provide a law enforcement officer from the department of the chief of police, constable, or sheriff to:

(1) accompany the applicant to the residence covered by the order;

(2) inform the respondent that the court has ordered that the respondent be excluded from the residence;

(3) protect the applicant while the applicant takes possession of the residence and the respondent takes possession of the respondent's necessary personal property; and

(4) if the respondent refuses to vacate the residence:

(A) remove the respondent from the residence; and

(B) arrest the respondent for violating the court order.

History of Fam. Code §86.004: Acts 1997, 75th Leg., ch. 34, §1, eff. May 5, 1997. Amended by Acts 1997, 75th Leg., ch. 852, §2, eff. June 18, 1997. Source: Former Fam. Code §71.18(d).

See also *O'Connor's Texas Family Law Handbook* (2017), "Removing respondent from residence," ch. 6-E, §4.3, p. 773.

FAM §86.005. PROTECTIVE ORDER FROM ANOTHER JURISDICTION

To ensure that law enforcement officers responding to calls are aware of the existence and terms of a protective order from another jurisdiction, each law enforcement agency shall establish procedures in the agency to provide adequate information or access to information for law enforcement officers regarding the name of each person protected by an order rendered in another jurisdiction and of each person against whom the protective order is directed.

History of Fam. Code §86.005: Acts 1997, 75th Leg., ch. 1193, §17, eff. Sept. 1, 1997. Amended by Acts 2001, 77th Leg., ch. 48, §1, eff. Sept. 1, 2001.

CHAPTER 87. MODIFICATION OF PROTECTIVE ORDERS

FAM §87.001. MODIFICATION OF PROTECTIVE ORDER

On the motion of any party, the court, after notice and hearing, may modify an existing protective order to:

(1) exclude any item included in the order; or

(2) include any item that could have been included in the order.

History of Fam. Code §87.001: Acts 1997, 75th Leg., ch. 34, §1, eff. May 5, 1997. Source: Former Fam. Code §71.14(a).

See also *O'Connor's Texas Family Law Handbook* (2017), "Motion to Modify," ch. 6-C, §13, p. 757.

ANNOTATIONS

Culver v. Culver, 360 S.W.3d 526, 539 (Tex.App.—Texarkana 2011, no pet.). "Although this Court has held the judgments [in this case] are 'modified' judgments, this Court has not held they were modifications within the meaning of, and subject to the provisions of, [Fam. Code] Ch. 87.... We believe that a trial court may modify a protective order over which it still has plenary power in the same manner as any other judgment. If the trial court's plenary jurisdiction had expired, Ch. 87 might apply depending on the circumstances. Because the trial court's plenary jurisdiction had not expired, the trial court could modify the judgment without complying with [Fam. Code] §87.003. The judgment ... was not a modification of an existing protective order within the meaning of Ch. 87—it did not include new substantive changes based on new evidence of changed conditions—rather, it was a modification of the protective order within the plenary power of the trial court, based on the original evidence and hearing—an important distinction."

FAM §87.002. MODIFICATION MAY NOT EXTEND DURATION OF ORDER

A protective order may not be modified to extend the period of the order's validity beyond the second anniversary of the date the original order was rendered or beyond the date the order expires under Section 85.025(a-1) or (c), whichever date occurs later.

History of Fam. Code §87.002: Acts 1997, 75th Leg., ch. 34, §1, eff. May 5, 1997. Amended by Acts 1999, 76th Leg., ch. 1160, §5, eff. Sept. 1, 1999; Acts 2011, 82nd Leg., ch. 627, §3, eff. Sept. 1, 2011. Source: Former Fam. Code §71.14(b).

FAM §87.003. NOTIFICATION OF MOTION TO MODIFY

Notice of a motion to modify a protective order is sufficient if delivery of the motion is attempted on the respondent at the respondent's last known address by

registered or certified mail as provided by Rule 21a, Texas Rules of Civil Procedure.

History of Fam. Code §87.003: Acts 1997, 75th Leg., ch. 34, §1, eff. May 5, 1997. Source: Former Fam. Code §71.14(c).

FAM §87.004. CHANGE OF ADDRESS OR TELEPHONE NUMBER

(a) If a protective order contains the address or telephone number of a person protected by the order, of the place of employment or business of the person, or of the child-care facility or school of a child protected by the order and that information is not confidential under Section 85.007, the person protected by the order may file a notification of change of address or telephone number with the court that rendered the order to modify the information contained in the order.

(b) The clerk of the court shall attach the notification of change to the protective order and shall deliver a copy of the notification to the respondent by registered or certified mail as provided by Rule 21a, Texas Rules of Civil Procedure.

(c) The filing of a notification of change of address or telephone number and the attachment of the notification to a protective order does not affect the validity of the order.

History of Fam. Code §87.004: Acts 1997, 75th Leg., ch. 1193, §18, eff. Sept. 1, 1997.

CHAPTER 88. UNIFORM INTERSTATE ENFORCEMENT OF PROTECTIVE ORDERS ACT

NCCUSL Prefatory Comment*

I. Introduction

The Uniform Interstate Enforcement of Domestic-Violence Protection Orders Act ("the Act") provides a uniform mechanism for the interstate enforcement of domestic-violence protective orders. The need for such a mechanism is founded on the widespread understanding that States have not consistently or effectively enforced domestic-violence protection orders issued by other States. The Act, therefore, has two main purposes. First, it defines the meaning of interstate enforcement in the context of the enforcement of domestic-violence protection orders. Second, it establishes uniform procedures for the effective interstate enforcement of domestic-violence protection orders.

Many States, recognizing the severity of the problems regarding the interstate enforcement of domestic-violence protection orders, have enacted legislation requiring their courts to enforce the domestic-violence protection orders of other States. Many of these statutes, however, while mandating enforcement, are either silent or ambiguous regarding several important questions that must be answered in order to establish an effective system for the interstate enforcement of these orders. The Congress of the United States, as well, has enacted legislation requiring interstate enforcement of domestic-violence protection orders, but this legislation is also silent or ambiguous regarding these important questions.

First, many of the existing statutes do not sufficiently explain the core requirements of interstate enforcement of protection orders. For example, many of the state statutes, and the federal legislation, require courts and law enforcement officers to enforce the orders of other States as if they were the protection orders of the enforcing State. This provision, however, does not answer the question of whether state courts and officers are required to enforce provisions of foreign protection orders that would not be authorized by the law of the enforcing State. This question, and others, must be answered if there is to be effective uniform enforcement of protection orders. Second, many of the existing statutes do not specify the procedures state courts and officers must follow in enforcing foreign protection orders. For example, many of the statutes are silent on whether individuals seeking the enforcement of a protection order must register or file the order with the enforcing State before action can be taken on their behalf. This Act resolves the issues left unanswered in existing legislation and provides a uniform scheme for enforcement of these orders.

II. The Requirements of Interstate Enforcement

The Act first defines what it means to accord interstate enforcement to domestic-violence protection orders. These orders must be enforced if the issuing tribunals had jurisdiction over both the parties and the matter under the law of the issuing State and if the individuals against whom the order is enforced were given reasonable notice and had an opportunity to be heard consistent with the right to due process. If the order was obtained ex parte, this notice and opportunity to be heard must be provided within a reasonable time.

The Act makes it clear that all the terms of the orders of the issuing States must be enforced, including terms that provide relief that the courts of the enforcing State would lack power to provide. The Act also provides that all protection orders that both recognize the standing of the protected individual to seek enforcement of the order and satisfy the criteria of validity established by the Act must be enforced. In addition, provisions of protection orders governing custody and visitation matters are enforceable under this Act. Terms that concern support are not.[1] The terms of mutual protection orders which favor of a respondent are also not enforceable if they were not issued in response to a written pleading filed by the respondent and if the issuing tribunal did not make specific findings in favor of the respondent.

III. Enforcement Procedures

The Act also provides uniform procedures for the interstate enforcement of domestic-violence protection orders. The Act envisions that the enforcement of foreign protection orders will require law enforcement officers of enforcing States to rely on probable cause judgments that a valid order exists and has been violated. The Act, however, provides that if a protected individual can provide direct proof of the existence of a facially valid order, by, for example, presenting a paper copy or through an electronic registry, probable cause is conclusively established. If no such proof is forthcoming, the Act provides that if officers, relying on the totality of the circumstances, determine that there is probable cause to believe that a valid protection order exists and has been violated, the order will be enforced. The individual against whom the order is enforced will have sufficient opportunity to demonstrate that the order is invalid when the case is brought before the enforcing tribunal. Law enforcement officers, as well as other government agents, will be encouraged to rely on probable cause judgments by the Act's inclusion of an immunity provision, protecting agents of the government acting in good faith.

The Act does not require individuals seeking the enforcement of a protection order to register or file the order with the enforcing State. The Act does, however, include an optional registration process. This process permits individuals to register a protection order by presenting a copy of the order to a responsible state agency or any state officer or agency. The copy presented must

* **Editor's note:**

The NCCUSL comments have been edited to reflect the Texas Legislature's omission of sections, changing of text, and changing of section numbers from the original uniform act. The Texas Legislature did not adopt the NCCUSL comments when it adopted the Uniform Interstate Enforcement of Protective Orders Act. The full uniform act and comments can be found at www.uniformlaws.org.

FAM §87.004

be certified by the issuing State. The purpose of these procedures is to make it as easy as possible for the protected individual to register the protection order and thus facilitate its enforcement.

1. **Editor's note:** The Texas Legislature's enactment of the Act allows for enforcement of support.

FAM §88.001. SHORT TITLE

This chapter may be cited as the Uniform Interstate Enforcement of Domestic Violence Protection Orders Act.

History of Fam. Code §88.001: Acts 2001, 77th Leg., ch. 48, §2, eff. Sept. 1, 2001.

History of Former Fam. Code §88.001: Acts 1997, 75th Leg., ch. 1193, §19, eff. Sept. 1, 1997. Deleted by Acts 2001, 77th Leg., ch. 48, §2, eff. Sept. 1, 2001.

FAM §88.002. DEFINITIONS

In this chapter:

(1) "Foreign protective order" means a protective order issued by a tribunal of another state.

(2) "Issuing state" means the state in which a tribunal issues a protective order.

(3) "Mutual foreign protective order" means a foreign protective order that includes provisions issued in favor of both the protected individual seeking enforcement of the order and the respondent.

(4) "Protected individual" means an individual protected by a protective order.

(5) "Protective order" means an injunction or other order, issued by a tribunal under the domestic violence or family violence laws or another law of the issuing state, to prevent an individual from engaging in violent or threatening acts against, harassing, contacting or communicating with, or being in physical proximity to another individual.

(6) "Respondent" means the individual against whom enforcement of a protective order is sought.

(7) "State" means a state of the United States, the District of Columbia, the Commonwealth of Puerto Rico, the United States Virgin Islands, or a territory or insular possession subject to the jurisdiction of the United States. The term includes a military tribunal of the United States, an Indian tribe or band, and an Alaskan native village that has jurisdiction to issue protective orders.

(8) "Tribunal" means a court, agency, or other entity authorized by law to issue or modify a protective order.

History of Fam. Code §88.002: Acts 2001, 77th Leg., ch. 48, §2, eff. Sept. 1, 2001.

History of Former Fam. Code §88.002: Acts 1997, 75th Leg., ch. 1193, §19, eff. Sept. 1, 1997. Deleted by Acts 2001, 77th Leg., ch. 48, §2, eff. Sept. 1, 2001.

NCCUSL Comment*

The term "protective order" includes only those orders issued under the domestic-violence or family-violence laws of the issuing State. Protective orders issued outside of the domestic or family violence context are not enforceable under the provisions of this Act. The scope of enforceable protective orders is further limited by §88.003(b). In addition, the term "protective order" includes an order modifying a previous order. Thus, a modified order, is enforceable, under the Act, in the same manner as a newly issued order.

The terms "protected individual" and "respondent" refer to the relief sought by the parties in the action brought in the enforcing State. The Act recognizes that neither the protected individual nor the respondent may have been a named party in the action brought in the issuing State; the Act applies to individuals meeting the definition of protected individual or respondent whether they were named in the caption or the body of the protective order. The Act also recognizes that the parties may have been called by different terms, e.g. plaintiff, defendant, petitioner, in the issuing State.

The term "mutual foreign protective orders" refers to protective orders in which an issuing State includes provisions protecting both parties. Enforcement of these foreign protection orders is governed by §88.003(g).

The Violence Against Women Act, 18 U.S.C. §2265, requires that States accord full faith and credit to tribal protective orders. Like state orders, tribal orders must satisfy the criteria for validity, as defined in §88.003(d), in order to qualify for interstate enforcement across state or tribal lines.

The Act uses the term "tribunal," rather than "court," in order to accommodate States that rely upon administrative or other entities to issue or modify protective orders.

FAM §88.003. JUDICIAL ENFORCEMENT OF ORDER

(a) A tribunal of this state shall enforce the terms of a foreign protective order, including a term that provides relief that a tribunal of this state would not have power to provide but for this section. The tribunal shall enforce the order regardless of whether the order was obtained by independent action or in another proceeding, if the order is an order issued in response to a complaint, petition, or motion filed by or on behalf of an individual seeking protection. In a proceeding to enforce a foreign protective order, the tribunal shall follow the procedures of this state for the enforcement of protective orders.

(b) A tribunal of this state shall enforce the provisions of the foreign protective order that govern the possession of and access to a child if the provisions were issued in accordance with the jurisdictional requirements governing the issuance of possession and access orders in the issuing state.

(c) A tribunal of this state may enforce a provision of the foreign protective order relating to child support if the order was issued in accordance with the jurisdictional requirements of Chapter 159 and the federal Full Faith and Credit for Child Support Orders Act, 28 U.S.C. Section 1738B, as amended.

* See footnote on p. 365.

FAM §88.001

(d) A foreign protective order is valid if the order:

(1) names the protected individual and the respondent;

(2) is currently in effect;

(3) was rendered by a tribunal that had jurisdiction over the parties and the subject matter under the law of the issuing state; and

(4) was rendered after the respondent was given reasonable notice and an opportunity to be heard consistent with the right to due process, either:

(A) before the tribunal issued the order; or

(B) in the case of an ex parte order, within a reasonable time after the order was rendered.

(e) A protected individual seeking enforcement of a foreign protective order establishes a prima facie case for its validity by presenting an order that is valid on its face.

(f) It is an affirmative defense in an action seeking enforcement of a foreign protective order that the order does not meet the requirements for a valid order under Subsection (d).

(g) A tribunal of this state may enforce the provisions of a mutual foreign protective order that favor a respondent only if:

(1) the respondent filed a written pleading seeking a protective order from the tribunal of the issuing state; and

(2) the tribunal of the issuing state made specific findings in favor of the respondent.

History of Fam. Code §88.003: Acts 2001, 77th Leg., ch. 48, §2, eff. Sept. 1, 2001.

History of Former Fam. Code §88.003: Acts 1997, 75th Leg., ch. 1193, §19, eff. Sept. 1, 1997. Deleted by Acts 2001, 77th Leg., ch. 48, §2, eff. Sept. 1, 2001.

ANNOTATIONS

Harvey v. State, 78 S.W.3d 368, 373 (Tex.Crim.App. 2002). "We have not overlooked the portion of [Pen. Code] §25.07(a) that applies to an act that was 'in violation of an order ... issued by another jurisdiction as provided by [Fam. Code] ch. 88....' We think it likely that the laws of other jurisdictions require ... notice provisions [similar to those under Fam. Code ch. 82]. If prosecution is brought for violation of another jurisdiction's order that was issued without notice, and if the defendant in such a case had no actual notice of the order, there will be an issue whether such evidence establishes the offense."

NCCUSL Comment*

Subsection (a) implements the core purpose of the Act. Effective interstate enforcement of protective orders is founded on the principle that enforcing States must enforce all the substantive terms of a foreign protective order, including terms that provide relief that a tribunal of the enforcing State would lack power to provide, but for this Act. This provision means that the tribunals of enforcing States must enforce the specific terms of a foreign protective order even if their state law would not allow the relief in question. For example, if the law of the issuing State provides that a court may issue a protective order including terms that concern the possession of property, e.g., an order giving the protected individual possession of the family automobile, but the law of the enforcing State does not authorize such substantive relief, the tribunal of the enforcing State must enforce the order in its entirety. To give another example, if the law of the issuing State allows protective orders to remain effective for a longer period than is allowed by the enforcing State, the tribunal of the enforcing State should enforce the order for the time specified in the order of the issuing State. In a proceeding to enforce the substantive terms of the foreign protective order, however, the court of the enforcing State shall follow its own procedures.

Subsection (a) provides that only protective orders that were issued in response to a complaint, petition, or motion filed by or on behalf of an individual seeking protection can be enforced under this Act; orders issued sua sponte are not enforceable under this Act.

...

Subsection (b) further defines the scope of enforceable protective orders under the Act. Subsection (b) provides that the provisions of protective orders that govern custody and visitation rights must be enforced. Enforcement of these provisions is essential because, first, the award of custody is often essential for the protection of children from potential violence, and, second, because the protected individual will not seek a safe distance from a threatening individual if custody of a child is jeopardized. These provisions may only be enforced, however, if they were issued in accordance with the jurisdictional requirements for the issuance of all custody and visitation orders, contained, depending on the State, either in the Uniform Child Custody Jurisdiction Act or the Uniform Child Custody Jurisdiction and Enforcement Act, and the federal Parental Kidnapping Prevention Act. This Act, however, does not provide for the enforcement of orders governing custody and visitation rights that are not included in a protective order.

...

Subsection (d) requires that, to be valid for the purpose of enforcement under this Act, a foreign protective order must be "currently in effect." This provision includes orders that have been modified; the modified order is the one currently in effect. While the Act requires that a foreign protective order, to be valid, identify the protected individual and respondent, merely technical errors, such as an incorrect spelling of a name, should not preclude enforcement of the order. The question of the validity of an order is a question of law for the court of the enforcing State. Once an order is adjudged valid, the proceeding shall be governed by the established procedures of the enforcing State.

The respondent's constitutional right to due process is protected by the opportunity to raise defenses in the enforcement proceeding, as provided in subsection (f). If, for example, the respondent was not provided with reasonable notice and opportunity to be heard by the tribunal of the State issuing the protective order, the enforcing tribunal may not enforce the order. Thus, the interstate enforcement of a valid foreign protective order, even without a prior hearing, does not deprive the respondent of any rights to due process because the respondent was provided with reasonable notice and opportunity to be heard when the order was issued.

The enforcement mechanisms established by the Act do not require the presentation by the protected individual of an authenticated copy of the foreign protective order. While States, as required by the Constitution and federal statutes that articulate authentication requirements, including 28 U.S.C. §1738, must accord properly authenticated foreign judgments full faith and credit enforcement, they may choose to enforce foreign orders they would not be required to enforce under the provisions of the Constitution or other federal law. By adopting this Act, States have chosen to give that extra measure of full faith and credit to foreign protective orders.

In addition, in recent years, particularly with regard to the enforcement of domestic relations orders, the federal government has employed the power

* See footnote on p. 365.

granted to it by Article IV, Sec. 1 of the Constitution of the United States to prescribe the manner in which States give full faith and credit to the acts, records, and proceedings of other States to require States to enforce foreign orders in circumstances in which States have traditionally been reluctant to render such enforcement. For example, the federal Parental Kidnapping Prevention Act, 28 U.S.C. §1738a, requires greater interstate enforcement of child custody orders and the federal Personal Responsibility and Work Opportunity Reconciliation Act, 110 Stat. 2105 (1996), requires that States, in order to facilitate the enforcement of support orders, adopt the provisions of the Uniform Interstate Family Support Act. The Violence Against Women Act extends the principle of these laws to the subject of the interstate enforcement of domestic-violence protective orders.

Subsection (g), adapted from the federal Violence Against Women Act, 18 U.S.C. §2265(c), addresses the enforcement of mutual foreign protective orders, which contain provisions protecting both the protected individual and the respondent. Provisions of a mutual foreign protective order issued in favor of the respondent will not be enforced without proof that the respondent filed a written pleading seeking a protective order. If a respondent can prove that he or she made a specific request for relief and that the issuing tribunal made specific findings that the respondent was entitled to the requested relief, the protective orders will be enforced against the protected individual.

In order to facilitate the interstate enforcement of foreign protective orders, States should strongly consider requiring tribunals that issue protective orders to state clearly that these orders are entitled to interstate enforcement under both federal and state law. Such enforcement would also be greatly facilitated if issuing States provided each protected individual with a certified copy of the protective order. In addition, States should consider adopting a standard certification or confirmation form stating the protective order issued by their tribunals satisfies the criteria of validity articulated in subsection (d), thus qualifying the protective order for interstate enforcement. Use of the following certification form is recommended.

__________ (Name),	:	IN THE __________ COURT OF
Plaintiff	:	__________ (County/Judicial District)
	:	__________ (State/Territory)
vs.	:	CIVIL ACTION – LAW
	:	PROTECTION/RESTRAINING ORDER
__________ (Name),	:	
Defendant	:	Docket No. __________, 20___

Certification of Protection/Restraining Order

It is hereby certified that the attached is a true and correct copy of the order entered in the above-captioned action on (date) and that the original of the attached order was duly executed by the judicial authority whose signature appears thereon. The order expires on (date).

The order is: [ ] a civil protection/restraining order

OR [ ] a criminal protection/restraining order,

that recognizes the standing of the plaintiff to seek enforcement of the order.

It is further certified that:

(a) the issuing court determined that it had jurisdiction over the parties and the subject matter under the laws of (state or Indian tribe).

(b) the defendant was given reasonable notice and had opportunity to be heard before this order was issued; or if the order was issued ex parte, the defendant was given notice and had opportunity to be heard after the order was issued, consistent with the rights of the defendant to due process.

(c) the order was otherwise issued in accordance with the requirements of the Uniform Interstate Enforcement of Domestic-Violence Protection Orders Act, and the Violence Against Women Act, 18 U.S.C. §2265.

For custody and visitation orders:

the order was issued in accordance with the requirements of the Uniform Child Custody Jurisdiction Act or the Uniform Child Custody Jurisdiction and Enforcement Act of this state/territory and is consistent with the provisions of the Parental Kidnapping Prevention Act. 28 U.S.C. §1738A.

The attached order shall be presumed to be valid and enforceable in this and other jurisdictions.

Signature of Clerk of Court or other authorized official: __________
Judicial District: __________ Address __________
Phone: __________ Fax: __________ Date: __________
Seal:

FAM §88.004. NONJUDICIAL ENFORCEMENT OF ORDER

(a) A law enforcement officer of this state, on determining that there is probable cause to believe that a valid foreign protective order exists and that the order has been violated, shall enforce the foreign protective order as if it were an order of a tribunal of this state. A law enforcement officer has probable cause to believe that a foreign protective order exists if the protected individual presents a foreign protective order that identifies both the protected individual and the respondent and on its face, is currently in effect.

(b) For the purposes of this section, a foreign protective order may be inscribed on a tangible medium or may be stored in an electronic or other medium if it is retrievable in a perceivable form. Presentation of a certified copy of a protective order is not required for enforcement.

(c) If a protected individual does not present a foreign protective order, a law enforcement officer may determine that there is probable cause to believe that a valid foreign protective order exists by relying on any relevant information.

(d) A law enforcement officer of this state who determines that an otherwise valid foreign protective order cannot be enforced because the respondent has not been notified or served with the order shall inform the respondent of the order and make a reasonable effort to serve the order on the respondent. After informing the respondent and attempting to serve the order, the officer shall allow the respondent a reasonable opportunity to comply with the order before enforcing the order.

(e) The registration or filing of an order in this state is not required for the enforcement of a valid foreign protective order under this chapter.

History of Fam. Code §88.004: Acts 2001, 77th Leg., ch. 48, §2, eff. Sept. 1, 2001.

History of Former Fam. Code §88.004: Acts 1997, 75th Leg., ch. 1193, §19, eff. Sept. 1, 1997. Deleted by Acts 2001, 77th Leg., ch. 48, §2, eff. Sept. 1, 2001.

See also *O'Connor's Texas Family Law Handbook* (2017), "Enforcing foreign protective orders," ch. 6-E, §4.4, p. 773.

NCCUSL Comment*

The enforcement procedures in subsections (a)-(c) rely on the sound exercise of the judgment of law enforcement officers to determine whether there exists probable cause to believe that a valid foreign protective order exists and has been violated. These procedures anticipate that there will be many instances in which the protected individual does not have, or cannot, under the circumstances, produce a paper copy of the foreign protective order. Subsections (a) and (b) establish a per se rule for determining probable cause of the existence of an order. If the protected individual presents, whether by providing a paper copy (which need not be certified) of a protective order or through an electronic medium, such as access to a state registry of orders, proof of a facially valid order, the order should be enforced. In determining whether there is proof of a facially valid order, a law enforcement officer, where possible, may, and, indeed, should, search, using an electronic or other medium, a state or federal registry of orders.

Subsection (c) concerns the circumstance in which the protected individual cannot present direct proof of the protective order. In this situation, law enforcement officers are expected to obtain information from all available sources, including interviewing the parties and contacting other law enforcement agencies, to determine whether there is a valid protective order in effect. If the officer finds, after considering the totality of the circumstances, that there is probable cause to believe that a valid foreign protective order exists and has been violated, he or she should enforce the order. This probable cause determination must meet the constitutional standards for determining probable cause. If it is later determined that no such order was in place or the order was otherwise unenforceable, law enforcement agencies, officers, or other state officials will be protected by the immunity provision of §88.006 for actions taken in good faith.

Subsection (d) provides that if a law enforcement officer discovers in the course of a probable cause investigation that the respondent has not been notified of the issuance of or served with an otherwise valid foreign protective order, the officer must then inform the respondent of the terms and conditions of the protective order and make a reasonable effort to serve the order upon the respondent. The respondent must be allowed a reasonable opportunity to comply with the order before the order is enforced.

Subsection (e) makes clear that, if a State either adopts its own process for the registration or filing of foreign protective orders or adopts the process provided in §5, the State shall not require the registration or filing of a foreign protective order for enforcement.

FAM §88.005. REGISTRATION OF ORDER

(a) An individual may register a foreign protective order in this state. To register a foreign protective order, an individual shall:

(1) present a certified copy of the order to a sheriff, constable, or chief of police responsible for the registration of orders in the local computer records and in the statewide law enforcement system maintained by the Texas Department of Public Safety; or

(2) present a certified copy of the order to the Department of Public Safety and request that the order be registered in the statewide law enforcement system maintained by the Department of Public Safety.

(b) On receipt of a foreign protective order, the agency responsible for the registration of protective orders shall register the order in accordance with this section and furnish to the individual registering the order a certified copy of the registered order.

(c) The agency responsible for the registration of protective orders shall register a foreign protective order on presentation of a copy of a protective order that has been certified by the issuing state. A registered foreign protective order that is inaccurate or not currently in effect shall be corrected or removed from the registry in accordance with the law of this state.

(d) An individual registering a foreign protective order shall file an affidavit made by the protected individual that, to the best of the protected individual's knowledge, the order is in effect.

(e) A foreign protective order registered under this section may be entered in any existing state or federal registry of protective orders, in accordance with state or federal law.

(f) A fee may not be charged for the registration of a foreign protective order.

History of Fam. Code §88.005: Acts 2001, 77th Leg., ch. 48, §2, eff. Sept. 1, 2001.

NCCUSL Comment*

The federal Violence Against Women Act, as amended by the Violence Against Women Act of 2000 (Pub. L. No. 106-386), prohibits States that provide for the registration or filing of orders from, without the permission of the individual registering or filing the order, notifying other States of the registration or filing of the order.

Subsection (a) provides that any person, including a potential respondent, may register foreign protective orders. This reason behind this provision is to ensure that all parties have the opportunity to provide relevant information to the State. Orders, for example, may be modified with custody arrangements. Subsection (a) also requires that a person seeking to register a foreign protective order must present a certified copy of that order. The copy must be a writing on paper, thus exempting this requirement from the provisions of the Uniform Electronic Transactions Act.

Subsection (c) provides that if the State has registered orders that are no longer in effect or are inaccurate, these orders must be removed from the registry or, in the case of error, corrected. The precise method of how state and federal registries manage their registries, including the deletion of inaccurate information, is governed by each government's law regarding the management of records.

If an order is registered under this section, the individual who registered the order is expected to inform the enforcing State of any modifications to the registered protective order.

FAM §88.006. IMMUNITY

A state or local governmental agency, law enforcement officer, prosecuting attorney, clerk of court, or any state or local governmental official acting in an official capacity is immune from civil and criminal liability for an act or omission arising from the registration or enforcement of a foreign protective order or the detention or arrest of a person alleged to have violated a foreign protective order if the act or omission was done in good faith in an effort to comply with this chapter.

History of Fam. Code §88.006: Acts 2001, 77th Leg., ch. 48, §2, eff. Sept. 1, 2001.

* See footnote on p. 365.

NCCUSL Comment*

This immunity provision includes States, state and local governmental agencies, and all state and local government officials acting in their official capacity in order to prevent those seeking the imposition of criminal and civil liability for acts or omissions done in good faith in an effort to comply with the provisions of this Act from circumventing this immunity provision. The necessity for a generous immunity provision for the enforcement of foreign protective orders does not preclude state and local governments from using personnel and other internal sanctions in order to prevent and punish actions that, in the absence of this immunity provision, would have rendered the government agencies, officers, or officials civilly or criminally liable.

FAM §88.007. OTHER REMEDIES

A protected individual who pursues a remedy under this chapter is not precluded from pursuing other legal or equitable remedies against the respondent.

History of Fam. Code §88.007: Acts 2001, 77th Leg., ch. 48, §2, eff. Sept. 1, 2001.

NCCUSL Comment*

This section clarifies that the protective orders enforced under the Act are not the only means of protection available to victims of domestic violence. Other legal remedies, such as tort actions and criminal prosecution, are left undisturbed by this Act.

FAM §88.008. UNIFORMITY OF APPLICATION & CONSTRUCTION

In applying and construing this chapter, consideration shall be given to the need to promote uniformity of the law with respect to its subject matter among the states that enact the Uniform Interstate Enforcement of Domestic Violence Protection Orders Act.

History of Fam. Code §88.008: Acts 2001, 77th Leg., ch. 48, §2, eff. Sept. 1, 2001.

Chapters 89 & 90 blank

A SUBTITLE C. [REPORTING] FAMILY VIOLENCE REPORTING & SERVICES

CHAPTER 91. REPORTING FAMILY VIOLENCE

FAM §91.001. DEFINITIONS

In this subtitle:

(1) "Family violence" has the meaning assigned by Section 71.004.

(2) "Medical professional" means a licensed doctor, nurse, physician assistant, or emergency medical technician.

History of Fam. Code §91.001: Acts 1997, 75th Leg., ch. 34, §1, eff. May 5, 1997. Amended by H.B. 3649, §1, 85th Leg., eff. Sept. 1, 2017. Source: Former Fam. Code §73.01.

* See footnote on p. 365.

FAM §91.002. REPORTING BY WITNESSES ENCOURAGED

A person who witnesses family violence is encouraged to report the family violence to a local law enforcement agency.

History of Fam. Code §91.002: Acts 1997, 75th Leg., ch. 34, §1, eff. May 5, 1997. Source: Former Fam. Code §73.02.

See also *O'Connor's Texas Family Law Handbook* (2017), "Reporting Family Violence," ch. 1-G, §2, p. 82.

FAM §91.003. INFORMATION PROVIDED BY MEDICAL PROFESSIONALS

A medical professional who treats a person for injuries that the medical professional has reason to believe were caused by family violence shall:

(1) immediately provide the person with information regarding the nearest family violence shelter center;

(2) document in the person's medical file:

(A) the fact that the person has received the information provided under Subdivision (1); and

(B) the reasons for the medical professional's belief that the person's injuries were caused by family violence; and

(3) give the person a written notice in substantially the following form, completed with the required information, in both English and Spanish:

"NOTICE TO ADULT VICTIMS OF FAMILY VIOLENCE

"It is a crime for any person to cause you any physical injury or harm even if that person is a member or former member of your family or household.

"You may report family violence to a law enforcement officer by calling the following telephone numbers: __________________.

"If you, your child, or any other household resident has been injured or if you feel you are going to be in danger after a law enforcement officer investigating family violence leaves your residence or at a later time, you have the right to:

"Ask the local prosecutor to file a criminal complaint against the person committing family violence; and

"Apply to a court for an order to protect you. You may want to consult with a legal aid office, a prosecuting attorney, or a private attorney. A court can enter an order that:

"(1) prohibits the abuser from committing further acts of violence;

"(2) prohibits the abuser from threatening, harassing, or contacting you at home;

"(3) directs the abuser to leave your household; and

"(4) establishes temporary custody of the children or any property.

"A VIOLATION OF CERTAIN PROVISIONS OF COURT-ORDERED PROTECTION MAY BE A FELONY.

"CALL THE FOLLOWING VIOLENCE SHELTERS OR SOCIAL ORGANIZATIONS IF YOU NEED PROTECTION: ____________________."

History of Fam. Code §91.003: Acts 1997, 75th Leg., ch. 34, §1, eff. May 5, 1997. Source: Former Fam. Code §73.03.

FAM §91.004. APPLICATION OF SUBTITLE

This subtitle does not affect a duty to report child abuse under Chapter 261.

History of Fam. Code §91.004: Acts 1997, 75th Leg., ch. 34, §1, eff. May 5, 1997. Source: Former Fam. Code §73.05.

CHAPTER 92. IMMUNITY

FAM §92.001. IMMUNITY

(a) Except as provided by Subsection (b), a person who reports family violence under Section 91.002 or provides information under Section 91.003 is immune from civil liability that might otherwise be incurred or imposed.

(b) A person who reports the person's own conduct or who otherwise reports family violence in bad faith is not protected from liability under this section.

History of Fam. Code §92.001: Acts 1997, 75th Leg., ch. 34, §1, eff. May 5, 1997. Source: Former Fam. Code §73.04.

See also *O'Connor's Texas Family Law Handbook* (2017), "Immunity," ch. 1-G, §2.3, p. 82.

E CHAPTER 93. CONFIDENTIAL & PRIVILEGED COMMUNICATIONS

FAM §93.001. DEFINITIONS

In this chapter:

(1) "Advocate" means a person who has at least 20 hours of training in assisting victims of family violence and is an employee or volunteer of a family violence center.

(2) "Family violence center" means a public or private nonprofit organization that provides, as its primary purpose, services to victims of family violence, including the services described by Section 51.005(b)(3), Human Resources Code.

(3) "Victim" has the meaning assigned to "victim of family violence" by Section 51.002, Human Resources Code.

History of Fam. Code §93.001: Enacted by H.B. 3649, §2, 85th Leg., eff. Sept. 1, 2017.

FAM §93.002. CONFIDENTIAL COMMUNICATIONS

A written or oral communication between an advocate and a victim made in the course of advising, advocating for, counseling, or assisting the victim is confidential and may not be disclosed.

History of Fam. Code §93.002: Enacted by H.B. 3649, §2, 85th Leg., eff. Sept. 1, 2017.

FAM §93.003. PRIVILEGED COMMUNICATIONS

(a) A victim has a privilege to refuse to disclose and to prevent another from disclosing a confidential communication described by Section 93.002.

(b) The privilege may be claimed by:

(1) a victim or a victim's attorney on a victim's behalf;

(2) a parent, guardian, or conservator of a victim under 18 years of age; or

(3) an advocate or a family violence center on a victim's behalf.

History of Fam. Code §93.003: Enacted by H.B. 3649, §2, 85th Leg., eff. Sept. 1, 2017.

FAM §93.004. EXCEPTIONS

(a) A communication that is confidential under this chapter may be disclosed only:

(1) to another individual employed by or volunteering for a family violence center for the purpose of furthering the advocacy process;

(2) for the purpose of seeking evidence that is admissible under Article 38.49, Code of Criminal Procedure, following an in camera review and a determination that the communication is admissible under that article;

(3) to other persons in the context of a support group or group counseling in which a victim is a participant; or

(4) for the purposes of making a report under Chapter 261 of this code or Section 48.051, Human Resources Code.

(b) Notwithstanding Subsection (a), the Texas Rules of Evidence govern the disclosure of a communication that is confidential under this chapter in a criminal or civil proceeding by an expert witness who relies on facts or data from the communication to form the basis of the expert's opinion.

(c) If the family violence center, at the request of the victim, discloses a communication privileged under this chapter for the purpose of a criminal or civil proceeding, the family violence center shall disclose the communication to all parties to that criminal or civil proceeding.

History of Fam. Code §93.004: Enacted by H.B. 3649, §2, 85th Leg., eff. Sept. 1, 2017.

Chapters 94-100 blank

Family Code—Title 5
The Parent-Child Relationship & the SAPCR
Table of Contents

Title 5. The Parent-Child Relationship & the Suit Affecting the Parent-Child Relationship

Subtitle A. General Provisions

FAMILY CODE—TITLE 5
THE PARENT-CHILD RELATIONSHIP & THE SAPCR
TABLE OF CONTENTS

TABLE OF CONTENTS

TABLE OF CONTENTS

TABLE OF CONTENTS

TABLE OF CONTENTS

TABLE OF CONTENTS

Table of Contents

TITLE 5. THE PARENT-CHILD RELATIONSHIP & THE SUIT AFFECTING THE PARENT-CHILD RELATIONSHIP

SUBTITLE A. GENERAL PROVISIONS

CHAPTER 101. DEFINITIONS

FAM §101.001. APPLICABILITY OF DEFINITIONS

(a) Definitions in this subchapter[1] apply to this title.

(b) If, in another part of this title, a term defined by this chapter has a meaning different from the meaning provided by this chapter, the meaning of that other provision prevails.

1. **Editor's note:** Probably should be "chapter." ***Hughey v. Hughey***, 923 S.W.2d 778, 780 n.7 (Tex.App.—Tyler 1996, writ denied).

History of Fam. Code §101.001: Acts 1995, 74th Leg., ch. 20, §1, eff. Apr. 20, 1995. Source: Former Fam. Code §11.01.

FAM §101.0010. ACKNOWLEDGED FATHER

"Acknowledged father" means a man who has established a father-child relationship under Chapter 160.

History of Fam. Code §101.0010: Acts 2001, 77th Leg., ch. 821, §2.04, eff. June 14, 2001.

NCCUSL Comment*

Section 101.0010, "acknowledged father," directly responds to a 1996 federal mandate encouraging states to adopt nonjudicial means for a man to identify himself as the father of a child in order to achieve an early determination of paternity. The term "acknowledged father" is given a relatively narrow meaning, rather than the broader definition previously accorded to the term. Only a man who acknowledges paternity of a child in accordance with the formal requirements established in Subchapter D qualifies as an "acknowledged father." Because the mother of the child must concur in the formal acknowledgment, the federal mandate declares that the states must treat the action as the equivalent of an adjudication of paternity.

FAM §101.0011. ADMINISTRATIVE WRIT OF WITHHOLDING

"Administrative writ of withholding" means the document issued by the Title IV-D agency or domestic relations office and delivered to an employer directing that earnings be withheld for payment of child support as provided by Chapter 158.

History of Fam. Code §101.0011: Acts 1997, 75th Leg., ch. 911, §5, eff. Sept. 1, 1997. Amended by Acts 2005, 79th Leg., ch. 199, §1, eff. Sept. 1, 2005.

FAM §101.0015. ALLEGED FATHER

(a) "Alleged father" means a man who alleges himself to be, or is alleged to be, the genetic father or a possible genetic father of a child, but whose paternity has not been determined.

---

* **Editor's note:**

Sections 101.0010 and 101.0015 are provided by the Uniform Parentage Act (UPA), which was adopted in part by Texas. The NCCUSL comments have been edited to reflect the Texas Legislature's omission of sections, changing of text, and changing of section numbers from the original uniform act. The Texas Legislature did not adopt the NCCUSL comments when it adopted the UPA. For the complete prefatory NCCUSL comment for the UPA, see p. 715. The full uniform act and comments can be found at www.uniformlaws.org.

(b) The term does not include:

(1) a presumed father;

(2) a man whose parental rights have been terminated or declared to not exist; or

(3) a male donor.

History of Fam. Code §101.0015: Acts 2001, 77th Leg., ch. 821, §2.04, eff. June 14, 2001.

NCCUSL Comment*

Section 101.0015, "alleged father," is derived from the UPUFA [Uniform Putative and Unknown Fathers Act] §1(1), although much of the terminology has been changed. A man who is asserted to be, or asserts himself to be or possibly to be, the father of a child is the primary target of the Uniform Parentage Act.

FAM §101.0017. AMICUS ATTORNEY

"Amicus attorney" has the meaning assigned by Section 107.001.

History of Fam. Code §101.0017: Acts 2005, 79th Leg., ch. 172, §15, eff. Sept. 1, 2005.

FAM §101.0018. ATTORNEY AD LITEM

"Attorney ad litem" has the meaning assigned by Section 107.001.

History of Fam. Code §101.0018: Acts 2005, 79th Leg., ch. 172, §15, eff. Sept. 1, 2005.

FAM §101.002. REPEALED

Repealed by Acts 2015, 84th Leg., ch. 1, §1.203(1), eff. Apr. 2, 2015.

FAM §101.0021. RENUMBERED

Renumbered as §101.036 by Acts 2015, 84th Leg., ch. 1, §1.027, eff. Apr. 2, 2015.

FAM §101.003. CHILD OR MINOR; ADULT

(a) "Child" or "minor" means a person under 18 years of age who is not and has not been married or who has not had the disabilities of minority removed for general purposes.

(b) In the context of child support, "child" includes a person over 18 years of age for whom a person may be obligated to pay child support.

(c) "Adult" means a person who is not a child.

History of Fam. Code §101.003: Acts 1995, 74th Leg., ch. 20, §1, eff. Apr. 20, 1995. Source: Former Fam. Code §11.01(1).

FAM §101.004. CHILD SUPPORT AGENCY

"Child support agency" means:

(1) the Title IV-D agency;

(2) a county or district attorney or any other county officer or county agency that executes a cooperative agreement with the Title IV-D agency to provide child support services under Part D of Title IV of the federal Social Security Act (42 U.S.C. Section 651 et seq.) and Chapter 231; or

(3) a domestic relations office.

History of Fam. Code §101.004: Acts 1995, 74th Leg., ch. 20, §1, eff. Apr. 20, 1995. Source: Former Fam. Code §14.80(3).

FAM §101.005. CHILD SUPPORT REVIEW OFFICER

"Child support review officer" means an individual designated and trained by a child support agency to conduct reviews under this title.

History of Fam. Code §101.005: Acts 1995, 74th Leg., ch. 20, §1, eff. Apr. 20, 1995. Amended by Acts 1995, 74th Leg., ch. 341, §2.01, eff. Sept. 1, 1995. Source: Former Fam. Code §14.80(7).

FAM §101.006. CHILD SUPPORT SERVICES[1]

"Child support services" means administrative or court actions to:

(1) establish paternity;

(2) establish, modify, or enforce child support or medical support obligations;

(3) locate absent parents; or

(4) cooperate with other states in these actions and any other action authorized or required under Part D of Title IV of the federal Social Security Act (42 U.S.C. Section 651 et seq.) or Chapter 231.

1. **Editor's note:** In 2015, the Legislature amended §101.006 to require dental support for a child subject to a child-support order, but the amendments are not effective until Sept. 1, 2018. For the text of the prospective amendments, see Acts 2015, 84th Leg., ch. 1150, §2, eff. Sept. 1, 2018.

History of Fam. Code §101.006: Acts 1995, 74th Leg., ch. 20, §1, eff. Apr. 20, 1995. Source: Former Fam. Code §14.80(4).

FAM §101.007. CLEAR & CONVINCING EVIDENCE

"Clear and convincing evidence" means the measure or degree of proof that will produce in the mind of the trier of fact a firm belief or conviction as to the truth of the allegations sought to be established.

History of Fam. Code §101.007: Acts 1995, 74th Leg., ch. 20, §1, eff. Apr. 20, 1995. Source: Former Fam. Code §11.15(c).

ANNOTATIONS

In re G.M., 596 S.W.2d 846, 847 (Tex.1980). Clear and convincing "is an intermediate standard, falling between the preponderance standard of ordinary civil proceedings and the reasonable doubt standard of criminal proceedings."

FAM §101.008. COURT

"Court" means the district court, juvenile court having the same jurisdiction as a district court, or other court expressly given jurisdiction of a suit affecting the parent-child relationship.

* See footnote on p. 393.

History of Fam. Code §101.008: Acts 1995, 74th Leg., ch. 20, §1, eff. Apr. 20, 1995. Source: Former Fam. Code §11.01(2).

FAM §101.009. DANGER TO PHYSICAL HEALTH OR SAFETY OF CHILD

"Danger to the physical health or safety of a child" includes exposure of the child to loss or injury that jeopardizes the physical health or safety of the child without regard to whether there has been an actual prior injury to the child.

History of Fam. Code §101.009: Acts 1995, 74th Leg., ch. 20, §1, eff. Apr. 20, 1995. Source: Former Fam. Code §17.001.

FAM §§101.0094, 101.0095

In 2015, the Legislature enacted §§101.0094 and 101.0095 to require dental support for a child subject to a child-support order, but the enactments are not effective until Sept. 1, 2018. For the text of the prospective enactments, see Acts 2015, 84th Leg., ch. 1150, §3, eff. Sept. 1, 2018.

FAM §101.0096. DIGITIZED SIGNATURE

"Digitized signature" means a graphic image of a handwritten signature having the same legal force and effect for all purposes as a handwritten signature.

History of Fam. Code §101.0096: Acts 2013, 83rd Leg., ch. 790, §1, eff. Sept. 1, 2013.

FAM §101.010. DISPOSABLE EARNINGS

"Disposable earnings" means the part of the earnings of an individual remaining after the deduction from those earnings of any amount required by law to be withheld, union dues, nondiscretionary retirement contributions, and medical, hospitalization, and disability insurance coverage for the obligor and the obligor's children.

History of Fam. Code §101.010: Acts 1995, 74th Leg., ch. 20, §1, eff. Apr. 20, 1995. Source: Former Fam. Code §14.30(a)(2).

FAM §101.011. EARNINGS

"Earnings" means a payment to or due an individual, regardless of source and how denominated. The term includes a periodic or lump-sum payment for:

(1) wages, salary, compensation received as an independent contractor, overtime pay, severance pay, commission, bonus, and interest income;

(2) payments made under a pension, an annuity, workers' compensation, and a disability or retirement program; and

(3) unemployment benefits.

History of Fam. Code §101.011: Acts 1995, 74th Leg., ch. 20, §1, eff. Apr. 20, 1995. Amended by Acts 1997, 75th Leg., ch. 911, §1, eff. Sept. 1, 1997. Source: Former Fam. Code §14.30(a)(1).

FAM §101.012. EMPLOYER[1]

"Employer" means a person, corporation, partnership, workers' compensation insurance carrier, governmental entity, the United States, or any other entity that pays or owes earnings to an individual. The term includes, for the purposes of enrolling dependents in a group health insurance plan, a union, trade association, or other similar organization.

1. **Editor's note:** In 2015, the Legislature amended §101.012 to require dental support for a child subject to a child-support order, but the amendments are not effective until Sept. 1, 2018. For the text of the prospective amendments, see Acts 2015, 84th Leg., ch. 1150, §4, eff. Sept. 1, 2018.

History of Fam. Code §101.012: Acts 1995, 74th Leg., ch. 20, §1, eff. Apr. 20, 1995. Amended by Acts 1995, 74th Leg., ch. 341, §4.02, eff. Sept. 1, 1995; Acts 1997, 75th Leg., ch. 911, §2, eff. Sept. 1, 1997. Source: Former Fam. Code §14.30(a)(3).

FAM §101.0125. FAMILY VIOLENCE

"Family violence" has the meaning assigned by Section 71.004.

History of Fam. Code §101.0125: Acts 1999, 76th Leg., ch. 787, §1, eff. Sept. 1, 1999.

FAM §101.013. FILED

"Filed" means officially filed with the clerk of the court.

History of Fam. Code §101.013: Acts 1995, 74th Leg., ch. 20, §1, eff. Apr. 20, 1995.

A FAM §101.0133. FOSTER CARE

The amended text in §101.0133 is effective for service plans filed for a full adversary hearing held under Fam. Code §262.201 or a status hearing held under Fam. Code ch. 263 on or after Jan. 1, 2018. A hearing held before Jan. 1, 2018, is governed by the former law in effect at that time. Except as provided above, the amended text in §101.0133 is effective for SAPCRs filed on or after Sept. 1, 2017. SAPCRs filed before Sept. 1, 2017, are governed by the former law in effect at that time.

Foster homes or foster group homes licensed by TDFPS and agency foster group homes verified by a child-placing agency before Sept. 1, 2017, may continue to operate under the former law in effect at that time, until the foster home or foster group home converts to another residential child-care license or the license is relinquished, or the agency foster group home has been converted to a verified foster home or closed.

"Foster care" means the placement of a child who is in the conservatorship of the Department of Family and Protective Services and in care outside the child's home in a residential child-care facility, including an [agency

~~foster group home,~~] agency foster home, specialized child-care [~~foster group~~] home, cottage [~~foster~~] home operation, general residential operation, or another facility licensed or certified under Chapter 42, Human Resources Code, in which care is provided for 24 hours a day.

History of Fam. Code §101.0133: Acts 2015, 84th Leg., ch. 944, §7, eff. Sept. 1, 2015. Amended by H.B. 7, §4, 85th Leg., eff. Sept. 1, 2017.

FAM §101.0134. FOSTER CHILD

"Foster child" means a child who is in the managing conservatorship of the Department of Family and Protective Services.

History of Fam. Code §101.0134: Acts 2015, 84th Leg., ch. 944, §7, eff. Sept. 1, 2015.

FAM §101.014. GOVERNMENTAL ENTITY

"Governmental entity" means the state, a political subdivision of the state, or an agency of the state.

History of Fam. Code §101.014: Acts 1995, 74th Leg., ch. 20, §1, eff. Apr. 20, 1995. Source: Former Fam. Code §11.01(8).

FAM §101.0145. GUARDIAN AD LITEM

"Guardian ad litem" has the meaning assigned by Section 107.001.

History of Fam. Code §101.0145: Acts 2005, 79th Leg., ch. 172, §15, eff. Sept. 1, 2005.

FAM §101.015. HEALTH INSURANCE

"Health insurance" means insurance coverage that provides basic health care services, including usual physician services, office visits, hospitalization, and laboratory, X-ray, and emergency services, that may be provided through a health maintenance organization or other private or public organization, other than medical assistance under Chapter 32, Human Resources Code.

History of Fam. Code §101.015: Acts 1995, 74th Leg., ch. 20, §1, eff. Apr. 20, 1995. Amended by Acts 2001, 77th Leg., ch. 1023, §1, eff. Sept. 1, 2001. Source: Former Fam. Code §14.061(d).

FAM §101.016. JOINT MANAGING CONSERVATORSHIP

"Joint managing conservatorship" means the sharing of the rights and duties of a parent by two parties, ordinarily the parents, even if the exclusive right to make certain decisions may be awarded to one party.

History of Fam. Code §101.016: Acts 1995, 74th Leg., ch. 20, §1, eff. Apr. 20, 1995. Source: Former Fam. Code §14.021(b).

FAM §101.0161. JUDICIAL WRIT OF WITHHOLDING

"Judicial writ of withholding" means the document issued by the clerk of a court and delivered to an employer directing that earnings be withheld for payment of child support as provided by Chapter 158.

History of Fam. Code §101.0161: Acts 1997, 75th Leg., ch. 911, §5, eff. Sept. 1, 1997.

FAM §101.017. LICENSED CHILD PLACING AGENCY

The amended text in §101.017 is effective for service plans filed for a full adversary hearing held under Fam. Code §262.201 or a status hearing held under Fam. Code ch. 263 on or after Jan. 1, 2018. A hearing held before Jan. 1, 2018, is governed by the former law in effect at that time. Except as provided above, the amended text in §101.017 is effective for SAPCRs filed on or after Sept. 1, 2017. SAPCRs filed before Sept. 1, 2017, are governed by the former law in effect at that time.

Foster homes or foster group homes licensed by TDFPS and agency foster group homes verified by a child-placing agency before Sept. 1, 2017, may continue to operate under the former law in effect at that time, until the foster home or foster group home converts to another residential child-care license or the license is relinquished, or the agency foster group home has been converted to a verified foster home or closed.

"Licensed child placing agency" means a person, including an organization or corporation, licensed or certified under Chapter 42, Human Resources Code, by the Department of Family and Protective Services to place a child in an adoptive home or a residential child-care facility, including a child-care facility, agency foster home, cottage home operation, or general residential operation [~~agency foster group home, or adoptive home~~].

History of Fam. Code §101.017: Acts 1995, 74th Leg., ch. 20, §1, eff. Apr. 20, 1995. Amended by Acts 2011, 82nd Leg., ch. 110, §9, eff. May 21, 2011; Acts 2015, 84th Leg., ch. 1, §1.028, eff. Apr. 2, 2015; H.B. 7, §5, 85th Leg., eff. Sept. 1, 2017. Source: Former Fam. Code §11.01(7); former Hum. Res. Code §42.002(12).

FAM §101.018. LOCAL REGISTRY

"Local registry" means a county agency or public entity operated under the authority of a district clerk, county government, juvenile board, juvenile probation office, domestic relations office, or other county agency or public entity that serves a county or a court that has jurisdiction under this title and that:

(1) receives child support payments;

(2) maintains records of child support payments;

(3) distributes child support payments as required by law; and

(4) maintains custody of official child support payment records.

History of Fam. Code §101.018: Acts 1995, 74th Leg., ch. 20, §1, eff. Apr. 20, 1995. Amended by Acts 2005, 79th Leg., ch. 740, §1, eff. June 17, 2005. Source: Former Fam. Code §11.01(11).

FAM §101.019. MANAGING CONSERVATORSHIP

"Managing conservatorship" means the relationship between a child and a managing conservator appointed by court order.

History of Fam. Code §101.019: Acts 1995, 74th Leg., ch. 20, §1, eff. Apr. 20, 1995. Source: Former Fam. Code §11.01(6).

FAM §101.020. MEDICAL SUPPORT

"Medical support" means periodic payments or a lump-sum payment made under an order to cover medical expenses, including health insurance coverage, incurred for the benefit of a child.

History of Fam. Code §101.020: Acts 1995, 74th Leg., ch. 20, §1, eff. Apr. 20, 1995. Amended by Acts 1997, 75th Leg., ch. 911, §3, eff. Sept. 1, 1997. Source: Former Fam. Code §14.80(5).

FAM §101.0201. NOTICE OF APPLICATION FOR JUDICIAL WRIT OF WITHHOLDING

"Notice of application for judicial writ of withholding" means the document delivered to an obligor and filed with the court as required by Chapter 158 for the nonjudicial determination of arrears and initiation of withholding.

History of Fam. Code §101.0201: Acts 1997, 75th Leg., ch. 911, §5, eff. Sept. 1, 1997.

FAM §101.021. OBLIGEE

"Obligee" means a person or entity entitled to receive payments of child support, including an agency of this state or of another jurisdiction to which a person has assigned the person's right to support.

History of Fam. Code §101.021: Acts 1995, 74th Leg., ch. 20, §1, eff. Apr. 20, 1995. Amended by Acts 1999, 76th Leg., ch. 556, §1, eff. Sept. 1, 1999. Source: Former Fam. Code §11.01(10).

FAM §101.022. OBLIGOR

"Obligor" means a person required to make payments under the terms of a support order for a child.

History of Fam. Code §101.022: Acts 1995, 74th Leg., ch. 20, §1, eff. Apr. 20, 1995. Source: Former Fam. Code §11.01(9).

FAM §101.023. ORDER

"Order" means a final order unless identified as a temporary order or the context clearly requires a different meaning. The term includes a decree and a judgment.

History of Fam. Code §101.023: Acts 1995, 74th Leg., ch. 20, §1, eff. Apr. 20, 1995.

FAM §101.024. PARENT[1]

(a) "Parent" means the mother, a man presumed to be the father, a man legally determined to be the father, a man who has been adjudicated to be the father by a court of competent jurisdiction, a man who has acknowledged his paternity under applicable law, or an adoptive mother or father. Except as provided by Subsection (b), the term does not include a parent as to whom the parent-child relationship has been terminated.

(b) For purposes of establishing, determining the terms of, modifying, or enforcing an order, a reference in this title to a parent includes a person ordered to pay child support under Section 154.001(a-1) or to provide medical support for a child.

1. **Editor's note:** In 2015, the Legislature amended §101.024 to require dental support for a child subject to a child-support order, but the amendments are not effective until Sept. 1, 2018. For the text of the prospective amendments, see Acts 2015, 84th Leg., ch. 1150, §5, eff. Sept. 1, 2018.

History of Fam. Code §101.024: Acts 1995, 74th Leg., ch. 20, §1, eff. Apr. 20, 1995. Amended by Acts 1999, 76th Leg., ch. 556, §1, eff. Sept. 1, 1999; Acts 2001, 77th Leg., ch. 821, §2.05, eff. June 14, 2001; Acts 2005, 79th Leg., ch. 268, §1.03, eff. Sept. 1, 2005. Source: Former Fam. Code §11.01(3).

See also ***O'Connor's Texas Family Law Handbook*** (2017), "Bringing Conservatorship Suit," ch. 4-E, §2, p. 470.

FAM §101.025. PARENT-CHILD RELATIONSHIP

"Parent-child relationship" means the legal relationship between a child and the child's parents as provided by Chapter 160. The term includes the mother and child relationship and the father and child relationship.

History of Fam. Code §101.025: Acts 1995, 74th Leg., ch. 20, §1, eff. Apr. 20, 1995. Amended by Acts 2001, 77th Leg., ch. 821, §2.06, eff. June 14, 2001. Source: Former Fam. Code §11.01(4).

FAM §101.0255. RECORD

"Record" means information that is:

(1) inscribed on a tangible medium or stored in an electronic or other medium; and

(2) retrievable in a perceivable form.

History of Fam. Code §101.0255: Acts 2007, 80th Leg., ch. 972, §1, eff. Sept. 1, 2007.

FAM §101.026. RENDER

"Render" means the pronouncement by a judge of the court's ruling on a matter. The pronouncement may be made orally in the presence of the court reporter or in writing, including on the court's docket sheet or by a separate written instrument.

History of Fam. Code §101.026: Acts 1995, 74th Leg., ch. 20, §1, eff. Apr. 20, 1995.

ANNOTATIONS

In re M.G.F., No. 2-07-241-CV (Tex.App.—Fort Worth 2008, no pet.) (memo op.; 8-28-08). "The rendition of judgment is a present act … which decides the issues upon which the ruling is made. [¶] A trial

court's intention to render judgment in the future cannot be a present rendition of judgment. The words used by the trial court must clearly indicate the intent to render judgment at the time the words are expressed. Thus, the words, '[Y]our divorce *is* granted,' constitute a rendition of judgment, … but the words, 'I *am going to* grant the divorce in this case,' do not…."

FAM §101.027. PARENT LOCATOR SERVICE

"Parent locator service" means the service established under 42 U.S.C. Section 653.

History of Fam. Code §101.027: Acts 1995, 74th Leg., ch. 20, §1, eff. Apr. 20, 1995. Source: Former Fam. Code §15.051(a).

FAM §101.028. SCHOOL

"School" means an elementary or secondary school in which a child is enrolled or, if the child is not enrolled in an elementary or secondary school, the public school district in which the child primarily resides. For purposes of this section, a reference to elementary school includes prekindergarten.

History of Fam. Code §101.028: Acts 1995, 74th Leg., ch. 20, §1, eff. Apr. 20, 1995. Amended by Acts 2015, 84th Leg., ch. 1167, §2, eff. Sept. 1, 2015. Source: Former Fam. Code §14.033(a).

FAM §101.029. STANDARD POSSESSION ORDER

"Standard possession order" means an order that provides a parent with rights of possession of a child in accordance with the terms and conditions of Subchapter F, Chapter 153.

History of Fam. Code §101.029: Acts 1995, 74th Leg., ch. 20, §1, eff. Apr. 20, 1995. Source: Former Fam. Code §14.033(a)(2).

FAM §101.030. STATE

"State" means a state of the United States, the District of Columbia, the Commonwealth of Puerto Rico, or a territory or insular possession subject to the jurisdiction of the United States. The term includes an Indian tribe and a foreign jurisdiction that has established procedures for rendition and enforcement of an order that are substantially similar to the procedures of this title.

History of Fam. Code §101.030: Acts 1995, 74th Leg., ch. 20, §1, eff. Apr. 20, 1995. Source: Former Fam. Code §§14.80(6), 21.01(19).

FAM §101.0301. STATE CASE REGISTRY

"State case registry" means the registry established and operated by the Title IV-D agency under 42 U.S.C. Section 654a that has responsibility for maintaining records with respect to child support orders in all Title IV-D cases and in all other cases in which a support order is rendered or modified under this title on or after October 1, 1998.

History of Fam. Code §101.0301: Acts 1997, 75th Leg., ch. 911, §5, eff. Sept. 1, 1997.

FAM §101.0302. STATE DISBURSEMENT UNIT

"State disbursement unit" means the unit established and operated by the Title IV-D agency under 42 U.S.C. Section 654b that has responsibility for receiving, distributing, maintaining, and furnishing child support payments and records on or after October 1, 1999.

History of Fam. Code §101.0302: Acts 1999, 76th Leg., ch. 556, §1, eff. Sept. 1, 1999.

FAM §101.031. SUIT

"Suit" means a legal action under this title.

History of Fam. Code §101.031: Acts 1995, 74th Leg., ch. 20, §1, eff. Apr. 20, 1995. Amended by Acts 2015, 84th Leg., ch. 859, §2, eff. Sept. 1, 2015.

FAM §101.032. SUIT AFFECTING THE PARENT-CHILD RELATIONSHIP

(a) "Suit affecting the parent-child relationship" means a suit filed as provided by this title in which the appointment of a managing conservator or a possessory conservator, access to or support of a child, or establishment or termination of the parent-child relationship is requested.

(b) The following are not suits affecting the parent-child relationship:

(1) a habeas corpus proceeding under Chapter 157;

(2) a proceeding filed under Chapter 159 to determine parentage or to establish, enforce, or modify child support, whether this state is acting as the initiating or responding state; and

(3) a proceeding under Title 2.

History of Fam. Code §101.032: Acts 1995, 74th Leg., ch. 20, §1, eff. Apr. 20, 1995. Source: Former Fam. Code §11.01(5).

See also *O'Connor's Texas Family Law Handbook* (2017), "Original Suits Affecting the Parent-Child Relationship," ch. 4, p. 317.

ANNOTATIONS

Martin v. Martin, 776 S.W.2d 572, 574 (Tex.1989). "[A] suit to modify access rights constitutes a [Fam. Code §11.01(5), now §101.032, SAPCR]." *See also* ***Leonard v. Paxson***, 654 S.W.2d 440, 441 (Tex.1983) (suit to modify child support is SAPCR).

FAM §101.033. TITLE IV-D AGENCY

"Title IV-D agency" means the state agency designated under Chapter 231 to provide services under Part D of Title IV of the federal Social Security Act (42 U.S.C. Section 651 et seq.).

History of Fam. Code §101.033: Acts 1995, 74th Leg., ch. 20, §1, eff. Apr. 20, 1995. Source: Former Fam. Code §14.80(2); former Hum. Res. Code §76.001.

A FAM §101.034. TITLE IV-D CASE[1]

"Title IV-D case" means an action in which services are provided by the Title IV-D agency under Part D, Title IV, of the federal Social Security Act (42 U.S.C. Section 651 et seq.), relating to the location of an absent parent, determination of parentage, or establishment, modification, or enforcement of a child support or medical support obligation, including a suit for modification filed by the Title IV-D agency under Section 231.101(d) and any other action relating to the services that the Title IV-D agency is required or authorized to provide under Section 231.101.

1. **Editor's note:** In 2015, the Legislature amended §101.034 to require dental support for a child subject to a child-support order, but the amendments are not effective until Sept. 1, 2018. For the text of the prospective amendments, see Acts 2015, 84th Leg., ch. 1150, §6, eff. Sept. 1, 2018.

History of Fam. Code §101.034: Acts 1995, 74th Leg., ch. 20, §1, eff. Apr. 20, 1995. Amended by Acts 1997, 75th Leg., ch. 911, §4, eff. Sept. 1, 1997; S.B. 1329, §§1.01, 1.02, 85th Leg., eff. Sept. 1, 2017. Source: Former Fam. Code §14.80(2).

FAM §101.035. TRIBUNAL

"Tribunal" means a court, administrative agency, or quasi-judicial entity of a state authorized to establish, enforce, or modify support orders or to determine parentage.

History of Fam. Code §101.035: Acts 1995, 74th Leg., ch. 20, §1, eff. Apr. 20, 1995. Source: Former Fam. Code §21.01(22).

FAM §101.036. VITAL STATISTICS UNIT

"Vital statistics unit" means the vital statistics unit of the Department of State Health Services.

History of Fam. Code §101.036: Acts 1999, 76th Leg., ch. 556, §1, eff. Sept. 1, 1999. Renumbered from §101.0021 and amended by Acts 2015, 84th Leg., ch. 1, §1.027, eff. Apr. 2, 2015.

CHAPTER 102. FILING SUIT

FAM §102.001. SUIT AUTHORIZED; SCOPE OF SUIT

(a) A suit may be filed as provided in this title.

(b) One or more matters covered by this title may be determined in the suit. The court, on its own motion, may require the parties to replead in order that any issue affecting the parent-child relationship may be determined in the suit.

History of Fam. Code §102.001: Acts 1995, 74th Leg., ch. 20, §1, eff. Apr. 20, 1995. Source: Former Fam. Code §11.02.

FAM §102.002. COMMENCEMENT OF SUIT

An original suit begins by the filing of a petition as provided by this chapter.

History of Fam. Code §102.002: Acts 1995, 74th Leg., ch. 20, §1, eff. Apr. 20, 1995. Source: Former Fam. Code §11.07(a).

FAM §102.003. GENERAL STANDING TO FILE SUIT

(a) An original suit may be filed at any time by:

(1) a parent of the child;

(2) the child through a representative authorized by the court;

(3) a custodian or person having the right of visitation with or access to the child appointed by an order of a court of another state or country;

(4) a guardian of the person or of the estate of the child;

(5) a governmental entity;

(6) the Department of Family and Protective Services;

(7) a licensed child placing agency;

(8) a man alleging himself to be the father of a child filing in accordance with Chapter 160, subject to the limitations of that chapter, but not otherwise;

(9) a person, other than a foster parent, who has had actual care, control, and possession of the child for at least six months ending not more than 90 days preceding the date of the filing of the petition;

(10) a person designated as the managing conservator in a revoked or unrevoked affidavit of relinquish-

ment under Chapter 161 or to whom consent to adoption has been given in writing under Chapter 162;

(11) a person with whom the child and the child's guardian, managing conservator, or parent have resided for at least six months ending not more than 90 days preceding the date of the filing of the petition if the child's guardian, managing conservator, or parent is deceased at the time of the filing of the petition;

(12) a person who is the foster parent of a child placed by the Department of Family and Protective Services in the person's home for at least 12 months ending not more than 90 days preceding the date of the filing of the petition;

(13) a person who is a relative of the child within the third degree by consanguinity, as determined by Chapter 573, Government Code, if the child's parents are deceased at the time of the filing of the petition; or

(14) a person who has been named as a prospective adoptive parent of a child by a pregnant woman or the parent of the child, in a verified written statement to confer standing executed under Section 102.0035, regardless of whether the child has been born.

(b) In computing the time necessary for standing under Subsections (a)(9), (11), and (12), the court may not require that the time be continuous and uninterrupted but shall consider the child's principal residence during the relevant time preceding the date of commencement of the suit.

(c) Notwithstanding the time requirements of Subsection (a)(12), a person who is the foster parent of a child may file a suit to adopt a child for whom the person is providing foster care at any time after the person has been approved to adopt the child. The standing to file suit under this subsection applies only to the adoption of a child who is eligible to be adopted.

History of Fam. Code §102.003: Acts 1995, 74th Leg., ch. 20, §1, eff. Apr. 20, 1995. Amended by Acts 1995, 74th Leg., ch. 751, §8, eff. Sept. 1, 1995; Acts 1997, 75th Leg., ch. 575, §3, eff. Sept. 1, 1997; Acts 1999, 76th Leg., ch. 1048, §1 (eff. June 18, 1999), ch. 1390, §2 (eff. Sept. 1, 1999); Acts 2001, 77th Leg., ch. 821, §2.07, eff. June 14, 2001; Acts 2003, 78th Leg., ch. 37, §1 (eff. Sept. 1, 2003), ch. 573, §1 (eff. Sept. 1, 2003); Acts 2011, 82nd Leg., ch. 110, §10, eff. May 21, 2011; Acts 2015, 84th Leg., ch. 1, §1.029, eff. Apr. 2, 2015. Source: Former Fam. Code §11.03(a).

See also *O'Connor's Texas Family Law Handbook* (2017), "Who can file," ch. 4-E, §5.1, p. 478; "Intervenors," ch. 4-F, §8, p. 538.

ANNOTATIONS

Generally

Rivera v. Office of Atty. Gen., 960 S.W.2d 280, 281 (Tex.App.—Houston [1st Dist.] 1997, no pet.). "The [AG] has independent standing to bring a [SAPCR]."

§102.003(a)(4)

In re A.D.P., 281 S.W.3d 541, 549 (Tex.App.—El Paso 2008, no pet.). "Whether a temporary guardian [appointed under the Probate Code, now the Estates Code,] has standing under [Fam. Code] §102.003(a)(4) to file a SAPCR is an issue of first impression. [¶] The term 'guardian' in §102.003(a)(4) ... must be construed in accordance with the Probate Code's definition of 'guardian.' We thus conclude that ... the temporary guardians of [child] had standing to file the SAPCR."

§102.003(a)(9)

In re J.A.T., 502 S.W.3d 834, 836-37 (Tex.App.—Houston [14th Dist.] 2016, no pet.). "On appeal, [petitioner] contends that she had standing to intervene ... because as a result of the trial court's temporary orders, she had been [child's SMC] with actual care, control, and possession of him for the eight months immediately preceding [the] date [she filed the petition in intervention], and thus, she had standing to file an original SAPCR under [Fam. Code] §102.003(a)(9). [¶] We agree that a person who has standing to file an original petition under §102.003(a)(9) generally may instead file a petition in intervention; however, [petitioner] could not intervene in this lawsuit because [Fam. Code] §102.004(b) only permits the trial court to grant leave to intervene 'in a pending suit filed by a person authorized to do so under this subchapter.' Because [petitioner] lacked standing when she originally filed this SAPCR, this was not a 'suit filed by a person authorized to do so,' so she did not acquire standing to intervene in this suit while the case was pending."

In re I.I.G.T., 412 S.W.3d 803, 806-07 (Tex.App.—Dallas 2013, no pet.). Respondent "testified he had possession of the child and 'maintained care, custody, and control' of the child every weekend ... pursuant to a 'permanent arrangement' between him and Mother. He also picked up the child from daycare and school once or twice a week. He testified the child has her own bedroom at his house that she decorates herself. ... He said he did everything a father would do. *At 808:* In this case, there was no court order for [respondent's] possession of the child before he filed suit, and the evidence conflicts on whether [respondent] and Mother had an agreement for [respondent's] regular possession of the child. *At 809:* [T]he record does not show that, for the six months of [respondent's] possession of the child ending within 90 days of suit being filed, the

parties intended for the child to occupy [respondent's] home consistently over a substantial period of time and intended that [respondent's] home be a permanent rather than temporary abode for the child. Instead, Mother's testimony shows the periods of the child's residing with [respondent] for the various weekends, holidays, and summer breaks were each intended to be a temporary arrangement." *See also* ***In re M.K.S.-V.***, 301 S.W.3d 460, 465 (Tex.App.—Dallas 2009, pet. denied) (mother's ex-partner had standing because possession between mother and ex-partner shared characteristics of standard possession order and was not intended to be temporary arrangement).

In re Wells, 373 S.W.3d 174, 175 (Tex.App.—Beaumont 2012, orig. proceeding). Mother and mother's ex-partner "divided the responsibilities of caring for [child] by equally dividing their possession of him. *At 177-78:* While [mother] allowed [child] to live with [ex-partner] at times, [mother] was under no enforceable obligation to allow him to stay with [ex-partner]. [Mother] also made all decisions of legal significance for the child, such as her decision concerning [child's] education. We are also not persuaded that the medical consent that [mother] gave [ex-partner] is a delegation of sufficient legal authority because such consents, by statute, are only effective 'when the person having the right to consent ... cannot be contacted[.]' [¶] [T]he record shows that [mother] controlled where [child] would stay and for how long; therefore, the trial court's finding that [mother] abdicated her right of control over [child] is not supported by the record. [¶] In the absence of a finding that a child's parent is unfit, and in absence of any evidence showing that [ex-partner] actually exercised legal control over [child] during the period at issue, we ... conclude that [ex-partner] failed to demonstrate that she had standing [under §102.003(a)(9)] to file a SAPCR against [mother]." *See also* ***In re Crumbley***, 404 S.W.3d 156, 159-60 (Tex.App.—Texarkana 2013, orig. proceeding) (aunt had standing because she had possession of child two-thirds of each month; §102.003(a)(9) does not require possession to be exclusive); ***In re M.J.G.***, 248 S.W.3d 753, 758-59 (Tex.App.—Fort Worth 2008, no pet.) (even though children lived with grandparents who performed day-to-day caretaking duties for children, children's parents also lived with children in same home and did not abdicate their parental duties; grandparents did not have standing). *But see* ***Jasek v. TDFPS***, this page.

Jasek v. TDFPS, 348 S.W.3d 523, 532 (Tex.App.—Austin 2011, no pet.). "[T]he adjective 'actual' in the phrase 'actual care, control, and possession' modifies each of the three nouns that follows. Thus, a person asserting standing under §102.003(a)(9) must show actual care, actual control, and actual possession. *At 533:* '[A]ctual ... control ... of the child,' ... means the actual power or authority to guide or manage or the actual directing or restricting of the child, as opposed to legal or constructive power or authority to guide or manage the child. In sum, these words reflect the Legislature's intent to create standing for those who have, over time, developed and maintained a relationship with a child entailing the actual exercise of guidance, governance and direction similar to that typically exercised by parents with their children. *At 535:* To the extent that ... cases construe §102.003(a)(9) to require that either (1) a parent or conservator have relinquished rights over a child or (2) that the person seeking standing have ultimate legal authority to control a child, we respectfully disagree." *See also* ***In re Lankford***, 501 S.W.3d 681, 686-87 (Tex.App.—Tyler 2016, orig. proceeding); ***In re K.S.***, 492 S.W.3d 419, 424-25 (Tex. App.—Houston [14th Dist.] 2016, pet. denied); ***In re A.C.F.H.***, 373 S.W.3d 148, 153 (Tex.App.—San Antonio 2012, no pet.). *But see* ***In re Wells***, this page; ***In re K.K.C.***, this page.

In re K.K.C., 292 S.W.3d 788, 792-93 (Tex. App.—Beaumont 2009, orig. proceeding). Under §102.003(a)(9), "'control' ... must be understood in the context of the rights, duties, and responsibilities of a parent. 'Control' refers to the power or authority to guide and manage, and includes the authority to make decisions of legal significance for the child. The statute does not require that the person asserting standing demonstrate he had exclusive control of the child." *But see* ***Jasek v. TDFPS***, this page.

In re S.S.G., 208 S.W.3d 1, 3-4 (Tex.App.—Amarillo 2006, pet. denied). "The courts have carved out one exception to [§102.003(a)(9)]. If possession is maintained in violation of a valid court order, that possession does not confer standing to bring [a SAPCR]. [¶] However, as neither this court nor the trial court entered an order requiring [adopting couple] to turn over possession of [child] to [biological parents] prior to the issuance of mandate, we cannot say that [adopting couple's] continued possession of [child] was in violation of a court order. [¶] In the absence of authority for

a consent exception to standing through possession, we will not engraft one." *See also* ***In re E.N.C.***, No. 03-07-00099-CV (Tex.App.—Austin 2009, no pet.) (memo op.; 3-13-09).

Coons-Andersen v. Andersen, 104 S.W.3d 630, 636 (Tex.App.—Dallas 2003, no pet.). "[T]he person deemed to be standing in loco parentis [has] actual care and custody of a child in the parent's absence. [S]ection 102.003(a)(9) is in complete harmony with the common law doctrine of in loco parentis: a person who assumes the duties of a parent may be treated like a parent under the law and has the right to be a party in a lawsuit involving the child's custody. … Even though we have concluded [former lesbian partner] has not established that she was in loco parentis to the child, we also conclude … §102.003(a)(9) does not abrogate any cause of action [former lesbian partner] may have held under the common law doctrine of in loco parentis."

§102.003(a)(10)

In re A.T., No. 14-14-00071-CV (Tex.App.—Houston [14th Dist.] 2014, no pet.) (memo op.; 7-15-14). Foster parents "did not assert standing by filing an original suit under §102.003(a)(10). Instead, [foster parents] asserted standing by invoking §102.003(a)(10) as a basis for their request to intervene. Although §102.003 sets forth the statutory standing bases for filing an original suit rather than intervening, we cannot conclude that a person who satisfies the statutory standing requirements to file an original suit is nonetheless foreclosed from intervening. [¶] It was error for the trial court not to consider whether [foster parents] have standing to intervene under §102.003(a)(10) when standing to intervene under that section was raised by [foster parents'] pleadings and … arguments at the hearing on intervention."

§102.003(a)(11)

TDPRS v. Sherry, 46 S.W.3d 857, 861 (Tex.2001). "[M]ere 'legal residence' is not sufficient to satisfy the 'have resided' requirement in [§102.003(a)(11)]. Although the law sometimes gives a technical meaning to the noun 'residence,' it does not similarly interpret the verb 'resided,' and there is no indication that the Legislature meant anything more than the usual meaning of those words. We thus read 'have resided' to mean living together in the same household."

Doncer v. Dickerson, 81 S.W.3d 349, 358 (Tex.App.—El Paso 2002, no pet.). "Subsection 102.003(a)(11) was designed as a 'stepparent' statute, affording standing to, among others, a stepparent who helps raise a child when the stepparent's spouse—one of the child's parents—dies. A traditional application would indicate that upon the death of the mother, as a sole managing conservator of the child, her current husband would have standing. [Stepmother] contends this section should apply equally to the surviving spouse of the parent who, as a joint managing conservator of the child, does not have *de jure* primary possession but has *de facto* possession for approximately 50% of the time." Held: The court agreed.

§102.003(b)

In re Kelso, 266 S.W.3d 586, 590 (Tex.App.—Fort Worth 2008, orig. proceeding). "Courts should determine a child's principal residence by looking at the following factors: (1) whether the child has a fixed place of abode within the possession of the party, (2) occupied or intended to be occupied consistently over a substantial period of time, and (3) which is permanent rather than temporary."

FAM §102.0035. STATEMENT TO CONFER STANDING

(a) A pregnant woman or a parent of a child may execute a statement to confer standing to a prospective adoptive parent as provided by this section to assert standing under Section 102.003(a)(14). A statement to confer standing under this section may not be executed in a suit brought by a governmental entity under Chapter 262 or 263.

(b) A statement to confer standing must contain:

(1) the signature, name, age, and address of the person named as a prospective adoptive parent;

(2) the signature, name, age, and address of the pregnant woman or of the parent of the child who is consenting to the filing of a petition for adoption or to terminate the parent-child relationship as described by Subsection (a);

(3) the birth date of the child or the anticipated birth date if the child has not been born; and

(4) the name of the county in which the suit will be filed.

(c) The statement to confer standing must be attached to the petition in a suit affecting the parent-child relationship. The statement may not be used for any purpose other than to confer standing in a proceeding for adoption or to terminate the parent-child relationship.

(d) A statement to confer standing may be signed at any time during the pregnancy of the mother of the unborn child whose parental rights are to be terminated.

(e) A statement to confer standing is not required in a suit brought by a person who has standing to file a suit affecting the parent-child relationship under Sections 102.003(a)(1)-(13) or any other law under which the person has standing to file a suit.

(f) A person who executes a statement to confer standing may revoke the statement at any time before the person executes an affidavit for voluntary relinquishment of parental rights. The revocation of the statement must be in writing and must be sent by certified mail, return receipt requested, to the prospective adoptive parent.

(g) On filing with the court proof of the delivery of the revocation of a statement to confer standing under Subsection (f), the court shall dismiss any suit affecting the parent-child relationship filed by the prospective adoptive parent named in the statement.

History of Fam. Code §102.0035: Acts 2003, 78th Leg., ch. 37, §2, eff. Sept. 1, 2003.

A FAM §102.004. STANDING FOR GRANDPARENT OR OTHER PERSON

The amended text in §102.004 is effective for original SAPCRs filed on or after Sept. 1, 2017. Original SAPCRs filed before Sept. 1, 2017, are governed by the former law in effect at that time.

(a) In addition to the general standing to file suit provided by Section 102.003, a grandparent, or another relative of the child related within the third degree by consanguinity, may file an original suit requesting managing conservatorship if there is satisfactory proof to the court that:

(1) the order requested is necessary because the child's present circumstances would significantly impair the child's physical health or emotional development; or

(2) both parents, the surviving parent, or the managing conservator or custodian either filed the petition or consented to the suit.

(b) An original suit requesting possessory conservatorship may not be filed by a grandparent or other person. However, the court may grant a grandparent or other person, subject to the requirements of Subsection (b-1) if applicable, deemed by the court to have had substantial past contact with the child leave to intervene in a pending suit filed by a person authorized to do so under this chapter [~~subchapter~~] if there is satisfactory proof to the court that appointment of a parent as a sole managing conservator or both parents as joint managing conservators would significantly impair the child's physical health or emotional development.

(b-1) A foster parent may only be granted leave to intervene under Subsection (b) if the foster parent would have standing to file an original suit as provided by Section 102.003(a)(12).

(c) Possession of or access to a child by a grandparent is governed by the standards established by Chapter 153.

History of Fam. Code §102.004: Acts 1995, 74th Leg., ch. 20, §1, eff. Apr. 20, 1995. Amended by Acts 1999, 76th Leg., ch. 1048, §2, eff. June 19, 1999; Acts 2005, 79th Leg., ch. 916, §3, eff. June 18, 2005; Acts 2007, 80th Leg., ch. 1406, §2, eff. Sept. 1, 2007; H.B. 1410, §1, 85th Leg., eff. Sept. 1, 2017. Source: Former Fam. Code §11.03(b), (c).

See also ***O'Connor's Texas Family Law Handbook*** (2017), "Grandparent or person with substantial past contact," ch. 4-D, §7.1.2(2), p. 424; "Grandparent," ch. 4-E, §5.1.15, p. 483.

ANNOTATIONS

Shook v. Gray, 381 S.W.3d 540, 542-43 (Tex.2012). See annotation under Family Code §153.131, p. 516.

In re L.D.F., 445 S.W.3d 823, 828 (Tex.App.—El Paso 2014, no pet.). "In family law cases in which a petitioner must go beyond mere pleading allegations and provide 'satisfactory proof' of jurisdictional facts to establish statutory standing, the petitioner meets that burden where those predicate facts are proven by a preponderance of the evidence. *At 829-30:* [W]e refute [father's] contention that ... appointment of a parent in a limited conservatorship capacity somehow automatically precludes appointment of a grandparent as [JMC] by operation of law. The language in the Family Code is clear: if [SMC] by one parent or [JMC] by both parents would result in significant impairment of a child's physical health or emotional development, the court has wide discretion to appoint conservators in the child's best interest. While we agree with [father] that [Fam. Code] §102.004(b), a standing statute, does not grant the trial court power to appoint a parent and grandparent as [JMCs], [Fam. Code] §153.372 specifically authorizes a nonparent to serve as a [JMC] with a parent. Thus, when the statutory provisions are read as a whole, it becomes clear that once a non-parent surpasses the high bar set for intervenor standing under §102.004(b), the trial court may allow the grandparent 'to intervene and seek both managing and possessory conservatorship.' [¶] Where a trial court appoints a

parent and nonparent as [JMCs], it implicitly rules that parent's sole custody would significantly impair the child's physical health or emotional development. Here, because the trial court permitted grandparent intervention and joint custody in this case, we must assume it impliedly found that [father's SMC] *would* significantly impair [child's] physical health or emotional development." *See also* ***Mauldin v. Clements***, 428 S.W.3d 247, 263 (Tex.App.—Houston [1st Dist.] 2014, no pet.); ***Medrano v. Zapata***, this page. *But see* ***In re K.D.H.***, this page.

In re K.D.H., 426 S.W.3d 879, 881 (Tex.App.—Houston [14th Dist.] 2014, no pet.). "Today … this court addresses the legal standard for establishing standing under §102.004(a)(1)…. We conclude that, to have standing under [§102.004(a)(1)], a grandparent or other relative within the third degree by consanguinity must present proof that, when considered in the light most favorable to the petitioner, would enable reasonable and fair-minded people to find that the order requested is necessary because the child's circumstances on the date suit was filed would significantly impair the child's physical health or emotional development." *But see* ***In re L.D.F.***, p. 403; ***Medrano v. Zapata***, this page.

Medrano v. Zapata, No. 03-12-00131-CV (Tex. App.—Austin 2013, no pet.) (memo op.; 12-31-13). The term "'[s]atisfactory proof to the court' as used in [§102.004(a)(1)] denotes proof by a preponderance of the evidence. [¶] While [in this case] there may have been abundant reasons for the district court to credit [mother's] version of the facts rather than [son's], it remains that it impliedly did otherwise—and it is a fundamental limitation on our power that we must defer to such assessments by a fact-finder. We are likewise required to view the evidence in the light favorable to the district court's findings, drawing reasonable inferences in their favor, and presuming that the court resolved any evidentiary conflicts in a manner supporting its findings." *See also* ***In re L.D.F.***, p. 403. *But see* ***In re K.D.H.***, this page.

In re N.L.D., 412 S.W.3d 810, 815 (Tex.App.—Texarkana 2013, no pet.). Mother "does not contest that [intervenors] had substantial past contact with the child; instead, she argues that they only have substantial past contact with [child] because [temporary MC] 'simply left the child in the possession of [intervenors].' *At 816:* [Mother's] primary argument concerning standing is that the trial court should not have allowed conspiracy or conservatorship-by-proxy to establish standing under §102.004(b). However, there is no good-faith requirement in the rules on standing or intervention."

In re Lewis, 357 S.W.3d 396, 402 (Tex.App.—Fort Worth 2011, orig. proceeding). "[W]e hold that when both parents have been appointed [JMCs], the parent-managing conservators are collectively 'the managing conservator' and that each of the parent-managing conservators must consent to the grandparents' intervention before the grandparents have standing under [§]102.004(a)(2) based on the consent of 'the managing conservator.' Without consent from each managing conservator, the grandparents must have the consent of both parents or the child's surviving parent."

In re A.M.S., 277 S.W.3d 92, 98 (Tex.App.—Texarkana 2009, no pet.). "Section 102.004(a)(2) … should [not] be interpreted to prohibit consent after the filing of the suit. Section 102.004 does not specify when the consent must be given or whether the consent must be in writing. … Oral consent, given by the proper party and established in the record, is sufficient to grant standing under §102.004 even if consent is given after the filing of the petition." *See also* ***In re C.G.C.***, No. 12-08-00253-CV (Tex.App.—Tyler 2010, no pet.) (memo op.; 1-29-10) (parents' consent to entering temporary orders that appointed child's grandparents as JMCs "necessarily included" parents' consent to filing suit under §102.004(a)(2)).

Blackwell v. Humble, 241 S.W.3d 707, 722 (Tex. App.—Austin 2007, no pet.). "We agree … that [uncle] did not show that he had 'substantial past contact' with the children. [He] testified only that he had 'seen them regularly.' Without more, this does not show substantial past contact sufficient to warrant his intervention, especially in this case in which both parents are living and present and there is no testimony that the children are at risk living with [father]. [¶] [However,] we cannot hold that the trial court abused its discretion in allowing [grandmother] to intervene. She frequently cared for the children, lived nearby, and spent a great deal of time with the family, and the trial court reasonably could have determined that she showed substantial past contact with the children." *But see* ***In re M.A.M.***, 35 S.W.3d 788, 790 (Tex.App.—Beaumont 2001, no pet.) (grandparents, unlike "other persons,"

are not required to show substantial past contact with children to intervene under §102.004(b)).

FAM §102.0045. STANDING FOR SIBLING

(a) The sibling of a child may file an original suit requesting access to the child as provided by Section 153.551 if the sibling is at least 18 years of age.

(a-1) The sibling of a child who is separated from the sibling as the result of an action by the Department of Family and Protective Services may file an original suit as provided by Section 153.551 requesting access to the child, regardless of the age of the sibling. A court shall expedite a suit filed under this subsection.

(b) Access to a child by a sibling of the child is governed by the standards established by Section 153.551.

History of Fam. Code §102.0045: Acts 2005, 79th Leg., ch. 1191, §1, eff. Sept. 1, 2005. Amended by Acts 2009, 81st Leg., ch. 1113, §1, eff. Sept. 1, 2009; Acts 2015, 84th Leg., ch. 744, §1, eff. Sept. 1, 2015.

See also ***O'Connor's Texas Family Law Handbook*** (2017), "Suit for Sibling Access," ch. 4-I, p. 655.

FAM §102.005. STANDING TO REQUEST TERMINATION & ADOPTION

An original suit requesting only an adoption or for termination of the parent-child relationship joined with a petition for adoption may be filed by:

(1) a stepparent of the child;

(2) an adult who, as the result of a placement for adoption, has had actual possession and control of the child at any time during the 30-day period preceding the filing of the petition;

(3) an adult who has had actual possession and control of the child for not less than two months during the three-month period preceding the filing of the petition;

(4) an adult who has adopted, or is the foster parent of and has petitioned to adopt, a sibling of the child; or

(5) another adult whom the court determines to have had substantial past contact with the child sufficient to warrant standing to do so.

History of Fam. Code §102.005: Acts 1995, 74th Leg., ch. 20, §1, eff. Apr. 20, 1995. Amended by Acts 2007, 80th Leg., ch. 1406, §3(a), eff. Sept. 1, 2007. Source: Former Fam. Code §11.03(d).

ANNOTATIONS

In re J.C., 399 S.W.3d 235, 238 (Tex.App.—San Antonio 2012, no pet.). "Here, although the trial court found that the paternal grandparents had not established sufficient substantial past contact with [child] to confer standing pursuant to [Fam. Code] §102.005(5), it nonetheless held that the paternal grandparents had standing to bring their adoption suit pursuant to [Fam. Code] §102.006(c). Thus, we must determine whether §102.006(c), in and of itself, can confer standing. *At 239:* [I]n order for a party to have standing to bring an original petition for adoption, the party must first meet the standing requirements of §102.005. Section 102.006 does not confer standing, but instead limits which parties have standing to file a petition for adoption pursuant to §102.005."

In re C.M.C., 192 S.W.3d 866, 871 (Tex.App.—Texarkana 2006, no pet.). "The existence of 'substantial past contact' is inherently a fact-intensive inquiry for which it will be difficult, if not impossible, to formulate a concise standard or [list of] comprehensive factors. [T]he Legislature intended the standard to be flexible in order to deal with 'inevitable situations which could not be otherwise anticipated by the drafters.' [¶] Although [grandparents] presented evidence of the difficulties in maintaining contact with their grandchildren, we believe our inquiry should be focused on the amount of actual contact which occurred.... *At 872:* 'Substantial' is defined as 'of ample or considerable amount, quantity, size, etc.' ... Although there was evidence of telephone calls, cards, and letters, such interaction is too minimal under the circumstances of this case to create a fact issue concerning substantial contact." *See also* ***Rodarte v. Cox***, 828 S.W.2d 65, 69-70 (Tex.App.—Tyler 1991, writ denied) ("substantial contact" does not require possession and control).

FAM §102.006. LIMITATIONS ON STANDING

(a) Except as provided by Subsections (b) and (c), if the parent-child relationship between the child and every living parent of the child has been terminated, an original suit may not be filed by:

(1) a former parent whose parent-child relationship with the child has been terminated by court order;

(2) the father of the child; or

(3) a family member or relative by blood, adoption, or marriage of either a former parent whose parent-child relationship has been terminated or of the father of the child.

(b) The limitations on filing suit imposed by this section do not apply to a person who:

(1) has a continuing right to possession of or access to the child under an existing court order; or

(2) has the consent of the child's managing conservator, guardian, or legal custodian to bring the suit.

(c) The limitations on filing suit imposed by this section do not apply to an adult sibling of the child, a grandparent of the child, an aunt who is a sister of a parent of the child, or an uncle who is a brother of a parent of the child if the adult sibling, grandparent, aunt, or uncle files an original suit or a suit for modification requesting managing conservatorship of the child not later than the 90th day after the date the parent-child relationship between the child and the parent is terminated in a suit filed by the Department of Family and Protective Services requesting the termination of the parent-child relationship.

History of Fam. Code §102.006: Acts 1995, 74th Leg., ch. 20, §1, eff. Apr. 20, 1995. Amended by Acts 2001, 77th Leg., ch. 821, §2.08, eff. June 14, 2001; Acts 2007, 80th Leg., ch. 866, §1, eff. June 15, 2007. Source: Former Fam. Code §11.03(g), (h).

ANNOTATIONS

In re J.M.F., No. 13-12-00640-CV (Tex.App.—Corpus Christi 2013, no pet.) (memo op.; 9-26-13). "Even if standing is established, [Fam. Code] §102.006 can limit standing in cases where the parent-child relationship has been terminated, such as in [child's] case. [¶] [Petitioner] was [child's] natural uncle[, and he and his wife had adopted child's older siblings]. Therefore, he would be ineligible to bring suit under [§]102.006(a)(3).... [¶] The trial [court] held ... that the [§102.006](c) exception was inapplicable to [petitioners] because they did 'not have standing to file a SAPCR requesting managing conservatorship or possessory conservatorship,' presumably under [Fam. Code] §102.003. [Petitioners], though, did not file a SAPCR requesting managing conservatorship or possessory conservatorship under §102.003. Instead, they filed an original petition for adoption under [Fam. Code] §102.005. Section 102.006(c) is drafted disjunctively—persons can either file 'an original suit' *or* 'a suit for modification requesting managing conservatorship.' Here, [petitioners] timely filed 'an original suit' for adoption ... after the trial court terminated [child's] parents' parental rights. [¶] [Petitioners] fit 'within the parameters' of the exception established by §102.006(c) because [petitioner] was a natural uncle of [child] who filed an original petition within 90 days of the date [child's] parents' parental rights were terminated."

In re J.C., 399 S.W.3d 235, 238 (Tex.App.—San Antonio 2012, no pet.). See annotation under Family Code §102.005, p. 405.

In re A.M., 312 S.W.3d 76, 80 (Tex.App.—San Antonio 2010, pet. denied). "[W]e must decide whether a person seeking to adopt has the right to request an evidentiary hearing to determine whether the [TDFPS] wrongfully withheld its consent to adopt under [Fam. Code] §102.006(b)(2). *At 83-84:* [Maternal aunt and grandmother] contend that consent cannot be withheld without good cause and should be waived by the trial court if it is in the best interests of the children. We must determine whether §102.006(b)(2) should be read in conjunction with [Fam. Code] §162.010 governing adoptions. [¶] [S]ection 162.010's provision that the managing conservator's consent may not be refused absent good cause[] does not apply until *after* the movant has established standing under [Fam. Code] Ch. 102. [¶] [T]here ... is no statutory basis for an inquiry into the motivation of a managing conservator's refusal to consent to an adoption in §102.006, and we cannot import §162.010 to provide such a basis. [¶] Because the [TDFPS] was not required to give its consent and the good faith of such a decision is irrelevant to standing, the trial court did not err in refusing to hear evidence regarding whether the [TDFPS] wrongfully withheld its consent under §102.006(b)(2)."

FAM §102.007. STANDING OF TITLE IV-D AGENCY

In providing services authorized by Chapter 231, the Title IV-D agency or a political subdivision contracting with the attorney general to provide Title IV-D services under this title may file a child support action authorized under this title, including a suit for modification or a motion for enforcement.

History of Fam. Code §102.007: Acts 1995, 74th Leg., ch. 20, §1, eff. Apr. 20, 1995. Amended by Acts 1995, 74th Leg., ch. 341, §2.02, eff. Sept. 1, 1995. Source: Former Fam. Code §11.03(i).

ANNOTATIONS

In re A.M., 192 S.W.3d 570, 575 (Tex.2006). "The [AG], as the Title IV-D agency and [mother's] assignee, is fully authorized to sue for unpaid child support and defend against any claim that might affect that collection[, including a reimbursement claim]."

A FAM §102.008. CONTENTS OF PETITION

The amended text in §102.008 is effective for petitions filed and authorization agreements executed on or after Sept. 1, 2017. Petitions filed and authorization

agreements executed before Sept. 1, 2017, are governed by the former law in effect at that time.

(a) The petition and all other documents in a proceeding filed under this title, except a suit for adoption of an adult, shall be entitled "In the interest of __________, a child." In a suit in which adoption of a child is requested, the style shall be "In the interest of a child."

(b) The petition must include:

(1) a statement that the court in which the petition is filed has continuing, exclusive jurisdiction or that no court has continuing jurisdiction of the suit;

(2) the name and date of birth of the child, except that if adoption of a child is requested, the name of the child may be omitted;

(3) the full name of the petitioner and the petitioner's relationship to the child or the fact that no relationship exists;

(4) the names of the parents, except in a suit in which adoption is requested;

(5) the name of the managing conservator, if any, or the child's custodian, if any, appointed by order of a court of another state or country;

(6) the names of the guardians of the person and estate of the child, if any;

(7) the names of possessory conservators or other persons, if any, having possession of or access to the child under an order of the court;

(8) the name of an alleged father of the child or a statement that the identity of the father of the child is unknown;

(9) a full description and statement of value of all property owned or possessed by the child;

(10) a statement describing what action the court is requested to take concerning the child and the statutory grounds on which the request is made; [and]

(11) a statement as to whether, in regard to a party to the suit or a child of a party to the suit:

(A) there is in effect:

(i) a protective order under Title 4;

(ii) a protective order under Chapter 7A, Code of Criminal Procedure; or

(iii) an order for emergency protection under Article 17.292, Code of Criminal Procedure; or

(B) an application for an order described by Paragraph (A) is pending; and

(12) any other information required by this title.

(c) The petitioner shall attach a copy of each order described by Subsection (b)(11)(A) in which a party to the suit or a child of a party to the suit was the applicant or victim of the conduct alleged in the application or order and the other party was the respondent or defendant of an action regarding the conduct alleged in the application or order without regard to the date of the order. If a copy of the order is not available at the time of filing, the petition must state that a copy of the order will be filed with the court before any hearing.

(d) Notwithstanding any other provision of this section, if the Title IV-D agency files a petition in a suit affecting the parent-child relationship, the agency is not required to:

(1) include in the petition the statement described by Subsection (b)(11); or

(2) attach copies of the documentation described by Subsection (c).

History of Fam. Code §102.008: Acts 1995, 74th Leg., ch. 20, §1, eff. Apr. 20, 1995. Amended by Acts 2001, 77th Leg., ch. 296, §2, eff. Sept. 1, 2001; H.B. 3052, §6, 85th Leg., eff. Sept. 1, 2017. Source: Former Fam. Code §11.08(a), (b).

See also *O'Connor's Texas Family Law Handbook* (2017), "Contents," ch. 4-D, §2.4, p. 412.

ANNOTATIONS

Dohrn v. Delgado, 941 S.W.2d 244, 248 (Tex. App.—Corpus Christi 1996, orig. proceeding). "[W]e indulge a liberal construction of pleadings and pre-trial procedures in [SAPCRs], and technical rules of pleading and practice need not be strictly followed. The [SAPCR] petition need not specifically name the section of the Family Code on which the petitioner relies, as long as it makes the necessary allegations to support the relief afforded by that section." *See also* ***In re M.G.N.***, 491 S.W.3d 386, 408 (Tex.App.—San Antonio 2016, pet. denied) (trial courts possess "wide discretion" regarding sufficiency of pleadings in child-custody and control proceedings).

FAM §102.0085. REPEALED

Repealed by Acts 2003, 78th Leg., ch. 1313, §1, eff. Sept. 1, 2003.

FAM §102.0086. CONFIDENTIALITY OF PLEADINGS

(a) This section applies only in a county with a population of 3.4 million or more.

(b) Except as otherwise provided by law, all pleadings and other documents filed with the court in a suit affecting the parent-child relationship are confidential, are excepted from required public disclosure under

Chapter 552, Government Code, and may not be released to a person who is not a party to the suit until after the date of service of citation or the 31st day after the date of filing the suit, whichever date is sooner.

History of Fam. Code §102.0086: Acts 2003, 78th Leg., ch. 1314, §3, eff. Sept. 1, 2003.

FAM §102.009. SERVICE OF CITATION

(a) Except as provided by Subsection (b), the following are entitled to service of citation on the filing of a petition in an original suit:

(1) a managing conservator;

(2) a possessory conservator;

(3) a person having possession of or access to the child under an order;

(4) a person required by law or by order to provide for the support of the child;

(5) a guardian of the person of the child;

(6) a guardian of the estate of the child;

(7) each parent as to whom the parent-child relationship has not been terminated or process has not been waived under Chapter 161;

(8) an alleged father, unless there is attached to the petition an affidavit of waiver of interest in a child executed by the alleged father as provided by Chapter 161 or unless the petitioner has complied with the provisions of Section 161.002(b)(2), (3), or (4);

(9) a man who has filed a notice of intent to claim paternity as provided by Chapter 160;

(10) the Department of Family and Protective Services, if the petition requests that the department be appointed as managing conservator of the child;

(11) the Title IV-D agency, if the petition requests the termination of the parent-child relationship and support rights have been assigned to the Title IV-D agency under Chapter 231;

(12) a prospective adoptive parent to whom standing has been conferred under Section 102.0035; and

(13) a person designated as the managing conservator in a revoked or unrevoked affidavit of relinquishment under Chapter 161 or to whom consent to adoption has been given in writing under Chapter 162.

(b) Citation may be served on any other person who has or who may assert an interest in the child.

(c) Citation on the filing of an original petition in a suit shall be issued and served as in other civil cases.

(d) If the petition requests the establishment, termination, modification, or enforcement of a support right assigned to the Title IV-D agency under Chapter 231 or the rescission of a voluntary acknowledgment of paternity under Chapter 160, notice shall be given to the Title IV-D agency in a manner provided by Rule 21a, Texas Rules of Civil Procedure.

(e) In a proceeding under Chapter 233, the requirements imposed by Subsections (a) and (c) do not apply to the extent of any conflict between those requirements and the provisions in Chapter 233.

History of Fam. Code §102.009: Acts 1995, 74th Leg., ch. 20, §1, eff. Apr. 20, 1995. Amended by Acts 1995, 74th Leg., ch. 751, §10, eff. Sept. 1, 1995; Acts 1997, 75th Leg., ch. 561, §1 (eff. Sept. 1, 1997), ch. 599, §1 (eff. Sept. 1, 1997); Acts 1999, 76th Leg., ch. 62, §6.12 (eff. Sept. 1, 1999), ch. 556, §2 (eff. Sept. 1, 1999); Acts 2001, 77th Leg., ch. 821, §2.09, eff. June 14, 2001; Acts 2005, 79th Leg., ch. 916, §4, eff. June 17, 2005; Acts 2007, 80th Leg., ch. 972, §2 (eff. Sept. 1, 2007), ch. 1283, §1 (eff. Sept. 1, 2007); Acts 2009, 81st Leg., ch. 767, §1, eff. June 19, 2009. Source: Former Fam. Code §11.09(a)-(c), (f).

See also ***O'Connor's Texas Family Law Handbook*** (2017), "Service of Process," ch. 4-D, §5, p. 416.

ANNOTATIONS

TDPRS v. Sherry, 46 S.W.3d 857, 860 (Tex.2001). "Section 102.009 identifies those persons entitled to be served with citation in a SAPCR and includes 'an alleged father.' When the [AG] filed the … paternity suit, he alleged in the pleadings that [initially alleged father] was [child's] father. The [AG] did not allege that [petitioner] was [child's] father. Thus, [initially alleged father] was the only 'alleged father,' as the term is used in the statute, who was entitled to notice. *At 861:* [Section 102.009(b)] does not require service …; it merely allows voluntary service by the plaintiff or at the court's discretion." *But see* ***In re K.M.S.***, this page.

In re K.M.S., 68 S.W.3d 61, 68 (Tex.App.—Dallas 2001), *pet. denied*, 91 S.W.3d 331 (Tex.2002). "Implicit in [managing conservator's] testimony is that [petitioner] told [managing conservator's] mother and [managing conservator] that he believed he was [child's] father. Thus, [managing conservator] had notice that [petitioner] claimed to be [child's] father. Knowing that [petitioner] was an alleged father, [managing conservator] was required by … §102.009(a)(8) to serve [petitioner] with his petition to establish paternity. We … interpret 'alleged father' … to include a man who has informed the petitioner, either formally through service of process or informally by other means of communication, of his belief that he is the biological father of the child." *But see* ***TDPRS v. Sherry***, this page.

Roberson v. Pickett, 900 S.W.2d 112, 116 (Tex. App.—Houston [14th Dist.] 1995, no writ). "The issue presented ... is whether the statute intends for a person who has asserted an interest in a child by filing suit but has yet to have that right recognized is entitled to mandatory service. By filing suit to establish the relationship, the person moves from the group of those who have or may assert an interest who are not entitled to mandatory service to the group of those who are entitled to mandatory service. [A] person who has filed suit seeking guardianship fits within the meaning of guardian of the person or estate under [Fam. Code] §11.09(a)(5) and (a)(6) [now §102.009(a)(5) and (a)(6)]."

FAM §102.0091. WAIVER OF CITATION

(a) A party to a suit under this title may waive the issuance or service of citation after the suit is filed by filing with the clerk of the court in which the suit is filed the waiver of the party acknowledging receipt of a copy of the filed petition.

(b) The party executing the waiver may not sign the waiver using a digitized signature.

(c) The waiver must contain the mailing address of the party executing the waiver.

(d) Notwithstanding Section 132.001, Civil Practice and Remedies Code, the waiver must be sworn before a notary public who is not an attorney in the suit. This subsection does not apply if the party executing the waiver is incarcerated.

(e) The Texas Rules of Civil Procedure do not apply to a waiver executed under this section.

History of Fam. Code §102.0091: Acts 2015, 84th Leg., ch. 198, §5, eff. Sept. 1, 2015.

FAM §102.010. SERVICE OF CITATION BY PUBLICATION

(a) Citation may be served by publication as in other civil cases to persons entitled to service of citation who cannot be notified by personal service or registered or certified mail and to persons whose names are unknown.

(b) Citation by publication shall be published one time. If the name of a person entitled to service of citation is unknown, the notice to be published shall be addressed to "All Whom It May Concern." One or more causes to be heard on a certain day may be included in one notice and hearings may be continued from time to time without further notice.

(c) Citation by publication shall be sufficient if given in substantially the following form:

To (names of persons to be served with citation) and to all whom it may concern (if the name of any person to be served with citation is unknown), Respondent(s),

"STATE OF TEXAS

"You have been sued. You may employ an attorney. If you or your attorney do (does) not file a written answer with the clerk who issued this citation by 10 a.m. on the Monday next following the expiration of 20 days after you were served this citation and petition, a default judgment may be taken against you. The petition of ______________, Petitioner, was filed in the Court of ______________ County, Texas, on the ___ day of __________, _____, against __________, Respondent(s), numbered _____, and entitled 'In the interest of __________, a child (or children).' The suit requests (statement of relief requested, e.g., 'terminate the parent-child relationship'). The date and place of birth of the child (children) who is (are) the subject of the suit: ______________.

"The court has authority in this suit to render an order in the child's (children's) interest that will be binding on you, including the termination of the parent-child relationship, the determination of paternity, and the appointment of a conservator with authority to consent to the child's (children's) adoption.

"Issued and given under my hand and seal of the Court at __________, Texas, this the ___ day of _______, _____.

"______________ Clerk of the District Court of _________ County, Texas. By _________, Deputy."

(d) In any suit in which service of citation is by publication, a statement of the evidence of service, approved and signed by the court, must be filed with the papers of the suit as a part of the record.

(e) In a suit filed under Chapter 161 or 262 in which the last name of the respondent is unknown, the court may order substituted service of citation by publication, including publication by posting the citation at the courthouse door for a specified time, if the court finds and states in its order that the method of substituted service is as likely as citation by publication in a newspaper in the manner described by Subsection (b) to give the respondent actual notice of the suit. If the court orders that citation by publication shall be completed by posting the citation at the courthouse door for

a specified time, service must be completed on, and the answer date is computed from, the expiration date of the posting period. If the court orders another method of substituted service of citation by publication, service shall be completed as directed by the court.

History of Fam. Code §102.010: Acts 1995, 74th Leg., ch. 20, §1, eff. Apr. 20, 1995. Amended by Acts 2003, 78th Leg., ch. 1015, §1, eff. Sept. 1, 2003. Source: Former Fam. Code §11.09(d), (e).

See also ***O'Connor's Texas Family Law Handbook*** (2017), "Service by publication," ch. 4-D, §5.2.4, p. 418.

ANNOTATIONS

In re E.R., 385 S.W.3d 552, 564 (Tex.2012). "'[I]f personal service can be effected by the exercise of reasonable diligence, substituted service is not to be resorted to.' *At 565-66:* A diligent search must include inquiries that someone who really wants to find the defendant would make, and diligence is measured not by the quantity of the search but by its quality. [Caseworker] neglected 'obvious inquiries' a prudent investigator would have made. … When a known parent has not left the jurisdiction, when she has attended at least two court hearings and has come to the Department offices for a prescheduled, hour-long meeting with her children during the very period service was being attempted, and when the Department can reach her by telephone and can communicate with her family members, service by publication cannot provide the kind of process she is due. Sending a few faxes, checking websites, and making three phone calls—none of which were to [mother] or her family members—is not the type of diligent inquiry required before the Department may dispense with actual service in a case like this. … Here, it was both possible and practicable to more adequately warn [mother] of the impending termination of her parental rights, and notice by publication was therefore constitutionally inadequate."

In re P. RJ E., 499 S.W.3d 571, 576 (Tex.App.—Houston [1st Dist.] 2016, pet. filed 9-23-16). "The Texas Supreme Court in [***In re E.R.***, 385 S.W.3d 552 (Tex.2012),] stated that to fail to obtain personal service when the Department knows the location of a mother is 'poor, hopeless, and unjustif[ied]….' The same holds true for an alleged father that the Department identifies, locates, and names in the termination lawsuit. [¶] The Department knew of [alleged father's] identity and address at least one month before the termination hearing and his identity matched the descriptive information the mother gave the Department. Upon locating [alleged father], the Department specifically amended its petition to terminate [alleged father's] parental rights, joined [alleged father] as a party, sought a decree terminating [alleged father's] rights, and eventually obtained a judgment against him. It did so without personal service on [alleged father]. While a father's interest as a biological father may be insufficient in itself to require notice and an opportunity to be heard, the Department attempted to invoke the jurisdiction of the court over [alleged father] individually. Thus, due process requires here that the Department take the minimal burden of obtaining personal service on [alleged father] rather than relying on the earlier service by publication on 'unknown fathers.'"

Curley v. Curley, 511 S.W.3d 131, 134-35 (Tex. App.—El Paso 2014, no pet.). "'[N]otice of the nature of the suit is essential to a valid citation by publication.' At a minimum, this includes notice that the suit seeks to alter the parent-child relationship. [¶] Even if the instant citation had been given substantially in the form of §102.010(c), the record establishes that [H] was not duly diligent in attempting to locate [W] before resorting to service by publication. [¶] [W] testified that [H] knew how to contact several persons who knew her whereabouts…. She also testified that [H] could have obtained her current address from her telephone service provider, which listed [H] as an authorized user on the account, as well as her military insurance provider. [H] quickly and easily found [W's] correct address via the internet when he found and took possession of [child] 17 days after the default [divorce] judgment had been entered. [¶] [W]e conclude that [H] was not sufficiently diligent in attempting to locate [W] before resorting to service by publication. [H] neglected 'obvious inquiries' that a diligent litigant would have made."

FAM §102.011. ACQUIRING JURISDICTION OVER NONRESIDENT

(a) The court may exercise status or subject matter jurisdiction over the suit as provided by Chapter 152.

(b) The court may also exercise personal jurisdiction over a person on whom service of citation is required or over the person's personal representative, although the person is not a resident or domiciliary of this state, if:

(1) the person is personally served with citation in this state;

(2) the person submits to the jurisdiction of this state by consent, by entering a general appearance, or by filing a responsive document having the effect of waiving any contest to personal jurisdiction;

(3) the child resides in this state as a result of the acts or directives of the person;

(4) the person resided with the child in this state;

(5) the person resided in this state and provided prenatal expenses or support for the child;

(6) the person engaged in sexual intercourse in this state and the child may have been conceived by that act of intercourse;

(7) the person, as provided by Chapter 160:

(A) registered with the paternity registry maintained by the vital statistics unit; or

(B) signed an acknowledgment of paternity of a child born in this state; or

(8) there is any basis consistent with the constitutions of this state and the United States for the exercise of the personal jurisdiction.

History of Fam. Code §102.011: Acts 1995, 74th Leg., ch. 20, §1, eff. Apr. 20, 1995. Amended by Acts 1997, 75th Leg., ch. 561, §2, eff. Sept. 1, 1997; Acts 2009, 81st Leg., ch. 767, §2, eff. June 19, 2009; Acts 2015, 84th Leg., ch. 1, §1.030, eff. Apr. 2, 2015. Source: Former Fam. Code §11.051.

See also *O'Connor's Texas Family Law Handbook* (2017), "Child support & parentage – in personam jurisdiction," ch. 4-A, §2.2.2, p. 336.

ANNOTATIONS

In re S.A.V., 837 S.W.2d 80, 83 (Tex.1992). "Claims for child support and visitation expenses are like claims for debt in that they seek a personal judgment establishing a direct obligation to pay money. Therefore, a valid judgment for child support or visitation expenses may be rendered only by a court having jurisdiction over the person of the defendant. *At 84:* A 'custody determination' means a court decision providing for the custody of a child, including visitation rights. Unlike adjudications of child support and visitation expense, custody determinations are status adjudications not dependent upon personal jurisdiction over the parents. [¶] Generally, a family relationship is among those matters in which the forum state has such a strong interest that its courts may reasonably make an adjudication affecting that relationship even though one of the parties to the relationship may have had no personal contacts with the forum state. Consequently, due process permits adjudication of the custody and visitation of a child residing in the forum state without a showing of 'minimum contacts' on the part of the nonresident parent."

Flores v. Melo-Palacios, 921 S.W.2d 399, 404 (Tex. App.—Corpus Christi 1996, writ denied). "[T]he status or subject matter jurisdiction permitted by [Fam. Code] §11.051 [now §102.011] for [SAPCRs] is merely an alternative means of obtaining jurisdiction when the court is unable to obtain personal jurisdiction over the nonresident party. There is simply no requirement that there be both status and personal jurisdiction before a court may entertain a suit for child support. ... The jurisdictional principles used in child support determinations differ from the special jurisdictional principles used in child custody determinations which focus primarily on the 'status' of the child. It is well-settled that a court may only render a judgment for child support against a person if the court has [personal] jurisdiction over that person."

FAM §102.012. EXERCISING PARTIAL JURISDICTION

(a) A court in which a suit is filed may exercise its jurisdiction over those portions of the suit for which it has authority.

(b) The court's authority to resolve all issues in controversy between the parties may be restricted because the court lacks:

(1) the required personal jurisdiction over a nonresident party;

(2) the required jurisdiction under Chapter 152; or

(3) the required jurisdiction under Chapter 159.

(c) If a provision of Chapter 152 or Chapter 159 expressly conflicts with another provision of this title and the conflict cannot be reconciled, the provision of Chapter 152 or Chapter 159 prevails.

(d) In exercising jurisdiction, the court shall seek to harmonize the provisions of this code, the federal Parental Kidnapping Prevention Act (28 U.S.C. Section 1738A), and the federal Full Faith and Credit for Child Support Order Act (28 U.S.C. Section 1738B).

History of Fam. Code §102.012: Acts 1995, 74th Leg., ch. 20, §1, eff. Apr. 20, 1995. Amended by Acts 1999, 76th Leg., ch. 62, §6.13, eff. Sept. 1, 1999.

See also Fam. Code §6.308.

FAM §102.013. DOCKETING REQUIREMENTS

(a) In a suit for modification or a motion for enforcement, the clerk shall file the petition or motion and all related papers under the same docket number as the prior proceeding without additional letters, digits, or special designations.

(b) If a suit requests the adoption of a child, the clerk shall file the suit and all other papers relating to the suit in a new file having a new docket number.

(c) In a suit to determine parentage under this title in which the court has rendered an order relating to an earlier born child of the same parents, the clerk shall file the suit and all other papers relating to the suit under the same docket number as the prior parentage action. For all other purposes, including the assessment of fees and other costs, the suit is a separate suit.

History of Fam. Code §102.013: Acts 1995, 74th Leg., ch. 20, §1, eff. Apr. 20, 1995. Amended by Acts 2001, 77th Leg., ch. 1023, §2, eff. Sept. 1, 2001. Source: Former Fam. Code §11.07(c).

FAM §102.014. USE OF DIGITIZED SIGNATURE

(a) A digitized signature on an original petition under this chapter or any other pleading or order in a suit satisfies the requirements for and imposes the duties of signatories to pleadings, motions, and other papers identified under Rule 13, Texas Rules of Civil Procedure.

(b) A digitized signature under this section may be applied only by, and must remain under the sole control of, the person whose signature is represented.

History of Fam. Code §102.014: Acts 2013, 83rd Leg., ch. 790, §2, eff. Sept. 1, 2013.

CHAPTER 103. VENUE & TRANSFER OF ORIGINAL PROCEEDINGS

FAM §103.001. VENUE FOR ORIGINAL SUIT

(a) Except as otherwise provided by this title, an original suit shall be filed in the county where the child resides, unless:

(1) another court has continuing exclusive jurisdiction under Chapter 155; or

(2) venue is fixed in a suit for dissolution of a marriage under Subchapter D, Chapter 6.

(b) A suit in which adoption is requested may be filed in the county where the child resides or in the county where the petitioners reside, regardless of whether another court has continuing exclusive jurisdiction under Chapter 155. A court that has continuing exclusive jurisdiction is not required to transfer the suit affecting the parent-child relationship to the court in which the adoption suit is filed.

(c) A child resides in the county where the child's parents reside or the child's parent resides, if only one parent is living, except that:

(1) if a guardian of the person has been appointed by order of a county or probate court and a managing conservator has not been appointed, the child resides in the county where the guardian of the person resides;

(2) if the parents of the child do not reside in the same county and if a managing conservator, custodian, or guardian of the person has not been appointed, the child resides in the county where the parent having actual care, control, and possession of the child resides;

(3) if the child is in the care and control of an adult other than a parent and a managing conservator, custodian, or guardian of the person has not been appointed, the child resides where the adult having actual care, control, and possession of the child resides;

(4) if the child is in the actual care, control, and possession of an adult other than a parent and the whereabouts of the parent and the guardian of the person is unknown, the child resides where the adult having actual possession, care, and control of the child resides;

(5) if the person whose residence would otherwise determine venue has left the child in the care and control of the adult, the child resides where that adult resides;

(6) if a guardian or custodian of the child has been appointed by order of a court of another state or country, the child resides in the county where the guardian or custodian resides if that person resides in this state; or

(7) if it appears that the child is not under the actual care, control, and possession of an adult, the child resides where the child is found.

History of Fam. Code §103.001: Acts 1995, 74th Leg., ch. 20, §1, eff. Apr. 20, 1995. Amended by Acts 1999, 76th Leg., ch. 62, §6.14, eff. Sept. 1, 1999; Acts 2015, 84th Leg., ch. 944, §8, eff. Sept. 1, 2015. Source: Former Fam. Code §11.04.

See also *O'Connor's Texas Family Law Handbook* (2017), "Choosing the Court," ch. 4-A, p. 330.

ANNOTATIONS

In re Narvaiz, 193 S.W.3d 695, 699 (Tex.App.—Beaumont 2006, orig. proceeding). "In evaluating the Legislature's intent regarding the 'actual care, control, and possession' provision [in §103.001], we observe that the Family Code does not state whether the relevant time frame for the inquiry is the date the original

SAPCR is filed, or whether the relevant time frame for determining whether a party is in 'actual care, control, and possession' is an indeterminate time frame prior to the filing of the original SAPCR. *At 700:* We conclude that the Legislature's use of the term 'actual' rebuts any inference that it intended to incorporate a broader time frame other than the date of filing."

In re S.D., 980 S.W.2d 758, 760-61 (Tex.App.—San Antonio 1998, pet. denied). "Normally, children reside where their parents reside. ... Texas law is clear that an element of permanency is necessary before a party can be considered a resident of a particular county."

Arteaga v. TDPRS, 924 S.W.2d 756, 762 (Tex. App.—Austin 1996, writ denied). "The venue statute comes into play only after the trial court has determined that Texas courts have jurisdiction over the custody dispute."

FAM §103.002. TRANSFER OF ORIGINAL PROCEEDINGS WITHIN STATE

(a) If venue of a suit is improper in the court in which an original suit is filed and no other court has continuing, exclusive jurisdiction of the suit, on the timely motion of a party other than the petitioner, the court shall transfer the proceeding to the county where venue is proper.

(b) On a showing that a suit for dissolution of the marriage of the child's parents has been filed in another court, a court in which a suit is pending shall transfer the proceedings to the court where the dissolution of the marriage is pending.

(c) The procedures in Chapter 155 apply to a transfer of:

(1) an original suit under this section; or

(2) a suit for modification or a motion for enforcement under this title.

History of Fam. Code §103.002: Acts 1995, 74th Leg., ch. 20, §1, eff. Apr. 20, 1995. Source: Former Fam. Code §11.06(a), (c).

See also ***O'Connor's Texas Family Law Handbook*** (2017), "Challenging Venue," ch. 4-B, §3, p. 350.

FAM §103.003. TRANSFER OF ORIGINAL SUIT WITHIN STATE WHEN PARTY OR CHILD RESIDES OUTSIDE STATE

(a) A court of this state in which an original suit is filed or in which a suit for child support is filed under Chapter 159 shall transfer the suit to the county of residence of the party who is a resident of this state if all other parties and children affected by the proceedings reside outside this state.

(b) If one or more of the parties affected by the suit reside outside this state and if more than one party or one or more children affected by the proceeding reside in this state in different counties, the court shall transfer the suit according to the following priorities:

(1) to the court of continuing, exclusive jurisdiction, if any;

(2) to the county of residence of the child, if applicable, provided that:

(A) there is no court of continuing, exclusive jurisdiction; or

(B) the court of continuing, exclusive jurisdiction finds that neither a party nor a child affected by the proceeding resides in the county of the court of continuing jurisdiction; or

(3) if Subdivisions (1) and (2) are inapplicable, to the county most appropriate to serve the convenience of the resident parties, the witnesses, and the interest of justice.

(c) If a transfer of an original suit or suit for child support under Chapter 159 is sought under this section, Chapter 155 applies to the procedures for transfer of the suit.

History of Fam. Code §103.003: Acts 1995, 74th Leg., ch. 20, §1, eff. Apr. 20, 1995. Source: Former Fam. Code §11.061.

See also ***O'Connor's Texas Family Law Handbook*** (2017), "Challenging Venue," ch. 4-B, §3, p. 350.

CHAPTER 104. EVIDENCE

FAM §104.001. RULES OF EVIDENCE

Except as otherwise provided, the Texas Rules of Evidence apply as in other civil cases.

History of Fam. Code §104.001: Acts 1995, 74th Leg., ch. 20, §1, eff. Apr. 20, 1995. Amended by Acts 2005, 79th Leg., ch. 728, §6.002, eff. Sept. 1, 2005. Source: Former Fam. Code §11.14(e).

FAM §104.002. PRERECORDED STATEMENT OF CHILD

If a child 12 years of age or younger is alleged in a suit under this title to have been abused, the recording of an oral statement of the child recorded prior to the proceeding is admissible into evidence if:

(1) no attorney for a party was present when the statement was made;

(2) the recording is both visual and aural and is recorded on film or videotape or by other electronic means;

(3) the recording equipment was capable of making an accurate recording, the operator was competent, and the recording is accurate and has not been altered;

(4) the statement was not made in response to questioning calculated to lead the child to make a particular statement;

(5) each voice on the recording is identified;

(6) the person conducting the interview of the child in the recording is present at the proceeding and available to testify or be cross-examined by either party; and

(7) each party is afforded an opportunity to view the recording before it is offered into evidence.

History of Fam. Code §104.002: Acts 1995, 74th Leg., ch. 20, §1, eff. Apr. 20, 1995. Source: Former Fam. Code §11.21(a), (b).

See also *O'Connor's Texas Family Law Handbook* (2017), "Prerecorded statement of abused child," ch. 4-D, §12.4.1, p. 456.

ANNOTATIONS

In re S.P., 168 S.W.3d 197, 209-10 (Tex.App.—Dallas 2005, no pet.). "Unlike [Fam. Code] §104.006, [Fam. Code] §104.002 does not authorize the trial court to use the statement *in lieu of* testimony. While §104.002 may support admission of the videotape statement itself, it does not support the trial court's decision to allow the statement in lieu of the child's testimony. Both parents requested that [child] be made available and suggested that her testimony could be taken by alternative means, such as closed-circuit television under [Fam. Code] §104.004. The trial court refused these requests. Regardless of the admissibility of the videotaped statement under §104.002, that section does not authorize the trial court to admit [child's] videotaped statement in lieu of her testimony at trial without requiring the [TDPRS] to make the child available to testify."

In re R.V., 977 S.W.2d 777, 781 (Tex.App.—Fort Worth 1998, no pet.). An exception "to the right of face-to-face confrontation exists when the State shows that a special procedure is necessary to protect child witnesses from the trauma of testifying in court. [¶] The determination of whether such alternative forms of testimony [such as one-way, closed-circuit television] are necessary should be made on a case-by-case basis. In making such a determination, courts should consider whether: (1) use of a video is necessary to protect the welfare of the child; (2) the trauma to the child comes from exposure to the abuser, rather than from the courtroom generally; and (3) the emotional distress to the child would be more than minimal."

James v. Texas DHS, 836 S.W.2d 236, 239-41 (Tex. App.—Texarkana 1992, no writ). "By prohibiting leading questions in cases governed by [Fam. Code] §11.21(b)(4) [now §104.002(4)], the legislative branch adopted the common-law rule insofar as the uncross-examined videotaped testimony of children under the age of 12 is concerned. Under the strictures of ... §11.21, questions directed to a child must be open-ended and not suggestive of a response. We conclude that the videotape with these children's statements should have been excluded because the questioning was calculated to lead the children to a particular statement. The questioning itself was generally leading. In addition, [interviewer's] nonverbal communication, such as her approving, affectionate pats in response to desired answers and her active, demonstrative use of the dolls, coupled with her argumentative refusal to accept undesired answers, contributed to making a particular statement. Thus, the statement should not have been admitted as evidence."

FAM §104.003. PRERECORDED VIDEOTAPED TESTIMONY OF CHILD

(a) The court may, on the motion of a party to the proceeding, order that the testimony of the child be taken outside the courtroom and be recorded for showing in the courtroom before the court, the finder of fact, and the parties to the proceeding.

(b) Only an attorney for each party, an attorney ad litem for the child or other person whose presence would contribute to the welfare and well-being of the child, and persons necessary to operate the equipment may be present in the room with the child during the child's testimony.

(c) Only the attorneys for the parties may question the child.

(d) The persons operating the equipment shall be placed in a manner that prevents the child from seeing or hearing them.

(e) The court shall ensure that:

(1) the recording is both visual and aural and is recorded on film or videotape or by other electronic means;

(2) the recording equipment was capable of making an accurate recording, the operator was competent, and the recording is accurate and is not altered;

(3) each voice on the recording is identified; and

(4) each party to the proceeding is afforded an opportunity to view the recording before it is shown in the courtroom.

History of Fam. Code §104.003: Acts 1995, 74th Leg., ch. 20, §1, eff. Apr. 20, 1995. Source: Former Fam. Code §11.21(d).

FAM §104.004. REMOTE TELEVISED BROADCAST OF TESTIMONY OF CHILD

(a) If in a suit a child 12 years of age or younger is alleged to have been abused, the court may, on the motion of a party to the proceeding, order that the testimony of the child be taken in a room other than the courtroom and be televised by closed-circuit equipment in the courtroom to be viewed by the court and the parties.

(b) The procedures that apply to prerecorded videotaped testimony of a child apply to the remote broadcast of testimony of a child.

History of Fam. Code §104.004: Acts 1995, 74th Leg., ch. 20, §1, eff. Apr. 20, 1995. Source: Former Fam. Code §11.21(c).

FAM §104.005. SUBSTITUTION FOR IN-COURT TESTIMONY OF CHILD

(a) If the testimony of a child is taken as provided by this chapter, the child may not be compelled to testify in court during the proceeding.

(b) The court may allow the testimony of a child of any age to be taken in any manner provided by this chapter if the child, because of a medical condition, is incapable of testifying in open court.

History of Fam. Code §104.005: Acts 1995, 74th Leg., ch. 20, §1, eff. Apr. 20, 1995. Amended by Acts 1995, 74th Leg., ch. 751, §11, eff. Sept. 1, 1995. Source: Former Fam. Code §11.21(e).

FAM §104.006. HEARSAY STATEMENT OF CHILD ABUSE VICTIM

In a suit affecting the parent-child relationship, a statement made by a child 12 years of age or younger that describes alleged abuse against the child, without regard to whether the statement is otherwise inadmissible as hearsay, is admissible as evidence if, in a hearing conducted outside the presence of the jury, the court finds that the time, content, and circumstances of the statement provide sufficient indications of the statement's reliability and:

(1) the child testifies or is available to testify at the proceeding in court or in any other manner provided for by law; or

(2) the court determines that the use of the statement in lieu of the child's testimony is necessary to protect the welfare of the child.

History of Fam. Code §104.006: Acts 1997, 75th Leg., ch. 575, §4, eff. Sept. 1, 1997.

ANNOTATIONS

Ohio v. Clark, ___ U.S. ___, 135 S.Ct. 2173, 2180 (2015). "[A] statement cannot fall within the [Sixth Amendment] Confrontation Clause[, which gives the accused the right to confront a witness,] unless [the statement's] primary purpose was testimonial. *At 2181:* [Child's] statements occurred in the context of an ongoing emergency involving suspected child abuse. [T]he immediate concern was to protect a vulnerable child who needed help. [¶] There is no indication that the primary purpose of the conversation [between child and his teachers] was to gather evidence for [abuser's] prosecution. *At 2182:* Statements by very young children will rarely, if ever, implicate the Confrontation Clause. Few preschool students understand the details of our criminal justice system. ... Thus, it is extremely unlikely that a 3-year-old child ... would intend his statements to be a substitute for trial testimony. [¶] Statements made to someone who is not principally charged with uncovering and prosecuting criminal behavior are significantly less likely to be testimonial than statements given to law enforcement officers. It is common sense that the relationship between a student and his teacher is very different from that between a citizen and the police. ... In light of these circumstances, the Sixth Amendment did not prohibit the State from introducing [child's] statements at trial. *At 2183:* In any Confrontation Clause case, the individual who provided the out-of-court statement is not available as an in-court witness, but the testimony is admissible under an exception to the hearsay rules and is probative of the defendant's guilt. [¶] [Child's] statements to his teachers were not testimonial."

In re E.M., 494 S.W.3d 209, 218 (Tex.App.—Waco 2015, pet. denied). "[T]he analysis provided in case law ... relating to [CCP] art. 38.072 in determining reliability is an appropriate guide for courts to follow in determining reliability pursuant to [Fam. Code] §104.006. *At 219:* [T]he phrase[] 'time, content, and circumstances' in art. 38.072 'refers to the time the

child's statement was made to the outcry witness, the content of the child's statement, and the circumstances surrounding the making of that statement.' In making its determination of reliability pursuant to §104.006, just like in art. 38.072, we believe that the focus of the inquiry must remain upon the outcry statement, not the abuse itself. A child's outcry statement may be held reliable pursuant to art. 38.072 even when it contains vague or inconsistent statements about the actual details of the sexual abuse. We find the same to be true as it relates to §104.006."

In re M.R., 243 S.W.3d 807, 813 (Tex.App.—Fort Worth 2007, no pet.). Family Code §104.006 "is the civil analogue of [CCP] art. 38.072 ..., [and courts can use] the same type of analysis [when applying §104.006]. [¶] [A]rticle 38.072 ... provides a mechanism that requires that the trial court determine on a case-by-case basis if outcry testimony reaches the level of reliability required to be admissible as an exception to the hearsay rule. Indicia of reliability ... include (1) whether the child victim testifies at trial and admits making the out-of-court statement, (2) whether the child understands the need to tell the truth and has the ability to observe, recollect, and narrate, (3) whether the other evidence corroborates the statement, (4) whether the child made the statement spontaneously in his own terminology or whether evidence exists of prior prompting or manipulation by adults, (5) whether the child's statement is clear and unambiguous and rises to the needed level of certainty, (6) whether the statement is consistent with other evidence, (7) whether the statement describes an event that a child of the victim's age could not be expected to fabricate, (8) whether the child behaves abnormally after the contact, (9) whether the child has a motive to fabricate the statement, (10) whether the child expects punishment because of reporting the conduct, and (11) whether the accused had the opportunity to commit the offense. *At 814:* The reliability referred to in art. 38.072 is the reliability of the child's declaration, not the witness relaying the child's declaration."

In re K.L., 91 S.W.3d 1, 16 (Tex.App.—Fort Worth 2002, no pet.). "Section 104.006 does not require the trial court to make a finding that the witness' statement in lieu of the child's testimony is necessary to protect the child's welfare if the child does *not* testify. [¶] [O]nly if a child is *unavailable* to testify is the trial court required to make a finding that admission of the witness' statement in lieu of the child's testimony is necessary to protect the child's welfare."

FAM §104.007. VIDEO TESTIMONY OF CERTAIN PROFESSIONALS

(a) In this section, "professional" has the meaning assigned by Section 261.101(b).

(b) In a proceeding brought by the Department of Family and Protective Services concerning a child who is alleged in a suit to have been abused or neglected, the court may order that the testimony of a professional be taken outside the courtroom by videoconference:

(1) on the agreement of the department's counsel and respondent's counsel; or

(2) if good cause exists, on the court's own motion.

(c) In ordering testimony to be taken as provided by Subsection (b), the court shall ensure that the videoconference testimony allows:

(1) the parties and attorneys involved in the proceeding to be able to see and hear the professional as the professional testifies; and

(2) the professional to be able to see and hear the parties and attorneys examining the professional while the professional is testifying.

(d) If the court permits the testimony of a professional by videoconference as provided by this section to be admitted during the proceeding, the professional may not be compelled to be physically present in court during the same proceeding to provide the same testimony unless ordered by the court.

History of Fam. Code §104.007: Acts 2003, 78th Leg., ch. 266, §1, eff. Sept. 1, 2003. Amended by Acts 2015, 84th Leg., ch. 944, §9, eff. Sept. 1, 2015.

FAM §104.008. CERTAIN TESTIMONY PROHIBITED

(a) A person may not offer an expert opinion or recommendation relating to the conservatorship of or possession of or access to a child at issue in a suit unless the person has conducted a child custody evaluation relating to the child under Subchapter D, Chapter 107.

(b) In a contested suit, a mental health professional may provide other relevant information and opinions, other than those prohibited by Subsection (a), relating to any party that the mental health professional has personally evaluated.

(c) This section does not apply to a suit in which the Department of Family and Protective Services is a party.

History of Fam. Code §104.008: Acts 2015, 84th Leg., ch. 1252, §2.01, eff. Sept. 1, 2015.

CHAPTER 105. SETTINGS, HEARINGS, & ORDERS

FAM §105.001. TEMPORARY ORDERS BEFORE FINAL ORDER

(a) In a suit, the court may make a temporary order, including the modification of a prior temporary order, for the safety and welfare of the child, including an order:

(1) for the temporary conservatorship of the child;

(2) for the temporary support of the child;

(3) restraining a party from disturbing the peace of the child or another party;

(4) prohibiting a person from removing the child beyond a geographical area identified by the court; or

(5) for payment of reasonable attorney's fees and expenses.

(b) Except as provided by Subsection (c), temporary restraining orders and temporary injunctions under this section shall be granted without the necessity of an affidavit or verified pleading stating specific facts showing that immediate and irreparable injury, loss, or damage will result before notice can be served and a hearing can be held. Except as provided by Subsection (h), an order may not be rendered under Subsection (a)(1), (2), or (5) except after notice and a hearing. A temporary restraining order or temporary injunction granted under this section need not:

(1) define the injury or state why it is irreparable;

(2) state why the order was granted without notice; or

(3) include an order setting the cause for trial on the merits with respect to the ultimate relief requested.

(c) Except on a verified pleading or an affidavit in accordance with the Texas Rules of Civil Procedure, an order may not be rendered:

(1) attaching the body of the child;

(2) taking the child into the possession of the court or of a person designated by the court; or

(3) excluding a parent from possession of or access to a child.

(d) In a suit, the court may dispense with the necessity of a bond in connection with temporary orders on behalf of the child.

(e) Temporary orders rendered under this section are not subject to interlocutory appeal.

(f) The violation of a temporary restraining order, temporary injunction, or other temporary order rendered under this section is punishable by contempt and the order is subject to and enforceable under Chapter 157.

(g) The rebuttable presumptions established in favor of the application of the guidelines for a child support order and for the standard possession order under Chapters 153 and 154 apply to temporary orders. The presumptions do not limit the authority of the court to render other temporary orders.

(h) An order under Subsection (a)(1) may be rendered without notice and an adversary hearing if the order is an emergency order sought by a governmental entity under Chapter 262.

History of Fam. Code §105.001: Acts 1995, 74th Leg., ch. 20, §1, eff. Apr. 20, 1995. Amended by Acts 1997, 75th Leg., ch. 575, §5, eff. Sept. 1, 1997; Acts 1999, 76th Leg., ch. 1390, §3, eff. Sept. 1, 1999; Acts 2003, 78th Leg., ch. 1036, §1, eff. Sept. 1, 2003. Source: Former Fam. Code §§11.11(a)-(d), (g), (h), 14.033(*l*), 14.055(e).

See also *O'Connor's Texas Family Law Handbook* (2017), "Temporary Relief," ch. 5, p. 669.

ANNOTATIONS

Grigsby v. Coker, 904 S.W.2d 619, 620 (Tex.1995). "Gag orders in civil judicial proceedings are valid only when an imminent and irreparable harm to the judicial process will deprive litigants of a just resolution of their dispute, and the judicial action represents the least restrictive means to prevent that harm. *At 621:* While [Fam. Code] §11.11 [now §105.001] does give trial courts broad powers in family cases, it does not authorize them to invade constitutional guarantees. The trial court here could have adopted [a gag] order [that was less restrictive], but it failed to do so. This was a clear abuse of discretion. [¶] The faults in this gag order are likely a function of the procedure, or lack of procedure, used in adopting it: no formal motion, no prior notice, and no formal hearing or evidence."

Ex parte Hall, 854 S.W.2d 656, 658 (Tex.1993). "The temporary support order in this case was issued solely on the basis of the parties' prenuptial agreement and not on the authority of the Family Code. … For this reason the trial court did not consider it necessary to complete the hearing required by statute before granting temporary support. It did not determine whether the spousal support ordered was 'necessary and equitable,' as required by [Fam. Code] §3.58(c) [now §6.502], nor whether the temporary child support was 'for the safety and welfare of the child,' as required by [Fam. Code] §11.11(a) [now §105.001(a)(2)]. It did not take into account the guidelines and factors required for setting child support. … It calculated the arrearage due without any evidentiary basis. Under these circumstances, the temporary support order was not enforceable by contempt."

Ex parte Brown, 382 S.W.2d 97, 99 (Tex.1964). "In the ordinary case a temporary order … cannot remain in force after the entry of a final judgment, but a temporary custody order entered upon dismissal of the case which brought the child before the court necessarily continues in full force and effect until set aside by the issuing court or modified by another court of competent jurisdiction in an action instituted for the purpose of obtaining a final custody adjudication." *See also* ***Smelscer v. Smelscer***, 901 S.W.2d 708, 711 n.4 (Tex. App.—El Paso 1995, no writ).

In re Rogers, 370 S.W.3d 443, 445 (Tex.App.—Austin 2012, orig. proceeding). "Section 105.001(a)(5) does not authorize a trial court to make a temporary order for payment of attorney's fees 'for a purpose *other than* the safety and welfare of the child.' *At 447:* Although [mother's attorney testified] that the jury trial will have an adverse impact on the children and that the children are 'under assault' because their father does not see them as often as he is allowed, an award of interim attorney's fees will not affect those unfortunate situations either favorably or adversely—the trial will presumably still occur and [father] will remain free to interact with his children in the manner he chooses. But more important[ly] [mother's attorney] acknowledges that the temporary orders already in place adequately protect the safety and welfare of the … children and that no additional protections are necessary before the jury trial. [¶] Most importantly, [mother] did not explain how or even suggest that the award of interim attorney's fees were necessary for the safety and welfare of the children." *See also* ***In re Sartain***, No. 01-07-00920-CV (Tex.App.—Houston [1st Dist.] 2008, orig. proceeding) (memo op.; 4-3-08).

In re Mata, 212 S.W.3d 597, 605 (Tex.App.—Austin 2006, orig. proceeding). "Although a trial court need not make the same findings on temporary orders as it must in making a final order of termination, … neither should the court ignore the probable arrangements that will be imposed on final hearing in considering temporary orders. [¶] Therefore, in making temporary orders, the court should start with a presumption that a child's parent should be appointed managing conservator, as provided by the standard possession order. Only upon a verified pleading or affidavit and a showing that the placement of a child with his parent could endanger the child's well-being should a trial court grant temporary managing conservatorship to a non-parent." *See also* ***In re Aubin***, 29 S.W.3d 199, 203-04 (Tex.App.—Beaumont 2000, orig. proceeding) (appointing nonparents as temporary possessory conservators was abuse of discretion).

In re Vernor, 94 S.W.3d 201, 210 (Tex.App.—Austin 2002, orig. proceeding). A court abuses its discretion "in imposing temporary orders without due regard for the current living situations of the parties, *especially* the stability of the child's current living situation, and without regard for the financial or practical ability of the parties to comply with the court's orders."

Morse v. Baker-Olsen, 929 S.W.2d 659, 661-62 (Tex.App.—Houston [14th Dist.] 1996, orig. proceeding). Section 105.001 "primarily concerns the entry of orders for the child's welfare and protection. If we were to hold this section does not apply after the entry of a final decree of divorce or other final order, the trial court would have no authority to enter a post-judgment temporary order affecting a child's safety and welfare. Therefore, we decline relator's invitation to construe §105.001 as applicable only to cases where no final judgment has yet been rendered. *At 662 n.2:* Although there is no authority preventing issuance of a temporary injunction in situations where a parent tries to move to another geographical area, we believe there is potential for abuse if the trial court does not hold a hearing in a timely fashion following the issuance of the temporary injunction. The Family Code does not require a temporary injunction to include a date for the hearing on the ultimate relief requested."

FAM §105.0011. INFORMATION REGARDING PROTECTIVE ORDERS

At any time while a suit is pending, if the court believes, on the basis of any information received by the court, that a party to the suit or a member of the party's family or household may be a victim of family violence, the court shall inform that party of the party's right to apply for a protective order under Title 4.

History of Fam. Code §105.0011: Acts 2005, 79th Leg., ch. 361, §3, eff. June 17, 2005.

FAM §105.002. JURY

The amended text in §105.002 is effective for service plans filed for a full adversary hearing held under Fam. Code §262.201 or a status hearing held under Fam. Code ch. 263 on or after Jan. 1, 2018. A hearing held before Jan. 1, 2018, is governed by the former law in effect at that time. Except as provided above, the amended text in §105.002 is effective for SAPCRs filed on or after Sept. 1, 2017. SAPCRs filed before Sept. 1, 2017, are governed by the former law in effect at that time.

(a) Except as provided by Subsection (b), a party may demand a jury trial.

(b) A party may not demand a jury trial in:

(1) a suit in which adoption is sought, including a trial on the issue of denial or revocation of consent to the adoption by the managing conservator; or

(2) a suit to adjudicate parentage under Chapter 160.

(c) In a jury trial:

(1) a party is entitled to a verdict by the jury and the court may not contravene a jury verdict on the issues of:

(A) the appointment of a sole managing conservator;

(B) the appointment of joint managing conservators;

(C) the appointment of a possessory conservator;

(D) the determination of which joint managing conservator has the exclusive right to designate the primary residence of the child;

(E) the determination of whether to impose a restriction on the geographic area in which a joint managing conservator may designate the child's primary residence; and

(F) if a restriction described by Paragraph (E) is imposed, the determination of the geographic area within which the joint managing conservator must designate the child's primary residence; and

(2) the court may not submit to the jury questions on the issues of:

(A) support under Chapter 154 or Chapter 159;

(B) a specific term or condition of possession of or access to the child; or

(C) any right or duty of a conservator, other than the determination of which joint managing conservator has the exclusive right to designate the primary residence of the child under Subdivision (1)(D).

(d) The Department of Family and Protective Services in collaboration with interested parties, including the Permanent Judicial Commission for Children, Youth and Families, shall review the form of jury submissions in this state and make recommendations to the legislature not later than December 31, 2017, regarding whether broad-form or specific jury questions should be required in suits affecting the parent-child relationship filed by the department. This subsection expires September 1, 2019.

History of Fam. Code §105.002: Acts 1995, 74th Leg., ch. 20, §1, eff. Apr. 20, 1995. Amended by Acts 1995, 74th Leg., ch. 751, §12, eff. Sept. 1, 1995; Acts 1997, 75th Leg., ch. 180, §1, eff. Sept. 1, 1997; Acts 1999, 76th Leg., ch. 556, §3, eff. Sept. 1, 1999; Acts 2001, 77th Leg., ch. 821, §2.10, eff. June 14, 2001; Acts 2003, 78th Leg., ch. 1036, §§2, 22, eff. Sept. 1, 2003; H.B. 7, §6, 85th Leg., eff. Sept. 1, 2017. Source: Former Fam. Code §11.13.

See also *O'Connor's Texas Family Law Handbook* (2017), "Jury issues," ch. 4-D, §12.6, p. 457.

ANNOTATIONS

Danet v. Bhan, 436 S.W.3d 793, 796 (Tex.2014). "A jury verdict in a custody determination case is binding on the trial court if the evidence supports it. The jury's decision is entitled to substantial deference on appeal and is subject to ordinary evidentiary sufficiency review."

Lenz v. Lenz, 79 S.W.3d 10, 20 (Tex.2002). Family Code §105.002(d), now §105.002(c)(1)(E), "restricts the trial court's power to 'contravene a jury verdict' on the issue of primary residence. Therefore, [mother] is correct that the statute's plain language means that she was entitled to a jury verdict in this case, and the trial court was not authorized to contravene that verdict by imposing an additional geographical restriction."

Ex parte Sproull, 815 S.W.2d 250, 250 (Tex.1991). "An alleged contemnor has a constitutional right to a jury trial on a 'serious' charge of criminal contempt. A charge for which confinement may exceed six months is serious."

Martin v. Martin, 776 S.W.2d 572, 574 (Tex.1989). Under §105.002, "the court ... may grant or refuse a

jury trial in actions concerning the modification of specific details of administering a prior divorce decree. Inasmuch as the trial court determines the conditions of access, it is not reversible error to refuse a jury trial in actions involving only the modification of the conditions of access or the threshold requirements for the conditions of access."

In re Baker, 495 S.W.3d 393, 396 (Tex.App.—Houston [14th Dist.] 2016, orig. proceeding). See annotation under Family Code §6.703, p. 82.

FAM §105.003. PROCEDURE FOR CONTESTED HEARING

(a) Except as otherwise provided by this title, proceedings shall be as in civil cases generally.

(b) On the agreement of all parties to the suit, the court may limit attendance at the hearing to only those persons who have a direct interest in the suit or in the work of the court.

(c) A record shall be made as in civil cases generally unless waived by the parties with the consent of the court.

(d) When information contained in a report, study, or examination is before the court, the person making the report, study, or examination is subject to both direct examination and cross-examination as in civil cases generally.

(e) The hearing may be adjourned from time to time.

History of Fam. Code §105.003: Acts 1995, 74th Leg., ch. 20, §1, eff. Apr. 20, 1995. Source: Former Fam. Code §11.14(a), (b), (d), (f), (g).

Author's comment: Although many jurisdictions do not provide for the making of a record at a temporary hearing in front of an associate judge, this practice constitutes error in SAPCRs unless waived as provided by §105.003(c).

ANNOTATIONS

Duty to Make a Record

Stubbs v. Stubbs, 685 S.W.2d 643, 645 (Tex.1985). In a SAPCR, "all oral testimony must be recorded. It is the responsibility of the trial judge to see that the court reporter performs this duty." *See also* ***In re M.E.P.***, No. 2-05-148-CV (Tex.App.—Fort Worth 2006, no pet.) (memo op.; 2-23-06) (default judgment that modified child support and awarded attorney fees was reversed because no reporter's record was made at default hearing); ***Pringadi v. Heffern***, No. 03-05-00501-CV (Tex. App.—Austin 2005, no pet.) (memo op.; 11-3-05) (requirement of record is mandatory and not subject to harmless-error review).

Testimony on Reports, Studies & Examinations

Kates v. Smith, 556 S.W.2d 630, 632 (Tex.App.—Texarkana 1977, orig. proceeding). "To deny a party the opportunity to examine or cross-examine the author of [a report being considered by the court] deprives that party of a valuable right to deny, contradict or overcome by other evidence the matters contained in the report. Even if it can be said in such a case that the court's decision would have been the same without considering the report, the aggrieved party still has been deprived of information possibly valuable to him and has been denied the opportunity to properly present his case both in the trial court and in the appellate court."

Waiving the Record

Rogers v. Rogers, 561 S.W.2d 172, 173-74 (Tex. 1978). "'[I]f an appellant exercises due diligence and through no fault of his own is unable to obtain a proper record of the evidence introduced, this may require a new trial where his right to have the case reviewed on appeal can be preserved in no other way.'"

In re Vega, 10 S.W.3d 720, 722 (Tex.App.—Amarillo 1999, no pet.). "The order here contains a recitation that a 'record of the proceedings was waived.' However, where ... a party is not present nor represented by counsel at the hearing, the making of record cannot be waived as to the absent party and a trial court commits error in consenting to the waiver of a record." *See also* ***G.S.K. v. T.K.N.***, 940 S.W.2d 797, 799 (Tex.App.—El Paso 1997, no writ) (duty may not be waived upon consent of only those parties present in the courtroom at the time of hearing).

Henning v. Henning, 889 S.W.2d 611, 613 (Tex. App.—Houston [14th Dist.] 1994, writ denied). "[E]ven when there is no express waiver, the absence of a record does not warrant reversal unless appellant shows the record's absence is not a result of her own negligence or lack of due diligence. [Family Code] §11.14(d) [now §105.003(c)] has been clarified by case law to require a showing of diligence and responsibility on behalf of the complaining party to be certain a record is made. [U]nder §11.14(d), [a] party may waive the making of a record by express written agreement, or by not objecting to the lack of record during the hearing. ... When a party is present before the court, due diligence must be exercised in seeking a record. There is no requirement that a waiver of the record be made in writing." (Internal quotes omitted.)

See also ***In re D.J.M.***, 114 S.W.3d 637, 639 (Tex.App.—Fort Worth 2003, pet. denied). *But see* ***Ex parte Juarez***, this page.

Ex parte Juarez, 665 S.W.2d 200, 201 (Tex. App.—San Antonio 1984, orig. proceeding). "The language of [Fam. Code] §11.14(d) [now §105.003(c)] is mandatory and requires a record whether requested or not.... A mere showing that relator was present at the hearing and that he failed to object to the absence of a court reporter is not a showing that he waived his right to a statement of facts and that the court consented to this waiver. It is not the relator's burden to request a record. Section 11.14(d) requires that a record automatically be made in parent-child relationship matters *unless* the parties waive it *and* the court consents to that waiver." *But see* ***Henning v. Henning***, p. 420.

FAM §105.004. PREFERENTIAL SETTING

After a hearing, the court may:

(1) grant a motion filed by a party or by the amicus attorney or attorney ad litem for the child for a preferential setting for a trial on the merits; and

(2) give precedence to that hearing over other civil cases if the court finds that the delay created by ordinary scheduling practices will unreasonably affect the best interest of the child.

History of Fam. Code §105.004: Acts 1995, 74th Leg., ch. 20, §1, eff. Apr. 20, 1995. Amended by Acts 2005, 79th Leg., ch. 172, §16, eff. Sept. 1, 2005. Source: Former Fam. Code §11.14(i).

FAM §105.005. FINDINGS

Except as otherwise provided by this title, the court's findings shall be based on a preponderance of the evidence.

History of Fam. Code §105.005: Acts 1995, 74th Leg., ch. 20, §1, eff. Apr. 20, 1995. Source: Former Fam. Code §11.15(a).

FAM §105.006. CONTENTS OF FINAL ORDER

(a) A final order, other than in a proceeding under Chapter 161 or 162, must contain:

(1) the social security number and driver's license number of each party to the suit, including the child, except that the child's social security number or driver's license number is not required if the child has not been assigned a social security number or driver's license number; and

(2) each party's current residence address, mailing address, home telephone number, name of employer, address of employment, and work telephone number, except as provided by Subsection (c).

(b) Except as provided by Subsection (c), the court shall order each party to inform each other party, the court that rendered the order, and the state case registry under Chapter 234 of an intended change in any of the information required by this section as long as any person, as a result of the order, is under an obligation to pay child support or is entitled to possession of or access to a child. The court shall order that notice of the intended change be given at the earlier of:

(1) the 60th day before the date the party intends to make the change; or

(2) the fifth day after the date that the party knew of the change, if the party did not know or could not have known of the change in sufficient time to comply with Subdivision (1).

(c) If a court finds after notice and hearing that requiring a party to provide the information required by this section to another party is likely to cause the child or a conservator harassment, abuse, serious harm, or injury, or to subject the child or a conservator to family violence, as defined by Section 71.004, the court may:

(1) order the information not to be disclosed to another party; or

(2) render any other order the court considers necessary.

(d) An order in a suit that orders child support or possession of or access to a child must contain the following prominently displayed statement in boldfaced type, capital letters, or underlined:

"FAILURE TO OBEY A COURT ORDER FOR CHILD SUPPORT OR FOR POSSESSION OF OR ACCESS TO A CHILD MAY RESULT IN FURTHER LITIGATION TO ENFORCE THE ORDER, INCLUDING CONTEMPT OF COURT. A FINDING OF CONTEMPT MAY BE PUNISHED BY CONFINEMENT IN JAIL FOR UP TO SIX MONTHS, A FINE OF UP TO $500 FOR EACH VIOLATION, AND A MONEY JUDGMENT FOR PAYMENT OF ATTORNEY'S FEES AND COURT COSTS."

"FAILURE OF A PARTY TO MAKE A CHILD SUPPORT PAYMENT TO THE PLACE AND IN THE MANNER REQUIRED BY A COURT ORDER MAY RESULT IN THE PARTY NOT RECEIVING CREDIT FOR MAKING THE PAYMENT."

"FAILURE OF A PARTY TO PAY CHILD SUPPORT DOES NOT JUSTIFY DENYING THAT PARTY COURT-ORDERED POSSESSION OF OR ACCESS TO A CHILD. REFUSAL BY A PARTY TO ALLOW POSSESSION OF OR

ACCESS TO A CHILD DOES NOT JUSTIFY FAILURE TO PAY COURT-ORDERED CHILD SUPPORT TO THAT PARTY."

(e) Except as provided by Subsection (c), an order in a suit that orders child support or possession of or access to a child must also contain the following prominently displayed statement in boldfaced type, capital letters, or underlined:

"EACH PERSON WHO IS A PARTY TO THIS ORDER IS ORDERED TO NOTIFY EACH OTHER PARTY, THE COURT, AND THE STATE CASE REGISTRY OF ANY CHANGE IN THE PARTY'S CURRENT RESIDENCE ADDRESS, MAILING ADDRESS, HOME TELEPHONE NUMBER, NAME OF EMPLOYER, ADDRESS OF EMPLOYMENT, DRIVER'S LICENSE NUMBER, AND WORK TELEPHONE NUMBER. THE PARTY IS ORDERED TO GIVE NOTICE OF AN INTENDED CHANGE IN ANY OF THE REQUIRED INFORMATION TO EACH OTHER PARTY, THE COURT, AND THE STATE CASE REGISTRY ON OR BEFORE THE 60TH DAY BEFORE THE INTENDED CHANGE. IF THE PARTY DOES NOT KNOW OR COULD NOT HAVE KNOWN OF THE CHANGE IN SUFFICIENT TIME TO PROVIDE 60-DAY NOTICE, THE PARTY IS ORDERED TO GIVE NOTICE OF THE CHANGE ON OR BEFORE THE FIFTH DAY AFTER THE DATE THAT THE PARTY KNOWS OF THE CHANGE."

"THE DUTY TO FURNISH THIS INFORMATION TO EACH OTHER PARTY, THE COURT, AND THE STATE CASE REGISTRY CONTINUES AS LONG AS ANY PERSON, BY VIRTUE OF THIS ORDER, IS UNDER AN OBLIGATION TO PAY CHILD SUPPORT OR ENTITLED TO POSSESSION OF OR ACCESS TO A CHILD."

"FAILURE BY A PARTY TO OBEY THE ORDER OF THIS COURT TO PROVIDE EACH OTHER PARTY, THE COURT, AND THE STATE CASE REGISTRY WITH THE CHANGE IN THE REQUIRED INFORMATION MAY RESULT IN FURTHER LITIGATION TO ENFORCE THE ORDER, INCLUDING CONTEMPT OF COURT. A FINDING OF CONTEMPT MAY BE PUNISHED BY CONFINEMENT IN JAIL FOR UP TO SIX MONTHS, A FINE OF UP TO $500 FOR EACH VIOLATION, AND A MONEY JUDGMENT FOR PAYMENT OF ATTORNEY'S FEES AND COURT COSTS."

(e-1) An order in a suit that provides for the possession of or access to a child must contain the following prominently displayed statement in boldfaced type, in capital letters, or underlined:

"NOTICE TO ANY PEACE OFFICER OF THE STATE OF TEXAS: YOU MAY USE REASONABLE EFFORTS TO ENFORCE THE TERMS OF CHILD CUSTODY SPECIFIED IN THIS ORDER. A PEACE OFFICER WHO RELIES ON THE TERMS OF A COURT ORDER AND THE OFFICER'S AGENCY ARE ENTITLED TO THE APPLICABLE IMMUNITY AGAINST ANY CLAIM, CIVIL OR OTHERWISE, REGARDING THE OFFICER'S GOOD FAITH ACTS PERFORMED IN THE SCOPE OF THE OFFICER'S DUTIES IN ENFORCING THE TERMS OF THE ORDER THAT RELATE TO CHILD CUSTODY. ANY PERSON WHO KNOWINGLY PRESENTS FOR ENFORCEMENT AN ORDER THAT IS INVALID OR NO LONGER IN EFFECT COMMITS AN OFFENSE THAT MAY BE PUNISHABLE BY CONFINEMENT IN JAIL FOR AS LONG AS TWO YEARS AND A FINE OF AS MUCH AS $10,000."

(e-2) An order in a suit that orders child support must contain the following prominently displayed statement in boldfaced type, in capital letters, or underlined:

"THE COURT MAY MODIFY THIS ORDER THAT PROVIDES FOR THE SUPPORT OF A CHILD, IF:

(1) THE CIRCUMSTANCES OF THE CHILD OR A PERSON AFFECTED BY THE ORDER HAVE MATERIALLY AND SUBSTANTIALLY CHANGED; OR

(2) IT HAS BEEN THREE YEARS SINCE THE ORDER WAS RENDERED OR LAST MODIFIED AND THE MONTHLY AMOUNT OF THE CHILD SUPPORT AWARD UNDER THE ORDER DIFFERS BY EITHER 20 PERCENT OR $100 FROM THE AMOUNT THAT WOULD BE AWARDED IN ACCORDANCE WITH THE CHILD SUPPORT GUIDELINES."

(f) Except for an action in which contempt is sought, in any subsequent child support enforcement action, the court may, on a showing that diligent effort has been made to determine the location of a party, consider due process requirements for notice and service of process to be met with respect to that party on delivery of written notice to the most recent residential or employer address filed by that party with the court and the state case registry.

(g) The Title IV-D agency shall promulgate and provide forms for a party to use in reporting to the court and the state case registry under Chapter 234 the information required under this section.

(h) The court may include in a final order in a suit in which a party to the suit makes an allegation of child abuse or neglect a finding on whether the party who made the allegation knew that the allegation was false.

This finding shall not constitute collateral estoppel for any criminal proceeding. The court may impose on a party found to have made a false allegation of child abuse or neglect any civil sanction permitted under law, including attorney's fees, costs of experts, and any other costs.

History of Fam. Code §105.006: Acts 1995, 74th Leg., ch. 20, §1, eff. Apr. 20, 1995. Amended by Acts 1995, 74th Leg., ch. 751, §§13, 128, eff. Sept. 1, 1995; Acts 1997, 75th Leg., ch. 786, §1 (eff. Sept. 1, 1997), ch. 911, §6 (eff. Sept. 1, 1997); Acts 1999, 76th Leg., ch. 62, §19.01(21) (eff. Sept. 1, 1999), ch. 178, §5 (eff. Aug. 30, 1999); Acts 2001, 77th Leg., ch. 133, §1, eff. Sept. 1, 2001; Acts 2003, 78th Leg., ch. 184, §1, eff. Sept. 1, 2003; Acts 2007, 80th Leg., ch. 972, §3, eff. Sept. 1, 2007; Acts 2015, 84th Leg., ch. 280, §1 (eff. Sept. 1, 2015), ch. 859, §3 (eff. Sept. 1, 2015). Source: Former Fam. Code §11.155.

See also ***O'Connor's Texas Family Law Handbook*** (2017), "Judgment," ch. 4-D, §13, p. 458.

ANNOTATIONS

In re Office of the Atty. Gen., 456 S.W.3d 153, 156 (Tex.2015). "The Legislature has chosen to give OAG [Office of the Attorney General] discretion to designate a case with the family violence indicator, and has not chosen to allow trial courts to intervene, except to weigh the designation in considering a request for disclosure. [¶] Taken out of context, [§105.006(c)(2)'s] 'any other order' language might seem a sweeping provision of power, giving a trial court carte blanche to do as it pleases. But studied in context ... there is no question that 'any other order' cannot [grant discretion over the existence of the indicator]. Rather, a trial court may issue 'any other order' only to protect the parties likely to be harmed by disclosure of protected information. The trial court's misreading of subsection (c)(2) is foreclosed by statutory context because subsection (c)(2) is clearly limited to the risks of harm noted in subsection (c). *At 157:* In effect, the trial court in this case decided that the family violence indicator was not necessary and determined that it should be removed. But the trial court lacked authority to order OAG to remove the indicator from its files. OAG is assigned the indicator designation; the trial court is responsible for weighing that designation when asked to disclose protected information. These two lines do not intersect."

In re O'Donnell, No. 02-06-00002-CV (Tex.App.—Fort Worth 2006, orig. proceeding) (memo op.; 3-9-06). "[T]he items required to be included in a final order by ... §105.006 are clerical in nature, not substantive items that would preclude the 'Associate Judge's Report' from being a final judgment."

FAM §105.007. COMPLIANCE WITH ORDER REQUIRING NOTICE OF CHANGE OF REQUIRED INFORMATION

(a) A party shall comply with the order by giving written notice to each other party of an intended change in the party's current residence address, mailing address, home telephone number, name of employer, address of employment, and work telephone number.

(b) The party must give written notice by registered or certified mail of an intended change in the required information to each other party on or before the 60th day before the change is made. If the party does not know or could not have known of the change in sufficient time to provide 60-day notice, the party shall provide the written notice of the change on or before the fifth day after the date that the party knew of the change.

(c) The court may waive the notice required by this section on motion by a party if it finds that the giving of notice of a change of the required information would be likely to expose the child or the party to harassment, abuse, serious harm, or injury.

History of Fam. Code §105.007: Acts 1995, 74th Leg., ch. 20, §1, eff. Apr. 20, 1995. Amended by Acts 1995, 74th Leg., ch. 751, §14, eff. Sept. 1, 1995. Source: Former Fam. Code §14.045(a), (b).

FAM §105.008. RECORD OF SUPPORT ORDER FOR STATE CASE REGISTRY

(a) The clerk of the court shall provide the state case registry with a record of a court order for child support. The record of an order shall include information provided by the parties on a form developed by the Title IV-D agency. The form shall be completed by the petitioner and submitted to the clerk at the time the order is filed for record.

(b) To the extent federal funds are available, the Title IV-D agency shall reimburse the clerk of the court for the costs incurred in providing the record of support order required under this section.

History of Fam. Code §105.008: Acts 1997, 75th Leg., ch. 911, §7, eff. Sept. 1, 1997. Amended by Acts 2005, 79th Leg., ch. 916, §5, eff. June 17, 2005.

FAM §105.009. PARENT EDUCATION & FAMILY STABILIZATION COURSE

(a) In a suit affecting the parent-child relationship, including an action to modify an order in a suit affecting the parent-child relationship providing for possession of or access to a child, the court may order the parties to the suit to attend a parent education and fam-

ily stabilization course if the court determines that the order is in the best interest of the child.

(b) The parties to the suit may not be required to attend the course together. The court, on its own motion or the motion of either party, may prohibit the parties from taking the course together if there is a history of family violence in the marriage.

(c) A course under this section must be at least four hours, but not more than 12 hours, in length and be designed to educate and assist parents with regard to the consequences of divorce on parents and children. The course must include information on the following issues:

(1) the emotional effects of divorce on parents;

(2) the emotional and behavioral reactions to divorce by young children and adolescents;

(3) parenting issues relating to the concerns and needs of children at different development stages;

(4) stress indicators in young children and adolescents;

(5) conflict management;

(6) family stabilization through development of a coparenting relationship;

(7) the financial responsibilities of parenting;

(8) family violence, spousal abuse, and child abuse and neglect; and

(9) the availability of community services and resources.

(d) A course may not be designed to provide individual mental health therapy or individual legal advice.

(e) A course satisfies the requirements of this section if it is offered by:

(1) a mental health professional who has at least a master's degree with a background in family therapy or parent education; or

(2) a religious practitioner who performs counseling consistent with the laws of this state or another person designated as a program counselor by a church or religious institution if the litigant so chooses.

(f) Information obtained in a course or a statement made by a participant to a suit during a course may not be considered in the adjudication of the suit or in any subsequent legal proceeding. Any report that results from participation in the course may not become a record in the suit unless the parties stipulate to the record in writing.

(g) The court may take appropriate action with regard to a party who fails to attend or complete a course ordered by the court under this section, including holding the party in contempt of court, striking pleadings, or invoking any sanction provided by Rule 215, Texas Rules of Civil Procedure. The failure or refusal by a party to attend or complete a course required by this section may not delay the court from rendering a judgment in a suit affecting the parent-child relationship.

(h) The course required under this section may be completed by:

(1) personal instruction;

(2) videotape instruction;

(3) instruction through an electronic medium; or

(4) a combination of those methods.

(i) On completion of the course, the course provider shall issue a certificate of completion to each participant. The certificate must state:

(1) the name of the participant;

(2) the name of the course provider;

(3) the date the course was completed; and

(4) whether the course was provided by:

(A) personal instruction;

(B) videotape instruction;

(C) instruction through an electronic medium; or

(D) a combination of those methods.

(j) The county clerk in each county may establish a registry of course providers in the county and a list of locations at which courses are provided. The clerk shall include information in the registry identifying courses that are offered on a sliding fee scale or without charge.

(k) The court may not order the parties to a suit to attend a course under this section if the parties cannot afford to take the course. If the parties cannot afford to take a course, the court may direct the parties to a course that is offered on a sliding fee scale or without charge, if a course of that type is available. A party to a suit may not be required to pay more than $100 to attend a course ordered under this section.

(*l*) A person who has attended a course under this section may not be required to attend the course more than twice before the fifth anniversary of the date the person completes the course for the first time.

☠ *Subsection (m) was enacted by Acts 2005, 79th Leg., ch. 916, §6, enacted May 29, 2005, effective June 18, 2005, without reference to the conflicting enactment*

made by Acts 2005, 79th Leg., ch. 1171, §3, enacted May 25, 2005, effective Oct. 1, 2005. For harmonizing conflicts, see p. V.

(m) A course under this section must be available in both English and Spanish.

Subsection (m) was enacted by Acts 2005, 79th Leg., ch. 1171, §3, enacted May 25, 2005, effective Oct. 1, 2005, without reference to the conflicting enactment made by Acts 2005, 79th Leg., ch. 916, §6, enacted May 29, 2005, effective June 18, 2005. For harmonizing conflicts, see p. V.

(m) A course under this section in a suit filed in a county with a population of more than two million that is adjacent to a county with a population of more than one million must be available in both English and Spanish.

History of Fam. Code §105.009: Acts 1999, 76th Leg., ch. 946, §1, eff. Sept. 1, 1999. Amended by Acts 2005, 79th Leg., ch. 916, §6 (eff. June 18, 2005), ch. 1171, §3 (eff. Oct. 1, 2005).

CHAPTER 106. COSTS & ATTORNEY'S FEES

FAM §106.001. COSTS

The court may award costs in a suit or motion under this title and in a habeas corpus proceeding.

History of Fam. Code §106.001: Acts 1995, 74th Leg., ch. 20, §1, eff. Apr. 20, 1995. Amended by Acts 1997, 75th Leg., ch. 15, §1, eff. Sept. 1, 1997. Source: Former Fam. Code §11.18(a).

ANNOTATIONS

Campbell v. Wilder, 487 S.W.3d 146, 147 (Tex. 2016). See annotation under Family Code §6.708, p. 83.

Ex parte Williams, 866 S.W.2d 751, 753 (Tex. App.—Houston [1st Dist.] 1993, orig. proceeding). "'Costs' usually refer to fees and charges required by law to be paid to the courts or some of their officers, the amount of which is fixed by statute or the court's rules e.g. filing and service fees."

FAM §106.002. ATTORNEY'S FEES & EXPENSES

(a) In a suit under this title, the court may render judgment for reasonable attorney's fees and expenses and order the judgment and postjudgment interest to be paid directly to an attorney.

(b) A judgment for attorney's fees and expenses may be enforced in the attorney's name by any means available for the enforcement of a judgment for debt.

History of Fam. Code §106.002: Acts 1995, 74th Leg., ch. 20, §1, eff. Apr. 20, 1995. Amended by Acts 1997, 75th Leg., ch. 15, §2, eff. Sept. 1, 1997; Acts 2003, 78th Leg., ch. 478, §1, eff. Sept. 1, 2003. Source: Former Fam. Code §§11.18(a), 11.22(j).

See also ***O'Connor's Texas Family Law Handbook*** (2017), "Judgment for attorney fees & expenses," ch. 4-D, §13.6, p. 465.

ANNOTATIONS

Tucker v. Thomas, 419 S.W.3d 292, 293 (Tex.2013). "[A] trial court does not have discretion to characterize attorney's fees awarded in non-enforcement modification suits as necessaries or as additional child support. *At 300:* Except when a trial court finds that a party filed a non-enforcement modification suit frivolously or with the purpose of harassing the opposing party, no provision in [Fam. Code] Ch. 156 authorizes an award of attorney's fees in modification suits. Thus, trial courts must look to [Fam. Code] §106.002—Title 5's general attorney's fee provision—for authority to award attorney's fees in most non-enforcement modification suits. Noticeably absent from §106.002 is authority for a trial court to characterize an attorney's fee award as necessaries or as additional child support. In light of this absence of express authorization, we conclude that the Legislature did not intend to provide trial courts with discretion to assess attorney's fees awarded to a party in Ch. 156 modification suits as additional child support. Moreover, neither our precedent nor the plain language of [Fam. Code] §151.001(c) supports the court of appeals' conclusion that attorney's fees in non-enforcement modification suits may be characterized as necessaries, enforceable by contempt."

In re R.E.S., 482 S.W.3d 584, 586 (Tex.App.—San Antonio 2015, no pet.). Section 106.002 "does not designate to which party [attorney] fees may be awarded, nor does it limit the trial court's designation. The award of attorney's fees is within the sound discretion of the trial court. In the past, courts have analyzed the award of attorney's fees with an eye to the prevailing, or successful, party. However, the current language of … §106.002 does not impose a prevailing-party requirement. Rarely is either party a clear-cut victor in a [SAPCR], and the difficulty of determining which party prevailed in a family case has long been recognized. *At 587:* [T]he prevailing-party determination is but one factor in a trial court's analysis of an attorney's-fee award. In addition, a prevailing-party determination is not a conclusive or decisive factor." *See also* ***Coburn v. Moreland***, 433 S.W.3d 809, 838-41 (Tex.App.—Austin 2014, no pet.).

Watts v. Oliver, 396 S.W.3d 124, 133 (Tex.App.—Houston [14th Dist.] 2013, no pet.). "[A]lthough [§106.002] provides that a judgment for attorney's fees and expenses may be enforced in the attorney's name, nothing in the statutory language requires that the judgment be paid directly to an attorney. [Section 106.002] contains no terms which would prevent a trial court from awarding a judgment in the name of the party and giving them the right to enforce that judgment while ordering that any amounts recovered should be paid to the party's attorney."

Preston v. Dyer, No. 09-11-00200-CV (Tex.App.—Beaumont 2012, pet. denied) (memo op.; 11-29-12). Father "argues the arbitrator exceeded his authority by favoring [mother] with an award of attorney's fees. According to [father], the parties agreed to pay attorney's fees only if there was an attempt to obtain interest in the other party's property, and the party seeking to do so prevailed in that effort. Although the disputes that were arbitrated did not include any issues regarding the characterization of [either party's] property, the arbitrator awarded [mother] $25,000 in attorney's fees. According to [father], the arbitrator had no authority to do so because the premarital agreement contains no provision for fees based on a recovery of either spousal support or child support. [¶] [T]he scope of the disputes the parties agreed to submit to arbitration is broad. The [Texas Arbitration Act] provides that arbitrators 'shall award attorney's fees as additional sums required to be paid under the award only if the fees are provided for: (1) in the agreement to arbitrate; or (2) by law for a recovery in a civil action in the district court on a cause of action on which any part of the award is based.' [Family Code §106.002] allows [mother] to recover attorney's fees on a claim for child support. [CPRC §38.001(8)] provides for a party to recover fees when successfully recovering on a claim for breach of contract. [¶] In this case, the arbitrator's award of fees is authorized by law; therefore, the arbitrator had the authority to award attorney's fees."

In re M.A.N.M., 231 S.W.3d 562, 567-68 (Tex. App.—Dallas 2007, no pet.). "To support an award of reasonable attorney's fees, there should be evidence of the time spent by the attorney on the case, the nature of the preparation, the complexity of the case, the experience of the attorney, and the prevailing hourly rates. However, 'evidence on each of these factors is not necessary to determine the amount of an attorney's fee award.' The court may also consider the entire record and the common knowledge of the lawyers and judges. [¶] [Here, there] was no testimony about ... attorney's hourly rate or the number of hours he spent on the case. However, there is no rigid requirement that there must be evidence on both these facts to make a determination of attorney's fees. Rather, ... counsel testified as to the total fees incurred and that the fees were reasonable and necessary. [¶] [W]e cannot conclude the trial court abused its discretion...."

Moroch v. Collins, 174 S.W.3d 849, 870-71 (Tex. App.—Dallas 2005, pet. denied). "[S]ection 106.002 does not provide that conservatorship must be at issue at the time of trial in order for the court to award attorney's fees. Because this suit is a SAPCR, the trial court did not err in awarding attorney's fees against [H]. [¶] Also, [H] argues that any award of attorney's fees to [W] was error because the amount of the attorney's fees exceeds the value of the community estate, having the effect of divesting [H] of his separate property. [H] relies on ... the proposition that '[t]he award of attorney's fees in a divorce action not involving the parent-child relationship cannot exceed the value of the community property at issue before the court.' [However,] this case [involves] a SAPCR. Thus, [H's] argument that the attorney's fees award, by exceeding the value of the community estate, improperly divests him of his separate property fails."

Farish v. Farish, 921 S.W.2d 538, 546 (Tex.App.—Beaumont 1996, no writ). "In order to be entitled to a discretionary award of attorney's fees ..., a party must file with the court an affirmative pleading requesting them unless the issue is waived or tried by consent."

CHAPTER 107. SPECIAL APPOINTMENTS, CHILD CUSTODY EVALUATIONS, & ADOPTION EVALUATIONS

Subchapter A. Court-Ordered Representation in Suits Affecting the Parent-Child Relationship

SUBCHAPTER A. COURT-ORDERED REPRESENTATION IN SUITS AFFECTING THE PARENT-CHILD RELATIONSHIP

FAM §107.001. DEFINITIONS

In this chapter:

(1) "Amicus attorney" means an attorney appointed by the court in a suit, other than a suit filed by a governmental entity, whose role is to provide legal services necessary to assist the court in protecting a child's best interests rather than to provide legal services to the child.

(2) "Attorney ad litem" means an attorney who provides legal services to a person, including a child, and who owes to the person the duties of undivided loyalty, confidentiality, and competent representation.

(3) "Developmentally appropriate" means structured to account for a child's age, level of education, cultural background, and degree of language acquisition.

(4) "Dual role" means the role of an attorney who is appointed under Section 107.0125 to act as both guardian ad litem and attorney ad litem for a child in a suit filed by a governmental entity.

(5) "Guardian ad litem" means a person appointed to represent the best interests of a child. The term includes:

(A) a volunteer advocate from a charitable organization described by Subchapter C who is appointed by the court as the child's guardian ad litem;

(B) a professional, other than an attorney, who holds a relevant professional license and whose training relates to the determination of a child's best interests;

(C) an adult having the competence, training, and expertise determined by the court to be sufficient to represent the best interests of the child; or

(D) an attorney ad litem appointed to serve in the dual role.

History of Fam. Code §107.001: Acts 1995, 74th Leg., ch. 20, §1, eff. Apr. 20, 1995. Amended by Acts 1995, 74th Leg., ch. 751, §15, eff. Sept. 1, 1995; Acts 1997, 75th Leg., ch. 1294, §1, eff. Sept. 1, 1997; Acts 2003, 78th Leg., ch. 262, §1, eff. Sept. 1, 2003; Acts 2015, 84th Leg., ch. 1, §1.031 (eff. Apr. 2, 2015), ch. 1252, §1.01 (eff. Sept. 1, 2015). Source: Former Fam. Code §11.10(a), (b)(1).

ANNOTATIONS

In re Bradshaw, 273 S.W.3d 851, 860 (Tex.App.—Houston [14th Dist.] 2008, orig. proceeding). Father "maintains that, because purpose of the amicus attorney is to assist the trial court in determining the 'best interest of the child' and the 'best interest of the child' standard is not applicable to a habeas corpus proceeding, the trial court has erroneously ordered [father] to pay the amicus attorney's legal fees. [¶] [T]he trial court may not deny a writ of habeas corpus on the basis of the best interests of the child. *At 861:* [W]e conclude that [judge] abused his discretion in directing further participation of the amicus attorney during the hearing on the petition for a writ of habeas corpus."

Ⓐ FAM §107.002. POWERS & DUTIES OF GUARDIAN AD LITEM FOR CHILD

(a) A guardian ad litem appointed for a child under this chapter is not a party to the suit but may:

(1) conduct an investigation to the extent that the guardian ad litem considers necessary to determine the best interests of the child; and

(2) obtain and review copies of the child's relevant medical, psychological, and school records as provided by Section 107.006.

The amended text in subsection (b) is effective for service plans filed for a full adversary hearing held under Fam. Code §262.201 or a status hearing held under Fam. Code ch. 263 on or after Jan. 1, 2018. A hearing held before Jan. 1, 2018, is governed by the former law in effect at that time. Except as provided above, the amended text in subsection (b) is effective for SAPCRs filed on or after Sept. 1, 2017. SAPCRs filed before Sept. 1, 2017, are governed by the former law in effect at that time.

(b) A guardian ad litem appointed for the child under this chapter shall:

(1) within a reasonable time after the appointment, interview:

(A) the child in a developmentally appropriate manner, if the child is four years of age or older;

(B) each person who has significant knowledge of the child's history and condition, including educators, child welfare service providers, and any foster parent of the child; and

(C) the parties to the suit;

(2) seek to elicit in a developmentally appropriate manner the child's expressed objectives;

(3) consider the child's expressed objectives without being bound by those objectives;

(4) encourage settlement and the use of alternative forms of dispute resolution; and

(5) perform any specific task directed by the court.

(b-1) In addition to the duties required by Subsection (b), a guardian ad litem appointed for a child in a proceeding under Chapter 262 or 263 shall:

(1) review the medical care provided to the child; [and]

(2) in a developmentally appropriate manner, seek to elicit the child's opinion on the medical care provided; and

(3) for a child at least 16 years of age, ascertain whether the child has received the following documents:

(A) a certified copy of the child's birth certificate;

(B) a social security card or a replacement social security card;

(C) a driver's license or personal identification certificate under Chapter 521, Transportation Code; and

(D) any other personal document the Department of Family and Protective Services determines appropriate.

The amended text in subsection (c) is effective for service plans filed for a full adversary hearing held under Fam. Code §262.201 or a status hearing held under Fam. Code ch. 263 on or after Jan. 1, 2018. A hearing held before Jan. 1, 2018, is governed by the former law in effect at that time. Except as provided above, the amended text in subsection (c) is effective for SAPCRs filed on or after Sept. 1, 2017. SAPCRs filed before Sept. 1, 2017, are governed by the former law in effect at that time.

(c) A guardian ad litem appointed for the child under this chapter is entitled to:

(1) receive a copy of each pleading or other paper filed with the court in the case in which the guardian ad litem is appointed;

(2) receive notice of each hearing in the case;

(3) participate in case staffings by the Department of Family and Protective Services concerning the child;

(4) attend all legal proceedings in the case but may not call or question a witness or otherwise provide legal services unless the guardian ad litem is a licensed attorney who has been appointed in the dual role;

(5) review and sign, or decline to sign, an agreed order affecting the child; [and]

(6) explain the basis for the guardian ad litem's opposition to the agreed order if the guardian ad litem does not agree to the terms of a proposed order;

(7) have access to the child in the child's placement;

(8) be consulted and provide comments on decisions regarding placement, including kinship, foster care, and adoptive placements;

(9) evaluate whether the child welfare services providers are protecting the child's best interests regarding appropriate care, treatment, services, and all other foster children's rights listed in Section 263.008;

(10) receive notification regarding and an invitation to attend meetings related to the child's service plan and a copy of the plan; and

(11) attend court-ordered mediation regarding the child's case.

(d) The court may compel the guardian ad litem to attend a trial or hearing and to testify as necessary for the proper disposition of the suit.

(e) Unless the guardian ad litem is an attorney who has been appointed in the dual role and subject to the Texas Rules of Evidence, the court shall ensure in a hearing or in a trial on the merits that a guardian ad litem has an opportunity to testify regarding, and is permitted to submit a report regarding, the guardian ad litem's recommendations relating to:

(1) the best interests of the child; and

(2) the bases for the guardian ad litem's recommendations.

(f) In a nonjury trial, a party may call the guardian ad litem as a witness for the purpose of cross-examination regarding the guardian's report without the guardian ad litem being listed as a witness by a party. If the guardian ad litem is not called as a witness, the court shall permit the guardian ad litem to testify in the narrative.

(g) In a contested case, the guardian ad litem shall provide copies of the guardian ad litem's report, if any, to the attorneys for the parties as directed by the court, but not later than the earlier of:

(1) the date required by the scheduling order; or

(2) the 10th day before the date of the commencement of the trial.

(h) Disclosure to the jury of the contents of a guardian ad litem's report to the court is subject to the Texas Rules of Evidence.

(i) A guardian ad litem appointed to represent a child in the managing conservatorship of the Department of Family and Protective Services shall, before each scheduled hearing under Chapter 263, determine whether the child's educational needs and goals have been identified and addressed.

History of Fam. Code §107.002: Acts 1995, 74th Leg., ch. 20, §1, eff. Sept. 1, 1995. Amended by Acts 1995, 74th Leg., ch. 943, §10, eff. Sept. 1, 1995; Acts 1997, 75th Leg., ch. 1294, §2, eff. Sept. 1, 1997; Acts 2003, 78th Leg., ch. 262, §1, eff. Sept. 1, 2003; Acts 2005, 79th Leg., ch. 172, §1, eff. Sept. 1, 2005; Acts 2013, 83rd Leg., ch. 204, §1 (eff. Sept. 1, 2013), ch. 688, §1 (eff. Sept. 1, 2013); Acts 2015, 84th Leg., ch. 1, §1.032, eff. Apr. 2, 2015; H.B. 7, §7, 85th Leg., eff. Sept. 1, 2017; S.B. 11, §2, 85th Leg., eff. Sept. 1, 2017; S.B. 1758, §1, 85th Leg., eff. Sept. 1, 2017.

See also ***O'Connor's Texas Family Law Handbook*** (2017), "Guardian Ad Litem," ch. 4-C, §4, p. 390.

ANNOTATIONS

In re Scheller, 325 S.W.3d 640, 645 (Tex.2010). "The role of the psychologist in evaluating the children and parties is consistent with the role of a guardian ad litem because the psychologist gives the court recommendations about the children's best interests. *At 646:* [T]he trial court did not err in appointing an expert to serve as [both] guardian ad litem to the children and as a psychologist to evaluate the case and make recommendations to the court regarding the children's best interests."

Diamond v. San Soucie, 239 S.W.3d 428, 434 (Tex. App.—Dallas 2007, no pet.). "An ad litem is entitled to attend all legal proceedings. Because the ad litem is required to participate to the extent necessary to protect the ward, she 'should be allowed considerable latitude in determining what depositions, hearings, conferences or other activities are necessary to that effort.' [I]t was up to [ad litem] to determine when she needed to be present." *See also **In re K.C.P.***, 142 S.W.3d 574, 585 (Tex.App.—Texarkana 2004, no pet.) (Fam. Code §107.002(c)(4) and (6) prevail over TRCP 614, so guardian ad litem could be present during trial).

Ⓐ FAM §107.003. POWERS & DUTIES OF ATTORNEY AD LITEM FOR CHILD & AMICUS ATTORNEY

(a) An attorney ad litem appointed to represent a child or an amicus attorney appointed to assist the court:

(1) shall:

(A) subject to Rules 4.02, 4.03, and 4.04, Texas Disciplinary Rules of Professional Conduct, and within a reasonable time after the appointment, interview:

(i) the child in a developmentally appropriate manner, if the child is four years of age or older;

(ii) each person who has significant knowledge of the child's history and condition, including any foster parent of the child; and

(iii) the parties to the suit;

(B) seek to elicit in a developmentally appropriate manner the child's expressed objectives of representation;

(C) consider the impact on the child in formulating the attorney's presentation of the child's expressed objectives of representation to the court;

(D) investigate the facts of the case to the extent the attorney considers appropriate;

(E) obtain and review copies of relevant records relating to the child as provided by Section 107.006;

(F) participate in the conduct of the litigation to the same extent as an attorney for a party;

(G) take any action consistent with the child's interests that the attorney considers necessary to expedite the proceedings;

(H) encourage settlement and the use of alternative forms of dispute resolution; and

(I) review and sign, or decline to sign, a proposed or agreed order affecting the child;

(2) must be trained in child advocacy or have experience determined by the court to be equivalent to that training; and

(3) is entitled to:

(A) request clarification from the court if the role of the attorney is ambiguous;

(B) request a hearing or trial on the merits;

(C) consent or refuse to consent to an interview of the child by another attorney;

(D) receive a copy of each pleading or other paper filed with the court;

(E) receive notice of each hearing in the suit;

(F) participate in any case staffing concerning the child conducted by the Department of Family and Protective Services; and

(G) attend all legal proceedings in the suit.

(b) In addition to the duties required by Subsection (a), an attorney ad litem appointed for a child in a proceeding under Chapter 262 or 263 shall:

(1) review the medical care provided to the child;

(2) in a developmentally appropriate manner, seek to elicit the child's opinion on the medical care provided; and

(3) for a child at least 16 years of age:

(A) advise the child of the child's right to request the court to authorize the child to consent to the child's own medical care under Section 266.010; and

(B) ascertain whether the child has received the following documents:

(i) a certified copy of the child's birth certificate;

(ii) a social security card or a replacement social security card;

(iii) a driver's license or personal identification certificate under Chapter 521, Transportation Code; and

(iv) any other personal document the Department of Family and Protective Services determines appropriate.

History of Fam. Code §107.003. Acts 1997, 75th Leg., ch. 1294, §3, eff. Sept. 1, 1997. Amended by Acts 2003, 78th Leg., ch. 262, §1, eff. Sept. 1, 2003; Acts 2005, 79th Leg., ch. 172, §2, eff. Sept. 1, 2005; Acts 2013, 83rd Leg., ch. 204, §2, eff. Sept. 1, 2013; Acts 2015, 84th Leg., ch. 1, §1.033, eff. Apr. 2, 2015; S.B. 11, §3, 85th Leg., eff. Sept. 1, 2017; S.B. 1758, §2, 85th Leg., eff. Sept. 1, 2017.

History of Former Fam. Code §107.003: Acts 1995, 74th Leg., ch. 20, §1, eff. Apr. 20, 1995. Renumbered as §107.015 by Acts 1995, 74th Leg., ch. 75, §15, eff. Sept. 1, 1995.

See also *O'Connor's Texas Family Law Handbook* (2017), "Attorney Ad Litem," ch. 4-C, §2, p. 367; "Amicus Attorney," ch. 4-C, §3, p. 387.

ANNOTATIONS

O'Connor v. O'Connor, 245 S.W.3d 511, 515 (Tex. App.—Houston [1st Dist.] 2007, no pet.). "Under the Family Code, an amicus attorney and an attorney ad litem appointed to represent a child have the same duties. However, there is one important distinction. The attorney ad litem represents the child. The amicus attorney is appointed specifically to assist the court. And the plain language of the statutory definition of amicus attorney can mean only that the amicus attorney assists the court that appointed her. To whatever extent the trial court has a role during an appeal of the final decree, the amicus attorney may assist that court. But the amicus attorney represents neither an appellant nor an appellee and therefore has no basis for filing a brief in the appeal. [¶] [T]he trial court is, in effect, the amicus attorney's client for a limited purpose." ***But see In re S.A.G.***, 403 S.W.3d 907, 915 (Tex.App.—Texarkana 2013, pet. denied) (trial court is not amicus attorney's client).

In re Collins, 242 S.W.3d 837, 847 (Tex.App.—Houston [14th Dist.] 2007, orig. proceeding). Section 107.003(1)(G) "does not authorize an amicus attorney to expedite a SAPCR by using powers not conferred by statute, and the statute does not purport to expand the amicus attorney's powers to allow him to act as [child's] next friend in other lawsuits, to enter contracts on [child's] behalf, or to participate in other litigation on [child's] behalf."

In re P.A., No. 2-03-277-CV (Tex.App.—Fort Worth 2004, pet. denied) (memo op.; 10-21-04). "'No harm or violation of any Statute has been shown in allowing the attorney ad litem to make peremptory strikes, question the witnesses and argue to the jury.' Therefore, the trial court correctly allotted the ad litem her own peremptory strikes to exercise on behalf of the children. However, upon appellant's motion to equalize, the trial court, having allowed the ad litem strikes, was obligated to determine whether the ad litem was aligned with either side and then to equalize the strikes."

Ⓐ FAM §107.004. ADDITIONAL DUTIES OF ATTORNEY AD LITEM FOR CHILD

The amended text in §107.004 is effective for service plans filed for a full adversary hearing held under Fam. Code §262.201 or a status hearing held under Fam. Code ch. 263 on or after Jan. 1, 2018. A hearing held before Jan. 1, 2018, is governed by the former law in effect at that time. Except as provided above, the amended text in §107.004 is effective for SAPCRs filed on or after Sept. 1, 2017. SAPCRs filed before Sept. 1, 2017, are governed by the former law in effect at that time.

(a) Except as otherwise provided by this chapter, the attorney ad litem appointed for a child shall, in a developmentally appropriate manner:

(1) advise the child;

(2) represent the child's expressed objectives of representation and follow the child's expressed objectives of representation during the course of litigation if the attorney ad litem determines that the child is competent to understand the nature of an attorney-client re-

lationship and has formed that relationship with the attorney ad litem; and

(3) as appropriate, considering the nature of the appointment, become familiar with the American Bar Association's standards of practice for attorneys who represent children in abuse and neglect cases, the suggested amendments to those standards adopted by the National Association of Counsel for Children, and the American Bar Association's standards of practice for attorneys who represent children in custody cases.

(b) An attorney ad litem appointed for a child in a proceeding under Subtitle E shall complete at least three hours of continuing legal education relating to representing children in child protection cases as described by Subsection (c) as soon as practicable after the attorney ad litem is appointed. An attorney ad litem is not required to comply with this subsection if the court finds that the attorney ad litem has experience equivalent to the required education.

(b-1) An attorney who is on the list maintained by the court as being qualified for appointment as an attorney ad litem for a child in a child protection case must complete at least three hours of continuing legal education relating to the representation of a child in a proceeding under Subtitle E each year before the anniversary date of the attorney's listing.

(c) The continuing legal education required by Subsections (b) and (b-1) must:

(1) be low-cost and available to persons throughout this state, including on the Internet provided through the State Bar of Texas; and

(2) focus on the duties of an attorney ad litem in, and the procedures of and best practices for, representing a child in a proceeding under Subtitle E.

(d) Except as provided by Subsection (e), an attorney ad litem appointed for a child in a proceeding under Chapter 262 or 263 shall:

(1) meet before each court hearing with:

(A) the child, if the child is at least four years of age; or

(B) the individual with whom the child ordinarily resides, including the child's parent, conservator, guardian, caretaker, or custodian, if the child is younger than four years of age; and

(2) if the child or individual is not present at the court hearing, file a written statement with the court indicating that the attorney ad litem complied with Subdivision (1).

(d-1) A meeting required by Subsection (d) must take place:

(1) a sufficient time before the hearing to allow the attorney ad litem to prepare for the hearing in accordance with the child's expressed objectives of representation; and

(2) in a private setting that allows for confidential communications between the attorney ad litem and the child or individual with whom the child ordinarily resides, as applicable.

(d-2) An attorney ad litem appointed to represent a child in the managing conservatorship of the Department of Family and Protective Services shall, before each scheduled hearing under Chapter 263, determine whether the child's educational needs and goals have been identified and addressed.

(d-3) An attorney ad litem appointed to represent a child in the managing conservatorship of the Department of Family and Protective Services shall periodically continue to review the child's safety and well-being, including any effects of trauma to the child, and take appropriate action, including requesting a review hearing when necessary to address an issue of concern.

(e) An attorney ad litem appointed for a child in a proceeding under Chapter 262 or 263 is not required to comply with Subsection (d) before a hearing if the court finds at that hearing that the attorney ad litem has shown good cause why the attorney ad litem's compliance with that subsection is not feasible or in the best interest of the child. Additionally, a court may, on a showing of good cause, authorize an attorney ad litem to comply with Subsection (d) by conferring with the child or other individual, as appropriate, by telephone or video conference.

History of Fam. Code §107.004: Acts 2003, 78th Leg., ch. 262, §1, eff. Sept. 1, 2003. Amended by Acts 2005, 79th Leg., ch. 172, §3 (eff. Sept. 1, 2005), ch. 268, §1.04(a) (eff. Sept. 1, 2005); Acts 2007, 80th Leg., ch. 310, §1, eff. June 15, 2007; Acts 2011, 82nd Leg., ch. 572, §1 (eff. Sept. 1, 2011), ch. 573, §1 (eff. Sept. 1, 2011); Acts 2013, 83rd Leg., ch. 688, §2 (eff. Sept. 1, 2013), ch. 810, §1 (eff. Sept. 1, 2013); H.B. 7, §8, 85th Leg., eff. Sept. 1, 2017.

See also *O'Connor's Texas Family Law Handbook* (2017), "Duties of attorney ad litem," ch. 4-C, §2.10, p. 378.

FAM §107.0045. DISCIPLINE OF ATTORNEY AD LITEM

An attorney ad litem who fails to perform the duties required by Sections 107.003 and 107.004 is subject to disciplinary action under Subchapter E, Chapter 81, Government Code.

History of Fam. Code §107.0045: Acts 2005, 79th Leg., ch. 268, §1.05, eff. Sept. 1, 2005.

FAM §107.005. ADDITIONAL DUTIES OF AMICUS ATTORNEY

(a) Subject to any specific limitation in the order of appointment, an amicus attorney shall advocate the best interests of the child after reviewing the facts and circumstances of the case. Notwithstanding Subsection (b), in determining the best interests of the child, an amicus attorney is not bound by the child's expressed objectives of representation.

(b) An amicus attorney shall, in a developmentally appropriate manner:

(1) with the consent of the child, ensure that the child's expressed objectives of representation are made known to the court;

(2) explain the role of the amicus attorney to the child;

(3) inform the child that the amicus attorney may use information that the child provides in providing assistance to the court; and

(4) become familiar with the American Bar Association's standards of practice for attorneys who represent children in custody cases.

(c) An amicus attorney may not disclose confidential communications between the amicus attorney and the child unless the amicus attorney determines that disclosure is necessary to assist the court regarding the best interests of the child.

History of Fam. Code §107.005: Acts 2003, 78th Leg., ch. 262, §1, eff. Sept. 1, 2003. Amended by Acts 2005, 79th Leg., ch. 172, §4, eff. Sept. 1, 2005.

See also *O'Connor's Texas Family Law Handbook* (2017), "Duties," ch. 4-C, §3.8, p. 389.

FAM §107.006. ACCESS TO CHILD & INFORMATION RELATING TO CHILD

(a) In conjunction with an appointment under this chapter, other than an appointment of an attorney ad litem for an adult or a parent, the court shall issue an order authorizing the attorney ad litem, guardian ad litem for the child, or amicus attorney to have immediate access to the child and any information relating to the child.

(b) Without requiring a further order or release, the custodian of any relevant records relating to the child, including records regarding social services, law enforcement records, school records, records of a probate or court proceeding, and records of a trust or account for which the child is a beneficiary, shall provide access to a person authorized to access the records under Subsection (a).

(c) Without requiring a further order or release, the custodian of a medical, mental health, or drug or alcohol treatment record of a child that is privileged or confidential under other law shall release the record to a person authorized to access the record under Subsection (a), except that a child's drug or alcohol treatment record that is confidential under 42 U.S.C. Section 290dd-2 may only be released as provided under applicable federal regulations.

(d) The disclosure of a confidential record under this section does not affect the confidentiality of the record, and the person provided access to the record may not disclose the record further except as provided by court order or other law.

(e) Notwithstanding the provisions of this section, the requirements of Section 159.008, Occupations Code, apply.

(f) Repealed by Acts 2013, 83rd Leg., ch. 904, §1, eff. Sept. 1, 2013.

History of Fam. Code §107.006: Acts 1995, 74th Leg., ch. 943, §11, eff. Sept. 1, 1995. Amended by Acts 1997, 75th Leg., ch. 1294, §4, eff. Sept. 1, 1997; Acts 2003, 78th Leg., ch. 262, §1, eff. Sept. 1, 2003; Acts 2005, 79th Leg., ch. 172, §5, eff. Sept. 1, 2005; Acts 2011, 82nd Leg., ch. 206, §1, eff. May 30, 2011; Acts 2013, 83rd Leg., ch. 904, §1, eff. Sept. 1, 2013.

FAM §107.007. ATTORNEY WORK PRODUCT & TESTIMONY

(a) An attorney ad litem, an attorney serving in the dual role, or an amicus attorney may not:

(1) be compelled to produce attorney work product developed during the appointment as an attorney;

(2) be required to disclose the source of any information;

(3) submit a report into evidence; or

(4) testify in court except as authorized by Rule 3.08, Texas Disciplinary Rules of Professional Conduct.

(b) Subsection (a) does not apply to the duty of an attorney to report child abuse or neglect under Section 261.101.

History of Fam. Code §107.007: Acts 2003, 78th Leg., ch. 262, §1, eff. Sept. 1, 2003.

FAM §107.008. SUBSTITUTED JUDGMENT OF ATTORNEY FOR CHILD

(a) An attorney ad litem appointed to represent a child or an attorney appointed in the dual role may determine that the child cannot meaningfully formulate the child's objectives of representation in a case because the child:

(1) lacks sufficient maturity to understand and form an attorney-client relationship with the attorney;

(2) despite appropriate legal counseling, continues to express objectives of representation that would be seriously injurious to the child; or

(3) for any other reason is incapable of making reasonable judgments and engaging in meaningful communication.

(b) An attorney ad litem or an attorney appointed in the dual role who determines that the child cannot meaningfully formulate the child's expressed objectives of representation may present to the court a position that the attorney determines will serve the best interests of the child.

(c) If a guardian ad litem has been appointed for the child in a suit filed by a governmental entity requesting termination of the parent-child relationship or appointment of the entity as conservator of the child, an attorney ad litem who determines that the child cannot meaningfully formulate the child's expressed objectives of representation:

(1) shall consult with the guardian ad litem and, without being bound by the guardian ad litem's opinion or recommendation, ensure that the guardian ad litem's opinion and basis for any recommendation regarding the best interests of the child are presented to the court; and

(2) may present to the court a position that the attorney determines will serve the best interests of the child.

History of Fam. Code §107.008: Acts 2003, 78th Leg., ch. 262, §1, eff. Sept. 1, 2003. Amended by Acts 2005, 79th Leg., ch. 172, §6, eff. Sept. 1, 2005.

A FAM §107.009. IMMUNITY

The amended text in §107.009 is effective for SAPCRs filed on or after Sept. 1, 2017. SAPCRs filed before Sept. 1, 2017, are governed by the former law in effect at that time.

(a) A guardian ad litem, an attorney ad litem, a child custody evaluator, or an amicus attorney appointed under this chapter is not liable for civil damages arising from an action taken, a recommendation made, or an opinion given in the capacity of guardian ad litem, attorney ad litem, child custody evaluator, or amicus attorney.

(b) Subsection (a) does not apply to an action taken, a recommendation made, or an opinion given:

(1) with conscious indifference or reckless disregard to the safety of another;

(2) in bad faith or with malice; or

(3) that is grossly negligent or wilfully wrongful.

History of Fam. Code §107.009: Acts 2003, 78th Leg., ch. 262, §1, eff. Sept. 1, 2003. Amended by Acts 2005, 79th Leg., ch. 172, §7, eff. Sept. 1, 2005; H.B. 1501, §1, 85th Leg., eff. Sept. 1, 2017.

ANNOTATIONS

Kabbani v. Papadopolous, No. 01-07-00191-CV (Tex.App.—Houston [1st Dist.] 2009, pet. denied) (memo op.; 2-26-09). "[T]he provisions of §107.009(b) do not create a cause of action on which a claimant may state a claim for relief. Section 107.009(b) ... operates to limit ... the immunity ... under §107.009(a). [¶] We may not, therefore, construe [mother's claim for civil damages for actions taken by attorney ad litem] as contending that she stated a claim, but, rather, as contending that she invoked §107.009(b)'s exceptions to the affirmative defense of immunity...."

FAM §107.010. DISCRETIONARY APPOINTMENT OF ATTORNEY AD LITEM FOR INCAPACITATED PERSON

The court may appoint an attorney to serve as an attorney ad litem for a person entitled to service of citation in a suit if the court finds that the person is incapacitated. The attorney ad litem shall follow the person's expressed objectives of representation and, if appropriate, refer the proceeding to the proper court for guardianship proceedings.

History of Fam. Code §107.010: Acts 2003, 78th Leg., ch. 262, §1, eff. Sept. 1, 2003.

See also *O'Connor's Texas Family Law Handbook* (2017), "Appointment for incapacitated person," ch. 4-C, §2.2.1(3), p. 370.

SUBCHAPTER B. APPOINTMENTS IN CERTAIN SUITS

PART 1. APPOINTMENTS IN SUITS BY GOVERNMENTAL ENTITY

FAM §107.011. MANDATORY APPOINTMENT OF GUARDIAN AD LITEM

(a) Except as otherwise provided by this subchapter, in a suit filed by a governmental entity seeking termination of the parent-child relationship or the appointment of a conservator for a child, the court shall appoint a guardian ad litem to represent the best interests of the child immediately after the filing of the petition but before the full adversary hearing.

(b) The guardian ad litem appointed for a child under this section may be:

(1) a charitable organization composed of volunteer advocates or an individual volunteer advocate appointed under Subchapter C;

(2) an adult having the competence, training, and expertise determined by the court to be sufficient to represent the best interests of the child; or

(3) an attorney appointed in the dual role.

(c) The court may not appoint a guardian ad litem in a suit filed by a governmental entity if an attorney is appointed in the dual role unless the court appoints another person to serve as guardian ad litem for the child and restricts the role of the attorney to acting as an attorney ad litem for the child.

(d) The court may appoint an attorney to serve as guardian ad litem for a child without appointing the attorney to serve in the dual role only if the attorney is specifically appointed to serve only in the role of guardian ad litem. An attorney appointed solely as a guardian ad litem:

(1) may take only those actions that may be taken by a nonattorney guardian ad litem; and

(2) may not:

(A) perform legal services in the case; or

(B) take any action that is restricted to a licensed attorney, including engaging in discovery other than as a witness, making opening and closing statements, or examining witnesses.

History of Fam. Code §107.011: Acts 1995, 74th Leg., ch. 20, §1, eff. Apr. 20, 1995. Renumbered from §107.002(a), (b) by Acts 1995, 74th Leg., ch. 751, §15, eff. Sept. 1, 1995. Amended by Acts 2003, 78th Leg., ch. 262, §1, eff. Sept. 1, 2003. Source: Former Fam. Code §11.10(b)(2), (c).

See also *O'Connor's Texas Family Law Handbook* (2017), "Appointments in suits brought by governmental entities," ch. 4-C, §4.3.2, p. 391.

FAM §107.012. MANDATORY APPOINTMENT OF ATTORNEY AD LITEM FOR CHILD

In a suit filed by a governmental entity requesting termination of the parent-child relationship or to be named conservator of a child, the court shall appoint an attorney ad litem to represent the interests of the child immediately after the filing, but before the full adversary hearing, to ensure adequate representation of the child.

History of Fam. Code §107.012: Acts 1995, 74th Leg., ch. 20, §1, eff. Apr. 20, 1995. Renumbered from §107.002(c) by Acts 1995, 74th Leg., ch. 751, §15, eff. Sept. 1, 1995. Source: Former Fam. Code §11.10(d).

See also *O'Connor's Texas Family Law Handbook* (2017), "Grounds for suits brought by governmental entities," ch. 4-C, §2.2.2, p. 370.

FAM §107.0125. APPOINTMENT OF ATTORNEY IN DUAL ROLE

(a) In order to comply with the mandatory appointment of a guardian ad litem under Section 107.011 and the mandatory appointment of an attorney ad litem under Section 107.012, the court may appoint an attorney to serve in the dual role.

(b) If the court appoints an attorney to serve in the dual role under this section, the court may at any time during the pendency of the suit appoint another person to serve as guardian ad litem for the child and restrict the attorney to acting as an attorney ad litem for the child.

(c) An attorney appointed to serve in the dual role may request the court to appoint another person to serve as guardian ad litem for the child. If the court grants the attorney's request, the attorney shall serve only as the attorney ad litem for the child.

(d) Unless the court appoints another person as guardian ad litem in a suit filed by a governmental entity, an appointment of an attorney to serve as an attorney ad litem in a suit filed by a governmental entity is an appointment to serve in the dual role regardless of the terminology used in the appointing order.

History of Fam. Code §107.0125: Acts 2003, 78th Leg., ch. 262, §1, eff. Sept. 1, 2003.

See also *O'Connor's Texas Family Law Handbook* (2017), "Dual-Role Attorney Ad Litem," ch. 4-C, §5, p. 396.

FAM §107.013. MANDATORY APPOINTMENT OF ATTORNEY AD LITEM FOR PARENT

(a) In a suit filed by a governmental entity under Subtitle E in which termination of the parent-child relationship or the appointment of a conservator for a child is requested, the court shall appoint an attorney ad litem to represent the interests of:

(1) an indigent parent of the child who responds in opposition to the termination or appointment;

(2) a parent served by citation by publication;

(3) an alleged father who failed to register with the registry under Chapter 160 and whose identity or location is unknown; and

(4) an alleged father who registered with the paternity registry under Chapter 160, but the petitioner's attempt to personally serve citation at the address provided to the registry and at any other address for the alleged father known by the petitioner has been unsuccessful.

(a-1) In a suit described by Subsection (a), if a parent is not represented by an attorney at the parent's first appearance in court, the court shall inform the parent of:

(1) the right to be represented by an attorney; and

(2) if the parent is indigent and appears in opposition to the suit, the right to an attorney ad litem appointed by the court.

(b) If both parents of the child are entitled to the appointment of an attorney ad litem under this section and the court finds that the interests of the parents are not in conflict and that there is no history or pattern of past or present family violence by one parent directed against the other parent, a spouse, or a child of the parties, the court may appoint an attorney ad litem to represent the interests of both parents.

(c) Repealed by Acts 2013, 83rd Leg., ch. 810, §11, eff. Sept. 1, 2013.

(d) The court shall require a parent who claims indigence under Subsection (a) to file an affidavit of indigence in accordance with Rule 145(b) of the Texas Rules of Civil Procedure before the court may conduct a hearing to determine the parent's indigence under this section. The court may consider additional evidence at that hearing, including evidence relating to the parent's income, source of income, assets, property ownership, benefits paid in accordance with a federal, state, or local public assistance program, outstanding obligations, and necessary expenses and the number and ages of the parent's dependents. If the court determines the parent is indigent, the court shall appoint an attorney ad litem to represent the parent.

(e) A parent who the court has determined is indigent for purposes of this section is presumed to remain indigent for the duration of the suit and any subsequent appeal unless the court, after reconsideration on the motion of the parent, the attorney ad litem for the parent, or the attorney representing the governmental entity, determines that the parent is no longer indigent due to a material and substantial change in the parent's financial circumstances.

History of Fam. Code §107.013: Acts 1995, 74th Leg., ch. 20, §1, eff. Apr. 20, 1995. Renumbered from §107.002(d) by Acts 1995, 74th Leg., ch. 751, §15, eff. Sept. 1, 1995. Amended by Acts 1997, 75th Leg., ch. 561, §3, eff. Sept. 1, 1997; Acts 2001, 77th Leg., ch. 821, §2.11, eff. June 14, 2001; Acts 2003, 78th Leg., ch. 262, §1, eff. Sept. 1, 2003; Acts 2005, 79th Leg., ch. 268, §1.06, eff. Sept. 1, 2005; Acts 2007, 80th Leg., ch. 526, §1, eff. June 16, 2007; Acts 2011, 82nd Leg., ch. 75, §1, eff. Sept. 1, 2011; Acts 2013, 83rd Leg., ch. 810, §§2, 11, eff. Sept. 1, 2013; Acts 2015, 84th Leg., ch. 128, §1, eff. Sept. 1, 2015. Source: Former Fam. Code §11.10(d).

ANNOTATIONS

In re P.M., ___ S.W.3d ___ (Tex.2016) (No. 15-0171; 4-1-16). "[T]he right to counsel under [Fam. Code] §107.013(a)(1) through the exhaustion of appeals under [Fam. Code] §107.016(2)(B) includes all proceedings in this Court, including the filing of a petition for review. Once appointed by the trial court, counsel should be permitted to withdraw only for good cause and on appropriate terms and conditions. Mere dissatisfaction of counsel or client with each other is not good cause. Nor is counsel's belief that the client has no grounds to seek further review from the court of appeals' decision. Counsel's obligation to the client may still be satisfied by filing an appellate brief meeting the standards set in ***Anders v. California***[, 386 U.S. 738 (1967)], and its progeny. In light of our holding, however, an ***Anders*** motion to withdraw brought in the court of appeals, in the absence of additional grounds for withdrawal, may be premature. Courts have a duty to see that withdrawal of counsel will not result in foreseeable prejudice to the client. If a court of appeals allows an attorney to withdraw, it must provide for the appointment of new counsel to pursue a petition for review. In this Court, appointed counsel's obligations can be satisfied by filing a petition for review that satisfies the standards for an ***Anders*** brief. [¶] While an appellate court may be equipped to rule on a motion to withdraw in many instances, it may decide instead, as the court of appeals did in this case with a motion unrelated to any ***Anders*** claim, to refer the motion to the trial court for evidence and a hearing. An appellate court must ordinarily refer the matter of appointment of replacement counsel to the trial court."

In re M.S., 115 S.W.3d 534, 544 (Tex.2003). "We hold that the statutory right to counsel in parental-rights termination cases embodies the right to effective counsel. *At 545:* [To prove ineffective assistance of counsel], [f]irst, the defendant must show that counsel's performance was deficient. … Second, the defendant must show that the deficient performance prejudiced the defense. [¶] It is only when 'the conduct [is] so outrageous that no competent attorney would have engaged in it,' that the challenged conduct will constitute ineffective assistance. *At 550:* [I]f the court of appeals finds that the evidence to support termination was factually insufficient, and that counsel's failure to preserve a factual sufficiency complaint was unjustified and fell below being objectively reasonable, then it must hold that counsel's failure to preserve the factual sufficiency complaint by a motion for new trial constituted ineffective assistance of counsel." *See also* ***B.C. v. TDFPS***, 446 S.W.3d 869, 877 (Tex.App.—El Paso 2014,

no pet.) (strong presumption that counsel's conduct falls within wide range of reasonable professional assistance).

In re B.L.D., 113 S.W.3d 340, 347 (Tex.2003). "[A] trial court must determine whether there is a substantial risk that a lawyer's obligations to one parent would materially and adversely affect his or her obligations to the other parent when deciding whether there is a conflict of interest between parents opposing termination in a single suit. In evaluating whether there is a substantial risk of conflict of interest before trial, the trial court should consider the available record to determine the likelihood that the parents' positions will be adverse to each other. *At 348:* We acknowledge that a potential for conflicts of interest between parents challenging termination may always be present. However, the trial court's inquiry under the standard we articulate today is limited to whether there is an actual conflict of interest." *See also* ***In re K.M.H.***, 181 S.W.3d 1, 11 (Tex.App.—Houston [14th Dist.] 2005, no pet.).

In re S.R., 452 S.W.3d 351, 372 (Tex.App.—Houston [14th Dist.] 2014, pet. denied). "Unlike [Fam. Code] §107.012 requiring appointment of an attorney ad litem for a child, [Fam. Code] §107.013 contains no specific timetable for appointing an attorney ad litem to represent the parent's interests. Courts have found that the complete failure of a trial court to appoint counsel to represent the interests of indigent parents constitutes reversible error. [¶] Section 107.013(d) requires that a parent who claims indigence under §107.013(a) must file an affidavit of indigence before the court can conduct a hearing to determine the parent's indigence. Here, the Father signed a written request for appointment of counsel, with information supporting his indigence claim.... Counsel was appointed the same day. Assuming the Father's documents were sufficient to trigger the process for mandatory appointment of an attorney ad litem, the trial court completed that process promptly upon receiving the Father's documents. We hold the trial court did not err in appointing counsel for the Father after the adversary hearing." *See also* ***In re V.L.B.***, this page.

In re V.L.B., 445 S.W.3d 802, 806-07 (Tex.App.—Houston [1st Dist.] 2014, no pet.). "Complete failure of a trial court to appoint counsel for indigent parents constitutes reversible error. The question presented here is whether delaying that appointment until after the commencement of the termination trial does as well. [Family Code] §107.013 does not specify the time by which an indigent parent requesting representation must receive it. [¶] Considering the mandatory nature of the appointment of counsel upon a finding of indigency, and the appointed attorney's specific obligations [under Fam. Code §107.0131] in connection with representing an indigent parent, a trial court should address a parent's affidavit of indigence as soon as possible—before the next critical stage of the proceedings, whether it be a hearing, a mediation, a pretrial conference, or, in particular, a trial on the merits, and allow a reasonable time for appointed counsel to make necessary preparations. When an indigent parent seeks representation before a critical stage of the proceedings, and the trial court nonetheless proceeds with that stage, the delay may render the ultimate appointment a toothless exercise and irreparably impair the parent's ability to defend the case or regain custody of the child." *See also* ***In re S.R.***, this page; ***In re C.D.S.***, 172 S.W.3d 179, 185-86 (Tex.App.—Fort Worth 2005, no pet.) (failure to appoint attorney ad litem before trial, eight months after affidavit of indigence was filed, was error). *But see* ***In re M.J.M.L.***, p. 438.

In re J.M., 361 S.W.3d 734, 736 (Tex.App.—Amarillo 2012, no pet.). "[D]oes a trial court err in failing to appoint an attorney ad litem to represent a parent when the parent at issue has made no formal request for appointment of an attorney[?] *At 737:* From [the] record, it is apparent to the Court that [indigent mother] was responding in opposition to the termination. *At 738:* The [TDFPS] contends that [mother] answered ready for trial when asked by the trial court if she was ready to proceed. That announcement of ready, coupled with no affirmative request for appointment of an attorney would mean, according to the [TDFPS], that the trial court committed no error in failing to appoint her an attorney ad litem. Such a contention is an effort to place an additional requirement on §107.013(a), that being that when a parent appears in opposition to a termination *and* requests an attorney. However, such a requirement is not present in the statute. [¶] [The TDFPS also asserts] that [mother] voluntarily waived any rights to appointed counsel under §107.013(a). ... The record is devoid of any indication that [mother] knew of her rights to claim indigency and request counsel. *At 739:* In consideration of the recognized constitutional dimensions of the parent-child relationship, we see no reason why the trial court

should not make an inquiry into whether [mother] desired to proceed without benefit of counsel. Accordingly, we ... find that the trial court committed reversible error by proceeding without appointing an attorney to represent [mother]." *See also* ***In re V.L.B.***, 445 S.W.3d 802, 806 (Tex.App.—Houston [1st Dist.] 2014, no pet.) (mother who filed affidavit of indigence before trial and testified at trial about her attempts to obtain counsel did not waive right to counsel).

In re V.V., 349 S.W.3d 548, 559 (Tex.App.—Houston [1st Dist.] 2010, pet. denied). "[A]n ineffective assistance of counsel claim [in a civil parental-rights termination case] 'requires more than merely showing that appointed counsel was ineffective.' The parent must also show that 'counsel's deficient performance prejudiced the defense.' To show prejudice, the parent 'must show that there is a reasonable probability that, but for counsel's unprofessional errors, the result of the proceeding would have been different.'"

In re C.D.S., 172 S.W.3d 179, 185 (Tex.App.—Fort Worth 2005, no pet.). "[W]e hold that the term 'indigent' in §107.013(a)(1) ... means a person who does not have the resources, nor is able to obtain the resources, to hire and retain an attorney for representation in the termination case. In making this determination, the court can consider the purported indigent's income, source of income, assets, property owned, outstanding obligations, necessary expenses, number and ages of dependents, and spousal income available to the defendant." *See also* ***In re R.D.Y.***, 51 S.W.3d 314, 325 (Tex.App.—Houston [1st Dist.] 2001, pet. denied) (fact that mother was receiving government entitlement based on indigency was prima facie evidence that she was indigent).

In re M.J.M.L., 31 S.W.3d 347, 354 (Tex.App.—San Antonio 2000, pet. denied). Mother "urges us to interpret [Fam. Code] §107.013(a)(1) to require appointment of an attorney immediately after the filing of a petition to terminate the parent-child relationship, before any hearings are held in the case. [¶] The more open-ended language of §107.013(a)(1) directly contrasts with [Fam. Code §107.012] which mandates the appointment of an attorney ad litem for children involved in termination proceedings 'immediately after the filing [of the suit], but before the full adversary hearing.' Presumably, if the Legislature wished to impose a similar deadline for appointment of counsel for indigent parents, it would have done so. We decline to read such a deadline into the statute. The appointment of counsel six months after the case began was not in itself a violation of §107.013(a)(1)." *But see* ***In re V.L.B.***, p. 437.

FAM §107.0131. POWERS & DUTIES OF ATTORNEY AD LITEM FOR PARENT

(a) An attorney ad litem appointed under Section 107.013 to represent the interests of a parent:

(1) shall:

(A) subject to Rules 4.02, 4.03, and 4.04, Texas Disciplinary Rules of Professional Conduct, and within a reasonable time after the appointment, interview:

(i) the parent, unless the parent's location is unknown;

(ii) each person who has significant knowledge of the case; and

(iii) the parties to the suit;

(B) investigate the facts of the case;

(C) to ensure competent representation at hearings, mediations, pretrial matters, and the trial on the merits:

(i) obtain and review copies of all court files in the suit during the attorney ad litem's course of representation; and

(ii) when necessary, conduct formal discovery under the Texas Rules of Civil Procedure or the discovery control plan;

(D) take any action consistent with the parent's interests that the attorney ad litem considers necessary to expedite the proceedings;

(E) encourage settlement and the use of alternative forms of dispute resolution;

(F) review and sign, or decline to sign, a proposed or agreed order affecting the parent;

(G) meet before each court hearing with the parent, unless the court:

(i) finds at that hearing that the attorney ad litem has shown good cause why the attorney ad litem's compliance is not feasible; or

(ii) on a showing of good cause, authorizes the attorney ad litem to comply by conferring with the parent, as appropriate, by telephone or video conference;

(H) abide by the parent's objectives for representation;

(I) become familiar with the American Bar Association's standards of practice for attorneys who represent parents in abuse and neglect cases; and

(J) complete at least three hours of continuing legal education relating to representing parents in child protection cases as described by Subsection (b) as soon as practicable after the attorney ad litem is appointed, unless the court finds that the attorney ad litem has experience equivalent to that education; and

(2) is entitled to:

(A) request clarification from the court if the role of the attorney ad litem is ambiguous;

(B) request a hearing or trial on the merits;

(C) consent or refuse to consent to an interview of the parent by another attorney;

(D) receive a copy of each pleading or other paper filed with the court;

(E) receive notice of each hearing in the suit;

(F) participate in any case staffing conducted by the Department of Family and Protective Services in which the parent is invited to participate, including, as appropriate, a case staffing to develop a family plan of service, a family group conference, a permanency conference, a mediation, a case staffing to plan for the discharge and return of the child to the parent, and any other case staffing that the department determines would be appropriate for the parent to attend, but excluding any internal department staffing or staffing between the department and the department's legal representative; and

(G) attend all legal proceedings in the suit.

(b) The continuing legal education required by Subsection (a)(1)(J) must:

(1) be low-cost and available to persons throughout this state, including on the Internet provided through the State Bar of Texas; and

(2) focus on the duties of an attorney ad litem in, and the procedures of and best practices for, representing a parent in a proceeding under Subtitle E.

(c) An attorney who is on the list maintained by the court as being qualified for appointment as an attorney ad litem for a parent in a child protection case must complete at least three hours of continuing legal education relating to the representation of a parent in a proceeding under Subtitle E each year before the anniversary date of the attorney's listing.

History of Fam. Code §107.0131: Acts 2011, 82nd Leg., ch. 647, §1, eff. Sept. 1, 2011. Amended by Acts 2013, 83rd Leg., ch. 810, §3, eff. Sept. 1, 2013.

See also ***O'Connor's Texas Family Law Handbook*** (2017), "Qualifications – appointment for parent," ch. 4-C, §2.4.2, p. 373; "Attorney ad litem rights – general or temporary appointment for parent in government suit," ch. 4-C, §2.9.3, p. 377; "Attorney ad litem duties – appointment for parent in government suit," ch. 4-C, §2.10.4, p. 382.

FAM §107.0132. POWERS & DUTIES OF ATTORNEY AD LITEM FOR ALLEGED FATHER

(a) Except as provided by Subsections (b) and (d), an attorney ad litem appointed under Section 107.013 to represent the interests of an alleged father is only required to:

(1) conduct an investigation regarding the petitioner's due diligence in locating the alleged father, including by verifying that the petitioner has obtained a certificate of the results of a search of the paternity registry under Chapter 160;

(2) interview any party or other person who has significant knowledge of the case who may have information relating to the identity or location of the alleged father; and

(3) conduct an independent investigation to identify or locate the alleged father, as applicable.

(b) If the attorney ad litem identifies and locates the alleged father, the attorney ad litem shall:

(1) provide to each party and the court the alleged father's name and address and any other locating information; and

(2) if appropriate, request the court's approval for the attorney ad litem to assist the alleged father in establishing paternity.

(c) If the alleged father is adjudicated to be a parent of the child and is determined by the court to be indigent, the court may appoint the attorney ad litem to continue to represent the father's interests as a parent under Section 107.013(a)(1) or (c).

(d) If the attorney ad litem is unable to identify or locate the alleged father, the attorney ad litem shall submit to the court a written summary of the attorney ad litem's efforts to identify or locate the alleged father with a statement that the attorney ad litem was unable to identify or locate the alleged father. On receipt of the summary required by this subsection, the court shall discharge the attorney from the appointment.

History of Fam. Code §107.0132: Acts 2011, 82nd Leg., ch. 647, §1, eff. Sept. 1, 2011. Amended by Acts 2013, 83rd Leg., ch. 810, §4, eff. Sept. 1, 2013.

See also ***O'Connor's Texas Family Law Handbook*** (2017), "Appointment for alleged father," ch. 4-C, §2.2.2(5), p. 372; "Attorney ad litem duties – appointment for alleged father in government suit," ch. 4-C, §2.10.5, p. 384.

FAM §107.0133. DISCIPLINE OF ATTORNEY AD LITEM FOR PARENT OR ALLEGED FATHER

An attorney ad litem appointed for a parent or an alleged father who fails to perform the duties required by Section 107.0131 or 107.0132, as applicable, is subject to disciplinary action under Subchapter E, Chapter 81, Government Code.

History of Fam. Code §107.0133: Acts 2011, 82nd Leg., ch. 647, §1, eff. Sept. 1, 2011.

FAM §107.0135. DELETED

Deleted by Acts 2003, 78th Leg., ch. 262, §1, eff. Sept. 1, 2003.

FAM §107.014. POWERS & DUTIES OF ATTORNEY AD LITEM FOR CERTAIN PARENTS

(a) Except as provided by Subsections (b) and (e), an attorney ad litem appointed under Section 107.013 to represent the interests of a parent whose identity or location is unknown or who has been served by citation by publication is only required to:

(1) conduct an investigation regarding the petitioner's due diligence in locating the parent;

(2) interview any party or other person who has significant knowledge of the case who may have information relating to the identity or location of the parent; and

(3) conduct an independent investigation to identify or locate the parent, as applicable.

(b) If the attorney ad litem identifies and locates the parent, the attorney ad litem shall:

(1) provide to each party and the court the parent's name and address and any other available locating information unless the court finds that:

(A) disclosure of a parent's address is likely to cause that parent harassment, serious harm, or injury; or

(B) the parent has been a victim of family violence; and

(2) if appropriate, assist the parent in making a claim of indigence for the appointment of an attorney.

(c) If the court makes a finding described by Subsection (b)(1)(A) or (B), the court may:

(1) order that the information not be disclosed; or

(2) render any other order the court considers necessary.

(d) If the court determines the parent is indigent, the court may appoint the attorney ad litem to continue to represent the parent under Section 107.013(a)(1).

(e) If the attorney ad litem is unable to identify or locate the parent, the attorney ad litem shall submit to the court a written summary of the attorney ad litem's efforts to identify or locate the parent with a statement that the attorney ad litem was unable to identify or locate the parent. On receipt of the summary required by this subsection, the court shall discharge the attorney from the appointment.

History of Fam. Code §107.014: Acts 2013, 83rd Leg., ch. 810, §5, eff. Sept. 1, 2013.

History of Former Fam. Code §107.014: Deleted by Acts 2003, 78th Leg., ch. 262, §1, eff. Sept. 1, 2003.

FAM §107.0141. TEMPORARY APPOINTMENT OF ATTORNEY AD LITEM FOR CERTAIN PARENTS

(a) The court may appoint an attorney ad litem to represent the interests of a parent for a limited period beginning at the time the court issues a temporary restraining order or attachment of the parent's child under Chapter 262 and ending on the court's determination of whether the parent is indigent before commencement of the full adversary hearing.

(b) An attorney ad litem appointed for a parent under this section:

(1) has the powers and duties of an attorney ad litem appointed under Section 107.0131; and

(2) if applicable, shall:

(A) conduct an investigation regarding the petitioner's due diligence in locating and serving citation on the parent; and

(B) interview any party or other person who may have information relating to the identity or location of the parent.

(c) If the attorney ad litem identifies and locates the parent, the attorney ad litem shall:

(1) inform the parent of the parent's right to be represented by an attorney and of the parent's right to an attorney ad litem appointed by the court, if the parent is indigent and appears in opposition to the suit;

(2) if the parent claims indigence and requests an attorney ad litem beyond the period of the temporary appointment under this section, assist the parent in making a claim of indigence for the appointment of an attorney ad litem; and

(3) assist the parent in preparing for the full adversary hearing under Subchapter C, Chapter 262.

(d) If the court determines the parent is indigent, the court may appoint the attorney ad litem to continue to represent the parent under Section 107.013(a)(1).

(e) If the attorney ad litem is unable to identify or locate the parent, the attorney ad litem shall submit to the court a written summary of the attorney ad litem's efforts to identify or locate the parent with a statement that the attorney ad litem was unable to identify or locate the parent. On receipt of the summary required by this subsection, the court shall discharge the attorney ad litem from the appointment.

(f) If the attorney ad litem identifies or locates the parent, and the court determines that the parent is not indigent, the court shall discharge the attorney ad litem from the appointment.

History of Fam. Code §107.0141: Acts 2015, 84th Leg., ch. 128, §2, eff. Sept. 1, 2015.

FAM §107.015. ATTORNEY FEES

(a) An attorney appointed under this chapter to serve as an attorney ad litem for a child, an attorney in the dual role, or an attorney ad litem for a parent is entitled to reasonable fees and expenses in the amount set by the court to be paid by the parents of the child unless the parents are indigent.

(b) If the court determines that one or more of the parties are able to defray the fees and expenses of an attorney ad litem or guardian ad litem for the child as determined by the reasonable and customary fees for similar services in the county of jurisdiction, the fees and expenses may be ordered paid by one or more of those parties, or the court may order one or more of those parties, prior to final hearing, to pay the sums into the registry of the court or into an account authorized by the court for the use and benefit of the payee on order of the court. The sums may be taxed as costs to be assessed against one or more of the parties.

(c) If indigency of the parents is shown, an attorney ad litem appointed to represent a child or parent in a suit filed by a governmental entity shall be paid from the general funds of the county according to the fee schedule that applies to an attorney appointed to represent a child in a suit under Title 3 as provided by Chapter 51. The court may not award attorney ad litem fees under this chapter against the state, a state agency, or a political subdivision of the state except as provided by this subsection.

(d) A person appointed as a guardian ad litem or attorney ad litem shall complete and submit to the court a voucher or claim for payment that lists the fees charged and hours worked by the guardian ad litem or attorney ad litem. Information submitted under this section is subject to disclosure under Chapter 552, Government Code.

History of Fam. Code §107.015: Acts 1995, 74th Leg., ch. 20, §1, eff. Apr. 20, 1995. Renumbered from §107.003 by Acts 1995, 74th Leg., ch. 751, §15, eff. Sept. 1, 1995. Amended by Acts 1999, 76th Leg., ch. 1390, §6, eff. Sept. 1, 1999; Acts 2003, 78th Leg., ch. 262, §1, eff. Sept. 1, 2003; Acts 2005, 79th Leg., ch. 268, §1.07, eff. Sept. 1, 2005. Source: Former Fam. Code §11.10(a), (e).

See also ***O'Connor's Texas Family Law Handbook*** (2017), "Fees & expenses," ch. 4-C, §2.11, p. 385.

ANNOTATIONS

Brownsville-Valley Reg'l Med. Ctr., Inc. v. Gamez, 894 S.W.2d 753, 754 (Tex.1995). This court holds that "it is an abuse of discretion for a trial court to award ad litem fees for services performed after resolution of the conflict of interest which gave rise to the appointment."

A FAM §107.016. CONTINUED REPRESENTATION; DURATION OF APPOINTMENT

The amended text in §107.016 is effective for service plans filed for a full adversary hearing held under Fam. Code §262.201 or a status hearing held under Fam. Code ch. 263 on or after Jan. 1, 2018. A hearing held before Jan. 1, 2018, is governed by the former law in effect at that time. Except as provided above, the amended text in §107.016 is effective for SAPCRs filed on or after Sept. 1, 2017. SAPCRs filed before Sept. 1, 2017, are governed by the former law in effect at that time.

In a suit filed by a governmental entity in which termination of the parent-child relationship or appointment of the entity as conservator of the child is requested:

(1) an order appointing the Department of Family and Protective Services as the child's managing conservator may provide for the continuation of the appointment of the guardian ad litem [~~or attorney ad litem~~] for the child for any period during the time the child remains in the conservatorship of the department, as set by the court; [~~and~~]

(2) an order appointing the Department of Family and Protective Services as the child's managing conservator may provide for the continuation of the appointment of the attorney ad litem for the child as long as the child remains in the conservatorship of the department; and

(3) an attorney appointed under this subchapter to serve as an attorney ad litem for a parent or an alleged father continues to serve in that capacity until the earliest of:

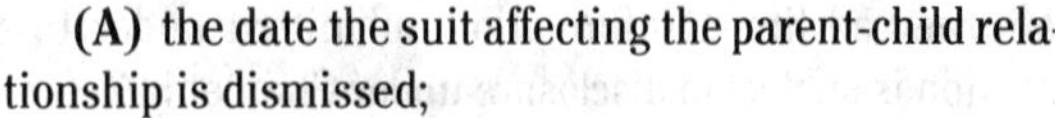

(A) the date the suit affecting the parent-child relationship is dismissed;

(B) the date all appeals in relation to any final order terminating parental rights are exhausted or waived; or

(C) the date the attorney is relieved of the attorney's duties or replaced by another attorney after a finding of good cause is rendered by the court on the record.

History of Fam. Code §107.016: Acts 1995, 74th Leg., ch. 751, §15, eff. Sept. 1, 1995. Amended by Acts 1997, 75th Leg., ch. 575, §6, eff. Sept. 1, 1997; Acts 2003, 78th Leg., ch. 262, §1, eff. Sept. 1, 2003; Acts 2011, 82nd Leg., ch. 75, §2, eff. Sept. 1, 2011; H.B. 7, §9, 85th Leg., eff. Sept. 1, 2017.

ANNOTATIONS

In re P.M., ___ S.W.3d ___ (Tex.2016) (No. 15-0171; 4-1-16). See annotation under Family Code §107.013, p. 436.

FAM §107.0161. AD LITEM APPOINTMENTS FOR CHILD COMMITTED TO TEXAS JUVENILE JUSTICE DEPARTMENT

If an order appointing the Department of Family and Protective Services as managing conservator of a child does not continue the appointment of the child's guardian ad litem or attorney ad litem and the child is committed to the Texas Juvenile Justice Department or released under supervision by the Texas Juvenile Justice Department, the court may appoint a guardian ad litem or attorney ad litem for the child.

History of Fam. Code §107.0161: Acts 2009, 81st Leg., ch. 108, §3, eff. May 23, 2009. Amended by Acts 2015, 84th Leg., ch. 734, §79, eff. Sept. 1, 2015.

FAM §107.017. APPOINTMENT OF AMICUS ATTORNEY PROHIBITED

The court may not appoint a person to serve as an amicus attorney in a suit filed by a governmental entity under this chapter.

History of Fam. Code §107.017: Acts 2003, 78th Leg., ch. 262, §1, eff. Sept. 1, 2003.

Sections 107.018-107.020 reserved for expansion

PART 2. APPOINTMENTS IN SUITS OTHER THAN SUITS BY GOVERNMENTAL ENTITY

FAM §107.021. DISCRETIONARY APPOINTMENTS

(a) In a suit in which the best interests of a child are at issue, other than a suit filed by a governmental entity requesting termination of the parent-child relationship or appointment of the entity as conservator of the child, the court may appoint one of the following:

(1) an amicus attorney;

(2) an attorney ad litem; or

(3) a guardian ad litem.

(a-1) In a suit requesting termination of the parent-child relationship that is not filed by a governmental entity, the court shall, unless the court finds that the interests of the child will be represented adequately by a party to the suit whose interests are not in conflict with the child's interests, appoint one of the following:

(1) an amicus attorney; or

(2) an attorney ad litem.

(b) In determining whether to make an appointment under this section, the court:

(1) shall:

(A) give due consideration to the ability of the parties to pay reasonable fees to the appointee; and

(B) balance the child's interests against the cost to the parties that would result from an appointment by taking into consideration the cost of available alternatives for resolving issues without making an appointment;

(2) may make an appointment only if the court finds that the appointment is necessary to ensure the determination of the best interests of the child, unless the appointment is otherwise required by this code; and

(3) may not require a person appointed under this section to serve without reasonable compensation for the services rendered by the person.

History of Fam. Code §107.021: Acts 2003, 78th Leg., ch. 262, §1, eff. Sept. 1, 2003. Amended by Acts 2005, 79th Leg., ch. 172, §8, eff. Sept. 1, 2005. Source: Former Fam. Code §107.011.

See also ***O'Connor's Texas Family Law Handbook*** (2017), "Court Appointments in SAPCRs," ch. 4-C, p. 365.

ANNOTATIONS

In re A.G.D., ___ S.W.3d ___ (Tex.App.—Amarillo 2015, order) (No. 07-15-00201-CV; 6-16-15). "The petition to terminate [incarcerated father's] parental rights was filed by the mother of the child and not by a governmental entity. Therefore, appointment of counsel [for father] is not mandatory. However, authority has interpreted §107.021 … as granting trial courts the discretion to appoint counsel in termination proceedings wherein the State … is not a party. [¶] If it is determined that [father] is indigent and is entitled to appointed counsel, the trial court may appoint him counsel…."

In re K.M.M., 326 S.W.3d 714, 715 (Tex.App.—Amarillo 2010, no pet.). "[M]issing from the [trial-court] record is any finding that [mother] would or could adequately represent [child]. [W]ithout such a finding, the appointment of either an amicus attorney or attorney ad litem was mandatory. [I]t has been recognized that where parents are adversaries in a suit to terminate one parent's rights, the trial court can seldom find that one party adequately represents the interests of the children involved or that their interests are not adverse. Moreover, the failure to abide by §107.021 may be raised for the first time on appeal. [¶] [Mother] urges us to imply that the trial court made the requisite finding and concluded that a home study conducted before the court terminated [father's] parental rights constituted the appointment of a disinterested party to represent [child]. Yet, we can do neither. Because no specific finding entered by the trial court encompassed an element of whether [mother] could adequately represent [child], no finding may be implied on the matter."

In re Villanueva, 292 S.W.3d 236, 246 (Tex.App.—Texarkana 2009, orig. proceeding). "[T]he trial court abused its discretion when it ordered [mother] to pay the costs and fees associated with the attorney ad litem ... when [mother] is indigent as a matter of law...."

FAM §107.022. CERTAIN PROHIBITED APPOINTMENTS

In a suit other than a suit filed by a governmental entity requesting termination of the parent-child relationship or appointment of the entity as conservator of the child, the court may not appoint:

(1) an attorney to serve in the dual role; or

(2) a volunteer advocate to serve as guardian ad litem for a child unless the training of the volunteer advocate is designed for participation in suits other than suits filed by a governmental entity requesting termination of the parent-child relationship or appointment of the entity as conservator of the child.

History of Fam. Code §107.022: Acts 2003, 78th Leg., ch. 262, §1, eff. Sept. 1, 2003. Amended by Acts 2005, 79th Leg., ch. 172, §9, eff. Sept. 1, 2005.

FAM §107.023. FEES IN SUITS OTHER THAN SUITS BY GOVERNMENTAL ENTITY

(a) In a suit other than a suit filed by a governmental entity requesting termination of the parent-child relationship or appointment of the entity as conservator of the child, in addition to the attorney's fees that may be awarded under Chapter 106, the following persons are entitled to reasonable fees and expenses in an amount set by the court and ordered to be paid by one or more parties to the suit:

(1) an attorney appointed as an amicus attorney or as an attorney ad litem for the child; and

(2) a professional who holds a relevant professional license and who is appointed as guardian ad litem for the child, other than a volunteer advocate.

(b) The court shall:

(1) determine the fees and expenses of an amicus attorney, an attorney ad litem, or a guardian ad litem by reference to the reasonable and customary fees for similar services in the county of jurisdiction;

(2) order a reasonable cost deposit to be made at the time the court makes the appointment; and

(3) before the final hearing, order an additional amount to be paid to the credit of a trust account for the use and benefit of the amicus attorney, attorney ad litem, or guardian ad litem.

(c) A court may not award costs, fees, or expenses to an amicus attorney, attorney ad litem, or guardian ad litem against the state, a state agency, or a political subdivision of the state under this part.

(d) The court may determine that fees awarded under this subchapter to an amicus attorney, an attorney ad litem for the child, or a guardian ad litem for the child are necessaries for the benefit of the child.

History of Fam. Code §107.023: Acts 2003, 78th Leg., ch. 262, §1, eff. Sept. 1, 2003. Amended by Acts 2005, 79th Leg., ch. 172, §10, eff. Sept. 1, 2005.

Sections 107.024-107.030 blank

SUBCHAPTER C. APPOINTMENT OF VOLUNTEER ADVOCATES

FAM §107.031. VOLUNTEER ADVOCATES

(a) In a suit filed by a governmental entity requesting termination of the parent-child relationship or appointment of the entity as conservator of the child, the court may appoint a charitable organization composed of volunteer advocates whose charter mandates the provision of services to allegedly abused and neglected children or an individual who has received the court's approved training regarding abused and neglected children and who has been certified by the court to appcar at court hearings as a guardian ad litem for the child or as a volunteer advocate for the child.

(b) In a suit other than a suit filed by a governmental entity requesting termination of the parent-child re-

lationship or appointment of the entity as conservator of the child, the court may appoint a charitable organization composed of volunteer advocates whose training provides for the provision of services in private custody disputes or a person who has received the court's approved training regarding the subject matter of the suit and who has been certified by the court to appear at court hearings as a guardian ad litem for the child or as a volunteer advocate for the child. A person appointed under this subsection is not entitled to fees under Section 107.023.

(c) A court-certified volunteer advocate appointed under this section may be assigned to act as a surrogate parent for the child, as provided by 20 U.S.C. Section 1415(b), if:

(1) the child is in the conservatorship of the Department of Family and Protective Services;

(2) the volunteer advocate is serving as guardian ad litem for the child; [~~and~~]

(3) a foster parent of the child is not acting as the child's parent under Section 29.015, Education Code; and

(4) the volunteer advocate completes a training program for surrogate parents that complies with minimum standards established by rule by the Texas Education Agency within the time specified by Section 29.015(b), Education Code.

History of Fam. Code §107.031: Acts 1995, 74th Leg., ch. 20, §1, eff. Apr. 20, 1995. Renumbered from §107.004 by Acts 1995, 74th Leg., ch. 751, §15, eff. Sept. 1, 1995. Amended by Acts 1997, 75th Leg., ch. 1294, §6, eff. Sept. 1, 1997; Acts 1999, 76th Leg., ch. 430, §3, eff. Sept. 1, 1999; Acts 2003, 78th Leg., ch. 262, §1, eff. Sept. 1, 2003; Acts 2005, 79th Leg., ch. 172, §11, eff. Sept. 1, 2005; H.B. 1556, §3, 85th Leg., eff. Sept. 1, 2017. Source: Former Fam. Code §11.101.

See also *O'Connor's Texas Family Law Handbook* (2017), "Volunteer Advocate," ch. 4-C, §6, p. 397.

Sections 107.032-107.050 reserved for expansion

SUBCHAPTER D. CHILD CUSTODY EVALUATION

FAM §§107.0501 TO 107.05145. RENUMBERED

Renumbered as §§107.101, 107.103, 107.104, 107.107-107.109, 107.111 by Acts 2015, 84th Leg., ch. 1252, §§1.03, 1.05, 1.06, 1.08-1.10, 1.13, eff. Sept. 1, 2015.

FAM §§107.0515 TO 107.053. REPEALED

Repealed by Acts 2015, 84th Leg., ch. 1252, §4.01, eff. Sept. 1, 2015.

FAM §§107.054 TO 107.056. RENUMBERED

Renumbered as §§107.113-107.115 by Acts 2015, 84th Leg., ch. 1252, §§1.15-1.17, eff. Sept. 1, 2015.

FAM §§107.061 TO 107.072. RENUMBERED

Renumbered as §§107.251-107.262 by S.B. 1488, §24.001(6), 85th Leg., eff. Sept. 1, 2017.

FAM §107.101. DEFINITIONS

In this subchapter:

(1) "Child custody evaluation" means an evaluative process ordered by a court in a contested case through which information, opinions, recommendations, and answers to specific questions asked by the court may be:

(A) made regarding:

(i) conservatorship of a child, including the terms and conditions of conservatorship;

(ii) possession of or access to a child, including the terms and conditions of possession or access; or

(iii) any other issue affecting the best interest of a child; and

(B) made to the court, the parties to the suit, the parties' attorneys, and any other person appointed under this chapter by the court in the suit.

(2) "Child custody evaluator" means an individual who conducts a child custody evaluation under this subchapter. The term includes a private child custody evaluator.

(3) "Department" means the Department of Family and Protective Services.

(4) "Person" includes an agency or a domestic relations office.

(5) "Private child custody evaluator" means a person conducting a child custody evaluation who is not conducting the evaluation as an employee of or contractor with a domestic relations office.

(6) "Supervision" means directing, regularly reviewing, and meeting with a person with respect to the completion of work for which the supervisor is responsible for the outcome. The term does not require the constant physical presence of the person providing supervision and may include telephonic or other electronic communication.

History of Fam. Code §107.101: Acts 2007, 80th Leg., ch. 832, §1, eff. Sept. 1, 2007. Renumbered from §107.0501 and amended by Acts 2015, 84th Leg., ch. 1252, §§1.02, 1.03, eff. Sept. 1, 2015.

FAM §107.102. APPLICABILITY

(a) For purposes of this subchapter, a child custody evaluation does not include services provided in accordance with the Interstate Compact on the Placement of Children adopted under Subchapter B, Chapter 162, or

an evaluation conducted in accordance with Section 262.114 by an employee of or contractor with the department.

(b) The department may not conduct a child custody evaluation.

(c) Except as provided by Subsections (a) and (b), this subchapter does not apply to the department or to a suit to which the department is a party.

History of Fam. Code §107.102: Acts 2015, 84th Leg., ch. 1252, §1.04, eff. Sept. 1, 2015.

FAM §107.1025. EFFECT OF MENTAL EXAMINATION

A mental examination described by Rule 204.4, Texas Rules of Civil Procedure, does not by itself satisfy the requirements for a child custody evaluation under this subchapter. A mental examination may be included in the report required under this subchapter and relied on by the child custody evaluator to the extent the evaluator considers appropriate under the circumstances.

History of Fam. Code §107.1025: Acts 2015, 84th Leg., ch. 1252, §1.04, eff. Sept. 1, 2015.

Ⓐ FAM §107.103. ORDER FOR CHILD CUSTODY EVALUATION

The amended text in §107.103 is effective for SAPCRs filed on or after Sept. 1, 2017. SAPCRs filed before Sept. 1, 2017, are governed by the former law in effect at that time.

(a) The court, after notice and hearing or on agreement of the parties, may order the preparation of a child custody evaluation regarding:

(1) the circumstances and condition of:

(A) a child who is the subject of a suit;

(B) a party to a suit; and

(C) if appropriate, the residence of any person requesting conservatorship of, possession of, or access to a child who is the subject of the suit; and

(2) any issue or question relating to the suit at the request of the court before or during the evaluation process.

(b) The court may not appoint a child custody evaluator in a suit involving a nonparent seeking conservatorship of a child unless, after notice and hearing or on agreement of the parties, the court makes a specific finding that good cause has been shown for the appointment of a child custody evaluator.

(c) Except for an order appointing a child custody evaluator who is qualified under Section 107.104(b)(3), an [An] order for a child custody evaluation must include:

(1) the name of each person who will conduct the evaluation;

(2) the purpose of the evaluation; [and]

(3) a list of the basic elements of an evaluation required by Section 107.109(c);

(4) a list of any additional elements of an evaluation required by the court to be completed, including any additional elements specified in Section 107.109(d); and

(5) the specific issues or questions to be addressed in the evaluation.

(d) Except as provided by Section 107.106, each individual who conducts a child custody evaluation must be qualified under Section 107.104.

History of Fam. Code §107.103: Acts 1995, 74th Leg., ch. 20, §1, eff. Apr. 20, 1995. Renumbered from §107.005(a), (b) by Acts 1995, 74th Leg., ch. 751, §15, eff. Sept. 1, 1995. Amended by Acts 1999, 76th Leg., ch. 1390, §7, eff. Sept. 1, 1999; Acts 2001, 77th Leg., ch. 133, §2 (eff. Sept. 1, 2001), ch. 488, §1 (eff. June 11, 2001); Acts 2007, 80th Leg., ch. 832, §2, eff. Sept. 1, 2007. Renumbered from §107.051 and amended by Acts 2015, 84th Leg., ch. 1252, §1.05, eff. Sept. 1, 2015. Amended by H.B. 1501, §2, 85th Leg., eff. Sept. 1, 2017. Source: Former Fam. Code §11.12(a), (b).

See also ***O'Connor's Texas Family Law Handbook*** (2017), "Social study, child-custody evaluation & adoption evaluation," ch. 4-D, §11.5, p. 430.

ANNOTATIONS

In re Villanueva, 292 S.W.3d 236, 242 (Tex.App.—Texarkana 2009, orig. proceeding). "The ... Family Code does not specifically address [whether] the trial court [can order] an indigent parent to pay for [a child-custody evaluation]. *At 243:* The trial court acts under clear instructions to consider first the best interest of the child. So, to the extent a [child-custody evaluation] would assist the trial court in so doing, the [child-custody evaluation] *could* be necessary. But ... while the trial court must make the determination of the best interest of the child, there is no evidence that, without [a child-custody evaluation], the trial court will be unable to make such determination. *At 246:* [Here, we] conclude that the trial court abused its discretion when it ordered [mother] to pay the costs and fees associated with the [child-custody evaluator] when [mother] is indigent as a matter of law...."

Chacon v. Chacon, 978 S.W.2d 633, 637-38 (Tex. App.—El Paso 1998, no pet.). "Generally speaking, the purpose of a [child-custody evaluation] is to interview the litigants and those individuals with knowledge of relevant facts, such as extended family members, neighbors, scout leaders, teachers, baby sitters, day-

care providers, doctors, sports coaches, and other individuals who have had the opportunity to observe the parenting abilities of the litigants, the relationship between the child and the parents, the living arrangements at both households, and the plans each litigant has adopted for the day-to-day caretaking of the child. It is designed to be comparative in nature, that is to compare the circumstances and conditions of all individuals seeking managing conservatorship or possession of a child, and to make recommendations to the court regarding the best interest of the child."

FAM §107.104. CHILD CUSTODY EVALUATOR: MINIMUM QUALIFICATIONS

(a) In this section:

(1) "Full-time experience" means a period during which an individual works at least 30 hours per week.

(2) "Human services field of study" means a field of study designed to prepare an individual in the disciplined application of counseling, family therapy, psychology, or social work values, principles, and methods.

(b) To be qualified to conduct a child custody evaluation, an individual must:

(1) have at least a master's degree from an accredited college or university in a human services field of study and a license to practice in this state as a social worker, professional counselor, marriage and family therapist, or psychologist, or have a license to practice medicine in this state and a board certification in psychiatry and:

(A) after completing any degree required by this subdivision, have two years of full-time experience or equivalent part-time experience under professional supervision during which the individual performed functions involving the evaluation of physical, intellectual, social, and psychological functioning and needs and developed an understanding of the social and physical environment, both present and prospective, to meet those needs; and

(B) after obtaining a license required by this subdivision, have performed at least 10 court-ordered child custody evaluations under the supervision of an individual qualified under this section;

(2) meet the requirements of Subdivision (1)(A) and be practicing under the direct supervision of an individual qualified under this section in order to complete at least 10 court-ordered child custody evaluations under supervision; or

(3) be employed by or under contract with a domestic relations office, provided that the individual conducts child custody evaluations relating only to families ordered by a court to participate in child custody evaluations conducted by the domestic relations office.

(c) Notwithstanding Subsections (b)(1) and (2), an individual with a doctoral degree and who holds a license in a human services field of study is qualified to conduct a child custody evaluation if the individual has completed a number of hours of professional development coursework and practice experience directly related to the performance of child custody evaluations as described by this chapter, satisfactory to the licensing agency that issues the individual's license.

(d) The licensing agency that issues a license to an individual described by Subsection (c) may determine by rule that internships, practicums, and other professional preparatory activities completed by the individual during the course of achieving the person's doctoral degree satisfy the requirements of Subsection (c) in whole or in part.

(e) In addition to the qualifications prescribed by this section, an individual must complete at least eight hours of family violence dynamics training provided by a family violence service provider to be qualified to conduct a child custody evaluation under this subchapter.

History of Fam. Code §107.104: Acts 2007, 80th Leg., ch. 832, §3, eff. Sept. 1, 2007. Amended by Acts 2009, 81st Leg., ch. 1113, §2, eff. Sept. 1, 2009. Renumbered from §107.0511 and amended by Acts 2015, 84th Leg., ch. 1252, §1.06, eff. Sept. 1, 2015.

History of Former Fam. Code §107.0511: Acts 2001, 77th Leg., ch. 133, §3, eff. Sept. 1, 2001. Renumbered as §107.0519 and amended by Acts 2007, 80th Leg., ch. 832, §3, eff. Sept. 1, 2007.

FAM §107.105.CHILD CUSTODY EVALUATION: SPECIALIZED TRAINING REQUIRED

(a) The court shall determine whether the qualifications of a child custody evaluator satisfy the requirements of this subchapter.

(b) A child custody evaluator must demonstrate, if requested, appropriate knowledge and competence in child custody evaluation services consistent with professional models, standards, and guidelines.

History of Fam. Code §107.105: Acts 2015, 84th Leg., ch. 1252, §1.07, eff. Sept. 1, 2015.

FAM §107.106. EXCEPTION TO QUALIFICATIONS REQUIRED TO CONDUCT CHILD CUSTODY EVALUATION

(a) In a county with a population of less than 500,000, if a court finds that an individual who meets

the requirements of Section 107.104 is not available in the county to conduct a child custody evaluation in a timely manner, the court, after notice and hearing or on agreement of the parties, may appoint an individual the court determines to be otherwise qualified to conduct the evaluation.

(b) An individual appointed under this section shall comply with all provisions of this subchapter, other than Section 107.104.

History of Fam. Code §107.106: Acts 2015, 84th Leg., ch. 1252, §1.07, eff. Sept. 1, 2015.

FAM §107.107. CHILD CUSTODY EVALUATOR: CONFLICTS OF INTEREST & BIAS

(a) Before accepting appointment as a child custody evaluator in a suit, a person must disclose to the court, each attorney for a party to the suit, any attorney for a child who is the subject of the suit, and any party to the suit who does not have an attorney:

(1) any conflict of interest that the person believes the person has with any party to the suit or a child who is the subject of the suit;

(2) any previous knowledge that the person has of a party to the suit or a child who is the subject of the suit, other than knowledge obtained in a court-ordered evaluation;

(3) any pecuniary relationship that the person believes the person has with an attorney in the suit;

(4) any relationship of confidence or trust that the person believes the person has with an attorney in the suit; and

(5) any other information relating to the person's relationship with an attorney in the suit that a reasonable, prudent person would believe would affect the ability of the person to act impartially in conducting a child custody evaluation.

(b) The court may not appoint a person as a child custody evaluator in a suit if the person makes any of the disclosures in Subsection (a) unless:

(1) the court finds that:

(A) the person has no conflict of interest with a party to the suit or a child who is the subject of the suit;

(B) the person's previous knowledge of a party to the suit or a child who is the subject of the suit is not relevant;

(C) the person does not have a pecuniary relationship with an attorney in the suit; and

(D) the person does not have a relationship of trust or confidence with an attorney in the suit; or

(2) the parties and any attorney for a child who is the subject of the suit agree in writing to the person's appointment as the child custody evaluator.

(c) After being appointed as a child custody evaluator in a suit, a person shall immediately disclose to the court, each attorney for a party to the suit, any attorney for a child who is the subject of the suit, and any party to the suit who does not have an attorney any discovery of:

(1) a conflict of interest that the person believes the person has with a party to the suit or a child who is the subject of the suit; and

(2) previous knowledge that the person has of a party to the suit or a child who is the subject of the suit, other than knowledge obtained in a court-ordered evaluation.

(d) A person shall resign from the person's appointment as a child custody evaluator in a suit if the person makes any of the disclosures in Subsection (c) unless:

(1) the court finds that:

(A) the person has no conflict of interest with a party to the suit or a child who is the subject of the suit; and

(B) the person's previous knowledge of a party to the suit or a child who is the subject of the suit is not relevant; or

(2) the parties and any attorney for a child who is the subject of the suit agree in writing to the person's continued appointment as the child custody evaluator.

(e) A child custody evaluator who has previously conducted a child custody evaluation for a suit may conduct all subsequent evaluations in the suit unless the court finds that the evaluator is biased.

(f) An individual may not be appointed as a child custody evaluator in a suit if the individual has worked in a professional capacity with a party to the suit, a child who is the subject of the suit, or a member of the party's or child's family who is involved in the suit. This subsection does not apply to an individual who has worked in a professional capacity with a party, a child, or a member of the party's or child's family only as a teacher of parenting skills in a group setting, with no individualized interaction with any party, the child, any party's family, or the child's family, or as a child custody

evaluator who performed a previous evaluation. A child custody evaluator who has worked as a teacher of parenting skills in a group setting that included a party, a child, or another person who will be the subject of an evaluation or has worked as a child custody evaluator for a previous evaluation must notify the court and the attorney of each represented party or, if a party is not represented, the evaluator must notify the party. For purposes of this subsection, "family" has the meaning assigned by Section 71.003.

History of Fam. Code §107.107: Acts 2007, 80th Leg., ch. 832, §3, eff. Sept. 1, 2007. Renumbered from §107.0512 and amended by Acts 2015, 84th Leg., ch. 1252, §1.08, eff. Sept. 1, 2015.

FAM §107.108. GENERAL PROVISIONS APPLICABLE TO CONDUCT OF CHILD CUSTODY EVALUATION & PREPARATION OF REPORT

(a) Unless otherwise directed by a court or prescribed by a provision of this title, a child custody evaluator's actions in conducting a child custody evaluation must be in conformance with the professional standard of care applicable to the evaluator's licensure and any administrative rules, ethical standards, or guidelines adopted by the licensing authority that licenses the evaluator.

(b) A court may impose requirements or adopt local rules applicable to a child custody evaluation or a child custody evaluator that do not conflict with this subchapter.

(c) A child custody evaluator shall follow evidence-based practice methods and make use of current best evidence in making assessments and recommendations.

(d) A child custody evaluator shall disclose to each attorney of record any communication regarding a substantive issue between the evaluator and an attorney of record representing a party in a contested suit. This subsection does not apply to a communication between a child custody evaluator and an attorney ad litem or amicus attorney.

(e) To the extent possible, a child custody evaluator shall verify each statement of fact pertinent to a child custody evaluation and shall note the sources of verification and information in the child custody evaluation report prepared under Section 107.113.

(f) A child custody evaluator shall state the basis for the evaluator's conclusions or recommendations, and the extent to which information obtained limits the reliability and validity of the opinion and the conclusions and recommendations of the evaluator, in the child custody evaluation report prepared under Section 107.113. A child custody evaluator who has evaluated only one side of a contested suit shall refrain from making a recommendation regarding conservatorship of a child or possession of or access to a child, but may state whether any information obtained regarding a child's placement with a party indicates concerns for:

(1) the safety of the child;

(2) the party's parenting skills or capability;

(3) the party's relationship with the child; or

(4) the mental health of the party.

(g) A child custody evaluation must be conducted in compliance with this subchapter, regardless of whether the child custody evaluation is conducted:

(1) by a single child custody evaluator or multiple evaluators working separately or together; or

(2) within a county served by the court with continuing jurisdiction or at a geographically distant location.

(h) A child custody evaluation report must include for each child custody evaluator who conducted any portion of the child custody evaluation:

(1) the name and license number of the child custody evaluator; and

(2) a statement that the child custody evaluator:

(A) has read and meets the requirements of Section 107.104; or

(B) was appointed under Section 107.106.

History of Fam. Code §107.108: Acts 2007, 80th Leg., ch. 832, §3, eff. Sept. 1, 2007. Renumbered from §107.0513 and amended by Acts 2015, 84th Leg., ch. 1252, §1.09, eff. Sept. 1, 2015.

A FAM §107.109. ELEMENTS OF CHILD CUSTODY EVALUATION

The amended text in §107.109 is effective for SAPCRs filed on or after Sept. 1, 2017. SAPCRs filed before Sept. 1, 2017, are governed by the former law in effect at that time.

(a) A child custody evaluator may not offer an opinion regarding conservatorship of a child who is the subject of a suit or possession of or access to the child unless each basic element of a child custody evaluation as specified in ~~[described by]~~ this section and each additional element ordered by the court, if any, has been completed, unless the failure to complete an element is satisfactorily explained as provided by Subsection (b).

(b) A child custody evaluator shall:

(1) identify in the report required by Section 107.113 any basic element or any additional element of a child custody evaluation described by this section that was not completed;

(2) explain the reasons the element was not completed; and

(3) include an explanation of the likely effect of the missing element on the confidence the child custody evaluator has in the evaluator's expert opinion.

(c) The basic elements of a child custody evaluation under this subchapter consist of:

(1) a personal interview of each party to the suit seeking conservatorship of, possession of, or access to the child;

(2) interviews, conducted in a developmentally appropriate manner, of each child who is the subject of the suit who is at least four years of age [~~, regardless of the age of the child,~~] during a period of possession of each party to the suit but outside the presence of the party;

(3) observation of each child who is the subject of the suit, regardless of the age of the child, in the presence of each party to the suit, including, as appropriate, during supervised visitation, unless contact between a party and a child is prohibited by court order or the person conducting the evaluation has good cause for not conducting the observation and states the good cause in writing provided to the parties to the suit before the completion of the evaluation;

(4) an observation and, if the child is at least four years of age [~~old~~], an interview of any child who is not a subject of the suit who lives on a full-time basis in a residence that is the subject of the evaluation, including with other children or parties who are subjects of the evaluation, where appropriate;

(5) the obtaining of information from relevant collateral sources, including the review of:

(A) relevant school records;

(B) relevant physical and mental health records of each party to the suit and each child who is the subject of the suit;

(C) relevant records of the department obtained under Section 107.111;

(D) criminal history information relating to each child who is the subject of the suit, each party to the suit, and each person who lives with a party to the suit; and

(E) notwithstanding other law, records or information from any other collateral source that may have relevant information;

(6) [~~evaluation of the home environment of each party seeking conservatorship of a child who is the subject of the suit or possession of or access to the child, unless the condition of the home environment is identified as not being in dispute in the court order requiring the child custody evaluation;~~]

[~~(7)~~] for each individual residing in a residence subject to the child custody evaluation, consideration of any criminal history information and any contact with the department or a law enforcement agency regarding abuse or neglect; and

(7) [~~(8)~~] assessment of the relationship between each child who is the subject of the suit and each party seeking possession of or access to the child.

(d) The court may order additional elements of a child custody evaluation under this subchapter, including the following [~~consist of~~]:

(1) balanced interviews and observations of each child who is the subject of the suit so that a child who is interviewed or observed while in the care of one party to the suit is also interviewed or observed while in the care of each other party to the suit;

(2) an interview of each individual, including a child who is at least four years of age, residing on a full-time or part-time basis in a residence subject to the child custody evaluation;

(3) evaluation of the residence [~~home environment~~] of each party seeking conservatorship of a child who is the subject of the suit or possession of or access to the child [~~, regardless of whether the home environment is in dispute~~];

(4) observation of a child who is the subject of the suit with each adult who lives in a residence that is the subject of the evaluation;

(5) an interview, if the child is at least four years of age, and observation of a child who is not the subject of the suit but who lives on a full-time or part-time basis in a residence that is the subject of the evaluation;

(6) psychometric testing, if necessary, consistent with Scction 107.110; and

(7) the performance of other tasks requested of the evaluator by the court, including:

(A) a joint interview of the parties to the suit; or

(B) the review of any other information that the court determines is relevant.

History of Fam. Code §107.109: Acts 2007, 80th Leg., ch. 832, §3, eff. Sept. 1, 2007. Renumbered from §107.0514 and amended by Acts 2015, 84th Leg., ch. 1252, §1.10, eff. Sept. 1, 2015. Amended by H.B. 1501, §3, 85th Leg., eff. Sept. 1, 2017.

A FAM §107.110. PSYCHOMETRIC TESTING

The amended text in §107.110 is effective for SAPCRs filed on or after Sept. 1, 2017. SAPCRs filed before Sept. 1, 2017, are governed by the former law in effect at that time.

(a) A child custody evaluator may conduct psychometric testing as part of a child custody evaluation if:

(1) ordered by the court or determined necessary by the child custody evaluator; and

(2) the child custody evaluator is:

(A) appropriately licensed and trained to administer and interpret the specific psychometric tests selected; and

(B) trained in the specialized forensic application of psychometric testing.

(b) Selection of a specific psychometric test is at the professional discretion of the child custody evaluator based on the specific issues raised in the suit.

(c) A child custody evaluator may only use psychometric tests if the evaluator is familiar with the reliability, validation, and related standardization or outcome studies of, and proper applications and use of, the tests within a forensic setting.

(d) If a child custody evaluator considers psychometric testing necessary but lacks specialized training or expertise to use the specific tests under this section, the evaluator may designate a licensed psychologist to conduct the testing and may request additional orders from the court.

History of Fam. Code §107.110: Acts 2015, 84th Leg., ch. 1252, §1.11, eff. Sept. 1, 2015. Amended by H.B. 1501, §4, 85th Leg., eff. Sept. 1, 2017.

A FAM §107.1101. EFFECT OF POTENTIALLY UNDIAGNOSED SERIOUS MENTAL ILLNESS

The amended text in §107.1101 is effective for SAPCRs filed on or after Sept. 1, 2017. SAPCRs filed before Sept. 1, 2017, are governed by the former law in effect at that time.

(a) In this section, "serious mental illness" has the meaning assigned by Section 1355.001, Insurance Code.

(b) If a child custody evaluator identifies the presence of a potentially undiagnosed serious mental illness experienced by an individual who is a subject of the child custody evaluation and the evaluator is not qualified by the evaluator's licensure, experience, and training to assess a serious mental illness, the evaluator shall make one or more appropriate referrals for a mental examination of the individual and may request additional orders from the court.

(c) The child custody evaluation report must include any information that the evaluator considers appropriate under the circumstances regarding the possible effects of an individual's potentially undiagnosed serious mental illness on the evaluation and the evaluator's recommendations.

History of Fam. Code §107.1101: Acts 2015, 84th Leg., ch. 1252, §1.12, eff. Sept. 1, 2015. Amended by H.B. 1501, §5, 85th Leg., eff. Sept. 1, 2017.

FAM §107.111. CHILD CUSTODY EVALUATOR ACCESS TO INVESTIGATIVE RECORDS OF DEPARTMENT; OFFENSE

(a) A child custody evaluator appointed by a court is entitled to obtain from the department a complete, unredacted copy of any investigative record regarding abuse or neglect that relates to any person residing in the residence subject to the child custody evaluation.

(b) Except as provided by this section, records obtained by a child custody evaluator from the department under this section are confidential and not subject to disclosure under Chapter 552, Government Code, or to disclosure in response to a subpoena or a discovery request.

(c) A child custody evaluator may disclose information obtained under Subsection (a) in the child custody evaluation report prepared under Section 107.113 only to the extent the evaluator determines that the information is relevant to the child custody evaluation or a recommendation made under this subchapter.

(d) A person commits an offense if the person recklessly discloses confidential information obtained from the department in violation of this section. An offense under this subsection is a Class A misdemeanor.

History of Fam. Code §107.111: Acts 2013, 83rd Leg., ch. 74, §1, eff. Sept. 1, 2013. Renumbered from §107.05145 and amended by Acts 2015, 84th Leg., ch. 1252, §1.13, eff. Sept. 1, 2015.

E FAM §107.1111. CHILD CUSTODY EVALUATOR ACCESS TO OTHER RECORDS

(a) Notwithstanding any other state law regarding confidentiality, a child custody evaluator appointed by a

court is entitled to obtain records that relate to any person residing in a residence subject to a child custody evaluation from:

(1) a local law enforcement authority;

(2) a criminal justice agency;

(3) a juvenile justice agency;

(4) a community supervision and corrections department created under Chapter 76, Government Code; or

(5) any other governmental entity.

(b) Except as provided by this section, records obtained by a child custody evaluator under this section are confidential and not subject to disclosure under Chapter 552, Government Code, or to disclosure in response to a subpoena or a discovery request.

(c) A child custody evaluator may disclose information obtained under Subsection (a) in the child custody evaluation report prepared under Section 107.113 only to the extent the evaluator determines that the information is relevant to the child custody evaluation or a recommendation made under this subchapter.

(d) A person commits an offense if the person recklessly discloses confidential information obtained under Subsection (a) in violation of this section. An offense under this subsection is a Class A misdemeanor.

History of Fam. Code §107.1111: Enacted by H.B. 1501, §6, 85th Leg., eff. Sept. 1, 2017.

FAM §107.112. COMMUNICATIONS & RECORDKEEPING OF CHILD CUSTODY EVALUATOR

(a) Notwithstanding any rule, standard of care, or privilege applicable to the professional license held by a child custody evaluator, a communication made by a participant in a child custody evaluation is subject to disclosure and may be offered in any judicial or administrative proceeding if otherwise admissible under the rules of evidence.

(b) A child custody evaluator shall:

(1) keep a detailed record of interviews that the evaluator conducts, observations that the evaluator makes, and substantive interactions that the evaluator has as part of a child custody evaluation; and

(2) maintain the evaluator's records consistent with applicable laws, including rules applicable to the evaluator's license.

(c) Except for records obtained from the department in accordance with Section 107.111, a private child custody evaluator shall, after completion of an evaluation and the preparation and filing of a child custody evaluation report under Section 107.113, make available in a reasonable time the evaluator's records relating to the evaluation on the written request of an attorney for a party, a party who does not have an attorney, and any person appointed under this chapter in the suit in which the evaluator conducted the evaluation, unless a court has issued an order restricting disclosure of the records.

(d) Except for records obtained from the department in accordance with Section 107.111, records relating to a child custody evaluation conducted by an employee of or contractor with a domestic relations office shall, after completion of the evaluation and the preparation and filing of a child custody evaluation report under Section 107.113, be made available on written request according to the local rules and policies of the office.

(e) A person maintaining records subject to disclosure under this section may charge a reasonable fee for producing the records before copying the records.

(f) A private child custody evaluator shall retain all records relating to a child custody evaluation conducted by the evaluator until the ending date of the retention period adopted by the licensing authority that issues the professional license held by the evaluator based on the date the evaluator filed the child custody evaluation report prepared under this section with the court.

(g) A domestic relations office shall retain records relating to a child custody evaluation conducted by a child custody evaluator acting as an employee of or contractor with the office for the retention period established by the office.

(h) A person who participates in a child custody evaluation is not a patient as that term is defined by Section 611.001(1), Health and Safety Code.

History of Fam. Code §107.112: Acts 2015, 84th Leg., ch. 1252, §1.14, eff. Sept. 1, 2015.

A FAM §107.113. CHILD CUSTODY EVALUATION REPORT REQUIRED

The amended text in §107.113 is effective for SAPCRs filed on or after Sept. 1, 2017. SAPCRs filed before Sept. 1, 2017, are governed by the former law in effect at that time.

(a) A child custody evaluator who conducts a child custody evaluation shall prepare [~~and file~~] a report containing the evaluator's findings, opinions, recom-

mendations, and answers to specific questions asked by the court relating to the evaluation.

(b) The person conducting a child custody evaluation shall file with the court on a date set by the court notice that the report under this section is complete. On the earlier of the date the notice is filed or the date required under Section 107.114, the person shall provide a copy of the report to:

(1) each party's attorney;

(2) each party who is not represented by an attorney; and

(3) each attorney ad litem, guardian ad litem, and amicus attorney appointed in the suit [~~a report containing the person's findings and conclusions. The report shall be made a part of the record of the suit~~].

(c) If the suit is settled before completion of the child custody evaluation report, the report under this section is not required.

(d) A report prepared under this section must include the information required by Section 107.108(h) for each child custody evaluator who conducted any portion of the evaluation.

History of Fam. Code §107.113: Acts 1995, 74th Leg., ch. 20, §1, eff. Apr. 20, 1995. Renumbered from §107.005(h) by Acts 1995, 74th Leg., ch. 751, §15, eff. Sept. 1, 1995. Renumbered from §107.054 and amended by Acts 2015, 84th Leg., ch. 1252, §1.15, eff. Sept. 1, 2015. Amended by H.B. 1501, §7, 85th Leg., eff. Sept. 1, 2017. Source: Former Fam. Code §11.12(c).

A FAM §107.114. INTRODUCTION & PROVISION OF CHILD CUSTODY EVALUATION REPORT

The amended text in §107.114 is effective for SAPCRs filed on or after Sept. 1, 2017. SAPCRs filed before Sept. 1, 2017, are governed by the former law in effect at that time.

(a) Disclosure to the court or the jury of the contents of a child custody evaluation report prepared under Section 107.113 is subject to the rules of evidence.

(b) Unless the court has rendered an order restricting disclosure, a private child custody evaluator shall provide to the attorneys of the parties to a suit, any party who does not have an attorney, and any other person appointed by the court under this chapter in a suit a copy of the child custody evaluation report before the earlier of:

(1) the third day after the date the child custody evaluation report is completed; or

(2) the 30th day before the date of commencement of the trial.

(c) A child custody evaluator who conducts a child custody evaluation as an employee of or under contract with a domestic relations office shall provide to the attorneys of the parties to a suit and any person appointed in the suit under this chapter a copy of the child custody evaluation report before the earlier of:

(1) the seventh day after the date the child custody evaluation report is completed; or

(2) the fifth day before the date the trial commences.

(d) A child custody evaluator who conducts a child custody evaluation as an employee of or under contract with a domestic relations office shall provide a copy of the report to a party to the suit as provided by the local rules and policies of the office or by a court order.

History of Fam. Code §107.114: Acts 1995, 74th Leg., ch. 20, §1, eff. Apr. 20, 1995. Renumbered from §107.005(i)-(k) by Acts 1995, 74th Leg., ch. 751, §15, eff. Sept. 1, 1995. Renumbered from §107.055 and amended by Acts 2015, 84th Leg., ch. 1252, §1.16, eff. Sept. 1, 2015. Amended by H.B. 1501, §8, 85th Leg., eff. Sept. 1, 2017. Source: Former Fam. Code §§11.12(c), 11.14(c).

FAM §107.115. CHILD CUSTODY EVALUATION FEE

If the court orders a child custody evaluation to be conducted, the court shall award the person appointed as the child custody evaluator a reasonable fee for the preparation of the child custody evaluation that shall be imposed in the form of a money judgment and paid directly to the person. The person may enforce the judgment for the fee by any means available under law for civil judgments.

History of Fam. Code §107.115: Acts 1995, 74th Leg., ch. 20, §1, eff. Apr. 20, 1995. Renumbered from §107.005(*l*) by Acts 1995, 74th Leg., ch. 751, §15, eff. Sept. 1, 1995. Amended by Acts 2007, 80th Leg., ch. 832, §5, eff. Sept. 1, 2007. Renumbered from §107.056 and amended by Acts 2015, 84th Leg., ch. 1252, §1.17, eff. Sept. 1, 2015. Source: Former Fam. Code §11.18(c).

SUBCHAPTER E. ADOPTION EVALUATION

FAM §107.151. DEFINITIONS

In this subchapter:

(1) "Adoption evaluation" means a pre-placement or post-placement evaluative process through which information and recommendations regarding adoption of a child may be made to the court, the parties, and the parties' attorneys.

(2) "Adoption evaluator" means a person who conducts an adoption evaluation under this subchapter.

(3) "Department" means the Department of Family and Protective Services.

(4) "Supervision" means directing, regularly reviewing, and meeting with a person with respect to the completion of work for which the supervisor is respon-

sible for the outcome. The term does not require the constant physical presence of the person providing supervision and may include telephonic or other electronic communication.

History of Fam. Code §107.151: Acts 2015, 84th Leg., ch. 1252, §1.18, eff. Sept. 1, 2015.

See also 40 T.A.C. §745.9041.

FAM §107.152. APPLICABILITY

(a) For purposes of this subchapter, an adoption evaluation does not include services provided in accordance with the Interstate Compact on the Placement of Children adopted under Subchapter B, Chapter 162, or an evaluation conducted in accordance with Section 262.114 by an employee of or contractor with the department.

(b) This subchapter does not apply to the pre-placement and post-placement parts of an adoption evaluation conducted by a licensed child-placing agency or the department.

(c) The pre-placement and post-placement parts of an adoption evaluation conducted by a licensed child-placing agency or the department are governed by rules adopted by the ~~[executive]~~ commissioner of the department ~~[Health and Human Services Commission]~~.

(d) In a suit involving a licensed child-placing agency or the department, a licensed child-placing agency or the department shall conduct the pre-placement and post-placement parts of the adoption evaluation and file reports on those parts with the court before the court renders a final order of adoption.

(e) A court may appoint the department to conduct the pre-placement and post-placement parts of an adoption evaluation in a suit only if the department is:

(1) a party to the suit; or

(2) the managing conservator of the child who is the subject of the suit.

History of Fam. Code §107.152: Acts 2015, 84th Leg., ch. 1252, §1.18, eff. Sept. 1, 2015. Amended by H.B. 5, §3, 85th Leg., eff. Sept. 1, 2017.

See also 40 T.A.C. §§745.9043, 745.9045.

FAM §107.153. ORDER FOR ADOPTION EVALUATION

(a) The court shall order the performance of an adoption evaluation to evaluate each party who requests termination of the parent-child relationship or an adoption in a suit for:

(1) termination of the parent-child relationship in which a person other than a parent may be appointed managing conservator of a child; or

(2) an adoption.

(b) The adoption evaluation required under Subsection (a) must include an evaluation of the circumstances and the condition of the home and social environment of any person requesting to adopt a child who is at issue in the suit.

(c) The court may appoint a qualified individual, a qualified private entity, or a domestic relations office to conduct the adoption evaluation.

(d) Except as provided by Section 107.155, a person who conducts an adoption evaluation must meet the requirements of Section 107.154.

(e) The costs of an adoption evaluation under this section shall be paid by the prospective adoptive parent.

History of Fam. Code §107.153: Acts 2015, 84th Leg., ch. 1252, §1.18, eff. Sept. 1, 2015.

See also 40 T.A.C. §745.9098.

FAM §107.154. ADOPTION EVALUATOR: MINIMUM QUALIFICATIONS

(a) In this section:

(1) "Full-time experience" means a period during which a person works at least 30 hours per week.

(2) "Human services field of study" means a field of study designed to prepare a person in the disciplined application of counseling, family therapy, psychology, or social work values, principles, and methods.

The amended text in subsection (b) is effective for adoption evaluations conducted on or after Sept. 1, 2017. Adoption evaluations conducted before Sept. 1, 2017, are governed by the former law in effect at that time.

(b) To be qualified to conduct an adoption evaluation under this subchapter, a person must:

(1) have a degree from an accredited college or university in a human services field of study and a license to practice in this state as a social worker, professional counselor, marriage and family therapist, or psychologist and:

(A) have one year of full-time experience working at a child-placing agency conducting child-placing activities; or

(B) be practicing under the direct supervision of a person qualified under this section to conduct adoption evaluations;

(2) be employed by or under contract with a domestic relations office, provided that the person conducts adoption evaluations relating only to families ordered to

participate in adoption evaluations conducted by the domestic relations office; or

(3) be qualified as a child custody evaluator under Section 107.104.

(c) In addition to the other qualifications prescribed by this section, an individual must complete at least eight hours of family violence dynamics training provided by a family violence service provider to be qualified to conduct an adoption evaluation under this subchapter.

History of Fam. Code §107.154: Acts 2015, 84th Leg., ch. 1252, §1.18, eff. Sept. 1, 2015. Amended by H.B. 5, §4(a), 85th Leg., eff. Sept. 1, 2017.

FAM §107.155. EXCEPTION TO QUALIFICATIONS REQUIRED TO CONDUCT ADOPTION EVALUATION

(a) In a county with a population of less than 500,000, if a court finds that an individual who meets the requirements of Section 107.154 is not available in the county to conduct an adoption evaluation in a timely manner, the court, after notice and hearing or on agreement of the parties, may appoint a person the court determines to be otherwise qualified to conduct the evaluation.

(b) An individual appointed under this section shall comply with all provisions of this subchapter, other than Section 107.154.

History of Fam. Code §107.155: Acts 2015, 84th Leg., ch. 1252, §1.18, eff. Sept. 1, 2015.

FAM §107.156. ADOPTION EVALUATOR: CONFLICTS OF INTEREST & BIAS

(a) Before accepting appointment as an adoption evaluator in a suit, a person must disclose to the court, each attorney for a party to the suit, any attorney for a child who is the subject of the suit, and any party to the suit who does not have an attorney:

(1) any conflict of interest that the person believes the person has with a party to the suit or a child who is the subject of the suit;

(2) any previous knowledge that the person has of a party to the suit or a child who is the subject of the suit;

(3) any pecuniary relationship that the person believes the person has with an attorney in the suit;

(4) any relationship of confidence or trust that the person believes the person has with an attorney in the suit; and

(5) any other information relating to the person's relationship with an attorney in the suit that a reasonable, prudent person would believe would affect the ability of the person to act impartially in conducting an adoption evaluation.

(b) The court may not appoint a person as an adoption evaluator in a suit if the person makes any of the disclosures in Subsection (a) unless:

(1) the court finds that:

(A) the person has no conflict of interest with a party to the suit or a child who is the subject of the suit;

(B) the person's previous knowledge of a party to the suit or a child who is the subject of the suit is not relevant;

(C) the person does not have a pecuniary relationship with an attorney in the suit; and

(D) the person does not have a relationship of trust or confidence with an attorney in the suit; or

(2) the parties and any attorney for a child who is the subject of the suit agree in writing to the person's appointment as the adoption evaluator.

(c) After being appointed as an adoption evaluator in a suit, a person shall immediately disclose to the court, each attorney for a party to the suit, any attorney for a child who is the subject of the suit, and any party to the suit who does not have an attorney any discovery of:

(1) a conflict of interest that the person believes the person has with a party to the suit or a child who is the subject of the suit; and

(2) previous knowledge that the person has of a party to the suit or a child who is the subject of the suit, other than knowledge obtained in a court-ordered evaluation.

(d) A person shall resign from the person's appointment as an adoption evaluator in a suit if the person makes any of the disclosures in Subsection (c) unless:

(1) the court finds that:

(A) the person has no conflict of interest with a party to the suit or a child who is the subject of the suit; and

(B) the person's previous knowledge of a party to the suit or a child who is the subject of the suit is not relevant; or

(2) the parties and any attorney for a child who is the subject of the suit agree in writing to the person's continued appointment as the adoption evaluator.

(e) An individual may not be appointed as an adoption evaluator in a suit if the individual has worked in a professional capacity with a party to the suit, a child who is the subject of the suit, or a member of the party's or child's family who is involved in the suit. This subsection does not apply to an individual who has worked in a professional capacity with a party, a child, or a member of the party's or child's family only as a teacher of parenting skills in a group setting, with no individualized interaction with any party, the child, any party's family, or the child's family, or as a child custody evaluator or adoption evaluator who performed a previous evaluation. For purposes of this subsection, "family" has the meaning assigned by Section 71.003.

History of Fam. Code §107.156: Acts 2015, 84th Leg., ch. 1252, §1.18, eff. Sept. 1, 2015.

FAM §107.157. REPORTING CERTAIN PLACEMENTS FOR ADOPTION

An adoption evaluator shall report to the department any adoptive placement that appears to have been made by someone other than a licensed child-placing agency or a child's parent or managing conservator.

History of Fam. Code §107.157: Acts 2015, 84th Leg., ch. 1252, §1.18, eff. Sept. 1, 2015.

See also 40 T.A.C. §745.9051.

FAM §107.158. GENERAL PROVISIONS APPLICABLE TO CONDUCT OF ADOPTION EVALUATOR & PREPARATION OF REPORTS

(a) Unless otherwise directed by a court or prescribed by this subchapter, an adoption evaluator's actions in conducting an adoption evaluation must be in conformance with the professional standard of care applicable to the evaluator's licensure and any administrative rules, ethical standards, or guidelines adopted by the licensing authority that licenses the evaluator.

(b) A court may impose requirements or adopt local rules applicable to an adoption evaluation or an adoption evaluator that do not conflict with this subchapter.

(c) An adoption evaluator shall follow evidence-based practice methods and make use of current best evidence in making assessments and recommendations.

(d) An adoption evaluator shall disclose to each attorney of record any communication regarding a substantive issue between the evaluator and an attorney of record representing a party in a contested suit. This subsection does not apply to a communication between an adoption evaluator and an amicus attorney.

(e) To the extent possible, an adoption evaluator shall verify each statement of fact pertinent to an adoption evaluation and shall note the sources of verification and information in any report prepared on the evaluation.

(f) An adoption evaluator shall state the basis for the evaluator's conclusions or recommendations in any report prepared on the evaluation.

(g) An adoption evaluation report must include for each adoption evaluator who conducted any portion of the adoption evaluation:

(1) the name and license number of the adoption evaluator; and

(2) a statement that the adoption evaluator:

(A) has read and meets the requirements of Section 107.154; or

(B) was appointed under Section 107.155.

History of Fam. Code §107.158: Acts 2015, 84th Leg., ch. 1252, §1.18, eff. Sept. 1, 2015.

See also 40 T.A.C. §§745.9047, 745.9049.

A FAM §107.159. REQUIREMENTS FOR PRE-PLACEMENT PORTION OF ADOPTION EVALUATION & REPORT

(a) Unless otherwise agreed to by the court, the pre-placement part of an adoption evaluation must comply with the minimum requirements for the pre-placement part of an adoption evaluation under rules adopted by the [~~executive~~] commissioner of the department [~~Health and Human Services Commission~~].

(b) Unless a child who is the subject of the suit begins to reside in a prospective adoptive home before the suit is commenced, an adoption evaluator shall file with the court a report containing the evaluator's findings and conclusions made after completion of the pre-placement portion of the adoption evaluation.

(c) In a suit filed after the date a child who is the subject of the suit begins to reside in a prospective adoptive home, the report required under this section and the post-placement adoption evaluation report required under Section 107.160 may be combined in a single report.

(d) The report required under this section must be filed with the court before the court may sign the final order for termination of the parent-child relationship. The report shall be included in the record of the suit.

(e) A copy of the report prepared under this section must be made available to the prospective adoptive parents before the court renders a final order of adoption.

History of Fam. Code §107.159: Acts 2015, 84th Leg., ch. 1252, §1.18, eff. Sept. 1, 2015. Amended by H.B. 5, §5, 85th Leg., eff. Sept. 1, 2017.

See also 40 T.A.C. §§745.9053-745.9079, 745.9093, 745.9097.

A FAM §107.160. REQUIREMENTS FOR POST-PLACEMENT PORTION OF ADOPTION EVALUATION & REPORT

(a) Unless otherwise agreed to by the court, the post-placement part of an adoption evaluation must comply with the minimum requirements for the post-placement part of an adoption evaluation under rules adopted by the [~~executive~~] commissioner of the department [~~Health and Human Services Commission~~].

(b) An adoption evaluator shall file with the court a report containing the evaluator's findings and conclusions made after a child who is the subject of the suit in which the evaluation is ordered begins to reside in a prospective adoptive home.

(c) The report required under this section must be filed with the court before the court renders a final order of adoption. The report shall be included in the record of the suit.

(d) A copy of the report prepared under this section must be made available to the prospective adoptive parents before the court renders a final order of adoption.

History of Fam. Code §107.160: Acts 2015, 84th Leg., ch. 1252, §1.18, eff. Sept. 1, 2015. Amended by H.B. 5, §6, 85th Leg., eff. Sept. 1, 2017.

See also 40 T.A.C. §§745.9081-745.9091, 745.9097.

FAM §107.161. INTRODUCTION & PROVISION OF ADOPTION EVALUATION REPORT & TESTIMONY RELATING TO ADOPTION EVALUATION

(a) Disclosure to the jury of the contents of an adoption evaluation report prepared under Section 107.159 or 107.160 is subject to the rules of evidence.

(b) The court may compel the attendance of witnesses necessary for the proper disposition of a suit, including a representative of an agency that conducts an adoption evaluation, who may be compelled to testify.

History of Fam. Code §107.161: Acts 2015, 84th Leg., ch. 1252, §1.18, eff. Sept. 1, 2015.

FAM §107.162. ADOPTION EVALUATION FEE

If the court orders an adoption evaluation to be conducted, the court shall award the adoption evaluator a reasonable fee for the preparation of the evaluation that shall be imposed in the form of a money judgment and paid directly to the evaluator. The evaluator may enforce the judgment for the fee by any means available under law for civil judgments.

History of Fam. Code §107.162: Acts 2015, 84th Leg., ch. 1252, §1.18, eff. Sept. 1, 2015.

FAM §107.163. ADOPTION EVALUATOR ACCESS TO INVESTIGATIVE RECORDS OF DEPARTMENT; OFFENSE

(a) An adoption evaluator is entitled to obtain from the department a complete, unredacted copy of any investigative record regarding abuse or neglect that relates to any person residing in the residence subject to the adoption evaluation.

(b) Except as provided by this section, records obtained by an adoption evaluator from the department under this section are confidential and not subject to disclosure under Chapter 552, Government Code, or to disclosure in response to a subpoena or a discovery request.

(c) An adoption evaluator may disclose information obtained under Subsection (a) in the adoption evaluation report prepared under Section 107.159 or 107.160 only to the extent the evaluator determines that the information is relevant to the adoption evaluation or a recommendation made under this subchapter.

(d) A person commits an offense if the person recklessly discloses confidential information obtained from the department in violation of this section. An offense under this subsection is a Class A misdemeanor.

History of Fam. Code §107.163: Acts 2015, 84th Leg., ch. 1252, §1.18, eff. Sept. 1, 2015.

See also 40 T.A.C. §745.9095.

SUBCHAPTER F. EVALUATIONS IN CONTESTED ADOPTIONS

FAM §107.201. APPLICABILITY

This subchapter does not apply to services provided in accordance with the Interstate Compact on the Placement of Children adopted under Subchapter B, Chapter 162, to an evaluation conducted in accordance with Section 262.114 by an employee of or contractor with the department, or to a suit in which the Department of Family and Protective Services is a party.

History of Fam. Code §107.201: Acts 2015, 84th Leg., ch. 1252, §1.18, eff. Sept. 1, 2015.

FAM §107.202. ASSIGNMENT OF EVALUATIONS IN CONTESTED ADOPTIONS

(a) In a suit in which the adoption of a child is being contested, the court shall determine the nature of

the questions posed before appointing an evaluator to conduct either a child custody evaluation or an adoption evaluation.

(b) If the court is attempting to determine whether termination of parental rights is in the best interest of a child who is the subject of the suit, the court shall order the evaluation as a child custody evaluation under Subchapter D and include termination as one of the specific issues to be addressed in the evaluation.

(c) When appointing an evaluator to assess the issue of termination of parental rights, the court may, through written order, modify the requirements of the child custody evaluation to take into account the circumstances of the family to be assessed. The court may also appoint the evaluator to concurrently address the requirements for an adoption evaluation under Subchapter E if the evaluator recommends that termination of parental rights is in the best interest of the child who is the subject of the suit.

(d) If the court is attempting to determine whether the parties seeking adoption would be suitable to adopt the child who is the subject of the suit if the termination of parental rights is granted, but the court is not attempting to determine whether such termination of parental rights is in the child's best interest, the court may order the evaluation as an adoption evaluation under Subchapter E.

History of Fam. Code §107.202: Acts 2015, 84th Leg., ch. 1252, §1.18, eff. Sept. 1, 2015.

SUBCHAPTER G. OFFICE OF CHILD REPRESENTATION & OFFICE OF PARENT REPRESENTATION

In 2017, subchapter G was redesignated from subchapter E by S.B. 1488, §24.001(6), 85th Leg., eff. Sept. 1, 2017.

FAM §107.251. DEFINITION

In this subchapter, "governmental entity" includes a county, a group of counties, a department of a county, an administrative judicial region created by Section 74.042, Government Code, and any entity created under the Interlocal Cooperation Act as permitted by Chapter 791, Government Code.

History of Fam. Code §107.251: Acts 2015, 84th Leg., ch. 571, §1, eff. Sept. 1, 2015. Renumbered from §107.061 by S.B. 1488, §24.001(6), 85th Leg., eff. Sept. 1, 2017.

FAM §107.252. APPLICABILITY

This subchapter applies to a suit filed by a governmental entity seeking termination of the parent-child relationship or the appointment of a conservator for a child in which appointment of an attorney is required under Section 107.012 or 107.013.

History of Fam. Code §107.252: Acts 2015, 84th Leg., ch. 571, §1, eff. Sept. 1, 2015. Renumbered from §107.062 by S.B. 1488, §24.001(6), 85th Leg., eff. Sept. 1, 2017.

FAM §107.253. NONPROFIT FUNDING

This subchapter does not limit or prevent a nonprofit corporation from receiving and using money obtained from other entities to provide legal representation and services as authorized by this subchapter.

History of Fam. Code §107.253: Acts 2015, 84th Leg., ch. 571, §1, eff. Sept. 1, 2015. Renumbered from §107.063 by S.B. 1488, §24.001(6), 85th Leg., eff. Sept. 1, 2017.

FAM §107.254. OFFICE OF CHILD REPRESENTATION

An office of child representation is an entity that uses public money to provide legal representation and services for a child in a suit filed by a governmental entity seeking termination of the parent-child relationship or the appointment of a conservator for the child in which appointment is mandatory for a child under Section 107.012.

History of Fam. Code §107.254: Acts 2015, 84th Leg., ch. 571, §1, eff. Sept. 1, 2015. Renumbered from §107.064 by S.B. 1488, §24.001(6), 85th Leg., eff. Sept. 1, 2017.

FAM §107.255. OFFICE OF PARENT REPRESENTATION

An office of parent representation is an entity that uses public money to provide legal representation and services for a parent in a suit filed by a governmental entity seeking termination of the parent-child relationship or the appointment of a conservator for a child in which appointment is mandatory for a parent under Section 107.013.

History of Fam. Code §107.255: Acts 2015, 84th Leg., ch. 571, §1, eff. Sept. 1, 2015. Renumbered from §107.065 by S.B. 1488, §24.001(6), 85th Leg., eff. Sept. 1, 2017.

FAM §107.256. CREATION OF OFFICE OF CHILD REPRESENTATION OR OFFICE OF PARENT REPRESENTATION

(a) An office described by Section 107.254 [~~107.064~~] or 107.255 [~~107.065~~] may be a governmental entity or a nonprofit corporation operating under a written agreement with a governmental entity, other than an individual judge or court.

(b) The commissioners court of any county, on written approval of a judge of a statutory county court or a district court having family law jurisdiction in the county, may create an office of child representation, an

office of parent representation, or both offices by establishing a department of the county or designating under a contract a nonprofit corporation to perform the duties of an office.

(c) The commissioners courts of two or more counties may enter into a written agreement to jointly create and jointly fund a regional office of child representation, a regional office of parent representation, or both regional offices.

(d) In creating an office of child representation or office of parent representation under this section, the commissioners court shall specify or the commissioners courts shall jointly specify, as applicable:

(1) the duties of the office;

(2) the types of cases to which the office may be appointed under this chapter and the courts in which an attorney employed by the office may be required to appear;

(3) if the office is a nonprofit corporation, the term during which the contract designating the office is effective and how that contract may be renewed on expiration of the term; and

(4) if an oversight board is established under Section 107.262 [~~107.072~~] for the office, the powers and duties that have been delegated to the oversight board.

History of Fam. Code §107.256: Acts 2015, 84th Leg., ch. 571, §1, eff. Sept. 1, 2015. Renumbered from §107.066 and amended by S.B. 1488, §§24.001(6), 24.002(2), 85th Leg., eff. Sept. 1, 2017.

FAM §107.257. NONPROFIT AS OFFICE

(a) Before contracting with a nonprofit corporation to serve as an office of child representation or office of parent representation, the commissioners court or commissioners courts, as applicable, must solicit proposals for the office.

(b) After considering each proposal for an office of child representation or office of parent representation submitted by a nonprofit corporation, the commissioners court or commissioners courts, as applicable, shall select a proposal that reasonably demonstrates that the office will provide adequate quality representation for children for whom appointed counsel is required under Section 107.012 or for parents for whom appointed counsel is required under Section 107.013, as applicable.

(c) The total cost of the proposal may not be the sole consideration in selecting a proposal.

History of Fam. Code §107.257: Acts 2015, 84th Leg., ch. 571, §1, eff. Sept. 1, 2015. Renumbered from §107.067 by S.B. 1488, §24.001(6), 85th Leg., eff. Sept. 1, 2017.

FAM §107.258. PLAN OF OPERATION FOR OFFICE

The applicable commissioners court or commissioners courts shall require a written plan of operation from an entity serving as an office of child representation or office of parent representation. The plan must include:

(1) a budget for the office, including salaries;

(2) a description of each personnel position, including the chief counsel position;

(3) the maximum allowable caseloads for each attorney employed by the office;

(4) provisions for training personnel and attorneys employed by the office;

(5) a description of anticipated overhead costs for the office;

(6) policies regarding the use of licensed investigators and expert witnesses by the office; and

(7) a policy to ensure that the chief of the office and other attorneys employed by the office do not provide representation to a child, a parent, or an alleged father, as applicable, if doing so would create a conflict of interest.

History of Fam. Code §107.258: Acts 2015, 84th Leg., ch. 571, §1, eff. Sept. 1, 2015. Renumbered from §107.068 by S.B. 1488, §24.001(6), 85th Leg., eff. Sept. 1, 2017.

FAM §107.259. OFFICE PERSONNEL

(a) An office of child representation or office of parent representation must be directed by a chief counsel who:

(1) is a member of the State Bar of Texas;

(2) has practiced law for at least three years; and

(3) has substantial experience in the practice of child welfare law.

(b) An office of child representation or office of parent representation may employ attorneys, licensed investigators, licensed social workers, and other personnel necessary to perform the duties of the office as specified by the commissioners court or commissioners courts.

(c) An attorney for the office of child representation or office of parent representation must comply with any applicable continuing education and training requirements of Sections 107.004 and 107.0131 before accepting representation.

(d) Except as authorized by this chapter, the chief counsel and other attorneys employed by an office of child representation or office of parent representation may not:

(1) engage in the private practice of child welfare law; or

(2) accept anything of value not authorized by this chapter for services rendered under this chapter.

(e) A judge may remove from a case a person who violates Subsection (d).

History of Fam. Code §107.259: Acts 2015, 84th Leg., ch. 571, §1, eff. Sept. 1, 2015. Renumbered from §107.069 by S.B. 1488, §24.001(6), 85th Leg., eff. Sept. 1, 2017.

Ⓐ FAM §107.260. APPOINTMENTS IN COUNTY IN WHICH OFFICE CREATED

(a) If there is an office of child representation or office of parent representation serving a county, a court in that county shall appoint for a child or parent, as applicable, an attorney from the office in a suit filed in the county by a governmental entity seeking termination of the parent-child relationship or the appointment of a conservator for the child, unless there is a conflict of interest or other reason to appoint a different attorney from the list maintained by the court of attorneys qualified for appointment under Section 107.012 or 107.013.

(b) An office of child representation or office of parent representation may not accept an appointment if:

(1) a conflict of interest exists;

(2) the office has insufficient resources to provide adequate representation;

(3) the office is incapable of providing representation in accordance with the rules of professional conduct;

(4) the appointment would require one or more attorneys at the office to have a caseload that exceeds the maximum allowable caseload; or

(5) the office shows other good cause for not accepting the appointment.

(c) An office of parent representation may investigate the financial condition of any person the office is appointed to represent under Section 107.013. The office shall report the results of the investigation to the appointing judge. The judge may hold a hearing to determine if the person is indigent and entitled to appointment of representation under Section 107.013.

(d) If it is necessary to appoint an attorney who is not employed by an office of child representation or office of parent representation for one or more parties, the attorney is entitled to the compensation provided by Section 107.015.

History of Fam. Code §107.260: Acts 2015, 84th Leg., ch. 571, §1, eff. Sept. 1, 2015. Renumbered from §107.070 by S.B. 1488, §24.001(6), 85th Leg., eff. Sept. 1, 2017.

Ⓐ FAM §107.261. FUNDING OF OFFICE

An office of child representation or office of parent representation is entitled to receive money for personnel costs and expenses incurred in operating as an office in amounts set by the commissioners court and paid out of the appropriate county fund, or jointly fixed by the commissioners courts and proportionately paid out of each appropriate county fund if the office serves more than one county.

History of Fam. Code §107.261: Acts 2015, 84th Leg., ch. 571, §1, eff. Sept. 1, 2015. Renumbered from §107.071 by S.B. 1488, §24.001(6), 85th Leg., eff. Sept. 1, 2017.

Ⓐ FAM §107.262. OVERSIGHT BOARD

(a) The commissioners court of a county or the commissioners courts of two or more counties may establish an oversight board for an office of child representation or office of parent representation created in accordance with this subchapter.

(b) A commissioners court that establishes an oversight board under this section shall appoint members of the board. Members may include one or more of the following:

(1) an attorney with substantial experience in child welfare law;

(2) the judge of a trial court having family law jurisdiction in the county or counties for which the office was created;

(3) a county commissioner; and

(4) a county judge.

(c) A commissioners court may delegate to the oversight board any power or duty of the commissioners court to provide oversight of an office of child representation or office of parent representation under this subchapter, including:

(1) recommending selection and removal of a chief counsel of the office;

(2) setting policy for the office; and

(3) developing a budget proposal for the office.

(d) An oversight board established under this section may not access privileged or confidential information.

(e) A judge who serves on an oversight board under this section has judicial immunity in a suit arising from the performance of a power or duty described by Subsection (c).

History of Fam. Code §107.262: Acts 2015, 84th Leg., ch. 571, §1, eff. Sept. 1, 2015. Renumbered from §107.072 by S.B. 1488, §24.001(6), 85th Leg., eff. Sept. 1, 2017.

A SUBCHAPTER H. MANAGED ASSIGNED COUNSEL PROGRAM FOR THE REPRESENTATION OF CERTAIN CHILDREN & PARENTS

In 2017, subchapter H was redesignated from subchapter F by S.B. 1488, §24.001(7), 85th Leg., eff. Sept. 1, 2017.

A FAM §107.301. DEFINITIONS

In this subchapter:

(1) "Governmental entity" includes a county, a group of counties, a department of a county, an administrative judicial region created by Section 74.042, Government Code, and any entity created under the Interlocal Cooperation Act as permitted by Chapter 791, Government Code.

(2) "Program" means a managed assigned counsel program created under this subchapter.

History of Fam. Code §107.301: Acts 2015, 84th Leg., ch. 571, §1, eff. Sept. 1, 2015. Renumbered from §107.101 by S.B. 1488, §24.001(7), 85th Leg., eff. Sept. 1, 2017.

A FAM §107.302. MANAGED ASSIGNED COUNSEL PROGRAM

(a) A managed assigned counsel program may be operated with public money for the purpose of appointing counsel to provide legal representation and services for a child or parent in a suit filed by a governmental entity seeking termination of the parent-child relationship or the appointment of a conservator for the child in which appointment is mandatory for a child under Section 107.012 or for a parent under Section 107.013.

(b) The program may be operated by a governmental entity, nonprofit corporation, or local bar association under a written agreement with a governmental entity, other than an individual judge or court.

History of Fam. Code §107.302: Acts 2015, 84th Leg., ch. 571, §1, eff. Sept. 1, 2015. Renumbered from §107.102 by S.B. 1488, §24.001(7), 85th Leg., eff. Sept. 1, 2017.

A FAM §107.303. CREATION OF MANAGED ASSIGNED COUNSEL PROGRAM

(a) The commissioners court of a county, on written approval of a judge of a statutory county court or a district court having family law jurisdiction in the county, may appoint a governmental entity, nonprofit corporation, or local bar association to operate a managed assigned counsel program for the legal representation of:

(1) a child in a suit in which appointment is mandatory under Section 107.012; or

(2) a parent in a suit in which appointment is mandatory under Section 107.013.

(b) The commissioners courts of two or more counties may enter into a written agreement to jointly appoint and fund a governmental entity, nonprofit corporation, or bar association to operate a program that provides legal representation for children, parents, or both children and parents.

(c) In appointing an entity to operate a program under this subchapter, the commissioners court shall specify or the commissioners courts shall jointly specify:

(1) the types of cases in which the program may appoint counsel under this section, and the courts in which the counsel appointed by the program may be required to appear; and

(2) the term of any agreement establishing a program and how the agreement may be terminated or renewed.

History of Fam. Code §107.303: Acts 2015, 84th Leg., ch. 571, §1, eff. Sept. 1, 2015. Renumbered from §107.103 by S.B. 1488, §24.001(7), 85th Leg., eff. Sept. 1, 2017.

A FAM §107.304. PLAN FOR PROGRAM REQUIRED

The commissioners court or commissioners courts shall require a written plan of operation from an entity operating a program under this subchapter. The plan of operation must include:

(1) a budget for the program, including salaries;

(2) a description of each personnel position, including the program's director;

(3) the maximum allowable caseload for each attorney appointed under the program;

(4) provisions for training personnel of the program and attorneys appointed under the program;

(5) a description of anticipated overhead costs for the program;

(6) a policy regarding licensed investigators and expert witnesses used by attorneys appointed under the program;

(7) a policy to ensure that appointments are reasonably and impartially allocated among qualified attorneys; and

(8) a policy to ensure that an attorney appointed under the program does not accept appointment in a case that involves a conflict of interest for the attorney.

History of Fam. Code §107.304: Acts 2015, 84th Leg., ch. 571, §1, eff. Sept. 1, 2015. Renumbered from §107.104 by S.B. 1488, §24.001(7), 85th Leg., eff. Sept. 1, 2017.

FAM §107.305. PROGRAM DIRECTOR; PERSONNEL

(a) Unless a program uses a review committee appointed under Section 107.306 [~~107.106~~], a program under this subchapter must be directed by a person who:

(1) is a member of the State Bar of Texas;

(2) has practiced law for at least three years; and

(3) has substantial experience in the practice of child welfare law.

(b) A program may employ personnel necessary to perform the duties of the program and enter into contracts necessary to perform the program's duties as specified by the commissioners court or commissioners courts under this subchapter.

History of Fam. Code §107.305: Acts 2015, 84th Leg., ch. 571, §1, eff. Sept. 1, 2015. Renumbered from §107.105 and amended by S.B. 1488, §§24.001(7), 24.002(3), 85th Leg., eff. Sept. 1, 2017.

FAM §107.306. REVIEW COMMITTEE

(a) The governmental entity, nonprofit corporation, or local bar association operating a program may appoint a review committee of three or more individuals to approve attorneys for inclusion on the program's public appointment list.

(b) Each member of the committee:

(1) must meet the requirements described by Section 107.305(a) [~~107.105(a)~~] for the program director;

(2) may not be employed as a prosecutor; and

(3) may not be included on or apply for inclusion on the public appointment list.

History of Fam. Code §107.306: Acts 2015, 84th Leg., ch. 571, §1, eff. Sept. 1, 2015. Renumbered from §107.106 and amended by S.B. 1488, §§24.001(7), 24.002(4), 85th Leg., eff. Sept. 1, 2017.

FAM §107.307. APPOINTMENT FROM PROGRAM'S PUBLIC APPOINTMENT LIST

(a) The judge of a county served by a program shall make any appointment required under Section 107.012 or 107.013 in a suit filed in the county by a governmental entity seeking termination of the parent-child relationship or the appointment of a conservator for the child from the program's public appointment list, unless there is a conflict of interest or other reason to appoint a different attorney from the list maintained by the court of attorneys qualified for appointment under Section 107.012 or 107.013.

(b) The program's public appointment list from which an attorney is appointed under this section must contain the names of qualified attorneys, each of whom:

(1) applies to be included on the list;

(2) meets any applicable requirements, including any education and training programs required under Sections 107.004 and 107.0131; and

(3) is approved by the program director or review committee, as applicable.

History of Fam. Code §107.307: Acts 2015, 84th Leg., ch. 571, §1, eff. Sept. 1, 2015. Renumbered from §107.107 by S.B. 1488, §24.001(7), 85th Leg., eff. Sept. 1, 2017.

FAM §107.308. FUNDING OF PROGRAM

(a) A program is entitled to receive money for personnel costs and expenses incurred in amounts set by the commissioners court and paid out of the appropriate county fund or jointly fixed by the commissioners courts and proportionately paid out of each appropriate county fund if the program serves more than one county.

(b) An attorney appointed under the program is entitled to reasonable fees as provided by Section 107.015.

History of Fam. Code §107.308: Acts 2015, 84th Leg., ch. 571, §1, eff. Sept. 1, 2015. Renumbered from §107.108 by S.B. 1488, §24.001(7), 85th Leg., eff. Sept. 1, 2017.

CHAPTER 108. CENTRAL RECORD FILE; VITAL STATISTICS

FAM §108.001. TRANSMITTAL OF RECORDS OF SUIT BY CLERK

(a) Except as provided by this chapter, the clerk of the court shall transmit to the vital statistics unit a certified record of the order rendered in a suit, together with the name and all prior names, birth date, and place of birth of the child on a form provided by the unit. The form shall be completed by the petitioner and submitted to the clerk at the time the order is filed for record.

(b) The vital statistics unit shall maintain these records in a central file according to the name, birth date, and place of birth of the child, the court that rendered the order, and the docket number of the suit.

(c) Except as otherwise provided by law, the records required under this section to be maintained by the vital statistics unit are confidential.

(d) In a Title IV-D case, the Title IV-D agency may transmit the record and information specified by Subsection (a) directly to the vital statistics unit. The record and information are not required to be certified if transmitted by the Title IV-D agency under this subsection.

History of Fam. Code §108.001: Acts 1995, 74th Leg., ch. 20, §1, eff. Apr. 20, 1995. Amended by Acts 1995, 74th Leg., ch. 751, §16, eff. Sept. 1, 1995; Acts 1999, 76th Leg., ch. 1390, §8, eff. Sept. 1, 1999; Acts 2007, 80th Leg., ch. 972, §4, eff. Sept. 1, 2007; Acts 2015, 84th Leg., ch. 1, §1.034 (eff. Apr. 2, 2015), ch. 963, §1 (eff. Sept. 1, 2015). Source: Former Fam. Code §11.17(a), (d).

FAM §108.002. DISSOLUTION OF MARRIAGE RECORDS MAINTAINED BY CLERK

A clerk may not transmit to the central record file the pleadings, papers, studies, and records relating to a suit for divorce or annulment or to declare a marriage void.

History of Fam. Code §108.002: Acts 1995, 74th Leg., ch. 20, §1, eff. Apr. 20, 1995. Source: Former Fam. Code §11.17(b).

FAM §108.003. TRANSMITTAL OF INFORMATION REGARDING ADOPTION

(a) The clerk of a court that renders a decree of adoption shall, not later than the 10th day of the first month after the month in which the adoption is rendered, transmit to the central registry of the vital statistics unit a certified report of adoption that includes:

(1) the name of the adopted child after adoption as shown in the adoption order;

(2) the birth date of the adopted child;

(3) the docket number of the adoption suit;

(4) the identity of the court rendering the adoption;

(5) the date of the adoption order;

(6) the name and address of each parent, guardian, managing conservator, or other person whose consent to adoption was required or waived under Chapter 162, or whose parental rights were terminated in the adoption suit;

(7) the identity of the licensed child placing agency, if any, through which the adopted child was placed for adoption; and

(8) the identity, address, and telephone number of the registry through which the adopted child may register as an adoptee.

(b) Except as otherwise provided by law, for good cause shown, or on an order of the court that granted the adoption or terminated the proceedings under Section 155.001, the records concerning a child maintained by the district clerk after rendition of a decree of adoption, the records of a child-placing agency that has ceased operations, and the records required under this section to be maintained by the vital statistics unit are confidential, and no person is entitled to access to or information from these records.

(c) If the vital statistics unit determines that a report filed with the unit under this section requires correction, the unit shall mail the report directly to an attorney of record with respect to the adoption. The attorney shall return the corrected report to the unit. If there is no attorney of record, the unit shall mail the report to the clerk of the court for correction.

History of Fam. Code §108.003: Acts 1995, 74th Leg., ch. 20, §1, eff. Apr. 20, 1995. Amended by Acts 1995, 74th Leg., ch. 751, §17, eff. Sept. 1, 1995; Acts 1999, 76th Leg., ch. 62, §6.16 (eff. Sept. 1, 1999), ch. 1390, §9 (eff. Sept. 1, 1999); Acts 2003, 78th Leg., ch. 1128, §3, eff. Sept. 1, 2003; Acts 2015, 84th Leg., ch. 1, §1.035, eff. Apr. 2, 2015. Source: Former Fam. Code §11.17(b); former Hum. Res. Code §§49.003(d), 49.005(d).

See also 25 T.A.C. §181.31.

FAM §108.004. TRANSMITTAL OF FILES ON LOSS OF JURISDICTION

On the loss of jurisdiction of a court under Chapter 155, 159, or 262, the clerk of the court shall transmit to the central registry of the vital statistics unit a certified record, on a form provided by the unit, stating that jurisdiction has been lost, the reason for the loss of jurisdiction, and the name and all previous names, date of birth, and place of birth of the child.

History of Fam. Code §108.004: Acts 1995, 74th Leg., ch. 20, §1, eff. Apr. 20, 1995. Amended by Acts 1995, 74th Leg., ch. 751, §18, eff. Sept. 1, 1995; Acts 2007, 80th Leg., ch. 972, §5, eff. Sept. 1, 2007; Acts 2015, 84th Leg., ch. 1, §1.036, eff. Apr. 2, 2015. Source: Former Fam. Code §11.17(b).

FAM §108.005. ADOPTION RECORDS RECEIVED BY VITAL STATISTICS UNIT

(a) When the vital statistics unit receives a record from the district clerk showing that continuing, exclusive jurisdiction of a child has been lost due to the adoption of the child, the unit shall close the records concerning that child.

(b) An inquiry concerning a child who has been adopted shall be handled as though the child had not previously been the subject of a suit affecting the parent-child relationship.

History of Fam. Code §108.005: Acts 1995, 74th Leg., ch. 20, §1, eff. Apr. 20, 1995. Amended by Acts 1995, 74th Leg., ch. 751, §19, eff. Sept. 1, 1995. Repealed by Acts 1995, 74th Leg., ch. 968, §11, eff. Sept. 1, 1995. Amended by Acts 1999, 76th Leg., ch. 1390, §10, eff. Sept. 1, 1999; Acts 2015, 84th Leg., ch. 1, §§1.037, 1.038, eff. Apr. 2, 2015. Source: Former Fam. Code §11.17(b).

FAM §108.006. FEES

(a) The Department of State Health Services may charge a reasonable fee to cover the cost of determining and sending information concerning the identity of the court with continuing, exclusive jurisdiction.

(b) On the filing of a suit requesting the adoption of a child, the clerk of the court shall collect an additional fee of $15.

(c) The clerk shall send the fees collected under Subsection (b) to the Department of State Health Services for deposit in a special fund in the state treasury from which the legislature may appropriate money only to operate and maintain the central file and central registry of the vital statistics unit.

(d) The receipts from the fees charged under Subsection (a) shall be deposited in a financial institution as determined by the Department of State Health Services and withdrawn as necessary for the sole purpose of operating and maintaining the central record file.

History of Fam. Code §108.006: Acts 1995, 74th Leg., ch. 20, §1, eff. Apr. 20, 1995. Amended by Acts 1995, 74th Leg., ch. 751, §20, eff. Sept. 1, 1995; Acts 2015, 84th Leg., ch. 1, §1.039, eff. Apr. 2, 2015. Source: Former Fam. Code §§11.17(c), 11.171.

FAM §108.007. MICROFILM

(a) The vital statistics unit may use microfilm or other suitable means for maintaining the central record file.

(b) A certified reproduction of a document maintained by the vital statistics unit is admissible in evidence as the original document.

History of Fam. Code §108.007: Acts 1995, 74th Leg., ch. 20, §1, eff. Apr. 20, 1995. Amended by Acts 1995, 74th Leg., ch. 751, §21, eff. Sept. 1, 1995; Acts 2015, 84th Leg., ch. 1, §1.040, eff. Apr. 2, 2015. Source: Former Fam. Code §11.17(e).

FAM §108.008. FILING INFORMATION AFTER DETERMINATION OF PATERNITY

(a) On a determination of paternity, the petitioner shall provide the clerk of the court in which the order was rendered the information necessary to prepare the report of determination of paternity. The clerk shall:

(1) prepare the report on a form provided by the vital statistics unit; and

(2) complete the report immediately after the order becomes final.

(b) On completion of the report, the clerk of the court shall forward to the state registrar a report for each order that became final in that court.

History of Fam. Code §108.008: Acts 1995, 74th Leg., ch. 20, §1, eff. Apr. 20, 1995. Amended by Acts 1999, 76th Leg., ch. 556, §4, eff. Sept. 1, 1999; Acts 2015, 84th Leg., ch. 1, §1.041, eff. Apr. 2, 2015. Source: Former Fam. Code §13.43(a)-(c).

FAM §108.009. BIRTH CERTIFICATE

(a) The state registrar shall substitute a new birth certificate for the original based on the order in accordance with laws or rules that permit the correction or substitution of a birth certificate for an adopted child or a child whose parents marry each other subsequent to the birth of the child.

(b) The new certificate may not show that the father and child relationship was established after the child's birth but may show the child's actual place and date of birth.

History of Fam. Code §108.009: Acts 1995, 74th Leg., ch. 20, §1, eff. Apr. 20, 1995. Amended by Acts 2001, 77th Leg., ch. 821, §2.12, eff. June 14, 2001. Source: Former Fam. Code §13.43(e), (f).

See also 25 T.A.C. §181.8.

FAM §108.110. RELEASE OF INFORMATION BY VITAL STATISTICS UNIT

(a) The vital statistics unit shall provide to the Department of Family and Protective Services:

(1) adoption information as necessary for the department to comply with federal law or regulations regarding the compilation or reporting of adoption information to federal officials; and

(2) other information as necessary for the department to administer its duties.

(b) The unit may release otherwise confidential information from the unit's central record files to another governmental entity that has a specific need for the information and maintains appropriate safeguards to prevent further dissemination of the information.

History of Fam. Code §108.110: Acts 1999, 76th Leg., ch. 1390, §11, eff. Sept. 1, 1999. Amended by Acts 2015, 84th Leg., ch. 1, §1.042, eff. Apr. 2, 2015.

CHAPTER 109. APPEALS

FAM §109.001. TEMPORARY ORDERS DURING PENDENCY OF APPEAL

The amended text in §109.001 is effective for orders rendered on or after Sept. 1, 2017. Orders rendered before Sept. 1, 2017, are governed by the former law in effect at that time.

(a) In a suit affecting the parent-child relationship [~~Not later than the 30th day after the date an appeal is perfected~~], on the motion of any party or on the court's own motion and after notice and hearing, the court may make any order necessary to preserve and protect the safety and welfare of the child during the pendency of an [~~the~~] appeal as the court may deem necessary and equitable. In addition to other matters, an order may:

(1) appoint temporary conservators for the child and provide for possession of the child;

(2) require the temporary support of the child by a party;

(3) enjoin [~~restrain~~] a party from molesting or disturbing the peace of the child or another party;

(4) prohibit a person from removing the child beyond a geographical area identified by the court;

(5) require payment of reasonable and necessary attorney's fees and expenses; or

(6) suspend the operation of the order or judgment that is being appealed.

(b) A temporary order under this section enjoining a party from molesting or disturbing the peace of the child or another party:

(1) may be rendered without:

(A) the issuance of a bond between the spouses; or

(B) an affidavit or a verified pleading stating specific facts showing that immediate and irreparable injury, loss, or damage will result; and

(2) is not required to:

(A) define the injury or state why the injury is irreparable; or

(B) include an order setting the suit for trial on the merits with respect to the ultimate relief sought.

(b-1) A motion seeking an original temporary order under this section:

(1) may be filed before trial; and

(2) may not be filed by a party after the date by which that party is required to file the party's notice of appeal under the Texas Rules of Appellate Procedure.

(b-2) The trial court retains jurisdiction to conduct a hearing and sign a temporary order under this section until the 60th day after the date any eligible party has filed a notice of appeal from final judgment under the Texas Rules of Appellate Procedure.

(b-3) The trial court retains jurisdiction to modify and enforce a temporary order [~~its orders rendered~~] under this section unless the appellate court, on a proper showing, supersedes the court's order.

(b-4) On the motion of a party or on the court's own motion, after notice and hearing, the trial court may modify a previous temporary order rendered under this section if:

(1) the circumstances of a party have materially and substantially changed since the rendition of the previous order; and

(2) modification is equitable and necessary for the safety and welfare of the child.

(b-5) A party may seek review of the trial court's temporary order under this section by:

(1) petition for writ of mandamus; or

(2) proper assignment in the party's brief.

(c) A temporary order rendered under this section is not subject to interlocutory appeal.

(d) The court may not suspend under Subsection (a)(6) the operation of an order or judgment terminating the parent-child relationship in a suit brought by the state or a political subdivision of the state permitted by law to bring the suit.

(e) The remedies provided in this section are cumulative of all other remedies allowed by law.

History of Fam. Code §109.001: Acts 1995, 74th Leg., ch. 20, §1, eff. Apr. 20, 1995. Amended by Acts 2001, 77th Leg., ch. 539, §1, eff. Sept. 1, 2001; S.B. 1237, §4, 85th Leg., eff. Sept. 1, 2017. Source: Former Fam. Code §11.11(e)-(g).

See also ***O'Connor's Texas Family Law Handbook*** (2017), "Temporary Orders," ch. 5-D, p. 695.

ANNOTATIONS

Dancy v. Daggett, 815 S.W.2d 548, 549 (Tex.1991). This court holds that "mandamus is an appropriate remedy ... since the trial court's issuance of temporary orders is not subject to interlocutory appeal."

In re Reardon, 514 S.W.3d 919, ___ (Tex.App.—Fort Worth 2017, n.p.h.). "Subsequent modification and [Fam. Code] §109.001 are not inconsistent[.] [¶] [D]uring the pendency of an appeal [under §109.001], a party may seek temporary relief from a SAPCR order—including the suspension of the order itself—as long as the modification sought is necessary to 'preserve and protect the safety and welfare of the child' during the appellate process. At the same time, a party may also seek to *permanently* modify that SAPCR order in a new suit, provided the petitioner can show sufficient statutory grounds to establish his or her right to do so. … Because [Fam. Code §§109.001 and 109.002 and the statutes governing modification suits] serve independent purposes—one type of modification providing temporary relief, the other type making permanent change—a simultaneous request for both would present neither conflict nor redundancy. Rather than meaningless or superfluous, §109.001 is merely one component in an overall statutory scheme designed to provide avenues of relief at multiple levels and in fluid circumstances, one part of an integrated approach to address the unique circumstances that arise in the ever-changing environment of family life." *See also* ***Blank v. Nuszen***, No. 01-13-01061-CV (Tex.App.—Houston [1st Dist.] 2015, no pet.) (memo op.; 8-11-15) (same); ***Hudson v. Markum***, 931 S.W.2d 336, 338 (Tex.App.—Dallas 1996, no writ) (trial court's continuing, exclusive jurisdiction to modify final order continues even while appeal of order is pending). *But see* ***In re E.W.N.***, this page.

In re Moore, 511 S.W.3d 278, 285 (Tex.App.—Dallas 2016, no pet.). "Father contends that '[m]andamus is the appropriate—and, indeed, only—means to challenge temporary orders pending appeal.' *At 286:* We respectfully disagree that subsection (c) deprives us of jurisdiction to review a §109.001 order in conjunction with the pending appeal from the final judgment. Those courts concluding otherwise did not distinguish between an accelerated interlocutory appeal and an appeal from a final judgment. [¶] Subsection (c) does not prohibit all appeals; it prohibits only interlocutory appeals from temporary orders. We construe this to mean only that an accelerated appeal of a temporary order, separate from the appeal from the final judgment, is statutorily prohibited. Subsection (b) supports this construction because it authorizes the appellate court to supersede the trial court's order. … 'Authorizing the appellate court to supersede enforcement of the order suggests the appellate court may do so to allow review of the order by the appellate court in the pending appeal. We see nothing in [§109.001] that deprives the appellate court of jurisdiction to consider the issue with the merits of the pending appeal from the final judgment.'" *But see* ***Marcus v. Smith***, 313 S.W.3d 408, 416 (Tex.App.—Houston [1st Dist.] 2009, orig. proceeding) (court declined to review temporary order for attorney fees with pending appeal from final judgment); ***Johnson v. Johnson***, 948 S.W.2d 835, 838 (Tex.App.—San Antonio 1997, writ denied) (same).

In re E.W.N., 482 S.W.3d 150, 152 (Tex.App.—El Paso 2015, no pet.). "Father argues that the trial court retained continuing, exclusive jurisdiction of the [modification] order and could modify that order even while Father's appeal was pending…. *At 154:* If a trial court's exclusive, continuing jurisdiction of a cause operated in the manner asserted by Father, §109.001's grant of limited authority to the trial court to enter temporary orders pending appeal would be completely unnecessary. … Section 109.001 implicitly, if not explicitly, recognizes an appellate court's exclusive plenary authority over the cause on appeal. *At 157:* Father filed his notice of appeal from the … modification order on December 20, 2011. He filed his petition to modify in the trial court on January 12, 2012, and a first amended petition to modify on February 5, 2013. In the interim, he sought temporary orders. The Second Court of Appeals acquired exclusive plenary jurisdiction over the cause once Father perfected his appeal and the trial court's plenary power to enter temporary orders pursuant to §109.001 expired on January 19, 2012. The trial court correctly dismissed Father's first amended petition to modify." *But see* ***In re Reardon***, this page.

Marcus v. Smith, 313 S.W.3d 408, 418 (Tex.App.—Houston [1st Dist.] 2009, orig. proceeding). "Evidence is sufficient to justify appellate attorney's fees to preserve and protect the safety and welfare of the child under §109.001 when the recipient of appellate attorney's fees 'has primary responsibility of the children and for the care and upkeep of and the debt on the children's principal home.' [¶] An unconditional award of appellant's appellate attorney's fees is improper, and a trial court must condition the award upon the appellant's unsuccessful appeal. However, an unconditional award of appellate attorney's fees does not require reversal; instead, the appellate court may modify the trial court's

judgment to make the attorney's fees contingent upon successful appeal." *See also* ***In re Garza***, 153 S.W.3d 97, 101 (Tex.App.—San Antonio 2004, orig. proceeding). *But see* ***In re Jafarzadeh***, No. 05-14-01576-CV (Tex. App.—Dallas 2015, orig. proceeding) (memo op.; 1-2-15) (unconditional award of attorney fees proper to promote best interest of child on appeal).

In re Gonzalez, 981 S.W.2d 313, 314 (Tex.App.—San Antonio 1998, pet. denied). In §109.001, "if the trial court has the authority to *suspend* an order or judgment that is being appealed, the court has jurisdiction to *enforce* an order or judgment that is being appealed. While this provision might appear to empower the court to act only within a 30-day window after an appeal is perfected, the [Family] Code clearly indicates in §109.001 that the court retains jurisdiction beyond 30 days even where the merits of the order is under appeal. [¶] We interpret [§109.001(b)'s] language to mean that the trial court retains jurisdiction to enforce temporary orders for child support whenever the payor-parent fails to pay."

A FAM §109.002. APPELLATE REVIEW ~~[APPEAL]~~

The amended text in §109.002 is effective for orders rendered on or after Sept. 1, 2017. Orders rendered before Sept. 1, 2017, are governed by the former law in effect at that time.

(a) An appeal from a final order rendered in a suit, when allowed under this section or under other provisions of law, shall be as in civil cases generally under the Texas Rules of Appellate Procedure, except that an appeal from a final order rendered under Subchapter D, Chapter 152, must comply with Section 152.314.

(a-1) An appeal in a suit in which termination of the parent-child relationship is ordered ~~[in issue]~~ shall be given precedence over other civil cases by the appellate courts, ~~[and]~~ shall be accelerated, and shall follow ~~[by]~~ the ~~[appellate courts. The]~~ procedures for an accelerated appeal under the Texas Rules of Appellate Procedure ~~[apply to an appeal in which the termination of the parent-child relationship is in issue]~~.

(b) An appeal may be taken by any party to a suit from a final order rendered under this title.

(c) An appeal from a final order, with or without a supersedeas bond, does not suspend the order unless suspension is ordered by the court rendering the order. The appellate court, on a proper showing, may permit the order to be suspended, unless the order provides for the termination of the parent-child relationship in a suit brought by the state or a political subdivision of the state permitted by law to bring the suit.

(d) On the motion of the parties or on the court's own motion, the appellate court in its opinion may identify the parties by fictitious names or by their initials only.

History of Fam. Code §109.002: Acts 1995, 74th Leg., ch. 20, §1, eff. Apr. 20, 1995. Amended by Acts 1999, 76th Leg., ch. 62, §6.17, eff. Sept. 1, 1999; Acts 2001, 77th Leg., ch. 421, §1 (eff. Sept. 1, 2001), ch. 539, §2 (eff. Sept. 1, 2001); Acts 2011, 82nd Leg., ch. 75, §3, eff. Sept. 1, 2011; S.B. 1237, §§5, 6, 85th Leg., eff. Sept. 1, 2017. Source: Former Fam. Code §11.19.

See also ***O'Connor's Texas Family Law Handbook*** (2017), "Must be accelerated," ch. 4-H, §17.2.3, p. 653; ***O'Connor's Texas Appeals***, "Appeals required by statute to be accelerated," ch. 1-B, §2.6.1(3), p. 24; "Motion to Accelerate Appeal or to Give Appeal Precedence," ch. 3-C, p. 99; "Motion to Extend Time," ch. 3-F, p. 116.

ANNOTATIONS

In re J.M., 396 S.W.3d 528, 529 (Tex.2013). "In this parental termination case, we determine whether a motion for new trial and notice of appeal combined in one document can invoke appellate jurisdiction. *At 530-31:* Nothing in our [TRAPs] or our jurisprudence prevents a party from combining a notice of appeal with a motion for new trial (or filing both the motion and notice simultaneously). [¶] In *K.A.F.* [below], we ... held that a combined filing of a motion for new trial and a motion to modify judgment did not qualify as a substitute for a notice of appeal, but there neither portion of the combined filing addressed the appellate court. ... Moreover, giving effect to the notice of appeal portion does not render the motion for new trial portion meaningless: the trial court retained plenary power over the case to grant or deny the motion for new trial. If the trial court does not grant the motion for new trial by the time its plenary power expires, the case is still within the appellate court's jurisdiction. [¶] The present filing expressed an intent to appeal to the court of appeals and was partially entitled a notice of appeal, which constituted a bona fide attempt to invoke appellate jurisdiction upon its filing with the trial court clerk."

In re K.A.F., 160 S.W.3d 923, 925 (Tex.2005). TRAP 26.1(b) "applies to an appeal in a parental rights termination case and requires that the notice of appeal be filed within 20 days after a judgment or order is signed. *At 927:* [I]n an accelerated appeal, absent a [TRAP] 26.3 motion, the deadline for filing a notice of appeal is strictly set at 20 days after the judgment is signed, with no exceptions, and filing a [TRAP] 26.1(a) motion for new trial, motion to modify the judgment, motion to re-

instate, or request for findings of fact and conclusions of law will not extend that deadline. Allowing such post-order motions to automatically delay the appellate deadline is simply inconsistent with the idea of accelerating the appeal in the first place." *See also* ***In re R.B.M.***, 338 S.W.3d 755, 756-57 (Tex.App.—Houston [14th Dist.] 2011, no pet.) (filing affidavit of indigency is not bona fide attempt to invoke appellate court's jurisdiction).

In re J.R.J., 357 S.W.3d 153, 156 (Tex.App.—Fort Worth 2011, orig. proceeding). "[T]he trial court ordered [father's court-appointed] counsel not to file a notice of appeal until [father, who could not be contacted,] communicated to counsel his desire to appeal. ... But the question of whether [father's] counsel has the authority to file a notice of appeal is one for this court, not the trial court. Therefore, the trial court abused its discretion by ordering [father's] counsel not to file a notice of appeal. *At 157:* It always has been and always will be that the client must decide whether to appeal a judgment. But to the extent there is a factual dispute concerning the lawyer's authority to file a notice of appeal on a client's behalf because the client may not have expressed a desire to appeal, the dispute must be resolved by the court of appeals, typically after an abatement, a limited remand to the trial court for an evidentiary hearing, and the filing of supplemental findings of fact or conclusions of law."

Jane Doe v. Brazoria Cty. Child Prot. Servs., 226 S.W.3d 563, 570-71 (Tex.App.—Houston [1st Dist.] 2007, no pet.). "In the accelerated appeal of a civil case, [t]he appellate court may [under TRAP 26.3] extend the time to file the notice of appeal, if, within 15 days after the deadline for filing the notice of appeal, the party (1) files the notice of appeal, and (2) files in the appellate court a motion complying with [TRAP] 10.5(b). A motion to extend time to file notice of appeal is necessarily implied when an appellant, acting in good faith, files a perfecting instrument beyond the time allowed for perfecting an appeal, but within the 15-day period in which appellant would be entitled to move to extend the filing deadline. [¶] Appellant must still, however, [provide] a reasonable explanation for late filing the notice of appeal."

In re N.J.G., 980 S.W.2d 764, 766-67 (Tex. App.—San Antonio 1998, no pet.). "The ... Family Code permits a party to appeal a final order in a [SAPCR]. To be final, a judgment must determine the rights of the parties and dispose of all the issues involved so no future action will be necessary in order to settle and determine the case. A judgment is interlocutory when it determines less than all issues as to all parties thereby leaving something to be determined and adjudicated by the court in disposing of the parties and their rights. Accordingly, an order is interlocutory if it leaves open the issue of permanent conservatorship." (Internal quotes omitted.) *See also* ***In re J.D.***, 304 S.W.3d 522, 524-25 (Tex.App.—Waco 2009, no pet.) (intent to finally dispose of case must be unequivocally expressed in words of order).

Ⓐ FAM §109.003. PAYMENT FOR COURT REPORTER'S RECORD ~~[STATEMENT OF FACTS]~~

The amended text in §109.003 is effective for orders rendered on or after Sept. 1, 2017. Orders rendered before Sept. 1, 2017, are governed by the former law in effect at that time.

(a) If the party requesting a court reporter's record ~~[statement of facts]~~ in an appeal of a suit has filed an affidavit stating the party's inability to pay costs as provided by Rule 20, Texas Rules of Appellate Procedure, and the affidavit is approved by the trial court, the trial court may order the county in which the trial was held to pay the costs of preparing the court reporter's record ~~[statement of facts]~~.

(b) Nothing in this section shall be construed to permit an official court reporter to be paid more than once for the preparation of the court reporter's record ~~[statement of facts]~~.

History of Fam. Code §109.003: Acts 1995, 74th Leg., ch. 20, §1, eff. Apr. 20, 1995. Amended by Acts 1995, 74th Leg., ch. 472, §1, eff. Sept. 1, 1995; Acts 2001, 77th Leg., ch. 1420, §5.0025, eff. Sept. 1, 2001; S.B. 1237, §7, 85th Leg., eff. Sept. 1, 2017. Source: Former Fam. Code §11.191.

CHAPTER 110. COURT FEES

FAM §110.001. GENERAL RULE

Except as provided by this chapter, fees in a matter covered by this title shall be as in civil cases generally.

History of Fam. Code §110.001: Acts 1995, 74th Leg., ch. 20, §1, eff. Apr. 20, 1995.

FAM §110.002. FILING FEES & DEPOSITS

(a) The clerk of the court may collect a filing fee of $15 in a suit for filing:

(1) a suit or motion for modification;

(2) a motion for enforcement;

(3) a notice of application for judicial writ of withholding;

(4) a motion to transfer;

(5) a petition for license suspension;

(6) a motion to revoke a stay of license suspension; or

(7) a motion for contempt.

(b) No other filing fee may be collected or required for an action described in this section.

(c) The clerk may collect a deposit as in other cases, in the amount set by the clerk for payment of expected costs and other expenses arising in the proceeding.

History of Fam. Code §110.002: Acts 1995, 74th Leg., ch. 20, §1, eff. Apr. 20, 1995. Amended by Acts 1997, 75th Leg., ch. 911, §8 (eff. Sept. 1, 1997), ch. 976, §6 (eff. Sept. 1, 1997); Acts 2003, 78th Leg., ch. 268, §1, eff. Sept. 1, 2003. Source: Former Fam. Code §14.13.

FAM §110.003. NO SEPARATE OR ADDITIONAL FILING FEE

The clerk of the court may not require:

(1) a separate filing fee in a suit joined with a suit for dissolution of marriage under Title 1; or

(2) an additional filing fee if more than one form of relief is requested in a suit.

History of Fam. Code §110.003: Acts 1995, 74th Leg., ch. 20, §1, eff. Apr. 20, 1995. Source: Former Fam. Code §11.18(b).

FAM §110.004. FEE FOR ISSUING & DELIVERING WITHHOLDING ORDER OR WRIT

The clerk of the court may charge a reasonable fee, not to exceed $15, for each order or writ of income withholding issued by the clerk and delivered to an employer.

History of Fam. Code §110.004: Acts 1995, 74th Leg., ch. 20, §1, eff. Apr. 20, 1995. Amended by Acts 1997, 75th Leg., ch. 911, §9, eff. Sept. 1, 1997. Source: Former Fam. Code §§14.43(i), 14.45(h).

FAM §110.005. TRANSFER FEE

(a) The fee for filing a transferred case is $45 payable to the clerk of the court to which the case is transferred. No portion of this fee may be sent to the state.

(b) A party may not be assessed any other fee, cost, charge, or expense by the clerk of the court or other public official in connection with filing of the transferred case.

(c) The fee limitation in this section does not affect a fee payable to the court transferring the case.

History of Fam. Code §110.005: Acts 1995, 74th Leg., ch. 20, §1, eff. Apr. 20, 1995. Source: Former Fam. Code §11.06(*l*).

FAM §110.006. DOMESTIC RELATIONS OFFICE OPERATIONS FEES & CHILD SUPPORT SERVICE FEES

(a) If an administering entity of a domestic relations office adopts an initial operations fee under Section 203.005(a)(1), the clerk of the court shall:

(1) collect the operations fee at the time the original suit, motion for modification, or motion for enforcement, as applicable, is filed; and

(2) send the fee to the domestic relations office.

(b) If an administering entity of a domestic relations office adopts an initial child support service fee under Section 203.005(a)(2), the clerk of the court shall:

(1) collect the child support service fee at the time the original suit is filed; and

(2) send the fee to the domestic relations office.

(c) The fees described by Subsections (a) and (b) are not filing fees for purposes of Section 110.002 or 110.003.

History of Fam. Code §110.006: Acts 1997, 75th Leg., ch. 702, §1, eff. Sept. 1, 1997. Amended by Acts 1999, 76th Leg., ch. 556, §5, eff. Sept. 1, 1999; Acts 2009, 81st Leg., ch. 767, §3 (eff. June 19, 2009), ch. 1035, §1 (eff. June 19, 2009).

CHAPTER 111. GUIDELINES FOR POSSESSION & CHILD SUPPORT

FAM §111.001. REVIEW OF GUIDELINES

(a) Prior to each regular legislative session, the standing committees of each house of the legislature having jurisdiction over family law issues shall review and, if necessary, recommend revisions to the guidelines for possession of and access to a child under Chapter 153. The committee shall report the results of the review and shall include any recommended revisions in the committee's report to the legislature.

(b) At least once every four years, the Title IV-D agency shall review the child support guidelines under Chapter 154 as required by 42 U.S.C. Section 667(a) and report the results of the review and any recommendations for any changes to the guidelines and their

manner of application to the standing committees of each house of the legislature having jurisdiction over family law issues.

History of Fam. Code §111.001: Acts 1995, 74th Leg., ch. 20, §1, eff. Apr. 20, 1995. Amended by Acts 1999, 76th Leg., ch. 556, §6, eff. Sept. 1, 1999; Acts 2011, 82nd Leg., ch. 8, §1, eff. Sept. 1, 2011. Source: Former Fam. Code §§14.03(j), 14.05(h), (i).

FAM §111.002. GUIDELINES SUPERSEDE COURT RULES

(a) The guidelines in this title supersede local court rules and rules of the supreme court that conflict with the guidelines.

(b) Notwithstanding other law, the guidelines may not be repealed or modified by a rule adopted by the supreme court.

History of Fam. Code §111.002: Acts 1995, 74th Leg., ch. 20, §1, eff. Apr. 20, 1995. Source: Former Fam. Code §§14.032(e), (f), 14.052(c), (d).

FAM §111.003. POSTING GUIDELINES

A copy of the guidelines for possession of and access to a child under Chapter 153 and a copy of the guidelines for the support of a child under Chapter 154 shall be prominently displayed at or near the entrance to the courtroom of every court having jurisdiction of a suit.

History of Fam. Code §111.003: Acts 1995, 74th Leg., ch. 20, §1, eff. Apr. 20, 1995. Source: Former Fam. Code §§14.033(p), 14.058.

Chapters 112-150 reserved for expansion

SUBTITLE B. SUITS AFFECTING THE PARENT-CHILD RELATIONSHIP

CHAPTER 151. RIGHTS & DUTIES IN PARENT-CHILD RELATIONSHIP

FAM §151.001. RIGHTS & DUTIES OF PARENT

(a) A parent of a child has the following rights and duties:

(1) the right to have physical possession, to direct the moral and religious training, and to designate the residence of the child;

(2) the duty of care, control, protection, and reasonable discipline of the child;

(3) the duty to support the child, including providing the child with clothing, food, shelter, medical and dental care, and education;

(4) the duty, except when a guardian of the child's estate has been appointed, to manage the estate of the child, including the right as an agent of the child to act in relation to the child's estate if the child's action is required by a state, the United States, or a foreign government;

(5) except as provided by Section 264.0111, the right to the services and earnings of the child;

(6) the right to consent to the child's marriage, enlistment in the armed forces of the United States, medical and dental care, and psychiatric, psychological, and surgical treatment;

(7) the right to represent the child in legal action and to make other decisions of substantial legal significance concerning the child;

(8) the right to receive and give receipt for payments for the support of the child and to hold or disburse funds for the benefit of the child;

(9) the right to inherit from and through the child;

(10) the right to make decisions concerning the child's education; and

(11) any other right or duty existing between a parent and child by virtue of law.

(b) The duty of a parent to support his or her child exists while the child is an unemancipated minor and continues as long as the child is fully enrolled in a secondary school in a program leading toward a high school diploma and complies with attendance requirements described by Section 154.002(a)(2).

(c) A parent who fails to discharge the duty of support is liable to a person who provides necessaries to those to whom support is owed.

(d) The rights and duties of a parent are subject to:

(1) a court order affecting the rights and duties;

(2) an affidavit of relinquishment of parental rights; and

(3) an affidavit by the parent designating another person or agency to act as managing conservator.

(e) Only the following persons may use corporal punishment for the reasonable discipline of a child:

(1) a parent or grandparent of the child;

(2) a stepparent of the child who has the duty of control and reasonable discipline of the child; and

(3) an individual who is a guardian of the child and who has the duty of control and reasonable discipline of the child.

History of Fam. Code §151.001: Acts 1995, 74th Leg., ch. 20, §1, eff. Apr. 20, 1995. Amended by Acts 1995, 74th Leg., ch. 751, §23, eff. Sept. 1, 1995; Acts 2001, 77th Leg., ch. 509, §2, eff. Sept. 1, 2001. Renumbered from §151.003 and amended by Acts 2001, 77th Leg., ch. 821, §2.13 (eff. June 14, 2001), ch. 964, §2 (eff. Sept. 1, 2001). Amended by Acts 2003, 78th Leg., ch. 1036, §3, eff. Sept. 1, 2003; Acts 2005, 79th Leg., ch. 924, §1, eff. Sept. 1, 2005; Acts 2007, 80th Leg., ch. 972, §6, eff. Sept. 1, 2007.

History of Former Fam. Code §151.001: Acts 1995, 74th Leg., ch. 20, §1, eff. Apr. 20, 1995. Deleted by Acts 2001, 77th Leg., ch. 821, §2.13, eff. June 14, 2001. Source: Former Fam. Code §§4.02, 12.04.

See also *O'Connor's Texas Family Law Handbook* (2017), "Parents' Rights & Duties," ch. 1-C, §3, p. 37; "Rights & Duties of Conservators," ch. 4-E, §4, p. 472.

ANNOTATIONS

Generally

R.W. v. TDPRS, 944 S.W.2d 437, 439-40 (Tex.App.—Houston [14th Dist.] 1997, no writ). "Under the ... Family Code, a presumed father is treated the same as all other parents, natural or adoptive. Just like all other parents, [presumed father] shouldered the duty to support the child, including providing the child with clothing, food, shelter, medical and dental care, and education and the duty of care, control, protection, and reasonable discipline of the child. And just like all other parents, these duties arose long before [presumed father] filed his voluntary statement of paternity and without regard to any adjudication by a court establishing his parentage. The duty existed from the moment [presumed father], by his actions, recognized the child as his own." (Internal quotes omitted.)

Care, Control & Protection

Rodriguez v. Spencer, 902 S.W.2d 37, 40-41 (Tex. App.—Houston [1st Dist.] 1995, no writ). Family Code §12.04, now §151.001(a)(2), "is limited to the parent-child relationship, not the parent-third party relationship. [T]he cases applying §12.04 have done so only when a parent faces criminal liability for acts or omissions toward his or her own child. [S]ection 12.04 does not establish a parent's duty to control or discipline children for the benefit of third parties."

Legal Representation

In re Bridgestone Americas Tire Opers., LLC, 459 S.W.3d 565, 577 (Tex.2015). "Texas law allows minors to sue by next friend [under TRCP 44] when they have a legal guardian who is not authorized to sue in Texas in that capacity. *At 572 n.9:* [Under Fam. Code §151.001(a)(4) and (7), a] parent ... typically qualifies as a legal guardian for purposes of Rule 44, and his minor child may not sue by next friend."

Patterson v. Planned Parenthood, Inc., 971 S.W.2d 439, 446 (Tex.1998). "[O]nly the parents or guardians of a minor may represent their legal interests."

In re Collins, 242 S.W.3d 837, 841 (Tex.App.—Houston [14th Dist.] 2007, orig. proceeding). Father "begins with the contention that, as [child's] father, he was authorized to assert [child's] wrongful death claims as [child's] next friend. The Grandparents respond that the prior court order granted [child's] mother the exclusive right to take legal action on [child's] behalf. *At 842:* Although a parent's right to 'possession' and issues of conservatorship (or the child's residence) are distinct legal concepts, we agree that the mother's rights to establish [child's] residence and to exercise [child's] legal rights were extinguished upon her death. At that time, the right to take legal action on [child's] behalf passed to [father] as her only surviving parent."

Medical Consent

Miller v. HCA, Inc., 118 S.W.3d 758, 766 (Tex. 2003). "[P]arents are presumed to be appropriate decision-makers, giving parents the right to consent to their infant's medical care and surgical treatment. A logical corollary of that right ... is that parents have the right not to consent to certain medical care for their infant, i.e., parents have the right to refuse certain medical care. [¶] Of course, this broad grant of parental decision-making authority is not without limits. The State's role as *parens patriae* permits it to intercede in parental decision-making under certain circumstances."

Support

Tucker v. Thomas, 419 S.W.3d 292, 300 (Tex.2013). Family Code "§151.001(c) may [not] be used as a vehicle for awarding attorney's fees in non-enforcement modification suits as necessaries or as additional child support. Section 151.001(c) conditions a parent's liability for necessaries upon a parent's *failure* to discharge the duty of support. Failure to support the child is not the basis for a non-enforcement modification suit under [Fam. Code] Ch. 156. In contrast, the failure to support a child is often the focus of enforcement proceedings under [Fam. Code] Ch. 157, and consistent with §151.001(c), the Legislature deliberately provided trial courts with authority to enforce an award of attorney's fees in enforcement suits by the same means available for enforcing a child support order. Further, the Legislature has specifically provided trial courts with discretion to characterize fees awarded to an amicus attor-

ney, attorney ad litem, or guardian ad litem appointed under [Fam. Code] Ch. 107 ... as necessaries, but it has not done the same for attorney's fees awarded to a party in a Ch. 156 modification suit. Because Ch. 156 is devoid of similar authorization, we conclude that the Legislature did not intend to provide trial courts with discretion to characterize attorney's fees incurred by a party in a non-enforcement modification suit as necessaries."

Harrington v. State, 547 S.W.2d 621, 624 (Tex. Crim.App.1977). "It is the duty of *each* parent to support his or her minor children. The fact that a father might entrust the care of his child to his wife or some other person does not relieve him of his responsibility to see that his child is properly cared for unless it is shown that some other person had *sole* and *exclusive* care, custody, and control of the minor child."

Bailey v. Bailey, 987 S.W.2d 206, 209 (Tex.App.—Amarillo 1999, no pet.). "[T]he scope of the duty to support was, and is, quite plenary. [I]t encompasses the rather boundless task of maintaining and educating, which at a minimum obligates the parents to provide the child those things necessary in sickness and health, such as clothing, food, shelter, medical and dental attention, and education." *See also* ***Woodruff v. Woodruff***, 487 S.W.2d 791, 793 (Tex.App.—Texarkana 1972, no writ) (college or university education is not general necessity, but special advantage).

Farish v. Farish, 982 S.W.2d 623, 628 (Tex.App.—Houston [1st Dist.] 1998, no pet.). "A child's right to be supported by his or her parents is a moral and legal right[,] the nature of which does not change upon remarriage by one or both of the parents."

Office of Atty. Gen. v. Carter, 977 S.W.2d 159, 160-61 (Tex.App.—Houston [14th Dist.] 1998, no pet.). "Each parent is obligated to support his or her child during the period of the child's minority, and is liable to *any person* who provides necessaries for that child. This duty is imposed at the birth of the child, and is not altered merely because the parents subsequently get divorced. Thus, *any person*, including the other parent, who provides necessaries for that child *may bring suit* to recover from a parent who fails to discharge that duty of support."

In re B.T., 954 S.W.2d 44, 49 (Tex.App.—San Antonio 1997, pet. denied). A parent's "duty of support exists regardless of whether a parent is court-ordered to support the child or not. [O]ccasional gifts are insufficient to fulfill a parent's obligation of support."

Klise v. Klise, 678 S.W.2d 545, 547 (Tex.App.—Houston [14th Dist.] 1984, no writ). Family Code §4.02, now §151.001, "does not require that the parents make mathematically equal contributions for the support of their children. It only provides that each parent has the equal obligation, in accordance with their respective ability, to contribute money or services to support and maintain the children. The fact that the parties have independent earning capacities is *not* to be included in this determination."

FAM §151.002. RIGHTS OF A LIVING CHILD AFTER AN ABORTION OR PREMATURE BIRTH

(a) A living human child born alive after an abortion or premature birth is entitled to the same rights, powers, and privileges as are granted by the laws of this state to any other child born alive after the normal gestation period.

(b) In this code, "born alive" means the complete expulsion or extraction from its mother of a product of conception, irrespective of the duration of pregnancy, which, after such separation, breathes or shows any other evidence of life such as beating of the heart, pulsation of the umbilical cord, or definite movement of voluntary muscles, whether or not the umbilical cord has been cut or the placenta is attached. Each product of the birth is considered born alive.

History of Fam. Code §151.002: Acts 1995, 74th Leg., ch. 20, §1, eff. Apr. 20, 1995. Renumbered from §151.004 by Acts 2001, 77th Leg., ch. 821, §2.13, eff. June 14, 2001.

History of Former Fam. Code §151.002: Acts 1995, 74th Leg., ch. 20, §1, eff. Apr. 20, 1995. Deleted by Acts 2001, 77th Leg., ch. 821, §2.13, eff. June 14, 2001. Source: Former Fam. Code §12.05.

FAM §151.003. LIMITATION ON STATE AGENCY ACTION

A state agency may not adopt rules or policies or take any other action that violates the fundamental right and duty of a parent to direct the upbringing of the parent's child.

History of Fam. Code §151.003: Acts 1999, 76th Leg., ch. 62, §6.18(a), eff. Sept. 1, 1999. Renumbered from §151.005 by Acts 2001, 77th Leg., ch. 821, §2.13, eff. June 14, 2001.

History of Former Fam. Code §151.003: Acts 1995, 74th Leg., ch. 20, §1, eff. Apr. 20, 1995. Amended by Acts 1995, 74th Leg., ch. 751, §23, eff. Sept. 1, 1995; Acts 2001, 77th Leg., ch. 509, §2, eff. Sept. 1, 2001. Renumbered as §151.001 by Acts 2001, 77th Leg., ch. 821, §2.13, eff. June 14, 2001.

FAM §§151.004, 151.005. RENUMBERED

Renumbered as §§151.002, 151.003 by Acts 2001, 77th Leg., ch. 821, §2.13, eff. June 14, 2001.

Sections 151.006-151.100 reserved for expansion

FAM §§151.101 TO 151.103. DELETED

Deleted by Acts 2001, 77th Leg., ch. 821, §2.13, eff. June 14, 2001.

CHAPTER 152. UNIFORM CHILD CUSTODY JURISDICTION & ENFORCEMENT ACT

NCCUSL Prefatory Comment*

This Act, the Uniform Child Custody Jurisdiction and Enforcement Act (UCCJEA), revisits the problem of the interstate child almost thirty years after the Conference promulgated the Uniform Child Custody Jurisdiction Act (UCCJA). The UCCJEA accomplishes two major purposes.

First, it revises the law on child custody jurisdiction in light of federal enactments and almost thirty years of inconsistent case law. Article 2 (Subchapter C) of this Act provides clearer standards for which states can exercise original jurisdiction over a child custody determination. It also, for the first time, enunciates a standard of continuing jurisdiction and clarifies modification jurisdiction. Other aspects of the article harmonize the law on simultaneous proceedings, clean hands, and forum non conveniens.

Second, this Act provides in Article 3 (Subchapter D) for a remedial process to enforce interstate child custody and visitation determinations. In doing so, it brings a uniform procedure to the law of interstate enforcement that is currently producing inconsistent results. In many respects, this Act accomplishes for custody and visitation determinations the same uniformity that has occurred in interstate child support with the promulgation of the Uniform Interstate Family Support Act (UIFSA).

Revision of Uniform Child Custody Jurisdiction Act

The UCCJA was adopted as law in all 50 states, the District of Columbia, and the Virgin Islands. A number of adoptions, however, significantly departed from the original text. In addition, almost thirty years of litigation since the promulgation of the UCCJA produced substantial inconsistency in interpretation by state courts. As a result, the goals of the UCCJA were rendered unobtainable in many cases.

In 1980, the federal government enacted the Parental Kidnapping Prevention Act (PKPA), 28 U.S.C. §1738A, to address the interstate custody jurisdictional problems that continued to exist after the adoption of the UCCJA. The PKPA mandates that state authorities give full faith and credit to other states' custody determinations, so long as those determinations were made in conformity with the provisions of the PKPA. The PKPA provisions regarding bases for jurisdiction, restrictions on modifications, preclusion of simultaneous proceedings, and notice requirements are similar to those in the UCCJA. There are, however, some significant differences. For example, the PKPA authorizes continuing exclusive jurisdiction in the original decree state so long as one parent or the child remains there and that state has continuing jurisdiction under its own law. The UCCJA did not directly address this issue. To further complicate the process, the PKPA partially incorporates state UCCJA law in its language. The relationship between these two statutes became "technical enough to delight a medieval property lawyer." Homer H. Clark, *Domestic Relations* §12.5 at 494 (2d ed. 1988).

As documented in an extensive study by the American Bar Association's Center on Children and the Law, *Obstacles to the Recovery and Return of Parentally Abducted Children* (1993) (*Obstacles Study*), inconsistency of interpretation of the UCCJA and the technicalities of applying the PKPA, resulted in a loss of uniformity among the states. The Obstacles Study suggested a number of amendments which would eliminate the inconsistent state interpretations and harmonize the UCCJA with the PKPA.

The revisions of the jurisdictional aspects of the UCCJA eliminate the inconsistent state interpretations and can be summarized as follows:

1. Home state priority. The PKPA prioritizes "home state" jurisdiction by requiring that full faith and credit cannot be given to a child custody determination by a state that exercises initial jurisdiction as a "significant connection state" when there is a "home state." Initial custody determinations based on "significant connections" are not entitled to PKPA enforcement unless there is no home state. The UCCJA, however, specifically authorizes four independent bases of jurisdiction without prioritization. Under the UCCJA, a signifi-

* **Editor's note:**

The NCCUSL comments have been edited to reflect the Texas Legislature's omission of sections, changing of text, and changing of section numbers from the original uniform act. The Texas Legislature did not adopt the NCCUSL comments when it adopted the Uniform Child Custody Jurisdiction Enforcement Act. The full uniform act and comments can be found at www.uniformlaws.org.

cant connection custody determination may have to be enforced even if it would be denied enforcement under the PKPA. The UCCJEA prioritizes home state jurisdiction in Section 152.201.

2. Clarification of emergency jurisdiction. There are several problems with the current emergency jurisdiction provision of the UCCJA §3(a)(3). First, the language of the UCCJA does not specify that emergency jurisdiction may be exercised only to protect the child on a temporary basis until the court with appropriate jurisdiction issues a permanent order. Some courts have interpreted the UCCJA language to so provide. Other courts, however, have held that there is no time limit on a custody determination based on emergency jurisdiction. Simultaneous proceedings and conflicting custody orders have resulted from these different interpretations.

Second, the emergency jurisdiction provisions predated the widespread enactment of state domestic violence statutes. Those statutes are often invoked to keep one parent away from the other parent and the children when there is a threat of violence. Whether these situations are sufficient to invoke the emergency jurisdiction provision of the UCCJA has been the subject of some confusion since the emergency jurisdiction provision does not specifically refer to violence directed against the parent of the child or against a sibling of the child.

The UCCJEA contains a separate section on emergency jurisdiction at Section 152.204 which addresses these issues.

3. Exclusive continuing jurisdiction for the state that entered the decree. The failure of the UCCJA to clearly enunciate that the decree-granting state retains exclusive continuing jurisdiction to modify a decree has resulted in two major problems. First, different interpretations of the UCCJA on continuing jurisdiction have produced conflicting custody decrees. States also have different interpretations as to how long continuing jurisdiction lasts. Some courts have held that modification jurisdiction continues until the last contestant leaves the state, regardless of how many years the child has lived outside the state or how tenuous the child's connections to the state have become. Other courts have held that continuing modification jurisdiction ends as soon as the child has established a new home state, regardless of how significant the child's connections to the decree state remain. Still other states distinguish between custody orders and visitation orders. This divergence of views leads to simultaneous proceedings and conflicting custody orders.

The second problem arises when it is necessary to determine whether the state with continuing jurisdiction has relinquished it. There should be a clear basis to determine when that court has relinquished jurisdiction. The UCCJA provided no guidance on this issue. The ambiguity regarding whether a court has declined jurisdiction can result in one court improperly exercising jurisdiction because it erroneously believes that the other court has declined jurisdiction. This caused simultaneous proceedings and conflicting custody orders. In addition, some courts have declined jurisdiction after only informal contact between courts with no opportunity for the parties to be heard. This raised significant due process concerns. The UCCJEA addresses these issues in Sections 152.110, 152.202, and 152.206.

4. Specification of what custody proceedings are covered. The definition of custody proceeding in the UCCJA is ambiguous. States have rendered conflicting decisions regarding certain types of proceedings. There is no general agreement on whether the UCCJA applies to neglect, abuse, dependency, wardship, guardianship, termination of parental rights, and protection from domestic violence proceedings. The UCCJEA includes a sweeping definition that, with the exception of adoption, includes virtually all cases that can involve custody of or visitation with a child as a "custody determination."

5. Role of "Best Interests." The jurisdictional scheme of the UCCJA was designed to promote the best interests of the children whose custody was at issue by discouraging parental abduction and providing that, in general, the state with the closest connections to, and the most evidence regarding, a child should decide that child's custody. The "best interest" language in the jurisdictional sections of the UCCJA was not intended to be an invitation to address the merits of the custody dispute in the jurisdictional determination or to otherwise provide that "best interests" considerations should override jurisdictional determinations or provide an additional jurisdictional basis.

The UCCJEA eliminates the term "best interests" in order to clearly distinguish between the jurisdictional standards and the substantive standards relating to custody and visitation of children.

6. Other changes. This draft also makes a number of additional amendments to the UCCJA. Many of these changes were made to harmonize the provisions of this Act with those of the Uniform Interstate Family Support Act. One of the policy bases underlying this Act is to make uniform the law of interstate family proceedings to the extent possible, given the very different jurisdictional foundations. It simplifies the life of the family law practitioner when the same or similar provisions are found in both Acts.

Enforcement Provisions

One of the major purposes of the revision of the UCCJA was to provide a remedy for interstate visitation and custody cases. As with child support, state borders have become one of the biggest obstacles to enforcement of custody and visitation orders. If either parent leaves the state where the custody determination was made, the other parent faces considerable difficulty in enforcing the visitation and custody provisions of the decree. Locating the child, making service of process, and preventing adverse modification in a new forum all present problems.

There is currently no uniform method of enforcing custody and visitation orders validly entered in another state. As documented by the *Obstacles Study*, despite the fact that both the UCCJA and the PKPA direct the enforcement of visitation and custody orders entered in accordance with mandated jurisdictional prerequisites and due process, neither act provides enforcement procedures or remedies.

As the *Obstacles Study* pointed out, the lack of specificity in enforcement procedures has resulted in the law of enforcement evolving differently in different jurisdictions. In one state, it might be common practice to file a Motion to Enforce or a Motion to Grant Full Faith and Credit to initiate an enforcement proceeding. In another state, a Writ of Habeas Corpus or a Citation for Contempt might be commonly used. In some states, Mandamus and Prohibition also may be utilized. All of these enforcement procedures differ from jurisdiction to jurisdiction. While many states tend to limit considerations in enforcement proceedings to whether the court which issued the decree had jurisdiction to make the custody determination, others broaden the considerations to scrutiny of whether enforcement would be in the best interests of the child.

Lack of uniformity complicates the enforcement process in several ways: (1) It increases the costs of the enforcement action in part because the services of more than one lawyer may be required—one in the original forum and one in the state where enforcement is sought; (2) It decreases the certainty of outcome; (3) It can turn enforcement into a long and drawn out procedure. A parent opposed to the provisions of a visitation determination may be able to delay implementation for many months, possibly even years, thereby frustrating not only the other parent, but also the process that led to the issuance of the original court order.

The provisions of Article 3 (Subchapter D) provide several remedies for the enforcement of a custody determination. First, there is a simple procedure for registering a custody determination in another state. This will allow a party to know in advance whether that state will recognize the party's custody determination. This is extremely important in estimating the risk of the child's non-return when the child is sent on visitation. The provision should prove to be very useful in international custody cases.

Second, the Act provides a swift remedy along the lines of habeas corpus. Time is extremely important in visitation and custody cases. If visitation rights cannot be enforced quickly, they often cannot be enforced at all. This is particularly true if there is a limited time within which visitation can be exercised such as may be the case when one parent has been granted visitation during the winter or spring holiday period. Without speedy consideration and resolution of the enforcement of such visitation rights, the ability to visit may be lost entirely. Similarly, a custodial parent must be able to obtain prompt enforcement when the noncustodial parent refuses to return a child at the end of authorized visitation, particularly when a summer visitation extension will infringe on the school year. A swift enforcement mechanism is desirable for violations of both custody and visitation provisions.

The scope of the enforcing court's inquiry is limited to the issue of whether the decree court had jurisdiction and complied with due process in rendering the original custody decree. No further inquiry is necessary because neither Article 2 (Subchapter C) nor the PKPA allows an enforcing court to modify a custody determination.

Third, the enforcing court will be able to utilize an extraordinary remedy. If the enforcing court is concerned that the parent, who has physical custody of the child, will flee or harm the child, a warrant to take physical possession of the child is available.

Finally, there is a role for public authorities, such as prosecutors, in the enforcement process. Their involvement will encourage the parties to abide by the terms of the custody determination. If the parties know that public authorities and law enforcement officers are available to help in securing compliance

with custody determinations, the parties may be deterred from interfering with the exercise of rights established by court order.

The involvement of public authorities will also prove more effective in remedying violations of custody determinations. Most parties do not have the resources to enforce a custody determination in another jurisdiction. The availability of the public authorities as an enforcement agency will help ensure that this remedy can be made available regardless of income level. In addition, the public authorities may have resources to draw on that are unavailable to the average litigant.

This Act does not authorize the public authorities to be involved in the action leading up to the making of the custody determination, except when requested by the court, when there is a violation of the Hague Convention on the Civil Aspects of International Child Abduction, or when the person holding the child has violated a criminal statute. The Act does not mandate that public authorities be involved in all cases. Not all states, or local authorities, have the funds necessary for an effective custody and visitation enforcement program.

SUBCHAPTER A. APPLICATION & CONSTRUCTION

FAM §152.001. APPLICATION & CONSTRUCTION

This chapter shall be applied and construed to promote the uniformity of the law among the states that enact it.

History of Fam. Code §152.001: Acts 1995, 74th Leg., ch. 20, §1, eff. Apr. 20, 1995. Renumbered from §152.001(a)(9), (b) by Acts 1999, 76th Leg., ch. 34, §1, eff. Sept. 1, 1999. Source: Former Fam. Code §11.51.

ANNOTATIONS

In re Forlenza, 140 S.W.3d 373, 375 (Tex.2004). "The UCCJEA was designed to eliminate inconsistent state interpretations of the UCCJA's jurisdictional aspects and to harmonize the UCCJA with the [Parental Kidnapping Prevention Act]."

McGuire v. McGuire, 18 S.W.3d 801, 806 (Tex. App.—El Paso 2000, no pet.). "[C]ase law under the former Texas version of the [UCCJA] regarding continuing jurisdiction will have little, if any, precedent value under the new act." (Internal quotes omitted.)

FAM §152.002. CONFLICTS BETWEEN PROVISIONS

If a provision of this chapter conflicts with a provision of this title or another statute or rule of this state and the conflict cannot be reconciled, this chapter prevails.

History of Fam. Code §152.002: Acts 1999, 76th Leg., ch. 34, §1, eff. Sept. 1, 1999.

ANNOTATIONS

In re Bellamy, 67 S.W.3d 482, 484 (Tex.App.—Texarkana 2002, no pet.), *disapproved on other grounds*, ***In re Forlenza***, 140 S.W.3d 373 (Tex.2004). "[W]e find that [Fam. Code] §§152.202 and 155.003(b)(1) conflict in this case. When a provision of Ch. 152 conflicts with another provision of the Family Code or another statute or rule of Texas and the conflict cannot be reconciled, Ch. 152 prevails. Under the UCCJEA, Texas retains jurisdiction even if Texas is no longer the home state of the child or of the custodial parent, so long as there is a significant connection with this state." *See also* ***In re McCormick***, 87 S.W.3d 746, 750 (Tex.App.—Amarillo 2002, orig. proceeding).

FAM §§152.003 TO 152.025. DELETED

Deleted by Acts 1999, 76th Leg., ch. 34, §1, eff. Sept. 1, 1999.

Sections 152.026-152.100 reserved for expansion

SUBCHAPTER B. GENERAL PROVISIONS

FAM §152.101. SHORT TITLE

This chapter may be cited as the Uniform Child Custody Jurisdiction and Enforcement Act.

History of Fam. Code §152.101: Acts 1995, 74th Leg., ch. 20, §1, eff. Apr. 20, 1995. Renumbered from §152.025 by Acts 1999, 76th Leg., ch. 34, §1, eff. Sept. 1, 1999. Source: Former Fam. Code §11.75.

NCCUSL Comment*

Section 1 of the UCCJA was a statement of the purposes of the Act. Although extensively cited by courts, it was eliminated because Uniform Acts no longer contain such a section. Nonetheless, this Act should be interpreted according to its purposes which are to:

(1) Avoid jurisdictional competition and conflict with courts of other states in matters of child custody which have in the past resulted in the shifting of children from state to state with harmful effects on their well-being;

(2) Promote cooperation with the courts of other states to the end that a custody decree is rendered in that state which can best decide the case in the interest of the child;

(3) Discourage the use of the interstate system for continuing controversies over child custody;

(4) Deter abductions of children;

(5) Avoid relitigation of custody decisions of other states in this state; and

(6) Facilitate the enforcement of custody decrees of other states.

FAM §152.102. DEFINITIONS

In this chapter:

(1) "Abandoned" means left without provision for reasonable and necessary care or supervision.

(2) "Child" means an individual who has not attained 18 years of age.

(3) "Child custody determination" means a judgment, decree, or other order of a court providing for legal custody, physical custody, or visitation with respect to a child. The term includes permanent, temporary, initial, and modification orders. The term does not include an order relating to child support or another monetary obligation of an individual.

(4) "Child custody proceeding" means a proceeding in which legal custody, physical custody, or visitation with respect to a child is an issue. The term includes a

* See footnote on p. 472.

FAM §152.001

proceeding for divorce, separation, neglect, abuse, dependency, guardianship, paternity, termination of parental rights, and protection from domestic violence in which the issue may appear. The term does not include a proceeding involving juvenile delinquency, contractual emancipation, or enforcement under Subchapter D.

(5) "Commencement" means the filing of the first pleading in a proceeding.

(6) "Court" means an entity authorized under the law of a state to establish, enforce, or modify a child custody determination.

(7) "Home state" means the state in which a child lived with a parent or a person acting as a parent for at least six consecutive months immediately before the commencement of a child custody proceeding. In the case of a child less than six months of age, the term means the state in which the child lived from birth with a parent or a person acting as a parent. A period of temporary absence of a parent or a person acting as a parent is part of the period.

(8) "Initial determination" means the first child custody determination concerning a particular child.

(9) "Issuing court" means the court that makes a child custody determination for which enforcement is sought under this chapter.

(10) "Issuing state" means the state in which a child custody determination is made.

(11) "Legal custody" means the managing conservatorship of a child.

(12) "Modification" means a child custody determination that changes, replaces, supersedes, or is otherwise made after a previous determination concerning the same child, whether or not it is made by the court that made the previous determination.

(13) "Person acting as a parent" means a person, other than a parent, who:

(A) has physical custody of the child or has had physical custody for a period of six consecutive months, including any temporary absence, within one year immediately before the commencement of a child custody proceeding; and

(B) has been awarded legal custody by a court or claims a right to legal custody under the law of this state.

(14) "Physical custody" means the physical care and supervision of a child.

(15) "Tribe" means an Indian tribe or band, or Alaskan Native village, that is recognized by federal law or formally acknowledged by a state.

(16) "Visitation" means the possession of or access to a child.

(17) "Warrant" means an order issued by a court authorizing law enforcement officers to take physical custody of a child.

History of Fam. Code §152.102: Acts 1995, 74th Leg., ch. 20, §1, eff. Apr. 20, 1995. Renumbered from §152.002 by Acts 1999, 76th Leg., ch. 34, §1, eff. Sept. 1, 1999. Source: Former Fam. Code §11.52.

ANNOTATIONS

In re Dean, 393 S.W.3d 741, 749 (Tex.2012). Father "asserts that the home state rule [unconstitutionally] violates [his equal-protection rights] because a woman controls where she lives prior to giving birth, and that [deprives the father] of immediate post-birth involvement. [¶] [Family Code] §152.201(a) is a procedural mechanism for determining jurisdiction. The statute defines home state to establish where the proceedings should take place, without a bias for either parent. The *place of birth* is not the relevant consideration. Instead, we look to 'the State in which the child lived *from* birth with [a parent or person acting as a parent].' Residence is determinative, and it favors neither women nor men. A child could live 'from birth' with his father or his mother, and [Fam. Code] §§152.102(7) and 152.201(a) would apply with equal force in either scenario." Held: Home-state rule did not violate father's equal-protection rights under either the Texas Equal Rights Amendment or the 14th Amendment to the U.S. Constitution.

Powell v. Stover, 165 S.W.3d 322, 323 (Tex.2005). "We hold that, because the child lived in Tennessee with his parents for at least six consecutive months immediately before the child-custody proceeding was commenced, Texas is not the child's home state and the trial court's exercise of jurisdiction was improper. *At 326:* The Family Code defines 'home state' as the state in which a child 'lived' with a parent. The word 'lived' strongly connotes physical presence. [¶] The purposes behind the UCCJEA further suggest that a child's physical location is the central factor to be considered when determining a child's home state. The UCCJEA was intended to give prominence to objective factors. *At 327:* [A] test based on the totality of the circumstances suffers from essentially the same weakness as a purely intent-based test; both seek to promote

flexibility at the expense of the jurisdictional certainty that the home-state provision was intended to provide. *At 328:* We therefore hold that in determining where a child lived for purposes of establishing home-state jurisdiction, the trial court must consider the child's physical presence in a state." *See also* ***Seligman-Hargis v. Hargis***, 186 S.W.3d 582, 586 (Tex.App.—Dallas 2006, no pet.) (evidence established children had never lived in Texas and had been in Germany since 1997, so Germany was home state).

In re Walker, 428 S.W.3d 212, 218 (Tex.App.—Houston [1st Dist.] 2014, orig. proceeding). Child "was born ... in Georgia and lived there the majority of her life. On May 25, 2012, [father] purportedly 'moved' to Texas with [child]; however, within a very short time [father] and [child] returned to Georgia where they lived at the same residence as they had prior to May 25, 2012. [Father], with [child], finally left Georgia for Texas on July 25, 2012. [Father] instituted this proceeding on November 27, 2012. Because [child] did not move from Georgia until July 25, 2012, and July 25, 2012 is within six months of November 27, 2012, Georgia was [child's] home state within six months of the initiation of this child custody proceeding. [¶] [A]lthough [child] was absent from Georgia from May 25, 2012 until June 2012, this does not affect Georgia's home state jurisdiction. 'A temporary absence from the state continues to count as though the child lived within the state for purposes of determining the home state.'" *See also* ***In re K.Y.***, 273 S.W.3d 703, 707 (Tex. App.—Houston [14th Dist.] 2008, no pet.) (Texas was considered children's home state even though they took frequent trips to Oklahoma to visit foster parent during six-month period before suit was filed; such visits do not show that children moved from Texas). *But see* ***In re Tieri***, this page.

Berwick v. Wagner, 336 S.W.3d 805, 811 (Tex. App.—Houston [1st Dist.] 2011, pet. denied). One of child's adoptive fathers "contends that a parentage order cannot be a child custody determination under the UCCJEA absent *express* adjudication of custody in the judgment. [¶] [W]e conclude the trial court correctly recognized the ... judgment as a child custody determination because it resulted from proceedings in which 'legal custody, physical custody, or visitation [was] an issue' between the presumptive and intended parents. While custody was not disputed between [the two fathers] in that proceeding, it was very much at issue with relation to [child's] surrogate mother and her husband.... *At 812:* [N]ot all proceedings related to parentage involve custody. But many do, either expressly or by implication. *At 813:* [W]e are unpersuaded by [the] argument that the judgment must expressly mention the word 'custody' to qualify as a child custody determination. *At 814:* Because the ... order both terminates [child's] presumptive parental rights and grants exclusive parental rights and—by implication—custody to [the fathers], the trial court correctly concluded it qualifies as a 'child custody determination' for purposes of [Fam. Code] §152.305."

In re Tieri, 283 S.W.3d 889, 894 (Tex.App.—Tyler 2008, orig. proceeding). "Although a temporary absence of a parent is part of the [six-month requirement to find a child's home state under §152.102(7)], there is no provision for the children's temporary absence from the state. ... However, the respondent court characterized the absence of the children from Texas ... as 'temporary.' [¶] In total, the children lived in Texas for seven months before [mother] filed for divorce and custody.... However, these months were not consecutive. ... Because the children did not live with [mother] in Texas for a period of six consecutive months before she filed for divorce and custody, Texas is not the children's home state. Therefore, the respondent court abused its discretion by including periods of absence from the state in calculating the length of the children's residence in Texas." *But see* ***In re Walker***, this page.

In re Burk, 252 S.W.3d 736, 740 (Tex.App.—Houston [14th Dist.] 2008, orig. proceeding). Mother "contends Texas is not the 'home state' because 'home state' is defined as 'the' state in which the child lived from birth. [She] contends this means the child must have lived in only one state from birth. [Mother] argues [child] has not lived in Texas, i.e., 'the state,' *from birth* because [child] lived in more than one state before commencement of the proceeding. [Father] claims the language requires only that Texas must have been the child's home state at some time *within six months before* commencement of the proceeding. *At 741:* There is no indication the legislature intended 'the home state ... within six months,' to apply only to children six months of age or older. [¶] We agree with [father's] interpretation."

NCCUSL Comment*

The UCCJA did not contain a definition of "child." The definition here is taken from the PKPA.

* See footnote on p. 472.

The definition of "child-custody determination" now closely tracks the PKPA definition. It encompasses any judgment, decree or other order which provides for the custody of, or visitation with, a child, regardless of local terminology, including such labels as "managing conservatorship" or "parenting plan."

The definition of "child-custody proceeding" has been expanded from the comparable definition in the UCCJA. These listed proceedings have generally been determined to be the type of proceeding to which the UCCJA and PKPA are applicable. The list of examples removes any controversy about the types of proceedings where a custody determination can occur. Proceedings that affect access to the child are subject to this Act. The inclusion of proceedings related to protection from domestic violence is necessary because in some states domestic violence proceedings may affect custody of and visitation with a child. Juvenile delinquency or proceedings to confer contractual rights are not "custody proceedings" because they do not relate to civil aspects of access to a child. While a determination of paternity is covered under the Uniform Interstate Family Support Act, the custody and visitation aspects of paternity cases are custody proceedings. Cases involving the Hague Convention on the Civil Aspects of International Child Abduction have not been included at this point because custody of the child is not determined in a proceeding under the International Child Abductions Remedies Act. Those proceedings are specially included in the Subchapter D enforcement process.

"Commencement" has been included in the definitions as a replacement for the term "pending" found in the UCCJA. Its inclusion simplifies some of the simultaneous proceedings provisions of this Act.

The definition of "home state" has been reworded slightly. No substantive change is intended from the UCCJA.

The term "issuing state" is borrowed from UIFSA. In UIFSA, it refers to the court that issued the support or parentage order. Here, it refers to the state, or the court, which made the custody determination that is sought to be enforced. It is used primarily in Subchapter D.

The term "person acting as a parent" has been slightly redefined. It has been broadened from the definition in the UCCJA to include a person who has acted as a parent for a significant period of time prior to the filing of the custody proceeding as well as a person who currently has physical custody of the child. In addition, a person acting as a parent must either have legal custody or claim a right to legal custody under the law of this state. The reference to the law of this state means that a court determines the issue of whether someone is a "person acting as a parent" under its own law. This reaffirms the traditional view that a court in a child custody case applies its own substantive law. The court does not have to undertake a choice-of-law analysis to determine whether the individual who is claiming to be a person acting as a parent has standing to seek custody of the child.

The definition of "tribe" is the one mandated for use in Uniform Acts. Should a state choose to apply this Act to tribal adjudications, this definition should be enacted as well as the entirety of Section 152.104.

The term "contestant" as has been omitted from this revision. It was defined in the UCCJA §2(1) as "a person, including a parent, who claims a right to custody or visitation rights with respect to a child." It seems to have served little purpose over the years, and whatever function it once had has been subsumed by state laws on who has standing to seek custody of or visitation with a child. In addition UCCJA §2(5) which defined "decree" and "custody decree" has been eliminated as duplicative of the definition of "custody determination."

FAM §152.103. PROCEEDINGS GOVERNED BY OTHER LAW

This chapter does not govern an adoption proceeding or a proceeding pertaining to the authorization of emergency medical care for a child.

History of Fam. Code §152.103: Acts 1999, 76th Leg., ch. 34, §1, eff. Sept. 1, 1999.

NCCUSL Comment*

Two proceedings are governed by other acts. Adoption cases are excluded from this Act because adoption is a specialized area which is thoroughly covered by the Uniform Adoption Act (UAA) (1994). Most states either will adopt that Act or will adopt the jurisdictional provisions of that Act. Therefore the jurisdictional provisions governing adoption proceeding are generally found elsewhere.

However, there are likely to be a number of instances where it will be necessary to apply this Act in an adoption proceeding. For example, if a state adopts the UAA then Section 3-101 of the Act specifically refers in places to the Uniform Child Custody Jurisdiction Act which will become a reference to this Act. Second, the UAA requires that if an adoption is denied or set aside, the court is to determine the child's custody. UAA §3-704. Those custody proceedings would be subject to this Act. See Joan Heifetz Hollinger, The Uniform Adoption Act: Reporter's Ruminations, 30 Fam.L.Q. 345 (1996).

Children that are the subject of interstate placements for adoption or foster care are governed by the Interstate Compact on the Placement of Children (ICPC). The UAA §2-107 provides that the provisions of the compact, although not jurisdictional, supply the governing rules for all children who are subject to it. As stated in the Comments to that section: "Once a court exercises jurisdiction, the ICPC helps determine the legality of an interstate placement." For a discussion of the relationship between the UCCJA and the ICPC see *J.D.S. v. Franks*, 893 P.2d 732 (Ariz. 1995). [Texas has not adopted the UAA.]

Proceedings pertaining to the authorization of emergency medical care for children are outside the scope of this Act since they are not custody determinations. All states have procedures which allow the state to temporarily supersede parental authority for purposes of emergency medical procedures. Those provisions will govern without regard to this Act.

FAM §152.104. APPLICATION TO INDIAN TRIBES

(a) A child custody proceeding that pertains to an Indian child as defined in the Indian Child Welfare Act of 1978 (25 U.S.C. Section 1901 et seq.) is not subject to this chapter to the extent that it is governed by the Indian Child Welfare Act.

(b) A court of this state shall treat a tribe as if it were a state of the United States for the purpose of applying this subchapter and Subchapter C.

(c) A child custody determination made by a tribe under factual circumstances in substantial conformity with the jurisdictional standards of this chapter must be recognized and enforced under Subchapter D.

History of Fam. Code §152.104: Acts 1999, 76th Leg., ch. 34, §1, eff. Sept. 1, 1999.

NCCUSL Comment*

The definition of "tribe" is found at Section 152.102(15). This Act does not purport to legislate custody jurisdiction for tribal courts. However, a Tribe could adopt this Act as enabling legislation by simply replacing references to "this state" with "this Tribe."

If the Indian Child Welfare Act requires that a case be heard in tribal court, then its provisions determine jurisdiction.

FAM §152.105. INTERNATIONAL APPLICATION OF CHAPTER

(a) A court of this state shall treat a foreign country as if it were a state of the United States for the purpose of applying this subchapter and Subchapter C.

(b) Except as otherwise provided in Subsection (c), a child custody determination made in a foreign country under factual circumstances in substantial conformity with the jurisdictional standards of this chapter must be recognized and enforced under Subchapter D.

* See footnote on p. 472.

(c) A court of this state need not apply this chapter if the child custody law of a foreign country violates fundamental principles of human rights.

(d) A record of all of the proceedings under this chapter relating to a child custody determination made in a foreign country or to the enforcement of an order for the return of the child made under the Hague Convention on the Civil Aspects of International Child Abduction shall be made by a court reporter or as provided by Section 201.009.

History of Fam. Code §152.105: Acts 1995, 74th Leg., ch. 20, §1, eff. Apr. 20, 1995. Renumbered from §152.023 by Acts 1999, 76th Leg., ch. 34, §1, eff. Sept. 1, 1999. Amended by Acts 2011, 82nd Leg., ch. 92, §1, eff. Sept. 1, 2011. Source: Former Fam. Code §11.73.

NCCUSL Comment*

The provisions of this Act have international application to child custody proceedings and determinations of other countries. Another country will be treated as if it were a state of the United States for purposes of applying Subchapters A, B, and C of this Act. Custody determinations of other countries will be enforced if the facts of the case indicate that jurisdiction was in substantial compliance with the requirements of this Act.

In this section, the term "child-custody determination" should be interpreted to include proceedings relating to custody or analogous institutions of the other country. See generally, Article 3 of The Hague Convention on Jurisdiction, Applicable Law, Recognition, Enforcement and Co-operation in Respect of Parental Responsibility and Measures for the Protection of Children. 35 I.L.M. 1391 (1996).

A court of this state may refuse to apply this Act when the child custody law of the other country violates basic principles relating to the protection of human rights and fundamental freedoms. The same concept is found in Section 20 of the Hague Convention on the Civil Aspects of International Child Abduction (return of the child may be refused if this would not be permitted by the fundamental principles of the requested state relating to the protection of human rights and fundamental freedoms). In applying subsection (c), the court's scrutiny should be on the child custody law of the foreign country and not on other aspects of the other legal system. This Act takes no position on what laws relating to child custody would violate fundamental freedoms. While the provision is a traditional one in international agreements, it is invoked only in the most egregious cases.

This section is derived from Section 23 of the UCCJA.

FAM §152.106. EFFECT OF CHILD CUSTODY DETERMINATION

A child custody determination made by a court of this state that had jurisdiction under this chapter binds all persons who have been served in accordance with the laws of this state or notified in accordance with Section 152.108 or who have submitted to the jurisdiction of the court and who have been given an opportunity to be heard. As to those persons, the determination is conclusive as to all decided issues of law and fact except to the extent the determination is modified.

History of Fam. Code §152.106: Acts 1995, 74th Leg., ch. 20, §1, eff. Apr. 20, 1995. Renumbered from §152.012 by Acts 1999, 76th Leg., ch. 34, §1, eff. Sept. 1, 1999. Source: Former Fam. Code §11.62.

NCCUSL Comment*

No substantive changes have been made to this section which was Section 12 of the UCCJA.

* See footnote on p. 472.

FAM §152.107. PRIORITY

If a question of existence or exercise of jurisdiction under this chapter is raised in a child custody proceeding, the question, upon request of a party, must be given priority on the calendar and handled expeditiously.

History of Fam. Code §152.107: Acts 1995, 74th Leg., ch. 20, §1, eff. Apr. 20, 1995. Renumbered from §152.024 by Acts 1999, 76th Leg., ch. 34, §1, eff. Sept. 1, 1999. Source: Former Fam. Code §11.74.

NCCUSL Comment*

No substantive change was made to this section which was Section 24 of the UCCJA. The section is placed toward the beginning of Subchapter B to emphasize its importance.

The language change from "case" to "question" is intended to clarify that it is the jurisdictional issue which must be expedited and not the entire custody case. Whether the entire custody case should be given priority is a matter of local law.

FAM §152.108. NOTICE TO PERSONS OUTSIDE STATE

(a) Notice required for the exercise of jurisdiction when a person is outside this state may be given in a manner prescribed by the law of this state for service of process or by the law of the state in which the service is made. Notice must be given in a manner reasonably calculated to give actual notice but may be by publication if other means are not effective.

(b) Proof of service may be made in the manner prescribed by the law of this state or by the law of the state in which the service is made.

(c) Notice is not required for the exercise of jurisdiction with respect to a person who submits to the jurisdiction of the court.

History of Fam. Code §152.108: Acts 1995, 74th Leg., ch. 20, §1, eff. Apr. 20, 1995. Amended by Acts 1999, 76th Leg., ch. 178, §6, eff. Aug. 30, 1999. Renumbered from §152.005 and amended by Acts 1999, 76th Leg., ch. 34, §1, eff. Sept. 1, 1999. Source: Former Fam. Code §11.55.

NCCUSL Comment*

This section authorizes notice and proof of service to be made by any method allowed by either the state which issues the notice or the state where the notice is received. This eliminates the need to specify the type of notice in the Act and therefore the provisions of Section 5 of the UCCJA which specified how notice was to be accomplished were eliminated. The change reflects an approach in this Act to use local law to determine many procedural issues. Thus, service by facsimile is permissible if allowed by local rule in either state. In addition, where special service or notice rules are available for some procedures, in either jurisdiction, they could be utilized under this Act. For example, if a case involves domestic violence and the statute of either state would authorize notice to be served by a peace officer, such service could be used under this Act.

Although Section 152.105 requires foreign countries to be treated as states for purposes of this Act, attorneys should be cautioned about service and notice in foreign countries. Countries have their own rules on service which must usually be followed. Attorneys should consult the Hague Convention on the Service Abroad of Judicial and Extrajudicial Documents in Civil or Commercial Matters, 20 U.S.T. 36, T.I.A.S. 6638 (1965).

FAM §152.109. APPEARANCE & LIMITED IMMUNITY

(a) A party to a child custody proceeding, including a modification proceeding, or a petitioner or respon-

dent in a proceeding to enforce or register a child custody determination, is not subject to personal jurisdiction in this state for another proceeding or purpose solely by reason of having participated, or of having been physically present for the purpose of participating, in the proceeding.

(b) A person who is subject to personal jurisdiction in this state on a basis other than physical presence is not immune from service of process in this state. A party present in this state who is subject to the jurisdiction of another state is not immune from service of process allowed under the laws of that state.

(c) The immunity granted by Subsection (a) does not extend to civil litigation based on acts unrelated to the participation in a proceeding under this chapter committed by an individual while present in this state.

History of Fam. Code §152.109: Acts 1999, 76th Leg., ch. 34, §1, eff. Sept. 1, 1999.

NCCUSL Comment*

This section establishes a general principle that participation in a custody proceeding does not, by itself, give the court jurisdiction over any issue for which personal jurisdiction over the individual is required. The term "participate" should be read broadly. For example, if jurisdiction is proper under Subchapter C, a respondent in an original custody determination, or a party in a modification determination, should be able to request custody without this constituting the seeking of affirmative relief that would waive personal jurisdictional objections. Once jurisdiction is proper under Subchapter C, a party should not be placed in the dilemma of choosing between seeking custody or protecting a right not to be subject to a monetary judgment by a court with no other relationship to the party.

This section is comparable to the immunity provision of UIFSA §314. A party who is otherwise not subject to personal jurisdiction can appear in a custody proceeding or an enforcement action without being subject to the general jurisdiction of the state by virtue of the appearance. However, if the petitioner would otherwise be subject to the jurisdiction of the state, appearing in a custody proceeding or filing an enforcement proceeding will not provide immunity. Thus, if the non-custodial parent moves from the state that decided the custody determination, that parent is still subject to the state's jurisdiction for enforcement of child support if the child or an individual obligee continues to reside there. See also UIFSA §205. If the non-custodial parent returns to enforce the visitation aspects of the custody determination, the state can utilize any appropriate means to collect the back-due child support. However, the situation is different if both parties move from State A after the determination, with the custodial parent and the child establishing a new home state in State B, and the non-custodial parent moving to State C. The non-custodial parent is not, at this point, subject to the jurisdiction of State B for monetary matters. See also *Kulko v. Superior Court*, 436 U.S. 84 (1978). If the non-custodial parent comes into State B to enforce the visitation aspects of the determination, the non-custodial parent is not subject to the jurisdiction of State B for those proceedings and issues requiring personal jurisdiction by filing the enforcement action.

A party also is immune from service of process during the time in the state for an enforcement action except for those claims for which jurisdiction could be based on contacts other than mere physical presence. Thus, when the non-custodial parent comes into State B to enforce the visitation aspects of the decree, State B cannot acquire jurisdiction over the child support aspects of the decree by serving the non-custodial parent in the state. *Cf.* UIFSA §611 (personally serving the obligor in the state of the residence of the obligee is not by itself a sufficient jurisdictional basis to authorize a modification of child support). However, a party who is in this state and subject to the jurisdiction of another state may be served with process to appear in that state, if allowable under the laws of that state.

As the Comments to UIFSA §314 note, the immunity provided by this section is limited. It does not provide immunity for civil litigation unrelated to the enforcement action. For example, a party to an enforcement action is not immune from service regarding a claim that involves an automobile accident occurring while the party is in the state.

FAM §152.110. COMMUNICATION BETWEEN COURTS

(a) In this section, "record" means information that is inscribed on a tangible medium or that is stored in an electronic or other medium and is retrievable in perceivable form.

(b) A court of this state may communicate with a court in another state concerning a proceeding arising under this chapter.

(c) The court may allow the parties to participate in the communication. If the parties are not able to participate in the communication, they must be given the opportunity to present facts and legal arguments before a decision on jurisdiction is made.

(d) If proceedings involving the same parties are pending simultaneously in a court of this state and a court of another state, the court of this state shall inform the other court of the simultaneous proceedings. The court of this state shall request that the other court hold the proceeding in that court in abeyance until the court in this state conducts a hearing to determine whether the court has jurisdiction over the proceeding.

(e) Communication between courts on schedules, calendars, court records, and similar matters may occur without informing the parties. A record need not be made of the communication.

(f) Except as otherwise provided in Subsection (e), a record must be made of any communication under this section. The parties must be informed promptly of the communication and granted access to the record.

History of Fam. Code §152.110: Acts 1999, 76th Leg., ch. 34, §1, eff. Sept. 1, 1999. Amended by Acts 2001, 77th Leg., ch. 329, §1, eff. May 25, 2001.

NCCUSL Comment*

This section emphasizes the role of judicial communications. It authorizes a court to communicate concerning any proceeding arising under this Act. This includes communication with foreign tribunals and tribal courts. Communication can occur in many different ways such as by telephonic conference and by on-line or other electronic communication. The Act does not preclude any method of communication and recognizes that there will be increasing use of modern communication techniques.

Communication between courts is required under Sections 152.204, 152.206, and 152.306 and strongly suggested in applying Section 152.207. Apart from those sections, there may be less need under this Act for courts to communicate concerning jurisdiction due to the prioritization of home state jurisdiction. Communication is authorized, however, whenever the court finds it would be helpful. The court may authorize the parties to participate in the communication. However, the Act does not mandate participation. Communication between courts is often difficult to schedule and participation by the parties may be impractical. Phone calls often have to be made after-hours or whenever the schedules of judges allow.

* See footnote on p. 472.

This section does require that a record be made of the conversation and that the parties have access to that record in order to be informed of the content of the conversation. The only exception to this requirement is when the communication involves relatively inconsequential matters such as scheduling, calendars, and court records. Included within this latter type of communication would be matters of cooperation between courts under Section 152.112. A record includes notes or transcripts of a court reporter who listened to a conference call between the courts, an electronic recording of a telephone call, a memorandum or an electronic record of the communication between the courts, or a memorandum or an electronic record made by a court after the communication.

The second sentence of subsection (c) protects the parties against unauthorized ex parte communications. The parties' participation in the communication may amount to a hearing if there is an opportunity to present facts and jurisdictional arguments. However, absent such an opportunity, the participation of the parties should not to be considered a substitute for a hearing and the parties must be given an opportunity to fairly and fully present facts and arguments on the jurisdictional issue before a determination is made. This may be done through a hearing or, if appropriate, by affidavit or memorandum. The court is expected to set forth the basis for its jurisdictional decision, including any court-to-court communication which may have been a factor in the decision.

FAM §152.111. TAKING TESTIMONY IN ANOTHER STATE

(a) In addition to other procedures available to a party, a party to a child custody proceeding may offer testimony of witnesses who are located in another state, including testimony of the parties and the child, by deposition or other means allowed in this state for testimony taken in another state. The court on its own motion may order that the testimony of a person be taken in another state and may prescribe the manner in which and the terms upon which the testimony is taken.

(b) A court of this state may permit an individual residing in another state to be deposed or to testify by telephone, audiovisual means, or other electronic means before a designated court or at another location in that state. A court of this state shall cooperate with courts of other states in designating an appropriate location for the deposition or testimony.

(c) Documentary evidence transmitted from another state to a court of this state by technological means that do not produce an original writing may not be excluded from evidence on an objection based on the means of transmission.

History of Fam. Code §152.111: Acts 1995, 74th Leg., ch. 20, §1, eff. Apr. 20, 1995. Renumbered from §152.018 by Acts 1999, 76th Leg., ch. 34, §1, eff. Sept. 1, 1999. Source: Former Fam. Code §11.68.

NCCUSL Comment*

No substantive changes have been made to subsection (a) which was Section 18 of the UCCJA.

Subsections (b) and (c) merely provide that modern modes of communication are permissible in the taking of testimony and the transmittal of documents. See also UIFSA §316.

* See footnote on p. 472.

FAM §152.112. COOPERATION BETWEEN COURTS; PRESERVATION OF RECORDS

(a) A court of this state may request the appropriate court of another state to:

(1) hold an evidentiary hearing;

(2) order a person to produce or give evidence pursuant to procedures of that state;

(3) order that an evaluation be made with respect to the custody of a child involved in a pending proceeding;

(4) forward to the court of this state a certified copy of the transcript of the record of the hearing, the evidence otherwise presented, and any evaluation prepared in compliance with the request; and

(5) order a party to a child custody proceeding or any person having physical custody of the child to appear in the proceeding with or without the child.

(b) Upon request of a court of another state, a court of this state may hold a hearing or enter an order described in Subsection (a).

(c) Travel and other necessary and reasonable expenses incurred under Subsections (a) and (b) may be assessed against the parties according to the law of this state.

(d) A court of this state shall preserve the pleadings, orders, decrees, records of hearings, evaluations, and other pertinent records with respect to a child custody proceeding until the child attains 18 years of age. Upon appropriate request by a court or law enforcement official of another state, the court shall forward a certified copy of those records.

History of Fam. Code §152.112: Acts 1995, 74th Leg., ch. 20, §1, eff. Apr. 20, 1995. Renumbered from §§152.019-152.021 by Acts 1999, 76th Leg., ch. 34, §1, eff. Sept. 1, 1999. Source: Former Fam. Code §§11.69-11.71.

NCCUSL Comment*

This section is the heart of judicial cooperation provision of this Act. It provides mechanisms for courts to cooperate with each other in order to decide cases in an efficient manner without causing undue expense to the parties. Courts may request assistance from courts of other states and may assist courts of other states.

The provision on the assessment of costs for travel provided in the UCCJA §19 has been changed. The UCCJA provided that the costs may be assessed against the parties or the state or county. Assessment of costs against a government entity in a case where the government is not involved is inappropriate and therefore that provision has been removed. In addition, if the state is involved as a party, assessment of costs and expenses against the state must be authorized by other law. It should be noted that the term "expenses" means out-of-pocket costs. Overhead costs should not be assessed as expenses.

No other substantive changes have been made. The term "social study" as used in the UCCJA was replaced with the modern term: "custody evaluation." The Act does not take a position on the admissibility of a custody evaluation

that was conducted in another state. It merely authorizes a court to seek assistance of, or render assistance to, a court of another state.

This section combines the text of Sections 19-22 of the UCCJA.

Sections 152.113-152.200 reserved for expansion

SUBCHAPTER C. JURISDICTION

FAM §152.201. INITIAL CHILD CUSTODY JURISDICTION

(a) Except as otherwise provided in Section 152.204, a court of this state has jurisdiction to make an initial child custody determination only if:

(1) this state is the home state of the child on the date of the commencement of the proceeding, or was the home state of the child within six months before the commencement of the proceeding and the child is absent from this state but a parent or person acting as a parent continues to live in this state;

(2) a court of another state does not have jurisdiction under Subdivision (1), or a court of the home state of the child has declined to exercise jurisdiction on the ground that this state is the more appropriate forum under Section 152.207 or 152.208, and:

(A) the child and the child's parents, or the child and at least one parent or a person acting as a parent, have a significant connection with this state other than mere physical presence; and

(B) substantial evidence is available in this state concerning the child's care, protection, training, and personal relationships;

(3) all courts having jurisdiction under Subdivision (1) or (2) have declined to exercise jurisdiction on the ground that a court of this state is the more appropriate forum to determine the custody of the child under Section 152.207 or 152.208; or

(4) no court of any other state would have jurisdiction under the criteria specified in Subdivision (1), (2), or (3).

(b) Subsection (a) is the exclusive jurisdictional basis for making a child custody determination by a court of this state.

(c) Physical presence of, or personal jurisdiction over, a party or a child is not necessary or sufficient to make a child custody determination.

History of Fam. Code §152.201: Acts 1995, 74th Leg., ch. 20, §1, eff. Apr. 20, 1995. Amended by Acts 1995, 74th Leg., ch. 751, §24, eff. Sept. 1, 1995; Acts 1997, 75th Leg., ch. 575, §7, eff. Sept. 1, 1997. Renumbered from §152.003 and amended by Acts 1999, 76th Leg., ch. 34, §1, eff. Sept. 1, 1999. Source: Former Fam. Code §11.53.

See also ***O'Connor's Texas Family Law Handbook*** (2017), "Jurisdiction to grant relief," ch. 4-A, §2.2, p. 331.

ANNOTATIONS

In re Dean, 393 S.W.3d 741, 747 (Tex.2012). "Whether the Texas divorce action was filed [before suit in New Mexico] is irrelevant in determining jurisdiction over custody matters, as the two proceedings involve different inquiries. Jurisdiction over custody determinations is governed by the [UCCJEA], regardless of whether there is an ongoing divorce. *At 750:* The New Mexico trial court ... had jurisdiction over the custody dispute because New Mexico is [child's] home state. Yet the New Mexico trial court deferred to Texas. ... As applied to the facts here, the [UCCJEA] would have allowed Texas to exercise jurisdiction only if New Mexico had declined jurisdiction 'on the ground that [Texas] ... is the more appropriate forum ... under §152.207 or [§]152.208.' But New Mexico's declination was not based on [either statute]. ... Rather, the New Mexico court dismissed the case solely because 'Texas has determined it will exercise jurisdiction.' We appreciate that trial court's effort to avoid an interstate conflict, but we do not believe the [UCCJEA] allows deferral on that basis."

Powell v. Stover, 165 S.W.3d 322, 323 (Tex.2005). See annotation under Family Code §152.102, p. 475.

In re S.J., ___ S.W.3d ___ (Tex.App.—Houston [14th Dist.] 2017, orig. proceeding) (No. 14-17-00054-CV; 2-23-17). "Father argues that even if the jurisdictional requirements of the UCCJEA ... were not met, the trial court still has inherent power to apply the equitable principles of *parens patriate* to issue orders, in its 'broad discretion ... for immediate protection of a child,' when it determines those orders to be necessary in the child's best interest.... Father cites no case or statute that indicates that the principle of *parens patriate* is a jurisdictional avenue independent of the [UCCJEA] for children whose home state is outside Texas. Rather, the UCCJEA is the 'exclusive jurisdictional basis' for Texas courts to make a child custody determination. Unless a court finds that it has jurisdiction under one of the four enumerated grounds in §152.201(b), it cannot exercise jurisdiction over a child custody determination."

In re S.A.H., 465 S.W.3d 662, 666 (Tex.App.—Houston [14th Dist.] 2014, no pet.). "'[T]he operative date for determining whether Texas has jurisdiction is the date the suit was filed in Texas.'"

Berwick v. Wagner, 336 S.W.3d 805, 814 (Tex. App.—Houston [1st Dist.] 2011, pet. denied). Peti-

tioner "argues that the [Texas] trial court should not have registered the California judgment [establishing the parent-child relationship] because ... the California court lacked jurisdiction to enter an order containing a custody determination before [child] was born. *At 815-16:* As the ***Waltenburg*** court [below] noted, interpreting the UCCJEA to permit a party to file a pre-birth suit so as to trump any post-birth proper jurisdiction of another state would run counter to the UCCJEA's preference for home-state jurisdiction. ... We agree.... We do not, however, read ***Waltenburg***'s refusal to recognize UCCJEA orders entered pre-birth simply because the petition is filed (or the judgment entered) before the child is born so broadly as to include cases where the court otherwise has proper jurisdiction over the matter upon the child's birth. In cases in which the pre-birth suit and the 'home state' of the child are one and the same, courts have recognized that UCCJEA petitions can be filed pre-birth with the jurisdictional analysis reserved for post-birth (if there is an issue at that point about jurisdictions or competing forums)."

In re S.J.A., 272 S.W.3d 678, 685 (Tex.App.—Dallas 2008, no pet.). "A high level of physical presence in Texas is not necessary to satisfy the significant-connection standard. Further, the question is not which state has *the most* significant connection with the children. Rather, in determining whether the record supports a finding the children and Mother have a significant connection with Texas, we look at the nature and quality of the children's contacts with Texas."

Waltenburg v. Waltenburg, 270 S.W.3d 308, 316 (Tex.App.—Dallas 2008, no pet.). "[T]he UCCJEA [does not] authorize jurisdiction over a child custody proceeding concerning an unborn child. *At 318:* [R]eading the UCCJEA to authorize jurisdiction over a custody matter concerning an unborn child would defeat the clear purpose underlying the legislature's enactment of the UCCJEA—to prioritize home-state jurisdiction. Under such a reading, a party could file suit pre-birth under the UCCJEA provision authorizing jurisdiction when 'no other court has jurisdiction,' and use the 'simultaneous proceeding' provision to control, post-birth, whether the child's home state can ever exercise that 'priority' jurisdiction. We reject this reading of the UCCJEA." *See also* ***Arnold v. Price***, 365 S.W.3d 455, 461 (Tex.App.—Fort Worth 2011, no pet.); ***Berwick v. Wagner***, p. 481.

In re Barnes, 127 S.W.3d 843, 847-48 (Tex. App.—San Antonio 2003, orig. proceeding). Section 152.201(a)(2)'s "significant connection jurisdiction should only be employed when Texas is not the home state and it appears that no other state could assert home state jurisdiction.... [Child] has never lived in this state; his only connection with Texas is that his father now resides here. Therefore, the trial court erred in taking jurisdiction over the custody dispute under §152.201(a)(2). [¶] [I]t does not appear the Utah court made a decision to decline jurisdiction over the custody matter. Even if it has, Virginia is still a proper forum for the custody matters. Until both Virginia and Utah have declined jurisdiction in favor of Texas, Texas is not authorized to take jurisdiction over [child's] custody determination." (Internal quotes omitted.) *See also* ***Ruffier v. Ruffier***, 190 S.W.3d 884, 890 (Tex. App.—El Paso 2006, no pet.) (until Belarus has declined jurisdiction in favor of Texas, Texas is not authorized to assert significant-connection jurisdiction over custody determination).

In re Y.M.A., 111 S.W.3d 790, 794 (Tex.App.—Fort Worth 2003, no pet.). "The family had lived in Egypt within the six months before commencement of [W's] proceeding. Although [H] had taken [child] to Texas approximately one month before [W] filed the Egyptian proceeding, [W] continued to live in Egypt despite [child's] absence. Thus, Egypt was the child's home state and had jurisdiction to make the initial child custody order. Because Egypt, which is considered a state of the U.S. for applying jurisdictional rules, had jurisdiction of the case under §152.201(a)(1), a Texas court would have no jurisdiction over the case."

NCCUSL Comment*

This section provides mandatory jurisdictional rules for the original child custody proceeding. It generally continues the provisions of the UCCJA §3. However, there have been a number of changes to the jurisdictional bases.

1. Home state jurisdiction. The jurisdiction of the home state has been prioritized over other jurisdictional bases. Section 3 of the UCCJA provided four independent and concurrent bases of jurisdiction. The PKPA provides that full faith and credit can only be given to an initial custody determination of a "significant connection" state when there is no home state. This Act prioritizes home state jurisdiction in the same manner as the PKPA thereby eliminating any potential conflict between the two acts.

The six-month extended home state provision of subsection (a)(1) has been modified slightly from the UCCJA. The UCCJA provided that home state jurisdiction continued for six months when the child had been removed by a person seeking the child's custody or for other reasons and a parent or a person acting as a parent continues to reside in the home state. Under this Act, it is no longer necessary to determine why the child has been removed. The only inquiry relates to the status of the person left behind. This change provides a slightly more refined home state standard than the UCCJA or the PKPA, which

* See footnote on p. 472.

also requires a determination that the child has been removed "by a contestant or for other reasons." The scope of the PKPA's provision is theoretically narrower than this Act. However, the phrase "or for other reasons" covers most fact situations where the child is not in the home state and, therefore, the difference has no substantive effect.

In another sense, the six-month extended home state jurisdiction provision in this Act is narrower than the comparable provision in the PKPA. The PKPA's definition of extended home state is more expansive because it applies whenever a "contestant" remains in the home state. That class of individuals has been eliminated in this Act. This Act retains the original UCCJA classification of "parent or person acting as parent" to define who must remain for a state to exercise the six-month extended home state jurisdiction. This eliminates the undesirable jurisdictional determinations which would occur as a result of differing state substantive laws on visitation involving grandparents and others. For example, if State A's law provided that grandparents could obtain visitation with a child after the death of one of the parents, then the grandparents, who would be considered "contestants" under the PKPA, could file a proceeding within six months after the remaining parent moved and have the case heard in State A. However, if State A did not provide that grandparents could seek visitation under such circumstances, the grandparents would not be considered "contestants" and State B where the child acquired a new home state would provide the only forum. This Act bases jurisdiction on the parent and child or person acting as a parent and child relationship without regard to grandparents or other potential seekers of custody or visitation. There is no conflict with the broader provision of the PKPA. The PKPA in §(c)(1) authorizes states to narrow the scope of their jurisdiction.

2. Significant connection jurisdiction. This jurisdictional basis has been amended in four particulars from the UCCJA. First, the "best interest" language of the UCCJA has been eliminated. This phrase tended to create confusion between the jurisdictional issue and the substantive custody determination. Since the language was not necessary for the jurisdictional issue, it has been removed.

Second, the UCCJA based jurisdiction on the presence of a significant connection between the child and the child's parents or the child and at least one contestant. This Act requires that the significant connections be between the child, the child's parents or the child and a person acting as a parent.

Third, a significant connection state may assume jurisdiction only when there is no home state or when the home state decides that the significant connection state would be a more appropriate forum under Section 152.207 or 152.208. Fourth, the determination of significant connections has been changed to eliminate the language of "present or future care." The jurisdictional determination should be made by determining whether there is sufficient evidence in the state for the court to make an informed custody determination. That evidence might relate to the past as well as to the "present or future."

Emergency jurisdiction has been moved to a separate section. This is to make it clear that the power to protect a child in crisis does not include the power to enter a permanent order for that child except as provided by that section.

Subsection (a)(3) provides for jurisdiction when all states with jurisdiction under subsections (a)(1) and (a)(2) determine that this state is a more appropriate forum. The determination would have to be made by all states with jurisdiction under subsections (a)(1) and (a)(2). Jurisdiction would not exist under this paragraph because the home state determined it is a more appropriate place to hear the case if there is another state that could exercise significant connection jurisdiction under subsection (a)(2).

Subsection (a)(4) retains the concept of jurisdiction by necessity as found in the UCCJA and in the PKPA. This default jurisdiction only occurs if no other state would have jurisdiction under subsections (a)(1) through (a)(3).

Subsections (b) and (c) clearly state the relationship between jurisdiction under this Act and other forms of jurisdiction. Personal jurisdiction over, or the physical presence of, a parent or the child is neither necessary nor required under this Act. In other words neither minimum contacts nor service within the state is required for the court to have jurisdiction to make a custody determination. Further, the presence of minimum contacts or service within the state does not confer jurisdiction to make a custody determination. Subject to Section 152.204, satisfaction of the requirements of subsection (a) is mandatory.

The requirements of this section, plus the notice and hearing provisions of the Act, are all that is necessary to satisfy due process. This Act, like the UCCJA and the PKPA is based on Justice Frankfurter's concurrence in *May v. Anderson*, 345 U.S. 528 (1953). As pointed out by Professor Bodenheimer, the reporter for the UCCJA, no "workable interstate custody law could be built around [Justice] Burton's plurality opinion...." Bridgette Bodenheimer, The Uniform Child Custody Jurisdiction Act: A Legislative Remedy for Children Caught in the Conflict of Laws, 22 Vand.L.Rev. 1207, 1233 (1969). It should also be noted that since jurisdiction to make a child custody determination is subject matter jurisdiction, an agreement of the parties to confer jurisdiction on a court that would not otherwise have jurisdiction under this Act is ineffective.

FAM §152.202. EXCLUSIVE CONTINUING JURISDICTION

(a) Except as otherwise provided in Section 152.204, a court of this state which has made a child custody determination consistent with Section 152.201 or 152.203 has exclusive continuing jurisdiction over the determination until:

(1) a court of this state determines that neither the child, nor the child and one parent, nor the child and a person acting as a parent, have a significant connection with this state and that substantial evidence is no longer available in this state concerning the child's care, protection, training, and personal relationships; or

(2) a court of this state or a court of another state determines that the child, the child's parents, and any person acting as a parent do not presently reside in this state.

(b) A court of this state which has made a child custody determination and does not have exclusive, continuing jurisdiction under this section may modify that determination only if it has jurisdiction to make an initial determination under Section 152.201.

History of Fam. Code §152.202: Acts 1995, 74th Leg., ch. 20, §1, eff. Apr. 20, 1995. Amended by Acts 1995, 74th Leg., ch. 751, §24, eff. Sept. 1, 1995; Acts 1997, 75th Leg., ch. 575, §7, eff. Sept. 1, 1997. Renumbered from §152.003(d) by Acts 1999, 76th Leg., ch. 34, §1, eff. Sept. 1, 1999. Source: Former Fam. Code §11.53.

See also ***O'Connor's Texas Family Law Handbook*** (2017), "Filing SAPCR after order rendered in earlier SAPCR," ch. 4-A, §3.2, p. 343; "Court loses CEJ," ch. 9-A, §2.1.2, p. 974.

ANNOTATIONS

In re Forlenza, 140 S.W.3d 373, 378-79 (Tex.2004). "[T]he UCCJEA does not premise the exclusive continuing jurisdiction determination on which state has the *most* significant connection with the child. This relative type of inquiry is appropriate under [Fam. Code] §152.207, which allows a court with exclusive continuing jurisdiction to decline it in favor of a more convenient forum, but it does not affect the initial [Fam. Code] §152.202 jurisdictional analysis. Importantly, the only issue before us is whether the Texas court retained jurisdiction; the court could still decline to exercise that jurisdiction if another forum was more convenient. In this case, though, the children's almost

continual change of residence supports the trial court's conclusion that the children had a significant connection with Texas based on their visits here and their personal relationships maintained in this state. [¶] [E]xclusive jurisdiction continues in the decree-granting state as long as a significant connection exists *or* substantial evidence is present."

In re Isquierdo, 426 S.W.3d 128, 133-34 (Tex. App.—Houston [1st Dist.] 2012, orig. proceeding). "The trial court, in its oral ruling and findings of fact, emphasized that [father] still resides in Texas. However, the mere fact that [father] continues to reside in Texas does not support the trial court's exercise of exclusive continuing jurisdiction over the [visitation] modification proceeding brought by [father]. *At 133 n.7:* [The Second Court of Appeals in ***In re K.B.A.*** has] interpreted §152.202(a) as providing for continuing exclusive jurisdiction merely by the fact that one parent continues to reside in Texas. [But] the supreme court in ***Forlenza*** acknowledged that the fact that one parent continues to reside in Texas is not 'determinative.'" *But see* ***In re K.B.A.***, 145 S.W.3d 685, 689 (Tex.App.—Fort Worth 2004, no pet.) (termination suit; "[b]ecause one litigant, the mother, still resides in Texas, the Texas trial court that made the original child custody determination is the only court that has jurisdiction").

In re Lewin, 149 S.W.3d 727, 740-41 (Tex.App.—Austin 2004, orig. proceeding). See annotation under Family Code §152.208, p. 491.

NCCUSL Comment*

This is a new section addressing continuing jurisdiction. Continuing jurisdiction was not specifically addressed in the UCCJA. Its absence caused considerable confusion, particularly because the PKPA, §1738(d), requires other states to give Full Faith and Credit to custody determinations made by the original decree state pursuant to the decree state's continuing jurisdiction so long as that state has jurisdiction under its own law and remains the residence of the child or any contestant.

This section provides the rules of continuing jurisdiction and borrows from UIFSA as well as recent UCCJA case law. The continuing jurisdiction of the original decree state is exclusive. It continues until one of two events occurs:

1. If a parent or a person acting as a parent remains in the original decree state, continuing jurisdiction is lost when neither the child, the child and a parent, nor the child and a person acting as a parent continue to have a significant connection with the original decree state and there is no longer substantial evidence concerning the child's care, protection, training and personal relations in that state. In other words, even if the child has acquired a new home state, the original decree state retains exclusive, continuing jurisdiction, so long as the general requisites of the "substantial connection" jurisdiction provisions of Section 152.201 are met. If the relationship between the child and the person remaining in the state with exclusive, continuing jurisdiction becomes so attenuated that the court could no longer find significant connections and substantial evidence, jurisdiction would no longer exist.

The use of the phrase "a court of this state" under subsection (a)(1) makes it clear that the original decree state is the sole determinant of whether jurisdiction continues. A party seeking to modify a custody determination must obtain an order from the original decree state stating that it no longer has jurisdiction.

2. Continuing jurisdiction is lost when the child, the child's parents, and any person acting as a parent no longer reside in the original decree state. The exact language of subsection (a)(2) was the subject of considerable debate. Ultimately the Conference settled on the phrase that "a court of this state or a court of another state determines that the child, the child's parents, and any person acting as a parent do not presently reside in this state" to determine when the exclusive, continuing jurisdiction of a state ended. The phrase is meant to be identical in meaning to the language of the PKPA which provides that full faith and credit is to be given to custody determinations made by a state in the exercise of its continuing jurisdiction when that "state remains the residence of...." The phrase is also the equivalent of the language "continues to reside" which occurs in UIFSA §205(a)(1) to determine the exclusive, continuing jurisdiction of the state that made a support order. The phrase "remains the residence of" in the PKPA has been the subject of conflicting case law. It is the intention of this Act that subsection (a)(2) of this section means that the named persons no longer continue to actually live within the state. Thus, unless a modification proceeding has been commenced, when the child, the parents, and all persons acting as parents physically leave the state to live elsewhere, the exclusive, continuing jurisdiction ceases.

The phrase "do not presently reside" is not used in the sense of a technical domicile. The fact that the original determination state still considers one parent a domiciliary does not prevent it from losing exclusive, continuing jurisdiction after the child, the parents, and all persons acting as parents have moved from the state.

If the child, the parents, and all persons acting as parents have all left the state which made the custody determination prior to the commencement of the modification proceeding, considerations of waste of resources dictate that a court in State B, as well as a court in State A, can decide that State A has lost exclusive, continuing jurisdiction.

The continuing jurisdiction provisions of this section are narrower than the comparable provisions of the PKPA. That statute authorizes continuing jurisdiction so long as any "contestant" remains in the original decree state and that state continues to have jurisdiction under its own law. This Act eliminates the contestant classification. The Conference decided that a remaining grandparent or other third party who claims a right to visitation, should not suffice to confer exclusive, continuing jurisdiction on the state that made the original custody determination after the departure of the child, the parents and any person acting as a parent. The significant connection to the original decree state must relate to the child, the child and a parent, or the child and a person acting as a parent. This revision does not present a conflict with the PKPA. The PKPA's reference in §1738(d) to §1738(c)(1) recognizes that states may narrow the class of cases that would be subject to exclusive, continuing jurisdiction. However, during the transition from the UCCJA to this Act, some states may continue to base continuing jurisdiction on the continued presence of a contestant, such as a grandparent. The PKPA will require that such decisions be enforced. The problem will disappear as states adopt this Act to replace the UCCJA.

Jurisdiction attaches at the commencement of a proceeding. If State A had jurisdiction under this section at the time a modification proceeding was commenced there, it would not be lost by all parties moving out of the state prior to the conclusion of proceeding. State B would not have jurisdiction to hear a modification unless State A decided that State B was more appropriate under Section 152.207.

Exclusive, continuing jurisdiction is not reestablished if, after the child, the parents, and all persons acting as parents leave the state, the non-custodial parent returns. As subsection (b) provides, once a state has lost exclusive, continuing jurisdiction, it can modify its own determination only if it has jurisdiction under the standards of Section 152.201. If another state acquires exclusive continuing jurisdiction under this section, then its orders cannot be modified even if this state has once again become the home state of the child.

In accordance with the majority of UCCJA case law, the state with exclusive, continuing jurisdiction may relinquish jurisdiction when it determines that another state would be a more convenient forum under the principles of Section 152.207.

* See footnote on p. 472.

FAM §152.203. JURISDICTION TO MODIFY DETERMINATION

Except as otherwise provided in Section 152.204, a court of this state may not modify a child custody determination made by a court of another state unless a court of this state has jurisdiction to make an initial determination under Section 152.201(a)(1) or (2) and:

(1) the court of the other state determines it no longer has exclusive continuing jurisdiction under Section 152.202 or that a court of this state would be a more convenient forum under Section 152.207; or

(2) a court of this state or a court of the other state determines that the child, the child's parents, and any person acting as a parent do not presently reside in the other state.

History of Fam. Code §152.203: Acts 1995, 74th Leg., ch. 20, §1, eff. Apr. 20, 1995. Amended by Acts 1995, 74th Leg., ch. 751, §24, eff. Sept. 1, 1995; Acts 1997, 75th Leg., ch. 575, §7, eff. Sept. 1, 1997. Renumbered from §152.003(d) by Acts 1999, 76th Leg., ch. 34, §1, eff. Sept. 1, 1999. Source: Former Fam. Code §11.64.

ANNOTATIONS

In re T.B., 497 S.W.3d 640, 649 (Tex.App.—Fort Worth 2016, pet. denied). "Although the nonexclusive statutory factors support the determination that Florida is an inconvenient forum for Mother's SAPCR and that Texas is a more appropriate forum, Father points out that the Florida court did not sign an order so holding. *At 652:* Under the unique facts presented here, we hold that the Florida court's failure to communicate with the trial court for over six months and the Florida court's failure to rule on Father's motion filed with it—for over six months before the trial court proceeded to a final hearing, for over eight months before the trial court signed a final judgment, and for over 14 months to date—constitutes an implied determination by the Florida court to decline to exercise its home-state jurisdiction and an implied determination by the Florida court that Texas is a more convenient forum for litigation of Mother's modification SAPCR. … Consequently, under the narrow facts presented here, we hold that the trial court possessed subject-matter jurisdiction to modify the Florida court's order concerning conservatorship and visitation issues."

Saavedra v. Schmidt, 96 S.W.3d 533, 541-42 (Tex. App.—Austin 2002, no pet.). "Absent the California court's relinquishment of … exclusive continuing jurisdiction, the Texas court was without jurisdiction to modify the California orders. … It is of no consequence that the Texas court determined that it was a more appropriate forum; the California court must make this determination before a court of this state may modify the California court's child custody determinations."

NCCUSL Comment*

This section complements Section 152.202 and is addressed to the court that is confronted with a proceeding to modify a custody determination of another state. It prohibits a court from modifying a custody determination made consistently with this Act by a court in another state unless a court of that state determines that it no longer has exclusive, continuing jurisdiction under Section 152.202 or that this state would be a more convenient forum under Section 152.207. The modification state is not authorized to determine that the original decree state has lost its jurisdiction. The only exception is when the child, the child's parents, and any person acting as a parent do not presently reside in the other state. In other words, a court of the modification state can determine that all parties have moved away from the original state. The court of the modification state must have jurisdiction under the standards of Section 152.201.

FAM §152.204. TEMPORARY EMERGENCY JURISDICTION

(a) A court of this state has temporary emergency jurisdiction if the child is present in this state and the child has been abandoned or it is necessary in an emergency to protect the child because the child, or a sibling or parent of the child, is subjected to or threatened with mistreatment or abuse.

(b) If there is no previous child custody determination that is entitled to be enforced under this chapter and a child custody proceeding has not been commenced in a court of a state having jurisdiction under Sections 152.201 through 152.203, a child custody determination made under this section remains in effect until an order is obtained from a court of a state having jurisdiction under Sections 152.201 through 152.203. If a child custody proceeding has not been or is not commenced in a court of a state having jurisdiction under Sections 152.201 through 152.203, a child custody determination made under this section becomes a final determination, if it so provides and this state becomes the home state of the child.

(c) If there is a previous child custody determination that is entitled to be enforced under this chapter, or a child custody proceeding has been commenced in a court of a state having jurisdiction under Sections 152.201 through 152.203, any order issued by a court of this state under this section must specify in the order a period that the court considers adequate to allow the person seeking an order to obtain an order from the state having jurisdiction under Sections 152.201 through 152.203. The order issued in this state remains in effect until an order is obtained from the other state within the period specified or the period expires.

* See footnote on p. 472.

(d) A court of this state which has been asked to make a child custody determination under this section, upon being informed that a child custody proceeding has been commenced in or a child custody determination has been made by a court of a state having jurisdiction under Sections 152.201 through 152.203, shall immediately communicate with the other court. A court of this state which is exercising jurisdiction pursuant to Sections 152.201 through 152.203, upon being informed that a child custody proceeding has been commenced in or a child custody determination has been made by a court of another state under a statute similar to this section shall immediately communicate with the court of that state to resolve the emergency, protect the safety of the parties and the child, and determine a period for the duration of the temporary order.

History of Fam. Code §152.204: Acts 1995, 74th Leg., ch. 20, §1, eff. Apr. 20, 1995. Amended by Acts 1995, 74th Leg., ch. 751, §24, eff. Sept. 1, 1995; Acts 1997, 75th Leg., ch. 575, §7, eff. Sept. 1, 1997. Renumbered from §152.003(e) by Acts 1999, 76th Leg., ch. 34, §1, eff. Sept. 1, 1999.

See also ***O'Connor's Texas Family Law Handbook*** (2017), "Emergency child-custody determination – TEJ," ch. 4-A, §2.2.3, p. 340; "Filing SAPCR for emergency custody," ch. 4-A, §3.4, p. 347.

ANNOTATIONS

In re S.J., ___ S.W.3d ___ (Tex.App.—Houston [14th Dist.] 2017, orig. proceeding) (No. 14-17-00054-CV; 2-23-17). Family Code "[c]h. 152 … does not define 'mistreatment' or 'abuse.' However, we find guidance from [Fam. Code] §261.001 …, which provides that 'abuse' includes, among other things, 'mental or emotional injury to a child that results in an observable and material impairment in the child's growth, development, or psychological functioning' or 'physical injury that results in substantial harm to the child, or the genuine threat of substantial harm from physical injury to the child.' [¶] [N]o language in [Fam. Code] §152.204 indicates that taking a child to Texas with the intent to move there without the other parent's knowledge or consent, by itself, constitutes mistreatment or abuse that would warrant the exercise of emergency jurisdiction under §152.204(a). Rather, §152.204(a) states that there must be an 'emergency' such that it is necessary to protect the child because of mistreatment or abuse. There is no evidence that Mother's taking the child to Texas caused the child any mental or emotional injury that resulted in an observable and material impairment in the child's growth, development, or psychological functioning that necessitated the exercise of emergency jurisdiction under §152.204. [¶] Because the trial court lacked jurisdiction under §152.204 …, it abused its discretion by issuing the Emergency Jurisdiction Order. Such order is therefore … void…."

In re Salminen, 492 S.W.3d 31, 41 (Tex.App.—Houston [1st Dist.] 2016, orig. proceeding). "Regarding the requirements of §152.204(a), [father] failed to provide evidence that [child] was present in Texas at the time the trial court rendered the Temporary Order…. [Mother and child] had returned to Finland [seven days before the hearing]. [Mother] was available to testify by phone, but she provided no evidence at the hearing. Although the amicus attorney testified that she had visited with [mother and child] in Texas 'recently,' neither she nor [father] provided any evidence that [child] was residing in Texas at the time of the … hearing."

In re J.C.B., 209 S.W.3d 821, 824 n.4 (Tex.App.—Amarillo 2006, no pet.). "[W]e … conclude that the concept of 'home state' differs [from Fam. Code §152.102(7)] when jurisdiction is invoked under [Fam. Code] §152.204(a) and omits the requirement that the six months of residence occur before the proceeding is commenced. If this were not so, then there could be no home state for purposes of finalizing orders rendered via emergency jurisdiction since the proceeding began before the child had resided with a parent or parent surrogate in Texas for six months."

In re M.G.M., 163 S.W.3d 191, 196 (Tex.App.—Beaumont 2005, no pet.). "The fact that the main focus at the time the application was filed was protection for the applicant and the children from family violence could not allow the trial court to apply [Fam. Code] Title 4 exclusively and to the exclusion of the procedures set out in [Fam. Code] ch. 152. *At 198-99:* [T]he proper course open to the trial court was to have exercised temporary emergency jurisdiction under [Fam. Code] §152.204(a) and issued the temporary ex parte protective order which could include all of the provisions listed under [Fam. Code] §85.022(b) as specifically tailored to the facts presented. Additionally, the trial court was authorized to [prohibit H] from removing the children from [W's] possession as this was also a reasonable condition for protection of the children and [W]. Having done this, it was incumbent for the trial court to have communicated with the Michigan court as soon as possible once the trial court was aware of the simultaneous proceeding pending there, after having stayed any further proceedings in its court. If the Michigan court indicates to the trial court that Michigan is the

more appropriate forum, the trial court shall dismiss the pending temporary ex parte protective order and application, but only when the trial court is satisfied that the Michigan court has entered a substantially similar order that would protect [W] and the children from family violence...."

Saavedra v. Schmidt, 96 S.W.3d 533, 544 (Tex. App.—Austin 2002, no pet.). "[T]he possibility that allegations of immediate harm might be true is sufficient for a court to assume temporary emergency jurisdiction in the best interests of the child under the UCCJEA. The duty of states to recognize and enforce a custody determination of another state must yield if circumstances require temporary emergency orders to protect the child. *At 545:* Temporary emergency jurisdiction is reserved for extraordinary circumstances. *At 548-49:* [T]he trial court's assumption of temporary emergency jurisdiction does not include jurisdiction to modify the child custody determination [of another state]. A court's exercise of temporary emergency jurisdiction is temporary in nature and may not be used as a vehicle to attain modification jurisdiction for an ongoing, indefinite period of time."

NCCUSL Comment*

The provisions of this section are an elaboration of what was formerly Section 3(a)(3) of the UCCJA. It remains, as Professor Bodenheimer's comments to that section noted, "an extraordinary jurisdiction reserved for extraordinary circumstances."

This section codifies and clarifies several aspects of what has become common practice in emergency jurisdiction cases under the UCCJA and PKPA. First, a court may take jurisdiction to protect the child even though it can claim neither home state nor significant connection jurisdiction. Second, the duties of states to recognize, enforce and not modify a custody determination of another state do not take precedence over the need to enter a temporary emergency order to protect the child. Third, a custody determination made under the emergency jurisdiction provisions of this section is a temporary order. The purpose of the order is to protect the child until the state that has jurisdiction under Sections 152.201-152.203 enters an order.

Under certain circumstances, however, subsection (b) provides that an emergency custody determination may become a final custody determination. If there is no existing custody determination, and no custody proceeding is filed in a state with jurisdiction under Sections 152.201-152.203, an emergency custody determination made under this section becomes a final determination, if it so provides, when the state that issues the order becomes the home state of the child.

Subsection (c) is concerned with the temporary nature of the order when there exists a prior custody order that is entitled to be enforced under this Act or when a subsequent custody proceeding is filed in a state with jurisdiction under Sections 152.201-152.203. Subsection (c) allows the temporary order to remain in effect only so long as is necessary for the person who obtained the determination under this section to present a case and obtain an order from the state with jurisdiction under Sections 152.201-152.203. That time period must be specified in the order. If there is an existing order by a state with jurisdiction under Sections 152.201-152.203, that order need not be reconfirmed. The temporary emergency determination would lapse by its own terms at the end of the specified period or when an order is obtained from the court with jurisdiction under Sections 152.202-152.203. The court with appropriate jurisdiction also may decide, under the provisions of 152.207, that the court that entered the emergency order is in a better position to address the safety of the person who obtained the emergency order, or the child, and decline jurisdiction under Section 152.207.

Any hearing in the state with jurisdiction under Sections 152.201-152.203 on the temporary emergency determination is subject to the provisions of Sections 152.111 and 152.112. These sections facilitate the presentation of testimony and evidence taken out of state. If there is a concern that the person obtaining the temporary emergency determination under this section would be in danger upon returning to the state with jurisdiction under Sections 152.201-152.203, these provisions should be used.

Subsection (d) requires communication between the court of the state that is exercising jurisdiction under this section and the court of another state that is exercising jurisdiction under Sections 152.201-152.203. The pleading rules of Section 152.209 apply fully to determinations made under this section. Therefore, a person seeking a temporary emergency custody determination is required to inform the court pursuant to Section 152.209(d) of any proceeding concerning the child that has been commenced elsewhere. The person commencing the custody proceeding under Sections 152.201-152.203 is required under Section 152.209(a) to inform the court about the temporary emergency proceeding. These pleading requirements are to be strictly followed so that the courts are able to resolve the emergency, protect the safety of the parties and the child, and determine a period for the duration of the temporary order.

Relationship to the PKPA. The definition of emergency has been modified to harmonize it with the PKPA. The PKPA's definition of emergency jurisdiction does not use the term "neglect." It defines an emergency as "mistreatment or abuse." Therefore "neglect" has been eliminated as a basis for the assumption of temporary emergency jurisdiction. Neglect is so elastic a concept that it could justify taking emergency jurisdiction in a wide variety of cases. Under the PKPA, if a state exercised temporary emergency jurisdiction based on a finding that the child was neglected without a finding of mistreatment or abuse, the order would not be entitled to federal enforcement in other states.

Relationship to Protective Order Proceedings. The UCCJA and the PKPA were enacted long before the advent of state procedures on the use of protective orders to alleviate problems of domestic violence. Issues of custody and visitation often arise within the context of protective order proceedings since the protective order is often invoked to keep one parent away from the other parent and the children when there is a threat of violence. This Act recognizes that a protective order proceeding will often be the procedural vehicle for invoking jurisdiction by authorizing a court to assume temporary emergency jurisdiction when the child's parent or sibling has been subjected to or threatened with mistreatment or abuse.

In order for a protective order that contains a custody determination to be enforceable in another state it must comply with the provisions of this Act and the PKPA. Although the Violence Against Women's Act (VAWA), 18 U.S.C. §2265, does provide an independent basis for the granting of full faith and credit to protective orders, it expressly excludes "custody" orders from the definition of "protective order," 22 U.S.C. §2266.

Many states authorize the issuance of protective orders in an emergency without notice and hearing. This Act does not address the propriety of that procedure. It is left to local law to determine the circumstances under which such an order could be issued, and the type of notice that is required, in a case without an interstate element. However, an order issued after the assumption of temporary emergency jurisdiction is entitled to interstate enforcement and nonmodification under this Act and the PKPA only if there has been notice and a reasonable opportunity to be heard as set out in Section 152.205. Although VAWA does require that full faith and credit be accorded to ex parte protective orders if notice will be given and there will be a reasonable opportunity to be heard, it does not include a "custody" order within the definition of "protective order."

VAWA does play an important role in determining whether an emergency exists. That Act requires a court to give full faith and credit to a protective order issued in another state if the order is made in accordance with the VAWA. This would include those findings of fact contained in the order. When a court is deciding whether an emergency exists under this section, it may not relitigate the existence of those factual findings.

* See footnote on p. 472.

FAM §152.205. NOTICE; OPPORTUNITY TO BE HEARD; JOINDER

(a) Before a child custody determination is made under this chapter, notice and an opportunity to be heard in accordance with the standards of Section 152.108 must be given to all persons entitled to notice under the law of this state as in child custody proceedings between residents of this state, any parent whose parental rights have not been previously terminated, and any person having physical custody of the child.

(b) This chapter does not govern the enforceability of a child custody determination made without notice or an opportunity to be heard.

(c) The obligation to join a party and the right to intervene as a party in a child custody proceeding under this chapter are governed by the law of this state as in child custody proceedings between residents of this state.

History of Fam. Code §152.205: Acts 1995, 74th Leg., ch. 20, §1, eff. Apr. 20, 1995. Renumbered from §§152.004, 152.010 by Acts 1999, 76th Leg., ch. 34, §1, eff. Sept. 1, 1999. Source: Former Fam. Code §§11.54, 11.60.

NCCUSL Comment*

This section generally continues the notice provisions of the UCCJA. However, it does not attempt to dictate who is entitled to notice. Local rules vary with regard to persons entitled to seek custody of a child. Therefore, this section simply indicates that persons entitled to seek custody should receive notice but leaves the rest of the determination to local law. Parents whose parental rights have not been previously terminated and persons having physical custody of the child are specifically mentioned as persons who must be given notice. The PKPA, §1738A(e), requires that they be given notice in order for the custody determination to be entitled to full faith and credit under that Act.

State laws also vary with regard to whether a court has the power to issue an enforceable temporary custody order without notice and hearing in a case without any interstate element. Such temporary orders may be enforceable, as against due process objections, for a short period of time if issued as a protective order or a temporary restraining order to protect a child from harm. Whether such orders are enforceable locally is beyond the scope of this Act. Subsection (b) clearly provides that the validity of such orders and the enforceability of such orders is governed by the law which authorizes them and not by this Act. An order is entitled to interstate enforcement and nonmodification under this Act only if there has been notice and an opportunity to be heard. The PKPA, §1738A(e), also requires that a custody determination is entitled to full faith and credit only if there has been notice and an opportunity to be heard.

Rules requiring joinder of people with an interest in the custody of and visitation with a child also vary widely throughout the country. The UCCJA has a separate section on joinder of parties which has been eliminated. The issue of who is entitled to intervene and who must be joined in a custody proceeding is to be determined by local state law.

A sentence of the UCCJA §4 which indicated that persons outside the state were to be given notice and an opportunity to be heard in accordance with the provision of that Act has been eliminated as redundant.

FAM §152.206. SIMULTANEOUS PROCEEDINGS

(a) Except as otherwise provided in Section 152.204, a court of this state may not exercise its jurisdiction under this subchapter if, at the time of the commencement of the proceeding, a proceeding concerning the custody of the child has been commenced in a court of another state having jurisdiction substantially in conformity with this chapter, unless the proceeding has been terminated or is stayed by the court of the other state because a court of this state is a more convenient forum under Section 152.207.

(b) Except as otherwise provided in Section 152.204, a court of this state, before hearing a child custody proceeding, shall examine the court documents and other information supplied by the parties pursuant to Section 152.209. If the court determines that a child custody proceeding has been commenced in a court in another state having jurisdiction substantially in accordance with this chapter, the court of this state shall stay its proceeding and communicate with the court of the other state. If the court of the state having jurisdiction substantially in accordance with this chapter does not determine that the court of this state is a more appropriate forum, the court of this state shall dismiss the proceeding.

(c) In a proceeding to modify a child custody determination, a court of this state shall determine whether a proceeding to enforce the determination has been commenced in another state. If a proceeding to enforce a child custody determination has been commenced in another state, the court may:

(1) stay the proceeding for modification pending the entry of an order of a court of the other state enforcing, staying, denying, or dismissing the proceeding for enforcement;

(2) enjoin the parties from continuing with the proceeding for enforcement; or

(3) proceed with the modification under conditions it considers appropriate.

History of Fam. Code §152.206: Acts 1995, 74th Leg., ch. 20, §1, eff. Apr. 20, 1995. Renumbered from §152.006 by Acts 1999, 76th Leg., ch. 34, §1, eff. Sept. 1, 1999. Source: Former Fam. Code §11.56.

See also *O'Connor's Texas Family Law Handbook* (2017), "Staying the Suit," ch. 4-B, §7, p. 363.

ANNOTATIONS

In re Brown, 203 S.W.3d 888, 891 (Tex.App.—Fort Worth 2006, orig. proceeding). "[W] filed for divorce first in Missouri, but the question remains whether Missouri's purported jurisdiction is 'substantially in conformity with this chapter.' Resolution of that question requires the determination of whether Texas is the children's home state because, under the Texas

* See footnote on p. 472.

UCCJEA, home-state jurisdiction trumps all other possible bases of jurisdiction in an initial child custody action; if Texas is the children's home state, Missouri could not be exercising jurisdiction 'substantially in conformity with this chapter.'" *See also* ***Powell v. Stover***, 165 S.W.3d 322, 328 (Tex.2005) (Tennessee's exercise of jurisdiction was "substantially in accordance" with UCCJEA because Tennessee was child's home state).

In re Presley, 166 S.W.3d 866, 868 (Tex.App.—Beaumont 2005, orig. proceeding). "When suit was filed, there was no 'home state.' [N]either Florida nor Texas was the home state. While both states may have significant connection jurisdiction under [Fam. Code] §152.201(a)(2), suit was filed first in Florida. Accordingly, [Fam. Code] §152.206(a) controls and the Texas court could not exercise jurisdiction unless the Florida proceeding had been terminated or stayed by the Florida court because Texas is a more convenient forum. The Texas court was required to stay its proceeding and communicate with the Florida court, and unless the Florida court determines the Texas court is a more appropriate forum, the Texas court is required to dismiss the proceeding."

NCCUSL Comment*

This section represents the remnants of the simultaneous proceedings provision of the UCCJA §6. The problem of simultaneous proceedings is no longer a significant issue. Most of the problems have been resolved by the prioritization of home state jurisdiction under Section 152.201; the exclusive, continuing jurisdiction provisions of Section 152.202; and the prohibitions on modification of Section 152.203. If there is a home state, there can be no exercise of significant connection jurisdiction in an initial child custody determination and, therefore, no simultaneous proceedings. If there is a state of exclusive, continuing jurisdiction, there cannot be another state with concurrent jurisdiction and, therefore, no simultaneous proceedings. Of course, the home state, as well as the state with exclusive, continuing jurisdiction, could defer to another state under Section 152.207. However, that decision is left entirely to the home state or the state with exclusive, continuing jurisdiction.

Under this Act, the simultaneous proceedings problem will arise only when there is no home state, no state with exclusive, continuing jurisdiction and more than one significant connection state. For those cases, this section retains the "first in time" rule of the UCCJA. Subsection (b) retains the UCCJA's policy favoring judicial communication. Communication between courts is required when it is determined that a proceeding has been commenced in another state.

Subsection (c) concerns the problem of simultaneous proceedings in the state with modification jurisdiction and enforcement proceedings under Subchapter D. This section authorizes the court with exclusive, continuing jurisdiction to stay the modification proceeding pending the outcome of the enforcement proceeding, to enjoin the parties from continuing with the enforcement proceeding, or to continue the modification proceeding under such conditions as it determines are appropriate. The court may wish to communicate with the enforcement court. However, communication is not mandatory. Although the enforcement state is required by the PKPA to enforce according to its terms a custody determination made consistently with the PKPA, that duty is subject to the decree being modified by a state with the power to do so under the PKPA. An order to enjoin the parties from enforcing the decree is the equivalent of a temporary modification by a state with the authority to do so. The concomitant provision addressed to the enforcement court is Section 152.306 of this Act. That section requires the enforcement court to communicate with the modification court in order to determine what action the modification court wishes the enforcement court to take.

The term "pending" that was utilized in the UCCJA section on simultaneous proceeding has been replaced. It has caused considerable confusion in the case law. It has been replaced with the term "commencement of the proceeding" as more accurately reflecting the policy behind this section. The latter term is defined in Section 152.102(5).

* See footnote on p. 472.

FAM §152.207. INCONVENIENT FORUM

(a) A court of this state which has jurisdiction under this chapter to make a child custody determination may decline to exercise its jurisdiction at any time if it determines that it is an inconvenient forum under the circumstances and that a court of another state is a more appropriate forum. The issue of inconvenient forum may be raised upon motion of a party, the court's own motion, or request of another court.

(b) Before determining whether it is an inconvenient forum, a court of this state shall consider whether it is appropriate for a court of another state to exercise jurisdiction. For this purpose, the court shall allow the parties to submit information and shall consider all relevant factors, including:

(1) whether domestic violence has occurred and is likely to continue in the future and which state could best protect the parties and the child;

(2) the length of time the child has resided outside this state;

(3) the distance between the court in this state and the court in the state that would assume jurisdiction;

(4) the relative financial circumstances of the parties;

(5) any agreement of the parties as to which state should assume jurisdiction;

(6) the nature and location of the evidence required to resolve the pending litigation, including testimony of the child;

(7) the ability of the court of each state to decide the issue expeditiously and the procedures necessary to present the evidence; and

(8) the familiarity of the court of each state with the facts and issues in the pending litigation.

(c) If a court of this state determines that it is an inconvenient forum and that a court of another state is a more appropriate forum, the court shall stay the pro-

ceedings upon condition that a child custody proceeding be promptly commenced in another designated state and may impose any other condition the court considers just and proper.

(d) A court of this state may decline to exercise its jurisdiction under this chapter if a child custody determination is incidental to an action for divorce or another proceeding while still retaining jurisdiction over the divorce or other proceeding.

History of Fam. Code §152.207: Acts 1995, 74th Leg., ch. 20, §1, eff. Apr. 20, 1995. Amended by Acts 1997, 75th Leg., ch. 15, §3, eff. Sept. 1, 1997. Renumbered from §152.007 by Acts 1999, 76th Leg., ch. 34, §1, eff. Sept. 1, 1999. Source: Former Fam. Code §11.57.

See also ***O'Connor's Texas Family Law Handbook*** (2017), "Challenging Texas Forum – Child Custody," ch. 4-B, §4, p. 357.

ANNOTATIONS

In re T.B., 497 S.W.3d 640, 649 (Tex.App.—Fort Worth 2016, pet. denied). "[A]pplication of the statutory factors in toto establish that Florida is an inconvenient forum for Mother's SAPCR and that Texas is a more convenient forum than Florida; the only factor supporting continuing jurisdiction in Florida is the parties' agreement. This single factor is not, however, conclusive and is considered along with the other listed nonexclusive factors, which show that Florida is an inconvenient forum and that Texas is a more convenient forum."

Lesem v. Mouradian, 445 S.W.3d 366, 376 (Tex. App.—Houston [1st Dist.] 2013, no pet.). "[S]ection 152.207 does not require the trial court to hold an evidentiary hearing before it makes a determination that Texas is an inconvenient forum."

Monk v. Pomberg, 263 S.W.3d 199, 206 (Tex. App.—Houston [1st Dist.] 2007, no pet.). "[M]ay a litigant pursue declaratory judgment to raise the issue of inconvenient forum under §152.207...? [¶] We conclude that a declaratory judgment may be used to declare rights under §152.207.... *At 207:* [T]he Declaratory Judgments Act allows [W] to have the trial court declare her rights, status and other legal relations under §152.207...."

NCCUSL Comment*

This section retains the focus of Section 7 of the UCCJA. It authorizes courts to decide that another state is in a better position to make the custody determination, taking into consideration the relative circumstances of the parties. If so, the court may defer to the other state.

The list of factors that the court may consider has been updated from the UCCJA. The list is not meant to be exclusive. Several provisions require comment. Subsection (1) is concerned specifically with domestic violence and other matters affecting the health and safety of the parties. For this purpose, the court should determine whether the parties are located in different states because one party is a victim of domestic violence or child abuse. If domestic violence or child abuse has occurred, this factor authorizes the court to consider which state can best protect the victim from further violence or abuse.

In applying subsection (3), courts should realize that distance concerns can be alleviated by applying the communication and cooperation provisions of Sections 152.111 and 152.112.

In applying subsection (7) on expeditious resolution of the controversy, the court could consider the different procedural and evidentiary laws of the two states, as well as the flexibility of the court dockets. It also should consider the ability of a court to arrive at a solution to all the legal issues surrounding the family. If one state has jurisdiction to decide both the custody and support issues, it would be desirable to determine that state to be the most convenient forum. The same is true when children of the same family live in different states. It would be inappropriate to require parents to have custody proceedings in several states when one state could resolve the custody of all the children.

Before determining whether to decline or retain jurisdiction, the court of this state may communicate, in accordance with Section 152.110, with a court of another state and exchange information pertinent to the assumption of jurisdiction by either court.

There are two departures from Section 7 of the UCCJA. First, the court may not simply dismiss the action. To do so would leave the case in limbo. Rather the court shall stay the case and direct the parties to file in the state that has been found to be the more convenient forum. The court is also authorized to impose any other conditions it considers appropriate. This might include the issuance of temporary custody orders during the time necessary to commence a proceeding in the designated state, dismissing the case if the custody proceeding is not commenced in the other state or resuming jurisdiction if a court of the other state refuses to take the case.

Second, UCCJA, §7(g) which allowed the court to assess fees and costs if it was a clearly inappropriate court, has been eliminated. If a court has jurisdiction under this Act, it could not be a clearly inappropriate court.

* See footnote on p. 472.

FAM §152.208. JURISDICTION DECLINED BY REASON OF CONDUCT

(a) Except as otherwise provided in Section 152.204 or other law of this state, if a court of this state has jurisdiction under this chapter because a person seeking to invoke its jurisdiction has engaged in unjustifiable conduct, the court shall decline to exercise its jurisdiction unless:

(1) the parents and all persons acting as parents have acquiesced in the exercise of jurisdiction;

(2) a court of the state otherwise having jurisdiction under Sections 152.201 through 152.203 determines that this state is a more appropriate forum under Section 152.207; or

(3) no court of any other state would have jurisdiction under the criteria specified in Sections 152.201 through 152.203.

(b) If a court of this state declines to exercise its jurisdiction pursuant to Subsection (a), it may fashion an appropriate remedy to ensure the safety of the child and prevent a repetition of the unjustifiable conduct, including staying the proceeding until a child custody proceeding is commenced in a court having jurisdiction under Sections 152.201 through 152.203.

(c) If a court dismisses a petition or stays a proceeding because it declines to exercise its jurisdiction pursuant to Subsection (a), it shall assess against the party seeking to invoke its jurisdiction necessary and reasonable expenses including costs, communication expenses, attorney's fees, investigative fees, expenses for witnesses, travel expenses, and child care during the course of the proceedings, unless the party from whom fees are sought establishes that the assessment would be clearly inappropriate. The court may not assess fees, costs, or expenses against this state unless authorized by law other than this chapter.

History of Fam. Code §152.208: Acts 1995, 74th Leg., ch. 20, §1, eff. Apr. 20, 1995. Renumbered from §152.008 by Acts 1999, 76th Leg., ch. 34, §1, eff. Sept. 1, 1999. Source: Former Fam. Code §11.58.

See also *O'Connor's Texas Family Law Handbook* (2017), "Petitioner engaged in unjustifiable conduct," ch. 4-B, §5.1.4, p. 361.

ANNOTATIONS

In re Lewin, 149 S.W.3d 727, 740-41 (Tex.App.—Austin 2004, orig. proceeding). Father "took the child from Canada to Texas for the purpose of obtaining another forum in which to litigate the custody issues he had already pursued in Canada. [Father] and the child's presence in Texas—the basis for the trial court's exercise of jurisdiction—was wholly due to the abduction. Even if there were an independent basis for the trial court's jurisdiction over [father's] modification suit ..., the trial court was required to decline its jurisdiction based on [father's] wrongful retention and later abduction of the child in search of a more favorable forum."

In re S.L.P., 123 S.W.3d 685, 689 (Tex.App.—Fort Worth 2003, no pet.). The purpose of §152.208 "is to ensure that when parents 'act in a reprehensible manner, such as removing, secreting, retaining, or restraining the child,' they will not receive an advantage for their unjustifiable conduct. [¶] [Mother] is the party seeking to invoke the trial court's jurisdiction. Therefore, it is [mother's] conduct that is examined under the standard set forth in the unjustifiable conduct provision." *See also* ***Dickerson v. Doyle***, 170 S.W.3d 713, 720 (Tex. App.—El Paso 2005, no pet.) (focus is on unjustified conduct of person who invoked court's jurisdiction); ***In re Presley***, 166 S.W.3d 866, 868 (Tex.App.—Beaumont 2005, orig. proceeding) (purpose of §152.208 is to ensure parents do not receive advantage for unjustifiable conduct).

NCCUSL Comment*

The "Clean Hands" section of the UCCJA has been truncated in this Act. Since there is no longer a multiplicity of jurisdictions which could take cognizance of a child-custody proceeding, there is less of a concern that one parent will take the child to another jurisdiction in an attempt to find a more favorable forum. Most of the jurisdictional problems generated by abducting parents should be solved by the prioritization of home state in Section 152.201; the exclusive, continuing jurisdiction provisions of Section 152.202; and the ban on modification in Section 152.203. For example, if a parent takes the child from the home state and seeks an original custody determination elsewhere, the stay-at-home parent has six months to file a custody petition under the extended home state jurisdictional provision of Section 152.201, which will ensure that the case is retained in the home state. If a petitioner for a modification determination takes the child from the state that issued the original custody determination, another state cannot assume jurisdiction as long as the first state exercises exclusive, continuing jurisdiction.

Nonetheless, there are still a number of cases where parents, or their surrogates, act in a reprehensible manner, such as removing, secreting, retaining, or restraining the child. This section ensures that abducting parents will not receive an advantage for their unjustifiable conduct. If the conduct that creates the jurisdiction is unjustified, courts must decline to exercise jurisdiction that is inappropriately invoked by one of the parties. For example, if one parent abducts the child pre-decree and establishes a new home state, that jurisdiction will decline to hear the case. There are exceptions. If the other party has acquiesced in the court's jurisdiction, the court may hear the case. Such acquiescence may occur by filing a pleading submitting to the jurisdiction, or by not filing in the court that would otherwise have jurisdiction under this Act. Similarly, if the court that would have jurisdiction finds that the court of this state is a more appropriate forum, the court may hear the case.

This section applies to those situations where jurisdiction exists because of the unjustified conduct of the person seeking to invoke it. If, for example, a parent in the state with exclusive, continuing jurisdiction under Section 152.202 has either restrained the child from visiting with the other parent, or has retained the child after visitation, and seeks to modify the decree, this section in inapplicable. The conduct of restraining or retaining the child did not create jurisdiction. Jurisdiction existed under this Act without regard to the parent's conduct. Whether a court should decline to hear the parent's request to modify is a matter of local law.

The focus in this section is on the unjustified conduct of the person who invokes the jurisdiction of the court. A technical illegality or wrong is insufficient to trigger the applicability of this section. This is particularly important in cases involving domestic violence and child abuse. Domestic violence victims should not be charged with unjustifiable conduct for conduct that occurred in the process of fleeing domestic violence, even if their conduct is technically illegal. Thus, if a parent flees with a child to escape domestic violence and in the process violates a joint custody decree, the case should not be automatically dismissed under this section. An inquiry must be made into whether the flight was justified under the circumstances of the case. However, an abusive parent who seizes the child and flees to another state to establish jurisdiction has engaged in unjustifiable conduct and the new state must decline to exercise jurisdiction under this section.

Subsection (b) authorizes the court to fashion an appropriate remedy for the safety of the child and to prevent a repetition of the unjustified conduct. Thus, it would be appropriate for the court to notify the other parent and to provide for foster care for the child until the child is returned to the other parent. The court could also stay the proceeding and require that a custody proceeding be instituted in another state that would have jurisdiction under this Act. It should be noted that the court is not making a forum non conveniens analysis in this section. If the conduct is unjustifiable, it must decline jurisdiction. It may, however, retain jurisdiction until a custody proceeding is commenced in the appropriate tribunal if such retention is necessary to prevent a repetition of the wrongful conduct or to ensure the safety of the child.

The attorney's fee standard for this section is patterned after the International Child Abduction Remedies Act, 42 U.S.C. §11607(b)(3). The assessed costs and fees are to be paid to the respondent who established that jurisdiction was based on unjustifiable conduct.

* See footnote on p. 472.

FAM §152.209. INFORMATION TO BE SUBMITTED TO COURT

(a) Except as provided by Subsection (e) or unless each party resides in this state, in a child custody proceeding, each party, in its first pleading or in an at-

tached affidavit, shall give information, if reasonably ascertainable, under oath as to the child's present address or whereabouts, the places where the child has lived during the last five years, and the names and present addresses of the persons with whom the child has lived during that period. The pleading or affidavit must state whether the party:

(1) has participated, as a party or witness or in any other capacity, in any other proceeding concerning the custody of or visitation with the child and, if so, identify the court, the case number, and the date of the child custody determination, if any;

(2) knows of any proceeding that could affect the current proceeding, including proceedings for enforcement and proceedings relating to domestic violence, protective orders, termination of parental rights, and adoptions and, if so, identify the court, the case number, and the nature of the proceeding; and

(3) knows the names and addresses of any person not a party to the proceeding who has physical custody of the child or claims rights of legal custody or physical custody of, or visitation with, the child and, if so, the names and addresses of those persons.

(b) If the information required by Subsection (a) is not furnished, the court, upon motion of a party or its own motion, may stay the proceeding until the information is furnished.

(c) If the declaration as to any of the items described in Subsections (a)(1) through (3) is in the affirmative, the declarant shall give additional information under oath as required by the court. The court may examine the parties under oath as to details of the information furnished and other matters pertinent to the court's jurisdiction and the disposition of the case.

(d) Each party has a continuing duty to inform the court of any proceeding in this or any other state that could affect the current proceeding.

(e) If a party alleges in an affidavit or a pleading under oath that the health, safety, or liberty of a party or child would be jeopardized by disclosure of identifying information, the information must be sealed and may not be disclosed to the other party or the public unless the court orders the disclosure to be made after a hearing in which the court takes into consideration the health, safety, or liberty of the party or child and determines that the disclosure is in the interest of justice.

History of Fam. Code §152.209: Acts 1995, 74th Leg., ch. 20, §1, eff. Apr. 20, 1995. Renumbered from §152.009 by Acts 1999, 76th Leg., ch. 34, §1, eff. Sept. 1, 1999. Amended by Acts 2003, 78th Leg., ch. 1036, §4, eff. Sept. 1, 2003. Source: Former Fam. Code §11.59.

NCCUSL Comment*

The pleading requirements from Section 9 of the UCCJA are generally carried over into this Act. Subsection (e) is based on the National Council of Juvenile and Family Court Judge's, Model Code on Domestic and Family Violence §304(c).

In subsection (a)(2), the term "proceedings" should be read broadly to include more than custody proceedings. Thus, if one parent was being criminally prosecuted for child abuse or custodial interference, those proceedings should be disclosed. If the child is subject to the Interstate Compact on the Placement of Children, facts relating to compliance with the Compact should be disclosed in the pleading or affidavit.

Subsection (b) has been added. It authorizes the court to stay the proceeding until the information required in subsection (a) has been disclosed, although failure to provide the information does not deprive the court of jurisdiction to hear the case. This follows the majority of jurisdictions which held that failure to comply with the pleading requirements of the UCCJA did not deprive the court of jurisdiction to make a custody determination.

FAM §152.210. APPEARANCE OF PARTIES & CHILD

(a) In a child custody proceeding in this state, the court may order a party to the proceeding who is in this state to appear before the court in person with or without the child. The court may order any person who is in this state and who has physical custody or control of the child to appear in person with the child.

(b) If a party to a child custody proceeding whose presence is desired by the court is outside this state, the court may order that a notice given pursuant to Section 152.108 include a statement directing the party to appear in person with or without the child and informing the party that failure to appear may result in a decision adverse to the party.

(c) The court may enter any orders necessary to ensure the safety of the child and of any person ordered to appear under this section.

(d) If a party to a child custody proceeding who is outside this state is directed to appear under Subsection (b) or desires to appear personally before the court with or without the child, the court may require another party to pay reasonable and necessary travel and other expenses of the party so appearing and of the child.

History of Fam. Code §152.210: Acts 1995, 74th Leg., ch. 20, §1, eff. Apr. 20, 1995. Renumbered from §152.011 by Acts 1999, 76th Leg., ch. 34, §1, eff. Sept. 1, 1999. Source: Former Fam. Code §11.61.

NCCUSL Comment*

No major changes have been made to this section which was Section 11 of the UCCJA. Language was added to subsection (a) to authorize the court to require a non-party who has physical custody of the child to produce the child.

Subsection (c) authorizes the court to enter orders providing for the safety of the child and the person ordered to appear with the child. If safety is a major concern, the court, as an alternative to ordering a party to appear with the child,

* See footnote on p. 472.

could order and arrange for the party's testimony to be taken in another state under Section 152.111. This alternative might be important when there are safety concerns regarding requiring victims of domestic violence or child abuse to travel to the jurisdiction where the abuser resides.

Sections 152.211-152.300 reserved for expansion

SUBCHAPTER D. ENFORCEMENT

FAM §152.301. DEFINITIONS

In this subchapter:

(1) "Petitioner" means a person who seeks enforcement of an order for return of a child under the Hague Convention on the Civil Aspects of International Child Abduction or enforcement of a child custody determination.

(2) "Respondent" means a person against whom a proceeding has been commenced for enforcement of an order for return of a child under the Hague Convention on the Civil Aspects of International Child Abduction or enforcement of a child custody determination.

History of Fam. Code §152.301: Acts 1999, 76th Leg., ch. 34, §1, eff. Sept. 1, 1999.

NCCUSL Comment*

For purposes of this article, "petitioner" and "respondent" are defined. The definitions clarify certain aspects of the notice and hearing sections.

FAM §152.302. ENFORCEMENT UNDER HAGUE CONVENTION

Under this subchapter a court of this state may enforce an order for the return of the child made under the Hague Convention on the Civil Aspects of International Child Abduction as if it were a child custody determination.

History of Fam. Code §152.302: Acts 1999, 76th Leg., ch. 34, §1, eff. Sept. 1, 1999.

NCCUSL Comment*

This section applies the enforcement remedies provided by this article to orders requiring the return of a child issued under the authority of the International Child Abduction Remedies Act (ICARA), 42 U.S.C. §11601 et seq., implementing the Hague Convention on the Civil Aspects of International Child Abduction. Specific mention of ICARA proceedings is necessary because they often occur prior to any formal custody determination. However, the need for a speedy enforcement remedy for an order to return the child is just as necessary.

FAM §152.303. DUTY TO ENFORCE

(a) A court of this state shall recognize and enforce a child custody determination of a court of another state if the latter court exercised jurisdiction in substantial conformity with this chapter or the determination was made under factual circumstances meeting the jurisdictional standards of this chapter and the determination has not been modified in accordance with this chapter.

(b) A court of this state may utilize any remedy available under other law of this state to enforce a child custody determination made by a court of another state. The remedies provided in this subchapter are cumulative and do not affect the availability of other remedies to enforce a child custody determination.

History of Fam. Code §152.303: Acts 1999, 76th Leg., ch. 34, §1, eff. Sept. 1, 1999.

NCCUSL Comment*

This section is based on Section 13 of the UCCJA which contained the basic duty to enforce. The language of the original section has been retained and the duty to enforce is generally the same.

Enforcement of custody determinations of issuing states is also required by federal law in the PKPA, 28 U.S.C. §1738A(a). The changes made in Subchapter C now make a state's duty to enforce and not modify a child custody determination of another state consistent with the enforcement and nonmodification provisions of the PKPA. Therefore custody determinations made by a state pursuant to the UCCJA that would be enforceable under the PKPA will generally be enforced under this Act. However, if a state custody determination made pursuant to the UCCJA would not be enforceable under the PKPA, it will also not be enforceable under this Act. Thus a custody determination made by a "significant connection" jurisdiction when there is a home state is not enforceable under the PKPA regardless of whether a proceeding was ever commenced in the home state. Even though such a determination would be enforceable under the UCCJA with its four concurrent bases of jurisdiction, it would not be enforceable under this Act. This carries out the policy of the PKPA of strongly discouraging a state from exercising its concurrent "significant connection" jurisdiction under the UCCJA when another state could exercise "home state" jurisdiction.

This section also incorporates the concept of Section 15 of the UCCJA to the effect that a custody determination of another state will be enforced in the same manner as a custody determination made by a court of this state. Whatever remedies are available to enforce a local determination can be utilized to enforce a custody determination of another state. However, it remains a custody determination of the state that issued it. A child-custody determination of another state is not subject to modification unless the state would have jurisdiction to modify the determination under Subchapter C.

The remedies provided by this subchapter for the enforcement of a custody determination will normally be used. This subchapter does not detract from other remedies available under other local law. There is often a need for a number of remedies to ensure that a child-custody determination is obeyed. If other remedies would easily facilitate enforcement, they are still available. The petitioner, for example, can still cite the respondent for contempt of court or file a tort claim for intentional interference with custodial relations if those remedies are available under local law.

FAM §152.304. TEMPORARY VISITATION

(a) A court of this state which does not have jurisdiction to modify a child custody determination may issue a temporary order enforcing:

(1) a visitation schedule made by a court of another state; or

(2) the visitation provisions of a child custody determination of another state that does not provide for a specific visitation schedule.

(b) If a court of this state makes an order under Subsection (a)(2), the court shall specify in the order a period that it considers adequate to allow the petitioner to obtain an order from a court having jurisdiction under the criteria specified in Subchapter C. The order re-

* See footnote on p. 472.

mains in effect until an order is obtained from the other court or the period expires.

History of Fam. Code §152.304: Acts 1999, 76th Leg., ch. 34, §1, eff. Sept. 1, 1999.

NCCUSL Comment*

This section authorizes a court to issue a temporary order if it is necessary to enforce visitation rights without violating the rules on nonmodification contained in Section 152.303. Therefore, if there is a visitation schedule provided in the custody determination that was made in accordance with Subchapter C, a court can issue an order under this section implementing the schedule. An implementing order may include make-up or substitute visitation.

A court may also issue a temporary order providing for visitation if visitation was authorized in the custody determination, but no specific schedule was included in the custody determination. Such an order could include a substitution of a specific visitation schedule for "reasonable and seasonable."

However, a court may not, under subsection (a)(2) provide for a permanent change in visitation. Therefore, requests for a permanent change in the visitation schedule must be addressed to the court with exclusive, continuing jurisdiction under Section 152.202 or modification jurisdiction under Section 152.203. As under Section 152.204, subsection (b) of this section requires that the temporary visitation order stay in effect only long enough to allow the person who obtained the order to obtain a permanent modification in the state with appropriate jurisdiction under Subchapter C.

FAM §152.305. REGISTRATION OF CHILD CUSTODY DETERMINATION

(a) A child custody determination issued by a court of another state may be registered in this state, with or without a simultaneous request for enforcement, by sending to the appropriate court in this state:

(1) a letter or other document requesting registration;

(2) two copies, including one certified copy, of the determination sought to be registered and a statement under penalty of perjury that to the best of the knowledge and belief of the person seeking registration the order has not been modified; and

(3) except as otherwise provided in Section 152.209, the name and address of the person seeking registration and any parent or person acting as a parent who has been awarded custody or visitation in the child custody determination sought to be registered.

(b) On receipt of the documents required by Subsection (a), the registering court shall:

(1) cause the determination to be filed as a foreign judgment, together with one copy of any accompanying documents and information, regardless of their form; and

(2) serve notice upon the persons named pursuant to Subsection (a)(3) and provide them with an opportunity to contest the registration in accordance with this section.

* See footnote on p. 472.

(c) The notice required by Subsection (b)(2) must state that:

(1) a registered determination is enforceable as of the date of the registration in the same manner as a determination issued by a court of this state;

(2) a hearing to contest the validity of the registered determination must be requested within 20 days after service of notice; and

(3) failure to contest the registration will result in confirmation of the child custody determination and preclude further contest of that determination with respect to any matter that could have been asserted.

(d) A person seeking to contest the validity of a registered order must request a hearing within 20 days after service of the notice. At that hearing, the court shall confirm the registered order unless the person contesting registration establishes that:

(1) the issuing court did not have jurisdiction under Subchapter C;

(2) the child custody determination sought to be registered has been vacated, stayed, or modified by a court having jurisdiction to do so under Subchapter C; or

(3) the person contesting registration was entitled to notice, but notice was not given in accordance with the standards of Section 152.108, in the proceedings before the court that issued the order for which registration is sought.

(e) If a timely request for a hearing to contest the validity of the registration is not made, the registration is confirmed as a matter of law and the person requesting registration and all persons served must be notified of the confirmation.

(f) Confirmation of a registered order, whether by operation of law or after notice and hearing, precludes further contest of the order with respect to any matter that could have been asserted at the time of registration.

History of Fam. Code §152.305: Acts 1995, 74th Leg., ch. 20, §1, eff. Apr. 20, 1995. Renumbered from §152.014 by Acts 1999, 76th Leg., ch. 34, §1, eff. Sept. 1, 1999. Source: Former Fam. Code §11.66.

ANNOTATIONS

Razo v. Vargas, 355 S.W.3d 866, 871-72 (Tex. App.—Houston [1st Dist.] 2011, no pet.). "Section 152.305 does not specifically require that the trial court hold an evidentiary hearing. [¶] In a situation in which an evidentiary hearing is not specifically required by statute, the issue turns on whether material facts necessary to determine the issue at hand are con-

troverted. If not, a trial court may summarily decide the issue; if so, 'the trial court must conduct an evidentiary hearing to determine the disputed material facts.' *At 874:* Although [in this case, mother's] request [to contest the validity of the registered child-custody decrees issued by a Mexican court] did not specifically state that [she] sought an 'evidentiary hearing,' she did specify two affirmative defenses to confirmation and enforcement.... [¶] We hold that by refusing to allow an evidentiary hearing before issuing its orders confirming the Mexican court's decrees [and] ordering their enforcement ... the trial court abused its discretion."

NCCUSL Comment*

The remainder of this subchapter provides enforcement mechanisms for interstate child custody determinations.

This section authorizes a simple registration procedure that can be used to predetermine the enforceability of a custody determination. It parallels the process in UIFSA for the registration of child support orders. It should be as much of an aid to pro se litigants as the registration procedure of UIFSA.

A custody determination can be registered without any accompanying request for enforcement. This may be of significant assistance in international cases. For example, the custodial parent under a foreign custody order can receive an advance determination of whether that order would be recognized and enforced before sending the child to the United States for visitation. Article 26 of the 1996 Hague Convention on Jurisdiction, Applicable Law, Recognition and Cooperation in Respect of Parental Responsibility and Measures for the Protection of Children, 35 I.L.M. 1391 (1996), requires those states which accede to the Convention to provide such a procedure.

FAM §152.306. ENFORCEMENT OF REGISTERED DETERMINATION

(a) A court of this state may grant any relief nor mally available under the law of this state to enforce a registered child custody determination made by a court of another state.

(b) A court of this state shall recognize and enforce, but may not modify, except in accordance with Subchapter C, a registered child custody determination of a court of another state.

History of Fam. Code §152.306: Acts 1995, 74th Leg., ch. 20, §1, eff. Apr. 20, 1995. Renumbered from §152.015 by Acts 1999, 76th Leg., ch. 34, §1, eff. Sept. 1, 1999. Source: Former Fam. Code §11.65.

NCCUSL Comment*

A registered child-custody determination can be enforced as if it was a child-custody determination of this state. However, it remains a custody determination of the state that issued it. A registered custody order is not subject to modification unless the state would have jurisdiction to modify the order under Subchapter C.

FAM §152.307. SIMULTANEOUS PROCEEDINGS

If a proceeding for enforcement under this subchapter is commenced in a court of this state and the court determines that a proceeding to modify the determination is pending in a court of another state having jurisdiction to modify the determination under Subchapter C, the enforcing court shall immediately communicate with the modifying court. The proceeding for enforcement continues unless the enforcing court, after consultation with the modifying court, stays or dismisses the proceeding.

History of Fam. Code §152.307: Acts 1995, 74th Leg., ch. 20, §1, eff. Apr. 20, 1995. Renumbered from §152.006 by Acts 1999, 76th Leg., ch. 34, §1, eff. Sept. 1, 1999. Source: Former Fam. Code §11.56.

NCCUSL Comment*

The pleading rules of Section 152.308, require the parties to disclose any pending proceedings. Normally, an enforcement proceeding will take precedence over a modification action since the PKPA requires enforcement of child custody determinations made in accordance with its terms. However, the enforcement court must communicate with the modification court in order to avoid duplicative litigation. The courts might decide that the court with jurisdiction under Subchapter C shall continue with the modification action and stay the enforcement proceeding. Or they might decide that the enforcement proceeding shall go forward. The ultimate decision rests with the court having exclusive, continuing jurisdiction under Section 152.202, or if there is no state with exclusive, continuing jurisdiction, then the decision rests with the state that would have jurisdiction to modify under Section 152.203. Therefore, if that court determines that the enforcement proceeding should be stayed or dismissed, the enforcement court should stay or dismiss the proceeding. If the enforcement court does not do so, the court with exclusive, continuing jurisdiction under Section 152.202, or with modification jurisdiction under Section 152.203, could enjoin the parties from continuing with the enforcement proceeding.

FAM §152.308. EXPEDITED ENFORCEMENT OF CHILD CUSTODY DETERMINATION

(a) A petition under this subchapter must be verified. Certified copies of all orders sought to be enforced and of any order confirming registration must be attached to the petition. A copy of a certified copy of an order may be attached instead of the original.

(b) A petition for enforcement of a child custody determination must state:

(1) whether the court that issued the determination identified the jurisdictional basis it relied upon in exercising jurisdiction and, if so, what the basis was;

(2) whether the determination for which enforcement is sought has been vacated, stayed, or modified by a court whose decision must be enforced under this chapter and, if so, identify the court, the case number, and the nature of the proceeding;

(3) whether any proceeding has been commenced that could affect the current proceeding, including proceedings relating to domestic violence, protective orders, termination of parental rights, and adoptions and, if so, identify the court, the case number, and the nature of the proceeding;

(4) the present physical address of the child and the respondent, if known;

* See footnote on p. 472.

(5) whether relief in addition to the immediate physical custody of the child and attorney's fees is sought, including a request for assistance from law enforcement officials and, if so, the relief sought; and

(6) if the child custody determination has been registered and confirmed under Section 152.305, the date and place of registration.

(c) Upon the filing of a petition, the court shall issue an order directing the respondent to appear in person with or without the child at a hearing and may enter any order necessary to ensure the safety of the parties and the child. The hearing must be held on the next judicial day after service of the order unless that date is impossible. In that event, the court shall hold the hearing on the first judicial day possible. The court may extend the date of hearing at the request of the petitioner.

(d) An order issued under Subsection (c) must state the time and place of the hearing and advise the respondent that at the hearing the court will award the petitioner immediate physical custody of the child and order the payment of fees, costs, and expenses under Section 152.312, and may schedule a hearing to determine whether further relief is appropriate, unless the respondent appears and establishes that:

(1) the child custody determination has not been registered and confirmed under Section 152.305 and that:

(A) the issuing court did not have jurisdiction under Subchapter C;

(B) the child custody determination for which enforcement is sought has been vacated, stayed, or modified by a court having jurisdiction to do so under Subchapter C; or

(C) the respondent was entitled to notice, but notice was not given in accordance with the standards of Section 152.108, in the proceedings before the court that issued the order for which enforcement is sought; or

(2) the child custody determination for which enforcement is sought was registered and confirmed under Section 152.305, but has been vacated, stayed, or modified by a court of a state having jurisdiction to do so under Subchapter C.

History of Fam. Code §152.308: Acts 1999, 76th Leg., ch. 34, §1, eff. Sept. 1, 1999.

NCCUSL Comment*

This section provides the normal remedy that will be used in interstate cases: the production of the child in a summary, remedial process based on habeas corpus.

The petition is intended to provide the court with as much information as possible. Attaching certified copies of all orders sought to be enforced allows the court to have the necessary information. Most of the information relates to the permissible scope of the court's inquiry. The petitioner has the responsibility to inform the court of all proceedings that would affect the current enforcement action. Specific mention is made of certain proceedings to ensure that they are disclosed. A "procedure relating to domestic violence" includes not only protective order proceedings but also criminal prosecutions for child abuse or domestic violence.

The order requires the respondent to appear at a hearing on the next judicial day. The term "next judicial day" in this section means the next day when a judge is at the courthouse. At the hearing, the court will order the child to be delivered to the petitioner unless the respondent is prepared to assert that the issuing state lacked jurisdiction, that notice was not given in accordance with Section 152.108, or that the order sought to be enforced has been vacated, modified, or stayed by a court with jurisdiction to do so under Subchapter C. The court is also to order payment of the fees and expenses set out in Section 152.312. The court may set another hearing to determine whether additional relief available under this state's law should be granted.

If the order has been registered and confirmed in accordance with Section 152.304, the only defense to enforcement is that the order has been vacated, stayed or modified since the registration proceeding by a court with jurisdiction to do so under Subchapter C.

FAM §152.309. SERVICE OF PETITION & ORDER

Except as otherwise provided in Section 152.311, the petition and order must be served, by any method authorized by the law of this state, upon the respondent and any person who has physical custody of the child.

History of Fam. Code §152.309: Acts 1999, 76th Leg., ch. 34, §1, eff. Sept. 1, 1999.

NCCUSL Comment*

In keeping with other sections of this Act, the question of how the petition and order should be served is left to local law.

FAM §152.310. HEARING & ORDER

(a) Unless the court issues a temporary emergency order pursuant to Section 152.204, upon a finding that a petitioner is entitled to immediate physical custody of the child, the court shall order that the petitioner may take immediate physical custody of the child unless the respondent establishes that:

(1) the child custody determination has not been registered and confirmed under Section 152.305 and that:

(A) the issuing court did not have jurisdiction under Subchapter C;

(B) the child custody determination for which enforcement is sought has been vacated, stayed, or modified by a court of a state having jurisdiction to do so under Subchapter C; or

(C) the respondent was entitled to notice, but notice was not given in accordance with the standards of Section 152.108, in the proceedings before the court that issued the order for which enforcement is sought; or

* See footnote on p. 472.

(2) the child custody determination for which enforcement is sought was registered and confirmed under Section 152.305 but has been vacated, stayed, or modified by a court of a state having jurisdiction to do so under Subchapter C.

(b) The court shall award the fees, costs, and expenses authorized under Section 152.312 and may grant additional relief, including a request for the assistance of law enforcement officials, and set a further hearing to determine whether additional relief is appropriate.

(c) If a party called to testify refuses to answer on the ground that the testimony may be self-incriminating, the court may draw an adverse inference from the refusal.

(d) A privilege against disclosure of communications between spouses and a defense of immunity based on the relationship of husband and wife or parent and child may not be invoked in a proceeding under this subchapter.

History of Fam. Code §152.310: Acts 1999, 76th Leg., ch. 34, §1, eff. Sept. 1, 1999.

NCCUSL Comment*

The scope of inquiry for the enforcing court is quite limited. Federal law requires the court to enforce the custody determination if the issuing state's decree was rendered in compliance with the PKPA. 28 U.S.C. §1738A(a). This Act requires enforcement of custody determinations that are made in conformity with Subchapter C's jurisdictional rules.

The certified copy, or a copy of the certified copy, of the custody determination entitling the petitioner to the child is prima facie evidence of the issuing court's jurisdiction to enter the order. If the order is one that is entitled to be enforced under Subchapter C and if it has been violated, the burden shifts to the respondent to show that the custody determination is not entitled to enforcement.

It is a defense to enforcement that another jurisdiction has issued a custody determination that is required to be enforced under Subchapter C. An example is when one court has based its original custody determination on the UCCJA §3(a)(2) (significant connections) and another jurisdiction has rendered an original custody determination based on the UCCJA §3(a)(1) (home state). When this occurs, Subchapter C, as well as the PKPA, mandate that the home state determination be enforced in all other states, including the state that rendered the significant connections determination.

Lack of notice in accordance with Section 152.108 by a person entitled to notice and opportunity to be heard at the original custody determination is a defense to enforcement of the custody determination. The scope of the defense under this Act is the same as the defense would be under the law of the state that issued the notice. Thus, if the defense of lack of notice would not be available under local law if the respondent purposely hid from the petitioner, took deliberate steps to avoid service of process or elected not to participate in the initial proceedings, the defense would also not be available under this Act.

There are no other defenses to an enforcement action. If the child would be endangered by the enforcement of a custody or visitation order, there may be a basis for the assumption of emergency jurisdiction under Section 152.204 of this Act. Upon the finding of an emergency, the court issues a temporary order and directs the parties to proceed either in the court that is exercising continuing jurisdiction over the custody proceeding under Section 152.202, or the court that would have jurisdiction to modify the custody determination under Section 152.203.

The court shall determine at the hearing whether fees should be awarded under Section 152.312. If so, it should order them paid. The court may determine if additional relief is appropriate, including requesting law enforcement officers to assist the petitioner in the enforcement of the order. The court may set a hearing to determine whether further relief should be granted.

The remainder of this section is derived from UIFSA §316 with regard to the privilege of self-incrimination, spousal privileges, and immunities. It is included to keep parallel the procedures for child support and child custody proceedings to the extent possible.

FAM §152.311. WARRANT TO TAKE PHYSICAL CUSTODY OF CHILD

(a) Upon the filing of a petition seeking enforcement of a child custody determination, the petitioner may file a verified application for the issuance of a warrant to take physical custody of the child if the child is imminently likely to suffer serious physical harm or be removed from this state.

(b) If the court, upon the testimony of the petitioner or other witness, finds that the child is imminently likely to suffer serious physical harm or be removed from this state, it may issue a warrant to take physical custody of the child. The petition must be heard on the next judicial day after the warrant is executed unless that date is impossible. In that event, the court shall hold the hearing on the first judicial day possible. The application for the warrant must include the statements required by Section 152.308(b).

(c) A warrant to take physical custody of a child must:

(1) recite the facts upon which a conclusion of imminent serious physical harm or removal from the jurisdiction is based;

(2) direct law enforcement officers to take physical custody of the child immediately;

(3) state the date for the hearing on the petition; and

(4) provide for the safe interim placement of the child pending further order of the court and impose conditions on placement of the child to ensure the appearance of the child and the child's custodian.

(c-1) If the petition seeks to enforce a child custody determination made in a foreign country or an order for the return of the child made under the Hague Convention on the Civil Aspects of International Child Abduction, the court may place a child with a parent or family member in accordance with Subsection (c)(4) only if the parent or family member has significant ties to the jurisdiction of the court. If a parent or family member of the child does not have significant ties to the jurisdiction of the court, the court shall provide for

* See footnote on p. 472.

the delivery of the child to the Department of Family and Protective Services in the manner provided for the delivery of a missing child by Section 262.007(c).

(d) The respondent must be served with the petition, warrant, and order immediately after the child is taken into physical custody.

(e) A warrant to take physical custody of a child is enforceable throughout this state. If the court finds on the basis of the testimony of the petitioner or other witness that a less intrusive remedy is not effective, it may authorize law enforcement officers to enter private property to take physical custody of the child. If required by exigent circumstances of the case, the court may authorize law enforcement officers to make a forcible entry at any hour.

(f) Repealed by Acts 2011, 82nd Leg., ch. 92, §4, eff. Sept. 1, 2011.

History of Fam. Code §152.311: Acts 1999, 76th Leg., ch. 34, §1, eff. Sept. 1, 1999. Amended by Acts 2011, 82nd Leg., ch. 92, §§2, 4, eff. Sept. 1, 2011.

NCCUSL Comment*

The section provides a remedy for emergency situations where there is a reason to believe that the child will suffer imminent, serious physical harm or be removed from the jurisdiction once the respondent learns that the petitioner has filed an enforcement proceeding. If the court finds such harm exists, it should temporarily waive the notice requirements and issue a warrant to take physical custody of the child. Immediately after the warrant is executed, the respondent is to receive notice of the proceedings.

The term "harm" cannot be totally defined and, as in the issuance of temporary restraining orders, the appropriate issuance of a warrant is left to the circumstances of the case. Those circumstances include cases where the respondent is the subject of a criminal proceeding as well as situations where the respondent is secreting the child in violation of a court order, abusing the child, a flight risk and other circumstances that the court concludes make the issuance of notice a danger to the child. The court must hear the testimony of the petitioner or another witness prior to issuing the warrant. The testimony may be heard in person, via telephone, or by any other means acceptable under local law. The court must state the reasons for the issuance of the warrant. The warrant can be enforced by law enforcement officers wherever the child is found in the state. The warrant may authorize entry upon private property to pick up the child if no less intrusive means are possible. In extraordinary cases, the warrant may authorize law enforcement to make a forcible entry at any hour.

The warrant must provide for the placement of the child pending the determination of the enforcement proceeding. Since the issuance of the warrant would not occur absent a risk of serious harm to the child, placement cannot be with the respondent. Normally, the child would be placed with the petitioner. However, if placement with the petitioner is not indicated, the court can order any other appropriate placement authorized under the laws of the court's state. Placement with the petitioner may not be indicated if there is a likelihood that the petitioner also will flee the jurisdiction. Placement with the petitioner may not be practical if the petitioner is proceeding through an attorney and is not present before the court.

This section authorizes the court to utilize whatever means are available under local law to ensure the appearance of the petitioner and child at the enforcement hearing. Such means might include cash bonds, a surrender of a passport, or whatever the court determines is necessary.

FAM §152.312. COSTS, FEES, & EXPENSES

(a) The court shall award the prevailing party, including a state, necessary and reasonable expenses incurred by or on behalf of the party, including costs, communication expenses, attorney's fees, investigative fees, expenses for witnesses, travel expenses, and child care during the course of the proceedings, unless the party from whom fees or expenses are sought establishes that the award would be clearly inappropriate.

(b) The court may not assess fees, costs, or expenses against a state unless authorized by law other than this chapter.

History of Fam. Code §152.312: Acts 1999, 76th Leg., ch. 34, §1, eff. Sept. 1, 1999.

NCCUSL Comment*

This section is derived from the International Child Abduction Remedies Act, 42 U.S.C. §11607(b)(3). Normally the court will award fees and costs against the non-prevailing party. Included as expenses are the amount of investigation fees incurred by private persons or by public officials as well as the cost of child placement during the proceedings.

The non-prevailing party has the burden of showing that such an award would be clearly inappropriate. Fees and costs may be inappropriate if their payment would cause the parent and child to seek public assistance.

This section implements the policies of Section 8(c) of Pub.L. 96-611 (part of the PKPA) which provides that:

In furtherance of the purposes of §1738A of title 28, United States Code [this section], as added by subsection (a) of this section, state courts are encouraged to—

(2) award to the person entitled to custody or visitation pursuant to a custody determination which is consistent with the provisions of such §1738A [this section], necessary travel expenses, attorneys' fees, costs of private investigations, witness fees or expenses, and other expenses incurred in connection with such custody determination....

The term "prevailing party" is not given a special definition for this Act. Each state will apply its own standard.

Subsection (b) was added to ensure that this section would not apply to the state unless otherwise authorized. The language is taken from UIFSA §313 (court may assess costs against obligee or support enforcement agency only if allowed by local law).

FAM §152.313. RECOGNITION & ENFORCEMENT

A court of this state shall accord full faith and credit to an order issued by another state and consistent with this chapter which enforces a child custody determination by a court of another state unless the order has been vacated, stayed, or modified by a court having jurisdiction to do so under Subchapter C.

History of Fam. Code §152.313: Acts 1995, 74th Leg., ch. 20, §1, eff. Apr. 20, 1995. Renumbered from §152.013 by Acts 1999, 76th Leg., ch. 34, §1, eff. Sept. 1, 1999. Source: Former Fam. Code §11.63.

NCCUSL Comment*

The enforcement order, to be effective, must also be enforced by other states. This section requires courts of this state to enforce and not modify enforcement orders issued by other states when made consistently with the provisions of this Act.

A FAM §152.314. ACCELERATED APPEALS

The amended text in §152.314 is effective for orders rendered on or after Sept. 1, 2017. Orders rendered before Sept. 1, 2017, are governed by the former law in effect at that time.

* See footnote on p. 472.

An appeal may be taken from a final order in a proceeding under this subchapter in accordance with accelerated [~~expedited~~] appellate procedures in other civil cases. Unless the court enters a temporary emergency order under Section 152.204, the enforcing court may not stay an order enforcing a child custody determination pending appeal.

History of Fam. Code §152.314: Acts 1999, 76th Leg., ch. 34, §1, eff. Sept. 1, 1999. Amended by S.B. 1237, §8, 85th Leg., eff. Sept. 1, 2017.

NCCUSL Comment*

The order may be appealed as an expedited civil matter. An enforcement order should not be stayed by the court. Provisions for a stay would defeat the purpose of having a quick enforcement procedure. If there is a risk of serious mistreatment or abuse to the child, a petition to assume emergency jurisdiction must be filed under Section 152.204. This section leaves intact the possibility of obtaining an extraordinary remedy such as mandamus or prohibition from an appellate court to stay the court's enforcement action. In many states, it is not possible to limit the constitutional authority of appellate courts to issue a stay. However, unless the information before the appellate panel indicates that emergency jurisdiction would be assumed under Section 152.204, there is no reason to stay the enforcement of the order pending appeal.

FAM §152.315. ROLE OF PROSECUTOR OR PUBLIC OFFICIAL

(a) In a case arising under this chapter or involving the Hague Convention on the Civil Aspects of International Child Abduction, the prosecutor or other appropriate public official may take any lawful action, including resorting to a proceeding under this subchapter or any other available civil proceeding to locate a child, obtain the return of a child, or enforce a child custody determination if there is:

(1) an existing child custody determination;

(2) a request to do so from a court in a pending child custody proceeding;

(3) a reasonable belief that a criminal statute has been violated; or

(4) a reasonable belief that the child has been wrongfully removed or retained in violation of the Hague Convention on the Civil Aspects of International Child Abduction.

(b) A prosecutor or appropriate public official acting under this section acts on behalf of the court and may not represent any party.

History of Fam. Code §152.315: Acts 1999, 76th Leg., ch. 34, §1, eff. Sept. 1, 1999.

NCCUSL Comment*

Sections 152.315-152.317 are derived from the recommendations of the *Obstacles Study* that urge a role for public authorities in civil enforcement of custody and visitation determinations. One of the basic policies behind this approach is that, as is the case with child support, the involvement of public authorities will encourage the parties to abide by the terms of the court order. The prosecutor usually would be the most appropriate public official to exercise authority under this section. However, states may locate the authority described in the section in the most appropriate public office for their governmental structure. The authority could be, for example, the Friend of the Court Office or the Attorney General. If the parties know that prosecutors and law enforcement officers are available to help secure the return of a child, the parties may be deterred from interfering with the exercise of rights established by court order.

The use of public authorities should provide a more effective method of remedying violations of the custody determination. Most parties do not have the resources to enforce a custody determination in another jurisdiction. The availability of the prosecutor or other government official as an enforcement agency will help ensure that remedies of this Act can be made available regardless of income level. In addition, the prosecutor may have resources to draw on that are unavailable to the average litigant.

The role of the public authorities should generally not begin until there is a custody determination that is sought to be enforced. The Act does not authorize the public authorities to be involved in the action leading up to the making of the custody determination, except when requested by the court, when there is a violation the Hague Convention on the Civil Aspects of International Child Abduction, or when the person holding the child has violated a criminal statute. This Act does not mandate that the public authorities be involved in all cases referred to it. There is only so much time and money available for enforcement proceedings. Therefore, the public authorities eventually will develop guidelines to determine which cases will receive priority.

The use of civil procedures instead of, or in addition to, filing and prosecuting criminal charges enlarges the prosecutor's options and may provide a more economical and less disruptive means of solving problems of criminal abduction and retention. With the use of criminal proceedings alone, the procedure may be inadequate to ensure the return of the child. The civil options would permit the prosecutor to resolve that recurring and often frustrating problem.

A concern was expressed about whether allowing the prosecutor to use civil means as a method of settling a child abduction violated either DR 7-105(A) of the Code of Professional Responsibility or Model Rule of Professional Responsibility 4.4. Both provisions either explicitly or implicitly disapprove of a lawyer threatening criminal action to gain an advantage in a civil case. However, the prohibition relates to threats that are solely to gain an advantage in a civil case. If the prosecutor has a good faith reason for pursuing the criminal action, there is no ethical violation. See also *Committee on Legal Ethics v. Printz*, 416 S.E. 2d 720 (W.Va.1992) (lawyer can threaten to press criminal charges against a client's former employee unless employee made restitution).

It must be emphasized that the public authorities do not become involved in the merits of the case. They are authorized only to locate the child and enforce the custody determination. The public authority is authorized by this section to utilize any civil proceeding to secure the enforcement of the custody determination. In most jurisdictions, that would be a proceeding under this Act. If the prosecutor proceeds pursuant to this Act, the prosecutor is subject to its provisions. There is nothing in this Act that would prevent a state from authorizing the prosecutor or other public official to use additional remedies beyond those provided in this Act.

The public authority does not represent any party to the custody determination. It acts as a "friend of the court." Its role is to ensure that the custody determination is enforced.

Sections 152.315-152.317 are limited to cases covered by this Act, i.e. interstate cases.

It should also be noted that the provisions of this section relate to the civil enforcement of child custody determinations. Nothing in this section is meant to detract from the ability of the prosecutor to use criminal provisions in child abduction cases.

FAM §152.316. ROLE OF LAW ENFORCEMENT

At the request of a prosecutor or other appropriate public official acting under Section 152.315, a law enforcement officer may take any lawful action reasonably necessary to locate a child or a party and assist a

* See footnote on p. 472.

prosecutor or appropriate public official with responsibilities under Section 152.315.

History of Fam. Code §152.316: Acts 1999, 76th Leg., ch. 34, §1, eff. Sept. 1, 1999.

NCCUSL Comment*

This section authorizes law enforcement officials to assist in locating a child and enforcing a custody determination when requested to do so by the public authorities. It is to be read as an enabling provision. Whether law enforcement officials have discretion in responding to a request by the prosecutor or other public official is a matter of local law.

FAM §152.317. COSTS & EXPENSES

If the respondent is not the prevailing party, the court may assess against the respondent all direct expenses and costs incurred by the prosecutor or other appropriate public official and law enforcement officers under Section 152.315 or 152.316.

History of Fam. Code §152.317: Acts 1999, 76th Leg., ch. 34, §1, eff. Sept. 1, 1999.

NCCUSL Comment*

One of the major problems of utilizing public officials to locate children and enforce custody and visitation determinations is cost. This section authorizes the prosecutor and law enforcement to recover costs against the non-prevailing party. The use of the term "direct" indicates that overhead is not a recoverable cost. This section cannot be used to recover the value of the time spent by the public authorities' attorneys.

CHAPTER 153. CONSERVATORSHIP, POSSESSION, & ACCESS

* See footnote on p. 472.

SUBCHAPTER A. GENERAL PROVISIONS

FAM §153.001. PUBLIC POLICY

(a) The public policy of this state is to:

(1) assure that children will have frequent and continuing contact with parents who have shown the ability to act in the best interest of the child;

(2) provide a safe, stable, and nonviolent environment for the child; and

(3) encourage parents to share in the rights and duties of raising their child after the parents have separated or dissolved their marriage.

(b) A court may not render an order that conditions the right of a conservator to possession of or access to a child on the payment of child support.

History of Fam. Code §153.001: Acts 1995, 74th Leg., ch. 20, §1, eff. Apr. 20, 1995. Amended by Acts 1995, 74th Leg., ch. 751, §25, eff. Sept. 1, 1995; Acts 1999, 76th Leg., ch. 787, §2, eff. Sept. 1, 1999. Source: Former Fam. Code §14.021(a).

FAM §153.002. BEST INTEREST OF CHILD

The best interest of the child shall always be the primary consideration of the court in determining the issues of conservatorship and possession of and access to the child.

History of Fam. Code §153.002: Acts 1995, 74th Leg., ch. 20, §1, eff. Apr. 20, 1995. Source: Former Fam. Code §14.07(a).

See also *O'Connor's Texas Family Law Handbook* (2017), "Best Interest of Child," ch. 4-E, §14, p. 491.

ANNOTATIONS

Troxel v. Granville, 530 U.S. 57, 68 (2000). "[T]here is a presumption that fit parents act in the best interests of their children."

Gillespie v. Gillespie, 644 S.W.2d 449, 451 (Tex. 1982). "The trial court is given wide latitude in determining the best interests of a minor child. The judgment of the trial court will be reversed only when it appears from the record as a whole that the court has abused its discretion."

Holley v. Adams, 544 S.W.2d 367, 371-72 (Tex. 1976). "An extended number of factors have been considered by the courts in ascertaining the best interest of the child. Included among these are the following: (A) the desires of the child; (B) the emotional and physical needs of the child now and in the future; (C) the emotional and physical danger to the child now and in the future; (D) the parental abilities of the individuals seeking custody; (E) the programs available to assist these individuals to promote the best interest of the child; (F) the plans for the child by these individuals or by the agency seeking custody; (G) the stability of the home or proposed placement; (H) the acts or omissions of the parent which may indicate that the existing parent-child relationship is not a proper one; and (I) any excuse for the acts or omissions of the parent. This listing is by no means exhaustive, but does indicate a number of considerations which either have been or would appear to be pertinent."

Bukovich v. Bukovich, 399 S.W.2d 528, 529 (Tex. 1966). "The controlling considerations are those changes of conditions affecting the welfare of the child. The desires, acts and claims of the respective parents are secondary considerations and material only as they bear upon the question of the best interest of the child."

Allen v. Allen, 475 S.W.3d 453, 458 (Tex.App.—Houston [14th Dist.] 2015, no pet.). "[T]he trial court ... determined that the best interest of the children was served by appointing [father] and not [mother] as the parent with the right to determine the primary residence. [¶] [T]he trial judge emphasized that [mother] had persisted and would likely continue to persist in preventing the children from having any chance at a relationship with their father. The judge further expressed doubt as to whether, if she were given the right to determine the children's primary residence, [mother] would ever allow the children to have a good relationship with [father]. Such persistent alienation of the other parent can be a guiding consideration in making possession and access determinations."

In re K.D., 471 S.W.3d 147, 165 (Tex.App.—Texarkana 2015, no pet.). See annotation under Family Code §153.0071, p. 508.

In re H.D.C., 474 S.W.3d 758, 764-65 (Tex.App.—Houston [14th Dist.] 2014, no pet.). "Although the trial court did not abuse its discretion in finding that the best interests of the children require them to be supervised and had ample evidence to support a restriction on who could supervise the children, ... the requirement that Mother herself be 'off work' and 'present' during her month of summer possession is unduly burdensome and unnecessarily restrictive. [This] restriction ... exceeds that which is required to protect the best interests of the children because a less burdensome restriction can serve the trial court's reasonable requirement that the children be properly supervised at all times."

In re Macalik, 13 S.W.3d 43, 45 (Tex.App.—Texarkana 1999, no pet.). In SAPCRs, "when the best interest of the child is always the overriding consideration, technical rules of pleading and practice are of little importance, and fair notice is afforded when the pleadings generally invoke the court's jurisdiction over custody and control of the children."

Fair v. Davis, 787 S.W.2d 422, 428-29 (Tex.App.—Dallas 1990, no writ). "*Weighing or taking into account* 'best interest' is different from requiring an affirmative finding of 'best interest.' Some courts have included 'best interests' as an element to be established in modifying visitation. We do not find a statutory requirement to do so. ... We hold that the requirement to *consider* best interest under [Fam. Code] §14.07(a) [now §153.002] is an instruction to give *deliberate thought to and weigh* all facts and circumstances that bear directly or indirectly on a child, including but not limited to, present or future physical, mental, emotional, educational, social, disciplinary and moral welfare, well-being, stability, and developmental needs. Likewise a finding of positive improvement is not a requirement under this section of the code."

FAM §153.003. NO DISCRIMINATION BASED ON SEX OR MARITAL STATUS

The court shall consider the qualifications of the parties without regard to their marital status or to the sex of the party or the child in determining:

(1) which party to appoint as sole managing conservator;

(2) whether to appoint a party as joint managing conservator; and

(3) the terms and conditions of conservatorship and possession of and access to the child.

History of Fam. Code §153.003: Acts 1995, 74th Leg., ch. 20, §1, eff. Apr. 20, 1995. Source: Former Fam. Code §§14.01(c)(1), 14.032(d).

ANNOTATIONS

In re McLean, 725 S.W.2d 696, 698 (Tex.1987). "The state no doubt has a significant interest in protecting the welfare of a child born to a mother not married to the child's father. [¶] Nevertheless, the state's interest can be protected without discriminating solely on the basis of sex. … A father who steps forward, willing and able to shoulder the responsibilities of raising a child should not be required to meet a higher burden of proof solely because he is male."

In re M.S.F., 383 S.W.3d 712, 716-17 (Tex.App.—Amarillo 2012, no pet.). Mother's "position regarding the evidence to support the trial court's finding of a material and substantial change of circumstances is that the trial court [improperly] considered evidence that centered almost exclusively on [mother's] marital status and religious beliefs. However, [§153.003] has not been held to bar a court from considering the effect of a parent's lifestyle and lifestyle choices upon the children when deciding matters of custody."

A FAM §153.004. HISTORY OF DOMESTIC VIOLENCE OR SEXUAL ABUSE

The amended text in §153.004 is effective for SAPCRs pending or filed on or after Sept. 1, 2017. SAPCRs in which a final order is rendered before Sept. 1, 2017, are governed by the former law in effect at that time.

(a) In determining whether to appoint a party as a sole or joint managing conservator, the court shall consider evidence of the intentional use of abusive physical force, or evidence of sexual abuse, by a party directed against the party's spouse, a parent of the child, or any person younger than 18 years of age committed within a two-year period preceding the filing of the suit or during the pendency of the suit.

(b) The court may not appoint joint managing conservators if credible evidence is presented of a history or pattern of past or present child neglect, or physical or sexual abuse by one parent directed against the other parent, a spouse, or a child, including a sexual assault in violation of Section 22.011 or 22.021, Penal Code, that results in the other parent becoming pregnant with the child. A history of sexual abuse includes a sexual assault that results in the other parent becoming pregnant with the child, regardless of the prior relationship of the parents. It is a rebuttable presumption that the appointment of a parent as the sole managing conservator of a child or as the conservator who has the exclusive right to determine the primary residence of a child is not in the best interest of the child if credible evidence is presented of a history or pattern of past or present child neglect, or physical or sexual abuse by that parent directed against the other parent, a spouse, or a child.

(c) The court shall consider the commission of family violence or sexual abuse in determining whether to deny, restrict, or limit the possession of a child by a parent who is appointed as a possessory conservator.

(d) The court may not allow a parent to have access to a child for whom it is shown by a preponderance of the evidence that:

(1) there is a history or pattern of committing family violence during the two years preceding the date of the filing of the suit or during the pendency of the suit; or

(2) the parent engaged in conduct that constitutes an offense under Section 21.02, 22.011, 22.021, or 25.02, Penal Code, and that as a direct result of the conduct, the victim of the conduct became pregnant with the parent's child.

(d-1) Notwithstanding Subsection (d), the court may allow a parent to have access to a child if the court:

(1) finds that awarding the parent access to the child would not endanger the child's physical health or emotional welfare and would be in the best interest of the child; and

(2) renders a possession order that is designed to protect the safety and well-being of the child and any other person who has been a victim of family violence committed by the parent and that may include a requirement that:

(A) the periods of access be continuously supervised by an entity or person chosen by the court;

(B) the exchange of possession of the child occur in a protective setting;

(C) the parent abstain from the consumption of alcohol or a controlled substance, as defined by Chapter 481, Health and Safety Code, within 12 hours prior to or during the period of access to the child; or

(D) the parent attend and complete a battering intervention and prevention program as provided by Article 42.141, Code of Criminal Procedure, or, if such a program is not available, complete a course of treatment under Section 153.010.

(e) It is a rebuttable presumption that it is not in the best interest of a child for a parent to have unsupervised visitation with the child if credible evidence is presented of a history or pattern of past or present child neglect or [~~physical or sexual~~] abuse or family violence by:

(1) that parent; or

(2) any person who resides in that parent's household or who is permitted by that parent to have unsupervised access to the child during that parent's periods of possession of or access to the child [~~directed against the other parent, a spouse, or a child~~].

(f) In determining under this section whether there is credible evidence of a history or pattern of past or present child neglect or [~~physical or sexual~~] abuse or family violence by a parent or other person, as applicable [~~directed against the other parent, a spouse, or a child~~], the court shall consider whether a protective order was rendered under Chapter 85, Title 4, against the parent or other person during the two-year period preceding the filing of the suit or during the pendency of the suit.

(g) In this section:

(1) "Abuse" and "neglect" have the meanings assigned by Section 261.001.

(2) "Family violence" has the meaning assigned by Section 71.004.

History of Fam. Code §153.004: Acts 1995, 74th Leg., ch. 20, §1, eff. Apr. 20, 1995. Amended by Acts 1999, 76th Leg., ch. 774, §1 (eff. Sept. 1, 1999), ch. 787, §3 (eff. Sept. 1, 1999); Acts 2001, 77th Leg., ch. 586, §1, eff. Sept. 1, 2001; Acts 2003, 78th Leg., ch. 642, §1, eff. Sept. 1, 2003; Acts 2013, 83rd Leg., ch. 907 §§1, 2, eff. Sept. 1, 2013; S.B. 495, §1, 85th Leg., eff. Sept. 1, 2017. Source: Former Fam. Code §§14.01(c)(2), 14.021(h), 14.03(d), (e)(3).

See also *O'Connor's Texas Family Law Handbook* (2017), "Domestic violence bars JMC," ch. 4-E, §15.3.1(2)(a), p. 498; "Family violence, sexual abuse & pregnancy caused by criminal act," ch. 4-E, §16.2.4(2), p. 511.

ANNOTATIONS

Peña v. Peña, 8 S.W.3d 639, 639 (Tex.1999). "[W]e disapprove of the following language in the court of appeals' opinion: 'In the present case, the two hitting incidents left [W] with a black eye each time. However, [W's] testimony only vaguely connects the two hitting incidents as both having been precipitated by arguments over [H's ex-W] and daughters. We do not know who initiated the arguments, whether the hittings were provoked in any manner, or what other factors may have contributed to either or both incidents, or any other relevant details that may show a relationship, connection or predictable pattern of physical abuse.' These considerations are not relevant to determining whether there was physical abuse or a history or pattern of domestic violence under the statute."

Lewelling v. Lewelling, 796 S.W.2d 164, 168 (Tex. 1990). Family Code §14.01(c)(2), now §153.004(a), "creates a preference that the non-violent parent, rather than the violent parent, be appointed managing conservator. Thus, in a custody dispute between two parents, §14.01(c)(2) allows evidence of spousal abuse to be considered only as a factor that weighs heavily against the abusive parent; such evidence does not weigh against the abused. As the abuser cannot take advantage of his acts of abuse in a custody battle with the abused, so the abuser's parents also may not benefit from that abuse. While expressing continued concern for the best interest of the child, the Legislature has also determined that removing a child from a parent simply because she has suffered physical abuse at the hands of her spouse is not in the best interest of our state."

Baker v. Baker, 469 S.W.3d 269, 274 (Tex.App.—Houston [14th Dist.] 2015, no pet.). Father "contends that §153.004(b) is applicable only when there is an express finding of a 'history or pattern of past or present child neglect, or physical or sexual abuse.' Father suggests that the trial court's more general finding of 'family violence' does not qualify under the statute. [¶] Based on the broad meanings of [family violence and abuse], we conclude that an act by one spouse that is intended to result in bodily injury to the other spouse, and actually results in bodily injury to the other spouse, qualifies as both family violence and physical abuse. We reject Father's argument that the trial court's finding of family violence is insufficient to trigger the effects of §153.004(b). [¶] Section 153.004(b) indicates that a history can be established by just a single incident. ... '[A] single act of violence can amount to a history of physical abuse.' *At 275-76:* Section 153.004 creates a presumption that it is not in the best interests of a child for a parent with a history of physical abuse to

be appointed [SMC]. However, that presumption is 'rebuttable.' Thus, Father is not rendered ineligible to be named [SMC], even though Mother proved that he has a history of being physically abusive towards her."

Kittman v. Miller, No. 12-13-00097-CV (Tex. App.—Tyler 2013, pet. denied) (memo op.; 8-29-13). "[T]he plain language of §153.004[(a)] indicates that evidence of the intentional use of abusive physical force must be used in determining whether to appoint a party as a sole or joint managing conservator. However, this statute applies to an original suit for conservatorship, possession, and access, not a modification suit. [Further], the plain language of §153.004 specifically states that its provision regarding evidence of the intentional use of abusive physical force applies to 'parties.' [Mother's] new husband and stepfather to her children[ ] was not a party to the original divorce and is not a party to this suit. Because §153.004 does not apply to this modification suit or to a nonparty, we conclude that the trial court abused its discretion by excluding evidence of [stepfather's] domestic violence that occurred more than two years prior to the filing of the suit."

Watts v. Watts, 396 S.W.3d 19, 22 (Tex.App.—San Antonio 2012, no pet.). Father argues "that [father] and [mother] could have been appointed [JMCs] if the jury found they both had been physically abusive against each other. This is a misunderstanding of the applicable law. [¶] [T]he trial court is prohibited from appointing [JMCs] where a history or pattern of abuse between the two parents exists regardless of whether the abuse is inflicted by one parent against the other or by both parents against each other. In other words, a history or pattern of physical abuse by both parents against each other necessarily includes a history or pattern of physical abuse by one parent against the other."

In re D.R., 177 S.W.3d 574, 582 (Tex.App.—Houston [1st Dist.] 2005, pet. denied). "Nothing in §153.004 automatically precluded [father] from being appointed as [child's] sole managing conservator upon a showing of a history or pattern of abuse or family violence. Moreover, §153.004(d) indicates that, even after a jury finding of family violence, [father] could still have been permitted 'access' to [child]. [T]he trial court's charge to the jury precluded the jury, once it made an affirmative finding [of a history of family violence], from considering whether [father] should have been appointed as [child's] sole managing conservator. We hold that the trial court erred in submitting [this jury charge]. *At 584:* [W]e further hold that the error constitutes reversible error...." *See also* ***In re M.M.M.***, 307 S.W.3d 846, 853-54 (Tex.App.—Fort Worth 2010, no pet.) (after finding of family violence, father was awarded supervised access to child).

FAM §153.005. APPOINTMENT OF SOLE OR JOINT MANAGING CONSERVATOR

(a) In a suit, except as provided by Section 153.004, the court:

(1) may appoint a sole managing conservator or may appoint joint managing conservators; and

(2) if the parents are or will be separated, shall appoint at least one managing conservator.

(b) A managing conservator must be a parent, a competent adult, the Department of Family and Protective Services, or a licensed child-placing agency.

(c) In making an appointment authorized by this section, the court shall consider whether, preceding the filing of the suit or during the pendency of the suit:

(1) a party engaged in a history or pattern of family violence, as defined by Section 71.004;

(2) a party engaged in a history or pattern of child abuse or child neglect; or

(3) a final protective order was rendered against a party.

History of Fam. Code §153.005: Acts 1995, 74th Leg., ch. 20, §1, eff. Apr. 20, 1995. Amended by Acts 2015, 84th Leg., ch. 1, §1.043 (eff. Apr. 2, 2015), ch. 117, §3 (eff. Sept. 1, 2015). Source: Former Fam. Code §14.01(a).

See also *O'Connor's Texas Family Law Handbook* (2017), "Appointing Conservators," ch. 4-E, §15, p. 496.

FAM §153.006. APPOINTMENT OF POSSESSORY CONSERVATOR

(a) If a managing conservator is appointed, the court may appoint one or more possessory conservators.

(b) The court shall specify the rights and duties of a person appointed possessory conservator.

(c) The court shall specify and expressly state in the order the times and conditions for possession of or access to the child, unless a party shows good cause why specific orders would not be in the best interest of the child.

History of Fam. Code §153.006: Acts 1995, 74th Leg., ch. 20, §1, eff. Apr. 20, 1995. Source: Former Fam. Code §14.03(a), (c).

See also *O'Connor's Texas Family Law Handbook* (2017), "Granting nonspecific order," ch. 4-E, §16.2.8, p. 515.

ANNOTATIONS

In re Marriage of Collier, 419 S.W.3d 390, 398-99 (Tex.App.—Amarillo 2011, no pet.). "[T]he trial court's possession order [gives SMC] complete discretion over [PC's] possession of [child] and, as such, is unenforceable by contempt. [¶] Because the order could deny [PC] access to [child], we must determine whether the trial court concluded that a complete denial of access is in the child's best interest. [T]he trial court had sufficient evidence to conclude that [PC] would pose some danger to [child] if he were given unrestricted possession; however, a complete denial of access was not warranted, and is inconsistent with the trial court's naming of [father] as possessory conservator. *At 400:* Although a judge can rightfully restrict the times and conditions of a parent's visitation, we ... disagree ... that giving total discretion, unenforceable by contempt, to one conservator constitutes a mere restriction on the conditions of visitation." *See also* ***In re M.A.H.***, 224 S.W.3d 838, 842-43 (Tex.App.—Texarkana 2007, pet. denied). *But see* ***In re R.D.Y.***, 51 S.W.3d 314, 324 (Tex.App.—Houston [1st Dist.] 2001, pet. denied) (court properly modified standard possession order to give primary JMC sole discretion to determine whether other JMC was mentally or physically capable of properly exercising visitation).

Hopkins v. Hopkins, 853 S.W.2d 134, 137 (Tex. App.—Corpus Christi 1993, no writ). The Family Code "gives trial courts only two options after appointing one parent sole managing conservator. If the trial court finds that the best interest of the child is served by granting the other parent possession of or access to the child, then it has no discretion and *must* appoint that parent a possessory conservator. If the trial court finds that it is *not* in the best interest of the child for the other parent to have possession of or access to the child and additionally finds that such possession of or access to the child would endanger the physical or emotional welfare of the child, then the court has discretion to either appoint or refuse to appoint that parent as a possessory conservator. *At 138:* [I]f the trial court *refuses* to appoint the parent a possessory conservator, it can do so only after finding neither possession nor access to be in the child's best interest and additionally finding that parental possession or access would endanger the physical or emotional welfare of the child. These findings preclude the trial court granting the parent any possession of or access to the child, whether supervised or not."

FAM §153.007. AGREED PARENTING PLAN

(a) To promote the amicable settlement of disputes between the parties to a suit, the parties may enter into a written agreed parenting plan containing provisions for conservatorship and possession of the child and for modification of the parenting plan, including variations from the standard possession order.

(b) If the court finds that the agreed parenting plan is in the child's best interest, the court shall render an order in accordance with the parenting plan.

(c) Terms of the agreed parenting plan contained in the order or incorporated by reference regarding conservatorship or support of or access to a child in an order may be enforced by all remedies available for enforcement of a judgment, including contempt, but are not enforceable as a contract.

(d) If the court finds the agreed parenting plan is not in the child's best interest, the court may request the parties to submit a revised parenting plan. If the parties do not submit a revised parenting plan satisfactory to the court, the court may, after notice and hearing, order a parenting plan that the court finds to be in the best interest of the child.

History of Fam. Code §153.007: Acts 1995, 74th Leg., ch. 20, §1, eff. Apr. 20, 1995. Amended by Acts 1995, 74th Leg., ch. 751, §26, eff. Sept. 1, 1995; Acts 2005, 79th Leg., ch. 482, §3, eff. Sept. 1, 2005; Acts 2007, 80th Leg., ch. 1181, §1, eff. Sept. 1, 2007. Source: Former Fam. Code §14.06.

See also Fam. Code §§153.133, 153.255, 154.124; ***O'Connor's Texas Family Law Handbook*** (2017), "Settlement – agreed parenting plan," ch. 4-E, §12.3, p. 489; "Modification of custody – generally," ch. 9-A, §3.1, p. 978.

ANNOTATIONS

Ex parte Gorena, 595 S.W.2d 841, 844 (Tex.1979). "Despite the fact that a judgment has its genesis in an agreement between the parties, the judgment itself has an independent status. Once the agreement of the parties has been approved by the court and made a part of its judgment, the agreement is no longer merely a contract between private individuals but is the judgment of the court."

Kendrick v. Seibert, 439 S.W.3d 408, 410 (Tex. App.—Houston [1st Dist.] 2014, no pet.). See annotation under Family Code §7.006, p. 97.

In re M.A.H., 365 S.W.3d 814, 820 (Tex.App.—Dallas 2012, no pet.). "Unlike agreements concerning the dissolution of marriage, which by statute are not revocable, the statutes concerning unmediated agree-

ments on child support, conservatorship, and possession of children lack similar language stating they are irrevocable. [Family Code] §§153.007 and 154.124 permit the trial court to render orders in accordance with an 'agreed parenting plan' or 'agreement.' In this case, [mother] revoked her consent to the agreement before the trial court rendered its orders on the agreement. Therefore, when the court rendered its orders, there was no longer an agreement in place. Accordingly, the trial court could not enter orders on child support, conservatorship, and possession in accordance with the rule 11 agreement based solely on that agreement."

In re Kubankin, 257 S.W.3d 852, 858 (Tex.App.—Waco 2008, orig. proceeding). "Parties to child custody orders doubtlessly effect de facto modifications of such orders by agreement and without court approval on a regular basis. … But court approval has always been required to make such agreements enforceable. [¶] [Family Code] §§153.007 and 154.124 are very similar in their language regarding the need for court approval of such agreements. But while there is little case law discussing this requirement under §153.007, there are some relevant decisions under §154.124 [that require parental agreements concerning child support to be approved by the court]. *At 859:* We hold that these decisions apply with equal force to agreements regarding conservatorship and possession of a child under §153.007."

Garcia-Udall v. Udall, 141 S.W.3d 323, 331 (Tex. App.—Dallas 2004, no pet.). Family Code §153.0071 "deals specifically with mediated settlement agreements, while [Fam. Code] §153.007 deals generally with agreements 'containing provisions for conservatorship and possession of the child.' Accordingly, we conclude §153.007 does not apply to mediated settlement agreements under §153.0071."

McLendon v. McLendon, 847 S.W.2d 601, 608 (Tex.App.—Dallas 1992, writ denied). "The court reporter's transcription of the dictated agreement results in a written agreement, and the sworn testimony of the parties given to the court reporter in open court memorializes the parties' consent and can also be reduced to writing. We hold that this procedure has the same legal effect as a written agreement signed by the parties and, in fact, results in a written agreement that meets the requirements of [Fam. Code] §3.631 [now §7.006], [Fam. Code] §14.06 [now §§153.007 and 154.124], and [Fam. Code] §14.021 [now §153.133]."

Ⓐ FAM §153.0071. ALTERNATE DISPUTE RESOLUTION PROCEDURES

The amended text in §153.0071 is effective for SAPCRs pending or filed on or after Sept. 1, 2017. SAPCRs in which a final order is rendered before Sept. 1, 2017, are governed by the former law in effect at that time.

(a) On written agreement of the parties, the court may refer a suit affecting the parent-child relationship to arbitration. The agreement must state whether the arbitration is binding or non-binding.

(b) If the parties agree to binding arbitration, the court shall render an order reflecting the arbitrator's award unless the court determines at a non-jury hearing that the award is not in the best interest of the child. The burden of proof at a hearing under this subsection is on the party seeking to avoid rendition of an order based on the arbitrator's award.

(c) On the written agreement of the parties or on the court's own motion, the court may refer a suit affecting the parent-child relationship to mediation.

(d) A mediated settlement agreement is binding on the parties if the agreement:

(1) provides, in a prominently displayed statement that is in boldfaced type or capital letters or underlined, that the agreement is not subject to revocation;

(2) is signed by each party to the agreement; and

(3) is signed by the party's attorney, if any, who is present at the time the agreement is signed.

(e) If a mediated settlement agreement meets the requirements of Subsection (d), a party is entitled to judgment on the mediated settlement agreement notwithstanding Rule 11, Texas Rules of Civil Procedure, or another rule of law.

(e-1) Notwithstanding Subsections (d) and (e), a court may decline to enter a judgment on a mediated settlement agreement if the court finds:

(1) that:

(A) [~~(1)~~] a party to the agreement was a victim of family violence, and that circumstance impaired the party's ability to make decisions; or

(B) the agreement would permit a person who is subject to registration under Chapter 62, Code of Criminal Procedure, on the basis of an offense committed by the person when the person was 17 years of age or older or who otherwise has a history or pattern

of past or present physical or sexual abuse directed against any person to:

(i) reside in the same household as the child; or

(ii) otherwise have unsupervised access to the child; and

(2) that the agreement is not in the child's best interest.

(f) A party may at any time prior to the final mediation order file a written objection to the referral of a suit affecting the parent-child relationship to mediation on the basis of family violence having been committed by another party against the objecting party or a child who is the subject of the suit. After an objection is filed, the suit may not be referred to mediation unless, on the request of a party, a hearing is held and the court finds that a preponderance of the evidence does not support the objection. If the suit is referred to mediation, the court shall order appropriate measures be taken to ensure the physical and emotional safety of the party who filed the objection. The order shall provide that the parties not be required to have face-to-face contact and that the parties be placed in separate rooms during mediation. This subsection does not apply to suits filed under Chapter 262.

(g) The provisions for confidentiality of alternative dispute resolution procedures under Chapter 154, Civil Practice and Remedies Code, apply equally to the work of a parenting coordinator, as defined by Section 153.601, and to the parties and any other person who participates in the parenting coordination. This subsection does not affect the duty of a person to report abuse or neglect under Section 261.101.

History of Fam. Code §153.0071: Acts 1995, 74th Leg., ch. 751, §27, eff. Sept. 1, 1995. Amended by Acts 1997, 75th Leg., ch. 937, §3, eff. Sept. 1, 1997; Acts 1999, 76th Leg., ch. 178, §7 (eff. Aug. 30, 1999), ch. 1351, §2 (eff. Sept. 1, 1999); Acts 2005, 79th Leg., ch. 916, §7, eff. June 17, 2005; Acts 2007, 80th Leg., ch. 1181, §2, eff. Sept. 1, 2007; S.B. 495, §2, 85th Leg., eff. Sept. 1, 2017.

See also ***O'Connor's Texas Family Law Handbook*** (2017), "ADR," ch. 4-D, §10.1, p. 425.

ANNOTATIONS

In re Lee, 411 S.W.3d 445, 453 (Tex.2013). Family Code "'does not authorize the trial court to substitute its judgment for the mediated settlement agreement entered by the parties unless the requirements of §153.0071(e-1) are met.' Subsection (e-1) … makes it absolutely clear that the Legislature limited the consideration of best interest in the context of entry of judgment on an MSA to cases involving family violence [or sex offenders]. Allowing a court to decline to enter judgment on a valid MSA on best interest grounds without [the required] findings would impermissibly render the … language in subsection (e-1) superfluous. *At 455:* Further, the specific statutory language of §153.0071(e) trumps [Fam. Code] §153.002's more general mandate [that the best interest of the child shall always be the primary consideration of the court in determining issues of conservatorship and possession]. [¶] [W]e hold that §153.0071(e) encourages parents to peaceably resolve their child-related disputes through mediation by foreclosing a broad best interest inquiry with respect to entry of judgment on properly executed MSAs, ensuring that the time and money spent on mediation will not have been wasted and that the benefits of successful mediation will be realized."

In re M.W.M., ___ S.W.3d ___ (Tex.App.—Dallas 2017, orig. proceeding) (No. 05-16-00797-CV; 4-5-17). "We do not believe that the Legislature intended the family code's arbitration provisions to stand on their own and in isolation. Rather, absent an irreconcilable conflict, where two or more separate statutory provisions pertain to the same subject, we are obliged to construe the provisions to the greatest extent reasonably possible so as to give effect to both. Thus, we conclude that the family code's rather skeletal arbitration provisions are augmented by and operate alongside the more general and vastly more detailed general arbitration regime in the [Texas General Arbitration Act]." *See also* ***Kilroy v. Kilroy***, 137 S.W.3d 780, 786 (Tex. App.—Houston [1st Dist.] 2004, orig. proceeding).

In re K.D., 471 S.W.3d 147, 165 (Tex.App.—Texarkana 2015, no pet.). Family Code "§§153.002 and 161.001(2) both require the trial court to determine the best interest of the child, and [***In re Lee***, 411 S.W.3d 445 (Tex.2013),] holds that [an MSA] obtained under [Fam. Code] §153.0071(e) forecloses the trial court's best-interest review under §153.002. Thus, we must decide whether §153.0071(e) also applies to the specific best-interest standard in §161.001(2). In other words, in this case, we must determine whether the trial court was bound by the parties' agreement that termination was in the best interest of [child]. *At 166:* [W]hile best interest is an element of the moving parties' proof regardless of whether the suit is brought under Ch. 153 or Ch. 161, different standards of review are applied to a trial court's best-interest finding under each chapter. [¶] Moreover, §153.002 only applies to cases involving

ongoing conservatorship and possession rights, neither of which are implicated in a parental-rights termination case. *At 168-69:* [W]e do not hold that a settlement agreement obtained through mediation under §153.0071 accomplishes nothing in a parental-rights termination case brought by the Department. [An MSA] and an affidavit of relinquishment in a parental-rights termination case may be binding between the parties, but it does not eliminate the Department's burden of proving ... under §161.001(2) that termination is in the child's best interest or the trial court's power to deny termination in the absence of such proof. *At 170-71:* [T]o hold that an agreement to terminate the parent-child relationship obtained via [an MSA] eliminates the Department's requirement to prove by clear and convincing evidence that the agreement is in the child's best interest would eliminate the due process protection which makes termination of parental rights by the State constitutional." *See also* ***In re Morris***, 498 S.W.3d 624, 631-32 (Tex.App.—Houston [14th Dist.] 2016, orig. proceeding).

In re Lovell-Osburn, 448 S.W.3d 616, 620 (Tex. App.—Houston [14th Dist.] 2014, orig. proceeding). "[T]he mere fact that the parties entered into a contractual agreement purporting to fix venue ... is not itself sufficient to override the mandatory venue provision at [Fam. Code] §155.201(b). Unless another statutory provision specifically authorizes a court to disregard the mandatory venue and transfer rule at §155.201(b), the trial court had a ministerial duty to transfer the underlying litigation ... notwithstanding the existence of a contractual agreement between the parties. *At 622:* Although [Fam. Code] §153.0071(e) requires courts to defer to certain decisions of parents agreed to in an MSA, ... that requirement is not unlimited. Were we to adopt the conclusion that the trial court was required to enter judgment on the parties' MSA containing the void venue provision, it would open the door to parties including within an MSA various provisions that otherwise would be void for being contrary to public policy. [¶] Therefore, because §153.0071(e) does not require a court to enter judgment on an MSA containing a void venue provision, §153.0071(e) does not provide a statutory basis for disregarding the mandatory venue rule at §155.201(b)."

Scruggs v. Linn, 443 S.W.3d 373, 378 (Tex.App.—Houston [14th Dist.] 2014, no pet.). "A trial court generally does not have discretion to decline to enter judgment on or deviate from an MSA. [¶] [Father] argues that the MSA reserved only the issue of retroactive child support for trial and thus the trial court abused its discretion in ordering him to pay some of [mother's] attorney's fees. ... Because the MSA, according to its own title—'Binding Mediated Settlement Agreement—Partial SAPCR'—and terms, is merely a partial settlement and does not address attorney's fees, and because the fees issue is related to retroactive child support—the issue expressly reserved for trial in the MSA—we conclude the trial court's award of attorney's fees to [mother] was not contrary to the MSA."

Byrd v. Byrd, No. 04-11-00700-CV (Tex.App.—San Antonio 2012, no pet.) (memo op.; 11-30-12). "[A] trial court ... has no authority to sign a judgment that varies from the terms of the mediated settlement agreement. [¶] We disagree that any claimed stipulation by [H's] counsel had the effect of altering the terms of the mediation agreement. ... By proceeding under §153.0071(d), the parties elect to make their agreement binding at the time of execution, thus creating a 'procedural shortcut' for the enforcement of the agreement. Thus, unlike standard contract situations, §153.0071(d) does not contemplate that the parties will have the ability to modify a mediated settlement agreement—whether by written amendment or oral stipulation—after execution, because the goal of the statute is to fast-track enforcement of mediated settlement agreements in divorce cases. [¶] Absent a finding that the agreement was illegal or violated public policy, or that [a] term ... was drafted in error or was ambiguous, the trial court thus had no discretion to render a judgment that varied from the terms of the Mediation Agreement." *See also* ***In re A.M.S.***, this page; ***Garcia-Udall v. Udall***, 141 S.W.3d 323, 332 (Tex. App.—Dallas 2004, no pet.) (trial court has no authority to enter judgment that varies from terms of settlement agreement).

In re A.M.S., No. 12-11-00218-CV (Tex.App.—Tyler 2012, no pet.) (memo op.; 7-31-12). "A final judgment rendered pursuant to a mediated settlement agreement must be in strict or literal compliance with that agreement. ... Modifications to settlement agreements are typically grounds for reversal, however, only where they add terms, significantly alter the original terms, or undermine the intent of the parties. [¶] [B]oth parties agreed in open court ... just four days after the medi-

ated settlement agreement had been signed, that it did not include [W's] contractual alimony claim. [¶] Therefore, when the trial judge made the … interlineation on the agreed order before signing it, she was not altering the terms of the mediated settlement agreement. She was only clarifying what the parties themselves had agreed to…. Thus, the trial judge was neither adding terms to nor altering the original terms of the mediated settlement agreement. She was merely establishing the parameters of the mediated settlement agreement. We hold that the trial judge did not abuse her discretion with the interlineation made in the agreed order." *See also* ***Byrd v. Byrd***, p. 509.

In re S.A.D.S., 413 S.W.3d 434, 438 (Tex.App.—Fort Worth 2010, no pet.). "[A]s long as a mediated settlement agreement complies with [Fam. Code] §153.0071, its failure to address the parental presumption or a trial court's finding of significant impairment under [Fam. Code] §153.131 [for appointing a managing conservator] does not render it void. Furthermore, as long as a mediated settlement agreement complies with §153.0071, the trial court must comply with the specific edicts of that section and not the more general §153.131. Therefore, a trial court does not need to add such a finding to a mediated settlement agreement, and it errs if it does place such a finding contrary to the parties' agreement in an order."

Beyers v. Roberts, 199 S.W.3d 354, 359 (Tex. App.—Houston [1st Dist.] 2006, pet. denied). "Nothing in [§153.0071] requires that a trial court conduct a best interest hearing before entering an order pursuant to a mediated settlement agreement. *At 360:* Furthermore, nothing in the common law creates a duty to determine best interest in every case in which the parents have reached a settlement of their child custody disputes. Trial courts have discretion to void all or part of a mediated settlement agreement if the court determines it is not in the child's best interest. However, courts have not held that the policy favoring children's best interest requires that trial courts determine best interest when the parties have settled their disputes, in every case. *At 361:* [S]ubsection (e-1) … allow[s] a trial court to conduct a best interest hearing in its discretion."

In re T.B.H.-H., 188 S.W.3d 312, 315 (Tex.App.—Waco 2006, no pet.). Section 153.0071(b) "indicates that the best interest hearing must occur before the time the trial court renders its order. In failing to file a motion to vacate the [arbitrator's] award and failing to present evidence concerning the child's best interest before the trial court rendered its order in accordance with the arbitrator's award, [mother] waived the right to a best interest hearing." *See also* ***In re C.A.K.***, 155 S.W.3d 554, 561 (Tex.App.—San Antonio 2004, pet. denied) (party challenging arbitration award must request best-interest hearing and obtain ruling in order to invoke right to hearing and preserve error).

Mailhot v. Mailhot, 124 S.W.3d 775, 777 (Tex. App.—Houston [1st Dist.] 2003, no pet.). See annotation under Family Code §6.602, p. 80.

Stieren v. McBroom, 103 S.W.3d 602, 605 (Tex. App.—San Antonio 2003, pet. denied). "An arbitration award has the same effect as the judgment of a court of last resort, and a trial court may not substitute its judgment for the arbitrator's merely because it would have reached a different decision. However, in [SAPCRs] the Texas Legislature has specifically granted the trial court the ability to substitute its judgment for that of the arbitrator when determining the best interest of a child. Yet, the Legislature has not articulated a standard by which to determine the 'best interest' of a child in a proceeding to vacate an arbitration award. *At 606:* Because the guiding principle in all [SAPCRs] is what is in the child's best interest and because Texas affords trial courts broad discretion in determining how the best interest of a child should be served, we conclude that our review here is limited to determining whether the trial court abused its discretion."

In re Calderon, 96 S.W.3d 711, 718 (Tex.App.—Tyler 2003, orig. proceeding). "[T]he phrase 'notwithstanding [TRCP] 11 or another rule of law' in [Fam. Code] §153.0071(e) means that Rule 11, [CPRC] ch. 154 …, and general contract law, insofar as they apply to the enforcement of settlement agreements, do not apply to the enforcement of a mediated settlement agreement in a SAPCR if the agreement meets the requirements of §153.0071(d)."

In re J.A.W.-N., 94 S.W.3d 119, 121 (Tex. App.—Corpus Christi 2002, no pet.). "Nothing in §153.0071(c) requires, nor should be construed to require, a written request or a written order of referral based on the request of the parties or the court's own motion as a prerequisite to parties agreeing to mediate their differences and reducing that agreement to writing. Such a requirement would have a chilling effect on

the mediation process. [Father] has directed us to no authority, and we find none, that precludes parties from agreeing to mediate without involving the court in making that decision." *See also* ***Kilroy v. Kilroy***, 137 S.W.3d 780, 789 (Tex.App.—Houston [1st Dist.] 2004, orig. proceeding) (TRCP 11 agreement did not require parties to petition trial court before initiating arbitration proceedings).

FAM §153.00715. DETERMINATION OF VALIDITY & ENFORCEABILITY OF CONTRACT CONTAINING AGREEMENT TO ARBITRATE

(a) If a party to a suit affecting the parent-child relationship opposes an application to compel arbitration or makes an application to stay arbitration and asserts that the contract containing the agreement to arbitrate is not valid or enforceable, notwithstanding any provision of the contract to the contrary, the court shall try the issue promptly and may order arbitration only if the court determines that the contract containing the agreement to arbitrate is valid and enforceable against the party seeking to avoid arbitration.

(b) A determination under this section that a contract is valid and enforceable does not affect the court's authority to stay arbitration or refuse to compel arbitration on any other ground provided by law.

(c) This section does not apply to:

(1) a court order;

(2) an agreed parenting plan described by Section 153.007;

(3) a mediated settlement agreement described by Section 153.0071;

(4) a collaborative law agreement described by Section 153.0072;[1] or

(5) any other agreement between the parties that is approved by a court.

1. **Editor's note:** Tex. Fam. Code §153.0072 was repealed by Acts 2011, 82nd Leg., ch. 1048, §2, eff. Sept. 1, 2011. Title 1-A, Collaborative Family Law, was enacted by Acts 2011, 82nd Leg., ch. 1048, §1, eff. Sept. 1, 2011.

History of Fam. Code §153.00715: Acts 2011, 82nd Leg., ch. 1088, §2, eff. June 17, 2011.

See also *O'Connor's Texas Family Law Handbook* (2017), "Effect of arbitration clause," ch. 2-D, §3.5.4, p. 171.

FAM §153.0072. REPEALED

Repealed by Acts 2011, 82nd Leg., ch. 1048, §2, eff. Sept. 1, 2011.

FAM §153.008. REPEALED

Repealed by Acts 2009, 81st Leg., ch. 1113, §31 (eff. Sept. 1, 2009), ch. 1118, §10 (eff. Sept. 1, 2009).

FAM §153.009. INTERVIEW OF CHILD IN CHAMBERS

(a) In a nonjury trial or at a hearing, on the application of a party, the amicus attorney, or the attorney ad litem for the child, the court shall interview in chambers a child 12 years of age or older and may interview in chambers a child under 12 years of age to determine the child's wishes as to conservatorship or as to the person who shall have the exclusive right to determine the child's primary residence. The court may also interview a child in chambers on the court's own motion for a purpose specified by this subsection.

(b) In a nonjury trial or at a hearing, on the application of a party, the amicus attorney, or the attorney ad litem for the child or on the court's own motion, the court may interview the child in chambers to determine the child's wishes as to possession, access, or any other issue in the suit affecting the parent-child relationship.

(c) Interviewing a child does not diminish the discretion of the court in determining the best interests of the child.

(d) In a jury trial, the court may not interview the child in chambers regarding an issue on which a party is entitled to a jury verdict.

(e) In any trial or hearing, the court may permit the attorney for a party, the amicus attorney, the guardian ad litem for the child, or the attorney ad litem for the child to be present at the interview.

(f) On the motion of a party, the amicus attorney, or the attorney ad litem for the child, or on the court's own motion, the court shall cause a record of the interview to be made when the child is 12 years of age or older. A record of the interview shall be part of the record in the case.

History of Fam. Code §153.009: Acts 1995, 74th Leg., ch. 20, §1, eff. Apr. 20, 1995. Amended by Acts 1997, 75th Leg., ch. 781, §1, eff. Sept. 1, 1997; Acts 2001, 77th Leg., ch. 1289, §2, eff. Sept. 1, 2001; Acts 2005, 79th Leg., ch. 916, §9, eff. June 17, 2005. Source: Former Fam. Code §14.07(c).

See also *O'Connor's Texas Family Law Handbook* (2017), "Child's preferences," ch. 4-E, §19.4.1, p. 522.

ANNOTATIONS

In re A.C., 387 S.W.3d 673, 676 (Tex.App.—Texarkana 2012, pet. denied). Father "contends that the trial court committed reversible error by failing to record its in-chamber interview with [child], despite having been requested to do so. *At 677:* [Generally,] to preserve this issue for appeal, the complaining party must object to the court reporter's failure to record the proceedings. No such objection was lodged by [father].

[¶] However, this circumstance is demonstrably different from the failure of a court reporter to record proceedings in open court. ... It may be that [father] assumed that a record of the interview was being made as it was taking place, raising the possibility that he would have had no opportunity to call it to the attention of the trial court until a post-interview discovery of the failure to make a record. [¶] We note that the information obtained by the trial court in such an interview is strictly supplemental to the evidence taken in court.... Nothing in the statute indicates that the child in such an interview is to be sworn and nothing reflects that anything resembling the [TREs] should apply during the interview. *At 678:* Because the trial court has the wide discretion ... and may choose to either take into account the information learned at such an interview or ignore it in its entirety, it is difficult to imagine that a failure to cause the interview to be recorded would cause a different outcome or result. ... Accordingly, although we agree with [father] that it was error to have failed to record the interview when his motion requested that it be recorded, the error was a harmless one."

In re C.B., No. 13-11-00472-CV (Tex.App.—Corpus Christi 2012, no pet.) (memo op.; 8-2-12). Mother "contends that the trial court had no discretion to deny the requests [for in-chamber interviews] because the term 'shall' used in §153.009(a) is mandatory, not discretionary. We agree. [¶] Nevertheless, we note that subsection (c) provides that '[i]nterviewing a child does not diminish the discretion of the court in determining the best interests of the child.' [¶] In light of the ... evidence concerning the preferences of the children and ... the trial court's statements that an interview in chambers would not assist the court in making the decision based on what it had already heard, we conclude that the trial court's refusal to interview [child] was consistent with the discretion recognized in subsection (c).... Although the trial court violated the mandatory language in subsection (a) by refusing to interview [child], we conclude based on the foregoing that the error was harmless and did not amount to reversible error."

In re S.L.L., No. 09-09-00429-CV (Tex.App.—Beaumont 2011, pet. denied) (memo op.; 3-31-11). Mother "argues that the trial court should have interviewed [child] and that she requested the interview at the hearing. ... In this case, there is no application for an interview contained in the clerk's record; the trial court had the discretion to deny the verbal request." *See also* ***In re J.L.C.***, No. 11-13-00252-CV (Tex.App.—Eastland 2014, no pet.) (memo op.; 8-29-14). *But see* ***In re C.B.***, No. 13-11-00472-CV (Tex.App.—Corpus Christi 2012, no pet.) (memo op.; 8-2-12) (§153.009 does not distinguish between written and oral applications).

FAM §153.010. ORDER FOR FAMILY COUNSELING

(a) If the court finds at the time of a hearing that the parties have a history of conflict in resolving an issue of conservatorship or possession of or access to the child, the court may order a party to:

(1) participate in counseling with a mental health professional who:

(A) has a background in family therapy;

(B) has a mental health license that requires as a minimum a master's degree; and

(C) has training in domestic violence if the court determines that the training is relevant to the type of counseling needed; and

(2) pay the cost of counseling.

(b) If a person possessing the requirements of Subsection (a)(1) is not available in the county in which the court presides, the court may appoint a person the court believes is qualified to conduct the counseling ordered under Subsection (a).

History of Fam. Code §153.010: Acts 1995, 74th Leg., ch. 20, §1, eff. Apr. 20, 1995. Amended by Acts 1997, 75th Leg., ch. 645, §1, eff. Sept. 1, 1997. Source: Former Fam. Code §14.03(h).

FAM §153.011. SECURITY BOND

If the court finds that a person who has a possessory interest in a child may violate the court order relating to the interest, the court may order the party to execute a bond or deposit security. The court shall set the amount and condition the bond or security on compliance with the order.

History of Fam. Code §153.011: Acts 1995, 74th Leg., ch. 20, §1, eff. Apr. 20, 1995. Source: Former Fam. Code §14.03(i).

FAM §153.012. RIGHT TO PRIVACY; DELETION OF PERSONAL INFORMATION IN RECORDS

The court may order the custodian of records to delete all references in the records to the place of residence of either party appointed as a conservator of the child before the release of the records to another party appointed as a conservator.

History of Fam. Code §153.012: Acts 1995, 74th Leg., ch. 20, §1, eff. Apr. 20, 1995. Source: Former Fam. Code §14.04(c).

FAM §153.013. FALSE REPORT OF CHILD ABUSE

(a) If a party to a pending suit affecting the parent-child relationship makes a report alleging child abuse by another party to the suit that the reporting party knows lacks a factual foundation, the court shall deem the report to be a knowingly false report.

(b) Evidence of a false report of child abuse is admissible in a suit between the involved parties regarding the terms of conservatorship of a child.

(c) If the court makes a finding under Subsection (a), the court shall impose a civil penalty not to exceed $500.

History of Fam. Code §153.013: Acts 1995, 74th Leg., ch. 751, §28, eff. Sept. 1, 1995. Amended by Acts 1997, 75th Leg., ch. 786, §2, eff. Sept. 1, 1997. Source: Former Fam. Code §34.031(b).

FAM §153.014. VISITATION CENTERS & VISITATION EXCHANGE FACILITIES

A county may establish a visitation center or a visitation exchange facility for the purpose of facilitating the terms of a court order providing for the possession of or access to a child.

History of Fam. Code §153.014: Acts 2001, 77th Leg., ch. 577, §1, eff. June 11, 2001.

FAM §153.015. ELECTRONIC COMMUNICATION WITH CHILD BY CONSERVATOR

(a) In this section, "electronic communication" means any communication facilitated by the use of any wired or wireless technology via the Internet or any other electronic media. The term includes communication facilitated by the use of a telephone, electronic mail, instant messaging, videoconferencing, or webcam.

(b) If a conservator of a child requests the court to order periods of electronic communication with the child under this section, the court may award the conservator reasonable periods of electronic communication with the child to supplement the conservator's periods of possession of the child. In determining whether to award electronic communication, the court shall consider:

(1) whether electronic communication is in the best interest of the child;

(2) whether equipment necessary to facilitate the electronic communication is reasonably available to all parties subject to the order; and

(3) any other factor the court considers appropriate.

(c) If a court awards a conservator periods of electronic communication with a child under this section, each conservator subject to the court's order shall:

(1) provide the other conservator with the e-mail address and other electronic communication access information of the child;

(2) notify the other conservator of any change in the e-mail address or other electronic communication access information not later than 24 hours after the date the change takes effect; and

(3) if necessary equipment is reasonably available, accommodate electronic communication with the child, with the same privacy, respect, and dignity accorded all other forms of access, at a reasonable time and for a reasonable duration subject to any limitation provided by the court in the court's order.

(d) The court may not consider the availability of electronic communication as a factor in determining child support. The availability of electronic communication under this section[1] is not intended as a substitute for physical possession of or access to the child,[1] where otherwise appropriate.

(e) In a suit in which the court's order contains provisions related to a finding of family violence in the suit, including supervised visitation, the court may award periods of electronic communication under this section only if:

(1) the award and terms of the award are mutually agreed to by the parties; and

(2) the terms of the award:

(A) are printed in the court's order in boldfaced, capitalized type; and

(B) include any specific restrictions relating to family violence or supervised visitation, as applicable, required by other law to be included in a possession or access order.

1. **Editor's note:** Acts 2007, 80th Leg., ch. 1041's enactment of §153.015 does not include the words "under this section" and has a comma before the words "where otherwise appropriate."

History of Fam. Code §153.015: Acts 2007, 80th Leg., ch. 972, §7 (eff. Sept. 1, 2007), ch. 1041, §1 (eff. June 15, 2007).

Sections 153.016-153.070 reserved for expansion

SUBCHAPTER B. PARENT APPOINTED AS CONSERVATOR: IN GENERAL

FAM §153.071. COURT TO SPECIFY RIGHTS & DUTIES OF PARENT APPOINTED A CONSERVATOR

If both parents are appointed as conservators of the child, the court shall specify the rights and duties of a parent that are to be exercised:

(1) by each parent independently;

(2) by the joint agreement of the parents; and

(3) exclusively by one parent.

History of Fam. Code §153.071: Acts 1995, 74th Leg., ch. 20, §1, eff. Apr. 20, 1995. Source: Former Fam. Code §14.02(a).

FAM §153.072. WRITTEN FINDING REQUIRED TO LIMIT PARENTAL RIGHTS & DUTIES

The court may limit the rights and duties of a parent appointed as a conservator if the court makes a written finding that the limitation is in the best interest of the child.

History of Fam. Code §153.072: Acts 1995, 74th Leg., ch. 20, §1, eff. Apr. 20, 1995. Source: Former Fam. Code §14.02(b).

ANNOTATIONS

King v. Lyons, 457 S.W.3d 122, 131 (Tex.App.—Houston [1st Dist.] 2014, no pet.). See annotation under TRCP 301, p. 1202.

Messier v. Messier, 389 S.W.3d 904, 909 (Tex. App.—Houston [14th Dist.] 2012, no pet.). "[T]he court clearly indicated that while there was insufficient evidence of a potential risk of international *abduction* by [mother], it was in the children's best interest for [father] to be in control of any international *travel* by the children. *At 910:* The evidence ... supports the conclusion that prohibiting [mother] from taking the children outside the U.S. or Texas without [father's] consent and prohibiting her from retaining or obtaining passports for the children appear to be reasonable restrictions of [her] rights as a possessory conservator and in the best interest of the children. [¶] But not all of the injunctions ... imposed appear rationally related to [father's] control of [children's] international travel.... The requirements [mirror] the 'Abduction Prevention Measures' listed in [Fam. Code] §153.503.... They go beyond merely providing [father] with control over the children's international travel.... The trial court abused its discretion in granting these injunctions absent a finding of a potential risk of international abduction; there was no evidence in this case supporting these measures as being in the children's best interest outside of a risk of international abduction."

FAM §153.073. RIGHTS OF PARENT AT ALL TIMES

(a) Unless limited by court order, a parent appointed as a conservator of a child has at all times the right:

(1) to receive information from any other conservator of the child concerning the health, education, and welfare of the child;

(2) to confer with the other parent to the extent possible before making a decision concerning the health, education, and welfare of the child;

(3) of access to medical, dental, psychological, and educational records of the child;

(4) to consult with a physician, dentist, or psychologist of the child;

(5) to consult with school officials concerning the child's welfare and educational status, including school activities;

(6) to attend school activities;

(7) to be designated on the child's records as a person to be notified in case of an emergency;

(8) to consent to medical, dental, and surgical treatment during an emergency involving an immediate danger to the health and safety of the child; and

(9) to manage the estate of the child to the extent the estate has been created by the parent or the parent's family.

(b) The court shall specify in the order the rights that a parent retains at all times.

History of Fam. Code §153.073: Acts 1995, 74th Leg., ch. 20, §1, eff. Apr. 20, 1995. Amended by Acts 1995, 74th Leg., ch. 751, §29, eff. Sept. 1, 1995; Acts 2003, 78th Leg., ch. 1036, §6, eff. Sept. 1, 2003. Source: Former Fam. Code §14.02(a), (b)(2).

See also ***O'Connor's Texas Family Law Handbook*** (2017), "Conservator," ch. 1-E, §2.2.1(2), p. 68; "Rights & Duties of Conservators," ch. 4-E, §4, p. 472.

ANNOTATIONS

Miller v. HCA, Inc., 118 S.W.3d 758, 766 (Tex. 2003). See annotation under Family Code §151.001, *Medical Consent*, p. 470.

Abrams v. Jones, 35 S.W.3d 620, 624 (Tex.2000). "We interpret [Fam. Code] §153.073 to ensure that a court may grant a parent who is divorced and who has been named a conservator the same rights of access to his or her child's psychological records as a parent who is not divorced. We do not interpret §153.073 to override the provisions of [H&SC] ch. 611 ... that specifically address parents' rights to the mental health records of their children. The legislative history of §153.073 indicates that it was enacted to equalize the rights of nonmanaging-conservator parents in comparison to managing-conservator parents. The Legislature did not intend in §153.073 to give greater rights to divorced parents than to parents who are not divorced."

FAM §153.074. RIGHTS & DUTIES DURING PERIOD OF POSSESSION

Unless limited by court order, a parent appointed as a conservator of a child has the following rights and duties during the period that the parent has possession of the child:

(1) the duty of care, control, protection, and reasonable discipline of the child;

(2) the duty to support the child, including providing the child with clothing, food, shelter, and medical and dental care not involving an invasive procedure;

(3) the right to consent for the child to medical and dental care not involving an invasive procedure; and

(4) the right to direct the moral and religious training of the child.

History of Fam. Code §153.074: Acts 1995, 74th Leg., ch. 20, §1, eff. Apr. 20, 1995. Amended by Acts 1995, 74th Leg., ch. 751, §30, eff. Sept. 1, 1995; Acts 2003, 78th Leg., ch. 1036, §7, eff. Sept. 1, 2003. Source: Former Fam. Code §14.02(b)(1).

FAM §153.075. DUTIES OF PARENT NOT APPOINTED CONSERVATOR

The court may order a parent not appointed as a managing or a possessory conservator to perform other parental duties, including paying child support.

History of Fam. Code §153.075: Acts 1995, 74th Leg., ch. 20, §1, eff. Apr. 20, 1995. Source: Former Fam. Code §14.03(d).

FAM §153.076. DUTY TO PROVIDE INFORMATION

(a) The court shall order that each conservator of a child has a duty to inform the other conservator of the child in a timely manner of significant information concerning the health, education, and welfare of the child.

(b) The court shall order that each conservator of a child has the duty to inform the other conservator of the child if the conservator resides with for at least 30 days, marries, or intends to marry a person who the conservator knows:

(1) is registered as a sex offender under Chapter 62, Code of Criminal Procedure; or

(2) is currently charged with an offense for which on conviction the person would be required to register under that chapter.

(b-1) The court shall order that each conservator of a child has the duty to inform the other conservator of the child if the conservator:

(1) establishes a residence with a person who the conservator knows is the subject of a final protective order sought by an individual other than the conservator that is in effect on the date the residence with the person is established;

(2) resides with, or allows unsupervised access to a child by, a person who is the subject of a final protective order sought by the conservator after the expiration of the 60-day period following the date the final protective order is issued; or

(3) is the subject of a final protective order issued after the date of the order establishing conservatorship.

(c) The notice required to be made under Subsection (b) must be made as soon as practicable but not later than the 40th day after the date the conservator of the child begins to reside with the person or the 10th day after the date the marriage occurs, as appropriate. The notice must include a description of the offense that is the basis of the person's requirement to register as a sex offender or of the offense with which the person is charged.

(c-1) The notice required to be made under Subsection (b-1) must be made as soon as practicable but not later than:

(1) the 30th day after the date the conservator establishes residence with the person who is the subject of the final protective order, if the notice is required by Subsection (b-1)(1);

(2) the 90th day after the date the final protective order was issued, if the notice is required by Subsection (b-1)(2); or

(3) the 30th day after the date the final protective order was issued, if the notice is required by Subsection (b-1)(3).

(d) A conservator commits an offense if the conservator fails to provide notice in the manner required by Subsections (b) and (c), or Subsections (b-1) and (c-1), as applicable. An offense under this subsection is a Class C misdemeanor.

History of Fam. Code §153.076: Acts 1995, 74th Leg., ch. 751, §31, eff. Sept. 1, 1995. Amended by Acts 1999, 76th Leg., ch. 330, §1, eff. Sept. 1, 1999; Acts 2003, 78th Leg., ch. 1036, §8, eff. Sept. 1, 2003; Acts 2015, 84th Leg., ch. 1166, §1, eff. Sept. 1, 2015. Source: Former Fam. Code §14.02(a).

ANNOTATIONS

Hodgson v. Minnesota, 497 U.S. 417, 450 (1990). "It is equally clear that the requirement that both parents be notified ... does not reasonably further any legitimate state interest. ... A statute requiring two-parent notification would not further any state interest in those instances. *At 452:* The second parent may well have an interest in the minor's abortion decision, making full communication among all members of a family desirable in some cases, but such communication may

not be decreed by the State. The State has no more interest in requiring all family members to talk with one another than it has in requiring certain of them to live together."

In re Doe 3, 19 S.W.3d 300, 320 (Tex.2000). "The constitutionality of §153.076 if applied in parental notification matters is questionable in light of ***Hodgson v. Minnesota***, 497 U.S. 417 (1990)."

Sections 153.077-153.130 reserved for expansion

SUBCHAPTER C. PARENT APPOINTED AS SOLE OR JOINT MANAGING CONSERVATOR

FAM §153.131. PRESUMPTION THAT PARENT TO BE APPOINTED MANAGING CONSERVATOR

(a) Subject to the prohibition in Section 153.004, unless the court finds that appointment of the parent or parents would not be in the best interest of the child because the appointment would significantly impair the child's physical health or emotional development, a parent shall be appointed sole managing conservator or both parents shall be appointed as joint managing conservators of the child.

(b) It is a rebuttable presumption that the appointment of the parents of a child as joint managing conservators is in the best interest of the child. A finding of a history of family violence involving the parents of a child removes the presumption under this subsection.

History of Fam. Code §153.131: Acts 1995, 74th Leg., ch. 20, §1, eff. Apr. 20, 1995. Amended by Acts 1995, 74th Leg., ch. 751, §32, eff. Sept. 1, 1995; Acts 1997, 75th Leg., ch. 1193, §20, eff. Sept. 1, 1997. Source: Former Fam. Code §14.01(b)(1).

See also ***O'Connor's Texas Family Law Handbook*** (2017), "Parent seeking conservatorship," ch. 4-E, §15.3, p. 496; "Nonparent seeking conservatorship," ch. 4-E, §15.4, p. 500.

ANNOTATIONS

Shook v. Gray, 381 S.W.3d 540, 542-43 (Tex.2012). "The court of appeals [held] that the trial court abused its discretion in naming [grandparent] as [child's SMC] because [grandparent] failed to ... overcome the presumption that a parent should be named as managing conservator. Additionally, the court of appeals remanded the case for the trial court to reconsider the conservatorship and access rights between [father] and [mother] only.... [¶] By foreclosing the trial court from considering [grandparent] on remand, the trial court may be unable to protect [child's] best interest. ... The trial court must be able to consider the changed circumstances. [O]ver four years have passed since the trial court issued its order. Even assuming [grandparent] previously failed to present evidence capable of overcoming the parental presumption, it does not follow that she will necessarily be unable to overcome the parental presumption under the present circumstances. [¶] [Grandparent's] inability to overcome the parental presumption does not deprive her of standing to be considered for conservatorship or access. If [grandparent] fails to overcome the presumption that a parent should be named managing conservator on remand, the trial court may still name [grandparent] as a [PC] or grant her access if that would be in [child's] best interest.[1]"

1. **Editor's note:** The last sentence in the annotation above—which was neither supported by law nor essential to the Court's decision in reversing the appellate court's judgment—is troubling for several reasons. First, it suggests that a nonparent may be appointed PC as a kind of consolation prize if the nonparent fails to rebut the parental presumption. The Family Code, however, explicitly requires that the parental presumption be rebutted if a nonparent seeks appointment as a PC over a parent. *See* Fam. Code §102.004(b). Second, for a grandparent who is not awarded conservatorship over a grandchild to be awarded possession or access, the Family Code requires a much higher burden than simply a best-interest showing. *See id.* §153.433.

In re J.A.J., 243 S.W.3d 611, 612-13 (Tex.2007). "We must decide the effect of a termination judgment's reversal on an unchallenged conservatorship appointment when the trial court finds that appointing a parent as conservator would significantly impair the child's physical health or emotional development, and that appointment of the [TDFPS] is in the child's best interest.... We conclude that reversal of a termination judgment in these circumstances does not affect the trial court's conservatorship appointment absent assigned error. *At 616-17:* In light of the differences in the factors that weigh in termination [under Fam. Code §161.001(1)] and conservatorship decisions [under Fam. Code §153.131(a)] and the differing burdens of proof and standards of appellate review, we conclude that a challenge to the [TDFPS's] appointment as [child's] managing conservator was not subsumed in [mother's] challenge to the termination order." *See also* ***In re D.N.C.***, 252 S.W.3d 317, 319 (Tex.2008) (***J.A.J.*** does not apply if conservatorship appointment was consequence of termination pursuant to Fam. Code §161.207); ***In re A.S.***, 261 S.W.3d 76, 92 (Tex.App.—Houston [14th Dist.] 2008, pet. denied) (even though TDFPS requested conservatorship under §153.131, trial court made no findings under that section to independently support conservatorship order; appointment was consequence of termination).

Lewelling v. Lewelling, 796 S.W.2d 164, 167 (Tex. 1990). "It is no longer adequate to offer evidence that the nonparent would be a better custodian of the child. Under [Fam. Code] §14.01 [now §153.131], the nonparent must affirmatively prove by a preponderance of the evidence that appointment of the parent as managing conservator would *significantly impair* the child, either physically or emotionally. This statute thus requires the nonparent to offer evidence of specific actions or omissions of the parent that demonstrate an award of custody to the parent would result in physical or emotional harm to the child."

In re S.T., 508 S.W.3d 482, 492-93 (Tex.App.—Fort Worth 2015, no pet.). "Acts or omissions that constitute significant impairment include, but are not limited to, physical abuse, severe neglect, abandonment, drug or alcohol abuse, or immoral behavior by the parent. The material time to consider is the present, and evidence of past conduct may not, by itself, be sufficient to show present unfitness. [¶] Other considerations may include parental irresponsibility, a history of mental disorders and suicidal thoughts, frequent moves, bad judgment, child abandonment, and an unstable, disorganized, and chaotic lifestyle that has put and will continue to put the child at risk. Likewise, the parent's treatment of other children may be relevant. The link between the parent's conduct and harm to the child may not be based on evidence that merely raises a surmise or speculation of possible harm." *See also* ***Taylor v. Taylor***, 254 S.W.3d 527, 536 (Tex.App.—Houston [1st Dist.] 2008, no pet.) (when nonparent and parent are both seeking managing conservatorship, close calls go to the parent).

In re N.T., 474 S.W.3d 465, 480 (Tex.App.—Dallas 2015, no pet.). See annotation under Family Code §161.207, p. 786.

Berwick v. Wagner, 509 S.W.3d 411, 420 (Tex. App.—Houston [1st Dist.] 2014, pet. denied). "Our recognition of [adjudicated father] as [child's] legal parent ... renders [biological father's] reliance on authority favoring parents over non-parents inapposite. Nothing under Texas law supports [biological father's] argument for applying a presumption in favor of a biological 'parent' over a parent acquiring 'parent' status through other legal channels (be it adoption, presumption, or assisted reproduction). [O]nly the difference between a parent and a non-parent has legal significance in determining who should be appointed sole or joint managing conservator of a child ...; the difference between a biological parent and a non-biological parent does not."

Compton v. Pfannenstiel, 428 S.W.3d 881, 883 (Tex.App.—Houston [1st Dist.] 2014, no pet.). "[T]he trial court appointed ... mother, father, and maternal grandmother as [JMCs]. *At 886:* [Mother] contends that the trial court's appointment of her mother as a [JMC] of [the] children is an abuse of its discretion, because parents are presumptively the managing conservators of their children. *At 887:* [Section 153.131] applies to the appointment of a non-parent in addition to both parents. [¶] The evidence in this case satisfies the statutory threshold, including evidence of [mother's] drug use, recent criminal arrests, and extreme neglect of her children while in her care; the trial court reasonably could find that the record demonstrated significant impairment of the children's health and emotional development. The father acceded to the necessity of the grandparent conservatorship in the children's interest. We hold that the trial court was within its discretion in naming a grandparent as a [JMC] to protect the children's physical health and emotional development."

In re S.A.D.S., 413 S.W.3d 434, 438 (Tex.App.—Fort Worth 2010, no pet.). See annotation under Family Code §153.0071, p. 510.

In re R.T.K., 324 S.W.3d 896, 902-03 (Tex.App.—Houston [14th Dist.] 2010, pet. denied). "Section 153.131(a) ... does not necessarily require proof of a parent's blameworthy conduct as a prerequisite to appointment of a nonparent as managing conservator. Instead, the statute plainly addresses only the *effect* of a parent's appointment on the child, as opposed to the myriad of circumstances—such as the parent's conduct—that might have *produced* that result. [¶] [E]vidence of a parent's 'blameworthy prior behavior,' by itself, may be sufficient to overcome the presumption in *some* cases. However, such proof may not be necessary in *all* cases if, as here, the record otherwise demonstrates that appointment of the parent would produce 'the statutorily required negative effect on the child.' [¶] In this case, [the] appointment of [mother] as [SMC] would uproot [child] 'from the only home he has known for the last eight years' and significantly impair his emotional development." *See also* ***In re J.G.***, No. 06-06-00114-CV (Tex.App.—Texarkana 2007, pet. denied) (memo op.; 6-13-07) ("Because safety, security, and stability are critical to child development, the

danger of uprooting a child may in some instances rise to a level that significantly impairs the child's emotional development."); ***Sotelo v. Gonzales***, 170 S.W.3d 783, 789 (Tex.App.—El Paso 2005, no pet.) (same); ***In re K.R.P.***, 80 S.W.3d 669, 677 (Tex.App.—Houston [1st Dist.] 2002, pet. denied) (court considered that uprooting child from only person who consistently cared for her for majority of her life would significantly impair her emotional development). *But see* ***In re B.B.M.***, this page.

Critz v. Critz, 297 S.W.3d 464, 471 (Tex.App.—Fort Worth 2009, no pet.). "Under §153.131, ... a non-parent may not be appointed a [JMC] without overcoming the presumption as to *both* parents. The plain wording of the statute makes clear that this presumption applies when a non-parent seeks managing conservatorship in lieu of or in addition to both parents. There is no language in §153.131 that indicates that the presumption is inapplicable to the appointment of non-parents as [JMCs] when the trial court also appoints one or both parents."

In re B.B.M., 291 S.W.3d 463, 467-68 (Tex.App.—Dallas 2009, pet. denied). "The evidence relied upon by the [adoptive parents] primarily relates to the potential impairment of the child's emotional development resulting from his removal from [their] home. This focus on potential harm caused by the child's removal is misplaced. The proper focus of the court's inquiry is solely upon whether the placement of the child with the natural parent would significantly impair the child's physical health or emotional development. [¶] [T]he negative effect on the child caused by his separation from the nonparents ..., standing alone, [is not] sufficient to deny a natural parent managing conservatorship...." *But see* ***In re R.T.K.***, p. 517.

In re Marriage of Bertram, 981 S.W.2d 820, 825 (Tex.App.—Texarkana 1998, no pet.). "The trial court must consider several factors in weighing the appointment of [JMCs]. These factors are: benefits to the child, the cooperative decision-making ability of the parents, geographical proximity, the parents' ability to promote a positive relationship with the other parent, the parents' prior child-rearing participation, and any other relevant factor. These factors are reviewed to determine whether the presumption in favor of [JMC] has been rebutted." *See also* ***Hinkle v. Hinkle***, 223 S.W.3d 773, 782 (Tex.App.—Dallas 2007, no pet.) (jury, as fact finder, was sole judge of credibility); ***Doyle v. Doyle***, 955 S.W.2d 478, 481-82 (Tex.App.—Austin 1997, no pet.) (trial judge, as fact finder, was sole judge of credibility).

FAM §153.132. RIGHTS & DUTIES OF PARENT APPOINTED SOLE MANAGING CONSERVATOR

Unless limited by court order, a parent appointed as sole managing conservator of a child has the rights and duties provided by Subchapter B and the following exclusive rights:

(1) the right to designate the primary residence of the child;

(2) the right to consent to medical, dental, and surgical treatment involving invasive procedures;

(3) the right to consent to psychiatric and psychological treatment;

(4) the right to receive and give receipt for periodic payments for the support of the child and to hold or disburse these funds for the benefit of the child;

(5) the right to represent the child in legal action and to make other decisions of substantial legal significance concerning the child;

(6) the right to consent to marriage and to enlistment in the armed forces of the United States;

(7) the right to make decisions concerning the child's education;

(8) the right to the services and earnings of the child; and

(9) except when a guardian of the child's estate or a guardian or attorney ad litem has been appointed for the child, the right to act as an agent of the child in relation to the child's estate if the child's action is required by a state, the United States, or a foreign government.

History of Fam. Code §153.132: Acts 1995, 74th Leg., ch. 20, §1, eff. Apr. 20, 1995. Amended by Acts 1995, 74th Leg., ch. 751, §33, eff. Sept. 1, 1995; Acts 2003, 78th Leg., ch. 1036, §9, eff. Sept. 1, 2003; Acts 2005, 79th Leg., ch. 916, §10, eff. June 17, 2005. Source: Former Fam. Code §14.02(b)(3).

ANNOTATIONS

In re S.M.D., 329 S.W.3d 8, 22 (Tex.App.—San Antonio 2010, pet. dism'd). "[T]he purpose of imposing a geographic residency restriction is to ensure those who have rights to possession of the child are able to effectively exercise such rights. No such purpose is served in this case. [T]here is no person other than [father] with a court-ordered right to possession of [child]. Under these circumstances, we hold the restriction [to benefit child's grandmother] unreason-

ably interferes with [father's] rights as a parent [SMC]." *See also* ***In re A.S.***, this page.

In re A.S., 298 S.W.3d 834, 835-36 (Tex.App.—Amarillo 2009, no pet.). Mother "asserts that the trial court could not lawfully [restrict her ability to choose child's residence] because it had appointed her [SMC] and, as such, she had the exclusive authority to select the child's primary residence. [¶] [S]ection 153.132(1) [does not deny a trial judge the authority to geographically restrict a child's residence even though it provides that an SMC] has the exclusive right to 'designate the primary residence of the child.' This is because that statute contains the preface '[u]nless limited by court order.' [In using] that phrase ..., the legislature made it clear that the itemized rights were not absolute but rather subject to limitation. [¶] [R]esidency restrictions may be imposed upon [an SMC] if warranted by the child's best interests." *See also* ***In re S.M.D.***, p. 518; ***In re Macalik***, 13 S.W.3d 43, 46 (Tex.App.—Texarkana 1999, no pet.) (§153.132 allows court to limit rights of SMCs).

In re J.E.P., 49 S.W.3d 380, 385 (Tex.App.—Fort Worth 2000, no pet.). "[T]he rights granted exclusively to [an SMC] under §153.132 do not include the right to have periods of possession in excess of those granted to the [PC], nor do they include the right to weekend possession of the child. While a managing conservator must necessarily enjoy sufficient access to and possession of the child to enable him to fully realize his rights and perform his duties, Father has made no allegation here that a Monday through Friday schedule deprives him of this opportunity. [¶] The only exclusive right previously held by Father that the court granted to Mother in the Order was the 'exclusive right to determine where the parties' two minor children attend school whether public or private.' In view of the fact that the family code gives courts the discretion to limit the rights ordinarily held by [an SMC] and to expressly grant rights to the [PC], we hold that this change alone is not the sort of drastic modification of the functions of the [SMC] that would create a de facto change in conservatorship."

FAM §153.133. PARENTING PLAN FOR JOINT MANAGING CONSERVATORSHIP

(a) If a written agreed parenting plan is filed with the court, the court shall render an order appointing the parents as joint managing conservators only if the parenting plan:

(1) designates the conservator who has the exclusive right to designate the primary residence of the child and:

(A) establishes, until modified by further order, the geographic area within which the conservator shall maintain the child's primary residence; or

(B) specifies that the conservator may designate the child's primary residence without regard to geographic location;

(2) specifies the rights and duties of each parent regarding the child's physical care, support, and education;

(3) includes provisions to minimize disruption of the child's education, daily routine, and association with friends;

(4) allocates between the parents, independently, jointly, or exclusively, all of the remaining rights and duties of a parent provided by Chapter 151;

(5) is voluntarily and knowingly made by each parent and has not been repudiated by either parent at the time the order is rendered; and

(6) is in the best interest of the child.

(b) The agreed parenting plan may contain an alternative dispute resolution procedure that the parties agree to use before requesting enforcement or modification of the terms and conditions of the joint conservatorship through litigation, except in an emergency.

(c) Notwithstanding Subsection (a)(1), the court shall render an order adopting the provisions of a written agreed parenting plan appointing the parents as joint managing conservators if the parenting plan:

(1) meets all the requirements of Subsections (a)(2) through (6); and

(2) provides that the child's primary residence shall be within a specified geographic area.

History of Fam. Code §153.133: Acts 1995, 74th Leg., ch. 20, §1, eff. Apr. 20, 1995. Amended by Acts 1999, 76th Leg., ch. 936, §1, eff. Sept. 1, 1999; Acts 2003, 78th Leg., ch. 1036, §10, eff. Sept. 1, 2003; Acts 2005, 79th Leg., ch. 482, §4, eff. Sept. 1, 2005; Acts 2007, 80th Leg., ch. 1181, §3, eff. Sept. 1, 2007; Acts 2009, 81st Leg., ch. 1113, §3, eff. Sept. 1, 2009. Source: Former Fam. Code §14.021(c), (d).

See also ***O'Connor's Texas Family Law Handbook*** (2017), "Settlement – agreed parenting plan," ch. 4-E, §12.3, p. 489.

ANNOTATIONS

McLendon v. McLendon, 847 S.W.2d 601, 608 (Tex.App.—Dallas 1992, writ denied). See annotation under Family Code §153.007, p. 507.

FAM §153.134. COURT-ORDERED JOINT CONSERVATORSHIP

(a) If a written agreed parenting plan is not filed with the court, the court may render an order appointing the parents joint managing conservators only if the appointment is in the best interest of the child, considering the following factors:

(1) whether the physical, psychological, or emotional needs and development of the child will benefit from the appointment of joint managing conservators;

(2) the ability of the parents to give first priority to the welfare of the child and reach shared decisions in the child's best interest;

(3) whether each parent can encourage and accept a positive relationship between the child and the other parent;

(4) whether both parents participated in child rearing before the filing of the suit;

(5) the geographical proximity of the parents' residences;

(6) if the child is 12 years of age or older, the child's preference, if any, regarding the person to have the exclusive right to designate the primary residence of the child; and

(7) any other relevant factor.

(b) In rendering an order appointing joint managing conservators, the court shall:

(1) designate the conservator who has the exclusive right to determine the primary residence of the child and:

(A) establish, until modified by further order, a geographic area within which the conservator shall maintain the child's primary residence; or

(B) specify that the conservator may determine the child's primary residence without regard to geographic location;

(2) specify the rights and duties of each parent regarding the child's physical care, support, and education;

(3) include provisions to minimize disruption of the child's education, daily routine, and association with friends;

(4) allocate between the parents, independently, jointly, or exclusively, all of the remaining rights and duties of a parent as provided by Chapter 151; and

(5) if feasible, recommend that the parties use an alternative dispute resolution method before requesting enforcement or modification of the terms and conditions of the joint conservatorship through litigation, except in an emergency.

History of Fam. Code §153.134: Acts 1995, 74th Leg., ch. 20, §1, eff. Apr. 20, 1995. Amended by Acts 1999, 76th Leg., ch. 936, §2, eff. Sept. 1, 1999; Acts 2003, 78th Leg., ch. 1036, §11, eff. Sept. 1, 2003; Acts 2005, 79th Leg., ch. 482, §5 (eff. Sept. 1, 2005), ch. 916, §11 (eff. June 17, 2005). Source: Former Fam. Code §14.021(e), (f).

See also *O'Connor's Texas Family Law Handbook* (2017), "Suit for Conservatorship," ch. 4-E, p. 469.

ANNOTATIONS

Gonzales v. Maggio, 500 S.W.3d 656, 660 (Tex. App.—Austin 2016, no pet.). Father "challenges ... the jury's finding ... that the geographic restriction to which [mother] was subject should be the boundaries of the State of Texas. He reasons that '[f]rom beginning to end of the jury trial ..., all of the evidence and argument was directed to the children either living in Travis County or in New York (or possibly Connecticut),' not 'anywhere in Texas.' *At 662-63:* While it is true that the parties at trial advocated competing sides of a Travis County-versus-New York debate ... the evidence they adduced collectively also lent support to the middle path that the jury ultimately determined to be in the children's best interests—permit [mother] to relocate out of Travis County with the children, if she saw fit, yet require that the children reside within Texas."

Berwick v. Wagner, 509 S.W.3d 411, 433 (Tex. App.—Houston [1st Dist.] 2014, pet. denied). "[W]hether appointment of one parent as [SMC] is in a child's best interest turns not on the parent's ability to parent individually, but instead on several statutory factors related to the parents' ability to effectively *co-parent.*"

In re K.L.D., No. 12-10-00386-CV (Tex.App.—Tyler 2012, no pet.) (memo op.; 6-13-12). In modification order, "[t]he court ... ordered the parents to mediate controversies before setting any hearing or initiating discovery in a suit for modification of the terms of the order, except in an emergency. [¶] [Mother] argues that the requirement is contrary to [§153.134(b)(5)], which authorizes only a recommendation that the parties mediate first. [¶] [A] trial judge has no authority to order mediation as a precondition to file in the future a motion to modify conservatorship issues pertaining to a minor child. Here, the trial court went beyond merely recommending mediation before litigating future modifications. The trial court abused its discretion by ordering the parties to mediate before setting any hearing or discovery in a suit for modification of the

terms and conditions of conservatorship, possession, or support of [child]."

In re K.L.W., 301 S.W.3d 423, 425-26 (Tex.App.—Dallas 2009, no pet.). Family Code "§153.134 is silent as to factors a trial court should consider when determining whether a domicile restriction is in the best interest of the child. [¶] In the context of residency restrictions and authorization of relocation, [the court must] consider the public policies outlined in [Fam. Code] §153.001(a). [And] a wide array of other factors can be relevant to the determination of a child's best interest after a parental relocation. These include the (1) reasons for and against the move, (2) education, health, and leisure opportunities afforded by the move, (3) accommodation of the child's special needs or talents, (4) effect of extended family relationships, (5) effect on visitation and communication with the noncustodial parent, (6) noncustodial parent's ability to relocate, and (7) the child's age. [The court] may also consider the general factors relevant to the best interest of a child, such as [the ***Holley*** factors under Fam. Code §153.002]." *See also* ***In re Cooper***, 333 S.W.3d 656, 661 (Tex.App.—Dallas 2009, orig. proceeding) (court could not force mother to make "extreme efforts" to find employment within residency-restricted area as requirement for modifying agreed order); ***Cisneros v. Dingbaum***, 224 S.W.3d 245, 258 (Tex.App.—El Paso 2005, no pet.) (primary custodial parent does not have burden to prove there should be no domicile restriction).

Lenz v. Lenz, 40 S.W.3d 111, 118 n.3 (Tex.App.—San Antonio 2000), *rev'd on other grounds*, 79 S.W.3d 10 (Tex.2002). "We find no merit to [primary custodial parent's] claim that the trial court's [residential restriction] infringes on her U.S. Constitutional right to travel. This right embraces three different components: the right to enter and leave another State; the right to be treated as a welcome visitor while temporarily present in another State; and, for those travelers who elect to become permanent residents, the right to be treated like other citizens of that State. Because the trial court's order in no way affects [primary custodial parent's] ability to return to Germany, the trial court's order does not interfere with: (1) her right to enter and leave another State; (2) her right to be treated as a welcome visitor in another State; or (3) her right to be treated like any other citizen of Texas who voluntarily subjects herself to the jurisdiction of the court system by filing a divorce proceeding." *See also* ***Morgan v. Morgan***, 254 S.W.3d 485, 491-92 (Tex.App.—Beaumont 2008, no pet.) (geographical restriction did not infringe on mother's right to travel or to make educational decisions for child); ***Bates v. Tesar***, 81 S.W.3d 411, 437-39 (Tex.App.—El Paso 2002, no pet.) (same).

Jenkins v. Jenkins, 16 S.W.3d 473, 482-83 (Tex. App.—El Paso 2000, no pet.). Section 153.134 "is mandatory, but it is only mandatory in the sense that any order entered by the trial court appointing a [JMC] must contain language delineating the various rights and duties of the conservators listed under §153.134(b). The list of rights and duties is not exclusive, nor does it define how the trial court shall assign or implement those rights and duties. The trial court retains broad discretion in crafting the rights and duties of each conservators so as to effectuate the best interest of the child."

FAM §153.135. EQUAL POSSESSION NOT REQUIRED

Joint managing conservatorship does not require the award of equal or nearly equal periods of physical possession of and access to the child to each of the joint conservators.

History of Fam. Code §153.135: Acts 1995, 74th Leg., ch. 20, §1, eff. Apr. 20, 1995. Source: Former Fam. Code §14.021(b).

FAM §153.136. REPEALED

Repealed by Acts 2003, 78th Leg., ch. 1036, §22, eff. Sept. 1, 2003.

FAM §153.137. REPEALED

Repealed by Acts 2009, 81st Leg., ch. 1113, §31, eff. Sept. 1, 2009.

FAM §153.138. CHILD SUPPORT ORDER AFFECTING JOINT CONSERVATORS

The appointment of joint managing conservators does not impair or limit the authority of the court to order a joint managing conservator to pay child support to another joint managing conservator.

History of Fam. Code §153.138: Acts 1995, 74th Leg., ch. 20, §1, eff. Apr. 20, 1995. Source: Former Fam. Code §14.021(g).

FAM §153.139. REPEALED

Repealed by Acts 1997, 75th Leg., ch. 561, §30, eff. Sept. 1, 1997.

Sections 153.140-153.190 reserved for expansion

SUBCHAPTER D. PARENT APPOINTED AS POSSESSORY CONSERVATOR

FAM §153.191. PRESUMPTION THAT PARENT TO BE APPOINTED POSSESSORY CONSERVATOR

The court shall appoint as a possessory conservator a parent who is not appointed as a sole or joint managing conservator unless it finds that the appointment is not in the best interest of the child and that parental posses-

sion or access would endanger the physical or emotional welfare of the child.

History of Fam. Code §153.191: Acts 1995, 74th Leg., ch. 20, §1, eff. Apr. 20, 1995. Source: Former Fam. Code §14.03(d).

ANNOTATIONS

In re Marriage of Collier, 419 S.W.3d 390, 398 (Tex.App.—Amarillo 2011, no pet.). "When a trial court appoints a parent [PC], it can conclude that unrestricted possession would endanger the physical or emotional welfare of the child, while restricted possession or access would not. The court can also conclude that access would not endanger the physical or emotional welfare of the child, but that access is not in the best interest of the child. However, the court cannot conclude[] that all access, even restricted access, would endanger the physical or emotional welfare of the child, because such a conclusion would prevent the trial court from appointing the parent [PC]."

In re Walters, 39 S.W.3d 280, 286-87 (Tex.App.—Texarkana 2001, no pet.). "[A] trial court has two options regarding possession and access when it appoints a parent [PC] and decides that the standard possession order is not in the best interest of the child: (1) fashion an order that restricts possession or access so as to eliminate any danger to the physical or emotional welfare of the child; or (2) deny that parent possession and access. However, because appointment of a parent as [PC] implies a finding that access by that parent will not endanger the physical or emotional welfare of the child, ... complete denial of access is limited to those situations in which the parent's access will not endanger the physical or emotional welfare of the child, but is not in the best interest of the child. So while [it] may be technically correct [to say] that a trial court may appoint a parent [PC] but deny that parent access to the child if it is in the best interest of the child to do so, complete denial of access should be rare." *See also* ***Elshafie v. Elshafie***, No. 13-10-00393-CV (Tex.App.—Corpus Christi 2011, no pet.) (memo op.; 11-22-11) (in best interest of child, court can grant, deny, restrict, or limit PC's possession of or access to child as well as PC's rights, privileges, duties, and responsibilities as to child).

FAM §153.192. RIGHTS & DUTIES OF PARENT APPOINTED POSSESSORY CONSERVATOR

(a) Unless limited by court order, a parent appointed as possessory conservator of a child has the rights and duties provided by Subchapter B and any other right or duty expressly granted to the possessory conservator in the order.

(b) In ordering the terms and conditions for possession of a child by a parent appointed possessory conservator, the court shall be guided by the guidelines in Subchapter E.

History of Fam. Code §153.192: Acts 1995, 74th Leg., ch. 20, §1, eff. Apr. 20, 1995. Source: Former Fam. Code §§14.03(b), 14.04.

ANNOTATIONS

In re Marriage of Collier, 419 S.W.3d 390, 398 (Tex.App.—Amarillo 2011, no pet.). See annotation under Family Code §153.191, this page.

In re Walters, 39 S.W.3d 280, 286-87 (Tex.App.—Texarkana 2001, no pet.). See annotation under Family Code §153.191, this page.

FAM §153.193. MINIMAL RESTRICTION ON PARENT'S POSSESSION OR ACCESS

The terms of an order that denies possession of a child to a parent or imposes restrictions or limitations on a parent's right to possession of or access to a child may not exceed those that are required to protect the best interest of the child.

History of Fam. Code §153.193: Acts 1995, 74th Leg., ch. 20, §1, eff. Apr. 20, 1995. Source: Former Fam. Code §14.03(d).

See also ***O'Connor's Texas Family Law Handbook*** (2017), "Restricting right to possession or access," ch. 4-E, §16.2.4, p. 510.

ANNOTATIONS

In re M.S.R., No. 13-05-493-CV (Tex.App.—Corpus Christi 2007, pet. denied) (memo op.; 11-1-07). "Complete denial of access should rarely be ordered. A parent appointed [PC] should at least have periodic visiting privileges with his or her child and should not be denied such privileges except in extreme circumstances. Therefore, this Court's review of any denial of parental access and visitation rights—be they conditional, temporary, or permanent—must be evaluated under an exacting standard: only 'extreme grounds' can warrant such a harsh remedy." *See also* ***In re I.C.N.***, No. 11-13-00105-CV (Tex.App.—Eastland 2014, no pet.) (memo op.; 6-5-14) (child visiting PC in prison is not contrary to child's best interest without evidence showing detriment to child). *But see* ***In re Walters***, 39 S.W.3d 280, 286 n.2 (Tex.App.—Texarkana 2001, no pet.) (severe limitation of access, even one amounting to complete denial of access, is permissible if in best interest of child).

Roosth v. Roosth, 889 S.W.2d 445, 451 (Tex.App.—Houston [14th Dist.] 1994, writ denied). "Because the trial court granted [father] status as a [PC], the trial court must have implicitly found that [father's] possession or access to the children would *not* endanger the physical or emotional welfare of the children. Limitations upon [father's] right to possession of or access to the children may not exceed that required to protect the children's best interest."

Sections 153.194-153.250 reserved for expansion

SUBCHAPTER E. GUIDELINES FOR THE POSSESSION OF A CHILD BY A PARENT NAMED AS POSSESSORY CONSERVATOR

FAM §153.251. POLICY & GENERAL APPLICATION OF GUIDELINES

(a) The guidelines established in the standard possession order are intended to guide the courts in ordering the terms and conditions for possession of a child by a parent named as a possessory conservator or as the minimum possession for a joint managing conservator.

(b) It is the policy of this state to encourage frequent contact between a child and each parent for periods of possession that optimize the development of a close and continuing relationship between each parent and child.

(c) It is preferable for all children in a family to be together during periods of possession.

(d) The standard possession order is designed to apply to a child three years of age or older.

History of Fam. Code §153.251: Acts 1995, 74th Leg., ch. 20, §1, eff. Apr. 20, 1995. Source: Former Fam. Code §14.032(a).

FAM §153.252. REBUTTABLE PRESUMPTION

In a suit, there is a rebuttable presumption that the standard possession order in Subchapter F:

(1) provides reasonable minimum possession of a child for a parent named as a possessory conservator or joint managing conservator; and

(2) is in the best interest of the child.

History of Fam. Code §153.252: Acts 1995, 74th Leg., ch. 20, §1, eff. Apr. 20, 1995. Source: Former Fam. Code §14.033(k).

FAM §153.253. STANDARD POSSESSION ORDER INAPPROPRIATE OR UNWORKABLE

The court shall render an order that grants periods of possession of the child as similar as possible to those provided by the standard possession order if the work schedule or other special circumstances of the managing conservator, the possessory conservator, or the child, or the year-round school schedule of the child, make the standard order unworkable or inappropriate.

History of Fam. Code §153.253: Acts 1995, 74th Leg., ch. 20, §1, eff. Apr. 20, 1995. Source: Former Fam. Code §14.033(k), (m).

A FAM §153.254. CHILD LESS THAN THREE YEARS OF AGE

(a) The court shall render an order appropriate under the circumstances for possession of a child less than three years of age. In rendering the order, the court shall consider evidence of all relevant factors, including:

(1) the caregiving provided to the child before and during the current suit;

(2) the effect on the child that may result from separation from either party;

(3) the availability of the parties as caregivers and the willingness of the parties to personally care for the child;

(4) the physical, medical, behavioral, and developmental needs of the child;

(5) the physical, medical, emotional, economic, and social conditions of the parties;

(6) the impact and influence of individuals, other than the parties, who will be present during periods of possession;

(7) the presence of siblings during periods of possession;

(8) the child's need to develop healthy attachments to both parents;

(9) the child's need for continuity of routine;

(10) the location and proximity of the residences of the parties;

(11) the need for a temporary possession schedule that incrementally shifts to the schedule provided in the prospective order under Subsection (d) based on:

(A) the age of the child; or

(B) minimal or inconsistent contact with the child by a party;

(12) the ability of the parties to share in the responsibilities, rights, and duties of parenting; and

(13) any other evidence of the best interest of the child.

The repealed text of former subsections (b) and (c) is effective for orders rendered before Sept. 1, 2017.

(b), (c) Repealed by S.B. 1237, §12(1), 85th Leg., eff. Sept. 1, 2017.

[~~(b)~~] [~~Notwithstanding the Texas Rules of Civil Procedure, in rendering an order under Subsection (a), the court shall make findings in support of the order if:~~]

[~~(1)~~] [~~a party files a written request with the court not later than the 10th day after the date of the hearing; or~~]

[~~(2)~~] [~~a party makes an oral request in court during the hearing on the order.~~]

[~~(c)~~] [~~The court shall make and enter the findings required by Subsection (b) not later than the 15th day after the date the party makes the request.~~]

(d) The court shall render a prospective order to take effect on the child's third birthday, which presumptively will be the standard possession order.

History of Fam. Code §153.254: Acts 1995, 74th Leg., ch. 20, §1, eff. Apr. 20, 1995. Amended by Acts 2011, 82nd Leg., ch. 86, §1, eff. Sept. 1, 2011; S.B. 1237, §12(1), 85th Leg., eff. Sept. 1, 2017. Source: Former Fam. Code §14.032(b).

ANNOTATIONS

In re Marriage of Bertram, 981 S.W.2d 820, 828-29 (Tex.App.—Texarkana 1998, no pet.). Section 153.254(a) "provides that when a child is less than three years of age, the court shall render an appropriate order under the circumstances for possession of the child. This section suggests that the trial court is not bound by the guidelines when the children are under three years of age. ... Section 153.254(b) [now §153.254(d)] provides that, at the same time, the trial court shall render a prospective order to take effect on the child's third birthday, which presumptively shall be the standard possession order. [¶] The judgment in the present case does not speak in terms of a prospective order to take effect after the children's third birthday. But because the order attempts to cover matters involving attendance at school, which is not applicable at this time, and situations in which the parents reside 100 miles or less apart, which is not the situation at this time, it can be assumed that this order was intended to apply after the children's third birthday. Thus, the presumptive application of the standard possession order should be applied [for any issues that are not already addressed in the order] for the time after the children reach their third birthday."

FAM §153.255. AGREEMENT

The court may render an order for periods of possession of a child that vary from the standard possession order based on the agreement of the parties.

History of Fam. Code §153.255: Acts 1995, 74th Leg., ch. 20, §1, eff. Apr. 20, 1995. Source: Former Fam. Code §14.033(n).

FAM §153.256. FACTORS FOR COURT TO CONSIDER

In ordering the terms of possession of a child under an order other than a standard possession order, the court shall be guided by the guidelines established by the standard possession order and may consider:

(1) the age, developmental status, circumstances, needs, and best interest of the child;

(2) the circumstances of the managing conservator and of the parent named as a possessory conservator; and

(3) any other relevant factor.

History of Fam. Code §153.256: Acts 1995, 74th Leg., ch. 20, §1, eff. Apr. 20, 1995. Amended by Acts 1995, 74th Leg., ch. 751, §35, eff. Sept. 1, 1995. Source: Former Fam. Code §14.032(c).

See also ***O'Connor's Texas Family Law Handbook*** (2017), "Alternative periods of possession," ch. 4-E, §16.2.5, p. 513.

ANNOTATIONS

In re D.R.S., 138 S.W.3d 467, 472 (Tex.App.—Houston [14th Dist.] 2004, pet. denied). "[T]he trial court's decision that the best interest of the child was to have a non-standard possession order was supported by its findings of fact and conclusions of law that: (1) [mother] had been irresponsible in numerous respects concerning herself and her children; (2) [child's aunt and uncle] had shown the ability to act in the best interest of the child; (3) the [JMCs] live 78 miles apart; and (4) a more stable environment for the child would be to spend three week periods with the respective [JMCs], rather than undergo the frequency of movement and disruption of daily schedule that would occur under a standard possession order." *See also* ***In re D.A.***, 307 S.W.3d 556, 562-63 (Tex.App.—Dallas 2010, no pet.) (deviating from standard possession order by requiring father to complete anger-management course before he could have access to child was not error).

Niskar v. Niskar, 136 S.W.3d 749, 756-57 (Tex. App.—Dallas 2004, no pet.). "The record supports the trial court's variance from the standard possession order in drafting the terms of the appellant's visitation. It is replete with testimony regarding the child's severe disabilities and the type of care she requires, and contains evidence of [father's] lack of involvement in her medical care prior to his divorce. We conclude that the trial court did not abuse its discretion in denying [father] overnight visitation or possession of his severely disabled daughter. [¶] Nevertheless, the trial court

cannot possibly know what is in the child's best interest in the future. ... We conclude that the portion of the trial court's order precluding [father] from applying to the trial court for overnight visitations or a change in the visitation schedule for two years is an abuse of the trial court's discretion."

FAM §153.257. MEANS OF TRAVEL

In an order providing for the terms and conditions of possession of a child, the court may restrict the means of travel of the child by a legal mode of transportation only after a showing of good cause contained in the record and a finding by the court that the restriction is in the best interest of the child. The court shall specify the duties of the conservators to provide transportation to and from the transportation facilities.

History of Fam. Code §153.257: Acts 1995, 74th Leg., ch. 20, §1, eff. Apr. 20, 1995. Source: Former Fam. Code §14.033(h).

ANNOTATIONS

Messier v. Messier, 389 S.W.3d 904, 909 (Tex. App.—Houston [14th Dist.] 2012, no pet.). See annotation under Family Code §153.072, p. 514.

In re M.A.S., 233 S.W.3d 915, 922-23 (Tex.App.—Dallas 2007, pet. denied). "When specifying a means of travel, even if optional, the trial court must specify the duties of the conservators to provide transportation to and from[, in this case,] the airport. The trial court's notice provision [requiring timely, written notice between parents] is merely part of those duties. It is prudent to require written notice when flight numbers and flight times are involved."

FAM §153.258. REQUEST FOR FINDINGS WHEN ORDER VARIES FROM STANDARD ORDER

The amended text in §153.258 is effective for orders rendered on or after Sept. 1, 2017. Orders rendered before Sept. 1, 2017, are governed by the former law in effect at that time.

(a) In ~~[Without regard to Rules 296 through 299, Texas Rules of Civil Procedure, in]~~ all cases in which possession of a child by a parent is contested and the possession of the child varies from the standard possession order, including a possession order for a child under three years of age, on ~~[written]~~ request by a party ~~[made or filed with the court not later than 10 days after the date of the hearing or on oral request made in open court during the hearing]~~, the court shall state in writing ~~[the order]~~ the specific reasons for the variance from the standard order.

(b) A request for findings of fact under this section must conform to the Texas Rules of Civil Procedure.

History of Fam. Code §153.258: Acts 1995, 74th Leg., ch. 20, §1, eff. Apr. 20, 1995. Amended by S.B. 1237, §9, 85th Leg., eff. Sept. 1, 2017. Source: Former Fam. Code §14.033(k).

See also ***O'Connor's Texas Family Law Handbook*** (2017), "Findings," ch. 4-E, §16.3, p. 516.

Sections 153.259-153.310 reserved for expansion

SUBCHAPTER F. STANDARD POSSESSION ORDER

FAM §153.3101. REFERENCE TO "SCHOOL" IN STANDARD POSSESSION ORDER

In a standard possession order, "school" means the elementary or secondary school in which the child is enrolled or, if the child is not enrolled in an elementary or secondary school, the public school district in which the child primarily resides.

History of Fam. Code §153.3101: Acts 2009, 81st Leg., ch. 1113, §4, eff. Sept. 1, 2009. Amended by Acts 2015, 84th Leg., ch. 1167, §3, eff. Sept. 1, 2015.

FAM §153.311. MUTUAL AGREEMENT OR SPECIFIED TERMS FOR POSSESSION

The court shall specify in a standard possession order that the parties may have possession of the child at times mutually agreed to in advance by the parties and, in the absence of mutual agreement, shall have possession of the child under the specified terms set out in the standard possession order.

History of Fam. Code §153.311: Acts 1995, 74th Leg., ch. 20, §1, eff. Apr. 20, 1995. Amended by Acts 2009, 81st Leg., ch. 1113, §5, eff. Sept. 1, 2009. Source: Former Fam. Code §14.033(b).

See also ***O'Connor's Texas Family Law Handbook*** (2017), "Possession & Access," ch. 4-E, §16, p. 505.

FAM §153.312. PARENTS WHO RESIDE 100 MILES OR LESS APART

(a) If the possessory conservator resides 100 miles or less from the primary residence of the child, the possessory conservator shall have the right to possession of the child as follows:

(1) on weekends throughout the year beginning at 6 p.m. on the first, third, and fifth Friday of each month and ending at 6 p.m. on the following Sunday; and

(2) on Thursdays of each week during the regular school term beginning at 6 p.m. and ending at 8 p.m., unless the court finds that visitation under this subdivision is not in the best interest of the child.

(b) The following provisions govern possession of the child for vacations and certain specific holidays and supersede conflicting weekend or Thursday periods of possession. The possessory conservator and the managing conservator shall have rights of possession of the child as follows:

(1) the possessory conservator shall have possession in even-numbered years, beginning at 6 p.m. on the day the child is dismissed from school for the school's spring vacation and ending at 6 p.m. on the day before school resumes after that vacation, and the managing conservator shall have possession for the same period in odd-numbered years;

(2) if a possessory conservator:

(A) gives the managing conservator written notice by April 1 of each year specifying an extended period or periods of summer possession, the possessory conservator shall have possession of the child for 30 days beginning not earlier than the day after the child's school is dismissed for the summer vacation and ending not later than seven days before school resumes at the end of the summer vacation, to be exercised in not more than two separate periods of at least seven consecutive days each, with each period of possession beginning and ending at 6 p.m. on each applicable day; or

(B) does not give the managing conservator written notice by April 1 of each year specifying an extended period or periods of summer possession, the possessory conservator shall have possession of the child for 30 consecutive days beginning at 6 p.m. on July 1 and ending at 6 p.m. on July 31;

(3) if the managing conservator gives the possessory conservator written notice by April 15 of each year, the managing conservator shall have possession of the child on any one weekend beginning Friday at 6 p.m. and ending at 6 p.m. on the following Sunday during one period of possession by the possessory conservator under Subdivision (2), provided that the managing conservator picks up the child from the possessory conservator and returns the child to that same place; and

(4) if the managing conservator gives the possessory conservator written notice by April 15 of each year or gives the possessory conservator 14 days' written notice on or after April 16 of each year, the managing conservator may designate one weekend beginning not earlier than the day after the child's school is dismissed for the summer vacation and ending not later than seven days before school resumes at the end of the summer vacation, during which an otherwise scheduled weekend period of possession by the possessory conservator will not take place, provided that the weekend designated does not interfere with the possessory conservator's period or periods of extended summer possession or with Father's Day if the possessory conservator is the father of the child.

History of Fam. Code §153.312: Acts 1995, 74th Leg., ch. 20, §1, eff. Apr. 20, 1995. Amended by Acts 1997, 75th Leg., ch. 802, §1, eff. Sept. 1, 1997; Acts 1999, 76th Leg., ch. 236, §1, eff. Sept. 1, 1999; Acts 2003, 78th Leg., ch. 1036, §13, eff. Sept. 1, 2003; Acts 2005, 79th Leg., ch. 916, §12, eff. June 17, 2005; Acts 2007, 80th Leg., ch. 1041, §2, eff. June 15, 2007; Acts 2009, 81st Leg., ch. 1113, §6, eff. Sept. 1, 2009. Source: Former Fam. Code §14.033(c), (e)(4)-(7).

ANNOTATIONS

Williams v. Williams, 407 S.W.3d 770, 772 (Tex. App.—El Paso 2012, no pet.). "The decree ... specifies that [mother] has a right to summer weekend access during [father's] extended summer possession.... *At 773:* [Father] had planned a trip to Yellowstone with the child and family friends during ... his extended summer possession. [Mother] requested her summer weekend possession [during that time]. [Father] claimed that [mother] should pick [child] up in Yellowstone while [mother] countered that the exchange had to occur at [child's] residence. *At 775-76:* The decree tracks the [§153.312(b)(3)] Standard Possession Order verbatim.... Without question, the trial court lacked authority to order [father] to bring the child back to North Texas for the weekend. By virtue of the MSA, the decree of divorce, and the Texas Family Code, [mother] must pick up [child] from [father] and return [child] to [father]. If [mother] as the custodial parent wants weekend access during [father's] vacation, that is her right. But she is bound by contract, judgment, and statute to travel to the site of the vacation."

FAM §153.313. PARENTS WHO RESIDE OVER 100 MILES APART

If the possessory conservator resides more than 100 miles from the residence of the child, the possessory conservator shall have the right to possession of the child as follows:

(1) either regular weekend possession beginning on the first, third, and fifth Friday as provided under the terms applicable to parents who reside 100 miles or less apart or not more than one weekend per month of the possessory conservator's choice beginning at 6 p.m. on the day school recesses for the weekend and ending at 6 p.m. on the day before school resumes after the week-

end, provided that the possessory conservator gives the managing conservator 14 days' written or telephonic notice preceding a designated weekend, and provided that the possessory conservator elects an option for this alternative period of possession by written notice given to the managing conservator within 90 days after the parties begin to reside more than 100 miles apart, as applicable;

(2) each year beginning at 6 p.m. on the day the child is dismissed from school for the school's spring vacation and ending at 6 p.m. on the day before school resumes after that vacation;

(3) if the possessory conservator:

(A) gives the managing conservator written notice by April 1 of each year specifying an extended period or periods of summer possession, the possessory conservator shall have possession of the child for 42 days beginning not earlier than the day after the child's school is dismissed for the summer vacation and ending not later than seven days before school resumes at the end of the summer vacation, to be exercised in not more than two separate periods of at least seven consecutive days each, with each period of possession beginning and ending at 6 p.m. on each applicable day; or

(B) does not give the managing conservator written notice by April 1 of each year specifying an extended period or periods of summer possession, the possessory conservator shall have possession of the child for 42 consecutive days beginning at 6 p.m. on June 15 and ending at 6 p.m. on July 27;

(4) if the managing conservator gives the possessory conservator written notice by April 15 of each year the managing conservator shall have possession of the child on one weekend beginning Friday at 6 p.m. and ending at 6 p.m. on the following Sunday during one period of possession by the possessory conservator under Subdivision (3), provided that if a period of possession by the possessory conservator exceeds 30 days, the managing conservator may have possession of the child under the terms of this subdivision on two nonconsecutive weekends during that time period, and further provided that the managing conservator picks up the child from the possessory conservator and returns the child to that same place; and

(5) if the managing conservator gives the possessory conservator written notice by April 15 of each year, the managing conservator may designate 21 days beginning not earlier than the day after the child's school is dismissed for the summer vacation and ending not later than seven days before school resumes at the end of the summer vacation, to be exercised in not more than two separate periods of at least seven consecutive days each, with each period of possession beginning and ending at 6 p.m. on each applicable day, during which the possessory conservator may not have possession of the child, provided that the period or periods so designated do not interfere with the possessory conservator's period or periods of extended summer possession or with Father's Day if the possessory conservator is the father of the child.

History of Fam. Code §153.313: Acts 1995, 74th Leg., ch. 20, §1, eff. Apr. 20, 1995. Amended by Acts 1995, 74th Leg., ch. 751, §36, eff. Sept. 1, 1995; Acts 1999, 76th Leg., ch. 236, §2, eff. Sept. 1, 1999; Acts 2009, 81st Leg., ch. 1113, §7, eff. Sept. 1, 2009. Source: Former Fam. Code §14.033(f).

FAM §153.314. HOLIDAY POSSESSION UNAFFECTED BY DISTANCE PARENTS RESIDE APART

The following provisions govern possession of the child for certain specific holidays and supersede conflicting weekend or Thursday periods of possession without regard to the distance the parents reside apart. The possessory conservator and the managing conservator shall have rights of possession of the child as follows:

(1) the possessory conservator shall have possession of the child in even-numbered years beginning at 6 p.m. on the day the child is dismissed from school for the Christmas school vacation and ending at noon on December 28, and the managing conservator shall have possession for the same period in odd-numbered years;

(2) the possessory conservator shall have possession of the child in odd-numbered years beginning at noon on December 28 and ending at 6 p.m. on the day before school resumes after that vacation, and the managing conservator shall have possession for the same period in even-numbered years;

(3) the possessory conservator shall have possession of the child in odd-numbered years, beginning at 6 p.m. on the day the child is dismissed from school before Thanksgiving and ending at 6 p.m. on the following Sunday, and the managing conservator shall have possession for the same period in even-numbered years;

(4) the parent not otherwise entitled under this standard possession order to present possession of a child on the child's birthday shall have possession of the child beginning at 6 p.m. and ending at 8 p.m. on

that day, provided that the parent picks up the child from the residence of the conservator entitled to possession and returns the child to that same place;

(5) if a conservator, the father shall have possession of the child beginning at 6 p.m. on the Friday preceding Father's Day and ending on Father's Day at 6 p.m., provided that, if he is not otherwise entitled under this standard possession order to present possession of the child, he picks up the child from the residence of the conservator entitled to possession and returns the child to that same place; and

(6) if a conservator, the mother shall have possession of the child beginning at 6 p.m. on the Friday preceding Mother's Day and ending on Mother's Day at 6 p.m., provided that, if she is not otherwise entitled under this standard possession order to present possession of the child, she picks up the child from the residence of the conservator entitled to possession and returns the child to that same place.

History of Fam. Code §153.314: Acts 1995, 74th Leg., ch. 20, §1, eff. Apr. 20, 1995. Amended by Acts 2003, 78th Leg., ch. 1036, §14, eff. Sept. 1, 2003; Acts 2007, 80th Leg., ch. 1041, §3, eff. June 15, 2007; Acts 2009, 81st Leg., ch. 1113, §8, eff. Sept. 1, 2009. Source: Former Fam. Code §14.033(e)(1)-(3), (8)-(10), (f)(2).

FAM §153.315. WEEKEND POSSESSION EXTENDED BY HOLIDAY

(a) If a weekend period of possession of the possessory conservator coincides with a student holiday or teacher in-service day that falls on a Monday during the regular school term, as determined by the school in which the child is enrolled, or with a federal, state, or local holiday that falls on a Monday during the summer months in which school is not in session, the weekend possession shall end at 6 p.m. on Monday.

(b) If a weekend period of possession of the possessory conservator coincides with a student holiday or teacher in-service day that falls on a Friday during the regular school term, as determined by the school in which the child is enrolled, or with a federal, state, or local holiday that falls on a Friday during the summer months in which school is not in session, the weekend possession shall begin at 6 p.m. on Thursday.

History of Fam. Code §153.315: Acts 1995, 74th Leg., ch. 20, §1, eff. Apr. 20, 1995. Amended by Acts 2009, 81st Leg., ch. 1113, §9, eff. Sept. 1, 2009. Source: Former Fam. Code §14.033(d).

FAM §153.316. GENERAL TERMS & CONDITIONS

The court shall order the following general terms and conditions of possession of a child to apply without regard to the distance between the residence of a parent and the child:

(1) the managing conservator shall surrender the child to the possessory conservator at the beginning of each period of the possessory conservator's possession at the residence of the managing conservator;

(2) if the possessory conservator elects to begin a period of possession at the time the child's school is regularly dismissed, the managing conservator shall surrender the child to the possessory conservator at the beginning of each period of possession at the school in which the child is enrolled;

(3) the possessory conservator shall be ordered to do one of the following:

(A) the possessory conservator shall surrender the child to the managing conservator at the end of each period of possession at the residence of the possessory conservator; or

(B) the possessory conservator shall return the child to the residence of the managing conservator at the end of each period of possession, except that the order shall provide that the possessory conservator shall surrender the child to the managing conservator at the end of each period of possession at the residence of the possessory conservator if:

(i) at the time the original order or a modification of an order establishing terms and conditions of possession or access the possessory conservator and the managing conservator lived in the same county, the possessory conservator's county of residence remains the same after the rendition of the order, and the managing conservator's county of residence changes, effective on the date of the change of residence by the managing conservator; or

(ii) the possessory conservator and managing conservator lived in the same residence at any time during a six-month period preceding the date on which a suit for dissolution of the marriage was filed and the possessory conservator's county of residence remains the same and the managing conservator's county of residence changes after they no longer live in the same residence, effective on the date the order is rendered;

(4) if the possessory conservator elects to end a period of possession at the time the child's school resumes, the possessory conservator shall surrender the child to the managing conservator at the end of each period of possession at the school in which the child is enrolled;

(5) each conservator shall return with the child the personal effects that the child brought at the beginning of the period of possession;

(6) either parent may designate a competent adult to pick up and return the child, as applicable; a parent or a designated competent adult shall be present when the child is picked up or returned;

(7) a parent shall give notice to the person in possession of the child on each occasion that the parent will be unable to exercise that parent's right of possession for a specified period;

(8) written notice, including notice provided by electronic mail or facsimile, shall be deemed to have been timely made if received or, if applicable, postmarked before or at the time that notice is due; and

(9) if a conservator's time of possession of a child ends at the time school resumes and for any reason the child is not or will not be returned to school, the conservator in possession of the child shall immediately notify the school and the other conservator that the child will not be or has not been returned to school.

History of Fam. Code §153.316: Acts 1995, 74th Leg., ch. 20, §1, eff. Apr. 20, 1995. Amended by Acts 1995, 74th Leg., ch. 751, §37, eff. Sept. 1, 1995; Acts 1997, 75th Leg., ch. 9, §1, eff. Sept. 1, 1997; Acts 2013, 83rd Leg., ch. 277, §1, eff. Sept. 1, 2013. Source: Former Fam. Code §14.033(g).

See also ***O'Connor's Texas Family Law Handbook*** (2017), "Possession pickup & surrender," ch. 4-E, §16.1.2, p. 508.

ANNOTATIONS

Weldon v. Weldon, 968 S.W.2d 515, 516 n.2 (Tex. App.—Texarkana 1998, no pet.). "Even though the standard possession order under [Fam. Code] §153.316 sets out the possessory rights of the [PC], the Section applies to [JMCs] not awarded primary physical residence of the child pursuant to [Fam. Code] §153.137."

FAM §153.3161. REPEALED

Repealed by Acts 2009, 81st Leg., ch. 727, §6 (eff. Sept. 1, 2009), ch. 1113, §31 (eff. Sept. 1, 2009).

FAM §153.3162. REPEALED

Repealed by Acts 2013, 83rd Leg., ch. 277, §3, eff. Sept. 1, 2013.

FAM §153.317. ALTERNATIVE BEGINNING & ENDING POSSESSION TIMES

(a) If elected by a conservator, the court shall alter the standard possession order under Sections 153.312, 153.314, and 153.315 to provide for one or more of the following alternative beginning and ending possession times for the described periods of possession, unless the court finds that the election is not in the best interest of the child:

(1) for weekend periods of possession under Section 153.312(a)(1) during the regular school term:

(A) beginning at the time the child's school is regularly dismissed;

(B) ending at the time the child's school resumes after the weekend; or

(C) beginning at the time described by Paragraph (A) and ending at the time described by Paragraph (B);

(2) for Thursday periods of possession under Section 153.312(a)(2):

(A) beginning at the time the child's school is regularly dismissed;

(B) ending at the time the child's school resumes on Friday; or

(C) beginning at the time described by Paragraph (A) and ending at the time described by Paragraph (B);

(3) for spring vacation periods of possession under Section 153.312(b)(1), beginning at the time the child's school is dismissed for those vacations;

(4) for Christmas school vacation periods of possession under Section 153.314(1), beginning at the time the child's school is dismissed for the vacation;

(5) for Thanksgiving holiday periods of possession under Section 153.314(3), beginning at the time the child's school is dismissed for the holiday;

(6) for Father's Day periods of possession under Section 153.314(5), ending at 8 a.m. on the Monday after Father's Day weekend;

(7) for Mother's Day periods of possession under Section 153.314(6):

(A) beginning at the time the child's school is regularly dismissed on the Friday preceding Mother's Day;

(B) ending at the time the child's school resumes after Mother's Day; or

(C) beginning at the time described by Paragraph (A) and ending at the time described by Paragraph (B); or

(8) for weekend periods of possession that are extended under Section 153.315(b) by a student holiday or teacher in-service day that falls on a Friday, beginning at the time the child's school is regularly dismissed on Thursday.

(b) A conservator must make an election under Subsection (a) before or at the time of the rendition of a possession order. The election may be made:

(1) in a written document filed with the court; or

(2) through an oral statement made in open court on the record.

History of Fam. Code §153.317: Acts 1995, 74th Leg., ch. 20, §1, eff. Apr. 20, 1995. Amended by Acts 1997, 75th Leg., ch. 9, §1, eff. Sept. 1, 1997; Acts 2003, 78th Leg., ch. 1036, §15, eff. Sept. 1, 2003; Acts 2009, 81st Leg., ch. 1113, §10, eff. Sept. 1, 2009; Acts 2013, 83rd Leg., ch. 277, §2, eff. Sept. 1, 2013. Source: Former Fam. Code §14.033(i).

See also *O'Connor's Texas Family Law Handbook* (2017), "Alternative times to begin or end possession," ch. 4-E, §16.2.2, p. 509.

ANNOTATIONS

Ruiz v. Ruiz, No. 02-12-00136-CV (Tex.App.—Fort Worth 2013, no pet.) (memo op.; 2-14-13). "[N]othing in §153.317 requires the trial court to make a formal or written finding that extended possession is not in the child's best interest before denying extended possession. [¶] Because no requirement exists that the trial court must make a formal, written not-in-the-best-interest-of-the-child finding before denying full extended possession, we hold that the trial court did not abuse its discretion [in this case] by denying [mother] full extended possession after implicitly finding that it was not in the child's best interest for [mother] to have extended possession."

Sections 153.318-153.370 reserved for expansion

SUBCHAPTER G. APPOINTMENT OF NONPARENT AS CONSERVATOR

FAM §153.371. RIGHTS & DUTIES OF NONPARENT APPOINTED AS SOLE MANAGING CONSERVATOR

Unless limited by court order or other provisions of this chapter, a nonparent, a licensed child-placing agency, or the Department of Family and Protective Services appointed as a managing conservator of the child has the following rights and duties:

(1) the right to have physical possession and to direct the moral and religious training of the child;

(2) the duty of care, control, protection, and reasonable discipline of the child;

(3) the duty to provide the child with clothing, food, shelter, education, and medical, psychological, and dental care;

(4) the right to consent for the child to medical, psychiatric, psychological, dental, and surgical treatment and to have access to the child's medical records;

(5) the right to receive and give receipt for payments for the support of the child and to hold or disburse funds for the benefit of the child;

(6) the right to the services and earnings of the child;

(7) the right to consent to marriage and to enlistment in the armed forces of the United States;

(8) the right to represent the child in legal action and to make other decisions of substantial legal significance concerning the child;

(9) except when a guardian of the child's estate or a guardian or attorney ad litem has been appointed for the child, the right to act as an agent of the child in relation to the child's estate if the child's action is required by a state, the United States, or a foreign government;

(10) the right to designate the primary residence of the child and to make decisions regarding the child's education; and

(11) if the parent-child relationship has been terminated with respect to the parents, or only living parent, or if there is no living parent, the right to consent to the adoption of the child and to make any other decision concerning the child that a parent could make.

History of Fam. Code §153.371: Acts 1995, 74th Leg., ch. 20, §1, eff. Apr. 20, 1995. Amended by Acts 1995, 74th Leg., ch. 751, §34, eff. Sept. 1, 1995; Acts 1999, 76th Leg., ch. 949, §1, eff. Sept. 1, 1999; Acts 2003, 78th Leg., ch. 1036, §16, eff. Sept. 1, 2003; Acts 2015, 84th Leg., ch. 1, §1.044, eff. Apr. 2, 2015. Source: Former Fam. Code §14.02(c).

See also *O'Connor's Texas Family Law Handbook* (2017), "Rights & Duties of Conservators," ch. 4-E, §4, p. 472.

ANNOTATIONS

In re V.L.K., 24 S.W.3d 338, 340 n.1 (Tex.2000). "A managing conservator has the right to establish the child's residence and has primary custody of the child."

FAM §153.372. NONPARENT APPOINTED AS JOINT MANAGING CONSERVATOR

(a) A nonparent, the Department of Family and Protective Services, or a licensed child-placing agency appointed as a joint managing conservator may serve in that capacity with either another nonparent or with a parent of the child.

(b) The procedural and substantive standards regarding an agreed or court-ordered joint managing conservatorship provided by Subchapter C apply to a nonparent joint managing conservator.

History of Fam. Code §153.372: Acts 1995, 74th Leg., ch. 20, §1, eff. Apr. 20, 1995. Amended by Acts 2015, 84th Leg., ch. 1, §1.045, eff. Apr. 2, 2015. Source: Former Fam. Code §14.021(j).

See also *O'Connor's Texas Family Law Handbook* (2017), "Nonparent seeking conservatorship," ch. 4-E, §15.4, p. 500.

ANNOTATIONS

In re De La Pena, 999 S.W.2d 521, 534-35 (Tex. App.—El Paso 1999, no pet.). "Section 153.372(b) provides that the procedural and substantive standards regarding a court-ordered [JMC] provided by Subch. C of [Ch. 153] apply to a nonparent joint managing conservator. The very first section of Subch. C contains the parental presumption. Accordingly, we conclude that as between a parent and nonparent, unless the court finds that appointment of the parent would not be in the best interest of the child because it would significantly impair the child's physical health or emotional development, the parent shall be appointed [SMC] or the parent and nonparent shall be appointed [JMCs]. If the court chooses the latter, the parent shall be awarded primary possession unless such an order would not be in the best interest of the child because it would significantly impair the child's physical health or emotional development. To hold otherwise would permit the court to apply the presumption in appointing the parent a [JMC] but nevertheless choose the primary residence of the child on the basis of a heads-up best interest test, with the court determining which of the parties is the 'better' choice. This results in the appointment of a parent as a managing conservator in name only, a paper title which eviscerates the purpose of the statute."

FAM §153.3721. ACCESS TO CERTAIN RECORDS BY NONPARENT JOINT MANAGING CONSERVATOR

Unless limited by court order or other provisions of this chapter, a nonparent joint managing conservator has the right of access to the medical records of the child, without regard to whether the right is specified in the order.

History of Fam. Code §153.3721: Acts 1999, 76th Leg., ch. 949, §2, eff. Sept. 1, 1999.

FAM §153.373. VOLUNTARY SURRENDER OF POSSESSION REBUTS PARENTAL PRESUMPTION

The presumption that a parent should be appointed or retained as managing conservator of the child is rebutted if the court finds that:

(1) the parent has voluntarily relinquished actual care, control, and possession of the child to a nonparent, a licensed child-placing agency, or the Department of Family and Protective Services for a period of one year or more, a portion of which was within 90 days preceding the date of intervention in or filing of the suit; and

(2) the appointment of the nonparent, agency, or Department of Family and Protective Services as managing conservator is in the best interest of the child.

History of Fam. Code §153.373: Acts 1995, 74th Leg., ch. 20, §1, eff. Apr. 20, 1995. Amended by Acts 2015, 84th Leg., ch. 1, §1.046, eff. Apr. 2, 2015. Source: Former Fam. Code §14.01(b)(2).

ANNOTATIONS

In re S.A.H., 420 S.W.3d 911, 922 (Tex.App.—Houston [14th Dist.] 2014, no pet.). "The Family Code does not define 'voluntarily relinquish' as that term is used in §153.373. *At 923-24:* [In this case, there] is extensive evidence that Great Aunt controlled all facets of [child's] life that a parent normally would control for ... 14 months, from school and extracurricular activities to medical treatment and birthday parties, and no appreciable evidence that Mother controlled any of these facets of [child's] life during that time period. Mother also did not financially support [child] during this time. [¶] Mother emphasizes that the arrangement was expressly intended to be temporary and not permanent, but she provides no citation or analysis for the proposition that, under §153.373, voluntary relinquishment must be intended to be permanent. [¶] Mother next contends that the Power of Attorney only granted limited rights to Great Aunt, such as enabling her to enroll [child] in school and obtain medical care for him, and argues that this limited grant of rights indicates Mother never ceded full control of [child] to Great Aunt. ... The allegedly limited nature of the Power of Attorney, however, does not indicate that Mother did not otherwise relinquish control regarding [child]. *At 925-26:* The record demonstrates Mother voluntarily relinquished care, control, and possession of [child] to Great Aunt for 12 months or more as required by §153.373...."

FAM §153.374. DESIGNATION OF MANAGING CONSERVATOR IN AFFIDAVIT OF RELINQUISHMENT

(a) A parent may designate a competent person, the Department of Family and Protective Services, or a licensed child-placing agency to serve as managing conservator of the child in an unrevoked or irrevocable affidavit of relinquishment of parental rights executed as provided by Chapter 161.

(b) The person, Department of Family and Protective Services, or agency designated to serve as manag-

ing conservator shall be appointed managing conservator unless the court finds that the appointment would not be in the best interest of the child.

History of Fam. Code §153.374: Acts 1995, 74th Leg., ch. 20, §1, eff. Apr. 20, 1995. Amended by Acts 1995, 74th Leg., ch. 751, §38, eff. Sept. 1, 1995; Acts 2015, 84th Leg., ch. 1, §1.047, eff. Apr. 2, 2015. Source: Former Fam. Code §14.01(d).

ANNOTATIONS

DFPS v. Alternatives in Motion, 210 S.W.3d 794, 801 (Tex.App.—Houston [1st Dist.] 2006, pet. denied). "[T]his case requires us to determine whether a trial court's temporary orders can preclude a parent from voluntarily relinquishing parental rights and designating a managing conservator pursuant to §153.374 when [TDFPS] has brought suit to terminate the parents' parental rights [and TDFPS had already been named temporary SMC]. *At 802:* [W]e conclude that the [parents' right to designate a managing conservator under §153.374] survives a trial court's temporary orders naming [TDFPS] managing conservator in a suit brought by the State to terminate parental rights. Here, however, the parents had been removed as managing conservators pending a hearing on involuntary termination of their parental rights. Thus, their affidavits that designated [placement agency] as managing conservator served only to transfer those rights the parents still possessed—in this instance, only possessory rights."

FAM §153.375. ANNUAL REPORT BY NONPARENT MANAGING CONSERVATOR

(a) A nonparent appointed as a managing conservator of a child shall each 12 months after the appointment file with the court a report of facts concerning the child's welfare, including the child's whereabouts and physical condition.

(b) The report may not be admitted in evidence in a subsequent suit.

History of Fam. Code §153.375: Acts 1995, 74th Leg., ch. 20, §1, eff. Apr. 20, 1995. Source: Former Fam. Code §14.01(e).

FAM §153.376. RIGHTS & DUTIES OF NONPARENT POSSESSORY CONSERVATOR

(a) Unless limited by court order or other provisions of this chapter, a nonparent, a licensed child-placing agency, or the Department of Family and Protective Services appointed as a possessory conservator has the following rights and duties during the period of possession:

(1) the duty of care, control, protection, and reasonable discipline of the child;

(2) the duty to provide the child with clothing, food, and shelter; and

(3) the right to consent to medical, dental, and surgical treatment during an emergency involving an immediate danger to the health and safety of the child.

(b) A nonparent possessory conservator has any other right or duty specified in the order.

History of Fam. Code §153.376: Acts 1995, 74th Leg., ch. 20, §1, eff. Apr. 20, 1995. Amended by Acts 2015, 84th Leg., ch. 1, §1.048, eff. Apr. 2, 2015. Source: Former Fam. Code §14.04(a), (b).

FAM §153.377. ACCESS TO CHILD'S RECORDS

A nonparent possessory conservator has the right of access to medical, dental, psychological, and educational records of the child to the same extent as the managing conservator, without regard to whether the right is specified in the order.

History of Fam. Code §153.377: Acts 1995, 74th Leg., ch. 20, §1, eff. Apr. 20, 1995. Source: Former Fam. Code §14.04(c).

Sections 153.378-153.430 reserved for expansion

SUBCHAPTER H. RIGHTS OF GRANDPARENT, AUNT, OR UNCLE

FAM §153.431. APPOINTMENT OF GRANDPARENT, AUNT, OR UNCLE AS MANAGING CONSERVATOR

If both of the parents of a child are deceased, the court may consider appointment of a parent, sister, or brother of a deceased parent as a managing conservator of the child, but that consideration does not alter or diminish the discretionary power of the court.

History of Fam. Code §153.431: Acts 1995, 74th Leg., ch. 20, §1, eff. Apr. 20, 1995. Amended by Acts 2005, 79th Leg., ch. 484, §§1, 2, eff. Sept. 1, 2005. Source: Former Fam. Code §14.07(b).

FAM §153.432. SUIT FOR POSSESSION OR ACCESS BY GRANDPARENT

(a) A biological or adoptive grandparent may request possession of or access to a grandchild by filing:

(1) an original suit; or

(2) a suit for modification as provided by Chapter 156.

(b) A grandparent may request possession of or access to a grandchild in a suit filed for the sole purpose of requesting the relief, without regard to whether the appointment of a managing conservator is an issue in the suit.

(c) In a suit described by Subsection (a), the person filing the suit must execute and attach an affidavit on knowledge or belief that contains, along with supporting facts, the allegation that denial of possession of or access to the child by the petitioner would significantly impair the child's physical health or emotional well-being. The court shall deny the relief sought and dismiss the suit unless the court determines that the facts stated in the affidavit, if true, would be sufficient to support the relief authorized under Section 153.433.

History of Fam. Code §153.432: Acts 1995, 74th Leg., ch. 20, §1, eff. Apr. 20, 1995. Amended by Acts 2005, 79th Leg., ch. 484, §3, eff. Sept. 1, 2005; Acts 2009, 81st Leg., ch. 1113, §11, eff. Sept. 1, 2009. Source: Former Fam. Code §14.03(e), (f)(1), (3).

See also ***O'Connor's Texas Family Law Handbook*** (2017), "Suit for Grandparent Possession or Access," ch. 4-J, p. 660.

ANNOTATIONS

In re Derzapf, 219 S.W.3d 327, 331 (Tex.2007). "[W]e must determine whether ... the children's step-grandfather[] has standing to pursue grandparent access. ... First, [grandparents' family argues] that although [Fam. Code] §153.432(a) states that a 'biological or adoptive grandparent' may file a suit for possession or access to their grandchildren, §153.432(b) refers only to 'a grandparent' as opposed to a 'biological or adoptive grandparent,' and thus even non-biological or adoptive grandparents may seek access under subsection (b). [¶] We disagree. Subsection (b) merely clarifies the circumstances in which a grandparent may request the possession or access described in subsection (a); it does not redefine who may seek access. *At 332-33:* Second, the trial court concluded that [step-grandfather] had 'general' standing to file a suit for access to the grandchildren under [Fam. Code] §102.003(a)(9).... [¶] Regardless of whether [step-grandfather] satisfied §102.003(a)(9)'s general standing requirements for filing a SAPCR—an issue we do not reach—the trial court awarded access based on the standards set forth in [Fam. Code] §153.433, the grandparent access statute. ... Concluding that [step-grandfather] had standing under §102.003(a)(9) when access was granted based on ch. 153 would permit an end run around the requirements of §153.432(a), a result the Legislature cannot have intended. [¶] Finally, [grandparents' family argues] that [step-grandfather] has a justiciable interest sufficient to confer standing.... [¶] The grandparent access statute explicitly sets forth who may sue for access, and [step-grandfather] did not meet those criteria. We cannot conclude that he has a justiciable interest in the controversy sufficient to override the statutory text permitting only biological or adoptive grandparents to seek access pursuant to the standards set forth in §153.433."

FAM §153.433. POSSESSION OF OR ACCESS TO GRANDCHILD

(a) The court may order reasonable possession of or access to a grandchild by a grandparent if:

(1) at the time the relief is requested, at least one biological or adoptive parent of the child has not had that parent's parental rights terminated;

(2) the grandparent requesting possession of or access to the child overcomes the presumption that a parent acts in the best interest of the parent's child by proving by a preponderance of the evidence that denial of possession of or access to the child would significantly impair the child's physical health or emotional well-being; and

(3) the grandparent requesting possession of or access to the child is a parent of a parent of the child and that parent of the child:

(A) has been incarcerated in jail or prison during the three-month period preceding the filing of the petition;

(B) has been found by a court to be incompetent;

(C) is dead; or

(D) does not have actual or court-ordered possession of or access to the child.

(b) An order granting possession of or access to a child by a grandparent that is rendered over a parent's objections must state, with specificity that:

(1) at the time the relief was requested, at least one biological or adoptive parent of the child had not had that parent's parental rights terminated;

(2) the grandparent requesting possession of or access to the child has overcome the presumption that a parent acts in the best interest of the parent's child by proving by a preponderance of the evidence that the denial of possession of or access to the child would significantly impair the child's physical health or emotional well-being; and

(3) the grandparent requesting possession of or access to the child is a parent of a parent of the child and that parent of the child:

(A) has been incarcerated in jail or prison during the three-month period preceding the filing of the petition;

(B) has been found by a court to be incompetent;

(C) is dead; or

(D) does not have actual or court-ordered possession of or access to the child.

History of Fam. Code §153.433: Acts 1995, 74th Leg., ch. 20, §1, eff. Apr. 20, 1995. Amended by Acts 1997, 75th Leg., ch. 1397, §1, eff. Sept. 1, 1997; Acts 2005, 79th Leg., ch. 484, §4, eff. Sept. 1, 2005; Acts 2009, 81st Leg., ch. 1113, §12, eff. Sept. 1, 2009. Source: Former Fam. Code §14.03(e).

Author's comment: From the Senate Committee on Jurisprudence, Bill Analysis, Tex. ch. 484, 79th Leg., R.S. (2005): "In 2000, the United States Supreme Court issued a ruling in ***Troxel v. Granville***, 530 U.S. 57 (2000), a case involving the visitation rights of grandparents. After several conflicting opinions by Texas appellate courts, [the] Texas Attorney General ... issued [***Tex. Atty. Gen. Op.***, No. GA-0260 (2004),] addressing the constitutionality of the Texas grandparent visitation statute following the ***Troxel*** decision. In that opinion, the attorney general concluded that in order for the Texas statute to be applied constitutionally, a court would have to require a grandparent to overcome a presumption that a parent acts in the best interest of his or her child by proving by a preponderance of the evidence that the parent is not fit or that denial of access by a grandparent would impair the child's well-being. [¶] [Chapter] 484 requires a court to grant reasonable possession of or access to a grandchild by a grandparent, if the grandparent can overcome the presumption that the parent acted in the best interest of the child. It also makes additional changes to comply with the ***Troxel*** ruling." Existing case law on this subject must be reviewed carefully in light of these amendments.

See also ***O'Connor's Texas Family Law Handbook*** (2017), "Grandparent's Burden," ch. 4-J, §2, p. 661; "Modification of possession & access for grandparent," ch. 9-A, §3.2, p. 986.

ANNOTATIONS

In re Chambless, 257 S.W.3d 698, 700 (Tex.2008). "A parent must be given a meaningful opportunity to be heard before a trial court awards temporary grandparental visitation. Thus, the trial court abused its discretion in awarding the paternal grandparents temporary visitation with [child] without affording [mother] a meaningful opportunity to be heard."

In re Derzapf, 219 S.W.3d 327, 333 (Tex.2007). "To succeed on her claim [for access, grandmother] must overcome the statutory presumption that denying the children access to her in particular—not [grandmother and step-grandfather] jointly or the ... family as a whole—would significantly impair the children's physical health or emotional well-being. [Grandmother] argues that ... there is sufficient evidence to prove that denying her access to her grandchildren would cause the grandchildren's emotional well-being to suffer.... *At 334:* The Legislature set a high threshold for a grandparent to overcome the presumption that a fit parent acts in his children's best interest: the grandparent must prove that denial of access would '*significantly* impair' the children's physical health or emotional well-being. There has been no such showing here. A court may not lightly interfere with child-rearing decisions made by [father]—a fit parent by all accounts—simply because a 'better decision' may have been made." *See also* ***In re Scheller***, 325 S.W.3d 640, 643-44 (Tex.2010) (evidence of children's behavior reflected children's sadness, but it did not overcome parental presumption); ***In re J.P.C.***, 261 S.W.3d 334, 340 (Tex.App.—Fort Worth 2008, no pet.) (mere testimony of grandparents and interested, nonexpert witness asserting that access should be granted did not overcome parental presumption).

In re J.M.T., 280 S.W.3d 490, 493 (Tex.App.—Eastland 2009, no pet.). "[T]here is no evidence that [adoptive parents] intended to deny [grandparents] possession of or access to the child. To the contrary, the evidence indicates that [adoptive parents] would continue to permit [grandparents] to have access to the child. [A]n order granting grandparent visitation cannot survive ... if there is no evidence that the parent intended to completely exclude the grandparent's access. [¶] [T]he 'denial of possession of or access to the child' by the grandparent is an express element in obtaining grandparent access under [§153.433(2)] in contravention of a parent's preference." *See also* ***In re D.K.B.***, No. 13-08-00177-CV (Tex.App.—Corpus Christi 2009, no pet.) (memo op.; 8-13-09) (grandparent access was denied in part because there was no evidence that mother would significantly restrict grandmother's access to child in absence of court intervention).

In re Smith, 260 S.W.3d 568, 573 (Tex.App.—Houston [14th Dist.] 2008, orig. proceeding). "Texas courts consistently have held that a grandparent's standing to request access is conferred by [Fam. Code] §153.432, not [Fam. Code] §153.433: 'Section 153.432 ... does give grandparents standing to petition the court for access to or possession of a child. Section 153.433 identifies the conditions under which such possession or access will be granted.' Although a successful access suit might require the grandparent to satisfy §153.433, whether the grandparent ultimately will succeed is a different question than whether the grandparent has the right simply to bring suit. [¶] Under the unambiguous language of §153.433, we conclude that this statute does not deal with standing."

FAM §153.434. LIMITATION ON RIGHT TO REQUEST POSSESSION OR ACCESS

A biological or adoptive grandparent may not request possession of or access to a grandchild if:

(1) each of the biological parents of the grandchild has:

(A) died;

(B) had the person's parental rights terminated; or

(C) executed an affidavit of waiver of interest in child or an affidavit of relinquishment of parental rights under Chapter 161 and the affidavit designates the Department of Family and Protective Services, a licensed child-placing agency, or a person other than the child's stepparent as the managing conservator of the child; and

(2) the grandchild has been adopted, or is the subject of a pending suit for adoption, by a person other than the child's stepparent.

History of Fam. Code §153.434: Acts 1995, 74th Leg., ch. 20, §1, eff. Apr. 20, 1995. Amended by Acts 1997, 75th Leg., ch. 561, §4, eff. Sept. 1, 1997; Acts 1999, 76th Leg., ch. 1390, §13, eff. Sept. 1, 1999; Acts 2005, 79th Leg., ch. 484, §5, eff. Sept. 1, 2005; Acts 2015, 84th Leg., ch. 1, §1.049, eff. Apr. 2, 2015. Source: Former Fam. Code §14.03(g).

ANNOTATIONS

In re Gonzalez, No. 04-14-00485-CV (Tex.App.—San Antonio 2014, orig. proceeding) (memo op.; 10-1-14). "[B]oth of the child's parents were dead and ... a suit for his adoption [by maternal grandparents] was pending at the time [paternal grandmother's] intervention and [paternal grandfather's] motion for grandparent access were filed.... Accordingly, the paternal grandparents lacked standing to bring their requests for possession and access [under §153.434]. [¶] The paternal grandparents appear to argue that the trial court's order denying the adoption petition somehow conferred standing because the adoption of the child was no longer pending. We disagree. Section 153.434 precludes a grandparent's standing to request possession or access under certain conditions. ... The trial court's denial of the adoption petition ... cannot operate to confer standing.... Nor does the denial of the adoption petition mean that the child is no longer 'the subject of a pending suit for adoption.' An appeal from the trial court's order denying the adoption is currently pending in this court. The suit for adoption will remain 'pending' until that appeal has been fully and finally resolved, or it is otherwise dismissed in the trial court."

Martinez v. Estrada, 392 S.W.3d 261, 264 (Tex. App.—San Antonio 2012, pet. denied). "Here, both the biological mother and father to the children had their parental rights terminated and the [maternal grandparents], persons other than a stepparent, had their petition for adoption granted at the outset of the hearing. ... Accordingly, [paternal grandmother] did not meet the standing requirements to pursue a claim under the grandparent access statute. [¶] Unfortunately, ... §153.434 dictated a winner-take-all result. Although [paternal grandmother] may have had standing to petition for adoption, she lost standing to request access the moment the [maternal grandparents'] petition for adoption was granted."

Sections 153.435-153.500 blank

SUBCHAPTER I. PREVENTION OF INTERNATIONAL PARENTAL CHILD ABDUCTION

FAM §153.501. NECESSITY OF MEASURES TO PREVENT INTERNATIONAL PARENTAL CHILD ABDUCTION

(a) In a suit, if credible evidence is presented to the court indicating a potential risk of the international abduction of a child by a parent of the child, the court, on its own motion or at the request of a party to the suit, shall determine under this section whether it is necessary for the court to take one or more of the measures described by Section 153.503 to protect the child from the risk of abduction by the parent.

(b) In determining whether to take any of the measures described by Section 153.503, the court shall consider:

(1) the public policies of this state described by Section 153.001(a) and the consideration of the best interest of the child under Section 153.002;

(2) the risk of international abduction of the child by a parent of the child based on the court's evaluation of the risk factors described by Section 153.502;

(3) any obstacles to locating, recovering, and returning the child if the child is abducted to a foreign country; and

(4) the potential physical or psychological harm to the child if the child is abducted to a foreign country.

History of Fam. Code §153.501: Acts 2003, 78th Leg., ch. 612, §1, eff. June 20, 2003.

See also *O'Connor's Texas Family Law Handbook* (2017), "Preventing International Child Abduction," ch. 4-E, §18, p. 518.

ANNOTATIONS

Messier v. Messier, 389 S.W.3d 904, 909 (Tex. App.—Houston [14th Dist.] 2012, no pet.). See annotation under Family Code §153.072, p. 514.

FAM §153.502. ABDUCTION RISK FACTORS

(a) To determine whether there is a risk of the international abduction of a child by a parent of the child, the court shall consider evidence that the parent:

(1) has taken, enticed away, kept, withheld, or concealed a child in violation of another person's right of possession of or access to the child, unless the parent presents evidence that the parent believed in good faith that the parent's conduct was necessary to avoid imminent harm to the child or the parent;

(2) has previously threatened to take, entice away, keep, withhold, or conceal a child in violation of another person's right of possession of or access to the child;

(3) lacks financial reason to stay in the United States, including evidence that the parent is financially independent, is able to work outside of the United States, or is unemployed;

(4) has recently engaged in planning activities that could facilitate the removal of the child from the United States by the parent, including:

(A) quitting a job;

(B) selling a primary residence;

(C) terminating a lease;

(D) closing bank accounts;

(E) liquidating other assets;

(F) hiding or destroying documents;

(G) applying for a passport or visa or obtaining other travel documents for the parent or the child; or

(H) applying to obtain the child's birth certificate or school or medical records;

(5) has a history of domestic violence that the court is required to consider under Section 153.004; or

(6) has a criminal history or a history of violating court orders.

(a-1) In considering evidence of planning activities under Subsection (a)(4), the court also shall consider any evidence that the parent was engaging in those activities as a part of a safety plan to flee from family violence.

(b) If the court finds that there is credible evidence of a risk of abduction of the child by a parent of the child based on the court's consideration of the factors in Subsection (a), the court shall also consider evidence regarding the following factors to evaluate the risk of international abduction of the child by a parent:

(1) whether the parent has strong familial, emotional, or cultural ties to another country, particularly a country that is not a signatory to or compliant with the Hague Convention on the Civil Aspects of International Child Abduction; and

(2) whether the parent lacks strong ties to the United States, regardless of whether the parent is a citizen or permanent resident of the United States.

(c) If the court finds that there is credible evidence of a risk of abduction of the child by a parent of the child based on the court's consideration of the factors in Subsection (a), the court may also consider evidence regarding the following factors to evaluate the risk of international abduction of the child by a parent:

(1) whether the parent is undergoing a change in status with the United States Immigration and Naturalization Service that would adversely affect that parent's ability to legally remain in the United States;

(2) whether the parent's application for United States citizenship has been denied by the United States Immigration and Naturalization Service;

(3) whether the parent has forged or presented misleading or false evidence to obtain a visa, a passport, a social security card, or any other identification card or has made any misrepresentation to the United States government; or

(4) whether the foreign country to which the parent has ties:

(A) presents obstacles to the recovery and return of a child who is abducted to the country from the United States;

(B) has any legal mechanisms for immediately and effectively enforcing an order regarding the possession of or access to the child issued by this state;

(C) has local laws or practices that would:

(i) enable the parent to prevent the child's other parent from contacting the child without due cause;

(ii) restrict the child's other parent from freely traveling to or exiting from the country because of that parent's gender, nationality, or religion; or

(iii) restrict the child's ability to legally leave the country after the child reaches the age of majority because of the child's gender, nationality, or religion;

(D) is included by the United States Department of State on a list of state sponsors of terrorism;

(E) is a country for which the United States Department of State has issued a travel warning to United States citizens regarding travel to the country;

(F) has an embassy of the United States in the country;

(G) is engaged in any active military action or war, including a civil war;

(H) is a party to and compliant with the Hague Convention on the Civil Aspects of International Child Abduction according to the most recent report on compliance issued by the United States Department of State;

(I) provides for the extradition of a parental abductor and the return of the child to the United States; or

(J) poses a risk that the child's physical health or safety would be endangered in the country because of specific circumstances relating to the child or because of human rights violations committed against children, including arranged marriages, lack of freedom of religion, child labor, lack of child abuse laws, female genital mutilation, and any form of slavery.

History of Fam. Code §153.502: Acts 2003, 78th Leg., ch. 612, §1, eff. June 20, 2003. Amended by Acts 2009, 81st Leg., ch. 1113, §13, eff. Sept. 1, 2009.

FAM §153.503. ABDUCTION PREVENTION MEASURES

If the court finds that it is necessary under Section 153.501 to take measures to protect a child from international abduction by a parent of the child, the court may take any of the following actions:

(1) appoint a person other than the parent of the child who presents a risk of abducting the child as the sole managing conservator of the child;

(2) require supervised visitation of the parent by a visitation center or independent organization until the court finds under Section 153.501 that supervised visitation is no longer necessary;

(3) enjoin the parent or any person acting on the parent's behalf from:

(A) disrupting or removing the child from the school or child-care facility in which the child is enrolled; or

(B) approaching the child at any location other than a site designated for supervised visitation;

(4) order passport and travel controls, including controls that:

(A) prohibit the parent and any person acting on the parent's behalf from removing the child from this state or the United States;

(B) require the parent to surrender any passport issued in the child's name, including any passport issued in the name of both the parent and the child; and

(C) prohibit the parent from applying on behalf of the child for a new or replacement passport or international travel visa;

(5) require the parent to provide:

(A) to the United States Department of State's Office of Children's Issues and the relevant foreign consulate or embassy:

(i) written notice of the court-ordered passport and travel restrictions for the child; and

(ii) a properly authenticated copy of the court order detailing the restrictions and documentation of the parent's agreement to the restrictions; and

(B) to the court proof of receipt of the written notice required by Paragraph (A)(i) by the United States Department of State's Office of Children's Issues and the relevant foreign consulate or embassy;

(6) order the parent to execute a bond or deposit security in an amount sufficient to offset the cost of recovering the child if the child is abducted by the parent to a foreign country;

(7) authorize the appropriate law enforcement agencies to take measures to prevent the abduction of the child by the parent; or

(8) include in the court's order provisions:

(A) identifying the United States as the country of habitual residence of the child;

(B) defining the basis for the court's exercise of jurisdiction; and

(C) stating that a party's violation of the order may subject the party to a civil penalty or criminal penalty or to both civil and criminal penalties.

History of Fam. Code §153.503: Acts 2003, 78th Leg., ch. 612, §1, eff. June 20, 2003.

ANNOTATIONS

Arredondo v. Betancourt, 383 S.W.3d 730, 741-42 (Tex.App.—Houston [14th Dist.] 2012, no pet.). "[T]he trial court's injunction permanently restricts [mother's] ability to travel outside 'the continental U.S.,' meaning she may not travel internationally ... at any time and for any reason without first obtaining [ex-H's] consent, whether or not she intends to have the child travel with her. *At 744:* [E]ach of the possible passport and travel controls listed [in §153.503(4)] are directed to controlling the *child's* whereabouts or the *child's* documents, reflecting the legislature's intent to prevent the international abduction of children by their parents. [¶] The trial court certainly has broad discretion to impose abduction-prevention measures and may order 'passport and travel controls' not limited to those specifically listed in §153.503(4). But ... the

travel restrictions imposed [in the court order] are not directed to international child-abduction prevention. Instead, the trial court has enjoined [mother's] ability to travel generally, even without the child. [W]e conclude that the trial court abused its discretion by ordering the injunction. [¶] Moreover, because the injunction is overly broad, unreasonably restrictive, and unrelated to either the child's best interest or the prevention of international child-abduction prevention, ... it violates [mother's] constitutional right to travel."

Sections 153.504-153.550 blank

SUBCHAPTER J. RIGHTS OF SIBLINGS

FAM §153.551. SUIT FOR ACCESS

(a) The sibling of a child who is separated from the child because of an action taken by the Department of Family and Protective Services may request access to the child by filing:

(1) an original suit; or

(2) a suit for modification as provided by Chapter 156.

(b) A sibling described by Subsection (a) may request access to the child in a suit filed for the sole purpose of requesting the relief, without regard to whether the appointment of a managing conservator is an issue in the suit.

(c) The court shall order reasonable access to the child by the child's sibling described by Subsection (a) if the court finds that access is in the best interest of the child.

History of Fam. Code §153.551: Acts 2005, 79th Leg., ch. 1191, §2, eff. Sept. 1, 2005. Amended by Acts 2009, 81st Leg., ch. 1113, §14, eff. Sept. 1, 2009.

See also ***O'Connor's Texas Family Law Handbook*** (2017), "Suit for Sibling Access," ch. 4-I, p. 655; "Modification of access for sibling," ch. 9-A, §3.3, p. 987.

FAM §153.552. REPEALED

Repealed by Acts 2009, 81st Leg., ch. 1113, §31, eff. Sept. 1, 2009.

Sections 153.553-153.600 blank

SUBCHAPTER K. PARENTING PLAN, PARENTING COORDINATOR, & PARENTING FACILITATOR

FAM §153.601. DEFINITIONS

In this subchapter:

(1) "Dispute resolution process" means:

(A) a process of alternative dispute resolution conducted in accordance with Section 153.0071 of this chapter and Chapter 154, Civil Practice and Remedies Code; or

(B) any other method of voluntary dispute resolution.

(2) "High-conflict case" means a suit affecting the parent-child relationship in which the court finds that the parties have demonstrated an unusual degree of:

(A) repetitiously resorting to the adjudicative process;

(B) anger and distrust; and

(C) difficulty in communicating about and cooperating in the care of their children.

(3) "Parenting coordinator" means an impartial third party:

(A) who, regardless of the title by which the person is designated by the court, performs any function described by Section 153.606 in a suit; and

(B) who:

(i) is appointed under this subchapter by the court on its own motion or on a motion or agreement of the parties to assist parties in resolving parenting issues through confidential procedures; and

(ii) is not appointed under another statute or a rule of civil procedure.

(3-a) "Parenting facilitator" means an impartial third party:

(A) who, regardless of the title by which the person is designated by the court, performs any function described by Section 153.6061 in a suit; and

(B) who:

(i) is appointed under this subchapter by the court on its own motion or on a motion or agreement of the parties to assist parties in resolving parenting issues through procedures that are not confidential; and

(ii) is not appointed under another statute or a rule of civil procedure.

(4) "Parenting plan" means the provisions of a final court order that:

(A) set out rights and duties of a parent or a person acting as a parent in relation to the child;

(B) provide for periods of possession of and access to the child, which may be the terms set out in the standard possession order under Subchapter F and any amendments to the standard possession order agreed to by the parties or found by the court to be in the best interest of the child;

(C) provide for child support; and

(D) optimize the development of a close and continuing relationship between each parent and the child.

History of Fam. Code §153.601: Acts 2005, 79th Leg., ch. 482, §2, eff. Sept. 1, 2005. Amended by Acts 2007, 80th Leg., ch. 1181, §4, eff. Sept. 1, 2007; Acts 2009, 81st Leg., ch. 1113, §16, eff. Sept. 1, 2009. Subchapter K amended by Acts 2009, 81st Leg., ch. 1113, §15, eff. Sept. 1, 2009.

FAM §153.602. PARENTING PLAN NOT REQUIRED IN TEMPORARY ORDER

A temporary order in a suit affecting the parent-child relationship rendered in accordance with Section 105.001 is not required to include a temporary parenting plan. The court may not require the submission of a temporary parenting plan in any case or by local rule or practice.

History of Fam. Code §153.602: Acts 2005, 79th Leg., ch. 482, §2, eff. Sept. 1, 2005. Amended by Acts 2007, 80th Leg., ch. 1181, §4, eff. Sept. 1, 2007.

See also ***O'Connor's Texas Family Law Handbook*** (2017), "No temporary parenting plan," ch. 5-D, §2.4.6, p. 699.

FAM §153.603. REQUIREMENT OF PARENTING PLAN IN FINAL ORDER

(a) Except as provided by Subsection (b), a final order in a suit affecting the parent-child relationship must include a parenting plan.

(b) The following orders are not required to include a parenting plan:

(1) an order that only modifies child support;

(2) an order that only terminates parental rights; or

(3) a final order described by Section 155.001(b).

(c) If the parties have not reached agreement on a final parenting plan on or before the 30th day before the date set for trial on the merits, a party may file with the court and serve a proposed parenting plan.

(d) This section does not preclude the parties from requesting the appointment of a parenting coordinator to resolve parental conflicts.

History of Fam. Code §153.603: Acts 2005, 79th Leg., ch. 482, §2, eff. Sept. 1, 2005. Amended by Acts 2007, 80th Leg., ch. 1181, §4, eff. Sept. 1, 2007.

FAM §153.6031. EXCEPTION TO DISPUTE RESOLUTION PROCESS REQUIREMENT

A requirement in a parenting plan that a party initiate or participate in a dispute resolution process before filing a court action does not apply to an action:

(1) to modify the parenting plan in an emergency;

(2) to modify child support;

(3) alleging that the child's present circumstances will significantly impair the child's physical health or significantly impair the child's emotional development;

(4) to enforce; or

(5) in which the party shows that enforcement of the requirement is precluded or limited by Section 153.0071.

History of Fam. Code §153.6031: Acts 2007, 80th Leg., ch. 1181, §4, eff. Sept. 1, 2007.

FAM §153.604. REPEALED

Repealed by Acts 2007, 80th Leg., ch. 1181, §11(1), eff. Sept. 1, 2007.

FAM §153.605. APPOINTMENT OF PARENTING COORDINATOR

(a) In a suit affecting the parent-child relationship, the court may, on its own motion or on a motion or agreement of the parties, appoint a parenting coordinator or assign a domestic relations office under Chapter 203 to appoint an employee or other person to serve as parenting coordinator.

(b) The court may not appoint a parenting coordinator unless, after notice and hearing, the court makes a specific finding that:

(1) the case is a high-conflict case or there is good cause shown for the appointment of a parenting coordinator and the appointment is in the best interest of any minor child in the suit; and

(2) the person appointed has the minimum qualifications required by Section 153.610, as documented by the person, unless those requirements have been waived by the court with the agreement of the parties in accordance with Section 153.610(c).

(c) Notwithstanding any other provision of this subchapter, a party may at any time file a written objection to the appointment of a parenting coordinator on the basis of family violence having been committed by another party against the objecting party or a child who is the subject of the suit. After an objection is filed, a parenting coordinator may not be appointed unless, on the request of a party, a hearing is held and the court finds that a preponderance of the evidence does not support the objection. If a parenting coordinator is appointed, the court shall order appropriate measures be taken to ensure the physical and emotional safety of the party who filed the objection. The order may provide that the parties not be required to have face-to-face contact and that the parties be placed in separate rooms during the parenting coordination.

(d) An individual appointed as a parenting coordinator may not serve in any nonconfidential capacity in the same case, including serving as an amicus attorney, guardian ad litem, child custody evaluator, or adoption evaluator under Chapter 107, as a friend of the court

under Chapter 202, or as a parenting facilitator under this subchapter.

History of Fam. Code §153.605: Acts 2005, 79th Leg., ch. 482, §2, eff. Sept. 1, 2005. Amended by Acts 2007, 80th Leg., ch. 1181, §5, eff. Sept. 1, 2007; Acts 2009, 81st Leg., ch. 1113, §17, eff. Sept. 1, 2009; Acts 2015, 84th Leg., ch. 1252, §3.01, eff. Sept. 1, 2015.

See also *O'Connor's Texas Family Law Handbook* (2017), "Parenting Coordinator," ch. 4-C, §7, p. 400.

FAM §153.6051. APPOINTMENT OF PARENTING FACILITATOR

(a) In a suit affecting the parent-child relationship, the court may, on its own motion or on a motion or agreement of the parties, appoint a parenting facilitator or assign a domestic relations office under Chapter 203 to appoint an employee or other person as a parenting facilitator.

(b) The court may not appoint a parenting facilitator unless, after notice and hearing, the court makes a specific finding that:

(1) the case is a high-conflict case or there is good cause shown for the appointment of a parenting facilitator and the appointment is in the best interest of any minor child in the suit; and

(2) the person appointed has the minimum qualifications required by Section 153.6101, as documented by the person.

(c) Notwithstanding any other provision of this subchapter, a party may at any time file a written objection to the appointment of a parenting facilitator on the basis of family violence having been committed by another party against the objecting party or a child who is the subject of the suit. After an objection is filed, a parenting facilitator may not be appointed unless, on the request of a party, a hearing is held and the court finds that a preponderance of the evidence does not support the objection. If a parenting facilitator is appointed, the court shall order appropriate measures be taken to ensure the physical and emotional safety of the party who filed the objection. The order may provide that the parties not be required to have face-to-face contact and that the parties be placed in separate rooms during the parenting facilitation.

History of Fam. Code §153.6051: Acts 2009, 81st Leg., ch. 1113, §18, eff. Sept. 1, 2009.

See also *O'Connor's Texas Family Law Handbook* (2017), "Parenting Facilitator," ch. 4-C, §8, p. 405.

FAM §153.606. DUTIES OF PARENTING COORDINATOR

(a) The court shall specify the duties of a parenting coordinator in the order appointing the parenting coordinator. The duties of the parenting coordinator are limited to matters that will aid the parties in:

(1) identifying disputed issues;

(2) reducing misunderstandings;

(3) clarifying priorities;

(4) exploring possibilities for problem solving;

(5) developing methods of collaboration in parenting;

(6) understanding parenting plans and reaching agreements about parenting issues to be included in a parenting plan;

(7) complying with the court's order regarding conservatorship or possession of and access to the child;

(8) implementing parenting plans;

(9) obtaining training regarding problem solving, conflict management, and parenting skills; and

(10) settling disputes regarding parenting issues and reaching a proposed joint resolution or statement of intent regarding those disputes.

(b) The appointment of a parenting coordinator does not divest the court of:

(1) its exclusive jurisdiction to determine issues of conservatorship, support, and possession of and access to the child; and

(2) the authority to exercise management and control of the suit.

(c) The parenting coordinator may not modify any order, judgment, or decree.

(d) Meetings between the parenting coordinator and the parties may be informal and are not required to follow any specific procedures unless otherwise provided by this subchapter.

(e) Repealed by Acts 2007, 80th Leg., ch. 1181, §11(2), eff. Sept. 1, 2007.

(f) A parenting coordinator appointed under this subchapter shall comply with the Ethical Guidelines for Mediators as adopted by the Supreme Court of Texas (Misc. Docket No. 05-9107, June 13, 2005). On request by the court, the parties, or the parties' attorneys, the parenting coordinator shall sign a statement of agreement to comply with those guidelines and submit the statement to the court on acceptance of the appointment. A failure to comply with the guidelines is grounds for removal of the parenting coordinator.

History of Fam. Code §153.606: Acts 2005, 79th Leg., ch. 482, §2, eff. Sept. 1, 2005. Amended by Acts 2007, 80th Leg., ch. 1181, §§6, 7, 11(2), eff. Sept. 1, 2007; Acts 2009, 81st Leg., ch. 1113, §19, eff. Sept. 1, 2009.

FAM §153.6061. DUTIES OF PARENTING FACILITATOR

(a) The court shall specify the duties of a parenting facilitator in the order appointing the parenting facilitator. The duties of the parenting facilitator are limited to those matters described with regard to a parenting coordinator under Section 153.606(a), except that the parenting facilitator may also monitor compliance with court orders.

(b) A parenting facilitator appointed under this subchapter shall comply with the standard of care applicable to the professional license held by the parenting facilitator in performing the parenting facilitator's duties.

(c) The appointment of a parenting facilitator does not divest the court of:

(1) the exclusive jurisdiction to determine issues of conservatorship, support, and possession of and access to the child; and

(2) the authority to exercise management and control of the suit.

(d) The parenting facilitator may not modify any order, judgment, or decree.

(e) Meetings between the parenting facilitator and the parties may be informal and are not required to follow any specific procedures unless otherwise provided by this subchapter or the standards of practice of the professional license held by the parenting facilitator.

History of Fam. Code §153.6061: Acts 2009, 81st Leg., ch. 1113, §20, eff. Sept. 1, 2009.

FAM §153.607. PRESUMPTION OF GOOD FAITH; REMOVAL OF PARENTING COORDINATOR

(a) It is a rebuttable presumption that a parenting coordinator is acting in good faith if the parenting coordinator's services have been conducted as provided by this subchapter and the Ethical Guidelines for Mediators described by Section 153.606(f).

(a-1) Except as otherwise provided by this section, the court may remove the parenting coordinator in the court's discretion.

(b) The court shall remove the parenting coordinator:

(1) on the request and agreement of all parties;

(2) on the request of the parenting coordinator;

(3) on the motion of a party, if good cause is shown; or

(4) if the parenting coordinator ceases to satisfy the minimum qualifications required by Section 153.610.

History of Fam. Code §153.607: Acts 2005, 79th Leg., ch. 482, §2, eff. Sept. 1, 2005. Amended by Acts 2007, 80th Leg., ch. 1181, §8, eff. Sept. 1, 2007; Acts 2009, 81st Leg., ch. 1113, §21, eff. Sept. 1, 2009.

FAM §153.6071. PRESUMPTION OF GOOD FAITH; REMOVAL OF PARENTING FACILITATOR

(a) It is a rebuttable presumption that a parenting facilitator is acting in good faith if the parenting facilitator's services have been conducted as provided by this subchapter and the standard of care applicable to the professional license held by the parenting facilitator.

(b) Except as otherwise provided by this section, the court may remove the parenting facilitator in the court's discretion.

(c) The court shall remove the parenting facilitator:

(1) on the request and agreement of all parties;

(2) on the request of the parenting facilitator;

(3) on the motion of a party, if good cause is shown; or

(4) if the parenting facilitator ceases to satisfy the minimum qualifications required by Section 153.6101.

History of Fam. Code §153.6071: Acts 2009, 81st Leg., ch. 1113, §22, eff. Sept. 1, 2009.

FAM §153.608. REPORT OF PARENTING COORDINATOR

A parenting coordinator shall submit a written report to the court and to the parties as often as ordered by the court. The report must be limited to a statement of whether the parenting coordination should continue.

History of Fam. Code §153.608: Acts 2005, 79th Leg., ch. 482, §2, eff. Sept. 1, 2005. Amended by Acts 2007, 80th Leg., ch. 1181, §9, eff. Sept. 1, 2007.

FAM §153.6081. REPORT OF PARENTING FACILITATOR

A parenting facilitator shall submit a written report to the court and to the parties as ordered by the court. The report may include a recommendation described by Section 153.6082(e) and any other information required by the court, except that the report may not include recommendations regarding the conservatorship of or the possession of or access to the child who is the subject of the suit.

History of Fam. Code §153.6081: Acts 2009, 81st Leg., ch. 1113, §22, eff. Sept. 1, 2009.

FAM §153.6082. REPORT OF JOINT PROPOSAL OR STATEMENT OF INTENT; AGREEMENTS & RECOMMENDATIONS

(a) If the parties have been ordered by the court to attempt to settle parenting issues with the assistance of a parenting coordinator or parenting facilitator and to attempt to reach a proposed joint resolution or statement of intent regarding the dispute, the parenting coordinator or parenting facilitator, as applicable, shall submit a written report describing the parties' joint proposal or statement to the parties, any attorneys for the parties, and any attorney for the child who is the subject of the suit.

(b) The proposed joint resolution or statement of intent is not an agreement unless the resolution or statement is:

(1) prepared by the parties' attorneys, if any, in a form that meets the applicable requirements of:

(A) Rule 11, Texas Rules of Civil Procedure;

(B) a mediated settlement agreement described by Section 153.0071;

(C) a collaborative law agreement described by Section 153.0072;[1]

(D) a settlement agreement described by Section 154.071, Civil Practice and Remedies Code; or

(E) a proposed court order; and

(2) incorporated into an order signed by the court.

(c) A parenting coordinator or parenting facilitator may not draft a document listed in Subsection (b)(1).

(d) The actions of a parenting coordinator or parenting facilitator under this section do not constitute the practice of law.

(e) If the parties have been ordered by the court to attempt to settle parenting issues with the assistance of a parenting facilitator and are unable to settle those issues, the parenting facilitator may make recommendations, other than recommendations regarding the conservatorship of or possession of or access to the child, to the parties and attorneys to implement or clarify provisions of an existing court order that are consistent with the substantive intent of the court order and in the best interest of the child who is the subject of the suit. A recommendation authorized by this subsection does not affect the terms of an existing court order.

1. **Editor's note:** Tex. Fam. Code §153.0072 was repealed by Acts 2011, 82nd Leg., ch. 1048, §2, eff. Sept. 1, 2011. Title 1-A, Collaborative Family Law, was enacted by Acts 2011, 82nd Leg., ch. 1048, §1, eff. Sept. 1, 2011.

History of Fam. Code §153.6082: Acts 2009, 81st Leg., ch. 1113, §22, eff. Sept. 1, 2009.

FAM §153.6083. COMMUNICATIONS & RECORDKEEPING OF PARENTING FACILITATOR

(a) Notwithstanding any rule, standard of care, or privilege applicable to the professional license held by a parenting facilitator, a communication made by a participant in parenting facilitation is subject to disclosure and may be offered in any judicial or administrative proceeding, if otherwise admissible under the rules of evidence. The parenting facilitator may be required to testify in any proceeding relating to or arising from the duties of the parenting facilitator, including as to the basis for any recommendation made to the parties that arises from the duties of the parenting facilitator.

(b) A parenting facilitator shall keep a detailed record regarding meetings and contacts with the parties, attorneys, or other persons involved in the suit.

(c) A person who participates in parenting facilitation is not a patient as defined by Section 611.001, Health and Safety Code, and no record created as part of the parenting facilitation that arises from the parenting facilitator's duties is confidential.

(d) On request, records of parenting facilitation shall be made available by the parenting facilitator to an attorney for a party, an attorney for a child who is the subject of the suit, and a party who does not have an attorney.

(e) A parenting facilitator shall keep parenting facilitation records from the suit until the seventh anniversary of the date the facilitator's services are terminated, unless a different retention period is established by a rule adopted by the licensing authority that issues the professional license held by the parenting facilitator.

History of Fam. Code §153.6083: Acts 2009, 81st Leg., ch. 1113, §22, eff. Sept. 1, 2009.

FAM §153.609. COMPENSATION OF PARENTING COORDINATOR

(a) A court may not appoint a parenting coordinator, other than a domestic relations office or a comparable county agency appointed under Subsection (c) or a volunteer appointed under Subsection (d), unless, after notice and hearing, the court finds that the parties have the means to pay the fees of the parenting coordinator.

(b) Any fees of a parenting coordinator appointed under Subsection (a) shall be allocated between the parties as determined by the court.

(c) Public funds may not be used to pay the fees of a parenting coordinator. Notwithstanding this prohibition, a court may appoint the domestic relations office or a comparable county agency to act as a parenting coordinator if personnel are available to serve that function.

(d) If due to hardship the parties are unable to pay the fees of a parenting coordinator, and a domestic relations office or a comparable county agency is not available under Subsection (c), the court, if feasible, may appoint a person who meets the minimum qualifications prescribed by Section 153.610, including an employee of the court, to act as a parenting coordinator on a volunteer basis and without compensation.

History of Fam. Code §153.609: Acts 2005, 79th Leg., ch. 482, §2, eff. Sept. 1, 2005. Amended by Acts 2007, 80th Leg., ch. 1181, §10, eff. Sept. 1, 2007; Acts 2011, 82nd Leg., ch. 682, §1, eff. June 17, 2011.

FAM §153.6091. COMPENSATION OF PARENTING FACILITATOR

Section 153.609 applies to a parenting facilitator in the same manner as provided for a parenting coordinator, except that a person appointed in accordance with Section 153.609(d) to act as a parenting facilitator must meet the minimum qualifications prescribed by Section 153.6101.

History of Fam. Code §153.6091: Acts 2009, 81st Leg., ch. 1113, §22, eff. Sept. 1, 2009. Amended by Acts 2011, 82nd Leg., ch. 682, §2, eff. June 17, 2011.

FAM §153.610. QUALIFICATIONS OF PARENTING COORDINATOR

(a) The court shall determine the required qualifications of a parenting coordinator, provided that a parenting coordinator must have experience working in a field relating to families, have practical experience with high-conflict cases or litigation between parents, and:

(1) hold at least:

(A) a bachelor's degree in counseling, education, family studies, psychology, or social work; or

(B) a graduate degree in a mental health profession, with an emphasis in family and children's issues; or

(2) be licensed in good standing as an attorney in this state.

(b) In addition to the qualifications prescribed by Subsection (a), a parenting coordinator must complete at least:

(1) eight hours of family violence dynamics training provided by a family violence service provider;

(2) 40 classroom hours of training in dispute resolution techniques in a course conducted by an alternative dispute resolution system or other dispute resolution organization approved by the court; and

(3) 24 classroom hours of training in the fields of family dynamics, child development, family law and the law governing parenting coordination, and parenting coordination styles and procedures.

(c) In appropriate circumstances, a court may, with the agreement of the parties, appoint a person as parenting coordinator who does not satisfy the requirements of Subsection (a) or Subsection (b)(2) or (3) if the court finds that the person has sufficient legal or other professional training or experience in dispute resolution processes to serve in that capacity.

(d) The actions of a parenting coordinator who is not an attorney do not constitute the practice of law.

History of Fam. Code §153.610: Acts 2005, 79th Leg., ch. 482, §2, eff. Sept. 1, 2005. Amended by Acts 2009, 81st Leg., ch. 1113, §23, eff. Sept. 1, 2009.

FAM §153.6101. QUALIFICATIONS OF PARENTING FACILITATOR

(a) The court shall determine whether the qualifications of a proposed parenting facilitator satisfy the requirements of this section. On request by a party, an attorney for a party, or any attorney for a child who is the subject of the suit, a person under consideration for appointment as a parenting facilitator in the suit shall provide proof that the person satisfies the minimum qualifications required by this section.

(b) A parenting facilitator must:

(1) hold a license to practice in this state as a social worker, licensed professional counselor, licensed marriage and family therapist, psychologist, or attorney; and

(2) have completed at least:

(A) eight hours of family violence dynamics training provided by a family violence service provider;

(B) 40 classroom hours of training in dispute resolution techniques in a course conducted by an alternative dispute resolution system or other dispute resolution organization approved by the court;

(C) 24 classroom hours of training in the fields of family dynamics, child development, and family law; and

(D) 16 hours of training in the laws governing parenting coordination and parenting facilitation and the multiple styles and procedures used in different models of service.

(c) The actions of a parenting facilitator who is not an attorney do not constitute the practice of law.

History of Fam. Code §153.6101: Acts 2009, 81st Leg., ch. 1113, §24, eff. Sept. 1, 2009.

FAM §153.6102. PARENTING FACILITATOR; CONFLICTS OF INTEREST & BIAS

(a) A person who has a conflict of interest with, or has previous knowledge of, a party or a child who is the subject of a suit must, before being appointed as parenting facilitator in a suit:

(1) disclose the conflict or previous knowledge to the court, each attorney for a party, any attorney for a child, and any party who does not have an attorney; and

(2) decline appointment in the suit unless, after the disclosure, the parties and the child's attorney, if any, agree in writing to the person's appointment as parenting facilitator.

(b) A parenting facilitator who, after being appointed in a suit, discovers that the parenting facilitator has a conflict of interest with, or has previous knowledge of, a party or a child who is the subject of the suit shall:

(1) immediately disclose the conflict or previous knowledge to the court, each attorney for a party, any attorney for a child, and any party who does not have an attorney; and

(2) withdraw from the suit unless, after the disclosure, the parties and the child's attorney, if any, agree in writing to the person's continuation as parenting facilitator.

(c) A parenting facilitator, before accepting appointment in a suit, must disclose to the court, each attorney for a party, any attorney for a child who is the subject of the suit, and any party who does not have an attorney:

(1) a pecuniary relationship with an attorney, party, or child in the suit;

(2) a relationship of confidence or trust with an attorney, party, or child in the suit; and

(3) other information regarding any relationship with an attorney, party, or child in the suit that might reasonably affect the ability of the person to act impartially during the person's service as parenting facilitator.

(d) A person who makes a disclosure required by Subsection (c) shall decline appointment as parenting facilitator unless, after the disclosure, the parties and the child's attorney, if any, agree in writing to the person's service as parenting facilitator in the suit.

(e) A parenting facilitator may not serve in any other professional capacity at any other time with any person who is a party to, or the subject of, the suit in which the person serves as parenting facilitator, or with any member of the family of a party or subject. A person who, before appointment as a parenting facilitator in a suit, served in any other professional capacity with a person who is a party to, or subject of, the suit, or with any member of the family of a party or subject, may not serve as parenting facilitator in a suit involving any family member who is a party to or subject of the suit. This subsection does not apply to a person whose only other service in a professional capacity with a family or any member of a family that is a party to or the subject of a suit to which this section applies is as a teacher of coparenting skills in a class conducted in a group setting. For purposes of this subsection, "family" has the meaning assigned by Section 71.003.

(f) A parenting facilitator shall promptly and simultaneously disclose to each party's attorney, any attorney for a child who is a subject of the suit, and any party who does not have an attorney the existence and substance of any communication between the parenting facilitator and another person, including a party, a party's attorney, a child who is the subject of the suit, and any attorney for a child who is the subject of the suit, if the communication occurred outside of a parenting facilitator session and involved the substance of parenting facilitation.

History of Fam. Code §153.6102: Acts 2009, 81st Leg., ch. 1113, §24, eff. Sept. 1, 2009.

FAM §153.611. EXCEPTION FOR CERTAIN TITLE IV-D PROCEEDINGS[1]

Notwithstanding any other provision of this subchapter, this subchapter does not apply to a proceeding in a Title IV-D case relating to the determination of parentage or establishment, modification, or enforcement of a child support or medical support obligation.

1. **Editor's note:** In 2015, the Legislature amended §153.611 to require dental support for a child subject to a child-support order, but the amendments are not effective until Sept. 1, 2018. For the text of the prospective amendments, see Acts 2015, 84th Leg., ch. 1150, §7, eff. Sept. 1, 2018.

History of Fam. Code §153.611: Acts 2005, 79th Leg., ch. 482, §2, eff. Sept. 1, 2005.

Sections 153.612-153.700 blank

SUBCHAPTER L. MILITARY DUTY

FAM §153.701. DEFINITIONS

In this subchapter:

(1) "Designated person" means the person ordered by the court to temporarily exercise a conservator's rights, duties, and periods of possession and access with regard to a child during the conservator's military deployment, military mobilization, or temporary military duty.

(2) "Military deployment" means the temporary transfer of a service member of the armed forces of this state or the United States serving in an active-duty status to another location in support of combat or some other military operation.

(3) "Military mobilization" means the call-up of a National Guard or Reserve service member of the armed forces of this state or the United States to extended active duty status. The term does not include National Guard or Reserve annual training.[1]

(4) "Temporary military duty" means the transfer of a service member of the armed forces of this state or the United States from one military base to a different location, usually another base, for a limited time for training or to assist in the performance of a noncombat mission.

1. **Editor's note:** Acts 2009, 81st Leg., ch. 727, §1 does not capitalize National Guard or Reserve.

History of Fam. Code §153.701: Acts 2009, 81st Leg., ch. 727, §1 (eff. Sept. 1, 2009), ch. 1113, §25 (eff. Sept. 1, 2009).

FAM §153.702. TEMPORARY ORDERS

(a) If a conservator is ordered to military deployment, military mobilization, or temporary military duty that involves moving a substantial distance from the conservator's residence so as to materially affect the conservator's ability to exercise the conservator's rights and duties in relation to a child, either conservator may file for an order under this subchapter without the necessity of showing a material and substantial change of circumstances other than the military deployment, military mobilization, or temporary military duty.

(b) The court may render a temporary order in a proceeding under this subchapter regarding:

(1) possession of or access to the child; or

(2) child support.

(c) A temporary order rendered by the court under this subchapter may grant rights to and impose duties on a designated person regarding the child, except that if the designated person is a nonparent, the court may not require the designated person to pay child support.

(d) After a conservator's military deployment, military mobilization, or temporary military duty is concluded, and the conservator returns to the conservator's usual residence, the temporary orders under this section terminate and the rights of all affected parties are governed by the terms of any court order applicable when the conservator is not ordered to military deployment, military mobilization, or temporary military duty.

History of Fam. Code §153.702: Acts 2009, 81st Leg., ch. 727, §1 (eff. Sept. 1, 2009), ch. 1113, §25 (eff. Sept. 1, 2009). Amended by Acts 2011, 82nd Leg., ch. 112, §1, eff. Sept. 1, 2011.

FAM §153.703. APPOINTING DESIGNATED PERSON FOR CONSERVATOR WITH EXCLUSIVE RIGHT TO DESIGNATE PRIMARY RESIDENCE OF CHILD

(a) If the conservator with the exclusive right to designate the primary residence of the child is ordered to military deployment, military mobilization, or temporary military duty, the court may render a temporary order to appoint a designated person to exercise the exclusive right to designate the primary residence of the child during the military deployment, military mobilization, or temporary military duty in the following order of preference:

(1) the conservator who does not have the exclusive right to designate the primary residence of the child;

(2) if appointing the conservator described by Subdivision (1) is not in the child's best interest, a designated person chosen by the conservator with the exclusive right to designate the primary residence of the child; or

(3) if appointing the conservator described by Subdivision (1) or the person chosen under Subdivision (2) is not in the child's best interest, another person chosen by the court.

(b) A nonparent appointed as a designated person in a temporary order rendered under this section has the rights and duties of a nonparent appointed as sole managing conservator under Section 153.371.

(c) The court may limit or expand the rights of a nonparent named as a designated person in a temporary order rendered under this section as appropriate to the best interest of the child.

History of Fam. Code §153.703: Acts 2009, 81st Leg., ch. 727, §1 (eff. Sept. 1, 2009), ch. 1113, §25 (eff. Sept. 1, 2009). Amended by Acts 2011, 82nd Leg., ch. 112, §2, eff. Sept. 1, 2011.

FAM §153.704. APPOINTING DESIGNATED PERSON TO EXERCISE VISITATION FOR CONSERVATOR WITH EXCLUSIVE RIGHT TO DESIGNATE PRIMARY RESIDENCE OF CHILD IN CERTAIN CIRCUMSTANCES

(a) If the court appoints the conservator without the exclusive right to designate the primary residence of the child under Section 153.703(a)(1), the court may award visitation with the child to a designated person chosen by the conservator with the exclusive right to designate the primary residence of the child.

(b) The periods of visitation shall be the same as the visitation to which the conservator without the exclusive right to designate the primary residence of the child was entitled under the court order in effect immediately before the date the temporary order is rendered.

(c) The temporary order for visitation must provide that:

(1) the designated person under this section has the right to possession of the child for the periods and in the manner in which the conservator without the exclusive right to designate the primary residence of the child is entitled under the court order in effect immediately before the date the temporary order is rendered;

(2) the child's other conservator and the designated person under this section are subject to the requirements of Section 153.316, with the designated person considered for purposes of that section to be the possessory conservator;

(3) the designated person under this section has the rights and duties of a nonparent possessory conservator under Section 153.376(a) during the period that the person has possession of the child; and

(4) the designated person under this section is subject to any provision in a court order restricting or prohibiting access to the child by any specified individual.

(d) The court may limit or expand the rights of a nonparent designated person named in a temporary order rendered under this section as appropriate to the best interest of the child.

History of Fam. Code §153.704: Acts 2009, 81st Leg., ch. 727, §1 (eff. Sept. 1, 2009), ch. 1113, §25 (eff. Sept. 1, 2009).

FAM §153.705. APPOINTING DESIGNATED PERSON TO EXERCISE VISITATION FOR CONSERVATOR WITHOUT EXCLUSIVE RIGHT TO DESIGNATE PRIMARY RESIDENCE OF CHILD

(a) If the conservator without the exclusive right to designate the primary residence of the child is ordered to military deployment, military mobilization, or temporary military duty, the court may award visitation with the child to a designated person chosen by the conservator, if the visitation is in the best interest of the child.

(b) The temporary order for visitation must provide that:

(1) the designated person under this section has the right to possession of the child for the periods and in the manner in which the conservator described by Subsection (a) would be entitled if not ordered to military deployment, military mobilization, or temporary military duty;

(2) the child's other conservator and the designated person under this section are subject to the requirements of Section 153.316, with the designated person considered for purposes of that section to be the possessory conservator;

(3) the designated person under this section has the rights and duties of a nonparent possessory conservator under Section 153.376(a) during the period that the designated person has possession of the child; and

(4) the designated person under this section is subject to any provision in a court order restricting or prohibiting access to the child by any specified individual.

(c) The court may limit or expand the rights of a nonparent designated person named in a temporary order rendered under this section as appropriate to the best interest of the child.

History of Fam. Code §153.705: Acts 2009, 81st Leg., ch. 727, §1 (eff. Sept. 1, 2009), ch. 1113, §25 (eff. Sept. 1, 2009).

FAM §153.706. REPEALED

Repealed by Acts 2011, 82nd Leg., ch. 112, §3, eff. Sept. 1, 2011.

FAM §153.707. EXPEDITED HEARING

(a) On a motion by the conservator who has been ordered to military deployment, military mobilization, or temporary military duty, the court shall, for good cause shown, hold an expedited hearing if the court finds that the conservator's military duties have a material effect on the conservator's ability to appear in person at a regularly scheduled hearing.

(b) A hearing under this section shall, if possible, take precedence over other suits affecting the parent-child relationship not involving a conservator who has been ordered to military deployment, military mobilization, or temporary military duty.

(c) On a motion by any party, the court shall, after reasonable advance notice and for good cause shown,

allow a party to present testimony and evidence by electronic means, including by teleconference or through the Internet.

History of Fam. Code §153.707: Acts 2009, 81st Leg., ch. 727, §1 (eff. Sept. 1, 2009), ch. 1113, §25 (eff. Sept. 1, 2009).

FAM §153.708. ENFORCEMENT

Temporary orders rendered under this subchapter may be enforced by or against the designated person to the same extent that an order would be enforceable against the conservator who has been ordered to military deployment, military mobilization, or temporary military duty.

History of Fam. Code §153.708: Acts 2009, 81st Leg., ch. 727, §1 (eff. Sept. 1, 2009), ch. 1113, §25 (eff. Sept. 1, 2009).

FAM §153.709. ADDITIONAL PERIODS OF POSSESSION OR ACCESS

(a) Not later than the 90th day after the date a conservator without the exclusive right to designate the primary residence of the child who is a member of the armed services concludes the conservator's military deployment, military mobilization, or temporary military duty, the conservator may petition the court to:

(1) compute the periods of possession of or access to the child to which the conservator would have otherwise been entitled during the conservator's deployment; and

(2) award the conservator additional periods of possession of or access to the child to compensate for the periods described by Subdivision (1).

(b) If the conservator described by Subsection (a) petitions the court under Subsection (a), the court:

(1) shall compute the periods of possession or access to the child described by Subsection (a)(1); and

(2) may award to the conservator additional periods of possession of or access to the child for a length of time and under terms the court considers reasonable, if the court determines that:

(A) the conservator was on military deployment, military mobilization, or temporary military duty in a location where access to the child was not reasonably possible; and

(B) the award of additional periods of possession of or access to the child is in the best interest of the child.

(c) In making the determination under Subsection (b)(2), the court:

(1) shall consider:

(A) the periods of possession of or access to the child to which the conservator would otherwise have been entitled during the conservator's military deployment, military mobilization, or temporary military duty, as computed under Subsection (b)(1);

(B) whether the court named a designated person under Section 153.705 to exercise limited possession of the child during the conservator's deployment; and

(C) any other factor the court considers appropriate; and

(2) is not required to award additional periods of possession of or access to the child that equals the possession or access to which the conservator would have been entitled during the conservator's military deployment, military mobilization, or temporary military duty, as computed under Subsection (b)(1).

(d) After the conservator described by Subsection (a) has exercised all additional periods of possession or access awarded under this section, the rights of all affected parties are governed by the terms of the court order applicable when the conservator is not ordered to military deployment, military mobilization, or temporary military duty.

History of Fam. Code §153.709: Acts 2009, 81st Leg., ch. 727, §1 (eff. Sept. 1, 2009), ch. 1113, §25 (eff. Sept. 1, 2009).

CHAPTER 154. CHILD SUPPORT

SUBCHAPTER A. COURT-ORDERED CHILD SUPPORT

A FAM §154.001. SUPPORT OF CHILD

The amended text in §154.001 is effective for SAPCRs filed on or after Sept. 1, 2017. SAPCRs filed before Sept. 1, 2017, are governed by the former law in effect at that time.

(a) The court may order either or both parents to support a child in the manner specified by the order:

(1) until the child is 18 years of age or until graduation from high school, whichever occurs later;

(2) until the child is emancipated through marriage, through removal of the disabilities of minority by court order, or by other operation of law;

(3) until the death of the child; or

(4) if the child is disabled as defined in this chapter, for an indefinite period.

(a-1) The court may order each person who is financially able and whose parental rights have been terminated with respect to [~~either~~] a child in substitute care for whom the department has been appointed managing conservator, a child for a reason described by Section 161.001(b)(1)(T)(iv) or (b)(1)(U), or a child who was conceived as a direct result of conduct that constitutes an offense under Section 21.02, 22.011, 22.021, or 25.02, Penal Code, to support the child in the manner specified by the order:

(1) until the earliest of:

(A) the child's adoption;

(B) the child's 18th birthday or graduation from high school, whichever occurs later;

(C) removal of the child's disabilities of minority by court order, marriage, or other operation of law; or

(D) the child's death; or

(2) if the child is disabled as defined in this chapter, for an indefinite period.

(b) The court may order either or both parents to make periodic payments for the support of a child in a proceeding in which the Department of Protective and Regulatory Services is named temporary managing conservator. In a proceeding in which the Department of Protective and Regulatory Services is named permanent managing conservator of a child whose parents' rights have not been terminated, the court shall order each parent that is financially able to make periodic payments for the support of the child.

(c) In a Title IV-D case, if neither parent has physical possession or conservatorship of the child, the court may render an order providing that a nonparent or agency having physical possession may receive, hold, or disburse child support payments for the benefit of the child.

History of Fam. Code §154.001: Acts 1995, 74th Leg., ch. 20, §1, eff. Apr. 20, 1995. Amended by Acts 1995, 74th Leg., ch. 751, §39, eff. Sept. 1, 1995; Acts 1999, 76th Leg., ch. 556, §8, eff. Sept. 1, 1999; Acts 2005, 79th Leg., ch. 268, §1.08(a), eff. Sept. 1, 2005; Acts 2013, 83rd Leg., ch. 907, §3, eff. Sept. 1, 2013; S.B. 77, §1, 85th Leg., eff. Sept. 1, 2017. Source: Former Fam. Code §14.05(a), (b), (d).

See also *O'Connor's Texas Family Law Handbook* (2017), "Suit for Child Support," ch. 4-F, p. 529.

ANNOTATIONS

Tucker v. Thomas, 419 S.W.3d 292, 293 (Tex.2013). See annotation under Family Code §106.002, p. 425.

Rodriguez v. Rodriguez, 860 S.W.2d 414, 415 (Tex. 1993). "A trial court has discretion to set child support within the parameters established by the child support guidelines set forth in the ... Family Code. A trial court's decision in this regard will not be overturned unless a clear abuse of discretion is shown."

FAM §154.002. CHILD SUPPORT THROUGH HIGH SCHOOL GRADUATION

(a) The court may render an original support order, or modify an existing order, providing child support past the 18th birthday of the child to be paid only if the child is:

(1) enrolled:

(A) under Chapter 25, Education Code, in an accredited secondary school in a program leading toward a high school diploma;

(B) under Section 130.008, Education Code, in courses for joint high school and junior college credit; or

(C) on a full-time basis in a private secondary school in a program leading toward a high school diploma; and

(2) complying with:

(A) the minimum attendance requirements of Subchapter C, Chapter 25, Education Code; or

(B) the minimum attendance requirements imposed by the school in which the child is enrolled, if the child is enrolled in a private secondary school.

(b) The request for a support order through high school graduation may be filed before or after the child's 18th birthday.

(c) The order for periodic support may provide that payments continue through the end of the month in which the child graduates.

History of Fam. Code §154.002: Acts 1995, 74th Leg., ch. 20, §1, eff. Apr. 20, 1995. Amended by Acts 1999, 76th Leg., ch. 506, §1, eff. Aug. 30, 1999; Acts 2003, 78th Leg., ch. 38, §1, eff. Sept. 1, 2003. Source: Former Fam. Code §14.05(a).

ANNOTATIONS

Roberts v. Swain, No. 01-13-00801-CV (Tex.App.—Houston [1st Dist.] 2014, no pet.) (memo op.; 5-13-14). Obligor "asserts that [child] had ... 36 unexcused absences for the entire school year. [¶] In support of [obligor's] assertion that [child] exceeded the number of permitted absences [allowed under Fam. Code §154.002(a)(2) and Educ. Code §25.085(e)], [obligor] relies on two ... report cards.... However, ... the report cards show only the number of [child's] absences during the school year but do not indicate which, if any, were unexcused. Further, the report cards reflect that [child] received credit and grades in each grading period of the ... school year, undermining [obligor's] contention that [child] did not meet minimum attendance requirements."

In re J.H., 264 S.W.3d 919, 925-26 (Tex.App.—Dallas 2008, no pet.). "The family code does not define 'private secondary school.' However, the other provisions of the statute do refer to the ... Education Code in determining the child's enrollment status. [T]he legislature has indicated in revisions to the [Education Code] that home schools are included within the purview of 'private or parochial schools.' Furthermore, the Texas Supreme Court has held that children enrolled in home school fall under the 'private school' exemption to the state compulsory public school attendance law. *At 927:* [In this case,] there is some evidence that [19-

year-old son] was enrolled on a full-time basis in [an Internet-based home-schooling program] leading toward a high school diploma and complying with the minimum attendance requirements."

FAM §154.003. MANNER OF PAYMENT

The court may order that child support be paid by:

(1) periodic payments;

(2) a lump-sum payment;

(3) an annuity purchase;

(4) the setting aside of property to be administered for the support of the child as specified in the order; or

(5) any combination of periodic payments, lump-sum payments, annuity purchases, or setting aside of property.

History of Fam. Code §154.003: Acts 1995, 74th Leg., ch. 20, §1, eff. Apr. 20, 1995. Source: Former Fam. Code §14.05(a).

FAM §154.004. PLACE OF PAYMENT

(a) The court shall order the payment of child support to the state disbursement unit as provided by Chapter 234.

(b) In a Title IV-D case, the court or the Title IV-D agency shall order that income withheld for child support be paid to the state disbursement unit of this state or, if appropriate, to the state disbursement unit of another state.

(c) This section does not apply to a child support order that:

(1) was initially rendered by a court before January 1, 1994; and

(2) is not being enforced by the Title IV-D agency.

History of Fam. Code §154.004: Acts 1995, 74th Leg., ch. 20, §1, eff. Apr. 20, 1995. Amended by Acts 1999, 76th Leg., ch. 556, §9, eff. Sept. 1, 1999; Acts 2003, 78th Leg., ch. 1247, §1, eff. Sept. 1, 2003. Source: Former Fam. Code §14.0503.

FAM §154.005. PAYMENTS OF SUPPORT OBLIGATION BY TRUST

(a) The court may order the trustees of a spendthrift or other trust to make disbursements for the support of a child to the extent the trustees are required to make payments to a beneficiary who is required to make child support payments as provided by this chapter.

(b) If disbursement of the assets of the trust is discretionary, the court may order child support payments from the income of the trust but not from the principal.

History of Fam. Code §154.005: Acts 1995, 74th Leg., ch. 20, §1, eff. Apr. 20, 1995. Source: Former Fam. Code §14.05(c).

ANNOTATIONS

Kolpack v. Torres, 829 S.W.2d 913, 916 (Tex. App.—Corpus Christi 1992, writ denied). "We do not find a provision in the Family Code that would place a duty on a discretionary trust to support its beneficiary-parent's child. The only provision in the Family Code relating directly to trusts is [Fam. Code] §14.05(c) [now §154.005], which we interpret allows a court to order a trustee to disburse income from a discretionary trust, to the extent that the trustee is required to make payments to a beneficiary who is required to make support payments under this section. [¶] The discretionary trust under §14.05(c) may be ordered by the trial court to make disbursements for child support if the beneficiary-parent is first obligated to the amount of child support." *See also* ***Robinson v. Robinson***, 694 S.W.2d 569, 572 (Tex.App.—Corpus Christi 1985, no writ).

Prewitt v. Smith, 528 S.W.2d 893, 896 (Tex.App.—Austin 1975, no writ). The provisions of Fam. Code §14.05(c), now §154.005, "are limited to 'spendthrift or other trust' of like nature and have no application to funds of public retirement system held by state officials for the benefit of members of the System.... Funds of a retirement system are part of a member's compensation or wages which are not subject to garnishment."

FAM §154.006. TERMINATION OF DUTY OF SUPPORT

(a) Unless otherwise agreed in writing or expressly provided in the order or as provided by Subsection (b), the child support order terminates on:

(1) the marriage of the child;

(2) the removal of the child's disabilities for general purposes;

(3) the death of the child;

(4) a finding by a court that the child:

(A) is 18 years of age or older; and

(B) has failed to comply with the enrollment or attendance requirements described by Section 154.002(a);

(5) the issuance under Section 161.005(h) of an order terminating the parent-child relationship between the obligor and the child based on the results of genetic testing that exclude the obligor as the child's genetic father; or

(6) if the child enlists in the armed forces of the United States, the date on which the child begins active service as defined by 10 U.S.C. Section 101.

(b) Unless a nonparent or agency has been appointed conservator of the child under Chapter 153, the order for current child support, and any provision relating to conservatorship, possession, or access terminates on the marriage or remarriage of the obligor and obligee to each other.

History of Fam. Code §154.006: Acts 1995, 74th Leg., ch. 20, §1, eff. Apr. 20, 1995. Amended by Acts 1999, 76th Leg., ch. 556, §9, eff. Sept. 1, 1999; Acts 2003, 78th Leg., ch. 38, §2, eff. Sept. 1, 2003; Acts 2007, 80th Leg., ch. 972, §9(a) (eff. Sept. 1, 2007), ch. 1404, §1 (eff. Sept. 1, 2007); Acts 2011, 82nd Leg., ch. 54, §1, eff. May 12, 2011. Source: Former Fam. Code §14.05(d).

ANNOTATIONS

Laird v. Swor, 737 S.W.2d 601, 603 (Tex.App.—Beaumont 1987, no writ). "The fact that the minor daughter later divorced and returned to her mother would not, we think, cancel her emancipation." *See also* ***Fernandez v. Fernandez***, 717 S.W.2d 781, 782-83 (Tex.App.—El Paso 1986, writ dism'd) (annulment of minor's 60-day marriage reinstated her minority and father's duty of support).

FAM §154.007. ORDER TO WITHHOLD CHILD SUPPORT FROM INCOME

(a) In a proceeding in which periodic payments of child support are ordered, modified, or enforced, the court or Title IV-D agency shall order that income be withheld from the disposable earnings of the obligor as provided by Chapter 158.

(b) If the court does not order income withholding, an order for support must contain a provision for income withholding to ensure that withholding may be effected if a delinquency occurs.

(c) A child support order must be construed to contain a withholding provision even if the provision has been omitted from the written order.

(d) If the order was rendered or last modified before January 1, 1987, the order is presumed to contain a provision for income withholding procedures to take effect in the event a delinquency occurs without further amendment to the order or future action by the court.

History of Fam. Code §154.007: Acts 1995, 74th Leg., ch. 20, §1, eff. Apr. 20, 1995. Amended by Acts 1997, 75th Leg., ch. 911, §10, eff. Sept. 1, 1997. Source: Former Fam. Code §14.05(e).

FAM §154.008. PROVISION FOR MEDICAL SUPPORT[1]

The court shall order medical support for the child as provided by Subchapters B and D.

1. **Editor's note:** In 2015, the Legislature amended §154.008 to require dental support for a child subject to a child-support order, but the amendments are not effective until Sept. 1, 2018. For the text of the prospective amendments, see Acts 2015, 84th Leg., ch. 1150, §8, eff. Sept. 1, 2018.

History of Fam. Code §154.008: Acts 1995, 74th Leg., ch. 20, §1, eff. Apr. 20, 1995. Amended by Acts 2001, 77th Leg., ch. 1023, §3, eff. Sept. 1, 2001. Source: Former Fam. Code §14.061(a).

FAM §154.009. RETROACTIVE CHILD SUPPORT

(a) The court may order a parent to pay retroactive child support if the parent:

(1) has not previously been ordered to pay support for the child; and

(2) was not a party to a suit in which support was ordered.

(b) In ordering retroactive child support, the court shall apply the child support guidelines provided by this chapter.

(c) Unless the Title IV-D agency is a party to an agreement concerning support or purporting to settle past, present, or future support obligations by prepayment or otherwise, an agreement between the parties does not reduce or terminate retroactive support that the agency may request.

(d) Notwithstanding Subsection (a), the court may order a parent subject to a previous child support order to pay retroactive child support if:

(1) the previous child support order terminated as a result of the marriage or remarriage of the child's parents;

(2) the child's parents separated after the marriage or remarriage; and

(3) a new child support order is sought after the date of the separation.

(e) In rendering an order under Subsection (d), the court may order retroactive child support back to the date of the separation of the child's parents.

History of Fam. Code §154.009: Acts 1995, 74th Leg., ch. 20, §1, eff. Apr. 20, 1995. Amended by Acts 2001, 77th Leg., ch. 1023, §4, eff. Sept. 1, 2001. Source: Former Fam. Code §14.062.

See also ***O'Connor's Texas Family Law Handbook*** (2017), "Calculating Retroactive Child Support," ch. 4-F, §16, p. 556.

ANNOTATIONS

In re Sanders, 159 S.W.3d 797, 803 (Tex.App.—Amarillo 2005, no pet.). Obligor argues the award of attorney fees was "error because [obligee's attorneys] did not segregate the amount incurred in prosecuting the action to establish parentage from that related to obtaining retroactive support. [¶] [B]ecause fees are recoverable in both a suit to establish parentage and to obtain retroactive fees and those were the two claims [obligee] pursued, neither she nor her attorney were obligated to segregate the fees as alleged by [obligor]."

FAM §154.010. NO DISCRIMINATION BASED ON MARITAL STATUS OF PARENTS OR SEX

The amount of support ordered for the benefit of a child shall be determined without regard to:

(1) the sex of the obligor, obligee, or child; or

(2) the marital status of the parents of the child.

History of Fam. Code §154.010: Acts 1995, 74th Leg., ch. 20, §1, eff. Apr. 20, 1995. Source: Former Fam. Code §§14.05(g), 14.053(i).

FAM §154.011. SUPPORT NOT CONDITIONED ON POSSESSION OR ACCESS

A court may not render an order that conditions the payment of child support on whether a managing conservator allows a possessory conservator to have possession of or access to a child.

History of Fam. Code §154.011: Acts 1995, 74th Leg., ch. 751, §40, eff. Sept. 1, 1995.

ANNOTATIONS

Seidel v. Seidel, 10 S.W.3d 365, 369 (Tex.App.—Dallas 1999, no pet.). "An order which makes one parent's visitation rights with the child contingent upon their timely payment of child support is 'coercive' and 'operatively null and void.' [¶] [S]ection 154.011 prohibits the trial court from rendering an order which provides for the release of the domicile restrictions imposed by the divorce decree on [obligee] and the children in the event [obligor] is deficient in the payment of the $38,000 child support judgment."

FAM §154.012. SUPPORT PAID IN EXCESS OF SUPPORT ORDER

(a) If an obligor is not in arrears and the obligor's child support obligation has terminated, the obligee shall return to the obligor a child support payment made by the obligor that exceeds the amount of support ordered, regardless of whether the payment was made before, on, or after the date the child support obligation terminated.

(b) An obligor may file a suit to recover a child support payment under Subsection (a). If the court finds that the obligee failed to return a child support payment under Subsection (a), the court shall order the obligee to pay to the obligor attorney's fees and all court costs in addition to the amount of support paid after the date the child support order terminated. For good cause shown, the court may waive the requirement that the obligee pay attorney's fees and costs if the court states the reasons supporting that finding.

History of Fam. Code §154.012: Acts 1999, 76th Leg., ch. 363, §1, eff. Sept. 1, 1999. Amended by Acts 2001, 77th Leg., ch. 1023, §5, eff. Sept. 1, 2001.

ANNOTATIONS

In re B.S.H., 308 S.W.3d 76, 81 (Tex.App.—Fort Worth 2009, no pet.). "The excess child support payments referred to in §154.012 ... do not refer to additional or increased payments that an obligor intends to make to meet the current needs of his or her child. Rather, they are excess payments mistakenly made or intended to be advances against future obligations."

Ⓐ FAM §154.013. CONTINUATION OF DUTY TO PAY SUPPORT AFTER DEATH OF OBLIGEE

(a) A child support obligation does not terminate on the death of the obligee but continues as an obligation to the child named in the support order, as required by this section.

(b) Notwithstanding any provision of the Estates ~~[Probate]~~ Code, a child support payment held by the Title IV-D agency, a local registry, or the state disbursement unit or any uncashed check or warrant representing a child support payment made before, on, or after the date of death of the obligee shall be paid proportionately for the benefit of each surviving child named in the support order and not to the estate of the obligee. The payment is free of any creditor's claim against the deceased obligee's estate and may be disbursed as provided by Subsection (c).

(c) On the death of the obligee, current child support owed by the obligor for the benefit of the child or any amount described by Subsection (b) shall be paid to:

(1) a person, other than a parent, who is appointed as managing conservator of the child;

(2) a person, including the obligor, who has assumed actual care, control, and possession of the child, if a managing conservator or guardian of the child has not been appointed;

(3) the county clerk, as provided by Chapter 1355, Estates ~~[Section 887, Texas Probate]~~ Code, in the name of and for the account of the child for whom the support is owed;

(4) a guardian of the child appointed under Title 3, Estates ~~[Chapter XIII, Texas Probate]~~ Code, as provided by that code; or

(5) the surviving child, if the child is an adult or has otherwise had the disabilities of minority removed.

(d) On presentation of the obligee's death certificate, the court shall render an order directing payment of child support paid but not disbursed to be made as provided by Subsection (c). A copy of the order shall be provided to:

(1) the obligor;

(2) as appropriate:

(A) the person having actual care, control, and possession of the child;

(B) the county clerk; or

(C) the managing conservator or guardian of the child, if one has been appointed;

(3) the local registry or state disbursement unit and, if appropriate, the Title IV-D agency; and

(4) the child named in the support order, if the child is an adult or has otherwise had the disabilities of minority removed.

(e) The order under Subsection (d) must contain:

(1) a statement that the obligee is deceased and that child support amounts otherwise payable to the obligee shall be paid for the benefit of a surviving child named in the support order as provided by Subsection (c);

(2) the name and age of each child named in the support order; and

(3) the name and mailing address of, as appropriate:

(A) the person having actual care, control, and possession of the child;

(B) the county clerk; or

(C) the managing conservator or guardian of the child, if one has been appointed.

(f) On receipt of the order required under this section, the local registry, state disbursement unit, or Title IV-D agency shall disburse payments as required by the order.

History of Fam. Code §154.013: Acts 2001, 77th Leg., ch. 1023, §6, eff. Sept. 1, 2001. Amended by S.B. 1488, §22.018, 85th Leg., eff. Sept. 1, 2017.

See also ***O'Connor's Texas Family Law Handbook*** (2017), "Disbursement Order – Death of Obligee," ch. 4-F, §20, p. 569.

ANNOTATIONS

Niskar v. Niskar, 136 S.W.3d 749, 759 (Tex.App.—Dallas 2004, no pet.). "A trial court has the authority to order that child support payments continue after the obligee's death. Also, a trial court has the authority to order a parent to maintain a life insurance policy for the child's benefit for so long as the child support obligation remains in effect. *At 760:* However, [absent evidence], there is no statute that authorizes the trial court to order [H] to maintain a life insurance policy for the payment of child support after his death."

FAM §154.014. PAYMENTS IN EXCESS OF COURT-ORDERED AMOUNT

(a) If a child support agency or local child support registry receives from an obligor who is not in arrears a child support payment in an amount that exceeds the court-ordered amount, the agency or registry, to the extent possible, shall give effect to any expressed intent of the obligor for the application of the amount that exceeds the court-ordered amount.

(b) If the obligor does not express an intent for the application of the amount paid in excess of the court-ordered amount, the agency or registry shall:

(1) credit the excess amount to the obligor's future child support obligation; and

(2) promptly disburse the excess amount to the obligee.

(c) This section does not apply to an obligee who is a recipient of public assistance under Chapter 31, Human Resources Code.

History of Fam. Code §154.014: Acts 2001, 77th Leg., ch. 1491, §2(a), eff. Sept. 1, 2001. Renumbered from §154.013 by Acts 2003, 78th Leg., ch. 1275, §2(52), eff. Sept. 1, 2003.

ANNOTATIONS

In re B.S.H., 308 S.W.3d 76, 79 (Tex.App.—Fort Worth 2009, no pet.). "[S]ection 154.014 ... regulates the manner by which excess child support payments to child support agencies or registries, not to individual obligees, must be applied. [¶] [However,] §154.014 ... offers guidance in determining how excess payments should be applied in a case where excess child support payments are made directly to individual obligees. Accordingly, we hold that in a case where an individual obligee receives from an obligor who is not in arrears a child support payment that exceeds the court-ordered amount, the trial court shall give effect to any expressed intent of the obligor to determine the proper application of the amount that exceeds the court-ordered amount." *See also* ***Bolton v. Bolton***, No. 01-10-00193-CV (Tex.App.—Houston [1st Dist.] 2011, no pet.) (memo op.; 1-27-11) (because H expressed intent to pay increased child support to meet children's current needs, court did not abuse its discretion by re-

fusing to credit excess payments as offset against his future child-support obligation).

A FAM §154.015. ACCELERATION OF UNPAID CHILD SUPPORT OBLIGATION[1]

(a) In this section, "estate" has the meaning assigned by Chapter 22, Estates ~~[Section 3, Texas Probate]~~ Code.

(b) If the child support obligor dies before the child support obligation terminates, the remaining unpaid balance of the child support obligation becomes payable on the date the obligor dies.

(c) For purposes of this section, the court of continuing jurisdiction shall determine the amount of the unpaid child support obligation for each child of the deceased obligor. In determining the amount of the unpaid child support obligation, the court shall consider all relevant factors, including:

(1) the present value of the total amount of monthly periodic child support payments that would become due between the month in which the obligor dies and the month in which the child turns 18 years of age, based on the amount of the periodic monthly child support payments under the child support order in effect on the date of the obligor's death;

(2) the present value of the total amount of health insurance premiums payable for the benefit of the child from the month in which the obligor dies until the month in which the child turns 18 years of age, based on the cost of health insurance for the child ordered to be paid on the date of the obligor's death;

(3) in the case of a disabled child under 18 years of age or an adult disabled child, an amount to be determined by the court under Section 154.306;

(4) the nature and amount of any benefit to which the child would be entitled as a result of the obligor's death, including life insurance proceeds, annuity payments, trust distributions, social security death benefits, and retirement survivor benefits; and

(5) any other financial resource available for the support of the child.

(d) If, after considering all relevant factors, the court finds that the child support obligation has been satisfied, the court shall render an order terminating the child support obligation. If the court finds that the child support obligation is not satisfied, the court shall render a judgment in favor of the obligee, for the benefit of the child, in the amount of the unpaid child support obligation determined under Subsection (c). The order must designate the obligee as constructive trustee, for the benefit of the child, of any money received in satisfaction of the judgment.

(e) The obligee has a claim, on behalf of the child, against the deceased obligor's estate for the unpaid child support obligation determined under Subsection (c). The obligee may present the claim in the manner provided by the Estates ~~[Texas Probate]~~ Code.

(f) If money paid to the obligee for the benefit of the child exceeds the amount of the unpaid child support obligation remaining at the time of the obligor's death, the obligee shall hold the excess amount as constructive trustee for the benefit of the deceased obligor's estate until the obligee delivers the excess amount to the legal representative of the deceased obligor's estate.

1. **Editor's note:** In 2015, the Legislature amended §154.015 to require dental support for a child subject to a child-support order, but the amendments are not effective until Sept. 1, 2018. For the text of the prospective amendments, see Acts 2015, 84th Leg., ch. 1150, §9, eff. Sept. 1, 2018.

History of Fam. Code §154.015: Acts 2007, 80th Leg., ch. 1404, §2, eff. Sept. 1, 2007. Amended by S.B. 1488, §22.019, 85th Leg., eff. Sept. 1, 2017.

See also Est. Code §355.102.

FAM §154.016. PROVISION OF SUPPORT IN EVENT OF DEATH OF PARENT[1]

(a) The court may order a child support obligor to obtain and maintain a life insurance policy, including a decreasing term life insurance policy, that will establish an insurance-funded trust or an annuity payable to the obligee for the benefit of the child that will satisfy the support obligation under the child support order in the event of the obligor's death.

(b) In determining the nature and extent of the obligation to provide for the support of the child in the event of the death of the obligor, the court shall consider all relevant factors, including:

(1) the present value of the total amount of monthly periodic child support payments from the date the child support order is rendered until the month in which the child turns 18 years of age, based on the amount of the periodic monthly child support payment under the child support order;

(2) the present value of the total amount of health insurance premiums payable for the benefit of the child from the date the child support order is rendered until the month in which the child turns 18 years of age,

based on the cost of health insurance for the child ordered to be paid; and

(3) in the case of a disabled child under 18 years of age or an adult disabled child, an amount to be determined by the court under Section 154.306.

(c) The court may, on its own motion or on a motion of the obligee, require the child support obligor to provide proof satisfactory to the court verifying compliance with the order rendered under this section.

1. **Editor's note:** In 2015, the Legislature amended §154.016 to require dental support for a child subject to a child-support order, but the amendments are not effective until Sept. 1, 2018. For the text of the prospective amendments, see Acts 2015, 84th Leg., ch. 1150, §10, eff. Sept. 1, 2018.

History of Fam. Code §154.016: Acts 2007, 80th Leg., ch. 1404, §2, eff. Sept. 1, 2007.

Sections 154.017-154.060 reserved for expansion

SUBCHAPTER B. COMPUTING NET RESOURCES AVAILABLE FOR PAYMENT OF CHILD SUPPORT

FAM §154.061. COMPUTING NET MONTHLY INCOME

(a) Whenever feasible, gross income should first be computed on an annual basis and then should be recalculated to determine average monthly gross income.

(b) The Title IV-D agency shall annually promulgate tax charts to compute net monthly income, subtracting from gross income social security taxes and federal income tax withholding for a single person claiming one personal exemption and the standard deduction.

History of Fam. Code §154.061: Acts 1995, 74th Leg., ch. 20, §1, eff. Apr. 20, 1995. Source: Former Fam. Code §14.053(a), (h).

ANNOTATIONS

Swaab v. Swaab, 282 S.W.3d 519, 526 (Tex.App.—Houston [14th Dist.] 2008, pet. dism'd). "The undisputed evidence of [father's] net resources included tax returns for the years 1996-2002 and 2004-2005. ... According to these returns, [father's] income varied from a high of $541,900 ... to a low of $10,360.... *At 527:* [G]iven the dramatic fluctuation in [father's] self-employment income, the trial court had the discretion to average [father's] past income to determine his approximate net monthly resources."

In re Sanders, 159 S.W.3d 797, 801 n.3 (Tex.App.—Amarillo 2005, no pet.). "[B]usiness losses (other than those suffered by a self-employed individual) are excluded when determining an obligor's net resources. So, while the tax returns indicated that [obligor] had little income for tax purposes due to losses he suffered, that does not mean that he had little income for purposes of determining his child support obligation."

Wright v. Wright, 867 S.W.2d 807, 814 (Tex. App.—El Paso 1993, writ denied). Obligor argues that Fam. Code §14.053(h), now §154.061, is inconsistent with Fam. Code §14.053(b), now §154.062, in that "it does not allow a deduction of health insurance costs from gross income in calculating net income. A careful reading of that statute, however, demonstrates that the purpose of [§14.053(h)] is to assist the courts in calculating the amount of deductions from gross income for taxes and social security to determine the obligor's net income as a single person claiming one personal exemption. Since many obligors may elect not to file their tax returns as single persons with one exemption, these charts serve as an aid in making the calculations for the courts. The net income calculation in [§14.053(h)] is not the same as the net resources calculation in [§14.053(b)]. Moreover, the 'Instructions for Use' included in the [§14.053(h)] tax charts clearly indicate that additional steps are required, after calculating net income, to determine net resources."

OFFICE OF THE ATTORNEY GENERAL 2017 TAX CHARTS

Pursuant to §154.061(b) of the Texas Family Code, the Office of the Attorney General of Texas, as the Title IV-D agency, has promulgated the following tax charts to assist courts in establishing the amount of a child support order. These tax charts are applicable to employed and self-employed persons in computing net monthly income.

INSTRUCTIONS FOR USE

To use these tables, first compute the obligor's annual gross income. Then recompute to determine the obligor's average monthly gross income. These tables provide a method for calculating "monthly net income" for child support purposes, subtracting from monthly gross income the social security taxes and the federal income tax withholding for a single person claiming one personal exemption and the standard deduction.

Thereafter, in many cases the guidelines call for a number of additional steps to complete the necessary calculations. For example, §§154.061-154.070 provide for appropriate additions to "income" as that term is defined for federal income tax purposes, and for certain subtractions from monthly net income, in order to arrive at the net resources of the obligor available for child support purposes. If necessary, one may compute an obligee's net resources using similar steps.

EMPLOYED PERSONS 2017 TAX CHART

Monthly Gross Wages	Social Security Taxes		Federal Income Taxes***	Net Monthly Income
	Old-Age, Survivors and Disability Insurance Taxes (6.2%)*	Hospital (Medicare) Insurance Taxes (1.45%)*, **		
$100.00	$6.20	$1.45	$0.00	$92.35
$200.00	$12.40	$2.90	$0.00	$184.70
$300.00	$18.60	$4.35	$0.00	$277.05
$400.00	$24.80	$5.80	$0.00	$369.40
$500.00	$31.00	$7.25	$0.00	$461.75
$600.00	$37.20	$8.70	$0.00	$554.10
$700.00	$43.40	$10.15	$0.00	$646.45
$800.00	$49.60	$11.60	$0.00	$738.80
$900.00	$55.80	$13.05	$3.33	$827.82
$1,000.00	$62.00	$14.50	$13.33	$910.17
$1,100.00	$68.20	$15.95	$23.33	$992.52
$1,200.00	$74.40	$17.40	$33.33	$1,074.87
$1,256.67****	$77.91	$18.22	$39.00	$1,121.54
$1,300.00	$80.60	$18.85	$43.33	$1,157.22
$1,400.00	$86.80	$20.30	$53.33	$1,239.57
$1,500.00	$93.00	$21.75	$63.33	$1,321.92
$1,600.00	$99.20	$23.20	$73.33	$1,404.27
$1,700.00	$105.40	$24.65	$86.16	$1,483.79
$1,800.00	$111.60	$26.10	$101.16	$1,561.14

EMPLOYED PERSONS 2017 TAX CHART				
	Social Security Taxes			
Monthly Gross Wages	Old-Age, Survivors and Disability Insurance Taxes (6.2%)*	Hospital (Medicare) Insurance Taxes (1.45%)*, **	Federal Income Taxes***	Net Monthly Income
$1,900.00	$117.80	$27.55	$116.16	$1,638.49
$2,000.00	$124.00	$29.00	$131.16	$1,715.84
$2,100.00	$130.20	$30.45	$146.16	$1,793.19
$2,200.00	$136.40	$31.90	$161.16	$1,870.54
$2,300.00	$142.60	$33.35	$176.16	$1,947.89
$2,400.00	$148.80	$34.80	$191.16	$2,025.24
$2,500.00	$155.00	$36.25	$206.16	$2,102.59
$2,600.00	$161.20	$37.70	$221.16	$2,179.94
$2,700.00	$167.40	$39.15	$236.16	$2,257.29
$2,800.00	$173.60	$40.60	$251.16	$2,334.64
$2,900.00	$179.80	$42.05	$266.16	$2,411.99
$3,000.00	$186.00	$43.50	$281.16	$2,489.34
$3,100.00	$192.20	$44.95	$296.16	$2,566.69
$3,200.00	$198.40	$46.40	$311.16	$2,644.04
$3,300.00	$204.60	$47.85	$326.16	$2,721.39
$3,400.00	$210.80	$49.30	$341.16	$2,798.74
$3,500.00	$217.00	$50.75	$356.16	$2,876.09
$3,600.00	$223.20	$52.20	$371.16	$2,953.44
$3,700.00	$229.40	$53.65	$386.16	$3,030.79
$3,800.00	$235.60	$55.10	$401.16	$3,108.14
$3,900.00	$241.80	$56.55	$416.16	$3,185.49
$4,000.00	$248.00	$58.00	$431.16	$3,262.84
$4,250.00	$263.50	$61.63	$490.75	$3,434.12
$4,500.00	$279.00	$65.25	$553.25	$3,602.50
$4,750.00	$294.50	$68.88	$615.75	$3,770.87
$5,000.00	$310.00	$72.50	$678.25	$3,939.25
$5,250.00	$325.50	$76.13	$740.75	$4,107.62
$5,500.00	$341.00	$79.75	$803.25	$4,276.00
$5,750.00	$356.50	$83.38	$865.75	$4,444.37
$6,000.00	$372.00	$87.00	$928.25	$4,612.75
$6,250.00	$387.50	$90.63	$990.75	$4,781.12
$6,500.00	$403.00	$94.25	$1,053.25	$4,949.50

EMPLOYED PERSONS 2017 TAX CHART				
	Social Security Taxes			
Monthly Gross Wages	Old-Age, Survivors and Disability Insurance Taxes (6.2%)*	Hospital (Medicare) Insurance Taxes (1.45%)*, **	Federal Income Taxes***	Net Monthly Income
$6,750.00	$418.50	$97.88	$1,115.75	$5,117.87
$7,000.00	$434.00	$101.50	$1,178.25	$5,286.25
$7,500.00	$465.00	$108.75	$1,303.25	$5,623.00
$8,000.00	$496.00	$116.00	$1,428.25	$5,959.75
$8,500.00	$527.00	$123.25	$1,553.25	$6,296.50
$9,000.00	$558.00	$130.50	$1,692.50	$6,619.00
$9,500.00	$589.00	$137.75	$1,832.50	$6,940.75
$10,000.00	$620.00	$145.00	$1,972.50	$7,262.50
$10,500.00	$651.00	$152.25	$2,112.50	$7,584.25
$11,000.00	$657.20*****	$159.50	$2,252.50	$7,930.80
$11,500.00	$657.20	$166.75	$2,392.50	$8,283.55
$11,877.69******	$657.20	$172.23	$2,498.26	$8,550.00
$12,000.00	$657.20	$174.00	$2,532.50	$8,636.30
$12,500.00	$657.20	$181.25	$2,672.50	$8,989.05
$13,000.00	$657.20	$188.50	$2,812.50	$9,341.80
$13,500.00	$657.20	$195.75	$2,952.50	$9,694.55
$14,000.00	$657.20	$203.00	$3,092.50	$10,047.30
$14,500.00	$657.20	$210.25	$3,232.50	$10,400.05
$15,000.00	$657.20	$217.50	$3,372.50	$10,752.80

FOOTNOTES TO EMPLOYED PERSONS 2017 TAX CHART:

* An employed person not subject to the Old-Age, Survivors and Disability Insurance/Hospital (Medicare) Insurance taxes will be allowed the reductions reflected in these columns, unless it is shown that such person has no similar contributory plan such as teacher retirement, federal railroad retirement, federal civil service retirement, etc.

** When income exceeds $200,000.00 per year there is an additional Medicare Tax of 0.9%. The additional Medicare Tax does not apply to any values shown on this chart because the highest gross income included is $15,000.00 per month ($180,000.00 per year).

*** These amounts represent one-twelfth (1/12) of the annual federal income tax calculated for a single taxpayer claiming one personal exemption ($4,050.00, subject to reduction in certain cases, as described below in this footnote) and taking the standard deduction ($6,350.00).

For a single taxpayer with an adjusted gross income in excess of $261,500.00, the deduction for the personal exemption is reduced by two percent (2%) for each $2,500.00 or fraction thereof by which adjusted gross income exceeds $261,500.00. The reduction is completed (i.e., the deduction for the personal exemption is eliminated) for adjusted gross income in excess of $384,000.00. In no case is the deduction for the personal exemption reduced by more than 100%. The phase out of the Personal Exemption does not apply to any values shown on this chart because the highest income included is $15,000.00 per month ($180,000.00 per year).

**** The amount represents one-twelfth (1/12) of the gross income of an individual earning the federal minimum wage ($7.25 per hour) for a 40-hour week for a full year. $7.25 per hour x 40 hours per week x 52 weeks per year equals $15,080.00 per year. One-twelfth (1/12) of $15,080.00 equals $1,256.67.

***** For annual gross wages above $127,200.00, this amount represents a monthly average of the Old-Age, Survivors and Disability Insurance tax based on the 2017 maximum Old-Age, Survivors and Disability Insurance tax of $7,886.40 per person (6.2% of the first $127,200.00 of annual gross wages equals $7,886.40). One-twelfth (1/12) of $7,886.40 equals $657.20.

****** This amount represents the point where the monthly gross wages of an employed individual would result in $8,550.00 of net resources. Texas Family Code section 154.125 provides "The guidelines for the support of a child in this section are specifically designed to apply to situations in which the obligor's monthly net resources are not greater than $7,500 or the adjusted amount determined under Subsection (a-1), whichever is greater." Effective September 1, 2013 the adjusted amount determined under Subsection (a-1) is $8,550.00.

REFERENCES RELATING TO EMPLOYED PERSONS 2017 TAX CHART:

1. Old-Age, Survivors and Disability Insurance Tax

(a) Contribution Base

(1) Social Security Administration's notice appearing in 81 Fed. Reg. 74854 (October 27, 2016)

(2) Section 3121(a) of the Internal Revenue Code of 1986, as amended (26 U.S.C. §3121(a))

(3) Section 230 of the Social Security Act, as amended (42 U.S.C. §430)

(b) Tax Rate

(1) Section 3101(a) of the Internal Revenue Code of 1986, as amended (26 U.S.C. §3101(a))

2. Hospital (Medicare) Insurance Tax

(a) Contribution Base

(1) Section 3121(a) of the Internal Revenue Code of 1986, as amended (26 U.S.C. §3121(a))

(2) Omnibus Budget Reconciliation Act of 1993, Pub. L. No. 103-66, §13207, 107 Stat. 312, 467-69 (1993)

(b) Tax Rate

(1) Section 3101(b) of the Internal Revenue Code of 1986, as amended (26 U.S.C. §3101(b))

3. Federal Income Tax

(a) Tax Rate Schedule for 2017 for Single Taxpayers

(1) Revenue Procedure 2016-55, Section 3.01, Table 3 which appears in Internal Revenue Bulletin 2016-45, dated November 7, 2016

(2) Section 1(c), (f) and (i) of the Internal Revenue Code of 1986, as amended (26 U.S.C. §1(c), 1(f), 1(i))

(b) Standard Deduction

(1) Revenue Procedure 2016-55, Section 3.14, which appears in Internal Revenue Bulletin 2016-45, dated November 7, 2016

(2) Section 63(c) of the Internal Revenue Code of 1986, as amended (26 U.S.C. §63(c))

(c) Personal Exemption

(1) Revenue Procedure 2016-55, Section 3.24, which appears in Internal Revenue Bulletin 2016-45, dated November 7, 2016

(2) Section 151(d) of the Internal Revenue Code of 1986, as amended (26 U.S.C. §151(d))

4. Adjusted amount determined under Subsection (a-1) of Texas Family Code section 154.125

Office of the Attorney General "Announcement of Adjustment Required by Texas Family Code section 154.125" appearing in 38 TexReg 4647 (July 19, 2013)

SELF-EMPLOYED PERSONS 2017 TAX CHART				
Monthly Net Earnings From Self-Employment*	Social Security Taxes		Federal Income Taxes****	Net Monthly Income
	Old-Age, Survivors and Disability Insurance Taxes (12.4%)**	Hospital (Medicare) Insurance Taxes (2.9%)**, ***		
$100.00	$11.45	$2.68	$0.00	$85.87
$200.00	$22.90	$5.36	$0.00	$171.74
$300.00	$34.35	$8.03	$0.00	$257.62
$400.00	$45.81	$10.71	$0.00	$343.48
$500.00	$57.26	$13.39	$0.00	$429.35
$600.00	$68.71	$16.07	$0.00	$515.22
$700.00	$80.16	$18.75	$0.00	$601.09
$800.00	$91.61	$21.43	$0.00	$686.96
$900.00	$103.06	$24.10	$0.00	$772.84
$1,000.00	$114.51	$26.78	$6.27	$852.44
$1,100.00	$125.97	$29.46	$15.56	$929.01
$1,200.00	$137.42	$32.14	$24.86	$1,005.58
$1,300.00	$148.87	$34.82	$34.15	$1,082.16
$1,400.00	$160.32	$37.49	$43.44	$1,158.75
$1,500.00	$171.77	$40.17	$52.74	$1,235.32
$1,600.00	$183.22	$42.85	$62.03	$1,311.90
$1,700.00	$194.67	$45.53	$71.32	$1,388.48
$1,800.00	$206.13	$48.21	$82.08	$1,463.58
$1,900.00	$217.58	$50.88	$96.02	$1,535.52
$2,000.00	$229.03	$53.56	$109.96	$1,607.45
$2,100.00	$240.48	$56.24	$123.90	$1,679.38
$2,200.00	$251.93	$58.92	$137.84	$1,751.31
$2,300.00	$263.38	$61.60	$151.78	$1,823.24
$2,400.00	$274.83	$64.28	$165.73	$1,895.16
$2,500.00	$286.29	$66.95	$179.67	$1,967.09
$2,600.00	$297.74	$69.63	$193.61	$2,039.02
$2,700.00	$309.19	$72.31	$207.55	$2,110.95
$2,800.00	$320.64	$74.99	$221.49	$2,182.88
$2,900.00	$332.09	$77.67	$235.43	$2,254.81
$3,000.00	$343.54	$80.34	$249.37	$2,326.75
$3,100.00	$354.99	$83.02	$263.31	$2,398.68
$3,200.00	$366.44	$85.70	$277.25	$2,470.61
$3,300.00	$377.90	$88.38	$291.19	$2,542.53

SELF-EMPLOYED PERSONS 2017 TAX CHART				
Monthly Net Earnings From Self-Employment*	Social Security Taxes		Federal Income Taxes****	Net Monthly Income
	Old-Age, Survivors and Disability Insurance Taxes (12.4%)**	Hospital (Medicare) Insurance Taxes (2.9%)**, ***		
$3,400.00	$389.35	$91.06	$305.13	$2,614.46
$3,500.00	$400.80	$93.74	$319.07	$2,686.39
$3,600.00	$412.25	$96.41	$333.01	$2,758.33
$3,700.00	$423.70	$99.09	$346.95	$2,830.26
$3,800.00	$435.15	$101.77	$360.89	$2,902.19
$3,900.00	$446.60	$104.45	$374.83	$2,974.12
$4,000.00	$458.06	$107.13	$388.77	$3,046.04
$4,250.00	$486.68	$113.82	$423.62	$3,225.88
$4,500.00	$515.31	$120.52	$473.77	$3,390.40
$4,750.00	$543.94	$127.21	$531.86	$3,546.99
$5,000.00	$572.57	$133.91	$589.94	$3,703.58
$5,250.00	$601.20	$140.60	$648.03	$3,860.17
$5,500.00	$629.83	$147.30	$706.11	$4,016.76
$5,750.00	$658.46	$153.99	$764.19	$4,173.36
$6,000.00	$687.08	$160.69	$822.28	$4,329.95
$6,250.00	$715.71	$167.38	$880.36	$4,486.55
$6,500.00	$744.34	$174.08	$938.45	$4,643.13
$6,750.00	$772.97	$180.78	$996.53	$4,799.72
$7,000.00	$801.60	$187.47	$1,054.62	$4,956.31
$7,500.00	$858.86	$200.86	$1,170.79	$5,269.49
$8,000.00	$916.11	$214.25	$1,286.96	$5,582.68
$8,500.00	$973.37	$227.64	$1,403.12	$5,895.87
$9,000.00	$1,030.63	$241.03	$1,519.29	$6,209.05
$9,500.00	$1,087.88	$254.42	$1,644.58	$6,513.12
$10,000.00	$1,145.14	$267.82	$1,774.69	$6,812.35
$10,500.00	$1,202.40	$281.21	$1,904.80	$7,111.59
$11,000.00	$1,259.65	$294.60	$2,034.91	$7,410.84
$11,500.00	$1,314.40*****	$307.99	$2,165.37	$7,712.24
$12,000.00	$1,314.40	$321.38	$2,303.49	$8,060.73
$12,500.00	$1,314.40	$334.77	$2,441.62	$8,409.21
$12,702.00******	$1,314.40	$340.18	$2,497.42	$8,550.00
$13,000.00	$1,314.40	$348.16	$2,579.74	$8,757.70

SELF-EMPLOYED PERSONS 2017 TAX CHART				
Monthly Net Earnings From Self-Employment*	Social Security Taxes		Federal Income Taxes****	Net Monthly Income
	Old-Age, Survivors and Disability Insurance Taxes (12.4%)**	Hospital (Medicare) Insurance Taxes (2.9%)**, ***		
$13,500.00	$1,314.40	$361.55	$2,717.87	$9,106.18
$14,000.00	$1,314.40	$374.94	$2,855.99	$9,454.67
$14,500.00	$1,314.40	$388.33	$2,994.12	$9,803.15
$15,000.00	$1,314.40	$401.72	$3,132.25	$10,151.63

FOOTNOTES TO SELF-EMPLOYED PERSONS 2017 TAX CHART:

* Determined without regard to Section 1402(a)(12) of the Internal Revenue Code of 1986, as amended (26 U.S.C. §1402(a)(12)) (the "Code").

** In calculating each of the Old-Age, Survivors and Disability Insurance tax and the Hospital (Medicare) Insurance tax, net earnings from self-employment are reduced by the deduction under Section 1402(a)(12) of the Code. The deduction under Section 1402(a)(12) of the Code is equal to net earnings from self-employment (determined without regard to Section 1402(a)(12) of the Code) multiplied by one-half (½) of the sum of the Old-Age, Survivors and Disability Insurance tax rate (12.4%) and the Hospital (Medicare) Insurance tax rate (2.9%). The sum of these rates is 15.3% (12.4% + 2.9% = 15.3%). One-half (½) of the combined rate is 7.65% (15.3% x ½ = 7.65%). The deduction can be computed by multiplying the net earnings from self-employment (determined without regard to Section 1402(a)(12) of the Code) by 92.35%. This gives the same deduction as multiplying the net earnings from self-employment (determined without regard to Section 1402(a)(12) of the Code) by 7.65% and then subtracting the result.

For example, the Social Security taxes imposed on monthly net earnings from self-employment (determined without regard to Section 1402(a)(12) of the Code) of $2,500.00 are calculated as follows:
(i) Old-Age, Survivors and Disability Insurance Taxes:
$2,500.00 x 92.35% x 12.4% = $286.29
(ii) Hospital (Medicare) Insurance Taxes:
$2,500.00 x 92.35% x 2.9% = $66.95

*** When income exceeds $200,000.00 per year there is an additional Medicare Tax of 0.9%. The additional Medicare Tax does not apply to any values shown on this chart because the highest gross income included is $15,000.00 per month ($180,000.00 per year).

**** These amounts represent one-twelfth (1/12) of the annual federal income tax calculated for a single taxpayer claiming one personal exemption ($4,050.00, subject to reduction in certain cases, as described below in this footnote) and taking the standard deduction ($6,350.00).

In calculating the annual federal income tax, gross income is reduced by the deduction under Section 164(f) of the Code. For example, monthly net earnings from self-employment of $8,500.00 times 12 months equals $102,000.00. The Old-Age, Survivors and Disability Insurance taxes imposed by Section 1401 of the Code for the taxable year equal $9,796.49 ($102,000.00 x .9235 x 12.4% = $11,680.43). The Hospital (Medicare) Insurance taxes imposed by Section 1401 of the Code for the taxable year equal $2,731.71 ($102,000.00 x .9235 x 2.9% = $2,731.71). The deduction under Section 164(f) of the Code for 2014 is equal to $7,206.08 (($11,680.43 x 0.5) + ($2,731.72 x 0.5) = $7,206.08).

For a single taxpayer with an adjusted gross income in excess of $261,500.00, the deduction for the personal exemption is reduced by two percent (2%) for each $2,500.00 or fraction thereof by which adjusted gross income exceeds $261,500.00. The reduction is completed (i.e., the deduction for the personal exemption is eliminated) for adjusted gross income in excess of $384,000.00. In no case is the deduction for the personal exemption reduced by more than 100%. The phase out of the Personal Exemption does not apply to any values shown on this chart because the highest income included is $15,000.00 per month ($180,000.00 per year).

***** For annual net earnings from self-employment (determined with regard to Section 1402(a)(12) of the Code) above $127,200.00, this amount represents a monthly average of the Old-Age, Survivors and Disability Insurance tax based on the 2017 maximum Old-Age, Survivors and Disability Insurance tax of $15,772.80 per person (12.4% of the first $127,200.00 of net earnings from self-employment (determined with regard to Section 1402(a)(12) of the Code) equals $15,772.80). One-twelfth (1/12) of $15,772.80 equals $1,314.40.

****** This amount represents the point where the monthly net earnings from self-employment of a self-employed individual would result in $8,550.00 of net resources. Texas Family Code section 154.125 provides "The guidelines for the support of a child in this section are specifically designed to apply to situations in which the obligor's monthly net resources are not greater than $7,500 or the adjusted amount determined under Subsection (a-1), whichever is greater." Effective September 1, 2013 the adjusted amount determined under Subsection (a-1) is $8,550.00.

REFERENCES RELATING TO SELF-EMPLOYED PERSONS 2017 TAX CHART:

1. Old-Age, Survivors and Disability Insurance Tax

(a) Contribution Base

(1) Social Security Administration's notice appearing in 81 Fed. Reg. 74854 (October 27, 2016)

(2) Section 1402(b) of the Internal Revenue Code of 1986, as amended (26 U.S.C. §1402(b))

(3) Section 230 of the Social Security Act, as amended (42 U.S.C. §430)

(b) Tax Rate

(1) Section 1401(a) of the Internal Revenue Code of 1986, as amended (26 U.S.C. §1401(a))

(c) Deduction Under Section 1402(a)(12)

(1) Section 1402(a)(12) of the Internal Revenue Code of 1986, as amended (26 U.S.C. §1402(a)(12))

2. Hospital (Medicare) Insurance Tax

(a) Contribution Base

(1) Section 1402(b) of the Internal Revenue Code of 1986, as amended (26 U.S.C. §1402(b))

(2) Omnibus Budget Reconciliation Act of 1993, Pub. L. No. 103-66, §13207, 107 Stat. 312, 467-69 (1993)

(b) Tax Rate

(1) Section 1401(b) of the Internal Revenue Code of 1986, as amended (26 U.S.C. §1401(b))

(c) Deduction Under Section 1402(a)(12)

(1) Section 1402(a)(12) of the Internal Revenue Code of 1986, as amended (26 U.S.C. §1402(a)(12))

3. Federal Income Tax

(a) Tax Rate Schedule for 2017 for Single Taxpayers

(1) Revenue Procedure 2016-55, Section 3.01, Table 3 which appears in Internal Revenue Bulletin 2016-45, dated November 7, 2016

(2) Section 1(c), (f) and (i) of the Internal Revenue Code of 1986, as amended (26 U.S.C. §1(c), 1(f), 1(i))

(b) Standard Deduction

(1) Revenue Procedure 2016-55, Section 3.14, which appears in Internal Revenue Bulletin 2016-45, dated November 7, 2016

(2) Section 63(c) of the Internal Revenue Code of 1986, as amended (26 U.S.C. §63(c))

(c) Personal Exemption

(1) Revenue Procedure 2016-55, Section 3.24, which appears in Internal Revenue Bulletin 2016-45, dated November 7, 2016

(2) Section 151(d) of the Internal Revenue Code of 1986, as amended (26 U.S.C. §151(d))

(d) Deduction Under Section 164(f)

(1) Section 164(f) of the Internal Revenue Code of 1986, as amended (26 U.S.C. §164(f))

4. Adjusted amount determined under Subsection (a-1) of Texas Family Code section 154.125

Office of the Attorney General "Announcement of Adjustment Required by Texas Family Code section 154.125" appearing in 38 TexReg 4647 (July 19, 2013)

FAM §154.062. NET RESOURCES[1]

(a) The court shall calculate net resources for the purpose of determining child support liability as provided by this section.

(b) Resources include:

(1) 100 percent of all wage and salary income and other compensation for personal services (including commissions, overtime pay, tips, and bonuses);

(2) interest, dividends, and royalty income;

(3) self-employment income;

(4) net rental income (defined as rent after deducting operating expenses and mortgage payments, but not including noncash items such as depreciation); and

(5) all other income actually being received, including severance pay, retirement benefits, pensions, trust income, annuities, capital gains, social security benefits other than supplemental security income, United States Department of Veterans Affairs disability benefits other than non-service-connected disability pension benefits, as defined by 38 U.S.C. Section 101(17), unemployment benefits, disability and workers' compensation benefits, interest income from notes regardless of the source, gifts and prizes, spousal maintenance, and alimony.

(c) Resources do not include:

(1) return of principal or capital;

(2) accounts receivable;

(3) benefits paid in accordance with the Temporary Assistance for Needy Families program or another federal public assistance program; or

(4) payments for foster care of a child.

(d) The court shall deduct the following items from resources to determine the net resources available for child support:

(1) social security taxes;

(2) federal income tax based on the tax rate for a single person claiming one personal exemption and the standard deduction;

(3) state income tax;

(4) union dues;

(5) expenses for the cost of health insurance or cash medical support for the obligor's child ordered by the court under Section 154.182; and

(6) if the obligor does not pay social security taxes, nondiscretionary retirement plan contributions.

(e) In calculating the amount of the deduction for health care coverage for a child under Subsection (d)(5), if the obligor has other minor dependents covered under the same health insurance plan, the court shall divide the total cost to the obligor for the insurance by the total number of minor dependents, including the child, covered under the plan.

(f) For purposes of Subsection (d)(6), a nondiscretionary retirement plan is a plan to which an employee is required to contribute as a condition of employment.

1. **Editor's note:** In 2015, the Legislature amended §154.062 to require dental support for a child subject to a child-support order, but the amendments are not effective until Sept. 1, 2018. For the text of the prospective amendments, see Acts 2015, 84th Leg., ch. 1150, §11, eff. Sept. 1, 2018.

History of Fam. Code §154.062: Acts 1995, 74th Leg., ch. 20, §1, eff. Apr. 20, 1995. Amended by Acts 1995, 74th Leg., ch. 751, §41, eff. Sept. 1, 1995; Acts 2007, 80th Leg., ch. 363, §1 (eff. Sept. 1, 2007), ch. 620, §1 (eff. Sept. 1, 2007); Acts 2009, 81st Leg., ch. 87, §9.001 (eff. Sept. 1, 2009), ch. 767, §4 (eff. June 19, 2009), ch. 834, §1 (eff. Sept. 1, 2009), ch. 1118, §1 (eff. Sept. 1, 2009); Acts 2011, 82nd Leg., ch. 91, §9.001 (eff. Sept. 1, 2011), ch. 932, §1 (eff. Sept. 1, 2012); Acts 2013, 83rd Leg., ch. 1046, §1, eff. Sept. 1, 2013. Source: Former Fam. Code §14.053(b).

See also *O'Connor's Texas Family Law Handbook* (2017), "Calculating Current Child Support," ch. 4-F, §13, p. 541.

ANNOTATIONS

Reagins v. Walker, ___ S.W.3d ___ (Tex.App.—Houston [14th Dist.] 2017, no pet.) (No. 14-15-00764-CV; 3-7-17). Mother "admitted to having to resort to internet searches to get any information regarding [father's] employment. She did not, however, offer any specifics regarding the types of searches she conducted 'on the Internet,' what search engines she may have used, or what websites she visited to obtain the information provided. She did not provide any specifics about [father's] employer, his position with the company, whether that work was on a full-time, part-time, or contract basis, or whether his job description was petroleum engineer. [¶] The defect in this testimony is not the fact that it was based on internet research. The problem here is that [mother] merely speculated regarding what [father] might make based on general information she obtained on the internet. [Mother's] testimony failed to establish that at the time of trial, [father] was currently employed, was employed as a petroleum engineer, or was employed earning any particular salary or even a salary within the stated range. [Mother's] testimony was simply too speculative to support the trial court's finding [of father's] salary…."

In re P.C.S., 320 S.W.3d 525, 537 (Tex.App.—Dallas 2010, pet. denied). "[W]e conclude the legislature's intent is that all receipts of money that are not specifically excluded by [§154.062(c)], whether nonrecurring or periodic, whether derived from the obligor's capital

or labor or from that of others, must be included in the definition of 'resources.' ... We conclude the language of [§154.062(b)(5)] creates a catch-all provision, and a cash inheritance is a 'resource' pursuant to that provision." *See also* ***In re A.M.P.***, 368 S.W.3d 842, 849 (Tex. App.—Houston [14th Dist.] 2012, no pet.) (modification suit; advance on inheritance was "resource" under §152.062(b)).

In re A.A.G., 303 S.W.3d 739, 739-40 (Tex.App.—Waco 2009, no pet.). "The sole issue ... is whether monies received as part of a structured settlement annuity are considered in the calculation of 'net resources' for purposes of calculating child support under [§154.062(b)(5) and (c)]. *At 741:* [T]he trial court needed to decide ... what portion of the payments being received represent a return of principal [not a resource] and what portion represents the interest being earned for the use or forbearance of the entire amount of the settlement proceeds [a resource]. *At 742:* [T]he exclusion of the entire annuity ... was erroneous...." *See also* ***Farish v. Farish***, 921 S.W.2d 538, 543 (Tex. App.—Beaumont 1996, no writ) (under §154.062(c), "the return of principal or capital" refers to return on a note, not to capital gains earned from sale of assets).

In re J.D.D., 242 S.W.3d 916, 922 (Tex.App.—Dallas 2008, pet. denied). Obligor's "duty to pay support is not limited to his ability to pay from current earnings, but also extends to his ability to pay from any and all sources that might be available."

In re L.R.P., 98 S.W.3d 312, 314 (Tex.App.—Houston [1st Dist.] 2003, pet. dism'd). Obligor "is not a working adult.... Rather, he is a college student. His father does not give him occasional gifts of money; he gives [obligor] a fixed amount of money each month to pay for his living expenses. We liken the monthly amount ... father sends to [obligor] to spousal maintenance; thus, we are persuaded that this kind of ongoing support falls within the purview of [§154.062]."

Norris v. Norris, 56 S.W.3d 333, 340 (Tex.App.—El Paso 2001, no pet.). "[W]hile it would be preferable for a trial court to find specific sums for net resources in the normal wage earner's or salaried person's case, where a person's income and net resources vary a great deal from month to month, it may only be possible to state a range of net resources. This is not prohibited provided the range is supported by the evidence." *See also* ***In re Marriage of Bertram***, 981 S.W.2d 820, 828 (Tex.App.—Texarkana 1998, no pet.) (trial court may predicate child support on former certain income as opposed to current uncertain income).

In re S.B.C., 952 S.W.2d 15, 19 (Tex.App.—San Antonio 1997, no writ). "Because courts may look to assets other than income when determining whether an obligor can reasonably afford the ordered child support, and a court may look to earning potential upon a finding of intentional unemployment, it was reasonable for the trial court ... to conclude that in light of his education, work experience, and ability to either sell or use his house as an income-producing asset, [obligor] could reasonably afford to pay the existing support order."

FAM §154.063. PARTY TO FURNISH INFORMATION

The court shall require a party to:

(1) furnish information sufficient to accurately identify that party's net resources and ability to pay child support; and

(2) produce copies of income tax returns for the past two years, a financial statement, and current pay stubs.

History of Fam. Code §154.063: Acts 1995, 74th Leg., ch. 20, §1, eff. Apr. 20, 1995. Source: Former Fam. Code §14.053(g).

FAM §154.064. MEDICAL SUPPORT FOR CHILD PRESUMPTIVELY PROVIDED BY OBLIGOR[1]

The guidelines for support of a child are based on the assumption that the court will order the obligor to provide medical support for the child in addition to the amount of child support calculated in accordance with those guidelines.

1. **Editor's note:** In 2015, the Legislature amended §154.064 to require dental support for a child subject to a child-support order, but the amendments are not effective until Sept. 1, 2018. For the text of the prospective amendments, see Acts 2015, 84th Leg., ch. 1150, §12, eff. Sept. 1, 2018.

History of Fam. Code §154.064: Acts 1995, 74th Leg., ch. 20, §1, eff. Apr. 20, 1995. Amended by Acts 2001, 77th Leg., ch. 1023, §7, eff. Sept. 1, 2001. Source: Former Fam. Code §14.053(d).

ANNOTATIONS

In re H.J.W., 302 S.W.3d 511, 514-15 (Tex.App.—Dallas 2009, no pet.). Father "argues that, because the amount of the monthly social security disability benefits [mother] now receives for the children is almost double the amount of his original child support obligation ..., the trial court should not have ordered him to continue to pay medical support. The child support guidelines assume the court will order an obligor to provide medical support in addition to the amount of

support calculated pursuant to the child support guidelines. The amount of medical support is thus separate and distinct from the amount required pursuant to the child support guidelines. ... Unlike [Fam. Code] §154.132, which requires the trial court to deduct the amount of disability payments the children receive from the amount due under the child support guidelines, the family code has no similar provision relating to medical support." *See also* ***Kish v. Kole***, 874 S.W.2d 835, 837 (Tex.App.—Beaumont 1994, no writ) (awarding offset against child support for providing health insurance was inappropriate because medical support is ordered in addition to child support under Fam. Code).

FAM §154.065. SELF-EMPLOYMENT INCOME

(a) Income from self-employment, whether positive or negative, includes benefits allocated to an individual from a business or undertaking in the form of a proprietorship, partnership, joint venture, close corporation, agency, or independent contractor, less ordinary and necessary expenses required to produce that income.

(b) In its discretion, the court may exclude from self-employment income amounts allowable under federal income tax law as depreciation, tax credits, or any other business expenses shown by the evidence to be inappropriate in making the determination of income available for the purpose of calculating child support.

History of Fam. Code §154.065: Acts 1995, 74th Leg., ch. 20, §1, eff. Apr. 20, 1995. Source: Former Fam. Code §14.053(c).

ANNOTATIONS

Powell v. Swanson, 893 S.W.2d 161, 164 (Tex. App.—Houston [1st Dist.] 1995, no writ). Obligee "contends that the deduction of business depreciation from [obligee's] adjusted gross income was erroneous. ... The Family Code provides that the trial court may decline deduction of depreciation if the evidence shows that the deduction is 'inappropriate to the determination of income for the purpose of calculating child support.' 'Net rental income' is defined in [Fam. Code] §14.053(b) [now §154.062] as 'rent after deducting operating expenses and mortgage payments, but not including noncash items such as depreciation.' We interpret these two sections to mean that depreciation is not to be included in the calculation of net rental income for the purpose of determining child support. [Obligor's] adjusted gross income should have been increased by the amount of the depreciation deducted from [obligor's] gross income on his federal income tax return."

FAM §154.066. INTENTIONAL UNEMPLOYMENT OR UNDEREMPLOYMENT

(a) If the actual income of the obligor is significantly less than what the obligor could earn because of intentional unemployment or underemployment, the court may apply the support guidelines to the earning potential of the obligor.

(b) In determining whether an obligor is intentionally unemployed or underemployed, the court may consider evidence that the obligor is a veteran, as defined by 38 U.S.C. Section 101(2), who is seeking or has been awarded:

(1) United States Department of Veterans Affairs disability benefits, as defined by 38 U.S.C. Section 101(16); or

(2) non-service-connected disability pension benefits, as defined by 38 U.S.C. Section 101(17).

History of Fam. Code §154.066: Acts 1995, 74th Leg., ch. 20, §1, eff. Apr. 20, 1995. Amended by Acts 2013, 83rd Leg., ch. 1046, §2, eff. Sept. 1, 2013. Source: Former Fam. Code §14.053(f).

See also ***O'Connor's Texas Family Law Handbook*** (2017), "Intentional unemployment or underemployment," ch. 4-F, §13.1.1(1)(a)[2], p. 542.

ANNOTATIONS

Iliff v. Iliff, 339 S.W.3d 74, 76 (Tex.2011). "[M]ay a trial court calculate child support based on earning potential, rather than actual earnings, when the obligor is intentionally unemployed or underemployed, but there is no proof that the obligor's unemployment or underemployment is for the purpose of avoiding child support? Because the language of ... §154.066 does not require such proof, we hold that intent to avoid child support need not be proven for the trial court to apply the child support guidelines to earning potential instead of actual earnings. However, a trial court may properly consider an obligor's intent to avoid child support as a factor, along with other relevant facts, in an intentional unemployment or underemployment analysis. *At 81-82:* A parent who is qualified to obtain gainful employment cannot evade his or her child support obligation by voluntarily remaining unemployed or underemployed. Concurrently, the court must consider 'a parent's right to pursue his or her own happiness,' ... with a parent's duty to support and provide for his or her child. The court must engage in a case-by-case determination to decide whether child support should be set based on

earning potential as opposed to actual earnings. [¶] Trial courts should be cautious of setting child support based on earning potential in every case where an obligor makes less money than he or she has in the past. [T]he statute [is limited] only to situations where the obligor makes 'significantly less' money because of intentional unemployment or underemployment."

In re N.T.P., 402 S.W.3d 13, 21 (Tex.App.—San Antonio 2012, no pet.). Father "voluntarily retired from the Air Force after 33 years of service and he voluntarily moved to England to be with his second wife. The question then becomes whether [father] is intentionally underemployed. ... As for a return to his former career as a nurse, [he] said nursing would not be 'well-suited to long-term' because of his disabilities. [Father] testified that one of the reasons he decided to retire was because he failed his last fitness test. ... He agreed that a nurse with his experience, training, and skills is capable of earning $60,000 to $90,000 per year. *At 22:* Here, on this record, we cannot say the trial court erred by granting [father's] petition based on [his] actual earnings rather than on his earning potential."

FAM §154.067. DEEMED INCOME

(a) When appropriate, in order to determine the net resources available for child support, the court may assign a reasonable amount of deemed income attributable to assets that do not currently produce income. The court shall also consider whether certain property that is not producing income can be liquidated without an unreasonable financial sacrifice because of cyclical or other market conditions. If there is no effective market for the property, the carrying costs of such an investment, including property taxes and note payments, shall be offset against the income attributed to the property.

(b) The court may assign a reasonable amount of deemed income to income-producing assets that a party has voluntarily transferred or on which earnings have intentionally been reduced.

History of Fam. Code §154.067: Acts 1995, 74th Leg., ch. 20, §1, eff. Apr. 20, 1995. Source: Former Fam. Code §14.053(e).

ANNOTATIONS

Roosth v. Roosth, 889 S.W.2d 445, 455 (Tex.App.—Houston [14th Dist.] 1994, writ denied). Obligor's inventory "indicates an ownership interest in four real estate rental partnerships and an interest in four oil & gas production partnerships. ... Although his income tax records indicate some distributions, [obligor] contended he did not physically receive cash distributions. Instead, [obligor] maintained that these distributions went directly to pay off tax liabilities. [¶] [Family Code] §14.053(e) [now §154.067] allows a trial court to assign a reasonable amount of income attributable to assets that do not currently produce income. Furthermore, the duty to support is not limited to a parent's ability to pay from current earnings, but extends to his financial ability to pay from any and all available sources. Based on the evidence, we find no abuse of discretion by the trial court in requiring [obligor] to pay $3,000.00 per month in child support." (Internal quotes omitted.)

FAM §154.068. WAGE & SALARY PRESUMPTION

(a) In the absence of evidence of a party's resources, as defined by Section 154.062(b), the court shall presume that the party has income equal to the federal minimum wage for a 40-hour week to which the support guidelines may be applied.

(b) The presumption required by Subsection (a) does not apply if the court finds that the party is subject to an order of confinement that exceeds 90 days and is incarcerated in a local, state, or federal jail or prison at the time the court makes the determination regarding the party's income.

History of Fam. Code §154.068: Acts 1995, 74th Leg., ch. 20, §1, eff. Apr. 20, 1995. Amended by Acts 2013, 83rd Leg., ch. 1046, §3, eff. Sept. 1, 2013; Acts 2015, 84th Leg., ch. 1249, §1, eff. Sept. 1, 2015. Source: Former Fam. Code §14.053(k).

See also *O'Connor's Texas Family Law Handbook* (2017), "Wage & salary income," ch. 4-F, §13.1.1(1)(a), p. 541.

FAM §154.069. NET RESOURCES OF SPOUSE

(a) The court may not add any portion of the net resources of a spouse to the net resources of an obligor or obligee in order to calculate the amount of child support to be ordered.

(b) The court may not subtract the needs of a spouse, or of a dependent of a spouse, from the net resources of the obligor or obligee.

History of Fam. Code §154.069: Acts 1995, 74th Leg., ch. 20, §1, eff. Apr. 20, 1995. Source: Former Fam. Code §14.056(c).

See also *O'Connor's Texas Family Law Handbook* (2017), "Not net resources," ch. 4-F, §13.1.1(2), p. 545.

ANNOTATIONS

In re Knott, 118 S.W.3d 899, 904 (Tex.App.—Texarkana 2003, no pet.). The Family Code "does not require the inclusion of a spouse's income from dividends, capital gains, and interest income, even though

these items might otherwise be characterized as community property absent a premarital agreement because (1) the Family Code defines 'resources' as one's salary, interest, dividends, and capital gains, and (2) the Family Code forbids inclusion of the net resources of the obligor's new spouse in computing the obligor's child support payment. Thus, a portion of the spouse's assets that might traditionally be labeled as community property but are derivative of the spouse's separate property or employment are outside the items which comprise the obligor's 'net resources' because they would fall entirely within the 'net resources' of the obligor's spouse." *See also* ***Koenig v. DeBerry***, No. 03-09-00252-CV (Tex.App.—Austin 2010, no pet.) (memo op.; 3-17-10) (community-property income that was subject to sole management and control of obligor spouse should have been included in calculating net resources); ***In re J.C.K.***, 143 S.W.3d 131, 138 (Tex.App.—Waco 2004, no pet.) (community-property income subject to sole management and control of nonobligor spouse should not be included in calculating net resources).

Starck v. Nelson, 878 S.W.2d 302, 305-06 (Tex. App.—Corpus Christi 1994, no writ). Obligor "claims that the trial court erred because it considered [his new W's] income. [T]he court did not use [his new W's] income to calculate [his] net resources; however, the court considered [his] remarriage in deviating from child support guidelines. The trial court found that [his new W's] contribution to their joint living expenses enabled [obligor] to pay more child support than if he were solely responsible for his living expenses. [¶] The precise language of [Fam. Code §14.056(c), now §154.069,] does not prohibit the trial court's action in this case. [However, permitting] the court to deviate from child support guidelines because the obligor's new spouse contributes to their joint living expenses allows the court to do indirectly what the statute directly prohibits." Held: Trial court should not have considered income of obligor's new W.

FAM §154.070. CHILD SUPPORT RECEIVED BY OBLIGOR

In a situation involving multiple households due child support, child support received by an obligor shall be added to the obligor's net resources to compute the net resources before determining the child support credit or applying the percentages in the multiple household table in this chapter.

History of Fam. Code §154.070: Acts 1995, 74th Leg., ch. 20, §1, eff. Apr. 20, 1995. Source: Former Fam. Code §14.055(i).

Sections 154.071-154.120 reserved for expansion

SUBCHAPTER C. CHILD SUPPORT GUIDELINES

FAM §154.121. GUIDELINES FOR THE SUPPORT OF A CHILD

The child support guidelines in this subchapter are intended to guide the court in determining an equitable amount of child support.

History of Fam. Code §154.121: Acts 1995, 74th Leg., ch. 20, §1, eff. Apr. 20, 1995. Source: Former Fam. Code §14.052(a).

FAM §154.122. APPLICATION OF GUIDELINES REBUTTABLY PRESUMED IN BEST INTEREST OF CHILD

(a) The amount of a periodic child support payment established by the child support guidelines in effect in this state at the time of the hearing is presumed to be reasonable, and an order of support conforming to the guidelines is presumed to be in the best interest of the child.

(b) A court may determine that the application of the guidelines would be unjust or inappropriate under the circumstances.

History of Fam. Code §154.122: Acts 1995, 74th Leg., ch. 20, §1, eff. Apr. 20, 1995. Source: Former Fam. Code §§14.05(j), 14.055(a).

FAM §154.123. ADDITIONAL FACTORS FOR COURT TO CONSIDER

(a) The court may order periodic child support payments in an amount other than that established by the guidelines if the evidence rebuts the presumption that application of the guidelines is in the best interest of the child and justifies a variance from the guidelines.

(b) In determining whether application of the guidelines would be unjust or inappropriate under the circumstances, the court shall consider evidence of all relevant factors, including:

(1) the age and needs of the child;

(2) the ability of the parents to contribute to the support of the child;

(3) any financial resources available for the support of the child;

(4) the amount of time of possession of and access to a child;

(5) the amount of the obligee's net resources, including the earning potential of the obligee if the actual

income of the obligee is significantly less than what the obligee could earn because the obligee is intentionally unemployed or underemployed and including an increase or decrease in the income of the obligee or income that may be attributed to the property and assets of the obligee;

(6) child care expenses incurred by either party in order to maintain gainful employment;

(7) whether either party has the managing conservatorship or actual physical custody of another child;

(8) the amount of alimony or spousal maintenance actually and currently being paid or received by a party;

(9) the expenses for a son or daughter for education beyond secondary school;

(10) whether the obligor or obligee has an automobile, housing, or other benefits furnished by his or her employer, another person, or a business entity;

(11) the amount of other deductions from the wage or salary income and from other compensation for personal services of the parties;

(12) provision for health care insurance and payment of uninsured medical expenses;

(13) special or extraordinary educational, health care, or other expenses of the parties or of the child;

(14) the cost of travel in order to exercise possession of and access to a child;

(15) positive or negative cash flow from any real and personal property and assets, including a business and investments;

(16) debts or debt service assumed by either party; and

(17) any other reason consistent with the best interest of the child, taking into consideration the circumstances of the parents.

History of Fam. Code §154.123: Acts 1995, 74th Leg., ch. 20, §1, eff. Apr. 20, 1995. Source: Former Fam. Code §§14.052(b), 14.054.

See also *O'Connor's Texas Family Law Handbook* (2017), "Deviating from child-support guidelines," ch. 4-F, §13.3, p. 550.

ANNOTATIONS

Rodriguez v. Rodriguez, 860 S.W.2d 414, 417 (Tex. 1993). The factors listed in Fam. Code §14.052(b), now §154.123(b)(1)-(4), and Fam. Code §14.054, now §154.123(b)(5)-(17), "provide bases for variance from strict application of the percentage guidelines, but only apply to the first $4,000 [now $7,500] of net resources."

Tran v. Nguyen, 480 S.W.3d 119, 127 (Tex.App.—Houston [14th Dist.] 2015, no pet.). "The court ... awarded to [mother the father's] share of the home equity as a lump sum payment of the child support obligation. [Father] urges ... that in the absence of any evidence regarding his income while in prison [for sexually assaulting his stepdaughter], the trial court should have based his child support obligation on the presumption that he made the federal minimum wage for a 40-hour workweek, which would have been less in aggregate than what the trial court awarded. *At 129:* Viewing the evidence in light of the factors set forth in §154.123, the trial court reasonably could have determined that [children] needed support; [father] would likely be unemployed for the duration of the children's minority years; [mother] would have possession of the children 100% of the time and had custody of another child; [father's] equity interest in the house was an available financial resource; and given [father's] incarceration, it was just and appropriate not to apply the child support guidelines to the minimum wage presumption, but instead to order his equity interest in the home as a lump sum child support payment."

Smith v. Smith, 143 S.W.3d 206, 217 (Tex.App.—Waco 2004, no pet.). "When a trial court establishes the amount of child support a parent must pay, the court must consider that parent's ability to contribute to the child's support. Each parent should support the child commensurate with his ability to pay; however, the amount paid should not be so great as to deny that parent the necessary expenses of living. The child support order implies a finding that the obligor has the ability to pay the amount ordered."

In re J.C.K., 143 S.W.3d 131, 138 (Tex.App.—Waco 2004, no pet.). "[R]esources of a non-obligor spouse should not be the sole basis to vary from the guidelines. However, if the obligee presents evidence that the obligor has intentionally or voluntarily reduced his earnings or earning potential, then the best interest of the child may dictate that the resources of a non-obligor spouse should be considered in deciding whether to vary from the guidelines."

Sanchez v. Sanchez, 915 S.W.2d 99, 102-03 (Tex. App.—San Antonio 1996, no writ). "The ... Family Code permits the court to render a final determination of support outside the range recommended by the guidelines if other relevant factors justify such a variance. Expressly included in the factors the court must consider in making its final determination are whether either party has the managing conservatorship or ac-

tual physical custody of another child and debts or debt service assumed by either party. Thus, consideration of the amount of debt service assumed by [father] and the split custody of the children are expressly authorized by [Fam. Code] §14.054 [now §154.123]. Since the note payments would clearly increase the amount of resources available to [mother], while decreasing the amount of resources available to [father], it cannot be said that considering the note payment to be a relevant factor is without reference to any guiding rules and principles. Although it is not a factor expressly listed in §14.054, it is clear that the list is not exclusive and the court may consider any factor it deems relevant." *See also* ***Roosth v. Roosth***, 889 S.W.2d 445, 454 (Tex. App.—Houston [14th Dist.] 1994, writ denied) (fact that father chose to live off gifts from father-in-law was relevant even though it was not factor listed under §154.123).

Belcher v. Belcher, 808 S.W.2d 202, 208 (Tex. App.—El Paso 1991, no writ), *overruled on other grounds*, ***Rodriguez v. Rodriguez***, 860 S.W.2d 414 (Tex. 1993). "[W]e believe the intent of the legislature in enacting [Fam. Code] §14.054(1) [now §154.123(5)] was to prevent an obligee from intentionally remaining unemployed or underemployed in order to gain an increase in child support, not to prevent an obligee from seeking to improve him or herself educationally so that he or she can hold a better or a permanent job. [Mother's] circumstances are distinguishable from a situation in which a woman decides on her own that her children need a full-time mother and quits working. Her unemployment was for a finite period of short duration while she completed her education which would presumably enable her to obtain steady and permanent employment. The evidence shows that she intended to maintain a full-time job as soon as she received her teaching certificate."

FAM §154.124. AGREEMENT CONCERNING SUPPORT

(a) To promote the amicable settlement of disputes between the parties to a suit, the parties may enter into a written agreement containing provisions for support of the child and for modification of the agreement, including variations from the child support guidelines provided by Subchapter C.

(b) If the court finds that the agreement is in the child's best interest, the court shall render an order in accordance with the agreement.

(c) Terms of the agreement pertaining to child support in the order may be enforced by all remedies available for enforcement of a judgment, including contempt, but are not enforceable as a contract.

(d) If the court finds the agreement is not in the child's best interest, the court may request the parties to submit a revised agreement or the court may render an order for the support of the child.

History of Fam. Code §154.124: Acts 1995, 74th Leg., ch. 20, §1, eff. Apr. 20, 1995. Amended by Acts 2003, 78th Leg., ch. 480, §1, eff. Sept. 1, 2003. Source: Former Fam. Code §§14.053(j), 14.06.

See also ***O'Connor's Texas Family Law Handbook*** (2017), "Settlement – support agreement," ch. 4-F, §11.3, p. 539.

ANNOTATIONS

Seabourne v. Seabourne, 493 S.W.3d 222, 225 (Tex.App.—Texarkana 2016, no pet.). Obligor "claims that the trial court lacked the authority to enter judgment because the provision of the final decree requiring that each party pay one-half of the children's college tuition constituted a postmajority support provision which was not established by a separate written agreement. *At 228:* The decree in this case ... includes a separate section for child support which requires periodic payments and which terminated under terms separate and distinct from the college-tuition provision. [T]he college-tuition provision in this case was ... included in a separate section of the decree. Here, that section was specifically listed as 'College Tuition.' We therefore conclude that the college-tuition provision of the decree here was not child support. [¶] Because the college-tuition provision here is not an agreement for child support, it is subject to enforcement as a contract. Here, the parties entered into an agreed divorce decree, which is a contract."

Bartlett v. Bartlett, 465 S.W.3d 745, 747 (Tex. App.—Houston [14th Dist.] 2015, no pet.). Mother "sued [father] for breach of contract after the couple divorced pursuant to an agreed decree and [father] refused to reimburse [mother] for their son's college expenses. *At 749-50:* [A] 'payment which is not to be made until after the child reaches the age of 18 is not child support.' ... 'Child support, by definition, applies only to a child under the age of 18 years who has not yet graduated from high school or a high-school equivalent program.' [C]hild support [can be distinguished] from 'post-majority support,' which 'applies only to a non-disabled child who is 18 years of age or older and is no longer enrolled in high school or a high-school equivalent program.' '[P]ost-majority support is not child sup-

port.' Consequently, ... §154.124(c), which prohibits enforcement of child support by a breach of contract action, [does] not apply to [a] claim for post-majority expenses (such as college expenses)." *See also* ***In re W.R.B.***, this page.

In re D.B.J., 459 S.W.3d 169, 172 (Tex.App.—Houston [14th Dist.] 2015, no pet.). Mother "maintains that the divorce decree was entered in accordance with an agreement between the parties for a continuation of support after [child] turned 18 and graduated; thus, such support could be enforced by contempt pursuant to [Fam. Code] §154.124(c). *At 174:* Family Code §§154.001 and 154.002 prohibit courts from ordering support for nondisabled children who have reached 18 and graduated from high school. Accordingly, the parties' agreement as set forth in the decree, requiring [father] to provide support for [child] past the child's 18th birthday and graduation from high school, does not meet the Family Code's other requirements for child support and therefore is not enforceable by contempt." *See also* ***In re W.R.B.***, this page.

Kendrick v. Seibert, 439 S.W.3d 408, 410 (Tex. App.—Houston [1st Dist.] 2014, no pet.). See annotation under Family Code §7.006, p. 97.

In re W.R.B., No. 05-12-00776-CV (Tex.App.—Dallas 2014, pet. denied) (memo op.; 2-20-14). "Section 154.124(c) does not prohibit the parties from entering into an agreement addressing post-majority support and enforcing it as a contract. In fact, ... a trial court may not order or enforce post-majority support without an agreement by the parties. Because [mother] did not seek contractual relief on the post-majority support issue, the trial court had no authority to order reimbursement of post-majority support." *See also* ***Bartlett v. Bartlett***, p. 570; ***In re D.B.J.***, this page.

In re M.A.H., 365 S.W.3d 814, 820 (Tex.App.—Dallas 2012, no pet.). See annotation under Family Code §153.007, p. 506.

In re D.S., 76 S.W.3d 512, 518 (Tex.App.—Houston [14th Dist.] 2002, no pet.). "Although a court may not arbitrarily impose automatic or formula increases in child support, if the parties agree on an automatic increase in child support upon the occurrence of a certain event, and the court has found that the agreement is in the best interest of the child, the parties may be ordered to perform in accordance with that agreement; and compliance may be enforced by all available remedies." *See also* ***Cisneros v. Cisneros***, 787 S.W.2d 550, 551-52 (Tex.App.—El Paso 1990, no writ).

McLendon v. McLendon, 847 S.W.2d 601, 608 (Tex.App.—Dallas 1992, writ denied). See annotation under Family Code §153.007, p. 507.

In re Marriage of Edwards, 804 S.W.2d 653, 655 (Tex.App.—Amarillo 1991, no writ). "[A]lthough the contractual agreement of [spouses] is incorporated in the decree of divorce pursuant to [Fam. Code] §14.06 [now §154.124], that section's provisions do not extinguish or limit the court's power to modify the support order to provide for the best interest of the child. Consequently, the trial court had the power to modify the child support provisions incorporated into the decree of divorce."

FAM §154.125. APPLICATION OF GUIDELINES TO NET RESOURCES

(a) The guidelines for the support of a child in this section are specifically designed to apply to situations in which the obligor's monthly net resources are not greater than $7,500 or the adjusted amount determined under Subsection (a-1), whichever is greater.

(a-1) The dollar amount prescribed by Subsection (a) is adjusted every six years as necessary to reflect inflation. The Title IV-D agency shall compute the adjusted amount, to take effect beginning September 1 of the year of the adjustment, based on the percentage change in the consumer price index during the 72-month period preceding March 1 of the year of the adjustment, as rounded to the nearest $50 increment. The Title IV-D agency shall publish the adjusted amount in the Texas Register before September 1 of the year in which the adjustment takes effect. For purposes of this subsection, "consumer price index" has the meaning assigned by Section 341.201, Finance Code.

(a-2) Expired.

(b) If the obligor's monthly net resources are not greater than the amount provided by Subsection (a), the court shall presumptively apply the following schedule in rendering the child support order:

CHILD SUPPORT GUIDELINES	
Based on the monthly net resources of the obligor	
1 child	20% of Obligor's Net Resources
2 children	25% of Obligor's Net Resources
3 children	30% of Obligor's Net Resources

4 children	35% of Obligor's Net Resources
5 children	40% of Obligor's Net Resources
6+ children	Not less than the amount for 5 children

History of Fam. Code §154.125: Acts 1995, 74th Leg., ch. 20, §1, eff. Apr. 20, 1995. Amended by Acts 2007, 80th Leg., ch. 620, §2, eff. Sept. 1, 2007; Acts 2009, 81st Leg., ch. 767, §5, eff. June 19, 2009. Source: Former Fam. Code §14.055(a), (b).

ANNOTATIONS

Escue v. Escue, 810 S.W.2d 845, 847 (Tex.App.—Texarkana 1991, no writ). Family Code §14.055(a), now §154.125, "creates a rebuttable presumption that an order for periodic child support payments established by [child-support guidelines] is reasonable and in the best interest of the child[.] *At 848:* The reference to the number of children in the guidelines is to the number of children involved in the particular suit before the court, not the obligor's total offspring."

FAM §154.126. APPLICATION OF GUIDELINES TO ADDITIONAL NET RESOURCES

(a) If the obligor's net resources exceed the amount provided by Section 154.125(a), the court shall presumptively apply the percentage guidelines to the portion of the obligor's net resources that does not exceed that amount. Without further reference to the percentage recommended by these guidelines, the court may order additional amounts of child support as appropriate, depending on the income of the parties and the proven needs of the child.

(b) The proper calculation of a child support order that exceeds the presumptive amount established for the portion of the obligor's net resources provided by Section 154.125(a) requires that the entire amount of the presumptive award be subtracted from the proven total needs of the child. After the presumptive award is subtracted, the court shall allocate between the parties the responsibility to meet the additional needs of the child according to the circumstances of the parties. However, in no event may the obligor be required to pay more child support than the greater of the presumptive amount or the amount equal to 100 percent of the proven needs of the child.

History of Fam. Code §154.126: Acts 1995, 74th Leg., ch. 20, §1, eff. Apr. 20, 1995. Amended by Acts 2007, 80th Leg., ch. 620, §3, eff. Sept. 1, 2007. Source: Former Fam. Code §14.055(c).

See also ***O'Connor's Texas Family Law Handbook*** (2017), "Determining amount of child support," ch. 4-F, §13.2, p. 547.

ANNOTATIONS

Rodriguez v. Rodriguez, 860 S.W.2d 414, 417 n.3 (Tex.1993). This court concludes "that 'needs of the child' includes more than the bare necessities of life, but is not determined by the parents' ability to pay or the lifestyle of the family. In determining the needs of the child, we direct courts to continue to follow the paramount guiding principle: *the best interest of the child.*"

Nordstrom v. Nordstrom, 965 S.W.2d 575, 579 n.4 (Tex.App.—Houston [1st Dist.] 1997, pet. denied). Based on the clear language of §154.126, "we hold that 'income of the parties' and 'proven needs of the child' are the only factors to be considered in awarding additional support over the presumptive amount for an obligor with over $6,000 [now $7,500 or an adjusted amount] in monthly net resources. *At 581:* Notwithstanding the needs [obligee] may have proven, §154.126 vests the court with the *discretion* to award additional amounts. It *mandates* only that the court consider the needs of the child and the parties' income in arriving at that decision, and that the amount allocated to the obligor not exceed the proven needs of the child. Therefore, even if [obligee] did conclusively prove the needs of the child, it was within the court's discretion to refuse to award additional support."

FAM §154.127. PARTIAL TERMINATION OF SUPPORT OBLIGATION

(a) A child support order for more than one child shall provide that, on the termination of support for a child, the level of support for the remaining child or children is in accordance with the child support guidelines.

(b) A child support order is in compliance with the requirement imposed by Subsection (a) if the order contains a provision that specifies:

(1) the events, including a child reaching the age of 18 years or otherwise having the disabilities of minority removed, that have the effect of terminating the obligor's obligation to pay child support for that child; and

(2) the reduced total amount that the obligor is required to pay each month after the occurrence of an event described by Subdivision (1).

History of Fam. Code §154.127: Acts 1995, 74th Leg., ch. 20, §1, eff. Apr. 20, 1995. Amended by Acts 2007, 80th Leg., ch. 972, §10, eff. Sept. 1, 2007. Source: Former Fam. Code §14.055(d).

ANNOTATIONS

Deltuva v. Deltuva, 113 S.W.3d 882, 886-87 (Tex. App.—Dallas 2003, no pet.). Father "contends the trial court erred by ordering him to pay a fixed amount of child support regardless of the number of children he is obligated to support. [¶] In this case, the divorce decree does not provide for a reduction in child support as [father's] children reach the age of 18 and leave high school. Therefore, we conclude [father] has shown the trial court abused its discretion in this regard…." *See also* ***Flores v. Cuevas***, No. 01-06-00257-CV (Tex. App.—Houston [1st Dist.] 2007, no pet.) (memo op.; 3-1-07) (even though amount awarded to support both children was lower than guideline amount for one child, court abused discretion by not including provision consistent with §154.127).

FAM §154.128. COMPUTING SUPPORT FOR CHILDREN IN MORE THAN ONE HOUSEHOLD

(a) In applying the child support guidelines for an obligor who has children in more than one household, the court shall apply the percentage guidelines in this subchapter by making the following computation:

(1) determine the amount of child support that would be ordered if all children whom the obligor has the legal duty to support lived in one household by applying the schedule in this subchapter;

(2) compute a child support credit for the obligor's children who are not before the court by dividing the amount determined under Subdivision (1) by the total number of children whom the obligor is obligated to support and multiplying that number by the number of the obligor's children who are not before the court;

(3) determine the adjusted net resources of the obligor by subtracting the child support credit computed under Subdivision (2) from the net resources of the obligor; and

(4) determine the child support amount for the children before the court by applying the percentage guidelines for one household for the number of children of the obligor before the court to the obligor's adjusted net resources.

(b) For the purpose of determining a child support credit, the total number of an obligor's children includes the children before the court for the establishment or modification of a support order and any other children, including children residing with the obligor, whom the obligor has the legal duty of support.

(c) The child support credit with respect to children for whom the obligor is obligated by an order to pay support is computed, regardless of whether the obligor is delinquent in child support payments, without regard to the amount of the order.

History of Fam. Code §154.128: Acts 1995, 74th Leg., ch. 20, §1, eff. Apr. 20, 1995. Source: Former Fam. Code §14.055(f)-(h).

FAM §154.129. ALTERNATIVE METHOD OF COMPUTING SUPPORT FOR CHILDREN IN MORE THAN ONE HOUSEHOLD

In lieu of performing the computation under the preceding section, the court may determine the child support amount for the children before the court by applying the percentages in the table below to the obligor's net resources:

MULTIPLE FAMILY ADJUSTED GUIDELINES (% OF NET RESOURCES)

		Number of children before the court						
		1	2	3	4	5	6	7
Number of other children for whom the obligor has a duty of support	0	20.00	25.00	30.00	35.00	40.00	40.00	40.00
	1	17.50	22.50	27.38	32.20	37.33	37.71	38.00
	2	16.00	20.63	25.20	30.33	35.43	36.00	36.44
	3	14.75	19.00	24.00	29.00	34.00	34.67	35.20
	4	13.60	18.33	23.14	28.00	32.89	33.60	34.18
	5	13.33	17.86	22.50	27.22	32.00	32.73	33.33
	6	13.14	17.50	22.00	26.60	31.27	32.00	32.62
	7	13.00	17.22	21.60	26.09	30.67	31.38	32.00

History of Fam. Code §154.129: Acts 1995, 74th Leg., ch. 20, §1, eff. Apr. 20, 1995. Source: Former Fam. Code §14.055(j).

FAM §154.130. FINDINGS IN CHILD SUPPORT ORDER

The amended text in §154.130 is effective for orders rendered on or after Sept. 1, 2017. Orders rendered before Sept. 1, 2017, are governed by the former law in effect at that time.

(a) Without regard to Rules 296 through 299, Texas Rules of Civil Procedure, in rendering an order of child support, the court shall make the findings required by Subsection (b) if:

(1) a party files a written request with the court before the final order is signed, but not later than 20 [~~10~~] days after the date of rendition of the order [~~the hearing~~];

(2) a party makes an oral request in open court during the hearing; or

(3) the amount of child support ordered by the court varies from the amount computed by applying the percentage guidelines under Section 154.125 or 154.129, as applicable.

(a-1) Repealed by S.B. 1237, §12(2), 85th Leg., eff. Sept. 1, 2017.

[~~(a-1)~~] [~~If findings under this section are required as a result of the request by a party under Subsection (a)(1) or (2), the court shall make and enter the findings not later than the 15th day after the date of the party's request.~~]

(b) If findings are required by this section, the court shall state whether the application of the guidelines would be unjust or inappropriate and shall state the following in the child support order:

"(1) the net resources of the obligor per month are $______;

"(2) the net resources of the obligee per month are $______;

"(3) the percentage applied to the obligor's net resources for child support is ______%; and

"(4) if applicable, the specific reasons that the amount of child support per month ordered by the court varies from the amount computed by applying the percentage guidelines under Section 154.125 or 154.129, as applicable."

(c) Findings under Subsection (b)(2) are required only if evidence of the monthly net resources of the obligee has been offered.

History of Fam. Code §154.130: Acts 1995, 74th Leg., ch. 20, §1, eff. Apr. 20, 1995. Amended by Acts 2001, 77th Leg., ch. 1023, §8, eff. Sept. 1, 2001; Acts 2007, 80th Leg., ch. 620, §4, eff. Sept. 1, 2007; Acts 2009, 81st Leg., ch. 767, §§6, 37, eff. June 19, 2009; S.B. 1237, §§10, 12(2), 85th Leg., eff. Sept. 1, 2017. Source: Former Fam. Code §14.057.

See also ***O'Connor's Texas Family Law Handbook*** (2017), "Findings," ch. 4-F, §18.3.8, p. 560; "Findings," ch. 9-D, §17.3.7, p. 1059.

ANNOTATIONS

Rodriguez v. Rodriguez, 860 S.W.2d 414, 418 n.4 (Tex.1993). Family Code §14.057, now §154.130, "does not require a trial court to make findings regarding its basis for the presumptive percentage award. We do not add such a requirement here. We note only that we do not have the benefit of any explanation by the trial court for determining what portion of its award out of the first $4,000 [now $7,500] of net resources are based on the needs of the child. It obviously would be helpful for appellate review of child support awards, when the obligor's net resources exceed [$4,000] per month, to have the benefit of the trial court's findings concerning the basis for the presumptive percentage award, and we commend this practice to our trial courts."

Rumscheidt v. Rumscheidt, 362 S.W.3d 661, 664-65 (Tex.App.—Houston [14th Dist.] 2011, no pet.). "The trial court did not grant [father's] motion to modify child support; therefore, the court was not required to make the specific statutory findings required under [Fam.] Code §154.130. But [father's] request for findings of fact and conclusions of law under [TRCP] 296 and 297 was directed to the trial court's findings and conclusions supporting its decision to *deny* [father's] request to modify his child-support obligation. [Father] timely and properly requested findings of fact and conclusions of law under Rules 296 and 297, and under these rules the trial court was required to file them." *See also* ***In re J.A.H.***, 311 S.W.3d 536, 543 (Tex. App.—El Paso 2009, no pet.) (§154.130 does not require findings on child's proven needs when motion to modify is denied).

Yarbrough v. Yarbrough, 151 S.W.3d 687, 692 (Tex.App.—Waco 2004, no pet.). "Because the percentage guidelines do not apply to net monthly resources exceeding $6,000 [now $7,500 or an adjusted amount], §154.130 does not apply to child support awarded from those resources. Thus, [father] did not fail to preserve this issue for review by failing to request findings under §154.130."

In re Guthrie, 45 S.W.3d 719, 723 (Tex.App.—Dallas 2001, pet. denied). "Retroactive support concerns payment of child support for a period before a child support order. Section 154.130 is directed to the setting of monthly support. Therefore, the refusal to award any retroactive support does not constitute a deviation from the guidelines such that a statutory finding is required."

Starck v. Nelson, 878 S.W.2d 302, 306-07 (Tex. App.—Corpus Christi 1994, no writ). Obligor "complains that the trial court erred by entering a child support order that deviates from child support guidelines without making the necessary findings that the application of the child support guidelines would be unjust or inappropriate as required by §14.057(b) [now §154.130(b)]. [Obligor] never brought the absence of §14.057(b) required findings to the trial court's attention. Although the statute requires the court to make

such a finding without requiring the procedures set out in [TRCP] 296-299, we hold that [obligor's] failure to bring that requirement to the court's attention constitutes a waiver of that complaint."

FAM §154.131. RETROACTIVE CHILD SUPPORT

(a) The child support guidelines are intended to guide the court in determining the amount of retroactive child support, if any, to be ordered.

(b) In ordering retroactive child support, the court shall consider the net resources of the obligor during the relevant time period and whether:

(1) the mother of the child had made any previous attempts to notify the obligor of his paternity or probable paternity;

(2) the obligor had knowledge of his paternity or probable paternity;

(3) the order of retroactive child support will impose an undue financial hardship on the obligor or the obligor's family; and

(4) the obligor has provided actual support or other necessaries before the filing of the action.

(c) It is presumed that a court order limiting the amount of retroactive child support to an amount that does not exceed the total amount of support that would have been due for the four years preceding the date the petition seeking support was filed is reasonable and in the best interest of the child.

(d) The presumption created under this section may be rebutted by evidence that the obligor:

(1) knew or should have known that the obligor was the father of the child for whom support is sought; and

(2) sought to avoid the establishment of a support obligation to the child.

(e) An order under this section limiting the amount of retroactive support does not constitute a variance from the guidelines requiring the court to make specific findings under Section 154.130.

(f) Notwithstanding any other provision of this subtitle, the court retains jurisdiction to render an order for retroactive child support in a suit if a petition requesting retroactive child support is filed not later than the fourth anniversary of the date of the child's 18th birthday.

History of Fam. Code §154.131: Acts 1995, 74th Leg., ch. 20, §1, eff. Apr. 20, 1995. Amended by Acts 2001, 77th Leg., ch. 329, §1 (eff. Sept. 1, 2001), ch. 821, §2.14 (eff. June 14, 2001), ch. 1023, §9 (eff. Sept. 1, 2001); Acts 2007, 80th Leg., ch. 972, §11(a), eff. Sept. 1, 2007. Source: Former Fam. Code §14.053(*l*).

See also ***O'Connor's Texas Family Law Handbook*** (2017), "Calculating Retroactive Child Support," ch. 4-F, §16, p. 556.

ANNOTATIONS

In re B.R., 327 S.W.3d 208, 212 (Tex.App.—San Antonio 2010, no pet.), *disapproved on other grounds*, ***Iliff v. Iliff***, 339 S.W.3d 74 (Tex.2011). "Section 154.131(c)'s presumption applies when the trial court's order *limits* the amount of retroactive child support to an amount not exceeding the total amount of support that would have been due for the four years preceding the date the petition seeking child support was filed. Nowhere does §154.131(c) prohibit a trial court from awarding an amount greater than four years of retroactive child support. That is, if a trial court limits the retroactive child support to the four year amount, the parent seeking more than that amount must rebut the presumption provided by §154.131(c) by proving that the obligor knew or should have known he was the father of the child and that the obligor sought to avoid the establishment of a support obligation to the child. Here, however, the trial court's order did not limit the retroactive child support to an amount representing four years of child support; therefore, §154.131(c)'s presumption was not triggered and does not apply to this case." *See also* ***In re A.B.***, 368 S.W.3d 850, 857-58 (Tex.App.—Houston [14th Dist.] 2012, no pet.) (because court's award of retroactive child support was based on ten years of nonpayments, the four-year presumption under §154.131(c) did not apply).

Randolph v. Randolph, No. 14-04-00180-CV (Tex. App.—Houston [14th Dist.] 2005, no pet.) (memo op.; 9-20-05). "In determining the amount of retroactive support, if any, a trial court must consider the obligor's net resources and certain factors. One factor is whether 'the obligor has provided actual support or other necessaries before the filing of the action.' Therefore, the trial court is allowed to consider an obligor's actions before compliance with any judicially-mandated support schemes. [¶] [T]he trial court could have concluded that [father] had paid a sufficient amount of support before the divorce action was filed. [¶] [E]ven if the amount of voluntary support was limited, the trial court acted within its discretion if it denied retroactive support because [father] had paid *some* [voluntary] support."

In re Valadez, 980 S.W.2d 910, 913 (Tex.App.—Corpus Christi 1998, pet. denied). "We agree with our sister courts that the guidelines are just that when ap-

plied to retroactive support; they are not mandatory, and [Fam. Code] §154.130(a)(3) & (b) requiring the court to specify why they are not being followed does not apply. [¶] 'Retroactive child support' is a repayment of monies expended for the care of the child in the past. It represents funds the nonsupporting parent owed to the child, as well as funds owed the supporting parent to discharge his or her proportionate duty of financial support to the child. In awarding retroactive support a trial court considers not only the support the errant parent should have provided to the child, but also the right to reimbursement afforded someone who has supported the child in the meantime. [¶] We hold a trial court has discretion in deciding whether to award retroactive child support and in deciding the amount of the award. Accordingly we will not reverse the trial court's judgment absent an abuse of discretion." *See also* ***Garza v. Blanton***, 55 S.W.3d 708, 710 (Tex.App.—Corpus Christi 2001, no pet.).

FAM §154.132. APPLICATION OF GUIDELINES TO CHILDREN OF CERTAIN DISABLED OBLIGORS

In applying the child support guidelines for an obligor who has a disability and who is required to pay support for a child who receives benefits as a result of the obligor's disability, the court shall apply the guidelines by determining the amount of child support that would be ordered under the child support guidelines and subtracting from that total the amount of benefits or the value of the benefits paid to or for the child as a result of the obligor's disability.

History of Fam. Code §154.132: Acts 1999, 76th Leg., ch. 891, §1, eff. Sept. 1, 1999.

ANNOTATIONS

In re H.J.W., 302 S.W.3d 511, 513-14 (Tex.App.—Dallas 2009, no pet.). Section 154.132 "entitles [obligor] to a credit for the children's social security payments contemporaneous with [obligor's] support obligation. ... This provision, however, does not require the trial court to order [obligee] to reimburse [obligor] for child support payments previously made once the children receive a lump sum disability award covering the same time period. ... The fact that [obligor] made his monthly child support payments suggests he was capable of meeting his support obligations despite his disability. [W]e have found [no authority] that would mandate reimbursement merely because the children received a lump sum disability payment covering the same time period."

In re G.L.S., 185 S.W.3d 56, 59 (Tex.App.—San Antonio 2005, no pet.). Family Code §154.132 "applies with equal force to the modification of support under [Fam. Code] ch. 156. [T]he record does not reflect that the trial court calculated the amount of child support [obligor] would be required to pay in the future in accordance with §154.132 [by calculating support owed and then deducting disability payments received]. Accordingly, we reverse the portion of the trial court's order establishing the amount of child support [obligor] is required to pay after the date of that order."

FAM §154.133. APPLICATION OF GUIDELINES TO CHILDREN OF OBLIGORS RECEIVING SOCIAL SECURITY

In applying the child support guidelines for an obligor who is receiving social security old age benefits and who is required to pay support for a child who receives benefits as a result of the obligor's receipt of social security old age benefits, the court shall apply the guidelines by determining the amount of child support that would be ordered under the child support guidelines and subtracting from that total the amount of benefits or the value of the benefits paid to or for the child as a result of the obligor's receipt of social security old age benefits.

History of Fam. Code §154.133: Acts 2001, 77th Leg., ch. 544, §1, eff. Sept. 1, 2001.

Sections 154.134-154.180 reserved for expansion

SUBCHAPTER D. MEDICAL SUPPORT FOR CHILD

Editor's note: ***In 2015, the Legislature amended the heading of subchapter D to include dental support for a child, but the amendment is not effective until Sept. 1, 2018. For the text of the prospective amendment, see Acts 2015, 84th Leg., ch. 1150, §13, eff. Sept. 1, 2018.***

FAM §154.181. MEDICAL SUPPORT ORDER

(a) The court shall render an order for the medical support of the child as provided by this section and Section 154.182 in:

(1) a proceeding in which periodic payments of child support are ordered under this chapter or modified under Chapter 156;

(2) any other suit affecting the parent-child relationship in which the court determines that medical support of the child must be established, modified, or clarified; or

(3) a proceeding under Chapter 159.

(b) Before a hearing on temporary orders or a final order, if no hearing on temporary orders is held, the court shall require the parties to the proceedings to disclose in a pleading or other statement:

(1) if private health insurance is in effect for the child, the identity of the insurance company providing the coverage, the policy number, which parent is responsible for payment of any insurance premium for the coverage, whether the coverage is provided through a parent's employment, and the cost of the premium; or

(2) if private health insurance is not in effect for the child, whether:

(A) the child is receiving medical assistance under Chapter 32, Human Resources Code;

(B) the child is receiving health benefits coverage under the state child health plan under Chapter 62, Health and Safety Code, and the cost of any premium; and

(C) either parent has access to private health insurance at reasonable cost to the obligor.

(c) In rendering temporary orders, the court shall, except for good cause shown, order that any health insurance coverage in effect for the child continue in effect pending the rendition of a final order, except that the court may not require the continuation of any health insurance that is not available to the parent at reasonable cost to the obligor. If there is no health insurance coverage in effect for the child or if the insurance in effect is not available at a reasonable cost to the obligor, the court shall, except for good cause shown, order health care coverage for the child as provided under Section 154.182.

(d) On rendering a final order the court shall:

(1) make specific findings with respect to the manner in which health care coverage is to be provided for the child, in accordance with the priorities identified under Section 154.182; and

(2) except for good cause shown or on agreement of the parties, require the parent ordered to provide health care coverage for the child as provided under Section 154.182 to produce evidence to the court's satisfaction that the parent has applied for or secured health insurance or has otherwise taken necessary action to provide for health care coverage for the child, as ordered by the court.

(e) In this section, "reasonable cost" means the cost of health insurance coverage for a child that does not exceed nine percent of the obligor's annual resources, as described by Section 154.062(b), if the obligor is responsible under a medical support order for the cost of health insurance coverage for only one child. If the obligor is responsible under a medical support order for the cost of health insurance coverage for more than one child, "reasonable cost" means the total cost of health insurance coverage for all children for which the obligor is responsible under a medical support order that does not exceed nine percent of the obligor's annual resources, as described by Section 154.062(b).

History of Fam. Code §154.181: Acts 1995, 74th Leg., ch. 20, §1, eff. Apr. 20, 1995. Amended by Acts 2001, 77th Leg., ch. 449, §1, eff. June 5, 2001; Acts 2003, 78th Leg., ch. 610, §1, eff. Sept. 1, 2003; Acts 2007, 80th Leg., ch. 363, §2, eff. Sept. 1, 2007; Acts 2009, 81st Leg., ch. 767, §7, eff. June 19, 2009. Source: Former Fam. Code §14.061.

FAM §154.1815

In 2015, the Legislature enacted §154.1815 to require dental support for a child subject to a child-support order, but the enactment is not effective until Sept. 1, 2018. For the text of the prospective enactment, see Acts 2015, 84th Leg., ch. 1150, §14, eff. Sept. 1, 2018.

FAM §154.182. HEALTH CARE COVERAGE FOR CHILD

(a) The court shall consider the cost, accessibility, and quality of health insurance coverage available to the parties and shall give priority to health insurance coverage available through the employment of one of the parties if the coverage is available at a reasonable cost to the obligor.

(b) In determining the manner in which health care coverage for the child is to be ordered, the court shall render its order in accordance with the following priorities, unless a party shows good cause why a particular order would not be in the best interest of the child:

(1) if health insurance is available for the child through a parent's employment or membership in a union, trade association, or other organization at reasonable cost, the court shall order that parent to include the child in the parent's health insurance;

(2) if health insurance is not available for the child under Subdivision (1) but is available to a parent at reasonable cost from another source, including the program under Section 154.1826 to provide health insurance in Title IV-D cases, the court may order that parent to provide health insurance for the child; or

(3) if health insurance coverage is not available for the child under Subdivision (1) or (2), the court shall

order the obligor to pay the obligee, in addition to any amount ordered under the guidelines for child support, an amount, not to exceed nine percent of the obligor's annual resources, as described by Section 154.062(b), as cash medical support for the child.

(b-1) If the parent ordered to provide health insurance under Subsection (b)(1) or (2) is the obligee, the court shall order the obligor to pay the obligee, as additional child support, an amount equal to the actual cost of health insurance for the child, but not to exceed a reasonable cost to the obligor. In calculating the actual cost of health insurance for the child, if the obligee has other minor dependents covered under the same health insurance plan, the court shall divide the total cost to the obligee for the insurance by the total number of minor dependents, including the child covered under the plan.

(b-2) If the court finds that neither parent has access to private health insurance at a reasonable cost to the obligor, the court shall order the parent awarded the exclusive right to designate the child's primary residence or, to the extent permitted by law, the other parent to apply immediately on behalf of the child for participation in a government medical assistance program or health plan. If the child participates in a government medical assistance program or health plan, the court shall order cash medical support under Subsection (b)(3).

(b-3) An order requiring the payment of cash medical support under Subsection (b)(3) must allow the obligor to discontinue payment of the cash medical support if:

(1) health insurance for the child becomes available to the obligor at a reasonable cost; and

(2) the obligor:

(A) enrolls the child in the insurance plan; and

(B) provides the obligee and, in a Title IV-D case, the Title IV-D agency, the information required under Section 154.185.

(c) In this section:

(1) "Accessibility" means the extent to which health insurance coverage for a child provides for the availability of medical care within a reasonable traveling distance and time from the child's primary residence, as determined by the court.

(2) "Reasonable cost" has the meaning assigned by Section 154.181(e).

(d) Repealed by Acts 2009, 81st Leg., ch. 767, §37, eff. June 19, 2009.

History of Fam. Code §154.182: Acts 1995, 74th Leg., ch. 20, §1, eff. Apr. 20, 1995. Amended by Acts 1997, 75th Leg., ch. 550, §2, eff. June 2, 1997; Acts 2001, 77th Leg., ch. 449, §2, eff. June 5, 2001; Acts 2003, 78th Leg., ch. 610, §2, eff. Sept. 1, 2003; Acts 2007, 80th Leg., ch. 363, §§3, 4 (eff. Sept. 1, 2007), ch. 620, §5 (eff. Sept. 1, 2007); Acts 2009, 81st Leg., ch. 767, §§8, 37, eff. June 19, 2009. Source: Former Fam. Code §14.061(a), (b).

See also 28 T.A.C. §§21.2001-21.2011; ***O'Connor's Texas Family Law Handbook*** (2017), "Calculating Medical Child Support," ch. 4-F, §15, p. 552.

ANNOTATIONS

Montes v. Filley, 359 S.W.3d 260, 264 (Tex. App.—El Paso 2011, no pet.). Mother "attacks the court's order requiring a non-parent third party to provide medical insurance [for] the children, contrary to the cost allocation priority order set out in §154.182…. *At 265:* We first disagree with the characterization of the order as requiring the children's stepfather to provide support. Health insurance coverage is available to the children through their stepfather's employment and the trial court's order simply required that [mother] include the children on that policy as long as the option is available. [¶] [Father] testified that while he had a private health insurance policy for himself, he did not have an employer-provided or group insurance policy. [Mother] testified that she was not employed outside of the home, but she was covered by health insurance through her husband's employer. We find no abuse of discretion in the order requiring that [mother] include the children on her husband's health insurance policy."

FAM §154.1825

In 2015, the Legislature enacted §154.1825 to require dental support for a child subject to a child-support order, but the enactment is not effective until Sept. 1, 2018. For the text of the prospective enactment, see Acts 2015, 84th Leg., ch. 1150, §15, eff. Sept. 1, 2018.

FAM §154.1826. HEALTH CARE PROGRAM FOR CERTAIN CHILDREN IN TITLE IV-D CASES

(a) In this section:

(1) "Health benefit plan issuer" means an insurer, health maintenance organization, or other entity authorized to provide health benefits coverage under the laws of this state.

(2) "Health care provider" means a physician or other person who is licensed, certified, or otherwise authorized to provide a health care service in this state.

(3) "Program" means the child health care program developed under this section.

(4) "Reasonable cost" has the meaning assigned by Section 154.181(e).

(5) "Third-party administrator" means a person who is not a health benefit plan issuer or agent of a health benefit plan issuer and who provides administrative services for the program, including processing enrollment of eligible children in the program and processing premium payments on behalf of the program.

(b) In consultation with the Texas Department of Insurance, the Health and Human Services Commission, and representatives of the insurance industry in this state, the Title IV-D agency shall develop and implement a statewide program to address the health care needs of children in Title IV-D cases for whom health insurance is not available to either parent at reasonable cost under Section 154.182(b)(1) or under Section 154.182(b)(2) from a source other than the program.

(c) The director of the Title IV-D agency may establish an advisory committee to consult with the director regarding the implementation and operation of the program. If the director establishes an advisory committee, the director may appoint any of the following persons to the advisory committee:

(1) representatives of appropriate public and private entities, including state agencies concerned with health care management;

(2) members of the judiciary;

(3) members of the legislature; and

(4) representatives of the insurance industry.

(d) The principal objective of the program is to provide basic health care services, including office visits with health care providers, hospitalization, and diagnostic and emergency services, to eligible children in Title IV-D cases at reasonable cost to the parents obligated by court order to provide medical support for the children.

(e) The Title IV-D agency may use available private resources, including gifts and grants, in administering the program.

(f) The Title IV-D agency shall adopt rules as necessary to implement the program. The Title IV-D agency shall consult with the Texas Department of Insurance and the Health and Human Services Commission in establishing policies and procedures for the administration of the program and in determining appropriate benefits to be provided under the program.

(g) A health benefit plan issuer that participates in the program may not deny health care coverage under the program to eligible children because of preexisting conditions or chronic illnesses. A child who is determined to be eligible for coverage under the program continues to be eligible until the termination of the parent's duty to pay child support as specified by Section 154.006. Enrollment of a child in the program does not preclude the subsequent enrollment of the child in another health care plan that becomes available to the child's parent at reasonable cost, including a health care plan available through the parent's employment or the state child health plan under Chapter 62, Health and Safety Code.

(h) The Title IV-D agency shall contract with an independent third-party administrator to provide necessary administrative services for operation of the program.

(i) A person acting as a third-party administrator under Subsection (h) is not considered an administrator for purposes of Chapter 4151, Insurance Code.

(j) The Title IV-D agency shall solicit applications for participation in the program from health benefit plan issuers that meet requirements specified by the agency. Each health benefit plan issuer that participates in the program must hold a certificate of authority issued by the Texas Department of Insurance.

(k) The Title IV-D agency shall promptly notify the courts of this state when the program has been implemented and is available to provide for the health care needs of children described by Subsection (b). The notification must specify a date beginning on which children may be enrolled in the program.

(*l*) On or after the date specified in the notification required by Subsection (k), a court that orders health care coverage for a child in a Title IV-D case shall order that the child be enrolled in the program authorized by this section unless other health insurance is available for the child at reasonable cost, including the state child health plan under Chapter 62, Health and Safety Code.

(m) Payment of premium costs for the enrollment of a child in the program may be enforced by the Title IV-D agency against the obligor by any means available for the enforcement of a child support obligation, including income withholding under Chapter 158.

(n) The program is not subject to any provision of the Insurance Code or other law that requires coverage or the offer of coverage of a health care service or benefit.

(o) Any health information obtained by the program, or by a third-party administrator providing program services, that is subject to the Health Insurance Portability and Accountability Act of 1996 (42 U.S.C. Section 1320d et seq.) or Chapter 181, Health and Safety Code, is confidential and not open to public inspection. Any personally identifiable financial information or supporting documentation of a parent whose child is enrolled in the program that is obtained by the program, or by a third-party administrator providing program services, is confidential and not open to public inspection.

History of Fam. Code §154.1826: Acts 2009, 81st Leg., ch. 767, §9, eff. June 19, 2009.

FAM §154.1827. ADMINISTRATIVE ADJUSTMENT OF MEDICAL SUPPORT ORDER

(a) In each Title IV-D case in which a medical support order requires that a child be enrolled in a health care program under Section 154.1826, the Title IV-D agency may administratively adjust the order as necessary on an annual basis to reflect changes in the amount of premium costs associated with the child's enrollment.

(b) The Title IV-D agency shall provide notice of the administrative adjustment to the obligor and the clerk of the court that rendered the order.

History of Fam. Code §154.1827: Acts 2009, 81st Leg., ch. 767, §9, eff. June 19, 2009.

FAM §154.183. MEDICAL SUPPORT ADDITIONAL SUPPORT DUTY OF OBLIGOR[1]

(a) An amount that an obligor is ordered to pay as medical support for the child under this chapter, including the costs of health insurance coverage or cash medical support under Section 154.182:

(1) is in addition to the amount that the obligor is required to pay for child support under the guidelines for child support;

(2) is a child support obligation; and

(3) may be enforced by any means available for the enforcement of child support, including withholding from earnings under Chapter 158.

(b) If the court finds and states in the child support order that the obligee will maintain health insurance coverage for the child at the obligee's expense, the court shall increase the amount of child support to be paid by the obligor in an amount not exceeding the actual cost to the obligee for maintaining health insurance coverage, as provided under Section 154.182(b-1).

(c) As additional child support, the court shall allocate between the parties, according to their circumstances:

(1) the reasonable and necessary health care expenses, including vision and dental expenses, of the child that are not reimbursed by health insurance or are not otherwise covered by the amount of cash medical support ordered under Section 154.182(b)(3); and

(2) amounts paid by either party as deductibles or copayments in obtaining health care services for the child covered under a health insurance policy.

1. **Editor's note:** In 2015, the Legislature amended §154.183 to require dental support for a child subject to a child-support order, but the amendments are not effective until Sept. 1, 2018. For the text of the prospective amendments, see Acts 2015, 84th Leg., ch. 1150, §16, eff. Sept. 1, 2018.

History of Fam. Code §154.183: Acts 1995, 74th Leg., ch. 20, §1, eff. Apr. 20, 1995. Amended by Acts 2007, 80th Leg., ch. 363, §5 (eff. Sept. 1, 2007), ch. 620, §6 (eff. Sept. 1, 2007); Acts 2009, 81st Leg., ch. 87, §9.002 (eff. Sept. 1, 2009), ch. 767, §10 (eff. June 19, 2009). Source: Former Fam. Code §§14.053(d), 14.061(c).

ANNOTATIONS

Wright v. Wright, 867 S.W.2d 807, 814 (Tex. App.—El Paso 1993, writ denied). The language in Fam. Code §14.053(d), now §154.183(c), "provides that 'the court will order the obligor to provide health insurance coverage for the child subject of the suit in addition to the amount of child support calculated pursuant to these guidelines.' We do not interpret that language to mean that the costs of such insurance can not be subtracted from the obligor's gross income to determine the amount of support due. The insurance costs paid by the obligor are to be paid in addition to the child support ordered by the trial court, in that the insurance costs are a separate obligation, not included within the amount of the child support ordered. [¶] [Obligor] was ordered to pay $618 per month in support. He was also ordered to maintain and pay for hospitalization insurance for the children. These insurance costs are not part of the $618; they are a separate obligation."

FAM §154.184. EFFECT OF ORDER[1]

(a) Receipt of a medical support order requiring that health insurance be provided for a child shall be considered a change in the family circumstances of the employee or member, for health insurance purposes, equivalent to the birth or adoption of a child.

(b) If the employee or member is eligible for dependent health coverage, the employer shall automatically enroll the child for the first 31 days after the receipt of the order or notice of the medical support order under Section 154.186 on the same terms and conditions as apply to any other dependent child.

(c) The employer shall notify the insurer of the automatic enrollment.

(d) During the 31-day period, the employer and insurer shall complete all necessary forms and procedures to make the enrollment permanent or shall report in accordance with this subchapter the reasons the coverage cannot be made permanent.

1. **Editor's note:** In 2015, the Legislature amended §154.184 to require dental support for a child subject to a child-support order, but the amendments are not effective until Sept. 1, 2018. For the text of the prospective amendments, see Acts 2015, 84th Leg., ch. 1150, §17, eff. Sept. 1, 2018.

History of Fam. Code §154.184: Acts 1995, 74th Leg., ch. 20, §1, eff. Apr. 20, 1995. Amended by Acts 1995, 74th Leg., ch. 341, §4.03, eff. Sept. 1, 1995; Acts 1997, 75th Leg., ch. 911, §11, eff. Sept. 1, 1997. Source: Former Fam. Code §14.061(r).

FAM §154.185. PARENT TO FURNISH INFORMATION[1]

(a) The court shall order a parent providing health insurance to furnish to either the obligee, obligor, or child support agency the following information not later than the 30th day after the date the notice of rendition of the order is received:

(1) the social security number of the parent;

(2) the name and address of the parent's employer;

(3) whether the employer is self-insured or has health insurance available;

(4) proof that health insurance has been provided for the child;

(5) if the employer has health insurance available, the name of the health insurance carrier, the number of the policy, a copy of the policy and schedule of benefits, a health insurance membership card, claim forms, and any other information necessary to submit a claim; and

(6) if the employer is self-insured, a copy of the schedule of benefits, a membership card, claim forms, and any other information necessary to submit a claim.

(b) The court shall also order a parent providing health insurance to furnish the obligor, obligee, or child support agency with additional information regarding health insurance coverage not later than the 15th day after the date the information is received by the parent.

1. **Editor's note:** In 2015, the Legislature amended §154.185 to require dental support for a child subject to a child-support order, but the amendments are not effective until Sept. 1, 2018. For the text of the prospective amendments, see Acts 2015, 84th Leg., ch. 1150, §18, eff. Sept. 1, 2018.

History of Fam. Code §154.185: Acts 1995, 74th Leg., ch. 20, §1, eff. Apr. 20, 1995. Amended by Acts 2001, 77th Leg., ch. 1023, §10, eff. Sept. 1, 2001. Source: Former Fam. Code §14.061(e), (f).

FAM §154.186. NOTICE TO EMPLOYER CONCERNING MEDICAL SUPPORT[1]

(a) The obligee, obligor, or a child support agency of this state or another state may send to the employer a copy of the order requiring an employee to provide health insurance coverage for a child or may include notice of the medical support order in an order or writ of withholding sent to the employer in accordance with Chapter 158.

(b) In an appropriate Title IV-D case, the Title IV-D agency of this state or another state shall send to the employer the national medical support notice required under Part D, Title IV of the federal Social Security Act (42 U.S.C. Section 651 et seq.), as amended. The notice may be used in any other suit in which an obligor is ordered to provide health insurance coverage for a child.

(c) The Title IV-D agency by rule shall establish procedures consistent with federal law for use of the national medical support notice and may prescribe forms for the efficient use of the notice. The agency shall provide the notice and forms, on request, to obligees, obligors, domestic relations offices, friends of the court, and attorneys.

1. **Editor's note:** In 2015, the Legislature amended §154.186 to require dental support for a child subject to a child-support order, but the amendments are not effective until Sept. 1, 2018. For the text of the prospective amendments, see Acts 2015, 84th Leg., ch. 1150, §§19, 20, eff. Sept. 1, 2018.

History of Fam. Code §154.186: Acts 1995, 74th Leg., ch. 20, §1, eff. Apr. 20, 1995. Amended by Acts 1995, 74th Leg., ch. 341, §4.04, eff. Sept. 1, 1995; Acts 1997, 75th Leg., ch. 911, §12, eff. Sept. 1, 1997; Acts 2003, 78th Leg., ch. 120, §1, eff. July 1, 2003; Acts 2007, 80th Leg., ch. 972, §12, eff. Sept. 1, 2007. Source: Former Fam. Code §14.061(g).

FAM §154.187. DUTIES OF EMPLOYER[1]

(a) An order or notice under this subchapter to an employer directing that health insurance coverage be provided to a child of an employee or member is binding on a current or subsequent employer on receipt without regard to the date the order was rendered. If the employee or member is eligible for dependent health coverage for the child, the employer shall immediately enroll the child in a health insurance plan regardless of whether the employee is enrolled in the plan. If dependent coverage is not available to the employee or member through the employer's health insurance plan or enrollment cannot be made permanent or if the employer is not responsible or otherwise liable for providing such

coverage, the employer shall provide notice to the sender in accordance with Subsection (c).

(b) If additional premiums are incurred as a result of adding the child to the health insurance plan, the employer shall deduct the health insurance premium from the earnings of the employee in accordance with Chapter 158 and apply the amount withheld to payment of the insurance premium.

(c) An employer who has received an order or notice under this subchapter shall provide to the sender, not later than the 40th day after the date the employer receives the order or notice, a statement that the child:

(1) has been enrolled in the employer's health insurance plan or is already enrolled in another health insurance plan in accordance with a previous child support or medical support order to which the employee is subject; or

(2) cannot be enrolled or cannot be enrolled permanently in the employer's health insurance plan and provide the reason why coverage or permanent coverage cannot be provided.

(d) If the employee ceases employment or if the health insurance coverage lapses, the employer shall provide to the sender, not later than the 15th day after the date of the termination of employment or the lapse of the coverage, notice of the termination or lapse and of the availability of any conversion privileges.

(e) On request, the employer shall release to the sender information concerning the available health insurance coverage, including the name of the health insurance carrier, the policy number, a copy of the policy and schedule of benefits, a health insurance membership card, and claim forms.

(f) In this section, "sender" means the person sending the order or notice under Section 154.186.

(g) An employer who fails to enroll a child, fails to withhold or remit premiums or cash medical support, or discriminates in hiring or employment on the basis of a medical support order or notice under this subchapter shall be subject to the penalties and fines in Subchapter C, Chapter 158.

(h) An employer who receives a national medical support notice under Section 154.186 shall comply with the requirements of the notice.

(i) The notices required by Subsections (c) and (d) must be provided to the sender by first class mail, unless the sender is the Title IV-D agency. Notices to the Title IV-D agency may be provided electronically or via first class mail.

1. **Editor's note:** In 2015, the Legislature amended §154.187 to require dental support for a child subject to a child-support order, but the amendments are not effective until Sept. 1, 2018. For the text of the prospective amendments, see Acts 2015, 84th Leg., ch. 1150, §21, eff. Sept. 1, 2018.

History of Fam. Code §154.187: Acts 1995, 74th Leg., ch. 20, §1, eff. Apr. 20, 1995. Amended by Acts 1995, 74th Leg., ch. 341, §4.05, eff. Sept. 1, 1995; Acts 1997, 75th Leg., ch. 911, §13, eff. Sept. 1, 1997; Acts 2003, 78th Leg., ch. 120, §2, eff. July 1, 2003; Acts 2009, 81st Leg., ch. 767, §11, eff. June 19, 2009; Acts 2011, 82nd Leg., ch. 508, §1, eff. Sept. 1, 2011; Acts 2015, 84th Leg., ch. 859, §4, eff. Sept. 1, 2015. Source: Former Fam. Code §14.061(h)-(k), (p).

See also *O'Connor's Texas Family Law Handbook* (2017), "On employer," ch. 4-F, §15.3.3, p. 554.

FAM §154.188. FAILURE TO PROVIDE OR PAY FOR REQUIRED HEALTH INSURANCE[1]

A parent ordered to provide health insurance or to pay the other parent additional child support for the cost of health insurance who fails to do so is liable for:

(1) necessary medical expenses of the child, without regard to whether the expenses would have been paid if health insurance had been provided; and

(2) the cost of health insurance premiums or contributions, if any, paid on behalf of the child.

1. **Editor's note:** In 2015, the Legislature amended §154.188 to require dental support for a child subject to a child-support order, but the amendments are not effective until Sept. 1, 2018. For the text of the prospective amendments, see Acts 2015, 84th Leg., ch. 1150, §22, eff. Sept. 1, 2018.

History of Fam. Code §154.188: Acts 1995, 74th Leg., ch. 20, §1, eff. Apr. 20, 1995. Amended by Acts 2001, 77th Leg., ch. 295, §1, eff. Sept. 1, 2001; Acts 2003, 78th Leg., ch. 610, §3, eff. Sept. 1, 2003. Source: Former Fam. Code §14.061(*l*).

FAM §154.189. NOTICE OF TERMINATION OR LAPSE OF INSURANCE COVERAGE[1]

(a) An obligor ordered to provide health insurance coverage for a child must notify the obligee and any child support agency enforcing a support obligation against the obligor of the:

(1) termination or lapse of health insurance coverage for the child not later than the 15th day after the date of a termination or lapse; and

(2) availability of additional health insurance to the obligor for the child after a termination or lapse of coverage not later than the 15th day after the date the insurance becomes available.

(b) If termination of coverage results from a change of employers, the obligor, the obligee, or the child support agency may send the new employer a copy of the order requiring the employee to provide health insurance for a child or notice of the medical support order as provided by this subchapter.

1. **Editor's note:** In 2015, the Legislature amended §154.189 to require dental support for a child subject to a child-support order, but the amendments are not effective until Sept. 1, 2018. For the text of the prospective amendments, see Acts 2015, 84th Leg., ch. 1150, §23, eff. Sept. 1, 2018.

History of Fam. Code §154.189: Acts 1995, 74th Leg., ch. 20, §1, eff. Apr. 20, 1995. Amended by Acts 1997, 75th Leg., ch. 911, §14, eff. Sept. 1, 1997. Source: Former Fam. Code §14.061(m).

FAM §154.190. REENROLLING CHILD FOR INSURANCE COVERAGE[1]

After health insurance has been terminated or has lapsed, an obligor ordered to provide health insurance coverage for the child must enroll the child in a health insurance plan at the next available enrollment period.

1. **Editor's note:** In 2015, the Legislature amended §154.190 to require dental support for a child subject to a child-support order, but the amendments are not effective until Sept. 1, 2018. For the text of the prospective amendments, see Acts 2015, 84th Leg., ch. 1150, §24, eff. Sept. 1, 2018.

History of Fam. Code §154.190: Acts 1995, 74th Leg., ch. 20, §1, eff. Apr. 20, 1995. Source: Former Fam. Code §14.061(m).

FAM §154.191. REMEDY NOT EXCLUSIVE[1]

(a) This subchapter does not limit the rights of the obligor, obligee, local domestic relations office, or Title IV-D agency to enforce, modify, or clarify the medical support order.

(b) This subchapter does not limit the authority of the court to render or modify a medical support order to provide for payment of uninsured health expenses, health care costs, or health insurance premiums in a manner consistent with this subchapter.

1. **Editor's note:** In 2015, the Legislature amended §154.191 to require dental support for a child subject to a child-support order, but the amendments are not effective until Sept. 1, 2018. For the text of the prospective amendments, see Acts 2015, 84th Leg., ch. 1150, §25, eff. Sept. 1, 2018.

History of Fam. Code §154.191: Acts 1995, 74th Leg., ch. 20, §1, eff. Apr. 20, 1995. Amended by Acts 2009, 81st Leg., ch. 767, §12, eff. June 19, 2009. Source: Former Fam. Code §14.061(n), (o).

ANNOTATIONS

Wright v. Wright, 867 S.W.2d 807, 813 (Tex.App.—El Paso 1993, writ denied). Family Code §14.061(o), now §154.191(b), "does not mandate an apportionment of uninsured medical expenses.... [¶] Section 14.061(o) leaves the issue of uncovered medical expenses to the discretion of the court, and as discussed above, the court's decision will be disturbed only if it acted without reference to guiding rules and principles. In the instant case, there was evidence before the trial court, in the form of testimony of both parties, that the parties wished to abide by the guidelines as found in the ... Family Code. We find that the trial court properly exercised its discretion in refusing to provide for the payment of uninsured medical expenses, as payment of such is left to the sound discretion of the trial court pursuant to §14.061(o)."

FAM §154.192. CANCELLATION OR ELIMINATION OF INSURANCE COVERAGE FOR CHILD[1]

(a) Unless the employee or member ceases to be eligible for dependent coverage, or the employer has eliminated dependent health coverage for all of the employer's employees or members, the employer may not cancel or eliminate coverage of a child enrolled under this subchapter until the employer is provided satisfactory written evidence that:

(1) the court order or administrative order requiring the coverage is no longer in effect; or

(2) the child is enrolled in comparable health insurance coverage or will be enrolled in comparable coverage that will take effect not later than the effective date of the cancellation or elimination of the employer's coverage.

1. **Editor's note:** In 2015, the Legislature amended §154.192 to require dental support for a child subject to a child-support order, but the amendments are not effective until Sept. 1, 2018. For the text of the prospective amendments, see Acts 2015, 84th Leg., ch. 1150, §26, eff. Sept. 1, 2018.

History of Fam. Code §154.192: Acts 1995, 74th Leg., ch. 20, §1, eff. Apr. 20, 1995. Amended by Acts 1995, 74th Leg., ch. 341, §4.06, eff. Sept. 1, 1995. Source: Former Fam. Code §14.061(q).

FAM §154.193. MEDICAL SUPPORT ORDER NOT QUALIFIED[1]

(a) If a plan administrator or other person acting in an equivalent position determines that a medical support order issued under this subchapter does not qualify for enforcement under federal law, the tribunal may, on its own motion or the motion of a party, render an order that qualifies for enforcement under federal law.

(b) The procedure for filing a motion for enforcement of a final order applies to a motion under this section. Service of citation is not required, and a person is not entitled to a jury in a proceeding under this section.

(c) The employer or plan administrator is not a necessary party to a proceeding under this section.

1. **Editor's note:** In 2015, the Legislature amended §154.193 to require dental support for a child subject to a child-support order, but the amendments are not effective until Sept. 1, 2018. For the text of the prospective amendments, see Acts 2015, 84th Leg., ch. 1150, §§27, 28, eff. Sept. 1, 2018.

History of Fam. Code §154.193: Acts 1997, 75th Leg., ch. 911, §15, eff. Sept. 1, 1997.

Sections 154.194-154.240 reserved for expansion

Subchapter E. Local Child Support Registry

FAM §154.241. LOCAL REGISTRY

(a) A local registry shall receive a court-ordered child support payment or a payment otherwise authorized by law and shall forward the payment, as appropri-

ate, to the Title IV-D agency, local domestic relations office, or obligee within two working days after the date the local registry receives the payment.

(b) A local registry may not require an obligor, obligee, or other party or entity to furnish a certified copy of a court order as a condition of processing child support payments and shall accept as sufficient authority to process the payments a photocopy, facsimile copy, or conformed copy of the court's order.

(c) A local registry shall include with each payment it forwards to the Title IV-D agency the date it received the payment and the withholding date furnished by the employer.

(d) A local registry shall accept child support payments made by personal check, money order, or cashier's check. A local registry may refuse payment by personal check if a pattern of abuse regarding the use of personal checks has been established. Abuse includes checks drawn on insufficient funds, abusive or offensive language written on the check, intentional mutilation of the instrument, or other actions that delay or disrupt the registry's operation.

(e) Subject to Section 154.004, at the request of an obligee, a local registry shall redirect and forward a child support payment to an address and in care of a person or entity designated by the obligee. A local registry may require that the obligee's request be in writing or be made on a form provided by the local registry for that purpose, but may not charge a fee for receiving the request or redirecting the payments as requested.

(f) A local registry may accept child support payments made by credit card, debit card, or automatic teller machine card.

(g) Notwithstanding any other law, a private entity may perform the duties and functions of a local registry under this section either under a contract with a county commissioners court or domestic relations office executed under Section 204.002 or under an appointment by a court.

History of Fam. Code §154.241: Acts 1995, 74th Leg., ch. 20, §1, eff. Apr. 20, 1995. Amended by Acts 1995, 74th Leg., ch. 751, §42, eff. Sept. 1, 1995; Acts 2003, 78th Leg., ch. 645, §1, eff. Sept. 1, 2003; Acts 2005, 79th Leg., ch. 740, §2, eff. June 17, 2005. Source: Former Fam. Code §14.0501.

FAM §154.242. PAYMENT OR TRANSFER OF CHILD SUPPORT PAYMENTS BY ELECTRONIC FUNDS TRANSFER

(a) A child support payment may be made by electronic funds transfer to:

(1) the Title IV-D agency;

(2) a local registry if the registry agrees to accept electronic payment; or

(3) the state disbursement unit.

(b) A local registry may transmit child support payments to the Title IV-D agency by electronic funds transfer. Unless support payments are required to be made to the state disbursement unit, an obligor may make payments, with the approval of the court entering the order, directly to the bank account of the obligee by electronic transfer and provide verification of the deposit to the local registry. A local registry in a county that makes deposits into personal bank accounts by electronic funds transfer as of April 1, 1995, may transmit a child support payment to an obligee by electronic funds transfer if the obligee maintains a bank account and provides the local registry with the necessary bank account information to complete electronic payment.

History of Fam. Code §154.242: Acts 1995, 74th Leg., ch. 20, §1, eff. Apr. 20, 1995. Amended by Acts 1995, 74th Leg., ch. 597, §1, eff. Jan. 1, 1996; Acts 1997, 75th Leg., ch. 702, §2 (eff. Jan. 1, 1998), ch. 1053, §2 (eff. Sept. 1, 1997); Acts 1999, 76th Leg., ch. 556, §10, eff. Sept. 1, 1999. Source: Former Fam. Code §14.0502.

FAM §154.243. PRODUCTION OF CHILD SUPPORT PAYMENT RECORD

The Title IV-D agency, a local registry, or the state disbursement unit may comply with a subpoena or other order directing the production of a child support payment record by sending a certified copy of the record or an affidavit regarding the payment record to the court that directed production of the record.

History of Fam. Code §154.243: Acts 1995, 74th Leg., ch. 20, §1, eff. Apr. 20, 1995. Amended by Acts 1999, 76th Leg., ch. 556, §10, eff. Sept. 1, 1999. Source: Former Fam. Code §14.0504.

Sections 154.244-154.300 reserved for expansion

SUBCHAPTER F. SUPPORT FOR A MINOR OR ADULT DISABLED CHILD

FAM §154.301. DEFINITIONS

In this subchapter:

(1) "Adult child" means a child 18 years of age or older.

(2) "Child" means a son or daughter of any age.

History of Fam. Code §154.301: Acts 1995, 74th Leg., ch. 20, §1, eff. Apr. 20, 1995. Source: Former Fam. Code §14.051(a).

FAM §154.302. COURT-ORDERED SUPPORT FOR DISABLED CHILD

(a) The court may order either or both parents to provide for the support of a child for an indefinite period and may determine the rights and duties of the parents if the court finds that:

(1) the child, whether institutionalized or not, requires substantial care and personal supervision because of a mental or physical disability and will not be capable of self-support; and

(2) the disability exists, or the cause of the disability is known to exist, on or before the 18th birthday of the child.

(b) A court that orders support under this section shall designate a parent of the child or another person having physical custody or guardianship of the child under a court order to receive the support for the child. The court may designate a child who is 18 years of age or older to receive the support directly.

History of Fam. Code §154.302: Acts 1995, 74th Leg., ch. 20, §1, eff. Apr. 20, 1995. Amended by Acts 1997, 75th Leg., ch. 1173, §1, eff. Sept. 1, 1997. Source: Former Fam. Code §14.051(b).

ANNOTATIONS

Worford v. Stamper, 801 S.W.2d 108, 108 (Tex. 1990). Obligee "filed a motion to modify the 1975 order in June 1986, requesting that the child support payments be increased and continued past the age of 18. It was undisputed by the parties that [son] would be unable to support himself after the age of 18 due to various physical and mental handicaps. When [son] was 15 years old, his developmental levels were between three and five years. His speech is unintelligible except to those closest to him and familiar with his responses. [Son] also suffers from a dentofacial deformity which makes it difficult for him to chew his food and maintain proper hygiene. *At 109:* The trial court entered a final modification order ..., increasing [obligor's] child support payments to $1350 per month and extending such payments beyond [son's] 18th birthday. *At 110:* Based upon [obligor's] net income and the special needs of the child in this case, we hold that the trial court did not abuse its discretion by entering an order of child support in the amount of $1350 per month."

Thompson v. Smith, 483 S.W.3d 87, 93-94 (Tex. App.—Houston [1st Dist.] 2015, no pet.). The "testimony demonstrates that [adult child], even with medication, has severe and unpredictable mood swings; is unguarded with strangers; engages in physical altercations and destructive behavior when angry; and lacks the ability to independently perform basic activities such as bathing, dressing herself, and preparing meals. [¶] The evidence that [adult child] has been unable to obtain employment and that she qualifies for [Supplemental Security Income (SSI)] benefits also supports the trial court's disability finding. SSI claimants must prove that they are disabled within the meaning of the Social Security Act. [42 U.S.C. §423(d)] defines 'disability' as an 'inability to engage in any substantial gainful activity by reason of any medically determinable physical or mental impairment which can be expected to result in death or which has lasted or can be expected to last for a continuous period of not less than 12 months.' [¶] To counter this evidence of disability, [father] points to evidence that [adult child] [1] is competent to testify in court, eligible to vote, and has sufficient intelligence and capability to execute a power of attorney; [2] can dress herself, does not need special equipment, and is able to communicate with others; [3] is able to read, write, perform basic math, and has a high school diploma; and [4] can use a computer and a telephone. [¶] These abilities, however, do not render the trial court's disability finding against the great weight and preponderance of the evidence. For instance, the standard for competency to testify does not correspond to the factors used to determine whether an adult child is disabled under the Family Code. [¶] [T]he trial court ... did not abuse its discretion in finding that [adult child] is disabled and incapable of self-support."

In re J.M.C., 395 S.W.3d 839, 846 (Tex.App.—Tyler 2013, no pet.). Under §154.302, "the trial court [is] required to consider all of the evidence of [adult child's] circumstances following his 18th birthday. Circumstances may exist after a disabled child turns 18 that could entirely relieve a parent of the duty to pay adult child support. *At 847:* [Mother] maintains that the trial court should have focused only on the [last eight years when son] lived in [Illinois] to determine whether [he] was eligible for adult child support. However, the trial court did not abuse its discretion in considering all of [son's] circumstances following his 18th birthday, including the [earlier] years [when] he lived in [Texas] and his capabilities [demonstrated he did not require substantial care or personal supervision and was capable of self-support]."

FAM §154.303. STANDING TO SUE

(a) A suit provided by this subchapter may be filed only by:

(1) a parent of the child or another person having physical custody or guardianship of the child under a court order; or

(2) the child if the child:

(A) is 18 years of age or older;

(B) does not have a mental disability; and

(C) is determined by the court to be capable of managing the child's financial affairs.

(b) The parent, the child, if the child is 18 years of age or older, or other person may not transfer or assign the cause of action to any person, including a governmental or private entity or agency, except for an assignment made to the Title IV-D agency under Section 231.104 or in the provision of child support enforcement services under Section 159.307.

History of Fam. Code §154.303: Acts 1995, 74th Leg., ch. 20, §1, eff. Apr. 20, 1995. Amended by Acts 1997, 75th Leg., ch. 1173, §2, eff. Sept. 1, 1997; Acts 2011, 82nd Leg., ch. 508, §2, eff. Sept. 1, 2011. Source: Former Fam. Code §14.051(c).

FAM §154.304. GENERAL PROCEDURE

Except as otherwise provided by this subchapter, the substantive and procedural rights and remedies in a suit affecting the parent-child relationship relating to the establishment, modification, or enforcement of a child support order apply to a suit filed and an order rendered under this subchapter.

History of Fam. Code §154.304: Acts 1995, 74th Leg., ch. 20, §1, eff. Apr. 20, 1995. Source: Former Fam. Code §14.051(i).

FAM §154.305. SPECIFIC PROCEDURES

(a) A suit under this subchapter may be filed:

(1) regardless of the age of the child; and

(2) as an independent cause of action or joined with any other claim or remedy provided by this code.

(b) If no court has continuing, exclusive jurisdiction of the child, an action under this subchapter may be filed as an original suit affecting the parent-child relationship.

(c) If there is a court of continuing, exclusive jurisdiction, an action under this subchapter may be filed as a suit for modification as provided by Chapter 156.

History of Fam. Code §154.305: Acts 1995, 74th Leg., ch. 20, §1, eff. Apr. 20, 1995. Source: Former Fam. Code §14.051(d)-(f).

FAM §154.306. AMOUNT OF SUPPORT AFTER AGE 18

In determining the amount of support to be paid after a child's 18th birthday, the specific terms and conditions of that support, and the rights and duties of both parents with respect to the support of the child, the court shall determine and give special consideration to:

(1) any existing or future needs of the adult child directly related to the adult child's mental or physical disability and the substantial care and personal supervision directly required by or related to that disability;

(2) whether the parent pays for or will pay for the care or supervision of the adult child or provides or will provide substantial care or personal supervision of the adult child;

(3) the financial resources available to both parents for the support, care, and supervision of the adult child; and

(4) any other financial resources or other resources or programs available for the support, care, and supervision of the adult child.

History of Fam. Code §154.306: Acts 1995, 74th Leg., ch. 20, §1, eff. Apr. 20, 1995. Source: Former Fam. Code §14.051(g).

ANNOTATIONS

Thompson v. Smith, 483 S.W.3d 87, 96 (Tex. App.—Houston [1st Dist.] 2015, no pet.). Father "asserts that [adult child's] general living expenses did not satisfy the statutory requirement that they meet a need stemming directly from her alleged disability. We disagree. The record shows that [adult child's] disabilities render her unable to work. She would not have qualified for [Supplemental Security Income] disability benefits if she had another source of significant financial support. She cannot independently meet her own daily living and health care expenses and requires substantial care and personal supervision. [Mother] provides [adult child] with substantial care and personal supervision in her own home; [father] was not asked to pay for [adult child] to receive care from a third party, such as a supervised living community or adult day care. The record shows that [mother] meets [adult child's] needs for support, care, and supervision, under circumstances that have remained more or less consistent since before [adult child] turned 18. This evidence supports a reasonable inference that [mother] will continue to care for [adult child] into the indefinite future."

In re J.M.W., 470 S.W.3d 544, 552 (Tex.App.—Houston [14th Dist.] 2014, no pet.). "[W]e discern no language in [Fam. Code] §154.306 indicating that these are the sole or exclusive factors for courts to consider when setting child support for an adult disabled child. *At 554:* While §154.306 provides for mandatory factors to be applied—indeed, 'specially considered'—after a disabled child reaches age 18, its application is not 'opposite' or 'incompatible' with the application of such other provisions. Here, the context of those sur-

rounding provisions consistently highlights the child support guidelines, and provides specific details, definitions, and prohibitions for applying them properly, as well as specific considerations for ultimately determining not to apply them. *At 555:* [W]hen determining child support for adult disabled children, courts must apply §154.306, but they continue to remain bound under [Fam. Code] §154.304 to consider and apply the substantive rights and remedies applicable to SAPCR suits '[e]xcept as otherwise provided.' In a modification suit involving an adult disabled child, these provisions may include, among others, those in [ch. 154,] subch. B ... related to computing net resources available for support; in [ch. 154,] subch. C related to the child support guidelines; in [ch. 154,] subch. F related to support for disabled children; and in [Fam. Code ch. 156,] subch. E ... related to modification of child support."

Wolk v. Wolk, No. 03-06-00595-CV (Tex.App.—Austin 2007, no pet.) (memo op.; 9-12-07). "Though evidence was presented that the child has Down syndrome, that [mother] has always been the primary caretaker, and that she has been taking care of the child for years, there was no evidence showing the child's current or future medical needs relating to his disability, the substantial care and supervision required relating to the child's disability, whether [mother] pays or will pay for the care or supervision of the child or will provide substantial care, or financial or other resources or programs available for the support and care of the child. We conclude that on the face of the record, the trial court did not have sufficient information 'to determine and give special consideration' to the statutorily required factors."

FAM §154.307. MODIFICATION & ENFORCEMENT

An order provided by this subchapter may contain provisions governing the rights and duties of both parents with respect to the support of the child and may be modified or enforced in the same manner as any other order provided by this title.

History of Fam. Code §154.307: Acts 1995, 74th Leg., ch. 20, §1, eff. Apr. 20, 1995. Source: Former Fam. Code §14.051(h).

FAM §154.308. REMEDY NOT EXCLUSIVE

(a) This subchapter does not affect a parent's:

(1) cause of action for the support of a disabled child under any other law; or

(2) ability to contract for the support of a disabled child.

(b) This subchapter does not affect the substantive or procedural rights or remedies of a person other than a parent, including a governmental or private entity or agency, with respect to the support of a disabled child under any other law.

History of Fam. Code §154.308: Acts 1995, 74th Leg., ch. 20, §1, eff. Apr. 20, 1995. Source: Former Fam. Code §14.051(j), (k).

FAM §154.309. POSSESSION OF OR ACCESS TO ADULT DISABLED CHILD

(a) A court may render an order for the possession of or access to an adult disabled child that is appropriate under the circumstances.

(b) Possession of or access to an adult disabled child is enforceable in the manner provided by Chapter 157. An adult disabled child may refuse possession or access if the adult disabled child is mentally competent.

(c) A court that obtains continuing, exclusive jurisdiction of a suit affecting the parent-child relationship involving a disabled person who is a child retains continuing, exclusive jurisdiction of subsequent proceedings involving the person, including proceedings after the person is an adult. Notwithstanding this subsection and any other law, a probate court may exercise jurisdiction in a guardianship proceeding for the person after the person is an adult.

History of Fam. Code §154.309: Acts 1995, 74th Leg., ch. 751, §43, eff. Sept. 1, 1995. Amended by Acts 2007, 80th Leg., ch. 453, §1, eff. June 16, 2007.

CHAPTER 155. CONTINUING, EXCLUSIVE JURISDICTION; TRANSFER

SUBCHAPTER A. CONTINUING, EXCLUSIVE JURISDICTION

FAM §155.001. ACQUIRING CONTINUING, EXCLUSIVE JURISDICTION

(a) Except as otherwise provided by this section, a court acquires continuing, exclusive jurisdiction over the matters provided for by this title in connection with a child on the rendition of a final order.

(b) The following final orders do not create continuing, exclusive jurisdiction in a court:

(1) a voluntary or involuntary dismissal of a suit affecting the parent-child relationship;

(2) in a suit to determine parentage, a final order finding that an alleged or presumed father is not the father of the child, except that the jurisdiction of the court is not affected if the child was subject to the jurisdiction of the court or some other court in a suit affecting the parent-child relationship before the commencement of the suit to adjudicate parentage; and

(3) a final order of adoption, after which a subsequent suit affecting the child must be commenced as though the child had not been the subject of a suit for adoption or any other suit affecting the parent-child relationship before the adoption.

(c) If a court of this state has acquired continuing, exclusive jurisdiction, no other court of this state has jurisdiction of a suit with regard to that child except as provided by this chapter, Section 103.001(b), or Chapter 262.

(d) Unless a final order has been rendered by a court of continuing, exclusive jurisdiction, a subsequent suit shall be commenced as an original proceeding.

History of Fam. Code §155.001: Acts 1995, 74th Leg., ch. 20, §1, eff. Apr. 20, 1995. Amended by Acts 1999, 76th Leg., ch. 62, §6.19, eff. Sept. 1, 1999; Acts 2001, 77th Leg., ch. 821, §2.15, eff. June 14, 2001; Acts 2015, 84th Leg., ch. 944, §10, eff. Sept. 1, 2015. Source: Former Fam. Code §11.05(a), (b), (d), (e).

See also ***O'Connor's Texas Family Law Handbook*** (2017), "Filing SAPCR after order rendered in earlier SAPCR," ch. 4-A, §3.2, p. 343.

ANNOTATIONS

In re C.G., 495 S.W.3d 40, 44-45 (Tex.App.—Corpus Christi 2016, pet. denied). "[T]he continuing, exclusive jurisdiction statutory scheme is 'truly jurisdictional'—that is, when one court has continuing and exclusive jurisdiction over a matter, any order or judgment issued by another court pertaining to the same matter is void." *See also* ***Celestine v. DFPS***, 321 S.W.3d 222, 230 (Tex. App.—Houston [1st Dist.] 2010, no pet.); ***In re Aguilera***, 37 S.W.3d 43, 48-49 (Tex.App.—El Paso 2000, orig. proceeding). *But see* ***Ramsey v. Ramsey***, this page.

Ramsey v. Ramsey, 19 S.W.3d 548, 554 n.7 (Tex. App.—Austin 2000, no pet.). Section 155.001 "is designed to operate more in the nature of dominant jurisdiction or venue, rather than true jurisdiction. For instance, on a showing that a suit for divorce has been filed in another court, the court having continuing, exclusive jurisdiction of a [SAPCR] *must* transfer the SAPCR proceedings to the divorce court. The task of transferring the case is a mandatory, ministerial duty. [¶] Additionally, if the court in which the divorce is pending renders a final judgment after being led by the bureau of vital statistics to believe erroneously that no court of continuing, exclusive jurisdiction existed, the first court is deemed to have lost its jurisdiction, and the divorce decree of the second court is enforceable—child custody and support issues included." *But see* ***In re C.G.***, this page.

Fleming v. Easton, 998 S.W.2d 252, 255 (Tex. App.—Dallas 1999, no pet.). Because mother's "claims involve matters pertaining to the parent-child relationship between [father] and their child, the district court that had previously acquired jurisdiction over the child through [couple's] divorce action, retains continuing and exclusive jurisdiction to decide these issues. [¶] The district court's acquisition of jurisdiction over the [parent-child] issues in this case preceded any jurisdiction that could have been acquired by the probate court. This case is distinguishable, therefore, from those in which the probate court acquired dominant jurisdiction by virtue of the administration of the estate being the 'first filed action.' Because jurisdiction vested in the district court before the probate court acquired jurisdiction over [father's] estate, the probate court would have had to *divest* the district court of its

jurisdiction before deciding this case. [¶] Furthermore, we have found no authority that would automatically divest the district court of its jurisdiction over the parent-child relationship upon [father's] death. Indeed, previously decided cases clearly indicate that the district court's continuing jurisdiction over the issues in this case was not affected by [father's] death."

Ex parte Holland, 807 S.W.2d 827, 827 (Tex. App.—Dallas 1991, writ dism'd). Father "contends that the [contempt] order is void because the visiting judge who signed it was without authority to preside in the contempt proceeding. *At 829:* Contempt proceedings brought to enforce child support obligations fall within [Fam. Code §11.05(a)'s, now §155.001's,] continuing jurisdiction. Thus we must consider whether, because of this continuing jurisdiction, [visiting judge] retained jurisdiction to enter the ... order of contempt and commitment. [¶] Opinions ... have distinguished between an individual judge's authority and the jurisdiction of the court in which he is sitting. *At 830:* [W]e conclude that the trial court's continuing jurisdiction in family law matters vested no jurisdiction in [visiting judge] that was independent of the ... order of assignment. Nor did the court's continuing jurisdiction extend the duration of his authority under that assignment. [Visiting judge's] assignment expired with the expiration of his plenary power.... Absent a new assignment, he was without authority to preside in the contempt proceedings leading to the ... order of contempt and commitment."

Ault v. Mulanax, 724 S.W.2d 824, 830 (Tex.App.—Texarkana 1986, no writ). "In the event that two different courts have a divorce action pending which include the parent-child relationship or two courts have matters which involve only the parent-child relationship, then when the court having dominant jurisdiction renders a final decree, the jurisdiction of the other court will terminate. When a final decree is entered by a court, it acquires continuing, exclusive jurisdiction pursuant to [Fam. Code] §11.05(e) [now §155.001]. This section further provides that a voluntary dismissal of a [SAPCR] prior to a final decree terminates all the jurisdiction of the court, and that unless a final decree has been entered by a court of continuing, exclusive jurisdiction, a subsequent suit shall be commenced as an original proceeding."

Crockett v. Crockett, 589 S.W.2d 759, 763 (Tex. App.—Dallas 1979, writ ref'd n.r.e.). Father "claims that the Ohio court which rendered the divorce decree has continuing and exclusive jurisdiction over all [SAPCRs], including modification of support and visitation. On the other hand, [mother] argues that 'continuing jurisdiction,' as defined in [Fam. Code] §11.05 [now §§155.001 and 155.002], relates only to Texas courts and has no extraterritorial effect. [¶] We ... hold that §11.05(a), when it mentions 'continuing jurisdiction,' refers only to courts within the State of Texas and has no extraterritorial application."

Ex parte Pepper, 544 S.W.2d 836, 839 (Tex.App.—Amarillo 1976), *writ dism'd*, 548 S.W.2d 884 (Tex.1977). "The paternal grandparents, possessing the order for visitation with the children, were given notice of the adoption proceedings. The final decree of adoption reserved no rights to them. The legal effect of the adoption decree was to end the trial court's continuing jurisdiction over the preadoption proceedings ... and, except for the children's right to inherit from their natural parents, to sever old legal ties and to create new legal relationships. Accordingly, the prior order for grandparental visitation ceased to have any legal effect upon entry of the final decree of adoption."

FAM §155.002. RETAINING CONTINUING, EXCLUSIVE JURISDICTION

Except as otherwise provided by this subchapter, a court with continuing, exclusive jurisdiction retains jurisdiction of the parties and matters provided by this title.

History of Fam. Code §155.002: Acts 1995, 74th Leg., ch. 20, §1, eff. Apr. 20, 1995. Amended by Acts 1999, 76th Leg., ch. 62, §6.20, eff. Sept. 1, 1999. Source: Former Fam. Code §11.05(a).

ANNOTATIONS

Trinidad v. Trinidad, No. 04-05-00062-CV (Tex. App.—San Antonio 2005, no pet.) (memo op.; 11-23-05). "While we find no Texas case speaking directly on a court's continuing, exclusive jurisdiction where the parents of a child marry for the first time after a child support order is entered, the situation is similar to a remarriage of the parents after a divorce. [The] Family Code treats the termination of the order of child support and the termination of the provisions relating to conservatorship on remarriage ... as ending the continuing, exclusive jurisdiction of the court in which the first divorce was obtained. We can find no logic for treating the remarriage after a divorce decree is entered differently from a marriage after a child support order is entered. Both the divorce decree and the

child support order are terminated, and since no action or order is pending subject to modification, the continuing, exclusive jurisdiction of the court that entered the divorce decree or child support order ends. This ensures that the district court that handles the divorce acquires dominant jurisdiction."

Hudson v. Markum, 931 S.W.2d 336, 337 (Tex. App.—Dallas 1996, no writ). A SAPCR "includes a suit to determine paternity. A motion to modify child support is also a [SAPCR]. A child support order 'may be modified only by the filing of a motion in the court having continuing, exclusive jurisdiction of the [SAPCR] as provided by [Fam. Code] §11.05 [now §156.002].' *At 338:* No one contests the trial court's jurisdiction to decide the paternity and support of the child who is the subject of this suit. Once the trial court decided the paternity and support of the child, it acquired continuing jurisdiction over the parent-child relationship. It retained continuing, exclusive jurisdiction to hear a new proceeding affecting that relationship."

Welsh v. Welsh, 905 S.W.2d 615, 616-17 (Tex. App.—Houston [14th Dist.] 1995, writ denied). P argues "that the case was transferred to an Impact Court in violation of the Family Code's specific provisions concerning how and when a case may be transferred to another court. Challenges to impact courts have arisen in numerous contexts, most frequently in criminal cases in which an appellant is contesting the legitimacy of the court itself. Such cases have been routinely resolved in favor of the legitimacy of these courts. ... All of these cases are resolved on the basis of the constitutional provision that authorizes district judges to hold court for each other when they deem it expedient. Out of this constitutional language comes the authorization for one district judge to try cases for another district judge, 'in the same court at the same time, each occupying a different courtroom.' These principles bear out [D's] contention that the Impact Court is a type of derivative court, a court acting as the 328th but with a different judge and in a different courtroom."

Lewis v. McCoy, 747 S.W.2d 48, 49 (Tex.App.—El Paso 1988, orig. proceeding). "What happens to the court's jurisdiction and order as to custody when the mother dies? In ***Greene v. Schuble***, 654 S.W.2d 436 (Tex.1983), the majority of the Court, in a mandamus proceeding, agreed that upon the death of the managing conservator the divorce decree no longer constituted a valid order governing possession of the child. *At 50:* We do not read the majority opinion in ***Greene*** ... to hold that the death of the managing conservator terminates the jurisdiction of the court which appointed the conservator. ... Since the Dallas County District Court originally had jurisdiction and the death of the managing conservator did not terminate that jurisdiction, another court could not obtain jurisdiction without a transfer order. This would include a probate court where an application was filed for appointment of a temporary guardian. [¶] We conclude that the Dallas County District Court had continuing jurisdiction to name a managing conservator for [minor child] after her mother died." *See also* ***Dohrn v. Delgado***, 941 S.W.2d 244, 248 (Tex.App.—Corpus Christi 1996, orig. proceeding) (death of party to divorce decree does not terminate continuing jurisdiction over children as long as they are minors).

FAM §155.003. EXERCISE OF CONTINUING, EXCLUSIVE JURISDICTION

(a) Except as otherwise provided by this section, a court with continuing, exclusive jurisdiction may exercise its jurisdiction to modify its order regarding managing conservatorship, possessory conservatorship, possession of and access to the child, and support of the child.

(b) A court of this state may not exercise its continuing, exclusive jurisdiction to modify managing conservatorship if:

(1) the child's home state is other than this state; or

(2) modification is precluded by Chapter 152.

(c) A court of this state may not exercise its continuing, exclusive jurisdiction to modify possessory conservatorship or possession of or access to a child if:

(1) the child's home state is other than this state and all parties have established and continue to maintain their principal residence outside this state; or

(2) each individual party has filed written consent with the tribunal of this state for a tribunal of another state to modify the order and assume continuing, exclusive jurisdiction of the suit.

(d) A court of this state may not exercise its continuing, exclusive jurisdiction to modify its child support order if modification is precluded by Chapter 159.

History of Fam. Code §155.003: Acts 1995, 74th Leg., ch. 20, §1, eff. Apr. 20, 1995. Source: Former Fam. Code §11.05(g).

ANNOTATIONS

In re Bellamy, 67 S.W.3d 482, 484 (Tex.App.—Texarkana 2002, no pet.). "[W]e find that [Fam. Code] §§152.202 and 155.003(b)(1) conflict in this case. When a provision of Ch. 152 conflicts with another provision of the Family Code or another statute or rule of Texas and the conflict cannot be reconciled, Ch. 152 prevails. Under the UCCJEA, Texas retains jurisdiction even if Texas is no longer the home state of the child or of the custodial parent, so long as there is a significant connection with this state."

FAM §155.004. LOSS OF CONTINUING, EXCLUSIVE JURISDICTION

(a) A court of this state loses its continuing, exclusive jurisdiction to modify its order if:

(1) an order of adoption is rendered after the court acquires continuing, exclusive jurisdiction of the suit;

(2) the parents of the child have remarried each other after the dissolution of a previous marriage between them and file a suit for the dissolution of their subsequent marriage combined with a suit affecting the parent-child relationship as if there had not been a prior court with continuing, exclusive jurisdiction over the child; or

(3) another court assumed jurisdiction over a suit and rendered a final order based on incorrect information received from the vital statistics unit that there was no court of continuing, exclusive jurisdiction.

(b) This section does not affect the power of the court to enforce its order for a violation that occurred before the time continuing, exclusive jurisdiction was lost under this section.

History of Fam. Code §155.004: Acts 1995, 74th Leg., ch. 20, §1, eff. Apr. 20, 1995. Amended by Acts 1997, 75th Leg., ch. 575, §8, eff. Sept. 1, 1997; Acts 2015, 84th Leg., ch. 1, §1.050, eff. Apr. 2, 2015. Source: Former Fam. Code §11.05(b), (f), (g).

ANNOTATIONS

Jones v. TDFPS, 400 S.W.3d 173, 178-79 (Tex. App.—Austin 2013, no pet.). See annotation under Family Code §155.104, p. 592.

FAM §155.005. JURISDICTION PENDING TRANSFER

(a) During the transfer of a suit from a court with continuing, exclusive jurisdiction, the transferring court retains jurisdiction to render temporary orders.

(b) The jurisdiction of the transferring court terminates on the docketing of the case in the transferee court.

History of Fam. Code §155.005: Acts 1995, 74th Leg., ch. 20, §1, eff. Apr. 20, 1995. Source: Former Fam. Code §11.05(h).

ANNOTATIONS

Bigham v. Dempster, 901 S.W.2d 424, 430 (Tex. 1995). "We cannot agree that the jurisdiction of the court turns on whether, or with what diligence, a clerk performs a ministerial duty to forward court documents. ... Although it refers to the receipt of all files, the apparent purpose of [Fam. Code] §11.06(m) [now §155.207(c)] is not to delay jurisdiction in the transferee court until it receives all files, but to require the clerk of the transferee court to declare the suit docketed after all files have been received. *At 431:* The term 'docketed' in our jurisprudence has the connotation not only of the clerk's formally placing the case on the list of cases pending in the court, but also of notice that the court is ready to act on the matter, to take jurisdiction over it. ... The rule is that the case is docketed when the court to which it is transferred has received a certified copy of the transfer order and asserts jurisdiction, or when all files have been transferred, whichever occurs first."

Sections 155.006-155.100 reserved for expansion

SUBCHAPTER B. IDENTIFICATION OF COURT OF CONTINUING, EXCLUSIVE JURISDICTION

FAM §155.101. REQUEST FOR IDENTIFICATION OF COURT OF CONTINUING, EXCLUSIVE JURISDICTION

(a) The petitioner or the court shall request from the vital statistics unit identification of the court that last had continuing, exclusive jurisdiction of the child in a suit unless:

(1) the petition alleges that no court has continuing, exclusive jurisdiction of the child and the issue is not disputed by the pleadings; or

(2) the petition alleges that the court in which the suit or petition to modify has been filed has acquired and retains continuing, exclusive jurisdiction of the child as the result of a prior proceeding and the issue is not disputed by the pleadings.

(b) The vital statistics unit shall, on the written request of the court, an attorney, or a party:

(1) identify the court that last had continuing, exclusive jurisdiction of the child in a suit and give the docket number of the suit; or

(2) state that the child has not been the subject of a suit.

(c) The child shall be identified in the request by name, birthdate, and place of birth.

(d) The vital statistics unit shall transmit the information not later than the 10th day after the date on which the request is received.

History of Fam. Code §155.101: Acts 1995, 74th Leg., ch. 20, §1, eff. Apr. 20, 1995. Amended by Acts 1995, 74th Leg., ch. 751, §44, eff. Sept. 1, 1995; Acts 1999, 76th Leg., ch. 178, §8, eff. Aug. 30, 1999; Acts 2015, 84th Leg., ch. 1, §1.051, eff. Apr. 2, 2015. Source: Former Fam. Code §11.071(a), (b).

ANNOTATIONS

In re M.R.M., 807 S.W.2d 779, 783 (Tex.App.—Houston [14th Dist.] 1991, writ denied). Father "contends the court erred when it failed to dismiss this suit without prejudice since 'it discovered another court was the court of continuing jurisdiction.' [¶] The petition filed by the Harris County Children's Protective Services specifically alleged that no other court had continuing jurisdiction. Both [mother] and the attorney ad litem for the children filed general denials. Furthermore, [father's] attorney appeared in this cause and never contested the transfer. We find that the issue of continuing jurisdiction was not disputed in the pleadings and, therefore, the Harris County Children's Protective Service was not required to make a request to the [DHS]. Thus, the court did not err in refusing to dismiss this suit." *See also* ***Brown v. Brown***, 555 S.W.2d 784, 786 (Tex.App.—El Paso 1977, no writ) (request for information was required because father's pleadings disputed allegation that no other court had continuing jurisdiction).

Crockett v. Crockett, 589 S.W.2d 759, 764 (Tex. App.—Dallas 1979, writ ref'd n.r.e.). "Obviously, the legislature did not expect the State Department of Public Welfare to maintain records on out-of-state courts having jurisdiction over every child that comes into Texas or every child that might be the subject of a [Texas SAPCR]. ... Thus, the only reasonable context in which the term 'continuing jurisdiction' can be read [in Fam. Code §11.071, now §155.101,] is as applying exclusively to Texas courts." *But see* ***Brown v. Brown***, 555 S.W.2d 784, 787 (Tex.App.—El Paso 1977, no writ) (Fam. Code §11.05(a), now §155.001, is extraterritorial in effect).

FAM §155.102. DISMISSAL

If a court in which a suit is filed determines that another court has continuing, exclusive jurisdiction of the child, the court in which the suit is filed shall dismiss the suit without prejudice.

History of Fam. Code §155.102: Acts 1995, 74th Leg., ch. 20, §1, eff. Apr. 20, 1995. Source: Former Fam. Code §11.071(d).

FAM §155.103. RELIANCE ON VITAL STATISTICS UNIT INFORMATION

(a) A court shall have jurisdiction over a suit if it has been, correctly or incorrectly, informed by the vital statistics unit that the child has not been the subject of a suit and the petition states that no other court has continuing, exclusive jurisdiction over the child.

(b) If the vital statistics unit notifies the court that the unit has furnished incorrect information regarding the existence of another court with continuing, exclusive jurisdiction before the rendition of a final order, the provisions of this chapter apply.

History of Fam. Code §155.103: Acts 1995, 74th Leg., ch. 20, §1, eff. Apr. 20, 1995. Amended by Acts 1995, 74th Leg., ch. 751, §45, eff. Sept. 1, 1995; Acts 2015, 84th Leg., ch. 1, §1.052, eff. Apr. 2, 2015. Source: Former Fam. Code §11.05(c).

ANNOTATIONS

Jones v. TDFPS, 400 S.W.3d 173, 178-79 (Tex. App.—Austin 2013, no pet.). See annotation under Family Code §155.104, this page.

FAM §155.104. VOIDABLE ORDER

(a) If a request for information from the vital statistics unit relating to the identity of the court having continuing, exclusive jurisdiction of the child has been made under this subchapter, a final order, except an order of dismissal, may not be rendered until the information is filed with the court.

(b) If a final order is rendered in the absence of the filing of the information from the vital statistics unit, the order is voidable on a showing that a court other than the court that rendered the order had continuing, exclusive jurisdiction.

History of Fam. Code §155.104: Acts 1995, 74th Leg., ch. 20, §1, eff. Apr. 20, 1995. Amended by Acts 1995, 74th Leg., ch. 751, §46, eff. Sept. 1, 1995; Acts 2015, 84th Leg., ch. 1, §1.053, eff. Apr. 2, 2015. Source: Former Fam. Code §11.071(c).

ANNOTATIONS

Jones v. TDFPS, 400 S.W.3d 173, 178-79 (Tex. App.—Austin 2013, no pet.). "[T]he Department did not file the bureau-of-vital-statistics [BVS] letter before the Williamson County court rendered a final order. Because the court did not render a final order [un-

der Fam. Code §155.004] *based on* incorrect information from the [BVS], the Travis County court did not lose its continuing, exclusive jurisdiction [CEJ] when the Williamson County court rendered its order. [Children's caretaker] argued at the hearing that, because the Department failed to file the [BVS] letter with the Williamson County court, the Travis County court never lost [CEJ], and the Williamson County order was therefore void. While we agree that the Travis County court did not lose its [CEJ], we disagree that the Williamson County order was void. ... In enacting [Fam. Code §155.104(b)], the legislature used the term 'voidable' rather than 'void.' ... Thus, we conclude that the Williamson County court order rendered prior to the Department's filing the [BVS] letter was merely voidable, not void."

In re T.S.L., 196 S.W.3d 233, 235 (Tex.App.—Fort Worth 2006, no pet.). "[W's] offer of proof at the ... hearing on her motion to identify the court of continuing, exclusive jurisdiction and plea to the jurisdiction included her [earlier] request for information with the BVS [bureau of vital statistics]. The 233rd District Court nevertheless rendered judgment in [H's] favor at the end of the hearing. ... Accordingly, we hold that the trial court violated §155.104(a) by rendering judgment in spite of its knowledge that [W] had filed a request with the BVS. We also hold that the BVS's determination that the 325th is the court of continuing jurisdiction in this case renders the trial court's judgment void under §155.104(b)."

Sections 155.105-155.200 reserved for expansion

SUBCHAPTER C. TRANSFER OF CONTINUING, EXCLUSIVE JURISDICTION

Ⓐ FAM §155.201. MANDATORY TRANSFER

(a) On the filing of a motion showing that a suit for dissolution of the marriage of the child's parents has been filed in another court and requesting a transfer to that court, the court having continuing, exclusive jurisdiction of a suit affecting the parent-child relationship shall, within the time required by Section 155.204, transfer the proceedings to the court in which the dissolution of the marriage is pending. The motion must comply with the requirements of Section 155.204(a).

(b) If a suit to modify or a motion to enforce an order is filed in the court having continuing, exclusive jurisdiction of a suit, on the timely motion of a party the court shall, within the time required by Section 155.204, transfer the proceeding to another county in this state if the child has resided in the other county for six months or longer.

(c) If a suit to modify or a motion to enforce an order is pending at the time a subsequent suit to modify or motion to enforce is filed, the court may transfer the proceeding as provided by Subsection (b) only if the court could have transferred the proceeding at the time the first motion or suit was filed.

☠ *Subsection (d) was enacted by H.B. 7, §10, 85th Leg., enacted May 26, 2017, effective Sept. 1, 2017, and S.B. 738, §1, 85th Leg., enacted May 24, 2017, effective Sept. 1, 2017, without reference to the conflicting enactment made by S.B. 999, §1, 85th Leg., enacted May 28, 2017, effective Sept. 1, 2017. For harmonizing conflicts, see p. V. Subsection (d) is effective for service plans filed for a full adversary hearing held under Fam. Code §262.201 or a status hearing held under Fam. Code ch. 263 on or after Jan. 1, 2018. Except as provided above, subsection (d) is effective for SAPCRs filed on or after Sept. 1, 2017.*

(d) On receiving notice that a court exercising jurisdiction under Chapter 262 has ordered the transfer of a suit under Section 262.203(a)(2), the court of continuing, exclusive jurisdiction shall, pursuant to the requirements of Section 155.204(i), transfer the proceedings to the court in which the suit under Chapter 262 is pending, within the time required by Section[1] 155.207(a).

☠ *Subsection (d) was enacted by S.B. 999, §1, 85th Leg., enacted May 28, 2017, effective Sept. 1, 2017, without reference to the conflicting enactments made by H.B. 7, §10, 85th Leg., enacted May 26, 2017, effective Sept. 1, 2017, and S.B. 738, §1, 85th Leg., enacted May 24, 2017, effective Sept. 1, 2017. For harmonizing conflicts, see p. V. Subsection (d) is effective for SAPCRs filed on or after Sept. 1, 2017.*

(d) On receiving notice that a court exercising jurisdiction under Chapter 262 has ordered the transfer of a suit under Section 262.203(a)(2), the court of continuing, exclusive jurisdiction shall, in accordance with the requirements of Section 155.204(i), transfer the proceedings to the court in which the suit under Chapter 262 is pending within the time required by Section 155.207(a).

1. **Editor's note:** In 2017, the Legislature enacted three versions of subsection (d). H.B. 7, §10, 85th Leg., enacted May 26, 2017, effective Sept. 1, 2017, and S.B. 999, §1, 85th Leg., enacted May 28, 2017, effective Sept. 1, 2017, use "Section," as shown here, and S.B. 738, §1, 85th Leg., enacted May 24, 2017, effective Sept. 1, 2017, uses "Subsection."

History of Fam. Code §155.201: Acts 1995, 74th Leg., ch. 20, §1, eff. Apr. 20, 1995. Amended by Acts 1999, 76th Leg., ch. 1135, §1, eff. Sept. 1, 1999; Acts 2005, 79th Leg., ch. 916, §14, eff. June 18, 2005; H.B. 7, §10, 85th Leg., eff. Sept. 1, 2017; S.B. 738, §1, 85th Leg., eff. Sept. 1, 2017; S.B. 999, §1, 85th Leg., eff. Sept. 1, 2017. Source: Former Fam. Code §11.06(b), (c).

See also *O'Connor's Texas Family Law Handbook* (2017), "Filing SAPCR with dissolution suit," ch. 4-A, §3.3, p. 347; "Family Code transfers," ch. 4-B, §3.2, p. 350.

ANNOTATIONS

Tippy v. Walker, 865 S.W.2d 928, 929 (Tex.1993). "This petition for writ of mandamus raises the issue of whether the six months residency period for mandatory transfer of venue in child custody modification motions under [Fam. Code] §11.06(b) [now §155.201(b)] only begins to run after the original custody decree is signed, or at the earlier date when the child's actual residency in the different county begins. [¶] We previously *implicitly* held that residency runs from the earlier date in holding that transfer was mandatory in ***Arias v. Spector***, 623 S.W.2d 312 (Tex.1981). In our computation in ***Arias*** we included part of the pre-judgment residency period to reach the required total residency then specified in §11.06(b). We now make that implicit holding explicit." *See also* ***In re Powell***, 79 S.W.3d 814, 816 (Tex.App.—Fort Worth 2002, no pet.).

Proffer v. Yates, 734 S.W.2d 671, 672 (Tex.1987). "The writ of mandamus has been available to compel mandatory transfer in [SAPCRs] for a number of years. *At 673:* Transfer of a case to a county where the child has resided for more than six months is a mandatory ministerial duty under [Fam. Code] §11.06(b) [now §155.201(b)]. And remedy by appeal, though available, is frequently inadequate to protect the rights of parents and children to a trial in a particular venue. Parents and children who have a right under the mandatory venue provisions to venue in a particular county should not be forced to go through a trial that is for naught. Justice demands a speedy resolution of child custody and child support issues."

Leonard v. Paxson, 654 S.W.2d 440, 441 (Tex. 1983). "The venue provisions of the Family Code remove [SAPCRs] from the operation of the general venue statute and the transfer provisions set forth in [Fam. Code] §11.06(b) [now §155.201] supplant the [TRCPs] governing pleas of privilege."

In re Lovell-Osburn, 448 S.W.3d 616, 620 (Tex. App.—Houston [14th Dist.] 2014, orig. proceeding). See annotation under Family Code §153.0071, p. 509.

In re Lawson, 357 S.W.3d 134, 136 (Tex.App.—San Antonio 2011, orig. proceeding). "It is undisputed that [child] has resided in McLennan County for six months or longer. [Father] argued that [child's] residence in McLennan County ... was temporary because the divorce decree required [mother] to move within 100 miles of his residence by August 1, 2011[, two days before mother filed motion to transfer]. However, it is mandatory under ... §155.201 for the trial court to transfer the suit to a county where the child has lived for six months or longer. [W]e can find [no exception] applicable to this case. [W]e conclude ... the trial court had a mandatory duty to transfer the proceeding to McLennan County."

In re Nabors, 276 S.W.3d 190, 196 (Tex.App.—Houston [14th Dist.] 2009, orig. proceeding). "The children resided with [foster parents] for approximately 17 months before TDFPS moved them to Harris County. They were placed in Harris County approximately two weeks before [foster parents] filed their motion to transfer venue. *At 197:* Under [Fam. Code] §155.201(b) the Legislature does not require that the children *currently reside* in the other county, only that they '*have resided*' there for six months or longer when the modification suit is filed. [¶] Our interpretation ... properly focuses on determination of the children's '*principal residence*' during the six month period. We duly regard the Legislature's instructions not to focus on time and location of the children on a particular day. In determining the county of principal residence we focus on elements of permanency for the children which are critical to establishing residency for venue purposes." *See also* ***In re Dozier***, No. 07-08-0491-CV (Tex. App.—Amarillo 2009, orig. proceeding) (memo op.; 1-29-09) (§155.201(b) does not require that child reside in county to which transfer is sought on date motion to transfer is filed).

In re Leder, 263 S.W.3d 283, 286 (Tex.App.—Houston [1st Dist.] 2007, orig. proceeding). "[T]he trial court concluded[] that [mother] waived venue by invoking the trial court's judicial power. [Father] claims that [mother] acted inconsistently with her desire to change venue when she filed a counter-claim, a jury demand, a motion to vacate the ex parte temporary orders, two motions for sanctions, and a certificate of

written discovery before obtaining a ruling on her motion for transfer. *At 287:* [W]e conclude that [mother's] actions did not waive her venue challenge. The affirmative relief requested by [mother] in tandem with her motion to transfer is expressly contemplated by the mandatory venue statute. [Mother's] preliminary motions and discovery are ancillary to the main action and did not invoke the power of the trial court in a manner inconsistent with [mother's] continuing intention to insist on a change of venue."

Huey v. Huey, 200 S.W.3d 851, 853 (Tex.App.—Dallas 2006, no pet.). "We conclude [mother's] act of [intentionally] removing the children to a county [in violation of the divorce decree] constitutes a waiver of the right to give notice of transfer under [Fam. Code] §155.204 and a forfeiture of the right to have the case transferred." *See also* ***In re Cooper***, 320 S.W.3d 905, 910 (Tex.App.—Texarkana 2010, orig. proceeding) (mother's act of removing child to county in violation of divorce decree was unintentional, so she did not forfeit her right to transfer under §155.201); ***In re M.A.S.***, 246 S.W.3d 182, 184 (Tex.App.—San Antonio 2007, no pet.) (mandatory transfer provisions in Family Code are not meant to be a tool to manipulate venue and play courts against each other).

In re Wheeler, 177 S.W.3d 350, 353 (Tex.App.—Houston [1st Dist.] 2005, orig. proceeding). The question is "whether the trial court was required to transfer venue to Brazos County, where one child has been living for the past seven years, while another child has been living in Harris County for the past eight months. [¶] [A] trial court has no discretion but to transfer venue as to one child if the child has been living in another county for at least six months prior to the proceedings and a controverting affidavit has not been filed in regard to that child. *At 354:* Because the real party in interest filed no controverting affidavit regarding the residence of [child in question], the trial court had a ministerial duty to sever and to transfer all proceedings pertaining to [child who had lived in Brazos County for the past seven years] to Brazos County." *See also* ***In re T.J.L.***, 97 S.W.3d 257, 264 (Tex.App.—Houston [14th Dist.] 2002, no pet.) (§155.201 requires court to transfer to county where child resides, even if court retains jurisdiction over another child of marriage who does not reside in that county).

FAM §155.202. DISCRETIONARY TRANSFER

(a) If the basis of a motion to transfer a proceeding under this subchapter is that the child resides in another county, the court may deny the motion if it is shown that the child has resided in that county for less than six months at the time the proceeding is commenced.

(b) For the convenience of the parties and witnesses and in the interest of justice, the court, on the timely motion of a party, may transfer the proceeding to a proper court in another county in the state.

History of Fam. Code §155.202: Acts 1995, 74th Leg., ch. 20, §1, eff. Apr. 20, 1995. Source: Former Fam. Code §11.06(b), (d).

See also ***O'Connor's Texas Family Law Handbook*** (2017), "Challenging Venue," ch. 4-B, §3, p. 350.

ANNOTATIONS

Hathorn v. Sivers, 962 S.W.2d 284, 286 n.3 (Tex.App.—Houston [14th Dist.] 1998, no writ). "We recognize that former [Fam. Code] §11.06(d) and [Fam. Code] §155.202(b) refer to transfers to other counties in the state, not intra-county transfers. The case law, however, refers to these sections of the Family Code when dealing with intra-county transfers. We see no reason to treat intra-county transfers differently, and therefore find §155.202(b) is applicable to this case. *At 287:* In this case, [mother's] motion specifically stated that the transfer was sought because she believed 'that the matters at hand may be handled more expeditiously for the parties and for the District Court, if this case is transferred to the county court.' We find that this is simply another way of stating that the request is for the convenience of the parties and in the interest of justice, a reason specifically authorizing transfers under §155.202 ... for discretionary transfers. Thus, ... we hold that the transfer to the county court at law was appropriate under §155.202(b) because there was a proper motion and order."

FAM §155.203. DETERMINING COUNTY OF CHILD'S RESIDENCE

In computing the time during which the child has resided in a county, the court may not require that the period of residence be continuous and uninterrupted but shall look to the child's principal residence during the six-month period preceding the commencement of the suit.

History of Fam. Code §155.203: Acts 1995, 74th Leg., ch. 20, §1, eff. Apr. 20, 1995. Source: Former Fam. Code §11.06(b).

ANNOTATIONS

In re Ferguson, 172 S.W.3d 122, 126 (Tex.App.—Beaumont 2005, orig. proceeding). "We do not deny that for purposes of construing other venue provisions

contained in various Texas codes and statutes the concept of 'dual residency' or of 'domicile versus residence' has its place. However, §155.203 requires the trial court to look to the child's 'principal residence' during the six-month period in question. *At 127:* We decline to embrace the concept of 'dual residences,' under the facts and circumstances of this case."

FAM §155.204. PROCEDURE FOR TRANSFER

In 2017, three bills amended §155.204. The amended text from H.B. 7, §11 is effective for service plans filed for a full adversary hearing held under Fam. Code §262.201 or a status hearing held under Fam. Code ch. 263 on or after Jan. 1, 2018. A hearing held before Jan. 1, 2018, is governed by the former law in effect at that time. Except as provided above, the amended text in §155.204 is effective for SAPCRs filed on or after Sept. 1, 2017. SAPCRs filed before Sept. 1, 2017, are governed by the former law in effect at that time.

(a) A motion to transfer under Section 155.201(a) may be filed at any time. The motion must contain a certification that all other parties, including the attorney general, if applicable, have been informed of the filing of the motion.

(b) Except as provided by Subsection (a) or Section 262.203, a motion to transfer by a petitioner or movant is timely if it is made at the time the initial pleadings are filed. A motion to transfer by another party is timely if it is made on or before the first Monday after the 20th day after the date of service of citation or notice of the suit or before the commencement of the hearing, whichever is sooner.

(c) If a timely motion to transfer has been filed and no controverting affidavit is filed within the period allowed for its filing, the proceeding shall, not later than the 21st day after the final date of the period allowed for the filing of a controverting affidavit, be transferred without a hearing to the proper court.

(d) On or before the first Monday after the 20th day after the date of notice of a motion to transfer is served, a party desiring to contest the motion must file a controverting affidavit denying that grounds for the transfer exist.

(e) If a controverting affidavit contesting the motion to transfer is filed, each party is entitled to notice not less than 10 days before the date of the hearing on the motion to transfer.

(f) Only evidence pertaining to the transfer may be taken at the hearing.

(g) If the court finds after the hearing on the motion to transfer that grounds for the transfer exist, the proceeding shall be transferred to the proper court not later than the 21st day after the date the hearing is concluded.

(h) An order transferring or refusing to transfer the proceeding is not subject to interlocutory appeal.

(i) If a transfer order has been signed by a court exercising jurisdiction under Chapter 262, the Department of Family and Protective Services shall [~~a party may~~] file the transfer order with the clerk of the court of continuing, exclusive jurisdiction. On receipt and without a hearing or further order from the court of continuing, exclusive jurisdiction, the clerk of the court of continuing, exclusive jurisdiction shall transfer the files as provided by this subchapter within the time required by Section[1] 155.207(a).

1. **Editor's note:** In 2017, three bills amended subsection (i). H.B. 7, §11, 85th Leg., enacted May 26, 2017, effective Sept. 1, 2017, and S.B. 999, §2, 85th Leg., enacted May 28, 2017, effective Sept. 1, 2017, use "Section," as shown here, and S.B. 738, §2, 85th Leg., enacted May 24, 2017, effective Sept. 1, 2017, uses "Subsection."

History of Fam. Code §155.204: Acts 1995, 74th Leg., ch. 20, §1, eff. Apr. 20, 1995. Amended by Acts 1999, 76th Leg., ch. 1150, §1 (eff. Sept. 1, 1999), ch. 1390, §14 (eff. Sept. 1, 1999); Acts 2005, 79th Leg., ch. 916, §15, eff. June 18, 2005; H.B. 7, §11, 85th Leg., eff. Sept. 1, 2017; S.B. 738, §2, 85th Leg., eff. Sept. 1, 2017; S.B. 999, §2, 85th Leg., eff. Sept. 1, 2017. Source: Former Fam. Code §11.06(f)-(i).

See also ***O'Connor's Texas Family Law Handbook*** (2017), "Procedures," ch. 4-B, §3.2.2, p. 352.

ANNOTATIONS

Alexander v. Russell, 699 S.W.2d 209, 210 (Tex. 1985). Family Code §11.06, now §155.204, "requires a timely motion by any party to the suit to transfer the proceedings. Absent a motion and order of transfer, the 243rd District Court retained exclusive jurisdiction. Despite what the conservatorship order says about the 327th District Court having jurisdiction, there is no order transferring the cause to the 327th District Court. Thus, the 243rd District Court retained jurisdiction. Any attempted transfer of this cause to the 327th District Court was not for a reason authorized under §11.06 and therefore the judge had no authority to transfer the cause. If the judge of the 243rd District Court found it necessary to recuse himself, the proper procedure was to have another district judge preside in the 243rd District Court, not to transfer the cause."

In re Thompson, 434 S.W.3d 624, 629 (Tex.App.—Houston [1st Dist.] 2014, orig. proceeding). "[A] motion is timely filed by a counter-petitioner if the motion

to transfer is filed with the counter-petition. [Father, however,] seeks no relief modifying matters affecting the parent-child relationship; he is not a counter-petitioner. The court in ***Bollard*** [***v. Berchelmann***, 921 S.W.2d 861 (Tex.App.—San Antonio 1996, orig. proceeding),] rejected the argument that any party filing a motion to transfer should be considered a 'movant' under §155.204(b).... [¶] [W]e hold that [father] was 'another party' under §155.204(b)...."

In re T.J.L., 97 S.W.3d 257, 262 (Tex.App.—Houston [14th Dist.] 2002, no pet.). "An order denying transfer under [Fam. Code §§155.201-155.207] is not subject to interlocutory appeal. However, an interlocutory order is appealable when it has merged into a subsequent final, appealable order. [Family Code §109.002(b)] allows appeal from a final order rendered in a [SAPCR]. The enforcement orders are final orders into which the denial of the motion to transfer could properly merge. [¶] [Mother] was not required to file a notice of appeal that explicitly referred to the order denying transfer or the date of this order. Instead, she properly challenges the order denying transfer as an issue in her appeal of the enforcement orders. Accordingly, [mother's] notices of appeal have invoked this court's jurisdiction to address the merits of her motion to transfer."

In re S.G.S., 53 S.W.3d 848, 851 (Tex.App.—Fort Worth 2001, no pet.). W argues that H's "motion to transfer was untimely because he did not move to transfer jurisdiction ... when he filed a proposed agreed order to modify their divorce decree to award [H] 100% of the [bank] account. [W] contends that [H's] filing of the proposed agreed order is the 'initial pleading' under §155.204(a) [now §155.204(b)]. Thus, she argues that [H], as the petitioner or movant, was required to file his motion to transfer venue then. [¶] Unlike [W's] petition that sought to modify the children's visitation schedules, [H's] proposed order sought only to modify their property settlement. Therefore, his proposed order was not a [SAPCR] and he was not required to file his transfer motion when he filed the proposed order."

FAM §155.205. TRANSFER OF CHILD SUPPORT REGISTRY

(a) On rendition of an order transferring continuing, exclusive jurisdiction to another court, the transferring court shall also order that all future payments of child support be made to the local registry of the transferee court or, if payments have previously been directed to the state disbursement unit, to the state disbursement unit.

(b) The transferring court's local registry or the state disbursement unit shall continue to receive, record, and forward child support payments to the payee until it receives notice that the transferred case has been docketed by the transferee court.

(c) After receiving notice of docketing from the transferee court, the transferring court's local registry shall send a certified copy of the child support payment record to the clerk of the transferee court and shall forward any payments received to the transferee court's local registry or to the state disbursement unit, as appropriate.

History of Fam. Code §155.205: Acts 1995, 74th Leg., ch. 20, §1, eff. Apr. 20, 1995. Amended by Acts 1999, 76th Leg., ch. 556, §11, eff. Sept. 1, 1999; Acts 2001, 77th Leg., ch. 1023, §11, eff. Sept. 1, 2001. Source: Former Fam. Code §§11.05(h), 11.06(j).

FAM §155.206. EFFECT OF TRANSFER

(a) A court to which a transfer is made becomes the court of continuing, exclusive jurisdiction and all proceedings in the suit are continued as if it were brought there originally.

(b) A judgment or order transferred has the same effect and shall be enforced as if originally rendered in the transferee court.

(c) The transferee court shall enforce a judgment or order of the transferring court by contempt or by any other means by which the transferring court could have enforced its judgment or order. The transferee court shall have the power to punish disobedience of the transferring court's order, whether occurring before or after the transfer, by contempt.

(d) After the transfer, the transferring court does not retain jurisdiction of the child who is the subject of the suit, nor does it have jurisdiction to enforce its order for a violation occurring before or after the transfer of jurisdiction.

History of Fam. Code §155.206: Acts 1995, 74th Leg., ch. 20, §1, eff. Apr. 20, 1995. Source: Former Fam. Code §11.06(k).

ANNOTATIONS

Ex parte Barnett, 600 S.W.2d 252, 255 (Tex.1980). "It would indeed be anomalous to permit courts to enforce by contempt proceedings the orders of another court in the circumstances described, but not permit the transferee court to enforce the orders of the trans-

ferring court in the face of the legislative intent clearly manifested in the Family Code that the new 'court of continuing jurisdiction' decide all matters relating to the subject matter of the case transferred. We hold that the district court of Collin County is empowered under the provisions of the Family Code to hear and decide pending and new contempt proceedings arising from the alleged failure to comply with orders of the transferring district court of Dallas County, regardless of whether all or some of the alleged contemptuous acts were committed before the transfer of the cause to the transferee court."

FAM §155.207. TRANSFER OF COURT FILES

(a) Not later than the 10th working day after the date an order of transfer is signed, the clerk of the court transferring a proceeding shall send to the proper court in the county to which transfer is being made:

(1) the pleadings in the pending proceeding and any other document specifically requested by a party;

(2) certified copies of all entries in the minutes;

(3) a certified copy of each final order; and

(4) a certified copy of the order of transfer signed by the transferring court.

(b) The clerk of the transferring court shall keep a copy of the transferred pleadings and other requested documents. If the transferring court retains jurisdiction of another child who was the subject of the suit, the clerk shall send a copy of the pleadings and other requested documents to the court to which the transfer is made and shall keep the original pleadings and other requested documents.

(c) On receipt of the pleadings, documents, and orders from the transferring court, the clerk of the transferee court shall docket the suit and shall notify the judge of the transferee court, all parties, the clerk of the transferring court, and, if appropriate, the transferring court's local registry that the suit has been docketed.

(d) The clerk of the transferring court shall send a certified copy of the order directing payments to the transferee court, to any party or employer affected by that order, and, if appropriate, to the local registry of the transferee court.

History of Fam. Code §155.207: Acts 1995, 74th Leg., ch. 20, §1, eff. Apr. 20, 1995. Amended by Acts 2001, 77th Leg., ch. 1023, §12, eff. Sept. 1, 2001; Acts 2005, 79th Leg., ch. 916, §16, eff. June 18, 2005; Acts 2015, 84th Leg., ch. 211, §1, eff. Sept. 1, 2015. Source: Former Fam. Code §11.06(j), (m).

ANNOTATIONS

Bigham v. Dempster, 901 S.W.2d 424, 430 (Tex. 1995). See annotation under Family Code §155.005, p. 591.

In re T.J.L., 97 S.W.3d 257, 264-65 (Tex.App.—Houston [14th Dist.] 2002, no pet.). Section 155.207 "does not state that a motion to sever is required to effect transfer as to one of several children. However, the statute clearly contemplates severance in those instances because it prescribes the procedure for handling the case files when one child is transferred and another child is not. [W]e have determined that the Legislature intended transfer as to one child when not all children live in the transferee county. Severance is the procedure to implement transfer in those instances. Therefore, because our primary aim is to give effect to legislative intent, we construe the statute as requiring severance to transfer the proceedings as to one of several children, even when the movant does not move to sever."

Sections 155.208-155.300 reserved for expansion

SUBCHAPTER D. TRANSFER OF PROCEEDINGS WITHIN THE STATE WHEN PARTY OR CHILD RESIDES OUTSIDE THE STATE

FAM §155.301. AUTHORITY TO TRANSFER

(a) A court of this state with continuing, exclusive jurisdiction over a child custody proceeding under Chapter 152 or a child support proceeding under Chapter 159 shall transfer the proceeding to the county of residence of the resident party if one party is a resident of this state and all other parties including the child or all of the children affected by the proceeding reside outside this state.

(b) If one or more of the parties affected by the proceedings reside outside the state and if more than one party or one or more children affected by the proceeding reside in this state in different counties, the court shall transfer the proceeding according to the following priorities:

(1) to the court of continuing, exclusive jurisdiction, if any;

(2) to the county of residence of the child, if applicable, provided that:

(A) Subdivision (1) is inapplicable; or

(B) the court of continuing, exclusive jurisdiction finds that neither a party nor a child affected by the proceeding resides in the county of the court of continuing, exclusive jurisdiction; or

(3) if Subdivisions (1) and (2) are inapplicable, to the county most appropriate to serve the convenience of the resident parties, the witnesses, and the interest of justice.

(c) Except as otherwise provided by this subsection, if a transfer of continuing, exclusive jurisdiction is sought under this section, the procedures for determining and effecting a transfer of proceedings provided by this chapter apply. If the parties submit to the court an agreed order for transfer, the court shall sign the order without the need for other pleadings.

History of Fam. Code §155.301: Acts 1995, 74th Leg., ch. 20, §1, eff. Apr. 20, 1995. Amended by Acts 2003, 78th Leg., ch. 1036, §17, eff. Sept. 1, 2003; Acts 2007, 80th Leg., ch. 972, §13, eff. Sept. 1, 2007. Source: Former Fam. Code §11.061.

See also ***O'Connor's Texas Family Law Handbook*** (2017), "Challenging venue – motion to transfer," ch. 9-A, §6.2.1(2), p. 997.

ANNOTATIONS

In re Casseb, 119 S.W.3d 841, 843 (Tex.App.—San Antonio 2003, no pet.). "We believe [Fam. Code] §155.301 was intended to apply whenever child support proceedings should be transferred within Texas because a party or a child resides outside of Texas regardless of whether a motion to modify support references [Fam. Code] ch. 156 or ch. 159. The phrase, 'a court of this state with continuing exclusive jurisdiction over a suit or action for child support under Ch. 159' can be read to mean that if a court in Texas has continuing exclusive jurisdiction over child support issues because [Fam. Code] §159.205 … provides that a court in Texas has continuing exclusive jurisdiction, then the transfer provision of §155.301 becomes mandatory." *See also* ***In re S.G.S.***, No. 2-05-211-CV (Tex.App.—Fort Worth 2006, pet. denied) (memo op.; 6-29-06) (predicate to applying Fam. Code §155.301(a) is not whether proceeding is brought under Fam. Code ch. 152 or ch. 159 but whether trial court has continuing, exclusive jurisdiction).

CHAPTER 156. MODIFICATION

SUBCHAPTER A. GENERAL PROVISIONS

FAM §156.001. ORDERS SUBJECT TO MODIFICATION

A court with continuing, exclusive jurisdiction may modify an order that provides for the conservatorship, support, or possession of and access to a child.

History of Fam. Code §156.001: Acts 1995, 74th Leg., ch. 20, §1, eff. Apr. 20, 1995. Source: Former Fam. Code §§11.05(g), 14.08(a).

ANNOTATIONS

In re P.D.M., 117 S.W.3d 453, 462 (Tex.App.—Fort Worth 2003, pet. denied). "Clearly, a custody order no longer governs the right to possession of a child when the managing conservator named in the order dies. Thus, the possessory conservator parent is free to seek a writ of habeas corpus compelling his 'present possession,' not necessarily 'custody,' of the children. But the fact that a prior order may no longer effectively govern the present right of possession to a child simply does not alter its status as a prior order or the reality of its prior existence, i.e., the effect it had on the subject children's lives. In other words, following the death of the manag-

ing conservator, a custody order is not a valid and subsisting order that operates to preclude issuance of a writ of habeas corpus to anyone other than the order's named, deceased managing conservator, but it nonetheless is a prior custody order for purposes of a ch. 156 suit to modify the parent-child relationship." *But see* ***Dohrn v. Delgado***, 941 S.W.2d 244, 248 (Tex.App.—Corpus Christi 1996, orig. proceeding) (suit filed after managing conservator's death that seeks change in custody order is original suit, not modification).

Considine v. Considine, 726 S.W.2d 253, 254 (Tex. App.—Austin 1987, no writ). "We note that before provisions relating to conservatorship, possession, and support in prior orders may be modified, the court must conduct a hearing. A 'hearing,' in this context, implies the admission and consideration of proof—the opposite of taking allegations of the motion for modification 'as confessed for want of an answer.' We conclude that the allegations in the motion to modify may not be taken as confessed for want of an answer. As a result, in a case of default by the respondent, the movant must prove up the required allegations of the motion to modify." *See also* ***Agraz v. Carnley***, 143 S.W.3d 547, 552-53 (Tex.App.—Dallas 2004, no pet.) (applying rationale of ***Considine*** court).

FAM §156.002. WHO CAN FILE

(a) A party affected by an order may file a suit for modification in the court with continuing, exclusive jurisdiction.

(b) A person or entity who, at the time of filing, has standing to sue under Chapter 102 may file a suit for modification in the court with continuing, exclusive jurisdiction.

(c) The sibling of a child who is separated from the child because of the actions of the Department of Family and Protective Services may file a suit for modification requesting access to the child in the court with continuing, exclusive jurisdiction.

History of Fam. Code §156.002: Acts 1995, 74th Leg., ch. 20, §1, eff. Apr. 20, 1995. Amended by Acts 2009, 81st Leg., ch. 1113, §26, eff. Sept. 1, 2009. Source: Former Fam. Code §§11.03(f), 14.08(a).

ANNOTATIONS

In re Martin, ___ S.W.3d ___ (Tex.App.—Dallas 2017, orig. proceeding) (No. 05-16-00987-CV; 2-3-17). "The parties do not dispute that Grandparents were parties to the [original] judgment, and the judgment recites that 'respondents ... appeared in person and through attorney of record....' To have standing, however, Grandparents must not only be parties to the order, but also be affected by the order. Although the term 'affected' is not defined by statute, the term is not ambiguous. The plain and ordinary meaning of 'affect' is 'to produce an effect upon.' Here, the agreed order awards Grandparents the right to 35 hours visitation and the right to be notified regarding extracurricular activities. Thus, it clearly affects Grandparents. Because Grandparents are parties to a judgment that affects them, Father's contention that Grandparents lack standing under §156.002 ... lacks merit." *See also* ***In re S.A.M.***, 321 S.W.3d 785, 789-90 (Tex.App.—Houston [14th Dist.] 2010, no pet.) (party need not have been granted conservatorship rights to be "party affected by an order"). *But see* ***Watts v. Watts***, 573 S.W.2d 864, 868 (Tex.App.—Fort Worth 1978, no writ) (under Fam. Code §14.08(a), now §156.002, a "party affected by the order" can be any person mentioned in context of conservatorship within decree being modified or any person who has "sufficient interest" in child who is subject of order).

In re Shifflet, 462 S.W.3d 528, 541 (Tex.App.—Houston [1st Dist.] 2015, orig. proceeding). In the original order, the paternal stepgrandfather and his wife "were given rights to telephone visitation with the children at least three days a week and were expressly permitted to enforce the order in their own name.... [¶] The record of the case shows that [father] was prohibited from seeing the children due to his domestic violence convictions. [Grandparents] effectively seek by their petition for intervention in this modification suit to step into his shoes. The record also shows both parents agreed for extended periods of time that the children should live with [grandparents], and they did so. It also shows that [mother] herself lived with [grandparents] for a period of time shortly before the filing of this suit. Under these circumstances, we conclude that [grandparents] have shown that they have substantial rights to the children that are affected by this suit and that their access to the children was important to the children's well-being. We therefore hold that they have a sufficient interest in both of the children to have standing to intervene in this suit by [mother] to modify the [original] Order, under §156.002(a), and to be named [SMCs] of the children."

In re C.A.M.M., 243 S.W.3d 211, 215 (Tex.App.—Houston [14th Dist.] 2007, pet. denied). Father "contends that upon [mother's] death, the prior conserva-

torship order was no longer a valid order governing conservatorship and possession. He reasons that because the prior order became invalid, the trial court erred by treating this action as a suit for modification, rather than an original [SAPCR]. *At 217-18:* [I]n accordance with the Legislature's preference for stability when modifying prior conservatorship orders, the trial court's treatment of the proceeding as a suit for modification is sanctioned by [Fam. Code §§102.003(11) and 156.002] permitting a non-parent to sue for modification upon the death of the managing conservator if the child and the conservator resided with the non-parent. [T]he parental presumption does not apply in a suit for modification." *See also* ***Guardianship of C.E.M.-K.***, 341 S.W.3d 68, 78-79 (Tex.App.—San Antonio 2011, pet. denied) (after original conservatorship determination has been made, any later custody proceeding, regardless of parties involved, is modification suit and parental presumption does not apply); ***In re P.D.M.***, 117 S.W.3d 453, 454 (Tex.App.—Fort Worth 2003, pet. denied) (father's suit for custody was considered modification of final divorce decree after mother, who was managing conservator, died; no parental presumption).

FAM §156.003. NOTICE

A party whose rights and duties may be affected by a suit for modification is entitled to receive notice by service of citation.

History of Fam. Code §156.003: Acts 1995, 74th Leg., ch. 20, §1, eff. Apr. 20, 1995. Amended by Acts 1999, 76th Leg., ch. 178, §9, eff. Aug. 30, 1999. Source: Former Fam. Code §§11.08(c), 14.08(b).

FAM §156.004. PROCEDURE

The Texas Rules of Civil Procedure applicable to the filing of an original lawsuit apply to a suit for modification under this chapter.

History of Fam. Code §156.004: Acts 1995, 74th Leg., ch. 20, §1, eff. Apr. 20, 1995. Source: Former Fam. Code §14.08(b).

A FAM §156.005. FRIVOLOUS FILING OF SUIT FOR MODIFICATION

The amended text in §156.005 is effective for orders rendered on or after Sept. 1, 2017. Orders rendered before Sept. 1, 2017, are governed by the former law in effect at that time.

Notwithstanding Rules 296 through 299, Texas Rules of Civil Procedure, if [If] the court finds that a suit for modification is filed frivolously or is designed to harass a party, the court shall state that finding in the order and assess [tax] attorney's fees as costs against the offending party.

History of Fam. Code §156.005: Acts 1995, 74th Leg., ch. 20, §1, eff. Apr. 20, 1995. Amended by S.B. 1237, §11, 85th Leg., eff. Sept. 1, 2017. Source: Former Fam. Code §14.082.

A FAM §156.006. TEMPORARY ORDERS

(a) Except as provided by Subsection (b), the court may render a temporary order in a suit for modification.

(b) While a suit for modification is pending, the court may not render a temporary order that has the effect of creating a designation, or changing the designation, of the person who has the exclusive right to designate the primary residence of the child, or the effect of creating a geographic area, or changing or eliminating the geographic area, within which a conservator must maintain the child's primary residence, under the final order unless the temporary order is in the best interest of the child and:

(1) the order is necessary because the child's present circumstances would significantly impair the child's physical health or emotional development;

(2) the person designated in the final order has voluntarily relinquished the primary care and possession of the child for more than six months; or

(3) the child is 12 years of age or older and has expressed to the court in chambers as provided by Section 153.009 the name of the person who is the child's preference to have the exclusive right to designate the primary residence of the child.

(b-1) A person who files a motion for a temporary order authorized by Subsection (b)(1) shall execute and attach to the motion an affidavit on the person's personal knowledge or the person's belief based on representations made to the person by a person with personal knowledge that contains facts that support the allegation that the child's present circumstances would significantly impair the child's physical health or emotional development. The court shall deny the relief sought and decline to schedule a hearing on the motion unless the court determines, on the basis of the affidavit, that facts adequate to support the allegation are stated in the affidavit. If the court determines that the facts stated are adequate to support the allegation, the court shall set a time and place for the hearing.

(c) Subsection (b)(2) does not apply to a conservator who has the exclusive right to designate the primary residence of the child and who has temporarily relinquished the primary care and possession of the child

to another person during the conservator's military deployment, military mobilization, or temporary military duty, as those terms are defined by Section 153.701.

History of Fam. Code §156.006: Acts 1995, 74th Leg., ch. 20, §1, eff. Apr. 20, 1995. Amended by Acts 1999, 76th Leg., ch. 1390, §15, eff. Sept. 1, 1999; Acts 2001, 77th Leg., ch. 1289, §3, eff. Sept. 1, 2001; Acts 2003, 78th Leg., ch. 1036, §18, eff. Sept. 1, 2003; Acts 2005, 79th Leg., ch. 916, §17, eff. June 18, 2005; Acts 2009, 81st Leg., ch. 727, §2 (eff. Sept. 1, 2009), ch. 1113, §27 (eff. Sept. 1, 2009), ch. 1118, §2 (eff. Sept. 1, 2009); Acts 2015, 84th Leg., ch. 397, §1, eff. Sept. 1, 2015; H.B. 1495, §1, 85th Leg., eff. Sept. 1, 2017. Source: Former Fam. Code §§11.11(a), 14.08(g).

ANNOTATIONS

In re G.P., 495 S.W.3d 927, 931 (Tex.App.—Fort Worth 2016, orig. proceeding). The "requirements for changing the person who has the exclusive right to designate the child's primary residence apply only when that designation has been previously set through a 'final order.' Here, as the trial court acknowledged in its docket entry, the … final order … did not name a person who had the exclusive right to designate the child's residence. Rather, the trial court's [later] temporary order was the first order to give any party the exclusive right to designate the child's primary residence. Thus, there is no 'final' designation to change, and Grandparents are not required to plead and prove one of the three circumstances described by [§156.006](b)(1)-(3)."

In re Strickland, 358 S.W.3d 818, 821 (Tex.App.—Fort Worth 2012, orig. proceeding). "A temporary order that deprives a custodial parent of any discretion inherent in the right to determine the child's primary residence has the effect of changing the designation of the person with the exclusive right to designate the child's primary residence. [A] trial court's temporary order imposing a geographic restriction on a child's residence when there is no geographic restriction in the decree is a change in the designation of the person who has the exclusive right to designate the primary residence in violation of §156.006(b). We … hold that the trial court's order that the children remain 'in the area' pending the preparation of social studies has the effect of changing the designation of the parent with the primary right to determine the children's residence under the decree because it imposes a restriction whereas the decree has none. *At 822-23:* Father contends that this case is unlike [others] because [mother is moving outside of] Texas. But §156.006 does not distinguish between geographical restrictions within or outside of the state, nor have we found any cases holding that a parent's move outside of the state constitutes *significant* impairment per se to a child's emotional development. [T]he trial court abused its discretion by ruling that the children must remain 'in the area' pending the preparation of a social study." *See also* ***In re Sanchez***, 228 S.W.3d 214, 217-18 (Tex.App.—San Antonio 2007, orig. proceeding) (temporary order effectively changed mother's exclusive right to designate primary residence by substantially reducing her overall possession time, restricting her possession rights, and being of an indefinite duration).

In re Rather, No. 14-11-00924-CV (Tex.App.—Houston [14th Dist.] 2011, orig. proceeding) (memo op.; 12-8-11). "Because … temporary orders [under §156.006] are not appealable, mandamus is an appropriate remedy."

Bolden v. Clapp, 751 S.W.2d 674, 676 (Tex.App.—Tyler 1988, orig. proceeding). "The question of law involved is what constitutes voluntary relinquishment of actual care, control, and possession so as to satisfy the requirement of [Fam. Code] §14.08(g)(2) [now §156.006(b)(2)] and thus empowering the trial court to enter temporary orders. [Mother] contends that relinquishment is the equivalent of abandonment and analogizes the requirements of §14.08(g)(2) to those for involuntary termination of parental rights under [Fam. Code] §15.02 [now §161.001]. That analogy is inapt. The statutes differ in their provisions and their purposes. *At 677:* We believe §14.08(g)(2) requires something less than the showing required by §15.02. Since the consequences of an action or order under ch. 14 are not as far-reaching, irrevocable and complete, we conclude that a lesser showing satisfies the voluntary relinquishment requirement of §14.08(g)(2)."

Sections 156.007-156.100 reserved for expansion

SUBCHAPTER B. MODIFICATION OF CONSERVATORSHIP, POSSESSION & ACCESS, OR DETERMINATION OF RESIDENCE

FAM §156.101. GROUNDS FOR MODIFICATION OF ORDER ESTABLISHING CONSERVATORSHIP OR POSSESSION & ACCESS

(a) The court may modify an order that provides for the appointment of a conservator of a child, that provides the terms and conditions of conservatorship, or that provides for the possession of or access to a child if modification would be in the best interest of the child and:

(1) the circumstances of the child, a conservator, or other party affected by the order have materially and substantially changed since the earlier of:

(A) the date of the rendition of the order; or

(B) the date of the signing of a mediated or collaborative law settlement agreement on which the order is based;

(2) the child is at least 12 years of age and has expressed to the court in chambers as provided by Section 153.009 the name of the person who is the child's preference to have the exclusive right to designate the primary residence of the child; or

(3) the conservator who has the exclusive right to designate the primary residence of the child has voluntarily relinquished the primary care and possession of the child to another person for at least six months.

(b) Subsection (a)(3) does not apply to a conservator who has the exclusive right to designate the primary residence of the child and who has temporarily relinquished the primary care and possession of the child to another person during the conservator's military deployment, military mobilization, or temporary military duty, as those terms are defined by Section 153.701.

History of Fam. Code §156.101: Acts 1995, 74th Leg., ch. 20, §1, eff. Apr. 20, 1995. Amended by Acts 1995, 74th Leg., ch. 751, §47, eff. Sept. 1, 1995; Acts 1999, 76th Leg., ch. 1390, §16, eff. Sept. 1, 1999; Acts 2001, 77th Leg., ch. 1289, §§4, 5, eff. Sept. 1, 2001; Acts 2003, 78th Leg., ch. 1036, §19, eff. Sept. 1, 2003; Acts 2009, 81st Leg., ch. 727, §3 (eff. Sept. 1, 2009), ch. 1113, §28 (eff. Sept. 1, 2009), ch. 1118, §3 (eff. Sept. 1, 2009). Source: Former Fam. Code §14.08(c)(1), (g)(3).

See also *O'Connor's Texas Family Law Handbook* (2017), "Modification of custody – generally," ch. 9-A, §3.1, p. 978.

ANNOTATIONS

Lenz v. Lenz, 79 S.W.3d 10, 14 (Tex.2002). "The Legislature has made clear that '[t]he best interest of the child shall always be the primary consideration of the court in determining the issues of conservatorship and possession of and access to the child.' Yet, the Family Code does not elaborate on the specific requirements for modification in the residency-restriction context, and we have no specific statute governing residency restrictions or their removal for purposes of relocation. Neither have Texas courts articulated any specific standards to apply in this context. Nonetheless, the Legislature has provided a basic framework upon which we may build guidelines for reviewing a modification that removes a residency restriction for purposes of relocation. Family Code §153.001 outlines this framework by pronouncing our public policy for all [SAPCRs]. We must endeavor to give meaning to these public policy imperatives as we interpret the Family Code modification standards in the relocation context." *See also* ***In re C.R.O.***, 96 S.W.3d 442, 448-52 (Tex. App.—Amarillo 2002, pet. denied).

In re V.L.K., 24 S.W.3d 338, 343 (Tex.2000). "A natural parent has the benefit of the parental presumption in an original proceeding, and the nonparent seeking conservatorship has a higher burden. However, the Legislature did not impose different burdens on parents and nonparents in modification suits. ... Because the Legislature did not express its intent to apply the presumption in [Fam. Code] ch. 156 modification suits, courts should not apply the presumption in those cases. *At 344:* We conclude that [Fam. Code] ch. 153's parental presumption does not apply in a Ch. 156 modification proceeding." *See also* ***Sotelo v. Gonzales***, 170 S.W.3d 783, 789 (Tex.App.—El Paso 2005, no pet.) (even when parties to modification suit are identical to those in original proceeding, presumption does not apply).

In re J.A., 482 S.W.3d 141, 145 (Tex.App.—El Paso 2015, no pet.). "The simple question we must first address is which order is controlling for the purpose of determining the timing of the modification action. If the [original] order—which specifies the terms and conditions of conservatorship—controls, then Father did not need to attach an affidavit. But if the child support review order controls, then the affidavit was required [under Fam. Code §156.102]. *At 146:* Other than reiterating the custodial designations, the [child-support-review] order does not address any specifics, nor does it incorporate the prior order by reference. We therefore conclude that the modification action was not filed within one year of the order sought to be modified and that no affidavit was required."

In re A.E.A., 406 S.W.3d 404, 410 (Tex.App.—Fort Worth 2013, no pet.). "[B]oth parties' modification claims required proof of the fact of changed circumstances of the child, a conservator, or other party affected by the order to be modified. But [H's] allegation of changed circumstances constituted a judicial admission of that fact and established that element of [W's] claim for modification, so [W] was not required to put on proof of this admitted fact. And because [H] judicially admitted this element of [W's] claim in his first amended petition to modify, [H] is barred on appeal from challenging the sufficiency of the evidence to support the fact he judicially admitted—a material and

substantial change in circumstances." *See also* ***In re L.C.L.***, 396 S.W.3d 712, 718-19 (Tex.App.—Dallas 2013, no pet.).

In re P.M.G., 405 S.W.3d 406, 412 (Tex.App.—Texarkana 2013, no pet.). "Moving a child from one location to another generally results in some change of the circumstances of the child or parents. The issue is whether such change is material and substantial. Some moves, depending on distance and other factors, may not materially alter or interfere with the relationship of the conservators with the child. Deciding whether the move causes a substantial and material change requires intensive examination of the facts of each case. Factors to be considered in such a determination include the distance involved, the quality of the relationship between the noncustodial parent and the child, the nature and quality of the child's contacts with the noncustodial parent, whether the relocation would deprive the noncustodial parent of regular and meaningful access to the child, the impact of the move on the quality and quantity of the child's contact with the noncustodial parent, the motive for the move, the motive for opposing the move, the feasibility of preserving the relationship between the noncustodial parent and the child through suitable visitation arrangements, and the proximity, availability, and safety of travel arrangements." *See also* ***In re A.N.O.***, 332 S.W.3d 673, 676-77 (Tex.App.—Eastland 2010, no pet.) (when parent who has right to designate child's residence moves child in violation of geographic restriction in divorce decree, material and substantial change occurs).

In re C.H.C., 392 S.W.3d 347, 352 (Tex.App.—Dallas 2013, no pet.). Father's "desire to [spend] more time with [child] is not a material and substantial change in circumstances. To conclude otherwise would allow any non-custodial parent, whose desire is often to spend more time with his or her child, to easily clear the material and substantial change hurdle of §156.101. This goes against the purpose of the 'significant hurdles' Texas law has imposed before a possession order may be modified."

In re H.N.T., 367 S.W.3d 901, 902 (Tex.App.—Dallas 2012, no pet.). "At the time of the final decree…, Mother was living in Houston. After she remarried, she moved … to Grayson County … with [child] from 2000 to 2010. [¶] In … 2010, Mother informed Father her family was experiencing financial difficulties, and she planned to return to Houston…. *At 903-04:* Father argues that [moving child] '… five hours away' from him is … a material and substantive change. *At 905:* Because the original divorce decree does not contain a geographic restriction and at the time it was entered Mother lived in Houston, her desire to move [child] back to Houston does not establish a material or substantial change in circumstances. If anything, it represents an anticipated circumstance because Father knew nothing within the decree prohibited Mother from moving with [child] at anytime to anywhere. … Thus, … a material and substantial change has not occurred from the conditions that existed at the time of the entry of the divorce decree with evidence of the conditions that existed at the time of the hearing on the petition to modify. The conditions at both points in time establish that Mother resided in Houston."

In re Cooper, 333 S.W.3d 656, 661 (Tex.App.—Dallas 2009, orig. proceeding). "No authority supports the trial court's requirement that [mother] make 'extreme efforts' to find employment within the residency-restricted area. To the contrary, courts favor modifying residency restrictions to allow the custodial parent to relocate when the proposed relocation will significantly improve the custodial parent's economic circumstances to the child's benefit. [¶] [T]he trial court imposed upon [mother] a greater burden than the law allows…."

In re S.R.O., 143 S.W.3d 237, 244 (Tex.App.—Waco 2004, no pet.). "[R]emarriage of a parent can constitute a material change in circumstances. *At 247 n.5:* [T]he fact of remarriage is not sufficient, standing alone, to justify the modification of a prior custody order. The movant must also meet the other statutory requisites necessary to obtain the requested modification, such as establishing that the requested modification would be in the best interest of the child."

FAM §156.102. MODIFICATION OF EXCLUSIVE RIGHT TO DETERMINE PRIMARY RESIDENCE OF CHILD WITHIN ONE YEAR OF ORDER

(a) If a suit seeking to modify the designation of the person having the exclusive right to designate the primary residence of a child is filed not later than one year after the earlier of the date of the rendition of the order or the date of the signing of a mediated or collaborative law settlement agreement on which the order is based, the person filing the suit shall execute and attach an affidavit as provided by Subsection (b).

(b) The affidavit must contain, along with supporting facts, at least one of the following allegations:

(1) that the child's present environment may endanger the child's physical health or significantly impair the child's emotional development;

(2) that the person who has the exclusive right to designate the primary residence of the child is the person seeking or consenting to the modification and the modification is in the best interest of the child; or

(3) that the person who has the exclusive right to designate the primary residence of the child has voluntarily relinquished the primary care and possession of the child for at least six months and the modification is in the best interest of the child.

(c) The court shall deny the relief sought and refuse to schedule a hearing for modification under this section unless the court determines, on the basis of the affidavit, that facts adequate to support an allegation listed in Subsection (b) are stated in the affidavit. If the court determines that the facts stated are adequate to support an allegation, the court shall set a time and place for the hearing.

(d) Subsection (b)(3) does not apply to a person who has the exclusive right to designate the primary residence of the child and who has temporarily relinquished the primary care and possession of the child to another person during the conservator's military deployment, military mobilization, or temporary military duty, as those terms are defined by Section 153.701.

History of Fam. Code §156.102: Acts 1995, 74th Leg., ch. 20, §1, eff. Apr. 20, 1995. Amended by Acts 2001, 77th Leg., ch. 1289, §6, eff. Sept. 1, 2001; Acts 2003, 78th Leg., ch. 1036, §20, eff. Sept. 1, 2003; Acts 2009, 81st Leg., ch. 727, §4 (eff. Sept. 1, 2009), ch. 1113, §29 (eff. Sept. 1, 2009). Source: Former Fam. Code §14.08(d), (e).

See also *O'Connor's Texas Family Law Handbook* (2017), "Affidavit supporting modification of primary conservator within one year," ch. 9-A, §4.5.2, p. 993.

ANNOTATIONS

In re McPeak, ___ S.W.3d ___ (Tex.App.—Houston [14th Dist.] 2017, orig. proceeding) (No. 14-17-00104-CV; 4-13-17). Family Code "§156.102 only applies to modification of final orders, not temporary orders. … Mother's motion to modify the Temporary Orders is governed by [Fam. Code] §105.001, not §156.102. [¶] Because Mother sought to modify *temporary* orders, not *final* orders, she was not required to file an affidavit that complied with §156.102." *See also* ***In re Casanova***, No. 05-14-01166-CV (Tex.App.—Dallas 2014, orig. proceeding) (memo op.; 11-20-14) (ch. 156 does not apply to modifications of temporary orders).

In re A.D., 474 S.W.3d 715, 720 (Tex.App.—Houston [14th Dist.] 2014, no pet.). "Section 156.102 was designed to promote stability in conservatorship of children by discouraging relitigation of custodial issues within a short period after the custody order, through a heightened standard of verified pleading. To evaluate the sufficiency of the affidavit, the trial court must determine whether the sworn facts, if true, justify a hearing on the motion to modify. *At 721 n.3:* [Father] filed his affidavit several months after his petition—but before [mother] filed her motion to dismiss. Regardless, the trial court properly construed the affidavit as amending the petition, as permitted under the procedural rules, and thus [father] 'attach[ed]' an affidavit to the petition."

In re N.A.D., 397 S.W.3d 747, 750 (Tex.App.—San Antonio 2013, no pet.). Grandparents "assert they were not required to file an affidavit because they are not [child's] parents, they were not parties to the termination suit, and the provisions of §156.102 apply only to divorcing parents and not to children in the Department's care. [¶] We believe the Legislature did not intend to limit §156.102's applicability solely to divorced parents or persons who were parties to an underlying termination suit. [¶] [Grandparents] next argue that §156.102 does not include the Department within the scope of the word 'person.' *At 751:* The [Texas Code Construction] Act provides that … the … definition of 'person' … include[s] a '… *government or governmental subdivision or agency*….' [W]e conclude §156.102's use of the word 'person' includes the Department."

In re D.W.J.B., 362 S.W.3d 777, 779 (Tex.App.—Texarkana 2012, no pet.). "[G]randmother filed an affidavit [under §156.102] claiming that she was 'deeply concerned for the safety and welfare' of the child, complaining of [father's] 'lengthy criminal history'[, and detailing information she had heard from the child and other family members]. *At 781:* An affidavit not explicitly based on personal knowledge is legally insufficient. Conclusions in the affidavits based upon the statements from others demonstrate the grandmother's lack of personal knowledge. Because the portion of the affi davit regarding [father's alleged endangering acts was] not within the grandmother's personal knowledge, these statements were not required consideration by the trial court during the initial examination of

whether the affidavit was sufficient to merit a hearing under §156.102...."

In re A.L.W., 356 S.W.3d 564, 566-67 (Tex.App.—Texarkana 2011, no pet.). "If [an] affidavit is not filed or is insufficient, §156.102(c) requires the trial court to deny the motion to modify and refuse to schedule a hearing on its merits. However, the trial court does not have to make a specific finding on the record that the affidavit was sufficient to warrant a hearing; the fact that the court set the hearing was, itself, proof that it regarded a filed affidavit as adequate. Even if a court erroneously holds a hearing despite the absence of an affidavit, any error is rendered harmless if the testimony admitted during the hearing would support an allegation that the children's environment may significantly impair their emotional development."

In re C.S., 264 S.W.3d 864, 870 (Tex.App.—Waco 2008, no pet.). "[W]e hold that a party is not entitled to 21 days' notice to respond to a dismissal motion under §156.102(c). *At 872:* [B]ecause of the unique provisions of §156.102(c), we hold that the rule regarding special exceptions does not apply. [¶] This statute permits a denial of relief (or dismissal) without any advance notice to the litigants, solely from the trial court's review of the pleadings."

In re A.S.M., 172 S.W.3d 710, 716 (Tex.App.—Fort Worth 2005, no pet.). "[W]e hold that a suit seeking to *eliminate* or modify the terms of a geographical restriction on a person having the exclusive right to determine a child's primary residence is a 'suit seeking to modify the designation of the person having the exclusive right to designate the primary residence of a child' for purposes of §156.102(a). [¶] Here, [because petition was filed within a year of the original order, mother] was required to file a §156.102 affidavit when she filed her original and first amended petitions seeking to eliminate the geographical restriction."

Mobley v. Mobley, 684 S.W.2d 226, 229 (Tex. App.—Fort Worth 1985, writ dism'd). Section 156.102(c) "requires that an initial determination be made by the court as to whether the facts sworn to in the affidavit supporting the motion to modify justify a hearing. [¶] To be entitled to have the motion set for a hearing in the instant case, [mother] had to state adequate facts to support the allegation that the child's physical health *may* be endangered or his emotional development significantly impaired. The facts alleged had to be sufficient to show the *possibility* of harm rather than the existence of harm."

FAM §156.103. INCREASED EXPENSES BECAUSE OF CHANGE OF RESIDENCE

(a) If a change of residence results in increased expenses for a party having possession of or access to a child, the court may render appropriate orders to allocate those increased expenses on a fair and equitable basis, taking into account the cause of the increased expenses and the best interest of the child.

(b) The payment of increased expenses by the party whose residence is changed is rebuttably presumed to be in the best interest of the child.

(c) The court may render an order without regard to whether another change in the terms and conditions for the possession of or access to the child is made.

History of Fam. Code §156.103: Acts 2001, 77th Leg., ch. 1289, §7, eff. Sept. 1, 2001.

History of Former Fam. Code §156.103: Acts 1995, 74th Leg., ch. 20, §1, eff. Apr. 20, 1995. Deleted by Acts 2001, 77th Leg., ch. 1289, §7, eff. Sept. 1, 2001. Source: Former Fam. Code §14.08(c)(4).

FAM §156.104. MODIFICATION OF ORDER ON CONVICTION FOR CHILD ABUSE; PENALTY

(a) Except as provided by Section 156.1045, the conviction of a conservator for an offense under Section 21.02, Penal Code, or the conviction of a conservator or an order deferring adjudication with regard to the conservator, for an offense involving the abuse of a child under Section 21.11, 22.011, or 22.021, Penal Code, is a material and substantial change of circumstances sufficient to justify a temporary order and modification of an existing court order or portion of a decree that provides for the appointment of a conservator or that sets the terms and conditions of conservatorship or for the possession of or access to a child.

(b) A person commits an offense if the person files a suit to modify an order or portion of a decree based on the grounds permitted under Subsection (a) and the person knows that the person against whom the motion is filed has not been convicted of an offense, or received deferred adjudication for an offense, under Section 21.02, 21.11, 22.011, or 22.021, Penal Code. An offense under this subsection is a Class B misdemeanor.

History of Fam. Code §156.104: Acts 2001, 77th Leg., ch. 1289, §8, eff. Sept. 1, 2001. Amended by Acts 2007, 80th Leg., ch. 593, §3.29, eff. Sept. 1, 2007.

History of Former Fam. Code §156.104: Acts 1995, 74th Leg., ch. 20, §1, eff. Apr. 20, 1995. Deleted by Acts 2001, 77th Leg., ch. 1289, §8, eff. Sept. 1, 2001. Source: Former Fam. Code §§14.021(g), 14.08(c)(5).

See also ***O'Connor's Texas Family Law Handbook*** (2017), "Material & substantial change – statutory," ch. 9-A, §3.1.4(1)(c), p. 980.

FAM §156.1045. MODIFICATION OF ORDER ON CONVICTION FOR FAMILY VIOLENCE

(a) The conviction or an order deferring adjudication of a person who is a possessory conservator or a sole or joint managing conservator for an offense involving family violence is a material and substantial change of circumstances sufficient to justify a temporary order and modification of an existing court order or portion of a decree that provides for the appointment of a conservator or that sets the terms and conditions of conservatorship or for the possession of or access to a child to conform the order to the requirements of Section 153.004(d).

(b) A person commits an offense if the person files a suit to modify an order or portion of a decree based on the grounds permitted under Subsection (a) and the person knows that the person against whom the motion is filed has not been convicted of an offense, or received deferred adjudication for an offense, involving family violence. An offense under this subsection is a Class B misdemeanor.

History of Fam. Code §156.1045: Acts 2001, 77th Leg., ch. 1289, §9, eff. Sept. 1, 2001.

ANNOTATIONS

In re R.T.H., 175 S.W.3d 519, 521-22 (Tex.App.—Fort Worth 2005, no pet.). "[I]f the trial court had named [father] as the parent with the exclusive right to determine [child's] primary residence, evidence that [mother] was placed on deferred adjudication for [assaulting father] would be sufficient to support the modification. But §156.1045 does not *compel* the trial court to modify an existing order in such a circumstance. In a modification proceeding, the best interest of the child must always be the trial court's primary concern."

FAM §156.105. MODIFICATION OF ORDER BASED ON MILITARY DUTY

The military duty of a conservator who is ordered to military deployment, military mobilization, or temporary military duty, as those terms are defined by Section 153.701, does not by itself constitute a material and substantial change of circumstances sufficient to justify a modification of an existing court order or portion of a decree that sets the terms and conditions for the possession of or access to a child except that the court may render a temporary order under Subchapter L, Chapter 153.

History of Fam. Code §156.105: Acts 2005, 79th Leg., ch. 916, §18, eff. June 18, 2005. Amended by Acts 2007, 80th Leg., ch. 972, §14 (eff. Sept. 1, 2007), ch. 1041, §5 (eff. June 15, 2007); Acts 2009, 81st Leg., ch. 727, §5 (eff. Sept. 1, 2009), ch. 1113, §30 (eff. Sept. 1, 2009).

History of Former Fam. Code §156.105: Repealed by Acts 2001, 77th Leg., ch. 1289, §12(1), eff. Sept. 1, 2001.

ANNOTATIONS

In re L.L., No. 04-08-00911-CV (Tex.App.—San Antonio 2010, pet. denied) (memo op.; 6-16-10). "Although ... recent statutory amendments preclude a trial court from modifying a conservatorship order based on voluntary relinquishment when the relinquishment is due to military deployment, the amended statute does not preclude a trial court from considering evidence of a parent's military deployment in determining whether circumstances have materially and substantially changed. Instead, the amended statute provides only that military deployment does not 'by itself' constitute a material and substantial change of circumstances."

Sections 156.106-156.200 reserved for expansion

FAM §§156.201 TO 156.203. REPEALED

Repealed by Acts 2001, 77th Leg., ch. 1289, §12(2), eff. Sept. 1, 2001.

Sections 156.204-156.300 reserved for expansion

FAM §§156.301 TO 156.304. REPEALED

Repealed by Acts 2001, 77th Leg., ch. 1289, §12(2), eff. Sept. 1, 2001.

Sections 156.305-156.400 reserved for expansion

SUBCHAPTER E. MODIFICATION OF CHILD SUPPORT

FAM §156.401. GROUNDS FOR MODIFICATION OF CHILD SUPPORT[1]

(a) Except as provided by Subsection (a-1), (a-2), or (b), the court may modify an order that provides for the support of a child, including an order for health care coverage under Section 154.182, if:

(1) the circumstances of the child or a person affected by the order have materially and substantially changed since the earlier of:

(A) the date of the order's rendition; or

(B) the date of the signing of a mediated or collaborative law settlement agreement on which the order is based; or

(2) it has been three years since the order was rendered or last modified and the monthly amount of the

child support award under the order differs by either 20 percent or $100 from the amount that would be awarded in accordance with the child support guidelines.

(a-1) If the parties agree to an order under which the amount of child support differs from the amount that would be awarded in accordance with the child support guidelines, the court may modify the order only if the circumstances of the child or a person affected by the order have materially and substantially changed since the date of the order's rendition.

(a-2) A court or administrative order for child support in a Title IV-D case may be modified at any time, and without a showing of material and substantial change in the circumstances of the child or a person affected by the order, to provide for medical support of the child if the order does not provide health care coverage as required under Section 154.182.

(b) A support order may be modified with regard to the amount of support ordered only as to obligations accruing after the earlier of:

(1) the date of service of citation; or

(2) an appearance in the suit to modify.

(c) An order of joint conservatorship, in and of itself, does not constitute grounds for modifying a support order.

(d) Release of a child support obligor from incarceration is a material and substantial change in circumstances for purposes of this section if the obligor's child support obligation was abated, reduced, or suspended during the period of the obligor's incarceration.

1. **Editor's note:** In 2015, the Legislature amended §156.401 to require dental support for a child subject to a child-support order, but the amendments are not effective until Sept. 1, 2018. For the text of the prospective amendments, see Acts 2015, ch. 1150, §29, 84th Leg., eff. Sept. 1, 2018.

History of Fam. Code §156.401: Acts 1995, 74th Leg., ch. 20, §1, eff. Apr. 20, 1995. Amended by Acts 1997, 75th Leg., ch. 911, §16, eff. Sept. 1, 1997; Acts 1999, 76th Leg., ch. 43, §1, eff. Sept. 1, 1999; Acts 2003, 78th Leg., ch. 1036, §21, eff. Sept. 1, 2003; Acts 2005, 79th Leg., ch. 916, §19, eff. June 18, 2005; Acts 2007, 80th Leg., ch. 363, §6 (eff. Sept. 1, 2007), ch. 972, §15 (eff. Sept. 1, 2007); Acts 2011, 82nd Leg., ch. 508, §3, eff. Sept. 1, 2011; Acts 2013, 83rd Leg., ch. 742, §5, eff. Sept. 1, 2013. Source: Former Fam. Code §§14.021(g), 14.08(c)(2).

See also ***O'Connor's Texas Family Law Handbook*** (2017), "Three-year modification rule," ch. 9-D, §3.2, p. 1032; "Material & substantial change," ch. 9-D, §3.3, p. 1032; "Accrued child support," ch. 9-D, §4.4.13(2)(b), p. 1042; "Calculating Modified Medical Child Support," ch. 9-D, §15, p. 1056.

ANNOTATIONS

Generally

In re Naylor, 160 S.W.3d 292, 294 (Tex.App.—Texarkana 2005, pet. denied). Obligee "contends the trial court erred in not retroactively applying the modification back to the time the petition was served. [A] support order may be modified only as to obligations accruing after the earlier of the date of service of citation or an appearance in the suit to modify. [¶] Nonetheless, a trial court has broad discretion under the Family Code to set the effective date of the modified order any time after the earlier of the date of service of citation or an appearance by the respondent." *See also* ***In re H.S.N.***, 69 S.W.3d 829, 833 (Tex.App.—Corpus Christi 2002, no pet.) (purpose of allowing retroactive modification is to remove obligor's motive to delay).

Rogers v. Griffin, 774 S.W.2d 706, 707 (Tex.App.—Texarkana 1989, no writ). "A court order that provides for the support of a child may be modified *only* by filing a motion in the court having continuing, exclusive jurisdiction of the [SAPCR]. Parents do not have the authority to reduce or modify court-ordered child support provisions without express court approval; such agreements violate public policy and are unenforceable."

Best Interest of Child

Trammell v. Trammell, 485 S.W.3d 571, 576 (Tex. App.—Houston [1st Dist.] 2016, no pet.). "Paramount to the trial court's determination of child support is the best interest of the child. *At 577:* [Father] stated that virtually all of his salary over the past several years had been paid to [mother] in accordance with his alimony and child support obligations under the final divorce decree. [Father] testified that … he secured a line of credit for his own living expenses and the children's private school tuition and extracurricular activities. … He further stated that he was insolvent and that if his child support obligations could not be modified he would be forced to declare bankruptcy. *At 578:* [T]here was sufficient evidence from which the trial court could have concluded that modifying [father's] child support to enable him to continue to meet his financial obligations under the decree without continuing to accumulate debt was in the best interest of the children."

Material & Substantial Change

Coburn v. Moreland, 433 S.W.3d 809, 830 (Tex. App.—Austin 2014, no pet.). Obligor "suggests that the relevant time period for determining whether there has been a material and substantial change of circumstances is fixed as the period of time between the date of the original divorce decree and the date the modification petition was filed. [¶] [A]nd as a result, he appears to be asserting that the trial court cannot con-

sider evidence arising after [the date of filing]. *At 831:* Section 156.401 authorizes the trial court to modify a child-support order in the event of changed circumstances '*since* ... the date of the order's rendition'.... [Here], the starting date prescribed by [§156.401] is the date of the order that is being modified, and the end date is ... when the trial court actually modifies the support order. Nothing in §156.401 limits the scope of relevant evidence to the circumstances in effect on the date a modification petition is filed, nor is any such limitation found elsewhere in Ch. 156." *See also* ***In re A.M.P.***, 368 S.W.3d 842, 846 (Tex.App.—Houston [14th Dist.] 2012, no pet.) (relevant end date is at time of trial); ***Melton v. Toomey***, 350 S.W.3d 235, 238 (Tex. App.—San Antonio 2011, no pet.) (relevant end date is at time of hearing).

In re L.R., 416 S.W.3d 675, 679 (Tex.App.—Houston [14th Dist.] 2013, no pet.). "[B]ecause the father's financial circumstances appear to have been immaterial to the parties' initial support order, ... an increase in the father's resources alone could not have been a *material* change in circumstances for purposes of a modification. [¶] When the parties initially divorced, both possessed significant resources, and neither was ordered to pay child support. There is no contention that the absence of child support resulted from either party's inability to afford it. [¶] As a result, an increase in the father's resources alone could not have justified modifying the support arrangement. [¶] Thus, even assuming that the denied discovery would have established an increase in the father's ability to pay, this would not mean that circumstances had '*materially* ... changed since the date of the order's rendition.' Rather, such evidence would only demonstrate that a factor not material to begin with—the father's ability to pay substantial child support—had changed."

In re N.T.P., 402 S.W.3d 13, 19 (Tex.App.—San Antonio 2012, no pet.). "If a circumstance was contemplated at the time of an original agreement, its eventuality is not a changed circumstance, but is instead an anticipated circumstance that cannot be evidence of a material or substantial change of circumstances. *At 20:* While we agree ... that international travel and [father's] eventual retirement were mentioned in the divorce decree, we do not agree that the specific date of his retirement some four years later or that he would reside in England after his retirement were contemplated under the decree. [¶] Therefore, at most, only an eventual retirement was contemplated, and there is no dispute that [father's] retirement resulted in a decrease in his pay. ... We conclude the reduction in [father's] pay due to his retirement constitutes a material and substantial change in circumstances."

Rooney v. Rooney, No. 14-10-01007-CV (Tex. App.—Houston [14th Dist.] 2011, no pet.) (memo op.; 8-23-11). "[A] court's determination as to whether a material change of circumstances has occurred is not guided by rigid or definite rules and is fact-specific. A breakdown of the children's expenses at the time of the initial order and at the time of the modification hearing is not necessary to show a material and substantial change of circumstances when evidence shows a substantial increase in the designated expenses for the children, in the absence of showing any decrease in expenses." *See also* ***In re J.A.R.***, No. 12-11-00025-CV (Tex.App.—Tyler 2011, no pet.) (memo op.; 8-24-11) (mother was not required to present evidence of financial circumstances at time of divorce because her testimony was presented in terms of how her expenses had changed since divorce); ***T.A.B. v. W.L.B.***, 598 S.W.2d 936, 939 (Tex.App.—El Paso 1980) (evidence of historical and current data is not only method of determining material and substantial change; any method of proof that shows change satisfies statute), *writ ref'd n.r.e.*, 606 S.W.2d 695 (Tex.1980). *But see* ***In re C.C.J.***, this page.

In re C.C.J., 244 S.W.3d 911, 917-18 (Tex.App.—Dallas 2008, no pet.). "In determining whether there has been a material and substantial change in circumstances, it is well-settled that the trial court must examine and compare the circumstances of the parents and any minor children at the time of the initial order with the circumstances existing at the time modification is sought. The record must contain both historical and current evidence of the relevant person's financial circumstances. Without both sets of data, the court has nothing to compare and cannot determine whether a material and substantial change has occurred. The movant has the burden to show the requisite material and substantial change in circumstances since the entry of the previous order." *But see* ***Rooney v. Rooney***, this page.

London v. London, 192 S.W.3d 6, 15 (Tex.App.—Houston [14th Dist.] 2005, pet. denied). "The trial court is given broad discretion in setting child support payments and in modifying those payments."

In re Z.B.P., 109 S.W.3d 772, 781-82 (Tex.App.—Fort Worth 2003, no pet.), *disapproved on other grounds*, ***Iliff v. Iliff***, 339 S.W.3d 74 (Tex.2011). "Because the children no longer live with [mother] during the week, she is no longer furnishing the degree of services to the children that she did at the time of the divorce; [father], on the other hand, is furnishing more services to the children than he did at the time of the divorce. This, in and of itself, constitutes a material and substantial change requiring the reallocation of financial obligations."

Three-Year Modification Rule

Njeako v. Njeako, No. 14-04-00991-CV (Tex.App.—Houston [14th Dist.] 2005, no pet.) (memo op.; 11-17-05). "[M]aterial and substantial change of circumstances is only one of two alternative reasons warranting a modification of a child support order. A trial court may also modify an order after three years if the amount under the order differs by specified amounts from the guideline award. [¶] [T]he trial court rendered the divorce decree setting [mother's] child support obligation at $180.... It rendered the order modifying that amount ... more than three years later. [¶] Twenty percent of [mother's net monthly income] is $381.14. Thus, the presumptive amount under the guidelines ... constitutes a difference of more than $100 from the amount awarded in the divorce decree. [¶] In modifying [mother's] child support obligation, the trial court followed the statutory requirements for modification and the relevant guidelines."

FAM §156.402. EFFECT OF GUIDELINES

(a) The court may consider the child support guidelines for single and multiple families under Chapter 154 to determine whether there has been a material or substantial change of circumstances under this chapter that warrants a modification of an existing child support order if the modification is in the best interest of the child.

(b) If the amount of support contained in the order does not substantially conform with the guidelines for single and multiple families under Chapter 154, the court may modify the order to substantially conform with the guidelines if the modification is in the best interest of the child. A court may consider other relevant evidence in addition to the factors listed in the guidelines.

History of Fam. Code §156.402: Acts 1995, 74th Leg., ch. 20, §1, eff. Apr. 20, 1995. Amended by Acts 1999, 76th Leg., ch. 62, §6.22 (eff. Sept. 1, 1999), ch. 556, §12 (eff. Sept. 1, 1999). Source: Former Fam. Code §14.056(a), (b).

ANNOTATIONS

Scott v. Younts, 926 S.W.2d 415, 418-19 (Tex. App.—Corpus Christi 1996, writ denied). "In determining whether a material and substantial change in circumstances warrants a modification, courts may refer to the child support guidelines listed elsewhere in the [Family] Code. The Code also specifically prevents courts from considering certain things as grounds for modification: namely, any increase in needs, standard of living or lifestyle of obligee, any history of voluntarily provided support, and net resources of new spouses. [¶] The 'guidelines' referred to in [Fam. Code] §14.056 [now §156.402] instruct the courts to consider various factors when ordering child support, based in part on the net resources and abilities of the parties, as well as the needs of the child. A court may deviate from the guidelines when their application would be inappropriate or unjust under the circumstances."

FAM §156.403. VOLUNTARY ADDITIONAL SUPPORT

A history of support voluntarily provided in excess of the court order does not constitute cause to increase the amount of an existing child support order.

History of Fam. Code §156.403: Acts 1995, 74th Leg., ch. 20, §1, eff. Apr. 20, 1995. Source: Former Fam. Code §14.056(b).

FAM §156.404. NET RESOURCES OF NEW SPOUSE

(a) The court may not add any portion of the net resources of a new spouse to the net resources of an obligor or obligee in order to calculate the amount of child support to be ordered in a suit for modification.

(b) The court may not subtract the needs of a new spouse, or of a dependent of a new spouse, from the net resources of the obligor or obligee in a suit for modification.

History of Fam. Code §156.404: Acts 1995, 74th Leg., ch. 20, §1, eff. Apr. 20, 1995. Source: Former Fam. Code §14.056(c).

See also *O'Connor's Texas Family Law Handbook* (2017), "Resources or needs of new spouse," ch. 9-D, §14.1.1, p. 1056.

ANNOTATIONS

Starck v. Nelson, 878 S.W.2d 302, 305-06 (Tex. App.—Corpus Christi 1994, no writ). "[T]he court did not use [obligor's W's] income to calculate [obligor's] net resources; however, the ... trial court found that [obligor's W's] contribution to their joint living expenses enabled [obligor] to pay more child support

than if he were solely responsible for his living expenses. [¶] In reading [Fam. Code §§14.053(b), (e) and 14.056(c), now §§154.062, 154.067, and 156.404,] together, the legislature has set forth what the court *must* consider (the definition of net resources), what the court *may* consider (the evidentiary and additional factors), and what the court *may not* consider (the new spouse's contribution). All three provisions should be read together and construed harmoniously if possible. Permitting the court to deviate from child support guidelines because the obligor's new spouse contributes to their joint living expenses allows the court to do indirectly what [§14.056(c)] directly prohibits."

FAM §156.405. CHANGE IN LIFESTYLE

An increase in the needs, standard of living, or lifestyle of the obligee since the rendition of the existing order does not warrant an increase in the obligor's child support obligation.

History of Fam. Code §156.405: Acts 1995, 74th Leg., ch. 20, §1, eff. Apr. 20, 1995. Source: Former Fam. Code §14.056(c).

FAM §156.406. USE OF GUIDELINES FOR CHILDREN IN MORE THAN ONE HOUSEHOLD

In applying the child support guidelines in a suit under this subchapter, if the obligor has the duty to support children in more than one household, the court shall apply the percentage guidelines for multiple families under Chapter 154.

History of Fam. Code §156.406: Acts 1995, 74th Leg., ch. 20, §1, eff. Apr. 20, 1995. Amended by Acts 1999, 76th Leg., ch. 62, §6.23 (eff. Sept. 1, 1999), ch. 556, §13 (eff. Sept. 1, 1999). Source: Former Fam. Code §14.056(d).

FAM §156.407. ASSIGNMENT OF CHILD SUPPORT RIGHT

A notice of assignment filed under Chapter 231 does not constitute a modification of an order to pay child support.

History of Fam. Code §156.407: Acts 1995, 74th Leg., ch. 20, §1, eff. Apr. 20, 1995. Source: Former Fam. Code §14.08(h).

FAM §156.408. MODIFICATION OF SUPPORT ORDER RENDERED BY ANOTHER STATE

(a) Unless both parties and the child reside in this state, a court of this state may modify an order of child support rendered by an appropriate tribunal of another state only as provided by Chapter 159.

(b) If both parties and the child reside in this state, a court of this state may modify an order of child support rendered by an appropriate tribunal of another state after registration of the order as provided by Chapter 159.

History of Fam. Code §156.408: Acts 1995, 74th Leg., ch. 20, §1, eff. Apr. 20, 1995. Amended by Acts 2001, 77th Leg., ch. 1023, §13, eff. Sept. 1, 2001.

FAM §156.409. CHANGE IN PHYSICAL POSSESSION

(a) The court shall, on the motion of a party or a person having physical possession of the child, modify an order providing for the support of the child to provide that the person having physical possession of the child for at least six months shall have the right to receive and give receipt for payments of support for the child and to hold or disburse money for the benefit of the child if the sole managing conservator of the child or the joint managing conservator who has the exclusive right to determine the primary residence of the child has:

(1) voluntarily relinquished the primary care and possession of the child;

(2) been incarcerated or sentenced to be incarcerated for at least 90 days; or

(3) relinquished the primary care and possession of the child in a proceeding under Title 3 or Chapter 262.

(a-1) If the court modifies a support order under this section, the court shall order the obligor to pay the person or entity having physical possession of the child any unpaid child support that is not subject to offset or reimbursement under Section 157.008 and that accrues after the date the sole or joint managing conservator:

(1) relinquishes possession and control of the child, whether voluntarily or in a proceeding under Title 3 or Chapter 262; or

(2) is incarcerated.

(a-2) This section does not affect the ability of the court to render a temporary order for the payment of child support that is in the best interest of the child.

(a-3) An order under this section that modifies a support order because of the incarceration of the sole or joint managing conservator of a child must provide that on the conservator's release from incarceration the conservator may file an affidavit with the court stating that the conservator has been released from incarceration, that there has not been a modification of the conservatorship of the child during the incarceration, and that the conservator has resumed physical possession of the child. A copy of the affidavit shall be delivered to the obligor and any other party, including the Title IV-D agency if appropriate. On receipt of the affidavit, the court on its own motion shall order the obligor to make support payments to the conservator.

(b) Notice of a motion for modification under this section may be served in the manner for serving a notice under Section 157.065.

History of Fam. Code §156.409: Acts 1999, 76th Leg., ch. 556, §14, eff. Sept. 1, 1999. Amended by Acts 2001, 77th Leg., ch. 1023, §14 (eff. Sept. 1, 2001), ch. 1289, §10 (eff. Sept. 1, 2001); Acts 2005, 79th Leg., ch. 261, §1, eff. May 30, 2005; Acts 2007, 80th Leg., ch. 972, §16, eff. Sept. 1, 2007.

FAM §156.410. REPEALED

Repealed by Acts 2009, 81st Leg., ch. 727, §6 (eff. Sept. 1, 2009), ch. 1113, §31 (eff. Sept. 1, 2009).

CHAPTER 157. ENFORCEMENT

SUBCHAPTER A. PLEADINGS & DEFENSES

FAM §157.001. MOTION FOR ENFORCEMENT

(a) A motion for enforcement as provided in this chapter may be filed to enforce any provision of a temporary or final order rendered in a suit.

(b) The court may enforce by contempt any provision of a temporary or final order.

(c) The court may enforce a temporary or final order for child support as provided in this chapter or Chapter 158.

(d) A motion for enforcement shall be filed in the court of continuing, exclusive jurisdiction.

(e) For purposes of this section, "temporary order" includes a temporary restraining order, standing order, injunction, and any other temporary order rendered by a court.

History of Fam. Code §157.001: Acts 1995, 74th Leg., ch. 20, §1, eff. Apr. 20, 1995. Amended by Acts 2015, 84th Leg., ch. 1105, §1, eff. Sept. 1, 2015. Source: Former Fam. Code §§14.30(b), 14.31, 14.40(a), 14.50(a).

See also *O'Connor's Texas Family Law Handbook* (2017), "Enforcing Child-Support Orders," ch. 10, p. 1063; "Enforcing Orders of Possession or Access," ch. 11, p. 1179.

ANNOTATIONS

In re Green, 221 S.W.3d 645, 649 (Tex.2007). "A failure to provide child support, including a failure to provide health insurance under a voluntary agreement, is punishable by contempt."

FAM §157.002. CONTENTS OF MOTION

(a) A motion for enforcement must, in ordinary and concise language:

(1) identify the provision of the order allegedly violated and sought to be enforced;

(2) state the manner of the respondent's alleged noncompliance;

(3) state the relief requested by the movant; and

(4) contain the signature of the movant or the movant's attorney.

(b) A motion for enforcement of child support:

(1) must include the amount owed as provided in the order, the amount paid, and the amount of arrearages;

(2) if contempt is requested, must include the portion of the order allegedly violated and, for each date of alleged contempt, the amount due and the amount paid, if any;

(3) may include as an attachment a copy of a record of child support payments maintained by the Title IV-D registry or a local registry; and

(4) if the obligor owes arrearages for a child receiving assistance under Part A of Title IV of the federal Social Security Act (42 U.S.C. Section 601 et seq.), may include a request that:

(A) the obligor pay the arrearages in accordance with a plan approved by the court; or

(B) if the obligor is already subject to a plan and is not incapacitated, the obligor participate in work activities, as defined under 42 U.S.C. Section 607(d), that the court determines appropriate.

(c) A motion for enforcement of the terms and conditions of conservatorship or possession of or access to a child must include the date, place, and, if applicable, the time of each occasion of the respondent's failure to comply with the order.

(d) The movant is not required to plead that the underlying order is enforceable by contempt to obtain other appropriate enforcement remedies.

(e) The movant may allege repeated past violations of the order and that future violations of a similar nature may occur before the date of the hearing.

History of Fam. Code §157.002: Acts 1995, 74th Leg., ch. 20, §1, eff. Apr. 20, 1995. Amended by Acts 1997, 75th Leg., ch. 911, §17, eff. Sept. 1, 1997. Source: Former Fam. Code §§14.311(a)-(e), 14.312.

See also *O'Connor's Texas Family Law Handbook* (2017), "Motion," ch. 10-A, §5, p. 1078; "Motion," ch. 11-A, §5, p. 1186.

ANNOTATIONS

In re Office of the Atty. Gen., 422 S.W.3d 623, 630 (Tex.2013). "[A] respondent may be found in contempt only for violations that are specifically pled in the motion for enforcement under §157.002."

In re H.G-J., 503 S.W.3d 679, 684-85 (Tex.App.—Houston [14th Dist.] 2016, no pet.). See annotation under Family Code §157.263, p. 634.

FAM §157.003. JOINDER OF CLAIMS & REMEDIES; NO ELECTION OF REMEDIES

(a) A party requesting enforcement may join in the same proceeding any claim and remedy provided for in this chapter, other provisions of this title, or other rules of law.

(b) A motion for enforcement does not constitute an election of remedies that limits or precludes:

(1) the use of any other civil or criminal proceeding to enforce a final order; or

(2) a suit for damages under Chapter 42.

History of Fam. Code §157.003: Acts 1995, 74th Leg., ch. 20, §1, eff. Apr. 20, 1995. Amended by Acts 1999, 76th Leg., ch. 62, §6.24, eff. Sept. 1, 1999. Source: Former Fam. Code §§14.30(d), 14.313(a), 14.33(d).

See also ***O'Connor's Texas Family Law Handbook*** (2017), "Other relief," ch. 10-A, §5.4.9(2), p. 1080; "Other relief," ch. 11-A, §5.4.9(2), p. 1188.

FAM §157.004. TIME LIMITATIONS; ENFORCEMENT OF POSSESSION

The court retains jurisdiction to render a contempt order for failure to comply with the order of possession and access if the motion for enforcement is filed not later than the sixth month after the date:

(1) the child becomes an adult; or

(2) on which the right of possession and access terminates under the order or by operation of law.

History of Fam. Code §157.004: Acts 1995, 74th Leg., ch. 20, §1, eff. Apr. 20, 1995. Source: Former Fam. Code §14.50(b).

See also ***O'Connor's Texas Family Law Handbook*** (2017), "Time limit to enforce by contempt," ch. 11-A, §3.1.3, p. 1184.

FAM §157.005. TIME LIMITATIONS; ENFORCEMENT OF CHILD SUPPORT

(a) The court retains jurisdiction to render a contempt order for failure to comply with the child support order if the motion for enforcement is filed not later than the second anniversary of the date:

(1) the child becomes an adult; or

(2) on which the child support obligation terminates under the order or by operation of law.

(b) The court retains jurisdiction to confirm the total amount of child support arrearages and render a cumulative money judgment for past-due child support, as provided by Section 157.263, if a motion for enforcement requesting a cumulative money judgment is filed not later than the 10th anniversary after the date:

(1) the child becomes an adult; or

(2) on which the child support obligation terminates under the child support order or by operation of law.

History of Fam. Code §157.005: Acts 1995, 74th Leg., ch. 20, §1, eff. Apr. 20, 1995. Amended by Acts 1999, 76th Leg., ch. 556, §15, eff. Sept. 1, 1999; Acts 2005, 79th Leg., ch. 916, §21, eff. June 18, 2005; Acts 2007, 80th Leg., ch. 972, §17, eff. Sept. 1, 2007; Acts 2009, 81st Leg., ch. 767, §13, eff. June 19, 2009. Source: Former Fam. Code §§14.40(b), 14.41(b).

See also ***O'Connor's Texas Family Law Handbook*** (2017), "Time limit to enforce by contempt," ch. 10-A, §3.1.3, p. 1073.

ANNOTATIONS

Dise v. Dise, 493 S.W.3d 704, 708 (Tex.App.—Houston [1st Dist.] 2016, no pet.). "Courts have held that §157.005 … is a jurisdictional provision that 'defin[es] the contours of the court's jurisdiction'; it is not a statute of limitations that sets a 'time frame within which a party must file a claim or forever lose the right to do so.'"

In re D.W.G., 391 S.W.3d 154, 160 (Tex.App.—San Antonio 2012, no pet.). "The Texas appellate courts that have been presented with the issue of whether [Fam. Code] §157.005(b) applies to child support enforcement remedies other than a cumulative money judgment, such as writs of withholding and child support liens, have concluded it does not. Similarly, … we conclude §157.005(b) only applies to cumulative money judgments for past-due child support as provided by [Fam. Code] §157.263, not to other child support enforcement remedies available under the Texas Family Code." *See also* ***Isaacs v. Isaacs***, 338 S.W.3d 184, 187-88 (Tex.App.—Houston [14th Dist.] 2011, pet. denied) (Fam. Code §§157.005, 157.323, and 158.309 do not irreconcilably conflict; they are each cumulative remedies with various limitations that can be used to seek payment of unpaid child support).

In re Radmacher, No. 14-08-00346-CV (Tex.App.—Houston [14th Dist.] 2008, orig. proceeding) (memo op.; 5-23-08). Father "argues that the trial court's jurisdiction to impose contempt should have expired two years after his youngest child turned 18. [Father] concedes that his child support obligations continued past his children's 18th birthdays, on an indefinite basis, because of the continuing needs of his disabled daughter.

[¶] Section 157.005(a) limits contempt jurisdiction to a fixed period after the expiration of the support obligation. [¶] Because [father's] child support obligation continues [indefinitely], the trial court retains jurisdiction to order criminal contempt."

In re Munks, 263 S.W.3d 270, 274 (Tex.App.—Houston [1st Dist.] 2007, orig. proceeding). "Although [father's] payments on the arrearage have extended beyond [child's] 18th birthday, the trial court's jurisdiction to enforce the obligation by contempt is not extended. '[T]o hold that contempt jurisdiction might be extended by ordering a payment schedule, on accrued arrearages, could result in contempt proceedings being brought at an almost infinite period of time after the child had reached adulthood, an obvious abrogation of the legislature's intent.'"

FAM §157.006. AFFIRMATIVE DEFENSE TO MOTION FOR ENFORCEMENT

(a) The issue of the existence of an affirmative defense to a motion for enforcement does not arise unless evidence is admitted supporting the defense.

(b) The respondent must prove the affirmative defense by a preponderance of the evidence.

History of Fam. Code §157.006: Acts 1995, 74th Leg., ch. 20, §1, eff. Apr. 20, 1995. Source: Former Fam. Code §§14.40(h), 14.50(e).

See also ***O'Connor's Texas Family Law Handbook*** (2017), "Affirmative defenses," ch. 10-A, §8.3.3(5), p. 1087; "Affirmative defenses," ch. 11-A, §8.3.3(5), p. 1190.

FAM §157.007. AFFIRMATIVE DEFENSE TO MOTION FOR ENFORCEMENT OF POSSESSION OR ACCESS

(a) The respondent may plead as an affirmative defense to contempt for failure to comply with an order for possession or access to a child that the movant voluntarily relinquished actual possession and control of the child.

(b) The voluntary relinquishment must have been for the time encompassed by the court-ordered periods during which the respondent is alleged to have interfered.

History of Fam. Code §157.007: Acts 1995, 74th Leg., ch. 20, §1, eff. Apr. 20, 1995. Source: Former Fam. Code §14.50(c).

See also ***O'Connor's Texas Family Law Handbook*** (2017), "Voluntary relinquishment," ch. 11-A, §8.3.3(5)(a), p. 1191.

ANNOTATIONS

Ex parte Rosser, 899 S.W.2d 382, 385 (Tex.App.—Houston [14th Dist.] 1995, orig. proceeding). "[T]he involuntary inability to comply with an order is a valid defense to contempt, for one's noncompliance cannot have been willful if the failure to comply was involuntary. Although the inability to comply defense technically rebuts the willfulness element of contempt liability, the relator nevertheless bears the burden to conclusively establish his inability to comply. [¶] All of the evidence ... indicates that [father] encouraged the visitation and did what he could to convince [daughter] to see her mother. *At 386:* Within the spectrum of visitation disputes, there may be instances in which: (1) a parent actively discourages or impedes visitation; (2) a parent passively fails to insist that a child comply with visitation; or (3) a parent is legitimately unable to compel a child to comply with visitation. We believe that the defense of involuntary inability to comply applies only to the third alternative, and not the first two." *But see* ***Ex parte Morgan***, 886 S.W.2d 829, 832 (Tex.App.—Amarillo 1994, orig. proceeding) (mother's passive conduct that denied visitation was not punishable by contempt).

FAM §157.008. AFFIRMATIVE DEFENSE TO MOTION FOR ENFORCEMENT OF CHILD SUPPORT

(a) An obligor may plead as an affirmative defense in whole or in part to a motion for enforcement of child support that the obligee voluntarily relinquished to the obligor actual possession and control of a child.

(b) The voluntary relinquishment must have been for a time period in excess of any court-ordered periods of possession of and access to the child and actual support must have been supplied by the obligor.

(c) An obligor may plead as an affirmative defense to an allegation of contempt or of the violation of a condition of community service requiring payment of child support that the obligor:

(1) lacked the ability to provide support in the amount ordered;

(2) lacked property that could be sold, mortgaged, or otherwise pledged to raise the funds needed;

(3) attempted unsuccessfully to borrow the funds needed; and

(4) knew of no source from which the money could have been borrowed or legally obtained.

(d) An obligor who has provided actual support to the child during a time subject to an affirmative defense under this section may request reimbursement for that support as a counterclaim or offset against the claim of the obligee.

(e) An action against the obligee for support supplied to a child is limited to the amount of periodic payments previously ordered by the court.

History of Fam. Code §157.008: Acts 1995, 74th Leg., ch. 20, §1, eff. Apr. 20, 1995. Source: Former Fam. Code §§14.40(c), (g), 14.41(c).

See also *O'Connor's Texas Family Law Handbook* (2017), "Affirmative defenses," ch. 10-A, §8.3.3(5), p. 1087; "Affirmative defense—relinquishment of possession + actual support," ch. 10-C, §7.3.3(5), p. 1128.

ANNOTATIONS

Generally

Office of the Atty. Gen. v. Scholer, 403 S.W.3d 859, 865 (Tex.2013). Family Code §157.008 "limits obligors to a single affirmative defense, and a court may not adjust arrearage amounts outside of the statutorily mandated exceptions, offsets, and counterclaims. Because courts are prohibited from making additional adjustments, affirmative defenses that are not included in the statute, like estoppel, are also prohibited because they would require courts to make discretionary determinations. *At 866:* Because payment of child support reflects a parent's duty to his child, furthering the child's welfare and best interests, estoppel is not an affirmative defense to a child support enforcement action."

In re A.M., 192 S.W.3d 570, 574 (Tex.2006). "Whether an obligor parent is entitled to an offset or to reimbursement will depend on whether such parent continued to pay the court-ordered support obligation during all or part of the period of excess possession. If support was paid during this period, the obligor must seek reimbursement; if it was not, the obligor must ask for an offset. In either event, §157.008's reimbursement remedies of offset or counterclaim are alternative, not cumulative. During any particular month, the obligor may be entitled to one or the other, but not both…. Moreover, the statute is purely defensive. It does not grant the obligor an independent right to seek reimbursement for support paid during periods of excess possession, but rather provides for reimbursement 'against the claim of the obligee.' Accordingly, we hold that the court of appeals erred in applying the statute to shift the support obligation from the obligor to the obligee during periods of excess possession. *At 575:* [Because] §157.008 operates only as a defense to a motion to enforce an existing order, [t]he [AG], as the Title IV-D agency and [mother's] assignee, is fully authorized to sue for unpaid child support and defend against any claim that might affect that collection. We therefore disagree with the court of appeals that the [AG] lacked standing in this matter."

Voluntary Relinquishment

Chenault v. Banks, 296 S.W.3d 186, 191 (Tex. App.—Houston [14th Dist.] 2009, no pet.). Father's estate "argues that because [father] paid for [son's boarding school], [mother] voluntarily relinquished actual possession and control of her son to [father] by allowing [son] to attend [boarding school]. We reject this argument. The obligor must prove that the obligee affirmatively agreed to relinquish possession and control of the child to the obligor. There is no evidence … to show that [mother] actually agreed to relinquish possession and control over her son to [father] simply by agreeing to allow [son] to attend boarding school."

In re W.J.B., 294 S.W.3d 873, 880 (Tex.App.—Beaumont 2009, no pet.). Section 157.008(b) "does not define the term 'relinquish,' [but] generally requires the trial court to compare the rights given each parent at the time of the divorce, usually found in the parties' divorce decree, with the circumstances present during the period in issue. This is generally a fact intensive inquiry…. [Here, the evidence showed] that [mother] 'voluntarily relinquished' [her rights to sole periods of possession] by allowing [father] to move into the home and to act as a full-time parent, which included paying for the children's actual support during that time. [¶] [Mother argues] that voluntary relinquishment occurs only when a child's domicile is separate from that of the obligee's. *At 882:* [But] periods of joint possession, along with sufficient evidence of actual support during such period, may be sufficient evidence to allow the statutory offset provision to apply…. *At 883:* [W]e decline … to construe the statute to interpret relinquish to mean giving up all rights of control and possession."

Actual Support

In re A.M., 192 S.W.3d 570, 575-76 (Tex.2006). "Because [father] had not provided evidence of his expenses, the [AG] contended that no offset could be awarded. [¶] There is disagreement among the courts of appeals regarding the proof needed to measure 'actual support' under §157.008. Some courts … have used the court-ordered support amount to measure the offset, stating that the obligor with actual possession is not required to make an exact accounting of actual expenditures. Other courts have held … the obligor to a more precise accounting. Still others have suggested that the level of proof may vary with the circumstances of the case. [¶] In this case, it was undisputed that [fa-

ther] solely supported his son and daughter, and later his son, during the two relevant periods of excess possession. [Mother testified] that she provided no support to [father] during these periods; nor was there evidence of support from anyone else during the relevant periods. Thus, the court of appeals could reasonably presume, as it did, that during the period of excess possession [father] was entitled to equate his monthly child support obligation to the actual support he provided each child. On this record, nothing more was required." *See also* ***Buzbee v. Buzbee***, this page.

In re M.P.M., 161 S.W.3d 650, 658-59 (Tex. App.—San Antonio 2005, no pet.). Obligee argues that "subsection (d) requires the obligor to construct a daily segregation of the amounts of actual support he provided the children, segregating the support provided on days during the period of voluntary relinquishment in which he would ordinarily be entitled to access and possession of the children. [¶] [T]he time subject to the affirmative defense is the period of voluntary relinquishment. [W]e do not read [§157.008(d)] to impose a segregation of actual costs incurred during the voluntary relinquishment period under subsection (d). ... We believe such [segregation] would lead to absurd results and be contrary to the statute's intent, *i.e.*, to allow reimbursement or offset for actual support provided by the obligor, who has acquired primary custody of the child through the obligee's voluntary relinquishment."

Buzbee v. Buzbee, 870 S.W.2d 335, 339 (Tex. App.—Waco 1994, no writ). "Under [Fam. Code] §14.41(c) [now §157.008], the amount of offset is limited to the amount of 'actual support' during periods of 'excess' possession. Therefore, [obligee] had the initial burden of establishing the amount of [obligor's] child-support arrearage. After this amount is established, [obligor] had the burden of establishing 'excess' possession and the amount of 'actual support.' *At 340-41:* By the plain language of the statute, the party claiming the benefit of the section must prove (1) that he had possession of the child for periods in excess of the court-ordered periods of possession (2) during which he incurred expenses for actual support of the child. Thus, to gain a credit against the arrearage, [obligor] was required to provide the court with some evidence of his expenditures on the child." *See also* ***In re A.M.***, p. 616; ***In re S.L.M.***, 97 S.W.3d 224, 234-35 (Tex.App.—Amarillo 2002, no pet.). *But see* ***Beck v. Walker***, 154 S.W.3d 895, 905 (Tex.App.—Dallas 2005, no pet.) (obligor who gained possession was under no greater obligation to file accountings for actual support than was obligee).

Inability to Pay

In re Mancha, 440 S.W.3d 158, 166-67 (Tex.App.—Houston [14th Dist.] 2013, orig. proceeding). "Mother ... suggests that the trial court's finding of indigence under [Fam. Code] §157.163 creates a 'presumption of indigence' for purposes of the [Fam. Code] §157.008(c) inability-to-pay affirmative defense. [¶] [T]he §157.008(c) factors are not the criteria for establishing §157.163 indigence because the purposes are different. Family law contempt proceedings are considered quasi-criminal in nature, and their proceedings should conform as nearly as practicable to those in criminal cases. ... In an indigence inquiry analogous to appointment of counsel, both the Court of Criminal Appeals and this court have forbidden trial court's consideration of an individual's ability to borrow funds to determine indigence for purposes of obtaining a free transcript. [¶] Because §157.008(c) specifically requires a showing that the child-support obligor is unable to borrow the funds to meet his or her obligations, the inability-to-pay threshold is necessarily higher than the indigence threshold. Mother is incorrect that the trial court's determination that she is 'legally indigent' for purposes of §157.163 creates either a constructive determination of §157.008(c) inability to pay or a legal presumption that shifts the burden to Father."

In re A.D.S., No. 14-08-00147-CV (Tex.App.—Houston [14th Dist.] 2009, no pet.) (memo op.; 9-22-09). "Because §157.008(c) only allows inability to pay as an affirmative defense to an allegation of contempt or of the violation of a condition of community service, the trial court erred by applying a credit against [father's] arrearage due to his incarceration." *See also* ***Office of Atty. Gen. v. McBee***, No. 01-08-00433-CV (Tex.App.—Houston [1st Dist.] 2009, no pet.) (memo op.; 9-17-09) (§157.008 does not authorize reduction of past-due arrearages to compensate for obligor's incarceration).

Contempt

Ex parte Rojo, 925 S.W.2d 654, 655 (Tex.1996). "A person cannot be incarcerated indefinitely for civil contempt if he or she does not have the ability to perform the condition required for release. Civil contempt is coercive, and is based on the notion that the contemnor carries the keys of his prison in his own pocket. *At 656:*

[Relator's ex-W] argues that he should have sought a regular job that would have paid more than the meager sums he was netting with his duct-cleaning business. This factor, while possibly relevant to the criminal contempt sanction, does not bear on the question of whether [relator] had the ability, when the trial court committed him, to purge himself of the civil contempt." (Internal quotes omitted.)

Ex parte Roosth, 881 S.W.2d 300, 300-01 (Tex. 1994). "Due process requires that an alleged criminal contemnor not shoulder the burden of persuasion to disprove an element of the offense of contempt. However, whether ability to pay court-ordered child support is an element of the offense of contempt, or is instead an affirmative defense to that charge, is a question left to state law. In Texas, inability to pay child support is an affirmative defense to the offense of contempt that must be proved by a preponderance of the evidence. The burden of proof and evidentiary standard imposed by the trial court under [Fam. Code] §14.40(g), (h) [now §§157.006, 157.008] are consistent with due process."

Ex parte Robertson, 880 S.W.2d 803, 803 (Tex. App.—Houston [1st Dist.] 1994, orig. proceeding). "A relator's current inability to pay does not affect his obligation to serve the criminal contempt portion of his sentence. The relator's current inability to pay the arrearage is therefore no defense to the criminal contempt."

FAM §157.009. CREDIT FOR PAYMENT OF DISABILITY BENEFITS

In addition to any other credit or offset available to an obligor under this title, if a child for whom the obligor owes child support receives a lump-sum payment as a result of the obligor's disability and that payment is made to the obligee as the representative payee of the child, the obligor is entitled to a credit. The credit under this section is equal to the amount of the lump-sum payment and shall be applied to any child support arrearage and interest owed by the obligor on behalf of that child at the time the payment is made.

History of Fam. Code §157.009: Acts 2009, 81st Leg., ch. 538, §1 (eff. June 19, 2009), ch. 767, §14 (eff. June 19, 2009).

Sections 157.010-157.060 reserved for expansion

SUBCHAPTER B. PROCEDURE

FAM §157.061. SETTING HEARING

(a) On filing a motion for enforcement requesting contempt, the court shall set the date, time, and place of the hearing and order the respondent to personally appear and respond to the motion.

(b) If the motion for enforcement does not request contempt, the court shall set the motion for hearing on the request of a party.

(c) The court shall give preference to a motion for enforcement of child support in setting a hearing date and may not delay the hearing because a suit for modification of the order requested to be enforced has been or may be filed.

History of Fam. Code §157.061: Acts 1995, 74th Leg., ch. 20, §1, eff. Apr. 20, 1995. Source: Former Fam. Code §§14.314(a), 14.32(d).

ANNOTATIONS

In re Taylor, 39 S.W.3d 406, 413 (Tex.App.—Waco 2001, orig. proceeding). "The provisions which govern notice of and appearance at hearings in which contempt is a requested remedy are found in [Fam. Code] §§105.006(f), 157.061(a), 157.062(a), 157.065, 157.066, 157.114, and 157.115.... These provisions read together require the following: (a) The court shall set a hearing date, and shall order the respondent ... to personally appear at the hearing and respond to the motion. This frequently is in the form of a 'show cause' order[;] (b) The movant ... should give written notice to the respondent ... of the date, time, and place of hearing, and a copy of the motion should be attached. The notice should be served at least ten days before the hearing[; and] (c) Although the notice may be sent by certified mail, if the respondent fails to appear, there is little remedy other than a resetting of the hearing. Therefore, the notice should be served in person on the respondent, after which if the respondent fails to appear, the court may not hold the respondent in contempt, but may render a default judgment in favor of movant, and order a capias to be issued for the arrest of the respondent."

FAM §157.062. NOTICE OF HEARING

(a) The notice of hearing must include the date, time, and place of the hearing.

(b) The notice of hearing need not repeat the allegations contained in the motion for enforcement.

(c) Notice of hearing on a motion for enforcement of a final order providing for child support or possession of or access to a child, any provision of a final order rendered against a party who has already appeared in a suit under this title, or any provision of a temporary order shall be given to the respondent by personal service

of a copy of the motion and notice not later than the 10th day before the date of the hearing. For purposes of this subsection, "temporary order" includes a temporary restraining order, standing order, injunction, and any other temporary order rendered by a court.

(d) If a motion for enforcement of a final order, other than a final order rendered against a party who has already appeared in a suit under this title, is joined with another claim:

(1) the hearing may not be held before 10 a.m. on the first Monday after the 20th day after the date of service; and

(2) the provisions of the Texas Rules of Civil Procedure applicable to the filing of an original lawsuit apply.

History of Fam. Code §157.062: Acts 1995, 74th Leg., ch. 20, §1, eff. Apr. 20, 1995. Amended by Acts 1995, 74th Leg., ch. 751, §49, eff. Sept. 1, 1995; Acts 2015, 84th Leg., ch. 1105, §2, eff. Sept. 1, 2015. Source: Former Fam. Code §§14.314(a), (b), 14.315(b), (c).

See also *O'Connor's Texas Family Law Handbook* (2017), "Notice of Hearing," ch. 10-A, §6, p. 1082; "Service," ch. 10-A, §7, p. 1083; "Service," ch. 11-A, §7, p. 1188.

ANNOTATIONS

Target Logistics, Inc. v. Office of the Atty. Gen., 465 S.W.3d 768, 770 (Tex.App.—El Paso 2015, no pet.). "[L]ate notice of a hearing given in contravention of the [TRCPs] mandates a new trial. [¶] It is undisputed by the parties that [employer] received notice two business days prior to the hearing. [Employer] contends such late notice under [Fam. Code] §157.062(c), which required at least ten days, constituted a deprival of its due process rights and the [AG] concedes this issue. We agree. [¶] We reverse the judgment and remand for a new trial." *See also* ***In re Aguilera***, this page; ***Ex parte Boyle***, this page.

In re Taylor, 39 S.W.3d 406, 413 (Tex.App.—Waco 2001, orig. proceeding). See annotation under Family Code §157.061, p. 618.

In re Aguilera, 37 S.W.3d 43, 53 (Tex.App.—El Paso 2000, orig. proceeding). "The failure to give the notice required by §157.062 does not render the proceeding void unless the lack of notice amounts to a denial of constitutional due process. *At 54:* When an obligor who has been personally served fails to appear, the court may not hold the obligor in contempt but may … issue a capias for his arrest. While finding the obligor in contempt on less than ten days' notice violates due process, there is no constitutional prohibition against compelling him to appear pursuant to the show cause order even if he has not been provided with the requisite notice. … Relator did not have the option of ignoring the show cause order as he might ignore citation in a civil suit because he is commanded by the court to appear, and if he ignores the command he may be brought in under a capias."

In re Hathcox, 981 S.W.2d 422, 425 (Tex.App.—Texarkana 1998, no pet.). "The obvious purpose of §157.062(d) is to allow a respondent extra time to answer and prepare for a hearing when a new claim has been joined with a motion for enforcement. [Petitioner's] argument that §157.062(d) applies only to original proceedings would defeat this purpose and would allow a petitioner to file only an original motion for enforcement of a support order and then amend that original motion to add new claims and avoid completely the additional time for answer and hearing provided by §157.062(d). We do not believe the legislature intended such a result."

Crawford v. Gardner, 690 S.W.2d 296, 297 (Tex. App.—Dallas 1985, no writ). "[T]he constitutional protections necessary in a proceeding based on a motion for contempt are not required in a proceeding that results solely in an order which reduces child support arrearage to money judgment…. [¶] Because [obligor] was not entitled to such constitutional protections, trial court did not err in rendering its money judgment award without greater notice than was afforded to [obligor] and the trial court's money judgment award is not void."

Ex parte Boyle, 545 S.W.2d 25, 27 (Tex.App.—Houston [1st Dist.] 1976, orig. proceeding). "The holding of a contempt hearing within less than ten days from the date of service of a show cause order is a procedural irregularity only. The court does not lack jurisdiction because the hearing was held within less than ten days. On the other hand, holding the hearing in less than ten days after service of notice may constitute a denial of due process. No clear and definite line can be drawn between that length of notice which will afford due process and that which will not. Each case must be evaluated on its own facts."

FAM §157.063. APPEARANCE

A party makes a general appearance for all purposes in an enforcement proceeding if:

(1) the party appears at the hearing or is present when the case is called; and

(2) the party does not object to the court's jurisdiction or the form or manner of the notice of hearing.

History of Fam. Code §157.063: Acts 1995, 74th Leg., ch. 20, §1, eff. Apr. 20, 1995. Source: Former Fam. Code §14.314(c).

See also *O'Connor's Texas Family Law Handbook* (2017), "Obligor appears," ch. 10-A, §12.1, p. 1092.

FAM §157.064. SPECIAL EXCEPTION

(a) If a respondent specially excepts to the motion for enforcement or moves to strike, the court shall rule on the exception or the motion to strike before it hears the motion for enforcement.

(b) If an exception is sustained, the court shall give the movant an opportunity to replead and continue the hearing to a designated date and time without the requirement of additional service.

History of Fam. Code §157.064: Acts 1995, 74th Leg., ch. 20, §1, eff. Apr. 20, 1995. Source: Former Fam. Code §14.311(f).

See also *O'Connor's Texas Family Law Handbook* (2017), "Rule on special exceptions," ch. 10-A, §12.1.2, p. 1093.

ANNOTATIONS

In re Mann, 162 S.W.3d 429, 433-34 (Tex.App.—Fort Worth 2005, orig. proceeding). Real party in interest (RPI) argues that relator "waived any complaint about her motion to enforce by failing to specially except to the motion in the trial court. We disagree. [¶] [RPI] cites as authority for her waiver argument [Fam. Code] §157.064 and [TRCP] 90 and 91. [¶] [In ***Ex parte Barlow***, 899 S.W.2d 791 (Tex.App.—Houston [14th Dist.] 1995, orig. proceeding), the court] specifically rejected a waiver argument identical to [RPI's]. The ***Barlow*** court noted that this argument has no place in an original proceeding. [¶] While [§157.064] does state that an alleged contemnor may file special exceptions to a motion to enforce, it does not require it, unlike [TRCP] 90 which does require an objection to preserve pleadings defects for appeal. The Texas Legislature purposefully placed precatory language in [§157.064]; if it had desired to make that section mandatory, it could have easily done so. [¶] We agree with ***Barlow***. We hold that a relator need not specially except to a defective motion to enforce to complain of lack of notice in a subsequent petition for writ of habeas corpus." (Internal quotes omitted.)

FAM §157.065. NOTICE OF HEARING, FIRST CLASS MAIL

(a) If a party has been ordered under Chapter 105 to provide the court and the state case registry with the party's current mailing address, notice of a hearing on a motion for enforcement of a final order or on a request for a court order implementing a postjudgment remedy for the collection of child support may be served by mailing a copy of the notice to the respondent, together with a copy of the motion or request, by first class mail to the last mailing address of the respondent on file with the court and the registry.

(b) The notice may be sent by the clerk of the court, the attorney for the movant or party requesting a court order, or any person entitled to the address information as provided in Chapter 105.

(c) A person who sends the notice shall file of record a certificate of service showing the date of mailing and the name of the person who sent the notice.

(d) Repealed by Acts 1997, 75th Leg., ch. 911, §97(a), eff. Sept. 1, 1997.

History of Fam. Code §157.065: Acts 1995, 74th Leg., ch. 20, §1, eff. Apr. 20, 1995. Amended by Acts 1997, 75th Leg., ch. 911, §18, eff. Sept. 1, 1997; Acts 2007, 80th Leg., ch. 972, §18, eff. Sept. 1, 2007; Acts 2015, 84th Leg., ch. 1105, §3 (eff. Sept. 1, 2015), ch. 859, §5 (eff. Sept. 1, 2015). Source: Former Fam. Code §14.314(c).

See also *O'Connor's Texas Family Law Handbook* (2017), "Method of service," ch. 10-A, §7.3, p. 1084.

FAM §157.066. FAILURE TO APPEAR

If a respondent who has been personally served with notice to appear at a hearing does not appear at the designated time, place, and date to respond to a motion for enforcement of an existing court order, regardless of whether the motion is joined with other claims or remedies, the court may not hold the respondent in contempt but may, on proper proof, grant a default judgment for the relief sought and issue a capias for the arrest of the respondent.

History of Fam. Code §157.066: Acts 1995, 74th Leg., ch. 20, §1, eff. Apr. 20, 1995. Amended by Acts 1995, 74th Leg., ch. 751, §50, eff. Sept. 1, 1995. Source: Former Fam. Code §14.317(a).

See also *O'Connor's Texas Family Law Handbook* (2017), "Effect of no answer," ch. 10-A, §8.3.2, p. 1086; "Obligor does not appear – served by personal delivery," ch. 10-A, §12.2, p. 1097.

ANNOTATIONS

In re Taylor, 39 S.W.3d 406, 413-14 (Tex.App.—Waco 2001, orig. proceeding). "[A]lthough the trial court is supposed to 'order' the respondent to appear, §157.066 makes it clear that even if that is done, failure to appear is not punishable by contempt, but rather, if and only if personal service has been obtained, the court can render a default judgment and order a capias for the arrest of the respondent. If Relator wants to preserve these remedies of default judgment and a capias, it is his responsibility to obtain personal service on [re-

spondent] of a proper notice of the hearing, and provide proof of same to the trial court."

Sections 157.067-157.100 reserved for expansion

SUBCHAPTER C. FAILURE TO APPEAR; BOND OR SECURITY

FAM §157.101. BOND OR SECURITY FOR RELEASE OF RESPONDENT

(a) When the court orders the issuance of a capias as provided in this chapter, the court shall also set an appearance bond or security, payable to the obligee or to a person designated by the court, in a reasonable amount.

(b) An appearance bond or security in the amount of $1,000 or a cash bond in the amount of $250 is presumed to be reasonable. Evidence that the respondent has attempted to evade service of process, has previously been found guilty of contempt, or has accrued arrearages over $1,000 is sufficient to rebut the presumption. If the presumption is rebutted, the court shall set a reasonable bond.

History of Fam. Code §157.101: Acts 1995, 74th Leg., ch. 20, §1, eff. Apr. 20, 1995. Source: Former Fam. Code §§14.318(a), 14.32(e).

See also ***O'Connor's Texas Family Law Handbook*** (2017), "Set amount of bond or security," ch. 10-A, §12.2.3, p. 1097.

ANNOTATIONS

In re Clark, 977 S.W.2d 152, 156-157 (Tex.App.—Houston [14th Dist.] 1998, orig. proceeding). "If the Legislature had not intended the factors listed in §157.101(b) to be exclusive it could have so stated in the statute. Nothing in §157.101(b) suggests the court can consider factors other than those enumerated in the statute for setting bond. ... Accordingly, we conclude that the factors listed in §157.101(b) are exclusive. [¶] [T]he trial court's finding that relator has 'avoided the execution of the capias,' is *not* the same as 'attempted to evade service of process' as that phrase is used in §157.101(b). ... Neither the [CCP] nor case law requires 'service' of an arrest warrant. ... Although avoiding execution of a capias is arguably worse than avoiding service of process, the statute simply does not make the former a consideration in setting bond. [¶] Likewise, the trial court's finding that relator was in arrears [for] the payment of court-ordered interim attorney's fees in excess of $1,000 does not satisfy §157.101(b). An 'arrearage' is 'money which is overdue and unpaid.' Although §157.101(b) does not specify the type of 'arrearage,' ch. 157 ... deals primarily with enforcement of child support and repeatedly refers to 'arrearages' in that context. ... Attorney's fees incurred in connection with the enforcement of child custody orders by motion or writ of habeas corpus are recoverable as costs. Such attorney's fees are plainly not 'arrearages' within the ordinary meaning of that term under §157.101(b)."

FAM §157.102. CAPIAS OR WARRANT; DUTY OF LAW ENFORCEMENT OFFICIALS

Law enforcement officials shall treat a capias or arrest warrant ordered under this chapter in the same manner as an arrest warrant for a criminal offense and shall enter the capias or warrant in the computer records for outstanding warrants maintained by the local police, sheriff, and Department of Public Safety. The capias or warrant shall be forwarded to and disseminated by the Texas Crime Information Center and the National Crime Information Center.

History of Fam. Code §157.102: Acts 1995, 74th Leg., ch. 20, §1, eff. Apr. 20, 1995. Amended by Acts 1997, 75th Leg., ch. 702, §3, eff. Sept. 1, 1997; Acts 1999, 76th Leg., ch. 556, §16, eff. Sept. 1, 1999; Acts 2007, 80th Leg., ch. 972, §19, eff. Sept. 1, 2007. Source: Former Fam. Code §14.317(d).

See also ***O'Connor's Texas Family Law Handbook*** (2017), "Law-enforcement duties," ch. 10-A, §12.2.4(1), p. 1098.

FAM §157.103. CAPIAS FEES

(a) The fee for issuing a capias as provided in this chapter is the same as the fee for issuance of a writ of attachment.

(b) The fee for serving a capias is the same as the fee for service of a writ in civil cases generally.

History of Fam. Code §157.103: Acts 1995, 74th Leg., ch. 20, §1, eff. Apr. 20, 1995. Source: Former Fam. Code §14.317(e).

FAM §157.104. CONDITIONAL RELEASE

If the respondent is taken into custody and released on bond, the court shall condition the bond on the respondent's promise to appear in court for a hearing as required by the court without the necessity of further personal service of notice on the respondent.

History of Fam. Code §157.104: Acts 1995, 74th Leg., ch. 20, §1, eff. Apr. 20, 1995. Source: Former Fam. Code §14.318(b).

See also ***O'Connor's Texas Family Law Handbook*** (2017), "Release subject to bond," ch. 10-A, §12.2.4(2)(b), p. 1098.

Ⓐ FAM §157.105. RELEASE HEARING

(a) If the respondent is taken into custody and not released on bond, the respondent shall be brought before the court that issued the capias on or before the third working day after the arrest. The court shall determine whether the respondent's appearance in court at a designated time and place can be assured by a

method other than by posting the bond or security previously established.

(a-1) The court may conduct the release hearing under Subsection (a) through the use of teleconferencing, videoconferencing, or other remote electronic means if the court determines that the method of appearance will facilitate the hearing.

(b) If the respondent is released without posting bond or security, the court shall set a hearing on the alleged contempt at a designated date, time, and place and give the respondent notice of hearing in open court. No other notice to the respondent is required.

(c) If the court is not satisfied that the respondent's appearance in court can be assured and the respondent remains in custody, a hearing on the alleged contempt shall be held as soon as practicable, but not later than the seventh day after the date that the respondent was taken into custody, unless the respondent and the respondent's attorney waive the accelerated hearing.

History of Fam. Code §157.105: Acts 1995, 74th Leg., ch. 20, §1, eff. Apr. 20, 1995. Amended by Acts 2007, 80th Leg., ch. 972, §21, eff. Sept. 1, 2007; S.B. 1965, §1, 85th Leg., eff. Sept. 1, 2017. Source: Former Fam. Code §14.318(c).

See also *O'Connor's Texas Family Law Handbook* (2017), "Release without bond," ch. 10-A, §12.2.4(2)(a), p. 1098; "No release," ch. 10-A, §12.2.4(2)(c), p. 1098.

FAM §157.106. CASH BOND AS SUPPORT

(a) If the respondent has posted a cash bond and is found to be in arrears in the payment of court-ordered child support, the court shall order that the proceeds of the cash bond be paid to the child support obligee or to a person designated by the court, not to exceed the amount of child support arrearages determined to exist.

(b) This section applies without regard to whether the respondent appears at the hearing.

History of Fam. Code §157.106: Acts 1995, 74th Leg., ch. 20, §1, eff. Apr. 20, 1995. Source: Former Fam. Code §14.318(d).

See also *O'Connor's Texas Family Law Handbook* (2017), "Forfeiture of cash bond," ch. 10-A, §12.2.5(2), p. 1098.

FAM §157.107. APPEARANCE BOND OR SECURITY OTHER THAN CASH BOND AS SUPPORT

(a) If the respondent fails to appear at the hearing as directed, the court shall order that the appearance bond or security be forfeited and that the proceeds of any judgment on the bond or security, not to exceed the amount of child support arrearages determined to exist, be paid to the obligee or to a person designated by the court.

(b) The obligee may file suit on the bond.

History of Fam. Code §157.107: Acts 1995, 74th Leg., ch. 20, §1, eff. Apr. 20, 1995. Source: Former Fam. Code §14.318(e).

See also *O'Connor's Texas Family Law Handbook* (2017), "Forfeiture of appearance bond or security," ch. 10-A, §12.2.5(1), p. 1098.

FAM §157.108. CASH BOND AS PROPERTY OF RESPONDENT

A court shall treat a cash bond posted for the benefit of the respondent as the property of the respondent. A person who posts the cash bond does not have recourse in relation to an order regarding the bond other than against the respondent.

History of Fam. Code §157.108: Acts 1995, 74th Leg., ch. 20, §1, eff. Apr. 20, 1995. Source: Former Fam. Code §14.318(f).

FAM §157.109. SECURITY FOR COMPLIANCE WITH ORDER

(a) The court may order the respondent to execute a bond or post security if the court finds that the respondent:

(1) has on two or more occasions denied possession of or access to a child who is the subject of the order; or

(2) is employed by an employer not subject to the jurisdiction of the court or for whom income withholding is unworkable or inappropriate.

(b) The court shall set the amount of the bond or security and condition the bond or security on compliance with the court order permitting possession or access or the payment of past-due or future child support.

(c) The court shall order the bond or security payable through the registry of the court:

(1) to the obligee or other person or entity entitled to receive child support payments designated by the court if enforcement of child support is requested; or

(2) to the person who is entitled to possession or access if enforcement of possession or access is requested.

History of Fam. Code §157.109: Acts 1995, 74th Leg., ch. 20, §1, eff. Apr. 20, 1995. Source: Former Fam. Code §§14.42(a), 14.51(a).

See also *O'Connor's Texas Family Law Handbook* (2017), "Bond," ch. 10-A, §5.4.9(2)(d), p. 1080; "Security bond," ch. 11-A, §13.2.9(4), p. 1194.

ANNOTATIONS

In re Gonzalez, 993 S.W.2d 147, 157 (Tex.App.—San Antonio 1999, no pet.). "By its terms, [§157.109] does not require the court to make a written finding."

FAM §157.110. FORFEITURE OF SECURITY FOR FAILURE TO COMPLY WITH ORDER

(a) On the motion of a person or entity for whose benefit a bond has been executed or security deposited,

the court may forfeit all or part of the bond or security deposit on a finding that the person who furnished the bond or security:

(1) has violated the court order for possession of and access to a child; or

(2) failed to make child support payments.

(b) The court shall order the registry to pay the funds from a forfeited bond or security deposit to the obligee or person or entity entitled to receive child support payments in an amount that does not exceed the child support arrearages or, in the case of possession of or access to a child, to the person entitled to possession or access.

(c) The court may order that all or part of the forfeited amount be applied to pay attorney's fees and costs incurred by the person or entity bringing the motion for contempt or motion for forfeiture.

History of Fam. Code §157.110: Acts 1995, 74th Leg., ch. 20, §1, eff. Apr. 20, 1995. Source: Former Fam. Code §§14.42(b), (c), (f), 14.51(b), (c), (f).

See also ***O'Connor's Texas Family Law Handbook*** (2017), "Bond forfeiture," ch. 11-A, §5.4.9(2)(d), p. 1188.

FAM §157.111. FORFEITURE NOT DEFENSE TO CONTEMPT

The forfeiture of bond or security is not a defense in a contempt proceeding.

History of Fam. Code §157.111: Acts 1995, 74th Leg., ch. 20, §1, eff. Apr. 20, 1995. Source: Former Fam. Code §§14.42(e), 14.51(e).

See also ***O'Connor's Texas Family Law Handbook*** (2017), "Not a defense," ch. 10-A, §8.3.3(6), p. 1089.

FAM §157.112. JOINDER OF FORFEITURE & CONTEMPT PROCEEDINGS

A motion for enforcement requesting contempt may be joined with a forfeiture proceeding.

History of Fam. Code §157.112: Acts 1995, 74th Leg., ch. 20, §1, eff. Apr. 20, 1995. Source: Former Fam. Code §§14.42(d), 14.51(d).

FAM §157.113. APPLICATION OF BOND PENDING WRIT

If the obligor requests to execute a bond or to post security pending a hearing by an appellate court on a writ, the bond or security on forfeiture shall be payable to the obligee.

History of Fam. Code §157.113: Acts 1995, 74th Leg., ch. 20, §1, eff. Apr. 20, 1995. Source: Former Fam. Code §§14.32(e), 14.40(f).

FAM §157.114. FAILURE TO APPEAR

The court may order a capias to be issued for the arrest of the respondent if:

(1) the motion for enforcement requests contempt;

(2) the respondent was personally served; and

(3) the respondent fails to appear.

History of Fam. Code §157.114: Acts 1995, 74th Leg., ch. 20, §1, eff. Apr. 20, 1995. Source: Former Fam. Code §14.317(a).

See also ***O'Connor's Texas Family Law Handbook*** (2017), "Issue capias," ch. 10-A, §12.2.2, p. 1097.

FAM §157.115. DEFAULT JUDGMENT

(a) The court may render a default order for the relief requested if the respondent:

(1) has been personally served, has filed an answer, or has entered an appearance; and

(2) does not appear at the designated time, place, and date to respond to the motion.

(b) If the respondent fails to appear, the court may not hold the respondent in contempt but may order a capias to be issued.

History of Fam. Code §157.115: Acts 1995, 74th Leg., ch. 20, §1, eff. Apr. 20, 1995. Amended by Acts 1995, 74th Leg., ch. 751, §51, eff. Sept. 1, 1995. Source: Former Fam. Code §14.317(a), (c).

See also ***O'Connor's Texas Family Law Handbook*** (2017), "Default judgment," ch. 10-A, §12.2.1, p. 1097.

Sections 157.116-157.160 reserved for expansion

SUBCHAPTER D. HEARING & ENFORCEMENT ORDER

FAM §157.161. RECORD

(a) Except as provided by Subsection (b), a record of the hearing in a motion for enforcement shall be made by a court reporter or as provided by Chapter 201.

(b) A record is not required if:

(1) the parties agree to an order; or

(2) the motion does not request incarceration and the parties waive the requirement of a record at the time of hearing, either in writing or in open court, and the court approves waiver.

History of Fam. Code §157.161: Acts 1995, 74th Leg., ch. 20, §1, eff. Apr. 20, 1995. Source: Former Fam. Code §14.32(b).

See also ***O'Connor's Texas Family Law Handbook*** (2017), "Make or waive record," ch. 10-A, §12.1.1, p. 1092.

FAM §157.162. PROOF

(a) The movant is not required to prove that the underlying order is enforceable by contempt to obtain other appropriate enforcement remedies.

(b) A finding that the respondent is not in contempt does not preclude the court from awarding the petitioner court costs and reasonable attorney's fees or ordering any other enforcement remedy, including rendering a money judgment, posting a bond or other security, or withholding income.

(c) The movant may attach to the motion a copy of a payment record. The movant may subsequently update that payment record at the hearing. If a payment

record was attached to the motion as authorized by this subsection, the payment record, as updated if applicable, is admissible to prove:

(1) the dates and in what amounts payments were made;

(2) the amount of any accrued interest;

(3) the cumulative arrearage over time; and

(4) the cumulative arrearage as of the final date of the record.

(c-1) A respondent may offer evidence controverting the contents of a payment record under Subsection (c).

(d), (e) Repealed by Acts 2013, 83rd Leg., ch. 649, §2, eff. June 14, 2013.

History of Fam. Code §157.162: Acts 1995, 74th Leg., ch. 20, §1, eff. Apr. 20, 1995. Amended by Acts 2007, 80th Leg., ch. 1189, §1, eff. June 15, 2007; Acts 2009, 81st Leg., ch. 767, §15, eff. June 19, 2009; Acts 2011, 82nd Leg., ch. 508, §4, eff. Sept. 1, 2011; Acts 2013, 83rd Leg., ch. 649, §§1, 2, eff. June 14, 2013. Source: Former Fam. Code §§14.311(b), (c), 14.33(d).

A FAM §157.163. APPOINTMENT OF ATTORNEY

(a) In a motion for enforcement or motion to revoke community service, the court must first determine whether incarceration of the respondent is a possible result of the proceedings.

(b) If the court determines that incarceration is a possible result of the proceedings, the court shall inform a respondent not represented by an attorney of the right to be represented by an attorney and, if the respondent is indigent, of the right to the appointment of an attorney.

(c) If the court determines that the respondent will not be incarcerated as a result of the proceedings, the court may require a respondent who is indigent to proceed without an attorney.

(d) If the respondent claims indigency and requests the appointment of an attorney, the court shall require the respondent to file an affidavit of indigency. The court may hear evidence to determine the issue of indigency.

(d-1) The court may conduct a hearing on the issue of indigency through the use of teleconferencing, videoconferencing, or other remote electronic means if the court determines that conducting the hearing in that manner will facilitate the hearing.

(e) Except as provided by Subsection (c), the court shall appoint an attorney to represent the respondent if the court determines that the respondent is indigent.

(f) If the respondent is not in custody, an appointed attorney is entitled to not less than 10 days from the date of the attorney's appointment to respond to the movant's pleadings and prepare for the hearing.

(g) If the respondent is in custody, an appointed attorney is entitled to not less than five days from the date the respondent was taken into custody to respond to the movant's pleadings and prepare for the hearing.

(h) The court may shorten or extend the time for preparation if the respondent and the respondent's attorney sign a waiver of the time limit.

(i) The scope of the court appointment of an attorney to represent the respondent is limited to the allegation of contempt or of violation of community supervision contained in the motion for enforcement or motion to revoke community supervision.

History of Fam. Code §157.163: Acts 1995, 74th Leg., ch. 20, §1, eff. Apr. 20, 1995. Amended by S.B. 1965, §2, 85th Leg., eff. Sept. 1, 2017. Source: Former Fam. Code §14.32(f).

See also ***O'Connor's Texas Family Law Handbook*** (2017), "Notify obligor of rights," ch. 10-A, §12.1.3, p. 1093.

ANNOTATIONS

Ex parte Acker, 949 S.W.2d 314, 316 (Tex.1997). "[S]ection 157.163 requires courts to admonish pro se litigants of their right to counsel, regardless of whether they are indigent or not." *See also* ***In re Aarons***, 10 S.W.3d 833, 833-34 (Tex.App.—Beaumont 2000, orig. proceeding) (court's failure to admonish petitioner of right to counsel rendered commitment arising from contempt order void).

Ex parte Keene, 909 S.W.2d 507, 507 (Tex.1995). Relator "contends that he is unlawfully confined because the trial court did not advise him of his right to counsel or of his right to appointed counsel under [Fam. Code] §14.32(f) [now §157.163]. We agree. *At 508:* In the absence of a knowing and intelligent waiver by [relator] of his right to counsel, made on the record, the trial court had no authority to hold him in contempt."

In re Mancha, 440 S.W.3d 158, 166-67 (Tex.App.—Houston [14th Dist.] 2013, orig. proceeding). See annotation under Family Code §157.008, *Inability to Pay*, p. 617.

In re Ohiri, 95 S.W.3d 413, 415 (Tex.App.—Houston [1st Dist.] 2002, orig. proceeding). "[W]ith his conditional liberty interest at stake, relator was instructed to appear before the trial court to determine whether he had violated the terms of the suspension of commitment order. The fact that the hearing was not

preceded by a new pleading denominated as a motion to revoke community service is immaterial. The nature of the proceeding, with one of its possible outcomes being relator's incarceration, was similar to a hearing on a motion to revoke community service and triggered the §157.163(b) requirement that the trial court admonish relator of his right to counsel."

FAM §157.164. PAYMENT OF APPOINTED ATTORNEY

(a) An attorney appointed to represent an indigent respondent is entitled to a reasonable fee for services within the scope of the appointment in the amount set by the court.

(b) The fee shall be paid from the general funds of the county according to the schedule for the compensation of counsel appointed to defend criminal defendants as provided in the Code of Criminal Procedure.

(c) For purposes of this section, a proceeding in a court of appeals or the Supreme Court of Texas is considered the equivalent of a bona fide appeal to the Texas Court of Criminal Appeals.

History of Fam. Code §157.164: Acts 1995, 74th Leg., ch. 20, §1, eff. Apr. 20, 1995. Source: Former Fam. Code §14.33(b).

See also ***O'Connor's Texas Family Law Handbook*** (2017), "Attorney fees," ch. 10-A, §12.1.3(2)(b)[2][c], p. 1096.

FAM §157.165. PROBATION OF CONTEMPT ORDER

The court may place the respondent on community supervision and suspend commitment if the court finds that the respondent is in contempt of court for failure or refusal to obey an order rendered as provided in this title.

History of Fam. Code §157.165: Acts 1995, 74th Leg., ch. 20, §1, eff. Apr. 20, 1995. Amended by Acts 1999, 76th Leg., ch. 62, §6.25, eff. Sept. 1, 1999. Source: Former Fam. Code §§14.40(e)(1), 14.50(d)(1).

See also ***O'Connor's Texas Family Law Handbook*** (2017), "Suspension of commitment for community supervision," ch. 10-A, §5.4.9(2)(a), p. 1080; "Suspend commitment – community supervision," ch. 10-A, §13.2.8(2), p. 1101.

FAM §157.166. CONTENTS OF ENFORCEMENT ORDER

(a) An enforcement order must include:

(1) in ordinary and concise language the provisions of the order for which enforcement was requested;

(2) the acts or omissions that are the subject of the order;

(3) the manner of the respondent's noncompliance; and

(4) the relief granted by the court.

(b) If the order imposes incarceration or a fine for criminal contempt, an enforcement order must contain findings identifying, setting out, or incorporating by reference the provisions of the order for which enforcement was requested and the date of each occasion when the respondent's failure to comply with the order was found to constitute criminal contempt.

(c) If the enforcement order imposes incarceration for civil contempt, the order must state the specific conditions on which the respondent may be released from confinement.

History of Fam. Code §157.166: Acts 1995, 74th Leg., ch. 20, §1, eff. Apr. 20, 1995. Amended by Acts 1999, 76th Leg., ch. 556, §17, eff. Sept. 1, 1999. Source: Former Fam. Code §14.33(a).

See also ***O'Connor's Texas Family Law Handbook*** (2017), "Findings," ch. 10-A, §13.2.7, p. 1099; "Contempt relief," ch. 10-A, §13.2.8, p. 1100; "Findings," ch. 11-A, §13.2.7, p. 1193; "Contempt relief," ch. 11-A, §13.2.8, p. 1193.

ANNOTATIONS

Generally

In re Phillips, 496 S.W.3d 769, 770 (Tex.2016). "The Tim Cole Act ('the Act') provides compensation for the time a person is wrongfully imprisoned and for child support owed but not paid by the person, plus interest, while imprisoned. [T]he Comptroller's authority to determine the compensation owed [under the Act] is exclusive, and ... the Comptroller therefore is not bound by a court's judgment in a child support enforcement proceeding."

In re Levingston, 996 S.W.2d 936, 938-39 (Tex. App.—Houston [14th Dist.] 1999, orig. proceeding). "The purpose of an enforcement order is to notify the offender of how he has violated its provisions and how he can purge himself of contempt, to notify the sheriff so that he can carry out enforcement, and to provide sufficient information for an adequate review."

Ex parte Coleman, 864 S.W.2d 573, 576 (Tex. App.—Tyler 1993, orig. proceeding). While Fam. Code §14.33(a), now §157.166, "does not prohibit stipulations in enforcement orders, it does require specificity and particularity. Thus, if a court relies upon the stipulation of parties, its order must either set out the stipulation in its entirety, or incorporate it sufficiently by reference in order to meet the requirements of §14.33(a)."

Order Being Enforced

Ex parte Chambers, 898 S.W.2d 257, 260 (Tex. 1995). "A court order is insufficient to support a judgment of contempt only if its interpretation requires inferences or conclusions about which *reasonable* per-

sons might differ. Only the existence of *reasonable* alternative constructions will prevent enforcement of the order. The order need not be full of superfluous terms and specifications adequate to counter any flight of fancy a contemnor may imagine in order to declare it vague."

Ex parte Slavin, 412 S.W.2d 43, 44 (Tex.1967). "It is an accepted rule of law that for a person to be held in contempt for disobeying a court decree, the decree must spell out the details of compliance in clear, specific and unambiguous terms so that such person will readily know exactly what duties or obligations are imposed upon him."

Ex parte Tanner, 904 S.W.2d 202, 204-05 (Tex. App.—Houston [14th Dist.] 1995, orig. proceeding). "[H] alleges that the divorce decree could not be enforced by contempt because it did not specify a location for payment of child support. [¶] Although providing a location or mailing address for payment might have been preferable, [H] has cited no actual difficulty or confusion concerning [W's] address. ... Under these circumstances, we are not persuaded that a failure to specify a location for payment of child support rendered the divorce decree so ambiguous as to be unenforceable by contempt." *See also* ***In re Sarabia***, No. 01-04-00263-CV (Tex.App.—Houston [1st Dist.] 2004, orig. proceeding) (memo op.; 7-21-04) (nothing in §157.166(b) explicitly requires place-of-payment provision).

Ex parte Grothe, 570 S.W.2d 183, 184 (Tex.App.—Austin 1978, orig. proceeding). An oral order "cannot comply with any of the requirements of ***Slavin***. It follows that the judgment of contempt for violation of the oral order ... cannot stand."

Contempt Order

Ex parte Shaklee, 939 S.W.2d 144, 145 (Tex.1997). "[T]o satisfy due process, the contempt order must clearly specify the punishment imposed by the court." *See also* ***Ex parte Kottwitz***, 8 S.W.2d 508, 509 (Tex. 1928) (judgment for contempt must be intelligible and certain, so defendant knows what is required).

Ex parte Hall, 854 S.W.2d 656, 658 (Tex.1993). "[T]he failure to comply with an order to pay a 'debt' is not contempt punishable by imprisonment because of the prohibition of [Tex. Const.] art. 1, §18 ..., which states: 'No person shall ever be imprisoned for debt.' Such an order may be enforced by other legal processes, such as execution or attachment of property, but not by imprisonment of the adjudicated debtor. The obligation which the law imposes on spouses to support one another and on parents to support their children is not considered a 'debt' within Art. 1, §18, but a legal duty arising out of the status of the parties."

Ex parte Garcia, 795 S.W.2d 740, 741 (Tex.1990). "The district court ordered relator jailed, finding that he was $4,151 in arrears. The court failed to specify, however, the time, date, and place of each occasion on which relator failed to pay such child support. [¶] Because the enforcement order does not contain the requisite specificity, it is not enforceable by contempt."

Ex parte Strickland, 723 S.W.2d 668, 669 (Tex. 1987). "Due process requires both a written judgment of contempt and a written order of commitment in order to punish a person for constructive contempt of court." *See also* ***Ex parte Littleton***, 97 S.W.3d 840, 842 (Tex.App.—Texarkana 2003, orig. proceeding).

Ex parte Davila, 718 S.W.2d 281, 282 (Tex.1986). "The order adjudging [father] in contempt makes no reference to any prior occasions when [he] failed to comply with the court's order. Nor does the order make any attempt to assess separate penalties for each separate contemptuous act. The judgment simply focuses on [father's] failure to pay a lump sum of $28,000 and assesses one penalty. The order also provides that [father] must pay the entire amount of $28,000 in order to purge himself of contempt. Since this lump sum plainly includes amounts which could not be the basis of a contempt finding at the time of the hearing, the entire judgment is tainted. If one punishment is assessed for multiple acts of contempt, and one of those acts is not punishable by contempt, the entire judgment is void." *See also* ***In re Newby***, this page.

Ex parte De Wees, 210 S.W.2d 145, 146-47 (Tex. 1948). "To order that one be imprisoned for an indefinite period in a civil contempt is purely a remedial measure. Its purpose is to coerce the contemnor to do an act within his or her power to perform. He must have the means by which he may purge himself of the contempt. [¶] Where it is not within the power of a person to perform the act which alone will purge him of contempt, the court is without power to imprison him for an indefinite term as punishment for an offense already committed."

In re Newby, 370 S.W.3d 463, 469 (Tex.App.—Fort Worth 2012, orig. proceeding). "[I]n this case, the trial court conditioned the relator's release on paying more

than the amount the trial court had found the relator in contempt for failing to pay. *At 470:* In [similar] cases, the appellate courts modified the civil coercive contempt parts of the orders to delete the additional amounts that the relators were required to pay to purge themselves of contempt, retaining only the amounts for which the relators were actually held in contempt, because the courts were able to calculate what the purging amounts should be. [¶] Therefore, having found error, we will modify the civil coercive contempt part of the order to reflect the correct ... arrearage for which relator was actually held in contempt...." *See also **In re Hall***, 433 S.W.3d 203, 207 (Tex.App.—Houston [14th Dist.] 2014, orig. proceeding) (when acts and punishments are listed separately in contempt order, invalid portions can be severed and valid portions can be retained and enforced).

In re Butler, 45 S.W.3d 268, 271 n.1 (Tex.App.—Houston [1st Dist.] 2001, orig. proceeding). "[T]he contempt order and order of commitment do not have to be signed at the same time. The ... Family Code contemplates situations such as the one here, when a contempt order providing for incarceration is conditionally suspended, but relator is later committed to jail if he does not comply with the conditions of suspension."

Ex parte Stanley, 826 S.W.2d 772, 772-73 (Tex. App.—Dallas 1992, orig. proceeding). "An enforcement order shall contain findings setting out in ordinary and concise language the provisions of the final order, decree, or judgment a party seeks to enforce. The enforcement order may do so by: (1) copying in their entirety the provisions for which enforcement was sought; (2) attaching a copy of the order for which enforcement was sought as an exhibit and incorporating it by reference; or (3) giving the volume and page numbers in the minutes of the court where one can find the order for which enforcement was sought. The punitive portion of an enforcement order that does not comply with the statutory requirements of [Fam. Code] §14.33(a) [now §157.166] is void. [¶] The least preferable method to attempt to comply with [§157.166] is solely by reference to the volume and page of the court minutes where the order can be found. That method requires a contemnor to look beyond the face of the enforcement order itself to determine what provisions of the earlier order he violated. [¶] Typographical errors do not necessarily invalidate contempt orders. When one seeking enforcement of an earlier court order chooses to draft a contempt order referencing the earlier order solely by volume and page of the court's minutes, we hold that strict compliance with [§157.166] requires that both the volume number and the page number be accurate." *See also **In re Luebe***, 404 S.W.3d 589, 595 (Tex.App.—Houston [1st Dist.] 2010, orig. proceeding) (§157.166 was satisfied because enforcement order implicated specific divorce-decree provisions); ***In re Anascavage***, 131 S.W.3d 108, 111 (Tex.App.—San Antonio 2004, orig. proceeding) (enforcement order complied with §157.166 by adequately setting forth provision of prior order sought to be enforced); ***Ex parte Tanner***, 904 S.W.2d 202, 205 (Tex.App.—Houston [14th Dist.] 1995, orig. proceeding) (***Stanley*** methods are not exclusive).

Right to Jury Trial

In re Newby, 370 S.W.3d 463, 466-67 (Tex.App.—Fort Worth 2012, orig. proceeding). "Although an absolute right to trial by jury in contempt proceedings does not exist, an alleged contemnor possesses such a right in criminal contempt cases in which the punishment assessed is 'serious.' Punishment assessed for criminal contempt beyond 180 days is considered 'serious' and may not be assessed unless there was a jury trial or a jury waiver. [¶] Even when the offenses are separate and the sentence for each act of contempt is less than six months, ... the alleged contemnor is nevertheless entitled to a jury trial if the sentences are aggregated to run consecutively, so as to result in punishment exceeding six months. [¶] Although the order finding [father] in contempt recites that [father] waived his Fifth Amendment rights after being admonished, it does not state that he waived his right to trial by jury. Moreover, the reporter's record from the hearing on the contempt motions shows that although the trial court did inform [father] of his right to a trial by jury, it did so midway through the hearing.... Additionally, the trial court did not ask [father] whether he specifically waived his right to trial by jury, and [father] only, clearly communicated his waiver of his Fifth Amendment right to testify, about the child support allegations. Accordingly, we ... hold that the record shows that the trial court sentenced [father] to greater than six months' confinement in violation of his right to a jury trial and that the criminal contempt part of the order is therefore void."

Commitment Order

In re Henry, 154 S.W.3d 594, 598 (Tex.2005). "[T]he commitment order here does not assess sepa-

rate penalties for each contemptuous act; rather, it requires [ex-H] to pay a ... lump sum to secure his freedom. ... 'If one punishment is assessed for multiple acts of contempt, and one of those acts is not punishable by contempt, the entire judgment is void.' Because the trial court did not allocate the ... judgment based on particular contemptuous acts, and because [ex-H's] failure to pay past-due property taxes ... is not punishable by coercive contempt, we hold that the trial court's entire civil commitment order is void."

Ex parte Hernandez, 827 S.W.2d 858, 858 (Tex. 1992). "A commitment order is the warrant, process or order by which a court directs a ministerial officer to take custody of a person. The order containing this directive need not take a particular form and may be a separate order issued by the court, an attachment or order issued by the clerk at the court's direction, or included in the contempt judgment. Although the form of the order is not important, the substance is. *At 859:* The contempt order does not direct the sheriff or other ministerial officer to take [contemnor] into custody and detain him under the terms of the judgment, nor does it direct the clerk to issue a written attachment or order of commitment to the proper officer. [¶] Accordingly, a majority of the Court grants the writ of habeas corpus, and orders [contemnor] discharged." *See also* ***Ex parte Ustick***, 9 S.W.3d 922, 925 (Tex.App.—Waco 2000, orig. proceeding).

Ex parte Amaya, 748 S.W.2d 224, 224-25 (Tex. 1988). "In order to satisfy due process requirements, both a written judgment of contempt and a written commitment order are necessary to imprison a person for civil constructive contempt of court. [¶] The trial court may cause a contemnor to be detained by the sheriff or other officer for a short and reasonable time while the judgment of contempt and the order of commitment are being prepared for the judge's signature. We hold that a three-day delay is not a 'short and reasonable time' while the documents are being prepared for signature. [¶] To hold otherwise would allow the trial court to place a person in jail indefinitely without any method for the prisoner to obtain his release by purging himself of the contempt and perhaps, without knowledge of why he was being held in contempt. Such proceedings would be in violation of due process." *See also* ***In re Linan***, 419 S.W.3d 694, 697-98 (Tex.App.—Houston [1st Dist.] 2013, orig. proceeding) (delay of four days following verbal order for confinement was not short and reasonable); ***In re Brown***, 114 S.W.3d 7, 10 (Tex. App.—Amarillo 2003, no pet.) (delay of one calendar day following verbal order for confinement was short and reasonable).

In re Markowitz, 25 S.W.3d 1, 3 (Tex.App.—Houston [14th Dist.] 1998, orig. proceeding). "Where the court does not sign a contempt judgment [coincidently] with a commitment order, the commitment order must contain the elements of a contempt judgment; that is, 'the order should clearly state in what respect the court's order has been violated.'" *See also* ***Ex parte Littleton***, 97 S.W.3d 840, 842 (Tex.App.—Texarkana 2003, orig. proceeding).

FAM §157.167. RESPONDENT TO PAY ATTORNEY'S FEES & COSTS

(a) If the court finds that the respondent has failed to make child support payments, the court shall order the respondent to pay the movant's reasonable attorney's fees and all court costs in addition to the arrearages. Fees and costs ordered under this subsection may be enforced by any means available for the enforcement of child support, including contempt.

(b) If the court finds that the respondent has failed to comply with the terms of an order providing for the possession of or access to a child, the court shall order the respondent to pay the movant's reasonable attorney's fees and all court costs in addition to any other remedy. If the court finds that the enforcement of the order with which the respondent failed to comply was necessary to ensure the child's physical or emotional health or welfare, the fees and costs ordered under this subsection may be enforced by any means available for the enforcement of child support, including contempt, but not including income withholding.

(c) Except as provided by Subsection (d), for good cause shown, the court may waive the requirement that the respondent pay attorney's fees and costs if the court states the reasons supporting that finding.

(d) If the court finds that the respondent is in contempt of court for failure or refusal to pay child support and that the respondent owes $20,000 or more in child support arrearages, the court may not waive the requirement that the respondent pay attorney's fees and costs unless the court also finds that the respondent:

(1) is involuntarily unemployed or is disabled; and

(2) lacks the financial resources to pay the attorney's fees and costs.

(e) Deleted by Acts 2005, 79th Leg., ch. 253, §1, eff. Sept. 1, 2005.

History of Fam. Code §157.167: Acts 1995, 74th Leg., ch. 20, §1, eff. Apr. 20, 1995. Amended by Acts 1999, 76th Leg., ch. 556, §18, eff. Sept. 1, 1999; Acts 2003, 78th Leg., ch. 477, §1 (eff. Sept. 1, 2003), ch. 1262, §1 (eff. Sept. 1, 2003); Acts 2005, 79th Leg., ch. 253, §1 (eff. Sept. 1, 2005), ch. 728, §6.003 (eff. Sept. 1, 2005). Source: Former Fam. Code §14.33(c).

See also ***O'Connor's Texas Family Law Handbook*** (2017), "Attorney fees & costs," ch. 10-A, §13.2.9(5), p. 1102; "Attorney fees & costs," ch. 11-A, §13.2.9(5), p. 1194.

ANNOTATIONS

In re Henry, 154 S.W.3d 594, 596 (Tex.2005). "A person may be confined under a court's contempt powers for failure to pay child support. But the obligation to support a child is viewed as a legal duty and not as a debt. Similarly, attorney's fees related to child-support contempt actions are viewed as costs and are not considered a debt. In this case, the trial court clearly had authority to order [obligor] confined for failure to pay past-due child support and related attorney's fees."

In re Braden, 483 S.W.3d 659, 665 (Tex.App.—Houston [14th Dist.] 2015, orig. proceeding). "Father's attorney did not attempt to segregate attorney's fees incurred for work performed in connection with the enforcement proceeding—fees that can be enforced through contempt—from attorney's fees incurred for work performed in connection with the modification proceeding—fees that cannot be enforced through contempt. *At 666:* Although there is evidence in the record to support an award of ... attorney's fees, in the absence of any segregation of fees incurred for enforcement from fees incurred for modification, there is no evidence that the trial court's ... award was solely for fees attributable to the enforcement action that can be enforced by contempt. We therefore hold that the ... award of attorney's fees is enforceable only as a debt, and the trial court abused its discretion by making the fee award enforceable by contempt."

Russell v. Russell, 478 S.W.3d 36, 44 (Tex.App.—Houston [14th Dist.] 2015, no pet.). "We disagree with [father] that §157.167 is not triggered if the requested fees are unreasonable. Section 157.167 expressly provides that the statute is triggered 'if the court finds that the respondent has failed to make child support payments,' not on a threshold finding of reasonableness. Absent a specific finding that the respondent has shown good cause to not pay attorney's fees, and the court stating the reasons supporting such a finding, the court is required to award reasonable attorney's fees to the movant. [¶] Because §157.167 requires that good cause be stated on the record and the trial judge rejected proposed finding supporting good cause, this court may not imply a finding of good cause to support the trial court's judgment. *At 46:* Further, §157.167 does not require that the trial court find contempt before awarding fees." *See also* ***In re T.L.K.***, 90 S.W.3d 833, 841 (Tex.App.—San Antonio 2002, no pet.) (reasonableness of attorney fees is fact question to be determined by the trier of fact and must be supported by competent evidence).

In re McLaurin, 467 S.W.3d 561, 565 (Tex.App.—Houston [1st Dist.] 2015, orig. proceeding). "Attorney's fees and costs awarded in proceedings to enforce child support payments are authorized by the Family Code, and the resulting obligation is not considered a debt and may be enforced through a contempt judgment. [¶] 'Although a trial court is clearly authorized to order the payment of costs and attorney's fees as sanctions ... the obligation to pay created thereby is a debt and the debtor may not be imprisoned for failing to pay it.' [¶] [C]ontempt judgments ordering imprisonment for disobeying a sanctions order to pay attorneys' fees or costs are void as an unconstitutional imprisonment for a debt."

Taylor v. Speck, 308 S.W.3d 81, 84 (Tex.App.—San Antonio 2010, no pet.). "[T]he trial court entered a cumulative money judgment ... for child support arrearages [that included additional] attorney's fees, payable to [mother's] attorneys in the event [father] filed a bankruptcy petition and the attorneys were required to collect child support through the bankruptcy process. *At 88:* [T]he trial court's decision to award conditional attorney's fees ... in the event of a bankruptcy does not preempt or otherwise intrude upon the jurisdiction of the trial court. Rather, such an award is akin to the conditional award of attorney's fees in the event of success on appeal, or in the event of a successful defense on appeal. Given that the trial court is mandated to award attorney's fees by §157.167, and a conditional award of post-judgment attorney's fees is recognized in Texas, we see no error in the trial court's award of additional attorney's fees in the event of a bankruptcy filing...."

FAM §157.168. ADDITIONAL PERIODS OF POSSESSION OR ACCESS

(a) A court may order additional periods of possession of or access to a child to compensate for the denial

of court-ordered possession or access. The additional periods of possession or access:

(1) must be of the same type and duration of the possession or access that was denied;

(2) may include weekend, holiday, and summer possession or access; and

(3) must occur on or before the second anniversary of the date the court finds that court-ordered possession or access has been denied.

(b) The person denied possession or access is entitled to decide the time of the additional possession or access, subject to the provisions of Subsection (a)(1).

History of Fam. Code §157.168: Acts 1995, 74th Leg., ch. 751, §52, eff. Sept. 1, 1995. Amended by Acts 1997, 75th Leg., ch. 974, §1, eff. Sept. 1, 1997; Acts 1999, 76th Leg., ch. 1034, §1, eff. Sept. 1, 1999.

See also ***O'Connor's Texas Family Law Handbook*** (2017), "Motion to Enforce by Additional Periods of Possession or Access," ch. 11-C, p. 1198.

ANNOTATIONS

In re Braden, 483 S.W.3d 659, 666 (Tex.App.—Houston [14th Dist.] 2015, orig. proceeding). "The 'same type and duration' means 'the same amount of time.' A trial court abuses its discretion under §157.168 by awarding make-up time that is greater than those periods for which possession or access was denied. [¶] The 62 days of additional possession … far exceeds the four days of possession that the trial court found relator had denied Father. Therefore, the trial court abused its discretion by awarding additional possession greater than that which relator had denied Father."

In re Zevallos, No. 14-11-01080-CV (Tex.App.—Houston [14th Dist.] 2012, orig. proceeding) (memo op.; 2-2-12). Mother "argues that the trial court violated §157.168 … by assessing an additional period of access or possession for the father that is not 'of the same type and duration of the possession or access that was denied.' [¶] [Mother] seems to argue that since she deprived the father of weekend and summer visitation, he should not receive Christmas visitation as an additional period of access. The statute does not require summer or weekend additional periods to be awarded for denial of summer or weekend visitation. In fact, if anything, the father has received less make-up possession than he was denied. The trial court did not abuse its discretion in awarding an additional two weeks to the father during the Christmas holiday as compensation for the denial of several weekends plus one month in the summer."

Sections 157.169-157.210 reserved for expansion

SUBCHAPTER E. COMMUNITY SUPERVISION

FAM §157.211. CONDITIONS OF COMMUNITY SUPERVISION

If the court places the respondent on community supervision and suspends commitment, the terms and conditions of community supervision may include the requirement that the respondent:

(1) report to the community supervision officer as directed;

(2) permit the community supervision officer to visit the respondent at the respondent's home or elsewhere;

(3) obtain counseling on financial planning, budget management, conflict resolution, parenting skills, alcohol or drug abuse, or other matters causing the respondent to fail to obey the order;

(4) pay required child support and any child support arrearages;

(5) pay court costs and attorney's fees ordered by the court;

(6) seek employment assistance services offered by the Texas Workforce Commission under Section 302.0035, Labor Code, if appropriate; and

(7) participate in mediation or other services to alleviate conditions that prevent the respondent from obeying the court's order.

History of Fam. Code §157.211: Acts 1995, 74th Leg., ch. 20, §1, eff. Apr. 20, 1995. Amended by Acts 1997, 75th Leg., ch. 702, §4, eff. Sept. 1, 1997; Acts 1999, 76th Leg., ch. 946, §2, eff. Sept. 1, 1999; Acts 2001, 77th Leg., ch. 311, §1, eff. Sept. 1, 2001. Source: Former Fam. Code §§14.40(e)(1), 14.50(d)(1).

See also ***O'Connor's Texas Family Law Handbook*** (2017), "Suspend commitment – community supervision," ch. 10-A, §13.2.8(2), p. 1101.

FAM §157.212. TERM OF COMMUNITY SUPERVISION

The initial period of community supervision may not exceed 10 years. The court may continue the community supervision beyond 10 years until the earlier of:

(1) the second anniversary of the date on which the community supervision first exceeded 10 years; or

(2) the date on which all child support, including arrearages and interest, has been paid.

History of Fam. Code §157.212: Acts 1995, 74th Leg., ch. 20, §1, eff. Apr. 20, 1995. Amended by Acts 1999, 76th Leg., ch. 1313, §1, eff. Sept. 1, 1999; Acts 2007, 80th Leg., ch. 972, §22, eff. Sept. 1, 2007. Source: Former Fam. Code §§14.40(e)(2), 14.50(d)(2).

See also ***O'Connor's Texas Family Law Handbook*** (2017), "Suspend commitment – community supervision," ch. 10-A, §13.2.8(2), p. 1101.

FAM §157.213. COMMUNITY SUPERVISION FEES

(a) The court may require the respondent to pay a fee to the court in an amount equal to that required of a criminal defendant subject to community supervision.

(b) The court may make payment of the fee a condition of granting or continuing community supervision.

(c) The court shall deposit the fees received under this subchapter as follows:

(1) if the community supervision officer is employed by a community supervision and corrections department, in the special fund of the county treasury provided by the Code of Criminal Procedure to be used for community supervision; or

(2) if the community supervision officer is employed by a domestic relations office, in one of the following funds, as determined by the office's administering entity:

(A) the general fund for the county in which the domestic relations office is located; or

(B) the office fund established by the administering entity for the domestic relations office.

History of Fam. Code §157.213: Acts 1995, 74th Leg., ch. 20, §1, eff. Apr. 20, 1995. Amended by Acts 2001, 77th Leg., ch. 311, §2, eff. Sept. 1, 2001. Source: Former Fam. Code §§14.40(e)(3), 14.50(d)(3).

See also *O'Connor's Texas Family Law Handbook* (2017), "Suspend commitment – community supervision," ch. 10-A, §13.2.8(2), p. 1101.

FAM §157.214. MOTION TO REVOKE COMMUNITY SUPERVISION

A prosecuting attorney, the Title IV-D agency, a domestic relations office, or a party affected by the order may file a verified motion alleging specifically that certain conduct of the respondent constitutes a violation of the terms and conditions of community supervision.

History of Fam. Code §157.214: Acts 1995, 74th Leg., ch. 20, §1, eff. Apr. 20, 1995. Amended by Acts 2001, 77th Leg., ch. 311, §3, eff. Sept. 1, 2001. Source: Former Fam. Code §§14.40(e)(4), 14.50(d)(4).

See also *O'Connor's Texas Family Law Handbook* (2017), "Motion to revoke," ch. 10-A, §15.1, p. 1104.

ANNOTATIONS

In re Zandi, 270 S.W.3d 76, 77 (Tex.2008). "[N]o motion [under §157.214] was filed to revoke [father's] suspension of commitment. [¶] [Mother] argues that the contempt order's requirement that [father] appear at a status hearing every six months was sufficient to put [father] on notice that he would be required to show compliance with the conditions of suspension at the status hearing. We disagree. [Mother] also argues that her complaints at the hearing were clear. But [father] was entitled to notice in advance of the hearing.... *At 78:* The purpose of notice is to apprise the respondent of the allegations he faces and provide him time to prepare to respond. Because that notice was lacking in this case, the court's order revoking suspension of commitment must be set aside."

In re Fountain, 433 S.W.3d 1, 7 (Tex.App.—Houston [1st Dist.] 2012, orig. proceeding). Parent "wrongly assumes that [possessory conservator's] motion to revoke [suspension of commitment] and the trial court's revocation order must satisfy all of the procedural safeguards for an enforcement motion under subch. D of ch. 157, as if a separate allegation, finding, and sentence for contempt of court were at issue. In other cases, these [subch. D] safeguards ... have been applied ... when ... a trial court made additional findings of contempt and imposed a different punishment [during a proceeding to revoke the suspension of commitment]. In such circumstances, with new allegations of contempt and enhanced sanctions, the motion to revoke ... functions as a separate enforcement motion for purposes of ch. 157. *At 8:* [But parent] provides no argument or authority for us to apply subch. D of ch. 157 and its detailed procedures applicable to an original enforcement hearing to the separate circumstance of a proceeding merely to determine whether to revoke the suspension of a valid prior order of commitment for contempt, and we decline to do so. ... A heightened procedural standard is justified for contempt proceedings in the first instance, especially when incarceration of the respondent is a potential result. But once there has been a judgment of contempt, there is no requirement that the same heightened measure of process be provided in order to adjudicate an allegation that the conditions of a suspended judgment have been violated. ... In the case of an order revoking community supervision, proof of any one violation of the conditions of suspension is sufficient to support the revocation order." *See also* ***In re B.C.C.***, 187 S.W.3d 721, 724 (Tex.App.—Tyler 2006, no pet.) (in appeal from order revoking community supervision, only question is whether trial court abused its discretion in revoking D's community supervision).

Ex parte Spikes, 909 S.W.2d 245, 247 (Tex.App.—Amarillo 1995, orig. proceeding). "It is our studied decision that the discretion the trial judge has to revoke the suspension of commitment for contempt and probation

ordered terminates when the period of probation has expired without a motion to revoke having been filed during the period of probation, and that the contemnor cannot afterwards be committed under the prior order of contempt. Our holding of the termination of the judge's discretion under such circumstances is the same holding applicable to revocation of probation in criminal cases under similar circumstances."

Ex parte Whitehead, 908 S.W.2d 68, 70 (Tex. App.—Houston [1st Dist.] 1995, orig. proceeding). "We hold that, as a general rule, failing to comply with conditions of probation does not constitute a new act of contempt. Rather, it exposes the offender to commitment for the acts adjudicated at the earlier hearing on the motion for contempt."

FAM §157.215. ARREST FOR ALLEGED VIOLATION OF COMMUNITY SUPERVISION

(a) If the motion to revoke community supervision alleges a prima facie case that the respondent has violated a term or condition of community supervision, the court may order the respondent's arrest by warrant.

(b) The respondent shall be brought promptly before the court ordering the arrest.

History of Fam. Code §157.215: Acts 1995, 74th Leg., ch. 20, §1, eff. Apr. 20, 1995. Source: Former Fam. Code §§14.40(e)(5), 14.50(d)(5).

See also ***O'Connor's Texas Family Law Handbook*** (2017), "Arrest," ch. 10-A, §15.2, p. 1105.

FAM §157.216. HEARING ON MOTION TO REVOKE COMMUNITY SUPERVISION

(a) The court shall hold a hearing without a jury not later than the third working day after the date the respondent is arrested under Section 157.215. If the court is unavailable for a hearing on that date, the hearing shall be held not later than the third working day after the date the court becomes available.

(b) The hearing under this section may not be held later than the seventh working day after the date the respondent is arrested.

(c) After the hearing, the court may continue, modify, or revoke the community supervision.

History of Fam. Code §157.216: Acts 1995, 74th Leg., ch. 20, §1, eff. Apr. 20, 1995. Amended by Acts 2007, 80th Leg., ch. 972, §23, eff. Sept. 1, 2007. Source: Former Fam. Code §§14.40(e)(6), 14.50(d)(6).

See also ***O'Connor's Texas Family Law Handbook*** (2017), "Hearing," ch. 10-A, §15.3, p. 1105; "Order modifying community supervision," ch. 10-A, §15.5, p. 1105.

FAM §157.217. DISCHARGE FROM COMMUNITY SUPERVISION

(a) When a community supervision period has been satisfactorily completed, the court on its own motion shall discharge the respondent from community supervision.

(b) The court may discharge the respondent from community supervision on the motion of the respondent if the court finds that the respondent:

(1) has satisfactorily completed one year of community supervision; and

(2) has fully complied with the community supervision order.

History of Fam. Code §157.217: Acts 1995, 74th Leg., ch. 20, §1, eff. Apr. 20, 1995. Source: Former Fam. Code §§14.40(e)(7), 14.50(d)(7).

See also ***O'Connor's Texas Family Law Handbook*** (2017), "Order modifying community supervision," ch. 10-A, §15.5, p. 1105.

Sections 157.218-157.260 reserved for expansion

SUBCHAPTER F. JUDGMENT & INTEREST

FAM §157.261. UNPAID CHILD SUPPORT AS JUDGMENT

(a) A child support payment not timely made constitutes a final judgment for the amount due and owing, including interest as provided in this chapter.

(b) For the purposes of this subchapter, interest begins to accrue on the date the judge signs the order for the judgment unless the order contains a statement that the order is rendered on another specific date.

History of Fam. Code §157.261: Acts 1995, 74th Leg., ch. 20, §1, eff. Apr. 20, 1995. Amended by Acts 1997, 75th Leg., ch. 702, §5, eff. Sept. 1, 1997. Source: Former Fam. Code §14.41(a).

See also ***O'Connor's Texas Family Law Handbook*** (2017), "Interest on unconfirmed support," ch. 10-C, §3.1.3, p. 1114; "Interest on confirmed support," ch. 10-C, §3.1.4, p. 1118.

ANNOTATIONS

Williams v. Patton, 821 S.W.2d 141, 141 (Tex. 1991). "[T]he question [is] whether [Fam. Code] §14.41(a) [now §157.261] prohibits parents from settling claims for child support arrearages before the unpaid amount has been reduced to a final judgment. We hold that §14.41(a) does prohibit such settlements. *At 144:* The purpose of §14.41(a) is to provide a custodial parent with remedies for nonpayment of child support in addition to contempt. Once the custodial parent obtains a money judgment for the amount of arrearages, this judgment may be enforced by any means normally available to a judgment creditor. Requiring that the trial court reduce arrearages to a final judgment before the parties can enter into a settlement and release

agreement shields the custodial parent from the financial pressures which frequently result when child support goes unpaid. *At 146:* Requiring that the trial court reduce arrearages to a final judgment before such agreements can be entered into protects the interests of the child by encouraging the payment of child support and protects the interests of the custodial parent by equalizing the bargaining positions of the parties."

Herzfeld v. Herzfeld, 285 S.W.3d 122, 129 (Tex. App.—Dallas 2009, no pet.). Father "concedes there were arrearages beginning ... when he failed to make the payments ordered by the decree and the obligation did not cease until [a later date]. ... Although the trial judge noted the divorce decree was silent regarding interest, [mother] argues the decree was entered after a trial and [it] was not her agreement that no interest would accrue on past due child support. [¶] [Under §157.261,] [t]he trial court does not have the discretion to increase or reduce the arrearage or the interest. ... '[A]ccrued interest is clearly part of the child support obligation which is to be reduced to a money judgment.' [¶] We conclude the trial judge erred by failing to award interest in her order confirming the child support arrearage."

In re Dickinson, 829 S.W.2d 919, 921 (Tex.App.—Amarillo 1992, no writ). "The remedies for delinquent child support [that] may be pursued by an obligee of either pursuing contempt under [Fam. Code] §14.40 [now §157.001] or obtaining a judgment for arrearage under [Fam. Code] §14.41 [now §157.261] are separate and distinct. However, pursuance of the remedy of a judgment for arrearage does not exclude enforcement of the same obligation by contempt."

FAM §157.262. REPEALED

Repealed by Acts 2011, 82nd Leg., ch. 508, §24, eff. Sept. 1, 2011.

FAM §157.263. CONFIRMATION OF ARREARAGES

(a) If a motion for enforcement of child support requests a money judgment for arrearages, the court shall confirm the amount of arrearages and render one cumulative money judgment.

(b) A cumulative money judgment includes:

(1) unpaid child support not previously confirmed;

(2) the balance owed on previously confirmed arrearages or lump sum or retroactive support judgments;

(3) interest on the arrearages; and

(4) a statement that it is a cumulative judgment.

(b-1) In rendering a money judgment under this section, the court may not reduce or modify the amount of child support arrearages but, in confirming the amount of arrearages, may allow a counterclaim or offset as provided by this title.

(c) If the amount of arrearages confirmed by the court reflects a credit to the obligor for support arrearages collected from a federal tax refund under 42 U.S.C. Section 664, and, subsequently, the amount of that credit is reduced because the refund was adjusted because of an injured spouse claim by a jointly filing spouse, the tax return was amended, the return was audited by the Internal Revenue Service, or for another reason permitted by law, the court shall render a new cumulative judgment to include as arrearages an amount equal to the amount by which the credit was reduced.

History of Fam. Code §157.263: Acts 1995, 74th Leg., ch. 20, §1, eff. Apr. 20, 1995. Amended by Acts 2003, 78th Leg., ch. 610, §4, eff. Sept. 1, 2003; Acts 2007, 80th Leg., ch. 972, §24, eff. Sept. 1, 2007; Acts 2011, 82nd Leg., ch. 508, §5, eff. Sept. 1, 2011. Source: Former Fam. Code §14.41(a), (e).

See also *O'Connor's Texas Family Law Handbook* (2017), "Motion to Reduce Child-Support Arrearages to Judgment," ch. 10-C, p. 1113.

ANNOTATIONS

Ochsner v. Ochsner, ___ S.W.3d ___ (Tex.2016) (No. 14-0638; 6-24-16). "[A]n arrearage in the child-support context occurs when an obligor has not satisfied his obligation. According to §157.263, however, the trial court is not merely to 'confirm the arrearages'; rather it must 'confirm *the amount* of arrearages.' An 'amount,' in the realm of arrearage, is 'a principal sum and the interest on it.' 'Amount' therefore denotes a quantity that can be broken into fractions and taken in the aggregate. The 'amount of arrearages' refers to the quantity, taken in the aggregate, of that fraction of the child-support obligation that remains unmet. Finally, the verb 'to confirm' means 'to give *new* assurance of the truth or validity' of some state of affairs. Thus a trial court instructed to 'confirm the amount of arrearages' is to determine the *quantity* of the child-support obligation that the obligor has failed to meet. The court that issued the support order in the first instance determined the total dollar value of the support obligation. The text of the enforcement statute indicates that the trial court must calculate which aggregated sub-fraction of this value stands unpaid. [¶] [I]n a child-support enforcement action, a trial court may consider the various payments made by the obligor, regardless of what precise manner an earlier court—presiding over

a distinct proceeding—specified in the child-support order. ... The statute requires the trial court to confirm the amount of arrearages, based on the amount the child-support order required the obligor to pay, and in light of various payments the court finds that the obligor made. There is no statutory requirement that child-support payments travel via registry, though the court that issued the support order thought it appropriate. The trial court in an enforcement action, therefore, may, in the appropriate case, consider the obligor's satisfaction of the obligee's tuition obligation in confirming the amount of arrearages."

In re H.G-J., 503 S.W.3d 679, 684-85 (Tex.App.—Houston [14th Dist.] 2016, no pet.). Family Code §157.263 imposes a mandatory duty "only when the proceedings involve a motion for enforcement. The proceedings here began when Father filed a motion to modify the parent-child relationship. Neither Father's pleadings nor Mother's pleadings sought enforcement. As set forth above, the OAG [Office of the Attorney General] filed only an answer, in which it generally denied the allegations in Father's pleadings and stated that '[t]he OAG urges that the Court confirm any outstanding arrears, render a judgment and appropriate payout.' [¶] The OAG's pleading does not contain the required allegations to constitute a motion for enforcement. To begin with, it does not actually allege that Father failed to pay any child support obligation; it merely 'urges that the Court confirm any outstanding arrears.' In other words, instead of alleging noncompliance, ... the OAG simply requested the court determine whether there was any noncompliance. Moreover, the OAG's answer does not 'include the amount owed as provided in the order, the amount paid, and the amount of arrearages' as required by [Fam. Code] §157.002(b)(1). Although the OAG introduced a Financial Activity Report into evidence during the hearing, it did not attach this document to its pleading as permitted under §157.002(b)(3). [¶] The OAG's answer did not provide Father with proper notice of any allegations of noncompliance; accordingly, the trial court was not required to enter an arrearage judgment under ... §157.263(a)."

In re A.C.B., 302 S.W.3d 560, 566-67 (Tex.App.—Amarillo 2009, no pet.). "Awarding interest on child support arrearages is mandatory and the trial court has no discretion to not award the full amount of interest due. Determining the date and the amount of the unpaid obligation is, therefore, necessary to calculate both the arrearage and the interest. [¶] Thus, because the modification order [in this case] did not state a due date for [father to pay for child's] tuition and fees or ... extracurricular activities, interest did not begin to accrue on these obligations until the date that the trial court signed the reformed judgment.... Therefore, ... the trial court abused its discretion in awarding prejudgment interest for the unpaid tuition and fees and extracurricular activities." *See also* ***Chenault v. Banks***, 296 S.W.3d 186, 193 (Tex.App.—Houston [14th Dist.] 2009, no pet.) (awarding interest on child-support arrearages is mandatory; trial court has no discretion to not award full amount of interest due).

Chenault v. Banks, 296 S.W.3d 186, 189-90 (Tex. App.—Houston [14th Dist.] 2009, no pet.). "In calculating child support arrearages, the trial court's discretion is very limited. ... The trial court 'acts as a mere scrivener in mechanically tallying up the amount of arrearage.' Although the trial court can award certain offsets and credits, the trial court has no discretion to forgive or decrease a past child support obligation. Thus, in a proceeding to confirm child support arrearages, the trial court's child support calculations must be based on the payment evidence presented, not the trial court's assessment of what is fair or reasonable. As with child support arrearages, the trial court also has no discretion to modify, forgive, or make equitable adjustments in awarding interest on child support arrearages." *See also* ***In re M.C.R.***, 55 S.W.3d 104, 109-10 (Tex. App.—San Antonio 2001, no pet.) (court had no discretion to reduce arrearage amount by awarding portion of accrued interest to obligor).

George v. Jeppeson, 238 S.W.3d 463, 473 (Tex. App.—Houston [1st Dist.] 2007, no pet.). "The requirement imposed on the trial court by §157.263(a) to 'confirm the amount of arrearages,' compels, at a minimum, that the movant substantiate 'the amount of arrearages.' No [§157.263(a)] duty arises, therefore, until the movant has met its burden to provide adequate proof to substantiate the arrearages alleged."

In re G.L.S., 185 S.W.3d 56, 59 (Tex.App.—San Antonio 2005, no pet.). "This court has never addressed whether an obligor is entitled to credit a lump sum social security disability payment received by his children against unconfirmed arrearages owed to the obligee. *At 61:* By adopting [Fam. Code] §154.132, [Application of Guidelines to Children of Certain Disabled Obligors,] the Legislature has recognized the equity in

granting a credit for social security disability benefits when establishing or modifying child support. However, the Legislature may have decided to only grant the credit prospectively because of the delays in the Administration's processing of disability claims. [T]he Administration may delay the processing for a year or more. The policy issues implicated in applying a lump-sum disability payment to unpaid, unconfirmed child support are more complicated than a credit for future benefits to be paid. Given the competing policies and equities, ... whether an obligor is entitled to an offset against past unconfirmed child support arrearages is an issue for the Legislature to decide. Until further action is taken by the Legislature, [Fam. Code] §157.262(a), (f) [now §157.263(b-1)] preclude[s] this court from finding that the trial court abused its discretion in refusing [to] credit the disability payment received by [obligor's child] against the unconfirmed child support arrearages." *See also* ***Attorney Gen. v. Stevens***, 84 S.W.3d 720, 723 (Tex.App.—Houston [1st Dist.] 2002, no pet.) (nothing in Family Code provides for disability-payment credit given by trial court, and §157.262(b) indicates counterclaims and offsets must be found exclusively in code).

In re Dryden, 52 S.W.3d 257, 262-63 (Tex.App.—Corpus Christi 2001, orig. proceeding). "We conclude that the 'error' complained of here—the granting of a judgment for past-due child support which may be executed upon at any time as long as the judgment is unsatisfied—is not erroneous at all. Even though [judge] stated in her ... letter that she did not intend for [obligee] to be able to execute on the child-support-arrearage judgment so long as [obligor] complied with the repayment orders, we conclude that [judge] had no authority to preclude [obligee] from attempting to collect the judgment. [Section 157.263] imposes an affirmative, mandatory duty on the trial court to reduce a child support arrearage to a money judgment upon request. [¶] [Because it] was mandatory that [judge] confirm and render the cumulative child-support-arrearage judgment, [judge] had no authority to preclude [obligee] from attempting to collect on the judgment."

FAM §157.264. ENFORCEMENT OF JUDGMENT

(a) A money judgment rendered as provided in this subchapter or a judgment for retroactive child support rendered under Chapter 154 may be enforced by any means available for the enforcement of a judgment for debts or the collection of child support.

(b) The court shall render an order requiring that the obligor make periodic payments on the judgment, including by income withholding under Chapter 158 if the obligor is subject to income withholding.

(c) An order rendered under Subsection (b) does not preclude or limit the use of any other means for enforcement of the judgment.

History of Fam. Code §157.264: Acts 1995, 74th Leg., ch. 20, §1, eff. Apr. 20, 1995. Amended by Acts 2001, 77th Leg., ch. 1023, §16, eff. Sept. 1, 2001; Acts 2007, 80th Leg., ch. 972, §25, eff. Sept. 1, 2007; Acts 2009, 81st Leg., ch. 767, §17, eff. June 19, 2009; Acts 2015, 84th Leg., ch. 859, §6, eff. Sept. 1, 2015. Source: Former Fam. Code §14.41(a).

FAM §157.265. ACCRUAL OF INTEREST ON CHILD SUPPORT

(a) Interest accrues on the portion of delinquent child support that is greater than the amount of the monthly periodic support obligation at the rate of six percent simple interest per year from the date the support is delinquent until the date the support is paid or the arrearages are confirmed and reduced to money judgment.

(b) Interest accrues on child support arrearages that have been confirmed and reduced to money judgment as provided in this subchapter at the rate of six percent simple interest per year from the date the order is rendered until the date the judgment is paid.

(c) Interest accrues on a money judgment for retroactive or lump-sum child support at the annual rate of six percent simple interest from the date the order is rendered until the judgment is paid.

(d) Subsection (a) applies to a child support payment that becomes due on or after January 1, 2002.

(e) Child support arrearages in existence on January 1, 2002, that were not confirmed and reduced to a money judgment on or before that date accrue interest as follows:

(1) before January 1, 2002, the arrearages are subject to the interest rate that applied to the arrearages before that date; and

(2) on and after January 1, 2002, the cumulative total of arrearages and interest accumulated on those arrearages described by Subdivision (1) is subject to Subsection (a).

(f) Subsections (b) and (c) apply to a money judgment for child support rendered on or after January 1, 2002. A money judgment for child support rendered be-

fore that date is governed by the law in effect on the date the judgment was rendered, and the former law is continued in effect for that purpose.

History of Fam. Code §157.265: Acts 1995, 74th Leg., ch. 20, §1, eff. Apr. 20, 1995. Amended by Acts 1995, 74th Leg., ch. 751, §53, eff. Sept. 1, 1995; Acts 1999, 76th Leg., ch. 943, §1, eff. Jan. 1, 2000; Acts 2001, 77th Leg., ch. 1491, §1, eff. Jan. 1, 2002; Acts 2005, 79th Leg., ch. 185, §1, eff. Sept. 1, 2005. Source: Former Fam. Code §14.34(a).

See also ***O'Connor's Texas Family Law Handbook*** (2017), "Unconfirmed support due between 9-1-91 and 12-31-99," ch. 10-C, §3.1.3(1)(a)[2], p. 1115; "Interest on confirmed support," ch. 10-C, §3.1.4, p. 1118.

ANNOTATIONS

In re M.C.C., 187 S.W.3d 383, 384 (Tex.2006). "We hold the language of the statute, the effective date language, and the statutory scheme, considered together, require prospective application of 2001 [Fam.] Code §157.265. *At 385:* The 2001 amendment to ... §157.265 does not indicate an intention by the Legislature to make the statute retroactive. ... We hold that the effective date language, when read in its entirety, does not require retroactive application of the interest rate in ... §157.265."

FAM §157.266. DATE OF DELINQUENCY

(a) A child support payment is delinquent for the purpose of accrual of interest if the payment is not received before the 31st day after the payment date stated in the order by:

(1) the local registry, Title IV-D registry, or state disbursement unit; or

(2) the obligee or entity specified in the order, if payments are not made through a registry.

(b) If a payment date is not stated in the order, a child support payment is delinquent if payment is not received by the registry or the obligee or entity specified in the order on the date that an amount equal to the support payable for one month becomes past due.

History of Fam. Code §157.266: Acts 1995, 74th Leg., ch. 20, §1, eff. Apr. 20, 1995. Amended by Acts 1999, 76th Leg., ch. 943, §2, eff. Jan. 1, 2000. Source: Former Fam. Code §14.34(b).

See also ***O'Connor's Texas Family Law Handbook*** (2017), "Unconfirmed support due between 9-1-91 and 12-31-99," ch. 10-C, §3.1.3(1)(a)[2], p. 1115.

FAM §157.267. INTEREST ENFORCED AS CHILD SUPPORT

Accrued interest is part of the child support obligation and may be enforced by any means provided for the collection of child support.

History of Fam. Code §157.267: Acts 1995, 74th Leg., ch. 20, §1, eff. Apr. 20, 1995. Source: Former Fam. Code §14.34(c).

See also ***O'Connor's Texas Family Law Handbook*** (2017), "Child-support obligation," ch. 10-A, §4.2.1(5)(a), p. 1076.

FAM §157.268. APPLICATION OF CHILD SUPPORT PAYMENT

Child support collected shall be applied in the following order of priority:

(1) current child support;

(2) non-delinquent child support owed;

(3) the principal amount of child support that has not been confirmed and reduced to money judgment;

(4) the principal amount of child support that has been confirmed and reduced to money judgment;

(5) interest on the principal amounts specified in Subdivisions (3) and (4); and

(6) the amount of any ordered attorney's fees or costs, or Title IV-D service fees authorized under Section 231.103 for which the obligor is responsible.

History of Fam. Code §157.268: Acts 1995, 74th Leg., ch. 20, §1, eff. Apr. 20, 1995. Amended by Acts 2001, 77th Leg., ch. 1023, §17, eff. Sept. 1, 2001; Acts 2007, 80th Leg., ch. 972, §20, eff. Sept. 1, 2007; Acts 2009, 81st Leg., ch. 767, §18, eff. Jan. 1, 2010. Source: Former Fam. Code §14.34(c).

See also ***O'Connor's Texas Family Law Handbook*** (2017), "Credit payments," ch. 10-C, §3.2 – Step 2, p. 1120; "How to calculate arrearages – payments collected on or after 1-1-10," ch. 10-C, §3.3, p. 1125.

FAM §157.269. RETENTION OF JURISDICTION[1]

A court that renders an order providing for the payment of child support retains continuing jurisdiction to enforce the order, including by adjusting the amount of the periodic payments to be made by the obligor or the amount to be withheld from the obligor's disposable earnings, until all current support and medical support and child support arrearages, including interest and any applicable fees and costs, have been paid.

1. **Editor's note:** In 2015, the Legislature amended §157.269 to require dental support for a child subject to a child-support order, but the amendments are not effective until Sept. 1, 2018. For the text of the prospective amendments, see Acts 2015, 84th Leg., ch. 1150, §30, eff. Sept. 1, 2018.

History of Fam. Code §157.269: Acts 1995, 74th Leg., ch. 751, §54, eff. Sept. 1, 1995. Amended by Acts 1999, 76th Leg., ch. 556, §19, eff. Sept. 1, 1999; Acts 2007, 80th Leg., ch. 972, §26, eff. Sept. 1, 2007.

ANNOTATIONS

In re Munks, 263 S.W.3d 270, 273 (Tex.App.—Houston [1st Dist.] 2007, orig. proceeding). Mother "contends that the trial court retained jurisdiction to issue a contempt order [after child turned 18], pursuant to [Fam. Code] §§101.003 and 157.269. Section 101.003 defines a 'child,' in the context of support.... Section 157.269 defines the jurisdiction of a court in terms of child support arrearages.... [Mother] contends that, pursuant to §157.269, the trial court retained jurisdiction to render a contempt order against [father] because the court maintains jurisdiction until

[father] has paid all amounts owed, without regard to whether [child] has become an adult, pursuant to §101.003(b). *At 274:* Although [father's] payments on the arrearage have extended beyond [child's] 18th birthday, the trial court's jurisdiction to enforce the obligation by contempt is not extended."

In re Dryden, 52 S.W.3d 257, 265 (Tex.App.—Corpus Christi 2001, orig. proceeding). This court holds "that §157.269 … does not empower a trial court to modify a judgment for child support arrearage after the court's plenary power has expired."

Sections 157.270-157.310 reserved for expansion

SUBCHAPTER G. CHILD SUPPORT LIEN

FAM §157.311. DEFINITIONS

In this subchapter:

(1) "Account" means:

(A) any type of a demand deposit account, checking or negotiable withdrawal order account, savings account, time deposit account, mutual fund account, certificate of deposit, or any other instrument of deposit in which an individual has a beneficial ownership either in its entirety or on a shared or multiple party basis, including any accrued interest and dividends; and

(B) an insurance policy, including a life insurance policy or annuity contract, in which an individual has a beneficial ownership or against which an individual may file a claim or counterclaim.

(2) "Claimant" means:

(A) the obligee or a private attorney representing the obligee;

(B) the Title IV-D agency providing child support services;

(C) a domestic relations office or local registry; or

(D) an attorney appointed as a friend of the court.

(3) "Court having continuing jurisdiction" is the court of continuing, exclusive jurisdiction in this state or a tribunal of another state having jurisdiction under the Uniform Interstate Family Support Act or a substantially similar act.

(4) "Financial institution" has the meaning assigned by 42 U.S.C. Section 669a(d)(1) and includes a depository institution, depository institution holding company as defined by 12 U.S.C. Section 1813(w), credit union, benefit association, insurance company, mutual fund, and any similar entity authorized to do business in this state.

(5) "Lien" means a child support lien issued in this or another state.

History of Fam. Code §157.311: Acts 1995, 74th Leg., ch. 20, §1, eff. Apr. 20, 1995. Amended by Acts 1997, 75th Leg., ch. 420, §1 (eff. Sept. 1, 1997), ch. 911, §19 (eff. Sept. 1, 1997); Acts 2001, 77th Leg., ch. 1023, §18, eff. Sept. 1, 2001; Acts 2003, 78th Leg., ch. 610, §5, eff. Sept. 1, 2003; Acts 2011, 82nd Leg., ch. 508, §6, eff. Sept. 1, 2011. Source: Former Fam. Code §14.971(a), (b).

FAM §157.312. GENERAL PROVISIONS

(a) A claimant may enforce child support by a lien as provided in this subchapter.

(b) The remedies provided by this subchapter do not affect the availability of other remedies provided by law.

(c) The lien is in addition to any other lien provided by law.

(d) A child support lien arises by operation of law against real and personal property of an obligor for all amounts of child support due and owing, including any accrued interest, regardless of whether the amounts have been adjudicated or otherwise determined, subject to the requirements of this subchapter for perfection of the lien.

(e) A child support lien arising in another state may be enforced in the same manner and to the same extent as a lien arising in this state.

(f) A foreclosure action under this subchapter is not required as a prerequisite to levy and execution on a judicial or administrative determination of arrearages as provided by Section 157.327.

(g) A child support lien under this subchapter may not be directed to an employer to attach to the disposable earnings of an obligor paid by the employer.

History of Fam. Code §157.312: Acts 1995, 74th Leg., ch. 20, §1, eff. Apr. 20, 1995. Amended by Acts 1997, 75th Leg., ch. 420, §2 (eff. Sept. 1, 1997), ch. 911, §20 (eff. Sept. 1, 1997); Acts 2001, 77th Leg., ch. 1023, §19, eff. Sept. 1, 2001; Acts 2003, 78th Leg., ch. 610, §6, eff. Sept. 1, 2003. Source: Former Fam. Code §§14.971(c), (d), 14.972(d).

ANNOTATIONS

In re C.A.T., 316 S.W.3d 202, 206 (Tex.App.—Dallas 2010, no pet.). "[T]he [AG] contends the trial court misconstrued [Fam. Code] §157.312(g) as prohibiting perfection of a child-support lien on a self-employed obligor's bank account. *At 208-09:* [W]hen a child-support lien is directed to a self-employed obligor's personal bank account, the lien is not directed to an 'employer' for purposes of attachment. Nor does the lien attach to the disposable earnings of the obligor paid or owed by an employer. Rather, the lien is directed to the obligor's financial institution 'possessing or controlling assets

or funds owned by, or owed to' the obligor as permitted under [Fam. Code] §157.327(a). The lien attaches to the disposable earnings allocated by the obligor directly from his own business and subject to his control. Disposable earnings under the control of an obligor have never been protected from child-support liens that arise as a matter of law. [¶] [S]ection 157.312(g) does not prohibit service of a child-support lien on the financial institution in this case in which [obligor] deposited all earnings and from which he paid all expenses, both personal and business."

In re R.C.T., 294 S.W.3d 238, 241 (Tex.App.—Houston [14th Dist.] 2009, pet. denied). "Is unpaid retroactive child support an amount that is 'due and owing,' thus creating a child-support lien, when the obligor is current in making court-ordered monthly payments on the retroactive support? [¶] [W]e conclude that the retroactive amount is an amount due and owing to [mother], and thus results in a child-support lien, regardless of whether [father] is current on the court-ordered payout schedule. *At 243:* The trial court ordered the [AG] to release the lien, reasoning that the retroactive support was not an arrearage or delinquency. But §157.312(d) does not require the debt to be an arrearage in order for a lien to arise. In fact, the lien arises by operation of law for all amounts due and owing, 'regardless of whether the amounts have been adjudicated or otherwise determined.' There is nothing in [§157.312(d)] requiring the debt to be an arrearage to trigger the attachment of the lien." *See also* ***Herzfeld v. Herzfeld***, 285 S.W.3d 122, 127 (Tex.App.—Dallas 2009, no pet.) (court erred by ruling child-support lien could not attach without court order that determined amount of arrearages).

FAM §157.313. CONTENTS OF CHILD SUPPORT LIEN NOTICE

(a) Except as provided by Subsection (e), a child support lien notice must contain:

(1) the name and address of the person to whom the notice is being sent;

(2) the style, docket or cause number, and identity of the tribunal of this or another state having continuing jurisdiction of the child support action and, if the case is a Title IV-D case, the case number;

(3) the full name, address, and, if known, the birth date, driver's license number, social security number, and any aliases of the obligor;

(4) the full name and, if known, social security number of the obligee;

(5) the amount of the current or prospective child support obligation, the frequency with which current or prospective child support is ordered to be paid, and the amount of child support arrearages owed by the obligor and the date of the signing of the court order, administrative order, or writ that determined the arrearages or the date and manner in which the arrearages were determined;

(6) the rate of interest specified in the court order, administrative order, or writ or, in the absence of a specified interest rate, the rate provided for by law;

(7) the name and address of the person or agency asserting the lien;

(8) the motor vehicle identification number as shown on the obligor's title if the property is a motor vehicle;

(9) a statement that the lien attaches to all nonexempt real and personal property of the obligor that is located or recorded in the state, including any property specifically identified in the notice and any property acquired after the date of filing or delivery of the notice;

(10) a statement that any ordered child support not timely paid in the future constitutes a final judgment for the amount due and owing, including interest, and accrues up to an amount that may not exceed the lien amount; and

(11) a statement that the obligor is being provided a copy of the lien notice and that the obligor may dispute the arrearage amount by filing suit under Section 157.323.

(b) A claimant may include any other information that the claimant considers necessary.

(c) Except as provided by Subsection (e), the lien notice must be verified.

(d) A claimant must file a notice for each after-acquired motor vehicle.

(e) A notice of a lien for child support under this section may be in the form authorized by federal law or regulation. The federal form of lien notice does not require verification when used by the Title IV-D agency.

(f) The requirement under Subsections (a)(3) and (4) to provide a social security number, if known, does not apply to a lien notice for a lien on real property.

History of Fam. Code §157.313: Acts 1995, 74th Leg., ch. 20, §1, eff. Apr. 20, 1995. Amended by Acts 1997, 75th Leg., ch. 420, §3 (eff. Sept. 1, 1997), ch. 911, §21 (eff. Sept. 1, 1997); Acts 2001, 77th Leg., ch. 1023, §20, eff. Sept. 1, 2001; Acts 2007, 80th Leg., ch. 972, §27, eff. Sept. 1, 2007. Source: Former Fam. Code §14.973.

See also 1 T.A.C. §55.119(a); *O'Connor's Texas Family Law Handbook* (2017), "Contents," ch. 10-E, §5.3.3, p. 1148.

FAM §157.314. FILING LIEN NOTICE OR ABSTRACT OF JUDGMENT; NOTICE TO OBLIGOR

(a) A child support lien notice or an abstract of judgment for past due child support may be filed by the claimant with the county clerk of:

(1) any county in which the obligor is believed to own nonexempt real or personal property;

(2) the county in which the obligor resides; or

(3) the county in which the court having continuing jurisdiction has venue of the suit affecting the parent-child relationship.

(b) A child support lien notice may be filed with or delivered to the following, as appropriate:

(1) the clerk of the court in which a claim, counterclaim, or suit by, or on behalf of, the obligor, including a claim or potential right to proceeds from an estate as an heir, beneficiary, or creditor, is pending, provided that a copy of the lien is mailed to the attorney of record for the obligor, if any;

(2) an attorney who represents the obligor in a claim or counterclaim that has not been filed with a court;

(3) any other individual or organization believed to be in possession of real or personal property of the obligor; or

(4) any governmental unit or agency that issues or records certificates, titles, or other indicia of property ownership.

(c) Not later than the 21st day after the date of filing or delivering the child support lien notice, the claimant shall provide a copy of the notice to the obligor by first class or certified mail, return receipt requested, addressed to the obligor at the obligor's last known address. If another person is known to have an ownership interest in the property subject to the lien, the claimant shall provide a copy of the lien notice to that person at the time notice is provided to the obligor.

(d) If a child support lien notice is delivered to a financial institution with respect to an account of the obligor, the institution shall immediately:

(1) provide the claimant with the last known address of the obligor; and

(2) notify any other person having an ownership interest in the account that the account has been frozen in an amount not to exceed the amount of the child support arrearage identified in the notice.

History of Fam. Code §157.314: Acts 1995, 74th Leg., ch. 20, §1, eff. Apr. 20, 1995. Amended by Acts 1997, 75th Leg., ch. 420, §4 (eff. Sept. 1, 1997), ch. 911, §22 (eff. Sept. 1, 1997); Acts 2001, 77th Leg., ch. 1023, §21, eff. Sept. 1, 2001. Source: Former Fam. Code §14.974.

See also *O'Connor's Texas Family Law Handbook* (2017), "Filing notice or abstract of judgment," ch. 10-E, §5.5, p. 1150.

ANNOTATIONS

Spates v. Office of the Atty. Gen., 485 S.W.3d 546, 554-56 (Tex.App.—Houston [14th Dist.] 2016, no pet.). Company 1 "argues that because [the Office of the Attorney General (OAG)] obtained its child support judgments in separate family courts[,] only those courts … had jurisdiction to grant the OAG's request for a charging order [to enforce the child-support judgments against obligor]. [Company 1] also argues that the liens are in the name of [obligor], who is not a party to the [breach-of-contract] case below, and [obligor's] status as an organizer and member of [company 1] does not entitle him to an interest in any specific property of the company. [¶] [Family Code §157.314(b)] provides that a child support lien notice may be filed with … the clerk of the court in which 'a claim, counterclaim, or suit by, or on behalf of, the obligor, including a claim or potential right to proceeds from an estate as an heir, beneficiary, or creditor, is pending….' [¶] Once [obligor's] child support arrearages were reduced to judgments in the respective family courts, they became enforceable as any other money judgment. [¶] Under [BOC §101.112(a)], '[o]n application by a judgment creditor of a member of a limited liability company … a court having jurisdiction may charge the membership interest of the judgment debtor to satisfy the judgment.' [¶] Here, [company 1] filed suit against [company 2] and obtained a settlement…. Once the OAG learned of [company 1's] lawsuit, it filed its application for a charging order…. The charging order recites that '[the OAG] has made a diligent search and has not been able to discover any assets of [obligor], subject to execution, and is entitled pursuant to statute to a charging order against [obligor's] interest in [company 1].' [¶] Only when—and if—[company 1] makes a distribution, will the distributed funds become [obligor's] nonexempt personal property. The charging order merely directs [company 1] to send any distributed funds up to the amounts owed by [obligor] directly to the OAG rather than to [obligor]. [¶] Be-

cause the Family Code authorizes the OAG to enforce and collect child-support judgments and expressly permits the OAG, as a judgment creditor, to enforce a money judgment in a court of competent jurisdiction in the same manner as any judgment creditor, we hold that the trial court had jurisdiction to enter the charging order against [obligor's] membership interest…."

FAM §157.3145. SERVICE ON FINANCIAL INSTITUTION

(a) Service of a child support lien notice on a financial institution relating to property held by the institution in the name of, or in behalf of, an obligor is governed by Section 59.008, Finance Code, if the institution is subject to that law, or may be delivered to the registered agent, the institution's main business office in this state, or another address provided by the institution under Section 231.307.

(b) A financial institution doing business in this state shall comply with the notice of lien and levy under this section regardless of whether the institution's corporate headquarters is located in this state.

History of Fam. Code §157.3145: Acts 2001, 77th Leg., ch. 1023, §22, eff. Sept. 1, 2001. Amended by Acts 2003, 78th Leg., ch. 610, §7, eff. Sept. 1, 2003.

See also *O'Connor's Texas Family Law Handbook* (2017), "Financial institution," ch. 10-E, §5.5.4, p. 1151.

FAM §157.315. RECORDING & INDEXING LIEN

(a) On receipt of a child support lien notice, the county clerk shall immediately record the notice in the county judgment records as provided in Chapter 52, Property Code.

(b) The county clerk may not charge the Title IV-D agency, a domestic relations office, a friend of the court, or any other party a fee for recording the notice of a lien. To qualify for this exemption, the lien notice must be styled "Notice of Child Support Lien" or be in the form authorized by federal law or regulation.

(c) The county clerk may not charge the Title IV-D agency, a domestic relations office, or a friend of the court a fee for recording the release of a child support lien. The lien release must be styled "Release of Child Support Lien."

History of Fam. Code §157.315: Acts 1995, 74th Leg., ch. 20, §1, eff. Apr. 20, 1995. Amended by Acts 1999, 76th Leg., ch. 595, §1 (eff. Sept. 1, 1999), ch. 769, §1 (eff. Sept. 1, 1999); Acts 2001, 77th Leg., ch. 1023, §23, eff. Sept. 1, 2001. Source: Former Fam. Code §14.975.

FAM §157.316. PERFECTION OF CHILD SUPPORT LIEN

(a) Except as provided by Subsection (b), a child support lien is perfected when an abstract of judgment for past due child support or a child support lien notice is filed or delivered as provided by Section 157.314.

(b) If a lien established under this subchapter attaches to a motor vehicle, the lien must be perfected in the manner provided by Chapter 501, Transportation Code, and the court or Title IV-D agency that rendered the order of child support shall include in the order a requirement that the obligor surrender to the court or Title IV-D agency evidence of the legal ownership of the motor vehicle against which the lien may attach. A lien against a motor vehicle under this subchapter is not perfected until the obligor's title to the vehicle has been surrendered to the court or Title IV-D agency and the Texas Department of Motor Vehicles has issued a subsequent title that discloses on its face the fact that the vehicle is subject to a child support lien under this subchapter.

History of Fam. Code §157.316: Acts 1995, 74th Leg., ch. 20, §1, eff. Apr. 20, 1995. Amended by Acts 1997, 75th Leg., ch. 420, §5 (eff. Sept. 1, 1997), ch. 911, §23 (eff. Sept. 1, 1997); Acts 2001, 77th Leg., ch. 1023, §23, eff. Sept. 1, 2001; Acts 2009, 81st Leg., ch. 933, §3C.01, eff. Sept. 1, 2009. Source: Former Fam. Code §14.972(a).

See also 43 T.A.C. §217.102; *O'Connor's Texas Family Law Handbook* (2017), "Perfecting Lien," ch. 10-E, §5, p. 1146.

Ⓐ FAM §157.317. PROPERTY TO WHICH LIEN ATTACHES

The amended text in §157.317 is effective for child-support lien notices issued on or after Sept. 1, 2017. Notices issued before Sept. 1, 2017, are governed by the former law in effect at that time.

(a) A child support lien attaches to all real and personal property not exempt under the Texas Constitution or other law, including:

(1) an account in a financial institution;

(2) a retirement plan, including an individual retirement account;

(3) the proceeds of an insurance policy, including the proceeds from a life insurance policy or annuity contract and the proceeds from the sale or assignment of life insurance or annuity benefits, a claim for compensation, or a settlement or award for the claim for compensation, due to or owned by the obligor; [and]

(4) property seized and subject to forfeiture under Chapter 59, Code of Criminal Procedure; and

(5) the proceeds derived from the sale of oil or gas production from an oil or gas well located in this state.

(a-1) A lien attaches to all property owned or acquired on or after the date the lien notice or abstract of judgment is filed with the county clerk of the county in

which the property is located, with the court clerk as to property or claims in litigation, or, as to property of the obligor in the possession or control of a third party, from the date the lien notice is delivered to that party.

(b) A lien attaches to all nonhomestead real property of the obligor but does not attach to a homestead exempt under the Texas Constitution or the Property Code.

History of Fam. Code §157.317: Acts 1995, 74th Leg., ch. 20, §1, eff. Apr. 20, 1995. Amended by Acts 1997, 75th Leg., ch. 420, §6 (eff. Sept. 1, 1997), ch. 911, §24 (eff. Sept. 1, 1997); Acts 1999, 76th Leg., ch. 344, §7.007 (eff. Sept. 1, 1999), ch. 556, §20 (eff. Sept. 1, 1999); Acts 2001, 77th Leg., ch. 1023, §25, eff. Sept. 1, 2001; Acts 2003, 78th Leg., ch. 610, §8, eff. Sept. 1, 2003; Acts 2007, 80th Leg., ch. 972, §28, eff. Sept. 1, 2007; Acts 2011, 82nd Leg., ch. 508, §7, eff. Sept. 1, 2011; S.B. 1965, §3, 85th Leg., eff. Sept. 1, 2017. Source: Former Fam. Code §14.972(b), (c).

See also *O'Connor's Texas Family Law Handbook* (2017), "Property Subject to Lien," ch. 10-E, §4, p. 1144.

FAM §157.3171. RELEASE OF LIEN ON HOMESTEAD PROPERTY

(a) An obligor who believes that a child support lien has attached to real property of the obligor that is the obligor's homestead, as defined by Section 41.002, Property Code, may file an affidavit to release the lien against the homestead in the same manner that a judgment debtor may file an affidavit under Section 52.0012, Property Code, to release a judgment lien against a homestead.

(b) Except as provided by Subsection (c), the obligor must comply with all requirements imposed by Section 52.0012, Property Code. For purposes of complying with that section, the obligor is considered to be a judgment debtor under that section and the claimant under the child support lien is considered to be a judgment creditor under that section.

(c) For purposes of Section 52.0012(d)(2), Property Code, and the associated text in the affidavit required by Section 52.0012(f), Property Code, the obligor is required only to send the letter and affidavit described in those provisions to the claimant under the child support lien at the claimant's last known address.

(d) The claimant under the child support lien may dispute the obligor's affidavit by filing a contradicting affidavit in the manner provided by Section 52.0012(e), Property Code.

(e) Subject to Subsection (f), an affidavit filed by an obligor under this section has the same effect with respect to a child support lien as an affidavit filed under Section 52.0012, Property Code, has with respect to a judgment lien.

(f) If the claimant files a contradicting affidavit as described by Subsection (d), the issue of whether the real property is subject to the lien must be resolved in an action brought for that purpose in the district court of the county in which the real property is located and the lien was filed.

History of Fam. Code §157.3171: Acts 2009, 81st Leg., ch. 164, §1, eff. May 26, 2009.

See also *O'Connor's Texas Family Law Handbook* (2017), "Lien is on homestead," ch. 10-E, §7.2.3, p. 1152.

FAM §157.318. DURATION & EFFECT OF CHILD SUPPORT LIEN

(a) Subject to Subsection (d), a lien is effective until all current support and child support arrearages, including interest, any costs and reasonable attorney's fees, and any Title IV-D service fees authorized under Section 231.103 for which the obligor is responsible, have been paid or the lien is otherwise released as provided by this subchapter.

(b) The lien secures payment of all child support arrearages owed by the obligor under the underlying child support order, including arrearages that accrue after the lien notice was filed or delivered as provided by Section 157.314.

(c) The filing of a lien notice or abstract of judgment with the county clerk is a record of the notice and has the same effect as any other lien notice with respect to real property records.

(d) A lien is effective with respect to real property until the 10th anniversary of the date on which the lien notice was filed with the county clerk. A lien subject to the limitation prescribed by this subsection may be renewed for subsequent 10-year periods by filing a renewed lien notice in the same manner as the original lien notice. For purposes of establishing priority, a renewed lien notice filed before the applicable 10th anniversary relates back to the date the original lien notice was filed. A renewed lien notice filed on or after the applicable 10th anniversary has priority over any other lien recorded with respect to the real property only on the basis of the date the renewed lien notice is filed.

History of Fam. Code §157.318: Acts 1995, 74th Leg., ch. 20, §1, eff. Apr. 20, 1995. Amended by Acts 1997, 75th Leg., ch. 420, §7 (eff. Sept. 1, 1997), ch. 911, §25 (eff. Sept. 1, 1997); Acts 2001, 77th Leg., ch. 1023, §26, eff. Sept. 1, 2001; Acts 2007, 80th Leg., ch. 972, §29, eff. Sept. 1, 2007; Acts 2009, 81st Leg., ch. 164, §2, eff. May 26, 2009. Source: Former Fam. Code §14.972(e).

See also *O'Connor's Texas Family Law Handbook* (2017), "Duration of Lien," ch. 10-E, §7, p. 1152.

FAM §157.319. EFFECT OF LIEN NOTICE

(a) If a person having actual notice of the lien possesses nonexempt personal property of the obligor that may be subject to the lien, the property may not be paid over, released, sold, transferred, encumbered, or conveyed unless:

(1) a release of lien signed by the claimant is delivered to the person in possession; or

(2) a court, after notice to the claimant and hearing, has ordered the release of the lien because arrearages do not exist.

(b) A person having notice of a child support lien who violates this section may be joined as a party to a foreclosure action under this chapter and is subject to the penalties provided by this subchapter.

(c) This section does not affect the validity or priority of a lien of a health care provider, a lien for attorney's fees, or a lien of a holder of a security interest. This section does not affect the assignment of rights or subrogation of a claim under Title XIX of the federal Social Security Act (42 U.S.C. Section 1396 et seq.), as amended.

History of Fam. Code §157.319: Acts 1995, 74th Leg., ch. 20, §1, eff. Apr. 20, 1995. Amended by Acts 1997, 75th Leg., ch. 420, §8 (eff. Sept. 1, 1997), ch. 911, §26 (eff. Sept. 1, 1997); Acts 2001, 77th Leg., ch. 1023, §27, eff. Sept. 1, 2001. Source: Former Fam. Code §14.976(b).

See also ***O'Connor's Texas Family Law Handbook*** (2017), "Perfecting Lien," ch. 10-E, §5, p. 1146.

FAM §157.320. PRIORITY OF LIEN AS TO REAL PROPERTY

(a) A lien created under this subchapter does not have priority over a lien or conveyance of an interest in the nonexempt real property recorded before the child support lien notice is recorded in the county where the real property is located.

(b) A lien created under this subchapter has priority over any lien or conveyance of an interest in the nonexempt real property recorded after the child support lien notice is recorded in the county clerk's office in the county where the property of the obligor is located.

(c) A conveyance of real property by the obligor after a lien notice has been recorded in the county where the real property is located is subject to the lien and may not impair the enforceability of the lien against the real property.

(d) A lien created under this subchapter is subordinate to a vendor's lien retained in a conveyance to the obligor.

History of Fam. Code §157.320: Acts 1995, 74th Leg., ch. 20, §1, eff. Apr. 20, 1995. Amended by Acts 1997, 75th Leg., ch. 911, §27, eff. Sept. 1, 1997. Source: Former Fam. Code §§14.976(c), 14.977.

See also ***O'Connor's Texas Family Law Handbook*** (2017), "Lien on real property," ch. 10-E, §5.1.2(2), p. 1147.

FAM §157.321. DISCRETIONARY RELEASE OF LIEN

A child support lien claimant may at any time release a lien on all or part of the property of the obligor or return seized property, without liability, if assurance of payment is considered adequate by the claimant or if the release or return will facilitate the collection of the arrearages. The release or return may not operate to prevent future action to collect from the same or other property owned by the obligor.

History of Fam. Code §157.321: Acts 1995, 74th Leg., ch. 20, §1, eff. Apr. 20, 1995. Amended by Acts 1997, 75th Leg., ch. 420, §9 (eff. Sept. 1, 1997), ch. 911, §28 (eff. Sept. 1, 1997); Acts 2001, 77th Leg., ch. 1023, §28, eff. Sept. 1, 2001. Source: Former Fam. Code §14.980.

See also ***O'Connor's Texas Family Law Handbook*** (2017), "Claimant agrees to release lien," ch. 10-E, §7.2.4, p. 1153.

FAM §157.322. MANDATORY RELEASE OF LIEN

(a) On payment in full of the amount of child support due, together with any costs and reasonable attorney's fees, the child support lien claimant shall execute and deliver to the obligor or the obligor's attorney a release of the child support lien.

(b) The release of the child support lien is effective when:

(1) filed with the county clerk with whom the lien notice or abstract of judgment was filed; or

(2) delivered to any other individual or organization that may have been served with a lien notice under this subchapter.

History of Fam. Code §157.322: Acts 1995, 74th Leg., ch. 20, §1, eff. Apr. 20, 1995. Amended by Acts 1997, 75th Leg., ch. 420, §10 (eff. Sept. 1, 1997), ch. 911, §§29, 97(a) (eff. Sept. 1, 1997); Acts 2001, 77th Leg., ch. 1023, §29, eff. Sept. 1, 2001. Source: Former Fam. Code §14.978.

See also ***O'Connor's Texas Family Law Handbook*** (2017), "Obligor makes complete payment," ch. 10-E, §7.2.1, p. 1152.

ANNOTATIONS

In re J.P., 296 S.W.3d 830, 835 (Tex.App.—Fort Worth 2009, no pet.). "A release [of a child-support lien] is a contract subject to the rules of contract construction. Accordingly, in order to establish the affirmative defense of release, the party asserting the defense ... is required to prove the elements of a contract. A release that is valid on its face, however, constitutes prima facie proof of payment; the burden of proving otherwise is on the party who denies its validity."

FAM §157.323. FORECLOSURE OR SUIT TO DETERMINE ARREARAGES

(a) In addition to any other remedy provided by law, an action to foreclose a child support lien, to dispute the amount of arrearages stated in the lien, or to resolve issues of ownership interest with respect to property subject to a child support lien may be brought in:

(1) the court in which the lien notice was filed under Section 157.314(b)(1);

(2) the district court of the county in which the property is or was located and the lien was filed; or

(3) the court of continuing jurisdiction.

(b) The procedures provided by Subchapter B apply to a foreclosure action under this section, except that a person or organization in possession of the property of the obligor or known to have an ownership interest in property that is subject to the lien may be joined as an additional respondent.

(c) If arrearages are owed by the obligor, the court shall:

(1) render judgment against the obligor for the amount due, plus costs and reasonable attorney's fees;

(2) order any official authorized to levy execution to satisfy the lien, costs, and attorney's fees by selling any property on which a lien is established under this subchapter; or

(3) order an individual or organization in possession of nonexempt personal property or cash owned by the obligor to dispose of the property as the court may direct.

(d) For execution and sale under this section, publication of notice is necessary only for three consecutive weeks in a newspaper published in the county where the property is located or, if there is no newspaper in that county, in the most convenient newspaper in circulation in the county.

History of Fam. Code §157.323: Acts 1995, 74th Leg., ch. 20, §1, eff. Apr. 20, 1995. Amended by Acts 1997, 75th Leg., ch. 420, §11 (eff. Sept. 1, 1997), ch. 911, §30 (eff. Sept. 1, 1997); Acts 2001, 77th Leg., ch. 1023, §30, eff. Sept. 1, 2001. Source: Former Fam. Code §14.979.

See also ***O'Connor's Texas Family Law Handbook*** (2017), "Permits seizure & sale," ch. 10-E, §5.1.3, p. 1147; "Foreclosing Lien," ch. 10-E, §9, p. 1158; "Contesting levy," ch. 10-F, §2.3, p. 1163.

ANNOTATIONS

Granado v. Meza, 398 S.W.3d 193, 193 (Tex.2013). "In this appeal, the trial court confirmed arrearages of $500. The proffered support for this finding is: (1) a clerical error by the Office of the Attorney General (OAG) mistakenly reflecting that the child-support obligation ended 12 years early, and (2) a statement in the OAG's ... Payment Record ... that the Record might not include payments made to local registries. The clerical error is no evidence of arrearages because the OAG could not modify this child-support obligation. And because the obligor testified that he only paid the OAG, the Payment Record's disclaimer that it might not include payments to local registries is no evidence of arrearages. Thus, while there is some evidence of arrearages, there is no evidence to support the trial court's $500 arrearage determination. Because a trial court's determination of child-support arrearages must be set aside if there is no evidence to support it, we reverse the judgment...."

In re C.D.E., ___ S.W.3d ___ (Tex.App.—Houston [14th Dist.] 2015, no pet.) (No. 14-14-00086-CV; 1-27-15). "The Family Code authorizes the OAG [Office of the Attorney General] to enforce child support orders and to collect and distribute support payments. As a child support claimant, the OAG is expressly authorized to enforce a child support obligation by filing a statutorily prescribed lien to collect all amounts of child support due and owing. [¶] [Section 157.323] does not provide an option authorizing the trial court to vacate or terminate a lien when arrearages are due and owing. [¶] [E]ven if the trial court found that Father was timely making payments on the arrearage in compliance with the [child-support] order, that portion of the trial court's order terminating the OAG's ... lien was contrary to the applicable provisions of the Family Code and the OAG's authority when, as here, an arrearage remained due and owing." *See also* ***In re H.G-J.***, 503 S.W.3d 679, 682-83 (Tex.App.—Houston [14th Dist.] 2016, no pet.) (trial court cannot order OAG to take funds that were collected for disbursement to obligee for benefit of children and use them to pay amicus attorney fees).

FAM §157.324. LIABILITY FOR FAILURE TO COMPLY WITH ORDER OR LIEN

A person who knowingly disposes of property subject to a child support lien or who, after a foreclosure hearing, fails to surrender on demand nonexempt personal property as directed by a court under this subchapter is liable to the claimant in an amount equal to

the value of the property disposed of or not surrendered, not to exceed the amount of the child support arrearages for which the lien or foreclosure judgment was issued.

History of Fam. Code §157.324: Acts 1995, 74th Leg., ch. 20, §1, eff. Apr. 20, 1995. Amended by Acts 1997, 75th Leg., ch. 420, §12 (eff. Sept. 1, 1997), ch. 911, §31 (eff. Sept. 1, 1997); Acts 2001, 77th Leg., ch. 1023, §31, eff. Sept. 1, 2001; Acts 2007, 80th Leg., ch. 972, §30, eff. Sept. 1, 2007. Source: Former Fam. Code §14.981.

See also ***O'Connor's Texas Family Law Handbook*** (2017), "Gives notice to third parties," ch. 10-E, §5.1.1, p. 1146; "Liability for not obeying order," ch. 10-E, §9.8, p. 1161.

FAM §157.325. RELEASE OF EXCESS FUNDS TO DEBTOR OR OBLIGOR

(a) If a person has in the person's possession earnings, deposits, accounts, balances, or other funds or assets of the obligor, including the proceeds of a judgment or other settlement of a claim or counterclaim due to the obligor that are in excess of the amount of arrearages specified in the child support lien, the holder of the nonexempt personal property or the obligor may request that the claimant release any excess amount from the lien. The claimant shall grant the request and discharge any lien on the excess amount unless the security for the arrearages would be impaired.

(b) If the claimant refuses the request, the holder of the personal property or the obligor may file suit under this subchapter for an order determining the amount of arrearages and discharging excess personal property or money from the lien.

History of Fam. Code §157.325: Acts 1995, 74th Leg., ch. 20, §1, eff. Apr. 20, 1995. Amended by Acts 1997, 75th Leg., ch. 420, §13 (eff. Sept. 1, 1997), ch. 911, §32 (eff. Sept. 1, 1997); Acts 2001, 77th Leg., ch. 1023, §32, eff. Sept. 1, 2001. Source: Former Fam. Code §14.982.

See also ***O'Connor's Texas Family Law Handbook*** (2017), "Personal property exceeds value of lien," ch. 10-E, §7.2.2, p. 1152; "Contesting Lien," ch. 10-E, §8, p. 1153.

FAM §157.326. INTEREST OF OBLIGOR'S SPOUSE OR ANOTHER PERSON HAVING OWNERSHIP INTEREST

(a) A spouse of an obligor or another person having an ownership interest in property that is subject to a child support lien may file suit under Section 157.323 to determine the extent, if any, of the spouse's or other person's interest in real or personal property that is subject to:

(1) a lien perfected under this subchapter; or

(2) an action to foreclose under this subchapter.

(b) After notice to the obligor, the obligor's spouse, any other person alleging an ownership interest, the claimant, and the obligee, the court shall conduct a hearing and determine the extent, if any, of the ownership interest in the property held by the obligor's spouse or other person. If the court finds that:

(1) the property is the separate property of the obligor's spouse or the other person, the court shall order that the lien against the property be released and that any action to foreclose on the property be dismissed;

(2) the property is jointly owned by the obligor and the obligor's spouse, the court shall determine whether the sale of the obligor's interest in the property would result in an unreasonable hardship on the obligor's spouse or family and:

(A) if so, the court shall render an order that the obligor's interest in the property not be sold and that the lien against the property should be released; or

(B) if not, the court shall render an order partitioning the property and directing that the property be sold and the proceeds applied to the child support arrearages; or

(3) the property is owned in part by another person, other than the obligor's spouse, the court shall render an order partitioning the property and directing that the obligor's share of the property be applied to the child support arrearages.

(c) In a proceeding under this section, the spouse or other person claiming an ownership interest in the property has the burden to prove the extent of that ownership interest.

History of Fam. Code §157.326: Acts 1995, 74th Leg., ch. 20, §1, eff. Apr. 20, 1995. Amended by Acts 1997, 75th Leg., ch. 420, §14 (eff. Sept. 1, 1997), ch. 911, §33 (eff. Sept. 1, 1997); Acts 2001, 77th Leg., ch. 1023, §33, eff. Sept. 1, 2001. Source: Former Fam. Code §14.983.

See also ***O'Connor's Texas Family Law Handbook*** (2017), "Petition to determine ownership," ch. 10-E, §8.2, p. 1156.

FAM §157.327. EXECUTION & LEVY ON FINANCIAL ASSETS OF OBLIGOR

(a) Notwithstanding any other provision of law, if a judgment or administrative determination of arrearages has been rendered, a claimant may deliver a notice of levy to any financial institution possessing or controlling assets or funds owned by, or owed to, an obligor and subject to a child support lien, including a lien for child support arising in another state.

(b) The notice under this section must:

(1) identify the amount of child support arrearages owing at the time the amount of arrearages was determined or, if the amount is less, the amount of arrear-

ages owing at the time the notice is prepared and delivered to the financial institution; and

(2) direct the financial institution to pay to the claimant, not earlier than the 15th day or later than the 21st day after the date of delivery of the notice, an amount from the assets of the obligor or from funds due to the obligor that are held or controlled by the institution, not to exceed the amount of the child support arrearages identified in the notice, unless:

(A) the institution is notified by the claimant that the obligor has paid the arrearages or made arrangements satisfactory to the claimant for the payment of the arrearages;

(B) the obligor or another person files a suit under Section 157.323 requesting a hearing by the court; or

(C) if the claimant is the Title IV-D agency, the obligor has requested an agency review under Section 157.328.

(c) A financial institution that receives a notice of levy under this section may not close an account in which the obligor has an ownership interest, permit a withdrawal from any account the obligor owns, in whole or in part, or pay funds to the obligor so that any amount remaining in the account is less than the amount of the arrearages identified in the notice, plus any fees due to the institution and any costs of the levy identified by the claimant.

(d) A financial institution that receives a notice of levy under this section shall notify any other person having an ownership interest in an account in which the obligor has an ownership interest that the account has been levied on in an amount not to exceed the amount of the child support arrearages identified in the notice of levy.

(e) The notice of levy may be delivered to a financial institution as provided by Section 59.008, Finance Code, if the institution is subject to that law or may be delivered to the registered agent, the institution's main business office in this state, or another address provided by the institution under Section 231.307.

(f) A financial institution may deduct the fees and costs identified in Subsection (c) from the obligor's assets before paying the appropriate amount to the claimant.

History of Fam. Code §157.327: Acts 2001, 77th Leg., ch. 1023, §34, eff. Sept. 1, 2001. Amended by Acts 2007, 80th Leg., ch. 972, §31, eff. Sept. 1, 2007.

See also ***O'Connor's Texas Family Law Handbook*** (2017), "Levying on Financial Institutions," ch. 10-F, p. 1162.

FAM §157.3271. LEVY ON FINANCIAL INSTITUTION ACCOUNT OF DECEASED OBLIGOR

(a) Subject to Subsection (b), the Title IV-D agency may, not earlier than the 90th day after the date of death of an obligor in a Title IV-D case, deliver a notice of levy to a financial institution in which the obligor was the sole owner of an account, regardless of whether the Title IV-D agency has issued a child support lien notice regarding the account.

(b) The Title IV-D agency may not deliver a notice of levy under this section if probate proceedings relating to the obligor's estate have commenced.

(c) The notice of levy must:

(1) identify the amount of child support arrearages determined by the Title IV-D agency to be owing and unpaid by the obligor on the date of the obligor's death; and

(2) direct the financial institution to pay to the Title IV-D agency, not earlier than the 45th day or later than the 60th day after the date of delivery of the notice, an amount from the assets of the obligor or from funds due to the obligor that are held or controlled by the institution, not to exceed the amount of the child support arrearages identified in the notice.

(d) Not later than the 35th day after the date of delivery of the notice, the financial institution must notify any other person asserting a claim against the account that:

(1) the account has been levied on for child support arrearages in the amount shown on the notice of levy; and

(2) the person may contest the levy by filing suit and requesting a court hearing in the same manner that a person may challenge a child support lien under Section 157.323.

(e) A person who contests a levy under this section, as authorized by Subsection (d)(2), may bring the suit in:

(1) the district court of the county in which the property is located or in which the obligor resided; or

(2) the court of continuing jurisdiction.

(f) The notice of levy may be delivered to a financial institution as provided by Section 59.008, Finance Code, if the institution is subject to that law or may be delivered to the registered agent, the institution's main business office in this state, or another address provided by the institution under Section 231.307.

(g) A financial institution may deduct its fees and costs, including any costs for complying with this section, from the deceased obligor's assets before paying the appropriate amount to the Title IV-D agency.

History of Fam. Code §157.3271: Acts 2011, 82nd Leg., ch. 508, §8, eff. Sept. 1, 2011.

See also *O'Connor's Texas Family Law Handbook* (2017), "Levy on Financial Institution of Deceased Obligor," ch. 10-F, §3, p. 1164.

FAM §157.328. NOTICE OF LEVY SENT TO OBLIGOR

(a) At the time the notice of levy under Section 157.327 is delivered to a financial institution, the claimant shall serve the obligor with a copy of the notice.

(b) The notice of levy delivered to the obligor must inform the obligor that:

(1) the claimant will not proceed with levy if, not later than the 10th day after the date of receipt of the notice, the obligor pays in full the amount of arrearages identified in the notice or otherwise makes arrangements acceptable to the claimant for the payment of the arrearage amounts; and

(2) the obligor may contest the levy by filing suit under Section 157.323 not later than the 10th day after the date of receipt of the notice.

(c) If the claimant is the Title IV-D agency, the obligor receiving a notice of levy may request review by the agency not later than the 10th day after the date of receipt of the notice to resolve any issue in dispute regarding the existence or amount of the arrearages. The agency shall provide an opportunity for a review, by telephone conference or in person, as appropriate to the circumstances, not later than the fifth business day after the date an oral or written request from the obligor for the review is received. If the review fails to resolve any issue in dispute, the obligor may file suit under Section 157.323 for a hearing by the court not later than the fifth day after the date of the conclusion of the agency review. If the obligor fails to timely file suit, the Title IV-D agency may request the financial institution to release and remit the funds subject to levy.

(d) The notice under this section may be delivered to the last known address of the obligor by first class mail, certified mail, or registered mail.

History of Fam. Code §157.328: Acts 2001, 77th Leg., ch. 1023, §34, eff. Sept. 1, 2001.

See also *O'Connor's Texas Family Law Handbook* (2017), "Notice of levy," ch. 10-F, §2.1, p. 1162.

FAM §157.329. NO LIABILITY FOR COMPLIANCE WITH NOTICE OF LEVY

A financial institution that possesses or has a right to an obligor's assets for which a notice of levy has been delivered and that surrenders the assets or right to assets to a child support lien claimant is not liable to the obligor or any other person for the property or rights surrendered.

History of Fam. Code §157.329: Acts 2001, 77th Leg., ch. 1023, §34, eff. Sept. 1, 2001.

See also *O'Connor's Texas Family Law Handbook* (2017), "Financial institution's liability," ch. 10-F, §2.4, p. 1164; "Financial institution's liability," ch. 10-F, §3.4, p. 1165.

FAM §157.330. FAILURE TO COMPLY WITH NOTICE OF LEVY

(a) A person who possesses or has a right to property that is the subject of a notice of levy delivered to the person and who refuses to surrender the property or right to property to the claimant on demand is liable to the claimant in an amount equal to the value of the property or right to property not surrendered but that does not exceed the amount of the child support arrearages for which the notice of levy has been filed.

(b) A claimant may recover costs and reasonable attorney's fees incurred in an action under this section.

History of Fam. Code §157.330: Acts 2001, 77th Leg., ch. 1023, §34, eff. Sept. 1, 2001. Amended by Acts 2007, 80th Leg., ch. 972, §32, eff. Sept. 1, 2007.

See also *O'Connor's Texas Family Law Handbook* (2017), "Liability to claimant," ch. 10-F, §2.4.2, p. 1164; "Liability to AG," ch. 10-F, §3.4.2, p. 1165.

FAM §157.331. ADDITIONAL LEVY TO SATISFY ARREARAGES

If the property or right to property on which a notice of levy has been filed does not produce money sufficient to satisfy the amount of child support arrearages identified in the notice of levy, the claimant may proceed to levy on other property of the obligor until the total amount of child support due is paid.

History of Fam. Code §157.331: Acts 2001, 77th Leg., ch. 1023, §34, eff. Sept. 1, 2001.

Sections 157.332-157.370 reserved for expansion

Subchapter H. Habeas Corpus

FAM §157.371. JURISDICTION

(a) The relator may file a petition for a writ of habeas corpus in either the court of continuing, exclusive jurisdiction or in a court with jurisdiction to issue a writ of habeas corpus in the county in which the child is found.

(b) Although a habeas corpus proceeding is not a suit affecting the parent-child relationship, the court

may refer to the provisions of this title for definitions and procedures as appropriate.

History of Fam. Code §157.371: Acts 1995, 74th Leg., ch. 20, §1, eff. Apr. 20, 1995.

See also *O'Connor's Texas Family Law Handbook* (2017), "Jurisdiction," ch. 11-D, §3, p. 1203.

FAM §157.372. RETURN OF CHILD

(a) Subject to Chapter 152 and the Parental Kidnapping Prevention Act (28 U.S.C. Section 1738A), if the right to possession of a child is governed by a court order, the court in a habeas corpus proceeding involving the right to possession of the child shall compel return of the child to the relator only if the court finds that the relator is entitled to possession under the order.

(b) If the court finds that the previous order was granted by a court that did not give the contestants reasonable notice of the proceeding and an opportunity to be heard, the court may not render an order in the habeas corpus proceeding compelling return of the child on the basis of that order.

History of Fam. Code §157.372: Acts 1995, 74th Leg., ch. 20, §1, eff. Apr. 20, 1995. Source: Former Fam. Code §14.10(a), (b).

See also *O'Connor's Texas Family Law Handbook* (2017), "Right of possession under court order," ch. 11-D, §5.1.1, p. 1205; "Return of child," ch. 11-D, §5.4.7(1), p. 1206; "Defenses – possession based on court order," ch. 11-D, §8.2.5, p. 1210; "Relator has superior right of possession," ch. 11-D, §10.2, p. 1213.

ANNOTATIONS

Greene v. Schuble, 654 S.W.2d 436, 437-38 (Tex. 1983). "In the absence of specific provisions to the contrary in an order establishing conservatorship, the death of the managing conservator ends the conservatorship order and it no longer constitutes a valid subsisting court order for purposes of [Fam. Code] §14.10 [now §§157.372-157.376]. [Section 14.10(e), now Fam. Code §157.376,] therefore applies. We adhere to the rule we stated prior to the adoption of the Family Code that in the event of the death of the managing conservator, the surviving parent has a right to possession of the children, and a court may enforce this right by issuance of a writ of habeas corpus."

Mergerson v. Daggett, 644 S.W.2d 451, 452 (Tex. 1982). Family Code §14.10(f), now §157.376, "applies only when the right to possession of a child is not governed by a court order. Since the … Court had previously issued temporary orders regarding [conservatorship], §14.10(a) [now Fam. Code §157.372] applies."

Lamphere v. Chrisman, 554 S.W.2d 935, 938 (Tex. 1977). The writ of habeas corpus "should be granted when the relator shows that he or she is entitled to custody of the child by virtue of a valid and subsisting court order. The right to possession may *not* be relitigated in the habeas corpus hearing; the relator is entitled to an issuance of the writ immediately on a showing of his or her right to custody."

In re Guerrero, 440 S.W.3d 917, 925-26 (Tex. App.—Amarillo 2014, orig. proceeding). See annotation under Family Code §157.374, p. 648.

In re deFilippi, 235 S.W.3d 319, 322 (Tex.App.—San Antonio 2007, orig. proceeding). "Upon proof of the bare legal right of possession, the grant of the writ of habeas corpus should be automatic, immediate, and ministerial. The trial court is not permitted to consider the child's best interest, nor go beyond the immediate welfare of the child, in a habeas corpus proceeding. Mandamus may issue to correct the erroneous denial of habeas corpus relief under the … Family Code. *At 323:* When a party such as [a parent] establishes his or her legal right to possession of a child, the trial court's authority to refuse habeas corpus relief is very limited. Evidence raising a serious immediate question concerning a child's welfare must be presented before the trial court has any discretion to deny the writ. A serious immediate question requires a situation that, without the court's immediate action, would subject the child to imminent danger of physical or emotional harm." *See also* ***In re Johnston***, 957 S.W.2d 945, 947 (Tex.App.—Beaumont 1997, orig. proceeding) (writ of habeas corpus should be automatic, immediate, and ministerial unless there is serious, immediate question concerning welfare of child).

FAM §157.373. RELATOR RELINQUISHED POSSESSION; TEMPORARY ORDERS

(a) If the relator has by consent or acquiescence relinquished actual possession and control of the child for not less than 6 months preceding the date of the filing of the petition for the writ, the court may either compel or refuse to order return of the child.

(b) The court may disregard brief periods of possession and control by the relator during the 6-month period.

(c) In a suit in which the court does not compel return of the child, the court may issue temporary orders under Chapter 105 if a suit affecting the parent-child relationship is pending and the parties have received notice of a hearing on temporary orders set for the same time as the habeas corpus proceeding.

History of Fam. Code §157.373: Acts 1995, 74th Leg., ch. 20, §1, eff. Apr. 20, 1995. Source: Former Fam. Code §14.10(c).

See also *O'Connor's Texas Family Law Handbook* (2017), "Relator relinquished possession," ch. 11-D, §8.2.5(3), p. 1210; "Relator has superior right of possession," ch. 11-D, §10.2, p. 1213; "Temporary Orders of Possession," ch. 11-D, §12, p. 1215.

FAM §157.374. WELFARE OF CHILD

Notwithstanding any other provision of this subchapter, the court may render an appropriate temporary order if there is a serious immediate question concerning the welfare of the child.

History of Fam. Code §157.374: Acts 1995, 74th Leg., ch. 20, §1, eff. Apr. 20, 1995. Source: Former Fam. Code §14.10(d).

See also *O'Connor's Texas Family Law Handbook* (2017), "Serious, immediate question of harm," ch. 11-D, §8.2.5(4), p. 1211; "Relator has superior right of possession," ch. 11-D, §10.2, p. 1213; "Temporary Orders of Possession," ch. 11-D, §12, p. 1215.

ANNOTATIONS

Whatley v. Bacon, 649 S.W.2d 297, 299 (Tex.1983). "[A]n order made pursuant to [Fam. Code] §14.10(c) [now §157.374] must include a court's finding of a serious and immediate question as is required by the plain language of the statute."

McElreath v. Stewart, 545 S.W.2d 955, 958 (Tex. 1977). Section 157.374 is for "a situation where the child was in imminent danger of physical or emotional harm and immediate action was necessary to protect the child." *See also* ***Brown v. Dixon***, 776 S.W.2d 599, 601 (Tex.App.—Tyler 1989, orig. proceeding).

In re Guerrero, 440 S.W.3d 917, 925-26 (Tex. App.—Amarillo 2014, orig. proceeding). Father "is both the surviving managing conservator of [child] and [child's] father. As against all others, either status gives to [father] superior rights to possess [child], in light of the death of [child's] mother. That being so, the record demonstrates [father's] bare legal right to possession of [child]. We need only determine now whether the evidence before the trial court raised a serious, immediate question concerning [child's] welfare in [father's] care. [¶] As [grandmother] testified, [child] may need time to adjust, but such periods of adjustment hardly seem avoidable as he adjusts to the tragic loss of his mother at such a tender age. It may be that the change in his routine will lead to instances of [child] acting out as he adjusts. This, however, does not rise to the level of a 'dire emergency' or an 'imminent danger' to [child's] physical or emotional well-being; 'it is well-established that merely removing a child from a familiar environment does not rise to the level of a serious and immediate question concerning a child's welfare in the habeas corpus context.'"

In re Bradshaw, 273 S.W.3d 851, 858-59 (Tex. App.—Houston [14th Dist.] 2008, orig. proceeding). "The fact that a child prefers to be with one parent over the other is not sufficient to support a finding that there is an immediate serious question concerning the child's welfare. The fact that a child has *merely* threatened to run away is not sufficient to support a finding that there is an immediate serious question concerning the child's welfare. [But the] fact that [child] had already run away twice ... supports ... finding that [child] is likely to run away again. ... We find that the evidence supports ... finding that a serious immediate question regarding the welfare of [child] exists."

FAM §157.375. IMMUNITY TO CIVIL PROCESS

(a) While in this state for the sole purpose of compelling the return of a child through a habeas corpus proceeding, the relator is not amenable to civil process and is not subject to the jurisdiction of any civil court except the court in which the writ is pending. The relator is subject to process and jurisdiction in that court only for the purpose of prosecuting the writ.

(b) A request by the relator for costs, attorney's fees, and necessary travel and other expenses under Chapter 106 or 152 is not a waiver of immunity to civil process.

History of Fam. Code §157.375: Acts 1995, 74th Leg., ch. 20, §1, eff. Apr. 20, 1995. Source: Former Fam. Code §14.10(e).

FAM §157.376. NO EXISTING ORDER

(a) If the right to possession of a child is not governed by an order, the court in a habeas corpus proceeding involving the right of possession of the child:

(1) shall compel return of the child to the parent if the right of possession is between a parent and a nonparent and a suit affecting the parent-child relationship has not been filed; or

(2) may either compel return of the child or issue temporary orders under Chapter 105 if a suit affecting the parent-child relationship is pending and the parties have received notice of a hearing on temporary orders set for the same time as the habeas corpus proceeding.

(b) The court may not use a habeas corpus proceeding to adjudicate the right of possession of a child between two parents or between two or more nonparents.

History of Fam. Code §157.376: Acts 1995, 74th Leg., ch. 20, §1, eff. Apr. 20, 1995. Source: Former Fam. Code §14.10(f).

See also ***O'Connor's Texas Family Law Handbook*** (2017), "No court order," ch. 11-D, §4.2.1, p. 1204; "Temporary Orders of Possession," ch. 11-D, §12, p. 1215.

ANNOTATIONS

Greene v. Schuble, 654 S.W.2d 436, 437-38 (Tex.1983). See annotation under Family Code §157.372, p. 647.

Sections 157.377-157.420 reserved for expansion

SUBCHAPTER I. CLARIFICATION OF ORDERS

FAM §157.421. CLARIFYING NONSPECIFIC ORDER

(a) A court may clarify an order rendered by the court in a proceeding under this title if the court finds, on the motion of a party or on the court's own motion, that the order is not specific enough to be enforced by contempt.

(b) The court shall clarify the order by rendering an order that is specific enough to be enforced by contempt.

(c) A clarified order does not affect the finality of the order that it clarifies.

History of Fam. Code §157.421: Acts 1995, 74th Leg., ch. 20, §1, eff. Apr. 20, 1995. Source: Former Fam. Code §11.22(a), (b), (g).

See also ***O'Connor's Texas Family Law Handbook*** (2017), "Motion to Clarify Child-Support Order," ch. 10-B, p. 1107; "Motion to Clarify Order of Possession or Access," ch. 11-B, p. 1195.

ANNOTATIONS

In re A.C.B., 103 S.W.3d 570, 577 (Tex.App.—San Antonio 2003, no pet.). "The only basis for clarifying a prior order is when a provision is ambiguous and nonspecific. In the absence of an ambiguity, the trial court is without authority to modify the judgment."

In re Hamilton, 975 S.W.2d 758, 762 (Tex.App.—Corpus Christi 1998, pet. denied). "A clarification order is analogous to a judgment *nunc pro tunc* in that it cannot substantively change a final order. Because of the confusion between the two competing orders, [obligor] properly sought clarification to learn which order he was expected to obey. The clarification order merely states that the [original] order is effective. Because the second order was never legally effective and could not be enforced, the sole effect of the district court's clarification order was to clarify [AG's] obligations and correct the erroneous entry of an unenforceable order. This is not outside the power of the district court as neither order was specific enough to be enforceable until the court clarified which was, in fact, effective."

FAM §157.422. PROCEDURE

(a) The procedure for filing a motion for enforcement of a final order applies to a motion for clarification.

(b) A person is not entitled to a jury in a proceeding under this subchapter.

History of Fam. Code §157.422: Acts 1995, 74th Leg., ch. 20, §1, eff. Apr. 20, 1995. Source: Former Fam. Code §11.22(h), (i).

See also ***O'Connor's Texas Family Law Handbook*** (2017), "Motion," ch. 10-B, §4, p. 1108; "Motion," ch. 11-B, §4, p. 1196.

FAM §157.423. SUBSTANTIVE CHANGE NOT ENFORCEABLE

(a) A court may not change the substantive provisions of an order to be clarified under this subchapter.

(b) A substantive change made by a clarification order is not enforceable.

History of Fam. Code §157.423: Acts 1995, 74th Leg., ch. 20, §1, eff. Apr. 20, 1995. Source: Former Fam. Code §11.22(c).

See also ***O'Connor's Texas Family Law Handbook*** (2017), "Ambiguity is nonsubstantive," ch. 10-B, §3.3, p. 1108; "Ambiguity is nonsubstantive," ch. 11-B, §3.3, p. 1195.

ANNOTATIONS

In re V.M.P., 185 S.W.3d 531, 534-35 (Tex.App.—Texarkana 2006, no pet.). "The trial court's 'clarification' order ordered [father] to pay only $97.50 per week, without providing for potential percentage increase that was clearly envisioned by the 1993 order. This is clearly a substantive change, which our [Family] Code expressly forbids—unless there is authority to modify. [¶] And, in this case, the trial court *did have authority* (pursuant to the parties' motions requesting modification) *and jurisdiction ... to modify* [father's] child support obligation. Thus, to the extent that the trial court's 'clarification' order ... amounted to a substantive modification, such change would certainly have been permissible if it were rendered as part of a 'modification' order. We, therefore, conclude the trial court, while mistaken in titling its order, did not err in entering the order."

Lundy v. Lundy, 973 S.W.2d 687, 688-89 (Tex.App.—Tyler 1998, pet. denied). "Although a court does retain the inherent power to clarify, interpret or enforce a provision of a divorce decree, a court may not set aside or alter a judgment after the expiration of its plenary power, and an order attempting to do so is void. A court may not change the substantive provisions of an order to be clarified, and a substantive change is not enforceable. The only basis for clarifying a prior decree is when a provision is ambiguous and non-specific. In

the absence of an ambiguity, the trial court is without authority to modify the judgment."

Dickens v. Willis, 957 S.W.2d 657, 659 (Tex.App.—Austin 1997, no pet.). "A substantive change occurs when a judicial error is corrected because such an error results from judicial reasoning and determination. On the other hand, when an error results from inaccurately recording the decision of the court, the error is *clerical.* [T]he correction of a clerical error does not effect a substantive change. [¶] Whether an error is clerical or judicial is a question of law. The question, however, becomes one of law only after the trial court factually determines whether it previously rendered judgment and the judgment's contents. ... Proof of a clerical error must be clear, satisfying, and convincing. Furthermore, [t]his Court must construe the original judgment as a whole toward the end of harmonizing and giving effect to all the court has written." (Internal quotes omitted.) *See also* ***In re Marriage of Ward***, 137 S.W.3d 910, 913 (Tex.App.—Texarkana 2004, no pet.); ***In re Dryden***, 52 S.W.3d 257, 263-64 (Tex.App.—Corpus Christi 2001, orig. proceeding).

FAM §157.424. RELATION TO MOTION FOR CONTEMPT

The court may render a clarification order before a motion for contempt is made or heard, in conjunction with a motion for contempt, or after the denial of a motion for contempt.

History of Fam. Code §157.424: Acts 1995, 74th Leg., ch. 20, §1, eff. Apr. 20, 1995. Source: Former Fam. Code §11.22(d).

See also ***O'Connor's Texas Family Law Handbook*** (2017), "With contempt motion," ch. 10-B, §4.2.2, p. 1109.

FAM §157.425. ORDER NOT RETROACTIVE

The court may not provide that a clarification order is retroactive for the purpose of enforcement by contempt.

History of Fam. Code §157.425: Acts 1995, 74th Leg., ch. 20, §1, eff. Apr. 20, 1995. Source: Former Fam. Code §11.22(e).

FAM §157.426. TIME ALLOWED TO COMPLY

(a) In a clarification order, the court shall provide a reasonable time for compliance.

(b) The clarification order may be enforced by contempt after the time for compliance has expired.

History of Fam. Code §157.426: Acts 1995, 74th Leg., ch. 20, §1, eff. Apr. 20, 1995. Source: Former Fam. Code §11.22(f).

See also ***O'Connor's Texas Family Law Handbook*** (2017), "Clarification," ch. 10-B, §12.8.1, p. 1111.

CHAPTER 158. WITHHOLDING FROM EARNINGS FOR CHILD SUPPORT

SUBCHAPTER A. INCOME WITHHOLDING REQUIRED; GENERAL PROVISIONS

FAM §158.001. INCOME WITHHOLDING; GENERAL RULE

In a proceeding in which periodic payments of child support are ordered, modified, or enforced, the court or the Title IV-D agency shall order that income be withheld from the disposable earnings of the obligor as provided by this chapter.

History of Fam. Code §158.001: Acts 1995, 74th Leg., ch. 20, §1, eff. Apr. 20, 1995. Amended by Acts 1997, 75th Leg., ch. 911, §34, eff. Sept. 1, 1997. Source: Former Fam. Code §§14.05(e), 14.43(a)(1).

See also ***O'Connor's Texas Family Law Handbook*** (2017), "Wage Withholding—Issuing Suspended Orders & Obtaining Judicial & Administrative Writs," ch. 10-D, p. 1135.

FAM §158.002. SUSPENSION OF INCOME WITHHOLDING

Except in a Title IV-D case, the court may provide, for good cause shown or on agreement of the parties, that the order withholding income need not be issued or delivered to an employer until:

(1) the obligor has been in arrears for an amount due for more than 30 days;

(2) the amount of the arrearages is an amount equal to or greater than the amount due for a one-month period; or

(3) any other violation of the child support order has occurred.

History of Fam. Code §158.002: Acts 1995, 74th Leg., ch. 20, §1, eff. Apr. 20, 1995. Amended by Acts 1997, 75th Leg., ch. 911, §35, eff. Sept. 1, 1997. Source: Former Fam. Code §14.43(a)(2), (3).

See also ***O'Connor's Texas Family Law Handbook*** (2017), "Issuing Suspended Wage-Withholding Order," ch. 10-D, §2, p. 1136.

FAM §158.003. WITHHOLDING FOR ARREARAGES IN ADDITION TO CURRENT SUPPORT

(a) In addition to income withheld for the current support of a child, income shall be withheld from the disposable earnings of the obligor to be applied toward the liquidation of any child support arrearages, including accrued interest as provided in Chapter 157.

(b) The additional amount to be withheld for arrearages shall be an amount sufficient to discharge those arrearages in not more than two years or an additional 20 percent added to the amount of the current monthly support order, whichever amount will result in the arrearages being discharged in the least amount of time.

History of Fam. Code §158.003: Acts 1995, 74th Leg., ch. 20, §1, eff. Apr. 20, 1995. Amended by Acts 1999, 76th Leg., ch. 556, §21, eff. Sept. 1, 1999. Source: Former Fam. Code §14.43(d).

FAM §158.004. WITHHOLDING FOR ARREARAGES WHEN NO CURRENT SUPPORT IS DUE

If current support is no longer owed, the court or the Title IV-D agency shall order that income be withheld for arrearages, including accrued interest as provided in Chapter 157, in an amount sufficient to discharge those arrearages in not more than two years.

History of Fam. Code §158.004: Acts 1995, 74th Leg., ch. 20, §1, eff. Apr. 20, 1995. Amended by Acts 1999, 76th Leg., ch. 556, §22, eff. Sept. 1, 1999. Source: Former Fam. Code §14.43(d).

FAM §158.005. WITHHOLDING TO SATISFY JUDGMENT FOR ARREARAGES

In rendering a cumulative judgment for arrearages, the court shall order that a reasonable amount of income be withheld from the disposable earnings of the obligor to be applied toward the satisfaction of the judgment.

History of Fam. Code §158.005: Acts 1995, 74th Leg., ch. 20, §1, eff. Apr. 20, 1995. Source: Former Fam. Code §§14.41(a), 14.43(d).

See also *O'Connor's Texas Family Law Handbook* (2017), "Wage withholding," ch. 10-C, §4.4.10(3), p. 1126.

ANNOTATIONS

Starck v. Nelson, 878 S.W.2d 302, 309 (Tex.App.—Corpus Christi 1994, no writ). "Disposable earnings are different and usually less than net resources."

FAM §158.0051. ORDER FOR WITHHOLDING FOR COSTS & FEES

(a) In addition to an order for income to be withheld for child support, including child support and child support arrearages, the court may render an order that income be withheld from the disposable earnings of the obligor to be applied towards the satisfaction of any ordered attorney's fees and costs resulting from an action to enforce child support under this title.

(b) An order rendered under this section is subordinate to an order or writ of withholding for child support under this chapter and is subject to the maximum amount allowed to be withheld under Section 158.009.

(c) The court shall order that amounts withheld for fees and costs under this section be remitted directly to the person entitled to the ordered attorney's fees or costs or be paid through a local registry for disbursement to that person.

History of Fam. Code §158.0051: Acts 2001, 77th Leg., ch. 1023, §35, eff. Sept. 1, 2001.

See also *O'Connor's Texas Family Law Handbook* (2017), "Attorney fees & costs," ch. 10-C, §12.8.2(2), p. 1132.

FAM §158.006. INCOME WITHHOLDING IN TITLE IV-D SUITS

In a Title IV-D case, the court or the Title IV-D agency shall order that income be withheld from the disposable earnings of the obligor and may not suspend, stay, or delay issuance of the order or of a judicial or administrative writ of withholding.

History of Fam. Code §158.006: Acts 1995, 74th Leg., ch. 20, §1, eff. Apr. 20, 1995. Amended by Acts 1997, 75th Leg., ch. 911, §36, eff. Sept. 1, 1997. Source: Former Fam. Code §14.43(b).

FAM §158.007. EXTENSION OF REPAYMENT SCHEDULE BY COURT OR TITLE IV-D AGENCY; UNREASONABLE HARDSHIP

If the court or the Title IV-D agency finds that the schedule for discharging arrearages would cause the obligor, the obligor's family, or children for whom support is due from the obligor to suffer unreasonable hardship, the court or agency may extend the payment period for a reasonable length of time.

History of Fam. Code §158.007: Acts 1995, 74th Leg., ch. 20, §1, eff. Apr. 20, 1995. Amended by Acts 1999, 76th Leg., ch. 556, §22, eff. Sept. 1, 1999. Source: Former Fam. Code §14.43(d).

ANNOTATIONS

In re D.C., 180 S.W.3d 647, 652 (Tex.App.—Waco 2005, no pet.). The appellate court's "review is limited to the issue of whether the court abused its discretion by permitting [obligor] to pay off the arrearages over a period which will exceed two years. *At 653:* [Obligor's] testimony suggests that his present financial circumstances permit him to pay $100 per week but he is concerned about the consequences of future financial difficulties. This is simply not an adequate factual basis to support a finding that requiring [obligor] to pay the arrearages off in two years will result in an 'unreasonable hardship.'"

In re Chambers, 5 S.W.3d 341, 343 (Tex.App.—Texarkana 1999, no pet.). "[T]he amount of arrearage to be paid each month is determined by the court and is subject to appellate review for an abuse of discretion. [¶] The Legislature chose to write [§158.007] to give the trial court discretion to make its decision based upon the facts of the particular case. [¶] Thus, if the trial court had facts before it from which it could conclude that a higher payment would cause the obligor to suffer an unreasonable hardship, it had the authority to extend the payment schedule. Further, the 'reasonable length of time' aspect of the statute is linked with the requirement that the amount of payment not cause an

'unreasonable hardship' upon the obligor or the obligor's family. This is a factually based question, which must be decided by each court based upon the particular case at bar."

FAM §158.008. PRIORITY OF WITHHOLDING

An order or writ of withholding has priority over any garnishment, attachment, execution, or other assignment or order affecting disposable earnings.

History of Fam. Code §158.008: Acts 1995, 74th Leg., ch. 20, §1, eff. Apr. 20, 1995. Source: Former Fam. Code §14.43(k).

FAM §158.009. MAXIMUM AMOUNT WITHHELD FROM EARNINGS

An order or writ of withholding shall direct that any employer of the obligor withhold from the obligor's disposable earnings the amount specified up to a maximum amount of 50 percent of the obligor's disposable earnings.

History of Fam. Code §158.009: Acts 1995, 74th Leg., ch. 20, §1, eff. Apr. 20, 1995. Amended by Acts 1997, 75th Leg., ch. 911, §37, eff. Sept. 1, 1997. Source: Former Fam. Code §14.43(f).

ANNOTATIONS

In re Chambers, 5 S.W.3d 341, 343 (Tex.App.—Texarkana 1999, no pet.). Section 158.009 "mandates that a court may order withholding of no more than the maximum amount of 50% of the obligor's disposable earnings. This Court will not impose a mandatory minimum payment as a matter of law when the Legislature has chosen not to write such a minimum into the statute and has provided other factors that must be considered in deciding the amount of monthly payments to be imposed upon the obligor."

FAM §158.010. ORDER OR WRIT BINDING ON EMPLOYER DOING BUSINESS IN STATE

An order or writ of withholding issued under this chapter and delivered to an employer doing business in this state is binding on the employer without regard to whether the obligor resides or works outside this state.

History of Fam. Code §158.010: Acts 1995, 74th Leg., ch. 20, §1, eff. Apr. 20, 1995. Amended by Acts 1997, 75th Leg., ch. 911, §38, eff. Sept. 1, 1997. Source: Former Fam. Code §14.43(h).

FAM §158.011. VOLUNTARY WITHHOLDING BY OBLIGOR

(a) An obligor may file with the clerk of the court a notarized or acknowledged request signed by the obligor and the obligee for the issuance and delivery to the obligor's employer of a writ of withholding. A notarized or acknowledged request may be filed under this section regardless of whether a writ or order has been served on any party or of the existence or amount of an arrearage.

(b) On receipt of a request under this section, the clerk shall issue and deliver a writ of withholding in the manner provided by this chapter.

(c) An employer that receives a writ of withholding issued under this section may request a hearing in the same manner and according to the same terms provided by Section 158.205.

(d) An obligor whose employer receives a writ of withholding issued under this section may request a hearing in the manner provided by Section 158.309.

(e) An obligee may contest a writ of withholding issued under this section by requesting, not later than the 180th day after the date on which the obligee discovers that the writ has been issued, a hearing in the manner provided by Section 158.309.

(f) A writ of withholding under this section may not reduce the total amount of child support, including arrearages, owed by the obligor.

History of Fam. Code §158.011: Acts 1995, 74th Leg., ch. 751, §55, eff. Sept. 1, 1995. Amended by Acts 1997, 75th Leg., ch. 911, §39, eff. Sept. 1, 1997.

Sections 158.012-158.100 reserved for expansion

SUBCHAPTER B. PROCEDURE

FAM §158.101. APPLICABILITY OF PROCEDURE

Except as otherwise provided in this chapter, the procedure for a motion for enforcement of child support as provided in Chapter 157 applies to an action for income withholding.

History of Fam. Code §158.101: Acts 1995, 74th Leg., ch. 20, §1, eff. Apr. 20, 1995.

FAM §158.102. TIME LIMITATIONS

An order or writ for income withholding under this chapter may be issued until all current support and child support arrearages, interest, and any applicable fees and costs, including ordered attorney's fees and court costs, have been paid.

History of Fam. Code §158.102: Acts 1995, 74th Leg., ch. 20, §1, eff. Apr. 20, 1995. Amended by Acts 1997, 75th Leg., ch. 911, §40, eff. Sept. 1, 1997; Acts 1999, 76th Leg., ch. 556, §23, eff. Sept. 1, 1999. Source: Former Fam. Code §14.43(r).

See also ***O'Connor's Texas Family Law Handbook*** (2017), "When to file," ch. 10-D, §3.2.2, p. 1137.

ANNOTATIONS

In re A.D., 73 S.W.3d 244, 246 (Tex.2002). "Like an order holding the obligor in contempt, a wage-withhold-

ing order is available to remedy past violations of a support order whether or not the court has reduced the delinquent amount to a single, cumulative judgment. *At 246 n.1:* A cumulative judgment for past-due child support increases the available enforcement methods, however, because such cumulative judgments are also enforceable 'by any means available for the enforcement of judgments for debts.' *At 249:* [S]tatutes providing time limits within which enforcement of an existing support liability may be effected concern the court's continuing enforcement jurisdiction and do not affect substantive rights."

Packard v. Davis, No. 2-08-022-CV (Tex.App.—Fort Worth 2008, no pet.) (memo op.; 11-13-08). "The trial court ... signed an enforcement order and an order for wage withholding under ch. 158[, but] it did not render a cumulative judgment for past-due child support.... [S]ection 158.102 ... contains no express deadline on the trial court's jurisdiction to enter an order that provides for income withholding and authorizes the entry of such an order 'until all current support and child support arrearages, interest, and any applicable fees and costs have been paid.' We thus hold that, based on the plain language of ... §158.102, the trial court possessed jurisdiction to sign an enforcement order and to order wage withholding. ... Thus, the trial court also had jurisdiction to award interest, attorney's fees, and costs. [¶] [When mother] filed her countermotion to enforce, the trial court had lost jurisdiction to enforce any past due child support payments owed ... via a money judgment. The trial court had not, however, lost jurisdiction to enforce past due child support via a wage withholding order. When entering such an order, the trial court is not required to also order wage withholding for attorney's fees. Consequently, even if the trial court erred or abused its discretion by ordering that each party bear his or her own attorney's fees, no harm occurred here because the trial court possessed discretion in any event to not include attorney's fees in the ordered wage withholding...."

FAM §158.103. CONTENTS OF ORDER OR WRIT OF WITHHOLDING

An order of withholding or writ of withholding issued under this chapter must contain the information required by the forms prescribed by the Title IV-D agency under Section 158.106.

History of Fam. Code §158.103: Acts 1995, 74th Leg., ch. 20, §1, eff. Apr. 20, 1995. Amended by Acts 1997, 75th Leg., ch. 911, §41, eff. Sept. 1, 1997; Acts 1999, 76th Leg., ch. 556, §23, eff. Sept. 1, 1999; Acts 2001, 77th Leg., ch. 1023, §36, eff. Sept. 1, 2001. Source: Former Fam. Code §14.43(e).

FAM §158.104. REQUEST FOR ISSUANCE OF ORDER OR JUDICIAL WRIT OF WITHHOLDING

A request for issuance of an order or judicial writ of withholding may be filed with the clerk of the court by the prosecuting attorney, the Title IV-D agency, the friend of the court, a domestic relations office, the obligor, the obligee, or an attorney representing the obligee or obligor.

History of Fam. Code §158.104: Acts 1995, 74th Leg., ch. 20, §1, eff. Apr. 20, 1995. Amended by Acts 1997, 75th Leg., ch. 702, §6, eff. Sept. 1, 1997; Acts 1999, 76th Leg., ch. 556, §23, eff. Sept. 1, 1999. Source: Former Fam. Code §14.43(g).

FAM §158.105. ISSUANCE & DELIVERY OF ORDER OR JUDICIAL WRIT OF WITHHOLDING

(a) On filing a request for issuance of an order or judicial writ of withholding, the clerk of the court shall cause a certified copy of the order or writ to be delivered to the obligor's current employer or to any subsequent employer of the obligor.

(b) The clerk shall issue and deliver the certified copy of the order or judicial writ not later than the fourth working day after the date the order is signed or the request is filed, whichever is later.

(c) An order or judicial writ of withholding shall be delivered to the employer by first class mail or, if requested, by certified or registered mail, return receipt requested, by electronic transmission, including electronic mail or facsimile transmission, or by service of citation to:

(1) the person authorized to receive service of process for the employer in civil cases generally; or

(2) a person designated by the employer, by written notice to the clerk, to receive orders or writs of withholding.

(d) The clerk may deliver an order or judicial writ of withholding under Subsection (c) by electronic mail if the employer has an electronic mail address or by facsimile transmission if the employer is capable of receiving documents transmitted in that manner. If delivery is accomplished by electronic mail, the clerk must request acknowledgment of receipt from the employer or use an electronic mail system with a read receipt capability. If delivery is accomplished by facsimile transmission, the clerk's facsimile machine must create a delivery confirmation report.

History of Fam. Code §158.105: Acts 1995, 74th Leg., ch. 20, §1, eff. Apr. 20, 1995. Amended by Acts 1997, 75th Leg., ch. 702, §7, eff. Sept. 1, 1997; Acts 1999, 76th Leg., ch. 556, §24, eff. Sept. 1, 1999; Acts 2001, 77th Leg., ch. 1023, §37, eff. Sept. 1, 2001; Acts 2005, 79th Leg., ch. 1113, §1, eff. Sept. 1, 2005. Source: Former Fam. Code §14.43(g), (h).

See also *O'Connor's Texas Family Law Handbook* (2017), "Delivery of writ," ch. 10-D, §3.6.4, p. 1140.

FAM §158.106. REQUIRED FORMS FOR INCOME WITHHOLDING

(a) The Title IV-D agency shall prescribe forms as required by federal law in a standard format entitled order or notice to withhold income for child support under this chapter.

(b) The Title IV-D agency shall make the required forms available to obligors, obligees, domestic relations offices, friends of the court, clerks of the court, and private attorneys.

(c) The Title IV-D agency may prescribe additional forms for the efficient collection of child support from earnings and to promote the administration of justice for all parties.

(d) The forms prescribed by the Title IV-D agency under this section shall be used:

(1) for an order or judicial writ of income withholding under this chapter; and

(2) to request voluntary withholding under Section 158.011.

History of Fam. Code §158.106: Acts 1995, 74th Leg., ch. 20, §1, eff. Apr. 20, 1995. Amended by Acts 1997, 75th Leg., ch. 911, §42, eff. Sept. 1, 1997; Acts 1999, 76th Leg., ch. 556, §25, eff. Sept. 1, 1999; Acts 2001, 77th Leg., ch. 1023, §38, eff. Sept. 1, 2001; Acts 2013, 83rd Leg., ch. 742, §6, eff. Sept. 1, 2013. Source: Former Fam. Code §§14.43(p), 14.44(f), 14.45(g).

See also 1 T.A.C. §§55.111-55.119.

FAM §158.107. REPEALED

Repealed by Acts 1997, 75th Leg., ch. 911, §97(a), eff. Sept. 1, 1997.

Sections 158.108-158.200 reserved for expansion

SUBCHAPTER C. RIGHTS & DUTIES OF EMPLOYER

FAM §158.201. ORDER OR WRIT BINDING ON EMPLOYER

(a) An employer required to withhold income from earnings is not entitled to notice of the proceedings before the order is rendered or writ of withholding is issued.

(b) An order or writ of withholding is binding on an employer regardless of whether the employer is specifically named in the order or writ.

History of Fam. Code §158.201: Acts 1995, 74th Leg., ch. 20, §1, eff. Apr. 20, 1995. Amended by Acts 1997, 75th Leg., ch. 911, §43, eff. Sept. 1, 1997. Source: Former Fam. Code §14.316.

See also *O'Connor's Texas Family Law Handbook* (2017), "Wage-Withholding Order – Employer Duties, Rights & Liabilities," ch. 4-F, §19, p. 565.

FAM §158.202. EFFECTIVE DATE OF & DURATION OF WITHHOLDING

An employer shall begin to withhold income in accordance with an order or writ of withholding not later than the first pay period following the date on which the order or writ was delivered to the employer and shall continue to withhold income as required by the order or writ as long as the obligor is employed by the employer.

History of Fam. Code §158.202: Acts 1995, 74th Leg., ch. 20, §1, eff. Apr. 20, 1995. Amended by Acts 1997, 75th Leg., ch. 911, §44, eff. Sept. 1, 1997. Source: Former Fam. Code §14.43(h).

FAM §158.203. REMITTING WITHHELD PAYMENTS

(a) The employer shall remit the amount to be withheld to the person or office named in the order or writ on each pay date. The payment must include the date on which the withholding occurred.

(b) An employer with 50 or more employees shall remit a payment required under this section by electronic funds transfer or electronic data interchange not later than the second business day after the pay date.

(b-1) An employer with fewer than 50 employees may remit a payment required under this section by electronic funds transfer or electronic data interchange. A payment remitted by the employer electronically must be remitted not later than the date specified by Subsection (b).

(c) The employer shall include with each payment transmitted:

(1) the number assigned by the Title IV-D agency, if available, and the county identification number, if available;

(2) the name of the county or the county's federal information processing standard code;

(3) the cause number of the suit under which withholding is required;

(4) the payor's name and social security number; and

(5) the payee's name and, if available, social security number, unless the payment is transmitted by electronic funds transfer.

(d) In a case in which an obligor's income is subject to withholding, the employer shall remit the payment of child support directly to the state disbursement unit.

(e) The state disbursement unit may impose on an employer described by Subsection (b) a payment processing surcharge in an amount of not more than $25 for each remittance made on behalf of an employee that is not made by electronic funds transfer or electronic data exchange. The payment processing surcharge un-

der this subsection may not be charged against the employee or taken from amounts withheld from the employee's wages.

(f) The state disbursement unit shall:

(1) notify an employer described by Subsection (b) who fails to remit withheld income by electronic funds transfer or electronic data exchange that the employer is subject to a payment processing surcharge under Subsection (e); and

(2) inform the employer of the amount of the surcharge owed and the manner in which the surcharge is required to be paid to the unit.

History of Fam. Code §158.203: Acts 1995, 74th Leg., ch. 20, §1, eff. Apr. 20, 1995. Amended by Acts 1997, 75th Leg., ch. 702, §8, eff. Jan. 1, 1998; Acts 1999, 76th Leg., ch. 556, §26, eff. Sept. 1, 1999; Acts 2009, 81st Leg., ch. 767, §19, eff. Sept. 1, 2009; Acts 2011, 82nd Leg., ch. 508, §9, eff. Sept. 1, 2011; Acts 2013, 83rd Leg., ch. 742, §7, eff. Sept. 1, 2013. Source: Former Fam. Code §14.43(h).

FAM §158.204. EMPLOYER MAY DEDUCT FEE FROM EARNINGS

An employer may deduct an administrative fee of not more than $10 each month from the obligor's disposable earnings in addition to the amount to be withheld as child support.

History of Fam. Code §158.204: Acts 1995, 74th Leg., ch. 20, §1, eff. Apr. 20, 1995. Amended by Acts 1999, 76th Leg., ch. 859, §1, eff. Sept. 1, 1999. Source: Former Fam. Code §14.43(i).

FAM §158.205. HEARING REQUESTED BY EMPLOYER

(a) Not later than the 20th day after the date an order or writ of withholding is delivered, the employer may, as appropriate, file a motion with the court or file a request with the Title IV-D agency for a hearing on the applicability of the order or writ to the employer. The Title IV-D agency by rule shall establish procedures for an agency hearing under this section.

(b) The hearing under this section shall be held not later than the 15th day after the date the motion or request was made.

(c) An order or writ of withholding remains binding and payments shall continue to be made pending further order of the court or, in the case of an administrative writ, action of the Title IV-D agency.

History of Fam. Code §158.205: Acts 1995, 74th Leg., ch. 20, §1, eff. Apr. 20, 1995. Amended by Acts 1997, 75th Leg., ch. 911, §45, eff. Sept. 1, 1997. Source: Former Fam. Code §14.43(d), (j).

See also 1 T.A.C. §55.115.

FAM §158.206. LIABILITY & OBLIGATION OF EMPLOYER; WORKERS' COMPENSATION CLAIMS[1]

(a) An employer receiving an order or a writ of withholding under this chapter, including an order or writ directing that health insurance be provided to a child, who complies with the order or writ is not liable to the obligor for the amount of income withheld and paid as required by the order or writ.

(b) An employer receiving an order or writ of withholding who does not comply with the order or writ is liable:

(1) to the obligee for the amount not paid in compliance with the order or writ, including the amount the obligor is required to pay for health insurance under Chapter 154;

(2) to the obligor for:

(A) the amount withheld and not paid as required by the order or writ; and

(B) an amount equal to the interest that accrues under Section 157.265 on the amount withheld and not paid; and

(3) for reasonable attorney's fees and court costs.

(c) If an obligor has filed a claim for workers' compensation, the obligor's employer shall send a copy of the income withholding order or writ to the insurance carrier with whom the claim has been filed in order to continue the ordered withholding of income.

1. **Editor's note:** In 2015, the Legislature amended §158.206 to require dental support for a child subject to a child-support order, but the amendments are not effective until Sept. 1, 2018. For the text of the prospective amendments, see Acts 2015, 84th Leg., ch. 1150, §31, eff. Sept. 1, 2018.

History of Fam. Code §158.206: Acts 1995, 74th Leg., ch. 20, §1, eff. Apr. 20, 1995. Amended by Acts 1995, 74th Leg., ch. 341, §4.07, eff. Sept. 1, 1995; Acts 1997, 75th Leg., ch. 911, §46, eff. Sept. 1, 1997; Acts 1999, 76th Leg., ch. 859, §2 (eff. Sept. 1, 1999), ch. 1580, §1 (eff. Sept. 1, 1999); Acts 2001, 77th Leg., ch. 1023, §39, eff. Sept. 1, 2001. Source: Former Fam. Code §14.43(*l*).

FAM §158.207. EMPLOYER RECEIVING MORE THAN ONE ORDER OR WRIT

(a) An employer receiving two or more orders or writs for one obligor shall comply with each order or writ to the extent possible.

(b) If the total amount due under the orders or writs exceeds the maximum amount allowed to be withheld under Section 158.009, the employer shall pay an equal amount towards the current support in each order or writ until the employer has complied fully with each current support obligation and, thereafter, equal amounts on the arrearages until the employer has complied with each order or writ, or until the maximum total amount of allowed withholding is reached, whichever occurs first.

(c) An employer who receives more than one order or writ of withholding that combines withholding for

child support and spousal maintenance as provided by Section 8.101 shall withhold income and pay the amount withheld in accordance with Section 8.207.

History of Fam. Code §158.207: Acts 1995, 74th Leg., ch. 20, §1, eff. Apr. 20, 1995. Amended by Acts 1997, 75th Leg., ch. 911, §47, eff. Sept. 1, 1997; Acts 2001, 77th Leg., ch. 807, §2, eff. Sept. 1, 2001. Source: Former Fam. Code §14.43(*l*).

FAM §158.208. EMPLOYER MAY COMBINE AMOUNTS WITHHELD

An employer required to withhold from more than one obligor may combine the amounts withheld and make a single payment to each agency designated if the employer separately identifies the amount of the payment that is attributable to each obligor.

History of Fam. Code §158.208: Acts 1995, 74th Leg., ch. 20, §1, eff. Apr. 20, 1995. Source: Former Fam. Code §14.43(*l*).

FAM §158.209. EMPLOYER'S PENALTY FOR DISCRIMINATORY HIRING OR DISCHARGE

(a) An employer may not use an order or writ of withholding as grounds in whole or part for the termination of employment or for any other disciplinary action against an employee.

(b) An employer may not refuse to hire an employee because of an order or writ of withholding.

(c) If an employer intentionally discharges an employee in violation of this section, the employer continues to be liable to the employee for current wages and other benefits and for reasonable attorney's fees and court costs incurred in enforcing the employee's rights as provided in this section.

(d) An action under this section may be brought by the employee, a friend of the court, the domestic relations office, or the Title IV-D agency.

History of Fam. Code §158.209: Acts 1995, 74th Leg., ch. 20, §1, eff. Apr. 20, 1995. Amended by Acts 1997, 75th Leg., ch. 911, §48, eff. Sept. 1, 1997. Source: Former Fam. Code §14.43(m).

FAM §158.210. FINE FOR NONCOMPLIANCE

(a) In addition to the civil remedies provided by this subchapter or any other remedy provided by law, an employer who knowingly violates the provisions of this chapter may be subject to a fine not to exceed $200 for each occurrence in which the employer fails to:

(1) withhold income for child support as instructed in an order or writ issued under this chapter; or

(2) remit withheld income within the time required by Section 158.203 to the payee identified in the order or writ or to the state disbursement unit.

(b) A fine recovered under this section shall be paid to the county in which the obligee resides and shall be used by the county to improve child support services.

History of Fam. Code §158.210: Acts 1995, 74th Leg., ch. 20, §1, eff. Apr. 20, 1995. Amended by Acts 1997, 75th Leg., ch. 420, §15, eff. Sept. 1, 1997; Acts 1999, 76th Leg., ch. 556, §27, eff. Sept. 1, 1999. Source: Former Fam. Code §14.43(n).

FAM §158.211. NOTICE OF TERMINATION OF EMPLOYMENT & OF NEW EMPLOYMENT

(a) If an obligor terminates employment with an employer who has been withholding income, both the obligor and the employer shall notify the court or the Title IV-D agency and the obligee of that fact not later than the seventh day after the date employment terminated and shall provide the obligor's last known address and the name and address of the obligor's new employer, if known.

(b) The obligor has a continuing duty to inform any subsequent employer of the order or writ of withholding after obtaining employment.

History of Fam. Code §158.211: Acts 1995, 74th Leg., ch. 20, §1, eff. Apr. 20, 1995. Amended by Acts 1999, 76th Leg., ch. 556, §28, eff. Sept. 1, 1999. Source: Former Fam. Code §14.43(o).

FAM §158.212. IMPROPER PAYMENT

An employer who remits a payment to an incorrect office or person shall remit the payment to the agency or person identified in the order of withholding not later than the second business day after the date the employer receives the returned payment.

History of Fam. Code §158.212: Acts 1999, 76th Leg., ch. 556, §29, eff. Sept. 1, 1999.

FAM §158.213. WITHHOLDING FROM WORKERS' COMPENSATION BENEFITS

(a) An insurance carrier that receives an order or writ of withholding under Section 158.206 for workers' compensation benefits payable to an obligor shall withhold an amount not to exceed the maximum amount allowed to be withheld from income under Section 158.009 regardless of whether the benefits payable to the obligor for lost income are paid as lump sum amounts or as periodic payments.

(b) An insurance carrier subject to this section shall send the amount withheld for child support to the place of payment designated in the order or writ of withholding.

History of Fam. Code §158.213: Acts 2003, 78th Leg., ch. 610, §9, eff. Sept. 1, 2003.

FAM §158.214. WITHHOLDING FROM SEVERANCE PAY

(a) In this section, "severance pay" means income paid on termination of employment in addition to the employee's usual earnings from the employer at the time of termination.

(b) An employer receiving an order or writ of withholding under this chapter shall withhold from any severance pay owed an obligor an amount equal to the amount the employer would have withheld under the order or writ if the severance pay had been paid as the obligor's usual earnings as a current employee.

(c) The total amount that may be withheld under this section is subject to the maximum amount allowed to be withheld under Section 158.009.

History of Fam. Code §158.214: Acts 2007, 80th Leg., ch. 972, §33, eff. Sept. 1, 2007.

FAM §158.215. WITHHOLDING FROM LUMP-SUM PAYMENTS

(a) In this section, "lump-sum payment" means income in the form of a bonus or an amount paid in lieu of vacation or other leave time. The term does not include an employee's usual earnings or an amount paid as severance pay on termination of employment.

(b) This section applies only to an employer who receives an administrative writ of withholding in a Title IV-D case.

(c) An employer to whom this section applies may not make a lump-sum payment to the obligor in the amount of $500 or more without first notifying the Title IV-D agency to determine whether all or a portion of the payment should be applied to child support arrearages owed by the obligor.

(d) After notifying the Title IV-D agency in compliance with Subsection (c), the employer may not make the lump-sum payment before the earlier of:

(1) the 10th day after the date on which the employer notified the Title IV-D agency; or

(2) the date on which the employer receives authorization from the Title IV-D agency to make the payment.

(e) If the employer receives a timely authorization from the Title IV-D agency under Subsection (d)(2), the employer may make the payment only in accordance with the terms of that authorization.

History of Fam. Code §158.215: Acts 2007, 80th Leg., ch. 972, §34, eff. Sept. 1, 2007. Amended by Acts 2009, 81st Leg., ch. 767, §20, eff. June 19, 2009.

Sections 158.216-158.300 reserved for expansion

SUBCHAPTER D. JUDICIAL WRIT OF WITHHOLDING ISSUED BY CLERK

FAM §158.301. NOTICE OF APPLICATION FOR JUDICIAL WRIT OF WITHHOLDING; FILING

(a) A notice of application for judicial writ of withholding may be filed if:

(1) a delinquency occurs in child support payments in an amount equal to or greater than the total support due for one month; or

(2) income withholding was not ordered at the time child support was ordered.

(b) The notice of application for judicial writ of withholding may be filed in the court of continuing jurisdiction by:

(1) the Title IV-D agency;

(2) the attorney representing the local domestic relations office;

(3) the attorney appointed a friend of the court as provided in Chapter 202;

(4) the obligor or obligee; or

(5) a private attorney representing the obligor or obligee.

(c) The Title IV-D agency may in a Title IV-D case file a notice of application for judicial writ of withholding on request of the obligor or obligee.

History of Fam. Code §158.301: Acts 1995, 74th Leg., ch. 20, §1, eff. Apr. 20, 1995. Amended by Acts 1995, 74th Leg., ch. 751, §57, eff. Sept. 1, 1995; Acts 1997, 75th Leg., ch. 911, §50, eff. Sept. 1, 1997. Source: Former Fam. Code §14.44(a).

See also *O'Connor's Texas Family Law Handbook* (2017), "Judicial Writ of Withholding," ch. 10-D, §3, p. 1136.

FAM §158.302. CONTENTS OF NOTICE OF APPLICATION FOR JUDICIAL WRIT OF WITHHOLDING[1]

The notice of application for judicial writ of withholding shall be verified and:

(1) state the amount of monthly support due, including medical support, the amount of arrearages or anticipated arrearages, including accrued interest, and the amount of wages that will be withheld in accordance with a judicial writ of withholding;

(2) state that the withholding applies to each current or subsequent employer or period of employment;

(3) state that if the obligor does not contest the withholding within 10 days after the date of receipt of the notice, the obligor's employer will be notified to begin the withholding;

(4) describe the procedures for contesting the issuance and delivery of a writ of withholding;

(5) state that if the obligor contests the withholding, the obligor will be afforded an opportunity for a hearing by the court not later than the 30th day after the date of receipt of the notice of contest;

(6) state that the sole ground for successfully contesting the issuance of a writ of withholding is a dispute concerning the identity of the obligor or the existence or amount of the arrearages, including accrued interest;

(7) describe the actions that may be taken if the obligor contests the notice of application for judicial writ of withholding, including the procedures for suspending issuance of a writ of withholding; and

(8) include with the notice a suggested form for the motion to stay issuance and delivery of the judicial writ of withholding that the obligor may file with the clerk of the appropriate court.

1. **Editor's note:** In 2015, the Legislature amended §158.302 to require dental support for a child subject to a child-support order, but the amendments are not effective until Sept. 1, 2018. For the text of the prospective amendments, see Acts 2015, 84th Leg., ch. 1150, §32, eff. Sept. 1, 2018.

History of Fam. Code §158.302: Acts 1995, 74th Leg., ch. 20, §1, eff. Apr. 20, 1995. Amended by Acts 1997, 75th Leg., ch. 911, §51, eff. Sept. 1, 1997. Source: Former Fam. Code §14.44(b).

See also 1 T.A.C. §55.111; ***O'Connor's Texas Family Law Handbook*** (2017), "Contents of notice," ch. 10-D, §3.2.4, p. 1137.

FAM §158.303. INTERSTATE REQUEST FOR INCOME WITHHOLDING

(a) The registration of a foreign support order as provided in Chapter 159 is sufficient for the filing of a notice of application for judicial writ of withholding.

(b) The notice shall be filed with the clerk of the court having venue as provided in Chapter 159.

(c) Notice of application for judicial writ of withholding may be delivered to the obligor at the same time that an order is filed for registration under Chapter 159.

History of Fam. Code §158.303: Acts 1995, 74th Leg., ch. 20, §1, eff. Apr. 20, 1995. Amended by Acts 1995, 74th Leg., ch. 751, §58, eff. Sept. 1, 1995; Acts 1997, 75th Leg., ch. 911, §52, eff. Sept. 1, 1997. Source: Former Fam. Code §14.44(h).

FAM §158.304. ADDITIONAL ARREARAGES

If the notice of application for judicial writ of withholding states that the obligor has repeatedly failed to pay support in accordance with the underlying support order, the judicial writ may include arrearages that accrue between the filing of the notice and the date of the hearing or the issuance of a judicial writ of withholding.

History of Fam. Code §158.304: Acts 1995, 74th Leg., ch. 20, §1, eff. Apr. 20, 1995. Amended by Acts 1997, 75th Leg., ch. 911, §53, eff. Sept. 1, 1997. Source: Former Fam. Code §14.44(d).

FAM §158.305. REPEALED

Repealed by Acts 1997, 75th Leg., ch. 911, §97(a), eff. Sept. 1, 1997.

FAM §158.306. DELIVERY OF NOTICE OF APPLICATION FOR JUDICIAL WRIT OF WITHHOLDING; TIME OF DELIVERY

(a) A notice of application for judicial writ of withholding may be delivered to the obligor by:

(1) hand delivery by a person designated by the Title IV-D agency or local domestic relations office;

(2) first-class or certified mail, return receipt requested, addressed to the obligor's last known address or place of employment; or

(3) by service of citation as in civil cases generally.

(b) If the notice is delivered by mailing or hand delivery, the party who filed the notice shall file with the court a certificate stating the name, address, and date on which the mailing or hand delivery was made.

(c) Notice is considered to have been received by the obligor:

(1) if hand delivered, on the date of delivery;

(2) if mailed by certified mail, on the date of receipt;

(3) if mailed by first-class mail, on the 10th day after the date the notice was mailed; or

(4) if delivered by service of citation, on the date of service.

History of Fam. Code §158.306: Acts 1995, 74th Leg., ch. 20, §1, eff. Apr. 20, 1995. Amended by Acts 1997, 75th Leg., ch. 911, §54, eff. Sept. 1, 1997. Source: Former Fam. Code §14.45(a).

See also ***O'Connor's Texas Family Law Handbook*** (2017), "Delivering notice," ch. 10-D, §3.3, p. 1138.

FAM §158.307. MOTION TO STAY ISSUANCE OF WRIT OF WITHHOLDING

(a) The obligor may stay issuance of a judicial writ of withholding by filing a motion to stay with the clerk of court not later than the 10th day after the date the notice of application for judicial writ of withholding was received.

(b) The grounds for filing a motion to stay issuance are limited to a dispute concerning the identity of the obligor or the existence or the amount of the arrearages.

(c) The obligor shall verify that statements of fact in the motion to stay issuance of the writ are true and correct.

History of Fam. Code §158.307: Acts 1995, 74th Leg., ch. 20, §1, eff. Apr. 20, 1995. Amended by Acts 1997, 75th Leg., ch. 911, §55, eff. Sept. 1, 1997. Source: Former Fam. Code §14.44(c).

See also 1 T.A.C. §55.112; *O'Connor's Texas Family Law Handbook* (2017), "Motion to stay," ch. 10-D, §3.4.1, p. 1139.

ANNOTATIONS

Glass v. Williamson, 137 S.W.3d 114, 116 (Tex. App.—Houston [1st Dist.] 2004, no pet.). "Because more than 20 days elapsed from when [W] mailed the notice, she argues that the trial court was without jurisdiction to consider whether the amounts reflected in the notice of application for writ of judicial withholding were incorrect. We disagree. *At 117:* [H's] failure to adhere to the procedural requirements of [§158.307] did not divest the district court of subject matter jurisdiction, but instead, only raised the issue of whether [H] was entitled to the relief he sought. Furthermore, because only the issue of whether [H] was entitled to the relief sought was raised, [H's] right to object to [W's] failure could be waived. [¶] We hold that by failing to object to [H's] failure to comply with the procedural requirements of §158 ..., [W] waived the right to assert that [H] was not entitled to contest the amount of arrearages reflected in the notice of application for writ of judicial withholding."

FAM §158.308. EFFECT OF FILING MOTION TO STAY

The filing of a motion to stay by an obligor in the manner provided by Section 158.307 prohibits the clerk of court from delivering the judicial writ of withholding to any employer of the obligor before a hearing is held.

History of Fam. Code §158.308: Acts 1995, 74th Leg., ch. 20, §1, eff. Apr. 20, 1995. Amended by Acts 1997, 75th Leg., ch. 911, §56, eff. Sept. 1, 1997. Source: Former Fam. Code §14.44(c).

See also *O'Connor's Texas Family Law Handbook* (2017), "Motion to stay," ch. 10-D, §3.4.1, p. 1139.

FAM §158.309. HEARING ON MOTION TO STAY[1]

(a) If a motion to stay is filed in the manner provided by Section 158.307, the court shall set a hearing on the motion and the clerk of court shall notify the obligor, obligee, or their authorized representatives, and the party who filed the application for judicial writ of withholding of the date, time, and place of the hearing.

(b) The court shall hold a hearing on the motion to stay not later than the 30th day after the date the motion was filed, except that a hearing may be held later than the 30th day after filing if both the obligor and obligee agree and waive the right to have the motion heard within 30 days.

(c) Upon hearing, the court shall:

(1) render an order for income withholding that includes a determination of the amount of child support arrearages, including medical support and interest; or

(2) grant the motion to stay.

1. **Editor's note:** In 2015, the Legislature amended §158.309 to require dental support for a child subject to a child-support order, but the amendments are not effective until Sept. 1, 2018. For the text of the prospective amendments, see Acts 2015, 84th Leg., ch. 1150, §33, eff. Sept. 1, 2018.

History of Fam. Code §158.309: Acts 1995, 74th Leg., ch. 20, §1, eff. Apr. 20, 1995. Amended by Acts 1995, 74th Leg., ch. 751, §59, eff. Sept. 1, 1995; Acts 1997, 75th Leg., ch. 911, §57, eff. Sept. 1, 1997. Source: Former Fam. Code §14.44(d).

See also *O'Connor's Texas Family Law Handbook* (2017), "Hearing – motion to stay filed," ch. 10-D, §3.5, p. 1139.

ANNOTATIONS

In re R.G., 362 S.W.3d 118, 122 (Tex.App.—San Antonio 2011, pet. denied). "[T]he issue ... is ... whether [Fam. Code] §158.309 imposes a duty on the trial court to conduct the hearing or requires the obligor to request the hearing. *At 123:* [Family Code] §157.061[, which contains similar statutory language,] reveals that the Texas Legislature has drawn a distinction, at least in cases seeking to enforce child support obligations, between imposing the obligation on the trial court to set a hearing and imposing the obligation on the party to request a hearing. The language in §157.061(a) imposes a 'statutorily required ministerial duty' on the trial court to set a hearing. Given that [Fam. Code] Ch. 157 and Ch. 158 both govern child support enforcement, there is no reason for this court to conclude that the Texas Legislature did not intend to impose the same obligation on the trial court under §158.309 ... as it imposed under §157.061(a)."

FAM §158.310. SPECIAL EXCEPTIONS

(a) A defect in a notice of application for judicial writ of withholding is waived unless the respondent specially excepts in writing and cites with particularity the alleged defect, obscurity, or other ambiguity in the notice.

(b) A special exception under this section must be heard by the court before hearing the motion to stay issuance.

(c) If the court sustains an exception, the court shall provide the party filing the notice an opportunity to refile and the court shall continue the hearing to a date certain without the requirement of additional service.

History of Fam. Code §158.310: Acts 1995, 74th Leg., ch. 20, §1, eff. Apr. 20, 1995. Amended by Acts 1997, 75th Leg., ch. 911, §58, eff. Sept. 1, 1997. Source: Former Fam. Code §14.44(d).

See also ***O'Connor's Texas Family Law Handbook*** (2017), "Special exceptions," ch. 10-D, §3.4.2, p. 1139; "Rule on special exceptions," ch. 10-D, §3.5.3, p. 1139.

FAM §158.311. ARREARAGES

(a) Payment of arrearages after receipt of notice of application for judicial writ of withholding may not be the sole basis for the court to refuse to order withholding.

(b) The court shall order that a reasonable amount of income be withheld to be applied toward the liquidation of arrearages, even though a judgment confirming arrearages has been rendered against the obligor.

History of Fam. Code §158.311: Acts 1995, 74th Leg., ch. 20, §1, eff. Apr. 20, 1995. Amended by Acts 1997, 75th Leg., ch. 911, §59, eff. Sept. 1, 1997. Source: Former Fam. Code §§14.43(a)(4), 14.44(a).

FAM §158.312. REQUEST FOR ISSUANCE & DELIVERY OF WRIT OF WITHHOLDING[1]

(a) If a notice of application for judicial writ of withholding is delivered and a motion to stay is not filed within the time limits provided by Section 158.307, the party who filed the notice shall file with the clerk of the court a request for issuance of the writ of withholding stating the amount of current support, including medical support, the amount of arrearages, and the amount to be withheld from the obligor's income.

(b) The request for issuance may not be filed before the 11th day after the date of receipt of the notice of application for judicial writ of withholding by the obligor.

1. **Editor's note:** In 2015, the Legislature amended §158.312 to require dental support for a child subject to a child-support order, but the amendments are not effective until Sept. 1, 2018. For the text of the prospective amendments, see Acts 2015, 84th Leg., ch. 1150, §34, eff. Sept. 1, 2018.

History of Fam. Code §158.312: Acts 1995, 74th Leg., ch. 20, §1, eff. Apr. 20, 1995. Amended by Acts 1997, 75th Leg., ch. 911, §60, eff. Sept. 1, 1997; Acts 1999, 76th Leg., ch. 307, §30, eff. Sept. 1, 1999. Source: Former Fam. Code §14.45(a).

See also ***O'Connor's Texas Family Law Handbook*** (2017), "Issuing writ – no motion to stay filed," ch. 10-D, §3.6, p. 1140.

FAM §158.313. ISSUANCE & DELIVERY OF WRIT OF WITHHOLDING

(a) On the filing of a request for issuance of a writ of withholding, the clerk of the court shall issue the writ.

(b) The writ shall be delivered as provided by Subchapter B.

(c) The clerk shall issue and mail the writ not later than the second working day after the date the request is filed.

History of Fam. Code §158.313: Acts 1995, 74th Leg., ch. 20, §1, eff. Apr. 20, 1995. Source: Former Fam. Code §14.45(a).

See also ***O'Connor's Texas Family Law Handbook*** (2017), "Delivery of writ," ch. 10-D, §3.6.4, p. 1140.

FAM §158.314. CONTENTS OF WRIT OF WITHHOLDING[1]

The judicial writ of income withholding issued by the clerk must direct that the employer or a subsequent employer withhold from the obligor's disposable income for current child support, including medical support, and child support arrearages an amount that is consistent with the provisions of this chapter regarding orders of withholding.

1. **Editor's note:** In 2015, the Legislature amended §158.314 to require dental support for a child subject to a child-support order, but the amendments are not effective until Sept. 1, 2018. For the text of the prospective amendments, see Acts 2015, 84th Leg., ch. 1150, §35, eff. Sept. 1, 2018.

History of Fam. Code §158.314: Acts 1995, 74th Leg., ch. 20, §1, eff. Apr. 20, 1995. Amended by Acts 1997, 75th Leg., ch. 911, §61, eff. Sept. 1, 1997. Source: Former Fam. Code §14.45(b).

See also ***O'Connor's Texas Family Law Handbook*** (2017), "Contents of writ," ch. 10-D, §3.6.3, p. 1140.

FAM §158.315. EXTENSION OF REPAYMENT SCHEDULE BY PARTY; UNREASONABLE HARDSHIP

If the party who filed the notice of application for judicial writ of withholding finds that the schedule for repaying arrearages would cause the obligor, the obligor's family, or the children for whom the support is due from the obligor to suffer unreasonable hardship, the party may extend the payment period in the writ.

History of Fam. Code §158.315: Acts 1995, 74th Leg., ch. 20, §1, eff. Apr. 20, 1995. Amended by Acts 1997, 75th Leg., ch. 911, §62, eff. Sept. 1, 1997. Source: Former Fam. Code §14.45(c).

See also ***O'Connor's Texas Family Law Handbook*** (2017), "Extension of repayment schedule," ch. 10-D, §3.6.3(2), p. 1140.

FAM §158.316. PAYMENT OF AMOUNT TO BE WITHHELD

The amount to be withheld shall be paid to the person or office named in the writ on each pay date and shall include with the payment the date on which the withholding occurred.

History of Fam. Code §158.316: Acts 1995, 74th Leg., ch. 20, §1, eff. Apr. 20, 1995. Source: Former Fam. Code §14.45(a).

FAM §158.317. FAILURE TO RECEIVE NOTICE OF APPLICATION FOR JUDICIAL WRIT OF WITHHOLDING

(a) Not later than the 30th day after the date of the first pay period following the date of delivery of the writ of withholding to the obligor's employer, the obligor may file an affidavit with the court that a motion to stay was not timely filed because the notice of application for judicial writ of withholding was not received by the obligor and that grounds exist for a motion to stay.

(b) Concurrently with the filing of the affidavit, the obligor may file a motion to withdraw the writ of withholding and request a hearing on the applicability of the writ.

(c) Income withholding may not be interrupted until after the hearing at which the court renders an order denying or modifying withholding.

History of Fam. Code §158.317: Acts 1995, 74th Leg., ch. 20, §1, eff. Apr. 20, 1995. Amended by Acts 1997, 75th Leg., ch. 911, §63, eff. Sept. 1, 1997. Source: Former Fam. Code §14.44(e).

See also ***O'Connor's Texas Family Law Handbook*** (2017), "Motion to withdraw writ," ch. 10-D, §3.8, p. 1141.

Section 158.318 reserved for expansion

FAM §158.319. ISSUANCE & DELIVERY OF JUDICIAL WRIT OF WITHHOLDING TO SUBSEQUENT EMPLOYER

(a) After the issuance of a judicial writ of withholding by the clerk, a party authorized to file a notice of application for judicial writ of withholding under this subchapter may issue the judicial writ of withholding to a subsequent employer of the obligor by delivering to the employer by certified mail a copy of the writ.

(b) The judicial writ of withholding must include the name, address, and signature of the party and clearly indicate that the writ is being issued to a subsequent employer.

(c) The party shall file a copy of the judicial writ of withholding with the clerk not later than the third working day following delivery of the writ to the subsequent employer. The party shall pay the clerk a fee of $15 at the time the copy of the writ is filed.

(d) The party shall file the postal return receipt from the delivery to the subsequent employer not later than the third working day after the party receives the receipt.

History of Fam. Code §158.319: Acts 1995, 74th Leg., ch. 751, §60, eff. Sept. 1, 1995. Amended by Acts 1997, 75th Leg., ch. 911, §64, eff. Sept. 1, 1997.

Sections 158.320-158.400 reserved for expansion

SUBCHAPTER E. MODIFICATION, REDUCTION, OR TERMINATION OF WITHHOLDING

FAM §158.401. MODIFICATIONS TO OR TERMINATION OF WITHHOLDING BY TITLE IV-D AGENCY

(a) The Title IV-D agency shall establish procedures for the reduction in the amount of or termination of withholding from income on the liquidation of an arrearages or the termination of the obligation of support in Title IV-D cases. The procedures shall provide that the payment of overdue support may not be used as the sole basis for terminating withholding.

(b) At the request of the Title IV-D agency, the clerk of the court shall issue a judicial writ of withholding to the obligor's employer reflecting any modification or changes in the amount to be withheld or the termination of withholding.

History of Fam. Code §158.401: Acts 1995, 74th Leg., ch. 20, §1, eff. Apr. 20, 1995. Amended by Acts 1997, 75th Leg., ch. 911, §65, eff. Sept. 1, 1997. Source: Former Fam. Code §§14.43(q), 14.45(f).

FAM §158.402. AGREEMENT BY PARTIES REGARDING AMOUNT OR DURATION OF WITHHOLDING

(a) An obligor and obligee may agree on a reduction in or termination of income withholding for child support on the occurrence of one of the following contingencies stated in the order:

(1) the child becomes 18 years of age or is graduated from high school, whichever is later;

(2) the child's disabilities of minority are removed by marriage, court order, or other operation of law; or

(3) the child dies.

(b) The obligor and obligee may file a notarized or acknowledged request with the clerk of the court under Section 158.011 for a revised judicial writ of withholding, including the termination of withholding.

(c) The clerk shall issue and deliver to an employer of the obligor a judicial writ of withholding that reflects the agreed revision or termination of withholding.

(d) An agreement by the parties under this section does not modify the terms of a support order.

History of Fam. Code §158.402: Acts 1995, 74th Leg., ch. 751, §61, eff. Sept. 1, 1995. Amended by Acts 1997, 75th Leg., ch. 911, §66, eff. Sept. 1, 1997.

FAM §158.403. MODIFICATIONS TO OR TERMINATION OF WITHHOLDING IN VOLUNTARY WITHHOLDING CASES

(a) If an obligor initiates voluntary withholding under Section 158.011, the obligee or an agency providing child support services may file with the clerk of the court a notarized request signed by the obligor and the obligee or agency, as appropriate, for the issuance and delivery to the obligor of a:

(1) modified writ of withholding that reduces the amount of withholding; or

(2) notice of termination of withholding.

(b) On receipt of a request under this section, the clerk shall issue and deliver a modified writ of with-

holding or notice of termination in the manner provided by Section 158.402.

(c) The clerk may charge a reasonable fee not to exceed $15 for filing the request.

(d) An obligee may contest a modified writ of withholding or notice of termination issued under this section by requesting a hearing in the manner provided by Section 158.309 not later than the 180th day after the date the obligee discovers that the writ or notice has been issued.

History of Fam. Code §158.403: Acts 1995, 74th Leg., ch. 751, §61, eff. Sept. 1, 1995.

FAM §158.404. DELIVERY OF ORDER OF REDUCTION OR TERMINATION OF WITHHOLDING

If a court has rendered an order that reduces the amount of child support to be withheld or terminates withholding for child support, any person or governmental entity may deliver to the employer a certified copy of the order without the requirement that the clerk of the court deliver the order.

History of Fam. Code §158.404: Acts 1995, 74th Leg., ch. 20, §1, eff. Apr. 20, 1995. Renumbered from §158.402 by Acts 1995, 74th Leg., ch. 751, §61, eff. Sept. 1, 1995. Source: Former Fam. Code §14.43(q).

FAM §158.405. LIABILITY OF EMPLOYERS

The provisions of this chapter regarding the liability of employers for withholding apply to an order that reduces or terminates withholding.

History of Fam. Code §158.405: Acts 1995, 74th Leg., ch. 20, §1, eff. Apr. 20, 1995. Renumbered from §158.403 by Acts 1995, 74th Leg., ch. 751, §61, eff. Sept. 1, 1995. Source: Former Fam. Code §14.43(q).

Sections 158.406-158.500 blank

SUBCHAPTER F. ADMINISTRATIVE WRIT OF WITHHOLDING

FAM §158.501. ISSUANCE OF ADMINISTRATIVE WRIT OF WITHHOLDING

(a) The Title IV-D agency may initiate income withholding by issuing an administrative writ of withholding for the enforcement of an existing order as authorized by this subchapter.

(b) Except as provided by Subsection (d), the Title IV-D agency is the only entity that may issue an administrative writ under this subchapter.

(c) The Title IV-D agency may use the procedures authorized by this subchapter to enforce a support order rendered by a tribunal of another state regardless of whether the order has been registered under Chapter 159.

(d) A domestic relations office may issue an administrative writ of withholding under this chapter in a proceeding in which the office is providing child support enforcement services. A reference in this code to the Title IV-D agency that relates to an administrative writ includes a domestic relations office, except that the writ must be in the form prescribed by the Title IV-D agency under Section 158.504.

History of Fam. Code §158.501: Acts 1997, 75th Leg., ch. 911, §67, eff. Sept. 1, 1997. Amended by Acts 1999, 76th Leg., ch. 556, §31, eff. Sept. 1, 1999; Acts 2001, 77th Leg., ch. 1023, §40, eff. Sept. 1, 2001; Acts 2005, 79th Leg., ch. 199, §§2-4, eff. Sept. 1, 2005.

See also ***O'Connor's Texas Family Law Handbook*** (2017), "Administrative Writ of Withholding," ch. 10-D, §4, p. 1141.

ANNOTATIONS

Attorney Gen. v. Redding, 60 S.W.3d 891, 895 (Tex.App.—Dallas 2001, no pet.). "Section 158.501(a) provides 'the [AG] may initiate income withholding by issuing an administrative writ of withholding for the enforcement of an existing order as authorized by this subchapter.' [Obligor] asserts an 'existing order' is limited to (1) a current support order, (2) an order holding an obligor in contempt, or (3) a *judgment* confirming arrearages. [Obligor] concludes that because the trial court lost jurisdiction to enter a judgment for arrearages, and such a judgment is a prerequisite to an administrative writ for arrears, the trial court properly withdrew the writ. The [AG] responds the definition of 'existing' order is not so limited and includes any enforceable order for support, including a child support order in which arrearages remain due. We agree with the [AG]."

FAM §158.502. WHEN ADMINISTRATIVE WRIT OF WITHHOLDING MAY BE ISSUED[1]

(a) An administrative writ of withholding under this subchapter may be issued by the Title IV-D agency at any time until all current support, including medical support, and child support arrearages, and Title IV-D service fees authorized under Section 231.103 for which the obligor is responsible, have been paid. The writ issued under this subsection may be based on an obligation in more than one support order.

(b) The Title IV-D agency may issue an administrative writ of withholding that directs that an amount be withheld for an arrearage or adjusts the amount to be withheld for an arrearage. An administrative writ issued under this subsection may be contested as provided by Section 158.506.

(c) The Title IV-D agency may issue an administrative writ of withholding as a reissuance of an existing withholding order on file with the court of continuing jurisdiction or a tribunal of another state. The administrative writ under this subsection is not subject to the contest provisions of Sections 158.505(a)(2) and 158.506.

(d) The Title IV-D agency may issue an administrative writ of withholding to direct child support payments to the state disbursement unit of another state.

1. **Editor's note:** In 2015, the Legislature amended §158.502 to require dental support for a child subject to a child-support order, but the amendments are not effective until Sept. 1, 2018. For the text of the prospective amendments, see Acts 2015, 84th Leg., ch. 1150, §36, eff. Sept. 1, 2018.

History of Fam. Code §158.502: Acts 1997, 75th Leg., ch. 911, §67, eff. Sept. 1, 1997. Amended by Acts 1999, 76th Leg., ch. 556, §31, eff. Sept. 1, 1999; Acts 2001, 77th Leg., ch. 1023, §41, eff. Sept. 1, 2001; Acts 2003, 78th Leg., ch. 1247, §2, eff. Sept. 1, 2003; Acts 2007, 80th Leg., ch. 972, §35, eff. Sept. 1, 2007.

See also ***O'Connor's Texas Family Law Handbook*** (2017), "Grounds," ch. 10-D, §4.1, p. 1141.

ANNOTATIONS

In re A.D., 73 S.W.3d 244, 246 (Tex.2002). See annotation under Family Code §158.102, p. 653.

FAM §158.503. DELIVERY OF ADMINISTRATIVE WRIT TO EMPLOYER; FILING WITH COURT OR MAINTAINING RECORD

(a) An administrative writ of withholding issued under this subchapter may be delivered to an employer by mail or by electronic transmission.

(b) The Title IV-D agency shall:

(1) not later than the third business day after the date of delivery of the administrative writ of withholding to an employer, file a copy of the writ, together with a signed certificate of service, in the court of continuing jurisdiction; or

(2) maintain a record of the writ until all support obligations of the obligor have been satisfied or income withholding has been terminated as provided by this chapter.

(b-1) The certificate of service required under Subsection (b)(1) may be signed electronically.

(c) The copy of the administrative writ of withholding filed with the clerk of court must include:

(1) the name, address, and signature of the authorized attorney or individual that issued the writ;

(2) the name and address of the employer served with the writ; and

(3) a true copy of the information provided to the employer.

(d) The clerk of the court may charge a reasonable fee not to exceed $15 for filing an administrative writ under this section.

History of Fam. Code §158.503: Acts 1997, 75th Leg., ch. 911, §67, eff. Sept. 1, 1997. Amended by Acts 1999, 76th Leg., ch. 556, §32, eff. Sept. 1, 1999; Acts 2001, 77th Leg., ch. 116, §1 (eff. Sept. 1, 2001), ch. 1023, §42 (eff. Sept. 1, 2001); Acts 2011, 82nd Leg., ch. 508, §§10, 11, eff. Sept. 1, 2011.

See also ***O'Connor's Texas Family Law Handbook*** (2017), "Delivering writ to employer," ch. 10-D, §4.3, p. 1142; "Filing or maintaining writ," ch. 10-D, §4.4, p. 1142.

FAM §158.504. CONTENTS OF ADMINISTRATIVE WRIT OF WITHHOLDING[1]

(a) The administrative writ of withholding must be in the form prescribed by the Title IV-D agency as required by this chapter and in a standard format authorized by the United States Department of Health and Human Services.

(b) An administrative writ of withholding issued under this subchapter may contain only the information that is necessary for the employer to withhold income for child support and medical support and shall specify the place where the withheld income is to be paid.

1. **Editor's note:** In 2015, the Legislature amended §158.504 to require dental support for a child subject to a child-support order, but the amendments are not effective until Sept. 1, 2018. For the text of the prospective amendments, see Acts 2015, 84th Leg., ch. 1150, §37, eff. Sept. 1, 2018.

History of Fam. Code §158.504: Acts 1997, 75th Leg., ch. 911, §67, eff. Sept. 1, 1997. Amended by Acts 1999, 76th Leg., ch. 556, §33, eff. Sept. 1, 1999; Acts 2001, 77th Leg., ch. 1023, §43, eff. Sept. 1, 2001.

See also ***O'Connor's Texas Family Law Handbook*** (2017), "Contents of writ," ch. 10-D, §4.2.2, p. 1142.

FAM §158.505. NOTICE TO OBLIGOR

(a) On issuance of an administrative writ of withholding, the Title IV-D agency shall send the obligor:

(1) notice that the withholding has commenced, including, if the writ is issued as provided by Section 158.502(b), the amount of the arrearages, including accrued interest;

(2) except as provided by Section 158.502(c), notice of the procedures to follow if the obligor desires to contest withholding on the grounds that the identity of the obligor or the existence or amount of arrearages is incorrect; and

(3) a copy of the administrative writ, including the information concerning income withholding provided to the employer.

(b) The notice required under this section may be sent to the obligor by:

(1) personal delivery by a person designated by the Title IV-D agency;

(2) first-class mail or certified mail, return receipt requested, addressed to the obligor's last known address; or

(3) service of citation as in civil cases generally.

(c) Repealed by Acts 1999, 76th Leg., ch. 556, §81, eff. Sept. 1, 1999.

History of Fam. Code §158.505: Acts 1997, 75th Leg., ch. 911, §67, eff. Sept. 1, 1997. Amended by Acts 1999, 76th Leg., ch. 556, §§34, 81, eff. Sept. 1, 1999; Acts 2001, 77th Leg., ch. 1023, §44, eff. Sept. 1, 2001.

See also *O'Connor's Texas Family Law Handbook* (2017), "Notice to obligor," ch. 10-D, §4.5, p. 1142.

FAM §158.506. CONTEST BY OBLIGOR TO ADMINISTRATIVE WRIT OF WITHHOLDING

(a) Except as provided by Section 158.502(c), an obligor receiving the notice under Section 158.505 may request a review by the Title IV-D agency to resolve any issue in dispute regarding the identity of the obligor or the existence or amount of arrearages. The Title IV-D agency shall provide an opportunity for a review, by telephonic conference or in person, as may be appropriate under the circumstances.

(b) After a review under this section, the Title IV-D agency may issue a new administrative writ of withholding to the employer, including a writ modifying the amount to be withheld or terminating withholding.

(c) If a review under this section fails to resolve any issue in dispute, the obligor may file a motion with the court to withdraw the administrative writ of withholding and request a hearing with the court not later than the 30th day after receiving notice of the agency's determination. Income withholding may not be interrupted pending a hearing by the court.

(d) If an administrative writ of withholding issued under this subchapter is based on an order of a tribunal of another state that has not been registered under Chapter 159, the obligor may file a motion with an appropriate court in accordance with Subsection (c).

History of Fam. Code §158.506: Acts 1997, 75th Leg., ch. 911, §67, eff. Sept. 1, 1997. Amended by Acts 1999, 76th Leg., ch. 556, §35, eff. Sept. 1, 1999; Acts 2007, 80th Leg., ch. 972, §36, eff. Sept. 1, 2007.

See also *O'Connor's Texas Family Law Handbook* (2017), "Contesting writ," ch. 10-D, §4.6, p. 1143.

FAM §158.507. ADMINISTRATIVE WRIT TERMINATING WITHHOLDING[1]

An administrative writ to terminate withholding may be issued and delivered to an employer by the Title IV-D agency when all current support, including medical support, and child support arrearages, and Title IV-D service fees authorized under Section 231.103 for which the obligor is responsible, have been paid.

1. **Editor's note:** In 2015, the Legislature amended §158.507 to require dental support for a child subject to a child-support order, but the amendments are not effective until Sept. 1, 2018. For the text of the prospective amendments, see Acts 2015, 84th Leg., ch. 1150, §38, eff. Sept. 1, 2018.

History of Fam. Code §158.507: Acts 1997, 75th Leg., ch. 911, §67, eff. Sept. 1, 1997. Amended by Acts 2007, 80th Leg., ch. 972, §37, eff. Sept. 1, 2007.

FAM §158.508. REPEALED

Repealed by Acts 2001, 77th Leg., ch. 1023, §76, eff. Sept. 1, 2001.

CHAPTER 159. UNIFORM INTERSTATE FAMILY SUPPORT ACT

NCCUSL Prefatory Comment*

I. History of Uniform Family Support Acts

A. URESA and RURESA

In 1950 the National Conference of Commissioners on Uniform State Laws (NCCUSL), now more commonly referred to as the Uniform Law Commission (ULC), began a series of uniform acts dealing with cases involving establishment, enforcement, and modification of orders for "any duty of support" across state lines. This evolving process started with a revolutionary idea entitled the Uniform Reciprocal Enforcement of Support Act (URESA), promulgated in 1950, and amended in 1952 and 1958. Further amendments in 1968 were so significant that the act was renamed the Revised Uniform Reciprocal Enforcement of Support Act (RURESA). Ultimately, all the states enacted one or more versions of the reciprocal support enforcement acts. A comprehensive history of the creation process from 1950 through 1968 is provided by William J. Brockelbank & Felix Infausto, Interstate Enforcement of Family Support (Bobbs-Merrill Co., 2d ed. 1971). As with most revolutions, without it subsequent development would not have been possible.

B. UIFSA (1992) (1996)

By 1988, however, problems had arisen regarding the application of RURESA in practice. After four iterations that lasted over four decades, revisiting the subject was deemed necessary. A drafting committee began to prepare amendments for RURESA, but the task proved more formidable than expected. The result was the promulgation of the Uniform Interstate Family Support Act, UIFSA (1992), which was designed to serve as a complete replacement for URESA and RURESA. In 1993 Arkansas and Texas were the first to enact the new act, and within three years thirty-five states had adopted it.

The year 1996 was an eventful one for UIFSA. First, a drafting committee was convened in spring 1996 in response to requests from representatives of employer groups for specific statutory directions regarding interstate child-support income withholding orders. Second, the child-support community (especially the state programs funded under title IV-D of the Social Security Act) requested a substantive and procedural review. As a result, the NCCUSL at its annual conference in July adopted significant amendments and promulgated

* **Editor's note:**

The NCCUSL comments have been edited to reflect the Texas Legislature's omission of sections and changing of section numbers from the original uniform act. The Texas Legislature did not adopt the NCCUSL comments when it adopted the Uniform Interstate Family Support Act. The full uniform act and comments can be found at www.uniformlaws.org.

UIFSA (1996). Less than one month later, the U.S. Congress assured that nationwide acceptance of the amended Act was virtually certain. In the "welfare reform" legislation passed in August 1996, officially known as the Personal Responsibility and Work Opportunity Reconciliation Act of 1996 (PRWORA), the enactment of UIFSA, as amended, was mandated as a condition of state eligibility for the federal funding of child support enforcement and even under exigent circumstances to continued receipt of subsidies for TANF (Temporary Assistance for Needy Families), as follows:

Sec. 321. Adoption of Uniform State Laws (42 U.S.C. §666) is amended by adding at the end the following new subsection:

(f) Uniform Interstate Family Support Act.—In order to satisfy (42 U.S.C. §654(20)(A)), on and after January 1, 1998, each state must have in effect the Uniform Interstate Family Support Act, as approved by the American Bar Association on February 9, 1993, together with any amendments officially adopted before January 1, 1998, by the National Conference of Commissioners on Uniform State Laws.

Personal Responsibility and Work Opportunity Reconciliation Act (PRWORA), Pub. L. 104-193, 110 Stat. 2105 (1996), as amended by the Welfare Reform Technical Corrections Act of 1997.

In accordance with this "federal mandate," all states enacted UIFSA (1996).

C. UIFSA (2001)

In 2000 the child-support community again requested that the act be reviewed and amended as appropriate in the light of the years of experience with the 1992 and 1996 versions. Further, beginning in 1993 there had been an extraordinary amount of comprehensive training on the act by the child-support enforcement agencies throughout the nation and associated agencies and organizations of those agencies, *e.g.*, U.S. Department of Health and Human Services (HHS), Office of Child Support Enforcement (OCSE); National Child Support Enforcement Association (NCSEA); Eastern Regional Interstate Child Support Association (ERICSA); and Western Interstate Child Support Enforcement Council (WICSEC). A significant consequence of this attention was that the provisions of UIFSA were far more familiar to those who administered it than ever was true of its predecessor acts, URESA and RURESA.

The drafting committee meeting in 2001 led to several substantive and procedural amendments, which clarified and extended the act without making any fundamental change in the earlier policies and procedures. The widespread acceptance of UIFSA has been due primarily to the fact that representatives of the child support enforcement community mentioned above participated actively in the drafting of every version of the act, including UIFSA (2008).

When Congress mandated that UIFSA (1996) must be in place in all states by 1998, most interested parties viewed that action as an unalloyed benefit for the promulgation of the uniform act. Although all states promptly adopted UIFSA (1996), in retrospect, the federal action became a mixed blessing when it partially froze further development of the act. Through the development of consecutively promulgated versions of the act, i.e., UIFSA (2001) and UIFSA (2008), UIFSA (1996) was withdrawn by NCCUSL as being no longer appropriate for enactment. The federal mandate, however, remains and as of January 1, 2015, UIFSA (1996) was in force in twenty five (25) states. The federal Office of Child Support Enforcement (OCSE) routinely granted waivers to any state requesting authority to enact UIFSA (2001), or, with a deferred effective date, UIFSA (2008). Using the waiver authority, as of January 1, 2015, seventeen states had enacted UIFSA (2001), and twelve states had approved UIFSA (2008), contingent upon the United States' ratification of the 2007 Convention. The current expectation is that all states, or at least a substantial majority of the remaining states will enact this version, UIFSA (2008), by the end of 2015.

For comprehensive discussions of many of the events described above, see Uniform Interstate Family Support Act, 9 Part IB U.L.A. 159, 291, 471 (2005); Symposium on International Enforcement of Child Support, 43 FAM. L.Q. No. 1, Spring 2009 (1-160 pp., John J. Sampson issue editor); John J. Sampson and Barry J. Brooks, Uniform Interstate Family Support Act (2001) with Prefatory Note and Comments (with Still More Unofficial Annotations), 36 FAM. L.Q. 329 (2002); John J. Sampson, Uniform Interstate Family Support Act (1996), Statutory Text, Prefatory Note, and Commissioners Comments (with More Unofficial Annotations), 32 FAM. L.Q. 385 (1998); John J. Sampson, Uniform Interstate Family Support Act with Unofficial Annotations, 27 FAM. L.Q. 91 (1993).

Case law developments are found in Kurtis D. Kemper, Construction and Application of Uniform Interstate Family Support Act, 18 A.L.R. 6th 97 (originally published in 2001); Kurtis D. Kemper, Validity, Construction, and Application of Full Faith and Credit for Child Support Orders Act (FFCCSOA), 28 U.S.C.A. §1738B—State Cases, 18 A.L.R. 6th 97 (originally published in 2006).

In sum, the original act, UIFSA (1992), was followed by two sets of amendments in 1996, and 2001. Throughout, the basic principles have remained constant, while the details have been refined by experience in the field. This version is the third set of significant amendments to the act, referred to in these comments as UIFSA (2008).

II. International Maintenance Orders

A. URESA and RURESA; Minimal Attention to International Orders

URESA (1950, 1952, and 1958) did not take into account enforcement of child-support or spousal-support orders that involved a foreign country. "State" was defined as one of the fifty states, the District of Columbia, or Puerto Rico. The 1958 amendments to URESA expanded the definition to "any state, territory or possession of the United States and the District of Columbia in which this or a substantially reciprocal law has been enacted."

RURESA (1968) made a significant change to the complete absence of attention to international support orders by expanding the definition of "state" to "any foreign jurisdiction in which this or substantially similar reciprocal law is in effect." Contemporaneous commentary indicated that the beneficiary of this amendment would be Canada, or at least certain Canadian provinces. The thought was expressed that the United States Department of State might negotiate a treaty with Canada, or that under a redefinition of the term "state" several Canadian provinces would be included as jurisdictions that would reciprocally enforce U.S. support orders.

B. UIFSA (1992) (1996); Minor Changes in Treatment of International Orders

The basic approach of UIFSA (1992) was to maintain the RURESA provision quoted above with the following minor modification: "State ... includes a foreign jurisdiction that has established procedures for issuance and enforcement of support orders which are substantially similar to the procedures under this [Act]." UIFSA (1996) continued the basic provisions by adding that the foreign jurisdiction might have enacted a law that was also "substantially similar" to URESA or RURESA. Further, an amendment to Section 304 recognized that courts in Canadian provinces entered provisional orders for support to accompany their outgoing requests for establishment and enforcement, and required a provisional order from a state of the United States in order to establish a support order in Canada.

C. UIFSA (2001); Bilateral Agreements Recognized

In August 1996 PRWORA was enacted just three weeks after the promulgation of UIFSA (1996), which continued the approach of RURESA and UIFSA (1992), i.e., define "state" as including a foreign country with a "substantially similar" law to UIFSA. Indeed, this approach remains the law on the statute books of those U.S. jurisdictions that continue UIFSA (1996) in effect. UIFSA (2001) deleted the reference to a foreign country having a "substantially similar law" to URESA or RURESA. Although the revised act did specifically recognize the existence of bilateral agreements between the United States and foreign countries or their political subdivisions, UIFSA (2008) is specifically designed to accommodate U.S. domestic law to international family support orders, especially those resulting under the new Hague Convention of November 23, 2007.

In short, the attention paid in the uniform support acts to issues involving foreign support orders initially was relatively limited until the advent of UIFSA (2001). Previously, in 1996 PRWORA tied the significant federal subsidy for child-support enforcement to the universal enactment of UIFSA (1996), and also laid the groundwork for greatly increased federal activity for reaching bilateral agreements on child support enforcement with foreign countries. The federal act authorized the Secretary of State, with the concurrence of the Secretary of Health and Human Services, to enter into international agreements with foreign reciprocating countries with support enforcement procedures substantially in conformity with such procedures in the United States. Individual U.S. states were also encouraged to enter into reciprocal arrangements with the foreign jurisdictions with which they had the greatest number of international cases.

In response, the U.S. State Department formed teams of negotiators to provide for bilateral agreements with a variety of foreign countries. Between 1998 and 2008, the United States entered into bilateral agreements with thirteen nations and eleven Canadian provinces (the federal government in Canada lacks jurisdiction over child-support orders). *See* www.acf.hhs.gov/programs/css/international.

To accommodate the new world of bilateral orders on the federal level, UIFSA (2001) redefined "state" to encompass foreign countries with bilateral agreements with the United States. Despite repeated requests to Congress to mandate adoption of that version in order to facilitate increased international activity in child-support enforcement, no congressional action was taken through the end of 2008; *see* §159.102(26), *infra*, for the text of UIFSA (2001) and the entirely new approach in UIFSA (2008).

As of June 1, 2003, there were several child support enforcement agreements among countries. One widely accepted agreement, which is largely hortatory and without practical effect, was sponsored by the United Nations in 1956 and referred to as the New York Convention. In addition, there are four agreements promulgated by The Hague Conference on Private International Law (HccH), two covering enforcement of child-support orders in 1958 and maintenance orders in 1973, and two dealing with applicable law in 1956 and 1973 (a civil law concept). These conventions operate primarily between European nations, and came to be viewed by HccH as out-of-date and relatively ineffective. In addition, there are a welter of regional agreements regarding enforcement of family maintenance orders. The United States is not a party to any of these multilateral agreements.

Beginning in June 2003, and continuing through November 2007, more than 70 countries met in The Hague, Netherlands, in five separate negotiating sessions to forge a new Hague Convention on the International Recovery of Child Support and Other Forms of Family Maintenance.

The United States delegation, headed by the U.S. State Department and including members from OCSE and other experts, was a crucial participant throughout the term of negotiations. It was clearly a goal of all the parties engaging in the negotiations that the United States be an active party and ultimately adopt the Convention.

As a first step, the Convention was signed by the United States at The Hague, Netherlands, on November 23, 2007. In context, this initial signature represents a commitment by the executive branch of the federal government to make a good faith effort to bring the Convention into force. The Senate has given its advice and consent to the Convention. When it is signed by the President, and the appropriate documents are filed in The Hague, the federal preemption of the issue via the treaty clause will be sufficient to make the Convention "the law of the land." *See* U.S. Const. art. VI. cl. 2. However, because this multilateral treaty is not selfexecuting, additional federal or state statutory enactments are necessary to enable the treaty and make it readily accessible to bench and bar. Because establishment, enforcement, and modification of family support are basically matters of state law, from the perspective of the Uniform Law Commission the vehicle for the acceptance into force of the new Convention is a revision of UIFSA (2001), hereafter called UIFSA (2008). In time, it is anticipated the new Hague Maintenance Convention will achieve a high level of integration with many other countries.

III. Drafting Principles for UIFSA (2008)

The basic principles underlying the drafting of UIFSA (2008) anticipated a strictly limited revision of the act in order to integrate the appropriate provisions of the new Convention into state law. Because UIFSA (2001) had such a wide influence on the text of the new Convention, in very many instances the principles, and sometimes almost the exact text, of the Convention were already contained in UIFSA (2001). The clear drafting goal was to integrate the Convention into state law, and not to revise UIFSA (2001) in a substantive manner. Most frequently the amendment to the existing text was merely to add "or a foreign country" to the directives about how a "tribunal of this state" should deal with an order or another action of a "state." Correspondingly, the definition of "state" no longer contains the legal fiction that a foreign country is a state of the United States.

Similarly, a significant portion of the language of the Convention need not be included in state law because that text speaks to the "Contracting States," that is, to the countries in which the Convention will come into force. A substantial percentage of the articles in the Convention are directed to the agreement between nation states or their political subdivisions, which do not implicate state tribunals. A majority of the provisions, however, do speak to the "competent authorities," which means to those tribunals charged with the obligation of applying the Convention to actual support orders. In sum, with relatively minimal amendments, the text of UIFSA (2008) combines the principles of UIFSA and the Convention with the required actions of a state tribunal to put the Convention into effect.

There are some instances in which the text of UIFSA (2008) and the Convention differ in a manner that cannot be reconciled by fiat. On these occasions it is necessary to accommodate the Convention language to state law in order to avoid conflict between the Convention and the uniform state law. A choice had to be made; either substantially amend the text of UIFSA (2001), or create an independent set of rules to accommodate the differences between UIFSA and the Convention. The latter was the preferred decision. An all-new Article 7 constitutes a stand-alone portion of the act designed to direct a "tribunal of this state" on limited special practices and handling deemed to be necessary for establishing or enforcing a Convention support order. This decision was based on the conclusion that a limited number of specialized rules for Convention orders would result in a simpler, smoother transition than attempting to integrate new rules into the millions of existing child-support orders.

UIFSA (2008) also may supply answers to some of the questions that the Convention leaves unresolved. This is particularly apt with regard to modification of existing orders when parties have moved from the issuing state or foreign country, or other factual circumstances have changed significantly. Regarding modification of orders, the Convention has only limited application, while UIFSA makes modification the subject of significant statutory effect. *See* §§159.609-159.616.

In sum, UIFSA (2008) constitutes a limited, rather than comprehensive, revision of the act. It is designed to integrate the Convention into state law, and not to amend UIFSA (2001) in any significant manner. The drafting principles are relatively simple:

(1) integrate the requirements of the Convention into the current text of UIFSA articles 1 through 6 by adding "or a foreign country" when the desired actions and goals of both acts are congruent;

(2) adapt the language of the Convention to the current text of UIFSA articles 1 through 6 in order to make that language more comprehensible to the American bench and bar;

(3) draft a stand-alone subchapter in UIFSA to direct a "tribunal of this state" on do's and don'ts unique to the Convention support orders containing issues only applicable under the Convention; and,

(4) omit the Convention text that need not be included in state law because it speaks only to "Contracting States," i.e., the United States and the other Convention countries.

The function of the comments to the act is not to serve as an annotated version of UIFSA (2008), but rather to provide the history and process involved in the drafting of the four iterations of a uniform act, one of which is in force in every jurisdiction of the United States. Other than key constitutional cases, most of the citations found in previous comments to earlier iterations of the act have been omitted.

IV. Federal Action Implicating UIFSA (2008)

The usual course for treaties entered into by the United States pursuant to the treaty power, U.S. CONST. art. II, §2, cl. 2, and which are not "self-executing," is for the treaty to be implemented through federal legislation. The states are, of course, required to comply with the treaty and the federal legislation, but, as noted above, the establishment, enforcement, and modification of family support orders are basically matters of state law. As UIFSA is the familiar and widely used tool for support determinations in cross-border situations, the Uniform Law Commission (ULC), in close consultation with the Department of State and the Department of Health and Human Service's Office of Child Support Enforcement (OCSE), incorporated applicable provisions of the Hague Maintenance Convention of November 23, 2007 into state law through amendments to UIFSA, now UIFSA (2008). In fact, the United States' negotiations team at The Hague included ULC representatives, and the 2007 treaty, in many important respects, parallels the UIFSA model of inter-jurisdictional cooperation.

While it includes specific new features for international case processing, UIFSA (2008) incorporates substantial provisions of state law which will already be familiar to attorneys, courts, support enforcement agencies, and litigants. Congress, which funds state child support programs through title IV-D of the Social Security Act has, since 1996, deemed it appropriate to require all states to adopt UIFSA as a condition for the continued receipt of federal funds. Adoption of UIFSA (2008) by the states, will ensure uniformity in implementation of the treaty throughout the country and will enable the United States to be in compliance with the Convention.

Obviously, federal action is also required, both to ratify the treaty and bring it into force. With respect to the Convention, federal legislation was necessary to implement parts of the Convention which do not directly implicate state tribunals, such as the provisions of Convention Chs. II and III dealing with

Central Authorities, use of the Federal Parent Locator Service, and collection of past-due support in international cases by offset of federal tax refunds.

The United States signed the treaty on November 23, 2007, signifying its intention to make good faith efforts to have the treaty adopted and implemented in this country. On September 29, 2010 the United States Senate gave its advice and consent to ratification of the treaty. Federal legislation which included provisions pertaining to the treaty was passed by both the House and Senate and was signed by the President on September 29, 2014, as Public Law 113-183. This legislation requires all states to adopt UIFSA (2008). The law further requires that UIFSA (2008) be in effect in each state no later "than the first day of the first calendar quarter beginning after the close of the first regular session of the State legislature that begins after the date of the enactment of this Act." If a state has a 2-year legislative session, "each year of the session shall be deemed to be a separate regular session of the State legislature." All states have regular legislative sessions during 2015 and, thus, all states must enact UIFSA (2008) in 2015.

Immediately following enactment of P.L. 113-183, the Commissioner of OCSE signed a policy Action Transmittal directed to all State Agencies Administering Child Support Plans under Title IV-D of the Social Security Act. This transmittal reiterates the legislative requirement that each state must have in effect the Uniform Interstate Family Support Act, "including any amendments adopted as of September 30, 2008." The transmittal is set forth in full below.

Adoption of UIFSA(2008) by the states is not only essential to the continued federal funding of state child support programs but is key to the United States' showing of good faith implementation of the Convention and the entry into force of the Convention in this country. That implementation will help assure that American support orders are fully and expeditiously accepted and enforced in other countries. At the beginning of 2015, thirty-two countries had already ratified, acceded to the Convention, or were bound by a Regional Economic Integration Organization mandate (i.e. the European Union's means of implementation of the Convention).

UNITED STATES DEPARTMENT OF HEALTH AND HUMAN SERVICES
OFFICE OF CHILD SUPPORT ENFORCEMENT
ACTION TRANSMITTAL
AT-14-11
DATE: October 9, 2014

TO: State Agencies Administering Child Support Plans under Title IV-D of the Social Security Act and Other Interested Individuals

SUBJECT: P.L. 113-183 UIFSA 2008 Enactment

On September 29, 2014 President Obama signed Public Law (P.L.) 113-183, the Preventing Sex Trafficking and Strengthening Families Act. This law amends section 466(f) of the Social Security Act, requiring all states to enact any amendments to the Uniform Interstate Family Support Act "officially adopted as of September 30, 2008 by the National Conference of Commissioners on Uniform State Laws" (referred to as UIFSA 2008). Among other changes, the UIFSA 2008 amendments integrate the appropriate provisions of The Hague Convention on the International Recovery of Child Support and Other Forms of Family Maintenance, which was adopted at the Hague Conference on Private International Law on November 23, 2007, referred to as the 2007 Family Maintenance Convention.

Section 301(f)(3)(A) of P.L. 113-183 requires that UIFSA 2008 must be in effect in every state "no later than the effective date of laws enacted by the legislature of the State implementing such paragraph, but in no event later than the first day of the first calendar quarter beginning after the close of the first regular session of the State legislature that begins after the date of the enactment of this Act." If a state has a 2-year legislative session, "each year of the session shall be deemed to be a separate regular session of the State legislature."

In 2008, after the National Conference of Commissioners on Uniform State Laws adopted the UIFSA 2008 amendments, several states asked OCSE if their state legislatures could enact UIFSA 2008. At that time, section 466(f) of the Social Security Act required states to adopt UIFSA 1996, a previous version to UIFSA 2008. OCSE issued DCL-08-41, which permitted states to enact UIFSA 2008 verbatim with a provision that the effective date of its enactment be delayed until the 2007 Family Maintenance Convention is ratified and the United States deposits its instrument of ratification. States that chose to follow this process did not need to request an exemption from OCSE. Eight states passed UIFSA 2008 using the effective date language described in DCL-08-41.

Due to the specific requirement in P.L. 113-183 that states enact UIFSA 2008 in their next state legislative session, OCSE rescinds DCL-08-41. The eight states that enacted UIFSA 2008 with a delayed implementation date must take the necessary legislative or administrative steps for UIFSA 2008 to be effective as directed in P.L. 113-183.

Now that the President has signed P.L. 113-183, the following steps must occur before the 2007 Family Maintenance convention can enter into force for the United States.

- All states must enact UIFSA 2008 verbatim by the effective date noted in P.L. 113-183. Where UIFSA 2008 has bracketed language, states may use terminology appropriate under state law. In addition, P.L. 113-183 requires states to make minor revisions to the state plan which OCSE will address in forthcoming guidance.
- The President must sign the instrument of ratification.
- Once these activities are completed, the United States will be able to deposit its instrument of ratification with the Ministry of Foreign Affairs of the Kingdom of the Netherlands, which is the depositary for the Hague Convention on the International Recovery of Child Support and Other Forms of Family Maintenance.

It is important to note that, once UIFSA 2008 is in effect in your state, international cases will not be processed under Article 7 of UIFSA 2008 until the 2007 Family Maintenance Convention enters into force for the United States. Once this occurs, Article 7 of UIFSA 2008 will be in effect for all cases transmitted and received under the 2007 Family Maintenance Convention.

OCSE expresses our sincere thanks to the entire child support community for the collaborative and monumental effort taken to reach this important milestone. We look forward to working together to enact UIFSA 2008 in all states, and to implement the 2007 Family Maintenance Convention in the United States.

Vicki Turetsky
Commissioner, Office of Child Support Enforcement

SUBCHAPTER A. CONFLICTS BETWEEN PROVISIONS

FAM §159.001. CONFLICTS BETWEEN PROVISIONS

If a provision of this chapter conflicts with a provision of this title or another statute or rule of this state and the conflict cannot be reconciled, this chapter prevails.

History of Fam. Code §159.001: Acts 1995, 74th Leg., ch. 20, §1, eff. Apr. 20, 1995.

ANNOTATIONS

Attorney Gen. v. Litten, 999 S.W.2d 74, 77 (Tex. App.—Houston [14th Dist.] 1999, no pet.). To "the extent any provision in [Fam. Code] ch. 157 conflicts with [Fam. Code] ch. 159, the provisions of Ch. 159 prevail. Because there is no statutory basis for applying the provisions of Ch. 157 to an action to register and enforce a foreign judgment for child support, we hold Ch. 157 is not applicable to this suit."

In re Chapman, 973 S.W.2d 346, 348 (Tex.App.—Amarillo 1998, no pet.). "In addition to the Uniform Enforcement of Foreign Judgments Act, the [UIFSA] provides the procedure for registering a foreign support order in Texas."

Sections 159.002-159.100 reserved for expansion

SUBCHAPTER B. GENERAL PROVISIONS

FAM §159.101. SHORT TITLE

This chapter may be cited as the Uniform Interstate Family Support Act.

History of Fam. Code §159.101: Acts 2003, 78th Leg., ch. 1247, §3, eff. Sept. 1, 2003.

FAM §159.102. DEFINITIONS

In this chapter:

(1) "Child" means an individual, whether over or under the age of majority, who:

(A) is or is alleged to be owed a duty of support by the individual's parent; or

(B) is or is alleged to be the beneficiary of a support order directed to the parent.

(2) "Child support order" means a support order for a child, including a child who has attained the age of majority under the law of the issuing state or foreign country.

(3) "Convention" means the Convention on the International Recovery of Child Support and Other Forms of Family Maintenance, concluded at The Hague on November 23, 2007.

(4) "Duty of support" means an obligation imposed or imposable by law to provide support for a child, spouse, or former spouse, including an unsatisfied obligation to provide support.

(5) "Foreign country" means a country, including a political subdivision thereof, other than the United States, that authorizes the issuance of support orders and:

(A) which has been declared under the law of the United States to be a foreign reciprocating country;

(B) which has established a reciprocal arrangement for child support with this state as provided in Section 159.308;

(C) which has enacted a law or established procedures for the issuance and enforcement of support orders which are substantially similar to the procedures under this chapter; or

(D) in which the Convention is in force with respect to the United States.

(6) "Foreign support order" means a support order of a foreign tribunal.

(7) "Foreign tribunal" means a court, administrative agency, or quasi-judicial entity of a foreign country which is authorized to establish, enforce, or modify support orders or to determine parentage of a child. The term includes a competent authority under the Convention.

(8) "Home state" means the state or foreign country in which a child lived with a parent or a person acting as parent for at least six consecutive months immediately preceding the time of filing of a petition or a comparable pleading for support and, if a child is less than six months old, the state or foreign country in which the child lived from birth with any of them. A period of temporary absence of any of them is counted as part of the six-month or other period.

(9) "Income" includes earnings or other periodic entitlements to money from any source and any other property subject to withholding for support under the law of this state.

(10) "Income-withholding order" means an order or other legal process directed to an obligor's employer, as provided in Chapter 158, to withhold support from the income of the obligor.

(11) "Initiating tribunal" means the tribunal of a state or foreign country from which a petition or comparable pleading is forwarded or a petition or comparable pleading is filed for forwarding to another state or foreign country.

(12) "Issuing foreign country" means the foreign country in which a tribunal issues a support order or a judgment determining parentage of a child.

(13) "Issuing state" means the state in which a tribunal issues a support order or a judgment determining parentage of a child.

(14) "Issuing tribunal" means the tribunal of a state or foreign country that issues a support order or a judgment determining parentage of a child.

(15) "Law" includes decisional and statutory law and rules and regulations having the force of law.

(16) "Obligee" means:

(A) an individual to whom a duty of support is or is alleged to be owed or in whose favor a support order or a judgment determining parentage of a child has been issued;

(B) a foreign country, state, or political subdivision of a state to which the rights under a duty of support or support order have been assigned or that has independent claims based on financial assistance provided to an individual obligee in place of child support;

(C) an individual seeking a judgment determining parentage of the individual's child; or

(D) a person that is a creditor in a proceeding under Subchapter H.

(17) "Obligor" means an individual, or the estate of a decedent, that:

(A) owes or is alleged to owe a duty of support;

(B) is alleged but has not been adjudicated to be a parent of a child;

(C) is liable under a support order; or

(D) is a debtor in a proceeding under Subchapter H.

(18) "Outside this state" means a location in another state or a country other than the United States, whether or not the country is a foreign country.

(19) "Person" means an individual, corporation, business trust, estate, trust, partnership, limited liability company, association, joint venture, public corporation, government or governmental subdivision, agency, or instrumentality, or any other legal or commercial entity.

(20) "Record" means information that is:

(A) inscribed on a tangible medium or that is stored in an electronic or other medium; and

(B) retrievable in a perceivable form.

(21) "Register" means to file in a tribunal of this state a support order or judgment determining parentage of a child issued in another state or a foreign country.

(22) "Registering tribunal" means a tribunal in which a support order or judgment determining parentage of a child is registered.

(23) "Responding state" means a state in which a petition or comparable pleading for support or to determine parentage of a child is filed or to which a petition or comparable pleading is forwarded for filing from another state or a foreign country.

(24) "Responding tribunal" means the authorized tribunal in a responding state or foreign country.

(25) "Spousal support order" means a support order for a spouse or former spouse of the obligor.

(26) "State" means a state of the United States, the District of Columbia, Puerto Rico, the United States Virgin Islands, or any territory or insular possession subject to the jurisdiction of the United States. The term includes an Indian nation or tribe.

(27) "Support enforcement agency" means a public official, governmental entity, or private agency authorized to:

(A) seek enforcement of support orders or laws relating to the duty of support;

(B) seek establishment or modification of child support;

(C) request determination of parentage of a child;

(D) attempt to locate obligors or their assets; or

(E) request determination of the controlling child support order.

"Support enforcement agency" does not include a domestic relations office unless that office has entered into a cooperative agreement with the Title IV-D agency to perform duties under this chapter.

(28) "Support order" means a judgment, decree, order, decision, or directive, whether temporary, final, or subject to modification, issued in a state or foreign country for the benefit of a child, a spouse, or a former spouse that provides for monetary support, health care, arrearages, retroactive support, or reimbursement for financial assistance provided to an individual obligee in place of child support. The term may include related costs and fees, interest, income withholding, automatic adjustment, reasonable attorney's fees, and other relief.

(29) "Tribunal" means a court, administrative agency, or quasi-judicial entity authorized to establish, enforce, or modify support orders or to determine parentage of a child.

History of Fam. Code §159.102: Acts 1995, 74th Leg., ch. 20, §1, eff. Apr. 20, 1995. Amended by Acts 1997, 75th Leg., ch. 607, §1, eff. Sept. 1, 1997. Renumbered from §159.101 and amended by Acts 2003, 78th Leg., ch. 1247, §3, eff. Sept. 1, 2003. Amended by Acts 2007, 80th Leg., ch. 972, §38, eff. Sept. 1, 2007; Acts 2015, 84th Leg., ch. 368, §1, eff. July 1, 2015. Source: Former Fam. Code §21.01.

ANNOTATIONS

Office of Atty. Gen. v. Carter, 977 S.W.2d 159, 161 (Tex.App.—Houston [14th Dist.] 1998, no pet.). "While it is true that a parent has a duty to support his or her child, under UIFSA, a nonparent seeking a support order to be established and enforced against a parent must have legal custody of the child. [T]he statute requires an 'obligor' to owe a duty of support to an 'obligee.' *At 162-63:* In this case, [grandparent] was not [child's] custodial parent or legal custodian. Thus, she was not an obligee under the statute's definition. Moreover, because [grandparent] had no right to receive support payments, she had no rights to assign to the State of Georgia's Department of Human Resources. Thus, Georgia's Department of Human Resources was not an obligee under the statute's definition. Conse-

quently, the trial court did not err in refusing to enter a child support order for [child]. [¶] [Family Code §102.003(9)] determines who has general standing to file suit in a [SAPCR]. A proceeding filed under UIFSA, however, is not a SAPCR. Thus, §102.003(9) does not apply in this case. *At 162 n.3:* We believe if the Texas Legislature had intended 'obligee' to include a non-parent without legal custody who is supporting the child, they would have so stated. *At 163:* We are not holding that [mother] is not liable to [grandparent] for the necessaries [grandparent] provided for [child]. However, [grandparent] may not seek support from [mother] under UIFSA because it requires that either (1) a support order exist or (2) [grandparent] have legal custody of [child]. [Grandparent] may sue [mother] to be reimbursed for the necessaries she has provided [child]. The [AG], however, cannot petition the trial court under UIFSA to issue a child support order withholding [mother's] income."

NCCUSL Comment*

The terms defined in UIFSA receive a major makeover in the now-realized expectation that the Convention will enter into force in the United States at a future time. Six definitions of terms are completely new, sixteen existing definitions are amended to a greater or lesser degree, seven definitions remain basically untouched albeit six of these are renumbered, and one term is deleted because it no longer appears in the act.

Many crucial definitions continue to be left to local law. For example, the definitions provided by subsections (1) "child," and (2) "child-support order," refer to "the age of majority" without further elaboration. The exact age at which a child becomes an adult for different purposes is a matter for the law of each state or foreign country as is the age at which a parent's duty to furnish child support terminates. Similarly, a wide variety of other terms of art are implicitly left to state law. The new Convention provides a more explicit definition of "child" that is entirely consistent with the laws of all states.

There is a divergence of opinion among the several states regarding the appropriate age for termination of child support. The overwhelming number of states set ages 18 (legal adulthood for most purposes), or 19, or one of those two ages and high-school graduation, whichever comes later. Relatively few states have retained the formerly popular age of 21. And, some states extend the support obligation past age 21 if the person to be supported is engaged in higher education. Allegedly some support enforcement agencies and some tribunals have been reluctant to enforce an ongoing child support obligation past age 21, but under UIFSA it is the law of the issuing state or foreign country that makes the determination of the appropriate age for termination of support from an obligor. Because the order has been established with personal jurisdiction over the parties, it is fully enforceable under the terms of the act.

Under the terms of the Convention, the standard obligation of a responding tribunal to enforce a child-support order is for a person "under the age of 21 years." *See* Convention art. 2. Scope. However, a contracting nation may make a reservation to limit enforcement of a child-support order to "persons who have not attained the age of 18 years." Id. This possibility will not affect this act domestically because the United States does not intend to make such a reservation. Currently states will enforce another jurisdiction's order even if such an order could not have been obtained in the responding state because the child was over 18. There is no requirement to establish an order for a child over the age of 18 if that cannot be done under the local jurisdiction's law.

Subsection (3) "Convention," identifies the Hague Maintenance Convention, the basis on which UIFSA (2008) was drafted. The text of the Convention may be accessed on the website of the Hague Convention on Private International Law, www.hcch.net/index_en.php. As noted above, the Convention was the result of negotiations involving more than 70 foreign nations or, in some instances political subdivisions of a foreign nation, conducted in a series of meetings from May 2003 to November 2007.

Subsection (4) "Duty of support," means the legal obligation to provide support, whether or not that duty has been the subject of an order by a tribunal. This broad definition includes both prospective and retrospective obligations to the extent they are imposed by the relevant state law.

The definitions in subsections (5) "foreign country," (6) "foreign support order," and (7) "foreign tribunal," are all new to UIFSA, and must be read in conjunction with the prior and the new definition of "state," now in subsection (26). Formerly, under certain circumstances a foreign country or political subdivision was declared to be a "state." Defining a foreign country or a political subdivision thereof, e.g., a Canadian province, as a "state" may be traced back to 1968, where this approach first appeared in the Revised Uniform Reciprocal Enforcement of Support Act (RURESA). That fiction created confusion because a foreign support order is not entitled to full faith and credit. Indeed, such orders of the sister states of the United States were only relatively recently accorded that treatment after congressional action in 1994 with the advent of the Full Faith and Credit for Child Support Orders Act (FFCCSOA), 28 U.S.C. §1738B. Thus, constitutional analysis is not required for enforcement of foreign support orders; only state statutory issues are involved.

The term "foreign judgment" is used only once in UIFSA (1996) and (2001) in a context that clearly intends to mean "from a sister state." If an international construction is intended, the text in UIFSA (2001) is uniformly "foreign country or political subdivision." The new definitions in UIFSA (2008) are fine-tuned to avoid ambiguity in order to ensure that "foreign" is used strictly to identify international proceedings and orders.

Subsection (5) requires additional careful reading; under the act "foreign country" by no means includes all foreign nations. *See* §159.102(5)(A)-(D). Countries identified by three of the four subsections are reasonably ascertainable. The list of reciprocating countries that have negotiated an executive agreement with the United States as described in subsection (5)(A), known as bilateral agreements, is found on the website of the federal Office of Child Support Enforcement (OCSE) at www.acf.hhs.gov/programs/css/international.

The countries described in §159.102(5)(B) have entered into an agreement with the forum state, which presumptively is known to officials of that state. A combined list of all such agreements of all states is not readily available.

Countries subject to §159.102(5)(C) theoretically could require individualized determinations on a case-by-case basis. An alternative might be for each state to create an efficient method for identifying foreign countries whose laws are "substantially similar" to UIFSA. On the other hand, the "substantially similar" test to measure the laws of foreign nations has been around since 1968 without eliciting much controversy.

In the future, assuming that there will be a number of countries with the Convention in force with the United States under §159.102(5)(D), the list of those countries will be well publicized.

Finally, there are very many foreign nations that do not, and will not, fit any of the definitions of "foreign country" established in the act. At present, there are 192 member states in the United Nations. Recognition and enforcement of support orders from nations that do not meet the definition of "foreign country" may be enforceable under the doctrine of comity. *See* §159.104.

Subsections (6) "foreign support order," (7) "foreign tribunal," and (12) "issuing foreign country" set down parallel tracks for a foreign support order, foreign tribunal, and foreign issuing country throughout the act.

Subsection (17) "obligor," and subsection (16) "obligee," are denominated in the Convention as "debtor" and "creditor." The terms inherently contain the legal obligation to pay or receive support, and implicitly refer to the individuals with a duty to support a child. "Obligor" includes an individual who is alleged to owe a duty of support as well as a person whose obligation has previously been determined. The one-order system of UIFSA can succeed only if the respective obligations of support are adjusted as the physical possession of a child changes between parents or involves a third-party caretaker. This must be accomplished in the context of modification, and not by the creation of multiple orders attempting to reflect each changing custody scenario. Obviously this issue is of concern not only to interstate and international child-support orders, but applies to intrastate orders as well.

* See footnote on p. 666.

Subsection (18) "outside this state," requires careful reading. This phrase is used in the act when the application of the provision is to be as broad as possible. Rather than limit the application of certain provisions of the act to other states, foreign countries as defined in subsection (5), or even countries whose orders are entitled to comity under §159.104, all nations and political subdivisions are truly "outside this state." For example, that term is found in §§159.316-159.318, which allow a tribunal of this state to accept information or assistance from everywhere in the world (in the court's discretion as to its effect).

The definitions in subsections (23) "responding state," and (24) "responding tribunal," accommodate the direct filing of a petition under UIFSA without the intervention of an initiating tribunal. Both definitions acknowledge the possibility that there may be a responding state and a responding tribunal in a situation where there is no initiating tribunal. Under current practice, the initial application for services most often will be generated by a support enforcement agency or a central authority of a foreign country and sent to the appropriate support enforcement agency in the responding state.

As discussed above in connection with subsections (5) through (7), the amended definition in subsection (26) "state," eliminates the legal fiction that a foreign country can be a state of the United States, and clarifies and implements the purpose of the act to enforce an international support order under state law. In UIFSA (2008), the term clearly is intended to refer only to a state of the United States or to other designated political entities subject to federal law.

The vast bulk of child support establishment, enforcement, and modification in the United States is performed by the state Title IV-D agencies. *See* Part IV-D, Social Security Act, 42 U.S.C. §651 et seq. Subsection (27) "support enforcement agency," includes not only those entities, but also any other state or local governmental entities, or private agencies acting under contract with such agencies, charged with establishing or enforcing child support. A private agency falls within the definition of a support enforcement agency only as an outsource of a Title IV-D agency or specifically identified as such under §159.103.

Subsection (28) "support order" is another definition that requires more careful reading than might be immediately clear. Virtually every financial aspect of a support order regarding child support or spousal support is covered. Throughout the act "support order" means both "child support" and "spousal support." "Child support" is used when the provision applies only to support for a child. The single provision applicable solely to spousal support is §159.211. Other forms of support that might be classified as "family support," are not dealt with by UIFSA.

Subsection (29) "tribunal," takes into account that a number of states have delegated various aspects of child-support establishment and enforcement to quasi-judicial bodies and administrative agencies. The term accounts for the breadth of state variations in dealing with support orders. This usage is standard in the child-support enforcement community; private practitioners who, only rarely, are involved in such cases may still find the term unfamiliar.

FAM §159.103. STATE TRIBUNAL & SUPPORT ENFORCEMENT AGENCY

(a) The court is the tribunal of this state.

(b) The office of the attorney general is the support enforcement agency of this state.

History of Fam. Code §159.103: Acts 1995, 74th Leg., ch. 20, §1, eff. Apr. 20, 1995. Amended by Acts 1997, 75th Leg., ch. 607, §2, eff. Sept. 1, 1997. Renumbered from §159.102 by Acts 2003, 78th Leg., ch. 1247, §3, eff. Sept. 1, 2003. Amended by Acts 2015, 84th Leg., ch. 368, §2, eff. July 1, 2015. Source: Former Fam. Code §21.02.

NCCUSL Comment*

Subsection (a) provides for the identification of the tribunal or tribunals to be charged with the application of this act.

Subsection (b) performs the same function for the support enforcement agency or agencies. By its terms it indicates the legislature may designate more than one entity as authorized to enforce a support order, including a private agency. To clarify, federal law and regulations require that each state designate a "single and separate organizational unit" as the state agency that is charged with administration of the state plan and is authorized, and funded under Title IV-D of the Social Security Act. Known throughout the United States as the as the "IV-D agency," it may delegate any of its functions to another state or local agency or may purchase services from any person or private agency. The IV-D agency, however, retains responsibility for ensuring compliance with the Title IV-D state plan. Moreover, by virtue of the receipt of a federal subsidy, the agency is subject to federal regulations. The legislature may also decide to provide services unrelated to, or not funded by the Title IV-D system. For example, the state legislature could identify (and fund) a private agency authorized to enforce a spousal-support order not involving child support, or could fund a public defender system to provide counsel for indigent defendants in IV-D cases.

FAM §159.104. REMEDIES CUMULATIVE

(a) Remedies provided by this chapter are cumulative and do not affect the availability of remedies under other law or the recognition of a foreign support order on the basis of comity.

(b) This chapter does not:

(1) provide the exclusive method of establishing or enforcing a support order under the law of this state; or

(2) grant a tribunal of this state jurisdiction to render judgment or issue an order relating to child custody or visitation in a proceeding under this chapter.

History of Fam. Code §159.104: Acts 1995, 74th Leg., ch. 20, §1, eff. Apr. 20, 1995. Renumbered from §159.103 and amended by Acts 2003, 78th Leg., ch. 1247, §3, eff. Sept. 1, 2003. Amended by Acts 2015, 84th Leg., ch. 368, §3, eff. July 1, 2015. Source: Former Fam. Code §21.03.

NCCUSL Comment*

The existence of procedures for interstate establishment, enforcement, or modification of support or a determination of parentage in UIFSA does not preclude the application of the general law of the forum. Even if the parents live in different states, for example, a petitioner may decide to file an original proceeding for child support (and most likely for other relief as well) directly in the state of residence of the respondent and proceed under that forum's generally applicable support law. In so doing, the out-of-state petitioner submits to the personal jurisdiction of the forum and, for the most part, is unaffected by UIFSA. Once a child-support order has been issued, this option is no longer available to interstate parties. Under UIFSA, a state may not permit a party to proceed to obtain a second support order; rather, in further litigation the tribunal must apply the act's provisions for enforcement of an existing order and limit modification to the strict standards of UIFSA.

This section facilitates the recognition and enforcement of a support order from a nation state that is entitled to have its orders recognized by comity, but is not a "foreign country" under §159.102(5). The insertion of the term "foreign support order" to replace "support order of a foreign country or political subdivision" in subsection (a) helps clarify application of "comity" for support enforcement cases. In UIFSA, four types of nation states are defined as "foreign countries": (1) Convention countries; (2) countries with bilateral agreements with the federal government; (3) countries with bilateral agreements with particular states; and (4) countries with similar support laws. However, orders of countries that do not fall within this definition may nevertheless be enforced under "comity". Applying comity to enforce a support order of a tribunal of another nation state intends courtesy and good will, and extends due regard for the legislative, executive, and judicial acts of another nation which is not a "foreign country" as defined in §159.102.

Although the determination by the United States Department of State that a foreign nation is a reciprocating country is binding on all states, recognition of a support order through comity is dependent on the law of each state. The reference to "remedies under other law" is intended to recognize the principle of comity as developed in the forum state by statutory or common law, rather than to create a substantive right independent of that law.

* See footnote on p. 666.

Subsection (b)(1) gives notice that UIFSA is not the only means for establishing or enforcing a support order with an interstate aspect. A potential child-support obligee may voluntarily submit to the jurisdiction of another state to seek the full range of desired relief under the law of that state using intrastate procedures, rather than resorting to the interstate procedure provided by UIFSA. A nonresident married parent may choose to file a proceeding in the forum state for dissolution of the marriage, including property division and spousal support, and in conjunction seek an order regarding child custody and visitation and child support. A parent may submit to the jurisdiction of another state for a determination of parentage and child support. A support order resulting from each of these scenarios implicates UIFSA. Invariably the issuing tribunal will have continuing, exclusive jurisdiction over its controlling child support or spousal-support order as provided by §§159.205, 159.207, and 159.211, *infra*, with all of the attendant application of the act to those orders. Likewise, the order or judgment of another state can be enforced without the necessity of registration under UIFSA by resort to other post-judgment enforcement remedies, such as lien, levy, execution, and filing claims in probate or bankruptcy actions.

On the other hand, subsection (b)(2) makes clear that jurisdiction to establish child custody and visitation orders is distinct from jurisdiction for child-support orders. For the former, jurisdiction generally rests on the child's connection with the state rather than personal jurisdiction over the respondent. *See* UCCJEA §201; *May v. Anderson*, 345 U.S. 528 (1953) (Frankfurter, J., concurring). Under the Supreme Court's case law, jurisdiction to establish a child-support order requires personal jurisdiction over the respondent. *See Kulko v. Superior Court*, 436 U.S. 84 (1978). If the child-support order is sought under the authority of UIFSA, the most important aspect of this rule is that a child-support obligee utilizing the provisions of UIFSA to establish child support across state lines submits to jurisdiction for child support only, and does not submit to the jurisdiction of the responding state with regard to child custody or visitation.

FAM §159.105. APPLICATION OF CHAPTER TO RESIDENT OF FOREIGN COUNTRY & FOREIGN SUPPORT PROCEEDING

(a) A tribunal of this state shall apply Subchapters B through G and, as applicable, Subchapter H to a support proceeding involving:

(1) a foreign support order;

(2) a foreign tribunal; or

(3) an obligee, obligor, or child residing in a foreign country.

(b) A tribunal of this state that is requested to recognize and enforce a support order on the basis of comity may apply the procedural and substantive provisions of Subchapters B through G.

(c) Subchapter H applies only to a support proceeding under the Convention. In such a proceeding, if a provision of Subchapter H is inconsistent with Subchapters B through G, Subchapter H controls.

History of Fam. Code §159.105: Acts 2015, 84th Leg., ch. 368, §4, eff. July 1, 2015.

NCCUSL Comment*

Four distinct entities are defined as a "foreign country" with tribunals that enter a "foreign support order." *See* §159.102(5). With regard to the three types of proceedings identified in subsection (a), all of the provisions in this act in Subchapters B through G apply. Note, however, that under subsection (c), only one of these, a country "in which the Convention is in force with respect to the United States," *see* §159.102(5)(D), will be subject to Subchapter H as well as Subchapters B through G. Thus, a support order from one of these countries may require special attention. After the Convention comes into force in the United States, a body of case law may develop if it becomes necessary to resolve unanticipated differences between this act and the Convention. As this extensive commentary and the many cross reference to provisions of the Convention indicate, significant efforts have been made to avoid any such conflicts.

Under subsection (b) a tribunal of this state may apply principles of comity if appropriate to recognize a support order from a foreign nation state that does not fit the definition of a "foreign country," *see* §159.102(5)(A)-(D), *supra*.

Subsection (c) resolves that if terms of the Convention and the terms of this act, including Subchapter H, are in conflict, the provision of the Convention controls. With regard to the other three statutory definitions of a "foreign country," all the terms, this act in Subchapters B through G control. After the Convention comes into force in the United States, a body of case law may develop to resolve unanticipated differences between this act and the Convention.

Sections 159.106-159.200 reserved for expansion

SUBCHAPTER C. JURISDICTION

FAM §159.201. BASES FOR JURISDICTION OVER NONRESIDENT

(a) In a proceeding to establish or enforce a support order or to determine parentage of a child, a tribunal of this state may exercise personal jurisdiction over a nonresident individual or the individual's guardian or conservator if:

(1) the individual is personally served with citation in this state;

(2) the individual submits to the jurisdiction of this state by consent in a record, by entering a general appearance, or by filing a responsive document having the effect of waiving any contest to personal jurisdiction;

(3) the individual resided with the child in this state;

(4) the individual resided in this state and provided prenatal expenses or support for the child;

(5) the child resides in this state as a result of the acts or directives of the individual;

(6) the individual engaged in sexual intercourse in this state and the child may have been conceived by that act of intercourse;

(7) the individual asserted parentage of a child in the paternity registry maintained in this state by the vital statistics unit; or

(8) there is any other basis consistent with the constitutions of this state and the United States for the exercise of personal jurisdiction.

(b) The bases of personal jurisdiction listed in Subsection (a) or in any other law of this state may not be used to acquire personal jurisdiction for a tribunal of this state to modify a child support order of another state

* See footnote on p. 666.

unless the requirements of Section 159.611 are met, or, in the case of a foreign support order, unless the requirements of Section 159.615 are met.

History of Fam. Code §159.201: Acts 1995, 74th Leg., ch. 20, §1, eff. Apr. 20, 1995. Amended by Acts 1997, 75th Leg., ch. 561, §5, eff. Sept. 1, 1997; Acts 2003, 78th Leg., ch. 1247, §4, eff. Sept. 1, 2003; Acts 2015, 84th Leg., ch. 368, §5 (eff. July 1, 2015), ch. 1, §1.054 (eff. Apr. 2, 2015). Source: Former Fam. Code §21.04.

See also ***O'Connor's Texas Family Law Handbook*** (2017), "Long-arm statute," ch. 4-A, §2.2.2(2)(a), p. 337.

NCCUSL Comment*

General Jurisdictional Principle: Sections 159.201 and 159.202 contain what is commonly described as long-arm jurisdiction over a nonresident respondent for purposes of establishing a support order or determining parentage. Read together, subsections (a) and (b) provide the basic jurisdictional rules established by the act for interstate application of a support order, and are designed to be as broad as is constitutionally permissible. To sustain enforceability of a family support order in the United States the tribunal must be able to assert personal jurisdiction over the parties. *See Estin v. Estin*, 334 U.S. 541, 68 S. Ct. 1213, 92 L. Ed. 1561 (1948), and *Vanderbilt v. Vanderbilt*, 354 U.S. 416, 77 S. Ct. 1360, 1 L. Ed. 2d 1456 (1957) (spousal support); *Kulko v. Superior Court*, 436 U.S. 84, 98 S. Ct. 1690, 56 L. Ed. 2d 132 (1978) (child support).

Long-arm Provisions: Inclusion of this long-arm provision in this interstate act is justified because residents of two separate states are involved in the litigation, both of whom must be subject to the personal jurisdiction of the forum. Thus, the case has a clear interstate aspect, despite the fact that the substantive and procedural law of the forum state is applicable to a lawsuit in what is a one-state case. This rationale is sufficient to invoke additional UIFSA provisions in an otherwise intrastate proceeding. *See* §§159.202, 159.316, and 159.318, as pertaining to special rules of evidence and discovery for UIFSA cases. The intent is to ensure that every enacting state has a long-arm statute that is as broad as constitutionally permitted.

In situations in which the long-arm statute can be satisfied, the petitioner (either the obligor or the obligee) has two options: (1) utilize the long-arm statute to obtain personal jurisdiction over the respondent, or, (2) initiate a two-state proceeding under the succeeding provisions of UIFSA seeking to establish a support order in the respondent's state of residence. Of course, a third option is also available that does not implicate UIFSA; a petitioner may initiate a proceeding in the respondent's state of residence by filing a proceeding to settle all issues between the parties in a single proceeding.

Under RURESA, multiple support orders affecting the same parties were commonplace. UIFSA created a structure designed to provide for only one support order at a time. The new one-order regime is facilitated and combined with a broad assertion of personal jurisdiction under this long-arm provision. The frequency of a two-state procedure involving the participation of tribunals in both states has been substantially reduced by the introduction of this long-arm statute.

Subsection by subsection analyses: Subsections (a)(1) through (a)(8) are derived from a variety of sources, including the Uniform Parentage Act (1973) §8, Texas Family Code §102.011, and New York Family Court Act §154.

Subsection (a)(1) codifies the holding of *Burnham v. Superior Court*, 495 U.S. 604 (1990), which reaffirms the constitutional validity of asserting personal jurisdiction based on personal service within a state.

Subsection (a)(2) expresses the principle that a nonresident party concedes personal jurisdiction by seeking affirmative relief or by submitting to the jurisdiction by answering or entering an appearance. However, the power to assert jurisdiction over an issue involving child support under the act does not necessarily extend the tribunal's jurisdiction to other matters. As noted above, family law is rife with instances of bifurcated jurisdiction. For example, a tribunal may have jurisdiction to establish a child-support order based on personal jurisdiction over the obligor under §159.201, but lack jurisdiction over child custody, which is a matter of status adjudication usually based on the home state of the child.

Subsections (a)(3) through (a)(6) identify specific fact situations justifying the assertion of long-arm jurisdiction over a nonresident. Each provides an appropriate affiliating nexus for such an assertion, when judged on a case-by-case basis with an eye on procedural and substantive due process. Further, each subsection does contain a possibility that an overly literal construction of the terms of the statute will overreach due process. For example, subsection (a)(3) provides that long-arm jurisdiction to establish a support order may be asserted if "the individual resided with the child in this state." The typical scenario contemplated by the statute is that the parties lived as a family unit in the forum state, separated, and one of the parents subsequently moved to another state while the other parent and the child continued to reside in the forum. No time frame is stated for filing a proceeding; this is based on the fact that the absent parent has a support obligation that extends for at least the minority of the child (and longer in some states).

On the other hand, suppose that the two parents and their child lived in State A for many years and then decided to move the family to State B to seek better employment opportunities. Those opportunities did not materialize and, after several weeks or a few months of frustration with the situation, one of the parents returned with the child to State A. Under these facts, a tribunal of State A may conclude it has long-arm jurisdiction to establish the support obligation of the absent parent. But, suppose that the family's sojourn in State B lasted for many years, and then one parent unilaterally decides to return to State A. It is reasonable to expect that a tribunal will conclude that assertion of personal jurisdiction over the absent parent immediately after the return based on subsection (a)(3) would offend due process. Note the provisions of UIFSA are available to the returning parent to establish child support in State B, and that state will have long-arm jurisdiction to establish support binding on the moving parent under §159.201. *See also* §159.204 for the resolution of simultaneous proceedings provided by the act.

Finally, subsection (a)(8) tracks the broad, catch-all provisions found in many state statutes, including Cal. Civ. Proc. Code §410.10 (1973), and Tex. Family Code §102.011. Note, however, that the California provision, standing alone, was found to be inadequate to sustain a child-support order under the facts presented in *Kulko v. Superior Court*, 436 U.S. 84 (1978).

Limit on Asserting Long-arm Jurisdiction to Modify Child-Support Order: Subsection (b) elaborates on the principle by providing that modification of an existing child-support order goes beyond the usual rules of personal jurisdiction over the parties. Amended in UIFSA (2001), subsection (b) makes clear long-arm personal jurisdiction over a respondent, standing alone, is not sufficient to grant subject matter jurisdiction to a responding tribunal of the state of residence of the petitioner for that tribunal to modify an existing child-support order. See the extended commentaries to §§159.609 through 159.616. The limitations on modification of a child support order provided by §159.611 must be observed irrespective of the existence of personal jurisdiction over the parties.

For tribunals of the United States, these sections integrate the concepts of personal jurisdiction and its progeny, continuing jurisdiction, and controlling orders. Note that the longarm provisions of UIFSA (1992) were originally written with only domestic cases in mind. If the tribunal of a state has personal jurisdiction over an individual residing in another state (or, by implication, a foreign country), the application of local law is entitled to recognition and enforcement. *See* Full Faith and Credit for Child Support Orders Act, a.k.a. FFCCSOA, 28 U.S.C. §1738B. Integrating this federal law based on the Constitution with the statutory rule of subject matter jurisdiction for modification of an existing child-support order is a major accomplishment of UIFSA. Obviously, the federal act is applicable to a child-support order issued by a state tribunal, but is not applicable to a foreign support order. Nor does FFCCSOA in any way affect a foreign country, which will apply its local law of recognition, enforcement, and modification to a child-support order originating from a state of the United States. When the Convention enters into force, the integration of UIFSA and the law of some foreign countries will be international in scope. At that time the jurisdictional rules of all concerned become significantly more complex. *See* §159.708. Nonetheless, it seems likely the complexity will be more theoretical than actually troublesome.

Applicability of Long-Arm Jurisdiction to Spousal Support: Although this long-arm statute applies to a spousal-support order, almost all of the specific provisions of this section relate to a child-support order or a determination of parentage. This derives from the fact that the focus of UIFSA is primarily on child support. Only subsections (a)(1), (a)(2), and (a)(8) are applicable to an action for spousal support asserting long-arm jurisdiction over a nonresident. The first two subsections are wholly noncontroversial insofar as an assertion of personal jurisdiction is concerned. Moreover, as a practical matter, an assertion of personal jurisdiction under UIFSA will almost always also yield jurisdiction over all matters to be decided between the spouses, including division of prop-

* See footnote on p. 666.

erty on divorce. Thus, the most obvious possible basis for asserting long-arm jurisdiction over spousal support, i.e., "last matrimonial domicile," is not included in §159.201 to avoid the potential problem of another instance of bifurcated jurisdiction. This restraint avoids a situation in which UIFSA would arguably grant long-arm jurisdiction for a spousal-support order when the forum state has no correlative statute for property division in divorce.

Potential Application of Long-arm Jurisdiction to Foreign Support Order: If the facts of a case warrant, whether in an interstate or an international context, a state tribunal shall apply long-arm jurisdiction to establish a support order without regard to the physical location or residence of a party outside the United States. Interestingly, under certain fact situations involving a request to recognize and enforce or modify a foreign support order, a state tribunal may be called upon to determine the applicability of long-arm jurisdiction under UIFSA to the facts of the case in order to decide the enforceability of the foreign support order.

For example, a challenge to a request for enforcement of a foreign support order may be made by a respondent based on an allegation that the foreign issuing tribunal lacked personal jurisdiction over the respondent. A respondent may acknowledge that the obligee or the child resides in France, and that a French tribunal issued a support order. But, in the *Kulko* decision the Court accepted the respondent's allegation that under the state law then available there was no nexus between himself and California and therefore no personal jurisdiction over him as required by the opinion. From the perspective of the French tribunal under the facts above, an asserted lack of personal jurisdiction is of no consequence. Under the law of France, like the law of virtually all other foreign nations, the child-based jurisdiction stemming from the residence of the obligee or child is sufficient to sustain a child-support order against the noncustodial parent. But, meshing the world-wide system of child-based jurisdiction with the U.S. requirement of in personam jurisdiction presented an easily resolved challenge to the drafters of the new Hague Maintenance Convention.

Thus, under the Convention, a state tribunal may be called upon to determine whether the facts underlying the support order would have provided the issuing foreign tribunal with personal jurisdiction over the respondent under the standards of this section. In effect, the question is whether the foreign tribunal would have been able to exercise jurisdiction in accordance with §159.201. The foregoing fact situation illustrates that it is for the state tribunal to determine if the order of the French tribunal would have complied with UIFSA §159.201 on the facts of the case. If so, the foreign support order is entitled to recognition and enforcement. For example, the facts of the case may show that the father lived with the child in France, supported the mother or child in France, or perhaps was responsible for, or agreed to the movement of the child to France.

On the other hand, if the issuing French tribunal would have lacked personal jurisdiction over the respondent if §159.201 had been applicable, the support order cannot be enforced because there was no nexus between France and the respondent. The United States will make a reservation to Convention article 20, declining to recognize or enforce a foreign support order on child-based jurisdiction founded solely on the location or residence of the obligee or the child in the foreign country.

Interestingly, if the responding state tribunal finds the French tribunal lacked personal jurisdiction over the respondent, additional action may be taken. In a Convention case, the responding state tribunal may establish a child-support order if it has personal jurisdiction over the respondent without requesting a separate application for establishment of a new order.

Related to Convention: art. 2. Scope; art. 19. Scope of the chapter; art. 20. Bases for recognition and enforcement; art. 32. Enforcement under internal law; art. 62. Reservations.

FAM §159.202. DURATION OF PERSONAL JURISDICTION

Personal jurisdiction acquired by a tribunal of this state in a proceeding under this chapter or other law of this state relating to a support order continues as long as the tribunal of this state has continuing, exclusive jurisdiction to modify its order or continuing jurisdiction to enforce its order as provided by Sections 159.205, 159.206, and 159.211.

History of Fam. Code §159.202: Acts 1995, 74th Leg., ch. 20, §1, eff. Apr. 20, 1995. Amended by Acts 2003, 78th Leg., ch. 1247, §5, eff. Sept. 1, 2003; Acts 2015, 84th Leg., ch. 368, §6, eff. July 1, 2015. Source: Former Fam. Code §21.05.

NCCUSL Comment*

It is a useful legal truism after a tribunal of a state issues a support order binding on the parties, which must be based on personal jurisdiction by virtue of *Kulko v. Superior Court*, 436 U.S. 84 (1978) and *Vanderbilt v. Vanderbilt*, 354 U.S. 416 (1957), jurisdiction in personam continues for the duration of the support obligation absent the statutorily specified reasons to terminate the order. The rule established by UIFSA is that the personal jurisdiction necessary to sustain enforcement or modification of an order of child support or spousal support persists as long as the order is in force and effect, even as to arrears, *see* §§159.205-159.207, 159.211, *infra*. This is true irrespective of the context in which the support order arose, *e.g.*, divorce, UIFSA support establishment, parentage establishment, modification of prior controlling order, etc. Insofar as a child-support order is concerned, depending on specific factual circumstances a distinction is made between retaining continuing, exclusive jurisdiction to modify an order and having continuing jurisdiction to enforce an order, *see* §§159.205 and 159.206, *infra*. Authority to modify a spousal-support order is permanently reserved to the issuing tribunal, §159.211, *infra*.

FAM §159.203. INITIATING & RESPONDING TRIBUNAL OF STATE

Under this chapter, a tribunal of this state may serve as an initiating tribunal to forward proceedings to a tribunal of another state and as a responding tribunal for proceedings initiated in another state or a foreign country.

History of Fam. Code §159.203: Acts 1995, 74th Leg., ch. 20, §1, eff. Apr. 20, 1995. Amended by Acts 1997, 75th Leg., ch. 607, §3, eff. Sept. 1, 1997; Acts 2015, 84th Leg., ch. 368, §7, eff. July 1, 2015. Source: Former Fam. Code §21.06.

NCCUSL Comment*

This section identifies the two roles a tribunal of the forum may serve: acting as either an initiating or a responding tribunal. See §§159.304 and 159.305 for the duties and powers of the tribunal in each of these capacities. Under UIFSA, a tribunal may serve as a responding tribunal even when there is no initiating tribunal. This accommodates the direct filing of a proceeding in a responding tribunal by a nonresident of the forum, whether residing in a state or anywhere else in the world. Note, however, that the section does not deal with whether an initiating tribunal of a state may forward a proceeding to a tribunal in a foreign country, which may be left to the individual support enforcement agency.

Related to Convention: art. 2. Scope; art. 37. Direct requests to competent authorities.

FAM §159.204. SIMULTANEOUS PROCEEDINGS

(a) A tribunal of this state may exercise jurisdiction to establish a support order if the petition or comparable pleading is filed after a pleading is filed in another state or a foreign country only if:

(1) the petition or comparable pleading in this state is filed before the expiration of the time allowed in the other state or the foreign country for filing a responsive pleading challenging the exercise of jurisdiction by the other state or the foreign country;

(2) the contesting party timely challenges the exercise of jurisdiction in the other state or the foreign country; and

---

* See footnote on p. 666.

(3) if relevant, this state is the home state of the child.

(b) A tribunal of this state may not exercise jurisdiction to establish a support order if the petition or comparable pleading is filed before a petition or comparable pleading is filed in another state or a foreign country if:

(1) the petition or comparable pleading in the other state or foreign country is filed before the expiration of the time allowed in this state for filing a responsive pleading challenging the exercise of jurisdiction by this state;

(2) the contesting party timely challenges the exercise of jurisdiction in this state; and

(3) if relevant, the other state or foreign country is the home state of the child.

History of Fam. Code §159.204: Acts 1995, 74th Leg., ch. 20, §1, eff. Apr. 20, 1995. Amended by Acts 2003, 78th Leg., ch. 1247, §6, eff. Sept. 1, 2003; Acts 2015, 84th Leg., ch. 368, §8, eff. July 1, 2015. Source: Former Fam. Code §21.07.

NCCUSL Comment*

Under the one-order system established by UIFSA, it was necessary to provide a procedure to eliminate the multiple orders so common under RURESA and URESA. This requires cooperation between, and deference by, state tribunals in order to avoid issuance of competing support orders. To this end, tribunals are expected to take an active role in seeking out information about support proceedings in another state or foreign country concerning the same child. Depending on the circumstances, one of the two tribunals considering the same support obligation should decide to defer to the other. The inclusion of a foreign country in this investigation facilitates the goal of a "one-order world" for a support obligation.

UIFSA (1992) took a significant departure from the approach adopted by the UCCJA (1986) ("first filing"), by choosing the "home state of the child" as the primary factual basis for resolving competing jurisdictional disputes. Not coincidentally, this had previously been the choice for resolving jurisdiction conflicts of the federal Parental Kidnapping Prevention Act, 28 U.S.C. Section 1738A (1980). Given the pre-emptive nature of the PKPA, and the possibility that custody and support will both be involved in some cases, the PKPA/UIFSA choice for resolving disputes between competing jurisdictional assertions was followed in 1997 by the decision of NCCUSL to replace the UCCJA with the UCCJEA. If the child has no home state, however, "first filing" will control.

FAM §159.205. CONTINUING, EXCLUSIVE JURISDICTION TO MODIFY CHILD SUPPORT ORDER

(a) A tribunal of this state that has issued a child support order consistent with the law of this state has and shall exercise continuing, exclusive jurisdiction to modify its child support order if the order is the controlling order and:

(1) at the time of the filing of a request for modification this state is the residence of the obligor, the individual obligee, or the child for whose benefit the support order is issued; or

(2) even if this state is not the residence of the obligor, the individual obligee, or the child for whose benefit the support order is issued, the parties consent in a record or in open court that the tribunal of this state may continue to exercise jurisdiction to modify its order.

(b) A tribunal of this state that has issued a child support order consistent with the law of this state may not exercise continuing, exclusive jurisdiction to modify the order if:

(1) all of the parties who are individuals file consent in a record with the tribunal of this state that a tribunal of another state that has jurisdiction over at least one of the parties who is an individual or that is located in the state of residence of the child may modify the order and assume continuing, exclusive jurisdiction; or

(2) the tribunal's order is not the controlling order.

(c) If a tribunal of another state has issued a child support order pursuant to the Uniform Interstate Family Support Act or a law substantially similar to that Act that modifies a child support order of a tribunal of this state, tribunals of this state shall recognize the continuing, exclusive jurisdiction of the tribunal of the other state.

(d) A tribunal of this state that lacks continuing, exclusive jurisdiction to modify a child support order may serve as an initiating tribunal to request a tribunal of another state to modify a support order issued in that state.

(e) A temporary support order issued ex parte or pending resolution of a jurisdictional conflict does not create continuing, exclusive jurisdiction in the issuing tribunal.

(f) Repealed by Acts 2003, 78th Leg., ch. 1247, §46, eff. Sept. 1, 2003.

History of Fam. Code §159.205: Acts 1995, 74th Leg., ch. 20, §1, eff. Apr. 20, 1995. Amended by Acts 1997, 75th Leg., ch. 607, §4, eff. Sept. 1, 1997; Acts 2003, 78th Leg., ch. 1247, §§7, 8, 46, eff. Sept. 1, 2003; Acts 2015, 84th Leg., ch. 368, §9, eff. July 1, 2015. Source: Former Fam. Code §21.08.

See also *O'Connor's Texas Family Law Handbook* (2017), "Jurisdiction to modify Texas order," ch. 9-D, §2.1.1, p. 1024.

ANNOTATIONS

In re Martinez, 450 S.W.3d 157, 163 (Tex. App.—San Antonio 2014, orig. proceeding). Obligee argues "the action she filed in the Texas trial court was an 'original' action as opposed to a modification. [S]he contends her action was *per force* an original action because the New York decree terminated pursuant to its own provisions before she filed suit in Texas. ... Thus, according to [obligee], there was no decree to modify. [¶] We disagree.... [S]ection 159.205 provides only

* See footnote on p. 666.

two ways in which a court may lose its continuing exclusive jurisdiction.... [D]espite the expiration of the New York decree by its terms, under UIFSA, New York never lost continuing, exclusive jurisdiction over this child support matter."

NCCUSL Comment*

This section is perhaps the most crucial provision in UIFSA. Consistent with the precedent of the federal PARENTAL KIDNAPPING PREVENTION ACT, 28 U.S.C. §1738A, except in very narrowly defined circumstances the issuing tribunal retains continuing, exclusive jurisdiction over a child-support order, commonly known as CEJ. First introduced by UIFSA in 1992, this principle is in force and widely accepted in all states. Indeed CEJ is fundamental to the principle of one-child-support-order-at-a-time.

As long as one of the individual parties or the child continues to reside in the issuing state, and as long as the parties do not agree to the contrary, the issuing tribunal has continuing, exclusive jurisdiction over its child-support order—which in practical terms means that it may modify its order. The statute takes an even-handed approach. The identity of the party remaining in the issuing state—obligor or obligee—does not matter. Indeed, if the individual parties have left the issuing state but the child remains behind, CEJ remains with the issuing tribunal. Even if the parties and the child no longer reside in the issuing state, the support order continues in existence and is fully enforceable unless and until a modification takes place in accordance with the requirements of Subchapter G, *infra*. Note, however, that the CEJ of the issuing tribunal over a spousal-support order is permanent, *see* §159.211, *infra*.

Subsection (a)(1) states the basic rule, and subsection (a)(2) states an exception to that rule. First, the time to measure whether the issuing tribunal has continuing, exclusive jurisdiction to modify its order, or whether the parties and the child have left the state, is explicitly stated to be at the time of filing a proceeding to modify the child-support order. Second, the term in subsection (a)(1) "is the residence" makes clear that any interruption of residence of a party between the date of the issuance of the order and the date of filing the request for modification does not affect jurisdiction to modify. Thus, if there is but one order, it is the controlling order in effect and enforceable throughout the United States, notwithstanding the fact that everyone at one time had left the issuing state. If the order is not modified during this time of mutual absence, a return to reside in the issuing state by a party or child immediately identifies the proper forum at the time of filing a proceeding for modification. Although the statute does not speak explicitly to the issue, temporary absence should be treated in a similar fashion. Temporary employment in another state may not forfeit a claim of residence in the issuing state. Of course, residence is a fact question for the trial court, keeping in mind that the question is residence, not domicile.

From the beginning of the implementation of the CEJ principle, questions have been raised about why a tribunal may not modify its own order if the parties agree that it should do so even after the parties have left the state. The move of the parties and the child from the state may have been of a very short distance and, although the parties no longer reside in the issuing state, they may prefer to continue to have the child-support order be governed by the same issuing tribunal because they continue to have a strong affiliation with it. For example, the child-support order may have been issued by a tribunal of Washington, D.C. Subsequently the obligee and child have moved to Virginia, the obligor now resides in Maryland, and perhaps one or both parties continue to be employed in Washington. Subsection (a)(2) authorizes retention of CEJ by the issuing state when the parties reasonably may prefer to continue to deal with the issuing tribunal even though the state is "not the residence" of the parties or child as an exception to the general rules of CEJ for modifications of a support order.

The other side of the coin follows logically. Just as subsection (a) defines the retention of continuing, exclusive jurisdiction, by clear implication the subsection also identifies how jurisdiction to modify may be lost. That is, if all the relevant persons—the obligor, the individual obligee, and the child—have permanently left the issuing state, absent an agreement the issuing tribunal no longer has an appropriate nexus with the parties or child to justify the exercise of jurisdiction to modify its child-support order. Further, the issuing tribunal will have no current evidence readily available to it about the factual circumstances of anyone involved, and the taxpayers of that state will have no reason to expend public funds on the process. Note, however, that the original order of the issuing tribunal remains valid and enforceable. That order is in effect not only in the issuing state, but also in those states in which the order has been registered. The order also may be registered and enforced in additional states even after the issuing tribunal has lost its power to modify its order, *see* §§159.601-159.604, *infra*. In sum, the original order remains in effect until it is properly modified in accordance with the narrow terms of §§159.609-159.612, *infra*.

Subsection (b)(1) explicitly provides that the parties may agree in a record that the issuing tribunal should relinquish its continuing, exclusive jurisdiction to modify so that a tribunal in another state may assume CEJ to modify the child-support order. It is believed that such consent seldom occurs because of the almost universal desire of each party to prefer his or her local tribunal. The principle that the parties should be allowed to agree upon an alternate forum if they so choose also extends to a situation in which all the parties and the child have left the issuing state and are in agreement that a tribunal of the state in which only the movant resides shall assume modification jurisdiction, *see* §159.611.

Although subsections (a) and (b) identify the methods for the retention and the loss of continuing, exclusive jurisdiction by the issuing tribunal, this section does not confer jurisdiction to modify on another tribunal. Modification requires that a tribunal have personal jurisdiction over the parties and meet other criteria as provided in §§159.609 through 159.615, *infra*.

Related to Convention: art. 18. Limit on proceedings.

FAM §159.206. CONTINUING JURISDICTION TO ENFORCE CHILD SUPPORT ORDER

(a) A tribunal of this state that has issued a child support order consistent with the law of this state may serve as an initiating tribunal to request a tribunal of another state to enforce:

(1) the order, if the order:

(A) is the controlling order; and

(B) has not been modified by a tribunal of another state that assumed jurisdiction under the Uniform Interstate Family Support Act; or

(2) a money judgment for arrears of support and interest on the order accrued before a determination that an order of a tribunal of another state is the controlling order.

(b) A tribunal of this state having continuing jurisdiction over a support order may act as a responding tribunal to enforce the order.

History of Fam. Code §159.206: Acts 1995, 74th Leg., ch. 20, §1, eff. Apr. 20, 1995. Amended by Acts 2003, 78th Leg., ch. 1247, §9, eff. Sept. 1, 2003; Acts 2015, 84th Leg., ch. 368, §10, eff. July 1, 2015. Source: Former Fam. Code §21.09.

NCCUSL Comment*

This section is the correlative of the continuing, exclusive jurisdiction described in the preceding section. It makes the relatively subtle distinction between the CEJ "to modify a support order" established in §159.205 and the "continuing jurisdiction to enforce" established in this section. A keystone of UIFSA is that the power to enforce the order of the issuing tribunal is not "exclusive" with that tribunal. Rather, on request one or more responding tribunals may also exercise authority to enforce the order of the issuing tribunal. Secondly, under the one-order-at-a-time system, the validity and enforceability of the controlling order continues unabated until it is fully complied with, unless it is replaced by a modified order issued in accordance with the standards

* See footnote on p. 666.

established by §§159.609-159.616. That is, even if the individual parties and the child no longer reside in the issuing state, the controlling order remains in effect and may be enforced by the issuing tribunal or any responding tribunal without regard to the fact that the potential for its modification and replacement exists.

Subsection (a) authorizes the issuing tribunal to initiate a request for enforcement of its order by a tribunal of another state if its order is controlling, *see* §159.207, or to request reconciliation of the arrears and interest due on its order if another order is controlling.

Subsection (b) reiterates that the issuing tribunal has jurisdiction to serve as a responding tribunal to enforce its own order at the request of another tribunal.

Related to Convention: art. 19. Scope of the Chapter.

FAM §159.207. DETERMINATION OF CONTROLLING CHILD SUPPORT ORDER

(a) If a proceeding is brought under this chapter and only one tribunal has issued a child support order, the order of that tribunal controls and must be recognized.

(b) If a proceeding is brought under this chapter and two or more child support orders have been issued by tribunals of this state, another state, or a foreign country with regard to the same obligor and same child, a tribunal of this state having personal jurisdiction over both the obligor and individual obligee shall apply the following rules and by order shall determine which order controls and must be recognized:

(1) if only one of the tribunals would have continuing, exclusive jurisdiction under this chapter, the order of that tribunal controls;

(2) if more than one of the tribunals would have continuing, exclusive jurisdiction under this chapter:

(A) an order issued by a tribunal in the current home state of the child controls; or

(B) if an order has not been issued in the current home state of the child, the order most recently issued controls; and

(3) if none of the tribunals would have continuing, exclusive jurisdiction under this chapter, the tribunal of this state shall issue a child support order that controls.

(c) If two or more child support orders have been issued for the same obligor and same child, on request of a party who is an individual or that is a support enforcement agency, a tribunal of this state having personal jurisdiction over both the obligor and the obligee who is an individual shall determine which order controls under Subsection (b). The request may be filed with a registration for enforcement or registration for modification under Subchapter G or may be filed as a separate proceeding.

(d) A request to determine which is the controlling order must be accompanied by a copy of every child support order in effect and the applicable record of payments. The requesting party shall give notice of the request to each party whose rights may be affected by the determination.

(e) The tribunal that issued the controlling order under Subsection (a), (b), or (c) has continuing jurisdiction to the extent provided by Section 159.205 or 159.206.

(f) A tribunal of this state that determines by order which is the controlling order under Subsection (b)(1) or (2) or Subsection (c), or that issues a new controlling order under Subsection (b)(3), shall state in that order:

(1) the basis upon which the tribunal made its determination;

(2) the amount of prospective support, if any; and

(3) the total amount of consolidated arrears and accrued interest, if any, under all of the orders after all payments made are credited as provided by Section 159.209.

(g) Within 30 days after issuance of an order determining which order is the controlling order, the party obtaining the order shall file a certified copy of the controlling order in each tribunal that issued or registered an earlier order of child support. A party or support enforcement agency obtaining the order that fails to file a certified copy is subject to appropriate sanctions by a tribunal in which the issue of failure to file arises. The failure to file does not affect the validity or enforceability of the controlling order.

(h) An order that has been determined to be the controlling order, or a judgment for consolidated arrears of support and interest, if any, made under this section, must be recognized in proceedings under this chapter.

History of Fam. Code §159.207: Acts 1995, 74th Leg., ch. 20, §1, eff. Apr. 20, 1995. Amended by Acts 1997, 75th Leg., ch. 607, §5, eff. Sept. 1, 1997; Acts 2003, 78th Leg., ch. 1247, §§10, 11, eff. Sept. 1, 2003; Acts 2015, 84th Leg., ch. 368, §11, eff. July 1, 2015. Source: Former Fam. Code §21.10.

NCCUSL Comment*

In addition to the introduction of the concepts of one-order and continuing, exclusive jurisdiction in §159.205, another dramatic founding principle of UIFSA was to establish a system whereby the multiple orders created by URESA and RURESA could be reconciled in the transition from a world with multiple child-support orders to a one-order-at-a-time world. This principle introduced by §159.207 was subsequently incorporated into the requirements of 28 USC 1738B, Full Faith and Credit for Child Support Orders, a.k.a. FFCCSOA.

* See footnote on p. 666.

The combination of FFCCSOA becoming effective on October 20, 1994 and the adoption of UIFSA (1996) being mandated for all states by January 1, 1998, has made this section almost never used. The existence of multiple, valid orders for ongoing support have all but disappeared.

Sections 159.207-159.210, and especially §159.207, are designed to span the gulf between the one-order system created by UIFSA and the multiple-order system previously in place under RURESA and URESA. These transitional procedures necessarily must provide for the eventual elimination of existing multiple support orders in an expeditious and efficient manner. Although FFCCSOA was effective October 20, 1994 and all U.S. jurisdictions enacted UIFSA by 1998, considerable time is required to pass before its one-order system could be completely in place. For example, multiple 21-year child-support orders issued for an infant in 1996 and 1997 would, by their terms, not end the conflict until the first expires 2017—absent resolution of the conflict by a tribunal under this section. Nonetheless, at least on the appellate level, the problem of multiple orders is fast disappearing. This section provides a relatively simple procedure to identify a single viable order that will be entitled to prospective enforcement in every state.

Subsection (a) declares that if only one child-support order exists, it is to be denominated the controlling order, irrespective of when and where it was issued and whether any of the individual parties or the child continue to reside in the issuing state.

Subsection (b) establishes the priority scheme for recognition and prospective enforcement of a single order among existing multiple orders regarding the same obligor, obligee, and child. A tribunal requested to sort out the multiple orders and determine which one will be prospectively controlling of future payments must have personal jurisdiction over the litigants in order to ensure that its decision is binding on all concerned. For UIFSA to function, one order must be denominated as the controlling order, and its issuing tribunal must be recognized as having continuing, exclusive jurisdiction. In choosing among existing multiple orders, none of which can be distinguished as being in conflict with the principles of UIFSA, subsection (b)(1) gives first priority to an order issued by the only tribunal that is entitled to continuing, exclusive jurisdiction under the terms of UIFSA, i.e., an individual party or the child continues to reside in that state and no other state meets this criterion. If two or more tribunals would have continuing, exclusive jurisdiction under the act, subsection (b)(2) first looks to the tribunal of the child's current home state. If that tribunal has not issued a support order, subsection (b)(2) looks next to the order most recently issued. Finally, subsection (b)(3) provides that if none of the existing multiple orders are entitled to be denominated as the controlling order because none of the preceding priorities apply, the forum tribunal is directed to issue a new order, given that it has personal jurisdiction over the obligor and obligee. The new order becomes the controlling order, establishes the continuing, exclusive jurisdiction of the tribunal, and fixes the support obligation and its nonmodifiable aspects, primarily duration of support, *see* §§159.604 and 159.611(c), *infra*. The rationale for creating a new order to replace existing multiple orders is that there is no valid reason to prefer the terms of any one of the multiple orders over another in the absence of a fact situation described in subsections (b)(1) or (b)(2).

As originally promulgated, UIFSA did not come to grips with whether existing multiple orders issued by different states might be entitled to full faith and credit without regard to the determination of the controlling order under the act. The drafters took the position that state law, however uniform, could not interfere with the ultimate interpretation of a constitutional directive. Fortunately, this question has almost certainly been mooted by the 1996 amendment to 28 U.S.C. §1738B, Full Faith and Credit for Child Support Orders. Congress incorporated the multiple order recognition provisions of §159.207 of UIFSA into FFCCSOA virtually word for word in the PERSONAL RESPONSIBILITY AND WORK OPPORTUNITY RECONCILIATION ACT OF 1996. Pub. L. 104-193, Aug. 22, 1996, 110 Stat. 2221.

It is not altogether clear whether the terms of UIFSA apply to a strictly intrastate case; that is, a situation in which multiple child-support orders have been issued by multiple tribunals of a single state and the parties and the child continue to reside in that state. This is not an uncommon situation, often traceable to the intrastate applicability of RURESA. A literal reading of the statutory language suggests the section applies. Further, FFCCSOA does not make a distinction regarding the tribunals that issued multiple orders. If multiple orders have been issued by different tribunals in the home state of the child, most likely the most recent will be recognized as the controlling order, notwithstanding the fact that UIFSA §159.207(b)(2)(B), and FFCCSOA 42 U.S.C. §1738B(f)(3), literally do not apply. At the very least, this section, together with FFCCSOA, provide a template for resolving such conflicts.

Subsection (c) clarifies that any party or a support enforcement agency may request a tribunal of the forum state to identify the controlling order. That party is directed to fully inform the tribunal of all existing child-support orders.

Subsection (d) seeks to assure the tribunal is furnished with all the information needed to make a proper determination of the controlling order, as well as the information needed to make a calculation of the consolidated arrears. The party or support enforcement agency requesting the determination of controlling order and determination of consolidated arrears is also required to notify all other parties and entities who may have an interest in either of those determinations. Those with such an interest most likely are support agencies and the obligee.

Subsection (e) provides that the determination of the controlling order under this section has the effect of establishing the tribunal with continuing, exclusive jurisdiction; only the order of that tribunal is entitled to prospective enforcement by a sister state.

Subsection (f) directs the forum tribunal to identify the details upon which it makes its determination of the controlling order. In addition, the tribunal is also directed to state specifically the amount of the prospective support, and to reconcile and consolidate the arrears and interest due on all of the multiple orders to the extent possible.

The party obtaining the determination is directed by subsection (g) to notify all interested tribunals of the decision after the fact. Although tribunals need not be given original notice of the proceeding, all tribunals that have contributed an order to the determination must be informed regarding which order was determined to be controlling, and should also be informed of the consolidated arrears and interest so that the extent of possible subsequent enforcement will be known with regard to each of the orders. The act does not deal with the resolution of potential conflicting claims regarding arrears; this is left to case-by-case decisions or to federal regulation.

Section 159.207 presumes that the parties are accorded notice and opportunity to be heard by the tribunal. It also presumes that the tribunal will be fully informed about all existing orders when it is requested to determine which one of the existing multiple child-support orders is to be accorded prospective enforcement. If this does not occur and one or more existing orders is not considered by the tribunal, the finality of its decision is likely to turn on principles of estoppel on a case-by-case basis.

Finally, subsection (h), affirms the concept that when a fully informed tribunal makes a determination of the controlling order for prospective enforcement, or renders a judgment for the amount of the consolidated arrears, the decision is entitled to full faith and credit.

FAM §159.208. CHILD SUPPORT ORDERS FOR TWO OR MORE OBLIGEES

In responding to registrations or petitions for enforcement of two or more child support orders in effect at the same time with regard to the same obligor and different individual obligees, at least one of which was issued by a tribunal of another state or a foreign country, a tribunal of this state shall enforce those orders in the same manner as if the orders had been issued by a tribunal of this state.

History of Fam. Code §159.208: Acts 1995, 74th Leg., ch. 20, §1, eff. Apr. 20, 1995. Amended by Acts 2003, 78th Leg., ch. 1247, §12, eff. Sept. 1, 2003; Acts 2015, 84th Leg., ch. 368, §12, eff. July 1, 2015. Source: Former Fam. Code §21.11.

NCCUSL Comment*

This section is concerned with those multiple orders that involve two or more families of the same obligor. Although all such orders are entitled to enforcement, practical difficulties frequently exist. For example, full enforcement

* See footnote on p. 666.

of each of the multiple orders may exceed the maximum allowed for income withholding. The federal statute, 42 U.S.C. §666(b)(1), requires that to be eligible for the federal funding for enforcement, states must provide a ceiling for child-support withholding expressed in a percentage that may not exceed the federal law limitations on wage garnishment, Consumer Credit Protection Act of 1968, 15 U.S.C. §1673(b). In order to allocate resources between competing families, UIFSA refers to state law. The basic principle is that one or more support orders for an out-of-state family of the obligor, and one or more orders for an in-state family, are of equal dignity. In allocating payments to different obligees, every child-support order should be treated as if it had been issued by a tribunal of the forum state, that is, preferential treatment for a local family over an out-of-state family is prohibited by local law. The addition of a foreign support order to the formula supplied by this section should assure that all children will have equal ability to obtain their share of child support.

FAM §159.209. CREDIT FOR PAYMENTS

A tribunal of this state shall credit amounts collected for a particular period under any child support order against the amounts owed for the same period under any other child support order for support of the same child issued by a tribunal of this state, another state, or a foreign country.

History of Fam. Code §159.209: Acts 1995, 74th Leg., ch. 20, §1, eff. Apr. 20, 1995. Amended by Acts 2003, 78th Leg., ch. 1247, §12, eff. Sept. 1, 2003; Acts 2015, 84th Leg., ch. 368, §13, eff. July 1, 2015. Source: Former Fam. Code §21.12.

NCCUSL Comment*

The issuing tribunal is ultimately responsible for the overall control of the enforcement methods employed and for accounting for the payments made on its order from multiple sources. Until that scheme is fully in place, however, it will be necessary to continue to mandate pro tanto credit for actual payments made against all existing orders. The addition to include a foreign support order in the calculation should assure all payments of support are properly credited. This section does not attempt to impact the way support paid in an individual case is apportioned or distributed between the obligee and one or more states asserting a claim to the monies.

FAM §159.210. APPLICATION OF CHAPTER TO NONRESIDENT SUBJECT TO PERSONAL JURISDICTION

A tribunal of this state exercising personal jurisdiction over a nonresident in a proceeding under this chapter or under other law of this state relating to a support order or recognizing a foreign support order may receive evidence from outside this state as provided by Section 159.316, communicate with a tribunal outside this state as provided by Section 159.317, and obtain discovery through a tribunal outside this state as provided by Section 159.318. In all other respects, Subchapters D, E, F, and G do not apply and the tribunal shall apply the procedural and substantive law of this state.

History of Fam. Code §159.210: Acts 2003, 78th Leg., ch. 1247, §12, 78th Leg., eff. Sept. 1, 2003. Amended by Acts 2015, 84th Leg., ch. 368, §14, eff. July 1, 2015.

NCCUSL Comment*

Assertion of long-arm jurisdiction over a nonresident results in a one-state proceeding without regard to the fact that one of the parties resides in a different state or in a foreign country. On obtaining personal jurisdiction the tribunal must apply the law of the forum. Once personal jurisdiction has been asserted over a nonresident, the issuing tribunal retains continuing, exclusive jurisdiction (CEJ) to modify, and continuing jurisdiction to enforce a support order in accordance with the provisions of the act. Of course, it is far more common for a support order to be issued in conjunction with a divorce or determination of parentage in which both the obligor and obligee are residents of the forum than to be issued as a result of an assertion of long-arm jurisdiction. Note that either the petitioner or the respondent may be the nonresident party (either of whom may be the obligor or the obligee). Also note that absent this provision, the ordinary intrastate substantive and procedural law of the forum would apply to either fact situation without reference to the fact that one of the parties is a nonresident. Thus, CEJ applies whether the matter at hand involves establishment of an original support order or enforcement or modification of an existing order. In any event, if one of the parties resides outside the forum state, the nonresident may avail himself or herself of the special evidentiary and discovery provisions provided by UIFSA.

This section makes clear that the special rules of evidence and procedure identified in §§159.316, 159.317, and 159.318 are applicable in a case involving a nonresident of the forum state. Section 159.316 facilitates decision-making when a party or a child resides "outside this state" by providing special rules to recognize the impediments to presenting evidence caused by nonresident status. Note the terminology has the broadest possible application, i.e., worldwide. The improved interstate and international exchange of information enables the nonresident to participate as fully as possible in the proceedings without the necessity of personally appearing in the forum state. The same considerations account for authorizing interstate and international communications between tribunals as per §159.317. Finally, the discovery procedures of §159.318 are made applicable in a one-state proceeding when another tribunal may assist in that process. Of course, "may assist" is entirely at the discretion of the other tribunal. Note, a foreign tribunal may be completely unfamiliar with discovery procedures as known in the United States.

Generally, however, the ordinary substantive and procedural law of the forum state applies in a one-state proceeding. In sum, the parties and the tribunal in a one-state case may utilize those procedures that contribute to economy, efficiency, and fair play.

Related to Convention: art. 20. Bases for recognition and enforcement.

FAM §159.211. CONTINUING, EXCLUSIVE JURISDICTION TO MODIFY SPOUSAL SUPPORT ORDER

(a) A tribunal of this state issuing a spousal support order consistent with the law of this state has continuing, exclusive jurisdiction to modify the spousal support order throughout the existence of the support obligation.

(b) A tribunal of this state may not modify a spousal support order issued by a tribunal of another state or a foreign country having continuing, exclusive jurisdiction over that order under the law of that state or foreign country.

(c) A tribunal of this state that has continuing, exclusive jurisdiction over a spousal support order may serve as:

(1) an initiating tribunal to request a tribunal of another state to enforce the spousal support order issued in this state; or

* See footnote on p. 666.

(2) a responding tribunal to enforce or modify its own spousal support order.

History of Fam. Code §159.211: Acts 2003, 78th Leg., ch. 1247, §12, eff. Sept. 1, 2003. Amended by Acts 2015, 84th Leg., ch. 368, §15, eff. July 1, 2015.

NCCUSL Comment*

The amendment to subsection (b) ensures that the restriction on modification of an out-of-state spousal-support order extends to a foreign order. At the same time, subsection (b) provides that the question of continuing, exclusive jurisdiction be resolved under the law of the issuing tribunal. Thus, if a foreign spousal-support order were subject to modification in another country by the law of the issuing tribunal, this section would permit modification in a tribunal of this state.

Related to Convention: art. 2. Scope.

Sections 159.212-159.300 reserved for expansion

SUBCHAPTER D. CIVIL PROVISIONS OF GENERAL APPLICATION

NCCUSL Introductory Comment

This subchapter adds a wide variety of procedural provisions to existing statutory and procedural rules for civil cases. If there is a conflict between those provisions found for other litigation and UIFSA rules set forth in this subchapter, obviously UIFSA rules prevail. For example, it is unlikely that a state will have a provision for testimony by telephone or audiovisual means in a final hearing. Section 159.316 of this act creates such a right for an out-of-state individual. Revisions in this subchapter shift the perspective slightly to accommodate the inclusion of a foreign support order in the equation. Many, but not all, of the provisions in this subchapter are based upon the fact that a party does not "reside in this state." Application of these provisions is not solely based on whether the absent party resides in "another state," as formerly was the case. Rather, three distinct formulations are employed depending on the intended application of the provisions: "residing in a state;" "residing in ... a foreign country;" or "residing outside this state." The third alternative is intentionally the broadest because it includes persons residing anywhere and is not limited to persons residing in a "foreign country" as defined in §159.102.

FAM §159.301. PROCEEDINGS UNDER CHAPTER

(a) Except as otherwise provided in this chapter, this subchapter applies to all proceedings under this chapter.

(b) Repealed by Acts 2003, 78th Leg., ch. 1247, §46, eff. Sept. 1, 2003.

(c) An individual petitioner or a support enforcement agency may initiate a proceeding authorized under this chapter by filing a petition in an initiating tribunal for forwarding to a responding tribunal or by filing a petition or a comparable pleading directly in a tribunal of another state or foreign country that has or can obtain personal jurisdiction over the respondent.

History of Fam. Code §159.301: Acts 1995, 74th Leg., ch. 20, §1, eff. Apr. 20, 1995. Amended by Acts 1997, 75th Leg., ch. 607, §6, eff. Sept. 1, 1997; Acts 2003, 78th Leg., ch. 1247, §§13, 46, eff. Sept. 1, 2003; Acts 2015, 84th Leg., ch. 368, §16, eff. July 1, 2015. Source: Former Fam. Code §21.13.

NCCUSL Comment*

Subsection (a) mandates application of the general provisions of this subchapter to all UIFSA proceedings, including those affecting a foreign support order.

The statement in subsection (c) is axiomatic that the tribunal in which a petition is filed for establishment or enforcement of a support order, or for modification of a child-support order, must be able to assert personal jurisdiction over the respondent. It is also axiomatic that an individual petitioner requesting affirmative relief under this act submits to the personal jurisdiction of the tribunal. Subsection (c) also continues reference to the basic two-state procedure long employed by the former reciprocal acts to establish a support order in the interstate context, but expands it to recognize foreign countries. Direct filing of a petition in a state tribunal by an individual or a support enforcement agency without reference to an initiating tribunal in another state was introduced by UIFSA (1992). UIFSA (2008) extends the direct filing capability to foreign countries as well.

Although the filing of a petition in an initiating tribunal to be forwarded to a responding tribunal is still recognized as an available procedure, the direct filing procedure has proven to be one of the most significant improvements in efficient interstate case management. The promulgation and use of the federally mandated, or substantially conforming, forms, §159.311(b), further serves to eliminate any role for the initiating tribunal. Incidentally, the Convention contains approved forms for use in Convention cases processed through a Central Authority.

Related to Convention: art. 2. Scope; art. 10. Available applications; art. 19. Scope of the chapter; art. 20. Bases for recognition and enforcement; art. 32. Enforcement under internal law; art. 33. Non-discrimination; art. 34. Enforcement measures; art. 37. Direct requests to competent authorities; Annex 1. Transmittal form under Article 12(2); Annex 2. Acknowledgement form under Article 12(3).

FAM §159.302. PROCEEDING BY MINOR PARENT

A minor parent or a guardian or other legal representative of a minor parent may maintain a proceeding on behalf of or for the benefit of the minor's child.

History of Fam. Code §159.302: Acts 1995, 74th Leg., ch. 20, §1, eff. Apr. 20, 1995. Amended by Acts 2003, 78th Leg., ch. 1247, §14, eff. Sept. 1, 2003. Source: Former Fam. Code §21.14.

NCCUSL Comment*

A minor parent may maintain a proceeding under UIFSA without the appointment of a guardian ad litem, even if the law of the forum jurisdiction requires a guardian for an in-state case. If a guardian or legal representative has been appointed, he or she may act on behalf of the minor's child in seeking support.

FAM §159.303. APPLICATION OF LAW OF STATE

Except as otherwise provided in this chapter, a responding tribunal of this state shall:

(1) apply the procedural and substantive law generally applicable to similar proceedings originating in this state and may exercise all powers and provide all remedies available in those proceedings; and

(2) determine the duty of support and the amount payable in accordance with the law and support guidelines of this state.

History of Fam. Code §159.303: Acts 1995, 74th Leg., ch. 20, §1, eff. Apr. 20, 1995. Amended by Acts 1997, 75th Leg., ch. 607, §7, eff. Sept. 1, 1997; Acts 2003, 78th Leg., ch. 1247, §15, eff. Sept. 1, 2003. Source: Former Fam. Code §21.15.

NCCUSL Comment*

Historically states have insisted that forum law be applied to support cases whenever possible. This continues to be a key principle of UIFSA. In general, a responding tribunal has the same powers in a proceeding involving parties in a case with interstate or international effect as it has in an intrastate case. This inevitably means that the act is not self-contained; rather, it is supplemented by

* See footnote on p. 666.

the forum's statutes and procedures governing support orders. To insure the efficient processing of the huge number of interstate support cases, it is vital that decision makers apply familiar rules of law to the maximum degree possible. This must be accomplished in a manner consistent with the overriding principle of UIFSA that enforcement is of the issuing tribunal's order, and that the responding state does not make the order its own as a condition of enforcing it.

FAM §159.304. DUTIES OF INITIATING TRIBUNAL

(a) On the filing of a petition authorized by this chapter, an initiating tribunal of this state shall forward the petition and its accompanying documents:

(1) to the responding tribunal or appropriate support enforcement agency in the responding state; or

(2) if the identity of the responding tribunal is unknown, to the state information agency of the responding state with a request that they be forwarded to the appropriate tribunal and that receipt be acknowledged.

(b) If requested by the responding tribunal, a tribunal of this state shall issue a certificate or other document and make findings required by the law of the responding state. If the responding tribunal is in a foreign country, on request the tribunal of this state shall specify the amount of support sought, convert that amount into the equivalent amount in the foreign currency under the applicable official or market exchange rate as publicly reported, and provide any other documents necessary to satisfy the requirements of the responding foreign tribunal.

History of Fam. Code §159.304: Acts 1995, 74th Leg., ch. 20, §1, eff. Apr. 20, 1995. Amended by Acts 1997, 75th Leg., ch. 607, §8, eff. Sept. 1, 1997; Acts 2003, 78th Leg., ch. 1247, §15, eff. Sept. 1, 2003; Acts 2015, 84th Leg., ch. 368, §17, eff. July 1, 2015. Source: Former Fam. Code §21.16.

NCCUSL Comment*

Subsection (a) was designed primarily to facilitate interstate enforcement between UIFSA states and URESA and RURESA states, with some applicability to cases involving foreign jurisdictions. Since 1998, by which time UIFSA had been enacted nationwide, the procedure described has gradually become an anachronism. Note, however, that the last RURESA child-support order may not expire until 2017 or 2018. *See* Prefatory Note.

Subsection (b), however, retains its utility with regard to a support order of a foreign nation. Supplying documentation required by a foreign jurisdiction, which is not otherwise required by UIFSA procedure, is appropriate in the international context. For example, a venerable process in British Commonwealth countries is known as provisional and confirming orders. A "provisional order" is a statement of the nonbinding amount of support being requested by a Canadian tribunal for establishment of a support order by a state responding tribunal. A state responding tribunal will receive information about the amount of support provisionally calculated by a tribunal in Canada. It needs to be borne in mind that a request to establish support from a Canadian tribunal will be accomplished in accordance with the law of the responding state. Thus, the Canadian provisional order is informative, but not binding on the responding tribunal. An order issued by the responding tribunal, whether for the amount suggested in the provisional order or another amount based on the local law of the responding tribunal, is known as a confirming order. Similarly, the initiating state's tribunal, knowing that a provisional order will be required by the Canadian tribunal, is directed to cooperate and provide a statement of the amount of support being provisionally requested.

The initiating tribunal of this state also has a duty to identify the amount of foreign currency equivalent to its request to the Canadian tribunal and a corresponding duty for a responding tribunal to convert the foreign currency into dollars if the foreign initiating tribunal has not done so, §159.305(f). The reference to "the applicable official or market exchange rate" takes into account the present practices of international money markets. A few countries continue to maintain an official exchange rate for their currency. The vast majority of countries recognize the fact that the value of their currency is subject to daily market fluctuations that are reported on the financial pages of many daily newspapers. Thus, in the example described above, a request for a specific amount of support in U.S. dollars, which is to be translated into Canadian dollars on a specific date, will inevitably have a variable value as the foreign currency rises or falls against the U.S. dollar.

Related to Convention: art. 31. Decisions produced by the combined effect of provisional and confirmation orders.

FAM §159.305. DUTIES & POWERS OF RESPONDING TRIBUNAL

(a) When a responding tribunal of this state receives a petition or comparable pleading from an initiating tribunal or directly under Section 159.301(c), the responding tribunal shall cause the petition or pleading to be filed and notify the petitioner where and when it was filed.

(b) A responding tribunal of this state, to the extent not prohibited by other law, may do one or more of the following:

(1) establish or enforce a support order, modify a child support order, determine the controlling child support order, or determine parentage of a child;

(2) order an obligor to comply with a support order, specifying the amount and the manner of compliance;

(3) order income withholding;

(4) determine the amount of any arrearages and specify a method of payment;

(5) enforce orders by civil or criminal contempt, or both;

(6) set aside property for satisfaction of the support order;

(7) place liens and order execution on the obligor's property;

(8) order an obligor to keep the tribunal informed of the obligor's current residential address, electronic mail address, telephone number, employer, address of employment, and telephone number at the place of employment;

(9) issue a bench warrant or capias for an obligor who has failed after proper notice to appear at a hearing ordered by thc tribunal and cnter the bench warrant or capias in any local and state computer systems for criminal warrants;

(10) order the obligor to seek appropriate employment by specified methods;

* See footnote on p. 666.

(11) award reasonable attorney's fees and other fees and costs; and

(12) grant any other available remedy.

(c) A responding tribunal of this state shall include in a support order issued under this chapter, or in the documents accompanying the order, the calculations on which the support order is based.

(d) A responding tribunal of this state may not condition the payment of a support order issued under this chapter on compliance by a party with provisions for visitation.

(e) If a responding tribunal of this state issues an order under this chapter, the tribunal shall send a copy of the order to the petitioner and the respondent and to the initiating tribunal, if any.

(f) If requested to enforce a support order, arrears, or judgment or modify a support order stated in a foreign currency, a responding tribunal of this state shall convert the amount stated in the foreign currency to the equivalent amount in dollars under the applicable official or market exchange rate as publicly reported.

History of Fam. Code §159.305: Acts 1995, 74th Leg., ch. 20, §1, eff. Apr. 20, 1995. Amended by Acts 1997, 75th Leg., ch. 607, §9, eff. Sept. 1, 1997; Acts 2003, 78th Leg., ch. 1247, §16, eff. Sept. 1, 2003; Acts 2015, 84th Leg., ch. 368, §18, eff. July 1, 2015. Source: Former Fam. Code §21.17.

NCCUSL Comment*

This section establishes a wide variety of duties for a responding tribunal. It contains: ministerial functions, subsection (a); judicial functions, subsection (b); and, substantive rules applicable to interstate cases, subsections (c)-(e). Because a responding tribunal may be an administrative agency rather than a court, the act explicitly states that a tribunal is not granted powers that it does not otherwise possess under state law. For example, authority to enforce a support order by contempt generally is limited to courts.

Subsection (a) directs the filing of the documents received without regard to whether an initiating tribunal in another state was involved in forwarding the documentation. It also directs that the individual or entity requesting the filing be notified, but leaves the means of that notification to local law. The advent of a variety of swifter, and perhaps even more reliable, forms of notice in the modern era justifies the deletion of a particular form of notice. For example, many states now authorize notice by telephone facsimile (FAX), or by an express delivery service, and many legal documents are transmitted by electronic mail (email).

Subsection (b) lists duties that, if possessed under state law in connection with intrastate cases, are extended to the responding tribunal in UIFSA cases. Thus, each subdivision purposefully avoids mention of substantive rules. For example, subsection (b)(7) does not identify the type, nature, or priority of liens that may be issued under UIFSA. As is generally true under the act, those details will be determined by applicable state law concerning support enforcement remedies of local orders.

Subsection (c) clarifies that the details of calculating the child-support order are to be included along with the order. Local law generally requires that variation from the child support guidelines must be explained, *see* 42 U.S.C. §667; this requirement is extended to interstate cases.

Subsection (d) states that an interstate support order may not be conditioned on compliance with a visitation order. While this may be at variance with state law governing intrastate cases, under a UIFSA proceeding the petitioner generally is not present before the tribunal. This distinction justifies prohibiting visitation issues from being litigated in the context of a support proceeding. All states have enacted some version of either the UCCJA or the UCCJEA providing for resolution of visitation issues in interstate cases.

Subsection (e) introduces the policy determination that the petitioner, the respondent, and the initiating tribunal, if any, shall be kept informed about actions taken by the responding tribunal.

Subsection (f) is designed to facilitate enforcement of a foreign support order. Note that the language directing a conversion to a monetary equivalence in dollars is intended to make clear the equivalence is not a modification of the original order to an absolute dollar figure; rather, satisfaction of the obligation is to be determined by the order-issuing tribunal based on the present dollar value of the currency in which the order is denominated.

Related to Convention: art. 19. Scope of the Chapter; art. 34. Enforcement measures; art. 35. Transfer of funds; art. 43. Recovery of costs.

FAM §159.306. INAPPROPRIATE TRIBUNAL

If a petition or comparable pleading is received by an inappropriate tribunal of this state, that tribunal shall forward the pleading and accompanying documents to an appropriate tribunal in this state or another state and notify the petitioner where and when the pleading was sent.

History of Fam. Code §159.306: Acts 1995, 74th Leg., ch. 20, §1, eff. Apr. 20, 1995. Amended by Acts 1997, 75th Leg., ch. 607, §10, eff. Sept. 1, 1997. Source: Former Fam. Code §21.18.

NCCUSL Comment*

If a [petition] or comparable pleading is received by an inappropriate tribunal of this state, the tribunal shall forward the pleading and accompanying documents to an appropriate tribunal of this state or another state and notify the [petitioner] where and when the pleading was sent. A tribunal receiving UIFSA documents in error is to forward the original documents to their proper destination without undue delay. This section was originally intended to apply both to initiating and responding tribunals receiving such documents, but the practical elimination of the role of initiating tribunals under modern practice now limits the notice requirement to the petitioner, i.e., the individual party or support enforcement agency, that filed (or misfiled) the document directly. For example, if a tribunal is inappropriately designated as the responding tribunal, it shall forward the petition to the appropriate responding tribunal wherever located, if known, and notify the petitioner of its action. Such a procedure is much to be preferred to returning the documents to the petitioner to begin the process anew.

Cooperation of this sort will facilitate the ultimate goals of the act. Although by its terms this section applies only to a tribunal of this state, it can be anticipated that the support enforcement agency will also assist in transferring documents to the appropriate tribunal. Note the section does not contemplate that a state tribunal will forward documents to a tribunal in a foreign country.

FAM §159.307. DUTIES OF SUPPORT ENFORCEMENT AGENCY

(a) A support enforcement agency of this state, on request, shall provide services to a petitioner in a proceeding under this chapter.

(b) A support enforcement agency of this state that is providing services to the petitioner shall:

(1) take all steps necessary to enable an appropriate tribunal of this state, another state, or a foreign country to obtain jurisdiction over the respondent;

(2) request an appropriate tribunal to set a date, time, and place for a hearing;

* See footnote on p. 666.

(3) make a reasonable effort to obtain all relevant information, including information as to income and property of the parties;

(4) within two days, exclusive of Saturdays, Sundays, and legal holidays, after receipt of notice in a record from an initiating, responding, or registering tribunal, send a copy of the notice to the petitioner;

(5) within two days, exclusive of Saturdays, Sundays, and legal holidays, after receipt of communication in a record from the respondent or the respondent's attorney, send a copy of the communication to the petitioner; and

(6) notify the petitioner if jurisdiction over the respondent cannot be obtained.

(c) A support enforcement agency of this state that requests registration of a child support order in this state for enforcement or for modification shall make reasonable efforts:

(1) to ensure that the order to be registered is the controlling order; or

(2) if two or more child support orders exist and the identity of the controlling order has not been determined, to ensure that a request for such a determination is made in a tribunal having jurisdiction to do so.

(d) A support enforcement agency of this state that requests registration and enforcement of a support order, arrears, or a judgment stated in a foreign currency shall convert the amount stated in the foreign currency into the equivalent amount in dollars under the applicable official or market exchange rate as publicly reported.

(e) A support enforcement agency of this state shall issue, or request a tribunal of this state to issue, a child support order and an income-withholding order that redirects payment of current support, arrears, and interest if requested to do so by a support enforcement agency of another state under Section 159.319.

(f) This chapter does not create or negate a relationship of attorney and client or other fiduciary relationship between a support enforcement agency or the attorney for the agency and the individual being assisted by the agency.

History of Fam. Code §159.307: Acts 1995, 74th Leg., ch. 20, §1, eff. Apr. 20, 1995. Amended by Acts 1997, 75th Leg., ch. 607, §11, eff. Sept. 1, 1997; Acts 2003, 78th Leg., ch. 1247, §17, eff. Sept. 1, 2003; Acts 2015, 84th Leg., ch. 368, §19, eff. July 1, 2015. Source: Former Fam. Code §21.19.

NCCUSL Comment*

Federal legislation signed on Sept. 29, 2014 (P.L. 113-183) authorizes states to enact Alternative A or Alternative B of subsection (a). The focus of subsection (a) is on providing services to a petitioner. Either the obligee or the obligor may request services, and that request may be in the context of the establishment of an initial child-support order, enforcement or review and adjustment of an existing child-support order, or a modification of that order (upward or downward). Note that the section does not distinguish between child support and spousal support for purposes of providing services. Note also, the services available may differ significantly; for example, modification of spousal support is limited to the issuing tribunal. *See* §159.205(e).

Alternative A continues the longstanding rule that this state's support enforcement agency shall provide services upon request to a petitioner seeking relief under this act. Under Alternative B, the support agency may exercise discretion to provide or not provide assistance to an applicant: (1) from a reciprocating country or Convention country who does not apply through the Central Authority of his or her own country, but rather applies directly to the support enforcement agency; and (2) residing overseas in a country other than a reciprocating country or Convention country. The lack of services, of course, may impact the means by which an individual is able to obtain assistance in pursuing an action in the appropriate tribunal.

Subsection (b) responds to the past complaints of many petitioners that they were not properly kept informed about the progress of their requests for services.

Subsection (c) is a procedural clarification reflecting actual practice of the support agencies developed after years of experience with the act. It imposes a duty on all support enforcement agencies to facilitate the UIFSA one-order world by actively searching for cases with multiple orders and obtaining a determination of the controlling order as expeditiously as possible. This agency duty correlates to new Subsection 159.602(d) regarding the registration process and cases with multiple orders.

Subsection (d) imposes a duty of currency conversion on a support enforcement agency similar to that imposed on an initiating tribunal in §159.304(b).

Read in conjunction with §159.319, subsection (e) requires the state support enforcement agency to facilitate redirection of the stream of child support in order that payments be more efficiently received by the obligee.

Subsection (f) explicitly states that UIFSA neither creates nor rejects the establishment of an attorney-client or fiduciary relationship between the support enforcement agency and a petitioner receiving services from that agency. This once-highly controversial issue is left to otherwise applicable state law, which generally has concluded that attorneys employed by a state support enforcement agency do not form an attorney-client relationship with either the parties or the child as the ultimate obligee.

Related to Convention: art. 35. Transfer of funds.

FAM §159.308. DUTY OF ATTORNEY GENERAL & GOVERNOR

(a) If the attorney general determines that the support enforcement agency is neglecting or refusing to provide services to an individual, the attorney general may order the agency to perform its duties under this chapter or may provide those services directly to the individual.

(b) The governor may determine that a foreign country has established a reciprocal arrangement for child support with this state and take appropriate action for notification of the determination.

History of Fam. Code §159.308: Acts 1995, 74th Leg., ch. 20, §1, eff. Apr. 20, 1995. Amended by Acts 2003, 78th Leg., ch. 1247, §18, eff. Sept. 1, 2003; Acts 2015, 84th Leg., ch. 368, §§20, 21, eff. July 1, 2015. Source: Former Fam. Code §21.20.

NCCUSL Comment*

Subsection (b) makes clear that a state has a variety of options in determining the international scope of its IV-D support enforcement program. Of course, a federal declaration that a foreign jurisdiction is a reciprocating country or political subdivision is controlling. *See* §159.102(5)(A). However, each

* See footnote on p. 666.

state may designate an official with authority to make a statewide, binding determination recognizing a foreign country, foreign nation state, or political subdivision as having a reciprocal arrangement with that state. *See* §159.102(5)(B).

FAM §159.309. PRIVATE COUNSEL

An individual may employ private counsel to represent the individual in proceedings authorized by this chapter.

History of Fam. Code §159.309: Acts 1995, 74th Leg., ch. 20, §1, eff. Apr. 20, 1995. Source: Former Fam. Code §21.21.

NCCUSL Comment*

The right of a party to retain private counsel in a proceeding brought under UIFSA is explicitly recognized. The failure to clearly recognize that power under the prior uniform acts led to confusion and inconsistent decisions. The Convention implicitly recognizes that the right to employ an attorney is to be available in every Convention country, but does not explicitly mention retaining private counsel. A "competent authority" in Convention terminology is equivalent to a tribunal.

Related to Convention: art. 37. Direct requests to competent authorities.

FAM §159.310. DUTIES OF STATE INFORMATION AGENCY

(a) The Title IV-D agency is the state information agency under this chapter.

(b) The state information agency shall:

(1) compile and maintain a current list, including addresses, of the tribunals in this state that have jurisdiction under this chapter and any support enforcement agencies in this state and transmit a copy to the state information agency of every other state;

(2) maintain a register of names and addresses of tribunals and support enforcement agencies received from other states;

(3) forward to the appropriate tribunal in the county in this state in which the obligee who is an individual or the obligor resides, or in which the obligor's property is believed to be located, all documents concerning a proceeding under this chapter received from another state or a foreign country; and

(4) obtain information concerning the location of the obligor and the obligor's property in this state not exempt from execution, by such means as postal verification and federal or state locator services, examination of telephone directories, requests for the obligor's address from employers, and examination of governmental records, including, to the extent not prohibited by other law, those relating to real property, vital statistics, law enforcement, taxation, motor vehicles, driver's licenses, and social security.

* See footnote on p. 666.

History of Fam. Code §159.310: Acts 1995, 74th Leg., ch. 20, §1, eff. Apr. 20, 1995. Amended by Acts 2003, 78th Leg., ch. 1247, §19, eff. Sept. 1, 2003; Acts 2015, 84th Leg., ch. 368, §22, eff. July 1, 2015. Source: Former Fam. Code §21.22.

NCCUSL Comment*

Subsection (a) identifies the state information agency.

Subsection (b) details the duties of that agency insofar as interstate proceedings are concerned. Subsection (b)(4) does not provide independent access to the information sources or to the governmental documents listed. Because states have different requirements and limitations concerning such access based on differing views of the privacy interests of individual citizens, the agency is directed to use all lawful means under the relevant state law to obtain and disseminate information.

FAM §159.311. PLEADINGS & ACCOMPANYING DOCUMENTS

(a) In a proceeding under this chapter, a petitioner seeking to establish a support order, to determine parentage of a child, or to register and modify a support order of a tribunal of another state or foreign country must file a petition. Unless otherwise ordered under Section 159.312, the petition or accompanying documents must provide, so far as known, the name, residential address, and social security numbers of the obligor and the obligee or the parent and alleged parent, and the name, sex, residential address, social security number, and date of birth of each child for whose benefit support is sought or whose parentage is to be determined. Unless filed at the time of registration, the petition must be accompanied by a copy of any support order known to have been issued by another tribunal. The petition may include any other information that may assist in locating or identifying the respondent.

(b) The petition must specify the relief sought. The petition and accompanying documents must conform substantially with the requirements imposed by the forms mandated by federal law for use in cases filed by a support enforcement agency.

History of Fam. Code §159.311: Acts 1995, 74th Leg., ch. 20, §1, eff. Apr. 20, 1995. Amended by Acts 2003, 78th Leg., ch. 1247, §20, eff. Sept. 1, 2003; Acts 2015, 84th Leg., ch. 368, §23, eff. July 1, 2015. Source: Former Fam. Code §21.23.

See also ***O'Connor's Texas Family Law Handbook*** (2017), "Non-Texas order," ch. 9-D, §4.4.13(2)(a)[2], p. 1041.

NCCUSL Comment*

This section establishes the basic requirements for drafting and filing interstate pleadings. Subsection (a) should be read in conjunction with §159.312, which provides for the confidentiality of certain information if disclosure is likely to result in harm to a party or a child. The goal of this section is to improve efficiency of the process by attaching all known support orders to the petition, coupled with the elimination of the requirement that such copies be certified. If a dispute arises over the authenticity of a purported order, the tribunal must, of necessity, sort out conflicting claims at that time. Another improvement is the deletion of the requirement for verified pleadings originated in URESA and carried forward in the original version of UIFSA. Note, however, that a request for registration of a foreign support order for which the Convention is in force is subject to §159.706. This is due to the fact that the list of documents comprising the required record in subsection (a) differs in a measurable degree with Convention articles 11 and 25.

Subsection (b) provides authorization for the use of the federally authorized forms to be used in interstate cases in connection with the IV-D child-support enforcement program and mandates substantial compliance with those forms. Although the use of other forms is not prohibited, standardized documents have resulted in substantial improvement in the efficient processing of UIFSA proceedings. The Convention also contains annexed forms for international use.

Related to Convention: art. 10. Available applications; art. 11. Application contents; art. 12. Transmission, receipt and processing of applications and cases through Central Authorities; art. 25. Documents; Annex 1. Transmittal form under Article 12(2); Annex 2. Acknowledgement form under Article 12(3).

FAM §159.312. NONDISCLOSURE OF INFORMATION IN EXCEPTIONAL CIRCUMSTANCES

If a party alleges in an affidavit or pleading under oath that the health, safety, or liberty of a party or child would be jeopardized by disclosure of specific identifying information, that information must be sealed and may not be disclosed to the other party or the public. After a hearing in which a tribunal takes into consideration the health, safety, or liberty of the party or child, the tribunal may order disclosure of information that the tribunal determines to be in the interest of justice.

History of Fam. Code §159.312: Acts 1995, 74th Leg., ch. 20, §1, eff. Apr. 20, 1995. Amended by Acts 2003, 78th Leg., ch. 1247, §21, eff. Sept. 1, 2003; Acts 2015, 84th Leg., ch. 368, §24, eff. July 1, 2015. Source: Former Fam. Code §21.24.

NCCUSL Comment*

UIFSA (1992) recognized that enforcement of child support across state lines might have an unintended consequence of putting a party or child at risk if domestic violence was involved in the past. This section is a substantial revision of the statutory formulation originally developed in UIFSA (1992). It conforms to the comparable provision in the Uniform Child Custody Jurisdiction and Enforcement Act Section 209. Public awareness of and sensitivity to the dangers of domestic violence has significantly increased since interstate enforcement of support originated. This section authorizes confidentiality in instances where there is a risk of domestic violence or child abduction. Section 159.712, *infra*, incorporates language from the Convention to restrict dissemination of personal jurisdiction to protect victims of domestic violence.

Although local law generally governs the conduct of the forum tribunal, state law may not provide for maintaining secrecy about the exact whereabouts of a litigant or other information ordinarily required to be disclosed under state law, i.e., Social Security number of the parties or the child. If so, this section creates a confidentiality provision that is particularly appropriate in light of the intractable problems associated with interstate parental kidnapping, *see* the Parental Kidnapping Prevention Act (PKPA), 28 U.S.C. §1738A.

Related to Convention: art. 38. Protection of personal data; art. 39. Confidentiality; art. 40. Non-disclosure of information.

FAM §159.313. COSTS & FEES

(a) The petitioner may not be required to pay a filing fee or other costs.

(b) If an obligee prevails, a responding tribunal of this state may assess against an obligor filing fees, reasonable attorney's fees, other costs, and necessary travel and other reasonable expenses incurred by the obligee and the obligee's witnesses. The tribunal may not assess fees, costs, or expenses against the obligee or the support enforcement agency of either the initiating or responding state or foreign country, except as provided by other law. Attorney's fees may be taxed as costs, and may be ordered paid directly to the attorney, who may enforce the order in the attorney's own name. Payment of support owed to the obligee has priority over fees, costs, and expenses.

(c) The tribunal shall order the payment of costs and reasonable attorney's fees if it determines that a hearing was requested primarily for delay. In a proceeding under Subchapter G, a hearing is presumed to have been requested primarily for delay if a registered support order is confirmed or enforced without change.

History of Fam. Code §159.313: Acts 1995, 74th Leg., ch. 20, §1, eff. Apr. 20, 1995. Amended by Acts 1997, 75th Leg., ch. 607, §12, eff. Sept. 1, 1997; Acts 2015, 84th Leg., ch. 368, §25, eff. July 1, 2015. Source: Former Fam. Code §21.25.

NCCUSL Comment*

Subsection (a) permits either party, i.e., as petitioner, to file without payment of a filing fee or other costs. This provision dates back to UIFSA (1992) when the term "unfunded mandate" was basically unknown.

Subsection (b), however, provides that only the support obligor may be assessed the authorized costs and fees by a tribunal. Federal law permits a state support enforcement agency to charge limited fees and to recover administrative costs from applicants for Title IV-D services, but many states have opted not to do so, or only to seek recovery from the obligor.

Subsection (c) provides a sanction to deal with a frivolous contest regarding compliance with an interstate withholding order, registration of a support order, or comparable delaying tactics regarding an appropriate enforcement remedy.

Related to Convention: art. 14. Effective access to procedures; art. 43. Recovery of costs.

FAM §159.314. LIMITED IMMUNITY OF PETITIONER

(a) Participation by a petitioner in a proceeding under this chapter before a responding tribunal, whether in person, by private attorney, or through services provided by the support enforcement agency, does not confer personal jurisdiction over the petitioner in another proceeding.

(b) A petitioner is not amenable to service of civil process while physically present in this state to participate in a proceeding under this chapter.

(c) The immunity granted by this section does not extend to civil litigation based on acts unrelated to a proceeding under this chapter committed by a party while physically present in this state to participate in the proceeding.

History of Fam. Code §159.314: Acts 1995, 74th Leg., ch. 20, §1, eff. Apr. 20, 1995. Amended by Acts 2003, 78th Leg., ch. 1247, §22, eff. Sept. 1, 2003; Acts 2015, 84th Leg., ch. 368, §26, eff. July 1, 2015. Source: Former Fam. Code §21.26.

* See footnote on p. 666.

NCCUSL Comment*

Under subsection (a), direct or indirect participation in a UIFSA proceeding does not subject a petitioner to an assertion of personal jurisdiction over the petitioner by the forum state in other litigation between the parties. The primary object of this prohibition is to preclude joining disputes over child custody and visitation with the establishment, enforcement, or modification of child support. This prohibition strengthens the ban on visitation litigation established in §159.305(d). A petition for affirmative relief under UIFSA limits the jurisdiction of the tribunal to the boundaries of the support proceeding. In sum, proceedings under UIFSA are not suitable vehicles for the relitigation of all of the issues arising out of a foreign divorce or custody case. Only enforcement or modification of the support portion of such decrees or orders are relevant. Other issues, such as custody and visitation, or matters relating to other aspect of the divorce decree, are collateral and have no place in a UIFSA proceeding.

Subsection (b) grants a litigant a variety of limited immunity from service of process during the time that party is physically present in a state for a UIFSA proceeding. The immunity provided is in no way comparable to diplomatic immunity, however, which should be clear from reading subsection (c) in conjunction with the other subsections.

Subsection (c) does not extend immunity to civil litigation unrelated to the support proceeding which stems from contemporaneous acts committed by a party while present in the state for the support litigation. For example, a petitioner involved in an automobile accident or a contract dispute over the cost of lodging while present in the state does not have immunity from a civil suit on those issues.

FAM §159.315. NONPARENTAGE AS DEFENSE

A party whose parentage of a child has been previously determined by or under law may not plead nonparentage as a defense to a proceeding under this chapter.

History of Fam. Code §159.315: Acts 1995, 74th Leg., ch. 20, §1, eff. Apr. 20, 1995. Source: Former Fam. Code §21.27.

NCCUSL Comment*

Arguably this section does no more than restate the basic principle of res judicata. However, there is a great variety of state law regarding presumptions of parentage and available defenses after a prior determination of parentage. As long as a proceeding is brought in an appropriate forum, this section is intended neither to discourage nor encourage collateral attacks in situations in which the law of another jurisdiction is at significant odds with local law. If a collateral attack on a parentage decree is permissible under the law of the issuing jurisdiction, such a proceeding must be pursued in that forum and not in a UIFSA proceeding.

This section mandates that a parentage decree rendered by another tribunal "pursuant to law" is not subject to collateral attack in a UIFSA proceeding. Of course, an attack on an alleged final order based on a fundamental constitutional defect in the parentage decree is permissible in the forum state. For example, a responding tribunal may find that another tribunal acted unconstitutionally by denying a party due process due to a failure of notice and opportunity to be heard or a lack of personal jurisdiction over a party who did not answer or appear. Insofar as the latter ground is concerned, the universal enactment of the long-arm statute asserting personal jurisdiction over a respondent if the child "may have been conceived" in the forum state may greatly reduce successful attacks on a parentage determination. *See* §159.201(a)(6).

Similarly, the law of the issuing state or foreign country may provide for a determination of parentage based on certain specific acts of the obligor, such as voluntarily acknowledging parentage as a substitute for a decree. UIFSA also is neutral regarding a collateral attack on such a parentage determination filed in the issuing tribunal. In the meantime, however, the responding tribunal must give effect to such an act of acknowledgment of parentage if it is recognized as determinative in the issuing state or foreign country. The consistent theme is that a collateral attack on a parentage determination cannot be made in a UIFSA proceeding other than on fundamental due-process grounds.

* See footnote on p. 666.

FAM §159.316. SPECIAL RULES OF EVIDENCE & PROCEDURE

(a) The physical presence of a nonresident party who is an individual in a tribunal of this state is not required for the establishment, enforcement, or modification of a support order or the rendition of a judgment determining parentage of a child.

(b) An affidavit, a document substantially complying with federally mandated forms, or a document incorporated by reference in an affidavit or document, that would not be excluded under the hearsay rule if given in person, is admissible in evidence if given under penalty of perjury by a party or witness residing outside this state.

(c) A copy of the record of child support payments certified as a true copy of the original by the custodian of the record may be forwarded to a responding tribunal. The copy is evidence of facts asserted in it and is admissible to show whether payments were made.

(d) Copies of bills for testing for parentage of a child, and for prenatal and postnatal health care of the mother and child furnished to the adverse party at least 10 days before trial are admissible in evidence to prove the amount of the charges billed and that the charges were reasonable, necessary, and customary.

(e) Documentary evidence transmitted from outside this state to a tribunal of this state by telephone, telecopier, or other electronic means that does not provide an original record may not be excluded from evidence on an objection based on the means of transmission.

(f) In a proceeding under this chapter, a tribunal of this state shall permit a party or witness residing outside this state to be deposed or to testify under penalty of perjury by telephone, audiovisual means, or other electronic means at a designated tribunal or other location. A tribunal of this state shall cooperate with other tribunals in designating an appropriate location for the deposition or testimony.

(g) If a party called to testify at a civil hearing refuses to answer on the ground that the testimony may be self-incriminating, the trier of fact may draw an adverse inference from the refusal.

(h) A privilege against disclosure of communications between spouses does not apply in a proceeding under this chapter.

(i) The defense of immunity based on the relationship of husband and wife or parent and child does not apply in a proceeding under this chapter.

(j) A voluntary acknowledgment of paternity, certified as a true copy, is admissible to establish parentage of the child.

History of Fam. Code §159.316: Acts 1995, 74th Leg., ch. 20, §1, eff. Apr. 20, 1995. Amended by Acts 2003, 78th Leg., ch. 1247, §23, eff. Sept. 1, 2003; Acts 2005, 79th Leg., ch. 344, §1, eff. June 17, 2005; Acts 2015, 84th Leg., ch. 368, §27, eff. July 1, 2015. Source: Former Fam. Code §21.28.

See also *O'Connor's Texas Family Law Handbook* (2017), "Nonresident party," ch. 9-D, §16.6.2, p. 1057.

NCCUSL Comment*

Note that the special rules of evidence and procedure are applicable to a party or witness "residing outside this state," substituting for "residing in another state." This is the broadest application possible because the utility of these special rules is not limited to parties in other states, or in foreign countries, as defined in the act, but extends to an individual residing anywhere. This extremely broad application of the special rules is to facilitate the processing of a support order in this state or elsewhere. This section combines many time-tested procedures with innovative methods for gathering evidence in interstate cases.

Subsection (a) ensures that a nonresident petitioner or a nonresident respondent may fully participate in a proceeding under the act without being required to appear personally. Subsection (b) recognizes the pervasive effect of the federal forms promulgated by the Office of Child Support Enforcement, which replace the necessity of swearing to a document "under oath" with the simpler requirement that the document be provided "under penalty of perjury," as has long been required by federal income tax Form 1040.

Subsections (b) through (f) provide special rules of evidence designed to take into account the virtually unique nature of the interstate proceedings under this act. These subsections provide exceptions to the otherwise guiding principle of UIFSA, i.e., local procedural and substantive law should apply. Because the out-of-state party, and that party's witnesses, necessarily do not ordinarily appear in person at the hearing, deviation from the ordinary rules of evidence is justified in order to assure that the tribunal will have available to it the maximum amount of information on which to base its decision. The intent throughout these subsections is to eliminate by statute as many potential hearsay problems as possible in interstate litigation, with the goal of providing each party with the means to present evidence, even if not physically present.

Subsection (d) provides a simplified means for proving health-care expenses related to the birth of a child. Because ordinarily the amount of these charges is not in dispute, this is designed to obviate the cost of having health-care providers appear in person or of obtaining affidavits of business records from each provider.

Subsections (e) and (f) encourage tribunals and litigants to take advantage of modern methods of communication in interstate support litigation; most dramatically, the out-of-state party is authorized to testify by the full panoply of audio and audiovisual technologies currently available for direct personal communication and to supply documents by fax, email, or direct transfer between computers or other electronic devices. One of the most useful applications of these subsections is to provide an enforcing tribunal with up-to-date information concerning the amount of arrears.

Subsection (f) unambiguously mandates that telephone or audiovisual testimony in depositions and hearings must be allowed. It anticipates that every courtroom is equipped with a speakerphone. In a day when laptop computers often come equipped with a video camera, live testimony from a remote location is not only possible, but almost as reliable as if the testimony was given in person. No doubt a demeanor is better judged in person than by viewing a video screen, but the latter is certainly preferable to only a disembodied voice.

Subsection (g) codifies the rule in effect in many states that in civil litigation an adverse inference may be drawn from a litigant's silence—that restriction of the Fifth Amendment does not apply. A related analogy is that a refusal to submit to genetic testing may be admitted into evidence and a trier of fact may resolve the question of parentage against the refusing party on the basis of an inference that the results of the test would have been unfavorable to the interest of that party.

Subsection (j), new in 2001, complies with the federally mandated procedure that every state must honor the "acknowledgment of paternity" validly made in another state.

Related to Convention: art. 13. Means of communication; art. 14. Effective access to procedures; art. 29. Physical presence of the child or the applicant not required.

FAM §159.317. COMMUNICATIONS BETWEEN TRIBUNALS

A tribunal of this state may communicate with a tribunal outside this state in a record or by telephone, electronic mail, or by other means, to obtain information concerning the laws, the legal effect of a judgment, decree, or order of that tribunal, and the status of a proceeding. A tribunal of this state may furnish similar information by similar means to a tribunal outside this state.

History of Fam. Code §159.317: Acts 1995, 74th Leg., ch. 20, §1, eff. Apr. 20, 1995. Amended by Acts 2003, 78th Leg., ch. 1247, §24, eff. Sept. 1, 2003; Acts 2015, 84th Leg., ch. 368, §28, eff. July 1, 2015. Source: Former Fam. Code §21.29.

NCCUSL Comment*

This section explicitly authorizes a state tribunal to communicate with a tribunal of another state, foreign country, or in a foreign nation state not defined as a foreign country. It was derived from UCCJA §110 authorizing such communications to facilitate a fully informed decision. The amendment in UIFSA (2008) not only expands the authorization to worldwide scope, i.e., "outside this state," but specifically adds email to the select modes of communication. Broad cooperation by tribunals is strongly encouraged in order to expedite establishment and enforcement of a support order. American judges are very familiar with this procedure. It remains to be seen whether overseas communication between judges will be received with similar cooperation.

FAM §159.318. ASSISTANCE WITH DISCOVERY

A tribunal of this state may:

(1) request a tribunal outside this state to assist in obtaining discovery; and

(2) on request, compel a person over whom the tribunal has jurisdiction to respond to a discovery order issued by a tribunal outside this state.

History of Fam. Code §159.318: Acts 1995, 74th Leg., ch. 20, §1, eff. Apr. 20, 1995. Amended by Acts 2015, 84th Leg., ch. 368, §29, eff. July 1, 2015. Source: Former Fam. Code §21.30.

NCCUSL Comment*

This section takes a logical step to facilitate interstate and international cooperation by enlisting the power of the forum to assist a tribunal of another state or country with the discovery process. The grant of authority is quite broad, enabling the tribunal of the enacting state to fashion its remedies to facilitate discovery consistent with local practice.

FAM §159.319. RECEIPT & DISBURSEMENT OF PAYMENTS

(a) A support enforcement agency or tribunal of this state shall disburse promptly any amounts received under a support order, as directed by the order. The

* See footnote on p. 666.

agency or tribunal shall furnish to a requesting party or tribunal of another state or a foreign country a certified statement by the custodian of the record of the amounts and dates of all payments received.

(b) If the obligor, the obligee who is an individual, and the child do not reside in this state, on request from the support enforcement agency of this state or another state, the support enforcement agency of this state or a tribunal of this state shall:

(1) direct that the support payment be made to the support enforcement agency in the state in which the obligee is receiving services; and

(2) issue and send to the obligor's employer a conforming income-withholding order or an administrative notice of change of payee reflecting the redirected payments.

(c) The support enforcement agency of this state on receiving redirected payments from another state under a law similar to Subsection (b) shall provide to a requesting party or a tribunal of the other state a certified statement by the custodian of the record of the amount and dates of all payments received.

History of Fam. Code §159.319: Acts 1995, 74th Leg., ch. 20, §1, eff. Apr. 20, 1995. Amended by Acts 2003, 78th Leg., ch. 1247, §25, eff. Sept. 1, 2003; Acts 2015, 84th Leg., ch. 368, §30, eff. July 1, 2015. Source: Former Fam. Code §21.31.

NCCUSL Comment*

The first sentence of subsection (a) is truly hortatory in nature, although its principle is implemented insofar as support enforcement agencies are required by federal regulations promulgated by the Office of Child Support Enforcement (OCSE). The second sentence confirms the duty of the agency or tribunal to furnish payment information in interstate or international cases.

As an exception to the usual provisions in Subchapter D, subsections (b) and (c) are applicable only to interstate cases. The procedure described was inspired by the Office of Child Support Enforcement (OCSE), U.S. Department of Health and Human Services, and is designed to speed up receipt of support payments. Support enforcement agencies are directed to cooperate in the efficient and expeditious collection and transfer of child support from obligor to obligee. Over two-thirds of all child support payments currently are made through direct income withholding actions, whereby an out-of-state IV-D agency sends direct notice to an employer in the obligor's state to withhold funds to satisfy the support obligation. Nonetheless, this section remains viable for those situation in which the direct withholding encounters a glitch. Further, there are ongoing problems in states not having income withholding payments go to the state disbursement unit. This section is intended to solve the problem by directing the payments to the most logical disbursement unit, i.e., the state with continuing exclusive jurisdiction.

Sections 159.320-159.400 reserved for expansion

SUBCHAPTER E. ESTABLISHMENT OF SUPPORT ORDER OR DETERMINATION OF PARENTAGE

NCCUSL Introductory Comment

A fundamental principle of U.S. jurisprudence is that our courts are open to litigants with a valid cause of action. This subchapter makes clear this principle applies to support actions, whether initiated by a resident of the United States or of a foreign nation.

FAM §159.401. ESTABLISHMENT OF SUPPORT ORDER

(a) If a support order entitled to recognition under this chapter has not been issued, a responding tribunal of this state with personal jurisdiction over the parties may issue a support order if:

(1) the individual seeking the order resides outside this state; or

(2) the support enforcement agency seeking the order is located outside this state.

(b) The tribunal may issue a temporary child support order if the tribunal determines that such an order is appropriate and the individual ordered to pay is:

(1) a presumed father of the child;

(2) petitioning to have his paternity adjudicated;

(3) identified as the father of the child through genetic testing;

(4) an alleged father who has declined to submit to genetic testing;

(5) shown by clear and convincing evidence to be the father of the child;

(6) an acknowledged father as provided by applicable state law;

(7) the mother of the child; or

(8) an individual who has been ordered to pay child support in a previous proceeding and the order has not been reversed or vacated.

(c) On finding, after notice and an opportunity to be heard, that an obligor owes a duty of support, the tribunal shall issue a support order directed to the obligor and may issue other orders under Section 159.305.

History of Fam. Code §159.401: Acts 1995, 74th Leg., ch. 20, §1, eff. Apr. 20, 1995. Amended by Acts 2003, 78th Leg., ch. 1247, §26, eff. Sept. 1, 2003; Acts 2015, 84th Leg., ch. 368, §§31, 32, eff. July 1, 2015. Source: Former Fam. Code §21.32.

ANNOTATIONS

Office of the Atty. Gen. v. Long, 401 S.W.3d 911, 912 (Tex.App.—Houston [14th Dist.] 2013, no pet.). "[A] North Carolina court entered a judgment of absolute divorce dissolving the marriage of [H] and [W]. [T]he North Carolina court issued findings stating that 'there are no claims for child support, alimony or equitable distribution of marital property between the parties.' [¶] We must determine whether a Texas court has jurisdiction to adjudicate [H's] child support obligation. *At 915:* [W]e conclude that the judgment of ab-

* See footnote on p. 666.

solute divorce makes no provision for child support. Without an existing order, the Attorney General's petition is properly classified as a petition to establish an order of support rather than a petition to modify an order of no support. Under UIFSA, the trial court had the authority to adjudicate [H's] child support obligation. [T]he North Carolina tribunal had not acquired continuing, exclusive jurisdiction...."

NCCUSL Comment*

This section authorizes a responding tribunal of this state to issue temporary and permanent support orders binding on an obligor over whom the tribunal has personal jurisdiction when the person or entity requesting the order is "outside this state," i.e., anywhere else in the world. UIFSA does not permit such orders to be issued when another support order entitled to recognition exists, thereby prohibiting a second tribunal from establishing another support order and the accompanying continuing, exclusive jurisdiction over the matter. *See* §§159.205 and 159.206.

Related to Convention: art. 11. Application contents; art. 14. Effective access to procedures; art. 15. Free legal assistance for child support applications; art. 16. Declaration to permit use of child-centered means test; art. 17. Applications not qualifying under 15 or 16; art. 20. Bases for recognition and enforcement; art. 25. Documents; art. 27. Findings of fact; art. 28. No review of the merits; art. 37. Direct requests to competent authorities; art. 56. Transitional provisions.

FAM §159.402. PROCEEDING TO DETERMINE PARENTAGE

A tribunal of this state authorized to determine parentage of a child may serve as a responding tribunal in a proceeding to determine parentage of a child brought under this chapter or a law or procedure substantially similar to this chapter.

History of Fam. Code §159.402: Acts 2015, 84th Leg., ch. 368, §33, eff. July 1, 2015.

NCCUSL Comment*

This subchapter authorizes a "pure" parentage action in the interstate context, i.e., an action not joined with a claim for support. The mother, an alleged father of a child, or a support enforcement agency may bring such an action. Typically an action to determine parentage across a state line or international border will also seek to establish a support order. *See* §159.401. An action to establish parentage under UIFSA is to be treated identically to such an action brought in the responding state.

In a departure from the rest of this act, in UIFSA (2001) the term "tribunal" was replaced by "court" in this section. The several states have a variety of combinations of judicial or administrative entities that are authorized to establish, enforce, and modify a child-support order. Because the Uniform Parentage Act (UPA) (2000) §104 restricts parentage determinations to "a court," *see* UPA (2000) §104, the drafters took the view that only a judicial officer should determine parentage as a matter of public policy. This conclusion was in error insofar as some states are concerned and is reversed in this iteration of the act.

Related to Convention: art. 2. Scope; art. 6. Specific functions of Central Authorities; art. 10. Available applications.

Sections 159.403-159.500 reserved for expansion

SUBCHAPTER F. ENFORCEMENT OF SUPPORT ORDER WITHOUT REGISTRATION

NCCUSL Introductory Comment

This subchapter governs direct filing of an income withholding order from one state to an employer in another state. Except as provided in §159.507, the provisions of this subchapter only apply to an interstate case and do not apply to an income-withholding order from a foreign country. While U.S. employers routinely enforce sister state income-withholding orders, enforcement of the wide variety of possible foreign support orders would provide too many complexities and challenges to justify requiring an employer to interpret and enforce an ostensible foreign income-withholding order. Indeed, income-withholding orders from a foreign country are quite rare at this time, although instances of that enforcement remedy probably will increase in the future.

* See footnote on p. 666.

FAM §159.501. EMPLOYER'S RECEIPT OF INCOME-WITHHOLDING ORDER OF ANOTHER STATE

An income-withholding order issued in another state may be sent by or on behalf of the obligee or by the support enforcement agency to the person defined as the obligor's employer under Chapter 158 without first filing a petition or comparable pleading or registering the order with a tribunal of this state.

History of Fam. Code §159.501: Acts 1995, 74th Leg., ch. 20, §1, eff. Apr. 20, 1995. Renumbered from §159.501(a) by Acts 1997, 75th Leg., ch. 607, §13, eff. Sept. 1, 1997. Amended by Acts 2003, 78th Leg., ch. 1247, §27, eff. Sept. 1, 2003; Acts 2015, 84th Leg., ch. 368, §34, eff. July 1, 2015. Source: Former Fam. Code §21.33(a).

NCCUSL Comment*

In 1984 Congress mandated that all states adopt procedures for enforcing income-withholding orders of sister states. Direct recognition by the out-of-state obligor's employer of a withholding order issued by another state long was sought by support enforcement associations and other advocacy groups. UIFSA (1992) recognized such a procedure. This subchapter was extensively amended in 1996, but was the subject only of clarifying amendments in 2001.

Section 159.501 is deliberately written in the passive voice; the act does not restrict those who may send an income-withholding order across state lines. Although the sender will ordinarily be a child support enforcement agency or the obligee, the obligor or any other person may supply an employer with the income-withholding order. "Sending a copy" of a withholding order to an employer is clearly distinguishable from "service" of that order on the same employer. Service of an order necessarily intends to invoke a tribunal's authority over an employer doing business in the state. Thus, for there to be valid "service" of a withholding order on an employer in a state, the tribunal must have authority to bind the employer. In most cases, this requires the assertion of the authority of a local responding tribunal in a "registration for enforcement" proceeding. In short, the formality of "service" defeats the whole purpose of direct income withholding across state lines.

The process contemplated in this subchapter is direct "notification" of an employer in another state of a withholding order without the involvement of initiating or responding tribunals. Therefore, receipt of a copy of a withholding order by facsimile, regular first class mail, registered or certified mail, or any other type of direct notice is sufficient to provide the requisite notice to trigger direct income withholding in the absence of a contest by the employee-obligor. This process is now widely used by not only child support enforcement agencies, but also by private collection agencies or private attorneys acting on behalf of obligees.

Except as provided in §159.507, Administrative Enforcement of Orders, none of the sections in Subchapter F are intended to apply to foreign support orders. While it is appropriate for U.S. employers to enforce sister state income-withholding orders routinely, enforcement of the wide variety of possible foreign support orders provides too many complexities and challenges to require an employer to interpret and enforce ostensible foreign income-withholding orders.

FAM §159.502. EMPLOYER'S COMPLIANCE WITH INCOME-WITHHOLDING ORDER OF ANOTHER STATE[1]

(a) On receipt of an income-withholding order, the obligor's employer shall immediately provide a copy of the order to the obligor.

(b) The employer shall treat an income-withholding order issued in another state that appears regular on its face as if the order had been issued by a tribunal of this state.

(c) Except as otherwise provided in Subsection (d) and Section 159.503, the employer shall withhold and distribute the funds as directed in the withholding order by complying with terms of the order that specify:

(1) the duration and amount of periodic payments of current child support, stated as a sum certain;

(2) the person designated to receive payments and the address to which the payments are to be forwarded;

(3) medical support, whether in the form of periodic cash payments, stated as a sum certain, or ordering the obligor to provide health insurance coverage for the child under a policy available through the obligor's employment;

(4) the amount of periodic payments of fees and costs for a support enforcement agency, the issuing tribunal, and the obligee's attorney, stated as sums certain; and

(5) the amount of periodic payments of arrearages and interest on arrearages, stated as sums certain.

(d) An employer shall comply with the law of the state of the obligor's principal place of employment for withholding from income with respect to:

(1) the employer's fee for processing an income-withholding order;

(2) the maximum amount permitted to be withheld from the obligor's income; and

(3) the times within which the employer must implement the withholding order and forward the child support payment.

1. **Editor's note:** In 2015, the Legislature amended §159.502 to require dental support for a child subject to a child-support order, but the amendments are not effective until Sept. 1, 2018. For the text of the prospective amendments, see Acts 2015, 84th Leg., ch. 1150, §39, eff. Sept. 1, 2018.

History of Fam. Code §159.502: Acts 1995, 74th Leg., ch. 20, §1, eff. Apr. 20, 1995. Renumbered from §159.501(a) by Acts 1997, 75th Leg., ch. 607, §13, eff. Sept. 1, 1997. Amended by Acts 2003, 78th Leg., ch. 1247, §28, eff. Sept. 1, 2003. Source: Former Fam. Code §21.33(a).

NCCUSL Comment*

In 1996 major employers and national payroll associations urged NCCUSL to supply more detail regarding the rights and duties of an employer on receipt of an income-withholding order from another state. The Conference obliged with amendments to UIFSA establishing a series of steps for employers to follow.

When an employer receives an income withholding order from another state, the first step is to notify the employee that an income withholding order has been received naming the employee as the obligor of child support, and that income withholding will begin within the time frame specified by local law. In other words, the employer will initially proceed just as if the withholding order had been received from a tribunal of the employer's state. It is the responsibility of the employee to take whatever protective measures are necessary to prevent the withholding if the employee asserts a defense as provided in §159.506, *infra*.

At this point neither an initiating nor a responding tribunal is directly involved. The withholding order may have been forwarded by the obligee, the obligee's attorney, or the out-of-state IV-D agency. In fact, there is no prohibition against anyone sending a valid copy of an income-withholding order, even a stranger to the litigation, such as the child's grandparent. Subsection (a) does not specify the method for sending this relatively informal notice for direct income withholding, but rather makes the assumption that the employer's communication to the employee regarding receipt of the order will cause an employee-obligor to act to prevent a wrongful invasion of his or her income if it is not owed as current child support or arrears.

Subsection (b) directs an employer of the enacting state to recognize a withholding order of a sister state, subject to the employee's right to contest the validity of the order or its enforcement. Prior to the promulgation of UIFSA, agencies in several states adopted a procedure of sending direct withholding requests to out-of-state employers. A contemporaneous study by the federal General Accounting Office reported that employers in a second state routinely recognized withholding orders of sister states despite an apparent lack of statutory authority to do so. UIFSA marked the first official sanction of this practice. Subsection (b) does not define "regular on its face," but the term should be liberally construed, *see **U.S. v. Morton***, 467 U.S. 822 (1984) ("legal process regular on its face"). The rules governing intrastate procedure and defenses for withholding orders will apply to interstate orders.

Subsection (c) answered employers' complaints that insufficient direction for action was given by the original UIFSA. Prior to the 1996 amendments an employer was merely told to "distribute the funds as directed in the withholding order." This section clarifies the terms of the out-of-state order with which the employer must strictly comply. As a general principle, an employer is directed to comply with the specific terms contained in the order, but there are exceptions. Moreover, many income-withholding orders received at that time did not provide the detail necessary for the employer to comply with every directive. Since then, however, the long-anticipated federal forms were promulgated throughout 1997 and 1998, with periodic updates to the present time. Most recently, the text of income withholding orders for child support is fast conforming to a nationwide norm. To the extent that an order is silent, the employer is not required to respond to unstated demands of the issuing tribunal. Formerly, employers often were so concerned about ambiguous or incomplete orders that they telephoned child support enforcement agencies in other states to attempt to understand and comply with unstated terms. Employers should not be expected to become investigators or shoulder the responsibility of learning the law of 50 states.

Subsection (c)(1) directs that the amount and duration of periodic payments of current child support must be stated in a sum certain in order to elicit compliance. The amount of current support and duration of the support obligation are fixed by the controlling order and should be stated in the withholding order so that the employer is informed of the date on which the withholding is anticipated to terminate. The "sum certain" requirement is crucial to facilitating the employer's compliance. For example, an order for a "percentage of the obligor's net income," does not satisfy this requirement and is not entitled to compliance from an employer receiving an interstate income-withholding order.

Subsection (c)(2) states the obvious: information necessary for compliance must be clearly stated. For example, the destination of the payments must correspond to the destination originally designated or subsequently authorized by the issuing tribunal, such as by the redirection of payments pursuant to §159.319, *supra*.

Subsection (c)(3) provides that medical support for the child must be stated either by a periodic cash payment or, alternatively, by an order directing the employee-obligor to provide health insurance coverage from his employment. In the absence of an order for payment of a sum certain, issuance of an order for medical support as child support is required to ensure the employer enrolls the obligor's child for coverage if medical insurance is available through the obligor's employment. Failure to enroll the child should elicit, at the least, registration of an order for enforcement in the responding state, to be implemented by an order of a tribunal directing either the employee or the employer to comply to furnish insurance coverage for the child. If the employer is so di-

* See footnote on p. 666.

rected by a medical support order, enrollment of the child in the health care plan at the employee-obligor's expense is not dependent on the obligor's consent, any more than withholding a sum certain from the obligor's income is subject to a veto. It is up to the employee-obligor to assert any defense to prevent the employer from abiding by the medical support order.

Subsection (c)(4) identifies certain costs and fees incurred in conjunction with the support enforcement that may be added to the withholding order.

Subsection (c)(5) requires that the amount of periodic payments for arrears and interest on arrears also must be stated as a sum certain. If the one-order system is to function properly, the issuing tribunal ultimately must be responsible to account for payments and maintain the record of arrears and interest rate on arrears. Full compliance with the support order will only be achieved when the issuing tribunal determines that the obligation no longer exists. The amount of periodic payments for arrears is also fixed by the controlling order unless the law of the issuing state or the state where the order is being enforced provides a procedure for redetermination of the amount.

Subsection (d) identifies those narrow provisions in which the law of the employee's work state applies, rather than the law of the issuing state. A large employer will almost certainly have a number of employees subject to income-withholding orders. From the employer's perspective, the procedural requirements for compliance should be uniform for all of those employees. Certain issues should be matters for the law of the employee's work state, such as the employer's fee for processing, the maximum amount to be withheld, and the time in which to comply. The latter necessarily includes the frequency with which income withholding must occur. This is also consistent with regard to the tax consideration imposed by choice of law considerations. The only element in the list of local laws identified in subsection (d) which stirred any controversy whatsoever was the fact that the maximum amount permitted to be withheld is to be subject to the law of the employee's work state. Demands of equal treatment for all obligees, plus the practical concern that large employers require uniform computer programming mandate this solution.

FAM §159.503. EMPLOYER'S COMPLIANCE WITH TWO OR MORE INCOME-WITHHOLDING ORDERS

If an obligor's employer receives two or more income-withholding orders with respect to the earnings of the same obligor, the employer satisfies the terms of the orders if the employer complies with the law of the state of the obligor's principal place of employment to establish the priorities for withholding and allocating income withheld for two or more child support obligees.

History of Fam. Code §159.503: Acts 1997, 75th Leg., ch. 607, §13, eff. Sept. 1, 1997. Amended by Acts 2003, 78th Leg., ch. 1247, §29, eff. Sept. 1, 2003.

NCCUSL Comment*

Consistent with the act's general problem-solving approach, the employer is directed to deal with multiple income orders for multiple families in the same manner as required by local law for orders of the forum state.

In addition to income withholding orders issued by tribunals of other states, state support enforcement agencies may also issue income withholding orders to enforce foreign child-support orders.

FAM §159.504. IMMUNITY FROM CIVIL LIABILITY

An employer who complies with an income-withholding order issued in another state in accordance with this subchapter is not subject to civil liability to an individual or agency with regard to the employer's withholding of child support from the obligor's income.

History of Fam. Code §159.504: Acts 1997, 75th Leg., ch. 607, §13, eff. Sept. 1, 1997.

NCCUSL Comment*

Because employer cooperation is a key element in interstate child support enforcement, it is sound policy to state explicitly that an employer who complies with an income-withholding order from another state is immune from civil liability.

FAM §159.505. PENALTIES FOR NONCOMPLIANCE

An employer who wilfully fails to comply with an income-withholding order issued by another state and received for enforcement is subject to the same penalties that may be imposed for noncompliance with an order issued by a tribunal of this state.

History of Fam. Code §159.505: Acts 1997, 75th Leg., ch. 607, §13, eff. Sept. 1, 1997.

NCCUSL Comment*

Only an employer who willfully fails to comply with an interstate order will be subject to enforcement procedures. Local law is the appropriate source for the applicable sanctions and other remedies available under state law.

FAM §159.506. CONTEST BY OBLIGOR

(a) An obligor may contest the validity or enforcement of an income-withholding order issued in another state and received directly by an employer in this state by registering the order in a tribunal of this state and filing a contest to that order as provided in Subchapter G or otherwise contesting the order in the same manner as if the order had been issued by a tribunal of this state.

(b) The obligor shall give notice of the contest to:

(1) a support enforcement agency providing services to the obligee;

(2) each employer that has directly received an income-withholding order relating to the obligor; and

(3) the person designated to receive payments in the income-withholding order or, if no person is designated, to the obligee.

History of Fam. Code §159.506: Acts 1995, 74th Leg., ch. 20, §1, eff. Apr. 20, 1995. Renumbered from §159.501(b) by Acts 1997, 75th Leg., ch. 607, §13, eff. Sept. 1, 1997. Amended by Acts 2003, 78th Leg., ch. 1247, §30, eff. Sept. 1, 2003; Acts 2015, 84th Leg., ch. 368, §35, eff. July 1, 2015. Source: Former Fam. Code §21.33(b).

NCCUSL Comment*

This section incorporates into the interstate context the local law regarding defenses an employee-obligor may raise to an income-withholding order. Generally, states have accepted the IV-D requirement that the only viable defense is a mistake of fact, 42 U.S.C. §666(b)(4)(A). This apparently includes errors in the amount of current support owed, in the amount of accrued arrearage, or mistaken identity of the alleged obligor. Other grounds are excluded, such as inappropriate amount of support ordered, changed financial circumstances of the obligor, or lack of visitation. H.R. Rep. No. 98-527, 98th Cong., 1st Sess. 33 (1983). The latter claims must be pursued in a separate proceeding in the appropriate state, not in a UIFSA proceeding.

This procedure is based on the assumption that valid defenses to income withholding for child support are few and far between. Experience has shown that in relatively few cases does an employee-obligor have a complete defense, e.g., the child has died, another contingency ending the support has occurred,

* See footnote on p. 666.

the order has been superseded, or there is a case of mistaken identity and the employee is not the obligor. An employee's complaint that "The child support is too high" must be ignored.

As noted frequently above, instances of multiple orders have become increasingly rare over the past two decades plus. Situations do arise, however, in which an employer has received multiple withholding notices regarding the obligor-employee and the same obligee. The notices may even allege conflicting amounts due, especially for payments on arrears. Additionally, many employees claim to have only learned of default orders when the withholding notice is delivered to the employer. This claim often is based on an assertion that the order being enforced through income withholding was entered without personal jurisdiction over the obligor-employee. A variety of similar fundamental defenses may be asserted, such as mistaken identity, full payment, another order controlling, etc.

Subsection (a) provides for a simple, efficient, and cost-effective method for an employee-alleged obligor to assert a defense. For example, if the existence of a support obligation is acknowledged but the details are at issue, the obligor may register the underlying "controlling" support order with a local tribunal and seek temporary protection pending resolution of the contest. This may be accomplished pro se, employment of private counsel, or by a request for services from the child support enforcement agency of the responding state. Some states provide administrative procedures for challenging the income withholding that may provide quicker resolution of a dispute than a judicially-based registration and hearing process. In the absence of expeditious action by the employee to assert a defense and contest the direct filing of a notice for withholding, however, the employer must begin income withholding in a timely fashion.

Another issue the employee-obligor may raise is that the withholding order received by the employer is not based on the controlling child-support order issued by the tribunal with continuing, exclusive jurisdiction, *see* §159.207, *supra*. Such a claim does not constitute a defense to the obligation of child support, but does put at issue the identity of the order to which the employer must respond.

The one order system initiated by UIFSA effectively has eliminated the multiple-order system of RURESA, which primarily involved multiple orders by different courts for the same child. At present most "duplicate income withholding orders" involve one state seeking state assigned arrears and another state also seeking arrears, and possibly ongoing support as well. Clearly the employer is in no position to make a decision on how to proceed to resolve such conflicting claims. When multiple orders involve the same employee-obligor and child, or multiple children (including those with other mothers), as a practical matter resort to a responding tribunal to resolve the resulting dispute almost certainly will be necessary.

FAM §159.507. ADMINISTRATIVE ENFORCEMENT OF ORDERS

(a) A party or support enforcement agency seeking to enforce a support order or an income-withholding order, or both, issued in another state or a foreign support order may send the documents required for registering the order to a support enforcement agency of this state.

(b) On receipt of the documents, the support enforcement agency, without initially seeking to register the order, shall consider and, if appropriate, use any administrative procedure authorized by the law of this state to enforce a support order or an income-withholding order, or both. If the obligor does not contest administrative enforcement, the order need not be registered. If the obligor contests the validity or administrative enforcement of the order, the support enforcement agency shall register the order under this chapter.

History of Fam. Code §159.507: Acts 1995, 74th Leg., ch. 20, §1, eff. Apr. 20, 1995. Renumbered from §159.502 by Acts 1997, 75th Leg., ch. 607, §13, eff. Sept. 1, 1997. Amended by Acts 2003, 78th Leg., ch. 1247, §31, eff. Sept. 1, 2003; Acts 2015, 84th Leg., ch. 368, §36, eff. July 1, 2015. Source: Former Fam. Code §21.34.

NCCUSL Comment*

Sections 159.501 through 159.506 are posited on the belief that U.S. employers ought not be burdened with enforcement of foreign income-withholding orders received directly from overseas. This view is inapplicable if a support enforcement agency is involved. The procedural safeguards built into the Title IV-D system of processing requests between Central Authorities provide reasonable assurance that the income withholding order to be enforced is genuine.

This section authorizes summary enforcement of an interstate or foreign child-support order through the administrative means available for intrastate orders if the agency deems it "appropriate" to do so. Under subsection (a), an interested party in another state or foreign country, which necessarily includes a private attorney or a support enforcement agency, may forward a support order or income-withholding order to a support enforcement agency of the responding state. The term "responding state" in this context does not necessarily contemplate resort to a tribunal as an initial step.

Subsection (b) directs the support enforcement agency in the responding state to consider and, if appropriate, to use that state's regular administrative procedures to process an out-of-state order. Thus, a local employer accustomed to dealing with the local agency need not change its procedure to comply with an out-of-state order. Similarly, the administrative agency is authorized to apply its ordinary rules equally to both intrastate and interstate orders. For example, if the administrative hearing procedure must be exhausted for an intrastate order before a contesting party may seek relief in a tribunal, the same rule applies to an interstate order received for administrative enforcement. This subsection also makes it clear that filing liens or submitting claims in legal actions do not require the initial registration of the order.

Sections 159.508-159.600 reserved for expansion

SUBCHAPTER G. REGISTRATION, ENFORCEMENT, & MODIFICATION OF SUPPORT ORDER

NCCUSL Introductory Comment

Sections 159.601 through 159.604 establish the basic procedure for the registration of a support order from another state or a foreign support order. Under RURESA when a tribunal of a responding state was requested to register and enforce an existing child-support order, the common practice was to ignore the request; rather, a separate proceeding would be initiated for the establishment of a new support order. This practice was specifically rejected by UIFSA; this practice under RURESA created the multiple support-order system that UIFSA was specifically designed to eliminate. Under §§159.205 through 159.207 the one-order system allows only one existing order to be enforced prospectively.

Sections 159.605 through 159.608 provide the procedure for the nonregistering party to contest registration of an order, either because the order is allegedly invalid, superseded, or no longer in effect, or because the enforcement remedy being sought is opposed by the nonregistering party. Other enforcement remedies may be available without resort to the UIFSA process under the law of the responding state. *See* §159.104.

The registration and enforcement provisions in §§159.601 through 159.608 are consistent with the "recognition and enforcement" provisions of the Convention. The terms of this subchapter and Subchapter H suffice to direct international support orders into the proper channels.

PART 1. REGISTRATION FOR ENFORCEMENT OF SUPPORT ORDER

FAM §159.601. REGISTRATION OF ORDER FOR ENFORCEMENT

A support order or income-withholding order issued in another state or a foreign support order may be registered in this state for enforcement.

* See footnote on p. 666.

History of Fam. Code §159.601: Acts 1995, 74th Leg., ch. 20, §1, eff. Apr. 20, 1995. Amended by Acts 2015, 84th Leg., ch. 368, §§37, 38, eff. July 1, 2015. Source: Former Fam. Code §21.35.

NCCUSL Comment*

Registration of an order in a tribunal of the responding state is the first step to enforce a support order from another state or foreign country. If a prior support order has been validly issued by a tribunal with continuing, exclusive jurisdiction, *see* §159.205, such an order is to be prospectively enforced against the obligor in the absence of narrow, strictly defined fact situations in which an existing order may be modified. *See* §§159.609 through 159.614. Until and unless that order is modified, however, it remains an order of the issuing tribunal and is fully enforceable in the responding state.

Although registration that is not accompanied by a request for the affirmative relief of enforcement is not prohibited, the act does not contemplate registration as serving a purpose in itself. In that regard, registration is a process, and the failure to register does not deprive an otherwise appropriate forum of subject matter jurisdiction. Note that either or both a state support order or a state income-withholding order may be registered. However, although a foreign support order also may be registered, this section does not contemplate recognition of a foreign income-withholding order.

Related to Convention: art. 23. Procedure on an application for recognition and enforcement; art. 26. Procedure on an application for recognition.

FAM §159.602. PROCEDURE TO REGISTER ORDER FOR ENFORCEMENT

(a) Except as otherwise provided by Section 159.706, a support order or income-withholding order of another state or a foreign support order may be registered in this state by sending the following records to the appropriate tribunal in this state:

(1) a letter of transmittal to the tribunal requesting registration and enforcement;

(2) two copies, including one certified copy, of the order to be registered, including any modification of the order;

(3) a sworn statement by the person requesting registration or a certified statement by the custodian of the records showing the amount of any arrearage;

(4) the name of the obligor and, if known:

(A) the obligor's address and social security number;

(B) the name and address of the obligor's employer and any other source of income of the obligor; and

(C) a description of and the location of property of the obligor in this state not exempt from execution; and

(5) except as otherwise provided by Section 159.312, the name and address of the obligee and, if applicable, the person to whom support payments are to be remitted.

(b) On receipt of a request for registration, the registering tribunal shall cause the order to be filed as an order of a tribunal of another state or a foreign support order, together with one copy of the documents and information, regardless of their form.

(c) A petition or comparable pleading seeking a remedy that must be affirmatively sought under other law of this state may be filed at the same time as the request for registration or later. The pleading must specify the grounds for the remedy sought.

(d) If two or more orders are in effect, the person requesting registration shall:

(1) furnish to the tribunal a copy of each support order asserted to be in effect in addition to the documents specified in this section;

(2) specify the order alleged to be the controlling order, if any; and

(3) specify the amount of consolidated arrears, if any.

(e) A request for a determination of which order is the controlling order may be filed separately from or with a request for registration and enforcement or for registration and modification. The person requesting registration shall give notice of the request to each party whose rights may be affected by the determination.

History of Fam. Code §159.602: Acts 1995, 74th Leg., ch. 20, §1, eff. Apr. 20, 1995. Amended by Acts 2001, 77th Leg., ch. 296, §3, eff. Sept. 1, 2001; Acts 2003, 78th Leg., ch. 1247, §33, eff. Sept. 1, 2003; Acts 2015, 84th Leg., ch. 368, §39, eff. July 1, 2015. Source: Former Fam. Code §21.36.

See also ***O'Connor's Texas Family Law Handbook*** (2017), "Registration of non-Texas orders," ch. 9-D, §2.2.2(1), p. 1030; "Registering non-Texas child-support order," ch. 9-D, §13.1, p. 1051.

ANNOTATIONS

Kendall v. Kendall, 340 S.W.3d 483, 498 (Tex. App.—Houston [1st Dist.] 2011, no pet.). "No Texas state court has squarely addressed the issue of whether failure to comply with a UIFSA registration requirement deprives a Texas court of subject-matter jurisdiction to enforce or modify a foreign support order. *At 500:* Generally, under Texas law, failure to establish a statutory procedural prerequisite does not deprive the trial court of subject-matter jurisdiction over a plaintiff's claim if the statutory prerequisite is merely a condition on which the plaintiff's right to relief depends. 'A statutory requirement is jurisdictional, as opposed to substantive, only when the Legislature's intent so indicates.' [¶] '[R]egistration of a foreign support order is simply a statutory prerequisite to enforcement of the order in Texas.' [A] 'court's action contrary to a statute' means the action is erroneous or voidable, but not void, so jurisdiction is not implicated."

* See footnote on p. 666.

NCCUSL Comment*

Subsection (a) outlines the mechanics for registration of an interstate or foreign support order. Substantial compliance with the requirements is expected. The procedure for registration and enforcement set forth in this section is basically unchanged for a foreign support order; indeed, all of §§159.601 through 159.608 apply. The requirement that the order be "issued by a tribunal" has been subtly modified. Although the vast majority of enforceable support orders will be from a tribunal, in relatively rare instances an enforceable "foreign support order" from a Convention country will not have been issued by a tribunal, *see e.g.*, §159.710, *infra*. Note, however, that a request for registration of a foreign support order for which the Convention is in force is subject to §159.706. This is because the list of documents comprising the required record in subsection (a) differs in a measurable degree with Convention art. 11 and 25.

Millions of interstate domestic cases have been, and will continue to be, processed under the procedure specified in this section. It has been estimated that only approximately one-tenth of one percent (0.1%) of the Title IV-D caseload involve a foreign support order. Thus, the documentation specified by this section is the same for interstate and non-Convention foreign support orders. A support order from a Convention country is covered by the separate list of specifications in §159.706 to accommodate the differences between this act and the Convention. Because child-support enforcement agencies have successfully dealt with foreign support orders with increasing frequency during the UIFSA era, this may well prove to be a distinction without much difference.

Subsection (b) confirms that the support order being registered is not converted into an order of the responding state; rather, it continues to be an order of the tribunal of the issuing state or foreign country.

Subsection (c) warns that if a particular enforcement remedy must be specifically sought under local law, the same rules of procedure and substantive law apply to an interstate or international case. For example, if license suspension or revocation is sought as a remedy for alleged noncompliance with an order, the substantive and procedural rules of the responding state apply. Whether the range of application of the remedy in the responding state is wider or narrower than that available in the issuing state or foreign country is irrelevant. The responding tribunal will apply the familiar law of its state, and is neither expected nor authorized to consider the enforcement laws of the issuing state or foreign country. In short, the responding tribunal follows the identical path for enforcing the order of a tribunal of another state or foreign country as it would when enforcing an order of the responding state. The authorization of a later filing to comply with local law contemplates that interstate or international pleadings may be liberally amended to conform to local practice.

Subsections (d) and (e) amplify the procedures to be followed when two or more child-support orders exist and registration for enforcement is sought. In such instances, the requester is directed to furnish the tribunal with sufficient information and documentation so that the tribunal may make a determination of the controlling order for prospective support and of the amount of consolidated arrears and interest accrued under all valid orders. *See* §159.207.

Related to Convention: art. 11. Application contents; art. 20. Bases for recognition and enforcement; art. 21. Severability and partial recognition and enforcement; art. 22. Grounds for refusing recognition and enforcement; art. 23. Procedure on an application for recognition and enforcement; art. 25. Documents.

FAM §159.603. EFFECT OF REGISTRATION FOR ENFORCEMENT

(a) A support order or income-withholding order issued in another state or a foreign support order is registered when the order is filed in the registering tribunal of this state.

(b) A registered support order issued in another state or a foreign country is enforceable in the same manner and is subject to the same procedures as an order issued by a tribunal of this state.

(c) Except as otherwise provided in this subchapter, a tribunal of this state shall recognize and enforce, but may not modify, a registered support order if the issuing tribunal had jurisdiction.

History of Fam. Code §159.603: Acts 1995, 74th Leg., ch. 20, §1, eff. Apr. 20, 1995. Amended by Acts 2015, 84th Leg., ch. 368, §40, eff. July 1, 2015. Source: Former Fam. Code §21.37.

ANNOTATIONS

In re A.W.D., 355 S.W.3d 914, 916 (Tex.App.—Amarillo 2011, no pet.). "[T]he trial court signed an 'order confirming registration of foreign support order.' ... The order does not contain language disposing of the affirmative claims alleged in the [AG's] motion for enforcement. Nor does it contain language indicating it is intended as a final judgment. [¶] [Obligor] filed a notice of appeal. [¶] Here the order of confirmation does not dispose of the claims raised in the motion for enforcement. The parties do not cite us to, nor are we aware of, any authority authorizing an immediate appeal of an interlocutory confirmation order while issues of contempt and enforcement remain pending. *At 917:* [There is] an exception to the general rule of finality ... specifying that 'a judgment otherwise disposing of all issues between the parties is not rendered interlocutory if further proceedings may be required to carry the judgment into effect or incidental matters remain to be settled.' [W]e find the exception ... inapplicable here."

NCCUSL Comment*

Initially the text of the registration procedure under UIFSA (1992) was nearly identical to that set forth in RURESA. But, the intent of UIFSA registration was always radically different. Under UIFSA, registration of a support order of State A continues to be an order of that state, which is to be enforced by a tribunal of State B. The ordinary rules of evidence and procedure of State B apply to hearings, except as local law may be supplemented or specifically superseded by other local law, i.e., UIFSA. The purpose of the registration procedure in §§159.601 through 159.604 is that the order being registered remains a State A order until modified.

First, note that subsection (a) is phrased in the passive voice; "A support order ... is registered when the order is filed in the registering tribunal...." This drafting is deliberate. By indirection, in effect UIFSA provides that either the obligor, the obligee, or a support enforcement agency, may register a support order of another state or a foreign support order. In fact, even a stranger to the litigation, for example a grandparent or an employer of an alleged obligor, may register a support order. Presumptively, the order registered is the valid, controlling order. If not, the act depends on the respondent to contest the registration. *See* §§159.605 through 159.608.

Subsection (b) provides that a support order of another state or a foreign support order is to be enforced and satisfied in the same manner as if it had been issued by a tribunal of the registering state. Conceptually, the responding tribunal is enforcing the order of a tribunal of another state or a foreign support order, not its own order.

Subsection (c) mandates enforcement of the registered order, but forbids modification unless the terms of §§159.609 through 159.614 are met. Under UIFSA there will be only one order in existence at any one time. That order is enforceable in a responding state irrespective of whether the order may be modified. In most instances, a child-support order will be subject to the continuing, exclusive jurisdiction of the issuing tribunal. Sometimes the issuing tribunal will not be able to exercise its authority to modify the order because

* See footnote on p. 666.

neither the child nor the parties reside in the issuing state. Nonetheless, the order may be registered and is fully enforceable in a responding state until the potential for modification actually occurs in accordance with the strict terms for such a proceeding. *See* §159.611. Thus, the registering tribunal always must bear in mind that the enforcement procedures taken, whether to enforce current support or to assist collecting current and future arrears and interest, are made on behalf of the issuing tribunal, and are not a modification of the controlling order.

Related to Convention: art. 11. Application contents; art. 20. Bases for recognition and enforcement; art. 21. Severability and partial recognition and enforcement; art. 22. Grounds for refusing recognition and enforcement; art. 23. Procedure on an application for recognition and enforcement; art. 25. Documents.

FAM §159.604. CHOICE OF LAW

(a) Except as otherwise provided by Subsection (d), the law of the issuing state or foreign country governs:

(1) the nature, extent, amount, and duration of current payments under a registered support order;

(2) the computation and payment of arrearages and accrual of interest on the arrearages under the support order; and

(3) the existence and satisfaction of other obligations under the support order.

(b) In a proceeding for arrears under a registered support order, the statute of limitation of this state, or of the issuing state or foreign country, whichever is longer, applies.

(c) A responding tribunal of this state shall apply the procedures and remedies of this state to enforce current support and collect arrears and interest due on a support order of another state or a foreign country registered in this state.

(d) After a tribunal of this state or another state determines which is the controlling order and issues an order consolidating arrears, if any, the tribunal of this state shall prospectively apply the law of the state or foreign country issuing the controlling order, including that state's or country's law on interest on arrears, on current and future support, and on consolidated arrears.

History of Fam. Code §159.604: Acts 1995, 74th Leg., ch. 20, §1, eff. Apr. 20, 1995. Amended by Acts 1997, 75th Leg., ch. 607, §14, eff. Sept. 1, 1997; Acts 2003, 78th Leg., ch. 1247, §34, eff. Sept. 1, 2003; Acts 2015, 84th Leg., ch. 368, §41, eff. July 1, 2015. Source: Former Fam. Code §21.38.

NCCUSL Comment*

Subsection (a) is intended to clarify the wide range of subjects that are governed by the choice-of-law rules established in this section. The task is to identify those aspects of the case for which local law is inapplicable. A basic principle of UIFSA is that throughout the process the controlling order remains the order of the tribunal of the issuing state or foreign country until a valid modification. The responding tribunal only assists in the enforcement of that order. Absent a loss of continuing, exclusive jurisdiction by the issuing tribunal and a subsequent modification of the order, the order never becomes an order of a responding tribunal.

Subsection (a) first identifies those aspects of the initial child-support order that are governed by the term's original decision and the function of the issuing tribunal. First and foremost, ultimate responsibility for enforcement and final resolution of the obligor's compliance with all aspects of the support order belongs to the issuing tribunal. Thus, calculation of whether the obligor has fully complied with the payment of current support, arrears, and interest on arrears is also the duty of the issuing tribunal.

In UIFSA (1992) the decision was made by NCCUSL that the duration of child support should be fixed by the initial controlling child-support order. *See* §159.611(c). This policy decision was somewhat controversial at the time, especially given the general rule that "local law controls." But, case law regarding issues created by movement from one state with one duration to a state with another policy was hopelessly muddled, so a solution was sought. Then, as now, the policies of states on this subject varied greatly: today, a few states continue to set the once most-common age of 21 as the cut-off date; some continue the obligation past 21, dependent on enrollment in higher education (often with limited time specified); at the other end of the spectrum, some states end the obligation of child support at age 18; in others at 19; and, most popularly, at one or the other of either age 18 or 19, plus graduation from high school, whichever is later.

Under subsection (a), if the initial issuing tribunal sets the age for termination of child support at 18, a responding state must recognize and enforce that child-support order. If the responding state sets its child support to age 21, the responding tribunal may not apply that time duration to require additional support to that age. The converse is also true. If the controlling order of another state ends the support obligation at 21, the responding tribunal in a state with 18 as the maximum duration for child support must enforce the controlling order until age 21. The dissent on this policy decision in UIFSA has abated over time. Interestingly, the Convention establishes age 21 as the hallmark. At the same time, under Convention art. 2(2), a country may reserve the right to limit the application of the Convention with regard to child support to persons who have not reached the age of 18. The United States does not intend to make such a reservation.

Similarly, subsection (a) directs that the law of the issuing state or foreign country governs the answer to questions such as whether a payment made for the benefit of a child, such as a Social Security benefit for a child of a disabled obligor, should be credited against the obligor's child support obligation. In sum, on these subjects the consistent rule is that a controlling order from State A is enforced in State B (and State C as well).

Note that as soon as a general proposition is identified, an exception may well be presented. Subsection (b) contains a choice-of-law provision that often diverges from other local law. In situations in which the statutes of limitation differ from state to state, the statute with the longer term is to be applied. In interstate cases, arrearages often will have accumulated over a considerable period of time before enforcement is perfected. The rationale for this exception to the general rule of "local law applies" is that the obligor should not gain an undue benefit from his or her choice of residence if the forum state, as the obligor's state of residence, has a shorter statute of limitations for arrearages than does the controlling order state. On the other side of the coin, i.e., if the forum has a longer statute of limitations, the obligor will be treated in an identical manner as all other obligors in that state. This choice of limitations also applies to the time period after the accrual of the arrears in which to bring an enforcement action.

Subsection (c) mandates that local law controls with regard to enforcement procedures. For example, if the issuing state or foreign country has enacted a wide variety of license suspension or revocation statutes, while the responding state has a much narrower list of licenses subject to suspension or revocation, local law prevails.

Subsection (d) may initially appear only to express a truism—the law of the issuing state is superior with regard to the terms of the support order. The last clause in the sentence, however, contains an important clarifying provision; that is, the law of the issuing state or foreign country is to be applied to the consolidated arrears, most particularly to the interest to be charged prospectively, even if the support orders of other states contributed a portion to those arrears. In sum, the local tribunal applies its own familiar procedures to enforce a support order, but it is clearly enforcing an order of a tribunal of another state and not an order of the forum.

* See footnote on p. 666.

Related to Convention: art. 2. Scope; art. 11. Application contents; art. 20. Bases for recognition and enforcement; art. 21. Severability and partial recognition and enforcement; art. 22. Grounds for refusing recognition and enforcement; art. 23. Procedure on an application for recognition and enforcement; art. 25. Documents.

PART 2. CONTEST OF VALIDITY OR ENFORCEMENT

FAM §159.605. NOTICE OF REGISTRATION OF ORDER

(a) When a support order or income-withholding order issued in another state or a foreign support order is registered, the registering tribunal of this state shall notify the nonregistering party. The notice must be accompanied by a copy of the registered order and the documents and relevant information accompanying the order.

(b) A notice must inform the nonregistering party:

(1) that a registered order is enforceable as of the date of registration in the same manner as an order issued by a tribunal of this state;

(2) that a hearing to contest the validity or enforcement of the registered order must be requested within 20 days after notice unless the registered order is under Section 159.707;

(3) that failure to contest the validity or enforcement of the registered order in a timely manner will result in confirmation of the order and enforcement of the order and the alleged arrearages; and

(4) of the amount of any alleged arrearages.

(c) If the registering party asserts that two or more orders are in effect, the notice must also:

(1) identify the two or more orders and the order alleged by the registering party to be the controlling order and the consolidated arrears, if any;

(2) notify the nonregistering party of the right to a determination of which is the controlling order;

(3) state that the procedures provided in Subsection (b) apply to the determination of which is the controlling order; and

(4) state that failure to contest the validity or enforcement of the order alleged to be the controlling order in a timely manner may result in confirmation that the order is the controlling order.

(d) On registration of an income-withholding order for enforcement, the support enforcement agency or the registering tribunal shall notify the obligor's employer under Chapter 158.

History of Fam. Code §159.605: Acts 1995, 74th Leg., ch. 20, §1, eff. Apr. 20, 1995. Amended by Acts 1997, 75th Leg., ch. 607, §15, eff. Sept. 1, 1997; Acts 2003, 78th Leg., ch. 1247, §35, eff. Sept. 1, 2003; Acts 2015, 84th Leg., ch. 368, §§42, 43, eff. July 1, 2015. Source: Former Fam. Code §21.39.

See also *O'Connor's Texas Family Law Handbook* (2017), "Notice of registration," ch. 9-D, §13.1.1(4), p. 1052; "Notice of registration," ch. 9-D, §13.1.2(4), p. 1053.

NCCUSL Comment*

Subsection (a) requires the registering tribunal to provide notice to the nonregistering party of the effect of registration. After such notice is given, absent a successful contest by the nonregistering party, the order will be confirmed and future contest will be precluded. The notice contemplates far more than merely announcing an intent to initiate enforcement of an existing support order. The registered order or orders and other relevant documents and information must accompany the notice, including details about the alleged arrears.

Subsection (b) provides the nonregistering party with a wealth of information about the proceeding, including that: (1) the order is immediately enforceable; (2) a hearing must be requested within a relatively short time; (3) failure to contest "will result" in a confirmation of the order (roughly the equivalent of a default judgment); and (4) the amount of arrears, if any. Initially subsection (b) made the suggestion, via brackets, that [20] days be the time within which a request for a hearing to contest the support order be made. The rationale for this relatively short period was that the matter had already been litigated, and the obligor had already had the requisite "day in court," and was allegedly in default of a known order. Moreover, advocates of child-support enforcement stressed the necessity of quick resolution of an instance of nonsupport.

On the other hand, the Convention requires notice of hearing to be within a fixed time of 30 days, and further a fixed time of 60 days if the respondent resides in a foreign country. *See* Convention art. 23(6). This difference between UIFSA and the Convention is accommodated in §159.707. The time frame for notice of registration for an interstate support order and a foreign support order not subject to the Convention will be established by local law.

Subsection (c) is the correlative to §159.602 regarding the notice to be given to the nonregistering party if determination of a controlling order must be made because of the existence of two or more child-support orders. The petitioner requesting this affirmative relief is directed to identify the order alleged to be controlling under §159.207.

Subsection (d) states the obvious; i.e., the obligor's employer also must be notified if income is to be withheld. Often this will not be necessary if the employer has already been notified by the responding state's enforcement agency via the administrative process established in §159.507.

Related to Convention: art. 20. Bases for recognition and enforcement; art. 23. Procedure on an application for recognition and enforcement.

FAM §159.606. PROCEDURE TO CONTEST VALIDITY OR ENFORCEMENT OF REGISTERED SUPPORT ORDER

(a) A nonregistering party seeking to contest the validity or enforcement of a registered support order in this state shall request a hearing within the time required by Section 159.605. The nonregistering party may seek to vacate the registration, to assert any defense to an allegation of noncompliance with the registered order, or to contest the remedies being sought or the amount of any alleged arrearages under Section 159.607.

(b) If the nonregistering party fails to contest the validity or enforcement of the registered support order

* See footnote on p. 666.

in a timely manner, the order is confirmed by operation of law.

(c) If a nonregistering party requests a hearing to contest the validity or enforcement of the registered support order, the registering tribunal shall schedule the matter for hearing and give notice to the parties of the date, time, and place of the hearing.

History of Fam. Code §159.606: Acts 1995, 74th Leg., ch. 20, §1, eff. Apr. 20, 1995. Amended by Acts 1997, 75th Leg., ch. 607, §16, eff. Sept. 1, 1997; Acts 2015, 84th Leg., ch. 368, §44, eff. July 1, 2015. Source: Former Fam. Code §21.40.

See also ***O'Connor's Texas Family Law Handbook*** (2017), "Contesting registration," ch. 9-D, §13.2, p. 1053.

NCCUSL Comment*

Subsection (a) directs the "nonregistering party" to contest the registration of an interstate support order or a foreign support order not subject to the Convention within a short period of time or forfeit the opportunity to contest. As noted in §159.605, that time frame is extended for cases subject to the Convention.

Notice of registration is the first step for enforcement or modification of another state's child-support order. Once the nonregistering party is put on notice of the registration, if an error allegedly has been made, the second step is crucial. The nonregistering party is required to assert any existing defense to the alleged controlling order, or forfeit the opportunity to contest the allegations. Note that either the obligor or the obligee may have objections to the registered order, although in the vast majority of cases the obligor is the nonregistering party.

On the other hand, there is a possibility that in multiple-order situations either party may register the order most favorable to that party rather than register the likely controlling order, thus triggering a contest. Deliberately furnishing misinformation regarding the controlling order doubtless constitutes chicanery, which is contrary to §159.605(c). When a support enforcement agency requests registration, §159.307(c) requires reasonable efforts to ensure registration of the proper controlling order. Nonetheless, there may be an honest difference of opinion as to which order controls. The nonregistering obligor has a significant stake in assuring that both the order and the arrears are correctly stated.

Under UIFSA a contest of the fundamental provisions of the registered order is not permitted in the responding state. The nonregistering party must return to the issuing state or foreign country to prosecute such a contest (only as the law of that state or foreign country permits). This approach is akin to the prohibition found in §159.315 against asserting a nonparentage defense in a UIFSA proceeding. There is no attempt by UIFSA to preclude a collateral attack on the support order from being litigated in the appropriate forum.

Subsection (b) precludes an untimely contest of a registered support order.

Subsection (c) directs that a hearing be scheduled when the nonregistering party contests some aspect of the registration.

Related to Convention: art. 20. Bases for recognition and enforcement; art. 22. Grounds for refusing recognition and enforcement; art. 23. Procedure on an application for recognition and enforcement; art. 26. Procedure on an application for recognition.

FAM §159.607. CONTEST OF REGISTRATION OR ENFORCEMENT

(a) A party contesting the validity or enforcement of a registered support order or seeking to vacate the registration has the burden of proving one or more of the following defenses:

(1) the issuing tribunal lacked personal jurisdiction over the contesting party;

(2) the order was obtained by fraud;

(3) the order has been vacated, suspended, or modified by a later order;

(4) the issuing tribunal has stayed the order pending appeal;

(5) there is a defense under the law of this state to the remedy sought;

(6) full or partial payment has been made;

(7) the statute of limitation under Section 159.604 precludes enforcement of some or all of the alleged arrearages; or

(8) the alleged controlling order is not the controlling order.

(b) If a party presents evidence establishing a full or partial defense under Subsection (a), a tribunal may stay enforcement of the registered support order, continue the proceeding to permit production of additional relevant evidence, and issue other appropriate orders. An uncontested portion of the registered support order may be enforced by all remedies available under the law of this state.

(c) If the contesting party does not establish a defense under Subsection (a) to the validity or enforcement of the registered support order, the registering tribunal shall issue an order confirming the order.

History of Fam. Code §159.607: Acts 1995, 74th Leg., ch. 20, §1, eff. Apr. 20, 1995. Amended by Acts 2003, 78th Leg., ch. 1247, §36, eff. Sept. 1, 2003; Acts 2015, 84th Leg., ch. 368, §45, eff. July 1, 2015. Source: Former Fam. Code §21.41.

See also ***O'Connor's Texas Family Law Handbook*** (2017), "Defenses," ch. 9-D, §13.2.3, p. 1054; "Confirming registration," ch. 9-D, §13.3.1, p. 1055.

NCCUSL Comment*

Subsection (a) places the burden on the nonregistering party to assert narrowly defined defenses to registration of a support order. The first of the listed defenses, lack of personal jurisdiction over the nonregistering party in the original proceeding, is undoubtedly the most widely discussed topic. It appears that at the appellate level, several of the other listed defenses are more commonly asserted. The decision in *Kulko v. Superior Court*, 436 U.S. 84 (1978) was somewhat controversial when delivered, and has remained so, at least in the international context. As a practical matter, however, the requirement that a support order be based on personal jurisdiction over both parties—but primarily the obligor—is a well-established fixture in the jurisprudence of the United States; relatively few appellate cases on this subject have been reported.

A nonregistering obligor may assert a wide variety of listed defenses, such as "payment" or "the obligation has terminated," in response to allegations of noncompliance with the registered order. There is no defense, however, to registration of a valid foreign support order. The nonregistering party also may contest the allegedly controlling order because its terms have been modified. Or, the defense may be based on the existence of a different controlling order. *See* §159.207. Presumably this defense must be substantiated by registration of the alleged controlling order to be effective.

While subsection (a)(6) is couched in terms that imply the defense to the amount of alleged arrears can only be that they are less, the converse is also available. For example, if the registering party is the obligor and asserts an amount of arrears that the obligee believes is too low, as the nonregistering party the obligee must contest to preclude confirmation of the alleged amount.

In the absence of a valid defense, if the obligor is found to be liable for current support, the registering tribunal must enter an order to enforce that obli-

* See footnote on p. 666.

gation. Additional proof of arrearages must also result in enforcement under the Bradley Amendment, 42 U.S.C. Section 666(a)(10), which requires all states to treat child-support payments as final judgments as they come due (or lose federal funding). Therefore, federal law precludes arrearages from being subject to retroactive modification. Future modification of a child support order from another state is governed by §§159.609-159.614, and §§159.615-159.616 regulate modification of foreign child support orders.

Subsection (c) provides that failure to contest a registered order successfully requires the tribunal to confirm the validity of the registered order.

Related to Convention: art. 26. Procedure on an application for recognition.

FAM §159.608. CONFIRMED ORDER

Confirmation of a registered support order, whether by operation of law or after notice and hearing, precludes further contest of the order with respect to any matter that could have been asserted at the time of registration.

History of Fam. Code §159.608: Acts 1995, 74th Leg., ch. 20, §1, eff. Apr. 20, 1995. Amended by Acts 2015, 84th Leg., ch. 368, §46, eff. July 1, 2015. Source: Former Fam. Code §21.42.

See also ***O'Connor's Texas Family Law Handbook*** (2017), "Confirming registration," ch. 9-D, §13.3.1, p. 1055.

NCCUSL Comment*

If, after notice, the nonregistering party fails to contest, the registered support order is confirmed by operation of law and no further action by a responding tribunal is necessary. Although the statute is not explicit on the subject, it seems likely in the absence of a contest both the registering and nonregistering party would be estopped from subsequently collaterally attacking the confirmed order, whether on the basis that "the wrong order was registered" or otherwise.

If contested, a registered support order must be confirmed by the responding tribunal if, after a hearing, the defenses authorized in §159.607 are rejected. Thus, either scenario precludes the nonregistering party from raising any issue that could have been asserted in a hearing. Confirmation of a support order, whether by action or as the result of inaction, validates both the terms of the order and the asserted arrearages.

Related to Convention: art. 22. Grounds for refusing recognition and enforcement; art. 26. Procedure on an application for recognition.

PART 3. REGISTRATION & MODIFICATION OF CHILD SUPPORT ORDER OF ANOTHER STATE

NCCUSL Introductory Comment

Authority to modify a child-support order of another state depends on the interaction of these sections with the continuing, exclusive jurisdiction of the issuing tribunal. *See* §§159.205 through 159.206. This also might involve the determination of the controlling order in a situation involving multiple child-support orders. These concepts are not present in the international context. *See* §§159.615, 159.616, and 159.711. Thus, modification of a support order from a foreign country other than a Convention country is not governed by §§159.609-159.614, but is subject to §§159.615-159.616, *infra*.

Sections 159.609 through 159.614 apply only to modification of an interstate child-support order. Most of the act applies to "a support order," which includes both child-support and spousal support. Both categories are generally subject to interstate enforcement under UIFSA. But, as a practical matter, the actual process of that enforcement is quite different. Child support is enforced almost exclusively by governmentally sponsored Title IV-D agencies, which also may enforce spousal support if it is included in the same order. In some states, local funds are appropriated for enforcement of spousal support as well. Only occasionally will a private attorney be involved in a child-support case, but spousal support not issued in conjunction with a child-support order generally requires representation pro se or by private counsel. More importantly, a tribunal of a responding state may enforce spousal support, but it does not have authority to modify a spousal-support order of another state or foreign country unless the law of that jurisdiction does not assert continuing, exclusive jurisdiction over its order. *See* §159.211.

FAM §159.609. PROCEDURE TO REGISTER CHILD SUPPORT ORDER OF ANOTHER STATE FOR MODIFICATION

A party or support enforcement agency seeking to modify, or to modify and enforce, a child support order issued in another state shall register that order in this state in the same manner provided in Sections 159.601 through 159.608 if the order has not been registered. A petition for modification may be filed at the same time as a request for registration, or later. The pleading must specify the grounds for modification.

History of Fam. Code §159.609: Acts 1995, 74th Leg., ch. 20, §1, eff. Apr. 20, 1995. Amended by Acts 2015, 84th Leg., ch. 368, §§47, 48, eff. July 1, 2015. Source: Former Fam. Code §21.43.

NCCUSL Comment*

Sections 159.609 through 159.614 deal with situations in which it is permissible for a registering state to modify the existing child-support order of another state. The first step for modification of another state's child-support order is registration in the responding tribunal under §§159.601 to 159.604. In some situations, this may also involve identification of the controlling order. A petitioner wishing to register a support order of another state for purposes of modification must conform to the general requirements for pleadings in §159.311, and follow the procedure for registration set forth in §159.602. If the tribunal has the requisite personal jurisdiction over the parties and may assume subject matter jurisdiction as provided in §§159.611 or 159.613, modification may be sought independently, in conjunction with registration and enforcement, or at a later date after the order has been registered and enforced if circumstances have changed.

FAM §159.610. EFFECT OF REGISTRATION FOR MODIFICATION

A tribunal of this state may enforce a child support order of another state registered for purposes of modification in the same manner as if the order had been issued by a tribunal of this state, but the registered support order may be modified only if the requirements of Section 159.611 or 159.613 have been met.

History of Fam. Code §159.610: Acts 1995, 74th Leg., ch. 20, §1, eff. Apr. 20, 1995. Amended by Acts 2003, 78th Leg., ch. 1247, §37, eff. Sept. 1, 2003; Acts 2015, 84th Leg., ch. 368, §49, eff. July 1, 2015. Source: Former Fam. Code §21.44.

NCCUSL Comment*

An order issued in another state registered for purposes of modification may be enforced in the same manner as an order registered for purposes of enforcement. But, the power of the forum tribunal to modify a child-support order of another tribunal is limited by the specific factual preconditions set forth in §§159.611 and 159.613.

FAM §159.611. MODIFICATION OF CHILD SUPPORT ORDER OF ANOTHER STATE

(a) If Section 159.613 does not apply, on petition a tribunal of this state may modify a child support order

* See footnote on p. 666.

issued in another state that is registered in this state if, after notice and hearing, the tribunal finds that:

(1) the following requirements are met:

(A) the child, the obligee who is an individual, and the obligor do not reside in the issuing state;

(B) a petitioner who is a nonresident of this state seeks modification; and

(C) the respondent is subject to the personal jurisdiction of the tribunal of this state; or

(2) this state is the residence of the child, or a party who is an individual is subject to the personal jurisdiction of the tribunal of this state, and all of the parties who are individuals have filed consents in a record in the issuing tribunal for a tribunal of this state to modify the support order and assume continuing, exclusive jurisdiction.

(b) Modification of a registered child support order is subject to the same requirements, procedures, and defenses that apply to the modification of an order issued by a tribunal of this state, and the order may be enforced and satisfied in the same manner.

(c) A tribunal of this state may not modify any aspect of a child support order that may not be modified under the law of the issuing state, including the duration of the obligation of support. If two or more tribunals have issued child support orders for the same obligor and same child, the order that controls and must be so recognized under Section 159.207 establishes the aspects of the support order that are nonmodifiable.

(d) In a proceeding to modify a child support order, the law of the state that is determined to have issued the initial controlling order governs the duration of the obligation of support. The obligor's fulfillment of the duty of support established by that order precludes imposition of a further obligation of support by a tribunal of this state.

(e) On issuance of an order by a tribunal of this state modifying a child support order issued in another state, the tribunal of this state becomes the tribunal of continuing, exclusive jurisdiction.

(f) Notwithstanding Subsections (a) through (e) of this section and Section 159.201(b), a tribunal of this state retains jurisdiction to modify an order issued by a tribunal of this state if:

(1) one party resides in another state; and

(2) the other party resides outside the United States.

History of Fam. Code §159.611: Acts 1995, 74th Leg., ch. 20, §1, eff. Apr. 20, 1995. Amended by Acts 1997, 75th Leg., ch. 607, §17, eff. Sept. 1, 1997; Acts 2001, 77th Leg., ch. 1420, §5.0026, eff. Sept. 1, 2001; Acts 2003, 78th Leg., ch. 1247, §38, eff. Sept. 1, 2003; Acts 2009, 81st Leg., ch. 767, §21, eff. June 19, 2009; Acts 2015, 84th Leg., ch. 368, §50, eff. July 1, 2015. Source: Former Fam. Code §21.45.

See also ***O'Connor's Texas Family Law Handbook*** (2017), "Non-Texas order," ch. 9-D, §4.4.13(2)(c)[2], p. 1042; "Choice of law for non-Texas order," ch. 9-D, §16.4, p. 1056.

ANNOTATIONS

In re Martinez, 450 S.W.3d 157, 160 (Tex. App.—San Antonio 2014, orig. proceeding). Obligee "filed a petition in Texas seeking ... to reinstate and extend [obligor's] child support obligation after it expired pursuant to the New York judgment.... *At 164:* [B]ased on [§159.611](c) and [(d)] and the comments thereto, the trial court in this case could not modify the duration of the New York decree to impose a further support obligation upon [obligor] or create a new obligation based on [child's] disability. The duration of the New York support decree is governed by New York law, which the parties stipulated does not provide for support of adult disabled children."

NCCUSL Comment*

The Play-away Rule. As long as the issuing tribunal has continuing, exclusive jurisdiction over its child-support order, a responding tribunal is precluded from modifying the controlling order. *See* §§159.205 through 159.207. UIFSA (1992) made critical choices regarding modification of an existing child-support order. First, the "one-order" rule was to be paramount. Second, the issuing tribunal had continuing, exclusive jurisdiction to modify its order as long as a party or the child continued to reside in the issuing state. The original order remained in force as the controlling order until modified by another tribunal. Third, a separate procedure was created for modification of an existing child-support order when all parties and the child moved from the issuing state and acquired new residences. The key was that the movant seeking modification be "a nonresident of this state." The deciding factor, determined after extended debate, centered on curbing or eliminating the undesirable effect of "ambush or tag" jurisdiction, e.g., the likelihood that the parties would vie to strike first to obtain a home-town advantage. Although constitutional under *Burnham v. Superior Court*, 495 U.S. 604 (1990), such lawsuits would discourage continued contact between the child and the obligor, or between the parties for fear of a lawsuit in a distant forum. Thus, the goal was to avoid the situation in which modification would be available in a forum having personal jurisdiction over both parties based solely on the ground that service of process was made in the would-be forum state.

Under subsection (a)(1), before a responding tribunal may modify the existing controlling order, three specific criteria must be satisfied. First, the individual parties and the child must no longer reside in the issuing state. Second, the party seeking modification, usually the obligee, must register the order as a nonresident of the forum. That forum is almost always the state of residence of the other party, usually the obligor. A colloquial (but easily understood) description is that the nonresident movant for modification must "play an away game on the other party's home field." Third, the forum must have personal jurisdiction over the parties. By registering the support order, the movant submits to the personal jurisdiction of the forum through seeking affirmative relief. On rare occasion, personal jurisdiction over the respondent may be supplied by long-arm jurisdiction. *See* §159.201.

The underlying policies of this procedure contemplate that the issuing tribunal no longer has an interest in exercising its continuing, exclusive jurisdiction to modify its order, nor information readily available to it to do so. The play-

* See footnote on p. 666.

away rule achieves rough justice between the parties in the majority of cases by preventing ambush in a local tribunal. Moreover, it takes into account the factual realities of the situation. In the overwhelming majority of cases the movant is the obligee who is receiving legal assistance in the issuing and responding states from Title IV-D support enforcement agencies. Further, evidence about the obligor's ability to pay child support and enforcement of the support order is best accomplished in the obligor's state of residence.

Fairness requires that an obligee seeking to modify the existing child-support order in the state of residence of the obligor will not be subject to a cross-motion to modify custody merely because the issuing tribunal has lost its continuing, exclusive jurisdiction over the support order. The same restriction applies to an obligor who moves to modify the support order in a state other than that of his or her residence.

There are exceptions to the play-away rule. Under subsection (a)(2), the parties may agree that a particular forum may serve to modify the order, even if the issuing tribunal has continuing, exclusive jurisdiction. Subsection (a)(2) also applies if the individual parties agree to submit the modification issue to a tribunal in the petitioner's state of residence. Implicit in this shift of jurisdiction is that the agreed tribunal has subject matter jurisdiction and personal jurisdiction over at least one of the parties or the child, and that the other party submits to the personal jurisdiction of that forum. UIFSA does not contemplate that parties may agree to confer jurisdiction on a tribunal without a nexus to the parties or the child.

Proof that neither individual party nor the child continues to reside in the issuing state is made directly in the responding tribunal. No purpose is served by requiring the movant to return to the original issuing tribunal for a hearing to elicit confirmation of fact that none of the relevant persons still lives in the issuing state. Thus, the issuing tribunal is not called upon to transfer or surrender its continuing, exclusive jurisdiction or otherwise participate in the process, nor does it have discretion to refuse to yield jurisdiction.

There is a distinction between the processes involved under subsection (a). Once the requirements of subsection (a)(1) are met for assumption of jurisdiction, the responding tribunal acts on the modification and then notifies the issuing tribunal that the prior controlling order has been replaced by a new controlling order. In contrast, for another tribunal to assume modification jurisdiction by agreement under subsection (a)(2), the individual parties first must agree in a record to modification in the responding tribunal and file the record with the issuing tribunal. Thereafter they may proceed in the responding tribunal.

A similar exception is found in §159.205(a)(2), which enables the parties to agree in a record of the original issuing tribunal that it may retain jurisdiction over the order even if all parties have left that state. Note that such an agreement can be incorporated in the initial order of the issuing tribunal.

Section 159.613 also is an exception to subsection (a)(1): it supplants the play-away rule if all parties have left the original issuing state and now reside in the same state, whether by chance or design.

Subsection (b) provides that when a responding tribunal assumes modification jurisdiction because the issuing tribunal has lost continuing, exclusive jurisdiction, the proceedings will generally follow local law with regard to modification of a child-support order, except as provided in subsections (c) and (d).

Duration of the Child Support Obligation. Prior to 1993 American case law was thoroughly in chaos over modification of the duration of a child-support obligation when an obligor or obligee moved from one state to another state and the states had different ages for the duration of child support. The existing duration usually was ignored by the issuance of a new order applying local law, which elicited a variety of appellate court opinions. UIFSA (1992) determined that a uniform rule should be proposed, to wit, duration of the child-support obligation would be fixed by the initial controlling order. Subsection (c) provides the original time frame for support is not modifiable unless the law of the issuing state provides for its modification. After UIFSA (1996) was universally enacted, some tribunals sought to subvert this policy by holding that completion of the obligation to support a child through age 18 established by a now-completed controlling order did not preclude the imposition of a new obligation to support the child through age 21, or beyond.

Subsection (d) prohibits imposition of multiple, albeit successive, support obligations. The initial controlling order may be modified and replaced by a new controlling order in accordance with the terms of §§159.609 through 159.614. But, the duration of the child support obligation remains constant, even though other aspects of the original order may be changed.

Sometimes a domestic-violence protective order includes a provision for child support that will be in force for a specific time. The duration of the protective order often is less than the general law of the state for duration of the child-support obligation. Under these facts the general law of the issuing state regarding duration controls a subsequent child-support order.

Subsection (e) provides that on modification the new child-support order becomes the controlling order to be recognized by all UIFSA states. Good practice mandates that the responding tribunal should explicitly state in its order that it is assuming responsibility for the controlling child-support order. Neither the parties nor other tribunals should be required to speculate about the effect of the action.

International Effect. Prohibiting modification based on the play-away principle in the international context is problematic. The issue arises because the United States is wedded to personal jurisdiction over the individual parties at a state level, rather than the child-based, national jurisdiction found virtually everywhere else. For example, a foreign country typically regards a support order to be of the country, not an order from a political subdivision, e.g., an order from Germany. In some important instances, however, a foreign support order is indeed made in a political subdivision, e.g., a support order from a Canadian province. Although consideration was given to labeling a support order issued in a state to be an order of the United States, conforming modification of child support to the general principles of state law through UIFSA is the only practical choice.

Subsection (f) creates a necessary exception to the play-away concept when the parties and the child no longer reside in the issuing state and one party resides outside the United States. The play-away principle makes sense when the tribunals involved have identical laws regarding continuing, exclusive jurisdiction to modify a child-support order. *See* §§159.205 through 159.207. If one party resides in a foreign country, a pure play-away rule would deny modification in a forum subject to UIFSA rules to the party or child who has moved from the issuing state, but continues to reside in the United States. This result does not occur under Convention art. 18, which places restrictions on modification of a support order in another Convention country if the obligee remains in the issuing Convention country. That article does not mention an effect when only the obligor remains in the issuing country, perhaps because the Convention makes clear that under a child-based system modification jurisdiction will follow the obligee and the child.

Subsection (f) identifies the tribunal that issued the controlling order as the logical choice for an available forum in which UIFSA will apply. This exception to the play-away rule provides assured personal jurisdiction over the parties, which in turn enables the issuing tribunal to retain continuing jurisdiction to modify its order. Of course, the party residing outside the United States has the option to pursue a modification in the state where the other party or child currently reside.

In sum, under this section personal service on either the custodial or noncustodial party found within the state borders, by itself, does not yield jurisdiction to modify. A party seeking to exercise rights of visitation, delivering or picking-up the child for such visitation, or engaging in unrelated business activity in the state, will not be involuntarily subjected to protracted litigation in an inconvenient forum. The play-away rule avoids the possible chilling effect on the exercise of parental contact with the child that the possibility of such litigation might have. The vast majority of disputes about whether a tribunal has jurisdiction will be eliminated. Moreover, submission by the petitioner to the state of residence of the respondent obviates this issue. Finally, because there is an existing order, the primary focus will shift to enforcement, thereby curtailing unnecessary modification efforts.

UIFSA Relationship to UCCJEA. Jurisdiction for modification of child support under subsections (a)(1) and (a)(2) is distinct from modification of custody under the federal Parental Kidnapping Prevention Act (PKPA), 42 U.S.C. §1738A, and the Uniform Child Custody Jurisdiction and Enforcement Act (UCCJEA) §§201-202. These acts provide that the court of exclusive, continuing jurisdiction may "decline jurisdiction." Declining jurisdiction, thereby creating a potential vacuum, is not authorized under UIFSA. Once a controlling child-support order is established under UIFSA, at all times thereafter there is an existing order in effect to be enforced. Even if the issuing tribunal no longer has continuing, exclusive jurisdiction, its order remains fully enforceable until a tribunal with modification jurisdiction issues a new order in conformance with this subchapter.

UIFSA and UCCJEA seek a world in which there is but one order at a time for child support and custody and visitation. Both have similar restrictions on the ability of a tribunal to modify the existing order. The major difference be-

tween the two acts is that the basic jurisdictional nexus of each is founded on different considerations. UIFSA has its focus on the personal jurisdiction necessary to bind the obligor to payment of a child-support order. UCCJEA places its focus on the factual circumstances of the child, primarily the "home state" of the child; personal jurisdiction to bind a party to the custody decree is not required. An example of the disparate consequences of this difference is the fact that a return to the decree state does not reestablish continuing, exclusive jurisdiction under the UCCJEA. *See* UCCJEA §202. Under similar facts UIFSA grants the issuing tribunal continuing, exclusive jurisdiction to modify its child-support order if, at the time the proceeding is filed, the issuing tribunal "is the residence" of one of the individual parties or the child. *See* §159.205.

Related to Convention: art. 18. Limit on proceedings.

FAM §159.612. RECOGNITION OF ORDER MODIFIED IN ANOTHER STATE

If a child support order issued by a tribunal of this state is modified by a tribunal of another state that assumed jurisdiction under the Uniform Interstate Family Support Act, a tribunal of this state:

(1) may enforce the order that was modified only as to arrears and interest accruing before the modification;

(2) may provide appropriate relief for violations of the order that occurred before the effective date of the modification; and

(3) shall recognize the modifying order of the other state, on registration, for the purpose of enforcement.

History of Fam. Code §159.612: Acts 1995, 74th Leg., ch. 20, §1, eff. Apr. 20, 1995. Amended by Acts 2003, 78th Leg., ch. 1247, §39, eff. Sept. 1, 2003; Acts 2015, 84th Leg., ch. 368, §51, eff. July 1, 2015. Source: Former Fam. Code §21.46.

NCCUSL Comment*

A key aspect of UIFSA is the deference to the controlling child-support order of a sister state demanded from a tribunal of the forum state. This applies not just to the original order, but also to a modified child-support order issued by a second state under the standards established by §§159.611 and 159.613. For the act to function properly, the original issuing tribunal must recognize and accept the modified order as controlling, and must regard its prior order as prospectively inoperative. Because the UIFSA system is based on an interlocking series of state laws, it is fundamental that a modifying tribunal of one state lacks the authority to direct the original issuing tribunal to release its continuing, exclusive jurisdiction. That result is accomplished through the enactment of UIFSA by all states, which empowers a modifying tribunal to assume continuing, exclusive jurisdiction from the original issuing tribunal and requires an issuing tribunal to recognize such an assumption of jurisdiction. This explains why the U.S. Congress took the extraordinary measure in PRWORA of mandating universal passage of UIFSA (1996), as amended. *See* Prefatory Note.

The original issuing tribunal retains authority post-modification to take remedial enforcement action directly connected to its now-modified order.

FAM §159.613. JURISDICTION TO MODIFY CHILD SUPPORT ORDER OF ANOTHER STATE WHEN INDIVIDUAL PARTIES RESIDE IN THIS STATE

(a) If all of the parties who are individuals reside in this state and the child does not reside in the issuing state, a tribunal of this state has jurisdiction to enforce and to modify the issuing state's child support order in a proceeding to register that order.

(b) A tribunal of this state exercising jurisdiction under this section shall apply the provisions of Subchapters B and C, this subchapter, and the procedural and substantive law of this state to the proceeding for enforcement or modification. Subchapters D, E, F, H, and I do not apply.

History of Fam. Code §159.613: Acts 1997, 75th Leg., ch. 607, §18, eff. Sept. 1, 1997. Amended by Acts 2015, 84th Leg., ch. 368, §52, eff. July 1, 2015.

NCCUSL Comment*

It is not unusual for the parties and the child subject to a child-support order to no longer reside in the issuing state, and for the individual parties to have moved to the same new state. The result is that the child-support order remains enforceable, but the issuing tribunal no longer has continuing, exclusive jurisdiction to modify its order. A tribunal of the state of mutual residence of the individual parties has jurisdiction to modify the child-support order and assume continuing, exclusive jurisdiction. Although the individual parties must reside in the forum state, there is no requirement that the child must also reside in the forum state (although the child must have moved from the issuing state).

Finally, because modification of the child-support order when all parties reside in the forum is essentially an intrastate matter, subsection (b) withdraws authority to apply most of the substantive and procedural provisions of UIFSA, i.e., those found in the act other than in Subchapters B, C, and G. Note the duration of the support obligation is a nonmodifiable aspect of the original controlling order, *see* §159.611(c)-(d).

FAM §159.614. NOTICE TO ISSUING TRIBUNAL OF MODIFICATION

Within 30 days after issuance of a modified child support order, the party obtaining the modification shall file a certified copy of the order with the issuing tribunal that had continuing, exclusive jurisdiction over the earlier order and in each tribunal in which the party knows the earlier order has been registered. A party who obtains the order and fails to file a certified copy is subject to appropriate sanctions by a tribunal in which the issue of failure to file arises. The failure to file does not affect the validity or enforceability of the modified order of the new tribunal having continuing, exclusive jurisdiction.

History of Fam. Code §159.614: Acts 1997, 75th Leg., ch. 607, §18, eff. Sept. 1, 1997.

NCCUSL Comment*

For the act to function properly, the prevailing party in a proceeding that modifies a controlling order must inform the original issuing tribunal about its loss of continuing, exclusive jurisdiction over its child-support order. Thereafter, the original tribunal may not modify, or review and adjust, the amount of child support. Notice to the issuing tribunal and other affected tribunals that the continuing, exclusive jurisdiction of the former controlling order has been modified is crucial to avoid the confusion and chaos of the multiple-order system UIFSA replaced.

The new issuing tribunal has authority to impose sanctions on a party who fails to comply with the requirement to give notice of a modification to all interested tribunals. Note, however, that failure to notify a displaced tribunal of the modification of its order does not affect the validity of the modified order.

* See footnote on p. 666.

PART 4. REGISTRATION & MODIFICATION OF FOREIGN CHILD SUPPORT ORDER

FAM §159.615. JURISDICTION TO MODIFY CHILD SUPPORT ORDER OF FOREIGN COUNTRY

(a) Except as otherwise provided by Section 159.711, if a foreign country lacks or refuses to exercise jurisdiction to modify its child support order pursuant to its laws, a tribunal of this state may assume jurisdiction to modify the child support order and bind all individuals subject to the personal jurisdiction of the tribunal regardless of whether the consent to modification of a child support order otherwise required of the individual under Section 159.611 has been given or whether the individual seeking modification is a resident of this state or of the foreign country.

(b) An order issued by a tribunal of this state modifying a foreign child support order under this section is the controlling order.

History of Fam. Code §159.615: Acts 2003, 78th Leg., ch. 1247, §40, eff. Sept. 1, 2003. Amended by Acts 2015, 84th Leg., ch. 368, §§53, 54, eff. July 1, 2015.

NCCUSL Comment*

Subsection (a) provides that a state tribunal may modify a foreign child-support order, other than a Convention order, when the foreign issuing tribunal lacks or refuses to exercise jurisdiction to modify its order. The standard example cited for the necessity of this special rule involved the conundrum posed when an obligor has moved to the responding state from the issuing country and the law of that country requires both parties to be physically present at a hearing before the tribunal in order to sustain a modification of child support. In that circumstance, the foreign issuing tribunal is unable to exercise jurisdiction to modify under its law. Ordinarily, under §159.611 the responding state tribunal is not authorized to issue a new order, in effect modifying the foreign support order, because the child or the obligee continues to reside in the issuing country. To remedy the perceived inequity in such a fact situation, this section provides an exception to the rule of §159.611. If both parties are subject to the personal jurisdiction of a state by the obligee's submission and the obligor's residence, or other grounds under §159.201, the responding state tribunal may modify the foreign child-support order. Modification of a Convention order is governed by §159.711.

The ability of a state tribunal to modify when the foreign country refuses to exercise its jurisdiction should be invoked with circumspection, as there may be a cogent reason for such refusal. Note, §159.317 empowers tribunals to communicate regarding this issue, rather than rely upon representations of one or more of the parties.

Subsection (b) states that if a new order is issued under subsection (a), it becomes the UIFSA controlling order insofar as other states are concerned. Obviously this act cannot dictate the same result to the issuing foreign tribunal, although it seems highly likely that either through child-based jurisdiction or an action filed by the obligee recognition by the foreign tribunal will occur.

Related to Convention: art. 18. Limit on proceedings.

FAM §159.616. PROCEDURE TO REGISTER CHILD SUPPORT ORDER OF FOREIGN COUNTRY FOR MODIFICATION

A party or support enforcement agency seeking to modify, or to modify and enforce, a foreign child support order not under the Convention may register that order in this state under Sections 159.601 through 159.608 if the order has not been registered. A petition for modification may be filed at the same time as a request for registration or at another time. The petition must specify the grounds for modification.

History of Fam. Code §159.616: Acts 2015, 84th Leg., ch. 368, §55, eff. July 1, 2015.

NCCUSL Comment*

The procedure for registration and enforcement set forth in §§159.601 through 159.608 is applicable to a child-support order from a non-Convention country. This section provides coverage for modification in that situation. Presumptively, the general law of the state regarding modification of a child-support order will apply because, by their terms, §§159.609 through 159.614 apply only to modification of a child-support order by a state tribunal. The rationale is that modification is available because the foreign order is not founded on the UIFSA principles of continuing, exclusive jurisdiction and a controlling order. *See* §§159.205-159.207.

Sections 159.617-159.700 reserved for expansion

SUBCHAPTER H. SUPPORT PROCEEDING UNDER CONVENTION

NCCUSL Introductory Comment

This subchapter contains provisions adapted from the Convention that could not be readily integrated into the existing body of Subchapters B through G. For the most part, extending the coverage of UIFSA (2008) to foreign countries was a satisfactory solution to merge the appropriate Convention terms into this act. In understanding this process, it must be clearly stated that the terms of the Convention are not substantive law.

The Convention is a multilateral treaty which binds the United States and the other Convention countries to assure compliance. As such, it will be the law of the land; but the treaty is not self-executing. *See, **Medellin v. Texas***, 552 U.S. 491, 128 S.Ct. 1346, 170 L.Ed.2d 190 (2008). Thus, the ultimate enforcement of the treaty in the United States is dependent on the key implementing federal law and the enactment of both federal and state legislation which provide the mechanism for enforcing the requirements of the Convention. This act is predicated on the principle that the enactment of UIFSA (2008) in all States and federal jurisdictions will effectively implement the Convention through state law by amending Subchapters B through G, plus the addition of this subchapter. The treaty, in essence, establishes the framework for a system of international cooperation by emulating the interstate effect of UIFSA for international cases, especially those affected by the Convention.

In relatively few instances, the provisions of the Convention are sufficiently specific that a choice was made between amending UIFSA accordingly, with a disproportionate effect on all support orders enforced under state law, or accommodating potential conflicts by creating a separate subchapter to apply only to Convention support orders. The choice was to draft this subchapter as state law to minimize disruption to interstate support orders, which constitute the vast majority of orders processed under UIFSA. Note that this act is the substantive and procedural state law for: (1) responding to an application for establishment, recognition and enforcement, or modification of a Convention support order; and, (2) initiating an application to a Convention country for similar action.

The four Hague maintenance conventions that preceded the 2007 Convention, and the three prior versions of UIFSA, have common goals. The distinctions between the jurisdictional rules in the common-law tradition in the United States, and the civil law systems in most of the countries that were parties to the earlier maintenance conventions, were obstacles to participation of the United States in any of the multilateral maintenance treaties. As the world has grown smaller and globalization has become the order of the day, reconciling the differences has become more and more important. Understanding the necessity for accommodation has made the task easier. This is not to say easy, as evidenced by the fact that the formal negotiations leading to the final text of the Convention spanned from May, 2003, to November, 2007.

The United States signed the Convention on November 23, 2007 and the Senate gave its advice and consent to ratification in 2010. Enabling federal legislation was enacted on September 29, 2014 which requires all states to enact

* See footnote on p. 666.

UIFSA (2008) by the end of 2015. At that point the United States will deposit its instrument of ratification and the Convention will enter into force in the United States.

UIFSA (2008) and the 2007 Convention have far more in common than did former uniform acts and maintenance conventions, and, in fact, many provisions of the Convention are modeled on UIFSA principles. The negotiations demonstrated that it is possible to draft an international convention, which incorporates core UIFSA principles into a system for the establishment and enforcement of child support and spousal-support orders across international borders, and creates an efficient, economical, and expeditious procedure to accomplish these goals. Matters in common, however, go far beyond identical goals. The negotiations provided an opportunity for an extended interchange of ideas about how to adapt legal mechanisms to facilitate child support enforcement between otherwise disparate legal systems.

International cross-border enforcement has been far more important in Western Europe, and more recently, throughout the countries of the European Union than has been the case in the United States. On the other hand, experience with establishment and enforcement of interstate child-support orders in the United States has been building since 1950, and accelerated rapidly with enactment of Title IV-D of the Social Security Act in 1975. Clearly, the issues are far easier to deal with nationally because of the common language, currency, and legal system, and, since 1996, with the Title IV-D requirement that all states enact the same version of UIFSA. In fact, since the advent of UIFSA and Title IV-D, millions of interstate cases have been processed through the child support enforcement system and thousands of support orders from other countries have also been registered and enforced in the United States because UIFSA treated such orders as if they had been entered by one of the states. In the future, in Convention countries, this country's orders will be entitled to similar treatment. The entry into force of the Convention is designed to further improve the process and will most certainly lead in a few years to a substantial increase in international cases, both incoming and outgoing.

To create UIFSA (2008), it was necessary to integrate the texts of UIFSA (2001) and the Convention. This did not present a significant drafting challenge for the most part. By far the most common amendment in Subchapters B through G is to substitute "state or foreign country" for the term "state." These simple amendments expanded a majority of this act to cover foreign support orders. In this subchapter statutory directions are given to "a tribunal of this state," and also to a "governmental entity, individual petitioner, support enforcement agency, or a party."

FAM §159.701. DEFINITIONS

In this subchapter:

(1) "Application" means a request under the Convention by an obligee or obligor, or on behalf of a child, made through a central authority for assistance from another central authority.

(2) "Central authority" means the entity designated by the United States or a foreign country described in Section 159.102(5)(D) to perform the functions specified in the Convention.

(3) "Convention support order" means a support order of a tribunal of a foreign country described in Section 159.102(5)(D).

(4) "Direct request" means a petition filed by an individual in a tribunal of this state in a proceeding involving an obligee, obligor, or child residing outside the United States.

(5) "Foreign central authority" means the entity designated by a foreign country described in Section 159.102(5)(D) to perform the functions specified in the Convention.

(6) "Foreign support agreement":

(A) means an agreement for support in a record that:

(i) is enforceable as a support order in the country of origin;

(ii) has been:

(a) formally drawn up or registered as an authentic instrument by a foreign tribunal; or

(b) authenticated by, or concluded, registered, or filed with a foreign tribunal; and

(iii) may be reviewed and modified by a foreign tribunal; and

(B) includes a maintenance arrangement or authentic instrument under the Convention.

(7) "United States central authority" means the secretary of the United States Department of Health and Human Services.

History of Fam. Code §159.701: Acts 1995, 74th Leg., ch. 20, §1, eff. Apr. 20, 1995. Amended by Acts 2003, 78th Leg., ch. 1247, §41, eff. Sept. 1, 2003; Acts 2015, 84th Leg., ch. 368, §§56, 57, eff. July 1, 2015. Source: Former Fam. Code §21.47.

NCCUSL Comment*

A readily apparent difference between UIFSA (2008) and the Convention is the perceived need for definitions in the former, and the very limited number of definitions in the latter. This act contains twenty-nine definitions in §159.102, and an additional seven for this subchapter. In contrast, the Convention contains only seven official definitions. Some of these are synonyms for definitions in UIFSA, i.e., "creditor and debtor" for "obligor and obligee," and "agreement in writing" for "record."

Subsection (1), "application" refers to the process for an individual obligor or obligee to request assistance from a central authority under the Convention.

Subsections (2) and (5) identify the governmental entities, i.e., central authority, in each contracting country or political subdivisions thereof, that will function as the operating agencies to facilitate contacts between Convention countries. The Convention is a treaty between the countries in which it is in force thus creating mutual obligations. The duties assigned in the Convention to the central authority of each country will be performed according to the choice of each country. It is crucial to recognize that in the United States it will be the Title IV-D agency of each state that will be designated by the U.S. central authority to perform most of the functions specified in the Convention. It appears likely that in many foreign countries the central authority will serve in the role of a clearinghouse, rather than as the operative enforcement entity, while some countries may assign all central authority functions to one agency.

Subsection (3), "Convention support order" narrows the term "foreign support order," as employed in Subchapters B through G. The provisions in those subchapters also apply to Convention support orders, but when this act is not congruent with the Convention, support orders under the Convention are subject to this subchapter. This subchapter has no application to a support order from a non-Convention foreign country, as defined in §159.102(5)(A) and (B) or a support order entitled to comity, §159.102(5)(C), except to the extent that a Convention country may request enforcement of a non-Convention support order that has been recognized in the United States under some other procedure, *see* §159.704.

Subsection (4) integrates the "direct request" authorized by the Convention with the provisions for filing a petition in Subchapters B through G.

The definition in the Convention for "maintenance arrangement" has been rephrased in Subsection (6), and must be read together with §159.710 to understand the process authorized in the Convention.

* See footnote on p. 666.

Convention source: art. 3. Definitions; art. 30. Maintenance arrangements.

Related to Convention: art. 4. Designation of Central Authorities; art. 37. Direct requests to competent authorities.

FAM §159.702. APPLICABILITY

This subchapter applies only to a support proceeding under the Convention. In such a proceeding, if a provision of this subchapter is inconsistent with Subchapters B through G, this subchapter controls.

History of Fam. Code §159.702: Acts 2015, 84th Leg., ch. 368, §58, eff. July 1, 2015.

NCCUSL Comment*

The first sentence definitively states that this subchapter applies only to a proceeding involving a Convention country, as defined in §159.102(5)(D). This subchapter does not generally apply to a support order from a non-Convention foreign country as defined in §159.102(5)(A) and (B) or to a support order entitled to comity. The second sentence resolves a situation in which there is a conflict between a section in this subchapter and a provision in Subchapters B through G, in which case this subchapter controls.

Related to Convention: art. 1. Object; art. 2. Scope; art. 4. Designation of Central Authorities.

FAM §159.703. RELATIONSHIP OF OFFICE OF ATTORNEY GENERAL TO UNITED STATES CENTRAL AUTHORITY

The office of the attorney general of this state is recognized as the agency designated by the United States central authority to perform specific functions under the Convention.

History of Fam. Code §159.703: Acts 2015, 84th Leg., ch. 368, §58, eff. July 1, 2015.

NCCUSL Comment*

The Secretary of Health and Human Services has designated the state Title IV-D child support agencies as the governmental entities that will carry out many of the central authority's functions under the Convention. Each state determines which public office or administrative agency will perform the Title IV-D services for child support enforcement. Because the federal government provides a significant subsidy for this effort, the actions of the agency must comply with federal statutes and regulations and the state legislature must enact certain mandatory laws. The relationship is symbiotic in that states choose to participate in the Title IV-D program, and do so by following their own state procedures and legislative enactments that recognize and authorize the state officer or agency to function under these conditions.

Related to Convention: ch. II. Administrative co-operation, arts. 4-8; ch. III. Applications through central authorities, arts. 9-17.

FAM §159.704. INITIATION BY OFFICE OF ATTORNEY GENERAL OF SUPPORT PROCEEDING UNDER CONVENTION

(a) In a support proceeding under this subchapter, the office of the attorney general of this state shall:

(1) transmit and receive applications; and

(2) initiate or facilitate the institution of a proceeding regarding an application in a tribunal of this state.

(b) The following support proceedings are available to an obligee under the Convention:

(1) recognition or recognition and enforcement of a foreign support order;

(2) enforcement of a support order issued or recognized in this state;

(3) establishment of a support order if there is no existing order, including, if necessary, determination of parentage of a child;

(4) establishment of a support order if recognition of a foreign support order is refused under Section 159.708(b)(2), (4), or (9);

(5) modification of a support order of a tribunal of this state; and

(6) modification of a support order of a tribunal of another state or a foreign country.

(c) The following support proceedings are available under the Convention to an obligor against which there is an existing support order:

(1) recognition of an order suspending or limiting enforcement of an existing support order of a tribunal of this state;

(2) modification of a support order of a tribunal of this state; and

(3) modification of a support order of a tribunal of another state or a foreign country.

(d) A tribunal of this state may not require security, bond, or deposit, however described, to guarantee the payment of costs and expenses in proceedings under the Convention.

History of Fam. Code §159.704: Acts 2015, 84th Leg., ch. 368, §58, eff. July 1, 2015.

NCCUSL Comment*

This section is designed to enable lawyers and non-lawyers to better understand proceedings under the Convention, which itself is written in terminology unfamiliar to legal proceedings in the United States.

Subsection (a) lists the rights and duties of a support enforcement agency.

Subsection (b) lists what rights and duties are available to an obligee, whether the proceeding is inbound from a Convention country or outbound to a Convention country.

In contrast to the general rule in UIFSA, which attempts to maintain something of parity between the obligor and obligee, subsection (c) limits the rights and duties available to an obligor under the Convention. This reflects the equal treatment ideal espoused by UIFSA in Subchapters B through G, and the pro-obligee philosophy of the Convention. In actual practice, the results may not be that different. Recall that until replaced by UIFSA, an informal subtitle given to URESA by its leading proponents was "The Runaway Pappy Act."

Subsection (d) tracks Convention art. 14 (5).

Convention source: art. 6. Specific functions of Central Authorities; art. 10. Available applications; art. 14. Effective access to procedures.

Related to Convention: ch. II. Administrative co-operation, arts. 4-7; ch. III. Applications through central authorities, arts. 9-17.

* See footnote on p. 666.

FAM §159.705. DIRECT REQUEST

(a) A petitioner may file a direct request seeking establishment or modification of a support order or determination of parentage of a child. In the proceeding, the law of this state applies.

(b) A petitioner may file a direct request seeking recognition and enforcement of a support order or support agreement. In the proceeding, Sections 159.706 through 159.713 apply.

(c) In a direct request for recognition and enforcement of a Convention support order or foreign support agreement:

(1) a security, bond, or deposit is not required to guarantee the payment of costs and expenses; and

(2) an obligee or obligor that in the issuing country has benefited from free legal assistance is entitled to benefit, at least to the same extent, from any free legal assistance provided for by the law of this state under the same circumstances.

(d) A petitioner filing a direct request is not entitled to assistance from the office of the attorney general.

(e) This subchapter does not prevent the application of laws of this state that provide simplified, more expeditious rules regarding a direct request for recognition and enforcement of a foreign support order or foreign support agreement.

History of Fam. Code §159.705: Acts 2015, 84th Leg., ch. 368, §58, eff. July 1, 2015.

NCCUSL Comment*

Given the long history of open courts in the United States, this section may seem axiomatic, redundant, or unnecessary. In fact, because this principle has not always been universal, it is important to recognize that the Convention confirms that an individual residing in a Convention country may file a petition directly in a tribunal of another Convention country without requesting the assistance of a central authority or a support enforcement agency. Given the variety of legal systems that may be involved under the Convention, this freedom of choice is explicitly protected. A person residing in a Convention county, whether a citizen or a noncitizen of the United States, may apply to a tribunal in the United States for establishment, recognition, and enforcement of a child-support order for enforcement of a spousal support order, for recognition and enforcement of a foreign support agreement, and in some situations, for modification of an existing support order. Of course, the freedom of an individual to petition for relief in a tribunal says nothing about the nature of legal representation, if any, implicit in the right of access to a tribunal, is that representation may be pro se or by private counsel. *See* §159.309.

Subsection (a) provides that an individual party may file a proceeding directly in a tribunal, thus submitting to the jurisdiction of the tribunal and to state law. The object of the proceeding may be establishment of a support order, determination of parentage of a child, or modification of an existing support order.

Subsection (b) recognizes that an individual party may file a proceeding in a tribunal requesting recognition and enforcement of a Convention support order, or a foreign support agreement as defined in §159.710. The party thereby chooses not to seek the services of a central authority or support enforcement agency. Nonetheless, the individual will be affected indirectly by the terms of the Convention because the proceeding is subject to §§159.706 through 159.713, which are drawn from the Convention. This effect applies to an individual residing in a Convention country and to an individual residing elsewhere who is seeking to enforce a Convention support order.

Subsection (c) contains two provisions drawn from the Convention specifically applicable to a petition for recognition and enforcement of a Convention support order. First, a guarantee of payment of costs may not be required. Second, if the individual has benefited from free legal assistance in a Convention country, that individual is entitled to free legal assistance if it is available in similar circumstances under the law of the responding state.

Under subsection (d) an individual party who files a direct request regarding a Convention support order in a tribunal is not entitled to assistance from the governmental entity, i.e. the support enforcement agency.

Subsection (e) echoes Article 52 of the Convention. An individual party who files a petition in a tribunal may take advantage of any "simplified, more expeditious rules" which may be available in the requested state, so long as they are "compatible with the protection offered to the parties under articles 23 and 24" of the Convention.

Convention source: art. 14. Effective access to procedures; art. 17. Applications not qualifying under Article 15 or Article 16; art. 37. Direct requests to competent authorities; art. 52, Most effective rule.

Related to Convention: ch. II. Administrative co-operation, arts. 4-8; ch. III. Applications through central authorities, arts. 9-17; art. 20. Bases for recognition and enforcement; art. 25. Documents; art. 27. Findings of fact; art. 28. No review of the merits; art. 37. Direct requests to competent authorities; art. 56. Transitional provisions.

FAM §159.706. REGISTRATION OF CONVENTION SUPPORT ORDER

(a) Except as otherwise provided in this subchapter, a party who is an individual or a support enforcement agency seeking recognition of a Convention support order shall register the order in this state as provided in Subchapter G.

(b) Notwithstanding Sections 159.311 and 159.602(a), a request for registration of a Convention support order must be accompanied by:

(1) the complete text of the support order or an abstract or extract of the support order drawn up by the issuing foreign tribunal, which may be in the form recommended by the Hague Conference on Private International Law;

(2) a record stating that the support order is enforceable in the issuing country;

(3) if the respondent did not appear and was not represented in the proceedings in the issuing country, a record attesting, as appropriate, either that the respondent had proper notice of the proceedings and an opportunity to be heard or that the respondent had proper notice of the support order and an opportunity to be heard in a challenge or appeal on fact or law before a tribunal;

(4) a record showing the amount of arrears, if any, and the date the amount was calculated;

* See footnote on p. 666.

(5) a record showing a requirement for automatic adjustment of the amount of support, if any, and the information necessary to make the appropriate calculations; and

(6) if necessary, a record showing the extent to which the applicant received free legal assistance in the issuing country.

(c) A request for registration of a Convention support order may seek recognition and partial enforcement of the order.

(d) A tribunal of this state may vacate the registration of a Convention support order without the filing of a contest under Section 159.707 only if, acting on its own motion, the tribunal finds that recognition and enforcement of the order would be manifestly incompatible with public policy.

(e) The tribunal shall promptly notify the parties of the registration or the order vacating the registration of a Convention support order.

History of Fam. Code §159.706: Acts 2015, 84th Leg., ch. 368, §58, eff. July 1, 2015.

NCCUSL Comment*

Subsection (a) integrates the Convention support order into the registration for enforcement procedure set forth in §§159.601 through 159.608. A state support enforcement agency and a tribunal will use basically the same procedures for a Convention order under this subchapter as would be used in a non-Convention proceeding.

From inception, UIFSA contained detailed provisions for substantive procedures for interstate child-support orders. To facilitate expedited processing, detailed statutory instructions have encouraged uniformity of legal documents. The Convention follows this precedent. The list of documents to be provided, however, is somewhat different than the documents described in §§159.311 and 159.602. In order to ensure that a document satisfying the requirements of the Convention will be accepted by a support enforcement agency or tribunal, subsection (a) identifies the documents required to accompany an application under the Convention.

Several of the required documents may be unfamiliar in the United States, e.g., the authority to provide an abstract or an extract of an order rather than the complete text of an order under subsection (b)(1); the requirement for a statement of enforceability of the order under subsection (b)(2); proof that the respondent had proper notice of the proceedings and an opportunity to be heard if the respondent did not appear and was not represented under subsection (b)(3); and proof that the applicant received free legal assistance in the issuing country under subsection (b)(6).

Subsection (c) provides that a petitioner may request only partial enforcement of a support order, *see* §159.709 *infra*, which speaks to partial enforcement by a tribunal.

Subsections (d) and (e) authorize action by a tribunal available under the Convention that may not be available under other state law. Subsection (d) permits the tribunal to vacate registration, acting on its own motion, under certain exceptional circumstances, and subsection (e) requires that notice be promptly provided of any such order vacating registration. Such ex officio review, if used to refuse recognition of an order, is in tension with the core UIFSA policy of requiring recognition. In any event, the subsections are not a vehicle for a review of the merits of the decision. An example would be useful here, but there is none in the Explanatory Report to the Convention, just the negative reference that a country could not use this to enforce a policy against ordering support for a child born out of wedlock. http://www.hcch.net/upload/expl38.pdf. Perhaps an example could be that the court might reject an application to establish support from a biological parent whose rights had been terminated and the child was subsequently adopted.

Convention source: art. 25. Documents; art. 21. Severability and partial recognition and enforcement; art. 22. Grounds for refusing recognition and enforcement; art. 23. Procedure on an application for recognition and enforcement; art. 25. Documents.

Related to Convention: art. 11. Application contents; art. 20. Bases for recognition and enforcement.

FAM §159.707. CONTEST OF REGISTERED CONVENTION SUPPORT ORDER

(a) Except as otherwise provided in this subchapter, Sections 159.605 through 159.608 apply to a contest of a registered Convention support order.

(b) A party contesting a registered Convention support order shall file a contest not later than 30 days after notice of the registration. If the contesting party does not reside in the United States, the contest must be filed not later than 60 days after notice of the registration.

(c) If the nonregistering party fails to contest the registered Convention support order by the time specified in Subsection (b), the order is enforceable.

(d) A contest of a registered Convention support order may be based only on grounds set forth in Section 159.708. The contesting party bears the burden of proof.

(e) In a contest of a registered Convention support order, a tribunal of this state:

(1) is bound by the findings of fact on which the foreign tribunal based its jurisdiction; and

(2) may not review the merits of the order.

(f) A tribunal of this state deciding a contest of a registered Convention support order shall promptly notify the parties of its decision.

(g) A challenge or appeal, if any, does not stay the enforcement of a Convention support order unless there are exceptional circumstances.

History of Fam. Code §159.707: Acts 2015, 84th Leg., ch. 368, §58, eff. July 1, 2015.

NCCUSL Comment*

Subsection (a) states the general rule that a contest of a registration is generally governed by §§159.605 through 159.608, *supra*. Subsection (b), however, establishes separate, longer time frames to contest the registration of a Convention support order than for filing a contest as established in §159.605. If notice of contest is to be given in the United States, the time difference is relatively modest, i.e., 30 days instead of 20. A more significant difference is created for out-of-country notice, i.e., 60 days instead of 20. Arguably this takes into account that providing notice to a party in a foreign country may take longer than ordinarily expected. In any event, the longer time frames are specifically required in connection with a Convention order. Note that while the principle may always be true that notice to a party situated in a foreign country may take longer, the additional times for notice apply only to an order subject to the Convention.

Subsections (c)-(g) transform Convention language into UIFSA terminology. Subsection (g), which prohibits a stay in enforcement pending a challenge

* See footnote on p. 666.

or appeal except in exceptional circumstances, is another substantive provision required by the Convention. It does not apply in non-Convention cases, in which domestic law determines whether a stay of enforcement should be granted pending an appeal or other challenge.

Convention source: art. 23. Procedure on an application for recognition and enforcement; art. 27. Findings of fact; art. 28. No review of the merits.

Related to Convention: art. 20. Bases for recognition and enforcement; art. 21. Severability and partial recognition and enforcement; art. 23. Procedure on an application for recognition and enforcement; art. 27. Findings of fact; art. 28. No review of the merits.

FAM §159.708. RECOGNITION & ENFORCEMENT OF REGISTERED CONVENTION SUPPORT ORDER

(a) Except as otherwise provided in Subsection (b), a tribunal of this state shall recognize and enforce a registered Convention support order.

(b) The following grounds are the only grounds on which a tribunal of this state may refuse recognition and enforcement of a registered Convention support order:

(1) recognition and enforcement of the order is manifestly incompatible with public policy, including the failure of the issuing tribunal to observe minimum standards of due process, which include notice and an opportunity to be heard;

(2) the issuing tribunal lacked personal jurisdiction consistent with Section 159.201;

(3) the order is not enforceable in the issuing country;

(4) the order was obtained by fraud in connection with a matter of procedure;

(5) a record transmitted in accordance with Section 159.706 lacks authenticity or integrity;

(6) a proceeding between the same parties and having the same purpose is pending before a tribunal of this state and that proceeding was the first to be filed;

(7) the order is incompatible with a more recent support order involving the same parties and having the same purpose if the more recent support order is entitled to recognition and enforcement under this chapter in this state;

(8) payment, to the extent alleged arrears have been paid in whole or in part;

(9) in a case in which the respondent neither appeared nor was represented in the proceeding in the issuing foreign country:

(A) if the law of that country provides for prior notice of proceedings, the respondent did not have proper notice of the proceedings and an opportunity to be heard; or

(B) if the law of that country does not provide for prior notice of the proceedings, the respondent did not have proper notice of the order and an opportunity to be heard in a challenge or appeal on fact or law before a tribunal; or

(10) the order was made in violation of Section 159.711.

(c) If a tribunal of this state does not recognize a Convention support order under Subsection (b)(2), (4), or (9):

(1) the tribunal may not dismiss the proceeding without allowing a reasonable time for a party to request the establishment of a new Convention support order; and

(2) the office of the attorney general shall take all appropriate measures to request a child support order for the obligee if the application for recognition and enforcement was received under Section 159.704.

History of Fam. Code §159.708: Acts 2015, 84th Leg., ch. 368, §58, eff. July 1, 2015.

NCCUSL Comment*

Enforceability; the general rule, with exceptions. Subsection (a) states the general proposition that if a child-support order is issued by a tribunal in a Convention country, except as otherwise provided in subsection (b), the order shall be recognized and enforced. In domestic cases UIFSA requires recognition of child-support order of a sister state, 28 U.S.C.A. §1738B, Full Faith and Credit for Child Support Orders Act (FFCCSOA). Receipt of a child-support order from a sister state is routinely processed and enforced. Critical examination of the sister state order for defects is not called for; it is the responsibility of the respondent to assert any defenses available. Moreover, experience has shown that child-support orders are generally valid, for relatively modest amounts, and seldom subject to claims of fraud. The most common defect is one of mistake, rather than deliberate misconduct.

Subsection (b) combines provisions from four separate articles in the Convention. These articles provide an extensive number of specific reasons for a tribunal or support enforcement agency of one Convention country to refuse to recognize a child-support order from another Convention country. For this act to be consistent with the Convention, it is necessary to identify the potential defects of a support order from a Convention country in which a defendant might raise a challenge based on lack of jurisdiction, due process, or enforceability of an order for arrearages. The majority of these defects arguably are self-explanatory, and almost all are subject to factual dispute to be resolved by the tribunal, to wit: (b)(1) "manifestly incompatible" with public policy, including violation of minimum standards of due process; (b)(2) issued without personal jurisdiction over the individual party (discussed at length below); (b)(3) unenforceable in the issuing country; (b)(4) obtained by fraud in connection with a matter of procedure; (b)(5) the record lacks authenticity or integrity, e.g., forged; (b)(6) a prior proceeding is pending; (b)(7) a more recent support order is controlling; (b)(8) full or partial payment; (b)(9)(A), (B), no appearance, notice, or opportunity to be heard (discussed below); and, (b)(10) exceeds limitations and restraints on modification. As with domestic cases, the norm will be to recognize and enforce a foreign order absent a challenge by the respondent. Three provisions most likely to trigger a tribunal to refuse to recognize and enforce a foreign support order require more attention, i.e., subsections (b)(2), (4) and (9)(A), (B).

Of particular note, subsection (c) applies to a refusal to recognize and enforce a Convention order under any of these grounds. From the perspective of the United States, subsection (b)(2) is likely to be the primary reason for a tri-

* See footnote on p. 666.

bunal to refuse to recognize and enforce a registered Convention support order. Key to its participation in the negotiations leading to the Convention, the United States insisted that a support order may be refused recognition by a tribunal if the issuing foreign tribunal lacked personal jurisdiction over the respondent. The facts underlying the Convention support order must be measured by a tribunal as consistent with the long-arm jurisdictional provisions of UIFSA. *See* §§159.201-159.202. A potential problem occurs only if a Convention support order cannot be enforced by a tribunal because there was no appropriate nexus between the foreign country and the respondent.

Subsection (c) provides that any of the reasons enumerated for not recognizing and enforcing a registered Convention support order, i.e., (b)(2), (4) and (9), will trigger the obligation of the tribunal not to dismiss the proceeding before allowing a reasonable time for a party to seek the establishment of a new child-support order. Moreover, if the Title IV-D support enforcement agency is involved, it must "take all appropriate measures to request a child-support order;" i.e., file a petition seeking to establish an initial child-support order by the tribunal. In that case, the tribunal shall treat the request for recognition and enforcement as a petition for establishment of a new order.

Two systems; direct and indirect jurisdiction. In drafting the Convention, the subject of the requisite jurisdiction to issue a support order generated considerable discussion. The choice divided itself into two distinct categories; rules of direct and indirect jurisdiction. Direct jurisdiction provides explicit bases on which a tribunal is vested with the power to assert its authority and enter a support order. *See* §159.201.

The UIFSA long-arm provisions are paradigm rules of direct jurisdiction. Section 159.201 identifies the bases on which a tribunal may assert personal jurisdiction over a nonresident individual, obligor or obligee, without regard to the current residence of the individual or child. As discussed in the comment to §159.201, *supra*, these long-arm jurisdictional rules for child support and spousal support orders were fashioned case-by-case by the Supreme Court, *see Estin v. Estin*, 334 U.S. 541, 68 S. Ct. 1213, 92 L.Ed. 1561 (1948); *Vanderbilt v. Vanderbilt*, 354 U.S. 416, 77 S. Ct. 1360, 1 L.Ed.2d 1456 (1957) (spousal support); *Kulko v. Superior Court*, 436 U.S. 84, 98 S.Ct. 1690, 56 L.Ed.2d 132 (1978) (child support).

An initial difficulty arose because some authorities from foreign countries expressed concern about the UIFSA long-arm statute. This was especially true regarding §159.201(a)(1), i.e., service of legal process that creates personal jurisdiction, sometimes called "tag or ambush jurisdiction." Some experts in civil law countries regard the claim that jurisdiction can be acquired merely by serving documents on an individual passing through, with no fundamental ties to the jurisdiction, as "exorbitant," and fundamentally unfair. Another provision eliciting criticism was §159.201(a)(6), which literally reads that an allegation of engaging in sexual intercourse in the state that "may have" resulted in conception will suffice to support a basis for issuing a child support-order.

Similarly, rules of jurisdiction recognized by civil law countries are contrary to the principles that apply to proceedings in the United States. The fact that residence of a child or an obligee in a forum is sufficient basis in most foreign countries to support a child-support order, even though the obligor has no personal nexus with the forum, is generally viewed as wholly inconsistent with notions of due process in the United States. Assuming the obligor has never been physically present in the forum and has not participated in any of the acts described in §159.201, an assertion of jurisdiction to establish a support order based solely on the residence of the obligee or child in that forum is widely regarded in the United States as unconstitutional.

The Convention adopts a rule of indirect jurisdiction which requires a tribunal to register and enforce the order of another tribunal if certain basic jurisdictional requirements have been satisfied. The Convention does not actually prescribe the bases on which the tribunal may assert jurisdiction, as UIFSA does in §159.201. Most commonly, in countries other than the United States if a child is a "habitual resident" of a country, a support order of a tribunal of that country will be recognized in another country. As a practical matter, although "habitual residence" of the obligee provides no basis for assertion of personal jurisdiction over the obligor in the United States, the home tribunal is almost always the preferred forum if the obligee has any basis under §159.201 to obtain long-arm jurisdiction over a non-resident obligor. That is, the actual custodian of the child is almost always the person who seeks to establish and enforce child support and, if possible, chooses to bring a proceeding in the state of residence of the obligee and the child. A tribunal that recognizes "habitual residence" as a basis for indirect jurisdiction would, accordingly, register and enforce an order from a tribunal in the "habitual residence" of the obligee or child without concern about whether the obligor has a nexus with that tribunal. Thus, most foreign concerns about the tenuous reaches of long-arm jurisdiction in the United States are obviated in practice.

The Convention eschews rules of direct jurisdiction, choosing instead to rely on half-a-dozen indirect rules of jurisdiction, "habitual residence" of any of the parties (respondent, creditor or child) being the most common. The focus of the Convention is to identify the bases on which a tribunal of one Convention country will be required to recognize the assertion of jurisdiction by a tribunal of another Convention country. When the Convention is in force in both countries, a support order issued by a tribunal of Country A will be enforced by a tribunal of Country B, provided that the order is enforceable in Country A, plus the host of other possible considerations discussed above. There are a limited number of exceptions, or "reservations," to such rules permitted under the Convention, which give rise to additional procedures noted below. Once recognition is accorded to a support order, the normal procedures available to enforce the order come into play. The routes to arrive at enforcement by way of direct or indirect jurisdiction are different, but the destination is the same.

Virtually all foreign countries recognize and enforce a child-support order based on the residence of the obligee or the child. The U.S. requirement of personal jurisdiction over the obligor is often regarded abroad as idiosyncratic. Nonetheless, the new Convention requires recognition of U.S. orders based on long-arm jurisdiction asserted over the obligor, a.k.a. "debtor" if the forum state is also the state of residence of the obligee, a.k.a. "creditor." From the perspective of a foreign tribunal, such an order should be considered valid, if only for creditor- or child-based jurisdictional reasons. The fact that the state tribunal requires a personal nexus between the parties and the tribunal is irrelevant to the foreign tribunal.

These distinct views of appropriate jurisdiction presented a genuine issue for resolution. The United States delegation took the position that, as a matter of constitutional law, its tribunals could not recognize and enforce creditor- or child-based support orders under certain factual circumstances accepted in other countries as providing appropriate jurisdiction. The conclusion of the delegation was that this approach conflicts with the *Kulko* decision, *supra*. The potential lack of nexus with the obligor, if jurisdiction was based solely on the "habitual residence" of the obligee, would present an impenetrable barrier to participation in the Convention by the United States.

Fairly early on in the Convention negotiations, a consensus developed that these different systems of jurisdiction could be accommodated. On the U.S. side, a challenge to a foreign child-support order will be rejected if the factual circumstances are sufficient to support an assertion of long-arm jurisdiction in the foreign tribunal. Rather obviously, the foreign tribunal need not, and almost certainly will not, consider whether there is a factual basis for establishing personal jurisdiction over the absent obligor based upon "minimum contacts" with the forum. This is not a part of the jurisprudence of the foreign tribunal. If a challenge to a support order is raised by the obligor when the order is sought for enforcement in a United States tribunal, however, that tribunal shall undertake a determination of whether the jurisdictional bases of §159.201 would have been applicable if that issue had been raised in the foreign tribunal. If so, the order is enforceable in this country, notwithstanding that the foreign tribunal based its decision on jurisdiction on the fact that the child or the obligee resided in that forum. *See* Convention art. 20(1)(c)-(d).

Asserting long-arm jurisdiction to establish a support order by a tribunal in a proceeding under UIFSA will be unaffected by the entry into force of the Convention. This will be true irrespective of whether the nonresident respondent resides in another state or in a foreign country, or even resides in a non-Convention foreign nation.

The term "habitually resident" is used in a number of private international law conventions, including the 2007 Maintenance Convention. The term is not defined in any of them. Rather, in common law countries its meaning is determined on a case-by-case basis by the practice and case law of each country. In the United States and elsewhere there is no consistent interpretation of the term by the courts considering it in the context of the 1980 Hague Convention on the Civil Aspects of International Child Abduction. The negotiators of the Convention from the United States made it clear that case law on the meaning of "habitually resident" in the child abduction context should not automatically be applied to child support cases. That is because the effect of the use of "habitual residence" in the 1980 Child Abduction Convention is intended to restrict the ability of a person to obtain a new custody order shortly after arriving in another country. In fact, one of the objects of the 1980 Convention is to limit the ability of a parent unhappy with the custody order of one court to "forum shop" by moving to another country and seeking a new order. In the 2007 Main-

tenance Convention, the object is to make it easier for an obligee to recover child support in an international case, not to restrict the ability of an obligee to apply for that support.

Due process under the Convention. Subsection (b)(9)(A) applies to a failure to give a party prior notice of the proceedings and an opportunity to be heard, which is the classic denial of due process in a proceeding in the United States.

Subsection (b)(9)(B) will be unfamiliar to practitioners in this country and requires some explanation. This provision recognizes the legitimacy of, and provides a method for challenge of, a support order which may be routinely entered in some administrative systems in an ex parte proceeding. The support order is issued without prior notice to the obligor or opportunity to be heard. The due process opportunity is provided after the ex parte decision. This system is currently in use in administrative proceedings in Australia and New Zealand. Because the respondent will not have participated in the original proceeding, the post facto due process allows the obligor an opportunity to challenge the decision on fact or law.

Convention source: art. 20. Bases for recognition and enforcement; art. 21. Severability and partial recognition and enforcement; art. 22. Grounds for refusing recognition and enforcement; art. 23. Procedure on an application for recognition and enforcement; art. 25. Documents.

Related to Convention: art. 11. Application contents.

FAM §159.709. PARTIAL ENFORCEMENT

If a tribunal of this state does not recognize and enforce a Convention support order in its entirety, it shall enforce any severable part of the order. An application or direct request may seek recognition and partial enforcement of a Convention support order.

History of Fam. Code §159.709: Acts 2015, 84th Leg., ch. 368, §58, eff. July 1, 2015.

NCCUSL Comment*

This section transforms Convention language into UIFSA terminology. If a responding tribunal is unable to enforce the entirety of a Convention support order, it shall enforce a severable part of the order. For example, a mother of a child may have another woman as her registered partner in a Convention country. If a support order provides support for both the mother and child support for the child, that part of the order awarding support to the mother from the registered partner may not be enforceable in some states. Nonetheless, a tribunal is obligated to recognize and enforce that part of the order for support of the child. The second sentence authorizes the mother to request enforcement only of the child support portion, *see also* §159.706(c), *supra*.

Convention source: art. 21. Severability and partial recognition and enforcement.

Related to Convention: art. 20. Bases for recognition and enforcement.

FAM §159.710. FOREIGN SUPPORT AGREEMENT

(a) Except as otherwise provided by Subsections (c) and (d), a tribunal of this state shall recognize and enforce a foreign support agreement registered in this state.

(b) An application or direct request for recognition and enforcement of a foreign support agreement must be accompanied by:

(1) the complete text of the foreign support agreement; and

(2) a record stating that the foreign support agreement is enforceable as an order of support in the issuing country.

(c) A tribunal of this state may vacate the registration of a foreign support agreement only if, acting on its own motion, the tribunal finds that recognition and enforcement would be manifestly incompatible with public policy.

(d) In a contest of a foreign support agreement, a tribunal of this state may refuse recognition and enforcement of the agreement if it finds:

(1) recognition and enforcement of the agreement is manifestly incompatible with public policy;

(2) the agreement was obtained by fraud or falsification;

(3) the agreement is incompatible with a support order involving the same parties and having the same purpose in this state, another state, or a foreign country if the support order is entitled to recognition and enforcement under this chapter in this state; or

(4) the record submitted under Subsection (b) lacks authenticity or integrity.

(e) A proceeding for recognition and enforcement of a foreign support agreement must be suspended during the pendency of a challenge to or appeal of the agreement before a tribunal of another state or a foreign country.

History of Fam. Code §159.710: Acts 2015, 84th Leg., ch. 368, §58, eff. July 1, 2015.

NCCUSL Comment*

Section 159.701(6) provides an extensive definition of a "foreign support agreement," which is UIFSA terminology to make more readily understandable for U.S. bench and bar a process that is denominated as a "maintenance arrangement" in the Convention. Subsection (a) requires a state tribunal to recognize and enforce a foreign support agreement if the terms of this section are met. Most crucially, such an agreement must be accompanied by a document stating that the foreign support agreement is as enforceable as a support order would be in the country of origin.

This section basically translates into common parlance the procedure identified in Convention art. 30, which was the result of a very extended discussions about "authentic instruments and private agreements" during the negotiations on the Convention. In many countries, such an agreement is unknown insofar as enforcement by a tribunal is concerned. In the United States, a purely private agreement is treated as a form of contract, rather than as an order of a tribunal. Under the Convention, however, a foreign support agreement meeting the standards established in this section, and as defined in §159.701(6), is entitled to enforcement by the tribunal. Advantages for enforcement of child support binding on the parties in the country of origin stem from the inclusion of a foreign support agreement because there is a growing tendency internationally to promote amicable solutions and avoid contentious procedures. In view of the movement towards alternative methods of dispute resolution in the United States, this mechanism provides for recognition and enforcement of a dispute resolution system in some of the likely Convention countries. The absence of this provision would have been a loss for the Convention, and limited its usefulness for support agreements, particularly in the Scandinavian countries. Although the possibility of a reservation is available, the United States has not indicated that it intends to make such a reservation.

* See footnote on p. 666.

To reiterate, the key to enforcement is that the foreign support agreement must be "enforceable as a decision" in the foreign country of its origin (quoting the Convention). If such an agreement is enforceable only as a contract, it will not fall within the scope of this section. Another key provision is that under subsection (e) the enforcement proceeding will be suspended if the respondent challenges the underlying agreement in a tribunal that has jurisdiction to hear challenges to the agreement.

Convention source: art. 3. Definitions; art. 30. Maintenance arrangements.

FAM §159.711. MODIFICATION OF CONVENTION CHILD SUPPORT ORDER

(a) A tribunal of this state may not modify a Convention child support order if the obligee remains a resident of the foreign country where the support order was issued unless:

(1) the obligee submits to the jurisdiction of a tribunal of this state, either expressly or by defending on the merits of the case without objecting to the jurisdiction at the first available opportunity; or

(2) the foreign tribunal lacks or refuses to exercise jurisdiction to modify its support order or issue a new support order.

(b) If a tribunal of this state does not modify a Convention child support order because the order is not recognized in this state, Section 159.708(c) applies.

History of Fam. Code §159.711: Acts 2015, 84th Leg., ch. 368, §58, eff. July 1, 2015.

NCCUSL Comment*

One goal of the Convention was to limit the number of multiple foreign orders with respect to the same parties to the extent possible. But, given differing laws and jurisdictional bases, consensus on limiting modification was reached only on the fact patterns presented by §159.711(a).

First, this section transforms Convention language into UIFSA terminology. The restriction identified on modification of a child-support order in subsection (a) strikes a familiar note. Similar to §159.611, *supra*, a restriction is placed on modification of a support order if the obligee remains in the issuing Convention country. Subsection (a)(1) provides an exception if, by failure to object, the obligee submits to the jurisdiction of another tribunal. Subsection (a)(2) is similar to §159.615, *supra*. From the perspective of the obligee, the restriction has virtually the same effect as found in §§159.205 and 159.611. That is, in effect the issuing foreign tribunal has a form of continuing, exclusive jurisdiction that it maintains over modification of the order so long as the obligee remains a resident of the country. The difference is that the protection against modification is accorded only to the obligee, and not to the obligor. Thus, under the Convention the obligee may be free to seek a modification in another forum notwithstanding the fact that the obligor remains in the issuing country but the obligee moves to another country, with the implicit requirement that the issuing foreign tribunal must have personal jurisdiction over the obligor to sustain the enforcement of modification by a state tribunal.

Subsection (b) requires a state tribunal to issue a new child-support order if the Convention order was founded on child-based jurisdiction, the foreign tribunal lacked personal jurisdiction over the obligor, and there is a request to establish an order in accordance with §159.708.

Convention source: art. 18. Limit on proceedings; art. 21. Severability and partial recognition and enforcement.

Related to Convention: art. 18. Limit on proceedings; art. 20. Bases for recognition and enforcement.

* See footnote on p. 666.

FAM §159.712. PERSONAL INFORMATION; LIMIT ON USE

Personal information gathered or transmitted under this subchapter may be used only for the purposes for which it was gathered or transmitted.

History of Fam. Code §159.712: Acts 2015, 84th Leg., ch. 368, §58, eff. July 1, 2015.

NCCUSL Comment*

This section is an almost word-for-word tracking of the Convention provision, rephrased in UIFSA terminology. This single sentence is illustrative of the different drafting rules for a uniform act and an international treaty. Although certainly not always adhered to, cardinal rules for drafting a uniform act include writing in the active voice, identifying the intended actor, and specifying the consequences for failure to follow the directive or ignore the proscription. Convention provisions, such as this one, are generally written in passive voice, the actor is not identified, and no penalty is specified for noncompliance. Insofar as the admirable goals of the provision are concerned, ambiguity in the statute, or an exception to the rule, must be resolved case-by-case.

Confidentiality is highly prized in the United States in many circumstances, e.g., the attorney-client privilege is protected to the maximum extent possible. Under other circumstances, the opposite is true, e.g., records of litigation are generally available, and a judicial decision is ordinarily in open court or public record. Neither goal is absolute. Section 159.312, *supra*, adds another exception, i.e., nondisclosure of information is sometimes required to protect the health, safety, or liberty of a party or a child. In a case in which there is a risk of domestic violence or parental kidnapping, nondisclosure may be crucial.

The anticipated breadth of application of this provision is to constrain individuals and entities subject to a Convention support order. Protection of personal information in this computerized world is increasingly important, whatever the medium or means of communication. Both the sender and recipient of personal information transmitted electronically are expected to take appropriate measures vis-à-vis their service providers to meet the requirements of this section. The exact meaning of the statutory phrase "for the purpose for which it was gathered or transmitted" will necessarily remain ambiguous until elaborated by statute, caselaw, or regulation.

Convention source: art. 38. Protection of personal data.

FAM §159.713. RECORD IN ORIGINAL LANGUAGE; ENGLISH TRANSLATION

A record filed with a tribunal of this state under this subchapter must be in the original language and, if not in English, must be accompanied by an English translation.

History of Fam. Code §159.713: Acts 2015, 84th Leg., ch. 368, §58, eff. July 1, 2015.

NCCUSL Comment*

The United States will declare that English is the official language for transmittals to this country. Further, the United States will make a reservation objecting to the use of French, the other official language of the Convention, as a default translation. Of course, the original order may be in French. The cost of translation is borne by the issuing state or Convention country.

Convention source: art. 44. Language requirements; art. 62. Reservations; art. 63. Declarations.

Related to Convention: art. 45. Means and costs of translation.

Sections 159.714-159.800 reserved for expansion

SUBCHAPTER I. INTERSTATE RENDITION

FAM §159.801. GROUNDS FOR RENDITION

(a) For purposes of this subchapter, "governor" includes an individual performing the functions of governor or the executive authority of a state covered by this chapter.

(b) The governor of this state may:

(1) demand that the governor of another state surrender an individual found in the other state who is charged criminally in this state with having failed to provide for the support of an obligee; or

(2) on the demand of the governor of another state, surrender an individual found in this state who is charged criminally in the other state with having failed to provide for the support of an obligee.

(c) A provision for extradition of individuals not inconsistent with this chapter applies to the demand even if the individual whose surrender is demanded was not in the demanding state when the crime was allegedly committed and has not fled from that state.

History of Fam. Code §159.801: Acts 1995, 74th Leg., ch. 20, §1, eff. Apr. 20, 1995. Amended by Acts 2003, 78th Leg., ch. 1247, §42, eff. Sept. 1, 2003; Acts 2015, 84th Leg., ch. 368, §59, eff. July 1, 2015. Source: Former Fam. Code §21.48.

NCCUSL Comment*

This section has not been amended substantively since 1968. Virtually no controversy has been generated regarding this procedure. Arguably application of subsection (c) is problematic in situations in which the obligor neither was present in the demanding state at the time of the commission of the crime nor fled from the demanding state. The possibility that an individual may commit a crime in a state without ever being physically present there has elicited considerable discussion and some case law. *See* L. BRILMAYER, AN INTRODUCTION TO JURISDICTION IN THE AMERICAN FEDERAL SYSTEM, 329-335 (1986) (discussing minimum contacts theory for criminal jurisdiction); Rotenberg, *Extraterritorial Legislative Jurisdiction and the State Criminal Law*, 38 TEX. L. REV. 763, 784-87 (1960) (due process requires that the behavior of the defendant must be predictably subject to state's criminal jurisdiction); *cf. Ex parte Boetscher*, 812 S.W.2d 600 (Tex. Crim. App. 1991) (Equal Protection Clause limits disparate treatment of nonresident defendants); *In re King*, 3 Cal.3d 226, 90 Cal. Rptr. 15, 474 P.2d 983 (1970), cert. denied 403 U.S. 931 (enhanced offense for nonresidents impacts constitutional right to travel).

FAM §159.802. CONDITIONS OF RENDITION

(a) Before making a demand that the governor of another state surrender an individual charged criminally in this state with having failed to provide for the support of an obligee, the governor of this state may require a prosecutor of this state to demonstrate that, not less than 60 days previously, the obligee had initiated proceedings for support under this chapter or that the proceeding would be of no avail.

(b) If, under this chapter or a law substantially similar to this chapter, the governor of another state makes a demand that the governor of this state surrender an individual charged criminally in that state with having failed to provide for the support of a child or other individual to whom a duty of support is owed, the governor may require a prosecutor to investigate the demand and report whether a proceeding for support has been initiated or would be effective. If it appears that a proceeding would be effective but has not been initiated, the governor may delay honoring the demand for a reasonable time to permit the initiation of a proceeding.

(c) If a proceeding for support has been initiated and the individual whose rendition is demanded prevails, the governor may decline to honor the demand. If the petitioner prevails and the individual whose rendition is demanded is subject to a support order, the governor may decline to honor the demand if the individual is complying with the support order.

History of Fam. Code §159.802: Acts 1995, 74th Leg., ch. 20, §1, eff. Apr. 20, 1995. Amended by Acts 2003, 78th Leg., ch. 1247, §43, eff. Sept. 1, 2003; Acts 2015, 84th Leg., ch. 368, §60, eff. July 1, 2015. Source: Former Fam. Code §21.49.

NCCUSL Comment*

This section has not undergone significant change since 1968. Interstate rendition remains the last resort for support enforcement, in part because a governor may exercise considerable discretion in deciding whether to honor a demand for rendition of an obligor.

Sections 159.803-159.900 reserved for expansion

SUBCHAPTER J. MISCELLANEOUS PROVISIONS

FAM §159.901. UNIFORMITY OF APPLICATION & CONSTRUCTION

In applying and construing this uniform act, consideration must be given to the need to promote uniformity of the law with respect to its subject matter among states that enact it.

History of Fam. Code §159.901: Acts 1995, 74th Leg., ch. 20, §1, eff. Apr. 20, 1995. Amended by Acts 2003, 78th Leg., ch. 1247, §44, eff. Sept. 1, 2003; Acts 2015, 84th Leg., ch. 368, §61, eff. July 1, 2015. Source: Former Fam. Code §21.50.

FAM §159.902. REPEALED

Repealed by Acts 2003, 78th Leg., ch. 1247, §46, eff. Sept. 1, 2003.

CHAPTER 160. UNIFORM PARENTAGE ACT

* See footnote on p. 666.

NCCUSL Prefatory Comment*

The National Conference of Commissioners on Uniform State Laws has addressed the subject of parentage throughout the 20th Century. In 1922, the Conference promulgated the "Uniform Illegitimacy Act," followed by the "Uniform Blood Tests To Determine Paternity Act" in 1952, the "Uniform Paternity Act" in 1960, and certain provisions in the "Uniform Probate Code" in 1969. The "Uniform Illegitimacy Act" was withdrawn by the Conference and none of the other Acts were widely adopted. As of June 1973, the Blood Tests to Determine Paternity Act had been enacted in nine states, the "Uniform Paternity Act" in four, and the "Uniform Probate Code" in five.

The most important uniform act addressing the status of the nonmarital child was the Uniform Parentage Act approved in 1973 [hereinafter referred to as UPA (1973)]. As of December, 2000, UPA (1973) was in effect in 19 states stretching from Delaware to California; in addition, many other states have enacted significant portions of it. Among the many notable features of this landmark Act was the declaration that all children should be treated equally without regard to marital status of the parents. In addition, the Act established a set of rules for presumptions of parentage, shunned the term "illegitimate," and chose instead to employ the term "child with no presumed father."

UPA (1973) had its genesis in a law review article, Harry D. Krause, *A Proposed Uniform Act on Legitimacy*, 44 Tex. L.Rev. 829 (1966); *see also* Krause, *Equal Protection for the Illegitimate*, 65 Mich. L.Rev. 477 (1967). Professor Krause followed with a pathfinding book, Illegitimacy: Law and Social Policy (1971), and then went on to serve as the reporter for UPA (1973). When work on the Act began, the notion of substantive legal equality of children regardless of the marital status of their parents seemed revolutionary. Even though the Conference had put itself on record in favor of equal rights of support and inheritance in the Paternity Act and the Probate Code, the law of many states continued to differentiate very significantly in the legal treatment of marital and nonmarital children. A series of United States Supreme Court decisions invalidating state inheritance, custody, and tort laws that disadvantaged out-of-wedlock children provided the both the impetus and a receptive climate for the Conference to promulgate UPA (1973).

Case law has not always reached consistent results in construing UPA (1973). Moreover, widely differing treatment on subjects not dealt with by the Act has been common. For example, California courts have held that a nonmarital father does not have standing to sue an intact family to assert his rights of fatherhood. Another UPA (1973) state, Colorado, has declared that under its state constitution the father may not be denied such rights. Texas, which has adopted many of the provisions of UPA (1973), reached much the same conclusion. Similarly, a judgment's binding effect on the child or on others seeking to claim a benefit of the judgment or to attack the judgment collaterally is confused in the case law. Adding to the confusion is the fact that UPA (1973) is entirely silent regarding the relationship between a divorce and a determination of parentage. Finally, the incredible scientific advances in parentage testing since 1973 warrant a thoroughgoing revision of the Act.

Beginning in the 1980s, states began to adopt paternity registries in an attempt to deal with the risk of a man's subsequent claim of paternity after the mother relinquishes a child for adoption. Although at that time the Conference rejected a paternity registry as a solution, it promulgated the Uniform Putative and Unknown Fathers Act in 1988 (UPUFA) to deal with the rights of such men. However, UPUFA has not been enacted by any state. In 1988 the Conference also adopted the Uniform Status of Children of Assisted Conception Act (USCACA). Assisted reproduction and gestational agreements became commonplace in the 1990s, long after the promulgation of UPA (1973). The USCACA resembled a model act more than a uniform act because it provided two opposing options regarding "gestational agreements." To date, only two states have enacted USCACA, each choosing a different option. [The Texas Legislature has not enacted the USCACA.]

The promulgation of the Uniform Parentage Act in 2000, as amended in 2002, is now the official recommendation of the Conference on the subject of parentage. This Act relegates to history all of the earlier uniform acts dealing with parentage, to wit, UPA (1973)[,] UPUFA (1988), and USCACA (1988). The amendments of 2002 are the end-result of objections lodged by the American Bar Association Section of Individual Rights and Responsibilities and the ABA Committee on the Unmet Legal Needs of Children, based on the view that in certain respects the 2000 version did not adequately treat a child of unmarried parents equally with a child of married parents. Because equal treatment of nonmarital children was a hallmark of the 1973 Act, the objections caused the drafters of the 2000 version to reconsider certain sections of the Act. Through extended discussion and a meeting of representatives of all the entities involved, a determination was made that the objections had merit. As a result of this process, the amendments shown in this Act were presented by mail ballot to the Commissioners and unanimously approved in November 2002.

In brief outline, UPA (2002) is structured as follows: Subchapter B, General Provisions, adds many new definitions to clarify the participants in determinations of parentage and adapt the Act to recent scientific developments. Subchapter C, Parent-Child Relationship, will look familiar to past users of UPA (1973) because it continues a number of the 1973 provisions with little or no change, while eliminating the ambiguous term "natural" to describe a genetic parent. Subchapter D, Voluntary Acknowledgment of Paternity, is entirely new and is driven by federal mandates that states provide simplified nonjudicial means to establish paternity, especially for newborns and young children. Subchapter E, Registry of Paternity, is entirely new and incorporates a tightly integrated registry law to deal with the rights of a man who is neither an acknowledged, presumed or adjudicated father. A primary goal of this article is to facilitate adoption proceedings. Subchapter F, Genetic Testing, comprehensively covers that subject in ten separate sections (the 1973 Act had one section on the subject). Subchapter G, Proceeding to Adjudicate Parentage, sets forth the parties to, and the procedures for, adjudicating parentage and challenging acknowledgments, presumptions, and judgments. Subchapter H, Child of Assisted Reproduction, recodifies USCACA (1988), but applies its provisions to nonmarital as well as marital children born as a result of assisted reproductive technologies. Subchapter I, Gestational Agreement, is based upon USCACA (1988), but follows only the option that permits enforcement of a gestational agreement. Moreover, the Act makes a number of important changes in that option.

UPA (1973) contained a number of other substantive provisions, including those applicable to child support and custody. These subjects are omitted from UPA (2002) because other state law adequately provides for them.

Finally, Uniform Parentage Act (2002) is consistent with the provisions of two other uniform acts of great significance, namely the Uniform Interstate Family Support Act [UIFSA (1996) and UIFSA (2001)] and the Uniform Child Custody Jurisdiction and Enforcement Act [UCCJEA (1997)].

SUBCHAPTER A. APPLICATION & CONSTRUCTION

FAM §160.001. APPLICATION & CONSTRUCTION

This chapter shall be applied and construed to promote the uniformity of the law among the states that enact the Uniform Parentage Act.

History of Fam. Code §160.001: Acts 2001, 77th Leg., ch. 821, §1.01, eff. June 14, 2001.

History of Former Fam. Code §160.001: Acts 1995, 74th Leg., ch. 20, §1, eff. Apr. 20, 1995. Amended by Acts 1999, 76th Leg., ch. 556, §36, eff. Sept. 1, 1999. Deleted by Acts 2001, 77th Leg., ch. 821, §1.01, eff. June 14, 2001.

FAM §160.002. CONFLICTS BETWEEN PROVISIONS

If a provision of this chapter conflicts with another provision of this title or another state statute or rule and the conflict cannot be reconciled, this chapter prevails.

History of Fam. Code §160.002: Acts 2001, 77th Leg., ch. 821, §1.01, eff. June 14, 2001.

---

* **Editor's note:**

The NCCUSL comments have been edited to reflect the Texas Legislature's omission of sections, changing of text, and changing of section numbers from the original uniform act. The Texas Legislature did not adopt the NCCUSL comments when it adopted the Uniform Parentage Act. The full uniform act and comments can be found at www.uniformlaws.org.

History of Former Fam. Code §160.002: Acts 1995, 74th Leg., ch. 20, §1, eff. Apr. 20, 1995. Amended by Acts 1999, 76th Leg., ch. 556, §81, eff. Sept. 1, 1999. Deleted by Acts 2001, 77th Leg., ch. 821, §1.01, eff. June 14, 2001. Source: Former Fam. Code §13.01.

Sections 160.003-160.100 reserved for expansion

SUBCHAPTER B. GENERAL PROVISIONS

FAM §160.101. SHORT TITLE

This chapter may be cited as the Uniform Parentage Act.

History of Fam. Code §160.101: Acts 2001, 77th Leg., ch. 821, §1.01, eff. June 14, 2001.

History of Former Fam. Code §160.101: Acts 1995, 74th Leg., ch. 20, §1, eff. Apr. 20, 1995. Amended by Acts 1995, 74th Leg., ch. 751, §62, eff. Sept. 1, 1995; Acts 1997, 75th Leg., ch. 962, §1, eff. Sept. 1, 1997. Deleted by Acts 2001, 77th Leg., ch. 821, §1.01, eff. June 14, 2001. Source: Former Fam. Code §12.06(a), (b).

FAM §160.102. DEFINITIONS

In this chapter:

(1) "Adjudicated father" means a man who has been adjudicated by a court to be the father of a child.

(2) "Assisted reproduction" means a method of causing pregnancy other than sexual intercourse. The term includes:

(A) intrauterine insemination;

(B) donation of eggs;

(C) donation of embryos;

(D) in vitro fertilization and transfer of embryos; and

(E) intracytoplasmic sperm injection.

(3) "Child" means an individual of any age whose parentage may be determined under this chapter.

(4) "Commence" means to file the initial pleading seeking an adjudication of parentage in a court of this state.

(5) "Determination of parentage" means the establishment of the parent-child relationship by the signing of a valid acknowledgment of paternity under Subchapter D or by an adjudication by a court.

(6) "Donor" means an individual who provides eggs or sperm to a licensed physician to be used for assisted reproduction, regardless of whether the eggs or sperm are provided for consideration. The term does not include:

(A) a husband who provides sperm or a wife who provides eggs to be used for assisted reproduction by the wife;

(B) a woman who gives birth to a child by means of assisted reproduction; or

(C) an unmarried man who, with the intent to be the father of the resulting child, provides sperm to be used for assisted reproduction by an unmarried woman, as provided by Section 160.7031.

(7) "Ethnic or racial group" means, for purposes of genetic testing, a recognized group that an individual identifies as all or part of the individual's ancestry or that is identified by other information.

(8) "Genetic testing" means an analysis of an individual's genetic markers to exclude or identify a man as the father of a child or a woman as the mother of a child. The term includes an analysis of one or more of the following:

(A) deoxyribonucleic acid; and

(B) blood-group antigens, red-cell antigens, human-leukocyte antigens, serum enzymes, serum proteins, or red-cell enzymes.

(9) "Intended parents" means individuals who enter into an agreement providing that the individuals will be the parents of a child born to a gestational mother by means of assisted reproduction, regardless of whether either individual has a genetic relationship with the child.

(10) "Man" means a male individual of any age.

(11) "Parent" means an individual who has established a parent-child relationship under Section 160.201.

(12) "Paternity index" means the likelihood of paternity determined by calculating the ratio between:

(A) the likelihood that the tested man is the father of the child, based on the genetic markers of the tested man, the mother of the child, and the child, conditioned on the hypothesis that the tested man is the father of the child; and

(B) the likelihood that the tested man is not the father of the child, based on the genetic markers of the tested man, the mother of the child, and the child, conditioned on the hypothesis that the tested man is not the father of the child and that the father of the child is of the same ethnic or racial group as the tested man.

(13) "Presumed father" means a man who, by operation of law under Section 160.204, is recognized as the father of a child until that status is rebutted or confirmed in a judicial proceeding.

(14) "Probability of paternity" means the probability, with respect to the ethnic or racial group to which the alleged father belongs, that the alleged father is the father of the child, compared to a random, unrelated

man of the same ethnic or racial group, expressed as a percentage incorporating the paternity index and a prior probability.

(15) "Record" means information that is inscribed on a tangible medium or that is stored in an electronic or other medium and is retrievable in a perceivable form.

(16) "Signatory" means an individual who authenticates a record and is bound by its terms.

(17) "Support enforcement agency" means a public official or public agency authorized to seek:

(A) the enforcement of child support orders or laws relating to the duty of support;

(B) the establishment or modification of child support;

(C) the determination of parentage;

(D) the location of child-support obligors and their income and assets; or

(E) the conservatorship of a child or the termination of parental rights.

History of Fam. Code §160.102: Acts 2001, 77th Leg., ch. 821, §1.01, eff. June 14, 2001. Amended by Acts 2007, 80th Leg., ch. 972, §39, eff. Sept. 1, 2007.

History of Former Fam. Code §160.102: Acts 1995, 74th Leg., ch. 20, §1, eff. Apr. 20, 1995. Deleted by Acts 2001, 77th Leg., ch. 821, §1.01, eff. June 14, 2001. Source: Former Fam. Code §13.02(a), (d).

ANNOTATIONS

In re P.S., 505 S.W.3d 106, 110 (Tex.App.—Fort Worth 2016, no pet.). "The evidence presented at trial conclusively established that Father did not provide his sperm donation to a licensed physician. Because Father did not provide sperm to a licensed physician, he does not meet the statutory definition of 'donor' in [Fam. Code] §160.102(6). Because Father is not a 'donor,' [Fam. Code] §160.702 does not prohibit Father from being named as a parent. Accordingly, based on the evidence presented, we hold that the trial court did not abuse its discretion by establishing a parent-child relationship between Father and [child]."

NCCUSL Comment*

Four separate definitions of "father" are provided by the Act to account for the permutations of a man who may be so classified. Section 101.0010, "acknowledged father," directly responds to a 1996 federal mandate encouraging states to adopt nonjudicial means for a man to identify himself as the father of a child in order to achieve an early determination of paternity. The term "acknowledged father" is given a relatively narrow meaning, rather than the broader definition previously accorded to the term. Only a man who acknowledges paternity of a child in accordance with the formal requirements established in Subchapter D qualifies as an "acknowledged father." Because the mother of the child must concur in the formal acknowledgment, the federal mandate declares that the states must treat the action as the equivalent of an adjudication of paternity.

Subsection (1), "adjudicated father," although self-defining, presents a policy choice reached by the Conference that contested parentage matters are reserved for courts to resolve. The definition is limited to judicial adjudication of parentage, rather than providing for an alternative of administrative determination of parentage.

Section 101.0015, "alleged father," is derived from the UPUFA §1(1), although much of the terminology has been changed. A man who is asserted to be, or asserts himself to be or possibly to be, the father of a child is the primary target of the Uniform Parentage Act.

Subsection (13), "presumed father," is more fully defined by the factual circumstances establishing a presumption of paternity in §160.204, *infra*.

Closely related to the definitions of "father," Subsection (10) is derived from the UPUFA §1(1). Defining "man" to include all male humans eliminates the connotation of adulthood, thereby satisfying the obvious need for the Act to cover under-age progenitors. Although objection to calling a 14-year-old father a "man" was raised when UPUFA was considered by the Conference, for purposes of procreation such a teen-age boy is a man.

Note that a wide variety of other terms historically employed to identify the male parent are not defined in this section. Specifically, the term "putative father" has been replaced by the broader term "alleged father." According to Webster's, "putative" means "commonly accepted or supposed." Clearly, many "alleged fathers" do not fit that definition. Further, UPUFA chose the term "biological father" over more ambiguous "natural father." Because one woman may be the genetic mother of a child while another woman is the gestational mother, for consistency the term "genetic father" was substituted for "biological." Definitions are not supplied for such terms as "unknown father, legal father, real father, and the like," either because the term is self-defining or because it is ambiguous.

Subsection (6) was amended in 2002 to clarify that an individual who becomes a parent through assisted reproduction as provided in Subchapter H is not a "donor." Similarly, an individual who is an intended parent through the procedure implemented in Subchapter I is not a "donor." No substantive change is intended by this clarification.

Subsection (7), "ethnic or racial group," relates to an individual only for purposes of genetic testing. The genetic tests themselves do not determine the race or ethnic group of the individual. Rather, if a tested individual is not excluded, his race or ethnic group provided is used in the paternity calculations because those calculations give the most conservative result, that is, those most favoring non-paternity.

Subsection (8), "genetic testing," contemplates that paternity testing must be broadly defined to include all of the traditional genetic tests, such as blood types and HLA (Human Leukocyte Antigen), as well as newer DNA technologies. In the past the term "blood test" was commonly applied to paternity testing. However, this usage actually referred to the sample collected; in fact, the tests were genetic tests performed on blood samples. The Act uses the scientific term "deoxyribonucleic acid." This is to accommodate the changes in technology used to evaluate the DNA. Early DNA testing involved RFLP technology (Restriction Fragment Length Polymorphism), followed by PCR techniques (Polymerase Chain Reaction); these may be replaced by newer technology, such as SNP (Single Nucleotide Polymorphisms). The type of DNA technology to be employed is best left to scientific bodies, such as accreditation agencies, *see* §160.503(a), *infra*.

Subsection (12), "paternity index," defines a complex scientific and mathematical concept. Note that the definition includes statistical measures of the mother and tested man. The tested man may be an alleged father, or any other potential biological father. In fact, under appropriate circumstances Subchapter F provides for testing without samples from the mother or the alleged father. In these cases the expert statistically reconstructs the missing potential mother or biological father from genetic testing of samples from their relatives. Therefore the definition is correct even in cases involving a missing parent.

Subsection (15) is derived from the Uniform Electronic Transactions Act §102(13), which establishes a standard for either paper or electronic record keeping.

FAM §160.103. SCOPE OF CHAPTER; CHOICE OF LAW

(a) Except as provided by Chapter 233, this chapter governs every determination of parentage in this state.

* See footnote on p. 715.

(b) The court shall apply the law of this state to adjudicate the parent-child relationship. The applicable law does not depend on:

(1) the place of birth of the child; or

(2) the past or present residence of the child.

(c) This chapter does not create, enlarge, or diminish parental rights or duties under another law of this state.

(d) Repealed by Acts 2003, 78th Leg., ch. 457, §3, eff. Sept. 1, 2003.

History of Fam. Code §160.103: Acts 2001, 77th Leg., ch. 821, §1.01, eff. June 14, 2001. Amended by Acts 2003, 78th Leg., ch. 457, §3, eff. Sept. 1, 2003; Acts 2009, 81st Leg., ch. 767, §22, eff. June 19, 2009.

History of Former Fam. Code §160.103: Acts 1995, 74th Leg., ch. 20, §1, eff. Apr. 20, 1995. Deleted by Acts 2001, 77th Leg., ch. 821, §1.01, eff. June 14, 2001. Source: Former Fam. Code §13.02(a).

NCCUSL Comment*

The new UPA conforms to the requirement of 42 U.S.C. §666(a)(5)(A), that a state must provide that parentage proceedings be available at any time before a child attains 18 years of age or suffer the potential penalty of forfeiture of the federal funds that subsidize child support enforcement by the state.

Subsection (b) is derived from the UIFSA (1996) §303 and UPA (1973) §8(b). This section simplifies choice of law principles; the local court is directed to apply local law. If in fact this state is an inappropriate forum, dismissal for forum non-conveniens may be appropriate.

FAM §160.104. AUTHORIZED COURTS

The following courts are authorized to adjudicate parentage under this chapter:

(1) a court with jurisdiction to hear a suit affecting the parent-child relationship under this title; or

(2) a court with jurisdiction to adjudicate parentage under another law of this state.

History of Fam. Code §160.104: Acts 2001, 77th Leg., ch. 821, §1.01, eff. June 14, 2001.

History of Former Fam. Code §160.104: Acts 1995, 74th Leg., ch. 20, §1, eff. Apr. 20, 1995. Deleted by Acts 2001, 77th Leg., ch. 821, §1.01, eff. June 14, 2001. Source: Former Fam. Code §13.03.

NCCUSL Comment*

Prior Uniform Statutory Source: UPA (1973) §8(a).

The court having jurisdiction over parentage proceedings under this Act should be identified here. Although a proceeding to determine parentage is most often associated with an action to establish a child support order, the Act departs from the choice made by the UIFSA (1996) §102, which allows for the establishment of a child support order by an administrative agency. Insofar as establishment of parentage is concerned, the new UPA reflects the deliberate decision by NCCUSL that an "adjudication" should require a judicial proceeding. This procedure is consistent with the practice of most states. In fact, very few states provide for the resolution of disputed paternity through administrative processes, which, of course, is a policy judgment for the state legislature to make.

The term "tribunal" found in UIFSA to describe both courts and agencies is not employed in the Act. Rather, the dispute resolution entity in UPA (2002) is limited to a "court." UPA (2002) conforms to the congressional determination that parentage may also be established by an acknowledgment of parentage under Subchapter D. Subchapter H allows parentage to be established in a written record that presumably could then be approved by an administrative officer. These exceptions create potential disputes that only a judicial proceeding can resolve.

Joinder of a parentage proceeding with an action for divorce, annulment, separate maintenance, or child support and custody is left to state law. This should be considered in choosing which court in a state is to be given jurisdiction over proceedings under this Act.

FAM §160.105. PROTECTION OF PARTICIPANTS

A proceeding under this chapter is subject to the other laws of this state governing the health, safety, privacy, and liberty of a child or any other individual who may be jeopardized by the disclosure of identifying information, including the person's address, telephone number, place of employment, and social security number and the name of the child's day-care facility and school.

History of Fam. Code §160.105: Acts 2001, 77th Leg., ch. 821, §1.01, eff. June 14, 2001.

History of Former Fam. Code §160.105: Acts 1995, 74th Leg., ch. 20, §1, eff. Apr. 20, 1995. Deleted by Acts 2001, 77th Leg., ch. 821, §1.01, eff. June 14, 2001. Source: Former Fam. Code §13.04(a)-(e), (g).

NCCUSL Comment*

Prior Uniform Statutory Source: UCCJEA (1997) §209(e).

FAM §160.106. DETERMINATION OF MATERNITY

The provisions of this chapter relating to the determination of paternity apply to a determination of maternity.

History of Fam. Code §160.106: Acts 2001, 77th Leg., ch. 821, §1.01, eff. June 14, 2001.

History of Former Fam. Code §160.106: Acts 1995, 74th Leg., ch. 20, §1, eff. Apr. 20, 1995. Deleted by Acts 2001, 77th Leg., ch. 821, §1.01, eff. June 14, 2001. Source: Former Fam. Code §13.05.

NCCUSL Comment*

Prior Uniform Statutory Source: UPA (1973) §21.

This section provides for a determination of the mother-child relationship if that issue is in dispute. Except in circumstances involving immigration, cases involving disputed maternity are extraordinarily rare. Therefore, the new UPA is otherwise written in terms applicable to the determination of paternity, while maintaining the possibility that a dispute may arise regarding whether a woman claiming maternity actually is the mother of a particular child.

Although certain provisions found in the balance of the Act logically do not apply in a proceeding to establish maternity, the Act continues the decision made in UPA (1973) not to burden these already complex provisions with unnecessary references to the ascertainment of maternity. Except for issues arising from assisted reproduction technologies or gestational agreements, see Subchapter H and Subchapter I, §160.201(a) is the sole provision in the Act that specifically relates to the mother-child relationship. In an actual case, a judge facing a claim for the determination of the mother-child relationship should have little difficulty deciding which portions of the Act should be applied.

Sections 160.107-160.200 reserved for expansion

SUBCHAPTER C. PARENT-CHILD RELATIONSHIP

FAM §160.201. ESTABLISHMENT OF PARENT-CHILD RELATIONSHIP

(a) The mother-child relationship is established between a woman and a child by:

* See footnote on p. 715.

(1) the woman giving birth to the child;

(2) an adjudication of the woman's maternity; or

(3) the adoption of the child by the woman.

(b) The father-child relationship is established between a man and a child by:

(1) an unrebutted presumption of the man's paternity of the child under Section 160.204;

(2) an effective acknowledgment of paternity by the man under Subchapter D, unless the acknowledgment has been rescinded or successfully challenged;

(3) an adjudication of the man's paternity;

(4) the adoption of the child by the man; or

(5) the man's consenting to assisted reproduction by his wife under Subchapter H, which resulted in the birth of the child.

History of Fam. Code §160.201: Acts 2001, 77th Leg., ch. 821, §1.01, eff. June 14, 2001.

History of Former Fam. Code §160.201: Acts 1995, 74th Leg., ch. 20, §1, eff. Apr. 20, 1995. Amended by Acts 1995, 74th Leg., ch. 751, §64, eff. Sept. 1, 1995; Acts 1999, 76th Leg., ch. 556, §37, eff. Sept. 1, 1999. Deleted by Acts 2001, 77th Leg., ch. 821, §1.01, eff. June 14, 2001. Source: Former Fam. Code §13.21(a), (b).

See also ***O'Connor's Texas Family Law Handbook*** (2017), "The Parent-Child Relationship," ch. 1-B, p. 21.

NCCUSL Comment*

Prior Uniform Statutory Source: UPA (1973), §4; expanded to include all possible bases of the parent-child relationship.

Subsection (b)(5) and Family Code §160.753 reflect the fact that Subchapter H provides that both a married and an unmarried couple are entitled to assisted reproductive technologies in order to become parents and to enter into a gestational agreement.

FAM §160.202. NO DISCRIMINATION BASED ON MARITAL STATUS

A child born to parents who are not married to each other has the same rights under the law as a child born to parents who are married to each other.

History of Fam. Code §160.202: Acts 2001, 77th Leg., ch. 821, §1.01, eff. June 14, 2001.

History of Former Fam. Code §160.202: Acts 1995, 74th Leg., ch. 20, §1, eff. Apr. 20, 1995. Amended by Acts 1995, 74th Leg., ch. 751, §64, eff. Sept. 1, 1995; Acts 1999, 76th Leg., ch. 556, §37, eff. Sept. 1, 1999. Deleted by Acts 2001, 77th Leg., ch. 821, §1.01, eff. June 14, 2001. Source: Former Fam. Code §13.22.

Author's comment: Texas courts no longer use terms such as "illegitimate" and "bastard" when referring to children.

NCCUSL Comment*

Prior Uniform Statutory Source: UPA (1973) §2 and Massachusetts Gen. Laws ch. 209C, §1.

From a legal and social policy perspective, this is one of the most significant substantive provisions of the Act, reaffirming the principle that regardless of the marital status of the parents, children and parents have equal rights with respect to each other. As discussed in the Prefatory Note, *supra*, U.S. Supreme Court decisions and lower federal and state court decisions require equal treatment of marital and nonmarital children without regard to the circumstances of their birth.

Nonetheless, the equal treatment principle does not necessarily eliminate all distinctions in the application of other substantive laws to different kinds of children. For example, as amended in 1991 the Uniform Probate Code §2-705(b), states:

In construing a dispositive provision of a transferor who is not a natural parent, an individual born to the natural parent is not considered a child of that parent unless the individual while a minor lived as a regular member of the household of that parent or of that parent's parent, brother, sister, spouse, or surviving spouse. 8 U.L.A. 188 (1998).

In short, the UPC provides that an individual is presumed not to be included in a class gift from someone other than the child's parent unless that individual lived as a member of the parent's family during childhood. This presumed intent of the donor is rebuttable. Although this provision probably has a disproportionate effect on nonmarital children, the disparity is not based on the circumstances of birth, but rather on post-birth living conditions.

FAM §160.203. CONSEQUENCES OF ESTABLISHMENT OF PARENTAGE

Unless parental rights are terminated, a parent-child relationship established under this chapter applies for all purposes, except as otherwise provided by another law of this state.

History of Fam. Code §160.203: Acts 2001, 77th Leg., ch. 821, §1.01, eff. June 14, 2001.

History of Former Fam. Code §160.203: Acts 1995, 74th Leg., ch. 20, §1, eff. Apr. 20, 1995. Amended by Acts 1995, 74th Leg., ch. 751, §64, eff. Sept. 1, 1995; Acts 1999, 76th Leg., ch. 556, §37, eff. Sept. 1, 1999. Deleted by Acts 2001, 77th Leg., ch. 821, §1.01, eff. June 14, 2001. Source: Former Fam. Code §13.23.

NCCUSL Comment*

Prior Uniform Statutory Source: USCACA (1988) §10.

This section may seem to state the obvious, but both the statement and the qualifier are necessary because without this explanation a literal reading of §§160.201-203 could lead to erroneous statutory constructions. The basic purpose of the section is to make clear that a mother, as defined in §160.201(a), is not a parent once her parental rights have been terminated. Similarly, a man whose paternity has been established by acknowledgment or by court adjudication may subsequently have his parental rights terminated.

The qualifier, "as otherwise provided by other law of this state," is necessary because other statutes may restrict rights of a parent. For example, UPC (1993) §2-114(c) precludes a parent of a child (and the parent's family) from inheriting from the child by intestate succession "unless that natural parent has openly treated the child as his [or hers] and has not refused to support the child." Similarly, as discussed in the preceding Comment, UPC (1993) §2-705(b) affects the right of a child to take under a class gift from a person who is not a parent of the child.

FAM §160.204. PRESUMPTION OF PATERNITY

(a) A man is presumed to be the father of a child if:

(1) he is married to the mother of the child and the child is born during the marriage;

(2) he is married to the mother of the child and the child is born before the 301st day after the date the marriage is terminated by death, annulment, declaration of invalidity, or divorce;

(3) he married the mother of the child before the birth of the child in apparent compliance with law, even if the attempted marriage is or could be declared invalid, and the child is born during the invalid marriage or before the 301st day after the date the marriage is terminated by death, annulment, declaration of invalidity, or divorce;

(4) he married the mother of the child after the birth of the child in apparent compliance with law, re-

* See footnote on p. 715.

gardless of whether the marriage is or could be declared invalid, he voluntarily asserted his paternity of the child, and:

(A) the assertion is in a record filed with the vital statistics unit;

(B) he is voluntarily named as the child's father on the child's birth certificate; or

(C) he promised in a record to support the child as his own; or

(5) during the first two years of the child's life, he continuously resided in the household in which the child resided and he represented to others that the child was his own.

(b) A presumption of paternity established under this section may be rebutted only by:

(1) an adjudication under Subchapter G; or

(2) the filing of a valid denial of paternity by a presumed father in conjunction with the filing by another person of a valid acknowledgment of paternity as provided by Section 160.305.

History of Fam. Code §160.204: Acts 2001, 77th Leg., ch. 821, §1.01, eff. June 14, 2001. Amended by Acts 2003, 78th Leg., ch. 610, §10 (eff. Sept. 1, 2003), ch. 1248, §1 (eff. Sept. 1, 2003); Acts 2015, 84th Leg., ch. 1, §1.055, eff. Apr. 2, 2015.

History of Former Fam. Code §160.204: Acts 1995, 74th Leg., ch. 20, §1, eff. Apr. 20, 1995. Renumbered from §160.205 by Acts 1995, 74th Leg., ch. 751, §64, eff. Sept. 1, 1995. Amended by Acts 1999, 76th Leg., ch. 556, §37, eff. Sept. 1, 1999. Deleted by Acts 2001, 77th Leg., ch. 821, §1.01, eff. June 14, 2001. Source: Former Fam. Code §13.22(a), (e).

See also ***O'Connor's Texas Family Law Handbook*** (2017), "Who Is a Father," ch. 1-B, §4, p. 28.

ANNOTATIONS

In re S.T., 467 S.W.3d 720, 728-29 (Tex.App.—Fort Worth 2015, orig. proceeding). See annotation under Family Code §160.607, p. 734.

NCCUSL Comment*

Prior Uniform Statutory Source: UPA (1973) §4.

A network of presumptions was established by UPA (1973) for application to cases in which proof of external circumstances indicate a particular man to be the probable father. The simplest of these is also the best known—birth of a child during the marriage between the mother and a man. When promulgated in 1973 the contemporaneous commentary noted that:

While perhaps no one state now includes all these presumptions in its law, the presumptions *are* based on existing presumptions of 'legitimacy' in state laws and do not represent a serious departure. Novel is that they have been collected under one roof. All presumptions of paternity are rebuttable in appropriate circumstances. Uniform Parentage Act (1973), Prefatory Note, 9B U.L.A. 379 (2001).

After amendments adopted in 2002, the Uniform Parentage Act retains all but one of the original presumptions of paternity contained in UPA §4 (1973). Originally the 2000 version of the new Act limited presumptions of paternity to those related to marriage. The objection by the ABA Steering Committee on the Unmet Legal Needs of Children and the Section of Individual Rights and Responsibilities that this could result in differential treatment of children born to unmarried parents resulted in the revision to this section.

Subsection (a)(1) deals with a child born during a marriage; subsection (a)(2) deals with a child conceived during marriage but born after its termination; subsection (a)(3) deals with a child conceived or born during an invalid marriage; and, subsection (a)(4) deals with a child born before a valid or invalid marriage, accompanied by other facts indicating the husband is the father.

Added by amendment in 2002, subsection (a)(5), is a significant revision of UPA §4(4) (1973), which created a presumption of paternity if a man "receives the child into his home and openly holds out the child as his natural child." Because there was no time frame specified in the 1973 act, the language fostered uncertainty about whether the presumption could arise if the receipt of the child into the man's home occurred for a short time or took place long after the child's birth. To more fully serve the goal of treating nonmarital and marital children equally, the "holding out" presumption is restored, subject to an express durational requirement that the man reside with the child for the first two years of the child's life. This mirrors the presumption applied to a married man established by §160.607, *infra*. Once this presumption arises, it is subject to attack only under the limited circumstances set forth in §160.607 for challenging a marital presumption, and is similarly subject to the estoppel principles of §160.608.

One presumption found in UPA (1973) is not repeated in the new Act. Former UPA §4(5) created a presumption of paternity if the man "acknowledges his paternity of the child in a writing filed with [named agency] [and] the mother does not dispute the acknowledgment within a reasonable time." This presumption was eliminated because it conflicts with Subchapter D, Voluntary Acknowledgment of Paternity, under which a valid acknowledgment establishes paternity rather than a presumption of paternity.

Finally, subsection (b) is a complete rewrite of UPA (1973) §4(b). The requirement that a presumption "may be rebutted only by clear and convincing evidence" was eliminated from the Act. The same fate was accorded the statement that: "If two or more presumptions arise which conflict with each other, the presumption which on the facts is founded on the weightier considerations of policy and logic controls." Nowadays the existence of modern genetic testing obviates this old approach to the problem of conflicting presumptions when a court is to determine paternity. Nowadays, genetic testing makes it possible in most cases to resolve competing claims to paternity. Moreover, courts may use the estoppel principles in §160.608 in appropriate circumstances to deny requests for genetic testing in the interests of preserving a child's ties to the presumed or acknowledged father who openly held himself out as the child's father regardless of whether he is in fact the biological father.

Sections 160.205-160.300 reserved for expansion

SUBCHAPTER D. VOLUNTARY ACKNOWLEDGMENT OF PATERNITY

NCCUSL Prefatory Comment*

Voluntary acknowledgment of paternity has long been an alternative to a contested paternity suit. Under UPA (1973) §4, the inclusion of a man's name on the child's birth certificate created a presumption of paternity, which could be rebutted. In order to improve the collection of child support, especially from unwed fathers, the U.S. Congress mandated a fundamental change in the acknowledgment procedure. The Personal Responsibility and Work Opportunity Reconciliation Act of 1996 (PRWORA, also known as the Welfare Reform Act) conditions receipt of federal child support enforcement funds on state enactment of laws that greatly strengthen the effect of a man's voluntary acknowledgment of paternity, 42 U.S.C. §666(a)(5)(C). In brief, it provides that a valid, unrescinded, unchallenged acknowledgment of paternity is to be treated as equivalent to a judicial determination of paternity.

Because in many respects the federal act is nonspecific, the new UPA contains clear and comprehensive procedures to comply with the federal mandate. Primary among the factual circumstances that Congress did not take into account was that a married woman may consent to an acknowledgment of paternity by a man who may indeed be her child's genetic father, but is not her husband. Under the new UPA, the mother's husband is the presumed father of the child, *see* §160.204, *supra*. By ignoring the real possibility that the child will have both an acknowledged father and a presumed father, Congress left it to the states to sort out which of the men should be recognized as the legal father.

* See footnote on p. 715.

Further, PRWORA does not require that a man acknowledging paternity must assert genetic paternity of the child. Section 160.301 is designed to prevent circumvention of adoption laws by requiring a sworn assertion of genetic parentage of the child.

Sections 160.302-305 clarify that, if a child has a presumed father, that man must file a denial of paternity in conjunction with another man's acknowledgment of paternity in order for the acknowledgment to be valid. If the presumed father is unwilling to cooperate, or his whereabouts are unknown, a court proceeding is necessary to resolve the issue of parentage.

Congress also directed that the acknowledgment can be "rescinded" within a particular timeframe, and subsequently can be "challenged" without stating a timeframe. Those procedures are dealt with in §§160.307-309.

Finally, the related issue of issuance or revision of birth certificates is left to other state law.

FAM §160.301. ACKNOWLEDGMENT OF PATERNITY

The mother of a child and a man claiming to be the biological father of the child may sign an acknowledgment of paternity with the intent to establish the man's paternity.

History of Fam. Code §160.301: Acts 2001, 77th Leg., ch. 821, §1.01, eff. June 14, 2001. Amended by Acts 2003, 78th Leg., ch. 1248, §2, eff. Sept. 1, 2003.

See also 1 T.A.C. §55.404; ***O'Connor's Texas Family Law Handbook*** (2017), "Father by acknowledged paternity," ch. 1-B, §4.2, p. 29; "Father by acknowledged paternity," ch. 4-G, §2.2.2, p. 574.

NCCUSL Comment*

Prior Uniform Statutory Source: 42 U.S.C. §666(a)(5)(C), see preceding comment.

PRWORA does not explicitly require that a man acknowledging parentage necessarily is asserting his biological parentage of the child. In order to prevent circumvention of adoption laws, §160.301 corrects this omission by requiring a sworn assertion of biological parentage of the child. A 2002 amendment provides that a man who signs an acknowledgment of paternity declares that he is the biological father of the child. Thus both the man and the mother acknowledge his paternity, under penalty of perjury, without requiring the parents to spell out the details of their sexual relations. Further, the amended language also takes into account a situation in which a man, who is unable to have sexual intercourse with his partner, may still have contributed to the conception of the child through the use of his own sperm. Henceforth, a man in that situation will be able to recognize legally his paternity through the voluntary acknowledgment procedure.

FAM §160.302. EXECUTION OF ACKNOWLEDGMENT OF PATERNITY

(a) An acknowledgment of paternity must:

(1) be in a record;

(2) be signed, or otherwise authenticated, under penalty of perjury by the mother and the man seeking to establish paternity;

(3) state that the child whose paternity is being acknowledged:

(A) does not have a presumed father or has a presumed father whose full name is stated; and

(B) does not have another acknowledged or adjudicated father;

(4) state whether there has been genetic testing and, if so, that the acknowledging man's claim of paternity is consistent with the results of the testing; and

(5) state that the signatories understand that the acknowledgment is the equivalent of a judicial adjudication of the paternity of the child and that a challenge to the acknowledgment is permitted only under limited circumstances.

(b) An acknowledgment of paternity is void if it:

(1) states that another man is a presumed father of the child, unless a denial of paternity signed or otherwise authenticated by the presumed father is filed with the vital statistics unit;

(2) states that another man is an acknowledged or adjudicated father of the child; or

(3) falsely denies the existence of a presumed, acknowledged, or adjudicated father of the child.

(c) A presumed father may sign or otherwise authenticate an acknowledgment of paternity.

(d) An acknowledgment of paternity constitutes an affidavit under Section 666(a)(5)(C), Social Security Act (42 U.S.C. Section 666(a)(5)(C)).

History of Fam. Code §160.302: Acts 2001, 77th Leg., ch. 821, §1.01, eff. June 14, 2001. Amended by Acts 2011, 82nd Leg., ch. 1221, §1, eff. Sept. 1, 2011; Acts 2015, 84th Leg., ch. 1, §1.056 (eff. Apr. 2, 2015), ch. 859, §7 (eff. Sept. 1, 2015).

See also ***O'Connor's Texas Family Law Handbook*** (2017), "Father by acknowledged paternity," ch. 1-B, §4.2, p. 29; "Father by acknowledged paternity," ch. 4-G, §2.2.2, p. 574.

NCCUSL Comment*

Prior Uniform Statutory Source: 42 U.S.C. §666(a)(5)(C).

The federal statute cited above provides that receipt of the federal subsidy by a state for its child support enforcement program is contingent on state enactment of laws establishing specific procedures for voluntary acknowledgment of paternity. This deceptively simple principle proved difficult to implement.

Problems most notably include fact situations in which the mother of the child is married to someone other than the man who intends to acknowledge his paternity. With an acknowledgment the child would then have both an acknowledged father and a presumed father. To deal with this circumstance, many states have passed laws allowing the presumed father to sign a denial of paternity, which must be filed as part of the acknowledgment. This Act adopts this common sense solution; otherwise the acknowledgment would have no legal consequence because it cannot affect the legal rights of the presumed father.

At least two other provisions of this section warrant special emphasis. Subsection (a)(2) requires that the acknowledgment be "signed, or otherwise authenticated, under penalty of perjury," just as income tax returns and many other government documents require. Clearly, the potential punishment for false swearing is substantial, and the benefits from avoiding the complication of requiring witnesses and a notary are significant in this context. Mandating greater formality would greatly discourage the in-hospital signatures so earnestly desired in 42 U.S.C. §666(a)(5)(C)(ii).

Similarly, in an attempt to ensure full disclosure and avoid false swearing, subsection (a)(4) requires that the results of genetic testing, if any, be reported along with confirmation that the acknowledgment is consistent with the results of that testing. This provision is also designed to avoid a possible subversion of the requirements for an adoption. A would-be "father" whose parentage of a child has been excluded by genetic testing may not validly sign an acknowledgment once that fact has been established.

* See footnote on p. 715.

FAM §160.303. DENIAL OF PATERNITY

A presumed father of a child may sign a denial of his paternity. The denial is valid only if:

(1) an acknowledgment of paternity signed or otherwise authenticated by another man is filed under Section 160.305;

(2) the denial is in a record and is signed or otherwise authenticated under penalty of perjury; and

(3) the presumed father has not previously:

(A) acknowledged paternity of the child, unless the previous acknowledgment has been rescinded under Section 160.307 or successfully challenged under Section 160.308; or

(B) been adjudicated to be the father of the child.

History of Fam. Code §160.303: Acts 2001, 77th Leg., ch. 821, §1.01, eff. June 14, 2001.

See also 1 T.A.C. §55.405.

FAM §160.304. RULES FOR ACKNOWLEDGMENT & DENIAL OF PATERNITY

(a) An acknowledgment of paternity and a denial of paternity may be contained in a single document or in different documents and may be filed separately or simultaneously. If the acknowledgment and denial are both necessary, neither document is valid until both documents are filed.

(b) An acknowledgment of paternity or a denial of paternity may be signed before the birth of the child.

(c) Subject to Subsection (a), an acknowledgment of paternity or denial of paternity takes effect on the date of the birth of the child or the filing of the document with the vital statistics unit, whichever occurs later.

(d) An acknowledgment of paternity or denial of paternity signed by a minor is valid if it otherwise complies with this chapter.

History of Fam. Code §160.304: Acts 2001, 77th Leg., ch. 821, §1.01, eff. June 14, 2001. Amended by Acts 2015, 84th Leg., ch. 1, §1.057, eff. Apr. 2, 2015.

NCCUSL Comment*

Prior Uniform Statutory Source: 42 U.S.C. §666(a)(5)(C)(i), requiring a "simple civil process" for voluntary acknowledgment of paternity.

FAM §160.305. EFFECT OF ACKNOWLEDGMENT OR DENIAL OF PATERNITY

(a) Except as provided by Sections 160.307 and 160.308, a valid acknowledgment of paternity filed with the vital statistics unit is the equivalent of an adjudication of the paternity of a child and confers on the acknowledged father all rights and duties of a parent.

(b) Except as provided by Sections 160.307 and 160.308, a valid denial of paternity filed with the vital statistics unit in conjunction with a valid acknowledgment of paternity is the equivalent of an adjudication of the nonpaternity of the presumed father and discharges the presumed father from all rights and duties of a parent.

History of Fam. Code §160.305: Acts 2001, 77th Leg., ch. 821, §1.01, eff. June 14, 2001. Amended by Acts 2015, 84th Leg., ch. 1, §1.058, eff. Apr. 2, 2015.

NCCUSL Comment*

Prior Uniform Statutory Source: 42 U.S.C. §666(a)(5)(D)(ii), requiring that an acknowledgment of paternity be "a legal finding of paternity," and 42 U.S.C. §666(a)(5)(M), directing that acknowledgments be "filed with the state registry of birth records…."

FAM §160.306. FILING FEE NOT REQUIRED

The Department of State Health Services may not charge a fee for filing:

(1) an acknowledgment of paternity;

(2) a denial of paternity; or

(3) a rescission of an acknowledgment of paternity or denial of paternity.

History of Fam. Code §160.306: Acts 2001, 77th Leg., ch. 821, §1.01, eff. June 14, 2001. Amended by Acts 2011, 82nd Leg., ch. 1221, §2, eff. Sept. 1, 2011; Acts 2015, 84th Leg., ch. 1, §1.059, eff. Apr. 2, 2015.

FAM §160.307. PROCEDURES FOR RESCISSION

(a) A signatory may rescind an acknowledgment of paternity or denial of paternity as provided by this section before the earlier of:

(1) the 60th day after the effective date of the acknowledgment or denial, as provided by Section 160.304; or

(2) the date a proceeding to which the signatory is a party is initiated before a court to adjudicate an issue relating to the child, including a proceeding that establishes child support.

(b) A signatory seeking to rescind an acknowledgment of paternity or denial of paternity must file with the vital statistics unit a completed rescission, on the form prescribed under Section 160.312, in which the signatory declares under penalty of perjury that:

(1) as of the date the rescission is filed, a proceeding has not been held affecting the child identified in the acknowledgment of paternity or denial of paternity, including a proceeding to establish child support;

---

* See footnote on p. 715.

(2) a copy of the completed rescission was sent by certified or registered mail, return receipt requested, to:

(A) if the rescission is of an acknowledgment of paternity, the other signatory of the acknowledgment of paternity and the signatory of any related denial of paternity; or

(B) if the rescission is of a denial of paternity, the signatories of the related acknowledgment of paternity; and

(3) if a signatory to the acknowledgment of paternity or denial of paternity is receiving services from the Title IV-D agency, a copy of the completed rescission was sent by certified or registered mail to the Title IV-D agency.

(c) On receipt of a completed rescission, the vital statistics unit shall void the acknowledgment of paternity or denial of paternity affected by the rescission and amend the birth record of the child, if appropriate.

(d) Any party affected by the rescission, including the Title IV-D agency, may contest the rescission by bringing a proceeding under Subchapter G to adjudicate the parentage of the child.

History of Fam. Code §160.307: Acts 2001, 77th Leg., ch. 821, §1.01, eff. June 14, 2001. Amended by Acts 2011, 82nd Leg., ch. 1221, §3, eff. Sept. 1, 2011; Acts 2015, 84th Leg., ch. 1, §1.060, eff. Apr. 2, 2015.

See also *O'Connor's Texas Family Law Handbook* (2017), "Rescinding acknowledgment or denial," ch. 1-B, §4.2.3(1), p. 30; "Rescinding denial," ch. 4-G, §2.2.1(2)(a), p. 574; "Rescinding AOP," ch. 4-G, §2.2.2(1), p. 575.

FAM §160.308. CHALLENGE AFTER EXPIRATION OF PERIOD FOR RESCISSION

(a) After the period for rescission under Section 160.307 has expired, a signatory of an acknowledgment of paternity or denial of paternity may commence a proceeding to challenge the acknowledgment or denial only on the basis of fraud, duress, or material mistake of fact. The proceeding may be commenced at any time before the issuance of an order affecting the child identified in the acknowledgment or denial, including an order relating to support of the child.

(b) A party challenging an acknowledgment of paternity or denial of paternity has the burden of proof.

(c) Notwithstanding any other provision of this chapter, a collateral attack on an acknowledgment of paternity signed under this chapter may not be maintained after the issuance of an order affecting the child identified in the acknowledgment, including an order relating to support of the child.

(d) For purposes of Subsection (a), evidence that, based on genetic testing, the man who is the signatory of an acknowledgement of paternity is not rebuttably identified as the father of a child in accordance with Section 160.505 constitutes a material mistake of fact.

History of Fam. Code §160.308: Acts 2001, 77th Leg., ch. 821, §1.01, eff. June 14, 2001. Amended by Acts 2005, 79th Leg., ch. 478, §1, eff. Sept. 1, 2005; Acts 2011, 82nd Leg., ch. 1221, §4, eff. Sept. 1, 2011.

See also *O'Connor's Texas Family Law Handbook* (2017), "Challenging acknowledgment or denial," ch. 1-B, §4.2.3(2), p. 32; "Suit to Adjudicate Parentage," ch. 4-G, p. 573.

NCCUSL Comment*

The federal statute also includes a provision for a "challenge" of an acknowledgment of paternity after the period for rescission of a voluntary acknowledgment of paternity has elapsed. Such a collateral attack is to be limited to a challenge based on alleged "fraud, duress, or material mistake of fact," and according to 42 U.S.C. §666(a)(5)(c)(D)(iii), must be made "in court."

FAM §160.309. PROCEDURE FOR CHALLENGE

(a) Each signatory to an acknowledgment of paternity and any related denial of paternity must be made a party to a proceeding to challenge the acknowledgment or denial of paternity.

(b) For purposes of a challenge to an acknowledgment of paternity or denial of paternity, a signatory submits to the personal jurisdiction of this state by signing the acknowledgment or denial. The jurisdiction is effective on the filing of the document with the vital statistics unit.

(c) Except for good cause shown, while a proceeding is pending to challenge an acknowledgment of paternity or a denial of paternity, the court may not suspend the legal responsibilities of a signatory arising from the acknowledgment, including the duty to pay child support.

(d) A proceeding to challenge an acknowledgment of paternity or a denial of paternity shall be conducted in the same manner as a proceeding to adjudicate parentage under Subchapter G.

(e) At the conclusion of a proceeding to challenge an acknowledgment of paternity or a denial of paternity, the court shall order the vital statistics unit to amend the birth record of the child, if appropriate.

History of Fam. Code §160.309: Acts 2001, 77th Leg., ch. 821, §1.01, eff. June 14, 2001. Amended by Acts 2011, 82nd Leg., ch. 1221, §5, eff. Sept. 1, 2011; Acts 2015, 84th Leg., ch. 1, §1.061, eff. Apr. 2, 2015.

FAM §160.310. RATIFICATION BARRED

A court or administrative agency conducting a judicial or administrative proceeding may not ratify an unchallenged acknowledgment of paternity.

* See footnote on p. 715.

History of Fam. Code §160.310: Acts 2001, 77th Leg., ch. 821, §1.01, eff. June 14, 2001.

NCCUSL Comment*

Prior Uniform Statutory Source: 42 U.S.C. §666(a)(5)(E).

FAM §160.311. FULL FAITH & CREDIT

A court of this state shall give full faith and credit to an acknowledgment of paternity or a denial of paternity that is effective in another state if the acknowledgment or denial has been signed and is otherwise in compliance with the law of the other state.

History of Fam. Code §160.311: Acts 2001, 77th Leg., ch. 821, §1.01, eff. June 14, 2001.

NCCUSL Comment*

Prior Uniform Statutory Source: 42 U.S.C. §666(a)(5)(C)(iv).

PRWORA requires states "to give full faith and credit to such an affidavit [of acknowledgment of paternity] signed in any other state according to its procedures." *Id.* And, §666(a)(5)(D)(ii) provides that a "signed voluntary acknowledgment is considered a legal finding of paternity." In sum, federal law requires that an acknowledgment of paternity has the same status as a "judgment," 28 U.S.C. §1738, a "child custody determination," 28 U.S.C. §1738A, and a "child support order," 28 U.S.C. §1738B. This section implements these mandates.

FAM §160.312. FORMS

(a) To facilitate compliance with this subchapter, the vital statistics unit shall prescribe forms for the:

(1) acknowledgment of paternity;

(2) denial of paternity; and

(3) rescission of an acknowledgment or denial of paternity.

(b) A valid acknowledgment of paternity, denial of paternity, or rescission of an acknowledgment or denial of paternity is not affected by a later modification of the prescribed form.

History of Fam. Code §160.312: Acts 2001, 77th Leg., ch. 821, §1.01, eff. June 14, 2001. Amended by Acts 2011, 82nd Leg., ch. 1221, §6, eff. Sept. 1, 2011; Acts 2015, 84th Leg., ch. 1, §1.062, eff. Apr. 2, 2015.

NCCUSL Comment*

Prior Uniform Statutory Source: 42 U.S.C. §666(a)(5)(C)(i), (iv).

The federal Office of Child Support Enforcement has issued an Action Transmittal to all IV-D agencies specifying how to insure that the forms comply with PRWORA, OCSE-AT-98-02, Required Data Elements for Paternity Acknowledgment Affidavits, www.acf.hhs.gov/programs/css/resource/required-data-elements-paternity-acknowledgement-affidavits.

FAM §160.313. RELEASE OF INFORMATION

The vital statistics unit may release information relating to the acknowledgment of paternity or denial of paternity to a signatory of the acknowledgment or denial and to the courts and Title IV-D agency of this or another state.

History of Fam. Code §160.313: Acts 2001, 77th Leg., ch. 821, §1.01, eff. June 14, 2001. Amended by Acts 2015, 84th Leg., ch. 1, §1.063, eff. Apr. 2, 2015.

FAM §160.314. ADOPTION OF RULES

The Title IV-D agency and the executive commissioner of the Health and Human Services Commission may adopt rules to implement this subchapter.

History of Fam. Code §160.314: Acts 2001, 77th Leg., ch. 821, §1.01, eff. June 14, 2001. Amended by Acts 2015, 84th Leg., ch. 1, §1.064, eff. Apr. 2, 2015.

FAM §160.315. MEMORANDUM OF UNDERSTANDING

(a) The Title IV-D agency and the vital statistics unit shall adopt a memorandum of understanding governing the collection and transfer of information for the voluntary acknowledgment of paternity.

(b) The Title IV-D agency and the vital statistics unit shall review the memorandum semiannually and renew or modify the memorandum as necessary.

History of Fam. Code §160.315: Acts 2001, 77th Leg., ch. 821, §1.01, eff. June 14, 2001. Amended by Acts 2015, 84th Leg., ch. 1, §1.065, eff. Apr. 2, 2015.

FAM §160.316. EXPIRED

Sections 160.317-160.400 reserved for expansion

SUBCHAPTER E. REGISTRY OF PATERNITY

NCCUSL Prefatory Comment*

In *Lehr v. Robertson*, 463 U.S. 248 (1983), the Supreme Court upheld the constitutionality of a New York "putative father registry." A New York statute required a father of a child born out-of-wedlock to register if he wished to be notified of a termination of parental rights or adoption proceeding. Thereafter, a series of well-publicized adoption cases occurred in which state courts held that nonmarital fathers had not been given proper notice of such proceedings and voided established adoptions. A substantial number of legislatures responded to these decisions by enacting paternity registries similar to the New York statute. As of May, 2000, at least 28 states had enacted legislation creating paternity registries.

Initially, in 1988 the Conference took a much different view, stating:

[The Uniform Putative and Unknown Fathers Act] does not include a putative fathers registry requirement for, essentially, three reasons: (1) while "ignorance of the law is no excuse," most fathers or potential fathers—even very responsible ones—are not likely to know about the registry as a means of protecting their rights, and the objective is providing some actual protection, not relying on a cliché more relevant to the criminal law; (2) individual state registries do not protect responsible fathers in interstate situations; and (3) since the registries rely on unsupported claims, their accuracy is in doubt and their potential for an invasion of privacy and for interference with matters of adoption, custody, and visitation is substantial. It has also been pointed out that such a registry could provide a means for blackmailing the mother. The registry can, however, provide a simple (albeit "hard-nosed" and potentially unjust) solution when a father fails to register, as in *Lehr v. Robertson*.

The new UPA reverses that approach by accepting the importance and utility of a parentage registry to facilitate infant adoptions. Under circumstances in which the mother consents to the adoption of her infant child, time is of the essence in placing an infant with the adoptive parents. Therefore, resort to the constitutionally approved paternity registry system is appropriate. But, the Act limits the effect of the registry to cases in which a child is less than one year of age at the time of the court hearing, *see* §405, *infra*. This recognizes the need to expedite infant adoptions, while properly protecting the rights of those nonmarital fathers who may not have registered, but instead have established some relationship with the child following birth. This gives the nonmarital father the opportunity to step forward to accept the responsibilities of parent-

* See footnote on p. 715.

hood, while not derailing infant adoptions. Requiring notification to the alleged father of a proceeding when the child has reached one year of age or more will not unduly delay the placement of an older child. Further, this Act excepts from the registration requirement a man who timely initiates a proceeding for paternity, notwithstanding his failure to register.

FAM §160.401. ESTABLISHMENT OF REGISTRY

A registry of paternity is established in the vital statistics unit.

History of Fam. Code §160.401: Acts 2001, 77th Leg., ch. 821, §1.01, eff. June 14, 2001. Amended by Acts 2015, 84th Leg., ch. 1, §1.066, eff. Apr. 2, 2015.

FAM §160.402. REGISTRATION FOR NOTIFICATION

(a) Except as otherwise provided by Subsection (b), a man who desires to be notified of a proceeding for the adoption of or the termination of parental rights regarding a child that he may have fathered may register with the registry of paternity:

(1) before the birth of the child; or

(2) not later than the 31st day after the date of the birth of the child.

(b) A man is entitled to notice of a proceeding described by Subsection (a) regardless of whether he registers with the registry of paternity if:

(1) a father-child relationship between the man and the child has been established under this chapter or another law; or

(2) the man commences a proceeding to adjudicate his paternity before the court has terminated his parental rights.

(c) A registrant shall promptly notify the registry in a record of any change in the information provided by the registrant. The vital statistics unit shall incorporate all new information received into its records but is not required to affirmatively seek to obtain current information for incorporation in the registry.

History of Fam. Code §160.402: Acts 2001, 77th Leg., ch. 821, §1.01, eff. June 14, 2001. Amended by Acts 2015, 84th Leg., ch. 1, §1.067, eff. Apr. 2, 2015.

See also ***O'Connor's Texas Family Law Handbook*** (2017), "Paternity Registry," ch. 4-H, §5, p. 608.

NCCUSL Comment*

A registry of paternity protects a claim of paternity from summary termination, but the primary advantage of such a registry is to facilitate infant adoptions. By registering, a registrant ensures that he will receive notice of the possible adoption of a child that he may have fathered if the birth occurs in the state of registration. In this manner, a man may seek to protect his right to assert parentage.

Limiting the consequence of a failure to register with a registry of paternity only to termination of paternal rights in cases of infant adoption seems appropriate. If an adoption is not commenced in the first year of the child's life, the nonmarital father and the mother remain responsible for support and eligible for custody or visitation throughout the minority of the child in the absence of an adoption or termination after notice to the alleged father. The latter fact situation distinguishes it from an infant adoption in which both parents lose those rights and duties for the benefit of the child.

The enactment of subsection (b)(2) eliminates one of the major criticisms of *Lehr v. Robertson*, 463 U.S. 248 (1983). In *Lehr*, although the genetic father did not avail himself of the New York putative fathers registry, he had filed a "visitation and paternity" petition in another local court. The trial judge in the adoption proceeding knew the identity of the biological father, where he could be located, and that he was seeking to establish his paternity in another court. Nonetheless, the court granted the adoption and terminated the genetic father's parental rights without notice to him. Subsection (b)(2) exempts an alleged father from the requirement of registration if the man "commences a proceeding to adjudicate his paternity before the court has terminated his parental rights."

The act of registration submits the man to the personal jurisdiction of the tribunals of the state of registration, *see* UIFSA (1996) §201(7).

FAM §160.403. NOTICE OF PROCEEDING

Except as provided by Sections 161.002(b)(2), (3), and (4) and (f), notice of a proceeding to adopt or to terminate parental rights regarding a child must be given to a registrant who has timely registered with regard to that child. Notice must be given in a manner prescribed for service of process in a civil action.

History of Fam. Code §160.403: Acts 2001, 77th Leg., ch. 821, §1.01, eff. June 14, 2001. Amended by Acts 2007, 80th Leg., ch. 1283, §2, eff. Sept. 1, 2007.

NCCUSL Comment*

This section is the logical conclusion to the legal rationale for establishing a paternity registry. In an adoption of a child or termination of parental rights proceeding, the registry provides a clear procedure for resolving whether a nonmarital father intends to assert his rights with regard to the child. If he registers, termination of his rights and adoption of his child may not proceed without notice to him; this affords him the opportunity to assert his paternity and his claims for custody or visitation.

FAM §160.404. TERMINATION OF PARENTAL RIGHTS: FAILURE TO REGISTER

The parental rights of a man alleged to be the father of a child may be terminated without notice as provided by Section 161.002 if the man:

(1) did not timely register with the vital statistics unit; and

(2) is not entitled to notice under Section 160.402 or 161.002.

History of Fam. Code §160.404: Acts 2001, 77th Leg., ch. 821, §1.01, eff. June 14, 2001. Amended by Acts 2015, 84th Leg., ch. 1, §1.068, eff. Apr. 2, 2015.

NCCUSL Comment*

This section is the obverse logical conclusion to the legal rationale for establishing a paternity registry. In an infant adoption or termination of the genetic father's parental rights, the registry provides a clear procedure for determining that a man does not intend to assert parental rights with regard to the infant. Although the registry protects a man's right to notice in a termination or adoption proceeding, his failure to register waives those rights. Thus, the registry is both a first step towards claiming parental rights and a means for terminating the rights of those men who do not register. If a man fails to register with the paternity registry, a termination and adoption may proceed without fear of a belated claim, most particularly a claim coming after adoptive parents have received custody of the infant. This expedited procedure greatly facilitates infant adoption, which in truth explains the existence—and popularity—of the registries with a majority of state legislatures.

* See footnote on p. 715.

Sections 160.405-160.410 reserved for expansion

FAM §160.411. REQUIRED FORM

The vital statistics unit shall adopt a form for registering with the registry. The form must require the signature of the registrant. The form must state that:

(1) the form is signed under penalty of perjury;

(2) a timely registration entitles the registrant to notice of a proceeding for adoption of the child or for termination of the registrant's parental rights;

(3) a timely registration does not commence a proceeding to establish paternity;

(4) the information disclosed on the form may be used against the registrant to establish paternity;

(5) services to assist in establishing paternity are available to the registrant through the support enforcement agency;

(6) the registrant should also register in another state if the conception or birth of the child occurred in the other state;

(7) information on registries in other states is available from the vital statistics unit; and

(8) procedures exist to rescind the registration of a claim of paternity.

History of Fam. Code §160.411: Acts 2001, 77th Leg., ch. 821, §1.01, eff. June 14, 2001. Amended by Acts 2015, 84th Leg., ch. 1, §1.069, eff. Apr. 2, 2015.

FAM §160.412. FURNISHING OF INFORMATION; CONFIDENTIALITY

(a) The vital statistics unit is not required to attempt to locate the mother of a child who is the subject of a registration. The vital statistics unit shall send a copy of the notice of the registration to a mother who has provided an address.

(b) Information contained in the registry is confidential and may be released on request only to:

(1) a court or a person designated by the court;

(2) the mother of the child who is the subject of the registration;

(3) an agency authorized by another law to receive the information;

(4) a licensed child-placing agency;

(5) a support enforcement agency;

(6) a party, or the party's attorney of record, to a proceeding under this chapter or a proceeding to adopt or to terminate parental rights regarding a child who is the subject of the registration; and

(7) the registry of paternity in another state.

History of Fam. Code §160.412: Acts 2001, 77th Leg., ch. 821, §1.01, eff. June 14, 2001. Amended by Acts 2015, 84th Leg., ch. 1, §1.070, eff. Apr. 2, 2015.

FAM §160.413. OFFENSE: UNAUTHORIZED RELEASE OF INFORMATION

(a) A person commits an offense if the person intentionally releases information from the registry of paternity to another person, including an agency, that is not authorized to receive the information under Section 160.412.

(b) An offense under this section is a Class A misdemeanor.

History of Fam. Code §160.413: Acts 2001, 77th Leg., ch. 821, §1.01, eff. June 14, 2001.

FAM §160.414. RESCISSION OF REGISTRATION

A registrant may rescind his registration at any time by sending to the registry a rescission in a record or another manner authenticated by him and witnessed or notarized.

History of Fam. Code §160.414: Acts 2001, 77th Leg., ch. 821, §1.01, eff. June 14, 2001.

FAM §160.415. UNTIMELY REGISTRATION

If a man registers later than the 31st day after the date of the birth of the child, the vital statistics unit shall notify the registrant that the registration was not timely filed.

History of Fam. Code §160.415: Acts 2001, 77th Leg., ch. 821, §1.01, eff. June 14, 2001. Amended by Acts 2007, 80th Leg., ch. 627, §1, eff. June 15, 2007; Acts 2015, 84th Leg., ch. 1, §1.071, eff. Apr. 2, 2015.

FAM §160.416. FEES FOR REGISTRY

(a) A fee may not be charged for filing a registration or to rescind a registration.

(b) Except as otherwise provided by Subsection (c), the vital statistics unit may charge a reasonable fee for making a search of the registry and for furnishing a certificate.

(c) A support enforcement agency is not required to pay a fee authorized by Subsection (b).

History of Fam. Code §160.416: Acts 2001, 77th Leg., ch. 821, §1.01, eff. June 14, 2001. Amended by Acts 2015, 84th Leg., ch. 1, §1.072, eff. Apr. 2, 2015.

Sections 160.417-160.420 reserved for expansion

FAM §160.421. SEARCH OF APPROPRIATE REGISTRY

(a) If a father-child relationship has not been established under this chapter, a petitioner for the adoption of or the termination of parental rights regarding

the child must obtain a certificate of the results of a search of the registry. The petitioner may request a search of the registry on or after the 32nd day after the date of the birth of the child, and the executive commissioner of the Health and Human Services Commission may not by rule impose a waiting period that must elapse before the vital statistics unit will conduct the requested search.

(b) If the petitioner for the adoption of or the termination of parental rights regarding a child has reason to believe that the conception or birth of the child may have occurred in another state, the petitioner must obtain a certificate of the results of a search of the paternity registry, if any, in the other state.

History of Fam. Code §160.421: Acts 2001, 77th Leg., ch. 821, §1.01, eff. June 14, 2001. Amended by Acts 2007, 80th Leg., ch. 627, §2, eff. June 15, 2007; Acts 2015, 84th Leg., ch. 1, §1.073, eff. Apr. 2, 2015.

FAM §160.422. CERTIFICATE OF SEARCH OF REGISTRY

(a) The vital statistics unit shall furnish a certificate of the results of a search of the registry on request by an individual, a court, or an agency listed in Section 160.412(b).

(b) The certificate of the results of a search must be signed on behalf of the unit and state that:

(1) a search has been made of the registry; and

(2) a registration containing the information required to identify the registrant:

(A) has been found and is attached to the certificate; or

(B) has not been found.

(c) A petitioner must file the certificate of the results of a search of the registry with the court before a proceeding for the adoption of or termination of parental rights regarding a child may be concluded.

(d) A search of the registry is not required if a parent-child relationship exists between a man and the child, as provided by Section 160.201(b), and that man:

(1) has been served with citation of the proceeding for termination of the parent-child relationship; or

(2) has signed a relinquishment of parental rights with regard to the child.

History of Fam. Code §160.422: Acts 2001, 77th Leg., ch. 821, §1.01, eff. June 14, 2001. Amended by Acts 2007, 80th Leg., ch. 1283, §3, eff. Sept. 1, 2007; Acts 2015, 84th Leg., ch. 1, §1.074, eff. Apr. 2, 2015.

FAM §160.423. ADMISSIBILITY OF CERTIFICATE

A certificate of the results of a search of the registry in this state or of a paternity registry in another state is admissible in a proceeding for the adoption of or the termination of parental rights regarding a child and, if relevant, in other legal proceedings.

History of Fam. Code §160.423: Acts 2001, 77th Leg., ch. 821, §1.01, eff. June 14, 2001.

Sections 160.424-160.500 reserved for expansion

SUBCHAPTER F. GENETIC TESTING

FAM §160.501. APPLICATION OF SUBCHAPTER

This subchapter governs genetic testing of an individual to determine parentage, regardless of whether the individual:

(1) voluntarily submits to testing; or

(2) is tested under an order of a court or a support enforcement agency.

History of Fam. Code §160.501: Acts 2001, 77th Leg., ch. 821, §1.01, eff. June 14, 2001.

NCCUSL Comment*

This section is intended to avoid problems with regard to the admissibility of the results of voluntary genetic testing. Testing is often agreed upon to avoid the cost and delay engendered by requiring a proceeding to be filed before the results of genetic testing can be admitted as evidence. If the test excludes the man's paternity, an unnecessary step has been avoided.

FAM §160.502. ORDER FOR TESTING

(a) Except as otherwise provided by this subchapter and by Subchapter G, a court shall order a child and other designated individuals to submit to genetic testing if the request is made by a party to a proceeding to determine parentage.

(b) If a request for genetic testing of a child is made before the birth of the child, the court or support enforcement agency may not order in utero testing.

(c) If two or more men are subject to court-ordered genetic testing, the testing may be ordered concurrently or sequentially.

History of Fam. Code §160.502: Acts 2001, 77th Leg., ch. 821, §1.01, eff. June 14, 2001.

See also ***O'Connor's Texas Family Law Handbook*** (2017), "Genetic Testing," ch. 4-G, §12, p. 589.

NCCUSL Comment*

Prior Uniform Statutory Source: UPA (1973) §11; 42 U.S.C. §666(a)(5)(B)(i) requiring genetic testing in certain cases.

The progress that science has made in understanding molecular genetics since the promulgation of UPA (1973) is phenomenal. Subsection (a) speaks to testing of a "designated individual" other than of the "mother, and alleged or presumed father" to take into account the fact that testing for paternity may

* See footnote on p. 715.

proceed without testing the mother. Further, testing may also proceed without testing the alleged father by testing close relatives of that man. Moreover, the right of the court to order testing is not absolute; §§160.607-160.609 place limitations on genetic testing if the child has a presumed, acknowledged, or adjudicated father.

Subsection (b) is intended to prevent the court from ordering the mother to undergo prenatal testing, such as through amniocentesis or other in utero collection method. These procedures pose a measurable risk to the life and health of both the fetus and the mother. If the mother volunteers for such testing, she may undergo prenatal sample collection for parentage determination.

Subsection (c) recognizes that multiple men may be participating in the establishment process. The laboratories prefer to evaluate all persons concurrently, as concurrent testing may prevent multiple sample collections from the child and in rare cases (such as evaluating two non-identical siblings) the laboratory can continue testing until one or both of the tested men are excluded. However, sequential testing is also acceptable.

FAM §160.503. REQUIREMENTS FOR GENETIC TESTING

(a) Genetic testing must be of a type reasonably relied on by experts in the field of genetic testing. The testing must be performed in a testing laboratory accredited by:

(1) the American Association of Blood Banks, or a successor to its functions;

(2) the American Society for Histocompatibility and Immunogenetics, or a successor to its functions; or

(3) an accrediting body designated by the federal secretary of health and human services.

(b) A specimen used in genetic testing may consist of one or more samples, or a combination of samples, of blood, buccal cells, bone, hair, or other body tissue or fluid. The specimen used in the testing is not required to be of the same kind for each individual undergoing genetic testing.

(c) Based on the ethnic or racial group of an individual, the testing laboratory shall determine the databases from which to select frequencies for use in the calculation of the probability of paternity of the individual. If there is disagreement as to the testing laboratory's choice:

(1) the objecting individual may require the testing laboratory, not later than the 30th day after the date of receipt of the report of the test, to recalculate the probability of paternity using an ethnic or racial group different from that used by the laboratory;

(2) the individual objecting to the testing laboratory's initial choice shall:

(A) if the frequencies are not available to the testing laboratory for the ethnic or racial group requested, provide the requested frequencies compiled in a manner recognized by accrediting bodies; or

(B) engage another testing laboratory to perform the calculations; and

(3) the testing laboratory may use its own statistical estimate if there is a question regarding which ethnic or racial group is appropriate and, if available, shall calculate the frequencies using statistics for any other ethnic or racial group requested.

(d) If, after recalculation using a different ethnic or racial group, genetic testing does not rebuttably identify a man as the father of a child under Section 160.505, an individual who has been tested may be required to submit to additional genetic testing.

History of Fam. Code §160.503: Acts 2001, 77th Leg., ch. 821, §1.01, eff. June 14, 2001.

See also *O'Connor's Texas Family Law Handbook* (2017), "Genetic Testing," ch. 4-G, §12, p. 589.

NCCUSL Comment*

Prior Uniform Statutory Source: 42 U.S.C. §666(a)(5)(B)(i)(I)(II) and §666(a)(5)(F)(i)(I)(II).

As of December 2000, the Secretary of Health and Human Services had not officially designated any accreditation bodies as referenced in subsection (a)(3). But, Information Memorandum O.C.S.E.-IM-97-03, Apr. 10, 1997, from the Deputy Director of the Office of Child Support Enforcement identifies the American Association of Blood Banks and American Society for Histocompatibility and Immunogenetics as meeting this requirement. The accreditation requirement assures that the testing will "be of a type reasonably relied upon by experts in the field of genetic testing."

Subsection (b) clarifies that a "specimen" suitable for genetic testing may be composed from one of a wide variety of constituent elements of "body tissue and fluids." This conforms the statutory language to biological terminology to assure common understanding between the scientific community and the legal profession. In states with statutes employing only the broad terms, bench and bar have evidenced confusion about the fact that blood, buccal cells, bone, hair, etc. are "body tissues."

Subsections (c) and (d) are designed to clarify the use of "race or ethnic group" in the paternity calculations. Generally, the individual tested provides the information regarding the ethnic or racial group to use in the calculations. These sections are designed to avoid last minute changes in the racial designation, a scientific version of "forum shopping," and to easily correct any misunderstanding about which race should be used.

FAM §160.504. REPORT OF GENETIC TESTING

(a) A report of the results of genetic testing must be in a record and signed under penalty of perjury by a designee of the testing laboratory. A report made under the requirements of this subchapter is self-authenticating.

(b) Documentation from the testing laboratory is sufficient to establish a reliable chain of custody that allows the results of genetic testing to be admissible without testimony if the documentation includes:

(1) the name and photograph of each individual whose specimens have been taken;

(2) the name of each individual who collected the specimens;

(3) the places in which the specimens were collected and the date of each collection;

* See footnote on p. 715.

(4) the name of each individual who received the specimens in the testing laboratory; and

(5) the dates the specimens were received.

History of Fam. Code §160.504: Acts 2001, 77th Leg., ch. 821, §1.01, eff. June 14, 2001.

See also *O'Connor's Texas Family Law Handbook* (2017), "Evidence," ch. 4-G, §13.4, p. 593.

NCCUSL Comment*

Prior Uniform Statutory Source: 42 U.S.C. §666(a)(5)(F) requiring genetic testing in certain cases.

Subsection (b) is designed to indicate that in civil trials only a minimal showing of reliability of the chain of custody is needed. This avoids evidentiary problems, such as arguments modeled on criminal cases in which the chain of evidence is crucial. If an element of the chain is missing, such a defect may be corrected by affidavit or other testimony as to the reliability of the sample. For example, samples from a deceased individual may be obtained from a coroner's office and a picture of the individual need not be taken. In this case, proof of the chain of custody of the body maintained by the coroner may be provided.

FAM §160.505. GENETIC TESTING RESULTS; REBUTTAL

(a) A man is rebuttably identified as the father of a child under this chapter if the genetic testing complies with this subchapter and the results disclose:

(1) that the man has at least a 99 percent probability of paternity, using a prior probability of 0.5, as calculated by using the combined paternity index obtained in the testing; and

(2) a combined paternity index of at least 100 to 1.

(b) A man identified as the father of a child under Subsection (a) may rebut the genetic testing results only by producing other genetic testing satisfying the requirements of this subchapter that:

(1) excludes the man as a genetic father of the child; or

(2) identifies another man as the possible father of the child.

(c) Except as otherwise provided by Section 160.510, if more than one man is identified by genetic testing as the possible father of the child, the court shall order each man to submit to further genetic testing to identify the genetic father.

History of Fam. Code §160.505: Acts 2001, 77th Leg., ch. 821, §1.01, eff. June 14, 2001.

NCCUSL Comment*

Prior Uniform Statutory Source: 42 U.S.C. §666(a)(5)(G) requiring genetic testing in certain cases.

The selection of a probability of paternity of 99.0% and a combined paternity index of 100 to 1 as the rebuttably identified man as father of the child is consistent with the year 2000 standard of practice in the genetic-testing community. Accrediting agencies require the reporting of both of these numbers. As of December, 2000, 27 states have established a presumption at less than this level. However, for several years the standard of practice in the scientific community has been 99.0%. Therefore, raising the genetic presumption to the 99.0% level should have no impact on those states. This number represents a reasonable level of testing, given the breadth of the Act and potential difficulty of working with some specimens in a probate case. It is not intended as a standard of practice for the laboratories, but as a legal presumption to satisfy the legal standard of proof. Given the rapid progress of science, it is likely that accrediting standards will rise over time. If the standard of practice becomes more strict, the newer standards will be made routine by the requirement that laboratories be accredited in order to perform testing under the Act. But, the legal significance of the genetic presumption stated in this section will be unaffected.

Genetic testing results will usually exceed the statutory minimum. During the drafting of the new UPA (2000) several statutory presumptions were considered, i.e., 95%, 99%, 99.9% and 99.99%. Genetic testing laboratory representatives presented quite persuasive arguments for a variety of choices. The Drafting Committee ultimately chose to settle on the 99% standard because:

(1) the 99% standard reflects the current standard of the American Association of Blood Banks (Standards for Parentage Testing Laboratories, 4th Edition 1999), and the proposed standards (5th Edition, 2001);

(2) the standards promulgated by the various accrediting bodies (American Association of Blood Banks and the American Society for Histocompatibility and Immunogenetics) will, in reality, set the benchmark for genetic testing;

(3) the 99% standard is consistent with the standards of the plurality of American jurisdictions as of December, 2000;

(4) a standard higher than 99% could cause evidentiary problems in probate proceedings because of degraded specimens. Similarly, that problem may arise in cases involving one or more missing individuals, e.g., the mother is not available, but the child and alleged father are available;

(5) the percentage is an evidentiary presumption that the respondent may always challenge by requesting a second test under Section 160.507; and

(6) a proceeding to adjudicate paternity is a civil action based on a preponderance of the evidence, not a criminal action based on evidence beyond reasonable doubt.

FAM §160.506. COSTS OF GENETIC TESTING

(a) Subject to the assessment of costs under Subchapter G, the cost of initial genetic testing must be advanced:

(1) by a support enforcement agency, if the agency is providing services in the proceeding;

(2) by the individual who made the request;

(3) as agreed by the parties; or

(4) as ordered by the court.

(b) In cases in which the cost of genetic testing is advanced by the support enforcement agency, the agency may seek reimbursement from a man who is rebuttably identified as the father.

History of Fam. Code §160.506: Acts 2001, 77th Leg., ch. 821, §1.01, eff. June 14, 2001.

NCCUSL Comment*

Prior Uniform Statutory Source: UPA (1973) §11; 42 U.S.C. §666(a)(5)(B)(ii)(I).

In general, the party seeking relief from a court must bear the cost of the initial genetic testing. The federal law mandates that the support enforcement agency pay the cost of testing, subject to recoupment. Subsection (a)(4) does present the possibility that a court might order a respondent to pay the initial cost.

FAM §160.507. ADDITIONAL GENETIC TESTING

The court or the support enforcement agency shall order additional genetic testing on the request of a party who contests the result of the original testing. If

* See footnote on p. 715.

the previous genetic testing identified a man as the father of the child under Section 160.505, the court or agency may not order additional testing unless the party provides advance payment for the testing.

History of Fam. Code §160.507: Acts 2001, 77th Leg., ch. 821, §1.01, eff. June 14, 2001.

NCCUSL Comment*

Prior Uniform Statutory Source: UPA (1973) §11; 42 U.S.C. §666(a)(5)(B)(ii)(II).

Obviously the opportunity for additional testing should be provided if the original testing is contested in good faith. The requirement that the contestant provide advance payment if prior testing has identified a man as the father is intended to discourage spurious contests. This section provides the most important mechanism for determining the accuracy of a paternity test. While extremely rare, even after initial tests indicate a probability of paternity greater than 99.99% it is theoretically possible that additional testing can result in exclusion of the tested man. Likewise, if there is an error in the chain of custody or testing procedures, exclusion is the expected outcome. The only way to reliably determine whether an error occurred is to obtain a second test.

FAM §160.508. GENETIC TESTING WHEN ALL INDIVIDUALS NOT AVAILABLE

(a) Subject to Subsection (b), if a genetic testing specimen for good cause and under circumstances the court considers to be just is not available from a man who may be the father of a child, a court may order the following individuals to submit specimens for genetic testing:

(1) the parents of the man;

(2) any brothers or sisters of the man;

(3) any other children of the man and their mothers; and

(4) other relatives of the man necessary to complete genetic testing.

(b) A court may not render an order under this section unless the court finds that the need for genetic testing outweighs the legitimate interests of the individual sought to be tested.

History of Fam. Code §160.508: Acts 2001, 77th Leg., ch. 821, §1.01, eff. June 14, 2001.

NCCUSL Comment*

In some cases, the alleged father may be unavailable for testing. Subsection (a) accommodates those cases by providing for testing of the man's relatives to establish his paternity or nonpaternity of a child. Depending on the proceeding, some of the individuals listed for testing in subsection (a) will be parties to the paternity proceeding and others will not. If an individual does not volunteer to participate in the testing and is not a party, in the absence of this provision the court would be required to decide whether it has the authority to order the testing and whether testing the objecting individual is necessary. This provision resolves the issues. Given the fact that genetic testing in the modern age is not invasive—use of the buccal swab method means that the intrusion into the privacy of the individual is relatively slight compared to the right of the child to have parentage established. Moreover, the alleged parent also has a right to have that fact determined.

Note that no provision is explicitly made for court-ordered testing of maternal relatives because the establishment of paternity by genetic testing is in no way dependent on testing the mother of the child. However, if maternity is at issue, §106, Determination of Maternity, directs that this section be construed to test the relatives of the mother.

FAM §160.509. DECEASED INDIVIDUAL

For good cause shown, the court may order genetic testing of a deceased individual.

History of Fam. Code §160.509: Acts 2001, 77th Leg., ch. 821, §1.01, eff. June 14, 2001.

NCCUSL Comment*

In some states, the court with jurisdiction to adjudicate parentage may lack authority to order disinterment of a deceased individual. If so, that authority is provided by this section.

FAM §160.510. IDENTICAL BROTHERS

(a) The court may order genetic testing of a brother of a man identified as the father of a child if the man is commonly believed to have an identical brother and evidence suggests that the brother may be the genetic father of the child.

(b) If each brother satisfies the requirements of Section 160.505 for being the identified father of the child and there is not another identical brother being identified as the father of the child, the court may rely on nongenetic evidence to adjudicate which brother is the father of the child.

History of Fam. Code §160.510: Acts 2001, 77th Leg., ch. 821, §1.01, eff. June 14, 2001.

NCCUSL Comment*

This section refers to "identical brothers" rather than "identical twins" to account for the possibility of identical triplets, etc. In some cases, non-identical brothers (and even other related men) will not be excluded after initial genetic testing. This section should not be used to resolve those cases because more sophisticated genetic testing can differentiate between non-identical siblings. If a case occurs in which, after initial testing, two men are not excluded, both men should be ordered to submit to additional testing as provided in Section 160.505(c) to determine which is the father. In the extremely rare case in which a competent laboratory exhausts all of its in-house testing and still cannot determine which non-identical sibling is excluded, the common practice is to provide the genetic material to another laboratory for more extensive testing to resolve the case.

Contrasting identical brothers with non-identical brothers, identical brothers can never be differentiated by additional genetic testing. This creates a completely different situation for the court. This section resolves the identical-brother conundrum as much as possible, and is designed to prevent the court from simply dismissing the case.

FAM §160.511. OFFENSE: UNAUTHORIZED RELEASE OF SPECIMEN

(a) A person commits an offense if the person intentionally releases an identifiable specimen of another person for any purpose not relevant to the parentage proceeding and without a court order or the written permission of the person who furnished the specimen.

* See footnote on p. 715.

(b) An offense under this section is a Class A misdemeanor.

History of Fam. Code §160.511: Acts 2001, 77th Leg., ch. 821, §1.01, eff. June 14, 2001.

NCCUSL Comment*

This section seeks to protect the privacy rights of persons who are tested for a parentage determination. Although the Drafting Committee was not informed of an instance in which a paternity-testing laboratory had released samples or performed unauthorized testing, several states have proposed or passed laws regulating the "genetic privacy" of paternity tests. This section is intended to provide some guidance in this area. The term "identifiable specimen" is included, as there are beneficial uses of samples for anonymous research purposes. For example, the frequency tables used to make calculations are compiled from anonymous data and provide a more precise calculation for all persons involved in paternity testing. On occasion, a court may order the laboratory to release samples. For instance, a man who had been tested in one paternity proceeding and then dies may have his samples utilized in another paternity proceeding if a court orders testing in the second action. Courts have also ordered the release of samples when the tested man has allegedly engaged in criminal conduct. This has occurred when the alleged father has sent an imposter for sample collection. If the state pursues criminal charges, a court might order the laboratory to release the samples to a state crime laboratory for further identification and possible criminal prosecution.

The Drafting Committee was informed that in one case, a grand jury brought indictments for multiple counts of a scheme to defraud, tampering with physical evidence and perjury against the alleged father and the impostor. The results of genetic testing for paternity purposes appear to have no medical or predictive value in any other context. Thus, regulation of the paternity-test results is left to the states. In some states, the records of paternity proceedings are open, thus allowing anyone to obtain the results. A more comprehensive treatment on this subject must necessarily be left to other laws.

The control of the records is left to other state law. In some states paternity records are open to the public, and a fundamental change in handling of the records is beyond the scope of this Act. The accreditation agencies provide guidance on this subject. For example, the American Association of Blood Banks requires that accredited laboratories maintain records for at least five years. Because a laboratory performing testing under this Act should be accredited, see Section 160.503(a), *supra*, protection is thus provided to the tested person's records under the accreditation standards.

FAM §160.512. OFFENSE: FALSIFICATION OF SPECIMEN

(a) A person commits an offense if the person alters, destroys, conceals, fabricates, or falsifies genetic evidence in a proceeding to adjudicate parentage, including inducing another person to provide a specimen with the intent to affect the outcome of the proceeding.

(b) An offense under this section is a felony of the third degree.

(c) An order excluding a man as the biological father of a child based on genetic evidence shown to be altered, fabricated, or falsified is void and unenforceable.

History of Fam. Code §160.512: Acts 2011, 82nd Leg., ch. 1221, §7, eff. Sept. 1, 2011.

Sections 160.513-160.600 reserved for expansion

* See footnote on p. 715.

SUBCHAPTER G. PROCEEDING TO ADJUDICATE PARENTAGE

FAM §160.601. PROCEEDING AUTHORIZED; RULES OF PROCEDURE

(a) A civil proceeding may be maintained to adjudicate the parentage of a child.

(b) The proceeding is governed by the Texas Rules of Civil Procedure, except as provided by Chapter 233.

History of Fam. Code §160.601: Acts 2001, 77th Leg., ch. 821, §1.01, eff. June 14, 2001. Amended by Acts 2009, 81st Leg., ch. 767, §23, eff. June 19, 2009.

NCCUSL Comment*

Prior Uniform Statutory Source: UPA (1973) §14.

A determination of paternity is governed by the ordinary rules of civil procedure. The party seeking to establish paternity is entitled to full discovery, to compel the testimony of all witnesses, and to have the case tried by a preponderance of the evidence. "The equipoise of the private interests that are at stake in a paternity proceeding supports the conclusion that the standard of proof normally applied in private litigation is also appropriate for these cases." *Rivera v. Minnich*, 483 U.S. 574, 581 (1987).

A corresponding amendment to UPC §2-114 was not made until the major revision of 1990 (as further revised in 1993). By that time, it had been recognized as illogical and unjust to impose discriminatory burdens on children born out-of-wedlock who were seeking paternal inheritance. It also had been ruled unconstitutional by application of the intermediate scrutiny test formulated under the 14th Amendment. *Reed v. Campbell*, 476 U.S. 852 (1986). Moreover, by 1990 the preponderance of the evidence standard had been widely applied to determinations of paternity and probate proceedings. Against this background, UPC (1993) abandoned the clear and convincing evidence standard for determining paternal relationships.

FAM §160.602. STANDING TO MAINTAIN PROCEEDING

(a) Subject to Subchapter D and Sections 160.607 and 160.609 and except as provided by Subsection (b), a proceeding to adjudicate parentage may be maintained by:

(1) the child;

(2) the mother of the child;

(3) a man whose paternity of the child is to be adjudicated;

(4) the support enforcement agency or another government agency authorized by other law;

(5) an authorized adoption agency or licensed child-placing agency;

(6) a representative authorized by law to act for an individual who would otherwise be entitled to maintain a proceeding but who is deceased, is incapacitated, or is a minor;

(7) a person related within the second degree by consanguinity to the mother of the child, if the mother is deceased; or

(8) a person who is an intended parent.

(b) After the date a child having no presumed, acknowledged, or adjudicated father becomes an adult, a

proceeding to adjudicate the parentage of the adult child may only be maintained by the adult child.

History of Fam. Code §160.602: Acts 2001, 77th Leg., ch. 821, §1.01, eff. June 14, 2001. Amended by Acts 2003, 78th Leg., ch. 457, §1 (eff. Sept. 1, 2003), ch. 1248, §3 (eff. Sept. 1, 2003).

See also *O'Connor's Texas Family Law Handbook* (2017), "Who can file," ch. 4-G, §3.1, p. 577.

ANNOTATIONS

In re Sandoval, No. 04-15-00244-CV (Tex. App.—San Antonio 2016, orig. proceeding) (memo op.; 1-27-16). Petitioner "obtained an Order Granting Change of Identity, which acknowledged his name change ... and included the following finding: '(3) Petitioner's sex is male.' Following the trial court's findings, the order concluded, 'IT IS ORDERED that Petitioner's identity is changed from female to male.' [¶] [Petitioner] contends that his Order Granting Change of Identity is legally sufficient to confer statutory standing to adjudicate his legal paternity to [mother's] adopted children under §160.602(a)(3). We disagree. [¶] [W]e conclude that [such an order] is not sufficient to confer statutory standing to maintain a suit to adjudicate parentage under §160.602(a)(3). The Order Granting Change of Identity is a recognized form of proof of [petitioner's] identity and age for the purpose of obtaining a marriage license. It may also be sufficient to acknowledge [petitioner's] legal status as a man. However, we need not reach such a conclusion in this case because, even if considered a man from birth for legal purposes, [petitioner's] status as a man is not sufficient to confer statutory standing as, 'a man whose paternity of the child is to be adjudicated.' If all that was required for standing was to be a man, then any man could maintain a suit to adjudicate parentage to any child. We do not believe that to be what the Texas Legislature intended. [¶] For a man to maintain a suit to adjudicate parentage, he must fall into one of the categories established by the statutory framework."

Gribble v. Layton, 389 S.W.3d 882, 884 (Tex. App.—Houston [14th Dist.] 2012, pet. denied). Mother, "individually and in her capacity as guardian of the person and estate of ... her disabled adult son, sued [son's] alleged biological father ... for a determination of parentage and child support. *At 887-88:* [Father] argues that a legal representative authorized to bring suit on behalf of an individual who is deceased, incapacitated, or a minor as provided in [§160.602](a)(6) is not authorized to bring suit on an adult child's behalf because subsection (b) provides that only the 'adult child' can maintain suit upon becoming an adult. [¶] [N]othing in the statute compels the conclusion that the legislature intended to divest a mentally disabled child of the ability to maintain an action to adjudicate parentage through a court-appointed guardian upon reaching adulthood. Indeed, such a conclusion would be contrary to the legislature's determination that a proceeding to adjudicate the parentage of a child having no presumed, acknowledged, or adjudicated father may be commenced at any time, including after the date the child becomes an adult. It would also lead to the absurd result of allowing a physically disabled adult child to maintain an action to adjudicate parentage while prohibiting a mentally disabled adult child from doing the same. [¶] We conclude that §160.602 does not preclude a mentally disabled adult child from maintaining an action to determine parentage through a court-appointed guardian."

In re Sullivan, 157 S.W.3d 911, 912 (Tex.App.—Houston [14th Dist.] 2005, orig. proceeding). "*Does an unmarried man who donated sperm to an unmarried woman for the conception of a child have standing to maintain a proceeding to adjudicate parentage of the resulting child? At 919:* [W]e conclude that, at a minimum, §160.602(a)(3) confers standing on a man alleging himself to be the biological father of the child in question and seeking an adjudication that he is the father of that child. *At 920:* The Texas Legislature ... has not made the determination of donor status part of the standing inquiry." *But see* ***In re H.C.S.***, 219 S.W.3d 33, 35-36 (Tex.App.—San Antonio 2006, no pet.) (male donor who did not sign acknowledgement of paternity cannot be "alleged father" because he does not have standing to bring original suit).

NCCUSL Comment*

Prior Uniform Statutory Source: UPA (1973) §6.

This section grants standing to a broad range of individuals and agencies to bring a parentage proceeding. But, several limitations on standing to sue are contained within the Act. Subchapter D details the procedures involved in a voluntary acknowledgment of parentage. Sections 160.607 and 160.609 establish the ground rules for proceedings involving children with, and without, a presumed father. Subchapter I regulates parentage determinations arising from a gestational agreement.

FAM §160.603. NECESSARY PARTIES TO PROCEEDING

The following individuals must be joined as parties in a proceeding to adjudicate parentage:

* See footnote on p. 715.

(1) the mother of the child; and

(2) a man whose paternity of the child is to be adjudicated.

History of Fam. Code §160.603: Acts 2001, 77th Leg., ch. 821, §1.01, eff. June 14, 2001.

NCCUSL Comment*

Prior Uniform Statutory Source: UPA (1973) §9.

This section partially follows and partially rejects the UPA (1973) requirements regarding who must be named as parties in a parentage proceeding. First, contra to UPA (1973), the child is not a necessary party. Few states require children as necessary parties. Further, with the widespread use of DNA testing, such a requirement has outlived its usefulness. On the other hand, failure to join a child as a party may later result in a child's successful collateral attack on the original determination of paternity to be filed by the child. This subject is discussed more fully in the comment to Section 160.637, *infra*.

Second, as far as can be ascertained, no state requires the children born to a woman during marriage to be named as parties in a divorce proceeding. Divorce decrees generally serve as res judicata in the event of a subsequent challenge to the decree's determination of parentage. *Id.*

E FAM §160.6035. CONTENTS OF PETITION; STATEMENT RELATING TO CERTAIN PROTECTIVE ORDERS REQUIRED

(a) The petition in a proceeding to adjudicate parentage must include a statement as to whether, in regard to a party to the proceeding or a child of a party to the proceeding:

(1) there is in effect:

(A) a protective order under Title 4;

(B) a protective order under Chapter 7A, Code of Criminal Procedure; or

(C) an order for emergency protection under Article 17.292, Code of Criminal Procedure; or

(2) an application for an order described by Subdivision (1) is pending.

(b) The petitioner shall attach a copy of each order described by Subsection (a)(1) in which a party to the proceeding or a child of a party to the proceeding was the applicant or victim of the conduct alleged in the application or order and the other party was the respondent or defendant of an action regarding the conduct alleged in the application or order without regard to the date of the order. If a copy of the order is not available at the time of filing, the petition must state that a copy of the order will be filed with the court before any hearing.

(c) Notwithstanding any other provision of this section, if the Title IV-D agency files a petition in a proceeding to adjudicate parentage, the agency is not required to:

(1) include in the petition the statement described by Subsection (a); or

(2) attach copies of the documentation described by Subsection (b).

History of Fam. Code §160.6035: Enacted by H.B. 3052, §7, 85th Leg., eff. Sept. 1, 2017.

FAM §160.604. PERSONAL JURISDICTION

(a) An individual may not be adjudicated to be a parent unless the court has personal jurisdiction over the individual.

(b) A court of this state having jurisdiction to adjudicate parentage may exercise personal jurisdiction over a nonresident individual or the guardian or conservator of the individual if the conditions in Section 159.201 are satisfied.

(c) Lack of jurisdiction over one individual does not preclude the court from making an adjudication of parentage binding on another individual over whom the court has personal jurisdiction.

History of Fam. Code §160.604: Acts 2001, 77th Leg., ch. 821, §1.01, eff. June 14, 2001.

See also ***O'Connor's Texas Family Law Handbook*** (2017), "Child support & parentage – in personam jurisdiction," ch. 4-A, §2.2.2, p. 336.

NCCUSL Comment*

Prior Uniform Statutory Source: UPA (1973) §6(b).

Although custody and visitation proceedings are considered to be status adjudications, and therefore do not require personal jurisdiction over both parents, subsection (a) confirms the long-standing view that paternity proceedings require personal jurisdiction.

Subsection (b) incorporates the long-arm provision for establishing personal jurisdiction over an absent respondent set forth in UIFSA (1996), which is in effect in every state.

Subsection (c) makes the best of a situation in which an adjudication will almost inevitably be incomplete because not all the necessary parties are subject to the personal jurisdiction of the court. The most likely scenario for this unfortunate circumstance is one in which the mother and alleged father of the child are subject to the court's jurisdiction, but the mother's absent husband is not. Even if the husband's whereabouts are known, if both the forum court and the court of his residence lack jurisdiction over all three parties, there still is no court with power to bind all of them to a parentage determination.

Subsection (c) takes the common sense approach that a court should not be dissuaded from making a parentage decision, even if it cannot bind all appropriate parties. In the scenario described above, binding the mother and alleged father to a decision of the man's parentage may not technically bind the husband (the presumed father), but more than likely it will end litigation on the subject.

FAM §160.605. VENUE

Venue for a proceeding to adjudicate parentage is in the county of this state in which:

(1) the child resides or is found;

(2) the respondent resides or is found if the child does not reside in this state; or

(3) a proceeding for probate or administration of the presumed or alleged father's estate has been commenced.

History of Fam. Code §160.605: Acts 2001, 77th Leg., ch. 821, §1.01, eff. June 14, 2001.

* See footnote on p. 715.

NCCUSL Comment*

Prior Uniform Statutory Source: UPA (1973) §8(c).

The venue provision provides choices proven to be reasonable and convenient since its inclusion in the 1973 Act.

FAM §160.606. NO TIME LIMITATION: CHILD HAVING NO PRESUMED, ACKNOWLEDGED, OR ADJUDICATED FATHER

A proceeding to adjudicate the parentage of a child having no presumed, acknowledged, or adjudicated father may be commenced at any time, including after the date:

(1) the child becomes an adult; or

(2) an earlier proceeding to adjudicate paternity has been dismissed based on the application of a statute of limitation then in effect.

History of Fam. Code §160.606: Acts 2001, 77th Leg., ch. 821, §1.01, eff. June 14, 2001.

NCCUSL Comment*

Prior Uniform Statutory Source: UPA (1973) §§6, 7.

For a state to retain the federal child support enforcement subsidy, 42 U.S.C. §666(a)(5)(A)(i) mandates that the states must have laws to "permit the establishment of the paternity of a child at any time before the child attains 18 years of age." States have chosen a wide range of age options: age 18 (20 states), age 19 (6 states), age 20 (2 states), age 21 (10 states), age 22 (2 states), age 23 (2 states), and no limitation (9 states). Several states limit the establishment of parental rights to a shorter period.

The new UPA directs that an individual whose parentage has not been determined has a civil right to determine his or her own parentage, which should not be subject to limitation except when an estate has been closed. Accordingly, this section allows a proceeding to adjudicate parentage after the child has reached the age of majority. Such a proceeding is the exclusive province of the child, however. This limitation prohibits the filing of an intrusive proceeding by an individual claiming to be a parent of an adult child, or by a legal stranger. There appear to be no reported problems encountered in states without a statute of limitations for such actions.

FAM §160.607. TIME LIMITATION: CHILD HAVING PRESUMED FATHER

(a) Except as otherwise provided by Subsection (b), a proceeding brought by a presumed father, the mother, or another individual to adjudicate the parentage of a child having a presumed father shall be commenced not later than the fourth anniversary of the date of the birth of the child.

(b) A proceeding seeking to adjudicate the parentage of a child having a presumed father may be maintained at any time if the court determines that:

(1) the presumed father and the mother of the child did not live together or engage in sexual intercourse with each other during the probable time of conception; or

(2) the presumed father was precluded from commencing a proceeding to adjudicate the parentage of the child before the expiration of the time prescribed by Subsection (a) because of the mistaken belief that he was the child's biological father based on misrepresentations that led him to that conclusion.

History of Fam. Code §160.607: Acts 2001, 77th Leg., ch. 821, §1.01, eff. June 14, 2001. Amended by Acts 2003, 78th Leg., ch. 1248, §4, eff. Sept. 1, 2003; Acts 2011, 82nd Leg., ch. 1221, §8, eff. Sept. 1, 2011.

ANNOTATIONS

In re S.T., 467 S.W.3d 720, 728-29 (Tex.App.—Fort Worth 2015, orig. proceeding). "Even though the agreed Order of Stipulations does not directly purport to impose liability on [alleged biological father], nor does it adjudicate him the child's biological father, the stipulation that '[f]acts exist that conclusively establish [presumed father's] right to the relief of being able to challenge his paternity of [the child], pursuant to [Fam. Code] §160.607(b)(2),' addresses and resolves [alleged biological father's] challenge to [presumed father's] suit on limitations grounds. [Presumed father] and [mother] cannot bind [alleged biological father], also a party to the underlying proceeding, to this stipulation, nor can they resolve this issue by stipulation. [¶] Moreover, the stipulations that [presumed father] is not the father or biological father attempt to adjudicate [presumed father's] nonpaternity by agreement contrary to [Fam. Code] §160.204(b), which provides that a presumption of paternity may be rebutted in only two ways.... The statutory scheme regarding the establishment of parentage ... contemplates that a child will not be left without a means of support, either by a presumed father or an adjudicated father. [Presumed father and mother's] agreements in the Order of Stipulations in this particular situation, therefore, contravene the statutory scheme and directly affect [alleged biological father]: once [presumed father] is no longer considered a presumed father without the necessity of an adjudication of paternity as required by the statute, no statute of limitations applies to a suit by the child or [mother] against [alleged biological father] to establish parentage. [W]e ... hold that the trial court abused its discretion by including the findings regarding [presumed father's] nonpaternity in the agreed Order of Stipulations."

Miles v. Peacock, 229 S.W.3d 384, 387-88 (Tex. App.—Houston [1st Dist.] 2007, no pet.). Adjudicated father "asserts that the four-year statute of limitations set forth in §160.607 bars [mother's] paternity suit because she did not bring it until [child] was nearly 14 years old. 'Limitations[, however,] is an affirmative de-

* See footnote on p. 715.

fense that is waived if not pleaded.' [¶] Here, [adjudicated father] failed to answer the lawsuit and thus did not plead a limitations defense. Nor did he ever appear in the lawsuit or in any way assert a limitations defense at any point in the proceedings. Accordingly, we conclude that [adjudicated father] has waived any limitations defense, and the trial court thus did not err in entering a default judgment adjudicating his paternity."

In re S.C.L., 175 S.W.3d 555, 558-60 (Tex.App.—Dallas 2005, no pet.). "Because the U.S. Supreme Court has determined that a biological father's right to establish parentage is not constitutionally protected and statutes limiting that right are a matter of legislative policy not constitutional law, we cannot conclude [biological father's] federal due process rights are violated by applying §160.607(a). [¶] We reach a similar conclusion with respect to [biological father's] rights under the Texas due course of law guarantee. [¶] [T]he purpose of §160.607(a) is to limit the time in which to establish a parent-child relationship when there is a presumptive father so as to protect the family unit. Here, there was no longer a family unit to protect once the parental rights of [presumptive father] and [mother] were terminated. Had there been no presumptive father, [biological father] would not be precluded from establishing a parent-child relationship with [child]."

In re R.O., No. 03-04-00506-CV (Tex.App.—Austin 2005, no pet.) (memo op.; 4-21-05). "We conclude that §160.607(a) ... applies to [child's] claim because a 'child' with a presumed father is 'another individual' included in the statute's definition of those who must bring suit within the four-year limitations period."

NCCUSL Comment*

Prior Uniform Statutory Source: UPA (1973) §6; *cf.* UPC (1993) §2-114(c).

This section deals with difficult issues. First, it establishes the right of a mother or a presumed marital or nonmarital father to challenge the presumption of his paternity established by §160.204. Second, it clarifies the right of a third-party male to claim paternity of a child who has an existing presumed father.

UPA (1973) §6(a) places a [five-year] limitation on the time in which a proceeding may be brought "for the purpose of declaring the non-existence of the father and child relationship presumed under [the Act]." At that time, the comment noted that:

"Ten states have denied standing to a man claiming to be the father when the mother was married to another at the time of the child's birth. In some of these states, even though a presumed father may seek to rebut his presumed paternity, a third-party male will be denied standing to raise that same issue."

As of the year 2000, the right of an "outsider" to claim paternity of a child born to a married woman varies considerably among the states. Thirty-three states allow a man alleging himself to be the father of a child with a presumed father to rebut the marital presumption. Some states have granted this right through legislation, while in other states case law has recognized the alleged father's right to rebut the presumption and establish his paternity. In some states, there is both statutory and common law support for the standing of a man alleging himself to be the father to assert his paternity of a child born to a married woman. Not that long ago, some states imposed an absolute bar on a man commencing a proceeding to establish his paternity if state law provides a statutory presumption of the paternity of another man. *See Michael H. v. Gerald D.*, 491 U.S. 110, (1989). It is increasingly clear that those days are coming to an end.

The new UPA attempts to establish a middle ground on these exceedingly complex issues. Subsection (a) establishes a four-year limitation for rebutting the presumption of paternity established under §160.204 if the mother and presumed father were living together at the time of conception. The presumption of paternity may be attacked by the mother, the presumed father, or a third-party male during this limited period; thereafter the presumption is immune from attack by any of those individuals except as provided in subsection (b).

The reverse fact situation is also clear in subsection (b)(1); a presumption of paternity may be challenged at any time if the mother and the presumed father were not cohabiting and did not engage in sexual intercourse at the probable time of conception.

FAM §160.608. AUTHORITY TO DENY MOTION FOR GENETIC TESTING

(a) In a proceeding to adjudicate parentage, a court may deny a motion for an order for the genetic testing of the mother, the child, and the presumed father if the court determines that:

(1) the conduct of the mother or the presumed father estops that party from denying parentage; and

(2) it would be inequitable to disprove the father-child relationship between the child and the presumed father.

(b) In determining whether to deny a motion for an order for genetic testing under this section, the court shall consider the best interest of the child, including the following factors:

(1) the length of time between the date of the proceeding to adjudicate parentage and the date the presumed father was placed on notice that he might not be the genetic father;

(2) the length of time during which the presumed father has assumed the role of father of the child;

(3) the facts surrounding the presumed father's discovery of his possible nonpaternity;

(4) the nature of the relationship between the child and the presumed father;

(5) the age of the child;

(6) any harm that may result to the child if presumed paternity is successfully disproved;

(7) the nature of the relationship between the child and the alleged father;

(8) the extent to which the passage of time reduces the chances of establishing the paternity of another man and a child support obligation in favor of the child; and

* See footnote on p. 715.

(9) other factors that may affect the equities arising from the disruption of the father-child relationship between the child and the presumed father or the chance of other harm to the child.

(c) In a proceeding involving the application of this section, a child who is a minor or is incapacitated must be represented by an amicus attorney or attorney ad litem.

(d) A denial of a motion for an order for genetic testing must be based on clear and convincing evidence.

(e) If the court denies a motion for an order for genetic testing, the court shall issue an order adjudicating the presumed father to be the father of the child.

(f) This section applies to a proceeding to challenge an acknowledgment of paternity or a denial of paternity as provided by Section 160.309(d).

History of Fam. Code §160.608: Acts 2001, 77th Leg., ch. 821, §1.01, eff. June 14, 2001. Amended by Acts 2003, 78th Leg., ch. 1248, §5, eff. Sept. 1, 2003; Acts 2005, 79th Leg., ch. 172, §17, eff. Sept. 1, 2005; Acts 2011, 82nd Leg., ch. 1221, §9, eff. Sept. 1, 2011.

See also *O'Connor's Texas Family Law Handbook* (2017), "Genetic testing inequitable," ch. 4-G, §12.3.2, p. 591.

ANNOTATIONS

Hausman v. Hausman, 199 S.W.3d 38, 42 (Tex. App.—San Antonio 2006, no pet.). "The only trial court action that §160.608 addresses is whether the trial court can deny a motion requesting genetic testing. Section 160.608 does not address the trial court's authority regarding orders determining parentage. [¶] [Mother] appears to be arguing that since §160.608 codified 'paternity by estoppel,' the trial court is without authority to find estoppel under other circumstances. In this case, the trial court found that [ex-H] was not the biological father of [child] but further found that [mother] was equitably estopped from denying [ex-H's] paternity. ... Although the theory of paternity by estoppel or equitable estoppel [is also] the theory that underlies §160.608, nothing in §160.608 or any other provision of the [Family] Code appears to broadly divest a trial court of its authority to apply the principles of equitable estoppel in paternity cases." *See also* ***Stamper v. Knox***, 254 S.W.3d 537, 544-45 (Tex. App.—Houston [1st Dist.] 2008, no pet.) (factors in §160.608(b) are relevant when person whose paternity has already been disproved by genetic testing seeks to estop another from denying paternity).

In re Shockley, 123 S.W.3d 642, 651-52 (Tex. App.—El Paso 2003, no pet.). "The application of estoppel in paternity actions is aimed at achieving fairness as between the parents by holding them, both mother and father, to their prior conduct regarding the paternity of the child. Estoppel is based on the public policy that children should be secure in knowing who their parents are. If a person has acted as the parent and bonded with the child, the child should not be required to suffer the potentially damaging trauma that may come from being told that the father she has known all her life is not in fact her father. In determining whether the doctrine should be applied to a particular case, the child's best interests are of paramount concern. To that end, the courts are more inclined to impose equitable estoppel to protect the status of a child in an already recognized and operative parent-child relationship. *At 652 n.7:* It is this theory that underlies new §160.608 which authorizes a trial court to deny a motion for genetic testing of a child with a presumed father if the court finds by clear and convincing evidence that the conduct of the mother or the presumed father estops that party from denying parentage and it would be inequitable to disprove the father-child relationship. This determination requires the court to consider the best interest of the child and nine enumerated factors, including the length of time during which the presumed father has assumed the role of father." (Internal quotes omitted.) *See also* ***In re K.B.H.***, No. 11-11-00233-CV (Tex.App.—Eastland 2013, pet. denied) (memo op.; 5-23-13) (biological father was equitably estopped from asserting paternity).

NCCUSL Comment*

This section incorporates the doctrine of paternity by estoppel. In appropriate circumstances, the court may deny genetic testing and find the presumed father to be the father of the child. The most common situation in which estoppel should be applied arises when a man knows that a child is not, or may not be, his genetic child, but the man has affirmatively accepted his role as child's father and both the mother and the child have relied on that acceptance. Similarly, the man may have relied on the mother's acceptance of him as the child's father and the mother is then estopped to deny the man's presumed parentage.

Subsection (b) delineates the standards for denying genetic testing. Subsection (c) requires the child to be independently represented. Subsection (d) requires an elevated standard of proof before the order for genetic testing can be denied.

Because §160.607 places a four-year limitation on challenging the presumption of parentage, the application of this section should be applied in those meritorious cases in which the best interest of the child compels the result and the conduct of the mother and presumed or acknowledged father is clear.

FAM §160.609. TIME LIMITATION: CHILD HAVING ACKNOWLEDGED OR ADJUDICATED FATHER

(a) If a child has an acknowledged father, a signatory to the acknowledgment or denial of paternity may

* See footnote on p. 715.

commence a proceeding under this chapter to challenge the paternity of the child only within the time allowed under Section 160.308.

(b) If a child has an acknowledged father or an adjudicated father, an individual, other than the child, who is not a signatory to the acknowledgment or a party to the adjudication and who seeks an adjudication of paternity of the child must commence a proceeding not later than the fourth anniversary of the effective date of the acknowledgment or adjudication.

History of Fam. Code §160.609: Acts 2001, 77th Leg., ch. 821, §1.01, eff. June 14, 2001. Amended by Acts 2011, 82nd Leg., ch. 1221, §10, eff. Sept. 1, 2011.

ANNOTATIONS

In re R.A.H., 130 S.W.3d 68, 69-70 (Tex.2004). "The court of appeals found [petitioner's] filing untimely based on a docket sheet entry from the earlier proceeding that indicates the trial court on August 27, 1997 (1) found [putative father] admitted paternity of [child], (2) established [putative father] as the possessory conservator of [child], and (3) arranged the visitation schedule for [child]. But no order was signed adjudicating paternity until September 26, 1997. 'When there is a question concerning the date judgment was rendered, the date the judgment was signed prevails over a conflicting docket sheet entry.' [¶] We agree with the court of appeals that the 'effective date' referenced in the [UPA] should be the date the prior adjudication was rendered and that judgment is rendered 'when the decision is officially announced orally in open court, by memorandum filed with the clerk, or otherwise announced publicly.' But in this case, there is no record or evidence of an oral pronouncement at the August 1997 paternity hearing, and the only written memorandum is the unsigned docket sheet. We hold judgment was rendered and paternity adjudicated on September 26, 1997 when the trial judge signed the paternity decree."

In re K.B.S., 172 S.W.3d 152, 155 (Tex.App.—Beaumont 2005, pet. denied). "We construe the term 'adjudicated father' in §160.609 to include an adoptive father as well as a father decreed to be a biological parent of the child. Prior to [putative father] filing his petition to adjudicate parentage, [adoptive father] was adjudicated to be [child's] father pursuant to the adoption order. Because [child] had an adjudicated father, [putative father] was not free to bring his action attempting to establish paternity at any time."

FAM §160.610. JOINDER OF PROCEEDINGS

(a) Except as provided by Subsection (b), a proceeding to adjudicate parentage may be joined with a proceeding for adoption, termination of parental rights, possession of or access to a child, child support, divorce, annulment, or probate or administration of an estate or another appropriate proceeding.

(b) A respondent may not join a proceeding described by Subsection (a) with a proceeding to adjudicate parentage brought under Chapter 159.

History of Fam. Code §160.610: Acts 2001, 77th Leg., ch. 821, §1.01, eff. June 14, 2001.

NCCUSL Comment*

Prior Uniform Statutory Source: UPA (1973) §8.

Joinder of paternity proceedings with related matters is common, especially when a child support agency seeks to establish paternity and fix child support.

Subsection (b) restricts counterclaims in those instances in which an initiating state sends a paternity suit to the responding state. Because petitioner is "appearing" in the other forum, to permit counterclaims would serve as a major deterrent to bringing such proceedings. This bar does not prevent a separate action for such matters, but there must be independent jurisdiction not arising from the petitioner's appearance in the paternity proceeding.

FAM §160.611. PROCEEDINGS BEFORE BIRTH

(a) A proceeding to determine parentage commenced before the birth of the child may not be concluded until after the birth of the child.

(b) In a proceeding described by Subsection (a), the following actions may be taken before the birth of the child:

(1) service of process;

(2) discovery; and

(3) except as prohibited by Section 160.502, collection of specimens for genetic testing.

History of Fam. Code §160.611: Acts 2001, 77th Leg., ch. 821, §1.01, eff. June 14, 2001.

NCCUSL Comment*

This section recognizes that establishing a parental relationship as quickly as possible may be in the best interest of a child. To facilitate that process, some initial steps may be completed prior to the birth of the child.

FAM §160.612. CHILD AS PARTY; REPRESENTATION

(a) A minor child is a permissible party, but is not a necessary party to a proceeding under this subchapter.

(b) The court shall appoint an amicus attorney or attorney ad litem to represent a child who is a minor or is incapacitated if the child is a party or the court finds that the interests of the child are not adequately represented.

* See footnote on p. 715.

History of Fam. Code §160.612: Acts 2001, 77th Leg., ch. 821, §1.01, eff. June 14, 2001. Amended by Acts 2005, 79th Leg., ch. 172, §18, eff. Sept. 1, 2005.

NCCUSL Comment*

This section rejects UPA (1973) §9. Consistent with Section 160.603, *supra*, this Act rejects the view that the child necessarily has independent standing in a parentage proceeding. On the other hand, if the court determines that the child in fact does have a position at variance with all the other litigants, an attorney may be appointed to represent that interest.

Sections 160.613-160.620 reserved for expansion

FAM §160.621. ADMISSIBILITY OF RESULTS OF GENETIC TESTING; EXPENSES

(a) Except as otherwise provided by Subsection (c), a report of a genetic testing expert is admissible as evidence of the truth of the facts asserted in the report. The admissibility of the report is not affected by whether the testing was performed:

(1) voluntarily or under an order of the court or a support enforcement agency; or

(2) before or after the date of commencement of the proceeding.

(b) A party objecting to the results of genetic testing may call one or more genetic testing experts to testify in person or by telephone, videoconference, deposition, or another method approved by the court. Unless otherwise ordered by the court, the party offering the testimony bears the expense for the expert testifying.

(c) If a child has a presumed, acknowledged, or adjudicated father, the results of genetic testing are inadmissible to adjudicate parentage unless performed:

(1) with the consent of both the mother and the presumed, acknowledged, or adjudicated father; or

(2) under an order of the court under Section 160.502.

(d) Copies of bills for genetic testing and for prenatal and postnatal health care for the mother and child that are furnished to the adverse party on or before the 10th day before the date of a hearing are admissible to establish:

(1) the amount of the charges billed; and

(2) that the charges were reasonable, necessary, and customary.

History of Fam. Code §160.621: Acts 2001, 77th Leg., ch. 821, §1.01, eff. June 14, 2001.

See also *O'Connor's Texas Family Law Handbook* (2017), "Evidence," ch. 4-G, §13.4, p. 593.

ANNOTATIONS

Miles v. Peacock, 229 S.W.3d 384, 388 (Tex.App.—Houston [1st Dist.] 2007, no pet.). Adjudicated father "observes that there is no evidence the trial court ordered genetic testing, and notes that [child's] presumed father ... did not offer testimony about consenting to a paternity test. [Adjudicated father], however, overlooks the fact that [presumed father] (like [mother]) requested paternity testing in his counterpetition for divorce. As such, we reject [the] contention that [presumed father] did not consent to paternity testing, and we hold that the paternity test results were admissible under §160.621(c)(1)."

NCCUSL Comment*

Prior Uniform Statutory Source: 42 U.S.C. §666(a)(5)(F)(ii).

Justification for additional testing is provided by subsection (a). If the objecting party can state with specificity the grounds for rejecting a genetic test, and those grounds cannot be clarified under Subchapter F, retesting should be ordered. For example, if the chain of custody is seriously flawed, or the testing laboratory is not accredited, errors of this sort may be corrected by collecting new specimens and repeating the testing. Unlike the samples collected in a potential criminal proceeding which cannot be replaced, such as a blood alcohol test, the samples in a paternity proceedings remain the same no matter when, or how often, the samples are collected. Any flaw in the original test can be corrected by collection of new samples and additional testing of the individuals.

FAM §160.622. CONSEQUENCES OF DECLINING GENETIC TESTING

(a) An order for genetic testing is enforceable by contempt.

(b) A court may adjudicate parentage contrary to the position of an individual whose paternity is being determined on the grounds that the individual declines to submit to genetic testing as ordered by the court.

(c) Genetic testing of the mother of a child is not a prerequisite to testing the child and a man whose paternity is being determined. If the mother is unavailable or declines to submit to genetic testing, the court may order the testing of the child and each man whose paternity is being adjudicated.

History of Fam. Code §160.622: Acts 2001, 77th Leg., ch. 821, §1.01, eff. June 14, 2001.

NCCUSL Comment*

Prior Uniform Statutory Source: UPA (1973) §10.

FAM §160.623. ADMISSION OF PATERNITY AUTHORIZED

(a) A respondent in a proceeding to adjudicate parentage may admit to the paternity of a child by filing a pleading to that effect or by admitting paternity under penalty of perjury when making an appearance or during a hearing.

(b) If the court finds that the admission of paternity satisfies the requirements of this section and that

* See footnote on p. 715.

there is no reason to question the admission, the court shall render an order adjudicating the child to be the child of the man admitting paternity.

History of Fam. Code §160.623: Acts 2001, 77th Leg., ch. 821, §1.01, eff. June 14, 2001.

NCCUSL Comment*

Prior Uniform Statutory Source: 42 U.S.C. §666(a)(5)(D)(i)(II).

FAM §160.624. TEMPORARY ORDER

(a) In a proceeding under this subchapter, the court shall render a temporary order for child support for a child if the order is appropriate and the individual ordered to pay child support:

(1) is a presumed father of the child;

(2) is petitioning to have his paternity adjudicated;

(3) is identified as the father through genetic testing under Section 160.505;

(4) is an alleged father who has declined to submit to genetic testing;

(5) is shown by clear and convincing evidence to be the father of the child; or

(6) is the mother of the child.

(b) A temporary order may include provisions for the possession of or access to the child as provided by other laws of this state.

History of Fam. Code §160.624: Acts 2001, 77th Leg., ch. 821, §1.01, eff. June 14, 2001.

NCCUSL Comment*

Prior Uniform Statutory Source: UIFSA (1996) §401; 42 U.S.C. §666(a)(5)(J).

Sections 160.625-160.630 reserved for expansion

FAM §160.631. RULES FOR ADJUDICATION OF PATERNITY

(a) The court shall apply the rules stated in this section to adjudicate the paternity of a child.

(b) The paternity of a child having a presumed, acknowledged, or adjudicated father may be disproved only by admissible results of genetic testing excluding that man as the father of the child or identifying another man as the father of the child.

(c) Unless the results of genetic testing are admitted to rebut other results of genetic testing, the man identified as the father of a child under Section 160.505 shall be adjudicated as being the father of the child.

(d) Unless the results of genetic testing are admitted to rebut other results of genetic testing, a man excluded as the father of a child by genetic testing shall be adjudicated as not being the father of the child.

(e) If the court finds that genetic testing under Section 160.505 does not identify or exclude a man as the father of a child, the court may not dismiss the proceeding. In that event, the results of genetic testing and other evidence are admissible to adjudicate the issue of paternity.

History of Fam. Code §160.631: Acts 2001, 77th Leg., ch. 821, §1.01, eff. June 14, 2001.

See also *O'Connor's Texas Family Law Handbook* (2017), "Suit to Adjudicate Parentage," ch. 4-G, p. 573.

NCCUSL Comment*

Prior Uniform Statutory Source: UPA (1973) §14.

This section establishes the controlling supremacy of admissible genetic test results in the adjudication of paternity. Other matters such as statute of limitations, equitable estoppel and res judicata may preclude the matter from reaching trial or the court denying genetic testing. However, if test results are admissible, those results control unless other test results create a conflict rebutting the admitted results.

The inclusion of the first clause in paragraph (d) indicates that although a genetic testing exclusion of paternity can be absolute, errors (and sometimes fraud) may occur in testing. Some courts have imposed a rule that a party must first show the test is in error before ordering another test. This imposes an impossible burden because the only accurate method to show that a test is in error is to repeat the testing. Without this clause, some litigants might argue that once an exclusion is obtained it is absolute and no other test can be ordered, even when the first test is shown to be wrong.

Paragraph (e) is included to ensure that the fact a genetic test does not reach the 99% level decreed in Section 160.505 will not be perceived as an indicator of an exclusion of paternity. Although test results that do not reach that level do not create a presumption of paternity, the testing should be evaluated as an indicator of paternity along with the other evidence of paternity presented in the proceeding. Presumably expert testimony will be required to provide information about the measure of the weight of a test that does not achieve "at least a 99 percent probability of paternity, using a prior probability of 0.50, as calculated by using the combined paternity index obtained in the testing, and a combined paternity index of at least 100 to 1."

FAM §160.632. JURY PROHIBITED

The court shall adjudicate paternity of a child without a jury.

History of Fam. Code §160.632: Acts 2001, 77th Leg., ch. 821, §1.01, eff. June 14, 2001.

NCCUSL Comment*

Prior Uniform Statutory Source: 42 U.S.C. §666(a)(5)(I), requiring state law to provide that "parties to an action to establish paternity are not entitled to trial by jury...."

UPA (1973) §14[(d)] prohibited jury trials in parentage proceedings on the basis that "The use of a jury is not desirable in the emotional atmosphere of cases of this nature." Congress agreed when it enacted an effectively identical prohibition in PRWORA (1996).

FAM §160.633. HEARINGS; INSPECTION OF RECORDS

(a) A proceeding under this subchapter is open to the public as in other civil cases.

(b) Papers and records in a proceeding under this subchapter are available for public inspection.

History of Fam. Code §160.633: Acts 2001, 77th Leg., ch. 821, §1.01, eff. June 14, 2001. Amended by Acts 2003, 78th Leg., ch. 610, §11, eff. Sept. 1, 2003.

* See footnote on p. 715.

NCCUSL Comment*

Prior Uniform Statutory Source: UPA (1973) §20.

UPA (1973) §20 was concerned with the privacy of the parties in a paternity proceeding and required closure of the proceedings. The high caseload and the desensitizing of such proceedings, however, lead to the conclusion that mandating closure of the proceedings is no longer appropriate.

FAM §160.634. ORDER ON DEFAULT

The court shall issue an order adjudicating the paternity of a man who:

(1) after service of process, is in default; and

(2) is found by the court to be the father of a child.

History of Fam. Code §160.634: Acts 2001, 77th Leg., ch. 821, §1.01, eff. June 14, 2001.

NCCUSL Comment*

Prior Uniform Statutory Source: 42 U.S.C. §666(a)(5)(H).

FAM §160.635. DISMISSAL FOR WANT OF PROSECUTION

The court may issue an order dismissing a proceeding commenced under this chapter for want of prosecution only without prejudice. An order of dismissal for want of prosecution purportedly with prejudice is void and has only the effect of a dismissal without prejudice.

History of Fam. Code §160.635: Acts 2001, 77th Leg., ch. 821, §1.01, eff. June 14, 2001.

NCCUSL Comment*

A major principle of the new UPA—and its predecessor—is that the child's right to have a determination of paternity is fundamental. This new section confirms this right by declaring that the delinquency of another person in prosecuting such a proceeding, *e.g.*, the mother or a support enforcement agency, may not permanently preclude the ultimate resolution of a parentage determination.

FAM §160.636. ORDER ADJUDICATING PARENTAGE; COSTS

(a) The court shall render an order adjudicating whether a man alleged or claiming to be the father is the parent of the child.

(b) An order adjudicating parentage must identify the child by name and date of birth.

(c) Except as otherwise provided by Subsection (d), the court may assess filing fees, reasonable attorney's fees, fees for genetic testing, other costs, and necessary travel and other reasonable expenses incurred in a proceeding under this subchapter. Attorney's fees awarded by the court may be paid directly to the attorney. An attorney who is awarded attorney's fees may enforce the order in the attorney's own name.

(d) The court may not assess fees, costs, or expenses against the support enforcement agency of this state or another state, except as provided by other law.

(e) On request of a party and for good cause shown, the court may order that the name of the child be changed.

(f) If the order of the court is at variance with the child's birth certificate, the court shall order the vital statistics unit to issue an amended birth record.

(g) On a finding of parentage, the court may order retroactive child support as provided by Chapter 154 and, on a proper showing, order a party to pay an equitable portion of all of the prenatal and postnatal health care expenses of the mother and the child.

(h) In rendering an order for retroactive child support under this section, the court shall use the child support guidelines provided by Chapter 154, together with any relevant factors.

History of Fam. Code §160.636: Acts 2001, 77th Leg., ch. 821, §1.01, eff. June 14, 2001. Amended by Acts 2015, 84th Leg., ch. 1, §1.075, eff. Apr. 2, 2015.

See also ***O'Connor's Texas Family Law Handbook*** (2017), "Judgment," ch. 4-G, §14, p. 595.

ANNOTATIONS

In re C.M.V., 479 S.W.3d 352, 358 (Tex.App.—El Paso 2015, no pet.). "A father does not have a constitutional right to have his children bear his last name. The ... Family Code permits a court to change the name of a child if the change is in the child's best interest. Additionally, in a case where the court has adjudicated parentage, a court may, on request of a party and for good cause shown, change the child's name. '[G]ood cause' and 'best interest' are distinct concepts and a parent seeking to change a child's name under §160.636(e) must establish both." *See also* ***In re S.M.V.***, 287 S.W.3d 435, 447-48 (Tex.App.—Dallas 2009, no pet.) (good cause is defined as "legally sufficient reason" for changing child's name); ***In re M.C.F.***, 121 S.W.3d 891, 895 (Tex.App.—Fort Worth 2003, no pet.) (court must determine whether good cause was shown for name change, and then whether change is in child's best interest). *But see* ***Anderson v. Dainard***, this page.

Anderson v. Dainard, 478 S.W.3d 147, 151 (Tex. App.—Houston [1st Dist.] 2015, no pet.). For a name change under Fam. Code §45.004 or §160.636, "[t]he child's best interest is the determinative issue; the interests of the parents are irrelevant. *At 151 n.1:* The good cause requirement in §160.636(e) is subsumed in the analysis of the best interest of the child, '[b]ecause the best interest of a child will necessarily be considered good cause for changing the child's name.' *At 152:* The evidence before the trial court was ... mixed. *At 153:* [I]t was not an abuse of discretion to determine

* See footnote on p. 715.

that it was in [child's] best interest to change her surname in order to facilitate the formation of a father-daughter bond with [father], who was meeting his obligations to [child] and expressed a desire to form a father-daughter bond that the trial court found sincere." *See also* ***In re H.S.B.***, 401 S.W.3d 77, 81 n.2 (Tex.App.—Houston [14th Dist.] 2011, no pet.) (best interest of child will necessarily be considered good cause for changing child's name; appellate court restricted analysis to best interest and presumed trial court found good cause on same ground). *But see* ***In re C.M.V.***, p. 740.

In re B.B.R., 188 S.W.3d 341, 345 (Tex.App.—Fort Worth 2006, no pet.). Adoption agency "argues that [§160.636] is intended to apply to parents only. However, [adoption agency] does not cite, and we have not found, any authority for this proposition when the parentage action is filed *by the father* in an effort to contest a nonparent's attempts to terminate his parental rights. While the statute does exclude governmental agencies from having attorney's fees assessed against them, … the mere fact that governmental agencies are excluded does not establish that the statute allows assessment of attorney's fees against parents alone. … The family code does not limit the parties against whom the trial court may assess reasonable attorney's fees in a parentage action, so we decline to hold that the trial court abused its discretion by assessing attorney's fees against [adoption agency]."

In re M.C.F., 121 S.W.3d 891, 895 (Tex.App.—Fort Worth 2003, no pet.). "While we recognize that a name change in connection with a paternity action under [Fam. Code] ch. 160 is not the same as a name change under [Fam. Code] ch. 45, we believe that the ch. 45 cases may be looked to in determining a child's best interest regarding the name change in a paternity action." *See also* ***In re A.J.P.***, No. 05-07-01772-CV (Tex. App.—Dallas 2009, no pet.) (memo op.; 2-17-09) (petition for name change under §160.636 must be verified as required by Fam. Code §45.002).

NCCUSL Comment*

Prior Uniform Statutory Source: UIFSA (1996) §313; UPA (1973) §§15, 16, 23.

This Act differs from UPA (1973), which attempted to do more than merely establish parentage. For example, UPA (1973) §15 provided for a wide range of court orders to be made relating to the child's support, custody, guardianship, visitation privileges, as well as to the payment by the father of the mother's expenses of pregnancy and confinement. This Act leaves such matters to other state law. Only in instances where other state law is likely to be inadequate does this Act specify special treatment for litigants. For example, subsections (c) and (d) may be required because ordinary civil litigation probably does not provide for the court to apportion the costs of litigation among the parties.

FAM §160.637. BINDING EFFECT OF DETERMINATION OF PARENTAGE

(a) Except as otherwise provided by Subsection (b) or Section 160.316, a determination of parentage is binding on:

(1) all signatories to an acknowledgment or denial of paternity as provided by Subchapter D; and

(2) all parties to an adjudication by a court acting under circumstances that satisfy the jurisdictional requirements of Section 159.201.

(b) A child is not bound by a determination of parentage under this chapter unless:

(1) the determination was based on an unrescinded acknowledgment of paternity and the acknowledgment is consistent with the results of genetic testing;

(2) the adjudication of parentage was based on a finding consistent with the results of genetic testing and the consistency is declared in the determination or is otherwise shown; or

(3) the child was a party or was represented in the proceeding determining parentage by an attorney ad litem.

(c) In a proceeding to dissolve a marriage, the court is considered to have made an adjudication of the parentage of a child if the court acts under circumstances that satisfy the jurisdictional requirements of Section 159.201, and the final order:

(1) expressly identifies the child as "a child of the marriage" or "issue of the marriage" or uses similar words indicating that the husband is the father of the child; or

(2) provides for the payment of child support for the child by the husband unless paternity is specifically disclaimed in the order.

(d) Except as otherwise provided by Subsection (b), a determination of parentage may be a defense in a subsequent proceeding seeking to adjudicate parentage by an individual who was not a party to the earlier proceeding.

(e) A party to an adjudication of paternity may challenge the adjudication only under the laws of this state relating to appeal, the vacating of judgments, or other judicial review.

History of Fam. Code §160.637: Acts 2001, 77th Leg., ch. 821, §1.01, eff. June 14, 2001.

* See footnote on p. 715.

ANNOTATIONS

In re R.J.P., 179 S.W.3d 181, 185 (Tex.App.—Houston [14th Dist.] 2005, no pet.). "Because [petitioner] did not challenge the 1998 order adjudicating his biological paternity 'under the laws of this state,' [according to §160.637(e),] we must determine whether the trial court was barred from relitigating [his] biological paternity in determining his child support obligation. *At 186:* We conclude collateral estoppel barred the issue of [petitioner's] biological paternity from being relitigated in this suit.... Thus, the trial court abused its discretion when it considered the paternity results in its determination of [petitioner's] child support obligation."

Baize v. Baize, 93 S.W.3d 197, 201-02 (Tex.App.—Houston [14th Dist.] 2002, pet. denied). "A finding of fact in a divorce decree that a child was born to the marriage of the parties is a binding determination that the husband is the father of the child. [¶] We must decide whether the trial court abused its discretion in determining that [mother's] paternity challenge was untimely because [mother] initiated this challenge after the trial court had decreed a divorce in accordance with the parties' settlement agreement. [¶] [Mother] had ample time and opportunity to contest paternity throughout the parties' divorce proceeding. She did not do so. Instead, she waited until after the trial court decreed divorce, a decree wholly in accordance with her settlement agreement and based in part on her testimony indicating that [child] is [father's] son. On the facts of this case, we conclude the trial court did not abuse its discretion...."

NCCUSL Comment*

A considerable amount of litigation involves exactly who is bound and who is not bound by a final order determining parentage. This section codifies rules regarding the effect of such orders. Subsection (a) provides that, if the order is issued under standards of personal jurisdiction of the UIFSA (1996), the order is binding on all parties to the proceeding. This solves the problem of an order issued without the appropriate jurisdiction, as would be the case of a divorce based on status jurisdiction in which the court lacked the requisite personal jurisdiction over a nonresident party.

Subsection (b) partially resolves the question of whether a child is bound by the terms of the order. UPA (1973) required that the child be made a party to a parentage proceeding, and be bound. However, the 1973 Act did not address whether a divorce decree had a legal impact on paternity. A majority of jurisdictions hold that the child is not bound by the divorce decree because the child was not a party to the proceeding. A minority of states hold that the child is bound by the order and that the child is in privity with the parents. In its present formulation, this subsection adopts the majority rule, which does not bind the child during minority unless the parentage order is based on genetic testing or the child was represented by an attorney ad litem.

Subsection (c) resolves whether a divorce decree constitutes a finding of paternity. This subsection provides that a decree is a determination of paternity if the decree states that the child was born of the marriage or grants the husband visitation or custody, or orders support. This is the majority rule in American jurisprudence.

Subsection (d) gives protection to third parties who may claim benefit of an earlier determination of parentage.

Finally, the section is silent on whether state IV-D agencies are bound by prior determinations of parentage. This controversial issue is left to other state law. Similarly, issues of collateral attack on final judgments are to be resolved by recourse to other state law, as in civil proceedings generally.

Sections 160.638-160.700 reserved for expansion

SUBCHAPTER H. CHILD OF ASSISTED REPRODUCTION

NCCUSL Prefatory Comment*

During the last thirty years, medical science has developed a wide array of assisted reproductive technology, often referred to as ART, which have enabled childless individuals and couples to become parents. Thousands of children are born in the United States each year as the result of ART. If a married couple uses their own eggs and sperm to conceive a child born to the wife, the parentage of the child is straightforward. The wife is the mother—by gestation and genetics, the husband is the father—by genetics and presumption. And, insofar as the Uniform Parentage Act is concerned, neither parent fits the definition of a "donor."

Current state laws and practices are not so straightforward, however. If a woman gives birth to a child conceived using sperm from a man other than her husband, she is the mother and her husband, if any, is the presumed father. However, the man who provided the sperm might assert his biological paternity, or the husband might seek to rebut the marital presumption of paternity by proving through genetic testing that he is not the genetic father. As was the case in UPA (1973), it is necessary for the new Act to clarify definitively the parentage of a child born under these circumstances.

Similarly, assisted reproduction may involve the eggs from a woman other than the mother—perhaps using the intended father's sperm, perhaps not. In either event, the new Act makes a policy decision to clearly exclude the egg donor from claiming maternity. Theoretically, it is even possible that absent appropriate legislation the mother could attempt to deny maternity based on her lack of genetic relationship.

Finally, many couples employ a common ART procedure that combines sperm and eggs to form a pre-zygote that is then frozen for future use. If the couple later divorces, or one of them dies, absent legislation there are no clear rules for determining the parentage of a child resulting from a pre-zygote implanted after divorce or after the death of the would-be father. Disposition of such pre-zygotes, or even issues of their "ownership," create not only broad publicity, but also are problems on which courts need guidance.

FAM §160.701. SCOPE OF SUBCHAPTER

This subchapter applies only to a child conceived by means of assisted reproduction.

History of Fam. Code §160.701: Acts 2001, 77th Leg., ch. 821, §1.01, eff. June 14, 2001.

NCCUSL Comment*

Subchapter H applies only to children born as the result of assisted reproduction technologies; a child conceived by sexual intercourse is not covered by this article, irrespective of the alleged intent of the parties.

FAM §160.702. PARENTAL STATUS OF DONOR

A donor is not a parent of a child conceived by means of assisted reproduction.

History of Fam. Code §160.702: Acts 2001, 77th Leg., ch. 821, §1.01, eff. June 14, 2001.

* See footnote on p. 715.

ANNOTATIONS

In re P.S., 505 S.W.3d 106, 110 (Tex.App.—Fort Worth 2016, no pet.). See annotation under Family Code §160.102, p. 717.

In re Sullivan, 157 S.W.3d 911, 919 (Tex.App.—Houston [14th Dist.] 2005, orig. proceeding). "If the Texas Legislature ... had intended to exclude donors from the class of those who have standing [under Fam. Code §160.602] to maintain a parentage proceeding, they easily could have excluded donors from the group of men 'whose paternity is to be adjudicated.' The omission of such an exclusion from the statute suggests that our lawmakers intended a sperm donor to have standing as a man 'whose paternity is to be adjudicated.' [¶] We ... conclude that under the statute, as drafted, the issue of the man's status as a donor under [Fam. Code] §160.702 is to be decided at the merits stage of the litigation rather than as part of the threshold issue of standing [under §160.602]." *But see* ***In re H.C.S.***, 219 S.W.3d 33, 35-36 (Tex.App.—San Antonio 2006, no pet.) (sperm donor does not have standing).

NCCUSL Comment*

Prior Uniform Statutory Source: UPA (1973) §5(b); USCACA (1988) §4(a).

If a child is conceived as the result of assisted reproduction, this section clarifies that a donor (whether of sperm or egg) is not a parent of the resulting child. The donor can neither sue to establish parental rights, nor be sued and required to support the resulting child. In sum, donors are eliminated from the parental equation.

The new UPA does not deal with many of the complex and serious legal problems raised by the practice of assisted reproduction. Issues such as ownership and disposition of embryos, regulation of the medical procedures, insurance coverage, etc., are left to other statutes or to the common law. Only the issue of parentage falls within the purview of this Act. This was also the case in UPA (1973), which wholly deferred speaking on the subject except to ensure the husband's paternal responsibility when he gave his consent to what was then called "artificial insemination" of his wife (now known in the scientific community as "intrauterine insemination"). The commentary to UPA (1973) stated: "It was thought useful, however, to single out and cover ... at least one fact situation that occurs frequently."

The new UPA goes well beyond that narrow view; it governs the parentage issues in all cases in which the birth mother is also the woman who intends to parent the child. It also ensures that if the mother is a married woman, her husband will be the father of the child if he gives his consent to assisted reproduction by his wife, regardless of which aspect of ART is utilized. Further, this section of the new UPA does not limit a donor's statutory exemption from becoming a legal parent of a child resulting from ART to a situation in which the donor provides sperm for assisted reproduction by a married woman. This requirement is not realistic in light of present ART practices and the constitutional protections of the procreative rights of unmarried as well as married women. Consequently, this section shields all donors, whether of sperm or eggs, (§160.102 (6), *supra*), from parenthood in all situations in which either a married woman or a single woman conceives a child through ART with the intent to be the child's parent, either by herself or with a man, as provided in sections 160.703 and 160.704.

If a married woman bears a child of assisted reproduction using a donor's sperm, the donor will not be the father in any event. Her husband will be the father unless and until the husband's lack of consent to the assisted reproduction is proven within four years of his learning of the birth, *see* §160.705, *infra*. This provides certainty of nonparentage for prospective donors.

The comment to now-withdrawn USCACA §4(a) states that "nonparenthood is also provided for those donors who provide sperm for assisted reproduction by unmarried women." Under those circumstances—called a "relatively rare situation" in the 1988 comment—"the child would have no legally recognized father." This result is retained in the new UPA, although the frequency of unmarried women using assisted reproduction appears to have grown significantly since 1988.

* See footnote on p. 715.

FAM §160.703. HUSBAND'S PATERNITY OF CHILD OF ASSISTED REPRODUCTION

If a husband provides sperm for or consents to assisted reproduction by his wife as provided by Section 160.704, he is the father of a resulting child.

History of Fam. Code §160.703: Acts 2001, 77th Leg., ch. 821, §1.01, eff. June 14, 2001.

NCCUSL Comment*

Prior Uniform Statutory Source: UPA (1973) §5; USCACA (1988) §§1, 3.

The father-child relationship is created between a man and the resulting child if the man provides sperm for, or consents to, assisted reproduction by his wife, *see* §160.704, *infra*. Given the dramatic increase in the use of ART in the United States during the past decade, it is crucial to clarify the parentage of all of the children born as a result of modern science.

FAM §160.7031. UNMARRIED MAN'S PATERNITY OF CHILD OF ASSISTED REPRODUCTION

(a) If an unmarried man, with the intent to be the father of a resulting child, provides sperm to a licensed physician and consents to the use of that sperm for assisted reproduction by an unmarried woman, he is the father of a resulting child.

(b) Consent by an unmarried man who intends to be the father of a resulting child in accordance with this section must be in a record signed by the man and the unmarried woman and kept by a licensed physician.

History of Fam. Code §160.7031: Acts 2007, 80th Leg., ch. 972, §40, eff. Sept. 1, 2007.

FAM §160.704. CONSENT TO ASSISTED REPRODUCTION

(a) Consent by a married woman to assisted reproduction must be in a record signed by the woman and her husband and kept by a licensed physician. This requirement does not apply to the donation of eggs by a married woman for assisted reproduction by another woman.

(b) Failure by the husband to sign a consent required by Subsection (a) before or after the birth of the child does not preclude a finding that the husband is the father of a child born to his wife if the wife and husband openly treated the child as their own.

History of Fam. Code §160.704: Acts 2001, 77th Leg., ch. 821, §1.01, eff. June 14, 2001. Amended by Acts 2007, 80th Leg., ch. 972, §41, eff. Sept. 1, 2007.

NCCUSL Comment*

Prior Uniform Statutory Source: UPA (1973) §5; UPC (1993) §2-114(c).

Subsection (b) provides that even if a husband did not consent to assisted reproduction, he may nonetheless be found to be the father of a child born through that means if he and the mother openly treat the child as their own. This principle is taken from the Uniform Probate Code §2C114(c) (1993), which provides that neither "natural parent" nor kindred may inherit from or through a child "unless that natural parent has openly treated the child as his [or hers], and has not refused to support the child." The treatment requirement substitutes evidence of the parties' conduct after the child is born for the requirement of formal consent in a record to prospective assisted reproduction. The "non-support" phrase in §2C114(c) was not carried forward in subsection (b) (and the term "natural parent" has been replaced by more accurate terminology).

FAM §160.705. LIMITATION ON HUSBAND'S DISPUTE OF PATERNITY

(a) Except as otherwise provided by Subsection (b), the husband of a wife who gives birth to a child by means of assisted reproduction may not challenge his paternity of the child unless:

(1) before the fourth anniversary of the date of learning of the birth of the child he commences a proceeding to adjudicate his paternity; and

(2) the court finds that he did not consent to the assisted reproduction before or after the birth of the child.

(b) A proceeding to adjudicate paternity may be maintained at any time if the court determines that:

(1) the husband did not provide sperm for or, before or after the birth of the child, consent to assisted reproduction by his wife;

(2) the husband and the mother of the child have not cohabited since the probable time of assisted reproduction; and

(3) the husband never openly treated the child as his own.

(c) The limitations provided by this section apply to a marriage declared invalid after assisted reproduction.

History of Fam. Code §160.705: Acts 2001, 77th Leg., ch. 821, §1.01, eff. June 14, 2001.

NCCUSL Comment*

Prior Uniform Statutory Source: USCACA (1988) §3; UPC (1993) §2-114(c).

Subsection (a) provides for a challenge to a husband's presumed paternity if the conception of the child was through assisted reproduction not consented to by the husband before or after the birth of the child. If a proceeding to establish nonpaternity is timely filed and the husband's lack of consent is demonstrated, the child will be without a legally-recognized father because the sperm donor is not the father under §160.702, *supra*. Because the filing of such a nonpaternity proceeding is permitted within four years of the husband's learning of the child's birth, the period of uncertainty concerning the identity of the child's father will be longer than four years in a situation in which an absent husband is not immediately made aware of the child's birth.

Subsection (b) provides an exception to the four-year time limit if the husband's sperm was not used, the couple has not cohabited since the probable time of the use of assisted reproduction, and the husband has never openly treated the child as his own.

FAM §160.706. EFFECT OF DISSOLUTION OF MARRIAGE

(a) If a marriage is dissolved before the placement of eggs, sperm, or embryos, the former spouse is not a parent of the resulting child unless the former spouse consented in a record kept by a licensed physician that if assisted reproduction were to occur after a divorce the former spouse would be a parent of the child.

(b) The consent of a former spouse to assisted reproduction may be withdrawn by that individual in a record kept by a licensed physician at any time before the placement of eggs, sperm, or embryos.

History of Fam. Code §160.706: Acts 2001, 77th Leg., ch. 821, §1.01, eff. June 14, 2001. Amended by Acts 2007, 80th Leg., ch. 972, §42, eff. Sept. 1, 2007.

ANNOTATIONS

Roman v. Roman, 193 S.W.3d 40, 44 (Tex.App.—Houston [1st Dist.] 2006, pet. denied). "In this case of first impression in Texas, we consider the merits of the trial court's award of frozen embryos to [W] as part of a 'just and right' division of community property in light of the parties' prior written agreement to discard the embryos. *At 50:* We believe that allowing the parties voluntarily to decide the disposition of frozen embryos in advance of cryopreservation, subject to mutual change of mind, jointly expressed, best serves the existing public policy of this State and the interests of the parties. We hold, therefore, that an embryo agreement that satisfies these criteria does not violate the public policy of the State of Texas. *At 54-55:* [Further, we] hold that the embryo agreement provides that the frozen embryos are to be discarded in the event of divorce. By awarding the frozen embryos to [W], the trial court improperly rewrote the parties' agreement instead of enforcing what the parties had voluntarily decided in the event of divorce."

NCCUSL Comment*

This section is entirely new to the Parentage Act, but its logic is derived from the policy stated in §160.707, *infra*. Subsection (a) applies only to married couples and posits that if there is to be no liability for a child conceived by assisted reproduction after death, then there should be no liability for a child conceived or implanted after divorce. If a former wife proceeds with assisted reproduction after a divorce, the former husband is not the legal parent of the resulting child unless he had previously consented in a record to post-divorce assisted reproduction. If such were the case, subsection (b) provides a mechanism for him to withdraw that consent, *i.e.*, by so stating in a record (presumably to be filed with the laboratory in which the sperm or embryos are stored).

A child born through assisted reproduction accomplished after consent has been voided by divorce or withdrawn in a record will have a legal mother

* See footnote on p. 715.

under §160.201(a)(1). However, the child will have a genetic father, but not a legal father. In this instance, intention, rather than biology, is the controlling factor. The section is intended to encourage careful drafting of assisted reproduction agreements. The attorney and the parties themselves should discuss the issue and clarify their intent before a problem arises.

This Act does not attempt to resolve issues as to control of frozen embryos following dissolution of marital or nonmarital relationships. As indicated in the prefatory note, those matters are left to other state laws.

FAM §160.707. PARENTAL STATUS OF DECEASED SPOUSE

If a spouse dies before the placement of eggs, sperm, or embryos, the deceased spouse is not a parent of the resulting child unless the deceased spouse consented in a record kept by a licensed physician that if assisted reproduction were to occur after death the deceased spouse would be a parent of the child.

History of Fam. Code §160.707: Acts 2001, 77th Leg., ch. 821, §1.01, eff. June 14, 2001. Amended by Acts 2007, 80th Leg., ch. 972, §43, eff. Sept. 1, 2007.

NCCUSL Comment*

Prior Uniform Statutory Source: USCACA (1988) §4[.]

Absent consent in a record, the death of a spouse whose genetic material is subsequently used either in conceiving an embryo or in implanting an already existing embryo into a womb ends the potential legal parenthood of the deceased. This section is designed primarily to avoid the problems of intestate succession which could arise if the posthumous use of a person's genetic material leads to the deceased being determined to be a parent. Of course, a spouse who wants to explicitly provide for such children in his or her will may do so.

Sections 160.708-160.750 blank

SUBCHAPTER I. GESTATIONAL AGREEMENTS

NCCUSL Prefatory Comment*

The longstanding shortage of adoptable children in this country has led many would-be parents to enlist a gestational mother (previously referred to as a "surrogate mother") to bear a child for them. As contrasted with the assisted reproduction regulated by Subchapter H, which involves the would-be parent or parents and most commonly one and sometimes two anonymous donors, the gestational agreement (previously known as a surrogacy agreement) provided in this subchapter is designed to involve at least three parties; the intended mother and father and the woman who agrees to bear a child for them through the use of assisted reproduction (the gestational mother). Additional people may be involved. For example, if the proposed gestational mother is married, her husband, if any, must be included in the agreement to dispense with his presumptive paternity of a child born to his wife. Further, an egg donor or a sperm donor, or both, may be involved, although neither will be joined as a party to the agreement. Thus, by definition, a child born pursuant to a gestational agreement will need to have maternity as well as paternity clarified.

The subject of gestational agreements was last addressed by the National Conference of Commissioners on Uniform State Laws in 1988 with the adoption of the Uniform Status of Children of Assisted Conception Act (USCACA). Because some Commissioners believed that such agreements should be prohibited, while others believed that such agreements should be allowed, but regulated, USCACA offered two alternatives on the subject; either to regulate such activities through a judicial review process or to void such contracts. As might have been predicted, the only two states to enact USCACA selected opposite options; Virginia chose to regulate such agreements, while North Dakota opted to void them.

In the years since the promulgation of USCACA (and virtual de facto rejection of that Act), approximately one-half of the states developed statutory or case law on the issue. Of those, about one-half recognized such agreements, and the other half rejected them. A survey in December, 2000, revealed a wide variety of approaches: eleven states allow gestational agreements by statute or case law; six states void such agreements by statute; eight states do not ban agreements per se, but statutorily ban compensation to the gestational mother, which as a practical matter limits the likelihood of agreement to close relatives; and two states judicially refuse to recognize such agreements. In states rejecting gestational agreements, the legal status of children born pursuant to such an agreement is uncertain. If gestational agreements are voided or criminalized, individuals determined to become parents through this method will seek a friendlier legal forum. This raises a host of legal issues. For example, a couple may return to their home state with a child born as the consequence of a gestational agreement recognized in another state. This presents a full faith and credit question if their home state has a statute declaring gestational agreements to be void or criminal.

Despite the legal uncertainties, thousands of children are born each year pursuant to gestational agreements. One thing is clear; a child born under these circumstances is entitled to have its status clarified. Therefore, NCCUSL once again ventured into this controversial subject, withdrawing USCACA and substituting Subchapter I of the new UPA. The subchapter incorporates many of the USCACA provisions allowing validation and enforcement of gestational agreements, along with some important modifications.

Subchapter I's replacement of the USCACA terminology, "surrogate mother," by "gestational mother" is important. First, labeling a woman who bears a child a "surrogate" does not comport with the dictionary definition of the term under any construction, to wit: "a person appointed to act in the place of another" or "something serving as a substitute." The term is especially misleading when "surrogate" refers to a woman who supplies both "egg and womb," that is, a woman who is a genetic as well as gestational mother. That combination is now typically avoided by the majority of ART practitioners in order to decrease the possibility that a genetic/gestational mother will be unwilling to relinquish her child to unrelated intended parents. Further, the term "surrogate" has acquired a negative connotation in American society, which confuses rather than enlightens the discussion.

In contrast, term "gestational mother" is both more accurate and more inclusive. It applies to both a woman who, through assisted reproduction, performs the gestational function without being genetically related to a child, and a woman is both the gestational and genetic mother. The key is that an agreement has been made that the child is to be raised by the intended parents. The latter practice has elicited disfavor in the ART community, which has concluded that the gestational mother's genetic link to the child too often creates additional emotional and psychological problems in enforcing a gestational agreement.

The new UPA treats entering into a gestational agreement as a significant legal act that should be approved by a court, just as an adoption is judicially approved. The procedure established generally follows that of USCACA, but departs from its terms in several important ways. First, nonvalidated gestational agreements are unenforceable (not void), thereby providing a strong incentive for the participants to seek judicial scrutiny. Second, there is no longer a requirement that at least one of the intended parents would be genetically related to the child born of the gestational agreement. Third, individuals who enter into nonvalidated gestational agreements and later refuse to adopt the resulting child may be liable for support of the child.

Although legal recognition of gestational agreements remains controversial, the plain fact is that medical technologies have raced ahead of the law without heed to the views of the general public—or legislators. Courts have recently come to acknowledge this reality when forced to render decisions regarding collaborative reproduction, noting that artificial insemination, gestational carriers, cloning and gene splicing are part of the present, as well as of the future. One court predicted that even if all forms of assisted reproduction were outlawed in a particular state, its courts would still be called upon to decide on the identity of the lawful parents of a child resulting from those procedures undertaken in less restrictive states. This court noted:

Again we must call on the Legislature to sort out the parental rights and responsibilities of those involved in artificial reproduction. No matter what one thinks of artificial insemination, traditional and gestational surrogacy (in all of its permutations) and as now appears in the not too distant future, cloning and even gene splicing—courts are still going to be faced with the problem of determining lawful parentage. A child cannot be ignored. Even if all the means of artificial reproduction were outlawed with draconian criminal penalties visited on the doctors and parties involved, courts would still be called upon to decide who the lawful parents are and who—other than the taxpayers—is obligated to provide maintenance and support for the child. These cases will not go

* See footnote on p. 715.

away. Again we must call on the Legislature to sort out the parental rights and responsibilities of those involved in artificial reproduction. Courts can continue to make decisions on an ad hoc basis without necessarily imposing some grand scheme. Or, the Legislature can act to impose a broader order which, even though it might not be perfect on a case-by-case basis, would bring some predictability to those who seek to make use of artificial reproductive techniques.

FAM §160.751. DEFINITION

In this subchapter, "gestational mother" means a woman who gives birth to a child conceived under a gestational agreement.

History of Fam. Code §160.751: Acts 2003, 78th Leg., ch. 457, §2, eff. Sept. 1, 2003.

NCCUSL Comment*

Section 160.751, "gestational mother," is derived from USCACA (1988) §1(4), which employed the now-discarded term "surrogate mother" to define the same factual circumstances dealt with in this subchapter. For purposes of this Act, a woman giving birth to her own genetic child, a.k.a. "birth mother," is distinguished from a "gestational mother." The former is both a gestational and genetic mother, while the latter also gives birth to a child, who may or may not be her genetic child. In the Act the term "gestational mother" is narrowly defined to restrict it to a situation in which a woman gives birth to a child pursuant to a gestational agreement validated under this subchapter.

FAM §160.752. SCOPE OF SUBCHAPTER; CHOICE OF LAW

(a) Notwithstanding any other provision of this chapter or another law, this subchapter authorizes an agreement between a woman and the intended parents of a child in which the woman relinquishes all rights as a parent of a child conceived by means of assisted reproduction and that provides that the intended parents become the parents of the child.

(b) This subchapter controls over any other law with respect to a child conceived under a gestational agreement under this subchapter.

History of Fam. Code §160.752: Acts 2003, 78th Leg., ch. 457, §2, Leg., eff. Sept. 1, 2003.

FAM §160.753. ESTABLISHMENT OF PARENT-CHILD RELATIONSHIP

(a) Notwithstanding any other provision of this chapter or another law, the mother-child relationship exists between a woman and a child by an adjudication confirming the woman as a parent of the child born to a gestational mother under a gestational agreement if the gestational agreement is validated under this subchapter or enforceable under other law, regardless of the fact that the gestational mother gave birth to the child.

(b) The father-child relationship exists between a child and a man by an adjudication confirming the man as a parent of the child born to a gestational mother under a gestational agreement if the gestational agreement is validated under this subchapter or enforceable under other law.

History of Fam. Code §160.753: Acts 2003, 78th Leg., ch. 457, §2, eff. Sept. 1, 2003.

FAM §160.754. GESTATIONAL AGREEMENT AUTHORIZED

(a) A prospective gestational mother, her husband if she is married, each donor, and each intended parent may enter into a written agreement providing that:

(1) the prospective gestational mother agrees to pregnancy by means of assisted reproduction;

(2) the prospective gestational mother, her husband if she is married, and each donor other than the intended parents, if applicable, relinquish all parental rights and duties with respect to a child conceived through assisted reproduction;

(3) the intended parents will be the parents of the child; and

(4) the gestational mother and each intended parent agree to exchange throughout the period covered by the agreement all relevant information regarding the health of the gestational mother and each intended parent.

(b) The intended parents must be married to each other. Each intended parent must be a party to the gestational agreement.

(c) The gestational agreement must require that the eggs used in the assisted reproduction procedure be retrieved from an intended parent or a donor. The gestational mother's eggs may not be used in the assisted reproduction procedure.

(d) The gestational agreement must state that the physician who will perform the assisted reproduction procedure as provided by the agreement has informed the parties to the agreement of:

(1) the rate of successful conceptions and births attributable to the procedure, including the most recent published outcome statistics of the procedure at the facility at which it will be performed;

(2) the potential for and risks associated with the implantation of multiple embryos and consequent multiple births resulting from the procedure;

(3) the nature of and expenses related to the procedure;

(4) the health risks associated with, as applicable, fertility drugs used in the procedure, egg retrieval procedures, and egg or embryo transfer procedures; and

* See footnote on p. 715.

(5) reasonably foreseeable psychological effects resulting from the procedure.

(e) The parties to a gestational agreement must enter into the agreement before the 14th day preceding the date the transfer of eggs, sperm, or embryos to the gestational mother occurs for the purpose of conception or implantation.

(f) A gestational agreement does not apply to the birth of a child conceived by means of sexual intercourse.

(g) A gestational agreement may not limit the right of the gestational mother to make decisions to safeguard her health or the health of an embryo.

History of Fam. Code §160.754: Acts 2003, 78th Leg., ch. 457, §2, eff. Sept. 1, 2003.

See also *O'Connor's Texas Family Law Handbook* (2017), "Mother by gestational agreement," ch. 1-B, §3.4, p. 23.

NCCUSL Comment*

Prior Uniform Statutory Source: USCACA §§1(3), 5, 9.

The previous uniform act on this subject, USCACA, proposed two alternatives, one of which was to declare that gestational agreements were void. Subsection (a) rejects that approach. The scientific state of the art and the medical facilities providing the technological capacity to utilize a woman other than the woman who intends to raise the child to be the gestational mother, guarantee that such agreements will continue to be written. Subsection (a) recognizes that certainty and initiates a procedure for its regulation by a judicial officer. This section permits all of the individuals directly involved in the procedure to enter into a written agreement; this includes the intended parents, the gestational mother, and her husband, if she is married. In addition, if known donors are involved, they also must sign the agreement. The agreement must provide that the intended parents will be the parents of any child born pursuant to the agreement while all of the others (gestational mother, her husband, if any, and the donors, as appropriate) relinquish all parental rights and duties.

Subsection (g) is intended to acknowledge that the gestational mother, as a pregnant woman, has a constitutionally-recognized right to decide issues regarding her prenatal care. In other words, the intended parents have no right to demand that the gestational mother undergo any particular medical regimen at their behest.

FAM §160.755. PETITION TO VALIDATE GESTATIONAL AGREEMENT

(a) The intended parents and the prospective gestational mother under a gestational agreement may commence a proceeding to validate the agreement.

(b) A person may maintain a proceeding to validate a gestational agreement only if:

(1) the prospective gestational mother or the intended parents have resided in this state for the 90 days preceding the date the proceeding is commenced;

(2) the prospective gestational mother's husband, if she is married, is joined as a party to the proceeding; and

(3) a copy of the gestational agreement is attached to the petition.

History of Fam. Code §160.755: Acts 2003, 78th Leg., ch. 457, §2, eff. Sept. 1, 2003.

NCCUSL Comment*

Prior Uniform Statutory Source: USCACA §6(a).

Sections 160.755 and 160.756, the core sections of this subchapter, provide for state involvement, through judicial oversight, of the gestational agreement before, during, and after the assisted reproduction process. The purpose of early involvement is to ensure that the parties are appropriate for a gestational agreement, that they understand the consequences of what they are about to do, and that the best interests of a child born of the gestational agreement are considered before the arrangement is validated. The trigger for state involvement is a petition brought by all the parties to the arrangement requesting a judicial order authorizing the assisted reproduction contemplated by their agreement. The agreement itself must be submitted to the court.

To discourage forum shopping, subsection (b)(1) requires that the petition may be filed only in a state in which the intended parents or the gestational mother have been residents for at least ninety days.

FAM §160.756. HEARING TO VALIDATE GESTATIONAL AGREEMENT

(a) A gestational agreement must be validated as provided by this section.

(b) The court may validate a gestational agreement as provided by Subsection (c) only if the court finds that:

(1) the parties have submitted to the jurisdiction of the court under the jurisdictional standards of this chapter;

(2) the medical evidence provided shows that the intended mother is unable to carry a pregnancy to term and give birth to the child or is unable to carry the pregnancy to term and give birth to the child without unreasonable risk to her physical or mental health or to the health of the unborn child;

(3) unless waived by the court, an agency or other person has conducted a home study of the intended parents and has determined that the intended parents meet the standards of fitness applicable to adoptive parents;

(4) each party to the agreement has voluntarily entered into and understands the terms of the agreement;

(5) the prospective gestational mother has had at least one previous pregnancy and delivery and carrying another pregnancy to term and giving birth to another child would not pose an unreasonable risk to the child's health or the physical or mental health of the prospective gestational mother; and

(6) the parties have adequately provided for which party is responsible for all reasonable health care expenses associated with the pregnancy, including pro-

* See footnote on p. 715.

viding for who is responsible for those expenses if the agreement is terminated.

(c) If the court finds that the requirements of Subsection (b) are satisfied, the court may render an order validating the gestational agreement and declaring that the intended parents will be the parents of a child born under the agreement.

(d) The court may validate the gestational agreement at the court's discretion. The court's determination of whether to validate the agreement is subject to review only for abuse of discretion.

History of Fam. Code §160.756: Acts 2003, 78th Leg., ch. 457, §2, eff. Sept. 1, 2003.

NCCUSL Comment*

Prior Uniform Statutory Source: USCACA §6(b).

This pre-conception authorization process for a gestational agreement is roughly analogous to prevailing adoption procedures in place in most states. Just as adoption contemplates the transfer of parentage of a child from the birth parents to the adoptive parents, a gestational agreement involves the transfer from the gestational mother to the intended parents. The Act is designed to protect the interests of the child to be born under the gestational agreement as well as the interests of the gestational mother and the intended parents.

In contrast to USCACA (1988) §1(3), there is no requirement that at least one of the intended parents be genetically related to the child born of a gestational agreement. Similarly, the likelihood that the gestational mother will also be the genetic mother is not directly addressed in the new Act, while USCACA (1988) apparently assumed that such a fact pattern would be typical. Experience with the intractable problems caused by such a combination has dissuaded the majority of fertility laboratories from following that practice. *See In re Matter of Baby M.*, 537 A.2d 1227 (N.J. 1988).

This section seeks to protect the interests of the child in several ways. The major protection of the child is the authorization procedure itself. The Act requires closely supervised gestational arrangements to ensure the security and well being of the child. Once a petition has been filed, subsections (c) and (d) permit—but do not require—the court to validate a gestational agreement. If it validates, the court must declare that the intended parents will be the parents of any child born pursuant to, and during the term of, the agreement.

Subsection (b) requires the court to make six separate findings before validating the agreement. Subsection (b)(1) requires the court to ensure that the 90-day residency requirement of §160.755 has been satisfied and that it has jurisdiction over the parties.

Under subsection (b)(3), the court will be informed of the results of a home study of the intended parents who must satisfy the suitability standards required of prospective adoptive parents.

The interests of all the parties are protected by subsection (b)(4), which is designed to protect the individuals involved from the possibility of overreaching or fraud. The court must find that all parties consented to the gestational agreement with full knowledge of what they agreed to do, which necessarily includes relinquishing the resulting child to the intended parents who are obligated to accept the child.

The requirement of assurance of health-care expenses until birth of the resulting child imposed by subsection (b)(6) further protects the gestational mother.

Section 160.756, spells out detailed requirements for the petition and the findings that must be made before an authorizing order can be issued, but nowhere states the consequences of violations of the rules. Because of the variety of types of violations that could possibly occur, a bright-line rule concerning the effect of such violations is inappropriate. The consequences of a failure to abide by the rules of this section are left to a case-by-case determination. A court should be guided by the Act's intention to permit gestational agreements and the equities of a particular situation. Note that §160.759 provides a period for termination of the agreement and vacating of the order. The discovery of a failure to abide by the rules of §160.756 would certainly provide an occasion for terminating the agreement. On the other hand, if a failure to abide by the rules of §160.756 is discovered by a party during a time when §160.759 termination is permissible, failure to seek termination might be an appropriate reason to estop the party from later seeking to overturn or ignore the §160.756 order.

* See footnote on p. 715.

FAM §160.757. INSPECTION OF RECORDS

The proceedings, records, and identities of the parties to a gestational agreement under this subchapter are subject to inspection under the same standards of confidentiality that apply to an adoption under the laws of this state.

History of Fam. Code §160.757: Acts 2003, 78th Leg., ch. 457, §2, eff. Sept. 1, 2003.

NCCUSL Comment*

The procedures involved in this subchapter are exceptionally personal, thereby warranting protection from invasions of privacy. Adoption records provide a suitable model for these records.

FAM §160.758. CONTINUING, EXCLUSIVE JURISDICTION

Subject to Section 152.201, a court that conducts a proceeding under this subchapter has continuing, exclusive jurisdiction of all matters arising out of the gestational agreement until the date a child born to the gestational mother during the period covered by the agreement reaches 180 days of age.

History of Fam. Code §160.758: Acts 2003, 78th Leg., ch. 457, §2, eff. Sept. 1, 2003.

NCCUSL Comment*

Prior Uniform Statutory Source: USCACA §6(e).

This section is designed to minimize the possibility of parallel litigation in different states and the consequent risk of childnapping for strategic purposes. The court that validated the gestational agreement will have authority to enforce the gestational agreement until the child is 180 days old. Note that only the parentage issues and enforcement issues are covered; collateral matters, such as custody, visitation, and child support are not covered by this Act.

FAM §160.759. TERMINATION OF GESTATIONAL AGREEMENT

(a) Before a prospective gestational mother becomes pregnant by means of assisted reproduction, the prospective gestational mother, her husband if she is married, or either intended parent may terminate a gestational agreement validated under Section 160.756 by giving written notice of the termination to each other party to the agreement.

(b) A person who terminates a gestational agreement under Subsection (a) shall file notice of the termination with the court. A person having the duty to notify the court who does not notify the court of the termination of the agreement is subject to appropriate sanctions.

(c) On receipt of the notice of termination, the court shall vacate the order rendered under Section 160.756 validating the gestational agreement.

(d) A prospective gestational mother and her husband, if she is married, may not be liable to an intended parent for terminating a gestational agreement if the termination is in accordance with this section.

History of Fam. Code §160.759: Acts 2003, 78th Leg., ch. 457, §2, eff. Sept. 1, 2003.

NCCUSL Comment*

Prior Uniform Statutory Source: USCACA §7.

Subsection (a) permits a party to terminate a gestational agreement by canceling the arrangement before the pregnancy has been established. This provides for cancellation during a time when the interests of the parties would not be unduly prejudiced by termination. By definition, the procreation process has not begun. The intended parents certainly have an expectation interest during this time, but the nature of this interest is little different from that which they would have while they were attempting to create a pregnancy through traditional means.

Under subsection (b) a party who wishes to terminate the agreement must inform the other parties in writing, and must also file notice with the court. The court must then vacate the order validating the agreement. An individual who does not notify the court of his/her termination of the agreement is subject to sanction.

USCACA §7(b) specifically dealt with termination of a "surrogacy agreement" by a gestational mother who provided the egg for the assisted conception. This possibility is not repeated in the new UPA because there is only a remote likelihood that an agreement for the gestational mother to furnish the egg will be countenanced. Assisted reproduction, as generally conducted by medical facilities today, disapproves of that practice.

Subsection (d) provides that before pregnancy a gestational mother is not liable to the intended parents for terminating the agreement. Although the new Act does not explicitly provide for termination of the agreement after pregnancy. Several sections deal with this issue under certain described circumstances. Section 160.754(g) recognizes that the gestational mother has plenary power to decide issues of her health and the health of the fetus. Sections 160.756(a) and 160.760(a) direct that the intended parents are in fact the parents of the child with an enforceable right to the possession of the child.

FAM §160.760. PARENTAGE UNDER VALIDATED GESTATIONAL AGREEMENT

(a) On the birth of a child to a gestational mother under a validated gestational agreement, the intended parents shall file a notice of the birth with the court not later than the 300th day after the date assisted reproduction occurred.

(b) After receiving notice of the birth, the court shall render an order that:

(1) confirms that the intended parents are the child's parents;

(2) requires the gestational mother to surrender the child to the intended parents, if necessary; and

(3) requires the vital statistics unit to issue a birth certificate naming the intended parents as the child's parents.

(c) If a person alleges that a child born to a gestational mother did not result from assisted reproduction, the court shall order that scientifically accepted parentage testing be conducted to determine the child's parentage.

(d) If the intended parents fail to file the notice required by Subsection (a), the gestational mother or an appropriate state agency may file the notice required by that subsection. On a showing that an order validating the gestational agreement was rendered in accordance with Section 160.756, the court shall order that the intended parents are the child's parents and are financially responsible for the child.

History of Fam. Code §160.760: Acts 2003, 78th Leg., ch. 457, §2, eff. Sept. 1, 2003. Amended by Acts 2005, 79th Leg., ch. 916, §22, eff. June 18, 2005; Acts 2015, 84th Leg., ch. 1, §1.076, eff. Apr. 2, 2015.

NCCUSL Comment*

Prior Uniform Statutory Source: USCACA §8.

Under subsection (a), the intended parents of a child born pursuant to an approved gestational agreement within 300 days of the use of assisted reproduction are deemed to be the legal parents if the order under §160.756 is still in effect. Notice of the birth of the child must be filed by the intended parents. On receipt of the notice under subsection (b), the court shall issue an order confirming that the intended parents are the legal parents of the child and direct the issuance of a birth certificate to confirm the court's determination. If necessary, the court may also order the gestational mother to surrender the child to the intended parents.

Subsection (d) clarifies the remedies available if the intended parents refuse to accept a child who is born as the result of a gestational agreement.

FAM §160.761. EFFECT OF GESTATIONAL MOTHER'S MARRIAGE AFTER VALIDATION OF AGREEMENT

If a gestational mother is married after the court renders an order validating a gestational agreement under this subchapter:

(1) the validity of the gestational agreement is not affected;

(2) the gestational mother's husband is not required to consent to the agreement; and

(3) the gestational mother's husband is not a presumed father of the child born under the terms of the agreement.

History of Fam. Code §160.761: Acts 2003, 78th Leg., ch. 457, §2, eff. Sept. 1, 2003.

NCCUSL Comment*

Prior Uniform Statutory Source: USCACA §9.

If, after the original court order validates the gestational agreement, the gestational mother marries, the gestational agreement continues to be valid and the consent of her new husband is not required. The new husband is neither a party to the original action nor the presumed father of a resulting child, and therefore ought not be burdened with the status of parent unless he is the genetic father or chooses to adopt the child.

* See footnote on p. 715.

FAM §160.762. EFFECT OF GESTATIONAL AGREEMENT THAT IS NOT VALIDATED

(a) A gestational agreement that is not validated as provided by this subchapter is unenforceable, regardless of whether the agreement is in a record.

(b) The parent-child relationship of a child born under a gestational agreement that is not validated as provided by this subchapter is determined as otherwise provided by this chapter.

(c) A party to a gestational agreement that is not validated as provided by this subchapter who is an intended parent under the agreement may be held liable for the support of a child born under the agreement, even if the agreement is otherwise unenforceable.

(d) The court may assess filing fees, reasonable attorney's fees, fees for genetic testing, other costs, and necessary travel and other reasonable expenses incurred in a proceeding under this section. Attorney's fees awarded by the court may be paid directly to the attorney. An attorney who is awarded attorney's fees may enforce the order in the attorney's own name.

History of Fam. Code §160.762: Acts 2003, 78th Leg., ch. 457, §2, eff. Sept. 1, 2003.

NCCUSL Comment*

Prior Uniform Statutory Source: USCACA §§5(b), 10.

This section distinguishes between an unenforceable agreement and a prohibited one. Given the widespread use of assisted reproductive technologies in modern society, the Act attempts only to regularize the parentage aspects of the science, not to regulate the practice of assisted reproduction. If individuals choose to ignore the protections afforded gestational agreements by the Act, parentage questions will remain when a child is born as a result of a nonvalidated gestational agreement. The Act provides no legal assistance to the intended parents. The gestational mother is denominated the mother irrespective of the source of the eggs, and donors of either eggs or sperm are not parents of the child. Notwithstanding the fact that the intended parents in a nonvalidated agreement may not enforce that agreement, subsection (c) provides that a court may hold the intended parents to an obligation to support the resulting child of the unenforceable agreement.

Under USCACA (1988), agreements that were not approved were declared "void." Under the new UPA, a nonapproved agreement is "unenforceable." The result may be virtually the same in some instances. As under the prior Act, the gestational mother is the mother of a child conceived through assisted reproduction if the gestational agreement has not been judicially approved as provided in this subchapter. Her husband, if he is a party to such agreement, is presumed to be the father. If the gestational mother's husband is not a party to the agreement, or if she is unmarried, paternity of the child will be left to existing law, if any. If the mother decides to keep the child, the intended parents have no recourse. If the parties agree that the intended parents will raise the child, adoption is the only means through which they may become the legal parents of the child will be through adoption.

FAM §160.763. HEALTH CARE FACILITY REPORTING REQUIREMENT

(a) The executive commissioner of the Health and Human Services Commission by rule shall develop and implement a confidential reporting system that requires each health care facility in this state at which assisted reproduction procedures are performed under gestational agreements to report statistics related to those procedures.

(b) In developing the reporting system, the executive commissioner shall require each health care facility described by Subsection (a) to annually report:

(1) the number of assisted reproduction procedures under a gestational agreement performed at the facility during the preceding year; and

(2) the number and current status of embryos created through assisted reproduction procedures described by Subdivision (1) that were not transferred for implantation.

History of Fam. Code §160.763: Acts 2003, 78th Leg., ch. 457, §2, eff. Sept. 1, 2003. Amended by Acts 2015, 84th Leg., ch. 1, §1.077, eff. Apr. 2, 2015.

CHAPTER 161. TERMINATION OF THE PARENT-CHILD RELATIONSHIP

* See footnote on p. 715.

SUBCHAPTER A. GROUNDS

A FAM §161.001. INVOLUNTARY TERMINATION OF PARENT-CHILD RELATIONSHIP

(a) In this section, "born addicted to alcohol or a controlled substance" means a child:

(1) who is born to a mother who during the pregnancy used a controlled substance, as defined by Chapter 481, Health and Safety Code, other than a controlled substance legally obtained by prescription, or alcohol; and

(2) who, after birth as a result of the mother's use of the controlled substance or alcohol:

(A) experiences observable withdrawal from the alcohol or controlled substance;

(B) exhibits observable or harmful effects in the child's physical appearance or functioning; or

(C) exhibits the demonstrable presence of alcohol or a controlled substance in the child's bodily fluids.

The amended text in subsection (b) is effective for SAPCRs filed on or after Sept. 1, 2017. SAPCRs filed before Sept. 1, 2017, are governed by the former law in effect at that time.

(b) The court may order termination of the parent-child relationship if the court finds by clear and convincing evidence:

(1) that the parent has:

(A) voluntarily left the child alone or in the possession of another not the parent and expressed an intent not to return;

(B) voluntarily left the child alone or in the possession of another not the parent without expressing an intent to return, without providing for the adequate support of the child, and remained away for a period of at least three months;

(C) voluntarily left the child alone or in the possession of another without providing adequate support of the child and remained away for a period of at least six months;

(D) knowingly placed or knowingly allowed the child to remain in conditions or surroundings which endanger the physical or emotional well-being of the child;

(E) engaged in conduct or knowingly placed the child with persons who engaged in conduct which endangers the physical or emotional well-being of the child;

(F) failed to support the child in accordance with the parent's ability during a period of one year ending within six months of the date of the filing of the petition;

(G) abandoned the child without identifying the child or furnishing means of identification, and the child's identity cannot be ascertained by the exercise of reasonable diligence;

(H) voluntarily, and with knowledge of the pregnancy, abandoned the mother of the child beginning at a time during her pregnancy with the child and continuing through the birth, failed to provide adequate support or medical care for the mother during the period of abandonment before the birth of the child, and remained apart from the child or failed to support the child since the birth;

(I) contumaciously refused to submit to a reasonable and lawful order of a court under Subchapter D, Chapter 261;

(J) been the major cause of:

(i) the failure of the child to be enrolled in school as required by the Education Code; or

(ii) the child's absence from the child's home without the consent of the parents or guardian for a substantial length of time or without the intent to return;

(K) executed before or after the suit is filed an unrevoked or irrevocable affidavit of relinquishment of parental rights as provided by this chapter;

(L) been convicted or has been placed on community supervision, including deferred adjudication community supervision, for being criminally responsible for the death or serious injury of a child under the fol-

lowing sections of the Penal Code, or under a law of another jurisdiction that contains elements that are substantially similar to the elements of an offense under one of the following Penal Code sections, or adjudicated under Title 3 for conduct that caused the death or serious injury of a child and that would constitute a violation of one of the following Penal Code sections:

(i) Section 19.02 (murder);

(ii) Section 19.03 (capital murder);

(iii) Section 19.04 (manslaughter);

(iv) Section 21.11 (indecency with a child);

(v) Section 22.01 (assault);

(vi) Section 22.011 (sexual assault);

(vii) Section 22.02 (aggravated assault);

(viii) Section 22.021 (aggravated sexual assault);

(ix) Section 22.04 (injury to a child, elderly individual, or disabled individual);

(x) Section 22.041 (abandoning or endangering child);

(xi) Section 25.02 (prohibited sexual conduct);

(xii) Section 43.25 (sexual performance by a child);

(xiii) Section 43.26 (possession or promotion of child pornography);

(xiv) Section 21.02 (continuous sexual abuse of young child or children);

(xv) Section 20A.02(a)(7) or (8) (trafficking of persons); and

(xvi) Section 43.05(a)(2) (compelling prostitution);

(M) had his or her parent-child relationship terminated with respect to another child based on a finding that the parent's conduct was in violation of Paragraph (D) or (E) or substantially equivalent provisions of the law of another state;

(N) constructively abandoned the child who has been in the permanent or temporary managing conservatorship of the Department of Family and Protective Services for not less than six months, and:

(i) the department has made reasonable efforts to return the child to the parent;

(ii) the parent has not regularly visited or maintained significant contact with the child; and

(iii) the parent has demonstrated an inability to provide the child with a safe environment;

(O) failed to comply with the provisions of a court order that specifically established the actions necessary for the parent to obtain the return of the child who has been in the permanent or temporary managing conservatorship of the Department of Family and Protective Services for not less than nine months as a result of the child's removal from the parent under Chapter 262 for the abuse or neglect of the child;

(P) used a controlled substance, as defined by Chapter 481, Health and Safety Code, in a manner that endangered the health or safety of the child, and:

(i) failed to complete a court-ordered substance abuse treatment program; or

(ii) after completion of a court-ordered substance abuse treatment program, continued to abuse a controlled substance;

(Q) knowingly engaged in criminal conduct that has resulted in the parent's:

(i) conviction of an offense; and

(ii) confinement or imprisonment and inability to care for the child for not less than two years from the date of filing the petition;

(R) been the cause of the child being born addicted to alcohol or a controlled substance, other than a controlled substance legally obtained by prescription;

(S) voluntarily delivered the child to a designated emergency infant care provider under Section 262.302 without expressing an intent to return for the child; [~~or~~]

(T) been convicted of:

(i) the murder of the other parent of the child under Section 19.02 or 19.03, Penal Code, or under a law of another state, federal law, the law of a foreign country, or the Uniform Code of Military Justice that contains elements that are substantially similar to the elements of an offense under Section 19.02 or 19.03, Penal Code;

(ii) criminal attempt under Section 15.01, Penal Code, or under a law of another state, federal law, the law of a foreign country, or the Uniform Code of Military Justice that contains elements that are substantially similar to the elements of an offense under Section 15.01, Penal Code, to commit the offense described by Subparagraph (i); [~~or~~]

(iii) criminal solicitation under Section 15.03, Penal Code, or under a law of another state, federal law, the law of a foreign country, or the Uniform Code of

Military Justice that contains elements that are substantially similar to the elements of an offense under Section 15.03, Penal Code, of the offense described by Subparagraph (i); or

(iv) the sexual assault of the other parent of the child under Section 22.011 or 22.021, Penal Code, or under a law of another state, federal law, or the Uniform Code of Military Justice that contains elements that are substantially similar to the elements of an offense under Section 22.011 or 22.021, Penal Code; or

(U) been placed on community supervision, including deferred adjudication community supervision, or another functionally equivalent form of community supervision or probation, for being criminally responsible for the sexual assault of the other parent of the child under Section 22.011 or 22.021, Penal Code, or under a law of another state, federal law, or the Uniform Code of Military Justice that contains elements that are substantially similar to the elements of an offense under Section 22.011 or 22.021, Penal Code; and

(2) that termination is in the best interest of the child.

Subsections (c) through (e) are effective for service plans filed for a full adversary hearing held under Fam. Code §262.201 or a status hearing held under Fam. Code ch. 263 on or after Jan. 1, 2018. Except as provided above, subsections (c) through (e) are effective for SAPCRs filed on or after Sept. 1, 2017.

(c) A court may not make a finding under Subsection (b) and order termination of the parent-child relationship based on evidence that the parent:

(1) homeschooled the child;

(2) is economically disadvantaged;

(3) has been charged with a nonviolent misdemeanor offense other than:

(A) an offense under Title 5, Penal Code;

(B) an offense under Title 6, Penal Code; or

(C) an offense that involves family violence, as defined by Section 71.004 of this code;

(4) provided or administered low-THC cannabis to a child for whom the low-THC cannabis was prescribed under Chapter 169, Occupations Code; or

(5) declined immunization for the child for reasons of conscience, including a religious belief.

(d) A court may not order termination under Subsection (b)(1)(O) based on the failure by the parent to comply with a specific provision of a court order if a parent proves by a preponderance of evidence that:

(1) the parent was unable to comply with specific provisions of the court order; and

(2) the parent made a good faith effort to comply with the order and the failure to comply with the order is not attributable to any fault of the parent.

(e) This section does not prohibit the Department of Family and Protective Services from offering evidence described by Subsection (c) as part of an action to terminate the parent-child relationship under this subchapter.

History of Fam. Code §161.001: Acts 1995, 74th Leg., ch. 20, §1, eff. Apr. 20, 1995. Amended by Acts 1995, 74th Leg., ch. 709, §1 (eff. Sept. 1, 1995), ch. 751, §65 (eff. Sept. 1, 1995); Acts 1997, 75th Leg., ch. 575, §9 (eff. Sept. 1, 1997), ch. 1022, §60 (eff. Sept. 1, 1997); Acts 1999, 76th Leg., ch. 1087, §1 (eff. Sept. 1, 1999), ch. 1390, §18 (eff. Sept. 1, 1999); Acts 2001, 77th Leg., ch. 1090, §1, eff. Sept. 1, 2001; Acts 2005, 79th Leg., ch. 508, §2, eff. Sept. 1, 2005; Acts 2007, 80th Leg., ch. 593, §3.30, eff. Sept. 1, 2007; Acts 2009, 81st Leg., ch. 86, §1, eff. Sept. 1, 2009; Acts 2011, 82nd Leg., ch. 1, §4.02, eff. Sept. 1, 2011; Acts 2015, 84th Leg., ch. 944, §11 (eff. Sept. 1, 2015), ch. 1, §1.078 (eff. Apr. 2, 2015); H.B. 7, §12, 85th Leg., eff. Sept. 1, 2017; S.B. 77, §2, 85th Leg., eff. Sept. 1, 2017. Source: Former Fam. Code §§11.15(b), 15.02(a).

See also ***O'Connor's Texas Family Law Handbook*** (2017), "Terminating the Parent-Child Relationship," ch. 4-H, §12, p. 617.

ANNOTATIONS

Generally

Holick v. Smith, 685 S.W.2d 18, 20 (Tex.1985). "The natural right existing between parents and their children is of constitutional dimensions. … A termination decree is complete, final, irrevocable and divests for all time that natural right as well as all legal rights, privileges, duties and powers with respect to each other except for the child's right to inherit. … Consequently, termination proceedings should be strictly scrutinized, and involuntary termination statutes are strictly construed in favor of the parent."

Wiley v. Spratlan, 543 S.W.2d 349, 352 (Tex.1976). "Actions which break the ties between a parent and child 'can never be justified without the most solid and substantial reasons.' Particularly in an action which permanently sunders those ties, should the proceedings be strictly scrutinized. This court has always recognized the strong presumption that the best interest of a minor is usually served by keeping custody in the natural parents. [¶] 'The presumption is based upon a logical belief that the ties of the natural relationship of parent and child ordinarily furnish strong assurance of genuine efforts on the part of the custodians to provide the child with the best care and opportunities possible,

and, as well, the best atmosphere for the mental, moral and emotional development of the child.'"

In re A.B.B., 482 S.W.3d 135, 140 (Tex.App.—El Paso 2015, no pet.). "No court in Texas has allowed a parent whose parental rights have been terminated to seek reversal based on ineffective assistance of **retained counsel.** *At 141:* We are sympathetic to the plight of a litigant who retains counsel in a private termination proceeding. Criminal defendants are granted the right to challenge the effectiveness of legal representation, regardless of whether counsel is retained or appointed. Inasmuch as the body of law surrounding parental terminations has equated the constitutional liberty interests in the parent-child relationship with liberty interests of criminal defendants, it is not a far leap for the courts to make. However, as an intermediate appellate court, it is not within our purview to legislate rights or create them by judicial fiat. We thus leave expansion of remedies in a private termination to the Legislature and the Supreme Court."

In re D.N., 405 S.W.3d 863, 870 (Tex.App.—Amarillo 2013, no pet.). "[A] trial court can terminate the parent-child relationship, even though it previously denied termination in another order, using [Fam. Code] §161.001 alone if termination is sought on *evidence of acts or omissions having occurred since the earlier order in which termination was denied*. But, to rely on acts or omissions evidence of which has been presented to the trial court prior to the earlier order denying termination, the Department must garner sufficient evidence of [Fam. Code] §161.004's elements, including a material and substantial change of the parties' circumstances."

Ruiz v. TDFPS, 212 S.W.3d 804, 813-14 (Tex.App.—Houston [1st Dist.] 2006, no pet.). "[T]his Court, in an en banc opinion, has specifically rejected DFPS's argument that we may affirm a trial court's termination order on the basis of a subsection of §161.001, which, although pleaded by DFPS in its original petition, was not expressly found to have been violated in the decree.... '[A] parental rights termination order can be upheld only on grounds both pleaded by [DFPS] and found by the trial court.'"

In re S.A.P., 169 S.W.3d 685, 695 (Tex.App.—Waco 2005, no pet.). "In a proceeding to terminate the parent-child relationship brought under §161.001, [petitioner] must establish by clear and convincing evidence two elements: (1) one or more acts or omissions enumerated under subsection (1) [now subsection (b)(1)] of §161.001 (termed a predicate violation); *and* (2) that termination is in the best interest of the child. The factfinder must find that *both* elements are established by clear and convincing evidence, and proof of one element does not relieve the petitioner of the burden of proving the other. If multiple predicate violations under §161.001(1) [now §161.001(b)(1)] were found in the trial court, we can affirm based on any one ground because only one predicate violation under §161.001(1) is necessary to a termination judgment."

In re J.T.G., 121 S.W.3d 117, 130 (Tex.App.—Fort Worth 2003, no pet.). Held: The entitlement in criminal proceedings of an indigent defendant to an expert in order to prepare and present a defense is not extended to parental-termination cases.

Avery v. State, 963 S.W.2d 550, 553 (Tex.App.—Houston [1st Dist.] 1997, no pet.). "The parental conduct to be examined in considering termination of parental rights includes what the parents did before and after the birth of the child."

Clear & Convincing Evidence

In re K.M.L., 443 S.W.3d 101, 112-13 (Tex.2014). "Our traditional legal sufficiency—or 'no evidence'—standard of review upholds a finding supported by '[a]nything more than a scintilla of evidence.' However, '[r]equiring only anything more than a mere scintilla of evidence does not equate to clear and convincing evidence.' Thus, our legal sufficiency review in a parental termination case must take into consideration whether the evidence is such that a factfinder could reasonably form a firm belief or conviction about the truth of the matter on which the State bears the burden of proof. [¶] In a legal sufficiency challenge, we credit evidence that supports the verdict if reasonable jurors could have done so and disregard contrary evidence unless reasonable jurors could not have done so. However, the reviewing court should not disregard undisputed facts that do not support the verdict to determine whether there is clear and convincing evidence. In cases requiring clear and convincing evidence, even evidence that does more than raise surmise and suspicion will not suffice unless that evidence is capable of producing a firm belief or conviction that the allegation is true. If the reviewing court determines that no reasonable factfinder could form a firm belief or conviction that the matter to be proven is true, then the court must conclude that the evidence is legally insufficient." *See*

also ***In re E.N.C.***, 384 S.W.3d 796, 802-03 (Tex.2012); ***In re J.F.C.***, 96 S.W.3d 256, 265-66 (Tex.2002).

In re A.B., 437 S.W.3d 498, 502-03 (Tex.2014). "Because the termination of parental rights implicates fundamental interests, a higher standard of proof—clear and convincing evidence—is required at trial. Given this higher burden at trial, … a proper factual sufficiency review requires the court of appeals to determine whether 'the evidence is such that a factfinder could reasonably form a firm belief or conviction about the truth of the State's allegations.' 'If, in light of the entire record, the disputed evidence that a reasonable factfinder could not have credited in favor of the finding is so significant that a factfinder could not reasonably have formed a firm belief or conviction, then the evidence is factually insufficient.' And in making this determination, the reviewing court must undertake 'an exacting review of the entire record with a healthy regard for the constitutional interests at stake.' [¶] [D]espite the heightened standard of review …, the court of appeals must nevertheless still provide due deference to the decisions of the factfinder, who, having full opportunity to observe witness testimony first-hand, is the sole arbiter when assessing the credibility and demeanor of witnesses. [I]f a court of appeals is *reversing* the jury's finding based on insufficient evidence, the reviewing court must 'detail the evidence relevant to the issue of parental termination and clearly state why the evidence is insufficient to support a termination finding by clear and convincing evidence.' *At 505:* But … we decline to mandate that courts of appeals detail the evidence when affirming a jury verdict."

In re E.W., 494 S.W.3d 287, 296-97 (Tex.App.—Texarkana 2015, no pet.). "The trial court specifically stated that it was relying on its own 'judicial knowledge' of the case in terminating [parents'] parental rights…. We have no doubt that the trial court may have been well acquainted through previous dealings with the parties with facts that may have supported termination on one of these grounds. However, it is inappropriate for a trial judge to take judicial notice of testimony even in a retrial of the same case. In order for testimony from a prior hearing or trial to be considered in a subsequent proceeding, the transcript of that testimony must be properly authenticated and entered into evidence. Thus, a trial judge may not even judicially notice testimony that was given at a temporary hearing in a family law case at a subsequent hearing in the same cause without admitting the prior testimony into evidence. The Department admitted no such transcripts into evidence at this termination hearing, and none were included in the clerk's record. [¶] Simply put, there was no evidence to support the trial court's finding that the Department proved the existence of either ground (D) or ground (E) by clear and convincing evidence." (Internal quotes omitted.)

Due Process

In re M.S., 115 S.W.3d 534, 549 (Tex.2003). The State's "initial interest in maintaining the familial bond versus its interest in maintaining procedural integrity weighs in favor of permitting a factual sufficiency review when counsel unjustifiably fails to [preserve error]. [¶] The parent's, child's and government's interest in a just and accurate decision dovetails with the third ***Eldridge*** factor—that of the risk of erroneous deprivation. [W]e cannot think of a more serious risk of erroneous deprivation of parental rights than when the evidence, though minimally existing, fails to clearly and convincingly establish in favor of jury findings that parental rights should be terminated." *See also* ***Mathews v. Eldridge***, 424 U.S. 319, 335 (1976).

In re B.L.D., 113 S.W.3d 340, 354 (Tex.2003). "As a general rule, due process does not mandate that appellate courts review unpreserved complaints of charge error in parental rights termination cases. [¶] [W]e acknowledge that in a given parental rights termination case, a different calibration of the ***Eldridge*** factors[, (1) private interests at stake, (2) the countervailing governmental interest, and (3) the risk of an erroneous deprivation of parental rights,] could require a court of appeals to review an unpreserved complaint of error to ensure that our procedures comport with due process." This could occur when a failure to preserve charge error constitutes ineffective assistance of counsel. *See also* ***Mathews v. Eldridge***, 424 U.S. 319, 335 (1976).

In re P. RJ E., 499 S.W.3d 571, 576 (Tex.App.—Houston [1st Dist.] 2016, pet. filed 9-23-16). See annotation under Family Code §102.010, p. 410.

In re A.M., 385 S.W.3d 74, 78 (Tex.App.—Waco 2012, pet. denied). "We … address the Department's assertion that [mother's] factual-sufficiency complaint is not preserved because she did not file a motion for new trial asserting factual insufficiency. [¶] The [Texas Supreme Court] has not directly addressed

whether the factual-sufficiency preservation requirement comports with due process in termination cases, though it has viewed the preservation requirement through the prism of an ineffective-assistance claim. *At 79:* [I]t appears to us that, in [***In re M.S.***, above], the supreme court implicitly declined to dispense with the factual-sufficiency preservation requirement in termination cases. We therefore ... hold that in termination cases, to raise a factual-sufficiency complaint on appeal, it must be preserved by including it in a motion for new trial."

Larson v. Giesenschlag, 368 S.W.3d 792, 796 (Tex. App.—Austin 2012, no pet.). "When a trial court's failure to act on an inmate's request for participation, in person or by other means, effectively bars the inmate from presenting his case, the trial court abuses its discretion. *At 797:* Litigants may not be denied reasonable access to the courts simply because they are inmates. However, this does not mean that an inmate has an absolute right to personally appear in every proceeding. An inmate's right to access 'entails not so much his personal presence as his opportunity to present evidence or contradict the evidence of the opposing party.' Thus, when an inmate requests a bench warrant for his personal appearance, he must include factual information demonstrating the necessity of his appearing at the proceeding. However, if a pro se inmate is not allowed to participate in a proceeding in person, a trial court should nevertheless afford the inmate an opportunity to proceed by affidavit, deposition, telephone, or other effective means. *At 798:* In this case, [father] had a right to be heard in this suit seeking to terminate his parental rights."

In re R.M.T., 352 S.W.3d 12, 18 (Tex.App.—Texarkana 2011, no pet.). "[T]here is no Texas authority which would permit a trial court to halt termination proceedings due to the incompetency of the parent. *At 19-20:* [Father] argues that because a parental rights termination proceeding is a quasi-criminal proceeding, procedural due process requires (as in criminal cases), that he not be subjected to trial until such time as he is competent to do so. [¶] We do not believe ... that classification of a termination proceeding as quasi-criminal can (or should) be a sole factor which is outcome determinative in resolving the question of whether [father's] termination of parental rights proceeding should have been continued until such time as he regained competency. Rather, we look to and weigh the ***Eldridge*** factors to determine if the termination proceeding in this case afforded [father] the measure of procedural due process to which he was entitled...." *See also* ***Mathews v. Eldridge***, 424 U.S. 319, 335 (1976).

Juries

Texas DHS v. E.B., 802 S.W.2d 647, 649 (Tex.1990). "The charge in parental rights cases should be the same as in other civil cases. The controlling question in this case was whether the parent-child relationship between the mother and each of her two children should be terminated, not what specific ground or grounds under [Fam. Code] §15.02 [now §161.001] the jury relied on to answer affirmatively the questions posed. All ten jurors agree that the mother had endangered the child by doing one or the other of the things listed in §15.02. [Respondent] argues that the charge, as presented to the jury, violates her due process right by depriving a natural mother of her fundamental right to the care, custody and management of her children. Recognizing her rights does not change the form of submission. The standard for review of the charge is abuse of discretion, and abuse of discretion occurs only when the trial court acts without reference to any guiding principle. Here the trial court tracked the statutory language in the instruction and then asked the controlling question. This simply does not amount to abuse of discretion." *See also* ***In re B.L.D.***, 113 S.W.3d 340, 354-55 (Tex.2003) (jury charge that included (1) two statutory grounds in the disjunctive and (2) broad-form jury questions regarding whether parents' rights should be terminated followed ***Texas DHS***, tracked Fam. Code language, and comported with TRCP 277 and 292).

In re J.T.G., 121 S.W.3d 117, 128 (Tex.App.—Fort Worth 2003, no pet.). "[W]hen multiple grounds for termination are sought and the trial court submits the issue using a broad-form question, we must uphold the jury's findings if any of the grounds for termination support the jury's finding; only one finding under §161.001(1) [now §161.001(b)(1)] is necessary to support a judgment of termination."

§161.001(b)(1)(A)

In re R.D.S., 902 S.W.2d 714, 718-19 (Tex.App.—Amarillo 1995, no writ). "[A] statute vests the trial judge with authority to end a parent-child relationship if it finds that 'the parent ... voluntarily left the child alone or in the possession of another not the parent and expressed an intent not to return.' There is no

specified time frame within which these pivotal indicia must arise. Though some authority suggests that the underlying misconduct may not be too remote in time, it is certain that it need not immediately precede the final hearing. [¶] Furthermore, discontinuing the misconduct does not necessarily prevent the court from acting. Once activity within the parameters of [Fam. Code] §15.02(a) [now §161.001(b)(1)] occurs, a parent's change of heart does not stay the court's hand. … Thus, if the evidence at bar established that [mother] voluntarily left her son with someone other than his biological father while expressing an intent not to return, the court was entitled to sever the parent-child relationship, notwithstanding her later attempt to renounce her decision." *See also* ***In re S.S.G.***, 153 S.W.3d 479, 484 (Tex.App.—Amarillo 2004, pet. denied) (having intent and expressing intent are not synonymous).

Swinney v. Mosher, 830 S.W.2d 187, 195 (Tex. App.—Fort Worth 1992, writ denied). There is no "evidence that [respondent] abandoned [daughter] as contemplated by [Fam. Code] §15.02(1)(A) [now §161.001(b)(1)(A)]. [Respondent's] actions of surrendering possession of [daughter] and execution of the affidavit relinquishing her parental rights were done in contemplation of her adoption …, not with an intent to abandon…. Also, there is [no] evidence that [respondent] expressed 'an intent not to return' as that language was intended to be applied by the legislature. [Respondent's] actions were done in furtherance of her original agreement to allow [petitioners] to adopt [daughter], which under [Fam. Code] §15.03(d)[, now §161.103, respondent] had a right to revoke. [Respondent's] prompt notice to [adopting couple] of her intent to revoke the affidavit coupled with her prompt retention of a lawyer, her attendance at all hearings concerning her termination, and her weekly visitation [with daughter], when it was permitted, establishes conclusively that [respondent] did not intend to abandon [daughter] under §15.02(1)(A). Any finding to the contrary would render §15.03(d) null and void. [¶] A finding that parental rights could be involuntarily terminated based on the actions consistent with an open adoption would be contrary to the history of Texas law prior to the Family Code and a subversion of the legislatures' intent…."

Smith v. McLin, 632 S.W.2d 390, 392 (Tex.App.—Austin 1982, writ ref'd n.r.e.). Adopting parents "provided [respondent] with an affidavit of relinquishment. The instrument, which [respondent] signed before a notary, manifested a clear intent to completely sever her ties with the child. Because the instrument was defective it could not, standing alone, serve as the proof necessary for termination. It is, however, evidentiary as to [respondent's] expressed intent not to return."

§161.001(b)(1)(B)

Brokenleg v. Butts, 559 S.W.2d 853, 856 (Tex. App.—El Paso 1977, writ ref'd n.r.e.). There are four elements to Fam. Code §15.02(1)(B), now §161.001(b)(1)(B): "(1) voluntarily leaving the child; (2) without expressing an intent to return; (3) without providing for the adequate support of the child; and (4) remaining away for a period of at least three months. [T]he standard for determining nonsupport under Subparagraph (B) is whether or not there is provision for adequate support of the child, rather than the parent's ability to support the child as in Subparagraph (F). The evidence in this case all reflects that the grandparents were able to and did in fact adequately support the child…. Since the test under this Subparagraph is not whether or not the parent actually supported the child, but whether or not arrangements were made for the adequate support of the child, and the evidence is undisputed that they were, we conclude that §15.02(1)(B) is not applicable…."

§161.001(b)(1)(C)

Holick v. Smith, 685 S.W.2d 18, 21 (Tex.1985). Respondents "argue that the legislature intended to require parents to personally 'provide adequate support' under (1)(C) [now (b)(1)(C)] because (1)(B) [now (b)(1)(B)] contains the language 'provide *for the* adequate support.' [¶] We believe that subsection (1)(C) is capable of two interpretations. 'Provide' is defined to mean 'to furnish; supply' or 'to fit out with means to an end.' Thus, subsection (1)(C) is susceptible to an interpretation which would merely require that the parent make arrangements for adequate support rather than personally support the child. [¶] We hold that under [Fam. Code] §15.02(1)(C) [now §161.001(b)(1)(C)], [mother] was required to make arrangements for the adequate support rather than personally support the children." *See also* ***In re R.M.***, 180 S.W.3d 874, 878 (Tex.App.—Texarkana 2005, no pet.) (physical delivery of child is not significant; controlling issue is whether parent was aware of, consented to, and participated in arrangement for child's support).

In re D.L.N., 958 S.W.2d 934, 937 (Tex.App.—Waco 1997, pet. denied), *disapproved on other grounds*, ***In re C.H.***, 89 S.W.3d 17 (Tex.2002). "We must look at the plain and common meaning of 'remained away for a period of at least six months' to determine if the law requires that these be six consecutive months of absence. The language used in this subsection indicates that a parent must remain away from a child for a minimum of six months, without providing adequate support, in order to have his or her parental rights terminated under this provision. Thus, because a parent should not face a termination on this ground until the minimum time-period of six months has passed, we believe the legislature intended that the six month time-period consist of six consecutive months. In addition to the plain language of the statute, other appellate courts have concluded that when a parent's rights are terminated for failing to support a child for one year under §161.001(1)(F) [now §161.001(b)(1)(F)] the 'year' referred to in the statute means 12 consecutive months. Finally, our interpretation of §161.001(1)(C) [now §161.001(b)(1)(C)] to require six consecutive months of absence is consistent with the Supreme Court's directive that involuntary termination statutes be strictly construed in favor of the parent." *See also* ***In re J.R.***, 319 S.W.3d 773, 777 (Tex.App.—El Paso 2010, no pet.) (period must last at least six consecutive months).

In re B.T., 954 S.W.2d 44, 49 (Tex.App.—San Antonio 1997, pet. denied). Respondent "claims in his brief that he did not voluntarily leave [child] with the Department since he was in jail most of the time. Mere imprisonment does not constitute intentional abandonment of the child as a matter of law. However, imprisonment is a factor to consider along with the other evidence." *See also* ***In re J.K.H.***, No. 06-09-00035-CV (Tex. App.—Texarkana 2009, no pet.) (memo op.; 9-16-09) (although father did not visit his children after divorce, he did not voluntarily leave children "in possession of another" because divorce decree required him to leave children in mother's possession).

In re S.K.S., 648 S.W.2d 402, 404 (Tex.App.—San Antonio 1983, no writ). Under §161.001(1)(C), now §161.001(b)(1)(C), "[i]n-ability to provide support during some months would not interrupt the running of the [limitations] period if no effort is made to pay support during other months in which there is clear ability to pay." *See also* ***In re Guillory***, 618 S.W.2d 948, 951 (Tex.App.—Houston [1st Dist.] 1981, no writ) (termination for nonsupport applies even when inability to pay is result of parent's conscious choice).

§161.001(b)(1)(D)

In re E.M., 494 S.W.3d 209, 222 (Tex.App.—Waco 2015, pet. denied). "A parent's illegal drug use and drug-related criminal activity may … support a finding that the child's surroundings endanger his or her physical or emotional well-being. … A factfinder may reasonably infer from a parent's refusal to take a drug test that the parent was using drugs. A parent's continued drug use demonstrates an inability to provide for the child's emotional and physical needs and to provide a stable environment for the child."

In re N.T., 474 S.W.3d 465, 476 (Tex.App.—Dallas 2015, no pet.). "'Endanger' means to expose to loss or injury or jeopardize a child's emotional or physical health. It is not necessary that the conduct be directed at the child or that the child actually suffer an injury. The primary distinction between subsections (D) and (E) is the source of the physical or emotional endangerment to the child. Subsection (D) addresses the child's surroundings and environment, while subsection (E) specifically addresses parental conduct. However, conduct of the parent or another can be relevant to the child's environment under subsection (D). That is, conduct of a parent or another person in the home can create an environment that endangers the physical and emotional well-being of a child as required for termination under subsection (D). Inappropriate, abusive, or unlawful conduct by persons who live in the child's home is part of the 'conditions or surroundings' of the child's home under subsection (D)." (Internal quotes omitted.) *See also* ***In re A.S.***, 261 S.W.3d 76, 83 (Tex. App.—Houston [14th Dist.] 2008, pet. denied) (living conditions that are merely "less-than-ideal" do not support finding under §161.001(1)(D), now §161.001(b)(1)(D)).

In re A.L.H., 468 S.W.3d 738, 746-47 (Tex.App.—Houston [14th Dist.] 2015, no pet.). "Subsection D is not a basis for terminating parental rights if the parent was unaware of the endangering environment. However, a parent need not know for certain that the child is in an endangering environment; awareness of such a potential is sufficient. The relevant time period is before the Department removes the child. [¶] No evidence was presented to support [caseworker's] opinion that the father had knowledge of the mother's drug use, either in the past or present. The record contains no

drug test results, criminal records, or prior termination decrees for either parent. ... Unsupported, conclusory opinions of a witness do not constitute evidence of probative force. A witness's belief is no more than mere surmise or suspicion, which is not the same as evidence. [¶] The record reflects the Department introduced no evidence of the actual physical surroundings or conditions of the child's environment prior to his removal. Moreover, the Department did not introduce legally-sufficient evidence that the father had knowledge of the child's environment at that time. Although there is some evidence of the father's suspected drug use, the record fails to reflect when it occurred or whether it posed a potential danger to the child. [¶] Subsection D unambiguously requires proof that the father knowingly exposed the child to an endangering environment. The record contains no evidence that the child was in an endangering environment before the child was taken into the Department's care or that the father knowingly exposed the child to such an environment." *See also* ***In re C.D.E.***, 391 S.W.3d 287, 296-97 (Tex. App.—Fort Worth 2012, no pet.) (no endangerment because incarcerated father was not aware of mother's drug use or condition of mother's home).

In re N.K., 399 S.W.3d 322, 330 (Tex.App.—Amarillo 2013, no pet.). "[E]ndangering conduct is not limited to actions directed toward the child.... A parent's conduct in the home, such as illegal drug use or unlawful conduct, can create an environment that endangers the child's physical and emotional well-being. Indeed, '[i]t is illogical to reason that inappropriate, debauching, unlawful, or unnatural conduct of persons who live in the home of a child, or with whom a child is compelled to associate on a regular basis in his home, are not inherently a part of the conditions and surroundings[ ] of that place or home.' *At 331:* Conduct which subjects a child to a life of uncertainty and instability endangers the physical and emotional well-being of a child. [¶] '[A]n environment which routinely subjects a child to the probability that she will be left alone because her parents are once again jailed, whether because of the continued violation of probationary conditions or because of a new offense growing out of a continued use of illegal drugs, or because the parents are once again committed to a rehabilitation program, endangers both the physical and emotional well-being of a child.'"

A.S. v. TDFPS, 394 S.W.3d 703, 713 (Tex.App.—El Paso 2012, no pet.). "[T]here are some distinctions in the application of subsections (D) and (E). Knowledge of paternity is a prerequisite to a showing of knowing placement of a child in an endangering environment under §161.001(1)(D) [now §161.001(b)(1)(D)], however it is not a prerequisite to a showing of a parental course of conduct which endangers a child under §161.001(1)(E) [now §161.001(b)(1)(E)]. Furthermore, termination [under] §161.001(1)(D) is permitted 'because of a single act or omission.' Conversely, termination under (E) requires a conscious course of conduct by the parent." *See also* ***In re Stevenson***, 27 S.W.3d 195, 203 (Tex.App.—San Antonio 2000, pet. denied) (to terminate parental rights under §161.001(1)(D), now §161.001(b)(1)(D), jury should have been instructed to limit consideration of father's acts and omissions to time after he learned that he was child's father).

In re H.L.F., No. 12-11-00243-CV (Tex.App.—Tyler 2012, pet. denied) (memo op.; 11-30-12). "[T]he fact that a mother used a controlled substance while she was pregnant and did not obtain routine prenatal care does not mean that termination is automatic. [¶] The Department did not present any evidence that [child] tested positive for any controlled substance, that she needed specialized medical treatment, or that she suffered from any birth defects, abnormalities, or complications as a result of [mother's] drug use during the first trimester of her pregnancy. At the time of the removal, [mother] had not had possession of [child]. Therefore, [mother] could not have exposed [child] to endangering conditions or surroundings between the time of [child's] birth and the time of her removal. [¶] [The Department] implicitly contend[s] that [methamphetamine use prior to and during the first trimester of mother's pregnancy] created an endangering condition or surrounding inside [mother's] womb before [child] was born. [But this is not a case involving] a mother who abused one or more controlled substances throughout her pregnancy and had a child who was born addicted to the controlled substance or with the controlled substance still in the child's system. [¶] [W]e hold that the evidence is legally insufficient to terminate [mother's] parental rights pursuant to subsection (D)."

In re J.R., 171 S.W.3d 558, 570 (Tex.App.—Houston [14th Dist.] 2005, no pet.). "Any alleged likelihood that [mother] will knowingly expose the children to a

dangerous environment in the future is not sufficient to prove a violation of §161.001(1)(D) [now §161.001(b)(1)(D)]. Such a likelihood would be relevant to the issue of whether termination is in the children's best interest and also would be relevant to the issue of how much contact [mother] should have with her children if her parental rights are not terminated, but it does not amount to proof of a past act of knowing environmental endangerment."

§161.001(b)(1)(E)

In re E.N.C., 384 S.W.3d 796, 805 (Tex.2012). "[D]eportation, like incarceration, is a factor that may be considered (albeit an insufficient one in and of itself to establish endangerment), [but] its relevance to endangerment depends on the circumstances. Under the [appellate] court's reasoning, the mere threat of deportation or incarceration resulting from an unlawful act, regardless of severity, would establish endangerment. We disagree with that analysis. ... The court's broad reasoning necessarily applies to citizens as well. Any offense committed by a citizen that could lead to imprisonment or confinement would also apparently establish endangerment, simply because the parent's ability to be present in his children's lives would be uncertain. Our nation's Constitution forbids such a far-reaching interpretation of our parental rights termination statutes. *At 806:* [T]here are similarities between incarceration and deportation in that the parent is no longer available to reside with the children in their home in the U.S. But, [u]nlike an incarcerated individual, a person who is deported is able to work, have a home, and support a family. More importantly, it is possible for the person's children to live with him. [¶] Deportation flowing from an unknown offense occurring many years earlier cannot satisfy the State's burden of proving by clear and convincing evidence that a parent engaged in an endangering course of conduct...." *See also **In re R.A.G.***, this page.

In re M.C., 917 S.W.2d 268, 270 (Tex.1996). "Although there is no evidence that [respondent] inflicted direct physical abuse on her children, there is evidence that she neglected their physical needs, and neglect can be just as dangerous to the well-being of a child as direct physical abuse."

Texas DHS v. Boyd, 727 S.W.2d 531, 533 (Tex. 1987). "While we agree that 'endanger' means more than a threat of metaphysical injury or the possible ill effects of a less-than-ideal family environment, it is not necessary that the conduct be directed at the child or that the child actually suffers injury. Rather, 'endanger' means to expose to loss or injury [or] to jeopardize[,] and imprisonment is certainly a factor to be considered by the trial court on the issue of endangerment. *At 534:* We hold that if the evidence, including the imprisonment, shows a course of conduct which has the effect of endangering the physical or emotional well-being of the child, a finding under [Fam. Code] §15.02(1)(E) [now §161.001(b)(1)(E)] is supportable."

In re R.A.G., ___ S.W.3d ___ (Tex.App.—El Paso 2017, no pet.) (No. 08-16-00178-CV; 1-11-17). Father "was incarcerated for the first four years of [child's] life.... Following his release from prison, [father] was deported to Mexico. It is understandable that [father], as a result of his deportation, has been unable to visit with [child] in person in the U.S., but the evidence showed that [father] has not had any other type of contact with [child] during the years following his deportation. According to [father's] sister, [father] has maintained the same telephone number and Facebook account since his release from prison ..., yet he made no effort to contact [child] even after he learned that the child had been removed from [mother's] care. [Father] has been absent from [child's] life to the extent that [child] did not even know that [he] is [child's] father. While incarceration and deportation are not sufficient, standing alone, to support a finding under §161.001(b)(1)(E), these facts are part of [father's] overall course of conduct. We conclude that the evidence is legally and factually sufficient to establish a firm conviction or belief in the mind of the trier of fact that [father] engaged in conduct that endangered [child's] physical or emotional well-being under §161.001(b)(1)(E)." *See also **In re E.N.C.***, this page.

In re B.C.S., 479 S.W.3d 918, 926-27 (Tex.App.—El Paso 2015, no pet.). "Under subsection (E), the cause of the danger to the child must be the parent's conduct alone, as evidenced not only by the parent's actions but also by the parent's omission or failure to act. The conduct to be examined includes what the parents did both before and after the child was born. To be relevant, the conduct does not have to have been directed at the child, nor must actual harm result to the child from the conduct. Additionally, termination under subsection (E) must be based on more than a single act or omission; a voluntary, deliberate, and conscious course of conduct by the parent is required. The specific danger

to the child's well-being need not be established as an independent proposition, but may be inferred from parental misconduct. Evidence of criminal conduct, convictions, and imprisonment and its effect on a parent's life and ability to parent may establish an endangering course of conduct. Imprisonment alone does not constitute an endangering course of conduct but it is a fact properly considered on the endangerment issue. Routinely subjecting a child to the probability that she will be left alone because her parent is in jail, endangers the child's physical and emotional well-being. However, the relationship of the parent and child, as well as efforts to improve or enhance parenting skills, are relevant in determining whether a parent's conduct results in 'endangerment' under §161.001(1)(E), even where the parent is incarcerated." (Internal quotes omitted.) *See also* ***In re S.M.***, 389 S.W.3d 483, 492 (Tex. App.—El Paso 2012, no pet.) (even though father committed multiple criminal offenses that led to incarceration before child was born, conduct could be considered to endanger child); ***In re H.L.F.***, No. 12-11-00243-CV (Tex.App.—Tyler 2012, pet. denied) (memo op.; 11-30-12) (endangering conduct before child's birth did not support termination because dangerous conduct stopped once child was born). *But see* ***In re T.C.C.H.***, No. 07-11-00179-CV (Tex.App.—Amarillo 2011, no pet.) (memo op.; 12-22-11) (termination can be based on single act or omission in extreme cases).

In re A.A.M., 464 S.W.3d 421, 426 (Tex.App.—Houston [1st Dist.] 2015, no pet.). "Drug abuse and its effect on the ability to parent can be part of an endangering course of conduct. Illegal drug use creates the possibility that the parent will be impaired or imprisoned and thus incapable of parenting. When a parent's imprisonment demonstrates a deliberate course of conduct, it too qualifies as endangering conduct. Drug use and the imprisonments relating to it harm the physical and emotional well-being of a child. [¶] The father observes that he merely exercised visitation during these periods of positive drug tests and criminal activity; he was not the custodial parent. Nevertheless, because they significantly harm the parenting relationship, criminal offenses and drug activity can constitute endangerment even if the criminal conduct transpires outside the child's presence." *See also* ***In re M.G.P.***, No. 02-11-00038-CV (Tex.App.—Fort Worth 2011, pet. denied) (memo op.; 12-22-11) (drug use before mother knew she was pregnant did not support termination because she stopped using drugs when she learned she was pregnant); ***In re A.S.***, 261 S.W.3d 76, 86 (Tex. App.—Houston [14th Dist.] 2008, pet. denied) (one-time use of marijuana during pregnancy did not support termination).

Burns v. Burns, 434 S.W.3d 223, 228 (Tex.App.—Houston [1st Dist.] 2014, no pet.). "According to [mother, father] judicially admitted that he endangered the child's emotional well-being by not visiting him [for several years], which conclusively proves that [father] engaged in conduct proscribed by §161.001(1)(E) [now §161.001(b)(1)(E)]. *At 229:* [Father's] acknowledgment that his absence from [child's] life 'endangers [child's] emotional well-being' is a testimonial admission, but it is not the kind of unequivocal statement that amounts to a judicial admission. *At 230:* Because the parties disputed both the reasons for, and effect of, [father's] absence from [child's] life, we hold [mother] cannot establish that [father's] rights must be terminated as a matter of law."

In re A.T., 406 S.W.3d 365, 371 (Tex.App.—Dallas 2013, pet. denied). "Unsanitary conditions can [qualify] as surroundings that endanger a child. [¶] [In this case], both parents [also] acknowledged they were possibly putting [child] in a dangerous situation by co-sleeping. [¶] [And] Mother's and Father's poor hygiene must certainly be considered. *At 372:* Evidence also supports Mother and Father hesitated in considering [child's] medical needs. [¶] [Mother] asserts that her low IQ rendered her incapable of knowing and recognizing any danger to [child]. We disagree. Courts have held that limited mental capacity does not, as a matter of law, negate a parent's ability to knowingly neglect their child. *At 374:* [T]he evidence supports the trial court's ruling that Mother and Father violated §§161.001(1)(D) and (E) [now §161.001(b)(1)(D) and (E)]." *See also* ***In re P.E.W.***, 105 S.W.3d 771, 777 (Tex.App.—Amarillo 2003, no pet.) (child can be endangered even if she does not "develop or succumb to a malady" due to unsanitary living conditions or lack of attention to medical needs).

In re T.G.R.-M., 404 S.W.3d 7, 14 (Tex.App.—Houston [1st Dist.] 2013, no pet.). "[A] factor that may contribute to an environment that endangers a child's well-being is a parent's abusive or violent criminal conduct. Evidence as to how a parent has treated another child is relevant regarding whether a course of endan-

gering conduct has been established. Evidence that a parent previously has engaged in abusive conduct allows an inference that the parent's violent behavior will continue in the future." *See also* ***In re E.A.G.***, 373 S.W.3d 129, 143 (Tex.App.—San Antonio 2012, pet. denied) (evidence that father had sexually assaulted stepdaughter was sufficient to show that his conduct endangered his other children who lived in same home, including unborn children).

Jordan v. Dossey, 325 S.W.3d 700, 723-24 (Tex. App.—Houston [1st Dist.] 2010, pet. denied). "A parent's mental state may be considered in determining whether a child is endangered if that mental state allows the parent to engage in conduct that jeopardizes the physical or emotional well-being of the child. A parent's mental instability and attempt to commit suicide may contribute to a finding that the parent engaged in a course of conduct that endangered a child's physical or emotional well-being." *See also* ***In re A.L.H.***, 515 S.W.3d 60, ___ (Tex.App.—Houston [14th Dist.] 2017, pet. denied) (mental illness alone is not ground for termination); ***In re C.J.S.***, 383 S.W.3d 682, 690 (Tex. App.—Houston [14th Dist.] 2012, no pet.) (mother's impaired judgment and lack of impulse control contributed to finding that her conduct endangered child).

In re C.A.B., 289 S.W.3d 874, 883 (Tex.App.—Houston [14th Dist.] 2009, no pet.). "[A] court may consider evidence establishing that a parent continued to engage in endangering conduct after the child's removal by the Department or after the child no longer was in the parent's care, thus showing the parent continued to engage in the course of conduct in question." *See also* ***Walker v. TDFPS***, 312 S.W.3d 608, 617 (Tex. App.—Houston [1st Dist.] 2009, pet. denied) (same as annotation); ***In re S.T.***, 263 S.W.3d 394, 402 (Tex. App.—Waco 2008, pet. denied) (father committed criminal acts before and after child's removal even though he knew his parental rights were in jeopardy; all conduct was evidence of endangerment). *But see* ***In re J.K.F.***, 345 S.W.3d 706, 711 (Tex.App.—Dallas 2011, no pet.) (relevant time frame to determine endangerment is before children are removed).

In re M.N.G., 147 S.W.3d 521, 536 (Tex.App.—Fort Worth 2004, pet. denied). "[S]cienter is only required under [§161.001(1)(E), now §161.001(b)(1)(E),] when a parent places the child *with others* who engage in an endangering course of conduct. As a general rule, conduct that subjects a child to a life of uncertainty and instability endangers the physical and emotional well-being of a child."

In re J.M.M., 80 S.W.3d 232, 242 (Tex.App.—Fort Worth 2002, pet. denied), *disapproved on other grounds*, ***In re J.F.C.***, 96 S.W.3d 256 (Tex.2002). "Placement with an abusive parent or relative is endangerment under [§161.001(1)(E), now §161.001(b)(1)(E)]." *See also* ***In re M.G.P.***, No. 02-11-00038-CV (Tex.App.—Fort Worth 2011, pet. denied) (memo op.; 12-22-11) (mother who was victim in abusive relationship did not endanger child because she tried to avoid contact with abuser and did not have pattern of being involved in multiple abusive relationships); ***In re J.J.S.***, 272 S.W.3d 74, 79 (Tex.App.—Waco 2008, pet. denied) (mother who was victim in abusive relationships exposed children to environment where physical violence was present); ***In re D.J.***, 100 S.W.3d 658, 669 (Tex.App.—Dallas 2003, pet. denied) (allegations of father's physical violence before child's birth were not enough to put mother on notice that father would abuse child).

Doyle v. TDPRS, 16 S.W.3d 390, 398 (Tex.App.—El Paso 2000, pet. denied). "The [TDPRS] urges that [respondent's] failure to locate and maintain stable employment so that she could provide for the children's needs and her failure to provide a stable home for the children violates §161.001(1)(E) [now §161.001(b)(1)(E)]. Ordinarily, the stability of the home is one of the factors that should be examined in ascertaining the best interest of a child. Depending on the evidence, it is possible that a parent's failure to provide a stable home and otherwise provide for the children's needs may contribute to a finding that termination is appropriate." *See also* ***In re J.R.***, 171 S.W.3d 558, 578 (Tex.App.—Houston [14th Dist.] 2005, no pet.) (§161.001(1)(E), now §161.001(b)(1)(E), finding cannot be based solely on failure to maintain stable housing).

§161.001(b)(1)(F)

In re D.M.D., 363 S.W.3d 916, 922 (Tex.App.—Houston [14th Dist.] 2012, no pet.). Mother's "primary support obligation was to pay … court-ordered child support. Nevertheless, [she] ignored this responsibility by providing certain necessities directly to the children—in the process circumventing the ability of the Department and the foster families to recoup money they were spending to support the children. Because [mother] had the ability but chose not to pay at least

some amount of child support, the trial court could have reasonably found [she] failed to support the child in accordance with her ability during a period of one year ending within six months of the date of the filing of the petition."

In re C.L., 322 S.W.3d 889, 892-93 (Tex.App.—Houston [14th Dist.] 2010, no pet.). "The undisputed evidence in the record shows that in [a] 12-month period ..., [father] gave no money whatsoever in [child] support.... [Father] had the ability to provide at least some support during these 12 months, but he provided none. [He] argues that DFPS must present evidence of his ability to pay during each month of the 12-month period. The evidence in the record regarding [his] income is not broken down on a monthly basis for the entire time period. However, even if [father] was unable to provide support during some of those months, that will not interrupt the running of the one-year period if he made no effort to pay during other months in which there is a clear ability to pay. It is undisputed that [father] had [some] income in the relevant time frame but provided no support at all. This is sufficient to support a finding ... of a violation of §161.001(1)(F) [now §161.001(b)(1)(F)]." *See also* ***In re C.M.C.***, No. 11-02-00270-CV (Tex.App.—Eastland 2003, no pet.) (memo op.; 3-6-03) (inability to provide support during some months will not interrupt running of one-year period if no effort is made to pay support during other months); ***In re T.B.D.***, this page.

In re N.A.F., 282 S.W.3d 113, 118 (Tex.App.—Waco 2009, no pet.). "While it is true that a child-support order contains an implied finding that the obligor was able to pay the ordered support, that 'support order only contains an implied finding as of the time the order is entered; it cannot predict the future.' Thus, a child-support order is no evidence of [father's] ability to pay support for the 12 consecutive months required by §161.001(1)(F) [now §161.001(b)(1)(F)]." *See also* ***In re D.M.D.***, 363 S.W.3d 916, 920 (Tex.App.—Houston [14th Dist.] 2012, no pet.).

In re E.M.E., 223 S.W.3d 71, 73-74 (Tex.App.—El Paso 2007, no pet.). "[W] argued at trial that the child support order contains an implied finding that [H] has the ability to pay the amount of child support ordered[, thus requiring H to prove as an affirmative defense that he did not have the ability to pay]. Section 161.001 does not create [an] affirmative defense in termination proceedings. To the contrary, §161.001(1)(F) [now §161.001(b)(1)(F)] squarely places the burden to prove ability to pay on the petitioner. [¶] [R]equiring the respondent to present evidence of inability to pay wrongfully shifts the burden and excuses the petitioner from proving that the parent failed to support in accordance with the parent's ability." *See also* ***In re L.J.N.***, 329 S.W.3d 667, 672 (Tex.App.—Corpus Christi 2010, no pet.) (managing conservators had burden to prove that incarcerated father had ability to pay child support); ***In re N.A.F.***, 282 S.W.3d 113, 117-18 (Tex.App.—Waco 2009, no pet.) (same as annotation). *But see* ***In re J.M.M.***, 80 S.W.3d 232, 251 (Tex.App.—Fort Worth 2002, pet. denied) (inability to pay court-ordered child support is affirmative defense in termination suit), *disapproved on other grounds*, ***In re J.F.C.***, 96 S.W.3d 256 (Tex.2002).

In re T.B.D., 223 S.W.3d 515, 518 (Tex.App.—Amarillo 2006, no pet.). "The one-year period means 12 consecutive months, and there must be proof the parent had the ability to pay support during each month of the 12-month period." *See also* ***In re R.M.***, 180 S.W.3d 874, 878 (Tex.App.—Texarkana 2005, no pet.) (termination was proper when father worked for 18-month period before suit was filed but did not pay any child support); ***Hellman v. Kincy***, 632 S.W.2d 216, 218 (Tex.App.—Fort Worth 1982, no writ) (12 consecutive months of not making arrearage payments supported termination even though father made current child-support payments during that period); ***In re C.L.***, this page.

§161.001(b)(1)(H)

In re D.M.F., 283 S.W.3d 124, 132 (Tex.App.—Fort Worth 2009, pet. granted, judgm't vacated w.r.m.). Section 161.001(1)(H), now §161.001(b)(1)(H), "requires scienter or prior knowledge of the pregnancy. [¶] [B]ecause there is no clear and convincing proof that [father] had knowledge that [mother] was carrying his child until ... *after* the child was born, the evidence could not show that he abandoned her *during* her pregnancy. [S]ubsection H cannot apply."

In re T.M.Z., 665 S.W.2d 184, 187 (Tex.App.—San Antonio 1984, no writ). "Although the evidence clearly shows it was the mother who left the scene when violence erupted during her seventh month of pregnancy, we do not agree there was no 'voluntary abandonment' by the father as the result of her departure. The father knew where his pregnant [W] went; he knew her parents and the location of their house. Testimony indicates he did go to that house on occasion, but he never

provided any support either to [W] or his child. He was not prohibited from tendering support through the [mail]. He was not prohibited from going to the attending doctor's office to arrange payment for prenatal care. Nor was he denied entrance to the business office of the hospital to arrange payment for hospital care for [W] and for delivery of his child. [¶] Abandonment can mean more than a physical leave-taking. It can also mean to turn one's back on a duty that one has."

Allred v. Harris Cty. Child Welfare Unit, 615 S.W.2d 803, 807 (Tex.App.—Houston [1st Dist.] 1980, writ ref'd n.r.e.). "The evidence that [father] entered into a course of wilful criminal activity with knowledge of [W's] pregnancy and of the possible consequences of his course of conduct implied a conscious disregard and indifference to his parental responsibilities and the subsequent imprisonment for such conduct constituted 'voluntary abandonment.'"

§161.001(b)(1)(J)

Yonko v. DFPS, 196 S.W.3d 236, 242 (Tex.App.—Houston [1st Dist.] 2006, no pet.). Mother "admits that she never enrolled [child] in school or otherwise provided him with a certified home-school education.... [Mother] further contends that she and [child] were never Texas residents for any relevant time period under the statute. [¶] The compulsory education statute does not state a residency requirement, and the case law indicates that moving frequently does not exempt a parent from the requirement of enrolling a child in school or otherwise providing for his education."

§161.001(b)(1)(K)

In re K.M.L., 443 S.W.3d 101, 113 (Tex.2014). "Family Code §161.001(1)(K) [now §161.001(b)(1)(K)] permits a trial court to terminate the parent-child relationship if it finds by clear and convincing evidence that the parent has executed an unrevoked or irrevocable affidavit of relinquishment of parental rights. The petitioner ... has the burden to prove the elements necessary to support termination of the parent-child relationship. [Family Code] §161.103 requires that the affidavit be for *voluntary* relinquishment, ... and implicit in §161.001(1)(K) is the requirement that the affidavit of parental rights be voluntarily executed. An involuntarily executed affidavit is a complete defense to a termination suit based on §161.001(1)(K)."

In re E.J.R., 503 S.W.3d 536, 543-44 (Tex.App.—Corpus Christi 2016, pet. filed 11-14-16). "[A]n affidavit of relinquishment *may* be a *sufficient* basis, in itself, to find the child's best interest; but ... such an affidavit [does not require] the trial court to order an involuntary termination.... [W]hile the execution of an affidavit of relinquishment of parental rights is relevant to the inquiry whether termination of parental rights is in the best interests of the child, such an affidavit 'is not *ipso facto* evidence that termination is in the child's best interest.' [¶] Even when an affidavit is irrevocable, public policy does not favor the conclusion that an affidavit of relinquishment makes termination mandatory. 'For instance, if termination would leave the child without financial support from a financially capable but disinterested parent, public policy would not favor letting the parent dispense with his obligation on the parent's whim.' Rather than being compelled to oblige a parent's desire for termination, the trial court may be better guided by a 'child's need for stability' and the recognition that 'a change in custody usually disrupts the child's living arrangements and the channels of a child's affection, and in effect alters the entire tenor of the child's life.'" *See also* ***In re K.S.L.***, 499 S.W.3d 109, 113-14 (Tex.App.—San Antonio 2016, pet. granted 6-23-17); ***In re Morris***, 498 S.W.3d 624, 628-29 (Tex.App.—Houston [14th Dist.] 2016, orig. proceeding); ***In re K.D.***, 471 S.W.3d 147, 164 (Tex.App.—Texarkana 2015, no pet.). *But see* ***In re J.H.***, p. 779.

In re B.B.F., 595 S.W.2d 873, 874 (Tex.App.—San Antonio 1980, no writ). "Since execution of an affidavit of relinquishment of parental rights is a proper basis for terminating those rights in a subsequent suit to terminate the parent-child relationship, and a waiver of process may be included in the affidavit, it is clear that a waiver of citation may be signed prior to the filing of suit. Thus, the Family Code provides an exception to the general rule that a waiver of citation is proper only if executed after suit is brought. There is a sound reason for this exception. After executing an unrevoked or irrevocable affidavit of relinquishment of parental rights, a natural parent is no longer an interested party in a suit to terminate the parent-child relationship. Consequently, neither due process nor logic require that a person who has voluntarily relinquished parental rights and waived service of citation be given notice of a subsequent suit to terminate the parent-child relationship."

§161.001(b)(1)(L)

In re L.S.R., 92 S.W.3d 529, 530 (Tex.2002). "The State presented evidence at trial showing that [father]

had received deferred adjudication for the offense of indecency with a child, an offense [father] committed against his four-year-old cousin when he was 16. The court of appeals held that there was no evidence to support termination under §161.001(1)(L)(iv) [now §161.001(b)(1)(L)(iv)] because there had been 'no showing that [father's] cousin suffered death or serious injury as a result of his conduct.' The court of appeals deleted this ground for termination from the judgment, but otherwise affirmed the judgment against [father]. [¶] We deny the petitions for review, but disavow any suggestion that molestation of a four-year-old, or indecency with a child, generally, does not cause serious injury."

R.F. v. TDFPS, 390 S.W.3d 63, 73 (Tex.App.—El Paso 2012, no pet.). Father "contends there is no evidence, or insufficient evidence, to prove that his [offense of indecency with a child] 'caused the death or serious injury of a child,' as required under [§161.001(1)(L), now §161.001(b)(1)(L)]. *At 75:* [He] complains that [child's therapist's] testimony did not make a causal connection between the sexual abuse and the child's hospitalization. We disagree. While [therapist] may not have specifically attributed all of Child['s] problems to the sexual abuse, she did testify that sexual abuse was a factor. [Father] cites no authority, and we have found none, suggesting that sexual indecency must be the sole cause of serious injury. [W]e find the evidence legally sufficient to support, by clear and convincing evidence, a determination that Child … suffered serious injury as a result of [father's] indecent conduct." *See also* ***In re L.S.R.***, p. 764.

In re A.L., 389 S.W.3d 896, 900-01 (Tex.App.—Houston [14th Dist.] 2012, no pet.). "The Family Code does not define 'serious injury,' and [mother] urges us to adopt the Penal Code's definition of 'serious bodily injury' as the standard required for [Fam. Code §161.001(1)(L), now §161.001(b)(1)(L),] to support termination. We decline to do so. [¶] 'Serious injury,' as used in subsection (L) modifies all the offenses listed thereunder. Not all offenses listed in subsection (L) require bodily injury. We conclude demonstrating 'serious injury' to a child under subsection (L) does not require a showing of 'serious bodily injury' as defined in the Penal Code. [¶] 'Serious' means 'having important or dangerous possible consequences,' while 'injury' means 'hurt, damage, or loss sustained.'" *See also* ***C.H. v. DFPS***, No. 01-11-00385-CV (Tex.App.—Houston [1st Dist.] 2012, pet. denied) (memo op.; 2-23-12) (§161.001(1)(L) requires showing of "serious injury" as defined by dictionary, not "serious bodily injury" as required by Pen. Code).

§161.001(b)(1)(M)

In re A.C., 394 S.W.3d 633, 640 (Tex.App.—Houston [1st Dist.] 2012, no pet.). "The mother challenges whether [prior termination] decree could be used to prove a prior termination because the decree, and therefore the termination, was on appeal and thus not necessarily final. The prior decree stated that 'this case is not final until [the trial court's] plenary jurisdiction from this final judgment expires, and all appeals, if any, have concluded.' While acknowledging that the 'case' was not final and accordingly maintaining the appointment of the attorneys ad litem and the guardian ad litem, the decree reiterated that 'this judgment is final.' But finality, in the sense of a complete exhaustion or waiver of all possible appellate remedies, is not expressly required by [§161.001(1)(M), now §161.001(b)(1)(M)]."

In re J.M.M., 80 S.W.3d 232, 243 (Tex.App.—Fort Worth 2002, pet. denied), *disapproved on other grounds*, ***In re J.F.C.***, 96 S.W.3d 256 (Tex.2002). "We hold that, when a prior decree of termination as to another child is properly admitted into evidence, the TDPRS need not reestablish that the parent's conduct with respect to that child was in violation of §161.001(1)(D) or (E) [now §161.001(b)(1)(D), (E)]. The TDPRS need only show that [parent's] rights were terminated as to her other children based on *findings* that she violated [sub-]sections (D) and (E)." *See also* ***Espinosa v. TDFPS***, No. 01-08-00309-CV (Tex.App.—Houston [1st Dist.] 2008, no pet.) (memo op.; 10-30-08).

§161.001(b)(1)(N)

In re G.P., 503 S.W.3d 531, 533-34 (Tex.App.—Waco 2016, pet. denied). "Under the second element, '[r]eturning the child to the parent, per §161.001(1)(N)(i) [now 161.001(b)(1)(N)(i)], does not necessarily mean that the child has to be physically delivered' to the individual. In fact, courts have previously held that this element can be satisfied by preparing and administering a service plan. [¶] There are several factors to indicate a parent's willingness and ability to provide the child with a safe environment: 'the child's age and physical and mental vulnerabilities; the willingness and ability of the child's family to seek out, accept, and complete counseling services and to cooperate with and facilitate

an appropriate agency's close supervision; the willingness and ability of the child's family to effect positive environmental and personal changes within a reasonable period of time; and whether the child's family demonstrates adequate parenting skills, including providing the child with minimally adequate health and nutritional care, a safe physical home environment, and an understanding of the child's needs and capabilities.'"

In re A.T.L., ___ S.W.3d ___ (Tex.App.—San Antonio 2015, pet. denied) (No. 04-15-00379-CV; 10-28-15). "A family service plan is designed to reunify a parent with a child who has been removed by the Department. Implementation of a family service plan by the Department is ordinarily considered a reasonable effort to return a child to its parent. [¶] '[T]he requirement that the Department has made reasonable efforts to return the child to the parent may be inapplicable when the parent is incarcerated.' However, reasonable efforts to return a child to a parent 'under §161.001(1)(N)(i) does not necessarily mean the child must be physically delivered to the incarcerated parent.' [¶] [Father] was confirmed as [child's] father during the ... termination hearing; he signed his plan [four months later]; he was incarcerated approximately three weeks later; and he remained incarcerated until the termination hearing. According to [father], there is no evidence in the record that he was provided a reasonable opportunity to enroll in, much less complete, any of his plan requirements. [¶] Although there appears to be no dispute that [mother] denied him any contact with [child], nothing in the record indicates [father] took any action to contact or gain access to his child in the more than eight months between her birth and his incarceration, or during the period of his incarceration. [Caseworker] testified [father] told her [that] doing the services was not imperative to him and [that] the plan was not important to him at that point in time because he wanted to get himself situated first. [¶] [T]he Department's preparation and administration of a service plan, in conjunction with its consideration of relative placements, supports the trial court's finding that the Department made reasonable efforts to return the child to [father]. [¶] Incarceration does not render 'it impossible for the parent to maintain significant contact with the child.' ... On this record, we conclude the evidence supports the trial court's finding that [father] did not regularly visit or maintain significant contact with [child]." *See also* ***In re M.V.G.***, 440 S.W.3d 54, 60-61 (Tex.App.—Waco 2010, no pet.) (Department must make "*reasonable* efforts," not ideal efforts).

Earvin v. DFPS, 229 S.W.3d 345, 348 (Tex.App.—Houston [1st Dist.] 2007, no pet.). "While we agree ... that the first three elements of constructive abandonment have been met, we do not agree that the [TDFPS] met its burden on the fourth element. *At 349:* The [TDFPS] cites no authority that a parent has an obligation to attempt to take custody of a child when the mother is in a treatment center and subsequently released. Nothing in the record indicates that [father] was aware of the severity of the mother's drug use or knew or should have known that the mother would resume drug use after being released from the treatment center. [¶] What the record does show, however, is that [father] cared for [child] while the mother was in the hospital and the treatment center, that [father] had access to a home to provide for [child], and that he had obtained a job three weeks before trial. Even if the trial court, as the trier of fact, chose to disbelieve [father's] testimony as not credible, this does not prove that the opposite is true."

In re D.S.A., 113 S.W.3d 567, 573-74 (Tex.App.—Amarillo 2003, no pet.). "[W]e disagree with the proposition that §161.001(1)(N) [now §161.001(b)(1)(N)] 'was never intended to apply to someone' in prison merely because the parent is in prison. ... Returning the child to the parent, per §161.001(1)(N)(i), does not necessarily mean that the child has to be physically delivered to the incarcerated individual. [I]t is quite conceivable that one in prison may still be able to [provide a good environment] by ... leaving the ward in the capable hands of a relative, friend or spouse. If such could be done, then it is conceivable that the State has the ability to relinquish its custody over the youth and, thereby, effectively return the child to the incarcerated parent. ... Nor can we say that incarceration renders it impossible for the parent to maintain significant contact with the child. While the child may not be able to live with the parent in a jail cell, ... the parent could nonetheless pursue a significant relationship [through] written correspondence. In sum, incarceration does not render sub-paragraph (N) inapplicable simply because of incarceration." *But see* ***In re D.T.***, 34 S.W.3d 625, 633 (Tex.App.—Fort Worth 2000, pet. denied) (requirement that Department return child to

parent under §161.001(1)(N), now §161.001(b)(1)(N), does not apply to parent who is incarcerated).

§161.001(b)(1)(O)

In re S.M.R., 434 S.W.3d 576, 584 (Tex.2014). "[W]hether a parent has done enough under the family-service plan to defeat termination under subpart (O) is ordinarily a fact question. [¶] While parents have generally had little success arguing substantial compliance to reverse a termination judgment under subpart (O), ... here the argument simply suggests a factual dispute. Conceivably, subpart (O) could be established as a termination ground as a matter of law. But when questions of compliance and degree are raised, and the trial court declines to terminate on this ground, the evidence is not conclusive; it is disputed."

In re E.C.R., 402 S.W.3d 239, 248 (Tex. 2013). "[W]hile [Fam. Code §161.001(1)(O), now §161.001(b)(1)(O),] requires removal under [Fam. Code] ch. 262 for abuse or neglect, those words are used broadly. '[A]buse or neglect of the child' necessarily includes the risks or threats of the environment in which the child is placed. Part of that calculus includes the harm suffered or the danger faced by other children under the parent's care. If a parent has neglected, sexually abused, or otherwise endangered her child's physical health or safety, such that initial and continued removal are appropriate, the child has been 'remov[ed] from the parent under Ch. 262 for the abuse or neglect of the child.'" *See also* ***In re S.M.R.***, 434 S.W.3d 576, 583 (Tex.2014) (acts or omissions listed in Fam. Code ch. 261 can be used to "inform" the terms abuse and neglect in ch. 262); ***In re K.N.D.***, 424 S.W.3d 8, 9-10 (Tex.2014) (evidence showed that child was removed for abuse and neglect under Fam. Code ch. 262 as required by §161.001(1)(O), now §161.001(b)(1)(O); mother's fight with roommates caused child's early birth, and mother had recently relinquished parental rights to her first child because she could not care for child).

D.F. v. TDFPS, 393 S.W.3d 821, 830 (Tex.App.—El Paso 2012, no pet.). "Children are removed from their parents under [Fam. Code] ch. 262 for the abuse or neglect of a child where the children may have been physically in the care of a relative, a medical or social services institution, or the Department. At the time of her removal, [child] was residing at the Child Crisis Center. While she was physically removed from that facility, we find for purposes of ch. 262, she was removed from her parent."

In re D.R.A., 374 S.W.3d 528, 532 (Tex.App.—Houston [14th Dist.] 2012, no pet.). Father "argues that DFPS cannot meet its burden of proof because [child] was not removed as the result of abuse or neglect on his part. [Child] was removed from [mother's] home. However, subsection (O) does not require that the parent who failed to comply with a court order be the same parent whose abuse or neglect of the child warranted the child's removal."

§161.001(b)(1)(P)

In re A.Q.W., 395 S.W.3d 285, 290-91 (Tex. App.—San Antonio 2013, no pet.). "Because [father] was incarcerated the six and one-half months from the time of [child's] birth to the time of the termination hearing, he could not have 'used a controlled substance ... in a manner that endangered the health or safety of the child.' And ... having received his service plan only 34[ ] days before the termination hearing, there is no evidence [father] was provided with an opportunity to enroll in, much less complete, 'a court-ordered substance abuse treatment program' while incarcerated. Finally, there is no evidence he has 'continued to abuse a controlled substance.' [¶] [T]he State argues [father's] drug use is a 'course of conduct' that has endangered [child's] health and safety. The State speculates this 'course of conduct' subjects a child to being left alone because his parent is once again jailed or once again committed to a drug treatment facility. But nothing in the record supports this speculation. There is no evidence [father] has been jailed repeatedly or been in and out of drug treatment of any type. Therefore, we conclude the evidence is legally insufficient to support a finding under §161.001(1)(P) [now §161.001(b)(1)(P)]."

In re J.E.H., 384 S.W.3d 864, 871 (Tex.App.—San Antonio 2012, no pet.). "[T]he Department had the burden of proving that [father] used a controlled substance *in a manner that endangered* [*child*]. ... The Department ... points out that [father] testified he tested positive for cocaine during the pendency of this suit. While [father] admitted that he tested positive for cocaine during the pendency of this suit, he denied having actually used cocaine and gave no testimony that would support a finding that his use of controlled substance endangered [child]. There is simply no evi-

dence in this record that supports the finding [father] used a controlled substance *in a manner that endangered [child]*."

§161.001(b)(1)(Q)

In re H.R.M., 209 S.W.3d 105, 108-09 (Tex.2006). "We recognize that a two-year sentence does not automatically meet subsection Q's two-year imprisonment requirement. In some cases, neither the length of the sentence nor the projected release date is dispositive of when the parent will in fact be released from prison. A parent sentenced to more than two years might well be paroled within two years. Thus, evidence of the availability of parole is relevant to determine whether the parent will be released within two years. Mere introduction of parole-related evidence, however, does not prevent a factfinder from forming a firm conviction or belief that the parent will remain incarcerated for at least two years. *At 110:* [Also,] [a]bsent evidence that the non-incarcerated parent agreed to care for the child on behalf of the incarcerated parent, merely leaving a child with a non-incarcerated parent does not constitute the ability to provide care." *See also* ***In re R.A.L.***, 291 S.W.3d 438, 443-44 (Tex.App.—Texarkana 2009, no pet.) (evidence that parents had been repeatedly denied parole in past was sufficient for jury to form belief that neither parent would be paroled within two years).

In re A.V., 113 S.W.3d 355, 356-57 (Tex.2003). "We hold that subsection Q's time period is prospective and that the subsection is constitutional even though applied to a parent incarcerated before the subsection's effective date. *At 360:* In reading subsection Q to apply prospectively, the subsection fills a gap left by other grounds for termination. A prospective reading of subsection Q allows the State to act in anticipation of a parent's abandonment of the child and not just in response to it. Thus, if the parent is convicted and sentenced to serve at least two years and will be unable to provide for his or her child during that time, the State may use subsection Q to ensure that the child will not be neglected."

In re H.B.C., 482 S.W.3d 696, 702 (Tex.App.—Texarkana 2016, no pet.). "'[W]hen the party seeking termination has established that the incarcerated parent will remain in confinement for the requisite period, the parent must then produce some evidence as to how [s]he would provide or arrange to provide care for the child during h[er] incarceration.' 'If the parent meets that burden of production, the [party seeking termination] then has the burden of persuasion to show that the parent's provision or arrangement would not satisfy the parent's duty to the child.' 'In other words, the [party seeking termination] must then persuade the trial court that the stated arrangements would not satisfy the parent's duty or obligation to the child.'" *See also* ***In re B.M.R.***, 84 S.W.3d 814, 818 (Tex.App.—Houston [1st Dist.] 2002, no pet.) (when deciding whether incarcerated parent is unable to care for child, court should consider parent's ability to provide financial and emotional support).

In re A.R., 497 S.W.3d 500, 503 (Tex.App.—Texarkana 2015, no pet.). "[I]n order to satisfy the elements of subsection (Q), the Department must present evidence that [father] knowingly engaged in the conduct that resulted in his conviction. ... DWI, third or more, [is] found in [Pen. Code] Ch. 49.... [Pen. Code] §49.11(a) ... provides, '[P]roof of a culpable mental state is not required for conviction of an offense under this chapter.' Thus, the holding in [***In re***] ***C.D.E.*** [below] is applicable here, and the Department could not establish that [father] knowingly engaged in the conduct that resulted in his conviction of the offense of DWI, third or more, by merely introducing evidence of the conviction. Instead, the Department was required to present proof of the facts surrounding the conviction to show that the father knowingly engaged in the conduct resulting in that conviction."

In re C.D.E., 391 S.W.3d 287, 299 (Tex.App.—Fort Worth 2012, no pet.). "Father's mere conviction for the strict-liability offense of intoxication manslaughter cannot automatically supply the knowing element required by subsection (Q). [¶] Given its common and ordinary meaning, the term 'knowingly' means 'in a knowing manner' and 'with awareness, deliberateness or intention.' *At 300:* [W]e hold that to establish that a parent 'knowingly engaged in criminal conduct' as set forth in subsection (Q), the Department must prove more than mere negligence. *At 301:* [T]he record contains no evidence from which the trial court could have formed a firm conviction or belief that Father '*knowingly* [as opposed to negligently] engaged in criminal conduct'...."

In re D.J.H., 381 S.W.3d 606, 612 (Tex.App.—San Antonio 2012, no pet.). Father "argues that the trial court erred in terminating his parental rights based on subsection (Q) ... because he will be released from prison less than two years from the date the State's

amended petition for termination was filed. According to [father], the date of the amended petition for termination should control because it was the amended petition that added subsection (Q) as a ground for termination. *At 613:* Given that the purpose of subsection (Q) is to protect children from being neglected, and not to provide notice, it is logical to conclude that when subsection (Q) refers to 'the petition,' it is referring to the original petition for termination, and not a subsequently amended one adding an allegation for termination under subsection (Q)."

§161.001(b)(1)(R)

In re L.G.R., 498 S.W.3d 195, 202-03 (Tex.App.—Houston [14th Dist.] 2016, pet. denied). "Mother argues the evidence is legally and factually insufficient to support the trial court's finding because there were no observable signs of marijuana, or withdrawal from marijuana in the Child at birth. The Family Code, however, does not require proof of signs of withdrawal. Under the Family Code definition, it is sufficient to show that the demonstrable presence of a controlled substance was observable in the Child's bodily fluids. [¶] Mother further argues that the Department presented no expert testimony that Mother was the cause of the Child being born addicted to a controlled substance. Mother does not cite, nor have we found, any legal authority supporting her argument that the Department was required to present expert testimony as to causation. A reasonable fact-finder could believe that a child's testing positive for a controlled substance at birth could be caused by its mother's use of the controlled substance during pregnancy. Mother's admission of marijuana use during pregnancy and the admission of the medical records showing marijuana in the Child's bodily fluids constitute sufficient evidence under the Family Code that Mother was the cause of the Child being born addicted to a controlled substance."

§161.001(b)(1)(T)

In re E.M.N., 221 S.W.3d 815, 825 (Tex.App.—Fort Worth 2007, no pet.). "Despite [mother's] conviction and imprisonment before subsection (T)'s enactment, [her] rights were not violated by its retroactive application. [Child] and [managing conservator], her grandmother, are part of the public whose interest subsection (T) advances. Subsection (T)'s underlying purpose is not to add additional punishment to [mother] for murdering [child's] father, but to safeguard the public welfare and advance the public interest by facilitating termination when one parent murders the other—an act previously used to support terminations under subsection (E). Therefore, [mother] cannot now claim surprise and damage to her settled expectations under these circumstances."

§161.001(b)(2)—Best Interest

Holley v. Adams, 544 S.W.2d 367, 371-72 (Tex. 1976). "An extended number of factors have been considered by the courts in ascertaining the best interest of the child. Included among these are the following: (A) the desires of the child; (B) the emotional and physical needs of the child now and in the future; (C) the emotional and physical danger to the child now and in the future; (D) the parental abilities of the individuals seeking custody; (E) the programs available to assist these individuals to promote the best interest of the child; (F) the plans for the child by these individuals or by the agency seeking custody; (G) the stability of the home or proposed placement; (H) the acts or omissions of the parent which may indicate that the existing parent-child relationship is not a proper one; and (I) any excuse for the acts or omissions of the parent. This listing is by no means exhaustive, but does indicate a number of considerations which either have been or would appear to be pertinent." *See also* ***Swate v. Swate***, 72 S.W.3d 763, 769 (Tex.App.—Waco 2002, pet. denied) (stepparent's desire to adopt is another factor); ***Salas v. TDPRS***, 71 S.W.3d 783, 792 (Tex. App.—El Paso 2002, no pet.) (child's young age is another factor).

In re J.K.V., 490 S.W.3d 250, 258 (Tex.App.—Texarkana 2016, no pet.). "[P]roof that a parent is outside the U.S. and cannot return should not automatically establish best interest. Still, there is evidence that [father] may not have done all he could to return and exercise parental duties over [child]. Accordingly, we find that [this] factor weighs slightly in favor of terminating [father's] parental rights."

In re K.D., 471 S.W.3d 147, 165 (Tex.App.—Texarkana 2015, no pet.). Family Code "§§153.002 and 161.001(2) both require the trial court to determine the best interest of the child, and [***In re Lee***, 411 S.W.3d 445 (Tex.2013),] holds that [an MSA] obtained under [Fam. Code] §153.0071(e) forecloses the trial court's best-interest review under §153.002. *At 171:* Having determined that ***Lee***'s interpretation of §153.0071(e) in the context of best-interest review under §153.002 does not apply to parental-rights termination cases brought

by the Department [see ***In re K.D.*** annotation under Family Code §153.0071, p. 508], we must now interpret §153.0071(e) in the context of best-interest review under §161.001(2). *At 172:* [O]nly cases for conservatorship, possession, and access to children that are referred to mediation under §153.0071(c) can produce [an MSA] that forecloses the trial court's best-interest review. Because termination cases are governed by [Fam. Code] Ch. 161, §153.0071(e) would not apply to such cases. Therefore, §153.0071(c) and (e) can be interpreted to mean that any suit under Title 5, including a parental-rights termination suit, may be referred to mediation, but only those suits for conservatorship, possession, and access that produce [an MSA] can eliminate the trial court's best-interest review. *At 174:* Section 153.0071(e) does not foreclose judicial review of the best-interest element of proof in a parental-rights termination case brought by the Department. Likewise, we hold that §153.0071(e) does not foreclose an appellate court from reviewing the legal and factual sufficiency of a trial court's finding that termination is in the child's best interest. Therefore, we are not bound by the MSA and or the Affidavit to find that termination of Mother's parental rights was in [child's] best interest; instead, the Department was required to prove best interest by clear and convincing evidence."

J.S. v. TDFPS, 511 S.W.3d 145, 160 (Tex.App.—El Paso 2014, no pet.). "The evidence supporting the predicate ground(s) [under §161.001(1), now §161.001(b)(1),] may also be used to support the finding that termination is in the best interests of the child. *At 161:* Mother urges this Court to weigh the evidence of her actual acts or omissions without reference to her guilty plea [to injury of a child] to determine whether there is legal or factual sufficiency to support the termination grounds. [Mother argues that] DFPS has waived the evidence of Mother's conviction because [§161.001(1)(L), now §161.001(b)(1)(L),] was not pleaded and DFPS induced Mother to plead guilty. [¶] It is uncontroverted Mother pled guilty to injury of a child and received four years' deferred adjudication supervision. … Mother denies she committed the injury to a child. Secondly, she asserts, her plea of guilty, presumably under oath, was motivated by her fear of Father coupled with DFPS's reassurance her children would be reunified with her. [T]here is no authority to collaterally attack a criminal conviction in a parental termination case. Therefore, we are not inclined to peer behind Mother's guilty plea to injury of [child] and will not disregard it in our sufficiency analysis."

T.W. v. TDFPS, 431 S.W.3d 645, 651 (Tex.App.—El Paso 2014, no pet.). "While it is presumed that it is in the child's best interest to preserve the parent-child relationship, the requirement to show that termination is in the child's best interest in addition to the clear and convincing standard of proof subsumes reunification issues and guarantees the constitutionality of termination proceedings. A separate consideration of alternatives to termination is not required. When determining the child's best interest, the focus is on the child and not the parent. Moreover, while the determination of where a child will be placed is a factor in determining the child's best interest, the fact that the placement will be with non-relatives is not a bar to termination."

In re E.D., 419 S.W.3d 615, 618 (Tex.App.—San Antonio 2013, pet. denied). In response to being asked why termination would be in the best interest of the children, CPS supervisor "explained that if both parents' parental rights were terminated, the children's maternal grandparents could get financial assistance after adopting the children. She said that if the parental rights were not terminated, the grandparents would not be entitled to a financial subsidy. *At 619:* We do not believe terminating a parent's rights to his children so that someone can obtain financial subsidies upon adoption is an appropriate basis on which to base a best interest finding."

In re A.H., 414 S.W.3d 802, 807 (Tex.App.—San Antonio 2013, no pet.). "The only evidence of best interest was offered by the caseworker who testified termination of all parental rights was in the children's best interest 'because the children need a loving family that will care for them and take care of their needs,' and the children were to be adopted by their current care givers. The State argues that although the evidence regarding best interest was 'limited,' no evidence was offered to contradict the caseworker's testimony and [mother] offered no proof that termination of her parental rights was not in the children's best interest. But due process and the Texas Family Code place the burden of proof on the Department to prove the necessary elements by the heightened burden of 'clear and convincing evidence.' Thus, conclusory testimony, such as the caseworker's, even if uncontradicted does not amount to more than a scintilla of evidence. And, '[a]lthough [a parent's] behavior may reasonably suggest

that a child would be better off with a new family, the best interest standard does not permit termination merely because a child might be better off living elsewhere.'"

In re N.L.D., 412 S.W.3d 810, 819 (Tex.App.—Texarkana 2013, no pet.). "Evidence supporting the termination of parental rights [under §161.001(1), now §161.001(b)(1),] is also probative of best interest. A parent's inability to provide adequate care for her child, lack of parenting skills, and poor judgment may be considered when looking at the child's best interests. Parental drug abuse is also a factor to be considered in determining a child's best interests. *At 823:* Evidence that a person has recently improved her life weighs against a finding that termination is in the best interest of the child."

In re S.R.L., 243 S.W.3d 232, 235-36 (Tex.App.—Houston [14th Dist.] 2007, no pet.). "The factfinder must find both a statutory violation and that termination is in the children's best interest. The trial judge may have believed DFPS conclusively established a statutory ground for termination under subsection Q, but the best interest determination is a separate inquiry. Because the trial judge did not actually form a firm conviction or belief that severing [father's] relationship with his children was in their best interest, we conclude the evidence is legally insufficient. [¶] That a parent is imprisoned does not automatically establish that termination of parental rights is in the child's best interest."

In re C.J.B., 137 S.W.3d 814, 820 (Tex.App.—Waco 2004, no pet.). "[T]he factors considered in termination cases are broader than those mentioned in [Fam. Code] §263.307, which is limited to the factors considered when 'determining whether the child's parents are willing and able to provide the child a safe environment....' Many, if not all, of the 13 factors listed in §263.307, one with six sub-parts, are subsumed within one of the broader ***Holley*** factors. [¶] Further, neither the Texas Supreme Court, nor this Court, has ever held that the ***Holley*** factors are exhaustive, or that all such considerations must be proved as a condition precedent to parental termination. The absence of evidence about some of these considerations does not preclude a factfinder from reasonably forming a firm belief or conviction that termination is in the child's best interest. The analysis of one factor may be adequate in a particular factual situation to support a finding that termination is in the best interest of the child." *See also* ***In re D.W.***, 445 S.W.3d 913, 925 (Tex.App.—Dallas 2014, pet. denied).

FAM §161.002. TERMINATION OF THE RIGHTS OF AN ALLEGED BIOLOGICAL FATHER

(a) Except as otherwise provided by this section, the procedural and substantive standards for termination of parental rights apply to the termination of the rights of an alleged father.

(b) The rights of an alleged father may be terminated if:

(1) after being served with citation, he does not respond by timely filing an admission of paternity or a counterclaim for paternity under Chapter 160;

(2) the child is over one year of age at the time the petition for termination of the parent-child relationship or for adoption is filed, he has not registered with the paternity registry under Chapter 160, and after the exercise of due diligence by the petitioner:

(A) his identity and location are unknown; or

(B) his identity is known but he cannot be located;

(3) the child is under one year of age at the time the petition for termination of the parent-child relationship or for adoption is filed and he has not registered with the paternity registry under Chapter 160; or

(4) he has registered with the paternity registry under Chapter 160, but the petitioner's attempt to personally serve citation at the address provided to the registry and at any other address for the alleged father known by the petitioner has been unsuccessful, despite the due diligence of the petitioner.

(c) Repealed by Acts 2015, 84th Leg., ch. 1, §1.203(2), eff. Apr. 2, 2015.

(c-1) The termination of the rights of an alleged father under Subsection (b)(2) or (3) rendered on or after January 1, 2008, does not require personal service of citation or citation by publication on the alleged father, and there is no requirement to identify or locate an alleged father who has not registered with the paternity registry under Chapter 160.

(d) The termination of rights of an alleged father under Subsection (b)(4) does not require service of citation by publication on the alleged father.

(e) The court shall not render an order terminating parental rights under Subsection (b)(2) or (3) unless the court receives evidence of a certificate of the re-

sults of a search of the paternity registry under Chapter 160 from the vital statistics unit indicating that no man has registered the intent to claim paternity.

(f) The court shall not render an order terminating parental rights under Subsection (b)(4) unless the court, after reviewing the petitioner's sworn affidavit describing the petitioner's effort to obtain personal service of citation on the alleged father and considering any evidence submitted by the attorney ad litem for the alleged father, has found that the petitioner exercised due diligence in attempting to obtain service on the alleged father. The order shall contain specific findings regarding the exercise of due diligence of the petitioner.

History of Fam. Code §161.002: Acts 1995, 74th Leg., ch. 20, §1, eff. Apr. 20, 1995. Amended by Acts 1995, 74th Leg., ch. 751, §66, eff. Sept. 1, 1995; Acts 1997, 75th Leg., ch. 561, §7, eff. Sept. 1, 1997; Acts 2001, 77th Leg., ch. 821, §2.16 (eff. June 14, 2001), ch. 1090, §1 (eff. Sept. 1, 2001); Acts 2007, 80th Leg., ch. 1283, §4, eff. Sept. 1, 2007; Acts 2015, 84th Leg., ch. 1, §§1.079, 1.203(2), eff. Apr. 2, 2015. Source: Former Fam. Code §15.023.

ANNOTATIONS

Attorney Gen. v. Lavan, 833 S.W.2d 952, 954 (Tex. 1992). "We ... find nothing in the [Family] Code that expressly prohibits the State from bringing a claim under [Fam. Code] ch. 12 [now ch. 151] to disestablish the paternity of a presumed father in the same suit in which it brings a claim under [Fam. Code] ch. 13 [now ch. 160] to establish paternity in an alleged biological father. To allow both claims ... to be joined in one suit advances the best interest of the child by eliminating any period of time a child would be left without the benefit of a legal father. ... Conversely, we find no countervailing benefit from a requirement that the paternity of a presumed father be disestablished in a final judgment in a separate proceeding before proceeding with a second suit to establish the paternity of an alleged biological father."

In re P. RJ E., 499 S.W.3d 571, 576 (Tex.App.—Houston [1st Dist.] 2016, pet. filed 9-23-16). See annotation under Family Code §102.010, p. 410.

In re C.M.D., 287 S.W.3d 510, 513 (Tex.App.—Houston [14th Dist.] 2009, no pet.). "The trial court refused to apply [§161.002(b)] and terminate the father's parental rights, instead declaring sua sponte that the statute was unconstitutional ... because it does not require (a) due diligence to locate the alleged father, (b) service of process on the alleged father, (c) appointment of an attorney ad litem to represent the alleged father's interests, or (d) a best interest finding. *At 516:* [W]e cannot agree with the trial court's determination that a constitutional violation has been established. An unwed father does not automatically have full constitutional paternal rights by virtue of a mere biological relationship. Rather, he must, early in the child's life, take some action to assert those rights. [¶] If the father had no intent to assert his parental rights, he could not have suffered a due process or equal protection violation based on a deprivation of those rights. ... Without evidence of an actual injury in the case before it, the trial court erred in declaring the paternity registry statute unconstitutional."

Toliver v. TDFPS, 217 S.W.3d 85, 105 (Tex.App.—Houston [1st Dist.] 2006, no pet.). Family Code §161.002(b)(1) "prescribes the filing of an admission of paternity, but there is no reference in the statute to any formalities that must be observed when 'filing' such an admission. Here, although [alleged father] did not file a document with the court clerk, he appeared at trial prior to the trial court's termination of his parental rights, unequivocally asserted that he was [child's] father, and requested that his parental rights not be terminated. [W]e hold that [alleged father] triggered his right to require DFPS to prove that he engaged in one of the types of conduct listed in [Fam. Code] §161.001(1) [now §161.001(b)(1)] before his parental rights could be terminated. Accordingly, we further hold that the trial court erred in finding [he] did not timely file an admission of paternity and in terminating his parental rights to [child]." *See also* ***In re U.B.***, No. 04-12-00687-CV (Tex.App.—San Antonio 2013, no pet.) (memo op.; 2-6-13) (man's actions of writing letter to judge stating that he was children's father and admitting paternity during trial testimony were sufficient to satisfy §161.002(b)(1)); ***In re K.W.***, No. 2-09-041-CV (Tex.App.—Fort Worth 2010, no pet.) (memo op.; 1-14-10) (man's actions of timely filing general denial and admitting paternity during trial testimony were sufficient to satisfy §161.002(b)(1)); ***In re C.M.C.***, 273 S.W.3d 862, 879-80 (Tex.App.—Houston [14th Dist.] 2008, no pet.) (man's actions of filing sworn affidavit that he was children's father and telling TDFPS that he did not want his parental rights terminated were sufficient to satisfy §161.002(b)(1)).

FAM §161.003. INVOLUNTARY TERMINATION: INABILITY TO CARE FOR CHILD

(a) The court may order termination of the parent-child relationship in a suit filed by the Department of Family and Protective Services if the court finds that:

(1) the parent has a mental or emotional illness or a mental deficiency that renders the parent unable to provide for the physical, emotional, and mental needs of the child;

(2) the illness or deficiency, in all reasonable probability, proved by clear and convincing evidence, will continue to render the parent unable to provide for the child's needs until the 18th birthday of the child;

(3) the department has been the temporary or sole managing conservator of the child of the parent for at least six months preceding the date of the hearing on the termination held in accordance with Subsection (c);

(4) the department has made reasonable efforts to return the child to the parent; and

(5) the termination is in the best interest of the child.

(b) Immediately after the filing of a suit under this section, the court shall appoint an attorney ad litem to represent the interests of the parent against whom the suit is brought.

(c) A hearing on the termination may not be held earlier than 180 days after the date on which the suit was filed.

(d) An attorney appointed under Subsection (b) shall represent the parent for the duration of the suit unless the parent, with the permission of the court, retains another attorney.

History of Fam. Code §161.003: Acts 1995, 74th Leg., ch. 20, §1, eff. Apr. 20, 1995. Amended by Acts 1995, 74th Leg., ch. 751, §67, eff. Sept. 1, 1995; Acts 2001, 77th Leg., ch. 496, §1 (eff. Sept. 1, 2001), ch. 1090, §2 (eff. Sept. 1, 2001); Acts 2015, 84th Leg., ch. 1, §1.080, eff. Apr. 2, 2015. Source: Former Fam. Code §15.024.

ANNOTATIONS

In re A.L.M., 300 S.W.3d 914, 919-20 (Tex.App.—Texarkana 2009, no pet.). "A trend ... seem[s] to appear [when courts consider termination under Fam. Code §161.003]. When the evidence is less convincing of the parent's complete inability to parent, appellate courts are still willing to affirm termination on this ground when the evidence establishes special, extensive medical or emotional needs of the children. Other cases make little or no mention of the specific needs of the child when evidence of the mental illness or deficiency make[s] it clear that the parent is unable to meet the needs of a child without severe problems. The needier the child, the more able the parent must be. [¶] [T]he elements of §161.003 [are] 'more stringent' than the elements of [Fam. Code] §161.001. [¶] [T]he State must prove that the parents are unable to meet the physical, mental, *and* emotional needs of the children. Realizing that often a child's needs are complex ... we do not propose that the State must set out examples of a parent's inability to meet each distinct need. *At 928-29:* [W]e must look at the parents' overall failure to provide for the needs of the children.... [¶] Section 161.003 ... requires more than a finding of mental deficiency. [I]t first requires proof that the [parents' inaction or actions were] not mere negligence, inattention, or poor parenting, but [occurred] because the parents were mentally deficient. Upon making that linkage, there must also be evidence to support a determination that the parents' mental deficiencies exclude them from now and in the future providing for their children." *See also* ***In re B.J.C.***, 495 S.W.3d 29, 37 (Tex.App.—Houston [14th Dist.] 2016, no pet.) (DFPS sufficiently focused on mother's complete inability to parent, rather than possible special needs of children, who did not have severe problems or need special care).

Liu v. DFPS, 273 S.W.3d 785, 791 (Tex.App.—Houston [1st Dist.] 2008, no pet.). "Mental illness of a parent is not, in and of itself, grounds for termination of the parent-child relationship. The issue is whether [mother's] mental illness renders her unable to provide for [child] now and, with reasonable probability, until his 18th birthday. DFPS need not prove with certainty that the parent's mental disease will continue to render the parent unable to provide for the child's needs until the child's 18th birthday; rather, DFPS must show, by clear and convincing evidence, that the mental illness in all probability will do so. 'In all reasonable probability' does not mean beyond a reasonable doubt and does not require 'scientific certainty' that the parent's mental illness will continue until the child is 18." *See also* ***In re B.L.M.***, 114 S.W.3d 641, 648 (Tex.App.—Fort Worth 2003, no pet.); ***Salas v. TDPRS***, 71 S.W.3d 783, 790 (Tex.App.—El Paso 2002, no pet.).

FAM §161.004. TERMINATION OF PARENTAL RIGHTS AFTER DENIAL OF PRIOR PETITION TO TERMINATE

(a) The court may terminate the parent-child relationship after rendition of an order that previously denied termination of the parent-child relationship if:

(1) the petition under this section is filed after the date the order denying termination was rendered;

(2) the circumstances of the child, parent, sole managing conservator, possessory conservator, or other

party affected by the order denying termination have materially and substantially changed since the date that the order was rendered;

(3) the parent committed an act listed under Section 161.001 before the date the order denying termination was rendered; and

(4) termination is in the best interest of the child.

(b) At a hearing under this section, the court may consider evidence presented at a previous hearing in a suit for termination of the parent-child relationship of the parent with respect to the same child.

History of Fam. Code §161.004: Acts 1995, 74th Leg., ch. 20, §1, eff. Apr. 20, 1995. Source: Former Fam. Code §15.025.

ANNOTATIONS

In re K.P., 498 S.W.3d 157, 170 (Tex.App.—Houston [1st Dist.] 2016, pet. denied). "We disagree with the Department that the trial court's termination of Mother's parental rights can be affirmed under [Fam. Code] §161.004 ... on the theory that the trial court 'could have' based its termination on Mother's pre-2012 failure to follow the pre-2012 service plan.... [¶] When the Department does not plead §161.004 as grounds for termination, it is error to admit evidence from before a prior decree denying termination. [¶] The Department states in its brief that 'the evidence conclusively establishes that the mother committed the act of [Fam. Code §161.001(b)(1)(O)] before the entry of the prior decree.' But the service plan the Department purports to rely upon was excluded from evidence. And, although the Department insists that the 'evidence conclusively establishes that the mother' failed to comply with her service plan pre-2012, nothing in the pleadings or trial would have put Mother on notice to put on evidence about whether she complied with the pre-2012 service plan. This issue was not tried by consent, as Mother's counsel successfully excluded the service plan on relevance grounds and the Department *affirmatively represented* to the trial court and Mother that it was *not* seeking termination under the very service plan upon which it now seeks to rely. We thus cannot affirm the trial court's termination of Mother's parental rights for failure to follow a service plan pre-2012, especially when the court refused to admit that service plan because it was not relevant to a pleaded claim." *See also* ***In re A.A.M.***, this page.

In re A.A.M., 464 S.W.3d 421, 425-26 (Tex.App.—Houston [1st Dist.] 2015, no pet.). "[F]ather argues that a trial court may terminate parental rights based on evidence introduced in prior termination proceedings only if the petitioner pleads §161.004. [¶] [A]lthough ... the Department did not expressly name the statute by its code number in its petitions, it pleaded the statutory elements for modification of an earlier order, including materially changed circumstances. [¶] [T]he trial court found in its termination orders that the circumstances of the parties had materially and substantially changed since its prior orders and that evidence relating to events occurring before the prior orders was admissible pursuant to §161.004. Accordingly, we hold that the trial court properly considered evidence presented in earlier termination proceedings."

In re D.N., 405 S.W.3d 863, 870 (Tex.App.—Amarillo 2013, no pet.). See annotation under Family Code §161.001, *Generally*, p. 754.

In re K.G., 350 S.W.3d 338, 346 (Tex.App.—Fort Worth 2011, pet. denied). "Because DFPS sought termination of Mother's parental rights after the trial court rendered an order denying termination after the first termination trial, did DFPS have to plead and prove the grounds in [Fam. Code] §161.004 in addition to the grounds for termination under [Fam. Code] §161.001, and did the trial court have to make findings thereon? *At 349:* Section 161.004 appears to be typically used when parents raise res judicata in a termination trial or argue that it should have been raised. [¶] [But it] is unclear from the case law whether ... §161.004 [is] the exclusive means to terminate a parent's rights after denial of a prior termination or just a means to admit evidence from a prior termination trial. *At 352:* Based on [statutory construction, legislative history, and public policy], we cannot agree with Mother's contention that the *only* way the trial court could terminate her parental rights here was under §161.004. [¶] Rather, using §161.004 is the only way that the trial court could terminate her parental rights based upon 'evidence presented at' the hearing before the trial court issued its ... denial of the first petition to terminate. Therefore, while the trial court erred by admitting evidence from before the ... denial of DFPS's first petition when DFPS did not plead §161.004 as a ground to terminate Mother's parental rights, the error was harmless because ... the trial court ordered the termination under §161.001(1)(N) and (O) [now §161.001(b)(1)(N) and (O)], ... the evidence [of which occurred] after the [denial of the first petition]." *See also* ***In re J.R.***, No.

07-12-00003-CV (Tex.App.—Amarillo 2012, no pet.) (memo op.; 5-8-12) (proof of material and substantial change as required by §161.004(a)(2) is mechanism used to defeat parent's res judicata claim).

FAM §161.005. TERMINATION WHEN PARENT IS PETITIONER

(a) A parent may file a suit for termination of the petitioner's parent-child relationship. Except as provided by Subsection (h), the court may order termination if termination is in the best interest of the child.

(b) If the petition designates the Department of Family and Protective Services as managing conservator, the department shall be given service of citation. The court shall notify the department if the court appoints the department as the managing conservator of the child.

(c) Subject to Subsection (d), a man may file a suit for termination of the parent-child relationship between the man and a child if, without obtaining genetic testing, the man signed an acknowledgment of paternity of the child in accordance with Subchapter D, Chapter 160, or was adjudicated to be the father of the child in a previous proceeding under this title in which genetic testing did not occur. The petition must be verified and must allege facts showing that the petitioner:

(1) is not the child's genetic father; and

(2) signed the acknowledgment of paternity or failed to contest parentage in the previous proceeding because of the mistaken belief, at the time the acknowledgment was signed or on the date the court order in the previous proceeding was rendered, that he was the child's genetic father based on misrepresentations that led him to that conclusion.

(d) A man may not file a petition under Subsection (c) if:

(1) the man is the child's adoptive father;

(2) the child was conceived by assisted reproduction and the man consented to assisted reproduction by his wife under Subchapter H, Chapter 160; or

(3) the man is the intended father of the child under a gestational agreement validated by a court under Subchapter I, Chapter 160.

(e) A petition under Subsection (c) must be filed not later than the second anniversary of the date on which the petitioner becomes aware of the facts alleged in the petition indicating that the petitioner is not the child's genetic father.

(e-1) Expired.

(f) In a proceeding initiated under Subsection (c), the court shall hold a pretrial hearing to determine whether the petitioner has established a meritorious prima facie case for termination of the parent-child relationship. If a meritorious prima facie claim is established, the court shall order the petitioner and the child to submit to genetic testing under Subchapter F, Chapter 160.

(g) If the results of genetic testing ordered under Subsection (f) identify the petitioner as the child's genetic father under the standards prescribed by Section 160.505 and the results of any further testing requested by the petitioner and ordered by the court under Subchapter F, Chapter 160, do not exclude the petitioner as the child's genetic father, the court shall deny the petitioner's request for termination of the parent-child relationship.

(h) If the results of genetic testing ordered under Subsection (f) exclude the petitioner as the child's genetic father, the court shall render an order terminating the parent-child relationship.

(i) An order under Subsection (h) terminating the parent-child relationship ends the petitioner's obligation for future support of the child as of the date the order is rendered, as well as the obligation to pay interest that accrues after that date on the basis of a child support arrearage or money judgment for a child support arrearage existing on that date. The order does not affect the petitioner's obligations for support of the child incurred before that date. Those obligations are enforceable until satisfied by any means available for the enforcement of child support other than contempt.

(j) An order under Subsection (h) terminating the parent-child relationship does not preclude:

(1) the initiation of a proceeding under Chapter 160 to adjudicate whether another man is the child's parent; or

(2) if the other man subject to a proceeding under Subdivision (1) is adjudicated as the child's parent, the rendition of an order requiring that man to pay child support for the child under Chapter 154, subject to Subsection (k).

(k) Notwithstanding Section 154.131, an order described by Subsection (j)(2) may not require the other man to pay retroactive child support for any period preceding the date on which the order under Subsection

(h) terminated the parent-child relationship between the child and the man seeking termination under this section.

(*l*) At any time before the court renders an order terminating the parent-child relationship under Subsection (h), the petitioner may request that the court also order periods of possession of or access to the child by the petitioner following termination of the parent-child relationship. If requested, the court may order periods of possession of or access to the child only if the court determines that denial of periods of possession of or access to the child would significantly impair the child's physical health or emotional well-being.

(m) The court may include provisions in an order under Subsection (*l*) that require:

(1) the child or any party to the proceeding to participate in counseling with a mental health professional who:

(A) has a background in family therapy; and

(B) holds a professional license that requires the person to possess at least a master's degree; and

(2) any party to pay the costs of the counseling described by Subdivision (1).

(n) Notwithstanding Subsection (m)(1), if a person who possesses the qualifications described by that subdivision is not available in the county in which the court is located, the court may require that the counseling be conducted by another person the court considers qualified for that purpose.

(o) During any period of possession of or access to the child ordered under Subsection (*l*) the petitioner has the rights and duties specified by Section 153.074, subject to any limitation specified by the court in its order.

History of Fam. Code §161.005: Acts 1995, 74th Leg., ch. 20, §1, eff. Apr. 20, 1995. Amended by Acts 1995, 74th Leg., ch. 751, §68, eff. Sept. 1, 1995; Acts 2011, 82nd Leg., ch. 54, §2, eff. May 12, 2011; Acts 2013, 83rd Leg., ch. 227, §1, eff. June 14, 2013; Acts 2015, 84th Leg., ch. 1, §1.081, eff. Apr. 2, 2015. Source: Former Fam. Code §15.01.

ANNOTATIONS

In re J.K.B., 439 S.W.3d 442, 451 (Tex.App.—Houston [1st Dist.] 2014, no pet.). "Although a parent may … seek termination of the parent-child relationship based on the best interest of the child under §161.005(a), termination sought under subsection (c) does not include a best-interest determination. If a petitioner makes a prima facie showing under subsection (f), entitling him to genetic testing, and the genetic testing excludes him as the father, then he is entitled to termination under subsection (h), irrespective of the child's best interest."

In re D.I.P., 421 S.W.3d 106, 110 (Tex.App.—San Antonio 2013, pet. denied). "[S]ection 161.005(e) was intended to prohibit acknowledged and adjudicated fathers from filing petitions to terminate based on mistaken paternity in cases such as the one before us, where the father became aware of facts that indicated the child was not biologically his own—due to differences in physical appearance, his former girlfriend's history of infidelity, and the results of a voluntary genetic test excluding him as the biological father—but waited seven years before filing the petition to terminate. [¶] [T]he statute in no way specifies by what means awareness may be garnered. Further, the statute provides that the petitioner must allege facts '*indicating* that the petitioner is not the child's genetic father.' There is no requirement that lack of paternity be conclusively *established* prior to filing the petition to terminate the parent-child relationship. [W]e disagree that the awareness contemplated in §161.005(e) must be established by means of verified genetic testing."

In re C.E., 391 S.W.3d 200, 203-04 (Tex.App.—Houston [1st Dist.] 2012, no pet.). "[T]o make a prima facie case for genetic testing [under §161.005(c)], [father] had to present evidence sufficient to support an inference that a misrepresentation caused him to believe that he was [child's] biological father. [¶] Although [father's] verified petition does not point to any particular misrepresentation, circumstantial evidence adduced at the pretrial hearing supports the allegations in his petition. [¶] We conclude that a verified petition alleging that a misrepresentation caused [father] to believe that he was [child's] biological father coupled with circumstantial evidence that a misrepresentation as to paternity was made constitutes a prima facie case for genetic testing under … §161.005(c)."

Dockery v. State, No. 03-05-00713-CV (Tex.App.—Austin 2006, pet. denied) (memo op.; 11-14-06). Father "acknowledges in his petition that he is the father of the child that is the subject of the suit. At the hearing, he made it clear that one of his purposes in seeking a termination was to eliminate his child support arrearage. [¶] [Father] provided no evidence that termination was in the child's best interest. Because his child is now 19, [father] argues that he should not have to prove termination is in his son's best interest. But this

contention is contrary to §161.005(a), and the trial court properly denied [father's] petition."

A FAM §161.006. TERMINATION AFTER ABORTION

(a) A petition requesting termination of the parent-child relationship with respect to a parent who is not the petitioner may be granted if the child was born alive as the result of an abortion.

(b) In this code, "abortion" has the meaning assigned by Section 245.002, Health and Safety Code ~~[means an intentional expulsion of a human fetus from the body of a woman induced by any means for the purpose of causing the death of the fetus]~~.

(c) The court or the jury may not terminate the parent-child relationship under this section with respect to a parent who:

(1) had no knowledge of the abortion; or

(2) participated in or consented to the abortion for the sole purpose of preventing the death of the mother.

History of Fam. Code §161.006: Acts 1995, 74th Leg., ch. 20, §1, eff. Apr. 20, 1995. Amended by S.B. 8, §2, 85th Leg., eff. Sept. 1, 2017. Source: Former Fam. Code §15.022.

FAM §161.007. TERMINATION WHEN PREGNANCY RESULTS FROM CRIMINAL ACT

(a) Except as provided by Subsection (b), the court shall order the termination of the parent-child relationship of a parent and a child if the court finds by clear and convincing evidence that:

(1) the parent has engaged in conduct that constitutes an offense under Section 21.02, 22.011, 22.021, or 25.02, Penal Code;

(2) as a direct result of the conduct described by Subdivision (1), the victim of the conduct became pregnant with the parent's child; and

(3) termination is in the best interest of the child.

(b) If, for the two years after the birth of the child, the parent was married to or cohabiting with the other parent of the child, the court may order the termination of the parent-child relationship of the parent and the child if the court finds that:

(1) the parent has been convicted of an offense committed under Section 21.02, 22.011, 22.021, or 25.02, Penal Code;

(2) as a direct result of the commission of the offense by the parent, the other parent became pregnant with the child; and

(3) termination is in the best interest of the child.

History of Fam. Code §161.007: Acts 1997, 75th Leg., ch. 561, §8, eff. Sept. 1, 1997. Amended by Acts 2007, 80th Leg., ch. 593, §3.31, eff. Sept. 1, 2007; Acts 2013, 83rd Leg., ch. 907, §4, eff. Sept. 1, 2013.

Sections 161.008-161.100 reserved for expansion

SUBCHAPTER B. PROCEDURES

FAM §161.101. PETITION ALLEGATIONS

A petition for the termination of the parent-child relationship is sufficient without the necessity of specifying the underlying facts if the petition alleges in the statutory language the ground for the termination and that termination is in the best interest of the child.

History of Fam. Code §161.101: Acts 1995, 74th Leg., ch. 20, §1, eff. Apr. 20, 1995. Source: Former Fam. Code §11.08(e).

FAM §161.102. FILING SUIT FOR TERMINATION BEFORE BIRTH

(a) A suit for termination may be filed before the birth of the child.

(b) If the suit is filed before the birth of the child, the petition shall be styled "In the Interest of an Unborn Child." After the birth, the clerk shall change the style of the case to conform to the requirements of Section 102.008.

History of Fam. Code §161.102: Acts 1995, 74th Leg., ch. 20, §1, eff. Apr. 20, 1995. Source: Former Fam. Code §15.021(a), (c).

FAM §161.103. AFFIDAVIT OF VOLUNTARY RELINQUISHMENT OF PARENTAL RIGHTS

(a) An affidavit for voluntary relinquishment of parental rights must be:

(1) signed after the birth of the child, but not before 48 hours after the birth of the child, by the parent, whether or not a minor, whose parental rights are to be relinquished;

(2) witnessed by two credible persons; and

(3) verified before a person authorized to take oaths.

(b) The affidavit must contain:

(1) the name, county of residence, and age of the parent whose parental rights are being relinquished;

(2) the name, age, and birth date of the child;

(3) the names and addresses of the guardians of the person and estate of the child, if any;

(4) a statement that the affiant is or is not presently obligated by court order to make payments for the support of the child;

(5) a full description and statement of value of all property owned or possessed by the child;

(6) an allegation that termination of the parent-child relationship is in the best interest of the child;

(7) one of the following, as applicable:

(A) the name and county of residence of the other parent;

(B) a statement that the parental rights of the other parent have been terminated by death or court order; or

(C) a statement that the child has no presumed father;

(8) a statement that the parent has been informed of parental rights and duties;

(9) a statement that the relinquishment is revocable, that the relinquishment is irrevocable, or that the relinquishment is irrevocable for a stated period of time;

(10) if the relinquishment is revocable, a statement in boldfaced type concerning the right of the parent signing the affidavit to revoke the relinquishment only if the revocation is made before the 11th day after the date the affidavit is executed;

(11) if the relinquishment is revocable, the name and address of a person to whom the revocation is to be delivered; and

(12) the designation of a prospective adoptive parent, the Department of Family and Protective Services, if the department has consented in writing to the designation, or a licensed child-placing agency to serve as managing conservator of the child and the address of the person or agency.

(c) The affidavit may contain:

(1) a waiver of process in a suit to terminate the parent-child relationship filed under this chapter or in a suit to terminate joined with a petition for adoption; and

(2) a consent to the placement of the child for adoption by the Department of Family and Protective Services or by a licensed child-placing agency.

(d) A copy of the affidavit shall be provided to the parent at the time the parent signs the affidavit.

(e) The relinquishment in an affidavit that designates the Department of Family and Protective Services or a licensed child-placing agency to serve as the managing conservator is irrevocable. A relinquishment in any other affidavit of relinquishment is revocable unless it expressly provides that it is irrevocable for a stated period of time not to exceed 60 days after the date of its execution.

(f) A relinquishment in an affidavit of relinquishment of parental rights that fails to state that the relinquishment is irrevocable for a stated time is revocable as provided by Section 161.1035.

(g) To revoke a relinquishment under Subsection (e) the parent must sign a statement witnessed by two credible persons and verified before a person authorized to take oaths. A copy of the revocation shall be delivered to the person designated in the affidavit. If a parent attempting to revoke a relinquishment under this subsection has knowledge that a suit for termination of the parent-child relationship has been filed based on the parent's affidavit of relinquishment of parental rights, the parent shall file a copy of the revocation with the clerk of the court.

(h) The affidavit may not contain terms for limited post-termination contact between the child and the parent whose parental rights are to be relinquished as a condition of the relinquishment of parental rights.

History of Fam. Code §161.103: Acts 1995, 74th Leg., ch. 20, §1, eff. Apr. 20, 1995. Amended by Acts 1995, 74th Leg., ch. 751, §69, eff. Sept. 1, 1995; Acts 1997, 75th Leg., ch. 561, §9, eff. Sept. 1, 1997; Acts 2003, 78th Leg., ch. 561, §3, eff. Sept. 1, 2003; Acts 2007, 80th Leg., ch. 1283, §5 (eff. Sept. 1, 2007), ch. 1412, §1 (eff. Sept. 1, 2007); Acts 2015, 84th Leg., ch. 1, §1.082, eff. Apr. 2, 2015. Source: Former Fam. Code §15.03.

See also *O'Connor's Texas Family Law Handbook* (2017), "Affidavit of voluntary relinquishment," ch. 4-H, §2.5.2, p. 603.

ANNOTATIONS

In re K.M.L., 443 S.W.3d 101, 108 (Tex.2014). Under §161.103, "the affidavit [of relinquishment] must be witnessed by two credible persons and verified before a person authorized to take oaths. [Mother] argues that her affidavit of voluntary relinquishment is deficient because it does not include a verification—that is, it does not include a statement ... that she swears to the truth of the document's contents. *At 111:* The affidavit here is verified—[mother] swore, under oath, to the contents of the affidavit. If 'verify' means to 'substantiate by oath or affidavit,' ... and 'verification' is 'an oath or affirmation that an authorized officer administers to an affiant or deponent,' ... surely [mother's] signature on the affidavit where the notary stated, '[Mother], known to me to be the person whose signature appears below, appeared in person before me and being by me *duly sworn*, in the presence of the undersigned credible witnesses, stated *under oath*,' ... and later, in the jurat, stated, 'Signed *under oath* before me in the presence of the above witnesses ...,' ... constitutes a verification."

Brown v. McLennan Cty. Children's Prot. Servs., 627 S.W.2d 390, 393 (Tex.1982). "Looking to [Fam. Code] §15.03(c)(2) [now §161.103(c)(1)], it provides for waiver of citation within the affidavit of relinquish-

ment if the suit for termination of relationship is brought under [Fam. Code] §15.02(1)(K) [now §161.001(b)(1)(K)]. Section 15.02(1)(K) is the provision creating the right to termination when the parent has executed an affidavit of relinquishment either before or after the suit is filed. [¶] These provisions have been upheld as a permissible exception to the prohibition against pre-suit waiver. [¶] In this cause, [respondent] voluntarily executed the affidavit in question in the presence of two witnesses, before a notary. The affidavit clearly sets out she is relinquishing all parental rights, that suit will be filed to terminate her rights, that she will not be further informed about the suit, and that this act is irrevocable. Certainly this Court recognizes the parent-child relationship as a basic civil right due a high degree of protection. However, when a parent voluntarily terminates this parent-child bond, the best interests of the child become paramount."

In re J.H., 486 S.W.3d 190, 198 (Tex.App.—Dallas 2016, no pet.). Mother "challenges whether sufficient evidence supports the trial court's finding that terminating Mother's parental rights was in the children's best interest. [F]amily code §161.211(c) bars Mother's argument. [¶] The order terminating Mother's parental rights is based on her relinquishment affidavit. Accordingly, Mother cannot make any arguments on appeal except arguments relating to fraud, duress, or coercion in the execution of the affidavit. Mother's [argument] does not relate to fraud, duress, or coercion in the execution of the affidavit. Accordingly, §161.211(c) defeats her [argument] on appeal." *But see* ***In re K.S.L.***, 499 S.W.3d 109, 112-13 (Tex.App.—San Antonio 2016, pet. granted 6-23-17) (State is not relieved of its burden to prove best interest merely because parent has executed voluntary and irrevocable affidavit of relinquishment of parental rights).

In re A.H., 414 S.W.3d 802, 805 (Tex.App.—San Antonio 2013, no pet.). Mother "asserts the Affidavit [of voluntary relinquishment of parental rights] does not satisfy the requirements of [Fam.] Code §161.103 that the Affidavit state the relinquishing parent's county of residence and the county of residence of other parents. [Mother] also points to other deficiencies in the Affidavit regarding the names of the children in relation to their fathers. [Mother] argues the requirements of [Fam.] Code §§161.001[(1)](K) [now §161.001(b)(1)(K)] and 161.103 should be strictly construed in her favor because, other than best interest, no other ground supported termination. [¶] '[A] direct or collateral attack on an order terminating parental rights based on an unrevoked affidavit of relinquishment of parental rights or affidavit of waiver of interest in a child is limited to issues relating to fraud, duress, or coercion in the execution of the affidavit.' *At 806:* Nothing in the record indicates [mother] signed the Affidavit due to fraud, duress, coercion, or that she involuntarily executed the affidavit. [W]e conclude the evidence supporting the trial court's finding that [mother] had 'executed ... an unrevoked or irrevocable affidavit of relinquishment of parental rights ...,' is supported by clear and convincing evidence."

Moore v. Brown, 408 S.W.3d 423, 433 (Tex.App.—Austin 2013, pet. denied). See annotation under Family Code §161.211, p. 788.

In re C.L., No. 10-11-00228-CV (Tex.App.—Waco 2011, no pet.) (memo op.; 11-16-11). Father "contends that due process requires that the burden of proof to establish the voluntariness of the affidavit should remain with the proponent of the affidavit.... [¶] [He] relies on a dissenting opinion from [***In re L.M.I.***, 119 S.W.3d 707 (Tex.2003),] that argues that because the termination of parental rights is of constitutional dimension that due process requires that the proponent of an affidavit of relinquishment should bear the burden of establishing that it was indeed voluntary. [Father] further contends that at least two courts of appeals[, ***In re R.B.***, 225 S.W.3d 798 (Tex.App.—Fort Worth 2007, no pet.), and ***In re N.P.T.***, 169 S.W.3d 677 (Tex.App.—Dallas 2005, pet. denied),] have concluded that the standard set forth in that dissent regarding a different standard has merit although neither court adopted that standard because the result would have been the same under either standard. However, we note that since those opinions were issued the Fort Worth Court of Appeals sitting *en banc*[, in ***In re D.E.H.***, 301 S.W.3d 825 (Tex.App.—Fort Worth 2009, pet. denied),] expressly declined altering the standard based on the dissent in ***L.M.I.*** We also decline to alter the existing standards and burdens of proof...."

Vallejo v. TDFPS, 280 S.W.3d 917, 921 (Tex.App.—Austin 2009, no pet.). "[A] voluntary relinquishment affidavit does not moot further proceedings in an involuntary termination proceeding. It does not strip the court of jurisdiction to consider other grounds for termination, and does not prevent the court from assess-

ing the child's best interest. [¶] [A]n affidavit of voluntary relinquishment does not automatically and immediately terminate a parental relationship…." *See also* ***In re K.W.***, No. 2-08-162-CV (Tex.App.—Fort Worth 2009, no pet.) (memo op.; 2-19-09).

In re A.G.C., 279 S.W.3d 441, 447 (Tex.App.—Houston [14th Dist.] 2009, no pet.). Section 161.103(b) "requires that an affidavit for voluntary relinquishments of paternal rights 'must contain' specific information about the child and the parents, including the designation of [a] prospective adoptive parent or consenting agency to serve as a managing conservator for the child. However, in the present situation no such person or agency is necessary. … Mother sought to terminate Father's parental rights, no adoption has been sought, and no change was contemplated in the relationship between Mother and [child]. [I]n this circumstance of a private agreement between the parents in which the child was to remain with the mother and no adoption was contemplated, no designation of anyone else under [§161.103(b)(12)] was necessary."

Monroe v. Alternatives in Motion, 234 S.W.3d 56, 61-62 (Tex.App.—Houston [1st Dist.] 2007, no pet.). "Implicit in the Family Code is the requirement that an affidavit of relinquishment of parental rights must be voluntarily executed. Moreover, because an affidavit of relinquishment waives a constitutional right, it must be made voluntarily, knowingly, intelligently, and with full awareness of its legal consequences. The proponent of the affidavit has the burden to establish by clear and convincing evidence that the affidavit was executed according to the terms of §161.103…. An affidavit of relinquishment in proper form is prima facie evidence of its validity. Once the proponent has met that burden, the burden then shifts to the affiant to establish by a preponderance of the evidence that the affidavit was executed as a result of fraud, duress, or coercion. An involuntarily executed affidavit is a complete defense to a termination decree." *See also* ***In re N.P.T.***, 169 S.W.3d 677, 681 (Tex.App.—Dallas 2005, pet. denied) (affidavit of relinquishment procured in exchange for plea bargain where father was represented by attorney was voluntarily executed); ***Jones v. TDPRS***, 85 S.W.3d 483, 491-93 (Tex.App.—Austin 2002, pet. denied) (voluntary relinquishment was procured by fraud and therefore involuntarily executed); ***In re D.R.L.M.***, 84 S.W.3d 281, 286 (Tex.App.—Fort Worth 2002, pet. denied) (voluntary relinquishment was not obtained by fraud even though court did not comply with designation of managing conservator in affidavit); ***Queen v. Goeddertz***, 48 S.W.3d 928, 931-32 (Tex.App.—Beaumont 2001, no pet.) (affidavit of relinquishment was involuntary because affidavit contained language reserving father's right to visit child).

Wall v. TDFPS, 173 S.W.3d 178, 181 (Tex.App.—Austin 2005, no pet.). "[W]e will not categorically ignore the irrevocable nature of a relinquishment of parental rights to the [TDFPS] simply because an affidavit lacks the magic words 'managing conservator.' We strictly scrutinize the language of [mother's] affidavit to determine whether it reflects her intent to designate the [TDFPS] managing conservator of her children. [Mother's] affidavit clearly and repeatedly states that [she] is permanently relinquishing her rights to her children and that the [TDFPS] 'will assume responsibility for [the] Children,' 'care for the Children,' and 'place the Children for adoption.' Only as managing conservator would the [TDFPS] have the authority to place the children for adoption. Viewing the affidavit as a whole, the only meaningful construction is that [mother] intended to designate the [TDFPS] as managing conservator."

Martinez v. TDPRS, 116 S.W.3d 266, 271 (Tex. App.—El Paso 2003, pet. denied). "Characterizing her right to revocation as a procedural safeguard, [respondent] argues that §161.103(e) violates her right to substantive due process. She emphasizes that a parent who relinquishes her parental rights to a private individual can reserve a right to revocation while a parent who relinquishes her parental rights to [TDPRS] or a licensed child-placing agency cannot. *At 272:* [Section 161.103] does not create a risk of erroneous deprivation of a constitutionally protected interest because a parent may move to have an affidavit set aside in the event of fraud or other improper procurement of the affidavit. … Due process does not require that the child's rights be sacrificed to preserve rights which the parent has waived. The legitimate and compelling state interest in protecting the child in this situation is advanced by giving effect to the express will of the parent. [Respondent's] execution of the irrevocable affidavit of relinquishment triggered the State's compelling interest in protecting the rights of the child. Consequently, we conclude there is no due process violation."

In re R.D.S., 902 S.W.2d 714, 721 (Tex.App.—Amarillo 1995, no writ). This court is not ready to say that "revoking an affidavit of voluntary relinquishment

under [Fam. Code] §15.03[, now §161.103, does not] *per se* strip[ ] the document of all probative value. If the parent truly intended to 'not return' when [he or she] signed the affidavit, the fact that the parent *had* that intent is frozen. Rescinding the document simply evinces a changed mind. It does not have the effect of creating a time gate through which the parent may travel back and erase established fact. The affidavit remains indicative of the preexisting intent."

FAM §161.1031. MEDICAL HISTORY REPORT

(a) A parent who signs an affidavit of voluntary relinquishment of parental rights under Section 161.103 regarding a biological child must also prepare a medical history report that addresses the medical history of the parent and the parent's ancestors.

(b) The Department of Family and Protective Services, in cooperation with the Department of State Health Services, shall adopt a form that a parent may use to comply with this section. The form must be designed to permit a parent to identify any medical condition of the parent or the parent's ancestors that could indicate a predisposition for the child to develop the condition.

(c) The medical history report shall be used in preparing the health, social, educational, and genetic history report required by Section 162.005 and shall be made available to persons granted access under Section 162.006 in the manner provided by that section.

History of Fam. Code §161.1031: Acts 2005, 79th Leg., ch. 1258, §1, eff. Sept. 1, 2005.

FAM §161.1035. REVOCABILITY OF CERTAIN AFFIDAVITS

An affidavit of relinquishment of parental rights that fails to state that the relinquishment or waiver is irrevocable for a stated time is:

(1) revocable only if the revocation is made before the 11th day after the date the affidavit is executed; and

(2) irrevocable on or after the 11th day after the date the affidavit is executed.

History of Fam. Code §161.1035: Acts 1997, 75th Leg., ch. 561, §10, eff. Sept. 1, 1997. Amended by Acts 2007, 80th Leg., ch. 1283, §6, eff. Sept. 1, 2007.

FAM §161.104. RIGHTS OF DESIGNATED MANAGING CONSERVATOR PENDING COURT APPOINTMENT

A person, licensed child-placing agency, or the Department of Family and Protective Services designated managing conservator of a child in an irrevocable or unrevoked affidavit of relinquishment has a right to possession of the child superior to the right of the person executing the affidavit, the right to consent to medical, surgical, dental, and psychological treatment of the child, and the rights and duties given by Chapter 153 to a possessory conservator until such time as these rights and duties are modified or terminated by court order.

History of Fam. Code §161.104: Acts 1995, 74th Leg., ch. 20, §1, eff. Apr. 20, 1995. Amended by Acts 1995, 74th Leg., ch. 751, §70, eff. Sept. 1, 1995; Acts 2015, 84th Leg., ch. 1, §1.083, eff. Apr. 2, 2015. Source: Former Fam. Code §14.02(d).

FAM §161.105. REPEALED

Repealed by Acts 2007, 80th Leg., ch. 1283, §13, eff. Sept. 1, 2007.

FAM §161.106. AFFIDAVIT OF WAIVER OF INTEREST IN CHILD

(a) A man may sign an affidavit disclaiming any interest in a child and waiving notice or the service of citation in any suit filed or to be filed affecting the parent-child relationship with respect to the child.

(b) The affidavit may be signed before the birth of the child.

(c) The affidavit shall be:

(1) signed by the man, whether or not a minor;

(2) witnessed by two credible persons; and

(3) verified before a person authorized to take oaths.

(d) The affidavit may contain a statement that the affiant does not admit being the father of the child or having had a sexual relationship with the mother of the child.

(e) An affidavit of waiver of interest in a child may be used in a suit in which the affiant attempts to establish an interest in the child. The affidavit may not be used in a suit brought by another person, licensed child-placing agency, or the Department of Family and Protective Services to establish the affiant's paternity of the child.

(f) A waiver in an affidavit under this section is irrevocable.

(g), (h) Repealed by Acts 2007, 80th Leg., ch. 1283, §13, eff. Sept. 1, 2007.

(i) A copy of the affidavit shall be provided to the person who executed the affidavit at the time the person signs the affidavit.

(j) Repealed by Acts 2007, 80th Leg., ch. 1283, §13, eff. Sept. 1, 2007.

History of Fam. Code §161.106: Acts 1995, 74th Leg., ch. 20, §1, eff. Apr. 20, 1995. Amended by Acts 1997, 75th Leg., ch. 561, §11, eff. Sept. 1, 1997; Acts 2007, 80th Leg., ch. 1283, §§7, 13, eff. Sept. 1, 2007; Acts 2015, 84th Leg., ch. 1, §1.084, eff. Apr. 2, 2015. Source: Former Fam. Code §15.041(a)-(d).

FAM §161.107. MISSING PARENT OR RELATIVE

(a) In this section:

(1) "Parent" means a parent, as defined by Section 160.102, whose parent-child relationship with a child has not been terminated. The term does not include a man who does not have a parent-child relationship established under Chapter 160.

(2) "Relative" means a parent, grandparent, or adult sibling or child.

(b) If a parent of the child has not been personally served in a suit in which the Department of Family and Protective Services seeks termination, the department must make a diligent effort to locate that parent.

(c) If a parent has not been personally served and cannot be located, the department shall make a diligent effort to locate a relative of the missing parent to give the relative an opportunity to request appointment as the child's managing conservator.

(d) If the department is not able to locate a missing parent or a relative of that parent and sufficient information is available concerning the physical whereabouts of the parent or relative, the department shall request the state agency designated to administer a statewide plan for child support to use the parental locator service established under 42 U.S.C. Section 653 to determine the location of the missing parent or relative.

(e) The department shall be required to provide evidence to the court to show what actions were taken by the department in making a diligent effort to locate the missing parent and relative of the missing parent.

History of Fam. Code §161.107: Acts 1995, 74th Leg., ch. 20, §1, eff. Apr. 20, 1995. Amended by Acts 1995, 74th Leg., ch. 751, §71, eff. Sept. 1, 1995; Acts 2007, 80th Leg., ch. 1283, §§8, 9, eff. Sept. 1, 2007. Source: Former Fam. Code §15.051.

FAM §161.108. RELEASE OF CHILD FROM HOSPITAL OR BIRTHING CENTER

(a) Before or at the time an affidavit of relinquishment of parental rights under Section 161.103 is executed, the mother of a newborn child may authorize the release of the child from the hospital or birthing center to a licensed child-placing agency, the Department of Family and Protective Services, or another designated person.

(b) A release under this section must be:

(1) executed in writing;

(2) witnessed by two credible adults; and

(3) verified before a person authorized to take oaths.

(c) A hospital or birthing center shall comply with the terms of a release executed under this section without requiring a court order.

History of Fam. Code §161.108: Acts 1997, 75th Leg., ch. 561, §12, eff. Sept. 1, 1997. Amended by Acts 2015, 84th Leg., ch. 1, §1.085, eff. Apr. 2, 2015.

FAM §161.109. REQUIREMENT OF PATERNITY REGISTRY CERTIFICATE

(a) If a parent-child relationship does not exist between the child and any man, a certificate from the vital statistics unit signed by the registrar that a diligent search has been made of the paternity registry maintained by the unit and that a registration has not been found pertaining to the father of the child in question must be filed with the court before a trial on the merits in the suit for termination may be held.

(b) In a proceeding to terminate parental rights in which the alleged or probable father has not been personally served with citation or signed an affidavit of relinquishment or an affidavit of waiver of interest, the court may not terminate the parental rights of the alleged or probable father, whether known or unknown, unless a certificate from the vital statistics unit signed by the registrar states that a diligent search has been made of the paternity registry maintained by the unit and that a filing or registration has not been found pertaining to the father of the child in question.

History of Fam. Code §161.109: Acts 1997, 75th Leg., ch. 561, §12, eff. Sept. 1, 1997. Amended by Acts 2007, 80th Leg., ch. 1283, §10, eff. Sept. 1, 2007; Acts 2015, 84th Leg., ch, 1, §1.086, eff. Apr. 2, 2015.

Sections 161.110-161.200 reserved for expansion

SUBCHAPTER C. HEARING & ORDER

FAM §161.201. REPEALED

Repealed by Acts 2001, 77th Leg., ch. 130, §1, eff. Sept. 1, 2001.

FAM §161.2011. CONTINUANCE; ACCESS TO CHILD

(a) A parent whose rights are subject to termination in a suit affecting the parent-child relationship and against whom criminal charges are filed that directly relate to the grounds for which termination is sought may file a motion requesting a continuance of the final trial in the suit until the criminal charges are resolved. The court may grant the motion only if the court finds

that a continuance is in the best interest of the child. Notwithstanding any continuance granted, the court shall conduct status and permanency hearings with respect to the child as required by Chapter 263 and shall comply with the dismissal date under Section 263.401.

(b) Nothing in this section precludes the court from issuing appropriate temporary orders as authorized in this code.

(c) The court in which a suit to terminate the parent-child relationship is pending may render an order denying a parent access to a child if the parent is indicted for criminal activity that constitutes a ground for terminating the parent-child relationship under Section 161.001. The denial of access under this section shall continue until the date the criminal charges for which the parent was indicted are resolved and the court renders an order providing for access to the child by the parent.

History of Fam. Code §161.2011: Acts 1997, 75th Leg., ch. 1022, §61, eff. Sept. 1, 1997. Amended by Acts 2001, 77th Leg., ch. 1090, §1.01, eff. June 14, 2001.

ANNOTATIONS

In re TDPRS, 71 S.W.3d 446, 450 (Tex.App.—Fort Worth 2002, orig. proceeding). TDPRS contends that "the amendment to [Fam. Code] §161.2011 that prohibits a continuance or stay of a termination proceeding beyond the 180-day time period in [Fam. Code] §263.401(b) applies retroactively, and that, therefore, the trial court abused its discretion in not granting the TDPRS's motion to vacate the stay, to the extent it continues the case beyond 180 days after the original deadline of August 13, 2001. *At 451:* If a statute is procedural or remedial in nature, '[i]t is the settled law that a litigant has no vested right in a remedy, and that remedial statutes are valid and control the litigation from the date they become a law, and all proceedings taken thereafter must be under the new law.' [¶] We hold that the 2001 amendment to §161.2011 ... does not involve a vested substantive right, but is procedural or remedial in nature. Accordingly, the amended statute controlled the underlying case from its effective date, September 1, 2001."

In re M.C.M., 57 S.W.3d 27, 36 (Tex.App.—Houston [1st Dist.] 2001, pet. denied). "[W]e believe that [Fam. Code] §161.2011 should be read as a stay provision. That is, the 18-month deadline will be stayed by the pendency of criminal charges against the parent. The effect of the stay is to halt all action in the SAPCR and toll the running of the applicable time limits. Once the criminal proceedings against the parent terminate, the time period for resolving the SAPCR continues. Under this interpretation, compliance with §161.2011 would not cause the trial court to miss the dismissal deadline imposed by [Fam. Code] §263.401."

FAM §161.202. PREFERENTIAL SETTING

In a termination suit, after a hearing, the court shall grant a motion for a preferential setting for a final hearing on the merits filed by a party to the suit or by the amicus attorney or attorney ad litem for the child and shall give precedence to that hearing over other civil cases if:

(1) termination would make the child eligible for adoption; and

(2) discovery has been completed or sufficient time has elapsed since the filing of the suit for the completion of all necessary and reasonable discovery if diligently pursued.

History of Fam. Code §161.202: Acts 1995, 74th Leg., ch. 20, §1, eff. Apr. 20, 1995. Amended by Acts 2001, 77th Leg., ch. 133, §5, eff. Sept. 1, 2001; Acts 2005, 79th Leg., ch. 172, §19, eff. Sept. 1, 2005. Source: Former Fam. Code §11.14(h).

FAM §161.2021. MEDICAL HISTORY REPORT

(a) In a termination suit, the court shall order each parent before the court to provide information regarding the medical history of the parent and the parent's ancestors.

(b) A parent may comply with the court's order under this section by completing the medical history report form adopted by the Department of Family and Protective Services under Section 161.1031.

(c) If the Department of Family and Protective Services is a party to the termination suit, the information provided under this section must be maintained in the department records relating to the child and made available to persons with whom the child is placed.

History of Fam. Code §161.2021: Acts 2005, 79th Leg., ch. 1258, §2, eff. Sept. 1, 2005.

FAM §161.203. DISMISSAL OF PETITION

A suit to terminate may not be dismissed nor may a nonsuit be taken unless the dismissal or nonsuit is approved by the court. The dismissal or nonsuit approved by the court is without prejudice.

History of Fam. Code §161.203: Acts 1995, 74th Leg., ch. 20, §1, eff. Apr. 20, 1995. Amended by Acts 2001, 77th Leg., ch. 1090, §4, eff. Sept. 1, 2001. Source: Former Fam. Code §15.06.

FAM §161.204. TERMINATION BASED ON AFFIDAVIT OF WAIVER OF INTEREST

In a suit for termination, the court may render an order terminating the parent-child relationship between a child and a man who has signed an affidavit of waiver of interest in the child, if the termination is in the best interest of the child.

History of Fam. Code §161.204: Acts 1995, 74th Leg., ch. 20, §1, eff. Apr. 20, 1995. Amended by Acts 2001, 77th Leg., ch. 1090, §6, eff. Sept. 1, 2001. Source: Former Fam. Code §15.041(e).

FAM §161.205. ORDER DENYING TERMINATION

If the court does not order termination of the parent-child relationship, the court shall:

(1) deny the petition; or

(2) render any order in the best interest of the child.

History of Fam. Code §161.205: Acts 1995, 74th Leg., ch. 20, §1, eff. Apr. 20, 1995. Amended by Acts 2001, 77th Leg., ch. 1090, §6, eff. Sept. 1, 2001. Source: Former Fam. Code §15.05(c).

Ⓐ FAM §161.206. ORDER TERMINATING PARENTAL RIGHTS

The amended text in §161.206 is effective for service plans filed for a full adversary hearing held under Fam. Code §262.201 or a status hearing held under Fam. Code ch. 263 on or after Jan. 1, 2018. A hearing held before Jan. 1, 2018, is governed by the former law in effect at that time. Except as provided above, the amended text in §161.206 is effective for SAPCRs filed on or after Sept. 1, 2017. SAPCRs filed before Sept. 1, 2017, are governed by the former law in effect at that time.

(a) If the court finds by clear and convincing evidence grounds for termination of the parent-child relationship, it shall render an order terminating the parent-child relationship.

(a-1) In a suit filed by the Department of Family and Protective Services seeking termination of the parent-child relationship for more than one parent of the child, the court may order termination of the parent-child relationship for the parent only if the court finds by clear and convincing evidence grounds for the termination of the parent-child relationship for that parent.

(b) Except as provided by Section 161.2061, an order terminating the parent-child relationship divests the parent and the child of all legal rights and duties with respect to each other, except that the child retains the right to inherit from and through the parent unless the court otherwise provides.

(c) Nothing in this chapter precludes or affects the rights of a biological or adoptive maternal or paternal grandparent to reasonable access under Chapter 153.

(d) An order rendered under this section must include a finding that:

(1) a request for identification of a court of continuing, exclusive jurisdiction has been made as required by Section 155.101; and

(2) all parties entitled to notice, including the Title IV-D agency, have been notified.

History of Fam. Code §161.206: Acts 1995, 74th Leg., ch. 20, §1, eff. Apr. 20, 1995. Amended by Acts 1995, 74th Leg., ch. 709, §2 (eff. Sept. 1, 1995), ch. 751, §72 (eff. Sept. 1, 1995); Acts 2003, 78th Leg., ch. 561, §1, eff. Sept. 1, 2003; Acts 2007, 80th Leg., ch. 972, §44, eff. Sept. 1, 2007; H.B. 7, §13, 85th Leg., eff. Sept. 1, 2017. Source: Former Fam. Code §§11.15(b), 15.05(a), 15.07.

See also *O'Connor's Texas Family Law Handbook* (2017), "Judgment," ch. 4-H, §15, p. 649.

ANNOTATIONS

Texas DHS v. E.B., 802 S.W.2d 647, 649 (Tex.1990). "The charge in parental rights cases should be the same as in other civil cases. The controlling question in this case was whether the parent-child relationship between the mother and each of her two children should be terminated, not what specific ground or grounds under [Fam. Code] §15.02 [now §161.001] the jury relied on to answer affirmatively the questions posed. All ten jurors agree that the mother had endangered the child by doing one or the other of the things listed in §15.02. [Respondent] argues that the charge, as presented to the jury, violates her due process right by depriving a natural mother of her fundamental right to the care, custody and management of her children. Recognizing her rights does not change the form of submission. The standard for review of the charge is abuse of discretion, and abuse of discretion occurs only when the trial court acts without reference to any guiding principle. Here the trial court tracked the statutory language in the instruction and then asked the controlling question. This simply does not amount to abuse of discretion."

Durham v. Barrow, 600 S.W.2d 756, 760 (Tex. 1980). The Family Code "provides that an individual who has been divested of parental rights by a termination decree loses all legal rights and interest in the children who were the subject of the termination proceeding [and] that a person whose parental rights have been terminated is not entitled to notice of a subsequent adoption. Therefore, if the termination judgment

was valid, [a biological parent] has no standing to bring a bill of review as a party to [an] adoption."

LG Elecs., USA, Inc. v. Grigg, 424 S.W.3d 804, 808-09 (Tex.App.—Tyler 2014, no pet.). "[Ps] are the deceased's biological children, his parental rights were terminated before his death, and [Ps] were never adopted. The termination decrees do not provide that the children retained any legal rights from [decedent father]. By statute, however, an order terminating the parent-child relationship divests the child of all legal rights with respect to the parent except the right to inherit from him. This court is not permitted to ignore the legal effect of the termination decrees. Nor are we permitted to contravene legislative intent by creating a new class of beneficiaries under the [Wrongful Death] Act. Wrongful death benefits are conferred by statute, not through inheritance. Therefore, we hold that [Ps] do not have standing to sue under the [Wrongful Death] Act for [decedent father's] death."

Swate v. Swate, 72 S.W.3d 763, 771 (Tex.App.—Waco 2002, pet. denied). Reading Fam. Code §161.206(b) to "absolve child support arrearage would eliminate the purpose of [Fam. Code] §151.001(c).... The delinquent parent could refuse to pay child support until termination of parental rights was ultimately ordered, thus defeating the statute and the court's original order to pay child support."

In re J.R., 991 S.W.2d 318, 320 (Tex.App.—Fort Worth 1999, no pet.). The standard of clear and convincing evidence "is an intermediate standard that falls between the preponderance standard of ordinary civil proceedings and the reasonable doubt standard of criminal proceedings. While the proof must weigh heavier than merely the greater weight of the credible evidence, there is no requirement that the evidence be unequivocal or undisputed. Termination proceedings should be strictly scrutinized, and involuntary termination statutes are strictly construed in favor of the parent. [¶] This higher burden of proof in the trial court does not alter the appellate standard of review for factual sufficiency. Accordingly, to prevail on an assertion that the evidence supporting the termination of parental rights is 'factually insufficient,' the evidence supporting the finding must be so weak or the evidence to the contrary must be so overwhelming that the finding should be set aside and a new trial ordered. We are required to consider all of the evidence in the case in making this determination."

FAM §161.2061. TERMS REGARDING LIMITED POST-TERMINATION CONTACT

(a) If the court finds it to be in the best interest of the child, the court may provide in an order terminating the parent-child relationship that the biological parent who filed an affidavit of voluntary relinquishment of parental rights under Section 161.103 shall have limited post-termination contact with the child as provided by Subsection (b) on the agreement of the biological parent and the Department of Family and Protective Services.

(b) The order of termination may include terms that allow the biological parent to:

(1) receive specified information regarding the child;

(2) provide written communications to the child; and

(3) have limited access to the child.

(c) The terms of an order of termination regarding limited post-termination contact may be enforced only if the party seeking enforcement pleads and proves that, before filing the motion for enforcement, the party attempted in good faith to resolve the disputed matters through mediation.

(d) The terms of an order of termination under this section are not enforceable by contempt.

(e) The terms of an order of termination regarding limited post-termination contact may not be modified.

(f) An order under this section does not:

(1) affect the finality of a termination order; or

(2) grant standing to a parent whose parental rights have been terminated to file any action under this title other than a motion to enforce the terms regarding limited post-termination contact until the court renders a subsequent adoption order with respect to the child.

History of Fam. Code §161.2061: Acts 2003, 78th Leg., ch. 561, §2, eff. Sept. 1, 2003. Amended by Acts 2015, 84th Leg., ch. 1, §1.087, eff. Apr. 2, 2015.

See also *O'Connor's Texas Family Law Handbook* (2017), "Post-termination Contact," ch. 4-H, §13, p. 644.

FAM §161.2062. PROVISION FOR LIMITED CONTACT BETWEEN BIOLOGICAL PARENT & CHILD

(a) An order terminating the parent-child relationship may not require that a subsequent adoption order include terms regarding limited post-termination contact between the child and a biological parent.

(b) The inclusion of a requirement for post-termination contact described by Subsection (a) in a termination order does not:

(1) affect the finality of a termination or subsequent adoption order; or

(2) grant standing to a parent whose parental rights have been terminated to file any action under this title after the court renders a subsequent adoption order with respect to the child.

History of Fam. Code §161.2062: Acts 2003, 78th Leg., ch. 561, §2, eff. Sept. 1, 2003.

FAM §161.207. APPOINTMENT OF MANAGING CONSERVATOR ON TERMINATION

(a) If the court terminates the parent-child relationship with respect to both parents or to the only living parent, the court shall appoint a suitable, competent adult, the Department of Family and Protective Services, or a licensed child-placing agency as managing conservator of the child. An agency designated managing conservator in an unrevoked or irrevocable affidavit of relinquishment shall be appointed managing conservator.

(b) The order of appointment may refer to the docket number of the suit and need not refer to the parties nor be accompanied by any other papers in the record.

History of Fam. Code §161.207: Acts 1995, 74th Leg., ch. 20, §1, eff. Apr. 20, 1995. Amended by Acts 2015, 84th Leg., ch. 1, §1.088, eff. Apr. 2, 2015. Source: Former Fam. Code §15.05(b).

ANNOTATIONS

In re D.N.C., 252 S.W.3d 317, 318 (Tex.2008). "On appeal, [mother] challenged the sufficiency of the evidence to support the termination order, but she did not separately challenge appointment of [DFPS] as the children's managing conservator. The court of appeals reversed the termination order on factual insufficiency grounds, and also reversed the trial court's conservatorship appointment. *At 319:* [DFPS] here contends reversal of the conservatorship order was erroneous under our recent decision in ***In the Interest of J.A.J.***, 243 S.W.3d 611 (Tex.2007). In *J.A.J.*, however, [DFPS] requested conservatorship pursuant to [Fam.] Code §153.131 and the trial court made the specific findings that the statute requires: that appointment of a parent as [child's] managing conservator would not be in his best interest because it would significantly impair his physical health or emotional development, and that appointment of [DFPS] was in [child's] best interest. In light of these findings, we emphasized that the differing elements and standards of review applied to conservatorship and termination orders required separate challenges on appeal. In this case, by comparison, the only available statutory mechanism for [DFPS's] appointment was as a consequence of the termination pursuant to [Fam. Code] §161.207. Accordingly, *J.A.J.* does not apply, and [mother's] challenge to the conservatorship appointment was subsumed in her appeal of the parental-rights termination order." *See also* ***In re A.L.M.***, 300 S.W.3d 914, 931 (Tex.App.—Texarkana 2009, no pet.) (because conservatorship determination was subsumed into termination determination, conservatorship order was reversed when termination was reversed); ***In re A.S.***, 261 S.W.3d 76, 91-92 (Tex.App.—Houston [14th Dist.] 2008, pet. denied) (even though DFPS requested conservatorship under Fam. Code §153.131, trial court made no findings under that section to independently support conservatorship order; appointment was consequence of termination).

In re J.A.J., 243 S.W.3d 611, 612-13 (Tex.2007). "We must decide the effect of a termination judgment's reversal on an unchallenged conservatorship appointment when the trial court finds that appointing a parent as conservator would significantly impair the child's physical health or emotional development, and that appointment of the [TDFPS] is in the child's best interest.... We conclude that reversal of a termination judgment in these circumstances does not affect the trial court's conservatorship appointment absent assigned error. *At 616-17:* In light of the differences in the factors that weigh in termination [under Fam. Code §161.001(1)] and conservatorship decisions [under Fam. Code §153.131(a)] and the differing burdens of proof and standards of appellate review, we conclude that a challenge to the [TDFPS's] appointment as [child's] managing conservator was not subsumed in [mother's] challenge to the termination order."

In re N.T., 474 S.W.3d 465, 480 (Tex.App.—Dallas 2015, no pet.). "In cases where a trial court's termination of the parent-child relationship is reversed, a parent is required to independently challenge a trial court's finding under [Fam. Code] §153.131(a) to obtain reversal of the conservatorship appointment. *At 481:* In the case before us, we have overruled [Mother's] challenge to the termination, and the trial court's appointment of the Department as [SMC] may be considered a consequence of the termination pursuant to

[Fam. Code] §161.207. Further, Mother provides no authority for the proposition that she is a 'suitable, competent adult' as contemplated by §161.207(a) or that the presumption in §153.131(a) applies to a parent whose parental rights have been terminated under Ch. 161. Accordingly, Mother's challenge to the trial court's appointment of the Department as [SMC], rather than Mother, is without merit." (Internal quotes omitted.)

In re A.C., 394 S.W.3d 633, 644 (Tex.App.—Houston [1st Dist.] 2012, no pet.). "In contrast to the presumption of appointment given to a child's parents, ... there is no statutory presumption that a grandparent should be preferred over other non-parents. [¶] The primary consideration in determining conservatorship is always the best interest of the child. In determining that appointment of a party as managing conservator [under Fam. Code §161.207] is in the child's best interest, the court must consider both the [Fam. Code] §263.307 factors and the ***Holley*** factors...."

FAM §161.208. APPOINTMENT OF DEPARTMENT OF FAMILY & PROTECTIVE SERVICES AS MANAGING CONSERVATOR

If a parent of the child has not been personally served in a suit in which the Department of Family and Protective Services seeks termination, the court that terminates a parent-child relationship may not appoint the Department of Family and Protective Services as permanent managing conservator of the child unless the court determines that:

(1) the department has made a diligent effort to locate a missing parent who has not been personally served and a relative of that parent; and

(2) a relative located by the department has had a reasonable opportunity to request appointment as managing conservator of the child or the department has not been able to locate the missing parent or a relative of the missing parent.

History of Fam. Code §161.208: Acts 1995, 74th Leg., ch. 20, §1, eff. Apr. 20, 1995. Amended by Acts 2015, 84th Leg., ch. 1, §1.089, eff. Apr. 2, 2015. Source: Former Fam. Code §15.051(b).

FAM §161.209. COPY OF ORDER OF TERMINATION

A copy of an order of termination rendered under Section 161.206 is not required to be mailed to parties as provided by Rules 119a and 239a, Texas Rules of Civil Procedure.

History of Fam. Code §161.209: Acts 1995, 74th Leg., ch. 20, §1, eff. Apr. 20, 1995. Source: Former Fam. Code §11.16.

FAM §161.210. SEALING OF FILE

The court, on the motion of a party or on the court's own motion, may order the sealing of the file, the minutes of the court, or both, in a suit for termination.

History of Fam. Code §161.210: Acts 1995, 74th Leg., ch. 20, §1, eff. Apr. 20, 1995. Source: Former Fam. Code §11.17(f).

ANNOTATIONS

In re D.R.L.M., 84 S.W.3d 281, 307 (Tex.App.—Fort Worth 2002, pet. denied). "The trial court's termination and adoption order provided, 'All papers and records in this case, including the minutes of the Court, are ordered sealed.' *At 308:* TDPRS ... contends that [Fam. Code §§161.210 and 161.021] do not authorize the trial court to seal the reporter's record. According to TDPRS, the reporter's record is not part of the 'file' and is not sealable at all by the trial court. [¶] TDPRS's construction of §§161.210 and 162.021 would render them meaningless. If the court reporter's stenographic notes, transcription of those notes, and the exhibits offered into evidence at trial are not subject to a sealing order such as the one at issue, then in effect, the entire trial record is not sealed and is available to the public. We will not construe §§161.210 and 162.021 in a manner that renders them meaningless and ineffectual."

FAM §161.211. DIRECT OR COLLATERAL ATTACK ON TERMINATION ORDER

(a) Notwithstanding Rule 329, Texas Rules of Civil Procedure, the validity of an order terminating the parental rights of a person who has been personally served or who has executed an affidavit of relinquishment of parental rights or an affidavit of waiver of interest in a child or whose rights have been terminated under Section 161.002(b) is not subject to collateral or direct attack after the sixth month after the date the order was signed.

(b) Notwithstanding Rule 329, Texas Rules of Civil Procedure, the validity of an order terminating the parental rights of a person who is served by citation by publication is not subject to collateral or direct attack after the sixth month after the date the order was signed.

(c) A direct or collateral attack on an order terminating parental rights based on an unrevoked affidavit of relinquishment of parental rights or affidavit of waiver of interest in a child is limited to issues relating to fraud, duress, or coercion in the execution of the affidavit.

History of Fam. Code §161.211: Acts 1997, 75th Leg., ch. 600, §1 (eff. Sept. 1, 1997), ch. 601, §2 (eff. Sept. 1, 1997). Amended by Acts 1999, 76th Leg., ch. 1390, §19, eff. Sept. 1, 1999.

ANNOTATIONS

In re E.R., 385 S.W.3d 552, 566 (Tex.2012). "A complete failure of service deprives a litigant of due process and a trial court of personal jurisdiction; the resulting judgment is void and may be challenged at any time. … Accordingly, [§161.211] cannot place a temporal limit on a challenge to a void judgment filed by a defendant who did not receive the type of notice to which she was constitutionally entitled. Despite the Legislature's intent to expedite termination proceedings, it cannot do so at the expense of a parent's constitutional right to notice."

In re J.H., 486 S.W.3d 190, 197 (Tex.App.—Dallas 2016, no pet.). "That a parent feels pressure or emotional upset when she signs an affidavit does not itself render the affidavit involuntary."

In re K.D., 471 S.W.3d 147, 160 (Tex.App.—Texarkana 2015, no pet.). "Mother … argues that the Affidavit [executed pursuant to Fam. Code §161.103] was obtained via constructive fraud…. [C]onstructive fraud requires proof of a fiduciary or confidential relationship between the parties. Neither the Department, nor its agents, nor the child's ad litem occupy a confidential or fiduciary relationship with a parent in a parental-rights termination case. While the Department may provide services to parents as part of a family service plan, the Department acts to secure the best interests of the child rather than the parent."

Moore v. Brown, 408 S.W.3d 423, 433 (Tex.App.—Austin 2013, pet. denied). Birth parents' "central contention … is that … they executed their affidavits relinquishing parental rights less than 48 hours after the child's birth, and contrary to the requirements of [Fam. Code] §161.103. [Birth parents] urge that this defect not only negates the sole statutory ground for the district court's termination order, but renders the affidavit a 'nullity' or 'void' for all purposes and effectively returns the parties to the status quo that existed before the affidavits were executed. *At 436:* Although [birth parents] insist that the phrase 'person who has executed an affidavit of relinquishment of parental rights' [under Fam. Code §161.211(a)] presumes and requires 'an affidavit of relinquishment of parental rights' that complies with each of the requirements of §161.103, subsection (a) does not actually say this…. *At 438:* [Further, §161.211(c)'s] limitation of … 'issues relating to fraud, duress, or coercion in the execution of the affidavit' proscribes challenges based solely on a complaint that the affidavit violated one of §161.103's requirements. Subsection (c) thus bars … claims seeking to invalidate or set aside the termination order on the ground that [the] affidavits of relinquishment were executed within the 48-hour waiting period. *At 439:* [Consequently,] we have concluded that [birth parents'] waivers of their parental rights to [child] must be given effect." *See also* ***In re C.O.G.***, No. 13-12-00577-CV (Tex.App.—Corpus Christi 2013, no pet.) (memo op.; 12-12-13) (termination order could not be challenged on the basis that it didn't comply with §161.103's two-credible-witnesses requirement).

In re Bullock, 146 S.W.3d 783, 790-91 (Tex.App.—Beaumont 2004, orig. proceeding). "Essentially, §161.211's six month limitation on attacks on termination rulings is an affirmative defense…. The defense of limitations does not bar a plaintiff from filing a lawsuit. As such, [mother] was required to plead and present the affirmative defense of limitations, but failed to do so. Coupled with our finding that §161.211 is not a jurisdictional prerequisite to suit, the procedural default by [mother] at the … bill of review hearing results in our concluding that [mother and stepfather] have failed to establish 'that the facts and law permit the trial court to make but one decision.'" *See also* ***In re M.Y.W.***, No. 14-06-00185-CV (Tex.App.—Houston [14th Dist.] 2006, pet. denied) (memo op.; 11-21-06). *But see* ***In re C.T.C.***, 365 S.W.3d 853, 858 (Tex.App.—Dallas 2012, pet. granted, judgment vacated w.r.m.) (six-month deadline in §161.211(a) is bar to or preclusion of challenge to termination order more than six months after termination order is signed; it is not plea in avoidance).

CHAPTER 162. ADOPTION

SUBCHAPTER A. ADOPTION OF A CHILD

FAM §162.001. WHO MAY ADOPT & BE ADOPTED

(a) Subject to the requirements for standing to sue in Chapter 102, an adult may petition to adopt a child who may be adopted.

(b) A child residing in this state may be adopted if:

(1) the parent-child relationship as to each living parent of the child has been terminated or a suit for termination is joined with the suit for adoption;

(2) the parent whose rights have not been terminated is presently the spouse of the petitioner and the proceeding is for a stepparent adoption;

(3) the child is at least two years old, the parent-child relationship has been terminated with respect to

one parent, the person seeking the adoption has been a managing conservator or has had actual care, possession, and control of the child for a period of six months preceding the adoption or is the child's former stepparent, and the nonterminated parent consents to the adoption; or

(4) the child is at least two years old, the parent-child relationship has been terminated with respect to one parent, and the person seeking the adoption is the child's former stepparent and has been a managing conservator or has had actual care, possession, and control of the child for a period of one year preceding the adoption.

(c) If an affidavit of relinquishment of parental rights contains a consent for the Department of Family and Protective Services or a licensed child-placing agency to place the child for adoption and appoints the department or agency managing conservator of the child, further consent by the parent is not required and the adoption order shall terminate all rights of the parent without further termination proceedings.

History of Fam. Code §162.001: Acts 1995, 74th Leg., ch. 20, §1, eff. Apr. 20, 1995. Amended by Acts 1997, 75th Leg., ch. 561, §14, eff. Sept. 1, 1997; Acts 2003, 78th Leg., ch. 493, §1, eff. Sept. 1, 2003; Acts 2015, 84th Leg., ch. 1, §1.090, eff. Apr. 2, 2015. Source: Former Fam. Code §§16.01, 16.02, 16.03(b)-(d).

ANNOTATIONS

Trevino v. Garcia, 627 S.W.2d 147, 148 (Tex.1982). Petitioners "claim they are entitled to custody of [child] because they have adopted her by estoppel. We disagree. *At 149:* [Family Code] §16.03 [now §162.001] provides that a valid adoption must be preceded by either a judicial termination of the rights of the natural parents, or an irrevocable relinquishment of parental rights by affidavit meeting the requirements of [Fam. Code] §15.03(b) [now §161.103]. The Family Code requires a judicial [termination or relinquishment] order for adoption."

Durham v. Barrow, 600 S.W.2d 756, 761 (Tex. 1980). "[P] has no standing to attack the adoption by virtue of his being guardian ad litem in the termination proceeding. A guardian ad litem's representation is limited to matters related to the suit for which he was appointed. Termination suits are separate from any other [SAPCR], and a termination judgment is a final, appealable judgment. Therefore, [P] does not have standing to attack the adoption as a necessary party to that suit, and he was not entitled to notice of those proceedings under [Fam. Code] §11.09 [now §102.009]. [¶] Although the children were the subject of the adoption suit, they were not participants in the suit, and were not necessary parties to the adoption. Since the children themselves were not necessary parties to the adoption, a next friend would not have standing to attack the adoption by bill of review. *At 761 n.6:* In Texas, as in other jurisdictions, a total stranger may not bring a bill of review to set aside an adoption."

In re D.G., 329 S.W.3d 893, 897 (Tex.App.—Houston [14th Dist.] 2010, orig. proceeding). "While 'actual care, possession, and control' has not been addressed with regard to [Fam. Code] §162.001(b)(4), this phrase has been addressed with regard to standing to file [a SAPCR] under [Fam. Code] §102.003(a)(9).... 'Control' means more than the control implicit in having care and possession of the child. [¶] [Stepfather] testified that he interacted with [child] more than 30 times [in the two years following his separation with child's mother before their divorce]. [In the year following the separation, he] continued to pick up [child] from daycare.... [He] took [child] to church ... without [mother] being present[, and] had [child] for 12 hours ... at his college graduation. [But the] last time [stepfather] had possession of [child] without [mother's] presence was [a year before stepfather filed for adoption]. [Child] has not stayed overnight with [stepfather] since the separation. This is not sufficient to establish that [stepfather] had actual care, possession, and control of [child] for a period of one year preceding the adoption."

FAM §162.002. PREREQUISITES TO PETITION

(a) If a petitioner is married, both spouses must join in the petition for adoption.

(b) A petition in a suit for adoption or a suit for appointment of a nonparent managing conservator with authority to consent to adoption of a child must include:

(1) a verified allegation that there has been compliance with Subchapter B; or

(2) if there has not been compliance with Subchapter B, a verified statement of the particular reasons for noncompliance.

History of Fam. Code §162.002: Acts 1995, 74th Leg., ch. 20, §1, eff. Apr. 20, 1995. Source: Former Fam. Code §§11.08(d), 16.03(a).

FAM §162.0025. ADOPTION SOUGHT BY MILITARY SERVICE MEMBER

In a suit for adoption, the fact that a petitioner is a member of the armed forces of the United States, a member of the Texas National Guard or the National

Guard of another state, or a member of a reserve component of the armed forces of the United States may not be considered by the court, or any person performing an adoption evaluation or home screening, as a negative factor in determining whether the adoption is in the best interest of the child or whether the petitioner would be a suitable parent.

History of Fam. Code §162.0025: Acts 2007, 80th Leg., ch. 768, §1, eff. June 15, 2007. Amended by Acts 2015, 84th Leg., ch. 1252, §3.02, eff. Sept. 1, 2015.

FAM §162.003. ADOPTION EVALUATION

In a suit for adoption, an adoption evaluation must be conducted as provided in Chapter 107.

History of Fam. Code §162.003: Acts 1995, 74th Leg., ch. 20, §1, eff. Apr. 20, 1995. Amended by Acts 1995, 74th Leg., ch. 751, §73 (eff. Sept. 1, 1995), ch. 800, §1 (eff. Sept. 1, 1995); Acts 2001, 77th Leg., ch. 133, §6, eff. Sept. 1, 2001; Acts 2007, 80th Leg., ch. 832, §6, eff. Sept. 1, 2007; Acts 2015, 84th Leg., ch. 1252, §3.03, eff. Sept. 1, 2015. Source: Former Fam. Code §16.031(a).

FAM §162.004. REPEALED

Repealed by Acts 2001, 77th Leg., ch. 133, §7, eff. Sept. 1, 2001.

FAM §162.0045. PREFERENTIAL SETTING

The court shall grant a motion for a preferential setting for a final hearing on an adoption and shall give precedence to that hearing over all other civil cases not given preference by other law if the adoption evaluation has been filed and the criminal history for the person seeking to adopt the child has been obtained.

History of Fam. Code §162.0045: Acts 1997, 75th Leg., ch. 561, §15, eff. Sept. 1, 1997. Amended by Acts 2015, 84th Leg., ch. 1252, §3.04, eff. Sept. 1, 2015.

A FAM §162.005. PREPARATION OF HEALTH, SOCIAL, EDUCATIONAL, & GENETIC HISTORY REPORT

(a) This section does not apply to an adoption by the child's:

(1) grandparent;

(2) aunt or uncle by birth, marriage, or prior adoption; or

(3) stepparent.

(b) Before placing a child for adoption, the Department of Family and Protective Services, a licensed child-placing agency, or the child's parent or guardian shall compile a report on the available health, social, educational, and genetic history of the child to be adopted.

(c) The department shall ensure that each licensed child-placing agency, single source continuum contractor, or other person placing a child for adoption receives a copy of any portion of the report prepared by the department.

(d) If the child has been placed for adoption by a person or entity other than the department, a licensed child-placing agency, or the child's parent or guardian, it is the duty of the person or entity who places the child for adoption to prepare the report.

(e) The person or entity who places the child for adoption shall provide the prospective adoptive parents a copy of the report as early as practicable before the first meeting of the adoptive parents with the child. The copy of the report shall be edited to protect the identity of birth parents and their families.

(f) The department, licensed child-placing agency, parent, guardian, person, or entity who prepares and files the original report is required to furnish supplemental medical, psychological, and psychiatric information to the adoptive parents if that information becomes available and to file the supplemental information where the original report is filed. The supplemental information shall be retained for as long as the original report is required to be retained.

History of Fam. Code §162.005: Acts 1995, 74th Leg., ch. 20, §1, eff. Apr. 20, 1995. Amended by Acts 2015, 84th Leg., ch. 944, §12 (eff. Sept. 1, 2015), ch. 1, 84th Leg., §1.091 (eff. Apr. 2, 2015); S.B. 11, §4, 85th Leg., eff. Sept. 1, 2017. Source: Former Fam. Code §16.032(a), (f), (*l*).

FAM §162.006. ACCESS TO HEALTH, SOCIAL, EDUCATIONAL, & GENETIC HISTORY REPORT; RETENTION

(a), (a-1) Renumbered as §162.0062(a), (b) by Acts 2015, 84th Leg., ch. 944, §15(a), eff. Sept. 1, 2015.

(b) The department, licensed child-placing agency, or court retaining a copy of the report shall provide a copy of the report that has been edited to protect the identity of the birth parents and any other person whose identity is confidential to the following persons on request:

(1) an adoptive parent of the adopted child;

(2) the managing conservator, guardian of the person, or legal custodian of the adopted child;

(3) the adopted child, after the child is an adult;

(4) the surviving spouse of the adopted child if the adopted child is dead and the spouse is the parent or guardian of a child of the deceased adopted child; or

(5) a progeny of the adopted child if the adopted child is dead and the progeny is an adult.

(c) A copy of the report may not be furnished to a person who cannot furnish satisfactory proof of identity and legal entitlement to receive a copy.

(d) A person requesting a copy of the report shall pay the actual and reasonable costs of providing a copy and verifying entitlement to the copy.

(e) The report shall be retained for 99 years from the date of the adoption by the department or licensed child-placing agency placing the child for adoption. If the agency ceases to function as a child-placing agency, the agency shall transfer all the reports to the department or, after giving notice to the department, to a transferee agency that is assuming responsibility for the preservation of the agency's adoption records. If the child has not been placed for adoption by the department or a licensed child-placing agency and if the child is being adopted by a person other than the child's stepparent, grandparent, aunt, or uncle by birth, marriage, or prior adoption, the person or entity who places the child for adoption shall file the report with the department, which shall retain the copies for 99 years from the date of the adoption.

History of Fam. Code §162.006: Acts 1995, 74th Leg., ch. 20, §1, eff. Apr. 20, 1995. Amended by Acts 2013, 83rd Leg., ch. 1069, §1, eff. Sept. 1, 2013; Acts 2015, 84th Leg., ch. 944, §§13, 15(a) (eff. Sept. 1, 2015), ch. 1, §1.092 (eff. Apr. 2, 2015). Source: Former Fam. Code §16.032(a), (g), (i)-(k).

See also 25 T.A.C. §181.32.

A FAM §162.0062. ACCESS TO INFORMATION

(a) Except as provided by Subsection (c), the prospective adoptive parents of a child are entitled to examine the records and other information relating to the history of the child. The Department of Family and Protective Services, licensed child-placing agency, or other person placing a child for adoption shall inform the prospective adoptive parents of their right to examine the records and other information relating to the history of the child. The department, licensed child-placing agency, or other person placing the child for adoption shall edit the records and information to protect the identity of the biological parents and any other person whose identity is confidential.

(a-1) If a child is placed with a prospective adoptive parent prior to adoption, the prospective adoptive parent is entitled to examine any record or other information relating to the child's health history, including the portion of the report prepared under Section 162.005 for the child that relates to the child's health. The department, licensed child-placing agency, single source continuum contractor, or other person placing a child for adoption shall inform the prospective adoptive parent of the prospective adoptive parent's right to examine the records and other information relating to the child's health history. The department, licensed child-placing agency, single source continuum contractor, or other person placing the child for adoption shall edit the records and information to protect the identity of the biological parents and any other person whose identity is confidential.

(b) The records described by Subsection (a) must include any records relating to an investigation of abuse in which the child was an alleged or confirmed victim of sexual abuse while residing in a foster home or other residential child-care facility. If the licensed child-placing agency or other person placing the child for adoption does not have the information required by this subsection, the department, at the request of the licensed child-placing agency or other person placing the child for adoption, shall provide the information to the prospective adoptive parents of the child.

(c) If the prospective adoptive parents of a child have reviewed the health, social, educational, and genetic history report for the child and indicated that they want to proceed with the adoption, the department may, but is not required to, allow the prospective adoptive parents of the child to examine the records and other information relating to the history of the child, unless the prospective adoptive parents request the child's case record. The department shall provide the child's case record to the prospective adoptive parents on the request of the prospective adoptive parents.

(c-1) If the prospective adoptive parents of a child indicate they want to proceed with the adoption under Subsection (c), the department, licensed child-placing agency, or single source continuum contractor shall provide the prospective adoptive parents with access to research regarding underlying health issues and other conditions of trauma that could impact child development and permanency.

(d) The adoptive parents and the adopted child, after the child is an adult, are entitled to receive copies of the records that have been edited to protect the identity of the biological parents and any other person whose identity is confidential and other information relating to the history of the child maintained by the department, licensed child-placing agency, person, or entity placing the child for adoption.

(e) It is the duty of the person or entity placing the child for adoption to edit the records and information to protect the identity of the biological parents and any other person whose identity is confidential.

(f) At the time an adoption order is rendered, the court shall provide to the parents of an adopted child information provided by the vital statistics unit that describes the functions of the voluntary adoption registry under Subchapter E. The licensed child-placing agency shall provide to each of the child's biological parents known to the agency, the information when the parent signs an affidavit of relinquishment of parental rights or affidavit of waiver of interest in a child. The information shall include the right of the child or biological parent to refuse to participate in the registry. If the adopted child is 14 years old or older the court shall provide the information to the child.

History of Fam. Code §162.0062: Acts 1995, 74th Leg., ch. 20, §1, eff. Apr. 20, 1995. Amended by Acts 1997, 75th Leg., ch. 561, §17, eff. Sept. 1, 1997; Acts 2007, 80th Leg., ch. 1283, §11, eff. Sept. 1, 2007; Acts 2013, 83rd Leg., ch. 1069, §1, eff. Sept. 1, 2013. Renumbered from §§162.006(a), (a-1), 162.018 and amended by Acts 2015, 84th Leg., ch. 944, §15(a), (b), eff. Sept. 1, 2015. Amended by Acts 2015, 84th Leg., ch. 1, §§1.092, 1.096, eff. Apr. 2, 2015; S.B. 11, §5, 85th Leg., eff. Sept. 1, 2017. Source: Former Fam. Code §§16.032(a), (f), (g), (i)-(k), 16.09(b), (c).

See also 25 T.A.C. §181.32.

FAM §162.0065. EDITING ADOPTION RECORDS IN DEPARTMENT PLACEMENT

Notwithstanding any other provision of this chapter, in an adoption in which a child is placed for adoption by the Department of Family and Protective Services, the department is not required to edit records to protect the identity of birth parents and other persons whose identity is confidential if the department determines that information is already known to the adoptive parents or is readily available through other sources, including the court records of a suit to terminate the parent-child relationship under Chapter 161.

History of Fam. Code §162.0065: Acts 2003, 78th Leg., ch. 68, §1, eff. Sept. 1, 2003. Amended by Acts 2015, 84th Leg., ch. 1, §1.093, eff. Apr. 2, 2015.

A FAM §162.007. CONTENTS OF HEALTH, SOCIAL, EDUCATIONAL, & GENETIC HISTORY REPORT

(a) The health history of the child must include information about:

(1) the child's health status at the time of placement;

(2) the child's birth, neonatal, and other medical, psychological, psychiatric, and dental history information, including to the extent known by the department:

(A) whether the child's birth mother consumed alcohol during pregnancy; and

(B) whether the child has been diagnosed with fetal alcohol spectrum disorder;

(3) a record of immunizations for the child; and

(4) the available results of medical, psychological, psychiatric, and dental examinations of the child.

(b) The social history of the child must include information, to the extent known, about past and existing relationships between the child and the child's siblings, parents by birth, extended family, and other persons who have had physical possession of or legal access to the child.

(c) The educational history of the child must include, to the extent known, information about:

(1) the enrollment and performance of the child in educational institutions;

(2) results of educational testing and standardized tests for the child; and

(3) special educational needs, if any, of the child.

(d) The genetic history of the child must include a description of the child's parents by birth and their parents, any other child born to either of the child's parents, and extended family members and must include, to the extent the information is available, information about:

(1) their health and medical history, including any genetic diseases and disorders;

(2) their health status at the time of placement;

(3) the cause of and their age at death;

(4) their height, weight, and eye and hair color;

(5) their nationality and ethnic background;

(6) their general levels of educational and professional achievements, if any;

(7) their religious backgrounds, if any;

(8) any psychological, psychiatric, or social evaluations, including the date of the evaluation, any diagnosis, and a summary of any findings;

(9) any criminal conviction records relating to a misdemeanor or felony classified as an offense against the person or family or public indecency or a felony violation of a statute intended to control the possession or distribution of a substance included in Chapter 481, Health and Safety Code; and

(10) any information necessary to determine whether the child is entitled to or otherwise eligible for state or federal financial, medical, or other assistance.

(e) The report shall include a history of physical, sexual, or emotional abuse suffered by the child, if any.

(f) Notwithstanding the other provisions of this section, the Department of Family and Protective Services may, in accordance with department rule, modify the form and contents of the health, social, educational, and genetic history report for a child as the department determines appropriate based on:

(1) the relationship between the prospective adoptive parents and the child or the child's birth family;

(2) the provision of the child's case record to the prospective adoptive parents; or

(3) any other factor specified by department rule.

(g) In this section, "fetal alcohol spectrum disorder" means any of a group of conditions that can occur in a person whose mother consumed alcohol during pregnancy.

History of Fam. Code §162.007: Acts 1995, 74th Leg., ch. 20, §1, eff. Apr. 20, 1995. Amended by Acts 2015, 84th Leg., ch. 944, §§12, 14, eff. Sept. 1, 2015; S.B. 11, §6, 85th Leg., eff. Sept. 1, 2017. Source: Former Fam. Code §16.032(b)-(e).

FAM §162.008. FILING OF HEALTH, SOCIAL, EDUCATIONAL, & GENETIC HISTORY REPORT

(a) This section does not apply to an adoption by the child's:

(1) grandparent;

(2) aunt or uncle by birth, marriage, or prior adoption; or

(3) stepparent.

(b) A petition for adoption may not be granted until the following documents have been filed:

(1) a copy of the health, social, educational, and genetic history report signed by the child's adoptive parents; and

(2) if the report is required to be submitted to the Department of Family and Protective Services under Section 162.006(e), a certificate from the department acknowledging receipt of the report.

(c) A court having jurisdiction of a suit affecting the parent-child relationship may by order waive the making and filing of a report under this section if the child's biological parents cannot be located and their absence results in insufficient information being available to compile the report.

History of Fam. Code §162.008: Acts 1995, 74th Leg., ch. 20, §1, eff. Apr. 20, 1995. Amended by Acts 1999, 76th Leg., ch. 1390, §20, eff. Sept. 1, 1999; Acts 2015, 84th Leg., ch. 1, §1.094, eff. Apr. 2, 2015. Source: Former Fam. Code §16.032(h), (m).

FAM §162.0085. CRIMINAL HISTORY REPORT REQUIRED

(a) In a suit affecting the parent-child relationship in which an adoption is sought, the court shall order each person seeking to adopt the child to obtain that person's own criminal history record information. The court shall accept under this section a person's criminal history record information that is provided by the Department of Family and Protective Services or by a licensed child-placing agency that received the information from the department if the information was obtained not more than one year before the date the court ordered the history to be obtained.

(b) A person required to obtain information under Subsection (a) shall obtain the information in the manner provided by Section 411.128, Government Code.

History of Fam. Code §162.0085: Acts 1995, 74th Leg., ch. 751, §75 (eff. Sept. 1, 1995), ch. 908, §2 (eff. Sept. 1, 1995). Amended by Acts 1997, 75th Leg., ch. 561, §16, eff. Sept. 1, 1997; Acts 2015, 84th Leg., ch. 1, §1.095, eff. Apr. 2, 2015.

E FAM §162.0086. INFORMATION REGARDING SIBLING ACCESS

(a) The Department of Family and Protective Services shall provide information to each person seeking to adopt a child placed for adoption by the department regarding the right of a child's sibling to file a suit for access to the child under Sections 102.0045 and 153.551.

(b) The department may provide the information required under Subsection (a) on any form or application provided to prospective adoptive parents.

History of Fam. Code §162.0086: Enacted by H.B. 5, §7, 85th Leg., eff. Sept. 1, 2017; S.B. 948, §1, 85th Leg., eff. Sept. 1, 2017.

FAM §162.009. RESIDENCE WITH PETITIONER

(a) The court may not grant an adoption until the child has resided with the petitioner for not less than six months.

(b) On request of the petitioner, the court may waive the residence requirement if the waiver is in the best interest of the child.

History of Fam. Code §162.009: Acts 1995, 74th Leg., ch. 20, §1, eff. Apr. 20, 1995. Source: Former Fam. Code §16.04.

ANNOTATIONS

Celestine v. DFPS, 321 S.W.3d 222, 233 (Tex. App.—Houston [1st Dist.] 2010, no pet.). Petitioner "alleges that because §162.009(b) allows the trial court to waive the six-month requirement if it finds that waiver is in the child's best interest, she was therefore

entitled to an opportunity to present evidence and be heard on the issue of whether waiver was indeed in the children's best interest. *At 234:* [W]e conclude that this argument is without merit. First, ... §162.009 does not expressly require the trial court to hold a hearing specifically on this issue before it determines whether wavier of the six-month requirement is in the children's best interest. Second, it is apparent from the record that the [adoption] hearing was not the first time [petitioner's] fitness to care for the children was called into question. The trial court had already heard substantial testimony regarding the reasons why DFPS removed the children from [petitioner's] home [two years earlier]."

FAM §162.010. CONSENT REQUIRED

(a) Unless the managing conservator is the petitioner, the written consent of a managing conservator to the adoption must be filed. The court may waive the requirement of consent by the managing conservator if the court finds that the consent is being refused or has been revoked without good cause. A hearing on the issue of consent shall be conducted by the court without a jury.

(b) If a parent of the child is presently the spouse of the petitioner, that parent must join in the petition for adoption and further consent of that parent is not required.

(c) A child 12 years of age or older must consent to the adoption in writing or in court. The court may waive this requirement if it would serve the child's best interest.

History of Fam. Code §162.010: Acts 1995, 74th Leg., ch. 20, §1, eff. Apr. 20, 1995. Amended by Acts 1995, 74th Leg., ch. 751, §76, eff. Sept. 1, 1995. Source: Former Fam. Code §16.05.

ANNOTATIONS

Chapman v. Home, 561 S.W.2d 265, 267 (Tex. App.—Fort Worth 1978, no writ). "In agency adoption situations, consent of the managing conservator must be expressed in writing pursuant to the literal terms of [Fam. Code] §16.05(a) [now §162.010(a)] and will not be inferred from the fact of placement or subsequent acts allowing a child to remain in the possession of would-be adoptive parents. [¶] The managing conservator has good cause for withholding consent whenever it has good reason to believe in good faith that the adoptive placement is not working out satisfactorily or that the best interest of the child requires that it withhold or revoke consent. [¶] The burden of proof of establishing the managing conservator's lack of good cause for withholding or revoking consent rests upon the party seeking waiver of the consent requirement. [¶] The trial court may, in one hearing, consider whether or not the managing conservator has withheld consent without good cause, whether or not the child should be restored to the possession of the prospective adoptive parents, whether or not the adoption should be granted, and, if not, whether or not the managing conservator should have authority to place the child in the home of third parties pending appeal of an adverse decision by the original prospective adoptive parents." *See also* ***In re A.M.***, 312 S.W.3d 76, 83 (Tex.App.—San Antonio 2010, pet. denied) (provision under §162.010 that allows managing conservator to refuse consent to adoption applies only after movant has established standing under Fam. Code ch. 102).

FAM §162.011. REVOCATION OF CONSENT

At any time before an order granting the adoption of the child is rendered, a consent required by Section 162.010 may be revoked by filing a signed revocation.

History of Fam. Code §162.011: Acts 1995, 74th Leg., ch. 20, §1, eff. Apr. 20, 1995. Source: Former Fam. Code §16.06.

FAM §162.012. DIRECT OR COLLATERAL ATTACK

(a) Notwithstanding Rule 329, Texas Rules of Civil Procedure, the validity of an adoption order is not subject to attack after six months after the date the order was signed.

(b) The validity of a final adoption order is not subject to attack because a health, social, educational, and genetic history was not filed.

History of Fam. Code §162.012: Acts 1995, 74th Leg., ch. 20, §1, eff. Apr. 20, 1995. Amended by Acts 1997, 75th Leg., ch. 600, §2 (eff. Jan. 1, 1998), ch. 601, §1 (eff. Sept. 1, 1997). Source: Former Fam. Code §16.12.

FAM §162.013. ABATEMENT OR DISMISSAL

(a) If the sole petitioner dies or the joint petitioners die, the court shall dismiss the suit for adoption.

(b) If one of the joint petitioners dies, the proceeding shall continue uninterrupted.

(c) If the joint petitioners divorce, the court shall abate the suit for adoption. The court shall dismiss the petition unless the petition is amended to request adoption by one of the original petitioners.

History of Fam. Code §162.013: Acts 1995, 74th Leg., ch. 20, §1, eff. Apr. 20, 1995. Source: Former Fam. Code §16.11.

FAM §162.014. ATTENDANCE AT HEARING REQUIRED

(a) If the joint petitioners are husband and wife and it would be unduly difficult for one of the petitioners to appear at the hearing, the court may waive the attendance of that petitioner if the other spouse is present.

(b) A child to be adopted who is 12 years of age or older shall attend the hearing. The court may waive this requirement in the best interest of the child.

History of Fam. Code §162.014: Acts 1995, 74th Leg., ch. 20, §1, eff. Apr. 20, 1995. Source: Former Fam. Code §16.07.

FAM §162.015. RACE OR ETHNICITY

(a) In determining the best interest of the child, the court may not deny or delay the adoption or otherwise discriminate on the basis of race or ethnicity of the child or the prospective adoptive parents.

(b) This section does not apply to a person, entity, tribe, organization, or child custody proceeding subject to the Indian Child Welfare Act of 1978 (25 U.S.C. Section 1901 et seq.). In this subsection "child custody proceeding" has the meaning provided by 25 U.S.C. Section 1903.

History of Fam. Code §162.015: Acts 1995, 74th Leg., ch. 20, §1, eff. Apr. 20, 1995. Amended by Acts 1995, 74th Leg., ch. 751, §77, eff. Sept. 1, 1995. Source: Former Fam. Code §16.081.

FAM §162.016. ADOPTION ORDER

(a) If a petition requesting termination has been joined with a petition requesting adoption, the court shall also terminate the parent-child relationship at the same time the adoption order is rendered. The court must make separate findings that the termination is in the best interest of the child and that the adoption is in the best interest of the child.

(b) If the court finds that the requirements for adoption have been met and the adoption is in the best interest of the child, the court shall grant the adoption.

(c) The name of the child may be changed in the order if requested.

History of Fam. Code §162.016: Acts 1995, 74th Leg., ch. 20, §1, eff. Apr. 20, 1995. Source: Former Fam. Code §16.08.

ANNOTATIONS

Green v. Remling, 608 S.W.2d 905, 907 (Tex.1980). "The paramount considerations in adoption proceedings are the rights and welfare of the children involved and these statutes are to be liberally construed in favor of the minor to effectuate their beneficial purpose. *At 908:* [Family Code] §16.08(a) [now §162.016] indicates that the court may decree an adoption only when it is satisfied that adoption is in the best interests of the child. To effectuate this provision, the trial court in adoption cases is invested with broad discretionary power in determining the best interests of the children. The trial judge is better situated to weigh all of the surrounding circumstances and arrive at a judgment which in his discretion will best protect the best interests of the child. No right to a jury exists in an adoption hearing. The judgment of the trial court should not be disturbed unless it appears from the record as a whole that there was an abuse of discretion."

FAM §162.017. EFFECT OF ADOPTION

(a) An order of adoption creates the parent-child relationship between the adoptive parent and the child for all purposes.

(b) An adopted child is entitled to inherit from and through the child's adoptive parents as though the child were the biological child of the parents.

(c) The terms "child," "descendant," "issue," and other terms indicating the relationship of parent and child include an adopted child unless the context or express language clearly indicates otherwise.

(d) Nothing in this chapter precludes or affects the rights of a biological or adoptive maternal or paternal grandparent to reasonable possession of or access to a grandchild, as provided in Chapter 153.

History of Fam. Code §162.017: Acts 1995, 74th Leg., ch. 20, §1, eff. Apr. 20, 1995. Amended by Acts 2005, 79th Leg., ch. 916, §23, eff. June 18, 2005. Source: Former Fam. Code §16.09(a), (d)-(f).

See also Est. Code §22.004(a) (definition of "child" includes adopted child).

FAM §162.018. RENUMBERED

Renumbered as §162.0062(d)-(f) by Acts 2015, 84th Leg., ch. 944, §15(b), eff. Sept. 1, 2015.

FAM §162.019. COPY OF ORDER

A copy of the adoption order is not required to be mailed to the parties as provided in Rules 119a and 239a, Texas Rules of Civil Procedure.

History of Fam. Code §162.019: Acts 1995, 74th Leg., ch. 20, §1, eff. Apr. 20, 1995. Source: Former Fam. Code §11.16.

FAM §162.020. WITHDRAWAL OR DENIAL OF PETITION

If a petition requesting adoption is withdrawn or denied, the court may order the removal of the child from the proposed adoptive home if removal is in the child's best interest and may enter any order necessary for the welfare of the child.

History of Fam. Code §162.020: Acts 1995, 74th Leg., ch. 20, §1, eff. Apr. 20, 1995. Source: Former Fam. Code §16.10.

FAM §162.021. SEALING FILE

(a) The court, on the motion of a party or on the court's own motion, may order the sealing of the file and the minutes of the court, or both, in a suit requesting an adoption.

(b) Rendition of the order does not relieve the clerk from the duty to send information regarding adoption to the vital statistics unit as required by this subchapter and Chapter 108.

History of Fam. Code §162.021: Acts 1995, 74th Leg., ch. 20, §1, eff. Apr. 20, 1995. Amended by Acts 1995, 74th Leg., ch. 751, §78, eff. Sept. 1, 1995; Acts 2015, 84th Leg., ch. 1, §1.097, eff. Apr. 2, 2015. Source: Former Fam. Code §11.17(f).

FAM §162.022. CONFIDENTIALITY MAINTAINED BY CLERK

The records concerning a child maintained by the district clerk after entry of an order of adoption are confidential. No person is entitled to access to the records or may obtain information from the records except for good cause under an order of the court that issued the order.

History of Fam. Code §162.022: Acts 1995, 74th Leg., ch. 20, §1, eff. Apr. 20, 1995. Source: Former Fam. Code §11.17(d).

FAM §162.023. ADOPTION ORDER FROM FOREIGN COUNTRY

(a) Except as otherwise provided by law, an adoption order rendered to a resident of this state that is made by a foreign country shall be accorded full faith and credit by the courts of this state and enforced as if the order were rendered by a court in this state unless the adoption law or process of the foreign country violates the fundamental principles of human rights or the laws or public policy of this state.

(b) A person who adopts a child in a foreign country may register the order in this state. A petition for registration of a foreign adoption order may be combined with a petition for a name change. If the court finds that the foreign adoption order meets the requirements of Subsection (a), the court shall order the state registrar to:

(1) register the order under Chapter 192, Health and Safety Code; and

(2) file a certificate of birth for the child under Section 192.006, Health and Safety Code.

History of Fam. Code §162.023: Acts 2003, 78th Leg., ch. 19, §1, eff. Sept. 1, 2003.

FAM §162.024. REPEALED

Repealed by Acts 1995, 74th Leg., ch. 751, §1.28, eff. Sept. 1, 1995.

FAM §162.025. PLACEMENT BY UNAUTHORIZED PERSON; OFFENSE

(a) A person who is not the natural or adoptive parent of the child, the legal guardian of the child, or a child-placing agency licensed under Chapter 42, Human Resources Code, commits an offense if the person:

(1) serves as an intermediary between a prospective adoptive parent and an expectant parent or parent of a minor child to identify the parties to each other; or

(2) places a child for adoption.

(b) It is not an offense under this section if a professional provides legal or medical services to:

(1) a parent who identifies the prospective adoptive parent and places the child for adoption without the assistance of the professional; or

(2) a prospective adoptive parent who identifies a parent and receives placement of a child for adoption without the assistance of the professional.

(c) An offense under this section is a Class B misdemeanor.

History of Fam. Code §162.025: Acts 1995, 74th Leg., ch. 411, §1, eff. Sept. 1, 1995. Amended by Acts 1997, 75th Leg., ch. 561, §18, eff. Sept. 1, 1997.

E FAM §162.026. REGULATED CUSTODY TRANSFER OF ADOPTED CHILD

A parent, managing conservator, or guardian of an adopted child may not transfer permanent physical custody of the child to any person who is not a relative or stepparent of the child or an adult who has a significant and long-standing relationship with the child unless:

(1) the parent, managing conservator, or guardian files a petition with a court of competent jurisdiction requesting a transfer of custody; and

(2) the court approves the petition.

History of Fam. Code §162.026: Enacted by H.B. 834, §1, 85th Leg., eff. Sept. 1, 2017.

Sections 162.027-162.100 reserved for expansion

SUBCHAPTER B. INTERSTATE COMPACT ON THE PLACEMENT OF CHILDREN

FAM §162.101. DEFINITIONS

In this subchapter:

(1) "Appropriate public authorities," with reference to this state, means the commissioner of the Department of Family and Protective Services.

(2) "Appropriate authority in the receiving state," with reference to this state, means the commissioner of the Department of Family and Protective Services.

(3) "Compact" means the Interstate Compact on the Placement of Children.

(4) "Executive head," with reference to this state, means the governor.

History of Fam. Code §162.101: Acts 1995, 74th Leg., ch. 20, §1, eff. Apr. 20, 1995. Amended by Acts 1995, 74th Leg., ch. 846, §2, eff. June 16, 1995; Acts 2015, 84th Leg., ch. 1, §1.098, eff. Apr. 2, 2015. Source: Former Hum. Res. Code §§45.001, 45.022.

FAM §162.102. ADOPTION OF COMPACT; TEXT

The Interstate Compact on the Placement of Children is adopted by this state and entered into with all other jurisdictions in form substantially as provided by this subchapter.

INTERSTATE COMPACT ON THE PLACEMENT OF CHILDREN

ARTICLE I. PURPOSE & POLICY

It is the purpose and policy of the party states to cooperate with each other in the interstate placement of children to the end that:

(a) Each child requiring placement shall receive the maximum opportunity to be placed in a suitable environment and with persons or institutions having appropriate qualifications and facilities to provide a necessary and desirable degree and type of care.

(b) The appropriate authorities in a state where a child is to be placed may have full opportunity to ascertain the circumstances of the proposed placement, thereby promoting full compliance with applicable requirements for the protection of the child.

(c) The proper authorities of the state from which the placement is made may obtain the most complete information on the basis on which to evaluate a projected placement before it is made.

(d) Appropriate jurisdictional arrangements for the care of children will be promoted.

ARTICLE II. DEFINITIONS

As used in this compact:

(a) "Child" means a person who, by reason of minority, is legally subject to parental, guardianship, or similar control.

(b) "Sending agency" means a party state, officer, or employee thereof; a subdivision of a party state, or officer or employee thereof; a court of a party state; a person, corporation, association, charitable agency, or other entity which sends, brings, or causes to be sent or brought any child to another party state.

(c) "Receiving state" means the state to which a child is sent, brought, or caused to be sent or brought, whether by public authorities or private persons or agencies, and whether for placement with state or local public authorities or for placement with private agencies or persons.

(d) "Placement" means the arrangement for the care of a child in a family free or boarding home or in a child-caring agency or institution but does not include any institution caring for the mentally ill, mentally defective, or epileptic or any institution primarily educational in character, and any hospital or other medical facility.

ARTICLE III. CONDITIONS FOR PLACEMENT

(a) No sending agency shall send, bring, or cause to be sent or brought into any other party state any child for placement in foster care or as a preliminary to a possible adoption unless the sending agency shall comply with each and every requirement set forth in this article and with the applicable laws of the receiving state governing the placement of children therein.

(b) Prior to sending, bringing, or causing any child to be sent or brought into a receiving state for placement in foster care or as a preliminary to a possible adoption, the sending agency shall furnish the appropriate public authorities in the receiving state written notice of the intention to send, bring, or place the child in the receiving state. The notice shall contain:

(1) the name, date, and place of birth of the child;

(2) the identity and address or addresses of the parents or legal guardian;

(3) the name and address of the person, agency, or institution to or with which the sending agency proposes to send, bring, or place the child;

(4) a full statement of the reasons for such proposed action and evidence of the authority pursuant to which the placement is proposed to be made.

(c) Any public officer or agency in a receiving state which is in receipt of a notice pursuant to Paragraph (b) of this article may request of the sending agency, or any other appropriate officer or agency of or in the sending agency's state, and shall be entitled to receive therefrom, such supporting or additional information as it may deem necessary under the circumstances to carry out the purpose and policy of this compact.

(d) The child shall not be sent, brought, or caused to be sent or brought into the receiving state until the

appropriate public authorities in the receiving state shall notify the sending agency, in writing, to the effect that the proposed placement does not appear to be contrary to the interests of the child.

ARTICLE IV. PENALTY FOR ILLEGAL PLACEMENT

The sending, bringing, or causing to be sent or brought into any receiving state of a child in violation of the terms of this compact shall constitute a violation of the laws respecting the placement of children of both the state in which the sending agency is located or from which it sends or brings the child and of the receiving state. Such violation may be punished or subjected to penalty in either jurisdiction in accordance with its laws. In addition to liability for any such punishment or penalty, any such violation shall constitute full and sufficient grounds for the suspension or revocation of any license, permit, or other legal authorization held by the sending agency which empowers or allows it to place or care for children.

ARTICLE V. RETENTION OF JURISDICTION

(a) The sending agency shall retain jurisdiction over the child sufficient to determine all matters in relation to the custody, supervision, care, treatment, and disposition of the child which it would have had if the child had remained in the sending agency's state, until the child is adopted, reaches majority, becomes self-supporting, or is discharged with the concurrence of the appropriate authority in the receiving state. Such jurisdiction shall also include the power to effect or cause the return of the child or its transfer to another location and custody pursuant to law. The sending agency shall continue to have financial responsibility for support and maintenance of the child during the period of the placement. Nothing contained herein shall defeat a claim of jurisdiction by a receiving state sufficient to deal with an act of delinquency or crime committed therein.

(b) When the sending agency is a public agency, it may enter into an agreement with an authorized public or private agency in the receiving state providing for the performance of one or more services in respect of such case by the latter as agent for the sending agency.

(c) Nothing in this compact shall be construed to prevent a private charitable agency authorized to place children in the receiving state from performing services or acting as agent in that state for a private charitable agency of the sending state; nor to prevent the agency in the receiving state from discharging financial responsibility for the support and maintenance of a child who has been placed on behalf of the sending agency without relieving the responsibility set forth in Paragraph (a) hereof.

ARTICLE VI. INSTITUTIONAL CARE OF DELINQUENT CHILDREN

A child adjudicated delinquent may be placed in an institution in another party jurisdiction pursuant to this compact but no such placement shall be made unless the child is given a court hearing on notice to the parent or guardian with opportunity to be heard, prior to his being sent to such other party jurisdiction for institutional care and the court finds that:

(1) equivalent facilities for the child are not available in the sending agency's jurisdiction; and

(2) institutional care in the other jurisdiction is in the best interest of the child and will not produce undue hardship.

ARTICLE VII. COMPACT ADMINISTRATOR

The executive head of each jurisdiction party to this compact shall designate an officer who shall be general coordinator of activities under this compact in his jurisdiction and who, acting jointly with like officers of other party jurisdictions, shall have power to promulgate rules and regulations to carry out more effectively the terms and provisions of this compact.

ARTICLE VIII. LIMITATIONS

This compact shall not apply to:

(a) the sending or bringing of a child into a receiving state by his parent, stepparent, grandparent, adult brother or sister, adult uncle or aunt, or his guardian and leaving the child with any such relative or non-agency guardian in the receiving state; or

(b) any placement, sending, or bringing of a child into a receiving state pursuant to any other interstate compact to which both the state from which the child is sent or brought and the receiving state are party, or to any other agreement between said states which has the force of law.

ARTICLE IX. ENACTMENT & WITHDRAWAL

This compact shall be open to joinder by any state, territory, or possession of the United States, the District of Columbia, the Commonwealth of Puerto Rico,

and, with the consent of congress, the government of Canada or any province thereof. It shall become effective with respect to any such jurisdiction when such jurisdiction has enacted the same into law. Withdrawal from this compact shall be by the enactment of a statute repealing the same, but shall not take effect until two years after the effective date of such statute and until written notice of the withdrawal has been given by the withdrawing state to the governor of each other party jurisdiction. Withdrawal of a party state shall not affect the rights, duties, and obligations under this compact of any sending agency therein with respect to a placement made prior to the effective date of withdrawal.

ARTICLE X. CONSTRUCTION & SEVERABILITY

The provisions of this compact shall be liberally construed to effectuate the purposes thereof. The provisions of this compact shall be severable and if any phrase, clause, sentence, or provision of this compact is declared to be contrary to the constitution of any party state or of the United States or the applicability thereof to any government, agency, person, or circumstance is held invalid, the validity of the remainder of this compact and the applicability thereof to any government, agency, person, or circumstance shall not be affected thereby. If this compact shall be held contrary to the constitution of any state party thereto, the compact shall remain in full force and effect as to the remaining states and in full force and effect as to the state affected as to all severable matters.

History of Fam. Code §162.102: Acts 1995, 74th Leg., ch. 20, §1, eff. Apr. 20, 1995. Renumbered from §162.108 and amended by Acts 1995, 74th Leg., ch. 846, §3, eff. June 16, 1995. Source: Former Hum. Res. Code §45.021.

History of Former Fam. Code §162.102: Acts 1995, 74th Leg., ch. 20, §1, eff. Apr. 20, 1995. Repealed by Acts 1995, 74th Leg., ch. 846, §10, eff. June 16, 1995. Source: Former Hum. Res. Code §45.002(a)-(c), (e).

See also 40 T.A.C. §§700.1901, 700.1902.

ANNOTATIONS

Broyles v. Ashworth, 782 S.W.2d 31, 33-34 (Tex. App.—Fort Worth 1989, orig. proceeding). "We interpret [§162.102, art. V(a)] as meaning that whatever authority the sending agency might have with respect to custody and disposition of the child, prior to one of the listed events, is to be determined according to the law of the sending agency's state. We do not interpret the section to mean that a natural mother, if she is the sending agency, has the absolute right to regain custody of a child which she has placed in another state for adoption, merely upon her demand."

FAM §162.103. FINANCIAL RESPONSIBILITY FOR CHILD

(a) Financial responsibility for a child placed as provided in the compact is determined, in the first instance, as provided in Article V of the compact. After partial or complete default of performance under the provisions of Article V assigning financial responsibility, the commissioner of the Department of Family and Protective Services may bring suit under Chapter 154 and may file a complaint with the appropriate prosecuting attorney, claiming a violation of Section 25.05, Penal Code.

(b) After default, if the commissioner of the Department of Family and Protective Services determines that financial responsibility is unlikely to be assumed by the sending agency or the child's parents, the commissioner may cause the child to be returned to the sending agency.

(c) After default, the Department of Family and Protective Services shall assume financial responsibility for the child until it is assumed by the child's parents or until the child is safely returned to the sending agency.

History of Fam. Code §162.103: Acts 1995, 74th Leg., ch. 20, §1, eff. Apr. 20, 1995. Renumbered from §162.109 and amended by Acts 1995, 74th Leg., ch. 846, §4, eff. June 16, 1995. Amended by Acts 2015, 84th Leg., ch. 1, §1.099, eff. Apr. 2, 2015. Source: Former Hum. Res. Code §45.023.

History of Former Fam. Code §162.103: Acts 1995, 74th Leg., ch. 20, §1, eff. Apr. 20, 1995. Repealed by Acts 1995, 74th Leg., ch. 846, §10, eff. June 16, 1995. Source: Former Hum. Res. Code §45.003(a)-(d).

FAM §162.104. APPROVAL OF PLACEMENT

The commissioner of the Department of Family and Protective Services may not approve the placement of a child in this state without the concurrence of the individuals with whom the child is proposed to be placed or the head of an institution with which the child is proposed to be placed.

History of Fam. Code §162.104: Acts 1995, 74th Leg., ch. 20, §1, eff. Apr. 20, 1995. Renumbered from §162.110 and amended by Acts 1995, 74th Leg., ch. 846, §5, eff. June 16, 1995. Amended by Acts 2015, 84th Leg., ch. 1, §1.100, eff. Apr. 2, 2015. Source: Former Hum. Res. Code §45.024.

History of Former Fam. Code §162.104: Acts 1995, 74th Leg., ch. 20, §1, eff. Apr. 20, 1995. Repealed by Acts 1995, 74th Leg., ch. 846, §10, eff. June 16, 1995. Source: Former Hum. Res. Code §45.004.

FAM §162.105. PLACEMENT IN ANOTHER STATE

A juvenile court may place a delinquent child in an institution in another state as provided by Article VI of the compact. After placement in another state, the court retains jurisdiction of the child as provided by Article V of the compact.

History of Fam. Code §162.105: Acts 1995, 74th Leg., ch. 20, §1, eff. Apr. 20, 1995. Renumbered from §162.111 by Acts 1995, 74th Leg., ch. 846, §6, eff. June 16, 1995. Source: Former Hum. Res. Code §45.025.

History of Former Fam. Code §162.105: Acts 1995, 74th Leg., ch. 20, §1, eff. Apr. 20, 1995. Repealed by Acts 1995, 74th Leg., ch. 846, §10, eff. June 16, 1995. Source: Former Hum. Res. Code §45.005.

FAM §162.106. COMPACT AUTHORITY

(a) The governor shall appoint the commissioner of the Department of Family and Protective Services as compact administrator.

(b) The commissioner of the Department of Family and Protective Services shall designate a deputy compact administrator and staff necessary to execute the terms of the compact in this state.

History of Fam. Code §162.106: Acts 1995, 74th Leg., ch. 20, §1, eff. Apr. 20, 1995. Renumbered from §162.112 and amended by Acts 1995, 74th Leg., ch. 846, §7, eff. June 16, 1995. Amended by Acts 2015, 84th Leg., ch. 1, §1.101, eff. Apr. 2, 2015. Source: Former Hum. Res. Code §45.026.

History of Former Fam. Code §162.106: Acts 1995, 74th Leg., ch. 20, §1, eff. Apr. 20, 1995. Repealed by Acts 1995, 74th Leg., ch. 846, §10, eff. June 16, 1995. Source: Former Hum. Res. Code §45.006.

FAM §162.107. OFFENSES; PENALTIES

(a) An individual, agency, corporation, or child-care facility that violates a provision of the compact commits an offense. An offense under this subsection is a Class B misdemeanor.

(b) An individual, agency, corporation, child-care facility, or general residential operation in this state that violates Article IV of the compact commits an offense. An offense under this subsection is a Class B misdemeanor. On conviction, the court shall revoke any license to operate as a child-care facility or general residential operation issued by the Department of Family and Protective Services to the entity convicted and shall revoke any license or certification of the individual, agency, or corporation necessary to practice in the state.

History of Fam. Code §162.107: Acts 1995, 74th Leg., ch. 20, §1, eff. Apr. 20, 1995. Renumbered from §162.113 and amended by Acts 1995, 74th Leg., ch. 846, §8, eff. June 16, 1995. Amended by Acts 2015, 84th Leg., ch. 1, §1.102, eff. Apr. 2, 2015.

History of Former Fam. Code §162.107: Acts 1995, 74th Leg., ch. 20, §1, eff. Apr. 20, 1995. Repealed by Acts 1995, 74th Leg., ch. 846, §10, eff. June 16, 1995. Source: Former Hum. Res. Code §45.007.

FAM §§162.108 TO 162.113. RENUMBERED

Renumbered as §§162.103-162.107 by Acts 1995, 74th Leg., ch. 846, §§2-8, eff. June 16, 1995.

FAM §162.114. REPEALED

Repealed by Acts 1995, 74th Leg., ch. 846, §10, eff. June 16, 1995.

Sections 162.115-162.200 reserved for expansion

SUBCHAPTER C. INTERSTATE COMPACT ON ADOPTION & MEDICAL ASSISTANCE

FAM §162.201. ADOPTION OF COMPACT; TEXT

The Interstate Compact on Adoption and Medical Assistance is adopted by this state and entered into with all other jurisdictions joining in the compact in form substantially as provided under this subchapter.

INTERSTATE COMPACT ON ADOPTION & MEDICAL ASSISTANCE

ARTICLE I. FINDINGS

The legislature finds that:

(a) Finding adoptive families for children for whom state assistance is desirable, under Subchapter D, Chapter 162, and assuring the protection of the interest of the children affected during the entire assistance period require special measures when the adoptive parents move to other states or are residents of another state.

(b) The provision of medical and other necessary services for children, with state assistance, encounters special difficulties when the provision of services takes place in other states.

ARTICLE II. PURPOSES

The purposes of the compact are to:

(a) authorize the Department of Family and Protective Services, with the concurrence of the Health and Human Services Commission, to enter into interstate agreements with agencies of other states for the protection of children on behalf of whom adoption assistance is being provided by the Department of Family and Protective Services; and

(b) provide procedures for interstate children's adoption assistance payments, including medical payments.

ARTICLE III. DEFINITIONS

In this compact:

(a) "Adoption assistance state" means the state that signs an adoption assistance agreement in a particular case.

(b) "Residence state" means the state in which the child resides by virtue of the residence of the adoptive parents.

(c) "State" means a state of the United States, the District of Columbia, the Commonwealth of Puerto

Rico, the Virgin Islands, Guam, the Commonwealth of the Northern Mariana Islands, or a territory or possession of or a territory or possession administered by the United States.

ARTICLE IV. COMPACTS AUTHORIZED

The Department of Family and Protective Services, through its commissioner, is authorized to develop, participate in the development of, negotiate, and enter into one or more interstate compacts on behalf of this state with other states to implement one or more of the purposes of this compact. An interstate compact authorized by this article has the force and effect of law.

ARTICLE V. CONTENTS OF COMPACTS

A compact entered into under the authority conferred by this compact shall contain:

(1) a provision making the compact available for joinder by all states;

(2) a provision for withdrawal from the compact on written notice to the parties, with a period of one year between the date of the notice and the effective date of the withdrawal;

(3) a requirement that protections under the compact continue for the duration of the adoption assistance and apply to all children and their adoptive parents who on the effective date of the withdrawal are receiving adoption assistance from a party state other than the one in which they reside and have their principal place of abode;

(4) a requirement that each case of adoption assistance to which the compact applies be covered by a written adoption assistance agreement between the adoptive parents and the state child welfare agency of the state that provides the adoption assistance and that the agreement be expressly for the benefit of the adopted child and enforceable by the adoptive parents and the state agency providing the adoption assistance; and

(5) other provisions that are appropriate for the proper administration of the compact.

ARTICLE VI. OPTIONAL CONTENTS OF COMPACTS

A compact entered into under the authority conferred by this compact may contain the following provisions, in addition to those required under Article V of this compact:

(1) provisions establishing procedures and entitlement to medical, developmental, child-care, or other social services for the child in accordance with applicable laws, even if the child and the adoptive parents are in a state other than the one responsible for or providing the services or the funds to defray part or all of the costs thereof; and

(2) other provisions that are appropriate or incidental to the proper administration of the compact.

ARTICLE VII. MEDICAL ASSISTANCE

(a) A child with special needs who resides in this state and who is the subject of an adoption assistance agreement with another state is entitled to receive a medical assistance identification from this state on the filing in the state medical assistance agency of a certified copy of the adoption assistance agreement obtained from the adoption assistance state. In accordance with rules of the state medical assistance agency, the adoptive parents, at least annually, shall show that the agreement is still in effect or has been renewed.

(b) The state medical assistance agency shall consider the holder of a medical assistance identification under this article as any other holder of a medical assistance identification under the laws of this state and shall process and make payment on claims on the holder's account in the same manner and under the same conditions and procedures as for other recipients of medical assistance.

(c) The state medical assistance agency shall provide coverage and benefits for a child who is in another state and who is covered by an adoption assistance agreement made by the Department of Family and Protective Services for the coverage or benefits, if any, not provided by the residence state. The adoptive parents acting for the child may submit evidence of payment for services or benefit amounts not payable in the residence state and shall be reimbursed for those amounts. Services or benefit amounts covered under any insurance or other third-party medical contract or arrangement held by the child or the adoptive parents may not be reimbursed. The state medical assistance agency shall adopt rules implementing this subsection. The additional coverage and benefit amounts provided under this subsection are for services for which there is no federal contribution or services that, if federally aided, are not provided by the residence state. The rules shall include procedures for obtaining prior approval for services in cases in which prior approval is required for the assistance.

(d) The submission of a false, misleading, or fraudulent claim for payment or reimbursement for services or benefits under this article or the making of a false, misleading, or fraudulent statement in connection with the claim is an offense under this subsection if the person submitting the claim or making the statement knows or should know that the claim or statement is false, misleading, or fraudulent. A person who commits an offense under this subsection may be liable for a fine not to exceed $10,000 or imprisonment for not more than two years, or both the fine and the imprisonment. An offense under this subsection that also constitutes an offense under other law may be punished under either this subsection or the other applicable law.

(e) This article applies only to medical assistance for children under adoption assistance agreements with states that have entered into a compact with this state under which the other state provides medical assistance to children with special needs under adoption assistance agreements made by this state. All other children entitled to medical assistance under adoption assistance agreements entered into by this state are eligible to receive the medical assistance in accordance with the laws and procedures that apply to the agreement.

ARTICLE VIII. FEDERAL PARTICIPATION

Consistent with federal law, the Department of Family and Protective Services and the Health and Human Services Commission, in connection with the administration of this compact or a compact authorized by this compact, shall include the provision of adoption assistance and medical assistance for which the federal government pays some or all of the cost in any state plan made under the Adoption Assistance and Child Welfare Act of 1980 (Pub. L. No. 96-272), Titles IV-E and XIX of the Social Security Act, and other applicable federal laws. The Department of Family and Protective Services and the Health and Human Services Commission shall apply for and administer all relevant federal aid in accordance with law.

History of Fam. Code §162.201: Acts 1995, 74th Leg., ch. 846, §9, eff. June 16, 1995. Amended by Acts 2015, 84th Leg., ch. 1, §1.103, eff. Apr. 2, 2015.

FAM §162.202. AUTHORITY OF DEPARTMENT OF FAMILY & PROTECTIVE SERVICES

The Department of Family and Protective Services, with the concurrence of the Health and Human Services Commission, may develop, participate in the development of, negotiate, and enter into one or more interstate compacts on behalf of this state with other states to implement one or more of the purposes of this subchapter. An interstate compact authorized by this subchapter has the force and effect of law.

History of Fam. Code §162.202: Acts 1995, 74th Leg., ch. 846, §9, eff. June 16, 1995. Amended by Acts 2015, 84th Leg., ch. 1, §1.104, eff. Apr. 2, 2015.

FAM §162.203. COMPACT ADMINISTRATION

The commissioner of the Department of Family and Protective Services shall serve as the compact administrator. The administrator shall cooperate with all departments, agencies, and officers of this state and its subdivisions in facilitating the proper administration of the compact and any supplemental agreements entered into by this state. The commissioner of the Department of Family and Protective Services and the executive commissioner of the Health and Human Services Commission shall designate deputy compact administrators to represent adoption assistance services and medical assistance services provided under Title XIX of the Social Security Act.

History of Fam. Code §162.203: Acts 1995, 74th Leg., ch. 846, §9, eff. June 16, 1995. Amended by Acts 2015, 84th Leg., ch. 1, §1.105, eff. Apr. 2, 2015.

FAM §162.204. SUPPLEMENTARY AGREEMENTS

The compact administrator may enter into supplementary agreements with appropriate officials of other states under the compact. If a supplementary agreement requires or authorizes the use of any institution or facility of this state or requires or authorizes the provision of a service by this state, the supplementary agreement does not take effect until approved by the head of the department or agency under whose jurisdiction the institution or facility is operated or whose department or agency will be charged with rendering the service.

History of Fam. Code §162.204: Acts 1995, 74th Leg., ch. 846, §9, eff. June 16, 1995.

FAM §162.205. PAYMENTS BY STATE

The compact administrator, subject to the approval of the chief state fiscal officer, may make or arrange for payments necessary to discharge financial obligations imposed on this state by the compact or by a supplementary agreement entered into under the compact.

History of Fam. Code §162.205: Acts 1995, 74th Leg., ch. 846, §9, eff. June 16, 1995.

FAM §162.206. PENALTIES

A person who, under a compact entered into under this subchapter, knowingly obtains or attempts to obtain or aids or abets any person in obtaining, by means of a wilfully false statement or representation or by impersonation or other fraudulent device, any assistance on behalf of a child or other person to which the child or other person is not entitled, or assistance in an amount greater than that to which the child or other person is entitled, commits an offense. An offense under this section is a Class B misdemeanor. An offense under this section that also constitutes an offense under other law may be punished under either this section or the other applicable law.

History of Fam. Code §162.206: Acts 1995, 74th Leg., ch. 846, §9, eff. June 16, 1995.

Sections 162.207-162.300 reserved for expansion

SUBCHAPTER D. ADOPTION SERVICES BY THE DEPARTMENT OF FAMILY & PROTECTIVE SERVICES

FAM §162.301. DEFINITIONS

In this subchapter:

(1) "Adoption assistance agreement" means a written agreement, binding on the parties to the agreement, between the Department of Family and Protective Services and the prospective adoptive parents that specifies the nature and amount of any payment, services, or assistance to be provided under the agreement and stipulates that the agreement will remain in effect without regard to the state in which the prospective adoptive parents reside at any particular time.

(2) "Child" means a child who cannot be placed for adoption with appropriate adoptive parents without the provision of adoption assistance because of factors including ethnic background, age, membership in a minority or sibling group, the presence of a medical condition, or a physical, mental, or emotional disability.

(3) "Department" means the Department of Family and Protective Services.

History of Fam. Code §162.301: Acts 1995, 74th Leg., ch. 20, §1, eff. Apr. 20, 1995. Amended by Acts 1995, 74th Leg., ch. 412, §1, eff. Aug. 28, 1995; Acts 2015, 84th Leg., ch. 1, §§1.106, 1.107, eff. Apr. 2, 2015. Source: Former Hum. Res. Code §47.001.

FAM §162.302. REPEALED

Repealed by Acts 2015, 84th Leg., ch. 944, §86(1), eff. Sept. 1, 2015.

FAM §162.303. REPEALED

Repealed by Acts 2015, 84th Leg., ch. 944, §86(2), eff. Sept. 1, 2015.

FAM §162.304. FINANCIAL & MEDICAL ASSISTANCE

(a) The department shall administer a program to provide adoption assistance for eligible children and enter into adoption assistance agreements with the adoptive parents of a child as authorized by Part E of Title IV of the federal Social Security Act, as amended (42 U.S.C. Section 673).

(b) The adoption of a child may be subsidized by the department. The need for and amount of the subsidy shall be determined by the department under its rules.

(b-1) Subject to the availability of funds, the department shall pay a $150 subsidy each month for the premiums for health benefits coverage for a child with respect to whom a court has entered a final order of adoption if the child:

(1) was in the conservatorship of the department at the time of the child's adoptive placement;

(2) after the adoption, is not eligible for medical assistance under Chapter 32, Human Resources Code; and

(3) is younger than 18 years of age.

(b-2) The [~~executive~~] commissioner of the department [~~Health and Human Services Commission~~] shall adopt rules necessary to implement Subsection (b-1), including rules that:

(1) limit eligibility for the subsidy under that subsection to a child whose adoptive family income is less than 300 percent of the federal poverty level;

(2) provide for the manner in which the department shall pay the subsidy under that subsection; and

(3) specify any documentation required to be provided by an adoptive parent as proof that the subsidy is used to obtain and maintain health benefits coverage for the adopted child.

(c) to **(e)** Repealed by Acts 2015, 84th Leg., ch. 944, §86(3), eff. Sept. 1, 2015.

(f) Subject to the availability of funds, the department shall work with the Health and Human Services Commission and the federal government to develop a program to provide medical assistance under Chapter 32, Human Resources Code, to children who were in the conservatorship of the department at the time of adoptive placement and need medical or rehabilitative care but do not qualify for adoption assistance.

(g) The [~~executive~~] commissioner of the department [~~Health and Human Services Commission~~] by

rule shall provide that the maximum amount of the subsidy under Subsection (b) that may be paid to an adoptive parent of a child under an adoption assistance agreement is an amount that is equal to the amount that would have been paid to the foster parent of the child, based on the child's foster care service level on the date the department and the adoptive parent enter into the adoption assistance agreement. This subsection applies only to a child who, based on factors specified in rules of the department, the department determines would otherwise have been expected to remain in foster care until the child's 18th birthday and for whom this state would have made foster care payments for that care. Factors the department may consider in determining whether a child is eligible for the amount of the subsidy authorized by this subsection include the following:

(1) the child's mental or physical disability, age, and membership in a sibling group; and

(2) the number of prior placement disruptions the child has experienced.

(h) In determining the amount that would have been paid to a foster parent for purposes of Subsection (g), the department:

(1) shall use the minimum amount required to be paid to a foster parent for a child assigned the same service level as the child who is the subject of the adoption assistance agreement; and

(2) may not include any amount that a child-placing agency is entitled to retain under the foster care rate structure in effect on the date the department and the adoptive parent enter into the agreement.

(i) A child for whom a subsidy is provided under Subsection (b-1) for premiums for health benefits coverage and who does not receive any other subsidy under this section is not considered to be the subject of an adoption assistance agreement for any other purpose, including for determining eligibility for the exemption from payment of tuition and fees for higher education under Section 54.367, Education Code.

(j) The department shall keep records necessary to evaluate the adoption assistance program's effectiveness in encouraging and promoting the adoption of children.

History of Fam. Code §162.304: Acts 1995, 74th Leg., ch. 20, §1, eff. Apr. 20, 1995. Amended by Acts 1995, 74th Leg., ch. 412, §4, eff. Aug. 28, 1995; Acts 2005, 79th Leg., ch. 268, §1.09, eff. Sept. 1, 2005; Acts 2007, 80th Leg., ch. 267, §2 (eff. Sept. 1, 2007), ch. 1406, §4 (eff. Sept. 1, 2007); Acts 2009, 81st Leg., ch. 87, §27.001(15), eff. Sept. 1, 2009; Acts 2011, 82nd Leg., ch. 359, §11, eff. Jan. 1, 2012; Acts 2015, 84th Leg., ch. 944, §§16, 86(3), eff. Sept. 1, 2015; H.B. 5, §8, 85th Leg., eff. Sept. 1, 2017. Source: Former Hum. Res. Code §47.004.

A FAM §162.3041. CONTINUATION OF ASSISTANCE AFTER CHILD'S 18TH BIRTHDAY

(a) The department shall, in accordance with department rules, offer adoption assistance after a child's 18th birthday to the child's adoptive parents under an existing adoption assistance agreement entered into under Section 162.304 until:

(1) the first day of the month of the child's 21st birthday if the department determines, as provided by department rules, that:

(A) the child has a mental or physical disability that warrants the continuation of that assistance;

(B) the child, or the child's adoptive parent on behalf of the child, has applied for federal benefits under the supplemental security income program (42 U.S.C. Section 1381 et seq.), as amended; and

(C) the child's adoptive parents are providing the child's financial support; or

(2) if the child does not meet the requirements of Subdivision (1), the earlier of:

(A) the date the child ceases to regularly attend high school or a vocational or technical program;

(B) the date the child obtains a high school diploma or high school equivalency certificate;

(C) the date the child's adoptive parents stop providing financial support to the child; or

(D) the first day of the month of the child's 19th birthday.

(a-1) Notwithstanding Subsection (a), if the department first entered into an adoption assistance agreement with a child's adoptive parents after the child's 16th birthday, the department shall, in accordance with rules adopted by the [~~executive~~] commissioner of the department [~~Health and Human Services Commission~~], offer adoption assistance after the child's 18th birthday to the child's adoptive parents under an existing adoption agreement until the last day of the month of the child's 21st birthday, provided the child is:

(1) regularly attending high school or enrolled in a program leading toward a high school diploma or high school equivalency certificate;

(2) regularly attending an institution of higher education or a postsecondary vocational or technical program;

(3) participating in a program or activity that promotes, or removes barriers to, employment;

(4) employed for at least 80 hours a month; or

(5) incapable of doing any of the activities described by Subdivisions (1)-(4) due to a documented medical condition.

(b) In determining whether a child meets the requirements of Subdivision (a)(1), the department may conduct an assessment of the child's mental or physical disability or may contract for the assessment to be conducted.

(c) The department and any person with whom the department contracts to conduct an assessment under Subsection (b) shall:

(1) inform the adoptive parents of the child for whom the assessment is conducted of the application requirement under Subsection (a)(1)(B) for federal benefits for the child under the supplemental security income program (42 U.S.C. Section 1381 et seq.), as amended;

(2) provide assistance to the adoptive parents and the child in preparing an application for benefits under that program; and

(3) provide ongoing consultation and guidance to the adoptive parents and the child throughout the eligibility determination process for benefits under that program.

(d) The department is not required to provide adoption assistance benefits under Subsection (a) or (a-1) unless funds are appropriated to the department specifically for purposes of those subsections. If the legislature does not appropriate sufficient money to provide adoption assistance to the adoptive parents of all children described by Subsection (a), the department shall provide adoption assistance only to the adoptive parents of children described by Subsection (a)(1).

History of Fam. Code §162.3041: Acts 2001, 77th Leg., ch. 1449, §1, eff. Sept. 1, 2001. Amended by Acts 2009, 81st Leg., ch. 1118, §4 (eff. Sept. 1, 2009), ch. 1238, §6(a) (eff. Oct. 1, 2010); Acts 2015, 84th Leg., ch. 944, §17, eff. Sept. 1, 2015; H.B. 5, §9, 85th Leg., eff. Sept. 1, 2017.

FAM §162.305. REPEALED

Repealed by Acts 2015, 84th Leg., ch. 1, §1.203(3), eff. Apr. 2, 2015.

FAM §162.306. POSTADOPTION SERVICES

(a) The department may provide services after adoption to adoptees and adoptive families for whom the department provided services before the adoption.

(b) The department may provide services under this section directly or through contract.

(c) The services may include financial assistance, respite care, placement services, parenting programs, support groups, counseling services, crisis intervention, and medical aid.

History of Fam. Code §162.306: Acts 1995, 74th Leg., ch. 20, §1, eff. Apr. 20, 1995. Amended by Acts 1995, 74th Leg., ch. 412, §6, eff. Aug. 28, 1995. Source: Former Hum. Res. Code §47.031.

See also 40 T.A.C. §§700.1726-700.1735.

FAM §162.307. REPEALED

Repealed by Acts 1995, 74th Leg., ch. 412, §7, eff. Aug. 28, 1995.

FAM §162.308. REPEALED

Repealed by Acts 2015, 84th Leg., ch. 944, §86(4), eff. Sept. 1, 2015.

FAM §162.3085. ADOPTIVE PLACEMENT IN COMPLIANCE WITH FEDERAL LAW REQUIRED

The department or a licensed child-placing agency making an adoptive placement shall comply with the Multiethnic Placement Act of 1994 (42 U.S.C. Section 1996b).

History of Fam. Code §162.3085: Acts 2015, 84th Leg., ch. 944, §18, eff. Sept. 1, 2015.

FAM §162.309. REPEALED

Repealed by Acts 2015, 84th Leg., ch. 944, §86(5) (eff. Sept. 1, 2015), ch. 946, §2.37(a) (eff. Jan. 1, 2016).

Sections 162.310-162.400 reserved for expansion

SUBCHAPTER E. VOLUNTARY ADOPTION REGISTRIES

FAM §162.401. PURPOSE

The purpose of this subchapter is to provide for the establishment of mutual consent voluntary adoption registries through which adoptees, birth parents, and biological siblings may voluntarily locate each other. It is not the purpose of this subchapter to inhibit or prohibit persons from locating each other through other legal means or to inhibit or affect in any way the provision of postadoptive services and education, by adoption agencies or others, that go further than the procedures set out for registries established under this subchapter.

History of Fam. Code §162.401: Acts 1995, 74th Leg., ch. 20, §1, eff. Apr. 20, 1995. Source: Former Hum. Res. Code §49.001.

ANNOTATIONS

Little v. Smith, 943 S.W.2d 414, 418-19 (Tex.1997). "An adoptee who wants to know the identity of his or her biological parents, a parent whose child has been adopted and wants to locate that child, or a biological sibling may file an application with a registry. The statute spells out processes for establishing these regis-

tries, for making application to them, and for determining if applications 'match.' When a 'match' is found, the registry is required by statute to remind the registrants that they may withdraw the registration before disclosure is made, and each registrant is required to sign a consent to disclosure. Even after the death of a registrant, identifying information will not be released unless the registrant had specifically consented in writing to a posthumous disclosure of a match and that consent remained in effect and valid at the time of death. [¶] These procedures are designed to maintain the confidentiality of the identities of adoptees, their natural parents, and biological siblings unless there is a *mutual* desire for that information to be disclosed. The statutes contain no indication that an adoptee can circumvent these procedures simply by asking a court to open the adoption records so that any inheritance rights can be asserted."

FAM §162.402. DEFINITIONS

In this subchapter:

(1) "Administrator" means the administrator of a mutual consent voluntary adoption registry established under this subchapter.

(2) "Adoptee" means a person 18 years of age or older who has been legally adopted in this state or another state or country.

(3) "Adoption" means the act of creating the legal relationship of parent and child between a person and a child who is not the biological child of that person. The term does not include the act of establishing the legal relationship of parent and child between a man and a child through proof of paternity or voluntary legitimation proceedings.

(4) "Adoption agency" means a person, other than a natural parent or guardian of a child, who plans for the placement of or places a child in the home of a prospective adoptive parent.

(5) "Adoptive parent" means an adult who is a parent of an adoptee through a legal process of adoption.

(6) "Alleged father" means a man who is not deemed by law to be or who has not been adjudicated to be the biological father of an adoptee and who claims or is alleged to be the adoptee's biological father.

(7) "Authorized agency" means a public agency authorized to care for or to place children for adoption or a private entity approved for that purpose by the department through a license, certification, or other means. The term includes a licensed child-placing agency or a previously licensed child-placing agency that has ceased operations and has transferred its adoption records to the vital statistics unit or an agency authorized by the department to place children for adoption and a licensed child-placing agency that has been acquired by, merged with, or otherwise succeeded by an agency authorized by the department to place children for adoption.

(8) "Biological parent" means a man or woman who is the father or mother of genetic origin of a child.

(9) "Biological siblings" means persons who share a common birth parent.

(10) "Birth parent" means:

(A) the biological mother of an adoptee;

(B) the man adjudicated or presumed under Chapter 151 to be the biological father of an adoptee; and

(C) a man who has signed a consent to adoption, affidavit of relinquishment, affidavit of waiver of interest in child, or other written instrument releasing the adoptee for adoption, unless the consent, affidavit, or other instrument includes a sworn refusal to admit or a denial of paternity. The term includes a birth mother and birth father but does not include a person adjudicated by a court of competent jurisdiction as not being the biological parent of an adoptee.

(11) "Central registry" means the mutual consent voluntary adoption registry established and maintained by the vital statistics unit under this subchapter.

(12) "Department" means the Department of Family and Protective Services.

(13) "Registry" means a mutual consent voluntary adoption registry established under this subchapter.

(14) "Vital statistics unit" means the vital statistics unit of the Department of State Health Services.

History of Fam. Code §162.402: Acts 1995, 74th Leg., ch. 20, §1, eff. Apr. 20, 1995. Amended by Acts 1995, 74th Leg., ch. 968, §§1, 11, eff. Sept. 1, 1995; Acts 1997, 75th Leg., ch. 561, §19, eff. Sept. 1, 1997; Acts 2015, 84th Leg., ch. 1, §1.110, eff. Apr. 2, 2015. Source: Former Hum. Res. Code §49.002.

FAM §162.403. ESTABLISHMENT OF VOLUNTARY ADOPTION REGISTRIES

(a) The vital statistics unit shall establish and maintain a mutual consent voluntary adoption registry.

(b) Except as provided by Subsection (c), an agency authorized by the department to place children for adoption and an association comprised exclusively of those agencies may establish a mutual consent voluntary adoption registry. An agency may contract with

any other agency authorized by the department to place children for adoption or with an association comprised exclusively of those agencies to perform registry services on its behalf.

(c) An authorized agency that did not directly or by contract provide registry services as required by this subchapter on January 1, 1984, may not provide its own registry service. The vital statistics unit shall operate through the central registry those services for agencies not permitted to provide a registry under this section.

History of Fam. Code §162.403: Acts 1995, 74th Leg., ch. 20, §1, eff. Apr. 20, 1995. Amended by Acts 1997, 75th Leg., ch. 561, §20, eff. Sept. 1, 1997; Acts 2015, 84th Leg., ch. 1, §1.111, eff. Apr. 2, 2015. Source: Former Hum. Res. Code §49.003(a)-(c).

FAM §162.404. REQUIREMENT TO SEND INFORMATION TO CENTRAL REGISTRY

An authorized agency that is permitted to provide a registry under this subchapter or that participates in a mutual consent voluntary adoption registry with an association of authorized agencies shall send to the central registry a duplicate of all information the registry maintains in the agency's registry or sends to the registry in which the agency participates.

History of Fam. Code §162.404: Acts 1997, 75th Leg., ch. 561, §21, eff. Sept. 1, 1997.

History of Former Fam. Code §162.404: Acts 1995, 74th Leg., ch. 20, §1, eff. Apr. 20, 1995. Repealed by Acts 1995, 74th Leg., ch. 968, §11, eff. Sept. 1, 1995. Source: Former Hum. Res. Code §49.004.

See also 25 T.A.C. §181.43.

FAM §162.405. DETERMINATION OF APPROPRIATE REGISTRY

(a) The administrator of the central registry shall determine the appropriate registry to which an applicant is entitled to apply.

(b) On receiving an inquiry by an adoptee, birth parent, or sibling who has provided satisfactory proof of age and identity and paid all required inquiry fees, the administrator of the central registry shall review the information on file in the central index and consult with the administrators of other registries in the state to determine the identity of any appropriate registry through which the adoptee, birth parent, or sibling may register.

(c) Each administrator shall, not later than the 30th day after the date of receiving an inquiry from the administrator of the central registry, respond in writing to the inquiry that the registrant was not placed for adoption by an agency served by that registry or that the registrant was placed for adoption by an agency served by that registry. If the registrant was placed for adoption by an agency served by the registry, the administrator shall file a report with the administrator of the central registry including:

(1) the name of the adopted child as shown in the final adoption decree;

(2) the birth date of the adopted child;

(3) the docket number of the adoption suit;

(4) the identity of the court that granted the adoption;

(5) the date of the final adoption decree;

(6) the identity of the agency, if any, through which the adopted child was placed; and

(7) the identity, address, and telephone number of the registry through which the adopted child may register as an adoptee.

(d) After completing the investigation, the administrator of the central registry shall issue an official certificate stating:

(1) the identity of the registry through which the adoptee, birth parent, or biological sibling may apply for registration, if known; or

(2) if the administrator cannot make a conclusive determination, that the adoptee, birth parent, or biological sibling is entitled to apply for registration through the central registry.

History of Fam. Code §162.405: Acts 1995, 74th Leg., ch. 20, §1, eff. Apr. 20, 1995. Amended by Acts 1995, 74th Leg., ch. 751, §79 (eff. Sept. 1, 1995), ch. 968, §2 (eff. Sept. 1, 1995). Source: Former Hum. Res. Code §49.005.

FAM §162.406. REGISTRATION ELIGIBILITY

(a) An adoptee who is 18 years of age or older may apply to a registry for information about the adoptee's birth parents and biological siblings.

(b) A birth parent who is 18 years of age or older may apply to a registry for information about an adoptee who is a child by birth of the birth parent.

(c) An alleged father who is 18 years of age or older and who acknowledges paternity but is not, at the time of application, a birth father may register as a birth father but may not otherwise be recognized as a birth father for the purposes of this subchapter unless:

(1) the adoptee's birth mother in her application identifies him as the adoptee's biological father; and

(2) additional information concerning the adoptee obtained from other sources is not inconsistent with his claim of paternity.

(d) A biological sibling who is 18 years of age or older may apply to a registry for information about the person's adopted biological siblings.

(e) Only birth parents, adoptees, and biological siblings may apply for information through a registry.

(f) A person, including an authorized agency, may not apply for information through a registry as an agent, attorney, or representative of an adoptee, birth parent, or biological sibling.

History of Fam. Code §162.406: Acts 1995, 74th Leg., ch. 20, §1, eff. Apr. 20, 1995. Amended by Acts 1995, 74th Leg., ch. 968, §3, eff. Sept. 1, 1995. Source: Former Hum. Res. Code §49.006.

See also 25 T.A.C. §181.45.

FAM §162.407. REGISTRATION

(a) The administrator shall require each registration applicant to sign a written application.

(b) An adoptee adopted or placed through an authorized agency may register through the registry maintained by that agency or the registry to which the agency has delegated registry services or through the central registry maintained by the vital statistics unit.

(c) Birth parents and biological siblings shall register through:

(1) the registry of the authorized agency through which the adoptee was adopted or placed; or

(2) the central registry.

(d) The administrator may not accept an application for registration unless the applicant:

(1) provides proof of identity as provided by Section 162.408;

(2) establishes the applicant's eligibility to register; and

(3) pays all required registration fees.

(e) A registration remains in effect until the 99th anniversary of the date the registration is accepted unless a shorter period is specified by the applicant or the registration is withdrawn before that time.

(f) A registrant may withdraw the registrant's registration in writing without charge at any time.

(g) After a registration is withdrawn or expires, the registrant shall be treated as if the person has not previously registered.

(h) A completed registry application must be accepted or rejected before the 46th day after the date the application is received. If an application is rejected, the administrator shall provide the applicant with a written statement of the reason for the rejection.

History of Fam. Code §162.407: Acts 1995, 74th Leg., ch. 20, §1, eff. Apr. 20, 1995. Amended by Acts 1995, 74th Leg., ch. 968, §4, eff. Sept. 1, 1995; Acts 1997, 75th Leg., ch. 561, §22, eff. Sept. 1, 1997; Acts 2015, 84th Leg., ch. 1, §1.112, eff. Apr. 2, 2015. Source: Former Hum. Res. Code §49.007(a)-(c).

See also 25 T.A.C. §181.45.

FAM §162.408. PROOF OF IDENTITY

The rules and minimum standards of the Department of State Health Services for the vital statistics unit must provide for proof of identity in order to facilitate the purposes of this subchapter and to protect the privacy rights of adoptees, adoptive parents, birth parents, biological siblings, and their families.

History of Fam. Code §162.408: Acts 1995, 74th Leg., ch. 20, §1, eff. Apr. 20, 1995. Amended by Acts 1997, 75th Leg., ch. 561, §23, eff. Sept. 1, 1997; Acts 2015, 84th Leg., ch. 1, §1.113, eff. Apr. 2, 2015. Source: Former Hum. Res. Code §49.008.

FAM §162.409. APPLICATION

(a) An application must contain:

(1) the name, address, and telephone number of the applicant;

(2) any other name or alias by which the applicant has been known;

(3) the age, date of birth, and place of birth of the applicant;

(4) the original name of the adoptee, if known;

(5) the adoptive name of the adoptee, if known;

(6) a statement that the applicant is willing to allow the applicant's identity to be disclosed to a registrant who is eligible to learn the applicant's identity;

(7) the name, address, and telephone number of the agency or other entity, organization, or person placing the adoptee for adoption, if known, or, if not known, a statement that the applicant does not know that information;

(8) an authorization to the administrator and the administrator's designees to inspect all vital statistics records, court records, and agency records, including confidential records, relating to the birth, adoption, marriage, and divorce of the applicant or to the birth and death of any child or sibling by birth or adoption of the applicant;

(9) the specific address to which the applicant wishes notice of a successful match to be mailed;

(10) a statement that the applicant either does or does not consent to disclosure of identifying information about the applicant after the applicant's death;

(11) a statement that the registration is to be effective for 99 years or for a stated shorter period selected by the applicant; and

(12) a statement that the adoptee applicant either does or does not desire to be informed that registry records indicate that the applicant has a biological sibling who has registered under this subchapter.

(b) The application may contain the applicant's social security number if the applicant, after being advised of the right not to supply the number, voluntarily furnishes it.

(c) The application of a birth parent must include:

(1) the original name and date of birth or approximate date of birth of each adoptee with respect to whom the parent is registering;

(2) the names of all other birth children, including maiden names, aliases, dates and places of birth, and names of the birth parents;

(3) each name known or thought by the applicant to have been used by the adoptee's other birth parent;

(4) the last known address of the adoptee's other birth parent; and

(5) other available information through which the other birth parent may be identified.

(d) The application of a biological sibling must include:

(1) a statement explaining the applicant's basis for believing that the applicant has one or more biological siblings;

(2) the names, including maiden and married names, and aliases of all the applicant's siblings by birth and adoption and their dates and places of birth, if known;

(3) the names of the applicant's legal parents;

(4) the names of the applicant's birth parents, if known; and

(5) any other information known to the applicant through which the existence and identity of the applicant's biological siblings can be confirmed.

(e) An application may also contain additional information through which the applicant's identity and eligibility to register may be ascertained.

(f) The administrator shall assist the applicant in filling out the application if the applicant is unable to complete the application without assistance, but the administrator may not furnish the applicant with any substantive information necessary to complete the application.

History of Fam. Code §162.409: Acts 1995, 74th Leg., ch. 20, §1, eff. Apr. 20, 1995. Amended by Acts 1995, 74th Leg., ch. 968, §5, eff. Sept. 1, 1995. Source: Former Hum. Res. Code §49.007(e).

FAM §162.410. REPEALED

Repealed by Acts 1995, 74th Leg., ch. 968, §11, eff. Sept. 1, 1995.

FAM §162.411. FEES

(a) The costs of establishing, operating, and maintaining a registry may be recovered in whole or in part through users' fees charged to applicants and registrants.

(b) Each registry shall establish a schedule of fees for services provided by the registry. The fees shall be reasonably related to the direct and indirect costs of establishing, operating, and maintaining the registry.

(c) A fee may not be charged for withdrawing a registration.

(d) The fees collected by the vital statistics unit shall be deposited in a special fund in the general revenue fund. Funds in the special fund may be appropriated only for the administration of the central registry.

(e) The administrator may waive users' fees in whole or in part if the applicant provides satisfactory proof of financial inability to pay the fees.

History of Fam. Code §162.411: Acts 1995, 74th Leg., ch. 20, §1, eff. Apr. 20, 1995. Amended by Acts 1995, 74th Leg., ch. 968, §6, eff. Sept. 1, 1995; Acts 1997, 75th Leg., ch. 561, §24, eff. Sept. 1, 1997; Acts 2015, 84th Leg., ch. 1, §1.114, eff. Apr. 2, 2015. Source: Former Hum. Res. Code §49.011.

See also 25 T.A.C. §§181.22, 181.44.

FAM §162.412. SUPPLEMENTAL INFORMATION

(a) A registrant may amend the registrant's registration and submit additional information to the administrator. A registrant shall notify the administrator of any change in the registrant's name or address that occurs after acceptance of the application.

(b) The administrator does not have a duty to search for a registrant who fails to register a change of name or address.

History of Fam. Code §162.412: Acts 1995, 74th Leg., ch. 20, §1, eff. Apr. 20, 1995. Source: Former Hum. Res. Code §49.012.

FAM §162.413. COUNSELING

The applicant must participate in counseling for not less than one hour with a social worker or mental health professional with expertise in postadoption counseling after the administrator has accepted the application for registration and before the release of confidential information.

History of Fam. Code §162.413: Acts 1995, 74th Leg., ch. 20, §1, eff. Apr. 20, 1995. Amended by Acts 1995, 74th Leg., ch. 968, §7, eff. Sept. 1, 1995. Source: Former Hum. Res. Code §49.013.

FAM §162.414. MATCHING PROCEDURES

(a) The administrator shall process each registration in an attempt to match the adoptee and the adoptee's birth parents or the adoptee and the adoptee's biological siblings.

(b) The administrator shall determine that there is a match if the adult adoptee and the birth mother or the birth father have registered or if a biological sibling has registered.

(c) To establish or corroborate a match, the administrator shall request confirmation of a possible match from the vital statistics unit. If the agency operating the registry has in its own records sufficient information through which the match may be confirmed, the administrator may, but is not required to, request confirmation from the vital statistics unit. The vital statistics unit may confirm or deny the match without breaching the duty of confidentiality to the adoptee, adoptive parents, birth parents, or biological siblings and without a court order.

(d) To establish a match, the administrator may also request confirmation of a possible match from the agency, if any, that has possession of records concerning the adoption of an adoptee or from the court that granted the adoption, the hospital where the adoptee or any biological sibling was born, the physician who delivered the adoptee or biological sibling, or any other person who has knowledge of the relevant facts. The agency, court, hospital, physician, or person with knowledge may confirm or deny the match without breaching any duty of confidentiality to the adoptee, adoptive parents, birth parents, or biological siblings.

(e) If a match is denied by a source contacted under Subsection (d), the administrator shall make a full and complete investigation into the reliability of the denial. If the match is corroborated by other reliable sources and the administrator is satisfied that the denial is erroneous, the administrator may make disclosures but shall report to the adoptee, birth parents, and biological siblings involved that the match was not confirmed by all information sources.

History of Fam. Code §162.414: Acts 1995, 74th Leg., ch. 20, §1, eff. Apr. 20, 1995. Amended by Acts 1995, 74th Leg., ch. 968, §8, eff. Sept. 1, 1995; Acts 1997, 75th Leg., ch. 561, §25, eff. Sept. 1, 1997; Acts 2015, 84th Leg., ch. 1, §1.115, eff. Apr. 2, 2015. Source: Former Hum. Res. Code §49.014.

FAM §162.415. REPEALED

Repealed by Acts 1995, 74th Leg., ch. 968, §11, eff. Sept. 1, 1995.

FAM §162.416. DISCLOSURE OF IDENTIFYING INFORMATION

(a) When a match has been made and confirmed to the administrator's satisfaction, the administrator shall mail to each registrant, at the registrant's last known address, by fax or registered or certified mail, return receipt requested, delivery restricted to addressee only, a written notice:

(1) informing the registrant that a match has been made and confirmed;

(2) reminding the registrant that the registrant may withdraw the registration before disclosures are made, if desired; and

(3) notifying the registrant that before any identifying disclosures are made, the registrant must:

(A) sign a written consent to disclosure that allows the disclosure of identifying information about the other registrants to the registrant and allows the disclosure of identifying information about the registrant to other registrants;

(B) participate in counseling for not less than one hour with a social worker or mental health professional who has expertise in postadoption counseling; and

(C) provide the administrator with written certification that the counseling required under Subdivision (B) has been completed.

(b) Identifying information about a registrant shall be released without the registrant's having consented after the match to disclosure if the registrant is dead, the registrant's registration was valid at the time of death, and the registrant had in writing specifically authorized the postdeath disclosure in the registrant's application or in a supplemental statement filed with the administrator.

(c) Identifying information about a deceased birth parent may not be released until each surviving child of the deceased birth parent is an adult or until each child's surviving parent, guardian, managing conservator, or legal custodian consents in writing to the disclosure.

(d) The administrator shall prepare and release written disclosure statements identifying information about each of the registrants if the registrants complied with Subsection (a) and, before the 60th day after the date notification of match was mailed, the registrant or registrants have not withdrawn their registrations.

(e) If the administrator establishes that a match cannot be made because of the death of an adoptee, birth parent, or biological sibling, the administrator shall promptly notify the affected registrant. The administrator shall disclose the reason why a match can-

not be made and may disclose nonidentifying information concerning the circumstances of the person's death.

History of Fam. Code §162.416: Acts 1995, 74th Leg., ch. 20, §1, eff. Apr. 20, 1995. Amended by Acts 1995, 74th Leg., ch. 968, §9, eff. Sept. 1, 1995. Source: Former Hum. Res. Code §49.016.

See also 25 T.A.C. §§181.46, 181.47.

FAM §§162.417, 162.418. REPEALED

Repealed by Acts 1995, 74th Leg., ch. 968, §11, eff. Sept. 1, 1995.

FAM §162.419. REGISTRY RECORDS CONFIDENTIAL

(a) All applications, registrations, records, and other information submitted to, obtained by, or otherwise acquired by a registry are confidential and may not be disclosed to any person or entity except in the manner authorized by this subchapter.

(b) Information acquired by a registry may not be disclosed under freedom of information or sunshine legislation, rules, or practice.

(c) A person may not file or prosecute a class action litigation to force a registry to disclose identifying information.

History of Fam. Code §162.419: Acts 1995, 74th Leg., ch. 20, §1, eff. Apr. 20, 1995. Source: Former Hum. Res. Code §49.020.

See also 25 T.A.C. §181.47.

FAM §162.420. RULEMAKING

(a) The executive commissioner of the Health and Human Services Commission shall make rules and adopt minimum standards for the Department of State Health Services to:

(1) administer the provisions of this subchapter; and

(2) ensure that each registry respects the right to privacy and confidentiality of an adoptee, birth parent, and biological sibling who does not desire to disclose the person's identity.

(b) The Department of State Health Services shall conduct a comprehensive review of all rules and standards adopted under this subchapter not less than every six years.

(c) In order to provide the administrators an opportunity to review proposed rules and standards and send written suggestions to the executive commissioner of the Health and Human Services Commission, the executive commissioner shall, before adopting rules and minimum standards, send a copy of the proposed rules and standards not less than 60 days before the date they take effect to:

(1) the administrator of each registry established under this subchapter; and

(2) the administrator of each agency authorized by the department to place children for adoption.

History of Fam. Code §162.420: Acts 1995, 74th Leg., ch. 20, §1, eff. Apr. 20, 1995. Amended by Acts 1997, 75th Leg., ch. 561, §26, eff. Sept. 1, 1997; Acts 2015, 84th Leg., ch. 1, §1.116, eff. Apr. 2, 2015. Source: Former Hum. Res. Code §49.021.

See also 25 T.A.C. §§181.41-181.47.

FAM §162.421. PROHIBITED ACTS; CRIMINAL PENALTIES

(a) This subchapter does not prevent the Department of State Health Services from making known to the public, by appropriate means, the existence of voluntary adoption registries.

(b) Information received by or in connection with the operation of a registry may not be stored in a data bank used for any purpose other than operation of the registry.

(c) A person commits an offense if the person knowingly or recklessly discloses information from a registry application, registration, record, or other information submitted to, obtained by, or otherwise acquired by a registry in violation of this subchapter. This subsection may not be construed to penalize the disclosure of information from adoption agency records. An offense under this subsection is a felony of the second degree.

(d) A person commits an offense if the person with criminal negligence causes or permits the disclosure of information from a registry application, registration, record, or other information submitted to, obtained by, or otherwise acquired by a registry in violation of this subchapter. This subsection may not be construed to penalize the disclosure of information from adoption agency records. An offense under this subsection is a Class A misdemeanor.

(e) A person commits an offense if the person impersonates an adoptee, birth parent, or biological sibling with the intent to secure confidential information from a registry established under this subchapter. An offense under this subsection is a felony of the second degree.

(f) A person commits an offense if the person impersonates an administrator, agent, or employee of a registry with the intent to secure confidential information from a registry established under this subchapter. An offense under this subsection is a felony of the second degree.

(g) A person commits an offense if the person, with intent to deceive and with knowledge of the statement's meaning, makes a false statement under oath in connection with the operation of a registry. An offense under this subsection is a felony of the third degree.

History of Fam. Code §162.421: Acts 1995, 74th Leg., ch. 20, §1, eff. Apr. 20, 1995. Amended by Acts 1995, 74th Leg., ch. 968, §10, eff. Sept. 1, 1995; Acts 1997, 75th Leg., ch. 561, §27, eff. Sept. 1, 1997; Acts 2015, 84th Leg., ch. 1, §1.117, eff. Apr. 2, 2015. Source: Former Hum. Res. Code §49.022.

FAM §162.422. IMMUNITY FROM LIABILITY

(a) The Department of State Health Services or authorized agency establishing or operating a registry is not liable to any person for obtaining or disclosing identifying information about a birth parent, adoptee, or biological sibling within the scope of this subchapter and under its provisions.

(b) An employee or agent of the Department of State Health Services or of an authorized agency establishing or operating a registry under this subchapter is not liable to any person for obtaining or disclosing identifying information about a birth parent, adoptee, or biological sibling within the scope of this subchapter and under its provisions.

(c) A person or entity furnishing information to the administrator or an employee or agent of a registry is not liable to any person for disclosing information about a birth parent, adoptee, or biological sibling within the scope of this subchapter and under its provisions.

(d) A person or entity is not immune from liability for performing an act prohibited by Section 162.421.

History of Fam. Code §162.422: Acts 1995, 74th Leg., ch. 20, §1, eff. Apr. 20, 1995. Amended by Acts 1997, 75th Leg., ch. 561, §28, eff. Sept. 1, 1997; Acts 2015, 84th Leg., ch. 1, §1.118, eff. Apr. 2, 2015. Source: Former Hum. Res. Code §49.023.

Sections 162.423-162.500 reserved for expansion

SUBCHAPTER F. ADOPTION OF AN ADULT

FAM §162.501. ADOPTION OF ADULT

The court may grant the petition of an adult residing in this state to adopt another adult according to this subchapter.

History of Fam. Code §162.501: Acts 1995, 74th Leg., ch. 20, §1, eff. Apr. 20, 1995. Source: Former Fam. Code §16.51.

ANNOTATIONS

Dampier v. Williams, 493 S.W.3d 118, 125 (Tex. App.—Houston [1st Dist.] 2016, no pet.). "With the legal procedures in place for an adoptive parent to either (1) legally adopt the adult or (2) provide for that adult in his will, we are unwilling … to hold that an adult may be adopted by estoppel."

FAM §162.502. JURISDICTION

The petitioner shall file a suit to adopt an adult in the district court or a statutory county court granted jurisdiction in family law cases and proceedings by Chapter 25, Government Code, in the county of the petitioner's residence.

History of Fam. Code §162.502: Acts 1995, 74th Leg., ch. 20, §1, eff. Apr. 20, 1995. Source: Former Fam. Code §16.51.

FAM §162.503. REQUIREMENTS OF PETITION

(a) A petition to adopt an adult shall be entitled "In the Interest of __________, An Adult."

(b) If the petitioner is married, both spouses must join in the petition for adoption.

History of Fam. Code §162.503: Acts 1995, 74th Leg., ch. 20, §1, eff. Apr. 20, 1995. Source: Former Fam. Code §16.53.

FAM §162.504. CONSENT

A court may not grant an adoption unless the adult consents in writing to be adopted by the petitioner.

History of Fam. Code §162.504: Acts 1995, 74th Leg., ch. 20, §1, eff. Apr. 20, 1995. Source: Former Fam. Code §16.52.

FAM §162.505. ATTENDANCE REQUIRED

The petitioner and the adult to be adopted must attend the hearing. For good cause shown, the court may waive this requirement, by written order, if the petitioner or adult to be adopted is unable to attend.

History of Fam. Code §162.505: Acts 1995, 74th Leg., ch. 20, §1, eff. Apr. 20, 1995. Source: Former Fam. Code §16.54.

FAM §162.506. ADOPTION ORDER

(a) The court shall grant the adoption if the court finds that the requirements for adoption of an adult are met.

(b) Notwithstanding that both spouses have joined in a petition for the adoption of an adult as required by Section 162.503(b), the court may grant the adoption of the adult to both spouses or, on request of the spouses, to only one spouse.

History of Fam. Code §162.506: Acts 1995, 74th Leg., ch. 20, §1, eff. Apr. 20, 1995. Amended by Acts 2003, 78th Leg., ch. 555, §1, eff. June 20, 2003.

FAM §162.507. EFFECT OF ADOPTION

(a) The adopted adult is the son or daughter of the adoptive parents for all purposes.

(b) The adopted adult is entitled to inherit from and through the adopted adult's adoptive parents as

though the adopted adult were the biological child of the adoptive parents.

(c) The adopted adult may not inherit from or through the adult's biological parent. A biological parent may not inherit from or through an adopted adult.

History of Fam. Code §162.507: Acts 1995, 74th Leg., ch. 20, §1, eff. Apr. 20, 1995. Amended by Acts 2005, 79th Leg., ch. 169, §1, eff. Sept. 1, 2005. Source: Former Fam. Code §16.55.

Sections 162.508-162.600 blank

SUBCHAPTER G. MISCELLANEOUS PROVISIONS

FAM §162.601. INCENTIVES FOR LICENSED CHILD-PLACING AGENCIES

(a) Subject to the availability of funds, the Department of Family and Protective Services shall pay, in addition to any other amounts due, a monetary incentive to a licensed child-placing agency for the completion of an adoption:

(1) of a child, as defined by Section 162.301, receiving or entitled to receive foster care at department expense; and

(2) arranged with the assistance of the agency.

(b) The incentive may not exceed 25 percent of the amount the department would have spent to provide one year of foster care for the child, determined according to the child's level of care at the time the adoption is completed.

(c) For purposes of this section, an adoption is completed on the date on which the court issues the adoption order.

History of Fam. Code §162.601: Acts 1997, 75th Leg., ch. 1309, §1, eff. Sept. 1, 1997. Amended by Acts 2015, 84th Leg., ch. 1, §1.119, eff. Apr. 2, 2015.

FAM §162.602. DOCUMENTATION TO ACCOMPANY PETITION FOR ADOPTION OR ANNULMENT OR REVOCATION OF ADOPTION

At the time a petition for adoption or annulment or revocation of adoption is filed, the petitioner shall also file completed documentation that may be used by the clerk of the court, at the time the petition is granted, to comply with Section 192.009, Health and Safety Code, and Section 108.003.

History of Fam. Code §162.602: Acts 2003, 78th Leg., ch. 1128, §5, eff. Sept. 1, 2003.

E FAM §162.603. POST-ADOPTION SUPPORT INFORMATION PROVIDED BY LICENSED CHILD-PLACING AGENCIES

A licensed child-placing agency shall provide prospective adoptive parents with information regarding:

(1) the community services and other resources available to support a parent who adopts a child; and

(2) the options available to the adoptive parent if the parent is unable to care for the adopted child.

History of Fam. Code §162.603: Enacted by H.B. 834, §2, 85th Leg., eff. Sept. 1, 2017.

Sections 162.604-162.700 blank

E SUBCHAPTER H. EMBRYO DONATION INFORMATION

FAM §162.701. DEFINITIONS

In this subchapter:

(1) "Department" means the Department of Family and Protective Services.

(2) "Embryo donation" has the meaning assigned by Section 159.011, Occupations Code.

History of Fam. Code §162.701: Enacted by H.B. 785, §2, 85th Leg., eff. Sept. 1, 2017.

FAM §162.702. INFORMATION REGARDING EMBRYO DONATION

The department shall post information regarding embryo donation on the department's Internet website. The information must include contact information for nonprofit organizations that facilitate embryo donation.

History of Fam. Code §162.702: Enacted by H.B. 785, §2, 85th Leg., eff. Sept. 1, 2017.

Chapters 163-200 reserved for expansion

SUBTITLE C. JUDICIAL RESOURCES & SERVICES

CHAPTER 201. ASSOCIATE JUDGE

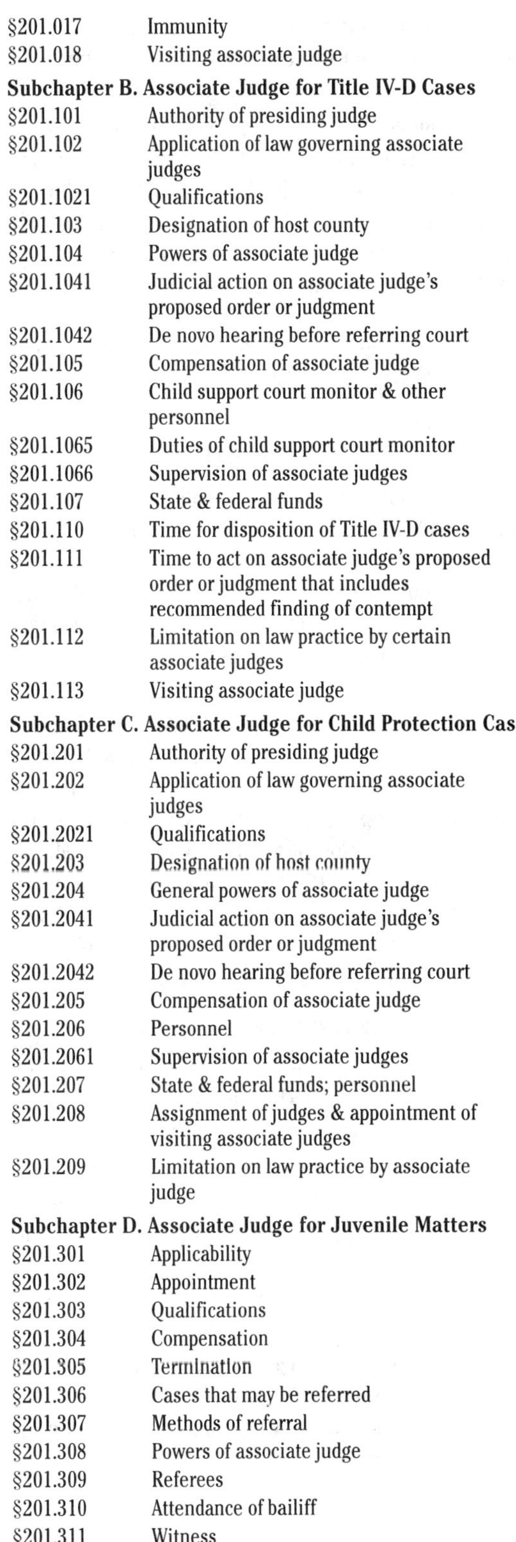

SUBCHAPTER A. ASSOCIATE JUDGE

FAM §201.001. APPOINTMENT

(a) A judge of a court having jurisdiction of a suit under this title, Title 1, Chapter 45, or Title 4 may appoint a full-time or part-time associate judge to perform the duties authorized by this chapter if the commissioners court of a county in which the court has jurisdiction authorizes the employment of an associate judge.

(b) If a court has jurisdiction in more than one county, an associate judge appointed by that court may serve only in a county in which the commissioners court has authorized the associate judge's appointment.

(c) If more than one court in a county has jurisdiction of a suit under this title, Title 1, Chapter 45, or Title 4 the commissioners court may authorize the appointment of an associate judge for each court or may authorize one or more associate judges to share service with two or more courts.

(d) If an associate judge serves more than one court, the associate judge's appointment must be made with the unanimous approval of all the judges under whom the associate judge serves.

(e) This section does not apply to an associate judge appointed under Subchapter B or C.

History of Fam. Code §201.001: Acts 1995, 74th Leg., ch. 20, §1, eff. Apr. 20, 1995. Amended by Acts 1999, 76th Leg., ch. 1302, §1, eff. Sept. 1, 1999; Acts 2003, 78th Leg., ch. 1258, §2, eff. Sept. 1, 2003; Acts 2015, 84th Leg., ch. 197, §1, eff. Sept. 1, 2015. Source: Former Gov't Code §54.001.

FAM §201.002. QUALIFICATIONS

(a) Except as provided by Subsection (b), to be eligible for appointment as an associate judge, a person must meet the requirements and qualifications to serve as a judge of the court or courts for which the associate judge is appointed.

(b) To be eligible for appointment as an associate judge under Subchapter B or C, a person must meet the requirements and qualifications established under those subchapters.

History of Fam. Code §201.002: Acts 1995, 74th Leg., ch. 20, §1, eff. Apr. 20, 1995. Amended by Acts 2007, 80th Leg., ch. 44, §1, eff. Sept. 1, 2007. Source: Former Gov't Code §54.002.

FAM §201.003. COMPENSATION

(a) An associate judge shall be paid a salary determined by the commissioners court of the county in which the associate judge serves.

(b) If an associate judge serves in more than one county, the associate judge shall be paid a salary as determined by agreement of the commissioners courts of the counties in which the associate judge serves.

(c) The associate judge's salary is paid from the county fund available for payment of officers' salaries.

(d) This section does not apply to an associate judge appointed under Subchapter B or C.

History of Fam. Code §201.003: Acts 1995, 74th Leg., ch. 20, §1, eff. Apr. 20, 1995. Amended by Acts 1999, 76th Leg., ch. 1302, §2, eff. Sept. 1, 1999; Acts 2003, 78th Leg., ch. 1258, §3, eff. Sept. 1, 2003. Source: Former Gov't Code §54.003.

FAM §201.004. TERMINATION OF ASSOCIATE JUDGE

(a) An associate judge who serves a single court serves at the will of the judge of that court.

(b) The employment of an associate judge who serves more than two courts may only be terminated by a majority vote of all the judges of the courts which the associate judge serves.

(c) The employment of an associate judge who serves two courts may be terminated by either of the judges of the courts which the associate judge serves.

(d) This section does not apply to an associate judge appointed under Subchapter B or C.

History of Fam. Code §201.004: Acts 1995, 74th Leg., ch. 20, §1, eff. Apr. 20, 1995. Amended by Acts 1999, 76th Leg., ch. 1302, §3, eff. Sept. 1, 1999; Acts 2003, 78th Leg., ch. 1258, §4, eff. Sept. 1, 2003. Source: Former Gov't Code §54.004.

FAM §201.005. CASES THAT MAY BE REFERRED

(a) Except as provided by this section, a judge of a court may refer to an associate judge any aspect of a suit over which the court has jurisdiction under this title, Title 1, Chapter 45, or Title 4, including any matter ancillary to the suit.

(b) Unless a party files a written objection to the associate judge hearing a trial on the merits, the judge may refer the trial to the associate judge. A trial on the merits is any final adjudication from which an appeal may be taken to a court of appeals.

(c) A party must file an objection to an associate judge hearing a trial on the merits or presiding at a jury trial not later than the 10th day after the date the party receives notice that the associate judge will hear the trial. If an objection is filed, the referring court shall hear the trial on the merits or preside at a jury trial.

(d) The requirements of Subsections (b) and (c) shall apply whenever a judge has authority to refer the trial of a suit under this title, Title 1, Chapter 45, or Title 4 to an associate judge, master, or other assistant judge regardless of whether the assistant judge is appointed under this subchapter.

History of Fam. Code §201.005: Acts 1995, 74th Leg., ch. 20, §1, eff. Apr. 20, 1995. Amended by Acts 1999, 76th Leg., ch. 1302, §4, eff. Sept. 1, 1999; Acts 2015, 84th Leg., ch. 197, §2, eff. Sept. 1, 2015. Source: Former Gov't Code §54.005.

ANNOTATIONS

In re Baker, 495 S.W.3d 393, 396-97 (Tex.App.—Houston [14th Dist.] 2016, orig. proceeding). "[W]e hold that the parties' waiver of objection to the associate judge hearing the original trial ... does not affect their statutory right to object to a trial by the associate judge after the case has been remanded for a partial new trial."

In re T.S., 191 S.W.3d 736, 737 (Tex.App.—Houston [14th Dist.] 2006, pet. denied). "[T]he failure to object under [Fam. Code] §201.005(c) ... did not deprive the parents of their right to appeal the associate judge's report under [Fam. Code] §§201.015 and 201.2042.... *At 739:* Section 201.015 allows an appeal by 'a party' who satisfies the procedural requirements of that section; it does not exclude parties who failed to object to the referral of the trial to an associate judge."

FAM §201.006. ORDER OF REFERRAL

(a) In referring a case to an associate judge, the judge of the referring court shall render:

(1) an individual order of referral; or

(2) a general order of referral specifying the class and type of cases to be heard by the associate judge.

(b) The order of referral may limit the power or duties of an associate judge.

History of Fam. Code §201.006: Acts 1995, 74th Leg., ch. 20, §1, eff. Apr. 20, 1995. Source: Former Gov't Code §54.006.

A FAM §201.007. POWERS OF ASSOCIATE JUDGE

(a) Except as limited by an order of referral, an associate judge may:

(1) conduct a hearing;

(2) hear evidence;

(3) compel production of relevant evidence;

(4) rule on the admissibility of evidence;

(5) issue a summons for:

(A) the appearance of witnesses; and

(B) the appearance of a parent who has failed to appear before an agency authorized to conduct an investigation of an allegation of abuse or neglect of a child after receiving proper notice;

(6) examine a witness;

(7) swear a witness for a hearing;

(8) make findings of fact on evidence;

(9) formulate conclusions of law;

(10) recommend an order to be rendered in a case;

(11) regulate all proceedings in a hearing before the associate judge;

(12) order the attachment of a witness or party who fails to obey a subpoena;

(13) order the detention of a witness or party found guilty of contempt, pending approval by the referring court as provided by Section 201.013;

(14) without prejudice to the right to a de novo hearing before the referring court [~~of appeal~~] under Section 201.015 and subject to Subsection (c), render and sign:

(A) a final order agreed to in writing as to both form and substance by all parties;

(B) a final default order;

(C) a temporary order; or

(D) a final order in a case in which a party files an unrevoked waiver made in accordance with Rule 119, Texas Rules of Civil Procedure, that waives notice to the party of the final hearing or waives the party's appearance at the final hearing;

(15) take action as necessary and proper for the efficient performance of the associate judge's duties; and

(16) render and sign a final order if the parties waive [~~that includes a waiver of~~] the right to a de novo hearing before the referring court under [~~of appeal pursuant to~~] Section 201.015 in writing before the start of a hearing conducted by the associate judge.

(b) An associate judge may, in the interest of justice, refer a case back to the referring court regardless of whether a timely objection to the associate judge hearing the trial on the merits or presiding at a jury trial has been made by any party.

(c) A final order described by Subsection (a)(14) becomes final after the expiration of the period described by Section 201.015(a) if a party does not request a de novo hearing in accordance with that section. An order described by Subsection (a)(14) or (16) that is rendered and signed by an associate judge constitutes an order of the referring court.

(d) An answer filed by or on behalf of a party who previously filed a waiver described in Subsection (a)(14)(D) shall revoke that waiver.

(e) An order signed before May 1, 2017, by an associate judge under Subsection (a)(16) is a final order rendered as of the date the order was signed.

History of Fam. Code §201.007: Acts 1995, 74th Leg., ch. 20, §1, eff. Apr. 20, 1995. Amended by Acts 1999, 76th Leg., ch. 1302, §5, eff. Sept. 1, 1999; Acts 2003, 78th Leg., ch. 476, §1, eff. Sept. 1, 2003; Acts 2005, 79th Leg., ch. 550, §1, eff. Sept. 1, 2005; Acts 2007, 80th Leg., ch. 839, §1 (eff. June 15, 2007), ch. 1406, §5 (eff. Sept. 1, 2007); H.B. 2927, §1, 85th Leg., eff. May 29, 2017; S.B. 1329, §1.03(a), 85th Leg., eff. Sept. 1, 2017. Source: Former Gov't Code §54.007.

ANNOTATIONS

In re M.K.R., 216 S.W.3d 58, 64 (Tex.App.—Fort Worth 2007, no pet.). "[W] argues that the report [for contempt] could not be a final order, despite the trial court's approval and signature, because [§201.007(a)(10)] contemplates that the order is a separate document beyond the associate judge's report. [W] refers us to nothing in the family code or the government code that specifically requires a separate document per se; instead, what is required is the separate *approval* of the district court.... Here, it is evident on the face of the report that the district court judge approved and signed the associate judge's report as the order of the court; the signature of the district court judge appears on the report under the words 'APPROVED AND SO ORDERED.' Nothing in this document states that an additional order will follow."

FAM §201.008. ATTENDANCE OF BAILIFF

A bailiff may attend a hearing by an associate judge if directed by the referring court.

History of Fam. Code §201.008: Acts 1995, 74th Leg., ch. 20, §1, eff. Apr. 20, 1995. Source: Former Gov't Code §54.008.

FAM §201.009. COURT REPORTER; RECORD

(a) A court reporter may be provided during a hearing held by an associate judge appointed under this chapter. A court reporter is required to be provided when the associate judge presides over a jury trial or a contested final termination hearing.

(b) A party, the associate judge, or the referring court may provide for a reporter during the hearing, if one is not otherwise provided.

(c) Except as provided by Subsection (a), in the absence of a court reporter or on agreement of the parties, the record may be preserved by any means approved by the associate judge.

(d) The referring court or associate judge may tax the expense of preserving the record under Subsection (c) as costs.

(e) On a request for a de novo hearing, the referring court may consider testimony or other evidence in the record in addition to witnesses or other matters presented under Section 201.015.

History of Fam. Code §201.009: Acts 1995, 74th Leg., ch. 20, §1, eff. Apr. 20, 1995. Amended by Acts 1999, 76th Leg., ch. 1302, §6, eff. Sept. 1, 1999; Acts 2007, 80th Leg., ch. 839, §§2, 3 (eff. June 15, 2007), ch. 1235, §1 (eff. Sept. 1, 2007); Acts 2009, 81st Leg., ch. 767, §24, eff. June 19, 2009. Source: Former Gov't Code §54.018.

FAM §201.010. WITNESS

(a) A witness appearing before an associate judge is subject to the penalties for perjury provided by law.

(b) A referring court may fine or imprison a witness who:

(1) failed to appear before an associate judge after being summoned; or

(2) improperly refused to answer questions if the refusal has been certified to the court by the associate judge.

History of Fam. Code §201.010: Acts 1995, 74th Leg., ch. 20, §1, eff. Apr. 20, 1995. Source: Former Gov't Code §54.009.

FAM §201.011. REPORT

(a) The associate judge's report may contain the associate judge's findings, conclusions, or recommendations and may be in the form of a proposed order. The associate judge's report must be in writing in the form directed by the referring court.

(b) After a hearing, the associate judge shall provide the parties participating in the hearing notice of the substance of the associate judge's report, including any proposed order.

(c) Notice may be given to the parties:

(1) in open court, by an oral statement or a copy of the associate judge's written report, including any proposed order;

(2) by certified mail, return receipt requested; or

(3) by facsimile transmission.

(d) There is a rebuttable presumption that notice is received on the date stated on:

(1) the signed return receipt, if notice was provided by certified mail; or

(2) the confirmation page produced by the facsimile machine, if notice was provided by facsimile transmission.

(e) After a hearing conducted by an associate judge, the associate judge shall send the associate judge's signed and dated report, including any proposed order, and all other papers relating to the case to the referring court.

History of Fam. Code §201.011: Acts 1995, 74th Leg., ch. 20, §1, eff. Apr. 20, 1995. Amended by Acts 1999, 76th Leg., ch. 1302, §7, eff. Sept. 1, 1999; Acts 2003, 78th Leg., ch. 464, §1, eff. Sept. 1, 2003; Acts 2007, 80th Leg., ch. 1235, §2, eff. Sept. 1, 2007. Source: Former Gov't Code §§54.010(a), (b), 54.012(c).

FAM §201.012. NOTICE OF RIGHT TO DE NOVO HEARING BEFORE REFERRING COURT

(a) Notice of the right to a de novo hearing before the referring court shall be given to all parties.

(b) The notice may be given:

(1) by oral statement in open court;

(2) by posting inside or outside the courtroom of the referring court; or

(3) as otherwise directed by the referring court.

History of Fam. Code §201.012: Acts 1995, 74th Leg., ch. 20, §1, eff. Apr. 20, 1995. Amended by Acts 2007, 80th Leg., ch. 1235, §§3, 4, eff. Sept. 1, 2007. Source: Former Gov't Code §54.010(c).

A FAM §201.013. ORDER OF COURT

(a) Pending a de novo hearing before the referring court, a proposed order or judgment of the associate judge is in full force and effect and is enforceable as an order or judgment of the referring court, except for an order providing for the appointment of a receiver.

(b) Except as provided by Section 201.007(c), if a request for a de novo hearing before the referring court is not timely filed ~~[or the right to a de novo hearing before the referring court is waived]~~, the proposed order or judgment of the associate judge becomes the order or judgment of the referring court only on the referring court's signing the proposed order or judgment.

(c) An order by an associate judge for the temporary detention or incarceration of a witness or party shall be presented to the referring court on the day the witness or party is detained or incarcerated. The referring court, without prejudice to the right to a de novo hearing provided by Section 201.015, may approve the temporary detention or incarceration or may order the release of the party or witness, with or without bond, pending a de novo hearing. If the referring court is not immediately available, the associate judge may order the release of the party or witness, with or without

bond, pending a de novo hearing or may continue the person's detention or incarceration for not more than 72 hours.

History of Fam. Code §201.013: Acts 1995, 74th Leg., ch. 20, §1, eff. Apr. 20, 1995. Amended by Acts 1999, 76th Leg., ch. 1302, §8, eff. Sept. 1, 1999; Acts 2003, 78th Leg., ch. 476, §2, eff. Sept. 1, 2003; Acts 2007, 80th Leg., ch. 1235, §5, eff. Sept. 1, 2007; H.B. 2927, §2, 85th Leg., eff. May 29, 2017; S.B. 1329, §1.03(b), 85th Leg., eff. Sept. 1, 2017. Source: Former Gov't Code §§54.013, 54.015.

ANNOTATIONS

Attorney Gen. v. Orr, 989 S.W.2d 464, 468 n.2 (Tex.App.—Austin 1999, no pet.). "We view the purpose of §201.013(a) to be allowing temporary orders to be in effect pending trial before the referring court. Despite the continuing validity of the associate judge's recommendations for that limited purpose, the judgment of the referring court on the issues appealed will be based solely on evidence presented at the de novo hearing."

A FAM §201.014. JUDICIAL ACTION ON ASSOCIATE JUDGE'S PROPOSED ORDER OR JUDGMENT

(a) Except as otherwise provided in this subchapter, unless ~~[Unless]~~ a party files a written request for a de novo hearing before the referring court, the referring court may:

(1) adopt, modify, or reject the associate judge's proposed order or judgment;

(2) hear further evidence; or

(3) recommit the matter to the associate judge for further proceedings.

(b) Regardless of whether a party files a written request for a de novo hearing before the referring court, a proposed order or judgment rendered by an associate judge in a suit filed by the Department of Family and Protective Services that meets the requirements of Section 263.401(d) is considered a final order for purposes of Section 263.401.

History of Fam. Code §201.014: Acts 1995, 74th Leg., ch. 20, §1, eff. Apr. 20, 1995. Amended by Acts 1999, 76th Leg., ch. 1302, §9, eff. Sept. 1, 1999; Acts 2007, 80th Leg., ch. 1235, §6, eff. Sept. 1, 2007; H.B. 2927, §3, 85th Leg., eff. May 29, 2017; S.B. 1329, §1.03(c), 85th Leg., eff. Sept. 1, 2017. Source: Former Gov't Code §54.011.

FAM §201.015. DE NOVO HEARING BEFORE REFERRING COURT

(a) A party may request a de novo hearing before the referring court by filing with the clerk of the referring court a written request not later than the third working day after the date the party receives notice of:

(1) the substance of the associate judge's report as provided by Section 201.011; or

(2) the rendering of the temporary order, if the request concerns a temporary order rendered by an associate judge under Section 201.007(a)(14)(C).

(b) A request for a de novo hearing under this section must specify the issues that will be presented to the referring court.

(c) In the de novo hearing before the referring court, the parties may present witnesses on the issues specified in the request for hearing. The referring court may also consider the record from the hearing before the associate judge, including the charge to and verdict returned by a jury.

(d) Notice of a request for a de novo hearing before the referring court shall be given to the opposing attorney under Rule 21a, Texas Rules of Civil Procedure.

(e) If a request for a de novo hearing before the referring court is filed by a party, any other party may file a request for a de novo hearing before the referring court not later than the third working day after the date the initial request was filed.

(f) The referring court, after notice to the parties, shall hold a de novo hearing not later than the 30th day after the date on which the initial request for a de novo hearing was filed with the clerk of the referring court.

(g) Before the start of a hearing by an associate judge, the parties may waive the right of a de novo hearing before the referring court in writing or on the record.

(h) The denial of relief to a party after a de novo hearing under this section or a party's waiver of the right to a de novo hearing before the referring court does not affect the right of a party to file a motion for new trial, motion for judgment notwithstanding the verdict, or other post-trial motion.

(i) A party may not demand a second jury in a de novo hearing before the referring court if the associate judge's proposed order or judgment resulted from a jury trial.

History of Fam. Code §201.015: Acts 1995, 74th Leg., ch. 20, §1, eff. Apr. 20, 1995. Amended by Acts 1999, 76th Leg., ch. 1302, §10, eff. Sept. 1, 1999; Acts 2007, 80th Leg., ch. 1043, §1 (eff. Sept. 1, 2007), ch. 1235, §7 (eff. Sept. 1, 2007); Acts 2009, 81st Leg., ch. 767, §25, eff. June 19, 2009; Acts 2013, 83rd Leg., ch. 916, §5, eff. Sept. 1, 2013; Acts 2015, 84th Leg., ch. 589, §1, eff. June 16, 2015. Source: Former Gov't Code §54.012(a), (d)-(i).

ANNOTATIONS

State v. Owens, 907 S.W.2d 484, 485 (Tex.1995). "Although the district court should have held a hearing on [respondent's] appeal before signing an order adopting the master's report, its failure to do so did not

deprive it of jurisdiction to issue the order or make the order void. A judgment is void only when it is clear that the court rendering the judgment had no jurisdiction over the parties or subject matter, no jurisdiction to render judgment, or no capacity to act as a court. Mere failure to follow proper procedure will not render a judgment void. [¶] An order which purports to dispose of all issues and all parties, like the district court's first order, is a final appealable order. Errors other than lack of jurisdiction must be attacked within the prescribed time limits. When [respondent] did not timely appeal from the first order, it became final."

In re J.A.P., 510 S.W.3d 722, 724 (Tex.App.—San Antonio 2016, no pet.). Respondent "argues the referring court erred in denying his request for a de novo hearing because such a hearing is mandatory when timely requested under [Fam. Code] §201.015, and because language purporting to waive the right to a de novo hearing is not effective when the order is merely 'approved as to form.' We agree. … The 'Order Waiving Jury' makes no mention whatsoever of a waiver of the de novo hearing. Instead, the 'Order Waiving Jury' includes language that merely provides [that] the parties agree to waive their objections to an associate judge hearing the termination trial on the merits as opposed to the referring court. The right to object to a referral under [Fam. Code] §201.005 is separate and distinct from the right to waive a de novo hearing under §201.015. Thus, because the record demonstrates that the purported 'waiver' did not comply with §201.015(g), we hold the referring district court erred in denying [respondent's] request for a de novo hearing. [¶] [E]ven if the right to object could be waived after the hearing, the waiver language included in the associate judge's order would not have been effective in this instance. [Respondent's] attorney merely signed the order as 'approved as to form' and the record does not support substantive approval of the waiver."

Chacon v. Chacon, 222 S.W.3d 909, 912 (Tex. App.—El Paso 2007, no pet.). "[H] argues that the referring court exceeded its jurisdiction by altering the associate judge's recommendations on issues he did not specifically raise on appeal. [¶] [H's] jurisdictional argument is based entirely on the language of §201.015(b).… *At 913:* [W]e hold that §201.015(b) is intended to limit the appealing party's ability to raise issues he has not specifically appealed in the *de novo* hearing. It is not a limit on the referring court's jurisdiction."

In re E.M., 54 S.W.3d 849, 852 (Tex.App.—Corpus Christi 2001, no pet.). To be entitled to "a *de novo* hearing on appeal of an associate judge's recommendations to the referring court, a party must timely file a written notice of appeal containing the associate judge's findings and conclusions to which the party objects. [¶] Although appellant's notice of appeal was timely filed, it did not contain his objections to any specific findings or conclusions. Because appellant failed to comply with the requirements under §201.015, we conclude he is not entitled to a *de novo* hearing of his appeal of the associate judge's recommendation."

Fountain v. Knebel, 45 S.W.3d 736, 739 (Tex. App.—Dallas 2001, no pet.). "The purpose of [§201.015] is to require the prompt resolution of appeals from an associate judge's rulings. Nonetheless, the referring court does not lose its jurisdiction if it fails to hear an appeal within 30 days after the appeal is filed. Rather, the 30-day provision affords a party the right to compel the district court to hear the case promptly. The requirement is a deadline for the trial court, not the parties. Once a party has filed a notice of appeal, the party has completed the prerequisites necessary to be entitled to a de novo hearing." *See also* ***In re L.R.***, 324 S.W.3d 885, 888-89 (Tex.App.—Austin 2010, orig. proceeding) (although court has jurisdiction to hold de novo hearing after 30-day window under §201.015(f) has passed, party can object to scheduled hearing date and compel court to comply with statute's requirement).

Attorney Gen. v. Orr, 989 S.W.2d 464, 467-68 (Tex. App.—Austin 1999, no pet.). "For purposes of the final determination of the merits of the case, … filing a notice of appeal to the referring court cuts off the earlier proceedings, and evidence is presented anew to the referring court; in making its decision, the referring court may not rely on what occurred before the associate judge. Although in the absence of a notice of appeal the referring court's action continues a process begun before the associate judge, filing a notice of appeal breaks that continuity and begins an entirely new process. [¶] [A] party whose case is heard by an associate judge and who files a notice of appeal from the report could fail to attend the de novo hearing before the referring court. Given that filing a notice of appeal initiates a new process before the referring court, such a defaulting party stands in the same position as one who fails to attend an ordinary trial on the merits after answering the petition."

A

FAM §201.016. APPELLATE REVIEW

(a) A party's failure to request a de novo hearing before the referring court or a party's waiver of the right to request a de novo hearing before the referring court does not deprive the party of the right to appeal to or request other relief from a court of appeals or the supreme court.

(b) Except as provided by Subsection (c), the date an order or judgment by the referring court is signed is the controlling date for the purposes of appeal to or request for other relief from a court of appeals or the supreme court.

(c) The date an agreed order, [or] a default order, or a final order described by Section 201.007(a)(16) is signed by an associate judge is the controlling date for the purpose of an appeal to, or a request for other relief relating to the order from, a court of appeals or the supreme court.

History of Fam. Code §201.016: Acts 1995, 74th Leg., ch. 20, §1, eff. Apr. 20, 1995. Amended by Acts 2003, 78th Leg., ch. 476, §3, eff. Sept. 1, 2003; Acts 2007, 80th Leg., ch. 1235, §8, eff. Sept. 1, 2007; H.B. 2927, §4, 85th Leg., eff. May 29, 2017; S.B. 1329, §1.03(d), 85th Leg., eff. Sept. 1, 2017. Source: Former Gov't Code §54.012(j).

ANNOTATIONS

In re N.R.C., 94 S.W.3d 799, 805 (Tex.App.—Houston [14th Dist.] 2002, pet. denied). "We conclude that the phrase 'other relief' refers to any and all relief other than relief obtained from the referring court. Any other reading of the statute would defeat the primary purpose of … §201.016, which is to allow litigants to appeal associate judges' rulings that they did not appeal to the referring court."

FAM §201.017. IMMUNITY

An associate judge appointed under this subchapter has the judicial immunity of a district judge. All existing immunity granted an associate judge by law, express or implied, continues in full force and effect.

History of Fam. Code §201.017: Acts 1995, 74th Leg., ch. 20, §1, eff. Apr. 20, 1995. Source: Former Gov't Code §54.017.

FAM §201.018. VISITING ASSOCIATE JUDGE

(a) If an associate judge appointed under this subchapter is temporarily unable to perform the judge's official duties because of absence or illness, injury, or other disability, a judge of a court having jurisdiction of a suit under this title, Title 1, Chapter 45, or Title 4 may appoint a visiting associate judge to perform the duties of the associate judge during the period of the associate judge's absence or disability if the commissioners court of a county in which the court has jurisdiction authorizes the employment of a visiting associate judge.

(b) To be eligible for appointment under this section, a person must have served as an associate judge for at least two years.

(c) Sections 201.001 through 201.017 apply to a visiting associate judge appointed under this section.

(d) This section does not apply to an associate judge appointed under Subchapter B.

History of Fam. Code §201.018: Acts 1999, 76th Leg., ch. 1355, §1, eff. Aug. 30, 1999. Amended by Acts 2001, 77th Leg., ch. 308, §1, eff. Sept. 1, 2001; Acts 2003, 78th Leg., ch. 1258, §5, eff. Sept. 1, 2003; Acts 2015, 84th Leg., ch. 197, §3, eff. Sept. 1, 2015.

Sections 201.019-201.100 reserved for expansion

SUBCHAPTER B. ASSOCIATE JUDGE FOR TITLE IV-D CASES

FAM §201.101. AUTHORITY OF PRESIDING JUDGE

(a) The presiding judge of each administrative judicial region, after conferring with the judges of courts in the region having jurisdiction of Title IV-D cases, shall determine which courts require the appointment of a full-time or part-time associate judge to complete each Title IV-D case within the time specified in this subchapter.

(b) If the presiding judge of an administrative judicial region determines under Subsection (a) that the courts in the region require the appointment of an associate judge, the presiding judge shall appoint an associate judge from a list of the qualified applicants who have submitted an application to the office of court administration. Before making the appointment, the presiding judge must provide the list to the judges of the courts from which cases will be referred to the associate judge. Each judge may recommend to the presiding judge the names of one or more applicants for appointment. An associate judge appointed under this subsection serves for a term of four years from the date the associate judge is appointed and qualifies for office. The appointment of an associate judge for a term does not affect the at-will employment status of the associate judge. The presiding judge may terminate an appointment at any time.

(b-1) Before reappointing an associate judge appointed under Subsection (b), the presiding judge must notify each judge of the courts from which cases will be referred to the associate judge of the presiding judge's

intent to reappoint the associate judge to another term. Each judge may submit to the presiding judge a recommendation on whether the associate judge should be reappointed.

(c) An associate judge appointed under this subchapter may be appointed to serve more than one court. Two or more judges of administrative judicial regions may jointly appoint one or more associate judges to serve the regions.

(d) Except as provided under Subsection (e), if an associate judge is appointed for a court under this subchapter, all Title IV-D cases shall be referred to the associate judge by a general order for each county issued by the judge of the court for which the associate judge is appointed, or, in the absence of that order, by a general order issued by the presiding judge who appointed the associate judge. Referral of Title IV-D cases may not be made for individual cases or case by case.

(e) If a county has entered into a contract with the Title IV-D agency under Section 231.0011, enforcement services may be directly provided in cases identified under the contract by county personnel as provided under Section 231.0011(d), including judges and associate judges of the courts of the county.

History of Fam. Code §201.101: Acts 1995, 74th Leg., ch. 20, §1, eff. Apr. 20, 1995. Amended by Acts 1999, 76th Leg., ch. 1072, §1, eff. Sept. 1, 1999; Acts 2003, 78th Leg., ch. 1258, §7, eff. Sept. 1, 2003; Acts 2013, 83rd Leg., ch. 742, §8, eff. Sept. 1, 2013; Acts 2015, 84th Leg., ch. 1182, §1.01, eff. Sept. 1, 2015. Source: Former Fam. Code §14.82(a), (b).

FAM §201.102. APPLICATION OF LAW GOVERNING ASSOCIATE JUDGES

Subchapter A applies to an associate judge appointed under this subchapter, except that, to the extent of any conflict between this subchapter and Subchapter A, this subchapter prevails.

History of Fam. Code §201.102: Acts 1995, 74th Leg., ch. 20, §1, eff. Apr. 20, 1995. Amended by Acts 1999, 76th Leg., ch. 556, §41 (eff. Sept. 1, 1999), ch. 1302, §11 (eff. Sept. 1, 1999); Acts 2003, 78th Leg., ch. 1258, §8, eff. Sept. 1, 2003; Acts 2007, 80th Leg., ch. 44, §2, eff. Sept. 1, 2007. Source: Former Fam. Code §14.82(c), (e).

FAM §201.1021. QUALIFICATIONS

(a) To be eligible for appointment under this subchapter, a person must be a citizen of the United States, have resided in this state for the two years preceding the date of appointment, and be:

(1) eligible for assignment under Section 74.054, Government Code, because the person is named on the list of retired and former judges maintained by the presiding judge of the administrative region under Section 74.055, Government Code; or

(2) licensed to practice law in this state and have been a practicing lawyer in this state, or a judge of a court in this state who is not otherwise eligible under Subdivision (1), for the four years preceding the date of appointment.

(b) An associate judge appointed under this subchapter shall during the term of appointment reside in the administrative judicial region, or a county adjacent to the region, in which the court to which the associate judge is appointed is located. An associate judge appointed to serve in two or more administrative judicial regions may reside anywhere in the regions.

History of Fam. Code §201.1021: Acts 2007, 80th Leg., ch. 44, §3, eff. Sept. 1, 2007. Amended by Acts 2009, 81st Leg., ch. 760, §1, eff. June 19, 2009.

FAM §201.103. DESIGNATION OF HOST COUNTY

(a) The presiding judges of the administrative judicial regions by majority vote shall determine the host county of an associate judge appointed under this subchapter.

(b) The host county shall provide an adequate courtroom and quarters, including furniture, necessary utilities, and telephone equipment and service, for the associate judge and other personnel assisting the associate judge.

(c) An associate judge is not required to reside in the host county.

History of Fam. Code §201.103: Acts 1995, 74th Leg., ch. 20, §1, eff. Apr. 20, 1995. Amended by Acts 2003, 78th Leg., ch. 1258, §8, eff. Sept. 1, 2003. Source: Former Fam. Code §14.82(d).

Ⓐ FAM §201.104. POWERS OF ASSOCIATE JUDGE

The amended text in §201.104 is effective for Title IV-D cases referred to an associate judge under Fam. Code ch. 201, subch. B on or after Sept. 1, 2017. Cases referred before Sept. 1, 2017, are governed by the former law in effect at that time.

(a) On the motion of a party or the associate judge, an associate judge may refer a complex case back to the judge for final disposition after the associate judge has recommended temporary support.

(b) An associate judge may render and sign any order that is not a final order on the merits of the case.

(c) An associate judge may recommend to the referring court any order after a trial on the merits.

(d) Only the referring court may hear and render an order on a motion for postjudgment relief, including a motion for a new trial or to vacate, correct, or reform a judgment.

(e) Notwithstanding Subsection (d) and subject to Section 201.1042(g), an associate judge may hear and render an order on any matter necessary to be decided in connection with a Title IV-D service, including:

(1) a suit to modify or clarify an existing child support order;

(2) a motion to enforce a child support order or revoke a respondent's community supervision and suspension of commitment;

(3) a respondent's compliance with the conditions provided in the associate judge's report for suspension of the respondent's commitment; [or]

(4) a motion for postjudgment relief, including a motion for a new trial or to vacate, correct, or reform a judgment, if neither party has requested a de novo hearing before the referring court;

(5) a suit affecting the parent-child relationship; and

(6) a suit for modification under Chapter 156.

History of Fam. Code §201.104: Acts 1995, 74th Leg., ch. 20, §1, eff. Apr. 20, 1995. Amended by Acts 1999, 76th Leg., ch. 556, §42, eff. Sept. 1, 1999; Acts 2001, 77th Leg., ch. 1023, §46, eff. Sept. 1, 2001; Acts 2003, 78th Leg., ch. 1258, §8, eff. Sept. 1, 2003; Acts 2009, 81st Leg., ch. 806, §1, eff. Sept. 1, 2009; H.B. 2048, §1, 85th Leg., eff. Sept. 1, 2017. Source: Former Fam. Code §14.82(f), (g).

FAM §201.1041. JUDICIAL ACTION ON ASSOCIATE JUDGE'S PROPOSED ORDER OR JUDGMENT

(a) If a request for a de novo hearing before the referring court is not timely filed or the right to a de novo hearing before the referring court is waived, the proposed order or judgment of the associate judge, other than a proposed order or judgment providing for enforcement by contempt or the immediate incarceration of a party, shall become the order or judgment of the referring court by operation of law without ratification by the referring court.

(b) An associate judge's proposed order or judgment providing for enforcement by contempt or the immediate incarceration of a party becomes an order of the referring court only if:

(1) the referring court signs an order adopting the associate judge's proposed order or judgment; and

(2) the order or judgment meets the requirements of Section 157.166.

(c) Except as provided by Subsection (b), a proposed order or judgment of the associate judge is in full force and effect and is enforceable as an order or judgment of the referring court pending a de novo hearing before the referring court.

History of Fam. Code §201.1041: Acts 1999, 76th Leg., ch. 556, §43, eff. Sept. 1, 1999. Amended by Acts 2001, 77th Leg., ch. 1023, §47, eff. Sept. 1, 2001; Acts 2003, 78th Leg., ch. 1258, §8, eff. Sept. 1, 2003; Acts 2007, 80th Leg., ch. 1235, §9, eff. Sept. 1, 2007.

ANNOTATIONS

Graham v. Graham, 414 S.W.3d 800, 801 (Tex. App.—Houston [1st Dist.] 2013, no pet.). "This appeal raises the question of [an appellate] court's jurisdiction over a contempt order issued by an associate judge that was never adopted by the referring trial court. *At 802:* Because the contempt order at issue in this appeal was not adopted by the referring court as a matter of law, the referring court retains the power to alter the order, reject it, or conduct further proceedings. [The appellate court lacks] jurisdiction to consider the appeal of an associate judge's order that is not final."

FAM §201.1042. DE NOVO HEARING BEFORE REFERRING COURT

(a) Except as provided by this section, Section 201.015 applies to a request for a de novo hearing before the referring court.

(b) The party requesting a de novo hearing before the referring court shall file notice with the clerk of the referring court not later than the third working day after the date the associate judge signs the proposed order or judgment.

(c) A respondent who timely files a request for a de novo hearing on an associate judge's proposed order or judgment providing for incarceration shall be brought before the referring court not later than the first working day after the date on which the respondent files the request for a de novo hearing. The referring court shall determine whether the respondent should be released on bond or whether the respondent's appearance in court at a designated time and place can be otherwise assured.

(d) If the respondent under Subsection (c) is released on bond or other security, the referring court shall condition the bond or other security on the respondent's promise to appear in court for a de novo hearing at a designated date, time, and place, and the referring court shall give the respondent notice of the hearing in open court. No other notice to the respondent is required.

(e) If the respondent under Subsection (c) is released without posting bond or security, the court shall set a de novo hearing at a designated date, time, and

place and give the respondent notice of the hearing in open court. No other notice to the respondent is required.

(f) If the referring court is not satisfied that the respondent's appearance in court can be assured and the respondent remains incarcerated, a de novo hearing shall be held as soon as practicable, but not later than the fifth day after the date the respondent's request for a de novo hearing before the referring court was filed, unless the respondent or, if represented, the respondent's attorney waives the accelerated hearing.

(g) Until a de novo hearing is held under this section and the referring court has signed an order or judgment or has ruled on a timely filed motion for new trial or a motion to vacate, correct, or reform a judgment, an associate judge may not hold a hearing on the respondent's compliance with conditions in the associate judge's proposed order or judgment for suspension of commitment or on a motion to revoke the respondent's community supervision and suspension of commitment.

History of Fam. Code §201.1042: Acts 1999, 76th Leg., ch. 556, §43, eff. Sept. 1, 1999. Amended by Acts 2001, 77th Leg., ch. 1023, §48, eff. Sept. 1, 2001; Acts 2003, 78th Leg., ch. 1258, §9, eff. Sept. 1, 2003; Acts 2007, 80th Leg., ch. 1235, §10, eff. Sept. 1, 2007; Acts 2013, 83rd Leg., ch. 916, §6, eff. Sept. 1, 2013.

FAM §201.105. COMPENSATION OF ASSOCIATE JUDGE

(a) An associate judge appointed under this subchapter is entitled to a salary to be determined by a majority vote of the presiding judges of the administrative judicial regions. The salary may not exceed 90 percent of the salary paid to a district judge as set by the General Appropriations Act.

(b) The associate judge's salary shall be paid from county funds available for payment of officers' salaries or from funds available from the state and federal government as provided by this subchapter.

History of Fam. Code §201.105: Acts 1995, 74th Leg., ch. 20, §1, eff. Apr. 20, 1995. Amended by Acts 2003, 78th Leg., ch. 1258, §10, eff. Sept. 1, 2003. Source: Former Fam. Code §14.83(a), (b).

FAM §201.106. CHILD SUPPORT COURT MONITOR & OTHER PERSONNEL

(a) The presiding judge of an administrative judicial region or the presiding judges of the administrative judicial regions, by majority vote, may appoint other personnel, including a child support court monitor for each associate judge appointed under this subchapter, as needed to implement and administer the provisions of this subchapter.

(b) The salaries of the personnel and court monitors shall be paid from county funds available for payment of officers' salaries or from funds available from the state and federal government as provided by this subchapter.

History of Fam. Code §201.106: Acts 1995, 74th Leg., ch. 20, §1, eff. Apr. 20, 1995. Amended by Acts 1999, 76th Leg., ch. 1072, §2, eff. Sept. 1, 1999; Acts 2003, 78th Leg., ch. 1258, §10, eff. Sept. 1, 2003. Source: Former Fam. Code §14.83(c).

FAM §201.1065. DUTIES OF CHILD SUPPORT COURT MONITOR

(a) A child support court monitor appointed under this subchapter shall monitor child support cases in which the obligor is placed on probation for failure to comply with the requirements of a child support order.

(b) In monitoring a child support case, a court monitor shall:

(1) conduct an intake assessment of the needs of an obligor that, if addressed, would enable the obligor to comply with a child support order;

(2) refer an obligor to employment services offered by the employment assistance program under Section 302.0035, Labor Code, if appropriate;

(3) provide mediation services or referrals to services, if appropriate;

(4) schedule periodic contacts with an obligor to assess compliance with the child support order and whether additional support services are required;

(5) monitor the amount and timeliness of child support payments owed and paid by an obligor; and

(6) if appropriate, recommend that the court:

(A) discharge an obligor from or modify the terms of the obligor's community supervision; or

(B) revoke an obligor's community supervision.

History of Fam. Code §201.1065: Acts 1999, 76th Leg., ch. 1072, §3, eff. Sept. 1, 1999. Amended by Acts 2003, 78th Leg., ch. 1258, §10, eff. Sept. 1, 2003.

FAM §201.1066. SUPERVISION OF ASSOCIATE JUDGES

(a) The office of court administration shall assist the presiding judges in:

(1) monitoring the associate judges' compliance with job performance standards and federal and state laws and policies;

(2) addressing the training needs and resource requirements of the associate judges;

(3) conducting annual performance evaluations for the associate judges and other personnel appointed under this subchapter based on written personnel perfor-

mance standards adopted by the presiding judges and performance information solicited from the referring courts and other relevant persons; and

(4) receiving, investigating, and resolving complaints about particular associate judges or the associate judge program under this subchapter based on a uniform process adopted by the presiding judges.

(b) The office of court administration shall develop procedures and a written evaluation form to be used by the presiding judges in conducting the annual performance evaluations under Subsection (a)(3).

(c) Each judge of a court that refers cases to an associate judge under this subchapter may submit to the presiding judge or the office of court administration information on the associate judge's performance during the preceding year based on a uniform process adopted by the presiding judges.

History of Fam. Code §201.1066: Acts 1999, 76th Leg., ch. 556, §44, eff. Sept. 1, 1999. Renumbered from §201.1065 by Acts 2001, 77th Leg., ch. 1420, §21.001(31), eff. Sept. 1, 2001. Amended by Acts 2003, 78th Leg., ch. 1258, §10, eff. Sept. 1, 2003; Acts 2015, 84th Leg., ch. 1182, §1.02, eff. Sept. 1, 2015.

FAM §201.107. STATE & FEDERAL FUNDS

(a) The office of court administration may contract with the Title IV-D agency for available state and federal funds under Title IV-D and may employ personnel needed to implement and administer this subchapter. An associate judge, a court monitor for each associate judge, and other personnel appointed under this subchapter are state employees for all purposes, including accrual of leave time, insurance benefits, retirement benefits, and travel regulations.

(b) The presiding judges of the administrative judicial regions, state agencies, and counties may contract with the Title IV-D agency for available federal funds under Title IV-D to reimburse costs and salaries associated with associate judges, court monitors, and personnel appointed under this subchapter and may also use available state funds and public or private grants.

(c) The presiding judges and the Title IV-D agency shall act and are authorized to take any action necessary to maximize the amount of federal funds available under the Title IV-D program.

History of Fam. Code §201.107: Acts 1995, 74th Leg., ch. 20, §1, eff. Apr. 20, 1995. Amended by Acts 1999, 76th Leg., ch. 556, §45 (eff. Sept. 1, 1999), ch. 1072, §4 (eff. Sept. 1, 1999); Acts 2003, 78th Leg., ch. 1258, §11, eff. Sept. 1, 2003. Source: Former Fam. Code §14.83(d), (e).

FAM §201.108. REPEALED

Repealed by Acts 2003, 78th Leg., ch. 1258, §27, eff. Sept. 1, 2003.

FAM §201.1085. REPEALED

Repealed by Acts 1999, 76th Leg., ch. 62, §6.26 (eff. Sept. 1, 1999), ch. 1302, §14 (eff. Sept. 1, 1999).

FAM §201.109. REPEALED

Repealed by Acts 2003, 78th Leg., ch. 1258, §27, eff. Sept. 1, 2003.

FAM §201.110. TIME FOR DISPOSITION OF TITLE IV-D CASES

(a) Title IV-D cases must be completed from the time of successful service to the time of disposition within the following time:

(1) 75 percent within six months; and

(2) 90 percent within one year.

(b) Title IV-D cases shall be given priority over other cases.

(c) A clerk or judge may not restrict the number of Title IV-D cases that are filed or heard in the courts.

History of Fam. Code §201.110: Acts 1995, 74th Leg., ch. 20, §1, eff. Apr. 20, 1995. Amended by Acts 2003, 78th Leg., ch. 1258, §12, eff. Sept. 1, 2003. Source: Former Fam. Code §14.81.

FAM §201.111. TIME TO ACT ON ASSOCIATE JUDGE'S PROPOSED ORDER OR JUDGMENT THAT INCLUDES RECOMMENDED FINDING OF CONTEMPT

(a) Not later than the 10th day after the date an associate judge's proposed order or judgment recommending a finding of contempt is signed, the referring court shall:

(1) adopt, modify, or reject the proposed order or judgment;

(2) hear further evidence; or

(3) recommit the matter for further proceedings.

(b) The time limit in Subsection (a) does not apply if a party has filed a written request for a de novo hearing before the referring court.

History of Fam. Code §201.111: Acts 1995, 74th Leg., ch. 751, §80, eff. Sept. 1, 1995. Amended by Acts 1999, 76th Leg., ch. 556, §46, eff. Sept. 1, 1999; Acts 2003, 78th Leg., ch. 1258, §§13, 14, eff. Sept. 1, 2003; Acts 2007, 80th Leg., ch. 1235, §11, eff. Sept. 1, 2007. Source: Former Fam. Code §14.82(h).

FAM §201.112. LIMITATION ON LAW PRACTICE BY CERTAIN ASSOCIATE JUDGES

A full-time associate judge appointed under this subchapter may not engage in the private practice of law.

History of Fam. Code §201.112: Acts 1999, 76th Leg., ch. 556, §47, eff. Sept. 1, 1999. Amended by Acts 2003, 78th Leg., ch. 1258, §15, eff. Sept. 1, 2003.

FAM §201.113. VISITING ASSOCIATE JUDGE

(a) If an associate judge appointed under this subchapter is temporarily unable to perform the associate

judge's official duties because of absence resulting from family circumstances, illness, injury, disability, or military service, or if there is a vacancy in the position of associate judge, the presiding judge of the administrative judicial region in which the associate judge serves or the vacancy occurs may appoint a visiting associate judge for Title IV-D cases to perform the duties of the associate judge during the period the associate judge is unable to perform the associate judge's duties or until another associate judge is appointed to fill the vacancy.

(b) A person is not eligible for appointment under this section unless the person has served as a master or associate judge under this chapter, a district judge, or a statutory county court judge for at least two years before the date of appointment.

(c) A visiting associate judge appointed under this section is subject to each provision of this chapter that applies to an associate judge serving under a regular appointment under this subchapter. A visiting associate judge appointed under this section is entitled to compensation to be determined by a majority vote of the presiding judges of the administrative judicial regions through use of funds under this subchapter. A visiting associate judge is not considered to be a state employee for any purpose.

(d) Section 2252.901, Government Code, does not apply to the appointment of a visiting associate judge under this section.

History of Fam. Code §201.113: Acts 2001, 77th Leg., ch. 1023, §49, eff. Sept. 1, 2001. Amended by Acts 2003, 78th Leg., ch. 1258, §15, eff. Sept. 1, 2003; Acts 2005, 79th Leg., ch. 343, §1, eff. June 17, 2005; Acts 2009, 81st Leg., ch. 760, §2, eff. June 19, 2009.

Sections 201.114-201.200 blank

SUBCHAPTER C. ASSOCIATE JUDGE FOR CHILD PROTECTION CASES

FAM §201.201. AUTHORITY OF PRESIDING JUDGE

(a) The presiding judge of each administrative judicial region, after conferring with the judges of courts in the region having family law jurisdiction and a child protection caseload, shall determine which courts require the appointment of a full-time or part-time associate judge to complete cases under Subtitle E within the times specified under that subtitle.

(b) If the presiding judge of an administrative judicial region determines under Subsection (a) that the courts in the region require the appointment of an associate judge, the presiding judge shall appoint an associate judge from a list of the qualified applicants who have submitted an application to the office of court administration. Before making the appointment, the presiding judge must provide the list to the judges of the courts from which cases will be referred to the associate judge. Each judge may recommend to the presiding judge the names of one or more applicants for appointment. An associate judge appointed under this subsection serves for a term of four years from the date the associate judge is appointed and qualifies for office. The appointment of an associate judge for a term does not affect the at-will employment status of the associate judge. The presiding judge may terminate an appointment at any time.

(b-1) Before reappointing an associate judge appointed under Subsection (b), the presiding judge must notify each judge of the courts from which cases will be referred to the associate judge of the presiding judge's intent to reappoint the associate judge to another term. Each judge may submit to the presiding judge a recommendation on whether the associate judge should be reappointed.

(c) An associate judge appointed under this subchapter may be appointed to serve more than one court. Two or more judges of administrative judicial regions may jointly appoint one or more associate judges to serve the regions.

(d) If an associate judge is appointed for a court, all child protection cases shall be referred to the associate judge by a general order for each county issued by the judge of the court for which the associate judge is appointed or, in the absence of that order, by a general order issued by the presiding judge who appointed the associate judge.

(e) This section does not limit the jurisdiction of a court to issue orders under Subtitle E.

History of Fam. Code §201.201: Acts 1999, 76th Leg., ch. 1302, §12, eff. Sept. 1, 1999. Amended by Acts 2003, 78th Leg., ch. 1258, §17, eff. Sept. 1, 2003; Acts 2011, 82nd Leg., ch. 377, §1, eff. June 17, 2011; Acts 2015, 84th Leg., ch. 1182, §1.03, eff. Sept. 1, 2015.

FAM §201.202. APPLICATION OF LAW GOVERNING ASSOCIATE JUDGES

Except as provided by this subchapter, Subchapter A applies to an associate judge appointed under this subchapter.

History of Fam. Code §201.202: Acts 1999, 76th Leg., ch. 1302, §12, eff. Sept. 1, 1999. Amended by Acts 2007, 80th Leg., ch. 44, §4, eff. Sept. 1, 2007.

FAM §201.2021. QUALIFICATIONS

(a) To be eligible for appointment under this subchapter, a person must be a citizen of the United States, have resided in this state for the two years preceding the date of appointment, and be:

(1) eligible for assignment under Section 74.054, Government Code, because the person is named on the list of retired and former judges maintained by the presiding judge of the administrative region under Section 74.055, Government Code; or

(2) licensed to practice law in this state and have been a practicing lawyer in this state, or a judge of a court in this state who is not otherwise eligible under Subdivision (1), for the four years preceding the date of appointment.

(b) An associate judge appointed under this subchapter shall during the term of appointment reside in the administrative judicial region, or a county adjacent to the region, in which the court to which the associate judge is appointed is located. An associate judge appointed to serve in two or more administrative judicial regions may reside anywhere in the regions.

History of Fam. Code §201.2021: Acts 2007, 80th Leg., ch. 44, §5, eff. Sept. 1, 2007. Amended by Acts 2009, 81st Leg., ch. 760, §3, eff. June 19, 2009.

FAM §201.203. DESIGNATION OF HOST COUNTY

(a) Subject to the approval of the commissioners court of the proposed host county, the presiding judges of the administrative judicial regions by majority vote shall determine the host county of an associate judge appointed under this subchapter.

(b) The host county shall provide an adequate courtroom and quarters, including furniture, necessary utilities, and telephone equipment and service, for the associate judge and other personnel assisting the associate judge.

(c) An associate judge is not required to reside in the host county.

History of Fam. Code §201.203: Acts 1999, 76th Leg., ch. 1302, §12, eff. Sept. 1, 1999.

A FAM §201.204. GENERAL POWERS OF ASSOCIATE JUDGE

(a) On the motion of a party or the associate judge, an associate judge may refer a complex case back to the referring court for final disposition after recommending temporary orders for the protection of a child.

(b) An associate judge may render and sign any pretrial order.

(c) An associate judge may recommend to the referring court any order after a trial on the merits.

(d) An associate judge may hear and render an order in a suit for the adoption of a child for whom the Texas Department of Family and Protective Services has been named managing conservator.

History of Fam. Code §201.204: Acts 1999, 76th Leg., ch. 1302, §12, eff. Sept. 1, 1999. Amended by Acts 2003, 78th Leg., ch. 1258, §18, eff. Sept. 1, 2003; S.B. 1329, §1.04, 85th Leg., eff. Sept. 1, 2017.

FAM §201.2041. JUDICIAL ACTION ON ASSOCIATE JUDGE'S PROPOSED ORDER OR JUDGMENT

(a) If a request for a de novo hearing before the referring court is not timely filed or the right to a de novo hearing before the referring court is waived, the proposed order or judgment of the associate judge becomes the order or judgment of the referring court by operation of law without ratification by the referring court.

(b) Regardless of whether a de novo hearing is requested before the referring court, a proposed order or judgment rendered by an associate judge that meets the requirements of Section 263.401(d) is considered a final order for purposes of Section 263.401.

History of Fam. Code §201.2041: Acts 2003, 78th Leg., ch. 1258, §19, eff. Sept. 1, 2003. Amended by Acts 2007, 80th Leg., ch. 1235, §12, eff. Sept. 1, 2007.

ANNOTATIONS

In re E.K.C., 486 S.W.3d 614, 617 (Tex.App.—San Antonio 2016, no pet.). "The associate judges who hear child protection cases in Bexar County appear to have adopted a practice of rendering and signing handwritten orders that terminate parental rights and award conservatorship soon following the trial on the merits. Frequently, as in this case, the handwritten order, called the 'Associate Judge's Report and Order,' is signed by the presiding judge of the district court as being 'so adopted and ordered.' Weeks and on occasion months later, a more formal and detailed typed 'Final Order' is signed. [¶] In [this] case …, this practice has caused unintended consequences. *At 618:* [T]he Associate Judge's Report and Order disposed of all issues and did not leave any issues for future determination. [¶] Because no motion extending the trial court's plenary power was filed, the [later] 'Final Order' was signed after the trial court lost plenary power, and it is a nullity. Because the Associate Judge's Report and Order … was final and started the appellate timetable, [father's] notice of appeal was due within 20 days after

the order was signed, or a motion for extension of time was due 15 days later."

FAM §201.2042. DE NOVO HEARING BEFORE REFERRING COURT

(a) Except as provided by this section, Section 201.015 applies to a request for a de novo hearing before the referring court.

(b) The party requesting a de novo hearing before the referring court shall file notice with the referring court and the clerk of the referring court.

History of Fam. Code §201.2042: Acts 2003, 78th Leg., ch. 1258, §19, eff. Sept. 1, 2003. Amended by Acts 2007, 80th Leg., ch. 1235, §13, eff. Sept. 1, 2007.

FAM §201.205. COMPENSATION OF ASSOCIATE JUDGE

(a) An associate judge appointed under this subchapter is entitled to a salary as determined by a majority vote of the presiding judges of the administrative judicial regions. The salary may not exceed 90 percent of the salary paid to a district judge as set by the state General Appropriations Act.

(b) The associate judge's salary shall be paid from county funds available for payment of officers' salaries subject to the approval of the commissioners court or from funds available from the state and federal governments as provided by this subchapter.

History of Fam. Code §201.205: Acts 1999, 76th Leg., ch. 1302, §12, eff. Sept. 1, 1999. Amended by Acts 2003, 78th Leg., ch. 1258, §20, eff. Sept. 1, 2003.

FAM §201.206. PERSONNEL

(a) The presiding judge of an administrative judicial region or the presiding judges of the administrative judicial regions, by majority vote, may appoint personnel as needed to implement and administer the provisions of this subchapter.

(b) The salaries of the personnel shall be paid from county funds available for payment of officers' salaries subject to the approval of the commissioners court or from funds available from the state and federal governments as provided by this subchapter.

History of Fam. Code §201.206: Acts 1999, 76th Leg., ch. 1302, §12, eff. Sept. 1, 1999. Amended by Acts 2003, 78th Leg., ch. 1258, §21, eff. Sept. 1, 2003.

FAM §201.2061. SUPERVISION OF ASSOCIATE JUDGES

(a) The office of court administration shall assist the presiding judges in:

(1) monitoring the associate judges' compliance with any applicable job performance standards, uniform practices adopted by the presiding judges, and federal and state laws and policies;

(2) addressing the training needs and resource requirements of the associate judges;

(3) conducting annual performance evaluations for the associate judges and other personnel appointed under this subchapter based on written personnel performance standards adopted by the presiding judges and performance information solicited from the referring courts and other relevant persons; and

(4) receiving, investigating, and resolving complaints about particular associate judges or the associate judge program under this subchapter based on a uniform process adopted by the presiding judges.

(b) The office of court administration shall develop procedures and a written evaluation form to be used by the presiding judges in conducting the annual performance evaluations under Subsection (a)(3).

(c) Each judge of a court that refers cases to an associate judge under this subchapter may submit to the presiding judge or the office of court administration information on the associate judge's performance during the preceding year based on a uniform process adopted by the presiding judges.

History of Fam. Code §201.2061: Acts 2003, 78th Leg., ch. 1258, §22, eff. Sept. 1, 2003. Amended by Acts 2015, 84th Leg., ch. 1182, §1.04, eff. Sept. 1, 2015.

FAM §201.207. STATE & FEDERAL FUNDS; PERSONNEL

(a) The office of court administration may contract for available state and federal funds from any source and may employ personnel needed to implement and administer this subchapter. An associate judge and other personnel appointed under this subsection are state employees for all purposes, including accrual of leave time, insurance benefits, retirement benefits, and travel regulations.

(b) The presiding judges of the administrative judicial regions, state agencies, and counties may contract for available federal funds from any source to reimburse costs and salaries associated with associate judges and personnel appointed under this section and may also use available state funds and public or private grants.

(c) The presiding judges and the office of court administration in cooperation with other agencies shall take action necessary to maximize the amount of federal money available to fund the use of associate judges under this subchapter.

History of Fam. Code §201.207: Acts 1999, 76th Leg., ch. 1302, §12, eff. Sept. 1, 1999.

FAM §201.208. ASSIGNMENT OF JUDGES & APPOINTMENT OF VISITING ASSOCIATE JUDGES

(a) This chapter does not limit the authority of a presiding judge to assign a judge eligible for assignment under Chapter 74, Government Code, to assist in processing cases in a reasonable time.

(b) If an associate judge appointed under this subchapter is temporarily unable to perform the associate judge's official duties because of absence resulting from family circumstances, illness, injury, disability, or military service, or if there is a vacancy in the position of associate judge, the presiding judge of the administrative judicial region in which the associate judge serves or the vacancy occurs may appoint a visiting associate judge to perform the duties of the associate judge during the period the associate judge is unable to perform the associate judge's duties or until another associate judge is appointed to fill the vacancy.

(c) A person is not eligible for appointment under this section unless the person has served as a master or associate judge under this chapter, a district judge, or a statutory county court judge for at least two years before the date of appointment.

(d) A visiting associate judge appointed under this section is subject to each provision of this chapter that applies to an associate judge serving under a regular appointment under this subchapter. A visiting associate judge appointed under this section is entitled to compensation, to be determined by a majority vote of the presiding judges of the administrative judicial regions, through use of funds under this subchapter. A visiting associate judge is not considered to be a state employee for any purpose.

(e) Section 2252.901, Government Code, does not apply to the appointment of a visiting associate judge under this section.

History of Fam. Code §201.208: Acts 1999, 76th Leg., ch. 1302, §12, eff. Sept. 1, 1999. Amended by Acts 2003, 78th Leg., ch. 1258, §23, eff. Sept. 1, 2003; Acts 2005, 79th Leg., ch. 343, §2, eff. June 17, 2005; Acts 2009, 81st Leg., ch. 760, §4, eff. June 19, 2009.

FAM §201.209. LIMITATION ON LAW PRACTICE BY ASSOCIATE JUDGE

An associate judge appointed under this subchapter may not engage in the private practice of law.

History of Fam. Code §201.209: Acts 2003, 78th Leg., ch. 1258, §24, eff. Sept. 1, 2003.

Sections 201.210-201.300 blank

SUBCHAPTER D. ASSOCIATE JUDGE FOR JUVENILE MATTERS

FAM §201.301. APPLICABILITY

This subchapter applies only to an associate judge appointed under this subchapter and does not apply to a juvenile court master appointed under Subchapter K, Chapter 54, Government Code.

History of Fam. Code §201.301: Acts 2011, 82nd Leg., 1st C.S., ch. 3, §6.03, eff. Jan. 1, 2012.

FAM §201.302. APPOINTMENT

(a) A judge of a court that is designated as a juvenile court may appoint a full-time or part-time associate judge to perform the duties authorized by this chapter if the commissioners court of a county in which the court has jurisdiction has authorized creation of an associate judge position.

(b) If a court has jurisdiction in more than one county, an associate judge appointed by that court may serve only in a county in which the commissioners court has authorized the appointment.

(c) If more than one court in a county has been designated as a juvenile court, the commissioners court may authorize the appointment of an associate judge for each court or may authorize one or more associate judges to share service with two or more courts.

(d) If an associate judge serves more than one court, the associate judge's appointment must be made as established by local rule, but in no event by less than a vote of two-thirds of the judges under whom the associate judge serves.

History of Fam. Code §201.302: Acts 2011, 82nd Leg., 1st C.S., ch. 3, §6.03, eff. Jan. 1, 2012.

FAM §201.303. QUALIFICATIONS

To qualify for appointment as an associate judge under this subchapter, a person must:

(1) be a resident of this state and one of the counties the person will serve;

(2) have been licensed to practice law in this state for at least four years;

(3) not have been removed from office by impeachment, by the supreme court, by the governor on address to the legislature, by a tribunal reviewing a recommendation of the State Commission on Judicial Conduct, or by the legislature's abolition of the judge's court; and

(4) not have resigned from office after having received notice that formal proceedings by the State Commission on Judicial Conduct had been instituted as pro-

vided in Section 33.022, Government Code, and before final disposition of the proceedings.

History of Fam. Code §201.303: Acts 2011, 82nd Leg., 1st C.S., ch. 3, §6.03, eff. Jan. 1, 2012.

FAM §201.304. COMPENSATION

(a) An associate judge shall be paid a salary determined by the commissioners court of the county in which the associate judge serves.

(b) If an associate judge serves in more than one county, the associate judge shall be paid a salary as determined by agreement of the commissioners courts of the counties in which the associate judge serves.

(c) The associate judge's salary is paid from the county fund available for payment of officers' salaries.

History of Fam. Code §201.304: Acts 2011, 82nd Leg., 1st C.S., ch. 3, §6.03, eff. Jan. 1, 2012.

FAM §201.305. TERMINATION

(a) An associate judge who serves a single court serves at the will of the judge of that court.

(b) The employment of an associate judge who serves more than two courts may only be terminated by a majority vote of all the judges of the courts which the associate judge serves.

(c) The employment of an associate judge who serves two courts may be terminated by either of the judges of the courts which the associate judge serves.

(d) To terminate an associate judge's employment, the appropriate judges must sign a written order of termination. The order must state:

(1) the associate judge's name and state bar identification number;

(2) each court ordering termination; and

(3) the date the associate judge's employment ends.

History of Fam. Code §201.305: Acts 2011, 82nd Leg., 1st C.S., ch. 3, §6.03, eff. Jan. 1, 2012.

FAM §201.306. CASES THAT MAY BE REFERRED

(a) Except as provided by this section, a judge of a juvenile court may refer to an associate judge any aspect of a juvenile matter brought:

(1) under this title or Title 3; or

(2) in connection with Rule 308a, Texas Rules of Civil Procedure.

(b) Unless a party files a written objection to the associate judge hearing a trial on the merits, the judge may refer the trial to the associate judge. A trial on the merits is any final adjudication from which an appeal may be taken to a court of appeals.

(c) A party must file an objection to an associate judge hearing a trial on the merits or presiding at a jury trial not later than the 10th day after the date the party receives notice that the associate judge will hear the trial. If an objection is filed, the referring court shall hear the trial on the merits or preside at a jury trial.

(d) The requirements of Subsections (b) and (c) apply when a judge has authority to refer the trial of a suit under this title, Title 1, or Title 4 to an associate judge, master, or other assistant judge regardless of whether the assistant judge is appointed under this subchapter.

History of Fam. Code §201.306: Acts 2011, 82nd Leg., 1st C.S., ch. 3, §6.03, eff. Jan. 1, 2012.

FAM §201.307. METHODS OF REFERRAL

(a) A case may be referred to an associate judge by an order of referral in a specific case or by an omnibus order.

(b) The order of referral may limit the power or duties of an associate judge.

History of Fam. Code §201.307: Acts 2011, 82nd Leg., 1st C.S., ch. 3, §6.03, eff. Jan. 1, 2012.

FAM §201.308. POWERS OF ASSOCIATE JUDGE

(a) Except as limited by an order of referral, an associate judge may:

(1) conduct a hearing;

(2) hear evidence;

(3) compel production of relevant evidence;

(4) rule on the admissibility of evidence;

(5) issue a summons for:

(A) the appearance of witnesses; and

(B) the appearance of a parent who has failed to appear before an agency authorized to conduct an investigation of an allegation of abuse or neglect of a child after receiving proper notice;

(6) examine a witness;

(7) swear a witness for a hearing;

(8) make findings of fact on evidence;

(9) formulate conclusions of law;

(10) recommend an order to be rendered in a case;

(11) regulate proceedings in a hearing;

(12) order the attachment of a witness or party who fails to obey a subpoena;

(13) order the detention of a witness or party found guilty of contempt, pending approval by the referring court; and

(14) take action as necessary and proper for the efficient performance of the associate judge's duties.

(b) An associate judge may, in the interest of justice, refer a case back to the referring court regardless of whether a timely objection to the associate judge hearing the trial on the merits or presiding at a jury trial has been made by any party.

History of Fam. Code §201.308: Acts 2011, 82nd Leg., 1st C.S., ch. 3, §6.03, eff. Jan. 1, 2012.

FAM §201.309. REFEREES

(a) An associate judge appointed under this subchapter may serve as a referee as provided by Sections 51.04(g) and 54.10.

(b) A referee appointed under Section 51.04(g) may be appointed to serve as an associate judge under this subchapter.

History of Fam. Code §201.309: Acts 2011, 82nd Leg., 1st C.S., ch. 3, §6.03, eff. Jan. 1, 2012.

FAM §201.310. ATTENDANCE OF BAILIFF

A bailiff may attend a hearing by an associate judge if directed by the referring court.

History of Fam. Code §201.310: Acts 2011, 82nd Leg., 1st C.S., ch. 3, §6.03, eff. Jan. 1, 2012.

FAM §201.311. WITNESS

(a) A witness appearing before an associate judge is subject to the penalties for perjury provided by law.

(b) A referring court may fine or imprison a witness who:

(1) failed to appear before an associate judge after being summoned; or

(2) improperly refused to answer questions if the refusal has been certified to the court by the associate judge.

History of Fam. Code §201.311: Acts 2011, 82nd Leg., 1st C.S., ch. 3, §6.03, eff. Jan. 1, 2012.

FAM §201.312. COURT REPORTER; RECORD

(a) A court reporter may be provided during a hearing held by an associate judge appointed under this subchapter. A court reporter is required to be provided when the associate judge presides over a jury trial or a contested final termination hearing.

(b) A party, the associate judge, or the referring court may provide for a reporter during the hearing if one is not otherwise provided.

(c) Except as provided by Subsection (a), in the absence of a court reporter or on agreement of the parties, the record may be preserved by any means approved by the associate judge.

(d) The referring court or associate judge may assess the expense of preserving the record as costs.

(e) On a request for a de novo hearing, the referring court may consider testimony or other evidence in the record, if the record is taken by a court reporter, in addition to witnesses or other matters presented under Section 201.317.

History of Fam. Code §201.312: Acts 2011, 82nd Leg., 1st C.S., ch. 3, §6.03, eff. Jan. 1, 2012.

FAM §201.313. REPORT

(a) The associate judge's report may contain the associate judge's findings, conclusions, or recommendations and may be in the form of a proposed order. The associate judge's report must be in writing and in the form directed by the referring court.

(b) After a hearing, the associate judge shall provide the parties participating in the hearing notice of the substance of the associate judge's report, including any proposed order.

(c) Notice may be given to the parties:

(1) in open court, by an oral statement or by providing a copy of the associate judge's written report, including any proposed order;

(2) by certified mail, return receipt requested; or

(3) by facsimile.

(d) A rebuttable presumption exists that notice is received on the date stated on:

(1) the signed return receipt, if notice was provided by certified mail; or

(2) the confirmation page produced by the facsimile machine, if notice was provided by facsimile.

(e) After a hearing conducted by an associate judge, the associate judge shall send the associate judge's signed and dated report, including any proposed order, and all other papers relating to the case to the referring court.

History of Fam. Code §201.313: Acts 2011, 82nd Leg., 1st C.S., ch. 3, §6.03, eff. Jan. 1, 2012.

FAM §201.314. NOTICE OF RIGHT TO DE NOVO HEARING; WAIVER

(a) An associate judge shall give all parties notice of the right to a de novo hearing to the judge of the referring court.

(b) The notice may be given:

(1) by oral statement in open court;

(2) by posting inside or outside the courtroom of the referring court; or

(3) as otherwise directed by the referring court.

(c) Before the start of a hearing by an associate judge, a party may waive the right of a de novo hearing before the referring court in writing or on the record.

History of Fam. Code §201.314: Acts 2011, 82nd Leg., 1st C.S., ch. 3, §6.03, eff. Jan. 1, 2012.

FAM §201.315. ORDER OF COURT

(a) Pending a de novo hearing before the referring court, a proposed order or judgment of the associate judge is in full force and effect and is enforceable as an order or judgment of the referring court, except for an order providing for the appointment of a receiver.

(b) If a request for a de novo hearing before the referring court is not timely filed or the right to a de novo hearing before the referring court is waived, the proposed order or judgment of the associate judge becomes the order or judgment of the referring court only on the referring court's signing the proposed order or judgment.

(c) An order by an associate judge for the temporary detention or incarceration of a witness or party shall be presented to the referring court on the day the witness or party is detained or incarcerated. The referring court, without prejudice to the right to a de novo hearing provided by Section 201.317, may approve the temporary detention or incarceration or may order the release of the party or witness, with or without bond, pending a de novo hearing. If the referring court is not immediately available, the associate judge may order the release of the party or witness, with or without bond, pending a de novo hearing or may continue the person's detention or incarceration for not more than 72 hours.

History of Fam. Code §201.315: Acts 2011, 82nd Leg., 1st C.S., ch. 3, §6.03, eff. Jan. 1, 2012.

FAM §201.316. JUDICIAL ACTION ON ASSOCIATE JUDGE'S PROPOSED ORDER OR JUDGMENT

Unless a party files a written request for a de novo hearing before the referring court, the referring court may:

(1) adopt, modify, or reject the associate judge's proposed order or judgment;

(2) hear additional evidence; or

(3) recommit the matter to the associate judge for further proceedings.

History of Fam. Code §201.316: Acts 2011, 82nd Leg., 1st C.S., ch. 3, §6.03, eff. Jan. 1, 2012.

FAM §201.317. DE NOVO HEARING

(a) A party may request a de novo hearing before the referring court by filing with the clerk of the referring court a written request not later than the third working day after the date the party receives notice of the substance of the associate judge's report as provided by Section 201.313.

(b) A request for a de novo hearing under this section must specify the issues that will be presented to the referring court. The de novo hearing is limited to the specified issues.

(c) Notice of a request for a de novo hearing before the referring court shall be given to the opposing attorney in the manner provided by Rule 21a, Texas Rules of Civil Procedure.

(d) If a request for a de novo hearing before the referring court is filed by a party, any other party may file a request for a de novo hearing before the referring court not later than the third working day after the date the initial request was filed.

(e) The referring court, after notice to the parties, shall hold a de novo hearing not later than the 30th day after the date the initial request for a de novo hearing was filed with the clerk of the referring court.

(f) In the de novo hearing before the referring court, the parties may present witnesses on the issues specified in the request for hearing. The referring court may also consider the record from the hearing before the associate judge, including the charge to and verdict returned by a jury, if the record was taken by a court reporter.

(g) The denial of relief to a party after a de novo hearing under this section or a party's waiver of the right to a de novo hearing before the referring court does not affect the right of a party to file a motion for new trial, a motion for judgment notwithstanding the verdict, or other posttrial motions.

(h) A party may not demand a second jury in a de novo hearing before the referring court if the associate judge's proposed order or judgment resulted from a jury trial.

History of Fam. Code §201.317: Acts 2011, 82nd Leg., 1st C.S., ch. 3, §6.03, eff. Jan. 1, 2012. Amended by Acts 2013, 83rd Leg., ch. 916, §7, eff. Sept. 1, 2013.

FAM §201.318. APPELLATE REVIEW

(a) A party's failure to request a de novo hearing before the referring court or a party's waiver of the right to request a de novo hearing before the referring court does not deprive the party of the right to appeal to or request other relief from a court of appeals or the supreme court.

(b) Except as provided by Subsection (c), the date an order or judgment by the referring court is signed is the controlling date for the purposes of appeal to or request for other relief from a court of appeals or the supreme court.

(c) The date an agreed order or a default order is signed by an associate judge is the controlling date for the purpose of an appeal to, or a request for other relief relating to the order from, a court of appeals or the supreme court.

History of Fam. Code §201.318: Acts 2011, 82nd Leg., 1st C.S., ch. 3, §6.03, eff. Jan. 1, 2012.

FAM §201.319. JUDICIAL IMMUNITY

An associate judge appointed under this subchapter has the judicial immunity of a district judge.

History of Fam. Code §201.319: Acts 2011, 82nd Leg., 1st C.S., ch. 3, §6.03, eff. Jan. 1, 2012.

FAM §201.320. VISITING ASSOCIATE JUDGE

(a) If an associate judge appointed under this subchapter is temporarily unable to perform the judge's official duties because of absence or illness, injury, or other disability, a judge of a court having jurisdiction of a suit under this title or Title 1 or 4 may appoint a visiting associate judge to perform the duties of the associate judge during the period of the associate judge's absence or disability if the commissioners court of a county in which the court has jurisdiction authorizes the employment of a visiting associate judge.

(b) To be eligible for appointment under this section, a person must have served as an associate judge for at least two years.

(c) Sections 201.001 through 201.017 apply to a visiting associate judge appointed under this section.

History of Fam. Code §201.320: Acts 2011, 82nd Leg., 1st C.S., ch. 3, §6.03, eff. Jan. 1, 2012.

CHAPTER 202. FRIEND OF THE COURT

FAM §202.001. APPOINTMENT

(a) After an order for child support or possession of or access to a child has been rendered, a court may appoint a friend of the court on:

(1) the request of a person alleging that the order has been violated; or

(2) its own motion.

(b) A court may appoint a friend of the court in a proceeding under Part D of Title IV of the federal Social Security Act (42 U.S.C. Section 651 et seq.) only if the Title IV-D agency agrees in writing to the appointment.

(c) The duration of the appointment of a friend of the court is as determined by the court.

(d) In the appointment of a friend of the court, the court shall give preference to:

(1) a local domestic relations office;

(2) a local child support collection office;

(3) the local court official designated to enforce actions as provided in Chapter 159; or

(4) an attorney in good standing with the State Bar of Texas.

(e) In the execution of a friend of the court's duties under this subchapter, a friend of the court shall represent the court to ensure compliance with the court's order.

History of Fam. Code §202.001: Acts 1995, 74th Leg., ch. 20, §1, eff. Apr. 20, 1995. Source: Former Fam. Code §14.91.

FAM §202.002. AUTHORITY & DUTIES

(a) A friend of the court may coordinate nonjudicial efforts to improve compliance with a court order relating to child support or possession of or access to a child by use of:

(1) telephone communication;

(2) written communication;

(3) one or more volunteer advocates under Chapter 107;

(4) informal pretrial consultation;

(5) one or more of the alternate dispute resolution methods under Chapter 154, Civil Practice and Remedies Code;

(6) a licensed social worker;

(7) a family mediator; and

(8) employment agencies, retraining programs, and any similar resources to ensure that both parents can meet their financial obligations to the child.

(b) A friend of the court, not later than the 15th day of the month following the reporting month:

(1) shall report to the court or monitor reports made to the court on:

(A) the amount of child support collected as a percentage of the amount ordered; and

(B) efforts to ensure compliance with orders relating to possession of or access to a child; and

(2) may file an action to enforce, clarify, or modify a court order relating to child support or possession of or access to a child.

(c) A friend of the court may file a notice of delinquency and a request for a writ of income withholding under Chapter 158 in order to enforce a child support order.

History of Fam. Code §202.002: Acts 1995, 74th Leg., ch. 20, §1, eff. Apr. 20, 1995. Amended by Acts 1995, 74th Leg., ch. 751, §81, eff. Sept. 1, 1995; Acts 1997, 75th Leg., ch. 702, §9, eff. Sept. 1, 1997; Acts 2003, 78th Leg., ch. 892, §21, eff. Sept. 1, 2003. Source: Former Fam. Code §14.92.

FAM §202.003. DUTY OF LOCAL OFFICES & OFFICIALS TO REPORT

A local domestic relations office, a local registry, or a court official designated to receive child support under a court order shall, if ordered by the court, report to the court or a friend of the court on a monthly basis:

(1) any delinquency and arrearage in child support payments; and

(2) any violation of an order relating to possession of or access to a child.

History of Fam. Code §202.003: Acts 1995, 74th Leg., ch. 20, §1, eff. Apr. 20, 1995. Source: Former Fam. Code §14.93.

FAM §202.004. ACCESS TO INFORMATION

A friend of the court may arrange access to child support payment records by electronic means if the records are computerized.

History of Fam. Code §202.004: Acts 1995, 74th Leg., ch. 20, §1, eff. Apr. 20, 1995. Source: Former Fam. Code §14.94.

FAM §202.005. COMPENSATION

(a) A friend of the court is entitled to compensation for services rendered and for expenses incurred in rendering the services.

(b) The court may assess the amount that the friend of the court receives in compensation against a party to the suit in the same manner as the court awards costs under Chapter 106.

(c) A friend of the court or a person who acts as the court's custodian of child support records, including the clerk of a court, may apply for and receive funds from the child support and court management account under Section 21.007, Government Code.

(d) A friend of the court who receives funds under Subsection (c) shall use the funds to reimburse any compensation the friend of the court received under Subsection (b).

History of Fam. Code §202.005: Acts 1995, 74th Leg., ch. 20, §1, eff. Apr. 20, 1995. Source: Former Fam. Code §14.95.

CHAPTER 203. DOMESTIC RELATIONS OFFICES

FAM §203.001. DEFINITIONS

In this chapter:

(1) "Administering entity" means a commissioners court, juvenile board, or other entity responsible for administering a domestic relations office under this chapter.

(2) "Domestic relations office" means a county office that serves families, county departments, and courts to ensure effective implementation of this title.

History of Fam. Code §203.001: Acts 1995, 74th Leg., ch. 20, §1, eff. Apr. 20, 1995. Amended by Acts 1995, 74th Leg., ch. 475, §1, eff. Sept. 1, 1995. Source: Former Hum. Res. Code §151.003(a).

FAM §203.002. ESTABLISHMENT OF DOMESTIC RELATIONS OFFICE

A commissioners court may establish a domestic relations office.

History of Fam. Code §203.002: Acts 1995, 74th Leg., ch. 20, §1, eff. Apr. 20, 1995. Renumbered from §203.003 and amended by Acts 1995, 74th Leg., ch. 475, §1, eff. Sept. 1, 1995. Source: Former Hum. Res. Code §151.001.

FAM §203.003. ADMINISTRATION

(a) A domestic relations office shall be administered:

(1) as provided by the commissioners court; or

(2) if the commissioners court does not otherwise provide for the administration of the office, by the juvenile board that serves the county in which the domestic relations office is located.

(b) The administering entity shall appoint and assign the duties of a director who shall be responsible for the day-to-day administration of the office. A director serves at the pleasure of the administering entity.

(c) The administering entity shall determine the amount of money needed to operate the office.

(d) A commissioners court that establishes a domestic relations office under this chapter may execute a bond for the office. A bond under this subsection must be:

(1) executed with a solvent surety company authorized to do business in the state; and

(2) conditioned on the faithful performance of the duties of the office.

(e) The administering entity shall establish procedures for the acceptance and use of a grant or donation to the office.

History of Fam. Code §203.003: Acts 1995, 74th Leg., ch. 20, §1, eff. Apr. 20, 1995. Renumbered from §203.004 and amended by Acts 1995, 74th Leg., ch. 475, §1, eff. Sept. 1, 1995. Source: Former Hum. Res. Code §151.002(a).

FAM §203.004. POWERS & DUTIES

(a) A domestic relations office may:

(1) collect and disburse child support payments that are ordered by a court to be paid through a domestic relations registry;

(2) maintain records of payments and disbursements made under Subdivision (1);

(3) file a suit, including a suit to:

(A) establish paternity;

(B) enforce a court order for child support or for possession of and access to a child; and

(C) modify or clarify an existing child support order;

(4) provide an informal forum in which alternative dispute resolution is used to resolve disputes under this code;

(5) prepare a court-ordered child custody evaluation or adoption evaluation under Chapter 107;

(6) represent a child as an amicus attorney, an attorney ad litem, or a guardian ad litem in a suit in which:

(A) termination of the parent-child relationship is sought; or

(B) conservatorship of or access to a child is contested;

(7) serve as a friend of the court;

(8) provide predivorce counseling ordered by a court;

(9) provide community supervision services under Chapter 157;

(10) provide information to assist a party in understanding, complying with, or enforcing the party's duties and obligations under Subdivision (3);

(11) provide, directly or through a contract, visitation services, including supervision of court-ordered visitation, visitation exchange, or other similar services;

(12) issue an administrative writ of withholding under Subchapter F, Chapter 158; and

(13) provide parenting coordinator services under Chapter 153.

(b) A court having jurisdiction in a proceeding under this title, Title 3, or Section 25.05, Penal Code, may order that child support payments be made through a domestic relations office.

(c) A domestic relations office may:

(1) hire or contract for the services of attorneys to assist the office in providing services under this chapter; and

(2) employ community supervision officers or court monitors.

History of Fam. Code §203.004: Acts 1995, 74th Leg., ch. 20, §1, eff. Apr. 20, 1995. Renumbered from §203.005 and amended by Acts 1995, 74th Leg., ch. 475, §1, eff. Sept. 1, 1995. Amended by Acts 1997, 75th Leg., ch. 702, §10, eff. Sept. 1, 1997; Acts 1999, 76th Leg., ch. 859, §3 (eff. Sept. 1, 1999), ch. 1191, §1 (eff. June 19, 1999); Acts 2001, 77th Leg., ch. 1023, §50, eff. Sept. 1, 2001; Acts 2005, 79th Leg., ch. 172, §20 (eff. Sept. 1, 2005), ch. 199, §5 (eff. Sept. 1, 2005); Acts 2007, 80th Leg., ch. 832, §7, eff. Sept. 1, 2007; Acts 2015, 84th Leg., ch. 1252, §3.05, eff. Sept. 1, 2015. Source: Former Hum. Res. Code §151.004.

FAM §203.005. FEES & CHARGES

(a) The administering entity may authorize a domestic relations office to assess and collect:

(1) an initial operations fee not to exceed $15 to be paid to the domestic relations office on each filing of an original suit, motion for modification, or motion for enforcement;

(2) in a county that has a child support enforcement cooperative agreement with the Title IV-D agency, an initial child support service fee not to exceed $36 to be paid to the domestic relations office on the filing of an original suit;

(3) a reasonable application fee to be paid by an applicant requesting services from the office;

(4) a reasonable attorney's fee and court costs incurred or ordered by the court;

(5) a monthly service fee not to exceed $3 to be paid annually in advance by a managing conservator and possessory conservator for whom the domestic relations office provides child support services;

(6) community supervision fees as provided by Chapter 157 if community supervision officers are employed by the domestic relations office;

(7) a reasonable fee for preparation of a court-ordered child custody evaluation or adoption evaluation;

(8) in a county that provides visitation services under Sections 153.014 and 203.004 a reasonable fee to be paid to the domestic relations office at the time the visitation services are provided;

(9) a fee to reimburse the domestic relations office for a fee required to be paid under Section 158.503(d) for filing an administrative writ of withholding;

(10) a reasonable fee for parenting coordinator services; and

(11) a reasonable fee for alternative dispute resolution services.

(b) The first payment of a fee under Subsection (a)(5) is due on the date that the person required to pay support is ordered to begin child support, alimony, or separate maintenance payments. Subsequent payments of the fee are due annually and in advance.

(c) The director of a domestic relations office shall attempt to collect all fees in an efficient manner.

(d) The administering entity may provide for an exemption from the payment of a fee authorized under this section if payment of the fee is not practical or in the interest of justice. Fees that may be exempted under this subsection include fees related to:

(1) spousal and child support payments made under an interstate pact;

(2) a suit brought by the Texas Department of Human Services;

(3) activities performed by the Department of Protective and Regulatory Services or another governmental agency, a private adoption agency, or a charitable organization; and

(4) services for a person who has applied for or who receives public assistance under the laws of this state.

(e) A fee authorized by this section for providing child support services is part of the child support obligation and may be enforced against both an obligor and obligee by any method available for the enforcement of child support, including contempt.

History of Fam. Code §203.005: Acts 1995, 74th Leg., ch. 20, §1, eff. Apr. 20, 1995. Renumbered from §203.009 and amended by Acts 1995, 74th Leg., ch. 475, §1, eff. Sept. 1, 1995. Amended by Acts 1999, 76th Leg., ch. 556, §48, eff. Sept. 1, 1999; Acts 2001, 77th Leg., ch. 1023, §51, eff. Sept. 1, 2001; Acts 2003, 78th Leg., ch. 707, §1 (eff. Sept. 1, 2003), ch. 1076, §1 (eff. Sept. 1, 2003); Acts 2005, 79th Leg., ch. 199, §6, eff. Sept. 1, 2005; Acts 2007, 80th Leg., ch. 832, §8, eff. Sept. 1, 2007; Acts 2009, 81st Leg., ch. 767, §26 (eff. June 19, 2009), ch. 1035, §2 (eff. June 19, 2009); Acts 2011, 82nd Leg., ch. 1341, §10, eff. June 17, 2011; Acts 2015, 84th Leg., ch. 1252, §3.06, eff. Sept. 1, 2015. Source: Former Hum. Res. Code §151.008.

FAM §203.006. FUND

(a) As determined by the administering entity, fees collected or received by a domestic relations office shall be deposited in:

(1) the general fund for the county in which the domestic relations office is located; or

(2) the office fund established for the domestic relations office.

(b) The administering entity shall use the domestic relations office fund to provide money for services authorized by this chapter.

(c) A domestic relations office fund may be supplemented as necessary from the county's general fund or from other money available from the county.

History of Fam. Code §203.006: Acts 1995, 74th Leg., ch. 20, §1, eff. Apr. 20, 1995. Renumbered from §203.010 and amended by Acts 1995, 74th Leg., ch. 475, §1, eff. Sept. 1, 1995. Amended by Acts 1997, 75th Leg., ch. 702, §11, eff. Sept. 1, 1997. Source: Former Hum. Res. Code §151.009.

FAM §203.007. ACCESS TO RECORDS; OFFENSE

(a) A domestic relations office may obtain the records described by Subsections (b), (c), (d), and (e) that relate to a person who has:

(1) been ordered to pay child support;

(2) been designated as a conservator of a child;

(3) been designated to be the father of a child;

(4) executed an acknowledgment of paternity;

(5) court-ordered possession of a child; or

(6) filed suit to adopt a child.

(b) A domestic relations office is entitled to obtain from the Department of Public Safety records that relate to:

(1) a person's date of birth;

(2) a person's most recent address;

(3) a person's current driver's license status;

(4) motor vehicle accidents involving a person;

(5) reported traffic-law violations of which a person has been convicted; and

(6) a person's criminal history record information.

(c) A domestic relations office is entitled to obtain from the Texas Workforce Commission records that relate to:

(1) a person's address;

(2) a person's employment status and earnings;

(3) the name and address of a person's current or former employer; and

(4) unemployment compensation benefits received by a person.

(d) To the extent permitted by federal law, a domestic relations office is entitled to obtain from the National Directory of New Hires[1] established under 42 U.S.C. Section 653(i), as amended, records that relate to a person described by Subsection (a), including records that relate to:

(1) the name, telephone number, and address of the person's employer;

(2) information provided by the person on a W-4 form; and

(3) information provided by the person's employer on a Title IV-D form.

(e) To the extent permitted by federal law, a domestic relations office is entitled to obtain from the state case registry records that relate to a person described by Subsection (a), including records that relate to:

(1) the street and mailing address and the social security number of the person;

(2) the name, telephone number, and address of the person's employer;

(3) the location and value of real and personal property owned by the person; and

(4) the name and address of each financial institution in which the person maintains an account and the account number for each account.

(f) An agency required to provide records under this section may charge a domestic relations office a fee for providing the records in an amount that does not exceed the amount paid for those records by the agency responsible for Title IV-D cases.

(g) The Department of Public Safety, the Texas Workforce Commission, or the office of the secretary of state may charge a domestic relations office a fee not to exceed the charge paid by the Title IV-D agency for furnishing records under this section.

(h) Information obtained by a domestic relations office under this section that is confidential under a constitution, statute, judicial decision, or rule is privileged and may be used only by that office.

(i) A person commits an offense if the person releases or discloses confidential information obtained under this section without the consent of the person to whom the information relates. An offense under this subsection is a Class C misdemeanor.

(j) A domestic relations office is entitled to obtain from the office of the secretary of state the following information about a registered voter to the extent that the information is available:

(1) complete name;

(2) current and former street and mailing address;

(3) sex;

(4) date of birth;

(5) social security number; and

(6) telephone number.

1. **Editor's note:** Acts 1999, 76th Leg., ch. 859, §4 does not capitalize "National Directory of New Hires."

History of Fam. Code §203.007: Acts 1995, 74th Leg., ch. 20, §1, eff. Apr. 20, 1995. Renumbered from §203.012 and amended by Acts 1995, 74th Leg., ch. 475, §1, eff. Sept. 1, 1995. Amended by Acts 1995, 74th Leg., ch. 803, §1, eff. Sept. 1, 1995; Acts 1997, 75th Leg., ch. 165, §7.18, eff. Sept. 1, 1997; Acts 1999, 76th Leg., ch. 556, §49 (eff. Sept. 1, 1999), ch. 859, §4 (eff. Sept. 1, 1999), ch. 1191, §2 (eff. June 19, 1999); Acts 2007, 80th Leg., ch. 832, §9, eff. Sept. 1, 2007. Source: Former Hum. Res. Code §151.011.

FAM §203.008. DELETED

Deleted by Acts 1995, 74th Leg., ch. 475, §1, eff. Sept. 1, 1995.

FAM §§203.009, 203.010. RENUMBERED

Renumbered as §§203.005, 203.006 by Acts 1995, 74th Leg., ch. 475, §1, eff. Sept. 1, 1995.

FAM §203.011. DELETED

Deleted by Acts 1995, 74th Leg., ch. 475, §1, eff. Sept. 1, 1995.

FAM §203.012. RENUMBERED

Renumbered as §203.007 by Acts 1995, 74th Leg., ch. 475, §1, eff. Sept. 1, 1995.

CHAPTER 204. CHILD SUPPORT COLLECTION BY PRIVATE ENTITY

FAM §204.001. APPLICABILITY

This chapter applies only to a commissioners court or domestic relations office of a county that did not have the authority to contract with a private entity to receive, disburse, and record payments or restitution of child support on January 1, 1997.

History of Fam. Code §204.001: Acts 1997, 75th Leg., ch. 1053, §1, eff. Sept. 1, 1997. Redesignated and amended by Acts 1999, 76th Leg., ch. 118, §1, eff. Sept. 1, 1999. Amended by Acts 2005, 79th Leg., ch. 740, §3, eff. June 17, 2005. Source: Former Hum. Res. Code §153.001.

FAM §204.002. AUTHORITY TO CONTRACT

A county, acting through its commissioners court or domestic relations office, may contract with a private entity to:

(1) enforce, collect, receive, and disburse:

(A) child support payments;

(B) other amounts due under a court order containing an order to pay child support; and

(C) fees, including fees provided by this chapter;

(2) maintain appropriate records, including records of child support and other amounts and fees that are due, past due, paid, or delinquent;

(3) locate absent parents;

(4) furnish statements to parents accounting for payments that are due, past due, paid, or delinquent;

(5) send billings and other appropriate notices to parents;

(6) perform any duty or function that a local registry is authorized to perform;

(7) perform any duty or function in connection with the state case registry; or

(8) provide another child support or visitation enforcement service authorized by the commissioners court, including mediation of disputes related to child support or visitation.

History of Fam. Code §204.002: Acts 1997, 75th Leg., ch. 1053, §1, eff. Sept. 1, 1997. Redesignated and amended by Acts 1999, 76th Leg., ch. 118, §1, eff. Sept. 1, 1999. Source: Former Hum. Res. Code §153.002.

FAM §204.003. TERMS & CONDITIONS OF CONTRACT

The commissioners court or domestic relations office shall include all appropriate terms and conditions in the contract that it determines are reasonable to secure the services of a private entity as provided by this chapter, including:

(1) provisions specifying the services to be provided by the entity;

(2) the method, conditions, and amount of compensation for the entity;

(3) provisions for the security of funds collected as child support, fees, or other amounts under the contract or that otherwise provide reasonable assurance to the county of the entity's full and faithful performance of the contract;

(4) provisions specifying the records to be kept by the entity, including any records necessary to fully account for all funds received and disbursed as child support, fees, or other amounts;

(5) requirements governing the inspection, verification, audit, or explanation of the entity's accounting or other records;

(6) the county's right to terminate the contract on 30 days' notice to the private entity if the private entity engages in an ongoing pattern of child support enforcement that constitutes wilful and gross misconduct subjecting delinquent obligors to unconscionable duress, abuse, or harassment;

(7) provisions permitting an obligor and obligee to jointly waive the monitoring procedure, if not required by law, by written request approved by order of the court having jurisdiction of the suit in which the child support order was issued; and

(8) provisions for the disclosure or nondisclosure of information or records maintained or known to the entity as a result of contract performance, including a requirement for the private entity to:

(A) disclose to any child support obligor that the private entity is attempting to enforce the obligor's child support obligation; and

(B) make no disclosure of the information or records other than in furtherance of the effort to enforce the child support order.

History of Fam. Code §204.003: Acts 1997, 75th Leg., ch. 1053, §1, eff. Sept. 1, 1997. Redesignated and amended by Acts 1999, 76th Leg., ch. 118, §1, eff. Sept. 1, 1999. Source: Former Hum. Res. Code §153.003.

FAM §204.004. FUNDING

(a) To provide or recover the costs of providing services authorized by this chapter, a commissioners court, on its behalf or on behalf of the domestic relations office, may:

(1) provide by order for the assessment and collection of a reasonable fee at the time a party files a suit affecting the parent-child relationship;

(2) provide by order for the assessment and collection of a fee of $3 per month at a time specified for payment of child support;

(3) provide by order for the assessment and collection of a late payment fee of $4 per month to be imposed if an obligor does not make a payment of child support in full when due;

(4) accept or receive funds from public grants or private sources available for providing services authorized by this chapter; or

(5) use any combination of funding sources specified by this subsection.

(b) The commissioners court, on its behalf or on behalf of the domestic relations office, may:

(1) provide by order for reasonable exemptions from the collection of fees authorized by Subsection (a); and

(2) require payment of a fee authorized by Subsection (a)(2) annually and in advance.

(c) The commissioners court may not charge a fee under Subsection (a)(2) if the amount of child support ordered to be paid is less than the equivalent of $100 per month.

(d) The fees established under Subsection (a) may be collected by any means provided for the collection of child support. The commissioners court may provide by order, on its behalf or on behalf of the domestic relations office, for the manner of collection of fees and the apportionment of payments received to meet fee obligations.

History of Fam. Code §204.004: Acts 1997, 75th Leg., ch. 1053, §1, eff. Sept. 1, 1997. Redesignated and amended by Acts 1999, 76th Leg., ch. 118, §1, eff. Sept. 1, 1999. Source: Former Hum. Res. Code §153.004.

FAM §204.005. CUMULATIVE EFFECT OF CHAPTER

A power or duty conferred on a county, county official, or county instrumentality by this chapter is cumulative of the powers and duties created or conferred by other law.

History of Fam. Code §204.005: Acts 1997, 75th Leg., ch. 1053, §1, eff. Sept. 1, 1997. Redesignated and amended by Acts 1999, 76th Leg., ch. 118, §1, eff. Sept. 1, 1999. Source: Former Hum. Res. Code §153.005.

Chapters 205-230 reserved for expansion

SUBTITLE D. ADMINISTRATIVE SERVICES

CHAPTER 231. TITLE IV-D SERVICES

SUBCHAPTER A. ADMINISTRATION OF TITLE IV-D PROGRAM

FAM §231.001. DESIGNATION OF TITLE IV-D AGENCY

The office of the attorney general is designated as the state's Title IV-D agency.

History of Fam. Code §231.001: Acts 1995, 74th Leg., ch. 20, §1, eff. Apr. 20, 1995. Source: Former Hum. Res. Code §76.001.

FAM §231.0011. DEVELOPMENT OF STATEWIDE INTEGRATED SYSTEM FOR CHILD SUPPORT & MEDICAL SUPPORT ENFORCEMENT[1]

(a) The Title IV-D agency shall have final approval authority on any contract or proposal for delivery of Title IV-D services under this section and in coordination with the Texas Judicial Council, the Office of Court Administration of the Texas Judicial System, the federal Office of Child Support Enforcement, and state, county, and local officials, shall develop and implement a statewide integrated system for child support and medical support enforcement, employing federal, state, local, and private resources to:

(1) unify child support registry functions;

(2) record and track all child support orders entered in the state;

(3) establish an automated enforcement process which will use delinquency monitoring, billing, and other enforcement techniques to ensure the payment of current support;

(4) incorporate existing enforcement resources into the system to obtain maximum benefit from state and federal funding; and

(5) ensure accountability for all participants in the process, including state, county, and local officials, private contractors, and the judiciary.

(b) Counties and other providers of child support services shall be required, as a condition of participation in the unified system, to enter into a contract with the Title IV-D agency, to comply with all federal requirements for the Title IV-D program, and to maintain at least the current level of funding for activities which are proposed to be included in the integrated child support system.

(c) The Title IV-D agency may contract with any county meeting technical system requirements necessary to comply with federal law for provision of Title IV-D services in that county. All new cases in which support orders are entered in such county after the effective date of a monitoring contract shall be Title IV-D cases. Any other case in the county, subject to federal requirements and the agreement of the county and the Title IV-D agency, may be included as a Title IV-D case. Any obligee under a support order may refuse Title IV-D enforcement services unless required to accept such services pursuant to other law.

(d) Counties participating in the unified enforcement system shall monitor all child support registry cases and on delinquency may, subject to the approval of the Title IV-D agency, provide enforcement services through:

(1) direct provision of services by county personnel;

(2) subcontracting all or portions of the services to private entities or attorneys; or

(3) such other methods as may be approved by the Title IV-D agency.

(e) The Title IV-D agency may phase in the integrated child support registry and enforcement system, and the requirement to implement the system shall be contingent on the receipt of locally generated funds and federal reimbursement. Locally generated funds include but are not limited to funds contributed by counties and cities.

(f) The Title IV-D agency shall adopt rules to implement this section.

(g) Participation in the statewide integrated system for child support and medical support enforcement by a county is voluntary, and nothing in this section shall be construed to mandate participation.

(h) This section does not limit the ability of the Title IV-D agency to enter into an agreement with a county for the provision of services as authorized under Section 231.002.

1. **Editor's note:** In 2015, the Legislature amended §231.0011 to require dental support for a child subject to a child-support order, but the amendments are not effective until Sept. 1, 2018. For the text of the prospective amendments, see Acts 2015, 84th Leg., ch. 1150, §§40, 41, eff. Sept. 1, 2018.

History of Fam. Code §231.0011: Acts 1995, 74th Leg., ch. 341, §1.01, eff. Sept. 1, 1995. Amended by Acts 1997, 75th Leg., ch. 702, §12, eff. Sept. 1, 1997; Acts 1999, 76th Leg., ch. 556, §50, eff. Sept. 1, 1999.

FAM §231.0012. CHILD SUPPORT ENFORCEMENT MANAGEMENT

The person appointed by the attorney general as the person responsible for managing the Title IV-D agency's child support enforcement duties shall report directly to the attorney general.

History of Fam. Code §231.0012: Acts 1997, 75th Leg., ch. 420, §16, eff. Sept. 1, 1997.

FAM §231.0013. DEDICATION OF FUNDS

Appropriations made to the Title IV-D agency for child support enforcement may be expended only for the purposes for which the money was appropriated.

History of Fam. Code §231.0013: Acts 1997, 75th Leg., ch. 420, §16, eff. Sept. 1, 1997.

FAM §231.002. POWERS & DUTIES[1]

(a) The Title IV-D agency may:

(1) accept, transfer, and expend funds, subject to the General Appropriations Act, made available by the federal or state government or by another public or private source for the purpose of carrying out this chapter;

(2) adopt rules for the provision of child support services;

(3) initiate legal actions needed to implement this chapter; and

(4) enter into contracts or agreements necessary to administer this chapter.

(b) The Title IV-D agency may perform the duties and functions necessary for locating children under agreements with the federal government as provided by 42 U.S.C. Section 663.

(c) The Title IV-D agency may enter into agreements or contracts with federal, state, or other public or private agencies or individuals for the purpose of carrying out the agency's responsibilities under federal or state law. The agreements or contracts between the agency and other state agencies or political subdivisions of this or another state, including a consortia of multiple states, and agreements or contracts with vendors for the delivery of program services are not subject to Chapter 771 or 783, Government Code.

(d) Consistent with federal law and any international treaty or convention to which the United States is a party and that has been ratified by the United States Congress, the Title IV-D agency may:

(1) on approval by and in cooperation with the governor, pursue negotiations and enter into reciprocal arrangements with the federal government, another state, or a foreign country or a political subdivision of the federal government, state, or foreign country to:

(A) establish and enforce child support obligations; and

(B) establish mechanisms to enforce an order providing for possession of or access to a child rendered under Chapter 153;

(2) spend money appropriated to the agency for child support enforcement to engage in international child support enforcement; and

(3) spend other money appropriated to the agency necessary for the agency to conduct the agency's activities under Subdivision (1).

(e) The Title IV-D agency may take the following administrative actions with respect to the location of a parent, the determination of parentage, and the establishment, modification, and enforcement of child support and medical support orders required by 42 U.S.C. Section 666(c), without obtaining an order from any other judicial or administrative tribunal:

(1) issue an administrative subpoena, as provided by Section 231.303, to obtain financial or other information;

(2) order genetic testing for parentage determination, as provided by Chapter 233;

(3) order income withholding, as provided by Chapter 233, and issue an administrative writ of withholding, as provided by Chapter 158; and

(4) take any action with respect to execution, collection, and release of a judgment or lien for child support necessary to satisfy the judgment or lien, as provided by Chapter 157.

(f) The Title IV-D agency shall recognize and enforce the authority of the Title IV-D agency of another state to take actions similar to the actions listed in this section.

(g) The Title IV-D agency shall develop and use procedures for the administrative enforcement of interstate cases meeting the requirements of 42 U.S.C. Section 666(a)(14) under which the agency:

(1) shall promptly respond to a request made by another state for assistance in a Title IV-D case; and

(2) may, by electronic or other means, transmit to another state a request for assistance in a Title IV-D case.

(h) Repealed by Acts 2009, 81st Leg., ch. 164, §3, eff. May 26, 2009.

(i) The Title IV-D agency may provide a release or satisfaction of a judgment for all or part of the amount of the arrearages assigned to the Title IV-D agency under Section 231.104(a).

(j) In the enforcement or modification of a child support order, the Title IV-D agency is not:

(1) subject to a mediation or arbitration clause or requirement in the order to which the Title IV-D agency was not a party; or

(2) liable for any costs associated with mediation or arbitration arising from provisions in the order or another agreement of the parties.

1. **Editor's note:** In 2015, the Legislature amended §231.002 to require dental support for a child subject to a child-support order, but the amendments are not effective until Sept. 1, 2018. For the text of the prospective amendments, see Acts 2015, 84th Leg., ch. 1150, §42, eff. Sept. 1, 2018.

History of Fam. Code §231.002: Acts 1995, 74th Leg., ch. 20, §1, eff. Apr. 20, 1995. Amended by Acts 1997, 75th Leg., ch. 874, §1 (eff. Sept. 1, 1997), ch. 911, §68 (eff. Sept. 1, 1997); Acts 1999, 76th Leg., ch. 62, §6.27 (eff. Sept. 1, 1999), ch. 556, §51 (eff. Sept. 1, 1999); Acts 2003, 78th Leg., ch. 310, §1 (eff. Sept. 1, 2003), ch. 610, §12 (eff. Sept. 1, 2003); Acts 2009, 81st Leg., ch. 164, §3, eff. May 26, 2009; Acts 2013, 83rd Leg., ch. 742, §9, eff. Sept. 1, 2013. Source: Former Hum. Res. Code §§76.002(a), (d), (f), 76.004(b).

See also 1 T.A.C. ch. 55.

FAM §231.003. FORMS & PROCEDURES

The Title IV-D agency shall by rule promulgate any forms and procedures necessary to comply fully with the intent of this chapter.

History of Fam. Code §231.003: Acts 1995, 74th Leg., ch. 20, §1, eff. Apr. 20, 1995. Source: Former Fam. Code §14.86.

See also 1 T.A.C. §§55.111-55.121.

FAM §231.004. REPEALED

Repealed by Acts 1997, 75th Leg., ch. 911, §97(a), eff. Sept. 1, 1997.

FAM §231.005. BIENNIAL REPORT REQUIRED

(a) The Title IV-D agency shall report to the legislature each biennium on:

(1) the effectiveness of the agency's child support enforcement activity in reducing the state's public assistance obligations; and

(2) the use and effectiveness of all enforcement tools authorized by state or federal law or otherwise available to the agency.

(b) The agency shall develop a method for estimating the costs and benefits of the child support enforcement program and the effect of the program on appropriations for public assistance.

History of Fam. Code §231.005: Acts 1995, 74th Leg., ch. 20, §1, eff. Apr. 20, 1995. Amended by Acts 1999, 76th Leg., ch. 556, §51, eff. Sept. 1, 1999; Acts 2011, 82nd Leg., ch. 990, §2, eff. June 17, 2011. Source: Former Hum. Res. Code §76.002(i).

FAM §231.006. INELIGIBILITY TO RECEIVE STATE GRANTS OR LOANS OR RECEIVE PAYMENT ON STATE CONTRACTS

(a) A child support obligor who is more than 30 days delinquent in paying child support and a business entity in which the obligor is a sole proprietor, partner, shareholder, or owner with an ownership interest of at least 25 percent is not eligible to:

(1) receive payments from state funds under a contract to provide property, materials, or services; or

(2) receive a state-funded grant or loan.

(a-1) Repealed by Acts 2007, 80th Leg., ch. 972, §65(1), eff. Sept. 1, 2007.

(b) A child support obligor or business entity ineligible to receive payments under Subsection (a) remains ineligible until:

(1) all arrearages have been paid;

(2) the obligor is in compliance with a written repayment agreement or court order as to any existing delinquency; or

(3) the court of continuing jurisdiction over the child support order has granted the obligor an exemption from Subsection (a) as part of a court-supervised effort to improve earnings and child support payments.

(c) A bid or an application for a contract, grant, or loan paid from state funds must include the name and social security number of the individual or sole proprietor and each partner, shareholder, or owner with an ownership interest of at least 25 percent of the business entity submitting the bid or application.

(d) A contract, bid, or application subject to the requirements of this section must include the following statement:

"Under Section 231.006, Family Code, the vendor or applicant certifies that the individual or business entity named in this contract, bid, or application is not ineligible to receive the specified grant, loan, or payment and acknowledges that this contract may be terminated and payment may be withheld if this certification is inaccurate."

(e) If a state agency determines that an individual or business entity holding a state contract is ineligible

to receive payment under Subsection (a), the contract may be terminated.

(f) If the certificate required under Subsection (d) is shown to be false, the vendor is liable to the state for attorney's fees, the costs necessary to complete the contract, including the cost of advertising and awarding a second contract, and any other damages provided by law or contract.

(g) This section does not create a cause of action to contest a bid or award of a state grant, loan, or contract. This section does not impose a duty on the Title IV-D agency to collect information to send to the comptroller to withhold a payment to a business entity. The Title IV-D agency and other affected agencies are encouraged to develop a system by which the Title IV-D agency may identify a business entity that is ineligible to receive a state payment under Subsection (a) and to ensure that a state payment to the entity is not made. This system should be implemented using existing funds and only if the Title IV-D agency, comptroller, and other affected agencies determine that it will be cost-effective.

(h) This section does not apply to a contract between governmental entities.

(i) The Title IV-D agency may adopt rules or prescribe forms to implement any provision of this section.

(j) A state agency may accept a bid that does not include the information required under Subsection (c) if the state agency collects the information before the contract, grant, or loan is executed.

History of Fam. Code §231.006: Acts 1995, 74th Leg., ch. 20, §1, eff. Apr. 20, 1995. Amended by Acts 1995, 74th Leg., ch. 751, §82, eff. Sept. 1, 1995; Acts 1999, 76th Leg., ch. 28, §1, eff. Sept. 1, 1999; Acts 2003, 78th Leg., ch. 437, §1 (eff. Sept. 1, 2003), ch. 1015, §2 (eff. Sept. 1, 2003); Acts 2007, 80th Leg., ch. 972, §§45, 65(1), eff. Sept. 1, 2007. Source: Former Fam. Code §14.52.

FAM §231.007. DEBTS TO STATE

(a) A person obligated to pay child support in a case in which the Title IV-D agency is providing services under this chapter who does not pay the required support is indebted to the state for the purposes of Section 403.055, Government Code, if the Title IV-D agency has reported the person to the comptroller under that section properly.

(b) The amount of a person's indebtedness to the state under Subsection (a) is equal to the sum of:

(1) the amount of the required child support that has not been paid; and

(2) any interest, fees, court costs, or other amounts owed by the person because the person has not paid the support.

(c) The Title IV-D agency is the sole assignee of all payments, including payments of compensation, by the state to a person indebted to the state under Subsection (a).

(d) On request of the Title IV-D agency:

(1) the comptroller shall make payable and deliver to the agency any payments for which the agency is the assignee under Subsection (c), if the comptroller is responsible for issuing warrants or initiating electronic funds transfers to make those payments; and

(2) a state agency shall make payable and deliver to the Title IV-D agency any payments for which the Title IV-D agency is the assignee under Subsection (c) if the comptroller is not responsible for issuing warrants or initiating electronic funds transfers to make those payments.

(e) A person indebted to the state under Subsection (a) may eliminate the debt by:

(1) paying the entire amount of the debt; or

(2) resolving the debt in a manner acceptable to the Title IV-D agency.

(f) The comptroller or a state agency may rely on a representation by the Title IV-D agency that:

(1) a person is indebted to the state under Subsection (a); or

(2) a person who was indebted to the state under Subsection (a) has eliminated the debt.

(g) Except as provided by Subsection (h), the payment of workers' compensation benefits to a person indebted to the state under Subsection (a) is the same for the purposes of this section as any other payment made to the person by the state. Notwithstanding Section 408.203, Labor Code, an order or writ to withhold income from workers' compensation benefits is not required before the benefits are withheld or assigned under this section.

(h) The amount of weekly workers' compensation benefits that may be withheld or assigned under this section may not exceed 50 percent of the person's weekly compensation benefits. The comptroller or a state agency may rely on a representation by the Title IV-D agency that a withholding or assignment under this section would not violate this subsection.

(i) Section 403.055(d), Government Code, does not authorize the comptroller to issue a warrant or initiate

an electronic funds transfer to pay the compensation or remuneration of an individual who is indebted to the state under Subsection (a).

(j) Section 2107.008(h), Government Code, does not authorize a state agency to pay the compensation or remuneration of an individual who is indebted to the state under Subsection (a).

(k) In this section, "compensation," "state agency," and "state officer or employee" have the meanings assigned by Section 403.055, Government Code.

History of Fam. Code §231.007: Acts 1995, 74th Leg., ch. 20, §1, eff. Apr. 20, 1995. Amended by Acts 1995, 74th Leg., ch. 751, §83, eff. Sept. 1, 1995; Acts 1997, 75th Leg., ch. 165, §7.19, eff. Sept. 1, 1997; Acts 1999, 76th Leg., ch. 1467, §1.07, eff. Jan. 1, 2000; Acts 2001, 77th Leg., ch. 1158, §6, eff. June 15, 2001; Acts 2003, 78th Leg., ch. 610, §13, eff. Sept. 1, 2003. Source: Former Hum. Res. Code §76.0041.

FAM §231.008. DISPOSITION OF FUNDS

(a) The Title IV-D agency shall deposit money received under assignments or as fees in a special fund in the state treasury. The agency may spend money in the fund for the administration of this chapter, subject to the General Appropriations Act.

(b) All other money received under this chapter shall be deposited in a special fund in the state treasury.

(c) Sections 403.094 and 403.095, Government Code, do not apply to a fund described by this section.

History of Fam. Code §231.008: Acts 1995, 74th Leg., ch. 20, §1, eff. Apr. 20, 1995. Source: Former Hum. Res. Code §76.005.

FAM §231.009. PAYMENT OF PENALTIES

From funds appropriated for the Title IV-D agency, the agency shall reimburse the Texas Department of Human Services for any penalty assessed under Title IV-A of the federal Social Security Act (42 U.S.C. Section 651 et seq.) that is assessed because of the agency's administration of this chapter.

History of Fam. Code §231.009: Acts 1995, 74th Leg., ch. 20, §1, eff. Apr. 20, 1995. Source: Former Hum. Res. Code §76.008.

FAM §231.010. COOPERATION WITH DEPARTMENT OF PROTECTIVE & REGULATORY SERVICES

(a) In this section, "department" means the Department of Protective and Regulatory Services.

(b) To the extent possible, the Title IV-D agency shall:

(1) provide to the department access to all of the Title IV-D agency's available child support locating resources;

(2) allow the department to use the Title IV-D agency's child support enforcement system to track child support payments and to have access to the agency's management reports that show payments made;

(3) make reports on Title IV-E, Social Security Act (42 U.S.C. Section 670 et seq.), foster care collections available to the department in a timely manner; and

(4) work with the department to obtain child support payments for protective services cases in which the department is responsible for providing care for children under temporary and final orders.

History of Fam. Code §231.010: Acts 1999, 76th Leg., ch. 228, §1, eff. Sept. 1, 1999. Amended by Acts 2001, 77th Leg., ch. 1420, §21.001(32), eff. Sept. 1, 2001. Renumbered from §231.011 by Acts 2003, 78th Leg., ch. 1275, §2(53), eff. Sept. 1, 2003.

History of Former Fam. Code §231.010: Repealed by Acts 2001, 77th Leg., ch. 1023, §76, eff. Sept. 1, 2001.

FAM §231.011. REPEALED

Repealed by Acts 2007, 80th Leg., ch. 972, §65(2), eff. Sept. 1, 2007.

FAM §231.012. CHILD SUPPORT WORK GROUP

(a) The director of the Title IV-D agency may convene a work group representing public and private entities with an interest in child support enforcement in this state to work with the director in developing strategies to improve child support enforcement in this state.

(b) The director of the Title IV-D agency shall appoint the members of the work group after consulting with appropriate public and private entities.

(c) The work group shall meet as convened by the director of the Title IV-D agency and consult with the director on matters relating to child support enforcement in this state, including the delivery of Title IV-D services.

(d) A work group member or the member's designee may not receive compensation but is entitled to reimbursement for actual and necessary expenses incurred in performing the member's duties under this section.

(e) The work group is not an advisory committee as defined by Section 2110.001, Government Code. Chapter 2110, Government Code, does not apply to the work group.

History of Fam. Code §231.012: Acts 1999, 76th Leg., ch. 556, §51, eff. Sept. 1, 1999. Amended by Acts 2003, 78th Leg., ch. 1258, §25, eff. Sept. 1, 2003; Acts 2007, 80th Leg., ch. 972, §§46, 47, eff. Sept. 1, 2007.

FAM §231.013. REPEALED

~~[INFORMATION RESOURCES STEERING COMMITTEE]~~

[~~(a)~~] [~~The Title IV-D agency shall create an information resources steering committee to:~~]

[~~(1)~~] [~~oversee information resource project development for the Title IV-D agency;~~]

[~~(2)~~] [~~make strategic prioritization recommendations;~~]

[~~(3)~~] [~~facilitate development of accurate information for the director of the Title IV-D agency; and~~]

[~~(4)~~] [~~perform other functions as determined by the director of the Title IV-D agency.~~]

[~~(b)~~] [~~The steering committee must include a senior management executive representing each significant function of the Title IV-D agency. The steering committee may include a person representing:~~]

[~~(1)~~] [~~counties; or~~]

[~~(2)~~] [~~a vendor contracting with the Title IV-D agency.~~]

[~~(c)~~] [~~The director of the Title IV-D agency shall appoint the members of the steering committee after consulting with the Department of Information Resources.~~]

Repealed by S.B. 526, §5(b), 85th Leg., eff. Sept. 1, 2017.

FAM §231.014. PERSONNEL

The director of the Title IV-D agency shall provide to the employees of the Title IV-D agency, as often as necessary, information regarding the requirements for employment under this title, including information regarding a person's responsibilities under applicable laws relating to standards of conduct for state employees.

History of Fam. Code §231.014: Acts 1999, 76th Leg., ch. 556, §51, eff. Sept. 1, 1999.

A

FAM §231.015. INSURANCE REPORTING PROGRAM

(a) In consultation with the Texas Department of Insurance and representatives of the insurance industry in this state, including insurance trade associations, the Title IV-D agency by rule shall operate a program under which insurers shall cooperate with the Title IV-D agency in identifying obligors who owe child support arrearages and are subject to liens for child support arrearages to intercept certain insurance settlements or awards for claims in satisfaction of the arrearage amounts.

(b) An insurer that provides information or responds to a notice of child support lien or levy under Subchapter G, Chapter 157, or acts in good faith to comply with procedures established by the Title IV-D agency under this section is not liable for those acts under any law to any person.

(c) An insurer may not be required to report or identify the following types of claims:

(1) a first-party property damage claim under:

(A) a personal automobile insurance policy for actual repair, replacement, or loss of use of an insured vehicle; or

(B) a residential or tenant property insurance policy for actual repair, replacement, or loss of use of an insured dwelling and contents, including additional living expenses actually incurred; [~~or~~]

(2) a third-party property damage claim:

(A) that will be paid to a vendor or repair facility for the actual repair, replacement, or loss of use of:

(i) a dwelling, condominium, or other improvements on real property;

(ii) a vehicle, including a motor vehicle, motorcycle, or recreational vehicle; or

(iii) other tangible personal property that has sustained actual damage or loss; or

(B) for the reimbursement to a claimant for payments made by the claimant to a vendor or repair facility for the actual repair, replacement, or loss of use of:

(i) a dwelling, condominium, or other improvements on real property;

(ii) a vehicle, including a motor vehicle, motorcycle, or recreational vehicle; or

(iii) other tangible personal property that has sustained actual damage or loss;

(3) a claim for benefits, or a portion of a claim for benefits, assigned to be paid to a funeral service provider or facility for actual funeral expenses owed by the insured that are not otherwise paid or reimbursed;

(4) a claim for benefits assigned to be paid to a health care provider or facility for actual medical expenses owed by the insured that are not otherwise paid or reimbursed; or

(5) a claim for benefits to be paid under a limited benefit insurance policy that provides:

(A) coverage for one or more specified diseases or illnesses;

(B) dental or vision benefits; or

(C) hospital indemnity or other fixed indemnity coverage.

History of Fam. Code §231.015: Acts 2001, 77th Leg., ch. 1023, §52, eff. Sept. 1, 2001. Amended by Acts 2009, 81st Leg., ch. 767, §27, eff. June 19, 2009; Acts 2011, 82nd Leg., ch. 508, §12, eff. Sept. 1, 2011; Acts 2015, 84th Leg., ch. 1185, §1, eff. June 19, 2015; H.B. 3845, §1, 85th Leg., eff. June 15, 2017.

Sections 231.016-231.100 reserved for expansion

SUBCHAPTER B. SERVICES PROVIDED BY TITLE IV-D PROGRAM

FAM §231.101. TITLE IV-D CHILD SUPPORT SERVICES[1]

(a) The Title IV-D agency may provide all services required or authorized to be provided by Part D of Title IV of the federal Social Security Act (42 U.S.C. Section 651 et seq.), including:

(1) parent locator services;

(2) paternity determination;

(3) child support and medical support establishment;

(4) review and adjustment of child support orders;

(5) enforcement of child support and medical support orders; and

(6) collection and distribution of child support payments.

(b) At the request of either the obligee or obligor, the Title IV-D agency shall review a child support order once every three years and, if appropriate, adjust the support amount to meet the requirements of the child support guidelines under Chapter 154.

(c) Except as notice is included in the child support order, a party subject to a support order shall be provided notice not less than once every three years of the party's right to request that the Title IV-D agency review and, if appropriate, adjust the amount of ordered support.

(d) The Title IV-D agency may review a support order at any time on a showing of a material and substantial change in circumstances, taking into consideration the best interests of the child. If the Title IV-D agency determines that the primary care and possession of the child has changed, the Title IV-D agency may file a petition for modification under Chapter 156.

(e) The Title IV-D agency shall distribute a child support payment received by the agency from an employer within two working days after the date the agency receives the payment.

1. **Editor's note:** In 2015, the Legislature amended §231.101 to require dental support for a child subject to a child-support order, but the amendments are not effective until Sept. 1, 2018. For the text of the prospective amendments, see Acts 2015, 84th Leg., ch. 1150, §43, eff. Sept. 1, 2018.

History of Fam. Code §231.101: Acts 1995, 74th Leg., ch. 20, §1, eff. Apr. 20, 1995. Amended by Acts 1997, 75th Leg., ch. 702, §13 (eff. Sept. 1, 1997), ch. 911, §69 (eff. Sept. 1, 1997); Acts 1999, 76th Leg., ch. 62, §19.01(22), eff. Sept. 1, 1999; Acts 2015, 84th Leg., ch. 963, §2, eff. Sept. 1, 2015. Source: Former Hum. Res. Code §76.002(e).

ANNOTATIONS

In re H.G-J., 503 S.W.3d 679, 682-84 (Tex.App.—Houston [14th Dist.] 2016, no pet.). "The [Office of the Attorney General's (OAG)] argument is ... that the portion of the trial court's final order requiring the OAG to disburse funds to the amicus attorney constituted an injunction—a form of relief that only the Texas Supreme Court is authorized to impose against the OAG [under Gov't Code §22.002]. [¶] Father does not point to any statutory provision providing the trial court with authority to order the OAG to take funds, which were collected for disbursement to Mother for support of the children, and use them to pay the amicus attorney's fees. [¶] Here, the order at issue was a prohibited injunction and did not flow necessarily from the trial court's inherent power over its own judgments. The trial court ordered the OAG to disburse funds to pay the amicus attorney's fees that were neither collected nor held for that purpose. The OAG's authority to collect and distribute child support is statutorily derived [from Fam. Code §231.101(a)(6)]. [S]ection 22.002(c) deprived the trial court of jurisdiction to compel the OAG to disburse child support funds to the amicus attorney. Accordingly, we ... modify the trial court's final order to remove the portion compelling the OAG to disburse child support funds to the amicus attorney."

FAM §231.102. ELIGIBILITY FOR CHILD SUPPORT SERVICES

The Title IV-D agency on application or as otherwise authorized by law may provide services for the benefit of a child without regard to whether the child has received public assistance.

History of Fam. Code §231.102: Acts 1995, 74th Leg., ch. 20, §1, eff. Apr. 20, 1995.

FAM §231.103. APPLICATION & SERVICE FEES

(a) The Title IV-D agency may:

(1) charge a reasonable application fee;

(2) charge a $25 annual service fee; and

(3) to the extent permitted by federal law, recover costs for the services provided in a Title IV-D case.

(b) An application fee may not be charged in a case in which the Title IV-D agency provides services because the family receives public assistance.

(c) An application fee may not exceed a maximum amount established by federal law.

(d) Repealed by Acts 2007, 80th Leg., ch. 972, §65(3), eff. Sept. 1, 2007.

(e) The Title IV-D agency may impose and collect a fee as authorized by federal law for each request for parent locator services under Section 231.101(a).

(f) The state disbursement unit established and operated by the Title IV-D agency under Chapter 234 may collect a monthly service fee of $3 in each case in which support payments are processed through the unit.

(g) The Title IV-D agency by rule shall establish procedures for the imposition of fees and recovery of costs authorized under this section.

(g-1) A fee authorized under this section for providing child support enforcement services is part of the child support obligation if the obligor is responsible for the fee, and may be enforced against the obligor through any method available for the enforcement of child support, including contempt.

(h) The attorney general child support application and service fee account is an account in the general revenue fund in the state treasury. The account consists of all fees and costs collected under this section. The Title IV-D agency may only use the money in the account for agency program expenditures.

History of Fam. Code §231.103: Acts 1995, 74th Leg., ch. 20, §1, eff. Apr. 20, 1995. Amended by Acts 2003, 78th Leg., ch. 1262, §§2, 3, eff. Sept. 1, 2003; Acts 2007, 80th Leg., ch. 972, §§48, 65(3), eff. Sept. 1, 2007. Source: Former Hum. Res. Code §76.004.

FAM §231.104. ASSIGNMENT OF RIGHT TO SUPPORT[1]

(a) To the extent authorized by federal law, the approval of an application for or the receipt of financial assistance as provided by Chapter 31, Human Resources Code, constitutes an assignment to the Title IV-D agency of any rights to support from any other person that the applicant or recipient may have personally or for a child for whom the applicant or recipient is claiming assistance.

(b) An application for child support services is an assignment of support rights to enable the Title IV-D agency to establish and enforce child support and medical support obligations, but an assignment is not a condition of eligibility for services.

1. **Editor's note:** In 2015, the Legislature amended §231.104 to require dental support for a child subject to a child-support order, but the amendments are not effective until Sept. 1, 2018. For the text of the prospective amendments, see Acts 2015, 84th Leg., ch. 1150, §44, eff. Sept. 1, 2018.

History of Fam. Code §231.104: Acts 1995, 74th Leg., ch. 20, §1, eff. Apr. 20, 1995. Amended by Acts 1997, 75th Leg., ch. 911, §70, eff. Sept. 1, 1997; Acts 2001, 77th Leg., ch. 1023, §53, eff. Sept. 1, 2001; Acts 2003, 78th Leg., ch. 610, §14, eff. Sept. 1, 2003. Source: Former Hum. Res. Code §76.003(a).

ANNOTATIONS

In re K.E.T., 974 S.W.2d 760, 762 (Tex.App.—San Antonio 1998, no pet.). "[D]uring the course of the four years that [obligee] was receiving public assistance, she received $11,645 from the State for the support of the children. The law provides that the State is entitled to recoup that amount from child support owed by [obligor]. The State argued that amounts paid to the children by the Social Security Administration can not be used to satisfy [obligor's] debt to the State. [¶] In this case, the arrearages at issue are owed to the State as assignee of [obligee's] right to receive child support obligations. However, under federal law, social security benefits are to be paid directly to the family and may not be assigned. Consequently, if [obligor's] arrearages were to be completely offset by the social security benefits in this case, the State would be left without a remedy because they never could have and cannot collect social security benefits in satisfaction of the assignment. Because [obligor] was obligated to pay his child support obligation directly to the State during the period of assignment, the social security benefits could not be used to satisfy his obligation to the State where those benefits have to be paid directly to the family and are unassignable."

FAM §231.105. NOTICE OF CHANGE OF PAYEE

(a) Child support payments for the benefit of a child whose support rights have been assigned to the Title IV-D agency under Section 231.104 shall be made payable to the Title IV-D agency and transmitted to the state disbursement unit as provided by Chapter 234.

(b) If a court has ordered support payments to be made to an applicant for or recipient of financial assistance or to an applicant for or recipient of Title IV-D services, the Title IV-D agency shall, on providing notice to the obligee and the obligor, direct the obligor or other payor to make support payments payable to the Title IV-D agency and to transmit the payments to the state disbursement unit. The Title IV-D agency shall file a copy of the notice with the court ordering the payments and with the child support registry. The notice must include:

(1) a statement that the child is an applicant for or recipient of financial assistance, or a child other than a recipient child for whom Title IV-D services are provided;

(2) the name of the child and the caretaker for whom support has been ordered by the court;

(3) the style and cause number of the case in which support was ordered; and

(4) instructions for the payment of ordered support to the agency.

(c) On receipt of a copy of the notice under Subsection (b), the clerk of the court shall file the notice in the appropriate case file.

History of Fam. Code §231.105: Acts 1995, 74th Leg., ch. 20, §1, eff. Apr. 20, 1995. Amended by Acts 1997, 75th Leg., ch. 911, §71, eff. Sept. 1, 1997; Acts 2001, 77th Leg., ch. 1023, §54, eff. Sept. 1, 2001. Source: Former Hum. Res. Code §76.003(b).

FAM §231.106. NOTICE OF TERMINATION OF ASSIGNMENT

(a) On termination of support rights to the Title IV-D agency, the Title IV-D agency shall, after providing notice to the obligee and the obligor, send a notice of termination of assignment to the obligor or other payor, which may direct that all or a portion of the payments be made payable to the agency and to other persons who are entitled to receive the payments.

(b) The Title IV-D agency shall send a copy of the notice of termination of assignment to the court ordering the support and to the child support registry, and on receipt of the notice the clerk of the court shall file the notice in the appropriate case file. The clerk may not require an order of the court to terminate the assignment and direct support payments to the person entitled to receive the payment.

History of Fam. Code §231.106: Acts 1995, 74th Leg., ch. 20, §1, eff. Apr. 20, 1995. Amended by Acts 1997, 75th Leg., ch. 911, §72, eff. Sept. 1, 1997; Acts 1999, 76th Leg., ch. 556, §52, eff. Sept. 1, 1999. Source: Former Hum. Res. Code §76.003(e).

FAM §231.107. CERTIFICATE OF ASSIGNMENT OR OF TERMINATION OF ASSIGNMENT

If an abstract of judgment or a child support lien on support amounts assigned to the Title IV-D agency under this chapter has previously been filed of record, the agency shall file for recordation, with the county clerk of each county in which such abstract or lien has been filed, a certificate that a notice of change of payee or a notice of termination of assignment has been issued by the agency.

History of Fam. Code §231.107: Acts 1995, 74th Leg., ch. 20, §1, eff. Apr. 20, 1995. Amended by Acts 1997, 75th Leg., ch. 911, §73, eff. Sept. 1, 1997. Source: Former Hum. Res. Code §76.003(f).

FAM §231.108. CONFIDENTIALITY OF RECORDS & PRIVILEGED COMMUNICATIONS

(a) Except as provided by Subsection (c), all files and records of services provided by the Title IV-D agency under this title, including information concerning a custodial parent, a noncustodial parent, a child, or an alleged or presumed father, are confidential.

(b) Except as provided by Subsection (c), all communications made by a recipient of financial assistance under Chapter 31, Human Resources Code, or an applicant for or recipient of services under this chapter are privileged.

(c) The Title IV-D agency may use or release information from the files and records, including information that results from a communication made by a recipient of financial assistance under Chapter 31, Human Resources Code, or by an applicant for or recipient of services under this chapter, for purposes directly connected with the administration of the child support, paternity determination, parent locator, or aid to families with dependent children programs. The Title IV-D agency may release information from the files and records to a consumer reporting agency in accordance with Section 231.114.

(d) The Title IV-D agency by rule may provide for the release of information to public officials.

(e) The Title IV-D agency may not release information on the physical location of a person if:

(1) a protective order has been entered with respect to the person; or

(2) there is reason to believe that the release of information may result in physical or emotional harm to the person.

(f) The Title IV-D agency, by rule, may provide for the release of information to persons for purposes not prohibited by federal law.

(g) The final order in a suit adjudicating parentage is available for public inspection as provided by Section 160.633.

History of Fam. Code §231.108: Acts 1995, 74th Leg., ch. 20, §1, eff. Apr. 20, 1995. Amended by Acts 1995, 74th Leg., ch. 341, §1.08, eff. Sept. 1, 1995; Acts 1997, 75th Leg., ch. 911, §74, eff. Sept. 1, 1997; Acts 1999, 76th Leg., ch. 556, §53, eff. Sept. 1, 1999; Acts 2003, 78th Leg., ch. 610, §15, eff. Sept. 1, 2003; Acts 2015, 84th Leg., ch. 963, §3, eff. Sept. 1, 2015. Source: Former Hum. Res. Code §76.006.

ANNOTATIONS

Jackson v. State Office of Admin. Hearings, 351 S.W.3d 290, 292 (Tex.2011). Petitioner "requested copies of 'each decision, opinion or order issued by [the

State Office of Administrative Hearings (SOAH)] during [specified] months ... for the Title IV-D Agency of the Office of the Attorney General['] pursuant to [Gov't Code] §552.022(a), which establishes categories of public information that must be disclosed unless an express exception renders the requested information confidential. *At 295:* SOAH argues [that Fam. Code §231.108] provides 'other law' as described in ... §552.022 and makes all the information [petitioner] seeks expressly confidential. [¶] [But petitioner] does not seek disclosure of 'files and records of services,' provided under [Fam. Code] ch. 231 as they are referenced in ... §231.108. Rather, he requested decisions and orders relating to license suspension proceedings. Family Code ch. 232, not 231, governs license suspension proceedings. And ch. 232 does not expressly except an agency's decisions, orders relating to the proceedings, or information in them, from public disclosure. [¶] But we conclude that while §231.108 does not provide a basis to withhold the decisions and orders in their entirety, the statute expressly provides that information obtained during provision of services under Ch. 231 is confidential, 'including information concerning a custodial parent, noncustodial parent, child, and an alleged or presumed father.' To the extent that such information appears within the decisions and orders requested by [petitioner], it must be redacted."

FAM §231.109. ATTORNEYS REPRESENTING STATE

(a) Attorneys employed by the Title IV-D agency may represent this state or another state in an action brought under the authority of federal law or this chapter.

(b) The Title IV-D agency may contract with private attorneys, other private entities, or political subdivisions of the state to provide services in Title IV-D cases.

(c) The Title IV-D agency shall provide copies of all contracts entered into under this section to the Legislative Budget Board and the Governor's Office of Budget and Planning, along with a written justification of the need for each contract, within 60 days after the execution of the contract.

(d) An attorney employed to provide Title IV-D services represents the interest of the state and not the interest of any other party. The provision of services by an attorney under this chapter does not create an attorney-client relationship between the attorney and any other party. The agency shall, at the time an application for child support services is made, inform the applicant that neither the Title IV-D agency nor any attorney who provides services under this chapter is the applicant's attorney and that the attorney providing services under this chapter does not provide legal representation to the applicant.

(e) An attorney employed by the Title IV-D agency or as otherwise provided by this chapter may not be appointed or act as an amicus attorney or attorney ad litem for a child or another party.

History of Fam. Code §231.109: Acts 1995, 74th Leg., ch. 20, §1, eff. Apr. 20, 1995. Amended by Acts 1995, 74th Leg., ch. 341, §1.02, eff. Sept. 1, 1995; Acts 2005, 79th Leg., ch. 172, §21, eff. Sept. 1, 2005. Source: Former Hum. Res. Code §76.007(a)-(e).

ANNOTATIONS

Office of the Atty. Gen. v. Scholer, 403 S.W.3d 859, 862 (Tex.2013). "Though the [Office of the Attorney General (OAG)] has general authority to initiate a suit on a parent's behalf, that authority does not explicitly make the OAG an assignee for purposes of collecting child support directly. Instead, [Fam. Code §231.104] gives the OAG a limited power of assignment in certain cases.... *At 865:* [Family Code §157.008] limits obligors to a single affirmative defense, and a court may not adjust arrearage amounts outside of the statutorily mandated exceptions, offsets, and counterclaims. Because courts are prohibited from making additional adjustments, affirmative defenses that are not included in the statute, like estoppel, are also prohibited because they would require courts to make discretionary determinations. *At 866-67:* A parent's duty of support ... is not a debt owed to the other parent. [¶] Because payment of child support reflects a parent's duty to his child, furthering the child's welfare and best interests, estoppel is not an affirmative defense to a child support enforcement action. A parent who owes that duty must diligently satisfy it. [E]xcept for the very narrow circumstance recognized by law ... he may not rely on the other parent's actions to extinguish his support duty."

FAM §231.110. AUTHORIZATION OF SERVICE

The provision of services by the Title IV-D agency under this chapter or Part D of Title IV of the federal Social Security Act (42 U.S.C. Section 651 et seq.) does not authorize service on the agency of any legal notice that is required to be served on any party other than the agency.

History of Fam. Code §231.110: Acts 1995, 74th Leg., ch. 20, §1, eff. Apr. 20, 1995. Source: Former Hum. Res. Code §76.007(f).

FAM §231.111. DISQUALIFICATION OF AGENCY

A court shall not disqualify the Title IV-D agency in a legal action filed under this chapter or Part D of Title IV of the federal Social Security Act (42 U.S.C. Section 651 et seq.) on the basis that the agency has previously provided services to a party whose interests may now be adverse to the relief requested.

History of Fam. Code §231.111: Acts 1995, 74th Leg., ch. 20, §1, eff. Apr. 20, 1995. Source: Former Hum. Res. Code §76.007(g).

FAM §231.112. INFORMATION ON PATERNITY ESTABLISHMENT

On notification by the state registrar under Section 192.005(d), Health and Safety Code, that the items relating to the child's father are not completed on a birth certificate filed with the state registrar, the Title IV-D agency may provide to:

(1) the child's mother and, if possible, the man claiming to be the child's biological father written information necessary for the man to complete an acknowledgment of paternity as provided by Chapter 160; and

(2) the child's mother written information:

(A) explaining the benefits of having the child's paternity established; and

(B) regarding the availability of paternity establishment and child support enforcement services.

History of Fam. Code §231.112: Acts 1995, 74th Leg., ch. 20, §1, eff. Apr. 20, 1995. Amended by Acts 1999, 76th Leg., ch. 556, §54, eff. Sept. 1, 1999. Source: Former Fam. Code §13.015.

FAM §231.113. ENFORCEMENT OF SUPPORT OBLIGATIONS IN PUBLIC ASSISTANCE CASES

To the extent possible, the Title IV-D agency shall enforce a child support obligation in a case involving a child who receives financial assistance under Chapter 31, Human Resources Code, not later than the first anniversary of the date the agency receives from the Texas Department of Human Services the information the department is required to provide to assist in the enforcement of that obligation.

History of Fam. Code §231.113: Acts 1995, 74th Leg., ch. 341, §1.03, eff. Sept. 1, 1995.

FAM §231.114. REPORTS OF CHILD SUPPORT PAYMENTS TO CONSUMER REPORTING AGENCIES

(a) The Title IV-D agency shall make information available in accordance with this section to a consumer reporting agency regarding the amount of child support owed and the amount paid by an obligor in a Title IV-D case.

(b) Before disclosing the information to consumer reporting agencies, the Title IV-D agency shall send the obligor a notice by mail to the obligor's last known address. The notice must include:

(1) the information to be released, including the amount of the obligor's child support obligation and delinquency, if any, that will be reported;

(2) the procedure available for the obligor to contest the accuracy of the information; and

(3) a statement that the information will be released if the obligor fails to contest the disclosure before the 30th day after the date of mailing of the notice.

(c) If the obligor does not contest the disclosure within the period specified by Subsection (b), the Title IV-D agency shall make the information available to the consumer reporting agency.

(d) The Title IV-D agency shall regularly update the information released to a consumer reporting agency under this section to ensure the accuracy of the released information.

(e) The Title IV-D agency may charge a consumer reporting agency a reasonable fee for making information available under this section, including all applicable mailing costs.

(f) In this section:

(1) "Consumer reporting agency" means any person that regularly engages in whole or in part in the practice of assembling or evaluating consumer credit information or other information on consumers for monetary fees, for dues, or on a cooperative nonprofit basis, to furnish consumer reports to third parties.

(2) "Obligor" means any person required to make payments under the terms of a support order for a child.

(3) "Title IV-D case" means a case in which services are being provided by the Title IV-D agency under Part D of Title IV of the federal Social Security Act (42 U.S.C. Section 651 et seq.) seeking to locate an absent parent, determine parentage, or establish, modify, enforce, or monitor a child support obligation.

History of Fam. Code §231.114: Acts 1995, 74th Leg., ch. 341, §1.03, eff. Sept. 1, 1995.

See also 1 T.A.C. §§55.102, 55.103.

FAM §231.115. NONCOOPERATION BY RECIPIENT OF PUBLIC ASSISTANCE

(a) The failure by a person who is a recipient of public assistance under Chapter 31, Human Resources Code, to provide accurate information as required by

Section 31.0315, Human Resources Code, shall serve as the basis for a determination by the Title IV-D agency that the person did not cooperate with the Title IV-D agency.

(b) The Title IV-D agency shall:

(1) identify the actions or failures to act by a recipient of public assistance that constitute noncooperation with the Title IV-D agency;

(2) adopt rules governing noncompliance; and

(3) send noncompliance determinations to the Texas Department of Human Services for immediate imposition of sanctions.

(c) In adopting rules under this section that establish the basis for determining that a person has failed to cooperate with the Title IV-D agency, the Title IV-D agency shall consider whether:

(1) good cause exists for the failure to cooperate;

(2) the person has failed to disclose the name and location of an alleged or probable parent of the child, if known by the person, at the time of applying for public assistance or at a subsequent time; and

(3) the person named a man as the alleged father and the man was subsequently excluded by parentage testing as being the father if the person has previously named another man as the child's father.

History of Fam. Code §231.115: Acts 1997, 75th Leg., ch. 911, §75, eff. Sept. 1, 1997. Amended by Acts 1999, 76th Leg., ch. 556, §54, eff. Sept. 1, 1999.

See also 1 T.A.C. §§55.3-55.5.

FAM §231.116. INFORMATION ON INTERNET

The Title IV-D agency shall place on the Internet for public access child support information to assist the public in child support matters, including application forms, child support collection in other states, and profiles of certain obligors who are in arrears in paying child support.

History of Fam. Code §231.116: Acts 1997, 75th Leg., ch. 420, §18, eff. Sept. 1, 1997.

FAM §231.1165. INFORMATION ON SERVICE OF CITATION

The Title IV-D agency shall update the agency's child support automated system to inform the parties in a suit of the service of citation in the suit not later than the first business day after the date the agency receives notice that citation has been served. The information required by this section must be available by telephone and on the Internet.

History of Fam. Code §231.1165: Acts 2001, 77th Leg., ch. 141, §1, eff. Sept. 1, 2001.

FAM §231.117. UNEMPLOYED & UNDEREMPLOYED OBLIGORS

(a) The Title IV-D agency shall refer to appropriate state and local entities that provide employment services any unemployed or underemployed obligor who is in arrears in court-ordered child support payments.

(b) A referral under Subsection (a) may include:

(1) skills training and job placement through:

(A) the Texas Workforce Commission; or

(B) the agency responsible for the food stamp employment and training program (7 U.S.C. Section 2015(d));

(2) referrals to education and literacy classes; and

(3) counseling regarding:

(A) substance abuse;

(B) parenting skills;

(C) life skills; and

(D) mediation techniques.

(c) The Title IV-D agency may require an unemployed or underemployed obligor to complete the training, classes, or counseling to which the obligor is referred under this section. The agency shall suspend under Chapter 232 the license of an obligor who fails to comply with the requirements of this subsection.

(d) A court or the Title IV-D agency may issue an order that requires the parent to either work, have a plan to pay overdue child support, or participate in work activities appropriate to pay the overdue support.

History of Fam. Code §231.117: Acts 1997, 75th Leg., ch. 165, §7.20(a), eff. Sept. 1, 1997. Renumbered from §231.115 by Acts 1999, 76th Leg., ch. 62, §19.01(23) (eff. Sept. 1, 1999), ch. 307, §54 (eff. Sept. 1, 1999). Amended by Acts 1999, 76th Leg., ch. 556, §54 (eff. Sept. 1, 1999), ch. 1072, §5 (eff. Sept. 1, 1999). Source: Former Hum. Res. Code §76.012.

A FAM §231.118. SERVICE OF CITATION

The amended text in §231.118 is effective for SAPCRs filed on or after Sept. 1, 2017. SAPCRs filed before Sept. 1, 2017, are governed by the former law in effect at that time.

(a) The Title IV-D agency may contract with private process servers to serve a citation, a subpoena, an order, or any other document required or appropriate under law to be served a party.

(b) For the purposes of Rule 103 of the Texas Rules of Civil Procedure, a person who serves a citation or any other document under this section is authorized to serve the document without a written court order authorizing the service.

(c) Issuance and return of the process shall be made in accordance with law and shall be verified by the person serving the document.

(d) Notwithstanding Subsection (c), a return of the process made under this section in a suit may not include the address served if:

(1) a pleading filed in the suit requests a finding under Section 105.006(c); or

(2) the court has previously made a finding and ordered nondisclosure under Section 105.006(c) relating to the parties and the order has not been superseded.

History of Fam. Code §231.118: Acts 1999, 76th Leg., ch. 556, §54, eff. Sept. 1, 1999. Amended by H.B. 2048, §2, 85th Leg., eff. Sept. 1, 2017.

FAM §231.119. OMBUDSMAN PROGRAM

(a) The Title IV-D agency shall establish an ombudsman program to process and track complaints against the Title IV-D agency. The director of the Title IV-D agency shall:

(1) designate an employee to serve as chief ombudsman to manage the ombudsman program; and

(2) designate an employee in each field office to act as the ombudsman for the office.

(b) The Title IV-D agency shall develop and implement a uniform process for receiving and resolving complaints against the Title IV-D agency throughout the state. The process shall include statewide procedures to inform the public and recipients of Title IV-D services of the right to file a complaint against the Title IV-D agency, including the mailing addresses and telephone numbers of appropriate Title IV-D agency personnel responsible for receiving complaints and providing related assistance.

(c) The ombudsman in each field office shall ensure that an employee in the field office responds to and attempts to resolve each complaint that is filed with the field office. If a complaint cannot be resolved at the field office level, the ombudsman in the field office shall refer the complaint to the chief ombudsman.

(d) The Title IV-D agency shall maintain a file on each written complaint filed with the Title IV-D agency. The file must include:

(1) the name of the person who filed the complaint;

(2) the date the complaint is received by the Title IV-D agency;

(3) the subject matter of the complaint;

(4) the name of each person contacted in relation to the complaint;

(5) a summary of the results of the review or investigation of the complaint; and

(6) an explanation of the reason the file was closed, if the agency closed the file without taking action other than to investigate the complaint.

(e) The Title IV-D agency, at least quarterly until final disposition of the complaint, shall notify the person filing the complaint and each person who is a subject of the complaint of the status of the investigation of the complaint unless the notice would jeopardize an undercover investigation.

(f) The Title IV-D agency shall provide to the person filing the complaint and to each person who is a subject of the complaint a copy of the Title IV-D agency's policies and procedures relating to complaint investigation and resolution.

History of Fam. Code §231.119: Acts 1999, 76th Leg., ch. 556, §54, eff. Sept. 1, 1999.

FAM §231.120. TOLL-FREE TELEPHONE NUMBER FOR EMPLOYERS

The Title IV-D agency shall maintain a toll-free telephone number at which personnel are available during normal business hours to answer questions from employers responsible for withholding child support. The Title IV-D agency shall inform employers about the toll-free telephone number.

History of Fam. Code §231.120: Acts 1999, 76th Leg., ch. 556, §54, eff. Sept. 1, 1999.

FAM §231.121. AVAILABILITY OF BROCHURES

The Title IV-D agency shall ensure that all Title IV-D brochures published by the agency are available to the public at courthouses where family law cases are heard in the state.

History of Fam. Code §231.121: Acts 2001, 77th Leg., ch. 141, §2, eff. Sept. 1, 2001.

FAM §231.122. MONITORING CHILD SUPPORT CASES; ENFORCEMENT

The Title IV-D agency shall monitor each Title IV-D case from the date the agency begins providing services on the case. If a child support obligor in a Title IV-D case becomes more than 60 days delinquent in paying child support, the Title IV-D agency shall expedite the commencement of an action to enforce the child support order.

History of Fam. Code §231.122: Acts 2005, 79th Leg., ch. 268, §1.10, eff. Sept. 1, 2005.

FAM §231.123. COOPERATION WITH VOLUNTEER INCOME TAX ASSISTANCE PROGRAMS[1]

(a) In order to maximize the amount of any tax refund to which an obligor may be entitled and which may be applied to child support and medical support obligations, the Title IV-D agency shall cooperate with volunteer income tax assistance programs in the state in informing obligors of the availability of the programs.

(b) The Title IV-D agency shall publicize the services of the volunteer income tax assistance programs by distributing printed materials regarding the programs and by placing information regarding the programs on the agency's Internet website.

(c) The Title IV-D agency is not responsible for producing or paying the costs of producing the printed materials distributed in accordance with Subsection (b).

1. **Editor's note:** In 2015, the Legislature amended §231.123 to require dental support for a child subject to a child-support order, but the amendments are not effective until Sept. 1, 2018. For the text of the prospective amendments, see Acts 2015, 84th Leg., ch. 1150, §45, eff. Sept. 1, 2018.

History of Fam. Code §231.123: Acts 2005, 79th Leg., ch. 925, §1, eff. Sept. 1, 2005. Renumbered from §231.122 by Acts 2007, 80th Leg., ch. 921, §17.001(22), eff. Sept. 1, 2007.

FAM §231.124. CHILD SUPPORT ARREARAGES PAYMENT INCENTIVE PROGRAM

(a) The Title IV-D agency may establish and administer a payment incentive program to promote payment by obligors who are delinquent in satisfying child support arrearages assigned to the Title IV-D agency under Section 231.104(a).

(b) A program established under this section must provide to a participating obligor a credit for every dollar amount paid by the obligor on interest and arrearages balances during each month of the obligor's voluntary enrollment in the program. In establishing a program under this section, the Title IV-D agency by rule must prescribe:

(1) criteria for a child support obligor's initial eligibility to participate in the program;

(2) the conditions for a child support obligor's continued participation in the program;

(3) procedures for enrollment in the program; and

(4) the terms of the financial incentives to be offered under the program.

(c) The Title IV-D agency shall provide eligible obligors with notice of the program and enrollment instructions.

History of Fam. Code §231.124: Acts 2011, 82nd Leg., ch. 508, §13, eff. Sept. 1, 2011.

See also *O'Connor's Texas Family Law Handbook* (2017), "Abating Enforcement & AG's Debt-Compromise Program," ch. 10-C, §13, p. 1133.

Sections 231.125-231.200 reserved for expansion

SUBCHAPTER C. PAYMENT OF FEES & COSTS

FAM §231.201. DEFINITIONS

In this subchapter:

(1) "Federal share" means the portion of allowable expenses for fees and other costs that will be reimbursed by the federal government under federal law and regulations regarding the administration of the Title IV-D program.

(2) "State share" means the portion of allowable expenses for fees and other costs that remain after receipt of the federal share of reimbursement and that is to be reimbursed by the state or may be contributed by certified public expenditure by a county.

History of Fam. Code §231.201: Acts 1995, 74th Leg., ch. 20, §1, eff. Apr. 20, 1995. Source: Former Hum. Res. Code §76.009(g).

FAM §231.202. AUTHORIZED COSTS & FEES IN TITLE IV-D CASES

In a Title IV-D case filed under this title, including a case filed under Chapter 159, the Title IV-D agency shall pay only the following costs and fees:

(1) filing fees and fees for issuance and service of process as provided by Chapter 110 of this code and by Sections 51.317(b)(1), (2), and (3) and (b-1), 51.318(b)(2), and 51.319(2), Government Code;

(2) fees for transfer as provided by Chapter 110;

(3) fees for the issuance and delivery of orders and writs of income withholding in the amounts provided by Chapter 110;

(4) the fee for services provided by sheriffs and constables, including:

(A) a fee authorized under Section 118.131, Local Government Code, for serving each item of process to each individual on whom service is required, including service by certified or registered mail; and

(B) a fee authorized under Section 157.103(b) for serving a capias;

(5) the fee for filing an administrative writ of withholding under Section 158.503(d);

(6) the fee for issuance of a subpoena as provided by Section 51.318(b)(1), Government Code; and

(7) a fee authorized by Section 72.031, Government Code, for the electronic filing of documents with a clerk.

History of Fam. Code §231.202: Acts 1995, 74th Leg., ch. 20, §1, eff. Apr. 20, 1995. Amended by Acts 1995, 74th Leg., ch. 341, §1.04 (eff. Sept. 1, 1995), ch. 641, §2.02 (eff. Sept. 1, 1995); Acts 1997, 75th Leg., ch. 165, §7.21(a), eff. Sept. 1, 1997; Acts 2001, 77th Leg., ch. 116, §2, eff. Sept. 1, 2001; Acts 2003, 78th Leg., ch. 1217, §1, eff. Sept. 1, 2003; Acts 2007, 80th Leg., ch. 972, §49, eff. Sept. 1, 2007; Acts 2009, 81st Leg., ch. 767, §28, eff. Sept. 1, 2009; Acts 2013, 83rd Leg., ch. 1290, §15, eff. Sept. 1, 2013. Source: Former Hum. Res. Code §76.009(a).

ANNOTATIONS

Attorney Gen. v. Lee, 92 S.W.3d 526, 528-29 (Tex. 2002). As a general rule, Fam. Code §231.204 "prohibits appellate courts from collecting fees for services rendered in a Title IV-D case except as provided by subch. C. [Family Code] §231.202 provides exceptions to the general rule. ... Although we agree that §231.202 requires the Title IV-D agency to pay some filing fees, we disagree that the section requires the agency to pay appellate filing fees."

FAM §231.2025. CONTINGENCY FEES

The Title IV-D agency may pay a contingency fee in a contract or agreement between the agency and a private agency or individual authorized under Section 231.002(c).

History of Fam. Code §231.2025: Acts 1997, 75th Leg., ch. 420, §19, eff. Sept. 1, 1997.

FAM §231.203. STATE EXEMPTION FROM BOND NOT AFFECTED

This subchapter does not affect, nor is this subchapter affected by, the exemption from bond provided by Section 6.001, Civil Practice and Remedies Code.

History of Fam. Code §231.203: Acts 1995, 74th Leg., ch. 20, §1, eff. Apr. 20, 1995. Source: Former Hum. Res. Code §76.009(h).

FAM §231.204. PROHIBITED FEES IN TITLE IV-D CASES

Except as provided by this subchapter, an appellate court, a clerk of an appellate court, a district or county clerk, sheriff, constable, or other government officer or employee may not charge the Title IV-D agency or a private attorney or political subdivision that has entered into a contract to provide Title IV-D services any fees or other amounts otherwise imposed by law for services rendered in, or in connection with, a Title IV-D case, including:

(1) a fee payable to a district clerk for:

(A) performing services related to the estates of deceased persons or minors;

(B) certifying copies; or

(C) comparing copies to originals;

(2) a court reporter fee, except as provided by Section 231.209;

(3) a judicial fund fee;

(4) a fee for a child support registry, enforcement office, or domestic relations office;

(5) a fee for alternative dispute resolution services;

(6) a filing fee or other costs payable to a clerk of an appellate court; and

(7) a statewide electronic filing system fund fee.

History of Fam. Code §231.204: Acts 1995, 74th Leg., ch. 20, §1, eff. Apr. 20, 1995. Amended by Acts 1999, 76th Leg., ch. 556, §55, eff. Sept. 1, 1999; Acts 2001, 77th Leg., ch. 1023, §55, eff. Sept. 1, 2001; Acts 2013, 83rd Leg., ch. 742, §10 (eff. Sept. 1, 2013), ch. 1290, §16 (eff. Sept. 1, 2013). Source: Former Hum. Res. Code §76.009(b).

ANNOTATIONS

Attorney Gen. v. Lee, 92 S.W.3d 526, 528-29 (Tex.2002). See annotation under Family Code §231.202, this page.

FAM §231.205. LIMITATIONS ON LIABILITY OF ATTORNEY GENERAL FOR AUTHORIZED FEES & COSTS

(a) The Title IV-D agency is liable for a fee or cost under this subchapter only to the extent that an express, specific appropriation is made to the agency exclusively for that purpose. To the extent that state funds are not available, the amount of costs and fees that are not reimbursed by the federal government and that represent the state share shall be paid by certified public expenditure by the county through the clerk of the court, sheriff, or constable. This section does not prohibit the agency from spending other funds appropriated for child support enforcement to provide the initial expenditures necessary to qualify for the federal share.

(b) The Title IV-D agency is liable for the payment of the federal share of reimbursement for fees and costs under this subchapter only to the extent that the federal share is received, and if an amount is paid by the agency and that amount is disallowed by the federal government or the federal share is not otherwise received, the clerk of the court, sheriff, or constable to whom the payment was made shall return the amount to the agency not later than the 30th day after the date on which notice is given by the agency.

History of Fam. Code §231.205: Acts 1995, 74th Leg., ch. 20, §1, eff. Apr. 20, 1995. Source: Former Hum. Res. Code §76.009(e), (f).

FAM §231.206. RESTRICTION ON FEES FOR CHILD SUPPORT OR REGISTRY SERVICES IN TITLE IV-D CASES

A district clerk, a county child support registry or enforcement office, or a domestic relations office may not

assess or collect fees for processing child support payments or for child support services from the Title IV-D agency, a managing conservator, or a possessory conservator in a Title IV-D case, except as provided by this subchapter.

History of Fam. Code §231.206: Acts 1995, 74th Leg., ch. 20, §1, eff. Apr. 20, 1995. Source: Former Hum. Res. Code §76.009(i).

FAM §231.207. METHOD OF BILLING FOR ALLOWABLE FEES

(a) To be entitled to reimbursement under this subchapter, the clerk of the court, sheriff, or constable must submit one monthly billing to the Title IV-D agency.

(b) The monthly billing must be in the form and manner prescribed by the Title IV-D agency and be approved by the clerk, sheriff, or constable.

History of Fam. Code §231.207: Acts 1995, 74th Leg., ch. 20, §1, eff. Apr. 20, 1995. Source: Former Hum. Res. Code §76.009(c).

FAM §231.208. AGREEMENTS FOR REIMBURSEMENT IN LIEU OF FEES

(a) The Title IV-D agency and a qualified county may enter into a written agreement under which reimbursement for salaries and certain other actual costs incurred by the clerk, sheriff, or constable in Title IV-D cases is provided to the county.

(b) A county may not enter into an agreement for reimbursement under this section unless the clerk, sheriff, or constable providing service has at least two full-time employees each devoted exclusively to providing services in Title IV-D cases.

(c) Reimbursement made under this section is in lieu of all costs and fees provided by this subchapter.

History of Fam. Code §231.208: Acts 1995, 74th Leg., ch. 20, §1, eff. Apr. 20, 1995. Source: Former Hum. Res. Code §76.009(d).

FAM §231.209. PAYMENT FOR SERVICES NOT AFFECTED BY THIS SUBCHAPTER

Without regard to this subchapter and specifically Section 231.205, the Title IV-D agency may pay the costs for:

(1) the services of an official court reporter for the preparation of statements of facts;

(2) the costs for the publication of citation served by publication; and

(3) mileage or other reasonable travel costs incurred by a sheriff or constable when traveling out of the county to execute an outstanding warrant or capias, to be reimbursed at a rate not to exceed the rate provided for mileage or other costs incurred by state employees in the General Appropriations Act.

History of Fam. Code §231.209: Acts 1995, 74th Leg., ch. 20, §1, eff. Apr. 20, 1995. Amended by Acts 1995, 74th Leg., ch. 341, §1.05, eff. Sept. 1, 1995. Source: Former Hum. Res. Code §76.009(i).

FAM §231.210. AUTHORITY TO PAY LITIGATION EXPENSES

(a) The Title IV-D agency may pay all fees, expenses, costs, and bills necessary to secure evidence and to take the testimony of a witness, including advance payments or purchases for transportation, lodging, meals, and incidental expenses of custodians of evidence or witnesses whose transportation is necessary and proper for the production of evidence or the taking of testimony in a Title IV-D case.

(b) In making payments under this section, the Title IV-D agency shall present vouchers to the comptroller that have been sworn to by the custodian or witness and approved by the agency. The voucher shall be sufficient to authorize payment without the necessity of a written contract.

(c) The Title IV-D agency may directly pay a commercial transportation company or commercial lodging establishment for the expense of transportation or lodging of a custodian or witness.

History of Fam. Code §231.210: Acts 1995, 74th Leg., ch. 20, §1, eff. Apr. 20, 1995. Source: Former Hum. Res. Code §76.002(g).

ANNOTATIONS

Attorney Gen. v. O'Quinn, 938 S.W.2d 542, 543-44 (Tex.App.—Beaumont 1997, no writ). "In a Title IV-D case, … 'the court may assess attorney fees and all court costs as authorized by law, except that the court may not assess those amounts against the [AG] or any party to whom the [AG] has provided services under this chapter.' [¶] [D] contends the award may be sustained pursuant to the statute which authorizes the [AG's] office to pay all fees, expenses, costs, and bills necessary to secure evidence and to take witness testimony. This statute authorizes submission of vouchers to the Comptroller's office for payment of expenses, but has nothing to do with civil liability for a respondent's attorney fees and court costs. As we have already noted, the statute regarding court costs specifically prohibits assessment of court costs."

FAM §231.211. AWARD OF COST AGAINST NONPREVAILING PARTY IN TITLE IV-D CASE

(a) At the conclusion of a Title IV-D case, the court may assess attorney's fees and all court costs as autho-

rized by law against the nonprevailing party, except that the court may not assess those amounts against the Title IV-D agency or a private attorney or political subdivision that has entered into a contract under this chapter or any party to whom the agency has provided services under this chapter. Such fees and costs may not exceed reasonable and necessary costs as determined by the court.

(b) The clerk of the court may take any action necessary to collect any fees or costs assessed under this section.

History of Fam. Code §231.211: Acts 1995, 74th Leg., ch. 20, §1, eff. Apr. 20, 1995. Source: Former Fam. Code §11.181.

Sections 231.212-231.300 reserved for expansion

SUBCHAPTER D. LOCATION OF PARENTS & RESOURCES

FAM §231.301. TITLE IV-D PARENT LOCATOR SERVICES[1]

(a) The parent locator service conducted by the Title IV-D agency shall be used to obtain information for:

(1) child support establishment and enforcement purposes regarding the identity, social security number, location, employer and employment benefits, income, and assets or debts of any individual under an obligation to pay child or medical support or to whom a support obligation is owed; or

(2) the establishment of paternity.

(b) As authorized by federal law, the following persons may receive information under this section:

(1) a person or entity that contracts with the Title IV-D agency to provide services authorized under Title IV-D or an employee of the Title IV-D agency;

(2) an attorney who has the duty or authority, by law, to enforce an order for possession of or access to a child;

(3) a court, or an agent of the court, having jurisdiction to render or enforce an order for possession of or access to a child;

(4) the resident parent, legal guardian, attorney, or agent of a child who is not receiving public assistance; and

(5) a state agency that administers a program operated under a state plan as provided by 42 U.S.C. Section 653(c).

1. **Editor's note:** In 2015, the Legislature amended §231.301 to require dental support for a child subject to a child-support order, but the amendments are not effective until Sept. 1, 2018. For the text of the prospective amendments, see Acts 2015, 84th Leg., ch. 1150, §46, eff. Sept. 1, 2018.

History of Fam. Code §231.301: Acts 1995, 74th Leg., ch. 20, §1, eff. Apr. 20, 1995. Amended by Acts 1997, 75th Leg., ch. 911, §76, eff. Sept. 1, 1997; Acts 1999, 76th Leg., ch. 556, §56, eff. Sept. 1, 1999. Source: Former Hum. Res. Code §77.001(a).

FAM §231.302. INFORMATION TO ASSIST IN LOCATION OF PERSONS OR PROPERTY

(a) The Title IV-D agency of this or another state may request and obtain information relating to the identity, location, employment, compensation, benefits, income, and property holdings or other assets of any person from a state or local government agency, private company, institution, or other entity as necessary to establish, modify, or enforce a support order.

(b) A government agency, private company, institution, or other entity shall provide the information requested under Subsection (a) directly to the Title IV-D agency not later than the seventh day after the request to obtain information is received, without the requirement of payment of a fee for the information, and shall, subject to safeguards on privacy and information security, provide the information in the most efficient and expeditious manner available, including electronic or automated transfer and interface. Any individual or entity disclosing information under this section in response to a request from a Title IV-D agency may not be held liable in any civil action or proceeding to any person for the disclosure of information under this subsection.

(c) Except as provided by Subsection (c-1) or (c-2), to assist in the administration of laws relating to child support enforcement under Parts A and D of Title IV of the federal Social Security Act (42 U.S.C. Section 601 et seq. and 42 U.S.C. Section 651 et seq.):

(1) each licensing authority shall request and each applicant for a license shall provide the applicant's social security number;

(2) each agency administering a contract that provides for a payment of state funds shall request and each individual or entity bidding on a state contract shall provide the individual's or entity's social security number as required by Section 231.006; and

(3) each agency administering a state-funded grant or loan program shall request and each applicant for a grant or loan shall provide the applicant's social security number as required by Section 231.006.

(c-1) For purposes of issuing a license to carry a concealed handgun under Subchapter H, Chapter 411, Government Code, the Department of Public Safety is

not required to request, and an applicant is not required to provide, the applicant's social security number.

(c-2) For purposes of issuing a fishing or hunting license, the Texas Parks and Wildlife Department is not required to request, and an applicant is not required to provide, the applicant's social security number if the applicant is 13 years of age or younger.

(d) This section does not limit the right of an agency or licensing authority to collect and use a social security number under another provision of law.

(e) Except as provided by Subsection (d), a social security number provided under this section is confidential and may be disclosed only for the purposes of responding to a request for information from an agency operating under the provisions of Part A or D of Title IV of the federal Social Security Act (42 U.S.C. Sections 601 et seq. and 651 et seq.).

(f) Information collected by the Title IV-D agency under this section may be used only for child support purposes.

(g) In this section, "licensing authority" has the meaning assigned by Section 232.001.

History of Fam. Code §231.302: Acts 1995, 74th Leg., ch. 20, §1, eff. Apr. 20, 1995. Amended by Acts 1995, 74th Leg., ch. 751, §84, eff. Sept. 1, 1995; Acts 1997, 75th Leg., ch. 420, §20 (eff. Sept. 1, 1997), ch. 911, §77 (eff. Sept. 1, 1997); Acts 1999, 76th Leg., ch. 62, §6.28, eff. Sept. 1, 1999; Acts 2001, 77th Leg., ch. 1023, §56, eff. Sept. 1, 2001; Acts 2013, 83rd Leg., ch. 665, §1, eff. Jan. 1, 2014; Acts 2015, 84th Leg., ch. 153, §1 (eff. Sept. 1, 2015), ch. 963, §4 (eff. Sept. 1, 2015). Source: Former Hum. Res. Code §77.001(b).

FAM §231.303. TITLE IV-D ADMINISTRATIVE SUBPOENA

(a) The Title IV-D agency of this state or another state may issue an administrative subpoena to any individual or private or public entity in this state to furnish information necessary to carry out the purposes of child support enforcement under 42 U.S.C. Section 651 et seq. or this chapter.

(b) An individual or entity receiving an administrative subpoena under this section shall comply with the subpoena. The Title IV-D agency may impose a fine in an amount not to exceed $500 on an individual or entity that fails without good cause to comply with an administrative subpoena. An alleged or presumed father or a parent who fails to comply with a subpoena without good cause may also be subject to license suspension under Chapter 232.

(c) A court may compel compliance with an administrative subpoena and with any administrative fine for failure to comply with the subpoena and may award attorney's fees and costs to the Title IV-D agency in enforcing an administrative subpoena on proof that an individual or organization failed without good cause to comply with the subpoena.

(d) An individual or organization may not be liable in a civil action or proceeding for disclosing financial or other information to a Title IV-D agency under this section. The Title IV-D agency may disclose information in a financial record obtained from a financial institution only to the extent necessary:

(1) to establish, modify, or enforce a child support obligation; or

(2) to comply with Section 233.001, as added by Chapter 420, Acts of the 75th Legislature, Regular Session, 1997.

History of Fam. Code §231.303: Acts 1995, 74th Leg., ch. 20, §1, eff. Apr. 20, 1995. Amended by Acts 1997, 75th Leg., ch. 911, §78, eff. Sept. 1, 1997; Acts 1999, 76th Leg., ch. 859, §5, eff. Sept. 1, 1999. Source: Former Hum. Res. Code §77.001(c).

FAM §231.304. REPEALED

Repealed by Acts 1997, 75th Leg., ch. 911, §97(b), eff. Oct. 1, 1998.

FAM §231.305. MEMORANDUM OF UNDERSTANDING ON CHILD SUPPORT FOR CHILDREN RECEIVING PUBLIC ASSISTANCE

(a) The Title IV-D agency and the Texas Department of Human Services by rule shall adopt a memorandum of understanding governing the establishment and enforcement of court-ordered child support in cases involving children who receive financial assistance under Chapter 31, Human Resources Code. The memorandum shall require the agency and the department to:

(1) develop procedures to ensure that the information the department is required to collect to establish and enforce child support:

(A) is collected from the person applying to receive the financial assistance at the time the application is filed;

(B) is accurate and complete when the department forwards the information to the agency;

(C) is not information previously reported to the agency; and

(D) is forwarded to the agency in an expeditious manner;

(2) develop procedures to ensure that the agency does not duplicate the efforts of the department in gathering necessary information;

(3) clarify each agency's responsibilities in the establishment and enforcement of child support;

(4) develop guidelines for use by eligibility workers and child support enforcement officers in obtaining from an applicant the information required to establish and enforce child support for that child;

(5) develop training programs for appropriate department personnel to enhance the collection of information for child support enforcement;

(6) develop a standard time, not to exceed 30 days, for the department to initiate a sanction on request from the agency;

(7) develop procedures for agency participation in department appeal hearings relating to noncompliance sanctions;

(8) develop performance measures regarding the timeliness and the number of sanctions resulting from agency requests for noncompliance sanctions; and

(9) prescribe:

(A) the time in which the department is required to forward information under Subdivision (1)(D); and

(B) what constitutes complete information under Subdivision (1)(B).

(b) The Title IV-D agency and the Texas Department of Human Services shall review and renew or modify the memorandum not later than January 1 of each even-numbered year.

History of Fam. Code §231.305: Acts 1995, 74th Leg., ch. 341, §1.07, eff. Sept. 1, 1995. Amended by Acts 1999, 76th Leg., ch. 556, §57, eff. Sept. 1, 1999.

FAM §231.306. MAXIMIZING MEDICAL SUPPORT ESTABLISHMENT & COLLECTION BY THE TITLE IV-D AGENCY[1]

(a) On the installation of an automated child support enforcement system, the Title IV-D agency is strongly encouraged to:

(1) maximize the collection of medical support; and

(2) establish cash medical support orders for children eligible for medical assistance under the state Medicaid program for whom private insurance coverage is not available.

(b) In this section, "medical support" has the meaning assigned by Section 101.020.

1. **Editor's note:** In 2015, the Legislature amended §231.306 to require dental support for a child subject to a child-support order, but the amendments are not effective until Sept. 1, 2018. For the text of the prospective amendments, see Acts 2015, 84th Leg., ch. 1150, §47, eff. Sept. 1, 2018.

History of Fam. Code §231.306: Acts 1995, 74th Leg., ch. 341, §2.03, eff. Sept. 1, 1995.

FAM §231.307. FINANCIAL INSTITUTION DATA MATCHES

(a) The Title IV-D agency shall develop a system meeting the requirements of federal law (42 U.S.C. Sections 666(a)(4) and (17)) for the exchange of data with financial institutions doing business in the state to identify an account of an obligor owing past-due child support and to enforce support obligations against the obligor, including the imposition of a lien and a levy and execution on an obligor's assets held in financial institutions as required by federal law (42 U.S.C. Section 666(c)(1)(G)).

(b) The Title IV-D agency by rule shall establish procedures for data matches authorized under this section.

(c) The Title IV-D agency may enter into an agreement with one or more states to create a consortium for data matches authorized under this section. The Title IV-D agency may contract with a vendor selected by the consortium to perform data matches with financial institutions.

(d) A financial institution providing information or responding to a notice of child support lien or levy provided under Subchapter G, Chapter 157, or otherwise acting in good faith to comply with the Title IV-D agency's procedures under this section may not be liable under any federal or state law for any damages that arise from those acts.

(e) In this section:

(1) "Financial institution" has the meaning assigned by Section 157.311; and

(2) "Account" has the meaning assigned by Section 157.311.

(f) A financial institution participating in data matches authorized by this section may provide the Title IV-D agency an address for the purpose of service of notices or process required in actions under this section or Subchapter G, Chapter 157.

(g) This section does not apply to an insurer subject to the reporting requirements under Section 231.015.

History of Fam. Code §231.307: Acts 1997, 75th Leg., ch. 911, §79, eff. Sept. 1, 1997. Amended by Acts 1999, 76th Leg., ch. 556, §58, eff. Sept. 1, 1999; Acts 2001, 77th Leg., ch. 1023, §57, eff. Sept. 1, 2001; Acts 2011, 82nd Leg., ch. 508, §14, eff. Sept. 1, 2011.

FAM §231.308. PUBLIC IDENTIFICATION OF CERTAIN OBLIGORS

(a) The Title IV-D agency shall develop a program to identify publicly certain child support obligors who

are delinquent in the payment of child support. The program shall include the displaying of photographs and profiles of obligors in public and private locations. The Title IV-D agency shall use posters, the news media, and other cost-effective methods to display photographs and profiles of certain obligors who are in arrears in paying child support. The Title IV-D agency shall divide the state into at least six regions for local identification of certain child support obligors who are delinquent in the payment of child support.

(b) The Title IV-D agency may not disclose information under this section that is by law required to remain confidential.

History of Fam. Code §231.308: Acts 1997, 75th Leg., ch. 420, §21, eff. Sept. 1, 1997.

FAM §231.309. REWARDS FOR INFORMATION

(a) The Title IV-D agency may offer a reward to an individual who provides information to the agency that leads to the collection of child support owed by an obligor who is delinquent in paying support.

(b) The Title IV-D agency shall adopt rules providing for the amounts of rewards offered under this section and the circumstances under which an individual providing information described in Subsection (a) is entitled to receive a reward.

(c) A reward paid under this section shall be paid from the child support retained collections account.

History of Fam. Code §231.309: Acts 1997, 75th Leg., ch. 420, §21, eff. Sept. 1, 1997.

FAM §231.310. REPEALED

Repealed by Acts 2007, 80th Leg., ch. 972, §65(4), eff. Sept. 1, 2007.

Sections 231.311-231.400 reserved for expansion

FAM §§231.401 TO 231.429. RENUMBERED

Renumbered as §§233.001-233.029 by Acts 1997, 75th Leg., ch. 911, §80, eff. Sept. 1, 1997.

FAM §§231.430, 231.431. REPEALED

Repealed by Acts 1997, 75th Leg., ch. 911, §97(a), eff. Sept. 1, 1997.

CHAPTER 232. SUSPENSION OF LICENSE

FAM §232.001. DEFINITIONS

In this chapter:

(1) "License" means a license, certificate, registration, permit, or other authorization that:

(A) is issued by a licensing authority;

(B) is subject before expiration to renewal, suspension, revocation, forfeiture, or termination by a licensing authority; and

(C) a person must obtain to:

(i) practice or engage in a particular business, occupation, or profession;

(ii) operate a motor vehicle on a public highway in this state; or

(iii) engage in any other regulated activity, including hunting, fishing, or other recreational activity for which a license or permit is required.

(2) "Licensing authority" means a department, commission, board, office, or other agency of the state or a political subdivision of the state that issues or renews a license or that otherwise has authority to suspend or refuse to renew a license.

(3) "Order suspending license" means an order issued by the Title IV-D agency or a court directing a licensing authority to suspend or refuse to renew a license.

(3-a) "Renewal" means any instance when a licensing authority:

(A) renews, extends, recertifies, or reissues a license; or

(B) periodically certifies a licensee to be in good standing with the licensing authority based on the required payment of fees or dues or the performance of some other mandated action or activity.

(4) "Subpoena" means a judicial or administrative subpoena issued in a parentage determination or child support proceeding under this title.

History of Fam. Code §232.001: Acts 1995, 74th Leg., ch. 655, §5.03 (eff. Sept. 1, 1995), ch. 751, §85 (eff. Sept. 1, 1995). Amended by Acts 1997, 75th Leg., ch. 911, §82, eff. Sept. 1, 1997; Acts 2001, 77th Leg., ch. 724, §1 (eff. Sept. 1, 2001), ch. 1023, §58 (eff. Sept. 1, 2001); Acts 2007, 80th Leg., ch. 972, §50, eff. Sept. 1, 2007; Acts 2015, 84th Leg., ch. 859, §8, eff. Sept. 1, 2015.

FAM §232.002. LICENSING AUTHORITIES SUBJECT TO CHAPTER

Unless otherwise restricted or exempted, all licensing authorities are subject to this chapter.

History of Fam. Code §232.002: Acts 1995, 74th Leg., ch. 655, §5.03 (eff. Sept. 1, 1995), ch. 751, §85 (eff. Sept. 1, 1995). Amended by Acts 1997, 75th Leg., ch. 165, §7.22 (eff. Sept. 1, 1997), ch. 1280, §1.02 (eff. Sept. 1, 1997), ch. 1288, §2 (eff. Sept. 1, 1997); Acts 1999, 76th Leg., ch. 1254, §4 (eff. Sept. 1, 1999), ch. 1477, §23 (eff. Sept. 1, 1999); Acts 2001, 77th Leg., ch. 394, §2 (eff. Sept. 1, 2001), ch. 1420, §14.744 (eff. Sept. 1, 2001); Acts 2003, 78th Leg., ch. 553, §2.003, eff. Feb. 1, 2004; Acts 2005, 79th Leg., ch. 798, §4.01, eff. Sept. 1, 2005; Acts 2007, 80th Leg., ch. 889, §53 (eff. Sept. 1, 2007), ch. 890, §2.02 (eff. Sept. 1, 2007), ch. 921, §6.001 (eff. Sept. 1, 2007), ch. 972, §51 (eff. Sept. 1, 2007).

FAM §232.0021. APPLICATION OF CHAPTER TO TEXAS LOTTERY COMMISSION

With respect to the Texas Lottery Commission, this chapter applies only to a lottery ticket sales agent license issued under Chapter 466, Government Code.

History of Fam. Code §232.0021: Acts 2001, 77th Leg., ch. 394, §3, eff. Sept. 1, 2001.

FAM §232.0022. SUSPENSION OR NONRENEWAL OF MOTOR VEHICLE REGISTRATION

(a) The Texas Department of Motor Vehicles is the appropriate licensing authority for suspension or nonrenewal of a motor vehicle registration under this chapter.

(b) The suspension or nonrenewal of a motor vehicle registration under this chapter does not:

(1) encumber the title to the motor vehicle or otherwise affect the transfer of the title to the vehicle; or

(2) affect the sale, purchase, or registration of the motor vehicle by a person who holds a general distinguishing number issued under Chapter 503, Transportation Code.

History of Fam. Code §232.0022: Acts 2007, 80th Leg., ch. 972, §52, eff. Sept. 1, 2007. Amended by Acts 2009, 81st Leg., ch. 933, §3C.02, eff. Sept. 1, 2009.

FAM §232.003. SUSPENSION OF LICENSE

(a) A court or the Title IV-D agency may issue an order suspending a license as provided by this chapter if an individual who is an obligor:

(1) owes overdue child support in an amount equal to or greater than the total support due for three months under a support order;

(2) has been provided an opportunity to make payments toward the overdue child support under a court-ordered or agreed repayment schedule; and

(3) has failed to comply with the repayment schedule.

(b) A court or the Title IV-D agency may issue an order suspending a license as provided by this chapter if a parent or alleged parent has failed, after receiving appropriate notice, to comply with a subpoena.

(c) A court may issue an order suspending license as provided by this chapter for an individual for whom a court has rendered an enforcement order under Chapter 157 finding that the individual has failed to comply with the terms of a court order providing for the possession of or access to a child.

History of Fam. Code §232.003: Acts 1995, 74th Leg., ch. 655, §5.03 (eff. Sept. 1, 1995), ch. 751, §85 (eff. Sept. 1, 1995). Amended by Acts 1997, 75th Leg., ch. 420, §§22, 23 (eff. Sept. 1, 1997), ch. 911, §83 (eff. Sept. 1, 1997); Acts 1999, 76th Leg., ch. 556, §59, eff. Sept. 1, 1999; Acts 2001, 77th Leg., ch. 724, §2 (eff. Sept. 1, 2001), ch. 1023, §59 (eff. Sept. 1, 2001).

See also *O'Connor's Texas Family Law Handbook* (2017), "Petition to Suspend License for Child Support," ch. 10-G, p. 1166; "Petition to Suspend License for Possession or Access," ch. 11-F, p. 1226.

FAM §232.004. PETITION FOR SUSPENSION OF LICENSE

(a) A child support agency or obligee may file a petition to suspend, as provided by this chapter, a license of an obligor who has an arrearage equal to or greater than the total support due for three months under a support order.

(b) In a Title IV-D case, the petition shall be filed with the Title IV-D agency, the court of continuing jurisdiction, or the tribunal in which a child support order has been registered under Chapter 159. The tribunal in which the petition is filed obtains jurisdiction over the matter.

(c) In a case other than a Title IV-D case, the petition shall be filed in the court of continuing jurisdiction or the court in which a child support order has been registered under Chapter 159.

(d) A proceeding in a case filed with the Title IV-D agency under this chapter is governed by the contested case provisions of Chapter 2001, Government Code, except that Section 2001.054 does not apply to the proceeding. The director of the Title IV-D agency or the director's designee may render a final decision in a contested case proceeding under this chapter.

History of Fam. Code §232.004: Acts 1995, 74th Leg., ch. 655, §5.03 (eff. Sept. 1, 1995), ch. 751, §85 (eff. Sept. 1, 1995). Amended by Acts 1997, 75th Leg., ch. 420, §24 (eff. Sept. 1, 1997), ch. 911, §84 (eff. Sept. 1, 1997); Acts 1999, 76th Leg., ch. 556, §60, eff. Sept. 1, 1999; Acts 2007, 80th Leg., ch. 972, §53, eff. Sept. 1, 2007.

See also 1 T.A.C. §§55.203(a), (b), 55.205; ***O'Connor's Texas Family Law Handbook*** (2017), "Petition," ch. 10-G, §4, p. 1168; "Petition," ch. 11-F, §4, p. 1226.

ANNOTATIONS

In re C.G., 261 S.W.3d 842, 849 (Tex.App.—Dallas 2008, no pet.). Mother "argues that [Fam. Code] §232.004 provides an independent basis, separate and apart from [Fam. Code] §232.003, for rendering an order suspending a license. *At 850:* We disagree. ... The fact that neither §232.004 nor [Fam. Code] §232.005 specifically requires the petition to allege facts complying with §232.003(a)(2) and (3) in a granulated, detailed manner does not transform §232.004 into a separate grant of authority to suspend licenses as a child support enforcement remedy. [¶] [S]ection 232.004 contains no language authorizing a court to order suspension of a license. It relates to who can 'file a petition to suspend, *as provided by this chapter*' and where the petition can be filed."

FAM §232.005. CONTENTS OF PETITION

(a) A petition under this chapter must state that license suspension is required under Section 232.003 and allege:

(1) the name and, if known, social security number of the individual;

(2) the name of the licensing authority that issued a license the individual is believed to hold; and

(3) the amount of arrearages owed under the child support order or the facts associated with the individual's failure to comply with:

(A) a subpoena; or

(B) the terms of a court order providing for the possession of or access to a child.

(b) A petition under this chapter may include as an attachment a copy of:

(1) the record of child support payments maintained by the Title IV-D registry or local registry;

(2) the subpoena with which the individual has failed to comply, together with proof of service of the subpoena; or

(3) with respect to a petition for suspension under Section 232.003(c):

(A) the enforcement order rendered under Chapter 157 describing the manner in which the individual was found to have not complied with the terms of a court order providing for the possession of or access to a child; and

(B) the court order containing the provisions that the individual was found to have violated.

History of Fam. Code §232.005: Acts 1995, 74th Leg., ch. 655, §5.03 (eff. Sept. 1, 1995), ch. 751, §85 (eff. Sept. 1, 1995). Amended by Acts 1997, 75th Leg., ch. 911, §85, eff. Sept. 1, 1997; Acts 2001, 77th Leg., ch. 724, §3 (eff. Sept. 1, 2001), ch. 1023, §60 (eff. Sept. 1, 2001); Acts 2009, 81st Leg., ch. 767, §29, eff. June 19, 2009.

See also ***O'Connor's Texas Family Law Handbook*** (2017), "Contents," ch. 10-G, §4.4, p. 1168; "Contents," ch. 11-F, §4.4, p. 1226.

FAM §232.006. NOTICE

(a) On the filing of a petition under Section 232.004, the clerk of the court or the Title IV-D agency shall deliver to the individual:

(1) notice of the individual's right to a hearing before the court or agency;

(2) notice of the deadline for requesting a hearing; and

(3) a hearing request form if the proceeding is in a Title IV-D case.

(b) Notice under this section may be served:

(1) if the party has been ordered under Chapter 105 to provide the court and registry with the party's current mailing address, by mailing a copy of the notice to the respondent, together with a copy of the petition, by first class mail to the last mailing address of the respondent on file with the court and the state case registry; or

(2) as in civil cases generally.

(c) The notice must contain the following prominently displayed statement in boldfaced type, capital letters, or underlined:

"AN ACTION TO SUSPEND ONE OR MORE LICENSES ISSUED TO YOU HAS BEEN FILED AS PROVIDED BY CHAPTER 232, TEXAS FAMILY CODE. YOU MAY EMPLOY AN ATTORNEY TO REPRESENT YOU IN THIS ACTION. IF YOU OR YOUR ATTORNEY DO NOT REQUEST A HEARING BEFORE THE 21ST DAY AFTER THE DATE OF SERVICE OF THIS NOTICE, AN ORDER SUSPENDING YOUR LICENSE MAY BE RENDERED."

History of Fam. Code §232.006: Acts 1995, 74th Leg., ch. 655, §5.03 (eff. Sept. 1, 1995), ch. 751, §85 (eff. Sept. 1, 1995). Amended by Acts 1997, 75th Leg., ch. 911, §86 (eff. Sept. 1, 1997), ch. 976, §7 (eff. Sept. 1, 1997); Acts 1999, 76th Leg., ch. 178, §11, eff. Aug. 30, 1999; Acts 2007, 80th Leg., ch. 972, §54, eff. Sept. 1, 2007.

See also ***O'Connor's Texas Family Law Handbook*** (2017), "Notice of Hearing," ch. 10-G, §5, p. 1170; "Notice of Hearing," ch. 11-F, §5, p. 1227.

FAM §232.007. HEARING ON PETITION TO SUSPEND LICENSE

(a) A request for a hearing and motion to stay suspension must be filed with the court or Title IV-D agency by the individual not later than the 20th day after the date of service of the notice under Section 232.006.

(b) If a request for a hearing is filed, the court or Title IV-D agency shall:

(1) promptly schedule a hearing;

(2) notify each party of the date, time, and location of the hearing; and

(3) stay suspension pending the hearing.

(c) In a case involving support arrearages, a record of child support payments made by the Title IV-D agency or a local registry is evidence of whether the payments were made. A copy of the record appearing regular on its face shall be admitted as evidence at a hearing under this chapter, including a hearing on a motion to revoke a stay. Either party may offer controverting evidence.

(d) In a case in which an individual has failed to comply with a subpoena, proof of service is evidence of delivery of the subpoena.

History of Fam. Code §232.007: Acts 1995, 74th Leg., ch. 655, §5.03 (eff. Sept. 1, 1995), ch. 751, §85 (eff. Sept. 1, 1995). Amended by Acts 1997, 75th Leg., ch. 911, §87, eff. Sept. 1, 1997.

See also 1 T.A.C. §§55.203(c), 55.207-55.212; ***O'Connor's Texas Family Law Handbook*** (2017), "Response," ch. 10-G, §7, p. 1171; "Prehearing Matters," ch. 10-G, §8, p. 1172; "Response," ch. 11-F, §7, p. 1227; "Prehearing Matters," ch. 11-F, §8, p. 1228.

FAM §232.008. ORDER SUSPENDING LICENSE FOR FAILURE TO PAY CHILD SUPPORT

(a) On making the findings required by Section 232.003, the court or Title IV-D agency shall render an order suspending the license unless the individual:

(1) proves that all arrearages and the current month's support have been paid;

(2) shows good cause for failure to comply with the subpoena or the terms of the court order providing for the possession of or access to a child; or

(3) establishes an affirmative defense as provided by Section 157.008(c).

(b) Subject to Subsection (b-1), the court or Title IV-D agency may stay an order suspending a license conditioned on the individual's compliance with:

(1) a reasonable repayment schedule that is incorporated in the order;

(2) the requirements of a reissued and delivered subpoena; or

(3) the requirements of any court order pertaining to the possession of or access to a child.

(b-1) The court or Title IV-D agency may not stay an order under Subsection (b)(1) unless the individual makes an immediate partial payment in an amount specified by the court or Title IV-D agency. The amount specified may not be less than $200.

(c) An order suspending a license with a stay of the suspension may not be served on the licensing authority unless the stay is revoked as provided by this chapter.

(d) A final order suspending license rendered by a court or the Title IV-D agency shall be forwarded to the appropriate licensing authority by the clerk of the court or Title IV-D agency. The clerk shall collect from an obligor a fee of $5 for each order mailed.

(e) If the court or Title IV-D agency renders an order suspending license, the individual may also be ordered not to engage in the licensed activity.

(f) If the court or Title IV-D agency finds that the petition for suspension should be denied, the petition shall be dismissed without prejudice, and an order suspending license may not be rendered.

History of Fam. Code §232.008: Acts 1995, 74th Leg., ch. 655, §5.03 (eff. Sept. 1, 1995), ch. 751, §85 (eff. Sept. 1, 1995). Amended by Acts 1997, 75th Leg., ch. 911, §88 (eff. Sept. 1, 1997), ch. 976, §8 (eff. Sept. 1, 1997); Acts 1999, 76th Leg., ch. 556, §61, eff. Sept. 1, 1999; Acts 2001, 77th Leg., ch. 724, §4, eff. Sept. 1, 2001; Acts 2013, 83rd Leg., ch. 674, §1, eff. Sept. 1, 2013.

See also ***O'Connor's Texas Family Law Handbook*** (2017), "Defense," ch. 10-G, §7.3.2(3), p. 1171; "Relief," ch. 10-G, §11.9, p. 1174; "Defenses," ch. 11-F, §7.3.3, p. 1228; "Relief," ch. 11-F, §11.8, p. 1229.

FAM §232.009. DEFAULT ORDER

The court or Title IV-D agency shall consider the allegations of the petition for suspension to be admitted and shall render an order suspending the license of an obligor without the requirement of a hearing if the court or Title IV-D agency determines that the individual failed to respond to a notice issued under Section 232.006 by:

(1) requesting a hearing; or

(2) appearing at a scheduled hearing.

History of Fam. Code §232.009: Acts 1995, 74th Leg., ch. 655, §5.03 (eff. Sept. 1, 1995), ch. 751, §85 (eff. Sept. 1, 1995). Amended by Acts 1997, 75th Leg., ch. 420, §25 (eff. Sept. 1, 1997), ch. 911, §89 (eff. Sept. 1, 1997); Acts 2001, 77th Leg., ch. 1023, §61, eff. Sept. 1, 2001.

See also ***O'Connor's Texas Family Law Handbook*** (2017), "Default judgment," ch. 10-G, §9.2, p. 1172; "Obligor does not appear," ch. 10-G, §10.1.1(1), p. 1173; "Response," ch. 11-F, §7, p. 1227.

FAM §232.010. REVIEW OF FINAL ADMINISTRATIVE ORDER

An order issued by a Title IV-D agency under this chapter is a final agency decision and is subject to review under the substantial evidence rule as provided by Chapter 2001, Government Code.

History of Fam. Code §232.010: Acts 1995, 74th Leg., ch. 655, §5.03 (eff. Sept. 1, 1995), ch. 751, §85 (eff. Sept. 1, 1995).

FAM §232.011. ACTION BY LICENSING AUTHORITY

(a) On receipt of a final order suspending license, the licensing authority shall immediately determine if the authority has issued a license to the individual named on the order and, if a license has been issued:

(1) record the suspension of the license in the licensing authority's records;

(2) report the suspension as appropriate; and

(3) demand surrender of the suspended license if required by law for other cases in which a license is suspended.

(b) A licensing authority shall implement the terms of a final order suspending license without additional review or hearing. The authority may provide notice as appropriate to the license holder or to others concerned with the license.

(c) A licensing authority may not modify, remand, reverse, vacate, or stay an order suspending license issued under this chapter and may not review, vacate, or reconsider the terms of a final order suspending license.

(d) An individual who is the subject of a final order suspending license is not entitled to a refund for any fee or deposit paid to the licensing authority.

(e) An individual who continues to engage in the business, occupation, profession, or other licensed activity after the implementation of the order suspending license by the licensing authority is liable for the same civil and criminal penalties provided for engaging in the licensed activity without a license or while a license is suspended that apply to any other license holder of that licensing authority.

(f) A licensing authority is exempt from liability to a license holder for any act authorized under this chapter performed by the authority.

(g) Except as provided by this chapter, an order suspending license or dismissing a petition for the suspension of a license does not affect the power of a licensing authority to grant, deny, suspend, revoke, terminate, or renew a license.

(h) The denial or suspension of a driver's license under this chapter is governed by this chapter and not by the general licensing provisions of Chapter 521, Transportation Code.

(i) An order issued under this chapter to suspend a license applies to each license issued by the licensing authority subject to the order for which the obligor is eligible. The licensing authority may not issue or renew any other license for the obligor until the court or the Title IV-D agency renders an order vacating or staying an order suspending license.

History of Fam. Code §232.011: Acts 1995, 74th Leg., ch. 655, §5.03 (eff. Sept. 1, 1995), ch. 751, §85 (eff. Sept. 1, 1995). Amended by Acts 1997, 75th Leg., ch. 165, §30.184 (eff. Sept. 1, 1997), ch. 911, §90 (eff. Sept. 1, 1997); Acts 2001, 77th Leg., ch. 1023, §62, eff. Sept. 1, 2001.

See also *O'Connor's Texas Family Law Handbook* (2017), "Suspension by Licensing Authority," ch. 10-G, §13, p. 1175.

FAM §232.012. MOTION TO REVOKE STAY

(a) The obligee, support enforcement agency, court, or Title IV-D agency may file a motion to revoke the stay of an order suspending license if the individual who is subject of an order suspending license does not comply with:

(1) the terms of a reasonable repayment plan entered into by the individual;

(2) the requirements of a reissued subpoena; or

(3) the terms of any court order pertaining to the possession of or access to a child.

(b) Notice to the individual of a motion to revoke stay under this section may be given by personal service or by mail to the address provided by the individual, if any, in the order suspending license. The notice must include a notice of hearing. The notice must be provided to the individual not less than 10 days before the date of the hearing.

(c) A motion to revoke stay must allege the manner in which the individual failed to comply with the repayment plan, the reissued subpoena, or the court order pertaining to possession of or access to a child.

(d) If the court or Title IV-D agency finds that the individual is not in compliance with the terms of the repayment plan, reissued subpoena, or court order pertaining to possession of or access to a child, the court or agency shall revoke the stay of the order suspending license and render a final order suspending license.

History of Fam. Code §232.012: Acts 1995, 74th Leg., ch. 655, §5.03 (eff. Sept. 1, 1995), ch. 751, §85 (eff. Sept. 1, 1995). Amended by Acts 1997, 75th Leg., ch. 911, §91, eff. Sept. 1, 1997; Acts 2001, 77th Leg., ch. 724, §5, eff. Sept. 1, 2001.

See also *O'Connor's Texas Family Law Handbook* (2017), "Motion to Revoke Stay," ch. 10-G, §15, p. 1176; "Motion to Revoke Stay," ch. 11-F, §15, p. 1230.

FAM §232.013. VACATING OR STAYING ORDER SUSPENDING LICENSE

(a) The court or Title IV-D agency may render an order vacating or staying an order suspending an individual's license if:

(1) the individual has:

(A) paid all delinquent child support or has established a satisfactory payment record;

(B) complied with the requirements of a reissued subpoena; or

(C) complied with the terms of any court order providing for the possession of or access to a child; or

(2) the court or Title IV-D agency determines that good cause exists for vacating or staying the order.

(b) The clerk of the court or Title IV-D agency shall promptly deliver an order vacating or staying an order suspending license to the appropriate licensing authority. The clerk shall collect from an obligor a fee of $5 for each order mailed.

(c) On receipt of an order vacating or staying an order suspending license, the licensing authority shall promptly issue the affected license to the individual if the individual is otherwise qualified for the license.

(d) An order rendered under this section does not affect the right of the child support agency or obligee to any other remedy provided by law, including the right to seek relief under this chapter. An order rendered under this section does not affect the power of a licensing authority to grant, deny, suspend, revoke, terminate, or renew a license as otherwise provided by law.

History of Fam. Code §232.013: Acts 1995, 74th Leg., ch. 655, §5.03 (eff. Sept. 1, 1995), ch. 751, §85 (eff. Sept. 1, 1995). Amended by Acts 1997, 75th Leg., ch. 911, §92 (eff. Sept. 1, 1997), ch. 976, §9 (eff. Sept. 1, 1997); Acts 2001, 77th Leg., ch. 724, §6, eff. Sept. 1, 2001; Acts 2003, 78th Leg., ch. 610, §16, eff. Sept. 1, 2003.

See also *O'Connor's Texas Family Law Handbook* (2017), "Motion to Stay or Vacate Order," ch. 10-G, §14, p. 1176; "Motion to Stay or Vacate Order," ch. 11-F, §14, p. 1230.

FAM §232.0135. DENIAL OF LICENSE ISSUANCE OR RENEWAL

(a) A child support agency, as defined by Section 101.004, may provide notice to a licensing authority concerning an obligor who has failed to pay child support under a support order for six months or more that requests the authority to refuse to approve an application for issuance of a license to the obligor or renewal of an existing license of the obligor.

(b) A licensing authority that receives the information described by Subsection (a) shall refuse to approve an application for issuance of a license to the obligor or renewal of an existing license of the obligor until the authority is notified by the child support agency that the obligor has:

(1) paid all child support arrearages;

(2) made an immediate payment of not less than $200 toward child support arrearages owed and established with the agency a satisfactory repayment schedule for the remainder or is in compliance with a court order for payment of the arrearages;

(3) been granted an exemption from this subsection as part of a court-supervised plan to improve the obligor's earnings and child support payments; or

(4) successfully contested the denial of issuance or renewal of license under Subsection (d).

(c) On providing a licensing authority with the notice described by Subsection (a), the child support agency shall send a copy to the obligor by first class mail and inform the obligor of the steps the obligor must take to permit the authority to approve the obligor's application for license issuance or renewal.

(d) An obligor receiving notice under Subsection (c) may request a review by the child support agency to resolve any issue in dispute regarding the identity of the obligor or the existence or amount of child support arrearages. The agency shall promptly provide an opportunity for a review, either by telephone or in person, as appropriate to the circumstances. After the review, if appropriate, the agency may notify the licensing authority that it may approve the obligor's application for issuance or renewal of license. If the agency and the obligor fail to resolve any issue in dispute, the obligor, not later than the 30th day after the date of receiving notice of the agency's determination from the review, may file a motion with the court to direct the agency to withdraw the notice under Subsection (a) and request a hearing on the motion. The obligor's application for license issuance or renewal may not be approved by the licensing authority until the court rules on the motion. If, after a review by the agency or a hearing by the court, the agency withdraws the notice under Subsec-

tion (a), the agency shall reimburse the obligor the amount of any fee charged the obligor under Section 232.014.

(e) If an obligor enters into a repayment agreement with the child support agency under this section, the agency may incorporate the agreement in an order to be filed with and confirmed by the court in the manner provided for agreed orders under Chapter 233.

(f) In this section, "licensing authority" does not include the State Securities Board.

History of Fam. Code §232.0135: Acts 2007, 80th Leg., ch. 972, §55, eff. Sept. 1, 2007. Amended by Acts 2011, 82nd Leg., ch. 508, §§15, 16, eff. Sept. 1, 2011; Acts 2013, 83rd Leg., ch. 674, §2 (eff. Sept. 1, 2013), ch. 742, §11 (eff. Sept. 1, 2013); Acts 2015, 84th Leg., ch. 859, §9, eff. Sept. 1, 2015.

FAM §232.014. FEE BY LICENSING AUTHORITY

(a) A licensing authority may charge a fee to an individual who is the subject of an order suspending license or of an action of a child support agency under Section 232.0135 to deny issuance or renewal of license in an amount sufficient to recover the administrative costs incurred by the authority under this chapter.

(b) A fee collected by the Texas Department of Motor Vehicles shall be deposited to the credit of the Texas Department of Motor Vehicles fund. A fee collected by the Department of Public Safety shall be deposited to the credit of the state highway fund.

History of Fam. Code §232.014: Acts 1995, 74th Leg., ch. 655, §5.03 (eff. Sept. 1, 1995), ch. 751, §85 (eff. Sept. 1, 1995). Amended by Acts 1997, 75th Leg., ch. 911, §93, eff. Sept. 1, 1997; Acts 2007, 80th Leg., ch. 972, §56, eff. Sept. 1, 2007; Acts 2009, 81st Leg., ch. 933, §3C.03, eff. Sept. 1, 2009; Acts 2011, 82nd Leg., ch. 508, §17, eff. Sept. 1, 2011; Acts 2013, 83rd Leg., ch. 1287, §1, eff. Sept. 1, 2013.

See also *O'Connor's Texas Family Law Handbook* (2017), "Fees for suspension," ch. 10-G, §13.3, p. 1176.

FAM §232.015. COOPERATION BETWEEN LICENSING AUTHORITIES & TITLE IV-D AGENCY

(a) The Title IV-D agency may request from each licensing authority the name, address, social security number, license renewal date, and other identifying information for each individual who holds, applies for, or renews a license issued by the authority.

(b) A licensing authority shall provide the requested information in the form and manner identified by the Title IV-D agency.

(c) The Title IV-D agency may enter into a cooperative agreement with a licensing authority to administer this chapter in a cost-effective manner.

(d) The Title IV-D agency may adopt a reasonable implementation schedule for the requirements of this section.

(e) The Title IV-D agency, the comptroller, and the Texas Alcoholic Beverage Commission shall by rule specify additional prerequisites for the suspension of licenses relating to state taxes collected under Title 2, Tax Code. The joint rules must be adopted not later than March 1, 1996.

History of Fam. Code §232.015: Acts 1995, 74th Leg., ch. 655, §5.03 (eff. Sept. 1, 1995), ch. 751, §85 (eff. Sept. 1, 1995). Amended by Acts 1997, 75th Leg., ch. 165, §7.23, eff. Sept. 1, 1997; Acts 2001, 77th Leg., ch. 1023, §63, eff. Sept. 1, 2001.

FAM §232.016. RULES, FORMS, & PROCEDURES

The Title IV-D agency by rule shall prescribe forms and procedures for the implementation of this chapter.

History of Fam. Code §232.016: Acts 1995, 74th Leg., ch. 655, §5.03 (eff. Sept. 1, 1995), ch. 751, §85 (eff. Sept. 1, 1995).

See also 1 T.A.C. §§55.201-55.216.

CHAPTER 233. CHILD SUPPORT REVIEW PROCESS TO ESTABLISH OR ENFORCE SUPPORT OBLIGATIONS

FAM §233.001. PURPOSE[1]

(a) The purpose of the procedures specified in the child support review process authorized by this chapter is to enable the Title IV-D agency to take expedited administrative actions to establish, modify, and enforce child support and medical support obligations, to determine parentage, or to take any other action authorized or required under Part D, Title IV, of the federal Social Security Act (42 U.S.C. Section 651 et seq.), and Chapter 231.

(b) A child support review order issued under this chapter and confirmed by a court constitutes an order of the court and is enforceable by any means available for the enforcement of child support obligations under this code, including withholding income, filing a child support lien, and suspending a license under Chapter 232.

1. **Editor's note:** In 2015, the Legislature amended §233.001 to require dental support for a child subject to a child-support order, but the amendments are not effective until Sept. 1, 2018. For the text of the prospective amendments, see Acts 2015, 84th Leg., ch. 1150, §48, eff. Sept. 1, 2018.

History of Fam. Code §233.001: Acts 1995, 74th Leg., ch. 20, §1, eff. Apr. 20, 1995. Amended by Acts 1995, 74th Leg., ch. 341, §2.04, eff. Sept. 1, 1995. Renumbered from §231.401 and amended by Acts 1997, 75th Leg., ch. 911, §80, eff. Sept. 1, 1997. Source: Former Fam. Code §14.802(a).

ANNOTATIONS

In re A.E.M., 455 S.W.3d 684, 688 (Tex.App.—Houston [1st Dist.] 2014, no pet.). "The purpose of the administrative conference between the parties 'is to provide an opportunity to reach an agreement on a child support order.' The child support review order is meant to cover topics such as 'current child support, medical support, a determination of any arrearages or retroactive support, and, if not otherwise ordered, income withholding.' [¶] Even if we concluded that the administrative conference can only cover matters [listed in Fam. Code §233.017], the hearing before the trial court on the unresolved issues is intended to allow matters beyond those limitations, including conservatorship and possession of a child. While it does not specifically include name changes as a matter that can be resolved by the trial court, [§233.017] also does not exclude it. Moreover, even if we interpreted [Fam. Code §§233.017 and 233.025] to restrict the considerations to be taken by the trial court, nothing in the statutory framework suggests the limitations are jurisdictional. [¶] At best, the fact that changing a child's name was not identified as a topic to be resolved in the Ch. 233 hearing before the trial court suggests that it was not generally intended to be resolved in the hearing. From there, there is no more than a weak inference to conclude that the legislature intended this to be a strict jurisdictional limitation. *At 689:* We hold there was no jurisdictional bar to the trial court's determination of the child's last name."

FAM §233.002. AGREEMENTS ENCOURAGED

To the extent permitted by this chapter, the Title IV-D agency shall encourage agreement of the parties.

History of Fam. Code §233.002: Acts 1995, 74th Leg., ch. 20, §1, eff. Apr. 20, 1995. Amended by Acts 1995, 74th Leg., ch. 341, §2.04, eff. Sept. 1, 1995. Renumbered from §231.402 and amended by Acts 1997, 75th Leg., ch. 911, §80, eff. Sept. 1, 1997. Source: Former Fam. Code §14.802(a).

FAM §233.003. BILINGUAL FORMS REQUIRED

A notice or other form used to implement administrative procedures under this chapter shall be printed in both Spanish and English.

History of Fam. Code §233.003: Acts 1995, 74th Leg., ch. 20, §1, eff. Apr. 20, 1995. Amended by Acts 1995, 74th Leg., ch. 341, §2.04, eff. Sept. 1, 1995. Renumbered from §231.403 and amended by Acts 1997, 75th Leg., ch. 911, §80, eff. Sept. 1, 1997. Source: Former Fam. Code §14.802(g).

FAM §233.004. INTERPRETER REQUIRED

If a party participating in an administrative proceeding under this chapter does not speak English or is hearing impaired, the Title IV-D agency shall provide for interpreter services at no charge to the party.

History of Fam. Code §233.004: Acts 1995, 74th Leg., ch. 20, §1, eff. Apr. 20, 1995. Amended by Acts 1995, 74th Leg., ch. 341, §2.04, eff. Sept. 1, 1995. Renumbered from §231.404 and amended by Acts 1997, 75th Leg., ch. 911, §80, eff. Sept. 1, 1997. Source: Former Fam. Code §14.802(g).

FAM §233.005. INITIATING ADMINISTRATIVE ACTIONS

An administrative action under this chapter may be initiated by issuing a notice of child support review under Section 233.006 or a notice of proposed child support review order under Section 233.009 or 233.0095 to each party entitled to notice.

History of Fam. Code §233.005: Acts 1995, 74th Leg., ch. 20, §1, eff. Apr. 20, 1995. Amended by Acts 1995, 74th Leg., ch. 341, §2.04, eff. Sept. 1, 1995. Renumbered from §231.405 and amended by Acts 1997, 75th Leg., ch. 911, §80, eff. Sept. 1, 1997. Amended by Acts 1999, 76th Leg., ch. 556, §63, eff. Sept. 1, 1999. Source: Former Fam. Code §§14.802(b), 14.803(a).

FAM §233.006. CONTENTS OF NOTICE OF CHILD SUPPORT REVIEW

(a) The notice of child support review issued by the Title IV-D agency must:

(1) describe the procedure for a child support review, including the procedures for requesting a negotiation conference;

(2) inform the recipient that the recipient may be represented by legal counsel during the review process or at a court hearing; and

(3) inform the recipient that the recipient may refuse to participate or cease participation in the child support review process, but that the refusal by the recipient to participate will not prevent the completion of the process or the filing of a child support review order.

(b) In addition to the information required by Subsection (a), the notice of child support review may inform the recipient that:

(1) an affidavit of financial resources included with the notice must be executed by the recipient and returned to the Title IV-D agency not later than the 15th day after the date the notice is received or delivered; and

(2) if the requested affidavit of financial resources is not returned as required, the agency may:

(A) proceed with the review using the information that is available to the agency; and

(B) file a legal action without further notice to the recipient, except as otherwise required by law.

History of Fam. Code §233.006: Acts 1995, 74th Leg., ch. 20, §1, eff. Apr. 20, 1995. Amended by Acts 1995, 74th Leg., ch. 341, §2.04, eff. Sept. 1, 1995. Renumbered from §231.406 and amended by Acts 1997, 75th Leg., ch. 911, §80, eff. Sept. 1, 1997. Amended by Acts 2001, 77th Leg., ch. 1023, §64, eff. Sept. 1, 2001. Source: Former Fam. Code §14.803(b), (c).

FAM §233.007. SERVICE OF NOTICE

(a) A notice required in an administrative action under this chapter may be delivered by personal service or first class mail on each party entitled to citation or notice as provided by Chapter 102.

(b) This section does not apply to notice required on filing of a child support review order or to later judicial actions.

History of Fam. Code §233.007: Acts 1995, 74th Leg., ch. 20, §1, eff. Apr. 20, 1995. Amended by Acts 1995, 74th Leg., ch. 341, §2.04, eff. Sept. 1, 1995. Renumbered from §231.407 and amended by Acts 1997, 75th Leg., ch. 911, §80, eff. Sept. 1, 1997. Source: Former Fam. Code §14.802(e), (f).

FAM §233.008. ADMINISTRATIVE SUBPOENA IN CHILD SUPPORT REVIEW

In a child support review under this chapter, the Title IV-D agency may issue an administrative subpoena authorized under Chapter 231 to any individual or organization believed to have financial or other information needed to establish, modify, or enforce a support order.

History of Fam. Code §233.008: Acts 1995, 74th Leg., ch. 20, §1, eff. Apr. 20, 1995. Amended by Acts 1995, 74th Leg., ch. 341, §2.04, eff. Sept. 1, 1995. Renumbered from §231.408 and amended by Acts 1997, 75th Leg., ch. 911, §80, eff. Sept. 1, 1997. Source: Former Fam. Code §14.802(c).

FAM §233.009. NOTICE OF PROPOSED CHILD SUPPORT REVIEW ORDER; NEGOTIATION CONFERENCE[1]

(a) After an investigation and assessment of financial resources, the Title IV-D agency may serve on the parties a notice of proposed child support review order in enforcing or modifying an existing order.

(b) The notice of proposed child support review order shall state:

(1) the amount of periodic payment of child support due, the amount of any overdue support that is owed as an arrearage as of the date of the notice, and the amounts that are to be paid by the obligor for current support due and in payment on the arrearage owed;

(2) that the person identified in the notice as the party responsible for payment of the support amounts may contest the notice order on the grounds that:

(A) the respondent is not the responsible party;

(B) the dependent child is no longer entitled to child support; or

(C) the amount of monthly support or arrearage is incorrectly stated; and

(3) that, if the person identified in the notice as the party responsible for payment of the support amounts does not contest the notice in writing or request a negotiation conference to discuss the notice not later than the 15th day after the date the notice was delivered, the Title IV-D agency may file a child support review order for child support and for medical support for the child as provided by Chapter 154 according to the information available to the agency.

(c) The Title IV-D agency may schedule a negotiation conference without a request from a party.

(d) The Title IV-D agency shall schedule a negotiation conference on the timely request of a party.

(e) The agency may conduct a negotiation conference, or any part of a negotiation conference, by telephone conference call, by video conference, as well as in person and may adjourn the conference for a reasonable time to permit mediation of issues that cannot be resolved by the parties and the agency.

(f) Notwithstanding any other provision of this chapter, if the parties have agreed to the terms of a proposed child support review order and each party has signed the order, including a waiver of the right to service of process as provided by Section 233.018, the Title IV-D agency may immediately present the order and waiver to the court for confirmation without conducting a negotiation conference or requiring the production of financial information.

1. **Editor's note:** In 2015, the Legislature amended §233.009 to require dental support for a child subject to a child-support order, but the amendments are not effective until Sept. 1, 2018. For the text of the prospective amendments, see Acts 2015, 84th Leg., ch. 1150, §49, eff. Sept. 1, 2018.

History of Fam. Code §233.009: Acts 1995, 74th Leg., ch. 20, §1, eff. Apr. 20, 1995. Amended by Acts 1995, 74th Leg., ch. 341, §2.04, eff. Sept. 1, 1995. Renumbered from §231.409 and amended by Acts 1997, 75th Leg., ch. 911, §80, eff. Sept. 1, 1997. Amended by Acts 2001, 77th Leg., ch. 1023, §65, eff. Sept. 1, 2001. Source: Former Fam. Code §14.804(a).

FAM §233.0095. NOTICE OF PROPOSED CHILD SUPPORT REVIEW ORDER IN CASES OF ACKNOWLEDGED PATERNITY[1]

(a) If an individual has signed the acknowledgment of paternity as the father of the child or executed a statement of paternity, the Title IV-D agency may serve on the parties a notice of proposed child support review order.

(b) The notice of proposed child support review order shall state:

(1) the amount of periodic payment of child support due;

(2) that the person identified in the notice as the party responsible for payment of the support amounts may only contest the amount of monthly support; and

(3) that, if the person identified in the notice as the party responsible for payment of the support amounts does not contest the notice in writing or request a negotiation conference to discuss the notice not later than the 15th day after the date the notice was delivered, the Title IV-D agency may file the child support order for child support and for medical support for the child as provided by Chapter 154 according to the information available to the agency.

(c) The Title IV-D agency may schedule a negotiation conference without a request from a party.

(d) The Title IV-D agency shall schedule a negotiation conference on the timely request of a party.

(e) The Title IV-D agency may conduct a negotiation conference, or any part of a negotiation conference, by telephone conference call, by video conference, or in person and may adjourn the conference for a reasonable time to permit mediation of issues that cannot be resolved by the parties and the agency.

(f) Notwithstanding any other provision of this chapter, if paternity has been acknowledged, the parties have agreed to the terms of a proposed child support review order, and each party has signed the order, including a waiver of the right to service of process as provided by Section 233.018, the Title IV-D agency may immediately present the order and waiver to the court for confirmation without conducting a negotiation conference or requiring the production of financial information.

1. **Editor's note:** In 2015, the Legislature amended §233.0095 to require dental support for a child subject to a child-support order, but the amendments are not effective until Sept. 1, 2018. For the text of the prospective amendments, see Acts 2015, 84th Leg., ch. 1150, §50, eff. Sept. 1, 2018.

History of Fam. Code §233.0095: Acts 1999, 76th Leg., ch. 556, §64, eff. Sept. 1, 1999. Amended by Acts 2001, 77th Leg., ch. 1023, §66, eff. Sept. 1, 2001.

FAM §233.010. NOTICE OF NEGOTIATION CONFERENCE; FAILURE TO ATTEND CONFERENCE

(a) The Title IV-D agency shall notify all parties entitled to notice of the negotiation conference of the date, time, and place of the conference not later than the 10th day before the date of the conference.

(b) If a party fails to attend the scheduled conference, the agency may proceed with the review and file a child support review order according to the information available to the agency.

History of Fam. Code §233.010: Acts 1995, 74th Leg., ch. 20, §1, eff. Apr. 20, 1995. Amended by Acts 1995, 74th Leg., ch. 341, §2.04, eff. Sept. 1, 1995. Renumbered from §231.410 and amended by Acts 1997, 75th Leg., ch. 911, §80, eff. Sept. 1, 1997. Source: Former Fam. Code §14.804(b), (c).

FAM §233.011. RESCHEDULING NEGOTIATION CONFERENCE; NOTICE REQUIRED

(a) The Title IV-D agency may reschedule or adjourn a negotiation conference on the request of any party.

(b) The Title IV-D agency shall give all parties notice of a rescheduled conference not later than the third day before the date of the rescheduled conference.

History of Fam. Code §233.011: Acts 1995, 74th Leg., ch. 20, §1, eff. Apr. 20, 1995. Amended by Acts 1995, 74th Leg., ch. 341, §2.04, eff. Sept. 1, 1995. Renumbered from §231.411 and amended by Acts 1997, 75th Leg., ch. 911, §80, eff. Sept. 1, 1997. Source: Former Fam. Code §14.804(d).

FAM §233.012. INFORMATION REQUIRED TO BE PROVIDED AT NEGOTIATION CONFERENCE

At the beginning of the negotiation conference, the child support review officer shall review with the parties participating in the conference information provided in the notice of child support review and inform the parties that:

(1) the purpose of the negotiation conference is to provide an opportunity to reach an agreement on a child support order;

(2) if the parties reach an agreement, the review officer will prepare an agreed review order to be effective immediately on being confirmed by the court, as provided by Section 233.024;

(3) a party does not have to sign a review order prepared by the child support review officer but that the Title IV-D agency may file a review order without the agreement of the parties;

(4) the parties may sign a waiver of the right to service of process;

(5) a party may file a request for a court hearing on a nonagreed order not later than the 20th day after the date a copy of the petition for confirmation of the order is delivered to the party; and

(6) a party may file a motion for a new trial not later than the 30th day after an order is confirmed by the court.

History of Fam. Code §233.012: Acts 1995, 74th Leg., ch. 20, §1, eff. Apr. 20, 1995. Amended by Acts 1995, 74th Leg., ch. 341, §2.04, eff. Sept. 1, 1995. Renumbered from §231.412 and amended by Acts 1997, 75th Leg., ch. 911, §80, eff. Sept. 1, 1997. Amended by Acts 2011, 82nd Leg., ch. 508, §19, eff. Sept. 1, 2011. Source: Former Fam. Code §14.804(e).

FAM §233.013. DETERMINING SUPPORT AMOUNT; MODIFICATION[1]

(a) The Title IV-D agency may use any information obtained by the agency from the parties or any other source and shall apply the child support guidelines provided by this code to determine the appropriate amount of child support. In determining the appropriate amount of child support, the agency may consider evidence of the factors a court is required to consider under Section 154.123(b), and, if the agency deviates from the guidelines in determining the amount of monthly child support, with or without the agreement of the parties, the child support review order must include the findings required to be made by a court under Section 154.130(b).

(b) If grounds exist for modification of a child support order under Subchapter E, Chapter 156, the Title IV-D agency may file an appropriate child support review order, including an order that has the effect of modifying an existing court or administrative order for child support without the necessity of filing a motion to modify.

(c) Notwithstanding Subsection (b), the Title IV-D agency may, at any time and without a showing of material and substantial change in the circumstances of the parties, file a child support review order that has the effect of modifying an existing order for child support to provide medical support for a child if the existing order does not provide health care coverage for the child as required under Section 154.182.

1. **Editor's note:** In 2015, the Legislature amended §233.013 to require dental support for a child subject to a child-support order, but the amendments are not effective until Sept. 1, 2018. For the text of the prospective amendments, see Acts 2015, 84th Leg., ch. 1150, §51, eff. Sept. 1, 2018.

History of Fam. Code §233.013: Acts 1995, 74th Leg., ch. 20, §1, eff. Apr. 20, 1995. Amended by Acts 1995, 74th Leg., ch. 341, §2.04, eff. Sept. 1, 1995. Renumbered from §231.413 and amended by Acts 1997, 75th Leg., ch. 911, §80, eff. Sept. 1, 1997. Amended by Acts 2011, 82nd Leg., ch. 508, §19, eff. Sept. 1, 2011; Acts 2013, 83rd Leg., ch. 742, §12, eff. Sept. 1, 2013; Acts 2015, 84th Leg., ch. 963, §5, eff. Sept. 1, 2015. Source: Former Fam. Code §14.802(d).

FAM §233.014. RECORD OF PROCEEDINGS

(a) For the purposes of this chapter, documentary evidence relied on by the child support review officer, including an affidavit of a party, together with the child support review order is a sufficient record of the proceedings.

(b) The Title IV-D agency is not required to make any other record or transcript of the negotiation conference.

History of Fam. Code §233.014: Acts 1995, 74th Leg., ch. 20, §1, eff. Apr. 20, 1995. Amended by Acts 1995, 74th Leg., ch. 341, §2.04, eff. Sept. 1, 1995. Renumbered from §231.414 and amended by Acts 1997, 75th Leg., ch. 911, §80, eff. Sept. 1, 1997. Source: Former Fam. Code §14.804(f).

FAM §233.015. ISSUANCE OF CHILD SUPPORT REVIEW ORDER OR FINDING THAT NO ORDER SHOULD BE ISSUED; EFFECT

(a) If a negotiation conference does not result in agreement by all parties to the child support review order, the Title IV-D agency shall render a final decision in the form of a child support review order or a determination that the agency should not issue a child support review order not later than the fifth day after the date of the negotiation conference.

(b) If the Title IV-D agency determines that the agency should not issue a child support order, the agency shall immediately provide each party with notice of the determination by personal delivery or by first class mail.

(c) A determination that a child support order should not be issued must include a statement of the reasons that an order is not being issued and a statement that the agency's determination does not affect the right of the Title IV-D agency or a party to request any other remedy provided by law.

History of Fam. Code §233.015: Acts 1995, 74th Leg., ch. 20, §1, eff. Apr. 20, 1995. Amended by Acts 1995, 74th Leg., ch. 341, §2.04, eff. Sept. 1, 1995. Renumbered from §231.415 and amended by Acts 1997, 75th Leg., ch. 911, §80, eff. Sept. 1, 1997. Source: Former Fam. Code §14.804(h)-(j).

FAM §233.016. VACATING CHILD SUPPORT REVIEW ORDER

(a) The Title IV-D agency may vacate a child support review order at any time before the order is filed with the court.

(b) A new negotiation conference, with notice to all parties, may be scheduled or the Title IV-D agency may make a determination that a child support review order should not be issued and give notice of that determination as provided by this chapter.

History of Fam. Code §233.016: Acts 1995, 74th Leg., ch. 20, §1, eff. Apr. 20, 1995. Amended by Acts 1995, 74th Leg., ch. 341, §2.04, eff. Sept. 1, 1995. Renumbered from §231.416 and amended by Acts 1997, 75th Leg., ch. 911, §80, eff. Sept. 1, 1997. Source: Former Fam. Code §14.804(k).

FAM §233.017. CONTENTS OF CHILD SUPPORT REVIEW ORDER[1]

(a) An order issued under this chapter must be reviewed and signed by an attorney of the Title IV-D agency and must contain all provisions that are appropriate for an order under this title, including current child support, medical support, a determination of any arrearages or retroactive support, and, if not otherwise ordered, income withholding.

(b) A child support review order providing for the enforcement of an order may not contain a provision that imposes incarceration or a fine or contains a finding of contempt.

(c) Repealed by Acts 2011, 82nd Leg., ch. 508, §25, eff. Sept. 1, 2011.

(d) A child support review order that is not agreed to by all the parties may specify and reserve for the court at the confirmation hearing unresolved issues relating to conservatorship or possession of a child.

1. **Editor's note:** In 2015, the Legislature amended §233.017 to require dental support for a child subject to a child-support order, but the amendments are not effective until Sept. 1, 2018. For the text of the prospective amendments, see Acts 2015, 84th Leg., ch. 1150, §52, eff. Sept. 1, 2018.

History of Fam. Code §233.017: Acts 1995, 74th Leg., ch. 20, §1, eff. Apr. 20, 1995. Amended by Acts 1995, 74th Leg., ch. 341, §2.04, eff. Sept. 1, 1995. Renumbered from §231.417 and amended by Acts 1997, 75th Leg., ch. 911, §80, eff. Sept. 1, 1997. Amended by Acts 2011, 82nd Leg., ch. 508, §25, eff. Sept. 1, 2011. Source: Former Fam. Code §14.805.

FAM §233.018. ADDITIONAL CONTENTS OF AGREED CHILD SUPPORT REVIEW ORDER

(a) If a negotiation conference results in an agreement of the parties, each party must sign the child support review order and the order must contain as to each party:

(1) a waiver by the party of the right to service of process and a court hearing;

(2) the mailing address of the party; and

(3) the following statement printed on the order in boldfaced type, in capital letters, or underlined:

"I ACKNOWLEDGE THAT I HAVE READ AND UNDERSTAND THIS CHILD SUPPORT REVIEW ORDER. I UNDERSTAND THAT IF I SIGN THIS ORDER, IT WILL BE CONFIRMED BY THE COURT WITHOUT FURTHER NOTICE TO ME. I KNOW THAT I HAVE A RIGHT TO REQUEST THAT A COURT RECONSIDER THE ORDER BY FILING A MOTION FOR A NEW TRIAL AT ANY TIME BEFORE THE 30TH DAY AFTER THE DATE OF THE CONFIRMATION OF THE ORDER BY THE COURT. I KNOW THAT IF I DO NOT OBEY THE TERMS OF THIS ORDER I MAY BE HELD IN CONTEMPT OF COURT."

(b) If a negotiation conference results in an agreement on some but not all issues in the case, the parties may sign a waiver of service along with an agreement to appear in court at a specified date and time for a determination by the court of all unresolved issues. Notice of the hearing is not required.

History of Fam. Code §233.018: Acts 1995, 74th Leg., ch. 20, §1, eff. Apr. 20, 1995. Amended by Acts 1995, 74th Leg., ch. 341, §2.04, eff. Sept. 1, 1995. Renumbered from §231.418 and amended by Acts 1997, 75th Leg., ch. 911, §80, eff. Sept. 1, 1997. Amended by Acts 1999, 76th Leg., ch. 556, §65, eff. Sept. 1, 1999; Acts 2001, 77th Leg., ch. 1023, §67, eff. Sept. 1, 2001; Acts 2003, 78th Leg., ch. 610, §17, eff. Sept. 1, 2003. Source: Former Fam. Code §14.804(g).

FAM §233.019. FILING OF AGREED REVIEW ORDER

(a) The Title IV-D agency shall file an agreed child support review order and a waiver of service signed by the parties with the clerk of the court having continuing jurisdiction of the child who is the subject of the order.

(b) If there is not a court of continuing jurisdiction, the Title IV-D agency shall file the agreed review order with the clerk of a court having jurisdiction under this title.

(c) If applicable, an acknowledgment of paternity or a written report of a parentage testing expert and

any documentary evidence relied upon by the agency shall be filed with the agreed review order as an exhibit to the order.

(d) A child support order issued by a tribunal of another state and filed with an agreed review order as an exhibit to the agreed review order shall be treated as a confirmed order without the necessity of registration under Subchapter G, Chapter 159.

(e) If a party timely files a motion for a new trial for reconsideration of an agreed review order and the court grants the motion, the agreed review order filed with the clerk constitutes a sufficient pleading by the Title IV-D agency for relief on any issue addressed in the order.

History of Fam. Code §233.019: Acts 1995, 74th Leg., ch. 20, §1, eff. Apr. 20, 1995. Amended by Acts 1995, 74th Leg., ch. 341, §2.04, eff. Sept. 1, 1995. Renumbered from §231.419 and amended by Acts 1997, 75th Leg., ch. 911, §80, eff. Sept. 1, 1997. Amended by Acts 1999, 76th Leg., ch. 556, §66, eff. Sept. 1, 1999; Acts 2007, 80th Leg., ch. 972, §57, eff. Sept. 1, 2007; Acts 2013, 83rd Leg., ch. 742, §13, eff. Sept. 1, 2013. Source: Former Fam. Code §14.806(a).

FAM §233.020. CONTENTS OF PETITION FOR CONFIRMATION OF NONAGREED ORDER

(a) A petition for confirmation of a child support review order not agreed to by the parties:

(1) must include the final review order as an attachment to the petition; and

(2) may include a waiver of service executed under Section 233.018(b) and an agreement to appear in court for a hearing.

(b) Documentary evidence relied on by the Title IV-D agency, including, if applicable, an acknowledgment of paternity or a written report of a parentage testing expert, shall be filed with the clerk as exhibits to the petition, but are not required to be served on the parties. The petition must identify the exhibits that are filed with the clerk.

History of Fam. Code §233.020: Acts 1995, 74th Leg., ch. 20, §1, eff. Apr. 20, 1995. Amended by Acts 1995, 74th Leg., ch. 341, §2.04, eff. Sept. 1, 1995. Renumbered from §231.420 and amended by Acts 1997, 75th Leg., ch. 911, §80, eff. Sept. 1, 1997. Amended by Acts 1999, 76th Leg., ch. 556, §67, eff. Sept. 1, 1999. Source: Former Fam. Code §14.806(b).

FAM §233.021. DUTIES OF CLERK OF COURT

(a) On the filing of an agreed child support review order or of a petition for confirmation of a nonagreed order issued by the Title IV-D agency, the clerk of court shall endorse on the order or petition the date and time the order or petition is filed.

(b) In an original action, the clerk shall endorse the appropriate court and cause number on the agreed review order or on the petition for confirmation of a nonagreed order.

(c) The clerk shall deliver by personal service a copy of the petition for confirmation of a nonagreed review order and a copy of the order, to each party entitled to service who has not waived service.

(d) A clerk of a district court is entitled to collect in a child support review case the fees authorized in a Title IV-D case by Chapter 231.

History of Fam. Code §233.021: Acts 1995, 74th Leg., ch. 20, §1, eff. Apr. 20, 1995. Amended by Acts 1995, 74th Leg., ch. 341, §2.04, eff. Sept. 1, 1995. Renumbered from §231.421 and amended by Acts 1997, 75th Leg., ch. 911, §80, eff. Sept. 1, 1997. Source: Former Fam. Code §14.806(c), (d).

ANNOTATIONS

In re S.B.S., 282 S.W.3d 711, 715 (Tex.App.—Amarillo 2009, pet. denied). "We construe the plain language of [Fam. Code §§233.021 and 233.0271] to provide a specific means of establishing parentage and child support obligations that deviates from the general rules of the [TRCPs]. While proper citation is necessary to support a default judgment in a civil case generally, … we believe that the interplay of the sections cited above establishes a process by which a default judgment may be taken in a child support review process proceeding without the issuance of a citation. [W]e believe that the legislature intended that service of the petition and proposed order, as directed under §233.021, would be sufficient service to support a default judgment against a party that failed to timely request a hearing."

FAM §233.022. FORM TO REQUEST A COURT HEARING ON NONAGREED ORDER

(a) A court shall consider any responsive pleading that is intended as an objection to confirmation of a child support review order not agreed to by the parties, including a general denial, as a request for a court hearing.

(b) The Title IV-D agency shall:

(1) make available to each clerk of court copies of the form to request a court hearing on a nonagreed review order; and

(2) provide the form to request a court hearing to a party to the child support review proceeding on request of the party.

(c) The clerk shall furnish the form to a party to the child support review proceeding on the request of the party.

History of Fam. Code §233.022: Acts 1995, 74th Leg., ch. 20, §1, eff. Apr. 20, 1995. Amended by Acts 1995, 74th Leg., ch. 341, §2.04, eff. Sept. 1, 1995. Renumbered from §231.422 and amended by Acts 1997, 75th Leg., ch. 911, §80, eff. Sept. 1, 1997. Source: Former Fam. Code §14.806(e).

FAM §233.023. TIME TO REQUEST A COURT HEARING

A party may file a request for a court hearing not later than the 20th day after the date the petition for confirmation of a nonagreed child support review order is delivered to the party.

History of Fam. Code §233.023: Acts 1995, 74th Leg., ch. 20, §1, eff. Apr. 20, 1995. Amended by Acts 1995, 74th Leg., ch. 341, §2.04, eff. Sept. 1, 1995. Renumbered from §231.423 and amended by Acts 1997, 75th Leg., ch. 911, §80, eff. Sept. 1, 1997. Source: Former Fam. Code §14.807(e).

A FAM §233.024. CONFIRMATION OF AGREED ORDER

(a) On the filing of an agreed child support review order signed by all parties, together with waiver of service, the court shall sign the order not later than the third day after the filing of the order. On expiration of the third day after the filing of the order, the order is considered confirmed by the court by operation of law, regardless of whether the court has signed the order. The court may sign the order before filing the order, but the signed order shall immediately be filed.

(b) On confirmation by the court, the Title IV-D agency shall immediately deliver to each party a copy of the signed agreed review order.

History of Fam. Code §233.024: Acts 1995, 74th Leg., ch. 20, §1, eff. Apr. 20, 1995. Amended by Acts 1995, 74th Leg., ch. 341, §2.04, eff. Sept. 1, 1995. Renumbered from §231.424 and amended by Acts 1997, 75th Leg., ch. 911, §80, eff. Sept. 1, 1997. Amended by Acts 2001, 77th Leg., ch. 1023, §68, eff. Sept. 1, 2001; Acts 2003, 78th Leg., ch. 610, §18, eff. Sept. 1, 2003; H.B. 2048, §3, 85th Leg., eff. Sept. 1, 2017. Source: Former Fam. Code §14.807(b), (c).

FAM §233.025. EFFECT OF REQUEST FOR HEARING ON NONAGREED ORDER; PLEADING

(a) A request for hearing or an order setting a hearing on confirmation of a nonagreed child support review order stays confirmation of the order pending the hearing.

(b) At a hearing on confirmation, any issues in dispute shall be heard in a trial de novo.

(c) The petition for confirmation and the child support review order constitute a sufficient pleading by the Title IV-D agency for relief on any issue addressed in the petition and order.

(d) The request for hearing may limit the scope of the de novo hearing by specifying the issues that are in dispute.

History of Fam. Code §233.025: Acts 1995, 74th Leg., ch. 20, §1, eff. Apr. 20, 1995. Amended by Acts 1995, 74th Leg., ch. 341, §2.04, eff. Sept. 1, 1995. Renumbered from §231.425 and amended by Acts 1997, 75th Leg., ch. 911, §80, eff. Sept. 1, 1997. Source: Former Fam. Code §14.807(d), (f).

FAM §233.026. TIME FOR COURT HEARING

(a) When a timely request for a court hearing has been filed as provided by Section 233.023, the court shall hold a hearing on the confirmation of a child support review order that has not been agreed to by the parties not later than the 30th day after the date the request was filed.

(b) A court may not hold a hearing on the confirmation of a nonagreed child support review order if a party does not timely request a hearing as provided by Section 233.023.

(c) If the court resets the time of the hearing, the reset hearing shall be held not later than the 30th day after the date set for the initial hearing.

History of Fam. Code §233.026: Acts 1995, 74th Leg., ch. 20, §1, eff. Apr. 20, 1995. Amended by Acts 1995, 74th Leg., ch. 341, §2.04, eff. Sept. 1, 1995. Renumbered from §231.426 and amended by Acts 1997, 75th Leg., ch. 911, §80, eff. Sept. 1, 1997. Amended by Acts 2003, 78th Leg., ch. 610, §19, eff. Sept. 1, 2003. Source: Former Fam. Code §14.807(g).

FAM §233.027. NONAGREED ORDER AFTER HEARING

(a) After the hearing on the confirmation of a nonagreed child support review order, the court shall:

(1) if the court finds that the nonagreed order should be confirmed, immediately sign the nonagreed order and enter the order as a final order of the court;

(2) if the court finds that the relief granted in the nonagreed child support review order is inappropriate, sign an appropriate order at the conclusion of the hearing or as soon after the conclusion of the hearing as is practical and enter the order as an order of the court; or

(3) if the court finds that all relief should be denied, enter an order that denies relief and includes specific findings explaining the reasons that relief is denied.

(b) Repealed by Acts 2013, 83rd Leg., ch. 742, §18, eff. Sept. 1, 2013.

(c) If the party who requested the hearing fails to appear at the hearing, the court shall sign the nonagreed order and enter the order as an order of the court.

History of Fam. Code §233.027: Acts 1995, 74th Leg., ch. 20, §1, eff. Apr. 20, 1995. Amended by Acts 1995, 74th Leg., ch. 341, §2.04, eff. Sept. 1, 1995. Renumbered from §231.427 and amended by Acts 1997, 75th Leg., ch. 911, §80, eff. Sept. 1, 1997. Amended by Acts 2003, 78th Leg., ch. 610, §20, eff. Sept. 1, 2003; Acts 2013, 83rd Leg., ch. 742, §§14, 15, 18, eff. Sept. 1, 2013. Source: Former Fam. Code §14.807(h), (i).

FAM §233.0271. CONFIRMATION OF NONAGREED ORDER WITHOUT HEARING

(a) If a request for hearing has not been timely received, the court shall confirm and sign a nonagreed child support review order not later than the 30th day after the date the petition for confirmation was delivered to the last party entitled to service.

(b) The Title IV-D agency shall immediately deliver a copy of the confirmed nonagreed review order to each party, together with notice of right to file a motion for a new trial not later than the 30th day after the date the order was confirmed by the court.

History of Fam. Code §233.0271: Acts 1997, 75th Leg., ch. 911, §80, eff. Sept. 1, 1997.

ANNOTATIONS

In re J.A.C., 362 S.W.3d 756, 760 (Tex.App.—Houston [14th Dist.] 2011, no pet.). "Section 233.0271(a) does not state whether it is jurisdictional. Further, §233.0271 does not provide any consequence for failure to sign a confirmation order within 30 days after delivery of the confirmation petition. [¶] Interpreting similar statutes prescribing expedited timelines for trial court action, other appellate courts have held that deadlines such as the requirement in §233.0271(a) are mandatory, but not jurisdictional, when the statute is silent regarding consequences of failure to comply. *At 761:* Chapter 233 was designed to allow agencies such as the [Office of the Attorney General (OAG)] to take expedited administrative action to establish, modify, and enforce child support obligations and determine parentage. This purpose is not 'well-served' if the trial court must dismiss any confirmation petition that is not heard within the required time, requiring the OAG to reinstitute the proceedings. Instead, the OAG, as the party who filed the confirmation petition, may seek mandamus relief to compel a confirmation order if the trial court fails to sign such an order within the 30-day period; however, the OAG may also acquiesce in the later ruling without affecting the court's subject-matter jurisdiction." *See also* ***In re Office of the Atty. Gen.***, 264 S.W.3d 800, 808-09 (Tex.App.—Houston [1st Dist.] 2008, orig. proceeding).

In re S.B.S., 282 S.W.3d 711, 715 (Tex.App.—Amarillo 2009, pet. denied). See annotation under Family Code §233.021, p. 871.

In re G.J.F., No. 03-07-00643-CV (Tex.App.—Austin 2008, no pet.) (memo op.; 8-29-08). "The [AG] asserts that the trial court abused its discretion by 'refusing to sign the child support review order that the [AG] had asked to be confirmed and by signing a different order instead.' The [AG] relies on §233.0271(a).... [¶] We do not find a basis for reversal in this record. ... The statute does not require that the court sign any non-agreed child support review order that is proposed to the court without review or alteration even if the order is not supported by required documentary evidence or statutory authority. ... The legislature must have envisioned that courts would, even in cases where no hearing is requested, examine the contents of the non-agreed child support order and the documentary evidence supporting the petition to be sure the order complies with statutory requirements."

FAM §233.028. SPECIAL CHILD SUPPORT REVIEW PROCEDURES RELATING TO ESTABLISHMENT OF PARENTAGE

(a) If the parentage of a child has not been established, the notice of child support review delivered to the parties must include an allegation that the recipient is a biological parent of the child. The notice shall inform the parties that:

(1) not later than the 15th day after the date of delivery of the notice, the alleged parent of the child shall either sign a statement of paternity or an acknowledgment of paternity or deny in writing that the alleged parent is the biological parent of the child;

(2) either party may request that scientifically accepted parentage testing be conducted to assist in determining the identities of the child's parents;

(3) if the alleged parent timely denies parentage of the child, the Title IV-D agency shall order parentage testing; and

(4) if the alleged parent does not deny parentage of the child, the Title IV-D agency may conduct a negotiation conference.

(b) If all parties agree to the child's parentage, the agency may file an agreed child support review order as provided by this chapter.

(c) If a party denies parentage of a child whose parentage has not previously been acknowledged or adjudicated, the Title IV-D agency shall order parentage testing and give each party notice of the time and place of testing. If either party fails or refuses to participate in administrative parentage testing, the Title IV-D agency may file a child support review order resolving the question of parentage against that party. The court shall confirm the child support review order as a temporary or final order of the court only after an opportunity for parentage testing has been provided.

(d) If genetic testing identifies the alleged parent as the parent of the child and the results of a verified written report of a genetic testing expert meet the requirements of Chapter 160 for issuing a temporary order, the Title IV-D agency may conduct a negotiation conference to resolve any issues of support and file with the court a child support review order.

(e) If the results of parentage testing exclude an alleged parent from being the biological parent of the child, the Title IV-D agency shall issue and provide to each party a child support review order that declares that the excluded person is not a parent of the child.

(f) Any party may file a petition for confirmation of a child support review order issued under this section.

History of Fam. Code §233.028: Acts 1995, 74th Leg., ch. 20, §1, eff. Apr. 20, 1995. Amended by Acts 1995, 74th Leg., ch. 341, §2.04, eff. Sept. 1, 1995. Renumbered from §231.428 and amended by Acts 1997, 75th Leg., ch. 911, §80, eff. Sept. 1, 1997. Amended by Acts 2001, 77th Leg., ch. 821, §2.17, eff. June 14, 2001; Acts 2015, 84th Leg., ch. 963, §6, eff. Sept. 1, 2015. Source: Former Fam. Code §14.808.

FAM §233.029. ADMINISTRATIVE PROCEDURE LAW NOT APPLICABLE

The child support review process under this chapter is not governed by Chapter 2001, Government Code.

History of Fam. Code §233.029: Acts 1995, 74th Leg., ch. 20, §1, eff. Apr. 20, 1995. Amended by Acts 1995, 74th Leg., ch. 341, §2.04, eff. Sept. 1, 1995. Renumbered from §231.429 and amended by Acts 1997, 75th Leg., ch. 911, §80, eff. Sept. 1, 1997. Source: Former Fam. Code §14.801.

CHAPTER 234. STATE CASE REGISTRY, DISBURSEMENT UNIT, & DIRECTORY OF NEW HIRES

SUBCHAPTER A. UNIFIED STATE CASE REGISTRY & DISBURSEMENT UNIT

FAM §234.001. ESTABLISHMENT & OPERATION OF STATE CASE REGISTRY & STATE DISBURSEMENT UNIT

(a) The Title IV-D agency shall establish and operate a state case registry and state disbursement unit meeting the requirements of 42 U.S.C. Sections 654a(e) and 654b and this subchapter.

(b) The state case registry shall maintain records of child support orders in Title IV-D cases and in other cases in which a child support order has been established or modified in this state on or after October 1, 1998.

(c) The state disbursement unit shall:

(1) receive, maintain, and furnish records of child support payments in Title IV-D cases and other cases as authorized by law;

(2) forward child support payments as authorized by law;

(3) maintain records of child support payments made through the state disbursement unit; and

(4) make available to a local registry each day in a manner determined by the Title IV-D agency the following information:

(A) the cause number of the suit under which withholding is required;

(B) the payor's name and social security number;

(C) the payee's name and, if available, social security number;

(D) the date the disbursement unit received the payment;

(E) the amount of the payment; and

(F) the instrument identification information.

(d) A certified child support payment record produced by the state disbursement unit is admissible as evidence of the truth of the information contained in the record and does not require further authentication or verification.

History of Fam. Code §234.001: Acts 1997, 75th Leg., ch. 911, §94, eff. Sept. 1, 1997. Amended by Acts 1999, 76th Leg., ch. 556, §68, eff. Sept. 1, 1999; Acts 2001, 77th Leg., ch. 1023, §69, eff. Sept. 1, 2001; Acts 2007, 80th Leg., ch. 972, §58, eff. Sept. 1, 2007.

FAM §234.002. INTEGRATED SYSTEM FOR CHILD SUPPORT & MEDICAL SUPPORT ENFORCEMENT[1]

The statewide integrated system for child support and medical support enforcement under Chapter 231 shall be part of the state case registry and state disbursement unit authorized by this subchapter.

1. **Editor's note:** In 2015, the Legislature amended §234.002 to require dental support for a child subject to a child-support order, but the amendments are not effective until Sept. 1, 2018. For the text of the prospective amendments, see Acts 2015, 84th Leg., ch. 1150, §53, eff. Sept. 1, 2018.

History of Fam. Code §234.002: Acts 1997, 75th Leg., ch. 911, §94, eff. Sept. 1, 1997. Amended by Acts 1999, 76th Leg., ch. 556, §68, eff. Sept. 1, 1999.

FAM §234.003. EXPIRED

FAM §234.004. CONTRACTS & COOPERATIVE AGREEMENTS

(a) The Title IV-D agency may enter into contracts and cooperative agreements as necessary to establish and operate the state case registry and state disbursement unit authorized under this subchapter.

(b) To the extent funds are available for this purpose, the Title IV-D agency may enter into contracts or cooperative agreements to process through the state disbursement unit child support collections in cases not otherwise eligible under 42 U.S.C. Section 654b.

History of Fam. Code §234.004: Acts 1997, 75th Leg., ch. 911, §94, eff. Sept. 1, 1997. Amended by Acts 2001, 77th Leg., ch. 1023, §70, eff. Sept. 1, 2001.

FAM §234.005. EXPIRED

FAM §234.006. RULEMAKING

The Title IV-D agency may adopt rules in compliance with federal law for the operation of the state case registry and the state disbursement unit.

History of Fam. Code §234.006: Acts 1999, 76th Leg., ch. 556, §68, eff. Sept. 1, 1999. Amended by Acts 2001, 77th Leg., ch. 1023, §71, eff. Sept. 1, 2001; Acts 2007, 80th Leg., ch. 972, §59, eff. Sept. 1, 2007.

FAM §234.007. NOTICE OF PLACE OF PAYMENT

(a) A court that orders income to be withheld for child support shall order that all income ordered withheld for child support shall be paid to the state disbursement unit.

(b) In order to redirect payments to the state disbursement unit, the Title IV-D agency shall issue a notice of place of payment informing the obligor, obligee, and employer that income withheld for child support is to be paid to the state disbursement unit and may not be remitted to a local registry, the obligee, or any other person or agency. If withheld support has been paid to a local registry, the Title IV-D agency shall send the notice to the registry to redirect any payments to the state disbursement unit.

(c) A copy of the notice under Subsection (b) shall be filed with the court of continuing jurisdiction.

(d) The notice under Subsection (b) must include:

(1) the name of the child for whom support is ordered and of the person to whom support is ordered by the court to be paid;

(2) the style and cause number of the case in which support is ordered; and

(3) instructions for the payment of ordered support to the state disbursement unit.

(e) On receipt of a copy of the notice under Subsection (b), the clerk of the court shall file the notice in the appropriate case file.

(f) The notice under Subsection (b) may be used by the Title IV-D agency to redirect child support payments from the state disbursement unit of this state to the state disbursement unit of another state.

History of Fam. Code §234.007: Acts 1999, 76th Leg., ch. 556, §68, eff. Sept. 1, 1999. Amended by Acts 2003, 78th Leg., ch. 1247, §45, eff. Sept. 1, 2003; Acts 2013, 83rd Leg., ch. 742, §16, eff. Sept. 1, 2013.

FAM §234.008. DEPOSIT, DISTRIBUTION, & ISSUANCE OF PAYMENTS

(a) Not later than the second business day after the date the state disbursement unit receives a child support payment, the state disbursement unit shall distribute the payment to the Title IV-D agency or the obligee.

(b) The state disbursement unit shall deposit daily all child support payments in a trust fund with the state comptroller. Subject to the agreement of the comptroller, the state disbursement unit may issue checks from the trust fund.

(c) to **(e)** Repealed by Acts 2007, 80th Leg., ch. 972, §65(5), eff. Sept. 1, 2007.

History of Fam. Code §234.008: Acts 1999, 76th Leg., ch. 556, §68, eff. Sept. 1, 1999. Amended by Acts 2003, 78th Leg., ch. 1262, §4, eff. Sept. 1, 2003; Acts 2005, 79th Leg., ch. 1232, §1, eff. Sept. 1, 2005; Acts 2007, 80th Leg., ch. 972, §§60, 65(5), eff. Sept. 1, 2007.

FAM §234.009. OFFICIAL CHILD SUPPORT PAYMENT RECORD

(a) The record of child support payments maintained by a local registry is the official record of a payment received directly by the local registry.

(b) The record of child support payments maintained by the state disbursement unit is the official record of a payment received directly by the unit.

(c) After the date child support payments formerly received by a local registry are redirected to the state disbursement unit, a local registry may accept a record of payments furnished by the state disbursement unit and may add the payments to the record of payments maintained by the local registry so that a complete payment record is available for use by the court.

(d) If the local registry does not add payments received by the state disbursement unit to the record maintained by the registry as provided by Subsection (c), the official record of child support payments consists of the record maintained by the local registry for payments received directly by the registry and the record maintained by the state disbursement unit for payments received directly by the unit.

History of Fam. Code §234.009: Acts 1999, 76th Leg., ch. 556, §68, eff. Sept. 1, 1999.

FAM §234.0091. ADMINISTRATIVE REVIEW OF CHILD SUPPORT PAYMENT RECORD

(a) On request, the state disbursement unit shall provide to an obligor or obligee a copy of the record of child support payments maintained by the unit. The record must include the amounts and dates of all payments received from or on behalf of the obligor and disbursed to the obligee.

(b) An obligor or obligee may request that the Title IV-D agency investigate an alleged discrepancy between the child support payment record provided by the state disbursement unit under Subsection (a) and the payment records maintained by the obligor or obligee. The obligor or obligee making the request must provide to the Title IV-D agency documentation of the alleged discrepancy, including a canceled check or other evidence of a payment or disbursement at issue.

(c) The Title IV-D agency shall respond to a request under Subsection (b) not later than the 20th day after the date the agency receives the request. If, after an investigation, the agency determines that the child support payment record maintained by the state disbursement unit should be amended, the state disbursement unit shall immediately make the required amendment to the record and notify the obligor or obligee who made the request under Subsection (b) of that amendment.

History of Fam. Code §234.0091: Acts 2003, 78th Leg., ch. 1085, §1, eff. June 20, 2003.

FAM §234.010. DIRECT DEPOSIT & ELECTRONIC BENEFITS TRANSFER OF CHILD SUPPORT PAYMENTS

(a) The state disbursement unit authorized under this chapter may make a direct deposit of a child support payment to an obligee by electronic funds transfer into an account with a financial institution maintained by the obligee. It is the responsibility of the obligee to notify the state disbursement unit of:

(1) the existence of an account;

(2) the appropriate routing information for direct deposit by electronic funds transfer into an account; and

(3) any modification to account information previously provided to the state disbursement unit, including information that an account has been closed.

(b) Except as provided by Subsection (d), the state disbursement unit shall deposit a child support payment by electronic funds transfer into a debit card account established for the obligee by the Title IV-D agency if the obligee:

(1) does not maintain an account with a financial institution;

(2) fails to notify the state disbursement unit of the existence of an account maintained with a financial institution; or

(3) closes an account maintained with a financial institution previously used to accept direct deposit of a child support payment without establishing a new account and notifying the state disbursement unit of the new account in accordance with Subsection (a).

(c) The Title IV-D agency shall:

(1) issue a debit card to each obligee for whom a debit card account is established under Subsection (b); and

(2) provide the obligee with instructions for activating and using the debit card.

(c-1) Chapter 604, Business & Commerce Code, does not apply to a debit card issued under Subsection (c).

(d) An obligee may decline in writing to receive child support payments by electronic funds transfer into an account with a financial institution or a debit card account and request that payments be provided by paper warrants if the obligee alleges that receiving payments by electronic funds transfer would impose a substantial hardship.

(e) A child support payment disbursed by the state disbursement unit by electronic funds transfer into an account with a financial institution maintained by the obligee or into a debit card account established for the obligee under Subsection (b) is solely the property of the obligee.

History of Fam. Code §234.010: Acts 1999, 76th Leg., ch. 1072, §6, eff. Sept. 1, 1999. Renumbered from §234.006 by Acts 2001, 77th Leg., ch. 1420, §21.001(33), eff. Sept. 1, 2001. Amended by Acts 2009, 81st Leg., ch. 551, §1 (eff. June 19, 2009), ch. 767, §30 (eff. June 19, 2009).

FAM §234.011. REPEALED

Repealed by Acts 2009, 81st Leg., ch. 551, §4 (eff. June 19, 2009), ch. 767, §37 (eff. June 19, 2009).

FAM §234.012. RELEASE OF INFORMATION FROM STATE CASE REGISTRY

Unless prohibited by a court in accordance with Section 105.006(c), the state case registry shall, on request and to the extent permitted by federal law, provide the information required under Sections 105.006 and 105.008 in any case included in the registry under Section 234.001(b) to:

(1) any party to the proceeding;

(2) an amicus attorney;

(3) an attorney ad litem;

(4) a friend of the court;

(5) a guardian ad litem;

(6) a domestic relations office;

(7) a prosecuting attorney or juvenile court acting in a proceeding under Title 3; or

(8) a governmental entity or court acting in a proceeding under Chapter 262.

History of Fam. Code §234.012: Acts 2007, 80th Leg., ch. 972, §61, eff. Sept. 1, 2007.

Sections 234.013-234.100 reserved for expansion

Subchapter B. State Directory of New Hires

FAM §234.101. DEFINITIONS

In this subchapter:

(1) "Employee" means an individual who is an employee within the meaning of Chapter 24 of the Internal Revenue Code of 1986 (26 U.S.C. Section 3401(c)) or an independent contractor as defined by the Internal Revenue Service. The term does not include an employee of a state agency performing intelligence or counterintelligence functions if the head of the agency has determined that reporting employee information under this subchapter could endanger the safety of the employee or compromise an ongoing investigation or intelligence activity.

(2) "Employer" has the meaning given that term by Section 3401(d) of the Internal Revenue Code of 1986 (26 U.S.C. Section 3401(d)) and includes a governmental entity and a labor organization, as that term is identified in Section 2(5) of the National Labor Relations Act (29 U.S.C. Section 152(5)), including an entity, also known as a "hiring hall," used by the labor organization and an employer to carry out requirements of an agreement between the organization and an employer described in Section 8(f)(3) of that Act (29 U.S.C. Section 158(f)(3)).

(3) "Newly hired employee" means an employee who:

(A) has not been previously employed by the employer; or

(B) was previously employed by the employer but has been separated from that employment for at least 60 consecutive days.

History of Fam. Code §234.101: Acts 1997, 75th Leg., ch. 911, §94, eff. Sept. 1, 1997. Amended by Acts 2013, 83rd Leg., ch. 742, §17, eff. Sept. 1, 2013; Acts 2015, 84th Leg., ch. 963, §7, eff. Sept. 1, 2015.

FAM §234.102. OPERATION OF NEW HIRE DIRECTORY

In cooperation with the Texas Workforce Commission, the Title IV-D agency shall develop and operate a state directory to which employers in the state shall report each newly hired or rehired employee in accordance with the requirements of 42 U.S.C. Section 653a.

History of Fam. Code §234.102: Acts 1997, 75th Leg., ch. 911, §94, eff. Sept. 1, 1997. Amended by Acts 1999, 76th Leg., ch. 178, §12, eff. Aug. 30, 1999.

FAM §234.103. CONTRACTS & COOPERATIVE AGREEMENTS

The Title IV-D agency may enter into cooperative agreements and contracts as necessary to create and operate the directory authorized under this subchapter.

History of Fam. Code §234.103: Acts 1997, 75th Leg., ch. 911, §94, eff. Sept. 1, 1997. Amended by Acts 1999, 76th Leg., ch. 178, §13, eff. Aug. 30, 1999.

FAM §234.104. PROCEDURES

The Title IV-D agency by rule shall establish procedures for reporting employee information and for operating a state directory of new hires meeting the requirements of federal law.

History of Fam. Code §234.104: Acts 1997, 75th Leg., ch. 911, §94, eff. Sept. 1, 1997. Amended by Acts 1999, 76th Leg., ch. 178, §14, eff. Aug. 30, 1999.

See also 1 T.A.C. §§55.301-55.308.

FAM §234.105. CIVIL PENALTY

(a) In addition to any other remedy provided by law, an employer who knowingly violates a procedure adopted under Section 234.104 for reporting employee information may be liable for a civil penalty as permitted by Section 453A(d) of the federal Social Security Act (42 U.S.C. Section 653a).

(b) The amount of the civil penalty may not exceed:

(1) $25 for each occurrence in which an employer fails to report an employee; or

(2) $500 for each occurrence in which the conduct described by Subdivision (1) is the result of a conspiracy between the employer and an employee to not supply a required report or to submit a false or incomplete report.

(c) The attorney general may sue to collect the civil penalty. A penalty collected under this section shall be deposited in a special fund in the state treasury.

History of Fam. Code §234.105: Acts 2007, 80th Leg., ch. 972, §62, eff. Sept. 1, 2007.

CHAPTER 235. REPEALED

Repealed by Acts 2007, 80th Leg., ch. 972, §65(6), eff. Sept. 1, 2007.

CHAPTER 236. REPEALED [~~COMPETITIVE BIDDING FOR CHILD SUPPORT COLLECTION SERVICES~~]

FAM §236.001. REPEALED [~~DEFINITION~~]

[~~In this chapter, "council" means the State Council on Competitive Government.~~]

Repealed by S.B. 706, §7(2), 85th Leg., eff. Sept. 1, 2017.

FAM §236.002. REPEALED [~~POWERS & DUTIES OF COUNCIL~~]

[~~(a)~~] [~~The council shall:~~]

[~~(1)~~] [~~establish an initiative called "Kids Can't Wait" to increase child support enforcement;~~]

[~~(2)~~] [~~identify child support enforcement functions performed by the Title IV-D agency that may be competitively bid;~~]

[~~(3)~~] [~~establish guidelines for referral of child support enforcement cases to a contractor;~~]

[~~(4)~~] [~~after consulting with the Title IV-D agency, make recommendations regarding competitive bidding of child support enforcement functions that are identified under Subdivision (2);~~]

[~~(5)~~] [~~consider the benefits of the state's participation in an electronic parent locator network or a similar national service designed to locate parents who owe child support;~~]

[~~(6)~~] [~~study the feasibility of cost recovery options in child support collection actions for children who do not receive public assistance; and~~]

[~~(7)~~] [~~engage in other activities necessary for the administration of this chapter.~~]

[~~(b)~~] [~~The Title IV-D agency shall coordinate with the council regarding competitive bidding of child support enforcement functions identified under this section.~~]

[~~(c)~~] [~~A member of the council may designate an employee of the state agency represented by the member to perform any of the member's powers or duties under this section.~~]

[~~(d)~~] [~~The Title IV-D agency shall cooperate with the council if requested by the council.~~]

[~~(e)~~] [~~Repealed by Acts 2011, 82nd Leg., ch. 990, §10(1) (eff. June 17, 2011), ch. 1083, §25(26) (eff. June 17, 2011).~~]

Repealed by S.B. 706, §7(2), 85th Leg., eff. Sept. 1, 2017.

FAM §236.003. REPEALED [~~CHILD SUPPORT COLLECTION AGREEMENT~~]

[~~The Title IV-D agency or a contractor awarded a contract under this chapter to collect child support may enter into an agreement with a person liable for the payment of child support. The agreement may relate to any matter that may be adjudicated by a court, including:~~]

[~~(1)~~] [~~the determination of paternity;~~]

[~~(2)~~] [~~the determination of the amount of child support due;~~]

[~~(3)~~] [~~the method of making child support payments;~~]

[~~(4)~~] [~~the imposition of income garnishment or withholding;~~]

[~~(5)~~] [~~the payment of fees;~~]

[~~(6)~~] [~~the reimbursement of costs; and~~]

~~[(7)] [other child support enforcement matters permitted by state or federal law.]~~

Repealed by S.B. 706, §7(2), 85th Leg., eff. Sept. 1, 2017.

Chapters 237-260 reserved for expansion

SUBTITLE E. PROTECTION OF THE CHILD

CHAPTER 261. INVESTIGATION OF REPORT OF CHILD ABUSE OR NEGLECT

SUBCHAPTER A. GENERAL PROVISIONS

Ⓐ FAM §261.001. DEFINITIONS

In 2017, three bills amended §261.001, but only one bill, H.B. 249, §2, saved the former law in effect at that time. The amended text from H.B. 249, §2 is effective for

reports of suspected abuse, neglect, or exploitation of a child made on or after Sept. 1, 2017. Reports made before Sept. 1, 2017, are governed by the former law in effect at that time. The amended text from H.B. 5, §36(1) and S.B. 11, §7 is effective Sept. 1, 2017.

In this chapter:

(1) "Abuse" includes the following acts or omissions by a person:

(A) mental or emotional injury to a child that results in an observable and material impairment in the child's growth, development, or psychological functioning;

(B) causing or permitting the child to be in a situation in which the child sustains a mental or emotional injury that results in an observable and material impairment in the child's growth, development, or psychological functioning;

(C) physical injury that results in substantial harm to the child, or the genuine threat of substantial harm from physical injury to the child, including an injury that is at variance with the history or explanation given and excluding an accident or reasonable discipline by a parent, guardian, or managing or possessory conservator that does not expose the child to a substantial risk of harm;

(D) failure to make a reasonable effort to prevent an action by another person that results in physical injury that results in substantial harm to the child;

(E) sexual conduct harmful to a child's mental, emotional, or physical welfare, including conduct that constitutes the offense of continuous sexual abuse of young child or children under Section 21.02, Penal Code, indecency with a child under Section 21.11, Penal Code, sexual assault under Section 22.011, Penal Code, or aggravated sexual assault under Section 22.021, Penal Code;

(F) failure to make a reasonable effort to prevent sexual conduct harmful to a child;

(G) compelling or encouraging the child to engage in sexual conduct as defined by Section 43.01, Penal Code, including compelling or encouraging the child in a manner that constitutes an offense of trafficking of persons under Section 20A.02(a)(7) or (8), Penal Code, prostitution under Section 43.02(b), Penal Code, or compelling prostitution under Section 43.05(a)(2), Penal Code;

(H) causing, permitting, encouraging, engaging in, or allowing the photographing, filming, or depicting of the child if the person knew or should have known that the resulting photograph, film, or depiction of the child is obscene as defined by Section 43.21, Penal Code, or pornographic;

(I) the current use by a person of a controlled substance as defined by Chapter 481, Health and Safety Code, in a manner or to the extent that the use results in physical, mental, or emotional injury to a child;

(J) causing, expressly permitting, or encouraging a child to use a controlled substance as defined by Chapter 481, Health and Safety Code;

(K) causing, permitting, encouraging, engaging in, or allowing a sexual performance by a child as defined by Section 43.25, Penal Code; [~~or~~]

(L) knowingly causing, permitting, encouraging, engaging in, or allowing a child to be trafficked in a manner punishable as an offense under Section 20A.02(a)(5), (6), (7), or (8), Penal Code, or the failure to make a reasonable effort to prevent a child from being trafficked in a manner punishable as an offense under any of those sections; or

(M) forcing or coercing a child to enter into a marriage.

(2) "Department" means the Department of Family and Protective Services.

(3) "Exploitation" means the illegal or improper use of a child or of the resources of a child for monetary or personal benefit, profit, or gain by an employee, volunteer, or other individual working under the auspices of a facility or program as further described by rule or policy.

(4) "Neglect":

(A) includes:

(i) the leaving of a child in a situation where the child would be exposed to a substantial risk of physical or mental harm, without arranging for necessary care for the child, and the demonstration of an intent not to return by a parent, guardian, or managing or possessory conservator of the child;

(ii) the following acts or omissions by a person:

(a) placing a child in or failing to remove a child from a situation that a reasonable person would realize requires judgment or actions beyond the child's level of maturity, physical condition, or mental abilities and that results in bodily injury or a substantial risk of immediate harm to the child;

(b) failing to seek, obtain, or follow through with medical care for a child, with the failure resulting in or

presenting a substantial risk of death, disfigurement, or bodily injury or with the failure resulting in an observable and material impairment to the growth, development, or functioning of the child;

(c) the failure to provide a child with food, clothing, or shelter necessary to sustain the life or health of the child, excluding failure caused primarily by financial inability unless relief services had been offered and refused;

(d) placing a child in or failing to remove the child from a situation in which the child would be exposed to a substantial risk of sexual conduct harmful to the child; or

(e) placing a child in or failing to remove the child from a situation in which the child would be exposed to acts or omissions that constitute abuse under Subdivision (1)(E), (F), (G), (H), or (K) committed against another child; [~~or~~]

(iii) the failure by the person responsible for a child's care, custody, or welfare to permit the child to return to the child's home without arranging for the necessary care for the child after the child has been absent from the home for any reason, including having been in residential placement or having run away; or

(iv) a negligent act or omission by an employee, volunteer, or other individual working under the auspices of a facility or program, including failurc to comply with an individual treatment plan, plan of care, or individualized service plan, that causes or may cause substantial emotional harm or physical injury to, or the death of, a child served by the facility or program as further described by rule or policy; and

(B) does not include the refusal by a person responsible for a child's care, custody, or welfare to permit the child to remain in or return to the child's home resulting in the placement of the child in the conservatorship of the department if:

(i) the child has a severe emotional disturbance;

(ii) the person's refusal is based solely on the person's inability to obtain mental health services necessary to protect the safety and well-being of the child; and

(iii) the person has exhausted all reasonable means available to the person to obtain the mental health services described by Subparagraph (ii).

(5) "Person responsible for a child's care, custody, or welfare" means a person who traditionally is responsible for a child's care, custody, or welfare, including:

(A) a parent, guardian, managing or possessory conservator, or foster parent of the child;

(B) a member of the child's family or household as defined by Chapter 71;

(C) a person with whom the child's parent cohabits;

(D) school personnel or a volunteer at the child's school; [~~or~~]

(E) personnel or a volunteer at a public or private child-care facility that provides services for the child or at a public or private residential institution or facility where the child resides; or

(F) an employee, volunteer, or other person working under the supervision of a licensed or unlicensed child-care facility, including a family home, residential child-care facility, employer-based day-care facility, or shelter day-care facility, as those terms are defined in Chapter 42, Human Resources Code.

(6) "Report" means a report that alleged or suspected abuse or neglect of a child has occurred or may occur.

(7) Repealed by H.B. 5, §36(1), 85th Leg., eff. Sept. 1, 2017.

[~~(7)~~] [~~"Executive commissioner" means the executive commissioner of the Health and Human Services Commission.~~]

(8) Repealed by Acts 2015, 84th Leg., ch. 1, §1.203(4), eff. Apr. 2, 2015.

(9) "Severe emotional disturbance" means a mental, behavioral, or emotional disorder of sufficient duration to result in functional impairment that substantially interferes with or limits a person's role or ability to function in family, school, or community activities.

History of Fam. Code §261.001: Acts 1995, 74th Leg., ch. 20, §1, eff. Apr. 20, 1995. Amended by Acts 1995, 74th Leg., ch. 751, §86, eff. Sept. 1, 1995; Acts 1997, 75th Leg., ch. 575, §10 (eff. Sept. 1, 1997), ch. 1022, §63 (eff. Sept. 1, 1997); Acts 1999, 76th Leg., ch. 62, §19.01(26), eff. Sept. 1, 1999; Acts 2001, 77th Leg., ch. 59, §1, eff. Sept. 1, 2001; Acts 2005, 79th Leg., ch. 268, §1.11, eff. Sept. 1, 2005; Acts 2007, 80th Leg., ch. 593, §3.32, eff. Sept. 1, 2007; Acts 2011, 82nd Leg., ch. 1, §4.03, eff. Sept. 1, 2011; Acts 2013, 83rd Leg., ch. 1142, §1, eff. Sept. 1, 2013; Acts 2015, 84th Leg., ch. 1, §§1.120, 1.203(4) (eff. Apr. 2, 2015), ch. 432, §1 (eff. Sept. 1, 2015), ch. 1273, §4 (eff. Sept. 1, 2015); H.B. 5, §36(1), 85th Leg., eff. Sept. 1, 2017; H.B. 249, §2, 85th Leg., eff. Sept. 1, 2017; S.B. 11, §7, 85th Leg., eff. Sept. 1, 2017. Source: Former Fam. Code §34.012.

See also 37 T.A.C. §§349.100, 350.100.

Ⓐ FAM §261.002. CENTRAL REGISTRY

(a) The department shall establish and maintain a central registry of the names of individuals found by the department to have abused or neglected a child.

(b) The executive commissioner shall adopt rules necessary to carry out this section. The rules shall:

(1) prohibit the department from making a finding of abuse or neglect against a person in a case in which the department is named managing conservator of a child who has a severe emotional disturbance only because the child's family is unable to obtain mental health services for the child; [~~and~~]

(2) establish guidelines for reviewing the records in the registry and removing those records in which the department was named managing conservator of a child who has a severe emotional disturbance only because the child's family was unable to obtain mental health services for the child;

(3) require the department to remove a person's name from the central registry maintained under this section not later than the 10th business day after the date the department receives notice that a finding of abuse and neglect against the person is overturned in:

(A) an administrative review or an appeal of the review conducted under Section 261.309(c);

(B) a review or an appeal of the review conducted by the office of consumer affairs of the department; or

(C) a hearing or an appeal conducted by the State Office of Administrative Hearings; and

(4) require the department to update any relevant department files to reflect an overturned finding of abuse or neglect against a person not later than the 10th business day after the date the finding is overturned in a review, hearing, or appeal described by Subdivision (3).

(c) The department may enter into agreements with other states to allow for the exchange of reports of child abuse and neglect in other states' central registry systems. The department shall use information obtained under this subsection in performing the background checks required under Section 42.056, Human Resources Code. The department shall cooperate with federal agencies and shall provide information and reports of child abuse and neglect to the appropriate federal agency that maintains the national registry for child abuse and neglect, if a national registry exists.

History of Fam. Code §261.002: Acts 1995, 74th Leg., ch. 20, §1, eff. Apr. 20, 1995. Amended by Acts 2005, 79th Leg., ch. 268, §1.12, eff. Sept. 1, 2005; Acts 2015, 84th Leg., ch. 1, §1.121 (eff. Apr. 2, 2015), ch. 432, §2 (eff. Sept. 1, 2015); H.B. 2849, §1, 85th Leg., eff. Sept. 1, 2017. Source: Former Fam. Code §34.06.

See also 40 T.A.C. §700.104.

FAM §261.003. APPLICATION TO STUDENTS IN SCHOOL FOR DEAF OR SCHOOL FOR BLIND & VISUALLY IMPAIRED

This chapter applies to the investigation of a report of abuse or neglect of a student, without regard to the age of the student, in the Texas School for the Deaf or the Texas School for the Blind and Visually Impaired.

History of Fam. Code §261.003: Acts 1995, 74th Leg., ch. 20, §1, eff. Apr. 20, 1995. Source: Former Fam. Code §34.013.

E FAM §261.004[A*]. TRACKING OF RECURRENCE OF CHILD ABUSE OR NEGLECT REPORTS

In 2017, the Legislature enacted two sections 261.004. This §261.004 was enacted by S.B. 11, §8, 85th Leg., effective Sept. 1, 2017. The [A] has been added by the editor to distinguish this §261.004 from the other, which is marked with [B*]. In 2019, the Legislature is expected to correct the duplicate numbering.*

(a) The department shall collect and monitor data regarding repeated reports of abuse or neglect:

(1) involving the same child, including reports of abuse or neglect of the child made while the child resided in other households and reports of abuse or neglect of the child by different alleged perpetrators made while the child resided in the same household; or

(2) by the same alleged perpetrator.

(b) In monitoring reports of abuse or neglect under Subsection (a), the department shall group together separate reports involving different children residing in the same household.

(c) The department shall consider any report collected under Subsection (a) involving any child or adult who is a part of a child's household when making case priority determinations or when conducting service or safety planning for the child or the child's family.

History of Fam. Code §261.004[A*]: Enacted by S.B. 11, §8, 85th Leg., eff. Sept. 1, 2017.

History of Former Fam. Code §261.004: Repealed by Acts 2015, 84th Leg., ch. 713, §4 (eff. Sept. 1, 2015), ch. 944, §86(6) (eff. Sept. 1, 2015).

E FAM §261.004[B*]. REFERENCE TO EXECUTIVE COMMISSIONER OR COMMISSION

In 2017, the Legislature enacted two sections 261.004. This §261.004 was enacted by H.B. 5, §10, 85th Leg., effective Sept. 1, 2017. The [B] has been added by the editor to distinguish this §261.004 from the other, which is marked with [A*]. In 2019, the Legislature is expected to correct the duplicate numbering.*

In this chapter:

(1) a reference to the executive commissioner or the executive commissioner of the Health and Human Services Commission means the commissioner of the department; and

(2) a reference to the Health and Human Services Commission means the department.

History of Fam. Code §261.004[B*]: Enacted by H.B. 5, §10, 85th Leg., eff. Sept. 1, 2017.

History of Former Fam. Code §261.004: Repealed by Acts 2015, 84th Leg., ch. 713, §4 (eff. Sept. 1, 2015), ch. 944, §86(6) (eff. Sept. 1, 2015).

Sections 261.005-261.100 reserved for expansion

SUBCHAPTER B. REPORT OF ABUSE OR NEGLECT; IMMUNITIES

A FAM §261.101. PERSONS REQUIRED TO REPORT; TIME TO REPORT

The amended text in §261.101 is effective for reports of suspected abuse, neglect, or exploitation of a child made on or after Sept. 1, 2017. Reports made before Sept. 1, 2017, are governed by the former law in effect at that time.

(a) A person having cause to believe that a child's physical or mental health or welfare has been adversely affected by abuse or neglect by any person shall immediately make a report as provided by this subchapter.

(b) If a professional has cause to believe that a child has been abused or neglected or may be abused or neglected, or that a child is a victim of an offense under Section 21.11, Penal Code, and the professional has cause to believe that the child has been abused as defined by Section 261.001 [~~or 261.401~~], the professional shall make a report not later than the 48th hour after the hour the professional first suspects that the child has been or may be abused or neglected or is a victim of an offense under Section 21.11, Penal Code. A professional may not delegate to or rely on another person to make the report. In this subsection, "professional" means an individual who is licensed or certified by the state or who is an employee of a facility licensed, certified, or operated by the state and who, in the normal course of official duties or duties for which a license or certification is required, has direct contact with children. The term includes teachers, nurses, doctors, day-care employees, employees of a clinic or health care facility that provides reproductive services, juvenile probation officers, and juvenile detention or correctional officers.

(b-1) In addition to the duty to make a report under Subsection (a) or (b), a person or professional shall make a report in the manner required by Subsection (a) or (b), as applicable, if the person or professional has cause to believe that an adult was a victim of abuse or neglect as a child and the person or professional determines in good faith that disclosure of the information is necessary to protect the health and safety of:

(1) another child; or

(2) an elderly person or person with a disability as defined by Section 48.002, Human Resources Code.

(c) The requirement to report under this section applies without exception to an individual whose personal communications may otherwise be privileged, including an attorney, a member of the clergy, a medical practitioner, a social worker, a mental health professional, an employee or member of a board that licenses or certifies a professional, and an employee of a clinic or health care facility that provides reproductive services.

(d) Unless waived in writing by the person making the report, the identity of an individual making a report under this chapter is confidential and may be disclosed only:

(1) as provided by Section 261.201; or

(2) to a law enforcement officer for the purposes of conducting a criminal investigation of the report.

History of Fam. Code §261.101: Acts 1995, 74th Leg., ch. 20, §1, eff. Apr. 20, 1995. Amended by Acts 1995, 74th Leg., ch. 751, §87, eff. Sept. 1, 1995; Acts 1997, 75th Leg., ch. 162, §1 (eff. Sept. 1, 1997), ch. 575, §11 (eff. Sept. 1, 1997), ch. 1022, §65 (eff. Sept. 1, 1997); Acts 1999, 76th Leg., ch. 62, §6.29 (eff. Sept. 1, 1999), ch. 1150, §2 (eff. Sept. 1, 1999), ch. 1390, §21 (eff. Sept. 1, 1999); Acts 2001, 77th Leg., ch. 1420, §5.003, eff. Sept. 1, 2001; Acts 2005, 79th Leg., ch. 949, §27, eff. Sept. 1, 2005; Acts 2013, 83rd Leg., ch. 395, §4, eff. June 14, 2013; Acts 2015, 84th Leg., ch. 1, §1.122, eff. Apr. 2, 2015; H.B. 249, §3, 85th Leg., eff. Sept. 1, 2017. Source: Former Fam. Code §§34.01, 34.02(d).

See also 19 T.A.C. §61.1051 (school employees); ***O'Connor's Texas Family Law Handbook*** (2017), "Duty to report," ch. 1-G, §3.2, p. 83.

ANNOTATIONS

Ohio v. Clark, ___ U.S. ___, 135 S.Ct. 2173, 2182-83 (2015). Abuser "emphasizes [state's] mandatory reporting obligations, in an attempt to equate [child's] teachers with the police and their caring questions with official interrogations. But the comparison is inapt. The teachers' pressing concern was to protect [child] and remove him from harm's way. Like all good teachers, they undoubtedly would have acted with the same purpose whether or not they had a state-law duty to report abuse. And mandatory reporting statutes alone cannot convert a conversation between a concerned teacher and her student into a law enforcement mission aimed primarily at gathering evidence for a prosecution. [¶] It is irrelevant that the teachers' questions and their duty to report the matter had the

natural tendency to result in [abuser's] prosecution. [¶] [Child's] statements to his teachers were not testimonial."

FAM §261.102. MATTERS TO BE REPORTED

A report should reflect the reporter's belief that a child has been or may be abused or neglected or has died of abuse or neglect.

History of Fam. Code §261.102: Acts 1995, 74th Leg., ch. 20, §1, eff. Apr. 20, 1995. Amended by Acts 1995, 74th Leg., ch. 751, §88, eff. Sept. 1, 1995. Source: Former Fam. Code §34.02(a).

FAM §261.103. REPORT MADE TO APPROPRIATE AGENCY

(a) Except as provided by Subsections (b) and (c) and Section 261.405, a report shall be made to:

(1) any local or state law enforcement agency;

(2) the department; or

(3) the state agency that operates, licenses, certifies, or registers the facility in which the alleged abuse or neglect occurred.

(b) A report may be made to the Texas Juvenile Justice Department instead of the entities listed under Subsection (a) if the report is based on information provided by a child while under the supervision of the Texas Juvenile Justice Department concerning the child's alleged abuse of another child.

(c) Notwithstanding Subsection (a), a report, other than a report under Subsection (a)(3) or Section 261.405, must be made to the department if the alleged or suspected abuse or neglect involves a person responsible for the care, custody, or welfare of the child.

History of Fam. Code §261.103: Acts 1995, 74th Leg., ch. 20, §1, eff. Apr. 20, 1995. Amended by Acts 1995, 74th Leg., ch. 751, §89, eff. Sept. 1, 1995; Acts 1999, 76th Leg., ch. 1477, §24, eff. Sept. 1, 1999; Acts 2001, 77th Leg., ch. 1297, §46, eff. Sept. 1, 2001; Acts 2005, 79th Leg., ch. 213, §1, eff. Sept. 1, 2005; Acts 2015, 84th Leg., ch. 1, §1.123 (eff. Apr. 2, 2015), ch. 734, §80 (eff. Sept. 1, 2015). Source: Former Fam. Code §34.02(a).

FAM §261.104. CONTENTS OF REPORT

The person making a report shall identify, if known:

(1) the name and address of the child;

(2) the name and address of the person responsible for the care, custody, or welfare of the child; and

(3) any other pertinent information concerning the alleged or suspected abuse or neglect.

History of Fam. Code §261.104: Acts 1995, 74th Leg., ch. 20, §1, eff. Apr. 20, 1995. Amended by Acts 1995, 74th Leg., ch. 751, §90, eff. Sept. 1, 1995. Source: Former Fam. Code §34.02(b).

ANNOTATIONS

Dominguez v. Kelly, 786 S.W.2d 749, 752 (Tex. App.—El Paso 1990, writ denied). "Imprecise compliance with form requirements, per se, will not vitiate an immunity provision. There was substantial compliance in this case."

FAM §261.105. REFERRAL OF REPORT BY DEPARTMENT OR LAW ENFORCEMENT

(a) All reports received by a local or state law enforcement agency that allege abuse or neglect by a person responsible for a child's care, custody, or welfare shall be referred immediately to the department.

(b) The department shall immediately notify the appropriate state or local law enforcement agency of any report it receives, other than a report from a law enforcement agency, that concerns the suspected abuse or neglect of a child or death of a child from abuse or neglect.

(c) In addition to notifying a law enforcement agency, if the report relates to a child in a facility operated, licensed, certified, or registered by a state agency, the department shall refer the report to the agency for investigation.

(c-1) Notwithstanding Subsections (b) and (c), if a report under this section relates to a child with an intellectual disability receiving services in a state supported living center as defined by Section 531.002, Health and Safety Code, or the ICF-IID component of the Rio Grande State Center, the department shall proceed with the investigation of the report as provided by Section 261.404.

(d) If the department initiates an investigation and determines that the abuse or neglect does not involve a person responsible for the child's care, custody, or welfare, the department shall refer the report to a law enforcement agency for further investigation. If the department determines that the abuse or neglect involves an employee of a public elementary or secondary school, and that the child is a student at the school, the department shall orally notify the superintendent of the school district in which the employee is employed about the investigation.

(e) In cooperation with the department, the Texas Juvenile Justice Department by rule shall adopt guidelines for identifying a report made to the Texas Juvenile Justice Department under Section 261.103(b) that

is appropriate to refer to the department or a law enforcement agency for investigation. Guidelines adopted under this subsection must require the Texas Juvenile Justice Department to consider the severity and immediacy of the alleged abuse or neglect of the child victim.

History of Fam. Code §261.105: Acts 1995, 74th Leg., ch. 20, §1, eff. Apr. 20, 1995. Amended by Acts 1997, 75th Leg., ch. 1022, §66, eff. Sept. 1, 1997; Acts 1999, 76th Leg., ch. 1477, §25, eff. Sept. 1, 1999; Acts 2003, 78th Leg., ch. 374, §3, eff. June 18, 2003; Acts 2009, 81st Leg., ch. 284, §4, eff. June 11, 2009; Acts 2015, 84th Leg., ch. 1, §1.124 (eff. Apr. 2, 2015), ch. 734, §81 (eff. Sept. 1, 2015), ch. 1167, §4 (eff. Sept. 1, 2015). Source: Former Fam. Code §34.02(c).

See also 40 T.A.C. §700.506.

FAM §261.1055. NOTIFICATION OF DISTRICT ATTORNEYS

(a) A district attorney may inform the department that the district attorney wishes to receive notification of some or all reports of suspected abuse or neglect of children who were in the county at the time the report was made or who were in the county at the time of the alleged abuse or neglect.

(b) If the district attorney makes the notification under this section, the department shall, on receipt of a report of suspected abuse or neglect, immediately notify the district attorney as requested and the department shall forward a copy of the reports to the district attorney on request.

History of Fam. Code §261.1055: Acts 1997, 75th Leg., ch. 1022, §67, eff. Sept. 1, 1997. Amended by Acts 2015, 84th Leg., ch. 1, §1.125, eff. Apr. 2, 2015.

FAM §261.106. IMMUNITIES

(a) A person acting in good faith who reports or assists in the investigation of a report of alleged child abuse or neglect or who testifies or otherwise participates in a judicial proceeding arising from a report, petition, or investigation of alleged child abuse or neglect is immune from civil or criminal liability that might otherwise be incurred or imposed.

(b) Immunity from civil and criminal liability extends to an authorized volunteer of the department or a law enforcement officer who participates at the request of the department in an investigation of alleged or suspected abuse or neglect or in an action arising from an investigation if the person was acting in good faith and in the scope of the person's responsibilities.

(c) A person who reports the person's own abuse or neglect of a child or who acts in bad faith or with malicious purpose in reporting alleged child abuse or neglect is not immune from civil or criminal liability.

History of Fam. Code §261.106: Acts 1995, 74th Leg., ch. 20, §1, eff. Apr. 20, 1995. Amended by Acts 1995, 74th Leg., ch. 751, §91, eff. Sept. 1, 1995. Source: Former Fam. Code §34.03.

ANNOTATIONS

Miranda v. Byles, 390 S.W.3d 543, 551 (Tex.App.—Houston [1st Dist.] 2012, pet. denied). "'Immunity from liability and immunity from suit are two distinct principles.' '[I]mmunity from liability is an affirmative defense, while immunity from suit deprives a court of subject matter jurisdiction.' [¶] Although it 'protects from judgment,' immunity from liability 'is not jurisdictional.' [A]sserting an affirmative defense does not convert it into a jurisdictional issue. *At 552:* Because [D] did not raise his affirmative defense of immunity from liability on appeal and because the issue is not jurisdictional, we cannot reach the merits of this argument and it cannot be a basis for reversing the trial court's judgment."

Nunez v. Jimenez, No. 04-07-00403-CV (Tex. App.—San Antonio 2007, no pet.) (memo op.; 12-12-07). "'Good faith' is the only element of immunity under §261.106(a); the statute does not require, as does official immunity, that a government employee prove he was acting within the scope of his authority in performing a discretionary duty. Like official immunity, immunity under §261.106(a) is an affirmative defense."

B.K. v. Cox, 116 S.W.3d 351, 361 (Tex.App.—Houston [14th Dist.] 2003, no pet.). "We find that the language of §261.106 ... unambiguously provides statutory immunity for certain persons who assist in the investigation of a report of alleged child abuse or neglect or who participate in a judicial proceeding arising from a report, petition or investigation of child abuse; however, we find no intent in the unambiguous language of this statute to abolish common-law derived judicial immunity. We conclude that the statutory privilege granted by §261.106 serves a different purpose than derived judicial immunity and that the Legislature, by enacting this statute, did not intend to abolish derived judicial immunity." *See also* ***Laub v. Pesikoff***, 979 S.W.2d 686, 690 n.2 (Tex.App.—Houston [1st Dist.] 1998, pet. denied).

FAM §261.107. FALSE REPORT; CRIMINAL PENALTY; CIVIL PENALTY

(a) A person commits an offense if, with the intent to deceive, the person knowingly makes a report as provided in this chapter that is false. An offense under this subsection is a state jail felony unless it is shown on the trial of the offense that the person has previously

been convicted under this section, in which case the offense is a felony of the third degree.

(b) A finding by a court in a suit affecting the parent-child relationship that a report made under this chapter before or during the suit was false or lacking factual foundation may be grounds for the court to modify an order providing for possession of or access to the child who was the subject of the report by restricting further access to the child by the person who made the report.

(c) The appropriate county prosecuting attorney shall be responsible for the prosecution of an offense under this section.

(d) The court shall order a person who is convicted of an offense under Subsection (a) to pay any reasonable attorney's fees incurred by the person who was falsely accused of abuse or neglect in any proceeding relating to the false report.

(e) A person who engages in conduct described by Subsection (a) is liable to the state for a civil penalty of $1,000. The attorney general shall bring an action to recover a civil penalty authorized by this subsection.

History of Fam. Code §261.107: Acts 1995, 74th Leg., ch. 20, §1, eff. Apr. 20, 1995. Amended by Acts 1995, 74th Leg., ch. 751, §92, eff. Sept. 1, 1995; Acts 1997, 75th Leg., ch. 575, §2 (eff. Sept. 1, 1997), ch. 1022, §68 (eff. Sept. 1, 1997); Acts 1999, 76th Leg., ch. 62, §6.30, eff. Sept. 1, 1999; Acts 2005, 79th Leg., ch. 268, §§1.13, 1.14(a), eff. Sept. 1, 2005. Source: Former Fam. Code §34.031.

ANNOTATIONS

Riley v. State, ___ S.W.3d ___ (Tex.App.—Houston [14th Dist.] 2014, pet. ref'd) (No. 14-12-00729-CR; 4-15-14). "A jury convicted [D] of making a false report with the [TDFPS] in violation of §261.107(a).... *At ___:* [D] claims the trial court erred in denying his motion for a directed verdict based on improper venue because ... he made the report by phone call from Harris County to the Department in Travis County, [so] no element of the offense occurred in Galveston County. [¶] There is no special venue statute applicable to the case at bar. Thus we must determine whether an element of the offense occurred in Galveston County. [¶] [A CPS] investigator ... testified that her CPS office in Galveston County receives reports 'through statewide intake' by 'the Intake Division.' Thus the Department[, a statewide agency,] acts as an agent of receipt for the local branch of CPS that will conduct the initial investigation. We therefore hold a Ch. 261 report is 'made' in the county of the CPS office that receives notification from the Department. Here, that office was in Galveston County. Accordingly, we hold Galveston County to be a proper county for the prosecution of the offense."

FAM §261.108. FRIVOLOUS CLAIMS AGAINST PERSON REPORTING

(a) In this section:

(1) "Claim" means an action or claim by a party, including a plaintiff, counterclaimant, cross-claimant, or third-party plaintiff, requesting recovery of damages.

(2) "Defendant" means a party against whom a claim is made.

(b) A court shall award a defendant reasonable attorney's fees and other expenses related to the defense of a claim filed against the defendant for damages or other relief arising from reporting or assisting in the investigation of a report under this chapter or participating in a judicial proceeding resulting from the report if:

(1) the court finds that the claim is frivolous, unreasonable, or without foundation because the defendant is immune from liability under Section 261.106; and

(2) the claim is dismissed or judgment is rendered for the defendant.

(c) To recover under this section, the defendant must, at any time after the filing of a claim, file a written motion stating that:

(1) the claim is frivolous, unreasonable, or without foundation because the defendant is immune from liability under Section 261.106; and

(2) the defendant requests the court to award reasonable attorney's fees and other expenses related to the defense of the claim.

History of Fam. Code §261.108: Acts 1995, 74th Leg., ch. 20, §1, eff. Apr. 20, 1995. Source: Former Fam. Code §34.032.

FAM §261.109. FAILURE TO REPORT; PENALTY

(a) A person commits an offense if the person is required to make a report under Section 261.101(a) and knowingly fails to make a report as provided in this chapter.

(a-1) A person who is a professional as defined by Section 261.101(b) commits an offense if the person is required to make a report under Section 261.101(b) and knowingly fails to make a report as provided in this chapter.

(b) An offense under Subsection (a) is a Class A misdemeanor, except that the offense is a state jail

felony if it is shown on the trial of the offense that the child was a person with an intellectual disability who resided in a state supported living center, the ICF-IID component of the Rio Grande State Center, or a facility licensed under Chapter 252, Health and Safety Code, and the actor knew that the child had suffered serious bodily injury as a result of the abuse or neglect.

(c) An offense under Subsection (a-1) is a Class A misdemeanor, except that the offense is a state jail felony if it is shown on the trial of the offense that the actor intended to conceal the abuse or neglect.

History of Fam. Code §261.109: Acts 1995, 74th Leg., ch. 20, §1, eff. Apr. 20, 1995. Amended by Acts 2009, 81st Leg., ch. 284, §5, eff. June 11, 2009; Acts 2013, 83rd Leg., ch. 290, §1, eff. Sept. 1, 2013; Acts 2015, 84th Leg., ch. 1, §1.126, eff. Apr. 2, 2015. Source: Former Fam. Code §34.07.

ANNOTATIONS

Perry v. S.N., 973 S.W.2d 301, 309 (Tex.1998). "Because a decision to impose negligence per se could not be limited to cases charging serious misconduct ..., but rather would impose immense potential liability under an ill-defined standard on a broad class of individuals whose relationship to the abuse was extremely indirect, we hold that it is not appropriate to adopt ... §261.109(a) as establishing a duty and standard of conduct in tort. Therefore, [parents] may not maintain a claim for negligence per se or gross negligence based on [Ds'] violation of the child abuse reporting statute."

FAM §261.110. EMPLOYER RETALIATION PROHIBITED

(a) In this section, "professional" has the meaning assigned by Section 261.101(b).

(b) An employer may not suspend or terminate the employment of, or otherwise discriminate against, a person who is a professional and who in good faith:

(1) reports child abuse or neglect to:

(A) the person's supervisor;

(B) an administrator of the facility where the person is employed;

(C) a state regulatory agency; or

(D) a law enforcement agency; or

(2) initiates or cooperates with an investigation or proceeding by a governmental entity relating to an allegation of child abuse or neglect.

(c) A person whose employment is suspended or terminated or who is otherwise discriminated against in violation of this section may sue for injunctive relief, damages, or both.

(d) A plaintiff who prevails in a suit under this section may recover:

(1) actual damages, including damages for mental anguish even if an injury other than mental anguish is not shown;

(2) exemplary damages under Chapter 41, Civil Practice and Remedies Code, if the employer is a private employer;

(3) court costs; and

(4) reasonable attorney's fees.

(e) In addition to amounts recovered under Subsection (d), a plaintiff who prevails in a suit under this section is entitled to:

(1) reinstatement to the person's former position or a position that is comparable in terms of compensation, benefits, and other conditions of employment;

(2) reinstatement of any fringe benefits and seniority rights lost because of the suspension, termination, or discrimination; and

(3) compensation for wages lost during the period of suspension or termination.

(f) A public employee who alleges a violation of this section may sue the employing state or local governmental entity for the relief provided for by this section. Sovereign immunity is waived and abolished to the extent of liability created by this section. A person having a claim under this section may sue a governmental unit for damages allowed by this section.

(g) In a suit under this section against an employing state or local governmental entity, a plaintiff may not recover compensatory damages for future pecuniary losses, emotional pain, suffering, inconvenience, mental anguish, loss of enjoyment of life, and other nonpecuniary losses in an amount that exceeds:

(1) $50,000, if the employing state or local governmental entity has fewer than 101 employees in each of 20 or more calendar weeks in the calendar year in which the suit is filed or in the preceding year;

(2) $100,000, if the employing state or local governmental entity has more than 100 and fewer than 201 employees in each of 20 or more calendar weeks in the calendar year in which the suit is filed or in the preceding year;

(3) $200,000, if the employing state or local governmental entity has more than 200 and fewer than 501 employees in each of 20 or more calendar weeks in the calendar year in which the suit is filed or in the preceding year; and

(4) $250,000, if the employing state or local governmental entity has more than 500 employees in each of 20 or more calendar weeks in the calendar year in which the suit is filed or in the preceding year.

(h) If more than one subdivision of Subsection (g) applies to an employing state or local governmental entity, the amount of monetary damages that may be recovered from the entity in a suit brought under this section is governed by the applicable provision that provides the highest damage award.

(i) A plaintiff suing under this section has the burden of proof, except that there is a rebuttable presumption that the plaintiff's employment was suspended or terminated or that the plaintiff was otherwise discriminated against for reporting abuse or neglect if the suspension, termination, or discrimination occurs before the 61st day after the date on which the person made a report in good faith.

(j) A suit under this section may be brought in a district or county court of the county in which:

(1) the plaintiff was employed by the defendant; or

(2) the defendant conducts business.

(k) It is an affirmative defense to a suit under Subsection (b) that an employer would have taken the action against the employee that forms the basis of the suit based solely on information, observation, or evidence that is not related to the fact that the employee reported child abuse or neglect or initiated or cooperated with an investigation or proceeding relating to an allegation of child abuse or neglect.

(*l*) A public employee who has a cause of action under Chapter 554, Government Code, based on conduct described by Subsection (b) may not bring an action based on that conduct under this section.

(m) This section does not apply to a person who reports the person's own abuse or neglect of a child or who initiates or cooperates with an investigation or proceeding by a governmental entity relating to an allegation of the person's own abuse or neglect of a child.

History of Fam. Code §261.110: Acts 2001, 77th Leg., ch. 896, §1, eff. Sept. 1, 2001.

ANNOTATIONS

Ysleta ISD v. Griego, 170 S.W.3d 792, 797 (Tex. App.—El Paso 2005, pet. denied). "We conclude that [petitioner] cannot maintain a cause of action for employer retaliation. The Legislature has specified that the administrative remedies set out in the Education Code apply to counselors who are contractual employees. Because [petitioner] was required to first exhaust his administrative remedies under [Educ. Code] ch. 21 … before pursuing his action for employer retaliation under the Family Code, the trial court lacked jurisdiction."

FAM §261.111. REFUSAL OF PSYCHIATRIC OR PSYCHOLOGICAL TREATMENT OF CHILD

(a) In this section, "psychotropic medication" has the meaning assigned by Section 266.001.

(b) The refusal of a parent, guardian, or managing or possessory conservator of a child to administer or consent to the administration of a psychotropic medication to the child, or to consent to any other psychiatric or psychological treatment of the child, does not by itself constitute neglect of the child unless the refusal to consent:

(1) presents a substantial risk of death, disfigurement, or bodily injury to the child; or

(2) has resulted in an observable and material impairment to the growth, development, or functioning of the child.

History of Fam. Code §261.111: Acts 2003, 78th Leg., ch. 1008, §3, eff. June 20, 2003. Amended by Acts 2015, 84th Leg., ch. 1, §1.127, eff. Apr. 2, 2015.

Sections 261.112-261.200 reserved for expansion

SUBCHAPTER C. CONFIDENTIALITY & PRIVILEGED COMMUNICATION

FAM §261.201. CONFIDENTIALITY & DISCLOSURE OF INFORMATION

(a) Except as provided by Section 261.203, the following information is confidential, is not subject to public release under Chapter 552, Government Code, and may be disclosed only for purposes consistent with this code and applicable federal or state law or under rules adopted by an investigating agency:

(1) a report of alleged or suspected abuse or neglect made under this chapter and the identity of the person making the report; and

(2) except as otherwise provided in this section, the files, reports, records, communications, audiotapes, videotapes, and working papers used or developed in an investigation under this chapter or in providing services as a result of an investigation.

(b) A court may order the disclosure of information that is confidential under this section if:

(1) a motion has been filed with the court requesting the release of the information;

(2) a notice of hearing has been served on the investigating agency and all other interested parties; and

(3) after hearing and an in camera review of the requested information, the court determines that the disclosure of the requested information is:

(A) essential to the administration of justice; and

(B) not likely to endanger the life or safety of:

(i) a child who is the subject of the report of alleged or suspected abuse or neglect;

(ii) a person who makes a report of alleged or suspected abuse or neglect; or

(iii) any other person who participates in an investigation of reported abuse or neglect or who provides care for the child.

(b-1) On a motion of one of the parties in a contested case before an administrative law judge relating to the license or certification of a professional, as defined by Section 261.101(b), or an educator, as defined by Section 5.001, Education Code, the administrative law judge may order the disclosure of information that is confidential under this section that relates to the matter before the administrative law judge after a hearing for which notice is provided as required by Subsection (b)(2) and making the review and determination required by Subsection (b)(3). Before the department may release information under this subsection, the department must edit the information to protect the confidentiality of the identity of any person who makes a report of abuse or neglect.

(c) In addition to Subsection (b), a court, on its own motion, may order disclosure of information that is confidential under this section if:

(1) the order is rendered at a hearing for which all parties have been given notice;

(2) the court finds that disclosure of the information is:

(A) essential to the administration of justice; and

(B) not likely to endanger the life or safety of:

(i) a child who is the subject of the report of alleged or suspected abuse or neglect;

(ii) a person who makes a report of alleged or suspected abuse or neglect; or

(iii) any other person who participates in an investigation of reported abuse or neglect or who provides care for the child; and

(3) the order is reduced to writing or made on the record in open court.

(d) The adoptive parents of a child who was the subject of an investigation and an adult who was the subject of an investigation as a child are entitled to examine and make copies of any report, record, working paper, or other information in the possession, custody, or control of the state that pertains to the history of the child. The department may edit the documents to protect the identity of the biological parents and any other person whose identity is confidential, unless this information is already known to the adoptive parents or is readily available through other sources, including the court records of a suit to terminate the parent-child relationship under Chapter 161.

(e) Before placing a child who was the subject of an investigation, the department shall notify the prospective adoptive parents of their right to examine any report, record, working paper, or other information in the possession, custody, or control of the department that pertains to the history of the child.

(f) The department shall provide prospective adoptive parents an opportunity to examine information under this section as early as practicable before placing a child.

(f-1) The department shall provide to a relative or other individual with whom a child is placed any information the department considers necessary to ensure that the relative or other individual is prepared to meet the needs of the child. The information required by this subsection may include information related to any abuse or neglect suffered by the child.

(g) Notwithstanding Subsection (b), the department, on request and subject to department rule, shall provide to the parent, managing conservator, or other legal representative of a child who is the subject of reported abuse or neglect information concerning the reported abuse or neglect that would otherwise be confidential under this section if the department has edited the information to protect the confidentiality of the identity of the person who made the report and any other person whose life or safety may be endangered by the disclosure.

(h) This section does not apply to an investigation of child abuse or neglect in a home or facility regulated under Chapter 42, Human Resources Code.

(i) Notwithstanding Subsection (a), the Texas Juvenile Justice Department shall release a report of alleged or suspected abuse or neglect made under this chapter if:

(1) the report relates to a report of abuse or neglect involving a child committed to the Texas Juvenile Justice Department during the period that the child is committed to that department; and

(2) the Texas Juvenile Justice Department is not prohibited by Chapter 552, Government Code, or other law from disclosing the report.

(j) The Texas Juvenile Justice Department shall edit any report disclosed under Subsection (i) to protect the identity of:

(1) a child who is the subject of the report of alleged or suspected abuse or neglect;

(2) the person who made the report; and

(3) any other person whose life or safety may be endangered by the disclosure.

(k) Notwithstanding Subsection (a), an investigating agency, other than the department or the Texas Juvenile Justice Department, on request, shall provide to the parent, managing conservator, or other legal representative of a child who is the subject of reported abuse or neglect, or to the child if the child is at least 18 years of age, information concerning the reported abuse or neglect that would otherwise be confidential under this section. The investigating agency shall withhold information under this subsection if the parent, managing conservator, or other legal representative of the child requesting the information is alleged to have committed the abuse or neglect.

(*l*) Before a child or a parent, managing conservator, or other legal representative of a child may inspect or copy a record or file concerning the child under Subsection (k), the custodian of the record or file must redact:

(1) any personally identifiable information about a victim or witness under 18 years of age unless that victim or witness is:

(A) the child who is the subject of the report; or

(B) another child of the parent, managing conservator, or other legal representative requesting the information;

(2) any information that is excepted from required disclosure under Chapter 552, Government Code, or other law; and

(3) the identity of the person who made the report.

History of Fam. Code §261.201: Acts 1995, 74th Leg., ch. 20, §1, eff. Apr. 20, 1995. Amended by Acts 1995, 74th Leg., ch. 751, §93, eff. Sept. 1, 1995; Acts 1997, 75th Leg., ch. 575, §12 (eff. Sept. 1, 1997), ch. 1022, §69 (eff. Sept. 1, 1997); Acts 1999, 76th Leg., ch. 1150, §3 (eff. Sept. 1, 1999), ch. 1390, §22 (eff. Sept. 1, 1999); Acts 2003, 78th Leg., ch. 68, §2, eff. Sept. 1, 2003; Acts 2005, 79th Leg., ch. 268, §1.15, eff. Sept. 1, 2005; Acts 2007, 80th Leg., ch. 263, §12, eff. June 8, 2007; Acts 2009, 81st Leg., ch. 713, §1 (eff. June 19, 2009), ch. 779, §1 (eff. Sept. 1, 2009), ch. 1377, §13 (eff. Sept. 1, 2009); Acts 2015, 84th Leg., ch. 1, §1.128 (eff. Apr. 2, 2015), ch. 734, §82 (eff. Sept. 1, 2015). Source: Former Fam. Code §34.08.

See also 37 T.A.C. §§349.500-349.540; 40 T.A.C. §§700.203-700.206.

ANNOTATIONS

Fears v. State, 479 S.W.3d 315, 327 (Tex.App.—Corpus Christi 2015, pet. ref'd). "Under U.S. Supreme Court precedent beginning with ***Brady*** [***v. Maryland***, 373 U.S. 83 (1963)], the State is required to disclose evidence known to it that is favorable or material to a defendant's guilt or punishment, whether or not the defendant requests it. *At 329:* [D] questions the relationship between the State's duty to disclose all favorable and material information under ***Brady*** and the confidentiality requirements of … §261.201. [¶] We reject [D's] argument that it was inappropriate for the trial court to conduct the … §261.201(b)(3) balancing test to determine whether to disclose material that [D] viewed as ***Brady*** evidence. The conflict that can arise between the State's need to keep information related to child abuse investigations confidential with a defendant's need for a fair trial is well recognized. *At 330:* [S]ection 261.201 provides for exactly the type of procedure approved [by U.S. Supreme Court precedent]: an *in camera* inspection of the material by the trial judge, and an ongoing duty to disclose any confidential material that is relevant or becomes relevant during the course of the trial."

Mason v. Glickman, 408 S.W.3d 691, 692-93 (Tex. App.—Dallas 2013, no pet.). "The Department initiated an investigation of [father] based on a report that he had hit his ten-year-old daughter three times…. After investigating, the Department … determined that … it was reasonable to conclude the alleged abuse did not occur. *At 694:* [Father] filed his Motion seeking disclosure of the identity of the reporter…. [T]he record contains no evidence that any person's life or safety could reasonably have been endangered by the disclosure sought. [¶] The dispositive issue became whether the disclosure was essential to the administration of justice[, as required under §261.201(b)(3)(A)]. … The trial court … had to determine whether [father] being able to litigate his [defamation] suit was essential to the administration of justice. *At 695-96:* Regardless of how the reporter … learned that [daughter said father hit her], the child's statement supports a statutory duty to report. The statute does not speak to a

duty to investigate; investigation is the Department's job. We conclude the trial court could have reasonably determined that the disclosure of the identity of the reporter in [father's] case was not essential to the administration of justice."

In re Fulgium, 150 S.W.3d 252, 254-55 (Tex.App.—Texarkana 2004, orig. proceeding). "The trial court is granted discretion under [Fam. Code] §§261.201, 264.408, and 264.613 ... to order disclosure of the information sought in this case, provided certain requirements have been met. Under §261.201, information relating to the investigation of child abuse may not be disclosed unless the court orders it disclosed after determining that disclosure is essential to the administration of justice and would not endanger the child, the person reporting the abuse, or any other person. While §261.201 does not specifically describe the entities to which it applies, §§264.408 and 264.613 provide that §261.201 applies to [court-appointed special advocates] and [the Children's Advocacy Center]. [¶] The exception allowing the trial court to order the disclosure is discretionary." *See also* ***S.C.S. v. TDFPS***, No. 02-09-341-CV (Tex.App.—Fort Worth 2010, no pet.) (memo op.; 7-22-10) (parents argued that disclosure of CPS records was essential to determine if civil or criminal action should be taken against person who made "false reports," but reports that are "ruled out" by CPS are not necessarily false; court found disclosure was not essential to administration of justice).

FAM §261.202. PRIVILEGED COMMUNICATION

In a proceeding regarding the abuse or neglect of a child, evidence may not be excluded on the ground of privileged communication except in the case of communications between an attorney and client.

History of Fam. Code §261.202: Acts 1995, 74th Leg., ch. 20, §1, eff. Apr. 20, 1995. Source: Former Fam. Code §34.04.

ANNOTATIONS

In re L.E.S., 471 S.W.3d 915, 927 (Tex.App.—Texarkana 2015, no pet.). "[T]he [jailhouse] conversation between [mother] and [father] was private and there is no evidence that either intended its disclosure to any other person, [so] we will treat it as covered by the [spousal communication] privilege. We must, therefore, determine if §261.202 ... removes that privilege in this case. *At 928:* The legislature chose the broad term 'proceeding' rather than the more specific term 'suit,' indicating the applicability of §261.202 to *any* proceeding, criminal or civil. ... Further, the termination proceeding involved the abuse or neglect of a child.... Given these broad parameters, there can be no question that this was a proceeding involving the abuse or neglect of a child. [Mother] and [father] were therefore not entitled to invoke the spousal communication privilege, and the trial court did not err in admitting the audio/video recording." (Internal quotes omitted.)

Almendarez v. State, 153 S.W.3d 727, 729 (Tex. App.—Dallas 2005, no pet.). The CCP "has no provision for a clergyman privilege; thus, [Fam. Code §261.202] takes precedence over [TRE] 505. [¶] [T]he court in ***Bordman v. State***, 56 S.W.3d 63 ... (Tex.App.—Houston [14th Dist.] 2001, pet. ref'd), held that, in a prosecution for aggravated sexual assault of three children, the trial court did not err in denying [D's] claim of clergy-communication privilege because §261.202 excepts the privilege in child abuse cases. We find the reasoning of the court in ***Bordman*** persuasive. Because this case involved abuse of a child, we conclude the trial court was correct in overruling appellant's objection that [church elder's] testimony involved privileged matters under [TRE] 505."

FAM §261.203. INFORMATION RELATING TO CHILD FATALITY

(a) Not later than the fifth day after the date the department receives a request for information about a child fatality with respect to which the department is conducting an investigation of alleged abuse or neglect, the department shall release:

(1) the age and sex of the child;

(2) the date of death;

(3) whether the state was the managing conservator of the child at the time of the child's death; and

(4) whether the child resided with the child's parent, managing conservator, guardian, or other person entitled to possession of the child at the time of the child's death.

(b) If, after a child abuse or neglect investigation described by Subsection (a) is completed, the department determines a child's death or a child's near fatality was caused by abuse or neglect, the department on request shall promptly release investigation information not prohibited from release under federal law, including the following information:

(1) the information described by Subsection (a), if not previously released to the person requesting the information;

(2) information on whether a child's death or near fatality:

(A) was determined by the department to be attributable to abuse or neglect; or

(B) resulted in a criminal investigation or the filing of criminal charges if known at the time the investigation is completed;

(3) for cases in which the child's death or near fatality occurred while the child was living with the child's parent, managing conservator, guardian, or other person entitled to possession of the child:

(A) a summary of any previous reports of abuse or neglect of the child or another child made while the child was living with that parent, managing conservator, guardian, or other person entitled to possession of the child;

(B) the disposition of any report under Paragraph (A);

(C) a description of any services, including family-based safety services, that were provided or offered by the department to the child or the child's family as a result of any report under Paragraph (A) and whether the services were accepted or declined; and

(D) the results of any risk or safety assessment completed by the department relating to the child; and

(4) for a case in which the child's death or near fatality occurred while the child was in substitute care with the department or with a residential child-care provider regulated under Chapter 42, Human Resources Code, the following information:

(A) the date the substitute care provider with whom the child was residing at the time of death or near fatality was licensed or verified;

(B) a summary of any previous reports of abuse or neglect investigated by the department relating to the substitute care provider, including the disposition of any investigation resulting from a report;

(C) any reported licensing violations, including notice of any action taken by the department regarding a violation; and

(D) records of any training completed by the substitute care provider while the child was placed with the provider.

(c) If the department is unable to release the information required by Subsection (b) before the 11th day after the date the department receives a request for the information or the date the investigation of the child fatality is completed, whichever is later, the department shall inform the person requesting the information of the date the department will release the information.

(d) Repealed by Acts 2015, 84th Leg., ch. 944, §86(7), eff. Sept. 1, 2015.

(e) Before the department releases any information under Subsection (b), the department shall redact from the records any information the release of which would:

(1) identify:

(A) the individual who reported the abuse or neglect; or

(B) any other individual other than the deceased child or an alleged perpetrator of the abuse or neglect;

(2) jeopardize an ongoing criminal investigation or prosecution;

(3) endanger the life or safety of any individual; or

(4) violate other state or federal law.

(f) The executive commissioner of the Health and Human Services Commission shall adopt rules to implement this section.

History of Fam. Code §261.203: Acts 2009, 81st Leg., ch. 779, §2, eff. Sept. 1, 2009. Amended by Acts 2015, 84th Leg., ch. 253, §1 (eff. Sept. 1, 2015), ch. 944, §86(7) (eff. Sept. 1, 2015).

Ⓐ FAM §261.204. ANNUAL CHILD FATALITY REPORT

(a) Not later than March 1 of each year, the [~~The~~] department shall publish an [~~annual~~] aggregated report using information compiled from each child fatality investigation for which the department made a finding regarding abuse or neglect, including cases in which the department determined the fatality was not the result of abuse or neglect. The report must protect the identity of individuals involved and contain the following information:

(1) the age and sex of the child and the county in which the fatality occurred;

(2) whether the state was the managing conservator of the child or whether the child resided with the child's parent, managing conservator, guardian, or other person entitled to the possession of the child at the time of the fatality;

(3) the relationship to the child of the individual alleged to have abused or neglected the child, if any;

(4) the number of any department abuse or neglect investigations involving the child or the individual alleged to have abused or neglected the child during the

two years preceding the date of the fatality and the results of the investigations;

(5) whether the department offered family-based safety services or conservatorship services to the child or family;

(6) the types of abuse and neglect alleged in the reported investigations, if any; and

(7) any trends identified in the investigations contained in the report.

(b) The report published under Subsection (a) must:

(1) accurately represent all abuse-related and neglect-related child fatalities in this state, including child fatalities investigated under Subchapter F, Chapter 264, and other child fatalities investigated by the department; and

(2) aggregate the fatalities by investigative findings and case disposition, including the following dispositions:

(A) abuse and neglect ruled out;

(B) unable to determine cause of death;

(C) reason to believe abuse or neglect occurred;

(D) reason to believe abuse or neglect contributed to child's death;

(E) unable to complete review; and

(F) administrative closure.

(c) The department may release additional information in the annual report if the release of the information is not prohibited by state or federal law.

(d) The department shall post the annual report on the department's Internet website and otherwise make the report available to the public.

(e) The executive commissioner of the Health and Human Services Commission may adopt rules to implement this section.

(f) At least once every 10 years, the department shall use the information reported under this section to provide guidance for possible department policy changes.

History of Fam. Code §261.204: Acts 2015, 84th Leg., ch. 253, §2, eff. Sept. 1, 2015. Amended by H.B. 1549, §1, 85th Leg., eff. Sept. 1, 2017.

Sections 261.205-261.300 reserved for expansion

SUBCHAPTER D. INVESTIGATIONS

A FAM §261.301. INVESTIGATION OF REPORT

(a) With assistance from the appropriate state or local law enforcement agency as provided by this section, the department shall make a prompt and thorough investigation of a report of child abuse or neglect allegedly committed by a person responsible for a child's care, custody, or welfare. The investigation shall be conducted without regard to any pending suit affecting the parent-child relationship.

In 2017, two bills amended subsections (b) and (c), but only one bill, H.B. 249, §4, saved the former law in effect at that time. The amended text from H.B. 249, §4 is effective for reports of suspected abuse, neglect, or exploitation of a child made on or after Sept. 1, 2017. Reports made before Sept. 1, 2017, are governed by the former law in effect at that time. The amended text from S.B. 11, §9 is effective Sept. 1, 2017.

(b) A state agency shall investigate a report that alleges abuse, [~~or~~] neglect, or exploitation occurred in a facility operated, licensed, certified, or registered by that agency as provided by Subchapter E. In conducting an investigation for a facility operated, licensed, certified, registered, or listed by the department, the department shall perform the investigation as provided by:

(1) Subchapter E; and

(2) the Human Resources Code.

(c) The department is not required to investigate a report that alleges child abuse, [~~or~~] neglect, or exploitation by a person other than a person responsible for a child's care, custody, or welfare. The appropriate state or local law enforcement agency shall investigate that report if the agency determines an investigation should be conducted.

(d) The executive commissioner shall by rule assign priorities and prescribe investigative procedures for investigations based on the severity and immediacy of the alleged harm to the child. The primary purpose of the investigation shall be the protection of the child. The rules must require the department, subject to the availability of funds, to:

(1) immediately respond to a report of abuse and neglect that involves circumstances in which the death of the child or substantial bodily harm to the child would result unless the department immediately intervenes;

(2) respond within 24 hours to a report of abuse and neglect that is assigned the highest priority, other than a report described by Subdivision (1); and

(3) respond within 72 hours to a report of abuse and neglect that is assigned the second highest priority.

(e) As necessary to provide for the protection of the child, the department shall determine:

(1) the nature, extent, and cause of the abuse or neglect;

(2) the identity of the person responsible for the abuse or neglect;

(3) the names and conditions of the other children in the home;

(4) an evaluation of the parents or persons responsible for the care of the child;

(5) the adequacy of the home environment;

(6) the relationship of the child to the persons responsible for the care, custody, or welfare of the child; and

(7) all other pertinent data.

(f) An investigation of a report to the department that alleges that a child has been or may be the victim of conduct that constitutes a criminal offense that poses an immediate risk of physical or sexual abuse of a child that could result in the death of or serious harm to the child shall be conducted jointly by a peace officer, as defined by Article 2.12, Code of Criminal Procedure, from the appropriate local law enforcement agency and the department or the agency responsible for conducting an investigation under Subchapter E.

(g) The inability or unwillingness of a local law enforcement agency to conduct a joint investigation under this section does not constitute grounds to prevent or prohibit the department from performing its duties under this subtitle. The department shall document any instance in which a law enforcement agency is unable or unwilling to conduct a joint investigation under this section.

(h) The department and the appropriate local law enforcement agency shall conduct an investigation, other than an investigation under Subchapter E, as provided by this section and Article 2.27, Code of Criminal Procedure, if the investigation is of a report that alleges that a child has been or may be the victim of conduct that constitutes a criminal offense that poses an immediate risk of physical or sexual abuse of a child that could result in the death of or serious harm to the child. Immediately on receipt of a report described by this subsection, the department shall notify the appropriate local law enforcement agency of the report.

(i) If at any time during an investigation of a report of child abuse or neglect to which the department has assigned the highest priority the department is unable to locate the child who is the subject of the report of abuse or neglect or the child's family, the department shall notify the Department of Public Safety that the location of the child and the child's family is unknown. If the Department of Public Safety locates the child and the child's family, the Department of Public Safety shall notify the department of the location of the child and the child's family.

☠ *Subsection (j) was enacted by H.B. 2124, §1, 85th Leg., enacted May 19, 2017, effective Sept. 1, 2017, without reference to the conflicting enactment made by H.B. 1549, §2, 85th Leg., enacted May 28, 2017, effective Sept. 1, 2017. For harmonizing conflicts, see p. V. The enacted text in subsection (j) is effective for reports of abuse or neglect made on or after Sept. 1, 2017.*

(j) In an investigation of a report of abuse or neglect allegedly committed by a person responsible for a child's care, custody, or welfare, the department shall determine whether the person is an active duty member of the United States armed forces or the spouse of a member on active duty. If the department determines the person is an active duty member of the United States armed forces or the spouse of a member on active duty, the department shall notify the United States Department of Defense Family Advocacy Program at the closest active duty military installation of the investigation.

☠ *Subsection (j) was enacted by H.B. 1549, §2, 85th Leg., enacted May 28, 2017, effective Sept. 1, 2017, without reference to the conflicting enactment made by H.B. 2124, §1, 85th Leg., enacted May 19, 2017, effective Sept. 1, 2017. For harmonizing conflicts, see p. V.*

(j) In geographic areas with demonstrated need, the department shall designate employees to serve specifically as investigators and responders for after-hours reports of child abuse or neglect.

History of Fam. Code §261.301: Acts 1995, 74th Leg., ch. 20, §1, eff. Apr. 20, 1995. Amended by Acts 1995, 74th Leg., ch. 751, §94 (eff. Sept. 1, 1995), ch. 943, §2 (eff. Sept. 1, 1995); Acts 1997, 75th Leg., ch. 1022, §70 (eff. Sept. 1, 1997), ch. 1137, §1 (eff. Sept. 1, 1997); Acts 1999, 76th Leg., ch. 1150, §4 (eff. Sept. 1, 1999), ch. 1390, §23 (eff. Sept. 1, 1999); Acts 2003, 78th Leg., ch. 867, §1, eff. Sept. 1, 2003; Acts 2005, 79th Leg., ch. 268, §1.16(a), eff. Sept. 1, 2005; Acts 2015, 84th Leg., ch. 1, §1.129 (eff. Apr. 2, 2015), ch. 1056, §1 (eff. Sept. 1, 2015); H.B. 249, §4, 85th Leg., eff. Sept. 1, 2017; H.B. 1549, §2, 85th Leg., eff. Sept. 1, 2017; H.B. 2124, §1, 85th Leg., eff. Sept. 1, 2017; S.B. 11, §9, 85th Leg., eff. Sept. 1, 2017. Source: Former Fam. Code §34.05(a), (b).

See also 40 T.A.C. §§700.505-700.523.

ANNOTATIONS

TDPRS v. Schutz, 101 S.W.3d 512, 521-22 (Tex. App.—Houston [1st Dist.] 2002, no pet.). Family Code

§261.309(e) "does not confer a right on [foster parents] to resort to filing suit in district court without submitting to a formal administrative hearing. [¶] Further, at least with respect to allegations of abuse or neglect that occurred in a foster home, [Fam. Code §261.301(b)] governs.... In conducting an investigation for such a facility, the department shall perform the investigation as provided by [Fam. Code] Subch. E (not Subch. D, the subchapter on which [foster parents] rely) and the Human Resources Code. [T]he definition of 'child-care facility' includes a 'foster home.' In other words, when the alleged abuse occurred in a foster home, the department conducts the investigation under [Fam.] Code §§261.401-261.409 *and* [Hum. Res. Code] ch. 42. Because the Family Code provision that deals with investigations of abuse or neglect in a foster home refers back to the Human Resources Code (and therefore incorporates the exhaustion-of-remedies requirement), [foster parents] were required to submit to an administrative hearing regardless of whether the Human Resources Code or the Family Code applies."

FAM §261.3011. JOINT INVESTIGATION GUIDELINES & TRAINING

(a) The department shall, in consultation with the appropriate law enforcement agencies, develop guide lines and protocols for joint investigations by the department and the law enforcement agency under Section 261.301. The guidelines and protocols must:

(1) clarify the respective roles of the department and law enforcement agency in conducting the investigation;

(2) require that mutual child protective services and law enforcement training and agreements be implemented by both entities to ensure the integrity and best outcomes of joint investigations; and

(3) incorporate the use of forensic methods in determining the occurrence of child abuse and neglect.

(b) The department shall collaborate with law enforcement agencies to provide to department investigators and law enforcement officers responsible for investigating reports of abuse and neglect joint training relating to methods to effectively conduct joint investigations under Section 261.301. The training must include information on interviewing techniques, evidence gathering, and testifying in court for criminal investigations, as well as instruction on rights provided by the Fourth Amendment to the United States Constitution.

History of Fam. Code §261.3011: Acts 2005, 79th Leg., ch. 268, §1.17, eff. Sept. 1, 2005.

FAM §261.3012. REPEALED

Repealed by Acts 2015, 84th Leg., ch. 944, §86(8), eff. Sept. 1, 2015.

FAM §261.3013. CASE CLOSURE AGREEMENTS PROHIBITED

(a) Except as provided by Subsection (b), on closing a case, the department may not enter into a written agreement with a child's parent or another adult with whom the child resides that requires the parent or other adult to take certain actions after the case is closed to ensure the child's safety.

(b) This section does not apply to an agreement that is entered into by a parent or other adult:

(1) following the removal of a child and that is subject to the approval of a court with continuing jurisdiction over the child;

(2) as a result of the person's participation in family group conferencing; or

(3) as part of a formal case closure plan agreed to by the person who will continue to care for a child as a result of a parental child safety placement.

(c) The department shall develop policies to guide caseworkers in the development of case closure agree ments authorized under Subsections (b)(2) and (3).

History of Fam. Code §261.3013: Acts 2011, 82nd Leg., ch. 598, §1, eff. Sept. 1, 2011.

FAM §261.3015. ALTERNATIVE RESPONSE SYSTEM

(a) In assigning priorities and prescribing investigative procedures based on the severity and immediacy of the alleged harm to a child under Section 261.301(d), the department shall establish an alternative response system to allow the department to make the most effective use of resources to investigate and respond to reported cases of abuse and neglect.

(b) Notwithstanding Section 261.301, the department may, in accordance with this section and department rules, conduct an alternative response to a report of abuse or neglect if the report does not:

(1) allege sexual abuse of a child;

(2) allege abuse or neglect that caused the death of a child; or

(3) indicate a risk of serious physical injury or immediate serious harm to a child.

(c) The department may administratively close a reported case of abuse or neglect without completing the investigation or alternative response and without providing services or making a referral to another entity for assistance if the department determines, after contacting a professional or other credible source, that the child's safety can be assured without further investigation, response, services, or assistance.

(d) In determining how to classify a reported case of abuse or neglect under the alternative response system, the child's safety is the primary concern. The classification of a case may be changed as warranted by the circumstances.

(e) An alternative response to a report of abuse or neglect must include:

(1) a safety assessment of the child who is the subject of the report;

(2) an assessment of the child's family; and

(3) in collaboration with the child's family, identification of any necessary and appropriate service or support to reduce the risk of future harm to the child.

(f) An alternative response to a report of abuse or neglect may not include a formal determination of whether the alleged abuse or neglect occurred.

(g) The department may implement the alternative response in one or more of the department's administrative regions before implementing the system statewide. The department shall study the results of the system in the regions where the system has been implemented in determining the method by which to implement the system statewide.

History of Fam. Code §261.3015: Acts 1997, 75th Leg., ch. 1022, §71, eff. Sept. 1, 1997. Amended by Acts 2005, 79th Leg., ch. 268, §1.19(a), eff. Sept. 1, 2005; Acts 2013, 83rd Leg., ch. 420, §1, eff. Sept. 1, 2013; Acts 2015, 84th Leg., ch. 1, §§1.130, 1.131, eff. Apr. 2, 2015.

FAM §261.3016. TRAINING OF PERSONNEL RECEIVING REPORTS OF ABUSE & NEGLECT

The department shall develop, in cooperation with local law enforcement officials and the Commission on State Emergency Communications, a training program for department personnel who receive reports of abuse and neglect. The training program must include information on:

(1) the proper methods of screening reports of abuse and neglect; and

(2) ways to determine the seriousness of a report, including determining whether a report alleges circumstances that could result in the death of or serious harm to a child or whether the report is less serious in nature.

History of Fam. Code §261.3016: Acts 2005, 79th Leg., ch. 54, §1 (eff. Sept. 1, 2005), ch. 268, §1.20 (eff. Sept. 1, 2005).

E FAM §261.3017[A*]. ABBREVIATED INVESTIGATION & ADMINISTRATIVE CLOSURE OF CERTAIN CASES

In 2017, the Legislature enacted two sections 261.3017. This §261.3017 was enacted by S.B. 190, §1, 85th Leg., effective June 9, 2017. The [A] has been added by the editor to distinguish this §261.3017 from the other, which is marked with [B*]. In 2019, the Legislature is expected to correct the duplicate numbering.*

(a) A department caseworker may refer a reported case of child abuse or neglect to a department supervisor for abbreviated investigation or administrative closure at any time before the 60th day after the date the report is received if:

(1) there is no prior report of abuse or neglect of the child who is the subject of the report;

(2) the department has not received an additional report of abuse or neglect of the child following the initial report;

(3) after contacting a professional or other credible source, the caseworker determines that the child's safety can be assured without further investigation, response, services, or assistance; and

(4) the caseworker determines that no abuse or neglect occurred.

(b) A department supervisor shall review each reported case of child abuse or neglect that has remained open for more than 60 days and administratively close the case if:

(1) the supervisor determines that:

(A) the circumstances described by Subsections (a)(1)-(4) exist; and

(B) closing the case would not expose the child to an undue risk of harm; and

(2) the department director grants approval for the administrative closure of the case.

(c) A department supervisor may reassign a reported case of child abuse or neglect that does not qualify for abbreviated investigation or administrative closure under Subsection (a) or (b) to a different department caseworker if the supervisor determines that

reassignment would allow the department to make the most effective use of resources to investigate and respond to reported cases of abuse or neglect.

(d) The executive commissioner shall adopt rules necessary to implement this section.

(e) In this section, "professional" means an individual who is licensed or certified by the state or who is an employee of a facility licensed, certified, or operated by the state and who, in the normal course of official duties or duties for which a license or certification is required, has direct contact with children. The term includes teachers, nurses, doctors, day-care employees, employees of a clinic or health care facility that provides reproductive services, juvenile probation officers, and juvenile detention or correctional officers.

History of Fam. Code §261.3017[A*]: Enacted by S.B. 190, §1, 85th Leg., eff. June 9, 2017.

E FAM §261.3017[B*]. CONSULTATION WITH PHYSICIAN NETWORKS & SYSTEMS REGARDING CERTAIN MEDICAL CONDITIONS

☠ *In 2017, the Legislature enacted two sections 261.3017. This §261.3017 was enacted by H.B. 2848, §1, 85th Leg., effective Sept. 1, 2017. The [B*] has been added by the editor to distinguish this §261.3017 from the other, which is marked with [A*]. In 2019, the Legislature is expected to correct the duplicate numbering.*

(a) In this section:

(1) "Network" means the Forensic Assessment Center Network.

(2) "System" means the entities that receive grants under the Texas Medical Child Abuse Resources and Education System (MEDCARES) authorized by Chapter 1001, Health and Safety Code.

(b) Any agreement between the department and the network or between the Department of State Health Services and the system to provide assistance in connection with abuse and neglect investigations conducted by the department must require the network and the system to have the ability to obtain consultations with physicians, including radiologists, geneticists, and endocrinologists, who specialize in identifying unique health conditions, including:

(1) rickets;

(2) Ehlers-Danlos Syndrome;

(3) osteogenesis imperfecta;

(4) vitamin D deficiency; and

(5) other similar metabolic bone diseases or connective tissue disorders.

(c) If, during an abuse or neglect investigation or an assessment provided under Subsection (b), the department or a physician in the network determines that a child requires a specialty consultation with a physician, the department or the physician shall refer the child's case to the system for the consultation, if the system has available capacity to take the child's case.

(d) In providing assessments to the department as provided by Subsection (b), the network and the system must use a blind peer review process to resolve cases where physicians in the network or system disagree in the assessment of the causes of a child's injuries or in the presence of a condition listed under Subsection (b).

History of Fam. Code §261.3017[B*]: Enacted by H.B. 2848, §1, 85th Leg., eff. Sept. 1, 2017.

FAM §261.3019. EXPIRED

FAM §261.302. CONDUCT OF INVESTIGATION

(a) The investigation may include:

(1) a visit to the child's home, unless the alleged abuse or neglect can be confirmed or clearly ruled out without a home visit; and

(2) an interview with and examination of the subject child, which may include a medical, psychological, or psychiatric examination.

(b) The interview with and examination of the child may:

(1) be conducted at any reasonable time and place, including the child's home or the child's school;

(2) include the presence of persons the department determines are necessary; and

(3) include transporting the child for purposes relating to the interview or investigation.

(b-1) Before the department may transport a child as provided by Subsection (b)(3), the department shall attempt to notify the parent or other person having custody of the child of the transport.

(c) The investigation may include an interview with the child's parents and an interview with and medical, psychological, or psychiatric examination of any child in the home.

(d) If, before an investigation is completed, the investigating agency believes that the immediate removal of a child from the child's home is necessary to protect the child from further abuse or neglect, the in-

vestigating agency shall file a petition or take other action under Chapter 262 to provide for the temporary care and protection of the child.

(e) An interview with a child in which the allegations of the current investigation are discussed and that is conducted by the department during the investigation stage shall be audiotaped or videotaped unless:

(1) the recording equipment malfunctions and the malfunction is not the result of a failure to maintain the equipment or bring adequate supplies for the equipment;

(2) the child is unwilling to allow the interview to be recorded after the department makes a reasonable effort consistent with the child's age and development and the circumstances of the case to convince the child to allow the recording; or

(3) due to circumstances that could not have been reasonably foreseen or prevented by the department, the department does not have the necessary recording equipment because the department employee conducting the interview does not ordinarily conduct interviews.

(e-1) An interview with a child alleged to be a victim of physical abuse or sexual abuse conducted by an investigating agency other than the department shall be audiotaped or videotaped unless the investigating agency determines that good cause exists for not audiotaping or videotaping the interview in accordance with rules of the agency. Good cause may include, but is not limited to, such considerations as the age of the child and the nature and seriousness of the allegations under investigation. Nothing in this subsection shall be construed as prohibiting the investigating agency from audiotaping or videotaping an interview of a child on any case for which such audiotaping or videotaping is not required under this subsection. The fact that the investigating agency failed to audiotape or videotape an interview is admissible at the trial of the offense that is the subject of the interview.

(f) A person commits an offense if the person is notified of the time of the transport of a child by the department and the location from which the transport is initiated and the person is present at the location when the transport is initiated and attempts to interfere with the department's investigation. An offense under this subsection is a Class B misdemeanor. It is an exception to the application of this subsection that the department requested the person to be present at the site of the transport.

History of Fam. Code §261.302: Acts 1995, 74th Leg., ch. 20, §1, eff. Apr. 20, 1995. Amended by Acts 1995, 74th Leg., ch. 751, §95, eff. Sept. 1, 1995; Acts 1997, 75th Leg., ch. 575, §§13, 14 (eff. Sept. 1, 1997), ch. 1022, §73 (eff. Sept. 1, 1997); Acts 2005, 79th Leg., ch. 268, §1.21, eff. Sept. 1, 2005; Acts 2015, 84th Leg., ch. 1, §1.132 (eff. Apr. 2, 2015), ch. 944, §19 (eff. Sept. 1, 2015). Source: Former Fam. Code §34.05(c), (d).

See also 40 T.A.C. §§700.507, 700.508, 700.519.

ANNOTATIONS

Bays v. State, 396 S.W.3d 580, 588-89 (Tex.Crim. App.2013). "The admissibility of a child-victim's pre-trial recorded statements is ... governed by [CCP] art. 38.071, which we refer to as the 'video statute.' The video statute creates a hearsay exception for a child's video- or audio-recorded pre-trial statements, but only if stringent requirements are met, including that the child is unavailable to testify at trial and that the interviewer is a neutral person experienced in child-abuse cases or a child-abuse expert. *At n.12:* Pursuant to [Fam. Code §261.302(e)], an interview conducted by TDFPS must be audio- or video-recorded if conducted during an active investigation. Admissibility of such recorded interviews at trial is governed by the video statute, which specifically applies to pretrial videotaped statements from a victim."

FAM §261.3021. CASEWORK DOCUMENTATION & MANAGEMENT

Subject to the appropriation of money, the department shall identify critical investigation actions that impact child safety and require department caseworkers to document those actions in a child's case file not later than the day after the action occurs.

History of Fam. Code §261.3021: Acts 2005, 79th Leg., ch. 268, §1.22, eff. Sept. 1, 2005. Amended by Acts 2015, 84th Leg., ch. 944, §20, eff. Sept. 1, 2015.

FAM §261.3022. CHILD SAFETY CHECK ALERT LIST

(a) The Department of Public Safety of the State of Texas shall maintain a child safety check alert list as part of the Texas Crime Information Center to help locate a child or the child's family for purposes of:

(1) investigating a report of child abuse or neglect;

(2) providing protective services to a family receiving family-based support services; or

(3) providing protective services to the family of a child in the managing conservatorship of the department.

(b) If the department is unable to locate a child or the child's family for a purpose described by Subsection

(a) after the department has attempted to locate the child for not more than 20 days, the department shall notify the Texas Department of Public Safety that the department is unable to locate the child or the child's family. The notice must include the information required by Subsections (c)(1)-(10).

(c) On receipt of the notice from the department, the Texas Department of Public Safety shall notify the Texas Crime Information Center to place the child and the child's family on a child safety check alert list. The alert list must include the following information if known or readily available:

(1) the name, sex, race, date of birth, any known identifying numbers, including social security number and driver's license number, and personal descriptions of the family member alleged to have abused or neglected a child according to the report the department is attempting to investigate;

(2) the name, sex, race, date of birth, any known identifying numbers, including social security number and driver's license number, and personal descriptions of any parent, managing conservator, or guardian of the child who cannot be located for the purposes described by Subsection (a);

(3) the name, sex, race, date of birth, any known identifying numbers, including social security number and driver's license number, and personal descriptions of the child who is the subject of the report or is receiving services described by Subsection (a)(2) or (3);

(4) if applicable, a code identifying the type of child abuse or neglect alleged or determined to have been committed against the child;

(5) the family's last known address;

(6) any known description of the motor vehicle, including the vehicle's make, color, style of body, model year, and vehicle identification number, in which the child is suspected to be transported;

(7) the case number assigned by the department;

(8) the department's dedicated law-enforcement telephone number for statewide intake;

(9) the date and time when and the location where the child was last seen; and

(10) any other information required for an entry as established by the center.

History of Fam. Code §261.3022: Acts 2005, 79th Leg., ch. 268, §1.22, eff. Sept. 1, 2005. Amended by Acts 2015, 84th Leg., ch. 1056, §2 (eff. Sept. 1, 2015), ch. 1202, §1 (eff. Sept. 1, 2015).

A FAM §261.3023. LAW ENFORCEMENT RESPONSE TO CHILD SAFETY CHECK ALERT

If a law enforcement officer encounters a child or other person [~~, including a child,~~] listed on the Texas Crime Information Center's child safety check alert list, the law enforcement officer shall follow the procedures described by Article 2.272, Code of Criminal Procedure.

History of Fam. Code §261.3023: Acts 2005, 79th Leg., ch. 268, §1.22, eff. Sept. 1, 2005. Amended by Acts 2015, 84th Leg., ch. 1056, §3 (eff. Sept. 1, 2015), ch. 1202, §2 (eff. Sept. 1, 2015). Reenacted and amended by S.B. 1488, §7.006, 85th Leg., eff. Sept. 1, 2017.

A FAM §261.3024. REMOVAL FROM CHILD SAFETY CHECK ALERT LIST

Subsection (a) was reenacted by S.B. 1488, §7.007, 85th Leg., eff. Sept. 1, 2017.

(a) A law enforcement officer who locates a child listed on the Texas Crime Information Center's child safety check alert list shall report that the child has been located in the manner prescribed by Article 2.272, Code of Criminal Procedure.

(b) If the department locates a child who has been placed on the child safety check alert list established under Section 261.3022 through a means other than information reported to the department by a law enforcement officer under Article 2.272, Code of Criminal Procedure, the department shall report to the Texas Crime Information Center that the child has been located.

(c) On receipt of notice that a child has been located, the Texas Crime Information Center shall remove the child and the child's family from the child safety check alert list.

History of Fam. Code §261.3024: Acts 2005, 79th Leg., ch. 268, §1.22, eff. Sept. 1, 2005. Amended by Acts 2015, 84th Leg., ch. 1056, §4 (eff. Sept. 1, 2015), ch. 1202, §3 (eff. Sept. 1, 2015); S.B. 1488, §7.007, 85th Leg., eff. Sept. 1, 2017.

A FAM §261.3025. CHILD SAFETY CHECK ALERT LIST PROGRESS REPORT

(a) Not later than February 1 of each year, the Department of Public Safety, with the assistance of the department, shall prepare and submit a report on the use of the Texas Crime Information Center's child safety check alert list to the standing committees of the senate and the house of representatives with primary jurisdiction over child protective services.

(b) The report must include the following information for the preceding calendar year:

(1) the number of law enforcement officers who completed the training program established under Section 1701.266 [~~1701.262~~], Occupations Code;

(2) the number of children who have been placed on the child safety check alert list and the number of those children who have been located; and

(3) the number of families who have been placed on the child safety check alert list and the number of those families who have been located.

(c) This section expires February 2, 2021.

History of Fam. Code §261.3025: Acts 2015, 84th Leg., ch. 1056, §5, eff. Mar. 1, 2016. Amended by S.B. 1488, §24.002(5), 85th Leg., eff. Sept. 1, 2017.

FAM §261.303. INTERFERENCE WITH INVESTIGATION; COURT ORDER

(a) A person may not interfere with an investigation of a report of child abuse or neglect conducted by the department.

(b) If admission to the home, school, or any place where the child may be cannot be obtained, then for good cause shown the court having family law jurisdiction shall order the parent, the person responsible for the care of the children, or the person in charge of any place where the child may be to allow entrance for the interview, examination, and investigation.

(c) If a parent or person responsible for the child's care does not consent to release of the child's prior medical, psychological, or psychiatric records or to a medical, psychological, or psychiatric examination of the child that is requested by the department, the court having family law jurisdiction shall, for good cause shown, order the records to be released or the examination to be made at the times and places designated by the court.

(d) A person, including a medical facility, that makes a report under Subchapter B shall release to the department, as part of the required report under Section 261.103, records that directly relate to the suspected abuse or neglect without requiring parental consent or a court order. If a child is transferred from a reporting medical facility to another medical facility to treat the injury or condition that formed the basis for the original report, the transferee medical facility shall, at the department's request, release to the department records relating to the injury or condition without requiring parental consent or a court order.

(e) A person, including a utility company, that has confidential locating or identifying information regarding a family that is the subject of an investigation under this chapter shall release that information to the department on request. The release of information to the department as required by this subsection by a person, including a utility company, is not subject to Section 552.352, Government Code, or any other law providing liability for the release of confidential information.

History of Fam. Code §261.303: Acts 1995, 74th Leg., ch. 20, §1, eff. Apr. 20, 1995. Amended by Acts 1995, 74th Leg., ch. 751, §96, eff. Sept. 1, 1995; Acts 1999, 76th Leg., ch. 1150, §5 (eff. Sept. 1, 1999), ch. 1390, §24 (eff. Sept. 1, 1999); Acts 2007, 80th Leg., ch. 1406, §6, eff. Sept. 1, 2007; Acts 2015, 84th Leg., ch. 1, §1.133, eff. Apr. 2, 2015. Source: Former Fam. Code §34.05(c).

ANNOTATIONS

Ross v. State, 507 S.W.3d 881, 901-02 (Tex.App.—Texarkana 2016, pet. granted 4-26-17). "Section 261.303(b) contemplates that the order only authorizes entry into a place where the child 'may be,' i.e., where the child is located. [¶] Although the order listed eight separate addresses where the child might be located, it only authorized entry into the residence where the unknown child was located. ... After the child is located in the residence, the order states what the Department may do: it may interview and examine the child, and it may 'observ[e] ... the premises or immediate surroundings where the [child] is located or where the alleged abuse or neglect occurred.' These actions, like the entry authorized under the order, are dependent on the child being located in the residence. [¶] In this case, both [DFPS investigator 1] and the State maintain that the initial entry into the residence and the actions taken in the bedroom were necessary to verify that the child was not located in the residence. [W]e find that the subsequent search of the kitchen and its contents was not authorized under the order or the statute. [DFPS investigator 2] testified that, based on what they saw in the bedroom, she and [DFPS investigator 1] concluded that the child had been there at one time, but that she was no longer there. [¶] She also testified that [DFPS investigator 1] told her she wanted to search other areas for evidence that the parents had been making drugs. ... Therefore, we find that there was sufficient evidence for the trial court to find that the search of the kitchen and its contents occurred after [DFPS investigator 1] determined that the child was not located in the residence. Since that search occurred after it was determined that the child was not present in the residence, it was not authorized under the order or the statute and was, therefore, unlawful, unless an emergency justified the search."

FAM §261.3031. FAILURE TO COOPERATE WITH INVESTIGATION; DEPARTMENT RESPONSE

(a) If a parent or other person refuses to cooperate with the department's investigation of the alleged abuse or neglect of a child and the refusal poses a risk to the child's safety, the department shall seek assistance from the appropriate attorney with responsibility for representing the department as provided by Section 264.009 to obtain a court order as described by Section 261.303.

(b) A person's failure to report to an agency authorized to investigate abuse or neglect of a child within a reasonable time after receiving proper notice constitutes a refusal by the person to cooperate with the department's investigation. A summons may be issued to locate the person.

History of Fam. Code §261.3031: Acts 2005, 79th Leg., ch. 268, §1.23, eff. Sept. 1, 2005. Amended by Acts 2007, 80th Leg., ch. 1406, §7, eff. Sept. 1, 2007; Acts 2015, 84th Leg., ch. 1, §1.134, eff. Apr. 2, 2015.

FAM §261.3032. INTERFERENCE WITH INVESTIGATION; CRIMINAL PENALTY

(a) A person commits an offense if, with the intent to interfere with the department's investigation of a report of abuse or neglect of a child, the person relocates the person's residence, either temporarily or permanently, without notifying the department of the address of the person's new residence or conceals the child and the person's relocation or concealment interferes with the department's investigation.

(b) An offense under this section is a Class B misdemeanor.

(c) If conduct that constitutes an offense under this section also constitutes an offense under any other law, the actor may be prosecuted under this section or the other law.

History of Fam. Code §261.3032: Acts 2005, 79th Leg., ch. 268, §1.24, eff. Sept. 1, 2005.

A FAM §261.304. INVESTIGATION OF ANONYMOUS REPORT

(a) If the department receives an anonymous report of child abuse or neglect by a person responsible for a child's care, custody, or welfare, the department shall conduct a preliminary investigation to determine whether there is any evidence to corroborate the report.

(b) An investigation under this section may include a visit to the child's home, unless the alleged abuse or neglect can be confirmed or clearly ruled out without a home visit, [and] an interview with and examination of the child, and an interview with the child's parents. In addition, the department may interview any other person the department believes may have relevant information.

(c) Unless the department determines that there is some evidence to corroborate the report of abuse, the department may not conduct the thorough investigation required by this chapter or take any action against the person accused of abuse.

History of Fam. Code §261.304: Acts 1995, 74th Leg., ch. 20, §1, eff. Apr. 20, 1995. Amended by S.B. 1063, §1, 85th Leg., eff. Sept. 1, 2017. Source: Former Fam. Code §34.053.

FAM §261.305. ACCESS TO MENTAL HEALTH RECORDS

(a) An investigation may include an inquiry into the possibility that a parent or a person responsible for the care of a child who is the subject of a report under Subchapter B has a history of medical or mental illness.

(b) If the parent or person does not consent to an examination or allow the department to have access to medical or mental health records requested by the department, the court having family law jurisdiction, for good cause shown, shall order the examination to be made or that the department be permitted to have access to the records under terms and conditions prescribed by the court.

(c) If the court determines that the parent or person is indigent, the court shall appoint an attorney to represent the parent or person at the hearing. The fees for the appointed attorney shall be paid as provided by Chapter 107.

(d) A parent or person responsible for the child's care is entitled to notice and a hearing when the department seeks a court order to allow a medical, psychological, or psychiatric examination or access to medical or mental health records.

(e) This access does not constitute a waiver of confidentiality.

History of Fam. Code §261.305: Acts 1995, 74th Leg., ch. 20, §1, eff. Apr. 20, 1995. Amended by Acts 1997, 75th Leg., ch. 575, §15, eff. Sept. 1, 1997; Acts 1999, 76th Leg., ch. 1150, §6 (eff. Sept. 1, 1999), ch. 1390, §25 (eff. Sept. 1, 1999); Acts 2015, 84th Leg., ch. 1, §1.135, eff. Apr. 2, 2015. Source: Former Fam. Code §34.05(c).

See also 40 T.A.C. §700.509.

FAM §261.306. REMOVAL OF CHILD FROM STATE

(a) If the department has reason to believe that a person responsible for the care, custody, or welfare of the child may remove the child from the state before the

investigation is completed, the department may file an application for a temporary restraining order in a district court without regard to continuing jurisdiction of the child as provided in Chapter 155.

(b) The court may render a temporary restraining order prohibiting the person from removing the child from the state pending completion of the investigation if the court:

(1) finds that the department has probable cause to conduct the investigation; and

(2) has reason to believe that the person may remove the child from the state.

History of Fam. Code §261.306: Acts 1995, 74th Leg., ch. 20, §1, eff. Apr. 20, 1995. Amended by Acts 2015, 84th Leg., ch. 1, §1.136, eff. Apr. 2, 2015. Source: Former Fam. Code §34.05(g).

FAM §261.307. INFORMATION RELATING TO INVESTIGATION PROCEDURE

(a) As soon as possible after initiating an investigation of a parent or other person having legal custody of a child, the department shall provide to the person:

(1) a summary that:

(A) is brief and easily understood;

(B) is written in a language that the person understands, or if the person is illiterate, is read to the person in a language that the person understands; and

(C) contains the following information:

(i) the department's procedures for conducting an investigation of alleged child abuse or neglect, including:

(a) a description of the circumstances under which the department would request to remove the child from the home through the judicial system; and

(b) an explanation that the law requires the department to refer all reports of alleged child abuse or neglect to a law enforcement agency for a separate determination of whether a criminal violation occurred;

(ii) the person's right to file a complaint with the department or to request a review of the findings made by the department in the investigation;

(iii) the person's right to review all records of the investigation unless the review would jeopardize an ongoing criminal investigation or the child's safety;

(iv) the person's right to seek legal counsel;

(v) references to the statutory and regulatory provisions governing child abuse and neglect and how the person may obtain copies of those provisions; and

(vi) the process the person may use to acquire access to the child if the child is removed from the home;

(2) if the department determines that removal of the child may be warranted, a proposed child placement resources form that:

(A) instructs the parent or other person having legal custody of the child to:

(i) complete and return the form to the department or agency; and

(ii) identify in the form three individuals who could be relative caregivers or designated caregivers, as those terms are defined by Section 264.751; and

(B) informs the parent or other person of a location that is available to the parent or other person to submit the information in the form 24 hours a day either in person or by facsimile machine or e-mail; and

(3) an informational manual required by Section 261.3071.

(b) The child placement resources form described by Subsection (a)(2) must include information on the periods of time by which the department must complete a background check.

History of Fam. Code §261.307: Acts 1995, 74th Leg., ch. 20, §1, eff. Apr. 20, 1995. Amended by Acts 2005, 79th Leg., ch. 268, §1.25, eff. Sept. 1, 2005; Acts 2009, 81st Leg., ch. 825, §1, eff. June 19, 2009. Source: Former Fam. Code §34.051.

FAM §261.3071. INFORMATIONAL MANUALS

(a) In this section:

(1) "Designated caregiver" and "relative caregiver" have the meanings assigned those terms by Section 264.751.

(2) "Voluntary caregiver" means a person who voluntarily agrees to provide temporary care for a child:

(A) who is the subject of an investigation by the department or whose parent, managing conservator, possessory conservator, guardian, caretaker, or custodian is receiving family-based safety services from the department;

(B) who is not in the conservatorship of the department; and

(C) who is placed in the care of the person by the parent or other person having legal custody of the child.

(b) The department shall develop and publish informational manuals that provide information for:

(1) a parent or other person having custody of a child who is the subject of an investigation under this chapter;

(2) a person who is selected by the department to be the child's relative or designated caregiver; and

(3) a voluntary caregiver.

(c) Information provided in the manuals must be in both English and Spanish and must include, as appropriate:

(1) useful indexes of information such as telephone numbers;

(2) the information required to be provided under Section 261.307(a)(1);

(3) information describing the rights and duties of a relative or designated caregiver;

(4) information regarding the relative and other designated caregiver program under Subchapter I, Chapter 264; and

(5) information regarding the role of a voluntary caregiver, including information on how to obtain any documentation necessary to provide for a child's needs.

History of Fam. Code §261.3071: Acts 2005, 79th Leg., ch. 268, §1.26, eff. Sept. 1, 2005. Amended by Acts 2009, 81st Leg., ch. 825, §1, eff. June 19, 2009.

FAM §261.308. SUBMISSION OF INVESTIGATION REPORT

(a) The department shall make a complete written report of the investigation.

(b), (c) Repealed by Acts 2015, 84th Leg., ch. 944, §86(9), eff. Sept. 1, 2015.

(d) The department shall release information regarding a person alleged to have committed abuse or neglect to persons who have control over the person's access to children, including, as appropriate, the Texas Education Agency, the State Board for Educator Certification, the local school board or the school's governing body, the superintendent of the school district, or the school principal or director if the department determines that:

(1) the person alleged to have committed abuse or neglect poses a substantial and immediate risk of harm to one or more children outside the family of a child who is the subject of the investigation; and

(2) the release of the information is necessary to assist in protecting one or more children from the person alleged to have committed abuse or neglect.

(e) On request, the department shall release information about a person alleged to have committed abuse or neglect to the State Board for Educator Certification if the board has a reasonable basis for believing that the information is necessary to assist the board in protecting children from the person alleged to have committed abuse or neglect.

History of Fam. Code §261.308: Acts 1995, 74th Leg., ch. 20, §1, eff. Apr. 20, 1995. Amended by Acts 1995, 74th Leg., ch. 751, §97, eff. Sept. 1, 1995; Acts 2007, 80th Leg., ch. 1372, §13, eff. June 15, 2007; Acts 2015, 84th Leg., ch. 1, §1.137 (eff. Apr. 2, 2015), ch. 944, §86(9) (eff. Sept. 1, 2015). Source: Former Fam. Code §34.05(e), (f).

FAM §261.309. REVIEW OF DEPARTMENT INVESTIGATIONS

(a) The executive commissioner shall by rule establish policies and procedures to resolve complaints relating to and conduct reviews of child abuse or neglect investigations conducted by the department.

(b) If a person under investigation for allegedly abusing or neglecting a child requests clarification of the status of the person's case or files a complaint relating to the conduct of the department's staff or to department policy, the department shall conduct an informal review to clarify the person's status or resolve the complaint. The division of the department responsible for investigating complaints shall conduct the informal review as soon as possible but not later than the 14th day after the date the request or complaint is received.

(c) If, after the department's investigation, the person who is alleged to have abused or neglected a child disputes the department's determination of whether child abuse or neglect occurred, the person may request an administrative review of the findings. A department employee in administration who was not involved in or did not directly supervise the investigation shall conduct the review. The review must sustain, alter, or reverse the department's original findings in the investigation.

(d) The department employee shall conduct the review prescribed by Subsection (c) as soon as possible but not later than the 45th day after the date the department receives the request, unless the department has good cause for extending the deadline. If a civil or criminal court proceeding or an ongoing criminal investigation relating to the alleged abuse or neglect investigated by the department is pending, the department may postpone the review until the court proceeding is completed.

(e) A person is not required to exhaust the remedies provided by this section before pursuing a judicial remedy provided by law.

(f) This section does not provide for a review of an order rendered by a court.

History of Fam. Code §261.309: Acts 1995, 74th Leg., ch. 20, §1, eff. Apr. 20, 1995. Amended by Acts 2015, 84th Leg., ch. 1, §1.138 (eff. Apr. 2, 2015), ch. 944, §21 (eff. Sept. 1, 2015). Source: Former Fam. Code §34.052.

ANNOTATIONS

Gates v. TDFPS, 252 S.W.3d 90, 94 (Tex.App.—Austin 2008, no pet.). Mother "timely requested an [administrative review of investigative findings (ARIF)], a step that ordinarily would have triggered the 45-day deadline [in Fam. Code §261.309(d)] for the Department to conduct the review. However, the Department, purporting to rely on the 'pending litigation' exception to the 45-day deadline, declined to schedule the ARIF until [six years later]. *At 97:* In §261.309 ... the legislature explicitly provided that the ARIF remedy is *not* exclusive of any judicial remedies.... The Department does not dispute this, but instead urges that its purported 'waiver' of the pending ARIF in favor of a [State Office of Administrative Hearings (SOAH)] contested-case proceeding somehow confers exclusive jurisdiction on itself, through SOAH, to adjudicate [mother's] claims. We reject that premise. [¶] [T.A.C.] §700.516(j) does not authorize the agency to unilaterally 'waive' [mother's Fam. Code] ARIF remedy and force her into a SOAH contested-case proceeding...."

TDPRS v. Schutz, 101 S.W.3d 512, 521-22 (Tex. App.—Houston [1st Dist.] 2002, no pet.). See annotation under Family Code §261.301, p. 894.

FAM §261.310. INVESTIGATION STANDARDS

(a) The executive commissioner shall by rule develop and adopt standards for persons who investigate suspected child abuse or neglect at the state or local level. The standards shall encourage professionalism and consistency in the investigation of suspected child abuse or neglect.

(b) The standards must provide for a minimum number of hours of annual professional training for interviewers and investigators of suspected child abuse or neglect.

(c) Repealed by Acts 2015, 84th Leg., ch. 944, §86(10), eff. Sept. 1, 2015.

(d) The standards shall:

(1) recommend that videotaped and audiotaped interviews be uninterrupted;

(2) recommend a maximum number of interviews with and examinations of a suspected victim;

(3) provide procedures to preserve evidence, including the original recordings of the intake telephone calls, original notes, videotapes, and audiotapes, for one year; and

(4) provide that an investigator of suspected child abuse or neglect make a reasonable effort to locate and inform each parent of a child of any report of abuse or neglect relating to the child.

(e) The department, in conjunction with the Department of Public Safety, shall provide to the department's residential child-care facility licensing investigators advanced training in investigative protocols and techniques.

History of Fam. Code §261.310: Acts 1995, 74th Leg., ch. 20, §1, eff. Apr. 20, 1995. Amended by Acts 2005, 79th Leg., ch. 268, §1.27, eff. Sept. 1, 2005; Acts 2015, 84th Leg., ch. 1, §1.139 (eff. Apr. 2, 2015), ch. 944, §86(10) (eff. Sept. 1, 2015). Source: Former Fam. Code §34.054.

See also 40 T.A.C. §700.519.

FAM §261.3101. REPEALED

Repealed by Acts 2015, 84th Leg., ch. 944, §86(11), eff. Sept. 1, 2015.

FAM §261.311. NOTICE OF REPORT

(a) When during an investigation of a report of suspected child abuse or neglect a representative of the department conducts an interview with or an examination of a child, the department shall make a reasonable effort before 24 hours after the time of the interview or examination to notify each parent of the child and the child's legal guardian, if one has been appointed, of the nature of the allegation and of the fact that the interview or examination was conducted.

(b) If a report of suspected child abuse or neglect is administratively closed by the department as a result of a preliminary investigation that did not include an interview or examination of the child, the department shall make a reasonable effort before the expiration of 24 hours after the time the investigation is closed to notify each parent and legal guardian of the child of the disposition of the investigation.

(c) The notice required by Subsection (a) or (b) is not required if the department or agency determines that the notice is likely to endanger the safety of the child who is the subject of the report, the person who made the report, or any other person who participates in the investigation of the report.

(d) The notice required by Subsection (a) or (b) may be delayed at the request of a law enforcement agency if notification during the required time would interfere with an ongoing criminal investigation.

History of Fam. Code §261.311: Acts 1995, 74th Leg., ch. 20, §1, eff. Apr. 20, 1995. Amended by Acts 1997, 75th Leg., ch. 1022, §74, eff. Sept. 1, 1997; Acts 2015, 84th Leg., ch. 1, §1.140, eff. Apr. 2, 2015. Source: Former Fam. Code §34.055.

FAM §261.312. REVIEW TEAMS; OFFENSE

(a) The department shall establish review teams to evaluate department casework and decision-making related to investigations by the department of child abuse or neglect. The department may create one or more review teams for each region of the department for child protective services. A review team is a citizen review panel or a similar entity for the purposes of federal law relating to a state's child protection standards.

(b) A review team consists of at least five members who serve staggered two-year terms. Review team members are appointed by the commissioner of the department and consist of volunteers who live in and are broadly representative of the region in which the review team is established and have expertise in the prevention and treatment of child abuse and neglect. At least two members of a review team must be parents who have not been convicted of or indicted for an offense involving child abuse or neglect, have not been determined by the department to have engaged in child abuse or neglect, and are not under investigation by the department for child abuse or neglect. A member of a review team is a department volunteer for the purposes of Section 411.114, Government Code.

(c) A review team conducting a review of an investigation may conduct the review by examining the facts of the case as outlined by the department caseworker and law enforcement personnel. A review team member acting in the member's official capacity may receive information made confidential under Section 40.005, Human Resources Code, or Section 261.201.

(d) A review team shall report to the department the results of the team's review of an investigation. The review team's report may not include confidential information. The findings contained in a review team's report are subject to disclosure under Chapter 552, Government Code. This section does not require a law enforcement agency to divulge information to a review team that the agency believes would compromise an ongoing criminal case, investigation, or proceeding.

(e) A member of a review team commits an offense if the member discloses confidential information. An offense under this subsection is a Class C misdemeanor.

History of Fam. Code §261.312: Acts 1995, 74th Leg., ch. 943, §3, eff. Sept. 1, 1995. Amended by Acts 1997, 75th Leg., ch. 575, §16, eff. Sept. 1, 1997; Acts 2009, 81st Leg., ch. 1372, §3, eff. June 19, 2009; Acts 2015, 84th Leg., ch. 1, §1.141, eff. Apr. 2, 2015.

FAM §261.3125. CHILD SAFETY SPECIALISTS

(a) The department shall employ in each of the department's administrative regions at least one child safety specialist. The job responsibilities of the child safety specialist must focus on child abuse and neglect investigation issues, including reports of child abuse required by Section 261.101, to achieve a greater compliance with that section, and on assessing and improving the effectiveness of the department in providing for the protection of children in the region.

(b) The duties of a child safety specialist must include the duty to:

(1) conduct staff reviews and evaluations of cases determined to involve a high risk to the health or safety of a child, including cases of abuse reported under Section 261.101, to ensure that risk assessment tools are fully and correctly used;

(2) review and evaluate cases in which there have been multiple referrals to the department of child abuse or neglect involving the same family, child, or person alleged to have committed the abuse or neglect; and

(3) approve decisions and assessments related to investigations of cases of child abuse or neglect that involve a high risk to the health or safety of a child.

History of Fam. Code §261.3125: Acts 1999, 76th Leg., ch. 1490, §1, eff. Sept. 1, 1999. Amended by Acts 2005, 79th Leg., ch. 268, §1.29, eff. Sept. 1, 2005; Acts 2009, 81st Leg., ch. 1372, §3, eff. June 19, 2009.

FAM §261.3126. COLOCATION OF INVESTIGATORS

(a) In each county, to the extent possible, the department and the local law enforcement agencies that investigate child abuse in the county shall colocate in the same offices investigators from the department and the law enforcement agencies to improve the efficiency of child abuse investigations. With approval of the local children's advocacy center and its partner agencies, in each county in which a children's advocacy center established under Section 264.402 is located, the department shall attempt to locate investigators from the department and county and municipal law enforcement agencies at the center.

(b) A law enforcement agency is not required to comply with the colocation requirements of this section if the law enforcement agency does not have a full-time

peace officer solely assigned to investigate reports of child abuse and neglect.

(c) If a county does not have a children's advocacy center, the department shall work with the local community to encourage one as provided by Section 264.402.

History of Fam. Code §261.3126: Acts 2005, 79th Leg., ch. 268, §1.30, eff. Sept. 1, 2005.

Section 261.313 reserved for expansion

FAM §261.314. TESTING

(a) The department shall provide testing as necessary for the welfare of a child who the department believes, after an investigation under this chapter, has been sexually abused, including human immunodeficiency virus (HIV) testing of a child who was abused in a manner by which HIV may be transmitted.

(b) Except as provided by Subsection (c), the results of a test under this section are confidential.

(c) If requested, the department shall report the results of a test under this section to:

(1) a court having jurisdiction of a proceeding involving the child or a proceeding involving a person suspected of abusing the child;

(2) a person responsible for the care and custody of the child as a foster parent; and

(3) a person seeking to adopt the child.

History of Fam. Code §261.314: Acts 1995, 74th Leg., ch. 943, §7, eff. Sept. 1, 1995.

FAM §261.315. REMOVAL OF CERTAIN INVESTIGATION INFORMATION FROM RECORDS

(a) At the conclusion of an investigation in which the department determines that the person alleged to have abused or neglected a child did not commit abuse or neglect, the department shall notify the person of the person's right to request the department to remove information about the person's alleged role in the abuse or neglect report from the department's records.

(b) On request under Subsection (a) by a person whom the department has determined did not commit abuse or neglect, the department shall remove information from the department's records concerning the person's alleged role in the abuse or neglect report.

(c) The executive commissioner shall adopt rules necessary to administer this section.

History of Fam. Code §261.315: Acts 1997, 75th Leg., ch. 1022, §75, eff. Sept. 1, 1997. Amended by Acts 2015, 84th Leg., ch. 1, §1.142, eff. Apr. 2, 2015.

See also 40 T.A.C. §700.523.

FAM §261.316. EXEMPTION FROM FEES FOR MEDICAL RECORDS

The department is exempt from the payment of a fee otherwise required or authorized by law to obtain a medical record from a hospital or health care provider if the request for a record is made in the course of an investigation by the department.

History of Fam. Code §261.316: Acts 1997, 75th Leg., ch. 575, §17, eff. Sept. 1, 1997. Renumbered from §261.315 by Acts 1999, 76th Leg., ch. 62, §19.01(27), eff. Sept. 1, 1999.

Sections 261.317-261.400 reserved for expansion

SUBCHAPTER E. INVESTIGATIONS OF ABUSE, NEGLECT, OR EXPLOITATION IN CERTAIN FACILITIES

A FAM §261.401. AGENCY INVESTIGATION

The repealed text of former subsection (a) is effective for reports of suspected abuse, neglect, or exploitation of a child made before Sept. 1, 2017.

(a) Repealed by H.B. 249, §14, 85th Leg., eff. Sept. 1, 2017; S.B. 11, §32, 85th Leg., eff. Sept. 1, 2017.

[~~(a)~~] [~~Notwithstanding Section 261.001, in this section:~~]

[~~(1)~~] [~~"Abuse" means an intentional, knowing, or reckless act or omission by an employee, volunteer, or other individual working under the auspices of a facility or program that causes or may cause emotional harm or physical injury to, or the death of, a child served by the facility or program as further described by rule or policy.~~]

[~~(2)~~] [~~"Exploitation" means the illegal or improper use of a child or of the resources of a child for monetary or personal benefit, profit, or gain by an employee, volunteer, or other individual working under the auspices of a facility or program as further described by rule or policy.~~]

[~~(3)~~] [~~"Neglect" means a negligent act or omission by an employee, volunteer, or other individual working under the auspices of a facility or program, including failure to comply with an individual treatment plan, plan of care, or individualized service plan, that causes or may cause substantial emotional harm or physical injury to, or the death of, a child served by the facility or program as further described by rule or policy.~~]

In 2017, two bills amended subsection (b), but only one bill, H.B. 249, §5, saved the former law in effect at

that time. The amended text from H.B. 249, §5 is effective for reports of suspected abuse, neglect, or exploitation of a child made on or after Sept. 1, 2017. Reports made before Sept. 1, 2017, are governed by the former law in effect at that time. The amended text from S.B. 11, §10 is effective Sept. 1, 2017.

(b) Except as provided by Section 261.404 of this code and Section 531.02013(1)(D), Government Code, a state agency that operates, licenses, certifies, registers, or lists a facility in which children are located or provides oversight of a program that serves children shall make a prompt, thorough investigation of a report that a child has been or may be abused, neglected, or exploited in the facility or program. The primary purpose of the investigation shall be the protection of the child.

(c) A state agency shall adopt rules relating to the investigation and resolution of reports received as provided by this subchapter. The executive commissioner shall review and approve the rules of agencies other than the Texas Department of Criminal Justice or the Texas Juvenile Justice Department to ensure that those agencies implement appropriate standards for the conduct of investigations and that uniformity exists among agencies in the investigation and resolution of reports.

(d) The Texas School for the Blind and Visually Impaired and the Texas School for the Deaf shall adopt policies relating to the investigation and resolution of reports received as provided by this subchapter. The executive commissioner shall review and approve the policies to ensure that the Texas School for the Blind and Visually Impaired and the Texas School for the Deaf adopt those policies in a manner consistent with the minimum standards adopted by the executive commissioner under Section 261.407.

History of Fam. Code §261.401: Acts 1995, 74th Leg., ch. 20, §1, eff. Apr. 20, 1995. Amended by Acts 1995, 74th Leg., ch. 751, §98, eff. Sept. 1, 1995; Acts 2001, 77th Leg., ch. 355, §2, eff. Sept. 1, 2001; Acts 2007, 80th Leg., ch. 908, §29, eff. Sept. 1, 2007; Acts 2009, 81st Leg., ch. 284, §6 (eff. June 11, 2009), ch. 720, §18 (eff. Sept. 1, 2009); Acts 2015, 84th Leg., ch. 1, §1.143, eff. Apr. 2, 2015; H.B. 249, §§5, 14, 85th Leg., eff. Sept. 1, 2017; S.B. 11, §§10, 32, 85th Leg., eff. Sept. 1, 2017. Source: Former Fam. Code §34.22.

See also 25 T.A.C. §§1.201-1.207.

FAM §261.402. INVESTIGATIVE REPORTS

(a) A state agency shall prepare and keep on file a complete written report of each investigation conducted by the agency under this subchapter.

(b) A state agency shall immediately notify the appropriate state or local law enforcement agency of any report the agency receives, other than a report from a law enforcement agency, that concerns the suspected abuse, neglect, or exploitation of a child or the death of a child from abuse or neglect. If the state agency finds evidence indicating that a child may have been abused, neglected, or exploited, the agency shall report the evidence to the appropriate law enforcement agency.

(c) A state agency that licenses, certifies, or registers a facility in which children are located shall compile, maintain, and make available statistics on the incidence in the facility of child abuse, neglect, and exploitation that is investigated by the agency.

(d) A state agency shall compile, maintain, and make available statistics on the incidence of child abuse, neglect, and exploitation in a facility operated by the state agency.

History of Fam. Code §261.402: Acts 1995, 74th Leg., ch. 20, §1, eff. Apr. 20, 1995. Amended by Acts 1995, 74th Leg., ch. 751, §99, eff. Sept. 1, 1995; Acts 2001, 77th Leg., ch. 355, §3, eff. Sept. 1, 2001; Acts 2015, 84th Leg., ch. 1, §1.144, eff. Apr. 2, 2015. Source: Former Fam. Code §34.23.

FAM §261.403. COMPLAINTS

(a) If a state agency receives a complaint relating to an investigation conducted by the agency concerning a facility operated by that agency in which children are located, the agency shall refer the complaint to the agency's governing body.

(b) The governing body of a state agency that operates a facility in which children are located shall ensure that the procedure for investigating abuse, neglect, and exploitation allegations and inquiries in the agency's facility is periodically reviewed under the agency's internal audit program required by Chapter 2102, Government Code.

History of Fam. Code §261.403: Acts 1995, 74th Leg., ch. 20, §1, eff. Apr. 20, 1995. Amended by Acts 2001, 77th Leg., ch. 355, §4, eff. Sept. 1, 2001; Acts 2015, 84th Leg., ch. 1, §1.145, eff. Apr. 2, 2015. Source: Former Fam. Code §34.24.

FAM §261.404. INVESTIGATIONS REGARDING CERTAIN CHILDREN RECEIVING SERVICES FROM CERTAIN PROVIDERS

(a) The department shall investigate a report of abuse, neglect, or exploitation of a child receiving services from a provider, as those terms are defined by Section 48.251, Human Resources Code, or as otherwise defined by rule. The department shall also investigate, under Subchapter F, Chapter 48, Human Resources Code, a report of abuse, neglect, or exploitation of a child receiving services from an officer, employee, agent, contractor, or subcontractor of a home and community support services agency licensed under Chapter

142, Health and Safety Code, if the officer, employee, agent, contractor, or subcontractor is or may be the person alleged to have committed the abuse, neglect, or exploitation.

(a-1) For an investigation of a child living in a residence owned, operated, or controlled by a provider of services under the home and community-based services waiver program described by Section 534.001(11)(B), Government Code, the department, in accordance with Subchapter E, Chapter 48, Human Resources Code, may provide emergency protective services necessary to immediately protect the child from serious physical harm or death and, if necessary, obtain an emergency order for protective services under Section 48.208, Human Resources Code.

(a-2) For an investigation of a child living in a residence owned, operated, or controlled by a provider of services under the home and community-based services waiver program described by Section 534.001(11)(B), Government Code, regardless of whether the child is receiving services under that waiver program from the provider, the department shall provide protective services to the child in accordance with Subchapter E, Chapter 48, Human Resources Code.

(a-3) For purposes of this section, Subchapters E and F, Chapter 48, Human Resources Code, apply to an investigation of a child and to the provision of protective services to that child in the same manner those subchapters apply to an investigation of an elderly person or person with a disability and the provision of protective services to that person.

(b) The department shall investigate the report under rules developed by the executive commissioner.

(c) If a report under this section relates to a child with an intellectual disability receiving services in a state supported living center or the ICF-IID component of the Rio Grande State Center, the department shall, within one hour of receiving the report, notify the facility in which the child is receiving services of the allegations in the report.

(d) If during the course of the department's investigation of reported abuse, neglect, or exploitation a caseworker of the department or the caseworker's supervisor has cause to believe that a child with an intellectual disability described by Subsection (c) has been abused, neglected, or exploited by another person in a manner that constitutes a criminal offense under any law, including Section 22.04, Penal Code, the caseworker shall immediately notify the Health and Human Services Commission's office of inspector general and promptly provide the commission's office of inspector general with a copy of the department's investigation report.

(e) The definitions of "abuse" and "neglect" prescribed by Section 261.001 do not apply to an investigation under this section.

(f) Repealed by Acts 2015, 84th Leg., ch. 860, §15(1) (eff. Sept. 1, 2015), ch. 1272, §19(1) (eff. Sept. 1, 2015).

History of Fam. Code §261.404: Acts 1995, 74th Leg., ch. 751, §100, eff. Sept. 1, 1995. Amended by Acts 1999, 76th Leg., ch. 907, §39, eff. Sept. 1, 1999; Acts 2009, 81st Leg., ch. 284, §7, eff. June 11, 2009; Acts 2015, 84th Leg., ch. 1, §1.146 (eff. Apr. 2, 2015), ch. 860, §§11, 12, 15(1) (eff. Sept. 1, 2015), ch. 1272, §§1, 2, 19(1) (eff. Sept. 1, 2015).

A FAM §261.405. INVESTIGATIONS IN JUVENILE JUSTICE PROGRAMS & FACILITIES

The amended text in §261.405 is effective for reports of suspected abuse, neglect, or exploitation of a child made on or after Sept. 1, 2017. Reports made before Sept. 1, 2017, are governed by the former law in effect at that time.

(a) Notwithstanding Section 261.001, in [In] this section:

(1) "Abuse" means an intentional, knowing, or reckless act or omission by an employee, volunteer, or other individual working under the auspices of a facility or program that causes or may cause emotional harm or physical injury to, or the death of, a child served by the facility or program as further described by rule or policy.

(2) "Exploitation" means the illegal or improper use of a child or of the resources of a child for monetary or personal benefit, profit, or gain by an employee, volunteer, or other individual working under the auspices of a facility or program as further described by rule or policy.

(3) "Juvenile justice facility" means a facility operated wholly or partly by the juvenile board, by another governmental unit, or by a private vendor under a contract with the juvenile board, county, or other governmental unit that serves juveniles under juvenile court jurisdiction. The term includes:

(A) a public or private juvenile pre-adjudication secure detention facility, including a holdover facility;

(B) a public or private juvenile post-adjudication secure correctional facility except for a facility operated solely for children committed to the Texas Juvenile Justice Department; and

(C) a public or private non-secure juvenile post-adjudication residential treatment facility that is not licensed by the Department of Family and Protective Services or the Department of State Health Services.

(4) [~~(2)~~] "Juvenile justice program" means a program or department operated wholly or partly by the juvenile board or by a private vendor under a contract with a juvenile board that serves juveniles under juvenile court jurisdiction. The term includes:

(A) a juvenile justice alternative education program;

(B) a non-residential program that serves juvenile offenders under the jurisdiction of the juvenile court; and

(C) a juvenile probation department.

(5) "Neglect" means a negligent act or omission by an employee, volunteer, or other individual working under the auspices of a facility or program, including failure to comply with an individual treatment plan, plan of care, or individualized service plan, that causes or may cause substantial emotional harm or physical injury to, or the death of, a child served by the facility or program as further described by rule or policy.

(b) A report of alleged abuse, neglect, or exploitation in any juvenile justice program or facility shall be made to the Texas Juvenile Justice Department and a local law enforcement agency for investigation.

(c) The Texas Juvenile Justice Department shall make a prompt, thorough [~~conduct an~~] investigation as provided by this chapter if that department receives a report of alleged abuse, neglect, or exploitation in any juvenile justice program or facility. The primary purpose of the investigation shall be the protection of the child.

(d) In an investigation required under this section, the investigating agency shall have access to medical and mental health records as provided by Subchapter D.

(e) As soon as practicable after a child is taken into custody or placed in a juvenile justice facility or juvenile justice program, the facility or program shall provide the child's parents with:

(1) information regarding the reporting of suspected abuse, neglect, or exploitation of a child in a juvenile justice facility or juvenile justice program to the Texas Juvenile Justice Department; and

(2) the Texas Juvenile Justice Department's toll-free number for this reporting.

History of Fam. Code §261.405: Acts 1995, 74th Leg., ch. 751, §100, eff. Sept. 1, 1995. Amended by Acts 1997, 75th Leg., ch. 162, §2 (eff. Sept. 1, 1997), ch. 1374, §8 (eff. Sept. 1, 1997); Acts 1999, 76th Leg., ch. 1150, §7 (eff. Sept. 1, 1999), ch. 1390, §26 (eff. Sept. 1, 1999), ch. 1477, §26 (eff. Sept. 1, 1999); Acts 2001, 77th Leg., ch. 1297, §47, eff. Sept. 1, 2001; Acts 2003, 78th Leg., ch. 283, §29, eff. Sept. 1, 2003; Acts 2005, 79th Leg., ch. 949, §28, eff. Sept. 1, 2005; Acts 2007, 80th Leg., ch. 908, §30, eff. Sept. 1, 2007; Acts 2015, 84th Leg., ch. 1, §1.147 (eff. Apr. 2, 2015), ch. 734, §83 (eff. Sept. 1, 2015); H.B. 249, §6, 85th Leg., eff. Sept. 1, 2017; S.B. 11, §11, 85th Leg., eff. Sept. 1, 2017.

See also 37 T.A.C. chs. 349, 350, 358.

FAM §261.406. INVESTIGATIONS IN SCHOOLS

(a) On receipt of a report of alleged or suspected abuse or neglect of a child in a public or private school under the jurisdiction of the Texas Education Agency, the department shall perform an investigation as provided by this chapter.

(b) The department shall send a copy of the completed report of the department's investigation to the Texas Education Agency. On request, the department shall provide a copy of the completed report of the department's investigation to the State Board for Educator Certification, the local school board or the school's governing body, the superintendent of the school district, and the school principal or director, unless the principal or director is alleged to have committed the abuse or neglect, for appropriate action. On request, the department shall provide a copy of the report of investigation to the parent, managing conservator, or legal guardian of a child who is the subject of the investigation and to the person alleged to have committed the abuse or neglect. The report of investigation shall be edited to protect the identity of the persons who made the report of abuse or neglect. Other than the persons authorized by the section to receive a copy of the report, Section 261.201(b) applies to the release of the report relating to the investigation of abuse or neglect under this section and to the identity of the person who made the report of abuse or neglect.

(c) Nothing in this section may prevent a law enforcement agency from conducting an investigation of a report made under this section.

(d) The executive commissioner shall adopt rules necessary to implement this section.

History of Fam. Code §261.406: Acts 1995, 74th Leg., ch. 751, §100, eff. Sept. 1, 1995. Amended by Acts 1997, 75th Leg., ch. 575, §18, eff. Sept. 1, 1997;

Acts 1999, 76th Leg., ch. 1150, §8 (eff. Sept. 1, 1999), ch. 1390, §27 (eff. Sept. 1, 1999); Acts 2005, 79th Leg., ch. 213, §2, eff. Sept. 1, 2005; Acts 2007, 80th Leg., ch. 1372, §14, eff. June 15, 2007; Acts 2015, 84th Leg., ch. 1, §1.148 (eff. Apr. 2, 2015), ch. 944, §22 (eff. Sept. 1, 2015).

See also 40 T.A.C. §§700.401-700.412.

FAM §261.407. MINIMUM STANDARDS

(a) The executive commissioner by rule shall adopt minimum standards for the investigation under Section 261.401 of suspected child abuse, neglect, or exploitation in a facility.

(b) A rule or policy adopted by a state agency or institution under Section 261.401 must be consistent with the minimum standards adopted by the executive commissioner.

(c) This section does not apply to a facility under the jurisdiction of the Texas Department of Criminal Justice or the Texas Juvenile Justice Department.

History of Fam. Code §261.407: Acts 2001, 77th Leg., ch. 355, §5, eff. Sept. 1, 2001. Renumbered from §261.405 by Acts 2003, 78th Leg., ch. 1275, §2(54), eff. Sept. 1, 2003. Amended by Acts 2015, 84th Leg., ch. 1, §1.149, eff. Apr. 2, 2015.

FAM §261.408. INFORMATION COLLECTION

(a) The executive commissioner by rule shall adopt uniform procedures for collecting information under Section 261.401, including procedures for collecting information on deaths that occur in facilities.

(b) The department shall receive and compile information on investigations in facilities. An agency submitting information to the department is responsible for ensuring the timeliness, accuracy, completeness, and retention of the agency's reports.

(c) This section does not apply to a facility under the jurisdiction of the Texas Department of Criminal Justice or the Texas Juvenile Justice Department.

History of Fam. Code §261.408: Acts 2001, 77th Leg., ch. 355, §5, eff. Sept. 1, 2001. Amended by Acts 2015, 84th Leg., ch. 1, §1.150, eff. Apr. 2, 2015.

FAM §261.409. INVESTIGATIONS IN FACILITIES UNDER TEXAS JUVENILE JUSTICE DEPARTMENT JURISDICTION

The board of the Texas Juvenile Justice Department by rule shall adopt standards for:

(1) the investigation under Section 261.401 of suspected child abuse, neglect, or exploitation in a facility under the jurisdiction of the Texas Juvenile Justice Department; and

(2) compiling information on those investigations.

History of Fam. Code §261.409: Acts 2001, 77th Leg., ch. 355, §6, eff. Sept. 1, 2001. Amended by Acts 2015, 84th Leg., ch. 734, §84, eff. Sept. 1, 2015.

FAM §261.410. REPORT OF ABUSE BY OTHER CHILDREN

(a) In this section:

(1) "Physical abuse" means:

(A) physical injury that results in substantial harm to the child requiring emergency medical treatment and excluding an accident or reasonable discipline by a parent, guardian, or managing or possessory conservator that does not expose the child to a substantial risk of harm; or

(B) failure to make a reasonable effort to prevent an action by another person that results in physical injury that results in substantial harm to the child.

(2) "Sexual abuse" means:

(A) sexual conduct harmful to a child's mental, emotional, or physical welfare; or

(B) failure to make a reasonable effort to prevent sexual conduct harmful to a child.

(b) An agency that operates, licenses, certifies, or registers a facility shall require a residential child-care facility to report each incident of physical or sexual abuse committed by a child against another child.

(c) Using information received under Subsection (b), the agency that operates, licenses, certifies, or registers a facility shall, subject to the availability of funds, compile a report that includes information:

(1) regarding the number of cases of physical and sexual abuse committed by a child against another child;

(2) identifying the residential child-care facility;

(3) regarding the date each allegation of abuse was made;

(4) regarding the date each investigation was started and concluded;

(5) regarding the findings and results of each investigation; and

(6) regarding the number of children involved in each incident investigated.

History of Fam. Code §261.410: Acts 2005, 79th Leg., ch. 268, §1.31, eff. Sept. 1, 2005.

Sections 261.411-261.500 blank

E Subchapter F. Protective Order in Certain Cases of Abuse or Neglect

FAM §261.501. Filing Application for Protective Order in Certain Cases of Abuse or Neglect

The department may file an application for a protective order for a child's protection under this subchapter on the department's own initiative or jointly with a parent, relative, or caregiver of the child who requests the filing of the application if the department:

(1) has temporary managing conservatorship of the child;

(2) determines that:

(A) the child:

(i) is a victim of abuse or neglect; or

(ii) has a history of being abused or neglected; and

(B) there is a threat of:

(i) immediate or continued abuse or neglect to the child;

(ii) someone illegally taking the child from the home in which the child is placed;

(iii) behavior that poses a threat to the caregiver with whom the child is placed; or

(iv) someone committing an act of violence against the child or the child's caregiver; and

(3) is not otherwise authorized to apply for a protective order for the child's protection under Chapter 82.

History of Fam. Code §261.501: Enacted by H.B. 7, §14, 85th Leg., eff. Sept. 1, 2017.

FAM §261.502. Certification of Findings

(a) In making the application under this subchapter, the department must certify that:

(1) the department has diligently searched for and:

(A) was unable to locate the child's parent, legal guardian, or custodian, other than the respondent to the application; or

(B) located and provided notice of the proposed application to the child's parent, legal guardian, or custodian, other than the respondent to the application; and

(2) if applicable, the relative or caregiver who is jointly filing the petition, or with whom the child would reside following an entry of the protective order, has not abused or neglected the child and does not have a history of abuse or neglect.

(b) An application for a temporary ex parte order under Section 261.503 may be filed without making the findings required by Subsection (a) if the department certifies that the department believes there is an immediate danger of abuse or neglect to the child.

History of Fam. Code §261.502: Enacted by H.B. 7, §14, 85th Leg., eff. Sept. 1, 2017.

FAM §261.503. Temporary Ex Parte Order

If the court finds from the information contained in an application for a protective order that there is an immediate danger of abuse or neglect to the child, the court, without further notice to the respondent and without a hearing, may enter a temporary ex parte order for the protection of the child.

History of Fam. Code §261.503: Enacted by H.B. 7, §14, 85th Leg., eff. Sept. 1, 2017.

FAM §261.504. Required Findings; Issuance of Protective Order

(a) At the close of a hearing on an application for a protective order under this subchapter, the court shall find whether there are reasonable grounds to believe that:

(1) the child:

(A) is a victim of abuse or neglect; or

(B) has a history of being abused or neglected; and

(2) there is a threat of:

(A) immediate or continued abuse or neglect to the child;

(B) someone illegally taking the child from the home in which the child is placed;

(C) behavior that poses a threat to the caregiver with whom the child is placed; or

(D) someone committing an act of violence against the child or the child's caregiver.

(b) If the court makes an affirmative finding under Subsection (a), the court shall issue a protective order that includes a statement of that finding.

History of Fam. Code §261.504: Enacted by H.B. 7, §14, 85th Leg., eff. Sept. 1, 2017.

FAM §261.505. Application of Other Law

To the extent applicable, except as otherwise provided by this subchapter, Title 4 applies to a protective order issued under this subchapter.

History of Fam. Code §261.505: Enacted by H.B. 7, §14, 85th Leg., eff. Sept. 1, 2017.

CHAPTER 262. PROCEDURES IN SUIT BY GOVERNMENTAL ENTITY TO PROTECT HEALTH & SAFETY OF CHILD

SUBCHAPTER A. GENERAL PROVISIONS

FAM §262.001. AUTHORIZED ACTIONS BY GOVERNMENTAL ENTITY

(a) A governmental entity with an interest in the child may file a suit affecting the parent-child relationship requesting an order or take possession of a child without a court order as provided by this chapter.

(b) In determining the reasonable efforts that are required to be made with respect to preventing or eliminating the need to remove a child from the child's home or to make it possible to return a child to the child's home, the child's health and safety is the paramount concern.

History of Fam. Code §262.001: Acts 1995, 74th Leg., ch. 20, §1, eff. Apr. 20, 1995. Amended by Acts 1999, 76th Leg., ch. 1150, §10 (eff. Sept. 1, 1999), ch. 1390, §29 (eff. Sept. 1, 1999). Source: Former Fam. Code §17.01.

FAM §262.002. JURISDICTION

A suit brought by a governmental entity requesting an order under this chapter may be filed in a court with jurisdiction to hear the suit in the county in which the child is found.

History of Fam. Code §262.002: Acts 1995, 74th Leg., ch. 20, §1, eff. Apr. 20, 1995. Amended by Acts 1999, 76th Leg., ch. 1150, §11 (eff. Sept. 1, 1999), ch. 1390, §30 (eff. Sept. 1, 1999). Source: Former Fam. Code §17.05(a).

E FAM §262.0022. REVIEW OF PLACEMENT; FINDINGS

At each hearing under this chapter, the court shall review the placement of each child in the temporary or permanent managing conservatorship of the Department of Family and Protective Services who is not placed with a relative caregiver or designated caregiver as defined by Section 264.751. The court shall include in its findings a statement on whether the department has the option of placing the child with a relative or other designated caregiver.

History of Fam. Code §262.0022: Enacted by H.B. 7, §15, 85th Leg., eff. Sept. 1, 2017.

FAM §262.003. CIVIL LIABILITY

A person who takes possession of a child without a court order is immune from civil liability if, at the time possession is taken, there is reasonable cause to believe there is an immediate danger to the physical health or safety of the child.

History of Fam. Code §262.003: Acts 1995, 74th Leg., ch. 20, §1, eff. Apr. 20, 1995. Source: Former Fam. Code §17.08.

FAM §262.004. ACCEPTING VOLUNTARY DELIVERY OF POSSESSION OF CHILD

A law enforcement officer or a juvenile probation officer may take possession of a child without a court order on the voluntary delivery of the child by the parent, managing conservator, possessory conservator, guardian, caretaker, or custodian who is presently entitled to possession of the child.

History of Fam. Code §262.004: Acts 1995, 74th Leg., ch. 20, §1, eff. Apr. 20, 1995. Amended by Acts 1995, 74th Leg., ch. 751, §101, eff. Sept. 1, 1995. Source: Former Fam. Code §17.03(a)(2).

FAM §262.005. FILING PETITION AFTER ACCEPTING VOLUNTARY DELIVERY OF POSSESSION OF CHILD

When possession of the child has been acquired through voluntary delivery of the child to a law enforcement officer or juvenile probation officer, the law enforcement officer or juvenile probation officer taking the child into possession shall cause a suit to be filed not later than the 60th day after the date the child is taken into possession.

History of Fam. Code §262.005: Acts 1995, 74th Leg., ch. 20, §1, eff. Apr. 20, 1995. Amended by Acts 1995, 74th Leg., ch. 751, §102, eff. Sept. 1, 1995. Source: Former Fam. Code §17.03(g).

FAM §262.006. LIVING CHILD AFTER ABORTION

(a) An authorized representative of the Department of Family and Protective Services may assume the care, control, and custody of a child born alive as the result of an abortion as defined by Chapter 161.

(b) The department shall file a suit and request an emergency order under this chapter.

(c) A child for whom possession is assumed under this section need not be delivered to the court except on the order of the court.

History of Fam. Code §262.006: Acts 1995, 74th Leg., ch. 20, §1, eff. Apr. 20, 1995. Amended by Acts 2015, 84th Leg., ch. 1, §1.151, eff. Apr. 2, 2015. Source: Former Fam. Code §17.011.

FAM §262.007. POSSESSION & DELIVERY OF MISSING CHILD

(a) A law enforcement officer who, during a criminal investigation relating to a child's custody, discovers that a child is a missing child and believes that a person may flee with or conceal the child shall take possession of the child and provide for the delivery of the child as provided by Subsection (b).

(b) An officer who takes possession of a child under Subsection (a) shall deliver or arrange for the delivery of the child to a person entitled to possession of the child.

(c) If a person entitled to possession of the child is not immediately available to take possession of the child, the law enforcement officer shall deliver the child to the Department of Family and Protective Services. Until a person entitled to possession of the child takes possession of the child, the department may, without a court order, retain possession of the child not longer than five days after the date the child is delivered to the department. While the department retains possession of a child under this subsection, the department may place the child in foster care. If a parent or other person entitled to possession of the child does not take possession of the child before the sixth day after the date the child is delivered to the department, the department shall proceed under this chapter as if the law enforcement officer took possession of the child under Section 262.104.

History of Fam. Code §262.007: Acts 1995, 74th Leg., ch. 776, §1, eff. Sept. 1, 1995. Amended by Acts 1999, 76th Leg., ch. 685, §6 (eff. Sept. 1, 1999), ch. 1150, §12 (eff. Sept. 1, 1999), ch. 1390, §31 (eff. Sept. 1, 1999); Acts 2015, 84th Leg., ch. 1, §1.152, eff. Apr. 2, 2015.

FAM §262.008. ABANDONED CHILDREN

(a) An authorized representative of the Department of Family and Protective Services may assume the care, control, and custody of a child:

(1) who is abandoned without identification or a means for identifying the child; and

(2) whose identity cannot be ascertained by the exercise of reasonable diligence.

(b) The department shall immediately file a suit to terminate the parent-child relationship of a child under Subsection (a).

(c) Repealed by Acts 2015, 84th Leg., ch. 1, §1.203(5), eff. Apr. 2, 2015.

History of Fam. Code §262.008: Acts 1997, 75th Leg., ch. 600, §4, eff. Jan. 1, 1998. Amended by Acts 2015, 84th Leg., ch. 1, §§1.153, 1.203(5), eff. Apr. 2, 2015.

FAM §262.009. TEMPORARY CARE OF CHILD TAKEN INTO POSSESSION

An employee of or volunteer with a law enforcement agency who successfully completes a background and criminal history check approved by the law enforcement agency may assist a law enforcement officer or juvenile probation officer with the temporary care of a child who is taken into possession by a governmental entity without a court order under this chapter until further arrangements regarding the custody of the child can be made.

History of Fam. Code §262.009: Acts 2003, 78th Leg., ch. 970, §1, eff. June 20, 2003.

FAM §262.010. CHILD WITH SEXUALLY TRANSMITTED DISEASE

(a) If during an investigation by the Department of Family and Protective Services the department discovers that a child younger than 11 years of age has a sexually transmitted disease, the department shall:

(1) appoint a special investigator to assist in the investigation of the case; and

(2) file an original suit requesting an emergency order under this chapter for possession of the child unless the department determines, after taking the following actions, that emergency removal is not necessary for the protection of the child:

(A) reviewing the medical evidence to determine whether the medical evidence supports a finding that abuse likely occurred;

(B) interviewing the child and other persons residing in the child's home;

(C) conferring with law enforcement;

(D) determining whether any other child in the home has a sexually transmitted disease and, if so, referring the child for a sexual abuse examination;

(E) if the department determines a forensic interview is appropriate based on the child's age and development, ensuring that each child alleged to have been abused undergoes a forensic interview by a children's advocacy center established under Section 264.402 or another professional with specialized training in conducting forensic interviews if a children's advocacy center is not available in the county in which the child resides;

(F) consulting with a department staff nurse or other medical expert to obtain additional information regarding the nature of the sexually transmitted disease and the ways the disease is transmitted and an opinion as to whether abuse occurred based on the facts of the case;

(G) contacting any additional witness who may have information relevant to the investigation, including other individuals who had access to the child; and

(H) if the department determines after taking the actions described by Paragraphs (A)-(G) that a finding of sexual abuse is not supported, obtaining an opinion from the Forensic Assessment Center Network as to whether the evidence in the case supports a finding that abuse likely occurred.

(b) If the department determines that abuse likely occurred, the department shall work with law enforcement to obtain a search warrant to require an individual the department reasonably believes may have sexually abused the child to undergo medically appropriate diagnostic testing for sexually transmitted diseases.

History of Fam. Code §262.010: Acts 2011, 82nd Leg., ch. 598, §2, eff. Sept. 1, 2011.

Ⓐ FAM §262.011. PLACEMENT IN SECURE AGENCY FOSTER HOME ~~[OR SECURE AGENCY FOSTER GROUP HOME]~~

The amended text in §262.011 is effective for service plans filed for a full adversary hearing held under Fam. Code §262.201 or a status hearing held under Fam. Code ch. 263 on or after Jan. 1, 2018. A hearing held before Jan. 1, 2018, is governed by the former law in effect at that time. Except as provided above, the amended text in §262.011 is effective for SAPCRs filed on or after Sept. 1,

2017. SAPCRs filed before Sept. 1, 2017, are governed by the former law in effect at that time.

Foster homes or foster group homes licensed by TDFPS and agency foster group homes verified by a child-placing agency before Sept. 1, 2017, may continue to operate under the former law in effect at that time, until the foster home or foster group home converts to another residential child-care license or the license is relinquished, or the agency foster group home has been converted to a verified foster home or closed.

A court in an emergency, initial, or full adversary hearing conducted under this chapter may order that the child who is the subject of the hearing be placed in a secure agency foster home [~~or secure agency foster group home~~] verified in accordance with Section 42.0531, Human Resources Code, if the court finds that:

(1) the placement is in the best interest of the child; and

(2) the child's physical health or safety is in danger because the child has been recruited, harbored, transported, provided, or obtained for forced labor or commercial sexual activity, including any child subjected to an act specified in Section 20A.02 or 20A.03, Penal Code.

History of Fam. Code §262.011: Acts 2015, 84th Leg., ch. 338, §1, eff. Sept. 1, 2015. Amended by H.B. 7, §16, 85th Leg., eff. Sept. 1, 2017.

A FAM §262.012. SEALING OF COURT RECORDS FILED ELECTRONICALLY

Section 262.012 was renumbered from §262.011 by S.B. 1488, §24.001(8), 85th Leg., eff. Sept. 1, 2017.

For purposes of determining whether to seal documents in accordance with Rule 76a, Texas Rules of Civil Procedure, in a suit under this subtitle, the court shall consider documents filed through an electronic filing system in the same manner as any other document filed with the court.

History of Fam. Code §262.012: Acts 2015, 84th Leg., ch. 455, §1, eff. June 15, 2015. Renumbered from §262.011 by S.B. 1488, §24.001(8), 85th Leg., eff. Sept. 1, 2017.

E FAM §262.013[A*]. FILING REQUIREMENT FOR PETITION REGARDING MORE THAN ONE CHILD

☠ *In 2017, the Legislature enacted two sections 262.013. This §262.013 was enacted by S.B. 999, §3, 85th Leg., effective Sept. 1, 2017. The [A*] has been added by the editor to distinguish this §262.013 from the other, which is marked with [B*]. In 2019, the Legislature is expected to correct the duplicate numbering.*

Each suit under this chapter based on allegations of abuse or neglect arising from the same incident or occurrence and involving children that live in the same home must be filed in the same court.

History of Fam. Code §262.013[A*]: Enacted by S.B. 999, §3, 85th Leg., eff. Sept. 1, 2017.

E FAM §262.013[B*]. VOLUNTARY TEMPORARY MANAGING CONSERVATORSHIP

☠ *In 2017, the Legislature enacted two sections 262.013. This §262.013 was enacted by H.B. 7, §17, 85th Leg., effective Sept. 1, 2017. The [B*] has been added by the editor to distinguish this §262.013 from the other, which is marked with [A*]. In 2019, the Legislature is expected to correct the duplicate numbering.*

In a suit affecting the parent-child relationship filed by the Department of Family and Protective Services, the existence of a parent's voluntary agreement to temporarily place the parent's child in the managing conservatorship of the department is not an admission by the parent that the parent engaged in conduct that endangered the child.

History of Fam. Code §262.013[B*]: Enacted by H.B. 7, §17, 85th Leg., eff. Sept. 1, 2017.

E FAM §262.014. DISCLOSURE OF CERTAIN EVIDENCE

On the request of the attorney for a parent who is a party in a suit affecting the parent-child relationship filed under this chapter, or the attorney ad litem for the parent's child, the Department of Family and Protective Services shall, before the full adversary hearing, provide:

(1) the name of any person, excluding a department employee, whom the department will call as a witness to any of the allegations contained in the petition filed by the department;

(2) a copy of any offense report relating to the allegations contained in the petition filed by the department that will be used in court to refresh a witness's memory; and

(3) a copy of any photograph, video, or recording that will be presented as evidence.

History of Fam. Code §262.014: Enacted by H.B. 7, §17, 85th Leg., eff. Sept. 1, 2017.

Sections 262.015-262.100 reserved for expansion

SUBCHAPTER B. TAKING POSSESSION OF CHILD

FAM §262.101. FILING PETITION BEFORE TAKING POSSESSION OF CHILD

The amended text in §262.101 is effective for SAPCRs filed on or after Sept. 1, 2017. SAPCRs filed before Sept. 1, 2017, are governed by the former law in effect at that time.

An original suit filed by a governmental entity that requests permission to take possession of a child without prior notice and a hearing must be supported by an affidavit sworn to by a person with personal knowledge and stating facts sufficient to satisfy a person of ordinary prudence and caution that:

(1) there is an immediate danger to the physical health or safety of the child or the child has been a victim of neglect or sexual abuse;

(2) [~~and that~~] continuation in the home would be contrary to the child's welfare;

(3) [~~(2)~~] there is no time, consistent with the physical health or safety of the child, for a full adversary hearing under Subchapter C; and

(4) [~~(3)~~] reasonable efforts, consistent with the circumstances and providing for the safety of the child, were made to prevent or eliminate the need for the removal of the child.

History of Fam. Code §262.101: Acts 1995, 74th Leg., ch. 20, §1, eff. Apr. 20, 1995. Amended by Acts 1995, 74th Leg., ch. 751, §103, eff. Sept. 1, 1995; Acts 1997, 75th Leg., ch. 752, §1, eff. June 17, 1997; Acts 1999, 76th Leg., ch. 1150, §§13, 14 (eff. Sept. 1, 1999), ch. 1390, §32 (eff. Sept. 1, 1999); Acts 2001, 77th Leg., ch. 849, §1, eff. Sept. 1, 2001; S.B. 999, §4, 85th Leg., eff. Sept. 1, 2017. Source: Former Fam. Code §17.02(b).

FAM §262.1015. REMOVAL OF ALLEGED PERPETRATOR; OFFENSE

The amended text in §262.1015 is effective for SAPCRs filed on or after Sept. 1, 2017. SAPCRs filed before Sept. 1, 2017, are governed by the former law in effect at that time.

(a) If the Department of Family and Protective Services determines after an investigation that child abuse has occurred and that the child would be protected in the child's home by the removal of the alleged perpetrator of the abuse, the department shall file a petition for the removal of the alleged perpetrator from the residence of the child rather than attempt to remove the child from the residence.

(a-1) Notwithstanding Subsection (a), if the Department of Family and Protective Services determines that a protective order issued under Title 4 provides a reasonable alternative to obtaining an order under that subsection, the department may:

(1) file an application for a protective order on behalf of the child instead of or in addition to obtaining a temporary restraining order under this section; or

(2) assist a parent or other adult with whom a child resides in obtaining a protective order.

(b) A court may issue a temporary restraining order in a suit by the department for the removal of an alleged perpetrator under Subsection (a) if the department's petition states facts sufficient to satisfy the court that:

(1) there is an immediate danger to the physical health or safety of the child or the child has been a victim of sexual abuse;

(2) there is no time, consistent with the physical health or safety of the child, for an adversary hearing;

(3) the child is not in danger of abuse from a parent or other adult with whom the child will continue to reside in the residence of the child;

(4) the parent or other adult with whom the child will continue to reside in the child's home is likely to:

(A) make a reasonable effort to monitor the residence; and

(B) report to the department and the appropriate law enforcement agency any attempt by the alleged perpetrator to return to the residence; and

(5) the issuance of the order is in the best interest of the child.

(c) The order shall be served on the alleged perpetrator and on the parent or other adult with whom the child will continue to reside.

(d) A temporary restraining order under this section expires not later than the 14th day after the date the order was rendered, unless the court grants an extension under Section 262.201(e) [~~262.201(a-3)~~].

(e) A temporary restraining order under this section and any other order requiring the removal of an alleged perpetrator from the residence of a child shall require that the parent or other adult with whom the child will continue to reside in the child's home make a reasonable effort to monitor the residence and report to the department and the appropriate law enforcement agency any attempt by the alleged perpetrator to return to the residence.

(f) The court shall order the removal of an alleged perpetrator if the court finds that the child is not in danger of abuse from a parent or other adult with whom the child will continue to reside in the child's residence and that:

(1) the presence of the alleged perpetrator in the child's residence constitutes a continuing danger to the physical health or safety of the child; or

(2) the child has been the victim of sexual abuse and there is a substantial risk that the child will be the victim of sexual abuse in the future if the alleged perpetrator remains in the residence.

(g) A person commits an offense if the person is a parent or other person with whom a child resides, the person is served with an order containing the requirement specified by Subsection (e), and the person fails to make a reasonable effort to monitor the residence of the child or to report to the department and the appropriate law enforcement agency an attempt by the alleged perpetrator to return to the residence. An offense under this section is a Class A misdemeanor.

(h) A person commits an offense if, in violation of a court order under this section, the person returns to the residence of the child the person is alleged to have abused. An offense under this subsection is a Class A misdemeanor, except that the offense is a felony of the third degree if the person has previously been convicted under this subsection.

History of Fam. Code §262.1015: Acts 1995, 74th Leg., ch. 943, §4, eff. Sept. 1, 1995. Amended by Acts 1997, 75th Leg., ch. 575, §19, eff. Sept. 1, 1997; Acts 2011, 82nd Leg., ch. 222, §2 (eff. Sept. 1, 2011), ch. 598, §3 (eff. Sept. 1, 2011); Acts 2013, 83rd Leg., ch. 810, §6, eff. Sept. 1, 2013; Acts 2015, 84th Leg., ch. 1, §1.154, eff. Apr. 2, 2015; S.B. 999, §5, 85th Leg., eff. Sept. 1, 2017.

A FAM §262.102. EMERGENCY ORDER AUTHORIZING POSSESSION OF CHILD

The amended text in §262.102 is effective for SAPCRs filed on or after Sept. 1, 2017. SAPCRs filed before Sept. 1, 2017, are governed by the former law in effect at that time.

(a) Before a court may, without prior notice and a hearing, issue a temporary order for the conservatorship of a child under Section 105.001(a)(1) or a temporary restraining order or attachment of a child authorizing a governmental entity to take possession of a child in a suit brought by a governmental entity, the court must find that:

(1) there is an immediate danger to the physical health or safety of the child or the child has been a victim of neglect or sexual abuse;

(2) [~~and that~~] continuation in the home would be contrary to the child's welfare;

(3) [~~(2)~~] there is no time, consistent with the physical health or safety of the child and the nature of the emergency, for a full adversary hearing under Subchapter C; and

(4) [~~(3)~~] reasonable efforts, consistent with the circumstances and providing for the safety of the child, were made to prevent or eliminate the need for removal of the child.

(b) In determining whether there is an immediate danger to the physical health or safety of a child, the court may consider whether the child's household includes a person who has:

(1) abused or neglected another child in a manner that caused serious injury to or the death of the other child; or

(2) sexually abused another child.

(c) If, based on the recommendation of or a request by the Department of Family and Protective Services, the court finds that child abuse or neglect has occurred and that the child requires protection from family violence by a member of the child's family or household, the court shall render a temporary order under Title 4 for the protection of the child. In this subsection, "family violence" has the meaning assigned by Section 71.004.

(d) The temporary order, temporary restraining order, or attachment of a child rendered by the court under Subsection (a) must contain the following statement prominently displayed in boldface type, capital letters, or underlined:

"YOU HAVE THE RIGHT TO BE REPRESENTED BY AN ATTORNEY. IF YOU ARE INDIGENT AND UNABLE TO AFFORD AN ATTORNEY, YOU HAVE THE RIGHT TO REQUEST THE APPOINTMENT OF AN ATTORNEY BY CONTACTING THE COURT AT [ADDRESS], [TELEPHONE NUMBER]. IF YOU APPEAR IN OPPOSITION TO THE SUIT, CLAIM INDIGENCE, AND REQUEST THE APPOINTMENT OF AN ATTORNEY, THE COURT WILL REQUIRE YOU TO SIGN AN AFFIDAVIT OF INDIGENCE AND THE COURT MAY HEAR EVIDENCE TO DETERMINE IF YOU ARE INDIGENT. IF THE COURT DETERMINES YOU ARE INDIGENT AND ELIGIBLE FOR APPOINTMENT OF AN ATTORNEY, THE COURT WILL APPOINT AN ATTORNEY TO REPRESENT YOU."

History of Fam. Code §262.102: Acts 1995, 74th Leg., ch. 20, §1, eff. Apr. 20, 1995. Amended by Acts 1995, 74th Leg., ch. 751, §104, eff. Sept. 1, 1995; Acts 1997, 75th Leg., ch. 752, §2, eff. June 17, 1997; Acts 1999, 76th Leg., ch. 1150, §15

(eff. Sept. 1, 1999), ch. 1390, §34 (eff. Sept. 1, 1999); Acts 2001, 77th Leg., ch. 849, §2, eff. Sept. 1, 2001; Acts 2003, 78th Leg., ch. 1276, §7.002(m), eff. Sept. 1, 2003; Acts 2013, 83rd Leg., ch. 810, §7, eff. Sept. 1, 2013; Acts 2015, 84th Leg., ch. 1, §1.155, eff. Apr. 2, 2015; S.B. 999, §6, 85th Leg., eff. Sept. 1, 2017. Source: Former Fam. Code §17.02(a), (d).

A FAM §262.103. DURATION OF TEMPORARY ORDER, TEMPORARY RESTRAINING ORDER, & ATTACHMENT

The amended text in §262.103 is effective for SAPCRs filed on or after Sept. 1, 2017. SAPCRs filed before Sept. 1, 2017, are governed by the former law in effect at that time.

A temporary order, temporary restraining order, or attachment of the child issued under Section 262.102(a) expires not later than 14 days after the date it is issued unless it is extended as provided by the Texas Rules of Civil Procedure or Section 262.201(e) [~~262.201(a-3)~~].

History of Fam. Code §262.103: Acts 1995, 74th Leg., ch. 20, §1, eff. Apr. 20, 1995. Amended by Acts 2013, 83rd Leg., ch. 810, §8, eff. Sept. 1, 2013; Acts 2015, 84th Leg., ch. 1, §1.156, eff. Apr. 2, 2015; S.B. 999, §7, 85th Leg., eff. Sept. 1, 2017. Source: Former Fam. Code §17.02(c).

FAM §262.104. TAKING POSSESSION OF A CHILD IN EMERGENCY WITHOUT A COURT ORDER

(a) If there is no time to obtain a temporary order, temporary restraining order, or attachment under Section 262.102(a) before taking possession of a child consistent with the health and safety of that child, an authorized representative of the Department of Family and Protective Services, a law enforcement officer, or a juvenile probation officer may take possession of a child without a court order under the following conditions, only:

(1) on personal knowledge of facts that would lead a person of ordinary prudence and caution to believe that there is an immediate danger to the physical health or safety of the child;

(2) on information furnished by another that has been corroborated by personal knowledge of facts and all of which taken together would lead a person of ordinary prudence and caution to believe that there is an immediate danger to the physical health or safety of the child;

(3) on personal knowledge of facts that would lead a person of ordinary prudence and caution to believe that the child has been the victim of sexual abuse or of trafficking under Section 20A.02 or 20A.03, Penal Code;

(4) on information furnished by another that has been corroborated by personal knowledge of facts and all of which taken together would lead a person of ordinary prudence and caution to believe that the child has been the victim of sexual abuse or of trafficking under Section 20A.02 or 20A.03, Penal Code; or

(5) on information furnished by another that has been corroborated by personal knowledge of facts and all of which taken together would lead a person of ordinary prudence and caution to believe that the parent or person who has possession of the child is currently using a controlled substance as defined by Chapter 481, Health and Safety Code, and the use constitutes an immediate danger to the physical health or safety of the child.

(b) An authorized representative of the Department of Family and Protective Services, a law enforcement officer, or a juvenile probation officer may take possession of a child under Subsection (a) on personal knowledge or information furnished by another, that has been corroborated by personal knowledge, that would lead a person of ordinary prudence and caution to believe that the parent or person who has possession of the child has permitted the child to remain on premises used for the manufacture of methamphetamine.

History of Fam. Code §262.104: Acts 1995, 74th Leg., ch. 20, §1, eff. Apr. 20, 1995. Amended by Acts 1997, 75th Leg., ch. 575, §20, eff. Sept. 1, 1997; Acts 2005, 79th Leg., ch. 282, §2, eff. Aug. 1, 2005; Acts 2015, 84th Leg., ch. 338, §2 (eff. Sept. 1, 2015), ch. 1, §1.157 (eff. Apr. 2, 2015). Source: Former Fam. Code §17.03(a)(3)-(6).

FAM §262.1041. REPEALED

Repealed by Acts 2015, 84th Leg., ch. 944, §86(12), eff. Sept. 1, 2015.

A FAM §262.105. FILING PETITION AFTER TAKING POSSESSION OF CHILD IN EMERGENCY

The amended text in §262.105 is effective for SAPCRs filed on or after Sept. 1, 2017. SAPCRs filed before Sept. 1, 2017, are governed by the former law in effect at that time.

(a) When a child is taken into possession without a court order, the person taking the child into possession, without unnecessary delay, shall:

(1) file a suit affecting the parent-child relationship;

(2) request the court to appoint an attorney ad litem for the child; and

(3) request an initial hearing to be held by no later than the first business [~~working~~] day after the date the child is taken into possession.

(b) An original suit filed by a governmental entity after taking possession of a child under Section 262.104

must be supported by an affidavit stating facts sufficient to satisfy a person of ordinary prudence and caution that:

(1) based on the affiant's personal knowledge or on information furnished by another person corroborated by the affiant's personal knowledge, one of the following circumstances existed at the time the child was taken into possession:

(A) there was an immediate danger to the physical health or safety of the child;

(B) the child was the victim of sexual abuse or of trafficking under Section 20A.02 or 20A.03, Penal Code;

(C) the parent or person who had possession of the child was using a controlled substance as defined by Chapter 481, Health and Safety Code, and the use constituted an immediate danger to the physical health or safety of the child; or

(D) the parent or person who had possession of the child permitted the child to remain on premises used for the manufacture of methamphetamine; and

(2) based on the affiant's personal knowledge:

(A) continuation of the child in the home would have been contrary to the child's welfare;

(B) there was no time, consistent with the physical health or safety of the child, for a full adversary hearing under Subchapter C; and

(C) reasonable efforts, consistent with the circumstances and providing for the safety of the child, were made to prevent or eliminate the need for the removal of the child.

History of Fam. Code §262.105: Acts 1995, 74th Leg., ch. 20, §1, eff. Apr. 20, 1995. Amended by Acts 2001, 77th Leg., ch. 809, §2, eff. Sept. 1, 2001; Acts 2015, 84th Leg., ch. 1, §1.158 (eff. Apr. 2, 2015), ch. 944, §86(13) (eff. Sept. 1, 2015); S.B. 999, §8, 85th Leg., eff. Sept. 1, 2017. Source: Former Fam. Code §17.03(b).

Ⓐ FAM §262.106. INITIAL HEARING AFTER TAKING POSSESSION OF CHILD IN EMERGENCY WITHOUT COURT ORDER

The amended text in §262.106 is effective for SAPCRs filed on or after Sept. 1, 2017. SAPCRs filed before Sept. 1, 2017, are governed by the former law in effect at that time.

(a) The court in which a suit has been filed after a child has been taken into possession without a court order by a governmental entity shall hold an initial hearing on or before the first business [~~working~~] day after the date the child is taken into possession. The court shall render orders that are necessary to protect the physical health and safety of the child. If the court is unavailable for a hearing on the first business [~~working~~] day, then, and only in that event, the hearing shall be held no later than the first business [~~working~~] day after the court becomes available, provided that the hearing is held no later than the third business [~~working~~] day after the child is taken into possession.

(b) The initial hearing may be ex parte and proof may be by sworn petition or affidavit if a full adversary hearing is not practicable.

(c) If the initial hearing is not held within the time required, the child shall be returned to the parent, managing conservator, possessory conservator, guardian, caretaker, or custodian who is presently entitled to possession of the child.

(d) For the purpose of determining under Subsection (a) the first business [~~working~~] day after the date the child is taken into possession, the child is considered to have been taken into possession by the Department of Family and Protective Services on the expiration of the five-day period permitted under Section 262.007(c) or 262.110(b), as appropriate.

History of Fam. Code §262.106: Acts 1995, 74th Leg., ch. 20, §1, eff. Apr. 20, 1995. Amended by Acts 1999, 76th Leg., ch. 1150, §16 (eff. Sept. 1, 1999), ch. 1390, §35 (eff. Sept. 1, 1999); Acts 2015, 84th Leg., ch. 1, §1.159, eff. Apr. 2, 2015; S.B. 999, §9, 85th Leg., eff. Sept. 1, 2017. Source: Former Fam. Code §17.03(c).

Ⓐ FAM §262.107. STANDARD FOR DECISION AT INITIAL HEARING AFTER TAKING POSSESSION OF CHILD WITHOUT A COURT ORDER IN EMERGENCY

The amended text in §262.107 is effective for SAPCRs filed on or after Sept. 1, 2017. SAPCRs filed before Sept. 1, 2017, are governed by the former law in effect at that time.

(a) The court shall order the return of the child at the initial hearing regarding a child taken in possession without a court order by a governmental entity unless the court is satisfied that:

(1) the evidence shows that one of the following circumstances exists:

(A) there is a continuing danger to the physical health or safety of the child if the child is returned to the parent, managing conservator, possessory conservator, guardian, caretaker, or custodian who is presently entitled to possession of the child;

(B) [~~or the evidence shows that~~] the child has been the victim of sexual abuse or of trafficking under

Section 20A.02 or 20A.03, Penal Code, on one or more occasions and that there is a substantial risk that the child will be the victim of sexual abuse or of trafficking in the future;

(C) the parent or person who has possession of the child is currently using a controlled substance as defined by Chapter 481, Health and Safety Code, and the use constitutes an immediate danger to the physical health or safety of the child; or

(D) the parent or person who has possession of the child has permitted the child to remain on premises used for the manufacture of methamphetamine;

(2) continuation of the child in the home would be contrary to the child's welfare; and

(3) reasonable efforts, consistent with the circumstances and providing for the safety of the child, were made to prevent or eliminate the need for removal of the child.

(b) In determining whether there is a continuing danger to the physical health or safety of a child, the court may consider whether the household to which the child would be returned includes a person who has:

(1) abused or neglected another child in a manner that caused serious injury to or the death of the other child; or

(2) sexually abused another child.

History of Fam. Code §262.107: Acts 1995, 74th Leg., ch. 20, §1, eff. Apr. 20, 1995. Amended by Acts 1995, 74th Leg., ch. 751, §105, eff. Sept. 1, 1995; Acts 2001, 77th Leg., ch. 849, §3, eff. Sept. 1, 2001; Acts 2015, 84th Leg., ch. 338, §3, eff. Sept. 1, 2015; S.B. 999, §10, 85th Leg., eff. Sept. 1, 2017. Source: Former Fam. Code §17.03(d), (e), (i).

FAM §262.108. UNACCEPTABLE FACILITIES FOR HOUSING CHILD

When a child is taken into possession under this chapter, that child may not be held in isolation or in a jail, juvenile detention facility, or other secure detention facility.

History of Fam. Code §262.108: Acts 1995, 74th Leg., ch. 20, §1, eff. Apr. 20, 1995. Amended by Acts 1997, 75th Leg., ch. 1374, §9, eff. Sept. 1, 1997. Source: Former Fam. Code §17.03(h).

FAM §262.109. NOTICE TO PARENT, CONSERVATOR, OR GUARDIAN

The amended text in §262.109 is effective for SAPCRs filed on or after Sept. 1, 2017. SAPCRs filed before Sept. 1, 2017, are governed by the former law in effect at that time.

(a) The Department of Family and Protective Services or other agency must give written notice as prescribed by this section to each parent of the child or to the child's conservator or legal guardian when a representative of the department or other agency takes possession of a child under this chapter.

(b) The written notice must be given as soon as practicable, but in any event not later than the first business [~~working~~] day after the date the child is taken into possession.

(c) The written notice must include:

(1) the reasons why the department or agency is taking possession of the child and the facts that led the department to believe that the child should be taken into custody;

(2) the name of the person at the department or agency that the parent, conservator, or other custodian may contact for information relating to the child or a legal proceeding relating to the child;

(3) a summary of legal rights of a parent, conservator, guardian, or other custodian under this chapter and an explanation of the probable legal procedures relating to the child; and

(4) a statement that the parent, conservator, or other custodian has the right to hire an attorney.

(d) The written notice may be waived by the court at the initial hearing:

(1) on a showing that:

(A) the parents, conservators, or other custodians of the child could not be located; or

(B) the department took possession of the child under Subchapter D; or

(2) for other good cause.

History of Fam. Code §262.109: Acts 1995, 74th Leg., ch. 20, §1, eff. Apr. 20, 1995. Amended by Acts 1997, 75th Leg., ch. 1022, §76, eff. Jan. 1, 1998; Acts 1999, 76th Leg., ch. 1150, §17 (eff. Sept. 1, 1999), ch. 1390, §36 (eff. Sept. 1, 1999); Acts 2001, 77th Leg., ch. 809, §3, eff. Sept. 1, 2001; Acts 2015, 84th Leg., ch. 1, §1.160, eff. Apr. 2, 2015; S.B. 999, §11, 85th Leg., eff. Sept. 1, 2017. Source: Former Fam. Code §17.031(b).

FAM §262.1095. INFORMATION PROVIDED TO RELATIVES & CERTAIN INDIVIDUALS; INVESTIGATION

(a) When the Department of Family and Protective Services or another agency takes possession of a child under this chapter, the department:

(1) shall provide information as prescribed by this section to each adult the department is able to identify and locate who is:

(A) related to the child within the third degree by consanguinity as determined under Chapter 573, Government Code;

(B) an adult relative of the alleged father of the child if the department has a reasonable basis to believe the alleged father is the child's biological father; or

(C) identified as a potential relative or designated caregiver, as defined by Section 264.751, on the proposed child placement resources form provided under Section 261.307; and

(2) may provide information as prescribed by this section to each adult the department is able to identify and locate who has a long-standing and significant relationship with the child.

(b) The information provided under Subsection (a) must:

(1) state that the child has been removed from the child's home and is in the temporary managing conservatorship of the department;

(2) explain the options available to the individual to participate in the care and placement of the child and the support of the child's family;

(3) state that some options available to the individual may be lost if the individual fails to respond in a timely manner; and

(4) include, if applicable, the date, time, and location of the hearing under Subchapter C, Chapter 263.

(c) The department is not required to provide information to an individual if the individual has received service of citation under Section 102.009 or if the department determines providing information is inappropriate because the individual has a criminal history or a history of family violence.

(d) The department shall use due diligence to identify and locate all individuals described by Subsection (a) not later than the 30th day after the date the department files a suit affecting the parent-child relationship. In order to identify and locate the individuals described by Subsection (a), the department shall seek information from:

(1) each parent, relative, and alleged father of the child; and

(2) the child in an age-appropriate manner.

(e) The failure of a parent or alleged father of the child to complete the proposed child placement resources form does not relieve the department of its duty to seek information about the person under Subsection (d).

History of Fam. Code §262.1095: Acts 2011, 82nd Leg., ch. 1071, §2, eff. Sept. 1, 2011. Amended by Acts 2015, 84th Leg., ch. 944, §23, eff. Sept. 1, 2015.

FAM §262.110. TAKING POSSESSION OF CHILD IN EMERGENCY WITH INTENT TO RETURN HOME

(a) An authorized representative of the Department of Family and Protective Services, a law enforcement officer, or a juvenile probation officer may take temporary possession of a child without a court order on discovery of a child in a situation of danger to the child's physical health or safety when the sole purpose is to deliver the child without unnecessary delay to the parent, managing conservator, possessory conservator, guardian, caretaker, or custodian who is presently entitled to possession of the child.

(b) Until a parent or other person entitled to possession of the child takes possession of the child, the department may retain possession of the child without a court order for not more than five days. On the expiration of the fifth day, if a parent or other person entitled to possession does not take possession of the child, the department shall take action under this chapter as if the department took possession of the child under Section 262.104.

History of Fam. Code §262.110: Acts 1995, 74th Leg., ch. 20, §1, eff. Apr. 20, 1995. Amended by Acts 1999, 76th Leg., ch. 1150, §18 (eff. Sept. 1, 1999), ch. 1390, §37 (eff. Sept. 1, 1999); Acts 2015, 84th Leg., ch. 1, §1.161, eff. Apr. 2, 2015. Source: Former Fam. Code §17.03(a)(1).

FAM §262.111. REPEALED

Repealed by Acts 2001, 77th Leg., ch. 849, §10, eff. Sept. 1, 2001.

FAM §262.112. EXPEDITED HEARING & APPEAL

(a) The Department of Family and Protective Services is entitled to an expedited hearing under this chapter in any proceeding in which a hearing is required if the department determines that a child should be removed from the child's home because of an immediate danger to the physical health or safety of the child.

(b) In any proceeding in which an expedited hearing is held under Subsection (a), the department, parent, guardian, or other party to the proceeding is entitled to an expedited appeal on a ruling by a court that the child may not be removed from the child's home.

(c) If a child is returned to the child's home after a removal in which the department was entitled to an expedited hearing under this section and the child is the subject of a subsequent allegation of abuse or neglect,

the department or any other interested party is entitled to an expedited hearing on the removal of the child from the child's home in the manner provided by Subsection (a) and to an expedited appeal in the manner provided by Subsection (b).

History of Fam. Code §262.112: Acts 1995, 74th Leg., ch. 943, §1, eff. Sept. 1, 1995. Renumbered from §262.111 by Acts 1997, 75th Leg., ch. 165, §31.01(29), eff. Sept. 1, 1997. Amended by Acts 2015, 84th Leg., ch. 1, §1.162, eff. Apr. 2, 2015.

FAM §262.113. FILING SUIT WITHOUT TAKING POSSESSION OF CHILD

The amended text in §262.113 is effective for service plans filed for a full adversary hearing held under Fam. Code §262.201 or a status hearing held under Fam. Code ch. 263 on or after Jan. 1, 2018. A hearing held before Jan. 1, 2018, is governed by the former law in effect at that time. Except as provided above, the amended text in §262.113 is effective for SAPCRs filed on or after Sept. 1, 2017. SAPCRs filed before Sept. 1, 2017, are governed by the former law in effect at that time.

An original suit filed by a governmental entity that requests to take possession of a child after notice and a hearing must be supported by an affidavit sworn to by a person with personal knowledge and stating facts sufficient to satisfy a person of ordinary prudence and caution that:

(1) there is a continuing danger to the physical health or safety of the child caused by an act or failure to act of the person entitled to possession of the child and that allowing the child to remain in the home would be contrary to the child's welfare; and

(2) reasonable efforts, consistent with the circumstances and providing for the safety of the child, have been made to prevent or eliminate the need to remove the child from the child's home [~~; and~~]

[~~(2)~~] [~~allowing the child to remain in the home would be contrary to the child's welfare~~].

History of Fam. Code §262.113: Acts 1999, 76th Leg., ch. 1150, §19 (eff. Sept. 1, 1999), ch. 1390, §38 (eff. Sept. 1, 1999). Amended by H.B. 7, §18, 85th Leg., eff. Sept. 1, 2017.

FAM §262.1131. TEMPORARY RESTRAINING ORDER BEFORE FULL ADVERSARY HEARING

In a suit filed under Section 262.113, the court may render a temporary restraining order as provided by Section 105.001.

History of Fam. Code §262.1131: Enacted by S.B. 999, §12, 85th Leg., eff. Sept. 1, 2017.

FAM §262.114. EVALUATION OF IDENTIFIED RELATIVES & OTHER DESIGNATED INDIVIDUALS; PLACEMENT

(a) Before a full adversary hearing under Subchapter C, the Department of Family and Protective Services must perform a background and criminal history check of the relatives or other designated individuals identified as a potential relative or designated caregiver, as defined by Section 264.751, on the proposed child placement resources form provided under Section 261.307. The department shall evaluate each person listed on the form to determine the relative or other designated individual who would be the most appropriate substitute caregiver for the child and must complete a home study of the most appropriate substitute caregiver, if any, before the full adversary hearing. Until the department identifies a relative or other designated individual qualified to be a substitute caregiver, the department must continue to explore substitute caregiver options. The time frames in this subsection do not apply to a relative or other designated individual located in another state.

(a-1) At the full adversary hearing under Section 262.201, the department shall, after redacting any social security numbers, file with the court:

(1) a copy of each proposed child placement resources form completed by the parent or other person having legal custody of the child;

(2) a copy of any completed home study performed under Subsection (a); and

(3) the name of the relative or other designated caregiver, if any, with whom the child has been placed.

(a-2) If the child has not been placed with a relative or other designated caregiver by the time of the full adversary hearing under Section 262.201, the department shall file with the court a statement that explains:

(1) the reasons why the department has not placed the child with a relative or other designated caregiver listed on the proposed child placement resources form; and

(2) the actions the department is taking, if any, to place the child with a relative or other designated caregiver.

(b) The department may place a child with a relative or other designated caregiver identified on the proposed child placement resources form if the department determines that the placement is in the best in-

terest of the child. The department must complete the background and criminal history check and conduct a preliminary evaluation of the relative or other designated caregiver's home before the child is placed with the relative or other designated caregiver. The department may place the child with the relative or designated caregiver before conducting the home study required under Subsection (a). Not later than 48 hours after the time that the child is placed with the relative or other designated caregiver, the department shall begin the home study of the relative or other designated caregiver. The department shall complete the home study as soon as possible unless otherwise ordered by a court. The department shall provide a copy of an informational manual required under Section 261.3071 to the relative or other designated caregiver at the time of the child's placement.

(c) The department shall consider placing a child who has previously been in the managing conservatorship of the department with a foster parent with whom the child previously resided if:

(1) the department determines that placement of the child with a relative or designated caregiver is not in the child's best interest; and

(2) the placement is available and in the child's best interest.

History of Fam. Code §262.114: Acts 2005, 79th Leg., ch. 268, §1.33, eff. Sept. 1, 2005. Amended by Acts 2009, 81st Leg., ch. 527, §1 (eff. Sept. 1, 2009), ch. 856, §1 (eff. Sept. 1, 2009); Acts 2015, 84th Leg., ch. 944, §24, eff. Sept. 1, 2015.

ANNOTATIONS

In re G.B. II, 357 S.W.3d 382, 384 (Tex.App.—Waco 2011, no pet.). "[F]ailure to conduct or obtain a home study pursuant to §262.114 is not a bar to termination. Additionally, a trial court does not abuse its discretion in determining that it would be against the children's best interest to delay the suit to evaluate a relative, risking dismissal of the case. Further, [mother] provides no authority, and we have found none, that suggests there is either a statutory or a common-law duty imposed on the Department to make a placement with a relative before a party's parental rights may be terminated." *See also* ***In re J.F.***, No. 02-07-007-CV (Tex.App.—Fort Worth 2007, pet. denied) (memo op.; 10-11-07) (§262.114 does not provide sanction for DFPS's failure to conduct home study; because children's safety is of paramount importance, court should still consider termination even if home study is not conducted).

FAM §262.115. VISITATION WITH CERTAIN CHILDREN; TEMPORARY VISITATION SCHEDULE

(a) In this section, "department" means the Department of Family and Protective Services.

(b) This section applies only to a child:

(1) who is in the temporary managing conservatorship of the department; and

(2) for whom the department's goal is reunification of the child with the child's parent.

(c) The department shall ensure that a parent who is otherwise entitled to possession of the child has an opportunity to visit the child not later than the fifth day after the date the department is named temporary managing conservator of the child unless:

(1) the department determines that visitation is not in the child's best interest; or

(2) visitation with the parent would conflict with a court order relating to possession of or access to the child.

(d) Before a hearing conducted under Subchapter C, the department in collaboration with each parent of the child must develop a temporary visitation schedule for the child's visits with each parent. The visitation schedule may conform to the department's minimum visitation policies. The department shall consider the factors listed in Section 263.107(c) in developing the temporary visitation schedule. Unless modified by court order, the schedule remains in effect until a visitation plan is developed under Section 263.107.

(e) The department may include the temporary visitation schedule in any report the department submits to the court before or during a hearing under Subchapter C. The court may render any necessary order regarding the temporary visitation schedule.

History of Fam. Code §262.115: Acts 2013, 83rd Leg., ch. 191, §1, eff. Sept. 1, 2013. Amended by Acts 2015, 84th Leg., ch. 944, §25, eff. Sept. 1, 2015.

E FAM §262.116. LIMITS ON REMOVAL

(a) The Department of Family and Protective Services may not take possession of a child under this subchapter based on evidence that the parent:

(1) homeschooled the child;

(2) is economically disadvantaged;

(3) has been charged with a nonviolent misdemeanor offense other than:

(A) an offense under Title 5, Penal Code;

(B) an offense under Title 6, Penal Code; or

(C) an offense that involves family violence, as defined by Section 71.004 of this code;

(4) provided or administered low-THC cannabis to a child for whom the low-THC cannabis was prescribed under Chapter 169, Occupations Code; or

(5) declined immunization for the child for reasons of conscience, including a religious belief.

(b) The department shall train child protective services caseworkers regarding the prohibitions on removal provided under Subsection (a).

(c) The executive commissioner of the Health and Human Services Commission may adopt rules to implement this section.

(d) This section does not prohibit the department from gathering or offering evidence described by Subsection (a) as part of an action to take possession of a child under this subchapter.

History of Fam. Code §262.116: Enacted by H.B. 7, §19, 85th Leg., eff. Sept. 1, 2017.

Sections 262.117-262.200 reserved for expansion

SUBCHAPTER C. ADVERSARY HEARING

Ⓐ FAM §262.201. FULL ADVERSARY HEARING; FINDINGS OF THE COURT

The amended text in §262.201 is effective for SAPCRs filed on or after Sept. 1, 2017. SAPCRs filed before Sept. 1, 2017, are governed by the former law in effect at that time.

☠ *Subsection (a) was amended by S.B. 999, §13, 85th Leg., enacted May 28, 2017, effective Sept. 1, 2017, without reference to the conflicting amendment made by H.B. 7, §20, 85th Leg., enacted May 26, 2017, effective Sept. 1, 2017. For harmonizing conflicts, see p. V.*

(a) In a suit filed under Section 262.101 or 262.105, unless [Unless] the child has already been returned to the parent, managing conservator, possessory conservator, guardian, caretaker, or custodian entitled to possession and the temporary order, if any, has been dissolved, a full adversary hearing shall be held not later than the 14th day after the date the child was taken into possession by the governmental entity, unless the court grants an extension under Subsection (e) or (e-1) [(a-3)].

☠ *Subsection (a) was amended by H.B. 7, §20, 85th Leg., enacted May 26, 2017, effective Sept. 1, 2017, without reference to the conflicting amendment made by S.B. 999, §13, 85th Leg., enacted May 28, 2017, effective Sept. 1, 2017. For harmonizing conflicts, see p. V. The amended text in subsection (a) is effective for service plans filed for a full adversary hearing held under Fam. Code §262.201 or a status hearing held under Fam. Code ch. 263 on or after Jan. 1, 2018. A hearing held before Jan. 1, 2018, is governed by the former law in effect at that time. Except as provided above, the amended text in subsection (a) is effective for SAPCRs filed on or after Sept. 1, 2017. SAPCRs filed before Sept. 1, 2017, are governed by the former law in effect at that time.*

(a) Unless the child has already been returned to the parent, managing conservator, possessory conservator, guardian, caretaker, or custodian entitled to possession and the temporary order, if any, has been dissolved, a full adversary hearing shall be held not later than the 14th day after the date the child was taken into possession by the governmental entity, unless the court grants an extension under Subsection (a-3) or (a-5).

☠ *Subsection (a-5) was enacted by H.B. 7, §20, 85th Leg., enacted May 26, 2017, effective Sept. 1, 2017, without reference to the conflicting renumbering made by S.B. 999, §13, 85th Leg., enacted May 28, 2017, effective Sept. 1, 2017. For harmonizing conflicts, see p. V. Subsection (a-5) is effective for service plans filed for a full adversary hearing held under Fam. Code §262.201 or a status hearing held under Fam. Code ch. 263 on or after Jan. 1, 2018. Except as provided above, subsection (a-5) is effective for SAPCRs filed on or after Sept. 1, 2017.*

(a-5) If a parent who is not indigent appears in opposition to the suit, the court may, for good cause shown, postpone the full adversary hearing for not more than seven days from the date of the parent's appearance to allow the parent to hire an attorney or to provide the parent's attorney time to respond to the petition and prepare for the hearing. A postponement under this subsection is subject to the limits and requirements prescribed by Subsection (a-3) and Section 155.207.

(b) A full adversary hearing in a suit filed under Section 262.113 requesting possession of a child shall be held not later than the 30th day after the date the suit is filed.

(c) [(a-1)] Before commencement of the full adversary hearing, the court must inform each parent not represented by an attorney of:

(1) the right to be represented by an attorney; and

(2) if a parent is indigent and appears in opposition to the suit, the right to a court-appointed attorney.

(d) [(a-2)] If a parent claims indigence and requests the appointment of an attorney before the full adversary hearing, the court shall require the parent to complete and file with the court an affidavit of indigence. The court may consider additional evidence to determine whether the parent is indigent, including evidence relating to the parent's income, source of income, assets, property ownership, benefits paid in accordance with a federal, state, or local public assistance program, outstanding obligations, and necessary expenses and the number and ages of the parent's dependents. If the appointment of an attorney for the parent is requested, the court shall make a determination of indigence before commencement of the full adversary hearing. If the court determines the parent is indigent, the court shall appoint an attorney to represent the parent.

(e) [(a-3)] The court may, for good cause shown, postpone the full adversary hearing for not more than seven days from the date of the attorney's appointment to provide the attorney time to respond to the petition and prepare for the hearing. The court may shorten or lengthen the extension granted under this subsection if the parent and the appointed attorney agree in writing. If the court postpones the full adversary hearing, the court shall extend a temporary order, temporary restraining order, or attachment issued by the court under Section 262.102(a) or Section 262.1131 for the protection of the child until the date of the rescheduled full adversary hearing.

(e-1) If a parent who is not indigent appears in opposition to the suit, the court may, for good cause shown, postpone the full adversary hearing for not more than seven days from the date of the parent's appearance to allow the parent to hire an attorney or to provide the parent's attorney time to respond to the petition and prepare for the hearing. A postponement under this subsection is subject to the limits and requirements prescribed by Subsection (e).

(f) [(a-4)] The court shall ask all parties present at the full adversary hearing whether the child or the child's family has a Native American heritage and identify any Native American tribe with which the child may be associated.

(g) In a suit filed under Section 262.101 or 262.105, at [(b) At] the conclusion of the full adversary hearing, the court shall order the return of the child to the parent, managing conservator, possessory conservator, guardian, caretaker, or custodian entitled to possession unless the court finds sufficient evidence to satisfy a person of ordinary prudence and caution that:

(1) there was a danger to the physical health or safety of the child, including a danger that the child would be a victim of trafficking under Section 20A.02 or 20A.03, Penal Code, which was caused by an act or failure to act of the person entitled to possession and for the child to remain in the home is contrary to the welfare of the child;

(2) the urgent need for protection required the immediate removal of the child and reasonable efforts, consistent with the circumstances and providing for the safety of the child, were made to eliminate or prevent the child's removal; and

(3) reasonable efforts have been made to enable the child to return home, but there is a substantial risk of a continuing danger if the child is returned home.

(h) In a suit filed under Section 262.101 or 262.105, if [(c) If] the court finds sufficient evidence to satisfy a person of ordinary prudence and caution that there is a continuing danger to the physical health or safety of the child and for the child to remain in the home is contrary to the welfare of the child, the court shall issue an appropriate temporary order under Chapter 105.

(i) In determining whether there is a continuing danger to the physical health or safety of the child under Subsection (g), the court may consider whether the household to which the child would be returned includes a person who:

(1) has abused or neglected another child in a manner that caused serious injury to or the death of the other child; or

(2) has sexually abused another child.

(j) In a suit filed under Section 262.113, at the conclusion of the full adversary hearing, the court shall issue an appropriate temporary order under Chapter 105 if the court finds sufficient evidence to satisfy a person of ordinary prudence and caution that:

(1) there is a continuing danger to the physical health or safety of the child caused by an act or failure to act of the person entitled to possession of the child and continuation of the child in the home would be contrary to the child's welfare; and

(2) reasonable efforts, consistent with the circumstances and providing for the safety of the child, were made to prevent or eliminate the need for the removal of the child.

(k) If the court finds that the child requires protection from family violence, as that term is defined by Section 71.004, by a member of the child's family or household, the court shall render a protective order for the child under Title 4.

(*l*) The court shall require each parent, alleged father, or relative of the child before the court to complete the proposed child placement resources form provided under Section 261.307 and file the form with the court, if the form has not been previously filed with the court, and provide the Department of Family and Protective Services with information necessary to locate any other absent parent, alleged father, or relative of the child. The court shall inform each parent, alleged father, or relative of the child before the court that the person's failure to submit the proposed child placement resources form will not delay any court proceedings relating to the child.

(m) The court shall inform each parent in open court that parental and custodial rights and duties may be subject to restriction or to termination unless the parent or parents are willing and able to provide the child with a safe environment. [~~If the court finds that the child requires protection from family violence by a member of the child's family or household, the court shall render a protective order under Title 4 for the child. In this subsection, "family violence" has the meaning assigned by Section 71.004.~~]

[~~(d)~~] [~~In determining whether there is a continuing danger to the physical health or safety of the child, the court may consider whether the household to which the child would be returned includes a person who:~~]

[~~(1)~~] [~~has abused or neglected another child in a manner that caused serious injury to or the death of the other child; or~~]

[~~(2)~~] [~~has sexually abused another child.~~]

(n) [~~(e)~~] The court shall place a child removed from the child's custodial parent with the child's noncustodial parent or with a relative of the child if placement with the noncustodial parent is inappropriate, unless placement with the noncustodial parent or a relative is not in the best interest of the child.

(o) [~~(f)~~] When citation by publication is needed for a parent or alleged or probable father in an action brought under this chapter because the location of the parent, alleged father, or probable father is unknown, the court may render a temporary order without delay at any time after the filing of the action without regard to whether notice of the citation by publication has been published.

(p) [~~(g)~~] For the purpose of determining under Subsection (a) the 14th day after the date the child is taken into possession, a child is considered to have been taken into possession by the Department of Family and Protective Services on the expiration of the five-day period permitted under Section 262.007(c) or 262.110(b), as appropriate.

History of Fam. Code §262.201: Acts 1995, 74th Leg., ch. 20, §1, eff. Apr. 20, 1995. Amended by Acts 1995, 74th Leg., ch. 751, §107, eff. Sept. 1, 1995; Acts 1997, 75th Leg., ch. 575, §21 (eff. Sept. 1, 1997), ch. 600, §5 (eff. Jan. 1, 1998), ch. 603, §1 (eff. Jan. 1, 1998), ch. 752, §3 (eff. June 17, 1997), ch. 1022, §77 (eff. Jan. 1, 1998), ch. 1022, §78 (eff. Sept. 1, 1997); Acts 1999, 76th Leg., ch. 62, §6.31(a), (b) (eff. Sept. 1, 1999), ch. 1150, §20 (eff. Sept. 1, 1999), ch. 1390, §39 (eff. Sept. 1, 1999); Acts 2001, 77th Leg., ch. 306, §1 (eff. Sept. 1, 2001), ch. 849, §4 (eff. Sept. 1, 2001); Acts 2005, 79th Leg., ch. 268, §1.34, eff. Nov. 1, 2005; Acts 2009, 81st Leg., ch. 856, §2, eff. Sept. 1, 2009; Acts 2013, 83rd Leg., ch. 810, §9, eff. Sept. 1, 2013; Acts 2015, 84th Leg., ch. 1, §1.163 (eff. Apr. 2, 2015), ch. 128, §3 (eff. Sept. 1, 2015), ch. 338, §4 (eff. Sept. 1, 2015), ch. 697, §1 (eff. Sept. 1, 2015); H.B. 7, §20, 85th Leg., eff. Sept. 1, 2017; S.B. 999, §13, 85th Leg., eff. Sept. 1, 2017. Source: Former Fam. Code §§17.03(f), 17.04.

ANNOTATIONS

In re Pate, 407 S.W.3d 416, 419 (Tex.App.—Houston [14th Dist.] 2013, orig. proceeding). "Removing a child from his home and parents on an emergency basis before fully litigating the issue of whether the parents should continue to have custody of the child is an extreme measure that may be taken only when the circumstances indicate a danger to the physical health and welfare of the child and the need for his protection is so urgent that immediate removal from the home is necessary. Unless evidence demonstrates the existence of each of the requirements of §262.201(b) [now §262.201(g)], the court is required to return the child to the custody of his parents pending litigation."

In re Cochran, 151 S.W.3d 275, 277 (Tex.App.—Texarkana 2004, orig. proceeding). "On direct examination, [caseworker who removed child] conceded that 'risk,' based on the prior terminations, had 'a large bearing' on the departmental decision to seek termination of [respondents'] parental rights. *At 280:* In the absence of any *current* conditions or actions that would constitute a danger to [child's] health or safety, the trial court could not have reasonably based its findings on the prior [parental-rights] terminations alone. We conclude that the trial court could not have found that the parents' prior terminations were acts or omissions

under §262.201(b)(1) [now §262.201(g)(1)] which posed a danger to [child] when the conduct resulting in the prior terminations was committed before her conception." *See also* ***In re Steed***, No. 03-08-00235-CV (Tex.App.—Austin 2008, orig. proceeding) (memo op.; 5-22-08) (evidence that children's physical health and safety may someday be threatened is not evidence that danger is imminent enough to warrant immediate removal under §262.201). *But see* ***In re B.W.B.***, No. 07-08-00487-CV (Tex.App.—Amarillo 2009, pet. dism'd) (memo op.; 10-29-09) (mother's prior criminal act was appropriate consideration under §262.201 because she had pleaded guilty to felony offense of injuring child under Fam. Code §161.001(1)(L)).

In re J.M.C., 109 S.W.3d 591, 595 (Tex.App.—Fort Worth 2003, no pet.). Family Code §262.201(a)'s "requirement that the trial court hold a full adversary hearing within 14 days of issuing an ex parte possession order is procedural, not jurisdictional. If a full adversary hearing is not held within 14 days, the remedy for both the parents and TDPRS is to compel the trial court by mandamus to conduct the adversary hearing promptly. The trial court does not, however, lose jurisdiction over the case. [¶] [N]othing in [Fam. Code] §§262.201, 263.401, or [TRCP] 680 deprives a trial court of jurisdiction over a termination proceeding simply because a temporary possession order has expired or the trial court does not hold a full adversary hearing."

In re E.D.L., 105 S.W.3d 679, 688 (Tex.App.—Fort Worth 2003, pet. denied). "We agree with TDPRS that the purpose of [§262.201] is to afford parents the opportunity to challenge TDPRS's right to retain any children whom TDPRS has taken into custody under an ex parte order from the court. A full adversary hearing thereby requires that the court enter temporary orders governing any children taken into custody, pending a full adjudication of parental rights at the termination hearing."

FAM §262.2015. AGGRAVATED CIRCUMSTANCES

(a) The court may waive the requirement of a service plan and the requirement to make reasonable efforts to return the child to a parent and may accelerate the trial schedule to result in a final order for a child under the care of the Department of Family and Protective Services at an earlier date than provided by Subchapter D, Chapter 263, if the court finds that the parent has subjected the child to aggravated circumstances.

(b) The court may find under Subsection (a) that a parent has subjected the child to aggravated circumstances if:

(1) the parent abandoned the child without identification or a means for identifying the child;

(2) the child or another child of the parent is a victim of serious bodily injury or sexual abuse inflicted by the parent or by another person with the parent's consent;

(3) the parent has engaged in conduct against the child or another child of the parent that would constitute an offense under the following provisions of the Penal Code:

(A) Section 19.02 (murder);

(B) Section 19.03 (capital murder);

(C) Section 19.04 (manslaughter);

(D) Section 21.11 (indecency with a child);

(E) Section 22.011 (sexual assault);

(F) Section 22.02 (aggravated assault);

(G) Section 22.021 (aggravated sexual assault);

(H) Section 22.04 (injury to a child, elderly individual, or disabled individual);

(I) Section 22.041 (abandoning or endangering child);

(J) Section 25.02 (prohibited sexual conduct);

(K) Section 43.25 (sexual performance by a child);

(L) Section 43.26 (possession or promotion of child pornography);

(M) Section 21.02 (continuous sexual abuse of young child or children);

(N) Section 43.05(a)(2) (compelling prostitution); or

(O) Section 20A.02(a)(7) or (8) (trafficking of persons);

(4) the parent voluntarily left the child alone or in the possession of another person not the parent of the child for at least six months without expressing an intent to return and without providing adequate support for the child;

(5) the parent's parental rights with regard to another child have been involuntarily terminated based on a finding that the parent's conduct violated Section 161.001(b)(1)(D) or (E) or a substantially equivalent provision of another state's law;

(6) the parent has been convicted for:

(A) the murder of another child of the parent and the offense would have been an offense under 18 U.S.C. Section 1111(a) if the offense had occurred in the special maritime or territorial jurisdiction of the United States;

(B) the voluntary manslaughter of another child of the parent and the offense would have been an offense under 18 U.S.C. Section 1112(a) if the offense had occurred in the special maritime or territorial jurisdiction of the United States;

(C) aiding or abetting, attempting, conspiring, or soliciting an offense under Paragraph (A) or (B); or

(D) the felony assault of the child or another child of the parent that resulted in serious bodily injury to the child or another child of the parent;

(7) the parent's parental rights with regard to another child of the parent have been involuntarily terminated; or

(8) the parent is required under any state or federal law to register with a sex offender registry.

(c) On finding that reasonable efforts to make it possible for the child to safely return to the child's home are not required, the court shall at any time before the 30th day after the date of the finding, conduct an initial permanency hearing under Subchapter D, Chapter 263. Separate notice of the permanency plan is not required but may be given with a notice of a hearing under this section.

(d) The Department of Family and Protective Services shall make reasonable efforts to finalize the permanent placement of a child for whom the court has made the finding described by Subsection (c). The court shall set the suit for trial on the merits as required by Subchapter D, Chapter 263, in order to facilitate final placement of the child.

History of Fam. Code §262.2015: Acts 1997, 75th Leg., ch. 1022, §79, eff. Sept. 1, 1997. Amended by Acts 1999, 76th Leg., ch. 1150, §21 (eff. Sept. 1, 1999), ch. 1390, §40 (eff. Sept. 1, 1999); Acts 2001, 77th Leg., ch. 849, §5, eff. Sept. 1, 2001; Acts 2005, 79th Leg., ch. 268, §1.35, eff. Sept. 1, 2005; Acts 2007, 80th Leg., ch. 593, §3.33, eff. Sept. 1, 2007; Acts 2011, 82nd Leg., ch. 1, §4.04, eff. Sept. 1, 2011; Acts 2015, 84th Leg., ch. 1, §1.164 (eff. Apr. 2, 2015), ch. 944, §26 (eff. Sept. 1, 2015).

ANNOTATIONS

In re Pate, 407 S.W.3d 416, 419 (Tex.App.—Houston [14th Dist.] 2013, orig. proceeding). Section 262.2015(a)(3) "affords the trial court discretion to determine what efforts are 'reasonable' to enable the child to return home. *At 420:* In this case, there was evidence of a prior removal, but no evidence of a prior termination. There is no evidence of other aggravated circumstances as defined by §262.2015.... At the hearing, the Department argued that no safety plan was necessary because of [mother's] history with the child's previous removal. In its response filed in this court, the Department continues to rely on [mother's] positive drug tests and her previous history with removal of the child. Although previous termination of another child is considered an aggravating circumstance, we find no authority holding that a previous temporary removal is sufficient to waive the requirement that the Department make reasonable attempts to enable the child to return home. Therefore, ... the Department was required to provide evidence that it had made reasonable efforts to enable the child to return home...."

In re Allen, 359 S.W.3d 284, 290 (Tex.App.—Texarkana 2012, orig. proceeding). "[T]here was evidence of a prior termination ... based on 'the well-being of the child' and 'the inability of [mother] to understand basic parenting skills and child development....' [But because] the stated reasons for the prior termination do not fit within subsections (D) and (E) of [Fam. Code] §161.001 [as required under Fam. Code §262.2015(b)(5)], there is no proof of 'aggravated circumstances' relating to the prior termination."

FAM §262.202. IDENTIFICATION OF COURT OF CONTINUING, EXCLUSIVE JURISDICTION

If at the conclusion of the full adversary hearing the court renders a temporary order, the governmental entity shall request identification of a court of continuing, exclusive jurisdiction as provided by Chapter 155.

History of Fam. Code §262.202: Acts 1995, 74th Leg., ch. 20, §1, eff. Apr. 20, 1995. Source: Former Fam. Code §17.05(b).

A FAM §262.203. TRANSFER OF SUIT

The amended text in §262.203 is effective for service plans filed for a full adversary hearing held under Fam. Code §262.201 or a status hearing held under Fam. Code ch. 263 on or after Jan. 1, 2018. A hearing held before Jan. 1, 2018, is governed by the former law in effect at that time. Except as provided above, the amended text in §262.203 is effective for SAPCRs filed on or after Sept. 1, 2017. SAPCRs filed before Sept. 1, 2017, are governed by the former law in effect at that time.

(a) On the motion of a party or the court's own motion, if applicable, the court that rendered the tempo-

rary order shall in accordance with procedures provided by Chapter 155:

(1) transfer the suit to the court of continuing, exclusive jurisdiction, if any, within the time required by Section[1] 155.207(a), if the court finds that the transfer is:

(A) necessary for the convenience of the parties; and

(B) in the best interest of the child;

(2) [~~if grounds exist for mandatory transfer from the court of continuing, exclusive jurisdiction under Section 155.201,~~] order transfer of the suit from the [~~that~~] court of continuing, exclusive jurisdiction; or

(3) if grounds exist for transfer based on improper venue, order transfer of the suit to the court having venue of the suit under Chapter 103.

(b) Notwithstanding Section 155.204, a motion to transfer relating to a suit filed under this chapter may be filed separately from the petition and is timely if filed while the case is pending.

(c) Notwithstanding Sections 6.407 and 103.002, a court exercising jurisdiction under this chapter is not required to transfer the suit to a court in which a parent has filed a suit for dissolution of marriage before a final order for the protection of the child has been rendered under Subchapter E, Chapter 263.

(d) An order of transfer must include:

(1) the date of any future hearings in the case that have been scheduled by the transferring court;

(2) any date scheduled by the transferring court for the dismissal of the suit under Section 263.401; and

(3) the name and contact information of each attorney ad litem or guardian ad litem appointed in the suit.

(e) The court to which a suit is transferred may retain an attorney ad litem or guardian ad litem appointed by the transferring court. If the court finds that the appointment of a new attorney ad litem or guardian ad litem is appropriate, the court shall appoint that attorney ad litem or guardian ad litem before the earlier of:

(1) the 10th day after the date of receiving the order of transfer; or

(2) the date of the first scheduled hearing after the transfer.

1. **Editor's note:** In 2017, three bills amended subsection (a)(1). H.B. 7, §21, 85th Leg., enacted May 26, 2017, effective Sept. 1, 2017, and S.B. 999, §14, 85th Leg., enacted May 28, 2017, effective Sept. 1, 2017, use "Section," as shown here, and S.B. 738, §3, 85th Leg., enacted May 24, 2017, effective Sept. 1, 2017, uses "Subsection."

History of Fam. Code §262.203: Acts 1995, 74th Leg., ch. 20, §1, eff. Apr. 20, 1995. Amended by Acts 1997, 75th Leg., ch. 575, §22, eff. Sept. 1, 1997; Acts 1999, 76th Leg., ch. 1150, §22 (eff. Sept. 1, 1999), ch. 1390, §41 (eff. Sept. 1, 1999); Acts 2015, 84th Leg., ch. 211, §2, eff. Sept. 1, 2015; H.B. 7, §21, 85th Leg., eff. Sept. 1, 2017; S.B. 738, §3, 85th Leg., eff. Sept. 1, 2017; S.B. 999, §14, 85th Leg., eff. Sept. 1, 2017. Source: Former Fam. Code §17.06(a).

FAM §262.204. TEMPORARY ORDER IN EFFECT UNTIL SUPERSEDED

(a) A temporary order rendered under this chapter is valid and enforceable until properly superseded by a court with jurisdiction to do so.

(b) A court to which the suit has been transferred may enforce by contempt or otherwise a temporary order properly issued under this chapter.

History of Fam. Code §262.204: Acts 1995, 74th Leg., ch. 20, §1, eff. Apr. 20, 1995. Source: Former Fam. Code §17.06(b), (c).

FAM §262.205. REPEALED [~~HEARING WHEN CHILD NOT IN POSSESSION OF GOVERNMENTAL ENTITY~~]

The repealed text of former §262.205 is effective for SAPCRs filed before Sept. 1, 2017.

[~~(a)~~] [~~In a suit requesting possession of a child after notice and hearing, the court may render a temporary restraining order as provided by Section 105.001. The suit shall be promptly set for hearing.~~]

[~~(b)~~] [~~After the hearing, the court may grant the request to remove the child from the parent, managing conservator, possessory conservator, guardian, caretaker, or custodian entitled to possession of the child if the court finds sufficient evidence to satisfy a person of ordinary prudence and caution that:~~]

[~~(1)~~] [~~reasonable efforts have been made to prevent or eliminate the need to remove the child from the child's home; and~~]

[~~(2)~~] [~~allowing the child to remain in the home would be contrary to the child's welfare.~~]

[~~(c)~~] [~~If the court orders removal of the child from the child's home, the court shall:~~]

[~~(1)~~] [~~issue an appropriate temporary order under Chapter 105; and~~]

[~~(2)~~] [~~inform each parent in open court that parental and custodial rights and duties may be subject to restriction or termination unless the parent is willing and able to provide a safe environment for the child.~~]

[~~(d)~~] [~~If citation by publication is required for a parent or alleged or probable father in an action under~~]

~~this chapter because the location of the person is unknown, the court may render a temporary order without regard to whether notice of the citation has been published.~~]

[~~(e)~~] [~~Unless it is not in the best interest of the child, the court shall place a child who has been removed under this section with:~~]

[~~(1)~~] [~~the child's noncustodial parent; or~~]

[~~(2)~~] [~~another relative of the child if placement with the noncustodial parent is inappropriate.~~]

[~~(f)~~] [~~If the court finds that the child requires protection from family violence by a member of the child's family or household, the court shall render a protective order for the child under Title 4.~~]

Repealed by S.B. 999, §15, 85th Leg., eff. Sept. 1, 2017.

E FAM §262.206. EX PARTE HEARINGS PROHIBITED

Unless otherwise authorized by this chapter or other law, a hearing held by a court in a suit under this chapter may not be ex parte.

History of Fam. Code §262.206: Enacted by H.B. 7, §22, 85th Leg., eff. Sept. 1, 2017.

Sections 262.207-262.300 blank

SUBCHAPTER D. EMERGENCY POSSESSION OF CERTAIN ABANDONED CHILDREN

FAM §262.301. DEFINITIONS

In this chapter:

(1) "Designated emergency infant care provider" means:

(A) an emergency medical services provider;

(B) a hospital;

(C) a freestanding emergency medical care facility licensed under Chapter 254, Health and Safety Code; or

(D) a child-placing agency licensed by the Department of Family and Protective Services under Chapter 42, Human Resources Code, that:

(i) agrees to act as a designated emergency infant care provider under this subchapter; and

(ii) has on staff a person who is licensed as a registered nurse under Chapter 301, Occupations Code, or who provides emergency medical services under Chapter 773, Health and Safety Code, and who will examine and provide emergency medical services to a child taken into possession by the agency under this subchapter.

(2) "Emergency medical services provider" has the meaning assigned that term by Section 773.003, Health and Safety Code.

History of Fam. Code §262.301: Acts 2001, 77th Leg., ch. 809, §4, eff. Sept. 1, 2001. Amended by Acts 2015, 84th Leg., ch. 1, §1.165 (eff. Apr. 2, 2015), ch. 260, §1 (eff. Sept. 1, 2015).

FAM §262.302. ACCEPTING POSSESSION OF CERTAIN ABANDONED CHILDREN

(a) A designated emergency infant care provider shall, without a court order, take possession of a child who appears to be 60 days old or younger if the child is voluntarily delivered to the provider by the child's parent and the parent did not express an intent to return for the child.

(b) A designated emergency infant care provider who takes possession of a child under this section has no legal duty to detain or pursue the parent and may not do so unless the child appears to have been abused or neglected. The designated emergency infant care provider has no legal duty to ascertain the parent's identity and the parent may remain anonymous. However, the parent may be given a form for voluntary disclosure of the child's medical facts and history.

(c) A designated emergency infant care provider who takes possession of a child under this section shall perform any act necessary to protect the physical health or safety of the child. The designated emergency infant care provider is not liable for damages related to the provider's taking possession of, examining, or treating the child, except for damages related to the provider's negligence.

History of Fam. Code §262.302: Acts 1999, 76th Leg., ch. 1087, §2, eff. Sept. 1, 1999. Renumbered from §262.301 and amended by Acts 2001, 77th Leg., ch. 809, §4, eff. Sept. 1, 2001.

FAM §262.303. NOTIFICATION OF POSSESSION OF ABANDONED CHILD

(a) Not later than the close of the first business day after the date on which a designated emergency infant care provider takes possession of a child under Section 262.302, the provider shall notify the Department of Family and Protective Services that the provider has taken possession of the child.

(b) The department shall assume the care, control, and custody of the child immediately on receipt of notice under Subsection (a).

History of Fam. Code §262.303: Acts 1999, 76th Leg., ch. 1087, §2, eff. Sept. 1, 1999. Renumbered from §262.302 and amended by Acts 2001, 77th Leg., ch. 809, §4, eff. Sept. 1, 2001. Amended by Acts 2015, 84th Leg., ch. 1, §1.166, eff. Apr. 2, 2015.

FAM §262.304. FILING PETITION AFTER ACCEPTING POSSESSION OF ABANDONED CHILD

A child for whom the Department of Family and Protective Services assumes care, control, and custody under Section 262.303 shall be treated as a child taken into possession without a court order, and the department shall take action as required by Section 262.105 with regard to the child.

History of Fam. Code §262.304: Acts 1999, 76th Leg., ch. 1087, §2, eff. Sept. 1, 1999. Renumbered from §262.303 and amended by Acts 2001, 77th Leg., ch. 809, §4, eff. Sept. 1, 2001. Amended by Acts 2015, 84th Leg., ch. 1, §1.167, eff. Apr. 2, 2015.

FAM §262.305. REPORT TO LAW ENFORCEMENT AGENCY; INVESTIGATION

(a) Immediately after assuming care, control, and custody of a child under Section 262.303, the Department of Family and Protective Services shall report the child to appropriate state and local law enforcement agencies as a potential missing child.

(b) A law enforcement agency that receives a report under Subsection (a) shall investigate whether the child is reported as missing.

History of Fam. Code §262.305: Acts 2001, 77th Leg., ch. 809, §4, eff. Sept. 1, 2001. Amended by Acts 2015, 84th Leg., ch. 1, §1.168, eff. Apr. 2, 2015.

FAM §262.306. NOTICE

Each designated emergency infant care provider shall post in a conspicuous location a notice stating that the provider is a designated emergency infant care provider location and will accept possession of a child in accordance with this subchapter.

History of Fam. Code §262.306: Acts 2001, 77th Leg., ch. 809, §4, eff. Sept. 1, 2001.

FAM §262.307. REIMBURSEMENT FOR CARE OF ABANDONED CHILD

The Department of Family and Protective Services shall reimburse a designated emergency infant care provider that takes possession of a child under Section 262.302 for the cost to the provider of assuming the care, control, and custody of the child.

History of Fam. Code §262.307: Acts 2001, 77th Leg., ch. 809, §4, eff. Sept. 1, 2001. Amended by Acts 2015, 84th Leg., ch. 1, §1.169, eff. Apr. 2, 2015.

FAM §262.308. CONFIDENTIALITY

(a) All identifying information, documentation, or other records regarding a person who voluntarily delivers a child to a designated emergency infant care provider under this subchapter is confidential and not subject to release to any individual or entity except as provided by Subsection (b).

(b) Any pleading or other document filed with a court under this subchapter is confidential, is not public information for purposes of Chapter 552, Government Code, and may not be released to a person other than to a party in a suit regarding the child, the party's attorney, or an attorney ad litem or guardian ad litem appointed in the suit.

(c) In a suit concerning a child for whom the Department of Family and Protective Services assumes care, control, and custody under this subchapter, the court shall close the hearing to the public unless the court finds that the interests of the child or the public would be better served by opening the hearing to the public.

(d) Unless the disclosure, receipt, or use is permitted by this section, a person commits an offense if the person knowingly discloses, receives, uses, or permits the use of information derived from records or files described by this section or knowingly discloses identifying information concerning a person who voluntarily delivers a child to a designated emergency infant care provider. An offense under this subsection is a Class B misdemeanor.

History of Fam. Code §262.308: Acts 2005, 79th Leg., ch. 620, §1, eff. Sept. 1, 2005.

FAM §262.309. SEARCH FOR RELATIVES NOT REQUIRED

The Department of Family and Protective Services is not required to conduct a search for the relatives of a child for whom the department assumes care, control, and custody under this subchapter.

History of Fam. Code §262.309: Acts 2005, 79th Leg., ch. 620, §1, eff. Sept. 1, 2005.

Sections 262.310-262.350 blank

SUBCHAPTER E. RELINQUISHING CHILD TO OBTAIN CERTAIN SERVICES

FAM §262.351. DEFINITIONS

In this subchapter:

(1) "Department" means the Department of Family and Protective Services.

(2) "Severe emotional disturbance" has the meaning assigned by Section 261.001.

History of Fam. Code §262.351: Acts 2013, 83rd Leg., ch. 1142, §3, eff. Sept. 1, 2013.

FAM §262.352. JOINT MANAGING CONSERVATORSHIP OF CHILD

(a) Before the department files a suit affecting the parent-child relationship requesting managing conser-

vatorship of a child who suffers from a severe emotional disturbance in order to obtain mental health services for the child, the department must, unless it is not in the best interest of the child, discuss with the child's parent or legal guardian the option of seeking a court order for joint managing conservatorship of the child with the department.

(b) Not later than November 1 of each even-numbered year, the department shall report the following information to the legislature:

(1) with respect to children described by Subsection (a):

(A) the number of children for whom the department has been appointed managing conservator;

(B) the number of children for whom the department has been appointed joint managing conservator; and

(C) the number of children who were diverted to community or residential mental health services through another agency; and

(2) the number of persons whose names were entered into the central registry of cases of child abuse and neglect only because the department was named managing conservator of a child who has a severe emotional disturbance because the child's family was unable to obtain mental health services for the child.

(c) Subsection (b) and this subsection expire September 1, 2019.

History of Fam. Code §262.352: Acts 2013, 83rd Leg., ch. 1142, §3, eff. Sept. 1, 2013. Amended by Acts 2015, 84th Leg., ch. 432, §3, eff. Sept. 1, 2015.

FAM §262.353. REPEALED [~~STUDY TO DEVELOP ALTERNATIVES TO RELINQUISHMENT OF CUSTODY TO OBTAIN MENTAL HEALTH SERVICES~~]

(a) to **(c)** Repealed by Acts 2015, 84th Leg., ch. 432, §4, eff. Sept. 1, 2015.

(d) Repealed by Acts 2015, 84th Leg., ch. 432, §4, eff. Sept. 1, 2015; S.B. 1488, §7.008, 85th Leg., eff. Sept. 1, 2017.

[~~(d)~~] [~~Not later than September 30, 2014, the department and the Department of State Health Services shall file a report with the legislature on the results of the study required by Subsection (a). The report must include:~~]

[~~(1)~~] [~~each option to prevent relinquishment of parental custody that was considered during the study;~~]

[~~(2)~~] [~~each option recommended for implementation, if any;~~]

[~~(3)~~] [~~each option that is implemented using existing resources;~~]

[~~(4)~~] [~~any policy or statutory change needed to implement a recommended option;~~]

[~~(5)~~] [~~the fiscal impact of implementing each option, if any;~~]

[~~(6)~~] [~~the estimated number of children and families that may be affected by the implementation of each option; and~~]

[~~(7)~~] [~~any other significant information relating to the study.~~]

(e) Repealed by Acts 2015, 84th Leg., ch. 432, §4, eff. Sept. 1, 2015.

Repealed by Acts 2015, 84th Leg., ch. 432, §4, eff. Sept. 1, 2015; S.B. 1488, §7.008, 85th Leg., eff. Sept. 1, 2017.

CHAPTER 263. REVIEW OF PLACEMENT OF CHILDREN UNDER CARE OF DEPARTMENT OF FAMILY & PROTECTIVE SERVICES

SUBCHAPTER A. GENERAL PROVISIONS

A FAM §263.001. DEFINITIONS

(a) In this chapter:

(1) "Advanced practice nurse" has the meaning assigned by Section 157.051, Occupations Code.

(1-a) "Age-appropriate normalcy activity" has the meaning assigned by Section 264.001.

(1-b) "Department" means the Department of Family and Protective Services.

(2) "Child's home" means the place of residence of at least one of the child's parents.

(3) "Household" means a unit composed of persons living together in the same dwelling, without regard to whether they are related to each other.

(3-a) "Least restrictive setting" means a placement for a child that, in comparison to all other available placements, is the most family-like setting.

(3-b) "Physician assistant" has the meaning assigned by Section 157.051, Occupations Code.

(4) "Substitute care" means the placement of a child who is in the conservatorship of the department in care outside the child's home. The term includes foster care, institutional care, adoption, placement with a relative of the child, or commitment to the Texas Juvenile Justice Department.

(b) In the preparation and review of a service plan under this chapter, a reference to the parents of the child includes both parents of the child unless the child has only one parent or unless, after due diligence by the department in attempting to locate a parent, only one parent is located, in which case the reference is to the remaining parent.

(c) With respect to a child who is older than six years of age and who is removed from the child's home, if a suitable relative or other designated caregiver is not available as a placement for the child, placing the child in a foster home or a general residential operation operating as a cottage home is considered the least restrictive setting.

(d) With respect to a child who is six years of age or younger and who is removed from the child's home, if a suitable relative or other designated caregiver is not available as a placement for the child, the least restrictive setting for the child is placement in:

(1) a foster home; or

(2) a general residential operation operating as a cottage home, only if the department determines it is in the best interest of the child.

History of Fam. Code §263.001: Acts 1995, 74th Leg., ch. 20, §1, eff. Apr. 20, 1995. Amended by Acts 1995, 74th Leg., ch. 751, §108, eff. Sept. 1, 1995; Acts 2005, 79th Leg., ch. 268, §1.36, eff. Sept. 1, 2005; Acts 2009, 81st Leg., ch. 108, §4, eff. May 23, 2009; Acts 2013, 83rd Leg., ch. 191, §2 (eff. Sept. 1, 2013), ch. 204, §3 (eff. Sept. 1, 2013), ch. 1324, §1 (eff. Sept. 1, 2013); Acts 2015, 84th Leg., ch. 1, §1.170 (eff. Apr. 2, 2015), ch. 262, §1 (eff. Sept. 1, 2015); H.B. 1542, §§1, 2, 85th Leg., eff. Sept. 1, 2017. Source: Former Fam. Code §18.01.

A FAM §263.002. REVIEW OF PLACEMENTS BY COURT; FINDINGS

The amended text in §263.002 is effective for service plans filed for a full adversary hearing held under Fam. Code §262.201 or a status hearing held under Fam. Code ch. 263 on or after Jan. 1, 2018. A hearing held before Jan. 1, 2018, is governed by the former law in effect at that time. Except as provided above, the amended text in §263.002 is effective for SAPCRs filed on or after Sept. 1, 2017. SAPCRs filed before Sept. 1, 2017, are governed by the former law in effect at that time.

(a) In a suit affecting the parent-child relationship in which the department has been appointed by the court or designated in an affidavit of relinquishment of parental rights as the temporary or permanent managing conservator of a child, the court shall hold a hearing to review:

(1) the conservatorship appointment and substitute care; and

(2) for a child committed to the Texas Juvenile Justice Department, the child's commitment in the Texas Juvenile Justice Department or release under supervision by the Texas Juvenile Justice Department.

(b) At each permanency hearing under this chapter, the court shall review the placement of each child in the temporary managing conservatorship of the department who is not placed with a relative caregiver or designated caregiver as defined by Section 264.751. The court shall include in its findings a statement whether the department placed the child with a relative or other designated caregiver.

(c) At each permanency hearing before the final order, the court shall review the placement of each child in the temporary managing conservatorship of the department who has not been returned to the child's home. The court shall make a finding on whether returning the child to the child's home is safe and appropriate, whether the return is in the best interest of the child, and whether it is contrary to the welfare of the child for the child to return home.

History of Fam. Code §263.002: Acts 1995, 74th Leg., ch. 20, §1, eff. Apr. 20, 1995. Amended by Acts 1995, 74th Leg., ch. 751, §109, eff. Sept. 1, 1995; Acts 2009, 81st Leg., ch. 108, §5, eff. May 23, 2009; Acts 2015, 84th Leg., ch. 1, §1.171, eff. Apr. 2, 2015; H.B. 7, §23, 85th Leg., eff. Sept. 1, 2017. Source: Former Fam. Code §18.02.

A FAM §263.0021. NOTICE OF HEARING; PRESENTATION OF EVIDENCE

The amended text in §263.0021 is effective for service plans filed for a full adversary hearing held under Fam. Code §262.201 or a status hearing held under Fam. Code ch. 263 on or after Jan. 1, 2018. A hearing held before Jan. 1, 2018, is governed by the former law in effect at that time. Except as provided above, the amended text in §263.0021 is effective for SAPCRs filed on or after Sept. 1, 2017. SAPCRs filed before Sept. 1, 2017, are governed by the former law in effect at that time.

Foster homes or foster group homes licensed by TDFPS and agency foster group homes verified by a child-placing agency before Sept. 1, 2017, may continue to operate under the former law in effect at that time, until the foster home or foster group home converts to another residential child-care license or the license is relinquished, or the agency foster group home has been converted to a verified foster home or closed.

(a) Notice of a hearing under this chapter shall be given to all persons entitled to notice of the hearing.

(b) The following persons are entitled to at least 10 days' notice of a hearing under this chapter and are entitled to present evidence and be heard at the hearing:

(1) the department;

(2) the foster parent, preadoptive parent, relative of the child providing care, or director or director's designee of the group home or general residential operation where the child is residing;

(3) each parent of the child;

(4) the managing conservator or guardian of the child;

(5) an attorney ad litem appointed for the child under Chapter 107, if the appointment was not dismissed in the final order;

(6) a guardian ad litem appointed for the child under Chapter 107, if the appointment was not dismissed in the final order;

(7) a volunteer advocate appointed for the child under Chapter 107, if the appointment was not dismissed in the final order;

(8) the child if:

(A) the child is 10 years of age or older; or

(B) the court determines it is appropriate for the child to receive notice; and

(9) any other person or agency named by the court to have an interest in the child's welfare.

(c) Notice of a hearing under this chapter may be given:

(1) as provided by Rule 21a, Texas Rules of Civil Procedure;

(2) in a temporary order following a full adversary hearing;

(3) in an order following a hearing under this chapter;

(4) in open court; or

(5) in any manner that would provide actual notice to a person entitled to notice.

(d) The licensed administrator of the child-placing agency responsible for placing the child or the licensed administrator's designee is entitled to at least 10 days' notice of a permanency hearing after final order.

(e) Notice of a hearing under this chapter provided to an individual listed under Subsection (b)(2) must state that the individual may, but is not required to, attend the hearing and may request to be heard at the hearing.

(f) In a hearing under this chapter, the court shall determine whether the child's caregiver is present at the hearing and allow the caregiver to testify if the caregiver wishes to provide information about the child.

History of Fam. Code §263.0021: Acts 1995, 74th Leg., ch. 20, §1, eff. Apr. 20, 1995. Amended by Acts 1997, 75th Leg., ch. 600, §10 (eff. Jan. 1, 1998), ch. 603, §5 (eff. Jan. 1, 1998), ch. 1022, §83 (eff. Jan. 1, 1998); Acts 2001, 77th Leg., ch. 849, §6, eff. Sept. 1, 2001; Acts 2013, 83rd Leg., ch. 885, §1, eff. Sept. 1, 2013. Renumbered from §263.301 and amended by Acts 2015, 84th Leg., ch. 944, §28, eff. Sept. 1, 2015. Amended by Acts 2015, 84th Leg., ch. 1, §1.178, eff. Apr. 2, 2015; H.B. 7, §24, 85th Leg., eff. Sept. 1, 2017. Source: Former Fam. Code §§18.08(b), (c), 18.12.

A FAM §263.0025. SPECIAL EDUCATION DECISION-MAKING FOR CHILDREN IN FOSTER CARE [~~APPOINTMENT OF SURROGATE PARENT~~]

(a) In this section, "child" means a child in the temporary or permanent managing conservatorship of the department who is eligible under Section 29.003, Education Code, to participate in a school district's special education program. [~~If a child in the temporary or permanent conservatorship of the department is eligible under Section 29.003, Education Code, to participate in a school district's special education program, the court may, when necessary to ensure that the educational rights of the child are protected, appoint a surrogate parent who:~~]

[~~(1)~~] [~~is willing to serve in that capacity; and~~]

[~~(2)~~] [~~meets the requirements of 20 U.S.C. Section 1415(b) and Section 29.001(10), Education Code.~~]

(a-1) A foster parent for a child may act as a parent for the child, as authorized under 20 U.S.C. Section 1415(b), if:

(1) the rights and duties of the department to make decisions regarding the child's education under Section 153.371 have not been limited by court order; and

(2) the foster parent agrees to the requirements of Sections 29.015(a)(3) and (b), Education Code.

(a-2) Sections 29.015(b-1), (c), and (d), Education Code, apply to a foster parent who acts or desires to act as a parent for a child for the purpose of making special education decisions.

(b) To ensure the educational rights of a child are protected in the special education process, the court may appoint a surrogate parent for the child if:

(1) the child's school district is unable to identify or locate a parent for the child; or

(2) the foster parent of the child is unwilling or unable to serve as a parent for the purposes of this subchapter [~~In appointing a surrogate parent for a child, the court shall give preferential consideration to a foster parent of the child as required under Section 29.015, Education Code~~].

(c) Except as provided by Subsection (d), the court may appoint a person to serve as a child's surrogate parent if the person:

(1) is willing to serve in that capacity; and

(2) meets the requirements of 20 U.S.C. Section 1415(b) [~~If the court does not appoint a child's foster parent to serve as the child's surrogate parent, the court shall give consideration to:~~]

[~~(1)~~] [~~a relative or other designated caregiver as defined by Section 264.751; or~~]

[~~(2)~~] [~~a court-appointed volunteer advocate who has been appointed to serve as the child's guardian ad litem, as provided by Section 107.031(c)~~].

(d) The following persons may not be appointed as a surrogate parent for the child:

(1) an employee of the department;

(2) an employee of the Texas Education Agency;

FAM §263.0025

(3) an employee of a school or school district; or

(4) an employee of any other agency that is involved in the education or care of the child.

(e) The court may appoint a child's guardian ad litem or court-certified volunteer advocate, as provided by Section 107.031(c), as the child's surrogate parent.

(f) In appointing a person to serve as the surrogate parent for a child, the court may consider the person's ability to meet the qualifications listed under Sections 29.0151(d)(2)-(8), Education Code.

(g) If the court prescribes training for a person who is appointed as the surrogate parent for a child, the training program must comply with the minimum standards for training established by rule by the Texas Education Agency.

History of Fam. Code §263.0025: Acts 2013, 83rd Leg., ch. 688, §3, eff. Sept. 1, 2013. Amended by H.B. 1556, §4, 85th Leg., eff. Sept. 1, 2017.

FAM §263.003. INFORMATION RELATING TO PLACEMENT OF CHILD

(a) Except as provided by Subsection (b), not later than the 10th day before the date set for a hearing under this chapter, the department shall file with the court any document described by Sections 262.114(a-1) and (a-2) that has not been filed with the court.

(b) The department is not required to file the documents required by Subsection (a) if the child is in an adoptive placement or another placement that is intended to be permanent.

History of Fam. Code §263.003: Acts 2009, 81st Leg., ch. 856, §3, eff. Sept. 1, 2009.

FAM §263.004. NOTICE TO COURT REGARDING EDUCATION DECISION-MAKING

(a) Unless the rights and duties of the department under Section 153.371(10) to make decisions regarding the child's education have been limited by court order, the department shall file with the court the name and contact information for each person who has been:

(1) designated by the department to make educational decisions on behalf of the child; and

(2) assigned to serve as the child's surrogate parent in accordance with 20 U.S.C. Section 1415(b) and Section 29.001(10), Education Code, for purposes of decision-making regarding special education services, if applicable.

(b) Not later than the fifth day after the date an adversary hearing under Section 262.201 or 262.205[1] is concluded, the information required by Subsection (a) shall be filed with the court and a copy shall be provided to the school the child attends.

(c) If a person other than a person identified under Subsection (a) is designated to make educational decisions or assigned to serve as a surrogate parent, the department shall include the updated information in a permanency progress report filed under Section 263.303 or 263.502. The updated information must be provided to the school the child attends not later than the fifth day after the date of designation or assignment.

1. **Editor's note:** Family Code §262.205 was repealed by S.B. 999, §15, 85th Leg., eff. Sept. 1, 2017.

History of Fam. Code §263.004: Acts 2013, 83rd Leg., ch. 688, §4, eff. Sept. 1, 2013. Amended by Acts 2015, 84th Leg., ch. 944, §29, eff. Sept. 1, 2015.

History of Former Fam. Code §263.004: Repealed by Acts 1999, 76th Leg., ch. 1150, §31 (eff. Sept. 1, 1999), ch. 1390, §50 (eff. Sept. 1, 1999).

FAM §263.0045. EDUCATION IN HOME SETTING FOR FOSTER CHILDREN

On request of a person providing substitute care for a child who is in the managing conservatorship of the department, the department shall allow the person to provide the child with an education in a home setting unless:

(1) the right of the department to allow the education of the child in a home setting has been specifically limited by court order;

(2) a court at a hearing conducted under this chapter finds, on good cause shown through evidence presented by the department in accordance with the applicable provisions in the department's child protective services handbook (CPS August 2013), that education in the home setting is not in the best interest of the child; or

(3) the department determines that federal law requires another school setting.

History of Fam. Code §263.0045: Acts 2015, 84th Leg., ch. 944, §27, eff. Sept. 1, 2015.

FAM §263.005. ENFORCEMENT OF FAMILY SERVICE PLAN

The department shall designate existing department personnel to ensure that the parties to a family service plan comply with the plan.

History of Fam. Code §263.005: Acts 1995, 74th Leg., ch. 943, §5, eff. Sept. 1, 1995.

FAM §263.006. WARNING TO PARENTS

At the status hearing under Subchapter C and at each permanency hearing under Subchapter D held after the court has rendered a temporary order appointing

the department as temporary managing conservator, the court shall inform each parent in open court that parental and custodial rights and duties may be subject to restriction or to termination unless the parent or parents are willing and able to provide the child with a safe environment.

History of Fam. Code §263.006: Acts 1997, 75th Leg., ch. 600, §6 (eff. Jan. 1, 1998), ch. 603, §2 (eff. Jan. 1, 1998), ch. 1022, §80 (eff. Jan. 1, 1998).

FAM §263.0061. NOTICE TO PARENTS OF RIGHT TO COUNSEL

(a) At the status hearing under Subchapter C and at each permanency hearing under Subchapter D held after the date the court renders a temporary order appointing the department as temporary managing conservator of a child, the court shall inform each parent not represented by an attorney of:

(1) the right to be represented by an attorney; and

(2) if a parent is indigent and appears in opposition to the suit, the right to a court-appointed attorney.

(b) If a parent claims indigence and requests the appointment of an attorney in a proceeding described by Subsection (a), the court shall require the parent to complete and file with the court an affidavit of indigence. The court may hear evidence to determine whether the parent is indigent. If the court determines the parent is indigent, the court shall appoint an attorney to represent the parent.

History of Fam. Code §263.0061: Acts 2013, 83rd Leg., ch. 810, §10, eff. Sept. 1, 2013.

FAM §263.007. REPORT REGARDING NOTIFICATION OF RELATIVES

Not later than the 10th day before the date set for a hearing under Subchapter C, the department shall file with the court a report regarding:

(1) the efforts the department made to identify, locate, and provide information to the individuals described by Section 262.1095;

(2) the name of each individual the department identified, located, or provided with information; and

(3) if applicable, an explanation of why the department was unable to identify, locate, or provide information to an individual described by Section 262.1095.

History of Fam. Code §263.007: Acts 2011, 82nd Leg., ch. 1071, §3, eff. Sept. 1, 2011.

A FAM §263.008. FOSTER CHILDREN'S BILL OF RIGHTS

The amended text in §263.008 is effective for service plans filed for a full adversary hearing held under Fam. Code §262.201 or a status hearing held under Fam. Code ch. 263 on or after Jan. 1, 2018. A hearing held before Jan. 1, 2018, is governed by the former law in effect at that time. Except as provided above, the amended text in §263.008 is effective for SAPCRs filed on or after Sept. 1, 2017. SAPCRs filed before Sept. 1, 2017, are governed by the former law in effect at that time.

Foster homes or foster group homes licensed by TDFPS and agency foster group homes verified by a child-placing agency before Sept. 1, 2017, may continue to operate under the former law in effect at that time, until the foster home or foster group home converts to another residential child-care license or the license is relinquished, or the agency foster group home has been converted to a verified foster home or closed.

(a) In this section:

(1) "Agency foster ~~[group]~~ home~~[,]~~" and ~~["agency foster home,"]~~ "facility~~[,]~~" ~~["foster group home," and "foster home"]~~ have the meanings assigned by Section 42.002, Human Resources Code.

(2) Repealed by Acts 2015, 84th Leg., ch. 944, §86(14), eff. Sept. 1, 2015.

(3) "Foster children's bill of rights" means the rights described by Subsection (b).

(b) It is the policy of this state that each child in foster care be informed of the child's rights provided by state or federal law or policy that relate to:

(1) abuse, neglect, exploitation, discrimination, and harassment;

(2) food, clothing, shelter, and education;

(3) medical, dental, vision, and mental health services, including the right of the child to consent to treatment;

(4) emergency behavioral intervention, including what methods are permitted, the conditions under which it may be used, and the precautions that must be taken when administering it;

(5) placement with the child's siblings and contact with members of the child's family;

(6) privacy and searches, including the use of storage space, mail, and the telephone;

(7) participation in school-related extracurricular or community activities;

(8) interaction with persons outside the foster care system, including teachers, church members, mentors, and friends;

FAM §263.008

(9) contact and communication with caseworkers, attorneys ad litem, guardians ad litem, and court-appointed special advocates;

(10) religious services and activities;

(11) confidentiality of the child's records;

(12) job skills, personal finances, and preparation for adulthood;

(13) participation in a court hearing that involves the child;

(14) participation in the development of service and treatment plans;

(15) if the child has a disability, the advocacy and protection of the rights of a person with that disability; and

(16) any other matter affecting the child's ability to receive care and treatment in the least restrictive environment that is most like a family setting, consistent with the best interests and needs of the child.

(c) The department shall provide a written copy of the foster children's bill of rights to each child placed in foster care in the child's primary language, if possible, and shall inform the child of the rights described by the foster children's bill of rights:

(1) orally in the child's primary language, if possible, and in simple, nontechnical terms; or

(2) for a child who has a disability, including an impairment of vision or hearing, through any means that can reasonably be expected to result in successful communication with the child.

(d) A child placed in foster care may, at the child's option, sign a document acknowledging the child's understanding of the foster children's bill of rights after the department provides a written copy of the foster children's bill of rights to the child and informs the child of the rights described by the foster children's bill of rights in accordance with Subsection (c). If a child signs a document acknowledging the child's understanding of the foster children's bill of rights, the document must be placed in the child's case file.

(e) An [~~agency foster group home,~~] agency foster home [~~, foster group home, foster home,~~] or other residential child-care facility in which a child is placed in foster care shall provide a copy of the foster children's bill of rights to a child on the child's request. The foster children's bill of rights must be printed in English and in a second language.

(f) The department shall promote the participation of foster children and former foster children in educating other foster children about the foster children's bill of rights.

(g) The department shall develop and implement a policy for receiving and handling reports that the rights of a child in foster care are not being observed. The department shall inform a child in foster care and, if appropriate, the child's parent, managing conservator, or guardian of the method for filing a report with the department under this subsection.

(h) This section does not create a cause of action.

History of Fam. Code §263.008: Acts 2011, 82nd Leg., ch. 791, §1, eff. Sept. 1, 2011. Renumbered from Fam. Code §263.007 by Acts 2013, 83rd Leg., ch. 161, §22.001(17), eff. Sept. 1, 2013. Amended by Acts 2015, 84th Leg., ch. 1, §1.172 (eff. Apr. 2, 2015), ch. 944, §86(14) (eff. Sept. 1, 2015); H.B. 7, §§25, 26, 85th Leg., eff. Sept. 1, 2017.

Author's comment: A more expansive list of rights for foster children is included in 40 T.A.C. §§748.1101-748.1119.

A FAM §263.009. PERMANENCY PLANNING MEETINGS

(a) The department shall hold a permanency planning meeting for each child for whom the department is appointed temporary managing conservator in accordance with a schedule adopted by the [~~executive~~] commissioner of the department [~~Health and Human Services Commission~~] by rule that is designed to allow the child to exit the managing conservatorship of the department safely and as soon as possible and be placed with an appropriate adult caregiver who will permanently assume legal responsibility for the child.

(b) At each permanency planning meeting, the department shall:

(1) identify any barriers to achieving a timely permanent placement for the child;

(2) develop strategies and determine actions that will increase the probability of achieving a timely permanent placement for the child; and

(3) use the family group decision-making model whenever possible.

(c) to **(f)** Repealed by Acts 2015, 84th Leg., ch. 944, §86(15), eff. Sept. 1, 2015.

History of Fam. Code §263.009: Acts 2013, 83rd Leg., ch. 1324, §2, eff. Sept. 1, 2013. Amended by Acts 2015, 84th Leg., ch. 944, §§30, 86(15), eff. Sept. 1, 2015; H.B. 5, §11, 85th Leg., eff. Sept. 1, 2017.

See also 40 T.A.C. §§700.1210, 700.1212.

Sections 263.010-263.100 reserved for expansion

SUBCHAPTER B. SERVICE PLAN & VISITATION PLAN

FAM §263.101. DEPARTMENT TO FILE SERVICE PLAN

Except as provided by Section 262.2015, not later than the 45th day after the date the court renders a temporary order appointing the department as temporary managing conservator of a child under Chapter 262, the department shall file a service plan.

History of Fam. Code §263.101: Acts 1995, 74th Leg., ch. 20, §1, eff. Apr. 20, 1995. Amended by Acts 1999, 76th Leg., ch. 1150, §24 (eff. Sept. 1, 1999), ch. 1390, §43 (eff. Sept. 1, 1999); Acts 2013, 83rd Leg., ch. 191, §3, eff. Sept. 1, 2013; Acts 2015, 84th Leg., ch. 1, §1.173 (eff. Apr. 2, 2015), ch. 944, §31 (eff. Sept. 1, 2015). Source: Former Fam. Code §18.03(a).

See also 40 T.A.C. §§700.1319-700.1325.

FAM §263.1015. REPEALED

Repealed by Acts 2015, 84th Leg., ch. 1, §1.203(6), eff. Apr. 2, 2015.

FAM §263.102. SERVICE PLAN; CONTENTS

(a) The service plan must:

(1) be specific;

(2) be in writing in a language that the parents understand, or made otherwise available;

(3) be prepared by the department in conference with the child's parents;

(4) state appropriate deadlines;

(5) specify the primary permanency goal and at least one alternative permanency goal;

(6) state steps that are necessary to:

(A) return the child to the child's home if the placement is in foster care;

(B) enable the child to remain in the child's home with the assistance of a service plan if the placement is in the home under the department's supervision; or

(C) otherwise provide a permanent safe placement for the child;

(7) state the actions and responsibilities that are necessary for the child's parents to take to achieve the plan goal during the period of the service plan and the assistance to be provided to the parents by the department or other agency toward meeting that goal;

(8) state any specific skills or knowledge that the child's parents must acquire or learn, as well as any behavioral changes the parents must exhibit, to achieve the plan goal;

(9) state the actions and responsibilities that are necessary for the child's parents to take to ensure that the child attends school and maintains or improves the child's academic compliance;

(10) state the name of the person with the department whom the child's parents may contact for information relating to the child if other than the person preparing the plan; and

(11) prescribe any other term or condition that the department determines to be necessary to the service plan's success.

(b) The service plan shall include the following statement:

TO THE PARENT: THIS IS A VERY IMPORTANT DOCUMENT. ITS PURPOSE IS TO HELP YOU PROVIDE YOUR CHILD WITH A SAFE ENVIRONMENT WITHIN THE REASONABLE PERIOD SPECIFIED IN THE PLAN. IF YOU ARE UNWILLING OR UNABLE TO PROVIDE YOUR CHILD WITH A SAFE ENVIRONMENT, YOUR PARENTAL AND CUSTODIAL DUTIES AND RIGHTS MAY BE RESTRICTED OR TERMINATED OR YOUR CHILD MAY NOT BE RETURNED TO YOU. THERE WILL BE A COURT HEARING AT WHICH A JUDGE WILL REVIEW THIS SERVICE PLAN.

(c) Repealed by Acts 2015, 84th Leg., ch. 944, §86(16), eff. Sept. 1, 2015.

(d) The department or other authorized entity must write the service plan in a manner that is clear and understandable to the parent in order to facilitate the parent's ability to follow the requirements of the service plan.

(e) Regardless of whether the goal stated in a child's service plan as required under Subsection (a)(5) is to return the child to the child's parents or to terminate parental rights and place the child for adoption, the department shall concurrently provide to the child and the child's family, as applicable:

(1) time-limited family reunification services as defined by 42 U.S.C. Section 629a for a period not to exceed the period within which the court must render a final order in or dismiss the suit affecting the parent-child relationship with respect to the child as provided by Subchapter E; and

(2) adoption promotion and support services as defined by 42 U.S.C. Section 629a.

(f) The department shall consult with relevant professionals to determine the skills or knowledge that the parents of a child under two years of age should learn or acquire to provide a safe placement for the child. The department shall incorporate those skills and abilities into the department's service plans, as appropriate.

(g) Repealed by Acts 2015, 84th Leg., ch. 944, §86(16), eff. Sept. 1, 2015.

History of Fam. Code §263.102: Acts 1995, 74th Leg., ch. 20, §1, eff. Apr. 20, 1995. Amended by Acts 2005, 79th Leg., ch. 268, §1.38(a), eff. Sept. 1, 2005; Acts 2007, 80th Leg., ch. 1406, §8, eff. Sept. 1, 2007; Acts 2015, 84th Leg., ch. 1, §1.174 (eff. Apr. 2, 2015), ch. 944, §§32, 86(16) (eff. Sept. 1, 2015). Source: Former Fam. Code §18.03(b)-(d).

See also 40 T.A.C. §§700.1319-700.1325.

FAM §263.103. ORIGINAL SERVICE PLAN: SIGNING & TAKING EFFECT

(a) The original service plan shall be developed jointly by the child's parents and a representative of the department, including informing the parents of their rights in connection with the service plan process. If a parent is not able or willing to participate in the development of the service plan, it should be so noted in the plan.

(a-1) Before the original service plan is signed, the child's parents and the representative of the department shall discuss each term and condition of the plan.

(b) The child's parents and the person preparing the original service plan shall sign the plan, and the department shall give each parent a copy of the service plan.

(c) If the department determines that the child's parents are unable or unwilling to participate in the development of the original service plan or sign the plan, the department may file the plan without the parents' signatures.

(d) The original service plan takes effect when:

(1) the child's parents and the appropriate representative of the department sign the plan; or

(2) the court issues an order giving effect to the plan without the parents' signatures.

(e) The original service plan is in effect until amended by the court or as provided under Section 263.104.

History of Fam. Code §263.103: Acts 1995, 74th Leg., ch. 20, §1, eff. Apr. 20, 1995. Amended by Acts 2011, 82nd Leg., ch. 598, §4, eff. Sept. 1, 2011; Acts 2015, 84th Leg., ch. 1, §1.175, eff. Apr. 2, 2015. Source: Former Fam. Code §18.04.

FAM §263.104. AMENDED SERVICE PLAN

(a) The service plan may be amended at any time. The department shall work with the parents to jointly develop any amendment to the service plan, including informing the parents of their rights in connection with the amended service plan process.

(b) The amended service plan supersedes the previously filed service plan and takes effect when:

(1) the child's parents and the appropriate representative of the department sign the plan; or

(2) the department determines that the child's parents are unable or unwilling to sign the amended plan and files it without the parents' signatures.

(c) A parent may file a motion with the court at any time to request a review and modification of the amended service plan.

(d) An amended service plan remains in effect until:

(1) superseded by a later-amended service plan that goes into effect as provided by Subsection (b); or

(2) modified by the court.

History of Fam. Code §263.104: Acts 1995, 74th Leg., ch. 20, §1, eff. Apr. 20, 1995. Amended by Acts 2011, 82nd Leg., ch. 598, §5, eff. Sept. 1, 2011; Acts 2015, 84th Leg., ch. 1, §1.176, eff. Apr. 2, 2015. Source: Former Fam. Code §18.05.

FAM §263.105. REVIEW OF SERVICE PLAN; MODIFICATION

(a) The service plan currently in effect shall be filed with the court.

(b) The court shall review the plan at the next required hearing under this chapter after the plan is filed.

(c) The court may modify an original or amended service plan at any time.

History of Fam. Code §263.105: Acts 1995, 74th Leg., ch. 20, §1, eff. Apr. 20, 1995. Amended by Acts 1999, 76th Leg., ch. 1150, §25 (eff. Sept. 1, 1999), ch. 1390, §44 (eff. Sept. 1, 1999); Acts 2011, 82nd Leg., ch. 1071, §§4, 5, eff. Sept. 1, 2011. Source: Former Fam. Code §18.06.

See also 40 T.A.C. §700.1325.

FAM §263.106. COURT IMPLEMENTATION OF SERVICE PLAN

After reviewing the original or any amended service plan and making any changes or modifications it deems necessary, the court shall incorporate the original and any amended service plan into the orders of the court and may render additional appropriate orders to implement or require compliance with an original or amended service plan.

History of Fam. Code §263.106: Acts 1995, 74th Leg., ch. 20, §1, eff. Apr. 20, 1995. Amended by Acts 2011, 82nd Leg., ch. 598, §6, eff. Sept. 1, 2011.

FAM §263.107. VISITATION PLAN

(a) This section applies only to a child in the temporary managing conservatorship of the department for whom the department's goal is reunification of the child with the child's parent.

(b) Not later than the 30th day after the date the department is named temporary managing conservator

of a child, the department in collaboration with each parent of the child shall develop a visitation plan.

(c) In determining the frequency and circumstances of visitation under this section, the department must consider:

(1) the safety and best interest of the child;

(2) the age of the child;

(3) the desires of each parent regarding visitation with the child;

(4) the location of each parent and the child; and

(5) the resources available to the department, including the resources to:

(A) ensure that visitation is properly supervised by a department employee or an available and willing volunteer the department determines suitable after conducting a background and criminal history check; and

(B) provide transportation to and from visits.

(d) Not later than the 10th day before the date of a status hearing under Section 263.201, the department shall file with the court a copy of the visitation plan developed under this section.

(e) The department may amend the visitation plan on mutual agreement of the child's parents and the department or as the department considers necessary to ensure the safety of the child. An amendment to the visitation plan must be in the child's best interest. The department shall file a copy of any amended visitation plan with the court.

(f) A visitation plan developed under this section may not conflict with a court order relating to possession of or access to the child.

History of Fam. Code §263.107: Acts 2013, 83rd Leg., ch. 191, §4, eff. Sept. 1, 2013.

FAM §263.108. REVIEW OF VISITATION PLAN; MODIFICATION

(a) At the first hearing held under this chapter after the date an original or amended visitation plan is filed with the court under Section 263.107, the court shall review the visitation plan, taking into consideration the factors specified in Section 263.107(c).

(b) The court may modify, or order the department to modify, an original or amended visitation plan at any time.

(c) A parent who is entitled to visitation under a visitation plan may at any time file a motion with the court to request review and modification of an original or amended visitation plan.

History of Fam. Code §263.108: Acts 2013, 83rd Leg., ch. 191, §4, eff. Sept. 1, 2013.

FAM §263.109. COURT IMPLEMENTATION OF VISITATION PLAN

(a) After reviewing an original or amended visitation plan, the court shall render an order regarding a parent's visitation with a child that the court determines appropriate.

(b) If the court finds that visitation between a child and a parent is not in the child's best interest, the court shall render an order that:

(1) states the reasons for finding that visitation is not in the child's best interest; and

(2) outlines specific steps the parent must take to be allowed to have visitation with the child.

(c) If the order regarding visitation between a child and a parent requires supervised visitation to protect the health and safety of the child, the order must outline specific steps the parent must take to have the level of supervision reduced.

History of Fam. Code §263.109: Acts 2013, 83rd Leg., ch. 191, §4, eff. Sept. 1, 2013.

Sections 263.110-263.200 reserved for expansion

SUBCHAPTER C. STATUS HEARING

FAM §263.201. STATUS HEARING; TIME

(a) Not later than the 60th day after the date the court renders a temporary order appointing the department as temporary managing conservator of a child, the court shall hold a status hearing to review the child's status and the service plan developed for the child.

(b) A status hearing is not required if the court holds an initial permanency hearing under Section 262.2015 and makes findings required by Section 263.202 before the date a status hearing is required by this section.

(c) The court shall require each parent, alleged father, or relative of the child before the court to submit the proposed child placement resources form provided under Section 261.307 at the status hearing, if the form has not previously been submitted.

History of Fam. Code §263.201: Acts 1995, 74th Leg., ch. 20, §1, eff. Apr. 20, 1995. Amended by Acts 1997, 75th Leg., ch. 600, §8 (eff. Jan. 1, 1998), ch. 603, §3 (eff. Jan. 1, 1998), ch. 1022, §81 (eff. Jan. 1, 1998); Acts 1999, 76th Leg., ch. 1150, §26 (eff. Sept. 1, 1999), ch. 1390, §45 (eff. Sept. 1, 1999); Acts 2005, 79th Leg., ch. 268, §1.37(a), eff. Nov. 1, 2005; Acts 2011, 82nd Leg., ch. 1071, §6, eff. Sept. 1, 2011. Source: Former Fam. Code §18.07(a).

ANNOTATIONS

In re T.T.F., 331 S.W.3d 461, 479-80 (Tex.App.—Fort Worth 2010, no pet.). Family Code "§§263.201 and 263.305 do not contain remedies for the failure to timely hold a status hearing or a subsequent permanency hearing, and [Fam. Code] §263.304(b) specifically provides that any party to the suit may compel the trial court, by mandamus, to comply with its obligation to conduct an initial permanency hearing within the statutory deadline. Thus, under ... §263.304(b) ..., [mother] could have sought to enforce her procedural right to a timely status hearing, a timely initial permanency hearing, and timely subsequent permanency hearings by mandamus. [A parent] cannot complain on appeal that she was denied procedural due process in the trial court when she did not seek to enforce her procedural rights in a timely manner...."

FAM §263.202. STATUS HEARING; FINDINGS

(a) If all persons entitled to citation and notice of a status hearing under this chapter were not served, the court shall make findings as to whether:

(1) the department has exercised due diligence to locate all necessary persons, including an alleged father of the child, regardless of whether the alleged father is registered with the registry of paternity under Section 160.402; and

(2) the child and each parent, alleged father, or relative of the child before the court have furnished to the department all available information necessary to locate an absent parent, alleged father, or relative of the child through exercise of due diligence.

(b) Except as otherwise provided by this subchapter, a status hearing shall be limited to matters related to the contents and execution of the service plan filed with the court. The court shall review the service plan that the department filed under this chapter for reasonableness, accuracy, and compliance with requirements of court orders and make findings as to whether:

(1) a plan that has the goal of returning the child to the child's parents adequately ensures that reasonable efforts are made to enable the child's parents to provide a safe environment for the child;

(2) the child's parents have reviewed and understand the plan and have been advised that unless the parents are willing and able to provide the child with a safe environment, even with the assistance of a service plan, within the reasonable period of time specified in the plan, the parents' parental and custodial duties and rights may be subject to restriction or to termination under this code or the child may not be returned to the parents;

(3) the plan is reasonably tailored to address any specific issues identified by the department; and

(4) the child's parents and the representative of the department have signed the plan.

(b-1) After reviewing the service plan and making any necessary modifications, the court shall incorporate the service plan into the orders of the court and may render additional appropriate orders to implement or require compliance with the plan.

(c), (d) Repealed by Acts 2011, 82nd Leg., ch. 1071, §9, eff. Sept. 1, 2011.

(e) At the status hearing, the court shall make a finding as to whether the court has identified the individual who has the right to consent for the child under Section 266.003.

(f) The court shall review the report filed by the department under Section 263.007 and inquire into the sufficiency of the department's efforts to identify, locate, and provide information to each adult described by Section 262.1095(a). The court shall order the department to make further efforts to identify, locate, and provide information to each adult described by Section 262.1095(a) if the court determines that the department's efforts have not been sufficient.

(f-1) The court shall ask all parties present at the status hearing whether the child or the child's family has a Native American heritage and identify any Native American tribe with which the child may be associated.

(g) The court shall give the child's parents an opportunity to comment on the service plan.

(h) If a proposed child placement resources form as described by Section 261.307 has not been submitted, the court shall require each parent, alleged father, or other person to whom the department is required to provide a form to submit a completed form.

History of Fam. Code §263.202: Acts 1995, 74th Leg., ch. 20, §1, eff. Apr. 20, 1995. Amended by Acts 1995, 74th Leg., ch. 751, §111, eff. Sept. 1, 1995; Acts 1999, 76th Leg., ch. 1150, §27 (eff. Sept. 1, 1999), ch. 1390, §46 (eff. Sept. 1, 1999); Acts 2001, 77th Leg., ch. 306, §2, eff. Sept. 1, 2001; Acts 2005, 79th Leg., ch. 268, §§1.38(b), 1.39, eff. Sept. 1, 2005; Acts 2011, 82nd Leg., ch. 1071, §§7, 9, eff. Sept. 1, 2011; Acts 2015, 84th Leg., ch. 1, §1.177 (eff. Apr. 2, 2015), ch. 697, §2 (eff. Sept. 1, 2015). Source: Former Fam. Code §18.07(b)-(d).

FAM §263.203. APPOINTMENT OF ATTORNEY AD LITEM; ADMONISHMENTS

(a) The court shall advise the parties of the provisions regarding the mandatory appointment of an attorney ad litem under Subchapter A, Chapter 107, and shall appoint an attorney ad litem to represent the interests of any person eligible if the appointment is required by that subchapter.

(b) The court shall advise the parties that progress under the service plan will be reviewed at all subsequent hearings, including a review of whether the parties have acquired or learned any specific skills or knowledge stated in the plan.

History of Fam. Code §263.203: Acts 2011, 82nd Leg., ch. 1071, §8, eff. Sept. 1, 2011.

Sections 263.204-263.300 reserved for expansion

SUBCHAPTER D. PERMANENCY HEARINGS

FAM §263.301. RENUMBERED

Renumbered as §263.0021 by Acts 2015, 84th Leg., ch. 944, §28, eff. Sept. 1, 2015.

FAM §263.302. CHILD'S ATTENDANCE AT HEARING

The child shall attend each permanency hearing unless the court specifically excuses the child's attendance. A child committed to the Texas Juvenile Justice Department may attend a permanency hearing in person, by telephone, or by videoconference. The court shall consult with the child in a developmentally appropriate manner regarding the child's permanency plan, if the child is four years of age or older and if the court determines it is in the best interest of the child. Failure by the child to attend a hearing does not affect the validity of an order rendered at the hearing.

History of Fam. Code §263.302: Acts 1995, 74th Leg., ch. 20, §1, eff. Apr. 20, 1995. Amended by Acts 1997, 75th Leg., ch. 600, §11 (eff. Jan. 1, 1998), ch. 603, §6 (eff. Jan. 1, 1998), ch. 1022, §84 (eff. Jan. 1, 1998); Acts 2007, 80th Leg., ch. 1304, §1, eff. June 15, 2007; Acts 2009, 81st Leg., ch. 108, §6, eff. May 23, 2009; Acts 2015, 84th Leg., ch. 734, §85, eff. Sept. 1, 2015. Source: Former Fam. Code §18.14.

FAM §263.3025. PERMANENCY PLAN

(a) The department shall prepare a permanency plan for a child for whom the department has been appointed temporary managing conservator. The department shall give a copy of the plan to each person entitled to notice under Section 263.0021(b) not later than the 10th day before the date of the child's first permanency hearing.

(b) In addition to the requirements of the department rules governing permanency planning, the permanency plan must contain the information required to be included in a permanency progress report under Section 263.303.

(c) The department shall modify the permanency plan for a child as required by the circumstances and needs of the child.

(d) In accordance with department rules, a child's permanency plan must include concurrent permanency goals consisting of a primary permanency goal and at least one alternate permanency goal.

History of Fam. Code §263.3025: Acts 1997, 75th Leg., ch. 600, §12 (eff. Jan. 1, 1998), ch. 603, §7 (eff. Jan. 1, 1998), ch. 1022, §85 (eff. Jan. 1, 1998). Amended by Acts 2001, 77th Leg., ch. 809, §5, eff. Sept. 1, 2001; Acts 2005, 79th Leg., ch. 620, §3, eff. Sept. 1, 2005; Acts 2009, 81st Leg., ch. 1372, §4, eff. June 19, 2009; Acts 2015, 84th Leg., ch. 944, §33, eff. Sept. 1, 2015.

See also 40 T.A.C. §§700.1201-700.1208.

FAM §263.3026. PERMANENCY GOALS; LIMITATION

(a) The department's permanency plan for a child may include as a goal:

(1) the reunification of the child with a parent or other individual from whom the child was removed;

(2) the termination of parental rights and adoption of the child by a relative or other suitable individual;

(3) the award of permanent managing conservatorship of the child to a relative or other suitable individual; or

(4) another planned, permanent living arrangement for the child.

(b) If the goal of the department's permanency plan for a child is to find another planned, permanent living arrangement for the child, the department shall document that there is a compelling reason why the other permanency goals identified in Subsection (a) are not in the child's best interest.

History of Fam. Code §263.3026: Acts 2009, 81st Leg., ch. 1372, §5, eff. June 19, 2009.

FAM §263.303. PERMANENCY PROGRESS REPORT BEFORE FINAL ORDER

(a) Not later than the 10th day before the date set for each permanency hearing before a final order is rendered, the department shall file with the court and provide to each party, the child's attorney ad litem, the child's guardian ad litem, and the child's volunteer advocate a permanency progress report unless the court orders a different period for providing the report.

(b) The permanency progress report must contain:

(1) information necessary for the court to conduct the permanency hearing and make its findings and determinations under Section 263.306;

(2) information on significant events, as defined by Section 264.018; and

(3) any additional information the department determines is appropriate or that is requested by the court and relevant to the court's findings and determinations under Section 263.306.

(c) A parent whose parental rights are the subject of a suit affecting the parent-child relationship, the attorney for that parent, or the child's attorney ad litem or guardian ad litem may file a response to the department's report filed under this section. A response must be filed not later than the third day before the date of the hearing.

History of Fam. Code §263.303: Acts 1995, 74th Leg., ch. 20, §1, eff. Apr. 20, 1995. Amended by Acts 1995, 74th Leg., ch. 751, §112, eff. Sept. 1, 1995; Acts 1997, 75th Leg., ch. 600, §13 (eff. Jan. 1, 1998), ch. 603, §8 (eff. Jan. 1, 1998), ch. 1022, §86 (eff. Jan. 1, 1998); Acts 2005, 79th Leg., ch. 172, §24, eff. Sept. 1, 2005; Acts 2009, 81st Leg., ch. 108, §7 (eff. May 23, 2009), ch. 1372, §6 (eff. June 19, 2009); Acts 2015, 84th Leg., ch. 1, §1.179 (eff. Apr. 2, 2015), ch. 944, §34 (eff. Sept. 1, 2015). Source: Former Fam. Code §18.10(b), (c).

FAM §263.304. INITIAL PERMANENCY HEARING; TIME

(a) Not later than the 180th day after the date the court renders a temporary order appointing the department as temporary managing conservator of a child, the court shall hold a permanency hearing to review the status of, and permanency plan for, the child to ensure that a final order consistent with that permanency plan is rendered before the date for dismissal of the suit under this chapter.

(b) The court shall set a final hearing under this chapter on a date that allows the court to render a final order before the date for dismissal of the suit under this chapter. Any party to the suit or an attorney ad litem for the child may seek a writ of mandamus to compel the court to comply with the duties imposed by this subsection.

History of Fam. Code §263.304: Acts 1995, 74th Leg., ch. 20, §1, eff. Apr. 20, 1995. Amended by Acts 1995, 74th Leg., ch. 751, §113, eff. Sept. 1, 1995; Acts 1997, 75th Leg., ch. 600, §14 (eff. Jan. 1, 1998), ch. 603, §9 (eff. Jan. 1, 1998), ch. 1022, §87 (eff. Jan. 1, 1998); Acts 2001, 77th Leg., ch. 1090, §7, eff. Sept. 1, 2001. Source: Former Fam. Code §18.08(a).

ANNOTATIONS

In re T.T.F., 331 S.W.3d 461, 479-80 (Tex.App.—Fort Worth 2010, no pet.). See annotation under Family Code §263.201, p. 942.

FAM §263.305. SUBSEQUENT PERMANENCY HEARINGS

A subsequent permanency hearing before entry of a final order shall be held not later than the 120th day after the date of the last permanency hearing in the suit. For good cause shown or on the court's own motion, the court may order more frequent hearings.

History of Fam. Code §263.305: Acts 1995, 74th Leg., ch. 20, §1, eff. Apr. 20, 1995. Amended by Acts 1997, 75th Leg., ch. 600, §15 (eff. Jan. 1, 1998), ch. 603, §10 (eff. Jan. 1, 1998), ch. 1022, §88 (eff. Jan. 1, 1998). Source: Former Fam. Code §18.10(a).

ANNOTATIONS

In re T.T.F., 331 S.W.3d 461, 479-80 (Tex.App.—Fort Worth 2010, no pet.). See annotation under Family Code §263.201, p. 942.

A FAM §263.306. PERMANENCY HEARINGS BEFORE FINAL ORDER

(a) Repealed by Acts 2015, 84th Leg., ch. 944, §86(17), eff. Sept. 1, 2015; S.B. 1488, §7.009(c), 85th Leg., eff. Sept. 1, 2017.

[~~(a)~~] [~~At each permanency hearing the court shall:~~]

[~~(1)~~] [~~identify all persons or parties present at the hearing or those given notice but failing to appear;~~]

[~~(2)~~] [~~review the efforts of the department in:~~]

[~~(A)~~] [~~attempting to locate all necessary persons;~~]

[~~(B)~~] [~~requesting service of citation; and~~]

[~~(C)~~] [~~obtaining the assistance of a parent in providing information necessary to locate an absent parent, alleged father, or relative of the child;~~]

[~~(3)~~] [~~review the efforts of each custodial parent, alleged father, or relative of the child before the court in providing information necessary to locate another absent parent, alleged father, or relative of the child;~~]

[~~(4)~~] [~~review any visitation plan or amended plan required under Section 263.107 and render any orders for visitation the court determines necessary;~~]

[~~(5)~~] [~~return the child to the parent or parents if the child's parent or parents are willing and able to provide the child with a safe environment and the return of the child is in the child's best interest;~~]

[~~(6)~~] [~~place the child with a person or entity, other than a parent, entitled to service under Chapter 102 if the person or entity is willing and able to provide the child with a safe environment and the placement of the child is in the child's best interest;~~]

[~~(7)~~] [~~evaluate the department's efforts to identify relatives who could provide the child with a safe envi-~~

~~ronment, if the child is not returned to a parent or another person or entity entitled to service under Chapter 102;~~]

[~~(8)~~] [~~evaluate the parties' compliance with temporary orders and the service plan;~~]

[~~(9)~~] [~~ask all parties present whether the child or the child's family has a Native American heritage and identify any Native American tribe with which the child may be associated;~~]

[~~(10)~~] [~~identify an education decision-maker for the child if one has not previously been identified;~~]

[~~(11)~~] [~~review the medical care provided to the child as required by Section 266.007;~~]

[~~(12)~~] [~~ensure the child has been provided the opportunity, in a developmentally appropriate manner, to express the child's opinion on the medical care provided;~~]

[~~(13)~~] [~~for a child receiving psychotropic medication, determine whether the child:~~]

[~~(A)~~] [~~has been provided appropriate psychosocial therapies, behavior strategies, and other non-pharmacological interventions; and~~]

[~~(B)~~] [~~has been seen by the prescribing physician, physician assistant, or advanced practice nurse at least once every 90 days for purposes of the review required by Section 266.011;~~]

[~~(14)~~] [~~determine whether:~~]

[~~(A)~~] [~~the child continues to need substitute care;~~]

[~~(B)~~] [~~the child's current placement is appropriate for meeting the child's needs, including with respect to a child who has been placed outside of the state, whether that placement continues to be in the best interest of the child; and~~]

[~~(C)~~] [~~other plans or services are needed to meet the child's special needs or circumstances;~~]

[~~(15)~~] [~~if the child is placed in institutional care, determine whether efforts have been made to ensure placement of the child in the least restrictive environment consistent with the best interest and special needs of the child;~~]

[~~(16)~~] [~~if the child is 16 years of age or older, order services that are needed to assist the child in making the transition from substitute care to independent living if the services are available in the community;~~]

[~~(17)~~] [~~determine plans, services, and further temporary orders necessary to ensure that a final order is rendered before the date for dismissal of the suit under this chapter;~~]

[~~(18)~~] [~~if the child is committed to the Texas Juvenile Justice Department or released under supervision by the Texas Juvenile Justice Department, determine whether the child's needs for treatment, rehabilitation, and education are being met; and~~]

[~~(19)~~] [~~determine the date for dismissal of the suit under this chapter and give notice in open court to all parties of:~~]

[~~(A)~~] [~~the dismissal date;~~]

[~~(B)~~] [~~the date of the next permanency hearing; and~~]

[~~(C)~~] [~~the date the suit is set for trial.~~]

(a-1) At each permanency hearing before a final order is rendered, the court shall:

(1) identify all persons and parties present at the hearing;

(2) review the efforts of the department or other agency in:

(A) locating and requesting service of citation on all persons entitled to service of citation under Section 102.009; and

(B) obtaining the assistance of a parent in providing information necessary to locate an absent parent, alleged father, or relative of the child;

(3) ask all parties present whether the child or the child's family has a Native American heritage and identify any Native American tribe with which the child may be associated;

(4) review the extent of the parties' compliance with temporary orders and the service plan and the extent to which progress has been made toward alleviating or mitigating the causes necessitating the placement of the child in foster care;

(5) [~~(4)~~] review the permanency progress report to determine:

(A) the safety and well-being of the child and whether the child's needs, including any medical or special needs, are being adequately addressed;

(B) the continuing necessity and appropriateness of the placement of the child, including with respect to a child who has been placed outside of this state, whether the placement continues to be in the best interest of the child;

(C) the appropriateness of the primary and alternative permanency goals for the child developed in accordance with department rule and whether the department has made reasonable efforts to finalize the permanency plan, including the concurrent permanency goals, in effect for the child;

(D) whether the child has been provided the opportunity, in a developmentally appropriate manner, to express the child's opinion on any medical care provided;

(E) for a child receiving psychotropic medication, whether the child:

(i) has been provided appropriate nonpharmacological interventions, therapies, or strategies to meet the child's needs; or

(ii) has been seen by the prescribing physician, physician assistant, or advanced practice nurse at least once every 90 days;

(F) whether an education decision-maker for the child has been identified, the child's education needs and goals have been identified and addressed, and there have been major changes in the child's school performance or there have been serious disciplinary events;

(G) for a child 14 years of age or older, whether services that are needed to assist the child in transitioning from substitute care to independent living are available in the child's community; and

(H) for a child whose permanency goal is another planned permanent living arrangement:

(i) the desired permanency outcome for the child, by asking the child; [and]

(ii) whether, as of the date of the hearing, another planned permanent living arrangement is the best permanency plan for the child and, if so, provide compelling reasons why it continues to not be in the best interest of the child to:

(a) return home;

(b) be placed for adoption;

(c) be placed with a legal guardian; or

(d) be placed with a fit and willing relative;

(iii) whether the department has conducted an independent living skills assessment under Section 264.121(a-3);

(iv) whether the department has addressed the goals identified in the child's permanency plan, including the child's housing plan, and the results of the independent living skills assessment;

(v) if the youth is 16 years of age or older, whether there is evidence that the department has provided the youth with the documents and information listed in Section 264.121(e); and

(vi) if the youth is 18 years of age or older or has had the disabilities of minority removed, whether there is evidence that the department has provided the youth with the documents and information listed in Section 264.121(e-1);

(6) [(5)] determine whether to return the child to the child's parents if the child's parents are willing and able to provide the child with a safe environment and the return of the child is in the child's best interest;

(7) [(6)] estimate a likely date by which the child may be returned to and safely maintained in the child's home, placed for adoption, or placed in permanent managing conservatorship; and

(8) [(7)] announce in open court the dismissal date and the date of any upcoming hearings.

(b) Repealed by Acts 2015, 84th Leg., ch. 944, §86(18), eff. Sept. 1, 2015.

(c) In addition to the requirements of Subsection (a-1) [(a)], at each permanency hearing before a final order is rendered the court shall review the department's efforts to ensure that the child has regular, ongoing opportunities to engage in age-appropriate normalcy activities, including activities not listed in the child's service plan.

History of Fam. Code §263.306: Acts 1995, 74th Leg., ch. 20, §1, eff. Apr. 20, 1995. Amended by Acts 1995, 74th Leg., ch. 751, §114, eff. Sept. 1, 1995; Acts 1997, 75th Leg., ch. 600, §16 (eff. Jan. 1, 1998), ch. 603, §11 (eff. Jan. 1, 1998), ch. 1022, §89 (eff. Jan. 1, 1998); Acts 1999, 76th Leg., ch. 1390, §47, eff. Sept. 1, 1999; Acts 2001, 77th Leg., ch. 306, §3 (eff. Sept. 1, 2001), ch. 849, §7 (eff. Sept. 1, 2001); Acts 2009, 81st Leg., ch. 108, §8 (eff. May 23, 2009), ch. 1372, §7 (eff. June 19, 2009); Acts 2013, 83rd Leg., ch. 191, §5 (eff. Sept. 1, 2013), ch. 204, §4 (eff. Sept. 1, 2013), ch. 688, §5 (eff. Sept. 1, 2013); Acts 2015, 84th Leg., ch. 1, §1.180 (eff. Apr. 2, 2015), ch. 262, §2 (eff. Sept. 1, 2015), ch. 697, §3 (eff. Sept. 1, 2015), ch. 944, §§35, 36, 86(17), (18) (eff. Sept. 1, 2015); S.B. 1488, §7.009, 85th Leg., eff. Sept. 1, 2017; S.B. 1758, §3, 85th Leg., eff. Sept. 1, 2017. Source: Former Fam. Code §18.09(a), (b).

FAM §263.307. FACTORS IN DETERMINING BEST INTEREST OF CHILD

(a) In considering the factors established by this section, the prompt and permanent placement of the child in a safe environment is presumed to be in the child's best interest.

(b) The following factors should be considered by the court and the department in determining whether the child's parents are willing and able to provide the child with a safe environment:

(1) the child's age and physical and mental vulnerabilities;

(2) the frequency and nature of out-of-home placements;

(3) the magnitude, frequency, and circumstances of the harm to the child;

(4) whether the child has been the victim of repeated harm after the initial report and intervention by the department;

(5) whether the child is fearful of living in or returning to the child's home;

(6) the results of psychiatric, psychological, or developmental evaluations of the child, the child's parents, other family members, or others who have access to the child's home;

(7) whether there is a history of abusive or assaultive conduct by the child's family or others who have access to the child's home;

(8) whether there is a history of substance abuse by the child's family or others who have access to the child's home;

(9) whether the perpetrator of the harm to the child is identified;

(10) the willingness and ability of the child's family to seek out, accept, and complete counseling services and to cooperate with and facilitate an appropriate agency's close supervision;

(11) the willingness and ability of the child's family to effect positive environmental and personal changes within a reasonable period of time;

(12) whether the child's family demonstrates adequate parenting skills, including providing the child and other children under the family's care with:

(A) minimally adequate health and nutritional care;

(B) care, nurturance, and appropriate discipline consistent with the child's physical and psychological development;

(C) guidance and supervision consistent with the child's safety;

(D) a safe physical home environment;

(E) protection from repeated exposure to violence even though the violence may not be directed at the child; and

(F) an understanding of the child's needs and capabilities; and

(13) whether an adequate social support system consisting of an extended family and friends is available to the child.

(c) In the case of a child 16 years of age or older, the following guidelines should be considered by the court in determining whether to adopt the permanency plan submitted by the department:

(1) whether the permanency plan submitted to the court includes the services planned for the child to make the transition from foster care to independent living; and

(2) whether this transition is in the best interest of the child.

History of Fam. Code §263.307: Acts 1995, 74th Leg., ch. 20, §1, eff. Apr. 20, 1995. Amended by Acts 2015, 84th Leg., ch. 1, §1.181, eff. Apr. 2, 2015. Source: Former Fam. Code §18.15.

ANNOTATIONS

In re J.I.T.P., 99 S.W.3d 841, 848 (Tex.App.—Houston [14th Dist.] 2003, no pet.). "We do not believe ... that the State must prove all 13 factors in §263.307 to determine the best interest of the child."

FAM §§263.308, 263.309. REPEALED

Repealed by Acts 1997, 75th Leg., ch. 603, §13, eff. Jan. 1, 1998; Acts 1997, 75th Leg., ch. 1022, §104(a), eff. Sept. 1, 1997.

Sections 263.310-263.400 blank

Subchapter E. Final Order for Child Under Department Care

Ⓐ FAM §263.401. DISMISSAL AFTER ONE YEAR; NEW TRIALS; EXTENSION

In 2017, two bills amended §263.401. The amended text from H.B. 7, §27, 85th Leg., eff. Sept. 1, 2017, is effective for SAPCRs filed on or after Sept. 1, 2017. SAPCRs filed before Sept. 1, 2017, are governed by the former law in effect at that time. The amended text from S.B. 11, §12, 85th Leg., eff. Sept. 1, 2017, is effective for SAPCRs pending or filed on or after Sept. 1, 2017. SAPCRs in which a final order is rendered before Sept. 1, 2017, are governed by the former law in effect at that time.

(a) Unless the court has commenced the trial on the merits or granted an extension under Subsection (b) or (b-1), on the first Monday after the first anniversary of the date the court rendered a temporary order appointing the department as temporary managing conservator, the court's jurisdiction over [~~court shall dismiss~~] the suit affecting the parent-child relationship filed by the department that requests termination

of the parent-child relationship or requests that the department be named conservator of the child is terminated and the suit is automatically dismissed without a court order. Not later than the 60th day before the day the suit is automatically dismissed, the court shall notify all parties to the suit of the automatic dismissal date.

(b) Unless the court has commenced the trial on the merits, the court may not retain the suit on the court's docket after the time described by Subsection (a) unless the court finds that extraordinary circumstances necessitate the child remaining in the temporary managing conservatorship of the department and that continuing the appointment of the department as temporary managing conservator is in the best interest of the child. If the court makes those findings, the court may retain the suit on the court's docket for a period not to exceed 180 days after the time described by Subsection (a). If the court retains the suit on the court's docket, the court shall render an order in which the court:

(1) schedules the new date on which the suit will be automatically dismissed if the trial on the merits has not commenced, which date must be not later than the 180th day after the time described by Subsection (a);

(2) makes further temporary orders for the safety and welfare of the child as necessary to avoid further delay in resolving the suit; and

(3) sets the trial on the merits on a date not later than the date specified under Subdivision (1).

(b-1) If, after commencement of the initial trial on the merits within the time required by Subsection (a) or (b), the court grants a motion for a new trial or mistrial, or the case is remanded to the court by an appellate court following an appeal of the court's final order, the court shall retain the suit on the court's docket and render an order in which the court:

(1) schedules a new date on which the suit will be automatically dismissed if the new trial has not commenced, which must be a date not later than the 180th day after the date on which:

(A) the motion for a new trial or mistrial is granted; or

(B) the appellate court remanded the case;

(2) makes further temporary orders for the safety and welfare of the child as necessary to avoid further delay in resolving the suit; and

(3) sets the new trial on the merits for a date not later than the date specified under Subdivision (1).

(c) If the court grants an extension under Subsection (b) or (b-1) but does not commence the trial on the merits before the dismissal date, the court's jurisdiction over [~~court shall dismiss~~] the suit is terminated and the suit is automatically dismissed without a court order. The court may not grant an additional extension that extends the suit beyond the required date for dismissal under Subsection (b) or (b-1), as applicable.

(d) Repealed by Acts 2007, 80th Leg., ch. 866, §5, eff. June 15, 2007.

History of Fam. Code §263.401: Acts 1997, 75th Leg., ch. 600, §17 (eff. Sept. 1, 1997), ch. 603, §12 (eff. Jan. 1, 1998), ch. 1022, §90 (eff. Jan. 1, 1998). Amended by Acts 2001, 77th Leg., ch. 1090, §8, eff. Sept. 1, 2001; Acts 2005, 79th Leg., ch. 268, §1.40, eff. Sept. 1, 2005; Acts 2007, 80th Leg., ch. 866, §§2, 5, eff. June 15, 2007; Acts 2015, 84th Leg., ch. 944, §§37, 38, eff. Sept. 1, 2015; H.B. 7, §27, 85th Leg., eff. Sept. 1, 2017; S.B. 11, §12, 85th Leg., eff. Sept. 1, 2017.

ANNOTATIONS

In re TDFPS, 210 S.W.3d 609, 612 (Tex.2006). "The Department argues that the January 23, 2003 ex parte order that gave the Department temporary conservatorship did not trigger the §263.401 time period. [¶] The Department obtained temporary managing conservatorship by order of the trial court on January 23, 2003. Thus, the statutory time period started on January 23rd.... Nothing in the statute excludes the Department's 14-day conservatorship obtained through the ex parte order from the calculation of the dismissal deadline in §263.401. *At 613-14:* Now we must determine whether the court of appeals correctly concluded that [mother and great-grandmother] had no adequate remedy by appeal and were therefore entitled to mandamus relief. [¶] Because the trial was underway when the dismissal deadline passed and because physical possession of the children had already transferred to the Department when the petition for writ of mandamus was filed with the court of appeals, we conclude that an accelerated appeal provided an adequate remedy in this case. ... Impending transfer of physical possession of the children or a trial court's unreasonable delay in entering a final decree might alter this conclusion, but this record raises neither concern."

In re D.S., 455 S.W.3d 750, 753 (Tex.App.—Amarillo 2015, no pet.). "[S]ection 263.401[, which turns on whether the trial on the merits has commenced,] requires more than a putative call of the case and an immediate recess in order to comply with the statute. We would suggest that at a minimum the par-

ties should be called upon to make their respective announcements and the trial court should ascertain whether there are any preliminary matters to be taken up."

In re C.M.D., No. 02-12-00237-CV (Tex.App.—Fort Worth 2012, no pet.) (memo op.; 11-29-12). "[T]he family code provisions that expedite termination proceedings must yield to due process. The family code's dismissal deadline must yield to Mother's and Father's constitutional due process right to participate in the termination trial after receiving constitutionally adequate notice."

In re T.T.F., 331 S.W.3d 461, 475 (Tex.App.—Fort Worth 2010, no pet.). "[S]ection 263.401 does not require the trial court to conduct a hearing before granting an extension. Thus, we must presume that the legislature did not intend to require a hearing before the trial court retains a case on its docket pursuant to §263.401(b). [Further,] §263.401(b) does not require a written extension order[;] an oral rendition is sufficient." *See also* ***Phillips v. TDPRS***, 149 S.W.3d 814, 817 (Tex.App.—Eastland 2004, no pet.) (oral rendition is sufficient under §263.401(b)).

In re K.Y., 273 S.W.3d 703, 708 (Tex.App.—Houston [14th Dist.] 2008, no pet.). "When DFPS files a [SAPCR], §263.401 allows a 12 month period in which to prosecute the suit, with a single 180 day extension. If a final order is not rendered within this time frame, the suit must be dismissed without prejudice. Once a suit is dismissed without prejudice, DFPS may refile the suit asserting the same grounds for termination originally alleged. However, DFPS cannot maintain temporary custody of the children without alleging new facts to support the termination. If a subsequent petition alleges new facts to support the termination, DFPS can maintain temporary custody." *See also* ***In re T.M.***, 33 S.W.3d 341, 347 (Tex.App.—Amarillo 2000, no pet.) (after dismissal under §263.401, TDPRS can refile suit asserting same grounds but must submit new facts to justify termination).

A FAM §263.402. LIMIT ON EXTENSION[; WAIVER]

The amended text in §263.402 is effective for service plans filed for a full adversary hearing held under Fam. Code §262.201 or a status hearing held under Fam. Code ch. 263 on or after Jan. 1, 2018. A hearing held before Jan. 1, 2018, is governed by the former law in effect at that time. Except as provided above, the amended text in §263.402 is effective for SAPCRs filed on or after Sept. 1, 2017. SAPCRs filed before Sept. 1, 2017, are governed by the former law in effect at that time.

[(a)] The parties to a suit under this chapter may not extend the deadlines set by the court under this subchapter by agreement or otherwise.

[(b)] [A party to a suit under this chapter who fails to make a timely motion to dismiss the suit under this subchapter waives the right to object to the court's failure to dismiss the suit. A motion to dismiss under this subsection is timely if the motion is made before the trial on the merits commences.]

History of Fam. Code §263.402: Acts 2001, 77th Leg., ch. 1090, §9, eff. Sept. 1, 2001. Amended by Acts 2007, 80th Leg., ch. 866, §3, eff. June 15, 2007; H.B. 7, §28, 85th Leg., eff. Sept. 1, 2017; S.B. 11, §13, 85th Leg., eff. Sept. 1, 2017.

A FAM §263.403. MONITORED RETURN OF CHILD TO PARENT

The amended text in §263.403 is effective for service plans filed for a full adversary hearing held under Fam. Code §262.201 or a status hearing held under Fam. Code ch. 263 on or after Jan. 1, 2018. A hearing held before Jan. 1, 2018, is governed by the former law in effect at that time. Except as provided above, the amended text in §263.403 is effective for SAPCRs filed on or after Sept. 1, 2017. SAPCRs filed before Sept. 1, 2017, are governed by the former law in effect at that time.

(a) Notwithstanding Section 263.401, the court may retain jurisdiction and not dismiss the suit or render a final order as required by that section if the court renders a temporary order that:

(1) finds that retaining jurisdiction under this section is in the best interest of the child;

(2) orders the department to:

(A) return the child to the child's parent; or

(B) transition the child, according to a schedule determined by the department or court, from substitute care to the parent while the parent completes the remaining requirements imposed under a service plan and specified in the temporary order that are necessary for the child's return;

(3) orders the department to continue to serve as temporary managing conservator of the child; and

(4) orders the department to monitor the child's placement to ensure that the child is in a safe environment.

(a-1) Unless the court has granted an extension under Section 263.401(b), the department or the parent

may request the court to retain jurisdiction for an additional six months as necessary for a parent to complete the remaining requirements in a service plan and specified in the temporary order that are mandatory for the child's return.

(b) If the court renders an order under this section, the court shall:

(1) include in the order specific findings regarding the grounds for the order; and

(2) schedule a new date, not later than the 180th day after the date the temporary order is rendered, for dismissal of the suit unless a trial on the merits has commenced.

(c) If before the dismissal of the suit or the commencement of the trial on the merits a child placed with a parent under this section must be moved from that home by the department or the court renders a temporary order terminating the transition order issued under Subsection (a)(2)(B) [~~before the dismissal of the suit or the commencement of the trial on the merits~~], the court shall, at the time of the move or order, schedule a new date for dismissal of the suit [~~unless a trial on the merits has commenced~~]. The new dismissal date may not be later than the original dismissal date established under Section 263.401 or the 180th day after the date the child is moved or the order is rendered under this subsection, whichever date is later.

(d) If the court renders an order under this section, the court must include in the order specific findings regarding the grounds for the order.

History of Fam. Code §263.403: Acts 1997, 75th Leg., ch. 600, §17 (eff. Sept. 1, 1997), ch. 603, §12 (eff. Jan. 1, 1997), ch. 1022, §90 (eff. Jan. 1, 1997). Amended by Acts 1999, 76th Leg., ch. 1390, §48, eff. Sept. 1, 1999. Renumbered from §263.402 by Acts 2001, 77th Leg., ch. 1090, §9, eff. Sept. 1, 2001. Amended by Acts 2007, 80th Leg., ch. 866, §4, eff. June 15, 2007; H.B. 7, §29, 85th Leg., eff. Sept. 1, 2017.

ANNOTATIONS

In re Neal, 4 S.W.3d 443, 445 (Tex.App.—Houston [1st Dist.] 1999, orig. proceeding). "There is no limit on the number of temporary orders that may be rendered under [Fam. Code] §263.402(a) [now §263.403(a)]. Any de facto extension in the 'one year final order or dismiss' rule of [Fam. Code] §263.401(a) that results from a §263.402(a) temporary order does not prevent a one-time extension under §263.401(b). *At 447:* Sections 263.401 and 263.402 represent a scheme adopted by the 1997 Legislature to ensure that children would remain under the temporary care of DPRS for no longer than one year, with an extension not to exceed 180 days beyond that under the two exceptions outlined above."

FAM §263.404. FINAL ORDER APPOINTING DEPARTMENT AS MANAGING CONSERVATOR WITHOUT TERMINATING PARENTAL RIGHTS

(a) The court may render a final order appointing the department as managing conservator of the child without terminating the rights of the parent of the child if the court finds that:

(1) appointment of a parent as managing conservator would not be in the best interest of the child because the appointment would significantly impair the child's physical health or emotional development; and

(2) it would not be in the best interest of the child to appoint a relative of the child or another person as managing conservator.

(b) In determining whether the department should be appointed as managing conservator of the child without terminating the rights of a parent of the child, the court shall take the following factors into consideration:

(1) that the child will reach 18 years of age in not less than three years;

(2) that the child is 12 years of age or older and has expressed a strong desire against termination or has continuously expressed a strong desire against being adopted; and

(3) the needs and desires of the child.

History of Fam. Code §263.404: Acts 1997, 75th Leg., ch. 600, §17 (eff. Sept. 1, 1997), ch. 603, §12 (eff. Jan. 1, 1998), ch. 1022, §90 (eff. Jan. 1, 1998). Renumbered from §263.403 by Acts 2001, 77th Leg., ch. 1090, §9, eff. Sept. 1, 2001. Amended by Acts 2015, 84th Leg., ch. 944, §39, eff. Sept. 1, 2015.

E FAM §263.4041. VERIFICATION OF TRANSITION PLAN

Notwithstanding Section 263.401, for a suit involving a child who is 14 years of age or older and whose permanency goal is another planned permanent living arrangement, the court shall verify that:

(1) the department has conducted an independent living skills assessment for the child as provided under Section 264.121(a-3);

(2) the department has addressed the goals identified in the child's permanency plan, including the child's housing plan, and the results of the independent living skills assessment;

(3) if the youth is 16 years of age or older, there is evidence that the department has provided the youth with the documents and information listed in Section 264.121(e); and

(4) if the youth is 18 years of age or older or has had the disabilities of minority removed, there is evidence that the department has provided the youth with the documents and information listed in Section 264.121(e-1).

History of Fam. Code §263.4041: Enacted by S.B. 1758, §4, 85th Leg., eff. Sept. 1, 2017.

FAM §263.405. APPEAL OF FINAL ORDER

(a) An appeal of a final order rendered under this subchapter is governed by the procedures for accelerated appeals in civil cases under the Texas Rules of Appellate Procedure. The appellate court shall render its final order or judgment with the least possible delay.

(b) A final order rendered under this subchapter must contain the following prominently displayed statement in boldfaced type, in capital letters, or underlined: "A PARTY AFFECTED BY THIS ORDER HAS THE RIGHT TO APPEAL. AN APPEAL IN A SUIT IN WHICH TERMINATION OF THE PARENT-CHILD RELATIONSHIP IS SOUGHT IS GOVERNED BY THE PROCEDURES FOR ACCELERATED APPEALS IN CIVIL CASES UNDER THE TEXAS RULES OF APPELLATE PROCEDURE. FAILURE TO FOLLOW THE TEXAS RULES OF APPELLATE PROCEDURE FOR ACCELERATED APPEALS MAY RESULT IN THE DISMISSAL OF THE APPEAL."

(b-1) Repealed by Acts 2011, 82nd Leg., ch. 75, §5, eff. Sept. 1, 2011.

(c) The supreme court shall adopt rules accelerating the disposition by the appellate court and the supreme court of an appeal of a final order granting termination of the parent-child relationship rendered under this subchapter.[1]

(d) to **(i)** Repealed by Acts 2011, 82nd Leg., ch. 75, §5, eff. Sept. 1, 2011.

1. **Editor's note:** Since Family Code §263.405(c) became effective in September 2011, the Texas Supreme Court has amended TRCP 306 and TRAP 20, 25, 28, 32, and 35. Tex.Sup.Ct. Order, Misc. Docket No. 12-9030 (eff. Mar. 1, 2012).

History of Fam. Code §263.405: Acts 2001, 77th Leg., ch. 1090, §9, eff. Sept. 1, 2001. Amended by Acts 2005, 79th Leg., ch. 176, §1, eff. Sept. 1, 2005; Acts 2007, 80th Leg., ch. 526, §2, eff. June 15, 2007; Acts 2011, 82nd Leg., ch. 75, §§4, 5, eff. Sept. 1, 2011.

ANNOTATIONS

In re A.W., 384 S.W.3d 872, 873 (Tex.App.—San Antonio 2012, no pet.). Father "argues that this court should not consider the Associate Judge's [handwritten] Report and Order to be a final, appealable order. *At 874:* [Father] asserts that the handwritten order cannot be considered final because it does not contain the prominently displayed statement required to be included in a final order under §263.405(b)…. Although it might be erroneous not to include this statement, we conclude that the absence of the statement does not affect the finality of the handwritten order."

E FAM §263.4055. SUPREME COURT RULES

The supreme court by rule shall establish civil and appellate procedures to address:

(1) conflicts between the filing of a motion for new trial and the filing of an appeal of a final order rendered under this chapter; and

(2) the period, including an extension of at least 20 days, for a court reporter to submit the reporter's record of a trial to an appellate court following a final order rendered under this chapter.

History of Fam. Code §263.4055: Enacted by H.B. 7, §30, 85th Leg., eff. Sept. 1, 2017.

FAM §263.406. COURT INFORMATION SYSTEM

The Office of Court Administration of the Texas Judicial System shall consult with the courts presiding over cases brought by the department for the protection of children to develop an information system to track compliance with the requirements of this subchapter for the timely disposition of those cases.

History of Fam. Code §263.406: Acts 1997, 75th Leg., ch. 600, §17, eff. Sept. 1, 1997. Renumbered from §263.404 by Acts 2001, 77th Leg., ch. 1090, §9, eff. Sept. 1, 2001.

FAM §263.407. FINAL ORDER APPOINTING DEPARTMENT AS MANAGING CONSERVATOR OF CERTAIN ABANDONED CHILDREN; TERMINATION OF PARENTAL RIGHTS

(a) There is a rebuttable presumption that a parent who delivers a child to a designated emergency infant care provider in accordance with Subchapter D, Chapter 262:

(1) is the child's biological parent;

(2) intends to relinquish parental rights and consents to the termination of parental rights with regard to the child; and

(3) intends to waive the right to notice of the suit terminating the parent-child relationship.

(a-1) A party that seeks to rebut a presumption in Subsection (a) may do so at any time before the parent-child relationship is terminated with regard to the child.

(b) If a person claims to be the parent of a child taken into possession under Subchapter D, Chapter 262, before the court renders a final order terminating the parental rights of the child's parents, the court shall order genetic testing for parentage determination unless parentage has previously been established. The court shall hold the petition for termination of the parent-child relationship in abeyance for a period not to exceed 60 days pending the results of the genetic testing.

(c) Before the court may render an order terminating parental rights with regard to a child taken into the department's custody under Section 262.303, the department must:

(1) verify with the National Crime Information Center and state and local law enforcement agencies that the child is not a missing child; and

(2) obtain a certificate of the search of the paternity registry under Subchapter E, Chapter 160, not earlier than the date the department estimates to be the 30th day after the child's date of birth.

History of Fam. Code §263.407: Acts 2001, 77th Leg., ch. 809, §6, eff. Sept. 1, 2001. Renumbered from §263.405 by Acts 2003, 78th Leg., ch. 1275, §2(54), eff. Sept. 1, 2003. Amended by Acts 2005, 79th Leg., ch. 620, §2, eff. Sept. 1, 2005; Acts 2007, 80th Leg., ch. 1035, §1 (eff. June 15, 2007), ch. 1283, §12 (eff. Sept. 1, 2007).

FAM §263.408. REQUIREMENTS FOR APPOINTMENT OF NONPARENT AS MANAGING CONSERVATOR

(a) In a suit in which the court appoints a nonparent as managing conservator of a child:

(1) the department must provide the nonparent with an explanation of the differences between appointment as a managing conservator of a child and adoption of a child, including specific statements informing the nonparent that:

(A) the nonparent's appointment conveys only the rights specified by the court order or applicable laws instead of the complete rights of a parent conveyed by adoption;

(B) a parent may be entitled to request visitation with the child or petition the court to appoint the parent as the child's managing conservator, notwithstanding the nonparent's appointment as managing conservator; and

(C) the nonparent's appointment as the child's managing conservator will not result in the eligibility of the nonparent and child for postadoption benefits; and

(2) in addition to the rights and duties provided under Section 153.371, the court order appointing the nonparent as managing conservator must include provisions that address the authority of the nonparent to:

(A) authorize immunization of the child or any other medical treatment that requires parental consent;

(B) obtain and maintain health insurance coverage for the child and automobile insurance coverage for the child, if appropriate;

(C) enroll the child in a day-care program or school, including prekindergarten;

(D) authorize the child to participate in school-related or extracurricular or social activities, including athletic activities;

(E) authorize the child to obtain a learner's permit, driver's license, or state-issued identification card;

(F) authorize employment of the child;

(G) apply for and receive public benefits for or on behalf of the child; and

(H) obtain legal services for the child and execute contracts or other legal documents for the child.

(b) The court must require evidence that the nonparent was informed of the rights and duties of a nonparent appointed as managing conservator of a child before the court renders an order appointing the nonparent as managing conservator of a child.

History of Fam. Code §263.408: Acts 2015, 84th Leg., ch. 182, §1, eff. Sept. 1, 2015.

Sections 263.409-263.500 reserved for expansion

SUBCHAPTER F. PERMANENCY HEARINGS AFTER FINAL ORDER

FAM §263.501. PERMANENCY HEARING AFTER FINAL ORDER

(a) If the department has been named as a child's managing conservator in a final order that does not include termination of parental rights, the court shall conduct a permanency hearing after the final order is rendered at least once every six months until the department is no longer the child's managing conservator.

(b) If the department has been named as a child's managing conservator in a final order that terminates a parent's parental rights, the court shall conduct a permanency hearing not later than the 90th day after the

date the court renders the final order. The court shall conduct additional permanency hearings at least once every six months until the department is no longer the child's managing conservator.

(c) Notice of each permanency hearing shall be given as provided by Section 263.0021 to each person entitled to notice of the hearing.

(d), **(e)** Repealed by Acts 2015, 84th Leg., ch. 944, §86(19), eff. Sept. 1, 2015.

(f) The child shall attend each permanency hearing in accordance with Section 263.302.

(g) A court required to conduct permanency hearings for a child for whom the department has been appointed permanent managing conservator may not dismiss a suit affecting the parent-child relationship filed by the department regarding the child while the child is committed to the Texas Juvenile Justice Department or released under the supervision of the Texas Juvenile Justice Department, unless the child is adopted or permanent managing conservatorship of the child is awarded to an individual other than the department.

History of Fam. Code §263.501: Acts 1997, 75th Leg., ch. 600, §17 (eff. Sept. 1, 1997), ch. 603, §12 (eff. Jan. 1, 1998), ch. 1022, §90 (eff. Jan. 1, 1997). Amended by Acts 2001, 77th Leg., ch. 849, §8, eff. Sept. 1, 2001; Acts 2007, 80th Leg., ch. 1304, §2, eff. June 15, 2007; Acts 2009, 81st Leg., ch. 108, §9 (eff. May 23, 2009), ch. 1372, §8 (eff. June 19, 2009); Acts 2013, 83rd Leg., ch. 885, §2, eff. Sept. 1, 2013; Acts 2015, 84th Leg., ch. 734, §86 (eff. Sept. 1, 2015), ch. 944, §§40-42, 86(19) (eff. Sept. 1, 2015).

FAM §263.502. PERMANENCY PROGRESS REPORT AFTER FINAL ORDER

(a) Not later than the 10th day before the date set for a permanency hearing after a final order is rendered, the department shall file a permanency progress report with the court and provide a copy to each person entitled to notice under Section 263.0021.

(a-1) The permanency progress report must contain:

(1) information necessary for the court to conduct the permanency hearing and make its findings and determinations under Section 263.5031;

(2) information on significant events, as defined by Section 264.018; and

(3) any additional information the department determines is appropriate or that is requested by the court and relevant to the court's findings and determinations under Section 263.5031.

(a-2) For good cause shown, the court may:

(1) order a different deadline for filing the permanency progress report; or

(2) waive the reporting requirement for a specific hearing.

(b) to **(d)** Repealed by Acts 2015, 84th Leg., ch. 944, §86(20), eff. Sept. 1, 2015.

History of Fam. Code §263.502: Acts 1997, 75th Leg., ch. 600, §17 (eff. Sept. 1, 1997), ch. 603, §12 (eff. Jan. 1, 1998), ch. 1022, §90 (eff. Jan. 1, 1998). Amended by Acts 2005, 79th Leg., ch. 268, §1.41(a), eff. Sept. 1, 2005; Acts 2009, 81st Leg., ch. 108, §10 (eff. May 23, 2009), ch. 1372, §9 (eff. June 19, 2009); Acts 2011, 82nd Leg., ch. 91, §9.002, eff. Sept. 1, 2011; Acts 2013, 83rd Leg., ch. 1324, §3, eff. Sept. 1, 2013; Acts 2015, 84th Leg., ch. 1, §1.182 (eff. Apr. 2, 2015), ch. 944, §§43, 44, 86(20) (eff. Sept. 1, 2015).

FAM §263.503. PLACEMENT REVIEW HEARINGS; PROCEDURE

(a), **(b)** Repealed by Acts 2015, 84th Leg., ch. 944, §86(21), eff. Sept. 1, 2015.

Subsection (c) was enacted by Acts 2015, 84th Leg., ch. 262, §3, enacted May 15, 2015, effective Sept. 1, 2015, without reference to the conflicting repeal of §263.503 made by Acts 2015, 84th Leg., ch. 944, §86(21), enacted May 29, 2015, effective Sept. 1, 2015. For harmonizing conflicts, see p. V. The enacted text in subsection (c) is effective for permanency or placement-review hearings conducted under chapter 263 on or after Sept. 1, 2015.

(c) In addition to the requirements of Subsection (a),[1] at each placement review hearing the court shall review the department's efforts to ensure that the child has regular, ongoing opportunities to engage in age-appropriate normalcy activities, including activities not listed in the child's service plan.

1. **Editor's note:** Subsection (a) was repealed by Acts 2015, 84th Leg., ch. 944, §86(21), effective Sept. 1, 2015.

History of Fam. Code §263.503: Acts 1997, 75th Leg., ch. 600, §17 (eff. Sept. 1, 1997), ch. 603, §12 (eff. Jan. 1, 1998), ch. 1022, §90 (eff. Jan. 1, 1998). Amended by Acts 2001, 77th Leg., ch. 849, §9, eff. Sept. 1, 2001; Acts 2009, 81st Leg., ch. 108, §11 (eff. May 23, 2009), ch. 1372, §10 (eff. June 19, 2009); Acts 2011, 82nd Leg., ch. 91, §9.003, eff. Sept. 1, 2011; Acts 2013, 83rd Leg., ch. 204, §5 (eff. Sept. 1, 2013), ch. 688, §6 (eff. Sept. 1, 2013); Acts 2015, 84th Leg., ch. 1, §1.183 (eff. Apr. 2, 2015), ch. 262, §3 (eff. Sept. 1, 2015), ch. 944, §86(21) (eff. Sept. 1, 2015).

A FAM §263.5031. PERMANENCY HEARINGS FOLLOWING FINAL ORDER

In 2017, two bills amended §263.5031, but only one bill, H.B. 7, §31, saved the former law in effect at that time. The amended text from H.B. 7, §31 is effective for service plans filed for a full adversary hearing held under Fam. Code §262.201 or a status hearing held under Fam. Code ch. 263 on or after Jan. 1, 2018. A hearing held before Jan. 1, 2018, is governed by the former law in effect at that time. Except as provided above, the amended text from H.B. 7, §31 is effective for SAPCRs

filed on or after Sept. 1, 2017. SAPCRs filed before Sept. 1, 2017, are governed by the former law in effect at that time. The amended text from S.B. 1758, §5 is effective Sept. 1, 2017.

At each permanency hearing after the court renders a final order, the court shall:

(1) identify all persons and parties present at the hearing;

(2) review the efforts of the department or other agency in notifying persons entitled to notice under Section 263.0021; and

(3) review the permanency progress report to determine:

(A) the safety and well-being of the child and whether the child's needs, including any medical or special needs, are being adequately addressed;

(B) whether the department placed the child with a relative or other designated caregiver and the continuing necessity and appropriateness of the placement of the child, including with respect to a child who has been placed outside of this state, whether the placement continues to be in the best interest of the child;

(C) if the child is placed in institutional care, whether efforts have been made to ensure that the child is placed in the least restrictive environment consistent with the child's best interest and special needs;

(D) the appropriateness of the primary and alternative permanency goals for the child, whether the department has made reasonable efforts to finalize the permanency plan, including the concurrent permanency goals, in effect for the child, and whether:

(i) the department has exercised due diligence in attempting to place the child for adoption if parental rights to the child have been terminated and the child is eligible for adoption; or

(ii) another permanent placement, including appointing a relative as permanent managing conservator or returning the child to a parent, is appropriate for the child;

(E) for a child whose permanency goal is another planned permanent living arrangement:

(i) the desired permanency outcome for the child, by asking the child; [and]

(ii) whether, as of the date of the hearing, another planned permanent living arrangement is the best permanency plan for the child and, if so, provide compelling reasons why it continues to not be in the best interest of the child to:

(a) return home;

(b) be placed for adoption;

(c) be placed with a legal guardian; or

(d) be placed with a fit and willing relative;

(iii) whether the department has conducted an independent living skills assessment under Section 264.121(a-3);

(iv) whether the department has addressed the goals identified in the child's permanency plan, including the child's housing plan, and the results of the independent living skills assessment;

(v) if the youth is 16 years of age or older, whether there is evidence that the department has provided the youth with the documents and information listed in Section 264.121(e); and

(vi) if the youth is 18 years of age or older or has had the disabilities of minority removed, whether there is evidence that the department has provided the youth with the documents and information listed in Section 264.121(e-1);

(F) if the child is 14 years of age or older, whether services that are needed to assist the child in transitioning from substitute care to independent living are available in the child's community;

(G) whether the child is receiving appropriate medical care and has been provided the opportunity, in a developmentally appropriate manner, to express the child's opinion on any medical care provided;

(H) for a child receiving psychotropic medication, whether the child:

(i) has been provided appropriate nonpharmacological interventions, therapies, or strategies to meet the child's needs; or

(ii) has been seen by the prescribing physician, physician assistant, or advanced practice nurse at least once every 90 days;

(I) whether an education decision-maker for the child has been identified, the child's education needs and goals have been identified and addressed, and there are major changes in the child's school performance or there have been serious disciplinary events;

(J) for a child for whom the department has been named managing conservator in a final order that does not include termination of parental rights, whether to

order the department to provide services to a parent for not more than six months after the date of the permanency hearing if:

(i) the child has not been placed with a relative or other individual, including a foster parent, who is seeking permanent managing conservatorship of the child; and

(ii) the court determines that further efforts at reunification with a parent are:

(a) in the best interest of the child; and

(b) likely to result in the child's safe return to the child's parent; and

(K) whether the department has identified a family or other caring adult who has made a permanent commitment to the child.

History of Fam. Code §263.5031: Acts 2015, 84th Leg., ch. 944, §45, eff. Sept. 1, 2015. Amended by H.B. 7, §31, 85th Leg., eff. Sept. 1, 2017; S.B. 1758, §5, 85th Leg., eff. Sept. 1, 2017.

Sections 263.504-263.600 blank

SUBCHAPTER G. EXTENDED JURISDICTION AFTER CHILD'S 18TH BIRTHDAY

FAM §263.601. DEFINITIONS

In this subchapter:

(1) "Extended foster care" means a residential living arrangement in which a young adult voluntarily delegates to the department responsibility for the young adult's placement and care and in which the young adult resides with a foster parent or other residential services provider that is:

(A) licensed or approved by the department or verified by a licensed or certified child-placing agency; and

(B) paid under a contract with the department.

(2) "Guardianship services" means the services provided by the Department of Aging and Disability Services under Subchapter E, Chapter 161, Human Resources Code.

(3) "Institution" means a residential facility that is operated, licensed, registered, certified, or verified by a state agency other than the department. The term includes a residential service provider under a Medicaid waiver program authorized under Section 1915(c) of the federal Social Security Act that provides services at a residence other than the young adult's own home.

(3-a) "Trial independence " means the status assigned to a young adult under Section 263.6015.

(4) "Young adult" means a person who was in the conservatorship of the department on the day before the person's 18th birthday.

History of Fam. Code §263.601: Acts 2009, 81st Leg., ch. 96, §1, eff. May 23, 2009. Amended by Acts 2011, 82nd Leg., 1st C.S., ch. 3, §11.01 (eff. Sept. 28, 2011), ch. 4, §63.01 (eff. Sept. 28, 2011); Acts 2013, 83rd Leg., ch. 456, §1, eff. Sept. 1, 2013.

FAM §263.6015. TRIAL INDEPENDENCE

(a) A young adult is assigned trial independence status when the young adult:

(1) does not enter extended foster care at the time of the young adult's 18th birthday; or

(2) exits extended foster care before the young adult's 21st birthday.

(b) Except as provided by Subsection (c), a court order is not required for a young adult to be assigned trial independence status. Trial independence is mandatory for a period of at least six months beginning on:

(1) the date of the young adult's 18th birthday for a young adult described by Subsection (a)(1); or

(2) the date the young adult exits extended foster care.

(c) A court may order trial independence status extended for a period that exceeds the mandatory period under Subsection (b) but does not exceed one year from the date the period under Subsection (b) commences.

(d) Except as provided by Subsection (e), a young adult who enters or reenters extended foster care after a period of trial independence must complete a new period of trial independence as provided by Subsection (b)(2).

(e) The trial independence status of a young adult ends on the young adult's 21st birthday.

History of Fam. Code §263.6015: Acts 2013, 83rd Leg., ch. 456, §2, eff. Sept. 1, 2013.

FAM §263.602. EXTENDED JURISDICTION

(a) Except as provided by Subsection (f), a court that had jurisdiction over a young adult on the day before the young adult's 18th birthday continues to have extended jurisdiction over the young adult and shall retain the case on the court's docket while the young adult is in extended foster care and during trial independence as described by Section 263.6015.

(b) A court with extended jurisdiction over a young adult in extended foster care shall conduct extended

foster care review hearings every six months for the purpose of reviewing and making findings regarding:

(1) whether the young adult's living arrangement is safe and appropriate and whether the department has made reasonable efforts to place the young adult in the least restrictive environment necessary to meet the young adult's needs;

(2) whether the department is making reasonable efforts to finalize the permanency plan that is in effect for the young adult, including a permanency plan for independent living;

(3) whether, for a young adult whose permanency plan is independent living:

(A) the young adult participated in the development of the plan of service;

(B) the young adult's plan of service reflects the independent living skills and appropriate services needed to achieve independence by the projected date; and

(C) the young adult continues to make reasonable progress in developing the skills needed to achieve independence by the projected date; and

(4) whether additional services that the department is authorized to provide are needed to meet the needs of the young adult.

(c) Not later than the 10th day before the date set for a hearing under this section, the department shall file with the court a copy of the young adult's plan of service and a report that addresses the issues described by Subsection (b).

(d) Notice of an extended foster care review hearing shall be given as provided by Rule 21a, Texas Rules of Civil Procedure, to the following persons, each of whom has a right to present evidence and be heard at the hearing:

(1) the young adult who is the subject of the suit;

(2) the department;

(3) the foster parent with whom the young adult is placed and the administrator of a child-placing agency responsible for placing the young adult, if applicable;

(4) the director of the residential child-care facility or other approved provider with whom the young adult is placed, if applicable;

(5) each parent of the young adult whose parental rights have not been terminated and who is still actively involved in the life of the young adult;

(6) a legal guardian of the young adult, if applicable; and

(7) the young adult's attorney ad litem, guardian ad litem, and volunteer advocate, the appointment of which has not been previously dismissed by the court.

(e) If, after reviewing the young adult's plan of service and the report filed under Subsection (c), and any additional testimony and evidence presented at the review hearing, the court determines that the young adult is entitled to additional services, the court may order the department to take appropriate action to ensure that the young adult receives those services.

(f) Unless the court extends its jurisdiction over a young adult beyond the end of trial independence as provided by Section 263.6021(a) or 263.603(a), the court's extended jurisdiction over a young adult as described in Subsection (a) terminates on the earlier of:

(1) the last day of the month in which trial independence ends; or

(2) the young adult's 21st birthday.

(g) A court with extended jurisdiction described by this section is not required to conduct periodic hearings described in this section for a young adult during trial independence and may not compel a young adult who has elected to not enter or has exited extended foster care to attend a court hearing. A court with extended jurisdiction during trial independence may, at the request of a young adult, conduct a hearing described by Subsection (b) or by Section 263.6021 to review any transitional living services the young adult is receiving during trial independence.

History of Fam. Code §263.602: Acts 2009, 81st Leg., ch. 96, §1, eff. May 23, 2009. Amended by Acts 2011, 82nd Leg., 1st C.S., ch. 3, §11.02 (eff. Sept. 28, 2011), ch. 4, §63.02 (eff. Sept. 28, 2011); Acts 2013, 83rd Leg., ch. 456, §3, eff. Sept. 1, 2013.

FAM §263.6021. VOLUNTARY EXTENDED JURISDICTION FOR YOUNG ADULT RECEIVING TRANSITIONAL LIVING SERVICES

(a) Notwithstanding Section 263.602, a court that had jurisdiction over a young adult on the day before the young adult's 18th birthday may, at the young adult's request, render an order that extends the court's jurisdiction beyond the end of trial independence if the young adult receives transitional living services from the department.

(b) Unless the young adult reenters extended foster care before the end of the court's extended jurisdiction described by Subsection (a), the extended jurisdiction of the court under this section terminates on the earlier of:

(1) the young adult's 21st birthday; or

(2) the date the young adult withdraws consent to the extension of the court's jurisdiction in writing or in court.

(c) At the request of a young adult who is receiving transitional living services from the department and who consents to voluntary extension of the court's jurisdiction under this section, the court may hold a hearing to review the services the young adult is receiving.

(d) Before a review hearing scheduled under this section, the department must file with the court a report summarizing the young adult's transitional living services plan, services being provided to the young adult under that plan, and the young adult's progress in achieving independence.

(e) If, after reviewing the report and any additional testimony and evidence presented at the hearing, the court determines that the young adult is entitled to additional services, the court may order the department to take appropriate action to ensure that the young adult receives those services.

History of Fam. Code §263.6021: Acts 2011, 82nd Leg., 1st C.S., ch. 3, §11.03 (eff. Sept. 28, 2011), ch. 4, §63.03 (eff. Sept. 28, 2011). Amended by Acts 2013, 83rd Leg., ch. 456, §4, eff. Sept. 1, 2013.

FAM §263.603. EXTENDED JURISDICTION TO DETERMINE GUARDIANSHIP

(a) Notwithstanding Section 263.6021, if the court believes that a young adult may be incapacitated as defined by Section 1002.017(2), Estates ~~[601(14)(B), Texas Probate]~~ Code, the court may extend its jurisdiction on its own motion without the young adult's consent to allow the department to refer the young adult to the Department of Aging and Disability Services for guardianship services as required by Section 48.209, Human Resources Code.

(b) The extended jurisdiction of the court under this section terminates on the earliest of the date:

(1) the Department of Aging and Disability Services determines a guardianship is not appropriate under Chapter 161, Human Resources Code;

(2) a court with probate jurisdiction denies the application to appoint a guardian; or

(3) a guardian is appointed and qualifies under the Estates ~~[Texas Probate]~~ Code.

(c) If the Department of Aging and Disability Services determines a guardianship is not appropriate, or the court with probate jurisdiction denies the application to appoint a guardian, the court under Subsection (a) may continue to extend its jurisdiction over the young adult only as provided by Section 263.602 or 263.6021.

(d) Notwithstanding any other provision of this subchapter, a young adult for whom a guardian is appointed and qualifies is not considered to be in extended foster care or trial independence and the court's jurisdiction ends on the date the guardian for the young adult is appointed and qualifies unless the guardian requests the extended jurisdiction of the court under Section 263.604.

History of Fam. Code §263.603: Acts 2009, 81st Leg., ch. 96, §1, eff. May 23, 2009. Amended by Acts 2011, 82nd Leg., 1st C.S., ch. 3, §11.04 (eff. Sept. 28, 2011), ch. 4, §63.04 (eff. Sept. 28, 2011); Acts 2013, 83rd Leg., ch. 456, §5, eff. Sept. 1, 2013; S.B. 1488, §22.020, 85th Leg., eff. Sept. 1, 2017.

FAM §263.604. GUARDIAN'S CONSENT TO EXTENDED JURISDICTION

(a) A guardian appointed for a young adult may request that the court extend the court's jurisdiction over the young adult.

(b) A court that extends its jurisdiction over a young adult for whom a guardian is appointed may not issue an order that conflicts with an order entered by the probate court that has jurisdiction over the guardianship proceeding.

History of Fam. Code §263.604: Acts 2009, 81st Leg., ch. 96, §1, eff. May 23, 2009.

FAM §263.605. CONTINUED OR RENEWED APPOINTMENT OF ATTORNEY AD LITEM, GUARDIAN AD LITEM, OR VOLUNTEER ADVOCATE

A court with extended jurisdiction under this subchapter may continue or renew the appointment of an attorney ad litem, guardian ad litem, or volunteer advocate for the young adult to assist the young adult in accessing services the young adult is entitled to receive from the department or any other public or private service provider.

History of Fam. Code §263.605: Acts 2009, 81st Leg., ch. 96, §1, eff. May 23, 2009.

FAM §263.606. DUTIES OF ATTORNEY OR GUARDIAN AD LITEM

An attorney ad litem or guardian ad litem appointed for a young adult who receives services in the young adult's own home from a service provider or resides in an institution that is licensed, certified, or verified by a state agency other than the department shall assist the

young adult as necessary to ensure that the young adult receives appropriate services from the service provider or institution, or the state agency that regulates the service provider or institution.

History of Fam. Code §263.606: Acts 2009, 81st Leg., ch. 96, §1, eff. May 23, 2009.

FAM §263.607. PROHIBITED APPOINTMENTS & ORDERS

(a) The court may not appoint the department or the Department of Aging and Disability Services as the managing conservator or guardian of a young adult.

(b) A court may not order the department to provide a service to a young adult unless the department:

(1) is authorized to provide the service under state law; and

(2) is appropriated money to provide the service in an amount sufficient to comply with the court order and the department's obligations to other young adults for whom the department is required to provide similar services.

History of Fam. Code §263.607: Acts 2009, 81st Leg., ch. 96, §1, eff. May 23, 2009.

FAM §263.608. RIGHTS OF YOUNG ADULT

A young adult who consents to the continued jurisdiction of the court has the same rights as any other adult of the same age.

History of Fam. Code §263.608: Acts 2009, 81st Leg., ch. 96, §1, eff. May 23, 2009.

FAM §263.609. REPEALED

Repealed by Acts 2011, 82nd Leg., 1st C.S., ch. 3, §11.05 (eff. Sept. 28, 2011), ch. 4, §63.05 (eff. Sept. 28, 2011).

CHAPTER 264. CHILD WELFARE SERVICES

SUBCHAPTER A. GENERAL PROVISIONS

A FAM §264.001. DEFINITIONS

In this chapter:

(1) "Age-appropriate normalcy activity" means an activity or experience:

(A) that is generally accepted as suitable for a child's age or level of maturity or that is determined to be developmentally appropriate for a child based on the development of cognitive, emotional, physical, and behavioral capacities that are typical for the age or age group; and

(B) in which a child who is not in the conservatorship of the state is generally allowed to participate, including extracurricular activities, in-school and out-of-school social activities, cultural and enrichment activities, and employment opportunities.

(1-a) "Department" means the Department of Family and Protective Services.

(2), (3) Repealed by H.B. 5, §36(1), 85th Leg., eff. Sept. 1, 2017.

~~[(2)] ["Commission" means the Health and Human Services Commission.]~~

~~[(3)] ["Executive commissioner" means the executive commissioner of the Health and Human Services Commission.]~~

(3-a) "Least restrictive setting" means a placement for a child that, in comparison to all other available placements, is the most family-like setting.

(4) "Residential child-care facility" has the meaning assigned by Section 42.002, Human Resources Code.

(5) "Standard of care of a reasonable and prudent parent" means the standard of care that a parent of reasonable judgment, skill, and caution would exercise in addressing the health, safety, and welfare of a child while encouraging the emotional and developmental growth of the child, taking into consideration:

(A) the overall health and safety of the child;

(B) the child's age, maturity, and development level;

(C) the best interest of the child based on the caregiver's knowledge of the child;

(D) the appropriateness of a proposed activity and any potential risk factors;

(E) the behavioral history of the child and the child's ability to safely participate in a proposed activity;

(F) the importance of encouraging the child's social, emotional, and developmental growth; and

(G) the importance of providing the child with the most family-like living experience possible.

History of Fam. Code §264.001: Acts 1995, 74th Leg., ch. 20, §1, eff. Apr. 20, 1995. Amended by Acts 2005, 79th Leg., ch. 268, §1.42, eff. Sept. 1, 2005; Acts 2015, 84th Leg., ch. 262, §4, eff. Sept. 1, 2015; H.B. 5, §36(1), 85th Leg., eff. Sept. 1, 2017; H.B. 1542, §3, 85th Leg., eff. Sept. 1, 2017. Source: Former Fam. Code §34.50; Hum. Res. Code §11.001(2).

E FAM §264.0011. REFERENCE TO EXECUTIVE COMMISSIONER OR COMMISSION

In this chapter:

(1) a reference to the executive commissioner or the executive commissioner of the Health and Human Services Commission means the commissioner of the department; and

(2) a reference to the commission or the Health and Human Services Commission means the department.

History of Fam. Code §264.0011: Enacted by H.B. 5, §12, 85th Leg., eff. Sept. 1, 2017.

FAM §264.002. SPECIFIC APPROPRIATION REQUIRED

(a) to **(d)** Repealed by Acts 2015, 84th Leg., ch. 944, §86(22), eff. Sept. 1, 2015.

(e) The department may not spend state funds to accomplish the purposes of this subtitle unless the funds have been specifically appropriated for those purposes.

History of Fam. Code §264.002: Acts 1995, 74th Leg., ch. 20, §1, eff. Apr. 20, 1995. Amended by Acts 2015, 84th Leg., ch. 944, §§46, 47, 86(22), eff. Sept. 1, 2015. Source: Former Hum. Res. Code §41.001.

FAM §264.003. REPEALED

Repealed by Acts 2001, 77th Leg., ch. 114, §3, eff. Sept. 1, 2001.

FAM §264.004. ALLOCATION OF STATE FUNDS

(a) The department shall establish a method of allocating state funds for children's protective services programs that encourages and rewards the contribution of funds or services from all persons, including local governmental entities.

(b) Except as provided by this subsection, if a contribution of funds or services is made to support a children's protective services program in a particular county, the department shall use the contribution to benefit that program. The department may use the contribution for another purpose only if the commissioners court of the county gives the department written permission.

(c) The department may use state and federal funds to provide benefits or services to children and families who are otherwise eligible for the benefits or services, including foster care, adoption assistance, medical assistance, family reunification services, and other child protective services and related benefits without regard to the immigration status of the child or the child's family.

History of Fam. Code §264.004: Acts 1995, 74th Leg., ch. 20, §1, eff. Apr. 20, 1995. Amended by Acts 1997, 75th Leg., ch. 575, §23, eff. Sept. 1, 1997. Source: Former Hum. Res. Code §41.0012.

FAM §264.005. COUNTY CHILD WELFARE BOARDS

(a) The commissioners court of a county may appoint a child welfare board for the county. The commissioners court and the department shall determine the size of the board and the qualifications of its members. However, a board must have not less than seven and not more than 15 members, and the members must be residents of the county. The members shall serve at the pleasure of the commissioners court and may be removed by the court for just cause. The members serve without compensation.

(b) With the approval of the department, two or more counties may establish a joint child welfare board if that action is found to be more practical in accomplishing the purposes of this chapter. A board representing more than one county has the same powers as a board representing a single county and is subject to the same conditions and liabilities.

(c) The members of a county child welfare board shall select a presiding officer and shall perform the duties required by the commissioners court and the department to accomplish the purposes of this chapter.

(d) A county child welfare board is an entity of the department for purposes of providing coordinated state and local public welfare services for children and their families and for the coordinated use of federal, state, and local funds for these services. The child welfare board shall work with the commissioners court.

(e) A county child welfare board is a governmental unit for the purposes of Chapter 101, Civil Practice and Remedies Code.

(f) A county child protective services board member may receive information that is confidential under Section 40.005, Human Resources Code, or Section 261.201 when the board member is acting in the member's official capacity.

(g) A child welfare board may conduct a closed meeting under Section 551.101, Government Code, to discuss, consider, or act on a matter that is confidential under Section 40.005, Human Resources Code, or Section 261.201.

History of Fam. Code §264.005: Acts 1995, 74th Leg., ch. 20, §1, eff. Apr. 20, 1995. Amended by Acts 1997, 75th Leg., ch. 575, §24, eff. Sept. 1, 1997. Source: Former Hum. Res. Code §41.002.

FAM §264.006. COUNTY FUNDS

The commissioners court of a county may appropriate funds from its general fund or any other fund for the administration of its county child welfare board. The court may provide for services to and support of children in need of protection and care without regard to the immigration status of the child or the child's family.

History of Fam. Code §264.006: Acts 1995, 74th Leg., ch. 20, §1, eff. Apr. 20, 1995. Amended by Acts 1997, 75th Leg., ch. 575, §25, eff. Sept. 1, 1997. Source: Former Hum. Res. Code §41.003.

FAM §264.007. REPEALED

Repealed by Acts 2015, 84th Leg., ch. 1, §1.203(7), eff. Apr. 2, 2015.

FAM §264.008. CHILD WELFARE SERVICE FUND

The child welfare service fund is a special fund in the state treasury. The fund shall be used to administer the child welfare services provided by the department.

History of Fam. Code §264.008: Acts 1995, 74th Leg., ch. 20, §1, eff. Apr. 20, 1995. Source: Former Hum. Res. Code §41.006.

FAM §264.009. LEGAL REPRESENTATION OF DEPARTMENT

(a) Except as provided by Subsection (b), (c), or (f), in any action under this code, the department shall

be represented in court by the county attorney of the county where the action is brought, unless the district attorney or criminal district attorney of the county elects to provide representation.

(b) If the county attorney, district attorney, or criminal district attorney is unable to represent the department in an action under this code because of a conflict of interest or because special circumstances exist, the attorney general shall represent the department in the action.

(c) If the attorney general is unable to represent the department in an action under this code, the attorney general shall deputize an attorney who has contracted with the department under Subsection (d) or an attorney employed by the department under Subsection (e) to represent the department in the action.

(d) Subject to the approval of the attorney general, the department may contract with a private attorney to represent the department in an action under this code.

(e) The department may employ attorneys to represent the department in an action under this code.

(f) In a county with a population of 2.8 million or more, in an action under this code, the department shall be represented in court by the attorney who represents the state in civil cases in the district or county court of the county where the action is brought. If such attorney is unable to represent the department in an action under this code because of a conflict of interest or because special circumstances exist, the attorney general shall represent the department in the action.

History of Fam. Code §264.009: Acts 1995, 74th Leg., ch. 20, §1, eff. Apr. 20, 1995. Amended by Acts 1995, 74th Leg., ch. 751, §116, eff. Sept. 1, 1995; Acts 1997, 75th Leg., ch. 1022, §91, eff. Sept. 1, 1997. Source: Former Fam. Code §11.20.

FAM §264.0091. USE OF TELECONFERENCING & VIDEOCONFERENCING TECHNOLOGY

Subject to the availability of funds, the department, in cooperation with district and county courts, shall expand the use of teleconferencing and videoconferencing to facilitate participation by medical experts, children, and other individuals in court proceedings, including children for whom the department or a licensed child-placing agency has been appointed managing conservator and who are committed to the Texas Juvenile Justice Department.

History of Fam. Code §264.0091: Acts 2005, 79th Leg., ch. 268, §1.43, eff. Sept. 1, 2005. Amended by Acts 2009, 81st Leg., ch. 108, §12, eff. May 23, 2009; Acts 2015, 84th Leg., ch. 1, §1.184, eff. Apr. 2, 2015.

FAM §264.010. CHILD ABUSE PLAN; LIMITATION ON EXPENDITURE OF FUNDS

(a) Funds appropriated for protective services, child and family services, and the purchased service system for the department may only be spent on or after March 1, 1996, in a county that provides the department with a child abuse prevention and protection plan. If a plan is not submitted to the department under this section, the department shall document the county's failure to submit a plan and may spend appropriated funds in the county to carry out the department's duties under this subtitle.

(b) A child abuse prevention and protection plan may be submitted by the governing body of a county or of a regional council of governments in which the county is an active participant.

(c) The department may not require a child abuse prevention and protection plan to exceed five double-spaced letter-size pages. The county or council of governments may voluntarily provide a longer plan.

(d) A child abuse prevention and protection plan must:

(1) specify the manner of communication between entities who are parties to the plan, including the department, the commission, local law enforcement agencies, the county and district attorneys, members of the medical and social service community, foster parents, and child advocacy groups; and

(2) provide other information concerning the prevention and investigation of child abuse in the area for which the plan is adopted.

History of Fam. Code §264.010: Acts 1995, 74th Leg., ch. 943, §6, eff. Sept. 1, 1995. Amended by Acts 2015, 84th Leg., ch. 1, §1.185, eff. Apr. 2, 2015.

FAM §264.011. LOCAL ACCOUNTS

(a) The department may establish and maintain local bank or savings accounts for a child who is under the managing conservatorship of the department as necessary to administer funds received in trust for or on behalf of the child.

(b) Funds maintained in an account under this section may be used by the department to support the child, including for the payment of foster care expenses, or may be paid to a person providing care for the child.

History of Fam. Code §264.011: Acts 1997, 75th Leg., ch. 575, §26, eff. Sept. 1, 1997.

FAM §264.0111. MONEY EARNED BY CHILD

The amended text in §264.0111 is effective for service plans filed for a full adversary hearing held under Fam. Code §262.201 or a status hearing held under Fam. Code ch. 263 on or after Jan. 1, 2018. A hearing held before Jan. 1, 2018, is governed by the former law in effect at that time. Except as provided above, the amended text in §264.0111 is effective for SAPCRs filed on or after Sept. 1, 2017. SAPCRs filed before Sept. 1, 2017, are governed by the former law in effect at that time.

Foster homes or foster group homes licensed by TDFPS and agency foster group homes verified by a child-placing agency before Sept. 1, 2017, may continue to operate under the former law in effect at that time, until the foster home or foster group home converts to another residential child-care license or the license is relinquished, or the agency foster group home has been converted to a verified foster home or closed.

(a) A child for whom the department has been appointed managing conservator and who has been placed by the department in a residential [~~foster home or~~] child-care facility [~~institution~~] as defined by Chapter 42, Human Resources Code, is entitled to keep any money earned by the child during the time of the child's placement.

(b) The child may deposit the money earned by the child in a bank or savings account subject to the sole management and control of the child as provided by Section 34.305, Finance Code. The child is the sole and absolute owner of the deposit account.

(c) If a child earns money as described by this section and is returned to the child's parent or guardian, the child's parent or guardian may not interfere with the child's authority to control, transfer, draft on, or make a withdrawal from the account.

(d) In this section, a reference to money earned by a child includes any interest that accrues on the money.

(e) The executive commissioner may adopt rules to implement this section.

History of Fam. Code §264.0111: Acts 2001, 77th Leg., ch. 964, §3, eff. Sept. 1, 2001. Amended by Acts 2015, 84th Leg., ch. 1, §1.186, eff. Apr. 2, 2015; H.B. 7, §32, 85th Leg., eff. Sept. 1, 2017.

FAM §264.012. REPEALED

Repealed by Acts 2015, 84th Leg., ch. 944, §86(23), eff. Sept. 1, 2015.

FAM §264.0121. NOTICE TO LEGISLATORS OF FOSTER CHILD'S DEATH

Not later than the fifth day after the date the department is notified of the death of a child for whom the department has been appointed managing conservator, the department shall provide the information described by Section 261.203(a) for the child to the state senators and state representatives who represent:

(1) the county in which the child's placement at the time of the child's death was located; and

(2) the county in which a suit affecting the parent-child relationship involving the child is pending.

History of Fam. Code §264.0121: Acts 2015, 84th Leg., ch. 722, §2, eff. June 17, 2015.

FAM §264.013. EXCHANGE OF INFORMATION WITH OTHER STATES

Subject to the availability of funds, the department shall enter into agreements with other states to allow for the exchange of information relating to a child for whom the department is or was the managing conservator. The information may include the child's health passport and education passport.

History of Fam. Code §264.013: Acts 2005, 79th Leg., ch. 268, §1.44, eff. Sept. 1, 2005.

FAM §264.014. RENUMBERED

Renumbered as §264.121(e-1) by Acts 2015, 84th Leg., ch. 944, §56, eff. Sept. 1, 2015.

FAM §264.0145. RELEASE OF CASE RECORD

(a) In this section, "case record" means those files, reports, records, communications, audio recordings, video recordings, or working papers under the custody and control of the department that are collected, developed, or used:

(1) in a child abuse or neglect investigation; or

(2) in providing services as a result of an investigation, including substitute care services for a child.

(b) The executive commissioner by rule shall establish guidelines that prioritize requests to release case records, including those made by an adult previously in the department's managing conservatorship.

(c) The department is not required to release a copy of the case record except as provided by law and department rule.

History of Fam. Code §264.0145: Acts 2011, 82nd Leg., ch. 568, §1, eff. Sept. 1, 2011. Amended by Acts 2013, 83rd Leg., ch. 1069, §2, eff. Sept. 1, 2013; Acts 2015, 84th Leg., ch. 1, §1.187, eff. Apr. 2, 2015.

FAM §264.015. TRAINING

(a) The department shall include training in trauma-informed programs and services in any training the department provides to foster parents, adoptive parents, kinship caregivers, department caseworkers, and department supervisors. The department shall pay for the training provided under this subsection with gifts, donations, and grants and any federal money available through the Fostering Connections to Success and Increasing Adoptions Act of 2008 (Pub. L. No. 110-351). The department shall annually evaluate the effectiveness of the training provided under this subsection to ensure progress toward a trauma-informed system of care.

(b) The department shall require department caseworkers and department supervisors to complete an annual refresher training course in trauma-informed programs and services.

(c) To the extent that resources are available, the department shall assist the following entities in developing training in trauma-informed programs and services and in locating money and other resources to assist the entities in providing trauma-informed programs and services:

(1) court-appointed special advocate programs;

(2) children's advocacy centers;

(3) local community mental health centers created under Section 534.001, Health and Safety Code; and

(4) domestic violence shelters.

History of Fam. Code §264.015: Acts 2009, 81st Leg., ch. 1118, §5, eff. Sept. 1, 2009. Amended by Acts 2011, 82nd Leg., ch. 371, §1, eff. Sept. 1, 2011.

FAM §264.016. REPEALED

Repealed by Acts 2015, 84th Leg., ch. 944, §86(24), eff. Sept. 1, 2015.

A FAM §264.017. REQUIRED REPORTING

Section 264.017 was amended by S.B. 1488, §7.010, 85th Leg., eff. Sept. 1, 2017, to correct the conflicting enactment of identical language in subsections (d) and (e).

(a) The department shall prepare and disseminate a report of statistics by county relating to key performance measures and data elements for child protection.

(b) The department shall provide the report required by Subsection (a) to the legislature and shall publish the report and make the report available electronically to the public not later than February 1 of each year. The report must include, with respect to the preceding year:

(1) information on the number and disposition of reports of child abuse and neglect received by the department;

(2) information on the number of clients for whom the department took protective action, including investigations, alternative responses, and court-ordered removals;

(3) information on the number of clients for whom the department provided services in each program administered by the child protective services division, including investigations, alternative responses, family-based safety services, conservatorship, post-adoption services, and transitional living services;

(4) the number of children in this state who died as a result of child abuse or neglect;

(5) the number of children described by Subdivision (4) for whom the department was the children's managing conservator at the time of death;

(6) information on the timeliness of the department's initial contact in an investigation or alternative response;

(7) information on the response time by the department in commencing services to families and children for whom an allegation of child abuse or neglect has been made;

(8) information regarding child protection staffing and caseloads by program area;

(9) information on the permanency goals in place and achieved for children in the managing conservatorship of the department, including information on the timeliness of achieving the goals, the stability of the children's placement in foster care, and the proximity of placements to the children's home counties;

(10) the number of children who suffer from a severe emotional disturbance and for whom the department is appointed managing conservator, including statistics on appointments as joint managing conservator, due to an individual voluntarily relinquishing custody of a child solely to obtain mental health services for the child;

(11) the number of children who are pregnant or a parent while in the managing conservatorship of the department and the number of the children born to a parent in the managing conservatorship of the department who are placed in the managing conservatorship of the department;

(12) the number of children who are missing from the children's substitute care provider while in the managing conservatorship of the department; and

(13) the number of children who were victims of trafficking under Chapter 20A, Penal Code, while in the managing conservatorship of the department.

(c) To the extent feasible, the report must also include, for each county, the amount of funding for child abuse and neglect prevention services and the rate of child abuse and neglect per 1,000 children in the county for the preceding year and for each of the preceding five years.

(d) Not later than September 1 of each year, the department shall seek public input regarding the usefulness of, and any proposed modifications to, existing reporting requirements and proposed additional reporting requirements. The department shall evaluate the public input provided under this subsection and seek to facilitate reporting to the maximum extent feasible within existing resources and in a manner that is most likely to assist public understanding of department functions.

(e) In addition to the information required under Subsections (a) and (b), the department shall annually publish information on the number of children who died during the preceding year whom the department determined had been abused or neglected but whose death was not the result of the abuse or neglect. The department may publish the information described by this subsection in the same report required by Subsection (a) or in another annual report published by the department.

History of Fam. Code §264.017: Acts 2015, 84th Leg., ch. 713, §1 (eff. Sept. 1, 2015), ch. 944, §48 (eff. Sept. 1, 2015). Amended by S.B. 1488, §7.010, 85th Leg., eff. Sept. 1, 2017.

Ⓐ FAM §264.018. REQUIRED NOTIFICATIONS

In 2017, two bills amended §264.018, but only one bill, H.B. 7, §33, saved the former law in effect at that time. The amended text from H.B. 7, §33 is effective for service plans filed for a full adversary hearing held under Fam. Code §262.201 or a status hearing held under Fam. Code ch. 263 on or after Jan. 1, 2018. A hearing held before Jan. 1, 2018, is governed by the former law in effect at that time. Except as provided above, the amended text from H.B. 7, §33 is effective for SAPCRs filed on or after Sept. 1, 2017. SAPCRs filed before Sept. 1, 2017, are governed by the former law in effect at that time. The amended text from S.B. 11, §14 is effective Sept. 1, 2017.

Foster homes or foster group homes licensed by TDFPS and agency foster group homes verified by a child-placing agency before Sept. 1, 2017, may continue to operate under the former law in effect at that time, until the foster home or foster group home converts to another residential child-care license or the license is relinquished, or the agency foster group home has been converted to a verified foster home or closed.

(a) In this section:

(1) "Child-placing agency" has the meaning assigned by Section 42.002, Human Resources Code.

☠ *Subsections (2) and (3) were enacted by Acts 2015, 84th Leg., ch. 722, §1, enacted May 26, 2015, effective June 17, 2015, without reference to the conflicting enactment of identical subsections in the opposite order by Acts 2015, 84th Leg., ch. 944, §48, enacted May 29, 2015, effective Sept. 1, 2015. For harmonizing conflicts, see p. V.*

(2) "Psychotropic medication" has the meaning assigned by Section 266.001.

(3) "Residential child-care facility" has the meaning assigned by Section 42.002, Human Resources Code.

(4) "Significant change in medical condition" means the occurrence of an injury or the onset of an illness that is life-threatening or may have serious long-term health consequences. The term includes the occurrence or onset of an injury or illness that requires hospitalization for surgery or another procedure that is not minor emergency care.

(5) "Significant event" means:

(A) a placement change, including failure by the department to locate an appropriate placement for at least one night;

(B) a significant change in medical condition;

(C) an initial prescription of a psychotropic medication or a change in dosage of a psychotropic medication;

(D) a major change in school performance or a serious disciplinary event at school; or

(E) any event determined to be significant under department rule.

(b) The notification requirements of this section are in addition to other notice requirements provided by law, including Sections 263.0021, 264.107(g), and 264.123.

(c) The department must provide notice under this section in a manner that would provide actual notice to a person entitled to the notice, including the use of electronic notice whenever possible.

(d) Not later than 24 hours after an event described by this subsection, the department shall make a reasonable effort to notify a parent of a child in the managing conservatorship of the department of:

(1) a significant change in medical condition of the child;

(2) the enrollment or participation of the child in a drug research program under Section 266.0041; and

(3) an initial prescription of a psychotropic medication.

(d-1) Except as provided by Subsection (d-2), as[1] soon as possible but not later than 24 hours after a change in placement of a child in the conservatorship of the department, the department shall give notice of the placement change to the managed care organization that contracts with the commission to provide health care services to the child under the STAR Health program. The managed care organization shall give notice of the placement change to the primary care physician listed in the child's health passport before the end of the second business day after the day the organization receives the notification from the department.

(d-2) In this subsection, "catchment area" has the meaning assigned by Section 264.152. In a catchment area in which community-based care has been implemented, the single source continuum contractor that has contracted with the commission to provide foster care services in that catchment area shall, as soon as possible but not later than 24 hours after a change in placement of a child in the conservatorship of the department, give notice of the placement change to the managed care organization that contracts with the commission to provide health care services to the child under the STAR Health program. The managed care organization shall give notice of the placement change to the child's primary care physician in accordance with Subsection (d-1).

(e) Not later than 48 hours before the department changes the residential child-care facility of a child in the managing conservatorship of the department, the department shall provide notice of the change to:

(1) the child's parent;

(2) an attorney ad litem appointed for the child under Chapter 107;

(3) a guardian ad litem appointed for the child under Chapter 107;

(4) a volunteer advocate appointed for the child under Chapter 107; and

(5) the licensed administrator of the child-placing agency responsible for placing the child or the licensed administrator's designee.

(f) Except as provided by Subsection (d-1), as [As] soon as possible but not later than the 10th day after the date the department becomes aware of a significant event affecting a child in the conservatorship of the department, the department shall provide notice of the significant event to:

(1) the child's parent;

(2) an attorney ad litem appointed for the child under Chapter 107;

(3) a guardian ad litem appointed for the child under Chapter 107;

(4) a volunteer advocate appointed for the child under Chapter 107;

(5) the licensed administrator of the child-placing agency responsible for placing the child or the licensed administrator's designee;

(6) a foster parent, prospective adoptive parent, relative of the child providing care to the child, or director of the group home or general residential operation where the child is residing; and

(7) any other person determined by a court to have an interest in the child's welfare.

(g) For purposes of Subsection (f), if a hearing for the child is conducted during the 10-day notice period described by that subsection, the department shall provide notice of the significant event at the hearing.

(h) The department is not required to provide notice under this section to a parent of a child in the managing conservatorship of the department if:

(1) the department cannot locate the parent;

(2) a court has restricted the parent's access to the information;

(3) the child is in the permanent managing conservatorship of the department and the parent has not participated in the child's case for at least six months despite the department's efforts to involve the parent;

(4) the parent's rights have been terminated; or

(5) the department has documented in the child's case file that it is not in the best interest of the child to involve the parent in case planning.

(i) The department is not required to provide notice of a significant event under this section to the child-placing agency responsible for the placement of a child in the managing conservatorship of the department, a foster parent, a prospective adoptive parent, a relative of the child providing care to the child, or the director of the group home or general residential operation where the child resides if that agency or individual is required under a contract or other agreement to provide notice of the significant event to the department.

(j) A person entitled to notice from the department under this section shall provide the department with current contact information, including the person's e-mail address and the telephone number at which the person may most easily be reached. The person shall update the person's contact information as soon as possible after a change to the information. The department is not required to provide notice under this section to a person who fails to provide contact information to the department. The department may rely on the most recently provided contact information in providing notice under this section.

(k) To facilitate timely notification under this section, a residential child-care facility contracting with the department for 24-hour care shall notify the department, in the time provided by the facility's contract, of a significant event for a child who is in the conservatorship of the department and residing in the facility.

(l) The executive commissioner of the Health and Human Services Commission shall adopt rules necessary to implement this section using a negotiated rulemaking process under Chapter 2008, Government Code.

1. **Editor's note:** In 2017, the Legislature enacted two versions of subsection (d-1). S.B. 11, §14, 85th Leg., enacted May 28, 2017, effective Sept. 1, 2017, uses "as," as shown here, and H.B. 7, §33, 85th Leg., enacted May 26, 2017, effective Sept. 1, 2017, uses "As."

History of Fam. Code §264.018: Acts 2015, 84th Leg., ch. 722, §1 (eff. June 17, 2015), ch. 944, §48 (eff. Sept. 1, 2015). Amended by H.B. 7, §33, 85th Leg., eff. Sept. 1, 2017; S.B. 11, §14, 85th Leg., eff. Sept. 1, 2017.

Sections 264.019-264.100 reserved for expansion

SUBCHAPTER B. FOSTER CARE

FAM §264.101. FOSTER CARE PAYMENTS

(a) The department may pay the cost of foster care for a child only if:

(1) the child has been placed by the department in a foster home or other residential child-care facility, as defined by Chapter 42, Human Resources Code, or in a comparable residential facility in another state; and

(2) the department:

(A) has initiated suit and been named conservator of the child; or

(B) has the duty of care, control, and custody after taking possession of the child in an emergency without a prior court order as authorized by this subtitle.

(a-1) The department shall continue to pay the cost of foster care for a child for whom the department provides care, including medical care, until the last day of the month in which the child attains the age of 18. The department shall continue to pay the cost of foster care for a child after the month in which the child attains the age of 18 as long as the child is:

(1) regularly attending high school or enrolled in a program leading toward a high school diploma or high school equivalency certificate;

(2) regularly attending an institution of higher education or a postsecondary vocational or technical program;

(3) participating in a program or activity that promotes, or removes barriers to, employment;

(4) employed for at least 80 hours a month; or

(5) incapable of performing the activities described by Subdivisions (1)-(4) due to a documented medical condition.

(a-2) The department shall continue to pay the cost of foster care under:

(1) Subsection (a-1)(1) until the last day of the month in which the child attains the age of 22; and

(2) Subsections (a-1)(2)-(5) until the last day of the month the child attains the age of 21.

(b) The department may not pay the cost of protective foster care for a child for whom the department has been named managing conservator under an order rendered solely under Section 161.001(b)(1)(J).

(c) The payment of foster care, including medical care, for a child as authorized under this subchapter

shall be made without regard to the child's eligibility for federally funded care.

(d) The executive commissioner may adopt rules that establish criteria and guidelines for the payment of foster care, including medical care, for a child and for providing care for a child after the child becomes 18 years of age if the child meets the requirements for continued foster care under Subsection (a-1).

(d-1) The executive commissioner may adopt rules that prescribe the maximum amount of state money that a residential child-care facility may spend on nondirect residential services, including administrative services. The commission shall recover the money that exceeds the maximum amount established under this subsection.

(e) The department may accept and spend funds available from any source to pay for foster care, including medical care, for a child in the department's care.

(f) In this section, "child" means a person who:

(1) is under 22 years of age and for whom the department has been appointed managing conservator of the child before the date the child became 18 years of age; or

(2) is the responsibility of an agency with which the department has entered into an agreement to provide care and supervision of the child.

History of Fam. Code §264.101: Acts 1995, 74th Leg., ch. 20, §1, eff. Apr. 20, 1995. Amended by Acts 1997, 75th Leg., ch. 575, §27, eff. Sept. 1, 1997; Acts 2005, 79th Leg., ch. 268, §1.45 (eff. Sept. 1, 2005), ch. 614, §1 (eff. May 27, 2005); Acts 2009, 81st Leg., ch. 1118, §6 (eff. Sept. 1, 2009), ch. 1238, §6(b) (eff. Oct. 1, 2010); Acts 2015, 84th Leg., ch. 1, §1.188 (eff. Apr. 2, 2015), ch. 944, §49 (eff. Sept. 1, 2015). Source: Former Hum. Res. Code §41.021.

See also 40 T.A.C. §§700.315-700.346.

FAM §264.1015. LIABILITY OF CHILD'S ESTATE FOR FOSTER CARE

(a) The cost of foster care provided for a child, including medical care, is an obligation of the estate of the child and the estate is liable to the department for the cost of the care.

(b) The department may take action to recover from the estate of the child the cost of foster care for the child.

History of Fam. Code §264.1015: Acts 1997, 75th Leg., ch. 575, §28, eff. Sept. 1, 1997.

FAM §264.102. COUNTY CONTRACTS

(a) The department may contract with a county commissioners court to administer the funds authorized by this subchapter for eligible children in the county and may require county participation.

(b) The payments provided by this subchapter do not abrogate the responsibility of a county to provide child welfare services.

History of Fam. Code §264.102: Acts 1995, 74th Leg., ch. 20, §1, eff. Apr. 20, 1995. Source: Former Hum. Res. Code §41.022.

FAM §264.103. DIRECT PAYMENTS

The department may make direct payments for foster care to a foster parent residing in a county with which the department does not have a contract authorized by Section 264.102.

History of Fam. Code §264.103: Acts 1995, 74th Leg., ch. 20, §1, eff. Apr. 20, 1995. Source: Former Hum. Res. Code §41.023.

FAM §264.104. PARENT OR GUARDIAN LIABILITY

(a) The parent or guardian of a child is liable to the state or to the county for a payment made by the state or county for foster care of a child under this subchapter.

(b) The cost of foster care for a child, including medical care, is a legal obligation of the child's parents, and the estate of a parent of the child is liable to the department for payment of the costs.

(c) The funds collected by the state under this section shall be used by the department for child welfare services.

History of Fam. Code §264.104: Acts 1995, 74th Leg., ch. 20, §1, eff. Apr. 20, 1995. Amended by Acts 1997, 75th Leg., ch. 575, §29, eff. Sept. 1, 1997. Source: Former Hum. Res. Code §41.024.

FAM §264.105. REPEALED

Repealed by Acts 2015, 84th Leg., ch. 1, §1.203(8), eff. Apr. 2, 2015.

FAM §264.106. REPEALED

Repealed by Acts 2015, 84th Leg., ch. 1, §1.203(9), eff. Apr. 2, 2015.

FAM §264.1061. FOSTER PARENT PERFORMANCE

The department shall monitor the performance of a foster parent who has been verified by the department in the department's capacity as a child-placing agency. The method under which performance is monitored must include the use of objective criteria by which the foster parent's performance may be assessed. The department shall include references to the criteria in a written agreement between the department and the foster parent concerning the foster parent's services.

History of Fam. Code §264.1061: Acts 1997, 75th Leg., ch. 1022, §92, eff. Sept. 1, 1997.

FAM §264.1062. REPEALED

Repealed by Acts 2007, 80th Leg., ch. 1406, §54(2), eff. Sept. 1, 2007.

FAM §264.1063. REPEALED

Repealed by Acts 2015, 84th Leg., ch. 1, §1.203(10), eff. Apr. 2, 2015.

A FAM §264.107. PLACEMENT OF CHILDREN

(a) Repealed by Acts 2015, 84th Leg., ch. 944, §86(25), eff. Sept. 1, 2015.

(b) The department shall use an application or assessment developed by the department in coordination with interested parties for the placement of children in contract residential care.

(b-1) Notwithstanding Subsection (b), the department shall use the standard application for the placement of children in contract residential care as adopted and maintained by the Health and Human Services Commission until the department develops an application or assessment under Subsection (b). Subject to the availability of funds, the department shall develop the application or assessment not later than December 1, 2016. This subsection expires September 1, 2017.

(c) In selecting a placement for a child, the department shall consider whether the placement is in the child's best interest. In determining whether a placement is in a child's best interest, the department shall consider whether the placement:

(1) is the least restrictive setting for the child;

(2) is the closest in geographic proximity to the child's home;

(3) is the most able to meet the identified needs of the child; and

(4) satisfies any expressed interests of the child relating to placement, when developmentally appropriate.

(d) Repealed by Acts 2015, 84th Leg., ch. 944, §86(25), eff. Sept. 1, 2015.

(e) In making placement decisions, the department shall:

(1) except when making an emergency placement that does not allow time for the required consultations, consult with the child's caseworker, attorney ad litem, and guardian ad litem and with any court-appointed volunteer advocate for the child; and

(2) use clinical protocols to match a child to the most appropriate placement resource.

(f) Repealed by Acts 2015, 84th Leg., ch. 1, §1.203(11), eff. Apr. 2, 2015.

(g) If the department is unable to find an appropriate placement for a child, an employee of the department who has on file a background and criminal history check may provide temporary emergency care for the child. An employee may not provide emergency care under this subsection in the employee's residence. The department shall provide notice to the court for a child placed in temporary care under this subsection not later than the next business day after the date the child is placed in temporary care.

History of Fam. Code §264.107: Acts 1995, 74th Leg., ch. 20, §1, eff. Apr. 20, 1995. Amended by Acts 2005, 79th Leg., ch. 268, §1.48, eff. Sept. 1, 2005; Acts 2007, 80th Leg., ch. 1406, §14, eff. Sept. 1, 2007; Acts 2013, 83rd Leg., ch. 193, §1, eff. Sept. 1, 2013; Acts 2015, 84th Leg., ch. 1, §§1.189, 1.203(11) (eff. Apr. 2, 2015), ch. 944, §§50, 86(25) (eff. Sept. 1, 2015); H.B. 1542, §4, 85th Leg., eff. Sept. 1, 2017. Source: Former Hum. Res. Code §41.027.

FAM §264.1071. REPEALED

Repealed by Acts 2015, 84th Leg., ch. 944, §86(26), eff. Sept. 1, 2015.

FAM §264.1072. EDUCATIONAL STABILITY

The department shall develop, in accordance with 42 U.S.C. Section 675, a plan to ensure the educational stability of a foster child.

History of Fam. Code §264.1072: Acts 2013, 83rd Leg., ch. 688, §7, eff. Sept. 1, 2013.

A FAM §264.1075. ASSESSING NEEDS OF CHILD

(a) On removing a child from the child's home, the department shall use assessment services provided by a child-care facility, a child-placing agency, or the child's medical home during the initial substitute care placement. The assessment may be used to determine the most appropriate substitute care placement for the child, if needed.

(b) As soon as possible after a child is placed in the managing conservatorship of the department [~~begins receiving foster care under this subchapter~~], the department shall assess whether the child has a developmental or intellectual disability.

(c) If the assessment required by Subsection (b) indicates that the child might have an intellectual disability, the department shall ensure that a referral for a determination of intellectual disability is made as soon as possible and that the determination is conducted by an authorized provider before the date of the child's 16th birthday, if practicable. If the child is placed in the managing conservatorship of the department after the child's 16th birthday, the determination of intellectual disability must be conducted as soon as possible after the assessment required by Subsection (b). In this subsection, "authorized provider" has the meaning assigned by Section 593.004, Health and Safety Code.

History of Fam. Code §264.1075: Acts 1997, 75th Leg., ch. 1022, §93, eff. Sept. 1, 1997. Amended by Acts 2005, 79th Leg., ch. 268, §1.49, eff. Sept. 1, 2005; Acts 2015, 84th Leg., ch. 1, §1.190 (eff. Apr. 2, 2015), ch. 944, §51 (eff. Sept. 1, 2015); H.B. 1549, §3, 85th Leg., eff. Sept. 1, 2017.

E FAM §264.1076. MEDICAL EXAMINATION REQUIRED

(a) This section applies only to a child who has been taken into the conservatorship of the department and remains in the conservatorship of the department for more than three business days.

(b) The department shall ensure that each child described by Subsection (a) receives an initial medical examination from a physician or other health care provider authorized under state law to conduct medical examinations not later than the end of the third business day after the date the child is removed from the child's home, if the child:

(1) is removed as the result of sexual abuse, physical abuse, or an obvious physical injury to the child; or

(2) has a chronic medical condition, a medically complex condition, or a diagnosed mental illness.

(c) Notwithstanding Subsection (b), the department shall ensure that any child who enters the conservatorship of the department receives any necessary emergency medical care as soon as possible.

(d) A physician or other health care provider conducting an examination under Subsection (b) may not administer a vaccination as part of the examination without parental consent, except that a physician or other health care provider may administer a tetanus vaccination to a child in a commercially available preparation if the physician or other health care provider determines that an emergency circumstance requires the administration of the vaccination. The prohibition on the administration of a vaccination under this subsection does not apply after the department has been named managing conservator of the child after a hearing conducted under Subchapter C, Chapter 262.

(e) Whenever possible, the department shall schedule the medical examination for a child before the last business day of the appropriate time frame provided under Subsection (b).

(f) The department shall collaborate with the commission and selected physicians and other health care providers authorized under state law to conduct medical examinations to develop guidelines for the medical examination conducted under this section, including guidelines on the components to be included in the examination. The guidelines developed under this subsection must provide assistance and guidance regarding:

(1) assessing a child for:

(A) signs and symptoms of child abuse and neglect;

(B) the presence of acute or chronic illness; and

(C) signs of acute or severe mental health conditions;

(2) monitoring a child's adjustment to being in the conservatorship of the department;

(3) ensuring a child has necessary medical equipment and any medication prescribed to the child or needed by the child; and

(4) providing appropriate support and education to a child's caregivers.

(g) Notwithstanding any other law, the guidelines developed under Subsection (f) do not create a standard of care for a physician or other health care provider authorized under state law to conduct medical examinations, and a physician or other health care provider may not be subject to criminal, civil, or administrative penalty or civil liability for failure to adhere to the guidelines.

(h) The department shall make a good faith effort to contact a child's primary care physician to ensure continuity of care for the child regarding medication prescribed to the child and the treatment of any chronic medical condition.

(i) Not later than December 31, 2019, the department shall submit a report to the standing committees of the house of representatives and the senate with primary jurisdiction over child protective services and foster care evaluating the statewide implementation of the medical examination required by this section. The report must include the level of compliance with the requirements of this section in each region of the state.

History of Fam. Code §264.1076: Enacted by S.B. 11, §15(a), 85th Leg., eff. Sept. 1, 2017.

FAM §264.108. REPEALED

Repealed by Acts 2015, 84th Leg., ch. 944, §86(27), eff. Sept. 1, 2015.

FAM §264.1085. FOSTER CARE PLACEMENT IN COMPLIANCE WITH FEDERAL LAW REQUIRED

The department or a licensed child-placing agency making a foster care placement shall comply with the Multiethnic Placement Act of 1994 (42 U.S.C. Section 1996b).

History of Fam. Code §264.1085: Acts 2015, 84th Leg., ch. 944, §52, eff. Sept. 1, 2015.

FAM §264.109. ASSIGNMENT OF SUPPORT RIGHTS IN SUBSTITUTE CARE CASES

(a) The placement of a child in substitute care by the department constitutes an assignment to the state of any support rights attributable to the child as of the date the child is placed in substitute care.

(b) If a child placed by the department in substitute care is entitled under federal law to Title IV-D child support enforcement services without the requirement of an application for services, the department shall immediately refer the case to the Title IV-D agency. If an application for Title IV-D services is required and the department has been named managing conservator of the child, then an authorized representative of the department shall be the designated individual entitled to apply for services on behalf of the child and shall promptly apply for the services.

(c) The department and the Title IV-D agency shall execute a memorandum of understanding for the implementation of the provisions of this section and for the allocation between the department and the agency, consistent with federal laws and regulations, of any child support funds recovered by the Title IV-D agency in substitute care cases. All child support funds recovered under this section and retained by the department or the Title IV-D agency and any federal matching or incentive funds resulting from child support collection efforts in substitute care cases shall be in excess of amounts otherwise appropriated to either the department or the Title IV-D agency by the legislature.

History of Fam. Code §264.109: Acts 1995, 74th Leg., ch. 751, §117, eff. Sept. 1, 1995.

FAM §264.110. PROSPECTIVE FOSTER OR ADOPTIVE PARENT STATEMENT

(a) to **(c)** Repealed by Acts 2015, 84th Leg., ch. 944, §86(28), eff. Sept. 1, 2015.

(d) Before a child may be placed with a foster or adoptive parent, the prospective foster or adoptive parent must sign a written statement in which the prospective foster or adoptive parent agrees to the immediate removal of the child by the department under circumstances determined by the department.

(e) to **(h)** Repealed by Acts 2015, 84th Leg., ch. 944, §86(28), eff. Sept. 1, 2015.

History of Fam. Code §264.110: Acts 1995, 74th Leg., ch. 943, §8, eff. Sept. 1, 1995. Renumbered from §264.109 by Acts 1997, 75th Leg., ch. 165, §31.01(30), eff. Sept. 1, 1997. Amended by Acts 2015, 84th Leg., ch. 1, §1.192 (eff. Apr. 2, 2015), ch. 944, §§53, 54, 86(28) (eff. Sept. 1, 2015).

FAM §264.111. REPEALED

Repealed by Acts 2015, 84th Leg., ch. 713, §4 (eff. Sept. 1, 2015), ch. 944, §86(29) (eff. Sept. 1, 2015).

FAM §264.112. REPORT ON CHILDREN IN SUBSTITUTE CARE

(a) The department shall report the status for children in substitute care to the executive commissioner at least once every 12 months.

(b) The report shall analyze the length of time each child has been in substitute care and the barriers to placing the child for adoption or returning the child to the child's parent or parents.

History of Fam. Code §264.112: Acts 1997, 75th Leg., ch. 600, §18, eff. Sept. 1, 1997. Amended by Acts 2015, 84th Leg., ch. 1, §1.193, eff. Apr. 2, 2015.

FAM §264.113. FOSTER PARENT RECRUITMENT

(a) In this section, "faith-based organization" means a religious or denominational institution or organization, including an organization operated for religious, educational, or charitable purposes and operated, supervised, or controlled, in whole or in part, by or in connection with a religious organization.

(b) The department shall develop a program to recruit and retain foster parents from faith-based organizations. As part of the program, the department shall:

(1) collaborate with faith-based organizations to inform prospective foster parents about the department's need for foster parents, the requirements for becoming a foster parent, and any other aspect of the foster care program that is necessary to recruit foster parents;

(2) provide training for prospective foster parents recruited under this section; and

(3) identify and recommend ways in which faith-based organizations may support persons as they are recruited, are trained, and serve as foster parents.

(c) The department shall work with OneStar Foundation to expand the program described by Subsection (b) to increase the number of foster families available for the department and its private providers. In cooperation with the department, OneStar Foundation may provide training and technical assistance to establish networks and services in faith-based organizations based on best practices for supporting prospective and current foster families.

(d) The department shall work with the Department of Assistive and Rehabilitative Services to recruit foster parents and adoptive parents who have skills,

training, or experience suitable to care for children with hearing impairments.

History of Fam. Code §264.113: Acts 2003, 78th Leg., ch. 957, §1, eff. June 20, 2003. Amended by Acts 2007, 80th Leg., ch. 1406, §16, eff. Sept. 1, 2007.

FAM §264.114. IMMUNITY FROM LIABILITY; ADVERSE DEPARTMENTAL ACTION PROHIBITED

(a) A faith-based organization, including the organization's employees and volunteers, that participates in a program under this chapter is subject to civil liability as provided by Chapter 84, Civil Practice and Remedies Code.

(b) A faith-based organization that provides financial or other assistance to a foster parent or to a member of the foster parent's household is not liable for damages arising out of the conduct of the foster parent or a member of the foster parent's household.

(c) A foster parent, other substitute caregiver, family relative or other designated caregiver, or licensed child placing agency caring for a child in the managing conservatorship of the department is not liable for harm caused to the child resulting from the child's participation in an age-appropriate normalcy activity approved by the caregiver if, in approving the child's participation in the activity, the caregiver exercised the standard of care of a reasonable and prudent parent.

(d) A licensed child placing agency is not subject to adverse action by the department, including contractual action or licensing or other regulatory action, arising out of the conduct of a foster parent who has exercised the standard of care of a reasonable and prudent parent.

History of Fam. Code §264.114: Acts 2003, 78th Leg., ch. 957, §1, eff. June 20, 2003. Amended by Acts 2015, 84th Leg., ch. 262, §§5, 6, eff. Sept. 1, 2015.

FAM §264.115. RETURNING CHILD TO SCHOOL

(a) If the department takes possession of a child under Chapter 262 during the school year, the department shall ensure that the child returns to school not later than the third school day after the date an order is rendered providing for possession of the child by the department, unless the child has a physical or mental condition of a temporary and remediable nature that makes the child's attendance infeasible.

(b) If a child has a physical or mental condition of a temporary and remediable nature that makes the child's attendance in school infeasible, the department shall notify the school in writing that the child is unable to attend school. If the child's physical or mental condition improves so that the child's attendance in school is feasible, the department shall ensure that the child immediately returns to school.

History of Fam. Code §264.115: Acts 2003, 78th Leg., ch. 234, §1, eff. Sept. 1, 2003. Renumbered from §264.113 by Acts 2005, 79th Leg., ch. 728, §23.001(25), eff. June 17, 2005.

FAM §264.116. TEXAS FOSTER GRANDPARENT MENTORS

(a) The department shall make the active recruitment and inclusion of senior citizens a priority in ongoing mentoring initiatives.

(b) An individual who volunteers as a mentor is subject to state and national criminal background checks in accordance with Sections 411.087 and 411.114, Government Code.

(c) The department shall require foster parents or employees of residential child-care facilities to provide appropriate supervision over individuals who serve as mentors during their participation in the mentoring initiative.

(d) Chapter 2109, Government Code, applies to the mentoring initiative described by this section.

History of Fam. Code §264.116: Acts 2005, 79th Leg., ch. 268, §1.50(a), eff. Sept. 1, 2005.

FAM §264.1165. EXPIRED

FAM §264.117. REPEALED

Repealed by Acts 2015, 84th Leg., ch. 722, §5 (eff. June 17, 2015), ch. 944, §86(30) (eff. Sept. 1, 2015).

FAM §264.118. ANNUAL SURVEY

(a) The department shall collect and report service and outcome information for certain current and former foster care youth for use in the National Youth in Transition Database as required by 42 U.S.C. Section 677(f) and 45 C.F.R. Section 1356.80 et seq.

(b) The identity of each child participating in a department survey is confidential and not subject to public disclosure under Chapter 552, Government Code. The department shall adopt procedures to ensure that the identity of each child participating in a department survey remains confidential.

History of Fam. Code §264.118: Acts 2005, 79th Leg., ch. 268, §1.50(a), eff. Sept. 1, 2005. Amended by Acts 2011, 82nd Leg., ch. 598, §7, eff. Sept. 1, 2011.

FAM §264.119. REPEALED

Repealed by Acts 2015, 84th Leg., ch. 722, §5 (eff. June 17, 2015), ch. 944, §86(31) (eff. Sept. 1, 2015).

FAM §264.120. DISCHARGE NOTICE

(a) Except as provided by Subsection (b), a substitute care provider with whom the department contracts

to provide substitute care services for a child shall include in a discharge notice the following information:

(1) the reason for the child's discharge; and

(2) the provider's recommendation regarding a future placement for the child that would increase the child's opportunity to attain a stable placement.

(b) In an emergency situation in which the department is required under the terms of the contract with the substitute care provider to remove a child within 24 hours after receiving the discharge notice, the provider must provide the information required by Subsection (a) to the department not later than 48 hours after the provider sends the discharge notice.

History of Fam. Code §264.120: Acts 2013, 83rd Leg., ch. 1324, §4, eff. Sept. 1, 2013.

A FAM §264.121. TRANSITIONAL LIVING SERVICES PROGRAM

(a) The department shall address the unique challenges facing foster children in the conservatorship of the department who must transition to independent living by:

(1) expanding efforts to improve transition planning and increasing the availability of transitional family group decision-making to all youth age 14 or older in the department's permanent managing conservatorship, including enrolling the youth in the Preparation for Adult Living Program before the age of 16;

(2) coordinating with the commission to obtain authority, to the extent allowed by federal law, the state Medicaid plan, the Title IV-E state plan, and any waiver or amendment to either plan, necessary to:

(A) extend foster care eligibility and transition services for youth up to age 21 and develop policy to permit eligible youth to return to foster care as necessary to achieve the goals of the Transitional Living Services Program; and

(B) extend Medicaid coverage for foster care youth and former foster care youth up to age 21 with a single application at the time the youth leaves foster care; and

(3) entering into cooperative agreements with the Texas Workforce Commission and local workforce development boards to further the objectives of the Preparation for Adult Living Program. The department, the Texas Workforce Commission, and the local workforce development boards shall ensure that services are prioritized and targeted to meet the needs of foster care and former foster care children and that such services will include, where feasible, referrals for short-term stays for youth needing housing.

(a-1) The department shall require a foster care provider to provide or assist youth who are age 14 or older in obtaining experiential life-skills training to improve their transition to independent living. Experiential life-skills training must be tailored to a youth's skills and abilities and must include training in practical activities that include grocery shopping, meal preparation and cooking, performing basic household tasks, and, when appropriate, using public transportation.

(a-2) The experiential life-skills training under Subsection (a-1) must include a financial literacy education program that:

(1) includes instruction on:

(A) obtaining and interpreting a credit score;

(B) protecting, repairing, and improving a credit score;

(C) avoiding predatory lending practices;

(D) saving money and accomplishing financial goals through prudent financial management practices;

(E) using basic banking and accounting skills, including balancing a checkbook;

(F) using debit and credit cards responsibly;

(G) understanding a paycheck and items withheld from a paycheck; and

(H) protecting financial, credit, and identifying information in personal and professional relationships; and

(2) assists a youth who has a source of income to establish a savings plan and, if available, a savings account that the youth can independently manage.

(a-3) The department shall conduct an independent living skills assessment for all youth in the department's conservatorship who are 16 years of age or older.

(a-4) The department shall conduct an independent living skills assessment for all youth in the department's permanent managing conservatorship who are at least 14 years of age but younger than 16 years of age.

(a-5) The department shall annually update the assessment for each youth assessed under Subsections (a-3) and (a-4) to determine the independent living skills the youth learned during the preceding year to ensure that the department's obligation to prepare the

youth for independent living has been met. The department shall conduct the annual update through the youth's plan of service in coordination with the youth, the youth's caseworker, the staff of the Preparation for Adult Living Program, and the youth's caregiver.

(a-6) The department, in coordination with stakeholders, shall develop a plan to standardize the curriculum for the Preparation for Adult Living Program that ensures that youth 14 years of age or older enrolled in the program receive relevant and age-appropriate information and training. The department shall report the plan to the legislature not later than December 1, 2018.

(b) In this section:

(1) "Local workforce development board" means a local workforce development board created under Chapter 2308, Government Code.

(2) "Preparation for Adult Living Program" means a program administered by the department as a component of the Transitional Living Services Program and includes independent living skills assessment, short-term financial assistance, basic self-help skills, and life-skills development and training regarding money management, health and wellness, job skills, planning for the future, housing and transportation, and interpersonal skills.

(3) "Transitional Living Services Program" means a program, administered by the department in accordance with department rules and state and federal law, for youth who are age 14 or older but not more than 21 years of age and are currently or were formerly in foster care, that assists youth in transitioning from foster care to independent living. The program provides transitional living services, Preparation for Adult Living Program services, and Education and Training Voucher Program services.

(c) At the time a child enters the Preparation for Adult Living Program, the department shall provide an information booklet to the child and the foster parent describing the program and the benefits available to the child, including extended Medicaid coverage until age 21, priority status with the Texas Workforce Commission, and the exemption from the payment of tuition and fees at institutions of higher education as defined by Section 61.003, Education Code. The information booklet provided to the child and the foster parent shall be provided in the primary language spoken by that individual.

(d) The department shall allow a youth who is at least 18 years of age to receive transitional living services, other than foster care benefits, while residing with a person who was previously designated as a perpetrator of abuse or neglect if the department determines that despite the person's prior history the person does not pose a threat to the health and safety of the youth.

(e) The department shall ensure that each youth acquires a copy and a certified copy of the youth's birth certificate, a social security card or replacement social security card, as appropriate, and a personal identification certificate under Chapter 521, Transportation Code, on or before the date on which the youth turns 16 years of age. The department shall designate one or more employees in the Preparation for Adult Living Program as the contact person to assist a youth who has not been able to obtain the documents described by this subsection in a timely manner from the youth's primary caseworker. The department shall ensure that:

(1) all youth who are age 16 or older are provided with the contact information for the designated employees; and

(2) a youth who misplaces a document provided under this subsection receives assistance in obtaining a replacement document or information on how to obtain a duplicate copy, as appropriate.

(e-1) If, at the time a youth is discharged from foster care, the youth is at least 18 years of age or has had the disabilities of minority removed, the department shall provide to the youth, not later than the 30th day before the date the youth is discharged from foster care, the following information and documents unless the youth already has the information or document:

(1) the youth's birth certificate;

(2) the youth's immunization records;

(3) the information contained in the youth's health passport;

(4) a personal identification certificate under Chapter 521, Transportation Code;

(5) a social security card or a replacement social security card, if appropriate; and

(6) proof of enrollment in Medicaid, if appropriate.

(e-2) When providing a youth with a document required by Subsection (e-1), the department shall provide the youth with a copy and a certified copy of the document or with the original document, as applicable.

(f) The department shall require a person with whom the department contracts for transitional living services for foster youth to provide or assist youth in obtaining:

(1) housing services;

(2) job training and employment services;

(3) college preparation services;

(4) services that will assist youth in obtaining a general education development certificate;

(5) services that will assist youth in developing skills in food preparation;

(6) nutrition education that promotes healthy food choices;

(7) a savings or checking account if the youth is at least 18 years of age and has a source of income; and

(8) any other appropriate transitional living service identified by the department.

(g) For a youth taking prescription medication, the department shall ensure that the youth's transition plan includes provisions to assist the youth in managing the use of the medication and in managing the child's long-term physical and mental health needs after leaving foster care, including provisions that inform the youth about:

(1) the use of the medication;

(2) the resources that are available to assist the youth in managing the use of the medication; and

(3) informed consent and the provision of medical care in accordance with Section 266.010(*l*).

(h) An entity with which the department contracts for transitional living services for foster youth shall, when appropriate, partner with a community-based organization to assist the entity in providing the transitional living services.

(i) The department shall ensure that the transition plan for each youth 16 years of age or older includes provisions to assist the youth in managing the youth's housing needs after the youth leaves foster care, including provisions that:

(1) identify the cost of housing in relation to the youth's sources of income, including any benefits or rental assistance available to the youth;

(2) if the youth's housing goals include residing with family or friends, state that the department has addressed the following with the youth:

(A) the length of time the youth expects to stay in the housing arrangement;

(B) expectations for the youth regarding paying rent and meeting other household obligations;

(C) the youth's psychological and emotional needs, as applicable; and

(D) any potential conflicts with other household members, or any difficulties connected to the type of housing the youth is seeking, that may arise based on the youth's psychological and emotional needs;

(3) inform the youth about emergency shelters and housing resources, including supervised independent living and housing at colleges and universities, such as dormitories;

(4) require the department to review a common rental application with the youth and ensure that the youth possesses all of the documentation required to obtain rental housing; and

(5) identify any individuals who are able to serve as cosigners or references on the youth's applications for housing.

History of Fam. Code §264.121: Acts 2005, 79th Leg., ch. 268, §1.51, eff. Sept. 1, 2005. Amended by Acts 2007, 80th Leg., ch. 1406, §17, eff. Sept. 1, 2007; Acts 2009, 81st Leg., ch. 407, §§1, 2, eff. Sept. 1, 2009; Acts 2013, 83rd Leg., ch. 168, §1 (eff. Sept. 1, 2013), ch. 204, §6 (eff. Sept. 1, 2013), ch. 342, §1 (eff. June 14, 2013); Acts 2015, 84th Leg., ch. 1, §1.194 (eff. Apr. 2, 2015), ch. 81, §1 (eff. Sept. 1, 2015), ch. 944, §§55, 56 (eff. Sept. 1, 2015), ch. 1236, §§7.004, 7.005, 21.001(18) (eff. Sept. 1, 2015); S.B. 1758, §6, 85th Leg., eff. Sept. 1, 2017.

E FAM §264.1211[A*]. CAREER DEVELOPMENT & EDUCATION PROGRAM

In 2017, the Legislature enacted three sections 264.1211. This §264.1211 was enacted by S.B. 1220, §3, 85th Leg., effective June 1, 2017. The [A] has been added by the editor to distinguish this §264.1211 from the others, which are marked with [B*] or [C*]. In 2019, the Legislature is expected to correct the identical numbering.*

(a) The department shall collaborate with local workforce development boards, foster care transition centers, community and technical colleges, schools, and any other appropriate workforce industry resources to create a program that:

(1) assists foster care youth and former foster care youth in obtaining:

(A) a high school diploma or a high school equivalency certificate; and

(B) industry certifications that are necessary for occupations that are in high demand;

(2) provides career guidance to foster care youth and former foster care youth; and

(3) informs foster care youth and former foster care youth about the tuition and fee waivers for institutions of higher education that are available under Section 54.366, Education Code.

(b) Not later than September 1, 2018, the department, in collaboration with the Texas Education Agency, shall produce a report on the program created under Subsection (a). The report must include recommendations for legislative or other action to further develop the program. The department shall submit the report to the governor, the lieutenant governor, the speaker of the house of representatives, and the standing committees of the legislature with jurisdiction over education. This subsection expires September 1, 2019.

History of Fam. Code §264.1211[A*]: Enacted by S.B. 1220, §3, 85th Leg., eff. June 1, 2017.

E FAM §264.1211[B*]. RECORDS & DOCUMENTS FOR CHILDREN AGING OUT OF FOSTER CARE

In 2017, the Legislature enacted three sections 264.1211. This §264.1211 was enacted by H.B. 3338, §1, 85th Leg., effective June 15, 2017. The [B] has been added by the editor to distinguish this §264.1211 from the others, which are marked with [A*] or [C*]. In 2019, the Legislature is expected to correct the identical numbering.*

The department in cooperation with volunteer advocates from a charitable organization described by Subchapter C, Chapter 107, and the Department of Public Safety shall develop procedures to ensure that a foster child obtains a driver's license or personal identification card before the child leaves the conservatorship of the department.

History of Fam. Code §264.1211[B*]: Enacted by H.B. 3338, §1, 85th Leg., eff. June 15, 2017.

E FAM §264.1211[C*]. FACILITATION OF TRANSITION TO INSTITUTION OF HIGHER EDUCATION

In 2017, the Legislature enacted three sections 264.1211. This §264.1211 was enacted by H.B. 928, §1, 85th Leg., effective June 1, 2017. The [C] has been added by the editor to distinguish this §264.1211 from the others, which are marked with [A*] or [B*]. In 2019, the Legislature is expected to correct the identical numbering.*

(a) In this section, "community resource coordination group" means a coordination group established under a memorandum of understanding under Section 531.055, Government Code.

(b) A department employee who is a member of a community resource coordination group shall inform the group about the tuition and fee waivers for institutions of higher education that are available to eligible children in foster care under Section 54.366, Education Code.

(c) Each school district, in coordination with the department, shall facilitate the transition of each child enrolled in the district who is eligible for a tuition and fee waiver under Section 54.366, Education Code, and who is likely to be in the conservatorship of the department on the day preceding the child's 18th birthday to an institution of higher education by:

(1) assisting the child with the completion of any applications for admission or for financial aid;

(2) arranging and accompanying the child on campus visits;

(3) assisting the child in researching and applying for private or institution-sponsored scholarships;

(4) identifying whether the child is a candidate for appointment to a military academy;

(5) assisting the child in registering and preparing for college entrance examinations, including, subject to the availability of funds, arranging for the payment of any examination fees by the department; and

(6) coordinating contact between the child and a liaison officer designated under Section 61.0908, Education Code, for students who were formerly in the department's conservatorship.

History of Fam. Code §264.1211[C*]: Enacted by H.B. 928, §1, 85th Leg., eff. June 1, 2017.

FAM §264.122. COURT APPROVAL REQUIRED FOR TRAVEL OUTSIDE UNITED STATES BY CHILD IN FOSTER CARE

(a) A child for whom the department has been appointed managing conservator and who has been placed in foster care may travel outside of the United States only if the person with whom the child has been placed has petitioned the court for, and the court has rendered an order granting, approval for the child to travel outside of the United States.

(b) The court shall provide notice to the department and to any other person entitled to notice in the

suit if the court renders an order granting approval for the child to travel outside of the United States under this section.

History of Fam. Code §264.122: Acts 2007, 80th Leg., ch. 1406, §18, eff. Sept. 1, 2007.

FAM §264.123. REPORTS CONCERNING CHILDREN WHO ARE MISSING OR VICTIMS OF SEX TRAFFICKING

(a) If a child in the department's managing conservatorship is missing from the child's substitute care provider, including a child who is abducted or is a runaway, the department shall notify the following persons that the child is missing:

(1) the appropriate law enforcement agencies;

(2) the court with jurisdiction over the department's managing conservatorship of the child;

(3) the child's attorney ad litem;

(4) the child's guardian ad litem; and

(5) the child's parent unless the parent:

(A) cannot be located or contacted;

(B) has had the parent's parental rights terminated; or

(C) has executed an affidavit of relinquishment of parental rights.

(b) The department shall provide the notice required by Subsection (a) not later than 24 hours after the time the department learns that the child is missing or as soon as possible if a person entitled to notice under that subsection cannot be notified within 24 hours.

(c) If a child has been reported as a missing child under Subsection (a), the department shall notify the persons described by Subsection (a) when the child returns to the child's substitute care provider not later than 24 hours after the time the department learns that the child has returned or as soon as possible if a person entitled to notice cannot be notified within 24 hours.

(d) The department shall make continuing efforts to determine the location of a missing child until the child returns to substitute care, including:

(1) contacting on a monthly basis:

(A) the appropriate law enforcement agencies;

(B) the child's relatives;

(C) the child's former caregivers; and

(D) any state or local social service agency that may be providing services to the child; and

(2) conducting a supervisory-level review of the case on a quarterly basis if the child is 15 years of age or younger to determine whether sufficient efforts have been made to locate the child and whether other action is needed.

(e) The department shall document in the missing child's case record:

(1) the actions taken by the department to:

(A) determine the location of the child; and

(B) persuade the child to return to substitute care;

(2) any discussion during, and determination resulting from, the supervisory-level review under Subsection (d)(2);

(3) any discussion with law enforcement officials following the return of the child regarding the child's absence; and

(4) any discussion with the child described by Subsection (f).

(f) After a missing child returns to the child's substitute care provider, the department shall interview the child to determine the reasons why the child was missing, where the child stayed during the time the child was missing, and whether, while missing, the child was a victim of conduct that constitutes an offense under Section 20A.02(a)(7), Penal Code. The department shall report to an appropriate law enforcement agency any disclosure made by a child that indicates that the child was the victim of a crime during the time the child was missing. The department shall make a report under this subsection not later than 24 hours after the time the disclosure is made. The department is not required to interview a missing child under this subsection if, at the time the child returns, the department knows that the child was abducted and another agency is investigating the abduction.

(g) The department shall collect information on each child in the department's managing conservatorship who is missing from the child's substitute care provider and on each child who, while in the department's managing conservatorship, is a victim of conduct that constitutes an offense under Section 20A.02(a)(7), Penal Code. The collected information must include information on:

(1) whether the managing conservatorship of the department is temporary or permanent;

(2) the type of substitute care in which the child is placed; and

(3) the child's sex, age, race, and ethnicity and the department region in which the child resides.

(h) The department shall prepare an annual report on the information collected under Subsection (g) and make the report available on the department's Internet website. The report may not include any individually identifiable information regarding a child who is the subject of information in the report.

History of Fam. Code §264.123: Acts 2011, 82nd Leg., ch. 1130, §1, eff. Sept. 1, 2011. Amended by Acts 2015, 84th Leg., ch. 713, §§2, 3, eff. Sept. 1, 2015.

FAM §264.124[A*]. FOSTER PARENT PILOT PROGRAM

In 2013, the Legislature enacted two sections 264.124. This §264.124 was enacted by Acts 2013, 83rd Leg., ch. 444, §1, effective Sept. 1, 2013. The [A] has been added by the editor to distinguish this §264.124 from the other, which is marked with [B*]. In 2015, Acts 2015, 84th Leg., ch. 1236, §21.001(19), effective Sept. 1, 2015, attempted to renumber this §264.124 to §264.125, but the enactment of §264.125 by Acts 2015, 84th Leg., ch. 262, §7, effective Sept. 1, 2015, prevailed.*

(a) The department shall establish a pilot program to provide specialized training to foster parents of children who have been traumatized or have serious mental health needs if the department or another state agency is able to provide the training using existing resources or a local governmental entity or charitable organization is able to provide the training at no cost to the state.

(b) The department shall:

(1) establish the pilot program in a county with a population of at least 1.5 million that is within 200 miles of an international border;

(2) coordinate the specialized training as part of community-based services and support provided under a Wraparound individualized planning process for foster children as prescribed by the Texas Integrated Funding Initiative Consortium; and

(3) evaluate the pilot program not later than the second anniversary of the date the program is established.

(c) The department shall prepare a report containing the evaluation required under Subsection (b)(3) and the department's recommendations on the feasibility and continuation of the pilot program. The department shall submit electronically a copy of the report to the governor, lieutenant governor, and speaker of the house of representatives not later than December 1, 2016.

(d) This section expires September 1, 2017.

History of Fam. Code §264.124[A*]: Acts 2013, 83rd Leg., ch. 444, §1, eff. Sept. 1, 2013. Amended by Acts 2015, 84th Leg., ch. 1236, §21.001(19), eff. Sept. 1, 2015.

FAM §264.124[B*]. DAY CARE FOR FOSTER CHILD

In 2013, the Legislature enacted two sections 264.124. This §264.124 was enacted by Acts 2013, 83rd Leg., ch. 423, §1, effective Sept. 1, 2013. The [B] has been added by the editor to distinguish this §264.124 from the other, which is marked with [A*].*

(a) In this section, "day care" means the assessment, care, training, education, custody, treatment, or supervision of a foster child by a person other than the child's foster parent for less than 24 hours a day, but at least two hours a day, three or more days a week.

(b) The department, in accordance with department rules, shall implement a process to verify that each foster parent who is seeking monetary assistance from the department for day care for a foster child has attempted to find appropriate day-care services for the foster child through community services, including Head Start programs, prekindergarten classes, and early education programs offered in public schools. The department shall specify the documentation the foster parent must provide to the department to demonstrate compliance with the requirements established under this subsection.

(c) Except as provided by Subsection (d), the department may not provide monetary assistance to a foster parent for day care for a foster child unless the department receives the verification required under Subsection (b).

(d) The department may provide monetary assistance to a foster parent for a foster child without the verification required under Subsection (b) if the department determines the verification would prevent an emergency placement that is in the child's best interest.

History of Fam. Code §264.124[B*]: Acts 2013, 83rd Leg., ch. 423, §1, eff. Sept. 1, 2013. Amended by Acts 2015, 84th Leg., ch. 1, §1.195, eff. Apr. 2, 2015.

FAM §264.125. AGE-APPROPRIATE NORMALCY ACTIVITIES; STANDARD OF CARE

(a) The department shall use its best efforts to normalize the lives of children in the managing conserva-

torship of the department by allowing substitute caregivers, without the department's prior approval, to make decisions similar to those a parent would be entitled to make regarding a child's participation in age-appropriate normalcy activities.

(b) In determining whether to allow a child in the managing conservatorship of the department to participate in an activity, a substitute caregiver must exercise the standard of care of a reasonable and prudent parent.

(c) The department shall adopt and implement policies consistent with this section promoting a substitute caregiver's ability to make decisions described by Subsection (a). The department shall identify and review any departmental policy or procedure that may impede a substitute caregiver's ability to make such decisions.

(d) The department shall require licensed child placing agency personnel, residential child care licensing staff, conservatorship caseworkers, and other persons as may be determined by the department to complete a course of training regarding:

(1) the importance of a child's participation in age-appropriate normalcy activities and the benefits of such activities to a child's well-being, mental health, and social, emotional, and developmental growth; and

(2) substitute caregiver decision-making under the standard of care of a reasonable and prudent parent.

History of Fam. Code §264.125: Acts 2015, 84th Leg., ch. 262, §7, eff. Sept. 1, 2015.

E FAM §264.1251. SUMMER INTERNSHIP PILOT PROGRAM

(a) The department shall establish a summer internship pilot program that provides foster youth with the opportunity to develop marketable job skills and obtain professional work experience through a summer internship with a participating business, nonprofit organization, or governmental entity.

(b) The department may collaborate with other state agencies, as appropriate, to establish the pilot program. The pilot program may be implemented in more than one department region.

(c) The department may enter into an agreement with one or more entities described by Subsection (a) to allow the entity to award internships to youth who participate in the pilot program. Internships provided under the pilot program may be paid or unpaid.

(d) Not later than April 1 of each year, the department shall select foster youth or former foster youth who are 15 years of age or older to participate in the pilot program. Each youth participating in the pilot program shall enter into an agreement with the organization awarding the internship and the department relating to the terms of the youth's internship.

(e) The department shall complete an evaluation of the pilot program not later than the second anniversary of the date the program begins.

(f) The department shall submit a report on the evaluation of the pilot program to the governor, the lieutenant governor, and the speaker of the house of representatives. The report must include:

(1) the number of youth who participated in the pilot program;

(2) the location and type of internships provided under the pilot program; and

(3) details of the department's efforts to recruit eligible youth to participate in the pilot program.

(g) The executive commissioner may adopt rules necessary to implement this section.

(h) This section expires September 1, 2021.

History of Fam. Code §264.1251: Enacted by H.B. 1608, §1, 85th Leg., eff. June 15, 2017.

E FAM §264.1252. FOSTER PARENT RECRUITMENT STUDY

(a) In this section, "young adult caregiver" means a person who:

(1) is at least 21 years of age but younger than 36 years of age; and

(2) provides foster care for children who are 14 years of age and older.

(b) The department shall conduct a study on the feasibility of developing a program to recruit and provide training for young adult caregivers.

(c) The department shall complete the study not later than December 31, 2018. In evaluating the feasibility of the program, the department shall consider methods to recruit young adult caregivers and the potential impact that the program will have on the foster children participating in the program, including whether the program may result in:

(1) increased placement stability;

(2) fewer behavioral issues;

(3) fewer instances of foster children running away from a placement;

(4) increased satisfactory academic progress in school;

(5) increased acquisition of independent living skills; and

(6) an improved sense of well-being.

(d) The department shall report the results of the study to the governor, lieutenant governor, speaker of the house of representatives, and members of the legislature as soon as possible after the study is completed.

(e) This section expires September 1, 2019.

History of Fam. Code §264.1252: Enacted by S.B. 11, §16(a), 85th Leg., eff. Sept. 1, 2017.

Ⓐ FAM §264.126. RENUMBERED

Renumbered as §264.153 by S.B. 11, §18(b), 85th Leg., eff. Sept. 1, 2017.

Ⓔ FAM §264.1261. FOSTER CARE CAPACITY NEEDS PLAN

☠ *Subsection (a) was enacted by H.B. 1549, §4, 85th Leg., enacted May 28, 2017, effective Sept. 1, 2017, without reference to the conflicting enactment made by S.B. 11, §17(a), 85th Leg., enacted May 28, 2017, effective Sept. 1, 2017. For harmonizing conflicts, see p. V.*

(a) In this section, "community-based foster care" means the redesigned foster care services system required by Chapter 598 (S.B. 218), Acts of the 82nd Legislature, Regular Session, 2011.

☠ *Subsection (a) was enacted by S.B. 11, §17(a), 85th Leg., enacted May 28, 2017, effective Sept. 1, 2017, without reference to the conflicting enactment made by H.B. 1549, §4, 85th Leg., enacted May 28, 2017, effective Sept. 1, 2017. For harmonizing conflicts, see p. V.*

(a) In this section, "community-based care" has the meaning assigned by Section 264.152.

(b) Appropriate department management personnel from a child protective services region in which community-based foster care has not been implemented, in collaboration with foster care providers, faith-based entities, and child advocates in that region, shall use data collected by the department on foster care capacity needs and availability of each type of foster care and kinship placement in the region to create a plan to address the substitute care capacity needs in the region. The plan must identify both short-term and long-term goals and strategies for addressing those capacity needs.

(c) A foster care capacity needs plan developed under Subsection (b) must be:

(1) submitted to and approved by the commissioner; and

(2) updated annually.

(d) The department shall publish each initial foster care capacity needs plan and each annual update to a plan on the department's Internet website.

History of Fam. Code §264.1261: Enacted by H.B. 1549, §4, 85th Leg., eff. Sept. 1, 2017; S.B. 11, §17(a), 85th Leg., eff. Sept. 1, 2017.

Ⓔ FAM §264.128. SINGLE CHILD PLAN OF SERVICE INITIATIVE

(a) In this section, "community-based care" has the meaning assigned by Section 264.152.

(b) In regions of the state where community-based care has not been implemented, the department shall:

(1) collaborate with child-placing agencies to implement the single child plan of service model developed under the single child plan of service initiative; and

(2) ensure that a single child plan of service is developed for each child in foster care in those regions.

History of Fam. Code §264.128: Enacted by S.B. 11, §17(a), 85th Leg., eff. Sept. 1, 2017.

Sections 264.129-264.150 reserved for expansion

Ⓔ SUBCHAPTER B-1. COMMUNITY-BASED CARE

FAM §264.151. LEGISLATIVE INTENT

(a) It is the intent of the legislature that the department contract with community-based nonprofit and local governmental entities that have the ability to provide child welfare services. The services provided by the entities must include direct case management to ensure child safety, permanency, and well-being, in accordance with state and federal child welfare goals.

(b) It is the intent of the legislature that the provision of community-based care for children be implemented with measurable goals relating to:

(1) the safety of children in placements;

(2) the placement of children in each child's home community;

(3) the provision of services to children in the least restrictive environment possible and, if possible, in a family home environment;

(4) minimal placement changes for children;

(5) the maintenance of contact between children and their families and other important persons;

(6) the placement of children with siblings;

(7) the provision of services that respect each child's culture;

(8) the preparation of children and youth in foster care for adulthood;

(9) the provision of opportunities, experiences, and activities for children and youth in foster care that are available to children and youth who are not in foster care;

(10) the participation by children and youth in making decisions relating to their own lives;

(11) the reunification of children with the biological parents of the children when possible; and

(12) the promotion of the placement of children with relative or kinship caregivers if reunification is not possible.

History of Fam. Code §264.151: Enacted by H.B. 5, §13, 85th Leg., eff. Sept. 1, 2017; S.B. 11, §18(a), 85th Leg., eff. Sept. 1, 2017.

FAM §264.152. DEFINITIONS

Except as otherwise provided, in this subchapter:

(1) "Alternative caregiver" means a person who is not the foster parent of the child and who provides temporary care for the child for more than 12 hours but less than 60 days.

(2) "Case management" means the provision of case management services to a child for whom the department has been appointed temporary or permanent managing conservator or to the child's family, a young adult in extended foster care, a relative or kinship caregiver, or a child who has been placed in the catchment area through the Interstate Compact on the Placement of Children, and includes:

(A) caseworker visits with the child;

(B) family and caregiver visits;

(C) convening and conducting permanency planning meetings;

(D) the development and revision of child and family plans of service, including a permanency plan and goals for a child or young adult in care;

(E) the coordination and monitoring of services required by the child and the child's family;

(F) the assumption of court-related duties regarding the child, including:

(i) providing any required notifications or consultations;

(ii) preparing court reports;

(iii) attending judicial and permanency hearings, trials, and mediations;

(iv) complying with applicable court orders; and

(v) ensuring the child is progressing toward the goal of permanency within state and federally mandated guidelines; and

(G) any other function or service that the department determines necessary to allow a single source continuum contractor to assume responsibility for case management.

(3) "Catchment area" means a geographic service area for providing child protective services that is identified as part of community-based care.

(4) "Community-based care" means the foster care redesign required by Chapter 598 (S.B. 218), Acts of the 82nd Legislature, Regular Session, 2011, as designed and implemented in accordance with the plan required by Section 264.153.

History of Fam. Code §264.152: Enacted by S.B. 11, §18(a), 85th Leg., eff. Sept. 1, 2017.

A FAM §264.153 [264.126]. COMMUNITY-BASED CARE [REDESIGN] IMPLEMENTATION PLAN

(a) The department shall develop and maintain a plan for implementing community-based [the foster] care [redesign required by Chapter 598 (S.B. 218), Acts of the 82nd Legislature, Regular Session, 2011]. The plan must:

(1) describe the department's expectations, goals, and approach to implementing community-based [foster] care [redesign];

(2) include a timeline for implementing community-based [the foster] care [redesign] throughout this state, any limitations related to the implementation, and a progressive intervention plan and a contingency plan to provide continuity of the delivery of foster care services and services for relative and kinship caregivers [service delivery] if a contract with a single source continuum contractor ends prematurely;

(3) delineate and define the case management roles and responsibilities of the department and the department's contractors and the duties, employees, and related funding that will be transferred to the contractor by the department;

(4) identify any training needs and include long-range and continuous plans for training and cross-training staff, including plans to train caseworkers using the standardized curriculum created by the human trafficking prevention task force under Section

FAM §264.153

402.035(d)(6), Government Code, as that section existed on August 31, 2017;

(5) include a plan for evaluating the costs and tasks associated with each contract procurement, including the initial and ongoing contract costs for the department and contractor;

(6) include the department's contract monitoring approach and a plan for evaluating the performance of each contractor and the community-based [~~foster~~] care [~~redesign~~] system as a whole that includes an independent evaluation of each contractor's processes and fiscal and qualitative outcomes; and

(7) include a report on transition issues resulting from implementation of community-based [~~the foster~~] care [~~redesign~~].

(b) The department shall annually:

(1) update the implementation plan developed under this section and post the updated plan on the department's Internet website; and

(2) post on the department's Internet website the progress the department has made toward its goals for implementing community-based [~~the foster~~] care [~~redesign~~].

History of Fam. Code §264.153: Acts 2015, 84th Leg., ch. 944, §57, eff. Sept. 1, 2015. Renumbered from §264.126 and amended by S.B. 11, §18(b), 85th Leg., eff. Sept. 1, 2017.

FAM §264.154. QUALIFICATIONS OF SINGLE SOURCE CONTINUUM CONTRACTOR; SELECTION

(a) To enter into a contract with the commission or department to serve as a single source continuum contractor to provide foster care service delivery, an entity must be a nonprofit entity that has an organizational mission focused on child welfare or a governmental entity.

(b) In selecting a single source continuum contractor, the department shall consider whether a prospective contractor for a catchment area has demonstrated experience in providing services to children and families in the catchment area.

History of Fam. Code §264.154: Enacted by S.B. 11, §18(a), 85th Leg., eff. Sept. 1, 2017.

FAM §264.155. REQUIRED CONTRACT PROVISIONS

A contract with a single source continuum contractor to provide community-based care services in a catchment area must include provisions that:

(1) establish a timeline for the implementation of community-based care in the catchment area, including a timeline for implementing:

(A) case management services for children, families, and relative and kinship caregivers receiving services in the catchment area; and

(B) family reunification support services to be provided after a child receiving services from the contractor is returned to the child's family;

(2) establish conditions for the single source continuum contractor's access to relevant department data and require the participation of the contractor in the data access and standards governance council created under Section 264.159;

(3) require the single source continuum contractor to create a single process for the training and use of alternative caregivers for all child-placing agencies in the catchment area to facilitate reciprocity of licenses for alternative caregivers between agencies, including respite and overnight care providers, as those terms are defined by department rule;

(4) require the single source continuum contractor to maintain a diverse network of service providers that offer a range of foster capacity options and that can accommodate children from diverse cultural backgrounds;

(5) allow the department to conduct a performance review of the contractor beginning 18 months after the contractor has begun providing case management and family reunification support services to all children and families in the catchment area and determine if the contractor has achieved any performance outcomes specified in the contract;

(6) following the review under Subdivision (5), allow the department to:

(A) impose financial penalties on the contractor for failing to meet any specified performance outcomes; or

(B) award financial incentives to the contractor for exceeding any specified performance outcomes;

(7) require the contractor to give preference for employment to employees of the department:

(A) whose position at the department is impacted by the implementation of community-based care; and

(B) who are considered by the department to be employees in good standing;

(8) require the contractor to provide preliminary and ongoing community engagement plans to ensure

communication and collaboration with local stakeholders in the catchment area, including any of the following:

(A) community faith-based entities;

(B) the judiciary;

(C) court-appointed special advocates;

(D) child advocacy centers;

(E) service providers;

(F) foster families;

(G) biological parents;

(H) foster youth and former foster youth;

(I) relative or kinship caregivers;

(J) child welfare boards, if applicable;

(K) attorneys ad litem;

(L) attorneys that represent parents involved in suits filed by the department; and

(M) any other stakeholders, as determined by the contractor; and

(9) require that the contractor comply with any applicable court order issued by a court of competent jurisdiction in the case of a child for whom the contractor has assumed case management responsibilities or an order imposing a requirement on the department that relates to functions assumed by the contractor.

History of Fam. Code §264.155: Enacted by S.B. 11, §18(a), 85th Leg., eff. Sept. 1, 2017.

FAM §264.156. READINESS REVIEW PROCESS FOR COMMUNITY-BASED CARE CONTRACTOR

(a) The department shall develop a formal review process to assess the ability of a single source continuum contractor to satisfy the responsibilities and administrative requirements of delivering foster care services and services for relative and kinship caregivers, including the contractor's ability to provide:

(1) case management services for children and families;

(2) evidence-based, promising practice, or evidence-informed supports for children and families; and

(3) sufficient available capacity for inpatient and outpatient services and supports for children at all service levels who have previously been placed in the catchment area.

(b) As part of the readiness review process, the single source continuum contractor must prepare a plan detailing the methods by which the contractor will avoid or eliminate conflicts of interest. The department may not transfer services to the contractor until the department has determined the plan is adequate.

(c) The department and commission must develop the review process under Subsection (a) before the department may expand community-based care outside of the initial catchment areas where community-based care has been implemented.

(d) If after conducting the review process developed under Subsection (a) the department determines that a single source continuum contractor is able to adequately deliver foster care services and services for relative and kinship caregivers in advance of the projected dates stated in the timeline included in the contract with the contractor, the department may adjust the timeline to allow for an earlier transition of service delivery to the contractor.

History of Fam. Code §264.156: Enacted by S.B. 11, §18(a), 85th Leg., eff. Sept. 1, 2017.

FAM §264.157. EXPANSION OF COMMUNITY-BASED CARE

(a) Not later than December 31, 2019, the department shall:

(1) identify not more than eight catchment areas in the state that are best suited to implement community-based care; and

(2) following the implementation of community-based care services in those catchment areas, evaluate the implementation process and single source continuum contractor performance in each catchment area.

(b) Notwithstanding the process for the expansion of community-based care described in Subsection (a), and in accordance with the community-based care implementation plan developed under Section 264.153, beginning September 1, 2017, the department shall begin accepting applications from entities to provide community-based care services in a designated catchment area.

(c) In expanding community-based care, the department may change the geographic boundaries of catchment areas as necessary to align with specific communities.

(d) The department shall ensure the continuity of services for children and families during the transition period to community-based care in a catchment area.

History of Fam. Code §264.157: Enacted by S.B. 11, §18(a), 85th Leg., eff. Sept. 1, 2017.

FAM §264.158. TRANSFER OF CASE MANAGEMENT SERVICES TO SINGLE SOURCE CONTINUUM CONTRACTOR

(a) In each initial catchment area where community-based care has been implemented or a contract with a single source continuum contractor has been executed before September 1, 2017, the department shall transfer to the single source continuum contractor providing foster care services in that area:

(1) the case management of children, relative and kinship caregivers, and families receiving services from that contractor; and

(2) family reunification support services to be provided after a child receiving services from the contractor is returned to the child's family for the period of time ordered by the court.

(b) The commission shall include a provision in a contract with a single source continuum contractor to provide foster care services and services for relative and kinship caregivers in a catchment area to which community-based care is expanded after September 1, 2017, that requires the transfer to the contractor of the provision of:

(1) the case management services for children, relative and kinship caregivers, and families in the catchment area where the contractor will be operating; and

(2) family reunification support services to be provided after a child receiving services from the contractor is returned to the child's family.

(c) The department shall collaborate with a single source continuum contractor to establish an initial case transfer planning team to:

(1) address any necessary data transfer;

(2) establish file transfer procedures; and

(3) notify relevant persons regarding the transfer of services to the contractor.

History of Fam. Code §264.158: Enacted by S.B. 11, §18(a), 85th Leg., eff. Sept. 1, 2017.

FAM §264.159. DATA ACCESS & STANDARDS GOVERNANCE COUNCIL

(a) The department shall create a data access and standards governance council to develop protocols for the electronic transfer of data from single source continuum contractors to the department to allow the contractors to perform case management functions.

(b) The council shall develop protocols for the access, management, and security of case data that is electronically shared by a single source continuum contractor with the department.

History of Fam. Code §264.159: Enacted by S.B. 11, §18(a), 85th Leg., eff. Sept. 1, 2017.

FAM §264.160. LIABILITY INSURANCE REQUIREMENTS

A single source continuum contractor and any subcontractor of the single source continuum contractor providing community-based care services shall maintain minimum insurance coverage, as required in the contract with the department, to minimize the risk of insolvency and protect against damages. The executive commissioner may adopt rules to implement this section.

History of Fam. Code §264.160: Enacted by S.B. 11, §18(a), 85th Leg., eff. Sept. 1, 2017.

FAM §264.161. STATUTORY DUTIES ASSUMED BY CONTRACTOR

Except as provided by Section 264.163, a single source continuum contractor providing foster care services and services for relative and kinship caregivers in a catchment area must, either directly or through subcontractors, assume the statutory duties of the department in connection with the delivery of foster care services and services for relative and kinship caregivers in that catchment area.

History of Fam. Code §264.161: Enacted by S.B. 11, §18(a), 85th Leg., eff. Sept. 1, 2017.

FAM §264.162. REVIEW OF CONTRACTOR PERFORMANCE

The department shall develop a formal review process to evaluate a single source continuum contractor's implementation of placement services and case management services in a catchment area.

History of Fam. Code §264.162: Enacted by S.B. 11, §18(a), 85th Leg., eff. Sept. 1, 2017.

FAM §264.163. CONTINUING DUTIES OF DEPARTMENT

In a catchment area in which a single source continuum contractor is providing family-based safety services or community-based care services, legal representation of the department in an action under this code shall be provided in accordance with Section 264.009.

History of Fam. Code §264.163: Enacted by S.B. 11, §18(a), 85th Leg., eff. Sept. 1, 2017.

FAM §264.164. CONFIDENTIALITY

(a) The records of a single source continuum contractor relating to the provision of community-based

care services in a catchment area are subject to Chapter 552, Government Code, in the same manner as the records of the department are subject to that chapter.

(b) Subchapter C, Chapter 261, regarding the confidentiality of certain case information, applies to the records of a single source continuum contractor in relation to the provision of services by the contractor.

History of Fam. Code §264.164: Enacted by S.B. 11, §18(a), 85th Leg., eff. Sept. 1, 2017.

FAM §264.165. NOTICE REQUIRED FOR EARLY TERMINATION OF CONTRACT

(a) A single source continuum contractor may terminate a contract entered into under this subchapter by providing notice to the department and the commission of the contractor's intent to terminate the contract not later than the 60th day before the date of the termination.

(b) The department may terminate a contract entered into with a single source continuum contractor under this subchapter by providing notice to the contractor of the department's intent to terminate the contract not later than the 30th day before the date of termination.

History of Fam. Code §264.165: Enacted by S.B. 11, §18(a), 85th Leg., eff. Sept. 1, 2017.

FAM §264.166. CONTINGENCY PLAN IN EVENT OF EARLY CONTRACT TERMINATION

(a) In each catchment area in which community-based care is implemented, the department shall create a contingency plan to ensure the continuity of services for children and families in the catchment area in the event of an early termination of the contract with the single source continuum contractor providing foster care services in that catchment area.

(b) To support each contingency plan, the single source continuum contractor providing foster care services in that catchment area, subject to approval by the department, shall develop a transfer plan to ensure the continuity of services for children and families in the catchment area in the event of an early termination of the contract with the department. The contractor shall submit an updated transfer plan each year and six months before the end of the contract period, including any extension. The department is not limited or restricted in requiring additional information from the contractor or requiring the contractor to modify the transfer plan as necessary.

(c) If a single source continuum contractor gives notice to the department of an early contract termination, the department may enter into a contract with a different contractor for the sole purpose of assuming the contract that is being terminated.

History of Fam. Code §264.166: Enacted by S.B. 11, §18(a), 85th Leg., eff. Sept. 1, 2017.

FAM §264.167. ATTORNEY-CLIENT PRIVILEGE

An employee, agent, or representative of a single source continuum contractor is considered to be a client's representative of the department for purposes of the privilege under Rule 503, Texas Rules of Evidence, as that privilege applies to communications with a prosecuting attorney or other attorney representing the department, or the attorney's representatives, in a proceeding under this subtitle.

History of Fam. Code §264.167: Enacted by S.B. 11, §18(a), 85th Leg., eff. Sept. 1, 2017.

FAM §264.168. REVIEW OF CONTRACTOR RECOMMENDATIONS BY DEPARTMENT

(a) Notwithstanding any other provision of this subchapter governing the transfer of case management authority to a single source continuum contractor, the department may review, approve, or disapprove a contractor's recommendation with respect to a child's permanency goal.

(b) Subsection (a) may not be construed to limit or restrict the authority of the department to include necessary oversight measures and review processes to maintain compliance with federal and state requirements in a contract with a single source continuum contractor.

(c) The department shall develop an internal dispute resolution process to decide disagreements between a single source continuum contractor and the department.

History of Fam. Code §264.168: Enacted by S.B. 11, §18(a), 85th Leg., eff. Sept. 1, 2017.

FAM §264.169. PILOT PROGRAM FOR FAMILY-BASED SAFETY SERVICES

(a) In this section, "case management services" means the direct delivery and coordination of a network of formal and informal activities and services in a catchment area where the department has entered into, or is in the process of entering into, a contract

with a single source continuum contractor to provide family-based safety services and case management and includes:

(1) caseworker visits with the child and all caregivers;

(2) family visits;

(3) family group conferencing or family group decision-making;

(4) development of the family plan of service;

(5) monitoring, developing, securing, and coordinating services;

(6) evaluating the progress of children, caregivers, and families receiving services;

(7) assuring that the rights of children, caregivers, and families receiving services are protected;

(8) duties relating to family-based safety services ordered by a court, including:

(A) providing any required notifications or consultations;

(B) preparing court reports;

(C) attending judicial hearings, trials, and mediations;

(D) complying with applicable court orders; and

(E) ensuring the child is progressing toward the goal of permanency within state and federally mandated guidelines; and

(9) any other function or service that the department determines is necessary to allow a single source continuum contractor to assume responsibility for case management.

(b) The department shall develop and implement in two child protective services regions of the state a pilot program under which the commission contracts with a single nonprofit entity that has an organizational mission focused on child welfare or a governmental entity in each region to provide family-based safety services and case management for children and families receiving family-based safety services. The contract must include a transition plan for the provision of services that ensures the continuity of services for children and families in the selected regions.

(c) The contract with an entity must include performance-based provisions that require the entity to achieve the following outcomes for families receiving services from the entity:

(1) a decrease in recidivism;

(2) an increase in protective factors; and

(3) any other performance-based outcome specified by the department.

(d) The commission may only contract for implementation of the pilot program with entities that the department considers to have the capacity to provide, either directly or through subcontractors, an array of evidence-based, promising practice, or evidence-informed services and support programs to children and families in the selected child protective services regions.

(e) The contracted entity must perform all statutory duties of the department in connection with the delivery of the services specified in Subsection (b).

(f) The contracted entity must give preference for employment to employees of the department:

(1) whose position at the department is impacted by the implementation of community-based care; and

(2) who are considered by the department to be employees in good standing.

(g) Not later than December 31, 2018, the department shall report to the appropriate standing committees of the legislature having jurisdiction over child protective services and foster care matters on the progress of the pilot program. The report must include:

(1) an evaluation of each contracted entity's success in achieving the outcomes described by Subsection (c); and

(2) a recommendation as to whether the pilot program should be continued, expanded, or terminated.

History of Fam. Code §264.169: Enacted by S.B. 11, §18(a), 85th Leg., eff. Sept. 1, 2017.

FAM §264.170. LIMITED LIABILITY FOR SINGLE SOURCE CONTINUUM CONTRACTOR & RELATED PERSONNEL

(a) A nonprofit entity that contracts with the department to provide services as a single source continuum contractor under this subchapter is considered to be a charitable organization for the purposes of Chapter 84, Civil Practice and Remedies Code, with respect to the provision of those services, and that chapter applies to the entity and any person who is an employee or volunteer of the entity.

(b) The limitations on liability provided by this section apply:

(1) only to an act or omission by the entity or person, as applicable, that occurs while the entity or person

is acting within the course and scope of the entity's contract with the department and the person's duties for the entity; and

(2) only if insurance coverage in the minimum amounts required by Chapter 84, Civil Practice and Remedies Code, is in force and effect at the time a cause of action for personal injury, death, or property damage accrues.

History of Fam. Code §264.170: Enacted by H.B. 5, §13, 85th Leg., eff. Sept. 1, 2017.

Sections 264.171-264.200 reserved for expansion

SUBCHAPTER C. CHILD & FAMILY SERVICES

A FAM §264.201. SERVICES BY DEPARTMENT

(a) When the department provides services directly or by contract to an abused or neglected child and the child's family, the services shall be designed to:

(1) prevent further abuse;

(2) alleviate the effects of the abuse suffered;

(3) prevent removal of the child from the home; and

(4) provide reunification services when appropriate for the return of the child to the home.

(b) The department shall emphasize ameliorative services for sexually abused children.

(c) The department shall provide or contract for necessary services to an abused or neglected child and the child's family without regard to whether the child remains in or is removed from the family home. If parental rights have been terminated, services may be provided only to the child.

(d) The services may include in-home programs, parenting skills training, youth coping skills, and individual and family counseling. If the department requires or a court orders parenting skills training services through a parenting education program, the program must be an evidence-based or promising practice parenting education program described by Section 265.151 [265.101] that is provided in the community in which the family resides, if available.

(e) The department may not provide and a court may not order the department to provide supervision for visitation in a child custody matter unless the department is a petitioner or intervener in the underlying suit.

History of Fam. Code §264.201: Acts 1995, 74th Leg., ch. 20, §1, eff. Apr. 20, 1995. Amended by Acts 1999, 76th Leg., ch. 1150, §28 (eff. Sept. 1, 1999), ch. 1390, §49 (eff. Sept. 1, 1999); Acts 2015, 84th Leg., ch. 1257, §1, eff. Sept. 1, 2015; S.B. 1488, §24.002(6), 85th Leg., eff. Sept. 1, 2017. Source: Former Fam. Code §34.51.

See also 40 T.A.C. §§700.701-700.706.

FAM §264.2011. ENHANCED IN-HOME SUPPORT PROGRAM

(a) To the extent that funding is available, the department shall develop a program to strengthen families through enhanced in-home support. The program shall assist certain low-income families and children in child neglect cases in which poverty is believed to be a significant underlying cause of the neglect and in which the enhancement of in-home support appears likely to prevent removal of the child from the home or to speed reunification of the child with the family.

(b) A family that meets eligibility criteria for inclusion in the program is eligible to receive limited funding from a flexible fund account to cover nonrecurring expenses that are designed to help the family accomplish the objectives included in the family's service plan.

(c) The executive commissioner shall adopt rules establishing:

(1) specific eligibility criteria for the program described in this section;

(2) the maximum amount of money that may be made available to a family through the flexible fund account; and

(3) the purposes for which money made available under the program may be spent.

(d) The department shall evaluate the results of the program to determine whether the program is successful in safely keeping families together. If the department determines that the program is successful, the department shall continue the program to the extent that funding is available.

History of Fam. Code §264.2011: Acts 2007, 80th Leg., ch. 1406, §19, eff. Sept. 1, 2007.

FAM §264.2015. FAMILY GROUP CONFERENCING

The department may collaborate with the courts and other appropriate local entities to develop and implement family group conferencing as a strategy for promoting family preservation and permanency for children.

History of Fam. Code §264.2015: Acts 2005, 79th Leg., ch. 268, §1.52, eff. Sept. 1, 2005.

FAM §264.202. STANDARDS & EFFECTIVENESS

(a) The department, with assistance from national organizations with expertise in child protective services, shall define a minimal baseline of in-home and foster care services for abused or neglected children that meets the professionally recognized standards for those services. The department shall attempt to provide services at a standard not lower than the minimal baseline standard.

(b) The department, with assistance from national organizations with expertise in child protective services, shall develop outcome measures to track and monitor the effectiveness of in-home and foster care services.

History of Fam. Code §264.202: Acts 1995, 74th Leg., ch. 20, §1, eff. Apr. 20, 1995. Source: Former Fam. Code §34.52.

FAM §264.203. REQUIRED PARTICIPATION

(a) Except as provided by Subsection (d), the court on request of the department may order the parent, managing conservator, guardian, or other member of the subject child's household to:

(1) participate in the services the department provides or purchases for:

(A) alleviating the effects of the abuse or neglect that has occurred; or

(B) reducing the reasonable likelihood that the child may be abused or neglected in the immediate or foreseeable future; and

(2) permit the child and any siblings of the child to receive the services.

(b) The department may request the court to order the parent, managing conservator, guardian, or other member of the child's household to participate in the services whether the child resides in the home or has been removed from the home.

(c) If the person ordered to participate in the services fails to follow the court's order, the court may impose appropriate sanctions in order to protect the health and safety of the child, including the removal of the child as specified by Chapter 262.

(d) If the court does not order the person to participate, the court in writing shall specify the reasons for not ordering participation.

History of Fam. Code §264.203: Acts 1995, 74th Leg., ch. 20, §1, eff. Apr. 20, 1995. Amended by Acts 2005, 79th Leg., ch. 268, §1.55, eff. Sept. 1, 2005; Acts 2007, 80th Leg., ch. 1406, §20, eff. Sept. 1, 2007. Source: Former Fam. Code §34.53.

FAM §264.204. COMMUNITY-BASED FAMILY SERVICES

(a) The department shall administer a grant program to provide funding to community organizations, including faith-based or county organizations, to respond to:

(1) low-priority, less serious cases of abuse and neglect; and

(2) cases in which an allegation of abuse or neglect of a child was unsubstantiated but involved a family that has been previously investigated for abuse or neglect of a child.

(b) The executive commissioner shall adopt rules to implement the grant program, including rules governing the submission and approval of grant requests and the cancellation of grants.

(c) To receive a grant, a community organization whose grant request is approved must execute an interagency agreement or a contract with the department. The contract must require the organization receiving the grant to perform the services as stated in the approved grant request. The contract must contain appropriate provisions for program and fiscal monitoring.

(d) In areas of the state in which community organizations receive grants under the program, the department shall refer low-priority, less serious cases of abuse and neglect to a community organization receiving a grant under the program.

(e) A community organization receiving a referral under Subsection (d) shall make a home visit and offer family social services to enhance the parents' ability to provide a safe and stable home environment for the child. If the family chooses to use the family services, a case manager from the organization shall monitor the case and ensure that the services are delivered.

(f) If after the home visit the community organization determines that the case is more serious than the department indicated, the community organization shall refer the case to the department for a full investigation.

(g) The department may not award a grant to a community organization in an area of the state in which a similar program is already providing effective family services in the community.

(h) For purposes of this section, a case is considered to be a less serious case of abuse or neglect if:

(1) the circumstances of the case do not appear to involve a reasonable likelihood that the child will be abused or neglected in the foreseeable future; or

(2) the allegations in the report of child abuse or neglect:

(A) are general in nature or vague and do not support a determination that the child who is the subject of the report has been abused or neglected or will likely be abused or neglected; or

(B) if substantiated, would not be considered abuse or neglect under this chapter.

History of Fam. Code §264.204: Acts 2005, 79th Leg., ch. 268, §1.53, eff. Sept. 1, 2005.

History of Former Fam. Code §264.204: Repealed by Acts 1995, 74th Leg., ch. 262, §100, eff. Jan. 1, 1996.

FAM §264.2041. CULTURAL AWARENESS

The department shall:

(1) develop and deliver cultural competency training to all service delivery staff;

(2) increase targeted recruitment efforts for foster and adoptive families who can meet the needs of children and youth who are waiting for permanent homes;

(3) target recruitment efforts to ensure diversity among department staff; and

(4) develop collaborative partnerships with community groups, agencies, faith-based organizations, and other community organizations to provide culturally competent services to children and families of every race and ethnicity.

History of Fam. Code §264.2041: Acts 2005, 79th Leg., ch. 268, §1.54(a), eff. Sept. 1, 2005.

E FAM §264.2042[A*]. GRANTS FOR FAITH-BASED COMMUNITY COLLABORATIVE PROGRAMS

☠ *In 2017, the Legislature enacted two sections 264.2042. This §264.2042 was enacted by S.B. 11, §19(a), 85th Leg., effective Sept. 1, 2017. The [A*] has been added by the editor to distinguish this §264.2042 from the other, which is marked with [B*]. In 2019, the Legislature is expected to correct the duplicate numbering.*

(a) Using available funds or private donations, the governor shall establish and administer an innovation grant program to award grants to support faith-based community programs that collaborate with the department and the commission to improve foster care and the placement of children in foster care.

(b) A faith-based community program is eligible for a grant under this section if:

(1) the effectiveness of the program is supported by empirical evidence; and

(2) the program has demonstrated the ability to build connections between faith-based, secular, and government stakeholders.

(c) The regional director for the department in the region where a grant recipient program is located, or the regional director's designee, shall serve as the liaison between the department and the program for collaborative purposes. For a program that operates in a larger region, the department may designate a liaison in each county where the program is operating. The department or the commission may not direct or manage the operation of the program.

(d) The initial duration of a grant under this section is two years. The governor may renew a grant awarded to a program under this section if funds are available and the governor determines that the program is successful.

(e) The governor may not award to a program grants under this section totaling more than $300,000.

(f) The governor shall adopt rules to implement the grant program created under this section.

History of Fam. Code §264.2042[A*]: Enacted by S.B. 11, §19(a), 85th Leg., eff. Sept. 1, 2017.

E FAM §264.2042[B*]. NONPROFIT ORGANIZATIONS PROVIDING CHILD & FAMILY SERVICES

☠ *In 2017, the Legislature enacted two sections 264.2042. This §264.2042 was enacted by H.B. 871, §11, 85th Leg., effective Sept. 1, 2017. The [B*] has been added by the editor to distinguish this §264.2042 from the other, which is marked with [A*]. In 2019, the Legislature is expected to correct the duplicate numbering.*

(a) The department shall cooperate with nonprofit organizations, including faith-based organizations, in providing information to families in crisis regarding child and family services, including respite care, voluntary guardianship, and other support services, available in the child's community.

(b) The department does not incur any obligation as a result of providing information as required by Subsection (a).

(c) The department is not liable for damages arising out of the provision of information as required by Subsection (a).

History of Fam. Code §264.2042[B*]: Enacted by H.B. 871, §11, 85th Leg., eff. Sept. 1, 2017.

E FAM §264.2043. PROHIBITION ON ABUSE OR NEGLECT INVESTIGATION BASED SOLELY ON REQUEST FOR INFORMATION

The department may not initiate an investigation of child abuse or neglect based solely on a request submitted to the department by a child's parent for information relating to child and family services available to families in crisis.

History of Fam. Code §264.2043: Enacted by H.B. 871, §11, 85th Leg., eff. Sept. 1, 2017.

FAM §264.205. SWIFT ADOPTION TEAMS

(a) The department shall develop swift adoption teams to expedite the process of placing a child under the jurisdiction of the department for adoption. Swift adoption teams developed under this section shall, in performing their duties, attempt to place a child for adoption with an appropriate relative of the child.

(b) A swift adoption team shall consist of department personnel who shall operate under policies adopted by rule by the executive commissioner. The department shall set priorities for the allocation of department resources to enable a swift adoption team to operate successfully under the policies adopted under this subsection.

(c) Repealed by Acts 2011, 82nd Leg., ch. 1050, §20 (eff. Sept. 1, 2011), ch. 1083, §25(27) (eff. June 17, 2011).

History of Fam. Code §264.205: Acts 1995, 74th Leg., ch. 943, §9, eff. Sept. 1, 1995. Amended by Acts 2001, 77th Leg., ch. 306, §4, eff. Sept. 1, 2001; Acts 2011, 82nd Leg., ch. 1050, §20 (eff. Sept. 1, 2011), ch. 1083, §25(27) (eff. June 17, 2011); Acts 2015, 84th Leg., ch. 1, §1.196, eff. Apr. 2, 2015.

FAM §264.206. REPEALED

Repealed by Acts 2015, 84th Leg., ch. 1, §1.203(12), eff. Apr. 2, 2015.

FAM §264.207. HOME STUDY REQUIRED BEFORE ADOPTION

(a) The department must complete a home study before the date an applicant is approved for an adoption.

(b) Repealed by Acts 2015, 84th Leg., ch. 944, §86(32), eff. Sept. 1, 2015.

History of Fam. Code §264.207: Acts 1997, 75th Leg., ch. 600, §19 (eff. Sept. 1, 1997), ch. 1022, §94 (eff. Sept. 1, 1997). Amended by Acts 2015, 84th Leg., ch. 944, §§58, 59, 86(32), eff. Sept. 1, 2015.

FAM §264.208. REPEALED

Repealed by Acts 2015, 84th Leg., ch. 944, §86(33), eff. Sept. 1, 2015.

Sections 264.209-264.300 reserved for expansion

SUBCHAPTER D. SERVICES TO AT-RISK YOUTH

FAM §264.301. SERVICES FOR AT-RISK YOUTH

(a) The department shall operate a program to provide services for children in at-risk situations and for the families of those children.

(b) The services under this section may include:

(1) crisis family intervention;

(2) emergency short-term residential care;

(3) family counseling;

(4) parenting skills training;

(5) youth coping skills training;

(6) mentoring; and

(7) advocacy training.

History of Fam. Code §264.301: Acts 1995, 74th Leg., ch. 20, §1, eff. Apr. 20, 1995. Amended by Acts 1995, 74th Leg., ch. 262, §58, eff. Jan. 1, 1996.

FAM §264.302. EARLY YOUTH INTERVENTION SERVICES

(a) This section applies to a child who:

(1) is seven years of age or older and under 17 years of age; and

(2) has not had the disabilities of minority for general purposes removed under Chapter 31.

(b) The department shall operate a program under this section to provide services for children in at-risk situations and for the families of those children.

(c) The department may not provide services under this section to a child who has:

(1) at any time been referred to juvenile court for engaging in conduct that violates a penal law of this state of the grade of felony other than a state jail felony; or

(2) been found to have engaged in delinquent conduct under Title 3.

(d) The department may provide services under this section to a child who engages in conduct for which the child may be found by a court to be an at-risk child, without regard to whether the conduct violates a penal law of this state of the grade of felony other than a state jail felony, if the child was younger than 10 years of age at the time the child engaged in the conduct.

(e) The department shall provide services for a child and the child's family if a contract to provide services under this section is available in the county and the child is referred to the department as an at-risk child by:

(1) a juvenile court or probation department as part of a progressive sanctions program under Chapter 59;

(2) a law enforcement officer or agency under Section 52.03; or

(3) a justice or municipal court under Article 45.057, Code of Criminal Procedure.

(f) The services under this section may include:

(1) crisis family intervention;

(2) emergency short-term residential care for children 10 years of age or older;

(3) family counseling;

(4) parenting skills training;

(5) youth coping skills training;

(6) advocacy training; and

(7) mentoring.

History of Fam. Code §264.302: Acts 1995, 74th Leg., ch. 262, §58, eff. Jan. 1, 1996. Amended by Acts 1997, 75th Leg., ch. 575, §31 (eff. Sept. 1, 1997), ch. 1086, §30 (eff. Sept. 1, 1997); Acts 2001, 77th Leg., ch. 1514, §16, eff. Sept. 1, 2001; Acts 2015, 84th Leg., ch. 944, §60, eff. Sept. 1, 2015.

FAM §264.303. REPEALED

Repealed by Acts 2015, 84th Leg., ch. 944, §86(34), eff. Sept. 1, 2015.

FAM §264.304. REPEALED [~~HEARING; DETERMINATION OF AT-RISK CHILD~~]

(a), **(b)** Repealed by Acts 2015, 84th Leg., ch. 944, §86(35), eff. Sept. 1, 2015.

(c) Repealed by Acts 2015, 84th Leg., ch. 944, §86(35), eff. Sept. 1, 2015; S.B. 1488, §7.011, 85th Leg., eff. Sept. 1, 2017.

[~~(c)~~] [~~The court shall determine that the child is an at-risk child if the court finds that the child has engaged in the following conduct:~~]

[~~(1)~~] [~~conduct, other than a traffic offense and except as provided by Subsection (d), that violates:~~]

[~~(A)~~] [~~the penal laws of this state; or~~]

[~~(B)~~] [~~the penal ordinances of any political subdivision of this state;~~]

[~~(2)~~] [~~the unexcused voluntary absence of the child on 10 or more days or parts of days within a six-month period from school without the consent of the child's parent, managing conservator, or guardian;~~]

[~~(3)~~] [~~the voluntary absence of the child from the child's home without the consent of the child's parent, managing conservator, or guardian for a substantial length of time or without intent to return;~~]

[~~(4)~~] [~~conduct that violates the laws of this state prohibiting driving while intoxicated or under the influence of intoxicating liquor (first or second offense) or driving while under the influence of any narcotic drug or of any other drug to a degree that renders the child incapable of safely driving a vehicle (first or second offense); or~~]

[~~(5)~~] [~~conduct that evidences a clear and substantial intent to engage in any behavior described by Subdivisions (1)-(4).~~]

(d) Repealed by Acts 2015, 84th Leg., ch. 944, §86(35), eff. Sept. 1, 2015.

Repealed by Acts 2015, 84th Leg., ch. 944, §86(35), eff. Sept. 1, 2015; S.B. 1488, §7.011, 85th Leg., eff. Sept. 1, 2017.

FAM §264.305. REPEALED

Repealed by Acts 2015, 84th Leg., ch. 944, §86(36), eff. Sept. 1, 2015.

FAM §264.306. REPEALED

Repealed by Acts 2015, 84th Leg., ch. 944, §86(37), eff. Sept. 1, 2015.

Sections 264.307-264.400 reserved for expansion

SUBCHAPTER E. CHILDREN'S ADVOCACY CENTERS

FAM §264.401. DEFINITION

In this subchapter, "center" means a children's advocacy center.

History of Fam. Code §264.401: Acts 1995, 74th Leg., ch. 255, §1, eff. Sept. 1, 1995.

FAM §264.402. ESTABLISHMENT OF CHILDREN'S ADVOCACY CENTER

On the execution of a memorandum of understanding under Section 264.403, a children's advocacy center may be established by community members and the participating entities described by Section 264.403(a) to serve a county or two or more contiguous counties.

History of Fam. Code §264.402: Acts 1995, 74th Leg., ch. 255, §1, eff. Sept. 1, 1995. Amended by Acts 2003, 78th Leg., ch. 185, §1, eff. Sept. 1, 2003.

FAM §264.403. INTERAGENCY MEMORANDUM OF UNDERSTANDING

(a) Before a center may be established under Section 264.402, a memorandum of understanding regarding participation in operation of the center must be executed among:

(1) the division of the department responsible for child abuse investigations;

(2) representatives of county and municipal law enforcement agencies that investigate child abuse in the area to be served by the center;

(3) the county or district attorney who routinely prosecutes child abuse cases in the area to be served by the center; and

(4) a representative of any other governmental entity that participates in child abuse investigations or offers services to child abuse victims that desires to participate in the operation of the center.

(b) A memorandum of understanding executed under this section shall include the agreement of each participating entity to cooperate in:

(1) developing a cooperative, team approach to investigating child abuse;

(2) reducing, to the greatest extent possible, the number of interviews required of a victim of child abuse to minimize the negative impact of the investigation on the child; and

(3) developing, maintaining, and supporting, through the center, an environment that emphasizes the best interests of children and that provides investigatory and rehabilitative services.

(c) A memorandum of understanding executed under this section may include the agreement of one or more participating entities to provide office space and administrative services necessary for the center's operation.

History of Fam. Code §264.403: Acts 1995, 74th Leg., ch. 255, §1, eff. Sept. 1, 1995.

FAM §264.404. BOARD REPRESENTATION

(a) In addition to any other persons appointed or elected to serve on the governing board of a children's advocacy center, the governing board must include an executive officer of, or an employee selected by an executive officer of:

(1) a law enforcement agency that investigates child abuse in the area served by the center;

(2) the child protective services division of the department; and

(3) the county or district attorney's office involved in the prosecution of child abuse cases in the area served by the center.

(b) Service on a center's board by an executive officer or employee under Subsection (a) is an additional duty of the person's office or employment.

History of Fam. Code §264.404: Acts 1995, 74th Leg., ch. 255, §1, eff. Sept. 1, 1995. Amended by Acts 2003, 78th Leg., ch. 185, §1, eff. Sept. 1, 2003.

FAM §264.405. DUTIES

A center shall:

(1) assess victims of child abuse and their families to determine their need for services relating to the investigation of child abuse;

(2) provide services determined to be needed under Subdivision (1);

(3) provide a facility at which a multidisciplinary team appointed under Section 264.406 can meet to facilitate the efficient and appropriate disposition of child abuse cases through the civil and criminal justice systems; and

(4) coordinate the activities of governmental entities relating to child abuse investigations and delivery of services to child abuse victims and their families.

History of Fam. Code §264.405: Acts 1995, 74th Leg., ch. 255, §1, eff. Sept. 1, 1995.

FAM §264.406. MULTIDISCIPLINARY TEAM

(a) A center's multidisciplinary team must include employees of the participating agencies who are professionals involved in the investigation or prosecution of child abuse cases.

(b) A center's multidisciplinary team may also include professionals involved in the delivery of services, including medical and mental health services, to child abuse victims and the victims' families.

(c) A multidisciplinary team shall meet at regularly scheduled intervals to:

(1) review child abuse cases determined to be appropriate for review by the multidisciplinary team; and

(2) coordinate the actions of the entities involved in the investigation and prosecution of the cases and the delivery of services to the child abuse victims and the victims' families.

(d) A multidisciplinary team may review a child abuse case in which the alleged perpetrator does not have custodial control or supervision of the child or is not responsible for the child's welfare or care.

(e) When acting in the member's official capacity, a multidisciplinary team member is authorized to receive information made confidential by Section 40.005, Human Resources Code, or Section 261.201 or 264.408.

History of Fam. Code §264.406: Acts 1995, 74th Leg., ch. 255, §1, eff. Sept. 1, 1995. Amended by Acts 1997, 75th Leg., ch. 575, §32, eff. Sept. 1, 1997; Acts 2003, 78th Leg., ch. 185, §1, eff. Sept. 1, 2003.

E FAM §264.4061. MULTIDISCIPLINARY TEAM RESPONSE REQUIRED

(a) The department shall refer a case to a center and the center shall initiate a response by a center's multidisciplinary team appointed under Section 264.406 when conducting an investigation of:

(1) a report of abuse that is made by a professional as defined by Section 261.101 and that:

(A) alleges sexual abuse of a child; or

(B) is a type of case handled by the center in accordance with the working protocol adopted for the center under Section 264.411(a)(9); or

(2) a child fatality in which there are surviving children in the deceased child's household or under the supervision of the caregiver involved in the child fatality.

(b) Any interview of a child conducted as part of the investigation under Subsection (a) must be a forensic interview conducted in accordance with the center's working protocol unless a forensic interview is not appropriate based on the child's age and development or the center's working protocol.

(c) Subsection (a) applies only to an investigation of abuse in a county served by a center that has executed an interagency memorandum of understanding under Section 264.403. If a county is not served by a center that has executed an interagency memorandum of understanding, the department may directly refer a case to a center in an adjacent county to initiate a response by that center's multidisciplinary team, if appropriate.

History of Fam. Code §264.4061: Enacted by S.B. 1806, §1, 85th Leg., eff. Sept. 1, 2017.

FAM §264.407. LIABILITY

(a) A person is not liable for civil damages for a recommendation made or an opinion rendered in good faith while acting in the official scope of the person's duties as a member of a multidisciplinary team or as a board member, staff member, or volunteer of a center.

(b) The limitation on civil liability of Subsection (a) does not apply if a person's actions constitute gross negligence.

History of Fam. Code §264.407: Acts 1995, 74th Leg., ch. 255, §1, eff. Sept. 1, 1995.

FAM §264.408. USE OF INFORMATION & RECORDS; CONFIDENTIALITY & OWNERSHIP

(a) The files, reports, records, communications, and working papers used or developed in providing services under this chapter are confidential and not subject to public release under Chapter 552, Government Code, and may only be disclosed for purposes consistent with this chapter. Disclosure may be to:

(1) the department, department employees, law enforcement agencies, prosecuting attorneys, medical professionals, and other state or local agencies that provide services to children and families; and

(2) the attorney for the child who is the subject of the records and a court-appointed volunteer advocate appointed for the child under Section 107.031.

(b) Information related to the investigation of a report of abuse or neglect under Chapter 261 and services provided as a result of the investigation is confidential as provided by Section 261.201.

(c) The department, a law enforcement agency, and a prosecuting attorney may share with a center information that is confidential under Section 261.201 as needed to provide services under this chapter. Confidential information shared with or provided to a center remains the property of the agency that shared or provided the information to the center.

(d) A video recording of an interview of a child that is made by a center is the property of the prosecuting attorney involved in the criminal prosecution of the case involving the child. If no criminal prosecution occurs, the video recording is the property of the attorney involved in representing the department in a civil action alleging child abuse or neglect. If the matter involving the child is not prosecuted, the video recording is the property of the department if the matter is an investigation by the department of abuse or neglect. If the department is not investigating or has not investigated the matter, the video recording is the property of the agency that referred the matter to the center.

(d-1) A video recording of an interview described by Subsection (d) is subject to production under Article 39.14, Code of Criminal Procedure, and Rule 615, Texas Rules of Evidence. A court shall deny any request by a defendant to copy, photograph, duplicate, or otherwise reproduce a video recording of an interview described by Subsection (d), provided that the prosecuting attorney makes the video recording reasonably available to the defendant in the same manner as property or material may be made available to defendants, attorneys, and expert witnesses under Article 39.15(d), Code of Criminal Procedure.

(e) The department shall be allowed access to a center's video recordings of interviews of children.

History of Fam. Code §264.408: Acts 1997, 75th Leg., ch. 575, §33, eff. Sept. 1, 1997. Amended by Acts 2011, 82nd Leg., ch. 653, §4, eff. June 17, 2011; Acts 2013, 83rd Leg., ch. 1069, §3, eff. Sept. 1, 2013; Acts 2015, 84th Leg., ch. 299, §1, eff. Sept. 1, 2015.

FAM §264.409. ADMINISTRATIVE CONTRACTS

(a) The department or the commission shall contract with a statewide organization that is exempt from federal income taxation under Section 501(a), Internal Revenue Code of 1986, as an organization described by Section 501(c)(3) of that code and designated as a supporting organization under Section 509(a)(3) of that code and that is composed of individuals or groups of individuals who have expertise in the establishment and operation of children's advocacy center programs. The statewide organization shall provide training, technical assistance, evaluation services, and funds administration to support contractual requirements under Section 264.411 for local children's advocacy center programs.

(b) If the commission enters into a contract under this section, the contract must provide that the statewide organization may not spend annually in the performance of duties under Subsection (a) more than 12 percent of the annual amount appropriated to the commission for purposes of this section.

History of Fam. Code §264.409: Acts 1997, 75th Leg., ch. 575, §33, eff. Sept. 1, 1997. Amended by Acts 1999, 76th Leg., ch. 347, §1, eff. Sept. 1, 1999; Acts 2015, 84th Leg., ch. 597, §1, eff. Sept. 1, 2015.

FAM §264.410. CONTRACTS WITH CHILDREN'S ADVOCACY CENTERS

(a) The statewide organization with which the department or the commission contracts under Section 264.409 shall contract for services with eligible centers to enhance the existing services of the programs.

(b) The contract under this section may not result in reducing the financial support a local center receives from another source.

(c) If the commission enters into a contract with a statewide organization under Section 264.409, the executive commissioner by rule shall adopt standards for eligible local centers. The statewide organization shall assist the executive commissioner in developing the standards.

History of Fam. Code §264.410: Acts 1997, 75th Leg., ch. 575, §33, eff. Sept. 1, 1997. Amended by Acts 1999, 76th Leg., ch. 347, §2, eff. Sept. 1, 1999; Acts 2015, 84th Leg., ch. 597, §2, eff. Sept. 1, 2015.

FAM §264.411. ELIGIBILITY FOR CONTRACTS

(a) A public entity that operated as a center under this subchapter before November 1, 1995, or a nonprofit entity is eligible for a contract under Section 264.410 if the entity:

(1) has a signed memorandum of understanding as provided by Section 264.403;

(2) operates under the authority of a governing board as provided by Section 264.404;

(3) has a multidisciplinary team of persons involved in the investigation or prosecution of child abuse cases or the delivery of services as provided by Section 264.406;

(4) holds regularly scheduled case reviews as provided by Section 264.406;

(5) operates in a neutral and physically separate space from the day-to-day operations of any public agency partner;

(6) has developed a method of statistical information gathering on children receiving services through the center and shares such statistical information with the statewide organization, the department, and the commission when requested;

(7) has an in-house volunteer program;

(8) employs an executive director who is answerable to the board of directors of the entity and who is not the exclusive salaried employee of any public agency partner;

(9) operates under a working protocol that includes a statement of:

(A) the center's mission;

(B) each agency's role and commitment to the center;

(C) the type of cases to be handled by the center;

(D) the center's procedures for conducting case reviews and forensic interviews and for ensuring access to specialized medical and mental health services; and

(E) the center's policies regarding confidentiality and conflict resolution; and

(10) implements at the center the following program components:

(A) a case tracking system that monitors statistical information on each child and nonoffending family member or other caregiver who receives services through the center and that includes progress and disposition information for each service the multidisciplinary team determines should be provided to the client;

(B) a child-focused setting that is comfortable, private, and physically and psychologically safe for diverse populations of children and nonoffending family members and other caregivers;

(C) family advocacy and victim support services that include comprehensive case management and victim support services available to each child and the child's nonoffending family members or other caregivers as part of the services the multidisciplinary team determines should be provided to a client;

(D) forensic interviews conducted in a neutral, fact-finding manner and coordinated to avoid duplicative interviewing;

(E) specialized medical evaluation and treatment services that are available to all children who receive services through the center and coordinated with the services the multidisciplinary team determines should be provided to a child;

(F) specialized trauma-focused mental health services that are designed to meet the unique needs of child abuse victims and the victims' nonoffending family members or other caregivers and that are available as part of the services the multidisciplinary team determines should be provided to a client; and

(G) a system to ensure that all services available to center clients are culturally competent and diverse and are coordinated with the services the multidisciplinary team determines should be provided to a client.

(b) The statewide organization may waive the requirements specified in Subsection (a) if it determines that the waiver will not adversely affect the center's ability to carry out its duties under Section 264.405.

History of Fam. Code §264.411: Acts 1997, 75th Leg., ch. 575, §33, eff. Sept. 1, 1997. Amended by Acts 1999, 76th Leg., ch. 347, §3, eff. Sept. 1, 1999; Acts 2003, 78th Leg., ch. 185, §2, eff. Sept. 1, 2003; Acts 2013, 83rd Leg., ch. 136, §1, eff. Sept. 1, 2013; Acts 2015, 84th Leg., ch. 597, §3, eff. Sept. 1, 2015.

Sections 264.412-264.500 reserved for expansion

SUBCHAPTER F. CHILD FATALITY REVIEW & INVESTIGATION

FAM §264.501. DEFINITIONS

In this subchapter:

(1) "Autopsy" and "inquest" have the meanings assigned by Article 49.01, Code of Criminal Procedure.

(2) Repealed by Acts 2015, 84th Leg., ch. 1, §1.203(13), eff. Apr. 2, 2015.

(3) "Child" means a person younger than 18 years of age.

(4) "Committee" means the child fatality review team committee.

(5) Repealed by Acts 2015, 84th Leg., ch. 1, §1.203(13), eff. Apr. 2, 2015.

(6) "Health care provider" means any health care practitioner or facility that provides medical evaluation or treatment, including dental and mental health evaluation or treatment.

(7) "Meeting" means an in-person meeting or a meeting held by telephone or other electronic medium.

(8) "Preventable death" means a death that may have been prevented by reasonable medical, social, legal, psychological, or educational intervention. The term includes the death of a child from:

(A) intentional or unintentional injuries;

(B) medical neglect;

(C) lack of access to medical care;

(D) neglect and reckless conduct, including failure to supervise and failure to seek medical care; and

(E) premature birth associated with any factor described by Paragraphs (A) through (D).

(9) "Review" means a reexamination of information regarding a deceased child from relevant agencies, professionals, and health care providers.

(10) "Review team" means a child fatality review team established under this subchapter.

(11) "Unexpected death" includes a death of a child that, before investigation:

(A) appears to have occurred without anticipation or forewarning; and

(B) was caused by trauma, suspicious or obscure circumstances, sudden infant death syndrome, abuse or neglect, or an unknown cause.

History of Fam. Code §264.501: Acts 1995, 74th Leg., ch. 255, §2 (eff. Sept. 1, 1995), ch. 878, §1 (eff. Sept. 1, 1995). Amended by Acts 2001, 77th Leg., ch. 957, §2, eff. Sept. 1, 2001; Acts 2015, 84th Leg., ch. 1, §1.203(13), eff. Apr. 2, 2015.

A FAM §264.502. COMMITTEE

(a) The child fatality review team committee is composed of:

(1) a person appointed by and representing the state registrar of vital statistics;

(2) a person appointed by and representing the commissioner of the department;

(3) a person appointed by and representing the Title V director of the Department of State Health Services; [and]

(4) a person appointed by and representing the speaker of the house of representatives;

(5) a person appointed by and representing the lieutenant governor;

(6) a person appointed by and representing the governor; and

(7) individuals selected under Subsection (b).

(b) The members of the committee who serve under Subsections (a)(1) through (6) [(3)] shall select the following additional committee members:

(1) a criminal prosecutor involved in prosecuting crimes against children;

(2) a sheriff;

(3) a justice of the peace;

(4) a medical examiner;

(5) a police chief;

(6) a pediatrician experienced in diagnosing and treating child abuse and neglect;

(7) a child educator;

(8) a child mental health provider;

(9) a public health professional;

(10) a child protective services specialist;

(11) a sudden infant death syndrome family service provider;

(12) a neonatologist;

(13) a child advocate;

(14) a chief juvenile probation officer;

(15) a child abuse prevention specialist;

(16) a representative of the Department of Public Safety;

(17) a representative of the Texas Department of Transportation;

(18) an emergency medical services provider; and

(19) a provider of services to, or an advocate for, victims of family violence.

(c) Members of the committee selected under Subsection (b) serve three-year terms with the terms of six or seven members, as appropriate, expiring February 1 each year.

(d) Members selected under Subsection (b) must reflect the geographical, cultural, racial, and ethnic diversity of the state.

(e) An appointment to a vacancy on the committee shall be made in the same manner as the original appointment. A member is eligible for reappointment.

(f) Members of the committee shall select a presiding officer from the members of the committee.

(g) The presiding officer of the committee shall call the meetings of the committee, which shall be held at least quarterly.

(h) A member of the committee is not entitled to compensation for serving on the committee but is entitled to reimbursement for the member's travel expenses as provided in the General Appropriations Act. Reimbursement under this subsection for a person serving on the committee under Subsection (a)(2) shall be paid from funds appropriated to the department. Reimbursement for other persons serving on the committee shall be paid from funds appropriated to the Department of State Health Services.

History of Fam. Code §264.502: Acts 1995, 74th Leg., ch. 255, §2 (eff. Sept. 1, 1995), ch. 878, §1 (eff. Sept. 1, 1995). Amended by Acts 2001, 77th Leg., ch. 957, §3, eff. Sept. 1, 2001; Acts 2005, 79th Leg., ch. 268, §1.56, eff. Sept. 1, 2005; Acts 2007, 80th Leg., ch. 396, §1, eff. Sept. 1, 2007; Acts 2009, 81st Leg., ch. 933, §3C.04, eff. Sept. 1, 2009; Acts 2011, 82nd Leg., ch. 1290, §42, eff. Sept. 1, 2011; Acts 2013, 83rd Leg., ch. 1145, §1, eff. Sept. 1, 2013; H.B. 1549, §5, 85th Leg., eff. Sept. 1, 2017.

FAM §264.503. PURPOSE & DUTIES OF COMMITTEE & SPECIFIED STATE AGENCIES

(a) The purpose of the committee is to:

(1) develop an understanding of the causes and incidence of child deaths in this state;

(2) identify procedures within the agencies represented on the committee to reduce the number of preventable child deaths; and

(3) promote public awareness and make recommendations to the governor and the legislature for changes in law, policy, and practice to reduce the number of preventable child deaths.

(b) To ensure that the committee achieves its purpose, the department and the Department of State Health Services shall perform the duties specified by this section.

(c) The department shall work cooperatively with:

(1) the Department of State Health Services;

(2) the committee; and

(3) individual child fatality review teams.

(d) The Department of State Health Services shall:

(1) recognize the creation and participation of review teams;

(2) promote and coordinate training to assist the review teams in carrying out their duties;

(3) assist the committee in developing model protocols for:

(A) the reporting and investigating of child fatalities for law enforcement agencies, child protective services, justices of the peace and medical examiners, and other professionals involved in the investigations of child deaths;

(B) the collection of data regarding child deaths; and

(C) the operation of the review teams;

(4) develop and implement procedures necessary for the operation of the committee; [and]

(5) develop and make available training for justices of the peace and medical examiners regarding inquests in child death cases; and

(6) promote education of the public regarding the incidence and causes of child deaths, the public role in preventing child deaths, and specific steps the public can undertake to prevent child deaths.

(d-1) The committee shall enlist the support and assistance of civic, philanthropic, and public service organizations in the performance of the duties imposed under Subsection (d).

(e) In addition to the duties under Subsection (d), the Department of State Health Services shall:

(1) collect data under this subchapter and coordinate the collection of data under this subchapter with other data collection activities; [and]

(2) perform annual statistical studies of the incidence and causes of child fatalities using the data collected under this subchapter; and

(3) evaluate the available child fatality data and use the data to create public health strategies for the prevention of child fatalities.

(f) Not later than April 1 of each even-numbered year, the committee shall publish a report that contains aggregate child fatality data collected by local child fatality review teams, recommendations to prevent child fatalities and injuries, and recommendations to the department on child protective services operations based on input from the child safety review subcommittee. The committee shall submit a copy of the report to the governor, lieutenant governor, speaker of the house of representatives, Department of State Health Services, and department and make the report available to the public. Not later than October 1 of each even-numbered year, the department shall submit a written response to the committee's recommendations to the committee, governor, lieutenant governor, speaker of the house of representatives, and Department of State Health Services describing which of the committee's recommendations regarding the operation of the child protective services system the department will implement and the methods of implementation.

(g) The committee shall perform the functions and duties required of a citizen review panel under 42 U.S.C. Section 5106a(c)(4)(A).

(h) Each member of the committee must be a member of the child fatality review team in the county where the committee member resides unless the committee member is an appointed representative of a state agency.

History of Fam. Code §264.503: Acts 1995, 74th Leg., ch. 255, §2 (eff. Sept. 1, 1995), ch. 878, §1 (eff. Sept. 1, 1995). Amended by Acts 2001, 77th Leg., ch. 957, §4, eff. Sept. 1, 2001; Acts 2005, 79th Leg., ch. 268, §1.57, eff. Sept. 1, 2005; Acts 2007, 80th Leg., ch. 396, §2, eff. Sept. 1, 2007; Acts 2013, 83rd Leg., ch. 1145, §2, eff. Sept. 1, 2013; H.B. 1549, §6, 85th Leg., eff. Sept. 1, 2017.

FAM §264.5031. COLLECTION OF NEAR FATALITY DATA

(a) In this section, "near fatality" means a case where a physician has certified that a child is in critical or serious condition, and a caseworker determines that the child's condition was caused by the abuse or neglect of the child.

(b) The department shall include near fatality child abuse or neglect cases in the child fatality case database, for cases in which child abuse or neglect is determined to have been the cause of the near fatality. The department must also develop a data collection strategy for near fatality child abuse or neglect cases.

History of Fam. Code §264.5031: Enacted by H.B. 1549, §7, 85th Leg., eff. Sept. 1, 2017.

FAM §264.5032. REPORT OF CHILD FATALITY & NEAR FATALITY DATA

(a) The department shall produce an aggregated report relating to child fatality and near fatality cases resulting from child abuse or neglect containing the following information:

(1) any prior contact the department had with the child's family and the manner in which the case was disposed, including cases in which the department made the following dispositions:

(A) priority none or administrative closure;

(B) call screened out;

(C) alternative or differential response provided;

(D) unable to complete the investigation;

(E) unable to determine whether abuse or neglect occurred;

(F) reason to believe abuse or neglect occurred; or

(G) child removed and placed into substitute care;

(2) for any case investigated by the department involving the child or the child's family:

(A) the number of caseworkers assigned to the case before the fatality or near fatality occurred; and

(B) the caseworker's caseload at the time the case was opened and at the time the case was closed;

(3) for any case in which the department investigation concluded that there was reason to believe that abuse or neglect occurred, and the family was referred to family-based safety services:

(A) the safety plan provided to the family;

(B) the services offered to the family; and

(C) the level of compliance with the safety plan or completion of the services by the family;

(4) the number of contacts the department made with children and families in family-based safety services cases; and

(5) the initial and attempted contacts the department made with child abuse and neglect victims.

(b) In preparing the part of the report required by Subsection (a)(1), the department shall include information contained in department records retained in accordance with the department's records retention schedule.

(c) The report produced under this section must protect the identity of individuals involved in a case that is included in the report.

(d) The department may combine the report required under this section with the annual child fatality report required to be produced under Section 261.204.

History of Fam. Code §264.5032: Enacted by H.B. 1549, §7, 85th Leg., eff. Sept. 1, 2017.

FAM §264.504. MEETINGS OF COMMITTEE

(a) Except as provided by Subsections (b), (c), and (d), meetings of the committee are subject to the open meetings law, Chapter 551, Government Code, as if the committee were a governmental body under that chapter.

(b) Any portion of a meeting of the committee during which the committee discusses an individual child's death is closed to the public and is not subject to the open meetings law, Chapter 551, Government Code.

(c) Information identifying a deceased child, a member of the child's family, a guardian or caretaker of the child, or an alleged or suspected perpetrator of abuse or neglect of the child may not be disclosed during a public meeting. On a majority vote of the committee members, the members shall remove from the committee any member who discloses information described by this subsection in a public meeting.

(d) Information regarding the involvement of a state or local agency with the deceased child or another person described by Subsection (c) may not be disclosed during a public meeting.

(e) The committee may conduct an open or closed meeting by telephone conference call or other electronic medium. A meeting held under this subsection is subject to the notice requirements applicable to other meetings. The notice of the meeting must specify as the location of the meeting the location where meetings of the committee are usually held. Each part of the meeting by telephone conference call that is required to be open to the public shall be audible to the public at the location specified in the notice of the meeting as the location of the meeting and shall be tape-recorded. The tape recording shall be made available to the public.

(f) This section does not prohibit the committee from requesting the attendance at a closed meeting of a person who is not a member of the committee and who has information regarding a deceased child.

History of Fam. Code §264.504: Acts 1995, 74th Leg., ch. 255, §2 (eff. Sept. 1, 1995), ch. 878, §1 (eff. Sept. 1, 1995). Amended by Acts 2005, 79th Leg., ch. 268, §1.58, eff. Sept. 1, 2005.

Ⓐ FAM §264.505. ESTABLISHMENT OF REVIEW TEAM

(a) A multidisciplinary and multiagency child fatality review team may be established for a county to review child deaths in that county. A [~~review team for a~~] county [~~with a population of less than 50,000~~] may join with an adjacent county or counties to establish a combined review team.

(b) Any person who may be a member of a review team under Subsection (c) may initiate the establishment of a review team and call the first organizational meeting of the team.

(c) A review team must reflect the diversity of the county's population and may include:

(1) a criminal prosecutor involved in prosecuting crimes against children;

(2) a sheriff;

(3) a justice of the peace or medical examiner;

(4) a police chief;

(5) a pediatrician experienced in diagnosing and treating child abuse and neglect;

(6) a child educator;

(7) a child mental health provider;

(8) a public health professional;

(9) a child protective services specialist;

(10) a sudden infant death syndrome family service provider;

(11) a neonatologist;

(12) a child advocate;

(13) a chief juvenile probation officer; and

(14) a child abuse prevention specialist.

(d) Members of a review team may select additional team members according to community resources and needs.

(e) A review team shall select a presiding officer from its members.

History of Fam. Code §264.505: Acts 1995, 74th Leg., ch. 255, §2 (eff. Sept. 1, 1995), ch. 878, §1 (eff. Sept. 1, 1995). Amended by Acts 2005, 79th Leg., ch. 268, §1.59, eff. Sept. 1, 2005; H.B. 1549, §8, 85th Leg., eff. Sept. 1, 2017.

FAM §264.506. PURPOSE & DUTIES OF REVIEW TEAM

(a) The purpose of a review team is to decrease the incidence of preventable child deaths by:

(1) providing assistance, direction, and coordination to investigations of child deaths;

(2) promoting cooperation, communication, and coordination among agencies involved in responding to child fatalities;

(3) developing an understanding of the causes and incidence of child deaths in the county or counties in which the review team is located;

(4) recommending changes to agencies, through the agency's representative member, that will reduce the number of preventable child deaths; and

(5) advising the committee on changes to law, policy, or practice that will assist the team and the agencies represented on the team in fulfilling their duties.

(b) To achieve its purpose, a review team shall:

(1) adapt and implement, according to local needs and resources, the model protocols developed by the department and the committee;

(2) meet on a regular basis to review child fatality cases and recommend methods to improve coordination of services and investigations between agencies that are represented on the team;

(3) collect and maintain data as required by the committee; [~~and~~]

(4) review and analyze the collected data to identify any demographic trends in child fatality cases, including whether there is a disproportionate number of child fatalities in a particular population group or geographic area; and

(5) submit to the vital statistics unit data reports on deaths reviewed as specified by the committee.

(c) A review team shall initiate prevention measures as indicated by the review team's findings.

History of Fam. Code §264.506: Acts 1995, 74th Leg., ch. 255, §2 (eff. Sept. 1, 1995), ch. 878, §1 (eff. Sept. 1, 1995). Amended by Acts 2015, 84th Leg., ch. 1, §1.197, eff. Apr. 2, 2015; H.B. 1549, §9, 85th Leg., eff. Sept. 1, 2017.

FAM §264.507. DUTIES OF PRESIDING OFFICER

The presiding officer of a review team shall:

(1) send notices to the review team members of a meeting to review a child fatality;

(2) provide a list to the review team members of each child fatality to be reviewed at the meeting;

(3) submit data reports to the vital statistics unit not later than the 30th day after the date on which the review took place; and

(4) ensure that the review team operates according to the protocols developed by the department and the committee, as adapted by the review team.

History of Fam. Code §264.507: Acts 1995, 74th Leg., ch. 255, §2 (eff. Sept. 1, 1995), ch. 878, §1 (eff. Sept. 1, 1995). Amended by Acts 2015, 84th Leg., ch. 1, §1.198, eff. Apr. 2, 2015.

FAM §264.508. REVIEW PROCEDURE

(a) The review team of the county in which the injury, illness, or event that was the cause of the death of the child occurred, as stated on the child's death certificate, shall review the death.

(b) On receipt of the list of child fatalities under Section 264.507, each review team member shall review the member's records and the records of the member's agency for information regarding each listed child.

History of Fam. Code §264.508: Acts 1995, 74th Leg., ch. 255, §2 (eff. Sept. 1, 1995), ch. 878, §1 (eff. Sept. 1, 1995).

FAM §264.509. ACCESS TO INFORMATION

(a) A review team may request information and records regarding a deceased child as necessary to carry out the review team's purpose and duties. Records and information that may be requested under this section include:

(1) medical, dental, and mental health care information; and

(2) information and records maintained by any state or local government agency, including:

(A) a birth certificate;

(B) law enforcement investigative data;

(C) medical examiner investigative data;

(D) juvenile court records;

(E) parole and probation information and records; and

(F) child protective services information and records.

(b) On request of the presiding officer of a review team, the custodian of the relevant information and records relating to a deceased child shall provide those records to the review team at no cost to the review team.

(b-1) The Department of State Health Services shall provide a review team with electronic access to the preliminary death certificate for a deceased child.

(c) This subsection does not authorize the release of the original or copies of the mental health or medical records of any member of the child's family or the guardian or caretaker of the child or an alleged or suspected perpetrator of abuse or neglect of the child which are in the possession of any state or local government agency as provided in Subsection (a)(2). Information relating to the mental health or medical condition of a member of[1] the child's family or the guardian or caretaker of the child or the alleged or suspected perpetrator of abuse or neglect of the child acquired as part of an investigation by a state or local government agency as provided in Subsection (a)(2) may be provided to the review team.

1. **Editor's note:** Enacted as "member of of the child's family." Probably should include only one "of."

History of Fam. Code §264.509: Acts 1995, 74th Leg., ch. 255, §2 (eff. Sept. 1, 1995), ch. 878, §1 (eff. Sept. 1, 1995). Amended by Acts 2005, 79th Leg., ch. 268, §1.60, eff. Sept. 1, 2005; H.B. 1549, §10, 85th Leg., eff. Sept. 1, 2017.

FAM §264.510. MEETING OF REVIEW TEAM

(a) A meeting of a review team is closed to the public and not subject to the open meetings law, Chapter 551, Government Code.

(b) This section does not prohibit a review team from requesting the attendance at a closed meeting of a person who is not a member of the review team and who has information regarding a deceased child.

(c) Except as necessary to carry out a review team's purpose and duties, members of a review team and persons attending a review team meeting may not disclose what occurred at the meeting.

(d) A member of a review team participating in the review of a child death is immune from civil or criminal liability arising from information presented in or opinions formed as a result of a meeting.

History of Fam. Code §264.510: Acts 1995, 74th Leg., ch. 255, §2 (eff. Sept. 1, 1995), ch. 878, §1 (eff. Sept. 1, 1995).

FAM §264.511. USE OF INFORMATION & RECORDS; CONFIDENTIALITY

(a) Information and records acquired by the committee or by a review team in the exercise of its purpose and duties under this subchapter are confidential and exempt from disclosure under the open records law, Chapter 552, Government Code, and may only be disclosed as necessary to carry out the committee's or review team's purpose and duties.

(b) A report of the committee or of a review team or a statistical compilation of data reports is a public record subject to the open records law, Chapter 552, Government Code, as if the committee or review team were a governmental body under that chapter, if the report or statistical compilation does not contain any information that would permit the identification of an individual.

(c) A member of a review team may not disclose any information that is confidential under this section.

(d) Information, documents, and records of the committee or of a review team that are confidential under this section are not subject to subpoena or discovery and may not be introduced into evidence in any civil or criminal proceeding, except that information, documents, and records otherwise available from other sources are not immune from subpoena, discovery, or introduction into evidence solely because they were presented during proceedings of the committee or a review team or are maintained by the committee or a review team.

History of Fam. Code §264.511: Acts 1995, 74th Leg., ch. 255, §2 (eff. Sept. 1, 1995), ch. 878, §1 (eff. Sept. 1, 1995).

FAM §264.512. GOVERNMENTAL UNITS

The committee and a review team are governmental units for purposes of Chapter 101, Civil Practice and Remedies Code. A review team is a unit of local government under that chapter.

History of Fam. Code §264.512: Acts 1995, 74th Leg., ch. 255, §2 (eff. Sept. 1, 1995), ch. 878, §1 (eff. Sept. 1, 1995).

FAM §264.513. REPORT OF DEATH OF CHILD

(a) A person who knows of the death of a child younger than six years of age shall immediately report the death to the medical examiner of the county in which the death occurs or, if the death occurs in a county that does not have a medical examiner's office or that is not part of a medical examiner's district, to a justice of the peace in that county.

(b) The requirement of this section is in addition to any other reporting requirement imposed by law, including any requirement that a person report child abuse or neglect under this code.

(c) A person is not required to report a death under this section that is the result of a motor vehicle accident. This subsection does not affect a duty imposed by another law to report a death that is the result of a motor vehicle accident.

History of Fam. Code §264.513: Acts 1995, 74th Leg., ch. 255, §2 (eff. Sept. 1, 1995), ch. 878, §1 (eff. Sept. 1, 1995).

A

FAM §264.514. PROCEDURE IN THE EVENT OF REPORTABLE DEATH

(a) A medical examiner or justice of the peace notified of a death of a child under Section 264.513 shall hold an inquest under Chapter 49, Code of Criminal Procedure, to determine whether the death is unexpected or the result of abuse or neglect. An inquest is not required under this subchapter if the child's death is expected and is due to a congenital or neoplastic disease. A death caused by an infectious disease may be considered an expected death if:

(1) the disease was not acquired as a result of trauma or poisoning;

(2) the infectious organism is identified using standard medical procedures; and

(3) the death is not reportable to the Department of State Health Services under Chapter 81, Health and Safety Code.

(a-1) The commissioners court of a county shall adopt regulations relating to the timeliness for conducting an inquest into the death of a child. The regulations adopted under this subsection must be as stringent as the standards issued by the National Association of Medical Examiners unless the commissioners court determines that it would be cost prohibitive for the county to comply with those standards.

(b) The medical examiner or justice of the peace shall immediately notify an appropriate local law enforcement agency if the medical examiner or justice of the peace determines that the death is unexpected or the result of abuse or neglect, and that agency shall investigate the child's death. The medical examiner or justice of the peace shall notify the appropriate county child fatality review team of the child's death not later than the 120th day after the date the death is reported.

(c) In this section, the terms "abuse" and "neglect" have the meaning assigned those terms by Section 261.001.

History of Fam. Code §264.514: Acts 1995, 74th Leg., ch. 255, §2 (eff. Sept. 1, 1995), ch. 878, §1 (eff. Sept. 1, 1995). Amended by Acts 1997, 75th Leg., ch. 1022, §95 (eff. Sept. 1, 1997), ch. 1301, §2 (eff. Sept. 1, 1997); Acts 1999, 76th Leg., ch. 785, §3, eff. Sept. 1, 1999; Acts 2015, 84th Leg., ch. 1, §1.199, eff. Apr. 2, 2015; H.B. 1549, §11(a), 85th Leg., eff. Sept. 1, 2017.

FAM §264.515. INVESTIGATION

(a) The investigation required by Section 264.514 must include:

(1) an autopsy, unless an autopsy was conducted as part of the inquest;

(2) an inquiry into the circumstances of the death, including an investigation of the scene of the death and interviews with the parents of the child, any guardian or caretaker of the child, and the person who reported the child's death; and

(3) a review of relevant information regarding the child from an agency, professional, or health care provider.

(b) The review required by Subsection (a)(3) must include a review of any applicable medical record, child protective services record, record maintained by an emergency medical services provider, and law enforcement report.

(c) The committee shall develop a protocol relating to investigation of an unexpected death of a child under this section. In developing the protocol, the committee shall consult with individuals and organizations that have knowledge and experience in the issues of child abuse and child deaths.

History of Fam. Code §264.515: Acts 1995, 74th Leg., ch. 255, §2 (eff. Sept. 1, 1995), ch. 878, §1 (eff. Sept. 1, 1995).

Sections 264.516-264.600 reserved for expansion

SUBCHAPTER G. COURT-APPOINTED VOLUNTEER ADVOCATE PROGRAMS

FAM §264.601. DEFINITIONS

In this subchapter:

(1) "Abused or neglected child" means a child who is:

(A) the subject of a suit affecting the parent-child relationship filed by a governmental entity; and

(B) under the control or supervision of the department.

(2) "Volunteer advocate program" means a volunteer-based, nonprofit program that:

(A) provides advocacy services to abused or neglected children with the goal of obtaining a permanent placement for a child that is in the child's best interest; and

(B) complies with recognized standards for volunteer advocate programs.

History of Fam. Code §264.601: Acts 1995, 74th Leg., ch. 20, §1, eff. Apr. 20, 1995. Amended by Acts 2009, 81st Leg., ch. 1224, §3, eff. Sept. 1, 2009. Source: Former Fam. Code §34.601.

FAM §264.602. CONTRACTS WITH ADVOCATE PROGRAMS

(a) The statewide organization with which the commission contracts under Section 264.603 shall contract for services with eligible volunteer advocate programs to provide advocacy services to abused or neglected children.

(b) The contract under this section may not result in reducing the financial support a volunteer advocate program receives from another source.

(c) The commission shall develop a scale of state financial support for volunteer advocate programs that declines over a six-year period beginning on the date each individual contract takes effect. After the end of the six-year period, the commission may not provide more than 50 percent of the volunteer advocate program's funding.

(d) The executive commissioner by rule shall adopt standards for a local volunteer advocate program. The statewide organization shall assist the executive commissioner in developing the standards.

(e) The department, in cooperation with the statewide organization with which the commission contracts under Section 264.603 and other interested agencies, shall support the expansion of court-appointed volunteer advocate programs into counties in which there is a need for the programs. In expanding into a county, a program shall work to ensure the independence of the program, to the extent possible, by establishing community support and accessing private funding from the community for the program.

(f) Expenses incurred by a volunteer advocate program to promote public awareness of the need for volunteer advocates or to explain the work performed by volunteer advocates that are paid with money from the commission volunteer advocate program account under Section 504.611, Transportation Code, are not considered administrative expenses for the purpose of Section 264.603(b).

History of Fam. Code §264.602: Acts 1995, 74th Leg., ch. 20, §1, eff. Apr. 20, 1995. Amended by Acts 1995, 74th Leg., ch. 751, §118, eff. Sept. 1, 1995; Acts 1997, 75th Leg., ch. 1294, §7, eff. Sept. 1, 1997; Acts 2005, 79th Leg., ch. 268, §1.61, eff. Sept. 1, 2005; Acts 2009, 81st Leg., ch. 1224, §4, eff. Sept. 1, 2009; Acts 2015, 84th Leg., ch. 597, §4, eff. Sept. 1, 2015. Source: Former Fam. Code §34.602.

FAM §264.603. ADMINISTRATIVE CONTRACTS

(a) The commission shall contract with one statewide organization that is exempt from federal income taxation under Section 501(a), Internal Revenue Code of 1986, as an organization described by Section 501(c)(3) of that code and designated as a supporting organization under Section 509(a)(3) of that code, and that is composed of individuals or groups of individuals who have expertise in the dynamics of child abuse and neglect and experience in operating volunteer advocate programs to provide training, technical assistance, and evaluation services for the benefit of local volunteer advocate programs. The contract shall:

(1) include measurable goals and objectives relating to the number of:

(A) volunteer advocates in the program; and

(B) children receiving services from the program; and

(2) follow practices designed to ensure compliance with standards referenced in the contract.

(b) The contract under this section shall provide that not more than 12 percent of the annual legislative appropriation to implement this subchapter may be spent for administrative purposes by the statewide organization with which the commission contracts under this section.

History of Fam. Code §264.603: Acts 1995, 74th Leg., ch. 20, §1, eff. Apr. 20, 1995. Amended by Acts 1995, 74th Leg., ch. 751, §119, eff. Sept. 1, 1995; Acts 1997, 75th Leg., ch. 600, §20, eff. Sept. 1, 1997; Acts 2009, 81st Leg., ch. 1224, §5, eff. Sept. 1, 2009; Acts 2015, 84th Leg., ch. 597, §5, eff. Sept. 1, 2015. Source: Former Fam. Code §34.603.

FAM §264.604. ELIGIBILITY FOR CONTRACTS

(a) A person is eligible for a contract under Section 264.602 only if the person is a public or private nonprofit entity that operates a volunteer advocate program that:

(1) uses individuals appointed as volunteer advocates or guardians ad litem by the court to provide for the needs of abused or neglected children;

(2) has provided court-appointed advocacy services for at least six months;

(3) provides court-appointed advocacy services for at least 10 children each month; and

(4) has demonstrated that the program has local judicial support.

(b) The statewide organization with which the commission contracts under Section 264.603 may not contract with a person that is not eligible under this section. However, the statewide organization may waive the requirement in Subsection (a)(3) for an established program in a rural area or under other special circumstances.

History of Fam. Code §264.604: Acts 1995, 74th Leg., ch. 20, §1, eff. Apr. 20, 1995. Amended by Acts 1995, 74th Leg., ch. 751, §120, eff. Sept. 1, 1995; Acts 1997, 75th Leg., ch. 1294, §8, eff. Sept. 1, 1997; Acts 2009, 81st Leg., ch. 1224, §6, eff. Sept. 1, 2009; Acts 2015, 84th Leg., ch. 597, §6, eff. Sept. 1, 2015. Source: Former Fam. Code §34.604.

FAM §264.605. CONTRACT FORM

A person shall apply for a contract under Section 264.602 on a form provided by the commission.

History of Fam. Code §264.605: Acts 1995, 74th Leg., ch. 20, §1, eff. Apr. 20, 1995. Amended by Acts 2015, 84th Leg., ch. 597, §7, eff. Sept. 1, 2015. Source: Former Fam. Code §34.605.

FAM §264.606. CRITERIA FOR AWARD OF CONTRACTS

The statewide organization with which the commission contracts under Section 264.603 shall consider the following in awarding a contract under Section 264.602:

(1) the volunteer advocate program's eligibility for and use of funds from local, state, or federal governmental sources, philanthropic organizations, and other sources;

(2) community support for the volunteer advocate program as indicated by financial contributions from civic organizations, individuals, and other community resources;

(3) whether the volunteer advocate program provides services that encourage the permanent placement of children through reunification with their families or timely placement with an adoptive family; and

(4) whether the volunteer advocate program has the endorsement and cooperation of the local juvenile court system.

History of Fam. Code §264.606: Acts 1995, 74th Leg., ch. 20, §1, eff. Apr. 20, 1995. Amended by Acts 1995, 74th Leg., ch. 751, §121, eff. Sept. 1, 1995; Acts 2015, 84th Leg., ch. 597, §8, eff. Sept. 1, 2015. Source: Former Fam. Code §34.606.

FAM §264.607. CONTRACT REQUIREMENTS

The commission shall require that a contract under Section 264.602 require the volunteer advocate program to:

(1) make quarterly and annual financial reports on a form provided by the commission;

(2) cooperate with inspections and audits that the commission makes to ensure service standards and fiscal responsibility; and

(3) provide as a minimum:

(A) independent and factual information in writing to the court and to counsel for the parties involved regarding the child;

(B) advocacy through the courts for permanent home placement and rehabilitation services for the child;

(C) monitoring of the child to ensure the safety of the child and to prevent unnecessary movement of the child to multiple temporary placements;

(D) reports in writing to the presiding judge and to counsel for the parties involved;

(E) community education relating to child abuse and neglect;

(F) referral services to existing community services;

(G) a volunteer recruitment and training program, including adequate screening procedures for volunteers;

(H) procedures to assure the confidentiality of records or information relating to the child; and

(I) compliance with the standards adopted under Section 264.602.

History of Fam. Code §264.607: Acts 1995, 74th Leg., ch. 20, §1, eff. Apr. 20, 1995. Amended by Acts 1995, 74th Leg., ch. 751, §122, eff. Sept. 1, 1995; Acts 1997, 75th Leg., ch. 1294, §9, eff. Sept. 1, 1997; Acts 2009, 81st Leg., ch. 1224, §7, eff. Sept. 1, 2009; Acts 2015, 84th Leg., ch. 597, §9, eff. Sept. 1, 2015. Source: Former Fam. Code §34.607.

FAM §264.608. REPORT TO THE LEGISLATURE

(a) Not later than December 1 of each year, the commission shall publish a report that:

(1) summarizes reports from volunteer advocate programs under contract with the commission;

(2) analyzes the effectiveness of the contracts made by the commission under this chapter; and

(3) provides information on:

(A) the expenditure of funds under this chapter;

(B) services provided and the number of children for whom the services were provided; and

(C) any other information relating to the services provided by the volunteer advocate programs under this chapter.

(b) The commission shall submit copies of the report to the governor, lieutenant governor, speaker of the house of representatives, Legislative Budget Board, and members of the legislature.

History of Fam. Code §264.608: Acts 1995, 74th Leg., ch. 20, §1, eff. Apr. 20, 1995. Amended by Acts 2013, 83rd Leg., ch. 1312, §21, eff. Sept. 1, 2013; Acts 2015, 84th Leg., ch. 597, §10, eff. Sept. 1, 2015. Source: Former Fam. Code §34.608.

FAM §264.609. RULE-MAKING AUTHORITY

The executive commissioner may adopt rules necessary to implement this subchapter.

History of Fam. Code §264.609: Acts 1995, 74th Leg., ch. 20, §1, eff. Apr. 20, 1995. Amended by Acts 2015, 84th Leg., ch. 597, §11, eff. Sept. 1, 2015. Source: Former Fam. Code §34.609.

FAM §264.610. CONFIDENTIALITY

The commission may not disclose information gained through reports, collected case data, or inspections that would identify a person working at or receiving services from a volunteer advocate program.

History of Fam. Code §264.610: Acts 1995, 74th Leg., ch. 20, §1, eff. Apr. 20, 1995. Amended by Acts 2015, 84th Leg., ch. 597, §12, eff. Sept. 1, 2015. Source: Former Fam. Code §34.610.

FAM §264.611. CONSULTATIONS

In implementing this chapter, the commission shall consult with individuals or groups of individuals who have expertise in the dynamics of child abuse and neglect and experience in operating volunteer advocate programs.

History of Fam. Code §264.611: Acts 1995, 74th Leg., ch. 20, §1, eff. Apr. 20, 1995. Amended by Acts 2015, 84th Leg., ch. 597, §13, eff. Sept. 1, 2015. Source: Former Fam. Code §34.611.

FAM §264.612. FUNDING

(a) The commission may solicit and receive grants or money from either private or public sources, including by appropriation by the legislature from the general revenue fund, to implement this chapter.

(b) The need for and importance of the implementation of this chapter by the commission requires priority and preferential consideration for appropriation.

(c) Repealed by Acts 1995, 74th Leg., ch. 751, §128, eff. Sept. 1, 1995.

History of Fam. Code §264.612: Acts 1995, 74th Leg., ch. 20, §1, eff. Apr. 20, 1995. Amended by Acts 1995, 74th Leg., ch. 751, §128, eff. Sept. 1, 1995; Acts 2015, 84th Leg., ch. 597, §14, eff. Sept. 1, 2015. Source: Former Fam. Code §34.612.

FAM §264.613. USE OF INFORMATION & RECORDS; CONFIDENTIALITY

(a) The files, reports, records, communications, and working papers used or developed in providing services under this subchapter are confidential and not subject to disclosure under Chapter 552, Government Code, and may only be disclosed for purposes consistent with this subchapter.

(b) Information described by Subsection (a) may be disclosed to:

(1) the department, department employees, law enforcement agencies, prosecuting attorneys, medical professionals, and other state agencies that provide services to children and families;

(2) the attorney for the child who is the subject of the information; and

(3) eligible children's advocacy centers.

(c) Information related to the investigation of a report of abuse or neglect of a child under Chapter 261 and services provided as a result of the investigation are confidential as provided by Section 261.201.

History of Fam. Code §264.613: Acts 2001, 77th Leg., ch. 142, §1, eff. May 16, 2001.

FAM §264.614. INTERNET APPLICATION FOR CASE TRACKING & INFORMATION MANAGEMENT SYSTEM

(a) Subject to the availability of money as described by Subsection (c), the department shall develop an Internet application that allows a court-appointed volunteer advocate representing a child in the managing conservatorship of the department to access the child's case file through the department's automated case tracking and information management system and to add the volunteer advocate's findings and reports to the child's case file.

(b) The court-appointed volunteer advocate shall maintain the confidentiality required by this chapter and department rule for the information accessed by the advocate through the system described by Subsection (a).

(c) The department may use money appropriated to the department and money received as a gift, grant, or donation to pay for the costs of developing and maintaining the Internet application required by Subsection (a). The department may solicit and accept gifts, grants, and donations of any kind and from any source for purposes of this section.

(d) The executive commissioner shall adopt rules necessary to implement this section.

History of Fam. Code §264.614: Acts 2013, 83rd Leg., ch. 205, §1, eff. Sept. 1, 2013. Amended by Acts 2015, 84th Leg., ch. 1, §1.200, eff. Apr. 2, 2015.

Sections 264.615-264.700 blank

SUBCHAPTER H. REPEALED

Repealed by Acts 2015, 84th Leg., ch. 1, §1.203(14), eff. Apr. 2, 2015.

Sections 264.702-264.728 blank

SUBCHAPTER H-1. EXPIRED

Sections 264.729-264.750 blank

SUBCHAPTER I. RELATIVE & OTHER DESIGNATED CAREGIVER PLACEMENT PROGRAM

A

FAM §264.751. DEFINITIONS

The amended text in §264.751 is effective for service plans filed for a full adversary hearing held under Fam. Code §262.201 or a status hearing held under Fam. Code ch. 263 on or after Jan. 1, 2018. A hearing held before Jan. 1, 2018, is governed by the former law in effect at that time. Except as provided above, the amended text in §264.751 is effective for SAPCRs filed on or after Sept. 1, 2017. SAPCRs filed before Sept. 1, 2017, are governed by the former law in effect at that time.

Foster homes or foster group homes licensed by TDFPS and agency foster group homes verified by a child-placing agency before Sept. 1, 2017, may continue to operate under the former law in effect at that time, until the foster home or foster group home converts to another residential child-care license or the license is relinquished, or the agency foster group home has been converted to a verified foster home or closed.

In this subchapter:

(1) "Designated caregiver" means an individual who has a longstanding and significant relationship with a child for whom the department has been appointed managing conservator and who:

(A) is appointed to provide substitute care for the child, but is not [~~licensed by the department or~~] verified by a licensed child-placing agency [~~or the department~~] to operate an [~~a foster home, foster group home,~~] agency foster home [~~, or agency foster group home~~] under Chapter 42, Human Resources Code; or

(B) is subsequently appointed permanent managing conservator of the child after providing the care described by Paragraph (A).

(2) "Relative" means a person related to a child by consanguinity as determined under Section 573.022, Government Code.

(3) "Relative caregiver" means a relative who:

(A) provides substitute care for a child for whom the department has been appointed managing conservator, but who is not [~~licensed by the department or~~] verified by a licensed child-placing agency [~~or the department~~] to operate an [~~a foster home, foster group home,~~] agency foster home [~~, or agency foster group home~~] under Chapter 42, Human Resources Code; or

(B) is subsequently appointed permanent managing conservator of the child after providing the care described by Paragraph (A).

History of Fam. Code §264.751: Acts 2005, 79th Leg., ch. 268, §1.62(a), eff. Sept. 1, 2005. Amended by Acts 2009, 81st Leg., ch. 1118, §7 (eff. Sept. 1, 2009), ch. 1238, §6(c) (eff. Sept. 1, 2009); H.B. 7, §34, 85th Leg., eff. Sept. 1, 2017.

FAM §264.752. RELATIVE & OTHER DESIGNATED CAREGIVER PLACEMENT PROGRAM

(a) The department shall develop and procure a program to:

(1) promote continuity and stability for children for whom the department is appointed managing conservator by placing those children with relative or other designated caregivers; and

(2) facilitate relative or other designated caregiver placements by providing assistance and services to those caregivers in accordance with this subchapter and rules adopted by the executive commissioner.

(b) Repealed by Acts 2015, 84th Leg., ch. 944, §86(38), eff. Sept. 1, 2015.

(c) The executive commissioner shall adopt rules necessary to implement this subchapter. The rules must include eligibility criteria for receiving assistance and services under this subchapter.

History of Fam. Code §264.752: Acts 2005, 79th Leg., ch. 268, §1.62(a), eff. Sept. 1, 2005. Amended by Acts 2015, 84th Leg., ch. 944, §86(38), eff. Sept. 1, 2015.

FAM §264.753. EXPEDITED PLACEMENT

The department shall expedite the completion of the background and criminal history check, the home study, and any other administrative procedure to ensure that the child is placed with a qualified relative or caregiver as soon as possible after the date the caregiver is identified.

History of Fam. Code §264.753: Acts 2005, 79th Leg., ch. 268, §1.62, eff. Sept. 1, 2005. Amended by Acts 2015, 84th Leg., ch. 1, §1.201, eff. Apr. 2, 2015.

A FAM §264.754. ASSESSMENT [INVESTIGATION] OF PROPOSED PLACEMENT

(a) In this section, "low-risk criminal offense" means a nonviolent criminal offense, including a fraud-based offense, the department determines has a low risk of impacting:

(1) a child's safety or well-being; or

(2) the stability of a child's placement with a relative or other designated caregiver.

(b) Before placing a child with a proposed relative or other designated caregiver, the department must conduct an assessment [investigation] to determine whether the proposed placement is in the child's best interest.

(c) If the department disqualifies a person from serving as a relative or other designated caregiver for a child on the basis that the person has been convicted of a low-risk criminal offense, the person may appeal the disqualification in accordance with the procedure developed under Subsection (d).

(d) The department shall develop:

(1) a list of criminal offenses the department determines are low-risk criminal offenses; and

(2) a procedure for appropriate regional administration of the department to review a decision to disqualify a person from serving as a relative or other designated caregiver that includes the consideration of:

(A) when the person's conviction occurred;

(B) whether the person has multiple convictions for low-risk criminal offenses; and

(C) the likelihood that the person will commit fraudulent activity in the future.

(e) The department shall:

(1) publish the list of low-risk criminal offenses and information regarding the review procedure developed under Subsection (d) on the department's Internet website; and

(2) provide prospective relative and other designated caregivers information regarding the review procedure developed under Subsection (d).

History of Fam. Code §264.754: Acts 2005, 79th Leg., ch. 268, §1.62, eff. Sept. 1, 2005. Amended by S.B. 879, §1, 85th Leg., eff. Sept. 1, 2017.

FAM §264.7541. CAREGIVER VISIT WITH CHILD; INFORMATION

(a) Except as provided by Subsection (b), before placing a child with a proposed relative or other designated caregiver, the department must:

(1) arrange a visit between the child and the proposed caregiver; and

(2) provide the proposed caregiver with a form, which may be the same form the department provides to nonrelative caregivers, containing information, to the extent it is available, about the child that would enhance continuity of care for the child, including:

(A) the child's school information and educational needs;

(B) the child's medical, dental, and mental health care information;

(C) the child's social and family information; and

(D) any other information about the child the department determines will assist the proposed caregiver in meeting the child's needs.

(b) The department may waive the requirements of Subsection (a) if the proposed relative or other designated caregiver has a long-standing or significant relationship with the child and has provided care for the child at any time during the 12 months preceding the date of the proposed placement.

History of Fam. Code §264.7541: Acts 2013, 83rd Leg., ch. 426, §1, eff. Sept. 1, 2013.

A FAM §264.755. CAREGIVER ASSISTANCE AGREEMENT

(a) The department shall, subject to the availability of funds, enter into a caregiver assistance agreement with each relative or other designated caregiver to provide monetary assistance and additional support services to the caregiver. The monetary assistance and support services shall be based on a family's need, as determined by Subsection (b) and rules adopted by the executive commissioner.

(b) The department shall provide monetary [Monetary] assistance [provided] under this section to a caregiver who has a family income that is less than or equal to 300 percent of the federal poverty level. Monetary assistance provided to a caregiver under this section may not exceed 50 percent of the department's daily basic foster care rate for the child. A caregiver who has a family income greater than 300 percent of the federal poverty level is not eligible for monetary assistance under this section [must include a one-time cash payment to the caregiver on the initial placement of a child or a sibling group. The amount of the cash payment, as determined by the department, may not exceed $1,000 for each child. The payment for placement of a sibling group must be at least $1,000 for the group,

but may not exceed $1,000 for each child in the group. The cash payment must be provided on the initial placement of each child with the caregiver and is provided to assist the caregiver in purchasing essential child-care items such as furniture and clothing].

(b-1) The department shall disburse monetary assistance provided to a caregiver under Subsection (b) in the same manner as the department disburses payments to a foster parent. The department may not provide monetary assistance to an eligible caregiver under Subsection (b) after the first anniversary of the date the caregiver receives the first monetary assistance payment from the department under this section. The department, at its discretion and for good cause, may extend the monetary assistance payments for an additional six months.

(b-2) The department shall implement a process to verify the family income of a relative or other designated caregiver for the purpose of determining eligibility to receive monetary assistance under Subsection (b).

(c) Monetary assistance and additional support services provided under this section may include:

(1) case management services and training and information about the child's needs until the caregiver is appointed permanent managing conservator;

(2) referrals to appropriate state agencies administering public benefits or assistance programs for which the child, the caregiver, or the caregiver's family may qualify;

(3) family counseling not provided under the Medicaid program for the caregiver's family for a period not to exceed two years from the date of initial placement;

(4) if the caregiver meets the eligibility criteria determined by rules adopted by the executive commissioner, reimbursement of all child-care expenses incurred while the child is under 13 years of age, or under 18 years of age if the child has a developmental disability, and while the department is the child's managing conservator; and

(5) if the caregiver meets the eligibility criteria determined by rules adopted by the executive commissioner, reimbursement of 50 percent of child-care expenses incurred after the caregiver is appointed permanent managing conservator of the child while the child is under 13 years of age, or under 18 years of age if the child has a developmental disability [; and]

[(6)] [reimbursement of other expenses, as determined by rules adopted by the executive commissioner, not to exceed $500 per year for each child].

(d) The department, in accordance with department rules, shall implement a process to verify that each relative and designated caregiver who is seeking monetary assistance or additional support services from the department for day care as defined by Section 264.124[1] for a child under this section has attempted to find appropriate day-care services for the child through community services, including Head Start programs, prekindergarten classes, and early education programs offered in public schools. The department shall specify the documentation the relative or designated caregiver must provide to the department to demonstrate compliance with the requirements established under this subsection. The department may not provide monetary assistance or additional support services to the relative or designated caregiver for the day care unless the department receives the required verification.

(e) The department may provide monetary assistance or additional support services to a relative or designated caregiver for day care without the verification required under Subsection (d) if the department determines the verification would prevent an emergency placement that is in the child's best interest.

(f) If a person who has a family income that is less than or equal to 300 percent of the federal poverty level enters into a caregiver assistance agreement with the department, obtains permanent managing conservatorship of a child, and meets all other eligibility requirements, the person may receive an annual reimbursement of other expenses for the child, as determined by rules adopted by the executive commissioner, not to exceed $500 per year until the earlier of:

(1) the third anniversary of the date the person was awarded permanent managing conservatorship of the child; or

(2) the child's 18th birthday.

1. **Editor's note:** In 2013, the Legislature enacted two sections 264.124. The §264.124 referenced here was enacted by Acts 2013, 83rd Leg., ch. 423, §1, effective Sept. 1, 2013, and is marked with [B*] in this book.

History of Fam. Code §264.755: Acts 2005, 79th Leg., ch. 268, §1.62, eff. Sept. 1, 2005. Amended by Acts 2013, 83rd Leg., ch. 423, §2 (eff. Sept. 1, 2013), ch. 426, §2 (eff. Sept. 1, 2013); Acts 2015, 84th Leg., ch. 1, §1.202, eff. Apr. 2, 2015; H.B. 4, §1, 85th Leg., eff. Sept. 1, 2017.

E FAM §264.7551. FRAUDULENT AGREEMENT; CRIMINAL OFFENSE; CIVIL PENALTY

(a) A person commits an offense if, with intent to defraud or deceive the department, the person know-

ingly makes or causes to be made a false statement or misrepresentation of a material fact that allows a person to enter into a caregiver assistance agreement.

(b) An offense under this section is:

(1) a Class C misdemeanor if the person entered into a fraudulent caregiver assistance agreement and received no monetary assistance under the agreement or received monetary assistance under the agreement for less than 7 days;

(2) a Class B misdemeanor if the person entered into a fraudulent caregiver assistance agreement and received monetary assistance under the agreement for 7 days or more but less than 31 days;

(3) a Class A misdemeanor if the person entered into a fraudulent caregiver assistance agreement and received monetary assistance under the agreement for 31 days or more but less than 91 days; or

(4) a state jail felony if the person entered into a fraudulent caregiver assistance agreement and received monetary assistance under the agreement for 91 days or more.

(c) If conduct that constitutes an offense under this section also constitutes an offense under any other law, the actor may be prosecuted under this section, the other law, or both.

(d) The appropriate county prosecuting attorney shall be responsible for the prosecution of an offense under this section.

(e) A person who engaged in conduct described by Subsection (a) is liable to the state for a civil penalty of $1,000. The attorney general shall bring an action to recover a civil penalty as authorized by this subsection.

(f) The commissioner of the department may adopt rules necessary to determine whether fraudulent activity that violates Subsection (a) has occurred.

History of Fam. Code §264.7551: Enacted by H.B. 4, §2, 85th Leg., eff. Sept. 1, 2017.

FAM §264.756. ASSISTANCE WITH PERMANENT PLACEMENT

The department shall collaborate with the State Bar of Texas and local community partners to identify legal resources to assist relatives and other designated caregivers in obtaining conservatorship, adoption, or other permanent legal status for the child.

History of Fam. Code §264.756: Acts 2005, 79th Leg., ch. 268, §1.62, eff. Sept. 1, 2005.

FAM §264.757. COORDINATION WITH OTHER AGENCIES

The department shall coordinate with other health and human services agencies, as defined by Section 531.001, Government Code, to provide assistance and services under this subchapter.

History of Fam. Code §264.757: Acts 2005, 79th Leg., ch. 268, §1.62(a), eff. Sept. 1, 2005.

FAM §264.758. FUNDS

The department and other state agencies shall actively seek and use federal funds available for the purposes of this subchapter.

History of Fam. Code §264.758: Acts 2005, 79th Leg., ch. 268, §1.62, eff. Sept. 1, 2005.

FAM §264.759. REPEALED

Repealed by Acts 2013, 83rd Leg., ch. 1312, §99(10), eff. Sept. 1, 2013.

A FAM §264.760. ELIGIBILITY FOR FOSTER CARE PAYMENTS & PERMANENCY CARE ASSISTANCE

The amended text in §264.760 is effective for service plans filed for a full adversary hearing held under Fam. Code §262.201 or a status hearing held under Fam. Code ch. 263 on or after Jan. 1, 2018. A hearing held before Jan. 1, 2018, is governed by the former law in effect at that time. Except as provided above, the amended text in §264.760 is effective for SAPCRs filed on or after Sept. 1, 2017. SAPCRs filed before Sept. 1, 2017, are governed by the former law in effect at that time.

Foster homes or foster group homes licensed by TDFPS and agency foster group homes verified by a child-placing agency before Sept. 1, 2017, may continue to operate under the former law in effect at that time, until the foster home or foster group home converts to another residential child-care license or the license is relinquished, or the agency foster group home has been converted to a verified foster home or closed.

Notwithstanding any other provision of this subchapter, a relative or other designated caregiver who becomes [~~licensed by the department or~~] verified by a licensed child-placing agency [~~or the department~~] to operate an [~~a foster home, foster group home,~~] agency foster home[~~, or agency foster group home~~] under Chapter 42, Human Resources Code, may receive foster care payments in lieu of the benefits provided by this subchapter, beginning with the first month in which the relative or other designated caregiver becomes licensed or is verified.

History of Fam. Code §264.760: Acts 2009, 81st Leg., ch. 1118, §8 (eff. Sept. 1, 2009), ch. 1238, §6(d) (eff. Sept. 1, 2009). Amended by H.B. 7, §35, 85th Leg., eff. Sept. 1, 2017.

FAM §264.761. STUDY OF PROGRAM

(a) The department shall study the effectiveness of the relative and other designated caregiver placement program created by this subchapter and make recommendations to the legislature for improving the program. The recommended improvements must be designed to minimize the number of placements for each child, maximize efficiency in the distribution of any monetary or other assistance for which caregivers qualify, facilitate a safe and permanent exit from the managing conservatorship of the department in as timely a fashion as possible, and assist caregivers in obtaining the verification necessary to qualify for foster care maintenance reimbursement. The recommendations may include increases in the amount of assistance and the identification of automated or other processes designed to speed the payment of assistance.

(b) The department shall report its findings and recommendations to the legislature not later than January 1, 2017.

(c) This section expires September 1, 2017.

History of Fam. Code §264.761: Acts 2015, 84th Leg., ch. 790, §1, eff. Sept. 1, 2015.

E FAM §264.762. ANNUAL REPORT

Not later than September 1 of each year, the department shall publish a report on the relative and other designated caregiver placement program created under this subchapter. The report must include data on permanency outcomes for children placed with relative or other designated caregivers, including:

(1) the number of disruptions in a relative or other designated caregiver placement;

(2) the reasons for any disruption in a relative or other designated caregiver placement; and

(3) the length of time before a relative or other designated caregiver who receives monetary assistance from the department under this subchapter obtains permanent managing conservatorship of a child.

History of Fam. Code §264.762: Enacted by H.B. 4, §3, 85th Leg., eff. Sept. 1, 2017.

Sections 264.763-264.800 blank

SUBCHAPTER J. FAMILY DRUG COURT PROGRAM

In 2013, the Legislature transferred Family Code ch. 264, subch. J, to Government Code title 2, subtitle K, and redesignated it as Government Code ch. 122. See Acts 2013, 83rd Leg., ch. 747, §1.02, eff. Sept. 1, 2013. See also Gov't Code ch. 122, p. 1350.

Sections 264.806-264.850 blank

SUBCHAPTER K. PERMANENCY CARE ASSISTANCE PROGRAM

FAM §264.851. DEFINITIONS

In this subchapter:

(1) Repealed by Acts 2015, 84th Leg., ch. 944, §86(39), eff. Sept. 1, 2015.

(2) "Kinship provider" means a relative of a foster child, or another adult with a longstanding and significant relationship with a foster child before the child was placed with the person by the department, with whom the child resides for at least six consecutive months after the person becomes licensed by the department or verified by a licensed child-placing agency or the department to provide foster care.

(3) "Permanency care assistance agreement" means a written agreement between the department and a kinship provider for the payment of permanency care assistance benefits as provided by this subchapter.

(4) "Permanency care assistance benefits" means monthly payments paid by the department to a kinship provider under a permanency care assistance agreement.

(5) "Relative" means a person related to a foster child by consanguinity or affinity.

History of Fam. Code §264.851: Acts 2009, 81st Leg., ch. 1118, §9 (eff. Sept. 1, 2009), ch. 1238, §6(e) (eff. Sept. 1, 2009). Amended by Acts 2015, 84th Leg., ch. 944, §86(39), eff. Sept. 1, 2015.

FAM §264.852. PERMANENCY CARE ASSISTANCE AGREEMENTS

(a) The department shall enter into a permanency care assistance agreement with a kinship provider who is eligible to receive permanency care assistance benefits.

(b) The department may enter into a permanency care assistance agreement with a kinship provider who is the prospective managing conservator of a foster child only if the kinship provider meets the eligibility criteria under federal and state law and department rule.

(c) A court may not order the department to enter into a permanency care assistance agreement with a kinship provider unless the kinship provider meets the eligibility criteria under federal and state law and department rule, including requirements relating to the criminal history background check of a kinship provider.

(d) A permanency care assistance agreement may provide for reimbursement of the nonrecurring ex-

penses a kinship provider incurs in obtaining permanent managing conservatorship of a foster child, including attorney's fees and court costs. The reimbursement of the nonrecurring expenses under this subsection may not exceed $2,000.

History of Fam. Code §264.852: Acts 2009, 81st Leg., ch. 1118, §9 (eff. Sept. 1, 2009), ch. 1238, §6(e) (eff. Sept. 1, 2009).

A FAM §264.8521. NOTICE TO APPLICANTS

The amended text in §264.8521 is effective for service plans filed for a full adversary hearing held under Fam. Code §262.201 or a status hearing held under Fam. Code ch. 263 on or after Jan. 1, 2018. A hearing held before Jan. 1, 2018, is governed by the former law in effect at that time. Except as provided above, the amended text in §264.8521 is effective for SAPCRs filed on or after Sept. 1, 2017. SAPCRs filed before Sept. 1, 2017, are governed by the former law in effect at that time.

Foster homes or foster group homes licensed by TDFPS and agency foster group homes verified by a child-placing agency before Sept. 1, 2017, may continue to operate under the former law in effect at that time, until the foster home or foster group home converts to another residential child-care license or the license is relinquished, or the agency foster group home has been converted to a verified foster home or closed.

At the time a person applies to become [~~licensed by the department or~~] verified by a licensed child-placing agency [~~or the department~~] to provide foster care in order to qualify for the permanency care assistance program, the department or the child-placing agency shall:

(1) notify the applicant that a background check, including a criminal history record check, will be conducted on the individual; and

(2) inform the applicant about criminal convictions that:

(A) preclude an individual from becoming a [~~licensed foster home or~~] verified agency foster home; and

(B) may also be considered in evaluating the individual's application.

History of Fam. Code §264.8521: Acts 2011, 82nd Leg., ch. 318, §1, eff. Sept. 1, 2011. Amended by H.B. 7, §36, 85th Leg., eff. Sept. 1, 2017.

FAM §264.853. RULES

The executive commissioner shall adopt rules necessary to implement the permanency care assistance program. The rules must:

(1) establish eligibility requirements to receive permanency care assistance benefits under the program; and

(2) ensure that the program conforms to the requirements for federal assistance as required by the Fostering Connections to Success and Increasing Adoptions Act of 2008 (Pub. L. No. 110-351).

History of Fam. Code §264.853: Acts 2009, 81st Leg., ch. 1118, §9 (eff. Sept. 1, 2009), ch. 1238, §6(e) (eff. Sept. 1, 2009).

FAM §264.854. MAXIMUM PAYMENT AMOUNT

The executive commissioner shall set the maximum monthly amount of assistance payments under a permanency care assistance agreement in an amount that does not exceed the amount of the monthly foster care maintenance payment the department would pay to a foster care provider caring for the child for whom the kinship provider is caring.

History of Fam. Code §264.854: Acts 2009, 81st Leg., ch. 1118, §9 (eff. Sept. 1, 2009), ch. 1238, §6(e) (eff. Sept. 1, 2009).

FAM §264.855. CONTINUED ELIGIBILITY FOR PERMANENCY CARE ASSISTANCE BENEFITS AFTER AGE 18

If the department first entered into a permanency care assistance agreement with a foster child's kinship provider after the child's 16th birthday, the department may continue to provide permanency care assistance payments until the last day of the month of the child's 21st birthday, provided the child is:

(1) regularly attending high school or enrolled in a program leading toward a high school diploma or high school equivalency certificate;

(2) regularly attending an institution of higher education or a postsecondary vocational or technical program;

(3) participating in a program or activity that promotes, or removes barriers to, employment;

(4) employed for at least 80 hours a month; or

(5) incapable of any of the activities described by Subdivisions (1)-(4) due to a documented medical condition.

History of Fam. Code §264.855: Acts 2009, 81st Leg., ch. 1118, §9 (eff. Sept. 1, 2009), ch. 1238, §6(e) (eff. Oct. 1, 2010).

FAM §264.856. APPROPRIATION REQUIRED

The department is not required to provide permanency care assistance benefits under this subchapter unless the department is specifically appropriated money for purposes of this subchapter.

History of Fam. Code §264.856: Acts 2009, 81st Leg., ch. 1118, §9 (eff. Sept. 1, 2009), ch. 1238, §6(e) (eff. Sept. 1, 2009).

FAM §264.857. REPEALED

~~[DEADLINE FOR NEW AGREEMENTS]~~

~~[The department may not enter into a permanency care assistance agreement after August 31, 2017. The department shall continue to make payments after that date under a permanency care assistance agreement entered into on or before August 31, 2017, according to the terms of the agreement.]~~

Repealed by S.B. 203, §1, 85th Leg., eff. May 29, 2017.

Sections 264.858-264.900 blank

SUBCHAPTER L. PARENTAL CHILD SAFETY PLACEMENTS

FAM §264.901. DEFINITIONS

In this subchapter:

(1) "Caregiver" means an individual, other than a child's parent, conservator, or legal guardian, who is related to the child or has a long-standing and significant relationship with the child or the child's family.

(2) "Parental child safety placement" means a temporary out-of-home placement of a child with a caregiver that is made by a parent or other person with whom the child resides in accordance with a written agreement approved by the department that ensures the safety of the child:

(A) during an investigation by the department of alleged abuse or neglect of the child; or

(B) while the parent or other person is receiving services from the department.

(3) "Parental child safety placement agreement" means an agreement between a parent or other person making a parental child safety placement and the caregiver that contains the terms of the placement and is approved by the department.

History of Fam. Code §264.901: Acts 2011, 82nd Leg., ch. 1071, §1, eff. Sept. 1, 2011.

FAM §264.902. PARENTAL CHILD SAFETY PLACEMENT AGREEMENT

(a) A parental child safety placement agreement must include terms that clearly state:

(1) the respective duties of the person making the placement and the caregiver, including a plan for how the caregiver will access necessary medical treatment for the child and the caregiver's duty to ensure that a school-age child is enrolled in and attending school;

(2) conditions under which the person placing the child may have access to the child, including how often the person may visit and the circumstances under which the person's visit may occur;

(3) the duties of the department;

(4) the date on which the agreement will terminate unless terminated sooner or extended to a subsequent date as provided under department policy; and

(5) any other term the department determines necessary for the safety and welfare of the child.

(b) A parental child safety placement agreement must contain the following statement in boldface type and capital letters: "YOUR AGREEMENT TO THE PARENTAL CHILD SAFETY PLACEMENT IS NOT AN ADMISSION OF CHILD ABUSE OR NEGLECT ON YOUR PART AND CANNOT BE USED AGAINST YOU AS AN ADMISSION OF CHILD ABUSE OR NEGLECT."

(c) A parental child safety placement agreement must be in writing and signed by the person making the placement and the caregiver.

(d) The department must provide a written copy of the parental child safety placement agreement to the person making the placement and the caregiver.

History of Fam. Code §264.902: Acts 2011, 82nd Leg., ch. 1071, §1, eff. Sept. 1, 2011.

A FAM §264.903. CAREGIVER EVALUATION

(a) The department shall develop policies and procedures for evaluating a potential caregiver's qualifications to care for a child under this subchapter, including policies and procedures for evaluating:

(1) the criminal history of a caregiver;

(2) allegations of abuse or neglect against a caregiver; and

(3) a caregiver's home environment and ability to care for the child.

(a-1) The department shall expedite the evaluation of a potential caregiver under this section to ensure that the child is placed with a caregiver who has the ability to protect the child from the alleged perpetrator of abuse or neglect against the child.

(b) A department caseworker who performs an evaluation of a caregiver under this section shall document the results of the evaluation in the department's case records.

(c) If, after performing an evaluation of a potential caregiver, the department determines that it is not in the child's best interest to be placed with the caregiver, the department shall notify the person who proposed

the caregiver and the proposed caregiver of the reasons for the department's decision, but may not disclose the specifics of any criminal history or allegations of abuse or neglect unless the caregiver agrees to the disclosure.

History of Fam. Code §264.903: Acts 2011, 82nd Leg., ch. 1071, §1, eff. Sept. 1, 2011. Amended by H.B. 1549, §12, 85th Leg., eff. Sept. 1, 2017.

FAM §264.904. DEPARTMENT PROCEDURES FOR CLOSING CASE

(a) Before closing a case in which the department has approved a parental child safety placement, the department must develop a plan with the person who made the placement and the caregiver for the safe return of the child to the person who placed the child with the caregiver or to another person legally entitled to possession of the child, as appropriate.

(b) The department may close a case with a child still living with the caregiver in a parental child safety placement if the department has determined that the child could safely return to the parent or person who made the parental child safety placement but the parent or other person agrees in writing for the child to continue to reside with the caregiver.

(c) If the department determines that the child is unable to safely return to the parent or person who made the parental child safety placement, the department shall determine whether the child can remain safely in the home of the caregiver or whether the department must seek legal conservatorship of the child in order to ensure the child's safety.

(d) Before the department may close a case with a child still living in a parental child safety placement, the department must:

(1) determine and document in the case file that the child can safely remain in the placement without the department's supervision;

(2) obtain the written agreement of the parent or person who made the parental child safety placement, if possible;

(3) obtain the caregiver's agreement in writing that the child can continue living in the placement after the department closes the case; and

(4) develop a written plan for the child's care after the department closes the case.

(e) The department is not required to comply with Subsection (d) if the department has filed suit seeking to be named conservator of the child under Chapter 262 and been denied conservatorship of the child.

History of Fam. Code §264.904: Acts 2011, 82nd Leg., ch. 1071, §1, eff. Sept. 1, 2011.

FAM §264.905. REMOVAL OF CHILD BY DEPARTMENT

This subchapter does not prevent the department from removing a child at any time from a person who makes a parental child safety placement or from a caregiver if removal is determined to be necessary by the department for the safety and welfare of the child as provided by Chapter 262.

History of Fam. Code §264.905: Acts 2011, 82nd Leg., ch. 1071, §1, eff. Sept. 1, 2011.

FAM §264.906. PLACEMENT PREFERENCE DURING CONSERVATORSHIP

If, while a parental child safety placement agreement is in effect, the department files suit under Chapter 262 seeking to be named managing conservator of the child, the department shall give priority to placing the child with the parental child safety placement caregiver as long as the placement is safe and available.

History of Fam. Code §264.906: Acts 2011, 82nd Leg., ch. 1071, §1, eff. Sept. 1, 2011.

CHAPTER 265. PREVENTION & EARLY INTERVENTION SERVICES

Subchapter A. Prevention & Early Intervention Services

FAM §265.001. Definitions

In this chapter:

(1) "Department" means the Department of Family and Protective Services.

(2) "Division" means the prevention and early intervention services division within the department.

(3) "Prevention and early intervention services" means programs intended to provide early intervention or prevent at-risk behaviors that lead to child abuse, delinquency, running away, truancy, and dropping out of school.

History of Fam. Code §265.001: Acts 1999, 76th Leg., ch. 489, §2, eff. Sept. 1, 1999. Amended by Acts 2007, 80th Leg., ch. 632, §1, eff. June 15, 2007; Acts 2015, 84th Leg., ch. 837, §1.12 (eff. Sept. 1, 2015), ch. 944, §61 (eff. Sept. 1, 2015), ch. 1257, §2 (eff. Sept. 1, 2015).

FAM §265.002. Prevention & Early Intervention Services Division

(a) The department shall operate a division to provide services for children in at-risk situations and for the families of those children and to achieve the consolidation of prevention and early intervention services within the jurisdiction of a single agency in order to avoid fragmentation and duplication of services and to increase the accountability for the delivery and administration of these services. The division shall be called the prevention and early intervention services division and shall have the following duties:

(1) to plan, develop, and administer a comprehensive and unified delivery system of prevention and early intervention services to children and their families in at-risk situations;

(2) to improve the responsiveness of services for at-risk children and their families by facilitating greater coordination and flexibility in the use of funds by state and local service providers;

(3) to provide greater accountability for prevention and early intervention services in order to demonstrate the impact or public benefit of a program by adopting outcome measures; and

(4) to assist local communities in the coordination and development of prevention and early intervention services in order to maximize federal, state, and local resources.

(b) The department's prevention and early intervention services division must be organizationally separate from the department's divisions performing child protective services and adult protective services functions.

History of Fam. Code §265.002: Acts 1999, 76th Leg., ch. 489, §2, eff. Sept. 1, 1999. Amended by Acts 2015, 84th Leg., ch. 837, §1.13, eff. Sept. 1, 2015.

FAM §265.003. Consolidation of Programs

(a) In order to implement the duties provided in Section 265.002, the department shall consolidate into the division programs with the goal of providing early intervention or prevention of at-risk behavior that leads to child abuse, delinquency, running away, truancy, and dropping out of school.

(b) The division may provide additional prevention and early intervention services in accordance with Section 265.002.

History of Fam. Code §265.003: Acts 1999, 76th Leg., ch. 489, §2, eff. Sept. 1, 1999.

A FAM §265.004. Use of Evidence-Based Programs for At-Risk Families

(a) To the extent that money is appropriated for the purpose, the department shall fund evidence-based programs, including parenting education, home visitation, family support services, mentoring, positive youth development programs, and crisis counseling, offered by community-based organizations that are designed to prevent or ameliorate child abuse and neglect. The programs funded under this subsection may be offered by a child welfare board established under Section 264.005, a local governmental board granted the powers and duties of a child welfare board under state law, a children's advocacy center established under Section 264.402, or other persons determined appropriate by the department.

(a-1) The department shall ensure that not less than 75 percent of the money appropriated for parenting education programs under Subsection (a) funds evidence-based programs described by Section 265.151(b) [265.101(b)] and that the remainder of that money funds promising practice programs described by Section 265.151(c) [265.101(c)].

(a-2) The department shall actively seek and apply for any available federal funds to support parenting education programs provided under this section.

(b) The department shall place priority on programs that target children whose race or ethnicity is disproportionately represented in the child protective services system.

(c) The department shall periodically evaluate the evidence-based abuse and neglect prevention programs to determine the continued effectiveness of the programs.

History of Fam. Code §265.004: Acts 2005, 79th Leg., ch. 268, §1.64, eff. Sept. 1, 2005. Amended by Acts 2007, 80th Leg., ch. 526, §4, eff. June 16, 2007; Acts 2015, 84th Leg., ch. 1257, §3, eff. Sept. 1, 2015; S.B. 1488, §24.002(7), 85th Leg., eff. Sept. 1, 2017.

E FAM §265.0041. COLLABORATION WITH INSTITUTIONS OF HIGHER EDUCATION

(a) Subject to the availability of funds, the Health and Human Services Commission, on behalf of the department, shall enter into agreements with institutions of higher education to conduct efficacy reviews of any prevention and early intervention programs that have not previously been evaluated for effectiveness through a scientific research evaluation process.

(b) Subject to the availability of funds, the department shall collaborate with an institution of higher education to create and track indicators of child well-being to determine the effectiveness of prevention and early intervention services.

History of Fam. Code §265.0041: Enacted by S.B. 11, §20, 85th Leg., eff. Sept. 1, 2017.

A FAM §265.005. STRATEGIC PLAN

(a) The department shall develop and implement a five-year strategic plan for prevention and early intervention services. Not later than September 1 of the last fiscal year in each five-year period, the department shall issue a new strategic plan for the next five fiscal years beginning with the following fiscal year.

(b) A strategic plan required under this section must:

(1) identify methods to leverage other sources of funding or provide support for existing community-based prevention efforts;

(2) include a needs assessment that identifies programs to best target the needs of the highest risk populations and geographic areas;

(3) identify the goals and priorities for the department's overall prevention efforts;

(4) report the results of previous prevention efforts using available information in the plan;

(5) identify additional methods of measuring program effectiveness and results or outcomes;

(6) identify methods to collaborate with other state agencies on prevention efforts; [and]

(7) identify specific strategies to implement the plan and to develop measures for reporting on the overall progress toward the plan's goals; and

Subsection (8) was enacted by H.B. 1549, §13, 85th Leg., enacted May 28, 2017, effective Sept. 1, 2017, without reference to the conflicting enactment made by S.B. 11, §21, 85th Leg., enacted May 28, 2017, effective Sept. 1, 2017. For harmonizing conflicts, see p. V.

(8) identify strategies and goals for increasing the number of families receiving prevention and early intervention services each year, subject to the availability of funds, to reach targets set by the department for providing services to families that are eligible to receive services through parental education, family support, and community-based programs financed with federal, state, local, or private resources.

Subsection (8) was enacted by S.B. 11, §21, 85th Leg., enacted May 28, 2017, effective Sept. 1, 2017, without reference to the conflicting enactment made by H.B. 1549, §13, 85th Leg., enacted May 28, 2017, effective Sept. 1, 2017. For harmonizing conflicts, see p. V.

(8) identify specific strategies to increase local capacity for the delivery of prevention and early intervention services through collaboration with communities and stakeholders.

(c) The department shall coordinate with interested parties and communities in developing the strategic plan under this section.

(d) The department shall annually update the strategic plan developed under this section.

(e) The department shall post the strategic plan developed under this section and any update to the plan on its Internet website.

History of Fam. Code §265.005: Acts 2015, 84th Leg., ch. 944, §62 (eff. Sept. 1, 2015), ch. 1257, §4 (eff. Sept. 1, 2015). Amended by H.B. 1549, §13, 85th Leg., eff. Sept. 1, 2017; S.B. 11, §21, 85th Leg., eff. Sept. 1, 2017.

History of Former Fam. Code §265.005: Expired by its own terms Sept. 1, 2009.

FAM §265.006. PROHIBITION ON USE OF AGENCY NAME OR LOGO

The department may not allow the use of the department's name or identifying logo or insignia on forms or other materials related to the department's prevention and early intervention services that are:

(1) provided by the department's contractors; or

(2) distributed by the department's contractors to the department's clients.

History of Fam. Code §265.006: Acts 2015, 84th Leg., ch. 837, §1.14, eff. Sept. 1, 2015.

E FAM §265.007. IMPROVING PROVISION OF PREVENTION & EARLY INTERVENTION SERVICES

(a) To improve the effectiveness and delivery of prevention and early intervention services, the department shall:

(1) identify geographic areas that have a high need for prevention and early intervention services but do not have prevention and early intervention services available in the area or have only unevaluated prevention and early intervention services available in the area; and

(2) develop strategies for community partners to:

(A) improve the early recognition of child abuse or neglect;

(B) improve the reporting of child abuse and neglect; and

(C) reduce child fatalities.

(b) The department may not use data gathered under this section to identify a specific family or individual.

History of Fam. Code §265.007: Enacted by H.B. 1549, §14, 85th Leg., eff. Sept. 1, 2017.

E FAM §265.008. EVALUATION OF PREVENTION & EARLY INTERVENTION SERVICES

(a) The department may enter into agreements with institutions of higher education to conduct efficacy reviews of any prevention and early intervention services provided under this chapter that have not previously been evaluated for effectiveness in a research evaluation. The efficacy review shall include, when possible, a cost-benefit analysis of the program to the state and, when applicable, the return on investment of the program to the state.

(b) The department may not enter into an agreement to conduct a program efficacy evaluation under this section unless:

(1) the agreement with the institution of higher education is cost neutral; and

(2) the department and institution of higher education conducting the evaluation under this section protect the identity of individuals who are receiving services from the department that are being evaluated.

History of Fam. Code §265.008: Enacted by H.B. 1549, §14, 85th Leg., eff. Sept. 1, 2017.

Sections 265.009-265.050 blank

SUBCHAPTER B. CHILD ABUSE & NEGLECT PRIMARY PREVENTION PROGRAMS

FAM §265.051. DEFINITIONS

In this subchapter:

(1) "Children's trust fund" means a child abuse and neglect primary prevention program.

(2) "Primary prevention" means services and activities available to the community at large or to families to prevent child abuse and neglect before it occurs. The term includes infant mortality prevention education programs.

(3) "Operating fund" means the Department of Family and Protective Services child abuse and neglect prevention operating fund account.

(4) "State agency" means a board, commission, department, office, or other state agency that:

(A) is in the executive branch of the state government;

(B) was created by the constitution or a statute of this state; and

(C) has statewide jurisdiction.

(5) "Trust fund" means the child abuse and neglect prevention trust fund account.

History of Fam. Code §265.051: Transferred by Acts 2015, 84th Leg., ch. 944, §63 (eff. Sept. 1, 2015), ch. 1257, §5 (eff. Sept. 1, 2015). Amended by Acts 2015, 84th Leg., ch. 1, §4.208, eff. Apr. 2, 2015. Source: Former Hum. Res. Code §40.101.

FAM §265.052. CHILD ABUSE & NEGLECT PRIMARY PREVENTION PROGRAMS

(a) The department shall operate the children's trust fund to:

(1) set policy, offer resources for community primary prevention programs, and provide information and education on prevention of child abuse and neglect;

(2) develop a state plan for expending funds for child abuse and neglect primary prevention programs that includes an annual schedule of transfers of trust fund money to the operating fund;

(3) develop eligibility criteria for applicants requesting funding for child abuse and neglect primary prevention programs; and

(4) establish funding priorities for child abuse and neglect primary prevention programs.

(b) The children's trust fund shall accommodate the department's existing rules and policies in procuring, awarding, and monitoring contracts and grants.

(c) The department may:

(1) apply for and receive funds made available by the federal government or another public or private source for administering programs under this subchapter and for funding for child abuse and neglect primary prevention programs; and

(2) solicit donations for child abuse and neglect primary prevention programs.

History of Fam. Code §265.052: Transferred by Acts 2015, 84th Leg., ch. 944, §63 (eff. Sept. 1, 2015), ch. 1257, §5 (eff. Sept. 1, 2015). Source: Former Hum. Res. Code §40.102.

FAM §265.053. ADMINISTRATIVE & OTHER COSTS

(a) Administrative costs under this subchapter during any fiscal year may not exceed an amount equal to 50 percent of the interest credited to the trust fund during the preceding fiscal year.

(b) Funds expended under a special project grant from a governmental source or a nongovernmental source for public education or public awareness may not be counted as administrative costs for the purposes of this section.

History of Fam. Code §265.053: Transferred by Acts 2015, 84th Leg., ch. 944, §63 (eff. Sept. 1, 2015), ch. 1257, §5 (eff. Sept. 1, 2015). Source: Former Hum. Res. Code §40.104.

FAM §265.054. CHILD ABUSE & NEGLECT PREVENTION TRUST FUND ACCOUNT

(a) The child abuse and neglect prevention trust fund account is an account in the general revenue fund. Money in the trust fund is dedicated to child abuse and neglect primary prevention programs.

(b) The department may transfer money contained in the trust fund to the operating fund at any time. However, during a fiscal year the department may not transfer more than the amount appropriated for the operating fund for that fiscal year. Money transferred to the operating fund that was originally deposited to the credit of the trust fund under Section 118.022, Local Government Code, may be used only for child abuse and neglect primary prevention programs.

(c) Interest earned on the trust fund shall be credited to the trust fund.

(d) The trust fund is exempt from the application of Section 403.095, Government Code.

(e) All marriage license fees and other fees collected for and deposited in the trust fund and interest earned on the trust fund balance shall be appropriated each biennium only to the operating fund for child abuse and neglect primary prevention programs.

History of Fam. Code §265.054: Transferred and amended by Acts 2015, 84th Leg., ch. 944, §63 (eff. Sept. 1, 2015), ch. 1257, §5 (eff. Sept. 1, 2015). Amended by Acts 2015, 84th Leg., ch. 1, §4.209, eff. Apr. 2, 2015. Source: Former Hum. Res. Code §40.105.

FAM §265.055. DEPARTMENT OPERATING FUND ACCOUNT

(a) The operating fund is an account in the general revenue fund.

(b) Administrative and other costs allowed in Section 265.053 shall be taken from the operating fund. The department may transfer funds contained in the operating fund to the trust fund at any time.

(c) The legislature may appropriate the money in the operating fund to carry out the provisions of this subchapter.

(d) The operating fund is exempt from the application of Section 403.095, Government Code.

History of Fam. Code §265.055: Transferred and amended by Acts 2015, 84th Leg., ch. 944, §63 (eff. Sept. 1, 2015), ch. 1257, §5 (eff. Sept. 1, 2015). Amended by Acts 2015, 84th Leg., ch. 1, §4.210, eff. Apr. 2, 2015. Source: Former Hum. Res. Code §40.106.

FAM §265.056. CONTRIBUTIONS

(a) The department may solicit contributions from any appropriate source.

(b) Any other contributions for child abuse and neglect primary prevention or other prevention and early intervention programs shall be deposited into a separate designated fund in the state treasury and shall be used for that designated purpose.

(c) A person may contribute funds to either the trust fund, the operating fund, or a fund designated by the department for a specific child abuse and neglect primary prevention or other prevention or early intervention purpose.

(d) If a person designates that a contribution is intended as a donation to a specific fund, the contribution shall be deposited in the designated fund.

History of Fam. Code §265.056: Transferred by Acts 2015, 84th Leg., ch. 944, §63 (eff. Sept. 1, 2015), ch. 1257, §5 (eff. Sept. 1, 2015). Source: Former Hum. Res. Code §40.107.

FAM §265.057. COMMUNITY YOUTH DEVELOPMENT GRANTS

(a) Subject to available funding, the department shall award community youth development grants to communities identified by incidence of crime. The department shall give priority in awarding grants under this section to areas of the state in which there is a high incidence of juvenile crime.

(b) The purpose of a grant under this section is to assist a community in alleviating conditions in the family and community that lead to juvenile crime.

History of Fam. Code §265.057: Transferred by Acts 2015, 84th Leg., ch. 944, §64 (eff. Sept. 1, 2015), ch. 1257, §6 (eff. Sept. 1, 2015). Source: Former Hum. Res. Code §40.0561.

Sections 265.058-265.100 blank

Subchapter C. Nurse-Family Partnership Competitive Grant Program

FAM §265.101. DEFINITIONS

In this subchapter:

(1) "Competitive grant program" means the nurse-family partnership competitive grant program established under this subchapter.

(2) "Partnership program" means a nurse-family partnership program.

History of Fam. Code §265.101: Transferred by Acts 2015, 84th Leg., ch. 837, §1.15(a), eff. Sept. 1, 2015. Source: Former Gov't Code §531.651.

FAM §265.102. OPERATION OF NURSE-FAMILY PARTNERSHIP COMPETITIVE GRANT PROGRAM

(a) The department shall operate a nurse-family partnership competitive grant program through which the department will award grants for the implementation of nurse-family partnership programs, or the expansion of existing programs, and for the operation of those programs for a period of not less than two years.

(b) The department shall award grants under the program to applicants, including applicants operating existing programs, in a manner that ensures that the partnership programs collectively:

(1) operate in multiple communities that are geographically distributed throughout this state; and

(2) provide program services to approximately 2,000 families.

History of Fam. Code §265.102: Transferred and amended by Acts 2015, 84th Leg., ch. 837, §1.15(a), eff. Sept. 1, 2015. Amended by Acts 2015, 84th Leg., ch. 1, §§2.188, 2.189, eff. Apr. 2, 2015. Source: Former Gov't Code §531.652.

FAM §265.103. PARTNERSHIP PROGRAM REQUIREMENTS

A partnership program funded through a grant awarded under this subchapter must:

(1) strictly adhere to the program model developed by the Nurse-Family Partnership National Service Office, including any clinical, programmatic, and data collection requirements of that model;

(2) require that registered nurses regularly visit the homes of low-income, first-time mothers participating in the program to provide services designed to:

(A) improve pregnancy outcomes;

(B) improve child health and development;

(C) improve family economic self-sufficiency and stability; and

(D) reduce the incidence of child abuse and neglect;

(3) require that nurses who provide services through the program:

(A) receive training from the office of the attorney general at least once each year on procedures by which a person may voluntarily acknowledge the paternity of a child and on the availability of child support services from the office;

(B) provide a mother with information about the rights, responsibilities, and benefits of establishing the paternity of her child, if appropriate;

(C) provide assistance to a mother and the alleged father of her child if the mother and alleged father seek to voluntarily acknowledge paternity of the child, if appropriate; and

(D) provide information to a mother about the availability of child support services from the office of the attorney general; and

(4) require that the regular nurse visits described by Subdivision (2) begin not later than a mother's 28th week of gestation and end when her child reaches two years of age.

History of Fam. Code §265.103: Transferred by Acts 2015, 84th Leg., ch. 837, §1.15(a), eff. Sept. 1, 2015. Source: Former Gov't Code §531.653.

FAM §265.1035. EXPIRED

FAM §265.104. APPLICATION

(a) A public or private entity, including a county, municipality, or other political subdivision of this state, may apply for a grant under this subchapter.

(b) To apply for a grant, an applicant must submit a written application to the department on a form prescribed by the department in consultation with the Nurse-Family Partnership National Service Office.

(c) The application prescribed by the department must:

(1) require the applicant to provide data on the number of low-income, first-time mothers residing in the community in which the applicant proposes to operate or expand a partnership program and provide a description of existing services available to those mothers;

(2) describe the ongoing monitoring and evaluation process to which a grant recipient is subject under Section 265.109, including the recipient's obligation to collect and provide information requested by the department under Section 265.109(c); and

(3) require the applicant to provide other relevant information as determined by the department.

History of Fam. Code §265.104: Transferred and amended by Acts 2015, 84th Leg., ch. 837, §1.15(a), eff. Sept. 1, 2015. Source: Former Gov't Code §531.654.

FAM §265.105. ADDITIONAL CONSIDERATIONS IN AWARDING GRANTS

In addition to the factors described by Sections 265.102(b) and 265.103, in determining whether to award a grant to an applicant under this subchapter, the department shall consider:

(1) the demonstrated need for a partnership program in the community in which the applicant proposes to operate or expand the program, which may be determined by considering:

(A) the poverty rate, the crime rate, the number of births to Medicaid recipients, the rate of poor birth outcomes, and the incidence of child abuse and neglect during a prescribed period in the community; and

(B) the need to enhance school readiness in the community;

(2) the applicant's ability to participate in ongoing monitoring and performance evaluations under Section 265.109, including the applicant's ability to collect and provide information requested by the department under Section 265.109(c);

(3) the applicant's ability to adhere to the partnership program standards adopted under Section 265.106;

(4) the applicant's ability to develop broad-based community support for implementing or expanding a partnership program, as applicable; and

(5) the applicant's history of developing and sustaining innovative, high-quality programs that meet the needs of families and communities.

History of Fam. Code §265.105: Transferred and amended by Acts 2015, 84th Leg., ch. 837, §1.15(a), eff. Sept. 1, 2015. Source: Former Gov't Code §531.655.

A FAM §265.106. PARTNERSHIP PROGRAM STANDARDS

The [executive] commissioner, with the assistance of the Nurse-Family Partnership National Service Office, shall adopt standards for the partnership programs funded under this subchapter. The standards must adhere to the Nurse-Family Partnership National Service Office program model standards and guidelines that were developed in multiple, randomized clinical trials and have been tested and replicated in multiple communities.

History of Fam. Code §265.106: Transferred by Acts 2015, 84th Leg., ch. 837, §1.15(a), eff. Sept. 1, 2015. Amended by H.B. 5, §15, 85th Leg., eff. Sept. 1, 2017. Source: Former Gov't Code §531.656.

FAM §265.107. USE OF AWARDED GRANT FUNDS

The grant funds awarded under this subchapter may be used only to cover costs related to implementing or expanding and operating a partnership program, including costs related to:

(1) administering the program;

(2) training and managing registered nurses who participate in the program;

(3) paying the salaries and expenses of registered nurses who participate in the program;

(4) paying for facilities and equipment for the program; and

(5) paying for services provided by the Nurse-Family Partnership National Service Office to ensure a grant recipient adheres to the organization's program model.

History of Fam. Code §265.107: Transferred by Acts 2015, 84th Leg., ch. 837, §1.15(a), eff. Sept. 1, 2015. Source: Former Gov't Code §531.657.

FAM §265.108. STATE NURSE CONSULTANT

Using money appropriated for the competitive grant program, the department shall hire or contract with a state nurse consultant to assist grant recipients with implementing or expanding and operating the partnership programs in the applicable communities.

History of Fam. Code §265.108: Transferred and amended by Acts 2015, 84th Leg., ch. 837, §1.15(a), eff. Sept. 1, 2015. Source: Former Gov't Code §531.658.

FAM §265.109. PROGRAM MONITORING & EVALUATION; ANNUAL COMMITTEE REPORTS

(a) The department, with the assistance of the Nurse-Family Partnership National Service Office, shall:

(1) adopt performance indicators that are designed to measure a grant recipient's performance with respect to the partnership program standards adopted by the [executive] commissioner under Section 265.106;

(2) use the performance indicators to continuously monitor and formally evaluate on an annual basis the performance of each grant recipient; and

(3) prepare and submit an annual report, not later than December 1 of each year, to the Senate Health and Human Services Committee, or its successor, and the House Human Services Committee, or its successor, regarding the performance of each grant recipient during the preceding state fiscal year with respect to providing partnership program services.

(b) The report required under Subsection (a)(3) must include:

(1) the number of low-income, first-time mothers to whom each grant recipient provided partnership program services and, of that number, the number of mothers who established the paternity of an alleged father as a result of services provided under the program;

(2) the extent to which each grant recipient made regular visits to mothers during the period described by Section 265.103(4); and

(3) the extent to which each grant recipient adhered to the Nurse-Family Partnership National Service Office's program model, including the extent to which registered nurses:

(A) conducted home visitations comparable in frequency, duration, and content to those delivered in Nurse-Family Partnership National Service Office clinical trials; and

(B) assessed the health and well-being of mothers and children participating in the partnership programs in accordance with indicators of maternal, child, and family health defined by the department in consultation with the Nurse-Family Partnership National Service Office.

(c) On request, each grant recipient shall timely collect and provide data and any other information required by the department to monitor and evaluate the recipient or to prepare the report required by this section.

History of Fam. Code §265.109: Transferred and amended by Acts 2015, 84th Leg., ch. 837, §1.15(a), eff. Sept. 1, 2015. Amended by Acts 2015, 84th Leg., ch. 1, §2.190, eff. Apr. 2, 2015; H.B. 5, §16, 85th Leg., eff. Sept. 1, 2017. Source: Former Gov't Code §531.659.

FAM §265.110. COMPETITIVE GRANT PROGRAM FUNDING

(a) The department shall actively seek and apply for any available federal funds, including federal Medicaid and Temporary Assistance for Needy Families (TANF) funds, to assist in financing the competitive grant program established under this subchapter.

(b) The department may use appropriated funds from the state government and may accept gifts, donations, and grants of money from the federal government, local governments, private corporations, or other persons to assist in financing the competitive grant program.

History of Fam. Code §265.110: Transferred and amended by Acts 2015, 84th Leg., ch. 837, §1.15(a), eff. Sept. 1, 2015. Source: Former Gov't Code §531.660.

Sections 265.111-265.150 blank

SUBCHAPTER D. PARENTING EDUCATION

Subchapter D was redesignated from subchapter C by S.B. 1488, §24.001(9), 85th Leg., eff. Sept. 1, 2017.

FAM §265.151. PARENTING EDUCATION PROGRAMS

(a) A parenting education program provided by the department must be an evidence-based program or a promising practice program described by this section.

(b) An evidence-based program is a parenting education program that:

(1) is research-based and grounded in relevant, empirical knowledge and program-determined outcomes;

(2) has comprehensive standards ensuring the highest quality service delivery with continuous improvement in the quality of service delivery;

(3) has demonstrated significant positive short-term and long-term outcomes;

(4) has been evaluated by at least one rigorous, random, controlled research trial across heterogeneous populations or communities with research results that have been published in a peer-reviewed journal;

(5) substantially complies with a program manual or design that specifies the purpose, outcomes, duration, and frequency of the program services; and

(6) employs well-trained and competent staff and provides continual relevant professional development opportunities to the staff.

(c) A promising practice program is a parenting education program that:

(1) has an active impact evaluation program or demonstrates a schedule for implementing an active impact evaluation program;

(2) has been evaluated by at least one outcome-based study demonstrating effectiveness or random, controlled trial in a homogeneous sample;

(3) substantially complies with a program manual or design that specifies the purpose, outcomes, duration, and frequency of the program services;

(4) employs well-trained and competent staff and provides continual relevant professional development opportunities to the staff; and

(5) is research-based and grounded in relevant, empirical knowledge and program-determined outcomes.

History of Fam. Code §265.151: Acts 2015, 84th Leg., ch. 1257, §7, eff. Sept. 1, 2015. Renumbered from §265.101 by S.B. 1488, §24.001(9), 85th Leg., eff. Sept. 1, 2017.

Ⓐ FAM §265.152. OUTCOMES OF EVIDENCE-BASED PARENTING EDUCATION

The department shall ensure that a parenting education program provided under this chapter achieves favorable behavioral outcomes in at least two of the following areas:

(1) improved cognitive development of children;

(2) increased school readiness of children;

(3) reduced child abuse, neglect, and injury;

(4) improved child safety;

(5) improved social-emotional development of children;

(6) improved parenting skills, including nurturing and bonding;

(7) improved family economic self-sufficiency;

(8) reduced parental involvement with the criminal justice system; and

(9) increased paternal involvement and support.

History of Fam. Code §265.152: Acts 2015, 84th Leg., ch. 1257, §7, eff. Sept. 1, 2015. Renumbered from §265.102 by S.B. 1488, §24.001(9), 85th Leg., eff. Sept. 1, 2017.

Ⓐ FAM §265.153. EVALUATION OF EVIDENCE-BASED PARENTING EDUCATION

(a) The department shall adopt outcome indicators to measure the effectiveness of parenting education programs provided under this chapter in achieving desired outcomes.

(b) The department may work directly with the model developer of a parenting education program to identify appropriate outcome indicators for the program and to ensure that the program substantially complies with the model.

(c) The department shall develop internal processes to share information with parenting education programs to assist the department in analyzing the performance of the programs.

(d) The department shall use information obtained under this section to:

(1) monitor parenting education programs;

(2) continually improve the quality of the programs; and

(3) evaluate the effectiveness of the programs.

History of Fam. Code §265.153: Acts 2015, 84th Leg., ch. 1257, §7, eff. Sept. 1, 2015. Renumbered from §265.103 by S.B. 1488, §24.001(9), 85th Leg., eff. Sept. 1, 2017.

Ⓐ FAM §265.154. REPORTS TO LEGISLATURE

(a) Not later than December 1 of each even-numbered year, the department shall prepare and submit a report on state-funded parenting education programs to the standing committees of the senate and house of representatives with jurisdiction over child protective services.

(b) A report submitted under this section must include:

(1) a description of the parenting education programs implemented and of the models associated with the programs;

(2) information on the families served by the programs, including the number of families served and their demographic information;

(3) the goals and achieved outcomes of the programs;

(4) information on the cost for each family served, including any available third-party return-on-investment analysis; and

(5) information explaining the percentage of money spent on evidence-based programs and on promising practice programs.

History of Fam. Code §265.154: Acts 2015, 84th Leg., ch. 1257, §7, eff. Sept. 1, 2015. Renumbered from §265.104 by S.B. 1488, §24.001(9), 85th Leg., eff. Sept. 1, 2017.

A FAM §265.155. RULES

The [executive] commissioner of the department [Health and Human Services Commission] may adopt rules as necessary to implement this subchapter.

History of Fam. Code §265.155: Acts 2015, 84th Leg., ch. 1257, §7, eff. Sept. 1, 2015. Renumbered from §265.105 by S.B. 1488, §24.001(9), 85th Leg., eff. Sept. 1, 2017. Amended by H.B. 5, §14, 85th Leg., eff. Sept. 1, 2017.

A CHAPTER 266. MEDICAL CARE & EDUCATIONAL SERVICES FOR CHILDREN IN CONSERVATORSHIP OF DEPARTMENT OF FAMILY & PROTECTIVE SERVICES [FOSTER CARE]

A FAM §266.001. DEFINITIONS

In this chapter:

(1) "Advanced practice nurse" has the meaning assigned by Section 157.051, Occupations Code.

(1-a) "Commission" means the Health and Human Services Commission.

(1-b) "Commissioner" means the commissioner of the Department of Family and Protective Services.

(2) "Department" means the Department of Family and Protective Services.

(2-a) "Drug research program" means any clinical trial, clinical investigation, drug study, or active medical or clinical research that has been approved by an institutional review board in accordance with the standards provided in the Code of Federal Regulations, 45 C.F.R. Sections 46.404 through 46.407, regarding:

(A) an investigational new drug; or

(B) the efficacy of an approved drug.

(3) "Executive commissioner" means the executive commissioner of the Health and Human Services Commission.

(4) Repealed by Acts 2015, 84th Leg., ch. 944, §86(40), eff. Sept. 1, 2015.

(4-a) "Investigational new drug" has the meaning assigned by 21 C.F.R. Section 312.3(b).

(5) "Medical care" means all health care and related services provided under the medical assistance program under Chapter 32, Human Resources Code, and described by Section 32.003(4), Human Resources Code.

(6) "Physician assistant" has the meaning assigned by Section 157.051, Occupations Code.

(7) "Psychotropic medication" means a medication that is prescribed for the treatment of symptoms of psychosis or another mental, emotional, or behavioral disorder and that is used to exercise an effect on the central nervous system to influence and modify behavior, cognition, or affective state. The term includes the following categories when used as described by this subdivision:

(A) psychomotor stimulants;

(B) antidepressants;

(C) antipsychotics or neuroleptics;

(D) agents for control of mania or depression;

(E) antianxiety agents; and

(F) sedatives, hypnotics, or other sleep-promoting medications.

History of Fam. Code §266.001: Acts 2005, 79th Leg., ch. 268, §1.65(a), eff. Sept. 1, 2005. Amended by Acts 2007, 80th Leg., ch. 506, §1, eff. Sept. 1, 2007; Acts 2013, 83rd Leg., ch. 204, §§7, 15, eff. Sept. 1, 2013; Acts 2015, 84th Leg., ch. 944, §86(40), eff. Sept. 1, 2015; H.B. 5, §17, 85th Leg., eff. Sept. 1, 2017; H.B. 7, §37, 85th Leg., eff. Sept. 1, 2017.

FAM §266.002. CONSTRUCTION WITH OTHER LAW

This chapter does not limit the right to consent to medical, dental, psychological, and surgical treatment under Chapter 32.

History of Fam. Code §266.002: Acts 2005, 79th Leg., ch. 268, §1.65(a), eff. Sept. 1, 2005.

A FAM §266.003. MEDICAL SERVICES FOR CHILD ABUSE & NEGLECT VICTIMS

(a) The department [commission] shall collaborate with the commission and health care and child

welfare professionals to design a comprehensive, cost-effective medical services delivery model, either directly or by contract, to meet the needs of children served by the department. The medical services delivery model must include:

(1) the designation of health care facilities with expertise in the forensic assessment, diagnosis, and treatment of child abuse and neglect as pediatric centers of excellence;

(2) a statewide telemedicine system to link department investigators and caseworkers with pediatric centers of excellence or other medical experts for consultation;

(3) identification of a medical home for each foster child on entering foster care at which the child will receive an initial comprehensive assessment as well as preventive treatments, acute medical services, and therapeutic and rehabilitative care to meet the child's ongoing physical and mental health needs throughout the duration of the child's stay in foster care;

(4) the development and implementation of health passports as described in Section 266.006;

(5) establishment and use of a management information system that allows monitoring of medical care that is provided to all children in foster care;

(6) the use of medical advisory committees and medical review teams, as appropriate, to establish treatment guidelines and criteria by which individual cases of medical care provided to children in foster care will be identified for further, in-depth review;

(7) development of the training program described by Section 266.004(h);

(8) provision for the summary of medical care described by Section 266.007; and

(9) provision for the participation of the person authorized to consent to medical care for a child in foster care in each appointment of the child with the provider of medical care.

(b) The department [~~commission~~] shall collaborate with health and human services agencies, community partners, the health care community, and federal health and social services programs to maximize services and benefits available under this section.

(c) The [~~executive~~] commissioner shall adopt rules necessary to implement this chapter.

(d) The commission is responsible for administering contracts with managed care providers for the provision of medical care to children in foster care. The department shall collaborate with the commission to ensure that medical care services provided by managed care providers match the needs of children in foster care.

History of Fam. Code §266.003: Acts 2005, 79th Leg., ch. 268, §1.65(a), eff. Sept. 1, 2005. Amended by H.B. 5, §18, 85th Leg., eff. Sept. 1, 2017.

FAM §266.0031. EXPIRED

FAM §266.004. CONSENT FOR MEDICAL CARE

(a) Medical care may not be provided to a child in foster care unless the person authorized by this section has provided consent.

(b) Except as provided by Section 266.010, the court may authorize the following persons to consent to medical care for a foster child:

(1) an individual designated by name in an order of the court, including the child's foster parent or the child's parent, if the parent's rights have not been terminated and the court determines that it is in the best interest of the parent's child to allow the parent to make medical decisions on behalf of the child; or

(2) the department or an agent of the department.

(c) If the person authorized by the court to consent to medical care is the department or an agent of the department, the department shall, not later than the fifth business day after the date the court provides authorization, file with the court and each party the name of the individual who will exercise the duty and responsibility of providing consent on behalf of the department. The department may designate the child's foster parent or the child's parent, if the parent's rights have not been terminated, to exercise the duty and responsibility of providing consent on behalf of the department under this subsection. If the individual designated under this subsection changes, the department shall file notice of the change with the court and each party not later than the fifth business day after the date of the change.

(d) A physician or other provider of medical care acting in good faith may rely on the representation by a person that the person has the authority to consent to the provision of medical care to a foster child as provided by Subsection (b).

(e) The department, a person authorized to consent to medical care under Subsection (b), the child's parent if the parent's rights have not been terminated, a guardian ad litem or attorney ad litem if one has been

appointed, or the person providing foster care to the child may petition the court for any order related to medical care for a foster child that the department or other person believes is in the best interest of the child. Notice of the petition must be given to each person entitled to notice under Section 263.0021(b).

(f) If a physician who has examined or treated the foster child has concerns regarding the medical care provided to the foster child, the physician may file a letter with the court stating the reasons for the physician's concerns. The court shall provide a copy of the letter to each person entitled to notice under Section 263.0021(b).

(g) On its own motion or in response to a petition under Subsection (e) or Section 266.010, the court may issue any order related to the medical care of a foster child that the court determines is in the best interest of the child.

(h) Notwithstanding Subsection (b), a person may not be authorized to consent to medical care provided to a foster child unless the person has completed a department-approved training program related to informed consent and the provision of all areas of medical care as defined by Section 266.001. This subsection does not apply to a parent whose rights have not been terminated unless the court orders the parent to complete the training.

(h-1) The training required by Subsection (h) must include training related to informed consent for the administration of psychotropic medication and the appropriate use of psychosocial therapies, behavior strategies, and other non-pharmacological interventions that should be considered before or concurrently with the administration of psychotropic medications.

(h-2) Each person required to complete a training program under Subsection (h) must acknowledge in writing that the person:

(1) has received the training described by Subsection (h-1);

(2) understands the principles of informed consent for the administration of psychotropic medication; and

(3) understands that non-pharmacological interventions should be considered and discussed with the prescribing physician, physician assistant, or advanced practice nurse before consenting to the use of a psychotropic medication.

(i) The person authorized under Subsection (b) to consent to medical care of a foster child shall participate in each appointment of the child with the provider of the medical care.

(j) Nothing in this section requires the identity of a foster parent to be publicly disclosed.

(k) The department may consent to health care services ordered or prescribed by a health care provider authorized to order or prescribe health care services regardless of whether the services are provided under the medical assistance program under Chapter 32, Human Resources Code, if the department otherwise has the authority under this section to consent to health care services.

History of Fam. Code §266.004: Acts 2005, 79th Leg., ch. 268, §1.65(a), eff. Sept. 1, 2005. Amended by Acts 2007, 80th Leg., ch. 727, §1, eff. June 15, 2007; Acts 2013, 83rd Leg., ch. 204, §8, eff. Sept. 1, 2013; Acts 2015, 84th Leg., ch. 944, §65, eff. Sept. 1, 2015.

See also ***O'Connor's Texas Family Law Handbook*** (2017), "Child in foster care," ch. 1-E, §2.2.1(1)(b), p. 67.

FAM §266.0041. ENROLLMENT & PARTICIPATION IN CERTAIN RESEARCH PROGRAMS

(a) Notwithstanding Section 266.004, a person may not authorize the enrollment of a foster child or consent to the participation of a foster child in a drug research program without a court order as provided by this section, unless the person is the foster child's parent and the person has been authorized by the court to make medical decisions for the foster child in accordance with Section 266.004.

(b) Before issuing an order authorizing the enrollment or participation of a foster child in a drug research program, the court must:

(1) appoint an independent medical advocate;

(2) review the report filed by the independent medical advocate regarding the advocate's opinion and recommendations concerning the foster child's enrollment and participation in the drug research program;

(3) consider whether the person conducting the drug research program:

(A) informed the foster child in a developmentally appropriate manner of the expected benefits of the drug research program, any potential side effects, and any available alternative treatments and received the foster child's assent to enroll the child to participate in the drug research program as required by the Code of Federal Regulations, 45 C.F.R. Section 46.408; or

(B) received informed consent in accordance with Subsection (h); and

(4) determine whether enrollment and participation in the drug research program is in the foster

child's best interest and determine that the enrollment and participation in the drug research program will not interfere with the appropriate medical care of the foster child.

(c) An independent medical advocate appointed under Subsection (b) is not a party to the suit but may:

(1) conduct an investigation regarding the foster child's participation in a drug research program to the extent that the advocate considers necessary to determine:

(A) whether the foster child assented to or provided informed consent to the child's enrollment and participation in the drug research program; and

(B) the best interest of the child for whom the advocate is appointed; and

(2) obtain and review copies of the foster child's relevant medical and psychological records and information describing the risks and benefits of the child's enrollment and participation in the drug research program.

(d) An independent medical advocate shall, within a reasonable time after the appointment, interview:

(1) the foster child in a developmentally appropriate manner, if the child is four years of age or older;

(2) the foster child's parent, if the parent is entitled to notification under Section 264.018;

(3) an advocate appointed by an institutional review board in accordance with the Code of Federal Regulations, 45 C.F.R. Section 46.409(b), if an advocate has been appointed;

(4) the medical team treating the foster child as well as the medical team conducting the drug research program; and

(5) each individual who has significant knowledge of the foster child's medical history and condition, including any foster parent of the child.

(e) After reviewing the information collected under Subsections (c) and (d), the independent medical advocate shall:

(1) submit a report to the court presenting the advocate's opinion and recommendation regarding whether:

(A) the foster child assented to or provided informed consent to the child's enrollment and participation in the drug research program; and

(B) the foster child's best interest is served by enrollment and participation in the drug research program; and

(2) at the request of the court, testify regarding the basis for the advocate's opinion and recommendation concerning the foster child's enrollment and participation in a drug research program.

(f) The court may appoint any person eligible to serve as the foster child's guardian ad litem, as defined by Section 107.001, as the independent medical advocate, including a physician or nurse or an attorney who has experience in medical and health care, except that a foster parent, employee of a substitute care provider or child placing agency providing care for the foster child, representative of the department, medical professional affiliated with the drug research program, independent medical advocate appointed by an institutional review board, or any person the court determines has a conflict of interest may not serve as the foster child's independent medical advocate.

(g) A person otherwise authorized to consent to medical care for a foster child may petition the court for an order permitting the enrollment and participation of a foster child in a drug research program under this section.

(h) Before a foster child, who is at least 16 years of age and has been determined to have the capacity to consent to medical care in accordance with Section 266.010, may be enrolled to participate in a drug research program, the person conducting the drug research program must:

(1) inform the foster child in a developmentally appropriate manner of the expected benefits of participation in the drug research program, any potential side effects, and any available alternative treatments; and

(2) receive written informed consent to enroll the foster child for participation in the drug research program.

(i) A court may render an order approving the enrollment or participation of a foster child in a drug research program involving an investigational new drug before appointing an independent medical advocate if:

(1) a physician recommends the foster child's enrollment or participation in the drug research program to provide the foster child with treatment that will prevent the death or serious injury of the child; and

(2) the court determines that the foster child needs the treatment before an independent medical advocate could complete an investigation in accordance with this section.

(j) As soon as practicable after issuing an order under Subsection (i), the court shall appoint an independent medical advocate to complete a full investigation of the foster child's enrollment and participation in the drug research program in accordance with this section.

(k) This section does not apply to:

(1) a drug research study regarding the efficacy of an approved drug that is based only on medical records, claims data, or outcome data, including outcome data gathered through interviews with a child, caregiver of a child, or a child's treating professional;

(2) a retrospective drug research study based only on medical records, claims data, or outcome data; or

(3) the treatment of a foster child with an investigational new drug that does not require the child's enrollment or participation in a drug research program.

(*l*) The department shall annually submit to the governor, lieutenant governor, speaker of the house of representatives, and the relevant committees in both houses of the legislature, a report regarding:

(1) the number of foster children who enrolled or participated in a drug research program during the previous year;

(2) the purpose of each drug research program in which a foster child was enrolled or participated; and

(3) the number of foster children for whom an order was issued under Subsection (i).

(m) A foster parent or any other person may not receive a financial incentive or any other benefit for recommending or consenting to the enrollment and participation of a foster child in a drug research program.

History of Fam. Code §266.0041: Acts 2007, 80th Leg., ch. 506, §2, eff. Sept. 1, 2007. Amended by Acts 2015, 84th Leg., ch. 722, §3 (eff. June 17, 2015), ch. 944, §66 (eff. Sept. 1, 2015).

FAM §266.0042. CONSENT FOR PSYCHOTROPIC MEDICATION

Consent to the administration of a psychotropic medication is valid only if:

(1) the consent is given voluntarily and without undue influence; and

(2) the person authorized by law to consent for the foster child receives verbally or in writing information that describes:

(A) the specific condition to be treated;

(B) the beneficial effects on that condition expected from the medication;

(C) the probable health and mental health consequences of not consenting to the medication;

(D) the probable clinically significant side effects and risks associated with the medication; and

(E) the generally accepted alternative medications and non-pharmacological interventions to the medication, if any, and the reasons for the proposed course of treatment.

History of Fam. Code §266.0042: Acts 2013, 83rd Leg., ch. 204, §9, eff. Sept. 1, 2013.

E FAM §266.005. FINDING ON HEALTH CARE CONSULTATION

If a court finds that a health care professional has been consulted regarding a health care service, procedure, or treatment for a child in the conservatorship of the department and the court declines to follow the recommendation of the health care professional, the court shall make findings in the record supporting the court's order.

History of Fam. Code §266.005: Enacted by H.B. 7, §38, 85th Leg., eff. Sept. 1, 2017.

History of Former Fam. Code §266.005: Repealed by Acts 2015, 84th Leg., ch. 722, §5 (eff. June 17, 2015), ch. 944, §86(41) (eff. Sept. 1, 2015).

A FAM §266.006. HEALTH PASSPORT

(a) The commission, in conjunction with the department, and with the assistance of physicians and other health care providers experienced in the care of foster children and children with disabilities and with the use of electronic health records, shall develop and provide a health passport for each foster child. The passport must be maintained in an electronic format and use [~~the commission's and~~] the department's existing computer resources to the greatest extent possible.

(b) The executive commissioner, in collaboration with the commissioner, shall adopt rules specifying the information required to be included in the passport. The required information may include:

(1) the name and address of each of the child's physicians and health care providers;

(2) a record of each visit to a physician or other health care provider, including routine checkups conducted in accordance with the Texas Health Steps program;

(3) an immunization record that may be exchanged with ImmTrac;

(4) a list of the child's known health problems and allergies;

(5) information on all medications prescribed to the child in adequate detail to permit refill of prescriptions, including the disease or condition that the medication treats; and

(6) any other available health history that physicians and other health care providers who provide care for the child determine is important.

(c) The system used to access the health passport must be secure and maintain the confidentiality of the child's health records.

(d) Health passport information shall be part of the department's record for the child as long as the child remains in foster care.

(e) The commission, in collaboration with the department, shall provide training or instructional materials to foster parents, physicians, and other health care providers regarding use of the health passport.

(f) The department shall make health passport information available in printed and electronic formats to the following individuals when a child is discharged from foster care:

(1) the child's legal guardian, managing conservator, or parent; or

(2) the child, if the child is at least 18 years of age or has had the disabilities of minority removed.

History of Fam. Code §266.006: Acts 2005, 79th Leg., ch. 268, §1.65(a), eff. Sept. 1, 2005. Amended by H.B. 5, §19, 85th Leg., eff. Sept. 1, 2017.

FAM §266.007. JUDICIAL REVIEW OF MEDICAL CARE

(a) At each hearing under Chapter 263, or more frequently if ordered by the court, the court shall review a summary of the medical care provided to the foster child since the last hearing. The summary must include information regarding:

(1) the nature of any emergency medical care provided to the child and the circumstances necessitating emergency medical care, including any injury or acute illness suffered by the child;

(2) all medical and mental health treatment that the child is receiving and the child's progress with the treatment;

(3) any medication prescribed for the child, the condition, diagnosis, and symptoms for which the medication was prescribed, and the child's progress with the medication;

(4) for a child receiving a psychotropic medication:

(A) any psychosocial therapies, behavior strategies, or other non-pharmacological interventions that have been provided to the child; and

(B) the dates since the previous hearing of any office visits the child had with the prescribing physician, physician assistant, or advanced practice nurse as required by Section 266.011;

(5) the degree to which the child or foster care provider has complied or failed to comply with any plan of medical treatment for the child;

(6) any adverse reaction to or side effects of any medical treatment provided to the child;

(7) any specific medical condition of the child that has been diagnosed or for which tests are being conducted to make a diagnosis;

(8) any activity that the child should avoid or should engage in that might affect the effectiveness of the treatment, including physical activities, other medications, and diet; and

(9) other information required by department rule or by the court.

(b) At or before each hearing under Chapter 263, the department shall provide the summary of medical care described by Subsection (a) to:

(1) the court;

(2) the person authorized to consent to medical treatment for the child;

(3) the guardian ad litem or attorney ad litem, if one has been appointed by the court;

(4) the child's parent, if the parent's rights have not been terminated; and

(5) any other person determined by the department or the court to be necessary or appropriate for review of the provision of medical care to foster children.

(c) At each hearing under Chapter 263, the foster child shall be provided the opportunity to express to the court the child's views on the medical care being provided to the child.

History of Fam. Code §266.007: Acts 2005, 79th Leg., ch. 268, §1.65(a), eff. Sept. 1, 2005. Amended by Acts 2013, 83rd Leg., ch. 204, §12, eff. Sept. 1, 2013.

A FAM §266.008. EDUCATION PASSPORT

(a) The department [~~commission~~] shall develop an education passport for each foster child. The depart-

ment [~~commission, in conjunction with the department,~~] shall determine the format of the passport. The passport may be maintained in an electronic format. The passport must contain educational records of the child, including the names and addresses of educational providers, the child's grade-level performance, and any other educational information the department [~~commission~~] determines is important.

(b) The department shall maintain the passport as part of the department's records for the child as long as the child remains in foster care.

(c) The department shall make the passport available to:

(1) any person authorized by law to make educational decisions for the foster child;

(2) the person authorized to consent to medical care for the foster child; and

(3) a provider of medical care to the foster child if access to the foster child's educational information is necessary to the provision of medical care and is not prohibited by law.

(d) The department [~~and the commission~~] shall collaborate with the Texas Education Agency to develop policies and procedures to ensure that the needs of foster children are met in every school district.

History of Fam. Code §266.008: Acts 2005, 79th Leg., ch. 268, §1.65(a), eff. Sept. 1, 2005. Amended by Acts 2013, 83rd Leg., ch. 688, §8, eff. Sept. 1, 2013; H.B. 5, §20, 85th Leg., eff. Sept. 1, 2017.

FAM §266.009. PROVISION OF MEDICAL CARE IN EMERGENCY

(a) Consent or court authorization for the medical care of a foster child otherwise required by this chapter is not required in an emergency during which it is immediately necessary to provide medical care to the foster child to prevent the imminent probability of death or substantial bodily harm to the child or others, including circumstances in which:

(1) the child is overtly or continually threatening or attempting to commit suicide or cause serious bodily harm to the child or others; or

(2) the child is exhibiting the sudden onset of a medical condition manifesting itself by acute symptoms of sufficient severity, including severe pain, such that the absence of immediate medical attention could reasonably be expected to result in placing the child's health in serious jeopardy, serious impairment of bodily functions, or serious dysfunction of any bodily organ or part.

(b) The physician providing the medical care or designee shall notify the person authorized to consent to medical care for a foster child about the decision to provide medical care without consent or court authorization in an emergency not later than the second business day after the date of the provision of medical care under this section. This notification must be documented in the foster child's health passport.

(c) This section does not apply to the administration of medication under Subchapter G, Chapter 574, Health and Safety Code, to a foster child who is at least 16 years of age and who is placed in an inpatient mental health facility.

History of Fam. Code §266.009: Acts 2005, 79th Leg., ch. 268, §1.65(a), eff. Sept. 1, 2005.

FAM §266.010. CONSENT TO MEDICAL CARE BY FOSTER CHILD AT LEAST 16 YEARS OF AGE

(a) A foster child who is at least 16 years of age may consent to the provision of medical care, except as provided by Chapter 33, if the court with continuing jurisdiction determines that the child has the capacity to consent to medical care. If the child provides consent by signing a consent form, the form must be written in language the child can understand.

(b) A court with continuing jurisdiction may make the determination regarding the foster child's capacity to consent to medical care during a hearing under Chapter 263 or may hold a hearing to make the determination on its own motion. The court may issue an order authorizing the child to consent to all or some of the medical care as defined by Section 266.001. In addition, a foster child who is at least 16 years of age, or the foster child's attorney ad litem, may file a petition with the court for a hearing. If the court determines that the foster child lacks the capacity to consent to medical care, the court may consider whether the foster child has acquired the capacity to consent to medical care at subsequent hearings under Section 263.5031.

(c) If the court determines that a foster child lacks the capacity to consent to medical care, the person authorized by the court under Section 266.004 shall continue to provide consent for the medical care of the foster child.

(d) If a foster child who is at least 16 years of age and who has been determined to have the capacity to consent to medical care refuses to consent to medical care and the department or private agency providing substitute care or case management services to the

child believes that the medical care is appropriate, the department or the private agency may file a motion with the court requesting an order authorizing the provision of the medical care.

(e) The motion under Subsection (d) must include:

(1) the child's stated reasons for refusing the medical care; and

(2) a statement prepared and signed by the treating physician that the medical care is the proper course of treatment for the foster child.

(f) If a motion is filed under Subsection (d), the court shall appoint an attorney ad litem for the foster child if one has not already been appointed. The foster child's attorney ad litem shall:

(1) discuss the situation with the child;

(2) discuss the suitability of the medical care with the treating physician;

(3) review the child's medical and mental health records; and

(4) advocate to the court on behalf of the child's expressed preferences regarding the medical care.

(g) The court shall issue an order authorizing the provision of the medical care in accordance with a motion under Subsection (d) to the foster child only if the court finds, by clear and convincing evidence, after the hearing that the medical care is in the best interest of the foster child and:

(1) the foster child lacks the capacity to make a decision regarding the medical care;

(2) the failure to provide the medical care will result in an observable and material impairment to the growth, development, or functioning of the foster child; or

(3) the foster child is at risk of suffering substantial bodily harm or of inflicting substantial bodily harm to others.

(h) In making a decision under this section regarding whether a foster child has the capacity to consent to medical care, the court shall consider:

(1) the maturity of the child;

(2) whether the child is sufficiently well informed to make a decision regarding the medical care; and

(3) the child's intellectual functioning.

(i) In determining whether the medical care is in the best interest of the foster child, the court shall consider:

(1) the foster child's expressed preference regarding the medical care, including perceived risks and benefits of the medical care;

(2) likely consequences to the foster child if the child does not receive the medical care;

(3) the foster child's prognosis, if the child does receive the medical care; and

(4) whether there are alternative, less intrusive treatments that are likely to reach the same result as provision of the medical care.

(j) This section does not apply to emergency medical care. An emergency relating to a foster child who is at least 16 years of age, other than a child in an inpatient mental health facility, is governed by Section 266.009.

(k) This section does not apply to the administration of medication under Subchapter G, Chapter 574, Health and Safety Code, to a foster child who is at least 16 years of age and who is placed in an inpatient mental health facility.

(*l*) Before a foster child reaches the age of 16, the department or the private agency providing substitute care or case management services to the foster child shall advise the foster child of the right to a hearing under this section to determine whether the foster child may consent to medical care. The department or the private agency providing substitute care or case management services shall provide the foster child with training on informed consent and the provision of medical care as part of the Preparation for Adult Living Program.

History of Fam. Code §266.010: Acts 2005, 79th Leg., ch. 268, §1.65(a), eff. Sept. 1, 2005. Amended by Acts 2015, 84th Leg., ch. 944, §67, eff. Sept. 1, 2015.

FAM §266.011. MONITORING USE OF PSYCHOTROPIC DRUG

The person authorized to consent to medical treatment for a foster child prescribed a psychotropic medication shall ensure that the child has been seen by the prescribing physician, physician assistant, or advanced practice nurse at least once every 90 days to allow the physician, physician assistant, or advanced practice nurse to:

(1) appropriately monitor the side effects of the medication; and

(2) determine whether:

(A) the medication is helping the child achieve the treatment goals; and

(B) continued use of the medication is appropriate.

History of Fam. Code §266.011: Acts 2013, 83rd Leg., ch. 204, §13, eff. Sept. 1, 2013.

Ⓐ FAM §266.012. COMPREHENSIVE ASSESSMENTS

(a) Not later than the 45th day after the date a child enters the conservatorship of the department, the child shall receive a developmentally appropriate comprehensive assessment. The assessment must include:

(1) a screening for trauma; and

(2) interviews with individuals who have knowledge of the child's needs.

(b) The department shall develop guidelines regarding the contents of an assessment report.

(c) A single source continuum contractor under Subchapter B-1, Chapter 264, providing therapeutic foster care services to a child shall ensure that the child receives a comprehensive assessment under this section at least once every 90 days.

History of Fam. Code §266.012: Acts 2015, 84th Leg., ch. 11, §1, eff. Sept. 1, 2015. Amended by S.B. 11, §22, 85th Leg., eff. Sept. 1, 2017.

Ⓔ FAM §266.013. CONTINUITY OF SERVICES PROVIDED BY COMMISSION

(a) In addition to the requirements of Section 266.003(d), the commission shall continue to provide any services to children in the conservatorship of the department that the commission provided to those children before September 1, 2017.

(b) Subsection (a) does not apply to any services provided by the commission in relation to a child's education passport created under Section 266.008.

History of Fam. Code §266.013: Enacted by H.B. 5, §21, 85th Leg., eff. Sept. 1, 2017.

CHAPTER 267. EXPIRED

Texas Rules of Civil Procedure

Annotated Rules

Table of Contents

TEXAS RULES OF CIVIL PROCEDURE
ANNOTATED RULES
TABLE OF CONTENTS

TEXAS RULES OF CIVIL PROCEDURE

ANNOTATED RULES

TABLE OF CONTENTS

TEXAS RULES OF CIVIL PROCEDURE
ANNOTATED RULES
TABLE OF CONTENTS

TABLE OF CONTENTS

TEXAS RULES OF CIVIL PROCEDURE
ANNOTATED RULES
TABLE OF CONTENTS

PART I. GENERAL RULES

TRCP 1. OBJECTIVE OF RULES

The proper objective of rules of civil procedure is to obtain a just, fair, equitable and impartial adjudication of the rights of litigants under established principles of substantive law. To the end that this objective may be attained with as great expedition and dispatch and at the least expense both to the litigants and to the state as may be practicable, these rules shall be given a liberal construction.

See also *O'Connor's Texas Rules*, "Introduction to the Texas Rules," ch. 1-A, p. 5.

TRCP 2. SCOPE OF RULES

These rules shall govern the procedure in the justice, county, and district courts of the State of Texas in all actions of a civil nature, with such exceptions as may be hereinafter stated. Where any statute in effect immediately prior to September 1, 1941, prescribed a rule of procedure in lunacy, guardianship, or estates of decedents, or any other probate proceedings in the county court differing from these Rules, and not included in the "List of Repealed Statutes," such statute shall apply; and where any statute in effect immediately prior to September 1, 1941, and not included in the "List of Repealed Statutes," prescribed a rule of procedure in any special statutory proceeding differing from these rules, such statute shall apply. All statutes in effect immediately prior to September 1, 1941, prescribing rules of procedure in bond or recognizance forfeitures in criminal cases are hereby continued in effect as rules of procedure governing such cases, but where such statutes prescribed no rules of procedure in such cases, these rules shall apply. All statutes in effect immediately prior to September 1, 1941, prescribing rules of procedure in tax suits are hereby continued in effect as rules of procedure governing such cases, but where such statutes prescribed no rules of procedure in such cases, these rules shall apply; provided, however, that Rule 117a shall control with respect to citation in tax suits.

See also *O'Connor's Texas Rules*, "Introduction to the Texas Rules," ch. 1-A, p. 5.

ANNOTATIONS

In re J.D.H., 661 S.W.2d 744, 748 (Tex.App.—Beaumont 1983, no writ). "[T]he rule to be followed in child custody cases is that technical rules of civil procedure, as to practice and pleading, are not of controlling importance, since the controlling factor is the best interests of the child. It is because of our profound concern for the best interests of the child in issue that we have addressed this point of error, for we are not technically required to do so under [TRCP] 90 because appellant failed to preserve the alleged error by objection."

TRCP 3. CONSTRUCTION OF RULES

Unless otherwise expressly provided, the past, present or future tense shall each include the other; the masculine, feminine, or neuter gender shall each include the other; and the singular and plural number shall each include the other.

See also Gov't Code §312.003.

TRCP 3a. LOCAL RULES

Each administrative judicial region, district court, county court, county court at law, and probate court may make and amend local rules governing practice before such courts, provided:

(1) that any proposed rule or amendment shall not be inconsistent with these rules or with any rule of the administrative judicial region in which the court is located;

(2) no time period provided by these rules may be altered by local rules;

(3) any proposed local rule or amendment shall not become effective until it is submitted and approved by the Supreme Court of Texas;

(4) any proposed local rule or amendment shall not become effective until at least thirty days after its publication in a manner reasonably calculated to bring it to the attention of attorneys practicing before the court or courts for which it is made;

(5) all local rules or amendments adopted and approved in accordance herewith are made available upon request to the members of the bar;

(6) no local rule, order, or practice of any court, other than local rules and amendments which fully comply with all requirements of this Rule 3a, shall ever be applied to determine the merits of any matter.

See also Gov't Code §51.807 (local rules for fax filing); Local Rules, p. 1493; TRJA 10; *O'Connor's Texas Rules*, "Local Rules," ch. 1-A, §4, p. 5.

ANNOTATIONS

Approximately $1,589.00 v. State, 230 S.W.3d 871, 874 (Tex.App.—Houston [14th Dist.] 2007, no pet.). "Rule 3a(2) absolutely prohibits application of a local rule that alters a time period set forth in the [TRCPs]. Rule 3a(2) does not distinguish a local rule

that shortens a time period from a local rule that lengthens a time period."

TRCP 4. COMPUTATION OF TIME

In computing any period of time prescribed or allowed by these rules, by order of court, or by any applicable statute, the day of the act, event, or default after which the designated period of time begins to run is not to be included. The last day of the period so computed is to be included, unless it is a Saturday, Sunday, or legal holiday, in which event the period runs until the end of the next day which is not a Saturday, Sunday, or legal holiday. Saturdays, Sundays, and legal holidays shall not be counted for any purpose in any time period of five days or less in these rules, except that Saturdays, Sundays, and legal holidays shall be counted for purpose of the three-day periods in Rules 21 and 21a, extending other periods by three days when service is made by mail.

See also Gov't Code §311.014; ***O'Connor's Texas Rules***, "Rules for Filing Documents," ch. 1-C, p. 28; "Rules for Serving Documents," ch. 1-D, p. 45; "Motion for Summary Judgment—General Rules," ch. 7-B, p. 690.

ANNOTATIONS

Sosa v. Central Power & Light, 909 S.W.2d 893, 895 (Tex.1995). Ps filed their amended petition seven days before the hearing on the motion for summary judgment. "When Rule 4 is applied, the day on which [Ps] filed their amendment is not counted but the seventh day after it was filed is counted. … As we held in ***Lewis*** [below], the last day counted from the date of the filing may be the date of the hearing. Therefore, [Ps] timely filed their second amended original petition."

Lewis v. Blake, 876 S.W.2d 314, 316 (Tex.1994). TRCP 4 "applies to *any* period of time prescribed by the [TRCPs]. Applying Rule 4 to [TRCP] 166a(c), the … hearing on a motion for summary judgment may be set as early as the 21st day after the motion is served, or the 24th day if the motion is served by mail."

Peacock v. Humble, 933 S.W.2d 341, 342-43 (Tex. App.—Austin 1996, orig. proceeding). "The Code Construction Act [Gov't Code ch. 311] and [TRCP] 4 … are not consistent in the manner in which they address Saturdays, Sundays, and legal holidays when computing time periods of five days or less. [¶] When a rule of procedure conflicts with a statute, the rule yields to the legislative enactment. … Because the three-day filing period in the present case is statutory, the Code Construction Act's method for computing time applies rather than the method contained in Rule 4."

TRCP 5. ENLARGEMENT OF TIME

When by these rules or by a notice given thereunder or by order of court an act is required or allowed to be done at or within a specified time, the court for cause shown may, at any time in its discretion (a) with or without motion or notice, order the period enlarged if application therefor is made before the expiration of the period originally prescribed or as extended by a previous order; or (b) upon motion permit the act to be done after the expiration of the specified period where good cause is shown for the failure to act. The court may not enlarge the period for taking any action under the rules relating to new trials except as stated in these rules.

If any document is sent to the proper clerk by first-class United States mail in an envelope or wrapper properly addressed and stamped and is deposited in the mail on or before the last day for filing same, the same, if received by the clerk not more than ten days tardily, shall be filed by the clerk and be deemed filed in time. A legible postmark affixed by the United States Postal Service shall be prima facie evidence of the date of mailing.

See also TRAP 4; ***O'Connor's Texas Rules***, "Rules for Filing Documents," ch. 1-C, p. 28; "Motion for Continuance," ch. 5-D, p. 394; "General Rules for Discovery," ch. 6-A, p. 491; "Motion for New Trial," ch. 10-B, p. 891.

ANNOTATIONS

Morris v. Aguilar, 369 S.W.3d 168, 171 (Tex.2012). "By its own terms, Rule 5 only applies to deadlines in the [TRCPs]." *See also* ***Gutierrez v. B&B Landfill, Inc.***, No. 10-12-00219-CV (Tex.App.—Waco 2013, no pet.) (memo op.; 4-4-13) (filing deadline was under Labor Code, not TRCPs; thus, Rule 5 did not apply).

In re Brookshire Grocery Co., 250 S.W.3d 66, 73 (Tex.2008). "Rule 5 provides that a trial court 'may not enlarge the period for taking any action under the rules relating to new trial except as stated in these rules.' The [TRCPs] place no such limitation on motions relating to modifying, correcting, or reforming the judgment; treating such a motion as a motion for new trial—thereby extending the trial court's otherwise expired plenary power—would permit an end run around Rule 5's prohibition."

Ramos v. Richardson, 228 S.W.3d 671, 673 (Tex. 2007). "The respondents argue that, for purposes of [TRCP 5,] the 'mailbox rule,' placing the notices of ap-

peal into the outgoing prison mailbox is not the equivalent of placing them into the U.S. mail. But ... an inmate who does everything necessary to satisfy timeliness requirements must not be penalized if the document is ultimately filed tardily because of an error on the part of officials over whom the inmate has no control."

Stokes v. Aberdeen Ins., 917 S.W.2d 267, 268 (Tex. 1996). "[W]e hold that mailing the document to the proper court address is *conditionally effective* as mailing it to the proper court clerk's address. [¶] The clerk still must receive the document within ten days to perfect the filing."

Lofton v. Allstate Ins., 895 S.W.2d 693, 693-94 (Tex.1995). "While a postmark is *prima facie* evidence of mailing, no postmark is available in this case. In the absence of a proper postmark or certificate of mailing, an attorney's uncontroverted affidavit may be evidence of the date of mailing." *See also* ***Landers v. State Farm Lloyds***, 257 S.W.3d 740, 745 (Tex.App.—Houston [1st Dist.] 2008, no pet.); ***Arnold v. Shuck***, 24 S.W.3d 470, 472 (Tex.App.—Texarkana 2000, pet. denied).

Miller Brewing Co. v. Villarreal, 829 S.W.2d 770, 771-72 (Tex.1992). "[A] party who finds the courthouse closed on the last day that a document must be filed ... may mail the document that day, and if it is received by the clerk not more than ten days later it is timely filed. He may also locate the clerk or judge of the court and file the document with them. In some circumstances a party may also move for an enlargement of time." *See also* ***Garcia v. State Farm Lloyds***, 287 S.W.3d 809, 815 (Tex.App.—Corpus Christi 2009, pet. denied) ("not more than ten days tardily" requirement in Rule 5 refers to ten days past filing deadline).

Pediatrix Med. Servs. v. De La O, 368 S.W.3d 34, 38-39 (Tex.App.—El Paso 2012, no pet.). "Rule 5 does not enlarge the time in which to file a pleading, but instead defines when it is 'deemed filed in time.' Therefore, the U.S. Post Office acts as a branch of the court clerk's office for purposes of filing pleadings only when the provisions of Rule 5 are satisfied. The rule applies to filings that contemplate a filing deadline. Indeed, if the language of Rule 5 is construed under its plain meaning, it requires a pleading to be considered filed when it is deposited in the mail only if the pleading has to be filed on or before the last day for filing. [¶] [The] second amended petition was mailed on December 30, 2009 and it was received and filed by the court clerk on January 4, 2010. Because there was no preset deadline to file the second amended petition, the provisions of Rule 5 do not apply. Therefore, [the] second amended petition was filed on January 4, 2010, the date the court clerk actually received and filed it...." *See also* ***FP Asset Grp. v. Providence Bank***, No. 05-12-01728-CV (Tex. App.—Dallas 2014, no pet.) (memo op.; 7-22-14).

TRCP 6. SUITS COMMENCED ON SUNDAY

No civil suit shall be commenced nor process issued or served on Sunday, except in cases of injunction, attachment, garnishment, sequestration, or distress proceedings; provided that citation by publication published on Sunday shall be valid.

See also *O'Connor's Texas Rules*, "Serving the Defendant with Suit," ch. 2-H, p. 184.

TRCP 7. MAY APPEAR BY ATTORNEY

Any party to a suit may appear and prosecute or defend his rights therein, either in person or by an attorney of the court.

See also *O'Connor's Texas Rules*, "Rules for Serving Documents," ch. 1-D, p. 45; "The Attorney," ch. 1-H, p. 64; *O'Connor's Texas Forms*, FORM 1H:1.

ANNOTATIONS

Ayres v. Canales, 790 S.W.2d 554, 557 (Tex.1990). "Ordering a party to be represented by an attorney violates Rule 7." *See also* ***Assignees of Best Buy v. Combs***, 395 S.W.3d 847, 862 (Tex.App.—Austin 2013, pet. denied) (trial court does not have power to appoint attorney without statutory or procedural authorization).

TRCP 8. ATTORNEY IN CHARGE

On the occasion of a party's first appearance through counsel, the attorney whose signature first appears on the initial pleadings for any party shall be the attorney in charge, unless another attorney is specifically designated therein. Thereafter, until such designation is changed by written notice to the court and all other parties in accordance with Rule 21a, said attorney in charge shall be responsible for the suit as to such party.

All communications from the court or other counsel with respect to a suit shall be sent to the attorney in charge.

See also *O'Connor's Texas Rules*, "The Attorney," ch. 1-H, p. 64; *O'Connor's Texas Forms*, FORM 1H:1.

ANNOTATIONS

City of Tyler v. Beck, 196 S.W.3d 784, 787 (Tex. 2006). "[N]othing in [TRCP 8] indicates that a motion filed by an attorney other than the designated attorney in charge is void or that other attorneys are not authorized to act on behalf of the party." *See also* ***Sunbeam Envtl. Servs. v. Texas Workers' Comp. Ins. Facility***, 71 S.W.3d 846, 851 (Tex.App.—Austin 2002, no pet.).

Gem Vending, Inc. v. Walker, 918 S.W.2d 656, 658 (Tex.App.—Fort Worth 1996, orig. proceeding). "Notice to an attorney is notice to a party. [O]nce an attorney has entered an appearance in a case, all communications *must* be sent to that attorney."

Palmer v. Cantrell, 747 S.W.2d 39, 41 (Tex.App.—Houston [1st Dist.] 1988, no writ). "Where a single adverse party is represented by two attorneys who are not associated in a firm, we believe that it is sufficient to serve the attorney who is designated as lead counsel because he has 'control in the management of the cause....'"

TRCP 9. NUMBER OF COUNSEL HEARD

Not more than two counsel on each side shall be heard on any question or on the trial, except in important cases, and upon special leave of the court.

See also *O'Connor's Texas Rules*, "The Attorney," ch. 1-H, p. 64.

TRCP 10. WITHDRAWAL OF ATTORNEY

An attorney may withdraw from representing a party only upon written motion for good cause shown. If another attorney is to be substituted as attorney for the party, the motion shall state: the name, address, telephone number, telecopier number, if any, and State Bar of Texas identification number of the substitute attorney; that the party approves the substitution; and that the withdrawal is not sought for delay only. If another attorney is not to be substituted as attorney for the party, the motion shall state: that a copy of the motion has been delivered to the party; that the party has been notified in writing of his right to object to the motion; whether the party consents to the motion; the party's last known address and all pending settings and deadlines. If the motion is granted, the withdrawing attorney shall immediately notify the party in writing of any additional settings or deadlines of which the attorney has knowledge at the time of the withdrawal and has not already notified the party. The Court may impose further conditions upon granting leave to withdraw. Notice or delivery to a party shall be either made to the party in person or mailed to the party's last known address by both certified and regular first class mail. If the attorney in charge withdraws and another attorney remains or becomes substituted, another attorney in charge must be designated of record with notice to all other parties in accordance with Rule 21a.

See also *O'Connor's Texas Rules*, "The Attorney," ch. 1-H, p. 64; *O'Connor's Texas Forms*, FORMS 1H:6, 7.

ANNOTATIONS

Rogers v. Clinton, 794 S.W.2d 9, 10 n.1 (Tex.1990). "Although a client may discharge his attorney at any time even without cause, an attorney may withdraw from representation of a client only if he satisfies the requirements of [TRCP] 10." *See also* ***Sims v. Fitzpatrick***, 288 S.W.3d 93, 100 (Tex.App.—Houston [1st Dist.] 2009, no pet.) (granting motion to withdraw that does not comply with TRCP 10 may be harmless error if court allows time for party to secure new counsel and time for new counsel to investigate case and prepare for trial).

Harrison v. Harrison, 367 S.W.3d 822, 827 (Tex. App.—Houston [14th Dist.] 2012, pet. denied). TRCP 10 "does not define 'good cause.' However, the Texas Disciplinary Rules of Professional Conduct articulate considerations relevant to the consideration of Rule 10 motions. [¶] [The Disciplinary Rules] provide[], among other things, that a lawyer shall not withdraw from representing a client 'unless withdrawal can be accomplished without material adverse effect on the interests of the client'; the client 'fails substantially to fulfill an obligation to the lawyer regarding the lawyer's services, including an obligation to pay the lawyer's fee as agreed, and has been given reasonable warning that the lawyer will withdraw unless the obligation is fulfilled'; and the representation 'will result in an unreasonable financial burden on the lawyer or has been rendered unreasonably difficult by the client.'"

TRCP 11. AGREEMENTS TO BE IN WRITING

Unless otherwise provided in these rules, no agreement between attorneys or parties touching any suit pending will be enforced unless it be in writing, signed and filed with the papers as part of the record, or unless it be made in open court and entered of record.

Caution: TRCP 11 is affected by Fam. Code §§4.002, 4.104, 4.203, 7.006, 153.007, 153.133, and 154.124.

See also TRCP 191.1 (agreements in discovery matters); *O'Connor's Texas Rules*, "Agreements Between Attorneys – Rule 11," ch. 1-H, §9, p. 76; "Settlement of the Suit," ch. 7-I, p. 759; *O'Connor's Texas Forms*, FORM 1H:13.

ANNOTATIONS

In re Vaishangi, Inc., 442 S.W.3d 256, 259 (Tex. 2014). "We have generally treated Rule 11 agreements as separate and distinct from agreed judgments entered thereon. But nothing in the [TRCPs] prohibits a Rule 11 agreement from being, itself, an agreed judgment, so long as the agreement meets the requirements for a final judgment. *At 260:* Although fact issues about the scope and terms of the Rule 11 agreement may remain, those issues do not prevent the Court from determining as a matter of law whether the Rule 11 agreement constitutes an agreed judgment."

Exito Elecs. Co. v. Trejo, 142 S.W.3d 302, 305 (Tex. 2004). "A Rule 11 Agreement between the parties, in and of itself, is not a plea, pleading, or motion. *At 306:* [W]hile filing a Rule 11 Agreement with the trial court is a requirement for enforcement, it is not in and of itself a request for enforcement or any other affirmative action by the trial court."

Padilla v. LaFrance, 907 S.W.2d 454, 461 (Tex. 1995). "The ... filing requirement [in TRCP 11] is satisfied so long as the agreement is filed before it is sought to be enforced."

Coale v. Scott, 331 S.W.3d 829, 831-32 (Tex.App.—Amarillo 2011, no pet.). "[T]he trial court's authority to approve a Rule 11 agreement does not depend upon whether it has [plenary] jurisdiction. It may enforce a Rule 11 agreement touching upon the suit executed after the cause was tried and finally resolved via judgment. [A] settlement agreement ... executed while the parties were attempting to sway the trial court to enforce its judgment logically falls within the scope of 'any suit pending' for purposes of Rule 11. [¶] [Party argued] that the Rule 11 agreement was unenforceable because they allegedly withdrew their consent to it before the trial court ordered its enforcement. We disagree. [¶] Rule 11 requires that the agreement be filed of record before the court may enforce it. If the accord is in writing, signed by the parties or their attorneys, and filed of record, it does not matter whether a party no longer agrees to it when the trial court is finally asked to enforce it. This is so because the agreement becomes a contract when executed, not when the trial court attempts to enforce it." *See also* ***Lane-Valente Indus. (Nat'l), Inc. v. J.P. Morgan Chase***, 468 S.W.3d 200, 204 (Tex.App.—Houston [14th Dist.] 2015, no pet.) (Rule 11 agreement can be enforced as contract if one party withdraws consent before judgment is rendered, but party seeking enforcement must pursue separate breach-of-contract claim subject to normal rules of pleading and proof).

ExxonMobil Corp. v. Valence Oper. Co., 174 S.W.3d 303, 309 (Tex.App.—Houston [1st Dist.] 2005, pet. denied). "A trial court has a ministerial duty to enforce a valid Rule 11 agreement. [¶] However, it is not sufficient that a party's consent to a Rule 11 agreement may have been given at one time; consent must exist at the time that judgment is rendered." *See also* ***Baylor Coll. of Med. v. Camberg***, 247 S.W.3d 342, 346 (Tex. App.—Houston [14th Dist.] 2008, pet. denied).

TRCP 12. ATTORNEY TO SHOW AUTHORITY

A party in a suit or proceeding pending in a court of this state may, by sworn written motion stating that he believes the suit or proceeding is being prosecuted or defended without authority, cause the attorney to be cited to appear before the court and show his authority to act. The notice of the motion shall be served upon the challenged attorney at least ten days before the hearing on the motion. At the hearing on the motion, the burden of proof shall be upon the challenged attorney to show sufficient authority to prosecute or defend the suit on behalf of the other party. Upon his failure to show such authority, the court shall refuse to permit the attorney to appear in the cause, and shall strike the pleadings if no person who is authorized to prosecute or defend appears. The motion may be heard and determined at any time before the parties have announced ready for trial, but the trial shall not be unnecessarily continued or delayed for the hearing.

See also *O'Connor's Texas Rules*, "The Attorney," ch. 1-H, p. 64; *O'Connor's Texas Forms*, FORMS 1H:8-10.

ANNOTATIONS

In re Users Sys. Servs., 22 S.W.3d 331, 335 (Tex. 1999). "[T]he procedure prescribed by Rule 12 for requiring an attorney to show his authority to act for a party presupposes the possibility that an attorney can be counsel of record for a party he is not authorized to represent. The [TRCPs] contemplate that authorization may not have existed or may cease before the attorney has withdrawn from the case."

Nolana Open MRI Ctr., Inc. v. Pechero, No. 13-13-00552-CV (Tex.App.—Corpus Christi 2015, no pet.) (memo op.; 2-12-15). "Typically, a challenged attorney satisfies his burden [under TRCP 12] if he produces an affidavit or testimony from his client indicating the attorney was retained to provide representation in the case."

In re Guardianship of Benavides, 403 S.W.3d 370, 374 (Tex.App.—San Antonio 2013, pet. denied). "As a general rule, an order on a rule 12 motion is an interlocutory order that is not appealable until it is merged into a final judgment. Nevertheless, probate and guardianship proceedings are often exceptions to the 'one final judgment' rule."

Air Park-Dallas Zoning Cmte. v. Crow-Billingsley Airpark, Ltd., 109 S.W.3d 900, 906 (Tex.App.—Dallas 2003, no pet.). "[A] Rule 12 motion may be properly brought when a new and different attorney attempts to appear as attorney of record purporting to advance a motion for new trial after the trial has concluded."

TRCP 13. EFFECT OF SIGNING OF PLEADINGS, MOTIONS & OTHER PAPERS; SANCTIONS

The signatures of attorneys or parties constitute a certificate by them that they have read the pleading, motion, or other paper; that to the best of their knowledge, information, and belief formed after reasonable inquiry the instrument is not groundless and brought in bad faith or groundless and brought for the purpose of harassment. Attorneys or parties who shall bring a fictitious suit as an experiment to get an opinion of the court, or who shall file any fictitious pleading in a cause for such a purpose, or shall make statements in pleading which they know to be groundless and false, for the purpose of securing a delay of the trial of the cause, shall be held guilty of a contempt. If a pleading, motion or other paper is signed in violation of this rule, the court, upon motion or upon its own initiative, after notice and hearing, shall impose an appropriate sanction available under Rule 215-2b,[1] upon the person who signed it, a represented party, or both.

Courts shall presume that pleadings, motions, and other papers are filed in good faith. No sanctions under this rule may be imposed except for good cause, the particulars of which must be stated in the sanction order. "Groundless" for purposes of this rule means no basis in law or fact and not warranted by good faith argument for the extension, modification, or reversal of existing law. A general denial does not constitute a violation of this rule. The amount requested for damages does not constitute a violation of this rule.

1. **Editor's note:** Now TRCP 215.2(b).

See also CPRC chs. 9, 10; ***O'Connor's Texas Rules***, "Groundless or frivolous pleadings," ch. 1-B, §3.4, p. 20; "Motion for Sanctions," ch. 5-K, p. 439; ***O'Connor's Texas Forms***, FORMS 5K:1, 2, 5.

ANNOTATIONS

GTE Comms. Sys. v. Tanner, 856 S.W.2d 725, 731 (Tex.1993). TRCP 13 "prescribes that courts presume that papers are filed in good faith. Thus, the burden is on the party moving for sanctions to overcome this presumption. [¶] Rule 13 requires that sanctions imposed be 'appropriate,' which is the equivalent of 'just' under [TRCP] 215." *See also* ***Olibas v. Gomez***, 242 S.W.3d 527, 534 (Tex.App.—El Paso 2007, pet. denied).

In re J.A., 482 S.W.3d 141, 148-49 (Tex.App.—El Paso 2015, no pet.). Father "asserts that the trial court's failure to state with particularity the good cause underlying its finding that the petition was groundless and filed in bad faith or for the purpose of harassment is reversible error. [¶] Sanctions may be imposed under [TRCP] 13 only for 'good cause, the particulars of which must be stated in the sanction order.' This requirement is mandatory. A trial court abuses its discretion by failing to comply with this requirement. Here, the trial court's sanction order notes only that Mother's Rule 13 Motion was 'well taken.' The order provides no further insight into the trial court's reasoning for dismissing Father's action. As the moving party, Mother had the burden of showing that Father's petition was groundless and filed in bad faith or to harass. But without a Reporter's Record or findings of facts, we have nothing to review. [¶] Failing to fully comply with the particularity requirement of Rule 13 does not automatically warrant reversal. *At 150:* In the case at hand, Father made neither a timely objection to the form of the sanctions order nor did he file a request for findings of fact and conclusions of law as permitted by [TRCP] 296. [W]e conclude [Father] has waived error." *See also* ***Gomer v. Davis***, 419 S.W.3d 470, 477-78 (Tex. App.—Houston [1st Dist.] 2013, no pet.).

Parker v. Walton, 233 S.W.3d 535, 539-40 (Tex. App.—Houston [14th Dist.] 2007, no pet.). "When determining whether Rule 13 sanctions are proper, the trial court must examine the facts available to the litigant and the circumstances existing when the litigant filed the pleading. Rule 13 requires sanctions based on

the acts or omissions of the represented party or counsel and not merely on the legal merit of the pleading. The trial court must provide notice and hold an evidentiary hearing 'to make the necessary factual determinations about the motives and credibility of the person signing the groundless petition.' ... Bad faith is not simply bad judgment or negligence; rather, it is the conscious doing of a wrong for dishonest, discriminatory, or malicious purposes. Improper motive is an essential element of bad faith. Harassment means that the pleading was intended to annoy, alarm, and abuse another person." *See also* ***Zeifman v. Michels***, No. 03-12-00114-CV (Tex.App.—Austin 2013, no pet.) (memo op.; 8-22-13) (party acts in bad faith if she has been put on notice that her understanding of facts may be incorrect but does not make reasonable inquiry before further pursuing her claim); ***Thielemann v. Kethan***, 371 S.W.3d 286, 294 (Tex.App.—Houston [1st Dist.] 2012, pet. denied) (party moving for sanctions must prove pleading party's subjective state of mind).

Loeffler v. Lytle ISD, 211 S.W.3d 331, 349-50 (Tex. App.—San Antonio 2006, pet. denied). "At the time these pleadings and motions were filed, [P] at the most provided the factual basis for these claims. The decision of what legal claims, objections, and motions to file was part and parcel of [P's] legal representation and was entrusted to ... her attorney. Because a party should not be punished for their attorney's conduct unless the party is implicated apart from having entrusted its legal representation, we conclude the trial court abused its discretion in imposing sanctions against [P] under ... Rule 13." *See also* ***Metzger v. Sebek***, 892 S.W.2d 20, 52-53 (Tex.App.—Houston [1st Dist.] 1994, writ denied) (court was right to sanction P for lying in affidavit, but amount of sanction was excessive).

In re A.S.M., 172 S.W.3d 710, 717-18 (Tex.App.—Fort Worth 2005, no pet.). "The trial court's findings of fact and conclusions of law clearly state that [mother's] failure to file the [Fam. Code §156.102] affidavit even after having such failure called to her attention warranted the sanctions award. Based on the foregoing, we hold that the trial court did not abuse its discretion in awarding sanctions under [TRCP] 13. [¶] [P]roof of the necessity or reasonableness of attorney's fees is not required when the fees are assessed as sanctions. Instead, the amount of attorney's fees awarded as sanctions is within the sound discretion of the trial court."

TRCP 14. AFFIDAVIT BY AGENT

Whenever it may be necessary or proper for any party to a civil suit or proceeding to make an affidavit, it may be made by either the party or his agent or his attorney.

See also TRCP 197.2(d); ***O'Connor's Texas Rules***, "Affidavits," ch. 1-B, §3.2.17, p. 12; ***O'Connor's Texas Forms***, FORM 1B:8.

ANNOTATIONS

Cantu v. Holiday Inns, Inc., 910 S.W.2d 113, 116 (Tex.App.—Corpus Christi 1995, writ denied). "A party's attorney may verify the pleading where he has knowledge of the facts, but does not have authority to verify based merely on his status as counsel. Here, counsel does not show any basis in the pleading or in her affidavit for her personal knowledge of relevant facts."

TRCP 14a. REPEALED

TRCP 14b. RETURN OR OTHER DISPOSITION OF EXHIBITS

The clerk of the court in which the exhibits are filed shall retain and dispose of the same as directed by the Supreme Court.

See also TRCP 75b.

ORDER RELATING TO RETENTION & DISPOSITION OF EXHIBITS IN CIVIL CASES

In compliance with the provisions of Texas Rule of Civil Procedure 14b, the Supreme Court hereby directs that exhibits offered or admitted into evidence shall be retained and disposed of by the clerk of the court in which the exhibits are filed upon the following basis.

The order shall apply only to: (1) those cases in which judgment has been rendered on service of process by publication and in which no motion for new trial was filed within two years after judgment was signed; and (2) all other cases in which judgment has been signed for one year and in which no appeal was perfected or in which a perfected appeal was dismissed or concluded by a final judgment as to all parties and the issuance of the appellate court's mandate such that the case is no longer pending on appeal or in the trial court.

The party who offered an exhibit may withdraw it from the clerk's office within thirty days of the later of (1) a case becoming subject to this order, or (2) the effective date of this order. The clerk, unless otherwise directed by the court, may dispose of any exhibits remaining after such time period.

TRCP 14c. DEPOSIT IN LIEU OF SURETY BOND

Wherever these rules provide for the filing of a surety bond, the party may in lieu of filing the bond deposit cash or other negotiable obligation of the government of the United States of America or any agency thereof, or with leave of court, deposit a negotiable obligation of any bank or savings and loan association chartered by the government of the United States of America or any state thereof that is insured by the government of the United States of America or any agency thereof, in the amount fixed for the surety bond, conditioned in the same manner as would be a surety bond for the protection of other parties. Any interest thereon shall constitute a part of the deposit.

PART II. RULES OF PRACTICE IN DISTRICT & COUNTY COURTS

SECTION 1. GENERAL RULES

TRCP 15. WRITS & PROCESS

The style of all writs and process shall be "The State of Texas"; and unless otherwise specially provided by law or these rules every such writ and process shall be directed to any sheriff or any constable within the State of Texas, shall be made returnable on the Monday next after expiration of twenty days from the date of service thereof, and shall be dated and attested by the clerk with the seal of the court impressed thereon; and the date of issuance shall be noted thereon.

See also Loc. Gov't Code §86.021; *O'Connor's Texas Rules*, "Serving the Defendant with Suit," ch. 2-H, p. 184; "Default Judgment," ch. 7-A, p. 671; *O'Connor's Texas Forms*, FORMS 2H:2, 3.

ANNOTATIONS

Williams v. Williams, 150 S.W.3d 436, 445 (Tex. App.—Austin 2004, pet. denied). "[W]e ... hold that citations *must* be expressly directed to the defendant under [TRCP] 99 and *may* also be addressed to the sheriff or constable under [TRCP] 15, but failure to include the sheriff or constable on the form of the citation will not render it void." *See also* ***Barker CATV Constr., Inc. v. Ampro, Inc.***, 989 S.W.2d 789, 792 (Tex.App.—Houston [1st Dist.] 1999, no pet.).

TRCP 16. SHALL ENDORSE ALL PROCESS

Every officer or authorized person shall endorse on all process and precepts coming to his hand the day and hour on which he received them, the manner in which he executed them, and the time and place the process was served and shall sign the returns officially.

See also Loc. Gov't Code §§85.021, 86.021; TRCP 107; *O'Connor's Texas Rules*, "Serving the Defendant with Suit," ch. 2-H, p. 184; "Default Judgment," ch. 7-A, p. 671.

ANNOTATIONS

Deutsche Bank Trust Co. v. Hall, 400 S.W.3d 668, 670 (Tex.App.—Texarkana 2013, pet. denied). "[T]he ... clerk employed the attachment of a green card (which bears the clerk's stamp that incorporates a date and time) in lieu of fully completing the return. [A] 'filed for record' stamp [does not] constitute[ ] an endorsement."

TRCP 17. OFFICER TO EXECUTE PROCESS

Except where otherwise expressly provided by law or these rules, the officer receiving any process to be executed shall not be entitled in any case to demand his fee for executing the same in advance of such execution, but his fee shall be taxed and collected as other costs in the case.

See also *O'Connor's Texas Rules*, "Serving the Defendant with Suit," ch. 2-H, p. 184; "Default Judgment," ch. 7-A, p. 671.

TRCP 18. WHEN JUDGE DIES DURING TERM, RESIGNS OR IS DISABLED

If the judge dies, resigns, or becomes unable to hold court during the session of court duly convened for the term, and the time provided by law for the holding of said court has not expired, such death, resignation, or inability on the part of the judge shall not operate to adjourn said court for the term, but such court shall be deemed to continue in session. If a successor to such judge shall qualify and assume office during the term, or if a judge be transferred to said district from some other judicial district, he may continue to hold said court for the term provided, and all motions undisposed of shall be heard and determined by him, and statements of facts and bills of exception shall be approved by him. If the time for holding such court expires before a successor shall qualify, and before a judge can be transferred to said district from some other judicial district, then all motions pending, including those for new trial, shall stand as continued in force until such successor has qualified and assumed office, or a judge has been transferred to said district who can hold said court, and thereupon such judge shall have power to act thereon at the succeeding term, or on an earlier day in vacation, on notice to all parties to the motion, and such orders shall have the same effect as if rendered in

term time. The time for allowing statement of facts and bills of exception from such orders shall date from the time the motion was decided.

See also Gov't Code §74.053.

ANNOTATIONS

2900 Smith, Ltd. v. Constellation NewEnergy, Inc., 301 S.W.3d 741, 744 n.6 (Tex.App.—Houston [14th Dist.] 2009, no pet.). TRCP 18 "'allows successor judges to dispose of unresolved matters and enter various orders so long as the successor judge does not render judgment without hearing evidence.'" *See also* ***W.C. Banks, Inc. v. Team, Inc.***, 783 S.W.2d 783, 786 (Tex. App.—Houston [1st Dist.] 1990, no writ).

TRCP 18a. RECUSAL & DISQUALIFICATION OF JUDGES

(a) ***Motion; Form and Contents.*** A party in a case in any trial court other than a statutory probate court or justice court may seek to recuse or disqualify a judge who is sitting in the case by filing a motion with the clerk of the court in which the case is pending. The motion:

(1) must be verified;

(2) must assert one or more of the grounds listed in Rule 18b;

(3) must not be based solely on the judge's rulings in the case; and

(4) must state with detail and particularity facts that:

(A) are within the affiant's personal knowledge, except that facts may be stated on information and belief if the basis for that belief is specifically stated;

(B) would be admissible in evidence; and

(C) if proven, would be sufficient to justify recusal or disqualification.

(b) ***Time for Filing Motion.***

(1) *Motion to recuse.* A motion to recuse:

(A) must be filed as soon as practicable after the movant knows of the ground stated in the motion; and

(B) must not be filed after the tenth day before the date set for trial or other hearing unless, before that day, the movant neither knew nor reasonably should have known:

(i) that the judge whose recusal is sought would preside at the trial or hearing; or

(ii) that the ground stated in the motion existed.

(2) *Motion to disqualify.* A motion to disqualify should be filed as soon as practicable after the movant knows of the ground stated in the motion.

(c) ***Response to Motion.***

(1) *By another party.* Any other party in the case may, but need not, file a response to the motion. Any response must be filed before the motion is heard.

(2) *By the respondent judge.* The judge whose recusal or disqualification is sought should not file a response to the motion.

(d) ***Service of Motion or Response.*** A party who files a motion or response must serve a copy on every other party. The method of service must be the same as the method of filing, if possible.

(e) ***Duty of the Clerk.***

(1) *Delivery of a motion or response.* When a motion or response is filed, the clerk of the court must immediately deliver a copy to the respondent judge and to the presiding judge of the administrative judicial region in which the court is located ("the regional presiding judge").

(2) *Delivery of order of recusal or referral.* When a respondent judge signs and files an order of recusal or referral, the clerk of the court must immediately deliver a copy to the regional presiding judge.

(f) ***Duties of the Respondent Judge; Failure to Comply.***

(1) *Responding to the motion.* Regardless of whether the motion complies with this rule, the respondent judge, within three business days after the motion is filed, must either:

(A) sign and file with the clerk an order of recusal or disqualification; or

(B) sign and file with the clerk an order referring the motion to the regional presiding judge.

(2) *Restrictions on further action.*

(A) *Motion filed before evidence offered at trial.* If a motion is filed before evidence has been offered at trial, the respondent judge must take no further action in the case until the motion has been decided, except for good cause stated in writing or on the record.

(B) *Motion filed after evidence offered at trial.* If a motion is filed after evidence has been offered at trial, the respondent judge may proceed, subject to stay by the regional presiding judge.

(3) *Failure to comply.* If the respondent judge fails to comply with a duty imposed by this rule, the movant may notify the regional presiding judge.

(g) ***Duties of Regional Presiding Judge.***

(1) *Motion.* The regional presiding judge must rule on a referred motion or assign a judge to rule. If a party files a motion to recuse or disqualify the regional presiding judge, the regional presiding judge may still assign a judge to rule on the original, referred motion. Alternatively, the regional presiding judge may sign and file with the clerk an order referring the second motion to the Chief Justice for consideration.

(2) *Order.* The ruling must be by written order.

(3) *Summary denial for noncompliance.*

(A) *Motion to recuse.* A motion to recuse that does not comply with this rule may be denied without an oral hearing. The order must state the nature of the noncompliance. Even if the motion is amended to correct the stated noncompliance, the motion will count for purposes of determining whether a tertiary recusal motion has been filed under the Civil Practice and Remedies Code.

(B) *Motion to disqualify.* A motion to disqualify may not be denied on the ground that it was not filed or served in compliance with this rule.

(4) *Interim orders.* The regional presiding judge or judge assigned to decide the motion may issue interim or ancillary orders in the pending case as justice may require.

(5) *Discovery.* Except by order of the regional presiding judge or the judge assigned to decide the motion, a subpoena or discovery request may not issue to the respondent judge and may be disregarded unless accompanied by the order.

(6) *Hearing.*

(A) *Time.* The motion must be heard as soon as practicable and may be heard immediately after it is referred to the regional presiding judge or an assigned judge.

(B) *Notice.* Notice of the hearing must be given to all parties in the case.

(C) *By telephone.* The hearing may be conducted by telephone on the record. Documents submitted by facsimile or email, otherwise admissible under the rules of evidence, may be considered.

(7) *Reassignment of case if motion granted.* If the motion is granted, the regional presiding judge must transfer the case to another court or assign another judge to the case.

(h) ***Sanctions.*** After notice and hearing, the judge who hears the motion may order the party or attorney who filed the motion, or both, to pay the reasonable attorney fees and expenses incurred by other parties if the judge determines that the motion was:

(1) groundless and filed in bad faith or for the purpose of harassment, or

(2) clearly brought for unnecessary delay and without sufficient cause.

(i) ***Chief Justice.*** The Chief Justice of the Supreme Court of Texas may assign judges and issue any orders permitted by this rule or pursuant to statute.

(j) ***Appellate Review.***

(1) *Order on motion to recuse.*

(A) *Denying motion.* An order denying a motion to recuse may be reviewed only for abuse of discretion on appeal from the final judgment.

(B) *Granting motion.* An order granting a motion to recuse is final and cannot be reviewed by appeal, mandamus, or otherwise.

(2) *Order on motion to disqualify.* An order granting or denying a motion to disqualify may be reviewed by mandamus and may be appealed in accordance with other law.

See also Gov't Code §§74.053, 74.059(c)(3); TRAP 16; ***O'Connor's Texas Rules***, "Motion to Challenge the Judge," ch. 5-C, p. 383; ***O'Connor's Texas Forms***, FORMS 5C.

ANNOTATIONS

In re Perritt, 992 S.W.2d 444, 445 (Tex.1999). "[A] judge designated by the presiding judge of the administrative judicial district to hear a recusal motion under [TRCP] 18a is also an assigned judge subject to objection and mandatory disqualification under [Gov't Code] §74.053(b)...."

In re Union Pac. Res., 969 S.W.2d 427, 428 (Tex. 1998). Mandamus is not available to review the denial of a motion to recuse made under the TRCPs. TRCP 18a(f), now TRCP 18a(j)(1)(a), "expressly provide[s] for appellate review from a final judgment after denial of a recusal motion. If the appellate court determines ... the trial judge should have been recused, the appellate court can reverse the trial court's judgment and remand for a new trial before a different judge."

In re Beddingfield, No. 10-15-00280-CV (Tex. App.—Waco 2015, orig. proceeding) (memo op.; 8-20-15). "There is no prohibition against the parties to a proceeding requesting and the trial court personnel setting matters for submission while a motion to recuse the particular trial court judge is pending pursuant to Rule 18a. Not all procedures are required to stop in a trial court just because such a motion has been filed. The only thing that cannot occur once a motion to recuse a trial court judge is filed is that the trial court judge that is the target of the motion cannot conduct any hearings or render any orders or judgments until the motion to recuse is resolved."

McElwee v. McElwee, 911 S.W.2d 182, 186 (Tex. App.—Houston [1st Dist.] 1995, writ denied). "Unlike recusal, disqualification cannot be waived.... Disqualification may be raised at any time." *See also* ***Sparkman v. Microsoft Corp.***, No. 12-13-00175-CV (Tex.App.—Tyler 2015, pet. denied) (memo op.; 3-18-15) (recusal may be waived if not raised by proper motion).

TRCP 18b. GROUNDS FOR RECUSAL & DISQUALIFICATION OF JUDGES

(a) ***Grounds for Disqualification.*** A judge must disqualify in any proceeding in which:

(1) the judge has served as a lawyer in the matter in controversy, or a lawyer with whom the judge previously practiced law served during such association as a lawyer concerning the matter;

(2) the judge knows that, individually or as a fiduciary, the judge has an interest in the subject matter in controversy; or

(3) either of the parties may be related to the judge by affinity or consanguinity within the third degree.

(b) ***Grounds for Recusal.*** A judge must recuse in any proceeding in which:

(1) the judge's impartiality might reasonably be questioned;

(2) the judge has a personal bias or prejudice concerning the subject matter or a party;

(3) the judge has personal knowledge of disputed evidentiary facts concerning the proceeding;

(4) the judge or a lawyer with whom the judge previously practiced law has been a material witness concerning the proceeding;

(5) the judge participated as counsel, adviser, or material witness in the matter in controversy, or expressed an opinion concerning the merits of it, while acting as an attorney in government service;

(6) the judge knows that the judge, individually or as a fiduciary, or the judge's spouse or minor child residing in the judge's household, has a financial interest in the subject matter in controversy or in a party to the proceeding, or any other interest that could be substantially affected by the outcome of the proceeding;

(7) the judge or the judge's spouse, or a person within the third degree of relationship to either of them, or the spouse of such a person:

(A) is a party to the proceeding or an officer, director, or trustee of a party;

(B) is known by the judge to have an interest that could be substantially affected by the outcome of the proceeding; or

(C) is to the judge's knowledge likely to be a material witness in the proceeding.

(8) the judge or the judge's spouse, or a person within the first degree of relationship to either of them, or the spouse of such a person, is acting as a lawyer in the proceeding.

(c) ***Financial Interests.*** A judge should inform himself or herself about personal and fiduciary financial interests, and make a reasonable effort to inform himself or herself about the personal financial interests of his or her spouse and minor children residing in the household.

(d) ***Terminology and Standards.*** In this rule:

(1) "proceeding" includes pretrial, trial, or other stages of litigation;

(2) the degree of relationship is calculated according to the civil law system;

(3) "fiduciary" includes such relationships as executor, administrator, trustee, and guardian;

(4) "financial interest" means ownership of a legal or equitable interest, however small, or a relationship as director, adviser, or other active participant in the affairs of a party, except that:

(A) ownership in a mutual or common investment fund that holds securities is not a "financial interest" in such securities unless the judge participates in the management of the fund;

(B) an office in an educational, religious, charitable, fraternal, or civic organization is not a "financial interest" in securities held by the organization;

(C) the proprietary interest of a policyholder in a mutual insurance company, of a depositor in a mutual

savings association, or a similar proprietary interest, is a "financial interest" in the organization only if the outcome of the proceeding could substantially affect the value of the interest;

(D) ownership of government securities is a "financial interest" in the issuer only if the outcome of the proceeding could substantially affect the value of the securities;

(E) an interest as a taxpayer or utility ratepayer, or any similar interest, is not a "financial interest" unless the outcome of the proceeding could substantially affect the liability of the judge or a person related to him within the third degree more than other judges.

(e) ***Waiving a Ground for Recusal.*** The parties to a proceeding may waive any ground for recusal after it is fully disclosed on the record.

(f) ***Discovery and Divestiture.*** If a judge does not discover that the judge is recused under subparagraphs (b)(6) or (b)(7)(B) until after the judge has devoted substantial time to the matter, the judge is not required to recuse himself or herself if the judge or the person related to the judge divests himself or herself of the interest that would otherwise require recusal.

See also Tex. Const. art. 5, §11; Gov't Code §§21.005, 74.053, 74.059(c)(3), 573.022-573.025; TRAP 16; ***O'Connor's Texas Rules***, "Motion to Challenge the Judge," ch. 5-C, p. 383; ***O'Connor's Texas Forms***, FORMS 5C.

ANNOTATIONS

In re O'Connor, 92 S.W.3d 446, 450 (Tex.2002). A divorce action and a modification proceeding "can, and often will, involve the same matter in controversy. When they do, the trial judge is disqualified from presiding over the modification proceeding if a lawyer with whom the judge previously practiced law served during that association as a lawyer in the divorce action." *See also* ***Tesco Am., Inc. v. Strong Indus.***, 221 S.W.3d 550, 553 (Tex.2006) (vicarious disqualification of appellate judges); ***In re D.C.***, No. 07-09-00320-CV (Tex.App.—Amarillo 2010, no pet.) (memo op.; 9-23-10) (suit to terminate parental rights that were established in earlier SAPCR involved same matter in controversy; father could raise issue of disqualification for first time on appeal).

In re E.R.C., 496 S.W.3d 270, 280 (Tex.App.—Texarkana 2016, pet. denied). Petitioner "argued at the recusal hearing and on appeal that Judge ... was biased in favor of the lesbian, gay, bisexual, and transgender (LGBT) community and against Christians. At the hearing, [petitioner] introduced evidence that Judge ... had been endorsed in his election campaign by two groups representing the LGBT community and of the endorsement procedures of one of the groups. [N]o evidence was introduced regarding Judge['s] involvement with the LGBT community or LGBT activist groups, or of his written or oral statements concerning LGBT rights or his religious views. [Petitioner's] speculation that Judge ... was biased based merely on the fact that he received endorsements from LGBT activist groups in an election campaign is not sufficient to overcome the presumption of judicial impartiality. Further, a reasonable, disinterested observer would recognize the reality that a judge participating in a political campaign may receive many endorsements from politically active groups and individuals and that at the same time, a judge is under the ethical obligation to remain impartial."

In re Commitment of Winkle, 434 S.W.3d 300, 311 (Tex.App.—Beaumont 2014, pet. denied). "The standard for recusal is clear. When the party moving for recusal relies on bias to claim the trial judge should be recused, the party filing the motion to recuse must show that a reasonable person, with knowledge of the circumstances, would harbor doubts as to the impartiality of the trial judge, and that the bias is of such a nature and extent that allowing the judge to serve would deny the movant's right to receive due process of law." *See also* ***Humitech Dev. Corp. v. Perlman***, 424 S.W.3d 782, 797 (Tex.App.—Dallas 2014, no pet.), *overruled on other grounds*, ***Hoskins v. Hoskins***, 497 S.W.3d 490 (Tex.2016).

Ludlow v. DeBerry, 959 S.W.2d 265, 271 (Tex. App.—Houston [14th Dist.] 1997, no writ). "[O]pinions formed by the judge on the basis of facts introduced or events occurring during proceedings do not constitute a basis for a recusal motion unless they display a deep-seated favoritism or antagonism that would make fair judgment impossible. [J]udicial remarks during the course of a trial that are critical or disapproving or even hostile to counsel, parties, or their cases, ordinarily do not support recusal. Such remarks *may* do so if they reveal an opinion deriving from an extrajudicial source and such remarks *will* do so if they reveal such a high degree of favoritism or antagonism as to make fair judgment impossible." *See also* ***Hansen v. JP Morgan Chase Bank***, 346 S.W.3d 769, 776 (Tex. App.—Dallas 2011, no pet.).

TRCP 18c. RECORDING & BROADCASTING OF COURT PROCEEDINGS

A trial court may permit broadcasting, televising, recording, or photographing of proceedings in the courtroom only in the following circumstances:

(a) in accordance with guidelines promulgated by the Supreme Court for civil cases, or

(b) when broadcasting, televising, recording, or photographing will not unduly distract participants or impair the dignity of the proceedings and the parties have consented, and consent to being depicted or recorded is obtained from each witness whose testimony will be broadcast, televised, or photographed, or

(c) the broadcasting, televising, recording, or photographing of investiture, or ceremonial proceedings.

Caution: TRCP 18c is affected by Fam. Code §§104.002-104.005.

See also ***O'Connor's Texas Family Law Handbook*** (2017), "Children," ch. 4-D, §12.3.2, p. 451.

TRCP 19. NON-ADJOURNMENT OF TERM

Every term of court shall commence and convene by operation of law at the time fixed by statute without any act, order, or formal opening by a judge or other official thereof, and shall continue to be open at all times until and including the last day of the term unless sooner adjourned by the judge thereof.

TRCP 20. MINUTES READ & SIGNED

On the last day of the session, the minutes shall be read, corrected and signed in open court by the judge. Each special judge shall sign the minutes of such proceedings as were had by him.

TRCP 21. FILING & SERVING PLEADINGS & MOTIONS

(a) ***Filing and Service Required.*** Every pleading, plea, motion, or application to the court for an order, whether in the form of a motion, plea, or other form of request, unless presented during a hearing or trial, must be filed with the clerk of the court in writing, must state the grounds therefor, must set forth the relief or order sought, and at the same time a true copy must be served on all other parties, and must be noted on the docket.

(b) ***Service of Notice of Hearing.*** An application to the court for an order and notice of any hearing thereon, not presented during a hearing or trial, must be served upon all other parties not less than three days before the time specified for the hearing, unless otherwise provided by these rules or shortened by the court.

(c) ***Multiple Parties.*** If there is more than one other party represented by different attorneys, one copy of each pleading must be served on each attorney in charge.

(d) ***Certificate of Service.*** The party or attorney of record, must certify to the court compliance with this rule in writing over signature on the filed pleading, plea, motion, or application.

(e) ***Additional Copies.*** After one copy is served on a party, that party may obtain another copy of the same pleading upon tendering reasonable payment for copying and delivering.

(f) ***Electronic Filing.***

(1) *Requirement.* Except in juvenile cases under Title 3 of the Family Code and truancy cases under Title 3A of the Family Code, attorneys must electronically file documents in courts where electronic filing has been mandated. Attorneys practicing in courts where electronic filing is available but not mandated and unrepresented parties may electronically file documents, but it is not required.

(2) *Email address.* The email address of an attorney or unrepresented party who electronically files a document must be included on the document.

(3) *Mechanism.* Electronic filing must be done through the electronic filing manager established by the Office of Court Administration and an electronic filing service provider certified by the Office of Court Administration.

(4) *Exceptions.*

(A) Wills are not required to be filed electronically.

(B) The following documents must not be filed electronically:

(i) documents filed under seal or presented to the court in camera; and

(ii) documents to which access is otherwise restricted by law or court order.

(C) For good cause, a court may permit a party to file other documents in paper form in a particular case.

(5) *Timely filing.* Unless a document must be filed by a certain time of day, a document is considered timely filed if it is electronically filed at any time before midnight (in the court's time zone) on the filing deadline. An electronically filed document is deemed filed when transmitted to the filing party's electronic filing service provider, except:

(A) if a document is transmitted on a Saturday, Sunday, or legal holiday, it is deemed filed on the next day that is not a Saturday, Sunday, or legal holiday; and

(B) if a document requires a motion and an order allowing its filing, the document is deemed filed on the date that the motion is granted.

(6) *Technical failure.* If a document is untimely due to a technical failure or a system outage, the filing party may seek appropriate relief from the court. If the missed deadline is one imposed by these rules, the filing party must be given a reasonable extension of time to complete the filing.

(7) *Electronic signatures.* A document that is electronically served, filed, or issued by a court or clerk is considered signed if the document includes:

(A) a "/s/" and name typed in the space where the signature would otherwise appear, unless the document is notarized or sworn; or

(B) an electronic image or scanned image of the signature.

(8) *Format.* An electronically filed document must:

(A) be in text-searchable portable document format (PDF);

(B) be directly converted to PDF rather than scanned, if possible;

(C) not be locked; and

(D) otherwise comply with the Technology Standards set by the Judicial Committee on Information Technology and approved by the Supreme Court.

(9) *Paper copies.* Unless required by local rule, a party need not file a paper copy of an electronically filed document.

(10) *Electronic notices from the court.* The clerk may send notices, orders, or other communications about the case to the party electronically. A court seal may be electronic.

(11) *Non-conforming documents.* The clerk may not refuse to file a document that fails to conform with this rule. But the clerk may identify the error to be corrected and state a deadline for the party to resubmit the document in a conforming format.

(12) *Original wills.* When a party electronically files an application to probate a document as an original will, the original will must be filed with the clerk within three business days after the application is filed.

(13) *Official record.* The clerk may designate an electronically filed document or a scanned paper document as the official court record. The clerk is not required to keep both paper and electronic versions of the same document unless otherwise required by local rule. But the clerk must retain an original will filed for probate in a numbered file folder.

See also *O'Connor's Texas Rules*, "Rules of Pleading," ch. 1-B, p. 6; "Rules for Filing Documents," ch. 1-C, p. 28; "Rules for Serving Documents," ch. 1-D, p. 45; "Pretrial Motions," ch. 5, p. 369.

ANNOTATIONS

Jamar v. Patterson, 868 S.W.2d 318, 319 (Tex. 1993). "[T]he date of filing is when the document is first tendered to the clerk [even if no filing fee is paid]. The filing [of the motion for new trial] was completed ... when [D] paid the filing fee. *At 319 n.3:* The filing is not completed until the fee is paid, and absent emergency or other rare circumstances, the court should not consider it before then." *See also* ***Tate v. E.I. DuPont de Nemours & Co.***, 934 S.W.2d 83, 84 (Tex.1996).

Perkins v. City of San Antonio, 293 S.W.3d 650, 654-55 (Tex.App.—San Antonio 2009, no pet.). TRCP 21 "is inapplicable to a trial setting. [When] the trial court's hearing [is] dispositive of the merits of [the] underlying case, the hearing [is] effectively a trial setting [and should be governed by TRCP 245]."

Approximately $1,589.00 v. State, 230 S.W.3d 871, 873-74 (Tex.App.—Houston [14th Dist.] 2007, no pet.). "Rule 21 does not expressly require that a motion and notice of hearing be *filed* at least three days before hearing. However, Rule 21 expressly requires that a motion and notice of hearing be *served* on opposing parties at the time of filing. Therefore, Rule 21 effectively requires that a motion and notice of hearing be *filed* at least three days before hearing, unless otherwise provided by the [TRCPs] or shortened by the court."

TRCP 21a. METHODS OF SERVICE

(a) ***Methods of Service.*** Every notice required by these rules, and every pleading, plea, motion, or other form of request required to be served under Rule 21, other than the citation to be served upon the filing of a cause of action and except as otherwise expressly provided in these rules, may be served by delivering a copy to the party to be served, or the party's duly authorized agent or attorney of record in the manner specified below:

(1) *Documents filed electronically.* A document filed electronically under Rule 21 must be served elec-

tronically through the electronic filing manager if the email address of the party or attorney to be served is on file with the electronic filing manager. If the email address of the party or attorney to be served is not on file with the electronic filing manager, the document may be served on that party or attorney under subparagraph (2).

(2) *Documents not filed electronically.* A document not filed electronically may be served in person, by mail, by commercial delivery service, by fax, by email, or by such other manner as the court in its discretion may direct.

(b) ***When Complete.***

(1) Service by mail or commercial delivery service shall be complete upon deposit of the document, postpaid and properly addressed, in the mail or with a commercial delivery service.

(2) Service by fax is complete on receipt. Service completed after 5:00 p.m. local time of the recipient shall be deemed served on the following day.

(3) Electronic service is complete on transmission of the document to the serving party's electronic filing service provider. The electronic filing manager will send confirmation of service to the serving party.

(c) ***Time for Action After Service.*** Whenever a party has the right or is required to do some act within a prescribed period after the service of a notice or other paper upon him and the notice or paper is served upon him by mail, three days shall be added to the prescribed period.

(d) ***Who May Serve.*** Notice may be served by a party to the suit, an attorney of record, a sheriff or constable, or by any other person competent to testify.

(e) ***Proof of Service.*** The party or attorney of record shall certify to the court compliance with this rule in writing over signature and on the filed instrument. A certificate by a party or an attorney of record, or the return of the officer, or the affidavit of any other person showing service of a notice shall be prima facie evidence of the fact of service. Nothing herein shall preclude any party from offering proof that the document was not received, or, if service was by mail, that the document was not received within three days from the date that it was deposited in the mail, and upon so finding, the court may extend the time for taking the action required of such party or grant such other relief as it deems just.

(f) ***Procedures Cumulative.*** These provisions are cumulative of all other methods of service prescribed by these rules.

Caution: TRCP 21a is affected by Fam. Code §§6.4035 and 6.409.

See also *O'Connor's Texas Rules*, "Rules of Pleading," ch. 1-B, p. 6; "Rules for Filing Documents," ch. 1-C, p. 28; "Rules for Serving Documents," ch. 1-D, p. 45; *O'Connor's Texas Forms*, FORM 1B:13; *O'Connor's Texas Family Law Handbook* (2017), "Suit for Divorce," ch. 3-A, p. 205; "Suit to Dissolve Marriage with Children," ch. 4-D, p. 410; "Temporary Restraining Orders," ch. 5-B, p. 677; "Temporary Orders," ch. 5-D, p. 695; "Final Protective Orders," ch. 6-C, p. 735.

ANNOTATIONS

In re E.A., 287 S.W.3d 1, 4 (Tex.2009). "Nothing in the rules requires a plaintiff to serve a nonanswering defendant with new citation for a more onerous amended petition. While a nonanswering defendant must be served with a more onerous amended petition in order for a default judgment to stand, ... Rule 21a service satisfies that requirement. *At 6:* Service of new citation is no longer required."

Mathis v. Lockwood, 166 S.W.3d 743, 745 (Tex. 2005). "[N]otice properly sent pursuant to Rule 21a raises a presumption that notice was received. But we cannot presume that notice was properly sent; when that is challenged, it must be proved according to the rule. [¶] [T]he record contains no certificate of service, no return receipt from certified or registered mail, and no affidavit certifying service. Instead, the only evidence of service in the record was the oral assurance of counsel. As the rule's requirements are neither vague nor onerous, we decline to expand them this far." *See also* ***Thomas v. Ray***, 889 S.W.2d 237, 238-39 (Tex. 1994); ***L'Arte de la Mode, Inc. v. Neiman Marcus Grp.***, 395 S.W.3d 291, 295 (Tex.App.—Dallas 2013, no pet.).

Wembley Inv. v. Herrera, 11 S.W.3d 924, 928 (Tex. 1999). "[W]hen the sender of a document relies on office routine or custom to support an inference that the document was mailed, the sender must provide corroborating evidence that the practice was actually carried out. ... At best, [witness's] affidavit is only an 'opinion[] that the notice w[as] *probably* sent,' and does not controvert [D's] attorneys' affidavits attesting that the nonsuit motion was not received."

Lewis v. Blake, 876 S.W.2d 314, 315 (Tex.1994). "Rule 21a extends [the] minimum notice [of a hearing on a motion for summary judgment] by three days when the motion is served by mail. *At 316:* [The] hearing ... may be set as early as the 21st day after the motion is served, or the 24th day if the motion is served by mail."

Harrison v. Harrison, 363 S.W.3d 859, 860 (Tex. App.—Houston [14th Dist.] 2012, no pet.). Mother's "bill of review ... attacked the notice provided to her in proceedings that ultimately terminated her parental rights to her child.... *At 864:* Rule 21a specifies that notices be sent to the party's last known address, 'thus imposing a responsibility on the person to be notified to keep the court and parties apprised of their correct and current address.' *At 865:* [Mother] failed to apprise the court of continuing jurisdiction of her current address after her counsel's withdrawal. However, we find no case ... that such a failure, standing alone, supports dismissal of a bill of review on lack of notice where the petitioner avers no receipt of notice. Loss of the opportunity to contest a termination of parental rights is simply too steep a penalty for keeping a current address on file with a court in perpetuity."

Brown v. Ogbolu, 331 S.W.3d 530, 534 (Tex.App.—Dallas 2011, no pet.). "[P] argues the record shows the counterclaim was not served on him because [D] did not complete the blank for the day on the certificate of service. We disagree. [¶] [D] served the counterclaim under rule 21a and included a certificate of service. While it is normal—and better practice—to include the date and manner of service in the certificate of service, the text of the rule does not require either. We conclude the certificate of service on [D's] counterclaim sufficiently complied with the certification requirement to raise the presumption of service." *See also* ***Approximately $14,980.00 v. State***, 261 S.W.3d 182, 187 (Tex. App.—Houston [14th Dist.] 2008, no pet.).

Etheredge v. Hidden Valley Airpark Ass'n, 169 S.W.3d 378, 382 (Tex.App.—Fort Worth 2005, pet. denied). "[W]hen a party does not receive actual notice, if the serving party has complied with the requirements of Rule 21a, 'constructive notice' may be established if the serving party presents evidence that the intended recipient engaged in instances of selective acceptance or refusal of certified mail relating to the case, ... or that the intended recipient refused all deliveries of certified mail." *See also* ***Jacobs v. Jacobs***, 448 S.W.3d 626, 632 (Tex.App.—Houston [14th Dist.] 2014, no pet.).

TRCP 21b. SANCTIONS FOR FAILURE TO SERVE OR DELIVER COPY OF PLEADINGS & MOTIONS

If any party fails to serve on or deliver to the other parties a copy of any pleading, plea, motion, or other application to the court for an order in accordance with Rules 21 and 21a, the court may in its discretion, after notice and hearing, impose an appropriate sanction available under Rule 215-2b.[1]

1. **Editor's note:** Now TRCP 215.2(b).

See also *O'Connor's Texas Rules*, "Rules of Pleading," ch. 1-B, p. 6; "Rules for Filing Documents," ch. 1-C, p. 28; "Rules for Serving Documents," ch. 1-D, p. 45; "Motion for Sanctions," ch. 5-K, p. 439; ***O'Connor's Texas Forms***, FORMS 5K:3-5.

TRCP 21c. PRIVACY PROTECTION FOR FILED DOCUMENTS

(a) ***Sensitive Data Defined.*** Sensitive data consists of:

(1) a driver's license number, passport number, social security number, tax identification number, or similar government-issued personal identification number;

(2) a bank account number, credit card number, or other financial account number; and

(3) a birth date, home address, and the name of any person who was a minor when the underlying suit was filed.

(b) ***Filing of Documents Containing Sensitive Data Prohibited.*** Unless the inclusion of sensitive data is specifically required by a statute, court rule, or administrative regulation, an electronic or paper document, except for wills and documents filed under seal, containing sensitive data may not be filed with a court unless the sensitive data is redacted.

(c) ***Redaction of Sensitive Data; Retention Requirement.*** Sensitive data must be redacted by using the letter "X" in place of each omitted digit or character or by removing the sensitive data in a manner indicating that the data has been redacted. The filing party must retain an unredacted version of the filed document during the pendency of the case and any related appellate proceedings filed within six months of the date the judgment is signed.

(d) ***Notice to Clerk.*** If a document must contain sensitive data, the filing party must notify the clerk by:

(1) designating the document as containing sensitive data when the document is electronically filed; or

(2) if the document is not electronically filed, by including, on the upper left-hand side of the first page, the phrase: "NOTICE: THIS DOCUMENT CONTAINS SENSITIVE DATA."

(e) *Non-conforming Documents.* The clerk may not refuse to file a document that contains sensitive data in violation of this rule. But the clerk may identify the error to be corrected and state a deadline for the party to resubmit a redacted, substitute document.

(f) ***Restriction on Remote Access.*** Documents that contain sensitive data in violation of this rule must not be posted on the Internet.

See also *O'Connor's Texas Rules*, "Documents with sensitive data – privacy protection," ch. 1-C, §4.2, p. 34.

SECTION 2. INSTITUTION OF SUIT

TRCP 22. COMMENCED BY PETITION

A civil suit in the district or county court shall be commenced by a petition filed in the office of the clerk.

Caution: TRCP 22 is affected by Fam. Code §102.002.

See also *O'Connor's Texas Rules*, "Rules for Filing Documents," ch. 1-C, p. 28; "Plaintiff's Original Petition," ch. 2-B, p. 117; "Serving the Defendant with Suit," ch. 2-H, p. 184; *O'Connor's Texas Forms*, FORMS 2B.

TRCP 23. SUITS TO BE NUMBERED CONSECUTIVELY

It shall be the duty of the clerk to designate the suits by regular consecutive numbers, called file numbers, and he shall mark on each paper in every case the file number of the cause.

See also *O'Connor's Texas Rules*, "Rules for Filing Documents," ch. 1-C, p. 28.

TRCP 24. DUTY OF CLERK

When a petition is filed with the clerk he shall indorse thereon the file number, the day on which it was filed and the time of filing, and sign his name officially thereto.

See also TRCP 74; *O'Connor's Texas Rules*, "Rules for Filing Documents," ch. 1-C, p. 28.

ANNOTATIONS

Biffle v. Morton Rubber Indus., 785 S.W.2d 143, 144 (Tex.1990). "An instrument is deemed in law filed at the time it is delivered to the clerk, regardless of whether the instrument is filemarked."

TRCP 25. CLERK'S FILE DOCKET

Each clerk shall keep a file docket which shall show in convenient form the number of the suit, the names of the attorneys, the names of the parties to the suit, and the nature thereof, and, in brief form, the officer's return on the process, and all subsequent proceedings had in the case with the dates thereof.

See also *O'Connor's Texas Rules*, "Rules for Filing Documents," ch. 1-C, p. 28.

TRCP 26. CLERK'S COURT DOCKET

Each clerk shall also keep a court docket in a permanent record that shall include the number of the case and the names of parties, the names of the attorneys, the nature of the action, the pleas, the motions, and the ruling of the court as made.

See also *O'Connor's Texas Rules*, "Rules for Filing Documents," ch. 1-C, p. 28.

TRCP 27. ORDER OF CASES

The cases shall be placed on the docket as they are filed.

See also *O'Connor's Texas Rules*, "Rules for Filing Documents," ch. 1-C, p. 28.

SECTION 3. PARTIES TO SUITS

TRCP 28. SUITS IN ASSUMED NAME

Any partnership, unincorporated association, private corporation, or individual doing business under an assumed name may sue or be sued in its partnership, assumed or common name for the purpose of enforcing for or against it a substantive right, but on a motion by any party or on the court's own motion the true name may be substituted.

TRCP 29. SUIT ON CLAIM AGAINST DISSOLVED CORPORATION

When no receiver has been appointed for a corporation which has dissolved, suit may be instituted on any claim against said corporation as though the same had not been dissolved, and service of process may be obtained on the president, directors, general manager, trustee, assignee, or other person in charge of the affairs of the corporation at the time it was dissolved, and judgment may be rendered as though the corporation had not been dissolved.

See also BOC §11.356; TRCP 160.

TRCP 30. PARTIES TO SUITS

Assignors, endorsers and other parties not primarily liable upon any instruments named in the chapter of the Business and Commerce Code, dealing with commercial paper, may be jointly sued with their principal obligors, or may be sued alone in the cases provided for by statute.

See also *O'Connor's Texas Rules*, "Parties," ch. 2-B, §4, p. 118; *O'Connor's Texas Forms*, FORMS 2B:10-18.

ANNOTATIONS

Reed v. Buck, 370 S.W.2d 867, 872 (Tex.1963). "We hold that when a party signs a note in the capacity of a maker, the payee (or one standing in the shoes of a

payee) may sue such maker singly and proceed to judgment upon the note without joining in the suit another or others who may also appear upon the note as comakers."

TRCP 31. SURETY NOT TO BE SUED ALONE

No surety shall be sued unless his principal is joined with him, or unless a judgment has previously been rendered against his principal, except in cases otherwise provided for in the law and these rules.

See also CPRC §17.001; *O'Connor's Texas Rules*, "Secondary parties," ch. 2-E, §6.2.1(2), p. 158.

TRCP 32. MAY HAVE QUESTION OF SURETYSHIP TRIED

When any suit is brought against two or more defendants upon any contract, any one or more of the defendants being surety for the other, the surety may cause the question of suretyship to be tried and determined upon the issue made for the parties defendant at the trial of the cause, or at any time before or after the trial or at a subsequent term. Such proceedings shall not delay the suit of the plaintiff.

TRCP 33. SUITS BY OR AGAINST COUNTIES

Suits by or against a county or incorporated city, town or village shall be in its corporate name.

TRCP 34. AGAINST SHERIFF, ETC.

Whenever a sheriff, constable, or a deputy or either has been sued for damages for any act done in his official character, and has taken an indemnifying bond for the acts upon which the suit is based, he may make the principal and surety on such bond parties defendant in such suit, and the cause may be continued to obtain service on such parties.

TRCP 35. ON OFFICIAL BONDS

In suits brought by the State or any county, city, independent school district, irrigation district, or other political subdivision of the State, against any officer who has held an office for more than one term, or against any depository which has been such depository for more than one term, or has given more than one official bond, the sureties on each and all such bonds may be joined as defendants in the same suit whenever it is difficult to determine when the default sued for occurred and which set of sureties on such bonds is liable therefor.

TRCP 36. DIFFERENT OFFICIALS & BONDSMEN

In suits by the State upon the official bond of a State officer, any subordinate officer who has given bond, payable either to the State or such superior officer, to cover all or part of the default sued for, together with the sureties on his official bond, may be joined as defendants with such superior officer and his bondsmen whenever it is alleged in the petition that both of such officers are liable for the money sued for.

TRCP 37. ADDITIONAL PARTIES

Before a case is called for trial, additional parties, necessary or proper parties to the suit, may be brought in, either by the plaintiff or the defendant, upon such terms as the court may prescribe; but not at a time nor in a manner to unreasonably delay the trial of the case.

See also *O'Connor's Texas Rules*, "Parties & Claims," ch. 2-E, p. 154.

TRCP 38. THIRD-PARTY PRACTICE

(a) When defendant may bring in third party. At any time after commencement of the action a defending party, as a third-party plaintiff, may cause a citation and petition to be served upon a person not a party to the action who is or may be liable to him or to the plaintiff for all or part of the plaintiff's claim against him. The third-party plaintiff need not obtain leave to make the service if he files the third-party petition not later than thirty (30) days after he serves his original answer. Otherwise, he must obtain leave on motion upon notice to all parties to the action. The person served, hereinafter called the third-party defendant, shall make his defenses to the third-party plaintiff's claim under the rules applicable to the defendant, and his counterclaims against the third-party plaintiff and cross-claims against other third-party defendants as provided in Rule 97. The third-party defendant may assert against the plaintiff any defenses which the third-party plaintiff has to the plaintiff's claim. The third-party defendant may also assert any claim against the plaintiff arising out of the transaction or occurrence that is the subject matter of the plaintiff's claim against the third-party plaintiff. The plaintiff may assert any claim against the third-party defendant arising out of the transaction or occurrence that is the subject matter of the plaintiff's claim against the third-party plaintiff, and the third-party defendant thereupon shall assert his defenses and his counterclaims and cross-claims. Any party may move to strike the third-party claim, or for its severance or separate trial. A third-party defen-

dant may proceed under this rule against any person not a party to the action who is or who may be liable to him or to the third-party plaintiff for all or part of the claim made in the action against the third-party defendant.

(b) When plaintiff may bring in third party. When a counterclaim is asserted against a plaintiff, he may cause a third party to be brought in under circumstances which under this rule would entitle a defendant to do so.

(c) This rule shall not be applied, in tort cases, so as to permit the joinder of a liability or indemnity insurance company, unless such company is by statute or contract liable to the person injured or damaged.

(d) This rule shall not be applied so as to violate any venue statute, as venue would exist absent this rule.

See also CPRC §33.004 (responsible third parties); ***O'Connor's Texas Rules***, "Parties & Claims," ch. 2-E, p. 154; "The Answer—Denying Liability," ch. 3-E, p. 263.

TRCP 39. JOINDER OF PERSONS NEEDED FOR JUST ADJUDICATION

(a) Persons to be Joined if Feasible. A person who is subject to service of process shall be joined as a party in the action if (1) in his absence complete relief cannot be accorded among those already parties, or (2) he claims an interest relating to the subject of the action and is so situated that the disposition of the action in his absence may (i) as a practical matter impair or impede his ability to protect that interest or (ii) leave any of the persons already parties subject to a substantial risk of incurring double, multiple, or otherwise inconsistent obligations by reason of his claimed interest. If he has not been so joined, the court shall order that he be made a party. If he should join as a plaintiff but refuses to do so, he may be made a defendant, or, in a proper case, an involuntary plaintiff.

(b) Determination by Court Whenever Joinder Not Feasible. If a person as described in subdivision (a)(1)-(2) hereof cannot be made a party, the court shall determine whether in equity and good conscience the action should proceed among the parties before it, or should be dismissed, the absent person being thus regarded as indispensable. The factors to be considered by the court include: first, to what extent a judgment rendered in the person's absence might be prejudicial to him or those already parties; second, the extent to which, by protective provisions in the judgment, by the shaping of relief, or other measures, the prejudice can be lessened or avoided; third, whether a judgment rendered in the person's absence will be adequate; fourth, whether the plaintiff will have an adequate remedy if the action is dismissed for non-joinder.

(c) Pleading Reasons for Nonjoinder. A pleading asserting a claim for relief shall state the names, if known to the pleader, of any persons as described in subdivision (a)(1)-(2) hereof who are not joined, and the reasons why they are not joined.

(d) Exception of Class Actions. This rule is subject to the provisions of Rule 42.

Caution: TRCP 39 is affected by Fam. Code §§1.105 and 162.002.

See also TRCP 40, 41, 51, 174; ***O'Connor's Texas Rules***, "Plaintiff's Original Petition," ch. 2-B, p. 117; "Parties & Claims," ch. 2-E, p. 154; "The Answer—Denying Liability," ch. 3-E, p. 263; "Motion to Abate—Challenging the Suit," ch. 3-I, p. 299; "Motions for Severance & Separate Trials," ch. 5-I, p. 423.

ANNOTATIONS

Brooks v. Northglen Ass'n, 141 S.W.3d 158, 162 (Tex.2004). "Rule 39 determines whether a trial court has authority to proceed without joining a person whose presence in the litigation is made mandatory by the Declaratory Judgment Act. [¶] [N]othing in the rule precluded the trial court from rendering complete relief among [parties] who had sued for a declaration of rights. Although the parties continue to litigate its correctness, the trial court's judgment represents a final and complete adjudication of the dispute for the parties who were before the court."

Cooper v. Texas Gulf Indus., 513 S.W.2d 200, 204 (Tex.1974). "Under the provisions of our present Rule 39 it would be rare indeed if there were a person whose presence was so indispensable in the sense that his absence deprives the court of jurisdiction to adjudicate between the parties already joined." *See also* ***State Office of Risk Mgmt. v. Herrera***, 288 S.W.3d 543, 549 (Tex.App.—Amarillo 2009, no pet.) (City was indispensable).

Longoria v. Exxon Mobil Corp., 255 S.W.3d 174, 180 (Tex.App.—San Antonio 2008, pet. denied). "Although [TRCP 39] provides for joinder in mandatory terms, 'there is no arbitrary standard or precise formula for determining whether a particular person falls within its provision.' If the trial court determines an absent person falls within the provisions of the rule, the court has a duty to effect the person's joinder. If a person required to be joined under Rule 39(a) cannot be joined, the trial court must decide 'whether in equity

and in good conscience the action should proceed among the parties before it, or should be dismissed' by considering the factors listed in Rule 39(b)."

Griggs v. Latham, 98 S.W.3d 382, 385 (Tex.App.—Corpus Christi 2003, pet. denied). TRCP 39 "focuses not so much on whether the court has jurisdiction over the parties, but rather on whether the court ought to proceed with the parties before it. Generally, the trial court has broad discretion under the rules of civil procedure in questions regarding the joinder of parties, and its determination will not be disturbed on appeal except for abuse of discretion. Even under the rule regarding joinder of persons needed for just adjudication, there is 'no arbitrary standard or precise formula for determining whether a particular person falls within its provisions.' Cases involving joinder disputes must turn on an application of the particular facts involved."

TRCP 40. PERMISSIVE JOINDER OF PARTIES

(a) Permissive Joinder. All persons may join in one action as plaintiffs if they assert any right to relief jointly, severally, or in the alternative in respect of or arising out of the same transaction, occurrence, or series of transactions or occurrences and if any question of law or fact common to all of them will arise in the action. All persons may be joined in one action as defendants if there is asserted against them jointly, severally, or in the alternative any right to relief in respect of or arising out of the same transaction, occurrence, or series of transactions or occurrences and if any question of law or fact common to all of them will arise in the action. A plaintiff or defendant need not be interested in obtaining or defending against all the relief demanded. Judgment may be given for one or more of the plaintiffs according to their respective rights to relief, and against one or more defendants according to their respective liabilities.

(b) Separate Trials. The court may make such orders as will prevent a party from being embarrassed, delayed, or put to expense by the inclusion of a party against whom he asserts no claim and who asserts no claim against him, and may order separate trials or make other orders to prevent delay or prejudice.

Caution: TRCP 40 is affected by Fam. Code §1.105.

See also TRCP 39, 41, 51, 174; ***O'Connor's Texas Rules***, "Plaintiff's Original Petition," ch. 2-B, p. 117; "Parties & Claims," ch. 2-E, p. 154; "The Answer—Denying Liability," ch. 3-E, p. 263; "Motion to Abate—Challenging the Suit," ch. 3-I, p. 299; "Motions for Severance & Separate Trials," ch. 5-I, p. 423.

ANNOTATIONS

Landers v. East Tex. Salt Water Disposal Co., 248 S.W.2d 731, 734 (Tex.1952). "Where the tortious acts of two or more wrongdoers join to produce an indivisible injury, ... all of the wrongdoers will be held jointly and severally liable for the entire damages and the injured party may proceed to judgment against any one separately or against all in one suit. If fewer than the whole number of wrongdoers are joined as defendants ..., those joined may by proper cross action ... bring in those omitted."

TRCP 41. MISJOINDER & NON-JOINDER OF PARTIES

Misjoinder of parties is not ground for dismissal of an action. Parties may be dropped or added, or suits filed separately may be consolidated, or actions which have been improperly joined may be severed and each ground of recovery improperly joined may be docketed as a separate suit between the same parties, by order of the court on motion of any party or on its own initiative at any stage of the action, before the time of submission to the jury or to the court if trial is without a jury, on such terms as are just. Any claim against a party may be severed and proceeded with separately.

See also TRCP 39, 40, 51, 174; ***O'Connor's Texas Rules***, "Parties & Claims," ch. 2-E, p. 154; "The Answer—Denying Liability," ch. 3-E, p. 263.

ANNOTATIONS

F.F.P. Oper. Partners v. Duenez, 237 S.W.3d 680, 693 (Tex.2007). "'A claim is properly severable if (1) the controversy involves more than one cause of action, (2) the severed claim is one that would be the proper subject of a lawsuit if independently asserted, and (3) the severed claim is not so interwoven with the remaining action that they involve the same facts and issues.' [A]voiding prejudice, doing justice, and increasing convenience are the controlling reasons to allow a severance." *See also* ***Guaranty Fed. Sav. Bank v. Horseshoe Oper. Co.***, 793 S.W.2d 652, 658 (Tex.1990); ***In re A.C.***, No. 2-08-407-CV (Tex.App.—Fort Worth 2009, no pet.) (memo op.; 6-25-09).

State Dept. of Hwys. & Pub. Transp. v. Cotner, 845 S.W.2d 818, 819 (Tex.1993). TRCP 41 "does not 'permit a trial court to sever a case after it has been submitted to the trier of fact.' [¶] A partial new trial may be ordered notwithstanding the prohibition in Rule 41 against post-submission severances. [TRCP] 320 is thus an exception to Rule 41."

Nichols v. Nichols, 331 S.W.3d 800, 804 (Tex. App.—Fort Worth 2010, no pet.). "In contrast to [TRCP] 329b, [TRCP] 41 [does not require] that a severance be determined 'by *written* order.' Furthermore, unlike Rule 329b, which requires a motion for new trial to be granted in writing before the relevant time period expires, nothing in Rule 41 requires a severance order to be in writing and signed before the remaining case is submitted to the trier of fact. [¶] [S]ubmission of the remaining cause to the trier of fact does not prevent a severance because a properly severable cause of action, if not tried, may still be tried separately. There is no justification for treating a properly severable cause of action differently. [T]he controlling reason for severance is to do justice, avoid prejudice, and promote convenience, not to prevent the trial of potentially viable claims."

TRCP 42. CLASS ACTIONS

(a) Prerequisites to a Class Action. One or more members of a class may sue or be sued as representative parties on behalf of all only if (1) the class is so numerous that joinder of all members is impracticable, (2) there are questions of law or fact common to the class, (3) the claims or defenses of the representative parties are typical of the claims or defenses of the class, and (4) the representative parties will fairly and adequately protect the interests of the class.

(b) Class Actions Maintainable. An action may be maintained as a class action if the prerequisites of subdivision (a) are satisfied, and in addition:

(1) the prosecution of separate actions by or against individual members of the class would create a risk of

(A) inconsistent or varying adjudications with respect to individual members of the class which would establish incompatible standards of conduct for the party opposing the class, or

(B) adjudications with respect to individual members of the class which would as a practical matter be dispositive of the interests of the other members not parties to the adjudications or substantially impair or impede their ability to protect their interests; or

(2) the party opposing the class has acted or refused to act on grounds generally applicable to the class, thereby making appropriate final injunctive relief or corresponding declaratory relief with respect to the class as a whole; or

(3) the questions of law or fact common to the members of the class predominate over any questions affecting only individual members, and a class action is superior to other available methods for the fair and efficient adjudication of the controversy. The matters pertinent to these issues include:

(A) the interest of members of the class in individually controlling the prosecution or defense of separate actions;

(B) the extent and nature of any litigation concerning the controversy already commenced by or against members of the class;

(C) the desirability or undesirability of concentrating the litigation of the claims in the particular forum; and

(D) the difficulties likely to be encountered in the management of a class action.

(c) Determining by Order Whether to Certify a Class Action; Notice and Membership in Class.

(1)(A) When a person sues or is sued as a representative of a class, the court must—at an early practicable time—determine by order whether to certify the action as a class action.

(B) An order certifying a class action must define the class and the class claims, issues, or defenses, and must appoint class counsel under Rule 42(g).

(C) An order under Rule 42(c)(1) may be altered or amended before final judgment. The court may order the naming of additional parties in order to insure the adequacy of representation.

(D) An order granting or denying certification under Rule 42(b)(3) must state:

(i) the elements of each claim or defense asserted in the pleadings;

(ii) any issues of law or fact common to the class members;

(iii) any issues of law or fact affecting only individual class members;

(iv) the issues that will be the object of most of the efforts of the litigants and the court;

(v) other available methods of adjudication that exist for the controversy;

(vi) why the issues common to the members of the class do or do not predominate over individual issues;

(vii) why a class action is or is not superior to other available methods for the fair and efficient adjudication of the controversy; and

(viii) if a class is certified, how the class claims and any issues affecting only individual members, raised by the claims or defenses asserted in the pleadings, will be tried in a manageable, time efficient manner.

(2)(A) For any class certified under Rule 42(b)(1) or (2), the court may direct appropriate notice to the class.

(B) For any class certified under Rule 42(b)(3), the court must direct to class members the best notice practicable under the circumstances, including individual notice to all members who can be identified through reasonable effort. The notice must concisely and clearly state in plain, easily understood language:

(i) the nature of the action;

(ii) the definition of the class certified;

(iii) the class claims, issues, or defenses;

(iv) that a class member may enter an appearance through counsel if the member so desires;

(v) that the court will exclude from the class any member who requests exclusion, stating when and how members may elect to be excluded; and

(vi) the binding effect of a class judgment on class members under Rule 42(c)(3).

(3) The judgment in an action maintained as a class action under subdivision (b)(1) or (b)(2), whether or not favorable to the class, shall include and describe those whom the court finds to be members of the class. The judgment in an action maintained as a class action under subdivision (b)(3), whether or not favorable to the class, shall include and specify or describe those to whom the notice provided in subdivision (c)(2) was directed, and who have not requested exclusion, and whom the court finds to be members of the class.

(d) Actions Conducted Partially as Class Actions; Multiple Classes and Subclasses. When appropriate (1) an action may be brought or maintained as a class action with respect to particular issues, or (2) a class may be divided into subclasses and each subclass treated as a class, and the provisions of this rule shall then be construed and applied accordingly.

(e) Settlement, Dismissal, or Compromise.

(1)(A) The court must approve any settlement, dismissal, or compromise of the claims, issues, or defenses of a certified class.

(B) Notice of the material terms of the proposed settlement, dismissal or compromise, together with an explanation of when and how the members may elect to be excluded from the class, shall be given to all members in such manner as the court directs.

(C) The court may approve a settlement, dismissal, or compromise that would bind class members only after a hearing and on finding that the settlement, dismissal, or compromise is fair, reasonable, and adequate.

(2) The parties seeking approval of a settlement, dismissal, or compromise under Rule 42(e)(1) must file a statement identifying any agreement made in connection with the proposed settlement, dismissal, or compromise.

(3) In an action previously certified as a class action under Rule 42(b)(3), the court may not approve a settlement unless it affords a new opportunity to request exclusion to individual class members who had an earlier opportunity to request exclusion but did not do so.

(4)(A) Any class member may object to a proposed settlement, dismissal, or compromise that requires court approval under Rule 42(e)(1)(A).

(B) An objection made under Rule 42(e)(4)(A) may be withdrawn only with the court's approval.

(f) Discovery. Unnamed members of a class action are not to be considered as parties for purposes of discovery.

(g) Class Counsel.

(1) *Appointing Class Counsel.*

(A) Unless a statute provides otherwise, a court that certifies a class must appoint class counsel.

(B) An attorney appointed to serve as class counsel must fairly and adequately represent the interests of the class.

(C) In appointing class counsel, the court

(i) must consider:

- the work counsel has done in identifying or investigating potential claims in the action;
- counsel's experience in handling class actions, other complex litigation, and claims of the type asserted in the action;
- counsel's knowledge of the applicable law; and
- the resources counsel will commit to representing the class;

(ii) may consider any other matter pertinent to counsel's ability to fairly and adequately represent the interests of the class;

(iii) may direct potential class counsel to provide information on any subject pertinent to the appointment and to propose terms for attorney fees and nontaxable costs; and

(iv) may make further orders in connection with the appointment.

(2) *Appointment Procedure.*

(A) The court may designate interim counsel to act on behalf of the putative class before determining whether to certify the action as a class action.

(B) When there is one applicant for appointment as class counsel, the court may appoint that applicant only if the applicant is adequate under Rule 42(g)(1)(B) and (C). If more than one adequate applicant seeks appointment as class counsel, the court must appoint the applicant or applicants best able to represent the interests of the class.

(C) The order appointing class counsel may include provisions about the award of attorney fees or nontaxable costs under Rule 42(h) and (i).

(h) Procedure for Determining Attorney Fees Award. In an action certified as a class action, the court may award attorney fees in accordance with subdivision (i) and nontaxable costs authorized by law or by agreement of the parties as follows:

(1) *Motion for Award of Attorney Fees.* A claim for an award of attorney fees and nontaxable costs must be made by motion, subject to the provisions of this subdivision, at a time set by the court. Notice of the motion must be served on all parties and, for motions by class counsel, directed to class members in a reasonable manner.

(2) *Objections to Motion.* A class member, or a party from whom payment is sought, may object to the motion.

(3) *Hearing and Findings.* The court must hold a hearing in open court and must find the facts and state its conclusions of law on the motion. The court must state its findings and conclusions in writing or orally on the record.

(i) Attorney's Fees Award.

(1) In awarding attorney fees, the court must first determine a lodestar figure by multiplying the number of hours reasonably worked times a reasonable hourly rate. The attorney fees award must be in the range of 25% to 400% of the lodestar figure. In making these determinations, the court must consider the factors specified in Rule 1.04(b), Tex. Disciplinary R. Prof. Conduct.

(2) If any portion of the benefits recovered for the class are in the form of coupons or other noncash common benefits, the attorney fees awarded in the action must be in cash and noncash amounts in the same proportion as the recovery for the class.

(j) Effective Date. Rule 42(i) applies only in actions filed after September 1, 2003.

TRCP 43. INTERPLEADER

Persons having claims against the plaintiff may be joined as defendants and required to interplead when their claims are such that the plaintiff is or may be exposed to double or multiple liability. It is not ground for objection to the joinder that the claims of the several claimants or the titles on which their claims depend do not have a common origin or are not identical but are adverse to and independent of one another, or that the plaintiff avers that he is not liable in whole or in part to any or all of the claimants. A defendant exposed to similar liability may obtain such interpleader by way of cross-claim or counterclaim. The provisions of this rule supplement and do not in any way limit the joinder of parties permitted in any other rules.

See also *O'Connor's Texas Rules*, "Joining Parties or Claims," ch. 5-J, p. 431; *O'Connor's Texas Forms*, FORMS 5J:4-6.

TRCP 44. MAY APPEAR BY NEXT FRIEND

Minors, lunatics, idiots, or persons non compos mentis who have no legal guardian may sue and be represented by "next friend" under the following rules:

(1) Such next friend shall have the same rights concerning such suits as guardians have, but shall give security for costs, or affidavits in lieu thereof, when required.

(2) Such next friend or his attorney of record may with the approval of the court compromise suits and agree to judgments, and such judgments, agreements and compromises, when approved by the court, shall be forever binding and conclusive upon the party plaintiff in such suit.

See also TRCP 173; *O'Connor's Texas Rules*, "Guardian Ad Litem Under TRCP 173," ch. 1-I, p. 87; *O'Connor's Texas Forms*, FORMS 1I:1-3.

ANNOTATIONS

In re Bridgestone Americas Tire Opers., LLC, 459 S.W.3d 565, 570 (Tex.2015). "The significance of a minor's having a legal guardian in the context of Rule 44 is that, when a minor already has a guardian who may sue on his behalf, the minor does not need next-friend representation in order to litigate his claims. For Rule

44 to make sense, it must be construed to enable minors to prosecute their claims—through a next friend—when they otherwise could not through a legal guardian. It follows that, if a legal guardian has been appointed or recognized in another jurisdiction, but that guardian lacks authority to sue on the minor's behalf in Texas and has no legal basis for obtaining such authority, the minor may sue by next friend under Rule 44. *At 572:* [A] nonresident guardian of a nonresident ward with no connection to Texas beyond a possible lawsuit simply has no authority to sue on behalf of the ward in Texas in his capacity as guardian. [¶] Accordingly, in this case, although the children's grandparents are recognized as the children's guardians under the law of Nuevo Leon where they reside, they have no authority to sue in that capacity on the children's behalf in Texas. To avoid depriving the children of the ability to pursue their claims before they turn 18, Rule 44 allows them to do so by next friend."

American Gen. Fire & Cas. Co. v. Vandewater, 907 S.W.2d 491, 492-93 (Tex.1995). "[A]n appellate court should evaluate whether the minor's interests have been properly protected and whether a deficiency in notice or due process has been shown to determine whether a trial court has obtained personal jurisdiction over a minor. In this case, the answer of [mother] in her capacity as [minor's] next friend was sufficient indication that [minor's] legal representative knew about the proceedings and could therefore defend against them." *See also* ***Doe v. Texas Ass'n of Sch. Bds., Inc.***, 283 S.W.3d 451, 463 (Tex.App.—Fort Worth 2009, pet. denied).

Gracia v. RC Cola-7-Up Bottling Co., 667 S.W.2d 517, 519 (Tex.1984). "In a suit by a 'next friend,' the real party plaintiff is the child and not the next friend."

In re KC Greenhouse Patio Apts., LP, 445 S.W.3d 168, 172 (Tex.App.—Houston [1st Dist.] 2012, orig. proceeding). TRCP 44 "does not authorize a trial court to transfer [the right to represent a minor] from a minor's parent to a third party by unilaterally replacing the parent as the minor's 'next friend' when a conflict of interest arises. [¶] [TRCP] 173—not rule 44—is the rule that grants a trial court authority to address conflicts of interest, and it does so through the appointment of a guardian ad litem, not the replacement of the next friend. Neither rule 44 nor rule 173 permits another person to sue as next friend for a minor who has a legal guardian or permits a court to replace a legal guardian with another person to act as next friend for purposes of pursuing a lawsuit on behalf of a minor."

Saldarriaga v. Saldarriaga, 121 S.W.3d 493, 499 (Tex.App.—Austin 2003, no pet.). TRCP 44 "gives a next friend the same rights as a guardian, which necessarily include the ability to make any decision with respect to a lawsuit on behalf of the ward, including a settlement decision. We find it incongruous that a next friend would have the same *rights* as a guardian but not be bound by the same *procedure* for appointment. If there is no difference between the actions a next friend and a guardian may take, then there should correspondingly be no difference between the procedural safeguards that govern how, when, and under what circumstances a person may be appointed a next friend or a guardian based on the alleged incapacity of the proposed ward. *At 500:* [T]he district court did not have jurisdiction to consider a guardianship for [W]. 'In those counties in which there is a statutory probate court, all applications, petitions, and motions regarding guardianships, mental health matters, or other matters addressed by this chapter *shall be filed and heard in the statutory probate court*.' ... A district judge may not accomplish an unlawful end by merely calling a guardian a 'next friend.' If someone was going to act for [W] against her wishes in settling the long-pending divorce, it needed to be a guardian, properly appointed by the probate court after all due process had been afforded to her."

Massey v. Galvan, 822 S.W.2d 309, 319 (Tex. App.—Houston [14th Dist.] 1992, writ denied). TRCP 44 "clearly states that only when a minor has no legal guardian may that minor be represented by a next friend. [W]hen [appellant] contracted ... to represent the minors, the minors had a legal guardian, ... the natural mother. [T]he death of the managing conservator ends the conservatorship order and it no longer constitutes a valid subsisting order. [W]ithout an existing court order, conservatorship is vested in the natural parent to the exclusion of other interested parties. Thus, when ... the managing conservator died, conservatorship vested in ... the natural mother."

SECTION 4. PLEADING

A. GENERAL

TRCP 45. DEFINITION & SYSTEM

Pleadings in the district and county courts shall

(a) be by petition and answer;

(b) consist of a statement in plain and concise language of the plaintiff's cause of action or the defen-

dant's grounds of defense. That an allegation be evidentiary or be of legal conclusion shall not be grounds for an objection when fair notice to the opponent is given by the allegations as a whole; and

(c) contain any other matter which may be required by any law or rule authorizing or regulating any particular action or defense.

Pleadings that are not filed electronically must be in writing, on paper measuring approximately 8½ inches by 11 inches, and signed by the party or his attorney. The use of recycled paper is strongly encouraged.

All pleadings shall be construed so as to do substantial justice.

Caution: TRCP 45 is affected by Fam. Code §§6.401, 6.402, 102.008, and 161.101.

See also ***O'Connor's Texas Rules***, "Rules of Pleading," ch. 1-B, p. 6; "Rules for Filing Documents," ch. 1-C, p. 28; "Plaintiff's Original Petition," ch. 2-B, p. 117; "Special Exceptions—Challenging the Pleadings," ch. 3-G, p. 286; "Default Judgment," ch. 7-A, p. 671.

ANNOTATIONS

Paramount Pipe & Sup. Co. v. Muhr, 749 S.W.2d 491, 494-95 (Tex.1988). "The purpose of the fair notice requirement is to provide the opposing party with sufficient information to enable him to prepare a defense. [¶] Rule 45 does not require that the plaintiff set out in his pleadings the evidence upon which he relies to establish his asserted cause of action." *See also* ***Perez v. Briercroft Serv.***, 809 S.W.2d 216, 218 (Tex.1991); ***Roark v. Allen***, 633 S.W.2d 804, 810 (Tex.1982).

Coffey v. Johnson, 142 S.W.3d 414, 417 (Tex. App.—Eastland 2004, no pet.). TRCP 45 "requires that a petition give fair notice of the plaintiff's claims. The test of fair notice is whether an opposing attorney of reasonable competence, with the pleadings before him, can determine the nature of the controversy and the testimony that would probably be relevant. A court must be able, from an examination of the plaintiff's pleadings alone, to ascertain with reasonable certainty the elements of a cause of action and the relief sought with sufficient particularity…." *See also* ***Taylor v. Taylor***, 337 S.W.3d 398, 401 (Tex.App.—Fort Worth 2011, no pet.).

TRCP 46. PETITION & ANSWER; EACH ONE INSTRUMENT OF WRITING

The original petition, first supplemental petition, second supplemental petition, and every other, shall each be contained in one instrument of writing, and so with the original answer and each of the supplemental answers.

TRCP 47. CLAIMS FOR RELIEF

An original pleading which sets forth a claim for relief, whether an original petition, counterclaim, cross-claim, or third party claim, shall contain:

(a) a short statement of the cause of action sufficient to give fair notice of the claim involved;

(b) a statement that the damages sought are within the jurisdictional limits of the court;

(c) except in suits governed by the Family Code, a statement that the party seeks:

(1) only monetary relief of $100,000 or less, including damages of any kind, penalties, costs, expenses, pre-judgment interest, and attorney fees; or

(2) monetary relief of $100,000 or less and non-monetary relief; or

(3) monetary relief over $100,000 but not more than $200,000; or

(4) monetary relief over $200,000 but not more than $1,000,000; or

(5) monetary relief over $1,000,000; and

(d) a demand for judgment for all the other relief to which the party deems himself entitled.

Relief in the alternative or of several different types may be demanded; provided, further, that upon special exception the court shall require the pleader to amend so as to specify the maximum amount claimed. A party that fails to comply with (c) may not conduct discovery until the party's pleading is amended to comply.

Caution: TRCP 47 is affected by Fam. Code §§6.401, 6.402, 102.008, and 161.101.

See also ***O'Connor's Texas Rules***, "Rules of Pleading," ch. 1-B, p. 6; "Plaintiff's Original Petition," ch. 2-B, p. 117; "Special Exceptions—Challenging the Pleadings," ch. 3-G, p. 286; "Default Judgment," ch. 7-A, p. 671; ***O'Connor's Texas Forms***, FORMS 2B:1-8; ***O'Connor's Texas Family Law Handbook*** (2017), "Suit for Divorce," ch. 3-A, p. 205; "Suit to Dissolve Marriage with Children," ch. 4-D, p. 410; "Suit for Conservatorship," ch. 4-E, p. 469; "Temporary Orders," ch. 5-D, p. 695.

ANNOTATIONS

Boyles v. Kerr, 855 S.W.2d 593, 601 (Tex.1993). "A court should uphold the petition as to a cause of action that may be reasonably inferred from what is specifically stated, even if an element of the cause of action is not specifically alleged." *See also* ***Lone Star Air Sys. v. Powers***, 401 S.W.3d 855, 861 (Tex.App.—Houston [14th Dist.] 2013, no pet.); ***In re P.D.D.***, 256 S.W.3d 834, 839 (Tex.App.—Texarkana 2008, no pet.).

Maswoswe v. Nelson, 327 S.W.3d 889, 894 (Tex. App.—Beaumont 2010, no pet.). "A reviewing court should liberally construe the plaintiff's petition to as-

sert any claim that could reasonably be inferred from the specific language in the petition. However, 'a reviewing court cannot use a liberal construction of the petition as a license to read into the petition a claim that it does not contain.'"

In re Marriage of Richards, 991 S.W.2d 32, 35 (Tex.App.—Amarillo 1999, pet. dism'd). TRCP 47 "specifically applies to pleas seeking affirmative relief. It requires that such pleas shall contain a short statement of the cause of action sufficient to give fair notice of the claim involved. [¶] The legislature has elaborated on the requisites of a petition seeking the dissolution of a marriage. It has done this by enacting [Fam. Code] §6.402…."

TRCP 48. ALTERNATIVE CLAIMS FOR RELIEF

A party may set forth two or more statements of a claim or defense alternatively or hypothetically, either in one count or defense or in separate counts or defenses. When two or more statements are made in the alternative and one of them if made independently would be sufficient, the pleading is not made insufficient by the insufficiency of one or more of the alternative statements. A party may also state as many separate claims or defenses as he has regardless of consistency and whether based upon legal or equitable grounds or both.

See also *O'Connor's Texas Rules*, "Alternative claims or defenses," ch. 1-B, §3.2.10, p. 9.

ANNOTATIONS

Birchfield v. Texarkana Mem'l Hosp., 747 S.W.2d 361, 367 (Tex.1987). "[W]here the prevailing party fails to elect between alternative measures of damages, the court should utilize the findings affording the greater recovery and render judgment accordingly."

Household Credit Servs. v. Driscol, 989 S.W.2d 72, 80 (Tex.App.—El Paso 1998, pet. denied). "If a plaintiff pleads alternate theories of liability under Rule 48, a judgment that awards damages based upon more than one theory does not amount to a double recovery if the theories of liability arise from two separate and distinct injuries, and there has been a separate and distinct finding of damages on both theories of liability."

TRCP 49. WHERE SEVERAL COUNTS

Where there are several counts in the petition, and entire damages are given, the verdict or judgment, as the case may be, shall be good, notwithstanding one or more of such counts may be defective.

TRCP 50. PARAGRAPHS, SEPARATE STATEMENTS

All averments of claim or defense shall be made in numbered paragraphs, the contents of each of which shall be limited as far as practicable to a statement of a single set of circumstances; and a paragraph may be referred to by number in all succeeding pleadings, so long as the pleading containing such paragraph has not been superseded by an amendment as provided by Rule 65. Each claim founded upon a separate transaction or occurrence and each defense other than denials shall be stated in a separate count or defense whenever a separation facilitates the clear presentation of the matters set forth.

See also *O'Connor's Texas Rules*, "Rules of Pleading," ch. 1-B, p. 6; "Plaintiff's Original Petition," ch. 2-B, p. 117.

TRCP 51. JOINDER OF CLAIMS & REMEDIES

(a) Joinder of Claims. The plaintiff in his petition or in a reply setting forth a counterclaim and the defendant in an answer setting forth a counterclaim may join either as independent or as alternate claims as many claims either legal or equitable or both as he may have against an opposing party. There may be a like joinder of claims when there are multiple parties if the requirements of Rules 39, 40, and 43 are satisfied. There may be a like joinder of cross claims or third-party claims if the requirements of Rules 38 and 97, respectively, are satisfied.

(b) Joinder of Remedies. Whenever a claim is one heretofore cognizable only after another claim has been prosecuted to a conclusion, the two claims may be joined in a single action; but the court shall grant relief in that action only in accordance with the relative substantive rights of the parties. This rule shall not be applied in tort cases so as to permit the joinder of a liability or indemnity insurance company, unless such company is by statute or contract directly liable to the person injured or damaged.

Caution: TRCP 51 is affected by Fam. Code §§6.406, 102.001, and 157.003.

See also TRCP 39-41, 174; *O'Connor's Texas Family Law Handbook* (2017), "Filing SAPCR with dissolution suit," ch. 4-A, §3.3, p. 347.

TRCP 52. ALLEGING A CORPORATION

An allegation that a corporation is incorporated shall be taken as true, unless denied by the affidavit of the adverse party, his agent or attorney, whether such corporation is a public or private corporation and however created.

See also TRCP 93(6); *O'Connor's Texas Rules*, "The Answer—Denying Liability," ch. 3-E, p. 263; "Motion to Abate—Challenging the Suit," ch. 3-I, p. 299.

TRCP 53. SPECIAL ACT OR LAW

A pleading founded wholly or in part on any private or special act or law of this State or of the Republic of Texas need only recite the title thereof, the date of its approval, and set out in substance so much of such act or laws as may be pertinent to the cause of action or defense.

TRCP 54. CONDITIONS PRECEDENT

In pleading the performance or occurrence of conditions precedent, it shall be sufficient to aver generally that all conditions precedent have been performed or have occurred. When such performances or occurrences have been so plead, the party so pleading same shall be required to prove only such of them as are specifically denied by the opposite party.

See also *O'Connor's Texas Rules*, "Conditions Precedent," ch. 2-B, §12, p. 133; "Denial of conditions precedent," ch. 3-E, §6.1, p. 271; *O'Connor's Texas Forms*, FORMS 2B:1-8, 3E:1-11.

ANNOTATIONS

Associated Indem. Corp. v. CAT Contracting, Inc., 964 S.W.2d 276, 283 n.6 (Tex.1998). "Where a party avers generally that all conditions precedent have been performed or have occurred, he or she need only prove those that are specifically denied by the opposite party. This pleading rule, however, does not shift the burden of proof on those conditions which the opposite party denies."

TRCP 55. JUDGMENT

In pleading a judgment or decision of a domestic or foreign court, judicial or quasi-judicial tribunal, or of a board or officer, it shall be sufficient to aver the judgment or decision without setting forth matter showing jurisdiction to render it.

See also CPRC ch. 36A.

TRCP 56. SPECIAL DAMAGE

When items of special damage are claimed, they shall be specifically stated.

See also *O'Connor's Texas Rules*, "Special damages," ch. 2-B, §9.2.1(2), p. 132.

ANNOTATIONS

Arthur Andersen & Co. v. Perry Equip. Corp., 945 S.W.2d 812, 816 (Tex.1997). Special damages are also known as consequential damages. "Consequential damages ... result naturally, but not necessarily, from the defendant's wrongful acts." *See also* ***Archer v. DDK Holdings LLC***, 463 S.W.3d 597, 608-09 (Tex.App.—Houston [14th Dist.] 2015, no pet.).

TRCP 57. SIGNING OF PLEADINGS

Every pleading of a party represented by an attorney shall be signed by at least one attorney of record in his individual name, with his State Bar of Texas identification number, address, telephone number, email address, and if available, fax number. A party not represented by an attorney shall sign his pleadings, state his address, telephone number, email address, and, if available, fax number.

See also TRCP 191.3; *O'Connor's Texas Rules*, "Rules of Pleading," ch. 1-B, p. 6; "Plaintiff's Original Petition," ch. 2-B, p. 117; *O'Connor's Texas Forms*, FORM 1B:3.

ANNOTATIONS

W.C. Turnbow Pet. Co. v. Fulton, 194 S.W.2d 256, 257 (Tex.1946). "Counsel should sign their names to motions and pleadings 'to make themselves responsible for what is stated in them, and so as to leave no doubt as to the parties for whom they appear.' But ... the signature to a pleading is a formal requisite and ... failure to comply with the requirement is not fatal to the pleading."

TRCP 58. ADOPTION BY REFERENCE

Statements in a pleading may be adopted by reference in a different part of the same pleading or in another pleading or in any motion, so long as the pleading containing such statements has not been superseded by an amendment as provided by Rule 65.

See also *O'Connor's Texas Rules*, "Rules of Pleading," ch. 1-B, p. 6.

ANNOTATIONS

Fawcett v. Grosu, 498 S.W.3d 650, 659 (Tex.App.—Houston [14th Dist.] 2016, pet. filed 8-22-16). "[P] filed a second amended petition; hence, his original petition and exhibits A-E attached thereto[ ] were superseded. In his second amended petition, however, [P] incorporates by reference exhibits A-E of his original petition. This was improper under [TRCP] 58.... [Ds], however, did not file special exceptions, as is required by [TRCP] 90, to [P's] pleading defect. While we agree that the incorporation by reference was improper, we cannot agree that it precluded consideration of exhibits attached to the original petition and incorporated without objection into the second petition. [Ds'] failure to specifically except to [P's] pleading defects in writing

waived such defect. We therefore consider the exhibits as part of our analysis."

TRCP 59. EXHIBITS & PLEADING

Notes, accounts, bonds, mortgages, records, and all other written instruments, constituting, in whole or in part, the claim sued on, or the matter set up in defense, may be made a part of the pleadings by copies thereof, or the originals, being attached or filed and referred to as such, or by copying the same in the body of the pleading in aid and explanation of the allegations in the petition or answer made in reference to said instruments and shall be deemed a part thereof for all purposes. Such pleadings shall not be deemed defective because of the lack of any allegations which can be supplied from said exhibit. No other instrument of writing shall be made an exhibit in the pleading.

TRCP 60. INTERVENOR'S PLEADINGS

Any party may intervene by filing a pleading, subject to being stricken out by the court for sufficient cause on the motion of any party.

Caution: TRCP 60 is affected by Fam. Code §102.004.

See also ***O'Connor's Texas Rules***, "Joining Parties or Claims," ch. 5-J, p. 431; ***O'Connor's Texas Forms***, FORMS 5J:1-3; ***O'Connor's Texas Family Law Handbook*** (2017), "Intervenors," ch. 3-A, §10, p. 243 (suit for divorce); "Intervenors," ch. 4-D, §7, p. 423 (suit to dissolve marriage with children); "Intervenors," ch. 9-D, §8, p. 1050 (suit to modify child support).

ANNOTATIONS

In re Union Carbide Corp., 273 S.W.3d 152, 154-55 (Tex.2008). "Because intervention is allowed as a matter of right, the 'justiciable interest' requirement is of paramount importance: it defines the category of nonparties who may, without consultation with or permission from the original parties or the court, interject their interests into a pending suit to which the intervenors have not been invited. ... If any party to the pending suit moves to strike the intervention, the intervenors have the burden to show a justiciable interest in the pending suit. [¶] To constitute a justiciable interest, '[t]he intervenor's interest must be such that if the original action had never been commenced, and he had first brought it as the sole plaintiff, he would have been entitled to recover in his own name to the extent at least of a part of the relief sought' in the original suit."

Texas Mut. Ins. v. Ledbetter, 251 S.W.3d 31, 36 (Tex.2008). "There is no deadline for intervention in the [TRCPs]. Generally one cannot intervene after final judgment. But when a subrogee's interest has been adequately represented and then suddenly abandoned by someone else, it can intervene even after judgment or on appeal so long as there is neither unnecessary delay nor prejudice to the existing parties." *See also* ***State v. Naylor***, 466 S.W.3d 783, 788 (Tex.2015) (petition in intervention filed after judgment may not be considered until judgment is set aside).

Baker v. Monsanto Co., 111 S.W.3d 158, 160 (Tex. 2003). "Typically, an intervention involves a claim against persons who have already appeared. Under these circumstances, the plea in intervention is properly served by any of the methods provided in [TRCP] 21a. However, absent a subsequent appearance, service of citation is necessary against an original defendant when the intervenor seeks affirmative relief against a defendant who has not appeared at the time the intervention was filed. [¶] [I]ntervenors are required to serve citation on a defendant when that defendant fails to appear and answer the plaintiff's petition. [A]n intervenor must serve citation on any third-party defendant it seeks to bring into the suit. And if the intervenor's claim is against the plaintiff, it must serve citation on the plaintiff, if the plaintiff does not make any further appearance in the case after the intervention."

Guaranty Fed. Sav. Bank v. Horseshoe Oper. Co., 793 S.W.2d 652, 657 (Tex.1990). "An intervenor is not required to secure the court's permission to intervene; the party who opposed the intervention has the burden to challenge it by a motion to strike. [¶] [I]t is an abuse of discretion to strike a plea in intervention if (1) the intervenor meets [the requirements of the rule], (2) the intervention will not complicate the case by an excessive multiplication of the issues, and (3) the intervention is almost essential to effectively protect the intervenor's interest."

Quiroz v. Gray, 441 S.W.3d 588, 594 (Tex.App.—El Paso 2014, no pet.). "To intervene successfully, a party must generally show that he has standing to maintain an original suit. However, a party need not make such a showing in a [SAPCR]. To intervene successfully in a SAPCR, a party only needs to demonstrate sufficient interest in the child the subject of the suit even if he cannot institute an original SAPCR in his own right. '[T]his relaxed standing rule promotes the overriding policy in all SAPCR suits, that of protecting the best interest of the child.' [¶] That said, intervention in a SAPCR is appropriate only upon a proper factual showing. In determining whether the party has met that burden, the trial court should consider the factual allega-

tions in the motion to intervene on which the right to intervene is predicated and those set forth in the pleadings of the other parties. The trial court should also consider any evidence on the issue adduced by the parties. Moreover, a party seeking to intervene in a SAPCR must do so in a timely manner. If a party fails to intervene timely and offers no evidence to justify the late intervention, the trial court will not be held to have abused its discretion in striking the intervention."

TRCP 61. TRIAL: INTERVENORS: RULES APPLY TO ALL PARTIES

These rules of pleading shall apply equally, so far as it may be practicable to intervenors and to parties, when more than one, who may plead separately.

TRCP 62. AMENDMENT DEFINED

The object of an amendment, as contra-distinguished from a supplemental petition or answer, is to add something to, or withdraw something from, that which has been previously pleaded so as to perfect that which is or may be deficient, or to correct that which has been incorrectly stated by the party making the amendment, or to plead new matter, additional to that formerly pleaded by the amending party, which constitutes an additional claim or defense permissible to the suit.

TRCP 63. AMENDMENTS & RESPONSIVE PLEADINGS

Parties may amend their pleadings, respond to pleadings on file of other parties, file suggestions of death and make representative parties, and file such other pleas as they may desire by filing such pleas with the clerk at such time as not to operate as a surprise to the opposite party; provided, that any pleadings, responses or pleas offered for filing within seven days of the date of trial or thereafter, or after such time as may be ordered by the judge under Rule 166, shall be filed only after leave of the judge is obtained, which leave shall be granted by the judge unless there is a showing that such filing will operate as a surprise to the opposite party.

See also *O'Connor's Texas Rules*, "Motion to Amend Pleadings—Pretrial," ch. 5-F, p. 409; "Motion to Amend Pleadings—Trial & Post-trial," ch. 8-F, p. 815; *O'Connor's Texas Forms*, FORMS 5F, 8F.

ANNOTATIONS

Kelly v. General Interior Constr., Inc., 301 S.W.3d 653, 659 (Tex.2010). "When the pleading is wholly devoid of jurisdictional facts, the plaintiff should amend the pleading to include the necessary factual allegations, ... allowing jurisdiction to be decided based on evidence rather than allegations, as it should be."

Chapin & Chapin, Inc. v. Texas Sand & Gravel Co., 844 S.W.2d 664, 665 (Tex.1992). Under TRCP 63 and 66, "'a trial court has no discretion to refuse an amendment unless: (1) the opposing party presents evidence of surprise or prejudice ...; or (2) the amendment asserts a new cause of action or defense, and thus is prejudicial on its face....' [¶] [W]e conclude that the trial court's refusal to allow [D] to verify its denial [less than seven days before trial] was an abuse of discretion." *See also* ***Greenhalgh v. Service Lloyds Ins.***, 787 S.W.2d 938, 940 (Tex.1990).

Goswami v. Metropolitan S&L Ass'n, 751 S.W.2d 487, 490 (Tex.1988). "[I]n the absence of a sufficient showing of surprise by the opposing party, the failure to obtain leave of court when filing a late pleading may be cured by the trial court's action in considering the amended pleading. [¶] A summary judgment proceeding is a trial within the meaning of Rule 63." *See also* ***John C. Flood of DC, Inc. v. SuperMedia, L.L.C.***, 408 S.W.3d 645, 653-54 (Tex.App.—Dallas 2013, pet. denied).

Halmos v. Bombardier Aerospace Corp., 314 S.W.3d 606, 623 (Tex.App.—Dallas 2010, no pet.). "An amendment that is prejudicial on its face has three defining characteristics: (1) it asserts a new substantive matter that reshapes the nature of trial itself; (2) the opposing party could not have anticipated the new matter in light of the development of the case up to the time the amendment was requested; and (3) the amendment would detrimentally affect the opposing party's presentation of its case." *See also* ***Thomas v. Graham Mortg. Corp.***, 408 S.W.3d 581, 593 (Tex.App.—Austin 2013, pet. denied).

TRCP 64. AMENDED INSTRUMENT

The party amending shall point out the instrument amended, as "original petition," or "plaintiff's first supplemental petition," or as "original answer," or "defendant's first supplemental answer" or other instrument filed by the party and shall amend by filing a substitute therefor, entire and complete in itself, indorsed "amended original petition," or "amended first supplemental petition," or "amended original answer," or "amended first supplemental answer," accordingly as said instruments of pleading are designated.

TRCP 65. SUBSTITUTED INSTRUMENT TAKES PLACE OF ORIGINAL

Unless the substituted instrument shall be set aside on exceptions, the instrument for which it is substituted shall no longer be regarded as a part of the pleading in the record of the cause, unless some error of the court in deciding upon the necessity of the amendment, or otherwise in superseding it, be complained of, and exception be taken to the action of the court, or unless it be necessary to look to the superseded pleading upon a question of limitation.

See also *O'Connor's Texas Rules*, "Amended pleadings," ch. 1-B, §3.7.1(1), p. 23; "Nonsuit by amendment," ch. 7-F, §2.8.1, p. 740.

ANNOTATIONS

FKM Prtshp. v. Board of Regents of the Univ. of Houston Sys., 255 S.W.3d 619, 633 (Tex.2008). "[A]mended pleadings and their contents take the place of prior pleadings. So, causes of action not contained in amended pleadings are effectively dismissed at the time the amended pleading is filed…." *See also* ***Deadmon v. DART***, 347 S.W.3d 442, 444 (Tex.App.—Dallas 2011, no pet.) (omitting parties' names from amended pleading dismisses them as effectively as entry of formal order of dismissal); ***Kothmann v. F. Vosburg Hall & Marylou Hall Children's Crisis Found.***, No. 03-09-00081-CV (Tex.App.—Austin 2010, no pet.) (memo op.; 7-15-10) (footnote 3) (omitted claims are withdrawn even if summary judgment was already granted on those claims).

AAMCO Transmissions, Inc. v. Bova, 484 S.W.3d 520, 523 (Tex.App.—Houston [1st Dist.] 2016, no pet.). "Service of an amended petition on a party that has not appeared is necessary only when a plaintiff seeks a more onerous judgment than prayed for in the original pleading. [¶] A judgment is more onerous if it exposes the defendant to increased liability. Increases in potential liability may result, for example, from the addition of new causes of action, inclusion of new elements of damages, or an increase in the amount of damages previously pleaded." (Internal quotes omitted.)

TRCP 66. TRIAL AMENDMENT

If evidence is objected to at the trial on the ground that it is not within the issues made by the pleading, or if during the trial any defect, fault or omission in a pleading, either of form or substance, is called to the attention of the court, the court may allow the pleadings to be amended and shall do so freely when the presentation of the merits of the action will be subserved thereby and the objecting party fails to satisfy the court that the allowance of such amendment would prejudice him in maintaining his action or defense upon the merits. The court may grant a postponement to enable the objecting party to meet such evidence.

See also *O'Connor's Texas Rules*, "Motion to Amend Pleadings—Trial & Post-trial," ch. 8-F, p. 815; *O'Connor's Texas Forms*, FORMS 8F.

ANNOTATIONS

City of Fort Worth v. Zimlich, 29 S.W.3d 62, 73 (Tex.2000). "A trial amendment must be filed as a written pleading; an oral statement at trial is insufficient to modify the pleadings. However, a party waives its complaint of any defect, omission, or fault in the pleadings if the party fails to specifically object before the submission of the charge to the jury."

State Bar v. Kilpatrick, 874 S.W.2d 656, 658 (Tex. 1994). "A court may not refuse a trial amendment unless (1) the opposing party presents evidence of surprise or prejudice, or (2) the amendment asserts a new cause of action or defense, and thus is prejudicial on its face. The burden of showing surprise or prejudice rests on the party resisting the amendment." *See also* ***Greenhalgh v. Service Lloyds Ins.***, 787 S.W.2d 938, 941 (Tex. 1990); ***CA Partners v. Spears***, 274 S.W.3d 51, 70 (Tex. App.—Houston [14th Dist.] 2008, pet. denied).

Deutsch v. Hoover, Bax & Slovacek, L.L.P., 97 S.W.3d 179, 185-86 (Tex.App.—Houston [14th Dist.] 2002, no pet.). TRCP 66 "suggests a postponement may cure any prejudice from a trial amendment. [N]othing in the rule [suggests] an offer of a mistrial does so, especially when the trial is virtually completed. A party seeking leave to amend its pleadings after the trial has commenced should not be rewarded by forcing the judge, jury, and opposing party to either acquiesce in the tardy amendment or start over. [T]he mistrial was the trial court's suggestion…. [D's] decision to refuse the trial court's offer … did not amount to a relinquishment of his objection [to the trial amendment]."

TRCP 67. AMENDMENTS TO CONFORM TO ISSUES TRIED WITHOUT OBJECTION

When issues not raised by the pleadings are tried by express or implied consent of the parties, they shall be treated in all respects as if they had been raised in the pleadings. In such case such amendment of the pleadings as may be necessary to cause them to conform to the evidence and to raise these issues may be made by

leave of court upon motion of any party at any time up to the submission of the case to the Court or jury, but failure so to amend shall not affect the result of the trial of these issues; provided that written pleadings, before the time of submission, shall be necessary to the submission of questions, as is provided in Rules 277 and 279.

See also *O'Connor's Texas Rules*, "TRCP 67," ch. 8-F, §2.4.2, p. 817.

ANNOTATIONS

Bedgood v. Madalin, 600 S.W.2d 773, 775-76 (Tex. 1980). "Rule 67 ... requires that written pleadings, before the time of submission, shall be necessary to the submission of special issues even where issues are tried by implied consent. Since there were no proper pleadings, the trial court erred in overruling [Ds'] objections to the introduction of evidence and the submission of special issues...."

Oil Field Haulers Ass'n v. Railroad Comm'n, 381 S.W.2d 183, 191 (Tex.1964). "[A] plaintiff may not sustain a favorable judgment on an unpleaded cause of action[] in the absence of trial by consent...." *See also* ***Huff Energy Fund, L.P. v. Longview Energy Co.***, 482 S.W.3d 184, 194 (Tex.App.—San Antonio 2015) (objection to submission of jury question on unpleaded issue prevents trial of that issue by implied consent), *aff'd*, ___ S.W.3d ___ (Tex.2017) (No. 15-0968, 6-9-17).

Case Corp. v. Hi-Class Bus. Sys., 184 S.W.3d 760, 771 (Tex.App.—Dallas 2005, pet. denied). "To determine whether an issue was tried by consent, the trial court examines the record not for evidence of the issue, but rather for evidence of trial of the issue. A party's unpleaded issue may be deemed tried by consent when evidence on the issue is developed under circumstances indicating both parties understood the issue was in the case, and the other party failed to make an appropriate complaint. On the other hand, trial by consent is inapplicable when evidence relevant to an unpleaded matter is also relevant to a pleaded issue; in that case admission of the evidence would not be calculated to elicit an objection ..., and its admission ordinarily would not demonstrate a 'clear intent' on the part of all parties to try the unpleaded issue." *See also* ***Gamboa v. Gamboa***, 383 S.W.3d 263, 271 (Tex.App.—San Antonio 2012, no pet.); ***In re A.B.H.***, 266 S.W.3d 596, 600 (Tex.App.—Fort Worth 2008, no pet.).

TRCP 68. COURT MAY ORDER REPLEADER

The court, when deemed necessary in any case, may order a repleader on the part of one or both of the parties, in order to make their pleadings substantially conform to the rules.

Caution: TRCP 68 is affected by Fam. Code §102.001.

ANNOTATIONS

Miller v. Kossey, 802 S.W.2d 873, 877 (Tex.App.—Amarillo 1991, writ denied). "[W]hen [P] failed to comply with the court's ... order to send a new notice establishing a necessary element of her cause of action, the court was authorized to dismiss her DTPA action. Consequently, the court did not err in dismissing the action."

TRCP 69. SUPPLEMENTAL PETITION OR ANSWER

Each supplemental petition or answer, made by either party, shall be a response to the last preceding pleading by the other party, and shall not repeat allegations formerly pleaded further than is necessary as an introduction to that which is stated in the pleading then being drawn up. These instruments, to wit, the original petition and its several supplements, and the original answer and its several supplements, shall respectively, constitute separate and distinct parts of the pleadings of each party; and the position and identity, by number and name, with the indorsement of each instrument, shall be preserved throughout the pleadings of either party.

TRCP 70. PLEADING: SURPRISE: COST

When either a supplemental or amended pleading is of such character and is presented at such time as to take the opposite party by surprise, the court may charge the continuance of the cause, if granted, to the party causing the surprise if the other party satisfactorily shows that he is not ready for trial because of the allowance of the filing of such supplemental or amended pleading, and the court may, in such event, in its discretion require the party filing such pleading to pay to the surprised party the amount of reasonable costs and expenses incurred by the other party as a result of the continuance, including attorney fees, or make such other order with respect thereto as may be just.

See also *O'Connor's Texas Rules*, "Motion for Continuance," ch. 5-D, p. 394; "Motion to Amend Pleadings—Pretrial," ch. 5-F, p. 409; "Motion to Amend Pleadings—Trial & Post-trial," ch. 8-F, p. 815; ***O'Connor's Texas Forms***, FORMS 5F, 8F.

TRCP 71. MISNOMER OF PLEADING

When a party has mistakenly designated any plea or pleading, the court, if justice so requires, shall treat the plea or pleading as if it had been properly designated.

Pleadings shall be docketed as originally designated and shall remain identified as designated, unless the court orders redesignation. Upon court order filed with the clerk, the clerk shall modify the docket and all other clerk records to reflect redesignation.

See also *O'Connor's Texas Rules*, "Misnomer," ch. 2-B, §4.3.1(2)(a), p. 122.

ANNOTATIONS

In re J.Z.P., 484 S.W.3d 924, 925 (Tex.2016). "We have stressed that 'courts should acknowledge the substance of the relief sought despite the formal styling of the pleading.' [Mother's] motion plainly requested relief from the trial court's order on the grounds that she had not been served with citation and had not learned of the trial court's order until a few days before her motion was filed. Her motion stated that her attorney of record was given no notice of [father's] modification petition, and court records reflected that notice of the order was sent only to [father] and his attorney. It is a fair inference that [mother's] counsel learned of the order no earlier than [mother] did. Justice plainly required the trial court and court of appeals to treat [mother's] motion as extending post-judgment deadlines. Neither court explained its refusal to do so, [father] has not offered any reason not to do so, and we are unable to discern one. Based on the motion and [father's] response, [mother] was entitled to an extension of the time for appeal. Her notice of appeal was timely filed." *See also* ***Riner v. City of Hunters Creek***, 403 S.W.3d 919, 921-22 (Tex.App.—Houston [14th Dist.] 2013, no pet.) (D specially excepted to P's petition on ground that it failed to establish subject-matter jurisdiction; court disregarded misnomer and treated challenge as plea to the jurisdiction instead of special exception).

TRCP 72, 73. REPEALED

TRCP 74. FILING WITH THE COURT DEFINED

The filing of pleadings, other papers and exhibits as required by these rules shall be made by filing them with the clerk of the court, except that the judge may permit the papers to be filed with him, in which event he shall note thereon the filing date and time and forthwith transmit them to the office of the clerk.

See also TRCP 24; *O'Connor's Texas Rules*, "Rules for Filing Documents," ch. 1-C, p. 28.

ANNOTATIONS

Miller Brewing Co. v. Villarreal, 829 S.W.2d 770, 771 (Tex.1992). "Under our current rules, a party who finds the courthouse closed on the last day that a document must be filed … may also locate the clerk or judge of the court and file the document with them."

Standard Fire Ins. v. LaCoke, 585 S.W.2d 678, 680 (Tex.1979). "The rule is traditionally stated to be that an instrument is deemed in law filed at the time it is left with the clerk, regardless of whether or not a file mark is placed on the instrument and regardless of whether the file mark gives some other date of filing." *See also* ***Pipkin v. Kroger Tex., L.P.***, 383 S.W.3d 655, 663-64 (Tex.App.—Houston [14th Dist.] 2012, pet. denied) (despite court order making e-filing mandatory, hard copy of affidavit was filed when left with clerk because court cannot contradict Texas law on when document is deemed filed).

TRCP 75. FILED PLEADINGS; WITHDRAWAL

All filed pleadings shall remain at all times in the clerk's office or in the court or in custody of the clerk, except that the court may by order entered on the minutes allow a filed pleading to be withdrawn for a limited time whenever necessary, on leaving a certified copy on file. The party withdrawing such pleading shall pay the costs of such order and certified copy.

ANNOTATIONS

Trinity Indus. v. Rivera, 745 S.W.2d 525, 526 (Tex. App.—Corpus Christi 1988, no writ). A party cannot terminate a suit by withdrawing its pleadings. "Under [the TRCPs], a final order terminating a lawsuit may be accomplished by a judgment on the merits, a dismissal or a non-suit."

TRCP 75a. FILING EXHIBITS: COURT REPORTER TO FILE WITH CLERK

The court reporter or stenographer shall file with the clerk of the court all exhibits which were admitted in evidence or tendered on bill of exception during the course of any hearing, proceeding, or trial.

See also TRAP 13.1(b), (c).

TRCP 75b. FILED EXHIBITS: WITHDRAWAL

All filed exhibits admitted in evidence or tendered on bill of exception shall, until returned or otherwise disposed of as authorized by Rule 14b, remain at all times in the clerk's office or in the court or in the custody of the clerk except as follows:

(a) The court may by order entered on the minutes allow a filed exhibit to be withdrawn by any party only

upon such party's leaving on file a certified, photo, or other reproduced copy of such exhibit. The party withdrawing such exhibit shall pay the costs of such order and copy.

(b) The court reporter or stenographer of the court conducting the hearing, proceedings, or trial in which exhibits are admitted or offered in evidence, shall have the right to withdraw filed exhibits, upon giving the clerk proper receipt therefor, whenever necessary for the court reporter or stenographer to transmit such original exhibits to an appellate court under the provisions of Rule 379 or to otherwise discharge the duties imposed by law upon said court reporter or stenographer.

ANNOTATIONS

Perez v. Bagous, 833 S.W.2d 671, 674 (Tex.App.—Corpus Christi 1992, no writ). "Once a party has admitted an exhibit into evidence at trial, the exhibit may not be retrieved and used to create another during a jury recess without notifying opposing counsel or the court. It is wholly outside the scope of the rule to then enter this newly created exhibit into evidence without informing opposing counsel of the use of the entered exhibit."

TRCP 76. MAY INSPECT PAPERS

Each attorney at law practicing in any court shall be allowed at all reasonable times to inspect the papers and records relating to any suit or other matter in which he may be interested.

ANNOTATIONS

U.S. Gov't v. Marks, 949 S.W.2d 320, 326 (Tex. 1997). P argues that sealing the transcript of the ex parte hearing between the judge and federal prosecutor violated TRCP 76. "This general rule is not absolute. Although not stated in the rule, there are exceptions, such as documents submitted *in camera* under a claim of privilege, documents subject to a protective order, or materials sealed under [TRCP] 76a. Rule 76 does not give [P] an absolute right to the transcript of the *in camera* hearing. *At 327:* However, the district court's order was overly broad in sealing the entire record rather than those portions that pertained to the grand jury proceeding."

Davenport v. Garcia, 834 S.W.2d 4, 24 (Tex.1992). Access to court records "is separately guaranteed to '[e]ach attorney at law practicing in any court ... at all reasonable times to inspect.' ... A court may not escape the strict obligations of [TRCP 76 and 76a] by tacitly closing the record through an unwritten order."

TRCP 76a. SEALING COURT RECORDS

1. Standard for Sealing Court Records. Court records may not be removed from court files except as permitted by statute or rule. No court order or opinion issued in the adjudication of a case may be sealed. Other court records, as defined in this rule, are presumed to be open to the general public and may be sealed only upon a showing of all of the following:

(a) a specific, serious and substantial interest which clearly outweighs:

(1) this presumption of openness;

(2) any probable adverse effect that sealing will have upon the general public health or safety;

(b) no less restrictive means than sealing records will adequately and effectively protect the specific interest asserted.

2. Court Records. For purposes of this rule, court records means:

(a) all documents of any nature filed in connection with any matter before any civil court, except:

(1) documents filed with a court in camera, solely for the purpose of obtaining a ruling on the discoverability of such documents;

(2) documents in court files to which access is otherwise restricted by law;

(3) documents filed in an action originally arising under the Family Code.

(b) settlement agreements not filed of record, excluding all reference to any monetary consideration, that seek to restrict disclosure of information concerning matters that have a probable adverse effect upon the general public health or safety, or the administration of public office, or the operation of government.

(c) discovery, not filed of record, concerning matters that have a probable adverse effect upon the general public health or safety, or the administration of public office, or the operation of government, except discovery in cases originally initiated to preserve bona fide trade secrets or other intangible property rights.

3. Notice. Court records may be sealed only upon a party's written motion, which shall be open to public inspection. The movant shall post a public notice at the place where notices for meetings of county governmen-

tal bodies are required to be posted, stating: that a hearing will be held in open court on a motion to seal court records in the specific case; that any person may intervene and be heard concerning the sealing of court records; the specific time and place of the hearing; the style and number of the case; a brief but specific description of both the nature of the case and the records which are sought to be sealed; and the identity of the movant. Immediately after posting such notice, the movant shall file a verified copy of the posted notice with the clerk of the court in which the case is pending and with the Clerk of the Supreme Court of Texas.

4. Hearing. A hearing, open to the public, on a motion to seal court records shall be held in open court as soon as practicable, but not less than fourteen days after the motion is filed and notice is posted. Any party may participate in the hearing. Non-parties may intervene as a matter of right for the limited purpose of participating in the proceedings, upon payment of the fee required for filing a plea in intervention. The court may inspect records in camera when necessary. The court may determine a motion relating to sealing or unsealing court records in accordance with the procedures prescribed by Rule 120a.

5. Temporary Sealing Order. A temporary sealing order may issue upon motion and notice to any parties who have answered in the case pursuant to Rules 21 and 21a upon a showing of compelling need from specific facts shown by affidavit or by verified petition that immediate and irreparable injury will result to a specific interest of the applicant before notice can be posted and a hearing held as otherwise provided herein. The temporary order shall set the time for the hearing required by paragraph 4 and shall direct that the movant immediately give the public notice required by paragraph 3. The court may modify or withdraw any temporary order upon motion by any party or intervenor, notice to the parties, and hearing conducted as soon as practicable. Issuance of a temporary order shall not reduce in any way the burden of proof of a party requesting sealing at the hearing required by paragraph 4.

6. Order on Motion to Seal Court Records. A motion relating to sealing or unsealing court records shall be decided by written order, open to the public, which shall state: the style and number of the case; the specific reasons for finding and concluding whether the showing required by paragraph 1 has been made; the specific portions of court records which are to be sealed; and the time period for which the sealed portions of the court records are to be sealed. The order shall not be included in any judgment or other order but shall be a separate document in the case; however, the failure to comply with this requirement shall not affect its appealability.

7. Continuing Jurisdiction. Any person may intervene as a matter of right at any time before or after judgment to seal or unseal court records. A court that issues a sealing order retains continuing jurisdiction to enforce, alter, or vacate that order. An order sealing or unsealing court records shall not be reconsidered on motion of any party or intervenor who had actual notice of the hearing preceding issuance of the order, without first showing changed circumstances materially affecting the order. Such circumstances need not be related to the case in which the order was issued. However, the burden of making the showing required by paragraph 1 shall always be on the party seeking to seal records.

8. Appeal. Any order (or portion of an order or judgment) relating to sealing or unsealing court records shall be deemed to be severed from the case and a final judgment which may be appealed by any party or intervenor who participated in the hearing preceding issuance of such order. The appellate court may abate the appeal and order the trial court to direct that further public notice be given, or to hold further hearings, or to make additional findings.

9. Application. Access to documents in court files not defined as court records by this rule remains governed by existing law. This rule does not apply to any court records sealed in an action in which a final judgment has been entered before its effective date. This rule applies to cases already pending on its effective date only with regard to:

(a) all court records filed or exchanged after the effective date;

(b) any motion to alter or vacate an order restricting access to court records, issued before the effective date.

Caution: TRCP 76a is affected by Fam. Code §§108.001, 108.005, 161.210, and 264.509.

See also CPRC §134A.002(6) (definition of "trade secret"); ***O'Connor's Texas Rules***, "Motion to Seal Court Records," ch. 5-L, p. 458; "Scope of Discovery," ch. 6-B, p. 530; ***O'Connor's Texas Forms***, FORMS 5L:1-8.

ANNOTATIONS

In re M-I L.L.C., 505 S.W.3d 569, 579 (Tex.2016). Third-party D "asserts that exclusion of its designated

representative [from the temporary-injunction hearing] would be inconsistent with [TRCP] 76a. By its express terms, however, Rule 76a only governs the sealing of 'court records.' It does not implicate oral testimony…."

General Tire, Inc. v. Kepple, 970 S.W.2d 520, 525 (Tex.1998). "[W]e hold that when a party seeks a protective order under [TRCP] 166b(5)(c) [now TRCP 192.6] to restrict the dissemination of unfiled discovery, and no party or intervenor contends that the discovery is a 'court record,' a trial court need not conduct a hearing or render any findings on that issue. If a party or intervenor opposing a protective order claims that the discovery is a 'court record,' the court must make a threshold determination on that issue. However, public notice and a [TRCP] 76a hearing are mandated only if the court finds that the documents are court records."

State Bar v. Jefferson, 942 S.W.2d 575, 576 (Tex. 1997). "[T]he Bar requests that all papers filed in the district court case be unsealed. The district court ordered the papers temporarily sealed under Rule 76a(5)…. The order provides for further proceedings as required by Rule 76a. The Bar may yet obtain from the district court the relief it seeks, and if it does not, it may appeal under Rule 76a(8). Mandamus is therefore unavailable."

Dallas Morning News v. 5th Ct. of Appeals, 842 S.W.2d 655, 657 (Tex.1992). "The press and the public have a right to be present at all proceedings in the trial of the underlying case, and to report all that they observe."

In re Coastal Bend Coll., 276 S.W.3d 83, 86 (Tex. App.—San Antonio 2008, no pet.). "'It is the burden of the party claiming the documents are open to the public to prove by a preponderance of the evidence that the documents are court records as defined by Rule 76a'…. *At 87:* [A] party must be allowed to tender a document in camera when necessary, without converting the document to a 'court record.' 'Were it otherwise, trial courts could not review the documents themselves in determining how to apply Rule 76a without requiring [the party] to relinquish the very relief sought under the rule.' [¶] [In addition, inclusion of the words 'court records' in the title of the] pleading, absent a clear, deliberate and unequivocal statement within the pleading itself that the documents were 'court records' as defined by Rule 76a(2), is not a judicial admission."

Compaq Computer Corp. v. Lapray, 75 S.W.3d 669, 673 (Tex.App.—Beaumont 2002, no pet.). "Rule 76a contains no requirement that the trial court determine the discoverability of **court records** prior to determining whether to seal or unseal those records. Only under the 76a(2)(a)(1) exception—for documents filed in camera 'solely for the purpose of obtaining a ruling on the discoverability of such documents'—must the issue of discoverability be decided before the documents may become court records."

P.I.A., Inc. v. Sullivan, 837 S.W.2d 844, 845-46 (Tex.App.—Fort Worth 1992, orig. proceeding). "The Family Code mandates that when a family law case is voluntarily dismissed, the court does not retain any continuing jurisdiction. [¶] The real parties in interest contend that ***Ashpole*** [below] was overruled by the … recent enactment of [TRCP] 76a. This rule gives a court power and procedure to seal court records along with continuing jurisdiction to enforce, alter, or vacate a sealing order. However, rule 76a states that documents filed in an original action arising under the Family Code are not court records within rule 76a. The rule then specifically states: Access to documents in court files not defined as court records by this rule remains governed by existing law. This means that ***Ashpole*** is good law and governs these sealed documents because they were filed in an original action arising under the Family Code."

Ashpole v. Millard, 778 S.W.2d 169, 170 (Tex. App.—Houston [1st Dist.] 1989, orig. proceeding). "[T]he trial court's inherent power to control public access to its records does not extend beyond the period of its plenary power. *At 171:* After a court's plenary power over a judgment or order expires, it may only: (1) make nunc pro tunc corrections of clerical errors in a prior judgment or order; and (2) declare a previous judgment or order void because it was signed after the court's plenary power had expired."

TRCP 77. LOST RECORDS & PAPERS

When any papers or records are lost or destroyed during the pendency of a suit, the parties may, with the approval of the judge, agree in writing on a brief statement of the matters contained therein; or either party may supply such lost records or papers as follows:

a. After three days' notice to the adverse party or his attorney, make written sworn motion before the court stating the loss or destruction of such record or

papers, accompanied by certified copies of the originals if obtainable, or by substantial copies thereof.

b. If, upon hearing, the court be satisfied that they are substantial copies of the original, an order shall be made substituting such copies or brief statement for the originals.

c. Such substituted copies or brief statement shall be filed with the clerk, constitute a part of the cause, and have the force and effect of the originals.

See also TRAP 34.5(e), 34.6(f); TRE 1003, 1004; *O'Connor's Texas Rules*, "Lost pleadings," ch. 1-C, §10.4, p. 42.

ANNOTATIONS

Coke v. Coke, 802 S.W.2d 270, 275 (Tex.App.—Dallas 1990, writ denied). The court overruled the party's objection to the trial court's reconstruction of the lost file from the adverse party's documents. The party "testified that as far as he could tell, the copies were true duplicates of the originals."

B. PLEADINGS OF PLAINTIFF

TRCP 78. PETITION; ORIGINAL & SUPPLEMENTAL; INDORSEMENT

The pleading of plaintiff shall consist of an original petition, and such supplemental petitions as may be necessary in the course of pleading by the parties to the suit. The original petition and the supplemental petitions shall be indorsed, so as to show their respective positions in the process of pleading, as "original petition," "plaintiff's first supplemental petition," "plaintiff's second supplemental petition," and so on, to be successively numbered, named, and indorsed.

Caution: TRCP 78 is affected by Fam. Code §§6.401, 6.402, 45.002, 45.102, 102.008, and 161.101.

See also *O'Connor's Texas Family Law Handbook* (2017), "Suit for Divorce," ch. 3-A, p. 205; "Suit to Dissolve Marriage with Children," ch. 4-D, p. 410; "Suit for Conservatorship," ch. 4-E, p. 469; "Suit for Child Support," ch. 4-F, p. 529; "Temporary Orders," ch. 5-D, p. 695; "Suit to Modify Conservatorship, Possession, or Access," ch. 9-A, p. 973.

TRCP 78a. CASE INFORMATION SHEET

(a) ***Requirement.*** A civil case information sheet, in the form promulgated by the Supreme Court of Texas, must accompany the filing of:

(1) an original petition or application; and

(2) a post-judgment petition for modification or motion for enforcement in a case arising under the Family Code.

(b) ***Signature.*** The civil case information sheet must be signed by the attorney for the party filing the pleading or by the party.

(c) ***Enforcement.*** The court and clerk must take appropriate measures to enforce this rule. But the clerk may not reject a pleading because the pleading is not accompanied by a civil case information sheet.

(d) ***Limitation on Use.*** The civil case information sheet is for data collection for statistical and administrative purposes and does not affect any substantive right.

(e) ***Applicability.*** The civil case information sheet is not required in cases filed in justice courts or small-claims courts, or in cases arising under Title 3 of the Family Code.

Editor's note: *Instructions for Completing the Texas Civil Case Information Sheet* and a printable form of the Civil Case Information Sheet can be found at the Texas Office of Court Administration website, www.txcourts.gov/rules-forms/forms.

See also *O'Connor's Texas Rules*, "Case-information sheet," ch. 1-B, §3.2.21, p. 15; *O'Connor's Texas Forms*, FORM 1B:16.

TRCP 79. THE PETITION

The petition shall state the names of the parties and their residences, if known, together with the contents prescribed in Rule 47 above.

Caution: TRCP 79 is affected by Fam. Code §§6.401, 6.402, 45.002, 45.102, 102.008, and 161.101.

See also *O'Connor's Texas Rules*, "Plaintiff's Original Petition," ch. 2-B, p. 117; *O'Connor's Texas Forms*, FORMS 2B.

ANNOTATIONS

Enserch Corp. v. Parker, 794 S.W.2d 2, 4-5 (Tex. 1990). "If the plaintiff merely misnames the correct defendant (misnomer), limitations is tolled and a subsequent amendment ... relates back to the date of the original petition. If, however, the plaintiff is mistaken as to which of two defendants is the correct one and there is ... a corporation with the name of the erroneously named defendant (misidentification), then the plaintiff has sued the wrong party and limitations is not tolled."

TRCP 80. PLAINTIFF'S SUPPLEMENTAL PETITION

The plaintiff's supplemental petitions may contain special exceptions, general denials, and the allegations of new matter not before alleged by him, in reply to those which have been alleged by the defendant.

ANNOTATIONS

Moody-Rambin Interests v. Moore, 722 S.W.2d 790, 792 (Tex.App.—Houston [14th Dist.] 1987, no writ). "'The proper way to bring new parties into a suit is by an amended pleading, and not by a supplemental pleading.' An exception to this rule exists if the neces-

sity for adding a new party arises from facts pled in the defendant's answer."

TRCP 81. DEFENSIVE MATTERS

When the defendant sets up a counter claim, the plaintiff may plead thereto under rules prescribed for pleadings of defensive matter by the defendant, so far as applicable. Whenever the defendant is required to plead any matter of defense under oath, the plaintiff shall be required to plead such matters under oath when relied on by him.

ANNOTATIONS

Greater Fort Worth & Tarrant Cty. Cmty. Action Agency v. Mims, 627 S.W.2d 149, 152 (Tex.1982). "If the plaintiff contesting the counterclaim does not intend to urge any defensive theory which must be verified or any affirmative defense under [TRCP] 94, he is not required to answer the defendant's counterclaim."

TRCP 82. SPECIAL DEFENSES

The plaintiff need not deny any special matter of defense pleaded by the defendant, but the same shall be regarded as denied unless expressly admitted.

C. PLEADINGS OF DEFENDANT

TRCP 83. ANSWER; ORIGINAL & SUPPLEMENTAL; INDORSEMENT

The answer of defendant shall consist of an original answer, and such supplemental answers as may be necessary, in the course of pleading by the parties to the suit. The original answer and the supplemental answers shall be indorsed, so as to show their respective positions in the process of pleading, as "original answer," "defendant's first supplemental answer," "defendant's second supplemental answer," and so on, to be successively numbered, named and indorsed.

Caution: TRCP 83 is affected by Fam. Code §§6.403, 8.057, 9.001, 53.04, and 82.021.

See also ***O'Connor's Texas Rules***, "Defendant's Pleadings," ch. 3-A, p. 213.

ANNOTATIONS

Smith v. Lippmann, 826 S.W.2d 137, 138 (Tex. 1992). "[A] defendant, who timely files a pro se answer by a signed letter that identifies the parties, the case, and the defendant's current address, has sufficiently appeared by answer and deserves notice of any subsequent proceedings in the case."

TRCP 84. ANSWER MAY INCLUDE SEVERAL MATTERS

The defendant in his answer may plead as many several matters, whether of law or fact, as he may think necessary for his defense, and which may be pertinent to the cause, and such matters shall be heard in such order as may be directed by the court, special appearance and motion to transfer venue, and the practice thereunder being excepted herefrom.

See also ***O'Connor's Texas Rules***, "Defendant's Pleadings," ch. 3-A, p. 213.

TRCP 85. ORIGINAL ANSWER; CONTENTS

The original answer may consist of motions to transfer venue, pleas to the jurisdiction, in abatement, or any other dilatory pleas; of special exceptions, of general denial, and any defense by way of avoidance or estoppel, and it may present a cross-action, which to that extent will place defendant in the attitude of a plaintiff. Matters in avoidance and estoppel may be stated together, or in several special pleas, each presenting a distinct defense, and numbered so as to admit of separate issues to be formed on them.

Caution: TRCP 85 is affected by Fam. Code §6.403.

See also ***O'Connor's Texas Rules***, "Defendant's Response & Pleadings," ch. 3, p. 209; ***O'Connor's Texas Forms***, FORMS 3E; ***O'Connor's Texas Family Law Handbook*** (2017), "Suit for Divorce," ch. 3-A, p. 205; "Suit to Dissolve Marriage with Children," ch. 4-D, p. 410; "Suit for Conservatorship," ch. 4-E, p. 469; "Suit for Child Support," ch. 4-F, p. 529; "Suit to Modify Conservatorship, Possession, or Access," ch. 9-A, p. 973.

TRCP 86. MOTION TO TRANSFER VENUE

1. Time to File. An objection to improper venue is waived if not made by written motion filed prior to or concurrently with any other plea, pleading or motion except a special appearance motion provided for in Rule 120a. A written consent of the parties to transfer the case to another county may be filed with the clerk of the court at any time. A motion to transfer venue because an impartial trial cannot be had in the county where the action is pending is governed by the provisions of Rule 257.

2. How to File. The motion objecting to improper venue may be contained in a separate instrument filed concurrently with or prior to the filing of the movant's first responsive pleading or the motion may be combined with other objections and defenses and included in the movant's first responsive pleading.

3. Requisites of Motion. The motion, and any amendments to it, shall state that the action should be transferred to another specified county of proper venue because:

(a) The county where the action is pending is not a proper county; or

(b) Mandatory venue of the action in another county is prescribed by one or more specific statutory provisions which shall be clearly designated or indicated.

The motion shall state the legal and factual basis for the transfer of the action and request transfer of the action to a specific county of mandatory or proper venue. Verification of the motion is not required. The motion may be accompanied by supporting affidavits as provided in Rule 87.

4. Response and Reply. Except as provided in paragraph 3(a) of Rule 87, a response to the motion to transfer is not required. Verification of a response is not required.

5. Service. A copy of any instrument filed pursuant to Rule 86 shall be served in accordance with Rule 21a.

Caution: TRCP 86 is affected by Fam. Code §§6.407, 103.002, 103.003, 155.201 et seq., 155.301, and 262.203.

See also CPRC ch. 15; *O'Connor's Texas Rules*, "Motion to Transfer—Challenging Venue," ch. 3-C, p. 235; *O'Connor's Texas Forms*, FORMS 3C; *O'Connor's Texas Family Law Handbook* (2017), "Challenging the Court," ch. 4-B, p. 349; "Suit to Modify Conservatorship, Possession, or Access," ch. 9-A, p. 973.

ANNOTATIONS

Martinez v. Flores, 820 S.W.2d 937, 938 (Tex. App.—Corpus Christi 1991, orig. proceeding). "[T]he transfer procedures in the Family Code governing [SAPCRs] are the exclusive mechanism for transferring [a] case or challenging venue and were designed to supplant the regular rules dealing with transfer of venue applicable in ordinary civil cases." *See also* ***Mendez v. Attorney Gen.***, 761 S.W.2d 519, 521 (Tex.App.—Corpus Christi 1988, no writ).

TRCP 87. DETERMINATION OF MOTION TO TRANSFER

1. Consideration of Motion. The determination of a motion to transfer venue shall be made promptly by the court and such determination must be made in a reasonable time prior to commencement of the trial on the merits. The movant has the duty to request a setting on the motion to transfer. Except on leave of court each party is entitled to at least 45 days notice of a hearing on the motion to transfer.

Except on leave of court, any response or opposing affidavits shall be filed at least 30 days prior to the hearing of the motion to transfer. The movant is not required to file a reply to the response but any reply and any additional affidavits supporting the motion to transfer must, except on leave of court, be filed not later than 7 days prior to the hearing date.

2. Burden of Establishing Venue.

(a) *In General.* A party who seeks to maintain venue of the action in a particular county in reliance upon Section 15.001[1] (General Rule), Sections 15.011-15.017 (Mandatory Venue), Sections 15.031-15.040 (Permissive Venue), or Sections 15.061 and 15.062 (Multiple Claims), Civil Practice and Remedies Code, has the burden to make proof, as provided in paragraph 3 of this rule, that venue is maintainable in the county of suit. A party who seeks to transfer venue of the action to another specified county under Section 15.001[1] (General Rule), Sections 15.011-15.017 (Mandatory Venue), Sections 15.031-15.040 (Permissive Venue), or Sections 15.061 and 15.062 (Multiple Claims), Civil Practice and Remedies Code, has the burden to make proof, as provided in paragraph 3 of this rule, that venue is maintainable in the county to which transfer is sought. A party who seeks to transfer venue of the action to another specified county under Sections 15.011-15.017, Civil Practice and Remedies Code on the basis that a mandatory venue provision is applicable and controlling has the burden to make proof, as provided in paragraph 3 of this rule, that venue is maintainable in the county to which transfer is sought by virtue of one or more mandatory venue exceptions.

(b) *Cause of Action.* It shall not be necessary for a claimant to prove the merits of a cause of action, but the existence of a cause of action, when pleaded properly, shall be taken as established as alleged by the pleadings. When the defendant specifically denies the venue allegations, the claimant is required, by prima facie proof as provided in paragraph 3 of this rule, to support such pleading that the cause of action taken as established by the pleadings, or a part of such cause of action, accrued in the county of suit. If a defendant seeks transfer to a county where the cause of action or a part thereof accrued, it shall be sufficient for the defendant to plead that if a cause of action exists, then the cause of action or part thereof accrued in the spe-

cific county to which transfer is sought, and such allegation shall not constitute an admission that a cause of action in fact exists. But the defendant shall be required to support his pleading by prima facie proof as provided in paragraph 3 of this rule, that, if a cause of action exists, it or a part thereof accrued in the county to which transfer is sought.

(c) *Other Rules.* A motion to transfer venue based on the written consent of the parties shall be determined in accordance with Rule 255. A motion to transfer venue on the basis that an impartial trial cannot be had in the county where the action is pending shall be determined in accordance with Rules 258 and 259.

3. Proof.

(a) *Affidavit and Attachments.* All venue facts, when properly pleaded, shall be taken as true unless specifically denied by the adverse party. When a venue fact is specifically denied, the party pleading the venue fact must make prima facie proof of that venue fact; provided, however, that no party shall ever be required for venue purposes to support by prima facie proof the existence of a cause of action or part thereof, and at the hearing the pleadings of the parties shall be taken as conclusive on the issues of existence of a cause of action. Prima facie proof is made when the venue facts are properly pleaded and an affidavit, and any duly proved attachments to the affidavit, are filed fully and specifically setting forth the facts supporting such pleading. Affidavits shall be made on personal knowledge, shall set forth specific facts as would be admissible in evidence, and shall show affirmatively that the affiant is competent to testify.

(b) *The Hearing.* The court shall determine the motion to transfer venue on the basis of the pleadings, any stipulations made by and between the parties and such affidavits and attachments as may be filed by the parties in accordance with the preceding subdivision of this paragraph 3 or of Rule 88.

(c) If a claimant has adequately pleaded and made prima facie proof that venue is proper in the county of suit as provided in subdivision (a) of paragraph 3, then the cause shall not be transferred but shall be retained in the county of suit, unless the motion to transfer is based on the grounds that an impartial trial cannot be had in the county where the action is pending as provided in Rules 257-259 or on an established ground of mandatory venue. A ground of mandatory venue is established when the party relying upon a mandatory exception to the general rule makes prima facie proof as provided in subdivision (a) of paragraph 3 of this rule.

(d) In the event that the parties shall fail to make prima facie proof that the county of suit or the specific county to which transfer is sought is a county of proper venue, then the court may direct the parties to make further proof.

4. No Jury. All venue challenges shall be determined by the court without the aid of a jury.

5. Motion for Rehearing. If venue has been sustained as against a motion to transfer, or if an action has been transferred to a proper county in response to a motion to transfer, then no further motions to transfer shall be considered regardless of whether the movant was a party to the prior proceedings or was added as a party subsequent to the venue proceedings, unless the motion to transfer is based on the grounds that an impartial trial cannot be had under Rules 257-259 or on the ground of mandatory venue, provided that such claim was not available to the other movant or movants.

Parties who are added subsequently to an action and are precluded by this rule from having a motion to transfer considered may raise the propriety of venue on appeal, provided that the party has timely filed a motion to transfer.

6. There shall be no interlocutory appeals from such determination.

1. **Editor's note:** Now CPRC §15.002.

Caution: TRCP 87 is affected by Fam. Code §§6.407, 103.002, 103.003, 155.201 et seq., 155.301, and 262.203.

See also CPRC ch. 15; ***O'Connor's Texas Rules***, "Choosing the Court—Venue," ch. 2-G, p. 175; "Motion to Transfer—Challenging Venue," ch. 3-C, p. 235; ***O'Connor's Texas Forms***, FORMS 3C; ***O'Connor's Texas Family Law Handbook*** (2017), "Challenging the Court," ch. 4-B, p. 349.

ANNOTATIONS

Martinez v. Flores, 820 S.W.2d 937, 938 (Tex. App.—Corpus Christi 1991, orig. proceeding). See annotation under TRCP 86, p. 1074.

TRCP 88. DISCOVERY & VENUE

Discovery shall not be abated or otherwise affected by pendency of a motion to transfer venue. Issuing process for witnesses and taking depositions shall not constitute a waiver of a motion to transfer venue, but depositions taken in such case may be read in evidence in any subsequent suit between the same parties concerning the same subject matter in like manner as if taken in such subsequent suit. Deposition transcripts, responses to requests for admission, answers to interrogatories and other discovery products containing in-

formation relevant to a determination of proper venue may be considered by the court in making the venue determination when they are attached to, or incorporated by reference in, an affidavit of a party, a witness or an attorney who has knowledge of such discovery.

See also *O'Connor's Texas Rules*, "Motion to Transfer—Challenging Venue," ch. 3-C, p. 235.

ANNOTATIONS

Montalvo v. Fourth Ct. of Appeals, 917 S.W.2d 1, 2 (Tex.1995). "[T]he trial court set a shortened schedule for completing discovery related to venue, filing [Ps'] response to the motions to transfer, and the hearing. [Ps] offered no argument or evidence that the limitation on discovery or the abbreviated schedule deprived them of any ability to develop evidence pertinent to the venue issue. Without a showing of such harm, the record is wholly insufficient to establish that [Ps] lacked an adequate remedy by appeal."

Double Diamond-Del., Inc. v. Alfonso, 487 S.W.3d 265, 272-73 (Tex.App.—Corpus Christi 2016, no pet.). "[Ds] objected to [Ps'] use of their own discovery responses as venue evidence.... [Ds] cited [TRCP] 197.3, which provides that '[a]nswers to interrogatories may be used only against the responding party.' [TRCP] 88 does not provide any such limitation when it stipulates that discovery ... can be considered by the trial court in making its venue determination. [W]e conclude that the specific provisions in rule 88 allow a party to use its own discovery responses in the context of a venue determination."

TRCP 89. TRANSFERRED IF MOTION IS SUSTAINED

If a motion to transfer venue is sustained, the cause shall not be dismissed, but the court shall transfer said cause to the proper court; and the costs incurred prior to the time such suit is filed in the court to which said cause is transferred shall be taxed against the plaintiff. The clerk shall make up a transcript of all the orders made in said cause, certifying thereto officially under the seal of the court, and send it with the original papers in the cause to the clerk of the court to which the venue has been changed. Provided, however, if the cause be severable as to parties defendant and shall be ordered transferred as to one or more defendants but not as to all, the clerk, instead of sending the original papers, shall make certified copies of such filed papers as directed by the court and forward the same to the clerk of the court to which the venue has been changed. After the cause has been transferred, as above provided for the clerk of the court to which the cause has been transferred shall mail notification to the plaintiff or his attorney that transfer of the cause has been completed, that the filing fee in the proper court is due and payable within thirty days from the mailing of such notification, and that the case may be dismissed if the filing fee is not timely paid; and if such filing fee is timely paid, the cause will be subject to trial at the expiration of thirty days after the mailing of notification to the parties or their attorneys by the clerk that the papers have been filed in the court to which the cause has been transferred; and if the filing fee is not timely paid, any court of the transferee county to which the case might have been assigned, upon its own motion or the motion of a party, may dismiss the cause without prejudice to the refiling of same.

See also *O'Connor's Texas Rules*, "Motion to Transfer—Challenging Venue," ch. 3-C, p. 235.

ANNOTATIONS

WTFO, Inc. v. Braithwaite, 899 S.W.2d 709, 718 (Tex.App.—Dallas 1995, no writ). "Where a cause of action is against several defendants jointly and severally, the trial court shall transfer the action as to those defendants whose motions are sustained. Comakers on a note are jointly and severally liable. Accordingly, because venue was proper in Dallas County, the trial court did not abuse its discretion in severing [D's] cause of action and transferring it to Dallas County."

TRCP 90. WAIVER OF DEFECTS IN PLEADING

General demurrers shall not be used. Every defect, omission or fault in a pleading either of form or of substance, which is not specifically pointed out by exception in writing and brought to the attention of the judge in the trial court before the instruction or charge to the jury or, in a non-jury case, before the judgment is signed, shall be deemed to have been waived by the party seeking reversal on such account; provided that this rule shall not apply as to any party against whom default judgment is rendered.

See also *O'Connor's Texas Rules*, "Special Exceptions—Challenging the Pleadings," ch. 3-G, p. 286.

ANNOTATIONS

Crosstex Energy Servs. v. Pro Plus, Inc., 430 S.W.3d 384, 395 (Tex.2014). "If a defect in the pleadings is incurable by amendment, a special exception is unnecessary."

Shoemake v. Fogel, Ltd., 826 S.W.2d 933, 937 (Tex. 1992). "[D] filed no special exceptions to clarify [P's] claim. Thus, [D] cannot now complain that [P's] pleading was insufficiently specific." *See also* ***Steves Sash & Door Co. v. Ceco Corp.***, 751 S.W.2d 473, 476 (Tex. 1988).

Taylor v. Taylor, 337 S.W.3d 398, 402 (Tex.App.—Fort Worth 2011, no pet.). Mother "contends that the trial court abused its discretion by refusing to hear evidence concerning child support from the date of separation through the date of her original petition, but [mother's] petition does not mention or even refer to a request for child support for that period of time. [Mother] argues that [father] waived any complaint concerning the sufficiency of her pleading by failing to specially except. [¶] Requiring [father] to specially except to [mother's] petition to determine whether [mother] sought child support prior to the date of her original petition would be akin to requiring a defendant to specially except to a plaintiff's pleading because other theories or causes of action are available but not included in the plaintiff's pleading. We hold that [mother's] original petition did not provide [father] with fair notice of her request for retroactive child support from the date of separation through the date of [mother's] original petition and that [father] did not waive his complaint concerning the sufficiency of [mother's] pleading for retroactive child support from the date of separation through the date of her original petition by failing to specially except."

In re J.D.H., 661 S.W.2d 744, 748 (Tex.App.—Beaumont 1983, no writ). "[T]he rule to be followed in child custody cases is that technical rules of civil procedure, as to practice and pleading, are not of controlling importance, since the controlling factor is the best interests of the child. It is because of our profound concern for the best interests of the child in issue that we have addressed this point of error, for we are not technically required to do so under [TRCP] 90 because appellant failed to preserve the alleged error by objection."

TRCP 91. SPECIAL EXCEPTIONS

A special exception shall not only point out the particular pleading excepted to, but it shall also point out intelligibly and with particularity the defect, omission, obscurity, duplicity, generality, or other insufficiency in the allegations in the pleading excepted to.

Caution: TRCP 91 is affected by Fam. Code §6.402.

See also *O'Connor's Texas Rules*, "Special Exceptions—Challenging the Pleadings," ch. 3-G, p. 286; *O'Connor's Texas Forms*, FORMS 3G.

ANNOTATIONS

Parker v. Barefield, 206 S.W.3d 119, 120 (Tex. 2006). If the trial court does not allow the party an opportunity to amend its pleadings, "the aggrieved party must prove that the opportunity to replead was requested and denied to preserve the error for review."

Friesenhahn v. Ryan, 960 S.W.2d 656, 658 (Tex. 1998). "Special exceptions may be used to challenge the sufficiency of a pleading. When the trial court sustains special exceptions, it must give the pleader an opportunity to amend the pleading. If a party refuses to amend, or the amended pleading fails to state a cause of action, then summary judgment may be granted. Summary judgment may also be proper if a pleading deficiency is of the type that could not be cured by an amendment." *See also* ***James v. Underwood***, 438 S.W.3d 704, 715-16 (Tex.App.—Houston [1st Dist.] 2014, no pet.).

Peek v. Equipment Serv., 779 S.W.2d 802, 805 (Tex.1989). "[T]he omission of any allegation regarding the amount in controversy from [P's] petition did not deprive the court of jurisdiction, but was instead a defect in pleading subject to special exception and amendment."

Gallien v. Washington Mut. Home Loans, Inc., 209 S.W.3d 856, 862-63 (Tex.App.—Texarkana 2006, no pet.). "[A]s a general rule, the trial court cannot dismiss a suit with prejudice when the plaintiff does not cure the objections made by special exceptions. More specifically, a trial court cannot dismiss a plaintiff's entire case with prejudice if the pleadings state a valid cause of action, but are vague, overbroad, or otherwise susceptible to valid special exceptions."

TRCP 91a. DISMISSAL OF BASELESS CAUSES OF ACTION

91a.1 Motion and Grounds. Except in a case brought under the Family Code or a case governed by Chapter 14 of the Texas Civil Practice and Remedies Code, a party may move to dismiss a cause of action on the grounds that it has no basis in law or fact. A cause of action has no basis in law if the allegations, taken as true, together with inferences reasonably drawn from them, do not entitle the claimant to the relief sought. A cause of action has no basis in fact if no reasonable person could believe the facts pleaded.

91a.2 Contents of Motion. A motion to dismiss must state that it is made pursuant to this rule, must identify each cause of action to which it is addressed, and must state specifically the reasons the cause of action has no basis in law, no basis in fact, or both.

91a.3 Time for Motion and Ruling. A motion to dismiss must be:

(a) filed within 60 days after the first pleading containing the challenged cause of action is served on the movant;

(b) filed at least 21 days before the motion is heard; and

(c) granted or denied within 45 days after the motion is filed.

91a.4 Time for Response. Any response to the motion must be filed no later than 7 days before the date of the hearing.

91a.5 Effect of Nonsuit or Amendment; Withdrawal of Motion.

(a) The court may not rule on a motion to dismiss if, at least 3 days before the date of the hearing, the respondent files a nonsuit of the challenged cause of action, or the movant files a withdrawal of the motion.

(b) If the respondent amends the challenged cause of action at least 3 days before the date of the hearing, the movant may, before the date of the hearing, file a withdrawal of the motion or an amended motion directed to the amended cause of action.

(c) Except by agreement of the parties, the court must rule on a motion unless it has been withdrawn or the cause of action has been nonsuited in accordance with (a) or (b). In ruling on the motion, the court must not consider a nonsuit or amendment not filed as permitted by paragraphs (a) or (b).

(d) An amended motion filed in accordance with (b) restarts the time periods in this rule.

91a.6 Hearing; No Evidence Considered. Each party is entitled to at least 14 days' notice of the hearing on the motion to dismiss. The court may, but is not required to, conduct an oral hearing on the motion. Except as required by 91a.7, the court may not consider evidence in ruling on the motion and must decide the motion based solely on the pleading of the cause of action, together with any pleading exhibits permitted by Rule 59.

91a.7 Award of Costs and Attorney Fees Required. Except in an action by or against a governmental entity or a public official acting in his or her official capacity or under color of law, the court must award the prevailing party on the motion all costs and reasonable and necessary attorney fees incurred with respect to the challenged cause of action in the trial court. The court must consider evidence regarding costs and fees in determining the award.

91a.8 Effect on Venue and Personal Jurisdiction. This rule is not an exception to the pleading requirements of Rules 86 and 120a, but a party does not, by filing a motion to dismiss pursuant to this rule or obtaining a ruling on it, waive a special appearance or a motion to transfer venue. By filing a motion to dismiss, a party submits to the court's jurisdiction only in proceedings on the motion and is bound by the court's ruling, including an award of attorney fees and costs against the party.

91a.9 Dismissal Procedure Cumulative. This rule is in addition to, and does not supersede or affect, other procedures that authorize dismissal.

Editor's note: Rule 91a applies to all suits, except those brought under the Family Code or governed by CPRC chapter 14 (inmate litigation). TRCP 91a.1. *See* Tex.Sup.Ct. Order, Misc. Docket No. 13-9022 (eff. Mar. 1, 2013).

See also *O'Connor's Texas Rules*, "Motion to Dismiss—Baseless Cause of Action," ch. 3-H, p. 294.

TRCP 92. GENERAL DENIAL

A general denial of matters pleaded by the adverse party which are not required to be denied under oath, shall be sufficient to put the same in issue. When the defendant has pleaded a general denial, and the plaintiff shall afterward amend his pleading, such original denial shall be presumed to extend to all matters subsequently set up by the plaintiff.

When a counterclaim or cross-claim is served upon a party who has made an appearance in the action, the party so served, in the absence of a responsive pleading, shall be deemed to have pleaded a general denial of the counterclaim or cross-claim, but the party shall not be deemed to have waived any special appearance or motion to transfer venue. In all other respects the rules prescribed for pleadings of defensive matter are applicable to answers to counterclaims and cross-claims.

See also *O'Connor's Texas Rules*, "The Answer—Denying Liability," ch. 3-E, p. 263.

ANNOTATIONS

Shell Chem. Co. v. Lamb, 493 S.W.2d 742, 744 (Tex.1973). "[A] general denial puts [P] on proof of every fact essential to his case and issue is joined on all

material facts asserted by [P] except those which are required to be denied under oath."

In re T.R.B., 350 S.W.3d 227, 233 (Tex.App.—San Antonio 2011, orig. proceeding). The Family Code "does not require a child's only parent who has full parental rights to allege anything more than a general denial to give fair notice she wishes to retain those rights in a SAPCR filed to diminish those rights. *At 234:* [Mother's] general denial was sufficient to require the Department and [intervenor] to carry their burden [of rebutting the parental presumption] when seeking to reduce or eliminate [mother's] conservatorship status."

TRCP 93. CERTAIN PLEAS TO BE VERIFIED

A pleading setting up any of the following matters, unless the truth of such matters appear of record, shall be verified by affidavit.

1. That the plaintiff has not legal capacity to sue or that the defendant has not legal capacity to be sued.

2. That the plaintiff is not entitled to recover in the capacity in which he sues, or that the defendant is not liable in the capacity in which he is sued.

3. That there is another suit pending in this State between the same parties involving the same claim.

4. That there is a defect of parties, plaintiff or defendant.

5. A denial of partnership as alleged in any pleading as to any party to the suit.

6. That any party alleged in any pleading to be a corporation is not incorporated as alleged.

7. Denial of the execution by himself or by his authority of any instrument in writing, upon which any pleading is founded, in whole or in part and charged to have been executed by him or by his authority, and not alleged to be lost or destroyed. Where such instrument in writing is charged to have been executed by a person then deceased, the affidavit shall be sufficient if it states that the affiant has reason to believe and does believe that such instrument was not executed by the decedent or by his authority. In the absence of such a sworn plea, the instrument shall be received in evidence as fully proved.

8. A denial of the genuineness of the indorsement or assignment of a written instrument upon which suit is brought by an indorsee or assignee and in the absence of such a sworn plea, the indorsement or assignment thereof shall be held as fully proved. The denial required by this subdivision of the rule may be made upon information and belief.

9. That a written instrument upon which a pleading is founded is without consideration, or that the consideration of the same has failed in whole or in part.

10. A denial of an account which is the foundation of the plaintiff's action, and supported by affidavit.

11. That a contract sued upon is usurious. Unless such plea is filed, no evidence of usurious interest as a defense shall be received.

12. That notice and proof of loss or claim for damage has not been given as alleged. Unless such plea is filed such notice and proof shall be presumed and no evidence to the contrary shall be admitted. A denial of such notice or such proof shall be made specifically and with particularity.

13. In the trial of any case appealed to the court from the Industrial Accident Board[1] the following, if pleaded, shall be presumed to be true as pleaded and have been done and filed in legal time and manner, unless denied by verified pleadings:

(a) Notice of injury.

(b) Claim for compensation.

(c) Award of the Board.

(d) Notice of intention not to abide by the award of the Board.

(e) Filing of suit to set aside the award.

(f) That the insurance company alleged to have been the carrier of the workers' compensation insurance at the time of the alleged injury was in fact the carrier thereof.

(g) That there was good cause for not filing claim with the Industrial Accident Board within the one year period provided by statute.

(h) Wage rate.

A denial of any of the matters set forth in subdivisions (a) or (g) of paragraph 13 may be made on information and belief.

Any such denial may be made in original or amended pleadings; but if in amended pleadings the same must be filed not less than seven days before the case proceeds to trial. In case of such denial the things so denied shall not be presumed to be true, and if essential to the case of the party alleging them, must be proved.

14. That a party plaintiff or defendant is not doing business under an assumed name or trade name as alleged.

15. In the trial of any case brought against an automobile insurance company by an insured under the provisions of an insurance policy in force providing protection against uninsured motorists, an allegation that the insured has complied with all the terms of the policy as a condition precedent to bringing the suit shall be presumed to be true unless denied by verified pleadings which may be upon information and belief.

16. Any other matter required by statute to be pleaded under oath.

1. **Editor's note:** In 1989, the name of the Industrial Accident Board was changed to the Texas Workers' Compensation Commission. Acts 1989, 71st Leg., 2nd C.S., ch. 1, §17.01, eff. Apr. 1, 1990. In 2005, the Commission was abolished, and most of its functions were transferred to the newly created Division of Workers' Compensation, Texas Department of Insurance. Acts 2005, 79th Leg., ch. 265, §1.003, eff. Sept. 1, 2005.

See also ***O'Connor's Texas Rules***, "Verified Pleas," ch. 3-E, §4, p. 264; ***O'Connor's Texas Forms***, FORM 3E:10.

ANNOTATIONS

Sixth RMA Partners v. Sibley, 111 S.W.3d 46, 56 (Tex.2003). "When capacity is contested, [TRCP 93(1)] requires that a verified plea be filed unless the truth of the matter appears of record. [¶] An argument that an opposing party does not have the capacity to participate in a suit can be waived by [the] failure to properly raise the issue in the trial court. [D] never raised [P's] failure to file an assumed name certificate ... in the trial court. Therefore, [D] waived the complaint." *See also* ***Nootsie, Ltd. v. Williamson Cty. Appr. Dist.***, 925 S.W.2d 659, 662 (Tex.1996); ***Werner v. Colwell***, 909 S.W.2d 866, 870 (Tex.1995).

Alphaville Ventures, Inc. v. First Bank, 429 S.W.3d 150, 153-54 (Tex.App.—Houston [14th Dist.] 2014, no pet.). "Rule 93(4) includes the following as a matter on which the defendant must file a verified denial: 'That there is a defect of parties, plaintiff or defendant.' Generally, a 'defect of parties' refers to joinder problems involving necessary or indispensable parties."

TRCP 94. AFFIRMATIVE DEFENSES

In pleading to a preceding pleading, a party shall set forth affirmatively accord and satisfaction, arbitration and award, assumption of risk, contributory negligence, discharge in bankruptcy, duress, estoppel, failure of consideration, fraud, illegality, injury by fellow servant, laches, license, payment, release, res judicata, statute of frauds, statute of limitations, waiver, and any other matter constituting an avoidance or affirmative defense. Where the suit is on an insurance contract which insures against certain general hazards, but contains other provisions limiting such general liability, the party suing on such contract shall never be required to allege that the loss was not due to a risk or cause coming within any of the exceptions specified in the contract, nor shall the insurer be allowed to raise such issue unless it shall specifically allege that the loss was due to a risk or cause coming within a particular exception to the general liability; provided that nothing herein shall be construed to change the burden of proof on such issue as it now exists.

Caution: TRCP 94 is affected by Fam. Code §§4.006, 6.008, 8.059, 42.007, 88.003, and 157.006-157.008.

See also ***O'Connor's Texas Rules***, "Affirmative Defenses," ch. 3-E, §5, p. 266; ***O'Connor's Texas Forms***, FORM 3E:11; ***O'Connor's Texas Family Law Handbook*** (2017), "Affirmative defenses," ch. 3-A, §9.3.3(7), p. 241 (suit for divorce); "Affirmative defense," ch. 4-F, §7.2.3(6)(c), p. 538 (suit for child support); "Affirmative defenses," ch. 4-H, §6.2.3(6)(c), p. 612 (suit for termination).

ANNOTATIONS

Zorrilla v. Aypco Constr. II, LLC, 469 S.W.3d 143, 146 (Tex.2015). "[T]he paramount issue on appeal is whether the statutory cap on exemplary damages [under CPRC §41.008(b)] is waived if not pleaded as an affirmative defense or avoidance. Our courts of appeals are split on the issue.... We hold the exemplary damages cap is not a 'matter constituting an avoidance or affirmative defense' and need not be affirmatively pleaded because it applies automatically when invoked and does not require proof of additional facts."

State v. Lueck, 290 S.W.3d 876, 880 (Tex.2009). "[A]n affirmative defense ... cannot be raised by a plea to the jurisdiction."

Quantum Chem. Corp. v. Toennies, 47 S.W.3d 473, 481 (Tex.2001). "It is the defendant's burden to plead and request instructions on an affirmative defense." *See also* ***Superior Broad. Prods. v. Doud Media Grp.***, 392 S.W.3d 198, 205 (Tex.App.—Eastland 2012, no pet.); ***Rio Grande Reg'l Hosp., Inc. v. Villarreal***, 329 S.W.3d 594, 621 (Tex.App.—Corpus Christi 2010, pet. granted, judgm't vacated w.r.m.).

Texas Beef Cattle Co. v. Green, 921 S.W.2d 203, 212 (Tex.1996). "[A]n affirmative defense ... is one of confession and avoidance. An affirmative defense does not seek to defend by merely denying the plaintiff's claims, but rather seeks to establish 'an independent

reason why the plaintiff should not recover.'" *See also* ***Moncrief Oil Int'l v. OAO Gazprom***, 332 S.W.3d 1, 15 (Tex.App.—Fort Worth 2010), *rev'd in part on other grounds*, 414 S.W.3d 142 (Tex.2013); ***In re P.D.D.***, 256 S.W.3d 834, 839 (Tex.App.—Texarkana 2008, no pet.).

Shoemake v. Fogel, Ltd., 826 S.W.2d 933, 937 (Tex. 1992). "Rule 94's requirement of pleading is not absolute. [¶] [T]he defense of [parental] immunity ... is not waived by the failure to specifically plead it if it is apparent on the face of the petition and established as a matter of law."

Waggoner v. Sims, 401 S.W.3d 402, 404 n.1 (Tex. App.—Texarkana 2013, no pet.). "[P] suggests that because the limitations claim was not raised in the first responsive pleading to suit, it has been waived. Although [TRCP] 94 requires the claim to be pled, the Rule does not require the claim to be brought in the first responsive pleading on penalty of waiver."

Yanez v. Ducasson, No. 01-12-00173-CV (Tex. App.—Houston [1st Dist.] 2012, no pet.) (memo op.; 12-20-12). "While [TRCP 94] identifies 'failure of consideration' as an affirmative defense, it does not include lack of consideration. Failure of consideration is a legal principle distinct from lack of consideration. Moreover, the presence of consideration is a fundamental element to establish the existence of a contract. Accordingly, it is an element of the plaintiff's burden of proof in a breach of contract claim, not an affirmative defense or plea in avoidance." *See also* ***Construction Fin. Servs. v. Chicago Title Ins.***, No. 04-12-00375-CV (Tex.App.—San Antonio 2013, pet. denied) (memo op.; 5-1-13) (footnote 8) (lack of consideration is not affirmative defense because it does not provide independent cause of action; rather, it goes directly to P's cause of action).

SecurityComm Grp. v. Brocail, No. 14-09-00295-CV (Tex.App.—Houston [14th Dist.] 2010, pet. denied) (memo op.; 12-28-10). "Although, typically, affirmative defenses are pleaded by a party opposing a claim for recovery or relief, the language of Rule 94 clearly requires the pleading of any 'matter constituting an avoidance' of any other matter—claim for relief or defense—asserted in another pleading, regardless of the alignment of the parties. [I]n order for a plaintiff to rely on an affirmative defense, or 'matter in avoidance,' to defeat a defendant's affirmative defense, the plaintiff must allege it in a petition or supplemental petition."

TRCP 95. PLEAS OF PAYMENT

When a defendant shall desire to prove payment, he shall file with his plea an account stating distinctly the nature of such payment, and the several items thereof; failing to do so, he shall not be allowed to prove the same, unless it be so plainly and particularly described in the plea as to give the plaintiff full notice of the character thereof.

See also *O'Connor's Texas Rules*, "The Answer—Denying Liability," ch. 3-E, p. 263.

ANNOTATIONS

Texas Mut. Ins. v. Ledbetter, 251 S.W.3d 31, 37 (Tex.2008). "Rule 95 ... governs payment as an affirmative *defense*, not payment as an affirmative *claim*."

Southwestern Fire & Cas. Co. v. Larue, 367 S.W.2d 162, 163 (Tex.1963). Under TRCP 94 and 95, payment is "an affirmative defense on which the defendant has the burden of proof, which must be specially pleaded, and may not be shown under a general denial."

TRCP 96. NO DISCONTINUANCE

Where the defendant has filed a counterclaim seeking affirmative relief, the plaintiff shall not be permitted by a discontinuance of his suit, to prejudice the right of the defendant to be heard on such counterclaim.

See also TRCP 162; *O'Connor's Texas Rules*, "Effect on defendant's claims," ch. 7-F, §6.3, p. 743.

ANNOTATIONS

BHP Pet. Co. v. Millard, 800 S.W.2d 838, 840 (Tex. 1990). "The plaintiff's right to take a nonsuit is *unqualified and absolute* as long as the defendant has not made a claim for affirmative relief."

TRCP 97. COUNTERCLAIM & CROSS-CLAIM

(a) Compulsory Counterclaims. A pleading shall state as a counterclaim any claim within the jurisdiction of the court, not the subject of a pending action, which at the time of filing the pleading the pleader has against any opposing party, if it arises out of the transaction or occurrence that is the subject matter of the opposing party's claim and does not require for its adjudication the presence of third parties of whom the court cannot acquire jurisdiction; provided, however, that a judgment based upon a settlement or compromise of a claim of one party to the transaction or occurrence prior to a disposition on the merits shall not operate as a bar to the

continuation or assertion of the claims of any other party to the transaction or occurrence unless the latter has consented in writing that said judgment shall operate as a bar.

(b) Permissive Counterclaims. A pleading may state as a counterclaim any claim against an opposing party whether or not arising out of the transaction or occurrence that is the subject matter of the opposing party's claim.

(c) Counterclaim Exceeding Opposing Claim. A counterclaim may or may not diminish or defeat the recovery sought by the opposing party. It may claim relief exceeding in amount or different in kind from that sought in the pleading of the opposing party, so long as the subject matter is within the jurisdiction of the court.

(d) Counterclaim Maturing or Acquired After Pleading. A claim which either matured or was acquired by the pleader after filing his pleading may be presented as a counterclaim by amended pleading.

(e) Cross-Claim Against Co-party. A pleading may state as a cross-claim any claim by one party against a co-party arising out of the transaction or occurrence that is the subject matter either of the original action or of a counterclaim therein. Such cross-claim may include a claim that the party against whom it is asserted is or may be liable to the cross-claimant for all or part of a claim asserted in the action against the cross-claimant.

(f) Additional Parties. Persons other than those made parties to the original action may be made parties to a third party action, counterclaim or cross-claim in accordance with the provisions of Rules 38, 39 and 40.

(g) Tort shall not be the subject of set-off or counterclaim against a contractual demand nor a contractual demand against tort unless it arises out of or is incident to or is connected with same.

(h) Separate Trials; Separate Judgments. If the court orders separate trials as provided in Rule 174, judgment on a counterclaim or cross-claim may be rendered when the court has jurisdiction so to do, even if the claims of the opposing party have been dismissed or otherwise disposed of.

See also CPRC §33.004 (responsible third parties); ***O'Connor's Texas Rules***, "Parties & Claims," ch. 2-E, p. 154; "The Answer—Denying Liability," ch. 3-E, p. 263; ***O'Connor's Texas Forms***, FORMS 3E.

ANNOTATIONS

In re J.B. Hunt Transp., 492 S.W.3d 287, 292-93 (Tex.2016). In ***Wyatt v. Shaw Plumbing Co.***, 760 S.W.2d 245 (Tex.1988), "we said that a counterclaim is compulsory if, among other things, 'it is not at the time of filing the answer the subject of a pending action.' [¶] There are two mistakes in that rendition of the compulsory-counterclaim rule. One problem is that the compulsory-counterclaim rule, located in [TRCP] 97(a), refers to 'the time of filing the *pleading*,' not 'the time of filing the *answer*' as we suggested. We therefore clarify that Rule 97 refers to *pleadings*, not *answers*. [¶] But the second ... issue is that we erroneously conflated two distinct requirements in Rule 97(a). The first three clauses of Rule 97(a) read as follows: 'A pleading shall state as a counterclaim any claim within the jurisdiction of the court, not the subject of a pending action, which at the time of filing the pleading the pleader has against any opposing party[.]' Our decision in ***Wyatt*** combined 'at the time of filing the pleading ...' with 'not the subject of a pending action,' creating the phrase '[the claim] is not at the time of filing the [pleading] the subject of a pending action.' But the third clause plainly does not modify the second clause.... Instead, the third clause must modify the word 'claim' in the first clause. [¶] This means that the second clause—'not the subject of a pending action'—is a standalone, unmodified phrase that modifies 'claim' in the first clause as well. [T]he claim must not have been the subject of a pending action *when the original suit was commenced*. If courts were to look at any subsequent snapshot in time, a wily litigant could avoid the compulsory-counterclaim rule by filing a second suit before that point in time to ensure that the litigant's claims are 'the subject of a pending action.' [A] counterclaim is compulsory if, in addition to Rule 97(a)'s other requirements, it was not the subject of a pending action when the original suit was commenced."

State & Cty. Mut. Fire Ins. v. Miller, 52 S.W.3d 693, 696 (Tex.2001). "[W]hen the parties are co-parties rather than opposing parties, the compulsory counterclaim rule and res judicata only act as a bar to a co-party's claim in a subsequent action if the co-parties had 'issues drawn between them' in the first action. For the purposes of res judicata, co-parties have issues drawn between them and become adverse when one co-party files a cross-action against a second co-party." *See*

also ***Getty Oil Co. v. Insurance Co. of N. Am.***, 845 S.W.2d 794, 800 (Tex.1992).

TRCP 98. SUPPLEMENTAL ANSWERS

The defendant's supplemental answers may contain special exceptions, general denial, and the allegations of new matter not before alleged by him, in reply to that which has been alleged by the plaintiff.

ANNOTATIONS

State v. Texas Mun. Power Agency, 565 S.W.2d 258, 277 (Tex.App.—Houston [1st Dist.] 1978, writ dism'd). "A supplemental answer is properly filed in response to any pleading of the plaintiff, regardless of whether it is an amended petition or a supplemental petition."

SECTION 5. CITATION

TRCP 99. ISSUANCE & FORM OF CITATION

a. Issuance. Upon the filing of the petition, the clerk, when requested, shall forthwith issue a citation and deliver the citation as directed by the requesting party. The party requesting citation shall be responsible for obtaining service of the citation and a copy of the petition. Upon request, separate or additional citations shall be issued by the clerk. The clerk must retain a copy of the citation in the court's file.

b. Form. The citation shall (1) be styled "The State of Texas," (2) be signed by the clerk under seal of court, (3) contain name and location of the court, (4) show date of filing of the petition, (5) show date of issuance of citation, (6) show file number, (7) show names of parties, (8) be directed to the defendant, (9) show the name and address of attorney for plaintiff, otherwise the address of plaintiff, (10) contain the time within which these rules require the defendant to file a written answer with the clerk who issued citation, (11) contain address of the clerk, and (12) shall notify the defendant that in case of failure of defendant to file an answer, judgment by default may be rendered for the relief demanded in the petition. The citation shall direct the defendant to file a written answer to the plaintiff's petition on or before 10:00 a.m. on the Monday next after the expiration of twenty days after the date of service thereof. The requirement of subsections 10 and 12 of this section shall be in the form set forth in section c of this rule.

c. Notice. The citation shall include the following notice to the defendant: "You have been sued. You may employ an attorney. If you or your attorney do not file a written answer with the clerk who issued this citation by 10:00 a.m. on the Monday next following the expiration of twenty days after you were served this citation and petition, a default judgment may be taken against you."

d. Copies. The party filing any pleading upon which citation is to be issued and served shall furnish the clerk with a sufficient number of copies thereof for use in serving the parties to be served, and when copies are so furnished the clerk shall make no charge for the copies.

Caution: TRCP 99 is affected by Fam. Code §§3.304, 3.305, 5.105, 6.408, 6.409, 9.001, 9.102, 45.003, 82.043, 102.009, 102.010, 154.193, 156.003, 158.306, 158.505, 161.005, and 233.007.

See also ***O'Connor's Texas Rules***, "Serving the Defendant with Suit," ch. 2-H, p. 184; "Default Judgment," ch. 7-A, p. 671; ***O'Connor's Texas Forms***, FORMS 2H.

ANNOTATIONS

Primate Constr., Inc. v. Silver, 884 S.W.2d 151, 153 (Tex.1994). "It is the responsibility of the one requesting service, not the process server, to see that service is properly accomplished. This responsibility extends to seeing that service is properly reflected in the record." *See also* ***In re Buggs***, 166 S.W.3d 506, 508 (Tex.App.—Texarkana 2005, orig. proceeding).

Midstate Envtl. Servs. v. Peterson, 435 S.W.3d 287, 290 (Tex.App.—Waco 2014, no pet.). "One of the most glaring defects as to the citation [in this case] is the lack of a seal. While language in the citation recites that it was 'issued and given under my hand *and seal of said court*…,' there is no seal visible on the copy of the original citation in the clerk's record. … Because we cannot presume a seal exists on the citation, the absence of a seal renders the original citation invalid. Accordingly, we join those courts that have held the absence of a seal is a defect in service that would make a default judgment improper."

Williams v. Williams, 150 S.W.3d 436, 445 (Tex. App.—Austin 2004, pet. denied). See annotation under TRCP 15, p. 1044.

Roberts v. Padre Island Brewing Co., 28 S.W.3d 618, 621-22 (Tex.App.—Corpus Christi 2000, pet. denied). "Reliance on the process server does not constitute due diligence in attempting service of process. A reasonable person … would have employed an alternate process server, a constable, or would have attempted service through other alternative court approved methods such as service through a court ap-

pointed third party. ... Although the existence of diligence is usually a question of fact, a lack of diligence exists as a matter of law because it is clear that [P] did not exhaust all of the alternatives available to achieve proper service." *See also* ***Holmes v. Texas Mut. Ins.***, 335 S.W.3d 738, 742 (Tex.App.—El Paso 2011, pet. abated 4-8-11); ***Boyattia v. Hinojosa***, 18 S.W.3d 729, 734 (Tex.App.—Dallas 2000, pet. denied).

TRCP 100 TO 102. REPEALED

TRCP 103. WHO MAY SERVE

Process—including citation and other notices, writs, orders, and other papers issued by the court—may be served anywhere by (1) any sheriff or constable or other person authorized by law, (2) any person authorized by law or by written order of the court who is not less than eighteen years of age, or (3) any person certified under order of the Supreme Court. Service by registered or certified mail and citation by publication must, if requested, be made by the clerk of the court in which the case is pending. But no person who is a party to or interested in the outcome of a suit may serve any process in that suit, and, unless otherwise authorized by a written court order, only a sheriff or constable may serve a citation in an action of forcible entry and detainer, a writ that requires the actual taking of possession of a person, property or thing, or process requiring that an enforcement action be physically enforced by the person delivering the process. The order authorizing a person to serve process may be made without written motion and no fee may be imposed for issuance of such order.

Caution: TRCP 103 is affected by Fam. Code §231.118.

See also *O'Connor's Texas Rules*, "Serving the Defendant with Suit," ch. 2-H, p. 184; "Default Judgment," ch. 7-A, p. 671.

ANNOTATIONS

Garcia v. Tester, No. 13-15-00498-CV (Tex.App.—Corpus Christi 2016, no pet.) (memo op.; 9-1-16). "[D] argues that [process server's] affidavit is insufficient because it stated merely that [process server] was authorized by a written order of 'a court in this county' rather than by 'a written order of *the* court' as required by [TRCP 103]. [D] contends that, according to the plain language of [TRCP 103], a private process server in a given case must be authorized by a written order of the particular court in which that case is pending. [¶] We disagree with [D's] assertion.... [Process server's] averment that he is authorized 'to serve citations and other notices' is sufficient to show that he was, in fact, authorized under Rule 103 to serve process in this case." *See also* ***Mayfield v. Dean Witter Fin. Servs.***, 894 S.W.2d 502, 505-06 (Tex.App.—Austin 1995, writ denied).

TRCP 104. REPEALED

TRCP 105. DUTY OF OFFICER OR PERSON RECEIVING

The officer or authorized person to whom process is delivered shall endorse thereon the day and hour on which he received it, and shall execute and return the same without delay.

See also *O'Connor's Texas Rules*, "Serving the Defendant with Suit," ch. 2-H, p. 184; "Default Judgment," ch. 7-A, p. 671.

ANNOTATIONS

Insurance Co. of Pa. v. Lejeune, 297 S.W.3d 254, 256 (Tex.2009). "Strict compliance with the rules governing service of citation is mandatory if a default judgment is to withstand an attack on appeal. Failure to comply with these rules constitutes error on the face of the record. Here, although [P] served [D] by certified mail, the record shows that the return of citation lacks the required notation showing the hour of receipt of citation. [P's] default judgment, therefore, cannot stand." *See also* ***Business Staffing, Inc. v. Gonzalez***, 331 S.W.3d 791, 792 (Tex.App.—Eastland 2010, no pet.).

Melendez v. John R. Schatzman, Inc., 685 S.W.2d 137, 138 (Tex.App.—El Paso 1985, no writ). Service by certified mail "was attempted ...; however, it does not appear that the officer receiving delivery of the process for service endorsed thereon the day and hour of receipt, nor was the return completed showing the execution by certified mail, all as required by Rule 105...."

TRCP 106. METHOD OF SERVICE

(a) Unless the citation or an order of the court otherwise directs, the citation shall be served by any person authorized by Rule 103 by

(1) delivering to the defendant, in person, a true copy of the citation with the date of delivery endorsed thereon with a copy of the petition attached thereto, or

(2) mailing to the defendant by registered or certified mail, return receipt requested, a true copy of the citation with a copy of the petition attached thereto.

(b) Upon motion supported by affidavit stating the location of the defendant's usual place of business or usual place of abode or other place where the defendant

can probably be found and stating specifically the facts showing that service has been attempted under either (a)(1) or (a)(2) at the location named in such affidavit but has not been successful, the court may authorize service

(1) by leaving a true copy of the citation, with a copy of the petition attached, with anyone over sixteen years of age at the location specified in such affidavit, or

(2) in any other manner that the affidavit or other evidence before the court shows will be reasonably effective to give the defendant notice of the suit.

Caution: TRCP 106 is affected by Fam. Code §§3.304, 3.305, 5.105, 6.408, 6.409, 45.003, 82.043, 102.009, 102.010, 158.306, 158.505, and 233.007.

See also ***O'Connor's Texas Rules***, "Serving the Defendant with Suit," ch. 2-H, p. 184; "Default Judgment," ch. 7-A, p. 671; ***O'Connor's Texas Forms***, FORMS 2H:4-6; ***O'Connor's Texas Family Law Handbook*** (2017), "Service of Process," ch. 3-A, §8, p. 233 (suit for divorce); "Service of Process," ch. 4-D, §5, p. 416 (suit to dissolve marriage with children).

ANNOTATIONS

Zanchi v. Lane, 408 S.W.3d 373, 380 (Tex.2013). "[D] argues that in order to 'serve' an expert report on a defendant who has not yet been served with process, the claimant must comply with the service-of-citation requirements under [TRCP] 106. We disagree. Rule 106 by its terms applies solely to service of citation. If the Legislature had intended to require a claimant to serve an expert report in accordance with Rule 106, it clearly knew how to do so."

State Farm Fire & Cas. Co. v. Costley, 868 S.W.2d 298, 298-99 (Tex.1993). "Under Rule 106(b) a court may authorize substituted service only after a plaintiff has unsuccessfully tried to effect personal service or service by certified mail, return receipt requested, as required by Rule 106(a). ... Thus, to require proof of actual notice upon substituted service would frustrate Rule 106(b)'s purpose of providing alternate methods [of service]." *See also* ***Singh v. Trinity Mktg. & Distrib. Co.***, 397 S.W.3d 257, 263-64 (Tex.App.—El Paso 2013, no pet.).

Uvalde Country Club v. Martin Linen Sup. Co., 690 S.W.2d 884, 885 (Tex.1985). "There are no presumptions in favor of valid issuance, service, and return of citation in the face of a writ of error [now a restricted appeal] attack on a default judgment. Moreover, failure to affirmatively show strict compliance with the [TRCPs] renders the attempted service of process invalid and of no effect." *See also* ***Steinke v. Mann***, 276 S.W.3d 608, 609-10 (Tex.App.—Waco 2008, no pet.) (court must expressly authorize service in accordance with either Rule 106(b)(1) or (b)(2)).

Luby v. Wood, No. 03-12-00179-CV (Tex.App.—Austin 2014, no pet.) (memo op.; 4-2-14). "[W]e have been unable to find any case supporting the proposition that a single attempt at service at a post office box is enough to warrant substituted service of process. [¶] Similarly, we have been unable to find any case standing for the proposition that mailing by regular mail a copy of the citation and the petition to a post office box under these circumstances can qualify as effective substituted service of process establishing jurisdiction over an individual. [Here], although the process server swore that the post office box was 'in current use,' the server's affidavit does not clarify whether that meant that [D] was regularly checking his mail there or simply that rental period for the box had not yet expired. Accordingly, the statement in the process server's affidavit [did not satisfy the requirements of Rule 106(b)]."

In re M.C.B., 400 S.W.3d 630, 633 (Tex.App.—Dallas 2013, no pet.). "[W]hen a default judgment is attacked by motion for new trial or bill of review in the trial court, ... the parties may introduce affidavits, depositions, testimony, and exhibits to explain what happened. *At 634:* [T]he trial court could have considered the process server's testimony in concluding that the requirements in the order authorizing substitute service were strictly followed. *At 635:* [Process server] taped the service in this case to [father's] door, in strict compliance with the trial court's order authorizing substitute service. Thus, [father] failed to establish the return of service did not strictly comply with the [TRCP] because the trial court's order required the citation to be attached or affixed to his door, and the return stated it was executed 'by 106 to door.'"

James v. Commission for Lawyer Discipline, 310 S.W.3d 586, 591 (Tex.App.—Dallas 2010, no pet.). "Rule 106 does not require that personal service be attempted at multiple locations before the trial court may authorize substituted service...."

Coronado v. Norman, 111 S.W.3d 838, 842 (Tex. App.—Eastland 2003, pet. denied). The process server's "affidavit does not contain sufficient facts to satisfy Rule 106(b). While the ... inclusion of the dates and times of attempted service [is not specifically required,] the specific dates and times of attempted service are important to establish sufficient facts to uphold a default judgment under Rule 106(b). Every attempt at personal service in this case may have been while [D] was at work. When told that [D] 'was not there,' the process server apparently did not try to find out where [D] could be located or when he would return."

TRCP 107. RETURN OF SERVICE

(a) The officer or authorized person executing the citation must complete a return of service. The return may, but need not, be endorsed on or attached to the citation.

(b) The return, together with any document to which it is attached, must include the following information:

(1) the cause number and case name;

(2) the court in which the case is filed;

(3) a description of what was served;

(4) the date and time the process was received for service;

(5) the person or entity served;

(6) the address served;

(7) the date of service or attempted service;

(8) the manner of delivery of service or attempted service;

(9) the name of the person who served or attempted to serve the process;

(10) if the person named in (9) is a process server certified under order of the Supreme Court, his or her identification number and the expiration date of his or her certification; and

(11) any other information required by rule or law.

(c) When the citation was served by registered or certified mail as authorized by Rule 106, the return by the officer or authorized person must also contain the return receipt with the addressee's signature.

(d) When the officer or authorized person has not served the citation, the return shall show the diligence used by the officer or authorized person to execute the same and the cause of failure to execute it, and where the defendant is to be found, if ascertainable.

(e) The officer or authorized person who serves or attempts to serve a citation must sign the return. If the return is signed by a person other than a sheriff, constable, or the clerk of the court, the return must either be verified or be signed under penalty of perjury. A return signed under penalty of perjury must contain the statement below in substantially the following form:

"My name is _________ (First) _________ (Middle) _______ (Last), my date of birth is _______, and my address is ____________ (Street), _______ (City), _______ (State), _______ (Zip Code), and _______ (Country). I declare under penalty of perjury that the foregoing is true and correct.

Executed in _______ County, State of _______, on the ______ day of _______ (Month), _______ (Year).

____
Declarant"

(f) Where citation is executed by an alternative method as authorized by Rule 106, proof of service shall be made in the manner ordered by the court.

(g) The return and any document to which it is attached must be filed with the court and may be filed electronically or by facsimile, if those methods of filing are available.

(h) No default judgment shall be granted in any cause until proof of service as provided by this rule or by Rules 108 or 108a, or as ordered by the court in the event citation is executed by an alternative method under Rule 106, shall have been on file with the clerk of the court ten days, exclusive of the day of filing and the day of judgment.

See also TRCP 16; *O'Connor's Texas Rules*, "Proof of Service – The Return," ch. 2-H, §9, p. 195; "Default Judgment," ch. 7-A, p. 671.

ANNOTATIONS

Campus Invs. v. Cullever, 144 S.W.3d 464, 466 (Tex.2004). "When substituted service on a statutory agent is allowed, the designee is not an agent for *serving* but for *receiving* process on the defendant's behalf. A certificate ... from the Secretary of State *conclusively* establishes that process was served. As the purpose of Rule 107 is to establish whether there has been proper citation and service, the Secretary's certificate fulfills that purpose." *See also* ***El Paisano Nw. Hwy., Inc. v. Arzate***, No. 05-12-01457-CV (Tex.App.—Dallas 2014, no pet.) (memo op.; 4-14-14) (P who strictly complies with rules for substituted service on Secretary of State is not required to also strictly comply with TRCP 106 and 107).

Primate Constr., Inc. v. Silver, 884 S.W.2d 151, 152-53 (Tex.1994). "The return of service is not a trivial, formulaic document. It has long been considered prima facie evidence of the facts recited therein. [¶] The officer's return does not cease to be prima facie evidence of the facts of service simply because the facts are recited in a form rather than filled in by the officer. ... If the facts as recited in the sheriff's return, pre-printed or otherwise, are incorrect and do not show

proper service, the one requesting service must amend the return prior to judgment."

James v. Commission for Lawyer Discipline, 310 S.W.3d 586, 591 (Tex.App.—Dallas 2010, no pet.). "The trial court's order for substituted service did not prescribe a manner for the proof of service, and [D] argues that omission rendered the order for substituted service void. We disagree. '[I]n the absence of a specification in the trial court's [TRCP] 106 order of a *different* manner of proving service, proof of service in the normal manner authorized by [TRCP] 107 is sufficient.'"

Silver B & Laviolette, LLC v. GH Contracting, Inc., No. 03-10-00091-CV (Tex.App.—Austin 2010, no pet.) (memo op.; 10-12-10). "If any of the requirements of Rule 107 are not met, the return is fatally defective and will not support a default judgment under direct attack. Strict compliance, however, does not require obeisance to the minutest detail. As long as the record as a whole shows that the citation was served on the defendant, service of process will not be invalidated." (Internal quotes omitted.) *See also* ***In re S.C.***, No. 02-15-00191-CV (Tex.App.—Fort Worth 2015, no pet.) (memo op.; 12-23-15).

Myan Mgmt. Grp. v. Adam Sparks Family Revocable Trust, 292 S.W.3d 750, 753-54 (Tex.App.—Dallas 2009, no pet.). "Service is invalid if the name on the return alters the identity of the defendant, but a minor change in the name does not render the return defective. [¶] Examples of name differences held not to invalidate service include the removal of a middle initial on the return, the omission of the corporate designation 'Inc.,' the lack of an accent mark on a corporate name, and the substitution of '@' for 'at.' [¶] [Here, r]emoving periods from 'L.L.C.' is a variation as minor as the lack of an accent mark on a corporate name.... Similarly, dropping 'Group, L.L.C.' from the entity name is like dropping 'Inc.' from the entity name.... Neither omission suggests that a different entity was served than the one listed in the petition."

Redwood Grp. v. Louiseau, 113 S.W.3d 866, 869 (Tex.App.—Austin 2003, no pet.). "While a return is prima facie evidence of the facts recited *therein*, this does not mean that the return is prima facie evidence of anything about which it is silent. For example, the two returns in question here contain nothing about the contents of the two lost citations; we cannot presume they conformed to the requirements of [TRCP 99] specifying the contents of a valid citation."

All Commercial Floors, Inc. v. Barton & Rasor, 97 S.W.3d 723, 727 (Tex.App.—Fort Worth 2003, no pet.). "[A] corporation is not a person capable of accepting process, and it must be served through its agents. Therefore, because the record shows on its face that the return was not signed by the addressee or registered agent and [D] is not capable of receiving service, [P] has failed to strictly comply with Rule 107."

Union Pac. Corp. v. Legg, 49 S.W.3d 72, 78 (Tex. App.—Austin 2001, no pet.). "The clerk's return of the citation directed to [D] and the accompanying certified-mail receipt do not bear a file mark or other indication that they were in fact filed with the clerk on a particular day, or that they were, indeed, filed at all. Consequently, they do not show they were 'on file' for the requisite ten days before default judgment was granted. We hold this violates the strict-compliance requirement. *At 79:* Rule 107 also requires that the return receipt bear 'the addressee's signature' when service is by certified mail. The return receipt in this instance bears only a stamp rather than a handwritten signature.... We believe the return receipt does not bear the requisite addressee's signature. A stamped signature may be sufficient if shown to be authorized by proof in the record, but no such proof appears here. We hold the return fatally defective...."

TRCP 108. SERVICE IN ANOTHER STATE

Where the defendant is absent from the State, or is a nonresident of the State, the form of notice to such defendant of the institution of the suit shall be the same as prescribed for citation to a resident defendant; and such notice may be served by any disinterested person who is not less than eighteen years of age, in the same manner as provided in Rule 106 hereof. The return of service in such cases shall be completed in accordance with Rule 107. A defendant served with such notice shall be required to appear and answer in the same manner and time and under the same penalties as if he had been personally served with a citation within this State to the full extent that he may be required to appear and answer under the Constitution of the United States in an action either in rem or in personam.

See also *O'Connor's Texas Rules*, "Serving the Defendant with Suit," ch. 2-H, p. 184.

ANNOTATIONS

Paramount Pipe & Sup. Co. v. Muhr, 749 S.W.2d 491, 495-96 (Tex.1988). TRCP 108 "is a valid procedural alternative to service under the long-arm statute. ... So long as the allegations confronting [D] were sufficient to satisfy due process requirements, the trial court had jurisdiction to render judgment by default against him. The only question ... is whether the jurisdictional allegations in the petitions were sufficient, under the [U.S.] Constitution ..., to require [D] to answer."

TRCP 108a. SERVICE OF PROCESS IN FOREIGN COUNTRIES

(1) Manner. Service of process may be effected upon a party in a foreign country if service of the citation and petition is made: (a) in the manner prescribed by the law of the foreign country for service in that country in an action in any of its courts of general jurisdiction; or (b) as directed by the foreign authority in response to a letter rogatory or a letter of request; or (c) in the manner provided by Rule 106; or (d) pursuant to the terms and provisions of any applicable treaty or convention; or (e) by diplomatic or consular officials when authorized by the United States Department of State; or (f) by any other means directed by the court that is not prohibited by the law of the country where service is to be made. The method for service of process in a foreign country must be reasonably calculated, under all of the circumstances, to give actual notice of the proceedings to the defendant in time to answer and defend. A defendant served with process under this rule shall be required to appear and answer in the same manner and time and under the same penalties as if he had been personally served with citation within this state to the full extent that he may be required to appear and answer under the Constitution of the United States or under any applicable convention or treaty in an action either in rem or in personam.

(2) Return. Proof of service may be made as prescribed by the law of the foreign country, by order of the court, by Rule 107, or by a method provided in any applicable treaty or convention.

See also CPRC §§17.044, 17.045; *O'Connor's Texas Rules*, "Service Outside the United States," ch. 2-H, §11, p. 199.

ANNOTATIONS

Commission of Contracts v. Arriba, Ltd., 882 S.W.2d 576, 584 (Tex.App.—Houston [1st Dist.] 1994, no writ). "[Ps] argue that service on a resident of a foreign country under the long-arm statute is improper, and that a resident of a foreign country can only be served according to the methods of service prescribed in [TRCP] 108a. *At 585:* We find a party in a foreign country may be served under the long-arm statute."

TRCP 109. CITATION BY PUBLICATION

When a party to a suit, his agent or attorney, shall make oath that the residence of any party defendant is unknown to affiant, and to such party when the affidavit is made by his agent or attorney, or that such defendant is a transient person, and that after due diligence such party and the affiant have been unable to locate the whereabouts of such defendant, or that such defendant is absent from or is a nonresident of the State, and that the party applying for the citation has attempted to obtain personal service of nonresident notice as provided for in Rule 108, but has been unable to do so, the clerk shall issue citation for such defendant for service by publication. In such cases it shall be the duty of the court trying the case to inquire into the sufficiency of the diligence exercised in attempting to ascertain the residence or whereabouts of the defendant or to obtain service of nonresident notice, as the case may be, before granting any judgment on such service.

Caution: TRCP 109 is affected by Fam. Code §§3.305, 6.409, 82.043, and 102.010.

See also *O'Connor's Texas Rules*, "Serving the Defendant with Suit," ch. 2-H, p. 184; "Default Judgment," ch. 7-A, p. 671; "MNT After Service by Publication," ch. 10-B, §10, p. 902; *O'Connor's Texas Forms*, FORMS 2H:4-6; ***O'Connor's Texas Family Law Handbook*** (2017), "Service by publication," ch. 3-A, §8.2.4, p. 233 (suit for divorce); "Service by publication," ch. 4-D, §5.2.4, p. 418 (suit to dissolve marriage with children).

ANNOTATIONS

In re E.R., 385 S.W.3d 552, 564 (Tex.2012). See annotation under Family Code §102.010, p. 410.

TRCP 109a. OTHER SUBSTITUTED SERVICE

Whenever citation by publication is authorized, the court may, on motion, prescribe a different method of substituted service, if the court finds, and so recites in its order, that the method so prescribed would be as likely as publication to give defendant actual notice. When such method of substituted service is authorized, the return of the officer executing the citation shall state particularly the manner in which service is accomplished, and shall attach any return receipt, returned mail, or other evidence showing the result of such service. Failure of defendant to respond to such citation shall not render the service invalid. When such

substituted service has been obtained and the defendant has not appeared, the provisions of Rules 244 and 329 shall apply as if citation had been served by publication.

Caution: TRCP 109a is affected by Fam. Code §§3.305, 6.409, 82.043, and 102.010.

See also ***O'Connor's Texas Rules***, "Serving the Defendant with Suit," ch. 2-H, p. 184; ***O'Connor's Texas Forms***, FORMS 2H:4-6; ***O'Connor's Texas Family Law Handbook*** (2017), "Substituted service – courthouse posting," ch. 4-D, §5.2.4(3)(b), p. 418.

TRCP 110. EFFECT OF RULES ON OTHER STATUTES

Where by statute or these rules citation by publication is authorized and the statute or rules do not specify the requisites of such citation or the method of service thereof, or where they direct that such citation be issued or served as in other civil actions, the provisions of these rules shall govern. Where, however, the statute authorizing citation by publication provides expressly for requisites of such citation or service thereof, or both, differing from the provisions of Rules 114, 115, and 116, these rules shall not govern, but the special statutory procedure shall continue in force; provided, however, that Rule 117a shall control with respect to citation in tax suits.

Caution: TRCP 110 is affected by Fam. Code §§3.305, 6.409, 82.043, and 102.010.

TRCP 111. CITATION BY PUBLICATION IN ACTION AGAINST UNKNOWN HEIRS OR STOCKHOLDERS OF DEFUNCT CORPORATIONS

If the plaintiff, his agent, or attorney, shall make oath that the names of the heirs or stockholders against whom an action is authorized by Section 17.004, Civil Practice and Remedies Code, are unknown to the affiant, the clerk shall issue a citation for service by publication. Such citation shall be addressed to the defendants by a concise description of their classification, as "the Unknown Heirs of A.B., deceased," or "Unknown Stockholders of __________ Corporation," as the case may be, and shall contain the other requisites prescribed in Rules 114 and 115 and shall be served as provided by Rule 116.

See also ***O'Connor's Texas Rules***, "Serving the Defendant with Suit," ch. 2-H, p. 184; "MNT After Service by Publication," ch. 10-B, §10, p. 902.

TRCP 112. PARTIES TO ACTIONS AGAINST UNKNOWN OWNERS OR CLAIMANTS OF INTEREST IN LAND

In suits authorized by Section 17.005, Civil Practice and Remedies Code, all persons claiming under such conveyance whose names are known to plaintiff shall be made parties by name and cited to appear, in the manner now provided by law as in other suits; all other persons claiming any interest in such land under such conveyance may be made parties to the suit and cited by publication under the designation "all persons claiming any title or interest in land under deed heretofore given to ____________ of ________________ as grantee" (inserting in the blanks the name and residence of grantee as given in such conveyance). It shall be permissible to join in one suit all persons claiming under two or more conveyances affecting title to the same tract of land.

See also CPRC §17.005; TRCP 113; ***O'Connor's Texas Rules***, "Serving the Defendant with Suit," ch. 2-H, p. 184; "MNT After Service by Publication," ch. 10-B, §10, p. 902.

TRCP 113. CITATION BY PUBLICATION IN ACTIONS AGAINST UNKNOWN OWNERS OR CLAIMANTS OF INTEREST IN LAND

In suits authorized by Section 17.005, Civil Practice and Remedies Code, plaintiff, his agent or attorney shall make and file with the clerk of the court an affidavit, stating

(a) the name of the grantee as set out in the conveyance constituting source of title of defendants, and

(b) stating that affiant does not know the names of any persons claiming title or interest under such conveyance other than as stated in plaintiff's petition and

(c) if the conveyance is to a company or association name as grantee, further stating whether grantee is incorporated or unincorporated, if such fact is known, and if such fact is unknown, so stating.

Said clerk shall thereupon issue a citation for service upon all persons claiming any title or interest in such land under such conveyance. The citation in such cases shall contain the requisites and be served in the manner provided by Rules 114, 115 and 116.

See also CPRC §17.005; TRCP 112; ***O'Connor's Texas Rules***, "Serving the Defendant with Suit," ch. 2-H, p. 184; "MNT After Service by Publication," ch. 10-B, §10, p. 902.

ANNOTATIONS

Quarles v. Champion Int'l, 760 S.W.2d 792, 794 (Tex.App.—Beaumont 1988, writ denied). Service of citation by publication on a known party is improper, and "this notice requirement to a known party is of due process dimension."

TRCP 114. CITATION BY PUBLICATION; REQUISITES

Where citation by publication is authorized by these rules, the citation shall contain the requisites prescribed by Rules 15 and 99, in so far as they are not inconsistent herewith, provided that no copy of the plaintiff's petition shall accompany this citation, and the citation shall be styled "The State of Texas" and shall be directed to the defendant or defendants by name, if their names are known, or to the defendant or defendants as designated in the petition, if unknown, or such other classification as may be fixed by any statute or by these rules. Where there are two or more defendants or classes of defendants to be served by publication, the citation may be directed to all of them by name and classification, so that service may be completed by publication of the one citation for the required number of times. The citation shall contain the names of the parties, a brief statement of the nature of the suit (which need not contain the details and particulars of the claim) a description of any property involved and of the interest of the named or unknown defendant or defendants, and, where the suit involves land, the requisites of Rule 115. If issued from the district or county court, the citation shall command such parties to appear and answer at or before 10 o'clock a.m. of the first Monday after the expiration of 42 days from the date of issuance thereof, specifying the day of the week, the day of the month, and the time of day the defendant is required to answer. If issued from the justice of the peace court, such citation shall command such parties to appear and answer on or before the first day of the first term of court which convenes after the expiration of 42 days from the date of issue thereof, specifying the day of the week, and the day of the month, that such term will meet.

Caution: TRCP 114 is affected by Fam. Code §§3.305, 6.409, 82.043, and 102.010.

See also ***O'Connor's Texas Family Law Handbook*** (2017), "Suit for Divorce," ch. 3-A, p. 205; "Suit to Dissolve Marriage with Children," ch. 4-D, p. 410.

TRCP 115. FORM OF PUBLISHED CITATION IN ACTIONS INVOLVING LAND

In citations by publication involving land, it shall be sufficient in making the brief statement of the claim in such citation to state the kind of suit, the number of acres of land involved in the suit, or the number of the lot and block, or any other plat description that may be of record if the land is situated in a city or town, the survey on which and the county in which the land is situated, and any special pleas which are relied upon in such suit.

TRCP 116. SERVICE OF CITATION BY PUBLICATION

The citation, when issued, shall be served by the sheriff or any constable of any county of the State of Texas or by the clerk of the court in which the case is pending, by having the same published once each week for four (4) consecutive weeks, the first publication to be at least twenty-eight (28) days before the return day of the citation. In all suits which do not involve the title to land or the partition of real estate, such publication shall be made in the county where the suit is pending, if there be a newspaper published in said county, but if not, then in an adjoining county where a newspaper is published. In all suits which involve the title to land or partition of real estate, such publication shall be made in the county where the land, or a portion thereof, is situated, if there be a newspaper in such county, but if not, then in an adjoining county to the county where the land or a part thereof is situated, where a newspaper is published.

Caution: TRCP 116 is affected by Fam. Code §§3.305, 6.409, 82.043, and 102.010.

See also ***O'Connor's Texas Rules***, "Service by publication," ch. 2-H, §4.4, p. 189.

TRCP 117. RETURN OF CITATION BY PUBLICATION

The return of the officer executing such citation shall show how and when the citation was executed, specifying the dates of such publication, be signed by him officially and shall be accompanied by a printed copy of such publication.

TRCP 117a. CITATION IN SUITS FOR DELINQUENT AD VALOREM TAXES

In all suits for collection of delinquent ad valorem taxes, the rules of civil procedure governing issuance and service of citation shall control the issuance and service of citation therein, except as herein otherwise specially provided.

1. Personal Service: Owner and Residence Known, Within State: Where any defendant in a tax suit is a resident of the State of Texas and is not subject to citation by publication under subdivision 3 below, the process shall conform substantially to the form hereinafter set out for personal service and shall contain the essential elements and be served and returned

and otherwise regulated by the provisions of Rules 99 to 107, inclusive.

2. Personal Service: Owner and Residence Known, Out of State: Where any such defendant is absent from the State or is a nonresident of the State and is not subject to citation by publication under subdivision 3 below, the process shall conform substantially to the form hereinafter set out for personal service and shall contain the essential elements and be served and returned and otherwise regulated by the provisions of Rule 108.

3. Service by Publication: Nonresident, Absent from State, Transient, Name Unknown, Residence Unknown, Owner Unknown, Heirs Unknown, Corporate Officers, Trustees, Receivers or Stockholders Unknown, Any Other Unknown Persons Owing or Claiming or Having an Interest: Where any defendant in a tax suit is a nonresident of the State, or is absent from the State, or is a transient person, or the name or the residence of any owner of any interest in any property upon which a tax lien is sought to be foreclosed, is unknown to the attorney requesting the issuance of process or filing the suit for the taxing unit, and such attorney shall make affidavit that such defendant is a nonresident of the State, or is absent from the State, or is a transient person, or that the name or residence of such owner is unknown and cannot be ascertained after diligent inquiry, each such person in every such class above mentioned, together with any and all other persons, including adverse claimants, owning or claiming or having any legal or equitable interest in or lien upon such property, may be cited by publication. All unknown owners of any interest in any property upon which any taxing unit seeks to foreclose a lien for taxes, including stockholders of corporations—defunct or otherwise—their successors, heirs, and assigns, may be joined in such suit under the designation of "unknown owners" and citation be had upon them as such; provided, however, that record owners of such property or of any apparent interest therein, including, without limitation, record lien holders, shall not be included in the designation of "unknown owners"; and provided further that where any record owner has rendered the property involved within five years before the tax suit is filed, citation on such record owner may not be had by publication or posting unless citation for personal service has been issued as to such record owner, with a notation thereon setting forth the same address as is contained on the rendition sheet made within such five years, and the sheriff or other person to whom citation has been delivered makes his return thereon that he is unable to locate the defendant. Where any attorney filing a tax suit for a taxing unit, or requesting the issuance of process in such suit, shall make affidavit that a corporation is the record owner of any interest in any property upon which a tax lien is sought to be foreclosed, and that he does not know, and after diligent inquiry has been unable to ascertain, the location of the place of business, if any, of such corporation, or the name or place of residence of any officer of such corporation upon whom personal service may be had, such corporation may be cited by publication as herein provided. All defendants of the classes enumerated above may be joined in the same citation by publication.

An affidavit which complies with the foregoing requirements therefor shall be sufficient basis for the citation above mentioned in connection with it but shall be held to be made upon the criminal responsibility of affiant.

Such citation by publication shall be directed to the defendants by names or by designation as hereinabove provided, and shall be issued and signed by the clerk of the court in which such tax suit is pending. It shall be sufficient if it states the file number and style of the case, the date of the filing of the petition, the names of all parties by name or by designation as hereinabove provided, and the court in which the suit is pending; shall command such parties to appear and defend such suit at or before 10 o'clock a.m. of the first Monday after the expiration of forty-two days from the date of the issuance thereof, specifying such date when such parties are required to answer; shall state the place of holding the court, the nature of the suit, and the date of the issuance of the citation; and shall be signed and sealed by the clerk.

The citation shall be published in the English language one time a week for two weeks in some newspaper published in the county in which the property is located, which newspaper must have been in general circulation for at least one year immediately prior to the first publication and shall in every respect answer the requirements of the law applicable to newspapers which are employed for such a purpose, the first publication to be not less than twenty-eight days prior to the return day fixed in the citation; and the affidavit of the editor or publisher of the newspaper giving the date of

publication, together with a printed copy of the citation as published, shall constitute sufficient proof of due publication when returned and filed in court. If there is no newspaper published in the county, then the publication may be made in a newspaper in an adjoining county, which newspaper shall in every respect answer the requirements of the law applicable to newspapers which are employed for such a purpose. The maximum fee for publishing the citation shall be the lowest published word or line rate of that newspaper for classified advertising. If the publication of the citation cannot be had for this fee, chargeable as costs and payable upon sale of the property, as provided by law, and this fact is supported by the affidavit of the attorney for the plaintiff or the attorney requesting the issuance of the process, then service of the citation may be made by posting a copy at the courthouse door of the county in which the suit is pending, the citation to be posted at least twenty-eight days prior to the return day fixed in the citation. Proof of the posting of the citation shall be made by affidavit of the attorney for the plaintiff, or of the person posting it. When citation is served as here provided it shall be sufficient, and no other form of citation or notice to the named defendants therein shall be necessary.

4. Citation in Tax Suits: General Provisions: Any process authorized by this rule may issue jointly in behalf of all taxing units who are plaintiffs or intervenors in any tax suit. The statement of the nature of the suit, to be set out in the citation, shall be sufficient if it contains a brief general description of the property upon which the taxes are due and the amount of such taxes, exclusive of interest, penalties, and costs, and shall state, in substance, that in such suit the plaintiff and all other taxing units who may set up their claims therein seek recovery of the delinquent ad valorem taxes due on said property, and the (establishment and foreclosure) of liens, if any, securing the payment of same, as provided by law; that in addition to the taxes all interest, penalties, and costs allowed by law up to and including the day of judgment are included in the suit; and that all parties to the suit, including plaintiff, defendants, and intervenors, shall take notice that claims for any taxes on said property becoming delinquent subsequent to the filing of the suit and up to the day of judgment, together with all interest, penalties, and costs allowed by law thereon, may, upon request therefor, be recovered therein without further citation or notice to any parties thereto. Such citation need not be accompanied by a copy of plaintiff's petition and no such copy need be served. Such citation shall also show the names of all taxing units which assess and collect taxes on said property not made parties to such suit, and shall contain, in substance, a recitation that each party to such suit shall take notice of, and plead and answer to, all claims and pleadings then on file or thereafter filed in said cause by all other parties therein, or who may intervene therein and set up their respective tax claims against said property. After citation or notice has been given on behalf of any plaintiff or intervenor taxing unit, the court shall have jurisdiction to hear and determine the tax claims of all taxing units who are parties plaintiff, intervenor or defendant at the time such process is issued and of all taxing units intervening after such process is issued, not only for the taxes, interest, penalties, and costs which may be due on said property at the time the suit is filed, but those becoming delinquent thereon at any time thereafter up to and including the day of judgment, without the necessity of further citation or notice to any party to said suit; and any taxing unit having a tax claim against said property may, by answer or intervention, set up and have determined its tax claim without the necessity of further citation or notice to any parties to such suit.

5. Form of Citation by Publication or Posting: The form of citation by publication or posting shall be sufficient if it is in substantially the following form, with proper changes to make the same applicable to personal property, where necessary, and if the suit includes or is for the recovery of taxes assessed on personal property, a general description of such personal property shall be sufficient:

THE STATE OF TEXAS §

COUNTY OF __________ §

In the name and by the authority of the State of Texas

Notice is hereby given as follows:

To ______________________________

____

and any and all other persons, including adverse claimants, owning or having or claiming any legal or equitable interest in or lien upon the following described property delinquent to Plaintiff herein, for taxes, to-wit:

____

____

Which said property is delinquent to Plaintiff for taxes in the following amounts:

$_____, exclusive of interest, penalties, and costs, and there is included in this suit in addition to the taxes all said interest, penalties, and costs thereon, allowed by law up to and including the day of judgment herein.

You are hereby notified that suit has been brought by _____ as Plaintiffs, against ______ as Defendants, by petition filed on the ___ day of ____, 20__, in a certain suit styled _________ v. _________ for collection of the taxes on said property and that said suit is now pending in the District Court of _____ County, Texas, ____ Judicial District, and the file number of said suit is ___________, that the names of all taxing units which assess and collect taxes on the property hereinabove described, not made parties to this suit, are _______________.

Plaintiff and all other taxing units who may set up their tax claims herein seek recovery of delinquent ad valorem taxes on the property hereinabove described, and in addition to the taxes all interest, penalties, and costs allowed by law thereon up to and including the day of judgment herein, and the establishment and foreclosure of liens, if any, securing the payment of same, as provided by law.

All parties to this suit, including plaintiff, defendants, and intervenors, shall take notice that claims not only for any taxes which were delinquent on said property at the time this suit was filed but all taxes becoming delinquent thereon at any time thereafter up to the day of judgment, including all interest, penalties, and costs allowed by law thereon, may, upon request therefor, be recovered herein without further citation or notice to any parties herein, and all said parties shall take notice of and plead and answer to all claims and pleadings now on file and which may hereafter be filed in said cause by all other parties herein, and all of those taxing units above named who may intervene herein and set up their respective tax claims against said property.

You are hereby commanded to appear and defend such suit on the first Monday after the expiration of forty-two (42) days from and after the date of issuance hereof, the same being the ___ day of ________, A.D., 20___ (which is the return day of such citation), before the honorable District Court of ____________ County, Texas, to be held at the courthouse thereof, then and there to show cause why judgment shall not be rendered for such taxes, penalties, interest, and costs, and condemning said property and ordering foreclosure of the constitutional and statutory tax liens thereon for taxes due the plaintiff and the taxing units parties hereto, and those who may intervene herein, together with all interest, penalties, and costs allowed by law up to and including the day of judgment herein, and all costs of this suit.

Issued and given under my hand and seal of said court in the City of _________, _______ County, Texas, this ___ day of __________, A.D., 20__.

____

Clerk of the District Court
____________ County, Texas,
____________ Judicial District.

6. Form of Citation by Personal Service in or out of State: The form of citation for personal service shall be sufficient if it is in substantially the following form, with proper changes to make the same applicable to personal property, where necessary, and if the suit includes or is for the recovery of taxes assessed on personal property, a general description of such personal property shall be sufficient:

THE STATE OF TEXAS
To ________, Defendant,
GREETING:

YOU ARE HEREBY COMMANDED to appear and answer before the Honorable District Court, _______ Judicial District, ______ County, Texas, at the Courthouse of said county in ______, Texas, at or before 10 o'clock a.m. of the Monday next after the expiration of 20 days from the date of service of this citation, then and there to answer the petition of ____________, Plaintiff, filed in said Court on the ___ day of _____, A.D., 20__, against _____________, Defendant, said suit being number ________ on the docket of said Court, the nature of which demand is a suit to collect delinquent ad valorem taxes on the property hereinafter described.

The amount of taxes due Plaintiff, exclusive of interest, penalties, and costs, is the sum of $_________, said property being described as follows, to-wit: ______________________________

____

The names of all taxing units which assess and collect taxes on said property, not made parties to this suit, are:

____

Plaintiff and all other taxing units who may set up their tax claims herein seek recovery of delinquent ad valorem taxes on the property hereinabove described, and in addition to the taxes all interest, penalties, and costs allowed by law thereon up to and including the day of judgment herein, and the establishment and foreclosure of liens securing the payment of same, as provided by law.

All parties to this suit, including plaintiff, defendants, and intervenors, shall take notice that claims not only for any taxes which were delinquent on said property at the time this suit was filed but all taxes becoming delinquent thereon at any time thereafter up to the day of judgment, including all interest, penalties, and costs allowed by law thereon, may, upon request therefor, be recovered herein without further citation or notice to any parties herein, and all said parties shall take notice of and plead and answer to all claims and pleadings now on file and which may hereafter be filed in this cause by all other parties hereto, and by all of those taxing units above named, who may intervene herein and set up their respective tax claims against said property.

If this citation is not served within 90 days after the date of its issuance, it shall be returned unserved.

The officer executing this return shall promptly serve the same according to the requirements of law and the mandates hereof and make due return as the law directs.

Issued and given under my hand and seal of said Court at ____, Texas, this the ___ day of ______, A.D., 20__.

____

Clerk of the District Court

____________ County, Texas,

By ____________, Deputy

See also *O'Connor's Texas Rules*, "Serving the Defendant with Suit," ch. 2-H, p. 184.

TRCP 118. AMENDMENT

At any time in its discretion and upon such notice and on such terms as it deems just, the court may allow any process or proof of service thereof to be amended, unless it clearly appears that material prejudice would result to the substantial rights of the party against whom the process issued.

See also *O'Connor's Texas Rules*, "Serving the Defendant with Suit," ch. 2-H, p. 184.

ANNOTATIONS

Higginbotham v. General Life & Acc. Ins., 796 S.W.2d 695, 697 (Tex.1990). Because a trial court's order holding that service was proper was "tantamount to formal amendment of the return of citation, the record was sufficient to show valid service."

LEJ Dev. Corp. v. Southwest Bank, 407 S.W.3d 863, 867-68 (Tex.App.—Fort Worth 2013, no pet.). "[T]he trial court may enter a postjudgment order granting amendment of a return of citation pursuant to rule 118 while the trial court retains plenary power. [¶] '[W]hen a return is amended under Rule 118, the amended return relates back and is regarded as filed when the original return was filed.' [This] satisfies the requirement that a return of service be on file for at least ten days before entry of judgment." *See also* ***Gonzalez v. Tapia***, 287 S.W.3d 805, 808 (Tex.App.—Corpus Christi 2009, pet. denied) (trial court can amend proof of service after default judgment has become final and plenary power has expired).

TRCP 119. ACCEPTANCE OF SERVICE

The defendant may accept service of process, or waive the issuance or service thereof by a written memorandum signed by him, or by his duly authorized agent or attorney, after suit is brought, sworn to before a proper officer other than an attorney in the case, and filed among the papers of the cause, and such waiver or acceptance shall have the same force and effect as if the citation had been issued and served as provided by law. The party signing such memorandum shall be delivered a copy of plaintiff's petition, and the receipt of the same shall be acknowledged in such memorandum. In every divorce action such memorandum shall also include the defendant's mailing address.

Caution: TRCP 119 is affected by Fam. Code §§6.4035, 45.0031, 102.0091.

See also CPRC §30.001; *O'Connor's Texas Rules*, "Serving the Defendant with Suit," ch. 2-H, p. 184; *O'Connor's Texas Forms*, FORM 2H:1.

ANNOTATIONS

Deen v. Kirk, 508 S.W.2d 70, 71 (Tex.1974). "Under the provisions of [TRCP 119], a defendant may waive the issuance and service of citation by filing among the papers of the cause a verified written memorandum 'signed by him, or by his duly authorized agent or attorney, after suit is brought.' [TRCS] art. 2224 [now CPRC §30.001] prohibits the waiver of process by an instrument executed prior to institution of suit."

Approximately $58,641.00 v. State, 331 S.W.3d 579, 583 (Tex.App.—Houston [14th Dist.] 2011, no pet.). "A written recitation that the acceptance of service meets all requirements of Rule 119 satisfies the requirement of a written memorandum."

In re Bruno, 974 S.W.2d 401, 405 (Tex.App.—San Antonio 1998, no pet.). Mother "argues that, while she waived her right to receive service of citation, she was still entitled to receive a copy of the petition for termination pursuant to [TRCP] 119. However, by its very terms, Rule 119 requires the delivery of the original petition only when a party either accepts service or waives the issuance of citation *after suit is brought*. It does not apply in cases of pre-suit waiver."

TRCP 119a. COPY OF DECREE

The district clerk shall forthwith mail a certified copy of the final divorce decree or order of dismissal to the party signing a memorandum waiving issuance or service of process. Such divorce decree or order of dismissal shall be mailed to the signer of the memorandum at the address stated in such memorandum or to the office of his attorney of record.

Caution: TRCP 119a is affected by Fam. Code §161.209.

See also ***O'Connor's Texas Family Law Handbook*** (2017), "Copies of orders," ch. 4-H, §15.4, p. 650.

TRCP 120. ENTERING APPEARANCE

The defendant may, in person, or by attorney, or by his duly authorized agent, enter an appearance in open court. Such appearance shall be noted by the judge upon his docket and entered in the minutes, and shall have the same force and effect as if the citation had been duly issued and served as provided by law.

Caution: TRCP 120 is affected by Fam. Code §157.063.

See also ***O'Connor's Texas Rules***, "The Attorney," ch. 1-H, p. 64; "Special Appearance—Challenging Personal Jurisdiction," ch. 3-B, p. 218.

ANNOTATIONS

In re D.M.B., 467 S.W.3d 100, 103 (Tex.App.—San Antonio 2015, pet. denied). The TDFPS contends "that Father made a general appearance at the [Fam. Code] Ch. 262 hearing and thereby waived any complaint regarding lack of service or improper service. *At 104:* Although a responsive pleading was never filed on behalf of Father, Father's attorney ad litem attended the Ch. 262 hearing and participated in the proceeding. … Although the attorney ad litem announced not ready and did not question any witnesses, a review of the record indicates that by objecting to substantive issues, such as the admissibility of evidence, the attorney ad litem was more than a mere bystander or silent figurehead at the Ch. 262 hearing. [C]ounsel's objection to the admission of evidence 'invoked the judgment of the court on a question other than the court's jurisdiction, recognized that the action was properly pending in Texas, and sought affirmative action from this court.' [¶] [I]n determining whether a general appearance occurred, the emphasis is on affirmative action—not affirmative relief—and a party who objects to the admission of hearsay evidence seeks such an action even if the trial court does not rule on the objection. [¶] [W]e hold the attorney ad litem's actions, particularly his multiple objections to substantive issues, constituted a general appearance, establishing the court's personal jurisdiction over Father."

Mays v. Perkins, 927 S.W.2d 222, 225 (Tex.App.—Houston [1st Dist.] 1996, no writ). "A defendant's appearance before a court generally indicates a submission to the court's jurisdiction. However, the mere presence in court by an attorney, retained as counsel by a person formerly a party to the lawsuit, does not constitute a general appearance, unless the attorney seeks a judgment or an adjudication on some question." *See also* ***In re D.M.B.***, 467 S.W.3d 100, 103 (Tex.App.—San Antonio 2015, pet. denied).

TRCP 120a. SPECIAL APPEARANCE

1. Notwithstanding the provisions of Rules 121, 122 and 123, a special appearance may be made by any party either in person or by attorney for the purpose of objecting to the jurisdiction of the court over the person or property of the defendant on the ground that such party or property is not amenable to process issued by the courts of this State. A special appearance may be made as to an entire proceeding or as to any severable claim involved therein. Such special appearance shall be made by sworn motion filed prior to motion to transfer venue or any other plea, pleading or motion; provided however, that a motion to transfer venue and any other plea, pleading, or motion may be contained in the same instrument or filed subsequent thereto without waiver of such special appearance; and may be amended to cure defects. The issuance of process for witnesses, the taking of depositions, the serving of requests for admissions, and the use of discovery processes, shall not constitute a waiver of such special appearance. Every appearance, prior to judgment, not in compliance with this rule is a general appearance.

2. Any motion to challenge the jurisdiction provided for herein shall be heard and determined before a motion to transfer venue or any other plea or pleading may be heard. No determination of any issue of fact in connection with the objection to jurisdiction is a determination of the merits of the case or any aspect thereof.

3. The court shall determine the special appearance on the basis of the pleadings, any stipulations made by and between the parties, such affidavits and attachments as may be filed by the parties, the results of discovery processes, and any oral testimony. The affidavits, if any, shall be served at least seven days before the hearing, shall be made on personal knowledge, shall set forth specific facts as would be admissible in evidence, and shall show affirmatively that the affiant is competent to testify.

Should it appear from the affidavits of a party opposing the motion that he cannot for reasons stated present by affidavit facts essential to justify his opposition, the court may order a continuance to permit affidavits to be obtained or depositions to be taken or discovery to be had or may make such other order as is just.

Should it appear to the satisfaction of the court at any time that any of such affidavits are presented in violation of Rule 13, the court shall impose sanctions in accordance with that rule.

4. If the court sustains the objection to jurisdiction, an appropriate order shall be entered. If the objection to jurisdiction is overruled, the objecting party may thereafter appear generally for any purpose. Any such special appearance or such general appearance shall not be deemed a waiver of the objection to jurisdiction when the objecting party or subject matter is not amenable to process issued by the courts of this State.

See also CPRC §§17.041, 17.042, 51.014(a)(7); ***O'Connor's Texas Rules***, "Special Appearance—Challenging Personal Jurisdiction," ch. 3-B, p. 218; ***O'Connor's Texas Forms***, FORMS 3B; ***O'Connor's Texas Family Law Handbook*** (2017), "Suit for Divorce," ch. 3-A, p. 205; "Challenging the Court," ch. 4-B, p. 349; "Suit to Dissolve Marriage with Children," ch. 4-D, p. 410.

ANNOTATIONS

Generally

Daimler AG v. Bauman, ___ U.S. ___, 134 S.Ct. 746, 760-61 (2014). "For an individual, the paradigm forum for the exercise of general jurisdiction is the individual's domicile; for a corporation, it is an equivalent place, one in which the corporation is fairly regarded as at home. With respect to a corporation, the place of incorporation and principal place of business are paradigm bases for general jurisdiction. [¶] [Ps] would have us look beyond [those paradigm bases] and approve the exercise of general jurisdiction in every State in which a corporation engages in a substantial, continuous, and systematic course of business. That formulation … is unacceptably grasping. [¶] [T]he inquiry … is not whether a foreign corporation's in-forum contacts can be said to be in some sense 'continuous and systematic,' it is whether that corporation's affiliations with the State are so 'continuous and systematic' as to render it essentially at home in the forum State. *At ___ n.19:* We do not foreclose the possibility that in an exceptional case … a corporation's operations in a forum other than its formal place of incorporation or principal place of business may be so substantial and of such a nature as to render the corporation at home in that state." (Internal quotes omitted.) *See also* ***Searcy v. Parex Res.***, 496 S.W.3d 58, 72-73 (Tex.2016).

Moncrief Oil Int'l v. OAO Gazprom, 414 S.W.3d 142, 150-51 (Tex.2013). "[S]pecific jurisdiction requires us to analyze jurisdictional contacts on a claim-by-claim basis. [A] 'plaintiff bringing multiple claims that arise out of different forum contacts of the defendant must establish specific jurisdiction for each claim.' [A] court need not assess contacts on a claim-by-claim basis if all claims arise from the same forum contacts. Because we determine that the tortious interference claims arise from separate jurisdictional contacts than the trade secrets claim, we analyze those contacts separately."

PHC-Minden, L.P. v. Kimberly-Clark Corp., 235 S.W.3d 163, 169-70 (Tex.2007). "We first determine the appropriate time period for assessing contacts for purposes of general jurisdiction, an issue on which our courts of appeals are in conflict. [¶] We conclude that the relevant period ends at the time suit is filed. [G]eneral jurisdiction is dispute-blind; accordingly, and in contrast to specific jurisdiction, the incident made the basis of the suit should not be the focus in assessing continuous and systematic contacts—contacts on which jurisdiction over any claim may be based. We also agree that 'a mere one-time snapshot of the defendant's in-state activities' may not be sufficient, … and contacts should be assessed over a reasonable number of years, up to the date suit is filed…. This includes contacts at the time the cause of action arose…."

Michiana Easy Livin' Country, Inc. v. Holten, 168 S.W.3d 777, 785 (Tex.2005). There are "[t]hree aspects of [the purposeful-availment requirement that] are relevant.... First, it is only the defendant's contacts with the forum that count.... [¶] Second, the acts relied on must be 'purposeful' rather than fortuitous. [¶] Third, a defendant must seek some benefit, advantage, or profit by 'availing' itself of the jurisdiction. [A] nonresident may purposefully avoid a particular jurisdiction by structuring its transactions so as neither to profit from the forum's laws nor be subject to its jurisdiction." *See also* ***TV Azteca, S.A.B. de C.V. v. Ruiz***, 490 S.W.3d 29, 37-38 (Tex.2016); ***Moncrief Oil Int'l v. OAO Gazprom***, 414 S.W.3d 142, 151 (Tex.2013); ***Moki Mac River Expeditions v. Drugg***, 221 S.W.3d 569, 575 (Tex.2007).

BMC Software Belg., N.V. v. Marchand, 83 S.W.3d 789, 794 (Tex.2002). The "courts of appeals [should] review the trial court's factual findings for legal and factual sufficiency and review the trial court's legal conclusions *de novo*. [¶] Whether a court has personal jurisdiction over a defendant is a question of law. However, the trial court frequently must resolve questions of fact before deciding the jurisdiction question." *See also* ***Zinc Nacional, S.A. v. Bouché Trucking, Inc.***, 308 S.W.3d 395, 397 (Tex.2010); ***Moki Mac River Expeditions v. Drugg***, 221 S.W.3d 569, 574 (Tex.2007).

CSR Ltd. v. Link, 925 S.W.2d 591, 595-96 (Tex. 1996). "[D] should not be subject to the jurisdiction of a foreign court based upon 'random,' 'fortuitous,' or 'attenuated' contacts. Minimum contacts are particularly important when [D] is from a different country because of the unique and onerous burden placed on a party called upon to defend a suit in a foreign legal system."

In re S.A.V., 837 S.W.2d 80, 84-85 (Tex.1992). "In his special appearance, the father challenged the trial court's subject matter jurisdiction to adjudicate custody as well as the court's personal jurisdiction over the father. The court of appeals determined that, by raising the issue of subject matter jurisdiction in his special appearance, the father made a general appearance before the trial court. We disagree. [¶] By challenging the court's subject matter jurisdiction over custody, the father challenged the satisfaction of the jurisdictional statute. As discussed earlier, in adjudications of custody, satisfaction of the jurisdictional statute confers 'personal jurisdiction' over the nonresident. As a result, the father's challenge to the court's subject matter jurisdiction over custody issues served as a challenge to the court's 'personal jurisdiction' over the father. This type of challenge is properly raised in a special appearance."

In re Stern, 321 S.W.3d 828, 839-40 (Tex.App.—Houston [1st Dist.] 2010, orig. proceeding). "The trial court may permit a continuance so that the opposing party may obtain [any] necessary jurisdictional discovery. However, Rule 120a(3) does not authorize postponement of a special appearance hearing to allow a party to obtain discovery prior to the court's ruling on the special appearance that is unnecessary or irrelevant to the establishment of jurisdictional facts. [¶] We ... conclude that those cases holding that 'nothing in Rule 120a specifically limits discovery to matters relating to the special appearance' are limited to those situations in which the issue is whether a defendant waives a special appearance by participating in discovery and that they do not apply when the issue is ... whether a trial court abuses its discretion by ordering or failing to order discovery at the request of a party opposing a special appearance. Those cases are controlled by the plain language of Rule 120a(3) and by ***Dawson-Austin v. Austin***[, 968 S.W.2d 319 (Tex.1998),] and its progeny."

Mouso v. Alworth, 777 S.W.2d 795, 797 (Tex. App.—Beaumont 1989, orig. proceeding). "We think it is axiomatic that before a court has the power to transfer a case under state statute, even one in the Family Code, that the court would have to possess the proper jurisdiction of the litigation, including in personam jurisdiction. We hold that Rule 120a is paramount and that a hearing on the special appearance must be held first."

Pleadings

Exito Elecs. Co. v. Trejo, 142 S.W.3d 302, 305 (Tex. 2004). TRCP 120a "requires only that a special appearance be filed before any other 'plea, pleading or motion.' A [TRCP] 11 Agreement between the parties, in and of itself, is not a plea, pleading, or motion. *At 306:* [W]hile filing a Rule 11 Agreement with the trial court is a requirement for enforcement, it is not in and of itself a request for enforcement or any other affirmative action by the trial court. [A] Rule 11 Agreement that extends a defendant's time to file an initial responsive pleading and is filed in the trial court before the defendant files a special appearance, even if the agreement

is not expressly made subject to the special appearance, does not violate Rule 120a's 'due-order-of-pleading' requirement and ... does not constitute a general appearance."

Dawson-Austin v. Austin, 968 S.W.2d 319, 322-23 (Tex.1998). The Supreme Court held (1) an unverified special appearance may be amended to cure the defect, even after the trial court has overruled it, as long as the amendment is filed before the defendant enters a general appearance; and (2) it is not necessary for the answer and other motions filed in the same instrument as the special appearance to contain "subject to" language. *See also* ***Horowitz v. Berger***, 377 S.W.3d 115, 123 (Tex.App.—Houston [14th Dist.] 2012, no pet.) (amended special appearance relates back, curing and replacing the original special appearance).

Casino Magic Corp. v. King, 43 S.W.3d 14, 18 (Tex. App.—Dallas 2001, pet. denied). TRCP 120a "requires special appearances to be made by 'sworn motion.' Strict compliance with the rule is required. [¶] In this case, the special appearance was not sworn or verified. Although [D] attached an affidavit to the special appearance which set out various 'jurisdictional facts,' in that affidavit [D's] general counsel stated only that the allegations in the *affidavit* were true and correct, not that the facts set out in the *special appearance* were true and correct. [W]e conclude the affidavit did not strictly comply with rule 120a and it, therefore, could not serve to verify the special appearance."

Waiver

GFTA Trendanalysen v. Varme, 991 S.W.2d 785, 786 (Tex.1999). "[A] party [does not waive] a due process challenge for want of minimum contacts by challenging the method of service in the special appearance." *See also* ***Moore v. Pulmosan Safety Equip. Corp.***, 278 S.W.3d 27, 33 (Tex.App.—Houston [14th Dist.] 2008, pet. denied).

Nationwide Distrib. Servs. v. Jones, 496 S.W.3d 221, 227-28 (Tex.App.—Houston [1st Dist.] 2016, no pet.). "The case law shows that a specially appearing party does not waive its jurisdictional challenge by: (1) serving nonjurisdictional discovery requests; (2) filing a motion to compel nonjurisdictional discovery but not scheduling a hearing or obtaining a ruling on such motion; (3) litigating a jurisdictional discovery dispute; (4) litigating other disputes that are factually related to the special appearance; or (5) litigating opposition to merits-based discovery sought by another party. To the extent each of these examples involved a defendant's 'use of discovery processes,' none of them also involved a violation of the due order of pleading."

Grynberg v. M-I L.L.C., 398 S.W.3d 864, 877-78 (Tex.App.—Corpus Christi 2012, pet. denied). "[T]he mere filing of a motion for new trial or other pleadings, with or without 'subject to' language, does not necessarily waive a previously filed or a simultaneously filed special appearance. [A] defendant may include language in the motion for new trial that it is ready to proceed to trial without waiving the special appearance, as long as the motion does not acknowledge jurisdiction or ask for some action other than dismissal for lack of jurisdiction. [¶] [A]ppearing in matters ancillary and prior to the main suit does not constitute a general appearance in the main suit and will not waive a personal-jurisdiction challenge." *See also* ***Carey v. State***, No. 04-09-00809-CV (Tex.App.—San Antonio 2010, pet. denied) (memo op.; 7-21-10) (Ds' agreement to extension of temporary restraining and temporary-injunction orders was not general appearance because agreement was part of ancillary proceeding). *But see* ***Schoendienst v. Haug***, 399 S.W.3d 313, 321 n.8 (Tex. App.—Austin 2013, no pet.) (D appeared by agreeing to temporary injunction; categorical rule that appearing in matters "ancillary and prior to the main suit" does not constitute general appearance is overbroad oversimplification).

Milacron Inc. v. Performance Rail Tie, L.P., 262 S.W.3d 872, 875-76 (Tex.App.—Texarkana 2008, no pet.). "Rule 120a requires that the specially appearing defendant timely request a hearing, specifically bring that request to the trial court's attention, and secure a ruling on the preliminary question of personal jurisdiction. [¶] A defendant waives his special appearance by not timely pressing for a hearing. It is inappropriate, especially when considering judicial economy, to litigate the special appearance in connection with the trial of the matter." *See also* ***DeGeorge v. Luedike/Fabel***, No. 09-14-00517-CV (Tex.App.—Beaumont 2016, no pet.) (memo op.; 4-28-16).

TRCP 121. ANSWER IS APPEARANCE

An answer shall constitute an appearance of the defendant so as to dispense with the necessity for the issuance or service of citation upon him.

ANNOTATIONS

Torres v. Johnson, 91 S.W.3d 905, 910 (Tex.App.—Fort Worth 2002, no pet.). "[N]o new service was required because [D] entered an appearance in the suit by moving for summary judgment after [P] amended his pleadings."

TRCP 122. CONSTRUCTIVE APPEARANCE

If the citation or service thereof is quashed on motion of the defendant, such defendant shall be deemed to have entered his appearance at ten o'clock a.m. on the Monday next after the expiration of twenty (20) days after the day on which the citation or service is quashed, and such defendant shall be deemed to have been duly served so as to require him to appear and answer at that time, and if he fails to do so, judgment by default may be rendered against him.

See also *O'Connor's Texas Rules*, "Motion to Quash—Challenging the Service," ch. 3-J, p. 307.

ANNOTATIONS

Kawasaki Steel Corp. v. Middleton, 699 S.W.2d 199, 202 (Tex.1985). "[A] non-resident defendant, like any other defendant, may move to quash the citation for defects in the process, but his only relief is additional time to answer rather than dismissal of the cause."

Ramirez v. Consolidated HGM Corp., 124 S.W.3d 914, 917 (Tex.App.—Amarillo 2004, no pet.). The trial court does not have to "resolve a motion to quash as a condition to preserving a complaint about service."

TRCP 123. REVERSAL OF JUDGMENT

Where the judgment is reversed on appeal or writ of error for the want of service, or because of defective service of process, no new citation shall be issued or served, but the defendant shall be presumed to have entered his appearance to the term of the court at which the mandate shall be filed.

See also *O'Connor's Texas Rules*, "Motion to Quash—Challenging the Service," ch. 3-J, p. 307.

ANNOTATIONS

Boyd v. Kobierowski, 283 S.W.3d 19, 23 (Tex. App.—San Antonio 2009, no pet.). TRCP 123 "presumes the non-resident defendant's general appearance after reversal of a judgment based on defective or no service. *At 24:* [D] could have escaped Rule 123's presumption of a general appearance using [TRCP] 120a's special appearance."

TRCP 124. NO JUDGMENT WITHOUT SERVICE

In no case shall judgment be rendered against any defendant unless upon service, or acceptance or waiver of process, or upon an appearance by the defendant, as prescribed in these rules, except where otherwise expressly provided by law or these rules.

When a party asserts a counterclaim or a cross-claim against another party who has entered an appearance, the claim may be served in any manner prescribed for service of citation or as provided in Rule 21(a).[1]

1. **Editor's note:** This is TRCP 21a.

See also *O'Connor's Texas Rules*, "Serving the Defendant with Suit," ch. 2-H, p. 184; "Default Judgment," ch. 7-A, p. 671.

ANNOTATIONS

Werner v. Colwell, 909 S.W.2d 866, 869-70 (Tex. 1995). "Judgment shall not be rendered against one who was neither named nor served as a party defendant. An exception exists when a person waives service by making a general appearance before the court. [W]e have never held and decline to hold today, that merely appearing as a witness in a cause serves as a general appearance, subjecting one to the jurisdiction of the court."

In re D.A.P., 267 S.W.3d 485, 489 (Tex.App.—Houston [14th Dist.] 2008, no pet.). "The Texas Supreme Court has held that a party seeking … child custody relief against a former spouse need not show that the former spouse has sufficient minimum contacts with Texas such that the exercise of personal jurisdiction does not offend traditional notions of fair play and substantial justice. Nonetheless, even though due process may not require the minimum contacts analysis, Texas procedural law and constitutional due process require that [mother] be served, waive service, or voluntarily appear before judgment pertaining to custody of her minor child may be rendered."

Spivey v. Holloway, 902 S.W.2d 46, 48 (Tex.App.—Houston [1st Dist.] 1995, no writ). "[E]ven without service or waiver of process, a judgment may be rendered upon appearance by the defendant. An appearance constitutes waiver of service. [W]e hold that [D's] signing of the divorce decree constituted an appearance before the court pursuant to rule 124."

SECTION 6. COSTS & SECURITY THEREFOR

TRCP 125. PARTIES RESPONSIBLE

Each party to a suit shall be liable to the officers of the court for all costs incurred by himself.

Caution: TRCP 125 is affected by Fam. Code §§6.708, 9.013, 9.014, 9.205, 33.004, 33.007, 41.002, 41.0025, 42.009, 81.003, 85.064, 106.001, 106.002, 107.015, 107.115, 110.002, 152.312, 152.317, 154.012, 156.005, 157.167, 157.211, 157.323, 158.206, 159.305, 159.313, 231.202, 231.205, and 231.209-231.211.

ANNOTATIONS

Gross v. Gross, 808 S.W.2d 215, 221 (Tex.App.—Houston [14th Dist.] 1991, no writ). Unsuccessful party argues "that courts do not have unlimited discretion under [Fam. Code] §11.18 [now §§106.001, 106.002] to award attorney's fees and costs. He further argues that only a successful party can recover attorney's fees and costs, absent good cause. Initially, we note that not only is [he] not a successful party, but the provisions of the Family Code with respect to attorney's fees and costs were intended to supplant the [TRCPs]."

16 TRCP 126. FEE FOR SERVICE OF PROCESS IN A COUNTY OTHER THAN IN THE COUNTY OF SUIT

(a) ***General Rule: Fee Due Before Service.*** A sheriff or constable may require payment before serving process in a case pending in a county other than the county in which the sheriff or constable is an officer.

(b) ***Exception: Statement of Inability to Afford Payment of Court Costs Filed.*** If a Statement of Inability to Afford Payment of Court Costs has been filed in a case in which the declarant requests service of process in a county other than in the county of suit, the clerk must indicate on the document to be served that a Statement of Inability to Afford Payment of Court Costs has been filed. The sheriff or constable must execute the service without demanding payment.

2016 change: Amended eff. Sept. 1, 2016, by order of Aug. 31, 2016 (Tex. Sup.Ct. Order, Misc. Docket No. 16-9122).

TRCP 127. PARTIES LIABLE FOR OTHER COSTS

Each party to a suit shall be liable for all costs incurred by him. If the costs cannot be collected from the party against whom they have been adjudged, execution may issue against any party in such suit for the amount of costs incurred by such party, but no more.

Caution: TRCP 127 is affected by Fam. Code §§6.708, 9.013, 9.014, 9.205, 33.004, 33.007, 41.002, 41.0025, 42.009, 81.003, 85.064, 106.001, 106.002, 107.015, 107.115, 110.002, 152.312, 152.317, 154.012, 156.005, 157.167, 157.211, 157.323, 158.206, 159.305, 159.313, 231.202, 231.205, and 231.209-231.211.

ANNOTATIONS

Gross v. Gross, 808 S.W.2d 215, 221 (Tex.App.—Houston [14th Dist.] 1991, no writ). See annotation under TRCP 125, this page.

TRCP 128. REPEALED

TRCP 129. HOW COSTS COLLECTED

If any party responsible for costs fails or refuses to pay the same within ten days after demand for payment, the clerk or justice of the peace may make certified copy of the bill of costs then due, and place the same in the hands of the sheriff or constable for collection. All taxes imposed on law proceedings shall be included in the bill of costs. Such certified bill of costs shall have the force and effect of an execution. The removal of a case by appeal shall not prevent the issuance of an execution for costs.

TRCP 130. OFFICER TO LEVY

The sheriff or constable upon demand and failure to pay said bill of costs, may levy upon a sufficient amount of property of the person from whom said costs are due to satisfy the same, and sell such property as under execution. Where such party is not a resident of the county where such suit is pending, the payment of such costs may be demanded of his attorney of record; and neither the clerk nor justice of the peace shall be allowed to charge any fee for making out such certified bill of costs, unless he is compelled to make a levy.

TRCP 131. SUCCESSFUL PARTY TO RECOVER

The successful party to a suit shall recover of his adversary all costs incurred therein, except where otherwise provided.

Caution: TRCP 131 is affected by Fam. Code §§6.708, 85.064, 106.001, 106.002, 107.015, 152.312, 152.317, 154.012, 157.167, 158.206, and 159.313.

See also CPRC §31.007; ***O'Connor's Texas Rules***, "Judgment," ch. 9-C, p. 861; ***O'Connor's Texas Family Law Handbook*** (2017), "Costs," ch. 3-A, §5.4.12(4), p. 231; "Award to prevailing party," ch. 4-D, §13.4.12(4)(b), p. 463.

ANNOTATIONS

Gross v. Gross, 808 S.W.2d 215, 221 (Tex.App.—Houston [14th Dist.] 1991, no writ). See annotation under TRCP 125, this page.

TRCP 132. REPEALED

TRCP 133. COSTS OF MOTION

The court may give or refuse costs on motions at its discretion, except where otherwise provided by law or these rules.

TRCP 134, 135. REPEALED

TRCP 136. DEMAND REDUCED BY PAYMENTS

Where the plaintiff's demand is reduced by payment to an amount which would not have been within the jurisdiction of the court, the defendant shall recover his costs.

TRCP 137. IN ASSAULT & BATTERY, ETC.

In civil actions for assault and battery, slander and defamation of character, if the verdict or judgment shall be for the plaintiff, but for less than twenty dollars, the plaintiff shall not recover his costs, but each party shall be taxed with the costs incurred by him in such suit.

TRCP 138. COST OF NEW TRIALS

The costs of new trials may either abide the result of the suit or may be taxed against the party to whom the new trial is granted, as the court may adjudge when he grants such new trial.

TRCP 139. ON APPEAL & CERTIORARI

When a case is appealed, if the judgment of the higher court be against the appellant, but for less amount than the original judgment, such party shall recover the costs of the higher court but shall be adjudged to pay the costs of the court below; if the judgment be against him for the same or a greater amount than in the court below, the adverse party shall recover the costs of both courts. If the judgment of the court above be in favor of the party appealing and for more than the original judgment, such party shall recover the costs of both courts; if the judgment be in his favor, but for the same or a less amount than in the court below, he shall recover the costs of the court below, and pay the costs of the court above.

ANNOTATIONS

Keene Corp. v. Gardner, 837 S.W.2d 224, 232 (Tex. App.—Dallas 1992, writ denied). "Because the appellate relief given [D] is *de minimis* compared to [Ps'] overall award affirmed on appeal, we assess all costs of this appeal against [D]."

TRCP 140. NO FEE FOR COPY

No fee for a copy of a paper not required by law or these rules to be copied shall be taxed in the bill of costs.

ANNOTATIONS

Crescendo Invs. v. Brice, 61 S.W.3d 465, 481 (Tex. App.—San Antonio 2001, pet. denied). "Transcripts 'necessarily obtained for use in the suit' seems to obviously include depositions and trial testimony used to question witnesses and prepare for argument at trial. [Ds] are not recovering for 'making copies' as prohibited by Rule 140. The expense of depositions has long been recognized as a chargeable item of court costs. Awarding costs for certified copies of depositions which may be admitted at trial does not violate Rule 140." *But see* ***Gumpert v. ABF Freight Sys.***, 312 S.W.3d 237, 241 (Tex.App.—Dallas 2010, no pet.) (costs to videotape depositions and obtain copies of deposition transcripts are not recoverable as taxable costs).

TRCP 141. COURT MAY OTHERWISE ADJUDGE COSTS

The court may, for good cause, to be stated on the record, adjudge the costs otherwise than as provided by law or these rules.

ANNOTATIONS

Roberts v. Williamson, 111 S.W.3d 113, 124 (Tex. 2003). The trial court "observed that because an ad litem is there for the benefit of all parties, it is 'fair' to split costs between the losing and prevailing parties. ... Certainly, fairness can be good cause, but the record must substantiate the connection. [¶] [T]he trial court's finding of good cause is premised on the perception that the prevailing party incidentally [benefited] from the guardian ad litem's services. ... Rule 141 still requires that the trial court state its reasons 'on the record' and with more specificity than the court's general notion of fairness here. Grounds of perceived fairness, without more, are insufficient to constitute good cause."

Schreiber v. State Farm Lloyds, 474 S.W.3d 308, 319 (Tex.App.—Houston [14th Dist.] 2015, pet. denied). "[P] argues [CPRC] §31.007(b) ... changed Texas law and gave trial courts discretion to not award the successful party all of the taxable court costs that party incurred, without any requirement that the trial court state on the record good cause for doing so. *At 320:* The statute does not address the circumstances under which a trial court may order a successful party to bear taxable court costs the party incurred. We conclude that this statute does not conflict with, supersede, or modify, [TRCP] 131 or [TRCP] 141.... Thus, this statute does not change the rule that the trial court must award the successful party to a suit all of its taxable court costs from the adverse party, unless the trial court finds good cause to adjudge the costs otherwise and states its reasons for finding good cause on the record."

Diaz v. Diaz, 350 S.W.3d 251, 256 (Tex.App.—San Antonio 2011, pet. denied). "The provisions of the Family Code with respect to attorney's fees and costs were

intended to supplant the [TRCPs]. ... Trial courts in the family law context ... are not bound by [TRCP 141's] 'good cause' requirement." *See also* ***Billeaud v. Billeaud***, 697 S.W.2d 652, 655 (Tex.App.—Houston [1st Dist.] 1985, no writ).

Hatfield v. Solomon, 316 S.W.3d 50, 67 (Tex. App.—Houston [14th Dist.] 2010, no pet.). The "power to allocate costs in a manner different from the norm does not encompass the power to tax as costs items that are not normally allowed as taxable court costs." *See also* ***May v. Ticor Title Ins.***, 422 S.W.3d 93, 106 (Tex. App.—Houston [14th Dist.] 2014, no pet.) (expert fees are not generally recoverable as court costs).

TRCP 142. SECURITY FOR COSTS

The clerk shall require from the plaintiff fees for services rendered before issuing any process unless filing is requested pursuant to Rule 145 of these rules.

TRCP 143. RULE FOR COSTS

A party seeking affirmative relief may be ruled to give security for costs at any time before final judgment, upon motion of any party, or any officer of the court interested in the costs accruing in such suit, or by the court upon its own motion. If such rule be entered against any party and he failed to comply therewith on or before twenty (20) days after notice that such rule has been entered, the claim for affirmative relief of such party shall be dismissed.

ANNOTATIONS

TransAmerican Nat. Gas Corp. v. Mancias, 877 S.W.2d 840, 844 (Tex.App.—Corpus Christi 1994, orig. proceeding). TRCP 143 "generally allows the trial court to require a party to post security for costs that have already accrued, but not to fix a specific amount for anticipated costs which a party is required to pay or post security for prematurely." *See also* ***In re Pendragon Transp.***, 423 S.W.3d 537, 541 (Tex.App.—Dallas 2014, orig. proceeding); ***Hager v. Apollo Paper Corp.***, 856 S.W.2d 512, 515 (Tex.App.—Houston [1st Dist.] 1993, no writ).

TRCP 143a. COSTS ON APPEAL TO COUNTY COURT

If the appellant fails to pay the costs on appeal from a judgment of a justice of the peace or small claims court[1] within twenty (20) days after being notified to do so by the county clerk, the appeal shall be deemed not perfected and the county clerk shall return all papers in said cause to the justice of the peace having original jurisdiction and the justice of the peace shall proceed as though no appeal had been attempted.

1. **Editor's note:** The Texas Legislature abolished small-claims courts by repealing Gov't Code ch. 28. *See* Acts 2013, 83rd Leg., R.S., ch. 2, §2, eff. Apr. 10, 2013; Acts 2011, 82nd Leg., 1st C.S., ch. 3, §§5.06, 5.09, eff. May 1, 2013. Now small-claims proceedings must be conducted by justice courts. Gov't Code §27.060(a); *see* TRCP 500.3(a).

ANNOTATIONS

Farmer v. McGee Servs., 704 S.W.2d 927, 929 (Tex. App.—Tyler 1986, no writ). "Since no notice [of costs] had been given, the trial court erred in applying Rule 143a to dismiss [D's] appeal."

TRCP 144. JUDGMENT ON COST BOND

All bonds given as security for costs shall authorize judgment against all the obligors in such bond for the said costs, to be entered in the final judgment of the cause.

ANNOTATIONS

Mosher v. Tunnell, 400 S.W.2d 402, 404 (Tex. App.—Houston [1st Dist.] 1966, writ ref'd n.r.e.). TRCP 144 "provides the bond shall authorize judgment against the obligors for said costs. This means such costs as shall be adjudged against the principal whatever be the amount."

16 TRCP 145. PAYMENT OF COSTS NOT REQUIRED

(a) ***General Rule.*** A party who files a Statement of Inability to Afford Payment of Court Costs cannot be required to pay costs except by order of the court as provided by this rule. After the Statement is filed, the clerk must docket the case, issue citation, and provide any other service that is ordinarily provided to a party. The Statement must either be sworn to before a notary or made under penalty of perjury. In this rule, "declarant" means the party filing the Statement.

(b) ***Supreme Court Form; Clerk to Provide.*** The declarant must use the form Statement approved by the Supreme Court, or the Statement must include the information required by the Court-approved form. The clerk must make the form available to all persons without charge or request.

(c) ***Costs Defined.*** "Costs" mean any fee charged by the court or an officer of the court that could be taxed in a bill of costs, including, but not limited to, filing fees, fees for issuance and service of process, fees for a

court-appointed professional, and fees charged by the clerk or court reporter for preparation of the appellate record.

(d) ***Defects.*** The clerk may refuse to file a Statement that is not sworn to before a notary or made under penalty of perjury. No other defect is a ground for refusing to file a Statement or requiring the party to pay costs. If a defect or omission in a Statement is material, the court—on its own motion or on motion of the clerk or any party—may direct the declarant to correct or clarify the Statement.

(e) ***Evidence of Inability to Afford Costs Required.*** The Statement must say that the declarant cannot afford to pay costs. The declarant must provide in the Statement, and, if available, in attachments to the Statement, evidence of the declarant's inability to afford costs, such as evidence that the declarant:

(1) receives benefits from a government entitlement program, eligibility for which is dependent on the recipient's means;

(2) is being represented in the case by an attorney who is providing free legal services to the declarant, without contingency, through:

(A) a provider funded by the Texas Access to Justice Foundation;

(B) a provider funded by the Legal Services Corporation; or

(C) a nonprofit that provides civil legal services to persons living at or below 200% of the federal poverty guidelines published annually by the United States Department of Health and Human Services;

(3) has applied for free legal services for the case through a provider listed in (e)(2) and was determined to be financially eligible but was declined representation; or

(4) does not have funds to afford payment of costs.

(f) ***Requirement to Pay Costs Notwithstanding Statement.*** The court may order the declarant to pay costs only as follows:

(1) *On Motion by the Clerk or a Party.* The clerk or any party may move to require the declarant to pay costs only if the motion contains sworn evidence, not merely on information or belief:

(A) that the Statement was materially false when it was made; or

(B) that because of changed circumstances, the Statement is no longer true in material respects.

(2) *On Motion by the Attorney Ad Litem for a Parent in Certain Cases.* An attorney ad litem appointed to represent a parent under Section 107.013, Family Code, may move to require the parent to pay costs only if the motion complies with (f)(1).

(3) *On Motion by the Court Reporter.* When the declarant requests the preparation of a reporter's record but cannot make arrangements to pay for it, the court reporter may move to require the declarant to prove the inability to afford costs.

(4) *On the Court's Own Motion.* Whenever evidence comes before the court that the declarant may be able to afford costs, or when an officer or professional must be appointed in the case, the court may require the declarant to prove the inability to afford costs.

(5) *Notice and Hearing.* The declarant may not be required to pay costs without an oral evidentiary hearing. The declarant must be given 10 days' notice of the hearing. Notice must either be in writing and served in accordance with Rule 21a or given in open court. At the hearing, the burden is on the declarant to prove the inability to afford costs.

(6) *Findings Required.* An order requiring the declarant to pay costs must be supported by detailed findings that the declarant can afford to pay costs.

(7) *Partial and Delayed Payment.* The court may order that the declarant pay the part of the costs the declarant can afford or that payment be made in installments. But the court must not delay the case if payment is made in installments.

(g) ***Review of Trial Court Order.***

(1) *Only Declarant May Challenge; Motion.* Only the declarant may challenge an order issued by the trial court under this rule. The declarant may challenge the order by motion filed in the court of appeals with jurisdiction over an appeal from the judgment in the case. The declarant is not required to pay any filing fees related to the motion in the court of appeals.

(2) *Time for Filing; Extension.* The motion must be filed within 10 days after the trial court's order is signed. The court of appeals may extend the deadline by 15 days if the declarant demonstrates good cause for the extension in writing.

(3) *Record.* After a motion is filed, the court of appeals must promptly send notice to the trial court clerk and the court reporter requesting preparation of the record of all trial court proceedings on the declarant's

claim of indigence. The court may set a deadline for filing the record. The record must be provided without charge.

(4) *Court of Appeals to Rule Promptly.* The court of appeals must rule on the motion at the earliest practicable time.

(h) ***Judgment.*** The judgment must not require the declarant to pay costs, and a provision in the judgment purporting to do so is void, unless the court has issued an order under (f), or the declarant has obtained a monetary recovery, and the court orders the recovery to be applied toward payment of costs.

Editor's note: The Court-approved form "Statement of Inability to Afford Payment of Court Costs" can be found at the Texas Office of Court Administration website, www.txcourts.gov/rules-forms/forms.

Comment to 2016 change: The rule has been rewritten. Access to the civil justice system cannot be denied because a person cannot afford to pay court costs. Whether a particular fee is a court cost is governed by this rule, Civil Practice and Remedies Code Section 31.007, and case law.

The issue is not merely whether a person can pay costs, but whether the person can afford to pay costs. A person may have sufficient cash on hand to pay filing fees, but the person cannot afford the fees if paying them would preclude the person from paying for basic essentials, like housing or food. Experience indicates that almost all filers described in (e)(1)-(3), and most filers described in (e)(4), cannot in fact afford to pay costs.

Because costs to access the system—filing fees, fees for issuance of process and notices, and fees for service and return—are kept relatively small, the expense involved in challenging a claim of inability to afford costs often exceeds the costs themselves. Thus, the rule does not allow the clerk or a party to challenge a litigant's claim of inability to afford costs without sworn evidence that the claim is false. The filing of a Statement of Inability to Afford Payment of Court Costs—which may either be sworn to before a notary or made under penalty of perjury, as permitted by Civil Practice and Remedies Code Section 132.001—is all that is needed to require the clerk to provide ordinary services without payment of fees and costs. But evidence may come to light that the claim was false when made. And the declarant's circumstances may change, so that the claim is no longer true. Importantly, costs may increase with the appointment of officers or professionals in the case, or when a reporter's record must be prepared. The reporter is always allowed to challenge a claim of inability to afford costs before incurring the substantial expense of record preparation. The trial court always retains discretion to require evidence of an inability to afford costs.

2016 change: Amended eff. Sept. 1, 2016, by order of Aug. 31, 2016 (Tex. Sup.Ct. Order, Misc. Docket No. 16-9122).

See also CPRC chs. 13, 14; ***O'Connor's Texas Rules***, "Suit by Indigent," ch. 2-I, p. 200; ***O'Connor's Texas Forms***, FORMS 2I; ***O'Connor's Texas Family Law Handbook*** (2017), "Court Appointments in SAPCRs," ch. 4-C, p. 365.

ANNOTATIONS

Campbell v. Wilder, 487 S.W.3d 146, 147 (Tex. 2016). See annotation under Family Code §6.708, p. 83.

TRCP 146. DEPOSIT FOR COSTS

In lieu of a bond for costs, the party required to give the same may deposit with the clerk of court or the justice of the peace such sum as the court or justice from time to time may designate as sufficient to pay the accrued costs.

Caution: TRCP 146 is affected by Fam. Code §110.002.

TRCP 147. APPLIES TO ANY PARTY

The foregoing rules as to security and rule for costs shall apply to any party who seeks a judgment against any other party.

ANNOTATIONS

Ex parte Shaffer, 649 S.W.2d 300, 302 (Tex.1983). "[O]ne who involuntarily comes into court and does not seek any affirmative relief cannot be required to post a cost bond."

TRCP 148. SECURED BY OTHER BOND

No further security shall be required if the costs are secured by the provisions of an attachment or other bond filed by the party required to give security for costs.

TRCP 149. EXECUTION FOR COSTS

When costs have been adjudged against a party and are not paid, the clerk or justice of the court in which the suit was determined may issue execution, accompanied by an itemized bill of costs, against such party to be levied and collected as in other cases; and said officer, on demand of any party to whom any such costs are due, shall issue execution for costs at once. This rule shall not apply to executors, administrators or guardians in cases where costs are adjudged against the estate of a deceased person or of a ward. No execution shall issue in any case for costs until after judgment rendered therefor by the court.

SECTION 7. ABATEMENT & DISCONTINUANCE OF SUIT

TRCP 150. DEATH OF PARTY

Where the cause of action is one which survives, no suit shall abate because of the death of any party thereto before the verdict or decision of the court is rendered, but such suit may proceed to judgment as hereinafter provided.

Caution: TRCP 150 is affected by Fam. Code §162.013.

See also ***O'Connor's Texas Rules***, "Plea to the Jurisdiction—Challenging the Court," ch. 3-F, p. 276; "Motion to Abate—Challenging the Suit," ch. 3-I, p. 299; ***O'Connor's Texas Family Law Handbook*** (2017), "Effect of spouse's death," ch. 3-A, §16.6, p. 273 (suit for divorce); "Effect of party's death on judgment," ch. 4-D, §13.7, p. 466 (suit to dissolve marriage with children).

ANNOTATIONS

Palomino v. Palomino, 960 S.W.2d 899, 900-01 (Tex.App.—El Paso 1997, pet. denied). "The general rule in Texas is that a cause of action for divorce is purely personal and becomes moot and abates upon the death of either spouse. ... However, when a trial court

has rendered judgment on the merits in a divorce case, the cause does not abate when a party dies, and the cause cannot be dismissed." *See also* ***Pollard v. Pollard***, 316 S.W.3d 246, 250-51 (Tex.App.—Dallas 2010, no pet.).

TRCP 151. DEATH OF PLAINTIFF

If the plaintiff dies, the heirs, or the administrator or executor of such decedent may appear and upon suggestion of such death being entered of record in open court, may be made plaintiff, and the suit shall proceed in his or their name. If no such appearance and suggestion be made within a reasonable time after the death of the plaintiff, the clerk upon the application of defendant, his agent or attorney, shall issue a scire facias for the heirs or the administrator or executor of such decedent, requiring him to appear and prosecute such suit. After service of such scire facias, should such heir or administrator or executor fail to enter appearance within the time provided, the defendant may have the suit dismissed.

Caution: TRCP 151 is affected by Fam. Code §162.013.

See also ***O'Connor's Texas Rules***, "Plaintiff's Original Petition," ch. 2-B, p. 117; "Motion to Abate—Challenging the Suit," ch. 3-I, p. 299.

TRCP 152. DEATH OF DEFENDANT

Where the defendant shall die, upon the suggestion of death being entered of record in open court, or upon petition of the plaintiff, the clerk shall issue a scire facias for the administrator or executor or heir requiring him to appear and defend the suit and upon the return of such service, the suit shall proceed against such administrator or executor or heir.

See also ***O'Connor's Texas Rules***, "Motion to Abate—Challenging the Suit," ch. 3-I, p. 299.

TRCP 153. WHEN EXECUTOR, ETC., DIES

When an executor or administrator shall be a party to any suit, whether as plaintiff or as defendant, and shall die or cease to be such executor or administrator, the suit may be continued by or against the person succeeding him in the administration, or by or against the heirs, upon like proceedings being had as provided in the two preceding rules, or the suit may be dismissed, as provided in Rule 151.

TRCP 154. REQUISITES OF SCIRE FACIAS

The scire facias and returns thereon, provided for in this section, shall conform to the requisites of citations and the returns thereon, under the provisions of these rules.

TRCP 155. SURVIVING PARTIES

Where there are two or more plaintiffs or defendants, and one or more of them die, upon suggestion of such death being entered upon the record, the suit shall at the instance of either party proceed in the name of the surviving plaintiffs or against the surviving defendants, as the case may be.

TRCP 156. DEATH AFTER VERDICT OR CLOSE OF EVIDENCE

When a party in a jury case dies between verdict and judgment, or a party in a non-jury case dies after the evidence is closed and before judgment is pronounced, judgment shall be rendered and entered as if all parties were living.

TRCP 157. REPEALED

TRCP 158. SUIT FOR THE USE OF ANOTHER

When a plaintiff suing for the use of another shall die before verdict, the person for whose use such suit was brought, upon such death being suggested on the record in open court, may prosecute the suit in his own name, and shall be as responsible for costs as if he brought the suit.

TRCP 159. SUIT FOR INJURIES RESULTING IN DEATH

In cases arising under the provisions of the title relating to injuries resulting in death, the suit shall not abate by the death of either party pending the suit, but in such case, if the plaintiff dies, where there is only one plaintiff, some one or more of the parties entitled to the money recovered may be substituted and the suit prosecuted to judgment in the name of such party or parties, for the benefit of the person entitled; if the defendant dies, his executor, administrator or heir may be made a party, and the suit prosecuted to judgment.

TRCP 160. DISSOLUTION OF CORPORATION

The dissolution of a corporation shall not operate to abate any pending suit in which such corporation is a defendant, but such suit shall continue against such corporation and judgment shall be rendered as though the same were not dissolved.

See also BOC §11.356; TRCP 29.

TRCP 161. WHERE SOME DEFENDANTS NOT SERVED

When some of the several defendants in a suit are served with process in due time and others are not so served, the plaintiff may either dismiss as to those not

so served and proceed against those who are, or he may take new process against those not served, or may obtain severance of the case as between those served and those not served, but no dismissal shall be allowed as to a principal obligor without also dismissing the parties secondarily liable except in cases provided by statute. No defendant against whom any suit may be so dismissed shall be thereby exonerated from any liability, but may at any time be proceeded against as if no such suit had been brought and no such dismissal ordered.

See also TRCP 240.

ANNOTATIONS

Young v. Hunderup, 763 S.W.2d 611, 612-13 (Tex. App.—Austin 1989, no writ). "Where the judgment disposes of all named parties except those which have not been served and have not appeared, ... the judgment is considered final for purposes of appeal and the case stands as if there had been a discontinuance as to those parties not served." *See also* ***Osborne v. St. Luke's Episcopal Hosp.***, 915 S.W.2d 906, 908 (Tex.App.—Houston [1st Dist.] 1996, writ denied). *But see* ***Reed v. Gum Keepsake Diamond Ctr.***, 657 S.W.2d 524, 525 (Tex.App.—Corpus Christi 1983, no writ) (judgment was not final because co-D was not served, did not waive service, did not make appearance, and was not dismissed).

TRCP 162. DISMISSAL OR NON-SUIT

At any time before the plaintiff has introduced all of his evidence other than rebuttal evidence, the plaintiff may dismiss a case, or take a non-suit, which shall be entered in the minutes. Notice of the dismissal or non-suit shall be served in accordance with Rule 21a on any party who has answered or has been served with process without necessity of court order.

Any dismissal pursuant to this rule shall not prejudice the right of an adverse party to be heard on a pending claim for affirmative relief or excuse the payment of all costs taxed by the clerk. A dismissal under this rule shall have no effect on any motion for sanctions, attorney's fees or other costs, pending at the time of dismissal, as determined by the court. Any dismissal pursuant to this rule which terminates the case shall authorize the clerk to tax court costs against dismissing party unless otherwise ordered by the court.

See also TRCP 96; ***O'Connor's Texas Rules***, "Voluntary Dismissal—Nonsuit," ch. 7-F, p. 739; ***O'Connor's Texas Forms***, FORMS 7F.

ANNOTATIONS

CTL/Thompson Tex., LLC v. Starwood Homeowner's Ass'n, 390 S.W.3d 299, 300 (Tex.2013). "A motion for sanctions is a claim for affirmative relief that survives nonsuit if the nonsuit would defeat the purpose of sanctions. For example, a sanction excluding witnesses for failure to supplement discovery does not survive nonsuit because its purpose is fully served by protecting the fairness of the trial of the action in which it is imposed. But a sanction for filing a frivolous lawsuit does survive nonsuit, else its imposition would rest completely in the plaintiff's hands, defeating its purpose."

Epps v. Fowler, 351 S.W.3d 862, 868-69 (Tex.2011). "[W]e have no doubt that a defendant who is the beneficiary of a nonsuit with prejudice would be a prevailing party [and would be entitled to attorney fees]. ... The res judicata effect of a nonsuit with prejudice works a permanent, inalterable change in the parties' legal relationship to the defendant's benefit: the defendant can never again be sued by the plaintiff or its privies for claims arising out of the same subject matter. [¶] In contrast, a nonsuit without prejudice works no such change in the parties' legal relationship; typically, the plaintiff remains free to re-file the same claims seeking the same relief. *At 870:* [But] a defendant may be a prevailing party when a plaintiff nonsuits without prejudice if the trial court determines, on the defendant's motion, that the nonsuit was taken to avoid an unfavorable ruling on the merits."

In re Greater Houston Orthopaedic Specialists, Inc., 295 S.W.3d 323, 325 (Tex.2009). "Granting a nonsuit is a ministerial act, and a plaintiff's right to a nonsuit exists from the moment a written motion is filed or an oral motion is made in open court, unless the defendant has, prior to that time, sought affirmative relief."

Villafani v. Trejo, 251 S.W.3d 466, 469 (Tex.2008). "A nonsuit under Rule 162 ... has 'no effect on any motion for sanctions, attorney's fees or other costs, pending at the time of dismissal.' [P] argues that since the trial court denied [D's] motion [for sanctions] before [P] filed the nonsuit, the motion was not a *pending* claim for affirmative relief[, and therefore,] Rule 162 does not protect [D's] motion from the nullifying effect of the nonsuit. [¶] We disagree.... Rule 162 protects a party's 'pending claim for affirmative relief' from the general rule that a party is required to get a ruling (or a

refusal to rule) from a trial court to preserve a right to appeal. 'Rule 162 merely acknowledges that a nonsuit does not affect ... a pending sanctions motion; it does not purport to limit the trial court's power to act.' *At 470:* [W]e do not read Rule 162 to mean that a nonsuit prevents a non-moving party from appealing a trial court's ruling on claims for affirmative relief merely because the ruling occurred prior to the nonsuit." *See also* ***Unifund CCR Partners v. Villa***, 299 S.W.3d 92, 96 (Tex. 2009); ***Crites v. Collins***, 284 S.W.3d 839, 843 (Tex. 2009).

Texas Mut. Ins. v. Ledbetter, 251 S.W.3d 31, 37 (Tex.2008). "Parties have an absolute right to nonsuit *their own* claims, but not *someone else's* claims they are trying to avoid. *At 38:* Rule 162 ... provides that '[a]ny dismissal pursuant to this rule shall not prejudice the right of an adverse party to be heard on a pending claim for affirmative relief.' A claim for affirmative relief is one 'on which the claimant could recover compensation or relief even if the plaintiff abandons his cause of action.' A carrier's subrogation claim is just such a claim, as it can be prosecuted by a carrier even if an injured worker never does. [T]he carrier here sought no affirmative relief *from* [*Ps*], seeking instead reimbursement from the funds [Ds] were about to pay them. But Rule 162 is not limited to affirmative claims *against the nonsuiter*; it prohibits dismissal if the effect would be to prejudice any pending claim for affirmative relief, period. [¶] [T]he dismissal here prejudiced the carrier's pending claim for affirmative relief. ... While [Ps] were entitled to nonsuit their own affirmative claims, they were not entitled to dismissal from the case." *See also* ***General Land Office v. OXY U.S.A., Inc.***, 789 S.W.2d 569, 570 (Tex.1990).

UTMB v. Estate of Blackmon, 195 S.W.3d 98, 101 (Tex.2006). "Rule 162 permits the trial court to hold hearings and enter orders affecting costs, attorney's fees, and sanctions, even after notice of nonsuit is filed, while the court retains plenary power. Thus, the trial court has discretion to defer signing an order of dismissal so that it can 'allow a reasonable amount of time' for holding hearings on these matters which are 'collateral to the merits of the underlying case.' Although the Rule permits motions for costs, attorney's fees, and sanctions to remain viable in the trial court, it does not forestall the nonsuit's effect of rendering the merits of the case moot."

In re Bennett, 960 S.W.2d 35, 38 (Tex.1997). "[P]laintiffs have the right under [TRCP] 162 to take a nonsuit at any time until they have introduced all evidence other than rebuttal evidence. Such a nonsuit may have the effect of vitiating earlier interlocutory orders and of precluding further action by the trial court.... [¶] Appellate timetables do not run from the date a nonsuit is filed, but rather from the date the trial court signs an order of dismissal." *See also* ***Klein v. Hernandez***, 315 S.W.3d 1, 3 (Tex.2010); ***Farmer v. Ben E. Keith Co.***, 907 S.W.2d 495, 496 (Tex.1995); ***Hyundai Motor Co. v. Alvarado***, 892 S.W.2d 853, 854-55 (Tex. 1995).

Ex parte Brown, 382 S.W.2d 97, 98-99 (Tex.1964). "We agree with relators that the non-suit in the original divorce action did not deprive the Moore Court of power to make temporary orders for the protection of the interests of the child. [Tex. Const.] art. 5, §8 ... confers upon the District Court original jurisdiction and general control over minors under such regulations as may be prescribed by law. 'While it has been held that a court may not take jurisdiction to adjudicate the custody of a minor on its own motion, it has also been held that a child becomes a ward of the court when it is brought before the court for any purpose. One cannot invoke the jurisdiction of the court to deal with the personal status or the person of a child and at the same time deny the power of the court, in that proceeding, to do with the child's person or his status whatever appears to the court to be for the best interest of the child.'"

Estate of Purgason v. Good, No. 14-14-00334-CV (Tex.App.—Houston [14th Dist.] 2016, pet. denied) (memo op.; 2-11-16). "[Ps] filed a notice of nonsuit pursuant to [TRCP] 162.... [Ps] subsequently refiled the suit. [T]hey ... contend that Rule 162 authorizes the clerk to tax costs only if the dismissal 'terminates' the case, and by refiling the claim, they deprived the trial court of the ability to award the costs. [Ps] argue that the trial court *could not* award the costs as the nonsuit ... did not 'terminate' the case because it was refiled. We disagree. [¶] The nonsuit terminated the case upon its filing."

Energy Transfer Fuel, L.P. v. Trammell, No. 12-09-00059-CV (Tex.App.—Tyler 2010, no pet.) (memo op.; 8-31-10). "A nonsuit may be taken after a temporary restraining order has been obtained but before the hearing on the temporary injunction. But the

nonsuit does not defeat the right of a restrained party who is damaged by the temporary restraining order to sue for wrongful injunction."

C/S Solutions, Inc. v. Energy Maint. Servs. Grp., 274 S.W.3d 299, 306-07 (Tex.App.—Houston [1st Dist.] 2008, no pet.). "[T]reatises have drawn a distinction between a pure [TRCP] 162 nonsuit, which voluntarily dismisses the entire case, and a voluntary dismissal that abandons the case as to certain parties and/or claims. This distinction has no practical effect when a plaintiff files a written 'nonsuit' that abandons the case as to certain claims so long as the written 'nonsuit' does not run afoul of the time restrictions in [TRCP] 63. Under our liberal pleading rules, the document is in substance an amended pleading voluntarily dismissing the claims, notwithstanding the fact that the word 'nonsuit' appears. Similarly, the distinction between a pure Rule 162 nonsuit and a voluntary dismissal that abandons the case as to certain parties has no practical effect unless a plaintiff 'nonsuits' those parties in a situation in which another party is prejudiced under [TRCP] 163."

Reynolds v. Murphy, 266 S.W.3d 141, 145-46 (Tex. App.—Fort Worth 2008, pet. denied). "Although a nonsuit may have the effect of vitiating a trial court's earlier interlocutory orders, a nonsuit does not vitiate a trial court's previously-made decisions on the merits, such as a summary judgment, or even a partial summary judgment, which becomes final upon disposition of the other issues in the case. [¶] The parties disagree as to whether the trial court's rulings striking [P's] amended petition are equivalent to a decision on the merits as to the new claims in the amended petition. [D] contends that the rulings were merely incidental interlocutory rulings because they did not involve any judgments on the merits of those claims…. [¶] [B]y striking [P's] new causes of action in [the amended] petition, and by refusing to allow discovery on those causes of action, the trial court effected a dismissal of those causes of action with prejudice without affording [P] an opportunity to replead. In essence, … the trial court effected the same type of disposition as a dismissal or a partial summary judgment precluding consideration of those claims. [W]e conclude [P's] nonsuit of its sole remaining claim did not vitiate the trial court's rulings effectively barring him from pursuing his new claims…." *See also* ***Waterman S.S. Corp. v. Ruiz***, 355 S.W.3d 387, 400 (Tex.App.—Houston [1st Dist.] 2011, pet. denied).

Bailey v. Gardner, 154 S.W.3d 917, 920 (Tex. App.—Dallas 2005, no pet.). "[P] made a tactical decision to nonsuit his case rather than face trial without expert testimony to support his claim. Taking a voluntary nonsuit for tactical advantage will not support an equitable extension of the limitations period. [E]quitable tolling does not apply to give [P] an extension on the limitations period [to refile his suit]."

TRCP 163. DISMISSAL AS TO PARTIES SERVED, ETC.

When it will not prejudice another party, the plaintiff may dismiss his suit as to one or more of several parties who were served with process, or who have answered, but no such dismissal shall in any case, be allowed as to a principal obligor, except in the cases provided for by statute.

See also *O'Connor's Texas Rules*, "Voluntary Dismissal—Nonsuit," ch. 7-F, p. 739.

ANNOTATIONS

Texas Cab Co. v. Giles, 783 S.W.2d 695, 697 (Tex. App.—El Paso 1989, no writ). "Unless the settlement with the deleted [D] was properly presented to the trial court, there generally could have been no dismissal to that [D] under [TRCP] 162 or 163, as the dismissal would have prejudiced [co-D]."

TRCP 164. REPEALED

TRCP 165. ABANDONMENT

A party who abandons any part of his claim or defense, as contained in the pleadings, may have that fact entered of record, so as to show that the matters therein were not tried.

See also *O'Connor's Texas Rules*, "Voluntary Dismissal—Nonsuit," ch. 7-F, p. 739.

ANNOTATIONS

Alan Reuber Chevrolet, Inc. v. Grady Chevrolet, Ltd., 287 S.W.3d 877, 887 (Tex.App.—Dallas 2009, no pet.). "Rule 165 permits an abandonment of a part of a claim or defense before, but not after, trial of the cause and entry of the judgment. This is the same requirement as for a nonsuit."

In re Shaw, 966 S.W.2d 174, 177 (Tex.App.—El Paso 1998, no pet.). "Whether a pleading has been abandoned is a question of law which we review de novo. Formal amendment of the pleadings is not re-

quired in order to show abandonment. Indeed, a stipulation may form the basis for abandonment."

TRCP 165a. DISMISSAL FOR WANT OF PROSECUTION

1. **Failure to Appear.** A case may be dismissed for want of prosecution on failure of any party seeking affirmative relief to appear for any hearing or trial of which the party had notice. Notice of the court's intention to dismiss and the date and place of the dismissal hearing shall be sent by the clerk to each attorney of record, and to each party not represented by an attorney and whose address is shown on the docket or in the papers on file, by posting same in the United States Postal Service. At the dismissal hearing, the court shall dismiss for want of prosecution unless there is good cause for the case to be maintained on the docket. If the court determines to maintain the case on the docket, it shall render a pretrial order assigning a trial date for the case and setting deadlines for the joining of new parties, all discovery, filing of all pleadings, the making of a response or supplemental responses to discovery and other pretrial matters. The case may be continued thereafter only for valid and compelling reasons specifically determined by court order. Notice of the signing of the order of dismissal shall be given as provided in Rule 306a. Failure to mail notices as required by this rule shall not affect any of the periods mentioned in Rule 306a except as provided in that rule.

2. **Non-compliance with Time Standards.** Any case not disposed of within time standards promulgated by the Supreme Court under its Administrative Rules may be placed on a dismissal docket.

3. **Reinstatement.** A motion to reinstate shall set forth the grounds therefor and be verified by the movant or his attorney. It shall be filed with the clerk within 30 days after the order of dismissal is signed or within the period provided by Rule 306a. A copy of the motion to reinstate shall be served on each attorney of record and each party not represented by an attorney whose address is shown on the docket or in the papers on file. The clerk shall deliver a copy of the motion to the judge, who shall set a hearing on the motion as soon as practicable. The court shall notify all parties or their attorneys of record of the date, time and place of the hearing.

The court shall reinstate the case upon finding after a hearing that the failure of the party or his attorney was not intentional or the result of conscious indifference but was due to an accident or mistake or that the failure has been otherwise reasonably explained.

In the event for any reason a motion for reinstatement is not decided by signed written order within seventy-five days after the judgment is signed, or, within such other time as may be allowed by Rule 306a, the motion shall be deemed overruled by operation of law. If a motion to reinstate is timely filed by any party, the trial court, regardless of whether an appeal has been perfected, has plenary power to reinstate the case until 30 days after all such timely filed motions are overruled, either by a written and signed order or by operation of law, whichever occurs first.

4. **Cumulative Remedies.** This dismissal and reinstatement procedure shall be cumulative of the rules and laws governing any other procedures available to the parties in such cases. The same reinstatement procedures and timetable are applicable to all dismissals for want of prosecution including cases which are dismissed pursuant to the court's inherent power, whether or not a motion to dismiss has been filed.

See also *O'Connor's Texas Rules*, "Involuntary Dismissal," ch. 7-G, p. 747; "Motion to Reinstate After Dismissal for Want of Prosecution," ch. 10-F, p. 930; *O'Connor's Texas Forms*, FORMS 7G.

ANNOTATIONS

In re Conner, 458 S.W.3d 532, 534 (Tex.2015). "The issue here is whether a trial court abuses its discretion by refusing to grant a motion to dismiss for want of prosecution in the face of unmitigated and unexplained delay. We hold that it does. [¶] Trial courts are generally granted considerable discretion when it comes to managing their dockets. Such discretion, however, is not absolute. It has long been the case that 'a delay of an unreasonable duration ..., if not sufficiently explained, will raise a conclusive presumption of abandonment of the plaintiff's suit.' This presumption justifies the dismissal of a suit under either a court's inherent authority or Rule 165a.... *At 535:* [Ps'] failure to provide good cause for their nearly decade-long delay mandates dismissal under Rule 165a(2).... Absent any reasonable explanation for the delay, the trial court clearly abused its discretion by disregarding the conclusive presumption of abandonment."

Alexander v. Lynda's Boutique, 134 S.W.3d 845, 849-50 (Tex.2004). "[T]he clerk has an affirmative duty under Rule 165a to give notice, but no duty to affirmatively show in the record that such notice was given.... [¶] [T]he fact that the record is silent about

the sending of notices under Rule 165a does not establish error on the face of the record. [M]ere silence as to whether notice was sent does not establish that notice was not sent or that it was sent to the wrong address. *At 852:* Rule 165a(1) does not preclude a trial court from scheduling a pre-trial hearing, giving notice that failure to attend that hearing may result in dismissal for want of prosecution, and also deciding at that hearing whether the case should be dismissed for want of prosecution if a party seeking relief fails to attend. All Rule 165a(1) requires is notice of intent to dismiss and of a date, time, and place for the hearing."

Villarreal v. San Antonio Truck & Equip., 994 S.W.2d 628, 630 (Tex.1999). "The trial court's authority to dismiss for want of prosecution stems from two sources: (1) Rule 165a … and (2) the court's inherent power. [¶] [A] party must be provided with notice and an opportunity to be heard before a court may dismiss a case for want of prosecution under either Rule 165a or its inherent authority. The failure to provide adequate notice of the trial court's intent to dismiss for want of prosecution requires reversal." *See also* ***Ringer v. Kimball***, 274 S.W.3d 865, 867 (Tex.App.—Fort Worth 2008, no pet.).

Smith v. Babcock & Wilcox Constr. Co., 913 S.W.2d 467, 468 (Tex.1995). "A failure to appear is not intentional or due to conscious indifference within the meaning of [TRCP 165a] merely because it is deliberate; it must also be without adequate justification. Proof of such justification—accident, mistake or other reasonable explanation—negates the intent or conscious indifference for which reinstatement can be denied. Also, conscious indifference means more than mere negligence." *See also* ***Johnson v. Hawkins***, 255 S.W.3d 394, 398 (Tex.App.—Dallas 2008, pet. denied) (whether failure to appear was not intentional or result of conscious indifference is fact-finding within trial court's discretion).

Harris Cty. v. Gambichler, 479 S.W.3d 514, 516-17 (Tex.App.—Houston [14th Dist.] 2015, no pet.). "It is well-settled that dismissal of a case with prejudice functions as a final determination on the merits. But a dismissal for want of prosecution is not a determination on the merits, and therefore dismissal with prejudice in such circumstances is improper. An order of dismissal for want of prosecution should simply place the parties in the position they were in prior to filing the suit."

Ashley & Laird, L.C. v. Gilbert, No. 05-15-00707-CV (Tex.App.—Dallas 2015, no pet.) (memo op.; 7-31-15). "'Rule 165a(3) sets forth a complete and exclusive remedy by way of a verified motion to reinstate.' [¶] An affidavit may satisfy the verification requirement. [W]e have also concluded that an evidentiary hearing conducted within the 30 day period for filing a verified motion for reinstatement satisfies the purposes of the rule.… [F]ailure to file a verified motion to reinstate may be cured if an affidavit or other evidence supporting the motion is filed within the same 30-day period required for filing the motion to reinstate. Here, however, the trial court's hearing was non-evidentiary and was conducted after the trial court's plenary power had expired, more than 30 days after the judgment dismissing the case for want of prosecution was signed. Thus, there is no basis for arguing that [Ps] made any effort to cure the defective motion to reinstate."

In re Valliance Bank, 422 S.W.3d 729, 731 (Tex. App.—Fort Worth 2013, orig. proceeding). "If the unsworn signature of a licensed lawyer in good standing with the State Bar and well known to the trial judge or in the professional community were a sufficient substitute for the 'verification' of a motion to reinstate, then counsel of record's routine signature would, itself, suffice, and rule 165(a)'s requirement for verification would be rendered meaningless. For us to hold that the signature of counsel for a party, which is required on all pleadings, sworn or unsworn, is sufficient to satisfy the requirement of verification under rule 165a(3) would be tantamount to rewriting the rules of procedure to eliminate that requirement…."

United Residential Props., L.P. v. Theis, 378 S.W.3d 552, 557 (Tex.App.—Houston [14th Dist.] 2012, no pet.). The 30-day deadline to file a motion to reinstate "is jurisdictional, and a trial court loses jurisdiction to reinstate a dismissed case after the deadline."

In re R.C.R., 230 S.W.3d 423, 426-27 (Tex.App.—Fort Worth 2007, no pet.). "Here, the trial court's order states that the court dismissed [father's] case because he failed to appear at the … hearing. However, [father] was unable to appear personally because he was incarcerated and because the trial court denied his request for a bench warrant. In addition, [he] was unable to appear by alternative means, such as by telephone or affidavit, because the trial court denied his motion to appear by such alternative means. Thus, the trial court

dismissed [father's] case for failure to appear without providing [him] any means to appear. This is fundamentally unfair and denied [father] access to the courts."

In re Wal-Mart Stores, 20 S.W.3d 734, 740 (Tex. App.—El Paso 2000, orig. proceeding). "Rule 165a(3) requires that a case be reinstated by signed written order.... An oral pronouncement by the court reinstating the case, even when accompanied by a docket entry, is ordinarily inadequate to reinstate the case."

Maida v. Fire Ins. Exch., 990 S.W.2d 836, 840-41 (Tex.App.—Fort Worth 1999, no pet.). We agree with our sister courts that "have held [TRCP] 165a(3)'s standard for reinstatement only applies to cases dismissed for failure to appear. [¶] The standard set out in [TRCP] 165a(3) is essentially the same standard as that for setting aside a default judgment. Such a standard is well suited for analyzing specific instances of conduct. On the other hand, it does not easily lend itself to determining whether a party diligently prosecuted a case or whether the disposition of the case complies with the supreme court's time standards for disposition. [¶] Furthermore, [TRCP] 165a(4) is consistent with application of [TRCP 165a(3)] to only instances of dismissal based on a failure to appear. [TRCP] 165a(4) requires that the *procedures* and *timetable*, be applied to all dismissals for want of prosecution. Therefore, we hold that [TRCP] 165a(3)'s reinstatement standard, 'conscious indifference,' only applies to cases dismissed for failure to appear." *But see* ***Cappetta v. Hermes***, 222 S.W.3d 160, 167 (Tex.App.—San Antonio 2006, no pet.).

SECTION 8. PRETRIAL PROCEDURE

TRCP 166. PRETRIAL CONFERENCE

In an appropriate action, to assist in the disposition of the case without undue expense or burden to the parties, the court may in its discretion direct the attorneys for the parties and the parties or their duly authorized agents to appear before it for a conference to consider:

(a) All pending dilatory pleas, motions and exceptions;

(b) The necessity or desirability of amendments to the pleadings;

(c) A discovery schedule;

(d) Requiring written statements of the parties' contentions;

(e) Contested issues of fact and simplification of the issues;

(f) The possibility of obtaining stipulations of fact;

(g) The identification of legal matters to be ruled on or decided by the court;

(h) The exchange of a list of direct fact witnesses, other than rebuttal or impeaching witnesses the necessity of whose testimony cannot reasonably be anticipated before the time of trial, who will be called to testify at trial, stating their address and telephone number, and the subject of the testimony of each such witness;

(i) The exchange of a list of expert witnesses who will be called to testify at trial, stating their address and telephone number, and the subject of the testimony and opinions that will be proffered by each expert witness;

(j) Agreed applicable propositions of law and contested issues of law;

(k) Proposed jury charge questions, instructions, and definitions for a jury case or proposed findings of fact and conclusions of law for a nonjury case;

(*l*) The marking and exchanging of all exhibits that any party may use at trial and stipulation to the authenticity and admissibility of exhibits to be used at trial;

(m) Written trial objections to the opposite party's exhibits, stating the basis for each objection;

(n) The advisability of a preliminary reference of issues to a master or auditor for findings to be used as evidence when the trial is to be by jury;

(o) The settlement of the case, and to aid such consideration, the court may encourage settlement;

(p) Such other matters as may aid in the disposition of the action.

The court shall make an order that recites the action taken at the pretrial conference, the amendments allowed to the pleadings, the time within which same may be filed, and the agreements made by the parties as to any of the matters considered, and which limits the issues for trial to those not disposed of by admissions, agreements of counsel, or rulings of the court; and such order when issued shall control the subsequent course of the action, unless modified at the trial to prevent manifest injustice. The court in its discretion may establish by rule a pretrial calendar on which actions may be placed for consideration as above provided and may either confine the calendar to jury actions or extend it to all actions.

Pretrial proceedings in multidistrict litigation may also be governed by Rules 11 and 13 of the Rules of Judicial Administration.

See also Gov't Code §21.001(a); TRCP 248; TRJA 11, 13; ***O'Connor's Texas Rules***, "Pretrial Conference," ch. 5-A, p. 373; "Motion to Transfer to Multidistrict Litigation Pretrial Court," ch. 5-G, p. 414; ***O'Connor's Texas Forms***, FORM 5A:1.

ANNOTATIONS

Koslow's v. Mackie, 796 S.W.2d 700, 703 (Tex. 1990). TRCP 166 "includes the power to order the parties through their attorneys (or through themselves if appearing pro se) to confer to narrow the issues for the written pretrial conference report."

Provident Life & Acc. Ins. v. Hazlitt, 216 S.W.2d 805, 807 (Tex.1949). "The purpose of [TRCP 166] is to simplify and shorten the trial.... [N]o controverted issues of fact could be adjudicated at [the pretrial] conference, but orders could be entered disposing of issues which are founded upon admitted or undisputed facts."

Stamatis v. Methodist Willowbrook Hosp., No. 14-14-00492-CV (Tex.App.—Houston [14th Dist.] 2015, no pet.) (memo op.; 6-2-15). "[D]ismissal at a pretrial conference is allowed in limited situations when determination of a legal question is dispositive of a case in its entirety."

Taylor v. Taylor, 254 S.W.3d 527, 532 (Tex.App.—Houston [1st Dist.] 2008, no pet.). Rule 166 "permits a trial court 'to make an order that recites the action taken at the pretrial conference,' that is, the rule permits the trial court to sign pretrial orders. As we have previously noted, one of the purposes of the pretrial order is to aid in the orderly disposition of cases. [¶] Although Rule 166 does not expressly authorize the trial court to impose sanctions for violations of a pretrial order, the Texas Supreme Court[, in ***Koslow's***, above,] determined that such power is implicit in Rule 166. Nonetheless, the sanctions imposed must be just and appropriate."

In re Estate of Henry, 250 S.W.3d 518, 526 (Tex. App.—Dallas 2008, no pet.). "Rule 166 ... provides that an order made at a pretrial conference hearing 'shall control the subsequent course of the action.' However, the trial court retains authority under rule 166 to modify an order to prevent manifest injustice. 'Rule 166 recognizes the fundamental rule that a trial court has the inherent right to change or modify any interlocutory order or judgment until the time the judgment on the merits in the case becomes final.'"

Lindley v. Johnson, 936 S.W.2d 53, 55 (Tex.App.—Tyler 1996, writ denied). "When a trial court's pretrial scheduling order changes the deadlines set forth in a procedural rule, the trial court's order prevails."

TRCP 166a. SUMMARY JUDGMENT

(a) For Claimant. A party seeking to recover upon a claim, counterclaim, or cross-claim or to obtain a declaratory judgment may, at any time after the adverse party has appeared or answered, move with or without supporting affidavits for a summary judgment in his favor upon all or any part thereof. A summary judgment, interlocutory in character, may be rendered on the issue of liability alone although there is a genuine issue as to amount of damages.

(b) For Defending Party. A party against whom a claim, counterclaim, or cross-claim is asserted or a declaratory judgment is sought may, at any time, move with or without supporting affidavits for a summary judgment in his favor as to all or any part thereof.

(c) Motion and Proceedings Thereon. The motion for summary judgment shall state the specific grounds therefor. Except on leave of court, with notice to opposing counsel, the motion and any supporting affidavits shall be filed and served at least twenty-one days before the time specified for hearing. Except on leave of court, the adverse party, not later than seven days prior to the day of hearing may file and serve opposing affidavits or other written response. No oral testimony shall be received at the hearing. The judgment sought shall be rendered forthwith if (i) the deposition transcripts, interrogatory answers, and other discovery responses referenced or set forth in the motion or response, and (ii) the pleadings, admissions, affidavits, stipulations of the parties, and authenticated or certified public records, if any, on file at the time of the hearing, or filed thereafter and before judgment with permission of the court, show that, except as to the amount of damages, there is no genuine issue as to any material fact and the moving party is entitled to judgment as a matter of law on the issues expressly set out in the motion or in an answer or any other response. Issues not expressly presented to the trial court by written motion, answer or other response shall not be considered on appeal as grounds for reversal. A summary judgment may be based on uncontroverted testimonial evidence of an interested witness, or of an expert witness as to subject matter concerning which the trier of fact must be guided solely by the opinion testimony of

experts, if the evidence is clear, positive and direct, otherwise credible and free from contradictions and inconsistencies, and could have been readily controverted.

(d) Appendices, References and Other Use of Discovery Not Otherwise on File. Discovery products not on file with the clerk may be used as summary judgment evidence if copies of the material, appendices containing the evidence, or a notice containing specific references to the discovery or specific references to other instruments, are filed and served on all parties together with a statement of intent to use the specified discovery as summary judgment proofs: (i) at least twenty-one days before the hearing if such proofs are to be used to support the summary judgment; or (ii) at least seven days before the hearing if such proofs are to be used to oppose the summary judgment.

(e) Case Not Fully Adjudicated on Motion. If summary judgment is not rendered upon the whole case or for all the relief asked and a trial is necessary, the judge may at the hearing examine the pleadings and the evidence on file, interrogate counsel, ascertain what material fact issues exist and make an order specifying the facts that are established as a matter of law, and directing such further proceedings in the action as are just.

(f) Form of Affidavits; Further Testimony. Supporting and opposing affidavits shall be made on personal knowledge, shall set forth such facts as would be admissible in evidence, and shall show affirmatively that the affiant is competent to testify to the matters stated therein. Sworn or certified copies of all papers or parts thereof referred to in an affidavit shall be attached thereto or served therewith. The court may permit affidavits to be supplemented or opposed by depositions or by further affidavits. Defects in the form of affidavits or attachments will not be grounds for reversal unless specifically pointed out by objection by an opposing party with opportunity, but refusal, to amend.

(g) When Affidavits Are Unavailable. Should it appear from the affidavits of a party opposing the motion that he cannot for reasons stated present by affidavit facts essential to justify his opposition, the court may refuse the application for judgment or may order a continuance to permit affidavits to be obtained or depositions to be taken or discovery to be had or may make such other order as is just.

(h) Affidavits Made in Bad Faith. Should it appear to the satisfaction of the court at any time that any of the affidavits presented pursuant to this rule are presented in bad faith or solely for the purpose of delay, the court shall forthwith order the party employing them to pay to the other party the amount of the reasonable expenses which the filing of the affidavits caused him to incur, including reasonable attorney's fees, and any offending party or attorney may be adjudged guilty of contempt.

(i) No-Evidence Motion. After adequate time for discovery, a party without presenting summary judgment evidence may move for summary judgment on the ground that there is no evidence of one or more essential elements of a claim or defense on which an adverse party would have the burden of proof at trial. The motion must state the elements as to which there is no evidence. The court must grant the motion unless the respondent produces summary judgment evidence raising a genuine issue of material fact.

Notes & Comments to TRCP 166a(i): This comment is intended to inform the construction and application of the rule. Paragraph (i) authorizes a motion for summary judgment based on the assertion that, after adequate opportunity for discovery, there is no evidence to support one or more specified elements of an adverse party's claim or defense. A discovery period set by pretrial order should be adequate opportunity for discovery unless there is a showing to the contrary, and ordinarily a motion under paragraph (i) would be permitted after the period but not before. The motion must be specific in challenging the evidentiary support for an element of a claim or defense; paragraph (i) does not authorize conclusory motions or general no-evidence challenges to an opponent's case. Paragraph (i) does not apply to ordinary motions for summary judgment under paragraphs (a) or (b), in which the movant must prove it is entitled to judgment by establishing each element of its own claim or defense as a matter of law. To defeat a motion made under paragraph (i), the respondent is not required to marshal its proof; its response need only point out evidence that raises a fact issue on the challenged elements. The existing rules continue to govern the general requirements of summary judgment practice. A motion under paragraph (i) is subject to sanctions provided by existing law (CPRC §§9.001-10.006) and rules (TRCP 13). The denial of a motion under paragraph (i) is no more reviewable by appeal or mandamus than the denial of a motion under paragraph (c).

See also *O'Connor's Texas Rules*, "Motion for Summary Judgment—General Rules," ch. 7-B, p. 690; "Traditional Motion for Summary Judgment," ch. 7-C, p. 716; "No-Evidence Motion for Summary Judgment," ch. 7-D, p. 729; *O'Connor's Texas Forms*, FORMS 7B, 7C; *O'Connor's Texas Family Law Handbook* (2017), "Suit to Dissolve Marriage with Children," ch. 4-D, p. 410; "Suit to Adjudicate Parentage," ch. 4-G, p. 573; "Suit to Modify Conservatorship, Possession, or Access," ch. 9-A, p. 973; "Suit to Modify Child Support," ch. 9-D, p. 1023.

ANNOTATIONS

Traditional SJ

Amedisys, Inc. v. Kingwood Home Health Care, LLC, 437 S.W.3d 507, 511 (Tex.2014). "[T]he party moving for traditional summary judgment [has] the burden to submit sufficient evidence that establishe[s] on its face that 'there is no genuine issue as to any material fact' and that it is 'entitled to judgment as a matter of law.' When a movant meets that burden of estab-

lishing each element of the claim or defense on which it seeks summary judgment, the burden then shifts to the non-movant to disprove or raise an issue of fact as to at least one of those elements. But if the movant does not satisfy its initial burden, the burden does not shift and the non-movant need not respond or present any evidence." *See also* ***State v. $90,235***, 390 S.W.3d 289, 292 (Tex.2013).

Frost Nat'l Bank v. Fernandez, 315 S.W.3d 494, 508 (Tex.2010). "A defendant who conclusively negates at least one of the essential elements of a cause of action or conclusively establishes an affirmative defense is entitled to summary judgment." *See also* ***Stanfield v. Neubaum***, 494 S.W.3d 90, 96 (Tex.2016).

Proulx v. Wells, 235 S.W.3d 213, 215 (Tex.2007). "Our jurisprudence has at times been less than clear in explaining the summary-judgment burden that inheres when the diligent-service question is presented. *At 216:* [O]nce a defendant has affirmatively pled the limitations defense and shown that service was effected after limitations expired, the burden shifts to the plaintiff 'to explain the delay.' Thus, it is the plaintiff's burden to present evidence regarding the efforts that were made to serve the defendant, and to explain every lapse in effort or period of delay. In some instances, the plaintiff's explanation may be *legally* improper to raise the diligence issue and the defendant will bear no burden at all. In others, the plaintiff's explanation of its service efforts may demonstrate a lack of due diligence as a matter of law, as when one or more lapses between service efforts are unexplained or patently unreasonable. But if the plaintiff's explanation for the delay raises a material fact issue concerning the diligence of service efforts, the burden shifts back to the defendant to conclusively show why, as a matter of law, the explanation is insufficient." *See also* ***Farmers Ins. Exch. v. Rodriguez***, 366 S.W.3d 216, 221 (Tex.App.—Houston [14th Dist.] 2012, pet. denied).

Valence Oper. Co. v. Dorsett, 164 S.W.3d 656, 661 (Tex.2005). "When both parties move for partial summary judgment on the same issues and the trial court grants one motion and denies the other ..., the reviewing court considers the summary judgment evidence presented by both sides, determines all questions presented, and if the reviewing court determines that the trial court erred, renders the judgment the trial court should have rendered." *See also* ***BCCA Appeal Grp. v. City of Houston***, 496 S.W.3d 1, 7 (Tex.2016); ***Merriman v. XTO Energy, Inc.***, 407 S.W.3d 244, 248 (Tex. 2013).

Park Place Hosp. v. Estate of Milo, 909 S.W.2d 508, 510 (Tex.1995). For Ds "to prevail, they were required to prove that there was no genuine issue as to any material fact and that they were entitled to judgment as a matter of law. In reviewing a summary judgment, we must accept as true evidence favoring [P], indulging every reasonable inference and resolving all doubts in [P's] favor." *See also* ***Cantey Hanger, LLP v. Byrd***, 467 S.W.3d 477, 481 (Tex.2015); ***Western Invs. v. Urena***, 162 S.W.3d 547, 550 (Tex.2005).

Rush v. Barrios, 56 S.W.3d 88, 98 (Tex.App.—Houston [14th Dist.] 2001, pet. denied). "A trial court may ... properly grant summary judgment after having previously denied [it] without a motion by or prior notice to the parties, as long as the court retains jurisdiction over the case."

Michael v. Dyke, 41 S.W.3d 746, 751 (Tex.App.—Corpus Christi 2001, no pet.). "When it is not readily apparent to the trial court that summary judgment is sought under rule 166a(i), the court should presume that it is filed under the traditional summary judgment rule and analyze it according to those well-recognized standards. [The] order granting summary judgment should clarify whether the motion is granted on no-evidence grounds or traditional grounds. When an order fails to so clarify, a motion requesting such clarification should be filed with the trial court."

No-Evidence SJ

Mack Trucks, Inc. v. Tamez, 206 S.W.3d 572, 581-82 (Tex.2006). A no-evidence motion for "summary judgment ... is essentially a motion for a pretrial directed verdict. Once such a motion is filed, the burden shifts to the nonmoving party to present evidence raising an issue of material fact as to the elements specified in the motion. We review the evidence presented by the motion and response in the light most favorable to the party against whom the summary judgment was rendered, crediting evidence favorable to that party if reasonable jurors could, and disregarding contrary evidence unless reasonable jurors could not." *See also* ***Timpte Indus. v. Gish***, 286 S.W.3d 306, 310 (Tex.2009).

King Ranch, Inc. v. Chapman, 118 S.W.3d 742, 751 (Tex.2003). "'A no evidence point will be sustained when (a) there is a complete absence of evidence of a vital fact, (b) the court is barred by rules of law or of evi-

dence from giving weight to the only evidence offered to prove a vital fact, (c) the evidence offered to prove a vital fact is no more than a mere scintilla, or (d) the evidence conclusively establishes the opposite of the vital fact.' ... More than a scintilla of evidence exists when the evidence[ ] 'rises to a level that would enable reasonable and fair-minded people to differ in their conclusions.'" *See also* ***Ford Motor Co. v. Ridgway***, 135 S.W.3d 598, 601 (Tex.2004) (evidence that does no more than create mere suspicion of existence of a fact is, in legal effect, no evidence).

Neurodiagnostic Tex, L.L.C. v. Pierce, 506 S.W.3d 153, 172 (Tex.App.—Tyler 2016, no pet.). "When determining whether adequate time for discovery has elapsed, we consider (1) the nature of the cause of action; (2) the nature of the evidence necessary to controvert the no evidence motion; (3) the length of time the case has been active in the trial court; (4) the amount of time the no evidence motion has been on file; (5) whether the movant has requested stricter time deadlines for discovery; (6) the amount of discovery that has already taken place; and (7) whether the discovery deadlines that are in place are specific or vague." *See also* ***McInnis v. Mallia***, 261 S.W.3d 197, 202-03 (Tex.App.—Houston [14th Dist.] 2008, no pet.) (time allocated for discovery in docket-control order is strong indicator of adequate time).

Nelson v. SCI Tex. Funeral Servs., 484 S.W.3d 248, 252 (Tex.App.—Eastland 2016, pet. filed 6-9-16). "[D's] no-evidence ground ... is not an ordinary no-evidence ground because it is premised on a legal contention concerning the law applicable to [P's] claim. [¶] '[T]he court must determine the law which is applicable to the case with respect to any no-evidence motion for summary judgment in order to determine if the summary judgment evidence raises a genuine issue of material fact. The fact that a dispute exists with respect to the applicable law does not prevent the court from performing its function of analyzing the non-movant's evidence to determine if it raises a fact issue.' Other courts have not taken this approach. They have concluded that a question of law is not a proper subject of a no-evidence motion for summary judgment."

Hybrid Motion

Merriman v. XTO Energy, Inc., 407 S.W.3d 244, 248 (Tex.2013). "[P] contends that we should treat [D's] motion as only a traditional one because [D] did not sufficiently segregate the grounds for the different types of motions. But [D] labeled its motion as a combined traditional and no-evidence motion, and as long as a motion clearly sets forth its grounds and otherwise meets the requirements of a no-evidence summary judgment motion, as [D's] did, it is sufficient as one. When a party moves for summary judgment on both traditional and no-evidence grounds as [D] did here, we first address the no-evidence grounds. That is because if the non-movant fails to produce legally sufficient evidence to meet his burden as to the no-evidence motion, there is no need to analyze whether the movant satisfied its burden under the traditional motion." *See also* ***Ford Motor Co. v. Ridgway***, 135 S.W.3d 598, 600 (Tex. 2004).

Binur v. Jacobo, 135 S.W.3d 646, 650-51 (Tex. 2004). TRCP 166a "does not prohibit a party from combining in a single motion a request for summary judgment that utilizes the procedures under either subsection (a) or (b), with a request for summary judgment that utilizes subsection (i).... The fact that evidence may be attached to a motion ... under subsection (a) or (b) does not foreclose a party from also asserting that there is no evidence with regard to a particular element. Similarly, if a motion brought solely under subsection (i) attaches evidence, that evidence should not be considered unless it creates a fact question, but such a motion should not be disregarded or treated as a motion under subsection (a) or (b). [¶] [U]sing headings to clearly delineate the basis for summary judgment under subsection (a) or (b) from the basis for summary judgment under subsection (i) would be helpful ..., but the rule does not require it."

Waite v. Woodard, Hall & Primm, P.C., 137 S.W.3d 277, 281 (Tex.App.—Houston [1st Dist.] 2004, no pet.). "Although [TRCP] 166a does not prohibit a hybrid motion, the motion must give fair notice to the non-movant of the basis on which the summary judgment is sought. [P's] motion did not give fair notice that it was attempting to establish its entitlement to judgment as a matter of law...."

SJ Evidence

Morgan v. Anthony, 27 S.W.3d 928, 929 (Tex. 2000). "The summary judgment evidence includes excerpts from two depositions of [P] and her answer to an interrogatory. Generally, a party cannot rely on its own answer to an interrogatory as summary judgment evidence. However, [P] was questioned in one of her depositions about her seven-page interrogatory answer

..., and the interrogatory answer was attached to her deposition as an exhibit. ... The excerpts from her deposition about the interrogatory answer and the interrogatory answer itself were part of the summary judgment record. The interrogatory answer became competent summary judgment evidence when it became a deposition exhibit, [P] affirmed in her deposition that it was correct, and she was subject to cross-examination about the assertions in her interrogatory answer." *See also* ***Watson v. Henderson***, No. 05-08-01158-CV (Tex.App.—Dallas 2010, pet. denied) (memo op.; 1-20-10).

Wadewitz v. Montgomery, 951 S.W.2d 464, 466 (Tex.1997). "Conclusory statements by an expert are insufficient to support or defeat summary judgment." *See also* ***Elizondo v. Krist***, 415 S.W.3d 259, 264 (Tex. 2013) (same as annotation); ***United Blood Servs. v. Longoria***, 938 S.W.2d 29, 30 (Tex.1997) (qualification of witness as expert is within court's discretion).

Trico Techs. v. Montiel, 949 S.W.2d 308, 310 (Tex. 1997). "The mere fact that the affidavit is self-serving does not necessarily make the evidence an improper basis for summary judgment. Summary judgment based on the uncontroverted affidavit of an interested witness is proper if the evidence is clear, positive, direct, otherwise credible, free from contradictions and inconsistencies, and could have been readily controverted. 'Could have been readily controverted' does not mean that the summary judgment evidence could have been easily and conveniently rebutted, but rather indicates that the testimony could have been effectively countered by opposing evidence." *See also* ***Neely v. Wilson***, 418 S.W.3d 52, 67 n.22 (Tex.2013).

Laidlaw Waste Sys. v. City of Wilmer, 904 S.W.2d 656, 660 (Tex.1995). "Generally, pleadings are not competent evidence, even if sworn or verified."

Wilson v. Burford, 904 S.W.2d 628, 629 (Tex.1995). "Rule 166a(c) plainly includes in the record evidence attached either to the motion or to a response." *See also* ***Johnson v. Driver***, 198 S.W.3d 359, 363 (Tex.App.—Tyler 2006, no pet.).

McConathy v. McConathy, 869 S.W.2d 341, 341 (Tex.1994). "[D]eposition excerpts [and other discovery] submitted as summary judgment evidence need not be authenticated. *At 342:* All parties have ready access to depositions taken in a cause, and thus deposition excerpts submitted with a motion for summary judgment may be easily verified as to their accuracy." *See also* ***Gunville v. Gonzales***, 508 S.W.3d 547, 561-62 (Tex.App.—El Paso 2016, no pet.).

Casso v. Brand, 776 S.W.2d 551, 558 (Tex.1989). "If the credibility of the affiant ... is likely to be a dispositive factor in the resolution of the case, then summary judgment is inappropriate. On the other hand, if the non-movant must, in all likelihood, come forth with independent evidence to prevail, then summary judgment may well be proper in the absence of such controverting proof."

Rockwall Commons Assocs. v. MRC Mortg. Grantor Trust I, 331 S.W.3d 500, 507 (Tex.App.—El Paso 2010, no pet.). "Substantive defects include affidavits that include legal or factual conclusions. Among the objections that may be raised at trial regarding the form of an affidavit are: (1) lack of personal knowledge; (2) hearsay; (3) statement of an interested witness that is not clear, positive, direct, or free from contradiction; and (4) competence."

Kastner v. Jenkens & Gilchrist, P.C., 231 S.W.3d 571, 581 (Tex.App.—Dallas 2007, no pet.). "The [TRCPs] do not require that summary judgment evidence be physically attached to the motion. Instead, the rules embody an infinitely more practical requirement that evidence be 'filed and served' with the motion."

Chau v. Riddle, 212 S.W.3d 699, 704 (Tex.App.—Houston [1st Dist.] 2006), *rev'd on other grounds*, 254 S.W.3d 453 (Tex.2008). "The affidavit of an expert who is not properly designated may not be used as evidence in a summary judgment context. Where the expert's testimony will be excluded at trial on the merits, it will be excluded from a summary judgment proceeding."

Brown v. Brown, 145 S.W.3d 745, 751 (Tex.App.—Dallas 2004, pet. denied). "Defects in the form of an affidavit must be objected to, and the opposing party must have the opportunity to amend the affidavit. The failure to obtain a ruling on an objection to the form of the affidavit waives the objection. Defects in the substance of an affidavit are not waived by the failure to obtain a ruling from the trial court on the objection, and they may be raised for the first time on appeal." *See also* ***Stovall & Assocs. v. Hibbs Fin. Ctr., Ltd.***, 409 S.W.3d 790, 797 (Tex.App.—Dallas 2013, no pet.) (objection that affidavit contains hearsay is objection to defect in form of affidavit); ***Vega v. Autozone W., Inc.***, No. 04-12-00724-CV (Tex.App.—San Antonio 2013, no pet.) (memo op.; 6-5-13) (objection that deposition contained hearsay statements was objection to defect in form); ***Watts v.***

Hermann Hosp., 962 S.W.2d 102, 105 (Tex.App.—Houston [1st Dist.] 1997, no pet.) (without objection, defects in authentication of attachments supporting SJ motion or response are waived).

Goss v. Bobby D. Assocs., 94 S.W.3d 65, 71 (Tex. App.—Tyler 2002, no pet.). "The trial court cannot consider affidavits offered by the non-movant to contradict deemed admissions in cases involving summary judgment." *See also* ***Dallas Drain Co. v. Welsh***, No. 05-14-00831-CV (Tex.App.—Dallas 2015, no pet.) (memo op.; 7-8-15).

Final vs. Partial SJ

M.O. Dental Lab v. Rape, 139 S.W.3d 671, 674 (Tex. 2004). "The court of appeals ... held that the trial court's order granting summary judgment was final for purposes of this appeal [even though it did not dispose of one D] because [that D] was never served and the record contains no pleadings or motions filed by [that D]. ... We [previously] held [in a similar circumstance that] 'the case stands as if there had been a discontinuance as to [unserved party], and the judgment is to be regarded as final for the purposes of appeal.' [¶] [Here, P] stated '[t]he location for service of [unserved D] is unknown at this time, so no citation is requested.' [B]oth [P] and [served Ds] agreed ... that [unserved D] was never served with process.... *At 675:* [W]e conclude that the trial court's order granting summary judgment is final for the purposes of this appeal." *See also* ***In re Miranda***, 142 S.W.3d 354, 356-57 (Tex.App.—El Paso 2004, orig. proceeding).

Jacobs v. Satterwhite, 65 S.W.3d 653, 655 (Tex. 2001). "'[I]f a defendant moves for summary judgment on only one of [multiple] claims asserted by the plaintiff, but the trial court renders judgment that the plaintiff take nothing on all claims asserted, the judgment is final—erroneous, but final.'"

McNally v. Guevara, 52 S.W.3d 195, 196 (Tex. 2001). "[A] party's omission of one of his claims from a motion for summary judgment does not waive the claim because a party can always move for partial summary judgment, and thus there can be no presumption that a motion for summary judgment addresses all of the movant's claims. Nothing in the trial court's judgment, other than its award of costs to [Ds], suggests that it intended to deny [Ds'] claim for attorney fees. The award of costs, by itself, does not make the judgment final."

Lehmann v. Har-Con Corp., 39 S.W.3d 191, 192-93 (Tex.2001). "We no longer believe that a Mother Hubbard clause in an order or in a judgment issued without a full trial can be taken to indicate finality. We therefore hold that in cases in which only one final and appealable judgment can be rendered, a judgment issued without a conventional trial is final for purposes of appeal if and only if either it actually disposes of all claims and parties then before the court, regardless of its language, or it states with unmistakable clarity that it is a final judgment as to all claims and all parties." *See also* ***Farm Bur. Cty. Mut. Ins. v. Rogers***, 455 S.W.3d 161, 163-64 (Tex.2015).

Pleadings in SJ Cases

Sosa v. Central Power & Light, 909 S.W.2d 893, 895 (Tex.1995). "Because [Ps] timely filed their second amended original petition, it superseded their first amended original petition containing the statements on which [Ds] based their motion for summary judgment. Contrary to statements in live pleadings, those contained in superseded pleadings are not conclusive and indisputable judicial admissions. Therefore, the basis for [Ds'] motion no longer existed and summary judgment was improper."

Natividad v. Alexsis, Inc., 875 S.W.2d 695, 699 (Tex.1994). "A review of the pleadings [when an SJ is based on the pleadings] is de novo, with the reviewing court taking all allegations, facts, and inferences in the pleadings as true and viewing them in a light most favorable to the pleader. The reviewing court will affirm the summary judgment only if the pleadings are legally insufficient."

In re B.I.V., 870 S.W.2d 12, 13 (Tex.1994). "A summary judgment should not be based on a pleading deficiency that could be cured by amendment."

Burt v. Harwell, 369 S.W.3d 623, 625 (Tex.App.—Dallas 2012, no pet.). "Although summary judgment generally may not be granted on a claim not addressed in the summary judgment proceeding, it may be granted on later pleaded causes of action if the grounds asserted in the motion show that the plaintiff could not recover from the defendant on the later pleaded causes of action." *See also* ***Lamell v. OneWest Bank***, 485 S.W.3d 53, 58 (Tex.App.—Houston [14th Dist.] 2015, pet. denied) (court can grant SJ on later-pleaded claims if grounds expressly presented in motion are sufficiently broad to cover claims).

Austin v. Countrywide Homes Loans, 261 S.W.3d 68, 75 (Tex.App.—Houston [1st Dist.] 2008, pet. denied). "Once the hearing date for a motion for summary judgment has passed, the movant must secure a written order granting leave in order to file an amended pleading."

Motion for Continuance

Carpenter v. Cimarron Hydrocarbons Corp., 98 S.W.3d 682, 688 (Tex.2002). "[A] motion for leave to file a late summary-judgment response should be granted when a litigant establishes good cause for failing to timely respond by showing that (1) the failure to respond was not intentional or the result of conscious indifference, but the result of accident or mistake, and (2) allowing the late response will occasion no undue delay or otherwise injure the party seeking summary judgment." *See also* ***Wheeler v. Green***, 157 S.W.3d 439, 442-43 (Tex.2005).

Tenneco Inc. v. Enterprise Prods., 925 S.W.2d 640, 647 (Tex.1996). "When a party contends that it has not had an adequate opportunity for discovery before a summary judgment hearing, it must file either an affidavit explaining the need for further discovery or a verified motion for continuance. [¶] The determination to allow [Ps] more time for discovery was within the trial court's discretion." *See also* ***Stierwalt v. FFE Transp. Servs.***, 499 S.W.3d 181, 189 (Tex.App.—El Paso 2016, no pet.) (affidavit should specify evidence sought and explain why it was not obtained earlier to avoid need for continuance).

Notice

Rorie v. Goodwin, 171 S.W.3d 579, 583 (Tex. App.—Tyler 2005, no pet.). "A trial court must give notice of the submission date for a motion for summary judgment because this date determines the date the nonmovant's response is due. The date of submission has the same meaning as the day of hearing under [TRCP] 166a(c). *At 584:* Failure to give proper notice violates the most rudimentary demands of due process of law."

TRCP 166b, 166c. REPEALED

TRCP 167. OFFER OF SETTLEMENT; AWARD OF LITIGATION COSTS

167.1 Generally. Certain litigation costs may be awarded against a party who rejects an offer made substantially in accordance with this rule to settle a claim for monetary damages—including a counterclaim, crossclaim, or third-party claim—except in:

(a) a class action;

(b) a shareholder's derivative action;

(c) an action by or against the State, a unit of state government, or a political subdivision of the State;

(d) an action brought under the Family Code;

(e) an action to collect workers' compensation benefits under title 5, subtitle A of the Labor Code; or

(f) an action filed in a justice of the peace court or small claims court.[1]

167.2 Settlement Offer.

(a) ***Defendant's declaration a prerequisite; deadline.*** A settlement offer under this rule may not be made until a defendant—a party against whom a claim for monetary damages is made—files a declaration invoking this rule. When a defendant files such a declaration, an offer or offers may be made under this rule to settle only those claims by and against that defendant. The declaration must be filed no later than 45 days before the case is set for conventional trial on the merits.

(b) ***Requirements of an offer.*** A settlement offer must:

(1) be in writing;

(2) state that it is made under Rule 167 and Chapter 42 of the Texas Civil Practice and Remedies Code;

(3) identify the party or parties making the offer and the party or parties to whom the offer is made;

(4) state the terms by which all monetary claims—including any attorney fees, interest, and costs that would be recoverable up to the time of the offer—between the offeror or offerors on the one hand and the offeree or offerees on the other may be settled;

(5) state a deadline—no sooner than 14 days after the offer is served—by which the offer must be accepted;

(6) be served on all parties to whom the offer is made.

(c) ***Conditions of offer.*** An offer may be made subject to reasonable conditions, including the execution of appropriate releases, indemnities, and other documents. An offeree may object to a condition by written notice served on the offeror before the deadline stated in the offer. A condition to which no such objection is made is presumed to have been reasonable. Rejection of an offer made subject to a condition deter-

mined by the trial court to have been unreasonable cannot be the basis for an award of litigation costs under this rule.

(d) ***Non-monetary and excepted claims not included.*** An offer must not include non-monetary claims and other claims to which this rule does not apply.

(e) ***Time limitations.*** An offer may not be made:

(1) before a defendant's declaration is filed;

(2) within 60 days after the appearance in the case of the offeror or offeree, whichever is later;

(3) within 14 days before the date the case is set for a conventional trial on the merits, except that an offer may be made within that period if it is in response to, and within seven days of, a prior offer.

(f) ***Successive offers.*** A party may make an offer after having made or rejected a prior offer. A rejection of an offer is subject to imposition of litigation costs under this rule only if the offer is more favorable to the offeree than any prior offer.

167.3 Withdrawal, Acceptance, and Rejection of Offer.

(a) ***Withdrawal of offer.*** An offer can be withdrawn before it is accepted. Withdrawal is effective when written notice of the withdrawal is served on the offeree. Once an unaccepted offer has been withdrawn, it cannot be accepted or be the basis for awarding litigation costs under this rule.

(b) ***Acceptance of offer.*** An offer that has not been withdrawn can be accepted only by written notice served on the offeror by the deadline stated in the offer. When an offer is accepted, the offeror or offeree may file the offer and acceptance and may move the court to enforce the settlement.

(c) ***Rejection of offer.*** An offer that is not withdrawn or accepted is rejected. An offer may also be rejected by written notice served on the offeror by the deadline stated in the offer.

(d) ***Objection to offer made before an offeror's joinder or designation of responsible third party.*** An offer made before an offeror joins another party or designates a responsible third party may not be the basis for awarding litigation costs under this rule against an offeree who files an objection to the offer within 15 days after service of the offeror's pleading or designation.

167.4 Awarding Litigation Costs.

(a) ***Generally.*** If a settlement offer made under this rule is rejected, and the judgment to be awarded on the monetary claims covered by the offer is significantly less favorable to the offeree than was the offer, the court must award the offeror litigation costs against the offeree from the time the offer was rejected to the time of judgment.

(b) ***"Significantly less favorable" defined.*** A judgment award on monetary claims is significantly less favorable than an offer to settle those claims if:

(1) the offeree is a claimant and the judgment would be less than 80% of the offer; or

(2) the offeree is a defendant and the judgment would be more than 120% of the offer.

(c) ***Litigation costs.*** Litigation costs are the expenditures actually made and the obligations actually incurred—directly in relation to the claims covered by a settlement offer under this rule—for the following:

(1) court costs;

(2) reasonable deposition costs, in cases filed on or after September 1, 2011;

(3) reasonable fees for not more than two testifying expert witnesses; and

(4) reasonable attorney fees.

(d) ***Limits on litigation costs.***

(1) In cases filed before September 1, 2011, the litigation costs that may be awarded under this rule must not exceed the following amount:

(A) the sum of the noneconomic damages, the exemplary or additional damages, and one-half of the economic damages to be awarded to the claimant in the judgment; minus

(B) the amount of any statutory or contractual liens in connection with the occurrences or incidents giving rise to the claim.

(2) In cases filed on or after September 1, 2011, the litigation costs that may be awarded to any party under this rule must not exceed the total amount that the claimant recovers or would recover before adding an award of litigation costs under this rule in favor of the claimant or subtracting as an offset an award of litigation costs under this rule in favor of the defendant.

(e) ***No double recovery permitted.*** A party who is entitled to recover attorney fees and costs under another law may not recover those same attorney fees and costs as litigation costs under this rule.

(f) ***Limitation on attorney fees and costs recovered by a party against whom litigation costs are awarded.*** A party against whom litigation costs are awarded may not recover attorney fees and costs under another law incurred after the date the party rejected the settlement offer made the basis of the award.

(g) ***Litigation costs to be awarded to defendant as a setoff.*** Litigation costs awarded to a defendant must be made a setoff to the claimant's judgment against the defendant.

167.5 Procedures.

(a) ***Modification of time limits.*** On motion, and for good cause shown, the court may—by written order made before commencement of trial on the merits—modify the time limits for filing a declaration under Rule 167.2(a) or for making an offer.

(b) ***Discovery permitted.*** On motion, and for good cause shown, a party against whom litigation costs are to be awarded may conduct discovery to ascertain the reasonableness of the costs requested. If the court determines the costs to be reasonable, it must order the party requesting discovery to pay all attorney fees and expenses incurred by other parties in responding to such discovery.

(c) ***Hearing required.*** The court must, upon request, conduct a hearing on a request for an award of litigation costs, at which the affected parties may present evidence.

167.6 Evidence Not Admissible. Evidence relating to an offer made under this rule is not admissible except for purposes of enforcing a settlement agreement or obtaining litigation costs. The provisions of this rule may not be made known to the jury by any means.

167.7 Other Settlement Offers Not Affected. This rule does not apply to any offer made in a mediation or arbitration proceeding. A settlement offer not made in compliance with this rule, or a settlement offer not made under this rule, or made in an action to which this rule does not apply, cannot be the basis for awarding litigation costs under this rule as to any party. This rule does not limit or affect a party's right to make a settlement offer that does not comply with this rule, or in an action to which this rule does not apply.

1. **Editor's note:** The Texas Legislature abolished small-claims courts by repealing Gov't Code ch. 28. *See* Acts 2013, 83rd Leg., R.S., ch. 2, §2, eff. Apr. 10, 2013; Acts 2011, 82nd Leg., 1st C.S., ch. 3, §§5.06, 5.09, eff. May 1, 2013. Now small-claims proceedings must be conducted by justice courts. Gov't Code §27.060(a); *see* TRCP 500.3(a).

See also *O'Connor's Texas Rules*, "Offer of Settlement," ch. 7-H, p. 753.

ANNOTATIONS

Note Inv. Grp. v. Associates First Capital Corp., 476 S.W.3d 463, 478 (Tex.App.—Beaumont 2015, no pet.). "[N]othing in the plain language of [TRCP 167] indicates that a claim must be formally pled when the settlement offer is made in order to be included in a settlement offer under the rule, and we decline to read any such requirement into those words when … there is no indication … that the Texas Supreme Court intended that we do so."

United Parcel Serv. v. Rankin, 468 S.W.3d 609, 628 (Tex.App.—San Antonio 2015, pet. denied). "[P] argues that 'to the time of judgment' [under TRCP 167.4(a)] includes the time until an appellate judgment is signed and thus the trial court abused its discretion by failing to award him conditional appellate attorneys' fees. [D] responds that the trial court correctly interpreted 'to the time of judgment' to mean to the time the trial court's judgment was signed. We agree with [D]. Based on the language of Rule 167 as a whole, we conclude the trial court did not abuse its discretion by failing to award conditional appellate attorneys' fees."

TRCP 167a. REPEALED

TRCP 168. PERMISSION TO APPEAL

On a party's motion or on its own initiative, a trial court may permit an appeal from an interlocutory order that is not otherwise appealable, as provided by statute. Permission must be stated in the order to be appealed. An order previously issued may be amended to include such permission. The permission must identify the controlling question of law as to which there is a substantial ground for difference of opinion, and must state why an immediate appeal may materially advance the ultimate termination of the litigation.

ANNOTATIONS

Armour Pipe Line Co. v. Sandel Energy, Inc., No. 14-16-00010-CV (Tex.App.—Houston [14th Dist.] 2016, n.p.h.) (memo op.; 2-9-16). TRCP 168 uses "the singular, 'a controlling question of law,' which arguably reflects an intent to restrict permissive appeals to interlocutory judgments that involve one controlling question of law. Even assuming that an appellate court enjoys some measure of discretion in permitting the ap-

peal of more than one question in appropriate circumstances, it is not clear that appropriate circumstances exist here. [The] statement of the issues ... identifies ... four questions (and numerous sub-issues) to be decided on appeal, which appear to encompass a number of legal points in multiple summary judgment orders. Rule 168's purpose—to provide a means for expedited appellate disposition of focused and potentially dispositive legal questions—is not served if this procedure is used to obtain piecemeal appellate review of ordinary interlocutory summary judgment orders."

TRCP 169. EXPEDITED ACTIONS

(a) ***Application.***

(1) The expedited actions process in this rule applies to a suit in which all claimants, other than counter-claimants, affirmatively plead that they seek only monetary relief aggregating $100,000 or less, including damages of any kind, penalties, costs, expenses, pre-judgment interest, and attorney fees.

(2) The expedited actions process does not apply to a suit in which a party has filed a claim governed by the Family Code, the Property Code, the Tax Code, or Chapter 74 of the Civil Practice & Remedies Code.

(b) ***Recovery.*** In no event may a party who prosecutes a suit under this rule recover a judgment in excess of $100,000, excluding post-judgment interest.

(c) ***Removal from Process.***

(1) A court must remove a suit from the expedited actions process:

(A) on motion and a showing of good cause by any party; or

(B) if any claimant, other than a counter-claimant, files a pleading or an amended or supplemental pleading that seeks any relief other than the monetary relief allowed by (a)(1).

(2) A pleading, amended pleading, or supplemental pleading that removes a suit from the expedited actions process may not be filed without leave of court unless it is filed before the earlier of 30 days after the discovery period is closed or 30 days before the date set for trial. Leave to amend may be granted only if good cause for filing the pleading outweighs any prejudice to an opposing party.

(3) If a suit is removed from the expedited actions process, the court must reopen discovery under Rule 190.2(c).

(d) ***Expedited Actions Process.***

(1) *Discovery.* Discovery is governed by Rule 190.2.

(2) *Trial setting; continuances.* On any party's request, the court must set the case for a trial date that is within 90 days after the discovery period in Rule 190.2(b)(1) ends. The court may continue the case twice, not to exceed a total of 60 days.

(3) *Time limits for trial.* Each side is allowed no more than eight hours to complete jury selection, opening statements, presentation of evidence, examination and cross-examination of witnesses, and closing arguments. On motion and a showing of good cause by any party, the court may extend the time limit to no more than twelve hours per side.

(A) The term "side" has the same definition set out in Rule 233.

(B) Time spent on objections, bench conferences, bills of exception, and challenges for cause to a juror under Rule 228 are not included in the time limit.

(4) *Alternative dispute resolution.*

(A) Unless the parties have agreed not to engage in alternative dispute resolution, the court may refer the case to an alternative dispute resolution procedure once, and the procedure must:

(i) not exceed a half-day in duration, excluding scheduling time;

(ii) not exceed a total cost of twice the amount of applicable civil filing fees; and

(iii) be completed no later than 60 days before the initial trial setting.

(B) The court must consider objections to the referral unless prohibited by statute.

(C) The parties may agree to engage in alternative dispute resolution other than that provided for in (A).

(5) *Expert testimony.* Unless requested by the party sponsoring the expert, a party may only challenge the admissibility of expert testimony as an objection to summary judgment evidence under Rule 166a or during the trial on the merits. This paragraph does not apply to a motion to strike for late designation.

See also *O'Connor's Texas Rules*, "Expedited actions," ch. 1-B, §3.3, p. 16.

TRCP 170. REPEALED

TRCP 171. MASTER IN CHANCERY

The court may, in exceptional cases, for good cause appoint a master in chancery, who shall be a citizen of this State, and not an attorney for either party to the ac-

tion, nor related to either party, who shall perform all of the duties required of him by the court, and shall be under orders of the court, and have such power as the master of chancery has in a court of equity.

The order of reference to the master may specify or limit his powers, and may direct him to report only upon particular issues, or to do or perform particular acts, or to receive and report evidence only and may fix the time and place for beginning and closing the hearings, and for the filing of the master's report. Subject to the limitations and specifications stated in the order, the master has and shall exercise the power to regulate all proceedings in every hearing before him and to do all acts and take all measures necessary or proper for the efficient performance of his duties under the order. He may require the production before him of evidence upon all matters embraced in the reference, including the production of books, papers, vouchers, documents and other writings applicable thereto. He may rule upon the admissibility of evidence, unless otherwise directed by the order of reference and has the authority to put witnesses on oath, and may, himself, examine them, and may call the parties to the action and examine them upon oath. When a party so requests, the master shall make a record of the evidence offered and excluded in the same manner as provided for a court sitting in the trial of a case.

The clerk of the court shall forthwith furnish the master with a copy of the order of reference.

The parties may procure the attendance of witnesses before the master by the issuance and service of process as provided by law and these rules.

The court may confirm, modify, correct, reject, reverse or recommit the report, after it is filed, as the court may deem proper and necessary in the particular circumstances of the case. The court shall award reasonable compensation to such master to be taxed as costs of suit.

See also *O'Connor's Texas Rules*, "Master in Chancery," ch. 1-K, p. 101.

ANNOTATIONS

Simpson v. Canales, 806 S.W.2d 802, 811 (Tex. 1991). "Rule 171 permits appointment of a master only 'in exceptional cases, for good cause.' [T]his requirement cannot be met merely by showing that a case is complicated or time-consuming, or that the court is busy." *See also* ***Hourani v. Katzen***, 305 S.W.3d 239, 247 (Tex.App.—Houston [1st Dist.] 2009, pet. denied).

Mann v. Mann, 607 S.W.2d 243, 246 (Tex.1980). "The Master conducted lengthy hearings which included hearing evidence and inspecting the books and inventory of the salvage warehouse. The records and the unique nature of the salvage business were such that the Master had great difficulty in valuing the community property assets of the business. In addition, and because of the complex nature of the property involved in the divorce proceeding, the trial court appointed an auditor and a receiver. [¶] [A] trial court should be free to exercise its discretion in the appointments of a master and should be reversed only where there is a clear abuse of this discretion. [¶] The fact that [W] had requested a jury trial does not preclude the appointment of a Master. Either party is entitled to a jury trial after a Master has filed his report. The present case involved numerous complex issues which involved the valuation of many types of dissimilar inventory having no regular market value. It was to the advantage and in the interest of all parties, including [H], to have a complete accounting of all the community and separate property assets of the parties."

In re Harris, 315 S.W.3d 685, 705 (Tex.App.—Houston [1st Dist.] 2010, orig. proceeding). "[C]ourts have found sufficient justification for the appointment of a master to supervise 'discovery questions which require extensive examination of highly technical and complex documents by a person having both a technical and a legal background.' [¶] Here, the case is not of a 'highly technical nature.' The fact that production of some of the discovery sought by [P] might require expert forensic examination of electronic media is not sufficient to show that this is an 'exceptional case' requiring expertise in computer forensics. Electronic discovery is a common component of modern litigation, and its mere presence alone does not constitute a showing of good cause for appointing a special master." *See also* ***Chapa v. Chapa***, No. 04-12-00519-CV (Tex. App.—San Antonio 2012, no pet.) (memo op.; 12-28-12) (special master's powers generally include authority to contact parties, conduct hearings, require production of evidence, and make recommendations to court).

AIU Ins. v. Mehaffy, 942 S.W.2d 796, 803 (Tex. App.—Beaumont 1997, orig. proceeding). "The cases construing Rule 171 provide that if a party timely and formally objects to a master's ruling, that party is entitled to a de novo hearing before a judge or jury. We

conclude this right is automatic and is not subject to a harmless error analysis."

TRCP 172. AUDIT

When an investigation of accounts or examination of vouchers appears necessary for the purpose of justice between the parties to any suit, the court shall appoint an auditor or auditors to state the accounts between the parties and to make report thereof to the court as soon as possible. The auditor shall verify his report by his affidavit stating that he has carefully examined the state of the account between the parties, and that his report contains a true statement thereof, so far as the same has come within his knowledge. Exceptions to such report or of any item thereof must be filed within 30 days of the filing of such report. The court shall award reasonable compensation to such auditor to be taxed as costs of suit.

See also TRE 706.

TRCP 173. GUARDIAN AD LITEM

173.1 Appointment Governed by Statute or Other Rules.

This rule does not apply to an appointment of a guardian ad litem governed by statute or other rules.

173.2 Appointment of Guardian ad Litem.

(a) ***When Appointment Required or Prohibited.*** The court must appoint a guardian ad litem for a party represented by a next friend or guardian only if:

(1) the next friend or guardian appears to the court to have an interest adverse to the party, or

(2) the parties agree.

(b) ***Appointment of the Same Person for Different Parties.*** The court must appoint the same guardian ad litem for similarly situated parties unless the court finds that the appointment of different guardians ad litem is necessary.

173.3 Procedure.

(a) ***Motion Permitted But Not Required.*** The court may appoint a guardian ad litem on the motion of any party or on its own initiative.

(b) ***Written Order Required.*** An appointment must be made by written order.

(c) ***Objection.*** Any party may object to the appointment of a guardian ad litem.

173.4 Role of Guardian ad Litem.

(a) ***Court Officer and Advisor.*** A guardian ad litem acts as an officer and advisor to the court.

(b) ***Determination of Adverse Interest.*** A guardian ad litem must determine and advise the court whether a party's next friend or guardian has an interest adverse to the party.

(c) ***When Settlement Proposed.*** When an offer has been made to settle the claim of a party represented by a next friend or guardian, a guardian ad litem has the limited duty to determine and advise the court whether the settlement is in the party's best interest.

(d) ***Participation in Litigation Limited.*** A guardian ad litem:

(1) may participate in mediation or a similar proceeding to attempt to reach a settlement;

(2) must participate in any proceeding before the court whose purpose is to determine whether a party's next friend or guardian has an interest adverse to the party, or whether a settlement of the party's claim is in the party's best interest;

(3) must not participate in discovery, trial, or any other part of the litigation unless:

(A) further participation is necessary to protect the party's interest that is adverse to the next friend's or guardian's, and

(B) the participation is directed by the court in a written order stating sufficient reasons.

173.5 Communications Privileged.

Communications between the guardian ad litem and the party, the next friend or guardian, or their attorney are privileged as if the guardian ad litem were the attorney for the party.

173.6 Compensation.

(a) ***Amount.*** If a guardian ad litem requests compensation, he or she may be reimbursed for reasonable and necessary expenses incurred and may be paid a reasonable hourly fee for necessary services performed.

(b) ***Procedure.*** At the conclusion of the appointment, a guardian ad litem may file an application for compensation. The application must be verified and must detail the basis for the compensation requested. Unless all parties agree to the application, the court must conduct an evidentiary hearing to determine the total amount of fees and expenses that are reasonable and necessary. In making this determination, the court must not consider compensation as a percentage of any judgment or settlement.

(c) *Taxation as Costs.* The court may tax a guardian ad litem's compensation as costs of court.

(d) *Other Benefit Prohibited.* A guardian ad litem may not receive, directly or indirectly, anything of value in consideration of the appointment other than as provided by this rule.

173.7 Review.

(a) *Right of Appeal.* Any party may seek mandamus review of an order appointing a guardian ad litem or directing a guardian ad litem's participation in the litigation. Any party and a guardian ad litem may appeal an order awarding the guardian ad litem compensation.

(b) *Severance.* On motion of the guardian ad litem or any party, the court must sever any order awarding a guardian ad litem compensation to create a final, appealable order.

(c) *No Effect on Finality of Settlement or Judgment.* Appellate proceedings to review an order pertaining to a guardian ad litem do not affect the finality of a settlement or judgment.

Caution: TRCP 173 is affected by Fam. Code §§31.004, 33.003, 33.006, 51.11, 107.001-107.003, and 107.006.

See also *O'Connor's Texas Rules*, "Guardian Ad Litem Under TRCP 173," ch. 1-I, p. 87; *O'Connor's Texas Forms*, FORMS 1I; *O'Connor's Texas Family Law Handbook* (2017), "Court Appointments in SAPCRs," ch. 4-C, p. 365.

ANNOTATIONS

Ford Motor Co. v. Stewart, Cox & Hatcher, P.C., 390 S.W.3d 294, 297 (Tex.2013). "[D] argues that the trial court abused its discretion under [TRCP] 173 by appointing a guardian ad litem when there was no apparent conflict of interest between [P-minor] and [parent-next friend]. [¶] The guardian ad litem's initial role is to 'determine and advise the court whether a party's next friend ... has an interest adverse to the party.' The trial court should remove the guardian ad litem when the evidence presented fails to confirm that a conflict of interest exists. *At 298:* In this case, [guardian ad litem] was not specifically assigned any duties by the pretrial judge. The context of his appointment, however, indicates that [guardian ad litem] was appointed for the limited purpose of determining and advising the pretrial judge as to whether there was a conflict of interest between [P-minor] and [parent-next friend], and if so, whether the ... settlement [with D] was in [P-minor's] best interest. [T]he pretrial judge should have removed [guardian ad litem] because there was no evidence that [parent-next friend] had an interest adverse to [P-minor]. ... We hold that a parent's obligation to provide her child with medical care, standing alone, does not create a conflict of interest within the confines of Rule 173." *See also* ***Brownsville-Valley Reg'l Med. Ctr., Inc. v. Gamez***, 894 S.W.2d 753, 755 (Tex.1995) (when conflict of interest no longer exists, trial court should remove guardian ad litem); ***Owens v. Perez***, 158 S.W.3d 96, 111 (Tex.App.—Corpus Christi 2005, no pet.) (potential conflict sufficient for appointment; actual conflict not required).

Ford Motor Co. v. Chacon, 370 S.W.3d 359, 362 (Tex.2012). "A guardian ad litem has the burden to ensure that his services do not exceed the scope of the role assigned by the trial court. In the context of that appointment, a guardian ad litem 'may be reimbursed for reasonable and necessary expenses incurred and may be paid a reasonable hourly fee for necessary services performed.' The amount of the award is within the trial court's discretion. [¶] [I]n determining the nature and duties of an appointment, we look to the context of the appointment and the duties assigned to the ad litem. [¶] The context of [ad litem's] appointment as guardian ad litem clearly indicates that [ad litem] was appointed for the limited purpose of determining and advising the court whether the ... settlement [with D1] was in [minor's] best interest. ... After the ... settlement [with D1] was finalized and judgment was entered, [ad litem] filed an application for compensation for guardian ad litem services he provided in connection with the [D1] settlement, which the court awarded in full. There was no subsequent motion or request for appointment of a guardian ad litem in connection with the [D2] settlement, nor did the trial court enter an order appointing one. In light of the requirements of Rule 173, we conclude that [ad litem's] work regarding the [D2] settlement was beyond the scope of his original appointment."

Ford Motor Co. v. Garcia, 363 S.W.3d 573, 580 (Tex.2012). "Rule 173.6 does not preclude awarding compensation for persons other than the person designated in the trial court's order as guardian ad litem if the evidence shows particular, unusual circumstances making services of other persons necessary for the ad litem's duties to be fulfilled. Such circumstances might exist, for example, if paralegals or other staff under the supervision of the appointed guardian ad litem could perform tasks necessary for the ad litem to properly fulfill his or her appointed role, but at a lesser hourly rate than the ad litem, or an unexpected emergency requires the guardian ad litem to miss a mandatory hear-

ing and an associated attorney familiar with the matter appears instead. *At 580 n.5:* [A] Rule 173 guardian ad litem might need to incur unusual expenses in order to properly advise the court. For example, expenses for an actuary or accountant to evaluate the economics of a structured settlement may be necessary."

Land Rover U.K., Ltd. v. Hinojosa, 210 S.W.3d 604, 607 (Tex.2006). "A guardian ad litem is not an attorney for the child but an officer appointed by the court to assist in protecting the child's interests when a conflict of interest arises between the child and the child's guardian or next friend. As the personal representative of a minor, a guardian ad litem is required to participate in the case only to the extent necessary to protect the minor's interest and should not duplicate the work performed by the plaintiff's attorney. If a guardian ad litem performs work beyond the scope of this role, such work is non-compensable. [¶] An appointed guardian ad litem may request a reasonable fee for services performed. ... To determine a reasonable fee for a guardian ad litem's services, a trial court applies the factors used to determine the reasonableness of attorney's fees." *See also* ***Jocson v. Crabb***, 196 S.W.3d 302, 306 (Tex.App.—Houston [1st Dist.] 2006, no pet.) (guardian ad litem should not participate in litigation or review discovery unless necessary to determine division of settlement proceeds).

Jocson v. Crabb, 133 S.W.3d 268, 270 (Tex.2004). "[O]bjections to ad litem fees are timely if raised at the post-trial fee hearing.... [¶] While the parties would be wise to seek direction ... when they disagree about an ad litem's role, it could be expensive and disruptive ... to pursue every disagreement to a hearing throughout the pretrial process. The final fee hearing is an appropriate forum to assert any objections to the fee request and obtain a ruling."

TRCP 174. CONSOLIDATION; SEPARATE TRIALS

(a) Consolidation. When actions involving a common question of law or fact are pending before the court, it may order a joint hearing or trial of any or all the matters in issue in the actions; it may order all the actions consolidated; and it may make such orders concerning proceedings therein as may tend to avoid unnecessary costs or delay.

(b) Separate Trials. The court in furtherance of convenience or to avoid prejudice may order a separate trial of any claim, cross-claim, counterclaim, or third-party claim, or of any separate issue or of any number of claims, cross-claims, counterclaims, third-party claims, or issues.

See also TRCP 39-41, 51; *O'Connor's Texas Rules*, "Motions for Severance & Separate Trials," ch. 5-I, p. 423; "Joining Parties or Claims," ch. 5-J, p. 431; *O'Connor's Texas Forms*, FORMS 5I:4-7, 5J:7-9.

ANNOTATIONS

Tarrant Reg'l Water Dist. v. Gragg, 151 S.W.3d 546, 556 (Tex.2004). TRCP 174(b) "allows a trial court to order a separate trial on any issue in the interest of convenience or to avoid prejudice. *At 557:* [S]eparate trials would have resulted in considerable and unnecessary evidentiary repetition. [I]t is likely that many, if not most, of the same witnesses would have been called to testify in both the liability and compensation trials had the trial court bifurcated the proceedings. '[T]here were several weeks of common questions of law and of fact involved in the matters that would have been considered in the first phase and the second phase of a bifurcated trial.' ... Under these circumstances, we cannot say that the trial court abused its discretion in refusing to bifurcate the proceedings."

In re Ethyl Corp., 975 S.W.2d 606, 611-12 (Tex. 1998). "The maximum number of claims that can be aggregated is not an absolute, and the particular circumstances determine the outer limits beyond which trial courts cannot go. [¶] While considerations of judicial economy are a factor, '[c]onsiderations of convenience and economy must yield to a paramount concern for a fair and impartial trial.'" *See also* ***In re Shell Oil Co.***, 202 S.W.3d 286, 290-91 (Tex.App.—Beaumont 2006, orig. proceeding).

Liberty Nat'l Fire Ins. v. Akin, 927 S.W.2d 627, 630 (Tex.1996). "A severance may ... be necessary in some bad faith [and contract] cases. A trial court will ... confront instances in which evidence admissible only on the bad faith claim would prejudice the insurer to such an extent that a fair trial on the contract claim would become unlikely. One example would be when the insurer has made a settlement offer on the disputed contract claim."

Grocers Sup. v. Cabello, 390 S.W.3d 707, 726 (Tex. App.—Dallas 2012, no pet.). "An order for a separate trial leaves the lawsuit intact but enables the court to hear and determine one or more issues without trying all controverted issues at the same hearing. An issue that is tried separately under rule 174 need not constitute a complete lawsuit in itself."

In re Gulf Coast Bus. Dev. Corp., 247 S.W.3d 787, 794-95 (Tex.App.—Dallas 2008, orig. proceeding). "Rule 174 give[s] the trial court broad discretion to consolidate cases with common issues of law or fact. [¶] The trial court may consolidate actions that relate to substantially the same transaction, occurrence, subject matter, or question. The actions should be so related that the evidence presented will be material, relevant, and admissible in each case. [¶] Even if the cases share common questions of law and fact, an abuse of discretion may be found if the consolidation results in prejudice to the complaining party. However, we may not presume prejudice; it must be demonstrated. Where the cases do share common questions of law and fact, and the record does not reveal actual prejudice, the consolidation does not provide a basis for reversal." *See also* ***In re Woodard***, No. 12-16-00032-CV (Tex.App.—Tyler 2016, orig. proceeding) (memo op.; 4-29-16) (in deciding whether to consolidate, court must balance judicial economy and convenience gained by consolidation against possibility of delay, prejudice, or jury confusion).

TRCP 175. ISSUE OF LAW & DILATORY PLEAS

When a case is called for trial in which there has been no pretrial hearing as provided by Rule 166, the issues of law arising on the pleadings, all pleas in abatement and other dilatory pleas remaining undisposed of shall be determined; and it shall be no cause for postponement of a trial of the issues of law that a party is not prepared to try the issues of fact.

ANNOTATIONS

Garcia v. Texas Employers' Ins., 622 S.W.2d 626, 630 n.3 (Tex.App.—Amarillo 1981, writ ref'd n.r.e.). "The language of Rule 175 imposes on the party relying upon a dilatory plea a duty to demand action by the court thereon at the time the rule requires action by the court, and his failure to do so is a waiver of the plea."

SECTION 9. EVIDENCE & DISCOVERY

Explanatory Statement Accompanying the 1999 Amendments to the Rules of Civil Procedure Governing Discovery[1]

The rules pertaining to discovery have been substantively revised and reorganized to clarify and streamline discovery procedures and to reduce costs and delays associated with discovery practice. The notes and comments appended to the rules, unlike most other notes and comments in the Rules of Civil Procedure, are intended to inform their construction and application by both courts and practitioners.

Discovery in civil cases is founded on the principle that justice is best served when litigants may obtain information not in their possession to prosecute and defend claims. Discovery provides access to that information, but at a price. Recent years' experience has shown that discovery may be misused to deny justice to parties by driving up the costs of litigation until it is unaffordable and stalling resolution of cases. As any litigant on a budget knows, the benefits to be gained by discovery in a particular case must be weighed against its costs. The rules of procedure must provide both adequate access to information and effective means of curbing discovery when appropriate to preserve litigation as a viable, affordable, and expeditious dispute resolution mechanism.

These revisions recognize the importance of discovery as well as the necessity for reasonable limits. The scope of discovery, always broad, is unchanged. All the forms of discovery under the prior rules are retained, and a new one—disclosure—is added. Disclosure is not required unless requested and thus does not burden cases in which it is not sought. When requested, it provides ready access to basic information without objection. At the same time, the necessity of a discovery control plan in each case, whether by rule or by order, is intended to focus courts and parties on both the need for discovery and its costs in each case. The Level 1 plan allows a party seeking recovery of no more than $50,000 to insist that discovery be minimal. The Level 2 plan will provide adequate discovery in most cases, and Level 3 is available for cases needing special attention. No single set of rules can address so diverse and changing a practice as discovery, and thus the rules maintain the ability of parties by agreement and courts by order to tailor discovery to individual cases.

Presentation of objections and assertions of privilege are streamlined under these rules. A party who objects to only part of a discovery request must usually comply with the rest of the request. Assertions of privilege are not to be made prophylactically against the threat of waiver, but only when information is actually withheld. Documents produced in discovery are now presumed to be authentic for use against the party producing them, thus avoiding the cost of proving authentication when there is no dispute. Procedures for oral

depositions are revised to encourage focused examination by imposing time limits and to discourage colloquy between counsel.

An important aspect of these revisions has been the regrouping of provisions in a more logical sequence and the elimination of archaic and confusing language.

1. **Editor's note:** Adopted eff. Jan. 1, 1999, by order of Nov. 9, 1998 (977-78 S.W.3d [Tex.Cases] xxxv).

A. EVIDENCE

TRCP 176. SUBPOENAS

176.1 Form. Every subpoena must be issued in the name of "The State of Texas" and must:

(a) state the style of the suit and its cause number;

(b) state the court in which the suit is pending;

(c) state the date on which the subpoena is issued;

(d) identify the person to whom the subpoena is directed;

(e) state the time, place, and nature of the action required by the person to whom the subpoena is directed, as provided in Rule 176.2;

(f) identify the party at whose instance the subpoena is issued, and the party's attorney of record, if any;

(g) state the text of Rule 176.8(a); and

(h) be signed by the person issuing the subpoena.

176.2 Required Actions. A subpoena must command the person to whom it is directed to do either or both of the following:

(a) attend and give testimony at a deposition, hearing, or trial;

(b) produce and permit inspection and copying of designated documents or tangible things in the possession, custody, or control of that person.

176.3 Limitations.

(a) ***Range.*** A person may not be required by subpoena to appear or produce documents or other things in a county that is more than 150 miles from where the person resides or is served. However, a person whose appearance or production at a deposition may be compelled by notice alone under Rules 199.3 or 200.2 may be required to appear and produce documents or other things at any location permitted under Rules 199.2(b)(2).

(b) ***Use for discovery.*** A subpoena may not be used for discovery to an extent, in a manner, or at a time other than as provided by the rules governing discovery.

176.4 Who May Issue. A subpoena may be issued by:

(a) the clerk of the appropriate district, county, or justice court, who must provide the party requesting the subpoena with an original and a copy for each witness to be completed by the party;

(b) an attorney authorized to practice in the State of Texas, as an officer of the court; or

(c) an officer authorized to take depositions in this State, who must issue the subpoena immediately on a request accompanied by a notice to take a deposition under Rules 199 or 200, or a notice under Rule 205.3, and who may also serve the notice with the subpoena.

176.5 Service.

(a) ***Manner of service.*** A subpoena may be served at any place within the State of Texas by any sheriff or constable of the State of Texas, or any person who is not a party and is 18 years of age or older. A subpoena must be served by delivering a copy to the witness and tendering to that person any fees required by law. If the witness is a party and is represented by an attorney of record in the proceeding, the subpoena may be served on the witness's attorney of record.

(b) ***Proof of service.*** Proof of service must be made by filing either:

(1) the witness's signed written memorandum attached to the subpoena showing that the witness accepted the subpoena; or

(2) a statement by the person who made the service stating the date, time, and manner of service, and the name of the person served.

176.6 Response.

(a) ***Compliance required.*** Except as provided in this subdivision, a person served with a subpoena must comply with the command stated therein unless discharged by the court or by the party summoning such witness. A person commanded to appear and give testimony must remain at the place of deposition, hearing, or trial from day to day until discharged by the court or by the party summoning the witness.

(b) ***Organizations.*** If a subpoena commanding testimony is directed to a corporation, partnership, association, governmental agency, or other organization, and the matters on which examination is requested are described with reasonable particularity, the organization must designate one or more persons to testify on

its behalf as to matters known or reasonably available to the organization.

(c) ***Production of documents or tangible things.*** A person commanded to produce documents or tangible things need not appear in person at the time and place of production unless the person is also commanded to attend and give testimony, either in the same subpoena or a separate one. A person must produce documents as they are kept in the usual course of business or must organize and label them to correspond with the categories in the demand. A person may withhold material or information claimed to be privileged but must comply with Rule 193.3. A nonparty's production of a document authenticates the document for use against the nonparty to the same extent as a party's production of a document is authenticated for use against the party under Rule 193.7.

(d) ***Objections.*** A person commanded to produce and permit inspection or copying of designated documents and things may serve on the party requesting issuance of the subpoena—before the time specified for compliance—written objections to producing any or all of the designated materials. A person need not comply with the part of a subpoena to which objection is made as provided in this paragraph unless ordered to do so by the court. The party requesting the subpoena may move for such an order at any time after an objection is made.

(e) ***Protective orders.*** A person commanded to appear at a deposition, hearing, or trial, or to produce and permit inspection and copying of designated documents and things, and any other person affected by the subpoena, may move for a protective order under Rule 192.6(b)—before the time specified for compliance—either in the court in which the action is pending or in a district court in the county where the subpoena was served. The person must serve the motion on all parties in accordance with Rule 21a. A person need not comply with the part of a subpoena from which protection is sought under this paragraph unless ordered to do so by the court. The party requesting the subpoena may seek such an order at any time after the motion for protection is filed.

(f) ***Trial subpoenas.*** A person commanded to attend and give testimony, or to produce documents or things, at a hearing or trial, may object or move for protective order before the court at the time and place specified for compliance, rather than under paragraphs (d) and (e).

176.7 Protection of Person from Undue Burden and Expense. A party causing a subpoena to issue must take reasonable steps to avoid imposing undue burden or expense on the person served. In ruling on objections or motions for protection, the court must provide a person served with a subpoena an adequate time for compliance, protection from disclosure of privileged material or information, and protection from undue burden or expense. The court may impose reasonable conditions on compliance with a subpoena, including compensating the witness for undue hardship.

176.8 Enforcement of Subpoena.

(a) ***Contempt.*** Failure by any person without adequate excuse to obey a subpoena served upon that person may be deemed a contempt of the court from which the subpoena is issued or a district court in the county in which the subpoena is served, and may be punished by fine or confinement, or both.

(b) ***Proof of payment of fees required for fine or attachment.*** A fine may not be imposed, nor a person served with a subpoena attached, for failure to comply with a subpoena without proof by affidavit of the party requesting the subpoena or the party's attorney of record that all fees due the witness by law were paid or tendered.

See also CPRC §22.001; ***O'Connor's Texas Rules***, "Subpoenas," ch. 1-L, p. 105; "Depositions," ch. 6-F, p. 604; ***O'Connor's Texas Forms***, FORMS 1L, 6F.

ANNOTATIONS

Automatic Drilling Machs., Inc. v. Miller, 515 S.W.2d 256, 259 (Tex.1974). "On motion … the court is authorized by [TRCP] 177a [now 176.7] to quash or modify the subpoena if it is unreasonable or oppressive or condition denial of the motion on advancement of reasonable costs by the party in whose behalf the subpoena was issued."

St. Luke's Episcopal Hosp. v. Garcia, 928 S.W.2d 307, 310 (Tex.App.—Houston [14th Dist.] 1996, orig. proceeding). "In determining whether a deposition notice or subpoena duces tecum is unreasonable and oppressive, the following factors are relevant: '(1) the quantity of materials subpoenaed, (2) the ease or difficulty of collecting and transporting the materials, (3) the length of time before the deposition, (4) the availability of the information from other sources, and (5) the relevance of the materials.'"

TRCP 177 TO 179. REPEALED

TRCP 180. REFUSAL TO TESTIFY

Any witness refusing to give evidence may be committed to jail, there to remain without bail until such witness shall consent to give evidence.

Caution: TRCP 180 is affected by Fam. Code §§6.704 and 6.705.

See also TRCP 176; ***O'Connor's Texas Rules***, "Subpoenas," ch. 1-L, p. 105; "Depositions," ch. 6-F, p. 604.

TRCP 181. PARTY AS WITNESS

Either party to a suit may examine the opposing party as a witness, and shall have the same process to compel his attendance as in the case of any other witness.

Caution: TRCP 181 is affected by Fam. Code §§6.704 and 104.002 et seq.

See also TRCP 176, 199-201; ***O'Connor's Texas Rules***, "Subpoenas," ch. 1-L, p. 105; "Depositions," ch. 6-F, p. 604.

TRCP 182, 182a. REPEALED

TRCP 183. INTERPRETERS

The court may appoint an interpreter of its own selection and may fix the interpreter's reasonable compensation. The compensation shall be paid out of funds provided by law or by one or more of the parties as the court may direct, and may be taxed ultimately as costs, in the discretion of the court.

See also TRCP 200.4; TRE 604; ***O'Connor's Texas Rules***, "Depositions," ch. 6-F, p. 604.

TRCP 184, 184a. REPEALED

TRCP 185. SUIT ON ACCOUNT

When any action or defense is founded upon an open account or other claim for goods, wares and merchandise, including any claim for a liquidated money demand based upon written contract or founded on business dealings between the parties, or is for personal service rendered, or labor done or labor or materials furnished, on which a systematic record has been kept, and is supported by the affidavit of the party, his agent or attorney taken before some officer authorized to administer oaths, to the effect that such claim is, within the knowledge of affiant, just and true, that it is due, and that all just and lawful offsets, payments and credits have been allowed, the same shall be taken as prima facie evidence thereof, unless the party resisting such claim shall file a written denial, under oath. A party resisting such a sworn claim shall comply with the rules of pleading as are required in any other kind of suit, provided, however, that if he does not timely file a written denial, under oath, he shall not be permitted to deny the claim, or any item therein, as the case may be. No particularization or description of the nature of the component parts of the account or claim is necessary unless the trial court sustains special exceptions to the pleadings.

See also ***O'Connor's Texas COA***, "Suit on Sworn Account," ch. 5-E, p. 118; ***O'Connor's Texas Forms***, FORMS 2B:3, 4, 3E:3, 4, 10.

ANNOTATIONS

Tedder v. Gardner Aldrich, LLP, 421 S.W.3d 651, 653 (Tex.2013). "Rule 185 contemplates that the defendant has personal knowledge of the basis of the claim.... *At 654:* When it appears from the plaintiff's account itself that the defendant was a stranger to the account, the defendant need not file a sworn denial to contest liability. [In this case, H] had no agreement with [law firm], never promised to pay for its representation of [W], and because of the attorney-client privilege, had no way of knowing what charges had been made or what had been paid.... Rule 185 does not require a party to swear to what he does not and cannot know. We thus agree ... that [H] was not required to deny [law firm's] claim under oath in order to contest his liability for its fees."

Vance v. Holloway, 689 S.W.2d 403, 403-04 (Tex. 1985). "The petition and affidavit filed by [P] clearly met the requirements of [TRCP] 185. [D] answered by way of an unverified general denial only. He failed to meet the requirements of [TRCP] 185 and 93(10) which state that a written denial of the plaintiff's action must be verified. [¶] [D], therefore, waived his right to dispute the amount and ownership of the account." *See also* ***Rizk v. Financial Guardian Ins. Agency***, 584 S.W.2d 860, 862 (Tex.1979); ***Day Cruises Maritime, L.L.C. v. Christus Spohn Health Sys.***, 267 S.W.3d 42, 53 (Tex.App.—Corpus Christi 2008, pet. denied).

Southern Mgmt. Servs. v. SM Energy Co., 398 S.W.3d 350, 356 (Tex.App.—Houston [14th Dist.] 2013, no pet.). "The [TRCPs] do not establish a ... presumption that a sworn denial extends to new matters alleged in an amended pleading. This omission suggests ... that a denial requiring verification must generally be filed again if the plaintiff amends the pleadings. [¶] [W]hen an amended account substantially differs from the original account, the party resisting the account must file another sworn denial."

Worley v. Butler, 809 S.W.2d 242, 245 (Tex.App.—Corpus Christi 1990, no writ). "To prevail in a cause of action on sworn account, a party must show: (1) that there was a sale and delivery of the merchandise or per-

formance of the services; (2) that the amount of the account is just, that is, that the prices were charged in accordance with an agreement or in the absence of an agreement, they are the usual, customary and reasonable prices for that merchandise or services; and (3) that the amount is unpaid."

TRCP 186 TO 189. REPEALED

B. DISCOVERY

TRCP 190. DISCOVERY LIMITATIONS

190.1 Discovery Control Plan Required. Every case must be governed by a discovery control plan as provided in this Rule. A plaintiff must allege in the first numbered paragraph of the original petition whether discovery is intended to be conducted under Level 1, 2, or 3 of this Rule.

190.2 Discovery Control Plan—Expedited Actions and Divorces Involving $50,000 or Less (Level 1).

(a) ***Application.*** This subdivision applies to:

(1) any suit that is governed by the expedited actions process in Rule 169; and

(2) unless the parties agree that Rule 190.3 should apply or the court orders a discovery control plan under Rule 190.4, any suit for divorce not involving children in which a party pleads that the value of the marital estate is more than zero but not more than $50,000.

(b) ***Limitations.*** Discovery is subject to the limitations provided elsewhere in these rules and to the following additional limitations:

(1) *Discovery period.* All discovery must be conducted during the discovery period, which begins when the suit is filed and continues until 180 days after the date the first request for discovery of any kind is served on a party.

(2) *Total time for oral depositions.* Each party may have no more than six hours in total to examine and cross-examine all witnesses in oral depositions. The parties may agree to expand this limit up to ten hours in total, but not more except by court order. The court may modify the deposition hours so that no party is given unfair advantage.

(3) *Interrogatories.* Any party may serve on any other party no more than 15 written interrogatories, excluding interrogatories asking a party only to identify or authenticate specific documents. Each discrete subpart of an interrogatory is considered a separate interrogatory.

(4) *Requests for production.* Any party may serve on any other party no more than 15 written requests for production. Each discrete subpart of a request for production is considered a separate request for production.

(5) *Requests for admissions.* Any party may serve on any other party no more than 15 written requests for admissions. Each discrete subpart of a request for admission is considered a separate request for admission.

(6) *Requests for disclosure.* In addition to the content subject to disclosure under Rule 194.2, a party may request disclosure of all documents, electronic information, and tangible items that the disclosing party has in its possession, custody, or control and may use to support its claims or defenses. A request for disclosure made pursuant to this paragraph is not considered a request for production.

(c) ***Reopening Discovery.*** If a suit is removed from the expedited actions process in Rule 169 or, in a divorce, the filing of a pleading renders this subdivision no longer applicable, the discovery period reopens, and discovery must be completed within the limitations provided in Rules 190.3 or 190.4, whichever is applicable. Any person previously deposed may be redeposed. On motion of any party, the court should continue the trial date if necessary to permit completion of discovery.

190.3 Discovery Control Plan—By Rule (Level 2).

(a) ***Application.*** Unless a suit is governed by a discovery control plan under Rules 190.2 or 190.4, discovery must be conducted in accordance with this subdivision.

(b) ***Limitations.*** Discovery is subject to the limitations provided elsewhere in these rules and to the following additional limitations:

(1) *Discovery period.* All discovery must be conducted during the discovery period, which begins when suit is filed and continues until:

(A) 30 days before the date set for trial, in cases under the Family Code; or

(B) in other cases, the earlier of

(i) 30 days before the date set for trial, or

(ii) nine months after the earlier of the date of the first oral deposition or the due date of the first response to written discovery.

(2) *Total time for oral depositions.* Each side may have no more than 50 hours in oral depositions to ex-

amine and cross-examine parties on the opposing side, experts designated by those parties, and persons who are subject to those parties' control. "Side" refers to all the litigants with generally common interests in the litigation. If one side designates more than two experts, the opposing side may have an additional six hours of total deposition time for each additional expert designated. The court may modify the deposition hours and must do so when a side or party would be given unfair advantage.

(3) *Interrogatories.* Any party may serve on any other party no more than 25 written interrogatories, excluding interrogatories asking a party only to identify or authenticate specific documents. Each discrete subpart of an interrogatory is considered a separate interrogatory.

190.4 Discovery Control Plan—By Order (Level 3).

(a) ***Application.*** The court must, on a party's motion, and may, on its own initiative, order that discovery be conducted in accordance with a discovery control plan tailored to the circumstances of the specific suit. The parties may submit an agreed order to the court for its consideration. The court should act on a party's motion or agreed order under this subdivision as promptly as reasonably possible.

(b) ***Limitations.*** The discovery control plan ordered by the court may address any issue concerning discovery or the matters listed in Rule 166, and may change any limitation on the time for or amount of discovery set forth in these rules. The discovery limitations of Rule 190.2, if applicable, or otherwise of Rule 190.3 apply unless specifically changed in the discovery control plan ordered by the court. The plan must include:

(1) a date for trial or for a conference to determine a trial setting;

(2) a discovery period during which either all discovery must be conducted or all discovery requests must be sent, for the entire case or an appropriate phase of it;

(3) appropriate limits on the amount of discovery; and

(4) deadlines for joining additional parties, amending or supplementing pleadings, and designating expert witnesses.

190.5 Modification of Discovery Control Plan. The court may modify a discovery control plan at any time and must do so when the interest of justice requires. Unless a suit is governed by the expedited actions process in Rule 169, the court must allow additional discovery:

(a) related to new, amended or supplemental pleadings, or new information disclosed in a discovery response or in an amended or supplemental response, if:

(1) the pleadings or responses were made after the deadline for completion of discovery or so nearly before that deadline that an adverse party does not have an adequate opportunity to conduct discovery related to the new matters, and

(2) the adverse party would be unfairly prejudiced without such additional discovery;

(b) regarding matters that have changed materially after the discovery cutoff if trial is set or postponed so that the trial date is more than three months after the discovery period ends.

190.6 Certain Types of Discovery Excepted. This rule's limitations on discovery do not apply to or include discovery conducted under Rule 202 ("Depositions Before Suit or to Investigate Claims"), or Rule 621a ("Discovery and Enforcement of Judgment"). But Rule 202 cannot be used to circumvent the limitations of this rule.

See also ***O'Connor's Texas Rules***, "General Rules for Discovery," ch. 6-A, p. 491; ***O'Connor's Texas Forms***, FORMS 6A:6-9; ***O'Connor's Texas Family Law Handbook*** (2017), "Suit for Divorce," ch. 3-A, p. 205; "Suit for Child Support," ch. 4-F, p. 529; "Temporary Ex Parte Protective Orders," ch. 6-B, p. 721.

ANNOTATIONS

In re Alford Chevrolet-Geo, 997 S.W.2d 173, 181 (Tex.1999). "[C]ourts may limit discovery pending resolution of threshold issues like venue, jurisdiction, forum non conveniens, and official immunity."

Brescia v. Slack & Davis, L.L.P., No. 03-08-00042-CV (Tex.App.—Austin 2010, pet. denied) (memo op.; 11-19-10). "Rule 190.4 does not require that the court's order provide deadlines different from those under a Level-2 case. Rather, the decision to provide different deadlines is left to the court's discretion. [¶] Depending on the discovery plan level, the discovery rules establish a date certain for the completion of discovery. Under the discovery rules, no longer is there a concern that discovery will be incomplete at the summary judgment phase. The specific deadline established by the pretrial discovery rules ensures that the evidence pre-

sented at the summary judgment stage and at the trial stage remains the same."

In re SWEPI L.P., 103 S.W.3d 578, 589 (Tex. App.—San Antonio 2003, orig. proceeding). "A review of the interrogatories reveals none that have multiple 'discrete subparts.' Each question relates to a particular claim and asks [P] to provide certain details about the facts underlying that claim. The 'subparts' objected to by [P] simply identify the types of facts [D] would like to have disclosed so that it can understand the parameters of the claims and prepare its defenses. [T]he interrogatories do not exceed the number allowed by Rule 190.3(b)(3)...."

TRCP 191. MODIFYING DISCOVERY PROCEDURES & LIMITATIONS; CONFERENCE REQUIREMENT; SIGNING DISCLOSURES, DISCOVERY REQUESTS, RESPONSES, & OBJECTIONS; FILING REQUIREMENTS

191.1 Modification of Procedures. Except where specifically prohibited, the procedures and limitations set forth in the rules pertaining to discovery may be modified in any suit by the agreement of the parties or by court order for good cause. An agreement of the parties is enforceable if it complies with Rule 11 or, as it affects an oral deposition, if it is made a part of the record of the deposition.

191.2 Conference. Parties and their attorneys are expected to cooperate in discovery and to make any agreements reasonably necessary for the efficient disposition of the case. All discovery motions or requests for hearings relating to discovery must contain a certificate by the party filing the motion or request that a reasonable effort has been made to resolve the dispute without the necessity of court intervention and the effort failed.

191.3 Signing of Disclosures, Discovery Requests, Notices, Responses, and Objections.

(a) ***Signature required.*** Every disclosure, discovery request, notice, response, and objection must be signed:

(1) by an attorney, if the party is represented by an attorney, and must show the attorney's State Bar of Texas identification number, address, telephone number, and fax number, if any; or

(2) by the party, if the party is not represented by an attorney, and must show the party's address, telephone number, and fax number, if any.

(b) ***Effect of signature on disclosure.*** The signature of an attorney or party on a disclosure constitutes a certification that to the best of the signer's knowledge, information, and belief, formed after a reasonable inquiry, the disclosure is complete and correct as of the time it is made.

(c) ***Effect of signature on discovery request, notice, response, or objection.*** The signature of an attorney or party on a discovery request, notice, response, or objection constitutes a certification that to the best of the signer's knowledge, information, and belief, formed after a reasonable inquiry, the request, notice, response, or objection:

(1) is consistent with the rules of civil procedure and these discovery rules and warranted by existing law or a good faith argument for the extension, modification, or reversal of existing law;

(2) has a good faith factual basis;

(3) is not interposed for any improper purpose, such as to harass or to cause unnecessary delay or needless increase in the cost of litigation; and

(4) is not unreasonable or unduly burdensome or expensive, given the needs of the case, the discovery already had in the case, the amount in controversy, and the importance of the issues at stake in the litigation.

(d) ***Effect of failure to sign.*** If a request, notice, response, or objection is not signed, it must be stricken unless it is signed promptly after the omission is called to the attention of the party making the request, notice, response, or objection. A party is not required to take any action with respect to a request or notice that is not signed.

(e) ***Sanctions.*** If the certification is false without substantial justification, the court may, upon motion or its own initiative, impose on the person who made the certification, or the party on whose behalf the request, notice, response, or objection was made, or both, an appropriate sanction as for a frivolous pleading or motion under Chapter 10 of the Civil Practice and Remedies Code.

191.4 Filing of Discovery Materials.

(a) ***Discovery materials not to be filed.*** The following discovery materials must not be filed:

(1) discovery requests, deposition notices, and subpoenas required to be served only on parties;

(2) responses and objections to discovery requests and deposition notices, regardless on whom the requests or notices were served;

(3) documents and tangible things produced in discovery; and

(4) statements prepared in compliance with Rule 193.3(b) or (d).

(b) ***Discovery materials to be filed.*** The following discovery materials must be filed:

(1) discovery requests, deposition notices, and subpoenas required to be served on nonparties;

(2) motions and responses to motions pertaining to discovery matters; and

(3) agreements concerning discovery matters, to the extent necessary to comply with Rule 11.

(c) ***Exceptions.*** Notwithstanding paragraph (a)—

(1) the court may order discovery materials to be filed;

(2) a person may file discovery materials in support of or in opposition to a motion or for other use in a court proceeding; and

(3) a person may file discovery materials necessary for a proceeding in an appellate court.

(d) ***Retention requirement for persons.*** Any person required to serve discovery materials not required to be filed must retain the original or exact copy of the materials during the pendency of the case and any related appellate proceedings begun within six months after judgment is signed, unless otherwise provided by the trial court.

(e) ***Retention requirement for courts.*** The clerk of the court shall retain and dispose of deposition transcripts and depositions upon written questions as directed by the Supreme Court.

191.5 Service of Discovery Materials. Every disclosure, discovery request, notice, response, and objection required to be served on a party or person must be served on all parties of record.

See also CPRC §10.001; TRCP 11, 13, 57; *O'Connor's Texas Rules*, "General Rules for Discovery," ch. 6-A, p. 491.

ANNOTATIONS

In re BP Prods. N. Am., Inc., 244 S.W.3d 840, 846 (Tex.2008). "This Court has not previously addressed the scope of a trial court's power to set aside an otherwise enforceable Rule 191.1 agreement. Consistent with its powers over discovery, a trial court may modify discovery procedures and limitations for 'good cause.' This power, however, is not 'unbounded.' Wherever possible, a trial court should give effect to agreements between the parties. [¶] A court should be particularly reluctant to set aside a Rule 191.1 agreement after one party has acted in reliance on the agreed procedure and performed its obligations under the agreement. *At 847:* In the absence of a motion for sanctions, proper notice and opportunity to be heard, or the trial court's invocation of the court's power to sanction, the order striking the discovery agreement is not supportable as a sanctions order."

Groves v. Gabriel, 874 S.W.2d 660, 661 n.3 (Tex. 1994). "[P] complains that [D's] motion to compel discovery did not contain the certificate of conference required under [TRCP 166b(7), now TRCP 191.2]. Because this rule is for the benefit of the trial court, the court's failure to require a certificate of conference does not justify mandamus relief."

TRCP 192. PERMISSIBLE DISCOVERY: FORMS & SCOPE; WORK PRODUCT; PROTECTIVE ORDERS; DEFINITIONS

192.1 Forms of Discovery. Permissible forms of discovery are:

(a) requests for disclosure;

(b) requests for production and inspection of documents and tangible things;

(c) requests and motions for entry upon and examination of real property;

(d) interrogatories to a party;

(e) requests for admission;

(f) oral or written depositions; and

(g) motions for mental or physical examinations.

192.2 Sequence of Discovery. The permissible forms of discovery may be combined in the same document and may be taken in any order or sequence.

192.3 Scope of Discovery.

(a) ***Generally.*** In general, a party may obtain discovery regarding any matter that is not privileged and is relevant to the subject matter of the pending action, whether it relates to the claim or defense of the party seeking discovery or the claim or defense of any other party. It is not a ground for objection that the information sought will be inadmissible at trial if the information sought appears reasonably calculated to lead to the discovery of admissible evidence.

(b) ***Documents and tangible things.*** A party may obtain discovery of the existence, description, nature,

custody, condition, location, and contents of documents and tangible things (including papers, books, accounts, drawings, graphs, charts, photographs, electronic or videotape recordings, data, and data compilations) that constitute or contain matters relevant to the subject matter of the action. A person is required to produce a document or tangible thing that is within the person's possession, custody, or control.

(c) ***Persons with knowledge of relevant facts.*** A party may obtain discovery of the name, address, and telephone number of persons having knowledge of relevant facts, and a brief statement of each identified person's connection with the case. A person has knowledge of relevant facts when that person has or may have knowledge of any discoverable matter. The person need not have admissible information or personal knowledge of the facts. An expert is "a person with knowledge of relevant facts" only if that knowledge was obtained first-hand or if it was not obtained in preparation for trial or in anticipation of litigation.

(d) ***Trial witnesses.*** A party may obtain discovery of the name, address, and telephone number of any person who is expected to be called to testify at trial. This paragraph does not apply to rebuttal or impeaching witnesses the necessity of whose testimony cannot reasonably be anticipated before trial.

(e) ***Testifying and consulting experts.*** The identity, mental impressions, and opinions of a consulting expert whose mental impressions and opinions have not been reviewed by a testifying expert are not discoverable. A party may discover the following information regarding a testifying expert or regarding a consulting expert whose mental impressions or opinions have been reviewed by a testifying expert:

(1) the expert's name, address, and telephone number;

(2) the subject matter on which a testifying expert will testify;

(3) the facts known by the expert that relate to or form the basis of the expert's mental impressions and opinions formed or made in connection with the case in which the discovery is sought, regardless of when and how the factual information was acquired;

(4) the expert's mental impressions and opinions formed or made in connection with the case in which discovery is sought, and any methods used to derive them;

(5) any bias of the witness;

(6) all documents, tangible things, reports, models, or data compilations that have been provided to, reviewed by, or prepared by or for the expert in anticipation of a testifying expert's testimony;

(7) the expert's current resume and bibliography.

(f) ***Indemnity and insuring agreements.*** Except as otherwise provided by law, a party may obtain discovery of the existence and contents of any indemnity or insurance agreement under which any person may be liable to satisfy part or all of a judgment rendered in the action or to indemnify or reimburse for payments made to satisfy the judgment. Information concerning the indemnity or insurance agreement is not by reason of disclosure admissible in evidence at trial.

(g) ***Settlement agreements.*** A party may obtain discovery of the existence and contents of any relevant portions of a settlement agreement. Information concerning a settlement agreement is not by reason of disclosure admissible in evidence at trial.

(h) ***Statements of persons with knowledge of relevant facts.*** A party may obtain discovery of the statement of any person with knowledge of relevant facts—a "witness statement"—regardless of when the statement was made. A witness statement is (1) a written statement signed or otherwise adopted or approved in writing by the person making it, or (2) a stenographic, mechanical, electrical, or other type of recording of a witness's oral statement, or any substantially verbatim transcription of such a recording. Notes taken during a conversation or interview with a witness are not a witness statement. Any person may obtain, upon written request, his or her own statement concerning the lawsuit, which is in the possession, custody or control of any party.

(i) ***Potential parties.*** A party may obtain discovery of the name, address, and telephone number of any potential party.

(j) ***Contentions.*** A party may obtain discovery of any other party's legal contentions and the factual bases for those contentions.

192.4 Limitations on Scope of Discovery. The discovery methods permitted by these rules should be limited by the court if it determines, on motion or on its own initiative and on reasonable notice, that:

(a) the discovery sought is unreasonably cumulative or duplicative, or is obtainable from some other source that is more convenient, less burdensome, or less expensive; or

(b) the burden or expense of the proposed discovery outweighs its likely benefit, taking into account the needs of the case, the amount in controversy, the parties' resources, the importance of the issues at stake in the litigation, and the importance of the proposed discovery in resolving the issues.

192.5 Work Product.

(a) ***Work product defined.*** Work product comprises:

(1) material prepared or mental impressions developed in anticipation of litigation or for trial by or for a party or a party's representatives, including the party's attorneys, consultants, sureties, indemnitors, insurers, employees, or agents; or

(2) a communication made in anticipation of litigation or for trial between a party and the party's representatives or among a party's representatives, including the party's attorneys, consultants, sureties, indemnitors, insurers, employees, or agents.

(b) ***Protection of work product.***

(1) *Protection of core work product—attorney mental processes.* Core work product—the work product of an attorney or an attorney's representative that contains the attorney's or the attorney's representative's mental impressions, opinions, conclusions, or legal theories—is not discoverable.

(2) *Protection of other work product.* Any other work product is discoverable only upon a showing that the party seeking discovery has substantial need of the materials in the preparation of the party's case and that the party is unable without undue hardship to obtain the substantial equivalent of the material by other means.

(3) *Incidental disclosure of attorney mental processes.* It is not a violation of subparagraph (1) if disclosure ordered pursuant to subparagraph (2) incidentally discloses by inference attorney mental processes otherwise protected under subparagraph (1).

(4) *Limiting disclosure of mental processes.* If a court orders discovery of work product pursuant to subparagraph (2), the court must—insofar as possible—protect against disclosure of the mental impressions, opinions, conclusions, or legal theories not otherwise discoverable.

(c) ***Exceptions.*** Even if made or prepared in anticipation of litigation or for trial, the following is not work product protected from discovery:

(1) information discoverable under Rule 192.3 concerning experts, trial witnesses, witness statements, and contentions;

(2) trial exhibits ordered disclosed under Rule 166 or Rule 190.4;

(3) the name, address, and telephone number of any potential party or any person with knowledge of relevant facts;

(4) any photograph or electronic image of underlying facts (*e.g.*, a photograph of the accident scene) or a photograph or electronic image of any sort that a party intends to offer into evidence; and

(5) any work product created under circumstances within an exception to the attorney-client privilege in Rule 503(d) of the Rules of Evidence.

(d) ***Privilege.*** For purposes of these rules, an assertion that material or information is work product is an assertion of privilege.

192.6 Protective Orders.

(a) ***Motion.*** A person from whom discovery is sought, and any other person affected by the discovery request, may move within the time permitted for response to the discovery request for an order protecting that person from the discovery sought. A person should not move for protection when an objection to written discovery or an assertion of privilege is appropriate, but a motion does not waive the objection or assertion of privilege. If a person seeks protection regarding the time or place of discovery, the person must state a reasonable time and place for discovery with which the person will comply. A person must comply with a request to the extent protection is not sought unless it is unreasonable under the circumstances to do so before obtaining a ruling on the motion.

(b) ***Order.*** To protect the movant from undue burden, unnecessary expense, harassment, annoyance, or invasion of personal, constitutional, or property rights, the court may make any order in the interest of justice and may—among other things—order that:

(1) the requested discovery not be sought in whole or in part;

(2) the extent or subject matter of discovery be limited;

(3) the discovery not be undertaken at the time or place specified;

(4) the discovery be undertaken only by such method or upon such terms and conditions or at the time and place directed by the court;

(5) the results of discovery be sealed or otherwise protected, subject to the provisions of Rule 76a.

192.7 Definitions. As used in these rules—

(a) *Written discovery* means requests for disclosure, requests for production and inspection of documents and tangible things, requests for entry onto property, interrogatories, and requests for admission.

(b) *Possession, custody, or control* of an item means that the person either has physical possession of the item or has a right to possession of the item that is equal or superior to the person who has physical possession of the item.

(c) A *testifying expert* is an expert who may be called to testify as an expert witness at trial.

(d) A *consulting expert* is an expert who has been consulted, retained, or specially employed by a party in anticipation of litigation or in preparation for trial, but who is not a testifying expert.

See also ***O'Connor's Texas Rules***, "General Rules for Discovery," ch. 6-A, p. 491; "Scope of Discovery," ch. 6-B, p. 530; "Electronic Discovery," ch. 6-C, p. 559; ***O'Connor's Texas Forms***, FORMS 6A:10-14.

ANNOTATIONS

Definition

In re Kuntz, 124 S.W.3d 179, 183 (Tex.2003). "[D] argues that he 'should not be ordered to produce documents in the physical possession of his corporate employer in this suit brought against him individually.' *At 184:* [D's] access is strictly limited to use of the [documents] in furtherance of his employer's services.... [¶] [M]ere access to the [documents] does not constitute 'physical possession' of the documents under the definition of 'possession, custody, or control' set forth in [TRCP] 192.7(b)."

GTE Comms. Sys. v. Tanner, 856 S.W.2d 725, 729 (Tex.1993). "The phrase, 'possession, custody or control,' within the meaning of [TRCP 192.7(b)], includes not only actual physical possession, but constructive possession, and the right to obtain possession from a third party, such as an agent or representative." *See also* ***In re Summersett***, 438 S.W.3d 74, 81 (Tex.App.—Corpus Christi 2013, orig. proceeding).

Scope of Discovery

In re National Lloyds Ins., 449 S.W.3d 486, 489-90 (Tex.2014). "Essentially, [the purpose of P's request for the insurance-claim files is] to compare [D's] evaluation of the damage to her home with [D's] evaluation of the damage to other homes to support her contention that her claims were undervalued. ... Scouring claim files in hopes of finding similarly situated claimants whose claims were evaluated differently from [P's] is at best an 'impermissible fishing expedition.' [¶] [P] is correct that discovery must be reasonably limited in time and geographic scope. But such limits in and of themselves do not render the underlying information discoverable. Because the information [P] seeks is not reasonably calculated to lead to the discovery of admissible evidence, the trial court's order compelling discovery of such information is necessarily overbroad."

In re Ford Motor Co., 427 S.W.3d 396, 397 (Tex. 2014). This court has "expressed concerns about allowing overly expansive discovery about testifying experts that can 'permit witnesses to be subjected to harassment and might well discourage reputable experts' from participating in the litigation process. [¶] The particular deposition notices in this case highlight the danger of permitting such expansive discovery. In his deposition notices to [experts' employers], [P] seeks detailed financial and business information for all cases the companies have handled for [D-automobile manufacturer] or any other automobile manufacturer from 2000 to 2011. Such a fishing expedition, seeking sensitive information covering twelve years, is just the type of overbroad discovery the rules are intended to prevent." *See also* ***K Mart Corp. v. Sanderson***, 937 S.W.2d 429, 431 (Tex.1996); ***In re Siroosian***, 449 S.W.3d 920, 923 (Tex. App.—Fort Worth 2014, orig. proceeding).

In re Weekley Homes, L.P., 295 S.W.3d 309, 313-14 (Tex.2009). TRCP 192.3(b) "provides for discovery of documents, [including] electronic information that is relevant to the subject matter of the action." *See also* ***In re Honza***, 242 S.W.3d 578, 581 (Tex.App.—Waco 2008, orig. proceeding).

In re Dana Corp., 138 S.W.3d 298, 302 (Tex.2004). "Rule 192.3(f) does not foreclose discovery of insurance information beyond that identified in the rule; however, we also conclude that the plain language of Rule 192.3(f), by itself, does not provide a sufficient basis to order discovery beyond the production of the 'existence and contents' of the policies. [A] party may discover information beyond an insurance agreement's existence and contents only if the information is otherwise discoverable under our scope-of-discovery rule."

Ford Motor Co. v. Leggat, 904 S.W.2d 643, 649 (Tex.1995). "Settlement agreements are discoverable,

to the extent they are relevant. Settlement agreements themselves, of course, are not admissible at trial to prove liability." *See also* ***In re Univar USA, Inc.***, 311 S.W.3d 175, 180 (Tex.App.—Beaumont 2010, orig. proceeding).

Monsanto Co. v. May, 889 S.W.2d 274, 276 (Tex. 1994). "A party is entitled to discovery that is relevant to the subject matter of the claim, and which appears reasonably calculated to lead to the discovery of admissible evidence." *See also* ***Ford Motor Co. v. Castillo***, 279 S.W.3d 656, 664 (Tex.2009); ***Volkswagen, A.G. v. Valdez***, 909 S.W.2d 900, 902 (Tex.1995).

In re Summersett, 438 S.W.3d 74, 81 (Tex.App.—Corpus Christi 2013, orig. proceeding). "Because the discovery rules often apply to reach information not within a party's physical possession, a party may often not have actual knowledge of the existence of information or documents in the possession of others 'but may be nevertheless obligated to gain knowledge of them.' Thus, in evaluating the scope of a given request to produce, the duty to produce is not always satisfied by producing the documents that are in the party's immediate physical possession but 'may often extend to documents in the possession of persons or entities that are not parties to the suit.' The party seeking production has the burden of proving that the relator has constructive possession or the right to obtain possession of the requested documents."

In re Commitment of Young, 410 S.W.3d 542, 551 (Tex.App.—Beaumont 2013, no pet.). "'It is the discovery proponent's burden to demonstrate that the requested documents fall within the scope-of-discovery of Rule 192.3.' Trial courts have the discretion to refuse to compel discovery if the information being requested by the interrogatory or request at issue is so inclusive that responding would require matters to be included that are unlikely to fall within the scope of discovery that governs the parties' dispute."

Experts

In re Christus Spohn Hosp. Kleberg, 222 S.W.3d 434, 439 (Tex.2007). See annotation under TRCP 193, *TRCP 193.3—Privileges*, p. 1141.

Work Product

In re Bexar Cty. Crim. Dist. Atty's Office, 224 S.W.3d 182, 187-88 (Tex.2007). "Rule 192.5(b)(1) distinguishes everyday work product from 'core work product' and makes clear that the latter … is inviolate and flatly 'not discoverable[ ]'.… Core work product is sacrosanct and its protection impermeable."

Occidental Chem. Corp. v. Banales, 907 S.W.2d 488, 490 (Tex.1995). "The attorney work product privilege protects two related but different concepts. First, the privilege protects the attorney's thought process, which includes strategy decisions and issue formulation, and notes or writings evincing those mental processes. Second, the privilege protects the mechanical compilation of information to the extent such compilation reveals the attorney's thought processes. The work product exemption is of continuing duration." *See also* ***National Tank Co. v. Brotherton***, 851 S.W.2d 193, 200 (Tex.1993).

National Un. Fire Ins. v. Valdez, 863 S.W.2d 458, 461 (Tex.1993). "[N]o legitimate purpose is served by allowing a party to discover an opponent's litigation file. Our decision today does not prevent a party from requesting specific documents or categories of documents relevant to issues in a pending case, even though some or all of the documents may be contained in an attorney's files."

In re Baytown Nissan Inc., 451 S.W.3d 140, 149 (Tex.App.—Houston [1st Dist.] 2014, orig. proceeding). "'Compelling an attorney of record involved in the litigation of the case to testify concerning the suit's subject matter generally implicates work product concerns' and 'is inappropriate under most circumstances.' [¶] Deposition questions requesting [D's attorney's] mental impressions regarding his conversation with [witness] are core work product and not discoverable. Other questions requesting factual details of [D's attorney's] conversation with [witness] are non-core work product. With respect to those questions, [P] had the burden of demonstrating the substantial need and undue hardship requirements for discovery of non-core work product. This is a particularly heavy burden when a discovery request seeks to compel the deposition of a party's attorney…."

Protective Orders

General Tire, Inc. v. Kepple, 970 S.W.2d 520, 524 (Tex.1998). "To the extent that discovery, whether filed or unfiled, is a 'court record' under [TRCP] 76a, the court must follow the stricter standards of that rule to limit its dissemination. *At 525:* [W]e hold that when a party seeks a protective order under [TRCP 192.6] to restrict the dissemination of unfiled discovery, and no party or intervenor contends that the discovery is a

'court record,' a trial court need not conduct a hearing or render any findings on that issue. If a party or intervenor opposing a protective order claims that the discovery is a 'court record,' the court must make a threshold determination on that issue. However, public notice and a Rule 76a hearing are mandated only if the court finds that the documents are court records."

Crown Cent. Pet. Corp. v. Garcia, 904 S.W.2d 125, 128 (Tex.1995). "When a party seeks to depose a ... high level corporate official [i.e., an apex deposition] and that official (or the corporation) files a motion for protective order ... denying any knowledge of relevant facts, the trial court should first determine whether the party seeking the deposition has arguably shown that the official has any unique or superior personal knowledge of discoverable information. If the party seeking the deposition cannot [so] show ..., the trial court should grant the motion for protective order and first require the party seeking the deposition to attempt to obtain the discovery through less intrusive methods."

In re Shell E&P, Inc., 179 S.W.3d 125, 130 (Tex. App.—San Antonio 2005, orig. proceeding). "[T]he non-party owner of [a document has] the right under Rule 192.6(a) to seek protection from disclosure of its documents in the trial court, whether through an objection, assertion of privilege, motion for a protective order, or motion for enforcement of an existing protective order. The trial court's ... order holding that [non-party] lacks standing to object to the disclosure of its documents conflicts with Rule 192.6(a) ...; therefore, ... the trial court clearly abused its discretion."

In re Amaya, 34 S.W.3d 354, 356-57 (Tex.App.—Waco 2001, orig. proceeding). "A trial judge may exercise some discretion in the granting of a protective order and in controlling the nature and form of discovery. ... A party seeking to avoid discovery must show particular, specific and demonstrable injury by facts sufficient to justify a protective order. 'So long as the discovery sought is within the scope of [TRCP] 166b [now TRCP 192], a trial court may not grant a protective order limiting discovery unless the party seeking such protection has met this burden.' Conclusory allegations are not adequate. [¶] Any party who seeks to exclude matters from discovery on grounds that the requested information is unduly burdensome, costly or harassing to produce, has the affirmative duty to plead and prove the work necessary to comply with discovery."

TRCP 193. WRITTEN DISCOVERY: RESPONSE; OBJECTION; ASSERTION OF PRIVILEGE; SUPPLEMENTATION & AMENDMENT; FAILURE TO TIMELY RESPOND; PRESUMPTION OF AUTHENTICITY

193.1 Responding to Written Discovery; Duty to Make Complete Response. A party must respond to written discovery in writing within the time provided by court order or these rules. When responding to written discovery, a party must make a complete response, based on all information reasonably available to the responding party or its attorney at the time the response is made. The responding party's answers, objections, and other responses must be preceded by the request to which they apply.

193.2 Objecting to Written Discovery.

(a) ***Form and time for objections.*** A party must make any objection to written discovery in writing—either in the response or in a separate document—within the time for response. The party must state specifically the legal or factual basis for the objection and the extent to which the party is refusing to comply with the request.

(b) ***Duty to respond when partially objecting; objection to time or place of production.*** A party must comply with as much of the request to which the party has made no objection unless it is unreasonable under the circumstances to do so before obtaining a ruling on the objection. If the responding party objects to the requested time or place of production, the responding party must state a reasonable time and place for complying with the request and must comply at that time and place without further request or order.

(c) ***Good faith basis for objection.*** A party may object to written discovery only if a good faith factual and legal basis for the objection exists at the time the objection is made.

(d) ***Amendment.*** An objection or response to written discovery may be amended or supplemented to state an objection or basis that, at the time the objection or response initially was made, either was inapplicable or was unknown after reasonable inquiry.

(e) ***Waiver of objection.*** An objection that is not made within the time required, or that is obscured by numerous unfounded objections, is waived unless the court excuses the waiver for good cause shown.

(f) ***No objection to preserve privilege.*** A party should not object to a request for written discovery on

the grounds that it calls for production of material or information that is privileged but should instead comply with Rule 193.3. A party who objects to production of privileged material or information does not waive the privilege but must comply with Rule 193.3 when the error is pointed out.

193.3 Asserting a Privilege. A party may preserve a privilege from written discovery in accordance with this subdivision.

(a) ***Withholding privileged material or information.*** A party who claims that material or information responsive to written discovery is privileged may withhold the privileged material or information from the response. The party must state—in the response (or an amended or supplemental response) or in a separate document—that:

(1) information or material responsive to the request has been withheld,

(2) the request to which the information or material relates, and

(3) the privilege or privileges asserted.

(b) ***Description of withheld material or information.*** After receiving a response indicating that material or information has been withheld from production, the party seeking discovery may serve a written request that the withholding party identify the information and material withheld. Within 15 days of service of that request, the withholding party must serve a response that:

(1) describes the information or materials withheld that, without revealing the privileged information itself or otherwise waiving the privilege, enables other parties to assess the applicability of the privilege, and

(2) asserts a specific privilege for each item or group of items withheld.

(c) ***Exemption.*** Without complying with paragraphs (a) and (b), a party may withhold a privileged communication to or from a lawyer or lawyer's representative or a privileged document of a lawyer or lawyer's representative—

(1) created or made from the point at which a party consults a lawyer with a view to obtaining professional legal services from the lawyer in the prosecution or defense of a specific claim in the litigation in which discovery is requested, and

(2) concerning the litigation in which the discovery is requested.

(d) ***Privilege not waived by production.*** A party who produces material or information without intending to waive a claim of privilege does not waive that claim under these rules or the Rules of Evidence if—within ten days or a shorter time ordered by the court, after the producing party actually discovers that such production was made—the producing party amends the response, identifying the material or information produced and stating the privilege asserted. If the producing party thus amends the response to assert a privilege, the requesting party must promptly return the specified material or information and any copies pending any ruling by the court denying the privilege.

193.4 Hearing and Ruling on Objections and Assertions of Privilege.

(a) ***Hearing.*** Any party may at any reasonable time request a hearing on an objection or claim of privilege asserted under this rule. The party making the objection or asserting the privilege must present any evidence necessary to support the objection or privilege. The evidence may be testimony presented at the hearing or affidavits served at least seven days before the hearing or at such other reasonable time as the court permits. If the court determines that an *in camera* review of some or all of the requested discovery is necessary, that material or information must be segregated and produced to the court in a sealed wrapper within a reasonable time following the hearing.

(b) ***Ruling.*** To the extent the court sustains the objection or claim of privilege, the responding party has no further duty to respond to that request. To the extent the court overrules the objection or claim of privilege, the responding party must produce the requested material or information within 30 days after the court's ruling or at such time as the court orders. A party need not request a ruling on that party's own objection or assertion of privilege to preserve the objection or privilege.

(c) ***Use of material or information withheld under claim of privilege.*** A party may not use—at any hearing or trial—material or information withheld from discovery under a claim of privilege, including a claim sustained by the court, without timely amending or supplementing the party's response to that discovery.

193.5 Amending or Supplementing Responses to Written Discovery.

(a) ***Duty to amend or supplement.*** If a party learns that the party's response to written discovery was incomplete or incorrect when made, or, although

complete and correct when made, is no longer complete and correct, the party must amend or supplement the response:

(1) to the extent that the written discovery sought the identification of persons with knowledge of relevant facts, trial witnesses, or expert witnesses, and

(2) to the extent that the written discovery sought other information, unless the additional or corrective information has been made known to the other parties in writing, on the record at a deposition, or through other discovery responses.

(b) ***Time and form of amended or supplemental response.*** An amended or supplemental response must be made reasonably promptly after the party discovers the necessity for such a response. Except as otherwise provided by these rules, it is presumed that an amended or supplemental response made less than 30 days before trial was not made reasonably promptly. An amended or supplemental response must be in the same form as the initial response and must be verified by the party if the original response was required to be verified by the party, but the failure to comply with this requirement does not make the amended or supplemental response untimely unless the party making the response refuses to correct the defect within a reasonable time after it is pointed out.

193.6 Failing to Timely Respond—Effect on Trial.

(a) ***Exclusion of evidence and exceptions.*** A party who fails to make, amend, or supplement a discovery response in a timely manner may not introduce in evidence the material or information that was not timely disclosed, or offer the testimony of a witness (other than a named party) who was not timely identified, unless the court finds that:

(1) there was good cause for the failure to timely make, amend, or supplement the discovery response; or

(2) the failure to timely make, amend, or supplement the discovery response will not unfairly surprise or unfairly prejudice the other parties.

(b) ***Burden of establishing exception.*** The burden of establishing good cause or the lack of unfair surprise or unfair prejudice is on the party seeking to introduce the evidence or call the witness. A finding of good cause or of the lack of unfair surprise or unfair prejudice must be supported by the record.

(c) ***Continuance.*** Even if the party seeking to introduce the evidence or call the witness fails to carry the burden under paragraph (b), the court may grant a continuance or temporarily postpone the trial to allow a response to be made, amended, or supplemented, and to allow opposing parties to conduct discovery regarding any new information presented by that response.

193.7 Production of Documents Self-Authenticating. A party's production of a document in response to written discovery authenticates the document for use against that party in any pretrial proceeding or at trial unless—within ten days or a longer or shorter time ordered by the court, after the producing party has actual notice that the document will be used—the party objects to the authenticity of the document, or any part of it, stating the specific basis for objection. An objection must be either on the record or in writing and must have a good faith factual and legal basis. An objection made to the authenticity of only part of a document does not affect the authenticity of the remainder. If objection is made, the party attempting to use the document should be given a reasonable opportunity to establish its authenticity.

See also *O'Connor's Texas Rules*, "General Rules for Discovery," ch. 6-A, p. 491; "Scope of Discovery," ch. 6-B, p. 530; *O'Connor's Texas Forms*, FORMS 6A:9, 15, 16, 19-22.

ANNOTATIONS

TRCP 193.1—Duty

Lucas v. Clark, 347 S.W.3d 800, 805 (Tex.App.—Austin 2011, pet. denied). "[T]ypically any challenge to a request for admission must be in compliance with Rule 193.1, [but the] question of a deemed admission's overbreadth only arises when a request for admission has been deemed admitted, which, by definition, occurs after a party has failed to timely respond or object to the request. No request for admission would be deemed admitted if the responding party had objected in writing within the parameters of Rule 193.1. Therefore, were we to require a party to object in writing to a request for admission's overbreadth in order to preserve the issue on appeal, no appellate court would ever face the issue. [¶] [N]o objection was necessary to reach the merits of the issue in this Court. This is true because the question before us is one of evidentiary sufficiency rather than procedural error. In viewing the effect of an overly broad request for admission, our analysis centers on whether a trial court is permitted to find that the request for admission irrefutably established the facts therein such that no additional evidence is required."

TRCP 193.2—Objections

General Motors Corp. v. Tanner, 892 S.W.2d 862, 863 (Tex.1995). "As the party objecting to the request, [P] was required to provide evidence in support of his objection."

TRCP 193.3—Privileges

In re Christus Spohn Hosp. Kleberg, 222 S.W.3d 434, 439 (Tex.2007). "The snap-back provision [in TRCP 193.3(d)] has typically been applied when a party inadvertently produces privileged documents to an opposing party. In this case, however, the privileged material was produced by a party to its own testifying expert, invoking [TRCP] 192.3(e)(6)'s overlapping directive that all materials provided to a testifying expert must be produced. *At 440-41:* [TRCP] 192.3(e)(6) and 192.5(c)(1) prevail over Rule 193.3(d)'s snap-back provision so long as the expert intends to testify at trial despite the inadvertent document production. That is, once privileged documents are disclosed to a testifying expert, and the party who designated the expert continues to rely upon that designation for trial, the documents may not be retrieved even if they were inadvertently produced. Of course, inadvertently produced material that could not by its nature have influenced the expert's opinion does not evoke the concerns the expert-disclosure rule was designed to prevent and the policy concerns underlying the rule's disclosure requirement would presumably never arise. In that event, there would be nothing to prevent the snap-back rule's application, although we note that a party seeking snap-back under such circumstances would bear a heavy burden in light of the disclosure rule's underlying purpose. *At 445:* An attorney who discovers that privileged documents have been inadvertently provided to a testifying expert may presumably withdraw the expert's designation and name another."

In re E.I. DuPont de Nemours & Co., 136 S.W.3d 218, 223 (Tex.2004). "[A]n affidavit, even if it addresses groups of documents rather than each document individually, has been held to be sufficient to make a prima facie showing of attorney-client and/or work product privilege. *At 224:* However, an affidavit is of no probative value if it merely presents global allegations that documents come within the asserted privilege. [D's affidavit] sets forth the factual basis for the applicability of the attorney-client and/or work product privileges to the documents at issue. [T]he specificity of [D's] affidavit and the log taken together are reasonably adequate to establish a prima facie case of privilege...." *See also* ***In re BP Prods.***, 263 S.W.3d 106, 113-14 (Tex.App.—Houston [1st Dist.] 2006, orig. proceeding).

In re Union Pac. Res., 22 S.W.3d 338, 340 (Tex. 1999). "'Any party who seeks to deny the production of evidence must claim a specific privilege against such production. The burden is on the party asserting a privilege from discovery to produce evidence *concerning the applicability of a particular privilege.*'" *See also* ***In re Monsanto Co.***, 998 S.W.2d 917, 926 (Tex.App.—Waco 1999, orig. proceeding).

Humphreys v. Caldwell, 888 S.W.2d 469, 470 (Tex. 1994). "A party who seeks to exclude any matter from discovery on the basis of an exemption or immunity from discovery, must specifically plead the particular exemption or immunity relied on and produce evidence supporting such claim in the form of affidavits or live testimony at a hearing."

In re Certain Underwriters, 294 S.W.3d 891, 902 (Tex.App.—Beaumont 2009, orig. proceeding). "Because the rules do not expressly define the term 'party who produces,' it is not clear that Rule 193.3(d) is confined to reach only parties to a suit. *At 903:* Because the law allows privileged information to be shared for certain purposes with specific others, privilege rules are necessarily designed to apply to persons other than the privilege's holder. Should the 'snap-back' provision apply only to the parties to the suit, that interpretation would effectively negate the privilege holder's enforcement rights when nonparties to the suit produce privileged information. Thus, we conclude that an interpretation of Rule 193.3(d) to read 'party who produces' as meaning 'party to the lawsuit who produces' would allow, rather than discourage, efforts to obtain privileged information from nonparties."

Warrantech Corp. v. Computer Adapters Servs., 134 S.W.3d 516, 524-25 (Tex.App.—Fort Worth 2004, no pet.). "The focus of [TRCP] 193.3(d) is on the intent to waive the privilege, not the intent to produce the material or information. [A] party who fails to diligently screen documents before producing them does not waive a claim of privilege, and the ten-day period runs from the party's first awareness of the mistake, not from the date of production. [A] party may identify before trial the documents intended to be offered, thereby triggering the obligation to assert any overlooked privilege under this rule." *See also* ***In re Certain Under-***

writers, 294 S.W.3d 891, 904 (Tex.App.—Beaumont 2009, orig. proceeding).

TRCP 193.4—Hearing

In re CI Host, Inc., 92 S.W.3d 514, 517 (Tex.2002). "Our discovery rules do not require notice to third parties so that they might have an opportunity to be heard on their own objections."

TRCP 193.5—Supplementing Discovery

Titus Cty. Hosp. Dist. v. Lucas, 988 S.W.2d 740, 740 (Tex.1998). TRCP 166b(6), now 193.5, "requires supplementation of a 'response' to a 'request for discovery.' An interrogatory answer is a response to a request for discovery, but testimony in a deposition is not. A general duty to supplement deposition testimony (as opposed to a narrow duty for certain expert testimony, for example) would impose too great a burden on litigants. We therefore disapprove the court of appeals' holding that deposition testimony must be supplemented."

Exxon Corp. v. West Tex. Gathering Co., 868 S.W.2d 299, 304 (Tex.1993). "Our rules do not prevent experts from refining calculations and perfecting reports through the time of trial. The testimony of an expert should not be barred because a change in some minor detail of the person's work has not been disclosed a month before trial. The additional supplementation requirement of [TRCP 166b(6), now TRCP 193.5,] does require that opposing parties have sufficient information about an expert's opinion to prepare a rebuttal with their own experts and cross-examination, and that they be promptly and fully advised when further developments have rendered past information incorrect or misleading."

Christus Health Gulf Coast v. Carswell, 433 S.W.3d 585, 614 (Tex.App.—Houston [1st Dist.] 2013), *rev'd in part on other grounds*, 505 S.W.3d 528 (Tex. 2016). "The trial court may impose monetary sanctions on a party for its failure to supplement its discovery responses in a timely manner [under TRCP 193.5]."

Snider v. Stanley, 44 S.W.3d 713, 715 (Tex.App.—Beaumont 2001, pet. denied). "'An amended or supplemental response must be made reasonably promptly after the party discovers the necessity for such a response.' It is presumed that response made within 30 days of trial is not reasonably promptly made. [D's] response, made 30 days before trial, is not subject to the presumption. [Ps] argue that the opposite presumption applies, that is, the supplementation was made reasonably promptly. We disagree. Had such a presumption been intended, it would have been incorporated into the rules."

TRCP 193.6—Effect of Failing to Respond

Alvarado v. Farah Mfg. Co., 830 S.W.2d 911, 914 (Tex.1992). The salutary purpose of TRCP 193.6 "is to require complete responses to discovery so as to promote responsible assessment of settlement and prevent trial by ambush. The rule is mandatory, and its sole sanction—exclusion of evidence—is automatic, unless there is good cause to excuse its imposition. The good cause exception permits a trial court to excuse a failure to comply with discovery in difficult or impossible circumstances. The trial court has discretion to determine whether the offering party has met his burden of showing good cause to admit the testimony; but the trial court has no discretion to admit testimony excluded by the rule without a showing of good cause." *See also* ***Hydrogeo, LLC v. Quitman ISD***, ___ S.W.3d ___ (Tex.App.—Texarkana 2016, no pet.) (No. 06-15-00007-CV; 1-6-16); ***Reservoir Sys. v. TGS-NOPEC Geophysical Co.***, 335 S.W.3d 297, 310-11 (Tex.App.—Houston [14th Dist.] 2010, pet. denied).

Cornejo v. Jones, No. 05-12-01256-CV (Tex.App.—Dallas 2014, no pet.) (memo op.; 1-29-14). "[D] argues that the phrase 'other than a named party' [in rule 193.6(a)] means that the testimony of named parties can never be excluded under [the rule]. We disagree. In context, the parenthetical language [i.e., 'other than a named party'] in rule 193.6(a) essentially states that named parties can testify at trial even if they do not list themselves as a fact witness in response to requests for disclosure. It does not state or imply that parties are not required to respond to interrogatories or other types of discovery requests. Here the issue is [D's] failure to respond to interrogatories, not whether he was listed as a fact witness in response to requests for disclosure. As a result, [D] was not exempt from the penalty of having his testimony excluded at trial."

TRCP 193.7—Self-Authenticating

Blanche v. First Nationwide Mortg. Corp., 74 S.W.3d 444, 451-52 (Tex.App.—Dallas 2002, no pet.). TRCP 193.7 "alleviate[s] the burden on a party receiving documents through discovery from proving the authenticity of those documents when they are used against the party who produced them. Rule 193.7 does not help [Ps] here because the documents attached to their summary judgment response were not produced

to them by [D], the party against whom the documents were used. ... A party cannot authenticate a document for use in its own favor by merely producing it in response to a discovery request."

TRCP 194. REQUESTS FOR DISCLOSURE

194.1 Request. A party may obtain disclosure from another party of the information or material listed in Rule 194.2 by serving the other party—no later than 30 days before the end of any applicable discovery period—the following request: "Pursuant to Rule 194, you are requested to disclose, within 30 days of service of this request, the information or material described in Rule [state rule, e.g., 194.2, or 194.2(a), (c), and (f), or 194.2(d)-(g)]."

194.2 Content. A party may request disclosure of any or all of the following:

(a) the correct names of the parties to the lawsuit;

(b) the name, address, and telephone number of any potential parties;

(c) the legal theories and, in general, the factual bases of the responding party's claims or defenses (the responding party need not marshal all evidence that may be offered at trial);

(d) the amount and any method of calculating economic damages;

(e) the name, address, and telephone number of persons having knowledge of relevant facts, and a brief statement of each identified person's connection with the case;

(f) for any testifying expert:

(1) the expert's name, address, and telephone number;

(2) the subject matter on which the expert will testify;

(3) the general substance of the expert's mental impressions and opinions and a brief summary of the basis for them, or if the expert is not retained by, employed by, or otherwise subject to the control of the responding party, documents reflecting such information;

(4) if the expert is retained by, employed by, or otherwise subject to the control of the responding party:

(A) all documents, tangible things, reports, models, or data compilations that have been provided to, reviewed by, or prepared by or for the expert in anticipation of the expert's testimony; and

(B) the expert's current resume and bibliography;

(g) any indemnity and insuring agreements described in Rule 192.3(f);

(h) any settlement agreements described in Rule 192.3(g);

(i) any witness statements described in Rule 192.3(h);

(j) in a suit alleging physical or mental injury and damages from the occurrence that is the subject of the case, all medical records and bills that are reasonably related to the injuries or damages asserted or, in lieu thereof, an authorization permitting the disclosure of such medical records and bills;

(k) in a suit alleging physical or mental injury and damages from the occurrence that is the subject of the case, all medical records and bills obtained by the responding party by virtue of an authorization furnished by the requesting party;

(*l*) the name, address, and telephone number of any person who may be designated as a responsible third party.

194.3 Response. The responding party must serve a written response on the requesting party within 30 days after service of the request, except that:

(a) a defendant served with a request before the defendant's answer is due need not respond until 50 days after service of the request, and

(b) a response to a request under Rule 194.2(f) is governed by Rule 195.

194.4 Production. Copies of documents and other tangible items ordinarily must be served with the response. But if the responsive documents are voluminous, the response must state a reasonable time and place for the production of documents. The responding party must produce the documents at the time and place stated, unless otherwise agreed by the parties or ordered by the court, and must provide the requesting party a reasonable opportunity to inspect them.

194.5 No Objection or Assertion of Work Product. No objection or assertion of work product is permitted to a request under this rule.

194.6 Certain Responses Not Admissible. A response to requests under Rule 194.2(c) and (d) that has been changed by an amended or supplemental response is not admissible and may not be used for impeachment.

See also *O'Connor's Texas Rules*, "General Rules for Discovery," ch. 6-A, p. 491; "Securing Discovery from Experts," ch. 6-D, p. 579; "Requests for Disclosure," ch. 6-E, p. 593; *O'Connor's Texas Forms*, FORMS 6D, 6E, 6J:1.

ANNOTATIONS

In re Staff Care, Inc., 422 S.W.3d 876, 881 (Tex. App.—Dallas 2014, orig. proceeding). "[T]here is no presumption that an amended disclosure made more than 30 days prior to trial is timely."

$27,877.00 Current Money v. State, 331 S.W.3d 110, 120 (Tex.App.—Fort Worth 2010, pet. denied). "[F]ailure to respond to a request for the mental impressions and opinions of the expert [under TRCP 194.2(f)] is a complete failure to respond, triggering the automatic exclusion under [TRCP] 193.6, … not just an incomplete answer, which the Texas Supreme Court has held requires a pretrial objection or a pretrial motion to compel or for sanctions…."

Van Heerden v. Van Heerden, 321 S.W.3d 869, 876 (Tex.App.—Houston [14th Dist.] 2010, no pet.). "[I]t is not clear what information is needed to satisfy [TRCP] 194.2(e)'s requirement of a 'brief statement of each identified person's connection with the case.' [¶] [W's] disclosure responses of 'Petitioner's father' and 'Petitioner's sister' adequately identify those witnesses' connection to the case or identity as relevant to the lawsuit."

Moore v. Memorial Hermann Hosp. Sys., 140 S.W.3d 870, 875 (Tex.App.—Houston [14th Dist.] 2004, no pet.). "[P] claims that she was not required to disclose the information required under [TRCP] 194.2(f) because [P's expert] was a rebuttal witness and not a designated or retained expert. However, once [D] disclosed the opinions of … its testifying expert, [P] could reasonably have anticipated the need to rebut the testimony of [D's expert] at trial. Therefore, [P's expert] was simply an ordinary rebuttal witness whose use reasonably could have been anticipated; rebuttal witnesses as such are not exempt from the scope of the written discovery rules."

In re K.S., 76 S.W.3d 36, 40 (Tex.App.—Amarillo 2002, no pet.). "The record shows that the TRCP 194 Request for Disclosure on which [parents] based their objection to the TDPRS witnesses was served only on behalf of [mother]. At the time the request was served, [father] had not made an appearance in the lawsuit and the document specified that [mother] was making the discovery request. The trial court did not abuse its discretion in denying the objection of [father] to testimony of the TDPRS witnesses when the witnesses had not been disclosed in response to a TRCP 194 request made only by [mother]."

Castellanos v. Littlejohn, 945 S.W.2d 236, 239 (Tex.App.—San Antonio 1997, orig. proceeding). P's expert "was retained as a consulting-only expert and was designated as a testifying expert only because of a clerical error. The issue presented … is whether a party who has inadvertently listed a consulting-only expert as a testifying expert may 'de-designate' him to reflect his proper status. We believe the party can do so, so long as the 'de-designation' does not constitute 'an offensive and unacceptable use of discovery mechanisms' or 'violate[] the clear purpose and policy underlying the rules of discovery.'"

TRCP 195. DISCOVERY REGARDING TESTIFYING EXPERT WITNESSES

195.1 Permissible Discovery Tools. A party may request another party to designate and disclose information concerning testifying expert witnesses only through a request for disclosure under Rule 194 and through depositions and reports as permitted by this rule.

195.2 Schedule for Designating Experts. Unless otherwise ordered by the court, a party must designate experts—that is, furnish information requested under Rule 194.2(f)—by the later of the following two dates: 30 days after the request is served, or—

(a) with regard to all experts testifying for a party seeking affirmative relief, 90 days before the end of the discovery period;

(b) with regard to all other experts, 60 days before the end of the discovery period.

195.3 Scheduling Depositions.

(a) ***Experts for party seeking affirmative relief.*** A party seeking affirmative relief must make an expert retained by, employed by, or otherwise in the control of the party available for deposition as follows:

(1) *If no report furnished.* If a report of the expert's factual observations, tests, supporting data, calculations, photographs, and opinions is not produced when the expert is designated, then the party must make the expert available for deposition reasonably promptly after the expert is designated. If the deposition cannot—due to the actions of the tendering party—reasonably be concluded more than 15 days before the deadline for

designating other experts, that deadline must be extended for other experts testifying on the same subject.

(2) *If report furnished.* If a report of the expert's factual observations, tests, supporting data, calculations, photographs, and opinions is produced when the expert is designated, then the party need not make the expert available for deposition until reasonably promptly after all other experts have been designated.

(b) ***Other experts.*** A party not seeking affirmative relief must make an expert retained by, employed by, or otherwise in the control of the party available for deposition reasonably promptly after the expert is designated and the experts testifying on the same subject for the party seeking affirmative relief have been deposed.

195.4 Oral Deposition. In addition to disclosure under Rule 194, a party may obtain discovery concerning the subject matter on which the expert is expected to testify, the expert's mental impressions and opinions, the facts known to the expert (regardless of when the factual information was acquired) that relate to or form the basis of the testifying expert's mental impressions and opinions, and other discoverable matters, including documents not produced in disclosure, only by oral deposition of the expert and by a report prepared by the expert under this rule.

195.5 Court-Ordered Reports. If the discoverable factual observations, tests, supporting data, calculations, photographs, or opinions of an expert have not been recorded and reduced to tangible form, the court may order these matters reduced to tangible form and produced in addition to the deposition.

195.6 Amendment and Supplementation. A party's duty to amend and supplement written discovery regarding a testifying expert is governed by Rule 193.5. If an expert witness is retained by, employed by, or otherwise under the control of a party, that party must also amend or supplement any deposition testimony or written report by the expert, but only with regard to the expert's mental impressions or opinions and the basis for them.

195.7 Cost of Expert Witnesses. When a party takes the oral deposition of an expert witness retained by the opposing party, all reasonable fees charged by the expert for time spent in preparing for, giving, reviewing, and correcting the deposition must be paid by the party that retained the expert.

See also *O'Connor's Texas Rules*, "General Rules for Discovery," ch. 6-A, p. 491; "Securing Discovery from Experts," ch. 6-D, p. 579; "Requests for Disclosure," ch. 6-E, p. 593; "Depositions," ch. 6-F, p. 604; ***O'Connor's Texas Forms***, FORMS 6D, 6E, 6F:1-3.

ANNOTATIONS

In re Ford Motor Co., 427 S.W.3d 396, 397 (Tex. 2014). "In his deposition notices to [experts' employers], [P sought] sensitive information covering 12 years, [which was an] overbroad discovery [request]. [¶] By holding that the requested discovery is impermissible in this case, we do not unduly inhibit discovery of an expert's potential bias. *At 398:* Indeed, the most probative information regarding the bias of a testifying expert comes from the expert herself. [¶] [P] argues that we have recognized at least one instance in which deposing the expert's employer was justified. In ***Walker v. Packer***[, 827 S.W.2d 833 (Tex.1992)], we held that discovery beyond the individual expert's deposition might be permissible when extrinsic evidence, discovered after the expert's deposition, puts his credibility in doubt. [¶] Assuming that this aspect of our holding in ***Walker*** survived the adoption of Rule 195, we disagree that [it] compels the result [P] seeks. Unlike ***Walker***, neither expert's credibility has been impugned in this case. And [P] has not demonstrated any other circumstance to warrant deposing the [expert] witnesses' employers' corporate representatives."

In re C.C., 476 S.W.3d 632, 639 (Tex.App.—Amarillo 2015, no pet.). "Here, [expert] was called as an expert witness by the intervenors ... even though the intervenors had not designated her as a testifying expert. Yet, the record reveals that no one had propounded any discovery requests upon the intervenors. Thus, a condition precedent to the application of [TRCP] 195.2 never occurred. That is, no one requested that the intervenors disclose their testifying experts under [TRCP] 194.2(f). Nor do we find of record an order obligating the parties to disclose their testifying experts by any date irrespective of whether another party sought their disclosure. So, the intervenors had no obligation to disclose [expert] before trial, and the trial court did not err in permitting her to testify."

Snider v. Stanley, 44 S.W.3d 713, 716 (Tex.App.—Beaumont 2001, pet. denied). "[Ds] did not designate [their expert] as soon as he was retained, employed, or otherwise in their control. Instead, they waited until 30 days before trial. We hold the trial court did not abuse its discretion in finding [Ds] did not supplement their discovery responses 'reasonably promptly.'"

TRCP 196. REQUESTS FOR PRODUCTION & INSPECTION TO PARTIES; REQUESTS & MOTIONS FOR ENTRY UPON PROPERTY

196.1 Request for Production and Inspection to Parties.

(a) *Request.* A party may serve on another party—no later than 30 days before the end of the discovery period—a request for production or for inspection, to inspect, sample, test, photograph and copy documents or tangible things within the scope of discovery.

(b) *Contents of request.* The request must specify the items to be produced or inspected, either by individual item or by category, and describe with reasonable particularity each item and category. The request must specify a reasonable time (on or after the date on which the response is due) and place for production. If the requesting party will sample or test the requested items, the means, manner and procedure for testing or sampling must be described with sufficient specificity to inform the producing party of the means, manner, and procedure for testing or sampling.

(c) *Requests for production of medical or mental health records regarding nonparties.*

(1) *Service of request on nonparty.* If a party requests another party to produce medical or mental health records regarding a nonparty, the requesting party must serve the nonparty with the request for production under Rule 21a.

(2) *Exceptions.* A party is not required to serve the request for production on a nonparty whose medical records are sought if:

(A) the nonparty signs a release of the records that is effective as to the requesting party;

(B) the identity of the nonparty whose records are sought will not directly or indirectly be disclosed by production of the records; or

(C) the court, upon a showing of good cause by the party seeking the records, orders that service is not required.

(3) *Confidentiality.* Nothing in this rule excuses compliance with laws concerning the confidentiality of medical or mental health records.

196.2 Response to Request for Production and Inspection.

(a) *Time for response.* The responding party must serve a written response on the requesting party within 30 days after service of the request, except that a defendant served with a request before the defendant's answer is due need not respond until 50 days after service of the request.

(b) *Content of response.* With respect to each item or category of items, the responding party must state objections and assert privileges as required by these rules, and state, as appropriate, that:

(1) production, inspection, or other requested action will be permitted as requested;

(2) the requested items are being served on the requesting party with the response;

(3) production, inspection, or other requested action will take place at a specified time and place, if the responding party is objecting to the time and place of production; or

(4) no items have been identified—after a diligent search—that are responsive to the request.

196.3 Production.

(a) *Time and place of production.* Subject to any objections stated in the response, the responding party must produce the requested documents or tangible things within the person's possession, custody or control at either the time and place requested or the time and place stated in the response, unless otherwise agreed by the parties or ordered by the court, and must provide the requesting party a reasonable opportunity to inspect them.

(b) *Copies.* The responding party may produce copies in lieu of originals unless a question is raised as to the authenticity of the original or in the circumstances it would be unfair to produce copies in lieu of originals. If originals are produced, the responding party is entitled to retain the originals while the requesting party inspects and copies them.

(c) *Organization.* The responding party must either produce documents and tangible things as they are kept in the usual course of business or organize and label them to correspond with the categories in the request.

196.4 Electronic or Magnetic Data. To obtain discovery of data or information that exists in electronic or magnetic form, the requesting party must specifically request production of electronic or magnetic data and specify the form in which the requesting party wants it produced. The responding party must produce the electronic or magnetic data that is responsive to the

request and is reasonably available to the responding party in its ordinary course of business. If the responding party cannot—through reasonable efforts—retrieve the data or information requested or produce it in the form requested, the responding party must state an objection complying with these rules. If the court orders the responding party to comply with the request, the court must also order that the requesting party pay the reasonable expenses of any extraordinary steps required to retrieve and produce the information.

196.5 Destruction or Alteration. Testing, sampling or examination of an item may not destroy or materially alter an item unless previously authorized by the court.

196.6 Expenses of Production. Unless otherwise ordered by the court for good cause, the expense of producing items will be borne by the responding party and the expense of inspecting, sampling, testing, photographing, and copying items produced will be borne by the requesting party.

196.7 Request or Motion for Entry Upon Property.

(a) ***Request or motion.*** A party may gain entry on designated land or other property to inspect, measure, survey, photograph, test, or sample the property or any designated object or operation thereon by serving—no later than 30 days before the end of any applicable discovery period—

(1) a request on all parties if the land or property belongs to a party, or

(2) a motion and notice of hearing on all parties and the nonparty if the land or property belongs to a nonparty. If the identity or address of the nonparty is unknown and cannot be obtained through reasonable diligence, the court must permit service by means other than those specified in Rule 21a that are reasonably calculated to give the nonparty notice of the motion and hearing.

(b) ***Time, place, and other conditions.*** The request for entry upon a party's property, or the order for entry upon a nonparty's property, must state the time, place, manner, conditions, and scope of the inspection, and must specifically describe any desired means, manner, and procedure for testing or sampling, and the person or persons by whom the inspection, testing, or sampling is to be made.

(c) ***Response to request for entry.***

(1) *Time to respond.* The responding party must serve a written response on the requesting party within 30 days after service of the request, except that a defendant served with a request before the defendant's answer is due need not respond until 50 days after service of the request.

(2) *Content of response.* The responding party must state objections and assert privileges as required by these rules, and state, as appropriate, that:

(A) entry or other requested action will be permitted as requested;

(B) entry or other requested action will take place at a specified time and place, if the responding party is objecting to the time and place of production; or

(C) entry or other requested action cannot be permitted for reasons stated in the response.

(d) ***Requirements for order for entry on nonparty's property.*** An order for entry on a nonparty's property may issue only for good cause shown and only if the land, property, or object thereon as to which discovery is sought is relevant to the subject matter of the action.

See also *O'Connor's Texas Rules*, "Discovery," ch. 6, p. 485; *O'Connor's Texas Forms*, FORMS 6I, 6K.

ANNOTATIONS

In re Weekley Homes, L.P., 295 S.W.3d 309, 314-15 (Tex.2009). "[E-]mail communications constitute 'electronic data,' and their characterization as such does not change when they are deleted from a party's inbox. Thus, deleted emails are within Rule 196.4's purview.... [I]t is a simple matter to request emails that have been deleted; knowledge as to the particular method or means of retrieving them is not necessary at the requesting stage of discovery. Once a specific request is made the parties can, and should, communicate as to the particularities of a party's computer storage system and potential methods of retrieval to assess the feasibility of their recovery. But even though it was not stated in [P's] written request that deleted emails were included within its scope, that [P] thought they were and was seeking this form of electronic information became abundantly clear in the course of discovery and before the hearing on the motion to compel. The purpose of Rule 196.4's specificity requirement is to ensure that requests for electronic information are clearly understood and disputes avoided. Because the scope of [P's] requests was understood before trial court inter-

vention, [D] was not prejudiced by [P's] failure to follow the rule and the trial court did not abuse its discretion by ordering production of the deleted emails. To ensure compliance with the rules and avoid confusion, however, parties seeking production of deleted emails should expressly request them." *See also* ***In re Harris***, 315 S.W.3d 685, 700-01 (Tex.App.—Houston [1st Dist.] 2010, orig. proceeding).

In re Colonial Pipeline Co., 968 S.W.2d 938, 942 (Tex.1998). "While [Ps] may be entitled to production of any relevant discovery from the related cases 'as they are kept in the usual course of business,' [Ds] cannot be forced to prepare an inventory of the documents for [Ps]."

Dillard Dept. Stores v. Hall, 909 S.W.2d 491, 492 (Tex.1995). "[P] admits that he wants the document production to explore whether he can in good faith allege racial discrimination. This is the very kind of 'fishing expedition' that is not allowable under [TRCP 196.1]."

Sears, Roebuck & Co. v. Ramirez, 824 S.W.2d 558, 559 (Tex.1992). The trial court ordered D to produce its annual reports *and* its federal income-tax statements. The Texas Supreme Court held there was "no justification for requiring [D] to produce the same information in different form."

In re Waste Mgmt., 392 S.W.3d 861, 874-75 (Tex. App.—Texarkana 2013, orig. proceeding). "[P's] first and third requests [for electronic discovery] contained the following instruction: 'Any and all data or information which is in electronic or magnetic form should be produced in a reasonable manner.' [¶] [D] cites [***In re Weekley Homes, L.P.***, 295 S.W.3d 309 (Tex.2009),] for the proposition that requests for production of electronic records must be 'clearly understood' so that disputes can be avoided. The Texas Supreme Court, though, was not referring to specificity concerning the file format, but was referring to the subject matter being requested, 'deleted emails.' We do not read ***Weekley Homes*** as requiring ... that the requesting party must specify the exact computer file format. [¶] A request for reasonably useable or a reasonable manner is sufficient. It provides some flexibility to the producing party. For example, a request for docx file format used by Microsoft Word 2010 might require some producing parties to purchase the specific software requested and expend resources converting files to the requested format. On the other hand, if the request was simply for a 'reasonably useable' electronic discovery, the producing party could produce files in Word Perfect X4 format instead. [I]f a party feels a request is too ambiguous, that party should contact the opposing side. A small amount of ambiguity, though, does not give the producing party *carte blanche* to do whatever it wants. [W]e have not been directed to any communication in which [P] agreed PDF files would suffice. [P's] request that the form be a 'reasonable manner' is sufficiently specific."

In re Family Dollar Stores, No. 09-11-00432-CV (Tex.App.—Beaumont 2011, orig. proceeding) (memo op.; 11-3-11). "Rule 196.4 ... requires a specific request for production of electronic or magnetic data, and the request is required to specify the form in which the data is to be produced. [¶] [R]equiring a party to reduce raw data from an electronic database to a paper report or to a list in an electronic form requires [D] to make a list that does not currently exist. Because Rule 196.1 does not allow one party to require that others make lists, the trial court's amended discovery order is broader than the scope of discovery permitted by the [TRCPs]."

In re SWEPI L.P., 103 S.W.3d 578, 584 (Tex. App.—San Antonio 2003, orig. proceeding). "It does not appear any Texas court has directly addressed what constitutes 'good cause' for a discovery order allowing entry onto land. Generally, 'good cause' for a discovery order is shown where ... (1) the discovery sought is relevant and material, that is, the information will in some way aid the movant in the preparation or defense of the case; and (2) the substantial equivalent of the material cannot be obtained through other means."

In re Lincoln Elec. Co., 91 S.W.3d 432, 437 (Tex. App.—Beaumont 2002, orig. proceeding). "In keeping with the overall spirit of non-waiver apparent in the ... discovery rules ..., we believe [TRCP 196.2(b)] permits a responding party ... to make 'objections' to such things as vagueness, overbreadth, [and] relevance ..., have these 'objections' ruled upon, and then make any assertions of privilege ... at a later time."

TRCP 197. INTERROGATORIES TO PARTIES

197.1 Interrogatories. A party may serve on another party—no later than 30 days before the end of the discovery period—written interrogatories to inquire about any matter within the scope of discovery except matters covered by Rule 195. An interrogatory may in-

quire whether a party makes a specific legal or factual contention and may ask the responding party to state the legal theories and to describe in general the factual bases for the party's claims or defenses, but interrogatories may not be used to require the responding party to marshal all of its available proof or the proof the party intends to offer at trial.

197.2 Response to Interrogatories.

(a) ***Time for response.*** The responding party must serve a written response on the requesting party within 30 days after service of the interrogatories, except that a defendant served with interrogatories before the defendant's answer is due need not respond until 50 days after service of the interrogatories.

(b) ***Content of response.*** A response must include the party's answers to the interrogatories and may include objections and assertions of privilege as required under these rules.

(c) ***Option to produce records.*** If the answer to an interrogatory may be derived or ascertained from public records, from the responding party's business records, or from a compilation, abstract or summary of the responding party's business records, and the burden of deriving or ascertaining the answer is substantially the same for the requesting party as for the responding party, the responding party may answer the interrogatory by specifying and, if applicable, producing the records or compilation, abstract or summary of the records. The records from which the answer may be derived or ascertained must be specified in sufficient detail to permit the requesting party to locate and identify them as readily as can the responding party. If the responding party has specified business records, the responding party must state a reasonable time and place for examination of the documents. The responding party must produce the documents at the time and place stated, unless otherwise agreed by the parties or ordered by the court, and must provide the requesting party a reasonable opportunity to inspect them.

(d) ***Verification required; exceptions.*** A responding party—not an agent or attorney as otherwise permitted by Rule 14—must sign the answers under oath except that:

(1) when answers are based on information obtained from other persons, the party may so state, and

(2) a party need not sign answers to interrogatories about persons with knowledge of relevant facts, trial witnesses, and legal contentions.

197.3 Use. Answers to interrogatories may be used only against the responding party. An answer to an interrogatory inquiring about matters described in Rule 194.2(c) and (d) that has been amended or supplemented is not admissible and may not be used for impeachment.

See also *O'Connor's Texas Rules*, "General Rules for Discovery," ch. 6-A, p. 491; "Interrogatories," ch. 6-G, p. 630; *O'Connor's Texas Forms*, FORMS 6G.

ANNOTATIONS

Morgan v. Anthony, 27 S.W.3d 928, 929 (Tex. 2000). See annotation under TRCP 166a, *SJ Evidence*, p. 1115.

Ticor Title Ins. v. Lacy, 803 S.W.2d 265, 266 (Tex. 1991). "'A party must be able to rely on the interrogatories and answers of other parties in the same suit. Otherwise, a multiparty case would require redundant interrogatories with identical questions and answers.'"

Palmer v. Espey Huston & Assocs., 84 S.W.3d 345, 356 (Tex.App.—Corpus Christi 2002, pet. denied). "[I]nterrogatories may be used only against the responding party."

TRCP 198. REQUESTS FOR ADMISSIONS

198.1 Request for Admissions. A party may serve on another party—no later than 30 days before the end of the discovery period written requests that the other party admit the truth of any matter within the scope of discovery, including statements of opinion or of fact or of the application of law to fact, or the genuineness of any documents served with the request or otherwise made available for inspection and copying. Each matter for which an admission is requested must be stated separately.

198.2 Response to Requests for Admissions.

(a) ***Time for response.*** The responding party must serve a written response on the requesting party within 30 days after service of the request, except that a defendant served with a request before the defendant's answer is due need not respond until 50 days after service of the request.

(b) ***Content of response.*** Unless the responding party states an objection or asserts a privilege, the responding party must specifically admit or deny the request or explain in detail the reasons that the responding party cannot admit or deny the request. A response must fairly meet the substance of the request. The responding party may qualify an answer, or deny a re-

quest in part, only when good faith requires. Lack of information or knowledge is not a proper response unless the responding party states that a reasonable inquiry was made but that the information known or easily obtainable is insufficient to enable the responding party to admit or deny. An assertion that the request presents an issue for trial is not a proper response.

(c) ***Effect of failure to respond.*** If a response is not timely served, the request is considered admitted without the necessity of a court order.

198.3 Effect of Admissions; Withdrawal or Amendment. Any admission made by a party under this rule may be used solely in the pending action and not in any other proceeding. A matter admitted under this rule is conclusively established as to the party making the admission unless the court permits the party to withdraw or amend the admission. The court may permit the party to withdraw or amend the admission if:

(a) the party shows good cause for the withdrawal or amendment; and

(b) the court finds that the parties relying upon the responses and deemed admissions will not be unduly prejudiced and that the presentation of the merits of the action will be subserved by permitting the party to amend or withdraw the admission.

See also *O'Connor's Texas Rules*, "General Rules for Discovery," ch. 6-A, p. 491; "Requests for Admissions," ch. 6-H, p. 638; *O'Connor's Texas Forms*, FORMS 6H.

ANNOTATIONS

Wheeler v. Green, 157 S.W.3d 439, 442 (Tex.2005). "[W]ithdrawing deemed admissions ... is proper upon a showing of (1) good cause, and (2) no undue prejudice. Good cause is established by showing the failure [to respond] was an accident or mistake, not intentional or the result of conscious indifference. *At 443:* Undue prejudice depends on whether withdrawing an admission ... will delay trial or significantly hamper the opposing party's ability to prepare for [trial]." *See also* ***Marino v. King***, 355 S.W.3d 629, 633 (Tex.2011); ***Wal-Mart Stores v. Deggs***, 968 S.W.2d 354, 356 (Tex. 1998).

In re Sewell, 472 S.W.3d 449, 456 (Tex.App.—Texarkana 2015, orig. proceeding), *disapproved on other grounds*, ***In re Bayview Loan Servicing, LLC***, ___ S.W.3d ___ (Tex.App.—Texarkana 2017, orig. proceeding) (No. 06-17-00040-CV; 3-31-17). "[W]here a party moves to withdraw deemed admissions that are merit-preclusive, due-process requires the party opposing withdrawal to prove that the moving party's failure to answer the admissions resulted from flagrant bad faith or callous disregard of the rules. Thus, although a party moving to withdraw admissions ordinarily must prove the requirements of Rule 198.3, when the deemed admissions are merit-preclusive, good cause exists absent bad faith or callous disregard of the rules by the party seeking the withdrawal. Moreover, in such instances, it is presumed that presentation of the merits would be served by allowing withdrawal of the deemed admissions." (Internal quotes omitted.) *See also* ***Medina v. Raven***, 492 S.W.3d 53, 61-62 (Tex. App.—Houston [1st Dist.] 2016, no pet.).

Duff v. Spearman, 322 S.W.3d 869, 884 (Tex. App.—Beaumont 2010, pet. denied). "A party that, without objection, allows the trial court to admit evidence controverting a matter deemed admitted may waive his right to rely upon the matter."

TRCP 199. DEPOSITIONS UPON ORAL EXAMINATION

199.1 Oral Examination; Alternative Methods of Conducting or Recording.

(a) ***Generally.*** A party may take the testimony of any person or entity by deposition on oral examination before any officer authorized by law to take depositions. The testimony, objections, and any other statements during the deposition must be recorded at the time they are given or made.

(b) ***Depositions by telephone or other remote electronic means.*** A party may take an oral deposition by telephone or other remote electronic means if the party gives reasonable prior written notice of intent to do so. For the purposes of these rules, an oral deposition taken by telephone or other remote electronic means is considered as having been taken in the district and at the place where the witness is located when answering the questions. The officer taking the deposition may be located with the party noticing the deposition instead of with the witness if the witness is placed under oath by a person who is present with the witness and authorized to administer oaths in that jurisdiction.

(c) ***Nonstenographic recording.*** Any party may cause a deposition upon oral examination to be recorded by other than stenographic means, including videotape recording. The party requesting the nonstenographic recording will be responsible for obtaining a person authorized by law to administer the oath and for assuring that the recording will be intelligible,

accurate, and trustworthy. At least five days prior to the deposition, the party must serve on the witness and all parties a notice, either in the notice of deposition or separately, that the deposition will be recorded by other than stenographic means. This notice must state the method of nonstenographic recording to be used and whether the deposition will also be recorded stenographically. Any other party may then serve written notice designating another method of recording in addition to the method specified, at the expense of such other party unless the court orders otherwise.

199.2 Procedure for Noticing Oral Deposition.

(a) ***Time to notice deposition.*** A notice of intent to take an oral deposition must be served on the witness and all parties a reasonable time before the deposition is taken. An oral deposition may be taken outside the discovery period only by agreement of the parties or with leave of court.

(b) ***Content of notice.***

(1) *Identity of witness; organizations.* The notice must state the name of the witness, which may be either an individual or a public or private corporation, partnership, association, governmental agency, or other organization. If an organization is named as the witness, the notice must describe with reasonable particularity the matters on which examination is requested. In response, the organization named in the notice must—a reasonable time before the deposition—designate one or more individuals to testify on its behalf and set forth, for each individual designated, the matters on which the individual will testify. Each individual designated must testify as to matters that are known or reasonably available to the organization. This subdivision does not preclude taking a deposition by any other procedure authorized by these rules.

(2) *Time and place.* The notice must state a reasonable time and place for the oral deposition. The place may be in:

(A) the county of the witness's residence;

(B) the county where the witness is employed or regularly transacts business in person;

(C) the county of suit, if the witness is a party or a person designated by a party under Rule 199.2(b)(1);

(D) the county where the witness was served with the subpoena, or within 150 miles of the place of service, if the witness is not a resident of Texas or is a transient person; or

(E) subject to the foregoing, at any other convenient place directed by the court in which the cause is pending.

(3) *Alternative means of conducting and recording.* The notice must state whether the deposition is to be taken by telephone or other remote electronic means and identify the means. If the deposition is to be recorded by nonstenographic means, the notice may include the notice required by Rule 199.1(c).

(4) *Additional attendees.* The notice may include the notice concerning additional attendees required by Rule 199.5(a)(3).

(5) *Request for production of documents.* A notice may include a request that the witness produce at the deposition documents or tangible things within the scope of discovery and within the witness's possession, custody, or control. If the witness is a nonparty, the request must comply with Rule 205 and the designation of materials required to be identified in the subpoena must be attached to, or included in, the notice. The nonparty's response to the request is governed by Rules 176 and 205. When the witness is a party or subject to the control of a party, document requests under this subdivision are governed by Rules 193 and 196.

199.3 Compelling Witness to Attend. A party may compel the witness to attend the oral deposition by serving the witness with a subpoena under Rule 176. If the witness is a party or is retained by, employed by, or otherwise subject to the control of a party, however, service of the notice of oral deposition upon the party's attorney has the same effect as a subpoena served on the witness.

199.4 Objections to Time and Place of Oral Deposition. A party or witness may object to the time and place designated for an oral deposition by motion for protective order or by motion to quash the notice of deposition. If the motion is filed by the third business day after service of the notice of deposition, an objection to the time and place of a deposition stays the oral deposition until the motion can be determined.

199.5 Examination, Objection, and Conduct During Oral Depositions.

(a) ***Attendance.***

(1) *Witness.* The witness must remain in attendance from day to day until the deposition is begun and completed.

(2) *Attendance by party.* A party may attend an oral deposition in person, even if the deposition is taken by telephone or other remote electronic means. If a deposition is taken by telephone or other remote electronic means, the party noticing the deposition must make arrangements for all persons to attend by the same means. If the party noticing the deposition appears in person, any other party may appear by telephone or other remote electronic means if that party makes the necessary arrangements with the deposition officer and the party noticing the deposition.

(3) *Other attendees.* If any party intends to have in attendance any persons other than the witness, parties, spouses of parties, counsel, employees of counsel, and the officer taking the oral deposition, that party must give reasonable notice to all parties, either in the notice of deposition or separately, of the identity of the other persons.

(b) ***Oath; examination.*** Every person whose deposition is taken by oral examination must first be placed under oath. The parties may examine and cross-examine the witness. Any party, in lieu of participating in the examination, may serve written questions in a sealed envelope on the party noticing the oral deposition, who must deliver them to the deposition officer, who must open the envelope and propound them to the witness.

(c) ***Time limitation.*** No side may examine or cross-examine an individual witness for more than six hours. Breaks during depositions do not count against this limitation.

(d) ***Conduct during the oral deposition; conferences.*** The oral deposition must be conducted in the same manner as if the testimony were being obtained in court during trial. Counsel should cooperate with and be courteous to each other and to the witness. The witness should not be evasive and should not unduly delay the examination. Private conferences between the witness and the witness's attorney during the actual taking of the deposition are improper except for the purpose of determining whether a privilege should be asserted. Private conferences may be held, however, during agreed recesses and adjournments. If the lawyers and witnesses do not comply with this rule, the court may allow in evidence at trial statements, objections, discussions, and other occurrences during the oral deposition that reflect upon the credibility of the witness or the testimony.

(e) ***Objections.*** Objections to questions during the oral deposition are limited to "Objection, leading" and "Objection, form." Objections to testimony during the oral deposition are limited to "Objection, nonresponsive." These objections are waived if not stated as phrased during the oral deposition. All other objections need not be made or recorded during the oral deposition to be later raised with the court. The objecting party must give a clear and concise explanation of an objection if requested by the party taking the oral deposition, or the objection is waived. Argumentative or suggestive objections or explanations waive objection and may be grounds for terminating the oral deposition or assessing costs or other sanctions. The officer taking the oral deposition will not rule on objections but must record them for ruling by the court. The officer taking the oral deposition must not fail to record testimony because an objection has been made.

(f) ***Instructions not to answer.*** An attorney may instruct a witness not to answer a question during an oral deposition only if necessary to preserve a privilege, comply with a court order or these rules, protect a witness from an abusive question or one for which any answer would be misleading, or secure a ruling pursuant to paragraph (g). The attorney instructing the witness not to answer must give a concise, nonargumentative, nonsuggestive explanation of the grounds for the instruction if requested by the party who asked the question.

(g) ***Suspending the deposition.*** If the time limitations for the deposition have expired or the deposition is being conducted or defended in violation of these rules, a party or witness may suspend the oral deposition for the time necessary to obtain a ruling.

(h) ***Good faith required.*** An attorney must not ask a question at an oral deposition solely to harass or mislead the witness, for any other improper purpose, or without a good faith legal basis at the time. An attorney must not object to a question at an oral deposition, instruct the witness not to answer a question, or suspend the deposition unless there is a good faith factual and legal basis for doing so at the time.

199.6 Hearing on Objections. Any party may, at any reasonable time, request a hearing on an objection or privilege asserted by an instruction not to answer or suspension of the deposition; provided the failure of a party to obtain a ruling prior to trial does not waive any objection or privilege. The party seeking to avoid discov-

ery must present any evidence necessary to support the objection or privilege either by testimony at the hearing or by affidavits served on opposing parties at least seven days before the hearing. If the court determines that an *in camera* review of some or all of the requested discovery is necessary to rule, answers to the deposition questions may be made in camera, to be transcribed and sealed in the event the privilege is sustained, or made in an affidavit produced to the court in a sealed wrapper.

See also CPRC §20.001; Gov't Code §§52.059, 154.101, 154.112 (imposes joint and several liability for cost of deposition on attorney who asks first question and attorney's firm); TRE 603; ***O'Connor's Texas Rules***, "General Rules for Discovery," ch. 6-A, p. 491; "Depositions," ch. 6-F, p. 604; ***O'Connor's Texas Forms***, FORMS 6F:1-3. For important information about the deposition procedure, see Court Reporters Certification Board, *Uniform Format Manual for Texas Reporters' Records* (2010), §§3.4 cmt., 3.7 cmt., www.txcourts.gov/rules-forms/rules-standards.

ANNOTATIONS

In re Reaud, 286 S.W.3d 574, 580 (Tex.App.—Beaumont 2009, orig. proceeding). "The third category of nonparty witnesses [in TRCP 199.3] are those ... 'otherwise controlled,' [a term that] is not defined by the procedural rules. [The term is limited] to include only control of the same kind, class, or nature as the types of control parties would have over employees or retained experts. ... While [TRCP 199.3 and 205.1] contain language that allow them to reach beyond retained experts and employees, it is now clear that these two rules do not extend to nonparties over whom the party does not have the type of control as it has over an employee or a retained expert."

In re Turner, 243 S.W.3d 843, 846 (Tex.App.—Eastland 2008, orig. proceeding). "When a deposition takes place outside one of the counties specifically identified by Rule 199.2(b)(2), it must be at a *convenient place*. This imposes an additional requirement and may, therefore, alter the analysis. But because it is clearly easier for an international traveler to travel to Dallas than Stephenville, if the trial court was authorized to order [relator] to come to Stephenville for a deposition, it did not abuse its discretion by moving the deposition to Dallas." *See also* ***In re Alamex, NV***, No. 01-12-00037-CV (Tex.App.—Houston [1st Dist.] 2012, orig. proceeding) (memo op.; 5-3-12) (convenience is determined from witness's viewpoint).

TRCP 200. DEPOSITIONS UPON WRITTEN QUESTIONS

200.1 Procedure for Noticing Deposition Upon Written Questions.

(a) ***Who may be noticed; when.*** A party may take the testimony of any person or entity by deposition on written questions before any person authorized by law to take depositions on written questions. A notice of intent to take the deposition must be served on the witness and all parties at least 20 days before the deposition is taken. A deposition on written questions may be taken outside the discovery period only by agreement of the parties or with leave of court. The party noticing the deposition must also deliver to the deposition officer a copy of the notice and of all written questions to be asked during the deposition.

(b) ***Content of notice.*** The notice must comply with Rules 199.1(b), 199.2(b), and 199.5(a)(3). If the witness is an organization, the organization must comply with the requirements of that provision. The notice also may include a request for production of documents as permitted by Rule 199.2(b)(5), the provisions of which will govern the request, service, and response.

200.2 Compelling Witness to Attend. A party may compel the witness to attend the deposition on written questions by serving the witness with a subpoena under Rule 176. If the witness is a party or is retained by, employed by, or otherwise subject to the control of a party, however, service of the deposition notice upon the party's attorney has the same effect as a subpoena served on the witness.

200.3 Questions and Objections.

(a) ***Direct questions.*** The direct questions to be propounded to the witness must be attached to the notice.

(b) ***Objections and additional questions.*** Within ten days after the notice and direct questions are served, any party may object to the direct questions and serve cross-questions on all other parties. Within five days after cross-questions are served, any party may object to the cross-questions and serve redirect questions on all other parties. Within three days after redirect questions are served, any party may object to the redirect questions and serve recross questions on all other parties. Objections to recross questions must be served within five days after the earlier of when recross questions are served or the time of the deposition on written questions.

(c) ***Objections to form of questions.*** Objections to the form of a question are waived unless asserted in accordance with this subdivision.

200.4 Conducting the Deposition Upon Written Questions. The deposition officer must: take the

deposition on written questions at the time and place designated; record the testimony of the witness under oath in response to the questions; and prepare, certify, and deliver the deposition transcript in accordance with Rule 203. The deposition officer has authority when necessary to summon and swear an interpreter to facilitate the taking of the deposition.

See also CPRC §20.001; Gov't Code §§154.101, 154.112; *O'Connor's Texas Rules*, "General Rules for Discovery," ch. 6-A, p. 491; "Depositions," ch. 6-F, p. 604; *O'Connor's Texas Forms*, FORMS 6F:4-6.

ANNOTATIONS

In re Toyota Motor Corp., 191 S.W.3d 498, 503 (Tex.App.—Waco 2006, orig. proceeding). "[D's] counsel [was ordered not to] be present when the depositions on written questions are conducted. [D] objects to being forced to rely on 'canned interrogatory answers prepared by [P's] counsel.' However, attorneys are not to answer written depositions for their clients. Thus, a deposition officer, not [Ps'] counsel, will record [the] answers to [D's] deposition questions."

St. Luke's Episcopal Hosp. v. Garcia, 928 S.W.2d 307, 310 (Tex.App.—Houston [14th Dist.] 1996, orig. proceeding). "Because relator has no objection to the form of [the] written questions, relator claims the provision in [TRCP 200] regarding timeliness of objections is inapplicable. We agree. In its objections to the deposition notice and subpoena duces tecum, relator's primary objections are substantive objections relating to privilege. We hold that the ten-day limitation in [TRCP 200] is inapplicable to substantive objections."

TRCP 201. DEPOSITIONS IN FOREIGN JURISDICTIONS FOR USE IN TEXAS PROCEEDINGS; DEPOSITIONS IN TEXAS FOR USE IN FOREIGN PROCEEDINGS

201.1 Depositions in Foreign Jurisdictions for Use in Texas Proceedings.

(a) ***Generally.*** A party may take a deposition on oral examination or written questions of any person or entity located in another state or a foreign country for use in proceedings in this State. The deposition may be taken by:

(1) notice;

(2) letter rogatory, letter of request, or other such device;

(3) agreement of the parties; or

(4) court order.

(b) ***By notice.*** A party may take the deposition by notice in accordance with these rules as if the deposition were taken in this State, except that the deposition officer may be a person authorized to administer oaths in the place where the deposition is taken.

(c) ***By letter rogatory.*** On motion by a party, the court in which an action is pending must issue a letter rogatory on terms that are just and appropriate, regardless of whether any other manner of obtaining the deposition is impractical or inconvenient. The letter must:

(1) be addressed to the appropriate authority in the jurisdiction in which the deposition is to be taken;

(2) request and authorize that authority to summon the witness before the authority at a time and place stated in the letter for examination on oral or written questions; and

(3) request and authorize that authority to cause the witness's testimony to be reduced to writing and returned, together with any items marked as exhibits, to the party requesting the letter rogatory.

(d) ***By letter of request or other such device.*** On motion by a party, the court in which an action is pending, or the clerk of that court, must issue a letter of request or other such device in accordance with an applicable treaty or international convention on terms that are just and appropriate. The letter or other device must be issued regardless of whether any other manner of obtaining the deposition is impractical or inconvenient. The letter or other device must:

(1) be in the form prescribed by the treaty or convention under which it is issued, as presented by the movant to the court or clerk; and

(2) must state the time, place, and manner of the examination of the witness.

(e) ***Objections to form of letter rogatory, letter of request, or other such device.*** In issuing a letter rogatory, letter of request, or other such device, the court must set a time for objecting to the form of the device. A party must make any objection to the form of the device in writing and serve it on all other parties by the time set by the court, or the objection is waived.

(f) ***Admissibility of evidence.*** Evidence obtained in response to a letter rogatory, letter of request, or other such device is not inadmissible merely because it

is not a verbatim transcript, or the testimony was not taken under oath, or for any similar departure from the requirements for depositions taken within this State under these rules.

(g) *Deposition by electronic means.* A deposition in another jurisdiction may be taken by telephone, videoconference, teleconference, or other electronic means under the provisions of Rule 199.

201.2 Depositions in Texas for Use in Proceedings in Foreign Jurisdictions. If a court of record of any other state or foreign jurisdiction issues a mandate, writ, or commission that requires a witness's oral or written deposition testimony in this State, the witness may be compelled to appear and testify in the same manner and by the same process used for taking testimony in a proceeding pending in this State.

See also CPRC §§20.001, 20.002; *O'Connor's Texas Rules*, "General Rules for Discovery," ch. 6-A, p. 491; "Depositions," ch. 6-F, p. 604; *O'Connor's Texas Forms*, FORMS 6F:1-6.

ANNOTATIONS

In re Issuance of Subpoenas for the Depositions of Darrell D. Bennett et al., 502 S.W.3d 373, 377-78 (Tex.App.—Houston [14th Dist.] 2016, no pet.). "In ***Ex parte Taylor***, [220 S.W. 74 (Tex.1920),] the [Supreme Court] concluded that the court with jurisdiction over the underlying case is generally charged with determining the relevancy and materiality of evidence sought by a party seeking a deposition in Texas under letters rogatory, while the Texas court has the obligation to protect the witness's legal rights, including, for example, the witness's right to avoid compelled production of privileged evidence. [¶] The trial court did not have the authority to quash or limit the depositions of the [Texas residents] based on a belief that the discovery is irrelevant. To get relief on that basis, the [Texas residents] must seek relief from the Wyoming trial court [that issued the letters rogatory]."

Kugle v. DaimlerChrysler Corp., 88 S.W.3d 355, 362 (Tex.App.—San Antonio 2002, pet. denied). "[Ps] contend that the trial court erred in admitting the deposition testimony of [three deponents] because the depositions were taken in Mexico but the witnesses were only sworn in by a Texas notary public. However, a foreign deposition may be taken by any notary public. [T]he trial court did not abuse its discretion in admitting the depositions."

TRCP 202. DEPOSITIONS BEFORE SUIT OR TO INVESTIGATE CLAIMS

202.1 Generally. A person may petition the court for an order authorizing the taking of a deposition on oral examination or written questions either:

(a) to perpetuate or obtain the person's own testimony or that of any other person for use in an anticipated suit; or

(b) to investigate a potential claim or suit.

202.2 Petition. The petition must:

(a) be verified;

(b) be filed in a proper court of any county:

(1) where venue of the anticipated suit may lie, if suit is anticipated; or

(2) where the witness resides, if no suit is yet anticipated;

(c) be in the name of the petitioner;

(d) state either:

(1) that the petitioner anticipates the institution of a suit in which the petitioner may be a party; or

(2) that the petitioner seeks to investigate a potential claim by or against petitioner;

(e) state the subject matter of the anticipated action, if any, and the petitioner's interest therein;

(f) if suit is anticipated, either:

(1) state the names of the persons petitioner expects to have interests adverse to petitioner's in the anticipated suit, and the addresses and telephone numbers for such persons; or

(2) state that the names, addresses, and telephone numbers of persons petitioner expects to have interests adverse to petitioner's in the anticipated suit cannot be ascertained through diligent inquiry, and describe those persons;

(g) state the names, addresses and telephone numbers of the persons to be deposed, the substance of the testimony that the petitioner expects to elicit from each, and the petitioner's reasons for desiring to obtain the testimony of each; and

(h) request an order authorizing the petitioner to take the depositions of the persons named in the petition.

202.3 Notice and Service.

(a) ***Personal service on witnesses and persons named.*** At least 15 days before the date of the hearing on the petition, the petitioner must serve the petition

and a notice of the hearing—in accordance with Rule 21a—on all persons petitioner seeks to depose and, if suit is anticipated, on all persons petitioner expects to have interests adverse to petitioner's in the anticipated suit.

(b) *Service by publication on persons not named.*

(1) *Manner.* Unnamed persons described in the petition whom the petitioner expects to have interests adverse to petitioner's in the anticipated suit, if any, may be served by publication with the petition and notice of the hearing. The notice must state the place for the hearing and the time it will be held, which must be more than 14 days after the first publication of the notice. The petition and notice must be published once each week for two consecutive weeks in the newspaper of broadest circulation in the county in which the petition is filed, or if no such newspaper exists, in the newspaper of broadest circulation in the nearest county where a newspaper is published.

(2) *Objection to depositions taken on notice by publication.* Any interested party may move, in the proceeding or by bill of review, to suppress any deposition, in whole or in part, taken on notice by publication, and may also attack or oppose the deposition by any other means available.

(c) *Service in probate cases.* A petition to take a deposition in anticipation of an application for probate of a will, and notice of the hearing on the petition, may be served by posting as prescribed by Section 33(f)(2) of the Probate Code.[1] The notice and petition must be directed to all parties interested in the testator's estate and must comply with the requirements of Section 33(c) of the Probate Code[2] insofar as they may be applicable.

(d) *Modification by order.* As justice or necessity may require, the court may shorten or lengthen the notice periods under this rule and may extend the notice period to permit service on any expected adverse party.

202.4 Order.

(a) *Required findings.* The court must order a deposition to be taken if, but only if, it finds that:

(1) allowing the petitioner to take the requested deposition may prevent a failure or delay of justice in an anticipated suit; or

(2) the likely benefit of allowing the petitioner to take the requested deposition to investigate a potential claim outweighs the burden or expense of the procedure.

(b) *Contents.* The order must state whether a deposition will be taken on oral examination or written questions. The order may also state the time and place at which a deposition will be taken. If the order does not state the time and place at which a deposition will be taken, the petitioner must notice the deposition as required by Rules 199 or 200. The order must contain any protections the court finds necessary or appropriate to protect the witness or any person who may be affected by the procedure.

202.5 Manner of Taking and Use. Except as otherwise provided in this rule, depositions authorized by this rule are governed by the rules applicable to depositions of nonparties in a pending suit. The scope of discovery in depositions authorized by this rule is the same as if the anticipated suit or potential claim had been filed. A court may restrict or prohibit the use of a deposition taken under this rule in a subsequent suit to protect a person who was not served with notice of the deposition from any unfair prejudice or to prevent abuse of this rule.

1. **Editor's note:** Now Estates Code §51.053.
2. **Editor's note:** Now Estates Code §§51.002, 51.003.

See also CPRC §20.001; ***O'Connor's Texas Rules***, "General Rules for Discovery," ch. 6-A, p. 491; "Depositions," ch. 6-F, p. 604; ***O'Connor's Texas Forms***, FORMS 6F:8-11.

ANNOTATIONS

In re DePinho, 505 S.W.3d 621, 624 (Tex.2016). "Rule [202] does not broadly authorize investigation of *any* action the petitioner may have based on future events—the petition must seek 'to investigate a potential claim or suit.' [A] 'claim' denotes an *existing*—rather than future or speculative—right that may be presently asserted. [A] suit may generally be maintained (i.e., it is a '*potential* ... suit') only when a court has jurisdiction over the matter.... [¶] Stated differently, a 'potential claim or suit' must be ripe."

In re Doe, 444 S.W.3d 603, 604 (Tex.2014). "Rule 202 ... allows 'a proper court' to authorize a deposition to investigate a potential claim before suit is filed. *At 608:* While Rule 202 is silent on the subject, we think it implicit ... that the court must have subject-matter jurisdiction over the anticipated action. The rule cannot be used, for example, to investigate a potential federal antitrust suit or patent suit, which can be brought

only in federal court. We must determine whether a proper court must also have personal jurisdiction over the potential defendant. For two reasons, we think it must. [¶] *First*: To allow discovery of a potential claim against a defendant over which the court would not have personal jurisdiction denies him the protection Texas procedure would otherwise afford. *At 610: Second*: To allow a Rule 202 court to order discovery without personal jurisdiction over a potential defendant unreasonably expands the rule. [¶] The burden is on the plaintiff in an action to plead allegations showing personal jurisdiction over the defendant. The same burden should be on a potential plaintiff under Rule 202. We recognize that this burden may be heavier in a case like this, in which the potential defendant's identity is unknown and may even be impossible to ascertain. But even so, Rule 202 does not guarantee access to information for every petitioner who claims to need it." *See also* ***In re City of Dallas***, 501 S.W.3d 71, 73 (Tex.2016).

In re Wolfe, 341 S.W.3d 932, 933 (Tex.2011). "[P]re-suit discovery 'is not an end within itself'; rather, it 'is in aid of a suit which is anticipated' and 'ancillary to the anticipated suit.' To prevent an end-run around discovery limitations that would govern the anticipated suit, Rule 202 restricts discovery in depositions to 'the same as if the anticipated suit or potential claim had been filed.' [A potential party] cannot obtain by Rule 202 what it would be denied in the anticipated action. [¶] Rule 202 is not a license for forced interrogations. Courts must strictly limit and carefully supervise pre-suit discovery to prevent abuse of the rule." *See also* ***In re Akzo Nobel Chem., Inc.***, 24 S.W.3d 919, 921 (Tex.App.—Beaumont 2000, orig. proceeding) (Rule 202 does not authorize trial court, before suit is filed, to order any form of discovery but deposition).

In re Does 1&2, 337 S.W.3d 862, 863 (Tex.2011). "[A] court may not order pre-suit discovery by agreement of the witness over the objections of other interested parties without making the findings required by Rule 202.4(a).... *At 865:* [P] argues that compliance with Rule 202 was excused because of its agreement with [D]. ... But [P] and [D] were not the only parties to the proceeding. Rule 202.3(a) requires that 'all persons petitioner expects to have interests adverse to petitioner's in the anticipated suit' be served with the petition and given notice of hearing. [P] asserted that relators would be defendants in the anticipated lawsuit, and by their motions to quash, relators made an appearance in the proceeding. [P] and [D] could not modify the procedures prescribed by Rule 202 by an agreement that did not include relators. [¶] ... Rule 202 expressly requires that discovery may be ordered 'only if' the required findings are made. The rule does not permit the findings to be implied from support in the record. [¶] The trial court clearly abused its discretion in failing to follow Rule 202." *See also* ***In re Cauley***, 437 S.W.3d 650, 657-58 (Tex.App.—Tyler 2014, orig. proceeding) (memo op.; 7-23-14) (respondent does not waive appeal of Rule 202 order that lacks required findings if respondent approves form, but not substance, of order).

TRCP 203. SIGNING, CERTIFICATION & USE OF ORAL & WRITTEN DEPOSITIONS

203.1 Signature and Changes.

(a) ***Deposition transcript to be provided to witness.*** The deposition officer must provide the original deposition transcript to the witness for examination and signature. If the witness is represented by an attorney at the deposition, the deposition officer must provide the transcript to the attorney instead of the witness.

(b) ***Changes by witness; signature.*** The witness may change responses as reflected in the deposition transcript by indicating the desired changes, in writing, on a separate sheet of paper, together with a statement of the reasons for making the changes. No erasures or obliterations of any kind may be made to the original deposition transcript. The witness must then sign the transcript under oath and return it to the deposition officer. If the witness does not return the transcript to the deposition officer within 20 days of the date the transcript was provided to the witness or the witness's attorney, the witness may be deemed to have waived the right to make the changes.

(c) ***Exceptions.*** The requirements of presentation and signature under this subdivision do not apply:

(1) if the witness and all parties waive the signature requirement;

(2) to depositions on written questions; or

(3) to nonstenographic recordings of oral depositions.

203.2 Certification. The deposition officer must file with the court, serve on all parties, and attach as part of the deposition transcript or nonstenographic recording of an oral deposition a certificate duly sworn by the officer stating:

(a) that the witness was duly sworn by the officer and that the transcript or nonstenographic recording of the oral deposition is a true record of the testimony given by the witness;

(b) that the deposition transcript, if any, was submitted to the witness or to the attorney for the witness for examination and signature, the date on which the transcript was submitted, whether the witness returned the transcript, and if so, the date on which it was returned.

(c) that changes, if any, made by the witness are attached to the deposition transcript;

(d) that the deposition officer delivered the deposition transcript or nonstenographic recording of an oral deposition in accordance with Rule 203.3;

(e) the amount of time used by each party at the deposition;

(f) the amount of the deposition officer's charges for preparing the original deposition transcript, which the clerk of the court must tax as costs; and

(g) that a copy of the certificate was served on all parties and the date of service.

203.3 Delivery.

(a) ***Endorsement; to whom delivered.*** The deposition officer must endorse the title of the action and "Deposition of (name of witness)" on the original deposition transcript (or a copy, if the original was not returned) or the original nonstenographic recording of an oral deposition, and must return:

(1) the transcript to the party who asked the first question appearing in the transcript, or

(2) the recording to the party who requested it.

(b) ***Notice.*** The deposition officer must serve notice of delivery on all other parties.

(c) ***Inspection and copying; copies.*** The party receiving the original deposition transcript or nonstenographic recording must make it available upon reasonable request for inspection and copying by any other party. Any party or the witness is entitled to obtain a copy of the deposition transcript or nonstenographic recording from the deposition officer upon payment of a reasonable fee.

203.4 Exhibits. At the request of a party, the original documents and things produced for inspection during the examination of the witness must be marked for identification by the deposition officer and annexed to the deposition transcript or nonstenographic recording. The person producing the materials may produce copies instead of originals if the party gives all other parties fair opportunity at the deposition to compare the copies with the originals. If the person offers originals rather than copies, the deposition officer must, after the conclusion of the deposition, make copies to be attached to the original deposition transcript or nonstenographic recording, and then return the originals to the person who produced them. The person who produced the originals must preserve them for hearing or trial and make them available for inspection or copying by any other party upon seven days' notice. Copies annexed to the original deposition transcript or nonstenographic recording may be used for all purposes.

203.5 Motion to Suppress. A party may object to any errors and irregularities in the manner in which the testimony is transcribed, signed, delivered, or otherwise dealt with by the deposition officer by filing a motion to suppress all or part of the deposition. If the deposition officer complies with Rule 203.3 at least one day before the case is called to trial, with regard to a deposition transcript, or 30 days before the case is called to trial, with regard to a nonstenographic recording, the party must file and serve a motion to suppress before trial commences to preserve the objections.

203.6 Use.

(a) ***Nonstenographic recording; transcription.*** A nonstenographic recording of an oral deposition, or a written transcription of all or part of such a recording, may be used to the same extent as a deposition taken by stenographic means. However, the court, for good cause shown, may require that the party seeking to use a nonstenographic recording or written transcription first obtain a complete transcript of the deposition recording from a certified court reporter. The court reporter's transcription must be made from the original or a certified copy of the deposition recording. The court reporter must, to the extent applicable, comply with the provisions of this rule, except that the court reporter must deliver the original transcript to the attorney requesting the transcript, and the court reporter's certificate must include a statement that the transcript is a true record of the nonstenographic recording. The party to whom the court reporter delivers the original transcript must make the transcript available, upon reasonable request, for inspection and copying by the witness or any party.

(b) ***Same proceeding.*** All or part of a deposition may be used for any purpose in the same proceeding in which it was taken. If the original is not filed, a certified copy may be used. "Same proceeding" includes a proceeding in a different court but involving the same subject matter and the same parties or their representatives or successors in interest. A deposition is admissible against a party joined after the deposition was taken if:

(1) the deposition is admissible pursuant to Rule 804(b)(1) of the Rules of Evidence, or

(2) that party has had a reasonable opportunity to redepose the witness and has failed to do so.

(c) ***Different proceeding.*** Depositions taken in different proceedings may be used as permitted by the Rules of Evidence.

See also Gov't Code §154.101; ***O'Connor's Texas Rules***, "General Rules for Discovery," ch. 6-A, p. 491; "Depositions," ch. 6-F, p. 604.

For important information about the deposition procedure, see Court Reporters Certification Board, *Uniform Format Manual for Texas Reporters' Records* (2010), §§3.4 cmt., 3.7 cmt., www.txcourts.gov/rules-forms/rules-standards.

ANNOTATIONS

Jones v. Colley, 820 S.W.2d 863, 866 (Tex.App.—Texarkana 1991, writ denied). "No rule requires that a deposition be read into the record or played before the jury in chronological order. A party, as a matter of trial strategy, is entitled to present his evidence in the order he believes constitutes the most effective presentation of his case, provided that it does not convey a *distinctly false* impression."

Klorer v. Block, 717 S.W.2d 754, 759 (Tex.App.—San Antonio 1986, writ ref'd n.r.e.). "The statement in [TRCP 203.5] that a deposition shall have been filed at least one entire day before the day of trial is a condition precedent to the filing of a *written* motion to suppress. This rule does not require that *all* depositions must be filed at least one entire day before the day of trial."

TRCP 204. PHYSICAL & MENTAL EXAMINATIONS

204.1 Motion and Order Required.

(a) ***Motion.*** A party may—no later than 30 days before the end of any applicable discovery period—move for an order compelling another party to:

(1) submit to a physical or mental examination by a qualified physician or a mental examination by a qualified psychologist; or

(2) produce for such examination a person in the other party's custody, conservatorship or legal control.

(b) ***Service.*** The motion and notice of hearing must be served on the person to be examined and all parties.

(c) ***Requirements for obtaining order.*** The court may issue an order for examination only for good cause shown and only in the following circumstances:

(1) when the mental or physical condition (including the blood group) of a party, or of a person in the custody, conservatorship or under the legal control of a party, is in controversy; or

(2) except as provided in Rule 204.4, an examination by a psychologist may be ordered when the party responding to the motion has designated a psychologist as a testifying expert or has disclosed a psychologist's records for possible use at trial.

(d) ***Requirements of order.*** The order must be in writing and must specify the time, place, manner, conditions, and scope of the examination and the person or persons by whom it is to be made.

204.2 Report of Examining Physician or Psychologist.

(a) ***Right to report.*** Upon request of the person ordered to be examined, the party causing the examination to be made must deliver to the person a copy of a detailed written report of the examining physician or psychologist setting out the findings, including results of all tests made, diagnoses and conclusions, together with like reports of all earlier examinations of the same condition. After delivery of the report, upon request of the party causing the examination, the party against whom the order is made must produce a like report of any examination made before or after the ordered examination of the same condition, unless the person examined is not a party and the party shows that the party is unable to obtain it. The court on motion may limit delivery of a report on such terms as are just. If a physician or psychologist fails or refuses to make a report the court may exclude the testimony if offered at the trial.

(b) ***Agreements; relationship to other rules.*** This subdivision applies to examinations made by agreement of the parties, unless the agreement expressly provides otherwise. This subdivision does not preclude discovery of a report of an examining physician or psychologist or the taking of a deposition of the physician or psychologist in accordance with the provisions of any other rule.

204.3 Effect of No Examination. If no examination is sought either by agreement or under this subdivision, the party whose physical or mental condition is in controversy must not comment to the court or jury concerning the party's willingness to submit to an examination, or on the right or failure of any other party to seek an examination.

204.4 Cases Arising Under Titles II or V, Family Code. In cases arising under Family Code Titles II or V, the court may—on its own initiative or on motion of a party—appoint:

(a) one or more psychologists or psychiatrists to make any and all appropriate mental examinations of the children who are the subject of the suit or of any other parties, and may make such appointment irrespective of whether a psychologist or psychiatrist has been designated by any party as a testifying expert;

(b) one or more experts who are qualified in paternity testing to take blood, body fluid, or tissue samples to conduct paternity tests as ordered by the court.

204.5 Definition. For the purpose of this rule, a psychologist is a person licensed or certified by a state or the District of Columbia as a psychologist.

See also TRE 510(d)(5); ***O'Connor's Texas Rules***, "General Rules for Discovery," ch. 6-A, p. 491; "Medical Records," ch. 6-J, p. 659; ***O'Connor's Texas Forms***, FORMS 6J.

ANNOTATIONS

In re H.E.B. Grocery Co., 492 S.W.3d 300, 303 (Tex. 2016). "The purpose of Rule 204.1's good-cause requirement is to balance the movant's right to a fair trial and the other party's right to privacy. To show good cause, the movant must (1) show that the requested examination is relevant to issues in controversy and will produce or likely lead to relevant evidence, (2) establish a reasonable nexus between the requested examination and the condition in controversy, and (3) demonstrate that the desired information cannot be obtained by less intrusive means."

In re Ten Hagen Excavating, Inc., 435 S.W.3d 859, 867-68 (Tex.App.—Dallas 2014, orig. proceeding). Rule 204.1's in-controversy requirement is "not met 'by mere conclusory allegations of the pleadings—nor by mere relevance to the case.' In cases involving physical injury, there are situations, however, where the pleadings alone are sufficient to place a party's physical condition in controversy. For instance, the [U.S.] Supreme Court has suggested that a plaintiff in a negligence action who claims physical injury as the result of a party's negligence places his 'physical injury clearly in controversy and provides the defendant with good cause for an examination to determine the existence and extent of such asserted injury' simply by seeking recovery for the alleged physical injury. This same precept applies equally to a defendant who asserts his physical condition as a defense to a claim."

TRCP 205. DISCOVERY FROM NONPARTIES

205.1 Forms of Discovery; Subpoena Requirement. A party may compel discovery from a nonparty—that is, a person who is not a party or subject to a party's control—only by obtaining a court order under Rules 196.7, 202, or 204, or by serving a subpoena compelling:

(a) an oral deposition;

(b) a deposition on written questions;

(c) a request for production of documents or tangible things, pursuant to Rule 199.2(b)(5) or Rule 200.1(b), served with a notice of deposition on oral examination or written questions; and

(d) a request for production of documents and tangible things under this rule.

205.2 Notice. A party seeking discovery by subpoena from a nonparty must serve, on the nonparty and all parties, a copy of the form of notice required under the rules governing the applicable form of discovery. A notice of oral or written deposition must be served before or at the same time that a subpoena compelling attendance or production under the notice is served. A notice to produce documents or tangible things under Rule 205.3 must be served at least 10 days before the subpoena compelling production is served.

205.3 Production of Documents and Tangible Things Without Deposition.

(a) ***Notice; subpoena.*** A party may compel production of documents and tangible things from a nonparty by serving—a reasonable time before the response is due but no later than 30 days before the end of any applicable discovery period—the notice required in Rule 205.2 and a subpoena compelling production or inspection of documents or tangible things.

(b) ***Contents of notice.*** The notice must state:

(1) the name of the person from whom production or inspection is sought to be compelled;

(2) a reasonable time and place for the production or inspection; and

(3) the items to be produced or inspected, either by individual item or by category, describing each item and category with reasonable particularity, and, if applicable, describing the desired testing and sampling with sufficient specificity to inform the nonparty of the means, manner, and procedure for testing or sampling.

(c) ***Requests for production of medical or mental health records of other nonparties.*** If a party requests a nonparty to produce medical or mental health records of another nonparty, the requesting party must serve the nonparty whose records are sought with the notice required under this rule. This requirement does not apply under the circumstances set forth in Rule 196.1(c)(2).

(d) ***Response.*** The nonparty must respond to the notice and subpoena in accordance with Rule 176.6.

(e) ***Custody, inspection and copying.*** The party obtaining the production must make all materials produced available for inspection by any other party on reasonable notice, and must furnish copies to any party who requests at that party's expense.

(f) ***Cost of production.*** A party requiring production of documents by a nonparty must reimburse the nonparty's reasonable costs of production.

See also *O'Connor's Texas Rules*, "Securing discovery from nonparties," ch. 6-A, §9.2, p. 503; "Depositions," ch. 6-F, p. 604; "Securing Documents & Tangible Things," ch. 6-I, p. 648; *O'Connor's Texas Forms*, FORM 6I:12.

ANNOTATIONS

In re Diversicare Gen. Partner, 41 S.W.3d 788, 794 (Tex.App.—Corpus Christi 2001, orig. proceeding), *overruled on other grounds*, ***In re Arriola***, 159 S.W.3d 670 (Tex.App.—Corpus Christi 2004, orig. proceeding). "[P]ersonal and clinical records do not have to be in the nonparty's possession to be described as nonparty records, they only have to be personal and clinical records *regarding* the nonparty."

TRCP 206 TO 214. REPEALED

TRCP 215. ABUSE OF DISCOVERY; SANCTIONS

215.1 Motion for Sanctions or Order Compelling Discovery. A party, upon reasonable notice to other parties and all other persons affected thereby, may apply for sanctions or an order compelling discovery as follows:

(a) ***Appropriate court.*** On matters relating to a deposition, an application for an order to a party may be made to the court in which the action is pending, or to any district court in the district where the deposition is being taken. An application for an order to a deponent who is not a party shall be made to the court in the district where the deposition is being taken. As to all other discovery matters, an application for an order will be made to the court in which the action is pending.

(b) ***Motion.***

(1) If a party or other deponent which is a corporation or other entity fails to make a designation under Rules 199.2(b)(1) or 200.1(b); or

(2) If a party, or other deponent, or a person designated to testify on behalf of a party or other deponent fails:

(A) to appear before the officer who is to take his deposition, after being served with a proper notice; or

(B) to answer a question propounded or submitted upon oral examination or upon written questions; or

(3) if a party fails:

(A) to serve answers or objections to interrogatories submitted under Rule 197, after proper service of the interrogatories; or

(B) to answer an interrogatory submitted under Rule 197; or

(C) to serve a written response to a request for inspection submitted under Rule 196, after proper service of the request; or

(D) to respond that discovery will be permitted as requested or fails to permit discovery as requested in response to a request for inspection submitted under Rule 196;

the discovering party may move for an order compelling a designation, an appearance, an answer or answers, or inspection or production in accordance with the request, or apply to the court in which the action is pending for the imposition of any sanction authorized by Rule 215.2(b) without the necessity of first having obtained a court order compelling such discovery.

When taking a deposition on oral examination, the proponent of the question may complete or adjourn the examination before he applies for an order.

If the court denies the motion in whole or in part, it may make such protective order as it would have been empowered to make on a motion pursuant to Rule 192.6.

(c) ***Evasive or incomplete answer.*** For purposes of this subdivision an evasive or incomplete answer is to be treated as a failure to answer.

(d) ***Disposition of motion to compel: award of expenses.*** If the motion is granted, the court shall, after opportunity for hearing, require a party or deponent whose conduct necessitated the motion or the party or attorney advising such conduct or both of them to pay, at such time as ordered by the court, the moving party the reasonable expenses incurred in obtaining the order, including attorney fees, unless the court finds that the opposition to the motion was substantially justified or that other circumstances make an award of expenses unjust. Such an order shall be subject to review on appeal from the final judgment.

If the motion is denied, the court may, after opportunity for hearing, require the moving party or attorney advising such motion to pay to the party or deponent who opposed the motion the reasonable expenses incurred in opposing the motion, including attorney fees, unless the court finds that the making of the motion was substantially justified or that other circumstances make an award of expenses unjust.

If the motion is granted in part and denied in part, the court may apportion the reasonable expenses incurred in relation to the motion among the parties and persons in a just manner.

In determining the amount of reasonable expenses, including attorney fees, to be awarded in connection with a motion, the trial court shall award expenses which are reasonable in relation to the amount of work reasonably expended in obtaining an order compelling compliance or in opposing a motion which is denied.

(e) ***Providing person's own statement.*** If a party fails to comply with any person's written request for the person's own statement as provided in Rule 192.3(h), the person who made the request may move for an order compelling compliance. If the motion is granted, the movant may recover the expenses incurred in obtaining the order, including attorney fees, which are reasonable in relation to the amount of work reasonably expended in obtaining the order.

215.2 Failure to Comply with Order or with Discovery Request.

(a) ***Sanctions by court in district where deposition is taken.*** If a deponent fails to appear or to be sworn or to answer a question after being directed to do so by a district court in the district in which the deposition is being taken, the failure may be considered a contempt of that court.

(b) ***Sanctions by court in which action is pending.*** If a party or an officer, director, or managing agent of a party or a person designated under Rules 199.2(b)(1) or 200.1(b) to testify on behalf of a party fails to comply with proper discovery requests or to obey an order to provide or permit discovery, including an order made under Rules 204 or 215.1, the court in which the action is pending may, after notice and hearing, make such orders in regard to the failure as are just, and among others the following:

(1) an order disallowing any further discovery of any kind or of a particular kind by the disobedient party;

(2) an order charging all or any portion of the expenses of discovery or taxable court costs or both against the disobedient party or the attorney advising him;

(3) an order that the matters regarding which the order was made or any other designated facts shall be taken to be established for the purposes of the action in accordance with the claim of the party obtaining the order;

(4) an order refusing to allow the disobedient party to support or oppose designated claims or defenses, or prohibiting him from introducing designated matters in evidence;

(5) an order striking out pleadings or parts thereof, or staying further proceedings until the order is obeyed, or dismissing with or without prejudice the action or proceedings or any part thereof, or rendering a judgment by default against the disobedient party;

(6) in lieu of any of the foregoing orders or in addition thereto, an order treating as a contempt of court the failure to obey any orders except an order to submit to a physical or mental examination;

(7) when a party has failed to comply with an order under Rule 204 requiring him to appear or produce another for examination, such orders as are listed in paragraphs (1), (2), (3), (4) or (5) of this subdivision, unless the person failing to comply shows that he is unable to appear or to produce such person for examination.

(8) In lieu of any of the foregoing orders or in addition thereto, the court shall require the party failing to obey the order or the attorney advising him, or both, to pay, at such time as ordered by the court, the reasonable expenses, including attorney fees, caused by the failure, unless the court finds that the failure was substantially justified or that other circumstances make an

award of expenses unjust. Such an order shall be subject to review on appeal from the final judgment.

(c) ***Sanction against nonparty for violation of Rules 196.7 or 205.3.*** If a nonparty fails to comply with an order under Rules 196.7 or 205.3, the court which made the order may treat the failure to obey as contempt of court.

215.3 Abuse of Discovery Process in Seeking, Making, or Resisting Discovery. If the court finds a party is abusing the discovery process in seeking, making or resisting discovery or if the court finds that any interrogatory or request for inspection or production is unreasonably frivolous, oppressive, or harassing, or that a response or answer is unreasonably frivolous or made for purposes of delay, then the court in which the action is pending may, after notice and hearing, impose any appropriate sanction authorized by paragraphs (1), (2), (3), (4), (5), and (8) of Rule 215.2(b). Such order of sanction shall be subject to review on appeal from the final judgment.

215.4 Failure to Comply with Rule 198.

(a) ***Motion.*** A party who has requested an admission under Rule 198 may move to determine the sufficiency of the answer or objection. For purposes of this subdivision an evasive or incomplete answer may be treated as a failure to answer. Unless the court determines that an objection is justified, it shall order that an answer be served. If the court determines that an answer does not comply with the requirements of Rule 198, it may order either that the matter is admitted or that an amended answer be served. The provisions of Rule 215.1(d) apply to the award of expenses incurred in relation to the motion.

(b) ***Expenses on failure to admit.*** If a party fails to admit the genuineness of any document or the truth of any matter as requested under Rule 198 and if the party requesting the admissions thereafter proves the genuineness of the document or the truth of the matter, he may apply to the court for an order requiring the other party to pay him the reasonable expenses incurred in making that proof, including reasonable attorney fees. The court shall make the order unless it finds that (1) the request was held objectionable pursuant to Rule 193, or (2) the admission sought was of no substantial importance, or (3) the party failing to admit had a reasonable ground to believe that he might prevail on the matter, or (4) there was other good reason for the failure to admit.

215.5 Failure of Party or Witness to Attend or to Serve Subpoena; Expenses.

(a) ***Failure of party giving notice to attend.*** If the party giving the notice of the taking of an oral deposition fails to attend and proceed therewith and another party attends in person or by attorney pursuant to the notice, the court may order the party giving the notice to pay such other party the reasonable expenses incurred by him and his attorney in attending, including reasonable attorney fees.

(b) ***Failure of witness to attend.*** If a party gives notice of the taking of an oral deposition of a witness and the witness does not attend because of the fault of the party giving the notice, if another party attends in person or by attorney because he expects the deposition of that witness to be taken, the court may order the party giving the notice to pay such other party the reasonable expenses incurred by him and his attorney in attending, including reasonable attorney fees.

215.6 Exhibits to Motions and Responses. Motions or responses made under this rule may have exhibits attached including affidavits, discovery pleadings, or any other documents.

See also CPRC ch. 10; ***O'Connor's Texas Rules***, "Motion for Sanctions," ch. 5-K, p. 439; "General Rules for Discovery," ch. 6-A, p. 491; "Depositions," ch. 6-F, p. 604; "Interrogatories," ch. 6-G, p. 630; "Requests for Admissions," ch. 6-H, p. 638; "Securing Documents & Tangible Things," ch. 6-I, p. 648; ***O'Connor's Texas Forms***, FORMS 6A:24-32.

ANNOTATIONS

Petroleum Solutions, Inc. v. Head, 454 S.W.3d 482, 489 (Tex.2014). "[C]ourts generally follow a two-part test in determining whether a particular sanction for discovery abuse is just. First, a direct relationship must exist between the offensive conduct, the offender, and the sanction imposed. To meet this requirement, a sanction must be directed against the wrongful conduct and toward remedying the prejudice suffered by the innocent party. Second, a sanction must not be excessive, which means it should be no more severe than necessary to satisfy its legitimate purpose. This prong requires the trial court to consider the availability of lesser sanctions and, 'in all but the most exceptional cases, actually test the lesser sanctions.'" *See also* ***CHRISTUS Health Gulf Coast v. Carswell***, 505 S.W.3d 528, 540 (Tex.2016); ***Spohn Hosp. v. Mayer***, 104 S.W.3d 878, 882 (Tex.2003).

American Flood Research, Inc. v. Jones, 192 S.W.3d 581, 584 (Tex.2006). "While there is no direct evidence that the employees knew of the depositions

and deliberately failed to attend, in the context of an enduring attorney-client relationship, knowledge acquired by the attorney is imputed to the client. [Ds' attorney] was present when the trial judge ordered [the depositions] in open court ..., yet neither [attorney] nor the employees appeared. Thus, a Rule 215.2 prerequisite to imposing sanctions—a party's failure to comply with an order to permit discovery—was satisfied."

Meyer v. Cathey, 167 S.W.3d 327, 333 (Tex.2005). "[W]aiver bars a trial court from awarding posttrial sanctions based on pretrial conduct of which a party 'was aware' before trial; lack of 'conclusive evidence' is not an excuse." *See also* ***Remington Arms Co. v. Caldwell***, 850 S.W.2d 167, 170 (Tex.1993).

Cire v. Cummings, 134 S.W.3d 835, 842 (Tex.2004). "Nothing ... requires that a trial court test the effectiveness of lesser sanctions by actually implementing and ordering each and every sanction that could possibly be imposed before striking the pleadings of a disobedient party. [A] trial court [is not required] to list each possible lesser sanction in its order and then explain why each would be ineffective. [T]he record [must] reflect that the court 'consider' the availability of appropriate lesser sanctions, and cautions that in all but the most exceptional cases, the trial court must actually test the lesser sanctions before striking the pleadings. [I]n cases of exceptional misconduct ..., the trial court is not required to test lesser sanctions before striking pleadings ... so long as the record reflects that the trial court considered lesser sanctions before striking pleadings and the party's conduct justifies the presumption that its claims lack merit. [A] trial court must analyze the available sanctions and offer a reasoned explanation as to the appropriateness of the sanction imposed." *See also* ***Low v. Henry***, 221 S.W.3d 609, 620 (Tex.2007); ***Chrysler Corp. v. Blackmon***, 841 S.W.2d 844, 849 (Tex.1992); ***In re F.A.V.***, 284 S.W.3d 929, 931 (Tex.App.—Dallas 2009, no pet.).

Occidental Chem. Corp. v. Banales, 907 S.W.2d 488, 490 (Tex.1995). "The sanction imposed for discovery abuse should be no more severe than necessary to satisfy the legitimate purposes of the discovery process offended. The work product privilege is essential to the attorney-client relationship. Requiring the production of the attorney's notes from interviews of witnesses is a severe sanction and should receive an appropriately strict review. Piercing the work product privilege, like the 'death penalty' sanction, should apply only when lesser sanctions are inadequate to correct the discovery abuse that has occurred, i.e., when it is the only appropriate sanction. Here the record does not reflect why lesser traditional sanctions might not cure the discovery abuse."

Global Servs. v. Bianchi, 901 S.W.2d 934, 938 (Tex. 1995). "We recognize that it is often difficult to prove that a party has withheld documents from discovery. Direct evidence of such conduct is seldom available, and it may be necessary to rely entirely upon circumstantial evidence. But an imposition of sanctions cannot be based merely on a party's bald assertions. There must be some evidence to show an abuse of discovery before sanctions can be imposed. [The district] court ordered [D] to keep trying to produce all the documents requested, and prohibited [D] from conducting any discovery of its own until it complied. ... Thus, the effect of the sanction is to prohibit [D] from conducting any discovery."

TransAmerican Nat. Gas Corp. v. Powell, 811 S.W.2d 913, 917 (Tex.1991). The punishment for discovery abuse "should fit the crime. *At 918:* Discovery sanctions cannot be used to adjudicate the merits of a party's claims or defenses unless a party's hindrance of the discovery process justifies a presumption that its claims or defenses lack merit." *See also* ***Paradigm Oil, Inc. v. Retamco Oper., Inc.***, 372 S.W.3d 177, 184 (Tex. 2012); ***Hernandez v. Mid-Loop, Inc.***, 170 S.W.3d 138, 143 (Tex.App.—San Antonio 2005, no pet.).

Christus Health Gulf Coast v. Carswell, 433 S.W.3d 585, 615-16 (Tex.App.—Houston [1st Dist.] 2013), *rev'd in part on other grounds*, 505 S.W.3d 528 (Tex.2016). "When a monetary sanction awarded pursuant to Rule 215 'is not tied to any evidence in the record and the basis of calculating the amount is unknown, the sanction constitutes an impermissible arbitrary fine.' Arbitrary fines 'are not susceptible to meaningful review.' When we review a trial court's sanctions order for an abuse of discretion, 'we must be able to determine not only that the trial court's decision to sanction the conduct at issue was proper, but that the sanction the trial court chose was just.' [¶] Absent some evidence supporting the amount of the monetary sanction or some basis for calculating the amount, we have no way to determine whether the amount of the sanction is excessive. When the trial court imposes a monetary sanction, 'the sanctionable conduct alone does not prescribe the amount of the sanction.'"

JNS Enter. v. Dixie Demolition, LLC, 430 S.W.3d 444, 453 (Tex.App.—Austin 2013, no pet.). "Rule 215.3 authorizes a trial court to impose a variety of sanctions 'if the court finds a party is abusing the discovery process in seeking, making or resisting discovery.' ... Producing false documents in discovery and then lying about those documents in deposition undoubtedly qualifies as an abuse ... of the discovery process.... [¶] While it may be true that death-penalty sanctions cases in Texas *usually* involve discovery orders under rule 215, the absence of such orders does not necessarily preclude the imposition of death-penalty sanctions where ... the objectionable discovery conduct is fabricating evidence and lying about that evidence in deposition. In most discovery disputes, the objectionable conduct is something that can be corrected using a court order.... But when a party fabricates evidence and lies about that evidence in deposition, these typical discovery orders would be ineffective in addressing or punishing the objectionable discovery conduct. [Thus], it is both logical and reasonable that there were no underlying discovery orders. We are not inclined to hold that, as a matter of law, there must be underlying orders that gradually lead up to the death-penalty sanction."

In re Vossdale Townhouse Ass'n, 302 S.W.3d 890, 893-94 (Tex.App.—Houston [14th Dist.] 2009, orig. proceeding). "An order directing that counsel may no longer represent his clients in the subject litigation is not among those sanctions enumerated in Rule 215.2(b). While Rule 215.2(b) does not limit the types of discovery sanctions the trial court may impose to those enumerated in the rule, the imposition of a sanction that is not specifically authorized in derogation of a clearly established legal right cannot be just. The trial court's order ... was imposed in derogation of the clearly established right to counsel of choice." *See also* ***In re White***, 227 S.W.3d 234, 236 (Tex.App.—San Antonio 2007, orig. proceeding) (Rule 215.2(b) does not authorize trial court to impose sanctions on nonparty deponents).

In re P.M.B., 2 S.W.3d 618, 624-25 (Tex.App.—Houston [14th Dist.] 1999, no pet.). "Compared to the best interest of the child, technical rules of pleading and practice are of little importance in determining child custody issues. This is also true with regard to rule 215 discovery sanctions. Moreover, courts have recognized that the exclusion of essential evidence, like the striking of pleadings, can equate to a death penalty sanction, and should not be used without considering whether lesser sanctions are adequate to accomplish the needed compliance, deterrence and punishment. [¶] We believe that the best interest of a child can only be attained when a court's decision is as well-informed as the circumstances allow. A decision on custody, possession, or access can rarely be well-informed without consideration of the evidence and perspectives of both parents. Because the exclusion of any important evidence as a discovery sanction can only produce a less-informed decision, contrary to the best interest of the child, we believe that it should be resorted to only where lesser sanctions are either impracticable or have been attempted and proven unsuccessful."

Ismail v. Ismail, 702 S.W.2d 216, 224 (Tex.App.—Houston [1st Dist.] 1985, writ ref'd n.r.e.). "The Family Code provides that the trial court may issue temporary orders requiring either party to file a sworn inventory. If a party fails to comply with a temporary order, the party may be punished under the court's contempt power. We hold that the request for an inventory in a divorce case is a specie of discovery, and that the sanctions provided for in [TRCP] 215, as well as those granted in [Fam. Code] §3.58(c)(1) [now §6.502], are available to the trial court to punish or secure compliance with its order to furnish an inventory."

TRCP 215a TO 215c. REPEALED

SECTION 10. THE JURY IN COURT

TRCP 216. REQUEST & FEE FOR JURY TRIAL

a. Request. No jury trial shall be had in any civil suit, unless a written request for a jury trial is filed with the clerk of the court a reasonable time before the date set for trial of the cause on the non-jury docket, but not less than thirty days in advance.

b. Jury Fee. Unless otherwise provided by law, a fee of ten dollars if in the district court and five dollars if in the county court must be deposited with the clerk of the court within the time for making a written request for a jury trial. The clerk shall promptly enter a notation of the payment of such fee upon the court's docket sheet.

Caution: TRCP 216 is affected by Fam. Code §§6.703 and 105.002.

See also U.S. Const. amend. 7; Tex. Const. art. 1, §15; Gov't Code §51.604; ***O'Connor's Texas Rules***, "Request for Jury Trial," ch. 5-B, p. 378; ***O'Connor's Texas Forms***, FORMS 5B:1-4; ***O'Connor's Texas Family Law Handbook*** (2017), "Suit for Divorce," ch. 3-A, p. 205; "Suit to Dissolve Marriage with Children," ch. 4-D, p. 410.

ANNOTATIONS

General Motors Corp. v. Gayle, 951 S.W.2d 469, 476 (Tex.1997). "Even where a party does not timely pay the jury fee, … a trial court should accord the right to jury trial if it can be done without interfering with the court's docket, delaying the trial, or injuring the opposing party. *At 477:* [D] established that a 30-day continuance to perfect [D's] jury trial demand would not cause [Ps] any injury or delay. [T]he trial court's seriatim trial schedule seems only a sham to hold [D] to its mistake in not paying the jury fee without penalizing the other side." *See also* ***Crittenden v. Crittenden***, 52 S.W.3d 768, 769 (Tex.App.—San Antonio 2001, pet. denied).

Ricardo N., Inc. v. Turcios de Argueta, 907 S.W.2d 423, 429 (Tex.1995). "Assuming [D's] request for a jury in advance of the first trial setting was not timely made, that request had certainly become timely when the case was remanded from federal court four years later."

Halsell v. Dehoyos, 810 S.W.2d 371, 371 (Tex. 1991). "A [jury] request in advance of the 30-day deadline [of TRCP 216] is presumed to have been made a reasonable time before trial." *See also* ***Sims v. Fitzpatrick***, 288 S.W.3d 93, 102 (Tex.App.—Houston [1st Dist.] 2009, no pet.) (party may rebut presumption by showing that granting jury trial would injure adverse party, disrupt court's docket, or impede handling of court's business); ***Brockie v. Webb***, 244 S.W.3d 905, 908 (Tex.App.—Dallas 2008, pet. denied) (party may waive right to jury if request is made after case is certified for trial and less than 30 days before trial).

In re K.M.H., 181 S.W.3d 1, 8 (Tex.App.—Houston [14th Dist.] 2005, no pet.). "When a party has perfected its right to a jury trial … but the trial court proceeds to trial without a jury, the party must, to preserve error, either object on the record to the trial court's action or indicate affirmatively in the record it intends to stand on its perfected right to a jury trial." *See also* ***Stallworth v. Stallworth***, 201 S.W.3d 338, 346 (Tex.App.—Dallas 2006, no pet.).

In re J.C., 108 S.W.3d 914, 916-17 (Tex.App.—Texarkana 2003, no pet.). "After being served with notice of suit to terminate his parental rights, [respondent] promptly filed a single document in which he responded in opposition to the suit, requested the appointment of an attorney ad litem, and requested that he be bench warranted from prison to attend the termination hearing. … It is reasonable to assume that [respondent], as a nonlawyer, was not aware of [TRCP] 216 and that most people in [respondent's] situation would have thought that such a fundamental right as trial by jury would be automatic. [¶] Obviously, [respondent's] counsel never had an opportunity to comply with Rule 216. He filed a request for jury trial on behalf of his client at his first opportunity, but this was well within 30 days before the trial setting. In ***Bell Helicopter Textron, Inc. v. Abbott***, 863 S.W.2d 139 (Tex. App.—Texarkana 1993, writ denied), we held that, when compliance with Rule 216 is made impossible by failure to give the notice required by [TRCP] 245, a demand for a jury trial made within 30 days of the trial setting will be deemed timely. Here, compliance with Rule 216 was made impossible for [respondent's] court-appointed attorney ad litem by the lateness of his appointment."

TRCP 217. OATH OF INABILITY

The deposit for a jury fee shall not be required when the party shall within the time for making such deposit, file with the clerk his affidavit to the effect that he is unable to make such deposit, and that he cannot, by the pledge of property or otherwise, obtain the money necessary for that purpose; and the court shall then order the clerk to enter the suit on the jury docket.

See also *O'Connor's Texas Rules*, "Request for Jury Trial," ch. 5-B, p. 378.

TRCP 218. JURY DOCKET

The clerks of the district and county courts shall each keep a docket, styled, "The Jury Docket," in which shall be entered in their order the cases in which jury fees have been paid or affidavit in lieu thereof has been filed as provided in the two preceding rules.

TRCP 219. JURY TRIAL DAY

The court shall designate the days for taking up the jury docket and the trial of jury cases. Such order may be revoked or changed in the court's discretion.

TRCP 220. WITHDRAWING CAUSE FROM JURY DOCKET

When any party has paid the fee for a jury trial, he shall not be permitted to withdraw the cause from the jury docket over the objection of the parties adversely interested. If so permitted, the court in its discretion may by an order permit him to withdraw also his jury fee deposit. Failure of a party to appear for trial shall be deemed a waiver by him of the right to trial by jury.

See also *O'Connor's Texas Rules*, "Request for Jury Trial," ch. 5-B, p. 378; *O'Connor's Texas Forms*, FORMS 5B:5, 6.

ANNOTATIONS

Mercedes-Benz Credit Corp. v. Rhyne, 925 S.W.2d 664, 666 (Tex.1996). "Only when a party demands a jury *and* pays the fee can the opposing party rely on those actions. In such a case, the trial court may not remove the case from the jury docket over the objections of the opposing party." *See also* ***Green v. W.E. Grace Mfg.***, 422 S.W.2d 723, 726 (Tex.1968).

In re T.K., No. 09-09-00472-CV (Tex.App.—Beaumont 2010, no pet.) (memo op.; 3-11-10). "[F]or Rule 220 purposes, a party, although not personally present, appears for trial when his attorney is present. If counsel refuses to go forward with the trial, however, that refusal constitutes a jury waiver. Likewise, late arrival by both counsel and the litigant waives the right to trial by jury." (Internal quotes omitted.)

In re J.N.F., 116 S.W.3d 426, 434-35 (Tex.App.—Houston [14th Dist.] 2003, no pet.). "'[U]nless an objection is made to the withdrawal of a case from the jury docket, the non-requesting party has no right to a jury trial.' If a party who has requested a jury trial in an initial pleading could effectively withdraw the request simply by omitting it in subsequent pleadings, the non-requesting party would be forced to scrutinize all such pleadings in order to avoid waiving a jury trial by failing to object to the withdrawal. [¶] [O]mitting a jury request from subsequent pleadings does not rise to the level of inaction that has been held to constitute the requesting party's waiver of a jury trial."

TRCP 221. CHALLENGE TO THE ARRAY

When the jurors summoned have not been selected by jury commissioners or by drawing the names from a jury wheel, any party to a suit which is to be tried by a jury may, before the jury is drawn challenge the array upon the ground that the officer summoning the jury has acted corruptly, and has wilfully summoned jurors known to be prejudiced against the party challenging or biased in favor of the adverse party. All such challenges must be in writing setting forth distinctly the grounds of such challenge and supported by the affidavit of the party or some other credible person. When such challenge is made, the court shall hear evidence and decide without delay whether or not the challenge shall be sustained.

See also Gov't Code §62.001; ***O'Connor's Texas Rules***, "Jury Selection," ch. 8-A, p. 769.

TRCP 222. WHEN CHALLENGE IS SUSTAINED

If the challenge be sustained, the array of jurors summoned shall be discharged, and the court shall order other jurors summoned in their stead, and shall direct that the officer who summoned the persons so discharged, and on account of whose misconduct the challenge has been sustained, shall not summon any other jurors in the case.

See also Gov't Code §§62.101-62.110 (juror qualifications).

TRCP 223. JURY LIST IN CERTAIN COUNTIES

In counties governed as to juries by the laws providing for interchangeable juries, the names of the jurors shall be placed upon the general panel in the order in which they are randomly selected, and jurors shall be assigned for service from the top thereof, in the order in which they shall be needed, and jurors returned to the general panel after service in any of such courts shall be enrolled at the bottom of the list in the order of their respective return; provided, however, after such assignment to a particular court, the trial judge of such court, upon the demand prior to voir dire examination by any party or attorney in the case reached for trial in such court, shall cause the names of all members of such assigned jury panel in such case to be placed in a receptacle, shuffled, and drawn, and such names shall be transcribed in the order drawn on the jury list from which the jury is to be selected to try such case. There shall be only one shuffle and drawing by the trial judge in each case.

See also Gov't Code §§62.016, 62.017 (interchangeable juries in certain counties); ***O'Connor's Texas Rules***, "Jury Selection," ch. 8-A, p. 769.

ANNOTATIONS

Rivas v. Liberty Mut. Ins., 480 S.W.2d 610, 612 (Tex.1972). "The court of civil appeals recognized the listing and reshuffle provisions of Rule 223 are designed to insure a random selection of jurors. While the method used here did not conform to the method prescribed by the rule, it did insure a degree of randomness in the listing of the jurors."

BNSF Ry. v. Wipff, 408 S.W.3d 662, 666 (Tex. App.—Fort Worth 2013, no pet.). TRCP 223 "is clear that a shuffle demand must be made before voir dire begins. [A] shuffle demand is untimely in a civil case if done after counsel reviews case-specific questionnaires that give detailed information beyond the 'name, rank, and serial number' given on information cards.

[P] relies on the fact that [D] reviewed a case-specific questionnaire before demanding the shuffle. *At 667:* But it is clear that the trial court had not given the venire the prescribed instructions under [TRCP] 226a before the requested jury shuffle. The Texas Supreme Court, in ordering the form of the Rule 226a instructions, mandated that they 'shall be given by the court to the members of the jury panel after they have been sworn in as provided in Rule 226 and *before the voir dire examination*.' [Thus], voir dire is not to begin until after the admonitory instructions are given to the venire. While true that case-specific questionnaires were completed and received by counsel, counsel had not viewed the venire, and the trial court had not given the venire the prescribed instructions. … Therefore, voir dire had not begun in this case even though counsel had an opportunity to review the questionnaires. *At 668:* [D's] shuffle demand was timely under Rule 223 because it was made before voir dire began."

TRCP 224. PREPARING JURY LIST

In counties not governed as to juries by the laws providing for interchangeable juries, when the parties have announced ready for trial the clerk shall write the name of each regular juror entered of record for that week on separate slips of paper, as near the same size and appearance as may be, and shall place the slips in a box and mix them well. The clerk shall draw from the box, in the presence of the court, the names of twenty-four jurors, if in the district court, or so many as there may be, if there be a less number in the box; and the names of twelve jurors if in the county court, or so many as there may be, and write the names as drawn upon two slips of paper and deliver one slip to each party to the suit or his attorney.

See also *O'Connor's Texas Rules*, "Jury Selection," ch. 8-A, p. 769.

ANNOTATIONS

Southwestern Pub. Serv. v. Morris, 380 S.W.2d 648, 649 (Tex.App.—Amarillo 1964, no writ). "[E]rror was committed by the court in refusing condemnor's request that the jury panel be drawn before the selection of the jury." Such error may be harmless.

TRCP 225. SUMMONING TALESMAN

When there are not as many as twenty-four names drawn from the box, if in the district court, or as many as twelve, if in the county court, the court shall direct the sheriff to summon such number of qualified persons as the court deems necessary to complete the panel. The names of those thus summoned shall be placed in the box and drawn and entered upon the slips as provided in the preceding rules.

TRCP 226. OATH TO JURY PANEL

Before the parties or their attorneys begin the examination of the jurors whose names have thus been listed, the jurors shall be sworn by the court or under its direction, as follows: "You, and each of you, do solemnly swear that you will true answers give to all questions propounded to you concerning your qualifications as a juror, so help you God."

See also *O'Connor's Texas Rules*, "Jury Selection," ch. 8-A, p. 769.

ANNOTATIONS

Barron v. State, 378 S.W.2d 144, 147 (Tex. App.—San Antonio 1964, no writ). "[F]ailure to swear the jury panel prior to the voir dire examination as required by Rule 226 … was waived by [the] failure to timely complain of same."

TRCP 226a. INSTRUCTIONS TO JURY PANEL & JURY

The court must give instructions to the jury panel and the jury as prescribed by order of the Supreme Court under this rule.

APPROVED INSTRUCTIONS

I.

That the following oral instructions, with such modifications as the circumstances of the particular case may require, shall be given by the court to the members of the jury panel after they have been sworn in as provided in Rule 226 and before the voir dire examination:

Members of the Jury Panel [or Ladies and Gentlemen of the Jury Panel]:

Thank you for being here. We are here to select a jury. Twelve [six] of you will be chosen for the jury. Even if you are not chosen for the jury, you are performing a valuable service that is your right and duty as a citizen of a free country.

Before we begin: Turn off all phones and other electronic devices. While you are in the courtroom, do not communicate with anyone through any electronic device. [For example, do not communicate by phone, text message, email message, chat room, blog, or social networking websites such as Facebook, Twitter, or Myspace.] [I will give you a number where others may con-

tact you in case of an emergency.] Do not record or photograph any part of these court proceedings, because it is prohibited by law.

If you are chosen for the jury, your role as jurors will be to decide the disputed facts in this case. My role will be to ensure that this case is tried in accordance with the rules of law.

Here is some background about this case. This is a civil case. It is a lawsuit that is not a criminal case. The parties are as follows: The plaintiff is _______, and the defendant is _______. Representing the plaintiff is _______, and representing the defendant is _______. They will ask you some questions during jury selection. But before their questions begin, I must give you some instructions for jury selection.

Every juror must obey these instructions. You may be called into court to testify about any violations of these instructions. If you do not follow these instructions, you will be guilty of juror misconduct, and I might have to order a new trial and start this process over again. This would waste your time and the parties' money, and would require the taxpayers of this county to pay for another trial.

These are the instructions.

1. To avoid looking like you are friendly with one side of the case, do not mingle or talk with the lawyers, witnesses, parties, or anyone else involved in the case. You may exchange casual greetings like "hello" and "good morning." Other than that, do not talk with them at all. They have to follow these instructions too, so you should not be offended when they follow the instructions.

2. Do not accept any favors from the lawyers, witnesses, parties, or anyone else involved in the case, and do not do any favors for them. This includes favors such as giving rides and food.

3. Do not discuss this case with anyone, even your spouse or a friend, either in person or by any other means [including by phone, text message, email message, chat room, blog, or social networking websites such as Facebook, Twitter, or Myspace]. Do not allow anyone to discuss the case with you or in your hearing. If anyone tries to discuss the case with you or in your hearing, tell me immediately. We do not want you to be influenced by something other than the evidence admitted in court.

4. The parties, through their attorneys, have the right to ask you questions about your background, experiences, and attitudes. They are not trying to meddle in your affairs. They are just being thorough and trying to choose fair jurors who do not have any bias or prejudice in this particular case.

5. Remember that you took an oath that you will tell the truth, so be truthful when the lawyers ask you questions, and always give complete answers. If you do not answer a question that applies to you, that violates your oath. Sometimes a lawyer will ask a question of the whole panel instead of just one person. If the question applies to you, raise your hand and keep it raised until you are called on.

Do you understand these instructions? If you do not, please tell me now.

The lawyers will now begin to ask their questions.

II.

That the following oral and written instructions, with such modifications as the circumstances of the particular case may require, shall be given by the court to the jury immediately after the jurors are selected for the case:

Members of the Jury [or Ladies and Gentlemen]:

You have been chosen to serve on this jury. Because of the oath you have taken and your selection for the jury, you become officials of this court and active participants in our justice system.

[Hand out the written instructions.]

You have each received a set of written instructions. I am going to read them with you now. Some of them you have heard before and some are new.

1. Turn off all phones and other electronic devices. While you are in the courtroom and while you are deliberating, do not communicate with anyone through any electronic device. [For example, do not communicate by phone, text message, email message, chat room, blog, or social networking websites such as Facebook, Twitter, or Myspace.] [I will give you a number where others may contact you in case of an emergency.] Do not post information about the case on the Internet before these court proceedings end and you are released from jury duty. Do not record or photograph any part of these court proceedings, because it is prohibited by law.

2. To avoid looking like you are friendly with one side of the case, do not mingle or talk with the lawyers, witnesses, parties, or anyone else involved in the case. You may exchange casual greetings like "hello" and "good morning." Other than that, do not talk with them

at all. They have to follow these instructions too, so you should not be offended when they follow the instructions.

3. Do not accept any favors from the lawyers, witnesses, parties, or anyone else involved in the case, and do not do any favors for them. This includes favors such as giving rides and food.

4. Do not discuss this case with anyone, even your spouse or a friend, either in person or by any other means [including by phone, text message, email message, chat room, blog, or social networking websites such as Facebook, Twitter, or Myspace]. Do not allow anyone to discuss the case with you or in your hearing. If anyone tries to discuss the case with you or in your hearing, tell me immediately. We do not want you to be influenced by something other than the evidence admitted in court.

5. Do not discuss this case with anyone during the trial, not even with the other jurors, until the end of the trial. You should not discuss the case with your fellow jurors until the end of the trial so that you do not form opinions about the case before you have heard everything.

After you have heard all the evidence, received all of my instructions, and heard all of the lawyers' arguments, you will then go to the jury room to discuss the case with the other jurors and reach a verdict.

6. Do not investigate this case on your own. For example, do not:

a. try to get information about the case, lawyers, witnesses, or issues from outside this courtroom;

b. go to places mentioned in the case to inspect the places;

c. inspect items mentioned in this case unless they are presented as evidence in court;

d. look anything up in a law book, dictionary, or public record to try to learn more about the case;

e. look anything up on the Internet to try to learn more about the case; or

f. let anyone else do any of these things for you.

This rule is very important because we want a trial based only on evidence admitted in open court. Your conclusions about this case must be based only on what you see and hear in this courtroom because the law does not permit you to base your conclusions on information that has not been presented to you in open court. All the information must be presented in open court so the parties and their lawyers can test it and object to it. Information from other sources, like the Internet, will not go through this important process in the courtroom. In addition, information from other sources could be completely unreliable. As a result, if you investigate this case on your own, you could compromise the fairness to all parties in this case and jeopardize the results of this trial.

7. Do not tell other jurors about your own experiences or other people's experiences. For example, you may have special knowledge of something in the case, such as business, technical, or professional information. You may even have expert knowledge or opinions, or you may know what happened in this case or another similar case. Do not tell the other jurors about it. Telling other jurors about it is wrong because it means the jury will be considering things that were not admitted in court.

8. Do not consider attorneys' fees unless I tell you to. Do not guess about attorneys' fees.

9. Do not consider or guess whether any party is covered by insurance unless I tell you to.

10. During the trial, if taking notes will help focus your attention on the evidence, you may take notes using the materials the court has provided. Do not use any personal electronic devices to take notes. If taking notes will distract your attention from the evidence, you should not take notes. Your notes are for your own personal use. They are not evidence. Do not show or read your notes to anyone, including other jurors.

You must leave your notes in the jury room or with the bailiff. The bailiff is instructed not to read your notes and to give your notes to me promptly after collecting them from you. I will make sure your notes are kept in a safe, secure location and not disclosed to anyone.

[You may take your notes back into the jury room and consult them during deliberations. But keep in mind that your notes are not evidence. When you deliberate, each of you should rely on your independent recollection of the evidence and not be influenced by the fact that another juror has or has not taken notes. After you complete your deliberations, the bailiff will collect your notes.]

When you are released from jury duty, the bailiff will promptly destroy your notes so that nobody can read what you wrote.

11. I will decide matters of law in this case. It is your duty to listen to and consider the evidence and to deter-

mine fact issues that I may submit to you at the end of the trial. After you have heard all the evidence, I will give you instructions to follow as you make your decision. The instructions also will have questions for you to answer. You will not be asked and you should not consider which side will win. Instead, you will need to answer the specific questions I give you.

Every juror must obey my instructions. If you do not follow these instructions, you will be guilty of juror misconduct, and I may have to order a new trial and start this process over again. This would waste your time and the parties' money, and would require the taxpayers of this county to pay for another trial.

Do you understand these instructions? If you do not, please tell me now.

Please keep these instructions and review them as we go through this case. If anyone does not follow these instructions, tell me.

III.

COURT'S CHARGE

Before closing arguments begin, the court must give to each member of the jury a copy of the charge, which must include the following written instructions, with such modifications as the circumstances of the particular case may require:

Members of the Jury [or Ladies & Gentlemen of the Jury]:

After the closing arguments, you will go to the jury room to decide the case, answer the questions that are attached, and reach a verdict. You may discuss the case with other jurors only when you are all together in the jury room.

Remember my previous instructions: Do not discuss the case with anyone else, either in person or by any other means. Do not do any independent investigation about the case or conduct any research. Do not look up any words in dictionaries or on the Internet. Do not post information about the case on the Internet. Do not share any special knowledge or experiences with the other jurors. Do not use your phone or any other electronic device during your deliberations for any reason. [I will give you a number where others may contact you in case of an emergency.]

[Any notes you have taken are for your own personal use. You may take your notes back into the jury room and consult them during deliberations, but do not show or read your notes to your fellow jurors during your deliberations. Your notes are not evidence. Each of you should rely on your independent recollection of the evidence and not be influenced by the fact that another juror has or has not taken notes.]

[You must leave your notes with the bailiff when you are not deliberating. The bailiff will give your notes to me promptly after collecting them from you. I will make sure your notes are kept in a safe, secure location and not disclosed to anyone. After you complete your deliberations, the bailiff will collect your notes. When you are released from jury duty, the bailiff will promptly destroy your notes so that nobody can read what you wrote.]

Here are the instructions for answering the questions.

1. Do not let bias, prejudice, or sympathy play any part in your decision.

2. Base your answers only on the evidence admitted in court and on the law that is in these instructions and questions. Do not consider or discuss any evidence that was not admitted in the courtroom.

3. You are to make up your own minds about the facts. You are the sole judges of the credibility of the witnesses and the weight to give their testimony. But on matters of law, you must follow all of my instructions.

4. If my instructions use a word in a way that is different from its ordinary meaning, use the meaning I give you, which will be a proper legal definition.

5. All the questions and answers are important. No one should say that any question or answer is not important.

6. Answer "yes" or "no" to all questions unless you are told otherwise. A "yes" answer must be based on a preponderance of the evidence [unless you are told otherwise]. Whenever a question requires an answer other than "yes" or "no," your answer must be based on a preponderance of the evidence [unless you are told otherwise].

The term "preponderance of the evidence" means the greater weight of credible evidence presented in this case. If you do not find that a preponderance of the evidence supports a "yes" answer, then answer "no." A preponderance of the evidence is not measured by the number of witnesses or by the number of documents admitted in evidence. For a fact to be proved by a preponderance of the evidence, you must find that the fact is more likely true than not true.

7. Do not decide who you think should win before you answer the questions and then just answer the ques-

tions to match your decision. Answer each question carefully without considering who will win. Do not discuss or consider the effect your answers will have.

8. Do not answer questions by drawing straws or by any method of chance.

9. Some questions might ask you for a dollar amount. Do not agree in advance to decide on a dollar amount by adding up each juror's amount and then figuring the average.

10. Do not trade your answers. For example, do not say, "I will answer this question your way if you answer another question my way."

11. [Unless otherwise instructed] The answers to the questions must be based on the decision of at least 10 of the 12 [5 of the 6] jurors. The same 10 [5] jurors must agree on every answer. Do not agree to be bound by a vote of anything less than 10 [5] jurors, even if it would be a majority.

As I have said before, if you do not follow these instructions, you will be guilty of juror misconduct, and I might have to order a new trial and start this process over again. This would waste your time and the parties' money, and would require the taxpayers of this county to pay for another trial. If a juror breaks any of these rules, tell that person to stop and report it to me immediately.

[Definitions, questions, and special instructions given to the jury will be transcribed here. If exemplary damages are sought against a defendant, the jury must unanimously find, with respect to that defendant, (i) liability on at least one claim for actual damages that will support an award of exemplary damages, (ii) any additional conduct, such as malice or gross negligence, required for an award of exemplary damages, and (iii) the amount of exemplary damages to be awarded. The jury's answers to questions regarding (ii) and (iii) must be conditioned on a unanimous finding regarding (i), except in an extraordinary circumstance when the conditioning instruction would be erroneous. The jury need not be unanimous in finding the amount of actual damages. Thus, if questions regarding (ii) and (iii) are submitted to the jury for defendants D1 and D2, instructions in substantially the following form must immediately precede such questions:

Preceding question (ii):

Answer Question (ii) for D1 only if you unanimously answered "Yes" to Question[s] (i) regarding D1. Otherwise, do not answer Question (ii) for D1. [Repeat for D2.]

You are instructed that in order to answer "Yes" to [any part of] Question (ii), your answer must be unanimous. You may answer "No" to [any part of] Question (ii) only upon a vote of 10 [5] or more jurors. Otherwise, you must not answer [that part of] Question (ii).

Preceding question (iii):

Answer Question (iii) for D1 only if you answered "Yes" to Question (ii) for D1. Otherwise, do not answer Question (iii) for D1. [Repeat for D2.]

You are instructed that you must unanimously agree on the amount of any award of exemplary damages.

These examples are given by way of illustration.]

Presiding Juror:

1. When you go into the jury room to answer the questions, the first thing you will need to do is choose a presiding juror.

2. The presiding juror has these duties:

a. have the complete charge read aloud if it will be helpful to your deliberations;

b. preside over your deliberations, meaning manage the discussions, and see that you follow these instructions;

c. give written questions or comments to the bailiff who will give them to the judge;

d. write down the answers you agree on;

e. get the signatures for the verdict certificate; and

f. notify the bailiff that you have reached a verdict.

Do you understand the duties of the presiding juror? If you do not, please tell me now.

Instructions for Signing the Verdict Certificate:

1. [Unless otherwise instructed] You may answer the questions on a vote of 10 [5] jurors. The same 10 [5] jurors must agree on every answer in the charge. This means you may not have one group of 10 [5] jurors agree on one answer and a different group of 10 [5] jurors agree on another answer.

2. If 10 [5] jurors agree on every answer, those 10 [5] jurors sign the verdict.

If 11 jurors agree on every answer, those 11 jurors sign the verdict.

If all 12 [6] of you agree on every answer, you are unanimous and only the presiding juror signs the verdict.

3. All jurors should deliberate on every question. You may end up with all 12 [6] of you agreeing on some answers, while only 10 [5] or 11 of you agree on other an-

swers. But when you sign the verdict, only those 10 [5] who agree on every answer will sign the verdict.

4. [Added if the charge requires some unanimity] There are some special instructions before Questions ___ explaining how to answer those questions. Please follow the instructions. If all 12 [6] of you answer those questions, you will need to complete a second verdict certificate for those questions.

Do you understand these instructions? If you do not, please tell me now.

____

Judge Presiding

VERDICT CERTIFICATE

Check one:

___ Our verdict is unanimous. All 12 [6] of us have agreed to each and every answer. The presiding juror has signed the certificate for all 12 [6] of us.

____

Signature of Presiding Juror

____

Printed Name of Presiding Juror

___ Our verdict is not unanimous. Eleven of us have agreed to each and every answer and have signed the certificate below.

___ Our verdict is not unanimous. Ten [Five] of us have agreed to each and every answer and have signed the certificate below.

SIGNATURE	*NAME PRINTED*
1. ____________	____________
2. ____________	____________
3. ____________	____________
4. ____________	____________
5. ____________	____________
6. ____________	____________
7. ____________	____________
8. ____________	____________
9. ____________	____________
10. ____________	____________
11. ____________	____________

If you have answered Question No. ___ [the exemplary damages amount], then you must sign this certificate also.

ADDITIONAL CERTIFICATE

[Used when some questions require unanimous answers]

I certify that the jury was unanimous in answering the following questions. All 12 [6] of us agreed to each of the answers. The presiding juror has signed the certificate for all 12 [6] of us.

[Judge to list questions that require a unanimous answer, including the predicate liability question.]

____

Signature of Presiding Juror

____

Printed Name of Presiding Juror

IV.

That the following oral instructions shall be given by the court to the jury after the verdict has been accepted by the court and before the jurors are released from jury duty:

Thank you for your verdict.

I have told you that the only time you may discuss the case is with the other jurors in the jury room. I now release you from jury duty. Now you may discuss the case with anyone. But you may also choose not to discuss the case; that is your right.

After you are released from jury duty, the lawyers and others may ask you questions to see if the jury followed the instructions, and they may ask you to give a sworn statement. You are free to discuss the case with them and to give a sworn statement. But you may choose not to discuss the case and not to give a sworn statement; that is your right.

See also *O'Connor's Texas Rules*, "Jury Selection," ch. 8-A, p. 769; "Jury Charge," ch. 8-I, p. 826; *O'Connor's Texas Forms*, FORM 8I:1.

ANNOTATIONS

Woods v. Crane Carrier Co., 693 S.W.2d 377, 379 (Tex.1985). "[W]hen terms requiring definitions are used more than once in a charge, it is preferable that the definition or instruction occur immediately after the general instructions required by [TRCP] 226a...."

In re Commitment of Stevenson, No. 09-11-00601-CV (Tex.App.—Beaumont 2013, no pet.) (memo op.; 9-19-13). "[D] relies on Rule 226a ... to support his argument that the trial court is prohibited from talking with the jurors. However, the instruction the Texas Supreme Court promulgated for trial courts to provide to the venire under this rule requires that trial courts instruct that members of the venire 'not mingle

or talk with the lawyers, witnesses, parties, or anyone else involved in the case.' We disagree that the Texas Supreme Court has interpreted Rule 226a in a way that proscribes a trial court from communicating with potential jurors during voir dire."

TRCP 227. CHALLENGE TO JUROR

A challenge to a particular juror is either a challenge for cause or a peremptory challenge. The court shall decide without delay any such challenge, and if sustained, the juror shall be discharged from the particular case. Either such challenge may be made orally on the formation of a jury to try the case.

See also Gov't Code §§62.101-62.110 (juror qualifications); ***O'Connor's Texas Rules***, "Jury Selection," ch. 8-A, p. 769.

TRCP 228. "CHALLENGE FOR CAUSE" DEFINED

A challenge for cause is an objection made to a juror, alleging some fact which by law disqualifies him to serve as a juror in the case or in any case, or which in the opinion of the court, renders him an unfit person to sit on the jury. Upon such challenge the examination is not confined to the answers of the juror, but other evidence may be heard for or against the challenge.

See also ***O'Connor's Texas Rules***, "Challenges for Cause," ch. 8-A, §6, p. 777.

ANNOTATIONS

Compton v. Henrie, 364 S.W.2d 179, 182 (Tex. 1963). "[T]he statutory disqualification of bias or prejudice extends not only to the litigant personally, but to the subject matter of the litigation as well."

TRCP 229. CHALLENGE FOR CAUSE

When twenty-four or more jurors, if in the district court, or twelve or more, if in the county court, are drawn, and the lists of their names delivered to the parties, if either party desires to challenge any juror for cause, the challenge shall then be made. The name of a juror challenged and set aside for cause shall be erased from such lists.

See also Gov't Code §§62.101-62.110 (juror qualifications); ***O'Connor's Texas Rules***, "Challenges for Cause," ch. 8-A, §6, p. 777.

ANNOTATIONS

Cortez v. HCCI-San Antonio, Inc., 159 S.W.3d 87, 90-91 (Tex.2005). "[T]o preserve error when a challenge for cause is denied, a party must use a peremptory challenge against the veniremember involved, exhaust its remaining challenges, and notify the trial court that a specific objectionable veniremember will remain on the jury list. [¶] While it is unclear whether [P] gave his notice to the trial court before or after he delivered his strike list, it does appear that the two events were roughly contemporaneous. More importantly, notice was given before the jury was seated.... We therefore hold that error was preserved. [¶] The fact that [P] prevailed at trial is not relevant [to whether any error was harmless] because ... 'harm occurs' when 'the party uses all of his peremptory challenges and is thus prevented from striking other objectionable jurors from the list because he has no additional peremptory challenges.' ... Here, ... we presume harm." *See also* ***Hallett v. Houston Nw. Med. Ctr.***, 689 S.W.2d 888, 890 (Tex.1985).

TRCP 230. CERTAIN QUESTIONS NOT TO BE ASKED

In examining a juror, he shall not be asked a question the answer to which may show that he has been convicted of an offense which disqualifies him, or that he stands charged by some legal accusation with theft or any felony.

See also ***O'Connor's Texas Rules***, "Jury Selection," ch. 8-A, p. 769.

ANNOTATIONS

Palmer Well Servs. v. Mack Trucks, Inc., 776 S.W.2d 575, 576 (Tex.1989). Gov't Code §62.102 "disqualifies a person to serve as a petit juror if he is 'under indictment or other legal accusation of misdemeanor or felony theft, or any other felony.'"

TRCP 231. NUMBER REDUCED BY CHALLENGES

If the challenges reduce the number of jurors to less than twenty-four, if in the district court, or to less than twelve, if in the county court, the court shall order other jurors to be drawn from the wheel or from the central jury panel or summoned, as the practice may be in the particular county, and their names written upon the list instead of those set aside for cause. Such jurors so summoned may likewise be challenged for cause.

TRCP 232. MAKING PEREMPTORY CHALLENGES

If there remain on such lists not subject to challenge for cause, twenty-four names, if in the district court, or twelve names, if in the county court, the parties shall proceed to make their peremptory challenges. A peremptory challenge is made to a juror without assigning any reason therefor.

See also ***O'Connor's Texas Rules***, "Peremptory Challenges," ch. 8-A, §7, p. 779.

ANNOTATIONS

Davis v. Fisk Elec. Co., 268 S.W.3d 508, 518-19 (Tex.2008). "Nonverbal conduct or demeanor, often elusive and always subject to interpretation, may well mask a race-based strike. For that reason, trial courts must carefully examine such rationales. ... ***Batson*** requires a 'clear and reasonably specific explanation' of the legitimate reasons for a strike ... and merely stating that a juror nonverbally 'reacted' is insufficient. *At 525:* [C]ourts must consider 'all relevant circumstances' when reviewing ***Batson*** challenges. And here, the relevant circumstances include many [factors], including a statistical disparity and unequal treatment of comparable jurors."

Goode v. Shoukfeh, 943 S.W.2d 441, 445-46 (Tex. 1997). "At the first step of the [***Batson***] process, the opponent of the peremptory challenge must establish a prima facie case of racial discrimination. [¶] During the second step of the process, the burden shifts to the party who has exercised the strike to come forward with a race-neutral explanation. ... The issue ... at this juncture is the facial validity of the explanation. ... It is not until the third step that the persuasiveness of the justification for the challenge becomes relevant. At the third step of the process, the trial court must determine if the party challenging the strike has proven purposeful racial discrimination, and the trial court may believe or not believe the explanation offered by the party who exercised the peremptory challenge. It is at this stage that implausible justifications for striking potential jurors 'may (and probably will) be found [by the trial court] to be pretexts for purposeful discrimination.'"

Powers v. Palacios, 813 S.W.2d 489, 491 (Tex. 1991). "We hold that equal protection is denied when race is a factor in counsel's exercise of a peremptory challenge to a prospective juror."

TRCP 233. NUMBER OF PEREMPTORY CHALLENGES

Except as provided below, each party to a civil action is entitled to six peremptory challenges in a case tried in the district court, and to three in the county court.

Alignment of the Parties. In multiple party cases, it shall be the duty of the trial judge to decide whether any of the litigants aligned on the same side of the docket are antagonistic with respect to any issue to be submitted to the jury, before the exercise of peremptory challenges.

Definition of Side. The term "side" as used in this rule is not synonymous with "party," "litigant," or "person." Rather, "side" means one or more litigants who have common interests on the matters with which the jury is concerned.

Motion to Equalize. In multiple party cases, upon motion of any litigant made prior to the exercise of peremptory challenges, it shall be the duty of the trial judge to equalize the number of peremptory challenges so that no litigant or side is given unfair advantage as a result of the alignment of the litigants and the award of peremptory challenges to each litigant or side. In determining how the challenges should be allocated the court shall consider any matter brought to the attention of the trial judge concerning the ends of justice and the elimination of an unfair advantage.

See also *O'Connor's Texas Rules*, "Peremptory Challenges," ch. 8-A, §7, p. 779; *O'Connor's Texas Forms*, FORMS 8A:1, 2.

ANNOTATIONS

Garcia v. Central Power & Light Co., 704 S.W.2d 734, 736 (Tex.1986). "The existence of antagonism [between litigants on the same side of a lawsuit] is a question of law. If no antagonism exists, each side must receive the same number of strikes. *At 737:* [I]n determining whether antagonism exists, the trial court must consider the pleadings, information disclosed by pretrial discovery, information and representations made during voir dire of the jury panel, and any other information brought to the attention of the trial court before the exercise of the strikes by the parties." *See also* ***Moore v. Altra Energy Techs.***, 321 S.W.3d 727, 741 (Tex.App.—Houston [14th Dist.] 2010, pet. denied).

TRCP 234. LISTS RETURNED TO THE CLERK

When the parties have made or declined to make their peremptory challenges, they shall deliver their lists to the clerk. The clerk shall, if the case be in the district court, call off the first twelve names on the lists that have not been erased; and if the case be in the county court, he shall call off the first six names on the lists that have not been erased; those whose names are called shall be the jury.

See also *O'Connor's Texas Rules*, "Jury Selection," ch. 8-A, p. 769.

TRCP 235. IF JURY IS INCOMPLETE

When by peremptory challenges the jury is left incomplete, the court shall direct other jurors to be drawn or summoned to complete the jury; and such other jurors shall be impaneled as in the first instance.

See also *O'Connor's Texas Rules*, "Jury Selection," ch. 8-A, p. 769.

TRCP 236. OATH TO JURY

The jury shall be sworn by the court or under its direction, in substance as follows: "You, and each of you, do solemnly swear that in all cases between parties which shall be to you submitted, you will a true verdict render, according to the law, as it may be given you in charge by the court, and to the evidence submitted to you under the rulings of the court. So help you God."

SECTION 11. TRIAL OF CAUSES

A. APPEARANCE & PROCEDURE

TRCP 237. APPEARANCE DAY

If a defendant, who has been duly cited, is by the citation required to answer on a day which is in term time, such day is appearance day as to him. If he is so required to answer on a day in vacation, he shall plead or answer accordingly, and the first day of the next term is appearance day as to him.

See also *O'Connor's Texas Rules*, "Default Judgment," ch. 7-A, p. 671.

ANNOTATIONS

Texas Alcoholic Bev. Comm'n v. Wilson, 573 S.W.2d 832, 835 (Tex.App.—Beaumont 1978, writ ref'd n.r.e.). "[D] had no valid notice that a hearing would be held prior to appearance day.... Any judgment entered before the time at which a defendant is commanded by the citation to appear and answer is erroneous and must be set aside."

TRCP 237a. CASES REMANDED FROM FEDERAL COURT

When any cause is removed to the Federal Court and is afterwards remanded to the state court, the plaintiff shall file a certified copy of the order of remand with the clerk of the state court and shall forthwith give written notice of such filing to the attorneys of record for all adverse parties. All such adverse parties shall have fifteen days from the receipt of such notice within which to file an answer. No default judgment shall be rendered against a party in a removed action remanded from federal court if that party filed an answer in federal court during removal.

ANNOTATIONS

HBA E., Ltd. v. JEA Boxing Co., 796 S.W.2d 534, 538 (Tex.App.—Houston [1st Dist.] 1990, writ denied). "Reading [TRCP] 237a and 239 together, we conclude that a default judgment cannot be granted against a defendant following remand of a case from federal to state court until 15 days have expired from the defendant's receipt of the remand notice from the plaintiff." *See also* ***Kashan v. McLane Co.***, No. 03-11-00125-CV (Tex. App.—Austin 2012, no pet.) (memo op.; 6-7-12).

TRCP 238. CALL OF APPEARANCE DOCKET

On the appearance day of a particular defendant and at the hour named in the citation, or as soon thereafter as may be practicable, the court or clerk in open court shall call, in their order, all the cases on the docket in which such day is appearance day as to any defendant, or, the court or clerk failing therein, any such case shall be so called on request of the plaintiff's attorney.

TRCP 239. JUDGMENT BY DEFAULT

Upon such call of the docket, or at any time after a defendant is required to answer, the plaintiff may in term time take judgment by default against such defendant if he has not previously filed an answer, and provided that the return of service shall have been on file with the clerk for the length of time required by Rule 107.

Caution: TRCP 239 is affected by Fam. Code §§85.006, 157.066, 157.115, and 232.009.

See also *O'Connor's Texas Rules*, "Default Judgment," ch. 7-A, p. 671; "MNT After Default Judgment," ch. 10-B, §9, p. 897; *O'Connor's Texas Forms*, FORMS 7A; *O'Connor's Texas Family Law Handbook* (2017), "Default judgment," ch. 3-A, §13.3, p. 261 (suit for divorce); "Default judgment," ch. 4-D, §10.3, p. 428 (suit to dissolve marriage with children).

ANNOTATIONS

In re R.R., 209 S.W.3d 112, 114-15 (Tex.2006). Under ***Craddock***, a "default judgment should be set aside and a new trial granted if (1) the failure to answer was not intentional or the result of conscious indifference but was due to a mistake or accident, (2) the defendant sets up a meritorious defense, and (3) the motion is filed at such time that granting a new trial would not result in delay or otherwise injure the plaintiff. The defendant's burden as to the first ***Craddock*** element has been satisfied when the factual assertions, if true, negate intentional or consciously indifferent conduct by the defendant and the factual assertions are not controverted by the plaintiff. [¶] Failing to file an answer in-

tentionally or due to conscious indifference means 'the defendant knew it was sued but did not care.' ... Not understanding a citation and then doing nothing following service does not constitute a mistake of law that is sufficient to meet the ***Craddock*** requirements. [W]e have also held that some excuse, although not necessarily a good one, will suffice to show that a defendant's failure to file an answer was not because the defendant did not care. *At 116-17:* [Under ***Craddock***'s second prong, a] meritorious defense has been set up ... if the facts alleged in the movant's motion and supporting affidavits set forth facts which in law constitute a meritorious defense, regardless of whether those facts are controverted. In regard to [mother's] claim of having set up a meritorious defense, we note that parental rights may be terminated only if termination is in the best interest of the children. [¶] There are several factors that should be taken into account when determining whether termination of parental rights is in the best interest of the child.... [T]here is [also] a strong presumption that the best interest of a child is served by keeping the child with a parent. Based on all these considerations as well as [mother's] factual assertions, we conclude that [mother] set up a meritorious defense to CPS's claim that termination would be in the best interest of the children. [¶] [Under ***Craddock***'s third prong, mother's] motion for new trial was timely filed and urged that granting a new trial would not result in delay or otherwise injure CPS or the children. [¶] If a defendant alleges that granting a new trial will not injure the plaintiff, the burden then shifts to the plaintiff to present proof of injury. The use of equitable principles guides the determination as to injury. ... We conclude that [mother] met the third ***Craddock*** requirement. Because [mother] satisfied all three ***Craddock*** requirements, we do not consider her claim that the ***Craddock*** standard should be modified for parental termination proceedings." *See also* ***Craddock v. Sunshine Bus Lines, Inc.***, 133 S.W.2d 124, 126 (Tex.1939) (creating three-prong test for setting aside default judgment and granting new trial); ***Anderson v. Anderson***, 282 S.W.3d 150, 153 (Tex.App.—El Paso 2009, no pet.) (applying three-prong test in divorce suit); ***Lowe v. Lowe***, 971 S.W.2d 720, 725-27 (Tex.App.—Houston [14th Dist.] 1998, pet. denied) (outlining reasons why ***Craddock*** should not be applied in SAPCRs).

In re Burlington Coat Factory Whs., 167 S.W.3d 827, 830 (Tex.2005). "[A] default judgment that fails to dispose of all claims can be final only if 'intent to finally dispose of the case' is 'unequivocally expressed in the words of the order itself.'" *See also* ***Lehmann v. Har-Con Corp.***, 39 S.W.3d 191, 200 (Tex.2001).

Lopez v. Lopez, 757 S.W.2d 721, 723 (Tex.1988). "Because the record here establishes that [D] had no actual or constructive notice of the trial setting, the lower courts erred in requiring him to show that he had a meritorious defense as a condition to granting his motion for new trial." *See also* ***Thottumkal v. Sidhu***, No. 14-13-00966-CV (Tex.App.—Houston [14th Dist.] 2014, no pet.) (memo op.; 12-9-14).

In re Brilliant, 86 S.W.3d 680, 693 (Tex.App.—El Paso 2002, no pet.). "An original answer may consist of motions to transfer venue, pleas to the jurisdiction, pleas in abatement, or any other dilatory pleas. If a timely answer has been filed, or the respondent has otherwise made an appearance in a contested case, she is entitled to notice of the trial setting as a matter of due process. Even a *pro se* answer in the form of a signed letter that identifies the parties, the case, and the defendant's current address, constitutes a sufficient appearance to require notice to that party of any subsequent proceedings. [¶] [W's] plea to the jurisdiction constituted an appearance. When a party has appeared, she is entitled to notice of trial pursuant to [TRCP] 245. ... A trial court's failure to comply with the rules of notice in a contested case deprives a party of the constitutional right to be present at the hearing, to voice her objections in an appropriate manner, and results in a violation of fundamental due process. Thus, if the respondent does not have notice of the trial setting as required by Rule 245, the default judgment should be set aside because it is ineffectual."

TRCP 239a. NOTICE OF DEFAULT JUDGMENT

At or immediately prior to the time an interlocutory or final default judgment is rendered, the party taking the same or his attorney shall certify to the clerk in writing the last known mailing address of the party against whom the judgment is taken, which certificate shall be filed among the papers in the cause. Immediately upon the signing of the judgment, the clerk shall mail written notice thereof to the party against whom the judgment was rendered at the address shown in the certificate, and note the fact of such mailing on the docket. The notice shall state the number and style of the case, the court in which the case is pending, the names of the parties in whose favor and against whom

the judgment was rendered, and the date of the signing of the judgment. Failure to comply with the provisions of this rule shall not affect the finality of the judgment.

See also *O'Connor's Texas Rules*, "Certificate of last known address," ch. 7-A, §3.9.2(2), p. 676; "Notice of Default Judgment," ch. 7-A, §6, p. 682.

TRCP 240. WHERE ONLY SOME ANSWER

Where there are several defendants, some of whom have answered or have not been duly served and some of whom have been duly served and have made default, an interlocutory judgment by default may be entered against those who have made default, and the cause may proceed or be postponed as to the others.

See also TRCP 161; *O'Connor's Texas Rules*, "Default Judgment," ch. 7-A, p. 671.

TRCP 241. ASSESSING DAMAGES ON LIQUIDATED DEMANDS

When a judgment by default is rendered against the defendant, or all of several defendants, if the claim is liquidated and proved by an instrument in writing, the damages shall be assessed by the court, or under its direction, and final judgment shall be rendered therefor, unless the defendant shall demand and be entitled to a trial by jury.

See also *O'Connor's Texas Rules*, "Liquidated damages – hearing not required," ch. 7-A, §3.13.1, p. 678.

ANNOTATIONS

Sherman Acquisition II LP v. Garcia, 229 S.W.3d 802, 809 (Tex.App.—Waco 2007, no pet.). "A claim is liquidated if the amount of damages caused by the defendant can be accurately calculated from (1) the factual, as opposed to conclusory, allegations in the petition, and (2) an instrument in writing. Whether a claim is liquidated must be determined from the language of the petition, as a seemingly liquidated claim may be unliquidated because of pleading allegations which require proof for resolution." *See also* ***Novosad v. Brian K. Cunningham, P.C.***, 38 S.W.3d 767, 773 (Tex.App.—Houston [14th Dist.] 2001, no pet.).

TRCP 242. REPEALED

TRCP 243. UNLIQUIDATED DEMANDS

If the cause of action is unliquidated or be not proved by an instrument in writing, the court shall hear evidence as to damages and shall render judgment therefor, unless the defendant shall demand and be entitled to a trial by jury in which case the judgment by default shall be noted, a writ of inquiry awarded, and the cause entered on the jury docket.

See also *O'Connor's Texas Rules*, "Unliquidated damages – hearing required," ch. 7-A, §3.13.2, p. 678.

ANNOTATIONS

Paradigm Oil, Inc. v. Retamco Oper., Inc., 372 S.W.3d 177, 182 (Tex.2012). "[D] does not contest the trial court's decision to strike its answer as a discovery sanction or the default judgment rendered against it on liability. [D's] appeal focuses instead on its exclusion from the trial on damages. [A] defaulted[ ] defendant has the right to participate in such a trial when, as here, the plaintiff's damages are unliquidated. *At 186:* So what kind of abuse would justify barring a defaulted defendant's participation at the hearing on unliquidated damages? [S]poliation [i]s one [possible] example[, b]ut [that] is not at issue in this case. *At 187:* Given … the … sanction that ended the liability litigation, the additional sanction … precluding [D's participation in] the damages trial was excessive."

Texas Commerce Bank v. New, 3 S.W.3d 515, 516 (Tex.1999). "We conclude that because unobjected-to hearsay is, as a matter of law, probative evidence, affidavits can be evidence for purposes of an unliquidated-damages hearing pursuant to Rule 243."

Holt Atherton Indus. v. Heine, 835 S.W.2d 80, 86 (Tex.1992). "As a general matter, when we sustain a no evidence point of error after a trial on the merits, we render judgment on that point. [¶] [However,] when an appellate court sustains a no evidence point after an *uncontested* hearing on unliquidated damages following a no-answer default judgment, the appropriate disposition is a remand for a new trial on the issue of unliquidated damages."

Ingram Indus. v. U.S. Bolt Mfg., 121 S.W.3d 31, 37 (Tex.App.—Houston [1st Dist.] 2003, no pet.). "A trial court may award unliquidated damages based on affidavit testimony. [T]he trial court based the award of damages on its consideration of 'the pleadings and evidence on file.' The evidence on file contained [the affidavit of P's general manager, which] set out [P's] damages. The trial court thus considered [the] affidavit to be proof of [P's] damages. Therefore, the trial court satisfied Rule 243's hearing requirement without the need of holding an evidentiary hearing."

Marr v. Marr, 905 S.W.2d 331, 333-34 (Tex.App.—Waco 1995, no writ). "The question before us is whether Rule 243 applies in divorce cases…. Rule 243 recognizes, first, the importance of a party's right to a trial by jury, and, second, that the determination of the

amount of damages is a question primarily for the jury. It assures defaulting defendants, provided they properly request and do not waive a trial by jury, that they will be afforded their right to have a jury weigh the facts underlying the plaintiff's complaint for unliquidated damages and ascertain from those facts the amount of their damages. [¶] We believe Rule 243 applies in cases involving the division of marital property as well as the proper characterization of the parties' assets as either community or separate. The prominent role of a jury in divorce cases is readily apparent. Parties to divorce proceedings are entitled to a jury trial upon proper request; the jury alone decides whether contested assets will be characterized as either community or separate; and, while the question of a just and right division of the marital estate rests solely within the sound discretion of the court, the jury's findings on the factual issues underlying the division of the marital estate, including the valuation of the assets, are conclusive. Given the right of parties to a jury trial in divorce cases and the pronounced functions of the jury in the property division and characterization aspects of divorce cases, we believe the nature of the property division to be sufficiently akin to the unliquidated damages referred to in Rule 243 so as to require defaulting parties in divorce cases be provided sufficient notice of a hearing before a jury on the issue of the property division, unless, of course, the defaulting party somehow waives his request for a jury."

TRCP 244. ON SERVICE BY PUBLICATION

Where service has been made by publication, and no answer has been filed nor appearance entered within the prescribed time, the court shall appoint an attorney to defend the suit in behalf of the defendant, and judgment shall be rendered as in other cases; but, in every such case a statement of the evidence, approved and signed by the judge, shall be filed with the papers of the cause as a part of the record thereof. The court shall allow such attorney a reasonable fee for his services, to be taxed as part of the costs.

Caution: TRCP 244 is affected by Fam. Code §§6.409 and 102.010.

See also *O'Connor's Texas Rules*, "MNT After Service by Publication," ch. 10-B, §10, p. 902; *O'Connor's Texas Forms*, FORM 10B:5.

ANNOTATIONS

Cahill v. Lyda, 826 S.W.2d 932, 933 (Tex.1992). "Rule 244 … requires that a trial court appoint an attorney ad litem to represent defendants served with citation by publication who fail to file an answer or appear before the court. Rule 244 also requires that the attorney ad litem be paid a reasonable fee for his services, which is to be taxed as part of the costs. The attorney ad litem must exhaust all remedies available to his client and, if necessary, represent his client's interest on appeal." *See also* ***Atlantic Shippers v. Jefferson Cty.***, 363 S.W.3d 276, 286-87 (Tex.App.—Beaumont 2012, no pet.).

Barnes v. Domain, 875 S.W.2d 32, 33 (Tex.App.—Houston [14th Dist.] 1994, no writ). "Neither the case law nor the language of [TRCP 244] reveals any indication that the burden is on the attorney to move the court to make such appointment."

TRCP 245. ASSIGNMENT OF CASES FOR TRIAL

The Court may set contested cases on written request of any party, or on the court's own motion, with reasonable notice of not less than forty-five days to the parties of a first setting for trial, or by agreement of the parties; provided, however, that when a case previously has been set for trial, the Court may reset said contested case to a later date on any reasonable notice to the parties or by agreement of the parties. Noncontested cases may be tried or disposed of at any time whether set or not, and may be set at any time for any other time.

A request for trial setting constitutes a representation that the requesting party reasonably and in good faith expects to be ready for trial by the date requested, but no additional representation concerning the completion of pretrial proceedings or of current readiness for trial shall be required in order to obtain a trial setting in a contested case.

See also Tex. Const. art. 1, §19; *O'Connor's Texas Rules*, "Trial setting," ch. 5-A, §3.3, p. 373; "Notice of trial or dispositive hearing," ch. 7-A, §4.3, p. 681; "Motion for New Trial," ch. 10-B, p. 891.

ANNOTATIONS

Morales v. Marquis, No. 13-12-00407-CV (Tex. App.—Corpus Christi 2013, no pet.) (memo op.; 5-23-13). "Notice under Rule 245 can … be waived if a party who is actively litigating the case did not receive the full notice but proceeded to trial without objection. In this case, nothing in the record shows that [D] had notice of the hearing in order to object, so [D] took no action whatsoever between the time she filed her answer and the time she filed her notice of restricted appeal. In these circumstances—when a defendant an-

swers but takes no further action—many appellate courts, including this one, have held that a post-answer default should be set aside. [P] does not cite to any case where a defendant who answered but took no other action was deemed to have waived their right to notice under Rule 245, and we have found none." *See also* ***Szanyi v. Gibson***, No. 01-15-00895-CV (Tex. App.—Houston [1st Dist.] 2016, no pet.) (memo op.; 6-14-16) (objection to insufficiency of notice must be made before trial; Rule 245 objection made in motion for new trial is untimely and preserves nothing for review); ***Johnson v. Mohammed***, No. 03-10-00763-CV (Tex.App.—Austin 2013, pet. dism'd) (memo op.; 5-10-13) (45-day notice requirement can be waived by party's action or lack thereof).

Long v. Commission for Lawyer Discipline, No. 14-11-00059-CV (Tex.App.—Houston [14th Dist.] 2012, no pet.) (memo op.; 10-30-12). "A case is 'noncontested,' and thus is not subject to Rule 245's 45 day notice requirement, when the defendant does not file a written answer." *See also* ***Templeton Mortg. Corp. v. Poenisch***, No. 04-15-00041-CV (Tex.App.—San Antonio 2015, no pet.) (memo op.; 11-18-15).

In re Marriage of Hughes, No. 07-08-0292-CV (Tex.App.—Amarillo 2009, no pet.) (memo op.; 5-29-09). "[T]he trial court heard [W's] motion for temporary orders and *sua sponte* entered a final order dismissing her divorce action with no prior notice that the hearing was dispositive until the order issued. [W]e find the trial court's order dismissing [W's] action ... was issued in violation of the notice requirements of Rule 245. [¶] [H] asserts that two sentences in his pleadings and his proposed order of dismissal submitted at the end of the hearing constituted notice that the hearing would be a dispositive one. [H's] assertions represent a fundamental misunderstanding of Rule 245. Rule 245 does not permit a party to unilaterally set a hearing as dispositive. *Only* the trial court can set a case for trial and there must be no less than 45 days notice. Here, we have neither a written request from either party, an agreement, nor 45 day notice. [¶] [T]he trial court abused its discretion in denying [W's] motion for a new trial."

Custom-Crete, Inc. v. K-Bar Servs., 82 S.W.3d 655, 659 (Tex.App.—San Antonio 2002, no pet.). "A trial court's failure to comply with Rule 245 in a contested case deprives a party of its constitutional right to be present at the hearing, to voice its objections in an appropriate manner, and results in a violation of fundamental due process. Failure to give the required notice constitutes lack of due process and is grounds for reversal." *See also* ***In re E.A.W.S.***, No. 2-06-00031-CV (Tex. App.—Fort Worth 2006, pet. denied) (memo op.; 12-7-06) (trial court abused its discretion by disregarding 45-day notice requirement, but reversal was improper because error caused no harm); ***In re Brilliant***, 86 S.W.3d 680, 693 (Tex.App.—El Paso 2002, no pet.) (if respondent doesn't have notice as required by Rule 245, default judgment should be set aside because it is ineffectual).

Harmon v. Harmon, 879 S.W.2d 213, 215 (Tex. App.—Houston [14th Dist.] 1994, writ denied). "[D] complains that the case was tried without notice in violation of [TRCP] 245, which requires not less than 45-days notice of a first trial setting. [¶] Since [D] did not answer, this was a *noncontested* case, and [D] was vulnerable to a default judgment. [D] was not entitled notice of a trial setting. [¶] [D] contends that the case was 'contested' until the 60-day waiting period required by [Fam. Code] §3.60 [now §6.702] had elapsed. We disagree. ... It is true that the 60-day statutory waiting period precluded a divorce judgment, default or otherwise, from being rendered.... But this does not mean that the case was 'contested' for purposes of Rule 245. The case became noncontested when [D] failed to answer."

TRCP 246. CLERK TO GIVE NOTICE OF SETTINGS

The clerk shall keep a record in his office of all cases set for trial, and it shall be his duty to inform any nonresident attorney of the date of setting of any case upon request by mail from such attorney, accompanied by a return envelope properly addressed and stamped. Failure of the clerk to furnish such information on proper request shall be sufficient ground for continuance or for a new trial when it appears to the court that such failure has prevented the attorney from preparing or presenting his claim or defense.

ANNOTATIONS

Bruneio v. Bruneio, 890 S.W.2d 150, 156 n.2 (Tex. App.—Corpus Christi 1994, no writ). TRCP 246 "merely provides an additional vehicle for notice to any of the various attorneys who may be working on the case and want direct notification.... Accordingly, Rule 246 [expands] the requirements of notice to include non-resi-

dent attorneys who would not otherwise be entitled to direct notification of the setting under [TRCP] 245 as the attorney in charge."

TRCP 247. TRIED WHEN SET

Every suit shall be tried when it is called, unless continued or postponed to a future day or placed at the end of the docket to be called again for trial in its regular order. No cause which has been set upon the trial docket of the court shall be taken from the trial docket for the date set except by agreement of the parties or for good cause upon motion and notice to the opposing party.

See also *O'Connor's Texas Rules*, "Motion for Continuance," ch. 5-D, p. 394.

TRCP 248. JURY CASES

When a jury has been demanded, questions of law, motions, exceptions to pleadings, and other unresolved pending matters shall, as far as practicable, be heard and determined by the court before the trial commences, and jurors shall be summoned to appear on the day so designated.

See also TRCP 166.

TRCP 249. CALL OF NON-JURY DOCKET

The non-jury docket shall be taken up at such times as not unnecessarily to interfere with the dispatch of business on the jury docket.

TRCP 250. REPEALED

B. CONTINUANCE & CHANGE OF VENUE

TRCP 251. CONTINUANCE

No application for a continuance shall be heard before the defendant files his defense, nor shall any continuance be granted except for sufficient cause supported by affidavit, or by consent of the parties, or by operation of law.

Caution: TRCP 251 is affected by Fam. Code §161.2011.

See also *O'Connor's Texas Rules*, "Motion for Continuance," ch. 5-D, p. 394; *O'Connor's Texas Forms*, FORMS 5D; *O'Connor's Texas Family Law Handbook* (2017), "Continuance," ch. 4-H, §11.4.6, p. 616; "Temporary Injunctions," ch. 5-C, p. 688; "Final Protective Orders," ch. 6-C, p. 735.

ANNOTATIONS

Tenneco Inc. v. Enterprise Prods., 925 S.W.2d 640, 647 (Tex.1996). "When a party contends that it has not had an adequate opportunity for discovery before a summary judgment hearing, it must file either an affidavit explaining the need for further discovery or a verified motion for continuance."

Villegas v. Carter, 711 S.W.2d 624, 626 (Tex.1986). "Generally, when movants fail to comply with [TRCP] 251's requirement that the motion for continuance be 'supported by affidavit,' we presume that the trial court did not abuse its discretion in denying the motion. It would be unrealistic, however, to apply this presumption to lay movants who without fault have their attorney withdrawn." *See also* ***Garner v. Fidelity Bank***, 244 S.W.3d 855, 858-59 (Tex.App.—Dallas 2008, no pet.) (Rule 251 does not require party opposing motion for continuance to object to lack of verification; failure to object does not preclude party from raising objection for first time on appeal).

In re Guardianship of Cantu de Villarreal, 330 S.W.3d 11, 26-27 (Tex.App.—Corpus Christi 2010, no pet.). "[A] trial court is not required to grant a motion for continuance just because a party is unable to be present at trial. When a continuance is sought because of the unavailability of a party, we examine [TRCP] 252." *See also* ***Murphree v. Cooper***, No. 14-11-00416-CV (Tex.App.—Houston [14th Dist.] 2012, no pet.) (memo op.; 6-19-12).

TRCP 252. APPLICATION FOR CONTINUANCE

If the ground of such application be the want of testimony, the party applying therefor shall make affidavit that such testimony is material, showing the materiality thereof, and that he has used due diligence to procure such testimony, stating such diligence, and the cause of failure, if known; that such testimony cannot be procured from any other source; and, if it be for the absence of a witness, he shall state the name and residence of the witness, and what he expects to prove by him; and also state that the continuance is not sought for delay only, but that justice may be done; provided that, on a first application for a continuance, it shall not be necessary to show that the absent testimony cannot be procured from any other source.

The failure to obtain the deposition of any witness residing within 100 miles of the courthouse of the county in which the suit is pending shall not be regarded as want of diligence when diligence has been used to secure the personal attendance of such witness under the rules of law, unless by reason of age, infirmity or sickness, or official duty, the witness will be unable to attend the court, or unless such witness is about to leave, or has left, the State or county in which the

suit is pending and will not probably be present at the trial.

See also *O'Connor's Texas Rules*, "Motion for Continuance," ch. 5-D, p. 394; *O'Connor's Texas Forms*, FORMS 5D.

ANNOTATIONS

State v. Wood Oil Distrib., 751 S.W.2d 863, 865 (Tex.1988). "[T]he failure of a litigant to diligently utilize the rules of civil procedure for discovery purposes will not authorize the granting of a continuance."

In re Commitment of Winkle, 434 S.W.3d 300, 306 (Tex.App.—Beaumont 2014, pet. denied). "Rule 252 implies that sworn testimony may be considered an adequate substitute for a witness's personal appearance in a civil trial."

Ramirez v. State, 973 S.W.2d 388, 391 (Tex.App.—El Paso 1998, no pet.). D's continuance "motion failed to specify the information and testimony he sought or why it was material. [D] did not state the names of the witnesses from whom he sought testimony, nor did he state what he expected to prove from said witnesses." *See also* ***New York Party Shuttle, LLC v. Bilello***, 414 S.W.3d 206, 217 (Tex.App.—Houston [1st Dist.] 2013, pet. denied).

Verkin v. Southwest Ctr. One, Ltd., 784 S.W.2d 92, 94 (Tex.App.—Houston [1st Dist.] 1989, writ denied). When a motion for continuance is (1) in substantial compliance with the rule, (2) verified, and (3) uncontroverted, the court "must accept the statements in the motion as true."

TRCP 253. ABSENCE OF COUNSEL AS GROUND FOR CONTINUANCE

Except as provided elsewhere in these rules, absence of counsel will not be good cause for a continuance or postponement of the cause when called for trial, except it be allowed in the discretion of the court, upon cause shown or upon matters within the knowledge or information of the judge to be stated on the record.

See also *O'Connor's Texas Rules*, "Motion for Continuance," ch. 5-D, p. 394; *O'Connor's Texas Forms*, FORM 5D:2.

ANNOTATIONS

Villegas v. Carter, 711 S.W.2d 624, 626 (Tex.1986). "[T]he trial court abused its discretion because the evidence shows that [P] was not negligent or at fault in causing his attorney's withdrawal. The court granted [P's] attorney's motion to voluntarily withdraw two days before trial—too short a time for [P] to find a new attorney and for that new attorney to investigate the case and prepare for trial." *See also* ***Harrison v. Harrison***, 367 S.W.3d 822, 827 (Tex.App.—Houston [14th Dist.] 2012, pet. denied).

TRCP 254. ATTENDANCE ON LEGISLATURE

In all civil actions, including matters of probate, and in all matters ancillary to such suits which require action by or the attendance of an attorney, including appeals but excluding temporary restraining orders, at any time within thirty days of a date when the legislature is to be in session, or at any time the legislature is in session, or when the legislature sits as a Constitutional Convention, it shall be mandatory that the court continue the cause if it shall appear to the court, by affidavit, that any party applying for continuance, or any attorney for any party to the cause, is a member of either branch of the legislature, and will be or is in actual attendance on a session of the same. If the member of the legislature is an attorney for a party to the cause, his affidavit shall contain a declaration that it is his intention to participate actively in the preparation and/or presentation of the case. Where a party to any cause, or an attorney for any party to a cause, is a member of the legislature, his affidavit need not be corroborated. On the filing of such affidavit, the court shall continue the cause until thirty days after adjournment of the legislature and the affidavit shall be proof of the necessity for the continuance, and the continuance shall be deemed one of right and shall not be charged against the movant upon any subsequent application for continuance.

The right to a continuance shall be mandatory, except only where the attorney was employed within ten days of the date the suit is set for trial, the right to continuance shall be discretionary.

Caution: TRCP 254 is affected by Fam. Code §84.005.

See also CPRC §30.003 for other requirements of a legislative continuance; *O'Connor's Texas Rules*, "Motion for Continuance," ch. 5-D, p. 394; *O'Connor's Texas Forms*, FORM 5D:2; *O'Connor's Texas Family Law Handbook* (2017), "Legislator," ch. 6-C, §7.2.1(3), p. 745.

ANNOTATIONS

In re Ford Motor Co., 165 S.W.3d 315, 319 (Tex. 2005). "'[A] legislative continuance is mandatory except in those cases in which the party opposing the continuance alleges that a substantial existing right will be defeated or abridged by delay.' When a party opposes a legislative continuance in such circumstances, the trial

court must conduct a hearing on the allegations and deny the motion if the allegations are shown to be meritorious." *See also* ***Waites v. Sondock***, 561 S.W.2d 772, 776 (Tex.1977).

TRCP 255. CHANGE OF VENUE BY CONSENT

Upon the written consent of the parties filed with the papers of the cause, the court, by an order entered on the minutes, may transfer the same for trial to the court of any other county having jurisdiction of the subject matter of such suit.

See also CPRC §15.020; ***O'Connor's Texas Rules***, "Consent of the Parties," ch. 3-C, §4, p. 246; ***O'Connor's Texas Forms***, FORMS 3C:10, 11.

ANNOTATIONS

Farris v. Ray, 895 S.W.2d 351, 352 (Tex.1995). "[A] signed written agreement filed in the record of the *transferee* court meets all the requirements of [TRCP] 11. Such an agreement, enforceable against the signatories under the terms of the rule, operates as an express waiver of any error there may have been in the initial transfer."

TRCP 256. REPEALED

TRCP 257. GRANTED ON MOTION

A change of venue may be granted in civil causes upon motion of either party, supported by his own affidavit and the affidavit of at least three credible persons, residents of the county in which the suit is pending, for any following cause:

(a) That there exists in the county where the suit is pending so great a prejudice against him that he cannot obtain a fair and impartial trial.

(b) That there is a combination against him instigated by influential persons, by reason of which he cannot expect a fair and impartial trial.

(c) That an impartial trial cannot be had in the county where the action is pending.

(d) For other sufficient cause to be determined by the court.

Caution: TRCP 257 is affected by Fam. Code §§103.002 and 103.003.

See also ***O'Connor's Texas Rules***, "Motion to Transfer—Challenging Venue," ch. 3-C, p. 235; ***O'Connor's Texas Forms***, FORMS 3C:4, 8, 11; ***O'Connor's Texas Family Law Handbook*** (2017), "Family Code transfers," ch. 4-B, §3.2, p. 350.

TRCP 258. SHALL BE GRANTED

Where such motion to transfer venue is duly made, it shall be granted, unless the credibility of those making such application, or their means of knowledge or the truth of the facts set out in the said application are attacked by the affidavit of a credible person; when thus attacked, the issue thus formed shall be tried by the judge; and the application either granted or refused. Reasonable discovery in support of, or in opposition to, the application shall be permitted, and such discovery as is relevant, including deposition testimony on file, may be attached to, or incorporated by reference in, the affidavit of a party, a witness, or an attorney who has knowledge of such discovery.

See also ***O'Connor's Texas Rules***, "Motion to Transfer—Challenging Venue," ch. 3-C, p. 235.

ANNOTATIONS

City of Abilene v. Downs, 367 S.W.2d 153, 155 (Tex.1963). "Rule 258 by its terms is mandatorily operative. It provides the only means by which issue can be joined."

In re East Tex. Med. Ctr. Athens, 154 S.W.3d 933, 935 (Tex.App.—Tyler 2005, orig. proceeding). "A trial court can deny the motion to transfer if the movant does not comply with [TRCP] 257. If the motion is challenged as permitted by [TRCP] 258, the judge must try the issue. If the motion is not challenged in the manner provided by Rule 258, transfer is mandatory."

TRCP 259. TO WHAT COUNTY

If the motion under Rule 257 is granted, the cause shall be removed:

(a) If from a district court, to any county of proper venue in the same or an adjoining district;

(b) If from a county court, to any adjoining county of proper venue;

(c) If (a) or (b) are not applicable, to any county of proper venue;

(d) If a county of proper venue (other than the county of suit) cannot be found, then if from

(1) A district court, to any county in the same or an adjoining district or to any district where an impartial trial can be had;

(2) A county court, to any adjoining county or to any district where an impartial trial can be had;

but the parties may agree that venue shall be changed to some other county, and the order of the court shall conform to such agreement.

See also ***O'Connor's Texas Rules***, "Motion to Transfer—Challenging Venue," ch. 3-C, p. 235.

TRCP 260. REPEALED

TRCP 261. TRANSCRIPT ON CHANGE

When a change of venue has been granted, the clerk shall immediately make out a correct transcript of all the orders made in said cause, certifying thereto officially under the seal of the court, and send the same, with the original papers in the cause, to the clerk of the court to which the venue has been changed.

C. THE TRIAL

TRCP 262. TRIAL BY THE COURT

The rules governing the trial of causes before a jury shall govern in trials by the court in so far as applicable.

ANNOTATIONS

Qantel Bus. Sys. v. Custom Controls Co., 761 S.W.2d 302, 304-05 (Tex.1988). "When a plaintiff rests, he indicates that he does not desire to put on further evidence, except by rebuttal testimony, and that he has fully developed his case." In a nonjury case, the court is presumed to have ruled on the sufficiency of the evidence when it grants judgment for the defendant after the plaintiff rests.

TRCP 263. AGREED CASE

Parties may submit matters in controversy to the court upon an agreed statement of facts filed with the clerk, upon which judgment shall be rendered as in other cases; and such agreed statement signed and certified by the court to be correct and the judgment rendered thereon shall constitute the record of the cause.

See also *O'Connor's Texas Rules*, "Motion for Judgment on Agreed Statement of Facts," ch. 7-E, p. 736; *O'Connor's Texas Forms*, FORMS 7E.

ANNOTATIONS

Taylor v. First Cmty. Credit Un., 316 S.W.3d 863, 866 (Tex.App.—Houston [14th Dist.] 2010, no pet.). "Strict compliance with [TRCP 263] is not required. When ... the record indicates that the trial court heard the case on stipulated facts, a reviewing court may treat the case as one involving an agreed statement of facts under Rule 263." *See also* ***Addison Urban Dev. Partners v. Alan Ritchey Materials Co.***, 437 S.W.3d 597, 600-01 (Tex.App.—Dallas 2014, no pet.).

State Farm Lloyds v. Kessler, 932 S.W.2d 732, 735 (Tex.App.—Fort Worth 1996, writ denied). "An agreed statement of facts under rule 263 is similar to a special verdict; it is the parties' request for judgment under the applicable law. The only issue on appeal is whether the trial court properly applied the law to the agreed facts. The appellate court is limited to those facts unless other facts are necessarily implied from the express facts in the statement. In an appeal of an 'agreed' case, there are no presumed findings in favor of the judgment, and the pleadings are immaterial." *See also* ***Ultrasound Tech. Servs. v. Dallas Cent. Appr. Dist.***, 357 S.W.3d 174, 176 (Tex.App.—Dallas 2011, pet. denied).

City of Galveston v. Giles, 902 S.W.2d 167, 170 n.2 (Tex.App.—Houston [1st Dist.] 1995, no writ). "Findings of fact have no place in the trial of an agreed case. Once the parties stipulate to all the facts, the court may not make additional fact findings."

TRCP 264. VIDEOTAPE TRIAL

By agreement of the parties, the trial court may allow that all testimony and such other evidence as may be appropriate be presented at trial by videotape. The expenses of such videotape recordings shall be taxed as costs. If any party withdraws agreement to a videotape trial, the videotape costs that have accrued will be taxed against the party withdrawing from the agreement.

TRCP 265. ORDER OF PROCEEDINGS ON TRIAL BY JURY

The trial of cases before a jury shall proceed in the following order unless the court should, for good cause stated in the record, otherwise direct:

(a) The party upon whom rests the burden of proof on the whole case shall state to the jury briefly the nature of his claim or defense and what said party expects to prove and the relief sought. Immediately thereafter, the adverse party may make a similar statement, and intervenors and other parties will be accorded similar rights in the order determined by the court.

(b) The party upon whom rests the burden of proof on the whole case shall then introduce his evidence.

(c) The adverse party shall briefly state the nature of his claim or defense and what said party expects to prove and the relief sought unless he has already done so.

(d) He shall then introduce his evidence.

(e) The intervenor and other parties shall make their statement, unless they have already done so, and shall introduce their evidence.

(f) The parties shall then be confined to rebutting testimony on each side.

(g) But one counsel on each side shall examine and cross-examine the same witness, except on leave granted.

TRCP 266. OPEN & CLOSE—ADMISSION

Except as provided in Rule 269 the plaintiff shall have the right to open and conclude both in adducing his evidence and in the argument, unless the burden of proof on the whole case under the pleadings rests upon the defendant, or unless the defendant or all of the defendants, if there should be more than one, shall, after the issues of fact are settled and before the trial commences, admit that the plaintiff is entitled to recover as set forth in the petition, except so far as he may be defeated, in whole or in part, by the allegations of the answer constituting a good defense, which may be established on the trial; which admission shall be entered of record, whereupon the defendant, or the defendants, if more than one, shall have the right to open and conclude in adducing the evidence and in the argument of the cause. The admission shall not serve to admit any allegation which is inconsistent with such defense, which defense shall be one that defendant has the burden of establishing, as for example, and without excluding other defenses: accord and satisfaction, adverse possession, arbitration and award, contributory negligence, discharge in bankruptcy, duress, estoppel, failure of consideration, fraud, release, res judicata, statute of frauds, statute of limitations, waiver, and the like.

See also *O'Connor's Texas Rules*, "Opening Statement," ch. 8-B, p. 788; "Final Argument," ch. 8-J, p. 844; *O'Connor's Texas Forms*, FORMS 8B, 8J.

ANNOTATIONS

4M Linen & Unif. Sup. Co. v. W.P. Ballard & Co., 793 S.W.2d 320, 324 (Tex.App.—Houston [1st Dist.] 1990, writ denied). "Rule 266 ... provides that the plaintiff has the right to open and close argument. There are two exceptions.... First, a defendant has the right to open and close if the burden of proof for the entire case under the pleadings is on defendant. Second, a defendant has the right to open and close if, before trial begins, defendant admits that plaintiff is entitled to recover, subject to proof of defensive allegations...."

TRCP 267. WITNESSES PLACED UNDER RULE

a. At the request of either party, in a civil case, the witnesses on both sides shall be sworn and removed out of the courtroom to some place where they cannot hear the testimony as delivered by any other witness in the cause. This is termed placing witnesses under the rule.

b. This rule does not authorize exclusion of (1) a party who is a natural person or the spouse of such natural person, or (2) an officer or employee of a party that is not a natural person and who is designated as its representative by its attorney, or (3) a person whose presence is shown by a party to be essential to the presentation of the cause.

c. If any party be absent, the court in its discretion may exempt from the rule a representative of such party.

d. Witnesses, when placed under Rule 614 of the Texas Rules of Civil Evidence, shall be instructed by the court that they are not to converse with each other or with any other person about the case other than the attorneys in the case, except by permission of the court, and that they are not to read any report of or comment upon the testimony in the case while under the rule.

e. Any witness or other person violating such instructions may be punished for contempt of court.

See also TRE 614; *O'Connor's Texas Rules*, "Invoking 'the Rule'," ch. 8-C, §3, p. 790.

ANNOTATIONS

Drilex Sys. v. Flores, 1 S.W.3d 112, 118-19 (Tex. 1999). "Although an expert witness may *typically* be found exempt under the essential presence exception, experts are not *automatically* exempt. Instead, [TRE] 614 and [TRCP] 267 vest in trial judges broad discretion to determine whether a witness is essential. *At 120:* We acknowledge that the court never expressly placed [D's expert] under [TRE 614] and never instructed him not to discuss the case with others. However, a court may, in its discretion, exclude the testimony of a prospective witness who technically violates [TRE 614] even though the witness was never actually placed under [TRE 614]."

TRCP 268. MOTION FOR INSTRUCTED VERDICT

A motion for directed verdict shall state the specific grounds therefor.

See also *O'Connor's Texas Rules*, "Motion for Directed Verdict," ch. 8-G, p. 820; *O'Connor's Texas Forms*, FORMS 8G.

ANNOTATIONS

City of Keller v. Wilson, 168 S.W.3d 802, 827 (Tex. 2005). "As both the inclusive and exclusive standards for the scope of legal-sufficiency review have a long

history in Texas, as both have been used in other contexts to review matter-of-law motions, as the federal courts have decided the differences between the two are more semantic than real, and as both—properly applied—must arrive at the same result, we see no compelling reason to choose among them. [¶] The key qualifier, of course, is 'properly applied.' The final test for legal sufficiency must always be whether the evidence at trial would enable reasonable and fair-minded people to reach the verdict under review. Whether a reviewing court begins by considering all the evidence or only the evidence supporting the verdict, legal-sufficiency review [of the denial of a directed verdict] must credit favorable evidence if reasonable jurors could, and disregard contrary evidence unless reasonable jurors could not." *See also* ***Mauricio v. Castro***, 287 S.W.3d 476, 479 (Tex.App.—Dallas 2009, no pet.).

Szczepanik v. First S. Trust Co., 883 S.W.2d 648, 649 (Tex.1994). "In reviewing … an instructed verdict, we must determine whether there is any evidence of probative force to raise a fact issue on the material questions presented. We consider all of the evidence in a light most favorable to the party against whom the verdict was instructed and disregard all contrary evidence and inferences…. If there is any conflicting evidence of probative value on any theory of recovery, an instructed verdict is improper…." *See also* ***S.V. v. R.V.***, 933 S.W.2d 1, 8 (Tex.1996).

Johnson v. Swain, 787 S.W.2d 36, 36 n.1 (Tex. 1989). "While a partial instructed verdict is not expressly contemplated by our rules, this device has been employed by trial courts as a convenient way of removing certain parts of a case from the factfinder." *See also* ***In re Commitment of Scott***, No. 09-11-00555-CV (Tex.App.—Beaumont 2012, no pet.) (memo op.; 10-25-12).

Brewer v. Lowe's Home Ctrs., Inc., No. 12-14-00155-CV (Tex.App.—Tyler 2015, no pet.) (memo op.; 10-14-15). "A directed verdict is proper when (1) a defect in the opponent's pleadings makes them insufficient to support a judgment; (2) the evidence conclusively proves a fact that establishes a party's right to judgment as a matter of law; or (3) the evidence offered on a cause of action is insufficient to raise an issue of fact. Generally, a directed verdict in favor of a defendant may be proper in two situations: (1) when a plaintiff does not present evidence 'raising a fact issue essential to the plaintiff's right of recovery'; and (2) when a plaintiff 'admits or the evidence conclusively establishes a defense to the plaintiff's cause of action.'"

TRCP 269. ARGUMENT

(a) After the evidence is concluded and the charge is read, the parties may argue the case to the jury. The party having the burden of proof on the whole case, or on all matters which are submitted by the charge, shall be entitled to open and conclude the argument; where there are several parties having separate claims or defenses, the court shall prescribe the order of argument between them.

(b) In all arguments, and especially in arguments on the trial of the case, the counsel opening shall present his whole case as he relies on it, both of law and facts, and shall be heard in the concluding argument only in reply to the counsel on the other side.

(c) Counsel for an intervenor shall occupy the position in the argument assigned by the court according to the nature of the claim.

(d) Arguments on questions of law shall be addressed to the court, and counsel should state the substance of the authorities referred to without reading more from books than may be necessary to verify the statement. On a question on motions, exceptions to the evidence, and other incidental matters, the counsel will be allowed only such argument as may be necessary to present clearly the question raised, and refer to authorities on it, unless further discussion is invited by the court.

(e) Arguments on the facts should be addressed to the jury, when one is impaneled in a case that is being tried, under the supervision of the court. Counsel shall be required to confine the argument strictly to the evidence and to the arguments of opposing counsel. Mere personal criticism by counsel upon each other shall be avoided, and when indulged in shall be promptly corrected as a contempt of court.

(f) Side-bar remarks, and remarks by counsel of one side, not addressed to the court, while the counsel on the other side is examining a witness or arguing any question to the court, or addressing the jury, will be rigidly repressed by the court.

(g) The court will not be required to wait for objections to be made when the rules as to arguments are violated; but should they not be noticed and corrected by the court, opposing counsel may ask leave of the court to rise and present his point of objection. But the

court shall protect counsel from any unnecessary interruption made on frivolous and unimportant grounds.

(h) It shall be the duty of every counsel to address the court from his place at the bar, and in addressing the court to rise to his feet; and while engaged in the trial of a case, he shall remain at his place in the bar.

See also *O'Connor's Texas Rules*, "Final Argument," ch. 8-J, p. 844; *O'Connor's Texas Forms*, FORMS 8J.

ANNOTATIONS

Living Ctrs. v. Peñalver, 256 S.W.3d 678, 680-81 (Tex.2008). "Error as to improper jury argument must ordinarily be preserved by a timely objection which is overruled. The complaining party must not have invited or provoked the improper argument. Typically, retraction of the argument or instruction from the court can cure any probable harm, but in rare instances the probable harm or prejudice cannot be cured. In such instances the argument is incurable and complaint about the argument may be made even though objection was not timely made. To prevail on a claim that improper argument was incurable, the complaining party generally must show that the argument by its nature, degree, and extent constituted such error that an instruction from the court or retraction of the argument could not remove its effects. [¶] [J]ury argument that strikes at the appearance of and the actual impartiality, equality, and fairness of justice rendered by courts is incurably harmful not only because of its harm to the litigants involved, but also because of its capacity to damage the judicial system. Such argument is not subject to the general harmless error analysis." *See also* ***Standard Fire Ins. v. Reese***, 584 S.W.2d 835, 839 (Tex. 1979); ***Richmond Condos. v. Skipworth Commercial Plumbing, Inc.***, 245 S.W.3d 646, 667-68 (Tex. App.—Fort Worth 2008, pet. denied).

Jones v. Republic Waste Servs., 236 S.W.3d 390, 401 (Tex.App.—Houston [1st Dist.] 2007, pet. denied). "To obtain reversal, appellants must first prove 'an error' that was not 'invited or provoked.' Counsel must confine argument 'strictly to the evidence and to the arguments of opposing counsel.' Criticism, censure, or abuse of counsel is not permitted. Appeals to passion and prejudice are improper, as are calls to punish a litigant for the acts of counsel." *See also* ***Popcap Games, Inc. v. MumboJumbo, LLC***, 350 S.W.3d 699, 721 (Tex. App.—Dallas 2011, pet. denied).

Sanchez v. Espinoza, 60 S.W.3d 392, 395 (Tex. App.—Amarillo 2001, pet. denied). In the argument, counsel "may discuss the 'environments' or circumstances of the case, the reasonableness or unreasonableness of the evidence, and the probative effect (or lack thereof) of the evidence. So too does he have the leeway to 'present his case as to make the law contained in the charge applicable to the facts of the case.' This leeway also includes the opportunity to encourage the jury to weigh, evaluate, and test the evidence before it."

TRCP 270. ADDITIONAL TESTIMONY

When it clearly appears to be necessary to the due administration of justice, the court may permit additional evidence to be offered at any time; provided that in a jury case no evidence on a controversial matter shall be received after the verdict of the jury.

See also *O'Connor's Texas Rules*, "Motion to Reopen for Additional Evidence," ch. 8-H, p. 823; *O'Connor's Texas Forms*, FORMS 8H.

ANNOTATIONS

Holden v. Holden, 456 S.W.3d 642, 650 (Tex.App.—Tyler 2015, no pet.). "The language of [TRCP 270] does not require a motion by a party, nor have we discovered authority preventing a trial court from reopening the evidence sua sponte. Rather, the courts addressing this issue have held that the trial court may reopen the evidence on its own motion. We agree with the reasoning in those cases."

Moore v. Jet Stream Invs., 315 S.W.3d 195, 201 (Tex.App.—Texarkana 2010, pet. denied). "A trial court's discretion to permit additional evidence 'should be exercised liberally to allow both parties to fully present their case.' ... In deciding whether to permit additional evidence, a trial court may consider (1) whether the movant showed due diligence in obtaining the evidence; (2) whether the additional evidence is decisive; (3) whether reopening the evidence will cause undue delay; and (4) whether reopening the evidence will cause injustice." *See also* ***Naguib v. Naguib***, 137 S.W.3d 367, 372-73 (Tex.App.—Dallas 2004, pet. denied); ***Lopez v. Lopez***, 55 S.W.3d 194, 201 (Tex.App.—Corpus Christi 2001, no pet.).

D. CHARGE TO THE JURY

TRCP 271. CHARGE TO THE JURY

Unless expressly waived by the parties, the trial court shall prepare and in open court deliver a written charge to the jury.

See also *O'Connor's Texas Rules*, "Jury Charge," ch. 8-I, p. 826.

TRCP 272. REQUISITES

The charge shall be in writing, signed by the court, and filed with the clerk, and shall be a part of the record of the cause. It shall be submitted to the respective parties or their attorneys for their inspection, and a reasonable time given them in which to examine and present objections thereto outside the presence of the jury, which objections shall in every instance be presented to the court in writing, or be dictated to the court reporter in the presence of the court and opposing counsel, before the charge is read to the jury. All objections not so presented shall be considered as waived. The court shall announce its rulings thereon before reading the charge to the jury and shall endorse the rulings on the objections if written or dictate same to the court reporter in the presence of counsel. Objections to the charge and the court's rulings thereon may be included as a part of any transcript or statement of facts on appeal and, when so included in either, shall constitute a sufficient bill of exception to the rulings of the court thereon. It shall be presumed, unless otherwise noted in the record, that the party making such objections presented the same at the proper time and excepted to the ruling thereon.

See also *O'Connor's Texas Rules*, "Jury Charge," ch. 8-I, p. 826; *O'Connor's Texas Forms*, FORMS 8I.

ANNOTATIONS

Wackenhut Corp. v. Gutierrez, 453 S.W.3d 917, 919-20 (Tex.2015). "[D] argues that, by detailing its reasons for opposing spoliation sanctions generally and a spoliation instruction in particular in its response to [P's] pretrial motion for sanctions, it timely made the trial court aware of its complaint [about the inclusion of a spoliation instruction in the jury charge]. Because the trial court ruled on the motion, [D] contends that it was not required to later object to the jury charge. [¶] [W]e have previously explained that '[t]here should be but one test for determining if a party has preserved error in the jury charge, and that is whether the party made the trial court aware of the complaint, timely and plainly, and obtained a ruling.' [¶] In light of [D's] specific reasons in its pretrial briefing for opposing a spoliation instruction and the trial court's recognition that it submitted the instruction over [D's] objection, there is no doubt that [D] timely made the trial court aware of its complaint and obtained a ruling. ... Therefore, we conclude that [D] preserved error."

King Fisher Mar. Serv. v. Tamez, 443 S.W.3d 838, 843 (Tex.2014). Rule 272 "provides that a trial court may not consider any objections made after the charge is read to the jury. But it does not follow that a trial court is obligated to consider *every* objection made before the charge is read to the jury. Instead, the plain language of the rule sets an outside limit for charge objections. [¶] Rule 272 mandates trial courts to afford the parties a 'reasonable time' to inspect the charge and present objections outside the presence of the jury. Nothing in the rule prohibits a trial court from setting a deadline for charge objections that may expire before it charges the jury as long as the deadline affords the parties a 'reasonable time' to inspect and object to the charge. Rule 272's reliance on reasonableness invites, rather than restricts, trial-court discretion. Accordingly, while the rule strictly prohibits objections after the charge is read, it affords trial courts latitude in addressing objections made before."

Cruz v. Andrews Restoration, Inc., 364 S.W.3d 817, 829 (Tex.2012). "'There should be but one test for determining if a party has preserved error in the jury charge, and that is whether the party made the trial court aware of the complaint, timely and plainly, and obtained a ruling.' *At 830:* A proposed charge, whether drafted by a party or by the court, may misalign the parties; misstate the burden of proof; leave out essential elements; or omit a defense, cause of action, or (as here) a line for attorney's fees. Our procedural rules require the lawyers to tell the court about such errors before the charge is formally submitted to a jury. *At 831:* Here, the parties had ample time to review the draft charge and point out discrepancies to the trial court. [P] can complain on appeal only if it made the trial court aware, timely and plainly, of the purported problem and obtained a ruling. Filing a pretrial charge that includes a question containing [a] subpart [that was omitted by the court], when no other part of the record reflects a discussion of the issue or objection to the question ultimately submitted, does not sufficiently alert the trial court to the issue." *See also* ***State Dept. of Hwys. & Pub. Transp. v. Payne***, 838 S.W.2d 235, 241 (Tex.1992).

Reinhart v. Young, 906 S.W.2d 471, 473 (Tex.1995). "This was not a close case, where a superfluous instruction would be more likely to influence the jury improperly. *At 474:* [A]nd even more important, the charge contained an instruction concerning the doc-

trine of sudden emergency. [Ps] made no objection whatsoever to this instruction, even though it reiterates much of the unavoidable accident instruction."

City of Brownsville v. Alvarado, 897 S.W.2d 750, 752 (Tex.1995). "Submission of an improper jury question can be harmless error if the jury's answers to other questions render the improper question immaterial. A jury question is considered immaterial when its answer can be found elsewhere in the verdict or when its answer cannot alter the effect of the verdict."

TRCP 273. JURY SUBMISSIONS

Either party may present to the court and request written questions, definitions, and instructions to be given to the jury; and the court may give them or a part thereof, or may refuse to give them, as may be proper. Such requests shall be prepared and presented to the court and submitted to opposing counsel for examination and objection within a reasonable time after the charge is given to the parties or their attorneys for examination. A request by either party for any questions, definitions, or instructions shall be made separate and apart from such party's objections to the court's charge.

See also *O'Connor's Texas Rules*, "Jury Charge," ch. 8-I, p. 826; *O'Connor's Texas Forms*, FORMS 8I.

ANNOTATIONS

Cruz v. Andrews Restoration, Inc., 364 S.W.3d 817, 831 (Tex.2012). "A charge filed before trial begins rarely accounts fully for the inevitable developments during trial. For these reasons, [TRCP 273 requires] that requests be prepared and presented to the court 'within a reasonable time *after* the charge is given to the parties or their attorneys for examination.' Notwithstanding our rules, we have held that a party may rely on a pretrial charge as long as the record shows that the trial court knew of the written request and refused to submit it."

Alaniz v. Jones & Neuse, Inc., 907 S.W.2d 450, 451 (Tex.1995). TRCP 273 "does not prohibit including the request in a complete charge as long as it is not obscured."

TRCP 274. OBJECTIONS & REQUESTS

A party objecting to a charge must point out distinctly the objectionable matter and the grounds of the objection. Any complaint as to a question, definition, or instruction, on account of any defect, omission, or fault in pleading, is waived unless specifically included in the objections. When the complaining party's objection, or requested question, definition, or instruction is, in the opinion of the appellate court, obscured or concealed by voluminous unfounded objections, minute differentiations or numerous unnecessary requests, such objection or request shall be untenable. No objection to one part of the charge may be adopted and applied to any other part of the charge by reference only.

See also *O'Connor's Texas Rules*, "Jury Charge," ch. 8-I, p. 826.

ANNOTATIONS

In re B.L.D., 113 S.W.3d 340, 351 (Tex.2003). "We are aware of no precedent in either our criminal or civil jurisprudence that informs the court of appeals' conclusion that 'core' jury charge issues in termination cases should be reviewed even when not preserved. Further, we cannot see any reasonable, practical, and consistent way of reviewing unpreserved complaints of charge error in termination cases that satisfies our narrow fundamental-error doctrine. [T]he fundamental-error doctrine does not permit appellate review of the complaint of unpreserved charge error in this case."

Holubec v. Brandenberger, 111 S.W.3d 32, 39 (Tex. 2003). "[Ds] plainly sought the submission of their statutory defense. Because the question actually submitted was defective, however, [Ds] did not have to submit their own substantially correct question. [Ds'] objection was sufficient to preserve error." *See also* ***Moss v. Waste Mgmt.***, 305 S.W.3d 76, 80 (Tex.App.—Houston [1st Dist.] 2009, pet. denied).

Harris Cty. v. Smith, 96 S.W.3d 230, 236 (Tex. 2002). If an element of damages in a broad-form submission is not supported by evidence, the party must object and ask the court to either (1) not include that element in the broad-form damages question or (2) submit the elements separately.

Universal Servs. Co. v. Ung, 904 S.W.2d 638, 640 (Tex.1995). A party cannot complain on appeal that the trial court did not submit an instruction or definition with the correct cluster if the party did not request it as part of that cluster.

General Chem. Corp. v. De La Lastra, 852 S.W.2d 916, 920 (Tex.1993). "[D] requested the very issues that it now seeks to avoid. Parties may not invite error by requesting an issue and then objecting to its submission."

Power Reps, Inc. v. Cates, No. 01-13-00856-CV (Tex.App.—Houston [1st Dist.] 2015, no pet.) (memo op.; 8-11-15). "A party is not required … to object before submission of the jury charge to preserve a complaint that a jury question is immaterial."

Cleveland Reg'l Med. Ctr., L.P. v. Celtic Props., L.C., 323 S.W.3d 322, 342 (Tex.App.—Beaumont 2010, pet. denied). "Generally, a request for a different instruction is not a substitute for an objection and does not preserve error." *See also* ***Reliant Energy Servs. v. Cotton Valley Compression, L.L.C.***, 336 S.W.3d 764, 785 n.23 (Tex.App.—Houston [1st Dist.] 2011, no pet.) (general objection that instruction was "not raised by the evidence" was not specific enough complaint).

C.M. Asfahl Agency v. Tensor, Inc., 135 S.W.3d 768, 795 (Tex.App.—Houston [1st Dist.] 2004, no pet.). "Rule 274's prohibition against adopting by reference has generally been interpreted as prohibiting one party from incorporating by reference its own objections to another portion of the charge. Yet, nothing in the rule limits its application to that context. *At 796:* [Ds] did not preserve any error premised on erroneously submitting question … to the jury merely by 'joining' the six substantive objections lodged by [co-D]. Instead, [Ds] were required to present their own objections."

TRCP 275. CHARGE READ BEFORE ARGUMENT

Before the argument is begun, the trial court shall read the charge to the jury in the precise words in which it was written, including all questions, definitions, and instructions which the court may give.

See also *O'Connor's Texas Rules*, "Jury Charge," ch. 8-I, p. 826.

ANNOTATIONS

Board of Regents v. S&G Constr. Co., 529 S.W.2d 90, 98-99 (Tex.App.—Austin 1975, writ ref'd n.r.e.), *overruled on other grounds*, ***Federal Sign v. Texas S. Univ.***, 951 S.W.2d 401 (Tex.1997). Held: A trial court does not violate TRCP 275 by amending the written charge to correct errors after oral argument.

TRCP 276. REFUSAL OR MODIFICATION

When an instruction, question, or definition is requested and the provisions of the law have been complied with and the trial judge refuses the same, the judge shall endorse thereon "Refused," and sign the same officially. If the trial judge modifies the same the judge shall endorse thereon "Modified as follows: (stating in what particular the judge has modified the same) and given, and exception allowed" and sign the same officially. Such refused or modified instruction, question, or definition, when so endorsed shall constitute a bill of exceptions, and it shall be conclusively presumed that the party asking the same presented it at the proper time, excepted to its refusal or modification, and that all the requirements of law have been observed, and such procedure shall entitle the party requesting the same to have the action of the trial judge thereon reviewed without preparing a formal bill of exceptions.

See also *O'Connor's Texas Rules*, "Jury Charge," ch. 8-I, p. 826.

ANNOTATIONS

Dallas Mkt. Ctr. Dev. Co. v. Liedeker, 958 S.W.2d 382, 386-87 (Tex.1997), *overruled on other grounds*, ***Torrington Co. v. Stutzman***, 46 S.W.3d 829 (Tex. 2000). Although Rule 276 requires the trial court to endorse refused requests "Refused" and sign them officially, that is not the only way to preserve error. The court can state on the record that they are refused. *See also* ***City of Lufkin v. AKJ Props., Inc.***, No. 06-12-00005-CV (Tex.App.—Texarkana 2012, no pet.) (memo op.; 6-26-12).

TRCP 277. SUBMISSION TO THE JURY

In all jury cases the court shall, whenever feasible, submit the cause upon broad-form questions. The court shall submit such instructions and definitions as shall be proper to enable the jury to render a verdict.

Inferential rebuttal questions shall not be submitted in the charge. The placing of the burden of proof may be accomplished by instructions rather than by inclusion in the question.

In any cause in which the jury is required to apportion the loss among the parties the court shall submit a question or questions inquiring what percentage, if any, of the negligence or causation, as the case may be, that caused the occurrence or injury in question is attributable to each of the persons found to have been culpable. The court shall also instruct the jury to answer the damage question or questions without any reduction because of the percentage of negligence or causation, if any, of the person injured. The court may predicate the damage question or questions upon affirmative findings of liability.

The court may submit a question disjunctively when it is apparent from the evidence that one or the other of the conditions or facts inquired about necessarily exists.

The court shall not in its charge comment directly on the weight of the evidence or advise the jury of the effect of their answers, but the court's charge shall not be objectionable on the ground that it incidentally constitutes a comment on the weight of the evidence or advises the jury of the effect of their answers when it is properly a part of an instruction or definition.

See also *O'Connor's Texas Rules*, "Jury Charge," ch. 8-I, p. 826.

ANNOTATIONS

Diamond Offshore Mgmt. v. Guidry, 171 S.W.3d 840, 844 (Tex.2005). "Broad-form submission does not entail omitting elements of proof from the charge. While the trial court could certainly have inquired about the separate issues ... in a single question with proper instructions, [D] was not obligated to request such a question. It was required only to object to the absence of any inquiry, which the trial court acknowledged [D] had done with its requested questions."

Harris Cty. v. Smith, 96 S.W.3d 230, 234 (Tex. 2002). "[T]he trial court erred in overruling [D's] timely and specific objection to the charge, which mixed valid and invalid elements of damages in a single broad-form submission, and that such error was harmful because it prevented the appellate court from determining 'whether the jury based its verdict on an improperly submitted invalid' element of damage. *At 236:* We hold that ***Casteel***'s reasoning [as to broad-form liability questions] applies equally to broad-form damage questions, and under its rationale we conclude that the charge error in this case was harmful."

Crown Life Ins. v. Casteel, 22 S.W.3d 378, 389 (Tex.2000). "When a single broad-form liability question erroneously commingles valid and invalid liability theories and the appellant's objection is timely and specific, the error is harmful when it cannot be determined whether the improperly submitted theories formed the sole basis for the jury's finding. *At 390:* Rule 277 is not absolute; rather, it mandates broad-form submission 'whenever feasible.' [Submitting] 'alternative liability standards when the governing law is unsettled might very well be a situation where broad-form submission is not feasible.' Similarly, when the trial court is unsure whether it should submit a particular theory of liability, separating liability theories best serves the policy of judicial economy underlying Rule 277 by avoiding the need for a new trial when the basis for liability cannot be determined. Furthermore, Rule 277 mandates that '[t]he court shall submit such instructions and definitions as shall be proper to enable the jury to render a verdict.' It is implicit in this mandate that the jury be able to base its verdict on legally valid questions and instructions. Thus, it may not be feasible to submit a single broad-form liability question that incorporates wholly separate theories of liability." *See also* ***Texas Comm'n on Human Rights v. Morrison***, 381 S.W.3d 533, 536-37 (Tex.2012).

Hyundai Motor Co. v. Rodriguez, 995 S.W.2d 661, 664 (Tex.1999). "[S]ubmission of a single question relating to multiple theories may be necessary to avoid the risk that the jury will become confused and answer questions inconsistently. The goal of the charge is to submit to the jury the issues for decision logically, simply, clearly, fairly, correctly, and completely." *See also* ***Texas DHS v. E.B.***, 802 S.W.2d 647, 649 (Tex.1990).

Texas Mut. Ins. v. Boetsch, 307 S.W.3d 874, 879-80 (Tex.App.—Dallas 2010, pet. denied). "An impermissible comment on the weight of the evidence occurs when, after examining the entire charge, it is determined that the judge assumed the truth of a material controverted fact or exaggerated, minimized, or withdrew some pertinent evidence from the jury's consideration. An instruction also will be held to be an improper comment on the weight of the evidence if it suggests to the jury the trial judge's opinion concerning the matter about which the jury is asked. Reversal is required if an improper comment on the weight of the evidence is one that was calculated to cause and probably did cause the rendition of an improper judgment." *See also* ***Flying J Inc. v. Meda, Inc.***, 373 S.W.3d 680, 687 (Tex.App.—San Antonio 2012, no pet.).

Valence Oper. Co. v. Anadarko Pet. Corp., 303 S.W.3d 435, 442 (Tex.App.—Texarkana 2010, no pet.). "A definition may properly be submitted to the jury if a term used in the charge has a distinct legal meaning, or if it differs in meaning from the usual and commonly accepted meaning. If the meaning that the parties intended to give to a term is a question of fact for the jury, and there is conflicting evidence before the jury as to the meaning of the term, it should not be defined, and the jury may decide the question based on its view of the evidence."

In re M.E.C., 66 S.W.3d 449, 458 (Tex.App.—Waco 2001, no pet.). TRCP 277 "provides that '[t]he court shall not in its charge comment directly on the weight of the evidence.' Although Rule 277 concerns the court's charge, appellate courts have applied the principle expressed therein to a court's verbal statements. [¶] A trial judge's statement during the course of trial impermissibly comments on the weight of the evidence if 'it indicates the judge's opinion concerning a matter to be determined by the jury.'"

In re M.C.M., 57 S.W.3d 27, 30 (Tex.App.—Houston [1st Dist.] 2001, pet. denied). Parents argue "the broad-form submission of jury questions is not proper in [a SAPCR proceeding to terminate parental rights]. They claim that, unless the jury makes a specific finding for each ground alleged for termination, as well as a separate finding that termination would be in the best interest of the child, their parental rights cannot be terminated. *At 31:* [I]t is not necessary for the trial court to submit separate questions in parental termination cases."

TRCP 278. SUBMISSION OF QUESTIONS, DEFINITIONS, & INSTRUCTIONS

The court shall submit the questions, instructions and definitions in the form provided by Rule 277, which are raised by the written pleadings and the evidence. Except in trespass to try title, statutory partition proceedings, and other special proceedings in which the pleadings are specially defined by statutes or procedural rules, a party shall not be entitled to any submission of any question raised only by a general denial and not raised by affirmative written pleading by that party. Nothing herein shall change the burden of proof from what it would have been under a general denial. A judgment shall not be reversed because of the failure to submit other and various phases or different shades of the same question. Failure to submit a question shall not be deemed a ground for reversal of the judgment, unless its submission, in substantially correct wording, has been requested in writing and tendered by the party complaining of the judgment; provided, however, that objection to such failure shall suffice in such respect if the question is one relied upon by the opposing party. Failure to submit a definition or instruction shall not be deemed a ground for reversal of the judgment unless a substantially correct definition or instruction has been requested in writing and tendered by the party complaining of the judgment.

See also *O'Connor's Texas Rules*, "Jury Charge," ch. 8-I, p. 826; *O'Connor's Texas Forms*, FORM 8I:1.

ANNOTATIONS

Railroad Comm'n v. Gulf Energy Expl. Corp., 482 S.W.3d 559, 571 (Tex.2016). "[P] argues [D] waived any error relating to the trial court's refusal of its proposed good-faith question by failing to request a definition of good faith in conjunction with the question. We disagree. [¶] [P] does not dispute that [D's] proposed … question generally tracked the pertinent statutory language. [D] complied with Rule 278 and did not waive the trial court's error in refusing to submit that question by failing to request an accompanying extra-statutory definition. We are particularly loath to find waiver for failing to propose a definition of a statutory term when no case law provided explicit guidance on what the proper definition of that term should be."

Shupe v. Lingafelter, 192 S.W.3d 577, 579 (Tex. 2006). "When a trial court refuses to submit a requested instruction on an issue raised by the pleadings and evidence, the question on appeal is whether the request was reasonably necessary to enable the jury to render a proper verdict. The omission of an instruction is reversible error only if the omission probably caused the rendition of an improper judgment." *See also* ***Grohman v. Kahlig***, 318 S.W.3d 882, 888 (Tex.2010); ***Texas Workers' Comp. Ins. Fund v. Mandlbauer***, 34 S.W.3d 909, 912 (Tex.2000).

In re S.A.P., 156 S.W.3d 574, 577 (Tex.2005). "An unpleaded issue may be tried by consent, but it still must be submitted to the jury."

Union Pac. R.R. v. Williams, 85 S.W.3d 162, 166 (Tex.2002). "A party is entitled to a jury question, instruction, or definition if the pleadings and evidence raise an issue. An instruction is proper if it (1) assists the jury, (2) accurately states the law, and (3) finds support in the pleadings and evidence." *See also* ***Seger v. Yorkshire Ins. Co.***, 503 S.W.3d 388, 408 (Tex.2016); ***Transcontinental Ins. v. Crump***, 330 S.W.3d 211, 221 (Tex.2010).

Triplex Comms. v. Riley, 900 S.W.2d 716, 718 (Tex. 1995). "If an issue is properly pleaded and is supported by some evidence, a litigant is entitled to have controlling questions submitted to the jury." *See also* ***Elbaor v. Smith***, 845 S.W.2d 240, 243 (Tex.1992).

Southwestern Bell Tel. Co. v. John Carlo Tex., Inc., 843 S.W.2d 470, 472 (Tex.1992). "The court of ap-

peals … held the error [of refusing to define justification] harmless. We disagree. Virtually the entire factual dispute between the parties has been over whether [D's] conduct was justified. To ask the jury to resolve this dispute without a proper legal definition to the essential legal issue was reversible error."

Dernick Res. v. Wilstein, 471 S.W.3d 468, 495 (Tex.App.—Houston [1st Dist.] 2015, pet. denied). "The trial court has broad discretion in submitting the jury charge, subject only to the requirement that the questions submitted must (1) control the disposition of the case; (2) be raised by the pleadings and the evidence; and (3) properly submit the disputed issues for the jury's determination." *See also* ***Texas Disposal Sys. Landfill, Inc. v. Waste Mgmt. Holdings, Inc.***, 219 S.W.3d 563, 580 (Tex.App.—Austin 2007, pet. denied).

In re F.L.R., 293 S.W.3d 278, 281 (Tex.App.—Waco 2009, no pet.). An oral request for a jury instruction, even when dictated on the record, does not satisfy TRCP 278. *See also* ***Yzaguirre v. University of Tex. Health Sci. Ctr.***, No. 04-09-00550-CV (Tex.App.—San Antonio 2010, no pet.) (memo op.; 4-7-10) (dictating a requested instruction will not support an appeal). *But see* ***In re M.P.***, 126 S.W.3d 228, 230-31 (Tex.App.—San Antonio 2003, no pet.) (allowing attorney's oral request on record).

TRCP 279. OMISSIONS FROM THE CHARGE

Upon appeal all independent grounds of recovery or of defense not conclusively established under the evidence and no element of which is submitted or requested are waived. When a ground of recovery or defense consists of more than one element, if one or more of such elements necessary to sustain such ground of recovery or defense, and necessarily referable thereto, are submitted to and found by the jury, and one or more of such elements are omitted from the charge, without request or objection, and there is factually sufficient evidence to support a finding thereon, the trial court, at the request of either party, may after notice and hearing and at any time before the judgment is rendered, make and file written findings on such omitted element or elements in support of the judgment. If no such written findings are made, such omitted element or elements shall be deemed found by the court in such manner as to support the judgment. A claim that the evidence was legally or factually insufficient to warrant the submission of any question may be made for the first time after verdict, regardless of whether the submission of such question was requested by the complainant.

See also *O'Connor's Texas Rules*, "Jury Charge," ch. 8-I, p. 826.

ANNOTATIONS

DiGiuseppe v. Lawler, 269 S.W.3d 588, 599 (Tex. 2008). "The purpose of the 'necessarily referable' requirement in Rule 279 is to give parties, against whom issues are to be deemed, fair notice of a partial submission, so that they have an opportunity to object to the charge or request submission of the missing issues to the ground of recovery or defense. Once a party is on notice of the independent ground of recovery or defense due to the existence of an issue necessarily referable thereto, if that party fails to object or request submission of the missing issues, he cannot be heard to complain on appeal, as he is said to have consented to the court's findings on the missing issues." (Internal quotes omitted.)

Chon Tri v. J.T.T., 162 S.W.3d 552, 558 (Tex.2005). "If one or more elements of that cause of action was omitted from the charge, and there was no request to include the omitted element or objection to its exclusion, and no written findings were made by the trial court on the omitted element, then the omitted element must be deemed found by the trial court in a manner that supports its judgment." *See also* ***In re J.F.C.***, 96 S.W.3d 256, 262-63 (Tex.2002).

Gulf States Utils. Co. v. Low, 79 S.W.3d 561, 564 (Tex.2002). "Rule 279 may support a deemed finding only when it can be deemed found 'in such manner as to support the judgment.' … The court of appeals misapplied Rule 279 to deem a finding, not to support the trial court's judgment, but to render a new judgment for actual damages in an amount nearly 15 times the trial court's award."

T.O. Stanley Boot Co. v. Bank of El Paso, 847 S.W.2d 218, 222-23 (Tex.1992). "[P] failed to submit or request any element of its affirmative claim to the jury. Unless [P's] affirmative claim is conclusively established under the evidence, the ground of recovery is waived upon appeal." *See also* ***May v. Ticor Title Ins.***, 422 S.W.3d 93, 100 (Tex.App.—Houston [14th Dist.] 2014, no pet.); ***Bank of Tex. v. VR Elec., Inc.***, 276 S.W.3d 671, 676-77 (Tex.App.—Houston [1st Dist.] 2008, pet. denied).

E. CASE TO THE JURY

TRCP 280. PRESIDING JUROR OF JURY

Each jury shall appoint one of their body presiding juror.

TRCP 281. PAPERS TAKEN TO JURY ROOM

With the court's permission, the jury may take with them to the jury room any notes they took during the trial. In addition, the jury may, and on request shall, take with them in their retirement the charges and instructions, general or special, which were given and read to them, and any written evidence, except the depositions of witnesses, but shall not take with them any special charges which have been refused. Where only part of a paper has been read in evidence, the jury shall not take the same with them, unless the part so read to them is detached from that which was excluded.

See also *O'Connor's Texas Rules*, "Juror Note-Taking," ch. 8-A, §10, p. 785.

ANNOTATIONS

First Employees Ins. v. Skinner, 646 S.W.2d 170, 172 (Tex.1983). "Rule 281 is mandatory and … the trial court is required to send all exhibits admitted into evidence to the jury room during the deliberations of the jury. Furthermore, this rule is self-operative and requires no request from the jurors or counsel." *See also* ***Formosa Plastics Corp. v. Kajima Int'l***, 216 S.W.3d 436, 464 (Tex.App.—Corpus Christi 2006, pet. denied) (any error in failing to send exhibits to jury room during deliberations is not reversible unless error probably caused rendition of improper judgment).

TRCP 282. JURY KEPT TOGETHER

The jury may either decide a case in court or retire for deliberation. If they retire, they shall be kept together in some convenient place, under the charge of an officer, until they agree upon a verdict or are discharged by the court; but the court in its discretion may permit them to separate temporarily for the night and at their meals, and for other proper purposes.

TRCP 283. DUTY OF OFFICER ATTENDING JURY

The officer in charge of the jury shall not make nor permit any communication to be made to them, except to inquire if they have agreed upon a verdict, unless by order of the court; and he shall not before their verdict is rendered communicate to any person the state of their deliberations or the verdict agreed upon.

ANNOTATIONS

Logan v. Grady, 482 S.W.2d 313, 322 (Tex.App.—Fort Worth 1972, no writ). "[T]he jury bailiff violated [TRCP] 283 and 285 … when he did not make the jury's wish as communicated to him known to the court and also when he instructed the jury that its members already had in the jury room all that it needed in order to answer Issue No. 14."

TRCP 284. JUDGE TO CAUTION JURY

Immediately after jurors are selected for a case, the court must instruct them to turn off their phones and other electronic devices and not to communicate with anyone through any electronic device while they are in the courtroom or while they are deliberating. The court must also instruct them that, while they are serving as jurors, they must not post any information about the case on the Internet or search for any information outside of the courtroom, including on the Internet, to try to learn more about the case.

If jurors are permitted to separate before they are released from jury duty, either during the trial or after the case is submitted to them, the court must instruct them that it is their duty not to communicate with, or permit themselves to be addressed by, any other person about any subject relating to the case.

TRCP 285. JURY MAY COMMUNICATE WITH COURT

The jury may communicate with the court by making their wish known to the officer in charge, who shall inform the court, and they may then in open court, and through their presiding juror, communicate with the court, either verbally or in writing. If the communication is to request further instructions, Rule 286 shall be followed.

See also *O'Connor's Texas Rules*, "Supplemental Instructions to Jury," ch. 8-I, §8, p. 840.

TRCP 286. JURY MAY RECEIVE FURTHER INSTRUCTIONS

After having retired, the jury may receive further instructions from the court touching any matter of law, either at their request or upon the court's own motion. For this purpose they shall appear before the judge in open court in a body, and if the instruction is being given at their request, they shall through their presid-

ing juror state to the court, in writing, the particular question of law upon which they desire further instruction. The court shall give such instruction in writing, but no instruction shall be given except in conformity with the rules relating to the charge. Additional argument may be allowed in the discretion of the court.

See also *O'Connor's Texas Rules*, "Supplemental Instructions to Jury," ch. 8-I, §8, p. 840.

ANNOTATIONS

Stevens v. Travelers Ins., 563 S.W.2d 223, 229 (Tex.1978). "[E]ven though there is a latent danger of coercion, supplemental, verdict-urging instructions are not, in and of themselves, erroneous, so long as the particular charge given is not otherwise objectionable."

In re E.M., 494 S.W.3d 209, 230 (Tex.App.—Waco 2015, pet. denied). "Rule 286 ... authorizes a trial court to give further instructions to the jury during deliberations. These instructions are to be given in conformity with the rules relating to the charge, which requires submission to the parties or their attorneys for their inspection and that [there be] a reasonable time to review and object outside the presence of the jury. [¶] A party and their counsel have a right to be present in court for all proceedings. However, it is a right that can be waived. [W]hile it may be common practice to rely on the trial court or the clerk to contact the lawyers in the event of a jury note, the practice is not required or even contemplated by the [TRCPs]. Because the court remains open for all purposes, there is no requirement for additional notice to the parties not in the courtroom when issues such as the proper response to a jury note are presented to the trial court for determination, and we are not willing to impose a duty upon the trial court to provide further notice to absent parties in the absence of an agreement to do so. In such events, the court is authorized to proceed and rule on the issue."

Watts v. Watts, 396 S.W.3d 19, 21 (Tex.App.—San Antonio 2012, no pet.). "The jury was instructed, 'A person may not be appointed a joint managing conservator if that person has a history or pattern of past or present child neglect or of physical or sexual abuse directed against a parent, a spouse, or a child.' During deliberations, the jury sent the trial court the following question, 'If the jury finds there is a history or a pattern of past physical abuse against both spouses, can we still name both as joint managing conservators?' [Father's] attorney argued the trial court should respond 'yes' to the question because the jury was asking a legal question or for legal direction. ... The trial judge responded that she believed answering 'yes' or 'no' to the question would be a comment on the case or would change the instructions already provided. The trial court decided not to provide any further instructions but to instruct the jury to re-read the court's charge. *At 22:* [B]ecause the jury found one parent should be appointed as sole managing conservator, the jury properly applied the law as given. Accordingly, the trial court did not abuse its discretion in refusing to give any further instructions to the jury."

Lochinvar Corp. v. Meyers, 930 S.W.2d 182, 187 (Tex.App.—Dallas 1996, no writ). "[R]ule 286 allow[s] a court the opportunity to correct an error by modifying its charge. [¶] The instruction was given to the jury in writing[, but trial court did not] reassemble the jury in the courtroom. [D] did not object to the court's failure to reassemble the jury and read the modified charge."

TRCP 287. DISAGREEMENT AS TO EVIDENCE

If the jury disagree as to the statement of any witness, they may, upon applying to the court, have read to them from the court reporter's notes that part of such witness' testimony on the point in dispute; but, if there be no such reporter, or if his notes cannot be read to the jury, the court may cause such witness to be again brought upon the stand and the judge shall direct him to repeat his testimony as to the point in dispute, and no other, as nearly as he can in the language used on the trial; and on their notifying the court that they disagree as to any portion of a deposition or other paper not permitted to be carried with them in their retirement, the court may, in like manner, permit such portion of said deposition or paper to be again read to the jury.

ANNOTATIONS

Krishnan v. Ramirez, 42 S.W.3d 205, 225 (Tex. App.—Corpus Christi 2001, pet. denied). "The judge is given broad discretion in determining what portions of the testimony are relevant to the jury's request to have testimony re-read."

TRCP 288. COURT OPEN FOR JURY

The court, during the deliberations of the jury, may proceed with other business or recess from time to time, but shall be deemed open for all purposes connected with the case before the jury.

TRCP 289. DISCHARGE OF JURY

The jury to whom a case has been submitted may be discharged by the court when they cannot agree and the parties consent to their discharge, or when they have been kept together for such time as to render it altogether improbable that they can agree, or when any calamity or accident may, in the opinion of the court, require it, or when by sickness or other cause their number is reduced below the number constituting the jury in such court.

The cause shall again be placed on the jury docket and shall again be set for trial as the court directs.

See also *O'Connor's Texas Rules*, "Verdict-urging instructions," ch. 8-I, §8.3, p. 840.

ANNOTATIONS

Shaw v. Greater Houston Transp., 791 S.W.2d 204, 209 (Tex.App.—Corpus Christi 1990, no writ). It was coercive for the trial court to refuse to release the jury after they stated three times that they were deadlocked.

F. VERDICT

TRCP 290. DEFINITION & SUBSTANCE

A verdict is a written declaration by a jury of its decision, comprehending the whole or all the issues submitted to the jury, and shall be either a general or special verdict, as directed, which shall be signed by the presiding juror of the jury.

A general verdict is one whereby the jury pronounces generally in favor of one or more parties to the suit upon all or any of the issues submitted to it. A special verdict is one wherein the jury finds the facts only on issues made up and submitted to them under the direction of the court.

A special verdict shall, as between the parties, be conclusive as to the facts found.

ANNOTATIONS

Wal-Mart Stores v. Alexander, 868 S.W.2d 322, 328 (Tex.1993). "A jury's marginal notations generally may not be considered on appeal. They reflect the jury's mental processes, but they are not part of its verdict."

Houston Fire & Cas. Ins. v. Gerhardt, 281 S.W.2d 176, 178 (Tex.App.—San Antonio 1955, orig. proceeding). "A verdict form reflecting answers to special issues but not signed by the foreman may or may not be a verdict, and presents a question which must be determined by the hearing of evidence."

TRCP 291. FORM OF VERDICT

No special form of verdict is required, and the judgment shall not be arrested or reversed for mere want of form therein if there has been substantial compliance with the requirements of the law in rendering a verdict.

TRCP 292. VERDICT BY PORTION OF ORIGINAL JURY

(a) Except as provided in subsection (b), a verdict may be rendered in any cause by the concurrence, as to each and all answers made, of the same ten or more members of an original jury of twelve or of the same five or more members of an original jury of six. However, where as many as three jurors die or be disabled from sitting and there are only nine of the jurors remaining of an original jury of twelve, those remaining may render and return a verdict. If less than the original twelve or six jurors render a verdict, the verdict must be signed by each juror concurring therein.

(b) A verdict may be rendered awarding exemplary damages only if the jury was unanimous in finding liability for and the amount of exemplary damages.

See also *O'Connor's Texas Rules*, "Verdict," ch. 8-K, p. 849.

ANNOTATIONS

In re M.G.N., 441 S.W.3d 246, 248 (Tex.2014). "[A] trial court may substitute a regular juror with an alternate if the regular juror is unable to fulfill or is disqualified from fulfilling his duties, but a trial court may only dismiss a juror and proceed with fewer than 12 jurors if the dismissed juror is constitutionally disabled."

Yanes v. Sowards, 996 S.W.2d 849, 850 (Tex.1999). The Texas Constitution and TRCPs "require a district-court jury to consist of 12 original jurors, but as few as 9 may render and return a verdict if the others die or become disabled from sitting. [T]rial courts have broad discretion in determining whether a juror is disabled from sitting when there is evidence of constitutional disqualification. But not just any inconvenience or delay is a disability. A constitutional disability must be in the nature of an actual physical or mental incapacity." (Internal quotes omitted.) *See also* ***McDaniel v. Yarbrough***, 898 S.W.2d 251, 253 (Tex.1995).

Schlafly v. Schlafly, 33 S.W.3d 863, 870 (Tex. App.—Houston [14th Dist.] 2000, pet. denied). "The alternate juror hears the same evidence that a regular juror hears and ... 'has the same functions, powers and privileges.' There is no reason to treat a jury comprised

of 12 members, one of whom is an alternate, any differently than a jury comprised of 12 regular members. ... We find 'original jurors' means all the jurors empaneled, both regular members and alternates."

TRCP 293. WHEN THE JURY AGREE

When the jury agree upon a verdict, they shall be brought into court by the proper officer, and they shall deliver their verdict to the clerk; and if they state that they have agreed, the verdict shall be read aloud by the clerk. If the verdict is in proper form, no juror objects to its accuracy, no juror represented as agreeing thereto dissents therefrom, and neither party requests a poll of the jury, the verdict shall be entered upon the minutes of the court.

TRCP 294. POLLING THE JURY

Any party shall have the right to have the jury polled. A jury is polled by reading once to the jury collectively the general verdict, or the questions and answers thereto consecutively, and then calling the name of each juror separately and asking the juror if it is the juror's verdict. If any juror answers in the negative when the verdict is returned signed only by the presiding juror as a unanimous verdict, or if any juror shown by the juror's signature to agree to the verdict should answer in the negative, the jury shall be retired for further deliberation.

See also *O'Connor's Texas Rules*, "Request to Poll Jury," ch. 8-K, §5, p. 850.

ANNOTATIONS

Suggs v. Fitch, 64 S.W.3d 658, 660 (Tex.App.—Texarkana 2001, no pet.). "The right to poll the jury pursuant to [TRCP] 294 is a waivable right and must be requested in order to be invoked." *See also* ***Pate v. Texline Feed Mills, Inc.***, 689 S.W.2d 238, 243 (Tex.App.—Amarillo 1985, writ ref'd n.r.e.) (once proper request is made, court has no discretion but to poll jury).

TRCP 295. CORRECTION OF VERDICT

If the purported verdict is defective, the court may direct it to be reformed. If it is incomplete, or not responsive to the questions contained in the court's charge, or the answers to the questions are in conflict, the court shall in writing instruct the jury in open court of the nature of the incompleteness, unresponsiveness, or conflict, provide the jury such additional instructions as may be proper, and retire the jury for further deliberations.

ANNOTATIONS

Beltran v. Brookshire Grocery Co., 358 S.W.3d 263, 268 (Tex.App.—Dallas 2011, pet. denied). "Rule 295 provides a procedure for correcting conflicting jury answers. ... The court must be made aware of the conflict before the jury is discharged because, once the jury is discharged, 'a conflict in the jury's answers cannot be reformed.'" *See also* ***Meek v. Onstad***, 430 S.W.3d 601, 605-06 (Tex.App.—Houston [14th Dist.] 2014, no pet.) (party waives complaint about conflicting answers by failing to raise complaint before jury is discharged).

Archer Daniels Midland Co. v. Bohall, 114 S.W.3d 42, 46 (Tex.App.—Eastland 2003, no pet.). TRCP 295 "applies only to defective verdicts, not defective charges. Before Rule 295 would authorize further instruction to the jury, the verdict must be incomplete, non-responsive to the questions contained in the court's charge, or contain answers which are in conflict." *See also* ***Fish v. Dallas ISD***, 170 S.W.3d 226, 229 (Tex.App.—Dallas 2005, pet. denied).

G. FINDINGS BY COURT

TRCP 296. REQUESTS FOR FINDINGS OF FACTS & CONCLUSIONS OF LAW

In any case tried in the district or county court without a jury, any party may request the court to state in writing its findings of fact and conclusions of law. Such request shall be entitled "Request for Findings of Fact and Conclusions of Law" and shall be filed within twenty days after judgment is signed with the clerk of the court, who shall immediately call such request to the attention of the judge who tried the case. The party making the request shall serve it on all other parties in accordance with Rule 21a.

Caution: TRCP 296 is affected by Fam. Code §§6.711 and 154.130.

See also *O'Connor's Texas Rules*, "Request for Findings of Fact & Conclusions of Law," ch. 10-E, p. 921; *O'Connor's Texas Forms*, FORMS 10E:1, 2; *O'Connor's Texas Family Law Handbook* (2017), "Suit for Divorce," ch. 3-A, p. 205; "Suit to Dissolve Marriage with Children," ch. 4-D, p. 410; "Reimbursement Claims," ch. 7-F, p. 910.

ANNOTATIONS

Black v. Dallas Cty. Child Welfare Unit, 835 S.W.2d 626, 630 n.10 (Tex.1992). "If no findings of fact or conclusions of law are filed, the reviewing court must imply all necessary fact findings in support of the trial court's judgment."

Ezy-Lift v. Ezy Acquisition, LLC, No. 01-13-00058-CV (Tex.App.—Houston [1st Dist.] 2014, pet. denied) (memo op.; 4-17-14). "Parties generally may not obtain findings of fact and conclusions of law after a jury trial. Parties may be able to obtain findings, however, if fact issues were submitted to the trial court for determination without submission to the jury or if the trial court's judgment substantially differs from or exceeds the scope of the jury's verdict." *See also* ***Roberts v. Roberts***, 999 S.W.2d 424, 433 (Tex.App.—El Paso 1999, no pet.).

Liberty Mut. Fire Ins. v. Laca, 243 S.W.3d 791, 794 (Tex.App.—El Paso 2007, no pet.). A party "has been harmed if, under the circumstances of the case, he is forced to guess the reason(s) why the trial court ruled against him. If there is only a single ground of recovery or a single defense in the case, the record would show that [party] has suffered no harm, because he is not forced to guess the reasons for the trial court's judgment. On the other hand, when there are multiple grounds for recovery or multiple defenses, [party] is forced to guess what the trial court's findings were, unless they are provided to him. Putting [party] in the position of having to guess the trial court's reasons for rendering judgment against him defeats the inherent purpose of [TRCP] 296 and 297. The purpose of a request under the rules is to 'narrow the bases of the judgment to only a portion of [the multiple] claims and defenses, thereby reducing the number of contentions that … must [be raised] on appeal.'"

In re T.N.H., No. 2-06-074-CV (Tex.App.—Fort Worth 2007, pet. denied) (memo op.; 2-15-07). Under TRCP 296, "[h]arm occurs when the circumstances of the particular case force an appellant to guess the reason or reasons that the trial court ruled against it. Where an appellant's recovery or defense is predicated upon a single ground, the lack of findings or conclusions does not require the appellant to guess as to the reason for the trial court's ruling. But where an appellant's recovery or defense is predicated upon two or more possible grounds, the lack of findings or conclusions forces an appellant to guess as to basis for the trial court's ruling."

Willms v. Americas Tire Co., 190 S.W.3d 796, 810 (Tex.App.—Dallas 2006, pet. denied). "When a trial court grants summary judgment relief, … findings of fact are not appropriate because the summary judgment proceeding has not been 'tried' within the scope of rule 296. Findings of fact and conclusions of law have no place in a summary judgment proceeding. If summary judgment is proper, there are no facts to find, and the legal conclusions have already been stated in the motion and response." *See also* ***K2M3, LLC v. Cocoon Data Holding Pty. Ltd.***, No. 13-11-00194-CV (Tex. App.—Corpus Christi 2012, pet. denied) (memo op.; 6-28-12) (term "tried" includes trial court's disposition of a case rendered after evidentiary hearing on conflicting evidence; findings and conclusions have no purpose when judgment is rendered as a matter of law); ***In re Estate of Davis***, 216 S.W.3d 537, 542 (Tex.App.—Texarkana 2007, pet. denied) (no findings of fact and conclusions of law required for special appearance subject to interlocutory appeal).

Roberts v. Roberts, 999 S.W.2d 424, 433 (Tex. App.—El Paso 1999, no pet.). "Findings of fact and conclusions of law as a general rule are not available after a jury trial. [TRCP] 296 provides that findings and conclusions are available in any case tried in the district or county court without a jury. … Given the assumption that findings and conclusions are appropriate in a bench trial but not in a jury trial, what happens when the two are combined? Perhaps the suit involves domestic torts and the jury will determine the personal injury or fraud issues while the judge will decide the ultimate division of property. Also, it is not unusual for the court to permit separate trials on the issues of property and custody, with a jury deciding issues of conservatorship and the judge deciding issues of characterization, valuation, and division of property. If one party chooses to appeal from the property division, is s/he entitled to findings and conclusions? If the jury and nonjury portions of the case are conducted via separate trials, findings and conclusions are available in the nonjury trial. When the judgment of the court differs substantially from or exceeds the scope of the jury verdict, findings are also available. … If at least one of the issues tried in the court below was tried to the jury, the entire trial was to a jury within the meaning of the rules." *See also* ***Limbaugh v. Limbaugh***, 71 S.W.3d 1, 6 (Tex.App.—Waco 2002, no pet.).

TRCP 297. TIME TO FILE FINDINGS OF FACT & CONCLUSIONS OF LAW

The court shall file its findings of fact and conclusions of law within twenty days after a timely request is filed. The court shall cause a copy of its findings and conclusions to be mailed to each party in the suit.

If the court fails to file timely findings of fact and conclusions of law, the party making the request shall, within thirty days after filing the original request, file with the clerk and serve on all other parties in accordance with Rule 21a a "Notice of Past Due Findings of Fact and Conclusions of Law" which shall be immediately called to the attention of the court by the clerk. Such notice shall state the date the original request was filed and the date the findings and conclusions were due. Upon filing this notice, the time for the court to file findings of fact and conclusions of law is extended to forty days from the date the original request was filed.

See also *O'Connor's Texas Rules*, "Request for Findings of Fact & Conclusions of Law," ch. 10-E, p. 921; *O'Connor's Texas Forms*, FORM 10E:3.

ANNOTATIONS

Tenery v. Tenery, 932 S.W.2d 29, 30 (Tex.1996). "[H]arm to the complaining party is presumed unless the contrary appears on the face of the record when the party makes a proper and timely request for findings and the trial court fails to comply. Error is harmful if it prevents an appellant from properly presenting a case to the appellate court." *See also* ***Cherne Indus. v. Magallanes***, 763 S.W.2d 768, 772 (Tex.1989); ***Lopez v. Bailon***, ___ S.W.3d ___ (Tex.App.—Amarillo 2015, order) (No. 07-14-00442-CV; 5-20-15).

Sonnier v. Sonnier, 331 S.W.3d 211, 214-15 (Tex. App.—Beaumont 2011, no pet.). "When the trial court [signs] findings of fact and conclusions of law, it no longer [has] jurisdiction over [a] case. Some courts of appeals ... have suggested that the trial court may file 'belated' findings of fact and conclusions of law even after the case is on appeal and the trial court's plenary power has expired. In our view, the opinions in these cases do not adequately explain under what authority the trial court may act in making the belated findings and conclusions when the appellate court has exclusive jurisdiction over the case. Instead, in allowing belated findings, the appellate courts note that the only issue that arises with belated findings is the injury to the appellant and not the trial court's jurisdiction to make the findings. ... We decline to follow the suggestion ... that a trial court may make fact findings and conclusions of law while the appellate court has exclusive jurisdiction over the case." *But see* ***In re E.A.C.***, this page.

Teague v. Livingston, No. 01-10-00075-CV (Tex. App.—Houston [1st Dist.] 2010, no pet.) (memo op.; 10-14-10). "[T]here is no 'duty on [a] trial court to file findings of fact or conclusions of law where there has been no trial.' A plea to the jurisdiction is similar to a summary judgment, in which findings of fact and conclusions of law are not necessary, because 'there are no facts to find,' and the 'legal grounds are limited to those stated in the motion and response.'"

Liberty Mut. Fire Ins. v. Laca, 243 S.W.3d 791, 794 (Tex.App.—El Paso 2007, no pet.). See annotation under TRCP 296, p. 1198.

In re E.A.C., 162 S.W.3d 438, 443 (Tex.App.—Dallas 2005, no pet.). "When a trial court files belated findings, the only issue that arises is whether the appellant was harmed, not whether the trial court had jurisdiction to make the findings. This harm may be in two forms: (1) the litigant is unable to request additional findings, or (2) the litigant was prevented from properly presenting his appeal." *But see* ***Sonnier v. Sonnier***, this page.

In re A.C.S., 157 S.W.3d 9, 14-15 (Tex.App.—Waco 2004, no pet.). "[T]he rules of procedure do not expressly prohibit a court from issuing belated findings. If an appellant can show harm from untimely findings, the appeal may be abated so the appellant can request amended additional findings."

Curtis v. Commission for Lawyer Discipline, 20 S.W.3d 227, 232 (Tex.App.—Houston [14th Dist.] 2000, no pet.). "The failure to file a notice of past due findings of fact waives the right to complain about the trial court's failure to file findings of fact and conclusions of law." *See also* ***Haining v. Haining***, No. 01-08-00091-CV (Tex.App.—Houston [1st Dist.] 2010, pet. denied) (memo op.; 3-25-10).

TRCP 298. ADDITIONAL OR AMENDED FINDINGS OF FACT & CONCLUSIONS OF LAW

After the court files original findings of fact and conclusions of law, any party may file with the clerk of the court a request for specified additional or amended findings or conclusions. The request for these findings shall be made within ten days after the filing of the original findings and conclusions by the court. Each request made pursuant to this rule shall be served on each party to the suit in accordance with Rule 21a.

The court shall file any additional or amended findings and conclusions that are appropriate within ten days after such request is filed, and cause a copy to be mailed to each party to the suit. No findings or conclu-

sions shall be deemed or presumed by any failure of the court to make any additional findings or conclusions.

See also *O'Connor's Texas Rules*, "Request for Findings of Fact & Conclusions of Law," ch. 10-E, p. 921; *O'Connor's Texas Forms*, FORM 10E:4.

ANNOTATIONS

Villalpando v. Villalpando, 480 S.W.3d 801, 810 (Tex.App.—Houston [14th Dist.] 2015, no pet.). "The failure to request amended or additional findings or conclusions waives the right to complain on appeal about the trial court's failure to make the omitted findings or conclusions." *See also* ***In re Marriage of C.A.S.***, 405 S.W.3d 373, 381 (Tex.App.—Dallas 2013, no pet.).

Rich v. Olah, 274 S.W.3d 878, 886 (Tex.App.—Dallas 2008, no pet.). Under TRCP 298, "[a] trial court is not required to make additional findings of fact that are unsupported in the record, that are evidentiary, or that are contrary to other previous findings." *See also* ***Villarreal v. Guerra***, 446 S.W.3d 404, 414 (Tex. App.—San Antonio 2014, pet. denied).

Pakdimounivong v. City of Arlington, 219 S.W.3d 401, 412 (Tex.App.—Fort Worth 2006, pet. denied). "Additional findings are not required if the original findings and conclusions properly and succinctly relate the ultimate findings of fact and law necessary to apprise the party of adequate information for the preparation of the party's appeal. An ultimate fact is one that would have a direct effect on the judgment. If the refusal to file additional findings does not prevent a party from adequately presenting an argument on appeal, there is no reversible error. If the requested findings will not result in a different judgment, the findings need not be made." *See also* ***H.K. Global Trading, Ltd. v. Combs***, 429 S.W.3d 132, 141 (Tex.App.—Austin 2014, pet. denied).

In re R.D.Y., 51 S.W.3d 314, 322 (Tex.App.—Houston [1st Dist.] 2001, pet. denied). "Additional findings are not required if the original findings of fact and conclusions of law 'properly and succinctly relate the ultimate findings of fact and law necessary to apprise [party] of adequate information for the preparation of his or her appeal.' [D] must show the trial court's refusal to file the requested additional findings caused the rendition of an improper judgment. If the refusal to file additional findings does not prevent [D] from adequately presenting her argument on appeal, there is no reversible error."

Vickery v. Commission for Lawyer Discipline, 5 S.W.3d 241, 254 (Tex.App.—Houston [14th Dist.] 1999, pet. denied). "[B]efore the failure to grant additional findings will impede an appellate court from presuming implied findings, the omission must be made manifest to the trial court. ... If the trial court is not specifically made aware of the missing element, the omission is presumed to be inadvertent."

TRCP 299. OMITTED FINDINGS

When findings of fact are filed by the trial court they shall form the basis of the judgment upon all grounds of recovery and of defense embraced therein. The judgment may not be supported upon appeal by a presumed finding upon any ground of recovery or defense, no element of which has been included in the findings of fact; but when one or more elements thereof have been found by the trial court, omitted unrequested elements, when supported by evidence, will be supplied by presumption in support of the judgment. Refusal of the court to make a finding requested shall be reviewable on appeal.

See also *O'Connor's Texas Rules*, "Request for Findings of Fact & Conclusions of Law," ch. 10-E, p. 921.

ANNOTATIONS

Worford v. Stamper, 801 S.W.2d 108, 109 (Tex. 1990). "In this case, no findings of fact or conclusions of law were requested or filed. It is therefore implied that the trial court made all the findings necessary to support its judgment. In determining whether some evidence supports the judgment and the implied findings of fact, 'it is proper to consider only that evidence most favorable to the issue and to disregard entirely that which is opposed to it or contradictory in its nature.'" *See also* ***Black v. Dallas Cty. Child Welfare Unit***, 835 S.W.2d 626, 630 n.10 (Tex.1992).

RBS Mortg., LLC v. Gonzalez, No. 04-11-00681-CV (Tex.App.—San Antonio 2013, no pet.) (memo op.; 2-27-13). "When the court's findings do not address a defense and the party relying on the defense does not request additional findings, that defense is waived."

O'Brien v. Daboval, 388 S.W.3d 826, 838 (Tex. App.—Houston [1st Dist.] 2012, no pet.). "If the findings of fact and the judgment are in conflict, the unchallenged findings control over the judgment."

Vickery v. Commission for Lawyer Discipline, 5 S.W.3d 241, 252 (Tex.App.—Houston [14th Dist.] 1999, pet. denied). "When a court makes findings of fact, but inadvertently omits an essential element of a ground of

recovery or defense, the presumption of validity will supply the omitted element by implication. However, if the record demonstrates the trial judge deliberately omitted the element, the presumption is refuted and the element cannot logically be supplied by implication." *See also* ***Smith v. McDaniel***, No. 12-12-00165-CV (Tex.App.—Tyler 2013, no pet.) (memo op.; 9-18-13).

TRCP 299a. FINDINGS OF FACT TO BE SEPARATELY FILED & NOT RECITED IN A JUDGMENT

Findings of fact shall not be recited in a judgment. If there is a conflict between findings of fact recited in a judgment in violation of this rule and findings of fact made pursuant to Rules 297 and 298, the latter findings will control for appellate purposes. Findings of fact shall be filed with the clerk of the court as a document or documents separate and apart from the judgment.

See also *O'Connor's Texas Rules*, "Judgment," ch. 9-C, p. 861; "Request for Findings of Fact & Conclusions of Law," ch. 10-E, p. 921.

ANNOTATIONS

Colbert v. DFPS, 227 S.W.3d 799, 809 (Tex.App.—Houston [1st Dist.] 2006), *pet. denied sub nom.* ***In re D.N.C.***, 252 S.W.3d 317 (Tex.2008). DFPS "urges that, because the trial court did not file findings of fact separately, as required in [TRCP 299a], this Court must affirm the judgment if any legal theory pleaded by DFPS is supported by the evidence. [¶] [A] trial court's recitation in the judgment of its ground for termination of parental rights is not a fact-finding that is prohibited under rule 299a.... The trial court ... was simply stating the grounds for termination of parental rights, as required by [Fam. Code] §161.206...."

In re Estate of Jones, 197 S.W.3d 894, 900 n.4 (Tex.App.—Beaumont 2006, pet. denied). "[I]f findings are recited in the judgment, and no one complains or requests findings, and there is no conflict with separately filed findings of fact, the findings of fact in the judgment should not be ignored on appeal." *See also* ***South Plains Lamesa R.R. v. Heinrich***, 280 S.W.3d 357, 364-65 (Tex.App.—Amarillo 2008, no pet.). *But see* ***Sutherland v. Cobern***, this page. For a discussion of the split in the courts of appeals on this issue, see ***O'Connor's Texas Rules***, "Not in judgment," ch. 10-E, §5.1.2, p. 927.

In re E.A.C., 162 S.W.3d 438, 442-43 (Tex.App.—Dallas 2005, no pet.). H argues that "a trial court's findings of fact control over its judgment and that the findings of fact in this case awarded lump sum child support, not an arrearage, citing [TRCP] 299a. [¶] [W] argues the family code requires the court to recite facts in the judgment and rule 299a does not apply. We disagree. The legislature made it clear in enacting the family code that, unless expressly provided otherwise, suits affecting the parent-child relationship are to be governed by the same rules of procedure as those generally applied in other civil cases. [¶] [W] cites [Fam. Code] §§157.166 and 157.263 ... as requiring certain fact findings in a child support arrearage judgment. But these sections refer to an order entered pursuant to a [Fam. Code] Ch. 157 motion to enforce a final order of child support. Because this case is an original SAPCR proceeding, not a motion to enforce a child support order under Ch. 157, we conclude these sections do not apply. But even if they did, nothing in the language of these sections states that we should disregard rule 299a when findings of fact have been requested pursuant to [TRCP] 296. Accordingly, we reject [W's] argument that the family code prevents rule 299a from applying to this case. *At 444:* We conclude the trial court's finding of a lump sum child support award in its separately-filed findings of fact following a timely request under rule 296 controls over its finding of an arrearage in the SAPCR order."

Pena v. Garza, 61 S.W.3d 529, 531-32 (Tex.App.—San Antonio 2001, no pet.). TRCP 299a "states that findings of fact should not be recited in a judgment but should be filed as a separate document. In contrast, [Fam. Code] §85.001 ... directs the court to find whether family violence has occurred and is likely to occur in the future, and to include these findings in the protective order. The rules of procedure are general rules; statutes are specific. Thus, when the two conflict, the statute trumps the rule. In its protective order, the trial court found that [boyfriend] committed family violence, that such violence was likely to occur in the future, and that a protective order was in the best interest of the household. The recitation of these findings complied with §85.001, thus the trial court did not err in refusing to file additional findings of fact and conclusions of law."

Sutherland v. Cobern, 843 S.W.2d 127, 131 n.7 (Tex.App.—Texarkana 1992, writ denied). "Findings of fact contained in the body of a judgment may not be considered on appeal. Therefore, for our purposes, we review this case as one in which no findings of fact were made." *See also* ***Casino Magic Corp. v. King***, 43

S.W.3d 14, 19 n.6 (Tex.App.—Dallas 2001, pet. denied). *But see* ***In re Estate of Jones***, p. 1201. For a discussion of the split in the courts of appeals on this issue, see ***O'Connor's Texas Rules***, "Not in judgment," ch. 10-E, §5.1.2, p. 927.

H. JUDGMENTS

TRCP 300. COURT TO RENDER JUDGMENT

Where a special verdict is rendered, or the conclusions of fact found by the judge are separately stated the court shall render judgment thereon unless set aside or a new trial is granted, or judgment is rendered notwithstanding verdict or jury finding under these rules.

ANNOTATIONS

Astec Indus. v. Suarez, 921 S.W.2d 794, 798 (Tex. App.—Fort Worth 1996, no writ). "In order for a judge's ministerial duty to render judgment under rule 300 ... to arise, the jury must first return a sufficient verdict for the judge to receive."

TRCP 301. JUDGMENTS

The judgment of the court shall conform to the pleadings, the nature of the case proved and the verdict, if any, and shall be so framed as to give the party all the relief to which he may be entitled either in law or equity. Provided, that upon motion and reasonable notice the court may render judgment non obstante veredicto if a directed verdict would have been proper, and provided further that the court may, upon like motion and notice, disregard any jury finding on a question that has no support in the evidence. Only one final judgment shall be rendered in any cause except where it is otherwise specially provided by law. Judgment may, in a proper case, be given for or against one or more of several plaintiffs, and for or against one or more of several defendants or intervenors.

Caution: TRCP 301 is affected by Fam. Code §105.002.

See also ***O'Connor's Texas Rules***, "Motion for JNOV," ch. 9-B, p. 857; "Judgment," ch. 9-C, p. 861; ***O'Connor's Texas Forms***, FORMS 9B, 9C:1; ***O'Connor's Texas Family Law Handbook*** (2017), "Suit for Divorce," ch. 3-A, p. 205; "Suit to Dissolve Marriage with Children," ch. 4-D, p. 410.

ANNOTATIONS

Tanner v. Nationwide Mut. Fire Ins., 289 S.W.3d 828, 830 (Tex.2009). "We review a JNOV under a no-evidence standard, meaning we 'credit evidence favoring the jury verdict if reasonable jurors could, and disregard contrary evidence unless reasonable jurors could not.'"

Tiller v. McLure, 121 S.W.3d 709, 713 (Tex.2003). "A trial court may grant a [JNOV] if there is no evidence to support one or more of the jury findings on issues necessary to liability."

Spencer v. Eagle Star Ins., 876 S.W.2d 154, 157 (Tex.1994). "A trial court may disregard a jury finding only if it is unsupported by evidence ... or if the issue is immaterial. A question is immaterial when it should not have been submitted, or when it was properly submitted but has been rendered immaterial by other findings. A question which calls for a finding beyond the province of the jury, such as a question of law, may be deemed immaterial." *See also* ***Wal-Mart Stores v. McKenzie***, 997 S.W.2d 278, 280 (Tex.1999).

Stewart v. USA Custom Paint & Body Shop, Inc., 870 S.W.2d 18, 20 (Tex.1994). "A judgment must be sufficiently definite and certain to define and protect the rights of all litigants, or it should provide a definite means of ascertaining such rights, to the end that ministerial officers can carry the judgment into execution without ascertainment of facts not therein stated."

Moran v. Williamson, 498 S.W.3d 85, 93 (Tex. App.—Houston [1st Dist.] 2016, pet. denied). "In determining whether the judgment conforms to the pleadings, we must view the pleadings as a whole. A general prayer for relief will support any relief raised by the evidence that is consistent with the allegations and causes of action stated in the petition."

In re P.A.C., 498 S.W.3d 210, 215-16 (Tex.App.—Houston [14th Dist.] 2016, pet. denied). "Although [father] did not specifically request the exclusive rights to consent to the children's marriages and to represent the children in legal actions, he did request to be appointed [SMC] of the children. [Family Code] §153.132 ... lists the exclusive rights belonging to [an SMC] absent limitation by a court order, and includes 'the right to consent to marriage' and 'the right to represent the child in legal action.' [Father's] request that he be appointed [SMC] of the children therefore encompassed a request that he be awarded the exclusive rights to consent to the children's marriages and to represent the children in legal action. Accordingly, we conclude that [father] requested that he be awarded those rights in his petition, and the trial court's final order awarding those rights exclusively to [father] conformed to the pleadings and was not an abuse of discretion."

King v. Lyons, 457 S.W.3d 122, 131 (Tex.App.—Houston [1st Dist.] 2014, no pet.). "[I]n [SAPCRs], a

trial court may not grant injunctive relief against a party unless that party had notice by way of the pleadings or the issue was tried by consent. A court should read the pleadings liberally and not foreclose the grant of injunctive relief for lack of pleading formality so long as the pleading was sufficient to inform the party to be enjoined of the substance of the issue. In matters concerning custody, control, possession, and visitation, the trial court's foremost consideration is the best interest of the child, and the court has discretion to fashion orders including injunctive relief that are in the best interest of the child and consistent with the allegations, general prayers for relief, and evidence, without the need for strict proof of the existence of a wrongful act, imminent harm, irreparable injury, and the absence of an adequate remedy at law. But in cases in which the injunctive relief sought or granted does not concern custody, control, possession, or visitation of a child, the party seeking such relief must show his entitlement to a permanent injunction as in any civil case."

In re P.M.G., 405 S.W.3d 406, 417 (Tex.App.—Texarkana 2013, no pet.). "A judgment, absent issues tried by consent, must conform to the pleadings. [¶] In cases affecting the parent-child relationship, however, the pleading requirements are of lesser importance. [¶] '[I]n cases affecting the parent/child relationship, when the best interest of the child is always the overriding consideration, technical rules of pleading and practice are of little importance, and fair notice is afforded when the pleadings generally invoke the court's jurisdiction over custody and control of the children.'" *See also* ***In re L.D.F.***, 445 S.W.3d 823, 832 (Tex. App.—El Paso 2014, no pet.) (grandmother's pleadings asking for SMC properly placed father on notice that she intended to seek custody of child; trial court did not err by granting grandmother JMC); ***Flowers v. Flowers***, 407 S.W.3d 452, 457 (Tex.App.—Houston [14th Dist.] 2013, no pet.) (pleadings must give reasonable notice of claims asserted).

Pitts & Collard, L.L.P. v. Schechter, 369 S.W.3d 301, 320 (Tex.App.—Houston [1st Dist.] 2011, no pet.). "The motion [for JNOV] should be granted (1) when the evidence is conclusive, and one party is entitled to recover as a matter of law or (2) when a legal principle precludes recovery. A motion for [JNOV] based on a legal principle is appropriately granted when it is conclusively established that recovery is precluded even though all the allegations are proven."

Hartford Fire Ins. v. C. Springs 300, Ltd., 287 S.W.3d 771, 779-80 (Tex.App.—Houston [1st Dist.] 2009, pet. denied). "There are ... exceptions to rule 301. Unpleaded claims or defenses that are tried by express or implied consent of the parties are treated as if they had been raised by the pleadings. The party who allows an issue to be tried by consent and who fails to raise the lack of a pleading before submission of the case cannot later raise the pleading deficiency for the first time on appeal."

In re Marriage of Moore, 890 S.W.2d 821, 838 n.10 (Tex.App.—Amarillo 1994, no writ). "A motion to disregard the jury's findings, with notice, is usually required to enable a court to disregard a finding and to preserve alleged error if the court fails to do so. However, in a marital relations case, such a motion is only necessary when the trial court is attempting to disregard a jury's finding as to the value of certain community property or the character or status of property possessed by the parties. This is true because the jury's findings as to the characterization and valuation of property are binding upon the trial court."

TRCP 302. ON COUNTERCLAIM

If the defendant establishes a demand against the plaintiff upon a counterclaim exceeding that established against him by the plaintiff, the court shall render judgment for defendant for such excess.

TRCP 303. ON COUNTERCLAIM FOR COSTS

When a counterclaim is pleaded, the party in whose favor final judgment is rendered shall also recover the costs, unless it be made to appear on the trial that the counterclaim of the defendant was acquired after the commencement of the suit, in which case, if the plaintiff establishes a claim existing at the commencement of the suit, he shall recover his costs.

See also TRCP 131, 141.

ANNOTATIONS

Henry v. Masson, 453 S.W.3d 43, 50-51 (Tex. App.—Houston [1st Dist.] 2014, no pet.). "Several of our sister courts have held that when a party alleges a counterclaim[,] if neither party is wholly successful on its claims, it is within the trial court's discretion to order each party to bear its own costs. [¶] Here, neither party was wholly successful on its claims.... Under these facts, ... we conclude that the trial court did not

abuse its discretion when it did not assess court costs against either party."

Reyna v. First Nat'l Bank, 55 S.W.3d 58, 74 (Tex. App.—Corpus Christi 2001, no pet.). "[O]n appeal, [P] asserts that since [D] did not prevail on its counterclaim, then some of the costs should be assessed against [D]. Given that the counterclaim was ... acquired before the suit, and [P] did not prevail on any of his claims, we conclude ... the trial court correctly assessed all costs against [P]."

TRCP 304. JUDGMENT UPON RECORD

Judgments rendered upon questions raised upon citations, pleadings, and all other proceedings, constituting the record proper as known at common law, must be entered at the date of each term when pronounced.

TRCP 305. PROPOSED JUDGMENT

Any party may prepare and submit a proposed judgment to the court for signature.

Each party who submits a proposed judgment for signature shall serve the proposed judgment on all other parties to the suit who have appeared and remain in the case, in accordance with Rule 21a.

Failure to comply with this rule shall not affect the time for perfecting an appeal.

See also *O'Connor's Texas Rules*, "Judgment," ch. 9-C, p. 861; *O'Connor's Texas Forms*, FORM 9C:1.

ANNOTATIONS

First Nat'l Bank v. Fojtik, 775 S.W.2d 632, 633 (Tex.1989). A party's motion asking the trial court to enter judgment does not waive the party's right to complain about that judgment. "There must be a method by which a party who desires to initiate the appellate process may move the trial court to render judgment without being bound by its terms."

Dikeman v. Snell, 490 S.W.2d 183, 185-86 (Tex. 1973). Held: Even when a judgment is prepared by a party, a mistake in the rendered judgment is a judicial error.

Vann v. Brown, 244 S.W.3d 612, 617 (Tex.App.—Dallas 2008, no pet.). "We recognize that rule 305 suggests a party 'may' offer the trial court a proposed judgment, but that is not a requirement. We cannot agree with [P's] assertion that Rule 305 suggests [D] should have supplied a proposed judgment to the trial court. The parties even acknowledge in oral argument that it is customary for the party in whose favor the verdict was returned to provide a proposed judgment to the trial judge."

TRCP 306. RECITATION OF JUDGMENT

The entry of the judgment shall contain the full names of the parties, as stated in the pleadings, for and against whom the judgment is rendered. In a suit for termination of the parent-child relationship or a suit affecting the parent-child relationship filed by a governmental entity for managing conservatorship, the judgment must state the specific grounds for termination or for appointment of the managing conservator.

See also *O'Connor's Texas Rules*, "Judgment," ch. 9-C, p. 861.

ANNOTATIONS

Crystal City ISD v. Wagner, 605 S.W.2d 743, 747 (Tex.App.—San Antonio 1980, writ ref'd n.r.e.). "Undoubtedly, the better practice is to recite the names of all the parties in the judgment.... Nevertheless, when ... the names of all the parties and the relief each is entitled to is easily ascertainable from the record, it would be a useless thing to remand the entire cause for the purpose of amending the judgment to include the names of all the parties."

TRCP 306a. PERIODS TO RUN FROM SIGNING OF JUDGMENT

1. Beginning of periods. The date of judgment or order is signed as shown of record shall determine the beginning of the periods prescribed by these rules for the court's plenary power to grant a new trial or to vacate, modify, correct or reform a judgment or order and for filing in the trial court the various documents that these rules authorize a party to file within such periods including, but not limited to, motions for new trial, motions to modify judgment, motions to reinstate a case dismissed for want of prosecution, motions to vacate judgment and requests for findings of fact and conclusions of law; but this rule shall not determine what constitutes rendition of a judgment or order for any other purpose.

2. Date to be shown. Judges, attorneys and clerks are directed to use their best efforts to cause all judgments, decisions and orders of any kind to be reduced to writing and signed by the trial judge with the date of signing stated therein. If the date of signing is not recited in the judgment or order, it may be shown in the record by a certificate of the judge or otherwise;

provided, however, that the absence of a showing of the date in the record shall not invalidate any judgment or order.

3. Notice of judgment. When the final judgment or other appealable order is signed, the clerk of the court shall immediately give notice to the parties or their attorneys of record by first-class mail advising that the judgment or order was signed. Failure to comply with the provisions of this rule shall not affect the periods mentioned in paragraph (1) of this rule, except as provided in paragraph (4).

4. No notice of judgment. If within twenty days after the judgment or other appealable order is signed, a party adversely affected by it or his attorney has neither received the notice required by paragraph (3) of this rule nor acquired actual knowledge of the order, then with respect to that party all the periods mentioned in paragraph (1) shall begin on the date that such party or his attorney received such notice or acquired actual knowledge of the signing, whichever occurred first, but in no event shall such periods begin more than ninety days after the original judgment or other appealable order was signed.

5. Motion, notice and hearing. In order to establish the application of paragraph (4) of this rule, the party adversely affected is required to prove in the trial court, on sworn motion and notice, the date on which the party or his attorney first either received a notice of the judgment or acquired actual knowledge of the signing and that this date was more than twenty days after the judgment was signed.

6. Nunc pro tunc order. When a corrected judgment has been signed after expiration of the court's plenary power pursuant to Rule 316, the periods mentioned in paragraph (1) of this rule shall run from the date of signing the corrected judgment with respect to any complaint that would not be applicable to the original document.

7. When process served by publication. With respect to a motion for new trial filed more than thirty days after the judgment was signed pursuant to Rule 329 when process has been served by publication, the periods provided by paragraph (1) shall be computed as if the judgment were signed on the date of filing the motion.

See also ***O'Connor's Texas Rules***, "Default Judgment," ch. 7-A, p. 671; "Judgment," ch. 9-C, p. 861; "Motion for New Trial," ch. 10-B, p. 891; "Motion to Reinstate After Dismissal for Want of Prosecution," ch. 10-F, p. 930; "Motion to Extend Postjudgment Deadlines," ch. 10-G, p. 936; "Motion for Judgment Nunc Pro Tunc," ch. 10-H, p. 942.

ANNOTATIONS

Generally

Board of Trs. of Bastrop ISD v. Toungate, 958 S.W.2d 365, 367 (Tex.1997). "We note that the trial court should have submitted the modified judgment to the clerk immediately upon signing it to avoid the burden of a notification hearing."

Martinez v. Humble Sand & Gravel, Inc., 875 S.W.2d 311, 312 (Tex.1994). "When … an otherwise final judgment fails to dispose of all parties, the court may make the judgment final for purposes of appeal by severing the causes and parties disposed of by the judgment into a different cause. *At 313:* When a severance order takes effect, the appellate timetable runs from the signing date of the order that made the judgment severed 'final' and appealable."

Wells Fargo Bank v. Erickson, 267 S.W.3d 139, 149 (Tex.App.—Corpus Christi 2008, no pet.). "[P] argues that a trial court cannot reconsider its decision to deny a rule 306a motion. We find nothing in the [TRCPs] that precludes a trial court from reconsidering its prior ruling on such a motion within its plenary power or from entertaining a second motion filed for the same purpose."

Coinmach, Inc. v. Aspenwood Apt. Corp., 98 S.W.3d 377, 378 (Tex.App.—Houston [1st Dist.] 2003, no pet.). "The issue for this Court is whether the effective date of the order granting a new trial is (1) the date the trial court signs the order or (2) the date the trial court clerk file-stamps the signed order. … We hold that the order granting a new trial became effective on the date signed by the trial court…."

Burns v. Bishop, 48 S.W.3d 459, 465 (Tex.App.—Houston [14th Dist.] 2001, no pet.). "Signing and rendition are not synonymous. Signing an order is not among the official steps that would fall within the common meaning of 'proceedings.' Drafting and signing the judgment [are] preparatory, *administrative* acts that … authenticate the record of the court's rendition. Rendition occurs when the trial court officially announces its decision (1) in open court in a manner that objectively reflects its intention to render or (2) by written memorandum *filed with the clerk*."

No Notice of Judgment

Ginn v. Forrester, 282 S.W.3d 430, 433 (Tex.2009). TRCP 306a does "not impose upon the clerk an affirma-

tive duty to record the mailing of the required notice[ ]; accordingly, the absence of proof in the record that notice was provided does not establish error on the face of the record. [¶] We … see [no] distinction … between a record that is silent and a record that contains a written notation that the record is silent; either way, proof of error is absent."

In re Lynd Co., 195 S.W.3d 682, 686 (Tex.2006). "Rule 306a does not require that the trial court issue a signed order with … a finding [of actual notice of final judgment]. [W]hen the trial court fails to specifically find the date of notice, the finding may be implied from the trial court's judgment, unless there is no evidence supporting the implied finding or the party challenging the judgment establishes as a matter of law an alternate notice date."

John v. Marshall Health Servs., 58 S.W.3d 738, 741 (Tex.2001). "Rule 306a(5) does not prohibit a motion from being filed at any time within the trial court's plenary jurisdiction measured from the date determined under Rule 306a(4). Rule 306a simply imposes no deadline, and none can be added by decision, other than the deadline of the expiration of the trial court's jurisdiction."

Estate of Howley v. Haberman, 878 S.W.2d 139, 140 (Tex.1994). "A party who does not have actual knowledge of an order of dismissal within 90 days of the date it is signed cannot move for reinstatement. Since [P] did not learn of the dismissal within this period, the order of dismissal for want of prosecution was final…. [P's] only possible recourse is a bill of review." *See also* ***Levit v. Adams***, 850 S.W.2d 469, 470 (Tex. 1993).

Southwest Warren, Inc. v. Crawford, 464 S.W.3d 822, 827 (Tex.App.—Houston [1st Dist.] 2015, no pet.). "Here, the trial court granted the motion to extend the post-judgment deadlines. This had the effect of establishing the new date of the judgment—for post-judgment deadline purposes—as the date that [Ds] learned of the default judgment. [T]he order 'rescinding' the grant of the motion to extend did not void or otherwise render the extension order a nullity. Because the extension order still had effect, the post-judgment deadlines continued to run from the date set by that order. To the degree that the order rescinding the grant of the extension has any legal effect, that effect cannot be to set the post-judgment deadlines at an earlier time."

TRCP 306b. REPEALED

TRCP 306c. PREMATURELY FILED DOCUMENTS

No motion for new trial or request for findings of fact and conclusions of law shall be held ineffective because prematurely filed; but every such motion shall be deemed to have been filed on the date of but subsequent to the time of signing of the judgment the motion assails, and every such request for findings of fact and conclusions of law shall be deemed to have been filed on the date of but subsequent to the time of signing of the judgment.

See also TRAP 27; *O'Connor's Texas Rules*, "Motion for New Trial," ch. 10-B, p. 891; "Requesting Findings of Fact," ch. 10-E, §3, p. 925.

ANNOTATIONS

Ryland Enter. v. Weatherspoon, 355 S.W.3d 664, 666 (Tex.2011). "[T]he premature filing rules in [TRCP] 306c and [TRAP] 27.2 apply equally to motions for new trial or to modify the judgment. [T]he filing of a motion for new trial or to modify the judgment, before the judgment is signed or within 30 days after, extends the deadline for filing a notice of appeal to 90 days."

Wilkins v. Methodist Health Care Sys., 160 S.W.3d 559, 563 (Tex.2005). "When a motion for new trial is granted, it becomes moot as to any effect it may have on a subsequent judgment. *At 564:* [A] motion for new trial that has been granted cannot 'assail' a subsequent judgment for purposes of determining the deadline for filing a notice of appeal."

Fredonia State Bank v. General Am. Life Ins., 881 S.W.2d 279, 281 (Tex.1994). "[A] motion for new trial relating to an earlier judgment may be considered applicable to a second judgment when the substance of the motion could properly be raised with respect to the corrected judgment."

TRCP 306d. REPEALED

TRCP 307. EXCEPTIONS, ETC., TRANSCRIPT

In non-jury cases, where findings of fact and conclusions of law are requested and filed, and in jury cases, where a special verdict is returned, any party claiming that the findings of the court or the jury, as the case may be, do not support the judgment, may have noted in the record an exception to said judgment and thereupon take an appeal or writ of error, where such writ is allowed, without a statement of facts or further excep-

tions in the transcript, but the transcript in such cases shall contain the conclusions of law and fact or the special verdict and the judgment rendered thereon.

TRCP 308. COURT SHALL ENFORCE ITS DECREES

The court shall cause its judgments and decrees to be carried into execution; and where the judgment is for personal property, and it is shown by the pleadings and evidence and the verdict, if any, that such property has an especial value to the plaintiff, the court may award a special writ for the seizure and delivery of such property to the plaintiff; and in such case may enforce its judgment by attachment, fine and imprisonment.

ANNOTATIONS

Cook v. Stallcup, 170 S.W.3d 916, 920-21 (Tex. App.—Dallas 2005, no pet.). After the court's plenary power expired, "the trial court had power only to enforce its judgment, subject to the limitation that any enforcement may not be inconsistent with the original judgment and must not constitute a material change in substantial adjudicated portions of the judgment." *See also* ***Kennedy v. Hudnall***, 249 S.W.3d 520, 523 (Tex. App.—Texarkana 2008, no pet.); ***Bridas Corp. v. Unocal Corp.***, 16 S.W.3d 887, 889 (Tex.App.—Houston [14th Dist.] 2000, pet. dism'd).

TRCP 308a. IN SUITS AFFECTING THE PARENT-CHILD RELATIONSHIP

When the court has ordered child support or possession of or access to a child and it is claimed that the order has been violated, the person claiming that a violation has occurred shall make this known to the court. The court may appoint a member of the bar to investigate the claim to determine whether there is reason to believe that the court order has been violated. If the attorney in good faith believes that the order has been violated, the attorney shall take the necessary action as provided under Chapter 14, Family Code.[1] On a finding of a violation, the court may enforce its order as provided in Chapter 14, Family Code.[1]

Except by order of the court, no fee shall be charged by or paid to the attorney representing the claimant. If the court determines that an attorney's fee should be paid, the fee shall be adjudged against the party who violated the court's order. The fee may be assessed as costs of court, or awarded by judgment, or both.

1. **Editor's note:** Now Family Code ch. 157. For current provisions of ch. 14, see Disposition Table, p. 1546.

ANNOTATIONS

Ex parte Herring, 438 S.W.2d 801, 803 (Tex.1969). TRCP 308a "contemplates that service under any of the applicable portions of [TRCP] 21a including service upon the attorney would constitute a compliance with the [TRCPs]. [¶] [I]t is a denial of due process to commit a person to prison for contempt who is not shown to be avoiding deliberately the service of process, and who has had *no* personal notice or knowledge of the show-cause hearing...." Relator discharged.

Taylor v. Speck, 308 S.W.3d 81, 88 (Tex.App.—San Antonio 2010, no pet.). "Rule 308a applies only when the trial court appoints an attorney to 'determine whether there is a reason to believe that the court order has been violated.'"

In re A.M., 974 S.W.2d 857, 865 (Tex.App.—San Antonio 1998, no pet.). TRCP 308a "governs enforcement actions for [SAPCRs]. That rule states that, in an enforcement action, no fee shall be charged or paid to an attorney, except by order of the court. In the event that attorney's fees are ordered, the rule states, '[T]he fee shall be adjudged against the party who violated the court's order.' The Family Code states that, in enforcement proceedings on child support payments, the court 'shall' order respondent to pay the movant's reasonable attorney's fees, unless good cause is stated in the court's findings. [¶] Rule 308a speaks only to enforcement proceedings. We note that several courts have held that, in non-enforcement proceedings under the Family Code, the trial court need not state good cause for awarding fees to the non-prevailing party. We agree that, because in family law cases involving children, the best interests of the children are paramount, it may not always be appropriate to award costs and fees to the prevailing party."

TRCP 309. IN FORECLOSURE PROCEEDINGS

Judgments for the foreclosure of mortgages and other liens shall be that the plaintiff recover his debt, damages and costs, with a foreclosure of the plaintiff's lien on the property subject thereto, and, except in judgments against executors, administrators and guardians, that an order of sale shall issue to any sheriff or any constable within the State of Texas, directing him to seize and sell the same as under execution, in satisfaction of the judgment; and, if the property cannot be found, or if the proceeds of such sale be insufficient to

satisfy the judgment, then to take the money or any balance thereof remaining unpaid, out of any other property of the defendant, as in case of ordinary executions.

TRCP 310. WRIT OF POSSESSION

When an order foreclosing a lien upon real estate is made in a suit having for its object the foreclosure of such lien, such order shall have all the force and effect of a writ of possession as between the parties to the foreclosure suit and any person claiming under the defendant to such suit by any right acquired pending such suit; and the court shall so direct in the judgment providing for the issuance of such order. The sheriff or other officer executing such order of sale shall proceed by virtue of such order of sale to place the purchaser of the property sold thereunder in possession thereof within thirty days after the day of sale.

TRCP 311. ON APPEAL FROM PROBATE COURT

Judgment on appeal or certiorari from any county court sitting in probate shall be certified to such county court for observance.

TRCP 312. ON APPEAL FROM JUSTICE COURT

Judgments on appeal or certiorari from a justice court shall be enforced by the county or district court rendering the judgment.

TRCP 313. AGAINST EXECUTORS, ETC.

A judgment for the recovery of money against an executor, administrator or guardian, as such, shall state that it is to be paid in the due course of administration. No execution shall issue thereon, but it shall be certified to the county court, sitting in matters of probate, to be there enforced in accordance with law, but judgment against an executor appointed and acting under a will dispensing with the action of the county court in reference to such estate shall be enforced against the property of the testator in the hands of such executor, by execution, as in other cases.

TRCP 314. CONFESSION OF JUDGMENT

Any person against whom a cause of action exists may, without process, appear in person or by attorney, and confess judgment therefor in open court as follows:

(a) A petition shall be filed and the justness of the debt or cause of action be sworn to by the person in whose favor the judgment is confessed.

(b) If the judgment is confessed by attorney, the power of attorney shall be filed and its contents be recited in the judgment.

(c) Every such judgment duly made shall operate as a release of all errors in the record thereof, but such judgment may be impeached for fraud or other equitable cause.

I. REMITTITUR & CORRECTION

TRCP 315. REMITTITUR

Any party in whose favor a judgment has been rendered may remit any part thereof in open court, or by executing and filing with the clerk a written remittitur signed by the party or the party's attorney of record, and duly acknowledged by the party or the party's attorney. Such remittitur shall be a part of the record of the cause. Execution shall issue for the balance only of such judgment.

See also *O'Connor's Texas Rules*, "Motion for Remittitur," ch. 10-C, p. 915; *O'Connor's Texas Forms*, FORMS 10C.

ANNOTATIONS

Larson v. Cactus Util. Co., 730 S.W.2d 640, 641 (Tex.1987). "A court of appeals should uphold a trial court remittitur only when the evidence is factually insufficient to support the verdict. [¶] If a court of appeals holds that there is no evidence to support a damages verdict, it should render a take nothing judgment as to that amount. If part of a damage verdict lacks sufficient evidentiary support, the proper course is to suggest a remittitur of that part of the verdict."

TRCP 316. CORRECTION OF CLERICAL MISTAKES IN JUDGMENT RECORD

Clerical mistakes in the record of any judgment may be corrected by the judge in open court according to the truth or justice of the case after notice of the motion therefor has been given to the parties interested in such judgment, as provided in Rule 21a, and thereafter the execution shall conform to the judgment as amended.

See also *O'Connor's Texas Rules*, "Motion for Judgment Nunc Pro Tunc," ch. 10-H, p. 942; *O'Connor's Texas Forms*, FORMS 10H.

ANNOTATIONS

Texas DOT v. A.P.I. Pipe & Sup., 397 S.W.3d 162, 167 (Tex.2013). "'A clerical error is one which does not result from judicial reasoning or determination.' Even a significant alteration to the original judgment may be accomplished through a judgment nunc pro tunc so

long as it merely corrects a clerical error. If 'the signed judgment inaccurately reflects the true decision of the court,' then 'the error is clerical and may be corrected.'"

Escobar v. Escobar, 711 S.W.2d 230, 231 (Tex. 1986). "After the trial court loses its jurisdiction over a judgment, it can correct only clerical errors in the judgment by judgment nunc pro tunc. In this regard, the trial court has plenary power to correct a clerical error made in *entering* final judgment. [¶] A judicial error is an error which occurs in the *rendering* as opposed to the *entering* of a judgment." *See also* ***In re Daredia***, 317 S.W.3d 247, 249-50 (Tex.2010); ***Andrews v. Koch***, 702 S.W.2d 584, 585 (Tex.1986).

In re A.M.C., 491 S.W.3d 62, 67-68 (Tex.App.—Houston [14th Dist.] 2016, no pet.). "When deciding whether a correction is of a judicial or a clerical error, we look to the judgment actually rendered, not the judgment that should or might have been rendered. The trial court can only correct the entry of a final written judgment that incorrectly states the judgment actually rendered. [¶] Whether an error in a judgment is judicial or clerical is a question of law we review de novo. However, a trial court must make a factual determination regarding whether it previously rendered judgment and the judgment's contents before it may decide the nature of the error. We may review only a trial court's factual determination on whether a judgment has been rendered and its contents for legal and factual sufficiency of the evidence. … If the same trial judge who renders the judgment grants the nunc pro tunc motion, we presume that the judge's personal recollection supports the finding of clerical error. [¶] The only 'copy' of the original enforcement order in the record is the one that was scanned into the trial court's electronic filing system. It is clear from the record that the handwritten language was not scanned completely into the electronic record. … The trial court included the omitted language in the Nunc Pro Tunc Enforcement Order. We conclude that the trial court's factual determination that its rendition of the original enforcement order included the omitted handwritten language was supported by some probative evidence, particularly given the presumption in favor of the trial court's recollection. [¶] We further conclude that the omission of the language from the scanned document was a clerical and not judicial error. This error was a failure of the scanner to pick up the entire page of the enforcement order, as reflected on the order in the electronic record. This is precisely the type of clerical error that is envisioned by [TRCP] 329b."

In re Marriage of Snead, No. 13-11-00200-CV (Tex.App.—Corpus Christi 2012, no pet.) (memo op.; 8-16-12). "A judgment nunc pro tunc does not disturb the initial judgment rendered by the trial court; it merely brings the court records into conformity with it. Accordingly, a judgment nunc pro tunc, although signed later, relates back to the date of the original judgment and is effective as of the earlier date."

TRCP 317 TO 319. REPEALED

J. NEW TRIALS

TRCP 320. MOTION & ACTION OF COURT THEREON

New trials may be granted and judgment set aside for good cause, on motion or on the court's own motion on such terms as the court shall direct. New trials may be granted when the damages are manifestly too small or too large. When it appears to the court that a new trial should be granted on a point or points that affect only a part of the matters in controversy and that such part is clearly separable without unfairness to the parties, the court may grant a new trial as to that part only, provided that a separate trial on unliquidated damages alone shall not be ordered if liability issues are contested. Each motion for new trial shall be in writing and signed by the party or his attorney.

See also *O'Connor's Texas Rules*, "Motion for New Trial," ch. 10-B, p. 891; *O'Connor's Texas Forms*, FORMS 10B.

ANNOTATIONS

In re Columbia Med. Ctr., 290 S.W.3d 204, 206 (Tex.2009). "The issue before us is whether, after a jury has rendered its verdict, the trial court may disregard that verdict, grant a new trial, and explain its action only as being 'in the interests of justice and fairness.' We conclude that just as appellate courts that set aside jury verdicts are required to detail reasons for doing so, trial courts must give more explanation than 'in the interest of justice' for setting aside a jury verdict. *At 212-13:* We do not retreat from the position that trial courts have significant discretion in granting new trials. However, such discretion should not, and does not, permit a trial judge to substitute his or her own views for that of the jury without a valid basis. … The trial court's action in failing to give its reasons for disregarding the jury verdict as to [D] was arbitrary and an abuse of discretion." *See also* ***In re Bent***, 487 S.W.3d

170, 175-76 (Tex.2016); ***In re Toyota Motor Sales, U.S.A., Inc.***, 407 S.W.3d 746, 756-57 (Tex.2013); ***In re United Scaffolding, Inc.***, 377 S.W.3d 685, 688-89 (Tex. 2012).

Old Republic Ins. v. Scott, 846 S.W.2d 832, 833 (Tex.1993). "The **filing** of a motion for new trial in order to extend the appellate timetable is a matter of right, whether or not there is any sound or reasonable basis for the conclusion that a further motion is necessary."

State Dept. of Hwys. & Pub. Transp. v. Cotner, 845 S.W.2d 818, 819 (Tex.1993). "A partial new trial may be ordered notwithstanding the prohibition in [TRCP] 41 against post-submission severances. [TRCP] 320 is thus an exception to Rule 41."

Gathe v. Gathe, 376 S.W.3d 308, 314-15 (Tex. App.—Houston [14th Dist.] 2012, no pet.). See annotation under Family Code §7.001, *Generally*, p. 88.

TRCP 321. FORM

Each point relied upon in a motion for new trial or in arrest of judgment shall briefly refer to that part of the ruling of the court, charge given to the jury, or charge refused, admission or rejection of evidence, or other proceedings which are designated to be complained of, in such a way that the objection can be clearly identified and understood by the court.

See also ***O'Connor's Texas Rules***, "Motion for New Trial," ch. 10-B, p. 891; ***O'Connor's Texas Forms***, FORMS 10B.

TRCP 322. GENERALITY TO BE AVOIDED

Grounds of objections couched in general terms—as that the court erred in its charge, in sustaining or overruling exceptions to the pleadings, and in excluding or admitting evidence, the verdict of the jury is contrary to law, and the like—shall not be considered by the court.

See also ***O'Connor's Texas Rules***, "Points of error," ch. 10-B, §2.3, p. 892.

ANNOTATIONS

Arkoma Basin Expl. Co. v. FMF Assocs. 1990-A, Ltd., 249 S.W.3d 380, 388 (Tex.2008). "If a single jury question involves many issues, it is possible that a general objection may not tell the trial court where to start. But post-trial objections will rarely be as detailed as an appellate brief because time is short, the record may not be ready, and the trial court is already familiar with the case. In that context, an objection is not necessarily inadequate because it does not specify every reason the evidence was insufficient. Like all other procedural rules, those regarding the specificity of post-trial objections should be construed liberally so that the right to appeal is not lost unnecessarily."

TRCP 323. REPEALED

TRCP 324. PREREQUISITES OF APPEAL

(a) Motion for New Trial Not Required. A point in a motion for new trial is not a prerequisite to a complaint on appeal in either a jury or a nonjury case, except as provided in subdivision (b).

(b) Motion for New Trial Required. A point in a motion for new trial is a prerequisite to the following complaints on appeal:

(1) A complaint on which evidence must be heard such as one of jury misconduct or newly discovered evidence or failure to set aside a judgment by default;

(2) A complaint of factual insufficiency of the evidence to support a jury finding;

(3) A complaint that a jury finding is against the overwhelming weight of the evidence;

(4) A complaint of inadequacy or excessiveness of the damages found by the jury; or

(5) Incurable jury argument if not otherwise ruled on by the trial court.

(c) Judgment Notwithstanding Findings; Cross-Points. When judgment is rendered non obstante veredicto or notwithstanding the findings of a jury on one or more questions, the appellee may bring forward by cross-point contained in his brief filed in the Court of Appeals any ground which would have vitiated the verdict or would have prevented an affirmance of the judgment had one been rendered by the trial court in harmony with the verdict, including although not limited to the ground that one or more of the jury's findings have insufficient support in the evidence or are against the overwhelming preponderance of the evidence as a matter of fact, and the ground that the verdict and judgment based thereon should be set aside because of improper argument of counsel.

The failure to bring forward by cross-points such grounds as would vitiate the verdict shall be deemed a waiver thereof; provided, however, that if a cross-point is upon a ground which requires the taking of evidence in addition to that adduced upon the trial of the cause, it is not necessary that the evidentiary hearing be held until after the appellate court determines that the cause be remanded to consider such a cross-point.

See also *O'Connor's Texas Rules*, "Making & Preserving Objections," ch. 1-F, p. 55; "Motion for JNOV," ch. 9-B, p. 857; "Motion for New Trial," ch. 10-B, p. 891.

ANNOTATIONS

Office of Atty. Gen. v. Burton, 369 S.W.3d 173, 174 (Tex.2012). "In this appeal of a judgment to confirm child support arrearage, the [AG] complains solely that the evidence is legally insufficient to support a judgment of no arrearage. The court of appeals [concluded] that the [AG] had waived its no-evidence complaint by not first presenting the complaint to the trial court. Because we conclude that this procedural step was unnecessary to preserve the complaint for appellate review, we reverse and remand. *At 175:* A motion for new trial is not a prerequisite to an appellate complaint about the legal sufficiency of the evidence. As a general rule, an appellant must first complain to the trial court by a timely request, objection, or motion and obtain a ruling as a prerequisite for appellate review of that complaint, but the general rule does not apply to complaints about the sufficiency of the evidence in a trial to the court. Thus, [TRAP] 33.1(d) provides that '[i]n a nonjury case, a complaint regarding the legal or factual insufficiency of the evidence ... may be made for the first time on appeal in the complaining party's brief.'"

Phillips v. Bramlett, 288 S.W.3d 876, 883 (Tex. 2009). "A complaint of incurable argument may be asserted and preserved in a motion for new trial, even without a complaint and ruling during the trial. Incurable jury argument is rare, however, because '[t]ypically, retraction of the argument or instruction from the court can cure any probable harm....' The party claiming incurable harm must persuade the court that, based on the record as a whole, the offensive argument was so extreme that a 'juror of ordinary intelligence could have been persuaded by that argument to agree to a verdict contrary to that to which he would have agreed but for such argument.'"

State Farm Lloyds v. Nicolau, 951 S.W.2d 444, 452 (Tex.1997). D was not entitled to a new trial based on newly discovered evidence because it had "not shown any likelihood that the new evidence, if introduced at trial, would have resulted in a different verdict on any of [Ps'] claims."

Lee v. Braeburn Valley W. Civic Ass'n, 786 S.W.2d 262, 263 (Tex.1990). "[A] motion for new trial is not a prerequisite for an appeal of a summary judgment proceeding."

In re Calzadias, 484 S.W.3d 574, 576 (Tex.App.—Amarillo 2016, orig. proceeding). "[T]he standard for granting a new trial based on newly discovered evidence in a suit concerning child custody has been relaxed. *At 577:* 'In such cases the children are the primary parties in interest, and they are rarely represented by counsel. Counsel for the contending parents cannot always be relied upon to protect the interests of the children because the parents often attempt to promote their own interests and vindicate their own asserted rights rather than to protect the children's interests. Consequently, the court's duty to protect the children's interests should not be limited by technical rules. Pertinent facts which may directly affect the interests of the children should be heard and considered by the trial court regardless of the lack of diligence of the parties in their presentation of information to the court.' ... '[T]he court [is not required to] grant a new trial whenever the losing party brings forth new evidence bearing on the issue of the best interests of the children. No abuse of discretion is shown unless the evidence presented in support of the motion, and not offered at the original trial, strongly shows that the original custody order would have a seriously adverse effect on the interest and welfare of the children, and that presentation of such evidence at another trial would probably change the result.' [¶] '[I]n child custody cases, it can be error to refuse to grant a motion for new trial even though the evidence is not newly discovered when there is an extreme case and the evidence is sufficiently strong.'"

In re A.M., 385 S.W.3d 74, 78 (Tex.App.—Waco 2012, pet. denied). See annotation under Family Code §161.001, *Due Process*, p. 755.

TRCP 325. REPEALED

TRCP 326. NOT MORE THAN TWO

Not more than two new trials shall be granted either party in the same cause because of insufficiency or weight of the evidence.

TRCP 327. FOR JURY MISCONDUCT

a. When the ground of a motion for new trial, supported by affidavit, is misconduct of the jury or of the officer in charge of them, or because of any communication made to the jury, or that a juror gave an erroneous or incorrect answer on voir dire examination, the court shall hear evidence thereof from the jury or others in open court, and may grant a new trial if such

misconduct proved, or the communication made, or the erroneous or incorrect answer on voir dire examination, be material, and if it reasonably appears from the evidence both on the hearing of the motion and the trial of the case and from the record as a whole that injury probably resulted to the complaining party.

b. A juror may not testify as to any matter or statement occurring during the course of the jury's deliberations or to the effect of anything upon his or any other juror's mind or emotions as influencing him to assent to or dissent from the verdict concerning his mental processes in connection therewith, except that a juror may testify whether any outside influence was improperly brought to bear upon any juror. Nor may his affidavit or evidence of any statement by him concerning a matter about which he would be precluded from testifying be received for these purposes.

See also TRE 606(b); *O'Connor's Texas Rules*, "MNT Based on Jury or Bailiff Misconduct," ch. 10-B, §14, p. 907; *O'Connor's Texas Forms*, FORM 10B:1.

ANNOTATIONS

Ford Motor Co. v. Castillo, 279 S.W.3d 656, 666 (Tex.2009). "[B]y their plain language, [TRCP 327(b) and TRE 606(b)] apply to motions for new trials, reasons jurors voted for or against verdicts, and inquiries into the validity of verdicts or indictments. Even when those types of issues are involved, the rules specifically allow jurors to testify about outside influence brought to bear on any of them."

Golden Eagle Archery, Inc. v. Jackson, 24 S.W.3d 362, 370 (Tex.2000). "A juror may testify about jury misconduct provided it does not require delving into deliberations. [¶] [TRCP 327(b) and TRE 606(b)] contemplate that an 'outside influence' originates from sources other than the jurors themselves. *At 371:* [An] alleged conversation between [jurors] during a trial break ... should not be considered 'deliberations' and therefore barred by Rule 606(b) and Rule 327(b)." *See also* ***Vargas de Damian v. Bell Helicopter Textron, Inc.***, 352 S.W.3d 124, 161 (Tex.App.—Fort Worth 2011, pet. denied) (juror testimony that they traded answers was not evidence of outside influence); ***Hutton v. AER Mfg. II, Inc.***, 224 S.W.3d 459, 463 (Tex.App.—Dallas 2007, pet. denied) (claim that jurors changed their votes or bargained away their positions because of supplemental charge was not evidence of outside influence).

Pharo v. Chambers Cty., 922 S.W.2d 945, 950 (Tex. 1996). The bailiff's misconduct "justifies a new trial only if it reasonably appears from the record that injury probably resulted to the complaining party. To show probable injury, there must be some indication in the record that the alleged misconduct most likely caused a juror to vote differently than he would otherwise have done on one or more issues vital to the judgment. Determining the existence of probable injury is a question of law." (Internal quotes omitted.) *See also* ***In re Health Care Unlimited, Inc.***, 429 S.W.3d 600, 603 (Tex.2014) (juror's communication with party representative about church retreat did not cause probable injury); ***In re Whataburger Rests. LP***, 429 S.W.3d 597, 599 (Tex.2014) (juror's failure to disclose that she had been a D in past lawsuits did not cause probable injury).

In re Zimmer, Inc., 451 S.W.3d 893, 900 (Tex. App.—Dallas 2014, orig. proceeding). "Rule 327 ... plainly states the trial court 'shall hear evidence [of misconduct of the jury or the officer in charge of them] from the jury or others in open court....' [P] argues this evidentiary requirement applies only when one of the parties seeks to offer live testimony. He contends it exists solely so jurors or other persons who are not willing to sign affidavits may be subpoenaed and compelled to testify. We disagree.... *At 901-02:* A proceeding under rule 327 is not complete ... upon the filing of the affidavits. ... The trial court has no discretion to refuse to conduct an evidentiary hearing when a party comes forward with affidavits supporting a cognizable claim of material jury misconduct. [¶] [P] argues, however, that because here neither party sought an evidentiary hearing, the trial court was entitled to decide the question of jury misconduct on the basis of affidavits and argument alone. We disagree. [¶] [A]ffidavits attached to a motion for new trial alleging juror misconduct are 'neither evidence nor admissible as such on the hearing for a new trial on the ground of jury misconduct.' [A] trial court may properly deny a motion for new trial when a party alleging jury misconduct relies only on affidavits and fails to request a hearing on his motion and offer live testimony proving misconduct. Similarly, a trial court properly denies a new trial when it holds a hearing and the party asserting misconduct discusses the affidavits but never attempts to admit the affidavits into evidence or present any other evidence of juror misconduct through live testimony. In such a situation

there is no evidence to support the complaining party's allegations of juror misconduct. We see no reason why the evidentiary requirements of rule 327 should be interpreted any less stringently when the trial court grants new trial and sets aside the jury verdict."

Jefferson v. Fuller, No. 01-11-00199-CV (Tex. App.—Houston [1st Dist.] 2012, pet. denied) (memo op.; 6-21-12). "'A juror can commit misconduct if he lies in voir dire about a matter on which he was clearly biased or prejudiced.' For false answers to voir dire questions to entitle a party to a new trial, the concealment must be in response to a specific and direct question calling for disclosure. To establish jury misconduct on grounds that the juror concealed information during voir dire, a party must obtain proof of concealment from a source other than jury deliberations."

Brandt v. Surber, 194 S.W.3d 108, 134 (Tex.App.—Corpus Christi 2006, pet. denied). "An outside influence does not include 'information not in evidence, unknown to the jurors prior to trial, acquired by a juror and communicated to one or more other jurors between the time the jurors received their instructions from the court and the rendition of the verdict[ ]'.... [¶] [One juror's] affidavit stating that other jurors discussed newspaper articles during deliberations was not evidence of any outside influence, but only described matters on the minds of other jurors during deliberations. The affidavit is, therefore, incompetent to serve as evidence of juror misconduct."

TRCP 328. REPEALED

TRCP 329. MOTION FOR NEW TRIAL ON JUDGMENT FOLLOWING CITATION BY PUBLICATION

In cases in which judgment has been rendered on service of process by publication, when the defendant has not appeared in person or by attorney of his own selection:

(a) The court may grant a new trial upon petition of the defendant showing good cause, supported by affidavit, filed within two years after such judgment was signed. The parties adversely interested in such judgment shall be cited as in other cases.

(b) Execution of such judgment shall not be suspended unless the party applying therefor shall give a good and sufficient bond payable to the plaintiff in the judgment, in an amount fixed in accordance with Appellate Rule 47 relating to supersedeas bonds, to be approved by the clerk, and conditioned that the party will prosecute his petition for new trial to effect and will perform such judgment as may be rendered by the court should its decision be against him.

(c) If property has been sold under the judgment and execution before the process was suspended, the defendant shall not recover the property so sold, but shall have judgment against the plaintiff in the judgment for the proceeds of such sale.

(d) If the motion is filed more than thirty days after the judgment was signed, the time period shall be computed pursuant to Rule 306a(7).

See also *O'Connor's Texas Rules*, "MNT After Service by Publication," ch. 10-B, §10, p. 902; *O'Connor's Texas Forms*, FORM 10B:5.

ANNOTATIONS

In re E.R., 385 S.W.3d 552, 563 (Tex.2012). "When judgment is rendered on service of process by publication, a party has two years to move for a new trial, which the trial court may grant for 'good cause.' But if service was invalid, a party is entitled to a new trial without showing good cause."

In re Boshears, No. 09-10-00187-CV (Tex.App.—Beaumont 2010, orig. proceeding) (memo op.; 6-10-10). "A bill of review filed within the time for filing a Rule 329 motion may be treated as a motion for new trial."

TRCP 329a. COUNTY COURT CASES

If a case or other matter is on trial or in the process of hearing when the term of the county court expires, such trial, hearing or other matter may be proceeded with at the next or any subsequent term of court and no motion or plea shall be considered as waived or overruled, because not acted upon at the term of court at which it was filed, but may be acted upon at any time the judge may fix or at which it may have been postponed or continued by agreement of the parties with leave of the court. This subdivision is not applicable to original or amended motions for new trial which are governed by Rule 329b.

TRCP 329b. TIME FOR FILING MOTIONS

The following rules shall be applicable to motions for new trial and motions to modify, correct, or reform judgments (other than motions to correct the record under Rule 316) in all district and county courts:

(a) A motion for new trial, if filed, shall be filed prior to or within thirty days after the judgment or other order complained of is signed.

(b) One or more amended motions for new trial may be filed without leave of court before any preceding motion for new trial filed by the movant is overruled and within thirty days after the judgment or other order complained of is signed.

(c) In the event an original or amended motion for new trial or a motion to modify, correct or reform a judgment is not determined by written order signed within seventy-five days after the judgment was signed, it shall be considered overruled by operation of law on expiration of that period.

(d) The trial court, regardless of whether an appeal has been perfected, has plenary power to grant a new trial or to vacate, modify, correct, or reform the judgment within thirty days after the judgment is signed.

(e) If a motion for new trial is timely filed by any party, the trial court, regardless of whether an appeal has been perfected, has plenary power to grant a new trial or to vacate, modify, correct, or reform the judgment until thirty days after all such timely-filed motions are overruled, either by a written and signed order or by operation of law, whichever occurs first.

(f) On expiration of the time within which the trial court has plenary power, a judgment cannot be set aside by the trial court except by bill of review for sufficient cause, filed within the time allowed by law; provided that the court may at any time correct a clerical error in the record of a judgment and render judgment nunc pro tunc under Rule 316, and may also sign an order declaring a previous judgment or order to be void because signed after the court's plenary power had expired.

(g) A motion to modify, correct, or reform a judgment (as distinguished from motion to correct the record of a judgment under Rule 316), if filed, shall be filed and determined within the time prescribed by this rule for a motion for new trial and shall extend the trial court's plenary power and the time for perfecting an appeal in the same manner as a motion for new trial. Each such motion shall be in writing and signed by the party or his attorney and shall specify the respects in which the judgment should be modified, corrected, or reformed. The overruling of such a motion shall not preclude the filing of a motion for new trial, nor shall the overruling of a motion for new trial preclude the filing of a motion to modify, correct, or reform.

(h) If a judgment is modified, corrected or reformed in any respect, the time for appeal shall run from the time the modified, corrected, or reformed judgment is signed, but if a correction is made pursuant to Rule 316 after expiration of the period of plenary power provided by this rule, no complaint shall be heard on appeal that could have been presented in an appeal from the original judgment.

See also *O'Connor's Texas Rules*, "Rules for Filing Documents," ch. 1-C, p. 28; "Motion for JNOV," ch. 9-B, p. 857; "Judgment," ch. 9-C, p. 861; "Motion for New Trial," ch. 10-B, p. 891; "Motion to Modify the Judgment," ch. 10-D, p. 918; "Motion for Judgment Nunc Pro Tunc," ch. 10-H, p. 942.

ANNOTATIONS

Plenary Power

In re Baylor Med. Ctr., 280 S.W.3d 227, 230-31 (Tex.2008). Rule 329b "terminates the trial court's plenary power 30 days after all timely motions for new trial are *overruled*, but there is no provision limiting its plenary power if such motions are *granted*. Under the current rules, if no judgment is signed, no plenary-power clock is ticking. [¶] When a new trial is granted, the case stands on the trial court's docket 'the same as though no trial had been had.' Accordingly, the trial court should then have the power to set aside a new trial order 'any time before a final judgment is entered.' [¶] [W]e recently clarified that 'a trial judge who modifies a judgment and then withdraws the modification has modified the judgment *twice* rather than never.' Rule 329b(h) provides that if a judgment is modified '*in any respect*' the appellate timetables are restarted. Surely a judgment that is set aside by a new trial order has been modified in *some* respect, even if it is later reinstated. Thus, if a new trial is granted and later withdrawn, the appellate deadlines run from the later order granting reinstatement rather than the earlier order. *At 232:* 'There is no sound reason why the court may not reconsider its ruling [granting] a new trial' at any time." *See also* ***Hidalgo v. Hidalgo***, 310 S.W.3d 887, 889 (Tex.2010).

In re Brookshire Grocery Co., 250 S.W.3d 66, 69 (Tex.2008). "[A]n amended motion [for new trial] may be filed without leave of court when: (1) no preceding motion for new trial has been overruled *and* (2) it is filed within 30 days of judgment. 'And' is conjunctive: an amended new-trial motion is timely filed only *before* the court overrules a prior one. An amended motion filed afterwards: (1) need not be considered by the trial court and (2) does not extend the trial court's plenary power. *At 72:* [T]he trial court retains plenary power for 30 days after overruling a motion for new trial; thus, the losing party may ask the trial court to reconsider its or-

der denying a new trial—or the court may grant a new trial on its own initiative—so long as the court issues an order granting new trial within its period of plenary power. [¶] Additionally, under Rule 329b, a trial court's plenary power to grant a new trial expires 30 days after it overrules a motion for new trial, only provided no other *type* of 329b motion (such as a motion to modify, correct, or reform the judgment) is 'timely filed.' Thus, a party whose motion for new trial is overruled within 30 days of judgment may still file a motion to modify, correct, or reform the judgment—provided it is filed within 30 days of judgment—and thereby extend the trial court's plenary power."

Moritz v. Preiss, 121 S.W.3d 715, 720 (Tex.2003). "[A]n amended motion for new trial filed more than 30 days after the trial court signs a final judgment is untimely. [T]he trial court may, at its discretion, consider the grounds raised in an untimely motion and grant a new trial under its inherent authority before the court loses plenary power. [¶] 'If the trial court ignores the tardy motion, it is ineffectual for any purpose. [I]f the court denies a new trial, the belated motion is a nullity and supplies no basis for consideration upon appeal of grounds which were required to be set forth in a timely motion.' *At 721:* [A]n untimely amended motion for new trial does not preserve issues for appellate review, even if the trial court considers and denies the untimely motion within its plenary power period."

Lane Bank Equip. Co. v. Smith S. Equip., Inc., 10 S.W.3d 308, 312 (Tex.2000). "[A] motion made after judgment to incorporate a sanction as a part of the final judgment does propose a change to that judgment. Such a motion is, on its face, a motion to modify, correct or reform the existing judgment within the meaning of Rule 329b(g). *At 314:* We ... hold that [such a motion] qualifies as a motion to modify under Rule 329b(g), thus extending the trial court's plenary jurisdiction and the appellate timetable." *See also* ***Mann v. Kendall Home Builders Constr. Partners I, Ltd.***, 464 S.W.3d 84, 89-90 (Tex.App.—Houston [14th Dist.] 2015, no pet.).

Scott & White Mem'l Hosp. v. Schexnider, 940 S.W.2d 594, 596 (Tex.1996). "A trial court's power to decide a motion for sanctions pertaining to matters occurring before judgment is no different than its power to decide any other motion during its plenary jurisdiction. [T]he time during which the trial court has authority to impose sanctions on such a motion is limited to when it retains plenary jurisdiction...." *See also* ***Law Offices of Robert D. Wilson v. Texas Univest-Frisco, Ltd.***, 291 S.W.3d 110, 113 (Tex.App.—Dallas 2009, no pet.).

L.M. Healthcare, Inc. v. Childs, 929 S.W.2d 442, 443 (Tex.1996). "That the trial court overruled [P's] motion for new trial does not shorten the trial court's plenary power to resolve a motion to modify the judgment. *At 444:* [TRCP 329b(e) and (g)] provide that a timely filed motion to modify judgment extends the trial court's plenary power, separate and apart from a motion for new trial." *See also* ***Board of Trs. of Bastrop ISD v. Toungate***, 958 S.W.2d 365, 367 (Tex.1997).

In re A.M.C., 491 S.W.3d 62, 67-68 (Tex.App.—Houston [14th Dist.] 2016, no pet.). See annotation under TRCP 316, p. 1209.

PNS Stores v. Rivera, 335 S.W.3d 265, 279-80 (Tex. App.—San Antonio 2010), *rev'd on other grounds*, 379 S.W.3d 267 (Tex.2012). "Generally, only a timely filed bill of review is available to set aside a judgment when the trial court's plenary power has expired. However, in ***Middleton*** [***v. Murff***, 689 S.W.2d 212 (Tex.1985)], the supreme court recognized an exception to rule 329b(f). According to the supreme court, the rule's mandate that only a timely filed bill of review is available to set aside a trial court's judgment after the court's plenary power has expired does not apply where the court had no jurisdictional power to render judgment. Importantly, however, the court specifically defined 'jurisdictional power' to mean 'jurisdiction over the subject matter, the power to hear and determine cases of the general class to which the particular one belongs.' Any other direct attack on a void judgment must comply with rule 329b(f), i.e., must be an attack by a timely filed bill of review. [¶] Accordingly, under ***Middleton***, it appears that an untimely bill of review is proper only if there is an absence of subject matter jurisdiction." *See also* ***Smalley v. Smalley***, 436 S.W.3d 801, 806 (Tex.App.—Houston [14th Dist.] 2014, no pet.).

In re Naylor, 120 S.W.3d 498, 500 (Tex.App.—Texarkana 2003, no pet.). "[W] takes the position that, because [H] did not file a motion for new trial or for reconsideration of the dismissal within 30 days from the date the dismissal was granted, the trial court lacked jurisdiction to take any action after its plenary power period expired. [¶] [W's] initial position is essentially that any attempt to undo the dismissal of the contempt proceeding either had to be pursued by appeal or by the

address of a timely motion to the trial court and that, since neither occurred, everything that happened after the trial court's plenary power expired is essentially a nullity. Decisions in contempt proceedings are not appealable. Similarly, an order finding a party not in contempt is not a final, appealable judgment. We have found no cases, and have been directed to no cases, that apply [TRCP 329b] to rulings made in contempt proceedings. Thus, the plenary power constraints of the rule would not apply in this case. [¶] As a general rule, a trial court retains plenary power over its interlocutory orders until a final judgment is entered. A trial court thus has the inherent authority to change or modify any interlocutory order until its plenary power expires. Further, except as authorized by the Legislature for specific categories of interlocutory orders, such orders are by their very nature not appealable. *At 501:* This situation arguably requires a different result because, by its very nature, this type of contempt proceeding, though part of the continuing saga of the divorce, is a separate order, and finality will not accrue on entry of some final judgment. That position, however, flies in the face of the cases holding categorically that contempt may be addressed only through habeas or mandamus in the proper circumstances. We decline the invitation to treat this situation differently. [¶] Thus, appeal was not an available remedy in this case."

In re T.G., 68 S.W.3d 171, 176 (Tex.App.—Houston [1st Dist.] 2002, pet. denied). "Parties may extend the trial court's initial 30-day plenary power to change its judgment by filing an appropriate post-judgment motion within the 30 day period. Appropriate motions include a motion for new trial, pursuant to [TRCP] 329b(e) ..., which [Ds] filed, or a motion to modify, correct, or reform the judgment under rule 329b(g). Although any change in the trial court's judgment will restart the appellate-timetable and plenary-power rules under rule 329b(h), a rule 329b motion for new trial or to modify, correct, or reform the judgment, or a motion that has the same effect, is the only means by which a party may extend the appellate timetables and the trial court's plenary power over its judgment. Amending a rule 329b motion does not extend the trial court's plenary power."

Written Order

In re Lovito-Nelson, 278 S.W.3d 773, 775 (Tex. 2009). "We have been clear that Rule 329b(c) requires a written order to grant a new trial. ... Although we have never had occasion to apply the rule to scheduling orders, the courts of appeals have, and have mostly held that such orders do not grant new trials." *See also* ***Faulkner v. Culver***, 851 S.W.2d 187, 188 (Tex.1993) (trial judge's oral pronouncement cannot substitute for written order).

Appellate Deadlines

Ryland Enter. v. Weatherspoon, 355 S.W.3d 664, 665-66 (Tex.2011). TRCP "329b states that a motion for new trial is timely if filed '*prior to* or within 30 days after the judgment ... complained of is signed.' This 'prior to' language is supplemented and clarified by [TRCP] 306c, which provides that '[n]o motion for new trial ... shall be held ineffective because prematurely filed; but every such motion shall be deemed to have been filed on the date of but subsequent to the time of signing of the judgment the motion assails.' [R]ule 329b(g) states that a 'motion to modify ... shall be filed and determined ... and shall extend ... the time for perfecting an appeal in the same manner as a motion for new trial.'"

Arkoma Basin Expl. Co. v. FMF Assocs. 1990-A, Ltd., 249 S.W.3d 380, 390-91 (Tex.2008). "'If a judgment is modified in any respect,' appellate deadlines do not run from the original judgment but 'from the date when the modified judgment is signed.' [¶] [T]he deadlines are restarted by '*any* change, whether or not material or substantial.' Thus, appellate deadlines are restarted by an order that does nothing more than change the docket number or deny all relief not expressly granted." *See also* ***In re J.L.***, 163 S.W.3d 79, 82 (Tex.2005) (because trial court modified and corrected judgment while it retained plenary power, time for filing notice of appeal was calculated from date of new final judgment); ***Abercia v. Kingvision Pay-Per-View, Ltd.***, 217 S.W.3d 688, 706 (Tex.App.—El Paso 2007, pet. denied) (even when later judgment differs from original judgment only by signature date, later judgment vacates former judgment).

Garza v. Garcia, 137 S.W.3d 36, 37-38 (Tex.2004). "A motion for new trial is 'conditionally filed' if tendered without the requisite fee, and appellate deadlines run from and are extended by that date: '[T]he failure to pay the fee before the motion is overruled by operation of law may forfeit altogether the movant's opportunity to have the trial court consider the motion; it does not, however, retroactively invalidate the conditional filing for purposes of the appellate timetable.' [¶] Al-

though we have previously reserved ruling on a fee that was never paid, we now extend [this] rule in these circumstances. [¶] This is not to say filing fees are irrelevant. '[A]bsent emergency or other rare circumstances' a motion for new trial should not be considered until the filing fee is paid." *See also* ***Tate v. E.I. DuPont de Nemours & Co.***, 934 S.W.2d 83, 84 (Tex. 1996).

Thomas v. Oldham, 895 S.W.2d 352, 356 (Tex. 1995). "Under Texas procedure, [P's] suit does not end with rendition of judgment. Rather, the parties may file one or more motions for new trial within 30 days after rendition of judgment. The trial court may in its discretion grant such a motion within 75 days after the judgment is signed, continuing the action for a new trial. … If a motion for new trial or motion to modify the judgment is overruled, the trial court still retains plenary power to vacate, modify, correct or reform the judgment for an additional 30 day period."

In re P.J.P.R., 508 S.W.3d 588, 590-91 (Tex.App.—El Paso 2016, no pet.). "If a trial court's judgment is altered or amended within the period of its plenary power, … the appellate timetable starts anew. Thus we consider whether the associate judge's order … itself altered or amended the district court's … order and created a new appellate time table. The [associate judge's] order indeed recited changes to be made to the [district court's] order. But the text of the order convinces us that it was a proposal that the district court could accept or reject. [¶] Family Code [§201.013(b)] also compels the conclusion that the associate judge's … order does not itself modify the [district court's] order. An associate judge's proposed order is in full force and effect pending *de novo* review, but when no request for a *de novo* hearing is made, 'the proposed order or judgment of the associate judge becomes the order or judgment of the referring court *only on the referring court's signing* the proposed order or judgment.' The referring court never signed the [associate judge's] order though a signature blank was included on the order for that purpose. [¶] Because the amended order was not signed until after the trial court's plenary power had expired, the amended order was void."

Abercia v. Kingvision Pay-Per-View, Ltd., 217 S.W.3d 688, 706 (Tex.App.—El Paso 2007, pet. denied). "Even when a subsequent judgment differs from the original judgment only by the signature date, the subsequent judgment vacates the former judgment. Any change, whether or not material or substantial, made in the judgment while the trial court retains plenary power will restart the appellate timetable from the date the modified judgment is signed."

In re Boyd, 34 S.W.3d 708, 710 (Tex.App.—Fort Worth 2000, orig. proceeding). Relator contends that Fam. Code §6.709 provides "the exclusive authority for the trial court to render the [temporary] order, and that the order is void because, under §6.709, the trial court lost jurisdiction to render the order 30 days after he perfected his appeal. [Real party in interest] responds that the trial court had plenary power to render the order under TRCP 329b, and that the trial court did not abuse its discretion by rendering the order, even though it was rendered more than 30 days after [relator] perfected his appeal. *At 711:* The trial court's power to render the [temporary] order derived exclusively from §6.709, which requires that all such orders be entered within 30 days of the perfection of a party's appeal. Because the order was entered more than 30 days from the date [relator] perfected his appeal, the trial court's power to act under the statute had terminated."

Bill of Review

Temple v. Archambo, 161 S.W.3d 217, 223-24 (Tex. App.—Corpus Christi 2005, no pet.). "Before a litigant can … secure a bill of review to set aside a final judgment, he must allege and prove: (1) a meritorious defense to the cause of action alleged to support the judgment; (2) which he was prevented from making by the fraud, accident or wrongful act of the opposing party; (3) unmixed with any fault or negligence of his own. [¶] A petition for bill of review must be filed within four years of the date of the disputed judgment. The only exception to the four-year limitation is where the petitioner proves *extrinsic* fraud. *At 225:* The final judgment of divorce in this matter was entered in 1989. The decree adjudged the parent-child relationship between [petitioner] and the minor child and became final. [¶] In 2000, [petitioner] filed his application for a bill of review, in which he sought for the first time to challenge his paternity of the child. The petition was not filed within the four-year statute of limitations. [His] petition must therefore allege and prove a prima facie case that his complaint was not barred as a matter of law and that he would be entitled to judgment on retrial if no contrary evidence was offered. *At 227:* [Petitioner] could not proceed with his bill of review because: (1) he did not allege or prove extrinsic fraud; and (2) he did

not allege with particularity sworn facts sufficient to constitute a meritorious defense and thus, as a pretrial matter, did not present prima facie proof to support the defense."

K. CERTAIN DISTRICT COURTS

TRCP 330. RULES OF PRACTICE & PROCEDURE IN CERTAIN DISTRICT COURTS

The following rules of practice and procedure shall govern and be followed in all civil actions in district courts in counties where the only district court of said county vested with civil jurisdiction, or all the district courts thereof having civil jurisdiction, have successive terms in said county throughout the year, without more than two days intervening between any of such terms, whether or not any one or more of such district courts include one or more other counties within its jurisdiction.

(a) Appealed Cases. In cases appealed to said district courts from inferior courts, the appeal, including transcript, shall be filed in the district court within thirty (30) days after the rendition of the judgment or order appealed from, and the appellee shall enter his appearance on the docket or answer to said appeal on or before ten o'clock a.m. of the Monday next after the expiration of twenty (20) days from the date the appeal is filed in the district court.

(b) [Repealed by order of July 22, 1975, eff. Jan. 1, 1976 (525-26 S.W.2d (Tex. Cases) li).]

(c) Postponement or Continuance. Cases may be postponed or continued by agreement with the approval of the court, or upon the court's own motion or for cause. When a case is called for trial and only one party is ready, the court may for good cause either continue the case for the term or postpone and reset it for a later day in the same or succeeding term.

(d) Cases May Be Reset. A case that is set and reached for trial may be postponed for a later day in the term or continued and reset for a day certain in the succeeding term on the same grounds as an application for continuance would be granted in other district courts. After any case has been set and reached in its due order and called for trial two (2) or more times and not tried, the court may dismiss the same unless the parties agree to a postponement or continuance but the court shall respect written agreements of counsel for postponement and continuance if filed in the case when or before it is called for trial unless to do so will unreasonably delay or interfere with other business of the court.

(e) Exchange and Transfer. Where in such county there are two or more district courts having civil jurisdiction, the judges of such courts may, in their discretion, exchange benches or districts from time to time, and may transfer cases and other proceedings from one court to another, and any of them may in his own courtroom try and determine any case or proceeding pending in another court without having the case transferred, or may sit in any other of said courts and there hear and determine any case there pending, and every judgment and order shall be entered in the minutes of the court in which the case is pending and at the time the judgment or order is rendered, and two (2) or more judges may try different cases in the same court at the same time, and each may occupy his own courtroom or the room of any other court. The judge of any such court may issue restraining orders and injunctions returnable to any other judge or court, and any judge may transfer any case or proceeding pending in his court to any other of said courts, and the judge of any court to which a case or proceeding is transferred shall receive and try the same, and in turn shall have power in his discretion to transfer any such case to any other of said courts and any other judge may in his courtroom try any case pending in any other of such courts.

(f) Cases Transferred to Judges Not Occupied. Where in such counties there are two or more district courts having civil jurisdiction, when the judge of any such court shall become disengaged, he shall notify the presiding judge, and the presiding judge shall transfer to the court of the disengaged judge the next case which is ready for trial in any of said courts. Any judge not engaged in his own court may try any case in any other court.

(g) Judge May Hear Only Part of Case. Where in such counties there are two or more district courts having civil jurisdiction, any judge may hear any part of any case or proceeding pending in any of said courts and determine the same, or may hear and determine any question in any case, and any other judge may complete the hearing and render judgment in the case.

(h) Any Judge May Hear Dilatory Pleas. Where in such county there are two or more district courts having civil jurisdiction, any judge may hear and determine motions, petitions for injunction, applications for appointment of receivers, interventions, pleas of privilege,

pleas in abatement, all dilatory pleas and special exceptions, motions for a new trial and all preliminary matters, questions and proceedings and may enter judgment or order thereon in the court in which the case is pending without having the case transferred to the court of the judge acting, and the judge in whose court the case is pending may thereafter proceed to hear, complete and determine the case or other matter, or any part thereof, and render final judgment therein. Any judgment rendered or action taken by any judge in any of said courts in the county shall be valid and binding.

(i) Acts in Succeeding Terms. If a case or other matter is on trial, or in the process of hearing when the term of court expires, such trial, hearing or other matter may be proceeded with at the next or any subsequent term of court and no motion or plea shall be considered as waived or overruled, because not acted upon at the term of court at which it was filed, but may be acted upon at any time the judge may fix or at which it may have been postponed or continued by agreement of the parties with leave of the court. This subdivision is not applicable to original or amended motions for new trial which are governed by Rule 329b.

See also Gov't Code §24.003.

ANNOTATIONS

In re U.S. Silica Co., 157 S.W.3d 434, 438-39 (Tex. 2005). "We disagree that all orders signed by a transferring court after transfer are void; many are not. This is especially true here because the transfers involved district courts in a single county. [¶] Trial courts have broad discretion to exchange benches and enter orders on other cases in the same county, even without a formal order or transfer. Given the broad powers district courts have to act for one another, we do not agree that these [interim] orders were entered without jurisdiction." *See also* ***Celestine v. DFPS***, 321 S.W.3d 222, 227 (Tex.App.—Houston [1st Dist.] 2010, no pet.) (court's continuing, exclusive jurisdiction does not preclude application of exchange-of-benches doctrine).

Wilson v. Dunn, 800 S.W.2d 833, 835 n.6 (Tex. 1990). "The 236th District Court and the 67th District Court both sit in Tarrant County. They are permitted to, and do, hear each other's civil cases under Rule 330." *See also* ***Pinnacle Gas Treating, Inc. v. Read***, 160 S.W.3d 564, 566 (Tex.2005) (87th District Court and 278th District Court are both in Leon County and have concurrent jurisdiction).

Hull v. South Coast Catamarans, L.P., 365 S.W.3d 35, 41 (Tex.App.—Houston [1st Dist.] 2011, pet. denied). "[R]ule 330(g) does not authorize a district judge who heard none of the case to render judgment in a bench trial. *At 42:* But [this] exception to the free exchange of benches is a narrow one."

Polk v. Southwest Crossing Homeowners Ass'n, 165 S.W.3d 89, 93 (Tex.App.—Houston [14th Dist.] 2005, pet. denied). "[P] does not have a protected proprietary interest in having her case heard by a particular district judge. Counties may adopt local rules to further govern the transfer of cases from one district court to another if they are not inconsistent with Rule 330(e). *At 94:* [A] failure to comply with the local rule's *procedural* requirements does not deprive a court of its jurisdiction. While the transferring and receiving courts should have complied with their own local rules regarding the transfer of cases, their failure to do so did not deprive [the district court] of jurisdiction over [P's] case." *See also* ***In re Rio Grande Valley Gas Co.***, 987 S.W.2d 167, 173 (Tex.App.—Corpus Christi 1999, orig. proceeding).

TRCP 331 TO 351. REPEALED

PART III. RULES OF PROCEDURE FOR THE COURTS OF APPEALS

TRCP 352 TO 473. REPEALED

PART IV. RULES OF PRACTICE FOR THE SUPREME COURT

TRCP 474 TO 522. REPEALED

PART V. RULES OF PRACTICE IN JUSTICE COURTS

TRCP 500. GENERAL RULES

500.1 Construction of Rules. Unless otherwise expressly provided, in Part V of these Rules of Civil Procedure:

(a) the past, present, and future tense each includes the other;

(b) the term "it" includes a person of either gender or an entity; and

(c) the singular and plural each includes the other.

500.2 Definitions. In Part V of these Rules of Civil Procedure:

(a) "Answer" is the written response that a party who is sued must file with the court after being served with a citation.

(b) "Citation" is the court-issued document required to be served upon a party to inform the party that it has been sued.

(c) "Claim" is the legal theory and alleged facts that, if proven, entitle a party to relief against another party in court.

(d) "Clerk" is a person designated by the judge as a justice court clerk, or the judge if there is no clerk available.

(e) "Counterclaim" is a claim brought by a party who has been sued against the party who filed the lawsuit, for example, a defendant suing a plaintiff.

(f) "County court" is the county court, statutory county court, or district court in a particular county with jurisdiction over appeals of civil cases from justice court.

(g) "Cross-claim" is a claim brought by one party against another party on the same side of a lawsuit. For example, if a plaintiff sues two defendants, the defendants can seek relief against each other by means of a cross-claim.

(h) "Default judgment" is a judgment awarded to a plaintiff when the defendant fails to answer and dispute the plaintiff's claims in the lawsuit.

(i) "Defendant" is a party who is sued, including a plaintiff against whom a counterclaim is filed.

(j) "Defense" is an assertion by a defendant that the plaintiff is not entitled to relief from the court.

(k) "Discovery" is the process through which parties obtain information from each other in order to prepare for trial or enforce a judgment. The term does not refer to any information that a party is entitled to under applicable law.

(*l*) "Dismissed without prejudice" means a case has been dismissed but has not been finally decided and may be refiled.

(m) "Dismissed with prejudice" means a case has been dismissed and finally decided and may not be refiled.

(n) "Judge" is a justice of the peace.

(o) "Judgment" is a final order by the court that states the relief, if any, a party is entitled to or must provide.

(p) "Jurisdiction" is the authority of the court to hear and decide a case.

(q) "Motion" is a request that the court make a specified ruling or order.

(r) "Notice" is a document prepared and delivered by the court or a party stating that something is required of the party receiving the notice.

(s) "Party" is a person or entity involved in the case that is either suing or being sued, including all plaintiffs, defendants, and third parties that have been joined in the case.

(t) "Petition" is a formal written application stating a party's claims and requesting relief from the court. It is the first document filed with the court to begin a lawsuit.

(u) "Plaintiff" is a party who sues, including a defendant who files a counterclaim.

(v) "Pleading" is a written document filed by a party, including a petition and an answer, that states a claim or defense and outlines the relief sought.

(w) "Relief" is the remedy a party requests from the court, such as the recovery of money or the return of property.

(x) "Serve" and "service" are delivery of citation as required by Rule 501.2, or of a document as required by Rule 501.4.

(y) "Sworn" means signed in front of someone authorized to take oaths, such as a notary, or signed under penalty of perjury. Filing a false sworn document can result in criminal prosecution.

(z) "Third party claim" is a claim brought by a party being sued against someone who is not yet a party to the case.

500.3 Application of Rules in Justice Court Cases.

(a) ***Small Claims Case.*** A small claims case is a lawsuit brought for the recovery of money damages, civil penalties, personal property, or other relief allowed by law. The claim can be for no more than $10,000, excluding statutory interest and court costs but including attorney fees, if any. Small claims cases are governed by Rules 500-507 of Part V of the Rules of Civil Procedure.

(b) ***Debt Claim Case.*** A debt claim case is a lawsuit brought to recover a debt by an assignee of a claim, a debt collector or collection agency, a financial institution, or a person or entity primarily engaged in the business of lending money at interest. The claim can be for no more than $10,000, excluding statutory interest and court costs but including attorney fees, if any. Debt claim cases in justice court are governed by Rules 500-

507 and 508 of Part V of the Rules of Civil Procedure. To the extent of any conflict between Rule 508 and the rest of Part V, Rule 508 applies.

(c) ***Repair and Remedy Case.*** A repair and remedy case is a lawsuit filed by a residential tenant under Chapter 92, Subchapter B of the Texas Property Code to enforce the landlord's duty to repair or remedy a condition materially affecting the physical health or safety of an ordinary tenant. The relief sought can be for no more than $10,000, excluding statutory interest and court costs but including attorney fees, if any. Repair and remedy cases are governed by Rules 500-507 and 509 of Part V of the Rules of Civil Procedure. To the extent of any conflict between Rule 509 and the rest of Part V, Rule 509 applies.

(d) ***Eviction Case.*** An eviction case is a lawsuit brought to recover possession of real property under Chapter 24 of the Texas Property Code, often by a landlord against a tenant. A claim for rent may be joined with an eviction case if the amount of rent due and unpaid is not more than $10,000, excluding statutory interest and court costs but including attorney fees, if any. Eviction cases are governed by Rules 500-507 and 510 of Part V of the Rules of Civil Procedure. To the extent of any conflict between Rule 510 and the rest of Part V, Rule 510 applies.

(e) ***Application of Other Rules.*** The other Rules of Civil Procedure and the Rules of Evidence do not apply except:

(1) when the judge hearing the case determines that a particular rule must be followed to ensure that the proceedings are fair to all parties; or

(2) when otherwise specifically provided by law or these rules.

(f) ***Examination of Rules.*** The court must make the Rules of Civil Procedure and the Rules of Evidence available for examination, either in paper form or electronically, during the court's business hours.

500.4 Representation in Justice Court Cases.

(a) ***Representation of an Individual.*** An individual may:

(1) represent himself or herself;

(2) be represented by an authorized agent in an eviction case; or

(3) be represented by an attorney.

(b) ***Representation of a Corporation or Other Entity.*** A corporation or other entity may:

(1) be represented by an employee, owner, officer, or partner of the entity who is not an attorney;

(2) be represented by a property manager or other authorized agent in an eviction case; or

(3) be represented by an attorney.

(c) ***Assisted Representation.*** The court may, for good cause, allow an individual representing himself or herself to be assisted in court by a family member or other individual who is not being compensated.

500.5 Computation of Time; Timely Filing.

(a) ***Computation of Time.*** To compute a time period in these rules:

(1) exclude the day of the event that triggers the period;

(2) count every day, including Saturdays, Sundays, and legal holidays; and

(3) include the last day of the period, but

(A) if the last day is a Saturday, Sunday, or legal holiday, the time period is extended to the next day that is not a Saturday, Sunday, or legal holiday; and

(B) if the last day for filing falls on a day during which the court is closed before 5:00 p.m., the time period is extended to the court's next business day.

(b) ***Timely Filing by Mail.*** Any document required to be filed by a given date is considered timely filed if deposited in the U.S. mail on or before that date, and received within 10 days of the due date. A legible postmark affixed by the United States Postal Service is evidence of the date of mailing.

(c) ***Extensions.*** The judge may, for good cause shown, extend any time period under these rules except those relating to new trial and appeal.

500.6 Judge to Develop the Case. In order to develop the facts of the case, a judge may question a witness or party and may summon any person or party to appear as a witness when the judge considers it necessary to ensure a correct judgment and a speedy disposition.

500.7 Exclusion of Witnesses. The court must, on a party's request, or may, on its own initiative, order witnesses excluded so that they cannot hear the testimony of other witnesses. This rule does not authorize the exclusion of:

(a) a party who is a natural person or the spouse of such natural person;

(b) an officer or employee designated as a representative of a party who is not a natural person; or

(c) a person whose presence is shown by a party to be essential to the presentation of the party's case.

500.8 Subpoenas.

(a) ***Use.*** A subpoena may be used by a party or the judge to command a person or entity to attend and give testimony at a hearing or trial. A person may not be required by subpoena to appear in a county that is more than 150 miles from where the person resides or is served.

(b) ***Who Can Issue.*** A subpoena may be issued by the clerk of the justice court or an attorney authorized to practice in the State of Texas, as an officer of the court.

(c) ***Form.*** Every subpoena must be issued in the name of the "State of Texas" and must:

(1) state the style of the suit and its case number;

(2) state the court in which the suit is pending;

(3) state the date on which the subpoena is issued;

(4) identify the person to whom the subpoena is directed;

(5) state the date, time, place, and nature of the action required by the person to whom the subpoena is directed;

(6) identify the party at whose instance the subpoena is issued, and the party's attorney of record, if any;

(7) state that "Failure by any person without adequate excuse to obey a subpoena served upon that person may be deemed a contempt of court from which the subpoena is issued and may be punished by fine or confinement, or both"; and

(8) be signed by the person issuing the subpoena.

(d) ***Service: Where, by Whom, How.*** A subpoena may be served at any place within the State of Texas by any sheriff or constable of the State of Texas, or by any person who is not a party and is 18 years of age or older. A subpoena must be served by delivering a copy to the witness and tendering to that person any fees required by law. If the witness is a party and is represented by an attorney of record in the proceeding, the subpoena may be served on the witness's attorney of record. Proof of service must be made by filing either:

(1) the witness's signed written memorandum attached to the subpoena showing that the witness accepted the subpoena; or

(2) a statement by the person who made the service stating the date, time, and manner of service, and the name of the person served.

(e) ***Compliance Required.*** A person commanded by subpoena to appear and give testimony must remain at the hearing or trial from day to day until discharged by the court or by the party summoning the witness. If a subpoena commanding testimony is directed to a corporation, partnership, association, governmental agency, or other organization, and the matters on which examination is requested are described with reasonable particularity, the organization must designate one or more persons to testify on its behalf as to matters known or reasonably available to the organization.

(f) ***Objection.*** A person commanded to attend and give testimony at a hearing or trial may object or move for a protective order before the court at or before the time and place specified for compliance. A party causing a subpoena to issue must take reasonable steps to avoid imposing undue burden or expense on the person served. In ruling on objections or motions for protection, the court must provide a person served with a subpoena an adequate time for compliance and protection from undue burden or expense. The court may impose reasonable conditions on compliance with a subpoena, including compensating the witness for undue hardship.

(g) ***Enforcement.*** Failure by any person without adequate excuse to obey a subpoena served upon that person may be deemed a contempt of the court from which the subpoena is issued or of a district court in the county in which the subpoena is served, and may be punished by fine or confinement, or both. A fine may not be imposed, nor a person served with a subpoena attached, for failure to comply with a subpoena without proof of service and proof by affidavit of the party requesting the subpoena or the party's attorney of record that all fees due the witness by law were paid or tendered.

500.9 Discovery.

(a) ***Pretrial Discovery.*** Pretrial discovery is limited to that which the judge considers reasonable and necessary. Any requests for pretrial discovery must be presented to the court for approval by written motion. The motion must be served on the responding party. Unless a hearing is requested, the judge may rule on the motion without a hearing. The discovery request must not be served on the responding party unless the

judge issues a signed order approving the request. Failure to comply with a discovery order can result in sanctions, including dismissal of the case or an order to pay the other party's discovery expenses.

(b) ***Post-Judgment Discovery.*** Post-judgment discovery is not required to be filed with the court. The party requesting discovery must give the responding party at least 30 days to respond to a post-judgment discovery request. The responding party may file a written objection with the court within 30 days of receiving the request. If an objection is filed, the judge must hold a hearing to determine if the request is valid. If the objection is denied, the judge must order the party to respond to the request. If the objection is upheld, the judge may reform the request or dismiss it entirely.

TRCP 501. CITATION & SERVICE

501.1 Citation.

(a) ***Issuance.*** When a petition is filed with a justice court to initiate a suit, the clerk must promptly issue a citation and deliver the citation as directed by the plaintiff. The plaintiff is responsible for obtaining service on the defendant of the citation and a copy of the petition with any documents filed with the petition. Upon request, separate or additional citations must be issued by the clerk. The clerk must retain a copy of the citation in the court's file.

(b) ***Form.*** The citation must:

(1) be styled "The State of Texas";

(2) be signed by the clerk under seal of court or by the judge;

(3) contain the name, location, and address of the court;

(4) show the date of filing of the petition;

(5) show the date of issuance of the citation;

(6) show the file number and names of parties;

(7) be directed to the defendant;

(8) show the name and address of attorney for plaintiff, or if the plaintiff does not have an attorney, the address of plaintiff; and

(9) notify defendant that if the defendant fails to file an answer, judgment by default may be rendered for the relief demanded in the petition.

(c) ***Notice.*** The citation must include the following notice to the defendant in boldface type: "You have been sued. You may employ an attorney to help you in defending against this lawsuit. But you are not required to employ an attorney. You or your attorney must file an answer with the court. Your answer is due by the end of the 14th day after the day you were served with these papers. If the 14th day is a Saturday, Sunday, or legal holiday, your answer is due by the end of the first day following the 14th day that is not a Saturday, Sunday, or legal holiday. Do not ignore these papers. If you do not file an answer by the due date, a default judgment may be taken against you. For further information, consult Part V of the Texas Rules of Civil Procedure, which is available online and also at the court listed on this citation."

(d) ***Copies.*** The plaintiff must provide enough copies to be served on each defendant. If the plaintiff fails to do so, the clerk may make copies and charge the plaintiff the allowable copying cost.

16 **501.2 Service of Citation.**

(a) ***Who May Serve.*** No person who is a party to or interested in the outcome of the suit may serve citation in that suit, and, unless otherwise authorized by written court order, only a sheriff or constable may serve a citation in an eviction case, a writ that requires the actual taking of possession of a person, property or thing, or process requiring that an enforcement action be physically enforced by the person delivering the process. Other citations may be served by:

(1) a sheriff or constable;

(2) a process server certified under order of the Supreme Court;

(3) the clerk of the court, if the citation is served by registered or certified mail; or

(4) a person authorized by court order who is 18 years of age or older.

(b) ***Method of Service.*** Citation must be served by:

(1) delivering a copy of the citation with a copy of the petition attached to the defendant in person, after endorsing the date of delivery on the citation; or

(2) mailing a copy of the citation with a copy of the petition attached to the defendant by registered or certified mail, restricted delivery, with return receipt or electronic return receipt requested.

(c) ***Service Fees.*** A plaintiff must pay all fees for service unless the plaintiff has filed a Statement of Inability to Afford Payment of Court Costs with the court. If the plaintiff has filed a Statement, the plaintiff must

arrange for the citation to be served by a sheriff, constable, or court clerk.

(d) ***Service on Sunday.*** A citation cannot be served on a Sunday except in attachment, garnishment, sequestration, or distress proceedings.

(e) ***Alternative Service of Citation.*** If the methods under (b) are insufficient to serve the defendant, the plaintiff, or the constable, sheriff, process server certified under order of the Supreme Court, or other person authorized to serve process, may make a request for alternative service. This request must include a sworn statement describing the methods attempted under (b) and stating the defendant's usual place of business or residence, or other place where the defendant can probably be found. The court may authorize the following types of alternative service:

(1) mailing a copy of the citation with a copy of the petition attached by first class mail to the defendant at a specified address, and also leaving a copy of the citation with petition attached at the defendant's residence or other place where the defendant can probably be found with any person found there who is at least 16 years of age; or

(2) mailing a copy of the citation with a copy of the petition attached by first class mail to the defendant at a specified address, and also serving by any other method that the court finds is reasonably likely to provide the defendant with notice of the suit.

(f) ***Service by Publication.*** In the event that service of citation by publication is necessary, the process is governed by the rules in county and district court.

501.3 Duties of Officer or Person Receiving Citation; Return of Service.

(a) ***Endorsement; Execution; Return.*** The officer or authorized person to whom process is delivered must:

(1) endorse on the process the date and hour on which he or she received it;

(2) execute and return the same without delay; and

(3) complete a return of service, which may, but need not, be endorsed on or attached to the citation.

(b) ***Contents of Return.*** The return, together with any document to which it is attached, must include the following information:

(1) the case number and case name;

(2) the court in which the case is filed;

(3) a description of what was served;

(4) the date and time the process was received for service;

(5) the person or entity served;

(6) the address served;

(7) the date of service or attempted service;

(8) the manner of delivery of service or attempted service;

(9) the name of the person who served or attempted service;

(10) if the person named in (9) is a process server certified under Supreme Court Order, his or her identification number and the expiration date of his or her certification; and

(11) any other information required by rule or law.

(c) ***Citation by Mail.*** When the citation is served by registered or certified mail as authorized by Rule 501.2(b)(2), the return by the officer or authorized person must also contain the receipt with the addressee's signature.

(d) ***Failure to Serve.*** When the officer or authorized person has not served the citation, the return must show the diligence used by the officer or authorized person to execute the same and the cause of failure to execute it, and where the defendant is to be found, if ascertainable.

(e) ***Signature.*** The officer or authorized person who serves or attempts to serve a citation must sign the return. If the return is signed by a person other than a sheriff, constable, or clerk of the court, the return must either be verified or be signed under penalty of perjury. A return signed under penalty of perjury must contain the statement below in substantially the following form:

"My name is _______ (First) _______ (Middle) _______ (Last), my date of birth is _______ (Month) ____ (Day), ____ (Year), and my address is _______ (Street), _______ (City), _______ (State) _______ (Zip Code), ___________ (Country). I declare under penalty of perjury that the foregoing is true and correct.

Executed in _______ County, State of _______, on the ______ day of ______ (Month), ______ (Year).

____
Declarant"

(f) ***Alternative Service.*** Where citation is executed by an alternative method as authorized by 501.2(e), proof of service must be made in the manner ordered by the court.

(g) ***Filing Return.*** The return and any document to which it is attached must be filed with the court and may be filed electronically or by fax, if those methods of filing are available.

(h) ***Prerequisite for Default Judgment.*** No default judgment may be granted in any case until proof of service as provided by this rule, or as ordered by the court in the event citation is executed by an alternative method under 501.2(e), has been on file with the clerk of the court 3 days, exclusive of the day of filing and the day of judgment.

501.4 Service of Papers Other than Citation.

(a) ***Method of Service.*** Other than a citation or oral motions made during trial or when all parties are present, every notice required by these rules, and every pleading, plea, motion, application to the court for an order, or other form of request, must be served on all other parties in one of the following ways:

(1) *In person.* A copy may be delivered to the party to be served, or the party's duly authorized agent or attorney of record, in person or by agent.

(2) *Mail or courier.* A copy may be sent by courier-receipted delivery or by certified or registered mail, to the party's last known address. Service by certified or registered mail is complete when the document is properly addressed and deposited in the United States mail, postage prepaid.

(3) *Fax.* A copy may be faxed to the recipient's current fax number. Service by fax after 5:00 p.m. local time of the recipient will be deemed to have been served on the following day.

(4) *Email.* A copy may be sent to an email address expressly provided by the receiving party, if the party has consented to email service in writing. Service by email after 5:00 p.m. local time of the recipient will be deemed to have been served on the following day.

(5) *Other.* A copy may be delivered in any other manner directed by the court.

(b) ***Timing.*** If a document is served by mail, 3 days will be added to the length of time a party has to respond to the document. Notice of any hearing requested by a party must be served on all other parties not less than 3 days before the time specified for the hearing.

(c) ***Who May Serve.*** Documents other than a citation may be served by a party to the suit, an attorney of record, a sheriff or constable, or by any other person competent to testify.

(d) ***Certificate of Service.*** The party or the party's attorney of record must include in writing on all documents filed a signed statement describing the manner in which the document was served on the other party or parties and the date of service. A certificate by a party or the party's attorney of record, or the return of the officer, or the sworn statement of any other person showing service of a notice is proof of service.

(e) ***Failure to Serve.*** A party may offer evidence or testimony that a notice or document was not received, or, if service was by mail, that it was not received within 3 days from the date of mailing, and upon so finding, the court may extend the time for taking the action required of the party or grant other relief as it deems just.

2016 change: Amended eff. Sept. 1, 2016, by order of Aug. 31, 2016 (Tex. Sup.Ct. Order, Misc. Docket No. 16-9122).

TRCP 502. INSTITUTION OF SUIT

502.1 Pleadings and Motions Must Be Written, Signed, and Filed. Except for oral motions made during trial or when all parties are present, every pleading, plea, motion, application to the court for an order, or other form of request must be written and signed by the party or its attorney and must be filed with the court. A document may be filed with the court by personal or commercial delivery, by mail, or electronically, if the court allows electronic filing. Electronic filing is governed by Rule 21.

502.2 Petition.

(a) ***Contents.*** To initiate a lawsuit, a petition must be filed with the court. A petition must contain:

(1) the name of the plaintiff;

(2) the name, address, telephone number, and fax number, if any, of the plaintiff's attorney, if applicable, or the address, telephone number, and fax number, if any, of the plaintiff;

(3) the name, address, and telephone number, if known, of the defendant;

(4) the amount of money, if any, the plaintiff seeks;

(5) a description and claimed value of any personal property the plaintiff seeks;

(6) a description of any other relief requested;

(7) the basis for the plaintiff's claim against the defendant; and

(8) if the plaintiff consents to email service of the answer and any other motions or pleadings, a statement consenting to email service and email contact information.

(b) *Justice Court Civil Case Information Sheet.* A justice court civil case information sheet, in the form promulgated by the Supreme Court of Texas, must accompany the filing of a petition and must be signed by the plaintiff or the plaintiff's attorney. The justice court civil case information sheet is for data collection for statistical and administrative purposes and does not affect any substantive right. The court may not reject a pleading because the pleading is not accompanied by a justice court civil case information sheet.

16 **502.3 Fees; Inability to Afford Fees.**

(a) *Fees and Statement of Inability to Afford Payment of Court Costs.* On filing the petition, the plaintiff must pay the appropriate filing fee and service fees, if any, with the court. A plaintiff who is unable to afford to pay the fees must file a Statement of Inability to Afford Payment of Court Costs. The Statement must either be sworn to before a notary or made under penalty of perjury. Upon filing the Statement, the clerk must docket the action, issue citation, and provide any other customary services.

(b) *Supreme Court Form; Contents of Statement.* The plaintiff must use the form Statement approved by the Supreme Court, or the Statement must include the information required by the Court-approved form. The clerk must make the form available to all persons without charge or request.

(c) *Certificate of Legal-Aid Provider.* If the party is represented by an attorney who is providing free legal services because of the party's indigence, without contingency, and the attorney is providing services either directly or by referral from a legal-aid provider described in Rule 145(e)(2), the attorney may file a certificate confirming that the provider screened the party for eligibility under the income and asset guidelines established by the provider. A Statement that is accompanied by the certificate of a legal-aid provider may not be contested under (d).

(d) *Contest.* Unless a certificate is filed under (c), the defendant may file a contest of the Statement at any time within 7 days after the day the defendant's answer is due. If the Statement attests to receipt of government entitlement based on indigence, the Statement may only be contested with regard to the veracity of the attestation. If contested, the judge must hold a hearing to determine the plaintiff's ability to afford the fees. At the hearing, the burden is on the plaintiff to prove the inability to afford fees. The judge may, regardless of whether the defendant contests the Statement, examine the Statement and conduct a hearing to determine the plaintiff's ability to afford fees. If the judge determines that the plaintiff is able to afford the fees, the judge must enter a written order listing the reasons for the determination, and the plaintiff must pay the fees in the time specified in the order or the case will be dismissed without prejudice.

16 **502.4 Venue—Where a Lawsuit May Be Brought.**

(a) *Applicable Law.* Laws specifying the venue—the county and precinct where a lawsuit may be brought—are found in Chapter 15, Subchapter E of the Texas Civil Practice and Remedies Code, which is available online and for examination during the court's business hours.

(b) *General Rule.* Generally, a defendant in a small claims case as described in Rule 500.3(a) or a debt claim case as described in Rule 500.3(b) is entitled to be sued in one of the following venues:

(1) the county and precinct where the defendant resides;

(2) the county and precinct where the incident, or the majority of incidents, that gave rise to the claim occurred;

(3) the county and precinct where the contract or agreement, if any, that gave rise to the claim was to be performed; or

(4) the county and precinct where the property is located, in a suit to recover personal property.

(c) *Non-resident Defendant; Defendant's Residence Unknown.* If the defendant is a non-resident of Texas, or if defendant's residence is unknown, the plaintiff may file the suit in the county and precinct where the plaintiff resides.

(d) *Motion to Transfer Venue.* If a plaintiff files suit in an improper venue, a defendant may challenge the venue selected by filing a motion to transfer venue. The motion must be filed before trial, no later than 21 days after the day the defendant's answer is filed, and must contain a sworn statement that the venue chosen by the plaintiff is improper and a specific county and precinct of proper venue to which transfer is sought. If the defendant fails to name a county and precinct, the court must instruct the defendant to do so and allow the defendant 7 days to cure the defect. If the defendant fails to correct the defect, the motion will be denied,

and the case will proceed in the county and precinct where it was originally filed.

(1) *Procedure.*[1]

(A) Judge to Set Hearing. If a defendant files a motion to transfer venue, the judge must set a hearing on the motion.

(B) Response. A plaintiff may file a response to a defendant's motion to transfer venue.

(C) Hearing. The parties may present evidence at the hearing. A witness may testify at a hearing, either in person or, with permission of the court, by means of telephone or an electronic communication system.

(D) Judge's Decision. If the motion is granted, the judge must sign an order designating the court to which the case will be transferred. If the motion is denied, the case will be heard in the court in which the plaintiff initially filed suit.

(E) Review. Motions for rehearing and interlocutory appeals of the judge's ruling on venue are not permitted.

(F) Time for Trial of the Case. No trial may be held until at least the 14th day after the judge's ruling on the motion to transfer venue.

(G) Order. An order granting a motion to transfer venue must state the reason for the transfer and the name of the court to which the transfer is made. When such an order of transfer is made, the judge who issued the order must immediately make out a true and correct transcript of all the entries made on the docket in the case, certify the transcript, and send the transcript, with a certified copy of the bill of costs and the original papers in the case, to the court in the precinct to which the case has been transferred. The court receiving the case must then notify the plaintiff that the case has been received and, if the case is transferred to a different county, that the plaintiff has 14 days after receiving the notice to pay the filing fee in the new court, or file a Statement of Inability to Afford Payment of Court Costs. The plaintiff is not entitled to a refund of any fees already paid. Failure to pay the fee or file a Statement will result in dismissal of the case without prejudice.

(e) ***Fair Trial Venue Change.*** If a party believes it cannot get a fair trial in a specific precinct or before a specific judge, the party may file a sworn motion stating such, supported by the sworn statements of two other credible persons, and specifying if the party is requesting a change of location or a change of judge. Except for good cause shown, this motion must be filed no less than 7 days before trial. If the party seeks a change of judge, the judge must exchange benches with another qualified justice of the peace, or if no judge is available to exchange benches, the county judge must appoint a visiting judge to hear the case. If the party seeks a change in location, the case must be transferred to the nearest justice court in the county that is not subject to the same or some other disqualification. If there is only one justice of the peace precinct in the county, then the judge must exchange benches with another qualified justice of the peace, or if no judge is available to exchange benches, the county judge must appoint a visiting judge to hear the case. In cases where exclusive jurisdiction is within a specific precinct, as in eviction cases, the only remedy available is a change of judge. A party may apply for relief under this rule only one time in any given lawsuit.

(f) ***Transfer of Venue by Consent.*** On the written consent of all parties or their attorneys, filed with the court, venue must be transferred to the court of any other justice of the peace of the county, or any other county.

502.5 Answer.

(a) ***Requirements.*** A defendant must file with the court a written answer to a lawsuit as directed by the citation and must also serve a copy of the answer on the plaintiff. The answer must contain:

(1) the name of the defendant;

(2) the name, address, telephone number, and fax number, if any, of the defendant's attorney, if applicable, or the address, telephone number, and fax number, if any, of the defendant; and

(3) if the defendant consents to email service, a statement consenting to email service and email contact information.

(b) ***General Denial.*** An answer that denies all of the plaintiff's allegations without specifying the reasons is sufficient to constitute an answer or appearance and does not bar the defendant from raising any defense at trial.

(c) ***Answer Docketed.*** The defendant's appearance must be noted on the court's docket.

(d) ***Due Date.*** Unless the defendant is served by publication, the defendant's answer is due by the end of

the 14th day after the day the defendant was served with the citation and petition, but

(1) if the 14th day is a Saturday, Sunday, or legal holiday, the answer is due on the next day that is not a Saturday, Sunday, or legal holiday; and

(2) if the 14th day falls on a day during which the court is closed before 5:00 p.m., the answer is due on the court's next business day.

(e) ***Due Date When Defendant Served by Publication.*** If a defendant is served by publication, the defendant's answer is due by the end of the 42nd day after the day the citation was issued, but

(1) if the 42nd day is a Saturday, Sunday, or legal holiday, the answer is due on the next day that is not a Saturday, Sunday, or legal holiday; and

(2) if the 42nd day falls on a day during which the court is closed before 5:00 p.m., the answer is due on the court's next business day.

16 **502.6 Counterclaim; Cross-Claim; Third Party Claim.**

(a) ***Counterclaim.*** A defendant may file a petition stating as a counterclaim any claim against a plaintiff that is within the jurisdiction of the justice court, whether or not related to the claims in the plaintiff's petition. The defendant must file a counterclaim petition as provided in Rule 502.2, and must pay a filing fee or provide a Statement of Inability to Afford Payment of Court Costs. The court need not generate a citation for a counterclaim and no answer to the counterclaim need be filed. The defendant must serve a copy of the counterclaim as provided by Rule 501.4.

(b) ***Cross-Claim.*** A plaintiff seeking relief against another plaintiff, or a defendant seeking relief against another defendant may file a cross-claim. The filing party must file a cross-claim petition as provided in Rule 502.2, and must pay a filing fee or provide a Statement of Inability to Afford Payment of Court Costs. A citation must be issued and served as provided by Rule 501.2 on any party that has not yet filed a petition or an answer, as appropriate. If the party filed against has filed a petition or an answer, the filing party must serve the cross-claim as provided by Rule 501.4.

(c) ***Third Party Claim.*** A defendant seeking to bring another party into a lawsuit who may be liable for all or part of the plaintiff's claim against the defendant may file a petition as provided in Rule 502.2, and must pay a filing fee or provide a Statement of Inability to Afford Payment of Court Costs. A citation must be issued and served as provided by Rule 501.2.

502.7 Amending and Clarifying Pleadings.

(a) ***Amending Pleadings.*** A party may withdraw something from or add something to a pleading, as long as the amended pleading is filed and served as provided by Rule 501.4 not less than 7 days before trial. The court may allow a pleading to be amended less than 7 days before trial if the amendment will not operate as a surprise to the opposing party.

(b) ***Insufficient Pleadings.*** A party may file a motion with the court asking that another party be required to clarify a pleading. The court must determine if the pleading is sufficient to place all parties on notice of the issues in the lawsuit, and may hold a hearing to make that determination. If the court determines a pleading is insufficient, the court must order the party to amend the pleading and set a date by which the party must amend. If a party fails to comply with the court's order, the pleading may be stricken.

1. **Editor's note:** There is no TRCP 502.4(d)(2); the original includes only (d)(1).

2016 change: Amended eff. Sept. 1, 2016, by order of Aug. 31, 2016 (Tex. Sup.Ct. Order, Misc. Docket No. 16-9122).

See also *O'Connor's Texas Rules*, "Case-information sheet," ch. 1-B, §3.2.21, p. 15; *O'Connor's Texas Forms*, FORM 1B:17.

TRCP 503. DEFAULT JUDGMENT; PRE-TRIAL MATTERS; TRIAL

503.1 If Defendant Fails to Answer.

(a) ***Default Judgment.*** If the defendant fails to file an answer by the date stated in Rule 502.5, the judge must ensure that service was proper, and may hold a hearing for this purpose. If it is determined that service was proper, the judge must render a default judgment in the following manner:

(1) *Claim Based on Written Document.* If the claim is based on a written document signed by the defendant, and a copy of the document has been filed with the court and served on the defendant, along with a sworn statement from the plaintiff that this is a true and accurate copy of the document and the relief sought is owed, and all payments, offsets or credits due to the defendant have been accounted for, the judge must render judgment for the plaintiff in the requested amount, without any necessity for a hearing. The plaintiff's attorney may also submit affidavits supporting an award of attorney fees to which the plaintiff is entitled, if any.

(2) *Other Cases.* Except as provided in (1), a plaintiff who seeks a default judgment against a defendant

must request a hearing, orally or in writing. The plaintiff must appear at the hearing and provide evidence of its damages. If the plaintiff proves its damages, the judge must render judgment for the plaintiff in the amount proven. If the plaintiff is unable to prove its damages, the judge must render judgment in favor of the defendant. With the permission of the court, a party may appear at a hearing by means of telephone or an electronic communication system.

(b) ***Appearance.*** If a defendant files an answer or otherwise appears in a case before a default judgment is signed by the judge, the judge must not enter a default judgment and the case must be set for trial as described in Rule 503.3.

(c) ***Post-answer Default.*** If a defendant who has answered fails to appear for trial, the court may proceed to hear evidence on liability and damages and render judgment accordingly.

(d) ***Notice.*** The plaintiff requesting a default judgment must provide to the clerk in writing the last known mailing address of the defendant at or before the time the judgment is signed. When a default judgment is signed, the clerk must immediately mail written notice of the judgment to the defendant at the address provided by the plaintiff, and note the fact of such mailing on the docket. The notice must state the number and style of the case, the court in which the case is pending, the names of the parties in whose favor and against whom the judgment was rendered, and the date the judgment was signed. Failure to comply with the provisions of this rule does not affect the finality of the judgment.

503.2 Summary Disposition.

(a) ***Motion.*** A party may file a sworn motion for summary disposition of all or part of a claim or defense without a trial. The motion must set out all supporting facts. All documents on which the motion relies must be attached. The motion must be granted if it shows that:

(1) there are no genuinely disputed facts that would prevent a judgment in favor of the party;

(2) there is no evidence of one or more essential elements of a defense which the defendant must prove to defeat the plaintiff's claim; or

(3) there is no evidence of one or more essential elements of the plaintiff's claim.

(b) ***Response.*** The party opposing the motion may file a sworn written response to the motion.

(c) ***Hearing.*** The court must not consider a motion for summary disposition until it has been on file for at least 14 days. The judge may consider evidence offered by the parties at the hearing. By agreement of the parties, the judge may decide the motion and response without a hearing.

(d) ***Order.*** The judge may enter judgment as to the entire case or may specify the facts that are established and direct such further proceedings in the case as are just.

503.3 Settings and Notice; Postponing Trial.

(a) ***Settings and Notice.*** After the defendant answers, the case will be set on a trial docket at the discretion of the judge. The court must send a notice of the date, time, and place of this setting to all parties at their address of record no less than 45 days before the setting date, unless the judge determines that an earlier setting is required in the interest of justice. Reasonable notice of all subsequent settings must be sent to all parties at their addresses of record.

(b) ***Postponing Trial.*** A party may file a motion requesting that the trial be postponed. The motion must state why a postponement is necessary. The judge, for good cause, may postpone any trial for a reasonable time.

503.4 Pretrial Conference.

(a) ***Conference Set; Issues.*** If all parties have appeared in a lawsuit, the court, at any party's request or on its own, may set a case for a pretrial conference. Reasonable notice must be sent to all parties at their addresses of record. Appropriate issues for the pretrial conference include:

(1) discovery;

(2) the amendment or clarification of pleadings;

(3) the admission of facts and documents to streamline the trial process;

(4) a limitation on the number of witnesses at trial;

(5) the identification of facts, if any, which are not in dispute between the parties;

(6) mediation or other alternative dispute resolution services;

(7) the possibility of settlement;

(8) trial setting dates that are amenable to the court and all parties;

(9) the appointment of interpreters, if needed;

(10) the application of a Rule of Civil Procedure not in Part V or a Rule of Evidence; and

(11) any other issue that the court deems appropriate.

(b) ***Eviction Cases.*** The court must not schedule a pretrial conference in an eviction case if it would delay trial.

503.5 Alternative Dispute Resolution.

(a) ***State Policy.*** The policy of this state is to encourage the peaceable resolution of disputes through alternative dispute resolution, including mediation, and the early settlement of pending litigation through voluntary settlement procedures. For that purpose, the judge may order any case to mediation or another appropriate and generally accepted alternative dispute resolution process.

(b) ***Eviction Cases.*** The court must not order mediation or any other alternative dispute resolution process in an eviction case if it would delay trial.

503.6 Trial.

(a) ***Docket Called.*** On the day of the trial setting, the judge must call all of the cases set for trial that day.

(b) ***If Plaintiff Fails to Appear.*** If the plaintiff fails to appear when the case is called for trial, the judge may postpone or dismiss the suit.

(c) ***If Defendant Fails to Appear.*** If the defendant fails to appear when the case is called for trial, the judge may postpone the case, or may proceed to take evidence. If the plaintiff proves its case, judgment must be awarded for the relief proven. If the plaintiff fails to prove its case, judgment must be rendered against the plaintiff.

TRCP 504. JURY

16 **504.1 Jury Trial Demanded.**

(a) ***Demand.*** Any party is entitled to a trial by jury. A written demand for a jury must be filed no later than 14 days before the date a case is set for trial. If the demand is not timely, the right to a jury is waived unless the late filing is excused by the judge for good cause.

(b) ***Jury Fee.*** Unless otherwise provided by law, a party demanding a jury must pay a fee of $22.00 or must file a Statement of Inability to Afford Payment of Court Costs at or before the time the party files a written request for a jury.

(c) ***Withdrawal of Demand.*** If a party who demands a jury and pays the fee withdraws the demand, the case will remain on the jury docket unless all other parties present agree to try the case without a jury. A party that withdraws its jury demand is not entitled to a refund of the jury fee.

(d) ***No Demand.*** If no party timely demands a jury and pays the fee, the judge will try the case without a jury.

504.2 Empaneling the Jury.

(a) ***Drawing Jury and Oath.*** If no method of electronic draw has been implemented, the judge must write the names of all prospective jurors present on separate slips of paper as nearly alike as may be, place them in a box, mix them well, and then draw the names one by one from the box. The judge must list the names drawn and deliver a copy to each of the parties or their attorneys.

(b) ***Oath.*** After the draw, the judge must swear the panel as follows: "You solemnly swear or affirm that you will give true and correct answers to all questions asked of you concerning your qualifications as a juror."

(c) ***Questioning the Jury.*** The judge, the parties, or their attorneys will be allowed to question jurors as to their ability to serve impartially in the trial but may not ask the jurors how they will rule in the case. The judge will have discretion to allow or disallow specific questions and determine the amount of time each side will have for this process.

(d) ***Challenge for Cause.*** A party may challenge any juror for cause. A challenge for cause is an objection made to a juror alleging some fact, such as a bias or prejudice, that disqualifies the juror from serving in the case or that renders the juror unfit to sit on the jury. The challenge must be made during jury questioning. The party must explain to the judge why the juror should be excluded from the jury. The judge must evaluate the questions and answers given and either grant or deny the challenge. When a challenge for cause has been sustained, the juror must be excused.

(e) ***Challenges Not for Cause.*** After the judge determines any challenges for cause, each party may select up to 3 jurors to excuse for any reason or no reason at all. But no prospective juror may be excused for membership in a constitutionally protected class.

(f) ***The Jury.*** After all challenges, the first 6 prospective jurors remaining on the list constitute the jury to try the case.

(g) ***If Jury Is Incomplete.*** If challenges reduce the number of prospective jurors below 6, the judge

may direct the sheriff or constable to summon others and allow them to be questioned and challenged by the parties as before, until at least 6 remain.

(h) ***Jury Sworn.*** When the jury has been selected, the judge must require them to take substantially the following oath: "You solemnly swear or affirm that you will render a true verdict according to the law and the evidence presented."

504.3 Jury Not Charged. The judge must not charge the jury.

504.4 Jury Verdict for Specific Articles. When the suit is for the recovery of specific articles and the jury finds for the plaintiff, the jury must assess the value of each article separately, according to the evidence presented at trial.

2016 change: Amended eff. Sept. 1, 2016, by order of Aug. 31, 2016 (Tex. Sup.Ct. Order, Misc. Docket No. 16-9122).

TRCP 505. JUDGMENT; NEW TRIAL

505.1 Judgment.

(a) ***Judgment upon Jury Verdict.*** Where a jury has returned a verdict, the judge must announce the verdict in open court, note it in the court's docket, and render judgment accordingly. The judge may render judgment on the verdict or, if the verdict is contrary to the law or the evidence, judgment notwithstanding the verdict.

(b) ***Case Tried by Judge.*** When a case has been tried before the judge without a jury, the judge must announce the decision in open court, note the decision in the court's docket, and render judgment accordingly.

(c) ***Form.*** A judgment must:

(1) clearly state the determination of the rights of the parties in the case;

(2) state who must pay the costs;

(3) be signed by the judge; and

(4) be dated the date of the judge's signature.

(d) ***Costs.*** The judge must award costs allowed by law to the successful party.

(e) ***Judgment for Specific Articles.*** Where the judgment is for the recovery of specific articles, the judgment must order that the plaintiff recover such specific articles, if they can be found, and if not, then their value as assessed by the judge or jury with interest at the prevailing post-judgment interest rate.

505.2 Enforcement of Judgment. Justice court judgments are enforceable in the same method as in county and district court, except as provided by law. When the judgment is for personal property, the court may award a special writ for the seizure and delivery of such property to the plaintiff, and may, in addition to the other relief granted in such cases, enforce its judgment by attachment or fine.

505.3 Motion to Set Aside; Motion to Reinstate; Motion for New Trial.

(a) ***Motion to Reinstate after Dismissal.*** A plaintiff whose case is dismissed may file a motion to reinstate the case no later than 14 days after the dismissal order is signed. The plaintiff must serve the defendant with a copy of the motion no later than the next business day using a method approved under Rule 501.4. The court may reinstate the case for good cause shown.

(b) ***Motion to Set Aside Default.*** A defendant against whom a default judgment is granted may file a motion to set aside the judgment no later than 14 days after the judgment is signed. The defendant must serve the plaintiff with a copy of the motion no later than the next business day using a method approved under Rule 501.4. The court may set aside the judgment and set the case for trial for good cause shown.

(c) ***Motion for New Trial.*** A party may file a motion for a new trial no later than 14 days after the judgment is signed. The party must serve all other parties with a copy of the motion no later than the next business day using a method approved under Rule 501.4. The judge may grant a new trial upon a showing that justice was not done in the trial of the case. Only one new trial may be granted to either party.

(d) ***Motion Not Required.*** Failure to file a motion under this rule does not affect a party's right to appeal the underlying judgment.

(e) ***Motion Denied as a Matter of Law.*** If the judge has not ruled on a motion to set aside, motion to reinstate, or motion for new trial, the motion is automatically denied at 5:00 p.m. on the 21st day after the day the judgment was signed.

TRCP 506. APPEAL

16 **506.1 Appeal.**

(a) ***How Taken; Time.*** A party may appeal a judgment by filing a bond, making a cash deposit, or filing a Statement of Inability to Afford Payment of Court Costs with the justice court within 21 days after the judgment is signed or the motion to reinstate, motion to set aside, or motion for new trial, if any, is denied.

(b) *Amount of Bond; Sureties; Terms.* A plaintiff must file a $500 bond. A defendant must file a bond in an amount equal to twice the amount of the judgment. The bond must be supported by a surety or sureties approved by the judge. The bond must be payable to the appellee and must be conditioned on the appellant's prosecution of its appeal to effect and payment of any judgment and all costs rendered against it on appeal.

(c) *Cash Deposit in Lieu of Bond.* In lieu of filing a bond, an appellant may deposit with the clerk of the court cash in the amount required of the bond. The deposit must be payable to the appellee and must be conditioned on the appellant's prosecution of its appeal to effect and payment of any judgment and all costs rendered against it on appeal.

(d) *Statement of Inability to Afford Payment of Court Costs.*

(1) *Filing.* An appellant who cannot furnish a bond or pay a cash deposit in the amount required may instead file a Statement of Inability to Afford Payment of Court Costs. The Statement must be on the form approved by the Supreme Court or include the information required by the Court-approved form and may be the same one that was filed with the petition.

(2) *Contest.* The Statement may be contested as provided in Rule 502.3(d) within 7 days after the opposing party receives notice that the Statement was filed.

(3) *Appeal If Contest Sustained.* If the contest is sustained, the appellant may appeal that decision by filing notice with the justice court within 7 days of that court's written order. The justice court must then forward all related documents to the county court for resolution. The county court must set the matter for hearing within 14 days and hear the contest de novo, as if there had been no previous hearing, and if the appeal is granted, must direct the justice court to transmit to the clerk of the county court the transcript, records, and papers of the case, as provided in these rules.

(4) *If No Appeal or If Appeal Overruled.* If the appellant does not appeal the ruling sustaining the contest, or if the county court denies the appeal, the appellant may, within five days, post an appeal bond or make a cash deposit in compliance with this rule.

(e) *Notice to Other Parties Required.* If a Statement of Inability to Afford Payment of Court Costs is filed, the court must provide notice to all other parties that the Statement was filed no later than the next business day. Within 7 days of filing a bond or making a cash deposit, an appellant must serve written notice of the appeal on all other parties using a method approved under Rule 501.4.

(f) *No Default on Appeal Without Compliance with Rule.* The county court to which an appeal is taken must not render default judgment against any party without first determining that the appellant has fully complied with this rule.

(g) *No Dismissal of Appeal Without Opportunity for Correction.* An appeal must not be dismissed for defects or irregularities in procedure, either of form or substance, without allowing the appellant, after 7 days' notice from the court, the opportunity to correct such defect.

(h) *Appeal Perfected.* An appeal is perfected when a bond, cash deposit, or Statement of Inability to Afford Payment of Court Costs is filed in accordance with this rule.

(i) *Costs.* The appellant must pay the costs on appeal to a county court in accordance with Rule 143a.

506.2 Record on Appeal. When an appeal has been perfected from the justice court, the judge must immediately send to the clerk of the county court a certified copy of all docket entries, a certified copy of the bill of costs, and the original papers in the case.

506.3 Trial de Novo. The case must be tried de novo in the county court. A trial de novo is a new trial in which the entire case is presented as if there had been no previous trial.

16 **506.4 Writ of Certiorari.**

(a) *Application.* Except in eviction cases, after final judgment in a case tried in justice court, a party may apply to the county court for a writ of certiorari.

(b) *Grounds.* An application must be granted only if it contains a sworn statement setting forth facts showing that either:

(1) the justice court did not have jurisdiction; or

(2) the final determination of the suit worked an injustice to the applicant that was not caused by the applicant's own inexcusable neglect.

(c) *Bond, Cash Deposit, or Sworn Statement of Indigency to Pay Required.* If the application is granted, a writ of certiorari must not issue until the applicant has filed a bond, made a cash deposit, or filed a Statement of Inability to Afford Payment of Court Costs that complies with Rule 145.

(d) ***Time for Filing.*** An application for writ of certiorari must be filed within 90 days after the date the final judgment is signed.

(e) ***Contents of Writ.*** The writ of certiorari must command the justice court to immediately make and certify a copy of the entries in the case on the docket, and immediately transmit the transcript of the proceedings in the justice court, together with the original papers and a bill of costs, to the proper court.

(f) ***Clerk to Issue Writ and Citation.*** When the application is granted and the bond, cash deposit, or Statement of Inability to Afford Payment of Court Costs has been filed, the clerk must issue a writ of certiorari to the justice court and citation to the adverse party.

(g) ***Stay of Proceedings.*** When the writ of certiorari is served on the justice court, the court must stay further proceedings on the judgment and comply with the writ.

(h) ***Cause Docketed.*** The action must be docketed in the name of the original plaintiff, as plaintiff, and of the original defendant, as defendant.

(i) ***Motion to Dismiss.*** Within 30 days after the service of citation on the writ of certiorari, the adverse party may move to dismiss the certiorari for want of sufficient cause appearing in the affidavit, or for want of sufficient bond. If the certiorari is dismissed, the judgment must direct the justice court to proceed with the execution of the judgment below.

(j) ***Amendment of Bond or Oath.*** The affidavit or bond may be amended at the discretion of the court in which it is filed.

(k) ***Trial de Novo.*** The case must be tried de novo in the county court and judgment must be rendered as in cases appealed from justice courts. A trial de novo is a new trial in which the entire case is presented as if there had been no previous trial.

2016 change: Amended eff. Sept. 1, 2016, by order of Aug. 31, 2016 (Tex. Sup.Ct. Order, Misc. Docket No. 16-9122).

ANNOTATIONS

Rowe v. Watkins, 340 S.W.3d 860, 863 (Tex. App.—El Paso 2011, no pet.). "When the appeal bond contains defects or irregularities, either of form or substance, the case should not be dismissed without first allowing the appealing party …, after notice of the defect, to correct or amend the defective appeal. Although the rules do not prescribe a specific type of notice, we have held that the notice must, in the very least, conform to due process which is met if the notice affords the party a fair opportunity to appear and defend her interests. As compliance with the appellate requirements of [TRCP] 571 [now 506.1] is jurisdictional, … if the appealing party fails to meet any one of the rule's prerequisites, and also fails to correct the defect within [the] notice [period], the appellate court, i.e., the county court, lacks jurisdiction to hear the appeal and must dismiss the same."

TRCP 507. ADMINISTRATIVE RULES FOR JUDGES & COURT PERSONNEL

507.1 Plenary Power. A justice court loses plenary power over a case when an appeal is perfected or if no appeal is perfected, 21 days after the later of the date judgment is signed or the date a motion to set aside, motion to reinstate, or motion for new trial, if any, is denied.

507.2 Forms. The court may provide forms to enable a party to file documents that comply with these rules. No party may be forced to use the court's forms.

507.3 Docket and Other Records.

(a) ***Docket.*** Each judge must keep a civil docket in a permanent record containing the following information:

(1) the title of all suits commenced before the court;

(2) the date when the first process was issued against the defendant, when returnable, and the nature of that process;

(3) the date when the parties, or either of them, appeared before the court, either with or without a citation;

(4) a description of the petition and any documents filed with the petition;

(5) every adjournment, stating at whose request and to what time;

(6) the date of the trial, stating whether the same was by a jury or by the judge;

(7) the verdict of the jury, if any;

(8) the judgment signed by the judge and the date the judgment was signed;

(9) all applications for setting aside judgments or granting new trials and the orders of the judge thereon, with the date;

(10) the date of issuing execution, to whom directed and delivered, and the amount of debt, damages

and costs and, when any execution is returned, the date of the return and the manner in which it was executed; and

(11) all stays and appeals that may be taken, and the date when taken, the amount of the bond and the names of the sureties.

(b) ***Other Records.*** The judge must also keep copies of all documents filed; other dockets, books, and records as may be required by law or these rules; and a fee book in which all costs accruing in every suit commenced before the court are taxed.

(c) ***Form of Records.*** All records required to be kept under this rule may be maintained electronically.

507.4 Issuance of Writs. Every writ from the justice courts must be in writing and be issued and signed by the judge officially. The style thereof must be "The State of Texas." It must, except where otherwise specially provided by law or these rules, be directed to the person or party upon whom it is to be served, be made returnable to the court, and note the date of its issuance.

TRCP 508. DEBT CLAIM CASES

508.1 Application. Rule 508 applies to a claim for the recovery of a debt brought by an assignee of a claim, a financial institution, a debt collector or collection agency, or a person or entity primarily engaged in the business of lending money at interest.

508.2 Petition.[1]

(a) ***Contents.*** In addition to the information required by Rule 502.2, a petition filed in a lawsuit governed by this rule must contain the following information:

(1) *Credit Accounts.* In a claim based upon a credit card, revolving credit, or open account, the petition must state:

(A) the account name or credit card name;

(B) the account number (which may be masked);

(C) the date of issue or origination of the account, if known;

(D) the date of charge-off or breach of the account, if known;

(E) the amount owed as of a date certain; and

(F) whether the plaintiff seeks ongoing interest.

(2) *Personal and Business Loans.* In a claim based upon a promissory note or other promise to pay a specific amount as of a date certain, the petition must state:

(A) the date and amount of the original loan;

(B) whether the repayment of the debt was accelerated, if known;

(C) the date final payment was due;

(D) the amount due as of the final payment date;

(E) the amount owed as of a date certain; and

(F) whether plaintiff seeks ongoing interest.

(3) *Ongoing Interest.* If a plaintiff seeks ongoing interest, the petition must state:

(A) the effective interest rate claimed;

(B) whether the interest rate is based upon contract or statute; and

(C) the dollar amount of interest claimed as of a date certain.

(4) *Assigned Debt.* If the debt that is the subject of the claim has been assigned or transferred, the petition must state:

(A) that the debt claim has been transferred or assigned;

(B) the date of the transfer or assignment;

(C) the name of any prior holders of the debt; and

(D) the name or a description of the original creditor.

508.3 Default Judgment.

(a) ***Generally.*** If the defendant does not file an answer to a claim by the answer date or otherwise appear in the case, the judge must promptly render a default judgment upon the plaintiff's proof of the amount of damages.

(b) ***Proof of the Amount of Damages.***

(1) *Evidence Must Be Served or Submitted.* Evidence of plaintiff's damages must either be attached to the petition and served on the defendant or submitted to the court after defendant's failure to answer by the answer date.

(2) *Form of Evidence.* Evidence of plaintiff's damages may be offered in a sworn statement or in live testimony. The evidence offered may include documentary evidence.

(3) *Establishment of the Amount of Damages.* The amount of damages is established by evidence:

(A) that the account or loan was issued to the defendant and the defendant is obligated to pay it;

(B) that the account was closed or the defendant breached the terms of the account or loan agreement;

(C) of the amount due on the account or loan as of a date certain after all payment credits and offsets have been applied; and

(D) that the plaintiff owns the account or loan and, if applicable, how the plaintiff acquired the account or loan.

(4) *Documentary Evidence Offered by Sworn Statement.* Documentary evidence may be considered if it is attached to a sworn statement made by the plaintiff or its representative, a prior holder of the debt or its representative, or the original creditor or its representative, that attests to the following:

(A) the documents were kept in the regular course of business;

(B) it was the regular course of business for an employee or representative with knowledge of the act recorded to make the record or to transmit information to be included in such record;

(C) the documents were created at or near the time or reasonably soon thereafter; and

(D) the documents attached are the original or exact duplicates of the original.

(5) *Consideration of Sworn Statement.* A judge is not required to accept a sworn statement if the source of information or the method or circumstances of preparation indicate lack of trustworthiness. But a judge may not reject a sworn statement only because it is not made by the original creditor or because the documents attested to were created by a third party and subsequently incorporated into and relied upon by the business of the plaintiff.

(c) ***Hearing.*** The judge may enter a default judgment without a hearing if the plaintiff submits sufficient written evidence of its damages and should do so to avoid undue expense and delay. Otherwise, the plaintiff may request a default judgment hearing at which the plaintiff must appear, in person or by telephonic or electronic means, and prove its damages. If the plaintiff proves its damages, the judge must render judgment for the plaintiff in the amount proven. If the plaintiff is unable to prove its damages, the judge must render judgment in favor of the defendant.

(d) ***Appearance.*** If the defendant files an answer or otherwise appears in a case before a default judgment is signed by the judge, the judge must not render a default judgment and must set the case for trial.

(e) ***Post-answer Default.*** If a defendant who has answered fails to appear for trial, the court may proceed to hear evidence on liability and damages and render judgment accordingly.

1. **Editor's note:** Rule 508.2 does not include a subsection (b). *See* Tex. Sup.Ct. Order, Misc. Docket No. 13-9049 (eff. Aug. 31, 2013).

TRCP 509. REPAIR & REMEDY CASES

509.1 Applicability of Rule. Rule 509 applies to a lawsuit filed in a justice court by a residential tenant under Chapter 92, Subchapter B of the Texas Property Code to enforce the landlord's duty to repair or remedy a condition materially affecting the physical health or safety of an ordinary tenant.

509.2 Contents of Petition; Copies; Forms and Amendments.

(a) ***Contents of Petition.*** The petition must be in writing and must include the following:

(1) the street address of the residential rental property;

(2) a statement indicating whether the tenant has received in writing the name and business street address of the landlord and landlord's management company;

(3) to the extent known and applicable, the name, business street address, and telephone number of the landlord and the landlord's management company, on-premises manager, and rent collector serving the residential rental property;

(4) for all notices the tenant gave to the landlord requesting that the condition be repaired or remedied:

(A) the date of the notice;

(B) the name of the person to whom the notice was given or the place where the notice was given;

(C) whether the tenant's lease is in writing and requires written notice;

(D) whether the notice was in writing or oral;

(E) whether any written notice was given by certified mail, return receipt requested, or by registered mail; and

(F) whether the rent was current or had been timely tendered at the time notice was given;

(5) a description of the property condition materially affecting the physical health or safety of an ordinary tenant that the tenant seeks to have repaired or remedied;

(6) a statement of the relief requested by the tenant, including an order to repair or remedy a condition, a reduction in rent, actual damages, civil penalties, attorney's fees, and court costs;

(7) if the petition includes a request to reduce the rent:

(A) the amount of rent paid by the tenant, the amount of rent paid by the government, if known, the rental period, and when the rent is due; and

(B) the amount of the requested rent reduction and the date it should begin;

(8) a statement that the total relief requested does not exceed $10,000, excluding interest and court costs but including attorney's fees; and

(9) the tenant's name, address, and telephone number.

(b) ***Copies.*** The tenant must provide the court with copies of the petition and any attachments to the petition for service on the landlord.

(c) ***Forms and Amendments.*** A petition substantially in the form promulgated by the Supreme Court is sufficient. A suit may not be dismissed for a defect in the petition unless the tenant is given an opportunity to correct the defect and does not promptly correct it.

509.3 Citation: Issuance; Appearance Date; Answer.

(a) ***Issuance.*** When the tenant files a written petition with a justice court, the judge must immediately issue citation directed to the landlord, commanding the landlord to appear before such judge at the time and place named in the citation.

(b) ***Appearance Date; Answer.*** The appearance date on the citation must not be less than 10 days nor more than 21 days after the petition is filed. For purposes of this rule, the appearance date on the citation is the trial date. The landlord may, but is not required to, file a written answer on or before the appearance date.

509.4 Service and Return of Citation; Alternative Service of Citation.

(a) ***Service and Return of Citation.*** The sheriff, constable, or other person authorized by Rule 501.2 who receives the citation must serve the citation by delivering a copy of it, along with a copy of the petition and any attachments, to the landlord at least 6 days before the appearance date. At least one day before the appearance date, the person serving the citation must file a return of service with the court that issued the citation. The citation must be issued, served, and returned in like manner as ordinary citations issued from a justice court.

(b) ***Alternative Service of Citation.***

(1) If the petition does not include the landlord's name and business street address, or if, after making diligent efforts on at least two occasions, the officer or authorized person is unsuccessful in serving the citation on the landlord under (a), the officer or authorized person must serve the citation by delivering a copy of the citation, petition, and any attachments to:

(A) the landlord's management company if the tenant has received written notice of the name and business street address of the landlord's management company; or

(B) if (b)(1)(A) does not apply and the tenant has not received the landlord's name and business street address in writing, the landlord's authorized agent for service of process, which may be the landlord's management company, on-premise manager, or rent collector serving the residential rental property.

(2) If the officer or authorized person is unsuccessful in serving citation under (b)(1) after making diligent efforts on at least two occasions at either the business street address of the landlord's management company, if (b)(1)(A) applies, or at each available business street address of the landlord's authorized agent for service of process, if (b)(1)(B) applies, the officer or authorized person must execute and file in the justice court a sworn statement that the officer or authorized person made diligent efforts to serve the citation on at least two occasions at all available business street addresses of the landlord and, to the extent applicable, the landlord's management company, on-premises manager, and rent collector serving the residential rental property, providing the times, dates, and places of each attempted service. The judge may then authorize the officer or authorized person to serve citation by:

(A) delivering a copy of the citation, petition, and any attachments to someone over the age of 16 years, at any business street address listed in the petition, or, if nobody answers the door at a business street address, either placing the citation, petition, and any attachments through a door mail chute or slipping them under the front door, and if neither of these latter methods is practical, affixing the citation, petition, and any at-

tachments to the front door or main entry to the business street address;

(B) within 24 hours of complying with (b)(2)(A), sending by first class mail a true copy of the citation, petition, and any attachments addressed to the landlord at the landlord's business street address provided in the petition; and

(C) noting on the return of the citation the date of delivery under (b)(2)(A) and the date of mailing under (b)(2)(B).

The delivery and mailing to the business street address under (b)(2)(A)-(B) must occur at least 6 days before the appearance date. At least one day before the appearance date, a return of service must be completed and filed in accordance with Rule 501.3 with the court that issued the citation. It is not necessary for the tenant to request the alternative service authorized by this rule.

509.5 Docketing and Trial; Failure to Appear.

(a) ***Docketing and Trial.*** The case must be docketed and tried as other cases. The judge may develop the facts of the case in order to ensure justice.

(b) ***Failure to Appear.***

(1) If the tenant appears at trial and the landlord has been duly served and fails to appear at trial, the judge may proceed to hear evidence. If the tenant establishes that the tenant is entitled to recover, the judge must render judgment against the landlord in accordance with the evidence.

(2) If the tenant fails to appear for trial, the judge may dismiss the lawsuit.

509.6 Judgment: Amount; Form and Content; Issuance and Service; Failure to Comply.

(a) ***Amount.*** Judgment may be rendered against the landlord for failure to repair or remedy a condition at the residential rental property if the total judgment does not exceed $10,000, excluding interest and court costs but including attorney's fees. Any party who prevails in a lawsuit brought under these rules may recover the party's court costs and reasonable attorney's fees as allowed by law.

(b) ***Form and Content.***

(1) The judgment must be in writing, signed, and dated and must include the names of the parties to the proceeding and the street address of the residential rental property where the condition is to be repaired or remedied.

(2) In the judgment, the judge may:

(A) order the landlord to take reasonable action to repair or remedy the condition;

(B) order a reduction in the tenant's rent, from the date of the first repair notice, in proportion to the reduced rental value resulting from the condition until the condition is repaired or remedied;

(C) award a civil penalty of one month's rent plus $500;

(D) award the tenant's actual damages; and

(E) award court costs and attorney's fees, excluding any attorney's fees for a claim for damages relating to a personal injury.

(3) If the judge orders the landlord to repair or remedy a condition, the judgment must include in reasonable detail the actions the landlord must take to repair or remedy the condition and the date when the repair or remedy must be completed.

(4) If the judge orders a reduction in the tenant's rent, the judgment must state:

(A) the amount of the rent the tenant must pay, if any;

(B) the frequency with which the tenant must pay the rent;

(C) the condition justifying the reduction of rent;

(D) the effective date of the order reducing rent;

(E) that the order reducing rent will terminate on the date the condition is repaired or remedied; and

(F) that on the day the condition is repaired or remedied, the landlord must give the tenant written notice, served in accordance with Rule 501.4, that the condition justifying the reduction of rent has been repaired or remedied and the rent will revert to the rent amount specified in the lease.

(c) ***Issuance and Service.*** The judge must issue the judgment. The judgment may be served on the landlord in open court or by any means provided in Rule 501.4 at an address listed in the citation, the address listed on any answer, or such other address the landlord furnishes to the court in writing. Unless the judge serves the landlord in open court or by other means provided in Rule 501.4, the sheriff, constable, or other authorized person who serves the landlord must promptly file a return of service in the justice court.

(d) ***Failure to Comply.*** If the landlord fails to comply with an order to repair or remedy a condition or reduce the tenant's rent, the failure is grounds for citing

the landlord for contempt of court under Section 21.002 of the Texas Government Code.

509.7 Counterclaims. Counterclaims and the joinder of suits against third parties are not permitted in suits under these rules. Compulsory counterclaims may be brought in a separate suit. Any potential causes of action, including a compulsory counterclaim, that are not asserted because of this rule are not precluded.

509.8 Appeal: Time and Manner; Perfection; Effect; Costs; Trial on Appeal.

(a) ***Time and Manner.*** Either party may appeal the decision of the justice court to a statutory county court or, if there is no statutory county court with jurisdiction, a county court or district court with jurisdiction by filing a written notice of appeal with the justice court within 21 days after the date the judge signs the judgment. If the judgment is amended in any respect, any party has the right to appeal within 21 days after the date the judge signs the new judgment, in the same manner set out in this rule.

(b) ***Perfection.*** The posting of an appeal bond is not required for an appeal under this rule, and the appeal is considered perfected with the filing of a notice of appeal. Otherwise, the appeal is in the manner provided by law for appeal from a justice court.

(c) ***Effect.*** The timely filing of a notice of appeal stays the enforcement of any order to repair or remedy a condition or reduce the tenant's rent, as well as any other actions.

(d) ***Costs.*** The appellant must pay the costs on appeal to a county court in accordance with Rule 143a.

(e) ***Trial on Appeal.*** On appeal, the parties are entitled to a trial de novo. A trial de novo is a new trial in which the entire case is presented as if there had been no previous trial. Either party is entitled to trial by jury on timely request and payment of a fee, if required. An appeal of a judgment of a justice court under these rules takes precedence in the county court and may be held at any time after the eighth day after the date the transcript is filed in the county court.

509.9 Effect of Writ of Possession. If a judgment for the landlord for possession of the residential rental property becomes final, any order to repair or remedy a condition is vacated and unenforceable.

See also *O'Connor's Texas COA*, "Failure to Repair or Remedy," ch. 16-F, p. 461.

TRCP 510. EVICTION CASES

510.1 Application. Rule 510 applies to a lawsuit to recover possession of real property under Chapter 24 of the Texas Property Code.

510.2 Computation of Time for Eviction Cases. Rule 500.5 applies to the computation of time in an eviction case. But if a document is filed by mail and not received by the court by the due date, the court may take any action authorized by these rules, including issuing a writ of possession requiring a tenant to leave the property.

510.3 Petition.

(a) ***Contents.*** In addition to the requirements of Rule 502.2, a petition in an eviction case must be sworn to by the plaintiff and must contain:

(1) a description, including the address, if any, of the premises that the plaintiff seeks possession of;

(2) a description of the facts and the grounds for eviction;

(3) a description of when and how notice to vacate was delivered;

(4) the total amount of rent due and unpaid at the time of filing, if any; and

(5) a statement that attorney fees are being sought, if applicable.

(b) ***Where Filed.*** The petition must be filed in the precinct where the premises is located. If it is filed elsewhere, the judge must dismiss the case. The plaintiff will not be entitled to a refund of the filing fee, but will be refunded any service fees paid if the case is dismissed before service is attempted.

(c) ***Defendants Named.*** If the eviction is based on a written residential lease, the plaintiff must name as defendants all tenants obligated under the lease residing at the premises whom plaintiff seeks to evict. No judgment or writ of possession may issue or be executed against a tenant obligated under a lease and residing at the premises who is not named in the petition and served with citation.

(d) ***Claim for Rent.*** A claim for rent within the justice court's jurisdiction may be asserted in an eviction case.

(e) ***Only Issue.*** The court must adjudicate the right to actual possession and not title. Counterclaims and the joinder of suits against third parties are not permitted in eviction cases. A claim that is not asserted

because of this rule can be brought in a separate suit in a court of proper jurisdiction.

510.4 Issuance, Service, and Return of Citation.

(a) ***Issuance of Citation; Contents.*** When a petition is filed, the court must immediately issue citation directed to each defendant. The citation must:

(1) be styled "The State of Texas";

(2) be signed by the clerk under seal of court or by the judge;

(3) contain the name, location, and address of the court;

(4) state the date of filing of the petition;

(5) state the date of issuance of the citation;

(6) state the file number and names of parties;

(7) state the plaintiff's cause of action and relief sought;

(8) be directed to the defendant;

(9) state the name and address of attorney for plaintiff, or if the plaintiff does not have an attorney, the address of plaintiff;

(10) state the day the defendant must appear in person for trial at the court issuing citation, which must not be less than 10 days nor more than 21 days after the petition is filed;

(11) notify the defendant that if the defendant fails to appear in person for trial, judgment by default may be rendered for the relief demanded in the petition;

(12) inform the defendant that, upon timely request and payment of a jury fee no later than 3 days before the day set for trial, the case will be heard by a jury;

(13) contain all warnings required by Chapter 24 of the Texas Property Code; and

(14) include the following statement: "For further information, consult Part V of the Texas Rules of Civil Procedure, which is available online and also at the court listed on this citation."

(b) ***Service and Return of Citation.***

(1) *Who May Serve.* Unless otherwise authorized by written court order, citation must be served by a sheriff or constable.

(2) *Method of Service.* The constable, sheriff, or other person authorized by written court order receiving the citation must execute it by delivering a copy with a copy of the petition attached to the defendant, or by leaving a copy with a copy of the petition attached with some person, other than the plaintiff, over the age of 16 years, at the defendant's usual place of residence, at least 6 days before the day set for trial.

(3) *Return of Service.* At least one day before the day set for trial, the constable, sheriff, or other person authorized by written court order must complete and file a return of service in accordance with Rule 501.3 with the court that issued the citation.

(c) ***Alternative Service by Delivery to the Premises.***

(1) *When Allowed.* The citation may be served by delivery to the premises if:

(A) the constable, sheriff, or other person authorized by written court order is unsuccessful in serving the citation under (b);

(B) the petition lists all home and work addresses of the defendant that are known to the plaintiff and states that the plaintiff knows of no other home or work addresses of the defendant in the county where the premises are located; and

(C) the constable, sheriff, or other person authorized files a sworn statement that it has made diligent efforts to serve such citation on at least two occasions at all addresses of the defendant in the county where the premises are located, stating the times and places of attempted service.

(2) *Authorization.* The judge must promptly consider a sworn statement filed under (1)(C) and determine whether citation may be served by delivery to the premises. The plaintiff is not required to make a request or motion for alternative service.

(3) *Method.* If the judge authorizes service by delivery to the premises, the constable, sheriff, or other person authorized by written court order must, at least 6 days before the day set for trial:

(A) deliver a copy of the citation with a copy of the petition attached to the premises by placing it through a door mail chute or slipping it under the front door; if neither method is possible, the officer may securely affix the citation to the front door or main entry to the premises; and

(B) deposit in the mail a copy of the citation with a copy of the petition attached, addressed to defendant at the premises and sent by first class mail.

(4) *Notation on Return.* The constable, sheriff, or other person authorized by written court order must

note on the return of service the date the citation was delivered and the date it was deposited in the mail.

510.5 Request for Immediate Possession.

(a) ***Immediate Possession Bond.*** The plaintiff may, at the time of filing the petition or at any time prior to final judgment, file a possession bond to be approved by the judge in the probable amount of costs of suit and damages that may result to defendant in the event that the suit has been improperly instituted, and conditioned that the plaintiff will pay defendant all such costs and damages that are adjudged against plaintiff.

(b) ***Notice to Defendant.*** The court must notify a defendant that the plaintiff has filed a possession bond. The notice must be served in the same manner as service of citation and must inform the defendant that if the defendant does not file an answer or appear for trial, and judgment for possession is granted by default, an officer will place the plaintiff in possession of the property on or after the 7th day after the date defendant is served with the notice.

(c) ***Time for Issuance and Execution of Writ.*** If judgment for possession is rendered by default and a possession bond has been filed, approved, and served under this rule, a writ of possession must issue immediately upon demand and payment of any required fees. The writ must not be executed before the 7th day after the date defendant is served with notice under (b).

(d) ***Effect of Appearance.*** If the defendant files an answer or appears at trial, no writ of possession may issue before the 6th day after the date a judgment for possession is signed or the day following the deadline for the defendant to appeal the judgment, whichever is later.

510.6 Trial Date; Answer; Default Judgment.

(a) ***Trial Date and Answer.*** The defendant must appear for trial on the day set for trial in the citation. The defendant may, but is not required to, file a written answer with the court on or before the day set for trial in the citation.

(b) ***Default Judgment.*** If the defendant fails to appear at trial and fails to file an answer before the case is called for trial, and proof of service has been filed in accordance with Rule 510.4, the allegations of the complaint must be taken as admitted and judgment by default rendered accordingly. If a defendant who has answered fails to appear for trial, the court may proceed to hear evidence and render judgment accordingly.

(c) ***Notice of Default.*** When a default judgment is signed, the clerk must immediately mail written notice of the judgment by first class mail to the defendant at the address of the premises.

16 **510.7 Trial.**

(a) ***Trial.*** An eviction case will be docketed and tried as other cases. No eviction trial may be held less than 6 days after service under Rule 510.4 has been obtained.

(b) ***Jury Trial Demanded.*** Any party may file a written demand for trial by jury by making a request to the court at least 3 days before the trial date. The demand must be accompanied by payment of a jury fee or by filing a Statement of Inability to Afford Payment of Court Costs. If a jury is demanded by either party, the jury will be impaneled and sworn as in other cases; and after hearing the evidence it will return its verdict in favor of the plaintiff or the defendant. If no jury is timely demanded by either party, the judge will try the case.

(c) ***Limit on Postponement.*** Trial in an eviction case must not be postponed for more than 7 days total unless both parties agree in writing.

510.8 Judgment; Writ; No New Trial.

(a) ***Judgment upon Jury Verdict.*** Where a jury has returned a verdict, the judge may render judgment on the verdict or, if the verdict is contrary to the law or the evidence, judgment notwithstanding the verdict.

(b) ***Judgment for Plaintiff.*** If the judgment is in favor of the plaintiff, the judge must render judgment for plaintiff for possession of the premises, costs, delinquent rent as of the date of entry of judgment, if any, and attorney fees if recoverable by law.

(c) ***Judgment for Defendant.*** If the judgment is in favor of the defendant, the judge must render judgment for defendant against the plaintiff for costs and attorney fees if recoverable by law.

(d) ***Writ.*** If the judgment or verdict is in favor of the plaintiff, the judge must award a writ of possession upon demand of the plaintiff and payment of any required fees.

(1) *Time to Issue.* Except as provided by Rule 510.5, no writ of possession may issue before the 6th day after the date a judgment for possession is signed or the day following the deadline for the defendant to appeal the judgment, whichever is later. A writ of possession may not issue more than 60 days after a judgment for possession is signed. For good cause, the court may extend

the deadline for issuance to 90 days after a judgment for possession is signed.

(2) *Time to Execute.* A writ of possession may not be executed after the 90th day after a judgment for possession is signed.

(3) *Effect of Appeal.* A writ of possession must not issue if an appeal is perfected and, if applicable, rent is paid into the registry, as required by these rules.

(e) ***No Motion for New Trial.*** No motion for new trial may be filed.

16 **510.9 Appeal.**

(a) ***How Taken; Time.*** A party may appeal a judgment in an eviction case by filing a bond, making a cash deposit, or filing a Statement of Inability to Afford Payment of Court Costs with the justice court within 5 days after the judgment is signed.

(b) ***Amount of Security; Terms.*** The justice court judge will set the amount of the bond or cash deposit to include the items enumerated in Rule 510.11. The bond or cash deposit must be payable to the appellee and must be conditioned on the appellant's prosecution of its appeal to effect and payment of any judgment and all costs rendered against it on appeal.

(c) ***Statement of Inability to Afford Payment of Court Costs.***

(1) *Filing.* An appellant who cannot furnish a bond or pay a cash deposit in the amount required may instead file a Statement of Inability to Afford Payment of Court Costs. The Statement must be on the form approved by the Supreme Court or include the information required by the Court-approved form.

(2) *Contest.* The Statement may be contested as provided in Rule 502.3(d) within 5 days after the opposing party receives notice that the Statement was filed.

(3) *Appeal If Contest Sustained.* If the contest is sustained, the appellant may appeal that decision by filing notice with the justice court within 5 days of that court's written order. The justice court must then forward all related documents to the county court for resolution. The county court must set the matter for hearing within 5 days and hear the contest de novo, as if there had been no previous hearing, and, if the appeal is granted, must direct the justice court to transmit to the clerk of the county court the transcript, records, and papers of the case, as provided in these rules.

(4) *If No Appeal or If Appeal Overruled.* If the appellant does not appeal the ruling sustaining the contest, or if the county court denies the appeal, the appellant may, within one business day, post an appeal bond or make a cash deposit in compliance with this rule.

(5) *Payment of Rent in Nonpayment of Rent Appeals.*

(A) Notice. If a defendant appeals an eviction for nonpayment of rent by filing a Statement of Inability to Afford Payment of Court Costs, the justice court must provide to the defendant a written notice at the time the Statement is filed that contains the following information in bold or conspicuous type:

(i) the amount of the initial deposit of rent, equal to one rental period's rent under the terms of the rental agreement, that the defendant must pay into the justice court registry;

(ii) whether the initial deposit must be paid in cash, cashier's check, or money order, and to whom the cashier's check or money order, if applicable, must be made payable;

(iii) the calendar date by which the initial deposit must be paid into the justice court registry, which must be within 5 days of the date the Statement is filed; and

(iv) a statement that failure to pay the required amount into the justice court registry by the required date may result in the court issuing a writ of possession without hearing.

(B) Defendant May Remain in Possession. A defendant who appeals an eviction for nonpayment of rent by filing a Statement of Inability to Afford Payment of Court Costs is entitled to stay in possession of the premises during the pendency of the appeal by complying with the following procedure:

(i) Within 5 days of the date that the defendant files a Statement of Inability to Afford Payment of Court Costs, it must pay into the justice court registry the amount set forth in the notice provided at the time the defendant filed the Statement. If the defendant was provided with notice and fails to pay the designated amount into the justice court registry within 5 days, and the transcript has not been transmitted to the county clerk, the plaintiff is entitled, upon request and payment of the applicable fee, to a writ of possession, which the justice court must issue immediately and without hearing.

(ii) During the appeal process as rent becomes due under the rental agreement, the defendant must pay the designated amount into the county court registry

within 5 days of the rental due date under the terms of the rental agreement.

(iii) If a government agency is responsible for all or a portion of the rent, the defendant must pay only that portion of the rent determined by the justice court to be paid during appeal. Either party may contest the portion of the rent that the justice court determines must be paid into the county court registry by filing a contest within 5 days after the judgment is signed. If a contest is filed, the justice court must notify the parties and hold a hearing on the contest within 5 days. If the defendant objects to the justice court's ruling at the hearing, the defendant is required to pay only the portion claimed to be owed by the defendant until the issue is tried in county court.

(iv) If the defendant fails to pay the designated amount into the court registry within the time limits prescribed by these rules, the plaintiff may file a sworn motion that the defendant is in default in county court. The plaintiff must notify the defendant of the motion and the hearing date. Upon a showing that the defendant is in default, the court must issue a writ of possession.

(v) The plaintiff may withdraw any or all rent in the county court registry upon sworn motion and hearing, prior to final determination of the case, showing just cause; dismissal of the appeal; or order of the court after final hearing.

(vi) All hearings and motions under this subparagraph are entitled to precedence in the county court.

(d) ***Notice to Other Parties Required.*** If a Statement of Inability to Afford Payment of Court Costs is filed, the court must provide notice to all other parties that the Statement was filed no later than the next business day. Within 5 days of filing a bond or making a cash deposit, an appellant must serve written notice of the appeal on all other parties using a method approved under Rule 501.4.

(e) ***No Default on Appeal Without Compliance with Rule.*** No judgment may be taken by default against the adverse party in the court to which the case has been appealed without first showing substantial compliance with this rule.

(f) ***Appeal Perfected.*** An appeal is perfected when a bond, cash deposit, or Statement of Inability to Afford Payment of Court Costs is filed in accordance with this rule.

510.10 Record on Appeal; Docketing; Trial de Novo.

(a) ***Preparation and Transmission of Record.*** Unless otherwise provided by law or these rules, when an appeal has been perfected, the judge must stay all further proceedings on the judgment and must immediately send to the clerk of the county court a certified copy of all docket entries, a certified copy of the bill of costs, and the original papers in the case together with any money in the court registry, including sums tendered pursuant to Rule 510.9(c)(5)(B).

(b) ***Docketing; Notice.*** The county clerk must docket the case and must immediately notify the parties of the date of receipt of the transcript and the docket number of the case. The notice must advise the defendant that it must file a written answer in the county court within 8 days if one was not filed in the justice court.

(c) ***Trial de Novo.*** The case must be tried de novo in the county court. A trial de novo is a new trial in which the entire case is presented as if there had been no previous trial. The trial, as well as any hearings and motions, is entitled to precedence in the county court.

510.11 Damages on Appeal. On the trial of the case in the county court the appellant or appellee will be permitted to plead, prove and recover his damages, if any, suffered for withholding or defending possession of the premises during the pendency of the appeal. Damages may include but are not limited to loss of rentals during the pendency of the appeal and attorney fees in the justice and county courts provided, as to attorney fees, that the requirements of Section 24.006 of the Texas Property Code have been met. Only the party prevailing in the county court will be entitled to recover damages against the adverse party. The prevailing party will also be entitled to recover court costs and to recover against the sureties on the appeal bond in cases where the adverse party has executed an appeal bond.

510.12 Judgment by Default on Appeal. An eviction case appealed to county court will be subject to trial at any time after the expiration of 8 days after the date the transcript is filed in the county court. If the defendant has filed a written answer in the justice court, it must be taken to constitute his appearance and answer in the county court and may be amended as in other cases. If the defendant made no answer in writing in the justice court and fails to file a written answer

within 8 days after the transcript is filed in the county court, the allegations of the complaint may be taken as admitted and judgment by default may be entered accordingly.

510.13 **Writ of Possession on Appeal.** The writ of possession, or execution, or both, will be issued by the clerk of the county court according to the judgment rendered, and the same will be executed by the sheriff or constable, as in other cases. The judgment of the county court may not be stayed unless within 10 days from the judgment the appellant files a supersedeas bond in an amount set by the county court pursuant to Section 24.007 of the Texas Property Code.

2016 change: Amended eff. Sept. 1, 2016, by order of Aug. 31, 2016 (Tex. Sup.Ct. Order, Misc. Docket No. 16-9122).

TRCP 523 TO 591. REPEALED

Editor's note: Rules 500-507 govern cases filed on or after August 31, 2013, and cases pending on August 31, 2013, unless the court determines that applying those rules to a case pending on August 31, 2013, would not be feasible or would work an injustice; in such a case, the procedure under the former rules applies. An action taken before August 31, 2013, in a case pending on August 31, 2013, that was done under any previously applicable procedure is treated as valid. If citation or other process was issued or served before August 31, 2013, in compliance with any previously applicable procedure, the party served has the time provided for under the former procedure to answer or otherwise respond. For the substance of the former rules and a comprehensive history of the amendments and repealers to those rules, see *O'Connor's Texas Rules * Civil Trials* (2013), p. 1031.

PART VI. RULES RELATING TO ANCILLARY PROCEEDINGS

SECTION 1. ATTACHMENT

TRCP 592. APPLICATION FOR WRIT OF ATTACHMENT & ORDER

Either at the commencement of a suit or at any time during its progress the plaintiff may file an application for the issuance of a writ of attachment. Such application shall be supported by affidavits of the plaintiff, his agent, his attorney, or other persons having knowledge of relevant facts. The application shall comply with all statutory requirements and shall state the grounds for issuing the writ and the specific facts relied upon by the plaintiff to warrant the required findings by the court. The writ shall not be quashed because two or more grounds are stated conjunctively or disjunctively. The application and any affidavits shall be made on personal knowledge and shall set forth such facts as would be admissible in evidence; provided that facts may be stated based upon information and belief if the grounds of such belief are specifically stated.

No writ shall issue except upon written order of the court after a hearing, which may be ex parte. The court, in its order granting the application, shall make specific findings of facts to support the statutory grounds found to exist, and shall specify the maximum value of property that may be attached, and the amount of bond required of plaintiff, and, further shall command that the attached property be kept safe and preserved subject to further orders of the court. Such bond shall be in an amount which, in the opinion of the court, will adequately compensate the defendant in the event plaintiff fails to prosecute his suit to effect, and to pay all damages and costs which may be adjudged against him for wrongfully suing out the writ of attachment. The court shall further find in its order the amount of bond required of defendant to replevy, which, unless the defendant chooses to exercise his option as provided in Rule 599, shall be the amount of plaintiff's claim, one year's accrual of interest if allowed by law on the claim, and the estimated costs of court. The order may direct the issuance of several writs at the same time, or in succession, to be sent to different counties.

TRCP 592a. BOND FOR ATTACHMENT

No writ of attachment shall issue until the party applying therefor has filed with the officer authorized to issue such writ a bond payable to the defendant in the amount fixed by the court's order, with sufficient surety or sureties as provided by statute to be approved by such officer, conditioned that the plaintiff will prosecute his suit to effect and pay to the extent of the penal amount of the bond all damages and costs as may be adjudged against him for wrongfully suing out such writ of attachment.

After notice to the opposite party, either before or after the issuance of the writ, the defendant or plaintiff may file a motion to increase or reduce the amount of such bond, or to question the sufficiency of the sureties thereon, in the court in which such suit is pending. Upon hearing, the court shall enter its order with respect to such bond and sufficiency of the sureties.

TRCP 592b. FORM OF ATTACHMENT BOND

The following form of bond may be used:

"The State of Texas,

County of ________,

"We, the undersigned, ________ as principal, and ________ and ________ as sureties, acknowledge ourselves bound to pay to C.D. the sum of ________ dollars, conditioned that the above bound

plaintiff in attachment against the said C.D., defendant, will prosecute his said suit to effect, and that he will pay all such damages and costs to the extent of the penal amount of this bond as shall be adjudged against him for wrongfully suing out such attachment. Witness our hands this ___ day of ________, 20__."

TRCP 593. REQUISITES FOR WRIT

A writ of attachment shall be directed to the sheriff or any constable within the State of Texas. It shall command him to attach and hold, unless replevied, subject to the further order of the court, so much of the property of the defendant, of a reasonable value in approximately the amount fixed by the court, as shall be found within his county.

TRCP 594. FORM OF WRIT

The following form of writ may be issued:

"The State of Texas.

"To the Sheriff or any Constable of any County of the State of Texas, greeting:

"We command you that you attach forthwith so much of the property of C.D., if it be found in your county, repleviable on security, as shall be of value sufficient to make the sum of ________ dollars, and the probable costs of suit, to satisfy the demand of A.B., and that you keep and secure in your hands the property so attached, unless replevied, that the same may be liable to further proceedings thereon to be had before our court in ________, County of ________. You will true return make of this writ on or before 10 a.m. of Monday, the ________ day of ________, 20___, showing how you have executed the same."

TRCP 595. SEVERAL WRITS

Several writs of attachment may, at the option of the plaintiff, be issued at the same time, or in succession, and sent to different counties, until sufficient property shall be attached to satisfy the writ.

TRCP 596. DELIVERY OF WRIT

The writ of attachment shall be dated and tested as other writs, and may be delivered to the sheriff or constable by the officer issuing it, or he may deliver it to the plaintiff, his agent or attorney, for that purpose.

TRCP 597. DUTY OF OFFICER

The sheriff or constable receiving the writ shall immediately proceed to execute the same by levying upon so much of the property of the defendant subject to the writ, and found within his county, as may be sufficient to satisfy the command of the writ.

TRCP 598. LEVY, HOW MADE

The writ of attachment shall be levied in the same manner as is, or may be, the writ of execution upon similar property.

TRCP 598a. SERVICE OF WRIT ON DEFENDANT

The defendant shall be served in any manner prescribed for service of citation, or as provided in Rule 21a, with a copy of the writ of attachment, the application, accompanying affidavits, and orders of the court as soon as practicable following the levy of the writ. There shall be prominently displayed on the face of the copy of the writ served on the defendant, in ten-point type and in a manner calculated to advise a reasonably attentive person of its contents, the following:

"To ________, Defendant:

You are hereby notified that certain properties alleged to be owned by you have been attached. If you claim any rights in such property, you are advised:

"YOU HAVE A RIGHT TO REGAIN POSSESSION OF THE PROPERTY BY FILING A REPLEVY BOND. YOU HAVE A RIGHT TO SEEK TO REGAIN POSSESSION OF THE PROPERTY BY FILING WITH THE COURT A MOTION TO DISSOLVE THIS WRIT."

TRCP 599. DEFENDANT MAY REPLEVY

At any time before judgment, should the attached property not have been previously claimed or sold, the defendant may replevy the same, or any part thereof, or the proceeds from the sale of the property if it has been sold under order of the court, by giving bond with sufficient surety or sureties as provided by statute, to be approved by the officer who levied the writ, payable to plaintiff, in the amount fixed by the court's order, or, at the defendant's option, for the value of the property sought to be replevied (to be estimated by the officer), plus one year's interest thereon at the legal rate from the date of the bond, conditioned that the defendant shall satisfy, to the extent of the penal amount of the bond, any judgment which may be rendered against him in such action.

On reasonable notice to the opposing party (which may be less than three days) either party shall have the right to prompt judicial review of the amount of bond required, denial of bond, sufficiency of sureties, and esti-

mated value of the property, by the court which authorized issuance of the writ. The court's determination may be made upon the basis of affidavits, if uncontroverted, setting forth such facts as would be admissible in evidence; otherwise, the parties shall submit evidence. The court shall forthwith enter its order either approving or modifying the requirements of the officer or of the court's prior order, and such order of the court shall supersede and control with respect to such matters.

On reasonable notice to the opposing party (which may be less than three days) the defendant shall have the right to move the court for a substitution of property, of equal value as that attached, for the property attached. Provided that there has been located sufficient property of the defendants to satisfy the order of attachment, the court may authorize substitution of one or more items of defendant's property for all or for part of the property attached. The court shall first make findings as to the value of the property to be substituted. If property is substituted, the property released from attachment shall be delivered to defendant, if such property is personal property, and all liens upon such property from the original order of attachment or modification thereof shall be terminated. Attachment of substituted property shall be deemed to have existed from the date of levy on the original property attached, and no property on which liens have become affixed since the date of levy on the original property may be substituted.

TRCP 600. SALE OF PERISHABLE PROPERTY

Whenever personal property which has been attached shall not have been claimed or replevied, the judge, or justice of the peace, out of whose court the writ was issued, may, either in term time or in vacation, order the same to be sold, when it shall be made to appear that such property is in danger of serious and immediate waste or decay, or that the keeping of the same until the trial will necessarily be attended with such expense or deterioration in value as greatly to lessen the amount likely to be realized therefrom.

TRCP 601. TO PROTECT INTERESTS

In determining whether the property attached is perishable, and the necessity or advantage of ordering a sale thereof, the judge or justice of the peace may act upon affidavits in writing or oral testimony, and may by a preliminary order entered of record, with or without notice to the parties as the urgency of the case in his opinion requires, direct the sheriff or constable to sell such property at public auction for cash, and thereupon the officer shall sell it accordingly.

TRCP 602. BOND OF APPLICANT FOR SALE

If the application for an order of sale be filed by any person or party other than the defendant from whose possession the property was taken by levy, the court shall not grant such order unless the applicant shall file with such court a bond payable to such defendant, with two or more good and sufficient sureties, to be approved by said court, conditioned that they will be responsible to the defendant for such damages as he may sustain in case such sale be illegally and unjustly applied for, or be illegally and unjustly made.

TRCP 603. PROCEDURE FOR SALE

Such sale of attached perishable personal property shall be conducted in the same manner as sales of personal property under execution; provided, however, that the time of the sale, and at the time of advertisement thereof, may be fixed by the judge or justice of the peace at a time earlier than ten days, according to the exigency of the case, and in such event notice thereof shall be given in such manner as directed by the order.

TRCP 604. RETURN OF SALE

The officer making such sale of perishable property shall promptly pay the proceeds of such sale to the clerk of such court or justice of the peace, as the case may be, and shall make written return of the order of sale signed by him officially, stating the time and place of the sale, the name of the purchaser, and the amount of money received, with an itemized account of the expenses attending the sale. Such return shall be filed with the papers of the case.

TRCP 605. JUDGE MAY MAKE NECESSARY ORDERS

When the perishable personal property levied on under the attachment writ has not been claimed or replevied, the judge or justice of the peace may make such orders, either in term time or vacation, as may be necessary for its preservation or use.

TRCP 606. RETURN OF WRIT

The officer executing the writ of attachment shall return the writ, with his action endorsed thereon, or attached thereto, signed by him officially, to the court from which it issued, at or before 10 o'clock a.m. of the Monday next after the expiration of fifteen days from

the date of issuance of the writ. Such return shall describe the property attached with sufficient certainty to identify it, and state when the same was attached, and whether any personal property attached remains still in his hands, and, if not, the disposition made of the same. When property has been replevied he shall deliver the replevy bond to the clerk or justice of the peace to be filed with the papers of the cause.

TRCP 607. REPORT OF DISPOSITION OF PROPERTY

When the property levied on is claimed, replevied or sold, or otherwise disposed of after the writ has been returned, the officer having the custody of the same shall immediately make a report in writing, signed by him officially, to the clerk, or justice of the peace, as the case may be, showing such disposition of the property. Such report shall be filed among the papers of the cause.

TRCP 608. DISSOLUTION OR MODIFICATION OF WRIT OF ATTACHMENT

A defendant whose property has been attached or any intervening party who claims an interest in such property, may by sworn written motion, seek to vacate, dissolve, or modify the writ, and the order directing its issuance, for any grounds or cause, extrinsic or intrinsic. Such motion shall admit or deny each finding of the order directing the issuance of the writ except where the movant is unable to admit or deny the finding, in which case movant shall set forth the reasons why he cannot admit or deny. Unless the parties agree to an extension of time, the motion shall be heard promptly, after reasonable notice to the plaintiff (which may be less than three days), and the issue shall be determined not later than ten days after the motion is filed. The filing of the motion shall stay any further proceedings under the writ, except for any orders concerning the care, preservation, or sale of perishable property, until a hearing is had and the issue is determined. The writ shall be dissolved unless at such hearing, the plaintiff shall prove the grounds relied upon for its issuance, but the court may modify its previous order granting the writ and the writ issued pursuant thereto. The movant shall, however, have the burden to prove that the reasonable value of the property attached exceeds the amount necessary to secure the debt, interest for one year, and probable costs. He shall also have the burden to prove the facts to justify substitution of property.

The court's determination may be made upon the basis of affidavits, if uncontroverted, setting forth such facts as would be admissible in evidence; otherwise, the parties shall submit evidence. The court may make all such orders, including orders concerning the care, preservation, or disposition of the property (or the proceeds therefrom if the same has been sold), as justice may require. If the movant has given a replevy bond, an order to vacate or dissolve the writ shall vacate the replevy bond and discharge the sureties thereon, and if the court modifies its order or the writ issued pursuant thereto, it shall make such further orders with respect to the bond as may be consistent with its modification.

TRCP 609. AMENDMENT

Clerical errors in the affidavit, bond, or writ of attachment, or the officer's return thereof, may upon application in writing to the judge or justice of the court in which the suit is filed, and after notice to the opponent, be amended in such manner and on such terms as the judge or justice shall authorize by an order entered in the minutes of the court or noted on the docket of the justice of the peace, provided the amendment does not change or add to the grounds of such attachment as stated in the affidavit, and provided such amendment appears to the judge or justice to be in furtherance of justice.

SECTION 2. DISTRESS WARRANT

TRCP 610. APPLICATION FOR DISTRESS WARRANT & ORDER

Either at the commencement of a suit or at any time during its progress the plaintiff may file an application for the issuance of a distress warrant with the justice of the peace. Such application may be supported by affidavits of the plaintiff, his agent, his attorney, or other persons having knowledge of relevant facts, but shall include a statement that the amount sued for is rent, or advances described by statute, or shall produce a writing signed by the tenant to that effect, and shall further swear that such warrant is not sued out for the purpose of vexing and harassing the defendant. The application shall comply with all statutory requirements and shall state the grounds for issuing the warrant and the specific facts relied upon by the plaintiff to warrant the required findings by the justice of the peace. The warrant shall not be quashed because two or more grounds are stated conjunctively or disjunctively. The application and any affidavits shall be made on personal knowledge

and shall set forth such facts as would be admissible in evidence provided that facts may be stated based upon information and belief if the grounds of such belief are specifically stated.

No warrant shall issue before final judgment except on written order of the justice of the peace after a hearing, which may be ex parte. Such warrant shall be made returnable to a court having jurisdiction of the amount in controversy. The justice of the peace in his order granting the application shall make specific findings of fact to support the statutory grounds found to exist, and shall specify the maximum value of property that may be seized, and the amount of bond required of plaintiff, and, further shall command that property be kept safe and preserved subject to further orders of the court having jurisdiction. Such bond shall be in an amount which, in the opinion of the court, shall adequately compensate defendant in the event plaintiff fails to prosecute his suit to effect, and pay all damages and costs as shall be adjudged against him for wrongfully suing out the warrant. The justice of the peace shall further find in his order the amount of bond required to replevy, which, unless the defendant chooses to exercise his option as provided in Rule 614, shall be the amount of plaintiff's claim, one year's accrual of interest if allowed by law on the claim, and the estimated costs of court. The order may direct the issuance of several warrants at the same time, or in succession, to be sent to different counties.

TRCP 611. BOND FOR DISTRESS WARRANT

No distress warrant shall issue before final judgment until the party applying therefor has filed with the justice of the peace authorized to issue such warrant a bond payable to the defendant in an amount approved by the justice of the peace, with sufficient surety or sureties as provided by statute, conditioned that the plaintiff will prosecute his suit to effect and pay all damages and costs as may be adjudged against him for wrongfully suing out such warrant.

After notice to the opposite party, either before or after the issuance of the warrant, the defendant or plaintiff may file a motion to increase or reduce the amount of such bond, or to question the sufficiency of the sureties thereon, in a court having jurisdiction of the subject matter. Upon hearing, the court shall enter its order with respect to such bond and sufficiency of the sureties.

TRCP 612. REQUISITES FOR WARRANT

A distress warrant shall be directed to the sheriff or any constable within the State of Texas. It shall command him to attach and hold, unless replevied, subject to the further orders of the court having jurisdiction, so much of the property of the defendant, not exempt by statute, of reasonable value in approximately the amount fixed by the justice of the peace, as shall be found within his county.

TRCP 613. SERVICE OF WARRANT ON DEFENDANT

The defendant shall be served in any manner prescribed for service of citation, or as provided in Rule 21a, with a copy of the distress warrant, the application, accompanying affidavits, and orders of the justice of the peace as soon as practicable following the levy of the warrant. There shall be prominently displayed on the face of the copy of the warrant served on the defendant, in 10-point type and in a manner calculated to advise a reasonably attentive person of its contents, the following:

To __________, Defendant:

You are hereby notified that certain properties alleged to be owned by you have been seized. If you claim any rights in such property, you are advised:

"YOU HAVE A RIGHT TO REGAIN POSSESSION OF THE PROPERTY BY FILING A REPLEVY BOND. YOU HAVE A RIGHT TO SEEK TO REGAIN POSSESSION OF THE PROPERTY BY FILING WITH THE COURT A MOTION TO DISSOLVE THIS WARRANT."

TRCP 614. DEFENDANT MAY REPLEVY

At any time before judgment, should the seized property not have been previously claimed or sold, the defendant may replevy the same, or any part thereof, or the proceeds from the sale of the property if it has been sold under order of the court, by giving bond with sufficient surety or sureties as provided by statute, to be approved by a court having jurisdiction of the amount in controversy payable to plaintiff in double the amount of the plaintiff's debt, or, at the defendant's option for not less than the value of the property sought to be replevied, plus one year's interest thereon at the legal rate from the date of the bond, conditioned that the defendant shall satisfy to the extent of the penal amount of the bond any judgment which may be rendered against him in such action.

On reasonable notice to the opposing party (which may be less than three days) either party shall have the right to prompt judicial review of the amount of bond required, denial of bond, sufficiency of sureties, and estimated value of the property, by a court having jurisdiction of the amount in controversy. The court's determination may be made upon the basis of affidavits if uncontroverted setting forth such facts as would be admissible in evidence, otherwise the parties shall submit evidence. The court shall forthwith enter its order either approving or modifying the requirements of the order of the justice of the peace, and such order of the court shall supersede and control with respect to such matters.

On reasonable notice to the opposing party (which may be less than three days) the defendant shall have the right to move the court for a substitution of property, of equal value as that attached, for the property seized. Provided that there has been located sufficient property of the defendant's to satisfy the order of seizure, the court may authorize substitution of one or more items of defendant's property for all or part of the property seized. The court shall first make findings as to the value of the property to be substituted. If property is substituted, the property released from seizure shall be delivered to defendant, if such property is personal property, and all liens upon such property from the original order of seizure or modification thereof shall be terminated. Seizure of substituted property shall be deemed to have existed from the date of levy on the original property seized, and no property on which liens have become affixed since the date of levy on the original property may be substituted.

TRCP 614a. DISSOLUTION OR MODIFICATION OF DISTRESS WARRANT

A defendant whose property has been seized or any intervening claimant who claims an interest in such property, may by sworn written motion, seek to vacate, dissolve, or modify the seizure, and the order directing its issuance, for any grounds or cause, extrinsic or intrinsic. Such motion shall admit or deny each finding of the order directing the issuance of the warrant except where the movant is unable to admit or deny the finding, in which case movant shall set forth the reasons why he cannot admit or deny. Unless the parties agree to an extension of time, the motion shall be heard promptly, after reasonable notice to the plaintiff (which may be less than three days), and the issue shall be determined not later than 10 days after the motion is filed. The filing of the motion shall stay any further proceedings under the warrant, except for any orders concerning the care, preservation, or sale of any perishable property, until a hearing is had, and the issue is determined. The warrant shall be dissolved unless, at such hearing, the plaintiff shall prove the specific facts alleged and the grounds relied upon for its issuance, but the court may modify the order of the justice of the peace granting the warrant and the warrant issued pursuant thereto. The movant shall however have the burden to prove that the reasonable value of the property seized exceeds the amount necessary to secure the debt, interest for one year, and probable costs. He shall also have the burden to prove the facts to justify substitution of property.

The court's determination may be made upon the basis of affidavits setting forth such facts as would be admissible in evidence, but additional evidence, if tendered by either party shall be received and considered. The court may make all such orders, including orders concerning the care, preservation, or disposition of the property (or the proceeds therefrom if the same has been sold), as justice may require. If the movant has given a replevy bond, an order to vacate or dissolve the warrant shall vacate the replevy bond and discharge the sureties thereon, and if the court modifies the order of the justice of the peace or the warrant issued pursuant thereto, it shall make such further orders with respect to the bond as may be consistent with its modification.

TRCP 615. SALE OF PERISHABLE PROPERTY

Whenever personal property which has been levied on under a distress warrant shall not have been claimed or replevied, the judge, or justice of the peace, to whose court such writ is made returnable may, either in term time or in vacation, order the same to be sold, when it shall be made to appear that such property is in danger of serious and immediate waste or decay, or that the keeping of the same until the trial will necessarily be attended with such expense or deterioration in value as greatly to lessen the amount likely to be realized therefrom.

TRCP 616. TO PROTECT INTERESTS

In determining whether the property levied upon is perishable, and the necessity or advantage of ordering a sale thereof, the judge or justice of the peace may act

upon affidavits in writing or oral testimony, and may by a preliminary order entered of record with or without notice to the parties as the urgency of the case in his opinion requires, direct the sheriff or constable to sell such property at public auction for cash, and thereupon the sheriff or constable shall sell it accordingly. If the application for an order of sale be filed by any person or party other than the defendant from whose possession the property was taken by levy, the court shall not grant such order, unless the applicant shall file with such court a bond payable to such defendant, with two or more good and sufficient sureties, to be approved by said court, conditioned that they will be responsible to the defendant for such damages as he may sustain in case such sale be illegally and unjustly applied for, or be illegally and unjustly made.

TRCP 617. PROCEDURE FOR SALE

Such sale of perishable personal property shall be conducted in the same manner as sales of personal property under execution; provided, however, that the time of the sale, and the time of advertisement thereof, may be fixed by the judge or justice of the peace at a time earlier than ten days, according to the exigency of the case, and in such event notice thereof shall be given in such manner as directed by the order.

TRCP 618. RETURN OF SALE

The officer making such sale of perishable property shall promptly pay the proceeds of such sale to the clerk of such court or to the justice of the peace, as the case may be, and shall make written return of the order of sale, signed by him officially, stating the time and place of the sale, the name of the purchaser, and the amount of money received, with an itemized account of the expenses attending the sale. Such return shall be filed with the papers of the case.

TRCP 619. CITATION FOR DEFENDANT

The justice at the time he issues the warrant shall issue a citation to the defendant requiring him to answer before such justice at the first day of the next succeeding term of court, stating the time and place of holding the same, if he has jurisdiction to finally try the cause, and upon its being returned served, to proceed to judgment as in ordinary cases; and, if he has not such jurisdiction, the citation shall require the defendant to answer before the court to which the warrant was made returnable at or before ten o'clock a.m. of the Monday next after the expiration of twenty days from the date of service thereof, stating the place of holding the court, and shall be returned with the other papers to such court. If the defendant has removed from the county without service, the proper officer shall state this fact in his return on the citation; and the court shall proceed to try the case ex parte, and may enter judgment.

TRCP 620. PETITION

When the warrant is made returnable to the district or county court, the plaintiff shall file his petition within ten days from the date of the issuance of the writ.

SECTION 3. EXECUTIONS

TRCP 621. ENFORCEMENT OF JUDGMENT

The judgments of the district, county, and justice courts shall be enforced by execution or other appropriate process. Such execution or other process shall be returnable in thirty, sixty, or ninety days as requested by the plaintiff, his agent or attorney.

TRCP 621a. DISCOVERY & ENFORCEMENT OF JUDGMENT

At any time after rendition of judgment, and so long as said judgment has not been suspended by a supersedeas bond or by order of a proper court and has not become dormant as provided by Article 3773, V.A.T.S., the successful party may, for the purpose of obtaining information to aid in the enforcement of such judgment, initiate and maintain in the trial court in the same suit in which said judgment was rendered any discovery proceeding authorized by these rules for pre-trial matters. Also, at any time after rendition of judgment, either party may, for the purpose of obtaining information relevant to motions allowed by Texas Rules of Appellate Procedure 47[1] and 49[1] initiate and maintain in the trial court in the same suit in which said judgment was rendered any discovery proceeding authorized by these rules for pre-trial matters. The rules governing and related to such pre-trial discovery proceedings shall apply in like manner to discovery proceedings after judgment. The rights herein granted to the parties shall inure to their successors or assignees, in whole or in part. Judicial supervision of such discovery proceedings after judgment shall be the same as that provided by law or these rules for pre-trial discovery and proceedings insofar as applicable.

1. **Editor's note:** Now TRAP 24.

TRCP 622. EXECUTION

An execution is a process of the court from which it is issued. The clerk of the district or county court or the justice of the peace, as the case may be, shall tax the costs in every case in which a final judgment has been rendered and shall issue execution to enforce such judgment and collect such costs. The execution and subsequent executions shall not be addressed to a particular county, but shall be addressed to any sheriff or any constable within the State of Texas.

TRCP 623. ON DEATH OF EXECUTOR

When an executor, administrator, guardian or trustee of an express trust dies, or ceases to be such executor, administrator, guardian or trustee after judgment, execution shall issue on such judgment in the name of his successor, upon an affidavit of such death or termination being filed with the clerk of the court or the justice of the peace, as the case may be, together with the certificate of the appointment of such successor under the hand and seal of the clerk of the court wherein the appointment was made.

TRCP 624. ON DEATH OF NOMINAL PLAINTIFF

When a person in whose favor a judgment is rendered for the use of another dies after judgment, execution shall issue in the name of the party for whose use the suit was brought upon an affidavit of such death being filed with the clerk of the court or the justice of the peace.

TRCP 625. ON MONEY OF DECEASED

If a sole defendant dies after judgment for money against him, execution shall not issue thereon, but the judgment may be proved up and paid in due course of administration.

TRCP 626. ON PROPERTY OF DECEASED

In any case of judgment other than a money judgment, where the sole defendant, or one or more of several joint defendants, shall die after judgment, upon an affidavit of such death being filed with the clerk, together with the certificate of the appointment of a representative of such decedent under the hand and seal of the clerk of the court wherein such appointment was made, the proper process on such judgment shall issue against such representative.

TRCP 627. TIME FOR ISSUANCE

If no supersedeas bond or notice of appeal, as required of agencies exempt from filing bonds, has been filed and approved, the clerk of the court or justice of the peace shall issue the execution upon such judgment upon application of the successful party or his attorney after the expiration of thirty days from the time a final judgment is signed. If a timely motion for new trial or in arrest of judgment is filed, the clerk shall issue the execution upon the judgment on application of the party or his attorney after the expiration of thirty days from the time the order overruling the motion is signed or from the time the motion is overruled by operation of law.

See also CPRC §§65.013, 65.014.

TRCP 628. EXECUTION WITHIN THIRTY DAYS

Such execution may be issued at any time before the thirtieth day upon the filing of an affidavit by the plaintiff in the judgment or his agent or attorney that the defendant is about to remove his personal property subject to execution by law out of the county, or is about to transfer or secrete such personal property for the purpose of defrauding his creditors.

See also CPRC §§65.013, 65.014.

TRCP 629. REQUISITES OF EXECUTION

The style of the execution shall be "The State of Texas." It shall be directed to any sheriff or any constable within the State of Texas. It shall be signed by the clerk or justice officially, and bear the seal of the court, if issued out of the district or county court, and shall require the officer to execute it according to its terms, and to make the costs which have been adjudged against the defendant in execution and the further costs of executing the writ. It shall describe the judgment, stating the court in which, and the time when, rendered, and the names of the parties in whose favor and against whom the judgment was rendered. A correct copy of the bill of costs taxed against the defendant in execution shall be attached to the writ. It shall require the officer to return it within thirty, sixty, or ninety days, as directed by the plaintiff or his attorney.

See also CPRC §§65.013, 65.014.

TRCP 630. EXECUTION ON JUDGMENT FOR MONEY

When an execution is issued upon a judgment for a sum of money, or directing the payment simply of a sum of money, it must specify in the body thereof the sum re-

covered or directed to be paid and the sum actually due when it is issued and the rate of interest upon the sum due. It must require the officer to satisfy the judgment and costs out of the property of the judgment debtor subject to execution by law.

See also CPRC §§65.013, 65.014.

TRCP 631. EXECUTION FOR SALE OF PARTICULAR PROPERTY

An execution issued upon a judgment for the sale of particular chattels or personal property or real estate, must particularly describe the property, and shall direct the officer to make the sale by previously giving the public notice of the time and place of sale required by law and these rules.

See also CPRC §§65.013, 65.014.

TRCP 632. EXECUTION FOR DELIVERY OF CERTAIN PROPERTY

An execution issued upon a judgment for the delivery of the possession of a chattel or personal property, or for the delivery of the possession of real property, shall particularly describe the property, and designate the party to whom the judgment awards the possession. The writ shall require the officer to deliver the possession of the property to the party entitled thereto.

See also CPRC §§65.013, 65.014.

TRCP 633. EXECUTION FOR POSSESSION OR VALUE OF PERSONAL PROPERTY

If the judgment be for the recovery of personal property or its value, the writ shall command the officer, in case a delivery thereof cannot be had, to levy and collect the value thereof for which the judgment was recovered, to be specified therein, out of any property of the party against whom judgment was rendered, liable to execution.

See also CPRC §§65.013, 65.014.

TRCP 634. EXECUTION SUPERSEDED

The clerk or justice of the peace shall immediately issue a writ of supersedeas suspending all further proceedings under any execution previously issued when a supersedeas bond is afterward filed and approved within the time prescribed by law or these rules.

See also CPRC §§65.013, 65.014.

TRCP 635. STAY OF EXECUTION IN JUSTICE COURT

At any time within ten days after the rendition of any judgment in a justice court, the justice may grant a stay of execution thereof for three months from the date of such judgment, if the person against whom such judgment was rendered shall, with one or more good and sufficient sureties, to be approved by the justice, appear before him and acknowledge themselves and each of them bound to the successful party in such judgment for the full amount thereof, with interest and costs, which acknowledgment shall be entered in writing on the docket, and signed by the persons binding themselves as sureties; provided, no such stay of execution shall be granted unless the party applying therefor shall first file an affidavit with the justice that he has not the money with which to pay such judgment, and that the enforcement of same by execution prior to three months would be a hardship upon him and would cause a sacrifice of his property which would not likely be caused should said execution be stayed. Such acknowledgment shall be entered by the justice on his docket and shall constitute a judgment against the defendant and such sureties, upon which execution shall issue in case the same is not paid on or before the expiration of such day.

See also CPRC §§65.013, 65.014.

TRCP 636. INDORSEMENTS BY OFFICER

The officer receiving the execution shall indorse thereon the exact hour and day when he received it. If he receives more than one on the same day against the same person he shall number them as received.

TRCP 637. LEVY OF EXECUTION

When an execution is delivered to an officer he shall proceed without delay to levy the same upon the property of the defendant found within his county not exempt from execution, unless otherwise directed by the plaintiff, his agent or attorney. The officer shall first call upon the defendant, if he can be found, or, if absent, upon his agent within the county, if known, to point out property to be levied upon, and the levy shall first be made upon the property designated by the defendant, or his agent. If in the opinion of the officer the property so designated will not sell for enough to satisfy the execution and costs of sale, he shall require an additional designation by the defendant. If no property be thus designated by the defendant, the officer shall levy the execution upon any property of the defendant subject to execution.

TRCP 638. PROPERTY NOT TO BE DESIGNATED

A defendant in execution shall not point out property which he has sold, mortgaged or conveyed in trust, or property exempt from forced sale.

TRCP 639. LEVY

In order to make a levy on real estate, it shall not be necessary for the officer to go upon the ground but it shall be sufficient for him to indorse such levy on the writ. Levy upon personal property is made by taking possession thereof, when the defendant in execution is entitled to the possession. Where the defendant in execution has an interest in personal property, but is not entitled to the possession thereof, a levy is made thereon by giving notice thereof to the person who is entitled to the possession, or one of them where there are several.

TRCP 640. LEVY ON STOCK RUNNING AT LARGE

A levy upon livestock running at large in a range, and which cannot be herded and penned without great inconvenience and expense, may be made by designating by reasonable estimate the number of animals and describing them by their marks and brands, or either; such levy shall be made in the presence of two or more credible persons, and notice thereof shall be given in writing to the owner or his herder or agent, if residing within the county and known to the officer.

TRCP 641. LEVY ON SHARES OF STOCK

A levy upon shares of stock of any corporation or joint stock company for which a certificate is outstanding is made by the officer seizing and taking possession of such certificate. Provided, however, that nothing herein shall be construed as restricting any rights granted under Section 8.317[1] of the Texas Uniform Commercial Code.

1. **Editor's note:** Deleted by Acts 1995, 74th Leg., ch. 962, §1, eff. Sept. 1, 1995. See Bus. & Com. Code §8.112.

TRCP 642. REPEALED

TRCP 643. LEVY ON GOODS PLEDGED OR MORTGAGED

Goods and chattels pledged, assigned or mortgaged as security for any debt or contract, may be levied upon and sold on execution against the person making the pledge, assignment or mortgage subject thereto; and the purchaser shall be entitled to the possession when it is held by the pledgee, assignee or mortgagee, on complying with the conditions of the pledge, assignment or mortgage.

ANNOTATIONS

Conseco Fin. Servicing Corp. v. J&J Mobile Homes, Inc., 120 S.W.3d 878, 886 (Tex.App.—Fort Worth 2003, pet. denied). "[P] reasons that under [TRCP] 643 a tax lien is the equivalent of a judicial lien created when an officer levies upon personal property under a writ of execution. [P] argues a tax lien is therefore subordinate to a security interest noted on the certificate of title. We disagree. [P] ignores the fact that tax liens are, by statute, given express priority status over security interests noted on certificates of title."

Grocers Sup. v. Intercity Inv. Props., 795 S.W.2d 225, 227 (Tex.App.—Houston [14th Dist.] 1990, no writ). "[T]he right of … a prior secured creditor, to take possession of its collateral was superior to the right of … a mere judgment creditor, and [the prior secured creditor] could regain possession of the collateral from the constable who had levied on the property."

TRCP 644. MAY GIVE DELIVERY BOND

Any personal property taken in execution may be returned to the defendant by the officer upon the delivery by the defendant to him of a bond, payable to the plaintiff, with two or more good and sufficient sureties, to be approved by the officer, conditioned that the property shall be delivered to the officer at the time and place named in the bond, to be sold according to law, or for the payment to the officer of a fair value thereof, which shall be stated in the bond.

TRCP 645. PROPERTY MAY BE SOLD BY DEFENDANT

Where property has been replevied, as provided in the preceding rule, the defendant may sell or dispose of the same, paying the officer the stipulated value thereof.

TRCP 646. FORFEITED DELIVERY BOND

In case of the non-delivery of the property according to the terms of the delivery bond, and non-payment of the value thereof, the officer shall forthwith indorse

the bond "Forfeited" and return the same to the clerk of the court or the justice of the peace from which the execution issued; whereupon, if the judgment remain unsatisfied in whole or in part, the clerk or justice shall issue execution against the principal debtor and the sureties on the bond for the amount due, not exceeding the stipulated value of the property, upon which execution no delivery bond shall be taken, which instruction shall be indorsed by the clerk or justice on the execution.

TRCP 646a. SALE OF REAL PROPERTY

Real property taken by virtue of any execution shall be sold at public auction, at the courthouse door of the county, unless the court orders that such sale be at the place where the real property is situated, on the first Tuesday of the month, between the hours of ten o'clock, a.m. and four o'clock, p.m.

TRCP 647. NOTICE OF SALE OF REAL ESTATE

The time and place of sale of real estate under execution, order of sale, or venditioni exponas, shall be advertised by the officer by having the notice thereof published in the English language once a week for three consecutive weeks preceding such sale, in some newspaper published in said county. The first of said publications shall appear not less than twenty days immediately preceding the day of sale. Said notice shall contain a statement of the authority by virtue of which the sale is to be made, the time of levy, and the time and place of sale; it shall also contain a brief description of the property to be sold, and shall give the number of acres, original survey, locality in the county, and the name by which the land is most generally known, but it shall not be necessary for it to contain field notes. Publishers of newspapers shall charge the legal rate of Two (2) Cents per word for the first insertion of such publication and One (1) Cent per word for such subsequent insertions, or such newspapers shall be entitled to charge for such publication at a rate equal to but not in excess of the published word or line rate of that newspaper for such class of advertising. If there be no newspaper published in the county, or none which will publish the notice of sale for the compensation herein fixed, the officer shall then post such notice in writing in three public places in the county, one of which shall be at the courthouse door of such county, for at least twenty days successively next before the day of sale. The officer making the levy shall give the defendant, or his attorney, written notice of such sale, either in person or by mail, which notice shall substantially conform to the foregoing requirements.

TRCP 648. "COURTHOUSE DOOR" DEFINED

By the term "courthouse door" of a county is meant either of the principal entrances to the house provided by the proper authority for the holding of the district court. If from any cause there is no such house, the door of the house where the district court was last held in that county shall be deemed to be the courthouse door. Where the courthouse, or house used by the court, has been destroyed by fire or other cause, and another has not been designated by the proper authority, the place where such house stood shall be deemed to be the courthouse door.

TRCP 649. SALE OF PERSONAL PROPERTY

Personal property levied on under execution shall be offered for sale on the premises where it is taken in execution, or at the courthouse door of the county, or at some other place if, owing to the nature of the property, it is more convenient to exhibit it to purchasers at such place. Personal property susceptible of being exhibited shall not be sold unless the same be present and subject to the view of those attending the sale, except shares of stock in joint stock or incorporated companies, and in cases where the defendant in execution has merely an interest without right to the exclusive possession in which case the interest of defendant may be sold and conveyed without the presence or delivery of the property. When a levy is made upon livestock running at large on the range, it is not necessary that such stock, or any part thereof, be present at the place of sale, and the purchaser at such sale is authorized to gather and pen such stock and select therefrom the number purchased by him.

TRCP 650. NOTICE OF SALE OF PERSONAL PROPERTY

Previous notice of the time and place of the sale of any personal property levied on under execution shall be given by posting notice thereof for ten days successively immediately prior to the day of sale at the courthouse door of any county and at the place where the sale is to be made.

TRCP 651. WHEN EXECUTION NOT SATISFIED

When the property levied upon does not sell for enough to satisfy the execution, the officer shall proceed anew, as in the first instance, to make the residue.

TRCP 652. PURCHASER FAILING TO COMPLY

If any person shall bid off property at any sale made by virtue of an execution, and shall fail to comply with the terms of the sale, he shall be liable to pay the plaintiff in execution twenty per cent on the value of the property thus bid off, besides costs, to be recovered on motion, five days notice of such motion being given to such purchaser; and should the property on a second sale bring less than on the former, he shall be liable to pay to the defendant in execution all loss which he sustains thereby, to be recovered on motion as above provided.

TRCP 653. RESALE OF PROPERTY

When the terms of the sale shall not be complied with by the bidder the levying officer shall proceed to sell the same property again on the same day, if there be sufficient time; but if not, he shall readvertise and sell the same as in the first instance.

TRCP 654. RETURN OF EXECUTION

The levying officer shall make due return of the execution, in writing and signed by him officially, stating concisely what such officer has done in pursuance of the requirements of the writ and of the law. The return shall be filed with the clerk of the court or the justice of the peace as the case may be. The execution shall be returned forthwith if satisfied by the collection of the money or if ordered by the plaintiff or his attorney indorsed thereon.

TRCP 655. RETURN OF EXECUTION BY MAIL

When an execution is placed in the hands of an officer of a county other than the one in which the judgment is rendered, return may be made by mail; but money cannot be thus sent except by direction of the party entitled to receive the same or his attorney of record.

TRCP 656. EXECUTION DOCKET

The clerk of each court shall keep an execution docket in which he shall enter a statement of all executions as they are issued by him, specifying the names of the parties, the amount of the judgment, the amount due thereon, the rate of interest when it exceeds six per cent, the costs, the date of issuing the execution, to whom delivered, and the return of the officer thereon, with the date of such return. Such docket entries shall be taken and deemed to be a record. The clerk shall keep an index and cross-index to the execution docket. When execution is in favor or against several persons, it shall be indexed in the name of each person. Any clerk who shall fail to keep said execution docket and index thereto, or shall neglect to make the entries therein, shall be liable upon his official bond to any person injured for the amount of damages sustained by such neglect.

SECTION 4. GARNISHMENT

TRCP 657. JUDGMENT FINAL FOR GARNISHMENT

In the case mentioned in subsection 3, section 63.001, Civil Practice and Remedies Code, the judgment whether based upon a liquidated demand or an unliquidated demand, shall be deemed final and subsisting for the purpose of garnishment from and after the date it is signed, unless a supersedeas bond shall have been approved and filed in accordance with Texas Rules of Appellate Procedure 47.[1]

1. Editor's note: Now TRAP 24.

TRCP 658. APPLICATION FOR WRIT OF GARNISHMENT & ORDER

Either at the commencement of a suit or at any time during its progress the plaintiff may file an application for a writ of garnishment. Such application shall be supported by affidavits of the plaintiff, his agent, his attorney, or other person having knowledge of relevant facts. The application shall comply with all statutory requirements and shall state the grounds for issuing the writ and the specific facts relied upon by the plaintiff to warrant the required findings by the court. The writ shall not be quashed because two or more grounds are stated conjunctively or disjunctively. The application and any affidavits shall be made on personal knowledge and shall set forth such facts as would be admissible in evidence; provided that facts may be stated based upon information and belief if the grounds of such belief are specifically stated.

No writ shall issue before final judgment except upon written order of the court after a hearing, which may be ex parte. The court in its order granting the application shall make specific findings of facts to support

the statutory grounds found to exist, and shall specify the maximum value of property or indebtedness that may be garnished and the amount of bond required of plaintiff. Such bond shall be in an amount which, in the opinion of the court, shall adequately compensate defendant in the event plaintiff fails to prosecute his suit to effect, and pay all damages and costs as shall be adjudged against him for wrongfully suing out the writ of garnishment. The court shall further find in its order the amount of bond required of defendant to replevy, which, unless defendant exercises his option as provided under Rule 664, shall be the amount of plaintiff's claim, one year's accrual of interest if allowed by law on the claim, and the estimated costs of court. The order may direct the issuance of several writs at the same time, or in succession, to be sent to different counties.

TRCP 658a. BOND FOR GARNISHMENT

No writ of garnishment shall issue before final judgment until the party applying therefor has filed with the officer authorized to issue such writ a bond payable to the defendant in the amount fixed by the court's order, with sufficient surety or sureties as provided by statute, conditioned that the plaintiff will prosecute his suit to effect and pay to the extent of the penal amount of the bond all damages and costs as may be adjudged against him for wrongfully suing out such writ of garnishment.

After notice to the opposite party, either before or after the issuance of the writ, the defendant or plaintiff may file a motion to increase or reduce the amount of such bond, or to question the sufficiency of the sureties. Upon hearing, the court shall enter its order with respect to such bond and the sufficiency of the sureties.

Should it be determined from the garnishee's answer if such is not controverted that the garnishee is indebted to the defendant, or has in his hands effects belonging to the defendant, in an amount or value less than the amount of the debt claimed by the plaintiff, then after notice to the defendant the court in which such garnishment is pending upon hearing may reduce the required amount of such bond to double the sum of the garnishee's indebtedness to the defendant plus the value of the effects in his hands belonging to the defendant.

TRCP 659. CASE DOCKETED

When the foregoing requirements of these rules have been complied with, the judge, or clerk, or justice of the peace, as the case may be, shall docket the case in the name of the plaintiff as plaintiff and of the garnishee as defendant; and shall immediately issue a writ of garnishment directed to the garnishee, commanding him to appear before the court out of which the same is issued at or before 10 o'clock a.m. of the Monday next following the expiration of twenty days from the date the writ was served, if the writ is issued out of the district or county court; or the Monday next after the expiration of ten days from the date the writ was served, if the writ is issued out of the justice court. The writ shall command the garnishee to answer under oath upon such return date what, if anything, he is indebted to the defendant, and was when the writ was served, and what effects, if any, of the defendant he has in his possession, and had when such writ was served, and what other persons, if any, within his knowledge, are indebted to the defendant or have effects belonging to him in their possession.

TRCP 660. REPEALED

TRCP 661. FORM OF WRIT

The following form of writ may be used:

"The State of Texas.

To E.F., Garnishee, greeting:

"Whereas, in the ______ Court of ____________ County (if a justice court, state also the number of the precinct), in a certain cause wherein A.B. is plaintiff and C.D. is defendant, the plaintiff, claiming an indebtedness against the said C.D. of ___________ dollars, besides interest and costs of suit, has applied for a writ of garnishment against you, E.F.; therefore you are hereby commanded to be and appear before said court at __________ in said county (if the writ is issued from the county or district court, here proceed: 'at 10 o'clock a.m. on the Monday next following the expiration of twenty days from the date of service hereof.' If the writ is issued from a justice of the peace court, here proceed: 'at or before 10 o'clock a.m. on the Monday next after the expiration of ten days from the date of service hereof.' In either event, proceed as follows:) then and there to answer upon oath what, if anything, you are indebted to the said C.D., and were when this writ was served upon you, and what effects, if any, of the said C.D. you have in your possession, and had when this writ was served, and what other persons, if any, within your knowledge, are indebted to the said C.D. or have effects belonging to him in their possession. You are further commanded NOT to pay to defendant any debt

or to deliver to him any effects, pending further order of this court. Herein fail not, but make due answer as the law directs."

TRCP 662. DELIVERY OF WRIT

The writ of garnishment shall be dated and tested as other writs, and may be delivered to the sheriff or constable by the officer who issued it, or he may deliver it to the plaintiff, his agent or attorney, for that purpose.

TRCP 663. EXECUTION & RETURN OF WRIT

The sheriff or constable receiving the writ of garnishment shall immediately proceed to execute the same by delivering a copy thereof to the garnishee, and shall make return thereof as of other citations.

TRCP 663a. SERVICE OF WRIT ON DEFENDANT

The defendant shall be served in any manner prescribed for service of citation or as provided in Rule 21a with a copy of the writ of garnishment, the application, accompanying affidavits and orders of the court as soon as practicable following the service of the writ. There shall be prominently displayed on the face of the copy of the writ served on the defendant, in ten-point type and in a manner calculated to advise a reasonably attentive person of its contents, the following:

"To __________, Defendant:

"You are hereby notified that certain properties alleged to be owned by you have been garnished. If you claim any rights in such property, you are advised:

"YOU HAVE A RIGHT TO REGAIN POSSESSION OF THE PROPERTY BY FILING A REPLEVY BOND. YOU HAVE A RIGHT TO SEEK TO REGAIN POSSESSION OF THE PROPERTY BY FILING WITH THE COURT A MOTION TO DISSOLVE THIS WRIT."

TRCP 664. DEFENDANT MAY REPLEVY

At any time before judgment, should the garnished property not have been previously claimed or sold, the defendant may replevy the same, or any part thereof, or the proceeds from the sale of the property if it has been sold under order of the court, by giving bond with sufficient surety or sureties as provided by statute, to be approved by the officer who levied the writ, payable to plaintiff, in the amount fixed by the court's order, or, at the defendant's option, for the value of the property or indebtedness sought to be replevied (to be estimated by the officer), plus one year's interest thereon at the legal rate from the date of the bond, conditioned that the defendant, garnishee, shall satisfy, to the extent of the penal amount of the bond, any judgment which may be rendered against him in such action.

On reasonable notice to the opposing party (which may be less than three days) either party shall have the right to prompt judicial review of the amount of bond required, denial of bond, sufficiency of sureties, and estimated value of the property, by the court which authorized issuance of the writ. The court's determination may be made upon the basis of affidavits, if uncontroverted, setting forth such facts as would be admissible in evidence; otherwise, the parties shall submit evidence. The court shall forthwith enter its order either approving or modifying the requirements of the officer or of the court's prior order, and such order of the court shall supersede and control with respect to such matters.

On reasonable notice to the opposing party (which may be less than three days) the defendant shall have the right to move the court for a substitution of property, of equal value as that garnished, for the property garnished. Provided that there has been located sufficient property of the defendant's to satisfy the order of garnishment, the court may authorize substitution of one or more items of defendant's property for all or for part of the property garnished. The court shall first make findings as to the value of the property to be substituted. If property is substituted, the property released from garnishment shall be delivered to defendant, if such property is personal property, and all liens upon such property from the original order of garnishment or modification thereof shall be terminated. Garnishment of substituted property shall be deemed to have existed from date of garnishment on the original property garnished, and no property on which liens have become affixed since the date of garnishment of the original property may be substituted.

TRCP 664a. DISSOLUTION OR MODIFICATION OF WRIT OF GARNISHMENT

A defendant whose property or account has been garnished or any intervening party who claims an interest in such property or account, may by sworn written motion, seek to vacate, dissolve or modify the writ of garnishment, and the order directing its issuance, for any grounds or cause, extrinsic or intrinsic. Such mo-

tion shall admit or deny each finding of the order directing the issuance of the writ except where the movant is unable to admit or deny the finding, in which case movant shall set forth the reasons why he cannot admit or deny. Unless the parties agree to an extension of time, the motion shall be heard promptly, after reasonable notice to the plaintiff (which may be less than three days), and the issue shall be determined not later than ten days after the motion is filed. The filing of the motion shall stay any further proceedings under the writ, except for any orders concerning the care, preservation or sale of any perishable property, until a hearing is had, and the issue is determined. The writ shall be dissolved unless, at such hearing, the plaintiff shall prove the grounds relied upon for its issuance, but the court may modify its previous order granting the writ and the writ issued pursuant thereto. The movant shall, however, have the burden to prove that the reasonable value of the property garnished exceeds the amount necessary to secure the debt, interest for one year, and probable costs. He shall also have the burden to prove facts to justify substitution of property.

The court's determination may be made upon the basis of affidavits, if uncontroverted, setting forth such facts as would be admissible in evidence; otherwise, the parties shall submit evidence. The court may make all such orders including orders concerning the care, preservation or disposition of the property (or the proceeds therefrom if the same has been sold), as justice may require. If the movant has given a replevy bond, an order to vacate or dissolve the writ shall vacate the replevy bond and discharge the sureties thereon, and if the court modifies its order or the writ issued pursuant thereto, it shall make such further orders with respect to the bond as may be consistent with its modification.

TRCP 665. ANSWER TO WRIT

The answer of the garnishee shall be under oath, in writing and signed by him, and shall make true answers to the several matters inquired of in the writ of garnishment.

See also *O'Connor's Texas Rules*, "The Answer—Denying Liability," ch. 3-E, p. 263.

TRCP 666. GARNISHEE DISCHARGED

If it appears from the answer of the garnishee that he is not indebted to the defendant, and was not so indebted when the writ of garnishment was served upon him, and that he has not in his possession any effects of the defendant and had not when the writ was served, and if he has either denied that any other persons within his knowledge are indebted to the defendant or have in their possession effects belonging to the defendant, or else has named such persons, should the answer of the garnishee not be controverted as hereinafter provided, the court shall enter judgment discharging the garnishee.

TRCP 667. JUDGMENT BY DEFAULT

If the garnishee fails to file an answer to the writ of garnishment at or before the time directed in the writ, it shall be lawful for the court, at any time after judgment shall have been rendered against the defendant, and on or after appearance day, to render judgment by default, as in other civil cases, against such garnishee for the full amount of such judgment against the defendant together with all interest and costs that may have accrued in the main case and also in the garnishment proceedings. The answer of the garnishee may be filed as in any other civil case at any time before such default judgment is rendered.

See also *O'Connor's Texas Rules*, "Default Judgment," ch. 7-A, p. 671.

TRCP 668. JUDGMENT WHEN GARNISHEE IS INDEBTED

Should it appear from the answer of the garnishee or should it be otherwise made to appear and be found by the court that the garnishee is indebted to the defendant in any amount, or was so indebted when the writ of garnishment was served, the court shall render judgment for the plaintiff against the garnishee for the amount so admitted or found to be due to the defendant from the garnishee, unless such amount is in excess of the amount of the plaintiff's judgment against the defendant with interest and costs, in which case, judgment shall be rendered against the garnishee for the full amount of the judgment already rendered against the defendant, together with interest and costs of the suit in the original case and also in the garnishment proceedings. If the garnishee fail or refuse to pay such judgment rendered against him, execution shall issue thereon in the same manner and under the same conditions as is or may be provided for the issuance of execution in other cases.

ANNOTATIONS

Wrigley v. First Nat'l Sec. Corp., 104 S.W.3d 259, 264 (Tex.App.—Beaumont 2003, no pet.). "The funds captured by the writ of garnishment are those held by

the garnishee in the account of the judgment debtor on the date the writ is served, and any additional funds deposited through the date the garnishee is required to answer. [P's] right to recover those funds from the garnishee is [not necessarily] fixed by whatever judgment [P] possesses on that date. The issuance and service of the writ of garnishment fixes the trial court's jurisdiction to determine whether the garnishee holds funds belonging to the judgment debtor, and necessarily that jurisdiction extends to a determination of title and ownership of the funds, regardless of how that ownership is placed in controversy. The garnishee may deposit the funds into the court, bring in all other claimants through interpleader, and the trial court may then adjudicate the conflicting claims of the parties."

TRCP 669. JUDGMENT FOR EFFECTS

Should it appear from the garnishee's answer, or otherwise, that the garnishee has in his possession, or had when the writ was served, any effects of the defendant liable to execution, including any certificates of stock in any corporation or joint stock company, the court shall render a decree ordering sale of such effects under execution in satisfaction of plaintiff's judgment and directing the garnishee to deliver them, or so much thereof as shall be necessary to satisfy plaintiff's judgment, to the proper officer for that purpose.

TRCP 670. REFUSAL TO DELIVER EFFECTS

Should the garnishee adjudged to have effects of the defendant in his possession, as provided in the preceding rule, fail or refuse to deliver them to the sheriff or constable on such demand, the officer shall immediately make return of such failure or refusal, whereupon on motion of the plaintiff, the garnishee shall be cited to show cause upon a date to be fixed by the court why he should not be attached for contempt of court for such failure or refusal. If the garnishee fails to show some good and sufficient excuse for such failure or refusal, he shall be fined for such contempt and imprisoned until he shall deliver such effects.

TRCP 671. REPEALED

TRCP 672. SALE OF EFFECTS

The sale so ordered shall be conducted in all respects as other sales of personal property under execution; and the officer making such sale shall execute a transfer of such effects or interest to the purchaser, with a brief recital of the judgment of the court under which the same was sold.

TRCP 673. MAY TRAVERSE ANSWER

If the plaintiff should not be satisfied with the answer of any garnishee, he may controvert the same by his affidavit stating that he has good reason to believe, and does believe, that the answer of the garnishee is incorrect, stating in what particular he believes the same to be incorrect. The defendant may also, in like manner, controvert the answer of the garnishee.

TRCP 674. TRIAL OF ISSUE

If the garnishee whose answer is controverted, is a resident of the county in which the proceeding is pending, an issue shall be formed under the direction of the court and tried as in other cases.

TRCP 675. DOCKET & NOTICE

The clerk of the court or the justice of the peace, on receiving certified copies filed in the county of the garnishee's residence under the provisions of the statutes, shall docket the case in the name of the plaintiff as plaintiff, and of the garnishee as defendant, and issue a notice to the garnishee, stating that his answer has been so controverted, and that such issue will stand for trial on the docket of such court. Such notice shall be directed to the garnishee, be dated and tested as other process from such court, and served by delivering a copy thereof to the garnishee. It shall be returnable, if issued from the district or county court, at ten o'clock a.m. of the Monday next after the expiration of twenty days from the date of its service; and if issued from the justice court, to the next term of such court convening after the expiration of twenty days after the service of such notice.

TRCP 676. ISSUE TRIED AS IN OTHER CASES

Upon the return of such notice served, an issue shall be formed under the direction of the court and tried as in other cases.

TRCP 677. COSTS

Where the garnishee is discharged upon his answer, the costs of the proceeding, including a reasonable compensation to the garnishee, shall be taxed against the plaintiff; where the answer of the garnishee has not been controverted and the garnishee is held thereon, such costs shall be taxed against the defen-

dant and included in the execution provided for in this section; where the answer is contested, the costs shall abide the issue of such contest.

TRCP 678. GARNISHEE DISCHARGED ON PROOF

It shall be a sufficient answer to any claim of the defendant against the garnishee founded on an indebtedness of such garnishee, or on the possession by him of any effects, for the garnishee to show that such indebtedness has been paid, or such effects, including any certificates of stock in any incorporated or joint stock company, have been delivered to any sheriff or constable as provided for in Rule 669.

TRCP 679. AMENDMENT

Clerical errors in the affidavit, bond, or writ of garnishment or the officer's return thereof, may upon application in writing to the judge or justice of the court in which the suit is filed, and after notice to the opponent, be amended in such manner and on such terms as the judge or justice shall authorize by an order entered in the minutes of the court (or noted on the docket of the justice of the peace), provided such amendment appears to the judge or justice to be in furtherance of justice.

SECTION 5. INJUNCTIONS

TRCP 680. TEMPORARY RESTRAINING ORDER

No temporary restraining order shall be granted without notice to the adverse party unless it clearly appears from specific facts shown by affidavit or by the verified complaint that immediate and irreparable injury, loss, or damage will result to the applicant before notice can be served and a hearing had thereon. Every temporary restraining order granted without notice shall be endorsed with the date and hour of issuance; shall be filed forthwith in the clerk's office and entered of record; shall define the injury and state why it is irreparable and why the order was granted without notice; and shall expire by its terms within such time after signing, not to exceed fourteen days, as the court fixes, unless within the time so fixed the order, for good cause shown, is extended for a like period or unless the party against whom the order is directed consents that it may be extended for a longer period. The reasons for the extension shall be entered of record. No more than one extension may be granted unless subsequent extensions are unopposed. In case a temporary restraining order is granted without notice, the application for a temporary injunction shall be set down for hearing at the earliest possible date and takes precedence of all matters except older matters of the same character; and when the application comes on for hearing the party who obtained the temporary restraining order shall proceed with the application for a temporary injunction and, if he does not do so, the court shall dissolve the temporary restraining order. On two days' notice to the party who obtained the temporary restraining order without notice or on such shorter notice to that party as the court may prescribe, the adverse party may appear and move its dissolution or modification and in that event the court shall proceed to hear and determine such motion as expeditiously as the ends of justice require.

Every restraining order shall include an order setting a certain date for hearing on the temporary or permanent injunction sought.

Author's comment: Temporary restraining orders under Family Code §§6.501 and 105.001 are not required to (1) define the injury, (2) state why it is irreparable, (3) state why the order was granted without notice, or (4) include an order setting the suit for trial on the merits. Fam. Code §§6.503, 105.001(b).

Caution: TRCP 680 is affected by Fam. Code §§6.501, 6.503, and 105.001.

See also CPRC ch. 65; ***O'Connor's Texas Rules***, "Injunctive Relief," ch. 2-C, p. 135; ***O'Connor's Texas Forms***, FORMS 2C:1-3; ***O'Connor's Texas Family Law Handbook*** (2017), "Temporary Restraining Orders," ch. 5-B, p. 677.

ANNOTATIONS

In re Office of the Atty. Gen., 257 S.W.3d 695, 697 (Tex.2008). TRCP 680 and 684 "require a trial court issuing a temporary restraining order to: (1) state why the order was granted without notice if it is granted *ex parte* …; (2) state the reasons for the issuance of the order by defining the injury and describing why it is irreparable …; (3) state the date the order expires and set a hearing on a temporary injunction …; and (4) set a bond…. Orders that fail to fulfill these requirements are void."

Ex parte Lesikar, 899 S.W.2d 654, 654 (Tex.1995). "Extensions of temporary restraining orders, absent some special statutory authority … must meet the limitations of [TRCP] 680, including in particular written orders and written extensions. An oral extension of a TRO is ineffective, and the contemnor must have notice of the actual written extension before he can be charged with contempt."

Davis v. Huey, 571 S.W.2d 859, 862 (Tex.1978). "At a hearing upon the request for a temporary injunction the only question before the trial court is whether the

applicant is entitled to preservation of the status quo of the subject matter of the suit pending trial on the merits. On appeal the reviewing court is limited in its consideration as to whether the trial court abused its discretion in making the foregoing determination." *See also* ***In re Newton***, 146 S.W.3d 648, 651 (Tex.2004) (status quo is defined as the last, actual, peaceable, noncontested status that preceded the pending controversy).

In re J.M.C., 109 S.W.3d 591, 595 (Tex.App.—Fort Worth 2003, no pet.). "[N]othing in [Fam. Code] §262.201, [Fam. Code] §263.401, or [TRCP] 680 deprives a trial court of jurisdiction over a termination proceeding simply because a temporary possession order has expired or the trial court does not hold a full adversary hearing."

Commonwealth Mortg. Corp. v. Wadkins, 709 S.W.2d 679, 680 (Tex.App.—Houston [14th Dist.] 1985, no writ). Family Code §3.58, now §6.501, "authorizes a domestic relations court to grant temporary orders for the 'preservation of the property and the protection of the parties.' The orders may be directed to one or both parties and need not define the injury or state why it is irreparable or state why the order was granted without notice."

TRCP 681. TEMPORARY INJUNCTIONS: NOTICE

No temporary injunction shall be issued without notice to the adverse party.

See also CPRC §51.014(a)(4) (interlocutory appeal of temporary injunction); ***O'Connor's Texas Rules***, "Injunctive Relief," ch. 2-C, p. 135; ***O'Connor's Texas Family Law Handbook*** (2017), "Temporary Restraining Orders," ch. 5-B, p. 677; "Temporary Injunctions," ch. 5-C, p. 688.

ANNOTATIONS

State v. Cook United, Inc., 469 S.W.2d 709, 712 (Tex.1971). "In the absence of notice to or service of citation upon the Attorney General of the State of Texas, ... the temporary injunction is hereby modified to enjoin only the county and district attorneys of Tarrant and McLennan Counties [who had notice], and shall have no effect on the Attorney General ... or the other district and county attorneys in this State."

RRE VIP Borrower, LLC v. Leisure Life Senior Apt. Hous., Ltd., No. 14-09-00923-CV (Tex.App.—Houston [14th Dist.] 2011, no pet.) (memo op.; 5-3-11). "The notice requirements of Rule 681 impliedly require that the adverse party have the right to be heard. The opportunity to be heard and present evidence must amount to more than the mere opportunity to cross-examine the other party's witnesses."

TRCP 682. SWORN PETITION

No writ of injunction shall be granted unless the applicant therefor shall present his petition to the judge verified by his affidavit and containing a plain and intelligible statement of the grounds for such relief.

Author's comment: Most temporary restraining orders and temporary injunctions under Family Code §§6.501, 6.502, and 105.001 do not require a sworn affidavit or a verified pleading stating specific facts showing immediate and irreparable injury. Fam. Code §§6.503, 105.001(b). However, temporary injunctions require a verified pleading or affidavit if they (1) attach the body of the child, (2) take the child into the possession of the court or a parent, or (3) exclude a parent from possession of or access to a child. Fam. Code §105.001(c).

Caution: TRCP 682 is affected by Fam. Code §§6.503 and 105.001.

See also ***O'Connor's Texas Rules***, "Injunctive Relief," ch. 2-C, p. 135; ***O'Connor's Texas Forms***, FORM 2C:1.

ANNOTATIONS

Butnaru v. Ford Motor Co., 84 S.W.3d 198, 204 (Tex.2002). "To obtain a temporary injunction, the applicant must plead and prove three specific elements: (1) a cause of action against the defendant; (2) a probable right to the relief sought; and (3) a probable, imminent, and irreparable injury in the interim."

Walling v. Metcalfe, 863 S.W.2d 56, 57 (Tex.1993). "A trial court may grant a temporary writ of injunction to preserve the status quo pending trial even though the applicant's prayer does not include a claim for equitable relief.... In such cases, however, a temporary injunction should only issue if the applicant establishes a probable right on final trial to the relief sought, and a probable injury in the interim."

Stewart Beach Condo. Homeowners Ass'n v. Gili N Prop Invs., 481 S.W.3d 336, 346 (Tex.App.—Houston [1st Dist.] 2015, no pet.). "'[T]he applicant for [a] temporary injunction [need not] offer evidence and persuade the judge to find from that evidence the adjudicative facts necessary for the applicant to prevail on the merits, based on probabilities.' A temporary injunction hearing is not a '*mini* trial' in which 'the judge predicts the applicant's chances of success at the real trial, based on the judge's estimate of where the truth probably lies concerning the adjudicative facts and the law made applicable thereto by the pleadings in the case.' '[T]o show a probable right of recovery,' the party applying for a temporary injunction[ ] 'must plead a cause of action and present some evidence that tends to sustain it. The evidence must be sufficient to raise a bona fide issue as to the applicant's right to ultimate relief.'"

In re MetroPCS Comms., 391 S.W.3d 329, 337 (Tex.App.—Dallas 2013, orig. proceeding). "[W]e cannot agree with [petitioner] that a temporary restraining order is not a 'writ of injunction' subject to the requirements of rule 682."

Mattox v. Jackson, 336 S.W.3d 759, 763 (Tex. App.—Houston [1st Dist.] 2011, no pet.). "A verified petition for injunctive relief is not required to grant a temporary injunction ... when a full evidentiary hearing on evidence independent of the petition has been held."

Crystal Media, Inc. v. HCI Acquisition Corp., 773 S.W.2d 732, 734 (Tex.App.—San Antonio 1989, no writ). "If the insufficiency of the verification is not objected to prior to the introduction of evidence the defect has been waived. [¶] Further, the court allowed an amendment of the verification...." *See also* ***Russell v. City of Dallas***, No. 05-13-00061-CV (Tex.App.—Dallas 2014, pet. denied) (memo op.; 5-16-14).

TRCP 683. FORM & SCOPE OF INJUNCTION OR RESTRAINING ORDER

Every order granting an injunction and every restraining order shall set forth the reasons for its issuance; shall be specific in terms; shall describe in reasonable detail and not by reference to the complaint or other document, the act or acts sought to be restrained; and is binding only upon the parties to the action, their officers, agents, servants, employees, and attorneys, and upon those persons in active concert or participation with them who receive actual notice of the order by personal service or otherwise.

Every order granting a temporary injunction shall include an order setting the cause for trial on the merits with respect to the ultimate relief sought. The appeal of a temporary injunction shall constitute no cause for delay of the trial.

Author's comment: Temporary restraining orders and injunctions under Family Code §§6.501, 6.502, and 105.001 do not require an order setting the suit for trial on the merits. Fam. Code §§6.503, 105.001(b)(3).

See also ***O'Connor's Texas Rules***, "Injunctive Relief," ch. 2-C, p. 135; "Request for Findings of Fact & Conclusions of Law," ch. 10-E, p. 921; ***O'Connor's Texas Forms***, FORMS 2C:3, 4; ***O'Connor's Texas Family Law Handbook*** (2017), "Temporary Restraining Orders," ch. 5-B, p. 677; "Temporary Injunctions," ch. 5-C, p. 688.

ANNOTATIONS

Qwest Comms. v. AT&T Corp., 24 S.W.3d 334, 337 (Tex.2000). The TRCPs "require that an order granting a temporary injunction set the cause for trial on the merits and fix the amount of security to be given by the applicant. These procedural requirements are mandatory, and an order granting a temporary injunction that does not meet them is subject to being declared void and dissolved." *See also* ***InterFirst Bank San Felipe v. Paz Constr. Co.***, 715 S.W.2d 640, 641 (Tex.1986).

Ex parte Slavin, 412 S.W.2d 43, 44 (Tex.1967). An injunction decree "must spell out the details of compliance in clear, specific and unambiguous terms so that such person will readily know exactly what duties or obligations are imposed upon him." *See also* ***RCI Entm't (San Antonio), Inc. v. City of San Antonio***, 373 S.W.3d 589, 603 (Tex.App.—San Antonio 2012, no pet.); ***Murray v. Epic Energy Res.***, 300 S.W.3d 461, 470-71 (Tex.App.—Beaumont 2009, no pet.).

Layton v. Ball, 396 S.W.3d 747, 753 (Tex.App.—Tyler 2013, no pet.). "Rule 683 is not violated when documents are attached to the injunction and referred to it as part of the injunction, because the attachments become part of the injunction itself."

RCI Entm't (San Antonio), Inc. v. City of San Antonio, 373 S.W.3d 589, 603 (Tex.App.—San Antonio 2012, no pet.). "An injunction should be broad enough to prevent a repetition of the wrong sought to be corrected. But, it must not be so broad as to enjoin a defendant from activities that are a lawful and proper exercise of his rights. Where a party's acts are divisible, and some acts are permissible and some are not, an injunction should not issue to restrain actions that are legal or about which there is no asserted complaint. Thus, the entry of an injunction that enjoins lawful as well as unlawful acts may constitute an abuse of discretion." *See also* ***Computek Computer & Office Sups. v. Walton***, 156 S.W.3d 217, 221 (Tex.App.—Dallas 2005, no pet.).

Senter Invs. v. Veerjee, 358 S.W.3d 841, 845-46 (Tex.App.—Dallas 2012, no pet.). Appellant "asserts the temporary injunction is void because it does not contain an order setting the case for trial on the merits. [TRCP] 683 requires every order granting a temporary injunction to include such an order. However, because this case involves a temporary injunction pending arbitration, we must also consider the application of the [Texas Arbitration Act (TAA)]. [¶] Once [appellant] decided to invoke the arbitration provision and the trial court compelled arbitration, the trial proceedings were governed by the TAA as well as the rules of civil procedure. Under the TAA, the trial court was required to stay the trial proceedings pending arbitration, subject to its

jurisdiction to grant orders under [CPRC] §171.086, including an injunction. [¶] The specific provisions of the TAA in this circumstance control over the rules of civil procedure; therefore, the temporary injunction order properly abated the trial court proceedings."

Intercontinental Terminals Co. v. Vopak N. Am., Inc., 354 S.W.3d 887, 899 (Tex.App.—Houston [1st Dist.] 2011, no pet.). "Rule 683 mandates that a trial court granting a temporary injunction must explain in the order its reasons for believing that the applicant has shown that it will suffer injury if interlocutory relief is not granted but does not require the trial court to provide reasons for believing that the applicant has shown a probable right to final relief. An explanation of the pending harm to the temporary injunction applicant, along with a specific recitation of the conduct enjoined, is all that is necessary to achieve Rule 683's purpose: 'to inform a party just what he is enjoined from doing and the reasons why he is so enjoined.' For these reasons, we hold that Rule 683 does not mandate that the trial court's order expressly state that the trial court found a probable right of recovery." *See also* ***Johnson-Todd v. Morgan***, No. 09-15-00073-CV (Tex.App.—Beaumont 2015, pet. denied) (memo op.; 5-14-15) (specificity requirement is not satisfied by mere recital of no adequate remedy at law and irreparable harm).

Emex Holdings, LLC v. Naim, No. 13-09-591-CV (Tex.App.—Corpus Christi 2010, no pet.) (memo op.; 5-27-10). "Requiring a trial date to be placed in every injunction order prevents a temporary injunction from effectively becoming permanent without a trial. [It] also places the onus upon the party requesting injunctive relief to renew the injunction if the trial is delayed beyond the trial date set forth in the order. [¶] [R]eference to an existing docket control order is not a substitute for stating a trial date in the order itself. Logically, if a pre-existing docket control order is insufficient to comply with rule 683, then a yet to be entered docket control order ... does not comply either." *See also* ***State Bd. for Educator Certification v. Montalvo***, No. 03-12-00723-CV (Tex.App.—Austin 2013, no pet.) (memo op.; 4-3-13) (temporary injunction order without trial date is void, not voidable); ***In re Marriage of Grossnickle***, 115 S.W.3d 238, 244 (Tex.App.—Texarkana 2003, no pet.) (requirement that injunction order set cause for trial on the merits is effectively same as requiring specific trial date to be set in the order).

Qaddura v. Indo-European Foods, Inc., 141 S.W.3d 882, 891-92 (Tex.App.—Dallas 2004, pet. denied). "Rule 683 provides that an order granting an injunction 'shall set forth the reasons for its issuance.' This rule, however, applies only to temporary restraining orders and temporary injunctions, not permanent injunctions."

Wells v. Wells, 539 S.W.2d 220, 222 (Tex.App.—Houston [1st Dist.] 1976, writ dism'd). "The trial court in a divorce proceeding is authorized by statute to grant temporary relief as it may deem necessary and equitable with respect to the parties and their property. The order in question recited that its provisions were necessary and equitable for the preservation of the parties' rights. This was sufficient compliance with Rule 683, ... requiring that every injunctive order set forth the reasons for its issuance."

TRCP 684. APPLICANT'S BOND

In the order granting any temporary restraining order or temporary injunction, the court shall fix the amount of security to be given by the applicant. Before the issuance of the temporary restraining order or temporary injunction the applicant shall execute and file with the clerk a bond to the adverse party, with two or more good and sufficient sureties, to be approved by the clerk, in the sum fixed by the judge, conditioned that the applicant will abide the decision which may be made in the cause, and that he will pay all sums of money and costs that may be adjudged against him if the restraining order or temporary injunction shall be dissolved in whole or in part.

Where the temporary restraining order or temporary injunction is against the State, a municipality, a State agency, or a subdivision of the State in its governmental capacity, and is such that the State, municipality, State agency, or subdivision of the State in its governmental capacity, has no pecuniary interest in the suit and no monetary damages can be shown, the bond shall be allowed in the sum fixed by the judge, and the liability of the applicant shall be for its face amount if the restraining order or temporary injunction shall be dissolved in whole or in part. The discretion of the trial court in fixing the amount of the bond shall be subject to review. Provided that under equitable circumstances and for good cause shown by affidavit or otherwise the court rendering judgment on the bond may allow recovery for less than its full face amount, the action of the court to be subject to review.

Author's comment: The court may dispense with the requirement of a bond involving temporary orders under Family Code §§6.501, 6.502, and 105.001. See TRCP 693a.

Caution: TRCP 684 is affected by Fam. Code §§6.503 and 105.001.

See also ***O'Connor's Texas Family Law Handbook*** (2017), "Temporary Restraining Orders," ch. 5-B, p. 677.

ANNOTATIONS

In re Office of the Atty. Gen., 257 S.W.3d 695, 697 (Tex.2008). See annotation under TRCP 680, p. 1259.

DeSantis v. Wackenhut Corp., 793 S.W.2d 670, 685-86 (Tex.1990). To prevail in a suit on a bond, "the claimant must prove that the [TRO] or temporary injunction was issued or perpetuated when it should not have been, and that it was later dissolved. The claimant need not prove that the [TRO] or temporary injunction was obtained maliciously or without probable cause." *See also* ***Goodin v. Jolliff***, 257 S.W.3d 341, 353 (Tex. App.—Fort Worth 2008, no pet.) (claimant must prove that issuance of injunction caused her damages).

Bay Fin. Sav. Bank v. Brown, 142 S.W.3d 586, 590 (Tex.App.—Texarkana 2004, no pet.). "[A]n order granting a temporary injunction [must] fix the amount of security to be given by the applicant. *At 591:* A bond for a temporary restraining order does not continue on and act as security for a temporary injunction unless expressly authorized by the trial court."

TRCP 685. FILING & DOCKETING

Upon the grant of a temporary restraining order or an order fixing a time for hearing upon an application for a temporary injunction, the party to whom the same is granted shall file his petition therefor, together with the order of the judge, with the clerk of the proper court; and, if such orders do not pertain to a pending suit in said court, the cause shall be entered on the docket of the court in its regular order in the name of the party applying for the writ as plaintiff and of the opposite party as defendant.

TRCP 686. CITATION

Upon the filing of such petition and order not pertaining to a suit pending in the court, the clerk of such court shall issue a citation to the defendant as in other civil cases, which shall be served and returned in like manner as ordinary citations issued from said court; provided, however, that when a temporary restraining order is issued and is accompanied with a true copy of plaintiff's petition, it shall not be necessary for the citation in the original suit to be accompanied with a copy of plaintiff's petition, nor contain a statement of the nature of plaintiff's demand, but it shall be sufficient for said citation to refer to plaintiff's claim as set forth in a true copy of plaintiff's petition which accompanies the temporary restraining order; and provided further that the court may have a hearing upon an application for a temporary restraining order or temporary injunction at such time and upon such reasonable notice given in such manner as the court may direct.

TRCP 687. REQUISITES OF WRIT

The writ of injunction shall be sufficient if it contains substantially the following requisites:

(a) Its style shall be, "The State of Texas."

(b) It shall be directed to the person or persons enjoined.

(c) It must state the names of the parties to the proceedings, plaintiff and defendant, and the nature of the plaintiff's application, with the action of the judge thereon.

(d) It must command the person or persons to whom it is directed to desist and refrain from the commission or continuance of the act enjoined, or to obey and execute such order as the judge has seen proper to make.

(e) If it is a temporary restraining order, it shall state the day and time set for hearing, which shall not exceed fourteen days from the date of the court's order granting such temporary restraining order; but if it is a temporary injunction, issued after notice, it shall be made returnable at or before ten o'clock a.m. of the Monday next after the expiration of twenty days from the date of service thereof, as in the case of ordinary citations.

(f) It shall be dated and signed by the clerk officially and attested with the seal of his office and the date of its issuance must be indorsed thereon.

TRCP 688. CLERK TO ISSUE WRIT

When the petition, order of the judge and bond have been filed, the clerk shall issue the temporary restraining order or temporary injunction, as the case may be, in conformity with the terms of the order, and deliver the same to the sheriff or any constable of the county of the residence of the person enjoined, or to the applicant, as the latter shall direct. If several persons are enjoined, residing in different counties, the clerk shall issue such additional copies of the writ as shall be requested by the applicant. The clerk must retain a copy

of the temporary restraining order or temporary injunction in the court's file.

TRCP 689. SERVICE & RETURN

The officer receiving a writ of injunction shall indorse thereon the date of its receipt by him, and shall forthwith execute the same by delivering to the party enjoined a true copy thereof. The officer must complete and file a return in accordance with Rule 107.

TRCP 690. THE ANSWER

The defendant to an injunction proceeding may answer as in other civil actions; but no injunction shall be dissolved before final hearing because of the denial of the material allegations of the plaintiff's petition, unless the answer denying the same is verified by the oath of the defendant.

See also ***O'Connor's Texas Rules***, "Verified Pleas," ch. 3-E, §4, p. 264; ***O'Connor's Texas Family Law Handbook*** (2017), "Temporary Injunctions," ch. 5-C, p. 688.

ANNOTATIONS

Executive Tele-Comm. Sys. v. Buchbaum, 669 S.W.2d 400, 403 (Tex.App.—Dallas 1984, no writ). "The only prescribed response for a defendant to a temporary injunction proceeding is pronounced in Rule 690, and the failure to answer does not impair the defendant's right to a full hearing. [A] party seeking an injunction cannot rely on the verified pleading rules to limit the defense of the nonmovant."

TRCP 691. BOND ON DISSOLUTION

Upon the dissolution of an injunction restraining the collection of money, by an interlocutory order of the court or judge, made in term time or vacation, if the petition be continued over for trial, the court or judge shall require of the defendant in such injunction proceedings a bond, with two or more good and sufficient sureties, to be approved by the clerk of the court, payable to the complainant in double the amount of the sum enjoined, and conditioned to refund to the complainant the amount of money, interest and costs which may be collected of him in the suit or proceeding enjoined if such injunction is made perpetual on final hearing. If such injunction is so perpetuated, the court, on motion of the complainant, may enter judgment against the principal and sureties in such bond for such amount as may be shown to have been collected from such defendant.

TRCP 692. DISOBEDIENCE

Disobedience of an injunction may be punished by the court or judge, in term time or in vacation, as a contempt. In case of such disobedience, the complainant, his agent or attorney, may file in the court in which such injunction is pending or with the judge in vacation, his affidavit stating what person is guilty of such disobedience and describing the acts constituting the same; and thereupon the court or judge shall cause to be issued an attachment for such person, directed to the sheriff or any constable of any county, and requiring such officer to arrest the person therein named if found within his county and have him before the court or judge at the time and place named in such writ; or said court or judge may issue a show cause order, directing and requiring such person to appear on such date as may be designated and show cause why he should not be adjudged in contempt of court. On return of such attachment or show cause order, the judge shall proceed to hear proof; and if satisfied that such person has disobeyed the injunction, either directly or indirectly, may commit such person to jail without bail until he purges himself of such contempt, in such manner and form as the court or judge may direct.

ANNOTATIONS

Ex parte Jackman, 663 S.W.2d 520, 524 (Tex. App.—Dallas 1983, orig. proceeding). "The injunction must be obeyed irrespective of the ultimate validity of the order, and a defendant cannot avoid compliance with the commands, or excuse his violation, of the injunction by simply moving to dissolve it or by the pendency of a motion to modify it."

TRCP 693. PRINCIPLES OF EQUITY APPLICABLE

The principles, practice and procedure governing courts of equity shall govern proceedings in injunctions when the same are not in conflict with these rules or the provisions of the statutes.

ANNOTATIONS

State v. Texas Pet Foods, Inc., 591 S.W.2d 800, 804 (Tex.1979). "[I]njunctive relief is proper when the trial court finds it justified under the rules of equity, notwithstanding a defendant's cessation of the activity or solemn promises to cease the activity. *At 805:* When it is determined that [a] statute is being violated, it is within the province of the district court to restrain it.

The doctrine of balancing the equities has no application to ... statutorily authorized injunctive relief."

TRCP 693a. BOND IN DIVORCE CASE

In a divorce case the court in its discretion may dispense with the necessity of a bond in connection with an ancillary injunction in behalf of one spouse against the other.

Author's comment: The court may dispense with the requirement of a bond for temporary orders under Family Code §§6.501, 6.502, and 105.001.

Caution: TRCP 693a is affected by Fam. Code §§6.503 and 105.001.

ANNOTATIONS

Lancaster v. Lancaster, 291 S.W.2d 303, 308 (Tex. 1956). After wife #2 filed divorce suit in one county, wife #1 filed suit in another county claiming interest in property subject to divorce. Wife #2 then got injunction without bond to prevent wife #1 from continuing her suit. "Rule 693a does not apply to [wife #1, a third party to divorce proceeding]; therefore, a bond should have been required before the issuance of any injunction [against wife #1]."

Eichelberger v. Hayton, 814 S.W.2d 179, 182 n.4 (Tex.App.—Houston [1st Dist.] 1991, writ denied). TRCP 693a "provides that in a divorce case, the court may dispense with the necessity of a bond in connection with an ancillary injunction in behalf of one spouse against the other. We note that the present cause of action is neither a divorce case, nor are the parties presently spouses. Thus, rule 693a is inapplicable."

Nationwide Life Ins. v. Nations, 654 S.W.2d 860, 861 (Tex.App.—Houston [14th Dist.] 1983, no writ). TRCP 693a "dispenses with the necessity of a bond for an ancillary injunction for one spouse against the other. Here the injunction was granted against a third party in favor of one of the spouses. Therefore, Rule 693a does not exempt appellees from posting a bond."

Hopkins v. Hopkins, 539 S.W.2d 242, 246 (Tex. App.—Fort Worth 1976, writ dism'd). Since there was a third-party D, "the provisions of law entitling the trial court to waive requirement of bond in connection with injunctions deemed necessary as applied to petitioners and respondents in divorce cases are without application."

SECTION 6. MANDAMUS

TRCP 694. NO MANDAMUS WITHOUT NOTICE

No mandamus shall be granted by the district or county court on ex parte hearing, and any peremptory mandamus granted without notice shall be abated on motion.

SECTION 7. RECEIVERS

TRCP 695. NO RECEIVER OF IMMOVABLE PROPERTY APPOINTED WITHOUT NOTICE

Except where otherwise provided by statute, no receiver shall be appointed without notice to take charge of property which is fixed and immovable. When an application for appointment of a receiver to take possession of property of this type is filed, the judge or court shall set the same down for hearing and notice of such hearing shall be given to the adverse party by serving notice thereof not less than three days prior to such hearing. If the order finds that the defendant is a nonresident or that his whereabouts is unknown, the notice may be served by affixing the same in a conspicuous manner and place upon the property or if that is impracticable it may be served in such other manner as the court or judge may require.

See also ***O'Connor's Texas Family Law Handbook*** (2017), "Temporary Orders," ch. 5-D, p. 695; "Dividing Community Assets & Liabilities," ch. 7-A, §7, p. 795.

ANNOTATIONS

Krumnow v. Krumnow, 174 S.W.3d 820, 829 (Tex. App.—Waco 2005, pet. denied). "Real estate is 'fixed and immovable property' within the meaning of Rule 695. Appointment of a receiver without giving notice to adverse parties to be heard ***on the application*** is reversible error."

TRCP 695a. BOND, & BOND IN DIVORCE CASE

No receiver shall be appointed with authority to take charge of property until the party applying therefor has filed with the clerk of the court a good and sufficient bond, to be approved by such clerk, payable to the defendant in the amount fixed by the court, conditioned for the payment of all damages and costs in such suit, in case it should be decided that such receiver was wrongfully appointed to take charge of such property. The amount of such bond shall be fixed at a sum sufficient to cover all such probable damages and costs. In a divorce case the court or judge, as a matter of discretion, may dispense with the necessity of a bond.

ANNOTATIONS

Ahmad v. Ahmed, 199 S.W.3d 573, 575 (Tex.App.—Houston [1st Dist.] 2006, no pet.). "The applicant's bond is a prerequisite to the appointment of a receiver, and the trial court's failure to require the bond necessi-

tates reversal of the order appointing the receiver. *At 576:* [T]he trial court's order does not require [P] to file a bond payable to [D]—nor does it indicate an appropriate amount for such a bond. ... Although the trial court properly required the receiver to post a bond [under CPRC §64.023], it did not incorporate the additional [TRCP] 695a bond requirement into its order. [T]he record does not indicate that [P] has posted the required Rule 695a bond. Therefore, ... the receivership must be dissolved."

In re Estate of Herring, 983 S.W.2d 61, 64 (Tex. App.—Corpus Christi 1998, no pet.). "[T]he bond requirements of Rule 695a do not apply to the appointment of a post-judgment receiver...."

SECTION 8. SEQUESTRATION

TRCP 696. APPLICATION FOR WRIT OF SEQUESTRATION & ORDER

Either at the commencement of a suit or at any time during its progress the plaintiff may file an application for a writ of sequestration. The application shall be supported by affidavits of the plaintiff, his agent, his attorney, or other persons having knowledge of relevant facts. The application shall comply with all statutory requirements and shall state the grounds for issuing the writ, including the description of the property to be sequestered with such certainty that it may be identified and distinguished from property of a like kind, giving the value of each article of the property and the county in which it is located, and the specific facts relied upon by the plaintiff to warrant the required findings by the court. The writ shall not be quashed because two or more grounds are stated conjunctively or disjunctively. The application and any affidavits shall be made on personal knowledge and shall set forth such facts as would be admissible in evidence; provided that facts may be stated based upon information and belief if the grounds of such belief are specifically stated.

No writ shall issue except upon written order of the court after a hearing, which may be ex parte. The court, in its order granting the application, shall make specific findings of facts to support the statutory grounds found to exist, and shall describe the property to be sequestered with such certainty that it may be identified and distinguished from property of a like kind, giving the value of each article of the property and the county in which it is located. Such order shall further specify the amount of bond required of plaintiff which shall be in an amount which, in the opinion of the court, shall adequately compensate defendant in the event plaintiff fails to prosecute his suit to effect and pay all damages and costs as shall be adjudged against him for wrongfully suing out the writ of sequestration including the elements of damages stated in Sections 62.044 and 62.045, Civil Practice and Remedies Code. The court shall further find in its order the amount of bond required of defendant to replevy, which shall be in an amount equivalent to the value of the property sequestered or to the amount of plaintiff's claim and one year's accrual of interest if allowed by law on the claim, whichever is the lesser amount, and the estimated costs of court. The order may direct the issuance of several writs at the same time, or in succession, to be sent to different counties.

See also CPRC §62.001.

TRCP 697. PETITION

If the suit be in the district or county court, no writ of sequestration shall issue, unless a petition shall have been first filed therein, as in other suits in said courts.

TRCP 698. BOND FOR SEQUESTRATION

No writ of sequestration shall issue until the party applying therefor has filed with the officer authorized to issue such writ a bond payable to the defendant in the amount fixed by the court's order, with sufficient surety or sureties as provided by statute to be approved by such officer, conditioned that the plaintiff will prosecute his suit to effect and pay to the extent of the penal amount of the bond all damages and costs as may be adjudged against him for wrongfully suing out such writ of sequestration, and plaintiff may further condition the bond pursuant to the provisions of Rule 708, in which case he shall not be required to give additional bond to replevy unless so ordered by the court.

After notice to the opposite party, either before or after the issuance of the writ, the defendant or plaintiff may file a motion to increase or reduce the amount of such bond, or to question the sufficiency of the sureties thereon, in the court in which such suit is pending. Upon hearing, the court shall enter its order with respect to such bond and sufficiency of the sureties as justice may require.

TRCP 699. REQUISITES OF WRIT

The writ of sequestration shall be directed "To the Sheriff or any Constable within the State of Texas" (not

naming a specific county) and shall command him to take into his possession the property, describing the same as it is described in the application or affidavits, if to be found in his county, and to keep the same subject to further orders of the court, unless the same is replevied. There shall be prominently displayed on the face of the writ, in ten-point type and in a manner calculated to advise a reasonably attentive person of its contents, the following:

"YOU HAVE A RIGHT TO REGAIN POSSESSION OF THE PROPERTY BY FILING A REPLEVY BOND. YOU HAVE A RIGHT TO SEEK TO REGAIN POSSESSION OF THE PROPERTY BY FILING WITH THE COURT A MOTION TO DISSOLVE THIS WRIT."

See also CPRC §§62.061-62.063.

TRCP 700. AMENDMENT

Clerical errors in the affidavit, bond, or writ of sequestration or the officer's return thereof may upon application in writing to the judge of the court in which the suit is filed and after notice to the opponent, be amended in such manner and on such terms as the judge shall authorize by an order entered in the minutes of the court, provided the amendment does not change or add to the grounds of such sequestration as stated in the affidavit, and provided such amendment appears to the judge to be in furtherance of justice.

TRCP 700a. SERVICE OF WRIT ON DEFENDANT

The defendant shall be served in any manner provided for service of citation or as provided in Rule 21a, with a copy of the writ of sequestration, the application, accompanying affidavits, and orders of the court as soon as practicable following the levy of the writ. There shall also be prominently displayed on the face of the copy of the writ served on defendant, in ten-point type and in a manner calculated to advise a reasonably attentive person of its contents, the following:

"To ____________________, Defendant:

You are hereby notified that certain properties alleged to be claimed by you have been sequestered. If you claim any rights in such property, you are advised:

"YOU HAVE A RIGHT TO REGAIN POSSESSION OF THE PROPERTY BY FILING A REPLEVY BOND. YOU HAVE A RIGHT TO SEEK TO REGAIN POSSESSION OF THE PROPERTY BY FILING WITH THE COURT A MOTION TO DISSOLVE THIS WRIT."

TRCP 701. DEFENDANT MAY REPLEVY

At any time before judgment, should the sequestered property not have been previously claimed, replevied, or sold, the defendant may replevy the same, or any part thereof, or the proceeds from the sale of the property if it has been sold under order of the court, by giving bond, with sufficient surety or sureties as provided by statute, to be approved by the officer who levied the writ, payable to plaintiff in the amount fixed by the court's order, conditioned as provided in Rule 702 or Rule 703.

On reasonable notice to the opposing party (which may be less than three days) either party shall have the right to prompt judicial review of the amount of bond required, denial of bond, sufficiency of sureties, and estimated value of the property, by the court which authorized issuance of the writ. The court's determination may be made upon the basis of affidavits, if uncontroverted, setting forth such facts as would be admissible in evidence; otherwise, the parties shall submit evidence. The court shall forthwith enter its order either approving or modifying the requirements of the officer or of the court's prior order, and such order of the court shall supersede and control with respect to such matters.

TRCP 702. BOND FOR PERSONAL PROPERTY

If the property to be replevied be personal property, the condition of the bond shall be that the defendant will not remove the same out of the county, or that he will not waste, ill-treat, injure, destroy, or dispose of the same, according to the plaintiff's affidavit, and that he will have such property, in the same condition as when it is replevied, together with the value of the fruits, hire or revenue thereof, forthcoming to abide the decision of the court, or that he will pay the value thereof, or the difference between its value at the time of replevy and the time of judgment and of the fruits, hire or revenue of the same in case he shall be condemned to do so.

TRCP 703. BOND FOR REAL ESTATE

If the property be real estate, the condition of such bond shall be that the defendant will not injure the property, and that he will pay the value of the rents of the same in case he shall be condemned so to do.

TRCP 704. RETURN OF BOND & ENTRY OF JUDGMENT

The bond provided for in the three preceding rules shall be returned with the writ to the court from whence

the writ issued. In case the suit is decided against the defendant, final judgment shall be rendered against all the obligors in such bond, jointly and severally, for the value of the property replevied as of the date of the execution of the replevy bond, and the value of the fruits, hire, revenue, or rent thereof, as the case may be.

TRCP 705. DEFENDANT MAY RETURN SEQUESTERED PROPERTY

Within ten days after final judgment for personal property the defendant may deliver to the plaintiff, or to the officer who levied the sequestration or to his successor in office the personal property in question, and such officer shall deliver same to plaintiff upon his demand therefor; or such defendant shall deliver such property to the officer demanding same under execution issued therefor upon a judgment for the title or possession of the same; and such officer shall receipt the defendant for such property; provided, however, that such delivery to the plaintiff or to such officer shall be without prejudice to any rights of the plaintiff under the replevy bond given by the defendant. Where a mortgage or other lien of any kind is foreclosed upon personal property sequestered and replevied, the defendant shall deliver such property to the officer calling for same under order of sale issued upon a judgment foreclosing such mortgage or other lien, either in the county of defendant's residence or in the county where sequestered, as demanded by such officer; provided, however, that such delivery by the defendant shall be without prejudice to any rights of the plaintiff under the replevy bond given by the defendant.

TRCP 706. DISPOSITION OF THE PROPERTY BY OFFICER

When the property is tendered back by the defendant to the officer who sequestered the same or to the officer calling for same under an order of sale, such officer shall receive said property and hold or dispose of the same as ordered by the court; provided, however, that such return to and receipt of same by the officer and any sale or disposition of said property by the officer under order or judgment of the court shall not affect or limit any rights of the plaintiff under the bond provided for in Rule 702.

TRCP 707. EXECUTION

If the property be not returned and received, as provided in the two preceding rules, execution shall issue upon said judgment for the amount due thereon, as in other cases.

TRCP 708. PLAINTIFF MAY REPLEVY

When the defendant fails to replevy the property within ten days after the levy of the writ and service of notice on defendant, the officer having the property in possession shall at any time thereafter and before final judgment, deliver the same to the plaintiff upon his giving bond payable to defendant in a sum of money not less than the amount fixed by the court's order, with sufficient surety or sureties as provided by statute to be approved by such officer. If the property to be replevied be personal property, the condition of the bond shall be that he will have such property, in the same condition as when it is replevied, together with the value of the fruits, hire or revenue thereof, forthcoming to abide the decision of the court, or that he will pay the value thereof, or the difference between its value at the time of replevy and the time of judgment (regardless of the cause of such difference in value, and of the fruits, hire or revenue of the same in case he shall be condemned to do so). If the property be real estate, the condition of such bond shall be that the plaintiff will not injure the property, and that he will pay the value of the rents of the same in case he shall be condemned to do so.

On reasonable notice to the opposing party (which may be less than three days) either party shall have the right to prompt judicial review of the amount of bond required, denial of bond, sufficiency of sureties, and estimated value of the property, by the court which authorized issuance of the writ. The court's determination may be made upon the basis of affidavits, if uncontroverted, setting forth such facts as would be admissible in evidence; otherwise, the parties shall submit evidence. The court shall forthwith enter its order either approving or modifying the requirements of the officer or of the court's prior order, and such order of the court shall supersede and control with respect to such matters.

TRCP 709. WHEN BOND FORFEITED

The bond provided for in the preceding rule shall be returned by the officer to the court issuing the writ immediately after he has approved same, and in case the suit is decided against the plaintiff, final judgment shall be entered against all the obligors in such bond, jointly and severally for the value of the property replevied as of the date of the execution of the replevy bond, and the value of the fruits, hire, revenue or rent thereof as the case may be. The same rules which govern the

discharge or enforcement of a judgment against the obligors in the defendant's replevy bond shall be applicable to and govern in case of a judgment against the obligors in the plaintiff's replevy bond.

TRCP 710. SALE OF PERISHABLE GOODS

If after the expiration of ten days from the levy of a writ of sequestration the defendant has failed to replevy the same, if the plaintiff or defendant shall make affidavit in writing that the property levied upon, or any portion thereof, is likely to be wasted or destroyed or greatly depreciated in value by keeping, and if the officer having possession of such property shall certify to the truth of such affidavit, it shall be the duty of the judge or justice of the peace to whose court the writ is returnable, upon the presentation of such affidavit and certificate, either in term time or vacation, to order the sale of said property or so much thereof as is likely to be so wasted, destroyed or depreciated in value by keeping, but either party may replevy the property at any time before such sale.

TRCP 711. ORDER OF SALE FOR

The judge or justice granting the order provided for in the preceding rule shall issue an order directed to the officer having such property in possession, commanding such officer to sell such property in the same manner as under execution.

TRCP 712. RETURN OF ORDER

The officer making such sale shall, within five days thereafter, return the order of sale to the court from whence the same issued, with his proceedings thereon, and shall, at the time of making such return, pay over to the clerk or justice of the peace the proceeds of such sale.

TRCP 712a. DISSOLUTION OR MODIFICATION OF WRIT OF SEQUESTRATION

A defendant whose property has been sequestered or any intervening party who claims an interest in such property, may by sworn written motion, seek to vacate, dissolve, or modify the writ and the order directing its issuance, for any grounds or cause, extrinsic or intrinsic, including a motion to reduce the amount of property sequestered when the total amount described and authorized by such order exceeds the amount necessary to secure the plaintiff's claim, one year's interest if allowed by law on the claim, and costs. Such motion shall admit or deny each finding of the order directing the issuance of the writ except where the movant is unable to admit or deny the finding, in which case movant shall set forth the reasons why he cannot admit or deny. Unless the parties agree to an extension of time, the motion shall be heard promptly, after reasonable notice to the plaintiff (which may be less than three days), and the issue shall be determined not later than ten days after the motion is filed. The filing of the motion shall stay any further proceedings under the writ, except for any orders concerning the care, preservation, or sale of any perishable property, until a hearing is had, and the issue is determined. The writ shall be dissolved unless, at such hearing, the plaintiff shall prove the grounds relied upon for its issuance, but the court may modify its previous order granting the writ and the writ issued pursuant thereto. The movant shall, however, have the burden to prove that the reasonable value of the property sequestered exceeds the amount necessary to secure the debt, interest for one year, and probable costs.

The court's determination may be made upon the basis of affidavits, if uncontroverted, setting forth such facts as would be admissible in evidence; otherwise, the parties shall submit evidence. The court may make all such orders, including orders concerning the care, preservation, or disposition of the property (or the proceeds therefrom if the same has been sold) as justice may require. If the movant has given a replevy bond, an order to vacate or dissolve the writ shall vacate the replevy bond and discharge the sureties thereon, and if the court modifies its order or the writ issued pursuant thereto, it shall make such further orders with respect to the bond as may be consistent with its modification.

See also CPRC §62.045.

TRCP 713. SALE ON DEBT NOT DUE

If the suit in which the sequestration issued be for a debt or demand not yet due, and the property sequestered be likely to be wasted, destroyed or greatly depreciated in value by keeping, the judge or justice of the peace shall, under the regulations hereinbefore provided, order the same to be sold, giving credit on such sale until such debt or demand shall become due.

See also CPRC §62.003.

TRCP 714. PURCHASER'S BOND

In the case of a sale as provided for in the preceding rule, the purchaser of the property shall execute his bond, with two or more good and sufficient sureties, to

be approved by the officer making the sale, and payable to such officer, in a sum not less than double the amount of the purchase money, conditioned that such purchaser shall pay such purchase money at the expiration of the time given.

TRCP 715. RETURN OF BOND

The bond provided for in the preceding rule shall be returned by the officer taking the same to the clerk or justice of the peace from whose court the order of sale issued, with such order, and shall be filed among the papers in the cause.

TRCP 716. RECOVERY ON BOND

In case the purchaser does not pay the purchase money at the expiration of the time given, judgment shall be rendered against all the obligors in such bond for the amount of such purchase money, interest thereon and all costs incurred in the enforcement and collection of the same; and execution shall issue thereon in the name of the plaintiff in the suit, as in other cases, and the money when collected shall be paid to the clerk or justice of the peace to abide the final decision of the cause.

SECTION 9. TRIAL OF RIGHT OF PROPERTY

TRCP 717. CLAIMANT MUST MAKE AFFIDAVIT

Whenever a distress warrant, writ of execution, sequestration, attachment, or other like writ is levied upon personal property, and such property, or any part thereof, shall be claimed by any claimant who is not a party to such writ, such claimant may make application that such claim is made in good faith, and file such application with the court in which such suit is pending. Such application may be supported by affidavits of the claimant, his agent, his attorney, or other persons having knowledge of relevant facts. The application shall comply with all statutory requirements and shall state the grounds for such claim and the specific facts relied upon by the claimant to warrant the required findings by the court.

The claim shall not be quashed because two or more grounds are stated conjunctively or disjunctively. The application and any affidavits shall be made on personal knowledge and shall set forth such facts as would be admissible in evidence; provided that facts may be stated based upon information and belief if the grounds of such belief are specifically stated.

No property shall be delivered to the claimant except on written order of the court after a hearing pursuant to Rule 718. The court in its order granting the application shall make specific findings of facts to support the statutory grounds found to exist and shall specify the amount of the bond required of the claimant.

TRCP 718. PROPERTY DELIVERED TO CLAIMANT

Any claimant who claims an interest in property on which a writ has been levied may, by sworn written motion, seek to obtain possession of such property. Such motion shall admit or deny each finding of the order directing the issuance of the writ except where the claimant is unable to admit or deny the finding, in which case claimant shall set forth the reasons why he cannot admit or deny. Such motion shall also contain the reasons why the claimant has superior right or title to the property claimed as against the plaintiff in the writ. Unless the parties agree to an extension of time, the motion shall be heard promptly, after reasonable notice to the plaintiff (which may be less than three days), and the issue shall be determined not later than 10 days after the motion is filed. The filing of the motion shall stay any further proceedings under the writ, except for any orders concerning the care, preservation, or sale of any perishable property, until a hearing is had, and the issue is determined. The claimant shall have the burden to show superior right or title to the property claimed as against the plaintiff and defendant in the writ.

The court's determination may be made upon the basis of affidavits, if uncontroverted, setting forth such facts as would be admissible in evidence, but additional evidence, if tendered by either party shall be received and considered. The court may make all such orders, including orders concerning the care, preservation, or disposition of the property, or the proceeds therefrom if the same has been sold, as justice may require, and if the court modifies its order or the writ issued pursuant thereto, it shall make such further orders with respect to the bond as may be consistent with its modification.

TRCP 719. BOND

No property shall be put in the custody of the claimant until the claimant has filed with the officer who made the levy, a bond in an amount fixed by the court's order equal to double the value of the property so claimed, payable to the plaintiff in the writ, with sufficient surety or sureties as provided by statute to be ap-

proved by such officer, conditioned that the claimant will return the same to the officer making the levy, or his successor, in as good condition as he received it, and shall also pay the reasonable value of the use, hire, increase and fruits thereof from the date of said bond, or, in case he fails so to return said property and pay for the use of the same, that he shall pay the plaintiff the value of said property, with legal interest thereon from the date of the bond, and shall also pay all damages and costs that may be awarded against him for wrongfully suing out such claim.

The plaintiff or claimant may file a motion to increase or reduce the amount of such bond, or to question the sufficiency of the sureties thereon, in the court in which such suit is pending. Upon hearing, the court shall enter its order with respect to such bond and sufficiency of the sureties.

TRCP 720. RETURN OF BOND

Whenever any person shall claim property and shall duly make the application and give the bond, if the writ under which the levy was made was issued by a justice of the peace or a court of the county where such levy was made, the officer receiving such application and bond shall endorse on the writ that such claim has been made and application and bond given, and by whom; and shall also endorse on such bond the value of the property as assessed by himself, and shall forthwith return such bond with a copy of the writ to the proper court having jurisdiction to try such claim.

TRCP 721. OUT-COUNTY LEVY

Whenever any person shall claim property and shall make the application and give the bond as provided for herein, if the writ under which such levy was made was issued by a justice of the peace or a court of another county than that in which such levy was made, then the officer receiving such bond shall endorse on such bond the value of the property as assessed by himself, and shall forthwith return such bond with a copy of the writ, to the proper court having jurisdiction to try such claim.

TRCP 722. RETURN OF ORIGINAL WRIT

The officer taking such bond shall also endorse on the original writ, if in his possession, that such claim has been made and application and bond given, stating by whom, the names of the surety or sureties, and to what justice or court the bond has been returned; and he shall forthwith return such original writ to the tribunal from which it issued.

TRCP 723. DOCKETING CAUSE

Whenever any bond for the trial of the right of property shall be returned, the clerk of the court, or such justice of the peace, shall docket the same in the original writ proceeding in the name of the plaintiff in the writ as the plaintiff, and the claimant of the property as intervening claimant.

TRCP 724. ISSUE MADE UP

After the claim proceedings have been docketed, and on the hearing day set by the court, then the court, or the justice of the peace, as the case may be, shall enter an order directing the making and joinder of issues by the parties. Such issues shall be in writing and signed by each party or his attorney. The plaintiff shall make a brief statement of the authority and right by which he seeks to subject the property levied on to the process, and it shall be sufficient for the claimant and other parties to make brief statements of the nature of their claims thereto.

TRCP 725. JUDGMENT BY DEFAULT

If the plaintiff appears and the claimant fails to ap pear or neglects or refuses to join issue under the direction of the court or justice within the time prescribed for pleading, the plaintiff shall have judgment by default.

TRCP 726. JUDGMENT OF NON-SUIT

If the plaintiff does not appear, he shall be nonsuited.

TRCP 727. PROCEEDINGS

The proceedings and practice on the trial shall be as nearly as may be the same as in other cases before such court or justice.

TRCP 728. BURDEN OF PROOF

If the property was taken from the possession of the claimant pursuant to the original writ, the burden of proof shall be on the plaintiff in the writ. If it was taken from the possession of the defendant in such writ, or any other person than the claimant, the burden of proof shall be on the claimant.

TRCP 729. COPY OF WRIT EVIDENCE

In all trials of the right of property, under the provisions of this section in any county other than that in which the writ issued under which the levy was made, the copy of the writ herein required to be returned by the officer making the levy shall be received in evidence in like manner as the original could be.

TRCP 730. FAILURE TO ESTABLISH TITLE

Where any claimant has obtained possession of property, and shall ultimately fail to establish his right thereto, judgment may be rendered against him and his sureties for the value of the property, with legal interest thereon from the date of such bond. Such judgment shall be rendered in favor of the plaintiff or defendant in the writ, or of the several plaintiffs or defendants, if more than one, and shall fix the amount of the claim of each.

TRCP 731. EXECUTION SHALL ISSUE

If such judgment should not be satisfied by a return of the property, then after the expiration of ten days from the date of the judgment, execution shall issue thereon in the name of the plaintiff or defendant for the amount of the claim, or of all the plaintiffs or defendants for the sum of their several claims, provided the amount of such judgment shall inure to the benefit of any person who shall show superior right or title to the property claimed as against the claimant; but if such judgment be for a less amount than the sum of the several plaintiffs' or defendants' claims, then the respective rights and priorities of the several plaintiffs or defendants shall be fixed and adjusted in the judgment.

TRCP 732. RETURN OF PROPERTY BY CLAIMANT

If, within ten days from the rendition of said judgment, the claimant shall return such property in as good condition as he received it, and pay for the use of the same together with the damages and costs, such delivery and payment shall operate as a satisfaction of such judgment.

TRCP 733. CLAIM IS A RELEASE OF DAMAGES

A claim made to the property, under the provisions of this section, shall operate as a release of all damages by the claimant against the officer who levied upon said property.

TRCP 734. LEVY ON OTHER PROPERTY

Proceedings for the trial of right of property under these rules shall in no case prevent the plaintiff in the writ from having a levy made upon any other property of the defendant.

PART VII. RULES RELATING TO SPECIAL PROCEEDINGS

SECTION 1. PROCEDURES RELATED TO FORECLOSURES OF CERTAIN LIENS

TRCP 735. FORECLOSURES REQUIRING A COURT ORDER

735.1 Liens Affected.

Rule 736 provides the procedure for obtaining a court order, when required, to allow foreclosure of a lien containing a power of sale in the security instrument, dedicatory instrument, or declaration creating the lien, including a lien securing any of the following:

(a) a home equity loan, reverse mortgage, or home equity line of credit under article XVI, sections 50(a)(6), 50(k), and 50(t) of the Texas Constitution;

(b) a tax lien transfer or property tax loan under sections 32.06 and 32.065 of the Tax Code; or

(c) a property owners' association assessment under section 209.0092 of the Property Code.

735.2 Other Statutory and Contractual Foreclosure Provisions Unaltered.

A Rule 736 order does not alter any foreclosure requirement or duty imposed under applicable law or the terms of the loan agreement, contract, or lien sought to be foreclosed. The only issue to be determined in a Rule 736 proceeding is whether a party may obtain an order under Rule 736 to proceed with foreclosure under applicable law and the terms of the loan agreement, contract, or lien sought to be foreclosed.

735.3 Judicial Foreclosure Unaffected.

A Rule 736 order is not a substitute for a judgment for judicial foreclosure, but any loan agreement, contract, or lien that may be foreclosed using Rule 736 procedures may also be foreclosed by judgment in an action for judicial foreclosure.

See also Tex. Const. art. 16, §50; Prop. Code §51.002.

TRCP 736. EXPEDITED ORDER PROCEEDING

736.1 Application.

(a) ***Where Filed.*** An application for an expedited order allowing the foreclosure of a lien listed in Rule

735 to proceed must be filed in a county where all or part of the real property encumbered by the loan agreement, contract, or lien sought to be foreclosed is located or in a probate court with jurisdiction over proceedings involving the property.

(b) ***Style.*** An application must be styled "In re: Order for Foreclosure Concerning [*state: property's mailing address*] under Tex. R. Civ. P. 736."

(c) ***When Filed.*** An application may not be filed until the opportunity to cure has expired under applicable law and the loan agreement, contract, or lien sought to be foreclosed.

(d) ***Contents.*** The application must:

(1) Identify by name and last known address each of the following parties:

(A) "Petitioner"—any person legally authorized to prosecute the foreclosure;

(B) "Respondent"—according to the records of the holder or servicer of the loan agreement, contract, or lien sought to be foreclosed:

(i) for a home equity loan, reverse mortgage, or home equity line of credit, each person obligated to pay the loan agreement, contract, or lien sought to be foreclosed and each mortgagor, if any, of the loan agreement, contract, or lien sought to be foreclosed;

(ii) for a tax lien transfer or property tax loan, each person obligated to pay the loan agreement, contract, or lien sought to be foreclosed, each mortgagor, if any, of the loan agreement, contract, or lien sought to be foreclosed, each owner of the property, and the holder of any recorded preexisting first lien secured by the property;

(iii) for a property owners' association assessment, each person obligated to pay the loan agreement, contract, or lien sought to be foreclosed who has a current ownership interest in the property.

(2) Identify the property encumbered by the loan agreement, contract, or lien sought to be foreclosed by its commonly known street address and legal description.

(3) Describe or state:

(A) the type of lien listed in Rule 735 sought to be foreclosed and its constitutional or statutory reference;

(B) the authority of the party seeking foreclosure, whether as the servicer, beneficiary, lender, investor, property owners' association, or other person with authority to prosecute the foreclosure;

(C) each person obligated to pay the loan agreement, contract, or lien sought to be foreclosed;

(D) each mortgagor, if any, of the loan agreement, contract, or lien sought to be foreclosed who is not a maker or assumer of the underlying debt;

(E) as of a date that is not more than sixty days prior to the date the application is filed:

(i) if the default is monetary, the number of unpaid scheduled payments,

(ii) if the default is monetary, the amount required to cure the default,

(iii) if the default is non-monetary, the facts creating the default, and

(iv) if applicable, the total amount required to pay off the loan agreement, contract, or lien;

(F) that the requisite notice or notices to cure the default has or have been mailed to each person as required under applicable law and the loan agreement, contract, or lien sought to be foreclosed and that the opportunity to cure has expired; and

(G) that before the application was filed, any other action required under applicable law and the loan agreement, contract, or lien sought to be foreclosed was performed.

(4) For a tax lien transfer or property tax loan, state all allegations required to be contained in the application in accordance with section 32.06(c-1)(1) of the Tax Code.

(5) Conspicuously state:

(A) that legal action is not being sought against the occupant of the property unless the occupant is also named as a respondent in the application; and

(B) that if the petitioner obtains a court order, the petitioner will proceed with a foreclosure of the property in accordance with applicable law and the terms of the loan agreement, contract, or lien sought to be foreclosed.

(6) Include an affidavit of material facts in accordance with Rule 166a(f) signed by the petitioner or the servicer describing the basis for foreclosure and, depending on the type of lien sought to be foreclosed, attach a legible copy of:

(A) the note, original recorded lien, or pertinent part of a property owners' association declaration or dedicatory instrument establishing the lien, and current assignment of the lien, if assigned;

(B) each notice required to be mailed to any person under applicable law and the loan agreement, contract, or lien sought to be foreclosed before the application was filed and proof of mailing of each notice; and

(C) for a tax lien transfer or property tax loan:

(i) the property owner's sworn document required under section 32.06(a-1) of the Tax Code; and

(ii) the taxing authority's certified statement attesting to the transfer of the lien, required under section 32.06(b) of the Tax Code.

736.2 Costs.

All filing, citation, mailing, service, and other court costs and fees are costs of court and must be paid by petitioner at the time of filing an application with the clerk of the court.

736.3 Citation.

(a) ***Issuance.***

(1) When the application is filed, the clerk must issue a separate citation for each respondent named in the application and one additional citation for the occupant of the property sought to be foreclosed.

(2) Each citation that is directed to a respondent must state that any response to the application is due the first Monday after the expiration of 38 days from the date the citation was placed in the custody of the U.S. Postal Service in accordance with the clerk's standard mailing procedures and state the date that the citation was placed in the custody of the U.S. Postal Service by the clerk.

(b) ***Service and Return.***

(1) The clerk of the court must serve each citation, with a copy of the application attached, by both first class mail and certified mail. A citation directed to a respondent must be mailed to the respondent's last known address that is stated in the application. A citation directed to the occupant of the property sought to be foreclosed must be mailed to Occupant of [*state: property's mailing address*] at the address of the property sought to be foreclosed that is stated in the application.

(2) Concurrently with service, the clerk must complete a return of service in accordance with Rule 107, except that the return of service need not contain a return receipt. For a citation mailed by the clerk in accordance with (b)(1), the date of service is the date and time the citation was placed in the custody of the U.S. Postal Service in a properly addressed, postage prepaid envelope in accordance with the clerk's standard mailing procedures.

(3) The clerk must only charge one fee per respondent or occupant served under this rule.

736.4 Discovery.

No discovery is permitted in a Rule 736 proceeding.

736.5 Response.

(a) ***Generally.*** A respondent may file a response contesting the application.

(b) ***Due Date.*** Any response to the application is due the first Monday after the expiration of 38 days from the date the citation was placed in the custody of the U.S. Postal Service in accordance with the clerk's standard mailing procedures, as stated on the citation.

(c) ***Form.*** A response must be signed in accordance with Rule 57 and may be in the form of a general denial under Rule 92, except that a respondent must affirmatively plead:

(1) why the respondent believes a respondent did not sign a loan agreement document, if applicable, that is specifically identified by the respondent;

(2) why the respondent is not obligated for payment of the lien;

(3) why the number of months of alleged default or the reinstatement or pay off amounts are materially incorrect;

(4) why any document attached to the application is not a true and correct copy of the original; or

(5) proof of payment in accordance with Rule 95.

(d) ***Other Claims.*** A response may not state an independent claim for relief. The court must, without a hearing, strike and dismiss any counterclaim, cross claim, third party claim, intervention, or cause of action filed by any person in a Rule 736 proceeding.

736.6 Hearing Required When Response Filed.

The court must not conduct a hearing under this rule unless a response is filed. If a response is filed, the court must hold a hearing after reasonable notice to the parties. The hearing on the application must not be held earlier than 20 days or later than 30 days after a request for a hearing is made by any party. At the hearing, the petitioner has the burden to prove by affidavits on file or evidence presented the grounds for granting the order sought in the application.

736.7 Default When No Response Filed.

(a) If no response to the application is filed by the due date, the petitioner may file a motion and proposed order to obtain a default order. For the purposes of obtaining a default order, all facts alleged in the application and supported by the affidavit of material facts constitute prima facie evidence of the truth of the matters alleged.

(b) The court must grant the application by default order no later than 30 days after a motion is filed under (a) if the application complies with the requirements of Rule 736.1 and was properly served in accordance with Rule 736.3. The petitioner need not appear in court to obtain a default order.

(c) The return of service must be on file with the clerk of the court for at least 10 days before the court may grant the application by default.

736.8 Order.

(a) The court must issue an order granting the application if the petitioner establishes the basis for the foreclosure. Otherwise, the court must deny the application.

(b) An order granting the application must describe:

(1) the material facts establishing the basis for foreclosure;

(2) the property to be foreclosed by commonly known mailing address and legal description;

(3) the name and last known address of each respondent subject to the order; and

(4) the recording or indexing information of each lien to be foreclosed.

(c) An order granting or denying the application is not subject to a motion for rehearing, new trial, bill of review, or appeal. Any challenge to a Rule 736 order must be made in a suit filed in a separate, independent, original proceeding in a court of competent jurisdiction.

736.9 Effect of the Order.

An order is without prejudice and has no res judicata, collateral estoppel, estoppel by judgment, or other effect in any other judicial proceeding. After an order is obtained, a person may proceed with the foreclosure process under applicable law and the terms of the lien sought to be foreclosed.

736.10 Bankruptcy.

If a respondent provides proof to the clerk of the court that respondent filed bankruptcy before an order is signed, the proceeding under this rule must be abated so long as the automatic stay is effective.

736.11 Automatic Stay and Dismissal if Independent Suit Filed.

(a) A proceeding or order under this rule is automatically stayed if a respondent files a separate, original proceeding in a court of competent jurisdiction that puts in issue any matter related to the origination, servicing, or enforcement of the loan agreement, contract, or lien sought to be foreclosed prior to 5:00 p.m. on the Monday before the scheduled foreclosure sale.

(b) Respondent must give prompt notice of the filing of the suit to petitioner or petitioner's attorney and the foreclosure trustee or substitute trustee by any reasonable means necessary to stop the scheduled foreclosure sale.

(c) Within ten days of filing suit, the respondent must file a motion and proposed order to dismiss or vacate with the clerk of the court in which the application was filed giving notice that respondent has filed an original proceeding contesting the right to foreclose in a court of competent jurisdiction. If no order has been signed, the court must dismiss a pending proceeding. If an order has been signed, the court must vacate the Rule 736 order.

(d) If the automatic stay under this rule is in effect, any foreclosure sale of the property is void. Within 10 business days of notice that the foreclosure sale was void, the trustee or substitute trustee must return to the buyer of the foreclosed property the purchase price paid by the buyer.

(e) The court may enforce the Rule 736 process under chapters 9 and 10 of the Civil Practices and Remedies Code.

736.12 Attachment of Order to Trustee's Deed.

A conformed copy of the order must be attached to the trustee or substitute trustee's foreclosure deed.

736.13 Promulgated Forms.

The Supreme Court of Texas may promulgate forms that conform to this rule.

See also Tex. Const. art. 16, §50; CPRC §§17.031, 154.028; Prop. Code §51.002.

SECTION 2. JUSTICE COURT PROCEEDINGS TO ENFORCE LANDLORD'S DUTY TO REPAIR OR REMEDY RESIDENTIAL RENTAL PROPERTY

TRCP 737. REPEALED

Editor's note: Rules 500-507 and 509 govern cases filed on or after August 31, 2013, and cases pending on August 31, 2013, unless the court determines that applying those rules to a case pending on August 31, 2013, would not be feasible or would work an injustice; in such a case, the procedure under the former rules applies. An action taken before August 31, 2013, in a case pending on August 31, 2013, that was done under any previously applicable procedure is treated as valid. If citation or other process was issued or served before August 31, 2013, in compliance with any previously applicable procedure, the party served has the time provided for under the former procedure to answer or otherwise respond. For the substance of the former rule and a comprehensive history of the amendments and repealers to that rule, see ***O'Connor's Texas Rules * Civil Trials*** (2013), p. 1083.

SECTION 3. FORCIBLE ENTRY & DETAINER

TRCP 738 TO 755. REPEALED

Editor's note: Rules 500-507 and 510 govern cases filed on or after August 31, 2013, and cases pending on August 31, 2013, unless the court determines that applying those rules to a case pending on August 31, 2013, would not be feasible or would work an injustice; in such a case, the procedure under the former rules applies. An action taken before August 31, 2013, in a case pending on August 31, 2013, that was done under any previously applicable procedure is treated as valid. If citation or other process was issued or served before August 31, 2013, in compliance with any previously applicable procedure, the party served has the time provided for under the former procedure to answer or otherwise respond. For the substance of the former rules and a comprehensive history of the amendments and repealers to those rules, see ***O'Connor's Texas Rules * Civil Trials*** (2013), p. 1086.

SECTION 4. PARTITION OF REAL ESTATE

TRCP 756. PETITION

The plaintiff's petition shall state:

(a) The names and residence, if known, of each of the other joint owners, or joint claimants, of such property.

(b) The share or interest which the plaintiff and the other joint owners, or joint claimants, of same own or claim so far as known to the plaintiff.

(c) The land sought to be partitioned shall be so described as that the same may be distinguished from any other and the estimated value thereof stated.

See also Prop. Code §23.001; ***O'Connor's Texas Family Law Handbook*** (2017), "Contents of petition," ch. 8-B, §4.4, p. 956.

ANNOTATIONS

Yoast v. Yoast, 649 S.W.2d 289, 292 (Tex.1983). "The court of appeals mischaracterized this case as a partition suit. [P's suit was for] trespass to try title. ... Partition issues may be resolved in a trespass to try title suit once the controversy as to title or right to possession is settled. That, however, does not convert the cause of action to a partition suit. [¶] A partition suit is based on the theory of common title, rather than disputed ownership."

TRCP 757. CITATION & SERVICE

Upon the filing of a petition for partition, the clerk shall issue citation for each of the joint owners, or joint claimants, named therein, as in other cases, and such citations shall be served in the manner and for the time provided for the service of citations in other cases.

ANNOTATIONS

Carper v. Halamicek, 610 S.W.2d 556, 557 (Tex. App.—Tyler 1980, writ ref'd n.r.e.). TRCP 757 "and past cases indicate that the joinder of all owners is mandatory and that no valid, binding decree of partition can be made in their absence."

TRCP 758. WHERE DEFENDANT IS UNKNOWN OR RESIDENCE IS UNKNOWN

If the plaintiff, his agent or attorney, at the commencement of any suit, or during the progress thereof, for the partition of land, shall make affidavit that an undivided portion of the land described in plaintiff's petition in said suit is owned by some person unknown to affiant, or that the place of residence of any known party owning an interest in land sought to be partitioned is unknown to affiant, the Clerk of the Court shall issue citation for publication, conforming to the requirements of Rules 114 and 115, and served in accordance with the directions of Rule 116. In case of unknown residence or party, the affidavit shall include a statement that after due diligence plaintiff and the affiant have been unable to ascertain the name or locate the residence of such party, as the case may be, and in such case it shall be the duty of the court trying the action to inquire into the sufficiency of the diligence so stated before granting any judgment.

See also ***O'Connor's Texas Family Law Handbook*** (2017), "Service by publication," ch. 8-B, §5.2.4, p. 958.

TRCP 759. JUDGMENT WHERE DEFENDANT CITED BY PUBLICATION

When the defendant has been duly cited by publication in accordance with the preceding rule, and no appearance is entered within the time prescribed for pleadings, the court shall appoint an attorney to defend in behalf of such owner or owners, and proceed as in other causes where service is made by publication. It

shall be the special duty of the court in all cases to see that its decree protects the rights of the unknown parties thereto. The judge of the court shall fix the fee of the attorney so appointed, which shall be entered and collected as costs against said unknown owner or owners.

TRCP 760. COURT SHALL DETERMINE, WHAT

Upon the hearing of the cause, the court shall determine the share or interest of each of the joint owners or claimants in the real estate sought to be divided, and all questions of law or equity affecting the title to such land which may arise.

ANNOTATIONS

Johnson v. Johnson-McHenry, 978 S.W.2d 142, 144 (Tex.App.—Austin 1998, no pet.). "[I]n a partition suit, the trial court determines whether the partition will be by sale or in kind, the share or interest of the joint owners or claimants, and all questions of law or equity affecting title. The court then allocates to the parties their rightful shares or tracts. A trial court may also exercise equitable powers in a partition suit."

TRCP 761. APPOINTMENT OF COMMISSIONERS

The court shall determine before entering the decree of partition whether the property, or any part thereof, is susceptible of partition; and, if the court determines that the whole, or any part of such property is susceptible of partition, then the court for that part of such property held to be susceptible of partition shall enter a decree directing the partition of such real estate, describing the same, to be made in accordance with the respective shares or interests of each of such parties entitled thereto, specify in such decree the share or interest of each party, and shall appoint three or more competent and disinterested persons as commissioners to make such partition in accordance with such decree and the law, a majority of which commissioners may act.

See also *O'Connor's Texas Family Law Handbook* (2017), "Partition in kind," ch. 8-B, §13.1.1, p. 964.

ANNOTATIONS

Goldberg v. Zinn, No. 14-11-01091-CV (Tex.App.—Houston [14th Dist.] 2013, no pet.) (memo op.; 6-6-13). "Unlike most other proceedings, a partition involves two final and appealable judgments. In the first judgment, the trial court (1) determines the interests of each of the joint owners or claimants in the real estate sought to be divided and decides all questions of law and equity affecting the title to such land; (2) determines whether the property is susceptible to partition or the subject of a sale; and (3) appoints commissioners to partition the property in accordance with the respective shares or interests of each of such parties entitled thereto. In the second judgment, the court approves of the commissioners' report and partitions the property in kind or by sale. [¶] [P] has not disputed the propriety of the appraisals in this case, and the record contains no evidence contradicting them. Without conflicting evidence, there was no need for the district court to 'try' the case for purposes of [TRCP] 296. [¶] As a result, findings of fact and conclusions of law were not required under Rule 296." *See also* ***Williams v. Mai***, 471 S.W.3d 16, 18 (Tex.App.—Houston [1st Dist.] 2015, no pet.).

Benson v. Fox, 589 S.W.2d 823, 826 (Tex.App.—Tyler 1979, no writ). "Rule 761 employs the word 'partition' in a restricted sense as synonymous with the phrase 'partition in kind.'"

TRCP 762. WRIT OF PARTITION

The clerk shall issue a writ of partition, directed to the sheriff or any constable of the county, commanding such sheriff or constable to notify each of the commissioners of their appointment as such, and shall accompany such writ with a certified copy of the decree of the court directing the partition.

TRCP 763. SERVICE OF WRIT OF PARTITION

The writ of partition shall be served by reading the same to each of the persons named therein as commissioners, and by delivering to any one of them the accompanying certified copy of the decree of the court.

See also *O'Connor's Texas Family Law Handbook* (2017), "Commissioners' Procedure for In-Kind Partition of Real Property," ch. 8-B, §14, p. 965.

TRCP 764. MAY APPOINT SURVEYOR

The court may, should it be deemed necessary, appoint a surveyor to assist the commissioners in making the partition, in which case the writ of partition shall name such surveyor, and shall be served upon him by reading the same to him.

TRCP 765. RETURN OF WRIT

A writ of partition, unless otherwise directed by the court, shall be made returnable twenty days from date of service on the commissioner last served; and the officer serving it shall endorse thereon the time and manner of such service.

TRCP 766. SHALL PROCEED TO PARTITION

The commissioners, or a majority of them, shall proceed to partition the real estate described in the decree of the court, in accordance with the directions contained in such decree and with the provisions of law and these rules.

See also *O'Connor's Texas Family Law Handbook* (2017), "Partition property," ch. 8-B, §14.2.1, p. 966.

ANNOTATIONS

Goldberg v. Zinn, No. 14-11-01091-CV (Tex.App.—Houston [14th Dist.] 2013, no pet.) (memo op.; 6-6-13). See annotation under TRCP 761, p. 1277.

TRCP 767. MAY CAUSE SURVEY

If the commissioners deem it necessary, they may cause to be surveyed the real estate to be partitioned into several tracts or parcels.

TRCP 768. SHALL DIVIDE REAL ESTATE

The commissioners shall divide the real estate to be partitioned into as many shares as there are persons entitled thereto, as determined by the court, each share to contain one or more tracts or parcels, as the commissioners may think proper, having due regard in the division to the situation, quantity and advantages of each share, so that the shares may be equal in value, as nearly as may be, in proportion to the respective interests of the parties entitled. The commissioners shall then proceed by lot to set apart to each of the parties entitled one of said shares, as determined by the decrees of the court.

ANNOTATIONS

Grimes v. Hall, 211 S.W.2d 956, 958 (Tex.App.—Eastland 1948, no writ). "Where the interests of the parties in the realty to be partitioned are unequal, selection of owners of shares by lot is not required."

TRCP 769. REPORT OF COMMISSIONERS

When the commissioners have completed the partition, they shall report the same in writing and under oath to the court, which report shall show:

(a) The property divided, describing the same.

(b) The several tracts or parcels into which the same was divided by them, describing each particularly.

(c) The number of shares and the land which constitutes each share, and the estimated value of each share.

(d) The allotment of each share.

(e) The report shall be accompanied by such field notes and maps as may be necessary to make the same intelligible.

The clerk shall immediately mail written notice of the filing of the report to all parties.

TRCP 770. PROPERTY INCAPABLE OF DIVISION

Should the court be of the opinion that a fair and equitable division of the real estate, or any part thereof, cannot be made, it shall order a sale of so much as is incapable of partition, which sale shall be for cash, or upon such other terms as the court may direct, and shall be made as under execution or by private or public sale through a receiver, if the court so order, and the proceeds thereof shall be returned into court and be partitioned among the persons entitled thereto, according to their respective interests.

ANNOTATIONS

Champion v. Robinson, 392 S.W.3d 118, 123 (Tex. App.—Texarkana 2012, pet. denied). "Texas law 'favors partition in kind over partition by sale.' [A]lthough [TRCP 770] seems to provide that the property must be 'incapable' of partition in kind, the Rule 'does not mean incapable in a physical sense.' Our inquiry is focused on whether partition in kind is 'fair and equitable,' which includes whether 'property can be divided in kind without materially impairing its value.' The party seeking partition by sale bears the burden of proving a partition in kind would not be fair and equitable." *See also* ***Daven Corp. v. TARH E&P Holdings, L.P.***, 441 S.W.3d 770, 776-77 (Tex.App.—San Antonio 2014, pet. denied).

TRCP 771. OBJECTIONS TO REPORT

Either party to the suit may file objections to any report of the commissioners in partition within thirty days of the date the report is filed, and in such case a trial of the issues thereon shall be had as in other cases. If the report be found to be erroneous in any material respect, or unequal and unjust, the same shall be rejected, and other commissioners shall be appointed by the Court, and the same proceedings had as in the first instance.

See also *O'Connor's Texas Family Law Handbook* (2017), "Contesting commissioners' report," ch. 8-B, §14.4, p. 966; "Second trial," ch. 8-B, §14.5, p. 967; "Rejection of report," ch. 8-B, §14.6, p. 967.

ANNOTATIONS

Williams v. Mai, 471 S.W.3d 16, 19 (Tex.App.—Houston [1st Dist.] 2015, no pet.). "Because the commissioners' report was not filed in the trial court, [D], who had objected to the preliminary replat before entry of judgment, was unable to object to the commissioners' report and have a trial of the issues as she is allowed to do under Rule 771. The trial court abused its discretion in depriving [D] of the right to object and to have a trial on the contested issues in the report."

Sand Point Ranch, Ltd. v. Smith, 363 S.W.3d 268, 272 (Tex.App.—Corpus Christi 2012, no pet.). "[A]ny complaint not made by a party in its rule 771 objection is waived on appeal."

Ellis v. First City Nat'l Bank, 864 S.W.2d 555, 557 (Tex.App.—Tyler 1993, no writ). "The party objecting to the commissioners' report [has] the burden of proving that it is materially erroneous or that it unequally and unjustly partitions the property."

SECTION 5. PARTITION OF PERSONAL PROPERTY

TRCP 772. PROCEDURE

An action seeking partition of personal property as authorized by Section 23.001, Texas Property Code, shall be commenced in the same manner as other civil suits, and the several owners or claimants of such property shall be cited as in other cases.

TRCP 773. VALUE ASCERTAINED

The separate value of each article of such personal property, and the allotment in kind to which each owner is entitled, shall be ascertained by the court, with or without a jury.

ANNOTATIONS

Price v. Price, 394 S.W.2d 855, 858 (Tex.App.—Tyler 1965, writ ref'd n.r.e.). "The fact that the property has now been transformed into personal property in the form of money would not alter the application rule, but would only make the property more susceptible to a partition in kind."

TRCP 774. DECREE OF COURT EXECUTED

When partition in kind of personal property is ordered by the judgment of the court, a writ shall be issued in accordance with such judgment, commanding the sheriff or constable of the county where the property may be to put the parties forthwith in possession of the property allotted to each respectively.

TRCP 775. PROPERTY SOLD

When personal property will not admit of a fair and equitable partition, the court shall ascertain the proportion to which each owner thereof is entitled, and order the property to be sold, and execution shall be issued to the sheriff or any constable of the county where the property may be describing such property and commanding such officer to sell the same as in other cases of execution, and pay over the proceeds of sale to the parties entitled thereto, in the proportion ascertained by the judgment of the court.

SECTION 6. PARTITION: MISCELLANEOUS PROVISIONS

TRCP 776. CONSTRUCTION

No provision of the statutes or rules relating to partition shall affect the mode of proceeding prescribed by law for the partition of estates of decedents among the heirs and legatees, nor preclude partition in any other manner authorized by the rules of equity, which rules shall govern in proceedings for partition in all respects not provided for by law or these rules.

TRCP 777. PLEADING & PRACTICE

The same rules of pleading, practice and evidence which govern in other civil actions shall govern in suits for partition, when not in conflict with any provisions of the law or these rules relating to partition.

ANNOTATIONS

Rayson v. Johns, 524 S.W.2d 380, 382 (Tex.App.—Texarkana 1975, writ ref'd n.r.e.). "[I]n whatever posture the question has arisen, the courts have treated disputed issues of fact in partition proceedings as being for the jury when one has been properly demanded. *At 383:* An issue of fact was ... raised on the question of the susceptibility of the land to division in kind, and since [Ds] properly requested it, they were entitled to a jury determination of the issue."

TRCP 778. COSTS

The court shall adjudge the costs in a partition suit to be paid by each party to whom a share has been allotted in proportion to the value of such share.

See also *O'Connor's Texas Family Law Handbook* (2017), "Court costs," ch. 8-B, §6.3.3(9), p. 961.

SECTION 7. QUO WARRANTO

TRCP 779. JOINDER OF PARTIES

When it appears to the court or judge that the several rights of diverse parties to the same office or franchise may properly be determined on one information, the court or judge may give leave to join all such persons in the same information in order to try their respective rights to such office or franchise.

TRCP 780. CITATION TO ISSUE

When such information is filed, the clerk shall issue citation as in civil actions, commanding the defendant to appear and answer the relator in an information in the nature of a quo warranto.

TRCP 781. PROCEEDINGS AS IN CIVIL CASES

Every person or corporation who shall be cited as hereinbefore provided shall be entitled to all the rights in the trial and investigation of the matters alleged against him, as in cases of trial in civil cases in this State. Either party may prosecute an appeal or writ of error from any judgment rendered, as in other civil cases, subject, however, to the provisions of Rule 42,[1] Texas Rules of Appellate Procedure, and the appellate court shall give preference to such case, and hear and determine the same as early as practicable.

1. **Editor's note:** Now TRAP 28.

TRCP 782. REMEDY CUMULATIVE

The remedy and mode of procedure hereby prescribed shall be construed to be cumulative of any now existing.

SECTION 8. TRESPASS TO TRY TITLE

TRCP 783. REQUISITES OF PETITION

The petition shall state:

(a) The real names of the plaintiff and defendant and their residences, if known.

(b) A description of the premises by metes and bounds, or with sufficient certainty to identify the same, so that from such description possession thereof may be delivered, and state the county or counties in which the same are situated.

(c) The interest which the plaintiff claims in the premises, whether it be a fee simple or other estate; and, if he claims an undivided interest, the petition shall state the same and the amount thereof.

(d) That the plaintiff was in possession of the premises or entitled to such possession.

(e) That the defendant afterward unlawfully entered upon and dispossessed him of such premises, stating the date, and withholds from him the possession thereof.

(f) If rents and profits or damages are claimed, such facts as show the plaintiff to be entitled thereto and the amount thereof.

(g) It shall conclude with a prayer for the relief sought.

TRCP 784. THE POSSESSOR SHALL BE DEFENDANT

The defendant in the action shall be the person in possession if the premises are occupied, or some person claiming title thereto in case they are unoccupied.

TRCP 785. MAY JOIN AS DEFENDANTS, WHEN

The plaintiff may join as a defendant with the person in possession, any other person who, as landlord, remainderman, reversioner or otherwise, may claim title to the premises, or any part thereof, adversely to the plaintiff.

TRCP 786. WARRANTOR, ETC., MAY BE MADE A PARTY

When a party is sued for lands, the real owner or warrantor may make himself, or may be made, a party defendant in the suit, and shall be entitled to make such defense as if he had been the original defendant in the action.

TRCP 787. LANDLORD MAY BECOME DEFENDANT

When such action shall be commenced against a tenant in possession, the landlord may enter himself as the defendant, or he may be made a party on motion of such tenant; and he shall be entitled to make the same defense as if the suit had been originally commenced against him.

TRCP 788. MAY FILE PLEA OF "NOT GUILTY" ONLY

The defendant in such action may file only the plea of "not guilty," which shall state in substance that he is not guilty of the injury complained of in the petition filed by the plaintiff against him, except that if he claims an allowance for improvements, he shall state the facts entitling him to the same.

TRCP 789. PROOF UNDER SUCH PLEA

Under such plea of "not guilty" the defendant may give in evidence any lawful defense to the action except the defense of limitations, which shall be specially pleaded.

TRCP 790. ANSWER TAKEN AS ADMITTING POSSESSION

Such plea or any other answer to the merits shall be an admission by the defendant, for the purpose of that action, that he was in possession of the premises sued for, or that he claimed title thereto at the time of commencing the action, unless he states distinctly in his answer the extent of his possession or claim, in which case it shall be an admission to such extent only.

TRCP 791. MAY DEMAND ABSTRACT OF TITLE

After answer filed, either party may, by notice in writing, duly served on the opposite party or his attorney of record, not less than ten days before the trial of the cause, demand an abstract in writing of the claim or title to the premises in question upon which he relies.

TRCP 792. TIME TO FILE ABSTRACT

Such abstract of title shall be filed with the papers of the cause that within thirty days after the service of the notice, or within such further time that the court on good cause shown may grant; and in default thereof, the court may, after notice and hearing prior to the beginning of trial, order that no written instruments which are evidence of the claim or title of such opposite party be given on trial.

TRCP 793. ABSTRACT SHALL STATE, WHAT

The abstract mentioned in the two preceding rules shall state:

(a) The nature of each document or written instrument intended to be used as evidence and its date; or

(b) If a contract or conveyance, its date, the parties thereto and the date of the proof of acknowledgment, and before what officer the same was made; and

(c) Where recorded, stating the book and page of the record.

(d) If not recorded in the county when the trial is had, copies of such instrument, with the names of the subscribing witnesses, shall be included. If such unrecorded instrument be lost or destroyed it shall be sufficient to state the nature of such instrument and its loss or destruction.

TRCP 794. AMENDED ABSTRACT

The court may allow either party to file an amended abstract of title, under the same rules, which authorize the amendment of pleadings so far as they are applicable; but in all cases the documentary evidence of title shall at the trial be confined to the matters contained in the abstract of title.

TRCP 795. RULES IN OTHER CASES OBSERVED

The trial shall be conducted according to the rules of pleading, practice and evidence in other cases in the district court and conformable to the principles of trial by ejectment, except as otherwise provided by these rules.

TRCP 796. SURVEYOR APPOINTED, ETC.

The judge of the court may, either in term time or in vacation, at his own discretion, or on motion of either party to the action appoint a surveyor, who shall survey the premises in controversy pursuant to the order of the court, and report his action under oath to such court. If said report be not rejected for good cause shown, the same shall be admitted as evidence on the trial.

TRCP 797. SURVEY UNNECESSARY, WHEN

Where there is no dispute as to the lines or boundaries of the land in controversy, or where the defendant admits that he is in possession of the lands or tenements included in the plaintiff's claim, or title, an order of survey shall be unnecessary.

TRCP 798. COMMON SOURCE OF TITLE

It shall not be necessary for the plaintiff to deraign title beyond a common source. Proof of a common source may be made by the plaintiff by certified copies of the deeds showing a chain of title to the defendant emanating from and under such common source. Before any such certified copies shall be read in evidence, they shall be filed with the papers of the suit three days before the trial, and the adverse party served with notice of such filing as in other cases. Such certified copies shall not be evidence of title in the defendant unless

offered in evidence by him. The plaintiff may make any legal objection to such certified copies, or the originals thereof, when introduced by the defendant.

TRCP 799. JUDGMENT BY DEFAULT

If the defendant, who has been personally served with citation according to law or these rules fails to appear and answer by himself or attorney within the time prescribed by law or these rules for other actions in the district court, then judgment by default may be entered against him and in favor of the plaintiff for the title to the premises, or the possession thereof, or for both, according to the petition, and for all costs, without any proof of title by the plaintiff.

TRCP 800. PROOF EX PARTE

If the defendant has been cited only by publication, and fails to appear and answer by himself, or by attorney of his own selection, or if any defendant, having answered, fails to appear by himself or attorney when the case is called for trial on its merits, the plaintiff shall make such proof as will entitle him prima facie to recover, whereupon the proper judgment shall be entered.

TRCP 801. WHEN DEFENDANT CLAIMS PART ONLY

Where the defendant claims part of the premises only, the answer shall be equivalent to a disclaimer of the balance.

TRCP 802. WHEN PLAINTIFF PROVES PART

Where the defendant claims the whole premises, and the plaintiff shows himself entitled to recover part, the plaintiff shall recover such part and costs.

TRCP 803. MAY RECOVER A PART

When there are two or more plaintiffs or defendants any one or more of the plaintiffs may recover against one or more of the defendants the premises, or any part thereof, or any interest therein, or damages, according to the rights of the parties.

TRCP 804. THE JUDGMENT

Upon the finding of the jury, or of the court where the case is tried by the court, in favor of the plaintiff for the whole or any part of the premises in controversy, the judgment shall be that the plaintiff recover of the defendant the title or possession, or both, as the case may be, of such premises, describing them, and where he recovers the possession, that he have his writ of possession.

TRCP 805. DAMAGES

Where it is alleged and proved that one of the parties is in possession of the premises, the court or jury, if they find for the adverse party, shall assess the damages for the use and occupation of the premises. If special injury to the property be alleged and proved, the damages for such injury shall also be assessed, and the proper judgment shall be entered therefor, on which execution may issue.

TRCP 806. CLAIM FOR IMPROVEMENTS

When the defendant or person in possession has claimed an allowance for improvements in accordance with Sections 22.021-22.024, Texas Property Code, the claim for use and occupation and damages mentioned in the preceding rule shall be considered and acted on in connection with such claim by the defendant or person in possession.

TRCP 807. JUDGMENT WHEN CLAIM FOR IMPROVEMENTS IS MADE

When a claim for improvements is successfully made under Sections 22.021-22.024, Texas Property Code, the judgment shall recite the estimated value of the premises without the improvements, and shall also include the conditions, stipulations and directions contained in Sections 22.021-22.024, Texas Property Code so far as applicable to the case before the court.

TRCP 808. THESE RULES SHALL NOT GOVERN, WHEN

Nothing in Sections 22.001-22.045, Texas Property Code, shall be so construed as to alter, impair or take away the rights of parties, as arising under the laws in force before the introduction of the common law, but the same shall be decided by the principles of the law under which the same accrued, or by which the same were regulated or in any manner affected.

TRCP 809. THESE RULES SHALL NOT GOVERN, WHEN

Nothing in these rules relating to trespass to try title shall be so construed as to alter, impair or take away the rights of parties, as arising under the laws in force before the introduction of the common law, but the same shall be decided by the principles of the law under which the same accrued, or by which the same were regulated or in any manner affected.

SECTION 9. SUITS AGAINST NON-RESIDENTS

TRCP 810. REQUISITES OF PLEADINGS

The petition in actions authorized by Section 17.003, Civil Practice and Remedies Code, shall state the real names of the plaintiff and defendant, and shall describe the property involved with sufficient certainty to identify the same, the interest which the plaintiff claims, and such proceedings shall be had in such action as may be necessary to fully settle and determine the question of right or title in and to said property between the parties to said suit, and to decree the title or right of the party entitled thereto; and the court may issue the appropriate order to carry such decree, judgment or order into effect; and whenever such petition has been duly filed and citation thereon has been duly served by publication as required by Rules 114-116, the plaintiff may, at any time prior to entering the decree by leave of court first had and obtained, file amended and supplemental pleadings that do not subject additional property to said suit without the necessity of reciting the defendants so cited as aforesaid.

TRCP 811. SERVICE BY PUBLICATION IN ACTIONS UNDER SECTION 17.003, CIVIL PRACTICE & REMEDIES CODE

In actions authorized by Section 17.003, Civil Practice and Remedies Code, service on the defendant or defendants may be made by publication as is provided by Rules 114-116 or by service of notice of the character and in the manner provided by Rule 108.

TRCP 812. NO JUDGMENT BY DEFAULT

No judgment by default shall be taken in such case when service has been had by publication, but in such case the facts entitling the plaintiff to judgment shall be exhibited to the court on the trial; and a statement of facts shall be filed as provided by law and these rules in suits against nonresidents of this State served by publication, where no appearance has been made by them.

TRCP 813. SUIT TO EXTINGUISH LIEN

If said suit shall be for the extinguishment of a lien or claim for money on said property that may be held by the defendant, the amount thereof, with interest, shall be ascertained by the court; and the same deposited in the registry of the court, subject to be drawn by the parties entitled thereto; but in such case no decree shall be entered until said sum is deposited; which fact shall be noted in said decree.

PART VIII. CLOSING RULES

TRCP 814. EFFECTIVE DATE

These rules shall take effect on September 1st, 1941. They shall govern all proceedings in actions brought after they take effect, and also all further proceedings in actions then pending, except to the extent that in the opinion of the court their application in a particular action pending when the rules take effect would not be feasible or would work injustice, in which event the former procedure shall apply. All things properly done under any previously existing rule or statutes prior to the taking effect of these rules shall be treated as valid. Where citation or other process is issued and served in compliance with existing rules or laws prior to the taking effect of these rules, the party upon whom such citation or other process has been served shall have the time provided for under such previously existing rules or laws in which to comply therewith.

TRCP 815. SUBSTANTIVE RIGHTS UNAFFECTED

These rules shall not be construed to enlarge or diminish any substantive rights or obligations of any parties to any civil action.

See also Gov't Code §22.004(a).

TRCP 816. JURISDICTION & VENUE UNAFFECTED

These rules shall not be construed to extend or limit the jurisdiction of the courts of the State of Texas nor the venue of actions therein.

TRCP 817. RENUMBERED

TRCP 818. REFERENCE TO FORMER STATUTES

Wherever any statute or rule refers to any practice or procedure in any law, laws, statute or statutes, or to a title, chapter, section, or article of the statutes, or contains any reference of any such nature, and the matter referred to has been supplanted in whole or in part by these rules, every such reference shall be deemed to be to the pertinent part or parts of these rules.

TRCP 819. PROCEDURE CONTINUED

All procedure prescribed by statutes of the State of Texas not specifically listed in the accompanying enumeration of repealed articles shall, insofar as the same

is not inconsistent with the provisions of these rules, continue in accordance with the provisions of such statutes as rules of court. In case of inconsistency between the provisions of these rules and any statutory procedure not specifically listed as repealed, these rules shall apply.

TRCP 820. WORKERS' COMPENSATION LAW

All portions of the Workers' Compensation Law, Articles 8306-8309-1, Revised Civil Statutes, and amendments thereto, which relate to matters of practice and procedure are hereby adopted and retained in force and effect as rules of court.

TRCP 821. PRIOR COURT RULES REPEALED

These rules shall supersede all Court Rules heretofore promulgated for any court; and all of said prior Court Rules are hereby repealed; provided, however, any rules of procedure heretofore adopted by a particular county or district court or by any Court of Appeals which were not of general application but were solely to regulate procedure in the particular court promulgating such rules are to remain in force and effect insofar as they are not inconsistent with these rules.

TRCP 822. TITLE

These rules may be known and cited as the Texas Rules of Civil Procedure.

Texas Rules of Evidence

Annotated Rules

Table of Contents

ARTICLE I. GENERAL PROVISIONS

TRE 101. TITLE, SCOPE, & APPLICABILITY OF THE RULES; DEFINITIONS

(a) Title. These rules may be cited as the Texas Rules of Evidence.

(b) Scope. These rules apply to proceedings in Texas courts except as otherwise provided in subdivisions (d)-(f).

(c) Rules on Privilege. The rules on privilege apply to all stages of a case or proceeding.

(d) Exception for Constitutional or Statutory Provisions or Other Rules. Despite these rules, a court must admit or exclude evidence if required to do so by the United States or Texas Constitution, a federal or Texas statute, or a rule prescribed by the United States or Texas Supreme Court or the Texas Court of Criminal Appeals. If possible, a court should resolve by reasonable construction any inconsistency between these rules and applicable constitutional or statutory provisions or other rules.

(e) Exceptions. These rules—except for those on privilege—do not apply to:

(1) the court's determination, under Rule 104(a), on a preliminary question of fact governing admissibility;

(2) grand jury proceedings; and

(3) the following miscellaneous proceedings:

(A) an application for habeas corpus in extradition, rendition, or interstate detainer proceedings;

(B) an inquiry by the court under Code of Criminal Procedure article 46B.004 to determine whether evidence exists that would support a finding that the defendant may be incompetent to stand trial;

(C) bail proceedings other than hearings to deny, revoke, or increase bail;

(D) hearings on justification for pretrial detention not involving bail;

(E) proceedings to issue a search or arrest warrant; and

(F) direct contempt determination proceedings.

(f) Exception for Justice Court Cases. These rules do not apply to justice court cases except as authorized by Texas Rule of Civil Procedure 500.3.

(g) Exception for Military Justice Hearings. The Texas Code of Military Justice, Tex. Gov't Code §§432.001-432.195, governs the admissibility of evidence in hearings held under that Code.

(h) Definitions. In these rules:

(1) "civil case" means a civil action or proceeding;

(2) "criminal case" means a criminal action or proceeding, including an examining trial;

(3) "public office" includes a public agency;

(4) "record" includes a memorandum, report, or data compilation;

(5) a "rule prescribed by the United States or Texas Supreme Court or the Texas Court of Criminal Appeals" means a rule adopted by any of those courts under statutory authority;

(6) "unsworn declaration" means an unsworn declaration made in accordance with Tex. Civ. Prac. & Rem. Code §132.001; and

(7) a reference to any kind of written material or any other medium includes electronically stored information.

See also Brown & Rondon, *Texas Rules of Evidence Handbook*, p. 43.

TRE 102. PURPOSE

These rules should be construed so as to administer every proceeding fairly, eliminate unjustifiable expense and delay, and promote the development of evidence law, to the end of ascertaining the truth and securing a just determination.

See also Brown & Rondon, *Texas Rules of Evidence Handbook*, p. 56.

TRE 103. RULINGS ON EVIDENCE

(a) Preserving a Claim of Error. A party may claim error in a ruling to admit or exclude evidence only if the error affects a substantial right of the party and:

(1) if the ruling admits evidence, a party, on the record:

(A) timely objects or moves to strike; and

(B) states the specific ground, unless it was apparent from the context; or

(2) if the ruling excludes evidence, a party informs the court of its substance by an offer of proof, unless the substance was apparent from the context.

(b) Not Needing to Renew an Objection. When the court hears a party's objections outside the presence of the jury and rules that evidence is admis-

sible, a party need not renew an objection to preserve a claim of error for appeal.

(c) **Court's Statement About the Ruling; Directing an Offer of Proof.** The court must allow a party to make an offer of proof outside the jury's presence as soon as practicable—and before the court reads its charge to the jury. The court may make any statement about the character or form of the evidence, the objection made, and the ruling. At a party's request, the court must direct that an offer of proof be made in question-and-answer form. Or the court may do so on its own.

(d) **Preventing the Jury from Hearing Inadmissible Evidence.** To the extent practicable, the court must conduct a jury trial so that inadmissible evidence is not suggested to the jury by any means.

(e) **Taking Notice of Fundamental Error in Criminal Cases.** In criminal cases, a court may take notice of a fundamental error affecting a substantial right, even if the claim of error was not properly preserved.

See also TRAP 44.1; *O'Connor's Texas Rules*, "Motion in Limine," ch. 5-E, p. 406; "Objecting to Evidence," ch. 8-D, p. 801; "Offer of Proof & Bill of Exception," ch. 8-E, p. 811; Brown & Rondon, *Texas Rules of Evidence Handbook*, p. 58.

ANNOTATIONS

In re Toyota Motor Sales, U.S.A., Inc., 407 S.W.3d 746, 760 (Tex.2013). "[W]here ... the party that requested the limine order *itself* introduces the evidence into the record, and then fails to immediately object, ask for a curative or limiting instruction or, alternatively, move for mistrial, the party waives any subsequent alleged error on the point."

PNS Stores v. Munguia, 484 S.W.3d 503, 511 (Tex. App.—Houston [14th Dist.] 2016, no pet.). "To adequately and effectively preserve error, an offer of proof must show the nature of the evidence specifically enough so that the reviewing court can determine its admissibility. The offer of proof may be made by counsel, who should reasonably and specifically summarize the evidence offered and state its relevance unless already apparent. If counsel makes such an offer, he must describe the actual content of the testimony and not merely comment on the reasons for it." *See also* ***PPC Transp. v. Metcalf***, 254 S.W.3d 636, 640-41 (Tex. App.—Tyler 2008, no pet.).

Bowman v. Patel, No. 01-10-00811-CV (Tex.App.—Houston [1st Dist.] 2012, no pet.) (memo op.; 2-16-12). "An offer of proof may be in the form of concise statement by counsel or in question-and-answer form. It is not required that the offer of proof show what specific facts the examination would reveal, but the appellant must clearly inform the trial court of the subject matter about which it wants to examine the witness."

Bobbora v. Unitrin Ins., 255 S.W.3d 331, 334-35 (Tex.App.—Dallas 2008, no pet.). "To preserve error concerning the exclusion of evidence, the complaining party must actually offer the evidence and secure an adverse ruling from the court. While the reviewing court may be able to discern from the record the nature of the evidence and the propriety of the trial court's ruling, without an offer of proof, we can never determine whether exclusion of the evidence was harmful. ... An offer of proof preserves error for appeal if: (1) it is made before the court, the court reporter, and opposing counsel, outside the presence of the jury; (2) it is preserved in the reporter's record; and (3) it is made before the charge is read to the jury. When no offer of proof is made before the trial court, the party must introduce the excluded testimony into the record by a formal bill of exception. A formal bill of exception must be presented to the trial court for its approval, and, if the parties agree to the contents of the bill, the trial court must sign the bill and file it with the trial court clerk. Failure to demonstrate the substance of the excluded evidence results in waiver." *See also* ***Perez v. Lopez***, 74 S.W.3d 60, 66 (Tex.App.—El Paso 2002, no pet.).

Benavides v. Cushman, Inc., 189 S.W.3d 875, 885 (Tex.App.—Houston [1st Dist.] 2006, no pet.). "'[A]ny error in admitting evidence is cured where the same evidence comes in elsewhere without objection.'"

Greenberg Traurig of N.Y., P.C. v. Moody, 161 S.W.3d 56, 91 (Tex.App.—Houston [14th Dist.] 2004, no pet.). "Because a trial court's ruling on a motion in limine preserves nothing for review, a party must object at trial when the testimony is offered to preserve error for appellate review. However, not all pretrial motions are motions in limine. There is a distinction between a motion in limine and a pretrial ruling on admissibility. The trial court has the authority to make a pretrial ruling on the admissibility of evidence."

Bean v. Baxter Healthcare Corp., 965 S.W.2d 656, 660 (Tex.App.—Houston [14th Dist.] 1998, no pet.). "[P] preserved error after its initial offer of the videotape. If exclusion of evidence is based on the substance

of the evidence, however, the offering party must reoffer it if it again becomes relevant. This may occur when the evidence is pertinent to rebuttal. Error is waived if the offering party fails to reoffer evidence for a limited purpose after it has been excluded pursuant to a general objection."

Chance v. Chance, 911 S.W.2d 40, 52 (Tex.App.—Beaumont 1995, writ denied). "[T]he rule requiring that proffered evidence be incorporated in a bill of exception does not apply to cross examination of an adverse witness. When cross-examination testimony is excluded, [D] need not show the answer to be expected but only need show that the substance of the evidence was apparent from the context within which the question was asked."

TRE 104. PRELIMINARY QUESTIONS

(a) **In General.** The court must decide any preliminary question about whether a witness is qualified, a privilege exists, or evidence is admissible. In so deciding, the court is not bound by evidence rules, except those on privilege.

(b) **Relevance That Depends on a Fact.** When the relevance of evidence depends on whether a fact exists, proof must be introduced sufficient to support a finding that the fact does exist. The court may admit the proposed evidence on the condition that the proof be introduced later.

(c) **Conducting a Hearing So That the Jury Cannot Hear It.** The court must conduct any hearing on a preliminary question so that the jury cannot hear it if:

(1) the hearing involves the admissibility of a confession in a criminal case;

(2) a defendant in a criminal case is a witness and so requests; or

(3) justice so requires.

(d) **Cross-Examining a Defendant in a Criminal Case.** By testifying outside the jury's hearing on a preliminary question, a defendant in a criminal case does not become subject to cross-examination on other issues in the case.

(e) **Evidence Relevant to Weight and Credibility.** This rule does not limit a party's right to introduce before the jury evidence that is relevant to the weight or credibility of other evidence.

See also *O'Connor's Texas Rules*, "Motion in Limine," ch. 5-E, p. 406; "Objecting to Evidence," ch. 8-D, p. 801; Brown & Rondon, ***Texas Rules of Evidence Handbook***, p. 85.

ANNOTATIONS

Broders v. Heise, 924 S.W.2d 148, 151 (Tex.1996). "The qualification of a witness as an expert is within the trial court's discretion. [T]he party offering the expert's testimony bears the burden to prove that the witness is qualified under [TRE] 702."

E.I. du Pont de Nemours & Co. v. Robinson, 923 S.W.2d 549, 556 (Tex.1995). "The trial court is responsible for making the preliminary determination of whether the proffered testimony meets the standards set forth [for experts]."

TRE 105. EVIDENCE THAT IS NOT ADMISSIBLE AGAINST OTHER PARTIES OR FOR OTHER PURPOSES

(a) **Limiting Admitted Evidence.** If the court admits evidence that is admissible against a party or for a purpose—but not against another party or for another purpose—the court, on request, must restrict the evidence to its proper scope and instruct the jury accordingly.

(b) **Preserving a Claim of Error.**

(1) ***Court Admits the Evidence Without Restriction.*** A party may claim error in a ruling to admit evidence that is admissible against a party or for a purpose—but not against another party or for another purpose—only if the party requests the court to restrict the evidence to its proper scope and instruct the jury accordingly.

(2) ***Court Excludes the Evidence.*** A party may claim error in a ruling to exclude evidence that is admissible against a party or for a purpose—but not against another party or for another purpose—only if the party limits its offer to the party against whom or the purpose for which the evidence is admissible.

See also *O'Connor's Texas Rules*, "Request for limited admissibility," ch. 8-D, §7.1.3(1), p. 809; Brown & Rondon, ***Texas Rules of Evidence Handbook***, p. 96.

ANNOTATIONS

Kia Motors Corp. v. Ruiz, 432 S.W.3d 865, 879 (Tex.2014). "[W]e disagree with the court of appeals' holding that, because the portion of the spreadsheet summarizing the ... claims was not hearsay, [D] waived its objection to the admission of the remainder of the spreadsheet by failing to request a limiting instruction. The court appeared to hold that, if one portion of a document is admissible, and another portion

is inadmissible, a party must request a limiting instruction to preserve error in the admission of the improper portion. This holding mischaracterizes the nature of a limiting instruction.... A limiting instruction does not provide a mechanism for the admission of a document that contains both admissible evidence and inadmissible, unredacted evidence. In other words, such an instruction does not allow for admission of evidence that is otherwise inadmissible for any purpose." *See also* ***U-Haul Int'l v. Waldrip***, 380 S.W.3d 118, 132 (Tex. 2012).

Larson v. Cactus Util. Co., 730 S.W.2d 640, 642 (Tex.1987). "Where tendered evidence should be considered for only one purpose, it is the opponent's burden to secure a limiting instruction. Absent a requested limiting instruction, [opponent of evidence] waived his grounds for complaint." *See also* ***Horizon/CMS Healthcare Corp. v. Auld***, 34 S.W.3d 887, 906 (Tex. 2000).

TRE 106. REMAINDER OF OR RELATED WRITINGS OR RECORDED STATEMENTS

If a party introduces all or part of a writing or recorded statement, an adverse party may introduce, at that time, any other part—or any other writing or recorded statement—that in fairness ought to be considered at the same time. "Writing or recorded statement" includes depositions.

See also Brown & Rondon, ***Texas Rules of Evidence Handbook***, p. 102.

ANNOTATIONS

Russell v. Beck, No. 06-11-00006-CV (Tex.App.—Texarkana 2011, no pet.) (memo op.; 6-7-11). "The rule of optional completeness only applies when one party introduces part of a statement or document, and in fairness, the opposing party is permitted to introduce as much of the balance as is necessary to explain the first part. It is permitted to correct any misleading impressions left when one party introduces only a portion of the evidence. A plain reading of [TRE] 106 and [TRE] 107 indicates their inapplicability when the same party seeks to offer an inadmissible omitted portion of a document it initially sought to introduce. [¶] Under the rule of optional completeness, additional material from a document or recording, part of which has been admitted into evidence, is admissible if that material 'ought in fairness to be considered contemporaneously.'"

Jones v. Colley, 820 S.W.2d 863, 866 (Tex.App.—Texarkana 1991, writ denied). "Rule 106 ... is not enforced by excluding the partial statement, but by allowing the opposing party to contemporaneously introduce any other part of the statement that should be considered with the portion introduced by the proponent."

TRE 107. RULE OF OPTIONAL COMPLETENESS

If a party introduces part of an act, declaration, conversation, writing, or recorded statement, an adverse party may inquire into any other part on the same subject. An adverse party may also introduce any other act, declaration, conversation, writing, or recorded statement that is necessary to explain or allow the trier of fact to fully understand the part offered by the opponent. "Writing or recorded statement" includes a deposition.

See also Brown & Rondon, ***Texas Rules of Evidence Handbook***, p. 105.

ANNOTATIONS

Russell v. Beck, No. 06-11-00006-CV (Tex.App.—Texarkana 2011, no pet.) (memo op.; 6-7-11). See annotation under TRE 106, this page.

Crosby v. Minyard Food Stores, 122 S.W.3d 899, 903 (Tex.App.—Dallas 2003, no pet.). "Rule 107 is designed to guard against the possibility of confusion, distortion, or false impression that could be created when only a portion of evidence is introduced. There are two threshold requirements for the application of the rule. First, some portion of the matter sought to be 'completed' must have actually been introduced into evidence. Merely referring to a statement does not invoke the rule. Second, the party seeking to complete the matter must show that the remainder being offered under rule 107 is on the same subject and is necessary to fully understand or explain the matter." *See also* ***In re C.C.***, 476 S.W.3d 632, 636 (Tex.App.—Amarillo 2015, no pet.).

ARTICLE II. JUDICIAL NOTICE

TRE 201. JUDICIAL NOTICE OF ADJUDICATIVE FACTS

(a) **Scope.** This rule governs judicial notice of an adjudicative fact only, not a legislative fact.

(b) **Kinds of Facts That May Be Judicially Noticed.** The court may judicially notice a fact that is not subject to reasonable dispute because it:

  (1) is generally known within the trial court's territorial jurisdiction; or

  (2) can be accurately and readily determined from sources whose accuracy cannot reasonably be questioned.

TRE 201

(c) Taking Notice. The court:
  (1) may take judicial notice on its own; or
  (2) must take judicial notice if a party requests it and the court is supplied with the necessary information.

(d) Timing. The court may take judicial notice at any stage of the proceeding.

(e) Opportunity to Be Heard. On timely request, a party is entitled to be heard on the propriety of taking judicial notice and the nature of the fact to be noticed. If the court takes judicial notice before notifying a party, the party, on request, is still entitled to be heard.

(f) Instructing the Jury. In a civil case, the court must instruct the jury to accept the noticed fact as conclusive. In a criminal case, the court must instruct the jury that it may or may not accept the noticed fact as conclusive.

See also CPRC §38.004; ***O'Connor's Texas Rules***, "Motion for Judicial Notice," ch. 5-M, p. 465; Brown & Rondon, ***Texas Rules of Evidence Handbook***, p. 112.

ANNOTATIONS

Freedom Comms. v. Coronado, 372 S.W.3d 621, 623 (Tex.2012). "[A] court will take judicial notice of another court's records if a party provides proof of the records."

In re J.L., 163 S.W.3d 79, 84 (Tex.2005). "If a fact is generally known, then obviously no expert is needed. [E]xpert testimony invariably concerns matters in dispute which are not capable of accurate resolution from outside, unquestioned sources. Because [expert's] testimony concerned disputed facts and opinions, it should not have been judicially noticed."

Office of Pub. Util. Counsel v. Public Util. Comm'n, 878 S.W.2d 598, 600 (Tex.1994). "A court of appeals has the power to take judicial notice for the first time on appeal."

In re Shifflet, 462 S.W.3d 528, 539 (Tex.App.—Houston [1st Dist.] 2015, orig. proceeding). "'A trial court may take judicial notice of its own records in matters that are generally known, easily proven, and not reasonably disputed.' 'Therefore, a court may take judicial notice that a pleading has been filed in the case, that it has signed an order, or of the law of another jurisdiction,' but '[a] court may not take judicial notice of the *truth* of allegations in its records.'" *See also* ***Barnard v. Barnard***, 133 S.W.3d 782, 789 (Tex.App.—Fort Worth 2004, pet. denied).

In re A.W.B., No. 14-11-00926-CV (Tex.App.—Houston [14th Dist.] 2012, no pet.) (memo op.; 3-27-12). "[W]e have held that 'we may presume that the trial court took ... judicial notice of the record without any request being made and without any announcement that it has done so.' More recently, we stated a 'trial court is presumed to judicially know what has previously taken place in the case tried before it, and the parties are not required to prove facts that the trial court judicially knows.' Here, the same judge who signed the order following an adversary hearing under [Fam. Code] Ch. 262 signed the decree for termination. The judge did not explicitly state that he was taking judicial notice of the Ch. 262 order, which is contained in the clerk's record on appeal and orders Mother 'to comply with each requirement set out in the [TDFPS's] original, or any amended, service plan during the pendency of this suit.' However, following our precedent, we presume that the judge took judicial notice." *See also* ***Sierad v. Barnett***, 164 S.W.3d 471, 481 (Tex. App.—Dallas 2005, no pet.) (trial court does not need to announce it is taking judicial notice). *But see* ***In re C.L.***, p. 1291.

Guyton v. Monteau, 332 S.W.3d 687, 692-93 (Tex. App.—Houston [14th Dist.] 2011, no pet.). "[T]he trial court's ruling was based on its judicial notice of all documents and testimony ever admitted in this case on any subject. [¶] Such sweeping judicial notice ... was an abuse of discretion.... A judicially-noticed fact 'must be one not subject to reasonable dispute in that it is either (1) generally known within the territorial jurisdiction of the trial court or (2) capable of accurate and ready determination by resort to sources whose accuracy cannot reasonably be questioned.' But '[p]ersonal knowledge is not judicial knowledge. The judge may personally know a fact of which he cannot take judicial notice.' Moreover, the trial court may not take judicial notice of the *truth* of factual statements and allegations contained in the pleadings, affidavits, or other documents in the file. [¶] It is inappropriate for a trial judge to take judicial notice of testimony even in a retrial of the same case." *See also* ***1.70 Acres v. State***, 935 S.W.2d 480, 489 (Tex.App.—Beaumont 1996, no writ) (variables such as vehicle's speed, road construction or repairs, weather, traffic, or accidents may be matters in someone's personal knowledge, but they are not necessarily matters subject to judicial review).

In re C.L., 304 S.W.3d 512, 515 (Tex.App.—Waco 2009, no pet.). "A court may take judicial notice of appropriate matters sua sponte. But when the court does so, it must at some point notify the parties that it has done so and give them an opportunity to challenge that decision. *At 516:* [P] did not ask the trial court to take judicial notice of any prior orders in its file or of any other matters. The court did not announce in open court that it was taking judicial notice, nor did it recite in the termination decree that it had done so. Thus, we hold that the court did not take judicial notice." *But see* ***In re A.W.B.***, p. 1290.

In re Sigmar, 270 S.W.3d 289, 302 (Tex.App.—Waco 2008, orig. proceeding). "[M]atters of legislative fact or of other non-adjudicative fact are subject to judicial notice but are not governed by Rule 201."

Apostolic Ch. v. American Honda Motor Co., 833 S.W.2d 553, 555-56 (Tex.App.—Tyler 1992, writ denied). "Highway nomenclature and designations within the trial court's jurisdiction are matters of common knowledge and proper subjects for judicial notice. ... In matters involving geographical knowledge, it is not necessary that a formal request for judicial notice be made by a party."

TRE 202. JUDICIAL NOTICE OF OTHER STATES' LAW

(a) **Scope.** This rule governs judicial notice of another state's, territory's, or federal jurisdiction's:

- Constitution;
- public statutes;
- rules;
- regulations;
- ordinances;
- court decisions; and
- common law.

(b) **Taking Notice.** The court:

(1) may take judicial notice on its own; or

(2) must take judicial notice if a party requests it and the court is supplied with the necessary information.

(c) **Notice and Opportunity to Be Heard.**

(1) ***Notice.*** The court may require a party requesting judicial notice to notify all other parties of the request so they may respond to it.

(2) ***Opportunity to Be Heard.*** On timely request, a party is entitled to be heard on the propriety of taking judicial notice and the nature of the matter to be noticed. If the court takes judicial notice before a party has been notified, the party, on request, is still entitled to be heard.

(d) **Timing.** The court may take judicial notice at any stage of the proceeding.

(e) **Determination and Review.** The court—not the jury—must determine the law of another state, territory, or federal jurisdiction. The court's determination must be treated as a ruling on a question of law.

See also *O'Connor's Texas Rules*, "Motion for Judicial Notice," ch. 5-M, p. 465; Brown & Rondon, *Texas Rules of Evidence Handbook*, p. 142.

ANNOTATIONS

Daugherty v. Southern Pac. Transp., 772 S.W.2d 81, 83 (Tex.1989). "The failure to plead sister-state law does not preclude a court from judicially noticing that law. ... Rule 202 requires the moving party to furnish sufficient information to the trial court for it to determine the foreign law's applicability to the case and to furnish all parties any notice that the court finds necessary." *See also* ***Colvin v. Colvin***, 291 S.W.3d 508, 514 (Tex.App.—Tyler 2009, no pet.) (preliminary motion required to assure application of laws from another jurisdiction).

Vince Poscente Int'l v. Compass Bank, 460 S.W.3d 211, 219 (Tex.App.—Dallas 2015, no pet.). "Unless a party requests the court to take judicial notice of or introduces proof of another state's law, or the court on its own motion takes judicial notice of another state's law, the court presumes the other state's law is the same as Texas law."

Burlington N. & Santa Fe Ry. v. Gunderson, Inc., 235 S.W.3d 287, 292 (Tex.App.—Fort Worth 2007, no pet.). "Rule 202 simply provides a mechanism by which a party may compel the trial court to judicially notice the law of another state; it does not force a party to make a definitive declaration as to which state's law applies."

TRE 203. DETERMINING FOREIGN LAW

(a) **Raising a Foreign Law Issue.** A party who intends to raise an issue about a foreign country's law must:

(1) give reasonable notice by a pleading or other writing; and

(2) at least 30 days before trial, supply all parties a copy of any written materials or sources the party intends to use to prove the foreign law.

(b) Translations. If the materials or sources were originally written in a language other than English, the party intending to rely on them must, at least 30 days before trial, supply all parties both a copy of the foreign language text and an English translation.

(c) Materials the Court May Consider; Notice. In determining foreign law, the court may consider any material or source, whether or not admissible. If the court considers any material or source not submitted by a party, it must give all parties notice and a reasonable opportunity to comment and submit additional materials.

(d) Determination and Review. The court—not the jury—must determine foreign law. The court's determination must be treated as a ruling on a question of law.

See also *O'Connor's Texas Rules*, "Motion for Judicial Notice," ch. 5-M, p. 465; Brown & Rondon, ***Texas Rules of Evidence Handbook***, p. 146.

ANNOTATIONS

Long Distance Int'l v. Telefonos de Mexico, S.A. de C.V., 49 S.W.3d 347, 351 (Tex.2001). "Rule 203 has been aptly characterized as a hybrid rule by which the presentation of the foreign law to the court resembles the presentment of evidence but which ultimately is decided as a question of law. Summary judgment is not precluded when experts disagree on the law's meaning if, as here, the parties do not dispute that all the pertinent foreign law was properly submitted in evidence. When experts disagree on how the foreign law applies to the facts, the court is presented with a question of law."

Petroleum Workers Un. v. Gomez, 503 S.W.3d 9, 33 (Tex.App.—Houston [14th Dist.] 2016, no pet.). "Rule 203 … contains no reference to a hearing, much less mandates one be held. [I]n interpreting Rule 203, … a trial court may consider any material or source, whether or not submitted by a party or admissible under the [TREs], including affidavits, testimony, briefs, and treatises. In other words, the foreign law determination can be addressed with or without an evidentiary hearing."

PennWell Corp. v. Ken Assocs., 123 S.W.3d 756, 760-61 (Tex.App.—Houston [14th Dist.] 2003, pet. denied). "Although appearing under the subtitle 'Judicial Notice' in the [TREs], the procedure established under Rule 203 for presentment of foreign law is not considered a judicial notice procedure because that term refers only to adjudicative facts and not to matters of law. Thus, the specific procedures set forth in Rule 203 must be followed for the determination of foreign law. [A] party requesting judicial notice must furnish the court with sufficient information to enable it to properly comply with the request; otherwise, the failure to provide adequate proof results in a presumption that the law of the foreign jurisdiction is identical to that of Texas." *See also* ***Gerdes v. Kennamer***, 155 S.W.3d 541, 548 (Tex.App.—Corpus Christi 2004, no pet.).

TRE 204. JUDICIAL NOTICE OF TEXAS MUNICIPAL & COUNTY ORDINANCES, TEXAS REGISTER CONTENTS, & PUBLISHED AGENCY RULES

(a) Scope. This rule governs judicial notice of Texas municipal and county ordinances, the contents of the Texas Register, and agency rules published in the Texas Administrative Code.

(b) Taking Notice. The court:

(1) may take judicial notice on its own; or

(2) must take judicial notice if a party requests it and the court is supplied with the necessary information.

(c) Notice and Opportunity to Be Heard.

(1) ***Notice.*** The court may require a party requesting judicial notice to notify all other parties of the request so they may respond to it.

(2) ***Opportunity to Be Heard.*** On timely request, a party is entitled to be heard on the propriety of taking judicial notice and the nature of the matter to be noticed. If the court takes judicial notice before a party has been notified, the party, on request, is still entitled to be heard.

(d) Determination and Review. The court—not the jury—must determine municipal and county ordinances, the contents of the Texas Register, and published agency rules. The court's determination must be treated as a ruling on a question of law.

See also *O'Connor's Texas Rules*, "Motion for Judicial Notice," ch. 5-M, p. 465; Brown & Rondon, ***Texas Rules of Evidence Handbook***, p. 149.

ARTICLE III. PRESUMPTIONS

[No rules adopted at this time.]

ARTICLE IV. RELEVANCE & ITS LIMITS

TRE 401. TEST FOR RELEVANT EVIDENCE

Evidence is relevant if:

(a) it has any tendency to make a fact more or less probable than it would be without the evidence; and

(b) the fact is of consequence in determining the action.

See also Brown & Rondon, *Texas Rules of Evidence Handbook*, p. 189.

ANNOTATIONS

Coastal Transp. Co. v. Crown Cent. Pet. Corp., 136 S.W.3d 227, 232 (Tex.2004). "Opinion testimony that is conclusory or speculative is not relevant evidence, because it does not tend to make the existence of a material fact 'more probable or less probable.'"

E.I. du Pont de Nemours & Co. v. Robinson, 923 S.W.2d 549, 556 (Tex.1995). "[T]o constitute scientific knowledge which will assist the trier of fact, the proposed [scientific] testimony must be relevant and reliable. [¶] The requirement that the proposed testimony be relevant incorporates traditional relevancy analysis under [TRE] 401 and 402.... To be relevant, the proposed testimony must be 'sufficiently tied to the facts of the case that it will aid the jury in resolving a factual dispute.'"

Transportation Ins. v. Moriel, 879 S.W.2d 10, 24-25 (Tex.1994). "Simply because a piece or pieces of evidence are material in the sense that they make a 'fact that is of consequence to the determination of the action more ... or less probable' does not render the evidence legally sufficient. As Professor McCormick succinctly put it, 'a brick is not a wall.'"

Rhey v. Redic, 408 S.W.3d 440, 460 (Tex.App.—El Paso 2013, no pet.). "To determine relevancy, the court must look at the purpose for offering the evidence. There must be some logical connection either directly or by inference between the fact offered and the fact to be proved."

TRE 402. GENERAL ADMISSIBILITY OF RELEVANT EVIDENCE

Relevant evidence is admissible unless any of the following provides otherwise:

- the United States or Texas Constitution;
- a statute;
- these rules; or
- other rules prescribed under statutory authority.

Irrelevant evidence is not admissible.

See also Brown & Rondon, *Texas Rules of Evidence Handbook*, p. 189.

ANNOTATIONS

E.I. du Pont de Nemours & Co. v. Robinson, 923 S.W.2d 549, 556 (Tex.1995). "Evidence that has no relationship to any of the issues in the case is irrelevant and does not satisfy [TRE] 702's requirement that the testimony be of assistance to the jury. It is thus inadmissible under Rule 702 as well as under [TRE] 401 and 402."

Lunsford v. Morris, 746 S.W.2d 471, 473 (Tex. 1988). The TREs do not "contemplate exclusion of otherwise relevant proof unless the evidence proffered is unfairly prejudicial, privileged, incompetent, or otherwise *legally* inadmissible."

Jampole v. Touchy, 673 S.W.2d 569, 573 (Tex. 1984), *disapproved on other grounds*, **Walker v. Packer**, 827 S.W.2d 833 (Tex.1992). "To increase the likelihood that all relevant evidence will be disclosed and brought before the trier of fact, the law circumscribes a significantly larger class of discoverable evidence [than admissible evidence] to include anything reasonably calculated to lead to the discovery of material evidence."

TRE 403. EXCLUDING RELEVANT EVIDENCE FOR PREJUDICE, CONFUSION, OR OTHER REASONS

The court may exclude relevant evidence if its probative value is substantially outweighed by a danger of one or more of the following: unfair prejudice, confusing the issues, misleading the jury, undue delay, or needlessly presenting cumulative evidence.

See also *O'Connor's Texas Rules*, "Objecting to Evidence," ch. 8-D, p. 801; Brown & Rondon, *Texas Rules of Evidence Handbook*, p. 206.

ANNOTATIONS

Bay Area Healthcare Grp. v. McShane, 239 S.W.3d 231, 234 (Tex.2007). "[T]estimony is not inadmissible on the sole ground that it is 'prejudicial' because in our adversarial system, much of a proponent's evidence is legitimately intended to wound the opponent."

Ford Motor Co. v. Miles, 967 S.W.2d 377, 389 (Tex. 1998). "[R]elevant photographic evidence is admissible unless it is merely calculated to arouse the sympathy, prejudice or passion [of] the jury where the photo-

graphs do not serve to illustrate disputed issues or aid the jury in understanding the case." (Internal quotes omitted.)

In re E.A.G., 373 S.W.3d 129, 147 (Tex.App.—San Antonio 2012, pet. denied). "The relevant criteria for determining whether the prejudice of admitting the evidence substantially outweighs the probative value include, but are not limited to, the following: (1) the probative value of the evidence; (2) the potential the evidence has to impress the jury in an irrational but nevertheless indelible way; (3) the time needed to develop the evidence; and (4) the proponent's need for the evidence to prove a fact of consequence."

In re J.B.C., 233 S.W.3d 88, 94-95 (Tex.App.—Fort Worth 2007, pet. denied). "A court may consider the following factors in determining whether the probative value of photographs is substantially outweighed by the danger of unfair prejudice: (1) the number of exhibits offered, (2) their gruesomeness, (3) their detail, (4) their size, (5) whether they are offered in color or in black and white, (6) whether they are close-up, and (7) whether the body depicted is clothed or naked. Autopsy photographs are generally admissible unless they depict mutilation caused by the autopsy itself. However, photographs that depict the nature, location, and extent of a wound have been declared probative enough to outweigh any prejudicial effect. Changes rendered by the autopsy process are of minor significance if the disturbing nature of the photograph is primarily due to the injuries caused by the appellant." *See also* ***In re K.Y.***, 273 S.W.3d 703, 710 (Tex.App.—Houston [14th Dist.] 2008, no pet.).

In re N.R.C., 94 S.W.3d 799, 807 (Tex.App.—Houston [14th Dist.] 2002, pet. denied). "The mere fact that another witness may have given the same or substantially the same testimony is not the decisive factor. Rather, we consider whether the excluded testimony would have added substantial weight to the complainant's case. [¶] As a litigant, [mother] retains the right to prove her case in the most persuasive manner possible. To defend herself, she may require several witnesses addressing the same material issue, as the testimony may come from disinterested sources or witnesses with differing vantage points. Indeed, litigants may, and often do, offer evidence from several different witnesses to prove one specific material fact. Often, the cumulative effect of the evidence heightens, rather than reduces, its probative force. Where, as here, different witnesses were to offer varying perspectives of the best interest of the children, the probative effect may likely have been heightened by the testimony of the stricken witnesses." *See also* ***Benavides v. Cushman, Inc.***, 189 S.W.3d 875, 883-84 (Tex.App.—Houston [1st Dist.] 2006, no pet.).

TRE 404. CHARACTER EVIDENCE; CRIMES OR OTHER ACTS

(a) Character Evidence.

(1) ***Prohibited Uses.*** Evidence of a person's character or character trait is not admissible to prove that on a particular occasion the person acted in accordance with the character or trait.

(2) ***Exceptions for an Accused.***

(A) In a criminal case, a defendant may offer evidence of the defendant's pertinent trait, and if the evidence is admitted, the prosecutor may offer evidence to rebut it.

(B) In a civil case, a party accused of conduct involving moral turpitude may offer evidence of the party's pertinent trait, and if the evidence is admitted, the accusing party may offer evidence to rebut it.

(3) ***Exceptions for a Victim.***

(A) In a criminal case, subject to the limitations in Rule 412, a defendant may offer evidence of a victim's pertinent trait, and if the evidence is admitted, the prosecutor may offer evidence to rebut it.

(B) In a homicide case, the prosecutor may offer evidence of the victim's trait of peacefulness to rebut evidence that the victim was the first aggressor.

(C) In a civil case, a party accused of assaultive conduct may offer evidence of the victim's trait of violence to prove self-defense, and if the evidence is admitted, the accusing party may offer evidence of the victim's trait of peacefulness.

(4) ***Exceptions for a Witness.*** Evidence of a witness's character may be admitted under Rules 607, 608, and 609.

(5) ***Definition of "Victim."*** In this rule, "victim" includes an alleged victim.

(b) Crimes, Wrongs, or Other Acts.

(1) ***Prohibited Uses.*** Evidence of a crime, wrong, or other act is not admissible to prove a per-

son's character in order to show that on a particular occasion the person acted in accordance with the character.

(2) ***Permitted Uses; Notice in Criminal Case.*** This evidence may be admissible for another purpose, such as proving motive, opportunity, intent, preparation, plan, knowledge, identity, absence of mistake, or lack of accident. On timely request by a defendant in a criminal case, the prosecutor must provide reasonable notice before trial that the prosecution intends to introduce such evidence—other than that arising in the same transaction—in its case-in-chief.

See also Brown & Rondon, ***Texas Rules of Evidence Handbook***, p. 238.

ANNOTATIONS

Service Corp. v. Guerra, 348 S.W.3d 221, 235 (Tex. 2011). "Evidence of other wrongs or acts is not admissible to prove character in order to show 'action in conformity therewith.' But it is admissible to show a party's intent, if material, provided the prior acts are 'so connected with the transaction at issue that they may all be parts of a system, scheme or plan.' This can be shown through evidence of similar acts temporally relevant and of the same substantive basis." *See also* ***In re K.L.R.***, 162 S.W.3d 291, 305-06 (Tex.App.—Tyler 2005, no pet.).

In re J.D., No. 03-14-00075-CV (Tex.App.—Austin 2016, no pet.) (memo op.; 2-3-16). "The exceptions listed under Rule 404(b) are neither mutually exclusive nor collectively exhaustive. Rule 404(b) is a rule of inclusion rather than exclusion. The rule excludes only that evidence that is offered (or will be used) solely for the purpose of proving bad character and hence conduct in conformity with that bad character. The proponent of uncharged misconduct evidence need not stuff a given set of facts into one of the laundry-list exceptions set out in Rule 404(b), but he must be able to explain to the trial court, and to the opponent, the logical and legal rationales that support its admission on a basis other than bad character or propensity purpose." (Internal quotes omitted.)

In re V.V., 349 S.W.3d 548, 557 n.3 (Tex.App.—Houston [1st Dist.] 2010, pet. denied). "Rule 404(b) does not require a final conviction as a predicate to admission of extraneous offense evidence of other 'wrongs or acts,' if that evidence is otherwise relevant and admissible."

TRE 405. METHODS OF PROVING CHARACTER

(a) By Reputation or Opinion.

(1) ***In General.*** When evidence of a person's character or character trait is admissible, it may be proved by testimony about the person's reputation or by testimony in the form of an opinion. On cross-examination of the character witness, inquiry may be made into relevant specific instances of the person's conduct.

(2) ***Accused's Character in a Criminal Case.*** In the guilt stage of a criminal case, a witness may testify to the defendant's character or character trait only if, before the day of the offense, the witness was familiar with the defendant's reputation or the facts or information that form the basis of the witness's opinion.

(b) By Specific Instances of Conduct. When a person's character or character trait is an essential element of a charge, claim, or defense, the character or trait may also be proved by relevant specific instances of the person's conduct.

See also Brown & Rondon, ***Texas Rules of Evidence Handbook***, p. 239.

ANNOTATIONS

In re G.M.P., 909 S.W.2d 198, 209 (Tex.App.—Houston [14th Dist.] 1995, no writ). "[W]hen a witness testifies as to the character of the accused, Rule 405(a) allows 'do you know' questions to be asked of the witness to test the basis for his personal opinion. Here, by making the statement 'My son wouldn't do that,' [D's father] became a character witness, espousing his opinion about [D's] propensity to commit the crime."

TRE 406. HABIT; ROUTINE PRACTICE

Evidence of a person's habit or an organization's routine practice may be admitted to prove that on a particular occasion the person or organization acted in accordance with the habit or routine practice. The court may admit this evidence regardless of whether it is corroborated or whether there was an eyewitness.

See also Brown & Rondon, ***Texas Rules of Evidence Handbook***, p. 293; ***O'Connor's Texas Forms***, FORM 5E:1.

ANNOTATIONS

Ortiz v. Glusman, 334 S.W.3d 812, 816 (Tex. App.—El Paso 2011, pet. denied). "To be admissible, the habit evidence must be 'a regular response to a re-

peated specific situation.' In other words, his response must be the same specific one to the same set of facts. One to two examples is insufficient to demonstrate a habit."

TRE 407. SUBSEQUENT REMEDIAL MEASURES; NOTIFICATION OF DEFECT

(a) Subsequent Remedial Measures. When measures are taken that would have made an earlier injury or harm less likely to occur, evidence of the subsequent measures is not admissible to prove:

- negligence;
- culpable conduct;
- a defect in a product or its design; or
- a need for a warning or instruction.

But the court may admit this evidence for another purpose, such as impeachment or—if disputed—proving ownership, control, or the feasibility of precautionary measures.

(b) Notification of Defect. A manufacturer's written notification to a purchaser of a defect in one of its products is admissible against the manufacturer to prove the defect.

See also Brown & Rondon, *Texas Rules of Evidence Handbook*, p. 300; *O'Connor's Texas Forms*, FORM 5E:1.

ANNOTATIONS

Beavers v. Northrop Worldwide Aircraft Servs., 821 S.W.2d 669, 677 (Tex.App.—Amarillo 1991, writ denied). "[W]e hold the exclusion under Rule 407(a) does not apply to evidence of subsequent remedial measures taken by third parties when offered to show that a defendant was not the cause of plaintiff's injury."

TRE 408. COMPROMISE OFFERS & NEGOTIATIONS

(a) Prohibited Uses. Evidence of the following is not admissible either to prove or disprove the validity or amount of a disputed claim:

(1) furnishing, promising, or offering—or accepting, promising to accept, or offering to accept—a valuable consideration in compromising or attempting to compromise the claim; and

(2) conduct or statements made during compromise negotiations about the claim.

(b) Permissible Uses. The court may admit this evidence for another purpose, such as proving a party's or witness's bias, prejudice, or interest, negating a contention of undue delay, or proving an effort to obstruct a criminal investigation or prosecution.

See also Brown & Rondon, *Texas Rules of Evidence Handbook*, p. 309.

ANNOTATIONS

Ford Motor Co. v. Leggat, 904 S.W.2d 643, 649 (Tex.1995). "Settlement agreements are discoverable ... to the extent they are relevant. Settlement agreements ... are not admissible at trial to prove liability." *See also* ***Birchfield v. Texarkana Mem'l Hosp.***, 747 S.W.2d 361, 365 (Tex.1987).

Vinson Minerals, Ltd. v. XTO Energy, Inc., 335 S.W.3d 344, 351-52 (Tex.App.—Fort Worth 2010, pet. denied). "Offers of settlement are not admissible to prove liability or invalidity of a claim or its amount. In an offer of settlement or compromise, a party concedes some right to which he believes he is entitled in order to bring about a mutual settlement. But rule 408 does not bar the admission of settlement offers when offered for another relevant purpose. Thus, an offer or demand for settlement may be admissible for another purpose, such as to demonstrate bias or prejudice. [¶] The burden is on the party objecting to evidence under rule 408 to show that it was a part of settlement negotiations and not offered for another purpose."

TRE 409. OFFERS TO PAY MEDICAL & SIMILAR EXPENSES

Evidence of furnishing, promising to pay, or offering to pay medical, hospital, or similar expenses resulting from an injury is not admissible to prove liability for the injury.

See also Brown & Rondon, *Texas Rules of Evidence Handbook*, p. 329; *O'Connor's Texas Forms*, FORM 5E:1.

TRE 410. PLEAS, PLEA DISCUSSIONS, & RELATED STATEMENTS

(a) Prohibited Uses in Civil Cases. In a civil case, evidence of the following is not admissible against the defendant who made the plea or was a participant in the plea discussions:

(1) a guilty plea that was later withdrawn;

(2) a nolo contendere plea;

(3) a statement made during a proceeding on either of those pleas under Federal Rule of Criminal Procedure 11 or a comparable state procedure; or

(4) a statement made during plea discussions with an attorney for the prosecuting authority if the

discussions did not result in a guilty plea or they resulted in a later-withdrawn guilty plea.

(b) Prohibited Uses in Criminal Cases. In a criminal case, evidence of the following is not admissible against the defendant who made the plea or was a participant in the plea discussions:

(1) a guilty plea that was later withdrawn;

(2) a nolo contendere plea that was later withdrawn;

(3) a statement made during a proceeding on either of those pleas under Federal Rule of Criminal Procedure 11 or a comparable state procedure; or

(4) a statement made during plea discussions with an attorney for the prosecuting authority if the discussions did not result in a guilty or nolo contendere plea or they resulted in a later-withdrawn guilty or nolo contendere plea.

(c) Exception. In a civil case, the court may admit a statement described in paragraph (a)(3) or (4) and in a criminal case, the court may admit a statement described in paragraph (b)(3) or (4), when another statement made during the same plea or plea discussions has been introduced and in fairness the statements ought to be considered together.

See also Brown & Rondon, *Texas Rules of Evidence Handbook*, p. 332.

TRE 411. LIABILITY INSURANCE

Evidence that a person was or was not insured against liability is not admissible to prove whether the person acted negligently or otherwise wrongfully. But the court may admit this evidence for another purpose, such as proving a witness's bias or prejudice or, if disputed, proving agency, ownership, or control.

See also Brown & Rondon, *Texas Rules of Evidence Handbook*, p. 345; *O'Connor's Texas Forms*, FORM 5E:1.

TRE 412. EVIDENCE OF PREVIOUS SEXUAL CONDUCT IN CRIMINAL CASES

(a) In General. The following evidence is not admissible in a prosecution for sexual assault, aggravated sexual assault, or attempt to commit sexual assault or aggravated sexual assault:

(1) reputation or opinion evidence of a victim's past sexual behavior; or

(2) specific instances of a victim's past sexual behavior.

(b) Exceptions for Specific Instances. Evidence of specific instances of a victim's past sexual behavior is admissible if:

(1) the court admits the evidence in accordance with subdivisions (c) and (d);

(2) the evidence:

(A) is necessary to rebut or explain scientific or medical evidence offered by the prosecutor;

(B) concerns past sexual behavior with the defendant and is offered by the defendant to prove consent;

(C) relates to the victim's motive or bias;

(D) is admissible under Rule 609; or

(E) is constitutionally required to be admitted; and

(3) the probative value of the evidence outweighs the danger of unfair prejudice.

(c) Procedure for Offering Evidence. Before offering any evidence of the victim's past sexual behavior, the defendant must inform the court outside the jury's presence. The court must then conduct an in camera hearing, recorded by a court reporter, and determine whether the proposed evidence is admissible. The defendant may not refer to any evidence ruled inadmissible without first requesting and gaining the court's approval outside the jury's presence.

(d) Record Sealed. The court must preserve the record of the in camera hearing, under seal, as part of the record.

(e) Definition of "Victim." In this rule, "victim" includes an alleged victim.

See also Brown & Rondon, *Texas Rules of Evidence Handbook*, p. 353.

ANNOTATIONS

In re Doe, 22 S.W.3d 601, 611-12 (Tex.App.—Austin 2000, orig. proceeding). "[P] argues that the 'rape victims shield laws,' incorporated in [TRE] 412, should apply despite the fact that the Rule specifically applies only in criminal cases. [¶] At this early stage of the litigation and considering the fact that [P] pleads that this was a forcible assault and thc grand jury indicted [D's employee] under the criminal statutes for the crime of sexual assault, we hold that until the record is more fully developed and these issues are clarified[,] the rape shield laws ought to protect the victim ... at this time. We hold that the trial court abused its discretion by failing to issue a protective or-

der preventing [D] from questioning [P] about her past and present sexual activity."

ARTICLE V. PRIVILEGES

TRE 501. PRIVILEGES IN GENERAL

Unless a Constitution, a statute, or these or other rules prescribed under statutory authority provide otherwise, no person has a privilege to:

(a) refuse to be a witness;

(b) refuse to disclose any matter;

(c) refuse to produce any object or writing; or

(d) prevent another from being a witness, disclosing any matter, or producing any object or writing.

Caution: TRE 501 is affected by Fam. Code §§6.704, 6.705, 152.310, 159.314, 159.316, 231.108, 261.101, 261.201, and 261.202.

See also *O'Connor's Texas Rules*, "Scope of Discovery," ch. 6-B, p. 530; Brown & Rondon, ***Texas Rules of Evidence Handbook***, p. 374; ***O'Connor's Texas Family Law Handbook*** (2017), "Testimony," ch. 3-A, §15.3, p. 265.

ANNOTATIONS

Volkswagen, A.G. v. Valdez, 909 S.W.2d 900, 902-03 (Tex.1995). The trial court must weigh the following factors when evaluating a privilege of a foreign country: (1) the importance of the discovery request to the investigation or litigation; (2) the degree of specificity of the request; (3) whether the information originated in the U.S.; (4) the availability of alternative means of securing the information; and (5) the extent to which noncompliance with the request would undermine important interests of the U.S., or the extent to which compliance would undermine important interests of the foreign jurisdiction where the information is located.

State v. Lowry, 802 S.W.2d 669, 671 (Tex.1991). "Only in certain narrow circumstances is it appropriate to obstruct the search for truth by denying discovery. Very limited exceptions to the strongly preferred policy of openness are recognized in our state procedural rules and statutes."

Oyster Creek Fin. Corp. v. Richwood Invs., 957 S.W.2d 640, 646 (Tex.App.—Amarillo 1997, pet. denied). "[B]ecause evidence is presumed discoverable, the party resisting discovery ... bears the burden of establishing the privilege and, therefore, must plead it and present evidence which establishes that the document(s) in question qualify for the privilege as a matter of law."

TRE 502. REQUIRED REPORTS PRIVILEGED BY STATUTE

(a) In General. If a law requiring a return or report to be made so provides:

(1) a person, corporation, association, or other organization or entity—whether public or private—that makes the required return or report has a privilege to refuse to disclose it and to prevent any other person from disclosing it; and

(2) a public officer or agency to whom the return or report must be made has a privilege to refuse to disclose it.

(b) Exceptions. This privilege does not apply in an action involving perjury, false statements, fraud in the return or report, or other failure to comply with the law in question.

See also *O'Connor's Texas Rules*, "Scope of Discovery," ch. 6-B, p. 530; Brown & Rondon, ***Texas Rules of Evidence Handbook***, p. 381; ***O'Connor's Texas Family Law Handbook*** (2017), "Reporting Family Violence, Child Abuse, Neglect, or History of Child Abuse," ch. 1-G, p. 82.

TRE 503. LAWYER-CLIENT PRIVILEGE

(a) Definitions. In this rule:

(1) A "client" is a person, public officer, or corporation, association, or other organization or entity—whether public or private—that:

(A) is rendered professional legal services by a lawyer; or

(B) consults a lawyer with a view to obtaining professional legal services from the lawyer.

(2) A "client's representative" is:

(A) a person who has authority to obtain professional legal services for the client or to act for the client on the legal advice rendered; or

(B) any other person who, to facilitate the rendition of professional legal services to the client, makes or receives a confidential communication while acting in the scope of employment for the client.

(3) A "lawyer" is a person authorized, or who the client reasonably believes is authorized, to practice law in any state or nation.

(4) A "lawyer's representative" is:

(A) one employed by the lawyer to assist in the rendition of professional legal services; or

(B) an accountant who is reasonably necessary for the lawyer's rendition of professional legal services.

(5) A communication is "confidential" if not intended to be disclosed to third persons other than those:

(A) to whom disclosure is made to further the rendition of professional legal services to the client; or

(B) reasonably necessary to transmit the communication.

(b) **Rules of Privilege.**

(1) ***General Rule.*** A client has a privilege to refuse to disclose and to prevent any other person from disclosing confidential communications made to facilitate the rendition of professional legal services to the client:

(A) between the client or the client's representative and the client's lawyer or the lawyer's representative;

(B) between the client's lawyer and the lawyer's representative;

(C) by the client, the client's representative, the client's lawyer, or the lawyer's representative to a lawyer representing another party in a pending action or that lawyer's representative, if the communications concern a matter of common interest in the pending action;

(D) between the client's representatives or between the client and the client's representative; or

(E) among lawyers and their representatives representing the same client.

(2) ***Special Rule in a Criminal Case.*** In a criminal case, a client has a privilege to prevent a lawyer or lawyer's representative from disclosing any other fact that came to the knowledge of the lawyer or the lawyer's representative by reason of the attorney-client relationship.

(c) **Who May Claim.** The privilege may be claimed by:

(1) the client;

(2) the client's guardian or conservator;

(3) a deceased client's personal representative; or

(4) the successor, trustee, or similar representative of a corporation, association, or other organization or entity—whether or not in existence.

The person who was the client's lawyer or the lawyer's representative when the communication was made may claim the privilege on the client's behalf—and is presumed to have authority to do so.

(d) **Exceptions.** This privilege does not apply:

(1) ***Furtherance of Crime or Fraud.*** If the lawyer's services were sought or obtained to enable or aid anyone to commit or plan to commit what the client knew or reasonably should have known to be a crime or fraud.

(2) ***Claimants Through Same Deceased Client.*** If the communication is relevant to an issue between parties claiming through the same deceased client.

(3) ***Breach of Duty by a Lawyer or Client.*** If the communication is relevant to an issue of breach of duty by a lawyer to the client or by a client to the lawyer.

(4) ***Document Attested by a Lawyer.*** If the communication is relevant to an issue concerning an attested document to which the lawyer is an attesting witness.

(5) ***Joint Clients.*** If the communication:

(A) is offered in an action between clients who retained or consulted a lawyer in common;

(B) was made by any of the clients to the lawyer; and

(C) is relevant to a matter of common interest between the clients.

Caution: TRE 503 is affected by Fam. Code §§261.101 and 261.202.

See also ***O'Connor's Texas Rules***, "Asserting privileges," ch. 6-A, §18.2, p. 510; "Scope of Discovery," ch. 6-B, p. 530; Brown & Rondon, ***Texas Rules of Evidence Handbook***, p. 384; ***O'Connor's Texas Forms***, FORM 5E:1; ***O'Connor's Texas Family Law Handbook*** (2017), "Attorney Ad Litem," ch. 4-C, §2, p. 367.

ANNOTATIONS

Generally

In re XL Specialty Ins., 373 S.W.3d 46, 50 (Tex. 2012). "[T]he privilege defined in Rule 503(b)(1)(C) ... has been variously described as the 'joint client' privilege, the 'joint defense' privilege, and the 'common interest' privilege. Courts sometimes use these terms interchangeably, but they involve distinct doctrines that serve different purposes. [¶] The joint client ... doctrine applies '[w]hen the same attorney simultaneously represents two or more clients on the same matter.' *At 51-53:* The joint defense rule applies [only in the context of litigation and] when multiple parties to a lawsuit, each represented by different attorneys, communicate among themselves for the purpose of forming

a common defense strategy. [¶] [Under t]he common interest rule[, t]he parties must share a mutual interest, but unlike the joint defense doctrine, the common interest rule applies to 'two or more separately represented persons whatever their denomination in pleadings and whether or not involved in litigation.' [¶] [Because] Texas requires that the communications be made in the context of a pending action[,] our privilege is not a 'common interest' privilege that extends beyond litigation. Nor is it a 'joint defense' privilege, as it applies not just to defendants but to any parties to a pending action. Rule 503(b)(1)(C)'s privilege is more appropriately termed an 'allied litigant' privilege. [¶] The allied litigant doctrine protects communications made between a client, or the client's lawyer, to another party's lawyer, not to the other party itself. This attorney-sharing requirement makes clear that the privilege applies only when the parties have separate counsel." *See also* ***In re Park Cities Bank***, 409 S.W.3d 859, 874 (Tex.App.—Tyler 2013, orig. proceeding).

In re Texas Health Res., 472 S.W.3d 895, 902 (Tex. App.—Dallas 2015, orig. proceeding). "The lawyer-client privilege protects not only confidential communications between the lawyer and client, but also the discourse among their representatives. Under Rule 503(a)(2), if a person authorized by the client to obtain legal services or act on legal advice on behalf of the client or to make or receive confidential communications with respect to legal services, that person is a client's representative even if the person is not an employee of the client. [¶] Insurance companies typically have the duty to conduct the defense of the insured under a liability policy, including the authority to select, employ, and pay the attorney. Such liability policies typically give the insurer complete and exclusive control of that defense, ... including the ability to obtain professional legal services on behalf of the insured. For that reason, under the proper circumstances, communications between an insurer and its insured may be shielded from discovery by the lawyer-client privilege." (Internal quotes omitted.)

Watson v. Kaminski, 51 S.W.3d 825, 827 (Tex. App.—Houston [1st Dist.] 2001, no pet.). "To be privileged, the communication must relate to pending or proposed litigation and must further the attorney's representation. [¶] The judge must consider the entire communication in its context and must extend the privilege to any statement that bears some relation to an existing or proposed judicial proceeding. All doubt should be resolved in favor of the communication's relation to the proceeding."

Boales v. Brighton Builders, Inc., 29 S.W.3d 159, 168 (Tex.App.—Houston [14th Dist.] 2000, pet. denied). "The [attorney-client] privilege extends to all matters concerning litigation or business transactions, regardless of whether the matters are pertinent to the matter for which the attorney was employed. The statements and advice of the attorney to the client are as protected as the communications of the client to the attorney." *See also* ***In re Small***, 346 S.W.3d 657, 663 (Tex. App.—El Paso 2009, orig. proceeding).

Perez v. Kirk & Carrigan, 822 S.W.2d 261, 265 (Tex.App.—Corpus Christi 1991, writ denied). "An agreement to form an attorney-client relationship may be implied from the conduct of the parties. Moreover, the relationship does not depend upon the payment of a fee, but may exist as a result of rendering services gratuitously."

Exceptions to Privilege

Granada Corp. v. First Ct. of Appeals, 844 S.W.2d 223, 227 (Tex.1992). "The crime-fraud exception [to the attorney-client privilege in TRE 503(d)(1)] applies only if a prima facie case is made of contemplated fraud. Additionally, there must be a relationship between the document for which the privilege is challenged and the prima facie proof offered."

In re Park Cities Bank, 409 S.W.3d 859, 869 (Tex. App.—Tyler 2013, orig. proceeding). "The party seeking discovery of an otherwise privileged communication bears the burden of proving the exception. [¶] The crime-fraud exception applies only if (1) the party asserting the exception makes a prima facie showing that a crime or fraud was ongoing or about to be committed, and (2) there is a relationship between the document for which the privilege is challenged and the prima facie proof offered. The prima facie requirement is met when the proponent offers evidence establishing the elements of fraud and that the fraud was ongoing, or about to be committed, at the time the document was prepared. The fraud alleged to have occurred must have happened at or during the time the document was prepared, and the document must have been created as part of perpetrating the fraud. [¶] In addition to the prima facie showing, the party asserting the crime-fraud exception must show that a nexus exists between the privileged documents and the alleged fraud. This

nexus must be established for each privileged document. Mere allegations of a connection between the alleged fraud and the document will not suffice." *See also* ***In re USA Waste Mgmt. Res.***, 387 S.W.3d 92, 98 (Tex. App.—Houston [14th Dist.] 2012, orig. proceeding); ***In re Small***, 346 S.W.3d 657, 666 (Tex.App.—El Paso 2009, orig. proceeding).

Offensive Use

Republic Ins. v. Davis, 856 S.W.2d 158, 163 (Tex. 1993). "In an instance in which the privilege is being used as a sword rather than a shield, the privilege may be waived. [T]he following factors should guide the trial court in determining whether a waiver has occurred. [¶] First, ... the party asserting the privilege must seek affirmative relief. Second, the privileged information sought must be such that, if believed by the fact finder, in all probability it would be outcome determinative of the cause of action asserted. Mere relevance is insufficient. A contradiction in position without more is insufficient. The confidential communication must go to the very heart of the affirmative relief sought. Third, disclosure of the confidential communication must be the only means by which the aggrieved party may obtain the evidence. If any one of these requirements is lacking, the trial court must uphold the privilege."

TRE 504. SPOUSAL PRIVILEGES

(a) Confidential Communication Privilege.

(1) ***Definition.*** A communication is "confidential" if a person makes it privately to the person's spouse and does not intend its disclosure to any other person.

(2) ***General Rule.*** A person has a privilege to refuse to disclose and to prevent any other person from disclosing a confidential communication made to the person's spouse while they were married. This privilege survives termination of the marriage.

(3) ***Who May Claim.*** The privilege may be claimed by:

(A) the communicating spouse;

(B) the guardian of a communicating spouse who is incompetent; or

(C) the personal representative of a communicating spouse who is deceased.

The other spouse may claim the privilege on the communicating spouse's behalf—and is presumed to have authority to do so.

(4) ***Exceptions.*** This privilege does not apply:

(A) ***Furtherance of Crime or Fraud.*** If the communication is made—wholly or partially—to enable or aid anyone to commit or plan to commit a crime or fraud.

(B) ***Proceeding Between Spouse and Other Spouse or Claimant Through Deceased Spouse.*** In a civil proceeding:

(i) brought by or on behalf of one spouse against the other; or

(ii) between a surviving spouse and a person claiming through the deceased spouse.

(C) ***Crime Against Family, Spouse, Household Member, or Minor Child.*** In a:

(i) proceeding in which a party is accused of conduct that, if proved, is a crime against the person of the other spouse, any member of the household of either spouse, or any minor child; or

(ii) criminal proceeding involving a charge of bigamy under Section 25.01 of the Penal Code.

(D) ***Commitment or Similar Proceeding.*** In a proceeding to commit either spouse or otherwise to place the spouse or the spouse's property under another's control because of a mental or physical condition.

(E) ***Proceeding to Establish Competence.*** In a proceeding brought by or on behalf of either spouse to establish competence.

(b) Privilege Not to Testify in a Criminal Case.

(1) ***General Rule.*** In a criminal case, an accused's spouse has a privilege not to be called to testify for the state. But this rule neither prohibits a spouse from testifying voluntarily for the state nor gives a spouse a privilege to refuse to be called to testify for the accused.

(2) ***Failure to Call Spouse.*** If other evidence indicates that the accused's spouse could testify to relevant matters, an accused's failure to call the spouse to testify is a proper subject of comment by counsel.

(3) ***Who May Claim.*** The privilege not to testify may be claimed by the accused's spouse or the spouse's guardian or representative, but not by the accused.

(4) ***Exceptions.*** This privilege does not apply:

(A) ***Certain Criminal Proceedings.*** In a criminal proceeding in which a spouse is charged with:

(i) a crime against the other spouse, any member of the household of either spouse, or any minor child; or

(ii) bigamy under Section 25.01 of the Penal Code.

(B) ***Matters That Occurred Before the Marriage.*** If the spouse is called to testify about matters that occurred before the marriage.

Caution: TRE 504 is affected by Fam. Code §§6.704, 152.310, and 159.316.

See also ***O'Connor's Texas Rules***, "Asserting privileges," ch. 6-A, §18.2, p. 510; "Scope of Discovery," ch. 6-B, p. 530; Brown & Rondon, ***Texas Rules of Evidence Handbook***, p. 432; ***O'Connor's Texas Family Law Handbook*** (2017), "Testimony," ch. 3-A, §15.3, p. 265; "No spousal privilege," ch. 9-D, §16.6.2(5), p. 1058.

ANNOTATIONS

Marshall v. Ryder Sys., 928 S.W.2d 190, 195 (Tex. App.—Houston [14th Dist.] 1996, writ denied). In civil cases, "[t]he marital privilege is limited to *confidential* communications between spouses. Only in criminal cases is there a broad, general privilege protecting a person from being a witness against his or her spouse."

TRE 505. PRIVILEGE FOR COMMUNICATIONS TO A CLERGY MEMBER

(a) **Definitions.** In this rule:

(1) A "clergy member" is a minister, priest, rabbi, accredited Christian Science Practitioner, or other similar functionary of a religious organization or someone whom a communicant reasonably believes is a clergy member.

(2) A "communicant" is a person who consults a clergy member in the clergy member's professional capacity as a spiritual adviser.

(3) A communication is "confidential" if made privately and not intended for further disclosure except to other persons present to further the purpose of the communication.

(b) **General Rule.** A communicant has a privilege to refuse to disclose and to prevent any other person from disclosing a confidential communication by the communicant to a clergy member in the clergy member's professional capacity as spiritual adviser.

(c) **Who May Claim.** The privilege may be claimed by:

(1) the communicant;

(2) the communicant's guardian or conservator; or

(3) a deceased communicant's personal representative.

The clergy member to whom the communication was made may claim the privilege on the communicant's behalf—and is presumed to have authority to do so.

Caution: TRE 505 is affected by Fam. Code §261.101.

See also ***O'Connor's Texas Rules***, "Asserting privileges," ch. 6-A, §18.2, p. 510; "Scope of Discovery," ch. 6-B, p. 530; Brown & Rondon, ***Texas Rules of Evidence Handbook***, p. 455; ***O'Connor's Texas Family Law Handbook*** (2017), "No exception for privileged communications," ch. 1-G, §3.2.3, p. 84.

ANNOTATIONS

Almendarez v. State, 153 S.W.3d 727, 729 (Tex. App.—Dallas 2005, no pet.). See annotation under Family Code §261.202, p. 891.

Nicholson v. Wittig, 832 S.W.2d 681, 685 (Tex. App.—Houston [1st Dist.] 1992, orig. proceeding). The clergy-communicant "privilege attaches when a person makes a communication with a reasonable expectation of confidentiality to a member of the clergy acting in his or her professional or spiritual capacity. [¶] An individual may invoke a privilege regardless of the nature of the underlying proceeding. *At 686:* Rule 505 makes no reference to the content of the communication; rather, the rule focuses on the counseling opportunity."

TRE 506. POLITICAL VOTE PRIVILEGE

A person has a privilege to refuse to disclose the person's vote at a political election conducted by secret ballot unless the vote was cast illegally.

See also ***O'Connor's Texas Rules***, "Asserting privileges," ch. 6-A, §18.2, p. 510; "Scope of Discovery," ch. 6-B, p. 530; Brown & Rondon, ***Texas Rules of Evidence Handbook***, p. 461.

TRE 507. TRADE SECRETS PRIVILEGE

(a) **General Rule.** A person has a privilege to refuse to disclose and to prevent other persons from disclosing a trade secret owned by the person, unless the court finds that nondisclosure will tend to conceal fraud or otherwise work injustice.

(b) **Who May Claim.** The privilege may be claimed by the person who owns the trade secret or the person's agent or employee.

(c) **Protective Measure.** If a court orders a person to disclose a trade secret, it must take any protective measure required by the interests of the privilege holder and the parties and to further justice.

See also Pen. Code §31.05(a)(4); ***O'Connor's Texas Rules***, "Asserting privileges," ch. 6-A, §18.2, p. 510; "Scope of Discovery," ch. 6-B, p. 530; Brown & Rondon, ***Texas Rules of Evidence Handbook***, p. 461.

TRE 508. INFORMER'S IDENTITY PRIVILEGE

(a) **General Rule.** The United States, a state, or a subdivision of either has a privilege to refuse to disclose a person's identity if:

(1) the person has furnished information to a law enforcement officer or a member of a legislative committee or its staff conducting an investigation of a possible violation of law; and

(2) the information relates to or assists in the investigation.

(b) **Who May Claim.** The privilege may be claimed by an appropriate representative of the public entity to which the informer furnished the information. The court in a criminal case must reject the privilege claim if the state objects.

(c) **Exceptions.**

(1) ***Voluntary Disclosure; Informer a Witness.*** This privilege does not apply if:

(A) the informer's identity or the informer's interest in the communication's subject matter has been disclosed—by a privilege holder or the informer's own action—to a person who would have cause to resent the communication; or

(B) the informer appears as a witness for the public entity.

(2) ***Testimony About the Merits.***

(A) ***Criminal Case.*** In a criminal case, this privilege does not apply if the court finds a reasonable probability exists that the informer can give testimony necessary to a fair determination of guilt or innocence. If the court so finds and the public entity elects not to disclose the informer's identity:

(i) on the defendant's motion, the court must dismiss the charges to which the testimony would relate; or

(ii) on its own motion, the court may dismiss the charges to which the testimony would relate.

(B) ***Certain Civil Cases.*** In a civil case in which the public entity is a party, this privilege does not apply if the court finds a reasonable probability exists that the informer can give testimony necessary to a fair determination of a material issue on the merits. If the court so finds and the public entity elects not to disclose the informer's identity, the court may make any order that justice requires.

(C) ***Procedures.***

(i) If it appears that an informer may be able to give the testimony required to invoke this exception and the public entity claims the privilege, the court must give the public entity an opportunity to show in camera facts relevant to determining whether this exception is met. The showing should ordinarily be made by affidavits, but the court may take testimony if it finds the matter cannot be satisfactorily resolved by affidavits.

(ii) No counsel or party may attend the in camera showing.

(iii) The court must seal and preserve for appeal evidence submitted under this subparagraph (2)(C). The evidence must not otherwise be revealed without the public entity's consent.

(3) ***Legality of Obtaining Evidence.***

(A) ***Court May Order Disclosure.*** The court may order the public entity to disclose an informer's identity if:

(i) information from an informer is relied on to establish the legality of the means by which evidence was obtained; and

(ii) the court is not satisfied that the information was received from an informer reasonably believed to be reliable or credible.

(B) ***Procedures.***

(i) On the public entity's request, the court must order the disclosure be made in camera.

(ii) No counsel or party may attend the in camera disclosure.

(iii) If the informer's identity is disclosed in camera, the court must seal and preserve for appeal the record of the in camera proceeding. The record of the in camera proceeding must not otherwise be revealed without the public entity's consent.

See also *O'Connor's Texas Rules*, "Asserting privileges," ch. 6-A, §18.2, p. 510; "Scope of Discovery," ch. 6-B, p. 530; Brown & Rondon, ***Texas Rules of Evidence Handbook***, p. 466.

TRE 509. PHYSICIAN-PATIENT PRIVILEGE

(a) Definitions. In this rule:

(1) A "patient" is a person who consults or is seen by a physician for medical care.

(2) A "physician" is a person licensed, or who the patient reasonably believes is licensed, to practice medicine in any state or nation.

(3) A communication is "confidential" if not intended to be disclosed to third persons other than those:

(A) present to further the patient's interest in the consultation, examination, or interview;

(B) reasonably necessary to transmit the communication; or

(C) participating in the diagnosis and treatment under the physician's direction, including members of the patient's family.

(b) Limited Privilege in a Criminal Case. There is no physician-patient privilege in a criminal case. But a confidential communication is not admissible in a criminal case if made:

(1) to a person involved in the treatment of or examination for alcohol or drug abuse; and

(2) by a person being treated voluntarily or being examined for admission to treatment for alcohol or drug abuse.

(c) General Rule in a Civil Case. In a civil case, a patient has a privilege to refuse to disclose and to prevent any other person from disclosing:

(1) a confidential communication between a physician and the patient that relates to or was made in connection with any professional services the physician rendered the patient; and

(2) a record of the patient's identity, diagnosis, evaluation, or treatment created or maintained by a physician.

(d) Who May Claim in a Civil Case. The privilege may be claimed by:

(1) the patient; or

(2) the patient's representative on the patient's behalf.

The physician may claim the privilege on the patient's behalf—and is presumed to have authority to do so.

(e) Exceptions in a Civil Case. This privilege does not apply:

(1) ***Proceeding Against Physician.*** If the communication or record is relevant to a claim or defense in:

(A) a proceeding the patient brings against a physician; or

(B) a license revocation proceeding in which the patient is a complaining witness.

(2) ***Consent.*** If the patient or a person authorized to act on the patient's behalf consents in writing to the release of any privileged information, as provided in subdivision (f).

(3) ***Action to Collect.*** In an action to collect a claim for medical services rendered to the patient.

(4) ***Party Relies on Patient's Condition.*** If any party relies on the patient's physical, mental, or emotional condition as a part of the party's claim or defense and the communication or record is relevant to that condition.

(5) ***Disciplinary Investigation or Proceeding.*** In a disciplinary investigation of or proceeding against a physician under the Medical Practice Act, Tex. Occ. Code §164.001 et seq., or a registered nurse under Tex. Occ. Code §301.451 et seq. But the board conducting the investigation or proceeding must protect the identity of any patient whose medical records are examined unless:

(A) the patient's records would be subject to disclosure under paragraph (e)(1); or

(B) the patient has consented in writing to the release of medical records, as provided in subdivision (f).

(6) ***Involuntary Civil Commitment or Similar Proceeding.*** In a proceeding for involuntary civil commitment or court-ordered treatment, or a probable cause hearing under Tex. Health & Safety Code:

(A) chapter 462 (Treatment of Persons With Chemical Dependencies);

(B) title 7, subtitle C (Texas Mental Health Code); or

(C) title 7, subtitle D (Persons With an Intellectual Disability Act).

(7) ***Abuse or Neglect of "Institution" Resident.*** In a proceeding regarding the abuse or neglect, or the cause of any abuse or neglect, of a resident of an "institution" as defined in Tex. Health & Safety Code §242.002.

(f) Consent for Release of Privileged Information.

(1) Consent for the release of privileged information must be in writing and signed by:

(A) the patient;

(B) a parent or legal guardian if the patient is a minor;

(C) a legal guardian if the patient has been adjudicated incompetent to manage personal affairs;

(D) an attorney appointed for the patient under Tex. Health & Safety Code title 7, subtitles C and D;

(E) an attorney ad litem appointed for the patient under Tex. Estates Code title 3, subtitle C;

(F) an attorney ad litem or guardian ad litem appointed for a minor under Tex. Fam. Code chapter 107, subchapter B; or

(G) a personal representative if the patient is deceased.

(2) The consent must specify:

(A) the information or medical records covered by the release;

(B) the reasons or purposes for the release; and

(C) the person to whom the information is to be released.

(3) The patient, or other person authorized to consent, may withdraw consent to the release of any information. But a withdrawal of consent does not affect any information disclosed before the patient or authorized person gave written notice of the withdrawal.

(4) Any person who receives information privileged under this rule may disclose the information only to the extent consistent with the purposes specified in the consent.

Caution: TRE 509 is affected by Fam. Code §261.101.

See also ***O'Connor's Texas Rules***, "Asserting privileges," ch. 6-A, §18.2, p. 510; "Scope of Discovery," ch. 6-B, p. 530; "Medical Records," ch. 6-J, p. 659; Brown & Rondon, ***Texas Rules of Evidence Handbook***, p. 476; ***O'Connor's Texas Forms***, FORM 5E:1; ***O'Connor's Texas Family Law Handbook*** (2017), "No exception for privileged communications," ch. 1-G, §3.2.3, p. 84.

ANNOTATIONS

R.K. v. Ramirez, 887 S.W.2d 836, 842 (Tex.1994). "[T]he patient-litigant exception to [TRE 509 and 510] privileges applies when a party's condition relates in a significant way to a party's claim or defense. *At 843 n.7:* Whether a condition is a part of a claim or defense should be determined on the face of the pleadings, without reference to the evidence that is allegedly privileged. *At 843:* [T]he exceptions to the medical and mental health privileges apply when (1) the records sought to be discovered are relevant to the condition at issue, and (2) the condition is relied upon as a part of a party's claim or defense, meaning that the condition itself is a fact that carries some legal significance."

Groves v. Gabriel, 874 S.W.2d 660, 661 (Tex.1994). "[A] trial court's order compelling release of medical records should be restrictively drawn so as to maintain the privilege with respect to records or communications not relevant to the underlying suit. The global release in this case does not meet the ***Mutter*** standard." *See also* ***In re Collins***, 286 S.W.3d 911, 916 (Tex.2009).

Mutter v. Wood, 744 S.W.2d 600, 600 (Tex.1988). "There are ... eight exceptions to the [physician-patient] privilege. *At 601:* In this case, the privilege was waived completely as to the defendant doctors and partially as to the treating doctors. To the extent, however, that the treating doctors had records or communications which were not relevant to the underlying suit, they remained privileged...."

In re Toyota Motor Corp., 191 S.W.3d 498, 502 (Tex.App.—Waco 2006, orig. proceeding). "A claim for mental anguish or emotional distress will not, standing alone, make a plaintiff's mental or emotional condition a part of the plaintiff's claim. [T]he allegation in [P's] petition that he suffered 'emotional shock' is not a sufficient basis to make his mental or emotional condition

an issue on which the jury will be required to make a factual determination. [¶] Therefore, [P's] communications ... are protected by the physician-patient privilege."

In re Arriola, 159 S.W.3d 670, 675-76 (Tex.App.—Corpus Christi 2004, orig. proceeding). "[Ds] contend the abuse-and-neglect exceptions [to TRE 509 and 510] apply only to proceedings brought by appropriate law enforcement agencies. [¶] However, the abuse-and-neglect exceptions ... contain no such limitation. [R]ules 509 and 510 state that the exceptions apply in administrative proceedings and civil proceedings in court. [¶] [Ds] contend numerous state statutes and administrative rules protect the records and medical information from disclosure.... [¶] However, each of the confidentiality and privilege provisions [Ds cite] contains an exception to nondisclosure where release of the information is required by law or ordered by the court. *At 677:* Here, the rules of evidence are the 'law' that requires release of the information."

James v. Kloos, 75 S.W.3d 153, 160 (Tex.App.—Fort Worth 2002, no pet.). "[A] party can be prejudiced when his doctor meets with opposing counsel, but ... such prejudice may not be severe enough to disallow the doctor's testimony. [P]rejudice due to an improper meeting does not necessarily mean prejudice at trial, and, therefore, does not mean that an improper verdict necessarily results when a doctor is allowed to testify after such a meeting. [T]here must be a showing that the ruling probably caused the rendition of an improper judgment." *See also* ***Durst v. Hill Country Mem'l Hosp.***, 70 S.W.3d 233, 237 (Tex.App.—San Antonio 2001, no pet.).

TRE 510. MENTAL HEALTH INFORMATION PRIVILEGE IN CIVIL CASES

(a) Definitions. In this rule:

(1) A "professional" is a person:

(A) authorized to practice medicine in any state or nation;

(B) licensed or certified by the State of Texas in the diagnosis, evaluation, or treatment of any mental or emotional disorder;

(C) involved in the treatment or examination of drug abusers; or

(D) who the patient reasonably believes to be a professional under this rule.

(2) A "patient" is a person who:

(A) consults or is interviewed by a professional for diagnosis, evaluation, or treatment of any mental or emotional condition or disorder, including alcoholism and drug addiction; or

(B) is being treated voluntarily or being examined for admission to voluntary treatment for drug abuse.

(3) A "patient's representative" is:

(A) any person who has the patient's written consent;

(B) the parent of a minor patient;

(C) the guardian of a patient who has been adjudicated incompetent to manage personal affairs; or

(D) the personal representative of a deceased patient.

(4) A communication is "confidential" if not intended to be disclosed to third persons other than those:

(A) present to further the patient's interest in the diagnosis, examination, evaluation, or treatment;

(B) reasonably necessary to transmit the communication; or

(C) participating in the diagnosis, examination, evaluation, or treatment under the professional's direction, including members of the patient's family.

(b) General Rule; Disclosure.

(1) In a civil case, a patient has a privilege to refuse to disclose and to prevent any other person from disclosing:

(A) a confidential communication between the patient and a professional; and

(B) a record of the patient's identity, diagnosis, evaluation, or treatment that is created or maintained by a professional.

(2) In a civil case, any person—other than a patient's representative acting on the patient's behalf—who receives information privileged under this rule may disclose the information only to the extent consistent with the purposes for which it was obtained.

(c) Who May Claim. The privilege may be claimed by:

(1) the patient; or

(2) the patient's representative on the patient's behalf.

The professional may claim the privilege on the patient's behalf—and is presumed to have authority to do so.

(d) Exceptions. This privilege does not apply:

(1) ***Proceeding Against Professional.*** If the communication or record is relevant to a claim or defense in:

(A) a proceeding the patient brings against a professional; or

(B) a license revocation proceeding in which the patient is a complaining witness.

(2) ***Written Waiver.*** If the patient or a person authorized to act on the patient's behalf waives the privilege in writing.

(3) ***Action to Collect.*** In an action to collect a claim for mental or emotional health services rendered to the patient.

(4) ***Communication Made in Court-Ordered Examination.*** To a communication the patient made to a professional during a court-ordered examination relating to the patient's mental or emotional condition or disorder if:

(A) the patient made the communication after being informed that it would not be privileged;

(B) the communication is offered to prove an issue involving the patient's mental or emotional health; and

(C) the court imposes appropriate safeguards against unauthorized disclosure.

(5) ***Party Relies on Patient's Condition.*** If any party relies on the patient's physical, mental, or emotional condition as a part of the party's claim or defense and the communication or record is relevant to that condition.

(6) ***Abuse or Neglect of "Institution" Resident.*** In a proceeding regarding the abuse or neglect, or the cause of any abuse or neglect, of a resident of an "institution" as defined in Tex. Health & Safety Code §242.002.

Caution: TRE 510 is affected by Fam. Code §261.101.

See also *O'Connor's Texas Rules*, "Asserting privileges," ch. 6-A, §18.2, p. 510; "Scope of Discovery," ch. 6-B, p. 530; "Medical Records," ch. 6-J, p. 659; Brown & Rondon, *Texas Rules of Evidence Handbook*, p. 496; *O'Connor's Texas Forms*, FORM 5E:1; *O'Connor's Texas Family Law Handbook* (2017), "No exception for privileged communications," ch. 1-G, §3.2.3, p. 84.

ANNOTATIONS

R.K. v. Ramirez, 887 S.W.2d 836, 843 (Tex.1994). "As a general rule, a mental condition will be a 'part' of a claim or defense if the pleadings indicate that the jury must make a factual determination concerning the condition itself."

Groves v. Gabriel, 874 S.W.2d 660, 661 (Tex.1994). "Because [P] alleges severe emotional damages, including 'post-traumatic stress disorder,' [she] waived the privilege as to any medical records relevant to her claim for emotional damages." *See also* ***Ginsberg v. Fifth Ct. of Appeals***, 686 S.W.2d 105, 107 (Tex.1985).

Garza v. Garza, 217 S.W.3d 538, 555 (Tex.App.—San Antonio 2006, no pet.). Mother's medical records were not privileged because mother's "medical condition relating to her personality and bipolar disorders was relevant to the issue of whether appointing her [SMC] was in her children's best interests. Both parties' medical and mental conditions were relevant to the jury's determination of which party should be named as the conservator."

In re Arriola, 159 S.W.3d 670, 675-76 (Tex.App.—Corpus Christi 2004, orig. proceeding). See annotation under TRE 509, p. 1306.

TRE 511. WAIVER BY VOLUNTARY DISCLOSURE

(a) General Rule.

A person upon whom these rules confer a privilege against disclosure waives the privilege if:

(1) the person or a predecessor of the person while holder of the privilege voluntarily discloses or consents to disclosure of any significant part of the privileged matter unless such disclosure itself is privileged; or

(2) the person or a representative of the person calls a person to whom privileged communications have been made to testify as to the person's character or character trait insofar as such communications are relevant to such character or character trait.

(b) Lawyer-Client Privilege and Work Product; Limitations on Waiver.

Notwithstanding paragraph (a), the following provisions apply, in the circumstances set out, to disclosure of a communication or information covered by the lawyer-client privilege or work-product protection.

(1) ***Disclosure Made in a Federal or State Proceeding or to a Federal or State Office or Agency; Scope of a Waiver.*** When the disclosure is made in a federal proceeding or state proceeding of any state or to a federal office or agency or state office or agency of any state and waives the lawyer-client privilege or work-product protection, the waiver extends to an undisclosed communication or information only if:

(A) the waiver is intentional;

(B) the disclosed and undisclosed communications or information concern the same subject matter; and

(C) they ought in fairness to be considered together.

(2) ***Inadvertent Disclosure in State Civil Proceedings.*** When made in a Texas state proceeding, an inadvertent disclosure does not operate as a waiver if the holder followed the procedures of Rule of Civil Procedure 193.3(d).

(3) ***Controlling Effect of a Court Order.*** A disclosure made in litigation pending before a federal court or a state court of any state that has entered an order that the privilege or protection is not waived by disclosure connected with the litigation pending before that court is also not a waiver in a Texas state proceeding.

(4) ***Controlling Effect of a Party Agreement.*** An agreement on the effect of disclosure in a state proceeding of any state is binding only on the parties to the agreement, unless it is incorporated into a court order.

See also *O'Connor's Texas Rules*, "Waiver of objections & privileges," ch. 6-A, §25.3, p. 526; Brown & Rondon, *Texas Rules of Evidence Handbook*, p. 526; *O'Connor's Texas Forms*, FORM 6A:23.

ANNOTATIONS

In re Bexar Cty. Crim. Dist. Atty's Office, 224 S.W.3d 182, 189 (Tex.2007). "Although the DA's Office turned over its prosecution file without objection, which waived the work-product privilege as to the file's contents, the record is devoid of any indication that by doing so the DA likewise enlisted its current and former personnel to testify in [P's] suit regarding their case materials and related impressions and communications. The DA's waiver here is limited, not limitless, and agreeing to produce a prosecution file does not in itself require the DA to produce its personnel so that their mental processes and related case preparation may be further probed."

In re Ford Motor Co., 211 S.W.3d 295, 301 (Tex. 2006). "The privilege to maintain a document's confidentiality belongs to the document owner, not to the trial court. … Mistaken document production by a court employee in violation of a court-signed protective order cannot constitute a party's voluntary waiver of confidentiality. … No matter how many people eventually [see] the materials, disclosures by a third-party, whether mistaken or malevolent, do not waive the privileged nature of the information. This principle should apply with particular force when documents are entrusted to a court."

Jordan v. Fourth Ct. of Appeals, 701 S.W.2d 644, 649 (Tex.1985). "If the matter for which a privilege is sought has been disclosed to a third party, thus raising the question of waiver of the privilege, the party asserting the privilege has the burden of proving that no waiver has occurred." *See also* ***In re E.C.***, 444 S.W.3d 760, 768 (Tex.App.—Fort Worth 2014, orig. proceeding).

In re Hicks, 252 S.W.3d 790, 794 (Tex.App.—Houston [14th Dist.] 2008, orig. proceeding). "An assignment of rights and claims does not automatically include a waiver of attorney-client privilege unless specifically stated in the language of the assignment." *See also* ***In re General Agents Ins. Co.***, 224 S.W.3d 806, 814 (Tex.App.—Houston [14th Dist.] 2007, orig. proceeding).

TRE 512. PRIVILEGED MATTER DISCLOSED UNDER COMPULSION OR WITHOUT OPPORTUNITY TO CLAIM PRIVILEGE

A privilege claim is not defeated by a disclosure that was:

(a) compelled erroneously; or

(b) made without opportunity to claim the privilege.

See also Brown & Rondon, *Texas Rules of Evidence Handbook*, p. 539.

ANNOTATIONS

In re Office of the Atty. Gen., No. 02-13-00455-CV (Tex.App.—Fort Worth 2014, orig. proceeding) (memo op.; 2-6-14). "We have found no support for the trial court's reasoning that because a right *may* be waived, the trial court can *make* the party waive it. [O]nly the holder of the privilege has the power to waive it. To al-

low a court to compel waiver would render any privilege ... vulnerable to forced waiver. [¶] [E]ven when a court can compel a party to produce privileged documents, it cannot waive the party's claim of privilege."

TRE 513. COMMENT ON OR INFERENCE FROM A PRIVILEGE CLAIM; INSTRUCTION

(a) Comment or Inference Not Permitted. Except as permitted in Rule 504(b)(2), neither the court nor counsel may comment on a privilege claim—whether made in the present proceeding or previously—and the factfinder may not draw an inference from the claim.

(b) Claiming Privilege Without the Jury's Knowledge. To the extent practicable, the court must conduct a jury trial so that the making of a privilege claim is not suggested to the jury by any means.

(c) Claim of Privilege Against Self-Incrimination in a Civil Case. Subdivisions (a) and (b) do not apply to a party's claim, in the present civil case, of the privilege against self-incrimination.

(d) Jury Instruction. When this rule forbids a jury from drawing an inference from a privilege claim, the court must, on request of a party against whom the jury might draw the inference, instruct the jury accordingly.

See also Brown & Rondon, ***Texas Rules of Evidence Handbook***, p. 542; ***O'Connor's Texas Forms***, FORM 5E:1.

ANNOTATIONS

Texas DPS Officers Ass'n v. Denton, 897 S.W.2d 757, 760 (Tex.1995). "[J]uries in civil cases [may] make negative inferences based upon the assertion of the privilege [against self-incrimination]. Also, when a plaintiff invokes the privilege, ... the trial court can subsequently prohibit the plaintiff from introducing evidence on the subject, and such an act of judicial discretion does not constitute penalizing the plaintiff's use of the privilege." *See also* ***Matbon, Inc. v. Gries***, 288 S.W.3d 471, 489-90 (Tex.App.—Eastland 2009, no pet.) (negative inference that jury may have drawn cannot rise beyond mere suspicion and cannot be considered as evidence at all, particularly under a clear-and-convincing-evidence standard); ***In re Moore***, 153 S.W.3d 527, 534 (Tex.App.—Tyler 2004, orig. proceeding) (when two equally consistent inferences can be made from an assertion of the Fifth Amendment so that neither inference is more probable than the other, neither inference can be made).

In re L.S., 748 S.W.2d 571, 575 (Tex.App.—Amarillo 1988, writ denied). TRE 513(b) "reflects a desire to protect the parties from any adverse inference drawn by the jurors who witness the invocation of the privilege against self-incrimination. 'It is reasonable to anticipate that in most instances, planned reliance upon the privilege will be known in advance and the mandate of rule 513(b) can be implemented through the use of motions in limine.'"

ARTICLE VI. WITNESSES

TRE 601. COMPETENCY TO TESTIFY IN GENERAL; "DEAD MAN'S RULE"

(a) In General. Every person is competent to be a witness unless these rules provide otherwise. The following witnesses are incompetent:

- **(1)** ***Insane Persons.*** A person who is now insane or was insane at the time of the events about which the person is called to testify.
- **(2)** ***Persons Lacking Sufficient Intellect.*** A child—or any other person—whom the court examines and finds lacks sufficient intellect to testify concerning the matters in issue.

(b) The "Dead Man's Rule."

- **(1)** ***Applicability.*** The "Dead Man's Rule" applies only in a civil case:
  - **(A)** by or against a party in the party's capacity as an executor, administrator, or guardian; or
  - **(B)** by or against a decedent's heirs or legal representatives and based in whole or in part on the decedent's oral statement.
- **(2)** ***General Rule.*** In cases described in subparagraph (b)(1)(A), a party may not testify against another party about an oral statement by the testator, intestate, or ward. In cases described in subparagraph (b)(1)(B), a party may not testify against another party about an oral statement by the decedent.
- **(3)** ***Exceptions.*** A party may testify against another party about an oral statement by the testator, intestate, ward, or decedent if:
  - **(A)** the party's testimony about the statement is corroborated; or
  - **(B)** the opposing party calls the party to testify at the trial about the statement.

(4) ***Instructions.*** If a court excludes evidence under paragraph (b)(2), the court must instruct the jury that the law prohibits a party from testifying about an oral statement by the testator, intestate, ward, or decedent unless the oral statement is corroborated or the opposing party calls the party to testify at the trial about the statement.

Caution: TRE 601 is affected by Fam. Code §§6.704 and 6.705.

See also Brown & Rondon, ***Texas Rules of Evidence Handbook***, p. 551; *O'Connor's Texas Forms*, FORM 5E:1.

ANNOTATIONS

Pipkin v. Kroger Tex., L.P., 383 S.W.3d 655, 668 (Tex.App.—Houston [14th Dist.] 2012, pet. denied). "[U]nder Rule 601, a child is considered competent to testify unless, after the child is examined by the court, it appears to the court that the child does not possess sufficient intellect to relate transactions about which he will testify. There is no age below which a child is automatically deemed incompetent to testify. When a trial court determines whether a child is competent to testify at trial, it considers (1) the competence of the child to observe intelligently the events in question at the time of the occurrence; (2) the child's capacity to recollect the events; and (3) the child's capacity to narrate the facts."

In re R.M.T., 352 S.W.3d 12, 24 (Tex.App.—Texarkana 2011, no pet.). In parental-rights termination proceeding, father argued "that the trial court erred when it allowed him to testify over his attorney's objection that he was not competent.... *At 25:* The burden of proof rests on the party who claims the witness is incompetent due to insanity to show the existence of insanity by a preponderance of the evidence. In order to demonstrate incompetency under Rule 601, it must be shown that the witness lacked the ability to perceive the relevant events, recall and narrate those events at the time of trial, or that the witness lacked the capacity to understand the obligation of the oath. Moreover, the adjudication of insanity creates a rebuttable presumption of insanity. *At 26:* State concedes [father] was incompetent to testify at trial, but maintains that because [father] has not demonstrated, argued, or even contended that the admission of his testimony resulted in an improper judgment, his Rule 601 argument must fail. We agree. [To reverse the judgment, father must have shown] that the error was reasonably calculated to cause, and probably did cause, rendition of an improper judgment."

Fraga v. Drake, 276 S.W.3d 55, 61 (Tex.App.—El Paso 2008, no pet.). "[C]ourts construe the Dead Man's Rule narrowly. [TRE 601(b)] does not prohibit testimony concerning statements by the deceased that are properly corroborated. Corroborating evidence must tend to support some of the material allegations or issues that are raised by the pleadings and testified to by the witness whose evidence is sought to be corroborated. It may come from any other competent witness or other legal source, including documentary evidence. Corroborating evidence ... must tend to confirm and strengthen the testimony of the witness and show the probability of its truth. For example, it is sufficient if the corroborating evidence shows conduct by the deceased that is generally consistent with the testimony concerning the deceased's statements."

TRE 602. NEED FOR PERSONAL KNOWLEDGE

A witness may testify to a matter only if evidence is introduced sufficient to support a finding that the witness has personal knowledge of the matter. Evidence to prove personal knowledge may consist of the witness's own testimony. This rule does not apply to a witness's expert testimony under Rule 703.

See also ***O'Connor's Texas Rules***, "Introducing Evidence," ch. 8-C, p. 790; "Objecting to Evidence," ch. 8-D, p. 801; Brown & Rondon, ***Texas Rules of Evidence Handbook***, p. 563.

ANNOTATIONS

Anderson Prod'g, Inc. v. Koch Oil Co., 929 S.W.2d 416, 425 (Tex.1996). "[D] argues that the trial court erred [because P's attorney] failed to demonstrate personal knowledge supporting the testimony. The record reflects that [P's attorney's] testimony was based on his review of the documents executed by [D], and that [D] had ample opportunity to cross-examine [him] regarding the basis of his conclusion. Under these circumstances, the trial court did not abuse its discretion in failing to strike the testimony." *See also* ***Marks v. St. Luke's Episcopal Hosp.***, 319 S.W.3d 658, 666 (Tex. 2010) (affidavits based on supposition are legally insufficient).

In re Valliance Bank, 422 S.W.3d 722, 726 n.1 (Tex.App.—Fort Worth 2012, orig. proceeding). "Verification must be based on personal knowledge. A party's attorney may verify the pleading when he has personal knowledge of the facts, but he does not have authority to verify based merely on his status as counsel."

TRE 603. OATH OR AFFIRMATION TO TESTIFY TRUTHFULLY

Before testifying, a witness must give an oath or affirmation to testify truthfully. It must be in a form designed to impress that duty on the witness's conscience.

See also Brown & Rondon, ***Texas Rules of Evidence Handbook***, p. 567.

ANNOTATIONS

Glenn v. C&G Elec., Inc., 977 S.W.2d 686, 689 (Tex.App.—Fort Worth 1998, pet. denied). The "requirement [to testify truthfully under oath] applies not only to those who will testify in person in the courtroom, but also to those whose testimony at the trial will be presented by deposition."

TRE 604. INTERPRETER

An interpreter must be qualified and must give an oath or affirmation to make a true translation.

See also TRCP 183, regarding appointment and compensation of interpreters; Brown & Rondon, ***Texas Rules of Evidence Handbook***, p. 569.

ANNOTATIONS

International Commercial Bank v. Hall-Fuston Corp., 767 S.W.2d 259, 261 (Tex.App.—Beaumont 1989, writ denied). When a foreign company attempts to introduce into evidence business records that are not written in English, one of its corporate representatives can orally interpret the documents under oath after being qualified as an expert.

TRE 605. JUDGE'S COMPETENCY AS A WITNESS

The presiding judge may not testify as a witness at the trial. A party need not object to preserve the issue.

See also Brown & Rondon, ***Texas Rules of Evidence Handbook***, p. 571.

ANNOTATIONS

In re M.S., 115 S.W.3d 534, 538 (Tex.2003). TDPRS offered two orders into evidence to show what mother was ordered to do to retain custody of her children and that she had not complied. Mother objected that admitting the orders violated TRE 605. The orders submitted to the jury permitted them "to see findings of fact made by the very judge presiding over the trial, and those facts were the very ones that the jury itself was being asked to find. [¶] [A]dmitting the orders as evidence ... that [mother] failed to comply with the orders of a court was not in itself inappropriate. However, the trial judge's factual findings that his order had, in fact, been violated, should have been redacted so that the jury could draw its own conclusions...." *See also* ***In re A.T.K.***, No. 02-11-00520-CV (Tex.App.—Fort Worth 2012, no pet.) (memo op.; 9-27-12).

In re C.C.K., No. 02-12-00347-CV (Tex.App.—Fort Worth 2013, no pet.) (memo op.; 2-7-13). "'The question should be whether the judge's statement of fact is essential to the exercise of some judicial function or is the functional equivalent of witness testimony.' [¶] Here, the trial judge's statement did not convey factual information not in evidence. Nor did the trial judge's statement seek to rebut any evidence adduced at trial. Instead, the trial judge's statement told the jurors what they would be asked to decide and was akin to a preview of the jury instructions that would be given at the conclusion of the trial.... The trial judge's instruction was not 'the functional equivalent of witness testimony,' nor did it 'convey factual information not in evidence.' The trial judge thus did not testify."

O'Quinn v. Hall, 77 S.W.3d 438, 448 (Tex.App.—Corpus Christi 2002, no pet.). "Rule 605 applies not only to members of the judiciary, 'but also to those performing judicial functions that conflict with a witness's role.'"

TRE 606. JUROR'S COMPETENCY AS A WITNESS

(a) **At the Trial.** A juror may not testify as a witness before the other jurors at the trial. If a juror is called to testify, the court must give a party an opportunity to object outside the jury's presence.

(b) **During an Inquiry into the Validity of a Verdict or Indictment.**

(1) ***Prohibited Testimony or Other Evidence.*** During an inquiry into the validity of a verdict or indictment, a juror may not testify about any statement made or incident that occurred during the jury's deliberations; the effect of anything on that juror's or another juror's vote; or any juror's mental processes concerning the verdict or indictment. The court may not receive a juror's affidavit or evidence of a juror's statement on these matters.

(2) ***Exceptions.*** A juror may testify:

(A) about whether an outside influence was improperly brought to bear on any juror; or

(B) to rebut a claim that the juror was not qualified to serve.

See also TRCP 327(b); ***O'Connor's Texas Rules***, "MNT Based on Jury or Bailiff Misconduct," ch. 10-B, §14, p. 907; Brown & Rondon, ***Texas Rules of Evidence Handbook***, p. 574.

ANNOTATIONS

Golden Eagle Archery, Inc. v. Jackson, 24 S.W.3d 362, 371 (Tex.2000). An "alleged conversation between [jurors] during a trial break ... should not be considered 'deliberations' and therefore barred by [TRE] 606(b) [now TRE 606(b)(1)] and [TRCP] 327(b). [The TRCPs] use the term 'deliberations' as meaning formal jury deliberations—when the jury weighs the evidence to arrive at a verdict."

Rosell v. Central W. Motor Stages, Inc., 89 S.W.3d 643, 661 (Tex.App.—Dallas 2002, pet. denied). "The essence of the 'outside influence' rule is to prevent outside information that affects the merits of the case from reaching the jury. The only evidence here is that the jury was told that they probably would be required to deliberate another day. ... Thus, the bailiff informing the jury of the court's schedule was not misconduct. Further, the juror testimony that jurors traded answers on issues is testimony about deliberations and is not evidence of outside influences."

Perry v. Safeco Ins., 821 S.W.2d 279, 281 (Tex. App.—Houston [1st Dist.] 1991, writ denied). "[T]he coercive influence of one juror upon the rest of the panel is not 'outside influence.' Proof of coercive statements and their effect on the jury is barred by the [TREs]."

TRE 607. WHO MAY IMPEACH A WITNESS

Any party, including the party that called the witness, may attack the witness's credibility.

See also *O'Connor's Texas Rules*, "Impeaching a Witness," ch. 8-C, §6, p. 794; Brown & Rondon, *Texas Rules of Evidence Handbook*, p. 591.

TRE 608. A WITNESS'S CHARACTER FOR TRUTHFULNESS OR UNTRUTHFULNESS

(a) Reputation or Opinion Evidence. A witness's credibility may be attacked or supported by testimony about the witness's reputation for having a character for truthfulness or untruthfulness, or by testimony in the form of an opinion about that character. But evidence of truthful character is admissible only after the witness's character for truthfulness has been attacked.

(b) Specific Instances of Conduct. Except for a criminal conviction under Rule 609, a party may not inquire into or offer extrinsic evidence to prove specific instances of the witness's conduct in order to attack or support the witness's character for truthfulness.

See also *O'Connor's Texas Rules*, "Rehabilitating a Witness," ch. 8-C, §7, p. 796; Brown & Rondon, *Texas Rules of Evidence Handbook*, p. 597; *O'Connor's Texas Forms*, FORM 5E:1.

ANNOTATIONS

Commerce & Indus. Ins. v. Ferguson-Stewart, 339 S.W.3d 744, 747 (Tex.App.—Houston [1st Dist.] 2011, no pet.). "Texas courts have consistently upheld the exclusion of evidence of a witness's prior drug use for general impeachment purposes."

Rose v. Intercontinental Bank, 705 S.W.2d 752, 757 (Tex.App.—Houston [1st Dist.] 1986, writ ref'd n.r.e.). Under TRE 608(a), "the witness' reputation for truthfulness must first be attacked before [the party] can offer rehabilitating evidence."

TRE 609. IMPEACHMENT BY EVIDENCE OF A CRIMINAL CONVICTION

(a) In General. Evidence of a criminal conviction offered to attack a witness's character for truthfulness must be admitted if:

- **(1)** the crime was a felony or involved moral turpitude, regardless of punishment;
- **(2)** the probative value of the evidence outweighs its prejudicial effect to a party; and
- **(3)** it is elicited from the witness or established by public record.

(b) Limit on Using the Evidence After 10 Years. This subdivision (b) applies if more than 10 years have passed since the witness's conviction or release from confinement for it, whichever is later. Evidence of the conviction is admissible only if its probative value, supported by specific facts and circumstances, substantially outweighs its prejudicial effect.

(c) Effect of a Pardon, Annulment, or Certificate of Rehabilitation. Evidence of a conviction is not admissible if:

- **(1)** the conviction has been the subject of a pardon, annulment, certificate of rehabilitation, or other equivalent procedure based on a finding that the person has been rehabilitated, and the person has not been convicted of a later crime that was classified as a felony or involved moral turpitude, regardless of punishment;
- **(2)** probation has been satisfactorily completed for the conviction, and the person has not been

convicted of a later crime that was classified as a felony or involved moral turpitude, regardless of punishment; or

(3) the conviction has been the subject of a pardon, annulment, or other equivalent procedure based on a finding of innocence.

(d) Juvenile Adjudications. Evidence of a juvenile adjudication is admissible under this rule only if:

(1) the witness is a party in a proceeding conducted under title 3 of the Texas Family Code; or

(2) the United States or Texas Constitution requires that it be admitted.

(e) Pendency of an Appeal. A conviction for which an appeal is pending is not admissible under this rule.

(f) Notice. Evidence of a witness's conviction is not admissible under this rule if, after receiving from the adverse party a timely written request specifying the witness, the proponent of the conviction fails to provide sufficient written notice of intent to use the conviction. Notice is sufficient if it provides a fair opportunity to contest the use of such evidence.

See also *O'Connor's Texas Rules*, "Impeaching by conviction," ch. 8-C, §6.4, p. 795; Brown & Rondon, ***Texas Rules of Evidence Handbook***, p. 608; *O'Connor's Texas Forms*, FORM 5E:1.

ANNOTATIONS

Cortez v. Wyche, No. 02-11-00364-CV (Tex.App.—Fort Worth 2012, no pet.) (memo op.; 5-3-12). "In ***Theus*** [***v. State***, 845 S.W.2d 874 (Tex.Crim.App. 1992)], the court of criminal appeals set out a nonexclusive list of factors to be considered in weighing the probative value of a conviction against its prejudicial effect under rule 609(a), including: (1) the impeachment value of the prior crime; (2) the temporal proximity of the past crime relative to the charged offense and the witness's subsequent history; (3) the similarity between the past crime and the offense being prosecuted; (4) the importance of the defendant's testimony; and (5) the importance of the credibility issue. [¶] [As] to the first factor, if the crime involves deception, it has a higher impeachment value. The second weighs in favor of admission if the past crime is recent and the witness has shown a 'propensity for running afoul of the law.' With regard to the third factor, ... 'in a civil case, if conduct is in issue that is similar to a past crime, then the third factor should weigh against admission.' As to the intertwined last factors, 'in a civil case, as the importance of a particular witness's testimony and credibility increases, so does the need to allow impeachment of that witness with evidence of a criminal conviction.'" *See also* ***Porter v. Nemir***, 900 S.W.2d 376, 382 (Tex. App.—Austin 1995, no writ).

Murray v. TDFPS, 294 S.W.3d 360, 369-70 (Tex. App.—Austin 2009, no pet.). "[R]ule 609 is not a categorical limitation on the introduction of convictions for any purpose. Rather, it applies only to convictions offered for purposes of impeachment. Here, the [TDFPS] offered [father's] convictions as evidence regarding the best interests of [child]. [Father's] use of illegal drugs and his prior convictions are relevant to several of the ***Holley*** factors used in determining the best interests of the child." *See also* ***Taylor v. TDPRS***, 160 S.W.3d 641, 653 (Tex.App.—Austin 2005, pet. denied).

U.S.A. Precision Mach. Co. v. Marshall, 95 S.W.3d 407, 410 (Tex.App.—Houston [1st Dist.] 2002, pet. denied). Held: A conviction is not final for purposes of impeachment under TRE 609 if it was reversed, it is pending on appeal, or the case was dismissed after a new trial was granted.

In re M.R., 975 S.W.2d 51, 55 (Tex.App.—San Antonio 1998, pet. denied). TRE 609 "exists to establish when and within what parameters a prior conviction may be introduced. It does not *require* a conviction in order to admit some testimony. [¶] [T]he Family Code itself does not require a conviction in order to introduce evidence of family violence. Instead, it requires that the evidence be 'credible.'"

TRE 610. RELIGIOUS BELIEFS OR OPINIONS

Evidence of a witness's religious beliefs or opinions is not admissible to attack or support the witness's credibility.

See also Brown & Rondon, ***Texas Rules of Evidence Handbook***, p. 627; *O'Connor's Texas Forms*, FORM 5E:1.

TRE 611. MODE & ORDER OF EXAMINING WITNESSES & PRESENTING EVIDENCE

(a) Control by the Court; Purposes. The court should exercise reasonable control over the mode and order of examining witnesses and presenting evidence so as to:

(1) make those procedures effective for determining the truth;

(2) avoid wasting time; and
(3) protect witnesses from harassment or undue embarrassment.

(b) Scope of Cross-Examination. A witness may be cross-examined on any relevant matter, including credibility.

(c) Leading Questions. Leading questions should not be used on direct examination except as necessary to develop the witness's testimony. Ordinarily, the court should allow leading questions:
(1) on cross-examination; and
(2) when a party calls a hostile witness, an adverse party, or a witness identified with an adverse party.

See also *O'Connor's Texas Rules*, "Scope of Examination," ch. 8-C, §4, p. 791; Brown & Rondon, *Texas Rules of Evidence Handbook*, p. 629.

ANNOTATIONS

State v. Gaylor Inv. Trust Prtshp., 322 S.W.3d 814, 819 (Tex.App.—Houston [14th Dist.] 2010, no pet.). "Every trial court has the inherent power to control the disposition of the cases on its docket with economy of time and effort for itself, for counsel, and for litigants. ... The trial court's inherent power, together with applicable rules of procedure and evidence, accord trial courts broad, but not unfettered, discretion in handling trials." (Internal quotes omitted.)

Torres v. Danny's Serv. Co., 266 S.W.3d 485, 487 (Tex.App.—Eastland 2008, pet. denied). "[A] witness may be cross-examined on any issue that is probative of her credibility. [¶] Texas courts have not adopted hard and fast rules for determining whether a witness's mental health history is relevant to a credibility analysis, choosing instead to consider this evidence on an ad hoc basis. *At 488:* Because Texas follows an ad hoc approach, trial courts have broad discretion. If mental health evidence is admissible for impeachment, the trial court also has considerable discretion to limit the scope of any cross-examination. But the trial court's discretion is not limitless. The mere fact that the witness has suffered from, or received treatment for, a mental illness or disturbance is insufficient to justify its admission. The trial court must have some evidence that the illness is such that 'it might tend to reflect upon the witness's credibility.' This evidence can take many forms, but it must show that the witness's perception of events was affected or that the witness was otherwise impaired."

State Office of Risk Mgmt. v. Escalante, 162 S.W.3d 619, 628 (Tex.App.—El Paso 2005, pet. dism'd). "The right to cross examine a witness is a substantial one, and it is error to so restrict it as to prevent the cross-examining party from going fully into all matters connected with the examination in chief. Due process requires an opportunity to confront and cross-examine adverse witnesses."

Stam v. Mack, 984 S.W.2d 747, 752 (Tex.App.—Texarkana 1999, no pet.). "The trial court interrupted [P's] cross-examination because it felt that [P] was questioning the witness on immaterial issues and he was going into areas that were improper. The trial court's interruption of the cross-examination was not improper, but was a proper action to maintain control and promote expedition."

TRE 612. WRITING USED TO REFRESH A WITNESS'S MEMORY

(a) Scope. This rule gives an adverse party certain options when a witness uses a writing to refresh memory:
(1) while testifying;
(2) before testifying, in civil cases, if the court decides that justice requires the party to have those options; or
(3) before testifying, in criminal cases.

(b) Adverse Party's Options; Deleting Unrelated Matter. An adverse party is entitled to have the writing produced at the hearing, to inspect it, to cross-examine the witness about it, and to introduce in evidence any portion that relates to the witness's testimony. If the producing party claims that the writing includes unrelated matter, the court must examine the writing in camera, delete any unrelated portion, and order that the rest be delivered to the adverse party. Any portion deleted over objection must be preserved for the record.

(c) Failure to Produce or Deliver the Writing. If a writing is not produced or is not delivered as ordered, the court may issue any appropriate order. But if the prosecution does not comply in a criminal case, the court must strike the witness's testimony or—if justice so requires—declare a mistrial.

See also Brown & Rondon, *Texas Rules of Evidence Handbook*, p. 637.

ANNOTATIONS

Goode v. Shoukfeh, 943 S.W.2d 441, 449 (Tex. 1997). "If a witness uses the writing while testifying[,] the adverse party must be given access to it, but if the

writing is used before the witness testifies, the court has the discretion to order the writing disclosed to the adverse party."

TRE 613. WITNESS'S PRIOR STATEMENT & BIAS OR INTEREST

(a) Witness's Prior Inconsistent Statement.

(1) ***Foundation Requirement.*** When examining a witness about the witness's prior inconsistent statement—whether oral or written—a party must first tell the witness:

(A) the contents of the statement;

(B) the time and place of the statement; and

(C) the person to whom the witness made the statement.

(2) ***Need Not Show Written Statement.*** If the witness's prior inconsistent statement is written, a party need not show it to the witness before inquiring about it, but must, upon request, show it to opposing counsel.

(3) ***Opportunity to Explain or Deny.*** A witness must be given the opportunity to explain or deny the prior inconsistent statement.

(4) ***Extrinsic Evidence.*** Extrinsic evidence of a witness's prior inconsistent statement is not admissible unless the witness is first examined about the statement and fails to unequivo cally admit making the statement.

(5) ***Opposing Party's Statement.*** This subdivision (a) does not apply to an opposing party's statement under Rule 801(e)(2).

(b) Witness's Bias or Interest.

(1) ***Foundation Requirement.*** When examining a witness about the witness's bias or interest, a party must first tell the witness the circumstances or statements that tend to show the witness's bias or interest. If examining a witness about a statement—whether oral or written—to prove the witness's bias or interest, a party must tell the witness:

(A) the contents of the statement;

(B) the time and place of the statement; and

(C) the person to whom the statement was made.

(2) ***Need Not Show Written Statement.*** If a party uses a written statement to prove the witness's bias or interest, a party need not show the statement to the witness before inquiring about it, but must, upon request, show it to opposing counsel.

(3) ***Opportunity to Explain or Deny.*** A witness must be given the opportunity to explain or deny the circumstances or statements that tend to show the witness's bias or interest. And the witness's proponent may present evidence to rebut the charge of bias or interest.

(4) ***Extrinsic Evidence.*** Extrinsic evidence of a witness's bias or interest is not admissible unless the witness is first examined about the bias or interest and fails to unequivocally admit it.

(c) Witness's Prior Consistent Statement. Unless Rule 801(e)(1)(B) provides otherwise, a witness's prior consistent statement is not admissible if offered solely to enhance the witness's credibility.

See also *O'Connor's Texas Rules*, "Impeaching a Witness," ch. 8-C, §6, p. 794; Brown & Rondon, ***Texas Rules of Evidence Handbook***, p. 644.

ANNOTATIONS

Walker v. Packer, 827 S.W.2d 833, 839 n.5 (Tex. 1992). "Evidence of bias is not admissible if the witness 'unequivocally admits such bias or interest' at trial. [Because D's witness] flatly denied [bias], such evidence should be discoverable."

In re Weir, 166 S.W.3d 861, 864 (Tcx.App.—Beaumont 2005, orig. proceeding). "Generally, an expert witness may be questioned regarding payment received for his work as an expert witness. However, pretrial discovery of all a witness's accounting and financial records, solely for the purpose of impeachment, may be denied. *At 865:* The parties' interests in obtaining discovery solely for impeachment must be weighed against the witness's legitimate interest in protecting unrelated financial information." *See also* ***In re Siroosian***, 449 S.W.3d 920, 923-26 (Tex.App.—Fort Worth 2014, orig. proceeding).

TRE 614. EXCLUDING WITNESSES

At a party's request, the court must order witnesses excluded so that they cannot hear other witnesses' testimony. Or the court may do so on its own. But this rule does not authorize excluding:

(a) a party who is a natural person and, in civil cases, that person's spouse;

(b) after being designated as the party's representative by its attorney:

(1) in a civil case, an officer or employee of a party that is not a natural person; or
(2) in a criminal case, a defendant that is not a natural person;

(c) a person whose presence a party shows to be essential to presenting the party's claim or defense; or

(d) the victim in a criminal case, unless the court determines that the victim's testimony would be materially affected by hearing other testimony at the trial.

See also TRCP 267; *O'Connor's Texas Rules*, "Invoking 'the Rule'," ch. 8-C, §3, p. 790; Brown & Rondon, *Texas Rules of Evidence Handbook*, p. 659.

ANNOTATIONS

Drilex Sys. v. Flores, 1 S.W.3d 112, 118-19 (Tex. 1999). "Although an expert witness may typically be found exempt under the essential presence exception, experts are not automatically exempt. Instead, [TRE] 614 and [TRCP] 267 vest in trial judges broad discretion to determine whether a witness is essential."

In re A.H.J., No. 05-15-00501-CV (Tex.App.—Dallas 2015, pet. denied) (memo op.; 10-8-15). "If the Rule is violated, … depending on the circumstances, the trial court may allow the testimony, exclude the testimony, or hold the violator in contempt."

In re H.M.S., 349 S.W.3d 250, 253 (Tex.App.—Dallas 2011, pet. denied). "Rule 614 …, commonly referred to as 'the rule,' requires the exclusion of witnesses from the courtroom upon the request of a party. Although there are four classes of witnesses that are exempt from the operation of the rule, 'officers of the court' are not among those exempted. Accordingly, [Judge] erred in refusing to exclude certain witnesses on the basis that they were court employees."

TRE 615. PRODUCING A WITNESS'S STATEMENT IN CRIMINAL CASES

(a) **Motion to Produce.** After a witness other than the defendant testifies on direct examination, the court, on motion of a party who did not call the witness, must order an attorney for the state or the defendant and the defendant's attorney to produce, for the examination and use of the moving party, any statement of the witness that:
(1) is in their possession;
(2) relates to the subject matter of the witness's testimony; and
(3) has not previously been produced.

(b) **Producing the Entire Statement.** If the entire statement relates to the subject matter of the witness's testimony, the court must order that the statement be delivered to the moving party.

(c) **Producing a Redacted Statement.** If the party who called the witness claims that the statement contains information that does not relate to the subject matter of the witness's testimony, the court must inspect the statement in camera. After excising any unrelated portions, the court must order delivery of the redacted statement to the moving party. If a party objects to an excision, the court must preserve the entire statement with the excised portion indicated, under seal, as part of the record.

(d) **Recess to Examine a Statement.** If the court orders production of a witness's statement, the court, on request, must recess the proceedings to allow the moving party time to examine the statement and prepare for its use.

(e) **Sanction for Failure to Produce or Deliver a Statement.** If the party who called the witness disobeys an order to produce or deliver a statement, the court must strike the witness's testimony from the record. If an attorney for the state disobeys the order, the court must declare a mistrial if justice so requires.

(f) **"Statement" Defined.** As used in this rule, a witness's "statement" means:
(1) a written statement that the witness makes and signs, or otherwise adopts or approves;
(2) a substantially verbatim, contemporaneously recorded recital of the witness's oral statement that is contained in any recording or any transcription of a recording; or
(3) the witness's statement to a grand jury, however taken or recorded, or a transcription of such a statement.

See also Brown & Rondon, *Texas Rules of Evidence Handbook*, p. 667.

ARTICLE VII. OPINIONS & EXPERT TESTIMONY

TRE 701. OPINION TESTIMONY BY LAY WITNESSES

If a witness is not testifying as an expert, testimony in the form of an opinion is limited to one that is:
(a) rationally based on the witness's perception; and

(b) helpful to clearly understanding the witness's testimony or to determining a fact in issue.

See also Brown & Rondon, ***Texas Rules of Evidence Handbook***, p. 676; ***O'Connor's Texas Family Law Handbook*** (2017), "Testimony," ch. 2-A, §6.1, p. 106; "Proving value of property," ch. 7-A, §5.3, p. 790; "Proving value of real property," ch. 7-B, §5.3, p. 820.

ANNOTATIONS

Natural Gas Pipeline Co. v. Justiss, 397 S.W.3d 150, 157 (Tex.2012). "Based on the presumption that an owner is familiar with his property and its value, the Property Owner Rule is an exception to the requirement that a witness must otherwise establish his qualifications to express an opinion on land values. Under the Rule, an owner's valuation testimony fulfills the same role that expert testimony does. *At 159:* Thus, as with expert testimony, property valuations may not be based solely on a property owner's *ipse dixit*. An owner may not simply echo the phrase 'market value' and state a number to substantiate his diminished value claim; he must provide the factual basis on which his opinion rests. [T]he owner's testimony may be challenged on cross-examination or refuted with independent evidence. But even if unchallenged, the testimony must support a verdict, and conclusory or speculative statements do not." *See also* ***Porras v. Craig***, 675 S.W.2d 503, 505 (Tex.1984).

Reid Rd. MUD v. Speedy Stop Food Stores, 337 S.W.3d 846, 851 52 (Tex.2011). "The line between who is a [TRE] 702 expert witness and who is a [TRE] 701 witness is not always bright. But when the main substance of the witness's testimony is based on application of the witness's specialized knowledge, skill, experience, training, or education to his familiarity with the property, then the testimony will generally be expert testimony within the scope of Rule 702. A witness giving such testimony must be properly disclosed and designated as an expert and the witness's testimony is subject to scrutiny under rules regarding experts and expert opinion. Any other principle would allow parties to conceal expert testimony by claiming the witness is one whose opinions are merely for the purpose of explaining the witness's perceptions and testimony. [¶] Accordingly, we do not categorically agree with [D's] contention that all persons with personal knowledge of real property can give opinion testimony as to the market value of that property without the testimony being considered and identified as expert testimony. Such a holding would allow circumvention of discovery and disclosure rules that allow parties to prepare for trial and protect themselves from trial by ambush. Instead, we hold that subject to the provisions of Rule 701, ... a witness who will be giving opinion evidence about a property's fair market value must be disclosed and designated as an expert pursuant to discovery and other applicable rules."

In re Z.R., No. 01-11-00715-CV (Tex.App.—Houston [1st Dist.] 2013, pet. denied) (memo op.; 8-29-13). "'Perceptions refer to a witness's interpretation of information acquired through his or her own senses or experiences at the time of the event (i.e., things the witness saw, heard, smelled, touched, felt, or tasted).' Thus, a Rule 701 witness may testify about his or her 'opinions, beliefs, or inferences as long as they are drawn from his or her own experiences or observations.'"

Rogers v. TDFPS, 175 S.W.3d 370, 377 (Tex.App.—Houston [1st Dist.] 2005, pet. dism'd). "A person with specialized knowledge may testify about his or her own observations under [TRE 701] and may also testify about the theories, facts, and data used in his or her area of expertise under [TRE] 702. A person who has professional social work training and experience, for example, can testify as both a lay and an expert witness. Although the caseworker here was asked if she had formed an opinion about what was in the best interest of the children, she did not voice that opinion, contrary to [respondent's] assertion that she expressed the 'collective opinion' of the agency. As such, she was not testifying as an expert witness, despite being able to testify as an expert, but only as a fact witness." *See also* ***Kilgore Mech. LLC v. Shafiee***, No. 14-10-00295-CV (Tex.App.—Houston [14th Dist.] 2011, no pet.) (memo op.; 5-12-11) (even if police officer qualifies as an expert under TRE 702, officer can also give lay opinions under TRE 701).

City of San Antonio v. Vela, 762 S.W.2d 314, 321 (Tex.App.—San Antonio 1988, writ denied). "'In general, a witness need not be an expert in medical matters to state an opinion as to his own physical health.'"

TRE 702. TESTIMONY BY EXPERT WITNESSES

A witness who is qualified as an expert by knowledge, skill, experience, training, or education may testify in the form of an opinion or otherwise if the expert's scientific, technical, or other specialized knowledge will help the trier of fact to understand the evidence or to determine a fact in issue.

See also *O'Connor's Texas Rules*, "Motion to Exclude Expert," ch. 5-N, p. 474; "Testimony from expert," ch. 8-C, §5.5, p. 793; "Objection to opinion of expert," ch. 8-D, §4.2, p. 804; Brown & Rondon, ***Texas Rules of Evidence Handbook***, p. 692; ***O'Connor's Texas Family Law Handbook*** (2017), "Testimony," ch. 2-A, §6.1, p. 106; "Valuing Assets & Liabilities," ch. 7-A, §5, p. 788; "Proving value of real property," ch. 7-B, §5.3, p. 820.

ANNOTATIONS

Generally

Reid Rd. MUD v. Speedy Stop Food Stores, 337 S.W.3d 846, 851-52 (Tex.2011). See annotation under TRE 701, p. 1317.

GTE Sw., Inc. v. Bruce, 998 S.W.2d 605, 620 (Tex. 1999). "Except in highly unusual circumstances, expert testimony concerning extreme and outrageous conduct would not meet [the standards of TRE 702]. Where ... the issue involves only general knowledge and experience rather than expertise, it is within the province of the jury to decide...." *See also* ***K-Mart Corp. v. Honeycutt***, 24 S.W.3d 357, 360 (Tex.2000).

In re G.M.P., 909 S.W.2d 198, 206 (Tex.App.—Houston [14th Dist.] 1995, no writ). "A determination of who is telling the truth is the sole province of the jury. [T]he trial court erred in allowing [expert] to testify that, in his expert opinion, [witness] was telling the truth."

Qualification of Expert

In re Commitment of Bohannan, 388 S.W.3d 296, 304-05 (Tex.2012). "That a witness has knowledge, skill, expertise, or training does not necessarily mean that the witness can assist the trier-of-fact. Expert testimony assists the trier-of-fact when the expert's knowledge and experience on a relevant issue are beyond that of the average juror and the testimony helps the trier-of-fact understand the evidence or determine a fact issue. [¶] Credentials are important, but credentials alone do not qualify an expert to testify. [F]or example, ... a medical license does not automatically qualify the holder to testify as an expert on every medical question. Trial courts must ensure that those who purport to be experts truly have expertise concerning the actual subject about which they are offering an opinion. The test is whether the offering party has established that the expert has knowledge, skill, experience, training, or education regarding the specific issue before the court which would qualify the expert to give an opinion on that particular subject." (Internal quotes omitted.) *See also* ***Broders v. Heise***, 924 S.W.2d 148, 152-53 (Tex.1996).

Havner v. E-Z Mart Stores, 825 S.W.2d 456, 460 n.4 (Tex.1992). "An investigating officer may properly testify as to causation." *See also* ***Gainsco Cty. Mut. Ins. v. Martinez***, 27 S.W.3d 97, 104 (Tex.App.—San Antonio 2000, pet. granted, judgm't vacated w.r.m.).

ExxonMobil Corp. v. Pagayon, 467 S.W.3d 36, 52 (Tex.App.—Houston [14th Dist.] 2015, pet. argued 12-6-16). "A physician from one school of practice may testify about the negligence of a physician of a different school of practice so long as the subject of inquiry is common to and equally recognized and developed in both fields. Thus, in determining whether a doctor is qualified to testify on the specific issue before it, the trial court should not focus on the specialty of the medical expert." (Internal quotes omitted.)

Yount v. State, 872 S.W.2d 706, 709-10 (Tex.Crim. App.1993). "We ... question whether a psychologist who specializes in child sexual abuse cases is an 'expert' on credibility. While a witness may possess 'scientific, technical, or other specialized knowledge' concerning sexually abused children, we seriously question whether any such person also possesses 'scientific, technical or other specialized knowledge,' beyond the realm of the jury, regarding the truthfulness of those children. 'Psychologists and psychiatrists are not, and do not claim to be, experts at discerning truth. Psychiatrists are trained to accept facts provided by their patients, not to act as judges of patients' credibility.' *At 711:* We ... conclude that expert testimony that a particular witness is truthful is inadmissible under Rule 702. [¶] The further question in this case is whether the same holds true for expert testimony as to the credibility of a *class* of persons to which the complainant belongs. ... An expert who testifies that a class of persons to which the victim belongs is truthful is essentially telling the jury that they can believe the victim in the instant case as well. This is not 'expert' testimony of the kind which will assist the jury under Rule 702. *At 712:* We hold that Rule 702 does not permit an expert to give an opinion that the complainant or class of persons to which the complainant belongs is truthful."

Estorque v. Schafer, 302 S.W.3d 19, 26 (Tex. App.—Fort Worth 2009, no pet.). "Qualifications must appear in the expert report and cannot be inferred." *See also* ***Philipp v. McCreedy***, 298 S.W.3d 682, 686 (Tex. App.—San Antonio 2009, no pet.).

In re M.D.S., 1 S.W.3d 190, 203 (Tex.App.—Amarillo 1999, no pet.). Doctor "testified that he was a medical doctor and had completed a full residency in psychiatry. He testified that his practice experience was in clinical psychiatry. He did not testify that he had any training or experience with termination of parent-child relationships. [Doctor] may well have been qualified to give expert opinion testimony in regard to termination of parent-child relationships. This record, however, does not demonstrate those qualifications. In the face of proper challenge, an expert must be proved to have qualification in the specific issue before the court."

Chance v. Chance, 911 S.W.2d 40, 51 (Tex.App.—Beaumont 1995, writ denied). Mother "contends that it was error to allow [doctor] to base his opinion, at least on part, on statements contained in a tape-recording of [child]. This tape-recording was made by [father] of a conversation between himself and his son.... [¶] For an expert's opinion to be admissible as evidence, the witness must be qualified in the area of his opinion, his opinion must have a sufficient evidentiary foundation, and the opinion must assist the fact finder. There is no contest that [doctor] qualified as an expert in the field of psychiatry. For the evidentiary base, [doctor] relied on [father's] history, which included [doctor's] interview of [father], another doctor's records, the tape recording in question, interviews with [father] during his office visits, tests, evaluations, and treatment. As an expert, [doctor] could base his opinion at least in part on inadmissible opinions if the facts are of a nature that other experts in the field reasonably rely on same. Even if the tape of the conversation with [child] is inadmissible[, doctor's] opinion would remain admissible."

Reliability of Opinion

Caffe Ribs, Inc. v. State, 487 S.W.3d 137, 144 (Tex. 2016). "When an expert's opinion is predicated on a particular set of facts, those facts need not be undisputed. An expert's opinion is only unreliable if it is contrary to actual, undisputed facts."

Gharda USA, Inc. v. Control Solutions, Inc., 464 S.W.3d 338, 349 (Tex.2015). "'[E]ach material part of an expert's theory must be reliable.' [¶] Whether an expert's testimony is reliable is based on more than whether the expert's methodology satisfies the ***Robinson*** factors. Reliable expert testimony must be based on a probability standard, rather than on mere possibility. Expert testimony is unreliable 'if there is too great an analytical gap between the data on which the expert relies and the opinion offered.' Whether an analytical gap exists is largely determined by comparing the facts the expert relied on, the facts in the record, and the expert's ultimate opinion. Analytical gaps may include circumstances in which the expert unreliably applies otherwise sound principles and methodologies, ... the expert's opinion is based on assumed facts that vary materially from the facts in the record, ... or the expert's opinion is based on tests or data that do not support the conclusions reached.... Regardless of the manner in which we determine reliability, we do not decide whether the expert's opinions are correct; rather, we determine whether the analysis used to form those opinions is reliable." *See also* ***Mack Trucks, Inc. v. Tamez***, 206 S.W.3d 572, 581 (Tex.2006).

Transcontinental Ins. v. Crump, 330 S.W.3d 211, 215-16 (Tex.2010). "In determining whether expert testimony is reliable, a court should consider the [***Robinson***] factors ... as well as the expert's experience, knowledge, and training. '[I]n very few cases will the evidence be such that the trial court's reliability determination can properly be based only on the experience of a qualified expert to the exclusion of factors such as those set out in ***Robinson***, or, on the other hand, properly be based only on factors such as those set out in ***Robinson*** to the exclusion of considerations based on a qualified expert's experience.'"

Whirlpool Corp. v. Camacho, 298 S.W.3d 631, 639-40 (Tex.2009). "The proponent [of expert testimony] must satisfy its burden regardless of the quality or quantity of the opposing party's evidence on the issue and regardless of whether the opposing party attempts to conclusively prove the expert testimony is wrong. [¶] Witnesses offered as experts in an area or subject will invariably have experience in that field. If courts merely accept 'experience' as a substitute for proof that an expert's opinions are reliable and then only examine the testimony for analytical gaps in the expert's logic and opinions, an expert can effectively insulate his or her conclusions from meaningful review by filling gaps in the testimony with almost any type of data or subjective opinions. We have recognized, and do recognize, that some subjects do not lend themselves to scientific testing and scientific methodology. But given the facts in this case, the analytical gap test was not the only factor that should have been considered.... This is

not one of the few cases in which appellate review of expert evidence should be limited to either an analysis focused solely on ***Robinson***-like factors or solely on an analytical gap test. [P]roper appellate legal sufficiency review ... requires evaluating [expert's] testimony by considering both ***Robinson***-type factors and examining for analytical gaps in his testimony." *See also* ***TXI Transp. v. Hughes***, 306 S.W.3d 230, 235 (Tex.2010) (factors are difficult to apply for vehicular-accident-reconstruction testimony).

Coastal Transp. Co. v. Crown Cent. Pet. Corp., 136 S.W.3d 227, 233 (Tex.2004). "When the expert's underlying methodology is challenged, the court 'necessarily looks beyond what the expert said' to evaluate the reliability of the expert's opinion. When the testimony is challenged as conclusory or speculative and therefore non-probative on its face, however, there is no need to go beyond the face of the record to test its reliability. [W]hen a reliability challenge requires the court to evaluate the underlying methodology, technique, or foundational data used by the expert, an objection must be timely made so that the trial court has the opportunity to conduct this analysis. However, when the challenge is restricted to the face of the record[,] a party may challenge the legal sufficiency of the evidence even in the absence of any objection to its admissibility."

Gammill v. Jack Williams Chevrolet, Inc., 972 S.W.2d 713, 726 (Tex.1998). "Nothing in the language of [TRE 702] suggests that opinions based on scientific knowledge should be treated any differently than opinions based on technical or other specialized knowledge. It would be an odd rule of evidence that insisted that some expert opinions be reliable but not others. All expert testimony should be shown to be reliable before it is admitted." *See also* ***Helena Chem. Co. v. Wilkins***, 47 S.W.3d 486, 499 (Tex.2001).

Merrell Dow Pharms. v. Havner, 953 S.W.2d 706, 714 (Tex.1997). "If the foundational data underlying opinion testimony are unreliable, ... any opinion drawn from that data is likewise unreliable. Further, an expert's testimony is unreliable even when the underlying data are sound if the expert draws conclusions from that data based on flawed methodology. A flaw in the expert's reasoning from the data may render reliance on a study unreasonable and render the inferences drawn therefrom dubious. Under that circumstance, the expert's scientific testimony is unreliable and, legally, no evidence." *See also* ***Cooper Tire & Rubber Co. v. Mendez***, 204 S.W.3d 797, 800-01 (Tex.2006).

E.I. du Pont de Nemours & Co. v. Robinson, 923 S.W.2d 549, 557 (Tex.1995). The factors to consider in determining the admissibility of scientific knowledge include "but are not limited to: (1) the extent to which the theory has been or can be tested; (2) the extent to which the technique relies upon the subjective interpretation of the expert; (3) whether the theory has been subjected to peer review and/or publication; (4) the technique's potential rate of error; (5) whether the underlying theory or technique has been generally accepted as valid by the relevant scientific community; and (6) the non-judicial uses which have been made of the theory or technique." *See also* ***Gomez v. American Honda Motor Co.***, No. 04-14-00398-CV (Tex.App.—San Antonio 2015, pet. denied) (memo op.; 4-22-15) (additional factors are whether expert has ruled out alternative causes of injury and whether expert's research and opinions were conducted and formed solely for purpose of litigation).

Taylor v. TDPRS, 160 S.W.3d 641, 650 (Tex.App.—Austin 2005, pet. denied). "[I]n fields other than the hard sciences, such as the social sciences, factors like an expert's education, training, and experience are more appropriate factors in testing reliability than the scientific method. Thus, when measuring the reliability of an expert's opinion in fields within the soft sciences, ... courts should consider whether: (1) the field of expertise is a legitimate one; (2) the subject matter of the expert's testimony is within the scope of that field; and (3) the expert's testimony properly relies upon the principles involved in that field of study." *See also* ***In re J.R.***, 501 S.W.3d 738, 748-49 (Tex.App.—Waco 2016, pet. denied).

Deadline to Object

General Motors Corp. v. Iracheta, 161 S.W.3d 462, 471 (Tex.2005). "The unreliability of expert opinions may be apparent as early as the discovery process but also may not emerge until trial, during or after the expert's testimony, or even later. An objection must be timely, but it need not anticipate a deficiency before it is apparent. [W]e cannot say that [D's] objection following cross-examination came too late."

TRE 703. BASES OF AN EXPERT'S OPINION TESTIMONY

An expert may base an opinion on facts or data in the case that the expert has been made aware of, reviewed, or personally observed. If experts in the par-

ticular field would reasonably rely on those kinds of facts or data in forming an opinion on the subject, they need not be admissible for the opinion to be admitted.

See also ***O'Connor's Texas Rules***, "Foundation test," ch. 5-N, §2.4, p. 479; Brown & Rondon, ***Texas Rules of Evidence Handbook***, p. 733.

ANNOTATIONS

Elizondo v. Krist, 415 S.W.3d 259, 263 (Tex.2013). "Under [TRE] 703, experts may base their testimony on facts or data that are 'of a type reasonably relied upon by experts in the particular field in forming opinions or inferences upon the subject.' That test is met when, in a mass tort litigation involving thousands of similar claimants and arising out of the same event, the expert measures the 'true' settlement value of a particular case by persuasively comparing all the circumstances of the case to the settlements obtained in other cases with similar circumstances arising from the event."

In re Christus Spohn Hosp. Kleberg, 222 S.W.3d 434, 440 (Tex.2007). "[I]n many instances, experts may rely on inadmissible hearsay, privileged communications, and other information that the ordinary witness may not." *See also* ***Gannon v. Wyche***, 321 S.W.3d 881, 889 (Tex.App.—Houston [14th Dist.] 2010, pet. denied); ***Sosa v. Koshy***, 961 S.W.2d 420, 427 (Tex. App.—Houston [1st Dist.] 1997, pet. denied).

Merrell Dow Pharms. v. Havner, 953 S.W.2d 706, 711 (Tex.1997). "The substance of the [expert's] testimony must be considered. *At 712:* [A]n expert's bald assurance of validity is not enough. *At 713:* The underlying data should be independently evaluated in determining if the opinion itself is reliable."

TRE 704. OPINION ON AN ULTIMATE ISSUE

An opinion is not objectionable just because it embraces an ultimate issue.

See also Brown & Rondon, ***Texas Rules of Evidence Handbook***, p. 746.

ANNOTATIONS

Birchfield v. Texarkana Mem'l Hosp., 747 S.W.2d 361, 365 (Tex.1987). "Fairness and efficiency dictate that an expert may state an opinion on a mixed question of law and fact as long as the opinion is confined to the relevant issues and is based on proper legal concepts." *See also* ***Dickerson v. DeBarbieris***, 964 S.W.2d 680, 690 (Tex.App.—Houston [14th Dist.] 1998, no pet.) (expert cannot state opinion or conclusion on pure question of law).

TRE 705. DISCLOSING THE UNDERLYING FACTS OR DATA & EXAMINING AN EXPERT ABOUT THEM

(a) **Stating an Opinion Without Disclosing the Underlying Facts or Data.** Unless the court orders otherwise, an expert may state an opinion—and give the reasons for it—without first testifying to the underlying facts or data. But the expert may be required to disclose those facts or data on cross-examination.

(b) **Voir Dire Examination of an Expert About the Underlying Facts or Data.** Before an expert states an opinion or discloses the underlying facts or data, an adverse party in a civil case may—or in a criminal case must—be permitted to examine the expert about the underlying facts or data. This examination must take place outside the jury's hearing.

(c) **Admissibility of Opinion.** An expert's opinion is inadmissible if the underlying facts or data do not provide a sufficient basis for the opinion.

(d) **When Otherwise Inadmissible Underlying Facts or Data May Be Disclosed; Instructing the Jury.** If the underlying facts or data would otherwise be inadmissible, the proponent of the opinion may not disclose them to the jury if their probative value in helping the jury evaluate the opinion is outweighed by their prejudicial effect. If the court allows the proponent to disclose those facts or data the court must, upon timely request, restrict the evidence to its proper scope and instruct the jury accordingly.

See also ***O'Connor's Texas Rules***, "Motion to Exclude Expert," ch. 5-N, p. 474; Brown & Rondon, ***Texas Rules of Evidence Handbook***, p. 752.

ANNOTATIONS

Arkoma Basin Expl. Co. v. FMF Assocs. 1990-A, Ltd., 249 S.W.3d 380, 389-90 (Tex.2008). "[E]xperts are not required to introduce ... foundational data at trial unless the opposing party or the court insists."

Kerr-McGee Corp. v. Helton, 133 S.W.3d 245, 252 (Tex.2004). "[B]ecause Rule 705(a) contemplates that the party against whom the evidence is offered may elicit testimony regarding the underlying facts or data on cross-examination, a motion to strike the testimony after such cross-examination is timely."

Weiss v. Mechanical Associated Servs., 989 S.W.2d 120, 124-25 (Tex.App.—San Antonio 1999, pet. denied). "The non-exclusive list of factors the court may consider in deciding admissibility [under TRE 705(c)] includes the extent to which the theory has been or can be tested, the extent to which the technique relies upon the subjective interpretation of the expert, whether the theory has been subjected to peer review and/or publication, the technique's potential rate of error, whether the underlying theory or technique has been generally accepted as valid by the relevant scientific community, and the non-judicial uses that have been made of the theory or technique."

TRE 706. AUDIT IN CIVIL CASES

Notwithstanding any other evidence rule, the court must admit an auditor's verified report prepared under Rule of Civil Procedure 172 and offered by a party. If a party files exceptions to the report, a party may offer evidence supporting the exceptions to contradict the report.

See also Brown & Rondon, *Texas Rules of Evidence Handbook*, p. 768.

ANNOTATIONS

Lovelace v. Sabine Consol., Inc., 733 S.W.2d 648, 656 (Tex.App.—Houston [14th Dist.] 1987, writ denied). "The audit report ... contains no such affidavit as is required by [TRCP] 172. ... Further, six days before trial [P] filed an objection to the audit. Therefore, the trial court did not err in admitting evidence that contradicted and supplemented the auditor's report."

ARTICLE VIII. HEARSAY

TRE 801. DEFINITIONS THAT APPLY TO THIS ARTICLE; EXCLUSIONS FROM HEARSAY

(a) **Statement.** "Statement" means a person's oral or written verbal expression, or nonverbal conduct that a person intended as a substitute for verbal expression.

(b) **Declarant.** "Declarant" means the person who made the statement.

(c) **Matter Asserted.** "Matter asserted" means:

- (1) any matter a declarant explicitly asserts; and
- (2) any matter implied by a statement, if the probative value of the statement as offered flows from the declarant's belief about the matter.

(d) **Hearsay.** "Hearsay" means a statement that:

- (1) the declarant does not make while testifying at the current trial or hearing; and
- (2) a party offers in evidence to prove the truth of the matter asserted in the statement.

(e) **Statements That Are Not Hearsay.** A statement that meets the following conditions is not hearsay:

- (1) ***A Declarant-Witness's Prior Statement.*** The declarant testifies and is subject to cross-examination about a prior statement, and the statement:
  - (A) is inconsistent with the declarant's testimony and:
    - (i) when offered in a civil case, was given under penalty of perjury at a trial, hearing, or other proceeding or in a deposition; or
    - (ii) when offered in a criminal case, was given under penalty of perjury at a trial, hearing, or other proceeding—except a grand jury proceeding—or in a deposition;
  - (B) is consistent with the declarant's testimony and is offered to rebut an express or implied charge that the declarant recently fabricated it or acted from a recent improper influence or motive in so testifying; or
  - (C) identifies a person as someone the declarant perceived earlier.
- (2) ***An Opposing Party's Statement.*** The statement is offered against an opposing party and:
  - (A) was made by the party in an individual or representative capacity;
  - (B) is one the party manifested that it adopted or believed to be true;
  - (C) was made by a person whom the party authorized to make a statement on the subject;
  - (D) was made by the party's agent or employee on a matter within the scope of that relationship and while it existed; or
  - (E) was made by the party's coconspirator during and in furtherance of the conspiracy.
- (3) ***A Deponent's Statement.*** In a civil case, the statement was made in a deposition taken in the same proceeding. "Same proceeding" is defined in Rule of Civil Procedure 203.6(b). The deponent's unavailability as a witness is not a requirement for admissibility.

Caution: TRE 801 is affected by Fam. Code §104.006.

See also *O'Connor's Texas Rules*, "Admissibility," ch. 6-F, §12.1, p. 618; Brown & Rondon, ***Texas Rules of Evidence Handbook***, p. 803; ***O'Connor's Texas Forms***, FORM 5E:1; ***O'Connor's Texas Family Law Handbook*** (2017), "Hearsay statement," ch. 4-D, §12.4.2, p. 456; "Sworn inventory & appraisement," ch. 7-A, §3.1, p. 784.

Comment: The definitions in TRE 801(a), (b), (c), and (d) combined bring within the hearsay rule four categories of conduct; these are described and illustrated below.

(1) A verbal (oral or written) explicit assertion. Illustration. Witness testifies that declarant said "A shot B." Declarant's conduct is a statement because it is an oral expression. Because it is an explicit assertion, the matter asserted is that A shot B. Finally, the statement is hearsay because it was not made while testifying at the trial and is offered to prove the truth of the matter asserted.

(2) A verbal (oral or written) explicit assertion, not offered to prove the matter explicitly asserted, but offered for the truth of a matter implied by the statement, the probative value of the statement flowing from declarant's belief as to the matter. Illustration. The only known remedy for X disease is medicine Y and the only known use of medicine Y is to cure X disease. To prove that Oglethorpe had X disease, witness testifies that declarant, a doctor, stated, "The best medicine for Oglethorpe is Y." The testimony is to a statement because it was a verbal expression. The matter asserted was that Oglethorpe had X disease because that matter is implied from the statement, the probative value of the statement as offered flowing from declarant's belief as to the matter. Finally, the statement is hearsay because it was not made while testifying at the trial and is offered to prove the truth of the matter asserted.

(3) Non-assertive verbal conduct offered for the truth of a matter implied by the statement, the probative value of the statement flowing from declarant's belief as to the matter. Illustration. In a rape prosecution to prove that Richard, the defendant, was in the room at the time of the rape, W testifies that declarant knocked on the door to the room and shouted, "Open the door, Richard." The testimony is to a statement because it was a verbal expression. The matter asserted was that Richard was in the room because that matter is implied from the statement, the probative value of the statement as offered flowing from declarant's belief as to the matter. Finally, the statement is hearsay because it was not made while testifying at the trial and is offered to prove the truth of the matter asserted.

(4) Nonverbal assertive conduct intended as a substitute for verbal expression. Illustration. W testifies that A asked declarant "Which way did X go?" and declarant pointed north. This nonverbal conduct of declarant was intended by him as a substitute for verbal expression and so is a statement. The matter asserted is that X went north because that is implied from the statement and the probative value of the statement as offered flows from declarant's belief that X went north. Finally, the statement is hearsay because it was not made at trial and is offered to prove the truth of the matter asserted.

ANNOTATIONS

TRE 801(d)

In re M.S., 115 S.W.3d 534, 543 (Tex.2003). "[T]he Agreement [between D and CPS] was not offered as proof of [D's] inability to care for her children, or as proof that her parental rights should be terminated, or as proof that termination was in the children's best interest. Rather, the Agreement was offered to show that an agreement had been made and what its terms were. The Agreement was not hearsay."

Marten v. Silva, 200 S.W.3d 297, 303 (Tex.App.—Dallas 2006, no pet.). "[N]either the document showing [car's] serial number nor the note from [D] was offered to prove the truth of the matters asserted.... Instead, the documents merely evidence an ongoing series of communications and faxes between [D] and [P] concerning [P's] purchase of [car]. Under these circumstances, ... the documents were not hearsay...."

City of Austin v. Houston Lighting & Power Co., 844 S.W.2d 773, 791 (Tex.App.—Dallas 1992, writ denied). "Generally, Texas courts consider newspaper articles inadmissible hearsay. [N]ewspaper articles not offered for the truth of the matters asserted but used merely to show notice of those matters are not hearsay."

TRE 801(e)

Tome v. U.S., 513 U.S. 150, 167 (1995) (criminal case interpreting federal rule). The federal rule "permits the introduction of a declarant's consistent out-of-court statements to rebut a charge of recent fabrication or improper influence or motive only when those statements were made before the charged recent fabrication or improper influence or motive."

Reid Rd. MUD v. Speedy Stop Food Stores, 337 S.W.3d 846, 858 (Tex.2011). "[A]dmissions by a party opponent can occur outside a judicial proceeding and are not inadmissible simply because they occur in an administrative hearing...."

Bay Area Healthcare Grp. v. McShane, 239 S.W.3d 231, 235 (Tex.2007). "Rule 801(e)(2) is straightforward: subject to other [TREs] that may limit admissibility, *any* statement by a party opponent is admissible against that party. [¶] Thus, the court of appeals erred in concluding that statements from [superseded] pleadings would only be admissible if they contained 'some statement relevant to a material issue in the case' that is 'inconsistent with the position taken by the party against whom it is introduced.' [T]he [TREs] no longer require inconsistency when it comes to admissibility of superseded pleadings. ... We hold that there is no requirement that the statement be inconsistent with the party's position at trial...." *See also* ***Quick v. Plastic Solutions***, 270 S.W.3d 173, 185 (Tex. App.—El Paso 2008, no pet.).

Direct Value, L.L.C. v. Stock Bldg. Sup., 388 S.W.3d 386, 391 n.5 (Tex.App.—Amarillo 2012, no pet.). "[E]-mail and its attachments were admissible as admissions of a party opponent."

Trencor, Inc. v. Cornech Mach. Co., 115 S.W.3d 145, 151 (Tex.App.—Fort Worth 2003, pet. denied). "A statement by a party's agent or servant concerning a matter within the scope of his agency or employment and made during the existence of the relationship may

be offered as an admission by the party itself. The fact of agency must, however, be established before the declaration can be admitted."

TRE 802. THE RULE AGAINST HEARSAY

Hearsay is not admissible unless any of the following provides otherwise:

- a statute;
- these rules; or
- other rules prescribed under statutory authority.

Inadmissible hearsay admitted without objection may not be denied probative value merely because it is hearsay.

Caution: TRE 802 is affected by Fam. Code §104.006.

See also Brown & Rondon, ***Texas Rules of Evidence Handbook***, p. 854; ***O'Connor's Texas Forms***, FORM 5E:1; ***O'Connor's Texas Family Law Handbook*** (2017), "Hearsay statement," ch. 4-D, §12.4.2, p. 456; "Sworn inventory & appraisement," ch. 7-A, §3.1, p. 784.

ANNOTATIONS

Texas Commerce Bank v. New, 3 S.W.3d 515, 517 (Tex.1999). "Nothing in rule 802 limits its application to contested hearings. The rule is not ambiguous and requires no explication." Thus, an affidavit containing unobjected-to hearsay can establish facts in a default-judgment case. *See also* ***Sherman Acquisition II LP v. Garcia***, 229 S.W.3d 802, 810-11 (Tex.App.—Waco 2007, no pet.).

Lee v. Dykes, 312 S.W.3d 191, 198 (Tex.App.—Houston [14th Dist.] 2010, no pet.). "[I]nadmissible evidence is [not] necessarily probative [even] if it is admitted without objection or is uncontroverted."

TRE 803. EXCEPTIONS TO THE RULE AGAINST HEARSAY—REGARDLESS OF WHETHER THE DECLARANT IS AVAILABLE AS A WITNESS

The following are not excluded by the rule against hearsay, regardless of whether the declarant is available as a witness:

(1) ***Present Sense Impression.*** A statement describing or explaining an event or condition, made while or immediately after the declarant perceived it.

(2) ***Excited Utterance.*** A statement relating to a startling event or condition, made while the declarant was under the stress of excitement that it caused.

(3) ***Then-Existing Mental, Emotional, or Physical Condition.*** A statement of the declarant's then-existing state of mind (such as motive, intent, or plan) or emotional, sensory, or physical condition (such as mental feeling, pain, or bodily health), but not including a statement of memory or belief to prove the fact remembered or believed unless it relates to the validity or terms of the declarant's will.

(4) ***Statement Made for Medical Diagnosis or Treatment.*** A statement that:

(A) is made for—and is reasonably pertinent to—medical diagnosis or treatment; and

(B) describes medical history; past or present symptoms or sensations; their inception; or their general cause.

(5) ***Recorded Recollection.*** A record that:

(A) is on a matter the witness once knew about but now cannot recall well enough to testify fully and accurately;

(B) was made or adopted by the witness when the matter was fresh in the witness's memory; and

(C) accurately reflects the witness's knowledge, unless the circumstances of the record's preparation cast doubt on its trustworthiness.

If admitted, the record may be read into evidence but may be received as an exhibit only if offered by an adverse party.

(6) ***Records of a Regularly Conducted Activity.*** A record of an act, event, condition, opinion, or diagnosis if:

(A) the record was made at or near the time by—or from information transmitted by—someone with knowledge;

(B) the record was kept in the course of a regularly conducted business activity;

(C) making the record was a regular practice of that activity;

(D) all these conditions are shown by the testimony of the custodian or another qualified witness, or by an affidavit or unsworn declaration that complies with Rule 902(10); and

(E) the opponent fails to demonstrate that the source of information or the method or circumstances of preparation indicate a lack of trustworthiness.

"Business" as used in this paragraph includes every kind of regular organized activity whether conducted for profit or not.

(7) ***Absence of a Record of a Regularly Conducted Activity.*** Evidence that a matter is not included in a record described in paragraph (6) if:

(A) the evidence is admitted to prove that the matter did not occur or exist;

(B) a record was regularly kept for a matter of that kind; and

(C) the opponent fails to show that the possible source of the information or other circumstances indicate a lack of trustworthiness.

(8) ***Public Records.*** A record or statement of a public office if:

(A) it sets out:

(i) the office's activities;

(ii) a matter observed while under a legal duty to report, but not including, in a criminal case, a matter observed by law-enforcement personnel; or

(iii) in a civil case or against the government in a criminal case, factual findings from a legally authorized investigation; and

(B) the opponent fails to demonstrate that the source of information or other circumstances indicate a lack of trustworthiness.

(9) ***Public Records of Vital Statistics.*** A record of a birth, death, or marriage, if reported to a public office in accordance with a legal duty.

(10) ***Absence of a Public Record.*** Testimony—or a certification under Rule 902—that a diligent search failed to disclose a public record or statement if the testimony or certification is admitted to prove that:

(A) the record or statement does not exist; or

(B) a matter did not occur or exist, if a public office regularly kept a record or statement for a matter of that kind.

(11) ***Records of Religious Organizations Concerning Personal or Family History.*** A statement of birth, legitimacy, ancestry, marriage, divorce, death, relationship by blood or marriage, or similar facts of personal or family history, contained in a regularly kept record of a religious organization.

(12) ***Certificates of Marriage, Baptism, and Similar Ceremonies.*** A statement of fact contained in a certificate:

(A) made by a person who is authorized by a religious organization or by law to perform the act certified;

(B) attesting that the person performed a marriage or similar ceremony or administered a sacrament; and

(C) purporting to have been issued at the time of the act or within a reasonable time after it.

(13) ***Family Records.*** A statement of fact about personal or family history contained in a family record, such as a Bible, genealogy, chart, engraving on a ring, inscription on a portrait, or engraving on an urn or burial marker.

(14) ***Records of Documents That Affect an Interest in Property.*** The record of a document that purports to establish or affect an interest in property if:

(A) the record is admitted to prove the content of the original recorded document, along with its signing and its delivery by each person who purports to have signed it;

(B) the record is kept in a public office; and

(C) a statute authorizes recording documents of that kind in that office.

(15) ***Statements in Documents That Affect an Interest in Property.*** A statement contained in a document that purports to establish or affect an interest in property if the matter stated was relevant to the document's purpose—unless later dealings with the property are inconsistent with the truth of the statement or the purport of the document.

(16) ***Statements in Ancient Documents.*** A statement in a document that is at least 20 years old and whose authenticity is established.

(17) ***Market Reports and Similar Commercial Publications.*** Market quotations, lists, directories, or other compilations that are generally relied on by the public or by persons in particular occupations.

(18) ***Statements in Learned Treatises, Periodicals, or Pamphlets.*** A statement contained in a treatise, periodical, or pamphlet if:

(A) the statement is called to the attention of an expert witness on cross-examination or relied on by the expert on direct examination; and

(B) the publication is established as a reliable authority by the expert's admission or testimony, by another expert's testimony, or by judicial notice.

If admitted, the statement may be read into evidence but not received as an exhibit.

(19) ***Reputation Concerning Personal or Family History.*** A reputation among a person's family by blood, adoption, or marriage—or among a person's associates or in the community—concerning the person's birth, adoption, legitimacy, ancestry, marriage, divorce, death, relationship by blood, adoption, or marriage, or similar facts of personal or family history.

(20) ***Reputation Concerning Boundaries or General History.*** A reputation in a community—arising before the controversy—concerning boundaries of land in the community or customs that affect the land, or concerning general historical events important to that community, state, or nation.

(21) ***Reputation Concerning Character.*** A reputation among a person's associates or in the community concerning the person's character.

(22) ***Judgment of a Previous Conviction.*** Evidence of a final judgment of conviction if:

(A) it is offered in a civil case and:

(i) the judgment was entered after a trial or guilty plea, but not a nolo contendere plea;

(ii) the conviction was for a felony;

(iii) the evidence is admitted to prove any fact essential to the judgment; and

(iv) an appeal of the conviction is not pending; or

(B) it is offered in a criminal case and:

(i) the judgment was entered after a trial or a guilty or nolo contendere plea;

(ii) the conviction was for a criminal offense;

(iii) the evidence is admitted to prove any fact essential to the judgment;

(iv) when offered by the prosecutor for a purpose other than impeachment, the judgment was against the defendant; and

(v) an appeal of the conviction is not pending.

(23) ***Judgments Involving Personal, Family, or General History or a Boundary.*** A judgment that is admitted to prove a matter of personal, family, or general history, or boundaries, if the matter:

(A) was essential to the judgment; and

(B) could be proved by evidence of reputation.

(24) ***Statement Against Interest.*** A statement that:

(A) a reasonable person in the declarant's position would have made only if the person believed it to be true because, when made, it was so contrary to the declarant's proprietary or pecuniary interest or had so great a tendency to invalidate the declarant's claim against someone else or to expose the declarant to civil or criminal liability or to make the declarant an object of hatred, ridicule, or disgrace; and

(B) is supported by corroborating circumstances that clearly indicate its trustworthiness, if it is offered in a criminal case as one that tends to expose the declarant to criminal liability.

Caution: TRE 803 is affected by Fam. Code §§54.031, 104.006, and 107.114.

See also ***O'Connor's Texas Rules***, "Introducing Evidence," ch. 8-C, p. 790; Brown & Rondon, ***Texas Rules of Evidence Handbook***, p. 857; ***O'Connor's Texas Family Law Handbook*** (2017), "Hearsay statement," ch. 4-D, §12.4.2, p. 456; "Sworn inventory & appraisement," ch. 7-A, §3.1, p. 784; "Hearsay rule for documents," ch. 9-D, §16.6.2(1), p. 1057.

ANNOTATIONS

Generally

Robinson v. Harkins & Co., 711 S.W.2d 619, 621 (Tex.1986). "All hearsay exceptions require a showing of trustworthiness."

Simien v. Unifund CCR Partners, 321 S.W.3d 235, 240 (Tex.App.—Houston [1st Dist.] 2010, no pet.). "The proponent of hearsay has the burden of showing that the testimony fits within an exception to the general rule prohibiting the admission of hearsay evidence." *See also* ***Reed v. Cook Children's Med. Ctr., Inc.***, No. 02-13-00405-CV (Tex.App.—Fort Worth 2014, no pet.) (memo op.; 5-29-14).

TRE 803(1)

1.70 Acres v. State, 935 S.W.2d 480, 488 (Tex. App.—Beaumont 1996, no writ). "Present sense impressions are those comments made at the time the declarant is receiving the impression or immediately thereafter. They possess the following safeguards which render them reliable: (1) the report at the moment of the thing then seen, heard, etc. is safe from any error from defect of memory of the declarant; (2) there

is little or no time for a calculated misstatement; (3) the statement will usually be made to another—the witness who reports it—who would have equal opportunity to observe and hence to check a misstatement." *See also* ***VIA Metro. Transit Auth. v. Barraza***, No. 04-13-00035-CV (Tex.App.—San Antonio 2013, pet. denied) (memo op.; 12-4-13).

TRE 803(2)

Volkswagen v. Ramirez, 159 S.W.3d 897, 908-09 (Tex.2004). "To be admissible as an excited utterance, a statement must be (1) a spontaneous reaction (2) to a personal observance of (3) a startling event (4) made while the declarant was still under the stress of excitement caused by the event. [¶] [The statement] must occur before the declarant has the opportunity to reflect on or ponder the shocking incident. Accordingly, we also consider the lapse in time between the startling event and the statement [as well as the] declarant's tone and tenor of voice...."

In re H.T.S., No. 04-11-00847-CV (Tex.App.—San Antonio 2012, pet. denied) (memo op.; 12-31-12). "To qualify as an excited utterance, the statement must be a product of a startling occurrence; the declarant must have been dominated by the emotion, excitement, fear, or pain of the occurrence; and the statement must be related to the circumstances of the startling occurrence. In determining whether a hearsay statement is admissible under the excited utterance exception, the reviewing court may look at: (1) the time that elapsed between the event and the statement, and (2) whether the statement was in response to a question. However, neither of these factors is dispositive; rather, '[t]he critical factor ... is whether the declarant was still dominated by the emotions, fear, excitement, or pain of the event at the time of the statement.'"

Felix v. Gonzalez, 87 S.W.3d 574, 578-79 (Tex. App.—San Antonio 2002, pet. denied). "The core of the excited utterance exception is reliability—a statement made by an out-of-court declarant during a state of excitement is more reliable than a statement made after time for reflection upon a startling event. Once the timing of the state of excitement is demonstrated, so long as the statement made *relates to* the startling event, it falls within the purview of the excited utterance exception."

Almaraz v. Burke, 827 S.W.2d 80, 83 (Tex.App.—Fort Worth 1992, writ denied). "Although [***First Sw. Lloyds Ins. v. MacDowell***, below,] states that the witness's statement was a narrative account, given after he had returned to the scene of the fire, the opinion does not reflect whether the witness was still excited from the fire and the chase at the time the statement was given, nor does it state whether that mattered in reaching the result. If the witness in that case were still excited from the event at the time he told the fire marshal what had just happened, we would have held that the evidence qualified as an exception to the hearsay rule in accordance with rule 803(2). On the other hand, if there were no evidence that the witness was still under the excitement of the preceding events, we would agree with the opinion."

First Sw. Lloyds Ins. v. MacDowell, 769 S.W.2d 954, 959 (Tex.App.—Texarkana 1989, writ denied). "A statement that is simply a narrative of past acts or events, as distinguished from a spontaneous utterance, does not qualify as an excited utterance regardless of how soon after the event that it is made. The circumstances must show that it was the event speaking through the person and not the person speaking about the event."

TRE 803(3)

Power v. Kelley, 70 S.W.3d 137, 141 (Tex.App.—San Antonio 2001, pet. denied). "'Statements admitted under [TRE 803(3)] are usually spontaneous remarks about pain or some other sensation, made by the declarant while the sensation, not readily observable by a third party, is being experienced.' 'The exception does not extend to statements of past external facts or conditions.'"

TRE 803(4)

In re H.L.A., No. 01-12-00912-CV (Tex.App.—Houston [1st Dist.] 2014, no pet.) (memo op.; 3-20-14). "The witness ... need not expressly state that the hearsay declarant recognized the need to be truthful in her statements for the medical treatment exception [in TRE 803(4)] to apply. Instead, the reviewing court must determine whether the record supports a conclusion that the declarant understood the importance of honesty in the context of medical diagnosis and treatment. [¶] The essential 'qualification' expressed in the rule is that the declarant believe that the information he conveys will ultimately be utilized in diagnosis or treatment of a condition from which the declarant is suffering, so that his selfish motive for truthfulness can be trusted. We conduct a two-part test for determining whether this requirement has been met. First, the

statement must be made for the purpose of diagnosis or treatment, and the declarant must know that it is made for the purpose of diagnosis and treatment. Second, the statements must actually be pertinent to diagnosis or treatment." (Internal quotes omitted.) *See also* ***In re C.B.L.***, No. 11-15-00227-CV (Tex.App.—Eastland 2016, pet. denied) (memo op.; 9-30-16) (if identity of perpetrator is part of hearsay statement, witness must outline how identity and relationship of perpetrator to declarant is information necessary for efficacy of treatment).

TRE 803(6)

Burroughs Wellcome Co. v. Crye, 907 S.W.2d 497, 500 (Tex.1995). "The diagnoses contained in [P's] medical and hospital records are admissible. However, to constitute evidence of causation, an expert opinion must rest in reasonable medical probability. [¶] The context of the opinions contained in the medical records ... indicates that these statements are merely recitations of medical history or opinion as to causation provided by other records, [P], or [her doctor]." Held: No evidence of causation.

Barnhart v. Morales, 459 S.W.3d 733, 744 (Tex. App.—Houston [14th Dist.] 2015, no pet.). "The fact that some parts of the challenged records were handwritten notes on preprinted forms designed to be filled in by the hospital's staff while evaluating and treating emergency room patients does not take them outside of the business records hearsay exception, so long as all requirements of that exception are met. [D] has not shown that the handwritten nature of these notes renders them untrustworthy."

Ortega v. CACH, LLC, 396 S.W.3d 622, 629-30 (Tex. App.—Houston [14th Dist.] 2013, no pet.). "[T]hird-party documents can become the business records of an organization and consequently admissible under rule 803(6) if the records are (1) incorporated and kept in the course of the testifying witness's business, (2) the business typically relies upon the accuracy of the contents of the documents, and (3) the circumstances otherwise indicate the trustworthiness of the documents. [¶] The theory underlying the business-records exception is that there is a certain probability of trustworthiness of records regularly kept by an organization while engaged in its activities and upon which it relies in the ordinary course of its activities. Therefore, if 'the source of information or the method or circumstances of preparation indicate lack of trustworthiness,' even a properly authenticated record may be inadmissible. Lack of trustworthiness is most frequently found when the record was prepared in anticipation of litigation." *See also* ***Freeman v. American Motorists Ins.***, 53 S.W.3d 710, 715 (Tex.App.—Houston [1st Dist.] 2001, no pet.).

Riddle v. Unifund CCR Partners, 298 S.W.3d 780, 782-83 (Tex.App.—El Paso 2009, no pet.). "Business records that have been created by one entity, but which have become another entity's primary record of the underlying transaction may be admissible pursuant to Rule 803(6). In addition, a document can comprise the records of another business if the second business determines the accuracy of the information generated by the first business. [¶] Although Rule 803(6) does not require the predicate witness to be the record's creator or have personal knowledge of the content of the record ..., the witness must have personal knowledge of the manner in which the records were prepared. Documents received from another entity are not admissible under Rule 803(6) if the witness is not qualified to testify about the entity's record keeping." *See also* ***Dodeka, L.L.C. v. Campos***, 377 S.W.3d 726, 732 (Tex. App.—San Antonio 2012, no pet.); ***In re E.A.K.***, 192 S.W.3d 133, 142 (Tex.App.—Houston [14th Dist.] 2006, pet. denied). *But see* ***Simien v. Unifund CCR Partners***, 321 S.W.3d 235, 244 (Tex.App.—Houston [1st Dist.] 2010, no pet.) (foundation witness's personal knowledge of recordkeeping by third party was not necessary).

Trantham v. Isaacks, 218 S.W.3d 750, 755 (Tex. App.—Fort Worth 2007, pet. denied). "The foundation for admission of a business record may be established by testimony or by affidavit." *See also* ***Benavides v. Cushman, Inc.***, 189 S.W.3d 875, 884 n.6 (Tex.App.—Houston [1st Dist.] 2006, no pet.).

In re K.C.P., 142 S.W.3d 574, 579 (Tex.App.—Texarkana 2004, no pet.). "There is a distinction in the treatment of [admissibility of drug-test results as business records] based on whether the case is civil or criminal in nature. Some civil cases have found business records containing laboratory tests are admissible by showing where the specimen was drawn, that it was sent to a laboratory, and that a medical doctor analyzed it and reported the results. [¶] Criminal cases require more.... *At 580:* [W]e believe the test for admissibility of [drug-test results in termination of parental rights cases] should comply with the rule as stated in crimi-

nal cases. [¶] We believe that admitting drug tests in a termination of parental rights case with no information as to the qualifications of the person or equipment used, the method of administering the test, and whether the test was a standard one for the particular substance indicates a lack of trustworthiness of the tests and that admission of such evidence is an abuse of discretion."

TRE 803(7)

Coleman v. United Sav. Ass'n, 846 S.W.2d 128, 131 (Tex.App.—Fort Worth 1993, no writ). "Testimony that is offered as evidence that a matter is not included in records to prove the nonoccurrence or nonexistence of the matter is inadmissible hearsay evidence unless rule 803(7) is satisfied. The initial foundational predicate of rule 803(7) is that the records that would include the matter, if it were not absent from those records, are kept in accordance with the provisions of rule 803(6). [D's] affidavit does not even attempt to satisfy the requirements of rule 803(6) and therefore cannot support the summary judgment."

TRE 803(8)

F-Star Socorro, L.P. v. City of El Paso, 281 S.W.3d 103, 106 (Tex.App.—El Paso 2008, no pet.). "[D] argues that the certified tax statement is not a public record under Rule 803(8).... The findings in the certified tax statement appear to result from the tax assessor-collector's investigation of [D], as outlined in Rule 803(8)(C) [now TRE 803(8)(A)(iii)]. Therefore, we find that the certified tax statement is a public record under the terms of Rule 803(8)."

Corrales v. TDFPS, 155 S.W.3d 478, 486 (Tex. App.—El Paso 2004, no pet.). "Generally speaking, the police reports were admissible as a public record. [¶] [T]he records also contained statements by witnesses which did not qualify as public records. Nevertheless, ... the reports are admissible unless the sources of information indicate a lack of trustworthiness. [T]here is a presumption of admissibility and the burden is placed on the party opposing the admission of a report to show its untrustworthiness." *See also* ***First Transit, Inc. v. Alfaro***, No. 14-14-00063-CV (Tex.App.—Houston [14th Dist.] 2015, pet. denied) (memo op.; 4-7-15).

In re T.T., 39 S.W.3d 355, 358 (Tex.App.—Houston [1st Dist.] 2001, no pet.). Parties "contend the trial judge's temporary order in this case, which was admitted in evidence upon final trial, was inadmissible hearsay and was an improper comment on the weight of the evidence. We agree. *At 359:* The State contends that the temporary order was not excluded by the hearsay rule because of the exception in [TRE] 803(8)(C) [now TRE 803(8)(A)(iii)]. [¶] We decline to hold that the exception in Rule 803(8)(C) would allow the admission of this temporary order. First, that rule was not meant to allow a jury to hear hearsay statements from the presiding judge about the merits of the case on trial. Even direct testimony by the presiding judge is expressly prohibited by [TRE] 605. It is inconceivable that the authors of the [TREs] would have meant to allow the presiding judge's hearsay statements into evidence while Rule 605 prohibits the judge from testifying in person. The prohibition in Rule 605 is stronger than any other in our rules of evidence; no other rule provides that objection is unnecessary to preserve the error for appellate review."

TRE 803(10)

Towne Square Assocs. v. Angelina Cty. Appr. Dist., 709 S.W.2d 776, 777 (Tex.App.—Beaumont 1986, no writ). "[Ds'] affidavits stated that, after a diligent search, [Ds] could find no notice of appeal filed in the records. [Ps] assert these affidavits are insufficient in that they contain hearsay and do not have some of the predicate language required for a business record in accordance with [TRE] 902. [Ps'] complete reliance on this rule is misplaced. The affidavits are controlled by [TRE] 803(10).... While it is true the affidavits do not meet the authentication requirements of Rule 902, they do contain testimony that a diligent search failed to disclose the notice of appeal."

TRE 803(14) & (15)

Tri-Steel Structures, Inc. v. Baptist Found., 166 S.W.3d 443, 451 (Tex.App.—Fort Worth 2005, pet. denied). TRE 803(15) requires "that the document have some sort of official or formal nature, which an unsigned letter does not possess. [D]ealings with the property [must] not be inconsistent with the statement after it was made."

Compton v. WWV Enters., 679 S.W.2d 668, 671 (Tex.App.—Eastland 1984, no writ). "Hearsay exceptions [TRE 803(14) and (15)] must ... be construed to relate to recitals or statements made in deeds, leases, mortgages and other such 'documents affecting an interest in property' and not to affidavits of heirship which more properly fall within the hearsay exception stated under [TRE] 804(b)(3)."

TRE 803(16)

Guthrie v. Suiter, 934 S.W.2d 820, 825 (Tex.App.—Houston [1st Dist.] 1996, no writ). "Statements contained in documents 20 years old or older qualify as an exception to the hearsay rule, provided the documents are properly authenticated. To qualify for this exception, the document must be shown (1) in such condition as to create no suspicion concerning its authenticity; (2) that it was in a place where it would likely be if it were authentic; and (3) that it has been in existence 20 years or more at the time it is offered."

TRE 803(17)

New Braunfels Factory Outlet Ctr. v. IHOP Rlty. Corp., 872 S.W.2d 303, 310 (Tex.App.—Austin 1994, no writ). "The hearsay exception provided by [TRE] 803(17) permits the admission of certain objective data.... At common law, survey results were also admissible *provided* that the party opposing admission was given the opportunity to cross-examine the person who had conducted the survey."

TRE 803(18)

King v. Bauer, 767 S.W.2d 197, 199-200 (Tex. App.—Corpus Christi 1989, writ denied). Under TRE 803(18), P introduced a medical textbook that was published two years after P's therapy, but the earlier edition of which was recognized by D as a learned treatise. "The fact that the third edition [of the textbook] was not published until 1980 does not serve to disqualify the evidence which was aimed at illustrating an appropriate treatment plan for [P] in 1978. Treatises which directly refer to the standard of care in use at the time of the occurrence are material, relevant and therefore admissible."

TRE 803(19)

Akers v. Stevenson, 54 S.W.3d 880, 885 (Tex. App.—Beaumont 2001, pet. denied). The hearsay exception for evidence concerning personal or family history arises "from necessity and [is] founded on the general reliability of statements by family members about family affairs when the statements by deceased persons regarding family history were made at a time when no pecuniary interest or other biased reason for the statements were present."

TRE 803(20)

Roberts v. Allison, 836 S.W.2d 185, 191 (Tex. App.—Tyler 1992, writ denied). "A reason for the exception [in TRE 803(20)] is '[t]he fact that a prolonged observation and discussion of certain matters of *general interest by a whole community will sift possible errors and bring the result down to us in a fairly trustworthy form furnishes a guarantee of correctness.*' [Ps'] proposed testimony pertains to an individual family's assertion of an easement; there is no contention of the ... community's knowledge of [Ps'] claim to access [D's] property. ... There was no proof of the recognized 'vehicles of reputation,' such as 'declarations of residents, old maps, surveys, deeds and leases' of the claimed easement. ... The trial court did not abuse its discretion in excluding [the] testimony of a claimed oral agreement granting an easement to [Ps] over the subject property."

TRE 803(22)

McCormick v. Texas Commerce Bank, 751 S.W.2d 887, 890 (Tex.App.—Houston [14th Dist.] 1988, writ denied). "Where (i) the issue at stake was identical to that in the criminal case, (ii) the issue had been actually litigated, and (iii) determination of the issue was a critical and necessary part of the prior judgment, the judgment is established by offensive collateral estoppel and is within the hearsay exception of [FRE] 803(22). [¶] Applying the standards of the federal judiciary to [TRE] 803(22), we hold that the trial court did not err in refusing to permit [D] to explain the circumstances of his criminal conviction."

TRE 803(24)

State v. Arnold, 778 S.W.2d 68, 69 (Tex.1989). Under TRE 803(24), a "statement may be self-serving in one respect but contrary to another interest. The court must balance these competing interests to determine their predominant nature and ultimately the level of trustworthiness to be accorded."

Green v. Reyes, 836 S.W.2d 203, 213 (Tex.App.—Houston [14th Dist.] 1992, no writ). "[A]ffidavits of persons who ... admit under oath an action which can subject them to criminal liability may be properly admitted at trial as an exception to the hearsay rule as statements against their interest."

TRE 804. EXCEPTIONS TO THE RULE AGAINST HEARSAY—WHEN THE DECLARANT IS UNAVAILABLE AS A WITNESS

(a) Criteria for Being Unavailable. A declarant is considered to be unavailable as a witness if the declarant:

(1) is exempted from testifying about the subject matter of the declarant's statement because the court rules that a privilege applies;

(2) refuses to testify about the subject matter despite a court order to do so;

(3) testifies to not remembering the subject matter;

(4) cannot be present or testify at the trial or hearing because of death or a then-existing infirmity, physical illness, or mental illness; or

(5) is absent from the trial or hearing and the statement's proponent has not been able, by process or other reasonable means, to procure the declarant's attendance or testimony.

But this subdivision (a) does not apply if the statement's proponent procured or wrongfully caused the declarant's unavailability as a witness in order to prevent the declarant from attending or testifying.

(b) The Exceptions. The following are not excluded by the rule against hearsay if the declarant is unavailable as a witness:

(1) ***Former Testimony.*** Testimony that:

(A) when offered in a civil case:

(i) was given as a witness at a trial or hearing of the current or a different proceeding or in a deposition in a different proceeding; and

(ii) is now offered against a party and the party—or a person with similar interest—had an opportunity and similar motive to develop the testimony by direct, cross-, or redirect examination.

(B) when offered in a criminal case:

(i) was given as a witness at a trial or hearing of the current or a different proceeding; and

(ii) is now offered against a party who had an opportunity and similar motive to develop it by direct, cross-, or redirect examination; or

(iii) was taken in a deposition under—and is now offered in accordance with—chapter 39 of the Code of Criminal Procedure.

(2) ***Statement Under the Belief of Imminent Death.*** A statement that the declarant, while believing the declarant's death to be imminent, made about its cause or circumstances.

(3) ***Statement of Personal or Family History.*** A statement about:

(A) the declarant's own birth, adoption, legitimacy, ancestry, marriage, divorce, relationship by blood, adoption or marriage, or similar facts of personal or family history, even though the declarant had no way of acquiring personal knowledge about that fact; or

(B) another person concerning any of these facts, as well as death, if the declarant was related to the person by blood, adoption, or marriage or was so intimately associated with the person's family that the declarant's information is likely to be accurate.

See also Brown & Rondon, *Texas Rules of Evidence Handbook*, p. 930.

ANNOTATIONS

Massey v. Allen Nat'l Prop., L.L.C., No. 02-11-00503-CV (Tex.App.—Fort Worth 2013, no pet.) (memo op.; 1-17-13). "A party offering the prior testimony of a witness must prove the witness is unavailable. Unavailability means that the witness is dead, that he had become insane or is physically unable to testify, that he is beyond the jurisdiction of the court, that his whereabouts are unknown and that a diligent search has been made to ascertain where he is, or that he has been kept away from the trial by the adverse party. Here, [P] did not prove that [witness] was unavailable. Instead, he argued that it was impossible to procure her testimony because [TRCP] 166a(c) does not allow oral testimony at a summary judgment hearing. However, [P] could have procured [witness's] testimony in the form of an affidavit or a deposition, which would have been acceptable summary judgment evidence. Therefore, the trial court did not abuse its discretion in excluding [witness's] prior testimony because [P] did not prove [witness] was unavailable."

Fuller-Austin Insulation Co. v. Bilder, 960 S.W.2d 914, 921 (Tex.App.—Beaumont 1998, pet. granted, judgm't vacated w.r.m.). "[T]he fact that [witness] was uncooperative in attending trial did not mean he could not give his deposition.... Although [witness] may have been beyond the subpoena power of the court, [D] did not establish it was unable to take his deposition or otherwise procure his testimony in this cause."

Thompson v. Mayes, 707 S.W.2d 951, 957 (Tex. App.—Eastland 1986, writ ref'd n.r.e.). Under TRE 804(b)(2), "dying declarations which concern the cause or the circumstances of what the declarant believed to be his impending death are admissible as exceptions to the hearsay rule."

TRE 805. HEARSAY WITHIN HEARSAY

Hearsay within hearsay is not excluded by the rule against hearsay if each part of the combined statements conforms with an exception to the rule.

See also Brown & Rondon, *Texas Rules of Evidence Handbook*, p. 945.

ANNOTATIONS

Houston Lighting & Power Co. v. Klein ISD, 739 S.W.2d 508, 519 (Tex.App.—Houston [14th Dist.] 1987, writ denied). "[C]harts summarizing studies of power lines and health effects [were] objected to ... as hearsay because the underlying studies were hearsay. [T]he error [in admitting the charts did not] cause the rendition of an improper verdict."

TRE 806. ATTACKING & SUPPORTING THE DECLARANT'S CREDIBILITY

When a hearsay statement—or a statement described in Rule 801(e)(2)(C), (D), or (E), or, in a civil case, a statement described in Rule 801(e)(3)—has been admitted in evidence, the declarant's credibility may be attacked, and then supported, by any evidence that would be admissible for those purposes if the declarant had testified as a witness. The court may admit evidence of the declarant's statement or conduct, offered to impeach the declarant, regardless of when it occurred or whether the declarant had an opportunity to explain or deny it. If the party against whom the statement was admitted calls the declarant as a witness, the party may examine the declarant on the statement as if on cross-examination.

See also Brown & Rondon, *Texas Rules of Evidence Handbook*, p. 947.

ANNOTATIONS

Anthony Pools, Inc. v. Charles & David, Inc., 797 S.W.2d 666, 676 (Tex.App.—Houston [14th Dist.] 1990, writ denied). "Texas courts long have allowed the use of affidavits to impeach a witness. The jury could have been allowed to consider any inconsistencies between the affidavit and the deposition as damaging to the credibility of [witness's] deposition, but not as substantive evidence. [¶] Upon timely request and objection, ... the court was required to instruct the jury of the limited use to be made of the affidavit."

Victor M. Solis Underground Util. & Paving Co. v. City of Laredo, 751 S.W.2d 532, 537 (Tex.App.—San Antonio 1988, writ denied). "If a declarant is unavailable as a witness, [TRE] 806 ... provides that testimony by that person at a former hearing is not excluded as hearsay if the party against whom the testimony is offered, 'or a person with similar interest, had an opportunity and similar motive to develop the testimony by direct, cross, or redirect examination.'"

ARTICLE IX. AUTHENTICATION & IDENTIFICATION

TRE 901. AUTHENTICATING OR IDENTIFYING EVIDENCE

(a) **In General.** To satisfy the requirement of authenticating or identifying an item of evidence, the proponent must produce evidence sufficient to support a finding that the item is what the proponent claims it is.

(b) **Examples.** The following are examples only—not a complete list—of evidence that satisfies the requirement:

(1) ***Testimony of a Witness with Knowledge.*** Testimony that an item is what it is claimed to be.

(2) ***Nonexpert Opinion About Handwriting.*** A nonexpert's opinion that handwriting is genuine, based on a familiarity with it that was not acquired for the current litigation.

(3) ***Comparison by an Expert Witness or the Trier of Fact.*** A comparison by an expert witness or the trier of fact with a specimen that the court has found is genuine.

(4) ***Distinctive Characteristics and the Like.*** The appearance, contents, substance, internal patterns, or other distinctive characteristics of the item, taken together with all the circumstances.

(5) ***Opinion About a Voice.*** An opinion identifying a person's voice—whether heard firsthand or through mechanical or electronic transmission or recording—based on hearing the voice at any time under circumstances that connect it with the alleged speaker.

(6) ***Evidence About a Telephone Conversation.*** For a telephone conversation, evidence that a call was made to the number assigned at the time to:

(A) a particular person, if circumstances, including self-identification, show that the person answering was the one called; or

(B) a particular business, if the call was made to a business and the call related to business reasonably transacted over the telephone.

(7) ***Evidence About Public Records.*** Evidence that:

(A) a document was recorded or filed in a public office as authorized by law; or

(B) a purported public record or statement is from the office where items of this kind are kept.

(8) ***Evidence About Ancient Documents or Data Compilations.*** For a document or data compilation, evidence that it:

(A) is in a condition that creates no suspicion about its authenticity;

(B) was in a place where, if authentic, it would likely be; and

(C) is at least 20 years old when offered.

(9) ***Evidence About a Process or System.*** Evidence describing a process or system and showing that it produces an accurate result.

(10) ***Methods Provided by a Statute or Rule.*** Any method of authentication or identification allowed by a statute or other rule prescribed under statutory authority.

See also *O'Connor's Texas Rules*, "Authenticity," ch. 8-C, §8.4, p. 797; Brown & Rondon, *Texas Rules of Evidence Handbook*, p. 954.

ANNOTATIONS

General Motors Corp. v. Gayle, 951 S.W.2d 469, 475 (Tex.1997). "Any tests that a party ... offer[s] at trial will be admissible only if the trial court determines that there is a substantial similarity between the test conditions and the accident conditions."

Kroger Co. v. Milanes, 474 S.W.3d 321, 342 (Tex. App.—Houston [14th Dist.] 2015, no pet.). "Generally, pictures or photographs relevant to any issue in a case are admissible. When a photograph or video portrays facts relevant to an issue, it is admissible if verified by a witness as being a correct representation of the facts. The verifying witness must know the object involved and be able to state that the photograph or video correctly represents it. The fact that the scene or the object portrayed in the photograph or video has changed since the time of the event in question in the litigation does not prevent the admission of the photograph or video into evidence if the changes are explained in such a manner that the photograph or video will help the jury in understanding the nature of the condition at the time of the event at issue." *See also* ***Kirwan v. City of Waco***, 249 S.W.3d 544, 549 (Tex.App.—Waco 2008) (not required that witness made photographs, observed their making, or knew when they were taken), *rev'd on other grounds*, 298 S.W.3d 618 (Tex.2009).

Sanchez v. Texas State Bd. of Med. Exam'rs, 229 S.W.3d 498, 509 (Tex.App.—Austin 2007, no pet.). "[T]he predicate for admissibility under rule 901 may be proven by circumstantial evidence." *See also* ***Gunville v. Gonzales***, 508 S.W.3d 547, 559 (Tex.App.—El Paso 2016, no pet.); ***Nicholas v. Environmental Sys. (Int'l)***, 499 S.W.3d 888, 900 (Tex.App.—Houston [14th Dist.] 2016, pet. denied).

In re G.F.O., 874 S.W.2d 729, 731 (Tex.App.—Houston [1st Dist.] 1994, no writ). "A document is considered authentic if a sponsoring witness vouches for its authenticity.... [T]he confession was properly authenticated because the [arresting] officer identified [D] and his confession." *See also* ***Baker v. City of Robinson***, 305 S.W.3d 783, 792 (Tex.App.—Waco 2009, pet. denied); ***Durkay v. Madco Oil Co.***, 862 S.W.2d 14, 24 (Tex.App.—Corpus Christi 1993, writ denied).

TRE 902. EVIDENCE THAT IS SELF-AUTHENTICATING

The following items of evidence are self-authenticating; they require no extrinsic evidence of authenticity in order to be admitted:

(1) ***Domestic Public Documents That Are Sealed and Signed.*** A document that bears:

(A) a seal purporting to be that of the United States; any state, district, commonwealth, territory, or insular possession of the United States; the former Panama Canal Zone; the Trust Territory of the Pacific Islands; a political subdivision of any of these entities; or a department, agency, or officer of any entity named above; and

(B) a signature purporting to be an execution or attestation.

(2) ***Domestic Public Documents That Are Not Sealed But Are Signed and Certified.*** A document that bears no seal if:

(A) it bears the signature of an officer or employee of an entity named in Rule 902(1)(A); and

(B) another public officer who has a seal and official duties within that same entity certifies under seal—or its equivalent—that the signer has the official capacity and that the signature is genuine.

(3) ***Foreign Public Documents.*** A document that purports to be signed or attested by a person who is authorized by a foreign country's law to do so.

(A) ***In General.*** The document must be accompanied by a final certification that certifies the genuineness of the signature and official position of the signer or attester—or of any foreign official whose certificate of genuineness relates to the signature or attestation or is in a chain of certificates of genuineness relating to the signature or attestation. The certification may be made by a secretary of a United States embassy or legation; by a consul general, vice consul, or consular agent of the United States; or by a diplomatic or consular official of the foreign country assigned or accredited to the United States.

(B) ***If Parties Have Reasonable Opportunity to Investigate.*** If all parties have been given a reasonable opportunity to investigate the document's authenticity and accuracy, the court may, for good cause, either:

(i) order that it be treated as presumptively authentic without final certification; or

(ii) allow it to be evidenced by an attested summary with or without final certification.

(C) ***If a Treaty Abolishes or Displaces the Final Certification Requirement.*** If the United States and the foreign country in which the official record is located are parties to a treaty or convention that abolishes or displaces the final certification requirement, the record and attestation must be certified under the terms of the treaty or convention.

(4) ***Certified Copies of Public Records.*** A copy of an official record—or a copy of a document that was recorded or filed in a public office as authorized by law—if the copy is certified as correct by:

(A) the custodian or another person authorized to make the certification; or

(B) a certificate that complies with Rule 902(1), (2), or (3), a statute, or a rule prescribed under statutory authority.

(5) ***Official Publications.*** A book, pamphlet, or other publication purporting to be issued by a public authority.

(6) ***Newspapers and Periodicals.*** Printed material purporting to be a newspaper or periodical.

(7) ***Trade Inscriptions and the Like.*** An inscription, sign, tag, or label purporting to have been affixed in the course of business and indicating origin, ownership, or control.

(8) ***Acknowledged Documents.*** A document accompanied by a certificate of acknowledgment that is lawfully executed by a notary public or another officer who is authorized to take acknowledgments.

(9) ***Commercial Paper and Related Documents.*** Commercial paper, a signature on it, and related documents, to the extent allowed by general commercial law.

(10) ***Business Records Accompanied by Affidavit.*** The original or a copy of a record that meets the requirements of Rule 803(6) or (7), if the record is accompanied by an affidavit that complies with subparagraph (B) of this rule and any other requirements of law, and the record and affidavit are served in accordance with subparagraph (A). For good cause shown, the court may order that a business record be treated as presumptively authentic even if the proponent fails to comply with subparagraph (A).

(A) ***Service Requirement.*** The proponent of a record must serve the record and the accompanying affidavit on each other party to the case at least 14 days before trial. The record and affidavit may be served by any method permitted by Rule of Civil Procedure 21a.

(B) ***Form of Affidavit.*** An affidavit is sufficient if it includes the following language, but this form is not exclusive. The proponent may use an unsworn declaration made under penalty of perjury in place of an affidavit.

1. I am the custodian of records [*or* I am an employee or owner] of __________ and am familiar with the manner in which its

records are created and maintained by virtue of my duties and responsibilities.

2. Attached are ____ pages of records. These are the original records or exact duplicates of the original records.
3. The records were made at or near the time of each act, event, condition, opinion, or diagnosis set forth. [*or* It is the regular practice of __________ to make this type of record at or near the time of each act, event, condition, opinion, or diagnosis set forth in the record.]
4. The records were made by, or from information transmitted by, persons with knowledge of the matters set forth. [*or* It is the regular practice of __________ for this type of record to be made by, or from information transmitted by, persons with knowledge of the matters set forth in them.]
5. The records were kept in the course of regularly conducted business activity. [*or* It is the regular practice of __________ to keep this type of record in the course of regularly conducted business activity.]
6. It is the regular practice of the business activity to make the records.

(11) ***Presumptions Under a Statute or Rule.*** A signature, document, or anything else that a statute or rule prescribed under statutory authority declares to be presumptively or prima facie genuine or authentic.

See also *O'Connor's Texas Rules*, "Documents that are self-authenticating," ch. 8-C, §8.4.4, p. 799; Brown & Rondon, ***Texas Rules of Evidence Handbook***, p. 997.

ANNOTATIONS

Williams Farms Produce Sales, Inc. v. R&G Produce Co., 443 S.W.3d 250, 259 (Tex.App.—Corpus Christi 2014, pet. abated 4-2-14). "[W]e hold that documents printed from government websites are self-authenticating under [TRE] 902(5). *At n.7:* [However], we also acknowledge that, because [the documents in this case] indicate they originated from government websites, they could also have been internally authenticated under [TRE] 901(b)(4)."

Al-Nayem Int'l Trading, Inc. v. Irving ISD, 159 S.W.3d 762, 764 (Tex.App.—Dallas 2005, no pet.). "Because … tax statements did not bear a seal or contain a certification under seal from a public officer, [they] were not self-authenticating as certified public records…."

Texas DPS v. Silva, 988 S.W.2d 873, 877 (Tex. App.—San Antonio 1999, pet. denied). "[D] cites no authority, nor have we found any requirement that the stamp state what the document is certifying or that the stamp be from the county where the documents were prepared."

TRE 903. SUBSCRIBING WITNESS'S TESTIMONY

A subscribing witness's testimony is necessary to authenticate a writing only if required by the law of the jurisdiction that governs its validity.

See also Brown & Rondon, ***Texas Rules of Evidence Handbook***, p. 1019.

ARTICLE X. CONTENTS OF WRITINGS, RECORDINGS, & PHOTOGRAPHS

TRE 1001. DEFINITIONS THAT APPLY TO THIS ARTICLE

In this article:

(a) A "writing" consists of letters, words, numbers, or their equivalent set down in any form.

(b) A "recording" consists of letters, words, numbers, or their equivalent recorded in any manner.

(c) A "photograph" means a photographic image or its equivalent stored in any form.

(d) An "original" of a writing or recording means the writing or recording itself or any counterpart intended to have the same effect by the person who executed or issued it. For electronically stored information, "original" means any printout—or other output readable by sight—if it accurately reflects the information. An "original" of a photograph includes the negative or a print from it.

(e) A "duplicate" means a counterpart produced by a mechanical, photographic, chemical, electronic, or other equivalent process or technique that accurately reproduces the original.

See also *O'Connor's Texas Rules*, "Documents authenticated by witness," ch. 8-C, §8.4.3, p. 797; Brown & Rondon, ***Texas Rules of Evidence Handbook***, p. 1024.

ANNOTATIONS

S.D.G. v. State, 936 S.W.2d 371, 381 (Tex.App.—Houston [14th Dist.] 1996, writ denied). "The predicate for introduction of a photograph and a videotape

TRE 1001

not accompanied by a sound recording requires proof of (1) its accuracy as a correct representation of the subject at a given time, and (2) its relevance to a material issue. ... Any witness who observed the object or the scene depicted in the photograph may lay the predicate."

TRE 1002. REQUIREMENT OF THE ORIGINAL

An original writing, recording, or photograph is required in order to prove its content unless these rules or other law provides otherwise.

See also Brown & Rondon, ***Texas Rules of Evidence Handbook***, p. 1024.

ANNOTATIONS

White v. Bath, 825 S.W.2d 227, 231 (Tex.App.—Houston [14th Dist.] 1992, writ denied). "[O]nly when one seeks to prove the contents of a document [does] the best evidence rule [apply]. When the document and its contents are only collaterally related to the issues in the case, the best evidence rule does not apply."

Ramsey v. Jones Enters., 810 S.W.2d 902, 905 (Tex.App.—Beaumont 1991, writ denied). "The best evidence of the content of documents is the documents themselves. The trial court erred in admitting hearsay testimony to prove up the content of documents without a proper showing that the subject documents were unavailable through no fault or failure on the part of the party offering same."

TRE 1003. ADMISSIBILITY OF DUPLICATES

A duplicate is admissible to the same extent as the original unless a question is raised about the original's authenticity or the circumstances make it unfair to admit the duplicate.

See also ***O'Connor's Texas Rules***, "Copy of document," ch. 8-C, §8.4.3(2), p. 797; Brown & Rondon, ***Texas Rules of Evidence Handbook***, p. 1025.

ANNOTATIONS

Ford Motor Co. v. Leggat, 904 S.W.2d 643, 646 (Tex.1995). "[I]n the absence of a challenge to the authenticity of the affidavit, submission of a copy is not grounds for rejecting it."

TRE 1004. ADMISSIBILITY OF OTHER EVIDENCE OF CONTENT

An original is not required and other evidence of the content of a writing, recording, or photograph is admissible if:

(a) all the originals are lost or destroyed, unless the proponent lost or destroyed them in bad faith;

(b) an original cannot be obtained by any available judicial process;

(c) an original is not located in Texas;

(d) the party against whom the original would be offered had control of the original; was at that time put on notice, by pleadings or otherwise, that the original would be a subject of proof at the trial or hearing; and fails to produce it at the trial or hearing; or

(e) the writing, recording, or photograph is not closely related to a controlling issue.

See also TRCP 77; ***O'Connor's Texas Rules***, "Copy of document," ch. 8-C, §8.4.3(2), p. 797; Brown & Rondon, ***Texas Rules of Evidence Handbook***, p. 1039.

ANNOTATIONS

Coke v. Coke, 802 S.W.2d 270, 275 (Tex.App.—Dallas 1990, writ denied). "Under rule 1004, an original document is not required if the original is lost or destroyed without the fault of the proponent. Copies are admissible if 'there is a reasonable account for [original's] absence or if there is no question of their authenticity.'"

TRE 1005. COPIES OF PUBLIC RECORDS TO PROVE CONTENT

The proponent may use a copy to prove the content of an official record—or of a document that was recorded or filed in a public office as authorized by law—if these conditions are met: the record or document is otherwise admissible; and the copy is certified as correct in accordance with Rule 902(4) or is testified to be correct by a witness who has compared it with the original. If no such copy can be obtained by reasonable diligence, then the proponent may use other evidence to prove the content.

See also ***O'Connor's Texas Rules***, "Documents that are self-authenticating," ch. 8-C, §8.4.4, p. 799; Brown & Rondon, ***Texas Rules of Evidence Handbook***, p. 1044.

ANNOTATIONS

ESIS, Inc. v. Johnson, 908 S.W.2d 554, 561 (Tex. App.—Fort Worth 1995, writ denied). "A copy of a public record is considered authentic if a sponsoring witness vouches for its authenticity or if the document meets the certification requirements for self-authentication contained in [TRE] 902."

TRE 1006. SUMMARIES TO PROVE CONTENT

The proponent may use a summary, chart, or calculation to prove the content of voluminous writings, recordings, or photographs that cannot be conveniently examined in court. The proponent must make the originals or duplicates available for examination or copying, or both, by other parties at a reasonable time and place. And the court may order the proponent to produce them in court.

See also Brown & Rondon, ***Texas Rules of Evidence Handbook***, p. 1047; ***O'Connor's Texas Family Law Handbook*** (2017), "Sworn inventory & appraisement," ch. 7-A, §3.1, p. 784.

ANNOTATIONS

Aquamarine Assocs. v. Burton Shipyard, Inc., 659 S.W.2d 820, 821 (Tex.1983). "In cases involving voluminous records, the trial court has discretion to relax the best evidence rule and allow the admission of summaries.... The party sponsoring the summary must, however, lay the proper predicate for its admission." *See also* ***Welder v. Welder***, 794 S.W.2d 420, 429 (Tex. App.—Corpus Christi 1990, no writ).

Shaw v. Lemon, 427 S.W.3d 536, 544-45 (Tex. App.—Dallas 2014, pet. denied). "Rule 1006 states that a summary's underlying records must have been made available to the opponent for inspection, but it does not state that the summary itself must be produced in discovery or disclosed within a certain time period of the trial. [P] has not cited, nor have we found, any case law requiring a rule 1006 summary to be produced in discovery or disclosed before trial. "

TRE 1007. TESTIMONY OR STATEMENT OF A PARTY TO PROVE CONTENT

The proponent may prove the content of a writing, recording, or photograph by the testimony, deposition, or written statement of the party against whom the evidence is offered. The proponent need not account for the original.

See also Brown & Rondon, ***Texas Rules of Evidence Handbook***, p. 1052.

TRE 1008. FUNCTIONS OF THE COURT & JURY

Ordinarily, the court determines whether the proponent has fulfilled the factual conditions for admitting other evidence of the content of a writing, recording, or photograph under Rule 1004 or 1005. But in a jury trial, the jury determines—in accordance with Rule 104(b)—any issue about whether:

(a) an asserted writing, recording, or photograph ever existed;

(b) another one produced at the trial or hearing is the original; or

(c) other evidence of content accurately reflects the content.

See also Brown & Rondon, ***Texas Rules of Evidence Handbook***, p. 1053.

TRE 1009. TRANSLATING A FOREIGN LANGUAGE DOCUMENT

(a) **Submitting a Translation.** A translation of a foreign language document is admissible if, at least 45 days before trial, the proponent serves on all parties:

(1) the translation and the underlying foreign language document; and

(2) a qualified translator's affidavit or unsworn declaration that sets forth the translator's qualifications and certifies that the translation is accurate.

(b) **Objection.** When objecting to a translation's accuracy, a party should specifically indicate its inaccuracies and offer an accurate translation. A party must serve the objection on all parties at least 15 days before trial.

(c) **Effect of Failing to Object or Submit a Conflicting Translation.** If the underlying foreign language document is otherwise admissible, the court must admit—and may not allow a party to attack the accuracy of—a translation submitted under subdivision (a) unless the party has:

(1) submitted a conflicting translation under subdivision (a); or

(2) objected to the translation under subdivision (b).

(d) **Effect of Objecting or Submitting a Conflicting Translation.** If conflicting translations are submitted under subdivision (a) or an objection is made under subdivision (b), the court must determine whether there is a genuine issue about the accuracy of a material part of the translation. If so, the trier of fact must resolve the issue.

(e) **Qualified Translator May Testify.** Except for subdivision (c), this rule does not preclude a party from offering the testimony of a qualified translator to translate a foreign language document.

(f) **Time Limits.** On a party's motion and for good cause, the court may alter this rule's time limits.

(g) **Court-Appointed Translator.** If necessary, the court may appoint a qualified translator. The reasonable value of the translator's services must be taxed as court costs.

See also Brown & Rondon, *Texas Rules of Evidence Handbook*, p. 1055.

ANNOTATIONS

In re DC, No. 01-11-00387-CV (Tex.App.—Houston [1st Dist.] 2012, pet. denied) (memo op.; 3-1-12). Father "complains that the initial return was in Spanish, and because it was not translated into English until after trial, it violated [TRE] 1009, which requires that all foreign documents to be admitted at trial must be translated 45 days before trial and be accompanied by an affidavit from a qualified translator. [¶] However, rule 1009 is a rule of evidence governing the admission of foreign documents of trial. [Father] has cited no cases in which rule 1009 requires the translation of foreign returns of service into English, or that such a translation could not be done in an amended return while the trial court still had plenary power. We have found no authority holding that rule 1009 trumps [TRCP] 118, which permits amended returns of service '[a]t any time.'"

Doncaster v. Hernaiz, 161 S.W.3d 594, 601 (Tex. App.—San Antonio 2005, no pet.). "[P] did file a copy of [foreign-language document] with a translation with her initial summary judgment motion, but failed to attach the translator's affidavit. Later, [P] supplemented her motion with an affidavit from the translator.... Because of [P's] late supplementation, the trial court provided [D] a one-week continuance before conducting the summary judgment hearing. Rule 1009 provides the court with authority to lengthen or shorten the time limits set by the rule. [A]ny error in failing to initially provide the affidavit of the translator was cured by its inclusion in the supplement, and it was therefore within the court's discretion to admit [document]."

For the complete Civil Practice & Remedies Code with annotations, see the current edition of ***O'Connor's Texas Civil Practice & Remedies Code Plus***. To order, call 1-800-OCONNOR (1-800-626-6667) or visit www.oconnors.com.

TITLE 2. TRIAL, JUDGMENT, & APPEAL

SUBTITLE B. TRIAL MATTERS

CHAPTER 16. LIMITATIONS

SUBCHAPTER A. LIMITATIONS OF PERSONAL ACTIONS

CPRC §16.003. TWO-YEAR LIMITATIONS PERIOD

(a) Except as provided by Sections 16.010, 16.0031, and 16.0045, a person must bring suit for trespass for injury to the estate or to the property of another, conversion of personal property, taking or detaining the personal property of another, personal injury, forcible entry and detainer, and forcible detainer not later than two years after the day the cause of action accrues.

(b) A person must bring suit not later than two years after the day the cause of action accrues in an action for injury resulting in death. The cause of action accrues on the death of the injured person.

SUBCHAPTER D. MISCELLANEOUS PROVISIONS

CPRC §16.068. AMENDED & SUPPLEMENTAL PLEADINGS

If a filed pleading relates to a cause of action, cross action, counterclaim, or defense that is not subject to a plea of limitation when the pleading is filed, a subsequent amendment or supplement to the pleading that changes the facts or grounds of liability or defense is not subject to a plea of limitation unless the amendment or supplement is wholly based on a new, distinct, or different transaction or occurrence.

CPRC §16.069. COUNTERCLAIM OR CROSS CLAIM

(a) If a counterclaim or cross claim arises out of the same transaction or occurrence that is the basis of an action, a party to the action may file the counterclaim or cross claim even though as a separate action it would be barred by limitation on the date the party's answer is required.

(b) The counterclaim or cross claim must be filed not later than the 30th day after the date on which the party's answer is required.

CPRC §16.072. SATURDAY, SUNDAY, OR HOLIDAY

If the last day of a limitations period under any statute of limitations falls on a Saturday, Sunday, or holiday, the period for filing suit is extended to include the next day that the county offices are open for business.

See also *O'Connor's Texas Rules*, "Computing Filing Deadlines," ch. 1-C, §7, p. 36.

SUBTITLE C. JUDGMENTS

CHAPTER 35. ENFORCEMENT OF JUDGMENTS OF OTHER STATES

CPRC §35.001. DEFINITION

In this chapter, "foreign judgment" means a judgment, decree, or order of a court of the United States or of any other court that is entitled to full faith and credit in this state.

CPRC §35.002. SHORT TITLE

This chapter may be cited as the Uniform Enforcement of Foreign Judgments Act.

CPRC §35.003. FILING & STATUS OF FOREIGN JUDGMENTS

(a) A copy of a foreign judgment authenticated in accordance with an act of congress or a statute of this state may be filed in the office of the clerk of any court of competent jurisdiction of this state.

(b) The clerk shall treat the foreign judgment in the same manner as a judgment of the court in which the foreign judgment is filed.

(c) A filed foreign judgment has the same effect and is subject to the same procedures, defenses, and proceedings for reopening, vacating, staying, enforcing, or satisfying a judgment as a judgment of the court in which it is filed.

CPRC §35.004. AFFIDAVIT; NOTICE OF FILING

(a) At the time a foreign judgment is filed, the judgment creditor or the judgment creditor's attorney shall file with the clerk of the court an affidavit showing the name and last known post office address of the judgment debtor and the judgment creditor.

(b) The judgment creditor or the judgment creditor's attorney shall:

(1) promptly mail notice of the filing of the foreign judgment to the judgment debtor at the address provided for the judgment debtor under Subsection (a); and

(2) file proof of mailing of the notice with the clerk of the court.

(c) The notice must include the name and post office address of the judgment creditor and if the judgment creditor has an attorney in this state, the attorney's name and address.

(d) On receipt of proof of mailing under Subsection (b), the clerk of the court shall note the mailing in the docket.

CPRC §35.005. REPEALED

CPRC §35.006. STAY

(a) If the judgment debtor shows the court that an appeal from the foreign judgment is pending or will be taken, that the time for taking an appeal has not expired, or that a stay of execution has been granted, has been requested, or will be requested, and proves that the judgment debtor has furnished or will furnish the security for the satisfaction of the judgment required by the state in which it was rendered, the court shall stay enforcement of the foreign judgment until the appeal is concluded, the time for appeal expires, or the stay of execution expires or is vacated.

(b) If the judgment debtor shows the court a ground on which enforcement of a judgment of the court of this state would be stayed, the court shall stay enforcement of the foreign judgment for an appropriate period and require the same security for suspending enforcement of the judgment that is required in this state in accordance with Section 52.006.

CPRC §35.007. FEES

(a) A person filing a foreign judgment shall pay to the clerk of the court the amount as otherwise provided by law for filing suit in the courts of this state.

(b) Filing fees are due and payable at the time of filing.

(c) Fees for other enforcement proceedings are as provided by law for judgments of the courts of this state.

CPRC §35.008. OPTIONAL PROCEDURE

A judgment creditor retains the right to bring an action to enforce a judgment instead of proceeding under this chapter.

CHAPTER 36. REPEALED

~~[ENFORCEMENT OF JUDGMENTS OF OTHER COUNTRIES]~~

In 2017, the Texas Legislature repealed Civil Practice & Remedies Code ch. 36 and enacted the Uniform Foreign-Country Money Judgments Recognition Act as Civil

Practice & Remedies Code ch. 36A. Chapter 36A, however, does not apply to foreign-country judgments for divorce, support, or maintenance, or other judgments rendered in connection with domestic relations, and is therefore not included in this book.

CPRC §36.001. REPEALED [DEFINITIONS]

[In this chapter:]

[(1)] ["Foreign country" means a governmental unit other than:]

[(A)] [the United States;]

[(B)] [a state, district, commonwealth, territory, or insular possession of the United States;]

[(C)] [the Panama Canal Zone; or]

[(D)] [the Trust Territory of the Pacific Islands.]

[(2)] ["Foreign country judgment" means a judgment of a foreign country granting or denying a sum of money other than a judgment for:]

[(A)] [taxes, a fine, or other penalty; or]

[(B)] [support in a matrimonial or family matter.]

Repealed by S.B. 944, §2, 85th Leg., eff. June 1, 2017.

CPRC §36.002. REPEALED [APPLICABILITY]

[(a)] [This chapter applies to a foreign country judgment:]

[(1)] [that is final and conclusive and enforceable where rendered, even though an appeal is pending or the judgment is subject to appeal; or]

[(2)] [that is in favor of the defendant on the merits of the cause of action and is final and conclusive where rendered, even though an appeal is pending or the judgment is subject to appeal.]

[(b)] [This chapter does not apply to a judgment rendered before June 17, 1981.]

Repealed by S.B. 944, §2, 85th Leg., eff. June 1, 2017.

CPRC §36.003. REPEALED [SHORT TITLE]

[This chapter may be cited as the Uniform Foreign Country Money-Judgment Recognition Act.]

Repealed by S.B. 944, §2, 85th Leg., eff. June 1, 2017.

CPRC §36.004. REPEALED [RECOGNITION & ENFORCEMENT]

[Except as provided by Section 36.005, a foreign country judgment that is filed with notice given as provided by this chapter, that meets the requirements of Section 36.002, and that is not refused recognition under Section 36.0044 is conclusive between the parties to the extent that it grants or denies recovery of a sum of money. The judgment is enforceable in the same manner as a judgment of a sister state that is entitled to full faith and credit.]

Repealed by S.B. 944, §2, 85th Leg., eff. June 1, 2017.

CPRC §36.0041. REPEALED [FILING]

[A copy of a foreign country judgment authenticated in accordance with an act of congress, a statute of this state, or a treaty or other international convention to which the United States is a party may be filed in the office of the clerk of a court in the county of residence of the party against whom recognition is sought or in any other court of competent jurisdiction as allowed under the Texas venue laws.]

Repealed by S.B. 944, §2, 85th Leg., eff. June 1, 2017.

CPRC §36.0042. REPEALED [AFFIDAVIT; NOTICE OF FILING]

[(a)] [At the time a foreign country judgment is filed, the party seeking recognition of the judgment or the party's attorney shall file with the clerk of the court an affidavit showing the name and last known post office address of the judgment debtor and the judgment creditor.]

[(b)] [The clerk shall promptly mail notice of the filing of the foreign country judgment to the party against whom recognition is sought at the address given and shall note the mailing in the docket.]

[(c)] [The notice must include the name and post office address of the party seeking recognition and that party's attorney, if any, in this state.]

Repealed by S.B. 944, §2, 85th Leg., eff. June 1, 2017.

CPRC §36.0043. REPEALED [ALTERNATE NOTICE OF FILING]

[(a)] [The party seeking recognition may mail a notice of the filing of the foreign country judgment to the other party and may file proof of mailing with the clerk.]

[(b)] [A clerk's lack of mailing the notice of filing does not affect the conclusive recognition of the foreign country judgment under this chapter if proof of mailing by the party seeking recognition has been filed.]

Repealed by S.B. 944, §2, 85th Leg., eff. June 1, 2017.

CPRC §36.0044. REPEALED [CONTESTING RECOGNITION]

[(a)] [A party against whom recognition of a foreign country judgment is sought may contest recogni-

CPRC

~~tion of the judgment if, not later than the 30th day after the date of service of the notice of filing, the party files with the court, and serves the opposing party with a copy of, a motion for nonrecognition of the judgment on the basis of one or more grounds under Section 36.005. If the party is domiciled in a foreign country, the party must file the motion for nonrecognition not later than the 60th day after the date of service of the notice of filing.~~]

[~~(b)~~] [~~The party filing the motion for nonrecognition shall include with the motion all supporting affidavits, briefs, and other documentation.~~]

[~~(c)~~] [~~A party opposing the motion must file any response, including supporting affidavits, briefs, and other documentation, not later than the 20th day after the date of service on that party of a copy of the motion for nonrecognition.~~]

[~~(d)~~] [~~The court may, on motion and notice, grant an extension of time, not to exceed 20 days unless good cause is shown, for the filing of a response or any document that is required to establish a ground for nonrecognition but that is not available within the time for filing the document.~~]

[~~(e)~~] [~~A party filing a motion for nonrecognition or responding to the motion may request an evidentiary hearing that the court may allow in its discretion.~~]

[~~(f)~~] [~~The court may at any time permit or require the submission of argument, authorities, or supporting material in addition to that provided for by this section.~~]

[~~(g)~~] [~~The court may refuse recognition of the foreign country judgment if the motions, affidavits, briefs, and other evidence before it establish grounds for nonrecognition as specified in Section 36.005, but the court may not, under any circumstances, review the foreign country judgment in relation to any matter not specified in Section 36.005.~~]

Repealed by S.B. 944, §2, 85th Leg., eff. June 1, 2017.

CPRC §36.005. REPEALED [~~GROUNDS FOR NONRECOGNITION~~]

[~~(a)~~] [~~A foreign country judgment is not conclusive if:~~]

[~~(1)~~] [~~the judgment was rendered under a system that does not provide impartial tribunals or procedures compatible with the requirements of due process of law;~~]

[~~(2)~~] [~~the foreign country court did not have personal jurisdiction over the defendant; or~~]

[~~(3)~~] [~~the foreign country court did not have jurisdiction over the subject matter.~~]

[~~(b)~~] [~~A foreign country judgment need not be recognized if:~~]

[~~(1)~~] [~~the defendant in the proceedings in the foreign country court did not receive notice of the proceedings in sufficient time to defend;~~]

[~~(2)~~] [~~the judgment was obtained by fraud;~~]

[~~(3)~~] [~~the cause of action on which the judgment is based is repugnant to the public policy of this state;~~]

[~~(4)~~] [~~the judgment conflicts with another final and conclusive judgment;~~]

[~~(5)~~] [~~the proceeding in the foreign country court was contrary to an agreement between the parties under which the dispute in question was to be settled otherwise than by proceedings in that court;~~]

[~~(6)~~] [~~in the case of jurisdiction based only on personal service, the foreign country court was a seriously inconvenient forum for the trial of the action; or~~]

[~~(7)~~] [~~it is established that the foreign country in which the judgment was rendered does not recognize judgments rendered in this state that, but for the fact that they are rendered in this state, conform to the definition of "foreign country judgment."~~]

Repealed by S.B. 944, §2, 85th Leg., eff. June 1, 2017.

CPRC §36.006. REPEALED [~~PERSONAL JURISDICTION~~]

[~~(a)~~] [~~A court may not refuse to recognize a foreign country judgment for lack of personal jurisdiction if:~~]

[~~(1)~~] [~~the defendant was served personally in the foreign country;~~]

[~~(2)~~] [~~the defendant voluntarily appeared in the proceedings, other than for the purpose of protecting property seized or threatened with seizure in the proceedings or of contesting the jurisdiction of the court over him;~~]

[~~(3)~~] [~~the defendant prior to the commencement of the proceedings had agreed to submit to the jurisdiction of the foreign country court with respect to the subject matter involved;~~]

[~~(4)~~] [~~the defendant was domiciled in the foreign country when the proceedings were instituted or, if the defendant is a body corporate, had its principal place of business, was incorporated, or had otherwise acquired corporate status in the foreign country;~~]

[~~(5)~~] [~~the defendant had a business office in the foreign country and the proceedings in the foreign~~

~~country court involved a cause of action arising out of business done by the defendant through that office in the foreign country; or~~]

[~~(6)~~] [~~the defendant operated a motor vehicle or airplane in the foreign country and the proceedings involved a cause of action arising out of operation of the motor vehicle or airplane.~~]

[~~(b)~~] [~~A court of this state may recognize other bases of jurisdiction.~~]

Repealed by S.B. 944, §2, 85th Leg., eff. June 1, 2017.

CPRC §36.007. REPEALED [~~STAY IN CASE OF APPEAL~~]

[~~If the defendant satisfies the court either that an appeal is pending or that the defendant is entitled and intends to appeal from the foreign country judgment, the court may stay the proceedings until the appeal has been determined or until a period of time sufficient to enable the defendant to prosecute the appeal has expired.~~]

Repealed by S.B. 944, §2, 85th Leg., eff. June 1, 2017.

CPRC §36.008. REPEALED [~~OTHER FOREIGN COUNTRY JUDGMENTS~~]

[~~This chapter does not prevent the recognition of a foreign country judgment in a situation not covered by this chapter.~~]

Repealed by S.B. 944, §2, 85th Leg., eff. June 1, 2017.

TITLE 7. ALTERNATE METHODS OF DISPUTE RESOLUTION

CHAPTER 154. ALTERNATIVE DISPUTE RESOLUTION PROCEDURES

SUBCHAPTER A. GENERAL PROVISIONS

CPRC §154.001. DEFINITIONS

In this chapter:

(1) "Court" includes an appellate court, district court, constitutional county court, statutory county court, family law court, probate court, municipal court, or justice of the peace court.

(2) "Dispute resolution organization" means a private profit or nonprofit corporation, political subdivision, or public corporation, or a combination of these, that offers alternative dispute resolution services to the public.

See also *O'Connor's Texas Family Law Handbook* (2017), "ADR," ch. 3-A, §13.1, p. 244; *O'Connor's Texas Rules*, "The ADR System," ch. 4-A, p. 325.

CPRC §154.002. POLICY

It is the policy of this state to encourage the peaceable resolution of disputes, with special consideration given to disputes involving the parent-child relationship, including the mediation of issues involving conservatorship, possession, and support of children, and the early settlement of pending litigation through voluntary settlement procedures.

See also *O'Connor's Texas Rules*, "Purpose," ch. 4-A, §1.2, p. 325.

CPRC §154.003. RESPONSIBILITY OF COURTS & COURT ADMINISTRATORS

It is the responsibility of all trial and appellate courts and their court administrators to carry out the policy under Section 154.002.

Sections 154.004-154.020 reserved for expansion

SUBCHAPTER B. ALTERNATIVE DISPUTE RESOLUTION PROCEDURES

CPRC §154.021. REFERRAL OF PENDING DISPUTES FOR ALTERNATIVE DISPUTE RESOLUTION PROCEDURE

(a) A court may, on its own motion or the motion of a party, refer a pending dispute for resolution by an alternative dispute resolution procedure including:

(1) an alternative dispute resolution system established under Chapter 26, Acts of the 68th Legislature, Regular Session, 1983 (Article 2372aa, Vernon's Texas Civil Statutes[1]);

(2) a dispute resolution organization; or

(3) a nonjudicial and informally conducted forum for the voluntary settlement of citizens' disputes through the intervention of an impartial third party, including those alternative dispute resolution procedures described under this subchapter.

(b) The court shall confer with the parties in the determination of the most appropriate alternative dispute resolution procedure.

(c) Except as provided by agreement of the parties, a court may not order mediation in an action that is subject to the Federal Arbitration Act (9 U.S.C. Sections 1-16).

1. **Editor's note:** Repealed. See generally CPRC ch. 152.

See also *O'Connor's Texas Family Law Handbook* (2017), "Referral," ch. 3-A, §13.1.1(1), p. 245; *O'Connor's Texas Rules*, "Referral Procedures for ADR," ch. 4-A, §3, p. 327; *O'Connor's Texas Forms*, FORM 4A:1.

CPRC §154.022. NOTIFICATION & OBJECTION

(a) If a court determines that a pending dispute is appropriate for referral under Section 154.021, the court shall notify the parties of its determination.

(b) Any party may, within 10 days after receiving the notice under Subsection (a), file a written objection to the referral.

(c) If the court finds that there is a reasonable basis for an objection filed under Subsection (b), the court may not refer the dispute under Section 154.021.

See also ***O'Connor's Texas Rules***, "Objecting to ADR," ch. 4-A, §4, p. 328; ***O'Connor's Texas Forms***, FORMS 4A:2, 3.

CPRC §154.023. MEDIATION

(a) Mediation is a forum in which an impartial person, the mediator, facilitates communication between parties to promote reconciliation, settlement, or understanding among them.

(b) A mediator may not impose his own judgment on the issues for that of the parties.

(c) Mediation includes victim-offender mediation by the Texas Department of Criminal Justice described in Article 56.13, Code of Criminal Procedure.

See also ***O'Connor's Texas Family Law Handbook*** (2017), "Mediation," ch. 3-A, §13.1.1, p. 244; ***O'Connor's Texas Rules***, "Mediation," ch. 4-A, §2.1.1, p. 325; "Mediation," ch. 4-B, p. 333; ***O'Connor's Texas Forms***, FORMS 4A:4, 4B.

CPRC §154.024. MINI-TRIAL

(a) A mini-trial is conducted under an agreement of the parties.

(b) Each party and counsel for the party present the position of the party, either before selected representatives for each party or before an impartial third party, to define the issues and develop a basis for realistic settlement negotiations.

(c) The impartial third party may issue an advisory opinion regarding the merits of the case.

(d) The advisory opinion is not binding on the parties unless the parties agree that it is binding and enter into a written settlement agreement.

See also ***O'Connor's Texas Rules***, "Minitrial," ch. 4-A, §2.2.1, p. 326; ***O'Connor's Texas Forms***, FORMS 4A:8, 9.

CPRC §154.025. MODERATED SETTLEMENT CONFERENCE

(a) A moderated settlement conference is a forum for case evaluation and realistic settlement negotiations.

(b) Each party and counsel for the party present the position of the party before a panel of impartial third parties.

(c) The panel may issue an advisory opinion regarding the liability or damages of the parties or both.

(d) The advisory opinion is not binding on the parties.

See also ***O'Connor's Texas Rules***, "Moderated settlement conference," ch. 4-A, §2.1.2, p. 325; ***O'Connor's Texas Forms***, FORM 4A:5.

CPRC §154.026. SUMMARY JURY TRIAL

(a) A summary jury trial is a forum for early case evaluation and development of realistic settlement negotiations.

(b) Each party and counsel for the party present the position of the party before a panel of jurors.

(c) The number of jurors on the panel is six unless the parties agree otherwise.

(d) The panel may issue an advisory opinion regarding the liability or damages of the parties or both.

(e) The advisory opinion is not binding on the parties.

See also ***O'Connor's Texas Rules***, "Summary jury trial," ch. 4-A, §2.1.4, p. 326; ***O'Connor's Texas Forms***, FORM 4A:6.

CPRC §154.027. ARBITRATION

(a) Nonbinding arbitration is a forum in which each party and counsel for the party present the position of the party before an impartial third party, who renders a specific award.

(b) If the parties stipulate in advance, the award is binding and is enforceable in the same manner as any contract obligation. If the parties do not stipulate in advance that the award is binding, the award is not binding and serves only as a basis for the parties' further settlement negotiations.

See also ***O'Connor's Texas Family Law Handbook*** (2017), "Arbitration," ch. 3-A, §13.1.4, p. 257; ***O'Connor's Texas Rules***, "Arbitration," ch. 4-A, §2.1.5, p. 326; "Arbitration," ch. 4-C, p. 335; ***O'Connor's Texas Forms***, FORMS 4A:7, 4C.

Section 154.028 omitted by editor

Sections 154.029-154.050 reserved for expansion

SUBCHAPTER C. IMPARTIAL THIRD PARTIES

CPRC §154.051. APPOINTMENT OF IMPARTIAL THIRD PARTIES

(a) If a court refers a pending dispute for resolution by an alternative dispute resolution procedure un-

der Section 154.021, the court may appoint an impartial third party to facilitate the procedure.

(b) The court may appoint a third party who is agreed on by the parties if the person qualifies for appointment under this subchapter.

(c) The court may appoint more than one third party under this section.

See also *O'Connor's Texas Rules*, "Appointment of Impartial Third Party," ch. 4-A, §6, p. 329.

A CPRC §154.052. QUALIFICATIONS OF IMPARTIAL THIRD PARTY

A person qualified to serve as an impartial third party immediately before Sept. 1, 2017, does not have to comply with the new requirements to serve as an impartial third party under amended subsection (b) until Jan. 1, 2018.

(a) Except as provided by Subsections (b) and (c), to qualify for an appointment as an impartial third party under this subchapter a person must have completed a minimum of 40 classroom hours of training in dispute resolution techniques in a course conducted by an alternative dispute resolution system or other dispute resolution organization approved by the court making the appointment.

(b) To qualify for an appointment as an impartial third party under this subchapter in a dispute relating to the parent-child relationship, a person must complete the training required by Subsection (a) and an additional 24 hours of training in the fields of family dynamics, child development, and family law, including a minimum of four hours of family violence dynamics training developed in consultation with a statewide family violence advocacy organization.

(c) In appropriate circumstances, a court may in its discretion appoint a person as an impartial third party who does not qualify under Subsection (a) or (b) if the court bases its appointment on legal or other professional training or experience in particular dispute resolution processes.

2017 Legislation: Amended by S.B. 539, §1, 85th Leg., eff. Sept. 1, 2017.
See also *O'Connor's Texas Rules*, "Qualifications," ch. 4-A, §6.1, p. 329.

CPRC §154.053. STANDARDS & DUTIES OF IMPARTIAL THIRD PARTIES

(a) A person appointed to facilitate an alternative dispute resolution procedure under this subchapter shall encourage and assist the parties in reaching a settlement of their dispute but may not compel or coerce the parties to enter into a settlement agreement.

(b) Unless expressly authorized by the disclosing party, the impartial third party may not disclose to either party information given in confidence by the other and shall at all times maintain confidentiality with respect to communications relating to the subject matter of the dispute.

(c) Unless the parties agree otherwise, all matters, including the conduct and demeanor of the parties and their counsel during the settlement process, are confidential and may never be disclosed to anyone, including the appointing court.

(d) Each participant, including the impartial third party, to an alternative dispute resolution procedure is subject to the requirements of Subchapter B, Chapter 261, Family Code, and Subchapter C, Chapter 48, Human Resources Code.

See also *O'Connor's Texas Rules*, "Standards & duties," ch. 4-A, §6.2, p. 329; "No disclosure by impartial third party," ch. 4-A, §7.1, p. 330.

CPRC §154.054. COMPENSATION OF IMPARTIAL THIRD PARTIES

(a) The court may set a reasonable fee for the services of an impartial third party appointed under this subchapter.

(b) Unless the parties agree to a method of payment, the court shall tax the fee for the services of an impartial third party as other costs of suit.

See also *O'Connor's Texas Rules*, "Fees," ch. 4-A, §6.3, p. 330.

CPRC §154.055. QUALIFIED IMMUNITY OF IMPARTIAL THIRD PARTIES

(a) A person appointed to facilitate an alternative dispute resolution procedure under this subchapter or under Chapter 152 relating to an alternative dispute resolution system established by counties, or appointed by the parties whether before or after the institution of formal judicial proceedings, who is a volunteer and who does not act with wanton and wilful disregard of the rights, safety, or property of another, is immune from civil liability for any act or omission within the course and scope of his or her duties or functions as an impartial third party. For purposes of this section, a volunteer impartial third party is a person who does not receive compensation in excess of reimbursement for expenses incurred or a stipend intended as reimbursement for expenses incurred.

(b) This section neither applies to nor is it intended to enlarge or diminish any rights or immunities enjoyed by an arbitrator participating in a binding arbitration pursuant to any applicable statute or treaty.

Sections 154.056-154.070 reserved for expansion

SUBCHAPTER D. MISCELLANEOUS PROVISIONS

CPRC §154.071. EFFECT OF WRITTEN SETTLEMENT AGREEMENT

(a) If the parties reach a settlement and execute a written agreement disposing of the dispute, the agreement is enforceable in the same manner as any other written contract.

(b) The court in its discretion may incorporate the terms of the agreement in the court's final decree disposing of the case.

(c) A settlement agreement does not affect an outstanding court order unless the terms of the agreement are incorporated into a subsequent decree.

See also Fam. Code §153.0071; ***O'Connor's Texas Family Law Handbook*** (2017), "Agreement incident to divorce," ch. 3-A, §13.2, p. 258; ***O'Connor's Texas Rules***, "Settlement Agreement," ch. 4-A, §10, p. 331; "Enforceable Settlement Agreements," ch. 7-I, §4, p. 763.

CPRC §154.072. STATISTICAL INFORMATION ON DISPUTES REFERRED

The Texas Supreme Court shall determine the need and method for statistical reporting of disputes referred by the courts to alternative dispute resolution procedures.

CPRC §154.073. CONFIDENTIALITY OF CERTAIN RECORDS & COMMUNICATIONS

(a) Except as provided by Subsections (c), (d), (e), and (f), a communication relating to the subject matter of any civil or criminal dispute made by a participant in an alternative dispute resolution procedure, whether before or after the institution of formal judicial proceedings, is confidential, is not subject to disclosure, and may not be used as evidence against the participant in any judicial or administrative proceeding.

(b) Any record made at an alternative dispute resolution procedure is confidential, and the participants or the third party facilitating the procedure may not be required to testify in any proceedings relating to or arising out of the matter in dispute or be subject to process requiring disclosure of confidential information or data relating to or arising out of the matter in dispute.

(c) An oral communication or written material used in or made a part of an alternative dispute resolution procedure is admissible or discoverable if it is admissible or discoverable independent of the procedure.

(d) A final written agreement to which a governmental body, as defined by Section 552.003, Government Code, is a signatory that is reached as a result of a dispute resolution procedure conducted under this chapter is subject to or excepted from required disclosure in accordance with Chapter 552, Government Code.

(e) If this section conflicts with other legal requirements for disclosure of communications, records, or materials, the issue of confidentiality may be presented to the court having jurisdiction of the proceedings to determine, in camera, whether the facts, circumstances, and context of the communications or materials sought to be disclosed warrant a protective order of the court or whether the communications or materials are subject to disclosure.

(f) This section does not affect the duty to report abuse or neglect under Subchapter B, Chapter 261, Family Code, and abuse, exploitation, or neglect under Subchapter C, Chapter 48, Human Resources Code.

(g) This section applies to a victim-offender mediation by the Texas Department of Criminal Justice as described in Article 56.13, Code of Criminal Procedure.

See also ***O'Connor's Texas Rules***, "Confidentiality," ch. 4-A, §7, p. 330.

Government Code

Selected Provisions
Table of Contents

TITLE 2. JUDICIAL BRANCH

SUBTITLE A. COURTS

CHAPTER 22. APPELLATE COURTS

SUBCHAPTER A. SUPREME COURT

E GOVT §22.0041. RULES REGARDING FOREIGN LAW & FOREIGN JUDGMENTS IN CERTAIN FAMILY LAW ACTIONS

(a) In this section:

(1) "Comity" means the recognition by a court of one jurisdiction of the laws and judicial decisions of a court of another jurisdiction.

(2) "Foreign judgment" means a judgment of a court, tribunal, or administrative adjudicator of a jurisdiction outside of the states and territories of the United States.

(3) "Foreign law" means a law, rule, or code of a jurisdiction outside of the states and territories of the United States.

(b) The supreme court shall adopt rules of evidence and procedure to implement the limitations on the granting of comity to a foreign judgment or an arbitration award involving a marriage relationship or a parent-child relationship under the Family Code to protect against violations of constitutional rights and public policy.

(c) The rules adopted under Subsection (b) must:

(1) require that any party who intends to seek enforcement of a judgment or an arbitration award based on foreign law that involves a marriage relationship or a parent-child relationship shall provide timely notice to the court and to each other party, including by providing information required by Rule 203, Texas Rules of Evidence, and by describing the court's authority to enforce or decide to enforce the judgment or award;

(2) require that any party who intends to oppose the enforcement of a judgment or an arbitration award based on foreign law that involves a marriage relationship or a parent-child relationship shall provide timely notice to the court and to each other party and include with the notice an explanation of the party's basis for opposition, including by stating whether the party asserts that the judgment or award violates constitutional rights or public policy;

(3) require a hearing on the record, after notice to the parties, to determine whether the proposed enforcement of a judgment or an arbitration award based on foreign law that involves a marriage relationship or a parent-child relationship violates constitutional rights or public policy;

(4) to facilitate appellate review, require that a court state its findings of fact and conclusions of law in a written order determining whether to enforce a foreign judgment or an arbitration award based on foreign law that involves a marriage relationship or a parent-child relationship;

(5) require that a court's determination under Subdivision (3) or (4) be made promptly so that the action may proceed expeditiously; and

(6) provide that a court may issue any orders the court considers necessary to preserve principles of comity or the freedom to contract for arbitration while protecting against violations of constitutional rights and public policy in the application of foreign law and the recognition and enforcement of foreign judgments and arbitration awards.

(d) In addition to the rules required under Subsection (b), the supreme court shall adopt any other rules the supreme court considers necessary or advisable to accomplish the purposes of this section.

(e) A rule adopted under this section does not apply to an action brought under the International Child Abduction Remedies Act (22 U.S.C. Section 9001 et seq.).

(f) In the event of a conflict between a rule adopted under this section and a federal or state law, the federal or state law prevails.

2017 Legislation: Enacted by H.B. 45, §2, 85th Leg., eff. Sept. 1, 2017.

E GOVT §22.022. JUDICIAL INSTRUCTION RELATED TO FOREIGN LAW & FOREIGN JUDGMENTS

(a) The supreme court shall provide for a course of instruction that relates to issues regarding foreign law, foreign judgments, and arbitration awards in relation to foreign law that arise in actions under the Family Code involving the marriage relationship and the parent-child relationship for judges involved in those actions.

(b) The course of instruction must include information about:

(1) the limits on comity and the freedom to contract for arbitration that protect against violations of constitutional rights and public policy in the application of foreign law and the recognition and enforce-

ment of foreign judgments and arbitration awards in actions brought under the Family Code; and

(2) the rules of evidence and procedure adopted under Section 22.0041.

(c) The supreme court shall adopt rules necessary to accomplish the purposes of this section.

2017 Legislation: Enacted by H.B. 45, §2, 85th Leg., eff. Sept. 1, 2017.

CHAPTER 24. DISTRICT COURTS

SUBCHAPTER A. GENERAL PROVISIONS

GOVT §24.022. EFFECT OF TRANSFER OF CERTAIN CASES FOLLOWING CREATION OF ADDITIONAL COURT

(a) On the creation of an additional district court in a county, an existing district court in the county may transfer to the new court a case regarding a child who is subject to the continuing exclusive jurisdiction of the existing court under Title 5, Family Code, regardless of whether the case is pending in the existing court or the existing court rendered a final order in the case.

(b) The district court to which the case is transferred under this section acquires continuing exclusive jurisdiction under Title 5, Family Code, over the child.

SUBTITLE B. JUDGES

CHAPTER 37. APPOINTMENTS OF ATTORNEYS AD LITEM, GUARDIANS AD LITEM, MEDIATORS, & GUARDIANS

GOVT §37.001. APPLICABILITY; CONFLICT OF LAW

(a) This chapter applies to a court in this state created by the Texas Constitution, by statute, or as authorized by statute that is located in a county with a population of 25,000 or more.

(b) To the extent of a conflict between this chapter and a specific provision relating to a court, this chapter controls.

GOVT §37.002. EXEMPTION

The appointment requirements of Section 37.004 do not apply to:

(1) a mediation conducted by an alternative dispute resolution system established under Chapter 152, Civil Practice and Remedies Code;

(2) a guardian ad litem or other person appointed under a program authorized by Section 107.031, Family Code;

(3) an attorney ad litem, guardian ad litem, amicus attorney, or mediator appointed under a domestic relations office established under Chapter 203, Family Code; or

(4) a person other than an attorney or a private professional guardian appointed to serve as a guardian as defined by Section 1002.012, Estates Code.

GOVT §37.003. LISTS OF ATTORNEYS AD LITEM, GUARDIANS AD LITEM, MEDIATORS, & GUARDIANS

(a) In addition to a list required by other state law or rule, each court in this state shall establish and maintain the following lists:

(1) a list of all attorneys who are qualified to serve as an attorney ad litem and are registered with the court;

(2) a list of all attorneys and other persons who are qualified to serve as a guardian ad litem and are registered with the court;

(3) a list of all persons who are registered with the court to serve as a mediator; and

(4) a list of all attorneys and private professional guardians who are qualified to serve as a guardian as defined by Section 1002.012, Estates Code, and are registered with the court.

(b) A court may establish and maintain more than one of a list required under Subsection (a) that is cat egorized by the type of case and the person's qualifications.

(c) A local administrative judge, at the request of one or more of the courts the judge serves, shall establish and maintain the lists required under Subsection (a) for those courts. The local administrative judge may establish and maintain one set of lists for all of the requesting courts and may maintain for the courts more than one of a list as provided in Subsection (b).

GOVT §37.004. APPOINTMENT OF ATTORNEYS AD LITEM, GUARDIANS AD LITEM, MEDIATORS, & GUARDIANS; MAINTENANCE OF LISTS

(a) Except as provided by Subsections (c) and (d), in each case in which the appointment of an attorney ad litem, guardian ad litem, or guardian is necessary, a court using a rotation system shall appoint the person whose name appears first on the applicable list maintained by the court as required by Section 37.003.

(b) In each case in which the appointment of a mediator is necessary because the parties to the case are

unable to agree on a mediator, a court using a rotation system shall appoint the person whose name appears first on the mediator list maintained by the court as required under Section 37.003.

(c) The court may appoint a person included on the applicable list whose name does not appear first on the list, or a person who meets statutory or other requirements to serve and who is not included on the list, if the appointment of that person as attorney ad litem, guardian ad litem, or guardian is agreed on by the parties and approved by the court.

(d) On finding good cause, the court may appoint a person included on the applicable list whose name does not appear first on the list, or a person who meets statutory or other requirements to serve on the case and who is not included on the list, if the appointment of that person as attorney ad litem, guardian ad litem, mediator, or guardian is required on a complex matter because the person:

(1) possesses relevant specialized education, training, certification, skill, language proficiency, or knowledge of the subject matter of the case;

(2) has relevant prior involvement with the parties or case; or

(3) is in a relevant geographic location.

(e) A person who is not appointed in the order in which the person's name appears on the applicable list shall remain next in order on the list.

(f) After a person has been appointed as an attorney ad litem, guardian ad litem, mediator, or guardian from the applicable list, the court shall place that person's name at the end of the list.

GOVT §37.005. POSTING OF LISTS

A court annually shall post each list established under Section 37.003 at the courthouse of the county in which the court is located and on any Internet website of the court.

SUBTITLE F. COURT ADMINISTRATION

CHAPTER 74. COURT ADMINISTRATION ACT

SUBCHAPTER C. ADMINISTRATIVE JUDICIAL REGIONS

GOVT §74.053. OBJECTION TO JUDGE ASSIGNED TO A TRIAL COURT

(a) When a judge is assigned to a trial court under this chapter:

(1) the order of assignment must state whether the judge is an active, former, retired, or senior judge; and

(2) the presiding judge shall, if it is reasonable and practicable and if time permits, give notice of the assignment to each attorney representing a party to the case that is to be heard in whole or part by the assigned judge.

(b) If a party to a civil case files a timely objection to the assignment, the judge shall not hear the case. Except as provided by Subsection (d), each party to the case is only entitled to one objection under this section for that case.

(c) An objection under this section must be filed not later than the seventh day after the date the party receives actual notice of the assignment or before the date the first hearing or trial, including pretrial hearings, commences, whichever date occurs earlier. The presiding judge may extend the time to file an objection under this section on written motion by a party who demonstrates good cause.

(d) An assigned judge or justice who was defeated in the last primary or general election for which the judge or justice was a candidate for the judicial office held by the judge or justice may not sit in a case if either party objects to the judge or justice.

(e) An active judge assigned under this chapter is not subject to an objection.

(f) For purposes of this section, notice of an assignment may be given and an objection to an assignment may be filed by electronic mail.

(g) In this section, "party" includes multiple parties aligned in a case as determined by the presiding judge.

SUBTITLE K. SPECIALTY COURTS

CHAPTER 122. FAMILY DRUG COURT PROGRAM

GOVT §122.001. FAMILY DRUG COURT PROGRAM DEFINED

In this chapter, "family drug court program" means a program that has the following essential characteristics:

(1) the integration of substance abuse treatment services in the processing of civil cases in the child welfare system with the goal of family reunification;

(2) the use of a comprehensive case management approach involving Department of Family and Protective Services caseworkers, court-appointed case managers, and court-appointed special advocates to rehabilitate a parent who has had a child removed from the parent's care by the department because of suspected child abuse or neglect and who is suspected of substance abuse;

(3) early identification and prompt placement of eligible parents who volunteer to participate in the program;

(4) comprehensive substance abuse needs assessment and referral to an appropriate substance abuse treatment agency;

(5) a progressive treatment approach with specific requirements that a parent must meet to advance to the next phase of the program;

(6) monitoring of abstinence through periodic alcohol or other drug testing;

(7) ongoing judicial interaction with program participants;

(8) monitoring and evaluation of program goals and effectiveness;

(9) continuing interdisciplinary education to promote effective program planning, implementation, and operations; and

(10) development of partnerships with public agencies and community organizations.

GOVT §122.002. AUTHORITY TO ESTABLISH PROGRAM

The commissioners court of a county may establish a family drug court program for persons who:

(1) have had a child removed from their care by the Department of Family and Protective Services; and

(2) are suspected by the Department of Family and Protective Services or a court of having a substance abuse problem.

GOVT §122.003. PARTICIPANT PAYMENT FOR TREATMENT & SERVICES

A family drug court program may require a participant to pay the cost of all treatment and services received while participating in the program, based on the participant's ability to pay.

GOVT §122.004. FUNDING

A county creating a family drug court under this chapter shall explore the possibility of using court improvement project funds to finance the family drug court in the county. The county shall also explore the availability of federal and state matching funds to finance the court.

TITLE 3. LEGISLATIVE BRANCH

SUBTITLE B. LEGISLATION

CHAPTER 311. CODE CONSTRUCTION ACT

SUBCHAPTER A. GENERAL PROVISIONS

GOVT §311.001. SHORT TITLE

This chapter may be cited as the Code Construction Act.

GOVT §311.002. APPLICATION

This chapter applies to:

(1) each code enacted by the 60th or a subsequent legislature as part of the state's continuing statutory revision program;

(2) each amendment, repeal, revision, and reenactment of a code or code provision by the 60th or a subsequent legislature;

(3) each repeal of a statute by a code; and

(4) each rule adopted under a code.

GOVT §311.003. RULES NOT EXCLUSIVE

The rules provided in this chapter are not exclusive but are meant to describe and clarify common situations in order to guide the preparation and construction of codes.

GOVT §311.004. CITATION OF CODES

A code may be cited by its name preceded by the specific part concerned. Examples of citations are:

(1) Title 1, Business & Commerce Code;

(2) Chapter 5, Business & Commerce Code;

(3) Section 9.304, Business & Commerce Code;

(4) Section 15.06(a), Business & Commerce Code; and

(5) Section 17.18(b)(1)(B)(ii), Business & Commerce Code.

GOVT §311.005. GENERAL DEFINITIONS

The following definitions apply unless the statute or context in which the word or phrase is used requires a different definition:

(1) "Oath" includes affirmation.

(2) "Person" includes corporation, organization, government or governmental subdivision or agency, business trust, estate, trust, partnership, association, and any other legal entity.

(3) "Population" means the population shown by the most recent federal decennial census.

(4) "Property" means real and personal property.

(5) "Rule" includes regulation.

(6) "Signed" includes any symbol executed or adopted by a person with present intention to authenticate a writing.

(7) "State," when referring to a part of the United States, includes any state, district, commonwealth, territory, and insular possession of the United States and any area subject to the legislative authority of the United States of America.

(8) "Swear" includes affirm.

(9) "United States" includes a department, bureau, or other agency of the United States of America.

(10) "Week" means seven consecutive days.

(11) "Written" includes any representation of words, letters, symbols, or figures.

(12) "Year" means 12 consecutive months.

(13) "Includes" and "including" are terms of enlargement and not of limitation or exclusive enumeration, and use of the terms does not create a presumption that components not expressed are excluded.

GOVT §311.006. INTERNAL REFERENCES

In a code:

(1) a reference to a title, chapter, or section without further identification is a reference to a title, chapter, or section of the code; and

(2) a reference to a subtitle, subchapter, subsection, subdivision, paragraph, or other numbered or lettered unit without further identification is a reference to a unit of the next larger unit of the code in which the reference appears.

Sections 311.007-311.010 reserved for expansion

SUBCHAPTER B. CONSTRUCTION OF WORDS & PHRASES

GOVT §311.011. COMMON & TECHNICAL USAGE OF WORDS

(a) Words and phrases shall be read in context and construed according to the rules of grammar and common usage.

(b) Words and phrases that have acquired a technical or particular meaning, whether by legislative definition or otherwise, shall be construed accordingly.

GOVT §311.012. TENSE, NUMBER, & GENDER

(a) Words in the present tense include the future tense.

(b) The singular includes the plural and the plural includes the singular.

(c) Words of one gender include the other genders.

GOVT §311.013. AUTHORITY & QUORUM OF PUBLIC BODY

(a) A grant of authority to three or more persons as a public body confers the authority on a majority of the number of members fixed by statute.

(b) A quorum of a public body is a majority of the number of members fixed by statute.

GOVT §311.014. COMPUTATION OF TIME

(a) In computing a period of days, the first day is excluded and the last day is included.

(b) If the last day of any period is a Saturday, Sunday, or legal holiday, the period is extended to include the next day that is not a Saturday, Sunday, or legal holiday.

(c) If a number of months is to be computed by counting the months from a particular day, the period ends on the same numerical day in the concluding month as the day of the month from which the computation is begun, unless there are not that many days in the concluding month, in which case the period ends on the last day of that month.

GOVT §311.015. REFERENCE TO A SERIES

If a statute refers to a series of numbers or letters, the first and last numbers or letters are included.

GOVT §311.016. "MAY," "SHALL," "MUST," ETC.

The following constructions apply unless the context in which the word or phrase appears necessarily requires a different construction or unless a different construction is expressly provided by statute:

(1) "May" creates discretionary authority or grants permission or a power.

(2) "Shall" imposes a duty.

(3) "Must" creates or recognizes a condition precedent.

(4) "Is entitled to" creates or recognizes a right.

(5) "May not" imposes a prohibition and is synonymous with "shall not."

(6) "Is not entitled to" negates a right.

(7) "Is not required to" negates a duty or condition precedent.

Sections 311.017-311.020 reserved for expansion

SUBCHAPTER C. CONSTRUCTION OF STATUTES

GOVT §311.021. INTENTION IN ENACTMENT OF STATUTES

In enacting a statute, it is presumed that:

(1) compliance with the constitutions of this state and the United States is intended;

(2) the entire statute is intended to be effective;

(3) a just and reasonable result is intended;

(4) a result feasible of execution is intended; and

(5) public interest is favored over any private interest.

GOVT §311.022. PROSPECTIVE OPERATION OF STATUTES

A statute is presumed to be prospective in its operation unless expressly made retrospective.

GOVT §311.023. STATUTE CONSTRUCTION AIDS

In construing a statute, whether or not the statute is considered ambiguous on its face, a court may consider among other matters the:

(1) object sought to be attained;

(2) circumstances under which the statute was enacted;

(3) legislative history;

(4) common law or former statutory provisions, including laws on the same or similar subjects;

(5) consequences of a particular construction;

(6) administrative construction of the statute; and

(7) title (caption), preamble, and emergency provision.

GOVT §311.024. HEADINGS

The heading of a title, subtitle, chapter, subchapter, or section does not limit or expand the meaning of a statute.

GOVT §311.025. IRRECONCILABLE STATUTES & AMENDMENTS

(a) Except as provided by Section 311.031(d), if statutes enacted at the same or different sessions of the legislature are irreconcilable, the statute latest in date of enactment prevails.

(b) Except as provided by Section 311.031(d), if amendments to the same statute are enacted at the same session of the legislature, one amendment without reference to another, the amendments shall be harmonized, if possible, so that effect may be given to each. If the amendments are irreconcilable, the latest in date of enactment prevails.

(c) In determining whether amendments are irreconcilable, text that is reenacted because of the requirement of Article III, Section 36, of the Texas Constitution is not considered to be irreconcilable with additions or omissions in the same text made by another amendment. Unless clearly indicated to the contrary, an amendment that reenacts text in compliance with that constitutional requirement does not indicate legislative intent that the reenacted text prevail over changes in the same text made by another amendment, regardless of the relative dates of enactment.

(d) In this section, the date of enactment is the date on which the last legislative vote is taken on the bill enacting the statute.

(e) If the journals or other legislative records fail to disclose which of two or more bills in conflict is latest in date of enactment, the date of enactment of the respective bills is considered to be, in order of priority:

(1) the date on which the last presiding officer signed the bill;

(2) the date on which the governor signed the bill; or

(3) the date on which the bill became law by operation of law.

GOVT §311.026. SPECIAL OR LOCAL PROVISION PREVAILS OVER GENERAL

(a) If a general provision conflicts with a special or local provision, the provisions shall be construed, if possible, so that effect is given to both.

(b) If the conflict between the general provision and the special or local provision is irreconcilable, the special or local provision prevails as an exception to the general provision, unless the general provision is the later enactment and the manifest intent is that the general provision prevail.

GOVT §311.027. STATUTORY REFERENCES

Unless expressly provided otherwise, a reference to any portion of a statute or rule applies to all reenactments, revisions, or amendments of the statute or rule.

GOVT §311.028. UNIFORM CONSTRUCTION OF UNIFORM ACTS

A uniform act included in a code shall be construed to effect its general purpose to make uniform the law of those states that enact it.

GOVT §311.029. ENROLLED BILL CONTROLS

If the language of the enrolled bill version of a statute conflicts with the language of any subsequent printing or reprinting of the statute, the language of the enrolled bill version controls.

GOVT §311.030. REPEAL OF REPEALING STATUTE

The repeal of a repealing statute does not revive the statute originally repealed nor impair the effect of any saving provision in it.

GOVT §311.031. SAVING PROVISIONS

(a) Except as provided by Subsection (b), the reenactment, revision, amendment, or repeal of a statute does not affect:

(1) the prior operation of the statute or any prior action taken under it;

(2) any validation, cure, right, privilege, obligation, or liability previously acquired, accrued, accorded, or incurred under it;

(3) any violation of the statute or any penalty, forfeiture, or punishment incurred under the statute before its amendment or repeal; or

(4) any investigation, proceeding, or remedy concerning any privilege, obligation, liability, penalty, forfeiture, or punishment; and the investigation, proceeding, or remedy may be instituted, continued, or enforced, and the penalty, forfeiture, or punishment imposed, as if the statute had not been repealed or amended.

(b) If the penalty, forfeiture, or punishment for any offense is reduced by a reenactment, revision, or amendment of a statute, the penalty, forfeiture, or punishment, if not already imposed, shall be imposed according to the statute as amended.

(c) The repeal of a statute by a code does not affect an amendment, revision, or reenactment of the statute by the same legislature that enacted the code. The amendment, revision, or reenactment is preserved and given effect as part of the code provision that revised the statute so amended, revised, or reenacted.

(d) If any provision of a code conflicts with a statute enacted by the same legislature that enacted the code, the statute controls.

GOVT §311.032. SEVERABILITY OF STATUTES

(a) If any statute contains a provision for severability, that provision prevails in interpreting that statute.

(b) If any statute contains a provision for nonseverability, that provision prevails in interpreting that statute.

(c) In a statute that does not contain a provision for severability or nonseverability, if any provision of the statute or its application to any person or circumstance is held invalid, the invalidity does not affect other provisions or applications of the statute that can be given effect without the invalid provision or application, and to this end the provisions of the statute are severable.

GOVT §311.034. WAIVER OF SOVEREIGN IMMUNITY

In order to preserve the legislature's interest in managing state fiscal matters through the appropriations process, a statute shall not be construed as a waiver of sovereign immunity unless the waiver is effected by clear and unambiguous language. In a statute, the use of "person," as defined by Section 311.005 to include governmental entities, does not indicate legislative intent to waive sovereign immunity unless the con-

text of the statute indicates no other reasonable construction. Statutory prerequisites to a suit, including the provision of notice, are jurisdictional requirements in all suits against a governmental entity.

GOVT §311.035. CONSTRUCTION OF STATUTE OR RULE INVOLVING CRIMINAL OFFENSE OR PENALTY

(a) In this section, "actor" and "element of offense" have the meanings assigned by Section 1.07, Penal Code.

(b) Except as provided by Subsection (c), a statute or rule that creates or defines a criminal offense or penalty shall be construed in favor of the actor if any part of the statute or rule is ambiguous on its face or as applied to the case, including:

(1) an element of offense; or

(2) the penalty to be imposed.

(c) Subsection (b) does not apply to a criminal offense or penalty under the Penal Code or under the Texas Controlled Substances Act.

(d) The ambiguity of a part of a statute or rule to which this section applies is a matter of law to be resolved by the judge.

TITLE 4. EXECUTIVE BRANCH

SUBTITLE A. EXECUTIVE OFFICERS

CHAPTER 402. ATTORNEY GENERAL

SUBCHAPTER A. GENERAL PROVISIONS

GOVT §402.010. LEGAL CHALLENGES TO CONSTITUTIONALITY OF STATE STATUTES

(a) In an action in which a party to the litigation files a petition, motion, or other pleading challenging the constitutionality of a statute of this state, the party shall file the form required by Subsection (a-1). The court shall, if the attorney general is not a party to or counsel involved in the litigation, serve notice of the constitutional challenge and a copy of the petition, motion, or other pleading that raises the challenge on the attorney general either by certified or registered mail or electronically to an e-mail address designated by the attorney general for the purposes of this section.

(a-1) The Office of Court Administration of the Texas Judicial System shall adopt the form that a party challenging the constitutionality of a statute of this state must file with the court in which the action is pending indicating which pleading should be served on the attorney general in accordance with this section.

(b) A court may not enter a final judgment holding a statute of this state unconstitutional before the 45th day after the date notice required by Subsection (a) is served on the attorney general.

(c) A party's failure to file as required by Subsection (a) or a court's failure to serve notice as required by Subsection (a) does not deprive the court of jurisdiction or forfeit an otherwise timely filed claim or defense based on the challenge to the constitutionality of a statute of this state.

(d) This section or the state's intervention in litigation in response to notice under this section does not constitute a waiver of sovereign immunity.

TITLE 8. PUBLIC RETIREMENT SYSTEMS

SUBTITLE A. PROVISIONS GENERALLY APPLICABLE TO PUBLIC RETIREMENT SYSTEMS

CHAPTER 804. DOMESTIC RELATIONS ORDERS & SPOUSAL CONSENT

SUBCHAPTER A. QUALIFIED DOMESTIC RELATIONS ORDERS

GOVT §804.001. DEFINITIONS

In this chapter:

(1) "Alternate payee" means a spouse, former spouse, child, or other dependent of a member or retiree who is recognized by a domestic relations order as having a right to receive all or a portion of the benefits payable by a public retirement system with respect to such member or retiree.

(2) "Domestic relations order" means any judgment, decree, or order, including approval of a property settlement agreement, which relates to the provision of child support, alimony payments, or marital property rights to a spouse, former spouse, child, or other dependent of a member or retiree, and is made pursuant to a domestic relations law, including a community property law of the State of Texas or of another state.

(3) "Public retirement system" means the Employees Retirement System of Texas, the Judicial Retirement System of Texas Plan One, the Judicial Retirement System of Texas Plan Two, the Teacher Retirement System of Texas, the Texas County and District Retirement System, the Texas Municipal Retirement System, and any other continuing, organized program of service retirement, disability retirement, or death

benefits for officers or employees of the state or a political subdivision or of an agency or instrumentality of the state or a political subdivision and includes the optional retirement program governed by Chapter 830. Public retirement system does not include:

(A) a program, other than the optional retirement program, for which benefits are administered by a life insurance company;

(B) a program providing only workers' compensation benefits;

(C) a program administered by the federal government;

(D) an individual retirement account or individual retirement annuity within the meaning of Section 408, or a retirement bond within the meaning of Section 409, of the Internal Revenue Code of 1986;

(E) a plan described by Subsection (d) of Section 401 of the Internal Revenue Code of 1986;

(F) a group or an individual account plan consisting of an annuity contract described by Subsection (b) of Section 403 of the Internal Revenue Code of 1986, other than a 403(b) contract or plan under the optional retirement program;

(G) an eligible state deferred compensation plan described by Subsection (b) of Section 457 of the Internal Revenue Code of 1986; or

(H) the program established by Chapter 615.

(4) "Qualified domestic relations order" means a domestic relations order which creates or recognizes the existence of an alternate payee's right or assigns to an alternate payee the right to receive all or a portion of the benefits payable with respect to a member or retiree under a public retirement system, which directs the public retirement system to disburse benefits to the alternate payee, and which meets the requirements of Section 804.003.

(5) "Statewide retirement system" means the Employees Retirement System of Texas, the Judicial Retirement System of Texas Plan One, the Judicial Retirement System of Texas Plan Two, the Teacher Retirement System of Texas, the Texas County and District Retirement System, or the Texas Municipal Retirement System.

GOVT §804.002. APPLICATION OF CHAPTERS

This subchapter and Subchapter C apply to each statewide retirement system and to the optional retirement program governed by Chapter 830. This subchapter and Subchapter C also apply to each other public retirement system for which the board of trustees of the system elects to adopt the provisions of this subchapter and Subchapter C. An election under this section must be by order or resolution and need not set out the text of this subchapter or Subchapter C. A board of trustees may not elect to adopt only this subchapter or Subchapter C.

GOVT §804.003. QUALIFIED DOMESTIC RELATIONS ORDERS

(a) Sections 811.005, 821.005, 831.004, 836.004, 841.006, and 851.006 and any similar antialienation provisions contained in any other public retirement system shall apply to the creation, assignment, recognition, or enforcement of a right to any benefit payable with respect to a member or retiree of a public retirement system to which the section applies pursuant to a domestic relations order unless the order is determined to be a qualified domestic relations order.

(b) Except as provided in Subsection (d), the administrative head of a public retirement system to which this chapter applies and to which a domestic relations order is submitted or his designee has exclusive authority to determine whether a domestic relations order is a qualified domestic relations order. A determination by the administrative head or his designee under this section may be appealed only to the board of trustees of the public retirement system. An appeal to the board of trustees of a statewide retirement system is a contested case under Chapter 2001. However, the board of a statewide retirement system by rule may waive the requirement of an appeal to the board. On appeal of a decision made by the board of trustees or by the administrative head if there is no appeal to the board under this section, the standard of review is by substantial evidence.

(c) Except as provided in Subsection (d), a court does not have jurisdiction over a public retirement system to which this chapter applies with respect to a divorce or other domestic relations action in which an alternate payee's right to receive all or a portion of the benefits payable to a member or retiree under the public retirement system is created or established. A party to such an action who attempts to make a public retirement system a party to the action contrary to the provision of this subsection shall be liable to the public retirement system for its costs and attorney's fees.

(d) Under the optional retirement program, applicable carriers shall determine whether a domestic relations order is a qualified domestic relations order. If a dispute arises over the determination of whether a domestic relations order is a qualified domestic relations order which cannot be resolved by the procedure described in Subsection (g), the court which issued the order or which otherwise has jurisdiction over the matter shall resolve the dispute with respect to a divorce or other domestic relations action in which an alternate payee's right to receive all or a portion of the benefits payable to a member or retiree under the optional retirement program is created or established.

(e) For the purposes of this section, benefits payable with respect to a member or retiree under the retirement system include the types of benefits payable by a public retirement system and a withdrawal of contributions from a public retirement system.

(f) A domestic relations order is a qualified domestic relations order only if such order:

(1) clearly specifies the:

(A) name and last known mailing address of:

(i) the member or retiree; and

(ii) each alternate payee covered by the order; and

(B) social security number, or an express authorization for the parties to use an alternate method acceptable to the public retirement system to verify the social security number, of the member or retiree and each alternate payee covered by the order;

(2) clearly specifies the amount or percentage of the member's or retiree's benefits to be paid by a public retirement system to each such alternate payee or the manner in which such amount or percentage is to be determined;

(3) clearly specifies the number of payments or the period to which such order applies;

(4) clearly specifies that such order applies to a designated public retirement system;

(5) does not require the public retirement system to provide any type or form of benefit or any option not otherwise provided under the plan;

(6) does not require the public retirement system to provide increased benefits determined on the basis of actuarial value;

(7) does not require the payment of benefits to an alternate payee which are required to be paid to another alternate payee under another order previously determined to be a qualified domestic relations order; and

(8) does not require the payment of benefits to an alternate payee before the retirement of a member, the distribution of a withdrawal of contributions to a member, or other distribution to a member required by law.

(g) A public retirement system may reject a domestic relations order as a qualified domestic relations order unless the order:

(1) provides for a proportional reduction of the amount awarded to an alternate payee in the event of the retirement of the member before normal retirement age;

(2) does not purport to require the designation of a particular person as the recipient of benefits in the event of a member's or annuitant's death;

(3) does not purport to require the selection of a particular benefit payment plan or option;

(4) provides clearly for each possible benefit distribution under plan provisions;

(5) does not require any action on the part of the retirement system contrary to its governing statutes or plan provision other than the direct payment of the benefit awarded to an alternate payee;

(6) does not make the award of an interest contingent on any condition other than those conditions resulting in the liability of a retirement system for payments under its plan provisions;

(7) does not purport to award any future benefit increases that are provided or required by the legislature;

(8) provides for a proportional reduction of the amount awarded to an alternate payee in the event that benefits available to the retiree or member are reduced by law; and

(9) if required by the retirement system, conforms to a model order adopted by the retirement system.

(h) The administrative head of a public retirement system to which this chapter applies or his designee (or applicable carrier, if under the optional retirement program), upon receipt of a certified copy of a domestic relations order, shall determine whether such order is a qualified domestic relations order and shall notify the member or retiree and each alternate payee of such determination. If the order is determined to be a qualified domestic relations order, the public retirement system (or applicable carrier, if under the optional retirement

program), shall pay benefits in accordance with the order. If the order is determined not to be a qualified domestic relations order, the member or retiree or any alternate payee named in the order may appeal the administrative head's determination in the manner specified in Subsection (b) or the optional retirement program carrier's determination in the manner specified in Subsection (d) and may petition the court which issued the order to amend the order so that it will be qualified. The court which issued the order or which would otherwise have jurisdiction over the matter has jurisdiction to amend the order so that it will be qualified even though all other matters incident to the action or proceeding have been fully and finally adjudicated.

(i) During any period in which the issue of whether a domestic relations order is a qualified domestic relations order is being determined by the agency administrative head, his designee, the board of trustees, a court of competent jurisdiction, optional retirement program carrier, or otherwise, the public retirement system shall separately account for the amounts, in this section referred to as the "segregated amounts," which would have been payable to the alternate payee during such period if the order had been determined to be a qualified domestic relations order.

(j) If a domestic relations order is determined to be a qualified domestic relations order, then the public retirement system (or applicable carrier, if under the optional retirement program) shall pay the segregated amounts without interest to the person or persons entitled thereto and shall thereafter pay benefits pursuant to the order.

(k) If a domestic relations order is determined not to be a qualified domestic relations order or if within 18 months of the date a domestic relations order is received by the public retirement system (or applicable carrier, if under the optional retirement program) the issue as to whether such order is a qualified domestic relations order is not resolved, then the public retirement system (or applicable carrier, if under the optional retirement program) shall pay the segregated amounts without interest and shall thereafter pay benefits to the person or persons who would have been entitled to such amounts if there had been no order. This subsection shall not be construed to limit or otherwise affect any liability, responsibility, or duty of a party with respect to any other party to the action out of which the order arose.

(*l*) Any determination that an order is a qualified domestic relations order which is made after the close of the 18-month period shall be applied prospectively only.

(m) The public retirement system, the board of trustees, and officers and employees of the public retirement system (or applicable carrier, if under the optional retirement program) shall not be liable to any person for making payments of any benefits in accordance with a domestic relations order in a cause in which a member or a retiree was a party or for making payments in accordance with Subsection (k).

(n) The board of trustees of a public retirement system may promulgate rules it deems necessary to implement the provisions of this section.

(o) Except as specifically provided in this subtitle or by any other statute, public employment does not confer special privileges or immunities on a public employee. An ownership or beneficial interest in any retirement, pension, or other financial plan not included in the definition of "public retirement system" as set forth in Section 804.001 held in whole or in part by an officer or employee of the state or a political subdivision or of an agency or an instrumentality of either, whether obtained in connection with that employment or otherwise, shall be subject to the requirements of the federal laws governing qualified domestic relations orders.

(p) A public retirement system may assess administrative fees on a party who is subject to a domestic relations order for the review of the order under this subchapter and, as applicable, for the administration of payments under an order that is determined to be qualified. In addition to other methods of collecting fees that a retirement system may establish, the retirement system may deduct fees from payments made under the order.

See also 34 T.A.C. ch. 74.

GOVT §804.004. LIFE ANNUITY OR LUMP-SUM PAYMENT IN LIEU OF BENEFITS AWARDED BY A QUALIFIED DOMESTIC RELATIONS ORDER

(a) The board of trustees of a public retirement system to which this chapter applies may by rule provide that, in lieu of paying an alternate beneficiary the interest awarded by a qualified domestic relations or-

der, the system may pay the alternate beneficiary an amount that is the actuarial equivalent of such interest in the form of:

(1) an annuity payable in equal monthly installments for the life of the alternate payee; or

(2) a lump sum.

(b) The determination of whether to pay an amount authorized by this section in lieu of the interest awarded by the qualified domestic relations order shall be at the sole discretion of the public retirement system.

(c) If a public retirement system elects to pay the alternate payee pursuant to this section, the benefit payable by the system to the member, retiree, or beneficiary shall be reduced by the interest in the benefit awarded to the alternate payee by the qualified domestic relations order.

(d) If the public retirement system pays the alternate payee pursuant to this section, the retirement system shall be entitled to rely on a beneficiary designation or benefit option selection made or changed pursuant to its plan without regard to any domestic relations order.

GOVT §804.005. PAYMENT IN CERTAIN CIRCUMSTANCES IN LIEU OF BENEFITS AWARDED BY QUALIFIED DOMESTIC RELATIONS ORDER

(a) This section applies only to the Employees Retirement System of Texas and the Teacher Retirement System of Texas.

(b) A public retirement system to which this section applies shall pay an alternate payee of a member of the retirement system who is described by Subsection (c), if the alternate payee so elects and in lieu of the interest awarded by a qualified domestic relations order on or after January 1, 1985, an amount that is the alternate payee's portion of the actuarial equivalent of the accrued retirement benefit of the member of the retirement system, determined as if the member retired on the date of the alternate payee's election. The amount becomes payable at the time the actuarial equivalent is determined, and the amount is payable in the form of an annuity payable in equal monthly installments for the life of the alternate payee.

(c) A member whose benefits are subject to partial payment under this section is one who has not retired from the retirement system, has attained the greater of the age of 62 or normal retirement age and the service requirements for service retirement, and retains credit and contributions in the retirement system attributable to that service.

(d) If an alternate payee elects to be paid under this section, the retirement system shall reduce the benefit payable by the system to the member or the member's beneficiary by the alternate payee's portion of the actuarial equivalent determined under Subsection (b).

(e) In determining under Subsection (b) the actuarial equivalent of an accrued retirement benefit, the system shall consider the member's benefit as a normal age standard service retirement annuity, without regard to any optional annuity chosen or beneficiary designated by the member.

(f) The beginning of monthly payments under this section terminates any interest that the alternate payee who receives the payment might otherwise have in benefits that accrue to the account of the member after the date the initial payment to the alternate payee is made.

(g) A public retirement system may adopt rules for administration of this section.

Sections 804.006-804.050 reserved for expansion

SUBCHAPTER B. SPOUSAL CONSENT REQUIREMENTS

GOVT §804.051. AUTHORITY TO REQUIRE SPOUSAL CONSENT

A public retirement system may adopt rules to require spousal consent for the selection of a service retirement annuity other than a joint and survivor annuity that pays benefits to the member's spouse on the death of the member or for the selection of a death benefits plan that pays benefits in the form of an annuity to a person other than the member's spouse on the death of the member.

Sections 804.052-804.100 reserved for expansion

SUBCHAPTER C. TERMINATION OF INTEREST IN PUBLIC RETIREMENT SYSTEM

GOVT §804.101. TERMINATION OF INTEREST IN PUBLIC RETIREMENT SYSTEM

The death of an alternate payee as defined in Section 804.001 or the death of a spouse of a member or retiree of a public retirement system to which this chap-

ter applies shall terminate the interest of the alternate payee or spouse in that public retirement system. This section shall not affect an interest in a public retirement system accrued to an individual as a member of the public retirement system.

For the complete Penal Code with annotations, see the current edition of ***O'Connor's Texas Criminal Codes Plus***. To order, call 1-800-OCONNOR (1-800-626-6667) or visit www.oconnors.com.

TITLE 6. OFFENSES AGAINST THE FAMILY

TITLE 6. OFFENSES AGAINST THE FAMILY

CHAPTER 25. OFFENSES AGAINST THE FAMILY

PEN §25.01. BIGAMY

(a) An individual commits an offense if:

(1) he is legally married and he:

(A) purports to marry or does marry a person other than his spouse in this state, or any other state or foreign country, under circumstances that would, but for the actor's prior marriage, constitute a marriage; or

(B) lives with a person other than his spouse in this state under the appearance of being married; or

(2) he knows that a married person other than his spouse is married and he:

(A) purports to marry or does marry that person in this state, or any other state or foreign country, under circumstances that would, but for the person's prior marriage, constitute a marriage; or

(B) lives with that person in this state under the appearance of being married.

(b) For purposes of this section, "under the appearance of being married" means holding out that the parties are married with cohabitation and an intent to be married by either party.

(c) It is a defense to prosecution under Subsection (a)(1) that the actor reasonably believed at the time of the commission of the offense that the actor and the person whom the actor married or purported to marry or with whom the actor lived under the appearance of being married were legally eligible to be married because the actor's prior marriage was void or had been dissolved by death, divorce, or annulment. For purposes of this subsection, an actor's belief is reasonable if the belief is substantiated by a certified copy of a death certificate or other signed document issued by a court.

(d) For the purposes of this section, the lawful wife or husband of the actor may testify both for or against the actor concerning proof of the original marriage.

(e) An offense under this section is a felony of the third degree, except that if at the time of the commission of the offense, the person whom the actor marries or purports to marry or with whom the actor lives under the appearance of being married is:

(1) 17 years of age, the offense is a felony of the second degree; or

(2) 16 years of age or younger, the offense is a felony of the first degree.

See also *O'Connor's Texas Family Law Handbook* (2017), "Bigamy," ch. 3-C, §3.2, p. 288.

PEN §25.02. PROHIBITED SEXUAL CONDUCT

(a) A person commits an offense if the person engages in sexual intercourse or deviate sexual intercourse with another person the actor knows to be, without regard to legitimacy:

(1) the actor's ancestor or descendant by blood or adoption;

(2) the actor's current or former stepchild or stepparent;

(3) the actor's parent's brother or sister of the whole or half blood;

(4) the actor's brother or sister of the whole or half blood or by adoption;

(5) the children of the actor's brother or sister of the whole or half blood or by adoption; or

(6) the son or daughter of the actor's aunt or uncle of the whole or half blood or by adoption.

(b) For purposes of this section:

(1) "Deviate sexual intercourse" means any contact between the genitals of one person and the mouth or anus of another person with intent to arouse or gratify the sexual desire of any person.

(2) "Sexual intercourse" means any penetration of the female sex organ by the male sex organ.

(c) An offense under this section is a felony of the third degree, unless the offense is committed under Subsection (a)(1), in which event the offense is a felony of the second degree.

See also CCP arts. 38.071, 38.072, 38.37; Pen. Code §3.03; *O'Connor's Texas Family Law Handbook* (2017), "Parent engages in criminal conduct," ch. 4-H, §12.1.4, p. 631.

PEN §25.03. INTERFERENCE WITH CHILD CUSTODY

(a) A person commits an offense if the person takes or retains a child younger than 18 years of age:

(1) when the person knows that the person's taking or retention violates the express terms of a judgment or order, including a temporary order, of a court disposing of the child's custody;

(2) when the person has not been awarded custody of the child by a court of competent jurisdiction, knows that a suit for divorce or a civil suit or application for habeas corpus to dispose of the child's custody has been filed, and takes the child out of the geographic area of the counties composing the judicial district if the court is a district court or the county if the court is a statutory county court, without the permission of the court and with the intent to deprive the court of authority over the child; or

(3) outside of the United States with the intent to deprive a person entitled to possession of or access to the child of that possession or access and without the permission of that person.

(b) A noncustodial parent commits an offense if, with the intent to interfere with the lawful custody of a child younger than 18 years, the noncustodial parent knowingly entices or persuades the child to leave the custody of the custodial parent, guardian, or person standing in the stead of the custodial parent or guardian of the child.

(c) It is a defense to prosecution under Subsection (a)(2) that the actor returned the child to the geographic area of the counties composing the judicial district if the court is a district court or the county if the court is a statutory county court, within three days after the date of the commission of the offense.

(c-1) It is an affirmative defense to prosecution under Subsection (a)(3) that:

(1) the taking or retention of the child was pursuant to a valid order providing for possession of or access to the child; or

(2) notwithstanding any violation of a valid order providing for possession of or access to the child, the actor's retention of the child was due only to circumstances beyond the actor's control and the actor promptly provided notice or made reasonable attempts to provide notice of those circumstances to the other person entitled to possession of or access to the child.

(c-2) Subsection (a)(3) does not apply if, at the time of the offense, the person taking or retaining the child:

(1) was entitled to possession of or access to the child; and

(2) was fleeing the commission or attempted commission of family violence, as defined by Section 71.004, Family Code, against the child or the person.

(d) An offense under this section is a state jail felony.

See also *O'Connor's Texas Family Law Handbook* (2017), "Interfering with child custody," ch. 1-D, §3.3.1(7), p. 58.

PEN §25.031. AGREEMENT TO ABDUCT FROM CUSTODY

(a) A person commits an offense if the person agrees, for remuneration or the promise of remuneration, to abduct a child younger than 18 years of age by force, threat of force, misrepresentation, stealth, or unlawful entry, knowing that the child is under the care and control of a person having custody or physical possession of the child under a court order, including a temporary order, or under the care and control of another person who is exercising care and control with the consent of a person having custody or physical possession under a court order, including a temporary order.

(b) An offense under this section is a state jail felony.

PEN §25.04. ENTICING A CHILD

(a) A person commits an offense if, with the intent to interfere with the lawful custody of a child younger than 18 years, he knowingly entices, persuades, or takes the child from the custody of the parent or guardian or person standing in the stead of the parent or guardian of such child.

(b) An offense under this section is a Class B misdemeanor, unless it is shown on the trial of the offense that the actor intended to commit a felony against the child, in which event an offense under this section is a felony of the third degree.

PEN §25.05. CRIMINAL NONSUPPORT

(a) An individual commits an offense if the individual intentionally or knowingly fails to provide support for the individual's child younger than 18 years of age, or for the individual's child who is the subject of a court order requiring the individual to support the child.

(b) For purposes of this section, "child" includes a child born out of wedlock whose paternity has either been acknowledged by the actor or has been established in a civil suit under the Family Code or the law of another state.

(c) Under this section, a conviction may be had on the uncorroborated testimony of a party to the offense.

(d) It is an affirmative defense to prosecution under this section that the actor could not provide support for the actor's child.

(e) The pendency of a prosecution under this section does not affect the power of a court to enter an order for child support under the Family Code.

(f) An offense under this section is a state jail felony.

See also Fam. Code chs. 157, 232; Gov't Code §21.002(f); 42 U.S.C. §651 et seq.

PEN §25.06. HARBORING RUNAWAY CHILD

(a) A person commits an offense if he knowingly harbors a child and he is criminally negligent about whether the child:

(1) is younger than 18 years; and

(2) has escaped from the custody of a peace officer, a probation officer, the Texas Youth Council, or a detention facility for children, or is voluntarily absent from the child's home without the consent of the child's parent or guardian for a substantial length of time or without the intent to return.

(b) It is a defense to prosecution under this section that the actor was related to the child within the second degree by consanguinity or affinity, as determined under Chapter 573, Government Code.

(c) It is a defense to prosecution under this section that the actor notified:

(1) the person or agency from which the child escaped or a law enforcement agency of the presence of the child within 24 hours after discovering that the child had escaped from custody; or

(2) a law enforcement agency or a person at the child's home of the presence of the child within 24 hours after discovering that the child was voluntarily absent from home without the consent of the child's parent or guardian.

(d) An offense under this section is a Class A misdemeanor.

(e) On the receipt of a report from a peace officer, probation officer, the Texas Youth Council, a foster home, or a detention facility for children that a child has escaped its custody or upon receipt of a report from a parent, guardian, conservator, or legal custodian that a child is missing, a law enforcement agency shall immediately enter a record of the child into the National Crime Information Center.

Ⓐ PEN §25.07. VIOLATION OF CERTAIN COURT ORDERS OR CONDITIONS OF BOND IN A FAMILY VIOLENCE, CHILD ABUSE OR NEGLECT, SEXUAL ASSAULT OR ABUSE, STALKING, OR TRAFFICKING CASE

(a) A person commits an offense if, in violation of a condition of bond set in a family violence, sexual assault or abuse, stalking, or trafficking case and related to the safety of a victim or the safety of the community, an order issued under Chapter 7A, Code of Criminal Procedure, an order issued under Article 17.292, Code of Criminal Procedure, an order issued under Section 6.504, Family Code, Chapter 83, Family Code, if the temporary ex parte order has been served on the person, [or] Chapter 85, Family Code, or Subchapter F, Chapter 261, Family Code, or an order issued by another jurisdiction as provided by Chapter 88, Family Code, the person knowingly or intentionally:

(1) commits family violence or an act in furtherance of an offense under Section 20A.02, 22.011, 22.021, or 42.072;

(2) communicates:

(A) directly with a protected individual or a member of the family or household in a threatening or harassing manner;

(B) a threat through any person to a protected individual or a member of the family or household; or

(C) in any manner with the protected individual or a member of the family or household except through the person's attorney or a person appointed by the court, if the violation is of an order described by this subsection and the order prohibits any communication with a protected individual or a member of the family or household;

(3) goes to or near any of the following places as specifically described in the order or condition of bond:

(A) the residence or place of employment or business of a protected individual or a member of the family or household; or

(B) any child care facility, residence, or school where a child protected by the order or condition of bond normally resides or attends;

(4) possesses a firearm;

(5) harms, threatens, or interferes with the care, custody, or control of a pet, companion animal, or assistance animal that is possessed by a person protected by the order or condition of bond; or

(6) removes, attempts to remove, or otherwise tampers with the normal functioning of a global positioning monitoring system.

(a-1) For purposes of Subsection (a)(5), possession of a pet, companion animal, or assistance animal by a person means:

(1) actual care, custody, control, or management of a pet, companion animal, or assistance animal by the person; or

(2) constructive possession of a pet, companion animal, or assistance animal owned by the person or for which the person has been the primary caregiver.

(b) For the purposes of this section:

(1) "Family violence," "family," "household," and "member of a household" have the meanings assigned by Chapter 71, Family Code.

(2) "Firearm" has the meaning assigned by Chapter 46.

(2-a) "Global positioning monitoring system" has the meaning assigned by Article 17.49, Code of Criminal Procedure.

(3) "Assistance animal" has the meaning assigned by Section 121.002, Human Resources Code.

(4) "Sexual abuse" means any act as described by Section 21.02 or 21.11.

(5) "Sexual assault" means any act as described by Section 22.011 or 22.021.

(6) "Stalking" means any conduct that constitutes an offense under Section 42.072.

(7) "Trafficking" means any conduct that constitutes an offense under Section 20A.02.

(c) If conduct constituting an offense under this section also constitutes an offense under another section of this code, the actor may be prosecuted under either section or under both sections.

(d) Reconciliatory actions or agreements made by persons affected by an order do not affect the validity of the order or the duty of a peace officer to enforce this section.

(e) A peace officer investigating conduct that may constitute an offense under this section for a violation of an order may not arrest a person protected by that order for a violation of that order.

(f) It is not a defense to prosecution under this section that certain information has been excluded, as provided by Section 85.007, Family Code, or Article 17.292, Code of Criminal Procedure, from an order to which this section applies.

(g) An offense under this section is a Class A misdemeanor, except the offense is a felony of the third degree if it is shown on the trial of the offense that the defendant:

(1) has previously been convicted two or more times of an offense under this section or two or more times of an offense under Section 25.072, or has previously been convicted of an offense under this section and an offense under Section 25.072; or

(2) has violated the order or condition of bond by committing an assault or the offense of stalking.

2017 Legislation: Amended by H.B. 7, §§68, 69, 85th Leg., eff. Sept. 1, 2017.

Section 25.071 omitted by editor

A PEN §25.072. REPEATED VIOLATION OF CERTAIN COURT ORDERS OR CONDITIONS OF BOND IN FAMILY VIOLENCE, CHILD ABUSE OR NEGLECT, SEXUAL ASSAULT OR ABUSE, STALKING, OR TRAFFICKING CASE

(a) A person commits an offense if, during a period that is 12 months or less in duration, the person two or more times engages in conduct that constitutes an offense under Section 25.07.

(b) If the jury is the trier of fact, members of the jury must agree unanimously that the defendant, during a period that is 12 months or less in duration, two or more times engaged in conduct that constituted an offense under Section 25.07.

(c) A defendant may not be convicted in the same criminal action of another offense an element of which is any conduct that is alleged as an element of the offense under Subsection (a) unless the other offense:

(1) is charged in the alternative;

(2) occurred outside the period in which the offense alleged under Subsection (a) was committed; or

(3) is considered by the trier of fact to be a lesser included offense of the offense alleged under Subsection (a).

(d) A defendant may not be charged with more than one count under Subsection (a) if all of the specific conduct that is alleged to have been engaged in is alleged to have been committed in violation of a single court order or single setting of bond.

(e) An offense under this section is a felony of the third degree.

2017 Legislation: Amended by H.B. 7, §70, 85th Leg., eff. Sept. 1, 2017.

PEN §25.08. SALE OR PURCHASE OF CHILD

(a) A person commits an offense if he:

(1) possesses a child younger than 18 years of age or has the custody, conservatorship, or guardianship of a child younger than 18 years of age, whether or not he has actual possession of the child, and he offers to accept, agrees to accept, or accepts a thing of value for the delivery of the child to another or for the possession of the child by another for purposes of adoption; or

(2) offers to give, agrees to give, or gives a thing of value to another for acquiring or maintaining the possession of a child for the purpose of adoption.

(b) It is an exception to the application of this section that the thing of value is:

(1) a fee or reimbursement paid to a child-placing agency as authorized by law;

(2) a fee paid to an attorney, social worker, mental health professional, or physician for services rendered in the usual course of legal or medical practice or in providing adoption counseling;

(3) a reimbursement of legal or medical expenses incurred by a person for the benefit of the child; or

(4) a necessary pregnancy-related expense paid by a child-placing agency for the benefit of the child's parent during the pregnancy or after the birth of the child as permitted by the minimum standards for child-placing agencies and Department of Protective and Regulatory Services rules.

(c) An offense under this section is a felony of the third degree, except that the offense is a felony of the second degree if the actor commits the offense with intent to commit an offense under Section 20A.02, 43.02, 43.05, or 43.25.

E PEN §25.081. UNREGULATED CUSTODY TRANSFER OF ADOPTED CHILD

(a) In this section:

(1) "Adopted child" means a person younger than 18 years of age who was legally adopted through a governmental entity or through private means, including a person who is in foster care or from a foreign country at the time of the adoption.

(2) "Unregulated custody transfer" means the transfer of the permanent physical custody of an adopted child by the parent, managing conservator, or guardian of the child without receiving approval of the transfer by a court as required by Section 162.026, Family Code.

(b) Except as otherwise provided by this section, a person commits an offense if the person knowingly:

(1) conducts an unregulated custody transfer of an adopted child; or

(2) facilitates or participates in the unregulated custody transfer of an adopted child, including by transferring, recruiting, harboring, transporting, providing, soliciting, or obtaining an adopted child for that purpose.

(c) An offense under this section is a felony of the third degree, except that the offense is a felony of the second degree if the actor commits the offense with intent to commit an offense under Section 20A.02, 43.02, 43.05, 43.25, 43.251, or 43.26.

(d) This section does not apply to:

(1) the placement of an adopted child with a licensed child-placing agency, the Department of Family and Protective Services, or an adult relative, stepparent, or other adult with a significant and long-standing relationship to the child;

(2) the placement of an adopted child by a licensed child-placing agency or the Department of Family and Protective Services;

(3) the temporary placement of an adopted child by the child's parent, managing conservator, or guardian for a designated short-term period with a specified intent and period for return of the child due to temporary circumstances, including:

(A) a vacation;

(B) a school-sponsored function or activity; or

(C) the incarceration, military service, medical treatment, or incapacity of the parent, managing conservator, or guardian;

(4) the placement of an adopted child in another state in accordance with the requirements of Subchapter B, Chapter 162, Family Code; or

(5) the voluntary delivery of an adopted child under Subchapter D, Chapter 262, Family Code.

2017 Legislation: Enacted by H.B. 834, §3, 85th Leg., eff. Sept. 1, 2017.

A PEN §25.09. ADVERTISING FOR PLACEMENT OF CHILD

The amended text in §25.09 is effective for offenses committed on or after Sept. 1, 2017. Offenses in which any element of the offense was committed before Sept. 1, 2017, are governed by the former law in effect at that time.

(a) A person commits an offense if the person advertises in the public media that the person will place, ~~[a child for adoption or will]~~ provide, or obtain a child for adoption or any other form of permanent physical custody of the child.

(b) This section does not apply to a licensed child-placing agency that is identified in the advertisement as a licensed child-placing agency.

(c) An offense under this section is a Class A misdemeanor unless the person has been convicted previously under this section, in which event the offense is a felony of the third degree.

(d) In this section:

(1) "Child" has the meaning assigned by Section 101.003, Family Code.

(2) "Public media" has the meaning assigned by Section 38.01. The term also includes communications through the use of the Internet or another public computer network.

2017 Legislation: Amended by H.B. 834, §4, 85th Leg., eff. Sept. 1, 2017.

Section 25.10 omitted by editor

PEN §25.11. CONTINUOUS VIOLENCE AGAINST THE FAMILY

(a) A person commits an offense if, during a period that is 12 months or less in duration, the person two or more times engages in conduct that constitutes an offense under Section 22.01(a)(1) against another person or persons whose relationship to or association with the defendant is described by Section 71.0021(b), 71.003, or 71.005, Family Code.

(b) If the jury is the trier of fact, members of the jury are not required to agree unanimously on the specific conduct in which the defendant engaged that constituted an offense under Section 22.01(a)(1) against the person or persons described by Subsection (a) or the exact date when that conduct occurred. The jury must agree unanimously that the defendant, during a period that is 12 months or less in duration, two or more times engaged in conduct that constituted an offense under Section 22.01(a)(1) against the person or persons described by Subsection (a).

(c) A defendant may not be convicted in the same criminal action of another offense the victim of which is an alleged victim of the offense under Subsection (a) and an element of which is any conduct that is alleged as an element of the offense under Subsection (a) unless the other offense:

(1) is charged in the alternative;

(2) occurred outside the period in which the offense alleged under Subsection (a) was committed; or

(3) is considered by the trier of fact to be a lesser included offense of the offense alleged under Subsection (a).

(d) A defendant may not be charged with more than one count under Subsection (a) if all of the specific conduct that is alleged to have been engaged in is alleged to have been committed against a single victim or members of the same household, as defined by Section 71.005, Family Code.

(e) An offense under this section is a felony of the third degree.

TITLE 9. OFFENSES AGAINST PUBLIC ORDER & DECENCY

CHAPTER 42. DISORDERLY CONDUCT & RELATED OFFENSES

A PEN §42.07. HARASSMENT

The amended text in §42.07 is effective for offenses committed or conduct violating a penal law on or after Sept. 1, 2017. Offenses committed or conduct that occurs in which any element of the offense was committed or the conduct occurred before Sept. 1, 2017, is governed by the former law in effect at that time.

(a) A person commits an offense if, with intent to harass, annoy, alarm, abuse, torment, or embarrass another, the person:

(1) initiates communication and in the course of the communication makes a comment, request, suggestion, or proposal that is obscene;

(2) threatens, in a manner reasonably likely to alarm the person receiving the threat, to inflict bodily injury on the person or to commit a felony against the person, a member of the person's family or household, or the person's property;

(3) conveys, in a manner reasonably likely to alarm the person receiving the report, a false report, which is known by the conveyor to be false, that another person has suffered death or serious bodily injury;

(4) causes the telephone of another to ring repeatedly or makes repeated telephone communications anonymously or in a manner reasonably likely to harass, annoy, alarm, abuse, torment, embarrass, or offend another;

(5) makes a telephone call and intentionally fails to hang up or disengage the connection;

(6) knowingly permits a telephone under the person's control to be used by another to commit an offense under this section; or

(7) sends repeated electronic communications in a manner reasonably likely to harass, annoy, alarm, abuse, torment, embarrass, or offend another.

(b) In this section:

(1) "Electronic communication" means a transfer of signs, signals, writing, images, sounds, data, or intelligence of any nature transmitted in whole or in part by a wire, radio, electromagnetic, photoelectronic, or photo-optical system. The term includes:

(A) a communication initiated through the use of [by] electronic mail, instant message, network call, a cellular or other type of telephone, a computer, a camera, text message, a social media platform or application, an Internet website, any other Internet-based communication tool, or facsimile machine; and

(B) a communication made to a pager.

(2) "Family" and "household" have the meaning assigned by Chapter 71, Family Code.

(3) "Obscene" means containing a patently offensive description of or a solicitation to commit an ultimate sex act, including sexual intercourse, masturbation, cunnilingus, fellatio, or anilingus, or a description of an excretory function.

(c) An offense under this section is a Class B misdemeanor, except that the offense is a Class A misdemeanor if:

(1) the actor has previously been convicted under this section; or

(2) the offense was committed under Subsection (a)(7) and:

(A) the offense was committed against a child under 18 years of age with the intent that the child:

(i) commit suicide; or

(ii) engage in conduct causing serious bodily injury to the child; or

(B) the actor has previously violated a temporary restraining order or injunction issued under Chapter 129A, Civil Practice and Remedies Code.

2017 Legislation: Amended by S.B. 179, §§13, 14, 85th Leg., eff. Sept. 1, 2017.

PEN §42.072. STALKING

(a) A person commits an offense if the person, on more than one occasion and pursuant to the same scheme or course of conduct that is directed specifically at another person, knowingly engages in conduct that:

(1) constitutes an offense under Section 42.07, or that the actor knows or reasonably should know the other person will regard as threatening:

(A) bodily injury or death for the other person;

(B) bodily injury or death for a member of the other person's family or household or for an individual with whom the other person has a dating relationship; or

(C) that an offense will be committed against the other person's property;

(2) causes the other person, a member of the other person's family or household, or an individual with

whom the other person has a dating relationship to be placed in fear of bodily injury or death or in fear that an offense will be committed against the other person's property, or to feel harassed, annoyed, alarmed, abused, tormented, embarrassed, or offended; and

(3) would cause a reasonable person to:

(A) fear bodily injury or death for himself or herself;

(B) fear bodily injury or death for a member of the person's family or household or for an individual with whom the person has a dating relationship;

(C) fear that an offense will be committed against the person's property; or

(D) feel harassed, annoyed, alarmed, abused, tormented, embarrassed, or offended.

(b) An offense under this section is a felony of the third degree, except that the offense is a felony of the second degree if the actor has previously been convicted of an offense under this section or of an offense under any of the following laws that contains elements that are substantially similar to the elements of an offense under this section:

(1) the laws of another state;

(2) the laws of a federally recognized Indian tribe;

(3) the laws of a territory of the United States; or

(4) federal law.

(c) For purposes of this section, a trier of fact may find that different types of conduct described by Subsection (a), if engaged in on more than one occasion, constitute conduct that is engaged in pursuant to the same scheme or course of conduct.

(d) In this section:

(1) "Dating relationship," "family," "household," and "member of a household" have the meanings assigned by Chapter 71, Family Code.

(2) "Property" includes a pet, companion animal, or assistance animal, as defined by Section 121.002, Human Resources Code.

TITLE 10. OFFENSES AGAINST PUBLIC HEALTH, SAFETY, & MORALS

CHAPTER 46. WEAPONS

PEN §46.04. UNLAWFUL POSSESSION OF FIREARM

(a) A person who has been convicted of a felony commits an offense if he possesses a firearm:

(1) after conviction and before the fifth anniversary of the person's release from confinement following conviction of the felony or the person's release from supervision under community supervision, parole, or mandatory supervision, whichever date is later; or

(2) after the period described by Subdivision (1), at any location other than the premises at which the person lives.

(b) A person who has been convicted of an offense under Section 22.01, punishable as a Class A misdemeanor and involving a member of the person's family or household, commits an offense if the person possesses a firearm before the fifth anniversary of the later of:

(1) the date of the person's release from confinement following conviction of the misdemeanor; or

(2) the date of the person's release from community supervision following conviction of the misdemeanor.

(c) A person, other than a peace officer, as defined by Section 1.07, actively engaged in employment as a sworn, full-time paid employee of a state agency or political subdivision, who is subject to an order issued under Section 6.504 or Chapter 85, Family Code, under Article 17.292 or Chapter 7A, Code of Criminal Procedure, or by another jurisdiction as provided by Chapter 88, Family Code, commits an offense if the person possesses a firearm after receiving notice of the order and before expiration of the order.

(d) In this section, "family," "household," and "member of a household" have the meanings assigned by Chapter 71, Family Code.

(e) An offense under Subsection (a) is a felony of the third degree. An offense under Subsection (b) or (c) is a Class A misdemeanor.

(f) For the purposes of this section, an offense under the laws of this state, another state, or the United States is, except as provided by Subsection (g), a felony if, at the time it is committed, the offense:

(1) is designated by a law of this state as a felony;

(2) contains all the elements of an offense designated by a law of this state as a felony; or

(3) is punishable by confinement for one year or more in a penitentiary.

(g) An offense is not considered a felony for purposes of Subsection (f) if, at the time the person possesses a firearm, the offense:

(1) is not designated by a law of this state as a felony; and

(2) does not contain all the elements of any offense designated by a law of this state as a felony.

For the complete Code of Criminal Procedure with annotations, see the current edition of ***O'Connor's Texas Criminal Codes Plus***. To order, call 1-800-OCONNOR (1-800-626-6667) or visit www.oconnors.com.

TITLE 1

TITLE 1

CHAPTER 5. FAMILY VIOLENCE PREVENTION

ART. 5.01. LEGISLATIVE STATEMENT

(a) Family violence is a serious danger and threat to society and its members. Victims of family violence are entitled to the maximum protection from harm or abuse or the threat of harm or abuse as is permitted by law.

(b) In any law enforcement, prosecutorial, or judicial response to allegations of family violence, the responding law enforcement or judicial officers shall protect the victim, without regard to the relationship between the alleged offender and victim.

ART. 5.02. DEFINITIONS

In this chapter, "family violence," "family," "household," and "member of a household" have the meanings assigned by Chapter 71, Family Code.

ART. 5.03. FAMILY OR HOUSEHOLD RELATIONSHIP DOES NOT CREATE AN EXCEPTION TO OFFICIAL DUTIES

A general duty prescribed for an officer by Chapter 2 of this code is not waived or excepted in any family violence case or investigation because of a family or household relationship between an alleged violator and the victim of family violence. A peace officer's or a magistrate's duty to prevent the commission of criminal offenses, including acts of family violence, is not waived or excepted because of a family or household relationship between the potential violator and victim.

ART. 5.04. DUTIES OF PEACE OFFICERS

(a) The primary duties of a peace officer who investigates a family violence allegation or who responds to a disturbance call that may involve family violence are to protect any potential victim of family violence, enforce the law of this state, enforce a protective order from another jurisdiction as provided by Chapter 88, Family Code, and make lawful arrests of violators.

(a-1) A peace officer who investigates a family violence allegation or who responds to a disturbance call that may involve family violence shall determine whether the address of the persons involved in the allegation or call matches the address of a current licensed foster home or verified agency foster home listed in the Texas Crime Information Center.

(b) A peace officer who investigates a family violence allegation or who responds to a disturbance call that may involve family violence shall advise any possible adult victim of all reasonable means to prevent further family violence, including giving written notice of a victim's legal rights and remedies and of the availability of shelter or other community services for family violence victims.

(c) A written notice required by Subsection (b) of this article is sufficient if it is in substantially the following form with the required information in English and in Spanish inserted in the notice:

"NOTICE TO ADULT VICTIMS OF FAMILY VIOLENCE

"It is a crime for any person to cause you any physical injury or harm EVEN IF THAT PERSON IS A MEMBER OR FORMER MEMBER OF YOUR FAMILY OR HOUSEHOLD.

"Please tell the investigating peace officer:

"IF you, your child, or any other household resident has been injured; or

"IF you feel you are going to be in danger when the officer leaves or later.

"You have the right to:

"ASK the local prosecutor to file a criminal complaint against the person committing family violence; and

"APPLY to a court for an order to protect you (you should consult a legal aid office, a prosecuting attorney, or a private attorney). If a family or household member assaults you and is arrested, you may request that a magistrate's order for emergency protection be issued. Please inform the investigating officer if you want an order for emergency protection. You need not be present when the order is issued. You cannot be charged a fee by a court in connection with filing, serving, or entering a protective order. For example, the court can enter an order that:

"(1) the abuser not commit further acts of violence;

"(2) the abuser not threaten, harass, or contact you at home;

"(3) directs the abuser to leave your household; and

"(4) establishes temporary custody of the children and directs the abuser not to interfere with the children or any property.

"A VIOLATION OF CERTAIN PROVISIONS OF COURT-ORDERED PROTECTION (such as (1) and (2) above) MAY BE A FELONY.

"CALL THE FOLLOWING VIOLENCE SHELTERS OR SOCIAL ORGANIZATIONS IF YOU NEED PROTECTION:

"________________

"________________."

See also *O'Connor's Texas Family Law Handbook* (2017), "Duties of Law Enforcement," ch. 6-E, p. 770.

ART. 5.045. STANDBY ASSISTANCE; LIABILITY

(a) In the discretion of a peace officer, the officer may stay with a victim of family violence to protect the victim and allow the victim to take the personal property of the victim or of a child in the care of the victim to a place of safety in an orderly manner.

(b) A peace officer who provides assistance under Subsection (a) of this article is not:

(1) civilly liable for an act or omission of the officer that arises in connection with providing the assistance or determining whether to provide the assistance; or

(2) civilly or criminally liable for the wrongful appropriation of any personal property by the victim.

ART. 5.05. REPORTS & RECORDS

(a) A peace officer who investigates a family violence incident or who responds to a disturbance call that may involve family violence shall make a written report, including but not limited to:

(1) the names of the suspect and complainant;

(2) the date, time, and location of the incident;

(3) any visible or reported injuries;

(4) a description of the incident and a statement of its disposition; and

(5) whether the suspect is a member of the state military forces or is serving in the armed forces of the United States in an active-duty status.

(a-1) In addition to the written report required under Subsection (a), a peace officer who investigates a family violence incident or who responds to a disturbance call that may involve family violence shall make a report to the Department of Family and Protective Services if the location of the incident or call, or the known address of a person involved in the incident or call, matches the address of a current licensed foster home or a verified agency foster home as listed in the Texas Crime Information Center. The report under this subsection may be made orally or electronically and must:

(1) include the information required by Subsection (a); and

(2) be filed with the Department of Family and Protective Services within 24 hours of the beginning of the investigation or receipt of the disturbance call.

(a-2) If a suspect is identified as being a member of the military, as described by Subsection (a)(5), the peace officer shall provide written notice of the incident or disturbance call to the staff judge advocate at Joint Force Headquarters or the provost marshal of the military installation to which the suspect is assigned with the intent that the commanding officer will be notified, as applicable.

(b) Each local law enforcement agency shall establish a departmental code for identifying and retrieving family violence reports as outlined in Subsection (a) of this section. A district or county attorney or an assistant district or county attorney exercising authority in the county where the law enforcement agency maintains records under this section is entitled to access to the records. The Department of Family and Protective Ser-

vices is entitled to access the records relating to any person who is 14 years of age or older and who resides in a licensed foster home or a verified agency foster home.

(c) In order to ensure that officers responding to calls are aware of the existence and terms of protective orders, each municipal police department and sheriff shall establish procedures within the department or office to provide adequate information or access to information for law enforcement officers of the names of persons protected by a protective order and of persons to whom protective orders are directed.

(d) Each law enforcement officer shall accept a certified copy of an original or modified protective order as proof of the validity of the order and it is presumed the order remains valid unless:

(1) the order contains a termination date that has passed;

(2) it is more than one year after the date the order was issued; or

(3) the law enforcement officer has been notified by the clerk of the court vacating the order that the order has been vacated.

(e) A peace officer who makes a report under Subsection (a) of this article shall provide information concerning the incident or disturbance to the bureau of identification and records of the Department of Public Safety for its recordkeeping function under Section 411.042, Government Code. The bureau shall prescribe the form and nature of the information required to be reported to the bureau by this article.

(f) On request of a victim of an incident of family violence, the local law enforcement agency responsible for investigating the incident shall provide the victim, at no cost to the victim, with any information that is:

(1) contained in the written report prepared under Subsection (a);

(2) described by Subsection (a)(1) or (2); and

(3) not exempt from disclosure under Chapter 552, Government Code, or other law.

See *O'Connor's Texas Family Law Handbook* (2017), "Report investigation," ch. 6-E, §2.4, p. 771.

ART. 5.06. DUTIES OF PROSECUTING ATTORNEYS & COURTS

(a) Neither a prosecuting attorney nor a court may:

(1) dismiss or delay any criminal proceeding that involves a prosecution for an offense that constitutes family violence because a civil proceeding is pending or not pending; or

(2) require proof that a complaining witness, victim, or defendant is a party to a suit for the dissolution of a marriage or a suit affecting the parent-child relationship before presenting a criminal allegation to a grand jury, filing an information, or otherwise proceeding with the prosecution of a criminal case.

(b) A prosecuting attorney's decision to file an application for a protective order under Chapter 71, Family Code, should be made without regard to whether a criminal complaint has been filed by the applicant. A prosecuting attorney may require the applicant to provide information for an offense report, relating to the facts alleged in the application, with a local law enforcement agency.

(c) The prosecuting attorney having responsibility under Section 71.04(c), Family Code, for filing applications for protective orders under Chapter 71, Family Code, shall provide notice of those responsibilities[1] to all law enforcement agencies within the jurisdiction of the prosecuting attorney for the prosecuting attorney.

1. **Editor's note:** Acts 1995, 74th Leg., ch. 564, §2 (eff. Sept. 1, 1995) uses "that responsibility."

ART. 5.07. VENUE FOR PROTECTIVE ORDER OFFENSES

The venue for an offense under Section 25.07 or 25.072, Penal Code, is in the county in which the order was issued or, without regard to the identity or location of the court that issued the protective order, in the county in which the offense was committed.

ART. 5.08. MEDIATION IN FAMILY VIOLENCE CASES

Notwithstanding Article 26.13(g) or 42A.301(15), in a criminal prosecution arising from family violence, as that term is defined by Section 71.004, Family Code, a court shall not refer or order the victim or the defendant involved to mediation, dispute resolution, arbitration, or other similar procedures.

CHAPTER 6. PREVENTING OFFENSES BY THE ACT OF MAGISTRATES & OTHER OFFICERS; EDUCATION CONCERNING CONSEQUENCES OF CERTAIN OFFENSES

ART. 6.09. STALKING PROTECTIVE ORDER

(a) At any proceeding related to an offense under Section 42.072, Penal Code, in which the defendant appears before the court, a person may request the court to render a protective order under Title 4, Family Code,

for the protection of the person. The request is made by filing "An Application for a Protective Order" in the same manner as an application for a protective order under Title 4, Family Code.

(b) The court shall render a protective order in the manner provided by Title 4, Family Code, if, in lieu of the finding that family violence occurred and is likely to occur in the future as required by Section 85.001, Family Code, the court finds that probable cause exists to believe that an offense under Section 42.072, Penal Code, occurred and that the nature of the scheme or course of conduct engaged in by the defendant in the commission of the offense indicates that the defendant is likely to engage in the future in conduct prohibited by Section 42.072(a)(1), (2), or (3), Penal Code.

(c) The procedure for the enforcement of a protective order under Title 4, Family Code, applies to the fullest extent practicable to the enforcement of a protective order under this article, including provisions relating to findings, contents, duration, warning, delivery, law enforcement duties, and modification.

See also *O'Connor's Texas Family Law Handbook* (2017), "Stalking," ch. 6-D, §2.4.5(5), p. 763.

CHAPTER 14. ARREST WITHOUT WARRANT

ART. 14.03. AUTHORITY OF PEACE OFFICERS

(a) Any peace officer may arrest, without warrant:

(1) persons found in suspicious places and under circumstances which reasonably show that such persons have been guilty of some felony, violation of Title 9, Chapter 42, Penal Code, breach of the peace, or offense under Section 49.02, Penal Code, or threaten, or are about to commit some offense against the laws;

(2) persons who the peace officer has probable cause to believe have committed an assault resulting in bodily injury to another person and the peace officer has probable cause to believe that there is danger of further bodily injury to that person;

(3) persons who the peace officer has probable cause to believe have committed an offense defined by Section 25.07, Penal Code, if the offense is not committed in the presence of the peace officer;

(4) persons who the peace officer has probable cause to believe have committed an offense involving family violence;

(5) persons who the peace officer has probable cause to believe have prevented or interfered with an individual's ability to place a telephone call in an emergency, as defined by Section 42.062(d), Penal Code, if the offense is not committed in the presence of the peace officer; or

(6) a person who makes a statement to the peace officer that would be admissible against the person under Article 38.21 and establishes probable cause to believe that the person has committed a felony.

(b) A peace officer shall arrest, without a warrant, a person the peace officer has probable cause to believe has committed an offense under Section 25.07, Penal Code, if the offense is committed in the presence of the peace officer.

(c) If reasonably necessary to verify an allegation of a violation of a protective order or of the commission of an offense involving family violence, a peace officer shall remain at the scene of the investigation to verify the allegation and to prevent the further commission of the violation or of family violence.

(d) A peace officer who is outside his jurisdiction may arrest, without warrant, a person who commits an offense within the officer's presence or view, if the offense is a felony, a violation of Chapter 42 or 49, Penal Code, or a breach of the peace. A peace officer making an arrest under this subsection shall, as soon as practicable after making the arrest, notify a law enforcement agency having jurisdiction where the arrest was made. The law enforcement agency shall then take custody of the person committing the offense and take the person before a magistrate in compliance with Article 14.06 of this code.

(e) The justification for conduct provided under Section 9.21, Penal Code, applies to a peace officer when the peace officer is performing a duty required by this article.

(f) In this article, "family violence" has the meaning assigned by Section 71.004, Family Code.

(g)(1) A peace officer listed in Subdivision (1), (2), or (5), Article 2.12, who is licensed under Chapter 1701, Occupations Code, and is outside of the officer's jurisdiction may arrest without a warrant a person who commits any offense within the officer's presence or view, other than a violation of Subtitle C, Title 7, Transportation Code.

(2) A peace officer listed in Subdivision (3), Article 2.12, who is licensed under Chapter 1701, Occupations Code, and is outside of the officer's jurisdiction may arrest without a warrant a person who commits any of-

fense within the officer's presence or view, except that an officer described in this subdivision who is outside of that officer's jurisdiction may arrest a person for a violation of Subtitle C, Title 7, Transportation Code, only if the offense is committed in the county or counties in which the municipality employing the peace officer is located.

(3) A peace officer making an arrest under this subsection shall as soon as practicable after making the arrest notify a law enforcement agency having jurisdiction where the arrest was made. The law enforcement agency shall then take custody of:

(A) the person committing the offense and take the person before a magistrate in compliance with Article 14.06; and

(B) any property seized during or after the arrest as if the property had been seized by a peace officer of that law enforcement agency.

CHAPTER 17. BAIL

ART. 17.29. ACCUSED LIBERATED

(a) When the accused has given the required bond, either to the magistrate or the officer having him in custody, he shall at once be set at liberty.

(b) Before releasing on bail a person arrested for an offense under Section 42.072, Penal Code, or a person arrested or held without warrant in the prevention of family violence, the law enforcement agency holding the person shall make a reasonable attempt to give personal notice of the imminent release to the victim of the alleged offense or to another person designated by the victim to receive the notice. An attempt by an agency to give notice to the victim or the person designated by the victim at the victim's or person's last known telephone number or address, as shown on the records of the agency, constitutes a reasonable attempt to give notice under this subsection. If possible, the arresting officer shall collect the address and telephone number of the victim at the time the arrest is made and shall communicate that information to the agency holding the person.

(c) A law enforcement agency or an employee of a law enforcement agency is not liable for damages arising from complying or failing to comply with Subsection (b) of this article.

(d) In this article, "family violence" has the meaning assigned by Section 71.004, Family Code.

ART. 17.291. FURTHER DETENTION OF CERTAIN PERSONS

(a) In this article:

(1) "family violence" has the meaning assigned to that phrase by Section 71.004, Family Code; and

(2) "magistrate" has the meaning assigned to it by Article 2.09 of this code.

(b) Article 17.29 does not apply when a person has been arrested or held without a warrant in the prevention of family violence if there is probable cause to believe the violence will continue if the person is immediately released. The head of the agency arresting or holding such a person may hold the person for a period of not more than four hours after bond has been posted. This detention period may be extended for an additional period not to exceed 48 hours, but only if authorized in a writing directed to the person having custody of the detained person by a magistrate who concludes that:

(1) the violence would continue if the person is released; and

(2) if the additional period exceeds 24 hours, probable cause exists to believe that the person committed the instant offense and that, during the 10-year period preceding the date of the instant offense, the person has been arrested:

(A) on more than one occasion for an offense involving family violence; or

(B) for any other offense, if a deadly weapon, as defined by Section 1.07, Penal Code, was used or exhibited during commission of the offense or during immediate flight after commission of the offense.

ART. 17.292. MAGISTRATE'S ORDER FOR EMERGENCY PROTECTION

(a) At a defendant's appearance before a magistrate after arrest for an offense involving family violence or an offense under Section 20A.02, 20A.03, 22.011, 22.021, or 42.072, Penal Code, the magistrate may issue an order for emergency protection on the magistrate's own motion or on the request of:

(1) the victim of the offense;

(2) the guardian of the victim;

(3) a peace officer; or

(4) the attorney representing the state.

(b) At a defendant's appearance before a magistrate after arrest for an offense involving family vio-

lence, the magistrate shall issue an order for emergency protection if the arrest is for an offense that also involves:

(1) serious bodily injury to the victim; or

(2) the use or exhibition of a deadly weapon during the commission of an assault.

(c) The magistrate in the order for emergency protection may prohibit the arrested party from:

(1) committing:

(A) family violence or an assault on the person protected under the order; or

(B) an act in furtherance of an offense under Section 20A.02 or 42.072, Penal Code;

(2) communicating:

(A) directly with a member of the family or household or with the person protected under the order in a threatening or harassing manner;

(B) a threat through any person to a member of the family or household or to the person protected under the order; or

(C) if the magistrate finds good cause, in any manner with a person protected under the order or a member of the family or household of a person protected under the order, except through the party's attorney or a person appointed by the court;

(3) going to or near:

(A) the residence, place of employment, or business of a member of the family or household or of the person protected under the order; or

(B) the residence, child care facility, or school where a child protected under the order resides or attends; or

(4) possessing a firearm, unless the person is a peace officer, as defined by Section 1.07, Penal Code, actively engaged in employment as a sworn, full-time paid employee of a state agency or political subdivision.

(c-1) In addition to the conditions described by Subsection (c), the magistrate in the order for emergency protection may impose a condition described by Article 17.49(b) in the manner provided by that article, including ordering a defendant's participation in a global positioning monitoring system or allowing participation in the system by an alleged victim or other person protected under the order.

(d) The victim of the offense need not be present when the order for emergency protection is issued.

(e) In the order for emergency protection the magistrate shall specifically describe the prohibited locations and the minimum distances, if any, that the party must maintain, unless the magistrate determines for the safety of the person or persons protected by the order that specific descriptions of the locations should be omitted.

(f) To the extent that a condition imposed by an order for emergency protection issued under this article conflicts with an existing court order granting possession of or access to a child, the condition imposed under this article prevails for the duration of the order for emergency protection.

(f-1) To the extent that a condition imposed by an order issued under this article conflicts with a condition imposed by an order subsequently issued under Chapter 85, Subtitle B, Title 4, Family Code, or under Title 1 or Title 5, Family Code, the condition imposed by the order issued under the Family Code prevails.

(f-2) To the extent that a condition imposed by an order issued under this article conflicts with a condition imposed by an order subsequently issued under Chapter 83, Subtitle B, Title 4, Family Code, the condition imposed by the order issued under this article prevails unless the court issuing the order under Chapter 83, Family Code:

(1) is informed of the existence of the order issued under this article; and

(2) makes a finding in the order issued under Chapter 83, Family Code, that the court is superseding the order issued under this article.

(g) An order for emergency protection issued under this article must contain the following statements printed in bold-face type or in capital letters:

"A VIOLATION OF THIS ORDER BY COMMISSION OF AN ACT PROHIBITED BY THE ORDER MAY BE PUNISHABLE BY A FINE OF AS MUCH AS $4,000 OR BY CONFINEMENT IN JAIL FOR AS LONG AS ONE YEAR OR BY BOTH. AN ACT THAT RESULTS IN FAMILY VIOLENCE OR A STALKING OR TRAFFICKING OFFENSE MAY BE PROSECUTED AS A SEPARATE MISDEMEANOR OR FELONY OFFENSE, AS APPLICABLE. IF THE ACT IS PROSECUTED AS A SEPARATE FELONY OFFENSE, IT IS PUNISHABLE BY CONFINEMENT IN PRISON FOR AT LEAST TWO YEARS. THE POSSESSION OF A FIREARM BY A PERSON, OTHER THAN A PEACE OFFICER, AS DEFINED BY SECTION 1.07, PENAL CODE, ACTIVELY ENGAGED IN EMPLOYMENT AS

A SWORN, FULL-TIME PAID EMPLOYEE OF A STATE AGENCY OR POLITICAL SUBDIVISION, WHO IS SUBJECT TO THIS ORDER MAY BE PROSECUTED AS A SEPARATE OFFENSE PUNISHABLE BY CONFINEMENT OR IMPRISONMENT.

"NO PERSON, INCLUDING A PERSON WHO IS PROTECTED BY THIS ORDER, MAY GIVE PERMISSION TO ANYONE TO IGNORE OR VIOLATE ANY PROVISION OF THIS ORDER. DURING THE TIME IN WHICH THIS ORDER IS VALID, EVERY PROVISION OF THIS ORDER IS IN FULL FORCE AND EFFECT UNLESS A COURT CHANGES THE ORDER."

(h) As soon as possible but not later than the next business day after the date the magistrate issues an order for emergency protection under this article, the magistrate shall send a copy of the order to the chief of police in the municipality where the member of the family or household or individual protected by the order resides, if the person resides in a municipality, or to the sheriff of the county where the person resides, if the person does not reside in a municipality. If the victim of the offense is not present when the order is issued, the magistrate issuing the order shall order an appropriate peace officer to make a good faith effort to notify, within 24 hours, the victim that the order has been issued by calling the victim's residence and place of employment. The clerk of the court shall send a copy of the order to the victim at the victim's last known address as soon as possible but not later than the next business day after the date the order is issued.

(h-1) A magistrate or clerk of the court may delay sending a copy of the order under Subsection (h) only if the magistrate or clerk lacks information necessary to ensure service and enforcement.

(i) If an order for emergency protection issued under this article prohibits a person from going to or near a child care facility or school, the magistrate shall send a copy of the order to the child care facility or school.

(i-1) The copy of the order and any related information may be sent under Subsection (h) or (i) electronically or in another manner that can be accessed by the recipient.

(j) An order for emergency protection issued under this article is effective on issuance, and the defendant shall be served a copy of the order by the magistrate or the magistrate's designee in person or electronically. The magistrate shall make a separate record of the service in written or electronic format. An order for emergency protection issued under Subsection (a) or (b)(1) of this article remains in effect up to the 61st day but not less than 31 days after the date of issuance. An order for emergency protection issued under Subsection (b)(2) of this article remains in effect up to the 91st day but not less than 61 days after the date of issuance. After notice to each affected party and a hearing, the issuing court may modify all or part of an order issued under this article if the court finds that:

(1) the order as originally issued is unworkable;

(2) the modification will not place the victim of the offense at greater risk than did the original order; and

(3) the modification will not in any way endanger a person protected under the order.

(k) To ensure that an officer responding to a call is aware of the existence and terms of an order for emergency protection issued under this article, not later than the third business day after the date of receipt of the copy of the order by the applicable law enforcement agency with jurisdiction over the municipality or county in which the victim resides, the law enforcement agency shall enter the information required under Section 411.042(b)(6), Government Code, into the statewide law enforcement information system maintained by the Department of Public Safety.

(k-1) A law enforcement agency may delay entering the information required under Subsection (k) only if the agency lacks information necessary to ensure service and enforcement.

(*l*) In the order for emergency protection, the magistrate shall suspend a license to carry a handgun issued under Subchapter H, Chapter 411, Government Code, that is held by the defendant.

(m) In this article:

(1) "Family," "family violence," and "household" have the meanings assigned by Chapter 71, Family Code.

(2) "Firearm" has the meaning assigned by Chapter 46, Penal Code.

(3) "Business day" means a day other than a Saturday, Sunday, or state or national holiday.

(n) On motion, notice, and hearing, or on agreement of the parties, an order for emergency protection issued under this article may be transferred to the court assuming jurisdiction over the criminal act giving rise to the issuance of the emergency order for protection. On transfer, the criminal court may modify all or part of

an order issued under this subsection in the same manner and under the same standards as the issuing court under Subsection (j).

See also *O'Connor's Texas Family Law Handbook* (2017), "Magistrate's Order for Emergency Protection," ch. 6-D, p. 760; "Duty Related to Magistrate's Orders for Emergency Protection – Entering Orders into Statewide System," ch. 6-E, §5, p. 774.

ART. 17.293. DELIVERY OF ORDER FOR EMERGENCY PROTECTION TO OTHER PERSONS

The magistrate or the clerk of the magistrate's court issuing an order for emergency protection under Article 17.292 that suspends a license to carry a handgun shall immediately send a copy of the order to the appropriate division of the Department of Public Safety at its Austin headquarters. On receipt of the order suspending the license, the department shall:

(1) record the suspension of the license in the records of the department;

(2) report the suspension to local law enforcement agencies, as appropriate; and

(3) demand surrender of the suspended license from the license holder.

ART. 17.49. CONDITIONS FOR DEFENDANT CHARGED WITH OFFENSE INVOLVING FAMILY VIOLENCE

(a) In this article:

(1) "Family violence" has the meaning assigned by Section 71.004, Family Code.

(2) "Global positioning monitoring system" means a system that electronically determines and reports the location of an individual through the use of a transmitter or similar device carried or worn by the individual that transmits latitude and longitude data to a monitoring entity through global positioning satellite technology. The term does not include a system that contains or operates global positioning system technology, radio frequency identification technology, or any other similar technology that is implanted in or otherwise invades or violates the individual's body.

(b) A magistrate may require as a condition of release on bond that a defendant charged with an offense involving family violence:

(1) refrain from going to or near a residence, school, place of employment, or other location, as specifically described in the bond, frequented by an alleged victim of the offense;

(2) carry or wear a global positioning monitoring system device and, except as provided by Subsection (h), pay the costs associated with operating that system in relation to the defendant; or

(3) except as provided by Subsection (h), if the alleged victim of the offense consents after receiving the information described by Subsection (d), pay the costs associated with providing the victim with an electronic receptor device that:

(A) is capable of receiving the global positioning monitoring system information from the device carried or worn by the defendant; and

(B) notifies the victim if the defendant is at or near a location that the defendant has been ordered to refrain from going to or near under Subdivision (1).

(c) Before imposing a condition described by Subsection (b)(1), a magistrate must afford an alleged victim an opportunity to provide the magistrate with a list of areas from which the victim would like the defendant excluded and shall consider the victim's request, if any, in determining the locations the defendant will be ordered to refrain from going to or near. If the magistrate imposes a condition described by Subsection (b)(1), the magistrate shall specifically describe the locations that the defendant has been ordered to refrain from going to or near and the minimum distances, if any, that the defendant must maintain from those locations.

(d) Before imposing a condition described by Subsection (b)(3), a magistrate must provide to an alleged victim information regarding:

(1) the victim's right to participate in a global positioning monitoring system or to refuse to participate in that system and the procedure for requesting that the magistrate terminate the victim's participation;

(2) the manner in which the global positioning monitoring system technology functions and the risks and limitations of that technology, and the extent to which the system will track and record the victim's location and movements;

(3) any locations that the defendant is ordered to refrain from going to or near and the minimum distances, if any, that the defendant must maintain from those locations;

(4) any sanctions that the court may impose on the defendant for violating a condition of bond imposed under this article;

(5) the procedure that the victim is to follow, and support services available to assist the victim, if the de-

fendant violates a condition of bond or if the global positioning monitoring system equipment fails;

(6) community services available to assist the victim in obtaining shelter, counseling, education, child care, legal representation, and other assistance available to address the consequences of family violence; and

(7) the fact that the victim's communications with the court concerning the global positioning monitoring system and any restrictions to be imposed on the defendant's movements are not confidential.

(e) In addition to the information described by Subsection (d), a magistrate shall provide to an alleged victim who participates in a global positioning monitoring system under this article the name and telephone number of an appropriate person employed by a local law enforcement agency whom the victim may call to request immediate assistance if the defendant violates a condition of bond imposed under this article.

(f) In determining whether to order a defendant's participation in a global positioning monitoring system under this article, the magistrate shall consider the likelihood that the defendant's participation will deter the defendant from seeking to kill, physically injure, stalk, or otherwise threaten the alleged victim before trial.

(g) An alleged victim may request that the magistrate terminate the victim's participation in a global positioning monitoring system at any time. The magistrate may not impose sanctions on the victim for requesting termination of the victim's participation in or refusing to participate in a global positioning monitoring system under this article.

(h) If the magistrate determines that a defendant is indigent, the magistrate may, based on a sliding scale established by local rule, require the defendant to pay costs under Subsection (b)(2) or (3) in an amount that is less than the full amount of the costs associated with operating the global positioning monitoring system in relation to the defendant or providing the victim with an electronic receptor device.

(i) If an indigent defendant pays to an entity that operates a global positioning monitoring system the partial amount ordered by a magistrate under Subsection (h), the entity shall accept the partial amount as payment in full. The county in which the magistrate who enters an order under Subsection (h) is located is not responsible for payment of any costs associated with operating the global positioning monitoring system in relation to an indigent defendant.

(j) A magistrate that imposes a condition described by Subsection (b)(1) or (2) shall order the entity that operates the global positioning monitoring system to notify the court and the appropriate local law enforcement agency if a defendant violates a condition of bond imposed under this article.

(k) A magistrate that imposes a condition described by Subsection (b) may only allow or require the defendant to execute or be released under a type of bond that is authorized by this chapter.

(*l*) This article does not limit the authority of a magistrate to impose any other reasonable conditions of bond or enter any orders of protection under other applicable statutes.

CHAPTER 42. JUDGMENT & SENTENCE

ART. 42.0373. MANDATORY RESTITUTION FOR CHILD WITNESS OF FAMILY VIOLENCE

(a) If after a conviction or a grant of deferred adjudication a court places a defendant on community supervision for an offense involving family violence, as defined by Section 71.004, Family Code, the court shall determine from the complaint, information, indictment, or other charging instrument, the presentence report, or other evidence before the court whether:

(1) the offense was committed in the physical presence of, or in the same habitation or vehicle occupied by, a person younger than 15 years of age; and

(2) at the time of the offense, the defendant had knowledge or reason to know that the person younger than 15 years of age was physically present or occupied the same habitation or vehicle.

(b) If the court determines both issues described by Subsection (a) in the affirmative, the court shall order the defendant to pay restitution in an amount equal to the cost of necessary rehabilitation, including medical, psychiatric, and psychological care and treatment, for a person described by Subsection (a)(1).

(c) The court shall, after considering the financial circumstances of the defendant, specify in a restitution order issued under Subsection (b) the manner in which the defendant must pay the restitution. The order must require restitution payments to be delivered in the manner described by Article 42.037(g)(4)(iii).

(d) A restitution order issued under Subsection (b) may be enforced by the state, or by a person or a parent or guardian of the person named in the order to receive the restitution, in the same manner as a judgment in a civil action.

(e) The court may hold a hearing, make findings of fact, and amend a restitution order issued under Subsection (b) if the defendant fails to pay the person named in the order in the manner specified by the court.

(f) A determination under this article may not be entered as an affirmative finding in the judgment for the offense for which the defendant was placed on community supervision.

ART. 42.23. NOTIFICATION OF COURT OF FAMILY VIOLENCE CONVICTION

(a) In this article, "family violence" has the meaning assigned by Section 71.004, Family Code.

(b) If the attorney representing the state in a criminal case involving family violence learns that the defendant is subject to the jurisdiction of another court relating to an order that provides for the appointment of a conservator or that sets the terms and conditions of conservatorship or for possession of or access to a child, the attorney representing the state shall notify the court in which the defendant is being tried of the existence of the order and the identity of the court of continuing jurisdiction.

(c) On the conviction or entry of an order deferring adjudication of a defendant for an offense involving family violence, the convicting court or the court entering the order shall notify the court of continuing jurisdiction of the conviction or deferred adjudication.

ART. 42.24. PROHIBITING CONTACT WITH VICTIM

If a defendant's sentence includes a term of confinement or imprisonment, the convicting court may, as part of the sentence, prohibit the defendant from contacting, during the term of the defendant's confinement or imprisonment, the victim of the offense of which the defendant is convicted or a member of the victim's family.

TITLE 7. MENTAL HEALTH & INTELLECTUAL DISABILITY

Subtitle E. Special Provisions Relating to Mental Illness & Mental Retardation

Chapter 611. Mental Health Records

TITLE 7. MENTAL HEALTH & INTELLECTUAL DISABILITY

SUBTITLE E. SPECIAL PROVISIONS RELATING TO MENTAL ILLNESS & MENTAL RETARDATION

CHAPTER 611. MENTAL HEALTH RECORDS

H&SC §611.001. DEFINITIONS

In this chapter:

(1) "Patient" means a person who consults or is interviewed by a professional for diagnosis, evaluation, or treatment of any mental or emotional condition or disorder, including alcoholism or drug addiction.

(2) "Professional" means:

(A) a person authorized to practice medicine in any state or nation;

(B) a person licensed or certified by this state to diagnose, evaluate, or treat any mental or emotional condition or disorder; or

(C) a person the patient reasonably believes is authorized, licensed, or certified as provided by this subsection.

H&SC §611.002. CONFIDENTIALITY OF INFORMATION & PROHIBITION AGAINST DISCLOSURE

(a) Communications between a patient and a professional, and records of the identity, diagnosis, evaluation, or treatment of a patient that are created or maintained by a professional, are confidential.

(b) Confidential communications or records may not be disclosed except as provided by Section 611.004 or 611.0045.

(c) This section applies regardless of when the patient received services from a professional.

H&SC §611.003. PERSONS WHO MAY CLAIM PRIVILEGE OF CONFIDENTIALITY

(a) The privilege of confidentiality may be claimed by:

(1) the patient;

(2) a person listed in Section 611.004(a)(4) or (a)(5) who is acting on the patient's behalf; or

(3) the professional, but only on behalf of the patient.

(b) The authority of a professional to claim the privilege of confidentiality on behalf of the patient is presumed in the absence of evidence to the contrary.

H&SC §611.004. AUTHORIZED DISCLOSURE OF CONFIDENTIAL INFORMATION OTHER THAN IN JUDICIAL OR ADMINISTRATIVE PROCEEDING

(a) A professional may disclose confidential information only:

(1) to a governmental agency if the disclosure is required or authorized by law;

(2) to medical or law enforcement personnel if the professional determines that there is a probability of imminent physical injury by the patient to the patient or others or there is a probability of immediate mental or emotional injury to the patient;

(3) to qualified personnel for management audits, financial audits, program evaluations, or research, in accordance with Subsection (b);

(4) to a person who has the written consent of the patient, or a parent if the patient is a minor, or a guardian if the patient has been adjudicated as incompetent to manage the patient's personal affairs;

(5) to the patient's personal representative if the patient is deceased;

(6) to individuals, corporations, or governmental agencies involved in paying or collecting fees for mental or emotional health services provided by a professional;

(7) to other professionals and personnel under the professionals' direction who participate in the diagnosis, evaluation, or treatment of the patient;

(8) in an official legislative inquiry relating to a state hospital or state school as provided by Subsection (c);

(9) to designated persons or personnel of a correctional facility in which a person is detained if the disclosure is for the sole purpose of providing treatment and health care to the person in custody;

(10) to an employee or agent of the professional who requires mental health care information to provide mental health care services or in complying with statutory, licensing, or accreditation requirements, if the professional has taken appropriate action to ensure that the employee or agent:

(A) will not use or disclose the information for any other purposes; and

(B) will take appropriate steps to protect the information; or

(11) to satisfy a request for medical records of a deceased or incompetent person pursuant to Section 74.051(e), Civil Practice and Remedies Code.

(b) Personnel who receive confidential information under Subsection (a)(3) may not directly or indirectly identify or otherwise disclose the identity of a patient in a report or in any other manner.

(c) The exception in Subsection (a)(8) applies only to records created by the state hospital or state school or by the employees of the hospital or school. Information or records that identify a patient may be released only with the patient's proper consent.

(d) A person who receives information from confidential communications or records may not disclose the information except to the extent that disclosure is consistent with the authorized purposes for which the person first obtained the information. This subsection does not apply to a person listed in Subsection (a)(4) or (a)(5) who is acting on the patient's behalf.

H&SC §611.0045. RIGHT TO MENTAL HEALTH RECORD

(a) Except as otherwise provided by this section, a patient is entitled to have access to the content of a confidential record made about the patient.

(b) The professional may deny access to any portion of a record if the professional determines that release of that portion would be harmful to the patient's physical, mental, or emotional health.

(c) If the professional denies access to any portion of a record, the professional shall give the patient a signed and dated written statement that having access to the record would be harmful to the patient's physical, mental, or emotional health and shall include a copy of the written statement in the patient's records. The statement must specify the portion of the record to which access is denied, the reason for denial, and the duration of the denial.

(d) The professional who denies access to a portion of a record under this section shall redetermine the necessity for the denial at each time a request for the denied portion is made. If the professional again denies access, the professional shall notify the patient of the denial and document the denial as prescribed by Subsection (c).

(e) If a professional denies access to a portion of a confidential record, the professional shall allow examination and copying of the record by another professional if the patient selects the professional to treat the patient for the same or a related condition as the professional denying access.

(f) The content of a confidential record shall be made available to a person listed by Section 611.004(a)(4) or (5) who is acting on the patient's behalf.

(g) A professional shall delete confidential information about another person who has not consented to the release, but may not delete information relating to the patient that another person has provided, the identity of the person responsible for that information, or the identity of any person who provided information that resulted in the patient's commitment.

(h) If a summary or narrative of a confidential record is requested by the patient or other person requesting release under this section, the professional shall prepare the summary or narrative.

(i) The professional or other entity that has possession or control of the record shall grant access to any portion of the record to which access is not specifically denied under this section within a reasonable time and may charge a reasonable fee.

(j) Notwithstanding Section 159.002, Occupations Code, this section applies to the release of a confidential record created or maintained by a professional, including a physician, that relates to the diagnosis, evaluation, or treatment of a mental or emotional condition or disorder, including alcoholism or drug addiction.

(k) The denial of a patient's access to any portion of a record by the professional or other entity that has

possession or control of the record suspends, until the release of that portion of the record, the running of an applicable statute of limitations on a cause of action in which evidence relevant to the cause of action is in that portion of the record.

H&SC §611.005. LEGAL REMEDIES FOR IMPROPER DISCLOSURE OR FAILURE TO DISCLOSE

(a) A person aggrieved by the improper disclosure of or failure to disclose confidential communications or records in violation of this chapter may petition the district court of the county in which the person resides for appropriate relief, including injunctive relief. The person may petition a district court of Travis County if the person is not a resident of this state.

(b) In a suit contesting the denial of access under Section 611.0045, the burden of proving that the denial was proper is on the professional who denied the access.

(c) The aggrieved person also has a civil cause of action for damages.

H&SC §611.006. AUTHORIZED DISCLOSURE OF CONFIDENTIAL INFORMATION IN JUDICIAL OR ADMINISTRATIVE PROCEEDING

(a) A professional may disclose confidential information in:

(1) a judicial or administrative proceeding brought by the patient or the patient's legally authorized representative against a professional, including malpractice proceedings;

(2) a license revocation proceeding in which the patient is a complaining witness and in which disclosure is relevant to the claim or defense of a professional;

(3) a judicial or administrative proceeding in which the patient waives the patient's right in writing to the privilege of confidentiality of information or when a representative of the patient acting on the patient's behalf submits a written waiver to the confidentiality privilege;

(4) a judicial or administrative proceeding to substantiate and collect on a claim for mental or emotional health services rendered to the patient;

(5) a judicial proceeding if the judge finds that the patient, after having been informed that communications would not be privileged, has made communications to a professional in the course of a court-ordered examination relating to the patient's mental or emotional condition or disorder, except that those communications may be disclosed only with respect to issues involving the patient's mental or emotional health;

(6) a judicial proceeding affecting the parent-child relationship;

(7) any criminal proceeding, as otherwise provided by law;

(8) a judicial or administrative proceeding regarding the abuse or neglect, or the cause of abuse or neglect, of a resident of an institution, as that term is defined by Chapter 242;

(9) a judicial proceeding relating to a will if the patient's physical or mental condition is relevant to the execution of the will;

(10) an involuntary commitment proceeding for court-ordered treatment or for a probable cause hearing under:

(A) Chapter 462;

(B) Chapter 574; or

(C) Chapter 593; or

(11) a judicial or administrative proceeding where the court or agency has issued an order or subpoena.

(b) On granting an order under Subsection (a)(5), the court, in determining the extent to which disclosure of all or any part of a communication is necessary, shall impose appropriate safeguards against unauthorized disclosure.

H&SC §611.007. REVOCATION OF CONSENT

(a) Except as provided by Subsection (b), a patient or a patient's legally authorized representative may revoke a disclosure consent to a professional at any time. A revocation is valid only if it is written, dated, and signed by the patient or legally authorized representative.

(b) A patient may not revoke a disclosure that is required for purposes of making payment to the professional for mental health care services provided to the patient.

(c) A patient may not maintain an action against a professional for a disclosure made by the professional in good faith reliance on an authorization if the professional did not have notice of the revocation of the consent.

H&SC §611.008. REQUEST BY PATIENT

(a) On receipt of a written request from a patient to examine or copy all or part of the patient's recorded mental health care information, a professional, as promptly as required under the circumstances but not later than the 15th day after the date of receiving the request, shall:

(1) make the information available for examination during regular business hours and provide a copy to the patient, if requested; or

(2) inform the patient if the information does not exist or cannot be found.

(b) Unless provided for by other state law, the professional may charge a reasonable fee for retrieving or copying mental health care information and is not required to permit examination or copying until the fee is paid unless there is a medical emergency.

(c) A professional may not charge a fee for copying mental health care information under Subsection (b) to the extent the fee is prohibited under Subchapter M, Chapter 161.

For the complete Property Code with annotations, see the current edition of ***O'Connor's Texas Property Code Plus***. To order, call 1-800-OCONNOR (1-800-626-6667) or visit www.oconnors.com.

TITLE 5. EXEMPT PROPERTY & LIENS

Subtitle A. Property Exempt from Creditors' Claims

TITLE 5. EXEMPT PROPERTY & LIENS

SUBTITLE A. PROPERTY EXEMPT FROM CREDITORS' CLAIMS

CHAPTER 41. INTERESTS IN LAND

SUBCHAPTER A. EXEMPTIONS IN LAND DEFINED

PROP §41.001. INTERESTS IN LAND EXEMPT FROM SEIZURE

(a) A homestead and one or more lots used for a place of burial of the dead are exempt from seizure for the claims of creditors except for encumbrances properly fixed on homestead property.

(b) Encumbrances may be properly fixed on homestead property for:

(1) purchase money;

(2) taxes on the property;

(3) work and material used in constructing improvements on the property if contracted for in writing as provided by Sections 53.254(a), (b), and (c);

(4) an owelty of partition imposed against the entirety of the property by a court order or by a written agreement of the parties to the partition, including a debt of one spouse in favor of the other spouse resulting from a division or an award of a family homestead in a divorce proceeding;

(5) the refinance of a lien against a homestead, including a federal tax lien resulting from the tax debt of both spouses, if the homestead is a family homestead, or from the tax debt of the owner;

(6) an extension of credit that meets the requirements of Section 50(a)(6), Article XVI, Texas Constitution; or

(7) a reverse mortgage that meets the requirements of Sections 50(k)-(p), Article XVI, Texas Constitution.

(c) The homestead claimant's proceeds of a sale of a homestead are not subject to seizure for a creditor's claim for six months after the date of sale.

See also ***O'Connor's Texas Family Law Handbook*** (2017), "Protection from forced sale for payment of debt," ch. 2-E, §3.2, p. 185.

PROP §41.002. DEFINITION OF HOMESTEAD

(a) If used for the purposes of an urban home or as both an urban home and a place to exercise a calling or business, the homestead of a family or a single, adult person, not otherwise entitled to a homestead, shall consist of not more than 10 acres of land which may be in one or more contiguous lots, together with any improvements thereon.

(b) If used for the purposes of a rural home, the homestead shall consist of:

(1) for a family, not more than 200 acres, which may be in one or more parcels, with the improvements thereon; or

(2) for a single, adult person, not otherwise entitled to a homestead, not more than 100 acres, which may be in one or more parcels, with the improvements thereon.

(c) A homestead is considered to be urban if, at the time the designation is made, the property is:

(1) located within the limits of a municipality or its extraterritorial jurisdiction or a platted subdivision; and

(2) served by police protection, paid or volunteer fire protection, and at least three of the following services provided by a municipality or under contract to a municipality:

(A) electric;

(B) natural gas;

(C) sewer;

(D) storm sewer; and

(E) water.

(d) The definition of a homestead as provided in this section applies to all homesteads in this state whenever created.

See also *O'Connor's Texas Family Law Handbook* (2017), "Homestead Property," ch. 2-E, p. 183.

Section 41.0021 omitted by editor

PROP §41.003. TEMPORARY RENTING OF A HOMESTEAD

Temporary renting of a homestead does not change its homestead character if the homestead claimant has not acquired another homestead.

PROP §41.004. ABANDONMENT OF A HOMESTEAD

If a homestead claimant is married, a homestead cannot be abandoned without the consent of the claimant's spouse.

PROP §41.005. VOLUNTARY DESIGNATION OF HOMESTEAD

(a) If a rural homestead of a family is part of one or more parcels containing a total of more than 200 acres, the head of the family and, if married, that person's spouse may voluntarily designate not more than 200 acres of the property as the homestead. If a rural homestead of a single adult person, not otherwise entitled to a homestead, is part of one or more parcels containing a total of more than 100 acres, the person may voluntarily designate not more than 100 acres of the property as the homestead.

(b) If an urban homestead of a family, or an urban homestead of a single adult person not otherwise entitled to a homestead, is part of one or more contiguous lots containing a total of more than 10 acres, the head of the family and, if married, that person's spouse or the single adult person, as applicable, may voluntarily designate not more than 10 acres of the property as the homestead.

(c) Except as provided by Subsection (e) or Subchapter B, to designate property as a homestead, a person or persons, as applicable, must make the designation in an instrument that is signed and acknowledged or proved in the manner required for the recording of other instruments. The person or persons must file the designation with the county clerk of the county in which all or part of the property is located. The clerk shall record the designation in the county deed records. The designation must contain:

(1) a description sufficient to identify the property designated;

(2) a statement by the person or persons who executed the instrument that the property is designated as the homestead of the person's family or as the homestead of a single adult person not otherwise entitled to a homestead;

(3) the name of the current record title holder of the property; and

(4) for a rural homestead, the number of acres designated and, if there is more than one survey, the number of acres in each.

(d) A person or persons, as applicable, may change the boundaries of a homestead designated under Subsection (c) by executing and recording an instrument in the manner required for a voluntary designation under that subsection. A change under this subsection does not impair rights acquired by a party before the change.

(e) Except as otherwise provided by this subsection, property on which a person receives an exemption from taxation under Section 11.43, Tax Code, is considered to have been designated as the person's homestead for purposes of this subchapter if the property is listed as the person's residence homestead on the most recent appraisal roll for the appraisal district established for the county in which the property is located. If a person designates property as a homestead under Subsection (c) or Subchapter B and a different property is considered to have been designated as the person's homestead under this subsection, the designation under Subsection (c) or Subchapter B, as applicable, prevails for purposes of this chapter.

(f) If a person or persons, as applicable, have not made a voluntary designation of a homestead under this section as of the time a writ of execution is issued against the person, any designation of the person's or persons' homestead must be made in accordance with Subchapter B.

(g) An instrument that made a voluntary designation of a homestead in accordance with prior law and that is on file with the county clerk on September 1,

1987, is considered a voluntary designation of a homestead under this section.

See also *O'Connor's Texas Family Law Handbook* (2017), "Voluntary designation," ch. 2-E, §5.1, p. 197.

PROP §41.0051. DISCLAIMER & DISCLOSURE REQUIRED

(a) A person may not deliver a written advertisement offering, for a fee, to designate property as a homestead as provided by Section 41.005 unless there is a disclaimer on the advertisement that is conspicuous and printed in 14-point boldface type or 14-point uppercase typewritten letters that makes the following statement or a substantially similar statement:

THIS DOCUMENT IS AN ADVERTISEMENT OF SERVICES. IT IS NOT AN OFFICIAL DOCUMENT OF THE STATE OF TEXAS.

(b) A person who solicits solely by mail or by telephone a homeowner to pay a fee for the service of applying for a property tax refund from a tax appraisal district or other governmental body on behalf of the homeowner shall, before accepting money from the homeowner or signing a contract with the homeowner for the person's services, disclose to the homeowner the name of the tax appraisal district or other governmental body that owes the homeowner a refund.

(c) A person's failure to provide a disclaimer on an advertisement as required by Subsection (a) or to provide the disclosure required by Subsection (b) is considered a false, misleading, or deceptive act or practice for purposes of Section 17.46(a), Business & Commerce Code, and is subject to action by the consumer protection division of the attorney general's office as provided by Section 17.46(a), Business & Commerce Code.

PROP §41.006. CERTAIN SALES OF HOMESTEAD

(a) Except as provided by Subsection (c), any sale or purported sale in whole or in part of a homestead at a fixed purchase price that is less than the appraised fair market value of the property at the time of the sale or purported sale, and in connection with which the buyer of the property executes a lease of the property to the seller at lease payments that exceed the fair rental value of the property, is considered to be a loan with all payments made from the seller to the buyer in excess of the sales price considered to be interest subject to Title 4, Finance Code.

(b) The taking of any deed in connection with a transaction described by this section is a deceptive trade practice under Subchapter E, Chapter 17, Business & Commerce Code, and the deed is void and no lien attaches to the homestead property as a result of the purported sale.

(c) This section does not apply to the sale of a family homestead to a parent, stepparent, grandparent, child, stepchild, brother, half brother, sister, half sister, or grandchild of an adult member of the family.

Section 41.007 omitted by editor

PROP §41.008. CONFLICT WITH FEDERAL LAW

To the extent of any conflict between this subchapter and any federal law that imposes an upper limit on the amount, including the monetary amount or acreage amount, of homestead property a person may exempt from seizure, this subchapter prevails to the extent allowed under federal law.

Sections 41.009-41.020 reserved for expansion

SUBCHAPTER B. DESIGNATION OF A HOMESTEAD IN AID OF ENFORCEMENT OF A JUDGMENT DEBT

PROP §41.021. NOTICE TO DESIGNATE

If an execution is issued against a holder of an interest in land of which a homestead may be a part and the judgment debtor has not made a voluntary designation of a homestead under Section 41.005, the judgment creditor may give the judgment debtor notice to designate the homestead as defined in Section 41.002. The notice shall state that if the judgment debtor fails to designate the homestead within the time allowed by Section 41.022, the court will appoint a commissioner to make the designation at the expense of the judgment debtor.

See also *O'Connor's Texas Family Law Handbook* (2017), "Notice to designate," ch. 2-E, §5.2.1, p. 198.

PROP §41.022. DESIGNATION BY HOMESTEAD CLAIMANT

At any time before 10 a.m. on the Monday next after the expiration of 20 days after the date of service of the notice to designate, the judgment debtor may designate the homestead as defined in Section 41.002 by filing a written designation, signed by the judgment debtor, with the justice or clerk of the court from which the writ of execution was issued, together with a plat of the area designated.

PROP §41.023. DESIGNATION BY COMMISSIONER

(a) If a judgment debtor who has not made a voluntary designation of a homestead under Section 41.005 does not designate a homestead as provided in Section 41.022, on motion of the judgment creditor, filed within 90 days after the issuance of the writ of execution, the court from which the writ of execution issued shall appoint a commissioner to designate the judgment debtor's homestead. The court may appoint a surveyor and others as may be necessary to assist the commissioner. The commissioner shall file his designation of the judgment debtor's homestead in a written report, together with a plat of the area designated, with the justice or clerk of the court not more than 60 days after the order of appointment is signed or within such time as the court may allow.

(b) Within 10 days after the commissioner's report is filed, the judgment debtor or the judgment creditor may request a hearing on the issue of whether the report should be confirmed, rejected, or modified as may be deemed appropriate in the particular circumstances of the case. The commissioner's report may be contradicted by evidence from either party, when exceptions to it or any item thereof have been filed before the hearing, but not otherwise. After the hearing, or if there is no hearing requested, the court shall designate the homestead as deemed appropriate and order sale of the excess.

(c) The commissioner, a surveyor, and others appointed to assist the commissioner are entitled to such fees and expenses as are deemed reasonable by the court. The court shall tax these fees and expenses against the judgment debtor as part of the costs of execution.

See also *O'Connor's Texas Family Law Handbook* (2017), "Motion to appoint commissioner," ch. 2-E, §5.2.2, p. 198.

PROP §41.024. SALE OF EXCESS

An officer holding an execution sale of property of a judgment debtor whose homestead has been designated under this chapter may sell the excess of the judgment debtor's interest in land not included in the homestead.

CHAPTER 42. PERSONAL PROPERTY

PROP §42.001. PERSONAL PROPERTY EXEMPTION

(a) Personal property, as described in Section 42.002, is exempt from garnishment, attachment, execution, or other seizure if:

(1) the property is provided for a family and has an aggregate fair market value of not more than $100,000, exclusive of the amount of any liens, security interests, or other charges encumbering the property; or

(2) the property is owned by a single adult, who is not a member of a family, and has an aggregate fair market value of not more than $50,000, exclusive of the amount of any liens, security interests, or other charges encumbering the property.

(b) The following personal property is exempt from seizure and is not included in the aggregate limitations prescribed by Subsection (a):

(1) current wages for personal services, except for the enforcement of court-ordered child support payments;

(2) professionally prescribed health aids of a debtor or a dependent of a debtor;

(3) alimony, support, or separate maintenance received or to be received by the debtor for the support of the debtor or a dependent of the debtor; and

(4) a religious bible or other book containing sacred writings of a religion that is seized by a creditor other than a lessor of real property who is exercising the lessor's contractual or statutory right to seize personal property after a tenant breaches a lease agreement for or abandons the real property.

(c) Except as provided by Subsection (b)(4), this section does not prevent seizure by a secured creditor with a contractual landlord's lien or other security in the property to be seized.

(d) Unpaid commissions for personal services not to exceed 25 percent of the aggregate limitations prescribed by Subsection (a) are exempt from seizure and are included in the aggregate.

(e) A religious bible or other book described by Subsection (b)(4) that is seized by a lessor of real property in the exercise of the lessor's contractual or statutory right to seize personal property after a tenant breaches a lease agreement for the real property or abandons the real property may not be included in the aggregate limitations prescribed by Subsection (a).

PROP §42.002. PERSONAL PROPERTY

(a) The following personal property is exempt under Section 42.001(a):

(1) home furnishings, including family heirlooms;

(2) provisions for consumption;

(3) farming or ranching vehicles and implements;

(4) tools, equipment, books, and apparatus, including boats and motor vehicles used in a trade or profession;

(5) wearing apparel;

(6) jewelry not to exceed 25 percent of the aggregate limitations prescribed by Section 42.001(a);

(7) two firearms;

(8) athletic and sporting equipment, including bicycles;

(9) a two-wheeled, three-wheeled, or four-wheeled motor vehicle for each member of a family or single adult who holds a driver's license or who does not hold a driver's license but who relies on another person to operate the vehicle for the benefit of the nonlicensed person;

(10) the following animals and forage on hand for their consumption:

(A) two horses, mules, or donkeys and a saddle, blanket, and bridle for each;

(B) 12 head of cattle;

(C) 60 head of other types of livestock; and

(D) 120 fowl; and

(11) household pets.

(b) Personal property, unless precluded from being encumbered by other law, may be encumbered by a security interest under Subchapter B, Chapter 9, Business & Commerce Code, or Subchapter F, Chapter 501, Transportation Code, or by a lien fixed by other law, and the security interest or lien may not be avoided on the ground that the property is exempt under this chapter.

PROP §42.0021. ADDITIONAL EXEMPTION FOR CERTAIN SAVINGS PLANS

(a) In addition to the exemption prescribed by Section 42.001, a person's right to the assets held in or to receive payments, whether vested or not, under any stock bonus, pension, annuity, deferred compensation, profit-sharing, or similar plan, including a retirement plan for self-employed individuals, or a simplified employee pension plan, an individual retirement account or individual retirement annuity, including an inherited individual retirement account, individual retirement annuity, Roth IRA, or inherited Roth IRA, or a health savings account, and under any annuity or similar contract purchased with assets distributed from that type of plan or account, is exempt from attachment, execution, and seizure for the satisfaction of debts to the extent the plan, contract, annuity, or account is exempt from federal income tax, or to the extent federal income tax on the person's interest is deferred until actual payment of benefits to the person under Section 223, 401(a), 403(a), 403(b), 408(a), 408A, 457(b), or 501(a), Internal Revenue Code of 1986, including a government plan or church plan described by Section 414(d) or (e), Internal Revenue Code of 1986. For purposes of this subsection, the interest of a person in a plan, annuity, account, or contract acquired by reason of the death of another person, whether as an owner, participant, beneficiary, survivor, coannuitant, heir, or legatee, is exempt to the same extent that the interest of the person from whom the plan, annuity, account, or contract was acquired was exempt on the date of the person's death. If this subsection is held invalid or preempted by federal law in whole or in part or in certain circumstances, the subsection remains in effect in all other respects to the maximum extent permitted by law.

(b) Contributions to an individual retirement account that exceed the amounts permitted under the applicable provisions of the Internal Revenue Code of 1986 and any accrued earnings on such contributions are not exempt under this section unless otherwise exempt by law. Amounts qualifying as nontaxable rollover contributions under Section 402(a)(5), 403(a)(4), 403(b)(8), or 408(d)(3) of the Internal Revenue Code of 1986 before January 1, 1993, are treated as exempt amounts under Subsection (a). Amounts treated as qualified rollover contributions under Section 408A, Internal Revenue Code of 1986, are treated as exempt amounts under Subsection (a). In addition, amounts qualifying as nontaxable rollover contributions under Section 402(c), 402(e)(6), 402(f), 403(a)(4), 403(a)(5), 403(b)(8), 403(b)(10), 408(d)(3), or 408A of the Internal Revenue Code of 1986 on or after January 1, 1993, are treated as exempt amounts under Subsection (a). Amounts qualifying as nontaxable rollover contributions under Section 223(f)(5) of the Internal Revenue Code of 1986 on or after January 1, 2004, are treated as exempt amounts under Subsection (a).

(c) Amounts distributed from a plan, annuity, account, or contract entitled to an exemption under Subsection (a) are not subject to seizure for a creditor's claim for 60 days after the date of distribution if the amounts qualify as a nontaxable rollover contribution under Subsection (b).

(d) A participant or beneficiary of a plan, annuity, account, or contract entitled to an exemption under Subsection (a), other than an individual retirement account or individual retirement annuity, is not prohibited from granting a valid and enforceable security interest in the participant's or beneficiary's right to the assets held in or to receive payments under the exempt plan, annuity, account, or contract to secure a loan to the participant or beneficiary from the exempt plan, annuity, account, or contract, and the right to the assets held in or to receive payments from the plan, annuity, account, or contract is subject to attachment, execution, and seizure for the satisfaction of the security interest or lien granted by the participant or beneficiary to secure the loan.

(e) If Subsection (a) is declared invalid or preempted by federal law, in whole or in part or in certain circumstances, as applied to a person who has not brought a proceeding under Title 11, United States Code, the subsection remains in effect, to the maximum extent permitted by law, as to any person who has filed that type of proceeding.

(f) A reference in this section to a specific provision of the Internal Revenue Code of 1986 includes a subsequent amendment of the substance of that provision.

PROP §42.0022. EXEMPTION FOR COLLEGE SAVINGS PLANS

(a) In addition to the exemption prescribed by Section 42.001, a person's right to the assets held in or to receive payments or benefits under any of the following is exempt from attachment, execution, and seizure for the satisfaction of debts:

(1) any fund or plan established under Subchapter F, Chapter 54, Education Code, including the person's interest in a prepaid tuition contract;

(2) any fund or plan established under Subchapter G, Chapter 54, Education Code, including the person's interest in a savings trust account; or

(3) any qualified tuition program of any state that meets the requirements of Section 529, Internal Revenue Code of 1986, as amended.

(b) If any portion of this section is held to be invalid or preempted by federal law in whole or in part or in certain circumstances, this section remains in effect in all other respects to the maximum extent permitted by law.

PROP §42.003. DESIGNATION OF EXEMPT PROPERTY

(a) If the number or amount of a type of personal property owned by a debtor exceeds the exemption allowed by Section 42.002 and the debtor can be found in the county where the property is located, the officer making a levy on the property shall ask the debtor to designate the personal property to be levied on. If the debtor cannot be found in the county or the debtor fails to make a designation within a reasonable time after the officer's request, the officer shall make the designation.

(b) If the aggregate value of a debtor's personal property exceeds the amount exempt from seizure under Section 42.001(a), the debtor may designate the portion of the property to be levied on. If, after a court's request, the debtor fails to make a designation within a reasonable time or if for any reason a creditor contests that the property is exempt, the court shall make the designation.

PROP §42.004. TRANSFER OF NONEXEMPT PROPERTY

(a) If a person uses the property not exempt under this chapter to acquire, obtain an interest in, make improvement to, or pay an indebtedness on personal property which would be exempt under this chapter with the intent to defraud, delay, or hinder an interested person from obtaining that to which the interested person is or may be entitled, the property, interest, or improvement acquired is not exempt from seizure for the satisfaction of liabilities. If the property, interest, or improvement is acquired by discharging an encumbrance held by a third person, a person defrauded, delayed, or hindered is subrogated to the rights of the third person.

(b) A creditor may not assert a claim under this section more than two years after the transaction from which the claim arises. A person with a claim that is unliquidated or contingent at the time of the transaction may not assert a claim under this section more than one year after the claim is reduced to judgment.

(c) It is a defense to a claim under this section that the transfer was made in the ordinary course of business by the person making the transfer.

PROP §42.005. CHILD SUPPORT LIENS

Sections 42.001, 42.002, and 42.0021 of this code do not apply to a child support lien established under Subchapter G, Chapter 157, Family Code.

ARTICLE 1. BILL OF RIGHTS

ARTICLE 16. GENERAL PROVISIONS

ARTICLE 1. BILL OF RIGHTS

ART. 1, §3a. EQUALITY UNDER THE LAW

Equality under the law shall not be denied or abridged because of sex, race, color, creed, or national origin. This amendment is self-operative.

ART. 1, §32. MARRIAGE

☠ *In* ***Obergefell v. Hodges****, ___ U.S. ___, 135 S.Ct. 2584 (2015), the U.S. Supreme Court held that same-sex couples may exercise the fundamental right to marry in all states, and that there is no lawful basis for a state to refuse to recognize a lawful same-sex marriage performed in another state on the ground of its same-sex character. See annotation under Family Code §6.204, p. 65.*

(a) Marriage in this state shall consist only of the union of one man and one woman.

(b) This state or a political subdivision of this state may not create or recognize any legal status identical or similar to marriage.

ARTICLE 16. GENERAL PROVISIONS

ART. 16, §15. SEPARATE & COMMUNITY PROPERTY

All property, both real and personal, of a spouse owned or claimed before marriage, and that acquired afterward by gift, devise or descent, shall be the separate property of that spouse; and laws shall be passed more clearly defining the rights of the spouses, in relation to separate and community property; provided that persons about to marry and spouses, without the intention to defraud pre-existing creditors, may by written instrument from time to time partition between themselves all or part of their property, then existing or to be acquired, or exchange between themselves the community interest of one spouse or future spouse in any property for the community interest of the other spouse or future spouse in other community property then existing or to be acquired, whereupon the portion or interest set aside to each spouse shall be and constitute a part of the separate property and estate of such spouse or future spouse; spouses also may from time to time, by written instrument, agree between themselves that the income or property from all or part of the separate property then owned or which thereafter might be acquired by only one of them, shall be the separate property of that spouse; if one spouse makes a gift of property to the other that gift is presumed to include all the income or property which might arise from that gift of property; spouses may agree in writing that all or part of their community property becomes the property of the surviving spouse on the death of a spouse; and spouses may agree in writing that all or part of the separate property owned by either or both of them shall be the spouses' community property.

ART. 16, §28. GARNISHMENT OF WAGES

No current wages for personal service shall ever be subject to garnishment, except for the enforcement of court-ordered:

(1) child support payments; or

(2) spousal maintenance.

18 ART. 16, §50. HOMESTEAD; PROTECTION FROM FORCED SALE; MORTGAGES, TRUST DEEDS, & LIENS

The amended text in subsection (a), proposed as a constitutional amendment by S.J.R. 60, §1, will be voted on during the Nov. 7, 2017 general election. If approved by the voters, the amendment will become effective Jan. 1, 2018.

(a) The homestead of a family, or of a single adult person, shall be, and is hereby protected from forced sale, for the payment of all debts except for:

(1) the purchase money thereof, or a part of such purchase money;

(2) the taxes due thereon;

(3) an owelty of partition imposed against the entirety of the property by a court order or by a written agreement of the parties to the partition, including a debt of one spouse in favor of the other spouse resulting from a division or an award of a family homestead in a divorce proceeding;

(4) the refinance of a lien against a homestead, including a federal tax lien resulting from the tax debt of

both spouses, if the homestead is a family homestead, or from the tax debt of the owner;

(5) work and material used in constructing new improvements thereon, if contracted for in writing, or work and material used to repair or renovate existing improvements thereon if:

(A) the work and material are contracted for in writing, with the consent of both spouses, in the case of a family homestead, given in the same manner as is required in making a sale and conveyance of the homestead;

(B) the contract for the work and material is not executed by the owner or the owner's spouse before the fifth day after the owner makes written application for any extension of credit for the work and material, unless the work and material are necessary to complete immediate repairs to conditions on the homestead property that materially affect the health or safety of the owner or person residing in the homestead and the owner of the homestead acknowledges such in writing;

(C) the contract for the work and material expressly provides that the owner may rescind the contract without penalty or charge within three days after the execution of the contract by all parties, unless the work and material are necessary to complete immediate repairs to conditions on the homestead property that materially affect the health or safety of the owner or person residing in the homestead and the owner of the homestead acknowledges such in writing; and

(D) the contract for the work and material is executed by the owner and the owner's spouse only at the office of a third-party lender making an extension of credit for the work and material, an attorney at law, or a title company;

(6) an extension of credit that:

(A) is secured by a voluntary lien on the homestead created under a written agreement with the consent of each owner and each owner's spouse;

(B) is of a principal amount that when added to the aggregate total of the outstanding principal balances of all other indebtedness secured by valid encumbrances of record against the homestead does not exceed 80 percent of the fair market value of the homestead on the date the extension of credit is made;

(C) is without recourse for personal liability against each owner and the spouse of each owner, unless the owner or spouse obtained the extension of credit by actual fraud;

(D) is secured by a lien that may be foreclosed upon only by a court order;

(E) does not require the owner or the owner's spouse to pay, in addition to any interest or any bona fide discount points used to buy down the interest rate, any fees to any person that are necessary to originate, evaluate, maintain, record, insure, or service the extension of credit that exceed, in the aggregate, two [~~three~~] percent of the original principal amount of the extension of credit, excluding fees for:

(i) an appraisal performed by a third party appraiser;

(ii) a property survey performed by a state registered or licensed surveyor;

(iii) a state base premium for a mortgagee policy of title insurance with endorsements established in accordance with state law; or

(iv) a title examination report if its cost is less than the state base premium for a mortgagee policy of title insurance without endorsements established in accordance with state law;

(F) is not a form of open-end account that may be debited from time to time or under which credit may be extended from time to time unless the open-end account is a home equity line of credit;

(G) is payable in advance without penalty or other charge;

(H) is not secured by any additional real or personal property other than the homestead;

(I) (repealed) [~~is not secured by homestead property that on the date of closing is designated for agricultural use as provided by statutes governing property tax, unless such homestead property is used primarily for the production of milk~~];

(J) may not be accelerated because of a decrease in the market value of the homestead or because of the owner's default under other indebtedness not secured by a prior valid encumbrance against the homestead;

(K) is the only debt secured by the homestead at the time the extension of credit is made unless the other debt was made for a purpose described by Subsections (a)(1)-(a)(5) or Subsection (a)(8) of this section;

(L) is scheduled to be repaid:

(i) in substantially equal successive periodic installments, not more often than every 14 days and not less often than monthly, beginning no later than two

months from the date the extension of credit is made, each of which equals or exceeds the amount of accrued interest as of the date of the scheduled installment; or

(ii) if the extension of credit is a home equity line of credit, in periodic payments described under Subsection (t)(8) of this section;

(M) is closed not before:

(i) the 12th day after the later of the date that the owner of the homestead submits a loan application to the lender for the extension of credit or the date that the lender provides the owner a copy of the notice prescribed by Subsection (g) of this section;

(ii) one business day after the date that the owner of the homestead receives a copy of the loan application if not previously provided and a final itemized disclosure of the actual fees, points, interest, costs, and charges that will be charged at closing. If a bona fide emergency or another good cause exists and the lender obtains the written consent of the owner, the lender may provide the documentation to the owner or the lender may modify previously provided documentation on the date of closing; and

(iii) the first anniversary of the closing date of any other extension of credit described by Subsection (a)(6) of this section secured by the same homestead property, except a refinance described by Paragraph (Q)(x)(f) of this subdivision, unless the owner on oath requests an earlier closing due to a state of emergency that:

(a) has been declared by the president of the United States or the governor as provided by law; and

(b) applies to the area where the homestead is located;

(N) is closed only at the office of the lender, an attorney at law, or a title company;

(O) permits a lender to contract for and receive any fixed or variable rate of interest authorized under statute;

(P) is made by one of the following that has not been found by a federal regulatory agency to have engaged in the practice of refusing to make loans because the applicants for the loans reside or the property proposed to secure the loans is located in a certain area:

(i) a bank, savings and loan association, savings bank, or credit union doing business under the laws of this state or the United States, including a subsidiary of a bank, savings and loan association, savings bank, or credit union described by this subparagraph;

(ii) a federally chartered lending instrumentality or a person approved as a mortgagee by the United States government to make federally insured loans;

(iii) a person licensed to make regulated loans, as provided by statute of this state;

(iv) a person who sold the homestead property to the current owner and who provided all or part of the financing for the purchase;

(v) a person who is related to the homestead property owner within the second degree of affinity or consanguinity; or

(vi) a person regulated by this state as a mortgage banker or mortgage company [~~broker~~]; and

(Q) is made on the condition that:

(i) the owner of the homestead is not required to apply the proceeds of the extension of credit to repay another debt except debt secured by the homestead or debt to another lender;

(ii) the owner of the homestead not assign wages as security for the extension of credit;

(iii) the owner of the homestead not sign any instrument in which blanks relating to substantive terms of agreement are left to be filled in;

(iv) the owner of the homestead not sign a confession of judgment or power of attorney to the lender or to a third person to confess judgment or to appear for the owner in a judicial proceeding;

(v) at the time the extension of credit is made, the owner of the homestead shall receive a copy of the final loan application and all executed documents signed by the owner at closing related to the extension of credit;

(vi) the security instruments securing the extension of credit contain a disclosure that the extension of credit is the type of credit defined by Subsection (a)(6) of this section [~~Section 50(a)(6), Article XVI, Texas Constitution~~];

(vii) within a reasonable time after termination and full payment of the extension of credit, the lender cancel and return the promissory note to the owner of the homestead and give the owner, in recordable form, a release of the lien securing the extension of credit or a copy of an endorsement and assignment of the lien to a lender that is refinancing the extension of credit;

(viii) the owner of the homestead and any spouse of the owner may, within three days after the extension of credit is made, rescind the extension of credit without penalty or charge;

(ix) the owner of the homestead and the lender sign a written acknowledgment as to the fair market value of the homestead property on the date the extension of credit is made;

(x) except as provided by Subparagraph (xi) of this paragraph, the lender or any holder of the note for the extension of credit shall forfeit all principal and interest of the extension of credit if the lender or holder fails to comply with the lender's or holder's obligations under the extension of credit and fails to correct the failure to comply not later than the 60th day after the date the lender or holder is notified by the borrower of the lender's failure to comply by:

(a) paying to the owner an amount equal to any overcharge paid by the owner under or related to the extension of credit if the owner has paid an amount that exceeds an amount stated in the applicable Paragraph (E), (G), or (O) of this subdivision;

(b) sending the owner a written acknowledgement that the lien is valid only in the amount that the extension of credit does not exceed the percentage described by Paragraph (B) of this subdivision, if applicable, or is not secured by property described under Paragraph (H) [~~or (I)~~] of this subdivision, if applicable;

(c) sending the owner a written notice modifying any other amount, percentage, term, or other provision prohibited by this section to a permitted amount, percentage, term, or other provision and adjusting the account of the borrower to ensure that the borrower is not required to pay more than an amount permitted by this section and is not subject to any other term or provision prohibited by this section;

(d) delivering the required documents to the borrower if the lender fails to comply with Subparagraph (v) of this paragraph or obtaining the appropriate signatures if the lender fails to comply with Subparagraph (ix) of this paragraph;

(e) sending the owner a written acknowledgement, if the failure to comply is prohibited by Paragraph (K) of this subdivision, that the accrual of interest and all of the owner's obligations under the extension of credit are abated while any prior lien prohibited under Paragraph (K) remains secured by the homestead; or

(f) if the failure to comply cannot be cured under Subparagraphs (x)(a)-(e) of this paragraph, curing the failure to comply by a refund or credit to the owner of $1,000 and offering the owner the right to refinance the extension of credit with the lender or holder for the remaining term of the loan at no cost to the owner on the same terms, including interest, as the original extension of credit with any modifications necessary to comply with this section or on terms on which the owner and the lender or holder otherwise agree that comply with this section; and

(xi) the lender or any holder of the note for the extension of credit shall forfeit all principal and interest of the extension of credit if the extension of credit is made by a person other than a person described under Paragraph (P) of this subdivision or if the lien was not created under a written agreement with the consent of each owner and each owner's spouse, unless each owner and each owner's spouse who did not initially consent subsequently consents;

(7) a reverse mortgage; or

(8) the conversion and refinance of a personal property lien secured by a manufactured home to a lien on real property, including the refinance of the purchase price of the manufactured home, the cost of installing the manufactured home on the real property, and the refinance of the purchase price of the real property.

(b) An owner or claimant of the property claimed as homestead may not sell or abandon the homestead without the consent of each owner and the spouse of each owner, given in such manner as may be prescribed by law.

(c) No mortgage, trust deed, or other lien on the homestead shall ever be valid unless it secures a debt described by this section, whether such mortgage, trust deed, or other lien, shall have been created by the owner alone, or together with his or her spouse, in case the owner is married. All pretended sales of the homestead involving any condition of defeasance shall be void.

(d) A purchaser or lender for value without actual knowledge may conclusively rely on an affidavit that designates other property as the homestead of the affiant and that states that the property to be conveyed or encumbered is not the homestead of the affiant.

(e) A refinance of debt secured by a homestead and described by any subsection under Subsections (a)(1)-(a)(5) that includes the advance of additional funds may not be secured by a valid lien against the homestead unless:

(1) the refinance of the debt is an extension of credit described by Subsection (a)(6) of this section; or

(2) the advance of all the additional funds is for reasonable costs necessary to refinance such debt or for a purpose described by Subsection (a)(2), (a)(3), or (a)(5) of this section.

The amended text in subsection (f), proposed as a constitutional amendment by S.J.R. 60, §1, will be voted on during the Nov. 7, 2017 general election. If approved by the voters, the amendment will become effective Jan. 1, 2018.

(f) A refinance of debt secured by the homestead, any portion of which is an extension of credit described by Subsection (a)(6) of this section, may not be secured by a valid lien against the homestead unless either:

(1) the refinance of the debt is an extension of credit described by Subsection (a)(6) or (a)(7) of this section; or

(2) all of the following conditions are met:

(A) the refinance is not closed before the first anniversary of the date the extension of credit was closed;

(B) the refinanced extension of credit does not include the advance of any additional funds other than:

(i) funds advanced to refinance a debt described by Subsections (a)(1) through (a)(7) of this section; or

(ii) actual costs and reserves required by the lender to refinance the debt;

(C) the refinance of the extension of credit is of a principal amount that when added to the aggregate total of the outstanding principal balances of all other indebtedness secured by valid encumbrances of record against the homestead does not exceed 80 percent of the fair market value of the homestead on the date the refinance of the extension of credit is made; and

(D) the lender provides the owner the following written notice on a separate document not later than the third business day after the date the owner submits the loan application to the lender and at least 12 days before the date the refinance of the extension of credit is closed:

"YOUR EXISTING LOAN THAT YOU DESIRE TO REFINANCE IS A HOME EQUITY LOAN. YOU MAY HAVE THE OPTION TO REFINANCE YOUR HOME EQUITY LOAN AS EITHER A HOME EQUITY LOAN OR AS A NON-HOME EQUITY LOAN, IF OFFERED BY YOUR LENDER.

"HOME EQUITY LOANS HAVE IMPORTANT CONSUMER PROTECTIONS. A LENDER MAY ONLY FORECLOSE A HOME EQUITY LOAN BASED ON A COURT ORDER. A HOME EQUITY LOAN MUST BE WITHOUT RECOURSE FOR PERSONAL LIABILITY AGAINST YOU AND YOUR SPOUSE.

"IF YOU HAVE APPLIED TO REFINANCE YOUR EXISTING HOME EQUITY LOAN AS A NON-HOME EQUITY LOAN, YOU WILL LOSE CERTAIN CONSUMER PROTECTIONS. A NON-HOME EQUITY REFINANCED LOAN:

"(1) WILL PERMIT THE LENDER TO FORECLOSE WITHOUT A COURT ORDER;

"(2) WILL BE WITH RECOURSE FOR PERSONAL LIABILITY AGAINST YOU AND YOUR SPOUSE; AND

"(3) MAY ALSO CONTAIN OTHER TERMS OR CONDITIONS THAT MAY NOT BE PERMITTED IN A TRADITIONAL HOME EQUITY LOAN.

"BEFORE YOU REFINANCE YOUR EXISTING HOME EQUITY LOAN TO MAKE IT A NON-HOME EQUITY LOAN, YOU SHOULD MAKE SURE YOU UNDERSTAND THAT YOU ARE WAIVING IMPORTANT PROTECTIONS THAT HOME EQUITY LOANS PROVIDE UNDER THE LAW AND SHOULD CONSIDER CONSULTING WITH AN ATTORNEY OF YOUR CHOOSING REGARDING THESE PROTECTIONS.

"YOU MAY WISH TO ASK YOUR LENDER TO REFINANCE YOUR LOAN AS A HOME EQUITY LOAN. HOWEVER, A HOME EQUITY LOAN MAY HAVE A HIGHER INTEREST RATE AND CLOSING COSTS THAN A NON-HOME EQUITY LOAN."

The enacted text in subsection (f-1), proposed as a constitutional amendment by S.J.R. 60, §1, will be voted on during the Nov. 7, 2017 general election. If approved by the voters, the enactment will become effective Jan. 1, 2018.

(f-1) A lien securing a refinance of debt under Subsection (f)(2) of this section is deemed to be a lien described by Subsection (a)(4) of this section. An affidavit executed by the owner or the owner's spouse acknowledging that the requirements of Subsection (f)(2) of this section have been met conclusively establishes that the requirements of Subsection (a)(4) of this section have been met.

The amended text in subsection (g), proposed as a constitutional amendment by S.J.R. 60, §1, will be voted

on during the Nov. 7, 2017 general election. If approved by the voters, the amendment will become effective Jan. 1, 2018.

(g) An extension of credit described by Subsection (a)(6) of this section may be secured by a valid lien against homestead property if the extension of credit is not closed before the 12th day after the lender provides the owner with the following written notice on a separate instrument:

"NOTICE CONCERNING EXTENSIONS OF CREDIT DEFINED BY SECTION 50(a)(6), ARTICLE XVI, TEXAS CONSTITUTION:

"SECTION 50(a)(6), ARTICLE XVI, OF THE TEXAS CONSTITUTION ALLOWS CERTAIN LOANS TO BE SECURED AGAINST THE EQUITY IN YOUR HOME. SUCH LOANS ARE COMMONLY KNOWN AS EQUITY LOANS. IF YOU DO NOT REPAY THE LOAN OR IF YOU FAIL TO MEET THE TERMS OF THE LOAN, THE LENDER MAY FORECLOSE AND SELL YOUR HOME. THE CONSTITUTION PROVIDES THAT:

"(A) THE LOAN MUST BE VOLUNTARILY CREATED WITH THE CONSENT OF EACH OWNER OF YOUR HOME AND EACH OWNER'S SPOUSE;

"(B) THE PRINCIPAL LOAN AMOUNT AT THE TIME THE LOAN IS MADE MUST NOT EXCEED AN AMOUNT THAT, WHEN ADDED TO THE PRINCIPAL BALANCES OF ALL OTHER LIENS AGAINST YOUR HOME, IS MORE THAN 80 PERCENT OF THE FAIR MARKET VALUE OF YOUR HOME;

"(C) THE LOAN MUST BE WITHOUT RECOURSE FOR PERSONAL LIABILITY AGAINST YOU AND YOUR SPOUSE UNLESS YOU OR YOUR SPOUSE OBTAINED THIS EXTENSION OF CREDIT BY ACTUAL FRAUD;

"(D) THE LIEN SECURING THE LOAN MAY BE FORECLOSED UPON ONLY WITH A COURT ORDER;

"(E) FEES AND CHARGES TO MAKE THE LOAN MAY NOT EXCEED 2 [3] PERCENT OF THE LOAN AMOUNT, EXCEPT FOR A FEE OR CHARGE FOR AN APPRAISAL PERFORMED BY A THIRD PARTY APPRAISER, A PROPERTY SURVEY PERFORMED BY A STATE REGISTERED OR LICENSED SURVEYOR, A STATE BASE PREMIUM FOR A MORTGAGEE POLICY OF TITLE INSURANCE WITH ENDORSEMENTS, OR A TITLE EXAMINATION REPORT;

"(F) THE LOAN MAY NOT BE AN OPEN-END ACCOUNT THAT MAY BE DEBITED FROM TIME TO TIME OR UNDER WHICH CREDIT MAY BE EXTENDED FROM TIME TO TIME UNLESS IT IS A HOME EQUITY LINE OF CREDIT;

"(G) YOU MAY PREPAY THE LOAN WITHOUT PENALTY OR CHARGE;

"(H) NO ADDITIONAL COLLATERAL MAY BE SECURITY FOR THE LOAN;

"(I) (repealed) [~~THE LOAN MAY NOT BE SECURED BY HOMESTEAD PROPERTY THAT IS DESIGNATED FOR AGRICULTURAL USE AS OF THE DATE OF CLOSING, UNLESS THE AGRICULTURAL HOMESTEAD PROPERTY IS USED PRIMARILY FOR THE PRODUCTION OF MILK~~];

"(J) YOU ARE NOT REQUIRED TO REPAY THE LOAN EARLIER THAN AGREED SOLELY BECAUSE THE FAIR MARKET VALUE OF YOUR HOME DECREASES OR BECAUSE YOU DEFAULT ON ANOTHER LOAN THAT IS NOT SECURED BY YOUR HOME;

"(K) ONLY ONE LOAN DESCRIBED BY SECTION 50(a)(6), ARTICLE XVI, OF THE TEXAS CONSTITUTION MAY BE SECURED WITH YOUR HOME AT ANY GIVEN TIME;

"(L) THE LOAN MUST BE SCHEDULED TO BE REPAID IN PAYMENTS THAT EQUAL OR EXCEED THE AMOUNT OF ACCRUED INTEREST FOR EACH PAYMENT PERIOD;

"(M) THE LOAN MAY NOT CLOSE BEFORE 12 DAYS AFTER YOU SUBMIT A LOAN APPLICATION TO THE LENDER OR BEFORE 12 DAYS AFTER YOU RECEIVE THIS NOTICE, WHICHEVER DATE IS LATER; AND MAY NOT WITHOUT YOUR CONSENT CLOSE BEFORE ONE BUSINESS DAY AFTER THE DATE ON WHICH YOU RECEIVE A COPY OF YOUR LOAN APPLICATION IF NOT PREVIOUSLY PROVIDED AND A FINAL ITEMIZED DISCLOSURE OF THE ACTUAL FEES, POINTS, INTEREST, COSTS, AND CHARGES THAT WILL BE CHARGED AT CLOSING; AND IF YOUR HOME WAS SECURITY FOR THE SAME TYPE OF LOAN WITHIN THE PAST YEAR, A NEW LOAN SECURED BY THE SAME PROPERTY MAY NOT CLOSE BEFORE ONE YEAR HAS PASSED FROM THE CLOSING DATE OF THE OTHER LOAN, UNLESS ON OATH YOU REQUEST AN EARLIER CLOSING DUE TO A DECLARED STATE OF EMERGENCY;

"(N) THE LOAN MAY CLOSE ONLY AT THE OFFICE OF THE LENDER, TITLE COMPANY, OR AN ATTORNEY AT LAW;

"(O) THE LENDER MAY CHARGE ANY FIXED OR VARIABLE RATE OF INTEREST AUTHORIZED BY STATUTE;

"(P) ONLY A LAWFULLY AUTHORIZED LENDER MAY MAKE LOANS DESCRIBED BY SECTION 50(a)(6), ARTICLE XVI, OF THE TEXAS CONSTITUTION;

"(Q) LOANS DESCRIBED BY SECTION 50(a)(6), ARTICLE XVI, OF THE TEXAS CONSTITUTION MUST:

"(1) NOT REQUIRE YOU TO APPLY THE PROCEEDS TO ANOTHER DEBT EXCEPT A DEBT THAT IS SECURED BY YOUR HOME OR OWED TO ANOTHER LENDER;

"(2) NOT REQUIRE THAT YOU ASSIGN WAGES AS SECURITY;

"(3) NOT REQUIRE THAT YOU EXECUTE INSTRUMENTS WHICH HAVE BLANKS FOR SUBSTANTIVE TERMS OF AGREEMENT LEFT TO BE FILLED IN;

"(4) NOT REQUIRE THAT YOU SIGN A CONFESSION OF JUDGMENT OR POWER OF ATTORNEY TO ANOTHER PERSON TO CONFESS JUDGMENT OR APPEAR IN A LEGAL PROCEEDING ON YOUR BEHALF;

"(5) PROVIDE THAT YOU RECEIVE A COPY OF YOUR FINAL LOAN APPLICATION AND ALL EXECUTED DOCUMENTS YOU SIGN AT CLOSING;

"(6) PROVIDE THAT THE SECURITY INSTRUMENTS CONTAIN A DISCLOSURE THAT THIS LOAN IS A LOAN DEFINED BY SECTION 50(a)(6), ARTICLE XVI, OF THE TEXAS CONSTITUTION;

"(7) PROVIDE THAT WHEN THE LOAN IS PAID IN FULL, THE LENDER WILL SIGN AND GIVE YOU A RELEASE OF LIEN OR AN ASSIGNMENT OF THE LIEN, WHICHEVER IS APPROPRIATE;

"(8) PROVIDE THAT YOU MAY, WITHIN 3 DAYS AFTER CLOSING, RESCIND THE LOAN WITHOUT PENALTY OR CHARGE;

"(9) PROVIDE THAT YOU AND THE LENDER ACKNOWLEDGE THE FAIR MARKET VALUE OF YOUR HOME ON THE DATE THE LOAN CLOSES; AND

"(10) PROVIDE THAT THE LENDER WILL FORFEIT ALL PRINCIPAL AND INTEREST IF THE LENDER FAILS TO COMPLY WITH THE LENDER'S OBLIGATIONS UNLESS THE LENDER CURES THE FAILURE TO COMPLY AS PROVIDED BY SECTION 50(a)(6)(Q)(x), ARTICLE XVI, OF THE TEXAS CONSTITUTION; AND

"(R) IF THE LOAN IS A HOME EQUITY LINE OF CREDIT:

"(1) YOU MAY REQUEST ADVANCES, REPAY MONEY, AND REBORROW MONEY UNDER THE LINE OF CREDIT;

"(2) EACH ADVANCE UNDER THE LINE OF CREDIT MUST BE IN AN AMOUNT OF AT LEAST $4,000;

"(3) YOU MAY NOT USE A CREDIT CARD, DEBIT CARD, OR SIMILAR DEVICE, OR PREPRINTED CHECK THAT YOU DID NOT SOLICIT, TO OBTAIN ADVANCES UNDER THE LINE OF CREDIT;

"(4) ANY FEES THE LENDER CHARGES MAY BE CHARGED AND COLLECTED ONLY AT THE TIME THE LINE OF CREDIT IS ESTABLISHED AND THE LENDER MAY NOT CHARGE A FEE IN CONNECTION WITH ANY ADVANCE;

"(5) THE MAXIMUM PRINCIPAL AMOUNT THAT MAY BE EXTENDED, WHEN ADDED TO ALL OTHER DEBTS SECURED BY YOUR HOME, MAY NOT EXCEED 80 PERCENT OF THE FAIR MARKET VALUE OF YOUR HOME ON THE DATE THE LINE OF CREDIT IS ESTABLISHED;

"(6) IF THE PRINCIPAL BALANCE UNDER THE LINE OF CREDIT AT ANY TIME EXCEEDS 80 [50] PERCENT OF THE FAIR MARKET VALUE OF YOUR HOME, AS DETERMINED ON THE DATE THE LINE OF CREDIT IS ESTABLISHED, YOU MAY NOT CONTINUE TO REQUEST ADVANCES UNDER THE LINE OF CREDIT UNTIL THE BALANCE IS LESS THAN 80 [50] PERCENT OF THE FAIR MARKET VALUE; AND

"(7) THE LENDER MAY NOT UNILATERALLY AMEND THE TERMS OF THE LINE OF CREDIT.

"THIS NOTICE IS ONLY A SUMMARY OF YOUR RIGHTS UNDER THE TEXAS CONSTITUTION. YOUR RIGHTS ARE GOVERNED BY SECTION 50, ARTICLE XVI, OF THE TEXAS CONSTITUTION, AND NOT BY THIS NOTICE."

If the discussions with the borrower are conducted primarily in a language other than English, the lender shall, before closing, provide an additional copy of the notice translated into the written language in which the discussions were conducted.

(h) A lender or assignee for value may conclusively rely on the written acknowledgment as to the fair market value of the homestead property made in accordance with Subsection (a)(6)(Q)(ix) of this section if:

(1) the value acknowledged to is the value estimate in an appraisal or evaluation prepared in accordance with a state or federal requirement applicable to an extension of credit under Subsection (a)(6); and

(2) the lender or assignee does not have actual knowledge at the time of the payment of value or advance of funds by the lender or assignee that the fair market value stated in the written acknowledgment was incorrect.

(i) This subsection shall not affect or impair any right of the borrower to recover damages from the lender or assignee under applicable law for wrongful foreclosure. A purchaser for value without actual knowledge may conclusively presume that a lien securing an extension of credit described by Subsection (a)(6) of this section was a valid lien securing the extension of credit with homestead property if:

(1) the security instruments securing the extension of credit contain a disclosure that the extension of credit secured by the lien was the type of credit defined by Section 50(a)(6), Article XVI, Texas Constitution;

(2) the purchaser acquires the title to the property pursuant to or after the foreclosure of the voluntary lien; and

(3) the purchaser is not the lender or assignee under the extension of credit.

(j) Subsection (a)(6) and Subsections (e)-(i) of this section are not severable, and none of those provisions would have been enacted without the others. If any of those provisions are held to be preempted by the laws of the United States, all of those provisions are invalid. This subsection shall not apply to any lien or extension of credit made after January 1, 1998, and before the date any provision under Subsection (a)(6) or Subsections (e)-(i) is held to be preempted.

(k) "Reverse mortgage" means an extension of credit:

(1) that is secured by a voluntary lien on homestead property created by a written agreement with the consent of each owner and each owner's spouse;

(2) that is made to a person who is or whose spouse is 62 years or older;

(3) that is made without recourse for personal liability against each owner and the spouse of each owner;

(4) under which advances are provided to a borrower:

(A) based on the equity in a borrower's homestead; or

(B) for the purchase of homestead property that the borrower will occupy as a principal residence;

(5) that does not permit the lender to reduce the amount or number of advances because of an adjustment in the interest rate if periodic advances are to be made;

(6) that requires no payment of principal or interest until:

(A) all borrowers have died;

(B) the homestead property securing the loan is sold or otherwise transferred;

(C) all borrowers cease occupying the homestead property for a period of longer than 12 consecutive months without prior written approval from the lender;

(C-1) if the extension of credit is used for the purchase of homestead property, the borrower fails to timely occupy the homestead property as the borrower's principal residence within a specified period after the date the extension of credit is made that is stipulated in the written agreement creating the lien on the property; or

(D) the borrower:

(i) defaults on an obligation specified in the loan documents to repair and maintain, pay taxes and assessments on, or insure the homestead property;

(ii) commits actual fraud in connection with the loan; or

(iii) fails to maintain the priority of the lender's lien on the homestead property, after the lender gives notice to the borrower, by promptly discharging any lien that has priority or may obtain priority over the lender's lien within 10 days after the date the borrower receives the notice, unless the borrower:

(a) agrees in writing to the payment of the obligation secured by the lien in a manner acceptable to the lender;

(b) contests in good faith the lien by, or defends against enforcement of the lien in, legal proceedings so as to prevent the enforcement of the lien or forfeiture of any part of the homestead property; or

(c) secures from the holder of the lien an agreement satisfactory to the lender subordinating the lien to all amounts secured by the lender's lien on the homestead property;

(7) that provides that if the lender fails to make loan advances as required in the loan documents and if the lender fails to cure the default as required in the loan documents after notice from the borrower, the lender forfeits all principal and interest of the reverse

mortgage, provided, however, that this subdivision does not apply when a governmental agency or instrumentality takes an assignment of the loan in order to cure the default;

(8) that is not made unless the prospective borrower and the spouse of the prospective borrower attest in writing that the prospective borrower and the prospective borrower's spouse received counseling regarding the advisability and availability of reverse mortgages and other financial alternatives that was completed not earlier than the 180th day nor later than the 5th day before the date the extension of credit is closed;

(9) that is not closed before the 12th day after the date the lender provides to the prospective borrower the following written notice on a separate instrument, which the lender or originator and the borrower must sign for the notice to take effect:

"IMPORTANT NOTICE TO BORROWERS

RELATED TO YOUR REVERSE MORTGAGE

"UNDER THE TEXAS TAX CODE, CERTAIN ELDERLY PERSONS MAY DEFER THE COLLECTION OF PROPERTY TAXES ON THEIR RESIDENCE HOMESTEAD. BY RECEIVING THIS REVERSE MORTGAGE YOU MAY BE REQUIRED TO FORGO ANY PREVIOUSLY APPROVED DEFERRAL OF PROPERTY TAX COLLECTION AND YOU MAY BE REQUIRED TO PAY PROPERTY TAXES ON AN ANNUAL BASIS ON THIS PROPERTY.

"THE LENDER MAY FORECLOSE THE REVERSE MORTGAGE AND YOU MAY LOSE YOUR HOME IF:

"(A) YOU DO NOT PAY THE TAXES OR OTHER ASSESSMENTS ON THE HOME EVEN IF YOU ARE ELIGIBLE TO DEFER PAYMENT OF PROPERTY TAXES;

"(B) YOU DO NOT MAINTAIN AND PAY FOR PROPERTY INSURANCE ON THE HOME AS REQUIRED BY THE LOAN DOCUMENTS;

"(C) YOU FAIL TO MAINTAIN THE HOME IN A STATE OF GOOD CONDITION AND REPAIR;

"(D) YOU CEASE OCCUPYING THE HOME FOR A PERIOD LONGER THAN 12 CONSECUTIVE MONTHS WITHOUT THE PRIOR WRITTEN APPROVAL FROM THE LENDER OR, IF THE EXTENSION OF CREDIT IS USED FOR THE PURCHASE OF THE HOME, YOU FAIL TO TIMELY OCCUPY THE HOME AS YOUR PRINCIPAL RESIDENCE WITHIN A PERIOD OF TIME AFTER THE EXTENSION OF CREDIT IS MADE THAT IS STIPULATED IN THE WRITTEN AGREEMENT CREATING THE LIEN ON THE HOME;

"(E) YOU SELL THE HOME OR OTHERWISE TRANSFER THE HOME WITHOUT PAYING OFF THE LOAN;

"(F) ALL BORROWERS HAVE DIED AND THE LOAN IS NOT REPAID;

"(G) YOU COMMIT ACTUAL FRAUD IN CONNECTION WITH THE LOAN; OR

"(H) YOU FAIL TO MAINTAIN THE PRIORITY OF THE LENDER'S LIEN ON THE HOME, AFTER THE LENDER GIVES NOTICE TO YOU, BY PROMPTLY DISCHARGING ANY LIEN THAT HAS PRIORITY OR MAY OBTAIN PRIORITY OVER THE LENDER'S LIEN WITHIN 10 DAYS AFTER THE DATE YOU RECEIVE THE NOTICE, UNLESS YOU:

"(1) AGREE IN WRITING TO THE PAYMENT OF THE OBLIGATION SECURED BY THE LIEN IN A MANNER ACCEPTABLE TO THE LENDER;

"(2) CONTEST IN GOOD FAITH THE LIEN BY, OR DEFEND AGAINST ENFORCEMENT OF THE LIEN IN, LEGAL PROCEEDINGS SO AS TO PREVENT THE ENFORCEMENT OF THE LIEN OR FORFEITURE OF ANY PART OF THE HOME; OR

"(3) SECURE FROM THE HOLDER OF THE LIEN AN AGREEMENT SATISFACTORY TO THE LENDER SUBORDINATING THE LIEN TO ALL AMOUNTS SECURED BY THE LENDER'S LIEN ON THE HOME.

"IF A GROUND FOR FORECLOSURE EXISTS, THE LENDER MAY NOT COMMENCE FORECLOSURE UNTIL THE LENDER GIVES YOU WRITTEN NOTICE BY MAIL THAT A GROUND FOR FORECLOSURE EXISTS AND GIVES YOU AN OPPORTUNITY TO REMEDY THE CONDITION CREATING THE GROUND FOR FORECLOSURE OR TO PAY THE REVERSE MORTGAGE DEBT WITHIN THE TIME PERMITTED BY SECTION 50(k)(10), ARTICLE XVI, OF THE TEXAS CONSTITUTION. THE LENDER MUST OBTAIN A COURT ORDER FOR FORECLOSURE EXCEPT THAT A COURT ORDER IS NOT REQUIRED IF THE FORECLOSURE OCCURS BECAUSE:

"(1) ALL BORROWERS HAVE DIED; OR

"(2) THE HOMESTEAD PROPERTY SECURING THE LOAN IS SOLD OR OTHERWISE TRANSFERRED."

"YOU SHOULD CONSULT WITH YOUR HOME COUNSELOR OR AN ATTORNEY IF YOU HAVE ANY CONCERNS ABOUT THESE OBLIGATIONS BEFORE YOU CLOSE YOUR REVERSE MORTGAGE LOAN. TO

LOCATE AN ATTORNEY IN YOUR AREA, YOU MAY WISH TO CONTACT THE STATE BAR OF TEXAS."

"THIS NOTICE IS ONLY A SUMMARY OF YOUR RIGHTS UNDER THE TEXAS CONSTITUTION. YOUR RIGHTS ARE GOVERNED IN PART BY SECTION 50, ARTICLE XVI, OF THE TEXAS CONSTITUTION, AND NOT BY THIS NOTICE.";

(10) that does not permit the lender to commence foreclosure until the lender gives notice to the borrower, in the manner provided for a notice by mail related to the foreclosure of liens under Subsection (a)(6) of this section, that a ground for foreclosure exists and gives the borrower at least 30 days, or at least 20 days in the event of a default under Subdivision (6)(D)(iii) of this subsection, to:

(A) remedy the condition creating the ground for foreclosure;

(B) pay the debt secured by the homestead property from proceeds of the sale of the homestead property by the borrower or from any other sources; or

(C) convey the homestead property to the lender by a deed in lieu of foreclosure; and

(11) that is secured by a lien that may be foreclosed upon only by a court order, if the foreclosure is for a ground other than a ground stated by Subdivision (6)(A) or (B) of this subsection.

(*l*) Advances made under a reverse mortgage and interest on those advances have priority over a lien filed for record in the real property records in the county where the homestead property is located after the reverse mortgage is filed for record in the real property records of that county.

(m) A reverse mortgage may provide for an interest rate that is fixed or adjustable and may also provide for interest that is contingent on appreciation in the fair market value of the homestead property. Although payment of principal or interest shall not be required under a reverse mortgage until the entire loan becomes due and payable, interest may accrue and be compounded during the term of the loan as provided by the reverse mortgage loan agreement.

(n) A reverse mortgage that is secured by a valid lien against homestead property may be made or acquired without regard to the following provisions of any other law of this state:

(1) a limitation on the purpose and use of future advances or other mortgage proceeds;

(2) a limitation on future advances to a term of years or a limitation on the term of open-end account advances;

(3) a limitation on the term during which future advances take priority over intervening advances;

(4) a requirement that a maximum loan amount be stated in the reverse mortgage loan documents;

(5) a prohibition on balloon payments;

(6) a prohibition on compound interest and interest on interest;

(7) a prohibition on contracting for, charging, or receiving any rate of interest authorized by any law of this state authorizing a lender to contract for a rate of interest; and

(8) a requirement that a percentage of the reverse mortgage proceeds be advanced before the assignment of the reverse mortgage.

(o) For the purposes of determining eligibility under any statute relating to payments, allowances, benefits, or services provided on a means-tested basis by this state, including supplemental security income, low-income energy assistance, property tax relief, medical assistance, and general assistance:

(1) reverse mortgage loan advances made to a borrower are considered proceeds from a loan and not income; and

(2) undisbursed funds under a reverse mortgage loan are considered equity in a borrower's home and not proceeds from a loan.

(p) The advances made on a reverse mortgage loan under which more than one advance is made must be made according to the terms established by the loan documents by one or more of the following methods:

(1) an initial advance at any time and future advances at regular intervals;

(2) an initial advance at any time and future advances at regular intervals in which the amounts advanced may be reduced, for one or more advances, at the request of the borrower;

(3) an initial advance at any time and future advances at times and in amounts requested by the borrower until the credit limit established by the loan documents is reached;

(4) an initial advance at any time, future advances at times and in amounts requested by the borrower until the credit limit established by the loan documents is reached, and subsequent advances at times and in

amounts requested by the borrower according to the terms established by the loan documents to the extent that the outstanding balance is repaid; or

(5) at any time by the lender, on behalf of the borrower, if the borrower fails to timely pay any of the following that the borrower is obligated to pay under the loan documents to the extent necessary to protect the lender's interest in or the value of the homestead property:

(A) taxes;

(B) insurance;

(C) costs of repairs or maintenance performed by a person or company that is not an employee of the lender or a person or company that directly or indirectly controls, is controlled by, or is under common control with the lender;

(D) assessments levied against the homestead property; and

(E) any lien that has, or may obtain, priority over the lender's lien as it is established in the loan documents.

(q) To the extent that any statutes of this state, including without limitation, Section 41.001 of the Texas Property Code, purport to limit encumbrances that may properly be fixed on homestead property in a manner that does not permit encumbrances for extensions of credit described in Subsection (a)(6) or (a)(7) of this section, the same shall be superseded to the extent that such encumbrances shall be permitted to be fixed upon homestead property in the manner provided for by this amendment.

(r) The supreme court shall promulgate rules of civil procedure for expedited foreclosure proceedings related to the foreclosure of liens under Subsection (a)(6) of this section and to foreclosure of a reverse mortgage lien that requires a court order.

(s) The Finance Commission of Texas shall appoint a director to conduct research on the availability, quality, and prices of financial services and research the practices of business entities in the state that provide financial services under this section. The director shall collect information and produce reports on lending activity of those making loans under this section. The director shall report his or her findings to the legislature not later than December 1 of each year.

The amended text in subsection (t), proposed as a constitutional amendment by S.J.R. 60, §1, will be voted on during the Nov. 7, 2017 general election. If approved by the voters, the amendment will become effective Jan. 1, 2018.

(t) A home equity line of credit is a form of an open-end account that may be debited from time to time, under which credit may be extended from time to time and under which:

(1) the owner requests advances, repays money, and reborrows money;

(2) any single debit or advance is not less than $4,000;

(3) the owner does not use a credit card, debit card, or similar device, or preprinted check unsolicited by the borrower, to obtain an advance;

(4) any fees described by Subsection (a)(6)(E) of this section are charged and collected only at the time the extension of credit is established and no fee is charged or collected in connection with any debit or advance;

(5) the maximum principal amount that may be extended under the account, when added to the aggregate total of the outstanding principal balances of all indebtedness secured by the homestead on the date the extension of credit is established, does not exceed an amount described under Subsection (a)(6)(B) of this section;

(6) <u>(repealed)</u> [~~no additional debits or advances are made if the total principal amount outstanding exceeds an amount equal to 50 percent of the fair market value of the homestead as determined on the date the account is established~~];

(7) the lender or holder may not unilaterally amend the extension of credit; and

(8) repayment is to be made in regular periodic installments, not more often than every 14 days and not less often than monthly, beginning not later than two months from the date the extension of credit is established, and:

(A) during the period during which the owner may request advances, each installment equals or exceeds the amount of accrued interest; and

(B) after the period during which the owner may request advances, installments are substantially equal.

(u) The legislature may by statute delegate one or more state agencies the power to interpret Subsections (a)(5)-(a)(7), (e)-(p), and (t), of this section. An act or omission does not violate a provision included in those

subsections if the act or omission conforms to an interpretation of the provision that is:

(1) in effect at the time of the act or omission; and

(2) made by a state agency to which the power of interpretation is delegated as provided by this subsection or by an appellate court of this state or the United States.

(v) A reverse mortgage must provide that:

(1) the owner does not use a credit card, debit card, preprinted solicitation check, or similar device to obtain an advance;

(2) after the time the extension of credit is established, no transaction fee is charged or collected solely in connection with any debit or advance; and

(3) the lender or holder may not unilaterally amend the extension of credit.

ART. 16, §51. AMOUNT OF HOMESTEAD; USES

The homestead, not in a town or city, shall consist of not more than two hundred acres of land, which may be in one or more parcels, with the improvements thereon; the homestead in a city, town or village, shall consist of lot or contiguous lots amounting to not more than 10 acres of land, together with any improvements on the land; provided, that the homestead in a city, town or village shall be used for the purposes of a home, or as both an urban home and a place to exercise a calling or business, of the homestead claimant, whether a single adult person, or the head of a family; provided also, that any temporary renting of the homestead shall not change the character of the same, when no other homestead has been acquired; provided further that a release or refinance of an existing lien against a homestead as to a part of the homestead does not create an additional burden on the part of the homestead property that is unreleased or subject to the refinance, and a new lien is not invalid only for that reason.

UNITED STATES CODE
SELECTED PROVISIONS
TABLE OF CONTENTS

SELECTED PROVISIONS
TABLE OF CONTENTS

TITLE 18. CRIMES & CRIMINAL PROCEDURE

PART I. CRIMES

CHAPTER 11A. CHILD SUPPORT

§228. FAILURE TO PAY LEGAL CHILD SUPPORT OBLIGATIONS

(a) Offense.—Any person who—

(1) willfully fails to pay a support obligation with respect to a child who resides in another State, if such obligation has remained unpaid for a period longer than 1 year, or is greater than $5,000;

(2) travels in interstate or foreign commerce with the intent to evade a support obligation, if such obligation has remained unpaid for a period longer than 1 year, or is greater than $5,000; or

(3) willfully fails to pay a support obligation with respect to a child who resides in another State, if such obligation has remained unpaid for a period longer than 2 years, or is greater than $10,000;

shall be punished as provided in subsection (c).

(b) Presumption.—The existence of a support obligation that was in effect for the time period charged in the indictment or information creates a rebuttable presumption that the obligor has the ability to pay the support obligation for that time period.

(c) Punishment. The punishment for an of fense under this section is—

(1) in the case of a first offense under subsection (a)(1), a fine under this title, imprisonment for not more than 6 months, or both; and

(2) in the case of an offense under paragraph (2) or (3) of subsection (a), or a second or subsequent offense under subsection (a)(1), a fine under this title, imprisonment for not more than 2 years, or both.

(d) Mandatory restitution.—Upon a conviction under this section, the court shall order restitution under section 3663A in an amount equal to the total unpaid support obligation as it exists at the time of sentencing.

(e) Venue.—With respect to an offense under this section, an action may be inquired of and prosecuted in a district court of the United States for—

(1) the district in which the child who is the subject of the support obligation involved resided during a period during which a person described in subsection (a) (referred to in this subsection as an "obliger") failed to meet that support obligation;

(2) the district in which the obliger resided during a period described in paragraph (1); or

(3) any other district with jurisdiction otherwise provided for by law.

(f) Definitions.—As used in this section—

(1) the term "Indian tribe" has the meaning given that term in section 102 of the Federally Recognized Indian Tribe List Act of 1994 (25 U.S.C. 479a);

(2) the term "State" includes any State of the United States, the District of Columbia, and any commonwealth, territory, or possession of the United States; and

(3) the term "support obligation" means any amount determined under a court order or an order of an administrative process pursuant to the law of a State or of an Indian tribe to be due from a person for the support and maintenance of a child or of a child and the parent with whom the child is living.

History of 18 U.S.C. §228: Oct. 25, 1992, P.L. 102-521, §2(a), 106 Stat. 3403; Oct. 11, 1996, P.L. 104-294, §607(1), 110 Stat. 3512; June 24, 1998, P.L. 105-187, §2, 112 Stat. 618.

CHAPTER 44. FIREARMS

§921. DEFINITIONS

(a) As used in this chapter—

(1) The term "person" and the term "whoever" include any individual, corporation, company, association, firm, partnership, society, or joint stock company.

(2) The term "interstate or foreign commerce" includes commerce between any place in a State and any place outside of that State, or within any possession of the United States (not including the Canal Zone) or the District of Columbia, but such term does not include commerce between places within the same State but through any place outside of that State. The term "State" includes the District of Columbia, the Commonwealth of Puerto Rico, and the possessions of the United States (not including the Canal Zone).

(3) The term "firearm" means (A) any weapon (including a starter gun) which will or is designed to or may readily be converted to expel a projectile by the action of an explosive; (B) the frame or receiver of any such weapon; (C) any firearm muffler or firearm silencer; or (D) any destructive device. Such term does not include an antique firearm.

(4) The term "destructive device" means—

(A) any explosive, incendiary, or poison gas—

(i) bomb,

(ii) grenade,

(iii) rocket having a propellant charge of more than four ounces,

(iv) missile having an explosive or incendiary charge of more than one-quarter ounce,

(v) mine, or

(vi) device similar to any of the devices described in the preceding clauses;

(B) any type of weapon (other than a shotgun or a shotgun shell which the Attorney General finds is generally recognized as particularly suitable for sporting purposes) by whatever name known which will, or which may be readily converted to, expel a projectile by the action of an explosive or other propellant, and which has any barrel with a bore of more than one-half inch in diameter; and

(C) any combination of parts either designed or intended for use in converting any device into any destructive device described in subparagraph (A) or (B) and from which a destructive device may be readily assembled.

The term "destructive device" shall not include any device which is neither designed nor redesigned for use as a weapon; any device, although originally designed for use as a weapon, which is redesigned for use as a signaling, pyrotechnic, line throwing, safety, or similar device; surplus ordnance sold, loaned, or given by the Secretary of the Army pursuant to the provisions of section 4684(2), 4685, or 4686 of title 10; or any other device which the Attorney General finds is not likely to be used as a weapon, is an antique, or is a rifle which the owner intends to use solely for sporting, recreational or cultural purposes.

(5) The term "shotgun" means a weapon designed or redesigned, made or remade, and intended to be fired from the shoulder and designed or redesigned and made or remade to use the energy of an explosive to fire through a smooth bore either a number of ball shot or a single projectile for each single pull of the trigger.

(6) The term "short-barreled shotgun" means a shotgun having one or more barrels less than eighteen inches in length and any weapon made from a shotgun (whether by alteration, modification, or otherwise) if such a weapon as modified has an overall length of less than twenty-six inches.

(7) The term "rifle" means a weapon designed or redesigned, made or remade, and intended to be fired from the shoulder and designed or redesigned and made or remade to use the energy of an explosive to fire only a single projectile through a rifled bore for each single pull of the trigger.

(8) The term "short-barreled rifle" means a rifle having one or more barrels less than sixteen inches in length and any weapon made from a rifle (whether by alteration, modification, or otherwise) if such weapon, as modified, has an overall length of less than twenty-six inches.

(9) to **(15)** *Omitted by editor.*

(16) The term "antique firearm" means—

(A) any firearm (including any firearm with a matchlock, flintlock, percussion cap, or similar type of ignition system) manufactured in or before 1898; or

(B) any replica of any firearm described in subparagraph (A) if such replica—

(i) is not designed or redesigned for using rimfire or conventional centerfire fixed ammunition, or

(ii) uses rimfire or conventional centerfire fixed ammunition which is no longer manufactured in the United States and which is not readily available in the ordinary channels of commercial trade; or

(C) any muzzle loading rifle, muzzle loading shotgun, or muzzle loading pistol, which is designed to use black powder, or a black powder substitute, and which cannot use fixed ammunition. For purposes of this subparagraph, the term "antique firearm" shall not include any weapon which incorporates a firearm frame or receiver, any firearm which is converted into a muzzle loading weapon, or any muzzle loading weapon which can be readily converted to fire fixed ammunition by replacing the barrel, bolt, breechblock, or any combination thereof.

(17)(A) The term "ammunition" means ammunition or cartridge cases, primers, bullets, or propellent powder designed for use in any firearm.

(17)(B) to **(23)** *Omitted by editor.*

(24) The terms "firearm silencer" and "firearm muffler" mean any device for silencing, muffling, or diminishing the report of a portable firearm, including any combination of parts, designed or redesigned, and intended for use in assembling or fabricating a firearm silencer or firearm muffler, and any part intended only for use in such assembly or fabrication.

(25) to **(29)** *Omitted by editor.*

(30), **(31)** Repealed by P.L. 103-322, §110105(2), 108 Stat. 2000, Sept. 13, 1994.

(32) The term "intimate partner" means, with respect to a person, the spouse of the person, a former spouse of the person, an individual who is a parent of a child of the person, and an individual who cohabitates or has cohabited with the person.

(33)(A) Except as provided in subparagraph (C),[1] the term "misdemeanor crime of domestic violence" means an offense that—

(i) is a misdemeanor under Federal, State, or Tribal law; and

(ii) has, as an element, the use or attempted use of physical force, or the threatened use of a deadly weapon, committed by a current or former spouse, parent, or guardian of the victim, by a person with whom the victim shares a child in common, by a person who is cohabiting with or has cohabited with the victim as a spouse, parent, or guardian, or by a person similarly situated to a spouse, parent, or guardian of the victim.

(B)(i) A person shall not be considered to have been convicted of such an offense for purposes of this chapter, unless—

(I) the person was represented by counsel in the case, or knowingly and intelligently waived the right to counsel in the case; and

(II) in the case of a prosecution for an offense described in this paragraph for which a person was entitled to a jury trial in the jurisdiction in which the case was tried, either

(aa) the case was tried by a jury, or

(bb) the person knowingly and intelligently waived the right to have the case tried by a jury, by guilty plea or otherwise.

(ii) A person shall not be considered to have been convicted of such an offense for purposes of this chapter if the conviction has been expunged or set aside, or is an offense for which the person has been pardoned or has had civil rights restored (if the law of the applicable jurisdiction provides for the loss of civil rights under such an offense) unless the pardon, expungement, or restoration of civil rights expressly provides that the person may not ship, transport, possess, or receive firearms.

(34), (35) *Omitted by editor.*

(b) *Omitted by editor.*

1. **Editor's note:** Enacted as such. No subparagraph (C) has been enacted.

History of 18 U.S.C. §921: June 19, 1968, P.L. 90-351, §902, 82 Stat. 226; Oct. 22, 1968, P.L. 90-618, §102, 82 Stat. 1214; Jan. 4, 1975, P.L. 93-639, §102, 88 Stat. 2217; May 19, 1986, P.L. 99-308, §101, 100 Stat. 449; July 8, 1986, P.L. 99-360, §1(b), 100 Stat. 766; Aug. 28, 1986, P.L. 99-408, §1, 100 Stat. 920; Nov. 29, 1990, P.L. 101-647, §§1702(b)(2), 2204(a), 104 Stat. 4845, 4857; Nov. 30, 1993, P.L. 103-159, §102(a)(2), 107 Stat. 1539; Sept. 13, 1994, P.L. 103-322, §§110102(b), 110103(b), 110105(2), 110401(a), 110519, 330021(1), 108 Stat. 1997, 1999, 2000, 2014, 2020, 2150; Dec. 29, 1995, P.L. 104-88, §303(1), 109 Stat. 943; Sept. 30, 1996, P.L. 104-208, §101(f) [§658(a)], 110 Stat. 3009-371; Oct. 21, 1998, P.L. 105-277, §101(b) [§119(a)], §101(h) [§115], 112 Stat. 2681-69, 2681-490; Nov. 2, 2002, P.L. 107-273, §11009(e)(1), 116 Stat. 1821; Nov. 25, 2002, P.L. 107-296, §1112(f)(1)-(3), (6), 116 Stat. 2276; Jan. 5, 2006, P.L. 109-162, §908(a), 119 Stat. 3083.

§922. UNLAWFUL ACTS

(a) to (c) *Omitted by editor.*

(d) It shall be unlawful for any person to sell or otherwise dispose of any firearm or ammunition to any person knowing or having reasonable cause to believe that such person—

(1) to (7) *Omitted by editor.*

(8) is subject to a court order that restrains such person from harassing, stalking, or threatening an intimate partner of such person or child of such intimate partner or person, or engaging in other conduct that would place an intimate partner in reasonable fear of bodily injury to the partner or child, except that this paragraph shall only apply to a court order that—

(A) was issued after a hearing of which such person received actual notice, and at which such person had the opportunity to participate; and

(B)(i) includes a finding that such person represents a credible threat to the physical safety of such intimate partner or child; or

(ii) by its terms explicitly prohibits the use, attempted use, or threatened use of physical force against such intimate partner or child that would reasonably be expected to cause bodily injury; or

(9) has been convicted in any court of a misdemeanor crime of domestic violence.

This subsection shall not apply with respect to the sale or disposition of a firearm or ammunition to a licensed importer, licensed manufacturer, licensed dealer, or licensed collector who pursuant to subsection (b) of section 925 of this chapter is not precluded from dealing in firearms or ammunition, or to a person who has been granted relief from disabilities pursuant to subsection (c) of section 925 of this chapter.

(e), (f) *Omitted by editor.*

(g) It shall be unlawful for any person—

(1) to (7) *Omitted by editor.*

(8) who is subject to a court order that—

(A) was issued after a hearing of which such person received actual notice, and at which such person had an opportunity to participate;

(B) *Omitted by editor.*

(C)(i) includes a finding that such person represents a credible threat to the physical safety of such intimate partner or child; or

(ii) by its terms explicitly prohibits the use, attempted use, or threatened use of physical force against such intimate partner or child that would reasonably be expected to cause bodily injury; or

(9) who has been convicted in any court of a misdemeanor crime of domestic violence,

to ship or transport in interstate or foreign commerce, or possess in or affecting commerce, any firearm or ammunition; or to receive any firearm or ammunition which has been shipped or transported in interstate or foreign commerce.

(h) It shall be unlawful for any individual, who to that individual's knowledge and while being employed for any person described in any paragraph of subsection (g) of this section, in the course of such employment—

(1) to receive, possess, or transport any firearm or ammunition in or affecting interstate or foreign commerce; or

(2) to receive any firearm or ammunition which has been shipped or transported in interstate or foreign commerce.

(i) to **(z)** *Omitted by editor.*

History of 18 U.S.C. §922: June 19, 1968, P.L. 90-351, §902, 82 Stat. 228; Oct. 22, 1968, P.L. 90-618, §102, 82 Stat. 1216; Dec. 21, 1982, P.L. 97-377, §165(a), 96 Stat. 1923; May 19, 1986, P.L. 99-308, §102, 100 Stat. 451; Aug. 28, 1986, P.L. 99-408, §2, 100 Stat. 920; Nov. 10, 1988, P.L. 100-649, §2(a), (f)(2)(A), 102 Stat. 3816, 3818; Nov. 18, 1988, P.L. 100-690, §7060(c), 102 Stat. 4404; Nov. 29, 1990, P.L. 101-647, §§1702(b)(1), 2201, 2202, 2204(b), 3524, 104 Stat. 4844, 4856, 4857, 4924; Nov. 30, 1993, P.L. 103-159, §§102(a)(1), (b), 302(a)-(c), 107 Stat. 1536, 1539, 1545; Sept. 13, 1994, P.L. 103-322, §§110102(a), 110103(a), 110106, 110201(a), 110401(b), (c), 110511, 110514, 320904, 320927, 330011(i), 108 Stat. 1996, 1998, 2000, 2010, 2014, 2019, 2125, 2131, 2145; Sept. 30, 1996, P.L. 104-208, §101(f) [§§657, 658(b)], 110 Stat. 3009-369, 3009-372; Oct. 11, 1996, P.L. 104-294, §603(b), (c)(1), (d), (e), (f)(1), (g), 110 Stat. 3503, 3504; Oct. 21, 1998, P.L. 105-277, §101(b), 112 Stat. 2681-71; Nov. 2, 2002, P.L. 107-273, §4003(a)(1), 116 Stat. 1811; Nov. 25, 2002, P.L. 107-296, §1112(f)(4), (6), 116 Stat. 2276; Oct. 26, 2005, P.L. 109-92, §§5(c)(1), 6(a), 119 Stat. 2099, 2101.

CHAPTER 55. KIDNAPPING

§1204. INTERNATIONAL PARENTAL KIDNAPPING

(a) Whoever removes a child from the United States, or attempts to do so, or retains a child (who has been in the United States) outside the United States with intent to obstruct the lawful exercise of parental rights shall be fined under this title or imprisoned not more than 3 years, or both.

(b) As used in this section—

(1) the term "child" means a person who has not attained the age of 16 years; and

(2) the term "parental rights," with respect to a child, means the right to physical custody of the child—

(A) whether joint or sole (and includes visiting rights); and

(B) whether arising by operation of law, court order, or legally binding agreement of the parties.

(c) It shall be an affirmative defense under this section that—

(1) the defendant acted within the provisions of a valid court order granting the defendant legal custody or visitation rights and that order was obtained pursuant to the Uniform Child Custody Jurisdiction Act or the Uniform Child Custody Jurisdiction and Enforcement Act and was in effect at the time of the offense;

(2) the defendant was fleeing an incidence or pattern of domestic violence; or

(3) the defendant had physical custody of the child pursuant to a court order granting legal custody or visitation rights and failed to return the child as a result of circumstances beyond the defendant's control, and the defendant notified or made reasonable attempts to notify the other parent or lawful custodian of the child of such circumstances within 24 hours after the visitation period had expired and returned the child as soon as possible.

(d) This section does not detract from The Hague Convention on the Civil Aspects of International Parental Child Abduction, done at The Hague on October 25, 1980.

History of 18 U.S.C. §1204: Dec. 2, 1993, P.L. 103-173, §2(a), 107 Stat. 1998; Apr. 30, 2003, P.L. 108-21, §107, 117 Stat. 655.

CHAPTER 110A. DOMESTIC VIOLENCE & STALKING

§2261. INTERSTATE DOMESTIC VIOLENCE

(a) Offenses—

(1) Travel or conduct of offender.—A person who travels in interstate or foreign commerce or enters or leaves Indian country or is present within the special maritime and territorial jurisdiction of the United States with the intent to kill, injure, harass, or intimidate a spouse, intimate partner, or dating partner and who, in the course of or as a result of such travel or presence, commits or attempts to commit a crime of violence

against that spouse, intimate partner, or dating partner, shall be punished as provided in subsection (b).

(2) Causing travel of victim.—A person who causes a spouse, intimate partner, or dating partner to travel in interstate or foreign commerce or to enter or leave Indian country by force, coercion, duress, or fraud, and who, in the course of, as a result of, or to facilitate such conduct or travel, commits or attempts to commit a crime of violence against that spouse, intimate partner, or dating partner shall be punished as provided in subsection (b).

(b) Penalties.—A person who violates this section or section 2261A shall be fined under this title, imprisoned—

(1) for life or any term of years, if death of the victim results;

(2) for not more than 20 years if permanent disfigurement or life threatening bodily injury to the victim results;

(3) for not more than 10 years, if serious bodily injury to the victim results or if the offender uses a dangerous weapon during the offense;

(4) as provided for the applicable conduct under chapter 109A if the offense would constitute an offense under chapter 109A (without regard to whether the offense was committed in the special maritime and territorial jurisdiction of the United States or in a Federal prison); and

(5) for not more than 5 years, in any other case,

or both fined and imprisoned.

(6) Whoever commits the crime of stalking in violation of a temporary or permanent civil or criminal injunction, restraining order, no-contact order, or other order described in section 2266 of title 18, United States Code, shall be punished by imprisonment for not less than 1 year.

History of 18 U.S.C. §2261: Sept. 13, 1994, P.L. 103-322, §40221(a), 108 Stat. 1926; Sept. 23, 1996, P.L. 104-201, §1069(b)(1), (2), 110 Stat. 2656; Oct. 28, 2000, P.L. 106-386, §1107(a), 114 Stat. 1497; Jan. 5, 2006, P.L. 109-162, §§114(b), 116(a), 117(a), 119 Stat. 2988, 2989; Mar. 7, 2013, P.L. 113-4, §107(a), 127 Stat. 77.

§2261A. STALKING

Whoever—

(1) travels in interstate or foreign commerce or is present within the special maritime and territorial jurisdiction of the United States, or enters or leaves Indian country, with the intent to kill, injure, harass, intimidate, or place under surveillance with intent to kill, injure, harass, or intimidate another person, and in the course of, or as a result of, such travel or presence engages in conduct that—

(A) places that person in reasonable fear of the death of, or serious bodily injury to—

(i) that person;

(ii) an immediate family member (as defined in section 115) of that person; or

(iii) a spouse or intimate partner of that person; or

(B) causes, attempts to cause, or would be reasonably expected to cause substantial emotional distress to a person described in clause (i), (ii), or (iii) of subparagraph (A); or

(2) with the intent to kill, injure, harass, intimidate, or place under surveillance with intent to kill, injure, harass, or intimidate another person, uses the mail, any interactive computer service or electronic communication service or electronic communication system of interstate commerce, or any other facility of interstate or foreign commerce to engage in a course of conduct that—

(A) places that person in reasonable fear of the death of or serious bodily injury to a person described in clause (i), (ii), or (iii) of paragraph (1)(A); or

(B) causes, attempts to cause, or would be reasonably expected to cause substantial emotional distress to a person described in clause (i), (ii), or (iii) of paragraph (1)(A),

shall be punished as provided in section 2261(b) of this title.

History of 18 U.S.C. §2261A: Sept. 23, 1996, P.L. 104-201, §1069(a), 110 Stat. 2655; Oct. 28, 2000, P.L. 106-386, §1107(b)(1), 114 Stat. 1498; Jan. 5, 2006, P.L. 109-162, §114(a), 119 Stat. 2987; Mar. 7, 2013, P.L. 113-4, §107(b), 127 Stat. 77.

§2262. INTERSTATE VIOLATION OF PROTECTION ORDER

(a) Offenses—

(1) Travel or conduct of offender.—A person who travels in interstate or foreign commerce, or enters or leaves Indian country or is present[1] within the special maritime and territorial jurisdiction of the United States, with the intent to engage in conduct that violates the portion of a protection order that prohibits or provides protection against violence, threats, or harassment against, contact or communication with, or physical proximity to, another person, or that would violate such a portion of a protection order in the jurisdiction in

which the order was issued, and subsequently engages in such conduct, shall be punished as provided in subsection (b).

(2) Causing travel of victim.—A person who causes another person to travel in interstate or foreign commerce or to enter or leave Indian country by force, coercion, duress, or fraud, and in the course of, as a result of, or to facilitate such conduct or travel engages in conduct that violates the portion of a protection order that prohibits or provides protection against violence, threats, or harassment against, contact or communication with, or physical proximity to, another person, or that would violate such a portion of a protection order in the jurisdiction in which the order was issued, shall be punished as provided in subsection (b).

(b) Penalties.—A person who violates this section shall be fined under this title, imprisoned—

(1) for life or any term of years, if death of the victim results;

(2) for not more than 20 years if permanent disfigurement or life threatening bodily injury to the victim results;

(3) for not more than 10 years, if serious bodily injury to the victim results or if the offender uses a dangerous weapon during the offense;

(4) as provided for the applicable conduct under chapter 109A if the offense would constitute an offense under chapter 109A (without regard to whether the offense was committed in the special maritime and territorial jurisdiction of the United States or in a Federal prison); and

(5) for not more than 5 years, in any other case,

or both fined and imprisoned.

1. **Editor's note:** P.L. 113-4, §107(c) purports to amend §2262(a)(2) by inserting "is present" after "Indian Country or." The insert probably should be made in §2262(a)(1) instead.

History of 18 U.S.C. §2262: Sept. 13, 1994, P.L. 103-322, §40221(a), 108 Stat. 1927; Sept. 23, 1996, P.L. 104-201, §1069(b)(2), 110 Stat. 2656; Oct. 11, 1996, P.L. 104-294, §605(d), 110 Stat. 3509; Oct. 28, 2000, P.L. 106-386, §1107(c), 114 Stat. 1498; Jan. 5, 2006, P.L. 109-162, §117(b), 119 Stat. 2989; Mar. 7, 2013, P.L. 113-4, §107(c), 127 Stat. 78.

Sections 2263 & 2264 omitted by editor

§2265. FULL FAITH & CREDIT GIVEN TO PROTECTION ORDERS

(a) Full Faith and Credit.—Any protection order issued that is consistent with subsection (b) of this section by the court of one State, Indian tribe, or territory (the issuing State, Indian tribe, or territory) shall be accorded full faith and credit by the court of another State, Indian tribe, or territory (the enforcing State, Indian tribe, or territory) and enforced by the court and law enforcement personnel of the other State, Indian tribal government or Territory as if it were the order of the enforcing State or tribe.

(b) Protection order.—A protection order issued by a State, tribal, or territorial court is consistent with this subsection if—

(1) such court has jurisdiction over the parties and matter under the law of such State, Indian tribe, or territory; and

(2) reasonable notice and opportunity to be heard is given to the person against whom the order is sought sufficient to protect that person's right to due process. In the case of ex parte orders, notice and opportunity to be heard must be provided within the time required by State, tribal, or territorial law, and in any event within a reasonable time after the order is issued, sufficient to protect the respondent's due process rights.

(c) Cross or counter petition.—A protection order issued by a State, tribal, or territorial court against one who has petitioned, filed a complaint, or otherwise filed a written pleading for protection against abuse by a spouse or intimate partner is not entitled to full faith and credit if—

(1) no cross or counter petition, complaint, or other written pleading was filed seeking such a protection order; or

(2) a cross or counter petition has been filed and the court did not make specific findings that each party was entitled to such an order.

(d) Notification and registration—

(1) Notification.—A State, Indian tribe, or territory according full faith and credit to an order by a court of another State, Indian tribe, or territory shall not notify or require notification of the party against whom a protection order has been issued that the protection order has been registered or filed in that enforcing State, tribal, or territorial jurisdiction unless requested to do so by the party protected under such order.

(2) No prior registration or filing as prerequisite for enforcement.—Any protection order that is otherwise consistent with this section shall be accorded full faith and credit, notwithstanding failure to

comply with any requirement that the order be registered or filed in the enforcing State, tribal, or territorial jurisdiction.

(3) Limits on internet publication of registration information.—A State, Indian tribe, or territory shall not make available publicly on the Internet any information regarding the registration, filing of a petition for, or issuance of a protection order, restraining order, or injunction[1] in either the issuing or enforcing State, tribal or territorial jurisdiction, if such publication would be likely to publicly reveal the identity or location of the party protected under such order. A State, Indian tribe, or territory may share court-generated and law enforcement-generated information contained in secure, governmental registries for protection order enforcement purposes.

(e) Tribal court jurisdiction.—For purposes of this section, a court of an Indian tribe shall have full civil jurisdiction to issue and enforce protection orders involving any person, including the authority to enforce any orders through civil contempt proceedings, to exclude violators from Indian land, and to use other appropriate mechanisms, in matters arising anywhere in the Indian country of the Indian tribe (as defined in section 1151) or otherwise within the authority of the Indian tribe.

1. **Editor's note:** Duplication of "restraining order, or injunction," as enacted by P.L. 109-271, §2(n), 120 Stat. 754, Aug. 12, 2006, has been omitted.

History of 18 U.S.C. §2265: Sept. 13, 1994, P.L. 103-322, §40221(a), 108 Stat. 1930; Oct. 28, 2000, P.L. 106-386, §1101(b)(4), 114 Stat. 1493; Jan. 5, 2006, P.L. 109-162, §106(a)-(c), 119 Stat. 2981, 2982; Aug. 12, 2006, P.L. 109-271, §2(n), 120 Stat. 754; Mar. 7, 2013, P.L. 113-4, §905, 127 Stat. 124.

§2265A. REPEAT OFFENDERS

(a) Maximum term of imprisonment.—The maximum term of imprisonment for a violation of this chapter after a prior domestic violence or stalking offense shall be twice the term otherwise provided under this chapter.

(b) Definition.—For purposes of this section—

(1) the term "prior domestic violence or stalking offense" means a conviction for an offense—

(A) under section 2261, 2261A, or 2262 of this chapter; or

(B) under State or tribal law for an offense consisting of conduct that would have been an offense under a section referred to in subparagraph (A) if the conduct had occurred within the special maritime and territorial jurisdiction of the United States, or in interstate or foreign commerce; and

(2) the term "State" means a State of the United States, the District of Columbia, or any commonwealth, territory, or possession of the United States.

History of 18 U.S.C. §2265A: Jan. 5, 2006, P.L. 109-162, §115, 119 Stat. 2988; Mar. 7, 2013, P.L. 113-4, §906(c), 127 Stat. 125.

§2266. DEFINITIONS

In this chapter:

(1) Bodily injury.—The term "bodily injury" means any act, except one done in self-defense, that results in physical injury or sexual abuse.

(2) Course of conduct.—The term "course of conduct" means a pattern of conduct composed of 2 or more acts, evidencing a continuity of purpose.

(3) Enter or leave Indian country.—The term "enter or leave Indian country" includes leaving the jurisdiction of 1 tribal government and entering the jurisdiction of another tribal government.

(4) Indian country.—The term "Indian country" has the meaning stated in section 1151 of this title.

(5) Protection order.—The term "protection order" includes—

(A) any injunction, restraining order, or any other order issued by a civil or criminal court for the purpose of preventing violent or threatening acts or harassment against, sexual violence, or contact or communication with or physical proximity to, another person, including any temporary or final order issued by a civil or criminal court whether obtained by filing an independent action or as a pendente lite order in another proceeding so long as any civil or criminal order was issued in response to a complaint, petition, or motion filed by or on behalf of a person seeking protection; and

(B) any support, child custody or visitation provisions, orders, remedies or relief issued as part of a protection order, restraining order, or injunction pursuant to State, tribal, territorial, or local law authorizing the issuance of protection orders, restraining orders, or injunctions for the protection of victims of domestic violence, sexual assault, dating violence, or stalking.

(6) Serious bodily injury.—The term "serious bodily injury" has the meaning stated in section 2119(2).

(7) Spouse or intimate partner.—The term "spouse or intimate partner" includes—

(A) for purposes of—

(i) sections other than 2261A—

(I) a spouse or former spouse of the abuser, a person who shares a child in common with the abuser, and a person who cohabits or has cohabited as a spouse with the abuser; or

(II) a person who is or has been in a social relationship of a romantic or intimate nature with the abuser, as determined by the length of the relationship, the type of relationship, and the frequency of interaction between the persons involved in the relationship; and

(ii) section 2261A—

(I) a spouse or former spouse of the target of the stalking, a person who shares a child in common with the target of the stalking, and a person who cohabits or has cohabited as a spouse with the target of the stalking; or

(II) a person who is or has been in a social relationship of a romantic or intimate nature with the target of the stalking, as determined by the length of the relationship, the type of the relationship, and the frequency of interaction between the persons involved in the relationship.

(B) any other person similarly situated to a spouse who is protected by the domestic or family violence laws of the State or tribal jurisdiction in which the injury occurred or where the victim resides.

(8) State.—The term "State" includes a State of the United States, the District of Columbia, and a commonwealth, territory, or possession of the United States.

(9) Travel in interstate or foreign commerce.—The term "travel in interstate or foreign commerce" does not include travel from 1 State to another by an individual who is a member of an Indian tribe and who remains at all times in the territory of the Indian tribe of which the individual is a member.

(10) Dating partner.—The term "dating partner" refers to a person who is or has been in a social relationship of a romantic or intimate nature with the abuser. The existence of such a relationship is based on a consideration of—

(A) the length of the relationship; and

(B) the type of relationship; and

(C) the frequency of interaction between the persons involved in the relationship.

History of 18 U.S.C. §2266: Sept. 13, 1994, P.L. 103-322, §40221(a), 108 Stat. 1931; Oct. 28, 2000, P.L. 106-386, §1107(d), 114 Stat. 1499; Jan. 5, 2006, P.L. 109-162, §§106(d), 116(b), 119 Stat. 2982, 2988; Aug. 12, 2006, P.L. 109-271, §2(c), (i), 120 Stat. 752.

TITLE 22. FOREIGN RELATIONS & INTERCOURSE

CHAPTER 97. INTERNATIONAL CHILD ABDUCTION REMEDIES

§9001. FINDINGS & DECLARATIONS

(a) Findings.—The Congress makes the following findings:

(1) The international abduction or wrongful retention of children is harmful to their well-being.

(2) Persons should not be permitted to obtain custody of children by virtue of their wrongful removal or retention.

(3) International abductions and retentions of children are increasing, and only concerted cooperation pursuant to an international agreement can effectively combat this problem.

(4) The Convention on the Civil Aspects of International Child Abduction, done at The Hague on October 25, 1980, establishes legal rights and procedures for the prompt return of children who have been wrongfully removed or retained, as well as for securing the exercise of visitation rights. Children who are wrongfully removed or retained within the meaning of the Convention are to be promptly returned unless one of the narrow exceptions set forth in the Convention applies. The Convention provides a sound treaty framework to help resolve the problem of international abduction and retention of children and will deter such wrongful removals and retentions.

(b) Declarations.—The Congress makes the following declarations:

(1) It is the purpose of this chapter to establish procedures for the implementation of the Convention in the United States.

(2) The provisions of this chapter are in addition to and not in lieu of the provisions of the Convention.

(3) In enacting this chapter the Congress recognizes—

(A) the international character of the Convention; and

(B) the need for uniform international interpretation of the Convention.

(4) The Convention and this chapter empower courts in the United States to determine only rights un-

der the Convention and not the merits of any underlying child custody claims.

History of 22 U.S.C. §9001: Apr. 29, 1988, P.L. 100-300, §2, 102 Stat. 437.

§9002. DEFINITIONS

For the purposes of this chapter—

(1) the term "applicant" means any person who, pursuant to the Convention, files an application with the United States Central Authority or a Central Authority of any other party to the Convention for the return of a child alleged to have been wrongfully removed or retained or for arrangements for organizing or securing the effective exercise of rights of access pursuant to the Convention;

(2) the term "Convention" means the Convention on the Civil Aspects of International Child Abduction, done at The Hague on October 25, 1980;

(3) the term "Parent Locator Service" means the service established by the Secretary of Health and Human Services under section 653 of title 42;

(4) the term "petitioner" means any person who, in accordance with this chapter, files a petition in court seeking relief under the Convention;

(5) the term "person" includes any individual, institution, or other legal entity or body;

(6) the term "respondent" means any person against whose interests a petition is filed in court, in accordance with this chapter, which seeks relief under the Convention;

(7) the term "rights of access" means visitation rights;

(8) the term "State" means any of the several States, the District of Columbia, and any commonwealth, territory, or possession of the United States; and

(9) the term "United States Central Authority" means the agency of the Federal Government designated by the President under section 9006(a) of this title.

History of 22 U.S.C. §9002: Apr. 29, 1988, P.L. 100-300, §3, 102 Stat. 437.

§9003. JUDICIAL REMEDIES

(a) Jurisdiction of courts.—The courts of the States and the United States district courts shall have concurrent original jurisdiction of actions arising under the Convention.

(b) Petitions.—Any person seeking to initiate judicial proceedings under the Convention for the return of a child or for arrangements for organizing or securing the effective exercise of rights of access to a child may do so by commencing a civil action by filing a petition for the relief sought in any court which has jurisdiction of such action and which is authorized to exercise its jurisdiction in the place where the child is located at the time the petition is filed.

(c) Notice.—Notice of an action brought under subsection (b) shall be given in accordance with the applicable law governing notice in interstate child custody proceedings.

(d) Determination of case.—The court in which an action is brought under subsection (b) shall decide the case in accordance with the Convention.

(e) Burdens of proof—

(1) A petitioner in an action brought under subsection (b) shall establish by a preponderance of the evidence—

(A) in the case of an action for the return of a child, that the child has been wrongfully removed or retained within the meaning of the Convention; and

(B) in the case of an action for arrangements for organizing or securing the effective exercise of rights of access, that the petitioner has such rights.

(2) In the case of an action for the return of a child, a respondent who opposes the return of the child has the burden of establishing—

(A) by clear and convincing evidence that one of the exceptions set forth in article 13b or 20 of the Convention applies; and

(B) by a preponderance of the evidence that any other exception set forth in article 12 or 13 of the Convention applies.

(f) Application of Convention.—For purposes of any action brought under this chapter—

(1) the term "authorities," as used in article 15 of the Convention to refer to the authorities of the state of the habitual residence of a child, includes courts and appropriate government agencies;

(2) the terms "wrongful removal or retention" and "wrongfully removed or retained," as used in the Convention, include a removal or retention of a child before the entry of a custody order regarding that child; and

(3) the term "commencement of proceedings," as used in article 12 of the Convention, means, with respect to the return of a child located in the United States, the filing of a petition in accordance with subsection (b) of this section.

(g) Full faith and credit.—Full faith and credit shall be accorded by the courts of the States and the courts of the United States to the judgment of any other such court ordering or denying the return of a child, pursuant to the Convention, in an action brought under this chapter.

(h) Remedies under Convention not exclusive.—The remedies established by the Convention and this chapter shall be in addition to remedies available under other laws or international agreements.

History of 22 U.S.C. §9003: Apr. 29, 1988, P.L. 100-300, §4, 102 Stat. 438.

§9004. PROVISIONAL REMEDIES

(a) Authority of courts.—In furtherance of the objectives of article 7(b) and other provisions of the Convention, and subject to the provisions of subsection (b) of this section, any court exercising jurisdiction of an action brought under section 9003(b) of this title may take or cause to be taken measures under Federal or State law, as appropriate, to protect the well-being of the child involved or to prevent the child's further removal or concealment before the final disposition of the petition.

(b) Limitation on authority.—No court exercising jurisdiction of an action brought under section 9003(b) of this title may, under subsection (a) of this section, order a child removed from a person having physical control of the child unless the applicable requirements of State law are satisfied.

History of 22 U.S.C. §9004: Apr. 29, 1988, P.L. 100-300, §5, 102 Stat. 439.

§9005. ADMISSIBILITY OF DOCUMENTS

With respect to any application to the United States Central Authority, or any petition to a court under section 9003 of this title, which seeks relief under the Convention, or any other documents or information included with such application or petition or provided after such submission which relates to the application or petition, as the case may be, no authentication of such application, petition, document, or information shall be required in order for the application, petition, document, or information to be admissible in court.

History of 22 U.S.C. §9005: Apr. 29, 1988, P.L. 100-300, §6, 102 Stat. 439.

§9006. UNITED STATES CENTRAL AUTHORITY

(a) Designation.—The President shall designate a Federal agency to serve as the Central Authority for the United States under the Convention.

(b) Functions.—The functions of the United States Central Authority are those ascribed to the Central Authority by the Convention and this chapter.

(c) Regulatory authority.—The United States Central Authority is authorized to issue such regulations as may be necessary to carry out its functions under the Convention and this chapter.

(d) Obtaining information from Parent Locator Service.—The United States Central Authority may, to the extent authorized by the Social Security Act [42 U.S.C. §301 et seq.], obtain information from the Parent Locator Service.

(e) Grant authority.—The United States Central Authority is authorized to make grants to, or enter into contracts or agreements with, any individual, corporation, other Federal, State, or local agency, or private entity or organization in the United States for purposes of accomplishing its responsibilities under the Convention and this chapter.

(f) Limited liability of private entities acting under the direction of the United States Central Authority—

(1) Limitation on liability.—Except as provided in paragraphs (2) and (3), a private entity or organization that receives a grant from or enters into a contract or agreement with the United States Central Authority under subsection (e) of this section for purposes of assisting the United States Central Authority in carrying out its responsibilities and functions under the Convention and this chapter, including any director, officer, employee, or agent of such entity or organization, shall not be liable in any civil action sounding in tort for damages directly related to the performance of such responsibilities and functions as defined by the regulations issued under subsection (c) of this section that are in effect on October 1, 2004.

(2) Exception for intentional, reckless, or other misconduct.—The limitation on liability under paragraph (1) shall not apply in any action in which the plaintiff proves that the private entity, organization, officer, employee, or agent described in paragraph (1), as the case may be, engaged in intentional misconduct or acted, or failed to act, with actual malice, with reckless disregard to a substantial risk of causing injury without legal justification, or for a purpose unrelated to the performance of responsibilities or functions under this chapter.

(3) Exception for ordinary business activities.—The limitation on liability under paragraph (1) shall not apply to any alleged act or omission related to an ordinary business activity, such as an activity involving general administration or operations, the use of motor vehicles, or personnel management.

History of 22 U.S.C. §9006: Apr. 29, 1988, P.L. 100-300, §7, 102 Stat. 439; Oct. 21, 1998, P.L. 105-277, §2213, 112 Stat. 2681-812; Oct. 25, 2004, P.L. 108-370, §2, 118 Stat. 1750.

§9007. COSTS & FEES

(a) Administrative costs.—No department, agency, or instrumentality of the Federal Government or of any State or local government may impose on an applicant any fee in relation to the administrative processing of applications submitted under the Convention.

(b) Costs incurred in civil actions—

(1) Petitioners may be required to bear the costs of legal counsel or advisors, court costs incurred in connection with their petitions, and travel costs for the return of the child involved and any accompanying persons, except as provided in paragraphs (2) and (3).

(2) Subject to paragraph (3), legal fees or court costs incurred in connection with an action brought under section 9003 of this title shall be borne by the petitioner unless they are covered by payments from Federal, State, or local legal assistance or other programs.

(3) Any court ordering the return of a child pursuant to an action brought under section 9003 of this title shall order the respondent to pay necessary expenses incurred by or on behalf of the petitioner, including court costs, legal fees, foster home or other care during the course of proceedings in the action, and transportation costs related to the return of the child, unless the respondent establishes that such order would be clearly inappropriate.

History of 22 U.S.C. §9007: Apr. 29, 1988, P.L. 100-300, §8, 102 Stat. 440.

§9008. COLLECTION, MAINTENANCE, & DISSEMINATION OF INFORMATION

(a) In general.—In performing its functions under the Convention, the United States Central Authority may, under such conditions as the Central Authority prescribes by regulation, but subject to subsection (c), receive from or transmit to any department, agency, or instrumentality of the Federal Government or of any State or foreign government, and receive from or transmit to any applicant, petitioner, or respondent, information necessary to locate a child or for the purpose of otherwise implementing the Convention with respect to a child, except that the United States Central Authority—

(1) may receive such information from a Federal or State department, agency, or instrumentality only pursuant to applicable Federal and State statutes; and

(2) may transmit any information received under this subsection notwithstanding any provision of law other than this chapter.

(b) Requests for information.—Requests for information under this section shall be submitted in such manner and form as the United States Central Authority may prescribe by regulation and shall be accompanied or supported by such documents as the United States Central Authority may require.

(c) Responsibility of government entities.—Whenever any department, agency, or instrumentality of the United States or of any State receives a request from the United States Central Authority for information authorized to be provided to such Central Authority under subsection (a), the head of such department, agency, or instrumentality shall promptly cause a search to be made of the files and records maintained by such department, agency, or instrumentality in order to determine whether the information requested is contained in any such files or records. If such search discloses the information requested, the head of such department, agency, or instrumentality shall immediately transmit such information to the United States Central Authority, except that any such information the disclosure of which—

(1) would adversely affect the national security interests of the United States or the law enforcement interests of the United States or of any State; or

(2) would be prohibited by section 9 of title 13;

shall not be transmitted to the Central Authority. The head of such department, agency, or instrumentality shall, immediately upon completion of the requested search, notify the Central Authority of the results of the search, and whether an exception set forth in paragraph (1) or (2) applies. In the event that the United States Central Authority receives information and the appropriate Federal or State department, agency, or instrumentality thereafter notifies the Central Authority that an exception set forth in paragraph (1) or (2) applies to that information, the Central Authority may not disclose that information under subsection (a).

(d) Information available from Parent Locator Service.—To the extent that information which the United States Central Authority is authorized to obtain under the provisions of subsection (c) can be obtained through the Parent Locator Service, the United States Central Authority shall first seek to obtain such information from the Parent Locator Service, before requesting such information directly under the provisions of subsection (c) of this section.

(e) Recordkeeping.—The United States Central Authority shall maintain appropriate records concerning its activities and the disposition of cases brought to its attention.

History of 22 U.S.C. §9008: Apr. 29, 1988, P.L. 100-300, §9, 102 Stat. 440.

§9009. OFFICE OF CHILDREN'S ISSUES

(a) Director requirements.—The Secretary of State shall fill the position of Director of the Office of Children's Issues of the Department of State (in this section referred to as the "Office") with an individual of senior rank who can ensure long-term continuity in the management and policy matters of the Office and has a strong background in consular affairs.

(b) Case officer staffing.—Effective April 1, 2000, there shall be assigned to the Office of Children's Issues of the Department of State a sufficient number of case officers to ensure that the average caseload for each officer does not exceed 75.

(c) Embassy contact.—The Secretary of State shall designate in each United States diplomatic mission an employee who shall serve as the point of contact for matters relating to international abductions of children by parents. The Director of the Office shall regularly inform the designated employee of children of United States citizens abducted by parents to that country.

(d) Reports to parents—

(1) In general.—Except as provided in paragraph (2), beginning 6 months after November 29, 1999, and at least once every 6 months thereafter, the Secretary of State shall report to each parent who has requested assistance regarding an abducted child overseas. Each such report shall include information on the current status of the abducted child's case and the efforts by the Department of State to resolve the case.

(2) Exception.—The requirement in paragraph (1) shall not apply in a case of an abducted child if—

(A) the case has been closed and the Secretary of State has reported the reason the case was closed to the parent who requested assistance; or

(B) the parent seeking assistance requests that such reports not be provided.

History of 22 U.S.C. §9009: Nov. 29, 1999, P.L. 106-113, §1000(a)(7) [App. G, §201], 113 Stat. 1536, 1501A-419.

§9010. INTERAGENCY COORDINATING GROUP

The Secretary of State, the Secretary of Health and Human Services, and the Attorney General shall designate Federal employees and may, from time to time, designate private citizens to serve on an interagency coordinating group to monitor the operation of the Convention and to provide advice on its implementation to the United States Central Authority and other Federal agencies. This group shall meet from time to time at the request of the United States Central Authority. The agency in which the United States Central Authority is located is authorized to reimburse such private citizens for travel and other expenses incurred in participating at meetings of the interagency coordinating group at rates not to exceed those authorized under subchapter I of chapter 57 of title 5 for employees of agencies.

History of 22 U.S.C. §9010: Apr. 29, 1988, P.L. 100-300, §10, 102 Stat. 441.

§9011. AUTHORIZATION OF APPROPRIATIONS

There are authorized to be appropriated for each fiscal year such sums as may be necessary to carry out the purposes of the Convention and this chapter.

History of 22 U.S.C. §9011: Apr. 29, 1988, P.L. 100-300, §12, 102 Stat. 442.

TITLE 25. INDIANS

CHAPTER 21. INDIAN CHILD WELFARE

§1901. CONGRESSIONAL FINDINGS

Recognizing the special relationship between the United States and the Indian tribes and their members and the Federal responsibility to Indian people, the Congress finds—

(1) that clause 3, section 8, article I of the United States Constitution provides that "The Congress shall have Power ... To regulate Commerce ... with Indian tribes" and, through this and other constitutional authority, Congress has plenary power over Indian affairs;

(2) that Congress, through statutes, treaties, and the general course of dealing with Indian tribes, has assumed the responsibility for the protection and preservation of Indian tribes and their resources;

(3) that there is no resource that is more vital to the continued existence and integrity of Indian tribes than their children and that the United States has a direct interest, as trustee, in protecting Indian children who are members of or are eligible for membership in an Indian tribe;

(4) that an alarmingly high percentage of Indian families are broken up by the removal, often unwarranted, of their children from them by nontribal public and private agencies and that an alarmingly high percentage of such children are placed in non-Indian foster and adoptive homes and institutions; and

(5) that the States, exercising their recognized jurisdiction over Indian child custody proceedings through administrative and judicial bodies, have often failed to recognize the essential tribal relations of Indian people and the cultural and social standards prevailing in Indian communities and families.

History of 25 U.S.C. §1901: Nov. 8, 1978, P.L. 95-608, §2, 92 Stat. 3069.

§1902. CONGRESSIONAL DECLARATION OF POLICY

The Congress hereby declares that it is the policy of this Nation to protect the best interests of Indian children and to promote the stability and security of Indian tribes and families by the establishment of minimum Federal standards for the removal of Indian children from their families and the placement of such children in foster or adoptive homes which will reflect the unique values of Indian culture, and by providing for assistance to Indian tribes in the operation of child and family service programs.

History of 25 U.S.C. §1902: Nov. 8, 1978, P.L. 95-608, §3, 92 Stat. 3069.

§1903. DEFINITIONS

For the purposes of this chapter, except as may be specifically provided otherwise, the term—

(1) "child custody proceeding" shall mean and include—

(i) "foster care placement" which shall mean any action removing an Indian child from its parent or Indian custodian for temporary placement in a foster home or institution or the home of a guardian or conservator where the parent or Indian custodian cannot have the child returned upon demand, but where parental rights have not been terminated;

(ii) "termination of parental rights" which shall mean any action resulting in the termination of the parent-child relationship;

(iii) "preadoptive placement" which shall mean the temporary placement of an Indian child in a foster home or institution after the termination of parental rights, but prior to or in lieu of adoptive placement; and

(iv) "adoptive placement" which shall mean the permanent placement of an Indian child for adoption, including any action resulting in a final decree of adoption.

Such term or terms shall not include a placement based upon an act which, if committed by an adult, would be deemed a crime or upon an award, in a divorce proceeding, of custody to one of the parents.

(2) "extended family member" shall be as defined by the law or custom of the Indian child's tribe or, in the absence of such law or custom, shall be a person who has reached the age of eighteen and who is the Indian child's grandparent, aunt or uncle, brother or sister, brother-in-law or sister-in-law, niece or nephew, first or second cousin, or stepparent;

(3) "Indian" means any person who is a member of an Indian tribe, or who is an Alaska Native and a member of a Regional Corporation as defined in [section] 1606 of title 43;

(4) "Indian child" means any unmarried person who is under age eighteen and is either (a) a member of an Indian tribe or (b) is eligible for membership in an Indian tribe and is the biological child of a member of an Indian tribe;

(5) "Indian child's tribe" means (a) the Indian tribe in which an Indian child is a member or eligible for membership or (b), in the case of an Indian child who is a member of or eligible for membership in more than one tribe, the Indian tribe with which the Indian child has the more significant contacts;

(6) "Indian custodian" means any Indian person who has legal custody of an Indian child under tribal law or custom or under State law or to whom temporary physical care, custody, and control has been transferred by the parent of such child;

(7) "Indian organization" means any group, association, partnership, corporation, or other legal entity owned or controlled by Indians, or a majority of whose members are Indians;

(8) "Indian tribe" means any Indian tribe, band, nation, or other organized group or community of Indians recognized as eligible for the services provided to Indi-

ans by the Secretary because of their status as Indians, including any Alaska Native village as defined in section 1602(c) of title 43;

(9) "parent" means any biological parent or parents of an Indian child or any Indian person who has lawfully adopted an Indian child, including adoptions under tribal law or custom. It does not include the unwed father where paternity has not been acknowledged or established;

(10) "reservation" means Indian country as defined in section 1151 of title 18 and any lands, not covered under such section, title to which is either held by the United States in trust for the benefit of any Indian tribe or individual or held by any Indian tribe or individual subject to a restriction by the United States against alienation;

(11) "Secretary" means the Secretary of the Interior; and

(12) "tribal court" means a court with jurisdiction over child custody proceedings and which is either a Court of Indian Offenses, a court established and operated under the code or custom of an Indian tribe, or any other administrative body of a tribe which is vested with authority over child custody proceedings.

History of 25 U.S.C. §1903: Nov. 8, 1978, P.L. 95-608, §4, 92 Stat. 3069.

SUBCHAPTER I. CHILD CUSTODY PROCEEDINGS

§1911. INDIAN TRIBE JURISDICTION OVER INDIAN CHILD CUSTODY PROCEEDINGS

(a) Exclusive jurisdiction.—An Indian tribe shall have jurisdiction exclusive as to any State over any child custody proceeding involving an Indian child who resides or is domiciled within the reservation of such tribe, except where such jurisdiction is otherwise vested in the State by existing Federal law. Where an Indian child is a ward of a tribal court, the Indian tribe shall retain exclusive jurisdiction, notwithstanding the residence or domicile of the child.

(b) Transfer of proceedings; declination by tribal court.—In any State court proceeding for the foster care placement of, or termination of parental rights to, an Indian child not domiciled or residing within the reservation of the Indian child's tribe, the court, in the absence of good cause to the contrary, shall transfer such proceeding to the jurisdiction of the tribe, absent objection by either parent, upon the petition of either parent or the Indian custodian or the Indian child's tribe: *Provided*, That such transfer shall be subject to declination by the tribal court of such tribe.

(c) State court proceedings; intervention.—In any State court proceeding for the foster care placement of, or termination of parental rights to, an Indian child, the Indian custodian of the child and the Indian child's tribe shall have a right to intervene at any point in the proceeding.

(d) Full faith and credit to public acts, records, and judicial proceedings of Indian tribes.—The United States, every State, every territory or possession of the United States, and every Indian tribe shall give full faith and credit to the public acts, records, and judicial proceedings of any Indian tribe applicable to Indian child custody proceedings to the same extent that such entities give full faith and credit to the public acts, records, and judicial proceedings of any other entity.

History of 25 U.S.C. §1911: Nov. 8, 1978, P.L. 95-608, §101, 92 Stat. 3071.

§1912. PENDING COURT PROCEEDINGS

(a) Notice; time for commencement of proceedings; additional time for preparation.—In any involuntary proceeding in a State court, where the court knows or has reason to know that an Indian child is involved, the party seeking the foster care placement of, or termination of parental rights to, an Indian child shall notify the parent or Indian custodian and the Indian child's tribe, by registered mail with return receipt requested, of the pending proceedings and of their right of intervention. If the identity or location of the parent or Indian custodian and the tribe cannot be determined, such notice shall be given to the Secretary in like manner, who shall have fifteen days after receipt to provide the requisite notice to the parent or Indian custodian and the tribe. No foster care placement or termination of parental rights proceeding shall be held until at least ten days after receipt of notice by the parent or Indian custodian and the tribe or the Secretary: *Provided*, That the parent or Indian custodian or the tribe shall, upon request, be granted up to twenty additional days to prepare for such proceeding.

(b) Appointment of counsel.—In any case in which the court determines indigency, the parent or Indian custodian shall have the right to court-appointed counsel in any removal, placement, or termination proceeding. The court may, in its discretion, appoint counsel for the child upon a finding that such appointment

is in the best interest of the child. Where State law makes no provision for appointment of counsel in such proceedings, the court shall promptly notify the Secretary upon appointment of counsel, and the Secretary, upon certification of the presiding judge, shall pay reasonable fees and expenses out of funds which may be appropriated pursuant to section 13 of this title.

(c) Examination of reports or other documents.—Each party to a foster care placement or termination of parental rights proceeding under State law involving an Indian child shall have the right to examine all reports or other documents filed with the court upon which any decision with respect to such action may be based.

(d) Remedial services and rehabilitative programs; preventive measures.—Any party seeking to effect a foster care placement of, or termination of parental rights to, an Indian child under State law shall satisfy the court that active efforts have been made to provide remedial services and rehabilitative programs designed to prevent the breakup of the Indian family and that these efforts have proved unsuccessful.

(e) Foster care placement orders; evidence; determination of damage to child.—No foster care placement may be ordered in such proceeding in the absence of a determination, supported by clear and convincing evidence, including testimony of qualified expert witnesses, that the continued custody of the child by the parent or Indian custodian is likely to result in serious emotional or physical damage to the child.

(f) Parental rights termination orders; evidence; determination of damage to child.—No termination of parental rights may be ordered in such proceeding in the absence of a determination, supported by evidence beyond a reasonable doubt, including testimony of qualified expert witnesses, that the continued custody of the child by the parent or Indian custodian is likely to result in serious emotional or physical damage to the child.

History of 25 U.S.C. §1912: Nov. 8, 1978, P.L. 95-608, §102, 92 Stat. 3071.

§1913. PARENTAL RIGHTS; VOLUNTARY TERMINATION

(a) Consent; record; certification matters; invalid consents.—Where any parent or Indian custodian voluntarily consents to a foster care placement or to termination of parental rights, such consent shall not be valid unless executed in writing and recorded before a judge of a court of competent jurisdiction and accompanied by the presiding judge's certificate that the terms and consequences of the consent were fully explained in detail and were fully understood by the parent or Indian custodian. The court shall also certify that either the parent or Indian custodian fully understood the explanation in English or that it was interpreted into a language that the parent or Indian custodian understood. Any consent given prior to, or within ten days after, birth of the Indian child shall not be valid.

(b) Foster care placement; withdrawal of consent.—Any parent or Indian custodian may withdraw consent to a foster care placement under State law at any time and, upon such withdrawal, the child shall be returned to the parent or Indian custodian.

(c) Voluntary termination of parental rights or adoptive placement; withdrawal of consent; return of custody.—In any voluntary proceeding for termination of parental rights to, or adoptive placement of, an Indian child, the consent of the parent may be withdrawn for any reason at any time prior to the entry of a final decree of termination or adoption, as the case may be, and the child shall be returned to the parent.

(d) Collateral attack; vacation of decree and return of custody; limitations.—After the entry of a final decree of adoption of an Indian child in any State court, the parent may withdraw consent thereto upon the grounds that consent was obtained through fraud or duress and may petition the court to vacate such decree. Upon a finding that such consent was obtained through fraud or duress, the court shall vacate such decree and return the child to the parent. No adoption which has been effective for at least two years may be invalidated under the provisions of this subsection unless otherwise permitted under State law.

History of 25 U.S.C. §1913: Nov. 8, 1978, P.L. 95-608, §103, 92 Stat. 3072.

§1914. PETITION TO COURT OF COMPETENT JURISDICTION TO INVALIDATE ACTION UPON SHOWING OF CERTAIN VIOLATIONS

Any Indian child who is the subject of any action for foster care placement or termination of parental rights under State law, any parent or Indian custodian from whose custody such child was removed, and the Indian child's tribe may petition any court of competent jurisdiction to invalidate such action upon a showing that such action violated any provision of sections 1911, 1912, and 1913 of this title.

History of 25 U.S.C. §1914: Nov. 8, 1978, P.L. 95-608, §104, 92 Stat. 3072.

§1915. PLACEMENT OF INDIAN CHILDREN

(a) Adoptive placements; preferences.—In any adoptive placement of an Indian child under State law, a preference shall be given, in the absence of good cause to the contrary, to a placement with—

(1) a member of the child's extended family;

(2) other members of the Indian child's tribe; or

(3) other Indian families.

(b) Foster care or preadoptive placements; criteria; preferences.—Any child accepted for foster care or preadoptive placement shall be placed in the least restrictive setting which most approximates a family and in which his special needs, if any, may be met. The child shall also be placed within reasonable proximity to his or her home, taking into account any special needs of the child. In any foster care or preadoptive placement, a preference shall be given, in the absence of good cause to the contrary, to a placement with—

(i) a member of the Indian child's extended family;

(ii) a foster home licensed, approved, or specified by the Indian child's tribe;

(iii) an Indian foster home licensed or approved by an authorized non-Indian licensing authority; or

(iv) an institution for children approved by an Indian tribe or operated by an Indian organization which has a program suitable to meet the Indian child's needs.

(c) Tribal resolution for different order of preference; personal preference considered; anonymity in application of preferences.—In the case of a placement under subsection (a) or (b) of this section, if the Indian child's tribe shall establish a different order of preference by resolution, the agency or court effecting the placement shall follow such order so long as the placement is the least restrictive setting appropriate to the particular needs of the child, as provided in subsection (b) of this section. Where appropriate, the preference of the Indian child or parent shall be considered:

Provided, That where a consenting parent evidences a desire for anonymity, the court or agency shall give weight to such desire in applying the preferences.

(d) Social and cultural standards applicable.—The standards to be applied in meeting the preference requirements of this section shall be the prevailing social and cultural standards of the Indian community in which the parent or extended family resides or with which the parent or extended family members maintain social and cultural ties.

(e) Record of placement; availability.—A record of each such placement, under State law, of an Indian child shall be maintained by the State in which the placement was made, evidencing the efforts to comply with the order of preference specified in this section. Such record shall be made available at any time upon the request of the Secretary or the Indian child's tribe.

History of 25 U.S.C. §1915: Nov. 8, 1978, P.L. 95-608, §105, 92 Stat. 3073.

§1916. RETURN OF CUSTODY

(a) Petition; best interests of child.—Notwithstanding State law to the contrary, whenever a final decree of adoption of an Indian child has been vacated or set aside or the adoptive parents voluntarily consent to the termination of their parental rights to the child, a biological parent or prior Indian custodian may petition for return of custody and the court shall grant such petition unless there is a showing, in a proceeding subject to the provisions of section 1912 of this title, that such return of custody is not in the best interests of the child.

(b) Removal from foster care home; placement procedure.—Whenever an Indian child is removed from a foster care home or institution for the purpose of further foster care, preadoptive, or adoptive placement, such placement shall be in accordance with the provisions of this chapter, except in the case where an Indian child is being returned to the parent or Indian custodian from whose custody the child was originally removed.

History of 25 U.S.C. §1916: Nov. 8, 1978, P.L. 95-608, §106, 92 Stat. 3073.

§1917. TRIBAL AFFILIATION INFORMATION & OTHER INFORMATION FOR PROTECTION OF RIGHTS FROM TRIBAL RELATIONSHIP; APPLICATION OF SUBJECT OF ADOPTIVE PLACEMENT; DISCLOSURE BY COURT

Upon application by an Indian individual who has reached the age of eighteen and who was the subject of an adoptive placement, the court which entered the final decree shall inform such individual of the tribal af-

filiation, if any, of the individual's biological parents and provide such other information as may be necessary to protect any rights flowing from the individual's tribal relationship.

History of 25 U.S.C. §1917: Nov. 8, 1978, P.L. 95-608, §107, 92 Stat. 3073.

§1918. REASSUMPTION OF JURISDICTION OVER CHILD CUSTODY PROCEEDINGS

(a) Petition; suitable plan; approval by Secretary.—Any Indian tribe which became subject to State jurisdiction pursuant to the provisions of the Act of August 15, 1953 (67 Stat. 588), as amended by title IV of the Act of April 11, 1968 (82 Stat. 73, 78), or pursuant to any other Federal law, may reassume jurisdiction over child custody proceedings. Before any Indian tribe may reassume jurisdiction over Indian child custody proceedings, such tribe shall present to the Secretary for approval a petition to reassume such jurisdiction which includes a suitable plan to exercise such jurisdiction.

(b) Criteria applicable to consideration by Secretary; partial retrocession—

(1) In considering the petition and feasibility of the plan of a tribe under subsection (a), the Secretary may consider, among other things:

(i) whether or not the tribe maintains a membership roll or alternative provision for clearly identifying the persons who will be affected by the reassumption of jurisdiction by the tribe;

(ii) the size of the reservation or former reservation area which will be affected by retrocession and reassumption of jurisdiction by the tribe;

(iii) the population base of the tribe, or distribution of the population in homogeneous communities or geographic areas; and

(iv) the feasibility of the plan in cases of multitribal occupation of a single reservation or geographic area.

(2) In those cases where the Secretary determines that the jurisdictional provisions of section 1911(a) of this title are not feasible, he is authorized to accept partial retrocession which will enable tribes to exercise referral jurisdiction as provided in section 1911(b) of this title, or, where appropriate, will allow them to exercise exclusive jurisdiction as provided in section 1911(a) of this title over limited community or geographic areas without regard for the reservation status of the area affected.

(c) Approval of petition; publication in Federal Register; notice; reassumption period; correction of causes for disapproval.—If the Secretary approves any petition under subsection (a), the Secretary shall publish notice of such approval in the Federal Register and shall notify the affected State or States of such approval. The Indian tribe concerned shall reassume jurisdiction sixty days after publication in the Federal Register of notice of approval. If the Secretary disapproves any petition under subsection (a), the Secretary shall provide such technical assistance as may be necessary to enable the tribe to correct any deficiency which the Secretary identified as a cause for disapproval.

(d) Pending actions or proceedings unaffected.—Assumption of jurisdiction under this section shall not affect any action or proceeding over which a court has already assumed jurisdiction, except as may be provided pursuant to any agreement under section 1919 of this title.

History of 25 U.S.C. §1918: Nov. 8, 1978, P.L. 95-608, §108, 92 Stat. 3074.

§1919. AGREEMENTS BETWEEN STATES & INDIAN TRIBES

(a) Subject coverage.—States and Indian tribes are authorized to enter into agreements with each other respecting care and custody of Indian children and jurisdiction over child custody proceedings, including agreements which may provide for orderly transfer of jurisdiction on a case-by-case basis and agreements which provide for concurrent jurisdiction between States and Indian tribes.

(b) Revocation; notice; actions or proceedings unaffected.—Such agreements may be revoked by either party upon one hundred and eighty days' written notice to the other party. Such revocation shall not affect any action or proceeding over which a court has already assumed jurisdiction, unless the agreement provides otherwise.

History of 25 U.S.C. §1919: Nov. 8, 1978, P.L. 95-608, §109, 92 Stat. 3074.

§1920. IMPROPER REMOVAL OF CHILD FROM CUSTODY; DECLINATION OF JURISDICTION; FORTHWITH RETURN OF CHILD: DANGER EXCEPTION

Where any petitioner in an Indian child custody proceeding before a State court has improperly removed the child from custody of the parent or Indian custodian or has improperly retained custody after a visit or other temporary relinquishment of custody, the court shall

decline jurisdiction over such petition and shall forthwith return the child to his parent or Indian custodian unless returning the child to his parent or custodian would subject the child to a substantial and immediate danger or threat of such danger.

History of 25 U.S.C. §1920: Nov. 8, 1978, P.L. 95-608, §110, 92 Stat. 3075.

§1921. HIGHER STATE OR FEDERAL STANDARD APPLICABLE TO PROTECT RIGHTS OF PARENT OR INDIAN CUSTODIAN OF INDIAN CHILD

In any case where State or Federal law applicable to a child custody proceeding under State or Federal law provides a higher standard of protection to the rights of the parent or Indian custodian of an Indian child than the rights provided under this subchapter, the State or Federal court shall apply the State or Federal standard.

History of 25 U.S.C. §1921: Nov. 8, 1978, P.L. 95-608, §111, 92 Stat. 3075.

§1922. EMERGENCY REMOVAL OR PLACEMENT OF CHILD; TERMINATION; APPROPRIATE ACTION

Nothing in this subchapter shall be construed to prevent the emergency removal of an Indian child who is a resident of or is domiciled on a reservation, but temporarily located off the reservation, from his parent or Indian custodian or the emergency placement of such child in a foster home or institution, under applicable State law, in order to prevent imminent physical damage or harm to the child. The State authority, official, or agency involved shall insure that the emergency removal or placement terminates immediately when such removal or placement is no longer necessary to prevent imminent physical damage or harm to the child and shall expeditiously initiate a child custody proceeding subject to the provisions of this subchapter, transfer the child to the jurisdiction of the appropriate Indian tribe, or restore the child to the parent or Indian custodian, as may be appropriate.

History of 25 U.S.C. §1922: Nov. 8, 1978, P.L. 95-608, §112, 92 Stat. 3075.

§1923. EFFECTIVE DATE

None of the provisions of this subchapter, except sections 1911(a), 1918, and 1919 of this title, shall affect a proceeding under State law for foster care placement, termination of parental rights, preadoptive placement, or adoptive placement which was initiated or completed prior to one hundred and eighty days after November 8, 1978, but shall apply to any subsequent proceeding in the same matter or subsequent proceedings affecting the custody or placement of the same child.

History of 25 U.S.C. §1923: Nov. 8, 1978, P.L. 95-608, §113, 92 Stat. 3075.

TITLE 26. INTERNAL REVENUE CODE

SUBTITLE A. INCOME TAXES

CHAPTER 1. NORMAL TAXES & SURTAXES

SUBCHAPTER B. COMPUTATION OF TAXABLE INCOME

PART I. DEFINITION OF GROSS INCOME, ADJUSTED GROSS INCOME, TAXABLE INCOME, ETC.

§66. TREATMENT OF COMMUNITY INCOME

(a) Treatment of community income where spouses live apart.—If—

(1) 2 individuals are married to each other at any time during a calendar year;

(2) such individuals—

(A) live apart at all times during the calendar year, and

(B) do not file a joint return under section 6013 with each other for a taxable year beginning or ending in the calendar year;

(3) one or both of such individuals have earned income for the calendar year which is community income; and

(4) no portion of such earned income is transferred (directly or indirectly) between such individuals before the close of the calendar year,

then, for purposes of this title, any community income of such individuals for the calendar year shall be treated in accordance with the rules provided by section 879(a).

(b) Secretary may disregard community property laws where spouse not notified of community income.—The Secretary may disallow the benefits of any community property law to any taxpayer with respect to any income if such taxpayer acted as if solely entitled to such income and failed to notify the taxpayer's spouse before the due date (including extensions) for filing the return for the taxable year in which the income was derived of the nature and amount of such income.

(c) Spouse relieved of liability in certain other cases.—Under regulations prescribed by the Secretary, if—

(1) an individual does not file a joint return for any taxable year,

(2) such individual does not include in gross income for such taxable year an item of community income properly includible therein which, in accordance with the rules contained in section 879(a), would be treated as the income of the other spouse,

(3) the individual establishes that he or she did not know of, and had no reason to know of, such item of community income, and

(4) taking into account all facts and circumstances, it is inequitable to include such item of community income in such individual's gross income,

then, for purposes of this title, such item of community income shall be included in the gross income of the other spouse (and not in the gross income of the individual). Under procedures prescribed by the Secretary, if, taking into account all the facts and circumstances, it is inequitable to hold the individual liable for any unpaid tax or any deficiency (or any portion of either) attributable to any item for which relief is not available under the preceding sentence, the Secretary may relieve such individual of such liability.

(d) Definitions.—For purposes of this section—

(1) Earned income.—The term "earned income" has the meaning given to such term by section 911(d)(2).

(2) Community income.—The term "community income" means income which, under applicable community property laws, is treated as community income.

(3) Community property laws.—The term "community property laws" means the community property laws of a State, a foreign country, or a possession of the United States.

History of 26 U.S.C. §66: Dec. 28, 1980, P.L. 96-605, §101(a), 94 Stat. 3521; July 18, 1984, P.L. 98-369, §424(b)(1), (2)(A), (B), 98 Stat. 802, 803; Dec. 19, 1989, P.L. 101-239, §7841(d)(8), 103 Stat. 2428; July 22, 1998, P.L. 105-206, §3201(b), 112 Stat. 739.

PART II. ITEMS SPECIFICALLY INCLUDED IN GROSS INCOME

§71. ALIMONY & SEPARATE MAINTENANCE PAYMENTS

(a) General rule.—Gross income includes amounts received as alimony or separate maintenance payments.

(b) Alimony or separate maintenance payments defined.—For purposes of this section—

(1) In general.—The term "alimony or separate maintenance payment" means any payment in cash if—

(A) such payment is received by (or on behalf of) a spouse under a divorce or separation instrument,

(B) the divorce or separation instrument does not designate such payment as a payment which is not includible in gross income under this section and not allowable as a deduction under section 215,

(C) in the case of an individual legally separated from his spouse under a decree of divorce or of separate maintenance, the payee spouse and the payor spouse are not members of the same household at the time such payment is made, and

(D) there is no liability to make any such payment for any period after the death of the payee spouse and there is no liability to make any payment (in cash or property) as a substitute for such payments after the death of the payee spouse.

(2) Divorce or separation instrument.—The term "divorce or separation instrument" means—

(A) a decree of divorce or separate maintenance or a written instrument incident to such a decree,

(B) a written separation agreement, or

(C) a decree (not described in subparagraph (A)) requiring a spouse to make payments for the support or maintenance of the other spouse.

(c) Payments to support children—

(1) In general.—Subsection (a) shall not apply to that part of any payment which the terms of the divorce or separation instrument fix (in terms of an amount of money or a part of the payment) as a sum which is payable for the support of children of the payor spouse.

(2) Treatment of certain reductions related to contingencies involving child.—For purposes of paragraph (1), if any amount specified in the instrument will be reduced—

(A) on the happening of a contingency specified in the instrument relating to a child (such as attaining a specified age, marrying, dying, leaving school, or a similar contingency), or

(B) at a time which can clearly be associated with a contingency of a kind specified in subparagraph (A),

an amount equal to the amount of such reduction will be treated as an amount fixed as payable for the support of children of the payor spouse.

(3) Special rule where payment is less than amount specified in instrument.—For purposes of this subsection, if any payment is less than the amount specified in the instrument, then so much of such payment as does not exceed the sum payable for support shall be considered a payment for such support.

(d) Spouse.—For purposes of this section, the term "spouse" includes a former spouse.

(e) Exception for joint returns.—This section and section 215 shall not apply if the spouses make a joint return with each other.

(f) Recomputation where excess front-loading of alimony payments—

(1) In general.—If there are excess alimony payments—

(A) the payor spouse shall include the amount of such excess payments in gross income for the payor spouse's taxable year beginning in the 3rd post-separation year, and

(B) the payee spouse shall be allowed a deduction in computing adjusted gross income for the amount of such excess payments for the payee's taxable year beginning in the 3rd post-separation year.

(2) Excess alimony payments.—For purposes of this subsection, the term "excess alimony payments" mean the sum of—

(A) the excess payments for the 1st post-separation year, and

(B) the excess payments for the 2nd post-separation year.

(3) Excess payments for 1st post-separation year.—For purposes of this subsection, the amount of the excess payments for the 1st post-separation year is the excess (if any) of—

(A) the amount of the alimony or separate maintenance payments paid by the payor spouse during the 1st post-separation year, over

(B) the sum of—

(i) the average of—

(I) the alimony or separate maintenance payments paid by the payor spouse during the 2nd post-separation year, reduced by the excess payments for the 2nd post-separation year, and

(II) the alimony or separate maintenance payments paid by the payor spouse during the 3rd post-separation year, plus

(ii) $15,000.

(4) Excess payments for 2nd post-separation year.—For purposes of this subsection, the amount of the excess payments for the 2nd post-separation year is the excess (if any) of—

(A) the amount of the alimony or separate maintenance payments paid by the payor spouse during the 2nd post-separation year, over

(B) the sum of—

(i) the amount of the alimony or separate maintenance payments paid by the payor spouse during the 3rd post-separation year, plus

(ii) $15,000.

(5) Exceptions—

(A) Where payment ceases by reason of death or remarriage.—Paragraph (1) shall not apply if—

(i) either spouse dies before the close of the 3rd post-separation year, or the payee spouse remarries before the close of the 3rd post-separation year, and

(ii) the alimony or separate maintenance payments cease by reason of such death or remarriage.

(B) Support payments.—For purposes of this subsection, the term "alimony or separate maintenance payment" shall not include any payment received under a decree described in subsection (b)(2)(C).

(C) Fluctuating payments not within control of payor spouse.—For purposes of this subsection, the term "alimony or separate maintenance payment" shall not include any payment to the extent it is made pursuant to a continuing liability (over a period of not less than 3 years) to pay a fixed portion or portions of the income from a business or property or from compensation for employment or self-employment.

(6) Post-separation years.—For purposes of this subsection, the term "1st post-separation years" means the 1st calendar year in which the payor spouse paid to the payee spouse alimony or separate maintenance payments to which this section applies. The 2nd and 3rd post-separation years shall be the 1st and 2nd succeeding calendar years, respectively.

(g) Cross references—

(1) For deduction of alimony or separate maintenance payments, see section 215.

(2) For taxable status of income of an estate or trust in the case of divorce, etc., see section 682.

History of 26 U.S.C. §71: Aug. 16, 1954, ch. 736, 68A Stat. 19; July 18, 1984, P.L. 98-369, §422(a), 98 Stat. 795; Oct. 22, 1986, P.L. 99-514, §1843(a)-(c)(1), (d), 100 Stat. 2853, 2855.

Regulation

C.F.R. §1.71-1T Alimony & Separate Maintenance Payments (temporary)

(a) In general.

Q-1 What is the income tax treatment of alimony or separate maintenance payments?

A-1 Alimony or separate maintenance payments are, under section 71, included in the gross income of the payee spouse and, under section 215, allowed as a deduction from the gross income of the payor spouse.

Q-2 What is an alimony or separate maintenance payment?

A-2 An alimony or separate maintenance payment is any payment received by or on behalf of a spouse (which for this purpose includes a former spouse) of the payor under a divorce or separation instrument that meets all of the following requirements:

(a) The payment is in cash (see A-5).

(b) The payment is not designated as a payment which is excludible from the gross income of the payee and nondeductible by the payor (see A-8).

(c) In the case of spouses legally separated under a decree of divorce or separate maintenance, the spouses are not members of the same household at the time the payment is made (see A-9).

(d) The payor has no liability to continue to make any payment after the death of the payee (or to make any payment as a substitute for such payment) and the divorce or separation instrument states that there is no such liability (see A-10).

(e) The payment is not treated as child support (see A-15).

(f) To the extent that one or more annual payments exceed $10,000 during any of the 6-post-separation years, the payor is obligated to make annual payments in each of the 6-post-separation years (see A-19).

Q-3 In order to be treated as alimony or separate maintenance payments, must the payments be "periodic" as that term was defined prior to enactment of the Tax Reform Act of 1984 or be made in discharge of a legal obligation of the payor to support the payee arising out of a marital or family relationship?

A-3 No. The Tax Reform Act of 1984 replaces the old requirements with the requirements described in A-2 above. Thus, the requirements that alimony or separate maintenance payments be "periodic" and be made in discharge of a legal obligation to support arising out of a marital or family relationship have been eliminated.

Q-4 Are the instruments described in section 71(a) of prior law the same as divorce or separation instruments described in section 71, as amended by the Tax Reform Act of 1984?

A-4 Yes.

(b) Specific requirements.

Q-5 May alimony or separate maintenance payments be made in a form other than cash?

A-5 No. Only cash payments (including checks and money orders payable on demand) qualify as alimony or separate maintenance payments. Transfers of services or property (including a debt instrument of a third party or an annuity contract), execution of a debt instrument by the payor, or the use of property of the payor do not qualify as alimony or separate maintenance payments.

Q-6 May payments of cash to a third party on behalf of a spouse qualify as alimony or separate maintenance payments if the payments are pursuant to the terms of a divorce or separation instrument?

A-6 Yes. Assuming all other requirements are satisfied, a payment of cash by the payor spouse to a third party under the terms of the divorce or separation instrument will qualify as a payment of cash which is received "on behalf of a spouse." For example, cash payments of rent, mortgage, tax, or tuition liabilities of the payee spouse made under the terms of the divorce or separation instrument will qualify as alimony or separate maintenance payments. Any payments to maintain property owned by the payor spouse and used by the payee spouse (including mortgage payments, real estate taxes and insurance premiums) are not payments on behalf of a spouse even if those payments are made pursuant to the terms of the divorce or separation instrument. Premiums paid by the payor spouse for term or whole life insurance on the payor's life made under the terms of the divorce or separation instrument will qualify as payments on behalf of the payee spouse to the extent that the payee spouse is the owner of the policy.

Q-7 May payments of cash to a third party on behalf of a spouse qualify as alimony or separate maintenance payments if the payments are made to the third party at the written request of the payee spouse?

A-7 Yes. For example, instead of making an alimony or separate maintenance payment directly to the payee, the payor spouse may make a cash payment to a charitable organization if such payment is pursuant to the written request, consent or ratification of the payee spouse. Such request, consent or ratification must state that the parties intend the payment to be treated as an alimony or separate maintenance payment to the payee spouse subject to the rules of section 71, and must be received by the payor spouse prior to the date of filing of the payor's first return of tax for the taxable year in which the payment was made.

Q-8 How may spouses designate that payments otherwise qualifying as alimony or separate maintenance payments shall be excludible from the gross income of the payee and nondeductible by the payor?

A-8 The spouses may designate that payments otherwise qualifying as alimony or separate maintenance payments shall be nondeductible by the payor and excludible from gross income by the payee by so providing in a divorce or separation instrument (as defined in section 71(b)(2)). If the spouses have executed a written separation agreement (as described in section 71(b)(2)(B)), any writing signed by both spouses which designates otherwise qualifying alimony or separate maintenance payments as nondeductible and excludible and which refers to the written separation agreement will be treated as a written separation agreement (and thus a divorce or separation instrument) for purposes of the preceding sentence. If the spouses are subject to temporary support orders (as described in section 71(b)(2)(C)), the designation of otherwise qualifying alimony or separate payments as nondeductible and excludible must be made in the original or a subsequent temporary support order. A copy of the instrument containing the designation of payments as not alimony or separate maintenance payments must be attached to the payee's first filed return of tax (Form 1040) for each year in which the designation applies.

Q-9 What are the consequences if, at the time a payment is made, the payor and payee spouses are members of the same household?

A-9 Generally, a payment made at the time when the payor and payee spouses are members of the same household cannot qualify as an alimony or separate maintenance payment if the spouses are legally separated under a decree of divorce or of separate maintenance. For purposes of the preceding sentence, a dwelling unit formerly shared by both spouses shall not be considered two separate households even if the spouses physically separate themselves within the dwelling unit. The spouses will not be treated as members of the same household if one spouse is preparing to depart from the household of the other spouse, and does depart not more than one month after the date the payment is made. If the spouses are not legally separated under a decree of divorce or separate maintenance, a payment under a written separation agreement or a decree described in section 71(b)(2)(C) may qualify as an alimony or separate maintenance payment notwithstanding that the payor and payee are members of the same household at the time the payment is made.

Q-10 Assuming all other requirements relating to the qualification of certain payments as alimony or separate maintenance payments are met, what are the consequences if the payor spouse is required to continue to make the payments after the death of the payee spouse?

A-10 None of the payments before (or after) the death of the payee spouse qualify as alimony or separate maintenance payments.

Q-11 What are the consequences if the divorce or separation instrument fails to state that there is no liability for any period after the death of the payee spouse to continue to make any payments which would otherwise qualify as alimony or separate maintenance payments?

A-11 If the instrument fails to include such a statement, none of the payments, whether made before or after the death of the payee spouse, will qualify as alimony or separate maintenance payments.

Example (1).—A is to pay B $10,000 in cash each year for a period of 10 years under a divorce or separation instrument which does not state that the payments will terminate upon the death of B. None of the payments will qualify as alimony or separate maintenance payments.

Example (2).—A is to pay B $10,000 in cash each year for a period of 10 years under a divorce or separation instrument which states that the payments will terminate upon the death of B. In addition, under the instrument, A is to pay B or B's estate $20,000 in cash each year for a period of 10 years. Because the $20,000 annual payments will not terminate upon the death of B, these pay-

ments will not qualify as alimony or separate maintenance payments. However, the separate $10,000 annual payments will qualify as alimony or separate maintenance payments.

Q-12 Will a divorce or separation instrument be treated as stating that there is no liability to make payments after the death of the payee spouse if the liability to make such payments terminates pursuant to applicable local law or oral agreement?

A-12 No. Termination of the liability to make payments must be stated in the terms of the divorce or separation instrument.

Q-13 What are the consequences if the payor spouse is required to make one or more payments (in cash or property) after the death of the payee spouse as a substitute for the continuation of pre-death payments which would otherwise qualify as alimony or separate maintenance payments?

A-13 If the payor spouse is required to make any such substitute payments, none of the otherwise qualifying payments will qualify as alimony or separate maintenance payments. The divorce or separation instrument need not state, however, that there is no liability to make any such substitute payment.

Q-14 Under what circumstances will one or more payments (in cash or property) which are to occur after the death of the payee spouse be treated as a substitute for the continuation of payments which would otherwise qualify as alimony or separate maintenance payments?

A-14 To the extent that one or more payments are to begin to be made, increase in amount, or become accelerated in time as a result of the death of the payee spouse, such payments may be treated as a substitute for the continuation of payments terminating on the death of the payee spouse which would otherwise qualify as alimony or separate maintenance payments. The determination of whether or not such payments are a substitute for the continuation of payments which would otherwise qualify as alimony or separate maintenance payments, and of the amount of the otherwise qualifying alimony or separate maintenance payments for which any such payments are a substitute, will depend on all of the facts and circumstances.

Example (1).—Under the terms of a divorce decree, A is obligated to make annual alimony payments to B of $30,000, terminating on the earlier of the expiration of 6 years or the death of B. B maintains custody of the minor children of A and B. The decree provides that at the death of B, if there are minor children of A and B remaining, A will be obligated to make annual payments of $10,000 to a trust, the income and corpus of which are to be used for the benefit of the children until the youngest child attains the age of majority. These facts indicate that A's liability to make annual $10,000 payments in trust for the benefit of his minor children upon the death of B is a substitute for $10,000 of the $30,000 annual payments to B. Accordingly, $10,000 of each of the $30,000 annual payments to B will not qualify as alimony or separate maintenance payments.

Example (2).—Under the terms of a divorce decree, A is obligated to make annual alimony payments to B of $30,000, terminating on the earlier of the expiration of 15 years or the death of B. The divorce decree provides that if B dies before the expiration of the 15 year period, A will pay to B's estate the difference between the total amount that A would have paid had B survived, minus the amount actually paid. For example, if B dies at the end of the 10th year in which payments are made, A will pay to B's estate $150,000 ($450,000-$300,000). These facts indicate that A's liability to make a lump sum payment to B's estate upon the death of B is a substitute for the full amount of each of the annual $30,000 payments to B. Accordingly, none of the annual $30,000 payments to B will qualify as alimony or separate maintenance payments. The result would be the same if the lump sum payable at B's death were discounted by an appropriate interest factor to account for the prepayment.

(c) Child support payments.

Q-15 What are the consequences of a payment which the terms of the divorce or separation instrument fix as payable for the support of a child of the payor spouse?

A-15 A payment which under the terms of the divorce or separation instrument is fixed (or treated as fixed) as payable for the support of a child of the payor spouse does not qualify as an alimony or separate maintenance payment. Thus, such a payment is not deductible by the payor spouse or includible in the income of the payee spouse.

Q-16 When is a payment fixed (or treated as fixed) as payable for the support of a child of the payor spouse?

A-16 A payment is fixed as payable for the support of a child of the payor spouse if the divorce or separation instrument specifically designates some sum or portion (which sum or portion may fluctuate) as payable for the support of a child of the payor spouse. A payment will be treated as fixed as payable for the support of a child of the payor spouse if the payment is reduced (a) on the happening of a contingency relating to a child of the payor, or (b) at a time which can clearly be associated with such a contingency. A payment may be treated as fixed as payable for the support of a child of the payor spouse even if other separate payments specifically are designated as payable for the support of a child of the payor spouse.

Q-17 When does a contingency relate to a child of the payor?

A-17 For this purpose, a contingency relates to a child of the payor if it depends on any event relating to that child, regardless of whether such event is certain or likely to occur. Events that relate to a child of the payor include the following: the child's attaining a specified age or income level, dying, marrying, leaving school, leaving the spouse's household, or gaining employment.

Q-18 When will a payment be treated as to be reduced at a time which can clearly be associated with the happening of a contingency relating to a child of the payor?

A-18 There are two situations, described below, in which payments which would otherwise qualify as alimony or separate maintenance payments will be presumed to be reduced at a time clearly associated with the happening of a contingency relating to a child of the payor. In all other situations, reductions in payments will not be treated as clearly associated with the happening of a contingency relating to a child of the payor.

The first situation referred to above is where the payments are to be reduced not more than 6 months before or after the date the child is to attain the age of 18, 21, or local age of majority. The second situation is where the payments are to be reduced on two or more occasions which occur not more than one year before or after a different child of the payor spouse attains a certain age between the ages of 18 and 24, inclusive. The certain age referred to in the preceding sentence must be the same for each such child, but need not be a whole number of years.

The presumption in the two situations described above that payments are to be reduced at a time clearly associated with the happening of a contingency relating to a child of the payor may be rebutted (either by the Service or by taxpayers) by showing that the time at which the payments are to be reduced was determined independently of any contingencies relating to the children of the payor. The presumption in the first situation will be rebutted conclusively if the reduction is a complete cessation of alimony or separate maintenance payments during the sixth post-separation year (described in A-21) or upon the expiration of a 72-month period. The presumption may also be rebutted in other circumstances, for example, by showing that alimony payments are to be made for a period customarily provided in the local jurisdiction, such as a period equal to one-half the duration of the marriage.

Example.—A and B are divorced on July 1, 1985, when their children, C (born July 15, 1970) and D (born September 23, 1972), are 14 and 12, respectively. Under the divorce decree, A is to make alimony payments to B of $2,000 per month. Such payments are to be reduced to $1,500 per month on January 1, 1991 and to $1,000 per month on January 1, 1995. On January 1, 1991, the date of the first reduction in payments, C will be 20 years 5 months and 17 days old. On January 1, 1995, the date of the second reduction in payments, D will be 22 years 3 months and 9 days old. Each of the reductions in payments is to occur not more than one year before or after a different child of A attains the age of 21 years and 4 months. (Actually, the reductions are to occur not more than one year before or after C and D attain any of the ages 21 years 3 months and 9 days through 21 years 5 months and 17 days.) Accordingly, the reductions will be presumed to clearly be associated with the happening of a contingency relating to C and D. Unless this presumption is rebutted, payments under the divorce decree equal to the sum of the reduction ($1,000 per month) will be treated as fixed for the support of the children of A and therefore will not qualify as alimony or separate maintenance payments.

(d) Excess front-loading rules.

Q-19 What are the excess front-loading rules?

A-19 The excess front-loading rules are two special rules which may apply to the extent that payments in any calendar year exceed $10,000. The first rule is a minimum term rule, which must be met in order for any annual payment, to the extent in excess of $10,000, to qualify as an alimony or separate maintenance payment (see A-2(f)). This rule requires that alimony or separate maintenance payments be called for, at a minimum, during the 6 "post-separation years." The second rule is a recapture rule which characterizes payments retrospectively by requiring a recalculation and inclusion in income by the

payor and deduction by the payee of previously paid alimony or separate maintenance payment to the extent that the amount of such payments during any of the 6 "post-separation years" falls short of the amount of payments during a prior year by more than $10,000.

Q-20 Do the excess front-loading rules apply to payments to the extent that annual payments never exceed $10,000?

A-20 No. For example, A is to make a single $10,000 payment to B. Provided that the other requirements of section 71 are met, the payment will qualify as an alimony or separate maintenance payment. If A were to make a single $15,000 payment to B, $10,000 of the payment would qualify as an alimony or separate maintenance payment and $5,000 of the payment would be disqualified under the minimum term rule because payments were not to be made for the minimum period.

Q-21 Do the excess front-loading rules apply to payments received under a decree described in section 71(b)(2)(C)?

A-21 No. Payments under decrees described in section 71(b)(2)(C) are to be disregarded entirely for purposes of applying the excess front-loading rules.

Q-22 Both the minimum term rule and the recapture rule refer to 6 "post-separation years." What are the 6 "post-separation years"?

A-22 The 6 "post-separation years" are the 6 consecutive calendar years beginning with the first calendar year in which the payor pays to the payee an alimony or separate maintenance payment (except a payment made under a decree described in section 71(b)(2)(C)). Each year within this period is referred to as a "post-separation year." The 6-year period need not commence with the year in which the spouses separate or divorce, or with the year in which payments under the divorce or separation instrument are made, if no payments during such year qualify as alimony or separate maintenance payments. For example, a decree for the divorce of A and B is entered in October, 1985. The decree requires A to make monthly payments to B commencing November 1, 1985, but A and B are members of the same household until February 15, 1986 (and as a result, the payments prior to January 16, 1986, do not qualify as alimony payments). For purposes of applying the excess front-loading rules to payments from A to B, the 6 calendar years 1986 through 1991 are post-separation years. If a spouse has been making payments pursuant to a divorce or separation instrument described in section 71(b)(2)(A) or (B), a modification of the instrument or the substitution of a new instrument (for example, the substitution of a divorce decree for a written separation agreement) will not result in the creation of additional post separation years. However, if a spouse has been making payments pursuant to a divorce or separation instrument described in section 71(b)(2)(C), the 6-year period does not begin until the first calendar year in which alimony or separate maintenance payments are made under a divorce or separation instrument described in section 71(b)(2)(A) or (B).

Q-23 How does the minimum term rule operate?

A-23 The minimum term rule operates in the following manner. To the extent payments are made in excess of $10,000, a payment will qualify as an alimony or separate maintenance payment only if alimony or separate maintenance payments are to be made in each of the 6 post-separation years. For example, pursuant to a divorce decree, A is to make alimony payments to B of $20,000 in each of the 5 calendar years 1985 through 1989. A is to make no payment in 1990. Under the minimum term rule, only $10,000 will qualify as an alimony payment in each of the calendar years 1985 through 1989. If the divorce decree also required A to make a $1 payment in 1990, the minimum term rule would be satisfied and $20,000 would be treated as an alimony payment in each of the calendar years 1985 through 1989. The recapture rule would, however, apply for 1990. For purposes of determining whether alimony or separate maintenance payments are to be made in any year, the possible termination of such payments upon the happening of a contingency (other than the passage of time) which has not yet occurred is ignored (unless such contingency may cause all or a portion of the payment to be treated as a child support payment).

Q-24 How does the recapture rule operate?

A-24 The recapture rule operates in the following manner. If the amount of alimony or separate maintenance payments paid in any post-separation year (referred to as the "computation year") falls short of the amount of alimony or separate maintenance payments paid in any prior post-separation year by more than $10,000, the payor must compute an "excess amount" for the computation year. The excess amount for any computation year is the sum of excess amounts determined with respect to each prior post-separation year. The excess amount determined with respect to a prior post-separation year is the excess of (1) the amount of alimony or separate maintenance payments paid by the payor spouse during such prior post-separation year, over (2) the amount of the alimony or separate maintenance payments paid by the payor spouse during the computation year plus $10,000. For purposes of this calculation, the amount of alimony or separate maintenance payments made by the payor spouse during any post-separation year preceding the computation year is reduced by any excess amount previously determined with respect to such year. The rules set forth above may be illustrated by the following example. A makes alimony payments to B of $25,000 in 1985 and $12,000 in 1986. The excess amount with respect to 1985 that is recaptured in 1986 is $3,000 ($25,000 - ($12,000 + $10,000)). For purposes of subsequent computation years, the amount deemed paid in 1985 is $22,000. If A makes alimony payments to B of $1,000 in 1987, the excess amount that is recaptured in 1987 will be $12,000. This is the sum of an $11,000 excess amount with respect to 1985 ($22,000 - ($1,000 + $10,000)) and a $1,000 excess amount with respect to 1986 ($12,000 - ($1,000 + $10,000)). If, prior to the end of 1990, payments decline further, additional recapture will occur. The payor spouse must include the excess amount in gross income for his/her taxable year beginning with or in the computation year. The payee spouse is allowed a deduction for the excess amount in computing adjusted gross income for his/her taxable year beginning with or in the computation year. However, the payee spouse must compute the excess amount by reference to the date when payments were made and not when payments were received.

Q-25 What are the exceptions to the recapture rule?

A-25 Apart from the $10,000 threshold for application of the recapture rule, there are three exceptions to the recapture rule. The first exception is for payments received under temporary support orders described in section 71(b)(2)(C) (see A-21). The second exception is for any payment made pursuant to a continuing liability over the period of the post-separation years to pay a fixed portion of the payor's income from a business or property or from compensation for employment or self-employment. The third exception is where the alimony or separate maintenance payments in any post-separation year cease by reason of the death of the payor or payee or the remarriage (as defined under applicable local law) of the payee before the close of the computation year. For example, pursuant to a divorce decree, A is to make cash payments to B of $30,000 in each of the calendar years 1985 through 1990. A makes cash payments of $30,000 in 1985 and $15,000 in 1986, in which year B remarries and A's alimony payments cease. The recapture rule does not apply for 1986 or any subsequent year. If alimony or separate maintenance payments made by A decline or cease during a post-separation year for any other reason (including a failure by the payor to make timely payments, a modification of the divorce or separation instrument, a reduction in the support needs of the payee, or a reduction in the ability of the payor to provide support) excess amounts with respect to prior post-separation years will be subject to recapture.

(e) Effective dates.

Q-26 When does section 71, as amended by the Tax Reform Act of 1984, become effective?

A-26 Generally, section 71, as amended, is effective with respect to divorce or separation instruments (as defined in section 71(b)(2)) executed after December 31, 1984. If a decree of divorce or separate maintenance executed after December 31, 1984, incorporates or adopts without change the terms of the alimony or separate maintenance payments under a divorce or separation instrument executed before January 1, 1985, such decree will be treated as executed before January 1, 1985. A change in the amount of alimony or separate maintenance payments or the time period over which such payments are to continue, or the addition or deletion of any contingencies or conditions relating to such payments is a change in the terms of the alimony or separate maintenance payments. For example, in November 1984, A and B executed a written separation agreement. In February 1985, a decree of divorce is entered in substitution for the written separation agreement. The decree of divorce does not change the terms of the alimony A pays to B. The decree of divorce will be treated as executed before January 1, 1985 and hence alimony payments under the decree will be subject to the rules of section 71 prior to amendment by the Tax Reform Act of 1984. If the amount or time period of the alimony or separate maintenance payments are not specified in the pre-1985 separation agreement or if the decree of divorce changes the amount or term of such payments, the decree of divorce will not be treated as executed before January 1, 1985, and alimony payments under the decree will be subject to the rules of section 71, as amended by the Tax Reform Act of 1984.

Section 71, as amended, also applies to any divorce or separation instrument executed (or treated as executed) before January 1, 1985 that has been

modified on or after January 1, 1985, if such modification expressly provides that section 71, as amended by the Tax Reform Act of 1984, shall apply to the instrument as modified. In this case, section 71, as amended, is effective with respect to payments made after the date the instrument is modified.

History of 26 C.F.R. §1.71-1T: 49 FR 34455, Aug. 31, 1984; 49 FR 36645, Sept. 19, 1984.

PART III. ITEMS SPECIFICALLY EXCLUDED FROM GROSS INCOME

§121. EXCLUSION OF GAIN FROM SALE OF PRINCIPAL RESIDENCE

(a) Exclusion.—Gross income shall not include gain from the sale or exchange of property if, during the 5-year period ending on the date of the sale or exchange, such property has been owned and used by the taxpayer as the taxpayer's principal residence for periods aggregating 2 years or more.

(b) Limitations—

(1) In general.—The amount of gain excluded from gross income under subsection (a) with respect to any sale or exchange shall not exceed $250,000.

(2) Special rules for joint returns.—In the case of a husband and wife who make a joint return for the taxable year of the sale or exchange of the property—

(A) $500,000 Limitation for certain joint returns.—Paragraph (1) shall be applied by substituting "$500,000" for "$250,000" if—

(i) either spouse meets the ownership requirements of subsection (a) with respect to such property;

(ii) both spouses meet the use requirements of subsection (a) with respect to such property; and

(iii) neither spouse is ineligible for the benefits of subsection (a) with respect to such property by reason of paragraph (3).

(B) Other joint returns.—If such spouses do not meet the requirements of subparagraph (A), the limitation under paragraph (1) shall be the sum of the limitations under paragraph (1) to which each spouse would be entitled if such spouses had not been married. For purposes of the preceding sentence, each spouse shall be treated as owning the property during the period that either spouse owned the property.

(3) Application to only 1 sale or exchange every 2 years.—Subsection (a) shall not apply to any sale or exchange by the taxpayer if, during the 2-year period ending on the date of such sale or exchange, there was any other sale or exchange by the taxpayer to which subsection (a) applied.

(4) Special rule for certain sales by surviving spouses.—In the case of a sale or exchange of property by an unmarried individual whose spouse is deceased on the date of such sale, paragraph (1) shall be applied by substituting '$500,000' for '$250,000' if such sale occurs not later than 2 years after the date of death of such spouse and the requirements of paragraph (2)(A) were met immediately before such date of death.

(5) Exclusion of gain allocated to nonqualified use—

(A) In general.—Subsection (a) shall not apply to so much of the gain from the sale or exchange of property as is allocated to periods of nonqualified use.

(B) Gain allocated to periods of nonqualified use.—For purposes of subparagraph (A), gain shall be allocated to periods of nonqualified use based on the ratio which—

(i) the aggregate periods of nonqualified use during the period such property was owned by the taxpayer, bears to

(ii) the period such property was owned by the taxpayer.

(C) Period of nonqualified use.—For purposes of this paragraph—

(i) In general.—The term "period of nonqualified use" means any period (other than the portion of any period preceding January 1, 2009) during which the property is not used as the principal residence of the taxpayer or the taxpayer's spouse or former spouse.

(ii) Exceptions.—The term "period of nonqualified use" does not include—

(I) any portion of the 5-year period described in subsection (a) which is after the last date that such property is used as the principal residence of the taxpayer or the taxpayer's spouse,

(II) any period (not to exceed an aggregate period of 10 years) during which the taxpayer or the taxpayer's spouse is serving on qualified official extended duty (as defined in subsection (d)(9)(C)) described in clause (i), (ii), or (iii) of subsection (d)(9)(A), and

(III) any other period of temporary absence (not to exceed an aggregate period of 2 years) due to change of employment, health conditions, or such other unforeseen circumstances as may be specified by the Secretary.

(D) Coordination with recognition of gain attributable to depreciation.—For purposes of this paragraph—

(i) subparagraph (A) shall be applied after the application of subsection (d)(6), and

(ii) subparagraph (B) shall be applied without regard to any gain to which subsection (d)(6) applies.

(c) Exclusion for taxpayers failing to meet certain requirements—

(1) In general.—In the case of a sale or exchange to which this subsection applies, the ownership and use requirements of subsection (a), and subsection (b)(3), shall not apply; but the dollar limitation under paragraph (1) or (2) of subsection (b), whichever is applicable, shall be equal to—

(A) the amount which bears the same ratio to such limitation (determined without regard to this paragraph) as

(B)(i) the shorter of—

(I) the aggregate periods, during the 5-year period ending on the date of such sale or exchange, such property has been owned and used by the taxpayer as the taxpayer's principal residence; or

(II) the period after the date of the most recent prior sale or exchange by the taxpayer to which subsection (a) applied and before the date of such sale or exchange, bears to

(ii) 2 years.

(2) Sales and exchanges to which subsection applies.—This subsection shall apply to any sale or exchange if—

(A) subsection (a) would not (but for this subsection) apply to such sale or exchange by reason of—

(i) a failure to meet the ownership and use requirements of subsection (a), or

(ii) subsection (b)(3), and

(B) such sale or exchange is by reason of a change in place of employment, health, or, to the extent provided in regulations, unforeseen circumstances.

(d) Special rules—

(1) Joint returns.—If a husband and wife make a joint return for the taxable year of the sale or exchange of the property, subsections (a) and (c) shall apply if either spouse meets the ownership and use requirements of subsection (a) with respect to such property.

(2) Property of deceased spouse.—For purposes of this section, in the case of an unmarried individual whose spouse is deceased on the date of the sale or exchange of property, the period such unmarried individual owned and used such property shall include the period such deceased spouse owned and used such property before death.

(3) Property owned by spouse or former spouse.—For purposes of this section—

(A) Property transferred to individual from spouse or former spouse.—In the case of an individual holding property transferred to such individual in a transaction described in section 1041(a), the period such individual owns such property shall include the period the transferor owned the property.

(B) Property used by former spouse pursuant to divorce decree, etc.—Solely for purposes of this section, an individual shall be treated as using property as such individual's principal residence during any period of ownership while such individual's spouse or former spouse is granted use of the property under a divorce or separation instrument (as defined in section 71(b)(2)).

(4) Tenant-stockholder in cooperative housing corporation.—For purposes of this section, if the taxpayer holds stock as a tenant-stockholder (as defined in section 216) in a cooperative housing corporation (as defined in such section), then—

(A) the holding requirements of subsection (a) shall be applied to the holding of such stock, and

(B) the use requirements of subsection (a) shall be applied to the house or apartment which the taxpayer was entitled to occupy as such stockholder.

(5) Involuntary conversions—

(A) In general.—For purposes of this section, the destruction, theft, seizure, requisition, or condemnation of property shall be treated as the sale of such property.

(B) Application of section 1033.—In applying section 1033 (relating to involuntary conversions), the amount realized from the sale or exchange of property shall be treated as being the amount determined without regard to this section, reduced by the amount of gain not included in gross income pursuant to this section.

(C) Property acquired after involuntary conversion.—If the basis of the property sold or exchanged is determined (in whole or in part) under section 1033(b) (relating to basis of property acquired through involuntary conversion), then the holding and use by the taxpayer of the converted property shall be treated as holding and use by the taxpayer of the property sold or exchanged.

(6) Recognition of gain attributable to depreciation.—Subsection (a) shall not apply to so much of the gain from the sale of any property as does not exceed the portion of the depreciation adjustments (as defined in section 1250(b)(3)) attributable to periods after May 6, 1997, in respect of such property.

(7) Determination of use during periods of out-of-residence care.—In the case of a taxpayer who—

(A) becomes physically or mentally incapable of self-care, and

(B) owns property and uses such property as the taxpayer's principal residence during the 5-year period described in subsection (a) for periods aggregating at least 1 year,

then the taxpayer shall be treated as using such property as the taxpayer's principal residence during any time during such 5-year period in which the taxpayer owns the property and resides in any facility (including a nursing home) licensed by a State or political subdivision to care for an individual in the taxpayer's condition.

(8) Sales of remainder interests.—For purposes of this section—

(A) In general.—At the election of the taxpayer, this section shall not fail to apply to the sale or exchange of an interest in a principal residence by reason of such interest being a remainder interest in such residence, but this section shall not apply to any other interest in such residence which is sold or exchanged separately.

(B) Exception for sales to related parties.—Subparagraph (A) shall not apply to any sale to, or exchange with, any person who bears a relationship to the taxpayer which is described in section 267(b) or 707(b).

(9) Uniformed services, foreign service, and intelligence community—

(A) In general.—At the election of an individual with respect to a property, the running of the 5-year period described in subsections (a) and (c)(1)(B) and paragraph (7) of this subsection with respect to such property shall be suspended during any period that such individual or such individual's spouse is serving on qualified official extended duty—

(i) as a member of the uniformed services,

(ii) as a member of the Foreign Service of the United States, or

(iii) as an employee of the intelligence community.

(B) Maximum period of suspension.—The 5-year period described in subsection (a) shall not be extended more than 10 years by reason of subparagraph (A).

(C) Qualified official extended duty.—For purposes of this paragraph—

(i) In general.—The term "qualified official extended duty" means any extended duty while serving at a duty station which is at least 50 miles from such property or while residing under Government orders in Government quarters.

(ii) Uniformed services.—The term "uniformed services" has the meaning given such term by section 101(a)(5) of title 10, United States Code, as in effect on the date of the enactment of this paragraph.

(iii) Foreign Service of the United States.—The term "member of the Foreign Service of the United States" has the meaning given the term "member of the Service" by paragraph (1), (2), (3), (4), or (5) of section 103 of the Foreign Service Act of 1980, as in effect on the date of the enactment of this paragraph.

(iv) Employee of intelligence community.—The term "employee of the intelligence community" means an employee (as defined by section 2105 of title 5, United States Code) of—

(I) the Office of the Director of National Intelligence,

(II) the Central Intelligence Agency,

(III) the National Security Agency,

(IV) the Defense Intelligence Agency,

(V) the National Geospatial Intelligence Agency,

(VI) the National Reconnaissance Office,

(VII) any other office within the Department of Defense for the collection of specialized national intelligence through reconnaissance programs,

(VIII) any of the intelligence elements of the Army, the Navy, the Air Force, the Marine Corps, the Federal Bureau of Investigation, the Department of Treasury, the Department of Energy, and the Coast Guard,

(IX) the Bureau of Intelligence and Research of the Department of State, or

(X) any of the elements of the Department of Homeland Security concerned with the analyses of foreign intelligence information.

(v) Extended duty.—The term "extended duty" means any period of active duty pursuant to a call or order to such duty for a period in excess of 90 days or for an indefinite period.

(vi) Repealed by P.L. 110-245, §113(b), 122 Stat. 1635, June 17, 2008.

(D) Special rules relating to election—

(i) Election limited to 1 property at a time.—An election under subparagraph (A) with respect to any property may not be made if such an election is in effect with respect to any other property.

(ii) Revocation of election.—An election under subparagraph (A) may be revoked at any time.

(E) Repealed by P.L. 110-245, §113(a), 122 Stat. 1635, June 17, 2008.

(10) Property acquired in like-kind exchange.—If a taxpayer acquires property in an exchange with respect to which gain is not recognized (in whole or in part) to the taxpayer under subsection (a) or (b) of section 1031, subsection (a) shall not apply to the sale or exchange of such property by such taxpayer (or by any person whose basis in such property is determined, in whole or in part, by reference to the basis in the hands of such taxpayer) during the 5-year period beginning with the date of such acquisition.

(11) Repealed by P.L. 111-312, §301(a), 124 Stat. 3300, Dec. 17, 2010.

(12) Peace Corps—

(A) In general.—At the election of an individual with respect to a property, the running of the 5-year period described in subsections (a) and (c)(1)(B) and paragraph (7) of this subsection with respect to such property shall be suspended during any period that such individual or such individual's spouse is serving outside the United States—

(i) on qualified official extended duty (as defined in paragraph (9)(C)) as an employee of the Peace Corps, or

(ii) as an enrolled volunteer or volunteer leader under section 5 or 6 (as the case may be) of the Peace Corps Act (22 U.S.C. 2504, 2505).

(B) Applicable rules.—For purposes of subparagraph (A), rules similar to the rules of subparagraphs (B) and (D) of paragraph (9) shall apply.

(e) Denial of exclusion for expatriates.—This section shall not apply to any sale or exchange by an individual if the treatment provided by section 877(a)(1) applies to such individual.

(f) Election to have section not apply.—This section shall not apply to any sale or exchange with respect to which the taxpayer elects not to have this section apply.

(g) Residences acquired in rollovers under section 1034.—For purposes of this section, in the case of property the acquisition of which by the taxpayer resulted under section 1034 (as in effect on the day before the date of the enactment of this section) in the nonrecognition of any part of the gain realized on the sale or exchange of another residence, in determining the period for which the taxpayer has owned and used such property as the taxpayer's principal residence, there shall be included the aggregate periods for which such other residence (and each prior residence taken into account under section 1223(6) in determining the holding period of such property) had been so owned and used.

History of 26 U.S.C. §121: Feb. 26, 1964, P.L. 88-272, §206(a), 78 Stat. 38; Oct. 4, 1976, P.L. 94-455, §§1404(a), 1906(b)(13)(A), 90 Stat. 1733, 1834; Nov. 6, 1978, P.L. 95-600, §404(a)-(c)(2), 92 Stat. 2869, 2870; Aug. 13, 1981, P.L. 97-34, §123(a), 95 Stat. 197; Nov. 10, 1988, P.L. 100-647, §6011(a), 102 Stat. 3691; Aug. 5, 1997, P.L. 105-34, §312(a), 111 Stat. 836; July 22, 1998, P.L. 105-206, §6005(e)(1), (2), 112 Stat. 805; June 7, 2001, P.L. 107-16, §542(c), 115 Stat. 84; Nov. 11, 2003, P.L. 108-121, §101(a), 117 Stat. 1336; Oct. 22, 2004, P.L. 108-357, §840(a), 118 Stat. 1597; Dec. 21, 2005, P.L. 109-135, §§402(a)(3), 403(ee), 119 Stat. 2610, 2631; Dec. 20, 2006, P.L. 109-432, §417(a)-(d), 120 Stat. 2965; Dec. 20, 2007, P.L. 110-142, §7(a), 121 Stat. 1806; Dec. 29, 2007, P.L. 110-172, §11(a)(11)(A), 121 Stat. 2485; June 17, 2008, P.L. 110-245, §§110(a), 113(a), (b), 122 Stat. 1633, 1635; July 30, 2008, P.L. 110-289, §3092(a), 122 Stat. 2911; Dec. 17, 2010, P.L. 111-312, §301(a), 124 Stat. 3300; Dec. 19, 2014, P.L. 113-295, §§212(c), 213(c)(1), 221(a)(20), 128 Stat. 4033, 4040.

PART V. DEDUCTIONS FOR PERSONAL EXEMPTIONS

§152. DEPENDENT DEFINED

(a) In general.—For purposes of this subtitle, the term "dependent" means—

(1) a qualifying child, or

(2) a qualifying relative.

(b) Exceptions.—For purposes of this section—

(1) Dependents ineligible.—If an individual is a dependent of a taxpayer for any taxable year of such taxpayer beginning in a calendar year, such individual shall be treated as having no dependents for any taxable year of such individual beginning in such calendar year.

(2) Married dependents.—An individual shall not be treated as a dependent of a taxpayer under subsection (a) if such individual has made a joint return with the individual's spouse under section 6013 for the taxable year beginning in the calendar year in which the taxable year of the taxpayer begins.

(3) Citizens or nationals of other countries—

(A) In general.—The term "dependent" does not include an individual who is not a citizen or national of the United States unless such individual is a resident of the United States or a country contiguous to the United States.

(B) Exception for adopted child.—Subparagraph (A) shall not exclude any child of a taxpayer (within the meaning of subsection (f)(1)(B)) from the definition of "dependent" if—

(i) for the taxable year of the taxpayer, the child has the same principal place of abode as the taxpayer and is a member of the taxpayer's household, and

(ii) the taxpayer is a citizen or national of the United States.

(c) Qualifying child.—For purposes of this section—

(1) In general.—The term "qualifying child" means, with respect to any taxpayer for any taxable year, an individual—

(A) who bears a relationship to the taxpayer described in paragraph (2),

(B) who has the same principal place of abode as the taxpayer for more than one-half of such taxable year,

(C) who meets the age requirements of paragraph (3),

(D) who has not provided over one-half of such individual's own support for the calendar year in which the taxable year of the taxpayer begins, and

(E) who has not filed a joint return (other than only for a claim of refund) with the individual's spouse under section 6013 for the taxable year beginning in the calendar year in which the taxable year of the taxpayer begins.

(2) Relationship.—For purposes of paragraph (1)(A), an individual bears a relationship to the taxpayer described in this paragraph if such individual is—

(A) a child of the taxpayer or a descendant of such a child, or

(B) a brother, sister, stepbrother, or stepsister of the taxpayer or a descendant of any such relative.

(3) Age requirements—

(A) In general.—For purposes of paragraph (1)(C), an individual meets the requirements of this paragraph if such individual is younger than the taxpayer claiming such individual as a qualifying child and—

(i) has not attained the age of 19 as of the close of the calendar year in which the taxable year of the taxpayer begins, or

(ii) is a student who has not attained the age of 24 as of the close of such calendar year.

(B) Special rule for disabled.—In the case of an individual who is permanently and totally disabled (as defined in section 22(e)(3)) at any time during such calendar year, the requirements of subparagraph (A) shall be treated as met with respect to such individual.

(4) Special rule relating to 2 or more who can claim the same qualifying child—

(A) In general.—Except as provided in subparagraphs (B) and (C), if (but for this paragraph) an individual may be claimed as a qualifying child by 2 or more taxpayers for a taxable year beginning in the same calendar year, such individual shall be treated as the qualifying child of the taxpayer who is—

(i) a parent of the individual, or

(ii) if clause (i) does not apply, the taxpayer with the highest adjusted gross income for such taxable year.

(B) More than 1 parent claiming qualifying child.—If the parents claiming any qualifying child do not file a joint return together, such child shall be treated as the qualifying child of—

(i) the parent with whom the child resided for the longest period of time during the taxable year, or

(ii) if the child resides with both parents for the same amount of time during such taxable year, the parent with the highest adjusted gross income.

(C) No parent claiming qualifying child.—If the parents of an individual may claim such individual as a qualifying child but no parent so claims the individual, such individual may be claimed as the qualifying child of another taxpayer but only if the adjusted gross income of such taxpayer is higher than the highest adjusted gross income of any parent of the individual.

(d) Qualifying relative.—For purposes of this section—

(1) In general.—The term "qualifying relative" means, with respect to any taxpayer for any taxable year, an individual—

(A) who bears a relationship to the taxpayer described in paragraph (2),

(B) whose gross income for the calendar year in which such taxable year begins is less than the exemption amount (as defined in section 151(d)),

(C) with respect to whom the taxpayer provides over one-half of the individual's support for the calendar year in which such taxable year begins, and

(D) who is not a qualifying child of such taxpayer or of any other taxpayer for any taxable year beginning in the calendar year in which such taxable year begins.

(2) Relationship.—For purposes of paragraph (1)(A), an individual bears a relationship to the taxpayer described in this paragraph if the individual is any of the following with respect to the taxpayer:

(A) A child or a descendant of a child.

(B) A brother, sister, stepbrother, or stepsister.

(C) The father or mother, or an ancestor of either.

(D) A stepfather or stepmother.

(E) A son or daughter of a brother or sister of the taxpayer.

(F) A brother or sister of the father or mother of the taxpayer.

(G) A son-in-law, daughter-in-law, father-in-law, mother-in-law, brother-in-law, or sister-in-law.

(H) An individual (other than an individual who at any time during the taxable year was the spouse, determined without regard to section 7703, of the taxpayer) who, for the taxable year of the taxpayer, has the same principal place of abode as the taxpayer and is a member of the taxpayer's household.

(3) Special rule relating to multiple support agreements.—For purposes of paragraph (1)(C), over one-half of the support of an individual for a calendar year shall be treated as received from the taxpayer if—

(A) no one person contributed over one-half of such support,

(B) over one-half of such support was received from 2 or more persons each of whom, but for the fact that any such person alone did not contribute over one-half of such support, would have been entitled to claim such individual as a dependent for a taxable year beginning in such calendar year,

(C) the taxpayer contributed over 10 percent of such support, and

(D) each person described in subparagraph (B) (other than the taxpayer) who contributed over 10 percent of such support files a written declaration (in such manner and form as the Secretary may by regulations prescribe) that such person will not claim such individual as a dependent for any taxable year beginning in such calendar year.

(4) Special rule relating to income of handicapped dependents—

(A) In general.—For purposes of paragraph (1)(B), the gross income of an individual who is permanently and totally disabled (as defined in section 22(e)(3)) at any time during the taxable year shall not include income attributable to services performed by the individual at a sheltered workshop if—

(i) the availability of medical care at such workshop is the principal reason for the individual's presence there, and

(ii) the income arises solely from activities at such workshop which are incident to such medical care.

(B) Sheltered workshop defined.—For purposes of subparagraph (A), the term "sheltered workshop" means a school—

(i) which provides special instruction or training designed to alleviate the disability of the individual, and

(ii) which is operated by an organization described in section 501(c)(3) and exempt from tax under section 501(a), or by a State, a possession of the United States, any political subdivision of any of the foregoing, the United States, or the District of Columbia.

(5) Special rules for support.—For purposes of this subsection—

(A) payments to a spouse which are includible in the gross income of such spouse under section 71 or 682 shall not be treated as a payment by the payor spouse for the support of any dependent, and

(B) in the case of the remarriage of a parent, support of a child received from the parent's spouse shall be treated as received from the parent.

(e) Special rule for divorced parents, etc.—

(1) In general.—Notwithstanding subsection (c)(1)(B), (c)(4), or (d)(1)(C), if—

(A) a child receives over one-half of the child's support during the calendar year from the child's parents—

(i) who are divorced or legally separated under a decree of divorce or separate maintenance,

(ii) who are separated under a written separation agreement, or

(iii) who live apart at all times during the last 6 months of the calendar year, and—

(B) such child is in the custody of 1 or both of the child's parents for more than one-half of the calendar year, such child shall be treated as being the qualifying child or qualifying relative of the noncustodial parent for a calendar year if the requirements described in paragraph (2) or (3) are met.

(2) Exception where custodial parent releases claim to exemption for the year.—For purposes of paragraph (1), the requirements described in this paragraph are met with respect to any calendar year if—

(A) the custodial parent signs a written declaration (in such manner and form as the Secretary may by regulations prescribe) that such custodial parent will not claim such child as a dependent for any taxable year beginning in such calendar year, and

(B) the noncustodial parent attaches such written declaration to the noncustodial parent's return for the taxable year beginning during such calendar year.

(3) Exception for certain pre-1985 instruments—

(A) In general.—For purposes of paragraph (1), the requirements described in this paragraph are met with respect to any calendar year if—

(i) a qualified pre-1985 instrument between the parents applicable to the taxable year beginning in such calendar year provides that the noncustodial parent shall be entitled to any deduction allowable under section 151 for such child, and

(ii) the noncustodial parent provides at least $600 for the support of such child during such calendar year. For purposes of this subparagraph, amounts expended for the support of a child or children shall be treated as received from the noncustodial parent to the extent that such parent provided amounts for such support.

(B) Qualified pre-1985 instrument.—For purposes of this paragraph, the term "qualified pre-1985 instrument" means any decree of divorce or separate maintenance or written agreement—

(i) which is executed before January 1, 1985,

(ii) which on such date contains the provision described in subparagraph (A)(i), and

(iii) which is not modified on or after such date in a modification which expressly provides that this paragraph shall not apply to such decree or agreement.

(4) Custodial parent and noncustodial parent.—For purposes of this subsection—

(A) Custodial parent.—The term "custodial parent" means the parent having custody for the greater portion of the calendar year.

(B) Noncustodial parent.—The term "noncustodial parent" means the parent who is not the custodial parent.

(5) Exception for multiple-support agreement.—This subsection shall not apply in any case where over one-half of the support of the child is treated as having been received from a taxpayer under the provision of subsection (d)(3).

(6) Special rule for support received from new spouse of parent.—For purposes of this subsection, in the case of the remarriage of a parent, support of a child received from the parent's spouse shall be treated as received from the parent.

(f) Other definitions and rules.—For purposes of this section—

(1) Child defined—

(A) In general.—The term "child" means an individual who is—

(i) a son, daughter, stepson, or stepdaughter of the taxpayer, or

(ii) an eligible foster child of the taxpayer.

(B) Adopted child.—In determining whether any of the relationships specified in subparagraph (A)(i) or paragraph (4) exists, a legally adopted individual of the taxpayer, or an individual who is lawfully placed with the taxpayer for legal adoption by the taxpayer, shall be treated as a child of such individual by blood.

(C) Eligible foster child.—For purposes of subparagraph (A)(ii), the term "eligible foster child" means an individual who is placed with the taxpayer by an authorized placement agency or by judgment, decree, or other order of any court of competent jurisdiction.

(2) Student defined.—The term "student" means an individual who during each of 5 calendar months during the calendar year in which the taxable year of the taxpayer begins—

(A) is a full-time student at an educational organization described in section 170(b)(1)(A)(ii), or

(B) is pursuing a full-time course of institutional on-farm training under the supervision of an accredited agent of an educational organization described in section 170(b)(1)(A)(ii) or of a State or political subdivision of a State.

(3) Determination of household status.—An individual shall not be treated as a member of the taxpayer's household if at any time during the taxable year of the taxpayer the relationship between such individual and the taxpayer is in violation of local law.

(4) Brother and sister.—The terms "brother" and "sister" include a brother or sister by the half blood.

(5) Special support test in case of students.—For purposes of subsections (c)(1)(D) and (d)(1)(C), in the case of an individual who is—

(A) a child of the taxpayer, and

(B) a student, amounts received as scholarships for study at an educational organization described in section 170(b)(1)(A)(ii) shall not be taken into account.

(6) Treatment of missing children—

(A) In general.—Solely for the purposes referred to in subparagraph (B), a child of the taxpayer—

(i) who is presumed by law enforcement authorities to have been kidnapped by someone who is not a member of the family of such child or the taxpayer, and

(ii) who had, for the taxable year in which the kidnapping occurred, the same principal place of abode as the taxpayer for more than one-half of the portion of such year before the date of the kidnapping,

shall be treated as meeting the requirement of subsection (c)(1)(B) with respect to a taxpayer for all taxable years ending during the period that the child is kidnapped.

(B) Purposes.—Subparagraph (A) shall apply solely for purposes of determining—

(i) the deduction under section 151(c),

(ii) the credit under section 24 (relating to child tax credit),

(iii) whether an individual is a surviving spouse or a head of a household (as such terms are defined in section 2), and

(iv) the earned income credit under section 32.

(C) Comparable treatment of certain qualifying relatives.—For purposes of this section, a child of the taxpayer—

(i) who is presumed by law enforcement authorities to have been kidnapped by someone who is not a member of the family of such child or the taxpayer, and

(ii) who was (without regard to this paragraph) a qualifying relative of the taxpayer for the portion of the taxable year before the date of the kidnapping,

shall be treated as a qualifying relative of the taxpayer for all taxable years ending during the period that the child is kidnapped.

(D) Termination of treatment.—Subparagraphs (A) and (C) shall cease to apply as of the first taxable year of the taxpayer beginning after the calendar year in which there is a determination that the child is dead (or, if earlier, in which the child would have attained age 18).

(7) Cross references.—For provision treating child as dependent of both parents for purposes of certain provisions, see sections 105(b), 132(h)(2)(B), and 213(d)(5).

History of 26 U.S.C. §152: Aug. 16, 1954, ch. 736, 68A Stat. 43; Aug. 9, 1955, ch. 693, §2, 69 Stat. 626; Sept. 2, 1958, P.L. 85-866, §4(a)-(c), 72 Stat. 1607; Sept. 23, 1959, P.L. 86-376, §1(a), 73 Stat. 699; Aug. 31, 1967, P.L. 90-78, §1, 81 Stat. 191; Dec. 30, 1969, P.L. 91-172, §912(a), 83 Stat. 722; Oct. 27, 1972, P.L. 92-580, §1(a), 86 Stat. 1276; Oct. 4, 1976, P.L. 94-455, §§1901(a)(24), (b)(7)(B), (8)(A), 1906(b)(13)(A), 2139(a), 90 Stat. 1767, 1794, 1834, 1932; July 18, 1984, P.L. 98-369, §§423(a), 482(b)(2), 98 Stat. 799, 848; Oct. 22, 1986, P.L. 99-514, §§104(b)(1)(B), (3), 1301(j)(8), 100 Stat. 2104, 2105, 2658; Oct. 4, 2004, P.L. 108-311, §201, 118 Stat. 1169; Dec. 21, 2005, P.L. 109-135, §404(a), 119 Stat. 2632; Oct. 7, 2008, P.L. 110-351, §501(a), (b), (c)(2), 122 Stat. 3979, 3980.

Regulation

C.F.R. §1.152-4 Special Rule for a Child of Divorced or Separated Parents or Parents Who Live Apart

(a) In general.—A taxpayer may claim a dependency deduction for a child (as defined in section 152(f)(1)) only if the child is the qualifying child of the taxpayer under section 152(c) or the qualifying relative of the taxpayer under section 152(d). Section 152(c)(4)(B) provides that a child who is claimed as a qualifying child by parents who do not file a joint return together is treated as the qualifying child of the parent with whom the child resides for a longer period of time during the taxable year or, if the child resides with both parents for an equal period of time, of the parent with the higher adjusted gross income. However, a child is treated as the qualifying child or qualifying relative of the noncustodial parent if the custodial parent releases a claim to the exemption under section 152(e) and this section.

(b) Release of claim by custodial parent—

(1) In general.—Under section 152(e)(1), notwithstanding section 152(c)(1)(B), (c)(4), or (d)(1)(C), a child is treated as the qualifying child or qualifying relative of the noncustodial parent (as defined in paragraph (d) of this section) if the requirements of paragraphs (b)(2) and (b)(3) of this section are met.

(2) Support, custody, and parental status—

(i) In general.—The requirements of this paragraph (b)(2) are met if the parents of the child provide over one-half of the child's support for the calendar year, the child is in the custody of one or both parents for more than one-half of the calendar year, and the parents—

(A) Are divorced or legally separated under a decree of divorce or separate maintenance;

(B) Are separated under a written separation agreement; or

(C) Live apart at all times during the last 6 months of the calendar year whether or not they are or were married.

(ii) Multiple support agreement.—The requirements of this paragraph (b)(2) are not met if over one-half of the support of the child is treated as having been received from a taxpayer under section 152(d)(3).

(3) Release of claim to child.—The requirements of this paragraph (b)(3) are met for a calendar year if—

(i) The custodial parent signs a written declaration that the custodial parent will not claim the child as a dependent for any taxable year beginning in that calendar year and the noncustodial parent attaches the declaration to the noncustodial parent's return for the taxable year; or

(ii) A qualified pre-1985 instrument, as defined in section 152(e)(3)(B), applicable to the taxable year beginning in that calendar year, provides that the noncustodial parent is entitled to the dependency exemption for the child and the noncustodial parent provides at least $600 for the support of the child during the calendar year.

(c) Custody.—A child is in the custody of one or both parents for more than one-half of the calendar year if one or both parents have the right under state law to physical custody of the child for more than one-half of the calendar year.

(d) Custodial parent—

(1) In general.—The *custodial parent* is the parent with whom the child resides for the greater number of nights during the calendar year, and the *noncustodial parent* is the parent who is not the custodial parent. A child is treated as residing with neither parent if the child is emancipated under state law. For purposes of this section, a child resides with a parent for a night if the child sleeps—

(i) At the residence of that parent (whether or not the parent is present); or

(ii) In the company of the parent, when the child does not sleep at a parent's residence (for example, the parent and child are on vacation together).

(2) Night straddling taxable years.—A night that extends over two taxable years is allocated to the taxable year in which the night begins.

(3) Absences—

(i) Except as provided in paragraph (d)(3)(ii) of this section, for purposes of this paragraph (d), a child who does not reside (within the meaning of paragraph (d)(1) of this section) with a parent for a night is treated as residing with the parent with whom the child would have resided for the night but for the absence.

(ii) A child who does not reside (within the meaning of paragraph (d)(1) of this section) with a parent for a night is treated as not residing with either parent for that night if it cannot be determined with which parent the child would have resided or if the child would not have resided with either parent for the night.

(4) Special rule for equal number of nights.—If a child is in the custody of one or both parents for more than one-half of the calendar year and the child resides with each parent for an equal number of nights during the calendar year, the parent with the higher adjusted gross income for the calendar year is treated as the custodial parent.

(5) Exception for a parent who works at night.—If, in a calendar year, due to a parent's nighttime work schedule, a child resides for a greater number of days but not nights with the parent who works at night, that parent is treated as the custodial parent. On a school day, the child is treated as residing at the primary residence registered with the school.

(e) Written declaration—

(1) Form of declaration—

(i) In general.—The written declaration under paragraph (b)(3)(i) of this section must be an unconditional release of the custodial parent's claim to the child as a dependent for the year or years for which the declaration is effective. A declaration is not unconditional if the custodial parent's release of the right to claim the child as a dependent requires the satisfaction of any condition, including the noncustodial parent's meeting of an obligation such as the payment of support. A written declaration must name the noncustodial parent to whom the exemption is released. A written declaration must specify the year or years for which it is effective. A written declaration that specifies all future years is treated as specifying the first taxable year after the taxable year of execution and all subsequent taxable years.

(ii) Form designated by IRS.—A written declaration may be made on Form 8332, Release/Revocation of Release of Claim to Exemption for Child by Custodial Parent, or successor form designated by the IRS. A written declaration not on the form designated by the IRS must conform to the substance of that form and must be a document executed for the sole purpose of serving as a written declaration under this section. A court order or decree or a separation agreement may not serve as a written declaration.

(2) Attachment to return.—A noncustodial parent must attach a copy of the written declaration to the parent's return for each taxable year in which the child is claimed as a dependent.

(3) Revocation of written declaration—

(i) In general.—A parent may revoke a written declaration described in paragraph (e)(1) of this section by providing written notice of the revocation to the other parent. The parent revoking the written declaration must make reasonable efforts to provide actual notice to the other parent. The revocation may be effective no earlier than the taxable year that begins in the first calendar year after the calendar year in which the parent revoking the written declaration provides, or makes reasonable efforts to provide, the written notice.

(ii) Form of revocation.—The revocation may be made on Form 8332, Release/Revocation of Release of Claim to Exemption for Child by Custodial Parent, or successor form designated by the IRS whether or not the written declaration was made on a form designated by the IRS. A revocation not on that form must conform to the substance of the form and must be a document executed for the sole purpose of serving as a revocation under this section. The revocation must specify the year or years for which the revocation is effective. A revocation that specifies all future years is treated as specifying the first taxable year after the taxable year the revocation is executed and all subsequent taxable years.

(iii) Attachment to return.—The parent revoking the written declaration must attach a copy of the revocation to the parent's return for each taxable year for which the parent claims a child as a dependent as a result of the revocation. The parent revoking the written declaration must keep a copy of the revocation and evidence of delivery of the notice to the other parent, or of the reasonable efforts to provide actual notice.

(4) Ineffective declaration or revocation.—A written declaration or revocation that fails to satisfy the requirements of this paragraph (e) has no effect.

(5) Written declaration executed in a taxable year beginning on or before July 2, 2008.—A written declaration executed in a taxable year beginning on or before July 2, 2008, that satisfies the requirements for the form of a written declaration in effect at the time the written declaration is executed, will be treated as meeting the requirements of paragraph (e)(1) of this section. Paragraph (e)(3) of this section applies without regard to whether a custodial parent executed the written declaration in a taxable year beginning on or before July 2, 2008.

(f) Coordination with other sections.—If section 152(e) and this section apply, a child is treated as the dependent of both parents for purposes of sections 105(b), 132(h)(2)(B), and 213(d)(5).

(g) Examples.—The provisions of this section are illustrated by the following examples that assume, unless otherwise provided, that each taxpayer's taxable year is the calendar year, one or both of the child's parents provide over one-half of the child's support for the calendar year, one or both parents have the right under state law to physical custody of the child for more than one-half of the calendar year, and the child otherwise meets the requirements of a qualifying child under section 152(c) or a qualifying relative under section 152(d). In addition, in each of the examples, no qualified pre-1985 instrument or multiple support agreement is in effect. The examples are as follows:

Example 1—

(i) B and C are the divorced parents of Child. In 2009, Child resides with B for 210 nights and with C for 155 nights. B executes a Form 8332 for 2009 releasing B's right to claim Child as a dependent for that year, which C attaches to C's 2009 return.

(ii) Under paragraph (d) of this section, B is the custodial parent of Child in 2009 because B is the parent with whom Child resides for the greater number of nights in 2009. Because the requirements of paragraphs (b)(2) and (3) of this section are met, C may claim Child as a dependent.

Example 2.—The facts are the same as in *Example 1* except that B does not execute a Form 8332 or similar declaration for 2009. Therefore, section 152(e) and this section do not apply. Whether Child is the qualifying child or qualifying relative of B or C is determined under section 152(c) or (d).

Example 3—

(i) D and E are the divorced parents of Child. Under a custody decree, Grandmother has the right under state law to physical custody of Child from January 1 to July 31, 2009.

(ii) Because D and E do not have the right under state law to physical custody of Child for over one-half of the 2009 calendar year, under paragraph (c) of this section, Child is not in the custody of one or both parents for over one-half of the calendar year. Therefore, section 152(e) and this section do not apply, and whether Child is the qualifying child or qualifying relative of D, E, or Grandmother is determined under section 152(c) or (d).

Example 4—

(i) The facts are the same as in *Example 3*, except that Grandmother has the right to physical custody of Child from January 1 to March 31, 2009, and, as a result, Child resides with Grandmother during this period. D and E jointly have the right to physical custody of Child from April 1 to December 31, 2009. During this period, Child resides with D for 180 nights and with E for 95 nights. D executes a Form 8332 for 2009 releasing D's right to claim Child as a dependent for that year, which E attaches to E's 2009 return.

(ii) Under paragraph (c) of this section, Child is in the custody of D and E for over one-half of the calendar year, because D and E have the right under state law to physical custody of Child for over one-half of the calendar year.

(iii) Under paragraph (d)(3)(ii) of this section, the nights that Child resides with Grandmother are not allocated to either parent. Child resides with D for a greater number of nights than with E during the calendar year and, under paragraph (d)(1) of this section, D is the custodial parent.

(iv) Because the requirements of paragraphs (b)(2) and (3) of this section are met, section 152(e) and this section apply, and E may claim Child as a dependent.

Example 5—

(i) The facts are the same as in *Example 4*, except that D is away on military service from April 10 to June 15, 2009, and September 6 to October 20, 2009. During these periods Child resides with Grandmother in Grandmother's residence. Child would have resided with D if D had not been away on military service. Grandmother claims Child as a dependent on Grandmother's 2009 return.

(ii) Under paragraph (d)(3)(i) of this section, Child is treated as residing with D for the nights that D is away on military service. Because the requirements of paragraphs (b)(2) and (3) of this section are met, section 152(e) and this section apply, and E, not Grandmother, may claim Child as a dependent.

Example 6.—F and G are the divorced parents of Child. In May of 2009, Child turns age 18 and is emancipated under the law of the state where Child resides. Therefore, in 2009 and later years, F and G do not have the right under state law to physical custody of Child for over one-half of the calendar year, and Child is not in the custody of F and G for over one-half of the calendar year. Section 152(e) and this section do not apply, and whether Child is the qualifying child or qualifying relative of F or G is determined under section 152(c) or (d).

Example 7—

(i) The facts are the same as in *Example 6*, except that Child turns age 18 and is emancipated under state law on August 1, 2009, resides with F from January 1, 2009, through May 31, 2009, and resides with G from June 1, 2009, through December 31, 2009. F executes a Form 8332 releasing F's right to claim Child as a dependent for 2009, which G attaches to G's 2009 return.

(ii) Under paragraph (c) of this section, Child is in the custody of F and G for over one-half of the calendar year.

(iii) Under paragraph (d)(1) of this section, Child is treated as not residing with either parent after Child's emancipation. Therefore, Child resides with F for 151 nights and with G for 61 nights. Because the requirements of paragraphs (b)(2) and (3) of this section are met, section 152(e) and this section apply, and G may claim Child as a dependent.

Example 8.—H and J are the divorced parents of Child. Child generally resides with H during the week and with J every other weekend. Child resides with J in H's residence for 10 consecutive nights while H is hospitalized. Under paragraph (d)(1)(i) of this section, Child resides with H for the 10 nights.

Example 9.—K and L, who are separated under a written separation agreement, are the parents of Child. In August 2009, K and Child spend 10 nights together in a hotel while on vacation. Under paragraph (d)(1)(ii) of this section, Child resides with K for the 10 nights that K and Child are on vacation.

Example 10.—M and N are the divorced parents of Child. On December 31, 2009, Child attends a party at M's residence. After midnight on January 1, 2010, Child travels to N's residence, where Child sleeps. Under paragraph (d)(1) of this section, Child resides with N for the night of December 31, 2009, to January 1, 2010, because Child sleeps at N's residence that night. However, under paragraph (d)(2) of this section, the night of December 31, 2009, to January 1, 2010, is allocated to taxable year 2009 for purposes of determining whether Child resides with M or N for a greater number of nights in 2009.

Example 11.—O and P, who never married, are the parents of Child. In 2009, Child spends alternate weeks residing with O and P. During a week that Child is residing with O, O gives Child permission to spend a night at the home of a friend. Under paragraph (d)(3)(i) of this section, the night Child spends at the friend's home is treated as a night that Child resides with O.

Example 12.—The facts are the same as in *Example 11*, except that Child also resides at summer camp for 6 weeks. Because Child resides with each parent for alternate weeks, Child would have resided with O for 3 weeks and with P for 3 weeks of the period that Child is at camp. Under paragraph (d)(3)(i) of this section, Child is treated as residing with O for 3 weeks and with P for 3 weeks.

Example 13.—The facts are the same as in *Example 12*, except that Child does not spend alternate weeks residing with O and P, and it cannot be determined whether Child would have resided with O or P for the period that Child is at camp. Under paragraph (d)(3)(ii) of this section, Child is treated as residing with neither parent for the 6 weeks.

Example 14—

(i) Q and R are the divorced parents of Child. Q works from 11 PM to 7 AM Sunday through Thursday nights. Because of Q's nighttime work schedule, Child resides with R Sunday through Thursday nights and with Q Friday and Saturday nights. Therefore, in 2009, Child resides with R for 261 nights and with Q for 104 nights. Child spends all daytime hours when Child is not in school with Q and Q's address is registered with Child's school as Child's primary residence. Q executes a Form 8332 for 2009 releasing Q's right to claim Child as a dependent for that year, which R attaches to R's 2009 return.

(ii) Under paragraph (d) of this section, Q is the custodial parent of Child in 2009. Child resides with R for a greater number of nights than with Q due to Q's nighttime work schedule, and Child spends a greater number of days with Q. Therefore, paragraph (d)(5) of this section applies rather than paragraph (d)(1) of this section. Because the requirements of paragraphs (b)(2) and (3) of this section are met, R may claim Child as a dependent.

Example 15—

(i) In 2009, S and T, the parents of Child, execute a written separation agreement. The agreement provides that Child will live with S and that T will make monthly child support payments to S. In 2009, Child resides with S for 335 nights and with T for 30 nights. S executes a letter declaring that S will not claim Child as a dependent in 2009 and in subsequent alternate years. The letter contains all the information requested on Form 8332, does not require the satisfaction of any condition such as T's payment of support, and has no purpose other than to serve as a written declaration under section 152(e) and this section. T attaches the letter to T's return for 2009 and 2011.

(ii) In 2010, T fails to provide support for Child, and S executes a Form 8332 revoking the release of S's right to claim Child as a dependent for 2011. S delivers a copy of the Form 8332 to T, attaches a copy of the Form 8332 to S's tax return for 2011, and keeps a copy of the Form 8332 and evidence of delivery of the written notice to T.

(iii) T may claim Child as a dependent for 2009 because S releases the right to claim Child as a dependent under paragraph (b)(3) of this section by executing the letter, which conforms to the requirements of paragraph (e)(1) of this section, and T attaches the letter to T's return in accordance with paragraph (e)(2) of this section. In 2010, S revokes the release of the claim in accordance with paragraph (e)(3) of this section, and the revocation takes effect in 2011, the taxable year that begins in the first calendar year after S provides written notice of the revocation to T. Therefore, in 2011, section 152(e) and this section do not apply, and whether Child is the qualifying child or qualifying relative of S or T is determined under section 152(c) or (d).

Example 16.—The facts are the same as *Example 15*, except that the letter expressly states that S releases the right to claim Child as a dependent only if T is current in the payment of support for Child at the end of the calendar year. The letter does not qualify as a written declaration under paragraph (b)(3) of this section because S's agreement not to claim Child as a dependent is conditioned on T's payment of support and, under paragraph (e)(1)(i) of this section, a writ-

ten declaration must be unconditional. Therefore, section 152(e) and this section do not apply, and whether Child is the qualifying child or qualifying relative of S or T for 2009 as well as 2011 is determined under section 152(c) or (d).

Example 17—

(i) U and V are the divorced parents of Child. Child resides with U for more nights than with V in 2009 through 2011. In 2009, U provides a written statement to V declaring that U will not claim Child as a dependent, but the statement does not specify the year or years it is effective. V attaches the statement to V's returns for 2009 through 2011.

(ii) Because the written statement does not specify a year or years, under paragraph (e)(1) of this section, it is not a written declaration that conforms to the substance of Form 8332. Under paragraph (e)(4) of this section, the statement has no effect. Section 152(e) and this section do not apply, and whether Child is the qualifying child or qualifying relative of U or V is determined under section 152(c) or (d).

Example 18—

(i) W and X are the divorced parents of Child. In 2009, Child resides solely with W. The divorce decree requires X to pay child support to W and requires W to execute a Form 8332 releasing W's right to claim Child as a dependent. W fails to sign a Form 8332 for 2009, and X attaches an unsigned Form 8332 to X's return for 2009.

(ii) The order in the divorce decree requiring W to execute a Form 8332 is ineffective to allocate the right to claim Child as a dependent to X. Furthermore, under paragraph (e)(1) of this section, the unsigned Form 8332 does not conform to the substance of Form 8332, and under paragraph (e)(4) of this section, the Form 8332 has no effect. Therefore, section 152(e) and this section do not apply, and whether Child is the qualifying child or qualifying relative of W or X is determined under section 152(c) or (d).

(iii) If, however, W executes a Form 8332 for 2009, and X attaches the Form 8332 to X's return, then X may claim Child as a dependent in 2009.

Example 19—

(i) Y and Z are the divorced parents of Child. In 2003, Y and Z enter into a separation agreement, which is incorporated into a divorce decree, under which Y, the custodial parent, releases Y's right to claim Child as a dependent for all future years. The separation agreement satisfies the requirements for the form of a written declaration in effect at the time it is executed. Z attaches a copy of the separation agreement to Z's returns for 2003 through 2009.

(ii) Under paragraph (e)(1)(ii) of this section, a separation agreement may not serve as a written declaration. However, under paragraph (e)(5) of this section, a written declaration executed in a taxable year beginning on or before July 2, 2008, that satisfies the requirements for the form of a written declaration in effect at the time the written declaration is executed, will be treated as meeting the requirements of paragraph (e)(1) of this section. Therefore, the separation agreement may serve as the written declaration required by paragraph (b)(3)(i) of this section for 2009, and Z may claim Child as a dependent in 2009 and later years.

Example 20—

(i) The facts are the same as in *Example 19*, except that in 2009 Y executes a Form 8332 revoking the release of Y's right to claim Child as a dependent for 2010. Y complies with all the requirements of paragraph (e)(3) of this section.

(ii) Although Y executes the separation agreement releasing Y's right to claim Child as a dependent in a taxable year beginning on or before July 2, 2008, under paragraph (e)(5) of this section, Y's execution of the Form 8332 in 2009 is effective to revoke the release. Therefore, section 152(e) and this section do not apply in 2010, and whether Child is the qualifying child or qualifying relative of Y or Z is determined under section 152(c) or (d).

(h) Effective/applicability date.—This section applies to taxable years beginning after July 2, 2008.

History of 26 C.F.R. §1.152-4: 36 FR 5337, Mar. 20, 1971; 36 FR 20039, Oct. 15, 1971; 44 FR 48674, Aug. 20, 1979; 73 FR 37801, July 2, 2008.

PART VII. ADDITIONAL ITEMIZED DEDUCTIONS FOR INDIVIDUALS

§215. ALIMONY, ETC., PAYMENTS

(a) General rule.—In the case of an individual, there shall be allowed as a deduction an amount equal to the alimony or separate maintenance payments paid during such individual's taxable year.

(b) Alimony or separate maintenance payments defined.—For purposes of this section, the term "alimony or separate maintenance payment" means any alimony or separate maintenance payment (as defined in section 71(b)) which is includible in the gross income of the recipient under section 71.

(c) Requirement of identification number.—The Secretary may prescribe regulations under which—

(1) any individual receiving alimony or separate maintenance payments is required to furnish such individual's taxpayer identification number to the individual making such payments, and

(2) the individual making such payments is required to include such taxpayer identification number on such individual's return for the taxable year in which such payments are made.

(d) Coordination with section 682.—No deduction shall be allowed under this section with respect to any payment if, by reason of section 682 (relating to income of alimony trusts), the amount thereof is not includible in such individual's gross income.

History of 26 U.S.C. §215: Aug. 16, 1954, ch. 736, 68A Stat. 71; July 18, 1984, P.L. 98-369, §422(b), 98 Stat. 797.

Regulations

C.F.R. §1.215-1 Periodic Alimony, Etc., Payments

(a) A deduction is allowable under section 215 with respect to periodic payments in the nature of, or in lieu of, alimony or an allowance for support actually paid by the taxpayer during his taxable year and required to be included in the income of the payee wife or former wife, as the case may be, under section 71. As to the amounts required to be included in the income of such wife or former wife, see section 71 and the regulations thereunder. For definition of husband and wife see section 7701(a)(17).

(b) The deduction under section 215 is allowed only to the obligor spouse. It is not allowed to an estate, trust, corporation, or any other person who may pay the alimony obligation of such obligor spouse. The obligor spouse, however, is not allowed a deduction for any periodic payment includible under section 71 in the income of the wife or former wife, which payment is attributable to property transferred in discharge of his obligation and which, under section 71(d) or section 682, is not includible in his gross income.

(c) The following examples, in which both H and W file their income tax returns on the basis of a calendar year, illustrate cases in which a deduction is or is not allowed under section 215:

Example (1).—Pursuant to the terms of a decree of divorce, H, in 1956, transferred securities valued at $100,000 in trust for the benefit of W, which fully discharged all his obligations to W. The periodic payments made by the trust to W are required to be included in W's income under section 71. Such payments are stated in section 71(d) not to be includible in H's income and, therefore, under section 215 are not deductible from his income.

Example (2).—A decree of divorce obtained by W from H incorporated a previous agreement of H to establish a trust, the trustees of which were instructed to pay W $5,000 a year for the remainder of her life. The court retained jurisdiction to order H to provide further payments if necessary for the support of W. In 1956 the trustee paid to W $4,000 from the income of the trust and $1,000 from the corpus of the trust. Under the provisions of sections 71 and 682(b), W

would include $5,000 in her income for 1956. H would not include any part of the $5,000 in his income nor take a deduction therefore. If H had paid the $1,000 to W pursuant to court order rather than allowing the trustees to pay it out of corpus, he would have been entitled to a deduction of $1,000 under the provisions of section 215.

(d) For other examples, see sections 71 and 682 and the regulations thereunder.

History of 26 C.F.R. §1.215-1: 25 FR 11402, Nov. 26, 1960.

C.F.R. §1.215-1T Alimony, Etc., Payments (temporary)

Q-1 What information is required by the Internal Revenue Service when an alimony or separate maintenance payment is claimed as a deduction by a payor?

A-1 The payor spouse must include on his/her first filed return of tax (Form 1040) for the taxable year in which the payment is made the payee's social security number, which the payee is required to furnish to the payor. For penalties applicable to a payor spouse who fails to include such information on his/her return of tax or to a payee spouse who fails to furnish his/her social security number to the payor spouse, see section 6676.

History of 26 C.F.R. §1.215-1T: 49 FR 34458, Aug. 31, 1984.

SUBCHAPTER O. GAIN OR LOSS ON DISPOSITION OF PROPERTY

PART III. COMMON NONTAXABLE EXCHANGES

§1041. TRANSFERS OF PROPERTY BETWEEN SPOUSES OR INCIDENT TO DIVORCE

(a) General rule.—No gain or loss shall be recognized on a transfer of property from an individual to (or in trust for the benefit of)—

(1) a spouse, or

(2) a former spouse, but only if the transfer is incident to the divorce.

(b) Transfer treated as gift; transferee has transferor's basis.—In the case of any transfer of property described in subsection (a)—

(1) for purposes of this subtitle, the property shall be treated as acquired by the transferee by gift, and

(2) the basis of the transferee in the property shall be the adjusted basis of the transferor.

(c) Incident to divorce.—For purposes of subsection (a)(2), a transfer of property is incident to the divorce if such transfer—

(1) occurs within 1 year after the date on which the marriage ceases, or

(2) is related to the cessation of the marriage.

(d) Special rule where spouse is nonresident alien.—Subsection (a) shall not apply if the spouse (or former spouse) of the individual making the transfer is a nonresident alien.

(e) Transfers in trust where liability exceeds basis.—Subsection (a) shall not apply to the transfer of property in trust to the extent that—

(1) the sum of the amount of the liabilities assumed, plus the amount of the liabilities to which the property is subject, exceeds

(2) the total of the adjusted basis of the property transferred.

Proper adjustment shall be made under subsection (b) in the basis of the transferee in such property to take into account gain recognized by reason of the preceding sentence.

History of 26 U.S.C. §1041: July 18, 1984, P.L. 98-369, §421(a), 98 Stat. 793; Oct. 22, 1986, P.L. 99-514, §1842(b), 100 Stat. 2853; Nov. 10, 1988, P.L. 100-647, §1018(1)(3), 102 Stat. 3584.

Regulation

C.F.R. §1.1041-1T Treatment of Transfer of Property Between Spouses or Incident to Divorce (temporary)

Q-1 How is the transfer of property between spouses treated under section 1041?

A-1 Generally, no gain or loss is recognized on a transfer of property from an individual to (or in trust for the benefit of) a spouse or, if the transfer is incident to a divorce, a former spouse. The following questions and answers describe more fully the scope, tax consequences and other rules which apply to transfers of property under section 1041.

(a) Scope of section 1041 in general.

Q-2 Does section 1041 apply only to transfers of property incident to divorce?

A-2 No. Section 1041 is not limited to transfers of property incident to divorce. Section 1041 applies to any transfer of property between spouses regardless of whether the transfer is a gift or is a sale or exchange between spouses acting at arm's length (including a transfer in exchange for the relinquishment of property or marital rights or an exchange otherwise governed by another nonrecognition provision of the Code). A divorce or legal separation need not be contemplated between the spouses at the time of the transfer nor must a divorce or legal separation ever occur.

Example (1).—A and B are married and file a joint return. A is the sole owner of a condominium unit. A sale or gift of the condominium from A to B is a transfer which is subject to the rules of section 1041.

Example (2).—A and B are married and file separate returns. A is the owner of an independent sole proprietorship, X Company. In the ordinary course of business, X Company makes a sale of property to B. This sale is a transfer of property between spouses and is subject to the rules of section 1041.

Example (3).—Assume the same facts as in example (2), except that X Company is a corporation wholly owned by A. This sale is not a sale between spouses subject to the rules of section 1041. However, in appropriate circumstances, general tax principles, including the step-transaction doctrine, may be applicable in recharacterizing the transaction.

Q-3 Do the rules of section 1041 apply to a transfer between spouses if the transferee spouse is a nonresident alien?

A-3 No. Gain or loss (if any) is recognized (assuming no other nonrecognition provision applies) at the time of a transfer of property if the property is transferred to a spouse who is a nonresident alien.

Q-4 What kinds of transfers are governed by section 1041?

A-4 Only transfers of property (whether real or personal, tangible or intangible) are governed by section 1041. Transfers of services are not subject to the rules of section 1041.

Q-5 Must the property transferred to a former spouse have been owned by the transferor spouse during the marriage?

A-5 No. A transfer of property acquired after the marriage ceases may be governed by section 1041.

(b) Transfer incident to the divorce.

Q-6 When is a transfer of property incident to the divorce?

A-6 A transfer of property is incident to the divorce in either of the following 2 circumstances—

(1) The transfer occurs not more than one year after the date on which the marriage ceases, or

(2) The transfer is related to the cessation of the marriage.

Thus, a transfer of property occurring not more than one year after the date on which the marriage ceases need not be related to the cessation of the marriage to qualify for section 1041 treatment. (See A-7 for transfers occurring more than one year after the cessation of the marriage.)

Q-7 When is a transfer of property related to the cessation of the marriage?

A-7 A transfer of property is treated as related to the cessation of the marriage if the transfer is pursuant to a divorce or separation instrument, as defined in section 71(b)(2), and the transfer occurs not more than 6 years after the date on which the marriage ceases. A divorce or separation instrument includes a modification or amendment to such decree or instrument. Any transfer not pursuant to a divorce or separation instrument and any transfer occurring more than 6 years after the cessation of the marriage is presumed to be not related to the cessation of the marriage. This presumption may be rebutted only by showing that the transfer was made to effect the division of property owned by the former spouses at the time of the cessation of the marriage. For example, the presumption may be rebutted by showing that (a) the transfer was not made within the one- and six-year periods described above because of factors which hampered an earlier transfer of the property, such as legal or business impediments to transfer or disputes concerning the value of the property owned at the time of the cessation of the marriage, and (b) the transfer is effected promptly after the impediment to transfer is removed.

Q-8 Do annulments and the cessations of marriages that are void ab initio due to violations of state law constitute divorces for purposes of section 1041?

A-8 Yes.

(c) Transfers on behalf of a spouse.

Q-9 May transfers of property to third parties on behalf of a spouse (or former spouse) qualify under section 1041?

A-9 Yes. There are three situations in which a transfer of property to a third party on behalf of a spouse (or former spouse) will qualify under section 1041, provided all other requirements of the section are satisfied. The first situation is where the transfer to the third party is required by a divorce or separation instrument. The second situation is where the transfer to the third party is pursuant to the written request of the other spouse (or former spouse). The third situation is where the transferor receives from the other spouse (or former spouse) a written consent or ratification of the transfer to the third party. Such consent or ratification must state that the parties intend the transfer to be treated as a transfer to the nontransferring spouse (or former spouse) subject to the rules of section 1041 and must be received by the transferor prior to the date of filing of the transferor's first return of tax for the taxable year in which the transfer was made. In the three situations described above, the transfer of property will be treated as made directly to the nontransferring spouse (or former spouse) and the nontransferring spouse will be treated as immediately transferring the property to the third party. The deemed transfer from the nontransferring spouse (or former spouse) to the third party is not a transaction that qualifies for nonrecognition of gain under section 1041. This A-9 shall not apply to transfers to which §1.1041-2 applies.

(d) Tax consequences of transfers subject to section 1041.

Q-10 How is the transferor of property under section 1041 treated for income tax purposes?

A-10 The transferor of property under section 1041 recognizes no gain or loss on the transfer even if the transfer was in exchange for the release of marital rights or other consideration. This rule applies regardless of whether the transfer is of property separately owned by the transferor or is a division (equal or unequal) of community property. Thus, the result under section 1041 differs from the result in *United States v. Davis*, 370 U.S. 65 (1962).

Q-11 How is the transferee of property under section 1041 treated for income tax purposes?

A-11 The transferee of property under section 1041 recognizes no gain or loss upon receipt of the transferred property. In all cases, the basis of the transferred property in the hands of the transferee is the adjusted basis of such property in the hands of the transferor immediately before the transfer. Even if the transfer is a bona fide sale, the transferee does not acquire a basis in the transferred property equal to the transferee's cost (the fair market value). This carryover basis rule applies whether the adjusted basis of the transferred property is less than, equal to, or greater than its fair market value at the time of transfer (or the value of any consideration provided by the transferee) and applies for purposes of determining loss as well as gain upon the subsequent disposition of the property by the transferee. Thus, this rule is different from the rule applied in section 1015(a) for determining the basis of property acquired by gift.

Q-12 Do the rules described in A-10 and A-11 apply even if the transferred property is subject to liabilities which exceed the adjusted basis of the property?

A-12 Yes. For example, assume A owns property having a fair market value of $10,000 and an adjusted basis of $1,000. In contemplation of making a transfer of this property incident to a divorce from B, A borrows $5,000 from a bank, using the property as security for the borrowing. A then transfers the property to B and B assumes, or takes the property subject to, the liability to pay the $5,000 debt. Under section 1041, A recognizes no gain or loss upon the transfer of the property, and the adjusted basis of the property in the hands of B is $1,000.

Q-13 Will a transfer under section 1041 result in a recapture of investment tax credits with respect to the property transferred?

A-13 In general, no. Property transferred under section 1041 will not be treated as being disposed of by, or ceasing to be section 38 property with respect to, the transferor. However, the transferee will be subject to investment tax credit recapture if, upon or after the transfer, the property is disposed of by, or ceases to be section 38 property with respect to, the transferee. For example, as part of a divorce property settlement, B receives a car from A that has been used in A's business for two years and for which an investment tax credit was taken by A. No part of A's business is transferred to B and B's use of the car is solely personal. B is subject to recapture of the investment tax credit previously taken by A.

(e) Notice and recordkeeping requirement with respect to transactions under section 1041.

Q-14 Does the transferor of property in a transaction described in section 1041 have to supply, at the time of the transfer, the transferee with records sufficient to determine the adjusted basis and holding period of the property at the time of the transfer and (if applicable) with notice that the property transferred under section 1041 is potentially subject to recapture of the investment tax credit?

A-14 Yes. A transferor of property under section 1041 must, at the time of the transfer, supply the transferee with records sufficient to determine the adjusted basis and holding period of the property as of the date of the transfer. In addition, in the case of a transfer of property which carries with it a potential liability for investment tax credit recapture, the transferor must, at the time of the transfer, supply the transferee with records sufficient to determine the amount and period of such potential liability. Such records must be preserved and kept accessible by the transferee.

(f) Property settlements—effective dates, transitional periods and elections.

Q-15 When does section 1041 become effective?

A-15 Generally, section 1041 applies to all transfers after July 18, 1984. However, it does not apply to transfers after July 18, 1984 pursuant to instruments in effect on or before July 18, 1984. (See A-16 with respect to exceptions to the general rule.)

Q-16 Are there any exceptions to the general rule stated in A-15 above?

A-16 Yes. Two transitional rules provide exceptions to the general rule stated in A-15. First, section 1041 will apply to transfers after July 18, 1984 under instruments that were in effect on or before July 18, 1984 if both spouses (or former spouses) elect to have section 1041 apply to such transfers. Second, section 1041 will apply to all transfers after December 31, 1983 (including transfers under instruments in effect on or before July 18, 1984) if both spouses (or former spouses) elect to have section 1041 apply. (See A-18 relating to the time and manner of making the elections under the first or second transitional rule.)

Q-17 Can an election be made to have section 1041 apply to some, but not all, transfers made after December 31, 1983, or some but not all, transfers made after July 18, 1984 under instruments in effect on or before July 18, 1984?

A-17 No. Partial elections are not allowed. An election under either of the two elective transitional rules applies to all transfers governed by that election whether before or after the election is made, and is irrevocable.

(g) Property settlements—time and manner of making the elections under section 1041.

Q-18 How do spouses (or former spouses) elect to have section 1041 apply to transfers after December 31, 1983, or to transfers after July 18, 1984 under instruments in effect on or before July 18, 1984?

A-18 In order to make an election under section 1041 for property transfers after December 31, 1983, or property transfers under instruments that were in effect on or before July 18, 1984, both spouses (or former spouses) must elect the application of the rules of section 1041 by attaching to the transferor's first

filed income tax return for the taxable year in which the first transfer occurs, a statement signed by both spouses (or former spouses) which includes each spouse's social security number and is in substantially the form set forth at the end of this answer.

In addition, the transferor must attach a copy of such statement to his or her return for each subsequent taxable year in which a transfer is made that is governed by the transitional election. A copy of the signed statement must be kept by both parties.

The election statements shall be in substantially the following form:

In the case of an election regarding transfers after 1983:

Section 1041 Election

The undersigned hereby elect to have the provisions of section 1041 of the Internal Revenue Code apply to all qualifying transfers of property after December 31, 1983. The undersigned understand that section 1041 applies to all property transferred between spouses, or former spouses incident to divorce. The parties further understand that the effects for Federal income tax purposes of having section 1041 apply are that (1) no gain or loss is recognized by the transferor spouse or former spouse as a result of this transfer; and (2) the basis of the transferred property in the hands of the transferee is the adjusted basis of the property in the hands of the transferor immediately before the transfer, whether or not the adjusted basis of the transferred property is less than, equal to, or greater than its fair market value at the time of the transfer. The undersigned understand that if the transferee spouse or former spouse disposes of the property in a transaction in which gain is recognized, the amount of gain which is taxable may be larger than it would have been if this election had not been made.

In the case of an election regarding preexisting decrees:

Section 1041 Election

The undersigned hereby elect to have the provisions of section 1041 of the Internal Revenue Code apply to all qualifying transfers of property after July 18, 1984 under any instrument in effect on or before July 18, 1984. The undersigned understand that section 1041 applies to all property transferred between spouses, or former spouses incident to the divorce. The parties further understand that the effects for Federal income tax purposes of having section 1041 apply are that (1) no gain or loss is recognized by the transferor spouse or former spouse as a result of this transfer; and (2) the basis of the transferred property in the hands of the transferee is the adjusted basis of the property in the hands of the transferor immediately before the transfer, whether or not the adjusted basis of the transferred property is less than, equal to, or greater than its fair market value at the time of the transfer. The undersigned understand that if the transferee spouse or former spouse disposes of the property in a transaction in which gain is recognized, the amount of gain which is taxable may be larger than it would have been if this election had not been made.

History of 26 C.F.R. §1.1041-1T: 49 FR 34452, Aug. 31, 1984; 68 FR 1536, Jan. 13, 2003.

SUBTITLE F. PROCEDURE & ADMINISTRATION

CHAPTER 61. INFORMATION & RETURNS

SUBCHAPTER A. RETURNS & RECORDS

PART II. TAX RETURNS OR STATEMENTS

SUBPART B. INCOME TAX RETURNS

§6015. RELIEF FROM JOINT & SEVERAL LIABILITY ON JOINT RETURN

(a) In general.—Notwithstanding section 6013(d)(3)—

(1) an individual who has made a joint return may elect to seek relief under the procedures prescribed under subsection (b); and

(2) if such individual is eligible to elect the application of subsection (c), such individual may, in addition to any election under paragraph (1), elect to limit such individual's liability for any deficiency with respect to such joint return in the manner prescribed under subsection (c).

Any determination under this section shall be made without regard to community property laws.

(b) Procedures for relief from liability applicable to all joint filers—

(1) In general.—Under procedures prescribed by the Secretary, if—

(A) a joint return has been made for a taxable year;

(B) on such return there is an understatement of tax attributable to erroneous items of one individual filing the joint return;

(C) the other individual filing the joint return establishes that in signing the return he or she did not know, and had no reason to know, that there was such understatement;

(D) taking into account all the facts and circumstances, it is inequitable to hold the other individual liable for the deficiency in tax for such taxable year attributable to such understatement; and

(E) the other individual elects (in such form as the Secretary may prescribe) the benefits of this subsection not later than the date which is 2 years after the date the Secretary has begun collection activities with respect to the individual making the election,

then the other individual shall be relieved of liability for tax (including interest, penalties, and other amounts) for such taxable year to the extent such liability is attributable to such understatement.

(2) Apportionment of relief.—If an individual who, but for paragraph (1)(C), would be relieved of liability under paragraph (1), establishes that in signing the return such individual did not know, and had no reason to know, the extent of such understatement, then such individual shall be relieved of liability for tax (including interest, penalties, and other amounts) for such taxable year to the extent that such liability is attributable to the portion of such understatement of which such individual did not know and had no reason to know.

(3) Understatement.—For purposes of this subsection, the term "understatement" has the meaning given to such term by section 6662(d)(2)(A).

(c) Procedures to limit liability for taxpayers no longer married or taxpayers legally separated or not living together—

(1) In general.—Except as provided in this subsection, if an individual who has made a joint return for any taxable year elects the application of this subsection, the individual's liability for any deficiency which is assessed with respect to the return shall not exceed the portion of such deficiency properly allocable to the individual under subsection (d).

(2) Burden of proof.—Except as provided in subparagraph (A)(ii) or (C) of paragraph (3), each individual who elects the application of this subsection shall have the burden of proof with respect to establishing the portion of any deficiency allocable to such individual.

(3) Election—

(A) Individuals eligible to make election—

(i) In general.—An individual shall only be eligible to elect the application of this subsection if—

(I) at the time such election is filed, such individual is no longer married to, or is legally separated from, the individual with whom such individual filed the joint return to which the election relates; or

(II) such individual was not a member of the same household as the individual with whom such joint return was filed at any time during the 12-month period ending on the date such election is filed.

(ii) Certain taxpayers ineligible to elect.—If the Secretary demonstrates that assets were transferred between individuals filing a joint return as part of a fraudulent scheme by such individuals, an election under this subsection by either individual shall be invalid (and section 6013(d)(3) shall apply to the joint return).

(B) Time for election.—An election under this subsection for any taxable year may be made at any time after a deficiency for such year is asserted but not later than 2 years after the date on which the Secretary has begun collection activities with respect to the individual making the election.

(C) Election not valid with respect to certain deficiencies.—If the Secretary demonstrates that an individual making an election under this subsection had actual knowledge, at the time such individual signed the return, of any item giving rise to a deficiency (or portion thereof) which is not allocable to such individual under subsection (d), such election shall not apply to such deficiency (or portion). This subparagraph shall not apply where the individual with actual knowledge establishes that such individual signed the return under duress.

(4) Liability increased by reason of transfers of property to avoid tax—

(A) In general.—Notwithstanding any other provision of this subsection, the portion of the deficiency for which the individual electing the application of this subsection is liable (without regard to this paragraph) shall be increased by the value of any disqualified asset transferred to the individual.

(B) Disqualified asset.—For purposes of this paragraph—

(i) In general.—The term "disqualified asset" means any property or right to property transferred to an individual making the election under this subsection with respect to a joint return by the other individual filing such joint return if the principal purpose of the transfer was the avoidance of tax or payment of tax.

(ii) Presumption—

(I) In general.—For purposes of clause (i), except as provided in subclause (II), any transfer which is made after the date which is 1 year before the date on which the first letter of proposed deficiency which allows the taxpayer an opportunity for administrative review in the Internal Revenue Service Office of Appeals is sent shall be presumed to have as its principal purpose the avoidance of tax or payment of tax.

(II) Exceptions.—Subclause (I) shall not apply to any transfer pursuant to a decree of divorce or separate maintenance or a written instrument incident to such a decree or to any transfer which an individual establishes did not have as its principal purpose the avoidance of tax or payment of tax.

(d) Allocation of deficiency.—For purposes of subsection (c)—

(1) In general.—The portion of any deficiency on a joint return allocated to an individual shall be the amount which bears the same ratio to such deficiency as the net amount of items taken into account in computing the deficiency and allocable to the individual under paragraph (3) bears to the net amount of all items taken into account in computing the deficiency.

(2) Separate treatment of certain items.—If a deficiency (or portion thereof) is attributable to—

(A) the disallowance of a credit; or

(B) any tax (other than tax imposed by section 1 or 55) required to be included with the joint return;

and such item is allocated to one individual under paragraph (3), such deficiency (or portion) shall be allocated to such individual. Any such item shall not be taken into account under paragraph (1).

(3) Allocation of items giving rise to the deficiency.—For purposes of this subsection—

(A) In general.—Except as provided in paragraphs (4) and (5), any item giving rise to a deficiency on a joint return shall be allocated to individuals filing the return in the same manner as it would have been allocated if the individuals had filed separate returns for the taxable year.

(B) Exception where other spouse benefits.—Under rules prescribed by the Secretary, an item otherwise allocable to an individual under subparagraph (A) shall be allocated to the other individual filing the joint return to the extent the item gave rise to a tax benefit on the joint return to the other individual.

(C) Exception for fraud.—The Secretary may provide for an allocation of any item in a manner not prescribed by subparagraph (A) if the Secretary establishes that such allocation is appropriate due to fraud of one or both individuals.

(4) Limitations on separate returns disregarded.—If an item of deduction or credit is disallowed in its entirety solely because a separate return is filed, such disallowance shall be disregarded and the item shall be computed as if a joint return had been filed and then allocated between the spouses appropriately. A similar rule shall apply for purposes of section 86.

(5) Child's liability.—If the liability of a child of a taxpayer is included on a joint return, such liability shall be disregarded in computing the separate liability of either spouse and such liability shall be allocated appropriately between the spouses.

(e) Petition for review by Tax Court—

(1) In general.—In the case of an individual against whom a deficiency has been asserted and who elects to have subsection (b) or (c) apply, or in the case of an individual who requests equitable relief under subsection (f)—

(A) In general.—In addition to any other remedy provided by law, the individual may petition the Tax Court (and the Tax Court shall have jurisdiction) to determine the appropriate relief available to the individual under this section if such petition is filed—

(i) at any time after the earlier of—

(I) the date the Secretary mails, by certified or registered mail to the taxpayer's last known address, notice of the Secretary's final determination of relief available to the individual, or

(II) the date which is 6 months after the date such election is filed or request is made with the Secretary, and

(ii) not later than the close of the 90th day after the date described in clause (i)(I).

(B) Restrictions applicable to collection of assessment—

(i) In general.—Except as otherwise provided in section 6851 or 6861, no levy or proceeding in court shall be made, begun, or prosecuted against the individual making an election under subsection (b) or (c) or requesting equitable relief under subsection (f) for collection of any assessment to which such election or request relates until the close of the 90th day referred to in subparagraph (A)(ii), or, if a petition has been filed with the Tax Court under subparagraph (A), until the decision of the Tax Court has become final. Rules similar to the rules of section 7485 shall apply with respect to the collection of such assessment.

(ii) Authority to enjoin collection actions.—Notwithstanding the provisions of section 7421(a), the beginning of such levy or proceeding during the time the prohibition under clause (i) is in force may be enjoined by a proceeding in the proper court, including the Tax Court. The Tax Court shall have no jurisdiction under this subparagraph to enjoin any action or proceeding unless a timely petition has been filed under subparagraph (A) and then only in respect of the amount of the assessment to which the election under subsection (b) or (c) relates or to which the request under subsection (f) relates.

(2) Suspension of running of period of limitations.—The running of the period of limitations in section 6502 on the collection of the assessment to which the petition under paragraph (1)(A) relates shall be suspended—

(A) for the period during which the Secretary is prohibited by paragraph (1)(B) from collecting by levy or a proceeding in court and for 60 days thereafter, and

(B) if a waiver under paragraph (5) is made, from the date the claim for relief was filed until 60 days after the waiver is filed with the Secretary.

(3) Limitation on Tax Court jurisdiction.—If a suit for refund is begun by either individual filing the joint return pursuant to section 6532—

(A) the Tax Court shall lose jurisdiction of the individual's action under this section to whatever extent jurisdiction is acquired by the district court or the United States Court of Federal Claims over the taxable years that are the subject of the suit for refund; and

(B) the court acquiring jurisdiction shall have jurisdiction over the petition filed under this subsection.

(4) Notice to other spouse.—The Tax Court shall establish rules which provide the individual filing a joint return but not making the election under subsection (b) or (c) or the request for equitable relief under subsection (f) with adequate notice and an opportunity to become a party to a proceeding under either such subsection.

(5) Waiver.—An individual who elects the application of subsection (b) or (c) or who requests equitable relief under subsection (f) (and who agrees with the Secretary's determination of relief) may waive in writing at any time the restrictions in paragraph (1)(B) with respect to collection of the outstanding assessment (whether or not a notice of the Secretary's final determination of relief has been mailed).

(6) Suspension of running of period for filing petition in title 11 cases.—In the case of a person who is prohibited by reason of a case under title 11, United States Code, from filing a petition under paragraph (1)(A) with respect to a final determination of relief under this section, the running of the period prescribed by such paragraph for filing such a petition with respect to such final determination shall be suspended for the period during which the person is so prohibited from filing such a petition, and for 60 days thereafter.

(f) Equitable relief.—Under procedures prescribed by the Secretary, if—

(1) taking into account all the facts and circumstances, it is inequitable to hold the individual liable for any unpaid tax or any deficiency (or any portion of either); and

(2) relief is not available to such individual under subsection (b) or (c), the Secretary may relieve such individual of such liability.

(g) Credits and refunds—

(1) In general.—Except as provided in paragraphs (2) and (3), notwithstanding any other law or rule of law (other than section 6511, 6512(b), 7121, or 7122), credit or refund shall be allowed or made to the extent attributable to the application of this section.

(2) Res judicata.—In the case of any election under subsection (b) or (c) or of any request for equitable relief under subsection (f), if a decision of a court in any prior proceeding for the same taxable year has become final, such decision shall be conclusive except with respect to the qualification of the individual for relief which was not an issue in such proceeding. The exception contained in the preceding sentence shall not apply if the court determines that the individual participated meaningfully in such prior proceeding.

(3) Credit and refund not allowed under subsection (c).—No credit or refund shall be allowed as a result of an election under subsection (c).

(h) Regulations.—The Secretary shall prescribe such regulations as are necessary to carry out the provisions of this section, including—

(1) regulations providing methods for allocation of items other than the methods under subsection (d)(3); and

(2) regulations providing the opportunity for an individual to have notice of, and an opportunity to participate in, any administrative proceeding with respect to an election made under subsection (b) or (c) or a request for equitable relief made under subsection (f) by the other individual filing the joint return.

History of 26 U.S.C. §6015: July 22, 1998, P.L. 105-206, §3201(a), 112 Stat. 734; Oct. 21, 1998, P.L. 105-277, §4002(c)(2), 112 Stat. 2681-906; Dec. 21, 2000, P.L. 106-554, §1(a)(7) [App. G, §313(a)], 114 Stat. 2763, 2763A-640; Dec. 20, 2006, P.L. 109-432, §408(a), (b), 120 Stat. 3061; Dec. 18, 2015, P.L. 114-113, §424(a)(1), 129 Stat. 3124.

TITLE 28. JUDICIARY & JUDICIAL PROCEDURE

PART V. PROCEDURE

CHAPTER 115. EVIDENCE; DOCUMENTARY

§1738. STATE & TERRITORIAL STATUTES & JUDICIAL PROCEEDINGS; FULL FAITH & CREDIT

The Acts of the legislature of any State, Territory, or Possession of the United States, or copies thereof, shall be authenticated by affixing the seal of such State, Territory or Possession thereto.

The records and judicial proceedings of any court of any such State, Territory or Possession, or copies thereof, shall be proved or admitted in other courts within the United States and its Territories and Possessions by the attestation of the clerk and seal of the court annexed, if a seal exists, together with a certificate of a judge of the court that the said attestation is in proper form.

Such Acts, records and judicial proceedings or copies thereof, so authenticated, shall have the same full faith and credit in every court within the United States and its Territories and Possessions as they have by law or usage in the courts of such State, Territory or Possession from which they are taken.

History of 28 U.S.C. §1738: June 25, 1948, ch. 646, 62 Stat. 947.

§1738A. FULL FAITH & CREDIT GIVEN TO CHILD CUSTODY DETERMINATIONS

(a) The appropriate authorities of every State shall enforce according to its terms, and shall not modify except as provided in subsections (f), (g), and (h) of this section, any custody determination or visitation determination made consistently with the provisions of this section by a court of another State.

(b) As used in this section, the term—

(1) "child" means a person under the age of eighteen;

(2) "contestant" means a person, including a parent or grandparent, who claims a right to custody or visitation of a child;

(3) "custody determination" means a judgment, decree, or other order of a court providing for the custody of a child, and includes permanent and temporary orders, and initial orders and modifications;

(4) "home State" means the State in which, immediately preceding the time involved, the child lived with his parents, a parent, or a person acting as parent, for at least six consecutive months, and in the case of a child less than six months old, the State in which the child lived from birth with any of such persons. Periods of temporary absence of any of such persons are counted as part of the six-month or other period;

(5) "modification" and "modify" refer to a custody or visitation determination which modifies, replaces, supersedes, or otherwise is made subsequent to, a prior custody or visitation determination concerning the same child, whether made by the same court or not;

(6) "person acting as a parent" means a person, other than a parent, who has physical custody of a child and who has either been awarded custody by a court or claims a right to custody;

(7) "physical custody" means actual possession and control of a child;

(8) "State" means a State of the United States, the District of Columbia, the Commonwealth of Puerto Rico, or a territory or possession of the United States; and

(9) "visitation determination" means a judgment, decree, or other order of a court providing for the visitation of a child and includes permanent and temporary orders and initial orders and modifications.

(c) A child custody or visitation determination made by a court of a State is consistent with the provisions of this section only if—

(1) such court has jurisdiction under the law of such State; and

(2) one of the following conditions is met:

(A) such State (i) is the home State of the child on the date of the commencement of the proceeding, or (ii) had been the child's home State within six months before the date of the commencement of the proceeding and the child is absent from such State because of his removal or retention by a contestant or for other reasons, and a contestant continues to live in such State;

(B)(i) it appears that no other State would have jurisdiction under subparagraph (A), and (ii) it is in the best interest of the child that a court of such State assume jurisdiction because (I) the child and his parents, or the child and at least one contestant, have a significant connection with such State other than mere physical presence in such State, and (II) there is available in such State substantial evidence concerning the child's present or future care, protection, training, and personal relationships;

(C) the child is physically present in such State and (i) the child has been abandoned, or (ii) it is necessary in an emergency to protect the child because the child, a sibling, or parent of the child has been subjected to or threatened with mistreatment or abuse;

(D)(i) it appears that no other State would have jurisdiction under subparagraph (A), (B), (C), or (E), or another State has declined to exercise jurisdiction on the ground that the State whose jurisdiction is in issue is the more appropriate forum to determine the custody

or visitation of the child, and (ii) it is in the best interest of the child that such court assume jurisdiction; or

(E) the court has continuing jurisdiction pursuant to subsection (d) of this section.

(d) The jurisdiction of a court of a State which has made a child custody or visitation determination consistently with the provisions of this section continues as long as the requirement of subsection (c)(1) of this section continues to be met and such State remains the residence of the child or of any contestant.

(e) Before a child custody or visitation determination is made, reasonable notice and opportunity to be heard shall be given to the contestants, any parent whose parental rights have not been previously terminated and any person who has physical custody of a child.

(f) A court of a State may modify a determination of the custody of the same child made by a court of another State, if—

(1) it has jurisdiction to make such a child custody determination; and

(2) the court of the other State no longer has jurisdiction, or it has declined to exercise such jurisdiction to modify such determination.

(g) A court of a State shall not exercise jurisdiction in any proceeding for a custody or visitation determination commenced during the pendency of a proceeding in a court of another State where such court of that other State is exercising jurisdiction consistently with the provisions of this section to make a custody or visitation determination.

(h) A court of a State may not modify a visitation determination made by a court of another State unless the court of the other State no longer has jurisdiction to modify such determination or has declined to exercise jurisdiction to modify such determination.

History of 28 U.S.C. §1738A: Dec. 28, 1980, P.L. 96-611, §8(a), 94 Stat. 3569; Nov. 12, 1998, P.L. 105-374, §1, 112 Stat. 3383; Oct. 28, 2000, P.L. 106-386, §1303(d), 114 Stat. 1512.

§1738B. FULL FAITH & CREDIT FOR CHILD SUPPORT ORDERS

(a) General rule.—The appropriate authorities of each State—

(1) shall enforce according to its terms a child support order made consistently with this section by a court of another State; and

(2) shall not seek or make a modification of such an order except in accordance with subsections (e), (f), and (i).

(b) Definitions.—In this section:

(1) The term "child" means—

(A) a person under 18 years of age; and

(B) a person 18 or more years of age with respect to whom a child support order has been issued pursuant to the laws of a State.

(2) The term "child's State" means the State in which a child resides.

(3) The term "child's home State" means the State in which a child lived with a parent or a person acting as parent for at least 6 consecutive months immediately preceding the time of filing of a petition or comparable pleading for support and, if a child is less than 6 months old, the State in which the child lived from birth with any of them. A period of temporary absence of any of them is counted as part of the 6-month period.

(4) The term "child support" means a payment of money, continuing support, or arrearages or the provision of a benefit (including payment of health insurance, child care, and educational expenses) for the support of a child.

(5) The term "child support order"—

(A) means a judgment, decree, or order of a court requiring the payment of child support in periodic amounts or in a lump sum; and

(B) includes—

(i) a permanent or temporary order; and

(ii) an initial order or a modification of an order.

(6) The term "contestant" means—

(A) a person (including a parent) who—

(i) claims a right to receive child support;

(ii) is a party to a proceeding that may result in the issuance of a child support order; or

(iii) is under a child support order; and

(B) a State or political subdivision of a State to which the right to obtain child support has been assigned.

(7) The term "court" means a court or administrative agency of a State that is authorized by State law to establish the amount of child support payable by a contestant or make a modification of a child support order.

(8) The term "modification" means a change in a child support order that affects the amount, scope, or duration of the order and modifies, replaces, supersedes, or otherwise is made subsequent to the child support order.

(9) The term "State" means a State of the United States, the District of Columbia, the Commonwealth of

Puerto Rico, the territories and possessions of the United States, and Indian country (as defined in section 1151 of title 18).

(c) Requirements of child support orders.—A child support order made by a court of a State is made consistently with this section if—

(1) a court that makes the order, pursuant to the laws of the State in which the court is located and subsections (e), (f), and (g)—

(A) has subject matter jurisdiction to hear the matter and enter such an order; and

(B) has personal jurisdiction over the contestants; and

(2) reasonable notice and opportunity to be heard is given to the contestants.

(d) Continuing jurisdiction.—A court of a State that has made a child support order consistently with this section has continuing, exclusive jurisdiction over the order if the State is the child's State or the residence of any individual contestant or the parties have consented in a record or open court that the tribunal of the State may continue to exercise jurisdiction to modify its order unless the court of another State, acting in accordance with subsections (e) and (f), has made a modification of the order.

(e) Authority to modify orders.—A court of a State may modify a child support order issued by a court of another State if—

(1) the court has jurisdiction to make such a child support order pursuant to subsection (i); and

(2)(A) the court of the other State no longer has continuing, exclusive jurisdiction of the child support order because that State no longer is the child's State or the residence of any individual contestant and the parties have not consented in a record or open court that the tribunal of the other State may continue to exercise jurisdiction to modify its order; or

(B) each individual contestant has filed written consent with the State of continuing, exclusive jurisdiction for a court of another State to modify the order and assume continuing, exclusive jurisdiction over the order.

(f) Recognition of child support orders.—If 1 or more child support orders have been issued with regard to an obligor and a child, a court shall apply the following rules in determining which order to recognize for purposes of continuing, exclusive jurisdiction and enforcement:

(1) If only 1 court has issued a child support order, the order of that court must be recognized.

(2) If 2 or more courts have issued child support orders for the same obligor and child, and only 1 of the courts would have continuing, exclusive jurisdiction under this section, the order of that court must be recognized.

(3) If 2 or more courts have issued child support orders for the same obligor and child, and more than 1 of the courts would have continuing, exclusive jurisdiction under this section, an order issued by a court in the current home State of the child must be recognized, but if an order has not been issued in the current home State of the child, the order most recently issued must be recognized.

(4) If 2 or more courts have issued child support orders for the same obligor and child, and none of the courts would have continuing, exclusive jurisdiction under this section, a court having jurisdiction over the parties shall issue a child support order, which must be recognized.

(5) The court that has issued an order recognized under this subsection is the court having continuing, exclusive jurisdiction under subsection (d).

(g) Enforcement of modified orders.—A court of a State that no longer has continuing, exclusive jurisdiction of a child support order may enforce the order with respect to nonmodifiable obligations and unsatisfied obligations that accrued before the date on which a modification of the order is made under subsections (e) and (f).

(h) Choice of law—

(1) In general.—In a proceeding to establish, modify, or enforce a child support order, the forum State's law shall apply except as provided in paragraphs (2) and (3).

(2) Law of state of issuance of order.—In interpreting a child support order including the duration of current payments and other obligations of support, a court shall apply the law of the State of the court that issued the order.

(3) Period of limitation.—In an action to enforce arrears under a child support order, a court shall apply the statute of limitation of the forum State or the State of the court that issued the order, whichever statute provides the longer period of limitation.

(i) Registration for modification.—If there is no individual contestant or child residing in the issuing

State, the party or support enforcement agency seeking to modify, or to modify and enforce, a child support order issued in another State shall register that order in a State with jurisdiction over the nonmovant for the purpose of modification.

History of 28 U.S.C. §1738B: Oct. 20, 1994, P.L. 103-383, §3(a), 108 Stat. 4064; Aug. 22, 1996, P.L. 104-193, §322, 110 Stat. 2221; Aug. 5, 1997, P.L. 105-33, §5554, 111 Stat. 636; Sept. 29, 2014, P.L. 113-183, §301(f)(2), 128 Stat. 1944.

§1738C. CERTAIN ACTS, RECORDS, & PROCEEDINGS & THE EFFECT THEREOF

☠ *In* ***Obergefell v. Hodges***, *___ U.S. ___, 135 S.Ct. 2584 (2015), the U.S. Supreme Court held that same-sex couples may exercise the fundamental right to marry in all states, and that there is no lawful basis for a state to refuse to recognize a lawful same-sex marriage performed in another state on the ground of its same-sex character. See annotation under Family Code §6.204, p. 65.*

No State, territory, or possession of the United States, or Indian tribe, shall be required to give effect to any public act, record, or judicial proceeding of any other State, territory, possession, or tribe respecting a relationship between persons of the same sex that is treated as a marriage under the laws of such other State, territory, possession, or tribe, or a right or claim arising from such relationship.

History of 28 U.S.C. §1738C: Sept. 21, 1996, P.L. 104-199, §2(a), 110 Stat. 2419.

TITLE 29. LABOR

CHAPTER 18. EMPLOYEE RETIREMENT INCOME SECURITY PROGRAM

For the complete text of ERISA with annotations, see the current edition of ***O'Connor's Federal Employment Codes Plus****. To order, call 1-800-OCONNOR (1-800-626-6667) or visit www.oconnors.com.*

TITLE 42. THE PUBLIC HEALTH & WELFARE

CHAPTER 21. CIVIL RIGHTS

SUBCHAPTER I. GENERALLY

§1996b. INTERETHNIC ADOPTION

(1) Prohibited conduct.—A person or government that is involved in adoption or foster care placements may not—

(A) deny to any individual the opportunity to become an adoptive or a foster parent, on the basis of the race, color, or national origin of the individual, or of the child, involved; or

(B) delay or deny the placement of a child for adoption or into foster care, on the basis of the race, color, or national origin of the adoptive or foster parent, or the child, involved.

(2) Enforcement.—Noncompliance with paragraph (1) is deemed a violation of title VI of the Civil Rights Act of 1964 [42 U.S.C. 2000d et seq.].

(3) No effect on the Indian Child Welfare Act of 1978.—This subsection shall not be construed to affect the application of the Indian Child Welfare Act of 1978 [25 U.S.C. 1901 et seq.].

History of 42 U.S.C. §1996b: Aug. 20, 1996, P.L. 104-188, title I, §1808(c), 110 Stat. 1904.

TITLE 50. WAR & NATIONAL DEFENSE

CHAPTER 50. SERVICEMEMBERS CIVIL RELIEF

SUBCHAPTER I. GENERAL PROVISIONS

§3911. DEFINITIONS

For the purposes of this chapter:

(1) Servicemember.—The term "servicemember" means a member of the uniformed services, as that term is defined in section 101(a)(5) of title 10.

(2) Military service.—The term "military service" means—

(A) in the case of a servicemember who is a member of the Army, Navy, Air Force, Marine Corps, or Coast Guard—

(i) active duty, as defined in section 101(d)(1) of title 10, and

(ii) in the case of a member of the National Guard, includes service under a call to active service authorized by the President or the Secretary of Defense for a period of more than 30 consecutive days under section 502(f) of title 32 for purposes of responding to a national emergency declared by the President and supported by Federal funds;

(B) in the case of a servicemember who is a commissioned officer of the Public Health Service or the National Oceanic and Atmospheric Administration, active service; and

(C) any period during which a servicemember is absent from duty on account of sickness, wounds, leave, or other lawful cause.

(3) Period of military service.—The term "period of military service" means the period beginning on the date on which a servicemember enters military ser-

vice and ending on the date on which the servicemember is released from military service or dies while in military service.

(4) Dependent.—The term "dependent," with respect to a servicemember, means—

(A) the servicemember's spouse;

(B) the servicemember's child (as defined in section 101(4) of title 38); or

(C) an individual for whom the servicemember provided more than one-half of the individual's support for 180 days immediately preceding an application for relief under this chapter.

(5) Court.—The term "court" means a court or an administrative agency of the United States or of any State (including any political subdivision of a State), whether or not a court or administrative agency of record.

(6) State.—The term "State" includes—

(A) a commonwealth, territory, or possession of the United States; and

(B) the District of Columbia.

(7) Secretary concerned.—The term "Secretary concerned"—

(A) with respect to a member of the armed forces, has the meaning given that term in section 101(a)(9) of title 10;

(B) with respect to a commissioned officer of the Public Health Service, means the Secretary of Health and Human Services; and

(C) with respect to a commissioned officer of the National Oceanic and Atmospheric Administration, means the Secretary of Commerce.

(8) Motor vehicle.—The term "motor vehicle" has the meaning given that term in section 30102(a)(6) of title 49.

(9) Judgment.—The term "judgment" means any judgment, decree, order, or ruling, final or temporary.

History of 50 U.S.C. §3911: Oct. 17, 1940, ch. 888, §101, as added Dec. 19, 2003, P.L. 108-189, §1, 117 Stat. 2836; Dec. 10, 2004, P.L. 108-454, §701, 118 Stat. 3624.

§3912. JURISDICTION & APPLICABILITY OF CHAPTER

(a) Jurisdiction.—This chapter applies to—

(1) the United States;

(2) each of the States, including the political subdivisions thereof; and

(3) all territory subject to the jurisdiction of the United States.

(b) Applicability to proceedings.—This chapter applies to any judicial or administrative proceeding commenced in any court or agency in any jurisdiction subject to this chapter. This chapter does not apply to criminal proceedings.

(c) Court in which application may be made.—When under this chapter any application is required to be made to a court in which no proceeding has already been commenced with respect to the matter, such application may be made to any court which would otherwise have jurisdiction over the matter.

History of 50 U.S.C. §3912: Oct. 17, 1940, ch. 888, §102, as added Dec. 19, 2003, P.L. 108-189, §1, 117 Stat. 2837.

Sections 3913 & 3914 omitted by editor

§3915. NOTIFICATION OF BENEFITS

The Secretary concerned shall ensure that notice of the benefits accorded by this chapter is provided in writing to persons in military service and to persons entering military service.

History of 50 U.S.C. §3915: Oct. 17, 1940, ch. 888, §105, as added Dec. 19, 2003, P.L. 108-189, §1, 117 Stat. 2839.

Sections 3916 & 3917 omitted by editor

§3918. WAIVER OF RIGHTS PURSUANT TO WRITTEN AGREEMENT

(a) In general.—A servicemember may waive any of the rights and protections provided by this chapter. Any such waiver that applies to an action listed in subsection (b) of this section is effective only if it is in writing and is executed as an instrument separate from the obligation or liability to which it applies. In the case of a waiver that permits an action described in subsection (b), the waiver is effective only if made pursuant to a written agreement of the parties that is executed during or after the servicemember's period of military service. The written agreement shall specify the legal instrument to which the waiver applies and, if the servicemember is not a party to that instrument, the servicemember concerned.

(b) Actions requiring waivers in writing.—The requirement in subsection (a) for a written waiver applies to the following:

(1) The modification, termination, or cancellation of—

(A) a contract, lease, or bailment; or

(B) an obligation secured by a mortgage, trust, deed, lien, or other security in the nature of a mortgage.

(2) The repossession, retention, foreclosure, sale, forfeiture, or taking possession of property that—

(A) is security for any obligation; or

(B) was purchased or received under a contract, lease, or bailment.

(c) Prominent display of certain contract rights waivers.—Any waiver in writing of a right or protection provided by this chapter that applies to a contract, lease, or similar legal instrument must be in at least 12 point type.

(d) Coverage of periods after orders received.—For the purposes of this section—

(1) a person to whom section 3917 of this title applies shall be considered to be a servicemember; and

(2) the period with respect to such a person specified in subsection (a) or (b), as the case may be, of section 3917 of this title shall be considered to be a period of military service.

History of 50 U.S.C. §3918: Oct. 17, 1940, ch. 888, §107, as added Dec. 19, 2003, P.L. 108-189, §1, 117 Stat. 2839; Dec. 10, 2004, P.L. 108-454, §702, 118 Stat. 3624.

Sections 3919 & 3920 omitted by editor

SUBCHAPTER II. GENERAL RELIEF

§3931. PROTECTION OF SERVICEMEMBERS AGAINST DEFAULT JUDGMENTS

(a) Applicability of section.—This section applies to any civil action or proceeding, including any child custody proceeding, in which the defendant does not make an appearance.

(b) Affidavit requirement—

(1) Plaintiff to file affidavit.—In any action or proceeding covered by this section, the court, before entering judgment for the plaintiff, shall require the plaintiff to file with the court an affidavit—

(A) stating whether or not the defendant is in military service and showing necessary facts to support the affidavit; or

(B) if the plaintiff is unable to determine whether or not the defendant is in military service, stating that the plaintiff is unable to determine whether or not the defendant is in military service.

(2) Appointment of attorney to represent defendant in military service.—If in an action covered by this section it appears that the defendant is in military service, the court may not enter a judgment until after the court appoints an attorney to represent the defendant. If an attorney appointed under this section to represent a servicemember cannot locate the servicemember, actions by the attorney in the case shall not waive any defense of the servicemember or otherwise bind the servicemember.

(3) Defendant's military status not ascertained by affidavit.—If based upon the affidavits filed in such an action, the court is unable to determine whether the defendant is in military service, the court, before entering judgment, may require the plaintiff to file a bond in an amount approved by the court. If the defendant is later found to be in military service, the bond shall be available to indemnify the defendant against any loss or damage the defendant may suffer by reason of any judgment for the plaintiff against the defendant, should the judgment be set aside in whole or in part. The bond shall remain in effect until expiration of the time for appeal and setting aside of a judgment under applicable Federal or State law or regulation or under any applicable ordinance of a political subdivision of a State. The court may issue such orders or enter such judgments as the court determines necessary to protect the rights of the defendant under this chapter.

(4) Satisfaction of requirement for affidavit.—The requirement for an affidavit under paragraph (1) may be satisfied by a statement, declaration, verification, or certificate, in writing, subscribed and certified or declared to be true under penalty of perjury.

(c) Penalty for making or using false affidavit.—A person who makes or uses an affidavit permitted under subsection (b) (or a statement, declaration, verification, or certificate as authorized under subsection (b)(4)) knowing it to be false, shall be fined as provided in title 18 or imprisoned for not more than one year, or both.

(d) Stay of proceedings.—In an action covered by this section in which the defendant is in military service, the court shall grant a stay of proceedings for a minimum period of 90 days under this subsection upon application of counsel, or on the court's own motion, if the court determines that—

(1) there may be a defense to the action and a defense cannot be presented without the presence of the defendant; or

(2) after due diligence, counsel has been unable to contact the defendant or otherwise determine if a meritorious defense exists.

(e) Inapplicability of section 3932 procedures.—A stay of proceedings under subsection (d) shall not be controlled by procedures or requirements under section 3932 of this title.

(f) Section 3932 protection.—If a servicemember who is a defendant in an action covered by this section receives actual notice of the action, the servicemember may request a stay of proceeding under section 3932 of this title.

(g) Vacation or setting aside of default judgments—

(1) Authority for court to vacate or set aside judgment.—If a default judgment is entered in an action covered by this section against a servicemember during the servicemember's period of military service (or within 60 days after termination of or release from such military service), the court entering the judgment shall, upon application by or on behalf of the servicemember, reopen the judgment for the purpose of allowing the servicemember to defend the action if it appears that—

(A) the servicemember was materially affected by reason of that military service in making a defense to the action; and

(B) the servicemember has a meritorious or legal defense to the action or some part of it.

(2) Time for filing application.—An application under this subsection must be filed not later than 90 days after the date of the termination of or release from military service.

(h) Protection of bona fide purchaser.—If a court vacates, sets aside, or reverses a default judgment against a servicemember and the vacating, setting aside, or reversing is because of a provision of this chapter, that action shall not impair a right or title acquired by a bona fide purchaser for value under the default judgment.

History of 50 U.S.C. §3931: Oct. 17, 1940, ch. 888, §201, as added Dec. 19, 2003, P.L. 108-189, §1, 117 Stat. 2840; Jan. 28, 2008, P.L. 110-181, §584(a), 122 Stat. 128.

§3932. STAY OF PROCEEDINGS WHEN SERVICEMEMBER HAS NOTICE

(a) Applicability of section.—This section applies to any civil action or proceeding, including any child custody proceeding, in which the plaintiff or defendant at the time of filing an application under this section—

(1) is in military service or is within 90 days after termination of or release from military service; and

(2) has received notice of the action or proceeding.

(b) Stay of proceedings—

(1) Authority for stay.—At any stage before final judgment in a civil action or proceeding in which a servicemember described in subsection (a) is a party, the court may on its own motion and shall, upon application by the servicemember, stay the action for a period of not less than 90 days, if the conditions in paragraph (2) are met.

(2) Conditions for stay.—An application for a stay under paragraph (1) shall include the following:

(A) A letter or other communication setting forth facts stating the manner in which current military duty requirements materially affect the servicemember's ability to appear and stating a date when the servicemember will be available to appear.

(B) A letter or other communication from the servicemember's commanding officer stating that the servicemember's current military duty prevents appearance and that military leave is not authorized for the servicemember at the time of the letter.

(c) Application not a waiver of defenses.—An application for a stay under this section does not constitute an appearance for jurisdictional purposes and does not constitute a waiver of any substantive or procedural defense (including a defense relating to lack of personal jurisdiction).

(d) Additional stay—

(1) Application.—A servicemember who is granted a stay of a civil action or proceeding under subsection (b) may apply for an additional stay based on continuing material affect of military duty on the servicemember's ability to appear. Such an application may be made by the servicemember at the time of the initial application under subsection (b) or when it appears that the servicemember is unavailable to prosecute or defend the action. The same information required under subsection (b)(2) shall be included in an application under this subsection.

(2) Appointment of counsel when additional stay refused.—If the court refuses to grant an additional stay of proceedings under paragraph (1), the court shall appoint counsel to represent the servicemember in the action or proceeding.

(e) Coordination with section 3931.—A servicemember who applies for a stay under this section

and is unsuccessful may not seek the protections afforded by section 3931 of this title.

(f) Inapplicability to section 3951.—The protections of this section do not apply to section 3951 of this title.

History of 50 U.S.C. §3932: Oct. 17, 1940, ch. 888, §202, as added Dec. 19, 2003, P.L. 108-189, §1, 117 Stat. 2842; Dec. 10, 2004, P.L. 108-454, §703, 118 Stat. 3624; Jan. 28, 2008, P.L. 110-181, §584(b), 122 Stat. 128.

Section 3933 omitted by editor

§3934. STAY OR VACATION OF EXECUTION OF JUDGMENTS, ATTACHMENTS, & GARNISHMENTS

(a) Court action upon material affect determination.—If a servicemember, in the opinion of the court, is materially affected by reason of military service in complying with a court judgment or order, the court may on its own motion and shall on application by the servicemember—

(1) stay the execution of any judgment or order entered against the servicemember; and

(2) vacate or stay an attachment or garnishment of property, money, or debts in the possession of the servicemember or a third party, whether before or after judgment.

(b) Applicability.—This section applies to an action or proceeding commenced in a court against a servicemember before or during the period of the servicemember's military service or within 90 days after such service terminates.

History of 50 U.S.C. §3934: Oct. 17, 1940, ch. 888, §204, as added Dec. 19, 2003, P.L. 108-189, §1, 117 Stat. 2843.

§3935. DURATION & TERM OF STAYS; CODEFENDANTS NOT IN SERVICE

(a) Period of stay.—A stay of an action, proceeding, attachment, or execution made pursuant to the provisions of this chapter by a court may be ordered for the period of military service and 90 days thereafter, or for any part of that period. The court may set the terms and amounts for such installment payments as is considered reasonable by the court.

(b) Codefendants.—If the servicemember is a codefendant with others who are not in military service and who are not entitled to the relief and protections provided under this chapter, the plaintiff may proceed against those other defendants with the approval of the court.

(c) Inapplicability of section.—This section does not apply to sections 3932 and 4021 of this title.

History of 50 U.S.C. §3935: Oct. 17, 1940, ch. 888, §205, as added Dec. 19, 2003, P.L. 108-189, §1, 117 Stat. 2844.

§3936. STATUTE OF LIMITATIONS

(a) Tolling of statutes of limitation during military service.—The period of a servicemember's military service may not be included in computing any period limited by law, regulation, or order for the bringing of any action or proceeding in a court, or in any board, bureau, commission, department, or other agency of a State (or political subdivision of a State) or the United States by or against the servicemember or the servicemember's heirs, executors, administrators, or assigns.

(b) Redemption of real property.—A period of military service may not be included in computing any period provided by law for the redemption of real property sold or forfeited to enforce an obligation, tax, or assessment.

(c) Inapplicability to internal revenue laws.—This section does not apply to any period of limitation prescribed by or under the internal revenue laws of the United States.

History of 50 U.S.C. §3936: Oct. 17, 1940, ch. 888, §206, as added Dec. 19, 2003, P.L. 108-189, §1, 117 Stat. 2844.

Sections 3937 & 3938 omitted by editor

HAGUE CONVENTION ON INTERNATIONAL CHILD ABDUCTION

The Convention on the Civil Aspects of International Child Abduction ("Child Abduction Convention") is an international treaty that provides a civil method to seek the return of a child who has been wrongfully removed or retained outside the country of the child's habitual residence. U.S. State Dept., *2010 Compliance Report*, p. 13, travel.state.gov/content/dam/childabduction/complianceReports/2010.pdf; *see* Hague Convention on the Civil Aspects of International Child Abduction, Oct. 25, 1980, art. 1. The Child Abduction Convention was adopted in 1980 and entered into force for the United States on July 1, 1988. U.S. State Dept., *2010 Compliance Report*, at 13. In the case of a child being abducted to or from the United States, relief under the Child Abduction Convention is available only between the United States and a Child Abduction Convention partner. *See* Hague Conv., arts. 37, 38; U.S. State Dept., *2010 Compliance Report*, at 13-14.

A Child Abduction Convention partner is a country that (1) has acceded to the Convention and has been accepted by the United States under Child Abduction Convention article 38 or (2) was a member of the Hague Conference on Private International Law during its 14th session and has signed and ratified the Child Abduction Convention or succeeded to it (as in the case of the states remaining after the breakup of the former Yugoslavia). *See* Hague Conv. on Child Abduction, arts. 37, 38. Each Child Abduction Convention partner has a designated government office, known as the Central Authority, to carry out specific Child Abduction Convention duties for that country. Hague Conv. on Child Abduction, art. 6. The Central Authority for the United States is the Department of State's Office of Children's Issues. travel.state.gov/content/childabduction/english/from.html. Even when a lawyer is representing an applicant, the application for the return of a child should always be routed through the Central Authority. Dyer, *To Celebrate a Score of Years!*, 33 N.Y.U. J. Int'l L. & Pol. 1, 13 (2000).

The Child Abduction Convention is implemented in the United States by the International Child Abduction Remedies Act ("ICARA"). 22 U.S.C. §§9001-9011. See "International Child Abduction Remedies," p. 1412. And in Texas, a court is authorized under the UCCJEA to enforce an order for the return of a child made under the Child Abduction Convention as if it were a child-custody determination. Tex. Fam. Code §152.302.

A summary of the United States' current Child Abduction Convention partners and effective dates is provided in the table below.

Country	Effective Date with U.S.	Method of Entry
Andorra	1/1/17	Acceded and accepted by U.S.
Argentina	6/1/91	Ratified
Australia	7/1/88	Ratified
Austria	10/1/88	Ratified
Bahamas	1/1/94	Acceded and accepted by U.S.
Belgium	5/1/99	Ratified
Belize	11/1/89	Acceded and accepted by U.S.
Bosnia and Herzegovina	12/1/91	Succeeded
Brazil	12/1/03	Acceded and accepted by U.S.
Bulgaria	1/1/05	Acceded and accepted by U.S.
Burkina Faso	11/1/92	Acceded and accepted by U.S.
Canada	7/1/88	Ratified
Chile	7/1/94	Acceded and accepted by U.S.
China, People's Republic of	Hong Kong 9/1/97; Macau 3/1/99	Continued (applies only in Hong Kong and Macau SARs)
Colombia	6/1/96	Acceded and accepted by U.S.
Costa Rica	1/1/08	Acceded and accepted by U.S.
Croatia	12/1/91	Succeeded
Cyprus	3/1/95	Acceded and accepted by U.S.
Czech Republic	3/1/98	Ratified

The Hague Conventions

The Hague Convention on International Child Abduction

Country	Effective Date with U.S.	Method of Entry
Denmark	7/1/91	Ratified
Dominican Republic	6/1/07	Acceded and accepted by U.S.
Ecuador	4/1/92	Acceded and accepted by U.S.
El Salvador	6/1/07	Acceded and accepted by U.S.
Estonia	5/1/07	Acceded and accepted by U.S.
Fiji	5/1/17	Acceded and accepted by U.S.
Finland	8/1/94	Ratified
France	7/1/88	Ratified
Germany	12/1/90	Ratified
Greece	6/1/93	Ratified
Guatemala	1/1/08	Acceded and accepted by U.S.
Honduras	6/1/94	Acceded and accepted by U.S.
Hungary	7/1/88	Acceded and accepted by U.S.
Iceland	12/1/96	Acceded and accepted by U.S.
Ireland	10/1/91	Ratified
Israel	12/1/91	Ratified
Italy	5/1/95	Ratified
Japan	4/1/14	Ratified
Korea, Republic of	11/1/13	Acceded and accepted by U.S.
Latvia	5/1/07	Acceded and accepted by U.S.
Lithuania	5/1/07	Acceded and accepted by U.S.
Luxembourg	7/1/88	Ratified
Macedonia, the former Yugoslav Republic of	12/1/91	Succeeded
Malta	2/1/03	Acceded and accepted by U.S.
Mauritius	10/1/93	Acceded and accepted by U.S.

Country	Effective Date with U.S.	Method of Entry
Mexico	10/1/91	Acceded and accepted by U.S.
Monaco	6/1/93	Acceded and accepted by U.S.
Montenegro	12/1/91	Succeeded
Morocco	12/1/12	Acceded and accepted by U.S.
Netherlands	9/1/90	Ratified
New Zealand	10/1/91	Acceded and accepted by U.S.
Norway	4/1/89	Ratified
Panama	6/1/94	Acceded and accepted by U.S.
Paraguay	1/1/08	Acceded and accepted by U.S.
Peru	6/1/07	Acceded and accepted by U.S.
Poland	11/1/92	Acceded and accepted by U.S.
Portugal	7/1/88	Ratified
Romania	6/1/93	Acceded and accepted by U.S.
Saint Kitts and Nevis	6/1/95	Acceded and accepted by U.S.
San Marino	1/1/08	Acceded and accepted by U.S.
Serbia	12/1/91	Succeeded
Singapore	5/1/12	Acceded and accepted by U.S.
Slovakia	2/1/01	Ratified
Slovenia	4/1/95	Acceded and accepted by U.S.
South Africa	11/1/97	Acceded and accepted by U.S.
Spain	7/1/88	Ratified
Sri Lanka	1/1/08	Acceded and accepted by U.S.
Sweden	6/1/89	Ratified
Switzerland	7/1/88	Ratified
Thailand	4/1/16	Acceded and accepted by U.S.

COUNTRY	EFFECTIVE DATE WITH U.S.	METHOD OF ENTRY
Trinidad and Tobago	8/1/13	Acceded and accepted by U.S.
Turkey	8/1/00	Ratified
Ukraine	9/1/07	Acceded and accepted by U.S.
United Kingdom of Great Britain and Northern Ireland	7/1/88	Ratified
U.K. – Anguilla	6/1/08	Extension of application and accepted by U.S.
U.K. – Bermuda	3/1/99	Extension of application and accepted by U.S.
U.K. – Cayman Islands	8/1/98	Extension of application and accepted by U.S.
U.K. – Falkland Islands	6/1/98	Extension of application and accepted by U.S.
U.K. – Isle of Man	9/1/91	Extension of application and accepted by U.S.
U.K. – Montserrat	3/1/99	Extension of application and accepted by U.S.
Uruguay	9/1/04	Acceded and accepted by U.S.
Venezuela	1/1/97	Ratified
Zimbabwe	8/1/95	Acceded and accepted by U.S.

Table Sources: Hague Conference on Private International Law, *Status Table, 28: Convention of 25 October 1980 on the Civil Aspects of International Child Abduction*, www.hcch.net/index_en.php?act=conventions.status&cid=24; U.S. State Department, *U.S. Hague Convention Treaty Partners*, travel.state.gov/content/childabduction/english/country/hague-party-countries.html.

CONVENTION ON THE CIVIL ASPECTS OF INTERNATIONAL CHILD ABDUCTION

(Concluded 25 October 1980)

The States signatory to the present Convention,

Firmly convinced that the interests of children are of paramount importance in matters relating to their custody,

Desiring to protect children internationally from the harmful effects of their wrongful removal or retention and to establish procedures to ensure their prompt return to the State of their habitual residence, as well as to secure protection for rights of access,

Have resolved to conclude a Convention to this effect, and have agreed upon the following provisions—

CHAPTER I—SCOPE OF THE CONVENTION

ARTICLE 1

The objects of the present Convention are—

(a) to secure the prompt return of children wrongfully removed to or retained in any Contracting State; and

(b) to ensure that rights of custody and of access under the law of one Contracting State are effectively respected in the other Contracting States.

ARTICLE 2

Contracting States shall take all appropriate measures to secure within their territories the implementation of the objects of the Convention. For this purpose they shall use the most expeditious procedures available.

ARTICLE 3

The removal or the retention of a child is to be considered wrongful where—

(a) it is in breach of rights of custody attributed to a person, an institution or any other body, either jointly or alone, under the law of the State in which the child was habitually resident immediately before the removal or retention; and

(b) at the time of removal or retention those rights were actually exercised, either jointly or alone, or would have been so exercised but for the removal or retention.

The rights of custody mentioned in sub-paragraph(a) above, may arise in particular by operation of law or by reason of a judicial or administrative decision, or by reason of an agreement having legal effect under the law of that State.

ARTICLE 4

The Convention shall apply to any child who was habitually resident in a Contracting State immediately before any breach of custody or access rights. The Convention shall cease to apply when the child attains the age of 16 years.

ARTICLE 5

For the purposes of this Convention—

(a) "rights of custody" shall include rights relating to the care of the person of the child and, in particular, the right to determine the child's place of residence;

(b) "rights of access" shall include the right to take a child for a limited period of time to a place other than the child's habitual residence.

CHAPTER II—CENTRAL AUTHORITIES

ARTICLE 6

A Contracting State shall designate a Central Authority to discharge the duties which are imposed by the Convention upon such authorities.

Federal States, States with more than one system of law or States having autonomous territorial organizations shall be free to appoint more than one Central Authority and to specify the territorial extent of their powers. Where a State has appointed more than one Central Authority, it shall designate the Central Authority to which applications may be addressed for transmission to the appropriate Central Authority within that State.

ARTICLE 7

Central Authorities shall co-operate with each other and promote co-operation amongst the competent authorities in their respective States to secure the prompt return of children and to achieve the other objects of this Convention.

In particular, either directly or through any intermediary, they shall take all appropriate measures—

(a) to discover the whereabouts of a child who has been wrongfully removed or retained;

(b) to prevent further harm to the child or prejudice to interested parties by taking or causing to be taken provisional measures;

(c) to secure the voluntary return of the child or to bring about an amicable resolution of the issues;

(d) to exchange, where desirable, information relating to the social background of the child;

(e) to provide information of a general character as to the law of their State in connection with the application of the Convention;

(f) to initiate or facilitate the institution of judicial or administrative proceedings with a view to obtaining the return of the child and, in a proper case, to make arrangements for organizing or securing the effective exercise of rights of access;

(g) where the circumstances so require, to provide or facilitate the provision of legal aid and advice, including the participation of legal counsel and advisers;

(h) to provide such administrative arrangements as may be necessary and appropriate to secure the safe return of the child;

(i) to keep each other informed with respect to the operation of this Convention and, as far as possible, to eliminate any obstacles to its application.

CHAPTER III—RETURN OF CHILDREN

ARTICLE 8

Any person, institution or other body claiming that a child has been removed or retained in breach of custody rights may apply either to the Central Authority of the child's habitual residence or to the Central Authority of any other Contracting State for assistance in securing the return of the child.

The application shall contain—

(a) information concerning the identity of the applicant, of the child and of the person alleged to have removed or retained the child;

(b) where available, the date of birth of the child;

(c) the grounds on which the applicant's claim for return of the child is based;

(d) all available information relating to the whereabouts of the child and the identity of the person with whom the child is presumed to be.

The application may be accompanied or supplemented by—

(e) an authenticated copy of any relevant decision or agreement;

(f) a certificate or an affidavit emanating from a Central Authority, or other competent authority of the State of the child's habitual residence, or from a qualified person, concerning the relevant law of that State;

(g) any other relevant document.

ARTICLE 9

If the Central Authority which receives an application referred to in Article 8 has reason to believe that the child is in another Contracting State, it shall directly and without delay transmit the application to the Central Authority of that Contracting State and inform the requesting Central Authority, or the applicant, as the case may be.

ARTICLE 10

The Central Authority of the State where the child is shall take or cause to be taken all appropriate measures in order to obtain the voluntary return of the child.

ARTICLE 11

The judicial or administrative authorities of Contracting States shall act expeditiously in proceedings for the return of children.

If the judicial or administrative authority concerned has not reached a decision within six weeks from the date of commencement of the proceedings, the applicant or the Central Authority of the requested State, on its own initiative or if asked by the Central Authority of the requesting State, shall have the right to request a statement of the reasons for the delay. If a reply is received by the Central Authority of the requested State, that Authority shall transmit the reply to the Central Authority of the requesting State, or to the applicant, as the case may be.

ARTICLE 12

Where a child has been wrongfully removed or retained in terms of Article 3 and, at the date of the commencement of the proceedings before the judicial or administrative authority of the Contracting State where the child is, a period of less than one year has elapsed from the date of the wrongful removal or retention, the authority concerned shall order the return of the child forthwith.

The judicial or administrative authority, even where the proceedings have been commenced after the expiration of the period of one year referred to in the preceding paragraph, shall also order the return of the child, unless it is demonstrated that the child is now settled in its new environment.

Where the judicial or administrative authority in the requested State has reason to believe that the child has been taken to another State, it may stay the proceedings or dismiss the application for the return of the child.

ARTICLE 13

Notwithstanding the provisions of the preceding Article, the judicial or administrative authority of the requested State is not bound to order the return of the child if the person, institution or other body which opposes its return establishes that—

(a) the person, institution or other body having the care of the person of the child was not actually exercising the custody rights at the time of removal or retention, or had consented to or subsequently acquiesced in the removal or retention; or

(b) there is a grave risk that his or her return would expose the child to physical or psychological harm or otherwise place the child in an intolerable situation.

The judicial or administrative authority may also refuse to order the return of the child if it finds that the child objects to being returned and has attained an age and degree of maturity at which it is appropriate to take account of its views.

In considering the circumstances referred to in this Article, the judicial and administrative authorities shall take into account the information relating to the social background of the child provided by the Central Authority or other competent authority of the child's habitual residence.

ARTICLE 14

In ascertaining whether there has been a wrongful removal or retention within the meaning of Article 3, the judicial or administrative authorities of the requested State may take notice directly of the law of, and of judicial or administrative decisions, formally recognized or not in the State of the habitual residence of the child, without recourse to the specific procedures for the proof of that law or for the recognition of foreign decisions which would otherwise be applicable.

ARTICLE 15

The judicial or administrative authorities of a Contracting State may, prior to the making of an order for the return of the child, request that the applicant obtain from the authorities of the State of the habitual residence of the child a decision or other determination that the removal or retention was wrongful within the meaning of Article 3 of the Convention, where such a decision or determination may be obtained in that State. The Central Authorities of the Contracting States shall so far as practicable assist applicants to obtain such a decision or determination.

ARTICLE 16

After receiving notice of a wrongful removal or retention of a child in the sense of Article 3, the judicial or administrative authorities of the Contracting State to which the child has been removed or in which it has been retained shall not decide on the merits of rights of

custody until it has been determined that the child is not to be returned under this Convention or unless an application under this Convention is not lodged within a reasonable time following receipt of the notice.

ARTICLE 17

The sole fact that a decision relating to custody has been given in or is entitled to recognition in the requested State shall not be a ground for refusing to return a child under this Convention, but the judicial or administrative authorities of the requested State may take account of the reasons for that decision in applying this Convention.

ARTICLE 18

The provisions of this Chapter do not limit the power of a judicial or administrative authority to order the return of the child at any time.

ARTICLE 19

A decision under this Convention concerning the return of the child shall not be taken to be a determination on the merits of any custody issue.

ARTICLE 20

The return of the child under the provisions of Article 12 may be refused if this would not be permitted by the fundamental principles of the requested State relating to the protection of human rights and fundamental freedoms.

CHAPTER IV—RIGHTS OF ACCESS

ARTICLE 21

An application to make arrangements for organizing or securing the effective exercise of rights of access may be presented to the Central Authorities of the Contracting States in the same way as an application for the return of a child.

The Central Authorities are bound by the obligations of co-operation which are set forth in Article 7 to promote the peaceful enjoyment of access rights and the fulfilment of any conditions to which the exercise of those rights may be subject. The Central Authorities shall take steps to remove, as far as possible, all obstacles to the exercise of such rights.

The Central Authorities, either directly or through intermediaries, may initiate or assist in the institution of proceedings with a view to organizing or protecting these rights and securing respect for the conditions to which the exercise of these rights may be subject.

CHAPTER V—GENERAL PROVISIONS

ARTICLE 22

No security, bond or deposit, however described, shall be required to guarantee the payment of costs and expenses in the judicial or administrative proceedings falling within the scope of this Convention.

ARTICLE 23

No legalization or similar formality may be required in the context of this Convention.

ARTICLE 24

Any application, communication or other document sent to the Central Authority of the requested State shall be in the original language, and shall be accompanied by a translation into the official language or one of the official languages of the requested State or, where that is not feasible, a translation into French or English.

However, a Contracting State may, by making a reservation in accordance with Article 42, object to the use of either French or English, but not both, in any application, communication or other document sent to its Central Authority.

ARTICLE 25

Nationals of the Contracting States and persons who are habitually resident within those States shall be entitled in matters concerned with the application of this Convention to legal aid and advice in any other Contracting State on the same conditions as if they themselves were nationals of and habitually resident in that State.

ARTICLE 26

Each Central Authority shall bear its own costs in applying this Convention.

Central Authorities and other public services of Contracting States shall not impose any charges in relation to applications submitted under this Convention. In particular, they may not require any payment from the applicant towards the costs and expenses of the proceedings or, where applicable, those arising from the participation of legal counsel or advisers. However, they may require the payment of the expenses incurred or to be incurred in implementing the return of the child.

However, a Contracting State may, by making a reservation in accordance with Article 42, declare that it

shall not be bound to assume any costs referred to in the preceding paragraph resulting from the participation of legal counsel or advisers or from court proceedings, except insofar as those costs may be covered by its system of legal aid and advice.

Upon ordering the return of a child or issuing an order concerning rights of access under this Convention, the judicial or administrative authorities may, where appropriate, direct the person who removed or retained the child, or who prevented the exercise of rights of access, to pay necessary expenses incurred by or on behalf of the applicant, including travel expenses, any costs incurred or payments made for locating the child, the costs of legal representation of the applicant, and those of returning the child.

ARTICLE 27

When it is manifest that the requirements of this Convention are not fulfilled or that the application is otherwise not well founded, a Central Authority is not bound to accept the application. In that case, the Central Authority shall forthwith inform the applicant or the Central Authority through which the application was submitted, as the case may be, of its reasons.

ARTICLE 28

A Central Authority may require that the application be accompanied by a written authorization empowering it to act on behalf of the applicant, or to designate a representative so to act.

ARTICLE 29

This Convention shall not preclude any person, institution or body who claims that there has been a breach of custody or access rights within the meaning of Article 3 or 21 from applying directly to the judicial or administrative authorities of a Contracting State, whether or not under the provisions of this Convention.

ARTICLE 30

Any application submitted to the Central Authorities or directly to the judicial or administrative authorities of a Contracting State in accordance with the terms of this Convention, together with documents and any other information appended thereto or provided by a Central Authority, shall be admissible in the courts or administrative authorities of the Contracting States.

ARTICLE 31

In relation to a State which in matters of custody of children has two or more systems of law applicable in different territorial units—

(a) any reference to habitual residence in that State shall be construed as referring to habitual residence in a territorial unit of that State;

(b) any reference to the law of the State of habitual residence shall be construed as referring to the law of the territorial unit in that State where the child habitually resides.

ARTICLE 32

In relation to a State which in matters of custody of children has two or more systems of law applicable to different categories of persons, any reference to the law of that State shall be construed as referring to the legal system specified by the law of that State.

ARTICLE 33

A State within which different territorial units have their own rules of law in respect of custody of children shall not be bound to apply this Convention where a State with a unified system of law would not be bound to do so.

ARTICLE 34

This Convention shall take priority in matters within its scope over the Convention of 5 October 1961 concerning the powers of authorities and the law applicable in respect of the protection of minors, as between Parties to both Conventions. Otherwise the present Convention shall not restrict the application of an international instrument in force between the State of origin and the State addressed or other law of the State addressed for the purposes of obtaining the return of a child who has been wrongfully removed or retained or of organizing access rights.

ARTICLE 35

This Convention shall apply as between Contracting States only to wrongful removals or retentions occurring after its entry into force in those States.

Where a declaration has been made under Article 39 or 40, the reference in the preceding paragraph to a Contracting State shall be taken to refer to the territorial unit or units in relation to which this Convention applies.

ARTICLE 36

Nothing in this Convention shall prevent two or more Contracting States, in order to limit the restrictions to which the return of the child may be subject, from agreeing among themselves to derogate from any provisions of this Convention which may imply such a restriction.

CHAPTER VI—FINAL CLAUSES

ARTICLE 37

The Convention shall be open for signature by the States which were Members of the Hague Conference on Private International Law at the time of its Fourteenth Session.

It shall be ratified, accepted or approved and the instruments of ratification, acceptance or approval shall be deposited with the Ministry of Foreign Affairs of the Kingdom of the Netherlands.

ARTICLE 38

Any other State may accede to the Convention.

The instrument of accession shall be deposited with the Ministry of Foreign Affairs of the Kingdom of the Netherlands.

The Convention shall enter into force for a State acceding to it on the first day of the third calendar month after the deposit of its instrument of accession.

The accession will have effect only as regards the relations between the acceding State and such Contracting States as will have declared their acceptance of the accession. Such a declaration will also have to be made by any Member State ratifying, accepting or approving the Convention after an accession. Such declaration shall be deposited at the Ministry of Foreign Affairs of the Kingdom of the Netherlands; this Ministry shall forward, through diplomatic channels, a certified copy to each of the Contracting States.

The Convention will enter into force as between the acceding State and the State that has declared its acceptance of the accession on the first day of the third calendar month after the deposit of the declaration of acceptance.

ARTICLE 39

Any State may, at the time of signature, ratification, acceptance, approval or accession, declare that the Convention shall extend to all the territories for the international relations of which it is responsible, or to one or more of them. Such a declaration shall take effect at the time the Convention enters into force for that State.

Such declaration, as well as any subsequent extension, shall be notified to the Ministry of Foreign Affairs of the Kingdom of the Netherlands.

ARTICLE 40

If a Contracting State has two or more territorial units in which different systems of law are applicable in relation to matters dealt with in this Convention, it may at the time of signature, ratification, acceptance, approval or accession declare that this Convention shall extend to all its territorial units or only to one or more of them and may modify this declaration by submitting another declaration at any time.

Any such declaration shall be notified to the Ministry of Foreign Affairs of the Kingdom of the Netherlands and shall state expressly the territorial units to which the Convention applies.

ARTICLE 41

Where a Contracting State has a system of government under which executive, judicial and legislative powers are distributed between central and other authorities within that State, its signature or ratification, acceptance or approval of, or accession to this Convention, or its making of any declaration in terms of Article 40 shall carry no implication as to the internal distribution of powers within that State.

ARTICLE 42

Any State may, not later than the time of ratification, acceptance, approval or accession, or at the time of making a declaration in terms of Article 39 or 40, make one or both of the reservations provided for in Article 24 and Article 26, third paragraph. No other reservation shall be permitted.

Any State may at any time withdraw a reservation it has made. The withdrawal shall be notified to the Ministry of Foreign Affairs of the Kingdom of the Netherlands.

The reservation shall cease to have effect on the first day of the third calendar month after the notification referred to in the preceding paragraph.

ARTICLE 43

The Convention shall enter into force on the first day of the third calendar month after the deposit of the third instrument of ratification, acceptance, approval or accession referred to in Articles 37 and 38.

Thereafter the Convention shall enter into force—

(1) for each State ratifying, accepting, approving or acceding to it subsequently, on the first day of the third calendar month after the deposit of its instrument of ratification, acceptance, approval or accession;

(2) for any territory or territorial unit to which the Convention has been extended in conformity with Article 39 or 40, on the first day of the third calendar month after the notification referred to in that Article.

ARTICLE 44

The Convention shall remain in force for five years from the date of its entry into force in accordance with the first paragraph of Article 43 even for States which subsequently have ratified, accepted, approved it or acceded to it.

If there has been no denunciation, it shall be renewed tacitly every five years.

Any denunciation shall be notified to the Ministry of Foreign Affairs of the Kingdom of the Netherlands at least six months before the expiry of the five year period. It may be limited to certain of the territories or territorial units to which the Convention applies.

The denunciation shall have effect only as regards the State which has notified it. The Convention shall remain in force for the other Contracting States.

ARTICLE 45

The Ministry of Foreign Affairs of the Kingdom of the Netherlands shall notify the States Members of the Conference, and the States which have acceded in accordance with Article 38, of the following—

(1) the signatures and ratifications, acceptances and approvals referred to in Article 37;

(2) the accessions referred to in Article 38;

(3) the date on which the Convention enters into force in accordance with Article 43;

(4) the extensions referred to in Article 39;

(5) the declarations referred to in Articles 38 and 40;

(6) the reservations referred to in Article 24 and Article 26, third paragraph, and the withdrawals referred to in Article 42;

(7) the denunciations referred to in Article 44.

In witness whereof the undersigned, being duly authorised thereto, have signed this Convention.

Done at The Hague, on the 25th day of October, 1980, in the English and French languages, both texts being equally authentic, in a single copy which shall be deposited in the archives of the Government of the Kingdom of the Netherlands, and of which a certified copy shall be sent, through diplomatic channels, to each of the States Members of the Hague Conference on Private International Law at the date of its Fourteenth Session.

HAGUE CONVENTION ON INTERNATIONAL RECOVERY OF CHILD SUPPORT & FAMILY MAINTENANCE

The Convention on the International Recovery of Child Support and Other Forms of Family Maintenance ("Child Support Convention") is an international treaty that ensures the effective international recovery of child support and other forms of family maintenance. *Explanatory Report on the Convention*, p. 5, assets.hcch.net/upload/expl38.pdf; *see* Hague Convention on the International Recovery of Child Support and Other Forms of Family Maintenance, November 23, 2007, art. 1. The Child Support Convention was adopted in 2007 and entered into force for the United States on January 1, 2017. *See Explanatory Report on the Convention,* at Preface n. 4; Hague Conference on Private International Law, *Status Table, 38: Convention of 23 November 2007 on the International Recovery of Child Support and Other Forms of Family Maintenance*, www.hcch.net/en/instruments/conventions/status-table/?cid=131.

Relief under the Child Support Convention is only available between the United States and a contracting state. *See* Hague Conv. on Child Support, arts. 1, 20. Each contracting state has a designated government office, known as the Central Authority, to carry out specific Child Support Convention duties for that country. Hague Conv. on Child Support, art. 4. The Central Authority for the United States is the Office of Child Support Enforcement in the Department of Health and Human Services. www.acf.hhs.gov/css/partners/international.

The Child Support Convention is implemented in the United States by the Uniform Interstate Family Support Act 2008, which was enacted by every state. *See Enactment Status Map*, www.uniformlaws.org/Act.aspx?title=Interstate%20Family%20Support%20Act%20Amendments%20(2008). The Child Support Convention provisions are primarily reflected in Texas Family Code chapter 159, subchapter H. *See* Tex. Fam. Code §§159.701-159.713.

A summary of the United States' current Child Support Convention contracting states and effective dates is provided in the table below.

Country	Effective Date with U.S.	Method of Entry
Albania	1/1/17	Ratified
Austria	1/1/17	Bound as result of approval by Regional Economic Integration Organisation*
Belgium	1/1/17	Bound as result of approval by Regional Economic Integration Organisation*
Bosnia and Herzegovina	1/1/17	Ratified
Bulgaria	1/1/17	Bound as result of approval by Regional Economic Integration Organisation*
Croatia	1/1/17	Bound as result of approval by Regional Economic Integration Organisation*
Cyprus	1/1/17	Bound as result of approval by Regional Economic Integration Organisation*
Czech Republic	1/1/17	Bound as result of approval by Regional Economic Integration Organisation*
Estonia	1/1/17	Bound as result of approval by Regional Economic Integration Organisation*
European Union	1/1/17	Approved by Regional Economic Integration Organisation
Finland	1/1/17	Bound as result of approval by Regional Economic Integration Organisation*
France	1/1/17	Bound as result of approval by Regional Economic Integration Organisation*
Germany	1/1/17	Bound as result of approval by Regional Economic Integration Organisation*

COUNTRY	EFFECTIVE DATE WITH U.S.	METHOD OF ENTRY
Greece	1/1/17	Bound as result of approval by Regional Economic Integration Organisation*
Hungary	1/1/17	Bound as result of approval by Regional Economic Integration Organisation*
Ireland	1/1/17	Bound as result of approval by Regional Economic Integration Organisation*
Italy	1/1/17	Bound as result of approval by Regional Economic Integration Organisation*
Kazakhstan	10/1/17	Acceded
Latvia	1/1/17	Bound as result of approval by Regional Economic Integration Organisation*
Lithuania	1/1/17	Bound as result of approval by Regional Economic Integration Organisation*
Luxembourg	1/1/17	Bound as result of approval by Regional Economic Integration Organisation*
Malta	1/1/17	Bound as result of approval by Regional Economic Integration Organisation*
Montenegro	1/1/17	Acceded
Netherlands	1/1/17	Bound as result of approval by Regional Economic Integration Organisation*
Norway	1/1/17	Ratified
Poland	1/1/17	Bound as result of approval by Regional Economic Integration Organisation*
Portugal	1/1/17	Bound as result of approval by Regional Economic Integration Organisation*
Romania	1/1/17	Bound as result of approval by Regional Economic Integration Organisation*
Slovakia	1/1/17	Bound as result of approval by Regional Economic Integration Organisation*
Slovenia	1/1/17	Bound as result of approval by Regional Economic Integration Organisation*
Spain	1/1/17	Bound as result of approval by Regional Economic Integration Organisation*
Sweden	1/1/17	Bound as result of approval by Regional Economic Integration Organisation*
Turkey	2/1/17	Ratified
Ukraine	1/1/17	Ratified
United Kingdom of Great Britain and Northern Ireland	1/1/17	Bound as result of approval by Regional Economic Integration Organisation*

* A Regional Economic Integration Organisation that is constituted solely by sovereign States and has competence over some or all of the matters governed by this Convention may similarly sign, accept, approve or accede to this Convention. Hague Conv. on Child Support, art. 59. The Regional Economic Integration Organisation shall in that case have the rights and obligations of a contracting state, to the extent that the Organisation has competence over matters governed by the Convention. *Id.*

Table source: Hague Conference on Private International Law, *Status Table, 38: Convention of 23 November 2007 on the International Recovery of Child Support and Other Forms of Family Maintenance, www.hcch.net/en/instruments/conventions/status-table/?cid=131.*

CONVENTION ON THE INTERNATIONAL RECOVERY OF CHILD SUPPORT & OTHER FORMS OF FAMILY MAINTENANCE

(Concluded 23 November 2007)

The States signatory to the present Convention,

Desiring to improve co-operation among States for the international recovery of child support and other forms of family maintenance,

Aware of the need for procedures which produce results and are accessible, prompt, efficient, cost-effective, responsive and fair,

Wishing to build upon the best features of existing Hague Conventions and other international instruments, in particular the United Nations *Convention on the Recovery Abroad of Maintenance* of 20 June 1956,

Seeking to take advantage of advances in technologies and to create a flexible system which can continue to evolve as needs change and further advances in technology create new opportunities,

Recalling that, in accordance with Articles 3 and 27 of the United Nations *Convention on the Rights of the Child* of 20 November 1989,

– in all actions concerning children the best interests of the child shall be a primary consideration,

– every child has a right to a standard of living adequate for the child's physical, mental, spiritual, moral and social development,

– the parent(s) or others responsible for the child have the primary responsibility to secure, within their abilities and financial capacities, the conditions of living necessary for the child's development, and

– States Parties should take all appropriate measures, including the conclusion of international agreements, to secure the recovery of maintenance for the child from the parent(s) or other responsible persons, in particular where such persons live in a State different from that of the child,

Have resolved to conclude this Convention and have agreed upon the following provisions—

CHAPTER I—OBJECT, SCOPE & DEFINITIONS

ARTICLE 1 OBJECT

The object of the present Convention is to ensure the effective international recovery of child support and other forms of family maintenance, in particular by—

(a) establishing a comprehensive system of co-operation between the authorities of the Contracting States;

(b) making available applications for the establishment of maintenance decisions;

(c) providing for the recognition and enforcement of maintenance decisions; and

(d) requiring effective measures for the prompt enforcement of maintenance decisions.

ARTICLE 2 SCOPE

(1) This Convention shall apply—

(a) to maintenance obligations arising from a parent-child relationship towards a person under the age of 21 years;

(b) to recognition and enforcement or enforcement of a decision for spousal support when the application is made with a claim within the scope of sub-paragraph (a); and

(c) with the exception of Chapters II and III, to spousal support.

(2) Any Contracting State may reserve, in accordance with Article 62, the right to limit the application of the Convention under sub-paragraph 1(a), to persons who have not attained the age of 18 years. A Contracting State which makes this reservation shall not be entitled to claim the application of the Convention to persons of the age excluded by its reservation.

(3) Any Contracting State may declare in accordance with Article 63 that it will extend the application of the whole or any part of the Convention to any maintenance obligation arising from a family relationship, parentage, marriage or affinity, including in particular obligations in respect of vulnerable persons. Any such declaration shall give rise to obligations between two Contracting States only in so far as their declarations cover the same maintenance obligations and parts of the Convention.

(4) The provisions of this Convention shall apply to children regardless of the marital status of the parents.

ARTICLE 3 DEFINITIONS

For the purposes of this Convention—

(a) "creditor" means an individual to whom maintenance is owed or is alleged to be owed;

(b) "debtor" means an individual who owes or who is alleged to owe maintenance;

(c) "legal assistance" means the assistance necessary to enable applicants to know and assert their rights and to ensure that applications are fully and effectively dealt with in the requested State. The means of providing such assistance may include as necessary legal advice, assistance in bringing a case before an au-

thority, legal representation and exemption from costs of proceedings;

(d) "agreement in writing" means an agreement recorded in any medium, the information contained in which is accessible so as to be usable for subsequent reference;

(e) "maintenance arrangement" means an agreement in writing relating to the payment of maintenance which—

(i) has been formally drawn up or registered as an authentic instrument by a competent authority; or

(ii) has been authenticated by, or concluded, registered or filed with a competent authority, and may be the subject of review and modification by a competent authority;

(f) "vulnerable person" means a person who, by reason of an impairment or insufficiency of his or her personal faculties, is not able to support him or herself.

CHAPTER II—ADMINISTRATIVE CO-OPERATION

ARTICLE 4 DESIGNATION OF CENTRAL AUTHORITIES

(1) A Contracting State shall designate a Central Authority to discharge the duties that are imposed by the Convention on such an authority.

(2) Federal States, States with more than one system of law or States having autonomous territorial units shall be free to appoint more than one Central Authority and shall specify the territorial or personal extent of their functions. Where a State has appointed more than one Central Authority, it shall designate the Central Authority to which any communication may be addressed for transmission to the appropriate Central Authority within that State.

(3) The designation of the Central Authority or Central Authorities, their contact details, and where appropriate the extent of their functions as specified in paragraph 2, shall be communicated by a Contracting State to the Permanent Bureau of the Hague Conference on Private International Law at the time when the instrument of ratification or accession is deposited or when a declaration is submitted in accordance with Article 61. Contracting States shall promptly inform the Permanent Bureau of any changes.

ARTICLE 5 GENERAL FUNCTIONS OF CENTRAL AUTHORITIES

Central Authorities shall—

(a) co-operate with each other and promote co-operation amongst the competent authorities in their States to achieve the purposes of the Convention;

(b) seek as far as possible solutions to difficulties which arise in the application of the Convention.

ARTICLE 6 SPECIFIC FUNCTIONS OF CENTRAL AUTHORITIES

(1) Central Authorities shall provide assistance in relation to applications under Chapter III. In particular they shall—

(a) transmit and receive such applications;

(b) initiate or facilitate the institution of proceedings in respect of such applications.

(2) In relation to such applications they shall take all appropriate measures—

(a) where the circumstances require, to provide or facilitate the provision of legal assistance;

(b) to help locate the debtor or the creditor;

(c) to help obtain relevant information concerning the income and, if necessary, other financial circumstances of the debtor or creditor, including the location of assets;

(d) to encourage amicable solutions with a view to obtaining voluntary payment of maintenance, where suitable by use of mediation, conciliation or similar processes;

(e) to facilitate the ongoing enforcement of maintenance decisions, including any arrears;

(f) to facilitate the collection and expeditious transfer of maintenance payments;

(g) to facilitate the obtaining of documentary or other evidence;

(h) to provide assistance in establishing parentage where necessary for the recovery of maintenance;

(i) to initiate or facilitate the institution of proceedings to obtain any necessary provisional measures that are territorial in nature and the purpose of which is to secure the outcome of a pending maintenance application;

(j) to facilitate service of documents.

(3) The functions of the Central Authority under this Article may, to the extent permitted under the law of its State, be performed by public bodies, or other bodies subject to the supervision of the competent authorities of that State. The designation of any such public bodies or other bodies, as well as their contact details and the extent of their functions, shall be communicated by a Contracting State to the Permanent Bureau of the Hague Conference on Private International Law. Contracting States shall promptly inform the Permanent Bureau of any changes.

(4) Nothing in this Article or Article 7 shall be interpreted as imposing an obligation on a Central Authority to exercise powers that can be exercised only by judicial authorities under the law of the requested State.

ARTICLE 7 REQUESTS FOR SPECIFIC MEASURES

(1) A Central Authority may make a request, supported by reasons, to another Central Authority to take appropriate specific measures under Article 6(2)(b), (c), (g), (h), (i) and (j) when no application under Article 10 is pending. The requested Central Authority shall take such measures as are appropriate if satisfied that they are necessary to assist a potential applicant in making an application under Article 10 or in determining whether such an application should be initiated.

(2) A Central Authority may also take specific measures on the request of another Central Authority in relation to a case having an international element concerning the recovery of maintenance pending in the requesting State.

ARTICLE 8 CENTRAL AUTHORITY COSTS

(1) Each Central Authority shall bear its own costs in applying this Convention.

(2) Central Authorities may not impose any charge on an applicant for the provision of their services under the Convention save for exceptional costs arising from a request for a specific measure under Article 7.

(3) The requested Central Authority may not recover the costs of the services referred to in paragraph 2 without the prior consent of the applicant to the provision of those services at such cost.

CHAPTER III—APPLICATIONS THROUGH CENTRAL AUTHORITIES

ARTICLE 9 APPLICATION THROUGH CENTRAL AUTHORITIES

An application under this Chapter shall be made through the Central Authority of the Contracting State in which the applicant resides to the Central Authority of the requested State. For the purpose of this provision, residence excludes mere presence.

ARTICLE 10 AVAILABLE APPLICATIONS

(1) The following categories of application shall be available to a creditor in a requesting State seeking to recover maintenance under this Convention—

(a) recognition or recognition and enforcement of a decision;

(b) enforcement of a decision made or recognised in the requested State;

(c) establishment of a decision in the requested State where there is no existing decision, including where necessary the establishment of parentage;

(d) establishment of a decision in the requested State where recognition and enforcement of a decision is not possible, or is refused, because of the lack of a basis for recognition and enforcement under Article 20, or on the grounds specified in Article 22 (b) or (e);

(e) modification of a decision made in the requested State;

(f) modification of a decision made in a State other than the requested State.

(2) The following categories of application shall be available to a debtor in a requesting State against whom there is an existing maintenance decision—

(a) recognition of a decision, or an equivalent procedure leading to the suspension, or limiting the enforcement, of a previous decision in the requested State;

(b) modification of a decision made in the requested State;

(c) modification of a decision made in a State other than the requested State.

(3) Save as otherwise provided in this Convention, the applications in paragraphs 1 and 2 shall be determined under the law of the requested State, and applications in paragraphs 1(c) to (f) and 2(b) and (c) shall

be subject to the jurisdictional rules applicable in the requested State.

ARTICLE 11
APPLICATION CONTENTS

(1) All applications under Article 10 shall as a minimum include—

(a) a statement of the nature of the application or applications;

(b) the name and contact details, including the address and date of birth of the applicant;

(c) the name and, if known, address and date of birth of the respondent;

(d) the name and date of birth of any person for whom maintenance is sought;

(e) the grounds upon which the application is based;

(f) in an application by a creditor, information concerning where the maintenance payment should be sent or electronically transmitted;

(g) save in an application under Article 10(1)(a) and (2)(a), any information or document specified by declaration in accordance with Article 63 by the requested State;

(h) the name and contact details of the person or unit from the Central Authority of the requesting State responsible for processing the application.

(2) As appropriate, and to the extent known, the application shall in addition in particular include—

(a) the financial circumstances of the creditor;

(b) the financial circumstances of the debtor, including the name and address of the employer of the debtor and the nature and location of the assets of the debtor;

(c) any other information that may assist with the location of the respondent.

(3) The application shall be accompanied by any necessary supporting information or documentation including documentation concerning the entitlement of the applicant to free legal assistance. In the case of applications under Article 10(1)(a) and (2)(a), the application shall be accompanied only by the documents listed in Article 25.

(4) An application under Article 10 may be made in the form recommended and published by the Hague Conference on Private International Law.

ARTICLE 12
TRANSMISSION, RECEIPT & PROCESSING OF APPLICATIONS & CASES THROUGH CENTRAL AUTHORITIES

(1) The Central Authority of the requesting State shall assist the applicant in ensuring that the application is accompanied by all the information and documents known by it to be necessary for consideration of the application.

(2) The Central Authority of the requesting State shall, when satisfied that the application complies with the requirements of the Convention, transmit the application on behalf of and with the consent of the applicant to the Central Authority of the requested State. The application shall be accompanied by the transmittal form set out in Annex 1. The Central Authority of the requesting State shall, when requested by the Central Authority of the requested State, provide a complete copy certified by the competent authority in the State of origin of any document specified under Articles 16(3), 25(1)(a), (b) and (d) and (3)(b) and 30(3).

(3) The requested Central Authority shall, within six weeks from the date of receipt of the application, acknowledge receipt in the form set out in Annex 2, and inform the Central Authority of the requesting State what initial steps have been or will be taken to deal with the application, and may request any further necessary documents and information. Within the same six-week period, the requested Central Authority shall provide to the requesting Central Authority the name and contact details of the person or unit responsible for responding to inquiries regarding the progress of the application.

(4) Within three months after the acknowledgement, the requested Central Authority shall inform the requesting Central Authority of the status of the application.

(5) Requesting and requested Central Authorities shall keep each other informed of—

(a) the person or unit responsible for a particular case;

(b) the progress of the case,

and shall provide timely responses to enquiries.

(6) Central Authorities shall process a case as quickly as a proper consideration of the issues will allow.

(7) Central Authorities shall employ the most rapid and efficient means of communication at their disposal.

(8) A requested Central Authority may refuse to process an application only if it is manifest that the requirements of the Convention are not fulfilled. In such case, that Central Authority shall promptly inform the requesting Central Authority of its reasons for refusal.

(9) The requested Central Authority may not reject an application solely on the basis that additional documents or information are needed. However, the requested Central Authority may ask the requesting Central Authority to provide these additional documents or information. If the requesting Central Authority does not do so within three months or a longer period specified by the requested Central Authority, the requested Central Authority may decide that it will no longer process the application. In this case, it shall inform the requesting Central Authority of this decision.

ARTICLE 13
MEANS OF COMMUNICATION

Any application made through Central Authorities of the Contracting States in accordance with this Chapter, and any document or information appended thereto or provided by a Central Authority, may not be challenged by the respondent by reason only of the medium or means of communication employed between the Central Authorities concerned.

ARTICLE 14
EFFECTIVE ACCESS TO PROCEDURES

(1) The requested State shall provide applicants with effective access to procedures, including enforcement and appeal procedures, arising from applications under this Chapter.

(2) To provide such effective access, the requested State shall provide free legal assistance in accordance with Articles 14 to 17 unless paragraph 3 applies.

(3) The requested State shall not be obliged to provide such free legal assistance if and to the extent that the procedures of that State enable the applicant to make the case without the need for such assistance, and the Central Authority provides such services as are necessary free of charge.

(4) Entitlements to free legal assistance shall not be less than those available in equivalent domestic cases.

(5) No security, bond or deposit, however described, shall be required to guarantee the payment of costs and expenses in proceedings under the Convention.

ARTICLE 15
FREE LEGAL ASSISTANCE FOR CHILD SUPPORT APPLICATIONS

(1) The requested State shall provide free legal assistance in respect of all applications by a creditor under this Chapter concerning maintenance obligations arising from a parent-child relationship towards a person under the age of 21 years.

(2) Notwithstanding paragraph 1, the requested State may, in relation to applications other than those under Article 10(1)(a) and (b) and the cases covered by Article 20(4), refuse free legal assistance if it considers that, on the merits, the application or any appeal is manifestly unfounded.

ARTICLE 16
DECLARATION TO PERMIT USE OF CHILD-CENTRED MEANS TEST

(1) Notwithstanding Article 15(1), a State may declare, in accordance with Article 63, that it will provide free legal assistance in respect of applications other than under Article 10(1)(a) and (b) and the cases covered by Article 20(4), subject to a test based on an assessment of the means of the child.

(2) A State shall, at the time of making such a declaration, provide information to the Permanent Bureau of the Hague Conference on Private International Law concerning the manner in which the assessment of the child's means will be carried out, including the financial criteria which would need to be met to satisfy the test.

(3) An application referred to in paragraph 1, addressed to a State which has made the declaration referred to in that paragraph, shall include a formal attestation by the applicant stating that the child's means meet the criteria referred to in paragraph 2. The requested State may only request further evidence of the child's means if it has reasonable grounds to believe that the information provided by the applicant is inaccurate.

(4) If the most favourable legal assistance provided for by the law of the requested State in respect of applications under this Chapter concerning maintenance

obligations arising from a parent-child relationship towards a child is more favourable than that provided for under paragraphs 1 to 3, the most favourable legal assistance shall be provided.

ARTICLE 17 APPLICATIONS NOT QUALIFYING UNDER ARTICLE 15 OR ARTICLE 16

In the case of all applications under this Convention other than those under Article 15 or Article 16—

(a) the provision of free legal assistance may be made subject to a means or a merits test;

(b) an applicant, who in the State of origin has benefited from free legal assistance, shall be entitled, in any proceedings for recognition or enforcement, to benefit, at least to the same extent, from free legal assistance as provided for by the law of the State addressed under the same circumstances.

CHAPTER IV—RESTRICTIONS ON BRINGING PROCEEDINGS

ARTICLE 18 LIMIT ON PROCEEDINGS

(1) Where a decision is made in a Contracting State where the creditor is habitually resident, proceedings to modify the decision or to make a new decision cannot be brought by the debtor in any other Contracting State as long as the creditor remains habitually resident in the State where the decision was made.

(2) Paragraph 1 shall not apply—

(a) where, except in disputes relating to maintenance obligations in respect of children, there is agreement in writing between the parties to the jurisdiction of that other Contracting State;

(b) where the creditor submits to the jurisdiction of that other Contracting State either expressly or by defending on the merits of the case without objecting to the jurisdiction at the first available opportunity;

(c) where the competent authority in the State of origin cannot, or refuses to, exercise jurisdiction to modify the decision or make a new decision; or

(d) where the decision made in the State of origin cannot be recognised or declared enforceable in the Contracting State where proceedings to modify the decision or make a new decision are contemplated.

CHAPTER V—RECOGNITION & ENFORCEMENT

ARTICLE 19 SCOPE OF THE CHAPTER

(1) This Chapter shall apply to a decision rendered by a judicial or administrative authority in respect of a maintenance obligation. The term "decision" also includes a settlement or agreement concluded before or approved by such an authority. A decision may include automatic adjustment by indexation and a requirement to pay arrears, retroactive maintenance or interest and a determination of costs or expenses.

(2) If a decision does not relate solely to a maintenance obligation, the effect of this Chapter is limited to the parts of the decision which concern maintenance obligations.

(3) For the purpose of paragraph 1, "administrative authority" means a public body whose decisions, under the law of the State where it is established—

(a) may be made the subject of an appeal to or review by a judicial authority; and

(b) have a similar force and effect to a decision of a judicial authority on the same matter.

(4) This Chapter also applies to maintenance arrangements in accordance with Article 30.

(5) The provisions of this Chapter shall apply to a request for recognition and enforcement made directly to a competent authority of the State addressed in accordance with Article 37.

ARTICLE 20 BASES FOR RECOGNITION & ENFORCEMENT

(1) A decision made in one Contracting State ("the State of origin") shall be recognised and enforced in other Contracting States if—

(a) the respondent was habitually resident in the State of origin at the time proceedings were instituted;

(b) the respondent has submitted to the jurisdiction either expressly or by defending on the merits of the case without objecting to the jurisdiction at the first available opportunity;

(c) the creditor was habitually resident in the State of origin at the time proceedings were instituted;

(d) the child for whom maintenance was ordered was habitually resident in the State of origin at the

time proceedings were instituted, provided that the respondent has lived with the child in that State or has resided in that State and provided support for the child there;

(e) except in disputes relating to maintenance obligations in respect of children, there has been agreement to the jurisdiction in writing by the parties; or

(f) the decision was made by an authority exercising jurisdiction on a matter of personal status or parental responsibility, unless that jurisdiction was based solely on the nationality of one of the parties.

(2) A Contracting State may make a reservation, in accordance with Article 62, in respect of paragraph 1(c), (e) or (f).

(3) A Contracting State making a reservation under paragraph 2 shall recognise and enforce a decision if its law would in similar factual circumstances confer or would have conferred jurisdiction on its authorities to make such a decision.

(4) A Contracting State shall, if recognition of a decision is not possible as a result of a reservation under paragraph 2, and if the debtor is habitually resident in that State, take all appropriate measures to establish a decision for the benefit of the creditor. The preceding sentence shall not apply to direct requests for recognition and enforcement under Article 19(5) or to claims for support referred to in Article 2(1)(b).

(5) A decision in favour of a child under the age of 18 years which cannot be recognised by virtue only of a reservation in respect of paragraph 1(c), (e) or (f) shall be accepted as establishing the eligibility of that child for maintenance in the State addressed.

(6) A decision shall be recognised only if it has effect in the State of origin, and shall be enforced only if it is enforceable in the State of origin.

ARTICLE 21
SEVERABILITY & PARTIAL RECOGNITION & ENFORCEMENT

(1) If the State addressed is unable to recognise or enforce the whole of the decision, it shall recognise or enforce any severable part of the decision which can be so recognised or enforced.

(2) Partial recognition or enforcement of a decision can always be applied for.

ARTICLE 22
GROUNDS FOR REFUSING RECOGNITION & ENFORCEMENT

Recognition and enforcement of a decision may be refused if—

(a) recognition and enforcement of the decision is manifestly incompatible with the public policy ("*ordre public*") of the State addressed;

(b) the decision was obtained by fraud in connection with a matter of procedure;

(c) proceedings between the same parties and having the same purpose are pending before an authority of the State addressed and those proceedings were the first to be instituted;

(d) the decision is incompatible with a decision rendered between the same parties and having the same purpose, either in the State addressed or in another State, provided that this latter decision fulfils the conditions necessary for its recognition and enforcement in the State addressed;

(e) in a case where the respondent has neither appeared nor was represented in proceedings in the State of origin—

(i) when the law of the State of origin provides for notice of proceedings, the respondent did not have proper notice of the proceedings and an opportunity to be heard; or

(ii) when the law of the State of origin does not provide for notice of the proceedings, the respondent did not have proper notice of the decision and an opportunity to challenge or appeal it on fact and law; or

(f) the decision was made in violation of Article 18.

ARTICLE 23
PROCEDURE ON AN APPLICATION FOR RECOGNITION & ENFORCEMENT

(1) Subject to the provisions of the Convention, the procedures for recognition and enforcement shall be governed by the law of the State addressed.

(2) Where an application for recognition and enforcement of a decision has been made through Central Authorities in accordance with Chapter III, the requested Central Authority shall promptly either—

(a) refer the application to the competent authority which shall without delay declare the decision enforceable or register the decision for enforcement; or

(b) if it is the competent authority take such steps itself.

(3) Where the request is made directly to a competent authority in the State addressed in accordance with Article 19(5), that authority shall without delay declare the decision enforceable or register the decision for enforcement.

(4) A declaration or registration may be refused only on the ground set out in Article 22(a). At this stage neither the applicant nor the respondent is entitled to make any submissions.

(5) The applicant and the respondent shall be promptly notified of the declaration or registration, made under paragraphs 2 and 3, or the refusal thereof in accordance with paragraph 4, and may bring a challenge or appeal on fact and on a point of law.

(6) A challenge or an appeal is to be lodged within 30 days of notification under paragraph 5. If the contesting party is not resident in the Contracting State in which the declaration or registration was made or refused, the challenge or appeal shall be lodged within 60 days of notification.

(7) A challenge or appeal may be founded only on the following—

(a) the grounds for refusing recognition and enforcement set out in Article 22;

(b) the bases for recognition and enforcement under Article 20;

(c) the authenticity or integrity of any document transmitted in accordance with Article 25(1)(a), (b) or (d) or (3)(b).

(8) A challenge or an appeal by a respondent may also be founded on the fulfilment of the debt to the extent that the recognition and enforcement relates to payments that fell due in the past.

(9) The applicant and the respondent shall be promptly notified of the decision following the challenge or the appeal.

(10) A further appeal, if permitted by the law of the State addressed, shall not have the effect of staying the enforcement of the decision unless there are exceptional circumstances.

(11) In taking any decision on recognition and enforcement, including any appeal, the competent authority shall act expeditiously.

ARTICLE 24
ALTERNATIVE PROCEDURE ON AN APPLICATION FOR RECOGNITION & ENFORCEMENT

(1) Notwithstanding Article 23(2) to (11), a State may declare, in accordance with Article 63, that it will apply the procedure for recognition and enforcement set out in this Article.

(2) Where an application for recognition and enforcement of a decision has been made through Central Authorities in accordance with Chapter III, the requested Central Authority shall promptly either—

(a) refer the application to the competent authority which shall decide on the application for recognition and enforcement; or

(b) if it is the competent authority, take such a decision itself.

(3) A decision on recognition and enforcement shall be given by the competent authority after the respondent has been duly and promptly notified of the proceedings and both parties have been given an adequate opportunity to be heard.

(4) The competent authority may review the grounds for refusing recognition and enforcement set out in Article 22(a), (c) and (d) of its own motion. It may review any grounds listed in Articles 20, 22 and 23(7)(c) if raised by the respondent or if concerns relating to those grounds arise from the face of the documents submitted in accordance with Article 25.

(5) A refusal of recognition and enforcement may also be founded on the fulfilment of the debt to the extent that the recognition and enforcement relates to payments that fell due in the past.

(6) Any appeal, if permitted by the law of the State addressed, shall not have the effect of staying the enforcement of the decision unless there are exceptional circumstances.

(7) In taking any decision on recognition and enforcement, including any appeal, the competent authority shall act expeditiously.

ARTICLE 25
DOCUMENTS

(1) An application for recognition and enforcement under Article 23 or Article 24 shall be accompanied by the following—

(a) a complete text of the decision;

(b) a document stating that the decision is enforceable in the State of origin and, in the case of a decision by an administrative authority, a document stating that the requirements of Article 19(3) are met unless that State has specified in accordance with Article 57 that decisions of its administrative authorities always meet those requirements;

(c) if the respondent did not appear and was not represented in the proceedings in the State of origin, a document or documents attesting, as appropriate, either that the respondent had proper notice of the proceedings and an opportunity to be heard, or that the respondent had proper notice of the decision and the opportunity to challenge or appeal it on fact and law;

(d) where necessary, a document showing the amount of any arrears and the date such amount was calculated;

(e) where necessary, in the case of a decision providing for automatic adjustment by indexation, a document providing the information necessary to make the appropriate calculations;

(f) where necessary, documentation showing the extent to which the applicant received free legal assistance in the State of origin.

(2) Upon a challenge or appeal under Article 23(7)(c) or upon request by the competent authority in the State addressed, a complete copy of the document concerned, certified by the competent authority in the State of origin, shall be provided promptly—

(a) by the Central Authority of the requesting State, where the application has been made in accordance with Chapter III;

(b) by the applicant, where the request has been made directly to a competent authority of the State addressed.

(3) A Contracting State may specify in accordance with Article 57—

(a) that a complete copy of the decision certified by the competent authority in the State of origin must accompany the application;

(b) circumstances in which it will accept, in lieu of a complete text of the decision, an abstract or extract of the decision drawn up by the competent authority of the State of origin, which may be made in the form recommended and published by the Hague Conference on Private International Law; or

(c) that it does not require a document stating that the requirements of Article 19(3) are met.

ARTICLE 26
PROCEDURE ON AN APPLICATION FOR RECOGNITION

This Chapter shall apply *mutatis mutandis* to an application for recognition of a decision, save that the requirement of enforceability is replaced by the requirement that the decision has effect in the State of origin.

ARTICLE 27
FINDINGS OF FACT

Any competent authority of the State addressed shall be bound by the findings of fact on which the authority of the State of origin based its jurisdiction.

ARTICLE 28
NO REVIEW OF THE MERITS

There shall be no review by any competent authority of the State addressed of the merits of a decision.

ARTICLE 29
PHYSICAL PRESENCE OF THE CHILD OR THE APPLICANT NOT REQUIRED

The physical presence of the child or the applicant shall not be required in any proceedings in the State addressed under this Chapter.

ARTICLE 30
MAINTENANCE ARRANGEMENTS

(1) A maintenance arrangement made in a Contracting State shall be entitled to recognition and enforcement as a decision under this Chapter provided that it is enforceable as a decision in the State of origin.

(2) For the purpose of Article 10(1)(a) and (b) and (2)(a), the term "decision" includes a maintenance arrangement.

(3) An application for recognition and enforcement of a maintenance arrangement shall be accompanied by the following—

(a) a complete text of the maintenance arrangement; and

(b) a document stating that the particular maintenance arrangement is enforceable as a decision in the State of origin.

(4) Recognition and enforcement of a maintenance arrangement may be refused if—

(a) the recognition and enforcement is manifestly incompatible with the public policy of the State addressed;

(b) the maintenance arrangement was obtained by fraud or falsification;

(c) the maintenance arrangement is incompatible with a decision rendered between the same parties and having the same purpose, either in the State addressed or in another State, provided that this latter decision fulfils the conditions necessary for its recognition and enforcement in the State addressed.

(5) The provisions of this Chapter, with the exception of Articles 20, 22, 23(7) and 25(1) and (3), shall apply *mutatis mutandis* to the recognition and enforcement of a maintenance arrangement save that—

(a) a declaration or registration in accordance with Article 23(2) and (3) may be refused only on the ground set out in paragraph 4(a);

(b) a challenge or appeal as referred to in Article 23(6) may be founded only on the following—

(i) the grounds for refusing recognition and enforcement set out in paragraph 4;

(ii) the authenticity or integrity of any document transmitted in accordance with paragraph 3;

(c) as regards the procedure under Article 24(4), the competent authority may review of its own motion the ground for refusing recognition and enforcement set out in paragraph 4(a) of this Article. It may review all grounds listed in paragraph 4 of this Article and the authenticity or integrity of any document transmitted in accordance with paragraph 3 if raised by the respondent or if concerns relating to those grounds arise from the face of those documents.

(6) Proceedings for recognition and enforcement of a maintenance arrangement shall be suspended if a challenge concerning the arrangement is pending before a competent authority of a Contracting State.

(7) A State may declare, in accordance with Article 63, that applications for recognition and enforcement of a maintenance arrangement shall only be made through Central Authorities.

(8) A Contracting State may, in accordance with Article 62, reserve the right not to recognise and enforce a maintenance arrangement.

ARTICLE 31
DECISIONS PRODUCED BY THE COMBINED EFFECT OF PROVISIONAL & CONFIRMATION ORDERS

Where a decision is produced by the combined effect of a provisional order made in one State and an order by an authority in another State ("the confirming State") confirming the provisional order—

(a) each of those States shall be deemed for the purposes of this Chapter to be a State of origin;

(b) the requirements of Article 22(e) shall be met if the respondent had proper notice of the proceedings in the confirming State and an opportunity to oppose the confirmation of the provisional order;

(c) the requirement of Article 20(6) that a decision be enforceable in the State of origin shall be met if the decision is enforceable in the confirming State; and

(d) Article 18 shall not prevent proceedings for the modification of the decision being commenced in either State.

CHAPTER VI—ENFORCEMENT BY THE STATE ADDRESSED

ARTICLE 32
ENFORCEMENT UNDER INTERNAL LAW

(1) Subject to the provisions of this Chapter, enforcement shall take place in accordance with the law of the State addressed.

(2) Enforcement shall be prompt.

(3) In the case of applications through Central Authorities, where a decision has been declared enforceable or registered for enforcement under Chapter V, enforcement shall proceed without the need for further action by the applicant.

(4) Effect shall be given to any rules applicable in the State of origin of the decision relating to the duration of the maintenance obligation.

(5) Any limitation on the period for which arrears may be enforced shall be determined either by the law of the State of origin of the decision or by the law of the State addressed, whichever provides for the longer limitation period.

ARTICLE 33 NON-DISCRIMINATION

The State addressed shall provide at least the same range of enforcement methods for cases under the Convention as are available in domestic cases.

ARTICLE 34 ENFORCEMENT MEASURES

(1) Contracting States shall make available in internal law effective measures to enforce decisions under this Convention.

(2) Such measures may include—

(a) wage withholding;

(b) garnishment from bank accounts and other sources;

(c) deductions from social security payments;

(d) lien on or forced sale of property;

(e) tax refund withholding;

(f) withholding or attachment of pension benefits;

(g) credit bureau reporting;

(h) denial, suspension or revocation of various licenses (for example, driving licenses);

(i) the use of mediation, conciliation or similar processes to bring about voluntary compliance.

ARTICLE 35 TRANSFER OF FUNDS

(1) Contracting States are encouraged to promote, including by means of international agreements, the use of the most cost-effective and efficient methods available to transfer funds payable as maintenance.

(2) A Contracting State, under whose law the transfer of funds is restricted, shall accord the highest priority to the transfer of funds payable under this Convention.

CHAPTER VII—PUBLIC BODIES

ARTICLE 36 PUBLIC BODIES AS APPLICANTS

(1) For the purposes of applications for recognition and enforcement under Article 10(1)(a) and (b) and cases covered by Article 20(4), "creditor" includes a public body acting in place of an individual to whom maintenance is owed or one to which reimbursement is owed for benefits provided in place of maintenance.

(2) The right of a public body to act in place of an individual to whom maintenance is owed or to seek reimbursement of benefits provided to the creditor in place of maintenance shall be governed by the law to which the body is subject.

(3) A public body may seek recognition or claim enforcement of—

(a) a decision rendered against a debtor on the application of a public body which claims payment of benefits provided in place of maintenance;

(b) a decision rendered between a creditor and debtor to the extent of the benefits provided to the creditor in place of maintenance.

(4) The public body seeking recognition or claiming enforcement of a decision shall upon request furnish any document necessary to establish its right under paragraph 2 and that benefits have been provided to the creditor.

CHAPTER VIII—GENERAL PROVISIONS

ARTICLE 37 DIRECT REQUESTS TO COMPETENT AUTHORITIES

(1) The Convention shall not exclude the possibility of recourse to such procedures as may be available under the internal law of a Contracting State allowing a person (an applicant) to seise directly a competent authority of that State in a matter governed by the Convention including, subject to Article 18, for the purpose of having a maintenance decision established or modified.

(2) Articles 14(5) and 17(b) and the provisions of Chapters V, VI, VII and this Chapter, with the exception of Articles 40(2), 42, 43(3), 44(3), 45 and 55, shall apply in relation to a request for recognition and enforcement made directly to a competent authority in a Contracting State.

(3) For the purpose of paragraph 2, Article 2(1)(a) shall apply to a decision granting maintenance to a vulnerable person over the age specified in that sub-paragraph where such decision was rendered before the person reached that age and provided for maintenance beyond that age by reason of the impairment.

ARTICLE 38 PROTECTION OF PERSONAL DATA

Personal data gathered or transmitted under the Convention shall be used only for the purposes for which they were gathered or transmitted.

ARTICLE 39 CONFIDENTIALITY

Any authority processing information shall ensure its confidentiality in accordance with the law of its State.

ARTICLE 40 NON-DISCLOSURE OF INFORMATION

(1) An authority shall not disclose or confirm information gathered or transmitted in application of this Convention if it determines that to do so could jeopardise the health, safety or liberty of a person.

(2) A determination to this effect made by one Central Authority shall be taken into account by another Central Authority, in particular in cases of family violence.

(3) Nothing in this Article shall impede the gathering and transmitting of information by and between authorities in so far as necessary to carry out the obligations under the Convention.

ARTICLE 41 NO LEGALISATION

No legalisation or similar formality may be required in the context of this Convention.

ARTICLE 42 POWER OF ATTORNEY

The Central Authority of the requested State may require a power of attorney from the applicant only if it acts on his or her behalf in judicial proceedings or before other authorities, or in order to designate a representative so to act.

ARTICLE 43 RECOVERY OF COSTS

(1) Recovery of any costs incurred in the application of this Convention shall not take precedence over the recovery of maintenance.

(2) A State may recover costs from an unsuccessful party.

(3) For the purposes of an application under Article 10(1)(b) to recover costs from an unsuccessful party in accordance with paragraph 2, the term "creditor" in Article 10(1) shall include a State.

(4) This Article shall be without prejudice to Article 8.

ARTICLE 44 LANGUAGE REQUIREMENTS

(1) Any application and related documents shall be in the original language, and shall be accompanied by a translation into an official language of the requested State or another language which the requested State has indicated, by way of declaration in accordance with Article 63, it will accept, unless the competent authority of that State dispenses with translation.

(2) A Contracting State which has more than one official language and cannot, for reasons of internal law, accept for the whole of its territory documents in one of those languages shall, by declaration in accordance with Article 63, specify the language in which such documents or translations thereof shall be drawn up for submission in the specified parts of its territory.

(3) Unless otherwise agreed by the Central Authorities, any other communications between such Authorities shall be in an official language of the requested State or in either English or French. However, a Contracting State may, by making a reservation in accordance with Article 62, object to the use of either English or French.

ARTICLE 45 MEANS & COSTS OF TRANSLATION

(1) In the case of applications under Chapter III, the Central Authorities may agree in an individual case or generally that the translation into an official language of the requested State may be made in the requested State from the original language or from any other agreed language. If there is no agreement and it is not possible for the requesting Central Authority to comply with the requirements of Article 44(1) and (2), then the application and related documents may be transmitted with translation into English or French for further translation into an official language of the requested State.

(2) The cost of translation arising from the application of paragraph 1 shall be borne by the requesting State unless otherwise agreed by Central Authorities of the States concerned.

(3) Notwithstanding Article 8, the requesting Central Authority may charge an applicant for the costs of translation of an application and related documents, except in so far as those costs may be covered by its system of legal assistance.

ARTICLE 46 NON-UNIFIED LEGAL SYSTEMS – INTERPRETATION

(1) In relation to a State in which two or more systems of law or sets of rules of law with regard to any matter dealt with in this Convention apply in different territorial units—

(a) any reference to the law or procedure of a State shall be construed as referring, where appropriate, to the law or procedure in force in the relevant territorial unit;

(b) any reference to a decision established, recognised, recognised and enforced, enforced or modified in that State shall be construed as referring, where appropriate, to a decision established, recognised, recognised and enforced, enforced or modified in the relevant territorial unit;

(c) any reference to a judicial or administrative authority in that State shall be construed as referring, where appropriate, to a judicial or administrative authority in the relevant territorial unit;

(d) any reference to competent authorities, public bodies, and other bodies of that State, other than Central Authorities, shall be construed as referring, where appropriate, to those authorised to act in the relevant territorial unit;

(e) any reference to residence or habitual residence in that State shall be construed as referring, where appropriate, to residence or habitual residence in the relevant territorial unit;

(f) any reference to location of assets in that State shall be construed as referring, where appropriate, to the location of assets in the relevant territorial unit;

(g) any reference to a reciprocity arrangement in force in a State shall be construed as referring, where appropriate, to a reciprocity arrangement in force in the relevant territorial unit;

(h) any reference to free legal assistance in that State shall be construed as referring, where appropriate, to free legal assistance in the relevant territorial unit;

(i) any reference to a maintenance arrangement made in a State shall be construed as referring, where appropriate, to a maintenance arrangement made in the relevant territorial unit;

(j) any reference to recovery of costs by a State shall be construed as referring, where appropriate, to the recovery of costs by the relevant territorial unit.

(2) This Article shall not apply to a Regional Economic Integration Organisation.

ARTICLE 47 NON-UNIFIED LEGAL SYSTEMS – SUBSTANTIVE RULES

(1) A Contracting State with two or more territorial units in which different systems of law apply shall not be bound to apply this Convention to situations which involve solely such different territorial units.

(2) A competent authority in a territorial unit of a Contracting State with two or more territorial units in which different systems of law apply shall not be bound to recognise or enforce a decision from another Contracting State solely because the decision has been recognised or enforced in another territorial unit of the same Contracting State under this Convention.

(3) This Article shall not apply to a Regional Economic Integration Organisation.

ARTICLE 48 CO-ORDINATION WITH PRIOR HAGUE MAINTENANCE CONVENTIONS

In relations between the Contracting States, this Convention replaces, subject to Article 56(2), the *Hague Convention of 2 October 1973 on the Recognition and Enforcement of Decisions Relating to Maintenance Obligations* and the Hague Convention of 15 April 1958 concerning the recognition and enforcement of decisions relating to maintenance obligations towards children in so far as their scope of application as between such States coincides with the scope of application of this Convention.

ARTICLE 49 CO-ORDINATION WITH THE 1956 NEW YORK CONVENTION

In relations between the Contracting States, this Convention replaces the United Nations *Convention on the Recovery Abroad of Maintenance* of 20 June 1956, in so far as its scope of application as between such States coincides with the scope of application of this Convention.

ARTICLE 50 RELATIONSHIP WITH PRIOR HAGUE CONVENTIONS ON SERVICE OF DOCUMENTS & TAKING OF EVIDENCE

This Convention does not affect the Hague Convention of 1 March 1954 on civil procedure, the *Hague Con-*

vention of 15 November 1965 on the Service Abroad of Judicial and Extrajudicial Documents in Civil or Commercial Matters and the *Hague Convention of 18 March 1970 on the Taking of Evidence Abroad in Civil or Commercial Matters*.

ARTICLE 51
CO-ORDINATION OF INSTRUMENTS & SUPPLEMENTARY AGREEMENTS

(1) This Convention does not affect any international instrument concluded before this Convention to which Contracting States are Parties and which contains provisions on matters governed by this Convention.

(2) Any Contracting State may conclude with one or more Contracting States agreements, which contain provisions on matters governed by the Convention, with a view to improving the application of the Convention between or among themselves, provided that such agreements are consistent with the objects and purpose of the Convention and do not affect, in the relationship of such States with other Contracting States, the application of the provisions of the Convention. The States which have concluded such an agreement shall transmit a copy to the depositary of the Convention.

(3) Paragraphs 1 and 2 shall also apply to reciprocity arrangements and to uniform laws based on special ties between the States concerned.

(4) This Convention shall not affect the application of instruments of a Regional Economic Integration Organisation that is a Party to this Convention, adopted after the conclusion of the Convention, on matters governed by the Convention provided that such instruments do not affect, in the relationship of Member States of the Regional Economic Integration Organisation with other Contracting States, the application of the provisions of the Convention. As concerns the recognition or enforcement of decisions as between Member States of the Regional Economic Integration Organisation, the Convention shall not affect the rules of the Regional Economic Integration Organisation, whether adopted before or after the conclusion of the Convention.

ARTICLE 52
MOST EFFECTIVE RULE

(1) This Convention shall not prevent the application of an agreement, arrangement or international instrument in force between the requesting State and the requested State, or a reciprocity arrangement in force in the requested State that provides for—

(a) broader bases for recognition of maintenance decisions, without prejudice to Article 22(f) of the Convention;

(b) simplified, more expeditious procedures on an application for recognition or recognition and enforcement of maintenance decisions;

(c) more beneficial legal assistance than that provided for under Articles 14 to 17; or

(d) procedures permitting an applicant from a requesting State to make a request directly to the Central Authority of the requested State.

(2) This Convention shall not prevent the application of a law in force in the requested State that provides for more effective rules as referred to in paragraph 1(a) to (c). However, as regards simplified, more expeditious procedures referred to in paragraph 1(b), they must be compatible with the protection offered to the parties under Articles 23 and 24, in particular as regards the rights of the parties to be duly notified of the proceedings and be given adequate opportunity to be heard and as regards the effects of any challenge or appeal.

ARTICLE 53
UNIFORM INTERPRETATION

In the interpretation of this Convention, regard shall be had to its international character and to the need to promote uniformity in its application.

ARTICLE 54
REVIEW OF PRACTICAL OPERATION OF THE CONVENTION

(1) The Secretary General of the Hague Conference on Private International Law shall at regular intervals convene a Special Commission in order to review the practical operation of the Convention and to encourage the development of good practices under the Convention.

(2) For the purpose of such review, Contracting States shall co-operate with the Permanent Bureau of the Hague Conference on Private International Law in the gathering of information, including statistics and case law, concerning the practical operation of the Convention.

ARTICLE 55
AMENDMENT OF FORMS

(1) The forms annexed to this Convention may be amended by a decision of a Special Commission con-

vened by the Secretary General of the Hague Conference on Private International Law to which all Contracting States and all Members shall be invited. Notice of the proposal to amend the forms shall be included in the agenda for the meeting.

(2) Amendments adopted by the Contracting States present at the Special Commission shall come into force for all Contracting States on the first day of the seventh calendar month after the date of their communication by the depositary to all Contracting States.

(3) During the period provided for in paragraph 2 any Contracting State may by notification in writing to the depositary make a reservation, in accordance with Article 62, with respect to the amendment. The State making such reservation shall, until the reservation is withdrawn, be treated as a State not Party to the present Convention with respect to that amendment.

ARTICLE 56
TRANSITIONAL PROVISIONS

(1) The Convention shall apply in every case where—

(a) a request pursuant to Article 7 or an application pursuant to Chapter III has been received by the Central Authority of the requested State after the Convention has entered into force between the requesting State and the requested State;

(b) a direct request for recognition and enforcement has been received by the competent authority of the State addressed after the Convention has entered into force between the State of origin and the State addressed.

(2) With regard to the recognition and enforcement of decisions between Contracting States to this Convention that are also Parties to either of the Hague Maintenance Conventions mentioned in Article 48, if the conditions for the recognition and enforcement under this Convention prevent the recognition and enforcement of a decision given in the State of origin before the entry into force of this Convention for that State, that would otherwise have been recognised and enforced under the terms of the Convention that was in effect at the time the decision was rendered, the conditions of that Convention shall apply.

(3) The State addressed shall not be bound under this Convention to enforce a decision or a maintenance arrangement, in respect of payments falling due prior to the entry into force of the Convention between the State of origin and the State addressed, except for maintenance obligations arising from a parent-child relationship towards a person under the age of 21 years.

ARTICLE 57
PROVISION OF INFORMATION CONCERNING LAWS, PROCEDURES & SERVICES

(1) A Contracting State, by the time its instrument of ratification or accession is deposited or a declaration is submitted in accordance with Article 61 of the Convention, shall provide the Permanent Bureau of the Hague Conference on Private International Law with—

(a) a description of its laws and procedures concerning maintenance obligations;

(b) a description of the measures it will take to meet the obligations under Article 6;

(c) a description of how it will provide applicants with effective access to procedures, as required under Article 14;

(d) a description of its enforcement rules and procedures, including any limitations on enforcement, in particular debtor protection rules and limitation periods;

(e) any specification referred to in Article 25(1)(b) and (3).

(2) Contracting States may, in fulfilling their obligations under paragraph 1, utilise a country profile form recommended and published by the Hague Conference on Private International Law.

(3) Information shall be kept up to date by the Contracting States.

CHAPTER IX—FINAL PROVISIONS

ARTICLE 58
SIGNATURE, RATIFICATION & ACCESSION

(1) The Convention shall be open for signature by the States which were Members of the Hague Conference on Private International Law at the time of its Twenty-First Session and by the other States which participated in that Session.

(2) It shall be ratified, accepted or approved and the instruments of ratification, acceptance or approval shall be deposited with the Ministry of Foreign Affairs of the Kingdom of the Netherlands, depositary of the Convention.

(3) Any other State or Regional Economic Integration Organisation may accede to the Convention after it has entered into force in accordance with Article 60(1).

(4) The instrument of accession shall be deposited with the depositary.

(5) Such accession shall have effect only as regards the relations between the acceding State and those Contracting States which have not raised an objection to its accession in the 12 months after the date of the notification referred to in Article 65. Such an objection may also be raised by States at the time when they ratify, accept or approve the Convention after an accession. Any such objection shall be notified to the depositary.

ARTICLE 59
REGIONAL ECONOMIC INTEGRATION ORGANISATIONS

(1) A Regional Economic Integration Organisation which is constituted solely by sovereign States and has competence over some or all of the matters governed by this Convention may similarly sign, accept, approve or accede to this Convention. The Regional Economic Integration Organisation shall in that case have the rights and obligations of a Contracting State, to the extent that the Organisation has competence over matters governed by the Convention.

(2) The Regional Economic Integration Organisation shall, at the time of signature, acceptance, approval or accession, notify the depositary in writing of the matters governed by this Convention in respect of which competence has been transferred to that Organisation by its Member States. The Organisation shall promptly notify the depositary in writing of any changes to its competence as specified in the most recent notice given under this paragraph.

(3) At the time of signature, acceptance, approval or accession, a Regional Economic Integration Organisation may declare in accordance with Article 63 that it exercises competence over all the matters governed by this Convention and that the Member States which have transferred competence to the Regional Economic Integration Organisation in respect of the matter in question shall be bound by this Convention by virtue of the signature, acceptance, approval or accession of the Organisation.

(4) For the purposes of the entry into force of this Convention, any instrument deposited by a Regional Economic Integration Organisation shall not be counted unless the Regional Economic Integration Organisation makes a declaration in accordance with paragraph 3.

(5) Any reference to a "Contracting State" or "State" in this Convention shall apply equally to a Regional Economic Integration Organisation that is a Party to it, where appropriate. In the event that a declaration is made by a Regional Economic Integration Organisation in accordance with paragraph 3, any reference to a "Contracting State" or "State" in this Convention shall apply equally to the relevant Member States of the Organisation, where appropriate.

ARTICLE 60
ENTRY INTO FORCE

(1) The Convention shall enter into force on the first day of the month following the expiration of three months after the deposit of the second instrument of ratification, acceptance or approval referred to in Article 58.

(2) Thereafter the Convention shall enter into force—

(a) for each State or Regional Economic Integration Organisation referred to in Article 59(1) subsequently ratifying, accepting or approving it, on the first day of the month following the expiration of three months after the deposit of its instrument of ratification, acceptance or approval;

(b) for each State or Regional Economic Integration Organisation referred to in Article 58(3) on the day after the end of the period during which objections may be raised in accordance with Article 58(5);

(c) for a territorial unit to which the Convention has been extended in accordance with Article 61, on the first day of the month following the expiration of three months after the notification referred to in that Article.

ARTICLE 61
DECLARATIONS WITH RESPECT TO NON-UNIFIED LEGAL SYSTEMS

(1) If a State has two or more territorial units in which different systems of law are applicable in relation to matters dealt with in the Convention, it may at the time of signature, ratification, acceptance, approval or accession declare in accordance with Article 63 that this Convention shall extend to all its territorial units or only to one or more of them and may modify this declaration by submitting another declaration at any time.

(2) Any such declaration shall be notified to the depositary and shall state expressly the territorial units to which the Convention applies.

(3) If a State makes no declaration under this Article, the Convention shall extend to all territorial units of that State.

(4) This Article shall not apply to a Regional Economic Integration Organisation.

ARTICLE 62 RESERVATIONS

(1) Any Contracting State may, not later than the time of ratification, acceptance, approval or accession, or at the time of making a declaration in terms of Article 61, make one or more of the reservations provided for in Articles 2(2), 20(2), 30(8), 44(3) and 55(3). No other reservation shall be permitted.

(2) Any State may at any time withdraw a reservation it has made. The withdrawal shall be notified to the depositary.

(3) The reservation shall cease to have effect on the first day of the third calendar month after the notification referred to in paragraph 2.

(4) Reservations under this Article shall have no reciprocal effect with the exception of the reservation provided for in Article 2(2).

ARTICLE 63 DECLARATIONS

(1) Declarations referred to in Articles 2(3), 11(1)(g), 16(1), 24(1), 30(7), 44(1) and (2), 59(3) and 61(1), may be made upon signature, ratification, acceptance, approval or accession or at any time thereafter, and may be modified or withdrawn at any time.

(2) Declarations, modifications and withdrawals shall be notified to the depositary.

(3) A declaration made at the time of signature, ratification, acceptance, approval or accession shall take effect simultaneously with the entry into force of this Convention for the State concerned.

(4) A declaration made at a subsequent time, and any modification or withdrawal of a declaration, shall take effect on the first day of the month following the expiration of three months after the date on which the notification is received by the depositary.

ARTICLE 64 DENUNCIATION

(1) A Contracting State to the Convention may denounce it by a notification in writing addressed to the depositary. The denunciation may be limited to certain territorial units of a multi-unit State to which the Convention applies.

(2) The denunciation shall take effect on the first day of the month following the expiration of 12 months after the date on which the notification is received by the depositary. Where a longer period for the denunciation to take effect is specified in the notification, the denunciation shall take effect upon the expiration of such longer period after the date on which the notification is received by the depositary.

ARTICLE 65 NOTIFICATION

The depositary shall notify the Members of the Hague Conference on Private International Law, and other States and Regional Economic Integration Organisations which have signed, ratified, accepted, approved or acceded in accordance with Articles 58 and 59 of the following—

(a) the signatures, ratifications, acceptances and approvals referred to in Articles 58 and 59;

(b) the accessions and objections raised to accessions referred to in Articles 58(3) and (5) and 59;

(c) the date on which the Convention enters into force in accordance with Article 60;

(d) the declarations referred to in Articles 2(3), 11(1)(g), 16(1), 24(1), 30(7), 44(1) and (2), 59(3) and 61(1);

(e) the agreements referred to in Article 51(2);

(f) the reservations referred to in Articles 2(2), 20(2), 30(8), 44(3) and 55(3), and the withdrawals referred to in Article 62(2);

(g) the denunciations referred to in Article 64.

In witness whereof the undersigned, being duly authorised thereto, have signed this Convention.

Done at The Hague, on the 23rd day of November 2007, in the English and French languages, both texts being equally authentic, in a single copy which shall be deposited in the archives of the Government of the Kingdom of the Netherlands, and of which a certified copy shall be sent, through diplomatic channels, to each of the Members of the Hague Conference on Private International Law at the date of its Twenty-First Session and to each of the other States which have participated in that Session.

RULES FOR A JUDICIAL BYPASS OF PARENTAL NOTICE & CONSENT UNDER CHAPTER 33 OF THE FAMILY CODE

RULES FOR A JUDICIAL BYPASS OF PARENTAL NOTICE & CONSENT UNDER CHAPTER 33 OF THE FAMILY CODE

Effective Jan. 1, 2016.

***Editor's note:** Judicial bypass forms referenced in the rules below are not included in this edition. Copies of these forms can be found at www.txcourts.gov/rules-forms/rules-standards.aspx.*

Explanatory Statement

Chapter 33 of the Texas Family Code provides for judicial authorization of an unemancipated minor to consent to an abortion in Texas without notice to, or the consent of, a parent, managing conservator, or guardian. Sections 33.003 and 33.004, which govern proceedings in the trial and appellate courts, authorize the Court to make rules to ensure that judicial bypass applications are decided confidentially and promptly. *See* Tex. Fam. Code §§33.003(*l*), 33.004(c). The statute also directs the Court to make forms for use in judicial bypass proceedings. *Id.* §§33.003(m), 33.004(d).

The Court approved the first set of rules and forms in 1999, following the enactment of Chapter 33. See Misc. Docket No. 99-9247 (Dec. 22, 1999); Act of May 25, 1999, 76th Leg., R.S., ch. 395, 1999 Tex. Gen. Laws 2466 (S.B. 30) (codified at Tex. Fam. Code §33.001 et seq.). The rules and forms have been amended to reflect the 2015 amendments to Chapter 33. *See* Act of June 1, 2015, 84th Leg., R.S., ch. 436 (H.B. 3994). The rules and forms track the statutory requirements. They do not reflect any judgment by the Court that Chapter 33, or any part of it, is constitutional. Constitutional questions should be resolved in an adversarial proceeding with full briefing and argument. Nor do the rules imply that abortion is—or is not—permitted in any specific situation. *See, e.g.*, ***Roe v. Wade***, 410 U.S. 113 (1973); Tex. Health & Safety Code §170.002 (restrictions on third trimester abortions of viable fetuses).

The notes and comments appended to the rules are intended to inform their construction and application by courts and practitioners.

RULE 1. GENERAL PROVISIONS

1.1 Applicability of These Rules. These rules govern proceedings for obtaining a court order authorizing a minor to consent to an abortion without notice to, or the consent of, a parent, managing conservator, or guardian under Chapter 33, Family Code. All references in these rules to "minor" refer to the minor applicant. Other Texas court rules—including the Rules of Civil Procedure, Rules of Evidence, Rules of Appellate Procedure, Rules of Judicial Administration, and local rules approved by the Supreme Court—also apply, but when the application of another rule would be inconsistent with the general framework or policy of Chapter 33, Family Code, or these rules, these rules control.

1.2 Expedition Required.

(a) ***Proceedings.*** A court must give proceedings under these rules precedence over all other pending matters to the extent necessary to ensure that applications and appeals are adjudicated as soon as possible and within the time required by Chapter 33, Family Code, and these rules.

(b) ***Prompt actual notice required.*** Without compromising the confidentiality required by statute and these rules, courts and clerks must serve orders, decisions, findings, and notices required under these rules in a manner designed to give prompt actual notice in order that the deadlines imposed by Chapter 33, Family Code, can be met.

1.3 Identity of Minor Protected.

(a) ***Generally.*** Proceedings under these rules must be conducted in a way that protects the confidentiality of the identity of the minor.

(b) ***No reference to minor's identity in proceeding.*** With the exception of the verification page required under Rule 2.1(c)(2) and the communications required under Rule 2.2(e), no reference may be made in any order, decision, finding, or notice, or on the record, to the name of the minor, her address, or other information by which she might be identified by persons not participating in the proceedings. Instead, the minor must be referred to as "Jane Doe" in a numbered cause.

(c) ***Notice.*** With the exception of orders and rulings released under Rule 1.4(b), all notices and communications from the court to the minor must be directed to the minor's attorney with a copy to the guardian ad litem. The minor's attorney must immediately serve on the guardian ad litem a copy of any document filed with the court. These requirements take effect when an attorney appears for the minor or when the clerk has notified the minor of the appointment of an attorney or a guardian ad litem.

1.4 Confidentiality of Proceedings Required; Exceptions.

(a) ***Generally.*** All officials and court personnel involved in the proceedings must ensure that the minor's contact with the clerk and the court is confidential and expeditious. Except as permitted by law, officials and court personnel must never disclose to anyone outside the proceeding—including the minor's parent, managing conservator, or legal guardian—that the minor is or

has ever been pregnant, or that she wants or has ever wanted an abortion.

(b) *Documents and information pertaining to the proceeding.*

(1) *General rule; disclosure prohibited.* As required by Chapter 33, Family Code, the application and all other court documents and information pertaining to the proceedings are confidential and privileged and are not subject to disclosure under Chapter 552, Government Code, or to discovery, subpoena, or other legal process.

(2) *Exception; disclosure to minor permitted.* The application and any other document in the court file may be disclosed to the minor.

(3) *Exception; disclosure of order to certain persons.* An order, ruling, opinion, or clerk's certificate may be released to:

- the minor;
- the minor's guardian ad litem;
- the minor's attorney;
- the physician who is to perform the abortion;
- a person designated in writing by the minor to receive the order, ruling, opinion, or certificate;
- a governmental agency or governmental attorney, in connection with a criminal or administrative action seeking to assert or protect the minor's interests; or
- another court, judge, or clerk in the same or related proceedings.

(c) *Filing of court reporter's notes required.* To ensure confidentiality, the court reporter's notes, in whatever form, must be filed with other court documents in the proceeding.

(d) *Duty to report possible abuse.*

(1) *Duty of the court.* A judge or justice who, as a result of a court proceeding governed by these rules, has reason to believe that a minor has been or may be physically or sexually abused must report the suspected abuse in accordance with Sections 33.0085 and 33.009, Family Code, and other law.

(2) *Duty of an attorney or guardian ad litem.* An attorney or a guardian ad litem who, as a result of a court proceeding governed by these rules, has reason to believe that a minor has been or may be physically or sexually abused must report the suspected abuse in accordance with Section 33.009, Family Code, and other law.

(e) *Department of Family and Protective Services or local law enforcement agency to disclose certain information in proceeding.* The Department of Family and Protective Services or a local law enforcement agency may disclose to the court, the minor's attorney, and the guardian ad litem any information obtained under Sections 33.008, 33.0085, and 33.009, Family Code, without being ordered to do so. The court may order the Department or a local law enforcement agency to disclose the information to the court, the minor's attorney, and the guardian ad litem, and the Department or agency must comply.

1.5 Methods of Transmitting Documents; Hearings Conducted By Remote Electronic Means; Electronic Record Allowed When Necessary.

(a) *Electronic filing through statewide portal prohibited.* Documents must not be filed through the electronic filing manager established by the Office of Court Administration.

(b) *Paper, fax, or email filing permitted.* Documents may be filed in paper form, by fax, or by email. The clerk of a court must designate an email address or a fax number for the filing of documents in proceedings governed by these rules and must take all reasonable steps to maintain the confidentiality of the filings. An attorney must notify the clerk by telephone before filing a document by email or fax.

(c) *Fax and email transmission by court and clerk.* The court and clerk may transmit orders, rulings, notices, and other documents by fax or email. But before the transmission is initiated, the sender must take all reasonable steps to maintain the confidentiality of the transmission. The time and date of a transmission by the court is the time and date when it was initiated.

(d) *Participation in hearings by electronic means.* Consistent with the confidentiality requirements of these rules, with the court's permission, a witness may participate in a hearing under these rules by video conferencing, telephone, or other remote electronic means. But the minor must appear before the court in person.

(e) *Record of hearing made by electronic means if necessary.* If the court determines that a court reporter is unavailable for a hearing, the court may have a record of the hearing made by audio recording or other electronic means. If a notice of appeal is filed, the court must have the recording transcribed if possible. The person transcribing the recording must

certify to the accuracy of the transcription. The court must transmit both the recording and the transcription to the court of appeals.

1.6 Disqualification, Recusal, or Objection to a Judge.

(a) ***Time for filing and ruling.*** A motion to recuse or disqualify a trial judge or an objection to a trial judge under Section 74.053, Government Code, must be filed before 10 a.m. of the first business day after an application is filed or promptly after the assignment of a judge to hear the case is made known to the minor's attorney, whichever is later. A motion to recuse or disqualify an appellate judge or an objection to an appellate judge under Section 75.551, Government Code, must be filed before 10 a.m. of the first business day after a notice of appeal is filed or promptly after the assignment of a judge is made known to the minor's attorney, whichever is later. A judge who chooses to withdraw voluntarily must do so immediately. A motion to disqualify or recuse or an objection to an assigned judge does not extend the deadline for ruling on the minor's application.

(b) ***Voluntary disqualification or recusal; objection.*** A judge who removes himself or herself voluntarily—whether in response to a motion or on the judge's own initiative—or to whom objection is made under Sections 74.053 or 75.551, Government Code, must immediately notify the appropriate authority under rule or statute for assigning another judge. That authority must immediately assign a judge or justice to the proceeding.

(c) ***Involuntary disqualification or recusal.*** A judge who refuses to remove himself or herself voluntarily from a proceeding in response to a motion must immediately refer the motion to the appropriate judge under rule or statute for determination. The judge to whom the motion is referred must rule on it as soon as possible and may do so with or without a hearing. If the motion is granted, the judge to whom the motion was referred must immediately assign another judge to the proceeding.

(d) ***Restrictions on the number of motions and objections.*** A minor who objects under Section 74.053 or Section 75.551, Government Code, to a judge assigned to the proceeding may not thereafter file a motion to recuse the judge assigned to replace the judge to whom the objection was made. A minor who files a motion to recuse or disqualify a judge may not thereafter object under Section 74.053 or Section 75.551, Government Code, to another judge assigned to the proceeding.

(e) ***Issues on appeal.*** Any error in the denial of a motion to recuse or disqualify, any error in the disallowance of an objection, or any challenge to a judge that a minor is precluded from making by subsections (a) or (d), may be raised only on appeal from the court's denial of the application.

1.7 Rules and Forms to be Made Available.

(a) ***Online.*** A complete set of these rules and forms must be posted on the Texas Judiciary website at www.txcourts.gov. Forms 1A, 2A, and 2B must be translated into Spanish.

(b) ***In clerks' offices.*** The clerk of a court in which an application or appeal may be filed must make the rules and forms—including the Spanish version of Form 1A, 2A, and 2B—and any applicable local rules available to a minor without charge.

1.8 Duties of Attorneys Ad Litem. An attorney ad litem must represent the minor in the trial court in the proceeding in which the attorney is assigned and in any appeal under these rules to the court of appeals or the Supreme Court. But an attorney ad litem is not required to represent the minor in any other court or any other proceeding.

1.9 Fees and Costs.

(a) ***No fees or costs charged to minor.*** No filing fee or court cost may be assessed against a minor for any proceeding in a trial or appellate court.

(b) ***State ordered to pay fees and costs.***

(1) *Fees and costs that may be paid.* The State may be ordered to pay the reasonable and necessary fees and expenses of the attorney ad litem, the reasonable and necessary fees and expenses of the guardian ad litem, the court reporter's fee as certified by the court reporter, and trial court filing fees and costs as certified by the clerk. Court costs include the expenses of an interpreter (Form 2H) and an evaluation by a licensed mental health counselor but do not include the fees or expenses of a witness. Court costs do not include fees that must be remitted to the state treasury.

(2) *To whom order directed and sent.* The order must be directed to the Comptroller of Public Accounts and sent to the Director, Fiscal Division, of the Texas Department of Health.

(3) *Form and contents of the order.* The order must state the amounts to be awarded the attorney ad litem

and the guardian ad litem. The order must be separate from any other order in the proceeding and must not address any subject other than the assessment of fees, expenses, and costs. A trial court may use Forms 2F and 2G, but it is not required to do so.

(4) *Time for signing and sending order.* The order must be signed by the judge and sent by the clerk to the Department of Health not later than the ninetieth day after the date of the final ruling in a proceeding.

(c) ***Motion to reconsider; time for filing.*** Within thirty days of actual receipt of the order, the Comptroller or any other person adversely affected by the order may file a motion in the trial court to reconsider the assessment of fees, expenses, or costs. The trial court retains jurisdiction of the case to hear and determine any timely filed motion to reconsider.

(d) ***Appeal.*** The Comptroller or any other person adversely affected by the order may appeal from the trial court's ruling on the motion to reconsider as from any other final judgment of the court.

(e) ***Report to the Office of Court Administration.*** The Department of Health must transmit to the Office of Court Administration a copy of every order assessing fees, expenses, or costs in a proceeding under Chapter 33, Family Code. Orders assessing fees, expenses, or costs are not subject to any order of the Supreme Court of Texas requiring mandatory reports of judicial appointments and fees or to the reporting requirements of Chapter 36, Government Code.

(f) ***Confidentiality.*** When transmitting an order awarding costs to the Department of Health, the clerk must take reasonable steps to preserve its confidentiality. The confidentiality of an order awarding costs—as prescribed by Chapter 33, Family Code—is not affected by its transmission to the Comptroller, Texas Department of Health, or the Office of Court Administration, nor is the order subject to public disclosure in response to a request under any statute, rule, or other law. But these rules do not preclude the Comptroller, the Texas Department of Health, or the Office of Court Administration from disclosing summary information from orders assessing costs for statistical or other such purposes.

1.10 Amicus Briefs. Amicus briefs may be submitted and received by a court—but not filed—under either of the following procedures.

(a) ***Confidential, case-specific briefs.*** A nonparty who is authorized to attend or participate in a particular proceeding under Chapter 33, Family Code, may submit an amicus brief addressing matters, including confidential matters, specific to the proceeding. The brief and the manner in which it is submitted must comply with Rules 1.3 and 1.4 and be directed to the court in which the proceeding is pending. If the brief is filed in paper form, the person must submit the original brief and the same number of copies required for other paper submissions to the court. The person must serve a copy of the brief on the minor's attorney and guardian ad litem. The court to which the brief is submitted must maintain the brief as part of the confidential case file in accordance with Rule 1.4.

(b) ***Public or general briefs.*** Any person may submit a brief addressing any matter relating to proceedings under Chapter 33, Family Code. The brief must not contain any information in violation of Rules 1.3 and 1.4. If the brief is filed in paper form, the person must submit the original brief and the same number of copies required for other paper submissions to the court. If the brief is submitted to a court of appeals, one copy of the brief must also be submitted to the Supreme Court of Texas. Upon receipt of an amicus brief submitted under this subsection, the Clerk of the Supreme Court must, as soon as practicable, have the brief posted on the Texas Judiciary website.

Notes & Comments

1. Rule 1.1 contemplates that other court rules of procedure and administration remain as a "default" governing matters not addressed in these rules. Thus, for example, these rules do not state a deadline for filing notices of appeal, so the ordinary 30-day deadline controls, *see* Tex. R. App. P. 26.1, but these rules control over inconsistent provisions in the appellate rules governing the docketing statement, the record, and briefing.

2. Rule 1.1 also contemplates that individual jurisdictions may enact local rules pursuant to Tex. R. Civ. P. 3a, Tex. R. App. P. 1.2, or Tex. R. Jud. Admin. 10, to the extent consistent with Chapter 33, Family Code, and with these rules, to tailor the implementation of the statute and these rules to local needs and preferences. Local rules may address, for example, the specific location or office where applications are to be filed, how applications are to be assigned for hearing, and whether an appellate court will permit or require briefing or oral argument. *See also* Rule 2, Comment 1.

3. Any judge involved in a proceeding—whether as the judge assigned to hear and decide the application; the judge assigned to hear and decide any disqualification, recusal, or objection; a judge authorized to transfer the application or assign another judge to it; or an appellate judge—may have access to all information (including the verification page) in the proceeding or any related proceeding, such as a prior filing by the minor. Similarly, a minor's attorney and guardian ad litem must, of course, have access to the case file to the extent necessary to perform their respective duties.

4. Sections 33.008, 33.0085, and 33.009, Family Code, require physicians, judges, attorneys, and guardians ad litem to report suspected physical or sexual abuse to the Texas Department of Family and Protective Services and to a local law enforcement agency. Section 33.010 makes confidential—"[n]otwithstanding any other law"—all information obtained by the Department or a law enforcement agency under Sections 33.008, 33.0085, and 33.009 except to the

extent necessary to prove certain criminal conduct. Rule 1.4(e) construes Section 33.010 in harmony with Section 33.003(i-2), which makes past or potential future abuse relevant to a claim that notifying or attempting to obtain the consent of a parent, managing conservator, or guardian would not be in the minor's best interest.

5. Rule 1.6 controls to the extent that it conflicts with other provisions regarding the disqualification or recusal of judges, such as Tex. R. Civ. P. 18a, Tex. R. App. P. 16, and Tex. Gov't Code 25.00255.

6. The archival requirements relating to proceedings under Chapter 33, Family Code, and these rules is governed by Sections 441.158 and 441.185, Government Code, and the schedules promulgated by the Texas State Library and Archives Commission pursuant to those authorities.

7. Orders awarding fees, expenses, and costs contain information that is made confidential by Chapter 33, Family Code. The confidentiality of the information should not be affected by the transmission of the order to the Texas Department of Health and to the Comptroller, which is necessary to effectuate payment, or to the Office of Court Administration, which is necessary to oversee the costs associated with the proceedings. Rule 1.9(f) does not preclude either the Comptroller, the Texas Department of Health, or the Office of Court Administration from disclosing total amounts paid for all proceedings, the average amount awarded per proceeding, or other statistical summaries or analyses that do not impair the confidentiality of the proceedings.

8. Rule 1.10 adds a procedure for filing amicus curiae briefs uniquely designed for the expedited and confidential nature of judicial bypass cases.

RULE 2. PROCEEDINGS IN THE TRIAL COURT

2.1 Where to File an Application; Court Assignment and Transfer; Application Form; Effect of a Nonsuit or Prior Determination.

(a) ***Counties in which an application may be filed.*** An application for an order under Section 33.003, Family Code, must be filed in the minor's county of residence, unless one of the following exceptions applies.

(1) *Minor's parent is a presiding judge.* If the minor's parent, managing conservator, or guardian is a presiding judge of a court described in (b)(1) in the county of the minor's residence, the application must be filed in:

(A) a contiguous county; or

(B) the county where the minor intends to obtain the abortion.

(2) *Residence in a county with a population of less than 10,000.* If the minor's county of residence has a population of less than 10,000, the application must be filed in:

(A) the minor's county of residence;

(B) a contiguous county; or

(C) the county where the minor intends to obtain the abortion.

(3) *Nonresident minor.* If the minor is not a Texas resident, the application must be filed in the county where the minor intends to obtain the abortion.

(b) ***Courts in which an application may be filed; assignment and transfer.***

(1) *Courts with jurisdiction.* An application may be filed in a district court (including a family district court), a county court at law, or a court having probate jurisdiction.

(2) *Application filed with district or county clerk.* An application must be filed with either the district clerk or the county clerk, who will assign the application to a court as provided by local rule or these rules. The clerk to whom the application is tendered cannot refuse to accept it because of any local rule or other rule or law that governs the filing and assignment of applications or cases. The clerk must accept the application and transfer it immediately to the proper clerk, advising the person tendering the application where it is being transferred.

(3) *Court assignment and transfer by local rule.* The courts in a county that have jurisdiction to hear applications may determine by local rule how applications will be assigned between or among them. A local rule must be approved by the Supreme Court under Rule 3a, Texas Rules of Civil Procedure.

(4) *Initial court assignment if no local rule.* Absent a local rule, the clerk who files an application—whether the district clerk or the county clerk—must assign it as follows:

(A) to a district court, if the active judge of the court, or a judge assigned to it, is available;

(B) if the application cannot be assigned under (A), then to a statutory county or probate court, if the active judge of the court, or a judge assigned to it, is available;

(C) if the application cannot be assigned under (A) or (B), then to the constitutional county court, if it has probate jurisdiction, and if the active judge of the court, or a judge assigned to it, is available;

(D) if the application cannot be assigned under (A), (B), or (C), then to the district court.

(5) *Judges who may hear and determine applications.* An application may be heard and determined by the active judge of the court to which the application is assigned, by any judge authorized to sit for the active judge, or by any judge who may be assigned to the court in which the application is pending. An application may not be heard or determined, or any proceedings under these rules conducted, by a master or magistrate.

(c) *Application form.* An application consists of two pages—a cover page and a separate verification page—if the minor is not represented by an attorney at the time of filing. If the minor is represented by an attorney at the time of filing, the application must include a third page, the attorney's sworn statement or declaration made under penalty of perjury.

(1) *Cover page.* The cover page may be submitted on Form 2A, but use of the form is not required. The cover page must be styled "In re Jane Doe" and must not disclose the name of the minor or any information from which the minor's identity could be derived. The cover page must state:

(A) that the minor is pregnant;

(B) that the minor is unmarried, is under 18 years of age, and has not had her disabilities removed under Chapter 31, Family Code;

(C) that the minor wishes to have an abortion without notifying or obtaining consent from either of her parents or a managing conservator or guardian, and the statutory ground or grounds on which she relies;

(D) that venue is proper in the county in which the application has been filed;

(E) whether the minor has retained an attorney, and if so, the attorney's name, email address, mailing address, and telephone number;

(F) whether the minor requests the court to appoint a particular person as her guardian ad litem; and

(G) that, concerning her current pregnancy, the minor has not previously filed an application that was denied; or

(H) if the minor has filed a previous application with respect to the current pregnancy that was denied, that this application is being filed in the same court that denied the previous application and that there has been a material change in circumstances since the time the previous application was denied.

(2) *Verification page.* The verification page may be submitted on Form 2B, but use of the form is not required. The verification page must be separate from the cover page, must be signed by the minor under oath or under penalty of perjury, and must state:

(A) the minor's full name, date of birth, physical address, mailing address, and telephone number;

(B) the name, address, telephone number, and relationship to the minor of any person the minor requests the court to appoint as her guardian ad litem;

(C) if the minor has not retained an attorney, a telephone number—whether that of the minor or someone else (such as a physician, friend, or relative)—at which the minor may be contacted immediately and confidentially until an attorney is appointed to represent her; and

(D) that all information contained in the application, including both the cover page and the verification page, is true.

(3) *Attorney's statement.* The minor's attorney must file with the application a sworn statement or unsworn declaration made under penalty of perjury that attests to the truth of the minor's claims regarding venue and prior applications.

(d) *Time of filing.* An application is filed when it is actually received by the district or county clerk.

(e) *Nonsuit requires permission.* A minor may not withdraw or nonsuit an application without permission of the court.

(f) *Res judicata effect of prior determination.*

(1) *General rule.* A minor who has filed an application and obtained a determination by the court under Rule 2.5 may not initiate a new application proceeding with respect to the same pregnancy, and the prior determination is res judicata on the issue whether the minor may consent to an abortion without notification to, or consent of, a parent, managing conservator, or guardian.

(2) *Exception for material change in circumstances.* A minor whose application is denied may submit a new application to the court that denied the application if the minor shows that there has been a material change in circumstances since the prior application was denied.

2.2 Clerk's Duties.

(a) *Assistance in filing.* The clerk must give prompt assistance—in a manner designed to protect the minor's confidentiality—to persons seeking to file an application. If requested, the clerk must administer the oath for the verification page or provide a person authorized to do so. The clerk must also redact from the cover page any information identifying the minor. The clerk must ensure that both the cover page and the separate verification page are completed in full.

(b) *Filing procedure.* The clerk must assign the application a cause number that does not identify the assigned judge and affix it to both the cover page and the verification page. The clerk must then provide a

certified copy of the verification page to the person filing the application. The clerk must file the verification page under seal in a secure place where access is limited to essential court personnel.

(c) ***Distribution.*** When an application is filed, the clerk must distribute the cover page and verification page, or a copy of them, to the appropriate court immediately. If appointment of a specific person as guardian ad litem has been requested, the clerk must also communicate the information to the appropriate court immediately.

(d) ***If judge of assigned court not available.*** The clerk must determine immediately whether the judge of the court to which the application is assigned is available to hear the application within the prescribed time period. If that judge is not available, the clerk must immediately notify the local administrative judge or judges and the presiding judge of the administrative judicial region and must send them any information requested, including the cover page and verification page.

(e) ***Notice of hearing and appointments.*** When the clerk is advised by the court of a time for the hearing or of the appointment of a guardian ad litem or an attorney ad litem, the clerk must immediately give notice—as directed in the verification page and to each appointee of the hearing time or appointment. A court coordinator or other court personnel may give notice instead of the clerk.

(f) ***Orders.*** The clerk must provide the minor's attorney and the guardian ad litem with copies of all court orders, including findings of fact and conclusions of law.

(g) ***Certificate of court's failure to rule within time prescribed by statute.*** If the court fails to rule on an application within the time required by Section 33.003(h), Family Code, then, upon the minor's request, the clerk must immediately issue a certificate to that effect, stating that the application is deemed to be denied. The clerk may use Form 2E but is not required to do so.

2.3 Court's Duties. Upon receipt of an application from the clerk, the court must promptly:

(a) appoint a qualified person to serve as guardian ad litem for the minor applicant;

(b) unless the minor has a retained attorney, appoint an attorney ad litem for the minor, who must not be the same person appointed as guardian ad litem;

(c) set a hearing on the application; and

(d) advise the clerk of the appointments and the hearing time.

2.4 Hearing.

(a) ***Time.***

(1) *General rule.* The court must conduct a hearing in time to rule on the application by the deadline stated in Rule 2.5(f).

(2) *Minor may request postponement.* The minor may postpone the hearing by written request to the clerk. The request may be submitted on Form 2C, but use of the form is not required. The request must either specify a date on which the minor will be ready for the hearing or state that the minor will later provide a date on which she will be ready for the hearing. Once the minor determines when she will be ready for the hearing, she must notify the clerk of that time in writing. The postponed hearing must be conducted in time for the court to rule on the application by the deadline stated in Rule 2.5(f).

(b) ***Place.*** The hearing should be held in a location, such as a judge's chambers, that will ensure confidentiality. The hearing may be held away from the courthouse.

(c) ***Persons attending.*** The hearing must be closed to the public. Only the judge, the court reporter, other essential court personnel, the minor, her attorney, her guardian ad litem, and witnesses on the minor's behalf may be present.

(d) ***Record.*** The court, the minor, the minor's attorney, or the guardian ad litem may request that the record—the clerk's record and reporter's record—be prepared. A request by the minor, the minor's attorney, or the guardian ad litem must be in writing and may be, but is not required to be, on Form 2I (if an appeal will be taken) or 2J (if an appeal will not be taken). The court reporter must provide an original and two copies of the reporter's record to the clerk. When the record has been prepared, the clerk must contact the minor, if she has requested the record; the minor's attorney; and the guardian ad litem at the telephone numbers shown on Form 2I or 2J and make it available to them. The record must be prepared and made available immediately if it has been requested for appeal or to demonstrate the past or potential abuse of the minor. When a notice of appeal is filed, the clerk must forward the record to the court of appeals in accordance with Rule 3.2(b).

(e) ***Hearing to be informal.*** The court should attempt to rule on the application without regard to tech-

nical defects in the application or the evidence. Affidavits of persons other than the minor are admissible. Statements in the application cannot be offered as evidence to support the application. If necessary, the court may assist the minor in remedying technical defects in the application and in presenting relevant and material facts.

2.5 Ruling.

(a) ***Form of ruling.*** The court's ruling on the application must include a signed order and written findings of fact and conclusions of law. The findings and conclusions may be included in the order. The court may use Form 2D, but it is not required to do so.

(b) ***Grounds for granting application.*** The court must grant the application if the minor establishes, by clear and convincing evidence:

(1) that the minor is mature and sufficiently well informed to make the decision to have an abortion performed without notice to, or consent of, a parent, managing conservator, or guardian; or

(2) that the notification or attempt to obtain consent would not be in the minor's best interest.

(c) ***The mature-and-informed inquiry.*** In determining whether the minor meets the requirements of (b)(1), the court must consider the experience, perspective, and judgment of the minor. The court may:

(1) consider all relevant factors, including:

(A) the minor's age;

(B) the minor's life experiences, such as working, traveling independently, or managing her own financial affairs; and

(C) steps taken by the minor to explore her options and the consequences of those options;

(2) inquire as to the minor's reasons for seeking an abortion;

(3) consider the degree to which the minor is informed about the state-published informational materials described by Chapter 171, Health and Safety Code; and

(4) require the minor to be evaluated by a licensed mental health counselor, who must return the evaluation to the court for review within three business days.

(d) ***The best-interest inquiry.*** In determining whether the minor meets the requirements of (b)(2), the court may inquire as to:

(1) the minor's reasons for not wanting to notify and obtain consent from a parent, managing conservator, or guardian;

(2) whether notification or the attempt to obtain consent may lead to physical or sexual abuse;

(3) whether the pregnancy was the result of sexual abuse by a parent, managing conservator, or guardian; and

(4) any history of physical or sexual abuse from a parent, managing conservator, or guardian.

(e) ***Grounds for denying the application.*** The court must deny the application if:

(1) the minor does not establish either ground in (b) by clear and convincing evidence; or

(2) the minor does not attend the hearing; and

(A) the minor had actual knowledge of the setting; or

(B) diligent attempts were made to notify the minor of the setting.

(f) ***Time for ruling.*** The court must rule on an application as soon as possible after it is filed, subject to any postponement requested by the minor, and immediately after the hearing is concluded. Section 33.003(h), Family Code, states that a court must rule on an application by 5 p.m. on the fifth business day after the day the application is filed, or if the minor requests a postponement, by 5 p.m. on the fifth business day after the date the minor states she is ready for the hearing.

(g) ***Failure to timely rule.*** If the court fails to timely rule on an application, the application is deemed to be denied.

(h) ***Notification of the right to appeal.*** If the court denies the application, it must inform the minor of her right to appeal under Rule 3 and furnish her with the notice of appeal form, Form 3A.

Notes & Comments

1. Section 33.003(b), Family Code, permits an application to be filed in "a county court at law, court having probate jurisdiction, or district court, including a family district court, in the minor's county of residence" or, if an exception applies, in a contiguous county or the county where the abortion would be performed. The initial assignment of an application to a specific court in a county is made by the clerk with whom the application is filed (not by the minor). Given the diversity of needs and circumstances among Texas courts, these rules allow the courts in each county to tailor the procedures for filing, handling, and assigning applications prescribed by these rules to best meet those needs and circumstances. Chapter 74, Subchapter C, Government Code, affords the presiding judge of an administrative judicial region broad discretion to assign active judges within the region, as well as visiting judges, to hear matters pending in courts within the region. *See* Tex. Govt. Code §§74.054, 74.056;

see also id. §74.056(b) (presiding judges may request judges from other judicial regions for assignment); §74.057 (Chief Justice may assign judges from one judicial region to another). Section 25.0022, Government Code, provides for assignment of probate judges. Furthermore, Chapter 74, Subchapter D, Government Code, authorizes district and statutory county court judges within a county to hear matters pending in any district or statutory county court in the county. *Id.* §74.094(a). Finally, Section 74.121, Government Code, permits courts within a county to transfer cases among courts having jurisdiction over the case. If no local rule governs assignments, then Rule 2.1(b)(4) controls.

2. Because an application is considered filed when it is actually received by the clerk, the timing provisions relating to filing by mail of Tex. R. Civ. P. 21a are inapplicable.

3. Section 33.003(f), Family Code, provides that a guardian ad litem may be (1) a person who may consent to treatment for the minor under Sections 32.001(a)(1)-(3), Family Code; (2) a psychiatrist or an individual licensed or certified as a psychologist under Chapter 501, Occupations Code; (3) an appropriate employee of the Department of Family and Protective Services; (4) a member of the clergy; or (5) another appropriate person selected by the court. The trial court may also consider appointing a qualified person requested by the minor. Although not directly applicable to these proceedings, the standards embodied in Chapter 107, Family Code, reflect legislative intent that competent and qualified persons be appointed to serve as ad litems and may provide general guidance concerning the nature of those qualifications. Appointment of an employee of the Department of Family and Protective Services to serve as guardian ad litem may give rise to a conflict of interest not immediately apparent at the time since the Department may be involved with the minor's family due to an abuse or neglect investigation, or may be party to a suit affecting the parent-child relationship, or may already be serving as the child's managing conservator.

4. The duties of guardians ad litem are not susceptible of precise definition. Generally, a guardian ad litem should interview the minor and conduct any investigation the guardian believes to be appropriate, without violating Rules 1.3 and 1.4, to assist the court in arriving at an opinion whether the minor is mature and sufficiently well informed to make the decision to have an abortion performed without notification to, or consent of, either of her parents or a managing conservator or guardian or whether notification or the attempt to obtain consent would not be in the best interest of the minor. Rule 2.5(c) and (d) list some nonexclusive factors outlined in Section 33.003(i-1)-(i-2), Family Code, that a court may consider in deciding whether the statutory criteria for a bypass have been met. Factors that have been considered in other jurisdictions with similar parental notification and consent statutes include:

- whether the minor has been examined by a doctor of medicine, doctor of osteopathy, or registered nurse—who is licensed to practice in Texas—and has given that health care provider an accurate and complete statement of her medical history;
- whether the minor has been provided with information or counseling bearing on her decision to have an abortion;
- whether the minor desires further counseling;
- whether, based on the information or counseling provided to the minor, she is able to give informed consent;
- whether the minor is attending school, or is or has been employed;
- whether the minor has previously filed an application that was denied;
- whether the minor lives with her parents;
- whether the minor desires an abortion or has been threatened, intimidated, or coerced into having an abortion;
- whether the pregnancy resulted from sexual assault, sexual abuse, or incest;
- whether there is a history or pattern of family violence; and
- whether the minor fears for her safety.

These considerations may not be relevant in every case, are not exclusive, and may not be sufficient to discharge the guardian ad litem's responsibilities in every case. Use of these factors as a basis for civil liability or as a statement of the standard of care is contrary to their intended purpose. Nothing in this comment alters existing standards of conduct under the Texas Disciplinary Rules of Professional Conduct, the Texas Rules of Disciplinary Procedure, or the Code of Judicial Conduct.

In addition to these general guidelines, Chapter 107, Family Code, sets forth duties of guardians and attorneys ad litem appointed in suits affecting the parent-child relationship. These duties are not directly applicable to proceedings under Chapter 33, Family Code, and may be incompatible with the confidential and expeditious nature of such proceedings, but they reflect general legislative intent concerning the responsibilities of ad litems.

5. Under Rule 2.5(b), once a court concludes that an application should be granted on a single ground, it need not address other grounds. But in addressing any ground, the court should attempt to ascertain, among other factors, whether the pregnancy resulted from sexual assault, sexual abuse, or incest. The legislative history of Chapter 33, Family Code, indicates that one of the principal purposes of the statute was to screen for sexual crimes and abuse of minors so as to protect them against further victimization.

RULE 3. APPEAL FROM DENIAL OF APPLICATION

3.1 How to Appeal. To appeal the denial of an application, the minor must file a notice of appeal with the clerk of the court that denied the application, file a copy of the notice of appeal with the clerk of the court of appeals to which an appeal is to be taken, and advise the clerk of the court of appeals by telephone that an appeal is being taken under Chapter 33, Family Code. The minor may use Form 3A but is not required to do so. The notice of appeal must:

(a) be styled "In re Jane Doe";

(b) state the number of the cause in the trial court;

(c) be addressed to a court of appeals with jurisdiction in the county in which the application was filed;

(d) state an intention to appeal; and

(e) be signed by the minor's attorney.

3.2 Clerk's Duties.

(a) ***Assistance in filing.*** The trial court clerk must give prompt assistance—in a manner designed to protect the minor's confidentiality—to persons seeking to file an appeal. The clerk must ensure that the notice of appeal is addressed to the proper court of appeals and that the minor's name and identifying information are not disclosed.

(b) ***Forwarding record to court of appeals.*** Upon receipt of a notice of appeal, the trial court clerk must immediately forward to the clerk of the court of appeals the notice of appeal, the clerk's record excluding the verification page, and the reporter's record. The trial court clerk must deliver the record to the clerk of the court of appeals by hand or send it by fax or email. The clerk must not send the record by mail.

(c) ***Certificate of court's failure to rule within time prescribed by statute.*** If the court of appeals fails to rule on an application within the time required by Section 33.004(b), Family Code, then, upon the minor's request, the clerk of the court of appeals must immediately issue a certificate to that effect, stating that the

trial court's order is affirmed. The clerk may use Form 3D but is not required to do so.

3.3 Proceedings in the Court of Appeals.

(a) ***Briefing and argument.*** A minor may request to be allowed to submit a brief and to present oral argument, but the court may decide to rule without a brief or oral argument.

(b) ***Ruling.*** The court of appeals—sitting in a three-judge panel—must issue a judgment affirming or reversing the trial court's order denying the application. The court may use Form 3C but is not required to do so.

(c) ***Time for ruling.*** The court of appeals must rule on an appeal as soon as possible, subject to any postponement requested by the minor. Section 33.004(b), Family Code, states that a court must rule on an appeal by 5 p.m. on the fifth business day after the notice of appeal is filed with the court that denied the application, or if the minor requests a postponement, by 5 p.m. on the fifth business day after the date the minor states she is ready to proceed.

(d) ***Postponement by minor.*** The minor may postpone the time of ruling by written request filed either with the trial court clerk at the time she files the notice of appeal or thereafter with the court of appeals clerk. The request may be submitted on Form 3B, but use of the form is not required. The request must either specify a date on which the minor will be ready to proceed to ruling, or state that the minor will later provide a date on which she will be ready to proceed to ruling. Once the minor determines when she will be ready to proceed to ruling, she must notify the court of appeals clerk of that date in writing.

(e) ***Opinion.***

(1) *Opinion optional; must preserve confidentiality.* A court of appeals may issue an opinion explaining its ruling, but it is not required to do so. An opinion that is designated for publication or public release must be written in a way to preserve the confidentiality of the identity of the minor.

(2) *Time.* Any opinion must issue not later than:

(A) ten business days after the day on which a notice of appeal is filed in the Supreme Court, if an appeal is taken to the Supreme Court; or

(B) sixty days after the day on which the court of appeals issued its judgment, if no appeal is taken to the Supreme Court.

(3) *Transmission to Supreme Court and trial court.* When the court of appeals issues an opinion, the clerk must transmit it immediately to the Supreme Court and to the trial court. If the opinion is not designated for publication or public release, the transmission must be confidential.

(f) ***Failure to timely rule.*** If the court of appeals fails to timely rule on the appeal, the trial court's judgment is deemed to be affirmed.

Notes & Comments

1. Chapter 33, Family Code, provides for no appeal from an order granting an application.

2. A request to postpone the ruling of the court of appeals may be used in conjunction with a request for oral argument or to submit briefing.

3. Neither Chapter 33, Family Code, nor these rules prescribe the appellate standard of review.

4. The 2015 amendments to Chapter 33, Family Code, permit the court of appeals to publish an opinion "if the opinion is written in a way to preserve the confidentiality of the identity of the pregnant minor." Tex. Fam. Code §33.004(c-1). Any opinion that is released to the public must not only omit the minor's name and other directly identifying information but it must also describe the facts in a way that those who know the minor would not be able to recognize her.

RULE 4. APPEAL TO THE SUPREME COURT

4.1 How to Appeal to the Supreme Court. To appeal from the court of appeals to the Supreme Court, the minor must file a notice of appeal with the clerk of the Supreme Court, file a copy of the notice of appeal with the clerk of the court of appeals, and advise the clerk of each court by telephone that an appeal is being taken under Chapter 33, Family Code. The minor may use Form 4A but is not required to do so. The notice of appeal must:

(a) be styled "In re Jane Doe";

(b) state the number of the cause in the court of appeals;

(c) state an intention to appeal; and

(d) be signed by the minor's attorney.

4.2 Clerk's Duties.

(a) ***Assistance in filing.*** The clerk of the Supreme Court must give prompt assistance—in a manner designed to protect the minor's confidentiality—to any person seeking to file an appeal. The clerk must ensure that the notice of appeal is addressed to the Supreme Court and that the minor's name and identifying information are not disclosed.

(b) ***Forwarding record to Supreme Court.*** Upon receipt of a notice of appeal to the Supreme Court, the clerks of the court of appeals and Supreme Court must

immediately forward to the Supreme Court the record that was before the court of appeals.

4.3 Proceedings in the Supreme Court. A minor may request to be allowed to submit a brief and to present oral argument, but the Court may decide to rule without a brief or oral argument. The Court must rule as soon as possible.

Editor's note: The local rules in this book are not complete sets of rules for the counties listed, but instead are specific to family-law cases. The rules are current as of the date of this book's publication. Because local rules for district courts are subject to amendment at any time, attorneys should contact the district clerk's office to determine if any amendments have been submitted to the Supreme Court for approval since the effective date. Also, some of the rules contain references to appendixes, exhibits, or addendums, most of which have not been included. Attorneys should contact the district clerk's office or visit the district clerk's website for these documents.

LOCAL RULES

DALLAS COUNTY

LOCAL RULES OF THE FAMILY DISTRICT COURTS

Effective May 11, 1999.

Editor's note: *In addition to the Local Rules of the Family District Courts of Dallas County, below, the 254th through the 256th, the 301st through the 303rd, and the 330th District Courts each have their own "Policies and Procedures." These can be printed from each court's website, which can be accessed through www.dallascounty.org/department/courts/family_district.php.*

PART I: FILING, ASSIGNMENT & TRANSFER

1.01. RANDOM ASSIGNMENT TO FAMILY COURTS

Except as provided in 1.02, the following cases shall be docketed numerically in order of filing and assigned in random order to the 301st, 302nd, 303rd, 330th, 254th, 255th and 256th District Courts (and Courts hereafter created giving preference to Family Law matters): divorce, annulment, suit to declare a marriage void, suits affecting the parent-child relationship concerning paternity/legitimation, managing conservatorship, termination and adoption, possessory conservatorship, possession and access to a child, support for a minor or disabled child, actions for breach, enforcement or interpretation of an agreement incident to divorce and/or decrees of divorce, pre-marital and partition agreements, protective orders (other than those filed by the District Attorney), uniform interstate family support cases, and all other cases arising under the Texas Family Code when there is no court of continuing jurisdiction, and all matters incident to or originating from such cases including suits for attorneys fees.

1.02. RANDOM ASSIGNMENT TO JUVENILE COURTS

When there is no court of continuing jurisdiction, the following cases shall be docketed numerically in order of filing and assigned in random order to the 304th and 305th District Courts (and district courts hereafter designated to handle juvenile matters): protection of children in an emergency, removal of infant from hospital, juvenile name change, minority disability removal, delinquency, children in need of supervision and, when Petitioner is the Texas Department of Protective & Regulatory Services, suits affecting the parent-child relationship concerning Managing Conservatorship, Paternity/Legitimation, Termination or Adoption.

1.03. ASSIGNMENT TO COURT OF CONTINUING JURISDICTION

If there is a court of continuing jurisdiction, all requests or petitions for further action, including but not limited to modification, habeas corpus, contempt or enforcement, clarification, protective orders or other relief under the Texas Family Code, shall be filed in the court of continuing jurisdiction.

1.04. BILLS OF REVIEW

Every suit or proceeding in the nature of a bill of review or otherwise, which seeks to attack, avoid or set aside any judgment, order or decree of a Family District Court of Dallas County, shall be assigned to the Court in which such judgment, order or decree was rendered.

1.05. ANCILLARY PROCEEDINGS

Every ancillary action suit shall be assigned to the Family District Court to which the matter is ancillary. Every garnishment, turnover or other collection-remedy after judgment or any action arising out of a decree/judgment or Agreement Incident to Divorce shall be filed in the Family District Court which rendered the judgment upon which the action is founded.

1.06. CASES SUBJECT TO TRANSFER

a. Every motion for transfer, consolidation or joint hearing of two or more cases under Rule 174(a), Texas Rules of Civil Procedure, shall be filed in the earliest

filed case. The Motion shall have the cause number and style of each applicable case. Notice of the hearing shall be given to all parties in all actions pursuant to Texas Rules of Civil Procedure 21 and 21a. If granted, the other District Court or Family District Court shall enter an order transferring all other actions into the earliest filed case, except in situations where a SAPCR is pending and a subsequent divorce is filed involving a parent of a child of the SAPCR. Upon motion, the SAPCR action shall be transferred and consolidated into the divorce action, in which case the transfer or consolidation shall be done pursuant to the Texas Family Code.

b. If any action is dismissed by any party or the Court, and is refiled within one hundred eighty (180) days of the date of dismissal and assigned to a different Court, either party or the Court may move within thirty (30) days of the filing of an answer to transfer the case to the first Court and, upon hearing, the transfer shall be granted.

1.07. CASES TRANSFERRED TO DALLAS COUNTY

Whenever a case is transferred to Dallas County by a Court of another county, and the order of transfer specifies the particular court to which the case is transferred, such specification shall be disregarded and the case shall be assigned in the manner provided in Part I of these rules.

1.08. SEVERED CASES

Whenever a motion to sever is granted, the severed claim shall be filed as a new case in the same Court and shall be assigned a new cause number by the District Clerk. A filing fee is required as in all new cases and the attorneys must provide copies of the severed pleadings at the time of filing.

PART II: EX PARTE ORDERS

2.01. PRESENTING EX PARTE ORDERS

All applications for ex parte orders shall first be presented for determination to the Court (Associate Judge) in which the case is pending, and only if the Court is unavailable to promptly review same may it be presented to another Court.

2.02. CERTIFICATES TO EX PARTE ORDERS

Prior to presentment, all applications for ex parte orders shall certify in writing, signed by the party or attorney, one of the following:

I hereby certify as follows: (check off and fill in blanks as required)

___ 1. To the best of my knowledge, there is no attorney of record representing any opposing party at this time; or

___ 2. Prior to presenting this matter to an Associate Judge for approval, I contacted all attorneys of record, transmitted a copy of the pleadings and proposed order in this matter, and notified them that I was requesting such ex parte relief, and:

___ A. After conferring, no attorney of record wishes to be heard prior to the presentment of this request for ex parte relief; or,

___ B. We were unable to reach an agreement, at which time I notified all attorneys of record that I would present this matter to the Associate Judge at _____ (time) on _____, (date) in the _____ (court) and invited them to attend and be heard prior to signing; or,

___ C. I was unable to speak with the opposing attorney(s) and I left word with a staff person for each attorney that I would present this matter to the Associate Judge at _____ (time) on _____ (date) in the _____ (court) and invited them to attend and be heard prior to signing; or,

___ D. After diligent attempts, I was unable to reach the opposing attorney(s) and was further unable to leave any message with counsel's office regarding the presentment of this matter to the Associate Judge.

For purposes of this rule, representation of prior counsel ends upon the entry of a final order.

PART III: SETTING HEARINGS

3.01. CERTIFICATES OF CONFERENCE

No motion or special exceptions, other than those listed in Rules 3.03, 3.04 and 3.06, will be set for hearing until the moving party shall first communicate with opposing counsel to determine whether a contemplated motion will be opposed. If not opposed, the moving party shall accompany the motion with a proposed order signed by all counsel indicating approval of same. If the motion will be opposed, the following certificate shall be attached to the motion and signed by the attorney in charge (or party pro se):

<u>CERTIFICATE OF CONFERENCE</u>

I, the undersigned attorney (or party pro se), hereby certify to the Court that:

___ 1. I have conferred with opposing counsel in an effort to resolve the issues contained in this motion without the necessity of Court intervention, or

___ 2. At _____ (time) on _____ (date), I attempted to reach opposing counsel and left a specific message that the purpose of my call was to attempt to resolve the issues contained in this motion without the necessity of Court intervention or could not leave a message because _____________________.

Such efforts have been unsuccessful, and it is necessary to set a hearing on this motion.

3.02. MOTIONS/ORDERS REQUIRING ASSOCIATE JUDGES' & JUDGES' SIGNATURES

The following documents require the approval of an Associate Judge and original signature of a Judge (but no certificate of conference) before it can be set by the Court Clerk/Administrator for hearing:

a. Show cause order on contempt;

b. Order granting a writ of habeas corpus;

c. Motion to modify filed within one year;

d. Any motion to modify in which a request for temporary orders is made at the time the motion to modify is filed;

e. Writ of attachment;

f. Writ of garnishment;

g. Application for any kind of injunctive relief;

h. Application for protective order;

i. Order Extending TRO;

j. Motion for continuance; and

k. Motion to reinstate

3.03. NOTICE FOR ALL OTHER HEARINGS

The following form should be used to set hearings on all matters (except as otherwise required by law):

<u>NOTICE OF HEARING</u>

The above motion is set for hearing on the Associate Judge's/Judge's docket of the Judicial District Court at _______ o'clock ___.m. on the ______ day of __________, ___________.

____

CLERK/ADMINISTRATOR OF COURT

By the Clerk's/Administrator's stamped signature, on the above Notice of Hearing, the Court Clerk/Administrator shall set the following matters for hearing, without a Judge's signature, Associate Judge's approval or certificate of conference:

a. Motion for summary judgment;

b. Rule 13 motions for sanctions;

c. Motion to show authority;

d. Motion to extend TRO;

e. Motion to transfer venue;

f. Special appearance;

g. Plea in bar;

h. Plea to the subject matter jurisdiction of the court;

i. Motion for new trial or to correct, modify or amend an order;

j. Motion for rehearing;

k. Appeal from associate judge's recommendation;

l. Motion for entry of order, with order sought attached if transmittal letter provided;

m. "Trial motions" (Motion in limine; motion affecting order of proceeding; motion related to strikes or challenges of jurors);

n. Motion for temporary orders; and

o. Motion for pretrial hearing

3.04. REMOVAL/RESET OF HEARINGS

A party or counsel setting a non-final or non-special set hearing may remove or reset such setting only (1) upon agreement of all opposing sides or (2) after reasonable notice to all opposing sides per Texas Rules of Civil Procedure Rule 21. Failure to comply with this rule may result in costs being assessed.

3.05. FINAL HEARINGS

a. A Clerk/Administrator may set final hearings on the merits without a certificate of conference or fiat.

b. Any person who obtains a setting for a final hearing before a District Judge or Associate Judge shall have the duty to send all opposing parties written notice of such setting within two (2) business days of the date they obtained such setting. This rule does not change the obligations for notice in the Texas Rules of Civil Procedure, including but not limited to Rules 12, 21, 21a, 166a and 245.

3.06. SPECIALLY SET CASE

Cases specially set shall take precedence over all other matters in all other Family District Courts, except matters entitled to preference by law and matters com-

menced but not completed in the preceding week. Other engagements of counsel or parties shall not be grounds for postponement of a case specially set, unless good cause is shown on a timely filed motion. No more than one case shall be specially set for any particular docket call. No party shall specially set a case that conflicts with another court setting of said party or his attorney. If a person with a special setting obtains a subsequent setting which conflicts with such special setting, that person must, within two (2) business days, notify the court setting the latter matter and opposing party of the conflict.

3.07. MOTIONS TO BE HEARD TEN OR MORE DAYS BEFORE TRIAL

Dilatory pleas, special exceptions and other motions or exceptions (excluding motions in limine and other trial motions) shall be heard no less than ten (10) days before the date on which the case is set for final hearing, provided that the pleadings to which same are directed are on file.

PART IV: SPECIAL EXCEPTIONS

4.01. SPECIAL EXCEPTIONS

The Court shall deny special exceptions complaining of a pleading which sets out its cause of action using language consistent with the Texas Family Code.

PART V: PRE-TRIAL CONFERENCE

5.01. PURPOSE OF PRE-TRIAL CONFERENCE

Counsel or parties pro se will be expected at pretrial to advise the Court which issues will be disputed and to be familiar with the authorities applicable to the questions of law raised at pre-trial. Failure to conform to this rule shall be ground for postponement of the trial, setting of further pre-trial hearings, or other appropriate action.

5.02. WHO SHALL ATTEND PRE-TRIAL CONFERENCE

Counsel attending the pre-trial shall either be the attorney in charge or shall be familiar with the case and be fully authorized to state the party's position on the law and the facts and to make stipulations of fact. Counsel may not send to pre-trial in his stead a legal assistant, paralegal, investigator, secretary or other nonattorney. Parties appearing pro se must attend pre-trial in person.

5.03. CONSEQUENCES FOR FAILURE TO ATTEND PRE-TRIAL CONFERENCE

When counsel or a party pro se, after notice, fails to appear at pre-trial the Court may:

a. Rule on all motions, dilatory pleas and exceptions in absence of such person;

b. Declare any motions, dilatory pleas, or exceptions of such absent party waived;

c. Advance or delay the trial setting according to the convenience of persons present;

d. Pass and reset the pre-trial;

e. Decline to set the case for trial, cancel a setting previously made; and/or[1]

f. Dismiss the case for want of prosecution or grant a default judgment, if attorneys were ordered to appear, especially where there has been a previous failure to appear or where no amendment has been filed after exceptions were previously sustained;

g. Grant sanctions or other relief.

1. **Editor's note:** Approved as such. The conjunction "and/or" probably should appear at the end of subsection (f).

PART VI: DISCOVERY

6.01. COMPLETION DATE FOR DISCOVERY

All parties shall complete discovery at least seven (7) days prior to the date said case is set for trial, unless otherwise ordered.

6.02. FILING OF DISCOVERY & RELATED MATERIALS

Requests for production or inspection and responses under TRCP Rule 167,[1] interrogatories and answers under TRCP Rule 168,[2] notices of depositions under TRCP Rules 220, 201, an[3] 208,[4] and business records accompanied by affidavit under Rule 902(10) TRE, shall be served as required by the Texas Rules of Civil Procedure but shall not be filed with the Clerk as follows:

a. The trial Court may order the materials to be filed;

b. A party sending a notice of oral deposition pursuant to the Texas Rules of Civil Procedure may file the notice if the deposition is to be taken out of state;

c. A party may file those portions of materials related to a request for relief under TRCP Rules 166b or 215,[5] or a response to such request, or to some other discovery dispute;

d. A party may file materials necessary for the determination of a motion for summary judgment, or for any response or reply to such a motion, or for any other pretrial motion or response or reply to such motion; or

e. A party may file materials necessary for a proceeding in an Appellate Court or for post-judgment purposes.

This local rule does not enlarge the type of documents that may be filed.

The party responsible for the service of such materials shall retain the original or an exact copy while the case and any related appellate proceedings are pending and for seven months thereafter.

1. **Editor's note:** Approved as such. Probably should be TRCP Rule 196.
2. **Editor's note:** Approved as such. Probably should be TRCP Rule 197.
3. **Editor's note:** Approved as such. Probably should be "and."
4. **Editor's note:** Approved as such. Probably should be TRCP Rules 220, 199, and 200.
5. **Editor's note:** Approved as such. Probably should be TRCP Rules 192 or 215.

6.03. WHERE DEPOSITIONS OF PARTIES & WITNESSES MAY BE TAKEN

Absent agreement of the parties, depositions of a party shall be taken in the office of the deposing counsel, provided that such office is in Dallas or contiguous counties. If a deposing party's counsel's office is not so located, the deposition shall be taken in the office of the deponent's counsel if it is located in Dallas or contiguous counties. If neither party's counsel is located in Dallas or contiguous counties, such parties' depositions shall be taken at an agreed upon location in Dallas County. Deposition of a non-party witness shall be taken at the office of the deposing party's counsel unless prohibited by the Texas Rules of Civil Procedure. For purposes of this subsection, counsel includes "party pro se."

6.04. WHO PAYS FOR DEPOSITION OF EXPERT WITNESS

The cost of an expert, for deposition, shall be paid prior to the deposition by the party who seeks to depose the expert, provided however, that the Court has the right to determine that the cost of deposition should be borne otherwise.

PART VII: ANNOUNCEMENT FOR TRIAL

7.01. APPEARANCE AT DOCKET CALL

Docket call is the trial setting. In all contested matters set for final hearing, at the time of docket call for a particular week, all counsel or parties pro se are required to appear at docket call and make their announcements to the Court concerning their readiness for trial unless they have previously appeared at the pre-trial and received a specific date and time for trial. Any unqualified announcement of "ready" or "ready subject to" another court engagement shall be made to the Judge, or if so instructed by the Judge, to the Court Coordinator.

7.02. CONTINUANCES

Every ground for postponement or continuance shall be brought to the Court's attention at or before the docket call on the date the case is set for trial. No request for pass, postponement or reset of any trial, pretrial, or other hearing shall be granted unless counsel for all parties involved consent, or unless all parties not joining in such request or their counsel have been notified and have had opportunity to object; provided however, that failure to make an announcement at docket call shall be taken as consent to pass, postpone, reset or dismiss for want of prosecution any case set for trial the following week. All motions for continuance shall be presented in the form and manner provided by the Texas Rules of Civil Procedure.

7.03. APPEARANCE FOR NON-FINAL MATTERS

For all non-final matters and cases set on either the Judge's daily docket or Associate Judge's docket, all parties and counsel shall appear at the time and place set for the hearing and make their announcement as provided in 7.01. Failure to appear shall be treated as failure to announce under 7.02.

7.04. CONFLICTING ENGAGEMENT OF COUNSEL

a. Where counsel for either party has a conflicting trial or appeal setting, the Court may hold the case over until the trial or appeal has been completed.

b. If counsel is engaged in trial or appeal in another court, counsel shall be obligated to advise the clerk of the Court in which he is set for trial or which is holding the case over of counsel's availability immediately upon completion of such other trial or appeal.

c. Mediation settings confirmed by letter from the Mediator and presented to the Court at docket call should take precedence over all cases except those cases previously given a special setting.

PART VIII: DISMISSAL FOR WANT OF PROSECUTION

8.01. ACTIONS RESULTING IN A CASE BEING DISMISSED FOR WANT OF PROSECUTION

a. Failure of a party to request a setting or take other appropriate action after notice from the Court Administrator that the case has been pending without action for more than 180 days, provided that upon giving the first notice (which shall be at least 30 days in advance of the date set for dismissal) of intent to dismiss for want of prosecution, the Court shall remove the matter from its dismissal docket if counsel for either side does contact the Court in person.

b. Failure of moving party or his counsel to appear for trial, pre-trial or other preliminary hearing.

c. Failure to comply with Rule 8.02; or

d. For any other reason provided for by these rules and/or the Texas Rules of Civil Procedure.

Subject to other provisions of these rules, the Clerk shall mail a written notice of such dismissal to all parties or their counsel of record.

8.02. DWP AFTER RENDITION OR ANNOUNCED SETTLEMENT

Unless ordered otherwise, within thirty days after rendition or an announced settlement by the parties, they shall cause decisions or settlements of any kind to be reduced to writing. Upon failure to furnish the Court Clerk/Administrator with such a judgment or order finally disposing of a case, or to request extension of the filing or to set a motion for entry, the Court shall enter an order of dismissal without prejudice with costs taxed at the Judge's discretion.

The Court will not sign an order that does not contain either the signature of all attorneys as to form or proof of notice that said order has been presented to all attorneys of record requesting same to file written objections within ten (10) days.

PART IX: WITHDRAWAL/SUBSTITUTION OF COUNSEL

9.01. CIRCUMSTANCES UNDER WHICH ATTORNEY MAY WITHDRAW

No attorney of record shall be permitted to withdraw from any case without presenting a motion and obtaining from the Court an order granting leave to withdraw pursuant to Texas Rules of Civil Procedure 10. The letter required under TRCP shall be sent to the client advising that the client has ten (10) days after the date of mailing the letter to make any objection to such withdrawal to the Court, in writing, and that if not done and no objection raised, the motion shall be granted. A copy of the motion shall be delivered or mailed to opposing counsel. No such motion shall be presented within thirty (30) days of the trial date or at such time as to require delay of the trial. After leave is granted, the withdrawing attorney shall send his client, the Court and opposing counsel a letter notifying of the last known mailing address of his client and of any settings. Notice to the client shall be by certified and regular mail.

9.02. ATTORNEY SUBSTITUTING FOR PRIOR ATTORNEY

If an attorney is substituting in as new counsel or attorney in charge for a party, the Court shall sign an order withdrawing the prior attorney in charge and substituting in the new counsel. Upon the filing of a motion requesting such relief signed by the party and the attorney substituting in as attorney in charge, the motion and order must be sent to all opposing parties and to the former attorney in charge, pursuant to Texas Rules if[1] Civil Procedure 21 and 21a.

1. **Editor's note:** Approved as such. Probably should be "of."

PART X: INFORMATION FROM CLERK

10.01. INFORMATION THE COURT CLERK WILL NOT PROVIDE TO PARTIES OR COUNSEL

a. The Court Clerk will not state whether a case has been filed.

b. No information will be given on a case unless a case number is known and provided. If the party or counsel does not know the case number, they will be referred to the public terminals in the records department of the District Clerk's Office.

10.02. INFORMATION THE COURT CLERK WILL PROVIDE TO PARTIES OR COUNSEL IF A CASE NUMBER IS GIVEN

a. What action is on file, the date of filing, the names addresses and telephone numbers of all attorneys in charge, and the specific court to which the case is assigned;

b. Returns of service and the dates of such returns;

c. Correct style of a case;

d. Any settings in a case.

10.03. COURT CLERK/ ADMINISTRATOR WILL TAKE MESSAGES FOR THE JUDGE

The Court Clerk/Administrator shall take and timely deliver messages, including those related to an attorney being delayed for an appearance, and shall promptly notify the Judge of same.

PART XI: FILING OF PLEADINGS

11.01. PLEADINGS MUST BE TITLED & HAVE HOLES PUNCHED

All pleadings, motions, orders and other papers, including exhibits attached thereto, when offered for filing or entry shall comply with TRCP Rule 45 and shall be descriptively titled and pre-punched at the top of the page to accommodate the Clerk's 2 3/4" center-to-center flat-filing system. Each instrument shall, at the bottom of each page, be numbered and titled, i.e. Petitioner's Original Petition-page 2. Motions shall be separate documents from orders and judgments. The Clerk may not sign or amend any instrument for a party or attorney.

11.02. USE OF FAX MACHINES

Any party pro se or attorney who does not have a fax machine but who uses one to send correspondence to the other party or parties must indicate the number of the facsimile machine they are using, and they shall thereafter in the case be deemed to have designated such fax number as a number for receiving same.

PART XII: ACCESS TO FILES

12.01. NO PART OF A FILE CAN BE REMOVED FROM COURT

No pleadings or paper belonging to the files of the Court shall be taken from the office or custody of the Clerk, except upon order of the Court or with the Court's permission.

12.02. ORDER LIMITING ACCESS TO A FILE

Any party or attorney may obtain an order limiting access to the files in any pending action by applying to the Court in which the action is filed and upon showing good cause for such action, the motion shall be granted. Upon the entry of an order limiting access to a file, the Clerk shall comply with the order and shall prevent all persons, except those therein designated, from having access to the file.

PART XIII: ATTORNEYS

13.01. AD LITEM ENTITLED TO ALL PLEADINGS

When the court appoints a guardian or attorney ad litem, all counsel shall provide such appointee with copies of their pleadings, orders, and reports filed with the Court, within five days (5) of notice of the appointment.

13.02. APPOINTMENT OF MEDIATOR

In a case selected for mediation, the Court encourages parties to choose their own mediator. The Court, if requested, shall appoint an attorney-mediator who has substantial family law litigation experience.

13.03. LAWYERS CREED & CODE OF JUDICIAL CONDUCT

Counsel and parties shall treat the Court, court personnel, each other and trial participants in a manner consistent with the Texas Lawyers Creed.

The Court and court personnel shall treat attorneys, parties and trial participants in a manner consistent with the Texas Code of Judicial Conduct.

13.04. VACATION LETTERS

Each attorney in charge shall have the right to designate vacation days and days of continuing legal education provided he notifies the clerk of the court and all opposing counsel in writing by separate letters in each case at least ten (10) days, prior to such designated dates, and provided said dates do not conflict with a current setting for trial, hearing, deposition, inspection, mediation or discovery deadline in the case. During the dates designated in said letter, opposing parties shall not set any matter for hearing in the case and any such setting is void. If a true emergency situation exists, the Court may grant ex parte emergency relief during the designated time period.

13.05. PRO SE LITIGANTS

Rules for attorneys apply equally to pro se litigants.

All requirements of these rules applicable to attorneys or counsel apply with equal force to pro se litigants. Pro se litigants are required to provide addresses and telephone listings at which they can be reached by court personnel and opposing counsel. Failure to accept delivery or to pick up mail addressed to the address provided by pro se litigants will be considered constructive receipt of the mail or delivered document which may be

established by postal service receipt, certified or registered mail receipt, or comparable proof of delivery.

PART XIV: COURTROOM DECORUM

14.01. ATTORNEYS TO INFORM CLIENT OF PROPER COURTROOM DECORUM

All attorneys shall be responsible for advising their clients and witnesses of appropriate courtroom conduct, attire, and policy regarding children.

14.02. PAGERS, BEEPERS & TELEPHONES

Pagers, beepers, and telephones should be turned off when a person is in the courtroom. If the beeper can be on without making a sound (except the vibration) it may remain on if kept in that mode. Failure to follow this rule may result in forfeiture of the device emitting sound.

14.03. APPROPRIATE DRESS FOR COURT APPEARANCES

The following shall not be acceptable in the courtroom: hats, bandannas or other headgear, shorts, bare midriffs, tank tops, tattered or dirty clothing.

14.04. CONDUCT IN THE COURTROOM

A. No magazines, newspapers or other such reading material may be read in the courtroom while court is in session.

B. There will be no eating, drinking or chewing gum in the courtroom unless the Court has expressly stated otherwise.

C. There will be no outbursts, disturbances, threats, obscene language, or gestures. Violation of this rule shall result in immediate expulsion and/or direct contempt.

14.05. CHILDREN IN THE COURTROOM

No child is to be brought to the courthouse unless the Judge or Associate Judge has specifically requested the child be brought at a time certain for interview or testimony.

14.06. CONSEQUENCES OF VIOLATING RULES UNDER PART XIV

Violation of the courtroom decorum rules of Part XIV will result in immediate expulsion of the person who is violating the same. They will not be permitted to return until they have conformed to these rules. Such expulsion will not be grounds for a continuance or delay, and the case will proceed.

PART XV: RULES

15.01. RULES

The numbering of Rule 15.01, below, approved by the Texas Supreme Court on May 11, 1999, Misc. Docket No. 99-9069, was duplicated in Rule 15, approved by the Texas Supreme Court on Apr. 24, 2007, Misc. Docket No. 07-9064.

These local rules shall supersede any other local rules and shall constitute the Local Rules of Practice for the Family District Courts of Dallas County, Texas, as adopted by the seven (7) Family District Courts but shall not in anyway supercede or pre-empt any standing order promulgated by any Family District Judge as to a particular policy of that court.

RULE 15. APPLICATION FOR & REFUSAL OF IV-D CHILD SUPPORT SERVICES

Effective Apr. 24, 2007.

15.01 As provided in Section 15.03, all final orders (judgments) that provide for child support to be paid through the State Disbursement Unit, excluding modifications of orders prior to the effective date of this rule, shall be deemed to include an application for IV-D child support services provided by Dallas County and the Office of the Attorney General of Texas, pursuant to Chapter 231 of the Texas Family Code.

15.02 Unless required to accept IV-D child support services pursuant to other laws, a child support obligee entitled to receive services pursuant to this rule may decline services by filing a written Refusal of Child Support Services with the Dallas County Child Support Office. Refusal of IV-D child support services pursuant to this rule does not preclude a subsequent written application for IV-D services, however, it does preclude an obligee from re-entering this "Local Rule" program.

15.03 A Dallas County Family District Court may implement this rule by written notice to the Presiding Family Judge, District Clerk, Child Support Office and the IV-D Agency. The rule is effective in that Court on the first (1st) day of the month following written notice and applies only to final orders signed after that date.

RULE 16. APPLICATION FOR & REFUSAL OF IV-D CHILD SUPPORT SERVICES—FORMER CASES INVOLVING GUARDIAN AD LITEM AND/OR FRIEND OF THE COURT

Effective Feb. 24, 2009.

16.01 All orders in which child support payments were being monitored by the Guardian Ad Litem and/or Friend of the Court but where the appointment of Guardian Ad Litem and/or Friend of the Court has been terminated by an Omnibus Order of the court, shall be deemed to include an application for IV-D child support services provided by Dallas County and the Office of the Attorney General of Texas, pursuant to Chapter 231 of the Texas Family Code.

16.02 Unless required to accept IV-D child support services pursuant to other laws, a child support obligee entitled to receive services pursuant to this rule may decline services by filing a written Refusal of Child Support Services with the Dallas County Child Support Office. Refusal of IV-D child support services pursuant to this rule does not preclude a subsequent written application for IV-D services; however, it does preclude an obligee from re-entering this "Local Rule" program.

16.03 A Dallas County Family District Court may implement this rule by written notice to the Presiding Family Judge, District Clerk, Domestic Relations Office, and the IV-D Agency. The rule is effective in that Court on the first (1st) day of the month following written notice and applies only to cases affected by orders set out in 16.01.

DALLAS COUNTY STANDING ORDER REGARDING CHILDREN, PETS, PROPERTY & CONDUCT OF THE PARTIES

Effective Jan. 5, 2017.

No party to this lawsuit has requested this order. Rather, this order is a standing order of the Dallas County District Courts that applies in every divorce suit and every suit affecting the parent-child relationship filed in Dallas County. The District Courts of Dallas County giving preference to family law matters have adopted this order because the parties, their children and the family pets should be protected and their property preserved while the lawsuit is pending before the court. Therefore, it is ORDERED:

1. NO DISRUPTION OF CHILDREN. All parties are ORDERED to refrain from doing the following acts concerning any children who are subjects of this case:

1.1 Removing the children from the State of Texas for the purpose of changing residence, acting directly or in concert with others, without the written agreement of both parties or an order of this Court.

1.2 Disrupting or withdrawing the children from the school or day-care facility where the children are presently enrolled, without the written agreement of both parents or an order of this Court.

1.3 Hiding or secreting the children from the other parent or changing the children's current place of abode, without the written agreement of both parents or an order of this Court.

1.4 Disturbing the peace of the children.

1.5 Making disparaging remarks regarding the other party in the presence or within the hearing of the children.

2. PROTECTION OF FAMILY PETS OR COMPANION ANIMALS. All parties are ORDERED to refrain from harming, threatening, interfering with the care, custody, or control of a pet or companion animal, possessed by a person protected by this order or by a member of the family or household of a person protected by this order.

3. CONDUCT OF THE PARTIES DURING THE CASE. All parties are ORDERED to refrain from doing the following acts:

3.1 Using vulgar, profane, obscene, or indecent language, or a coarse or offensive manner to communicate with the other party, whether in person or in any other manner, including by telephone or another electronic voice transmission, video chat, social media, in writing, or electronic messaging, with intent to annoy or alarm the other party.

3.2 Threatening the other party in person or in any other manner, including by telephone or another electronic voice transmission, video chat, social media, in writing, or electronic messaging, to take unlawful action against any person, intending by this action to annoy or alarm the other party.

3.3 Placing one or more telephone calls or text messages, at an unreasonable hour, in an offensive or repetitious manner, without a legitimate purpose of communication, or anonymously with the intent to alarm or annoy the other party.

3.4 Intentionally, knowing[1] or recklessly causing bodily injury to the other party or to a child of either party.

3.5 Threatening the other party or a child of either party with imminent bodily injury.

4. PRESERVATION OF PROPERTY AND USE OF FUNDS DURING DIVORCE CASE. If this is a divorce case, both parties to the marriage are ORDERED to refrain from intentionally and knowingly doing the following acts:

4.1 Destroying, removing, concealing, encumbering, transferring, or otherwise harming or reducing the value of the property of one or both of the parties.

4.2 Falsifying a writing or record including an electronic record, relating to the property of either party.

4.3 Misrepresenting or refusing to disclose to the other party or to the Court, on proper request, the existence, amount, or location of any tangible or intellectual property of one or both of the parties, including electronically stored or recorded information.

4.4 Damaging or destroying the tangible or intellectual property of one or both of the parties, including any document that represents or embodies anything of value, and causing pecuniary loss to the other party, including electronically stored or recorded information.

4.5 Tampering with the tangible or intellectual property of one or both of the parties, including any document, electronically stored or recorded information, that represents or embodies anything of value, and causing pecuniary loss to the other party.

4.6 Selling, transferring, assigning, mortgaging, encumbering, or in any other manner alienating any of the property of either party, whether personal property or real property or intellectual property, and whether separate or community, except as specifically authorized by this order.

4.7 Incurring any indebtedness, other than legal expenses in connection with this suit, except as specifically authorized by this order.

4.8 Making withdrawals from any checking or savings account in any financial institution for any purpose, except as specifically authorized by this order.

4.9 Spending any sum of cash in either party's possession or subject to either party's control for any purpose, except as specifically authorized by this order.

4.10 Withdrawing or borrowing in any manner for any purpose from any retirement, profit-sharing, pension, death, or other employee benefit plan or employee savings plan or from any individual retirement account or Keogh account, except as specifically authorized by this order.

4.11 Signing or endorsing the other party's name on any negotiable instrument, check, or draft, such as tax refunds, insurance payments, and dividends, or attempting to negotiate any negotiable instrument payable to the other party without the personal signature of the other party.

4.12 Destroying, disposing of, or altering, any financial records of the parties, including canceled checks, deposit slips, and other records from a financial institution, a record of credit purchases or cash advances, a tax return, and a financial statement.

4.13 Destroying, disposing of, or altering any email, text message, video message, or chat message or social media message or other electronic data or electronically stored information relevant to the subject matter of the suit for dissolution of marriage, regardless of whether the information is stored on a hard drive in a removable storage device, in cloud storage, or in another electronic storage medium.

4.14 Modifying, changing, or altering the native format or metadata of any electronic data or electronically stored information relevant to the subject matter of the suit for dissolution of marriage, regardless of whether the information is stored on a hard drive in a removable storage device, in cloud storage, or in another electronic storage medium.

4.15 Deleting any data or content from any social network profile used or created by either party or a child of the parties.

4.16 Using any password or personal identification number to gain access to the other party's email account, bank account, social media account, or any other electronic account.

4.17 Taking any action to terminate or limit credit or charge cards in the name of the other party.

4.18 Entering, operating, or exercising control over the motor vehicle in the possession of the other party.

4.19 Discontinuing or reducing the withholding for federal income taxes on wages or salary.

4.20 Terminating or in any manner affecting the service of water, electricity, gas, telephone, cable television, or other contractual services, such as security, pest control, landscaping, or yard maintenance at the other party's residence or in any manner attempting to withdraw any deposits for service in connection with such services.

4.21 Excluding the other party from the use and enjoyment of the other party's specifically identified residence.

4.22 Opening or redirecting mail, email or any other electronic communication addressed to the other party.

5. PERSONAL AND BUSINESS RECORDS IN DIVORCE CASE. "Records" means any tangible document or recording and includes e-mail or other digital or electronic data, whether stored on a computer hard drive, diskette or other electronic storage device. If this is a divorce case, both parties to the marriage are ORDERED to refrain from doing the following acts:

5.1[2] Concealing or destroying any family records, property records, financial records, business records or any records of income, debts, or other obligations.

5.2 Falsifying any writing or record relating to the property of either party.

6. INSURANCE IN DIVORCE CASE. If this is a divorce case, both parties to the marriage are ORDERED to refrain from doing the following acts:

6.1 Withdrawing or borrowing in any manner all or any part of the cash surrender value of life insurance policies on the life of either party, except as specifically authorized by this order.

6.2 Changing or in any manner altering the beneficiary designation on any life insurance on the life of either party or the parties' children.

6.3 Canceling, altering, or in any manner affecting any casualty, automobile, or health insurance policies insuring the parties' property or persons including the parties' minor children.

7. SPECIFIC AUTHORIZATIONS IN DIVORCE CASE. If this is a divorce case, both parties to the marriage are specifically authorized to do the following:

7.1 To engage in acts reasonable and necessary to the conduct of that party's usual business and occupation.

7.2 To make expenditures and incur indebtedness for reasonable attorney's fees and expenses in connection with this suit.

7.3 To make expenditures and incur indebtedness for reasonable and necessary living expenses for food, clothing, shelter, transportation and medical care.

7.4 To make withdrawals from accounts in financial institutions only for the purposes authorized by this order.

8. SERVICE AND APPLICATION OF THIS ORDER.

8.1 The Petitioner shall attach a copy of this order to the original petition and to each copy of the petition. At the time the petition is filed, if the Petitioner has failed to attach a copy of this order to the petition and any copy of the petition, the Clerk shall ensure that a copy of this order is attached to the petition and every copy of the petition presented.

8.2 This order is effective upon the filing of the original petition and shall remain in full force and effect as a temporary restraining order for fourteen days after the date of the filing of the original petition. If no party contests this order by presenting evidence at a hearing on or before fourteen days after the date of the filing of the original petition, this order shall continue in full force and effect as a temporary injunction until further order of the court. This entire order will terminate and will no longer be effective once the court signs a final order.

9. EFFECT OF OTHER COURT ORDERS. If any part of this order is different from any part of a protective order that has already been entered or is later entered, the protective order provisions prevail. Any part of this order not changed by some later order remains in full force and effect until the court signs a final decree.

10. PARTIES ENCOURAGED TO MEDIATE. The parties are encouraged to settle their disputes amicably without court intervention. The parties are encouraged to use alternative dispute resolution methods, such as mediation or informal settlement conferences (if appropriate), to resolve the conflicts that may arise in this lawsuit.

11. BOND WAIVED. It is **ORDERED** that the requirement of a bond is waived.

1. **Editor's note:** Approved as such. Probably should be "Intentionally, knowingly, or recklessly."

2. **Editor's note:** Numbering supplied by editor from Subsection 5.1 through end.

HARRIS COUNTY

RULES OF THE JUDICIAL DISTRICT COURTS—FAMILY TRIAL DIVISION

Effective Oct. 31, 2003.

RULE 1. OBJECTIVE

1.1 Purpose of the Rules. Obtaining a just, fair, and impartial adjudication of the parties' and the chil-

dren's rights is the purpose of these rules. To achieve this goal efficiently and inexpensively, while complying with procedural rules and substantive law, these rules encourage using alternate dispute resolution in all appropriate cases.

RULE 2. TRANSFER OF CASES

2.1 Multiple Suits. When a suit filed in a Family Trial Division court is in any way terminated (by nonsuit or otherwise), a subsequent suit or cause of action involving the same parties or the same subject matter shall be filed in, or transferred to, the court that first had jurisdiction of the parties or subject matter. This rule applies to all controversies, including divorce, support, conservatorship, and all matters incident to them, whether sought by original proceedings or by modification, clarification or enforcement of a former order, judgment or settlement agreement. When such a situation is disclosed for the first time after the hearing begins, the judge of the court shall immediately order the suit transferred to the court in which the prior suit was filed.

2.2 Enforcement of Consent Decree or Contract. In accordance with General Assignment Order of September 1, 1977, any action for the enforcement of a consent decree or contract arising out of or in conjunction with any action previously filed in any of the courts of the Family Trial Division shall be filed in the same court.

2.3 Transfer.

2.3.1 Continuing, Exclusive Jurisdiction. All provisions of the Texas Family Code ("Tex. Fam. Code") regarding continuing, exclusive jurisdiction and transfer shall take precedence over these rules.

2.3.2 Later Filed Case. If a case is filed in which there is a substantial identity of parties or subject matter as in a previously non-suited or dismissed case, the later case shall be assigned to the court where the prior case was pending. When such a situation is disclosed for the first time after the hearing begins, the judge of the court shall immediately order the suit transferred to the court in which the prior suit was pending.

2.4 Consolidation. A motion to consolidate cases shall be heard in the court where the lowest numbered case is pending. If the motion is granted, the consolidated case will be given the number of the lowest numbered case and assigned to that court.

2.5 Severance. If a severance is granted, the new case remains assigned to the court where the original case is pending, bearing the same file date and the same number as the original case with a letter designation; provided, however, that when a severed case has previously been consolidated from another court, the case shall upon severance be assigned to the court from which it was consolidated.

2.6 Presiding for Another. In all cases where a judge signs an order on behalf of another court, the case shall remain in the original court.

2.7 Improper Court. If a case is on the docket of a court by any manner other than as prescribed by these rules, the Administrative Judge of the Family Trial Division shall transfer the case to the proper court.

RULE 3. FLOW OF CASES

3.1 Appearances of Counsel. Any attorney representing a party in a case shall file an appropriate initial pleading with the court, be it a Petition, Answer, Notice of Appearance as Attorney of Record, or Motion and Order for Substitution of Counsel. The pleading shall contain all information required under Rule 57 of the Texas Rules of Civil Procedure ("T.R.C.P.").

3.2 Ancillary Matters.

3.2.1 Ancillary Docket. The ancillary docket consists of:

(1) Temporary injunctions;

(2) Temporary orders in original proceedings;

(3) Writs of habeas corpus;

(4) Motions for enforcement including contempts, except those brought under Title 5, Subtitle D, Chapter 231, Tex. Fam. Code;

(5) Temporary receiverships;

(6) Motions to transfer;

(7) In the discretion of the court, as may be limited by the Tex. Fam. Code, hearings for temporary orders in suits for modification of a final order; and

(8) All matters preliminary to trial on the merits.

3.2.2 Preference for ADR. In the discretion of the court, preference in setting hearings shall be given to matters in which the parties have participated in alternate dispute resolution procedures.

3.3 Docket Call Procedures.

3.3.1 Attorneys and pro se litigants who do not expect to be on time or present in the courtroom during docket call must notify the court and the opposing side of this fact.

3.3.2 Attorneys and pro se parties who will be late for docket call must give the court and opposing side

notice of their estimated time of arrival at court and the reason for the delay. If the attorney is late because he or she must appear in another court at the same time, the clerk must be notified not only that the attorney will be late (as above), but also the specific court(s) in which the attorney will be appearing.

3.3.3 If the moving party (if pro se) or the party's attorney does not appear in the courtroom within thirty (30) minutes of docket call, that party's motion may be passed by the court at the request of the responding party.

3.4 Telephone Conferences. Use of telephone conferences between judges or associate judges and all attorneys in a case is encouraged for non-evidentiary matters. Telephone conferences shall be scheduled through the court coordinator.

3.5 Interview of Child/Child's Testimony. In all cases in which the court deems testimony of a child to be necessary or required by statute, the attorney wishing to have the child interviewed shall arrange a specific time through the court coordinator for the court to interview the child. No party is to bring a child to the courthouse to testify without prior arrangement pursuant to this rule, unless the child's attendance is required by court order including a writ of habeas corpus or attachment. The attorney or pro se party who is responsible for the child's attendance at court shall immediately notify the court coordinator of the child's presence in the courthouse. The child shall not be brought into the courtroom without the express consent of the judge or associate judge.

3.6 Scheduling Orders. It shall be the duty of an attorney or pro se party entering a pending case to ascertain from the court whether a Scheduling Order has issued and if so, to obtain a copy of the Scheduling Order from the District Clerk's office. Notwithstanding the foregoing, it shall also be the duty of the Petitioner or Movant's attorney of record in a pending case in which a Scheduling Order has issued to provide a copy of the Scheduling Order to any pro se party who has made or makes a general appearance in the pending case.

3.7 Trials.

3.7.1 Manner of Setting. Cases shall be set for trial by order of the court.

3.7.2 Date of Setting. Cases shall be set for trial for a date certain. If a case is not assigned to trial by the second Friday after the date it was set, whether because of a continuance or because it was not reached, the court shall reset the case to a date certain. Unless all parties agree otherwise, the setting must comply with all requisites of T.R.C.P. 245.

3.7.3 Preference for ADR. In the discretion of the court, preference in setting cases for trial shall be given to matters in which the parties have participated in alternate dispute resolution procedures.

3.7.4 Assignment to Trial. A case is assigned to trial when counsel are called to the court to commence the jury or non-jury trial on the merits. For the purposes of engaged counsel, no court may have more than two cases assigned to trial at any one time, one before the judge and one before the associate judge.

3.7.5 Open Weeks. Except with the consent of all parties, and the court, no cases will be assigned to trial on the merits nor for ancillary hearings during:

(1) The week of the Second Administrative Judicial Region Conference (March);

(2) The week of the State Bar Convention (June);

(3) The week of the State Bar of Texas Advanced Family Law Course (August);

(4) The week of the Conference of the Judicial Section (September); and

(5) The last two weeks of December.

3.7.6 Continuances. Continuances shall be governed by T.R.C.P. 251 through 254.

3.8 Judgments and Orders. All judgments and orders must be submitted to the court for signing within ten (10) days from the date of rendition, unless otherwise directed by the court. The party who is directed to prepare the judgment or order shall furnish all opposing parties with a copy of the proposed judgment or order at least five (5) days prior to entry date. All judgments and orders submitted for entry must be signed by the judge within seven (7) working days from the date that the judgments or orders are submitted for entry, unless the judgment or order is rejected by the court. All judgments or orders in uncontested matters (except for settlements made pursuant to T.R.C.P. 11) and in default matters (where citation has been served and there has been no answer filed or other general appearance) must be presented at the time of hearing on the uncontested or default matter. All forms required by governmental entities shall be submitted at the time the judgment or order is submitted.

RULE 4. DISCLOSURE OF PROPERTY & FINANCIAL INFORMATION

4.1 Temporary Orders. In any hearing for temporary orders in which child support or spousal support is an issue, completion and exchange of Financial Information Statements, copies of income tax returns for the past two years, and the two most recent payroll stubs are required prior to the commencement of the hearing. This rule providing for the exchange of information shall constitute a discovery request under the T.R.C.P., and failure to comply with this rule may be grounds for sanctions, as provided by Rule 215 of the T.R.C.P. Sanctions shall not issue if the judge or associate judge determines that the failure to comply was not willful.

4.2 Final Information. A party's final Inventory, Financial Information Statement and financial information required under the Tex. Fam. Code including, but not limited to, the party's income tax returns for the past two years and the party's two most recent payroll stubs, as well as suggested findings regarding child support and a proposed division of property shall be exchanged no later than ten (10) days before trial, and shall be filed before the commencement of trial. If children are involved in the proceeding, the inventory shall contain sufficient information so the court may render a qualified medical child support order regarding health insurance for the children. This rule providing for the exchange of information shall constitute a discovery request under the T.R.C.P., and failure to comply with this rule may be grounds for sanctions.

4.3 Inventory. Each inventory shall list each item of property and its value, and shall also list each liability, together with the amount of the liability, the number of periodic payments in arrears, if any, the property securing its payment, and the name of the creditor. Any property or liability claimed to be separate property shall be so characterized. All beneficial interests in insurance and all benefits arising from a party's employment (such as pensions, profit sharing plans, savings or thrift plans, whether vested or non-vested) shall be identified. Each party shall incorporate as an exhibit to the inventory the last information furnished about to the employee's rights and monetary interest in the retirement and savings plans. Each party shall also furnish sufficient information so the court may render a qualified domestic relations order, if applicable. A summary attached to the inventory shall list and total, in columnar format, the property values and liabilities. Each inventory shall show the net worth of the community estate and the net worth of any claimed separate estate.

4.4 Duty of Disclosure. Without waiting for a discovery request, each party to a suit for divorce, annulment, or a suit in which child or spousal support is in issue, has a duty of disclosure of certain information to the other party. "Disclosure" includes providing for inspection and copying the information in the party's "possession, custody or control," as that phrase is defined in Rule 166b(2)(b) of the T.R.C.P. Different types of suits require disclosure of different information.

4.4.1 Disclosure in Suit for Divorce or Annulment. Each party to a suit for divorce or annulment shall, without waiting for a discovery request, provide to the other party the following information about property in which the party claims an interest:

(1) all documents pertaining to real estate;

(2) all documents pertaining to any pension, retirement, profit-sharing, or other employee benefit plan, together with the most recent account statement for any plan;

(3) all documents pertaining to any life, casualty, liability, and health insurance;

(4) the most recent account statement pertaining to any account located with any financial institution including, but not limited to, banks, savings & loans, credit unions, and brokerage firms.

4.4.2 Disclosure in Suit in Which Child or Spousal Support is in Issue. Each party to a suit in which child support or spousal support is in issue shall, without waiting for a discovery request, provide to the other party the following information:

(1) all policies, statements, and description of benefits which reflect any and all medical and health insurance coverage that is or would be available for the child or the spouse;

(2) Unless the information has previously been exchanged in connection with a temporary hearing (Rule 4.1), a Financial Information Statement for the party, together with that party's previous two years income tax returns and two most recent payroll check stubs, or, if no payroll check stubs are available, the party's latest Form W-2.

4.4.3 Failure to Comply. This rule providing for the duty of disclosure shall constitute a discovery request under T.R.C.P., and failure to comply with this rule (or any of its subparts) may be grounds for sanctions, as prescribed by Rule 215 of T.R.C.P.

4.4.4 Method of Disclosure.

(1) Timing of Disclosure. Disclosure required under this rule shall be made as follows:

(a) by a Petitioner or Movant within 30 days after the Respondent files Respondent's first pleading or makes a general appearance in the case;

(b) by a Respondent within 30 days after he or she files Respondent's first pleading or makes a general appearance in the case, whichever occurs first.

(2) Delivery of Disclosure. The disclosures required under this rule shall be made by furnishing the information to the opposing party's attorney of record or, if the opposing party is pro se, by furnishing the disclosures to the opposing party at the party's address. Each party making a disclosure shall promptly file a notice with the court advising that the required disclosure has taken place.

4.4.5 Duty to Supplement. After disclosure is made pursuant to this rule, each party shall be under a duty to reasonably supplement or to amend the information if the party obtains information on the basis of which he or she knows that the information disclosed was either incomplete or incorrect when made, or is no longer complete or true.

4.4.6 Rule 11. The provisions of this rule may be modified by agreement pursuant to Rule 11 of T.R.C.P.

RULE 5. REQUIREMENTS FOR CERTAIN DOCUMENTS

5.1 Certificate of Conference.

5.1.1 Unopposed motions shall be labeled "Unopposed" in the caption.

5.1.2 Opposed motions shall contain a certificate that:

(1) states that the movant and respondent have conferred with each other and in good faith have attempted to resolve the matter; and

(2) identifies the basis of disagreement between counsel; or

(3) states that the parties have not been able to confer, and states in detail all efforts made to confer, including dates and methods of attempted communication.

5.1.3 The clerk of each court is directed not to submit opposed motions to the judge which do not comply with this rule.

5.1.4 The provisions of subparts 5.1.2 and 5.1.3 do not apply to motions for summary judgment, default judgments, agreed judgments, motions for voluntary dismissal or non suit, and motions involving service of citation.

RULE 6. REFERRAL TO ASSOCIATE JUDGE

6.1 Referral. All pending cases and cases filed after the date of the adoption of these rules are hereby referred to the associate judge of each court pursuant to Chapter 201, Tex. Fam. Code, subject to limitations imposed by that same chapter.

6.2 Order of Referral. This Rule shall constitute the Order of Referral required by Section 201.006, Tex. Fam. Code, as to any pending or future cases under Title 1, 2, 4, or 5, Tex. Fam. Code.

RULE 7. ALTERNATE DISPUTE RESOLUTION

7.1 Temporary Hearings. In appropriate cases involving disputed custody or visitation issues, the court shall make referrals for mediation to Family Court Services or other private mediators agreed upon by the parties and attorneys. Additional issues may be mediated by agreement of the parties and attorneys. Attorneys may attend all mediations.

7.2 Final Trial. Except for good cause shown, cases shall be submitted for alternate dispute resolution procedures before trial.

7.3 Settlement Weeks. Referral of appropriate cases to alternate dispute resolution procedures shall be made at one or more settlement weeks each year as provided by law.

RULE 8. CONFLICTING ENGAGEMENTS

8.1 Inter-County. The Rules of the Second Administrative Judicial Region control conflicts in settings of all cases between of all cases between a Harris County court and a court not in Harris County.

8.2 Intra-County. Among the trial courts sitting in Harris County:

8.2.1 Trial/Trial. A trial setting not yet[1] assigned takes precedence over a conflicting trial setting not yet assigned;

8.2.2 Trial/Non-Trial. Trial settings take precedence over conflicting non-trial settings except as to court-ordered mediations which are scheduled prior to the assignment to trial;

8.2.3 Non-Trial/Pre-Trial. The matter which was first filed, regardless of cause number, shall take prece-

dence over non-trial settings, non-court-ordered alternate dispute resolution and non-court-ordered depositions.

8.3 Judge or Associate Judge. This rule is applicable whether the matter is assigned to the judge or the associate judge of a court.

8.4 Waiver. The court with precedence may yield.

8.5 Lead Counsel. This rule operates only where lead counsel, as defined by T.R.C.P. 8, is affected, unless the court expands coverage to other counsel.

8.6 Engaged Counsel. Counsel is deemed engaged and unavailable for trial if he or she participates in the actual trial or hearing of another case or in court-ordered alternate dispute resolution or court-ordered deposition.

8.7 Reporting of Conflicting Engagements. It is the duty of counsel to report promptly to the court immediately upon learning of a conflicting engagement that might preclude that counsel's availability for trial. Failure to do so may result in sanctions.

1. **Editor's note:** Approved as such. Probably should be "that is."

RULE 9. VACATIONS OF COUNSEL

9.1 General Rule. Subject to the provisions of 9.2 of this rule, an attorney may designate not more than four weeks of vacation during a calendar year as vacation, during which that attorney will not be assigned to trial or required to engage in any pretrial proceedings. This rule operates only where lead counsel, as defined by T.R.C.P. 8, is affected, unless the court expands coverage to other counsel. The vacation designation shall be honored only if it is made on the vacation letter form approved by the Board of District Judges of the Family Trial Division and is accompanied by the attorney's designation of at least one attorney who has consented to act for the vacationing attorney. The designated attorney shall be called upon to act only if the client consents to the designated attorney's representation, and then only if the court requests the designated attorney's participation due to an emergency.

9.2 Time for Designation. Written designation for vacation weeks during June, July, or August must be filed with the District Clerk by May 15. Written designation for vacation weeks in months other than June, July, or August must be filed with the District Clerk by February 1. Designated vacation weeks protect the attorney from trials or pretrial proceedings during those weeks, unless an order setting the case for trial was signed and the case was assigned to trial before the vacation designation was filed.

RULE 10. UNIFORMITY

10.1 Letters and Orders. In managing their dockets under T.R.C.P. 165a and 166, Family Trial Division judges shall use form letters and orders approved by the Board of District Judges of the Family Trial Division.

10.2 Policies and Procedures. The Board of District Judges of the Family Trial Division shall establish common policies and procedures on pertinent court business. If practical, policies and procedures shall be posted outside the entrance of each court.

RULE 11. ADMINISTRATION OF FAMILY TRIAL DIVISION

11.1 Presiding Judge. Each Family Trial Division judge, except the Administrative Judge, serves as Presiding Judge for a calendar month in rotation in order of judicial district numbers.

11.2 Administrative Judge of the Family Trial Division.

11.2.1 Term. At their regular May meeting, the Family Trial Division judges shall elect the Administrative Judge of the Family Trial Division for a one-year term beginning June 1 and ending the next May 31.

11.2.2 Substitute. The Administrative Judge of the Family Trial Division may, by written order, designate any other judge of the Division to act for the Administrative Judge if the judge is absent or unable to act. The substitute administrative judge shall have all the duties and authority granted by these rules to the Administrative Judge during the period of the designation.

11.3 Meetings. The Family Trial Division judges shall meet regularly each month at times and places as the Administrative Judge of the Family Trial Division may direct by a written notice distributed, except in case of emergency, at least 72 hours in advance of the meeting.

11.4 Reports to the Administrative Judge. On a monthly basis, the District Clerk shall supply to the Administrative Judge of the Family Trial Division information concerning the number of filings, dispositions, trials and other judicial activities in each Family Trial Division court.

RULE 12. PARENT EDUCATION & COUNSELING

12.1 Except for good cause shown, in all divorces joined with suits affecting the parent-child relation-

ship, the court shall require parents to attend an educational program for divorcing parents. In its discretion, the court may also refer parents involved in modification or enforcement litigation, or a child involved in any type of custody litigation, to an education course or for counseling. In protective order cases authorized by Chapter 85, Tex. Fam. Code the court may refer a party to a batterers' treatment program.

RULE 13. APPLICABILITY

13.1 Effective Date. These rules shall become effective on January 1, 1998, or upon their approval by the Texas Supreme Court pursuant to T.R.C.P. 3a, whichever comes later.

13.2 Cross-Reference. Any reference in these rules to a statute or a court rule shall also apply to any successor statute or court rule; whether recodification, revision or amendment.

13.3 Applicability. These rules are applicable to both jury and non-jury cases.

RULE 14. APPLICATION FOR & REFUSAL OF IV-D CHILD SUPPORT SERVICES

14.1 As provided in Section 14.3, all final divorce and paternity decrees, including any subsequent modification, that provides for child support paid through the Texas Child Support Disbursement Unit and all cases in which the Domestic Relations Office is currently appointed Friend of the Court, shall be deemed to include an application for IV-D child support services provided by Harris County and the Office of the Attorney General of Texas, pursuant to Chapter 231 of the Texas Family Code.

14.2 Unless required to accept IV-D child support services pursuant to other laws, a child support obligee entitled to receive services pursuant to this rule may decline services by filing a written Refusal of Child Support Services with the District Clerk. Refusal of IV-D child support services pursuant to this rule does not preclude a subsequent written application for services.

14.3 A Family District Court may implement this rule by written notice from the Presiding Judge to the Administrative Family Judge, District Clerk, Domestic Relations Office and the IV-D Agency. The rule is effective in that Court on the thirtieth (30) day following written notice and applies only to final orders signed after that date.

TARRANT COUNTY

LOCAL RULES OF COURT

Effective Nov. 29, 2006.

Parts 1-3 omitted by editor

PART 4. RULES FOR DISPOSITION OF FAMILY LAW CASES

RULE 4.01. GENERAL DISPOSITION RULES

(1) ADR. It shall be the policy of the family law courts of Tarrant County to encourage the amicable resolution of family law litigation, including the use of alternative dispute resolution. On its own motion, motion of a party or by agreement of the parties, the Court may refer a case to alternative dispute resolution pursuant to Chapter 154, Texas Civil Practice and Remedies Code, and 6.602 and 153.0071 of the Texas Family Code. On its own motion, motion of a party or by agreement of the parties, the Court may refer a case to access facilitation.

In a case selected for mediation, the Court encourages parties to choose their own mediator. The Court, if requested, shall appoint a mediator who has substantial family law mediation experience.

(2) Co-Parenting Education. Pursuant to Texas Family Code Sec. 153.001, it shall be the policy of the family law courts of Tarrant County to:

a. Assure that children will have frequent and continuing contact with parents who have shown the ability to act in the best interest of the child;

b. Provide a safe, stable, and nonviolent environment for the child; and

c. Encourage parents to share in the rights and duties of raising their child after the parents have separated or dissolved their marriage.

On its own motion, motion of a party or by agreement of the parties, the Court may order parties to attend co-parenting education for the purpose of promoting this policy. The courts hereby encourage all parties to suits affecting the parent-child relationship to attend these types of classes.

(3) Pre-Trial. Pre-trial hearings or orders will not be required in every case, but each Court may establish its own pre-trial procedures pursuant to Rule 166, Texas Rules of Civil Procedure. A pre-trial conference may be set on the Court's own motion or proper request of a party. If a pre-trial conference is set, counsel or par-

ties pro se will be expected at pre-trial to advise the Court which issues will be disputed and the time required for trial.

Counsel attending the pre-trial shall be the lead attorney or shall be familiar with the case and the party's position on the law and facts, and authorized to make stipulations of fact. Counsel shall not send a non-attorney to a pre-trial hearing. Parties appearing pro se must attend the pre-trial in person.

When counsel or a party pro se, after notice, fails to appear at pre-trial the Court may:

a. Rule on all motions, dilatory pleas and exceptions in the absence of such person, including declaring such to be waived;

d.[1] Advance or delay the trial setting according to the convenience of persons present;

e. Pass and reset the pre-trial;

f. Decline to set the case for trial or cancel a pending setting;

g. Dismiss the case for want of prosecution or grant a default judgment, as appropriate, provided counsel and pro se parties were properly notified to appear; and/or

h. Grant sanctions or other relief.

(4) Stipulations. It is the responsibility of each attorney to stipulate all accurate facts not in dispute, and to waive formal proof as to any document to be introduced about which there is no reasonable dispute as to authenticity.

(5) Notice. Unless otherwise ordered, all notice provisions and time periods provided by the Texas Rules of Civil Procedure, Family Code, Government Code, and any other applicable statute shall be followed. Unless specifically shortened by the court, a party responding to a request for temporary relief contained in an original action shall be entitled to at least 3 days notice of any hearing. No hearing for relief, temporary or final, shall be set prior to answer date in any Motion to Modify for child support and/or possession, unless special circumstances set forth by attached affidavit exist.

(6) Announcement of Time. When requested by the Court, it is the responsibility of each attorney to provide the Court with a reasonably accurate estimate of the time required for the Court to hear a matter. The Court may impose a reasonable time limitation upon counsel and pro se parties to present their cases, within the confines of due process.

(7) Child Support. Every temporary or final order submitted to the Court for approval, which contains provisions ordering the payment of child support, shall contain a paragraph ordering the parties to pay the appropriate fees that may be charged by the agency to whom child support is paid, in such language as may be approved by the Court.

(8) Medical Support Order. Every final order submitted to the Court for approval which contains provisions for child support shall be accompanied by a medical support order in conformance with the requirements of 154.181 of the Texas Family Code.

(9) Income Withholding. Every final order submitted to the Court for approval which contains provisions for child support shall be accompanied by a[2] order or writ for income withholding in accordance with Chapter 158 of the Texas Family Code and a completed Tarrant County Child Support Office Record of Support Form.

(10) Forms. All appropriate state and local forms shall be completed and delivered to the Court Clerk with all proposed Orders or Decrees to be left with the Clerk for consideration by the Court.

(11) Motion to Transfer, Consolidate, or Dismiss.

11.1 Within Tarrant County, Texas every motion for transfer, consolidation or joint hearing of two or more cases under Rule 174(a), Texas Rules of Civil Procedure, shall be filed in the earliest filed case. The Motion shall have the cause number and style of each applicable case. Notice of the hearing shall be given to all parties in all actions pursuant to Texas Rules of Civil Procedure 21 and 21a. If granted, the other Tarrant County Family District Court shall enter an order transferring all other actions into the earliest filed case, except in situations where a suit affecting parent child relationship is pending and a subsequent divorce is filed in which case the transfer or consolidation shall be done pursuant to the Texas Family Code.

11.2 If any action is dismissed or non-suited by any party, and is refiled within ninety (90) days and assigned to a different Court, either party or the Court may move to transfer the case to the Court in which the first suit was filed within the time limits provided by Section 155.204 of the Texas Family Code. Absent good cause shown, transfer shall be granted upon notice and hearing.

(12) Motion Practice.

12.1 Parties are directed to use all reasonable means to resolve pre-trial disputes to avoid the necessity of judicial intervention.

12.2 No motions, objections or special exceptions will be set for hearing unless the moving party shall have certified in such motion or in a letter substantially the following:

"A conference was held on (date) with (name of attorney for opposing party) on the merits of this motion. A reasonable effort has been made to resolve the dispute without the necessity of court intervention and the effort failed. Therefore it is presented to the Court for determination."

OR

"A conference was not held with (name of opposing attorney) on the merits of this motion because (explanation of inability to confer)."

12.3 Court Coordinators are responsible for scheduling the dates and times for hearings. The moving party shall attempt to secure agreed upon dates for hearing prior to setting the same. Upon receiving the date and time of hearing, the moving party shall immediately notify all other parties in writing as to the date, time and subject matter of the hearing. A copy of this communication shall be provided to the Court Coordinator.

12.4 On request of a party and with consent of the Judge, a matter not requiring a record by the Court Reporter may be conducted by telephone. The moving party shall be responsible for advising opposing parties of the method and time of hearing and shall be responsible for arranging the conference call.

12.5 By agreement, parties may submit matters for ruling by the Judge without a personal appearance and oral presentation. The Judge should be advised in writing when such procedure is desired.

(13) Ex Parte Orders.

13.1 All applications for ex parte orders shall first be presented for determination to the Court in which the case is pending, and only if the Court is unavailable to promptly review same, may it be presented to another Court.

13.2 Prior to presentment, all applications for ex parte orders shall certify in writing, signed by the party or attorney, one of the following which is to be completed as to each opposing counsel:

I hereby certify as follows: (check off and fill in blanks as required)

1. To the best of my knowledge, there is no attorney of record representing any opposing party at this time; or

2. Prior to presenting this matter to a Judge for approval, I contacted all attorneys of record, transmitted a copy of the pleadings and proposed order in this matter, and notified them that I was requesting such ex parte relief, and;

A. After conferring, no attorney of record wishes to be heard prior to the presentment of this request for ex parte relief; or,

B. We were unable to reach an agreement, at which time I notified all attorneys of record that I would present this matter to the Judge at (time) on (date) in the (court) and invited them to attend and be heard prior to signing; or,

C. I was unable to speak with the opposing attorney(s) and I left word with a staff person for each attorney that I would present this matter to the Judge at (time) on, (date) in the (court) and invited them to attend and be heard prior to signing; or,

D. After diligent attempts, I was unable to reach the opposing attorney(s).

For purposes of this rule, representation of counsel ends thirty-onc (31) days following cntry of a final order.

(14) Pleadings Must Be Titled & Have Holes Punched. All pleadings, motions, orders, and other papers, when offered for filing or entry shall comply with TRCP Rule 45 and shall be descriptively titled and prepunched at the top of the page to accommodate the Clerk's filing system. Each instrument shall be numbered and titled at the bottom of each page.

(15) Ad Litem Entitled to All Pleadings. When the court appoints an amicus attorney, attorney ad litem, or an attorney serving in a dual role, all counsel shall provide such appointee with copies of their pleadings, orders, and reports filed with the Court, within five days (5) of notice of the appointment.

(16) Lawyers Creed & Code of Judicial Conduct. Counsel and parties shall treat the Court, court personnel, each other and trial participants in a manner consistent with the Texas Lawyers Creed.

The Court and court personnel shall treat attorneys, parties and trial participants in a manner consistent with the Texas Code of Judicial Conduct.

(17) Vacation Letters. Each attorney in charge shall have the right to designate a reasonable number of vacation days and days of continuing legal education, provided he notifies the clerk of the Court and all opposing counsel in writing at least 30 days prior to such designated dates, and provided said dates do not conflict with a current setting for trial, hearing, deposition, inspection, mediation or discovery deadline in the case. During the dates designated in said letter, opposing counsel and parties shall not set any matter for deposition, inspection, mediation or hearing except for emergency situations requiring immediate action. If a matter is set during the dates designated in said letter, the Court may cancel the setting and/or reschedule it upon oral or written motion of a party or the Court's own motion.

(18) Proper Courtroom Decorum.

18.1 All attorneys shall be responsible for advising their clients and witnesses of appropriate courtroom conduct, attire, and policy regarding children.

18.2 Pagers, beepers, and telephones should be turned off when a person is in the courtroom. If the devise[3] can be on without making a sound (except the vibration) it may remain on if kept in that mode. Failure to follow this rule may result in a finding of contempt, fine or other sanction.

Absent medical necessity, the following shall not be acceptable in the courtroom: hats, bandanas or other headgear, shorts, bare midriffs, tank tops, tattered or dirty clothing.

18.3 There will be no eating, drinking or chewing gum in the courtroom unless the Court has expressly stated otherwise.

18.4 There will be no outbursts, disturbances, threats, obscene language, or gestures.

18.5 Violation of the courtroom decorum may result in immediate expulsion of the person who is violating the same or a finding of contempt, fine or other sanction.

(19) Pro Se Litigants. Rules for attorneys apply equally to pro se litigants. All requirements of these rules applicable to attorneys or counsel;[4] apply with equal force to pro se litigants. Pro se litigants are required to provide addresses and telephone listings at which they can be reached by court personnel and opposing counsel. Failure to accept delivery or to pick up mail addressed to the address provided by pro se litigants will be considered constructive receipt of the mail or delivered document which may be established by postal service receipt, certified or registered mail receipt, or comparable proof of delivery.

1. **Editor's note:** Approved as such. Subsections (b) and (c) do not exist in approved version.

2. **Editor's note:** Approved as such. Probably should be "an."

3. **Editor's note:** Approved as such. Probably should be "device."

4. **Editor's note:** Approved as such. The semicolon probably should not appear.

RULE 4.02. PROVE-UPS & DEFAULT HEARINGS

(1) Times. Each Court shall hear agreed cases and defaults daily, at times set by each Court. It will not be necessary to schedule agreed prove-ups and default hearings with the Court, and such are heard on a first-come-first-served basis, with the exception that the Court may first hear cases in which a party is appearing with counsel in order to minimize attorneys fees. A Court may cancel its daily uncontested hearings as may be required by other Court business. Notice of such cancellation shall be posted outside the Court, and parties and their attorneys may proceed as set forth in 4.02(2) below. Agreed prove ups and defaults maybe[1] heard at other times during the day if the court is available.

(2) Presiding Judge. Agreed cases and default hearings should normally be heard by the District Judge sitting in the Court to which the case is assigned. If that Judge is not available, then it may be heard by any other District Judge who so consents. Unless otherwise directed by the Court, multiple uncontested matters originating out of different Courts may be presented to one court for hearing. Once a case has been presented to a Judge, and the Judge has made a ruling or deferred ruling, the same matter may not be presented to a Judge other than the Judge to whom it was first presented without that Judge's approval. With the consent of the Court, agreed cases, not requiring a record, may be presented to the Associate Judge of the Court for hearing as permitted by 201.005, 201.007, and 201.104 of the Texas Family Code.

(3) Court's File. Any attorney presenting an uncontested matter to the Court for hearing shall obtain the Court's File of such case from the District Clerk's office prior to appearance before the Court. The Court's File shall be delivered to the Court's bailiff, or other person designated by the Court, for consideration by the Court. When the File is so delivered, it shall contain the

proposed Decree or Order, all other necessary pleadings, and all other documents required under Rule 4.01 above.

(4) Record. If a record of testimony is required, the attorney or pro se litigant shall so notify the bailiff, or other person designated by the Court, and shall complete any additional forms as may be required by the Court to be delivered to the court reporter prior to appearance before the Court.

1. **Editor's note:** Approved as such. Probably should be "may be."

RULE 4.03. TRIAL SETTINGS

(1) Final Trial. Cases will be set for final trial upon written request using the procedure and form as may be required by the specific Court. Each Court's procedure and setting request form shall be obtained from the Court's coordinator.

(2) Final Trial Before Associate Judges. Upon agreement of the parties and counsel of record, the Court may refer a case for final disposition by the Associate Judge of that court if the parties agree to waive their right of appeal to the referring court pursuant to 201.015 and 201.1042 of the Texas Family Code.

(3) Specially Set Case. Cases specially set shall take precedence over all other matters in all other Family District Courts, except matters entitled to preference by law and matters commenced but not completed in the preceding week. Other engagements of counsel or parties shall not be grounds for postponement of a case specially set, unless good cause is shown on a timely filed motion. No party shall specially set a case that conflicts with another court setting of said party or his or her attorney. If a person with a special setting obtains a subsequent setting which conflicts with such special setting, that person must, within two (2) business days, notify the court setting the later matter and opposing party of the conflict.

RULE 4.04. ASSOCIATE JUDGES & ASSOCIATE JUDGES FOR TITLE IV-D CASES

(1) Cases Referred. Each court may refer any aspect of a family law case to the Associate Judge or Associate Judges for Title IV-D Cases, that is consistent with Chapter 201 Sub-chapter A and B of the Texas Family Code. Unless otherwise ordered by the Court, the following matters will normally be so referred:

1.1 Requests for Temporary Orders in any case, including custody.

1.2 Motions to Modify on Temporary or Final Order, except for final custody modifications.

1.3 Motions to Transfer.

1.4 Motions for Enforcement or Contempt.

1.5 An action under Chapter 159 of the Texas Family Code.

1.6 Applications for Protective Orders.

1.7 Discovery matters.

1.8 Motions to Compel or for Sanctions.

1.9 Motions for Judgment, Entry, or to Sign Orders, if the hearing, the subject of the proposed Order, was heard by the Associate Judge.

1.10 Motions to Withdraw.

1.11 Pre-Trial Conferences.

1.12 Any other matter referred by the Court.

The Court will not refer to the Associate Judges for Title IV-D cases, and Associate Judges for Title IV-D cases shall not hear final trials involving divorce proceedings. The Court may decline to refer to the Associate Judges for Title IV-D cases, and the Associate Judges for Title IV-D cases shall not hear any matters listed above as is consistent with 201.104 of the Texas Family Code.

(2) Settings. Hearings before the Associate Judge shall be obtained from the coordinator of the appropriate Court and the appropriate written Order or Notice of Hearing shall be presented to the coordinator at the time the hearing is requested. The Court, in its discretion, may allow the setting or resetting of a hearing without a written Order or Notice, but the attorney requesting said setting or resetting shall send the coordinator and all parties written confirmation of the hearing date so set.

(3) Times. Hearings before the Associate Judge shall be held daily at a specific time and place as directed by the Court. Each attorney and party appearing before the Associate Judge shall timely report to the bailiff assigned to said Associate Judge on the date of the hearing, and the Associate Judge, at his or her discretion, may request an announcement from counsel or pro se parties as to the issues in controversy and estimates of time required.

RULE 4.05. TRIAL PROCEDURES

(1) Timely Appearance. It is the responsibility of every attorney to timely appear before the Judge or Associate Judge, as appropriate, at the time of any trial or

hearing. Unless otherwise directed by the Court, counsel shall check-in with the Court, or its bailiff, at or before the time the trial or hearing is set. If counsel is to be late for a trial or hearing or is in another Court, counsel or counsel's staff shall, by telephone or otherwise, notify the Court or its bailiff, giving the reason for the delay in appearance and specify which other Court(s) counsel is appearing before. Failure to appear or check-in with the Associate Judge or Court within 30 minutes of the scheduled hearing time shall result in a default being granted or the hearing being passed, as appropriate. Although it is the policy of the Courts to recognize the inevitable conflicts in an urban law practice and to be reasonably flexible, it is ultimately the responsibility of counsel to keep the Court accurately informed of counsel's whereabouts so that the Court's dockets will not be unduly disrupted. Violation of this rule may result in sanctions against counsel.

(2) Documents Required. In all cases in which support of a spouse and/or child(ren) is in issue, whether temporary or final, each party shall be required to furnish the Court and opposing party true and correct copies of the following, at or before the time of hearing, if available:

2.1 Summary statement of monthly income and expenses in a form substantially similar to any form that may be adopted by the Court.

2.2 All payroll stubs or wage statements for the past 3 months.

2.3 If self-employed, all profit and loss statements, balance sheets, income statements or other evidence of earnings for the previous 12 months.

2.4 Federal Income Tax Returns, including all attachments and schedules, for the two years immediately prior to the hearing, or if a return has not been prepared and filed for a particular year, all W-2's, 1099's, K-1's or other evidence of income for such a year.

2.5 Financial Statements filed by the parties with any financial institution within the past 2 years.

2.6 Any other documents as ordered by the Court, or properly subpoenaed by a party.

(3) Inventories. When ordered by the Court, each party shall file a sworn inventory and appraisement within 60 days of the Court's order, unless the Court or the parties extend or shorten such period. An Inventory and Appraisement may be ordered in any case in which the character, value or division of property or debts is in issue, and should be filed in a form substantially similar to the form provided in the Texas Family Practice Manual of the State Bar of Texas. Additionally, each party shall at the time of trial prepare for the Court and opposing counsel a written summary of that party's proposed division of property and debts.

(4) Orders. Within 60 days after rendition of a decision by the Judge or Associate Judge, counsel shall cause, unless ordered otherwise, all orders, decrees or judgments of any kind to be reduced to writing, approved as to form by opposing counsel, and to be delivered to the court for signature. If counsel is unable to secure the approval as to form from opposing counsel, counsel shall file a motion for entry of the proposed order and secure a hearing on same no sooner than 10 days from the date of filing of the Motion. The party or counsel responding to such a motion shall at least 3 days prior to the hearing present to opposing counsel an alternative proposed order or a written list of objections to the first order. Failure to furnish the Court with a proposed order, decree or judgment or to schedule a hearing for entry within the 60 day period may result in the Court's placing the case on the dismissal docket.

(5) Court Reporters. A court reporter will be furnished to the Associate Judges for hearings only on the days that Enforcement/Contempt matters are to be heard, unless special arrangements are made with the referring Judge. Counsel shall be required to furnish his or her own court reporter, if desired, for all other hearings before the Associate Judge.

RULE 4.06. CONTINUANCES & RESETS

(1) Associate Judges and Associate Judges for Title IV-D cases. Unless otherwise directed by the Court, motions for continuance and resets may be presented to the Associate Judge without the necessity of a written motion being filed. If not agreed by all parties, said motion for continuance or reset must be made to the Associate Judge after all parties have been given notice and an opportunity to object.

(2) Presiding Judges. No request for a continuance or resetting shall be granted by the presiding Judge of a Court without the filing of a written motion, notice and hearing, unless agreed by all parties, with the consent of the Court. All other requests shall be in writing pursuant to the Texas Rules of Civil Procedure, filed with the Court, and shall be heard as may be scheduled by the Court after proper notice to all parties.

Rules 4.07-4.10 reserved

RULE 4.11. DISCOVERY GUIDELINES

(1) Full Discovery. As provided in the Texas Rules of Civil Procedure and appellate court rulings, the Courts shall permit full, liberal and broad discovery, however such discovery shall not be unlimited, and the reasonable parameters contained in 192 of the Texas Rules of Civil Procedure, shall be applied in both letter and spirit.

(2) Disputes. Counsel shall attempt to resolve any discovery question, problem or dispute before intervention by the Court. Any discovery motion shall contain a certificate by the party or counsel filing the same in accordance with rule 4.01 (13) 13.2 above.

No discovery motion shall be set for hearing or heard unless it contains such certificate, signed by counsel or pro se party.

(3) Depositions. The following guidelines will generally be followed by the Courts on matters pertaining to oral depositions:

3.1 A party filing an action in Tarrant County must give his or her deposition in Tarrant County, if requested.

3.2 A Respondent properly sued in Tarrant County must give his or her deposition in Tarrant County, if requested.

3.3 The party initiating a deposition may elect to take the deposition orally or on written questions and the opposing party may elect to cross-examine orally or on written questions.

3.4 Unless agreed otherwise, fees charged by an expert for giving of deposition testimony shall be paid by the party requesting the deposition unless the expert is retained by the opposing party in which case fees shall be paid pursuant to 195.7 of the Texas Rules of Civil Procedure.

3.5 The following shall be presumed to be unreasonable unless otherwise agreed or ordered:

A. Notice of less than 10 days under Rules 21a and 199.2 Texas Rules of Civil Procedure.

B. Depositions scheduled for Saturday, Sunday or legal holidays in which the County Courthouse is closed.

C. Depositions scheduled to begin before 8:00 a.m. or to extend past 6:00 p.m.

3.6 A party initiating an oral deposition shall first attempt to communicate with all opposing counsels to determine whether agreement can be reached as to the date, time, place and materials to be furnished at the time of deposition. Any written notice of oral deposition shall state substantially as follows:

"A conference was held or attempted with the attorney for opposing party to agree on a date, time, place and materials to be furnished. Agreement could not be reached, or counsel will not respond, and the deposition is therefore being taken pursuant to this Notice (or) Agreement was reached and this Notice complies with the agreement."

Failure to hold such conference or to make adequate attempt to hold such conference prior to noticing a deposition shall be grounds to quash the deposition.

3.7 Notwithstanding the above guidelines, the parties may agree to a different procedure, and nothing shall preclude a party from submitting disputes as to such matters to the Court for determination by proper motion and hearing pursuant to the Texas Rules of Civil Procedure.

(4) Production. Unless otherwise ordered by the Court, or agreed by the parties, the following times and locations for production shall be presumed to be reasonable:

4.1 For non-voluminous production, counsel for the party from whom the production is requested shall make and deliver copies of the documents to the office of counsel for the requesting party in accordance with the request.

4.2 For voluminous production, counsel for the party from whom the production is requested shall gather the documents at his or her office and inform requesting counsel that they are available. Requesting counsel shall then, at the option of requesting counsel, either pick up the documents to examine, copy and return within 5 working days, or examine and copy the documents at the office of producing counsel, with the expense of copying to be paid by requesting counsel.

For purposes of this rule "voluminous production" shall be defined as the total documents produced, responsive to the request, being incapable of inclusion, in an orderly fashion, without overflow, within a "Bankers Box"; such being of the following dimensions: fifteen (15") inches long, twelve (12") inches wide, and ten (10") inches deep.

(5) Filing of Discovery. Notwithstanding Rule 1.07 of the Local Rules of Court, discovery matters shall

be filed or not filed in accordance with 191.4 of the Texas Rules of Civil Procedure.

Rules 4.12-4.99 reserved

APPLICATION FOR & REFUSAL OF TITLE IV-D CHILD SUPPORT SERVICES BY THE DOMESTIC RELATIONS OFFICE

Effective Jan. 30, 2007; amended subsection (a) effective May 25, 2010.

a. In each final divorce decree that orders child support and is signed on or after October 16, 2000 by the presiding judge of a Tarrant County Family District Court and any subsequent modification to that decree, and in each final parentage decree not based on an action initiated by a Title IV-D agency that orders child support and is signed on or after March 12, 2007 by the presiding judge of a Tarrant County Family District Court and any subsequent modification to that decree, the obligee in any such decree or modification to that decree shall be deemed to have made application for Title IV-D Child Support Services.

b. Unless required to accept such services pursuant to other laws, a recipient or obligee of child support entitled to receive Title IV-D child support services pursuant to this local rule may decline such services by filing a written Refusal of Child Support Services.

c. Refusal of Title IV-D child support services pursuant to this local rule does not preclude that person from making a subsequent written application to the Office of the Texas Attorney General for Title IV-D child support services.

d. The provisions of this local rule supercede in its entirety the Local Rule Regarding Application for and Refusal of Title IV-D Child Support Services, Tarrant County Family District Courts, Misc. Docket No. 00-9063, signed by the Supreme Court of Texas on April 12, 2000.

TRAVIS COUNTY

LOCAL RULES OF CIVIL PROCEDURE & RULES OF DECORUM

Effective June 2, 2014.

Chapters 1-6 omitted by editor

CHAPTER 7. UNCONTESTED & EMERGENCY MATTERS

7.1 Uncontested Docket. On Monday through Friday of each week from 8:30 a.m. until 9:20 a.m. and from 1:30 p.m. until 2:20 p.m., a Duty Judge will be available to sign orders and to hear uncontested divorces, uncontested name changes, agreed orders in pending cases, orders concerning service of citation, notices of hearing for temporary orders prior to answer day, orders to appear, friendly suits, and other such uncontested matters. These matters will ordinarily be considered in the order in which the proposed orders are brought to the courtroom clerk. Notice of the location of the Duty Judge presiding at the uncontested docket will be posted at the Courthouse and at traviscountycourts .org.[1] All agreed orders or other uncontested orders submitted to the Duty Judge for signature must be presented to the Duty Judge only at the times allotted for the uncontested docket.

7.2 Emergency Matters to be heard by Duty Judge and those to be heard by Judge Hearing CPS Docket. Requests for *ex parte* relief or any other emergency matter, except requests by the Department of Family Protective Services, must be presented to the Duty Judge. Requests for *ex parte* relief by the Department of Family & Protective Services must be presented to the Judge hearing the CPS Docket or that Judge's designee in the manner and at the times that Judge directs. Only when the Judge hearing the CPS Docket is unavailable to hear or designate a judge to hear an urgent matter may the Department seek *ex parte* relief from the Duty Judge.

7.3 Scheduling Appointment with Duty Judge for Emergency Matter. For requests for *ex parte* relief or any other emergency matter to be presented to the Duty Judge, the applicant must schedule an appointment with the Duty Judge unless the request meets the exception stated in Local Rule 23.2.

7.4 Fully Advise the Court. A party presenting any application for an *ex parte* order must fully advise the Court of the circumstances, particularly as to whether there has been any previous application for the same or similar relief or whether the relief sought will conflict with any previous order.

7.5 Request for Withdrawal of Minor's Funds. When a request is to be made for withdrawal of funds maintained in the Registry of the Court for the benefit of a minor who has not yet reached legal age, the applicant must bring to the Court with the motion and proposed Order a Summary of Minor's Bank Account obtained from the District Clerk reflecting the status of the mi-

nor's account and indicating previous withdrawals, if any.

1. **Editor's note:** Approved as such. Probably should be "www.traviscountytx.gov/courts."

Chapters 8-20 omitted by editor

CHAPTER 21. SETTING CASES ON THE FAMILY & CPS DOCKETS

21.1 Long Docket Cases. All longer than ½ day settings in family cases must be set on the Family Docket on any Monday at 8:30 a.m. Long Docket cases must be announced pursuant to Chapter 3.

21.2 Short Docket Settings. All shorter than ½ day settings in family cases must be set on the Family Docket at 8:30 a.m. on any Wednesday, Thursday, or Friday.

21.3 Continuances. Continuances for settings on the Family Docket are heard every Thursday at 1:30 p.m. Continuances of longer than ½ day merits settings are heard the Thursday one week before the setting. All others are heard the Thursday before the next week setting. This Rule does not relieve a movant of the burden of delivering a copy of the motion and giving notice of the hearing in the manner and within the time provided by the Texas Rules of Civil Procedure.

21.4 CPS Docket. The Judge hearing the CPS Docket will instruct litigants regarding the setting of hearings. The available written instructions and related documents are posted at: www.co.travis.tx.us/courts/files/documents_civilCPS.asp.[1] All contested termination merits trials must be set on the Central Docket. Agreed terminations must be set in accordance with the written instructions referred to above.

1. **Editor's note:** Approved as such. Probably should be "www.traviscountytx.gov/courts/files/cps."

CHAPTER 22. PROCEEDINGS BEFORE ASSOCIATE JUDGES IN FAMILY LAW CASES

22.1 Appointment of Associate Judges. Pursuant to statute, the District Courts have appointed Associate Judges to hear certain matters specified by these Local Rules and by these Local Rules do refer these matters to the Associate Judges.

22.2 Authority of Associate Judges. An Associate Judge may hear all matters relating to suits over which the District Courts have jurisdiction under TEX. FAM. CODE. ANN. Titles 1, 4 and 5.

22.3 Objections to Associate Judges.

(a) A party may file an objection to the assignment of an Associate Judge to hear any trial on the merits. A trial on the merits is any trial in which a party seeks a final adjudication from which an appeal may be taken to a Court of Appeals. The objection must be in writing. The time for filing an objection shall be:

(1) on or before ten days from receipt of a notice of setting on the Family docket; or

(2) on or before ten days from receipt of notice that a Judge referred a specific case to an Associate Judge for a trial on the merits.

(b) A person filing an objection shall deliver a copy of the objection to all parties and to the Court Administrator on the same day the objection is filed with the District Clerk.

(c) A party may file a motion to have any other matter heard originally before a Judge instead of an Associate Judge. The motion must be in writing and must specify the grounds in support of the motion. The party filing the motion must set the motion for hearing by a Judge with notice to all parties as required by the applicable rules of civil procedure.

22.4 Settings Before Associate Judges. Matters set before an Associate Judge will be set on the days and times reflected on the docket schedule published by the Court Administrator from time to time, and may include specialty dockets such as uncontested terminations of parental rights, adoptions and confirmations of foreign adoptions, and Domestic Relations Office cases, child protection cases, and County Attorney family violence cases. The current docket schedule may be obtained from the Court Administrator.

22.5 Request for *De Novo* Hearing. Any person requesting a *de novo* hearing before a Judge shall also deliver a copy of the request to the Court Administrator on the same day that the request is filed with the District Clerk.

CHAPTER 23. PRE-TRIAL PROCEDURE IN FAMILY LAW CASES

23.1 Standing Pre-Trial and Discovery Order. The parties in any divorce suit or suit affecting the parent-child relationship filed in Travis County are subject to the Travis County Standing Order regarding Children, Property and Conduct of Parties. This or-

der may be found on the Travis County website at traviscountycourts.org.[1] When requesting a temporary restraining order or temporary injunction, counsel should not repeat or otherwise address the subject matter contained in the standing order except to seek a modification of the standing order.

23.2 Application for TRO to be Served with Citation. Notwithstanding Chapter 7, in a family law case, a request for a TRO to be served with citation may be presented *ex parte* at the uncontested docket if supported by an affidavit *and* if the relief would not affect the possession of or access to a child. All other emergency relief is governed by Chapter 7.

23.3 Pre-Trial Procedure Before a Final Trial on the Merits. Before the final trial on the merits in any divorce suit, suit affecting the parent-child relationship, or suit to modify an order affecting the parent-child relationship, each party shall prepare and deliver pre-trial forms and any amended pleadings as follows:

(1) Forms Required Depend on Type of Suit and Issue at Trial.

(a) In a divorce suit, each party shall prepare and deliver a Proposed Property Division using the form posted at traviscountycourts.org,[1] fully completed and signed by the party, or a single agreed Proposed Property Division, signed by both parties.

(b) In any suit requiring a determination of child support or spousal maintenance, each party shall prepare and deliver a Proposed Support Decision using the form posted at traviscountycourts.org,[1] fully completed and signed by the party, or single agreed Proposed Support Decision signed by both parties.

(c) In any suit requiring a determination of conservatorship, or possession and access to a child, each party shall prepare and deliver a Proposed Parenting Plan, pursuant to TEX.FAM.CODE.ANN. §153.603, fully completed and signed by the party, or single agreed Proposed Parenting plan, signed by both parties. The form parenting plan posted on the Travis County website at traviscountycourts.org[1] is acceptable, and other forms may also be acceptable.

(d) In any suit subject to Section 3.3, each party shall also prepare and deliver a Proposed Disposition of Other Issues, which shall state separately in brief complete sentences each trial decision that is sought by the party that is not covered by the Proposed Property Division or Proposed Support Decision or Proposed Parenting Plan.

(2) Where to File. Each party shall file the required forms with the District Clerk and deliver a copy to the opposing party.

(3) When to File.

(a) Each party shall file the required pre-trial forms and any amendment to pleadings before 5:00 p.m. on the Monday two weeks before the week of the trial setting. (The Rule 166 Standing Order in Family Law Cases alters the pleading deadlines in Rule 63.)

(b) Amendments to pre-trial forms and amendments to pleadings may be filed after the deadline above only upon leave of court, which leave shall be granted unless there is a showing that the filing will operate as a surprise to the opposite party.

23.4 Pre-Trial Procedure Before a Temporary or Interim Orders Hearing. Before any hearing on temporary or interim orders in any divorce suit, suit affecting the parent-child relationship, or suit to modify an order affecting the parent-child relationship, each party shall prepare and deliver pre-trial forms as follows:

(1) Forms Required Determined by Issues at Hearing. In a hearing to determine child support or spousal maintenance, each party shall prepare and deliver and[2] Proposed Support Decision using the form posted at traviscountycourts.org,[1] fully completed.

(2) To Whom Form Is Delivered. Each party shall deliver the required form to the opposing party and to the Judge hearing the case.

(3) When Form Is Delivered. Each party shall deliver the required form before the case is called for hearing.

23.5 Not Required In DRO, DFPS, AG or County Attorney Protective Order Hearings. Pre-trial forms are not required for any hearing where the Travis County Domestic Relations Office, the Texas Department of Family and Protective Services, the Texas Attorney General's Office or the County Attorney Protective Order Division appear.

23.6 No Extensions or Waivers by Court Administrator or by Agreement. The Court Administrator is not authorized to extend the time for deliver-

ing pretrial forms. The parties may not by agreement waive or modify the provisions or requirements of these rules.

23.7 Use as Evidence. Subject to applicable rules of evidence, the pre-trial forms required by these rules may be used during the trial or hearing and may be marked as exhibits and offered in evidence.

23.8 Consequences for Failure to Comply.

(1) All Parties Fail to Comply. If all parties in a case fail to deliver pre-trial forms as required by these rules, the case will be required to be reset or will be moved to the bottom of the list of cases set for the same time and will be heard only after all announced cases are heard and only if time permits.

(2) A Party Fails to Comply. If it appears that any party in a case failed to deliver pre-trial forms as required by these rules, the Court may conduct a pre-trial conference and the Court may impose one or more of the sanctions authorized by TEX. R. CIV. PROC. 215 against any party or attorney responsible for such failure.

(3) Issues Waived. All issues not stated in pre-trial forms as required by these procedures will deemed[3] waived except upon a showing of good cause for failure to comply with these rules.

23.9 Motion to Confer with a Child. Litigants are discouraged from bringing a child to the courthouse, thereby removing the child from his or her daily routine, before the court decides whether and when to confer.

23.10 No Limitation on Texas Rules of Civil Procedure. These rules shall not be construed as a substitute for, or as any limitation on, any pre-trial or discovery provision(s) pursuant to the Texas Rules of Civil Procedure.

1. **Editor's note:** Approved as such. Probably should be "www.traviscountytx.gov/courts."
2. **Editor's note:** Approved as such. Probably should be "a."
3. **Editor's note:** Approved as such. Probably should be "will be deemed."

CHAPTER 24. CHILD SUPPORT & SPOUSAL MAINTENANCE ORDERS

24.1 Place of Payment. All child support required by any court order must be paid directly to the Texas Child Support State Disbursement Unit, P.O. Box 659791, San Antonio, Texas, 78265-9791.

All spousal maintenance required by any court order must be paid through the Travis County Domestic Relations Office, P.O. Box 1495, Austin, Texas 78767.

24.2[1] DRO as Registry. The Travis County Domestic Relations Office is hereby designated as the Registry of the Court for all District Courts for the purpose of receiving all spousal maintenance payments for the establishment and custody of records of child support payments.

24.3[1] Duty to Establish Account. At the time any spousal or child support is ordered, the party who is to receive the support must provide to the Domestic Relations Office a "Request To Establish An Account" containing the information required by that office. After the order or decree is signed, that party must deliver to the Domestic Relations Office a signed copy of the order or decree.

1. **Editor's note:** Numbering supplied by editor.

CHAPTER 25. ADOPTIONS & TERMINATIONS

25.1 Confidential Records. The District Clerk will maintain the files, docket sheets, and minutes as confidential records:

(a) In every suit in which the petition includes a prayer seeking adoption of a child;

(b) In every suit in which any authorized agency seeks termination of the parent-child relationship.

25.2 Non-Confidential Records. In all other suits seeking termination but not adoption, the files, docket sheets, and minutes will not be confidential or sealed unless otherwise ordered by the Court

All pre-adoptive home screening and post-placement adoptive reports will be maintained as confidential records.

25.2[1] Procedures. The District Courts have determined that the following procedures concerning the preparation of pre-adoptive home screenings and post-placement adoptive reports, and the appointments of guardians *ad litem* are necessary for the orderly disposition of suits seeking termination of the parent child relationship or adoption, or both. These procedures are subject to any order that may be made in a particular case.

(a) In every suit in which the petitioner seeks to terminate a parent-child relationship or seeks to adopt a child, the Clerk shall forward a copy of the petition as soon as practicable to the Manager of the Family Court Services Unit of the Travis County Domestic Relations Office (Family Court Services Manager).

(b) In each suit seeking adoption of a child placed for adoption by the Texas Department of Family and Protective Services (the Department), the pre-adoptive home screening and post-placement adoptive report shall be made by the Department.

(c) In each suit brought by a child placing agency (other than the Texas Department of Family and Protective Services) that seeks to terminate the parent-child relationship, and in each suit that seeks adoption of a child placed by a child placing agency, the child placing agency shall prepare the pre-adoptive home screening and post-placement adoptive report.

(d) In every other suit seeking termination of the parent-child Relationship or adoption of a child, the Family Court Services Manager shall prepare the pre-adoptive home screening and post-placement adoptive report. The Domestic Relations Office may designate private providers to prepare the pre-adoptive home screening and post-placement adoptive report. The fees for preparation of a pre-adoptive home screening and post-placement adoptive report shall be paid as directed by the Family Court Service Manager.

(e) In any case, any party or the Family Court Services Manager may request the appointment of the Family Court Services Manager as guardian *ad litem*, or the court on its own motion may appoint a guardian *ad litem*.

(f) In any case, the Family Court Services Manager may request that the case is set for trial or pretrial hearing.

25.4 Criteria. Each pre-adoptive home screening and post-placement adoptive report made pursuant to Section 25.3 (d) shall be prepared according to criteria established by the Family Court Services Manager under the supervision of the District Judges.

25.5 Pre-trial Information Form. In every termination suit, except those brought by the Texas Department of Family and Protective Services, and in all adoption suits, the petitioner shall file a completed pretrial information form with the District Clerk and serve a copy on the Family Court Services Manager fourteen days before the final hearing. Petitioner's Pretrial Form in Suit for Termination and Adoption, posted on the Travis County website at www.traviscountycourts.org,[2] is acceptable.

1. **Editor's note:** Approved as such. Probably should be numbered "25.3."

2. **Editor's note:** Approved as such. Probably should be "www.traviscountytx.gov/courts."

Editor's note: *Petitioner's Pretrial Form in Suit for Termination and/or Adoption has been omitted by the editor. It is available at www.traviscountytx.gov/images/courts/Docs/local_rules_civildistrict.pdf.*

CHAPTER 26. FAMILY LAW NOTICES & ORDERS TO APPEAR

26.1 Notice of Hearings for Appearance after Answer Day. Notices of Hearing for Temporary Orders that require appearance after answer day do not require an order and should not be presented to a judge for signature.

26.2 Orders to Appear. Orders to Appear before answer day must be on a separate page and must contain the following language:

"It is ordered that the Clerk shall issue notice to Respondent, ____________________, to appear, and the Respondent is hereby ordered to appear in court on the __________ day of ________________, 20__, at __________ __.m." At that time, the dockets posted at the courthouse will display the courtroom of the District Judge or Associate Judge assigned to hear the case, and the respondent is ordered to appear in that courtroom before the judge. The District Court number that appears at the top of the first page of the court documents ("in the _____ District Court of Travis County") is not necessarily the court that will hear the case. Rely on the docket displays and/or guidance from the Office of the Court Administrator at the courthouse.

TRAVIS COUNTY STANDING ORDER REGARDING CHILDREN, PROPERTY & CONDUCT OF THE PARTIES

Effective Jan. 1, 2005.

No party to this lawsuit has requested this order. Rather, this order is a standing order of the Travis County District Courts that applies in every divorce suit and every suit affecting the parent-child relationship filed in Travis County. The District Courts of Travis County have adopted this order because the parties and their children should be protected and their property preserved while the lawsuit is pending before the court. Therefore, it is ORDERED:

1. **NO DISRUPTION OF CHILDREN.** Both parties are ORDERED to refrain from doing the following acts concerning any children who are subjects of this case:

1.1 Removing the children from the State of Texas, acting directly or in concert with others, without the written agreement of both parties or an order of this Court.

1.2 Disrupting or withdrawing the children from the school or day-care facility where the children are presently enrolled, without the written agreement of both parents or an order of this Court.

1.3 Hiding or secreting the children from the other parent or changing the children's current place of abode, without the written agreement of both parents or an order of this Court.

1.4 Disturbing the peace of the children.

2. CONDUCT OF THE PARTIES DURING THE CASE. Both parties are ORDERED to refrain from doing the following acts:

2.1 Using vulgar, profane, obscene, or indecent language, or a coarse or offensive manner, to communicate with the other party, whether in person, by telephone, or in writing.

2.2 Threatening the other party in person, by telephone, or in writing to take unlawful action against any person.

2.3 Placing one or more telephone calls, at an unreasonable hour, in an offensive or repetitious manner, without a legitimate purpose of communication, or anonymously.

2.4 Opening or diverting mail addressed to the other party.

3. PRESERVATION OF PROPERTY AND USE OF FUNDS DURING DIVORCE CASE. If this is a divorce case, both parties to the marriage are ORDERED to refrain from doing the following acts:

3.1 Destroying, removing, concealing, encumbering, transferring, or otherwise harming or reducing the value of the property of one or both of the parties.

3.2 Misrepresenting or refusing to disclose to the other party or to the Court, on proper request, the existence, amount, or location of any property of one or both of the parties.

3.3 Damaging or destroying the tangible property of one or both of the parties, including any document that represents or embodies anything of value.

3.4 Tampering with the tangible property of one or both of the parties, including any document that represents or embodies anything of value, and causing pecuniary loss to the other party.

3.5 Selling, transferring, assigning, mortgaging, encumbering, or in any other manner alienating any of the property of either party, whether personal property or real estate property, and whether separate or community, except as specifically authorized by this order.

3.6 Incurring any indebtedness, other than legal expenses in connection with this suit, except as specifically authorized by this order.

3.7 Making withdrawals from any checking or savings account in any financial institution for any purpose, except as specifically authorized by this order.

3.8 Spending any sum of cash in either party's possession or subject to either party's control for any purpose, except as specifically authorized by this order.

3.9 Withdrawing or borrowing in any manner for any purpose from any retirement, profit-sharing, pension, death, or other employee benefit plan or employee savings plan or from any individual retirement account or Keogh account, except as specifically authorized by this order.

3.10 Signing or endorsing the other party's name on any negotiable instrument, check, or draft, such as tax refunds, insurance payments, and dividends, or attempting to negotiate any negotiable instrument payable to the other party without the personal signature of the other party.

3.11 Taking any action to terminate or limit credit or charge cards in the name of the other party.

3.12 Entering, operating, or exercising control over the motor vehicle in the possession of the other party.

3.13 Discontinuing or reducing the withholding for federal income taxes on wages or salary while this suit is pending.

3.14 Terminating or in any manner affecting the service of water, electricity, gas, telephone, cable television, or other contractual services, such as security, pest control, landscaping, or yard maintenance at the other party's residence or in any manner attempting to withdraw any deposits for service in connection with such services.

4. PERSONAL AND BUSINESS RECORDS IN DIVORCE CASE. If this is a divorce case, both parties to the marriage are ORDERED to refrain from doing the following acts:

4.1 Concealing or destroying any family records, property records, financial records, business records or any records of income, debts, or other obligations.

4.2 Falsifying any writing or record relating to the property of either party.

4.3 "Records" include e-mail or other digital or electronic data, whether stored on a computer hard drive, diskette or other electronic storage device.

5. INSURANCE IN DIVORCE CASE. If this is a divorce case, both parties to the marriage are ORDERED to refrain from doing the following acts:

5.1 Withdrawing or borrowing in any manner all or any part of the cash surrender value of life insurance policies on the life of either party, except as specifically authorized by this order.

5.2 Changing or in any manner altering the beneficiary designation on any life insurance on the life of either party or the parties' children.

5.3 Canceling, altering, or in any manner affecting any casualty, automobile, or health insurance policies insuring the parties' property of persons including the parties' minor children.

6. SPECIFIC AUTHORIZATIONS IN DIVORCE CASE. If this is a divorce case, both parties to the marriage are specifically authorized to do the following:

6.1 To engage in acts reasonable and necessary to the conduct of that party's usual business and occupation.

6.2 To make expenditures and incur indebtedness for reasonable attorney's fees and expenses in connection with this suit.

6.3 To make expenditures and incur indebtedness for reasonable and necessary living expenses for food, clothing, shelter, transportation and medical care.

6.4 To make withdrawals from accounts in financial institutions only for the purposes authorized by this order.

7. SERVICE AND APPLICATION OF THIS ORDER.

7.1 The Petitioner shall attach a copy of this order to the original petition and to each copy of the petition. At the time the petition is filed, if the Petitioner has failed to attach a copy of this order to the petition and any copy of the petition, the Clerk shall ensure that a copy of this order is attached to the petition and every copy of the petition presented.

7.2 This order is effective upon the filing of the original petition and shall remain in full force and effect as a temporary restraining order for fourteen days after the date of the filing of the original petition. If no party contests this order by presenting evidence at a hearing on or before fourteen days after the date of the filing of the original petition, this order shall continue in full force and effect as a temporary injunction until further order of the court. This entire order will terminate and will no longer be effective once the court signs a final order.

8. EFFECT OF OTHER COURT ORDERS. If any part of this order is different from any part of a protective order that has already been entered or is later entered, the protective order provisions prevail. Any part of this order not changed by some later order remains in full force and effect until the court signs a final decree.

9. PARTIES ENCOURAGED TO MEDIATE. The parties are encouraged to settle their disputes amicably without court intervention. The parties are encouraged to use alternative dispute resolution methods, such as mediation, to resolve the conflicts that may arise in this lawsuit.

IN THE DISTRICT COURTS OF TRAVIS COUNTY, TEXAS

RULE 166 STANDING ORDER IN FAMILY LAW CASES

Effective May 1, 2010.

In any divorce suit, suit affecting the parent-child relationship, or suit to modify an order affecting the parent-child relationship, pursuant to Texas Rules of Civil Procedure 63 and 166, amendments to pleadings may be filed after 5:00 p.m. on the Monday two weeks before the week of the trial setting only upon leave of court, which leave shall be granted unless there is a showing that the filing will operate as a surprise to the opposite party.

IN THE DISTRICT COURTS OF TRAVIS COUNTY, TEXAS

STANDING ORDER FOR APPLICATION FOR & REFUSAL OF IV-D CHILD SUPPORT SERVICES

Effective July 1, 2009.

All final orders, excluding modifications, that provide for child support to be paid through the local registry or the State Disbursement Unit shall be deemed to include an application for IV-D child support services provided by the County and the Office of the Attorney General of Texas, pursuant to Chapter 231 of the Texas

Family Code. This ORDER shall apply to final orders rendered by the Travis County District Courts after the effective date of this ORDER.

Unless required to accept IV-D child support services pursuant to other laws, a child support obligee entitled to receive services pursuant to this ORDER may decline services by filing a written Refusal of Child Support Services with the District Clerk.

Refusal of the IV-D Child Support Services pursuant to this ORDER does not preclude that person from making a subsequent written application for IV-D Child Support Services with the Office of the Attorney General of Texas.

TRAVIS COUNTY STANDING ORDER REGARDING TDFPS LITIGATION

Effective Nov. 1, 2007.

Editor's note: *This standing order applies to child-abuse and child-neglect cases that are "on file or to be filed" by TDFPS in Travis County as of Nov. 1, 2007. For the full text of this CPS Standing Order, see www.traviscountytx.gov/images/courts/Docs/StandingOrder_FirstAmended_CPS_CivilDistrictCPS.pdf.*

Charts & Tables

Table of Contents

Charts & Tables

1. Attorney Fees in Family-Law Proceedings

	Type of Action	Authority	When Permitted & Notes
	Dissolution of Marriage		
1	Division of property	*Carle*, 234 S.W.2d 1002, 1005 (Tex.1950); *see* FAM §7.001.	Allocation of attorney fees is factor to be considered by court in making equitable division of community estate.
2	Suit for dissolution of marriage	FAM §6.708(c).	Can be awarded reasonable fees. Can be ordered paid directly to attorney, who can enforce order in her own name.
3	Temporary orders before final order	FAM §6.502(a)(4).	Can be awarded reasonable fees for preservation of property and for protection of parties as deemed necessary and equitable.
4 17	Temporary orders during appeal	FAM §6.709(a)(2); ***Halleman***, 379 S.W.3d 443, 453 (F.W. 2012, no pet.) (protection of parties); ***In re Garza***, 153 S.W.3d 97, 101 (S.A. 2004, orig. proceeding) (preservation of property).	Can be awarded reasonable and necessary fees for preservation of property and for protection of parties as considered equitable and necessary.
	Enforcement		
5	Administrative subpoena issued by Title IV-D agency	FAM §231.303(c); *see id.* §231.303(a).	Administrative subpoena is used to obtain information about location and income of parent with support obligation. Attorney fees can be awarded if individual or organization, without good cause, did not comply with subpoena.
6	Agreements incident to divorce—breach of contract	CPRC §38.001(8); *see* ***De la Garza***, 185 S.W.3d 924, 931 (Dal. 2006, no pet.).	Must be awarded if claimant is prevailing party and recovers damages.
7	Child custody—generally	TRCP 308a.	Except by court order, no fee can be charged by or paid to attorney representing claimant. If fee is paid, it will be adjudged against party who violated order.
8	Child custody—interference with possessory interest in violation of temporary or final order	FAM §42.006(a)(1); *see id.* §42.009 (frivolous claim).	Can be awarded when (1) locating child who is subject to the order, recovering possession of child, and enforcing order or (2) suit is frivolous.
9	Child custody—UCCJEA	FAM §152.312(a).	Must be awarded to prevailing party unless clearly inappropriate.
10	Child or spousal support—UIFSA	FAM §§159.305(b)(11), 159.313(b), (c).	Can be awarded to prevailing obligee but not to prevailing obligor, except as provided by other law. Payment of fees by obligor is mandatory if hearing was requested primarily for delay.
11	Child support—failure to comply with notice of levy	FAM §157.330(b).	Can be awarded in an action under FAM §157.330.
12	Child support—foreclosure on lien or suit to address lien	FAM §157.323(c)(1).	Must be awarded if there is court judgment for arrearages.
13	Child support—motion to enforce	FAM §157.162(b).	Finding that respondent is not in contempt does not preclude court from awarding attorney fees.
14	Child support—wage-withholding order against employer	FAM §158.206(a), (b)(3).	Can be awarded when employer does not comply with wage-withholding order. Includes orders directing that health insurance be provided for child.

1. ATTORNEY FEES IN FAMILY-LAW PROCEEDINGS (CONT'D)

	TYPE OF ACTION	AUTHORITY	WHEN PERMITTED & NOTES
		Enforcement (continued)	
15	Child-support order	FAM §157.167(a), (c); ***Russell***, 478 S.W.3d 36, 45-46 (Hous. [14th] 2015, no pet.).	Must be awarded to movant if court finds respondent has not paid child support, unless respondent shows good cause and court states reasons supporting finding. Fees and costs ordered can be enforced by contempt.
16	Division of property—property divided in decree	***Jenkins***, 991 S.W.2d 440, 450 (F.W. 1999, denied); *see* FAM §9.014.	Nonprevailing party can be awarded attorney fees, but fee award must be reasonable under circumstances of case. When awarding attorney fees to nonprevailing party, court must state on the record or in its judgment the good cause substantiating award.
17	Possession of or access to child	FAM §157.167(b), (c).	Must be awarded to movant if court finds respondent has failed to comply with possession order, unless respondent shows good cause and court states reasons supporting finding. Fees and costs ordered can be enforced by contempt, but not by withholding income.
18	Premarital and postmarital agreements—breach of contract	See row 6, p. 1526.	
		Marital Property	
19	Agreements incident to divorce—enforcement	See row 6, p. 1526.	
20	Division of property—enforcement	See row 16, above.	
21	Division of property—equitable factor in dissolution	See row 1, p. 1526.	
22	Division of property—not previously divided	FAM §9.205.	Can be awarded in proceeding to divide property previously undivided in divorce decree or annulment. Can be ordered paid directly to attorney, who can enforce order in her own name.
23	Management of marital property under unusual circumstances	FAM §3.303.	Costs of suit for petitioning spouse include reasonable fees for attorney appointed either (1) at the court's discretion or (2) as required when respondent is reported to be prisoner of war or missing on public service.
24	Premarital and postmarital agreements—enforcement	See row 6, p. 1526.	
25	Sale of homestead under unusual circumstances	FAM §5.104.	Costs of suit for petitioning spouse include reasonable fees for attorney appointed either (1) at the court's discretion or (2) as required when respondent is reported to be prisoner of war or missing on public service.
		Post-decree Proceedings	
26	Division of property—not previously divided	See row 22, above.	
27	QDRO	FAM §9.106.	Can be awarded in proceeding to render enforceable QDRO or similar order. Can be ordered paid directly to attorney, who can enforce order in her own name.

1. ATTORNEY FEES IN FAMILY-LAW PROCEEDINGS (CONT'D)

	TYPE OF ACTION	AUTHORITY	WHEN PERMITTED & NOTES
	Protective Orders		
28	Application for protective order	FAM §81.005; ***In re Skero***, 253 S.W.3d 884, 886-87 (Beau. 2008, orig. proceeding).	Can be awarded for services of private or prosecuting attorney or attorney employed by TDFPS against (1) party found to have committed family violence or (2) party against whom agreed protective order is rendered.
	Suits Affecting the Parent-Child Relationship		
29	Attorney ad litem, amicus attorney, or guardian ad litem appointed to represent child	FAM §107.023 (suits not filed by governmental entity).	Entitled to reasonable fees and expenses. Court can determine that fees awarded are necessaries for child.
30	Attorney ad litem appointed to represent child or adult	FAM §107.015.	Entitled to reasonable fees and expenses. Unless parents of child are indigent, court can assess fees against one or both parties at its discretion.
31 ⑰	Attorney appointed under managed-assigned-counsel program	FAM §107.308(b); *see id.* §107.015.	Entitled to reasonable fees and expenses. Unless parents of child are indigent, court can assess fees against one or both parties at its discretion.
32	False report of child abuse or neglect	FAM §105.006(h).	Any party that knowingly makes false allegation of child abuse or neglect in SAPCR can be ordered to pay attorney fees.
33	Parentage suit—generally	FAM §160.636(c); *see* ***In re B.B.R.***, 188 S.W.3d 341, 345 (F.W. 2006, no pet.).	Can be awarded in order adjudicating parentage and paid directly to attorney, who can enforce order in her own name.
34	Parentage suit—gestational agreement not validated	FAM §160.762(d).	Can be awarded and paid directly to attorney, who can enforce order in her own name.
35	SAPCR—generally	FAM §106.002; ***In re R.E.S.***, 482 S.W.3d 584, 586-87 (S.A. 2015, no pet.); ***London***, 94 S.W.3d 139, 146 (Hous. [14th] 2002, no pet.).	Can be awarded as necessaries for child. No prevailing-party requirement.
36 ⑰	SAPCR—modification suit filed frivolously or designed to harass party	FAM §156.005; ***Tucker***, 419 S.W.3d 292, 296 (Tex.2013).	Must be assessed against offending party if suit is found to be frivolous or designed to harass. Court must state finding in order.
37	Temporary orders before final order	FAM §105.001(a)(5); ***In re Rogers***, 370 S.W.3d 443, 445 (Aus. 2012, orig. proceeding).	Can be awarded reasonable fees for safety and welfare of child.
38 ⑰	Temporary orders during appeal	FAM §109.001(a)(5).	Can be awarded reasonable and necessary fees for safety and welfare of child as deemed necessary and equitable.
39	Title IV-D suit	FAM §231.211.	Can be awarded against nonprevailing party except Title IV-D agency, private attorney, or political subdivision that has entered into contract to provide Title IV-D services.
	Temporary Orders		
40	SAPCR—before final order	See row 37, above.	
41	SAPCR—during appeal	See row 38, above.	
42	Suit for dissolution—before final order	See row 3, p. 1526.	
43	Suit for dissolution—during appeal	See row 4, p. 1526.	

1. ATTORNEY FEES IN FAMILY-LAW PROCEEDINGS (CONT'D)

	TYPE OF ACTION	AUTHORITY	WHEN PERMITTED & NOTES
	Miscellaneous Provisions		
44	Attorney ad litem appointed to represent child or adult	See row 30, p. 1528.	
45	Civil suit—generally	TRCP 131; ***Diaz***, 350 S.W.3d 251, 256 (S.A. 2011, denied).	Family Code provisions on attorney fees and costs were intended to supplant TRCPs, including Rule 131, which requires that prevailing party recover her costs.
46	Discrimination—wage-withholding order	FAM §§8.208(c), 158.209(c).	Applicant entitled to fees if employer intentionally discharges employee in violation of statute.
47	False report of child abuse or neglect	FAM §261.107(d).	Court shall order person convicted of offense under FAM §261.107(a) to pay reasonable fees of person falsely accused.
48	Frivolous claim against party reporting child abuse or neglect	FAM §261.108(b).	Must be awarded to defendant when (1) claim found to be frivolous, unreasonable, or without foundation and (2) claim is dismissed or judgment is rendered for defendant.
49	Interference with possessory interest in child	FAM §42.006(a)(1).	Can be included as damages.
50	Property damage caused by willful and malicious conduct of a child	FAM §41.001(2) (liability), §41.002 (limited damages), §41.0025 (inn or hotel).	Recoverable against parent or other person who had duty to control child between ages of 10 and 18.

Legend:

CPRC	Texas Civil Practice & Remedies Code
FAM	Texas Family Code
QDRO	Qualified domestic-relations order
SAPCR	Suit affecting the parent-child relationship
TDFPS	Texas Department of Family & Protective Services
TRCP	Texas Rules of Civil Procedure
UCCJEA	Uniform Child Custody Jurisdiction & Enforcement Act
UIFSA	Uniform Interstate Family Support Act

2. STATUTES OF LIMITATIONS IN FAMILY-LAW PROCEEDINGS

	SUIT	AUTHORITY	LIMITATIONS PERIOD	MISCELLANEOUS
	Dissolution of Marriage			
1	Annulment—marriage occurring less than 72 hours after issuance of license	FAM §6.110(b).	30 days from date of marriage	Except as provided by EST §§123.101-123.104, marriage subject to annulment cannot be challenged after death of spouse. FAM §6.111.
2	Annulment—underage marriage by person older than 16 but younger than 18 (by parent, guardian, managing conservator, or next friend)	FAM §§6.102(c), 6.103.	90 days from date of marriage if person is filing as next friend	Suit cannot be brought after underage person's 18th birthday.
3	Informal marriage	FAM §2.401(b).	Rebuttable presumption that parties did not agree to be married after 2 years from date when parties separated and ceased living together	Proof can still be attempted after 2 years to rebut presumption.
	Enforcement			
4	Child possession and access—contempt	FAM §157.004.	6 months after child becomes adult or 6 months after right of possession and access terminates	
5	Child support—contempt	FAM §157.005(a).	2 years after child becomes an adult or 2 years after support obligation terminates	Majority of Texas jurisdictions have found FAM §157.005 addresses how long court has jurisdiction and is not statute of limitations. ***In re S.C.S.***, 48 S.W.3d 831, 833-34 (Hous. [14th] 2001, denied) (discussing case law on issue).
6	Child-support arrearages—cumulative money judgment for	FAM §157.005(b); *see id.* §159.604(b) (UIFSA).	10 years after child becomes an adult or 10 years after support obligation terminates	Majority of Texas jurisdictions have found FAM §157.005 addresses how long court has jurisdiction and is not statute of limitations. ***In re S.C.S.***, 48 S.W.3d at 833-34 (discussing case law on issue).
7	Division of property—future property divided in decree	FAM §9.003(b).	2 years from date the right to property matures or accrues or the decree becomes final, whichever is later	
8	Division of property—property divided in decree	FAM §9.003(a).	2 years from date decree was signed or becomes final after appeal, whichever is later	Courts disagree on whether reducing monetary award to judgment is subject to limitations under FAM §9.003. *Compare* ***Morales***, 195 S.W.3d 188, 191-92 (S.A. 2006, denied) (subject to limitations), *with* ***Jenkins***, 991 S.W.2d 440, 445-46 & n.6 (F.W. 1999, denied) (not subject to limitations).

2. STATUTES OF LIMITATIONS IN FAMILY-LAW PROCEEDINGS (CONT'D)

	SUIT	AUTHORITY	LIMITATIONS PERIOD	MISCELLANEOUS
	Post-decree Division			
9	Division of property—not previously divided	FAM §9.202(a).	2 years from date former spouse communicates to other spouse an unequivocal repudiation of other spouse's ownership interest	Tolled for period that Texas court does not have jurisdiction over spouses or property. FAM §9.202(b). Section 9.202 does not bar otherwise valid partition under Property Code. ***Mayes***, 11 S.W.3d 440, 457 (Hous. [14th] 2000, denied).
10	Premarital agreements	*See* CPRC §16.004(a)(1) (conveyance of real property), §16.051 (residual); *see also* ***Stine***, 80 S.W.3d 586, 592 (Tex.2002) (breach of contract).	4 years	Tolled during marriage. FAM §4.008.
	Suits Affecting the Parent-Child Relationship			
11	Adoption—attacking validity	FAM §162.012(a).	6 months after date order was signed	
12	Adoption—revoking statement to confer standing	FAM §102.0035(f).	Anytime before affidavit of voluntary relinquishment of parental rights is executed	
13	Conservatorship—after termination	FAM §102.006(c).	90 days after parent-child relationship is terminated in suit brought by TDFPS	FAM §102.006(c) applies only to adult siblings, grandparent, or aunt or uncle of child if person files original or modification suit.
14	Parentage—adjudicating when child has acknowledged or adjudicated father (by nonsignatory other than child)	FAM §160.609(b).	4 years from effective date of acknowledgment or adjudication	
15	Parentage—adjudicating when child has no acknowledged, adjudicated, or presumed father	FAM §160.606.	Can be filed at any time	Can be filed even after date child becomes adult or after date an earlier proceeding to adjudicate paternity has been dismissed based on statute of limitations.
16	Parentage—adjudicating when child has presumed father	FAM §160.607.	4 years from date of child's birth or at any time if (1) presumed father and mother did not live together or have sex at probable time of conception or (2) presumed father could not timely commence proceeding because misrepresentations led him to mistakenly believe he was biological father	
17	Parentage—challenging acknowledgment or denial of paternity by signatory after period of rescission expires	FAM §160.308(a); *see id.* §160.609(a); *see also id.* §160.307.	Anytime before issuance of order affecting child, including child-support order	Basis of challenge must be fraud, duress, or material mistake of fact.

2. STATUTES OF LIMITATIONS IN FAMILY-LAW PROCEEDINGS (CONT'D)

	SUIT	AUTHORITY	LIMITATIONS PERIOD	MISCELLANEOUS
	Suits Affecting the Parent-Child Relationship (continued)			
18	Parentage—challenging paternity when birth of child is by means of assisted reproduction	FAM §160.705.	4 years from date husband learned of child's birth if husband did not consent to assisted reproduction	Paternity may be adjudicated at any time if husband (1) did not provide sperm or did not consent to assisted reproduction, (2) has not cohabited with mother since assisted reproduction, and (3) never openly treated child as his own.
19	Parentage—contesting voluntary statement of paternity executed before Sept. 1, 1999	FAM §160.316(a), (g).	Before Sept. 1, 2003	FAM §160.316 expired Sept. 1, 2004. For the language of the statute, see Acts 2001, 77th Leg., R.S., ch. 821, §1.01, eff. June 14, 2001.
20	Parentage—rescinding acknowledgment or denial of paternity by signatory	FAM §160.307; *see also id.* §160.308.	Earlier of (1) 60 days after effective date of acknowledgment or denial or (2) date proceeding is initiated to adjudicate issue relating to child, when signatory is party to proceeding	
21	Termination—attacking validity	FAM §161.211(a), (b).	6 months after date order was signed	Courts disagree on whether FAM §161.211 is bar to challenge of termination order or affirmative defense. *Compare **In re C.T.C.***, 365 S.W.3d 853, 858 (Dal. 2012, pet. granted, judgm't vacated w.r.m.) (bar to challenge of termination order), *with **In re Bullock***, 146 S.W.3d 783, 790-91 (Beau. 2004, orig. proceeding) (affirmative defense).
	Torts			
22	Assault. See ***O'Connor's Texas COA***, ch. 4, p. 33.	CPRC §16.003(a).	2 years (except sexual assault; see row 34, p. 1533)	
23	Breach of fiduciary duty. See ***O'Connor's Texas COA***, ch. 11, p. 261.	CPRC §16.004(a)(5).	4 years	Discovery rule applies. ***Slay***, 187 S.W.2d 377, 394 (Tex.1945). Cause accrues when claimant knew or should have known of facts that in exercise of reasonable diligence would have led to discovery of wrongful act. ***Little***, 943 S.W.2d 414, 420 (Tex.1997).
24	Breach of promise to marry	CPRC §16.002(a).	1 year	
25	Conversion of personal property. See ***O'Connor's Texas COA***, ch. 6, p. 159.	CPRC §16.003(a).	2 years	Discovery rule applies when possession was initially lawful and claimant makes no demand. ***Wells Fargo***, 360 S.W.3d 691, 702 (Dal. 2012, no pet.). Generally, cause accrues at time of unlawful taking. *Id.* at 700. If possession is initially lawful, cause accrues at earlier of demand and refusal or when unequivocal acts of conversion occur. *Id.*
26	Fraud. See ***O'Connor's Texas COA***, ch. 12-A, p. 281.	CPRC §16.004(a)(4).	4 years	Discovery rule applies. ***Hooks***, 457 S.W.3d 52, 57 (Tex.2015). Cause accrues when defendant makes false representation or omission. ***Hoover***, 835 S.W.2d 668, 676 (Dal. 1992, denied).

2. STATUTES OF LIMITATIONS IN FAMILY-LAW PROCEEDINGS (CONT'D)

	SUIT	AUTHORITY	LIMITATIONS PERIOD	MISCELLANEOUS
Torts (continued)				
27	Illegal wiretapping. See *O'Connor's Texas COA*, ch. 33-B, p. 1162.	*See* CPRC §16.003(a) (limitations period), §123.002 (wiretap as cause of action).	2 years	No statutory limitations period, but action may be categorized as invasion of privacy. *See* ***Collins***, 904 S.W.2d 792, 804 (Hous. [1st] 1995), *denied*, 923 S.W.2d 569 (Tex.1996). If interception cannot be detected immediately, discovery rule may apply and defer accrual until P discovers or reasonably should have discovered the interception. ***Parker***, 897 S.W.2d 918, 928-29 (F.W. 1995, denied), *disapproved on other grounds*, ***Formosa Plastics***, 960 S.W.2d 41 (Tex.1998); *see* ***Stephens***, 126 S.W.3d 120, 126-27 (Hous. [1st] 2003), *denied*, 181 S.W.3d 741 (Tex.2005).
28	Indecency with a child if conduct violates Pen §21.11	CPRC §16.0045(a)(6).	15 years	If victim dies, cause accrues on death. CPRC §16.0045(c). Limitations period tolled by "John Doe" pleading. *Id.* §16.0045(d).
29	Intentional infliction of emotional distress. See *O'Connor's Texas COA*, ch. 14, p. 389.	*See* CPRC §16.003(a).	2 years	Because IIED is considered a continuing tort, conduct throughout marriage can be considered. ***Toles***, 45 S.W.3d 252, 262 (Dal. 2001, denied). Under continuing-course-of-conduct doctrine, limitations period begins to run on date IIED ceased. ***Newton***, 895 S.W.2d 503, 506 (F.W. 1995, no writ).
30	Invasion of privacy. See *O'Connor's Texas COA*, ch. 15, p. 399.	*See* CPRC §16.003(a).	2 years	Discovery rule applies. *See* ***Stephens***, 126 S.W.3d at 126-27.
31	Prostitution (compelled) if conduct violates Pen §43.05(a)(1)	CPRC §16.0045(b)(4).	5 years	If victim dies, cause accrues on death. CPRC §16.0045(c). Limitations period tolled by "John Doe" pleading. *Id.* §16.0045(d).
32	Prostitution by a child (compelled) if conduct violates Pen §43.05(a)(2)	CPRC §16.0045(a)(5).	15 years	If victim dies, cause accrues on death. CPRC §16.0045(c). Limitations period tolled by "John Doe" pleading. *Id.* §16.0045(d).
33	Sexual abuse other than sexual assault or sexual abuse violating Pen §21.02	*See* CPRC §16.003(a).	2 years	
34	Sexual assault, aggravated sexual assault, or sexual abuse if conduct violates Pen §22.011(a)(1) or §22.021(a)(1)(A)	CPRC §16.0045(b)(1), (2).	5 years	If victim dies, cause accrues on death. CPRC §16.0045(c). Limitations period tolled by "John Doe" pleading. *Id.* §16.0045(d).
35	Sexual assault of a child, aggravated sexual assault of a child, or continuous sexual abuse of a young child or children if conduct violates Pen §21.02, §22.011(a)(2), or §22.021(a)(1)(B)	CPRC §16.0045(a)(1)-(3).	15 years	If victim dies, cause accrues on death. CPRC §16.0045(c). Limitations period tolled by "John Doe" pleading. *Id.* §16.0045(d).

2. Statutes of Limitations in Family-Law Proceedings (cont'd)

	Suit	Authority	Limitations Period	Miscellaneous
		Torts (continued)		
36	Sexual trafficking of a child if conduct violates Pen §20A.02(a)(7)(A), (B), (C), (D), or (H) or §20A.02(A)(8)	CPRC §16.0045(a)(4).	15 years	If victim dies, cause accrues on death. CPRC §16.0045(c). Limitations period tolled by "John Doe" pleading. *Id.* §16.0045(d).
37	Trafficking of person in violation of Pen §20A.02	CPRC §16.0045(b)(3).	5 years	If victim dies, cause accrues on death. CPRC §16.0045(c). Limitations period tolled by "John Doe" pleading. *Id.* §16.0045(d).

Legend:

CPRC	Texas Civil Practice & Remedies Code
EST	Texas Estates Code
FAM	Texas Family Code
IIED	Intentional infliction of emotional distress
Pen	Texas Penal Code
TDFPS	Texas Department of Family & Protective Services
UIFSA	Uniform Interstate Family Support Act
O'Connor's Texas COA	***O'Connor's Texas Causes of Action*** (2017)

3. DERIVATION TABLE—CURRENT TO FORMER

The derivation table covers the extensive renumbering of the Family Code that occurred before 1998. The year in parentheses indicates the year of enactment.

Unless otherwise noted, all references are to the Family Code.
GC = Texas Government Code HRC = Texas Human Resources Code p95 = Pre-1995

CURRENT	FORMER
§§1.101, 1.102	§2.01 (p95)
§1.103	§4.01 (p95)
§§1.104-1.107	§§4.03-4.06 (p95)
§§2.001, 2.002	§§1.01, 1.02 (p95)
§2.003	§1.02(2)(B) (p95)
§§2.004, 2.005	§§1.03, 1.04 (p95)
§2.006	§1.05(a), (b) (p95)
§2.007	§1.05(c) (p95)
§2.008	§1.06 (p95)
§2.009	§1.07 (p95)
§2.010	§1.07(e) (p95)
§2.012	§1.09 (p95)
§§2.101, 2.102	§§1.51, 1.52 (p95)
§2.103	§1.53 (p95)
§2.201	§1.81(a) (p95)
§2.202	§1.83(a), (b) (p95)
§2.203	§1.82(a), (b) (p95)
§2.204	§1.82(c), (d) (p95)
§2.205	§1.83(c), (d) (p95)
§2.206	§1.84 (p95)
§2.207	§1.81 (p95)
§§2.208, 2.209	§§1.85, 1.86 (p95)
§2.301	§2.02 (p95)
§2.302	§2.03 (p95)
§§2.401, 2.403	§§1.91, 1.93 (p95)
§§2.404, 2.405	§§1.94, 1.95 (p95)
§2.501	§4.02 (p95)
§3.001	§5.01(a) (p95)
§3.002	§5.01(b) (p95)

CURRENT	FORMER
§§3.003-3.005	§§5.02-5.04 (p95)
§§3.101-3.104	§§5.21-5.24 (p95)
§3.201	§4.031 (p95)
§§3.202, 3.203	§§5.61, 5.62 (p95)
§3.301	§5.25(a), (b) (p95)
§3.302	§5.26(a), (b) (p95)
§3.303	§§5.25(c), 5.26(c) (p95)
§3.304	§§5.25(d), 5.26(d) (p95)
§3.305	§5.25(e) (p95)
§3.306	§§5.25(f), 5.26(e) (p95)
§3.307	§§5.25(g), 5.26(f) (p95)
§3.308	§§5.25(h), 5.26(g) (p95)
§3.309	§5.27 (p95)
§§4.001-4.010	§§5.41-5.50 (p95)
§4.101	§5.51 (p95)
§4.102	§5.52 (p95)
§4.103	§5.53 (p95)
§4.104	§5.54 (p95)
§§4.105, 4.106	§§5.55, 5.56 (p95)
§§5.001, 5.002	§§5.81, 5.82 (p95)
§5.003 ('03)	§§5.84 (p95), 5.107 ('97)
§5.101	§§5.83(a), 5.831(a) (p95)
§5.102	§§5.85(a), 5.87(a) (p95)
§5.103	§§5.83(b), 5.831(b), 5.85(b), 5.87(b) (p95)

CURRENT	FORMER
§5.104	§§5.83(b), 5.831(b), 5.85(b), 5.87(b) (p95)
§5.105	§§5.83(b), 5.831(b), 5.85(b), 5.87(b) (p95)
§5.106	§§5.83(c), 5.831(c), 5.85(c), 5.87(c) (p95)
§5.108	§5.86 (p95)
§§6.001-6.008	§§3.01-3.08 (p95)
§6.102	§2.41(b) (p95)
§6.103	§2.41(a), (b) (p95)
§6.104	§2.41(c) (p95)
§§6.105-6.111	§§2.42-2.47 (p95)
§§6.201-6.203	§§2.21-2.23 (p95)
§§6.301-6.306	§§3.21-3.25 (p95)
§6.307	§§2.24, 3.25 (p95)
§§6.401-6.403	§§3.51-3.53 (p95)
§6.405	§3.522[B*] ('95)
§6.406	§3.55(a), (b) (p95)
§6.407	§3.55(b)-(d) (p95)
§6.409	§3.521 (p95)
§6.501	§3.58(a), (b) (p95)
§6.502	§§3.58(c), 3.59 (p95)
§6.503	§3.58(d), (e) (p95)
§6.504	§3.581 (p95)
§6.505	§3.54(a)-(c) (p95)
§6.506	§3.58(f) (p95)
§6.507	§3.58(g) (p95)
§6.701	§3.53 (p95)

3. DERIVATION TABLE—CURRENT TO FORMER (CONT'D)

CURRENT	FORMER
§6.702	§3.60 (p95)
§6.703	§3.61 (p95)
§6.704	§3.62 (p95)
§6.705	§3.54(b), (d) (p95)
§6.706	§3.64 (p95)
§6.707	§3.57 (p95)
§6.708	§§3.54(e), 3.65 (p95)
§6.709	§3.58(h), (i) (p95)
§6.801	§3.66(a), (b) (p95)
§6.802	§3.66(c) (p95)
§7.001	§3.63(a) (p95)
§7.002	§3.63(b) (p95)
§7.003	§3.633(a) (p95)
§7.004	§3.632(a) (p95)
§7.005	§3.632(d), (e) (p95)
§7.006	§3.631 (p95)
§8.001	§3.9601 (p95)
§8.051	§§3.9602 ('95), 8.002(a) ('97)
§8.052	§§3.9603 ('95), 8.003 ('97)
§8.053	§§3.9604 ('95), 8.004 ('97)
§8.054	§§3.9605 ('95), 8.005 ('97)
§8.055	§§3.9606 ('95), 8.006 ('97)
§8.056	§§3.9607 ('95), 8.007 ('97)
§8.057	§§3.9608 ('95), 8.008 ('97)
§8.059	§§3.9609 ('95), 8.009 ('97)
§8.060	§§3.9610 ('95), 8.010 ('97)
§8.061	§§3.9611 ('95), 8.011 ('97)
§9.001	§3.70(a), (b) (p95)
§9.002	§3.70(c) (p95)
§9.003	§3.70(c) (p95)
§9.004	§3.70(d) (p95)
§9.005	§3.70(e) (p95)
§9.006	§3.71(a) (p95)
§§9.007-9.014	§§3.71-3.77 (p95)
§9.101	§3.711(a), (b) ('95)
§9.102	§3.711(d) ('95)
§9.103	§3.711(a) ('95)
§9.104	§3.711(c) ('95)
§9.105	§3.711(e) ('95)
§9.201	§3.90(a), (b) (p95)
§9.202	§3.90(c) (p95)
§§9.203-9.205	§§3.91-3.93 (p95)
§9.301	§3.632(b), (c) (p95)
§9.302	§3.633(b)-(e) (p95)
§31.001	§31.01(a), (c) (p95)
§31.002	§31.02(a), (c) (p95)
§31.003	§31.03(a) (p95)
§31.004	§31.04 (p95)
§§31.005-31.007	§§31.06-31.08 (p95)
§§32.001, 32.002	§§35.01, 35.02 (p95)
§32.003	§35.03(a)-(f) (p95)
§32.004	§35.03(g) (p95)
§32.005	§35.04 (p95)
§32.101	§35.011 (p95)
§32.102	§§32.103 ('95), 35.013 (p95)
§32.103	§§32.104 ('95), 35.014 (p95)
§32.201	§35.05 (p95)
§§41.001, 41.002	§§33.01, 33.02 (p95)
§41.003	§33.03 (p95)
§42.001	§36.01 (p95)
§42.002	§36.02(a), (b) (p95)
§42.003	§36.02(c), (d) (p95)
§42.005	§36.05 (p95)
§42.006	§36.03 (p95)
§42.007	§36.04 (p95)
§42.008	§36.06 (p95)
§42.009	§36.08 (p95)
§45.001	§§32.01, 32.02(a) (p95)
§45.002	§32.02 (p95)
§45.003	§32.03 (p95)
§45.004	§32.04 (p95)
§45.005	§32.05 (p95)
§45.101	§32.21(a) (p95)
§45.102	§32.21(a), (b) (p95)
§45.103	§32.22 (p95)
§45.104	§32.23 (p95)
§71.001	§71.01(a) (p95)
§71.002	§71.01(b)(1) (p95)
§71.003	§71.01(b)(3) (p95)
§71.004	§71.01(b)(2) (p95)
§71.005	§71.01(b)(5) (p95)
§71.006	§71.01(b)(4), (6) (p95)
§81.001	§71.10(a), (b) (p95)
§81.002	§71.041(a) ('95)
§81.003	§71.041(b) ('95)
§81.004	§71.041(c) ('95)
§81.005	§71.041(d) ('95)
§81.006	§71.041(d) ('95)
§81.007	§71.04(c) (p95)
§81.008	§71.19 (p95)

3. DERIVATION TABLE—CURRENT TO FORMER (CONT'D)

CURRENT	FORMER
§82.001	§§71.02, 71.04(a) (p95)
§82.002	§71.04(b) (p95)
§82.003	§71.03 (p95)
§82.004	§71.05(a) (p95)
§82.005	§71.06 (p95)
§82.006	§71.05(c) (p95)
§82.007	§71.05(d) (p95)
§82.008	§71.05(f), (g) (p95)
§82.009	§71.05(e) (p95)
§82.021	§71.08 (p95)
§82.022	§71.121(a) ('95), (b) (p95)
§82.041	§71.07(d), (e) (p95)
§82.042	§71.07(b), (c) (p95)
§82.043	§§71.06(e) ('95), 71.07(a), (f)-(h) (p95)
§83.001	§71.15(a) (p95)
§83.002	§71.15(b), (c) (p95)
§83.003	§71.15(d) (p95)
§83.004	§71.15(e) (p95)
§83.005	§71.15(f) (p95)
§83.006	§71.15(g), (h) (p95)
§84.001	§§71.09(a), 71.121(c) (p95)
§84.002	§71.09(d) (p95)
§84.003	§71.09(c) (p95)
§84.004	§71.09(b) (p95)
§85.001	§§71.10(a), (b) (p95), 71.121(d) ('95)
§85.002	§71.10(c) (p95)
§85.003	§71.121(a) (p95), (e), (f) ('95)
§85.004	§71.06(f) ('95)
§85.005	§§71.10(d) ('95), 71.12(a), (b), (d), (e) (p95)
§85.006	§71.09(e) (p95)
§85.007	§71.111 (p95)
§85.009	§71.06(c) ('95)
§85.021	§71.11(a)(1)-(4), (6) (p95)
§85.022	§71.11(a)(5), (7), (b), (c) (p95)
§85.023	§71.11(d) (p95)
§85.024	§71.11(i) (p95)
§85.025	§71.13 (p95)
§85.026	§71.16 (p95)
§85.041	§71.17(a)-(d) ('95)
§85.042	§71.17(e)-(g) ('95)
§86.001	§71.18(a), (b) (p95)
§86.002	§71.18(c)[A*] ('95)
§86.003	§71.18(c)[B*] ('95)
§86.004	§71.18(d) ('95)
§87.001	§71.14(a) (p95)
§87.002	§71.14(b) (p95)
§87.003	§71.14(c) ('95)
§91.001	§73.01 ('95)
§91.002	§73.02 ('95)
§91.003	§73.03 ('95)
§91.004	§73.05 ('95)
§92.001	§73.04 ('95)
§101.001	§11.01 (p95)
§101.002	§11.01(7) (p95)
§101.003	§11.01(1) (p95)
§101.004	§14.80(3) (p95)
§101.005	§14.80(7) (p95)
§101.006	§14.80(4) (p95)
§101.007	§11.15(c) (p95)
§101.008	§11.01(2) (p95)
§101.009	§17.001 (p95)
§101.010	§14.30(a)(2) (p95)
§101.011	§14.30(a)(1) (p95)
§101.012	§14.30(a)(3) (p95)
§101.014	§11.01(8) (p95)
§101.015	§14.061(d) (p95)
§101.016	§14.021(b) (p95)
§101.017	§11.01(7); HRC §42.002(12) (p95)
§101.018	§11.01(11) (p95)
§101.019	§11.01(6) (p95)
§101.020	§14.80(5) (p95)
§101.021	§11.01(10) (p95)
§101.022	§11.01(9) (p95)
§101.024	§11.01(3) (p95)
§101.025	§11.01(4) (p95)
§101.027	§15.051(a)(1) (p95)
§101.028	§14.033(a)(1) (p95)
§101.029	§14.033(a)(2) (p95)
§101.030	§§14.80(6), 21.01(19) (p95)
§101.032	§11.01(5) (p95)
§101.033	§14.80(2); HRC §76.001 (p95)
§101.034	§14.80(2) (p95)
§101.035	§21.01(22) (p95)
§102.001	§11.02 (p95)
§102.002	§11.07(a) (p95)
§102.003	§11.03(a) (p95)
§102.004	§11.03(b), (c) (p95)
§102.005	§11.03(d) (p95)
§102.006	§11.03(g), (h) (p95)
§102.007	§11.03(i) (p95)
§102.008	§11.08(a), (b) (p95)

3. DERIVATION TABLE—CURRENT TO FORMER (CONT'D)

CURRENT	FORMER
§102.009	§11.09(a)-(c), (f) (p95)
§102.010	§11.09(d), (e) (p95)
§102.011	§11.051 (p95)
§102.013	§11.07(c) (p95)
§103.001	§11.04 (p95)
§103.002	§11.06(a), (c) (p95)
§103.003	§11.061 (p95)
§104.001	§11.14(e) (p95)
§104.002	§11.21(a), (b) (p95)
§104.003	§11.21(d) (p95)
§104.004	§11.21(c) (p95)
§104.005	§11.21(e) (p95)
§105.001	§§11.11(a)-(d), (g), (h), 14.033(1), 14.055(e) (p95)
§105.002	§11.13 (p95)
§105.003	§11.14(a), (b), (d), (f), (g) (p95)
§105.004	§11.14(i) (p95)
§105.005	§11.15(a) (p95)
§105.006	§11.155 (p95)
§105.007	§14.045(a), (b) (p95)
§106.001	§11.18(a) (p95)
§106.002	§§11.18(a), 11.22(j) (p95)
§107.001	§11.10(a), (b)(1) (p95)
§107.011	§11.10(b)(2), (c) (p95)
§107.012	§11.10(d) (p95)
§107.013	§11.10(d) (p95)
§107.015	§11.10(a), (e) (p95)
§107.031	§11.101 (p95)
§107.051	§11.12(a), (b) (p95)
§107.0511 ('07)	§107.0511 ('01)
§107.052	§11.12(b) (p95)
§107.053	§11.12(b) (p95)
§107.054	§11.12(c) (p95)
§107.055	§§11.12(c), 11.14(c) (p95)
§107.056	§11.18(c) (p95)
§108.001	§11.17(a), (d) (p95)
§108.002	§11.17(b) (p95)
§108.003	§11.17(b); HRC §§49.003(d), 49.005(d) (p95)
§108.004	§11.17(b) (p95)
§108.005	§11.17(b) (p95)
§108.006	§§11.17(c), 11.171 (p95)
§108.007	§11.17(e) (p95)
§108.008	§13.43(a)-(c) (p95)
§108.009	§13.43(e), (f) (p95)
§109.001	§11.11(e)-(g) (p95)
§109.002	§11.19 (p95)
§109.003	§11.191 (p95)
§110.002	§14.13 (p95)
§110.003	§11.18(b) (p95)
§110.004	§§14.43(i), 14.45(h) (p95)
§110.005	§11.06(*l*) (p95)
§111.001	§§14.03(j), 14.05(h), (i) (p95)
§111.002	§§14.032(e), (f), 14.052(c), (d) (p95)
§111.003	§§14.033(p), 14.058 (p95)
§151.001	§§4.02, 12.04 (p95), 151.003 ('95)
§151.002	§§12.05 (p95), 151.004 ('95)
§151.003	§151.005 ('99)
§152.001	§§11.51 (p95), 152.001(a)(9), (b) ('95)
§152.101	§§11.75 (p95), 152.025 ('95)
§152.102	§§11.52 (p95), 152.002 ('95)
§152.105	§§11.73 (p95), 152.023 ('95)
§152.106	§§11.62 (p95), 152.012 ('95)
§152.107	§§11.74 (p95), 152.024 ('95)
§152.108	§§11.55 (p95), 152.005 ('95)
§152.111	§§11.68 (p95), 152.018 ('95)
§152.112	§§11.69-11.71 (p95), 152.019-152.021 ('95)
§152.201	§§11.53 (p95), 152.003 ('95)
§152.202	§§11.53 (p95), 152.003(d) ('95)
§152.203	§§11.64 (p95), 152.003(d) ('95)
§152.204	§152.003(e) ('95)
§152.205	§§11.54, 11.60, 152.004 (p95), 152.010 ('95)
§152.206	§§11.56 (p95), 152.006 ('95)
§152.207	§§11.57 (p95), 152.007 ('95)
§152.208	§§11.58 (p95), 152.008 ('95)
§152.209	§§11.59 (p95), 152.009 ('95)
§152.210	§§11.61 (p95), 152.011 ('95)
§152.305	§§11.66, 152.014 (p95), 152.016 ('95)
§152.306	§§11.65 (p95), 152.015 ('95)

3. DERIVATION TABLE—CURRENT TO FORMER (CONT'D)

CURRENT	FORMER
§152.307	§§11.56 (p95), 152.006 ('95)
§152.313	§§11.63 (p95), 152.013 ('95)
§153.001	§14.021(a) (p95)
§153.002	§14.07(a) (p95)
§153.003	§§14.01(c)(1) (p95), 14.032(d) ('95)
§153.004	§§14.01(c)(2), 14.021(h), 14.03(d), (e)(3) (p95)
§153.005	§14.01(a) (p95)
§153.006	§14.03(a), (c) (p95)
§153.007	§14.06 (p95)
§153.009	§14.07(c) (p95)
§153.010	§14.03(h) (p95)
§153.011	§14.03(i) (p95)
§153.012	§14.04(c) (p95)
§153.013	§34.031(b) (p95)
§153.071	§14.02(a) (p95)
§153.072	§14.02(b) (p95)
§153.073	§14.02(a), (b)(2) (p95)
§153.074	§14.02(b)(1) (p95)
§153.075	§14.03(d) (p95)
§153.076	§14.02(a) (p95)
§153.131	§14.01(b)(1) (p95)
§153.132	§14.02(b)(3) (p95)
§153.133	§14.021(c), (d) (p95)
§153.134	§14.021(e), (f) (p95)
§153.135	§14.021(b) (p95)
§153.138	§14.021(g) (p95)
§153.191	§14.03(d) (p95)
§153.192	§§14.03(b), 14.04 (p95)
§153.193	§14.03(d) (p95)
§153.251	§14.032(a) (p95)
§153.252	§14.033(k) (p95)
§153.253	§14.033(k), (m) (p95)
§153.254	§14.032(b) (p95)
§153.255	§14.033(n) (p95)
§153.256	§14.032(c) (p95)
§153.257	§14.033(h) (p95)
§153.258	§14.033(k) (p95)
§153.311	§14.033(b) (p95)
§153.312	§14.033(c), (e)(4)-(7) (p95)
§153.313	§14.033(f) (p95)
§153.314	§14.033(e)(1)-(3), (8)-(10), (f)(2) (p95)
§153.315	§14.033(d) (p95)
§153.316	§14.033(g) (p95)
§153.317	§14.033(i) (p95)
§153.371	§14.02(c) (p95)
§153.372	§14.021(j) (p95)
§153.373	§14.01(b)(2) (p95)
§153.374	§14.01(d) (p95)
§153.375	§14.01(e) (p95)
§153.376	§14.04(a), (b) (p95)
§153.377	§14.04(c) (p95)
§153.431	§14.07(b) (p95)
§153.432	§14.03(e), (f)(1), (3) (p95)
§153.433	§14.03(e) (p95)
§153.434	§14.03(g) (p95)
§154.001	§14.05(a), (b), (d) (p95)
§154.002	§14.05(a) (p95)
§154.003	§14.05(a) (p95)
§154.004	§14.0503 (p95)
§154.005	§14.05(c) (p95)
§154.006	§14.05(d) (p95)
§154.007	§14.05(e) (p95)
§154.008	§14.061(a) (p95)
§154.009	§14.062 (p95)
§154.010	§§14.05(g), 14.053(i) (p95)
§154.061	§14.053(a), (h) (p95)
§154.062	§14.053(b) (p95)
§154.063	§14.053(g) (p95)
§154.064	§14.053(d) (p95)
§154.065	§14.053(c) (p95)
§154.066	§14.053(f) (p95)
§154.067	§14.053(e) (p95)
§154.068	§14.053(k) (p95)
§154.069	§14.056(c) (p95)
§154.070	§14.055(i) (p95)
§154.121	§14.052(a) (p95)
§154.122	§§14.05(j), 14.055(a) (p95)
§154.123	§§14.052(b), 14.054 (p95)
§154.124	§§14.053(j), 14.06 (p95)
§154.125	§14.055(a), (b) (p95)
§154.126	§14.055(c) (p95)
§154.127	§14.055(d) (p95)
§154.128	§14.055(f)-(h) (p95)
§154.129	§14.055(j) (p95)
§154.130	§14.057 (p95)
§154.131	§14.053(*l*) (p95)
§154.181	§14.061 (p95)
§154.182	§14.061(a), (b) (p95)
§154.183	§§14.053(d), 14.061(c) (p95)
§154.184	§14.061(r) (p95)
§154.185	§14.061(e), (f) (p95)

3. Derivation Table—Current to Former (cont'd)

Current	Former
§154.186	§14.061(g) (p95)
§154.187	§14.061(h)-(k), (p) (p95)
§154.188	§14.061(*l*) (p95)
§§154.189, 154.190	§14.061(m) (p95)
§154.191	§14.061(n), (o) (p95)
§154.192	§14.061(q) (p95)
§154.241	§14.0501 (p95)
§154.242	§14.0502 (p95)
§154.243	§14.0504 (p95)
§154.301	§14.051(a) (p95)
§154.302	§14.051(b) (p95)
§154.303	§14.051(c) (p95)
§154.304	§14.051(i) (p95)
§154.305	§14.051(d)-(f) (p95)
§154.306	§14.051(g) (p95)
§154.307	§14.051(h) (p95)
§154.308	§14.051(j), (k) (p95)
§155.001	§11.05(a), (b), (d), (e) (p95)
§155.002	§11.05(a) (p95)
§155.003	§11.05(g) (p95)
§155.004	§11.05(b), (f), (g) (p95)
§155.005	§11.05(h) (p95)
§155.101	§11.071(a), (b) (p95)
§155.102	§11.071(d) (p95)
§155.103	§11.05(c) (p95)
§155.104	§11.071(c) (p95)
§155.201	§11.06(b), (c) (p95)
§155.202	§11.06(b), (d) (p95)
§155.203	§11.06(b) (p95)

Current	Former
§155.204	§11.06(f)-(i) (p95)
§155.205	§§11.05(h), 11.06(j) (p95)
§155.206	§11.06(k) (p95)
§155.207	§11.06(j), (m) (p95)
§155.301	§11.061 (p95)
§156.001	§§11.05(g), 14.08(a) (p95)
§156.002	§§11.03(f), 14.08(a) (p95)
§156.003	§§11.09(c), 14.08(b) (p95)
§156.004	§14.08(b) (p95)
§156.005	§14.082 (p95)
§156.006	§§11.11(a), 14.08(g) (p95)
§156.101	§14.08(c)(1), (g)(3) (p95)
§156.102	§14.08(d), (e) (p95)
§156.401	§§14.021(g), 14.08(c)(2) (p95)
§156.402	§14.056(a), (b) (p95)
§156.403	§14.056(b) (p95)
§§156.404, 156.405	§14.056(c) (p95)
§156.406	§14.056(d) (p95)
§156.407	§14.08(h) (p95)
§157.001	§§14.30(b), 14.31, 14.40(a), 14.50(a) (p95)
§157.002	§§14.311(a)-(e), 14.312 (p95)
§157.003	§§14.30(d), 14.313(a), 14.33(d) (p95)
§157.004	§14.50(b) (p95)
§157.005	§§14.40(b), 14.41(b) (p95)
§157.006	§§14.40(h), 14.50(e) (p95)

Current	Former
§157.007	§14.50(c) (p95)
§157.008	§§14.40(c), (g), 14.41(c) (p95)
§157.061	§§14.314(a), 14.32(d) (p95)
§157.062	§§14.314(a), (b), 14.315(b), (c) (p95)
§157.063	§14.314(c) (p95)
§157.064	§14.311(f) (p95)
§157.065	§14.314(c) (p95)
§157.066	§14.317(a) (p95)
§157.101	§§14.318(a), 14.32(e) (p95)
§157.102	§14.317(d) (p95)
§157.103	§14.317(e) (p95)
§157.104	§14.318(b) (p95)
§157.105	§14.318(c) (p95)
§157.106	§14.318(d) (p95)
§157.107	§14.318(e) (p95)
§157.108	§14.318(f) (p95)
§157.109	§§14.42(a), 14.51(a) (p95)
§157.110	§§14.42(b), (c), (f), 14.51(b), (c), (f) (p95)
§157.111	§§14.42(e), 14.51(e) (p95)
§157.112	§§14.42(d), 14.51(d) (p95)
§157.113	§§14.32(e), 14.40(f) (p95)
§157.114	§14.317(a) (p95)
§157.115	§14.317(a), (c) (p95)
§157.161	§14.32(b) (p95)
§157.162	§§14.311(b), (c), 14.33(d) (p95)
§157.163	§14.32(f) (p95)
§157.164	§14.33(b) (p95)

3. DERIVATION TABLE—CURRENT TO FORMER (CONT'D)

CURRENT	FORMER
§157.165	§§14.40(e)(1), 14.50(d)(1) (p95)
§157.166	§14.33(a) (p95)
§157.167	§14.33(c) (p95)
§157.211	§§14.40(e)(1), 14.50(d)(1) (p95)
§157.212	§§14.40(e)(2), 14.50(d)(2) (p95)
§157.213	§§14.40(e)(3), 14.50(d)(3) (p95)
§157.214	§§14.40(e)(4), 14.50(d)(4) (p95)
§157.215	§§14.40(e)(5), 14.50(d)(5) (p95)
§157.216	§§14.40(e)(6), 14.50(d)(6) (p95)
§157.217	§§14.40(e)(7), 14.50(d)(7) (p95)
§157.261	§14.41(a) (p95)
§157.263	§14.41(a), (e) (p95)
§157.264	§14.41(a) (p95)
§157.265	§14.34(a) (p95)
§157.266	§14.34(b) (p95)
§§157.267, 157.268	§14.34(c) (p95)
§157.311	§14.971(a), (b) (p95)
§157.312	§§14.971(c), (d), 14.972(d) (p95)
§§157.313, 157.314	§§14.973, 14.974 (p95)
§157.315	§14.975 (p95)
§157.316	§14.972(a) (p95)
§157.317	§14.972(b), (c) (p95)
§157.318	§14.972(e) (p95)
§157.319	§14.976(b) (p95)
§157.320	§§14.976(c), 14.977 (p95)
§157.321	§14.980 (p95)
§157.322	§14.978 (p95)
§157.323	§14.979 (p95)
§157.324	§14.981 (p95)
§157.325	§14.982 (p95)
§157.326	§14.983 (p95)
§157.372	§14.10(a), (b) (p95)
§157.373	§14.10(c) (p95)
§157.374	§14.10(d) (p95)
§157.375	§14.10(e) (p95)
§157.376	§14.10(f) (p95)
§157.421	§11.22(a), (b), (g) (p95)
§157.422	§11.22(h), (i) (p95)
§157.423	§11.22(c) (p95)
§157.424	§11.22(d) (p95)
§157.425	§11.22(e) (p95)
§157.426	§11.22(f) (p95)
§158.001	§§14.05(e), 14.43(a)(1) (p95)
§158.002	§14.43(a)(2) (p95)
§§158.003, 158.004	§14.43(d) (p95)
§158.005	§§14.41(a), 14.43(d) (p95)
§158.006	§14.43(b) (p95)
§158.007	§14.43(d) (p95)
§158.008	§14.43(k) (p95)
§158.009	§14.43(f) (p95)
§158.010	§14.43(h) (p95)
§158.102	§14.43(r) (p95)
§158.103	§14.43(e) (p95)
§158.104	§14.43(g) (p95)
§158.105	§14.43(g), (h) (p95)
§158.106	§§14.43(p), 14.44(f), 14.45(g) (p95)
§158.201	§14.316 (p95)
§§158.202, 158.203	§14.43(h) (p95)
§158.204	§14.43(i) (p95)
§158.205	§§14.43(j), 14.45(d) (p95)
§§158.206-158.208	§14.43(*l*) (p95)
§158.209	§14.43(m) (p95)
§158.210	§14.43(n) (p95)
§158.211	§14.43(o) (p95)
§158.301	§14.44(a) (p95)
§158.302	§14.44(b) (p95)
§158.303	§14.44(h) (p95)
§158.304	§14.44(d) (p95)
§158.306	§14.45(a); *see* §14.44(a) (p95)
§§158.307, 158.308	§14.44(c) (p95)
§§158.309, 158.310	§14.44(d) (p95)
§158.311	§§14.43(a)(4), 14.44(a) (p95)
§§158.312, 158.313	§14.45(a) (p95)
§158.314	§14.45(b) (p95)
§158.315	§14.45(c) (p95)
§158.316	§14.45(a) (p95)
§158.317	§14.44(e) (p95)
§158.401	§§14.43(q), 14.45(f) (p95)
§158.404 ('95)	§14.43(q) (p95)
§158.405	§14.43(q) (p95)
§159.102	§21.01 (p95)
§159.103	§21.02 (p95)
§159.104	§21.03 (p95)
§159.201	§21.04 (p95)
§159.202	§21.05 (p95)
§159.203	§21.06 (p95)
§§159.204-159.209	§§21.07-21.12 (p95)
§§159.301-159.308	§§21.13-21.20 (p95)
§159.309	§21.21 (p95)

3. Derivation Table—Current to Former (cont'd)

Current	Former
§§159.310-159.312	§§21.22-21.24 (p95)
§159.313	§21.25 (p95)
§159.314	§21.26 (p95)
§159.315	§21.27 (p95)
§159.316	§21.28 (p95)
§159.317	§21.29 (p95)
§159.318	§21.30 (p95)
§159.319	§21.31 (p95)
§159.401	§21.32 (p95)
§§159.501, 159.502	§§21.33(a) (p95), 159.501(a) ('95)
§159.506	§§21.33(b) (p95), 159.501(b) ('95)
§159.507	§§21.34 (p95), 159.502 ('95)
§159.601	§21.35 (p95)
§159.602	§21.36 (p95)
§159.603	§21.37 (p95)
§§159.604, 159.605	§§21.38, 21.39 (p95)
§159.606	§21.40 (p95)
§159.607	§21.41 (p95)
§§159.608, 159.609	§§21.42, 21.43 (p95)
§§159.610-159.612	§§21.44-21.46 (p95)
§159.701	§21.47 (p95)
§§159.801, 159.802	§§21.48, 21.49 (p95)
§159.901	§21.50 (p95)
§161.001	§§11.15(b), 15.02(a) (p95)
§161.002	§15.023 (p95)
§161.003	§15.024 (p95)
§161.004	§15.025 (p95)
§161.005	§15.01 (p95)
§161.006	§15.022 (p95)
§161.101	§11.08(e) (p95)

Current	Former
§161.102	§15.021(a), (c) (p95)
§161.103	§15.03 (p95)
§161.104	§14.02(d) (p95)
§161.106	§15.041(a)-(d) (p95)
§161.107	§15.051 (p95)
§161.202	§11.14(h) (p95)
§161.203	§15.06 (p95)
§161.204	§15.041(e) (p95)
§161.205	§15.05(c) (p95)
§161.206	§§11.15(b), 15.05(a), 15.07 (p95)
§161.207	§15.05(b) (p95)
§161.208	§15.051(b) (p95)
§161.209	§11.16 (p95)
§161.210	§11.17(f) (p95)
§162.001	§§16.01, 16.02, 16.03(b)-(d) (p95)
§162.002	§§11.08(d), 16.03(a) (p95)
§162.003	§16.031(a) (p95)
§162.005	§16.032(a), (f), (*l*) (p95)
§162.006	§16.032(g), (i)-(k), (n) (p95)
§162.007	§16.032(b)-(e) (p95)
§162.008	§16.032(h), (m) (p95)
§§162.009-162.011	§§16.04-16.06 (p95)
§162.012	§16.12 (p95)
§162.013	§16.11 (p95)
§162.014	§16.07 (p95)
§162.015	§16.081 (p95)
§162.016	§16.08 (p95)
§162.017	§16.09(a), (d)-(f) (p95)
§162.018	§§16.032(f), (i), 16.09(b), (c) (p95)

Current	Former
§162.019	§11.16 (p95)
§162.020	§16.10 (p95)
§162.021	§11.17(f) (p95)
§162.022	§11.17(d) (p95)
§162.101	HRC §45.022 (p95)
§162.102	HRC §45.021 (p95)
§162.103	HRC §45.023 (p95)
§162.104	HRC §45.024 (p95)
§162.105	HRC §45.025 (p95)
§162.106	HRC §45.026 (p95)
§§162.301-162.303	HRC §§47.001-47.003 (p95)
§162.304	HRC §47.004 (p95)
§162.305	HRC §47.005 (p95)
§162.306	HRC §47.031 (p95)
§162.308	HRC §47.041 (p95)
§162.309	HRC §47.006 (p95)
§162.401	HRC §49.001 (p95)
§162.402	HRC §49.002 (p95)
§162.403	HRC §49.003(a)-(c) (p95)
§162.405	HRC §49.005 (p95)
§162.406	HRC §49.006 (p95)
§162.407	HRC §49.007(a)-(c) (p95)
§162.408	HRC §49.008 (p95)
§162.409	HRC §49.007(e) (p95)
§§162.411-162.414	HRC §§49.011-49.014 (p95)
§162.416	HRC §49.016 (p95)
§§162.419-162.422	HRC §§49.020-49.023 (p95)
§§162.501, 162.502	§§16.51, 16.52 (p95)
§162.503	§16.53 (p95)
§162.504	§16.52 (p95)
§162.505	§16.54 (p95)
§162.507	§16.55 (p95)

3. DERIVATION TABLE—CURRENT TO FORMER (CONT'D)

CURRENT	FORMER
§201.001	GC §54.001 (p95)
§201.002	GC §54.002 (p95)
§201.003	GC §54.003 (p95)
§201.004	GC §54.004 (p95)
§201.005	GC §54.005; *see* GC §54.014 (p95)
§201.006	GC §54.006 (p95)
§201.007	GC §54.007 (p95)
§201.008	GC §54.008 (p95)
§201.009	GC §54.018 (p95)
§201.010	GC §54.009 (p95)
§201.011	GC §§54.010(a), (b), 54.012(c) (p95)
§201.012	GC §54.010(c) (p95)
§201.013	GC §§54.013, 54.015 (p95)
§201.014	GC §54.011 (p95)
§201.015	GC §54.012(a), (d)-(i) (p95)
§201.016	GC §54.012(j) (p95)
§201.017	GC §54.017 (p95)
§201.101	§14.82(a), (b) (p95)
§201.102	§14.82(c), (e) (p95)
§201.103	§14.82(d) (p95)
§201.104	§14.82(f), (g) (p95)
§201.105	§14.83(a), (b) (p95)
§201.106	§14.83(c) (p95)
§201.107	§14.83(d), (e) (p95)
§201.110	§14.81 (p95)
§201.111	§14.82(h) (p95)
§202.001	§14.91 (p95)
§202.002	§14.92 (p95)
§202.003	§14.93 (p95)

CURRENT	FORMER
§§202.004, 202.005	§§14.94, 14.95 (p95)
§203.001	HRC §151.003(a) (p95)
§203.002	HRC §151.001 (p95)
§203.003	HRC §151.002(a) (p95)
§203.004	HRC §151.004 (p95)
§203.005	HRC §151.008 (p95)
§203.006	HRC §151.009 (p95)
§203.007	HRC §151.011 (p95)
§204.001	HRC §153.001 ('95)
§§204.002-204.005	HRC §§153.002-153.005 ('95)
§231.001	HRC §76.001 (p95)
§231.002	HRC §§76.002(a), (d), (f), 76.004(b) (p95)
§231.003	§14.86 (p95)
§231.005	HRC §76.002(i) (p95)
§231.006	§14.52 (p95)
§231.007	HRC §76.0041 (p95)
§231.008	HRC §76.005 (p95)
§231.009	HRC §76.008 (p95)
§231.101	HRC §76.002(e) (p95)
§231.103	HRC §76.004 (p95)
§231.104	HRC §76.003(a) (p95)
§231.105	HRC §76.003(b) (p95)
§231.106	HRC §76.003(e) (p95)
§231.107	HRC §76.003(f) (p95)
§231.108	HRC §76.006 (p95)

CURRENT	FORMER
§231.109	HRC §76.007(a)-(e) (p95)
§231.110	HRC §76.007(f) (p95)
§231.111	HRC §76.007(g) (p95)
§231.112	§13.015 (p95)
§231.117	§231.115 ('97); HRC §76.012 ('95)
§231.201	HRC §76.009(g) (p95)
§231.202	HRC §76.009(a) (p95)
§231.203	HRC §76.009(h) (p95)
§231.204	HRC §76.009(b) (p95)
§231.205	HRC §76.009(e), (f) (p95)
§231.206	HRC §76.009(i)[A*] (p95)
§231.207	HRC §76.009(c) (p95)
§231.208	HRC §76.009(d) (p95)
§231.209	HRC §76.009(i)[B*] (p95)
§231.210	HRC §76.002(g) (p95)
§231.211	§11.181 (p95)
§231.301	HRC §77.001(a) (p95)
§231.302	HRC §77.001(b) (p95)
§231.303	HRC §77.001(c) (p95)
§233.001	§§14.802(a) (p95), 231.401 ('95)
§233.002	§§14.802(a) (p95), 231.402 ('95)
§233.003	§§14.802(g) (p95), 231.403 ('95)
§233.004	§§14.802(g) (p95), 231.404 ('95)

3. DERIVATION TABLE—CURRENT TO FORMER (CONT'D)

CURRENT	FORMER
§233.005	§§14.802(b), 14.803(a) (p95), 231.405 ('95)
§233.006	§§14.803(b), (c) (p95), 231.406 ('95)
§233.007	§§14.802(e), (f) (p95), 231.407 ('95)
§233.008	§§14.802(c) (p95), 231.408 ('95)
§233.009	§§14.804(a) (p95), 231.409 ('95)
§233.010	§§14.804(b), (c) (p95), 231.410 ('95)
§233.011	§§14.804(d) (p95), 231.411 ('95)
§233.012	§§14.804(e) (p95), 231.412 ('95)
§233.013	§§14.802(d) (p95), 231.413 ('95)
§233.014	§§14.804(f) (p95), 231.414 ('95)
§233.015	§§14.804(h)-(j) (p95), 231.415 ('95)
§233.016	§§14.804(k) (p95), 231.416 ('95)
§233.017	§§14.805 (p95), 231.417 ('95)
§233.018	§§14.804(g) (p95), 231.418 ('95)
§233.019	§§14.806(a) (p95), 231.419 ('95)
§233.020	§§14.806(b) (p95), 231.420 ('95)
§233.021	§§14.806(c), (d) (p95), 231.421 ('95)
§233.022	§§14.806(e) (p95), 231.422 ('95)
§233.023	§§14.807(e) (p95), 231.423 ('95)
§233.024	§§14.807(b), (c) (p95), 231.424 ('95)

CURRENT	FORMER
§233.025	§§14.807(d), (f) (p95), 231.425 ('95)
§233.026	§§14.807(g) (p95), 231.426 ('95)
§233.027	§§14.807(h), (i) (p95), 231.427 ('95)
§233.028	§§14.808 (p95), 231.428 ('95)
§233.029	§§14.801 (p95), 231.429 ('95)
§261.001	§34.012 (p95)
§261.002	§34.06 (p95)
§261.003	§34.013 (p95)
§261.101	§§34.01, 34.02(d) (p95)
§261.102	§34.02(a) (p95)
§261.103	§34.02(a) (p95)
§261.104	§34.02(b) (p95)
§261.105	§34.02(c) (p95)
§261.106	§34.03 (p95)
§261.107	§34.031 (p95)
§261.108	§34.032 (p95)
§261.109	§34.07 (p95)
§261.201	§34.08 (p95)
§261.202	§34.04 (p95)
§261.301	§34.05(a), (b) (p95)
§261.302	§34.05(c), (d) (p95)
§261.303	§34.05(c) (p95)
§261.304	§34.053 (p95)
§261.305	§34.05(c) (p95)
§261.306	§34.05(g) (p95)
§261.307	§34.051 (p95)
§261.308	§34.05(e), (f) (p95)
§261.309	§34.052 (p95)
§261.310	§34.054 (p95)

CURRENT	FORMER
§261.311	§34.055 (p95)
§§261.401-261.403	§§34.22-34.24 (p95)
§262.001	§17.01 (p95)
§262.002	§17.05(a) (p95)
§262.003	§17.08 (p95)
§262.004	§17.03(a)(2) (p95)
§262.005	§17.03(g) (p95)
§262.006	§17.011 (p95)
§262.101	§17.02(b) (p95)
§262.102	§17.02(a), (d) (p95)
§262.103	§17.02(c) (p95)
§262.104	§17.03(a)(3)-(6) (p95)
§262.105	§17.03(b) (p95)
§262.106	§17.03(c) (p95)
§262.107	§17.03(d), (e), (i) (p95)
§262.108	§17.03(h) (p95)
§262.109	§17.031(b) (p95)
§262.110	§17.03(a)(1) (p95)
§262.112	§262.111 ('95)
§262.201	§§17.03(f), 17.04 (p95)
§262.202	§17.05(b) (p95)
§262.203	§17.06(a) (p95)
§262.204	§17.06(b), (c) (p95)
§263.001	§18.01 (p95)
§263.002	§18.02 (p95)
§263.101	§18.03(a) (p95)
§263.102	§18.03(b)-(d) (p95)
§§263.103-263.105	§§18.04-18.06 (p95)
§263.201	§18.07(a) (p95)
§263.202	§18.07(b)-(d) (p95)

3. Derivation Table—Current to Former (cont'd)

Current	Former
§263.301	§§18.08(b), (c), 18.12 (p95)
§263.302	§18.14 (p95)
§263.303	§18.10(b), (c) (p95)
§263.304	§18.08(a) (p95)
§263.305	§18.10(a) (p95)
§263.306	§18.09(a), (b) (p95)
§263.307	§18.15 (p95)
§263.403	§263.402 ('97)
§263.404	§263.403 ('97)
§263.406 ('01)	§263.404 ('97)
§264.001	§34.50; HRC §11.001(2) (p95)
§264.002	HRC §41.001 (p95)
§264.004	HRC §41.0012 (p95)
§264.005	HRC §41.002 (p95)
§264.006	HRC §41.003 (p95)
§264.007	HRC §41.004 (p95)
§264.008	HRC §41.006 (p95)
§264.009	§11.20 (p95)
§264.101	HRC §41.021 (p95)
§§264.102-264.105	HRC §§41.022-41.025 (p95)
§264.106	HRC §41.026
§264.107	HRC §41.027 (p95)
§264.108	HRC §41.028 (p95)
§264.110	§264.109 ('95)
§264.201 ('95)	§34.51 (p95)
§264.202	§34.52 (p95)
§264.203	§34.53 (p95)
§264.601	§34.601 (p95)
§264.602	§34.602 (p95)
§§264.603-264.612	§§34.603-34.612 (p95)
§264.71	GC §772.007 (p95)

4. DISPOSITION TABLE—FORMER TO CURRENT

The disposition table covers the extensive renumbering of the Family Code that occurred before 1998. The year in parentheses indicates the year of enactment.

Unless otherwise noted, all references are to the Family Code.
p95 = Pre-1995

FORMER	CURRENT
§1.01 (p95)	§2.001
§1.02 (p95)	§2.002
§1.02(2)(B) (p95)	§2.003
§§1.03, 1.04 (p95)	§§2.004, 2.005
§1.05(a), (b) (p95)	§2.006
§1.05(c) (p95)	§2.007
§§1.06, 1.07 (p95)	§§2.008, 2.009
§1.07(e) (p95)	§2.010
§1.08	Repealed ('09)
§1.09 (p95)	§2.012
§§1.51-1.53 (p95)	§§2.101-2.103
§1.81(a) (p95)	§2.201
§1.81(b) (p95)	§2.207
§1.82(a), (b) (p95)	§2.203
§1.82(c), (d) (p95)	§2.204
§1.83(a), (b) (p95)	§2.202
§1.83(c), (d) (p95)	§2.205
§§1.84-1.86 (p95)	§§2.206-2.209
§§1.91-1.95 (p95)	§§2.401-2.405
§2.01 (p95)	§§1.101, 1.102
§§2.02, 2.03 (p95)	§§2.301, 2.302
§§2.21-2.23 (p95)	§§6.201-6.203
§2.24	§6.307
§2.41(a) (p95)	Repealed ('07)
§2.41(a)	§6.103
§2.41(b) (p95)	§§6.102, 6.103
§2.41(c) (p95)	§6.104
§§2.42-2.44 (p95)	§§6.105-6.107
§§2.45, 2.46 (p95)	§§6.108, 6.109
§2.47 (p95)	§6.111
§2.48 (p95)	§6.110
§2.501 ('97)	§151.001
§§3.01-3.08 (p95)	§§6.001-6.008
§3.21 (p95)	§6.301
§§3.22, 3.23 (p95)	§§6.303, 6.304
§3.24 (p95)	§6.302
§3.25 (p95)	§§6.306, 6.307
§3.26 (p95)	§6.305
§§3.403, 3.404 ('99)	§§3.404, 3.405
§§3.51, 3.52 (p95)	§§6.401, 6.402
§3.521 (p95)	§6.409
§3.522[A*] ('95)	Repealed ('03)
§3.522[B*] ('95)	§6.405
§3.53 (p95)	§§6.403, 6.701
§3.54(a)-(c) (p95)	§6.505
§3.54(b), (d) (p95)	§6.705
§3.54(e)	§6.708
§3.55(a), (b)	§6.406
§3.55(b)-(d) (p95)	§6.407
§3.57 (p95)	§6.707
§3.58(a), (b) (p95)	§6.501
§3.58(c) (p95)	§6.502
§3.58(d), (e) (p95)	§6.503
§3.58(f) (p95)	§6.506
§3.58(g) (p95)	§6.507
§3.58(h), (i) (p95)	§6.709
§3.581 (p95)	§6.504
§3.59 (p95)	§6.502
§§3.60-3.62 (p95)	§§6.702-6.704
§3.63(a) (p95)	§7.001
§3.63(b) (p95)	§7.002
§3.631 (p95)	§7.006
§3.632(a) (p95)	§7.004
§3.632(b), (c) (p95)	§9.301
§3.632(d), (e) (p95)	§7.005
§3.633(a) (p95)	§7.003
§3.633(b)-(e) (p95)	§9.302
§3.64 (p95)	§6.706
§3.65 (p95)	§6.708
§3.66(a), (b) (p95)	§6.801
§3.66(c) (p95)	§6.802
§3.70(a), (b) (p95)	§9.001
§3.70(c) (p95)	§§9.002, 9.003
§3.70(d) (p95)	§9.004
§3.70(e) (p95)	§9.005
§3.71 (p95)	§9.007
§3.71(a) (p95)	§9.006
§3.711(a) ('95)	§§9.101, 9.103
§3.711(b) ('95)	§9.101
§3.711(c) ('95)	§9.104
§3.711(d) ('95)	§9.102
§3.711(e) ('95)	§9.105
§§3.72-3.76 (p95)	§§9.008-9.012
§3.77 (p95)	§§9.013, 9.014
§3.90(a), (b) (p95)	§9.201
§3.90(c) (p95)	§9.202
§§3.91-3.93 (p95)	§§9.203-9.205
§3.9601 ('95)	§8.001(1)
§§3.9602-3.9608 ('95)	§§8.051-8.057

4. DISPOSITION TABLE—FORMER TO CURRENT (CONT'D)

FORMER	CURRENT
§§3.9609-3.9611 ('95)	§§8.059-8.061
§4.01 (p95)	§1.103
§4.02 (p95)	§151.001
§4.03 (p95)	§1.104
§4.031 (p95)	§3.201
§§4.04-4.06 (p95)	§§1.105-1.107
§5.01(a) (p95)	§3.001
§5.01(b) (p95)	§3.002
§§5.02-5.04 (p95)	§§3.003-3.005
§5.107 ('97)	§5.003
§§5.21-5.24 (p95)	§§3.101-3.104
§5.25(a), (b) (p95)	§3.301
§5.25(c) (p95)	§3.303
§5.25(d) (p95)	§3.304
§5.25(e) (p95)	§3.305
§5.25(f) (p95)	§3.306
§5.25(g) (p95)	§3.307
§5.25(h) (p95)	§3.308
§5.26(a), (b) (p95)	§3.302
§5.26(c) (p95)	§3.303
§5.26(d) (p95)	§3.304
§5.26(e) (p95)	§3.306
§5.26(f) (p95)	§3.307
§5.26(g) (p95)	§3.308
§5.27 (p95)	§3.309
§§5.41-5.50 (p95)	§§4.001-4.010
§§5.51-5.56 (p95)	§§4.101-4.106
§§5.61, 5.62 (p95)	§§3.202, 3.203
§§5.81, 5.82 (p95)	§§5.001, 5.002
§5.83(a) (p95)	§5.101
§5.83(b) (p95)	§§5.103-5.105
§5.83(c) (p95)	§5.106
§5.831(a) (p95)	§5.101
§5.831(b) (p95)	§§5.103-5.105
§5.831(c) (p95)	§5.106

FORMER	CURRENT
§5.84 (p95)	§5.003
§5.85(a) (p95)	§5.102
§5.85(b) (p95)	§§5.103-5.105
§5.85(c) (p95)	§5.106
§5.86 (p95)	§5.108
§5.87(a) (p95)	§5.102
§5.87(b) (p95)	§§5.103-5.105
§5.87(c) (p95)	§5.106
§8.001 ('97)	§8.001(1)
§8.002(a) ('97)	§8.051
§8.002(b) ('97)	Omitted
§§8.003-8.008 ('97)	§§8.052-8.057
§8.009 ('97)	§8.059
§§8.010, 8.011 ('97)	§§8.060, 8.061
§11.01 (p95)	§101.001
§11.01(1) (p95)	§101.003
§11.01(2) (p95)	§101.008
§11.01(3) (p95)	§101.024
§11.01(4) (p95)	§101.025
§11.01(5) (p95)	§101.032
§11.01(6) (p95)	§101.019
§11.01(7) (p95)	§§101.002, 101.017
§11.01(8) (p95)	§101.014
§11.01(9) (p95)	§101.022
§11.01(10) (p95)	§101.021
§11.01(11) (p95)	§101.018
§11.02 (p95)	§102.001
§11.03(a) (p95)	§102.003
§11.03(b), (c) (p95)	§102.004
§11.03(d) (p95)	§102.005
§11.03(e) (p95)	Omitted
§11.03(f) (p95)	§156.002
§11.03(g), (h) (p95)	§102.006
§11.03(i) (p95)	§102.007

FORMER	CURRENT
§11.04 (p95)	§103.001
§11.05(a) (p95)	§§155.001, 155.002
§11.05(b) (p95)	§§155.001, 155.004
§11.05(c) (p95)	§155.103
§11.05(d), (e) (p95)	§155.001
§11.05(f) (p95)	§155.004
§11.05(g) (p95)	§§155.003, 155.004, 156.001
§11.05(h) (p95)	§§155.005, 155.205
§11.051 (p95)	§102.011
§11.06(a) (p95)	§103.002
§11.06(b) (p95)	§§155.201-155.203
§11.06(c) (p95)	§§103.002, 155.201(a)
§11.06(d) (p95)	§155.202
§11.06(e) (p95)	Omitted
§11.06(f)-(i) (p95)	§155.204
§11.06(j) (p95)	§§155.205, 155.207
§11.06(k) (p95)	§155.206
§11.06(*l*) (p95)	§110.005
§11.06(m) (p95)	§155.207
§11.061 (p95)	§§103.003, 155.301
§11.07(a) (p95)	§102.002
§11.07(b) (p95)	Omitted
§11.07(c) (p95)	§102.013
§11.071(a), (b) (p95)	§155.101
§11.071(c) (p95)	§155.104
§11.071(d) (p95)	§155.102
§11.08(a), (b) (p95)	§102.008
§11.08(d) (p95)	§162.002
§11.08(e) (p95)	§161.101
§11.09(a)-(c), (f) (p95)	§102.009
§11.09(c) (p95)	§156.003

4. DISPOSITION TABLE—FORMER TO CURRENT (CONT'D)

FORMER	CURRENT
§11.09(d), (e) (p95)	§102.010
§11.10(a) (p95)	§§107.011, 107.015
§11.10(b)(1) (p95)	§107.011
§11.10(b)(2), (c) (p95)	§107.021
§11.10(d) (p95)	§§107.012, 107.013
§11.10(e) (p95)	§107.015
§11.101 (p95)	§107.031
§11.11(a) (p95)	§156.006
§11.11(a)-(d), (g), (h) (p95)	§105.001
§11.11(e)-(g) (p95)	§109.001
§11.12(a) (p95)	§107.051
§11.12(b) (p95)	§§107.051-107.053
§11.12(c) (p95)	§§107.054, 107.055
§11.13 (p95)	§105.002
§11.14(a), (b), (d), (f), (g) (p95)	§105.003
§11.14(c) (p95)	§107.055
§11.14(e) (p95)	§104.001
§11.14(h) (p95)	§161.202
§11.14(i) (p95)	§105.004
§11.14(j) (p95)	Deleted ('01)
§11.15(a) (p95)	§105.005
§11.15(b) (p95)	§§161.001, 161.206
§11.15(c) (p95)	§101.007
§11.155 (p95)	§105.006
§11.16 (p95)	§§161.209, 162.019
§11.17(a) (p95)	§108.001
§11.17(b) (p95)	§§108.002-108.005
§11.17(c) (p95)	§108.006
§11.17(d) (p95)	§§108.001, 162.022
§11.17(e) (p95)	§108.007
§11.17(f) (p95)	§§161.210, 162.021
§11.171 (p95)	§108.006
§11.18(a) (p95)	§§106.001, 106.002
§11.18(b) (p95)	§110.003
§11.18(c) (p95)	§107.056
§11.181 (p95)	§231.211
§11.19 (p95)	§109.002
§11.191 (p95)	§109.003
§11.20 (p95)	§264.009
§11.21(a), (b) (p95)	§104.002
§11.21(c) (p95)	§104.004
§11.21(d) (p95)	§104.003
§11.21(e) (p95)	§104.005
§11.22(a), (b), (g) (p95)	§157.421
§11.22(c)-(f) (p95)	§§157.423-157.426
§11.22(h), (i) (p95)	§157.422
§11.22(j) (p95)	§106.002
§11.51 (p95)	§152.001
§11.52 (p95)	§152.102
§11.53 (p95)	§§152.201, 152.202
§11.54 (p95)	§152.205
§11.55 (p95)	§152.108
§11.56 (p95)	§§152.206, 152.307
§§11.57-11.59 (p95)	§§152.207-152.209
§11.60 (p95)	§152.205
§11.61 (p95)	§152.210
§11.62 (p95)	§152.106
§11.63 (p95)	§152.313
§11.64 (p95)	§152.203
§11.65 (p95)	§152.306
§11.66 (p95)	§152.305
§11.68 (p95)	§152.111
§§11.69-11.71 (p95)	§152.112
§11.73 (p95)	§152.105
§11.74 (p95)	§152.107
§11.75 (p95)	§152.101
§§12.01-12.03B (p95)	Deleted ('01)
§§12.04, 12.05 (p95)	§§151.001, 151.002
§12.06 (p95)	Deleted ('01)
§13.01 (p95)	Deleted ('01)
§13.015 (p95)	§231.112
§§13.02-13.09 (p95)	Deleted ('01)
§13.21(a), (b) (p95)	Deleted ('01)
§13.21(c), (d) (p95)	Omitted ('95)
§§13.22-13.24 (p95)	Deleted ('01)
§13.41 (p95)	*See* §103.001
§13.42(a) (p95)	Deleted ('01)
§13.42(b) (p95)	*See* §106.002(a)
§13.42(c) (p95)	Omitted ('95)
§13.42(d) (p95)	Deleted ('01)
§13.43(a)-(c) (p95)	§108.008
§13.43(d) (p95)	Deleted ('01)
§13.43(e), (f) (p95)	§108.009
§13.44 (p95)	Deleted ('01)
§14.01(a) (p95)	§153.005
§14.01(b)(1) (p95)	§153.131
§14.01(b)(2) (p95)	§153.373
§14.01(c)(1) (p95)	§153.003
§14.01(c)(2) (p95)	§153.004
§14.01(d) (p95)	§153.374
§14.01(e) (p95)	§153.375
§14.02(a) (p95)	§§153.071, 153.073, 153.076
§14.02(b) (p95)	§153.072
§14.02(b)(1) (p95)	§153.074
§14.02(b)(2) (p95)	§153.073
§14.02(b)(3) (p95)	§153.132

DISPOSITION TABLE

4. DISPOSITION TABLE—FORMER TO CURRENT (CONT'D)

FORMER	CURRENT
§14.02(c) (p95)	§153.371
§14.02(d) (p95)	§161.104
§14.02(e) (p95)	Repealed ('97)
§14.021(a) (p95)	§153.001
§14.021(b) (p95)	Repealed ('03)
§14.021(c), (d) (p95)	§153.133
§14.021(e), (f) (p95)	§153.134
§14.021(g) (p95)	§§153.138, 156.104, 156.401
§14.021(h) (p95)	§153.004
§14.021(i) (p95)	Omitted ('95)
§14.021(j) (p95)	§153.372
§14.03(a) (p95)	§153.006
§14.03(b) (p95)	§153.192
§14.03(c) (p95)	§153.006
§14.03(d) (p95)	§§153.004, 153.075, 153.191, 153.193
§14.03(e) (p95)	§§153.432, 153.433
§14.03(e)(3) (p95)	§153.004
§14.03(f)(1), (3) (p95)	§153.432
§14.03(g) (p95)	§153.434
§14.03(h) (p95)	§153.010
§14.03(i) (p95)	§153.011
§14.03(j) (p95)	§111.001
§14.032(a) (p95)	§153.251
§14.032(b) (p95)	§153.254
§14.032(c) (p95)	§153.256
§14.032(d) (p95)	§153.003
§14.032(e), (f) (p95)	§111.002
§14.033(a)(1) (p95)	§101.028
§14.033(a)(2) (p95)	§101.029
§14.033(b) (p95)	§153.311

FORMER	CURRENT
§14.033(c), (e)(4)-(7) (p95)	§153.312
§14.033(d) (p95)	§153.315
§14.033(e)(1)-(3) (p95)	§153.314
§14.033(e)(8)-(10) (p95)	§153.314
§14.033(f) (p95)	§153.313
§14.033(f)(2) (p95)	§153.314
§14.033(g) (p95)	§153.316
§14.033(g)(7) (p95)	Repealed ('01)
§14.033(h) (p95)	§153.257
§14.033(i) (p95)	§153.317
§14.033(k) (p95)	§§153.252, 153.253, 153.258
§14.033(*l*) (p95)	§105.001
§14.033(m) (p95)	§153.253
§14.033(n) (p95)	§153.255
§14.033(o) (p95)	Repealed ('01)
§14.033(p) (p95)	§111.003
§14.034 (p95)	Repealed ('09)
§14.04 (p95)	§153.192
§14.04(a), (b) (p95)	§153.376
§14.04(c) (p95)	§§153.012, 153.377
§14.045(a), (b) (p95)	§105.007
§14.045(c) (p95)	§105.007(b)
§14.05(a) (p95)	§§154.001-154.003
§14.05(b) (p95)	§154.001
§14.05(c) (p95)	§154.005
§14.05(d) (p95)	§§154.001, 154.006
§14.05(e) (p95)	§§154.007, 158.001
§14.05(f) (p95)	Omitted ('95)
§14.05(g) (p95)	§154.010
§14.05(h), (i) (p95)	§111.001

FORMER	CURRENT
§14.05(j) (p95)	§154.122
§§14.0501, 14.0502 (p95)	§§154.241, 154.242
§14.0503 (p95)	§154.004
§14.0504 (p95)	§154.243
§14.051(a)-(c) (p95)	§§154.301-154.303
§14.051(d)-(f) (p95)	§154.305
§14.051(g) (p95)	§154.306
§14.051(h) (p95)	§154.307
§14.051(i) (p95)	§154.304
§14.051(j), (k) (p95)	§154.308
§14.052(a) (p95)	§154.121
§14.052(b) (p95)	§154.123
§14.052(c), (d) (p95)	§111.002
§14.053(a) (p95)	§154.061
§14.053(b) (p95)	§154.062
§14.053(c) (p95)	§154.065
§14.053(d) (p95)	§§154.064, 154.183
§14.053(e) (p95)	§154.067
§14.053(f) (p95)	§154.066
§14.053(g) (p95)	§154.063
§14.053(h) (p95)	§154.061
§14.053(i) (p95)	§154.010
§14.053(j) (p95)	§154.124
§14.053(k) (p95)	§154.068
§14.053(*l*) (p95)	§154.131
§14.054 (p95)	§154.123
§14.055(a) (p95)	§§154.122, 154.125
§14.055(b)-(d) (p95)	§§154.125-154.127
§14.055(e) (p95)	§105.001
§14.055(f)-(h) (p95)	§154.128
§14.055(i) (p95)	§154.070

4. DISPOSITION TABLE—FORMER TO CURRENT (CONT'D)

FORMER	CURRENT
§14.055(j) (p95)	§154.129
§14.056(a) (p95)	§156.402
§14.056(b) (p95)	§§156.402, 156.403
§14.056(c) (p95)	§§154.069, 156.404, 156.405
§14.056(d) (p95)	§156.406
§14.057 (p95)	§154.130
§14.058 (p95)	§111.003
§14.06 (p95)	§§153.007, 154.124
§14.061 (p95)	§154.181
§14.061(a) (p95)	§§154.008, 154.182
§14.061(b), (c) (p95)	§§154.182, 154.183
§14.061(d) (p95)	§101.015
§14.061(e), (f) (p95)	§154.185
§14.061(g) (p95)	§154.186
§14.061(h)-(k) (p95)	§154.187
§14.061(*l*) (p95)	§154.188
§14.061(m) (p95)	§§154.189, 154.190
§14.061(n), (o) (p95)	§154.191
§14.061(p) (p95)	§154.187
§14.061(q) (p95)	§154.192
§14.061(r) (p95)	§154.184
§14.062 (p95)	§154.009
§14.07(a) (p95)	§153.002; §153.008 repealed ('09)
§14.07(b) (p95)	§153.431
§14.07(c) (p95)	§153.009
§14.08(a) (p95)	§§156.001, 156.002
§14.08(b) (p95)	§§156.003, 156.004
§14.08(c)(1) (p95)	§156.101
§14.08(c)(2) (p95)	§156.401
§14.08(c)(3) (p95)	Repealed ('01)
§14.08(c)(3)(C) (p95)	Repealed ('01)

FORMER	CURRENT
§14.08(c)(4), (5) (p95)	Deleted ('01)
§14.08(d), (e) (p95)	§156.102
§14.08(f) (p95)	Omitted ('95)
§14.08(g) (p95)	§156.006
§14.08(g)(3) (p95)	§156.101
§14.08(h) (p95)	§156.407
§14.08(i) (p95)	Repealed ('01)
§14.081(a) (p95)	Omitted ('95)
§14.081(b)-(d) (p95)	Repealed ('01)
§14.082 (p95)	§156.005
§14.10(a), (b) (p95)	§157.372
§14.10(c) (p95)	§157.373
§14.10(d) (p95)	§157.374
§14.10(e) (p95)	§157.375
§14.10(f) (p95)	§157.376
§14.11 (p95)	Omitted ('95)
§14.13 (p95)	§110.002
§14.30(a)(1) (p95)	§101.011
§14.30(a)(2) (p95)	§101.010
§14.30(a)(3) (p95)	§101.012
§14.30(b) (p95)	§157.001
§14.30(c) (p95)	*See* §§103.001, 103.002
§14.30(d) (p95)	§157.003
§14.31 (p95)	§157.001
§14.311(a)-(e) (p95)	§157.002
§14.311(b), (c) (p95)	§157.162
§14.311(f) (p95)	§157.064
§14.312 (p95)	§157.002
§14.313(a) (p95)	§157.003
§14.313(b) (p95)	Omitted ('95)
§14.314(a) (p95)	§§157.061, 157.062

FORMER	CURRENT
§14.314(b) (p95)	§157.062
§14.314(c) (p95)	§§157.063, 157.065
§14.315(b), (c) (p95)	§157.062
§14.316 (p95)	§158.201
§14.317(a) (p95)	§§157.066, 157.114, 157.115
§14.317(b) (p95)	Omitted ('95)
§14.317(c) (p95)	§157.115
§14.317(d), (e) (p95)	§§157.102, 157.103
§14.318(a) (p95)	§157.101
§14.318(b) (p95)	§157.104
§14.318(c)-(f) (p95)	§§157.105-157.108
§14.32(a) (p95)	Omitted ('95)
§14.32(b) (p95)	§157.161
§14.32(c) (p95)	Omitted ('95)
§14.32(d) (p95)	§157.061
§14.32(e) (p95)	§§157.101, 157.113
§14.32(f) (p95)	§157.163
§14.33(a) (p95)	§157.166
§14.33(b) (p95)	§157.164
§14.33(c) (p95)	§157.167
§14.33(d) (p95)	§§157.003, 157.162
§14.34(a) (p95)	§157.265
§14.34(b) (p95)	§157.266
§14.34(c) (p95)	§§157.267, 157.268
§14.40(a) (p95)	§157.001
§14.40(b) (p95)	§157.005
§14.40(c) (p95)	§157.008
§14.40(d) (p95)	Repealed ('11)
§14.40(e)(1) (p95)	§§157.165, 157.211
§14.40(e)(2)-(7) (p95)	§§157.212-157.217
§14.40(f) (p95)	§157.113
§14.40(g) (p95)	§157.008

4. DISPOSITION TABLE—FORMER TO CURRENT (CONT'D)

FORMER	CURRENT
§14.40(h) (p95)	§157.006
§14.41(a) (p95)	§§157.261, 157.263, 157.264, 158.005
§14.41(b) (p95)	§157.005
§14.41(c) (p95)	§157.008
§14.41(d) (p95)	Repealed ('11)
§14.41(e) (p95)	§157.263
§14.42(a) (p95)	§157.109
§14.42(b), (c), (f) (p95)	§157.110
§14.42(d) (p95)	§157.112
§14.42(e) (p95)	§157.111
§14.43(a)(1), (2) (p95)	§§158.001, 158.002
§14.43(a)(4) (p95)	§158.311
§14.43(b) (p95)	§158.006
§14.43(c) (p95)	Omitted ('95)
§14.43(d) (p95)	§§158.003-158.005, 158.007
§14.43(e) (p95)	§158.103
§14.43(f) (p95)	§158.009
§14.43(g) (p95)	§§158.104, 158.105
§14.43(h) (p95)	§§158.010, 158.105, 158.202, 158.203
§14.43(i) (p95)	§§110.004, 158.204
§14.43(j) (p95)	§158.205
§14.43(k) (p95)	§158.008
§14.43(*l*) (p95)	§§158.206-158.208
§14.43(m) (p95)	§158.209
§14.43(n) (p95)	§158.210
§14.43(o) (p95)	§158.211
§14.43(p) (p95)	§158.106
§14.43(q) (p95)	§§158.401, 158.404, 158.405
§14.43(r) (p95)	§158.102
§14.44(a) (p95)	§§158.301, 158.311
§14.44(b) (p95)	§158.302
§14.44(c) (p95)	§§158.307, 158.308
§14.44(d) (p95)	§§158.304, 158.309, 158.310
§14.44(e) (p95)	§158.317
§14.44(f) (p95)	§158.106
§14.44(g) (p95)	Repealed ('97)
§14.44(h) (p95)	§158.303
§14.45(a) (p95)	§§158.306, 158.312, 158.313, 158.316
§14.45(b) (p95)	§158.314
§14.45(c) (p95)	§158.315
§14.45(d) (p95)	§158.205
§14.45(e) (p95)	Omitted ('95)
§14.45(f) (p95)	§158.401
§14.45(g) (p95)	§158.106
§14.45(h) (p95)	§110.004
§14.50(a) (p95)	§157.001
§14.50(b) (p95)	§157.004
§14.50(c) (p95)	§157.007
§14.50(d)(1) (p95)	§§157.165, 157.211
§14.50(d)(2)-(7) (p95)	§§157.212-157.217
§14.50(e) (p95)	§157.006
§14.51(a) (p95)	§157.109
§14.51(b), (c), (f) (p95)	§157.110
§14.51(d) (p95)	§157.112
§14.51(e) (p95)	§157.111
§14.52 (p95)	§231.006
§14.80(1) (p95)	Omitted ('95)
§14.80(2) (p95)	§§101.033, 101.034
§14.80(3) (p95)	§101.004
§14.80(4) (p95)	§101.006
§14.80(5) (p95)	§101.020
§14.80(6) (p95)	§101.030
§14.80(7) (p95)	§101.005
§14.801 (p95)	§233.029
§14.802(a) (p95)	§§233.001, 233.002
§14.802(b) (p95)	§233.005
§14.802(c) (p95)	§233.008
§14.802(d) (p95)	§233.013
§14.802(e), (f) (p95)	§233.007
§14.802(g) (p95)	§§233.003, 233.004
§14.803(a) (p95)	§233.005
§14.803(b), (c) (p95)	§233.006
§14.804(a) (p95)	§233.009
§14.804(b), (c) (p95)	§233.010
§14.804(d) (p95)	§233.011
§14.804(e) (p95)	§233.012
§14.804(f) (p95)	§233.014
§14.804(g) (p95)	§233.018
§14.804(h)-(j) (p95)	§233.015
§14.804(k) (p95)	§233.016
§14.805 (p95)	§233.017
§14.806(a) (p95)	§233.019
§14.806(b) (p95)	§233.020
§14.806(c), (d) (p95)	§233.021
§14.806(e) (p95)	§233.022
§14.807(a) (p95)	Omitted ('95)
§14.807(b), (c) (p95)	§233.024
§14.807(d) (p95)	§233.025
§14.807(e) (p95)	§233.023
§14.807(f) (p95)	§233.025
§14.807(g) (p95)	§233.026
§14.807(h), (i) (p95)	§233.027
§14.808 (p95)	§233.028
§14.81 (p95)	§201.110
§14.82(a), (b) (p95)	§201.101

4. DISPOSITION TABLE—FORMER TO CURRENT (CONT'D)

FORMER	CURRENT
§14.82(c), (e) (p95)	§201.102
§14.82(d) (p95)	§201.103
§14.82(f), (g) (p95)	§201.104
§14.82(h) (p95)	§201.111
§14.83(a), (b) (p95)	§201.105
§14.83(c) (p95)	§201.106
§14.83(d), (e) (p95)	§201.107
§14.84 (p95)	Repealed ('03)
§14.85 (p95)	Repealed ('03)
§14.86 (p95)	§231.003
§14.91 (p95)	§202.001
§14.92 (p95)	§202.002
§14.93 (p95)	§202.003
§14.94 (p95)	§202.004
§14.95 (p95)	§202.005
§14.971(a), (b) (p95)	§157.311
§14.971(c), (d) (p95)	§157.312
§14.972(a) (p95)	§157.316
§14.972(b), (c) (p95)	§157.317
§14.972(d) (p95)	§157.312
§14.972(e) (p95)	§157.318
§§14.973-14.975 (p95)	§§157.313-157.315
§14.976(a) (p95)	§157.318(c)
§14.976(b) (p95)	§157.319
§14.976(c) (p95)	§157.320
§14.977 (p95)	§157.320
§§14.978, 14.979 (p95)	§§157.322, 157.323
§14.98 (p95)	§157.321
§§14.981-14.983 (p95)	§§157.324-157.326

FORMER	CURRENT
§15.01 (p95)	§161.005
§15.02(a) (p95)	§161.001
§15.021(a), (c) (p95)	§161.102
§15.021(b) (p95)	Deleted ('01)
§15.022 (p95)	§161.006
§§15.023-15.025 (p95)	§§161.002-161.004
§15.03 (p95)	§161.103
§15.04 (p95)	Repealed ('07)
§15.041(a)-(d) (p95)	§161.106
§15.041(e) (p95)	§161.204
§15.05(a) (p95)	§161.206
§15.05(b) (p95)	§161.207
§15.05(c) (p95)	§161.205
§15.051 (p95)	§161.107
§15.051(a)(1) (p95)	§101.027
§15.051(b) (p95)	§161.208
§15.06 (p95)	§161.203
§15.07 (p95)	§161.206
§§16.01, 16.02 (p95)	§§162.001, 162.002
§16.03(a) (p95)	§162.002
§16.03(b)-(d) (p95)	§162.001
§16.031(a) (p95)	§162.003
§16.031(b) (p95)	Repealed ('01)
§16.032(a) (p95)	§162.005
§16.032(b)-(e) (p95)	§162.007
§16.032(f) (p95)	§§162.005, 162.018
§16.032(g) (p95)	§162.006
§16.032(h), (m) (p95)	§162.008
§16.032(i) (p95)	§162.018
§16.032(i)-(k), (n) (p95)	§162.006

FORMER	CURRENT
§16.032(*l*) (p95)	§162.005
§§16.04-16.06 (p95)	§§162.009-162.011
§16.07 (p95)	§162.014
§16.08 (p95)	§162.016
§16.081 (p95)	§162.015
§16.09(a), (d)-(f) (p95)	§162.017
§16.09(b), (c) (p95)	§162.018
§16.10 (p95)	§162.020
§16.11 (p95)	§162.013
§16.12 (p95)	§162.012
§16.51 (p95)	§§162.501, 162.502
§16.52 (p95)	§162.504
§16.53 (p95)	§162.503
§16.54 (p95)	§162.505
§16.55 (p95)	§162.507
§17.001 (p95)	§101.009
§17.01 (p95)	§262.001
§17.011 (p95)	§262.006
§17.02(a), (d) (p95)	§262.102
§17.02(b) (p95)	§262.101
§17.02(c) (p95)	§262.103
§17.03(a)(1) (p95)	§262.110
§17.03(a)(2) (p95)	§262.004
§17.03(a)(3)-(6) (p95)	§262.104
§17.03(b) (p95)	§262.105
§17.03(c) (p95)	§262.106
§17.03(d), (e), (i) (p95)	§262.107
§17.03(f) (p95)	§262.201
§17.03(g) (p95)	§262.005
§17.03(h) (p95)	§262.108
§17.031(b) (p95)	§262.109

4. DISPOSITION TABLE—FORMER TO CURRENT (CONT'D)

FORMER	CURRENT
§17.04 (p95)	§262.201
§17.05(a) (p95)	§262.002
§17.05(b) (p95)	§262.202
§17.06(a) (p95)	§262.203
§17.06(b), (c) (p95)	§262.204
§17.08 (p95)	§262.003
§§18.01, 18.02 (p95)	§§263.001, 263.002
§18.03(a) (p95)	§263.101
§18.03(b)-(d) (p95)	§263.102
§§18.04-18.06 (p95)	§§263.103-263.105
§18.07(a) (p95)	§263.201
§18.07(b)-(d) (p95)	§263.202
§18.08(a) (p95)	§263.304
§18.08(b), (c) (p95)	§263.301
§18.09(a), (b) (p95)	§263.306
§18.09(c) (p95)	Repealed ('97)
§18.10(a) (p95)	§263.305
§18.10(b), (c) (p95)	§263.303
§18.12 (p95)	§263.301
§18.14 (p95)	§263.302
§18.15 (p95)	§263.307
§18.16 (p95)	Repealed ('97)
§21.01 (p95)	§159.101
§21.01(19) (p95)	§101.030
§21.01(22) (p95)	§101.035
§§21.02, 21.03 (p95)	§§159.102, 159.103
§§21.04-21.12 (p95)	§§159.201-159.209
§§21.13-21.31 (p95)	§§159.301-159.319
§21.32 (p95)	§159.401
§21.33(a) (p95)	§§159.501, 159.502

FORMER	CURRENT
§21.33(b) (p95)	§159.506
§21.34 (p95)	§159.507
§§21.35-21.46 (p95)	§§159.601-159.612
§21.47 (p95)	§159.701
§§21.48, 21.49 (p95)	§§159.801, 159.802
§21.50 (p95)	§159.901
§21.51 (p95)	Repealed ('03)
§21.52 (p95)	Omitted ('95)
§§25.01-25.09 (p95)	§§60.001-60.009
§31.01(a), (c) (p95)	§31.001
§31.01(b) (p95)	Omitted ('95)
§31.02(a), (c) (p95)	§31.002
§31.02(b) (p95)	Omitted ('95)
§31.03(a) (p95)	§31.003
§31.03(b) (p95)	Omitted ('95)
§§31.04-31.08 (p95)	§§31.004-31.007
§32.01 (p95)	§45.001
§32.02 (p95)	§45.002
§32.02(a) (p95)	§45.001
§§32.03-32.05 (p95)	§§45.003-45.005
§§32.103, 32.104 ('95)	§§32.102, 32.103
§32.21(a) (p95)	§§45.101, 45.102
§32.21(b) (p95)	§45.102
§32.21(c), (d) (p95)	Omitted ('95)
§§32.22, 32.23 (p95)	§§45.103, 45.104
§§33.01-33.03 (p95)	§§41.001-41.003
§34.01 (p95)	§261.101
§34.012 (p95)	§261.001
§34.013 (p95)	§261.003
§34.02(a) (p95)	§§261.102, 261.103

FORMER	CURRENT
§34.02(b), (c) (p95)	§§261.104, 261.105
§34.02(d) (p95)	§261.101
§34.03 (p95)	§261.106
§34.031 (p95)	§261.107
§34.031(b) (p95)	§153.013
§34.032 (p95)	§261.108
§34.04 (p95)	§261.202
§34.05(a), (b) (p95)	§261.301
§34.05(c) (p95)	§§261.303, 261.305
§34.05(c), (d) (p95)	§261.302
§34.05(e), (f) (p95)	§261.308
§34.05(g) (p95)	§261.306
§34.051 (p95)	§261.307
§34.052 (p95)	§261.309
§34.053 (p95)	§261.304
§§34.054, 34.055 (p95)	§§261.310, 261.311
§34.06 (p95)	§261.002
§34.07 (p95)	§261.109
§34.08 (p95)	§261.201
§§34.22-34.24 (p95)	§§261.401-261.403
§34.50 (p95)	§264.001
§§34.51-34.53 (p95)	§§264.201-264.203
§§34.601-34.612 (p95)	§§264.601-264.612
§35.01 (p95)	§32.001
§35.011 (p95)	§32.101
§§35.013, 35.014 (p95)	§§32.102, 32.103
§35.02 (p95)	§32.002
§35.03(a)-(f) (p95)	§32.003
§35.03(g) (p95)	§32.004
§35.04 (p95)	§32.005
§35.05 (p95)	§32.201

4. DISPOSITION TABLE—FORMER TO CURRENT (CONT'D)

FORMER	CURRENT
§36.01 (p95)	§42.001
§36.02(a), (b) (p95)	§42.002
§36.02(c), (d) (p95)	§42.003
§§36.03, 36.04 (p95)	§§42.006, 42.007
§36.05 (p95)	§42.005
§36.06 (p95)	§42.008
§36.08 (p95)	§42.009
§42.004 ('95)	Repealed ('99)
§71.008 ('97)	Repealed ('01)
§71.01(a) (p95)	§71.001
§71.01(b)(1) (p95)	§71.002
§71.01(b)(2) (p95)	§71.004
§71.01(b)(3) (p95)	§71.003
§71.01(b)(4), (6) (p95)	§71.006
§71.01(b)(5) (p95)	§71.005
§71.02 (p95)	§82.001
§71.03 (p95)	§82.003
§71.04(a) (p95)	§82.001
§71.04(b) (p95)	§82.002
§71.04(c) (p95)	§81.007
§71.04(d)-(f) (p95)	Repealed ('95)
§71.041(a) ('95)	§81.002
§71.041(b) ('95)	§81.003
§71.041(c) ('95)	§81.004
§71.041(d) ('95)	§§81.005, 81.006
§71.05(a) (p95)	§82.004
§71.05(b) (p95)	Omitted ('97)
§71.05(c) (p95)	§82.006
§71.05(d) (p95)	§82.007
§71.05(e) (p95)	§82.009
§71.05(f), (g) (p95)	§82.008
§71.06 (p95)	§82.005
§71.06(c) ('95)	§85.009

FORMER	CURRENT
§71.06(e) ('95)	§82.043
§71.06(f) ('95)	§85.004
§71.07(a) (p95)	§82.043
§71.07(b), (c) (p95)	§82.042
§71.07(d), (e) (p95)	§82.041
§71.07(f)-(h) (p95)	§82.043
§71.07(i) (p95)	Repealed ('95)
§71.08 (p95)	§82.021
§71.09(a) (p95)	§84.001
§71.09(b) (p95)	§84.004
§71.09(c) (p95)	§84.003
§71.09(d) (p95)	§84.002
§71.09(e) (p95)	§85.006
§71.10(a), (b) (p95)	§§81.001, 85.001
§71.10(c) (p95)	§85.002
§71.10(d) (p95)	§85.005
§71.11(a)(1)-(4), (6) (p95)	§85.021
§71.11(a)(5), (7), (b), (c) (p95)	§85.022
§71.11(d) (p95)	§85.023
§71.11(e)-(h) (p95)	Omitted ('95)
§71.11(i) (p95)	§85.024
§71.111 (p95)	§85.007
§71.12(a), (b) (p95)	§85.005
§71.12(c) (p95)	Omitted ('97)
§71.12(d), (e) (p95)	§85.005
§71.121(a) (p95)	§82.022
§71.121(a) ('95)	§85.003
§71.121(b) (p95)	§82.022
§71.121(c) (p95)	§84.001
§71.121(d) (p95)	§85.001

FORMER	CURRENT
§71.121(e), (f) (p95)	§85.003
§71.13(a) (p95)	§85.025
§71.13(b), (c) (p95)	Repealed ('95)
§71.14(a) (p95)	§87.001
§71.14(b) (p95)	§87.002
§71.14(c) ('95)	§87.003
§71.15(a) (p95)	§83.001
§71.15(b), (c) (p95)	§83.002
§71.15(d) (p95)	§83.003
§71.15(e) (p95)	§83.004
§71.15(f) (p95)	§83.005
§71.15(g), (h) (p95)	§83.006
§71.15(i) (p95)	§86.003
§71.15(j) (p95)	Repealed ('11)
§71.16 (p95)	§85.026
§71.17(a)-(d) (p95)	§85.041
§71.17(e)-(g) (p95)	§85.042
§71.18(a), (b) (p95)	§86.001
§71.18(c)[A*] (p95)	§86.002
§71.18(c)[B*] (p95)	§86.003
§71.18(d) (p95)	§86.004
§71.19 (p95)	§81.008
§§72.001-72.004 (p95)	Repealed ('95)
§§73.01-73.03 ('95)	§§91.001-91.003
§73.04 ('95)	§92.001
§73.05 ('95)	§91.004
§§88.001-88.004 ('97)	Deleted ('01)
§107.002(e) ('95)	Deleted ('03)
§§151.001, 151.002 ('95)	Deleted ('01)

4. DISPOSITION TABLE—FORMER TO CURRENT (CONT'D)

FORMER	CURRENT
§§151.003-151.005 ('95)	§§151.001-151.003
§§151.101-151.103 ('95)	Deleted ('01)
§152.001(a)(9), (b) ('95)	§152.001
§152.002 ('95)	§152.102
§152.003 ('95)	§152.201
§152.003(d) ('95)	§§152.202, 152.203
§152.003(e) ('95)	§152.204
§152.004 ('95)	§152.205
§152.005 ('95)	§152.108
§152.006 ('95)	§§152.206, 152.307
§§152.007-152.009 ('95)	§§152.207-152.209
§152.010 ('95)	§152.205
§152.011 ('95)	§152.210
§152.012 ('95)	§152.106
§152.013 ('95)	§152.313
§§152.014, 152.015 ('95)	§§152.305, 152.306
§152.016 ('95)	§152.305
§152.018 ('95)	§152.111
§§152.019-152.021 ('95)	§152.112
§152.023 ('95)	§152.105
§152.024 ('95)	§152.107
§152.025 ('95)	§152.101
§153.139 ('95)	Repealed ('01)
§§156.103, 156.104 ('95)	Deleted ('01)
§156.105 ('95)	Repealed ('01)
§§156.201-156.203 ('95)	Repealed ('01)
§§156.301-156.304 ('95)	Repealed ('01)
§158.107 ('95)	Repealed ('97)
§158.305 ('95)	Repealed ('97)
§158.508 ('97)	Repealed ('01)

FORMER	CURRENT
§159.501(a) ('95)	§§159.501, 159.502
§159.501(b) ('95)	§159.506
§159.502 ('95)	§159.507
§§160.001-160.007 ('95)	Deleted ('01)
§§160.101-160.110 ('95)	Deleted ('01)
§§160.201-160.206 ('95)	Deleted ('01)
§§160.207-160.216 ('99)	Deleted ('01)
§§160.251-160.263 ('97)	Deleted ('01)
§161.201 ('95)	Repealed ('01)
§162.0025 ('97)	Repealed ('01)
§162.004 ('95)	Repealed ('01)
§201.1085 ('97)	Repealed ('99)
§231.004 ('95)	Repealed ('97)
§231.010 ('97)	Repealed ('01)
§231.115 ('97)	§231.117
§231.304 ('95)	Repealed ('97)
§§231.401-231.429 ('95)	§§233.001-233.029
§§231.430, 231.431 ('95)	Repealed ('97)
§234.005 ('97)	Expired ('99)
§§235.001-235.004 ('97)	Repealed ('07)
§262.111[A*] ('95)	Repealed ('01)
§262.111[B*] ('95)	§262.112
§§263.003, 263.004 ('95)	Repealed ('99)
§§263.308, 263.309 ('95)	Repealed ('97)
§§263.402, 263.403 ('97)	§§263.403, 263.404
§264.003 ('95)	Repealed ('01)
§264.109 ('95)	§264.110
§§264.751-264.758 ('97)	Repealed ('03)

INDEX

INDEX

INDEX

INDEX

INDEX

INDEX

INDEX

NOTES

Notes

Notes

Notes

Notes

NOTES

NOTES

Notes

Notes

Notes

Notes

Notes